DATE DUE		

THE FIREFLY
FIVE LANGUAGE
VISUAL DICTIONARY

Jean-Claude **Corbeil**
Ariane **Archambault**

FIREFLY BOOKS

A FIREFLY BOOK

First Printing

Publisher Cataloging-in-Publication Data (U.S.)

Corbeil, Jean-Claude.

   The Firefly five language visual dictionary / English, Spanish, French, German, Italian / Jean-Claude Corbeil, Ariane Archambeault. —1st ed.

[1100] p. : col. ill. ; cm.

Includes index.

Summary: A comprehensive general reference visual dictionary featuring terms in English, Spanish French, German and Italian. Includes sections on astronomy, geography, the animal and vegetable kingdoms, human biology, the home, clothing and accessories, art and architecture, communication, transportation, energy, science, society and sports.

ISBN 1-55297-778-1

1. Dictionaries, Polyglot. 2. Picture dictionaries, Polyglot.

I. Archambeault, Ariane. II. Title.

413.21 dc22   PC2629.C67   2004

National Library of Canada Cataloguing in Publication

Corbeil, Jean-Claude, 1932-

   The Firefly five language visual dictionary : English, Spanish, French, German, Italian / Jean-Claude Corbeil, Ariane Archambault.

Includes index.

ISBN 1-55297-778-1

   1. Picture dictionaries, Polyglot. I. Archambault, Ariane, 1936-

II. Title.

AG250.C66372 2004   413'.1   C2004-901311-4

Published in the United States in 2004 by
Firefly Books (U.S.) Inc.
P.O. Box 1338, Ellicott Station
Buffalo, New York 14205

Published in Canada in 2004 by
Firefly Books Ltd.
66 Leek Crescent
Richmond Hill, Ontario L4B 1H1

Cover design: Gareth Lind

Printed in Singapore

ACKNOWLEDGMENTS

Our deepest gratitude to the individuals, institutions, companies and businesses that have provided us with the latest technical documentation for use in preparing *The Firefly Five Language Visual Dictionary*.

Arcand, Denys (réalisateur); Association Internationale de Signalisation Maritime; Association canadienne des paiements (Charlie Clarke); Association des banquiers canadiens (Lise Provost); Automobiles Citroën; Automobiles Peugeot; Banque du Canada (Lyse Brousseau); Banque Royale du Canada (Raymond Chouinard, Francine Morel, Carole Trottier); Barrett Xplore inc.; Bazarin, Christine;Bibliothèque du Parlement canadien (Service de renseignements); Bibliothèque nationale du Québec (Jean-François Palomino); Bluechip Kennels (Olga Gagne); Bombardier Aéronautique; Bridgestone-Firestone; Brother (Canada); Canadien National; Casavant Frères ltée; C.O.J.O. ATHENES 2004 (Bureau des Médias Internationaux); Centre Eaton de Montréal; Centre national du Costume (Recherche et de Diffusion); Cetacean Society International (William R. Rossiter); Chagnon, Daniel (architecte D.E.S. − M.E.Q.); Cohen et Rubin Architectes (Maggy Cohen); Commission Scolaire de Montréal (École St-Henri); Compagnie de la Baie d'Hudson (Nunzia Iavarone, Ron Oyama); Corporation d'hébergement du Québec (Céline Drolet); École nationale de théâtre du Canada (Bibliothèque); Élevage Le Grand Saphir (Stéphane Ayotte); Énergie atomique du Canada ltée; Eurocopter; Famous Players; Fédération bancaire française (Védi Hékiman); Fontaine, PierreHenry (biologiste); Future Shop; Garaga; Groupe Jean Coutu; Hôpital du Sacré-Cœur de Montréal; Hôtel Inter-Continental; Hydro-Québec; I.P.I.Q. (Serge Bouchard); IGA Barcelo; International Entomological Society (Dr. Michael Geisthardt); Irisbus; Jérôme, Danielle (O.D.); La Poste (Colette Gouts); Le Groupe Canam Manac inc.; Lévesque, Georges (urgentologue); Lévesque, Robert (chef machiniste); Manutan; Marriot Spring Hill suites; MATRA S.A.; Métro inc.; ministère canadien de la Défense nationale (Affaires publiques); ministère de la Défense, République Française; ministère de la Justice du Québec (Service de la gestion immobilière − Carol Sirois); ministère de l'Éducation du Québec (Direction de l'équipement scolaire- Daniel Chagnon); Muse Productions (Annick Barbery); National Aeronautics and Space Administration; National Oceanic and Atmospheric Administration; Nikon Canada inc.; Normand, Denis (consultant en télécommunications); Office de la langue française du Québec (Chantal Robinson); Paul Demers & Fils inc.; Phillips (France); Pratt & Whitney Canada inc.; Prévost Car inc.; Radio Shack Canada ltée; Réno-Dépôt inc.; Robitaille, Jean-François (Département de biologie, Université Laurentienne); Rocking T Ranch and Poultry Farm (Pete and Justine Theer); RONA inc.; Sears Canada inc.; Secrétariat d'État du Canada : Bureau de la traduction ; Service correctionnel du Canada; Société d'Entomologie Africaine (Alain Drumont); Société des musées québécois (Michel Perron); Société Radio-Canada; Sony du Canada ltée; Sûreté du Québec; Théâtre du Nouveau Monde; Transports Canada (Julie Poirier); Urgences-Santé (Éric Berry); Ville de Longueuil (Direction de la Police); Ville de Montréal (Service de la prévention des incendies); Vimont Lexus Toyota; Volvo Bus Corporation; Yamaha Motor Canada Ltd.

QA International wishes to extend a special thank you to the following people for their contribution to *The Firefly Five Language Visual Dictionary*:

Jean-Louis Martin, Marc Lalumière, Jacques Perrault, Stéphane Roy, Alice Comtois, Michel Blais, Christiane Beauregard, Mamadou Togola, Annie Maurice, Charles Campeau, Mivil Deschênes, Jonathan Jacques, Martin Lortie, Raymond Martin, Frédérick Simard, Yan Tremblay, Mathieu Blouin, Sébastien Dallaire, Hoang Khanh Le, Martin Desrosiers, Nicolas Oroc, François Escalmel, Danièle Lemay, Pierre Savoie, Benoît Bourdeau, Marie-Andrée Lemieux, Caroline Soucy, Yves Chabot, Anne-Marie Ouellette, Anne-Marie Villeneuve, Anne-Marie Brault, Nancy Lepage, Daniel Provost, François Vézina, Brad Wilson, Michael Worek, Lionel Koffler, Maraya Raduha, Dave Harvey, Mike Parkes, George Walker and Anna Simmons.

The Firefly Five Language Visual Dictionary was created and produced by

QA International
329, rue de la Commune Ouest, 3e étage
Montréal (Québec) H2Y 2E1 Canada
T 514.499.3000 F 514.499.3010
www.qa-international.com

EDITORIAL STAFF

Publisher: Jacques Fortin

Authors: Jean-Claude Corbeil and Ariane Archambault

Editorial Director: François Fortin

Editor-in-Chief: Serge D'Amico

Graphic Design: Anne Tremblay

PRODUCTION

Mac Thien Nguyen Hoang

Guylaine Houle

TERMINOLOGICAL RESEARCH

Jean Beaumont

Catherine Briand

Nathalie Guillo

ILLUSTRATIONS

Art Direction: Jocelyn Gardner

Jean-Yves Ahern

Rielle Lévesque

Alain Lemire

Mélanie Boivin

Yan Bohler

Claude Thivierge

Pascal Bilodeau

Michel Rouleau

Anouk Noël

Carl Pelletier

LAYOUT

Pascal Goyette

Janou-Ève LeGuerrier

Véronique Boisvert

Josée Gagnon

Karine Raymond

Geneviève Théroux Béliveau

DOCUMENTATION

Gilles Vézina

Kathleen Wynd

Stéphane Batigne

Sylvain Robichaud

Jessie Daigle

DATA MANAGEMENT

Programmer: Daniel Beaulieu

Nathalie Fréchette

REVISION

Marie-Nicole Cimon

PREPRESS

Sophie Pellerin

Kien Tang

Tony O'Riley

Jean-Claude Corbeil is an expert in linguistic planning, with a world-wide reputation in the fields of comparative terminology and socio-linguistics. He serves as a consultant to various international organizations and governments.

Ariane Archambault, a specialist in applied linguistics, has taught foreign languages and is now a terminologist and editor of dictionaries and reference books.

Introduction to
The Firefly Five Language Visual Dictionary

A DICTIONARY FOR ONE AND ALL

The Firefly Five Language Visual Dictionary uses pictures to define words. With thousands of illustrations and thousands of specialist and general terms, it provides a rich source of knowledge about the world around you.

Designed for the general reader and students of language, *The Firefly Five Language Visual Dictionary* responds to the needs of anyone seeking precise, correct terms for a wide range of objects. Using illustrations enables you to "see" immediately the meaning of each term.

You can use *The Firefly Five Language Visual Dictionary* in several ways:

By going from an idea to a word. If you are familiar with an object but do not know the correct name for it, you can look up the object in the dictionary and you will find the various parts correctly named.

By going from a word to an idea. If you want to check the meaning of a term, refer to the index where you will find the term and be directed to the appropriate illustration that defines the term.

For sheer pleasure. You can flip from one illustration to another or from one word to another, for the sole purpose of enjoying the illustrations and enriching your knowledge of the world around us.

STRUCTURE

The Firefly Five Language Visual Dictionary is divided into CHAPTERS, outlining subjects from astronomy to sports.

More complex subjects are divided into THEMES; for example, the Animal Kingdom chapter is divided into themes including insects and arachnids, mollusks, and crustaceans.

The TITLES name the object and, at times, the chief members of a class of objects are brought together under the same SUBTITLE.

The ILLUSTRATIONS show an object, a process or a phenomenon, and the most significant details from which they are constructed. It serves as a visual definition for each of the terms presented.

TERMINOLOGY

Each word in *The Firefly Five Language Visual Dictionary* has been carefully chosen and verified. Sometimes different words are used to name the same object, and in these cases the word most commonly used was chosen.

COLOR REFERENCE

On the spine and back of the book this identifies and accompanies each theme to facilitate quick access to the corresponding section in the book.

TITLE

It is highlighted in English, while the other languages are placed underneath in smaller characters. If the title runs over a number of pages, it is printed in gray on the pages subsequent to the first page on which it appears.

SUB-THEME

Most themes are subdivided into sub-themes. The sub-themes are multilingual.

ILLUSTRATION

Serves as a visual definition for each of the terms associated with it.

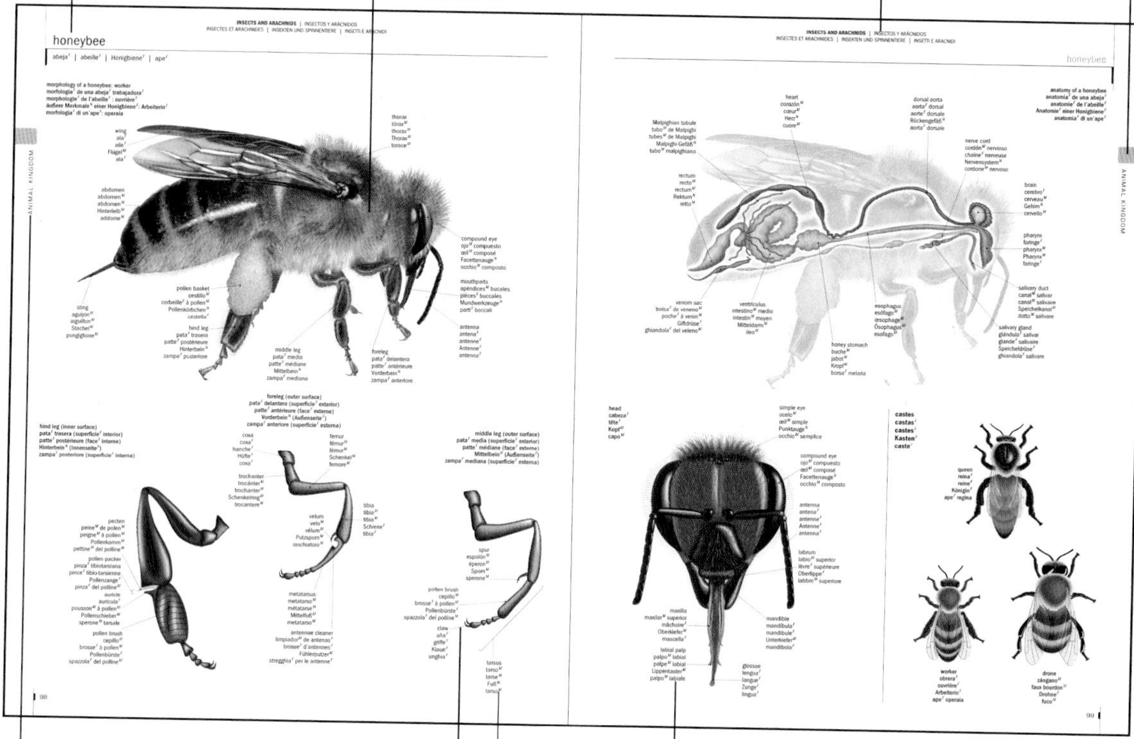

THEME

It is always in English. The equivalent in the other languages appears on the introduction page — the first double-page spread — for each theme.

TERM

Each term appears in the index with a reference to the pages on which it appears. It is given in all languages, with English as the main index entry.

NARROW LINES

These link the word to the item indicated. Where too many lines would make reading difficult, they have been replaced by color codes with captions or, in rare cases, by numbers.

GENDER INDICATION

F: feminine M: masculine N: neuter

The gender of each word in a term is indicated.

The characters shown in the dictionary are men or women when the function illustrated can be fulfilled by either. In these cases, the gender assigned to the word depends on the illustration; in fact, the word is either masculine or feminine depending on the sex of the person.

Contents

Contents

List of chapters

ASTRONOMY

ASTRONOMÍA | ASTRONOMIE | ASTRONOMIE | ASTRONOMIA

ASTRONOMY

solar system

sistema^M solar | système^M solaire | Sonnensystem^N | sistema^M solare

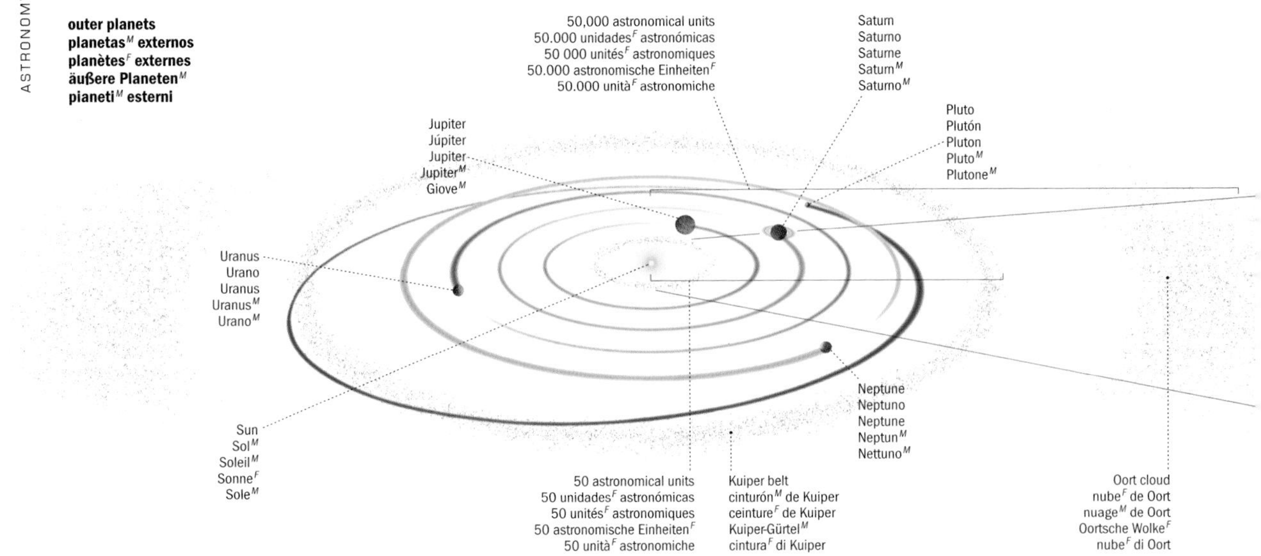

outer planets
planetas^M externos
planètes^F externes
äußere Planeten^M
pianeti^M esterni

50,000 astronomical units
50.000 unidades^F astronómicas
50 000 unités^F astronomiques
50.000 astronomische Einheiten^F
50.000 unità^F astronomiche

Satum
Saturno
Saturne
Saturn^M
Saturno^M

Pluto
Plutón
Pluton
Pluto^M
Plutone^M

Jupiter
Júpiter
Jupiter
Jupiter^M
Giove^M

Uranus
Urano
Uranus
Uranus^M
Urano^M

Neptune
Neptuno
Neptune
Neptun^M
Nettuno^M

Sun
Sol^M
Soleil^M
Sonne^F
Sole^M

50 astronomical units
50 unidades^F astronómicas
50 unités^F astronomiques
50 astronomische Einheiten^F
50 unità^F astronomiche

Kuiper belt
cinturón^M de Kuiper
ceinture^F de Kuiper
Kuiper-Gürtel^M
cintura^F di Kuiper

Oort cloud
nube^F de Oort
nuage^M de Oort
Oortsche Wolke^F
nube^F di Oort

planets and moons

planetas^M y satélites^M | planètes^F et satellites^M | Planeten^M und Monde^M | pianeti^M e satelliti^M

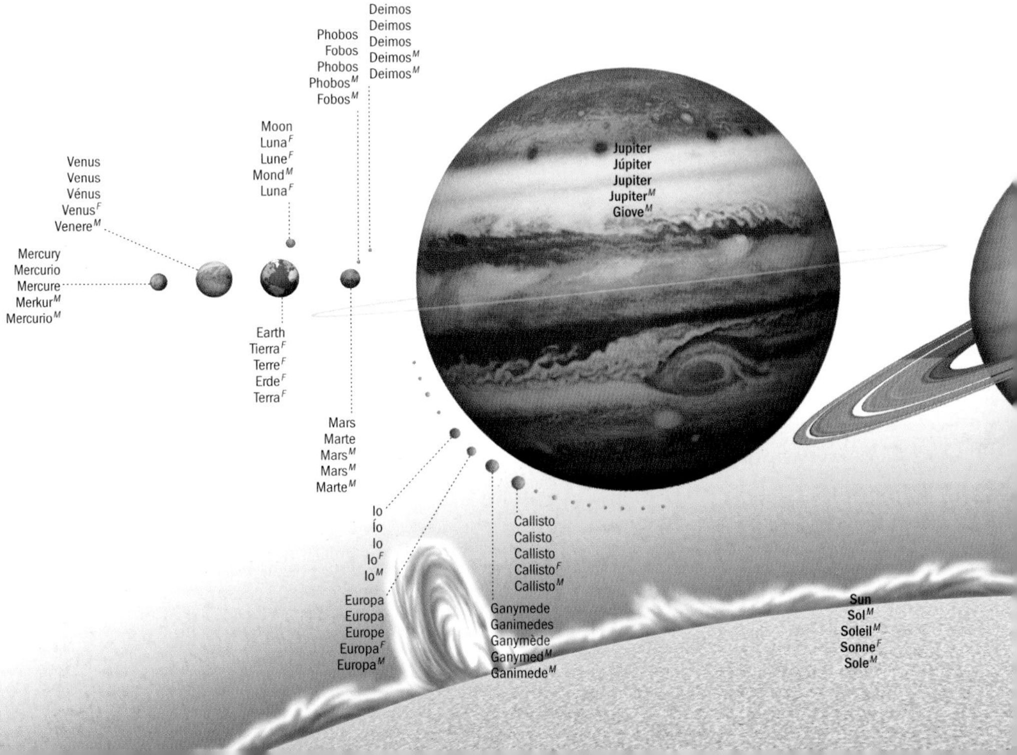

Deimos
Deimos
Deimos
Deimos^M
Deimos^M

Phobos
Fobos
Phobos
Phobos^M
Fobos^M

Moon
Luna^F
Lune^F
Mond^M
Luna^F

Venus
Venus
Vénus
Venus^F
Venere^M

Mercury
Mercurio
Mercure
Merkur^M
Mercurio^M

Jupiter
Júpiter
Jupiter
Jupiter^M
Giove^M

Earth
Tierra^F
Terre^F
Erde^F
Terra^F

Mars
Marte
Mars^M
Mars^M
Marte^M

Io
Io
Io
Io^F
Io^M

Callisto
Calisto
Callisto
Callisto^F
Callisto^M

Europa
Europa
Europe
Europa^F
Europa^M

Ganymede
Ganimedes
Ganymède
Ganymed^M
Ganimede^M

Sun
Sol^M
Soleil^M
Sonne^F
Sole^M

solar system

inner planets
planetas [M] **internos**
planètes [F] **internes**
innere Planeten [M]
pianeti [M] **interni**

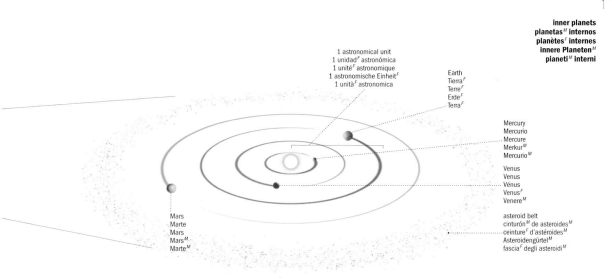

1 astronomical unit
1 unidad [F] astronómica
1 unité [F] astronomique
1 astronomische Einheit [F]
1 unità [F] astronomica

Earth
Tierra [F]
Terre [F]
Erde [F]
Terra [F]

Mercury
Mercurio
Mercure
Merkur [M]
Mercurio [M]

Venus
Venus
Vénus
Venus [F]
Venere [M]

asteroid belt
cinturón [M] de asteroides [M]
ceinture [F] d'astéroïdes [M]
Asteroidengürtel [M]
fascia [F] degli asteroidi [M]

Mars
Marte
Mars
Mars [M]
Marte [M]

planets and moons

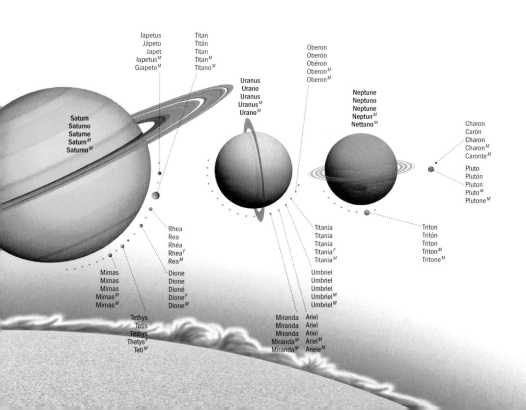

Iapetus
Jápeto
Japet
Iapetus [M]
Giapeto [M]

Titan
Titán
Titan
Titan [M]
Titano [M]

Oberon
Oberón
Obéron
Oberon [M]
Oberon [M]

Uranus
Urano
Uranus
Uranus [M]
Urano [M]

Neptune
Neptuno
Neptune
Neptun [M]
Nettuno [M]

Charon
Carón
Charon
Charon [M]
Caronte [M]

Saturn
Saturno
Saturne
Saturn [M]
Saturno [M]

Pluto
Plutón
Pluton
Pluto [M]
Plutone [M]

Rhea
Rea
Rhéa
Rhea [F]
Rea [M]

Titania
Titania
Titania
Titania [F]
Titania [M]

Triton
Tritón
Triton
Triton [M]
Tritone [M]

Mimas
Mimas
Mimas
Mimas [M]
Mimas [M]

Dione
Dione
Dioné
Dioné [F]
Dione [M]

Umbriel
Umbriel
Umbriel
Umbriel [M]
Umbriel [M]

Tethys
Tetis
Téthys
Thetys [F]
Teti [M]

Miranda
Miranda
Miranda
Miranda [M]
Miranda [M]

Ariel
Ariel
Ariel
Ariel [M]
Ariele [M]

Sun

Sol[M] | Soleil[M] | Sonne[F] | Sole[M]

ASTRONOMY

structure of the Sun
estructura[F] del Sol[M]
structure[F] du Soleil[M]
Aufbau[M] der Sonne[F]
struttura[F] del Sole[M]

spicules
espículas[F]
spicule[M]
Spikulen[F]
spicole[F]

chromosphere
cromosfera[F]
chromosphère[F]
Chromosphäre[F]
cromosfera[F]

flare
erupción[F]
éruption[F]
Flare[F]
brillamento[M]

corona
corona[F]
couronne[F]
Korona[F]
corona[F]

sunspot
mancha[F] solar
tache[F]
Sonnenfleck[M]
macchia[F] solare

granulation
granulación[F]
granulation[F]
Granulation[F]
granulazione[F]

convection zone
zona[F] de convección[F]
zone[F] de convection[F]
Konvektionszone[F]
zona[F] convettiva

photosphere
fotosfera[F]
photosphère[F]
Photosphäre[F]
fotosfera[F]

core
núcleo[M]
noyau[M]
Zentralbereich[M]
nucleo[M]

faculae
fáculas[F]
facule[F]
Fackeln[F]
facole[F]

radiation zone
zona[F] de radiación[F]
zone[F] de radiation[F]
Strahlungszone[F]
zona[F] radiativa

prominence
protuberancia[F]
protubérance[F]
Protuberanz[F]
protuberanza[F]

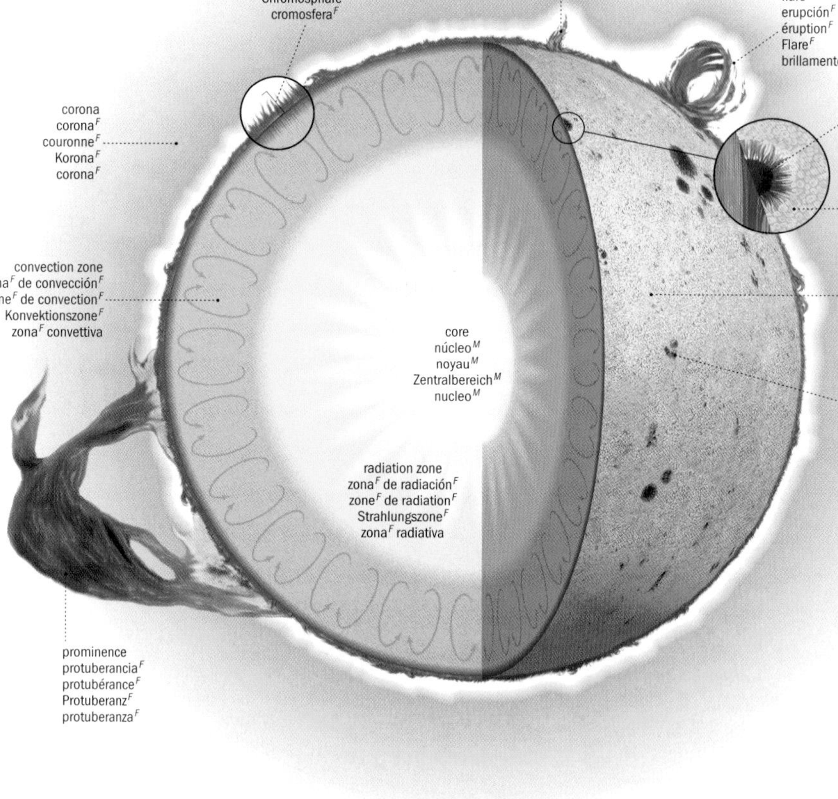

types of eclipses
tipos[M] de eclipses[M]
types[M] d'éclipses[F]
Finsternisarten[F]
tipi[M] di eclissi[F]

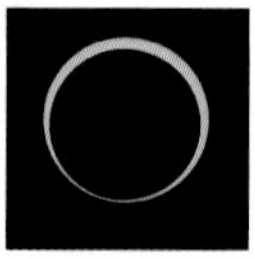

annular eclipse
eclipse[M] anular
éclipse[F] annulaire
ringförmige Finsternis[F]
eclissi[F] anulare

solar eclipse
eclipse[M] solar
éclipse[F] de Soleil[M]
Sonnenfinsternis[F]
eclissi[F] di Sole[M]

umbra shadow
cono[M] de sombra[F]
cône[M] d'ombre[F]
Kernschatten[M]
cono[M] d'ombra[F]

Earth's orbit
órbita[F] terrestre
orbite[F] terrestre
Erdbahn[F]
orbita[F] della Terra[F]

Moon
Luna[F]
Lune[F]
Mond[M]
Luna[F]

Sun
Sol[M]
Soleil[M]
Sonne[F]
Sole[M]

penumbra shadow
cono[M] de penumbra[F]
cône[M] de pénombre[F]
Halbschatten[M]
cono[M] di penombra[F]

Earth
Tierra[F]
Terre[F]
Erde[F]
Terra[F]

Moon's orbit
órbita[F] lunar
orbite[F] lunaire
Mondbahn[F]
orbita[F] della Luna[F]

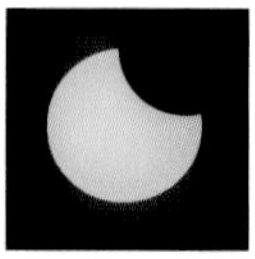

partial eclipse
eclipse[M] parcial
éclipse[F] partielle
partielle Finsternis[F]
eclissi[F] parziale

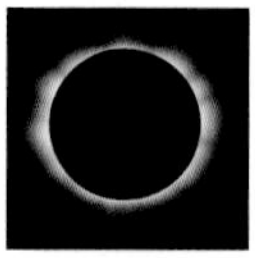

total eclipse
eclipse[M] total
éclipse[F] totale
totale Finsternis[F]
eclissi[F] totale

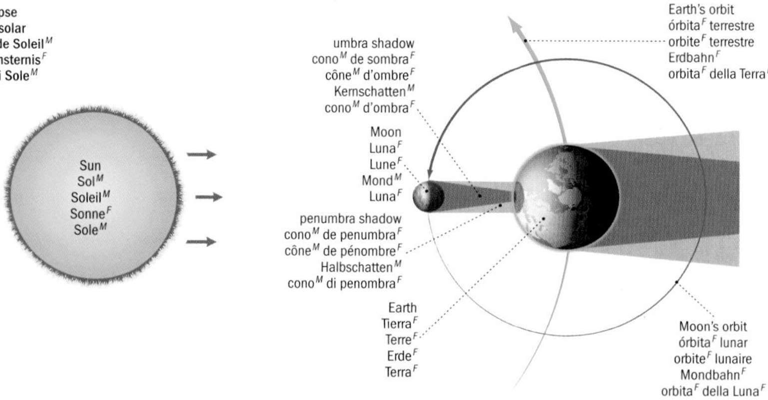

Moon

Luna[F] | Lune[F] | Mond[M] | Luna[F]

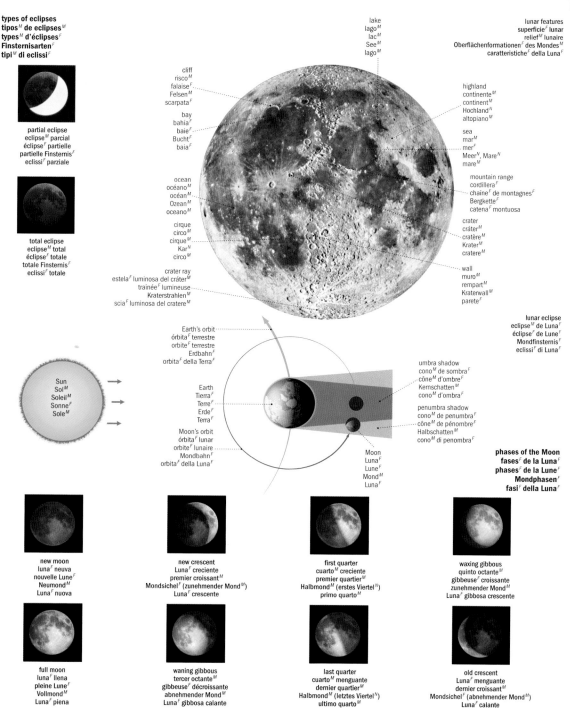

types of eclipses
tipos[M] de eclipses[M]
types[M] d'éclipses[F]
Finsternisarten[F]
tipi[M] di eclissi[F]

partial eclipse
eclipse[M] parcial
éclipse[F] partielle
partielle Finsternis[F]
eclissi[F] parziale

total eclipse
eclipse[M] total
éclipse[F] totale
totale Finsternis[F]
eclissi[F] totale

lake
lago[M]
lac[M]
See[M]
lago[M]

lunar features
superficie[F] lunar
relief[M] lunaire
Oberflächenformationen[F] des Mondes[M]
caratteristiche[F] della Luna[F]

cliff
risco[M]
falaise[F]
Felsen[M]
scarpata[F]

highland
continente[M]
continent[M]
Hochland[N]
altopiano[M]

bay
bahía[F]
baie[F]
Bucht[F]
baia[F]

sea
mar[M]
mer[F]
Meer[N], Mare[N]
mare[M]

ocean
océano[M]
océan[M]
Ozean[M]
oceano[M]

mountain range
cordillera[F]
chaîne[F] de montagnes[F]
Bergkette[F]
catena[F] montuosa

cirque
circo[M]
cirque[M]
Kar[N]
circo[M]

crater
cráter[M]
cratère[F]
Krater[M]
cratere[M]

crater ray
estela[F] luminosa del cráter[M]
traînée[F] lumineuse
Kraterstrahlen[M]
scia[F] luminosa del cratere[M]

wall
muro[M]
rempart[M]
Kraterwall[M]
parete[F]

lunar eclipse
eclipse[M] de Luna[F]
éclipse[F] de Lune[F]
Mondfinsternis[F]
eclissi[F] di Luna[F]

Earth's orbit
órbita[F] terrestre
orbite[F] terrestre
Erdbahn[F]
orbita[F] della Terra[F]

umbra shadow
cono[M] de sombra[F]
cône[M] d'ombre[F]
Kernschatten[M]
cono[M] d'ombra[F]

Sun
Sol[M]
Soleil[M]
Sonne[F]
Sole[M]

Earth
Tierra[F]
Terre[F]
Erde[F]
Terra[F]

penumbra shadow
cono[M] de penumbra[F]
cône[M] de pénombre[F]
Halbschatten[M]
cono[M] di penombra[F]

Moon's orbit
órbita[F] lunar
orbite[F] lunaire
Mondbahn[F]
orbita[F] della Luna[F]

Moon
Luna[F]
Lune[F]
Mond[M]
Luna[F]

phases of the Moon
fases[F] de la Luna[F]
phases[F] de la Lune[F]
Mondphasen[F]
fasi[F] della Luna[F]

new moon
luna[F] neuva
nouvelle Lune[F]
Neumond[M]
Luna[F] nuova

new crescent
Luna[F] creciente
premier croissant[M]
Mondsichel[F] (zunehmender Mond[M])
Luna[F] crescente

first quarter
cuarto[M] creciente
premier quartier[M]
Halbmond[M] (erstes Viertel[N])
primo quarto[M]

waxing gibbous
quinto octante[M]
gibbeuse[F] croissante
zunehmender Mond[M]
Luna[F] gibbosa crescente

full moon
luna[F] llena
pleine Lune[F]
Vollmond[M]
Luna[F] piena

waning gibbous
tercer octante[M]
gibbeuse[F] décroissante
abnehmender Mond[M]
Luna[F] gibbosa calante

last quarter
cuarto[M] menguante
dernier quartier[M]
Halbmond[M] (letztes Viertel[N])
ultimo quarto[M]

old crescent
Luna[F] menguante
dernier croissant[M]
Mondsichel[F] (abnehmender Mond[M])
Luna[F] calante

ASTRONOMY

meteorite

meteorito^M | météorite^F | Meteorit^M | meteorite$^{F/M}$

stony meteorites
meteoritos^M pétreos
météorites^F rocheuses
Steinmeteoriten^M
meteoriti$^{F/M}$ rocciose

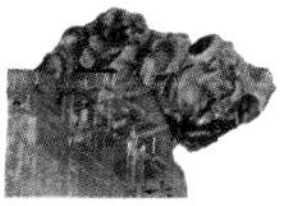

iron meteorite
meteorito^M ferroso
météorite^F ferreuse
Eisenmeteorit^M
meteorite$^{F/M}$ ferrosa

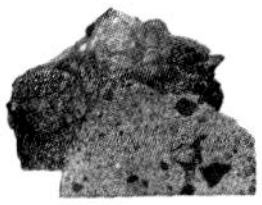

stony-iron meteorite
meteorito^M pétreo-ferroso
météorite^F métallo-rocheuse
Steineisenmeteorit^M
meteorite$^{F/M}$ ferro-rocciosa

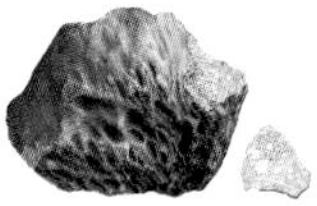

chondrite
condrito^M
chondrite^F
Chondrit^M
condrite^F

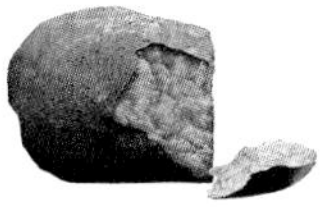

achondrite
acondrito^M
achondrite^F
Achondrit^M
acondrite^F

comet

cometa^M | comète^F | Komet^M | cometa^F

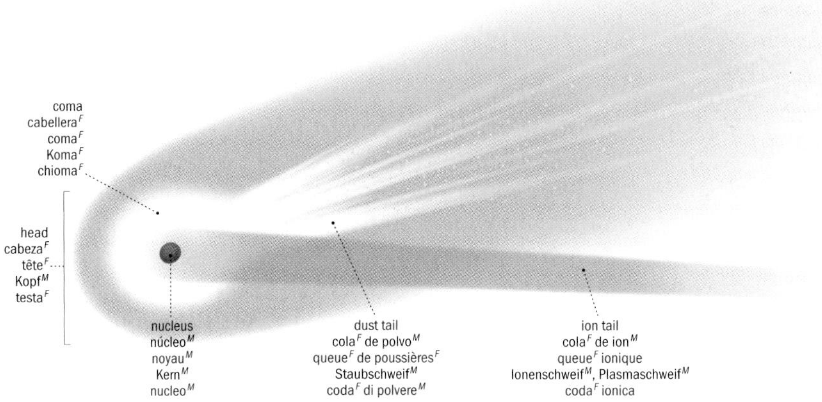

coma
cabellera^F
coma^F
Koma^F
chioma^F

head
cabeza^F
tête^F
Kopf^M
testa^F

nucleus
núcleo^M
noyau^M
Kern^M
nucleo^M

dust tail
cola^F de polvo^M
queue^F de poussières^F
Staubschweif^M
coda^F di polvere^M

ion tail
cola^F de ion^M
queue^F ionique
Ionenschweif^M, Plasmaschweif^M
coda^F ionica

star

estrella^F | étoile^F | Stern^M | stella^F

low-mass stars
estrellas^F de baja magnitud^F
étoiles^F de faible masse^F
kleine Sterne^M
stelle^F di massa^F minore

massive stars
estrellas de alta magnitud^F
étoiles^F massives
massereiche Sterne^M
stelle^F di massa^F maggiore

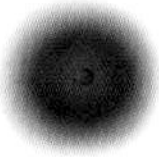

black dwarf
enana^F negra
naine^F noire
Schwarzer Zwerg^M
nana^F nera

supernova
supernova^F
supernova^F
Supernova^F
supernova^F

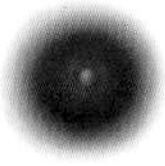

brown dwarf
enana^F parda
naine^F brune
Brauner Zwerg^M
nana^F bruna

nova
nova^F
nova^F
Nova^F
nova^F

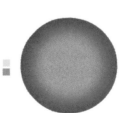

red giant
gigante^F roja
géante^F rouge
Roter Riese^M
gigante^F rossa

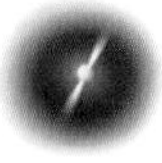

pulsar
pulsar^M
pulsar^M
Pulsar^M
pulsar^F

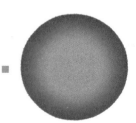

supergiant
supergigante^M
supergéante^F
Überriese^M
supergigante^F

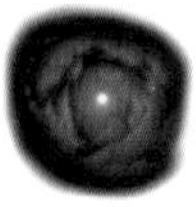

planetary nebula
nebulosa^F planetaria
nébuleuse^F planétaire
planetarischer Nebel^M
nebulosa^F planetaria

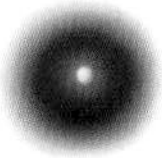

white dwarf
enana^F blanca
naine^F blanche
Weißer Zwerg^M
nana^F bianca

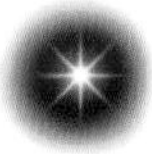

main-sequence star
estrella^F de secuencia^F principal
étoile^F de la séquence^F principale
Hauptreihenstern^M
stella^F della sequenza^F principale

black hole
agujero^M negro
trou^M noir
Schwarzes Loch^N
buco^M nero

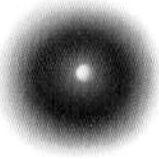

neutron star
estrella^F de neutrones^M
étoile^F à neutrons^M
Neutronenstern^M
stella^F di neutroni^M

galaxy

galaxia[F] | galaxie[F] | Galaxie[F] | galassia[F]

Hubble's classification
clasificación[F] de Hubble
classification[F] de Hubble
Hubblesche Klassifikation[F]
classificazione[F] di Hubble

Milky Way
Vía[F] Láctea
Voie[F] Lactée
Milchstraße[F]
Via[F] Lattea

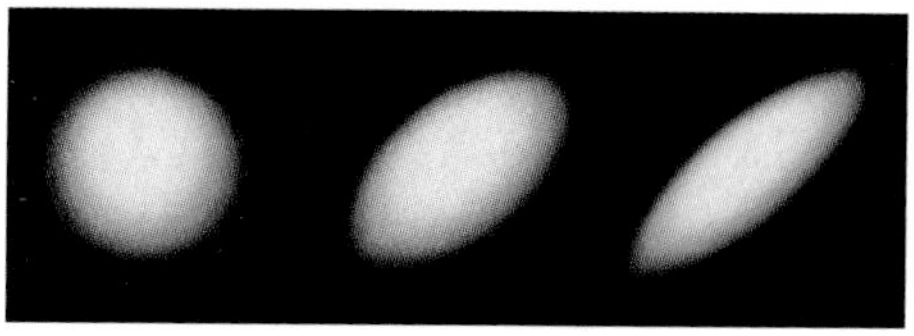

elliptical galaxy
galaxia[F] elíptica
galaxie[F] elliptique
elliptische Galaxie[F]
galassia[F] ellittica

Milky Way (seen from above)
Vía[F] Láctea (vista[F] desde arriba)
Voie[F] Lactée (vue[F] de dessus[M])
Milchstraße[F] (Ansicht[F] von oben)
Via[F] Lattea (vista[F] dall'alto)

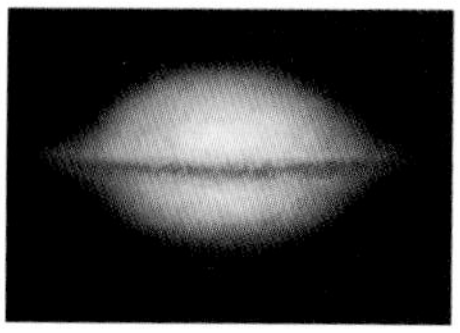

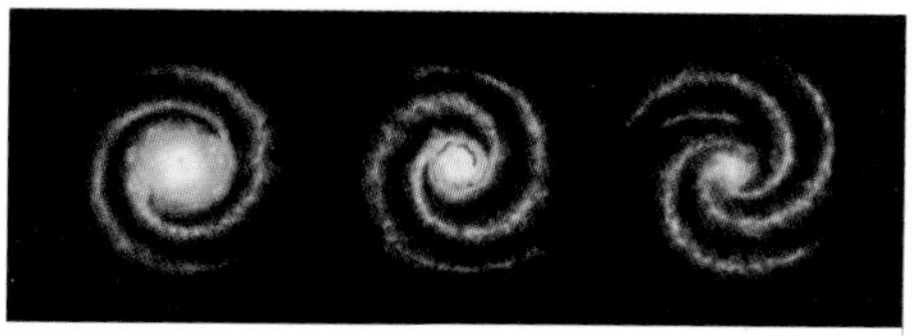

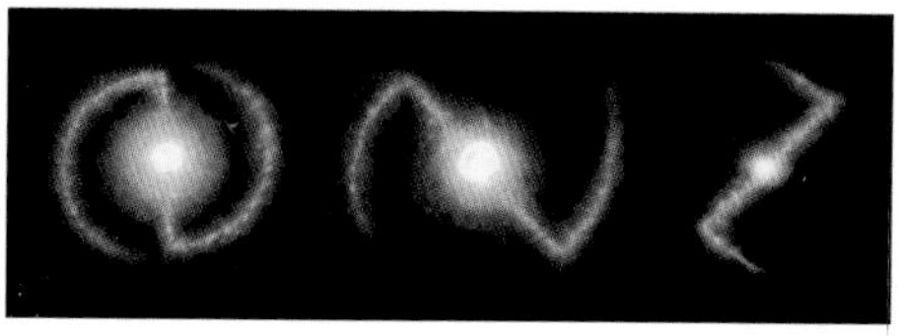

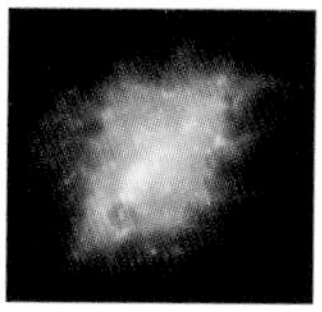

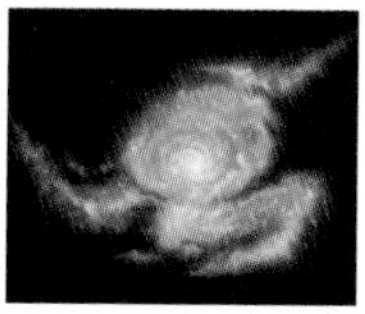

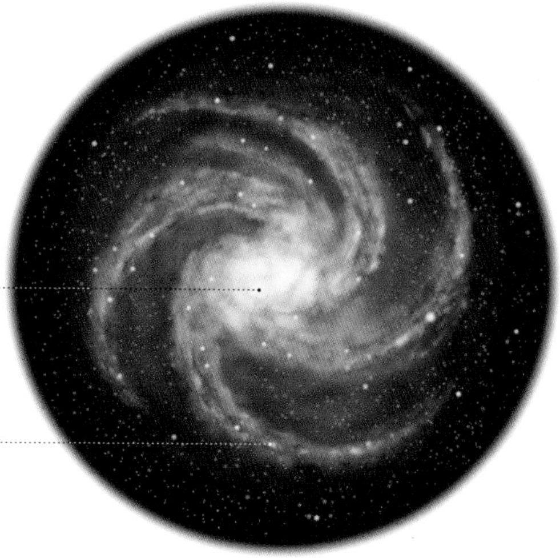

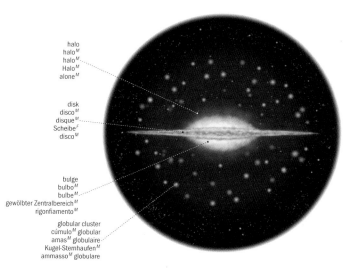

nucleus
núcleo[M]
noyau[M] galactique
Kern[M]
nucleo[M]

spiral arm
brazo[M] espiral
bras[M] spiral
Spiralarm[M]
braccio[M] della spirale[F]

lenticular galaxy
galaxia[F] lenticular
galaxie[F] lenticulaire
linsenförmige Galaxie[F]
galassia[F] lenticolare

Milky Way (side view)
Vía[F] Láctea (vista[F] lateral)
Voie[F] Lactée (vue[F] de profil[M])
Milchstraße[F] (Seitenansicht[F])
Via[F] Lattea (vista[F] laterale)

normal spiral galaxy
galaxia[F] espiral normal
galaxie[F] spirale normale
normale Spiralgalaxie[F]
galassia[F] a spirale[F] normale

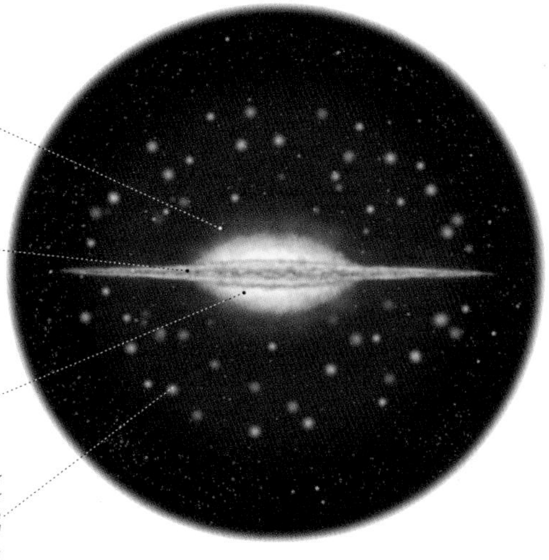

halo
halo[M]
halo[M]
Halo[M]
alone[M]

disk
disco[M]
disque[M]
Scheibe[F]
disco[M]

barred spiral galaxy
galaxia[F] espiral barrada
galaxie[F] spirale barrée
Balkenspiralgalaxie[F]
galassia[F] a spirale[F] barrata[F]

bulge
bulbo[M]
bulbe[M]
gewölbter Zentralbereich[M]
rigonfiamento[M]

globular cluster
cúmulo[M] globular
amas[M] globulaire
Kugel-Sternhaufen[M]
ammasso[M] globulare

type I irregular galaxy
galaxia[F] irregular de tipo[M] I
galaxie[F] irrégulière de type[M] I
irreguläre Galaxie[F] Typ[M] I
galassia[F] irregolare di tipo[M] I

type II irregular galaxy
galaxia[F] irregular de tipo[M] II
galaxie[F] irrégulière de type[M] II
irreguläre Galaxie[F] Typ[M] II
galassia[F] irregolare di tipo[M] II

ASTRONOMICAL OBSERVATION | OBSERVACIÓN ASTRONÓMICA
OBSERVATION ASTRONOMIQUE | BEOBACHTUNG DES WELTRAUMS | OSSERVAZIONE ASTRONOMICA

ASTRONOMY

planetarium

planetario[M] | planétarium[M] | Planetarium[N] | planetario[M]

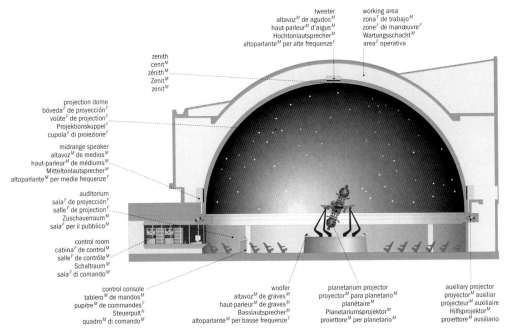

tweeter
altavoz[M] de agudos[M]
haut-parleur[M] d'aigus[M]
Hochtonlautsprecher[M]
altoparlante[M] per alte frequenze[F]

working area
zona[F] de trabajo[M]
zone[F] de manœuvre[F]
Wartungsschacht[M]
area[F] operativa

zenith
cenit[M]
zénith[M]
Zenit[M]
zenit[M]

projection dome
bóveda[F] de proyección[F]
voûte[F] de projection[F]
Projektionskuppel[F]
cupola[F] di proiezione[F]

midrange speaker
altavoz[M] de medios[M]
haut-parleur[M] de médiums[M]
Mitteltonlautsprecher[M]
altoparlante[M] per medie frequenze[F]

auditorium
sala[F] de proyección[F]
salle[F] de projection[F]
Zuschauerraum[M]
sala[F] per il pubblico[M]

control room
cabina[F] de control[M]
salle[F] de contrôle[M]
Schaltraum[M]
sala[F] di comando[M]

control console
tablero[M] de mandos[M]
pupitre[M] de commandes[F]
Steuerpult[N]
quadro[M] di comando[M]

woofer
altavoz[M] de graves[M]
haut-parleur[M] de graves[M]
Basslautsprecher[M]
altoparlante[M] per basse frequenze[F]

planetarium projector
proyector[M] para planetario[M]
planétaire[M]
Planetariumsprojektor[M]
proiettore[M] per planetario[M]

auxiliary projector
proyector[M] auxiliar
projecteur[M] auxiliaire
Hilfsprojektor[M]
proiettore[M] ausiliario

constellations of the southern hemisphere

constelaciones[F] del hemisferio[M] austral | constellations[F] de l'hémisphère[M] austral | Sternbilder[N] der südlichen Halbkugel[F] | costellazioni[F] dell'emisfero[M] meridionale

1
Whale
Ballena[F]
Baleine[F]
Walfisch[M]
Balena[F]

2
Aquarius
Acuario[M]
Verseau[M]
Wassermann[M]
Acquario[M]

3
Aquila, the Eagle
Águila[F]
Aigle[M]
Adler[M]
Aquila[F]

4
Capricorn
Capricornio[M]
Capricorne[M]
Steinbock[M]
Capricorno[M]

5
Microscope
Microscopio[M]
Microscope[M]
Mikroskop[N]
Microscopio[M]

6
Southern Fish
Pez[M] Austral
Poisson[M] austral
Südlicher Fisch[M]
Pesce[M] Australe

7
Grus, the Crane
Grulla[F]
Grue[F]
Kranich[M]
Gru[F]

8
Sculptor
Escultor[M]
Atelier[M] du Sculpteur[M]
Bildhauer[M]
Scultore[M]

9
Eridanus, the River
Eridano[M]
Éridan[M]
Eridanus[M]
Eridano[M]

10
Furnace
Horno[M]
Fourneau[M]
Ofen[M]
Fornace[F]

11
Clock
Reloj[M]
Horloge[F]
Pendeluhr[F]
Orologio[M]

12
Phoenix
Fénix[M]
Phénix[M]
Phönix[M]
Fenice[F]

13
Toucan
Tucán[M]
Toucan[M]
Tukan[M]
Tucano[M]

14
Peacock
Pavo[M]
Paon[M]
Pfau[M]
Pavone[M]

15
Indian
Indio[M]
Indien[M]
Inder[M]
Indiano[M]

16
Telescope
Telescopio[M]
Télescope[M]
Fernrohr[N]
Telescopio[M]

17
Southern Crown
Corona[F] Austral
Couronne[F] australe
Südliche Krone[F]
Corona[F] Australe

18
Sagittarius
Sagitario[M]
Sagittaire[M]
Schütze[M]
Sagittario[M]

19
Shield
Escudo[M]
Écu[M]
Schild[N]
Scudo[M]

20
Scorpio
Escorpión[M]
Scorpion[M]
Skorpion[M]
Scorpione[M]

21
Norma, the Square
Escuadra[F]
Équerre[F]
Winkelmaß[N]
Squadra[F]

22
Altar
Altar[M]
Autel[M]
Altar[M]
Altare[M]

23
Southern Triangle
Triángulo[M] Austral
Triangle[M] austral
Südliches Dreieck[N]
Triangolo[M] Australe

24
Bird of Paradise
Ave[F] del Paraíso[M]
Oiseau[M] du Paradis[M]
Paradiesvogel[M]
Uccello[M] del Paradiso[M]

25
Octant
Octante[M]
Octant[M]
Oktant[M]
Ottante[M]

26
Water Serpent (Hydrus)
Hidra[F] Macho
Hydre[F] mâle
Kleine Wasserschlange[F]
Idra[F] Maschio

27
Table
Mesa[F]
Table[F]
Tafelberg[M]
Mensa[F]

28
Net
Reticulo[M]
Réticule[M]
Netz[N]
Reticolo[M]

ASTRONOMICAL OBSERVATION | OBSERVACIÓN ASTRONÓMICA
OBSERVATION ASTRONOMIQUE | BEOBACHTUNG DES WELTRAUMS | OSSERVAZIONE ASTRONOMICA

constellations of the southern hemisphere

ASTRONOMY

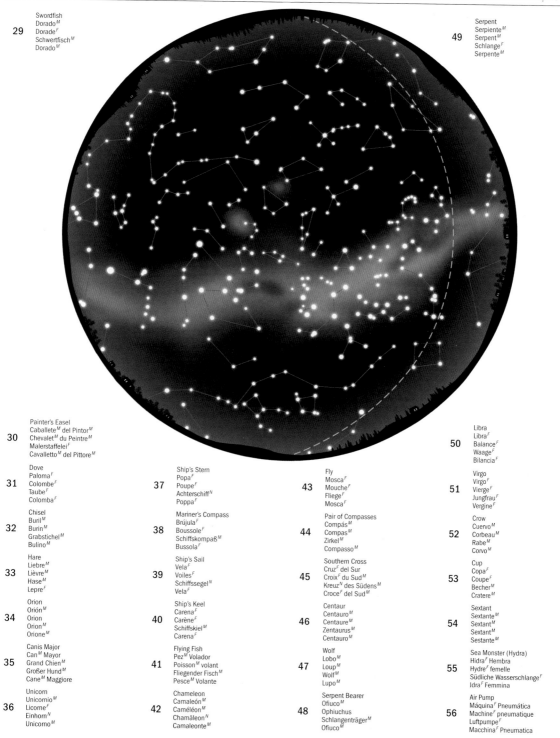

29
Swordfish
Dorado[M]
Dorade[F]
Schwertfisch[M]
Dorado[M]

49
Serpent
Serpiente[M]
Serpent[M]
Schlange[F]
Serpente[M]

30
Painter's Easel
Caballete[M] del Pintor[M]
Chevalet[M] du Peintre[M]
Malerstaffelei[F]
Cavalletto[M] del Pittore[M]

50
Libra
Libra[F]
Balance[F]
Waage[F]
Bilancia[F]

31
Dove
Paloma[F]
Colombe[F]
Taube[F]
Colomba[F]

37
Ship's Stern
Popa[F]
Poupe[F]
Achterschiff[N]
Poppa[F]

43
Fly
Mosca[F]
Mouche[F]
Fliege[F]
Mosca[F]

51
Virgo
Virgo[F]
Vierge[F]
Jungfrau[F]
Vergine[F]

32
Chisel
Buril[M]
Burin[M]
Grabstichel[M]
Bulino[M]

38
Mariner's Compass
Brújula[F]
Boussole[F]
Schiffskompaß[M]
Bussola[F]

44
Pair of Compasses
Compás[M]
Compas[M]
Zirkel[M]
Compasso[M]

52
Crow
Cuervo[M]
Corbeau[M]
Rabe[M]
Corvo[M]

33
Hare
Liebre[M]
Lièvre[M]
Hase[M]
Lepre[F]

39
Ship's Sail
Vela[F]
Voiles[F]
Schiffssegel[N]
Vela[F]

45
Southern Cross
Cruz[F] del Sur
Croix[F] du Sud[M]
Kreuz[N] des Südens[M]
Croce[F] del Sud[M]

53
Cup
Copa[F]
Coupe[F]
Becher[M]
Cratere[M]

34
Orion
Orión[M]
Orion[M]
Orion[M]
Orione[M]

40
Ship's Keel
Carena[F]
Carène[F]
Schiffskiel[M]
Carena[F]

46
Centaur
Centauro[M]
Centaure[M]
Zentaurus[M]
Centauro[M]

54
Sextant
Sextante[M]
Sextant[M]
Sextant[M]
Sestante[M]

35
Canis Major
Can[M] Mayor
Grand Chien[M]
Großer Hund[M]
Cane[M] Maggiore

41
Flying Fish
Pez[M] Volador
Poisson[M] volant
Fliegender Fisch[M]
Pesce[M] Volante

47
Wolf
Lobo[M]
Loup[M]
Wolf[M]
Lupo[M]

55
Sea Monster (Hydra)
Hidra[F] Hembra
Hydre[F] femelle
Südliche Wasserschlange[F]
Idra[F] Femmina

36
Unicorn
Unicornio[M]
Licorne[F]
Einhorn[N]
Unicorno[M]

42
Chameleon
Camaleón[M]
Caméléon[M]
Chamäleon[N]
Camaleonte[M]

48
Serpent Bearer
Ofiuco[M]
Ophiuchus
Schlangenträger[M]
Ofiuco[M]

56
Air Pump
Máquina[F] Pneumática
Machine[F] pneumatique
Luftpumpe[F]
Macchina[F] Pneumatica

ASTRONOMY

constellations of the northern hemisphere

constelaciones^F del hemisferio^M boreal | constellations^F de l'hémisphère^M boréal | Sternbilder^N der nördlichen Halbkugel^F | costellazioni^F dell'emisfero^M settentrionale

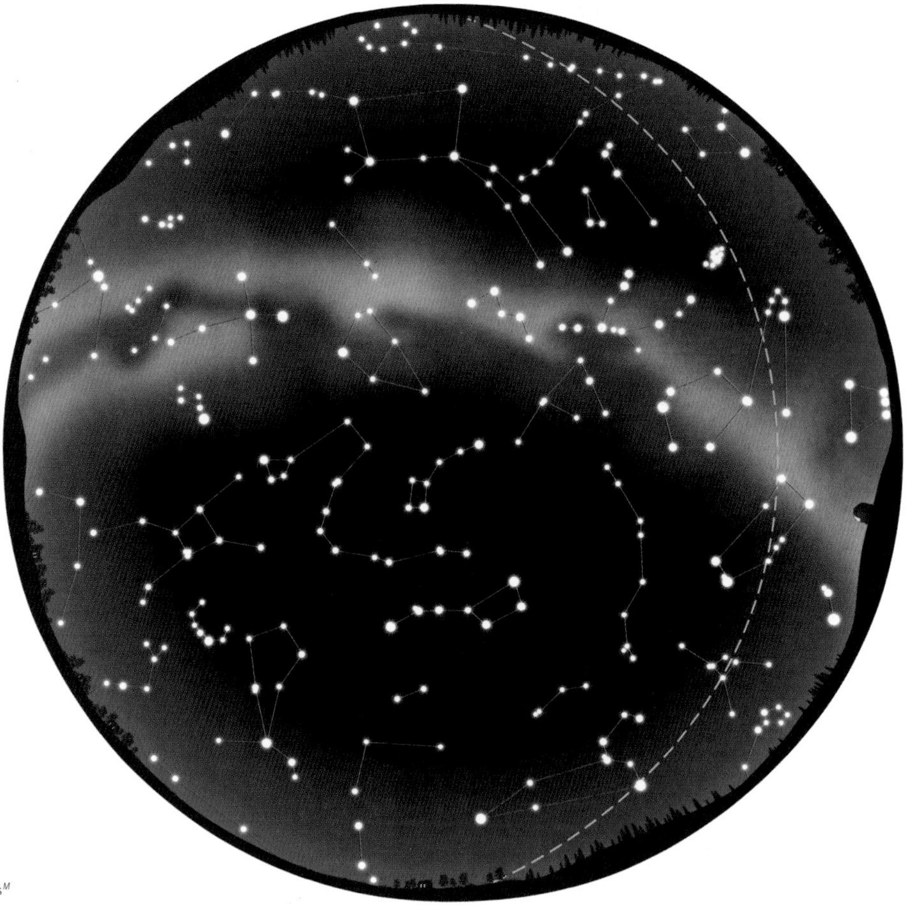

1
Pisces
Piscis^M
Poissons^M
Fische^M
Pesci^M

2
Whale
Ballena^F
Baleine^F
Walfisch^M
Balena^F

3
Aries
Aries^M
Bélier^M
Widder^M
Ariete^M

4
Triangle
Triángulo^M
Triangle^M
Dreieck^N
Triangolo^M Boreale

5
Andromeda
Andrómeda^F
Andromède
Andromeda^F
Andromeda^F

6
Pegasus
Pegaso^M
Pégase^M
Pegasus^M
Pegaso^M

7
Little Horse
Caballo^M Menor
Petit Cheval^M
Füllen^N
Cavalluccio^M

8
Dolphin
Delfín^M
Dauphin^M
Delphin^M
Delfino^M

9
Aquila, the Eagle
Águila^F
Aigle^M
Adler^M
Aquila^F

10
Arrow
Flecha^F
Flèche^F
Pfeil^M
Saetta^F

11
Swan
Cisne^M
Cygne^M
Schwan^M
Cigno^M

12
Lizard
Lagarto^M
Lézard^M
Eidechse^F
Lucertola^F

13
Cepheus
Cefeo^M
Céphée
Kepheus^M
Cefeo^M

14
Cassiopeia
Casiopea^F
Cassiopée
Kassiopeia^F
Cassiopea^F

15
Perseus
Perseo^M
Persée
Perseus^M
Perseo^M

16
Taurus
Tauro^M
Taureau^M
Stier^M
Toro^M

17
Orion
Orión^M
Orion
Orion^M
Orione^M

18
Charioteer
Cochero^M
Cocher^M
Fuhrmann^M
Cocchiere^M

19
Giraffe
Jirafa^F
Girafe^F
Giraffe^F
Giraffa^F

20
Lynx
Lince^M
Lynx^M
Luchs^M
Lince^F

21
Little Bear
Osa^F Menor
Petite Ourse^F
Kleiner Bär^M
Orsa^F Minore

constellations of the northern hemisphere

22
Dragon
Dragón[M]
Dragon[M]
Drache[M]
Dragone[M]

23
Lyre
Lira[F]
Lyre[F]
Leier[F]
Lira[F]

24
Serpent Bearer
Ofiuco[M]
Ophiuchus
Schlangenträger[M]
Ofiuco[M]

25
Hercules
Hércules[M]
Hercule
Herkules[M]
Ercole[M]

26
Serpent
Serpiente[F]
Serpent[M]
Schlange[F]
Serpente[M]

27
Northern Crown
Corona[F] Boreal
Couronne[F] boréale
Nördliche Krone[F]
Corona[F] Boreale

28
Herdsman
Boyero[M]
Bouvier[M]
Bärenhüter[M]
Boote[M]

29
Virgo
Virgo[F]
Vierge[F]
Jungfrau[F]
Vergine[F]

30
Berenice's Hair
Caballera[F] de Berenice[F]
Chevelure[F] de Bérénice
Haar[F] der Berenike[F]
Chioma[F] di Berenice

31
Hunting Dogs
Lebreles[M]
Chiens[M] de Chasse[F]
Jagdhunde[M]
Levrieri[M]

32
Great Bear
Osa[F] Mayor
Grande Ourse[F]
Großer Bär[M]
Orsa[F] Maggiore

33
Smaller Lion (Leo Minor)
León[M] Menor
Petit Lion[M]
Kleiner Löwe[M]
Leoncino[M]

34
Leo
León[M]
Lion[M]
Löwe[M]
Leone[M]

35
Water Monster (Hydra)
Hidra[F] Hembra
Hydre[F] femelle
Nördliche Wasserschlange[F]
Idra[F] Femmina

36
Cancer
Cáncer[M]
Cancer[M]
Krebs[M]
Cancro[M]

37
Little Dog (Canis Minor)
Can[M] Menor
Petit Chien[M]
Kleiner Hund[M]
Cane[M] Minore

38
Gemini
Géminis[F]
Gémeaux[M]
Zwillinge[M]
Gemelli[M]

39
Fox
Zorra[F]
Petit Renard[M]
Füchslein[M]
Volpetta[F]

40
Milky Way
Vía[F] Láctea
Voie[F] lactée
Milchstraße[F]
Via[F] Lattea

41
North Star (Polaris)
Estrella[F] Polar
Étoile[F] Polaire
Polarstern[M]
Stella[F] Polare

celestial coordinate system

sistema[M] de coordenadas[F] astronómicas | coordonnées[F] célestes | Koordinatensystem[N] der Himmelskugel[F] | sistema[M] di coordinate[F] celesti

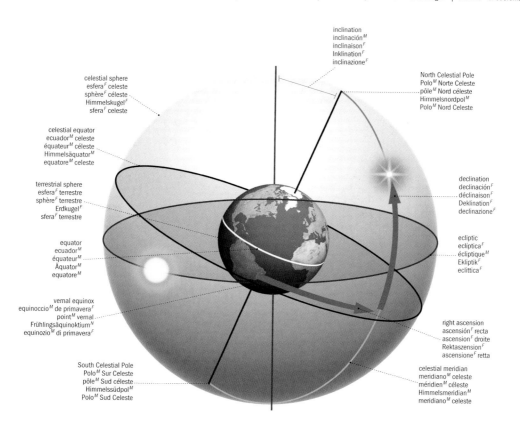

inclination
inclinación[M]
inclinaison[F]
Inklination[F]
inclinazione[F]

North Celestial Pole
Polo[M] Norte Celeste
pôle[M] Nord céleste
Himmelsnordpol[M]
Polo[M] Nord Celeste

celestial sphere
esfera[F] celeste
sphère[F] céleste
Himmelskugel[F]
sfera[F] celeste

celestial equator
ecuador[M] celeste
équateur[M] céleste
Himmelsäquator[M]
equatore[M] celeste

declination
declinación[F]
déclinaison[F]
Deklination[F]
declinazione[F]

terrestrial sphere
esfera[F] terrestre
sphère[F] terrestre
Erdkugel[F]
sfera[F] terrestre

ecliptic
ecliptica[F]
écliptique[M]
Ekliptik[F]
eclittica[F]

equator
ecuador[M]
équateur[M]
Äquator[M]
equatore[M]

vernal equinox
equinoccio[M] de primavera[F]
point[M] vernal
Frühlingsäquinoktium[N]
equinozio[M] di primavera[F]

right ascension
ascensión[F] recta
ascension[F] droite
Rektaszension[F]
ascensione[F] retta

South Celestial Pole
Polo[M] Sur Celeste
pôle[M] Sud céleste
Himmelssüdpol[M]
Polo[M] Sud Celeste

celestial meridian
meridiano[M] celeste
méridien[M] céleste
Himmelsmeridian[M]
meridiano[M] celeste

refracting telescope

telescopio^M refractor | lunette^F astronomique | Linsenfernrohr^N | cannocchiale^M

finderscope
anteojo^M buscador
chercheur^M
Suchfernrohr^N
cannocchiale^M cercatore

cradle
abrazadera^F
bride^F de fixation^F
Wiege^F
giogo^M di supporto^M

main tube
tubo^M principal
tube^M
Tubus^M
tubo^M principale

dew shield
parasol^M
pare-soleil^M
Sonnenblende^F
paraluce^M

eyepiece
ocular^M
oculaire^M
Okular^N
oculare^M

eyepiece holder
portaocular^M
tube^M porte-oculaire^M
Okularhalterung^F
portaoculare^M

declination setting scale
círculo^M graduado de declinación^F
cercle^M de déclinaison^F
Einstellung^F der Deklinationsachse^F
cerchio^M graduato della declinazione^F

star diagonal
ocular^M acodado
oculaire^M coudé
Zenitprisma^N
prisma^M astronomico

azimuth clamp
palanca^F de bloqueo^M del acimut^M
vis^F de blocage^F (azimut^M)
Azimutfeststeller^M
leva^F di bloccaggio^M dell'asse^M orizzontale

focusing knob
botón^M de enfoque^M
bouton^M de mise^F au point^M
Scharfeinstellung^F
manopola^F della messa^F a fuoco^M

altitude clamp
palanca^F de bloqueo^M de la altura^F
vis^F de blocage^F (latitude^F)
Höhenfeststeller^M
leva^F di bloccaggio^M dell'altezza^F

azimuth fine adjustment
ajuste^M fino del acimut^M
réglage^M micrométrique (azimut^M)
Azimutfeineinstellung^F
regolazione^F micrometrica dell'asse^M orizzontale

right ascension setting scale
anillo^M graduado^M de ascensión^F recta
cercle^M d'ascension^F droite
Einstellung^F der Rektaszensionsachse^F
cerchio^M graduato dell'ascensione^F retta

altitude fine adjustment
ajuste^M fino de la altura^F
réglage^M micrométrique (latitude^F)
Höhenfeineinstellung^F
regolazione^F micrometrica dell'altezza^F

counterweight
contrapeso^M
contrepoids^M
Gegengewicht^N
contrappeso^M

fork
horquilla^F
fourche^F
Gabel^F
forcella^F

tripod accessories shelf
repisa^F para accesorios^M
plateau^M pour accessoires^M
Stativablage^F
mensola^F portaccessori

tripod
tripode^M
trépied^M
Stativ^N
treppiede^M

cross section of a refracting telescope
sección^F transversal de un telescopio^M refractor
coupe^F d'une lunette^F astronomique
Linsenfernrohr^N im Querschnitt^M
sezione^F di un cannocchiale^M

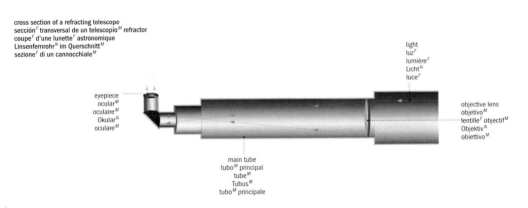

light
luz^F
lumière^F
Licht^N
luce^F

eyepiece
ocular^M
oculaire^M
Okular^N
oculare^M

objective lens
objetivo^M
lentille^F objectif^M
Objektiv^N
obiettivo^M

main tube
tubo^M principal
tube^M
Tubus^M
tubo^M principale

ASTRONOMY

reflecting telescope

telescopio^M reflector | télescope^M | Spiegelteleskop^N | telescopio^M

finderscope
anteojo^M buscador
chercheur^M
Suchfernrohr^N
cannocchiale^M cercatore

eyepiece
ocular^M
oculaire^M
Okular^N
oculare^M

cradle
abrazadera^F
bride^F de fixation^F
Wiege^F
giogo^M di supporto^M

support
soporte^M
support^M de fixation^F
Halterung^F
supporto^M

main tube
tubo^M principal
tube^M
Tubus^M
tubo^M principale

focusing knob
botón^M de enfoque^M
bouton^M de mise^F au point^M
Scharfeinstellung^F
manopola^F della messa^F a fuoco^M

declination setting scale
anillo^M graduado de declinación^F
cercle^M de déclinaison^F
Einstellung^F der Deklinationsachse^F
cerchio^M graduato della declinazione^F

right ascension setting scale
anillo^M graduado de ascensión^F recta
cercle^M d'ascension^F droite
Einstellung der Rektaszensionsachse^F
cerchio^M graduato dell'ascensione^F retta

azimuth fine adjustment
ajuste^M fino del acimut^M
réglage^M micrométrique (azimut^M)
Azimutfeineinstellung^F
regolazione^F micrometrica dell'asse^M orizzontale

azimuth clamp
palanca^F de bloqueo^M del acimut^M
vis^F de blocage^M (azimut^M)
Azimutfeststeller^M
leva^F di bloccaggio^M dell'asse^M orizzontale

altitude clamp
palanca^F de bloqueo^M de la altura^F
vis^F de blocage^M (latitude^F)
Höhenfeststeller^M
leva^F di bloccaggio^M dell'altezza^F

altitude fine adjustment
ajuste^M fino de la altura^F
réglage^M micrométrique (latitude^F)
Höhenfeineinstellung^F
regolazione^F micrometrica dell'altezza^F

cross section of a reflecting telescope
sección^F transversal de un telecopio^M reflector
coupe^F d'un télescope^M
Spiegelteleskop^N im Querschnitt^M
sezione^F di un telescopio^M

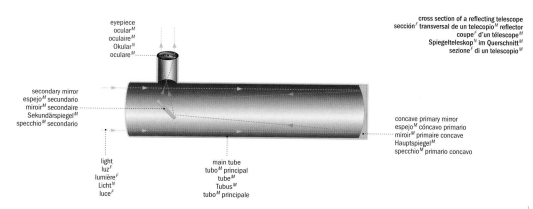

eyepiece
ocular^M
oculaire^M
Okular^N
oculare^M

secondary mirror
espejo^M secundario
miroir^M secondaire
Sekundärspiegel^M
specchio^M secondario

concave primary mirror
espejo^M cóncavo primario
miroir^M primaire concave
Hauptspiegel^M
specchio^M primario concavo

light
luz^F
lumière^F
Licht^N
luce^F

main tube
tubo^M principal
tube^M
Tubus^M
tubo^M principale

radio telescope

radiotelescopio^M | radiotélescope^M | Radioteleskop^N | radiotelescopio^M

ASTRONOMY

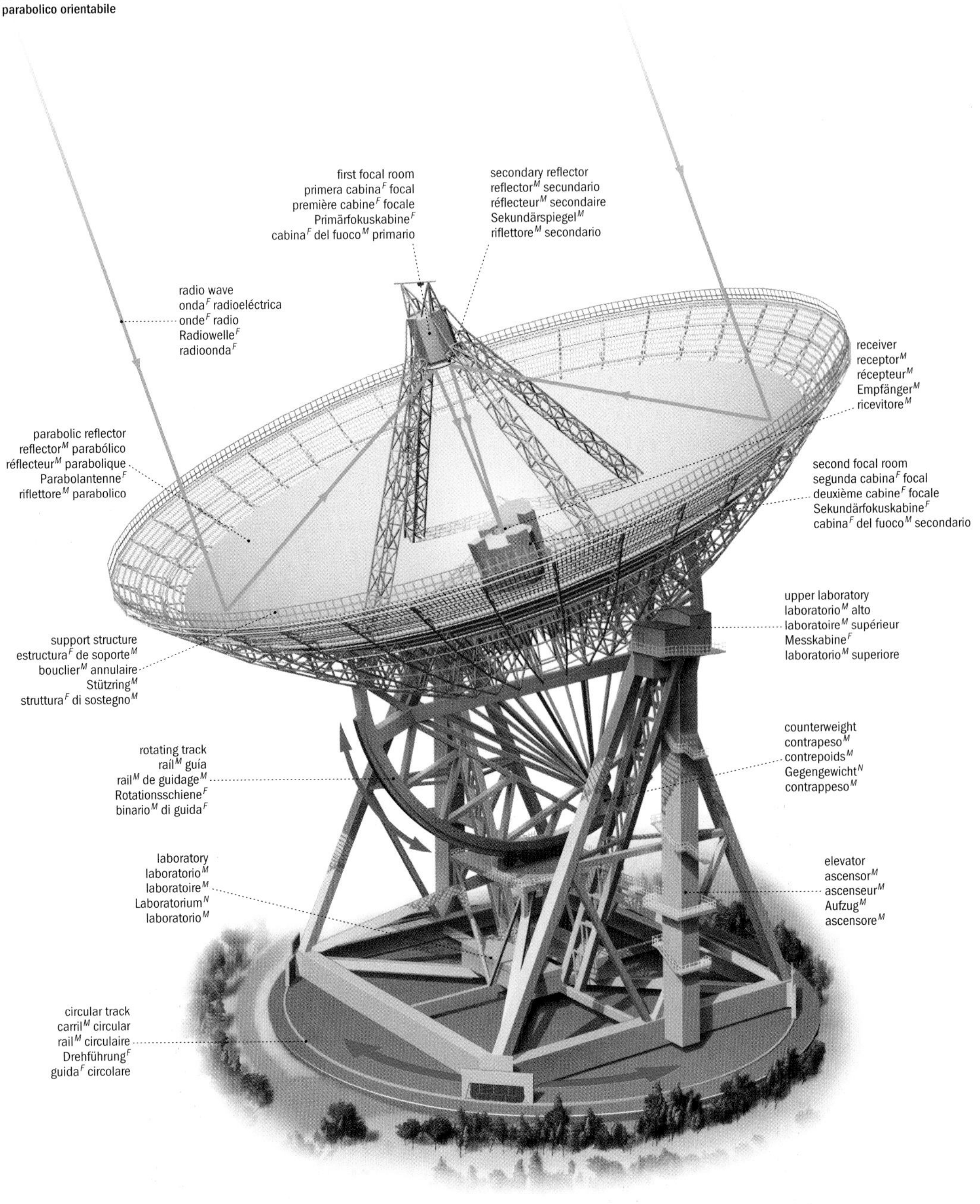

steerable parabolic reflector
reflector^M parabólico móvil
réflecteur^M parabolique orientable
schwenkbare Parabolantenne^F
riflettore^M parabolico orientabile

first focal room
primera cabina^F focal
première cabine^F focale
Primärfokuskabine^F
cabina^F del fuoco^M primario

secondary reflector
reflector^M secundario
réflecteur^M secondaire
Sekundärspiegel^M
riflettore^M secondario

radio wave
onda^F radioeléctrica
onde^F radio
Radiowelle^F
radioonda^F

receiver
receptor^M
récepteur^M
Empfänger^M
ricevitore^M

parabolic reflector
reflector^M parabólico
réflecteur^M parabolique
Parabolantenne^F
riflettore^M parabolico

second focal room
segunda cabina^F focal
deuxième cabine^F focale
Sekundärfokuskabine^F
cabina^F del fuoco^M secondario

support structure
estructura^F de soporte^M
bouclier^M annulaire
Stützring^M
struttura^F di sostegno^M

upper laboratory
laboratorio^M alto
laboratoire^M supérieur
Messkabine^F
laboratorio^M superiore

rotating track
rail^M guía
rail^M de guidage^M
Rotationsschiene^F
binario^M di guida^F

counterweight
contrapeso^M
contrepoids^M
Gegengewicht^N
contrappeso^M

laboratory
laboratorio^M
laboratoire^M
Laboratorium^N
laboratorio^M

elevator
ascensor^M
ascenseur^M
Aufzug^M
ascensore^M

circular track
carril^M circular
rail^M circulaire
Drehführung^F
guida^F circolare

ASTRONOMY

Hubble space telescope

telescopio[M] espacial Hubble | télescope[M] spatial Hubble | Hubble-Weltraumteleskop[N] | telescopio[M] spaziale Hubble

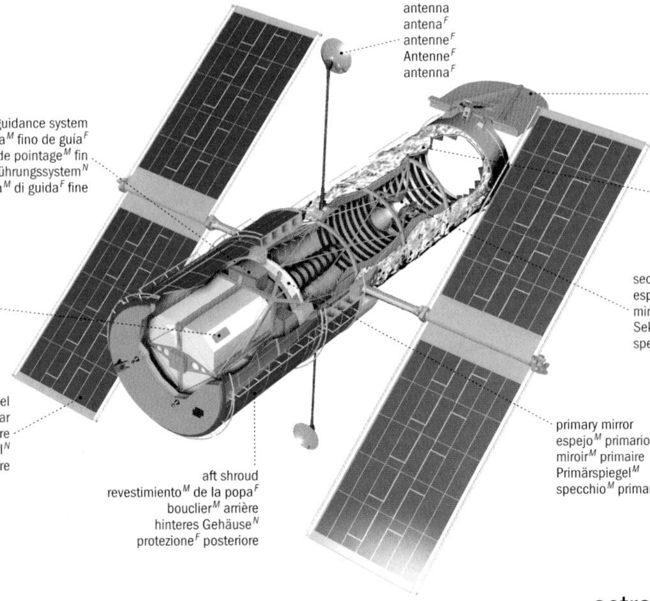

antenna
antena[F]
antenne[F]
Antenne[F]
antenna[F]

aperture door
puerta[F]
volet[M] mobile
Blendenöffnung[F]
portello[M] di apertura[F]

fine guidance system
sistema[M] fino de guía[F]
système[M] de pointage[M] fin
Feinnachführungssystem[N]
sistema[M] di guida[F] fine

light shield
escudo[M] solar
écran[M] protecteur
Lichtschutzschirm[M]
schermo[M]

secondary mirror
espejo[M] secundario
miroir[M] secondaire
Sekundärspiegel[M]
specchio[M] secondario

scientific instruments
instrumentos[M] científicos
appareils[M] scientifiques
Instrumente[N]
strumenti[M] scientifici

solar panel
panel[M] solar
panneau[M] solaire
Sonnensegel[N]
pannello[M] solare

primary mirror
espejo[M] primario
miroir[M] primaire
Primärspiegel[M]
specchio[M] primario

aft shroud
revestimiento[M] de la popa[F]
bouclier[M] arrière
hinteres Gehäuse[N]
protezione[F] posteriore

astronomical observatory

observatorio[M] astronómico | observatoire[M] astronomique | Sternwarte[F] | osservatorio[M] astronomico

cross section of an astronomical observatory
sección[M] transversal de un observatorio[M] astronómico
coupe[F] d'un observatoire[M] astronomique
Querschnitt[M] durch eine Sternwarte[F]
sezione[F] trasversale di un osservatorio[M] astronomico

secondary mirror
espejo[M] secundario
miroir[M] secondaire
Sekundärspiegel[M]
specchio[M] secondario

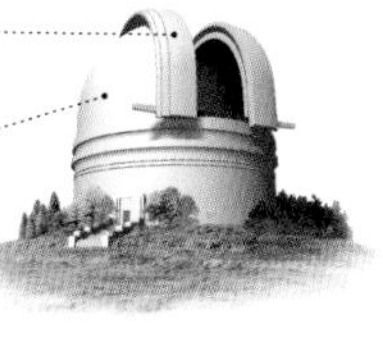

observatory
observatorio[M]
observatoire[M]
Sternwarte[F]
osservatorio[M]

dome shutter
obturador[M] de la cúpula[F]
cimier[M] mobile
Kuppelspaltabdeckung[F]
portellone[M] della cupola[F]

light
luz[F]
lumière[F]
Licht[N]
luce[F]

telescope
telescopio[M]
télescope[M]
Teleskop[N]
telescopio[M]

rotating dome
cúpula[F] giratoria
coupole[F] rotative
Drehkuppel[F]
cupola[F] rotante

flat mirror
espejo[M] plano
miroir[M] plan rétractable
ebener Spiegel[M]
specchio[M] piano

prime focus
foco[M] primario
foyer[M] primaire
Primärfokus[M]
fuoco[M] primario

horseshoe mount
montura[F] en herradura[F]
monture[F] en fer[M] à cheval[M]
Hufeisenmontierung[F]
montatura[F] a ferro di cavallo[M]

prime focus observing capsule
cabina[F] en el foco[M] primario
nacelle[F] d'observation[F]
Primärfokuskabine[F]
cabina[F] di osservazione[F] del fuoco[M] primario

hour angle gear
ángulo[M] horario
engrenage[M] horaire
Stundenwinkelantrieb[M]
ingranaggio[M] per il moto[M] orario

interior dome shell
cubierta[F] interior de la cúpula[F]
enveloppe[F] intérieure
innere Kuppelhülle[F]
volta[F] interna della cupola[F]

polar axis
eje[M] polar
axe[M] horaire
Polachse[F]
asse[M] polare

exterior dome shell
cubierta[F] exterior de la cúpula[F]
enveloppe[F] extérieure
äußere Kuppelhülle[F]
volta[F] esterna della cupola[F]

telescope base
base[F] del telescopio[M]
base[F]
Podest[N]
basamento[M] del telescopio[M]

observation post
puesto[M] de observación[F]
poste[F] d'observation[F]
Beobachtungsposten[M]
punto[M] di osservazione[F]

Cassegrain focus
foco[M] Cassegrain
foyer[M] Cassegrain
Cassegrain-Fokus[M]
fuoco[M] Cassegrain

primary mirror
espejo[M] primario
miroir[M] primaire concave
Hauptspiegel[M]
specchio[M] primario

coudé focus
foco[M] coudé
foyer[M] coudé
Coudé-Fokus[M]
fuoco[M] coudé

laboratory
laboratorio[M]
laboratoire[M]
Labor[N]
laboratorio[M]

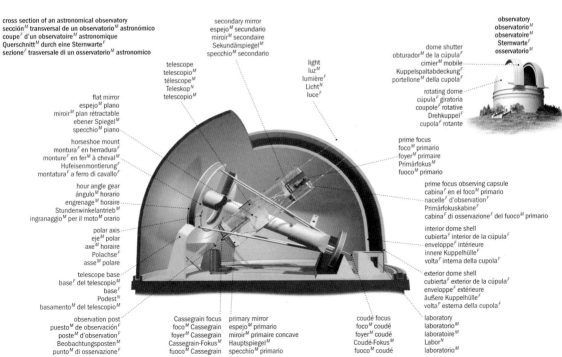

17

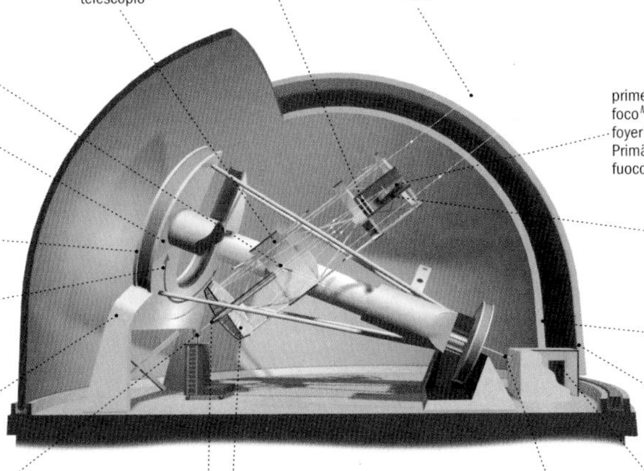

space probe

sonda^F espacial | sonde^F spatiale | Raumsonde^F | sonda^F spaziale

orbiter (Viking)
módulo^M orbital (Viking)
orbiteur^M (Viking)
Orbiter^M (Viking)
modulo^M orbitante (Viking)

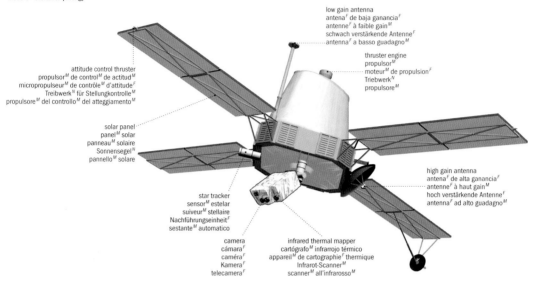

low gain antenna
antena^F de baja ganancia^F
antenne^F à faible gain^M
schwach verstärkende Antenne^F
antenna^F a basso guadagno^M

thruster engine
propulsor^M
moteur^M de propulsion^F
Triebwerk^N
propulsore^M

attitude control thruster
propulsor^M de control^M de actitud^M
micropropulseur^M de contrôle^M d'attitude^F
Treibwerk^N für Stellungkontrolle^M
propulsore^M del controllo^M del atteggiamento^M

solar panel
panel^M solar
panneau^M solaire
Sonnensegel^N
pannello^M solare

high gain antenna
antena^F de alta ganancia^F
antenne^F à haut gain^M
hoch verstärkende Antenne^F
antenna^F ad alto guadagno^M

star tracker
sensor^M estelar
suiveur^M stellaire
Nachführungseinheit^F
sestante^M automatico

camera
cámara^F
caméra^F
Kamera^F
telecamera^F

infrared thermal mapper
cartógrafo^M infrarrojo térmico
appareil^M de cartographie^F thermique
Infrarot-Scanner^M
scanner^M all'infrarosso^M

lander (Viking)
módulo^M de aterrizaje^M (Viking)
atterrisseur^M (Viking)
Landemodul^N (Viking)
modulo^M di atterraggio^M (Viking)

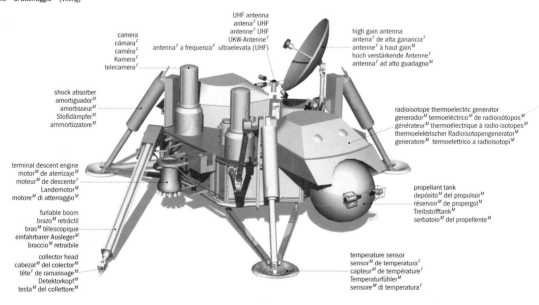

UHF antenna
antena^F UHF
antenne^F UHF
UKW-Antenne^F
antenna^F a frequenza^F ultraelevata (UHF)

camera
cámara^F
caméra^F
Kamera^F
telecamera^F

high gain antenna
antena^F de alta ganancia^F
antenne^F à haut gain^M
hoch verstärkende Antenne^F
antenna^F ad alto guadagno^M

shock absorber
amortiguador^M
amortisseur^M
Stoßdämpfer^M
ammortizzatore^M

radioisotope thermoelectric generator
generador^M termoeléctrico^M de radioisótopos^M
générateur^M thermoélectrique à radio-isotopes^M
thermoelektrischer Radioisotopengenerator^M
generatore^M termoelettrico a radioisotopi^M

terminal descent engine
motor^M de aterrizaje^M
moteur^M de descente^F
Landemotor^M
motore^M di atterraggio^M

furlable boom
brazo^M retráctil
bras^M télescopique
einfahrbarer Ausleger^M
braccio^M retraibile

propellant tank
depósito^M del propulsor^M
réservoir^M de propergol^M
Treibstofftank^M
serbatoio^M del propellente^M

collector head
cabezal^M del colector^M
tête^F de ramassage^M
Detektorkopf^M
testa^M del collettore^M

temperature sensor
sensor^M de temperatura^F
capteur^M de température^F
Temperaturfühler^M
sensore^M di temperatura^F

space probe

ASTRONOMY

examples of space probes
ejemplos[M] **de sondas**[F] **espaciales**
exemples[M] **de sondes**[F] **spatiales**
Beispiele[N] **für Raumsonden**[F]
esempi[M] **di sonde**[F] **spaziali**

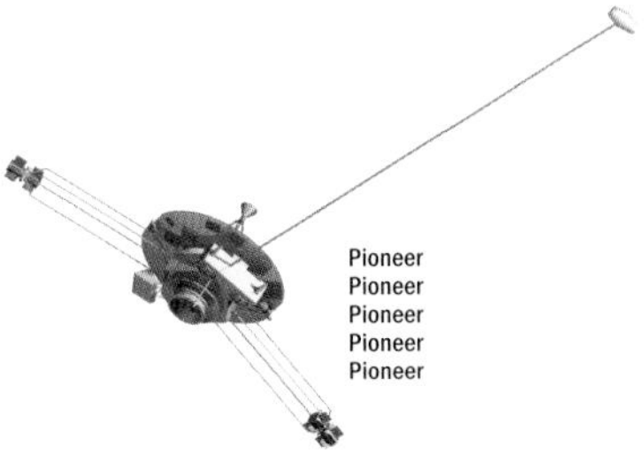

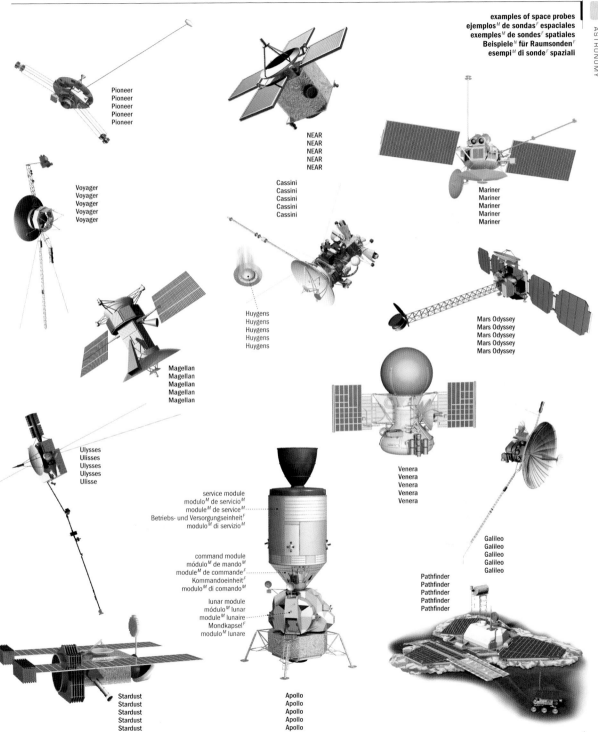

Pioneer
Pioneer
Pioneer
Pioneer
Pioneer

NEAR
NEAR
NEAR
NEAR
NEAR

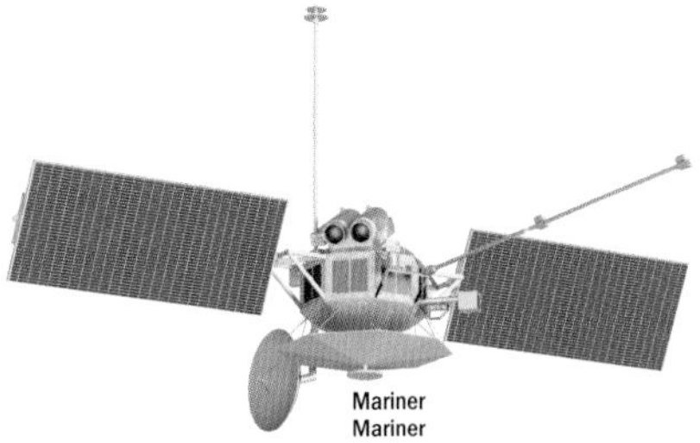

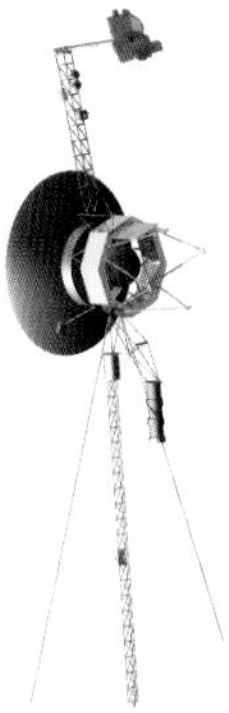

Voyager
Voyager
Voyager
Voyager
Voyager

Cassini
Cassini
Cassini
Cassini
Cassini

Mariner
Mariner
Mariner
Mariner
Mariner
Mariner

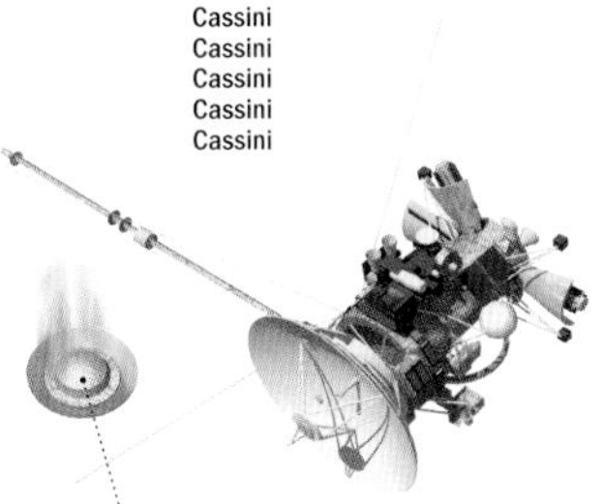

Huygens
Huygens
Huygens
Huygens
Huygens

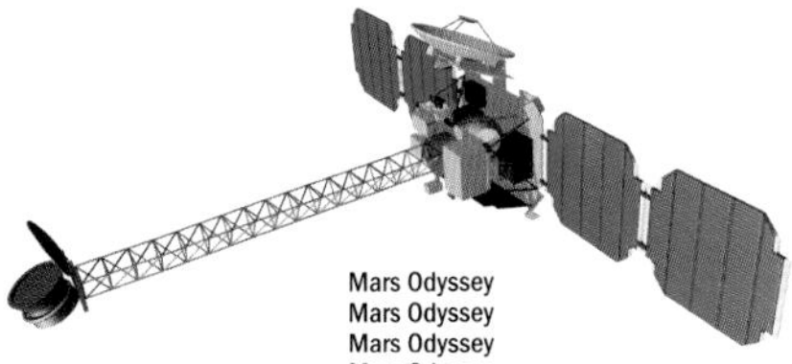

Mars Odyssey
Mars Odyssey
Mars Odyssey
Mars Odyssey
Mars Odyssey

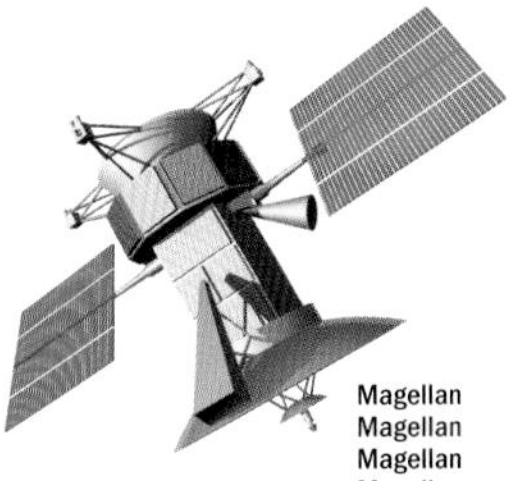

Magellan
Magellan
Magellan
Magellan
Magellan

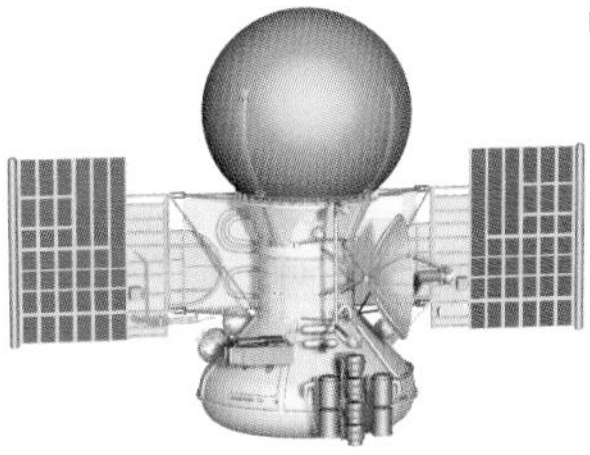

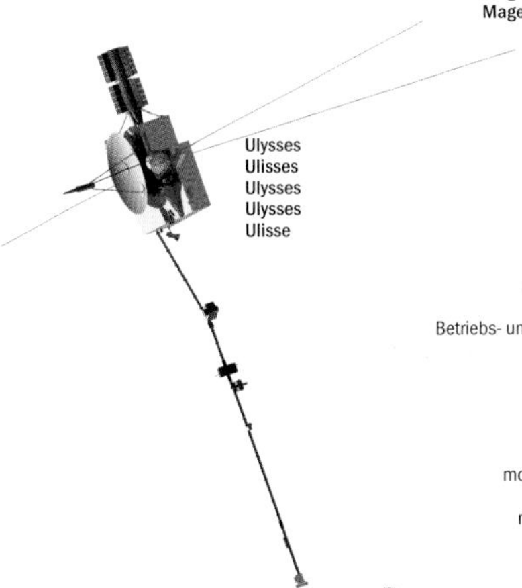

Ulysses
Ulisses
Ulysses
Ulysses
Ulisse

Venera
Venera
Venera
Venera
Venera

service module
modulo[M] de servicio[M]
module[M] de service[M]
Betriebs- und Versorgungseinheit[F]
modulo[M] di servizio[M]

command module
módulo[M] de mando[M]
module[M] de commande[F]
Kommandoeinheit[F]
modulo[M] di comando[M]

lunar module
módulo[M] lunar
module[M] lunaire
Mondkapsel[F]
modulo[M] lunare

Galileo
Galileo
Galileo
Galileo
Galileo

Pathfinder
Pathfinder
Pathfinder
Pathfinder
Pathfinder

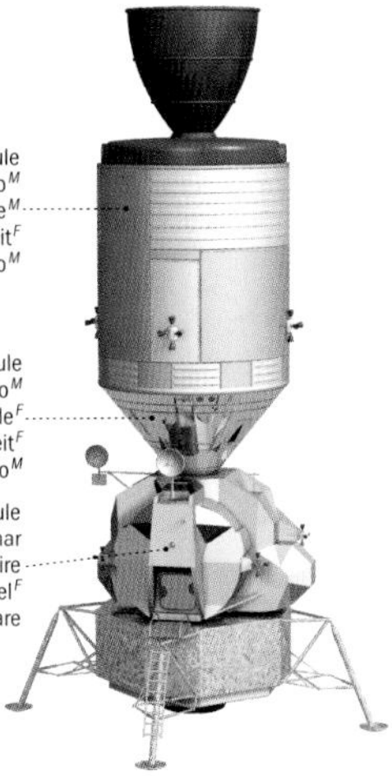

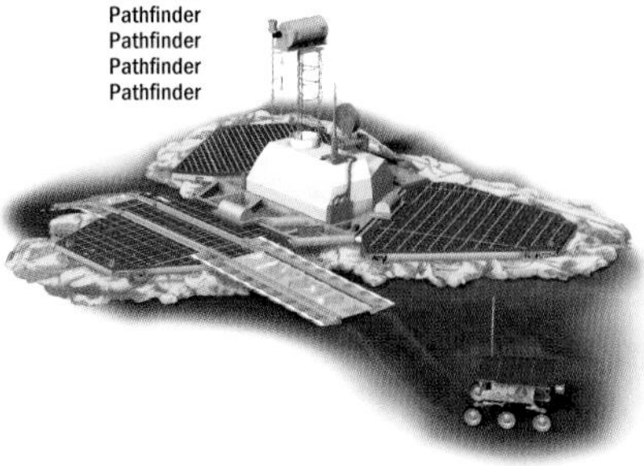

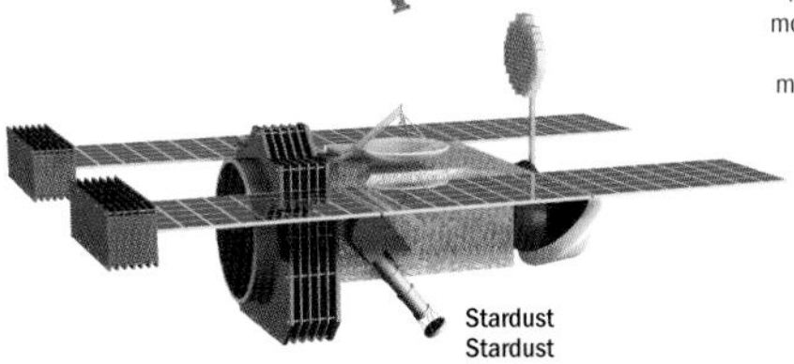

Stardust
Stardust
Stardust
Stardust
Stardust

Apollo
Apollo
Apollo
Apollo
Apollo

spacesuit

traje^M espacial | scaphandre^M spatial | Raumanzug^M | tuta^F spaziale

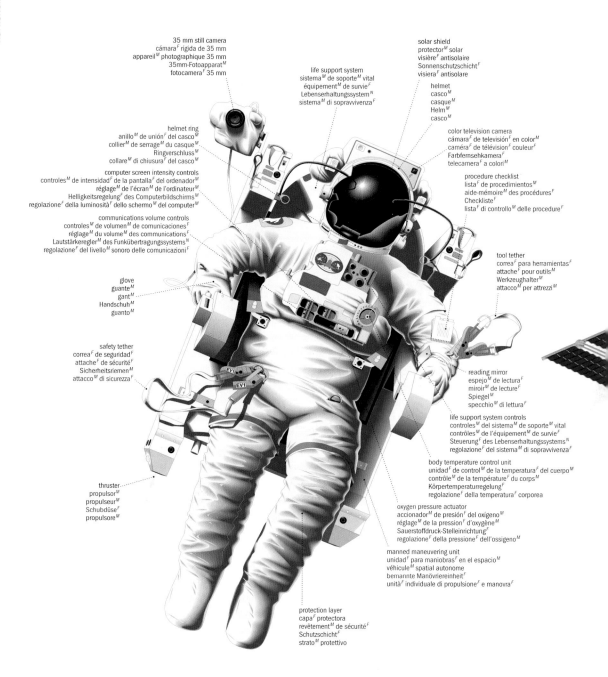

35 mm still camera
cámara^F rígida de 35 mm
appareil^M photographique 35 mm
35mm-Fotoapparat^M
fotocamera^F 35 mm

life support system
sistema^M de soporte^M vital
équipement^M de survie^F
Lebenserhaltungssystem^N
sistema^M di sopravvivenza^F

solar shield
protector^M solar
visière^F antisolaire
Sonnenschutzschicht^F
visiera^F antisolare

helmet
casco^M
casque^M
Helm^M
casco^M

helmet ring
anillo^M de unión^F del casco^M
collier^M de serrage^M du casque^M
Ringverschluss^M
collare^M di chiusura^F del casco^M

color television camera
cámara^F de televisión^F en color^M
caméra^F de télévision^F couleur^F
Farbfernsehkamera^F
telecamera^F a colori^M

computer screen intensity controls
controles^M de intensidad^F de la pantalla^F del ordenador^M
réglage^M de l'écran^M de l'ordinateur^M
Helligkeitsregelung^F des Computerbildschirms^M
regolazione^F della luminosità^F dello schermo^M del computer^M

procedure checklist
lista^F de procedimientos^M
aide-mémoire^M des procédures^F
Checkliste^F
lista^F di controllo^M delle procedure^F

communications volume controls
controles^M de volumen^M de comunicaciones^F
réglage^M du volume^M des communications^F
Lautstärkeregler^M des Funkübertragungssystems^N
regolazione^F del livello^M sonoro delle comunicazioni^F

tool tether
correa^F para herramientas^F
attache^F pour outils^M
Werkzeughalter^M
attacco^M per attrezzi^M

glove
guante^M
gant^M
Handschuh^M
guanto^M

reading mirror
espejo^M de lectura^F
miroir^M de lecture^F
Spiegel^M
specchio^M di lettura^F

safety tether
correa^F de seguridad^F
attache^F de sécurité^F
Sicherheitsriemen^M
attacco^M di sicurezza^F

life support system controls
controles^M del sistema^M de soporte^M vital
contrôles^M de l'équipement^M de survie^F
Steuerung^F des Lebenserhaltungssystems^N
regolazione^F del sistema^M di sopravvivenza^F

body temperature control unit
unidad^F de control^M de la temperatura^F del cuerpo^M
contrôle^M de la température^F du corps^M
Körpertemperaturregelung^F
regolazione^F della temperatura^F corporea

thruster
propulsor^M
propulseur^M
Schubdüse^F
propulsore^M

oxygen pressure actuator
accionador^M de presión^F del oxígeno^M
réglage^M de la pression^F d'oxygène^M
Sauerstoffdruck-Stelleinrichtung^F
regolazione^F della pressione^F dell'ossigeno^M

manned maneuvering unit
unidad^F para maniobras^F en el espacio^M
véhicule^M spatial autonome
bemannte Manövriereinheit^F
unità^F individuale di propulsione^F e manovra^F

protection layer
capa^F protectora
revêtement^M de sécurité^F
Schutzschicht^F
strato^M protettivo

international space station

estación^F espacial internacional | station^F spatiale internationale | internationale Raumstation^F | stazione^F spaziale internazionale

mobile remote servicer
unidad^F móvil de servicio^M por control^M remoto
unité^F mobile d'entretien^M télécommandée
ferngesteuertes Servicemodul^N
unità^F di servizio^M mobile a distanza^F

radiators
radiadores^M
radiateurs^M
Radiatoren^M
radiatori^M

truss structure
viga^F maestra
structure^F en treillis^M
Trägerstruktur^F
travatura^F reticolare

photovoltaic arrays
paneles^M fotovoltaicos
panneaux^M solaires
Solarzellengenerator^M
moduli^M fotovoltaici

Russian module
módulo^M ruso
module^M russe
russisches Modul^N
modulo^M russo

remote manipulator system
brazo^M por control^M remoto
télémanipulateur^M
Roboterarm^M
braccio^M telecomandato

centrifuge module
módulo^M centrifugo
centrifugeuse^F
Schwerkraftmodul^N
modulo^M centrifugo

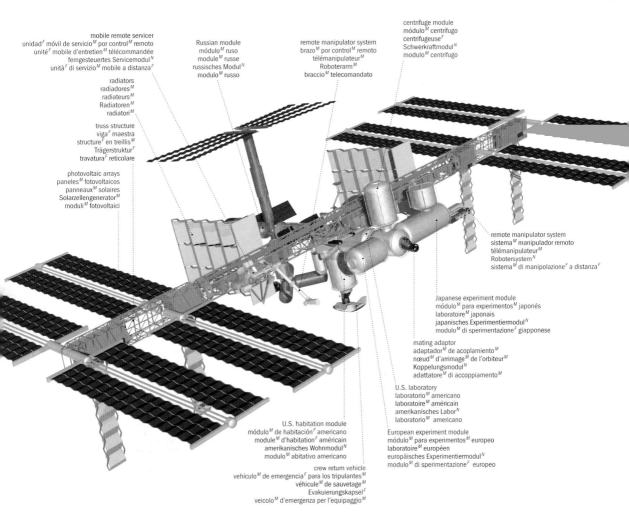

remote manipulator system
sistema^M manipulador remoto
télémanipulateur^M
Robotersystem^N
sistema^M di manipolazione^F a distanza^F

Japanese experiment module
módulo^M para experimentos^M japonés
laboratoire^M japonais
japanisches Experimentiermodul^N
modulo^M di sperimentazione^F giapponese

mating adaptor
adaptador^M de acoplamiento^M
nœud^M d'arrimage^M de l'orbiteur^M
Koppelungsmodul^N
adattatore^M di accoppiamento^M

U.S. laboratory
laboratorio^M americano
laboratoire^M américain
amerikanisches Labor^N
laboratorio^M americano

U.S. habitation module
módulo^M de habitación^F americano
module^M d'habitation^F américain
amerikanisches Wohnmodul^N
modulo^M abitativo americano

European experiment module
módulo^M para experimentos^M europeo
laboratoire^M européen
europäisches Experimentiermodul^N
modulo^M di sperimentazione^F europeo

crew return vehicle
vehículo^M de emergencia^F para los tripulantes^M
véhicule^M de sauvetage^M
Evakuierungskapsel^F
veicolo^M d'emergenza per l'equipaggio^M

space shuttle

ASTRONOMY

transbordador^M espacial | navette^F spatiale | Raumfähre^F | navetta^F spaziale

space shuttle at takeoff
transbordador^M espacial en posición^F de lanzamiento^M
navette^F spatiale au décollage^M
Raumfähre^F beim Start^M
navetta^F spaziale al decollo^M

external fuel tank
depósito^M externo de combustible^M
réservoir^M externe
Außentank^M
serbatoio^M esterno del combustibile^M

booster parachute
paracaídas^F auxiliar
parachute^M
Fallschirm^M für die Feststoffrakete^F
paracadute^M del booster^M

solid rocket booster
propulsor^M sólido
fusée^F à propergol^M solide
Feststoff^M-Booster^M
razzo^N a propellente^M solido

orbiter
orbitador^M
orbiteur^M
Orbiter^M
orbiter^M

remote manipulator system
sistema^M manipulador remoto
télémanipulateur^M
Roboterarm^M
braccio^M manipolatore^M telecomandato

cargo bay
bodega^F de carga^F
soute^F
Nutzlastraum^M
scomparto^M di carico^M

nozzle
propulsor^M
tuyère^F
Düse^F
ugello^M

flight deck
cabina^F de mando^M
habitacle^M
Cockpit^N
cabina^F di pilotaggio^M

surface insulation
recubrimiento^M aislante
revêtement^M thermique
Oberflächenisolierung^F
isolante^M termico

attitude control thrusters
propulsores^M de control^M de actitud^F
propulseurs^M de commande^M d'orientation^F
vorderes Rückstoßtriebwerk^N
propulsori^M per il controllo^M direzionale

heat shield
cubierta^F térmica
bouclier^M thermique
Hitzeschild^N
scudo^M termico

tile
loseta^F
tuile^F
Kachel^F
piastrella^F

side hatch
escotilla^F
écoutille^F d'accès^M
Seitenluke^F
portellone^M laterale

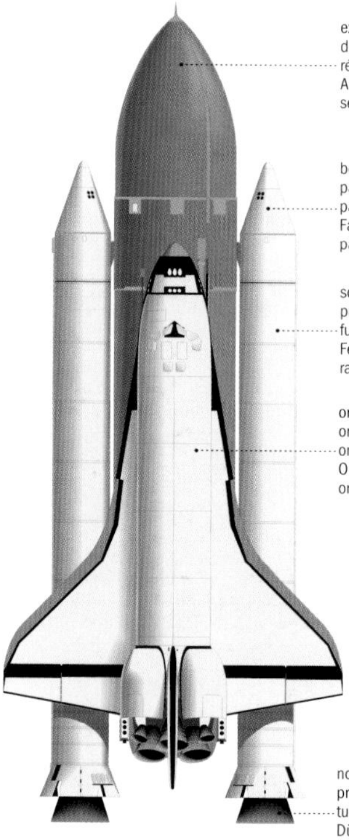

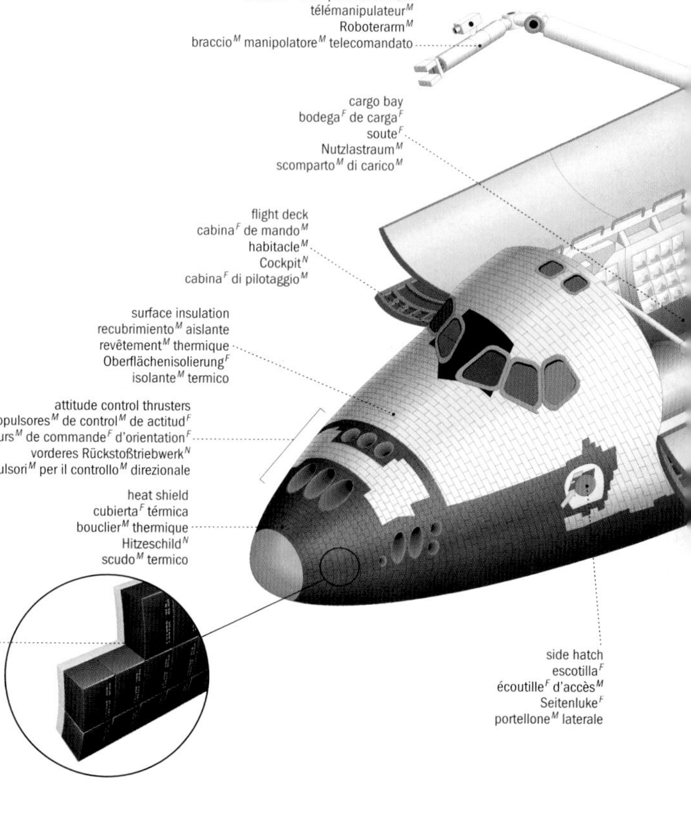

orbiter
orbitador[M]
orbiteur[M]
Orbiter[M]
orbiter[M]

scientific air lock
esclusa[F] científica de aire[M]
sas[M] du laboratoire[M]
Luftschleuse[F]
porta[F] del laboratorio[M] a tenuta[F] stagna

observation window
ventanilla[F] de observación[F]
hublot[M] d'observation[F]
Sichtfenster[N]
finestrino[M] di osservazione[F]

scientific instruments
instrumentos[M] científicos
instruments[M] scientifiques
wissenschaftliche Instrumente[N]
strumentazione[F] scientifica

hatch
escotilla[F]
écoutille[F]
Einstiegsluke[F]
boccaporto[M]

rudder
timón[M]
gouvernail[M]
Ruder[N]
timone[M]

main engine
motor[M] principal
moteur[M] principal
Haupttriebwerk[N]
motore[M] principale

maneuvering engine
propulsor[M] de maniobras[F]
moteur[M] de manœuvre[F]
Steuertriebwerk[N]
motore[M] di manovra[F]

tank
tanque[M]
réservoir[M]
Tank[M]
serbatoio[M]

body flap
aleta[F] de fuselaje[M]
volet[M]
hintere Klappe[F]
ipersostentatore[M]

elevon
alerón[M]
élevon[M]
Querruder[N]
elevone[M]

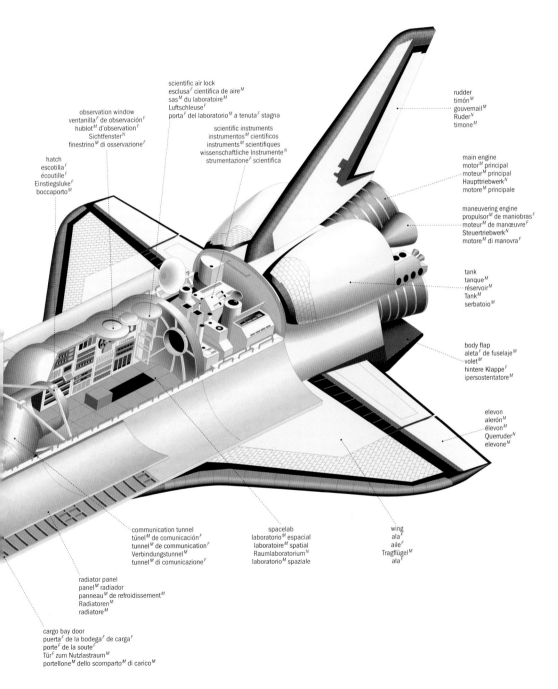

communication tunnel
túnel[M] de comunicación[F]
tunnel[M] de communication[F]
Verbindungstunnel[M]
tunnel[M] di comunicazione[F]

spacelab
laboratorio[M] espacial
laboratoire[M] spatial
Raumlaboratorium[N]
laboratorio[M] spaziale

wing
ala[F]
aile[F]
Tragflügel[M]
ala[F]

radiator panel
panel[M] radiador
panneau[M] de refroidissement[M]
Radiatoren[M]
radiatore[M]

cargo bay door
puerta[F] de la bodega[F] de carga[F]
porte[F] de la soute[F]
Tür[F] zum Nutzlastraum[M]
portellone[M] dello scomparto[M] di carico[M]

ASTRONOMY

space launcher

cohete^M espacial | lanceur^M spatial | Trägerrakete^F | razzo^M spaziale

cross section of a space launcher (Ariane V)
sección^M transversal de un lanzador^M espacial (Ariane V)
coupe^F d'un lanceur^M spatial (Ariane V)
Querschnitt^M durch eine Trägerrakete^F (Ariane V)
sezione^F trasversale di un razzo^M spaziale (Ariane V)

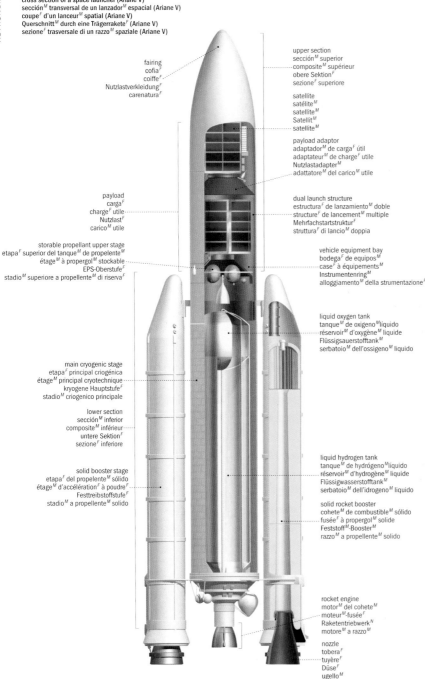

fairing
cofia^F
coiffe^F
Nutzlastverkleidung^F
carenatura^F

upper section
sección^M superior
composite^M supérieur
obere Sektion^F
sezione^F superiore

satellite
satélite^M
satellite^M
Satellit^M
satellite^M

payload adaptor
adaptador^M de carga^F útil
adaptateur^M de charge^F utile
Nutzlastadapter^M
adattatore^M del carico^M utile

payload
carga^F
charge^F utile
Nutzlast^F
carico^M utile

dual launch structure
estructura^F de lanzamiento^M doble
structure^F de lancement^M multiple
Mehrfachstartstruktur^F
struttura^F di lancio^M doppia

storable propellant upper stage
etapa^F superior del tanque^M de propelente^M
étage^M à propergol^M stockable
EPS-Oberstufe^F
stadio^M superiore a propellente^M di riserva^F

vehicle equipment bay
bodega^F de equipos^M
case^F à équipements^M
Instrumentenring^M
alloggiamento^M della strumentazione^F

liquid oxygen tank
tanque^M de oxígeno^M líquido
réservoir^M d'oxygène^M liquide
Flüssigsauerstofftank^M
serbatoio^M dell'ossigeno^M liquido

main cryogenic stage
etapa^F principal criogénica
étage^M principal cryotechnique
kryogene Hauptstufe^F
stadio^M criogenico principale

lower section
sección^M inferior
composite^M inférieur
untere Sektion^F
sezione^F inferiore

liquid hydrogen tank
tanque^M de hydrógeno^M líquido
réservoir^M d'hydrogène^M liquide
Flüssigwasserstofftank^M
serbatoio^M dell'idrogeno^M liquido

solid booster stage
etapa^F del propelente^M sólido
étage^M d'accélération^F à poudre^F
Festtreibstoffstufe^F
stadio^M a propellente^M solido

solid rocket booster
cohete^M de combustible^M sólido
fusée^F à propergol^M solide
Feststoff^M-Booster^M
razzo^M a propellente^M solido

rocket engine
motor^M del cohete^M
moteur^M-fusée^F
Raketentriebwerk^N
motore^M a razzo^M

nozzle
tobera^F
tuyère^F
Düse^F
ugello^M

examples of space launchers
ejemplos^M de lanzadores^M espaciales
exemples^M de lanceurs^M spatiaux
Beispiele^N für Trägerraketen^F
esempi^M di razzi^M spaziali

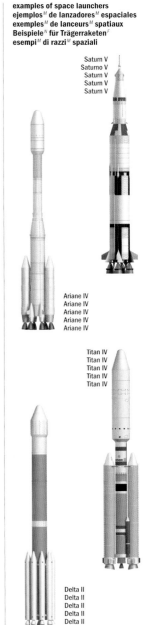

Saturn V
Saturno V
Saturn V
Saturn V
Saturn V

Ariane IV
Ariane IV
Ariane IV
Ariane IV
Ariane IV

Titan IV
Titan IV
Titan IV
Titan IV
Titan IV

Delta II
Delta II
Delta II
Delta II
Delta II

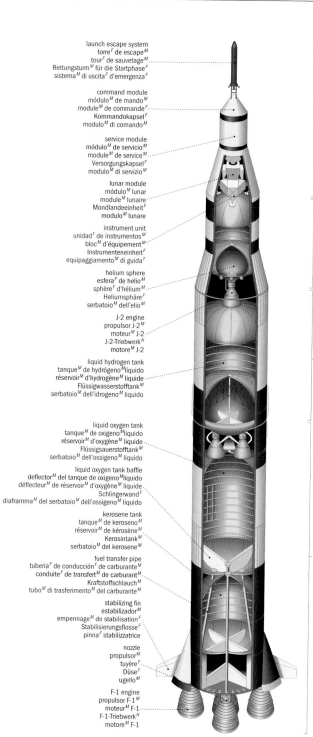

launch escape system
torre^F de escape^M
tour^F de sauvetage^M
Rettungsturm^M für die Startphase^F
sistema^M di uscita^F d'emergenza^F

command module
módulo^M de mando^M
module^M de commande^F
Kommandokapsel^F
modulo^M di comando^M

service module
módulo^M de servicio^M
module^M de service^M
Versorgungskapsel^F
modulo^M di servizio^M

lunar module
módulo^M lunar
module^M lunaire
Mondlandeeinheit^F
modulo^M lunare

instrument unit
unidad^F de instrumentos^M
bloc^F d'équipement^M
Instrumenteneinheit^F
equipaggiamento^M di guida^F

helium sphere
esfera^F de helio^M
sphère^F d'hélium^M
Heliumsphäre^F
serbatoio^M dell'elio^M

J-2 engine
propulsor J-2^M
moteur^M J-2
J-2-Triebwerk^N
motore^M J-2

liquid hydrogen tank
tanque^M de hydrógeno^{M}líquido
réservoir^M d'hydrogène^M liquide
Flüssigwasserstofftank^M
serbatoio^M dell'idrogeno^M liquido

liquid oxygen tank
tanque^M de oxigeno^{M}líquido
réservoir^M d'oxygène^M liquide
Flüssigsauerstofftank^M
serbatoio^M dell'ossigeno^M liquido

liquid oxygen tank baffle
deflector^M del tanque de oxigeno^{M}líquido
déflecteur^M de réservoir^M d'oxygène^M liquide
Schlingerwand^F
diaframma^M del serbatoio^M dell'ossigeno^M liquido

kerosene tank
tanque^M de keroseno^M
réservoir^M de kérosène^M
Kerosintank^M
serbatoio^M del kerosene^M

fuel transfer pipe
tubería^F de conducción^F de carburante^M
conduite^F de transfert^M de carburant^M
Kraftstoffschlauch^M
tubo^M di trasferimento^M del carburante^M

stabilizing fin
estabilizador^M
empennage^M de stabilisation^F
Stabilisierungsflosse^F
pinna^F stabilizzatrice

nozzle
propulsor^M
tuyère^F
Düse^F
ugello^M

F-1 engine
propulsor F-1^M
moteur^M F-1
F-1-Triebwerk^N
motore^M F-1

cross section of a space launcher (Saturn V)
sección^M transversal de un lanzador^M espacial (Saturno V)
coupe^F d'un lanceur^M spatial (Saturn V)
Querschnitt^M durch eine Trägerrakete^F (Saturn V)
sezione^F trasversale di un razzo^M spaziale (Saturn V)

payload
carga^F útil
charge^F utile
Nutzlast^F
carico^M utile

third stage
tercera etapa^F
troisième étage^M
dritte Stufe^F
terzo stadio^M

second stage
segunda etapa^F
deuxième étage^M
zweite Stufe^F
secondo stadio^M

first stage
primera etapa^F
premier étage^M
erste Stufe^F
primo stadio^M

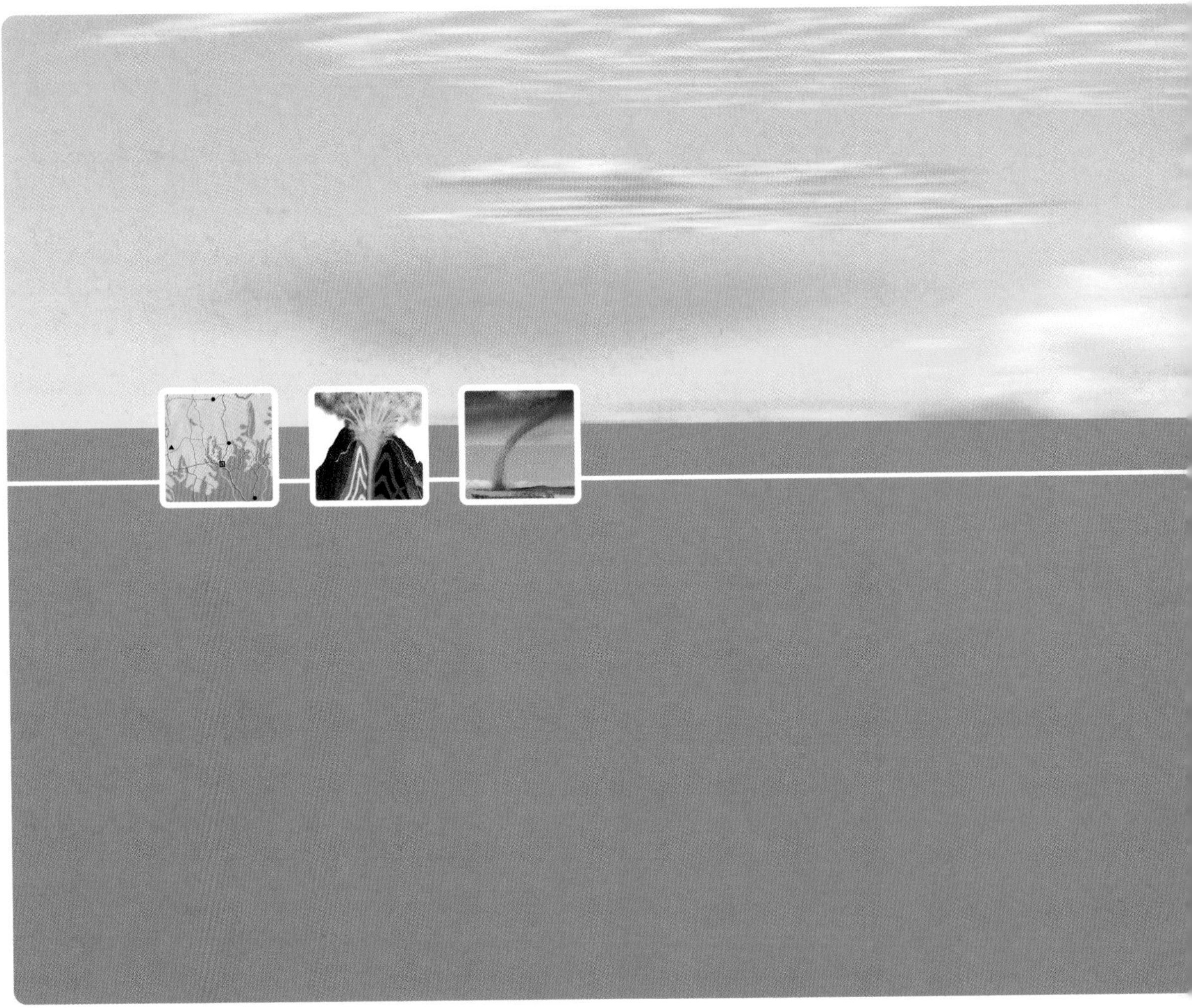

28 Geography

EARTH

TIERRA | TERRE | ERDE | TERRA

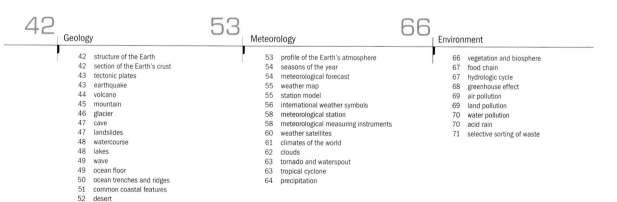

configuration of the continents

configuración^F de los continentes^M | configuration^F des continents^M | Lage^F der Kontinente^M | carta^F dei continenti^M

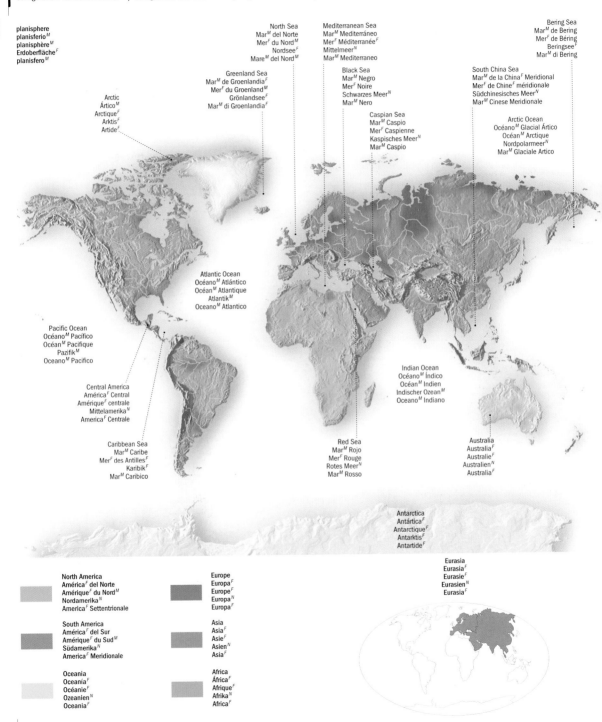

planisphere
planisferio^M
planisphère^M
Erdoberfläche^F
planisfero^M

North Sea
Mar^M del Norte
Mer^F du Nord^M
Nordsee^F
Mare^M del Nord^M

Mediterranean Sea
Mar^M Mediterráneo
Mer^F Méditerranée^F
Mittelmeer^N
Mar^M Mediterraneo

Bering Sea
Mar^M de Bering
Mer^F de Béring
Beringsee^F
Mar^M di Bering

Greenland Sea
Mar^M de Groenlandia^F
Mer^F du Groenland^M
Grönlandsee^F
Mar^M di Groenlandia^F

Black Sea
Mar^M Negro
Mer^F Noire
Schwarzes Meer^N
Mar^M Nero

South China Sea
Mar^M de la China^F Meridional
Mer^F de Chine^F méridionale
Südchinesisches Meer^N
Mar^M Cinese Meridionale

Arctic
Ártico^M
Arctique^F
Arktis^F
Artide^F

Caspian Sea
Mar^M Caspio
Mer^F Caspienne
Kaspisches Meer^N
Mar^M Caspio

Arctic Ocean
Océano^M Glacial Ártico
Océan^M Arctique
Nordpolarmeer^N
Mar^M Glaciale Artico

Atlantic Ocean
Océano^M Atlántico
Océan^M Atlantique
Atlantik^M
Oceano^M Atlantico

Pacific Ocean
Océano^M Pacífico
Océan^M Pacifique
Pazifik^M
Oceano^M Pacifico

Central America
América^F Central
Amérique^F centrale
Mittelamerika^N
America^F Centrale

Indian Ocean
Océano^M Índico
Océan^M Indien
Indischer Ozean^M
Oceano^M Indiano

Caribbean Sea
Mar^M Caribe
Mer^F des Antilles^F
Karibik^F
Mar^M Caribico

Red Sea
Mar^M Rojo
Mer^F Rouge
Rotes Meer^N
Mar^M Rosso

Australia
Australia^F
Australie^F
Australien^N
Australia^F

Antarctica
Antártica^F
Antarctique^F
Antarktis^F
Antartide^F

Eurasia
Eurasia^F
Eurasie^F
Eurasien^N
Eurasia^F

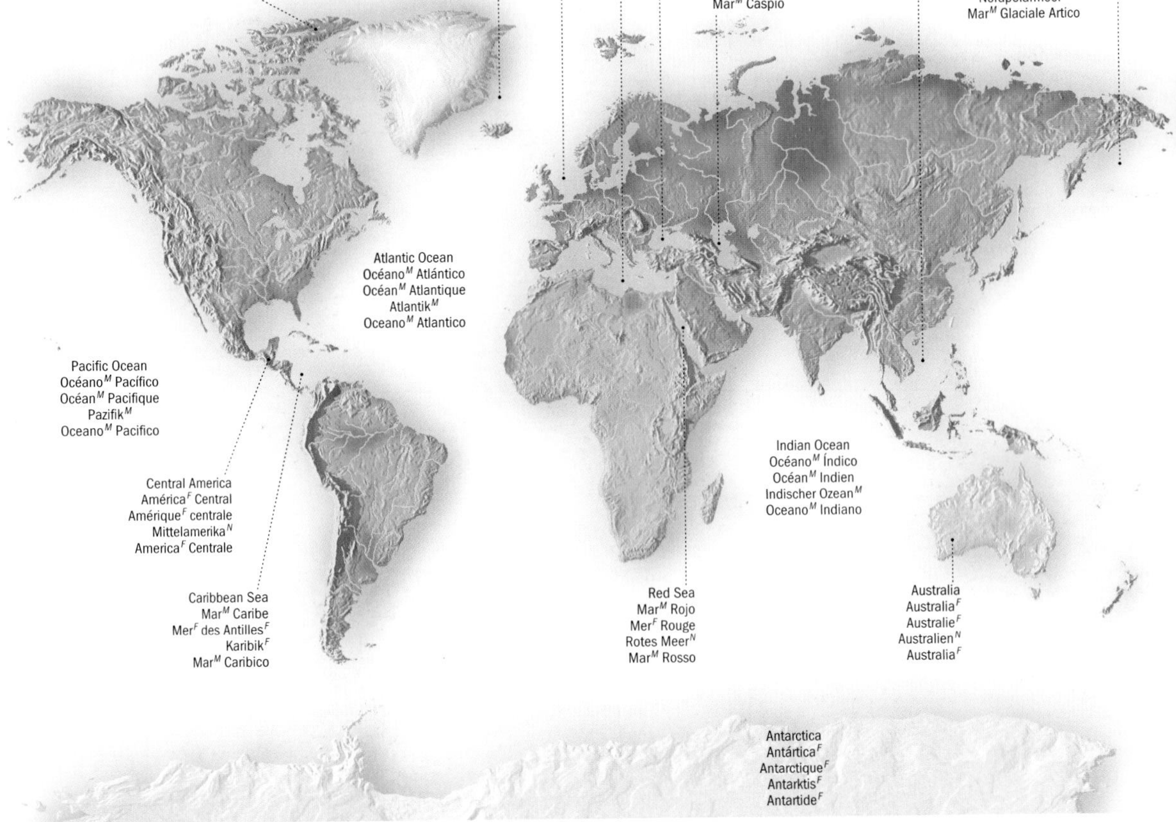

North America
América^F del Norte
Amérique^F du Nord^M
Nordamerika^N
America^F Settentrionale

Europe
Europa^F
Europe^F
Europa^N
Europa^F

South America
América^F del Sur
Amérique^F du Sud^M
Südamerika^N
America^F Meridionale

Asia
Asia^F
Asie^F
Asien^N
Asia^F

Oceania
Oceanía^F
Océanie^F
Ozeanien^N
Oceania^F

Africa
África^F
Afrique^F
Afrika^N
Africa^F

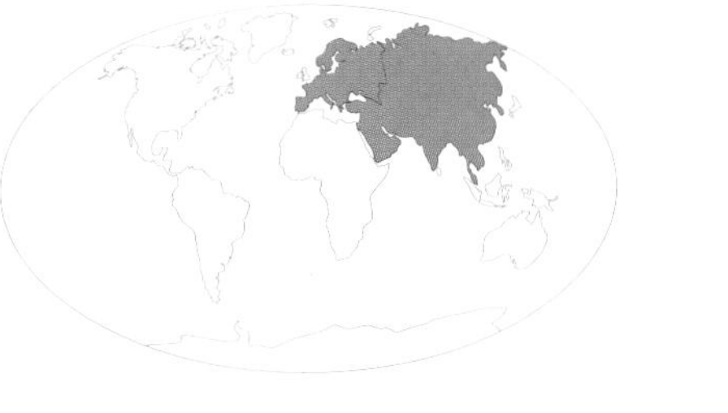

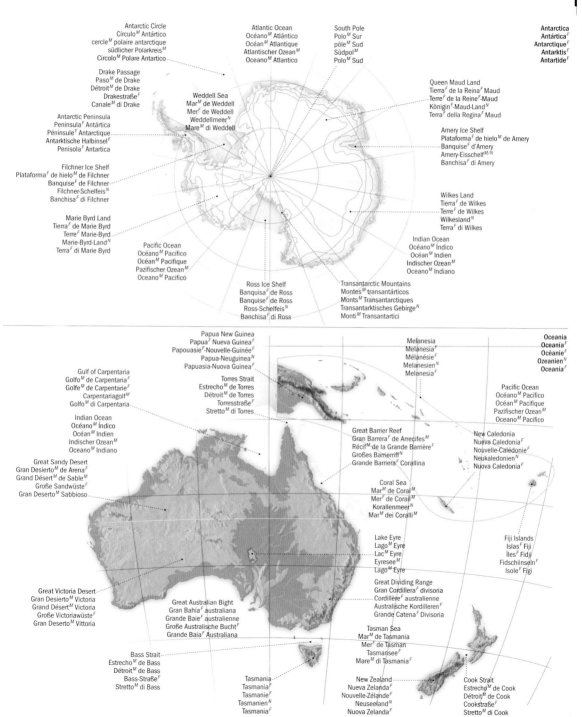

Antarctic Circle
Círculo M Antártico
cercle M polaire antarctique
südlicher Polarkreis M
Circolo M Polare Antartico

Atlantic Ocean
Océano M Atlántico
Océan M Atlantique
Atlantischer Ozean M
Oceano M Atlantico

South Pole
Polo M Sur
pôle M Sud
Südpol M
Polo M Sud

Antarctica
Antártica F
Antarctique F
Antarktis F
Antartide F

Drake Passage
Paso M de Drake
Détroit M de Drake
Drakestraße F
Canale M di Drake

Weddell Sea
Mar M de Weddell
Mer F de Weddell
Weddellmeer F
Mare M di Weddell

Queen Maud Land
Tierra F de la Reina F Maud
Terre F de la Reine F-Maud
Königin F-Maud-Land N
Terra F della Regina F Maud

Antarctic Peninsula
Península F Antártica
Péninsule F Antarctique
Antarktische Halbinsel F
Penisola F Antartica

Amery Ice Shelf
Plataforma F de hielo M de Amery
Banquise F d'Amery
Amery-Eisschelf M/N
Banchisa F di Amery

Filchner Ice Shelf
Plataforma F de hielo M de Filchner
Banquise F de Filchner
Filchner-Schelfeis N
Banchisa F di Filchner

Wilkes Land
Tierra F de Wilkes
Terre F de Wilkes
Wilkesland N
Terra F di Wilkes

Marie Byrd Land
Tierra F de Marie Byrd
Terre F Marie-Byrd
Marie-Byrd-Land N
Terra F di Marie Byrd

Pacific Ocean
Océano M Pacífico
Océan M Pacifique
Pazifischer Ozean M
Oceano M Pacifico

Indian Ocean
Océano M Índico
Océan M Indien
Indischer Ozean M
Oceano M Indiano

Ross Ice Shelf
Banquisa F de Ross
Banquise F de Ross
Ross-Schelfeis N
Banchisa F di Ross

Transantarctic Mountains
Montes M transantárticos
Monts M Transantarctiques
Transantarktisches Gebirge N
Monti M Transantartici

Papua New Guinea
Papua F Nueva Guinea F
Papouasie F-Nouvelle-Guinée F
Papua-Neuguinea N
Papuasia-Nuova Guinea F

Melanesia
Melanesia F
Mélanésie F
Melanesien N
Melanesia F

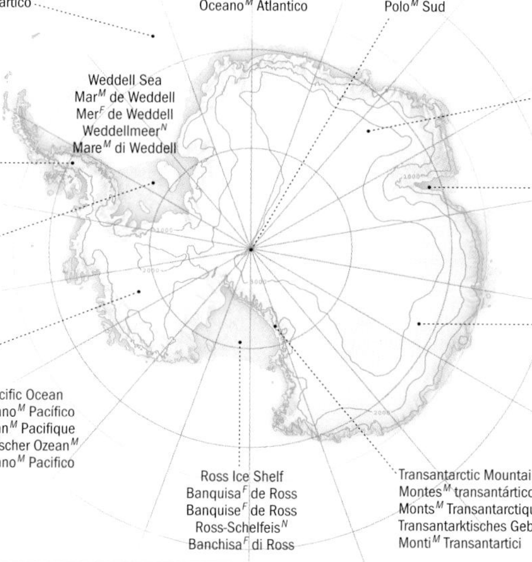

Oceania
Oceanía F
Océanie F
Ozeanien N
Oceania F

Gulf of Carpentaria
Golfo M de Carpentaria F
Golfe M de Carpentarie F
Carpentariagolf M
Golfo M di Carpentaria

Torres Strait
Estrecho M de Torres
Détroit M de Torres
Torresstraße F
Stretto M di Torres

Pacific Ocean
Océano M Pacífico
Océan M Pacifique
Pazifischer Ozean M
Oceano M Pacifico

Indian Ocean
Océano M Índico
Océan M Indien
Indischer Ozean M
Oceano M Indiano

Great Barrier Reef
Gran Barrera F de Arrecifes M
Récif M de la Grande Barrière F
Großes Barriereriff N
Grande Barriera F Corallina

New Caledonia
Nueva Caledonia F
Nouvelle-Calédonie F
Neukaledonien N
Nuova Caledonia F

Great Sandy Desert
Gran Desierto M de Arena F
Grand Désert M de Sable M
Große Sandwüste F
Gran Deserto M Sabbioso

Coral Sea
Mar M de Coral M
Mer F de Corail M
Korallenmeer N
Mar M dei Coralli M

Lake Eyre
Lago M Eyre
Lac M Eyre
Eyresee M
Lago M Eyre

Fiji Islands
Islas F Fiji
Îles F Fidji
Fidschiinseln F
Isole F Figi

Great Victoria Desert
Gran Desierto M Victoria
Grand Désert M Victoria
Große Victoriawüste F
Gran Deserto M Vittoria

Great Australian Bight
Gran Bahía F australiana
Grande Baie F australienne
Große Australische Bucht F
Grande Baia F Australiana

Great Dividing Range
Gran Cordillera F divisoria
Cordillère F australienne
Australische Kordilleren F
Grande Catena F Divisoria

Tasman Sea
Mar M de Tasmania
Mer F de Tasman
Tasmansee F
Mare M di Tasmania F

Bass Strait
Estrecho M de Bass
Détroit M de Bass
Bass-Straße F
Stretto M di Bass

Tasmania
Tasmania F
Tasmanie F
Tasmanien N
Tasmania F

New Zealand
Nueva Zelanda F
Nouvelle-Zélande F
Neuseeland N
Nuova Zelanda F

Cook Strait
Estrecho M de Cook
Détroit M de Cook
Cookstraße F
Stretto M di Cook

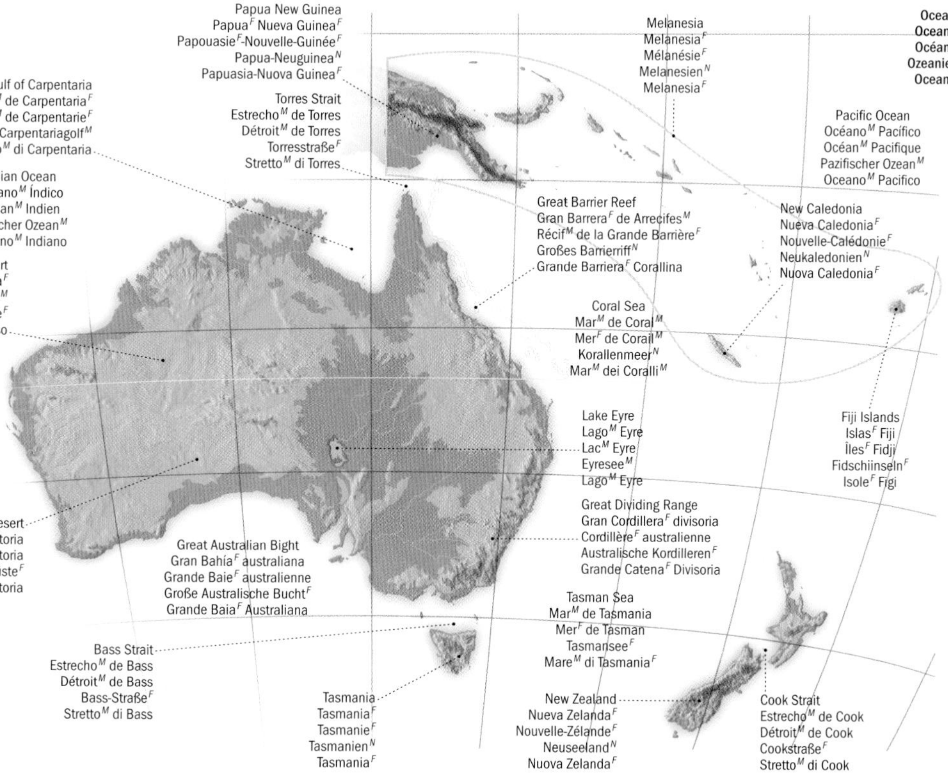

configuration of the continents

EARTH

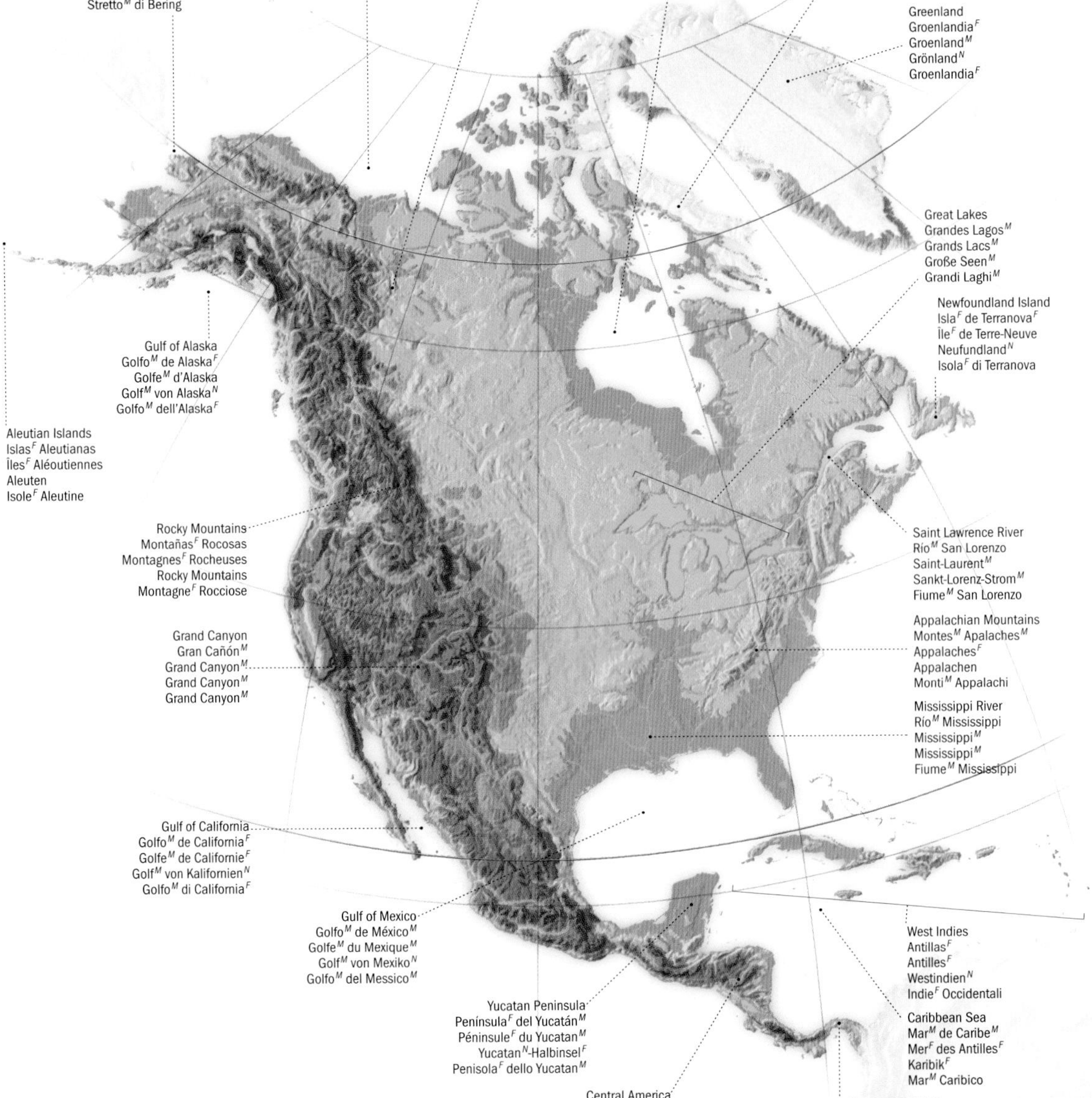

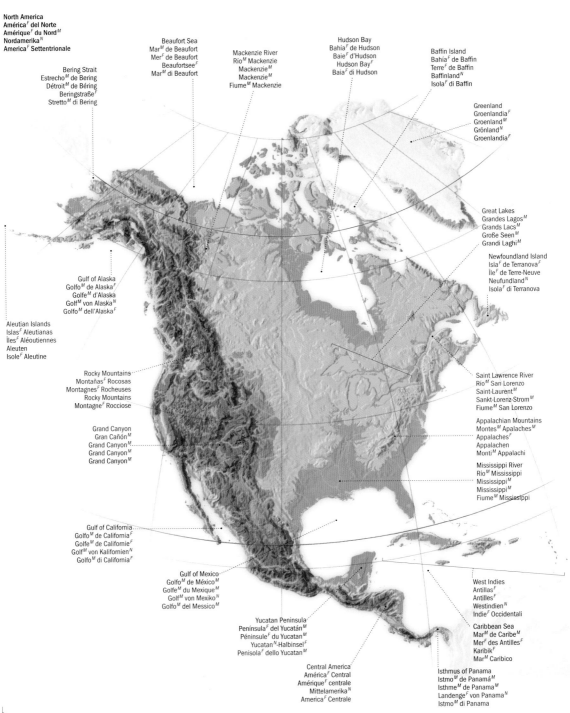

North America
América^F del Norte
Amérique^F du Nord^M
Nordamerika^N
America^F Settentrionale

Beaufort Sea
Mar^M de Beaufort
Mer^F de Beaufort
Beaufortsee^F
Mar^M di Beaufort

Mackenzie River
Río^M Mackenzie
Mackenzie^M
Mackenzie^M
Fiume^M Mackenzie

Hudson Bay
Bahía^F de Hudson
Baie^F d'Hudson
Hudson Bay^F
Baia^F di Hudson

Baffin Island
Bahía^F de Baffin
Terre^F de Baffin
Baffinland^N
Isola^F di Baffin

Bering Strait
Estrecho^M de Bering
Détroit^M de Béring
Beringstraße^F
Stretto^M di Bering

Greenland
Groenlandia^F
Groenland^M
Grönland^N
Groenlandia^F

Great Lakes
Grandes Lagos^M
Grands Lacs^M
Große Seen^M
Grandi Laghi^M

Newfoundland Island
Isla^F de Terranova^F
Île^F de Terre-Neuve
Neufundland^N
Isola^F di Terranova

Gulf of Alaska
Golfo^M de Alaska^F
Golfe^M d'Alaska
Golf^M von Alaska^N
Golfo^M dell'Alaska^F

Aleutian Islands
Islas^F Aleutianas
Îles^F Aléoutiennes
Aleuten
Isole^F Aleutine

Rocky Mountains
Montañas^F Rocosas
Montagnes^F Rocheuses
Rocky Mountains
Montagne^F Rocciose

Saint Lawrence River
Río^M San Lorenzo
Saint-Laurent^M
Sankt-Lorenz-Strom^M
Fiume^M San Lorenzo

Appalachian Mountains
Montes^M Apalaches^M
Appalaches^F
Appalachen
Monti^M Appalachi

Grand Canyon
Gran Cañón^M
Grand Canyon^M
Grand Canyon^M
Grand Canyon^M

Mississippi River
Río^M Mississippi
Mississippi^M
Mississippi^M
Fiume^M Mississippi

Gulf of California
Golfo^M de California^F
Golfe^M de Californie^F
Golf^M von Kalifornien^N
Golfo^M di California^F

West Indies
Antillas^F
Antilles^F
Westindien^N
Indie^F Occidentali

Gulf of Mexico
Golfo^M de México^M
Golfe^M du Mexique^M
Golf^M von Mexiko^N
Golfo^M del Messico

Yucatan Peninsula
Península^F del Yucatán^M
Péninsule^F du Yucatan^M
Yucatan^N-Halbinsel^F
Penisola^F dello Yucatan

Caribbean Sea
Mar^M de Caribe^M
Mer^F des Antilles^F
Karibik^F
Mar^M Caribico

Central America
América^F Central
Amérique^F centrale
Mittelamerika^N
America^F Centrale

Isthmus of Panama
Istmo^M de Panamá^M
Isthme^M de Panama^M
Landenge^F von Panama^N
Istmo^M di Panama

South America
América^F del Sur
Amérique^F du Sud^M
Südamerika^N
America^F Meridionale

Orinoco River
Río^M Orinoco
Orénoque^M
Orinoko^M
Fiume^M Orinoco

Amazon River
Río^M Amazonas
Amazone^F
Amazonas^M
Rio^M delle Amazzoni^F

Gulf of Panama
Golfo^M de Panamá^M
Golfe^M de Panama^M
Golf^M von Panama^N
Golfo^M di Panama

Equator
ecuador^M
équateur^M
Äquator^M
Equatore^M

Andes Cordillera
Cordillera^F de los Andes^M
Cordillère^F des Andes^F
Anden
Cordigliera^F delle Ande^F

Lake Titicaca
Lago^M Titicaca
Lac^M Titicaca
Titicacasee^M
Lago^M Titicaca

Atacama Desert
Desierto^M de Atacama
Désert^M d'Atacama
Atacama-Wüste^F
Deserto^M di Atacama

Paraná River
Río^M Paraná
Paraná^M
Paraná^M
Fiume^M Paranà

Patagonia
Patagonia^F
Patagonie^F
Patagonien^N
Patagonia^F

Falkland Islands
Islas^F Malvinas
Îles^F Falkland
Falkland-Inseln^F
Isole^F Falkland

Tierra del Fuego
Tierra^F del Fuego^M
Terre^F de Feu^M
Feuerland^N
Terra^F del Fuoco^M

Cape Horn
Cabo^M de Hornos
Cap^M Horn
Kap^N Horn
Capo^M Horn

Drake Passage
Paso^M de Drake
Détroit^M de Drake
Drakestraße^F
Canale^M di Drake

configuration of the continents

EARTH

Europe
Europa[F]
Europe[F]
Europa[N]
Europa[F]

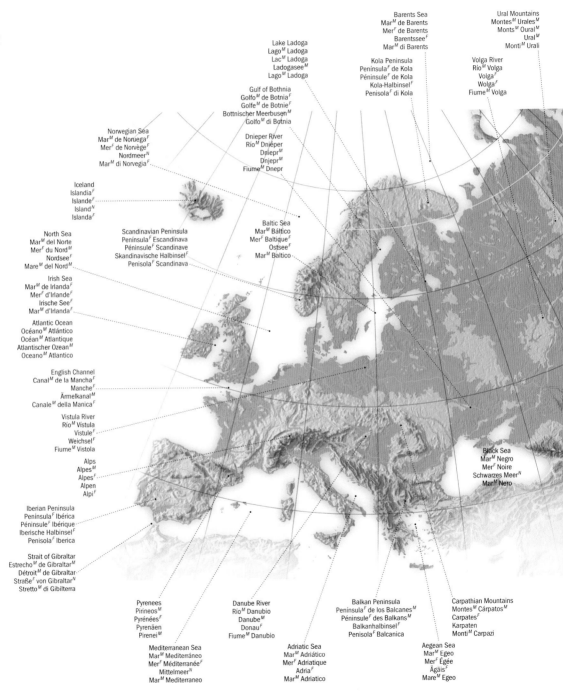

Barents Sea
Mar[M] de Barents
Mer[F] de Barents
Barentssee[F]
Mar[M] di Barents

Ural Mountains
Montes[M] Urales[M]
Monts[M] Oural[M]
Ural[M]
Monti[M] Urali

Lake Ladoga
Lago[M] Ladoga
Lac[M] Ladoga
Ladogasee[M]
Lago[M] Ladoga

Kola Peninsula
Península[F] de Kola
Péninsule[F] de Kola
Kola-Halbinsel[F]
Penisola[F] di Kola

Volga River
Río[M] Volga
Volga[F]
Wolga[F]
Fiume[M] Volga

Gulf of Bothnia
Golfo[M] de Botnia[F]
Golfe[M] de Botnie[F]
Bottnischer Meerbusen[M]
Golfo[M] di Botnia

Norwegian Sea
Mar[M] de Noruega[F]
Mer[F] de Norvège[F]
Nordmeer[N]
Mar[M] di Norvegia[F]

Dnieper River
Río[M] Dniéper
Dnjepr[M]
Dnjepr[M]
Fiume[M] Dnepr

Iceland
Islandia[F]
Islande[F]
Island[N]
Islanda[F]

Baltic Sea
Mar[M] Báltico
Mer[F] Baltique[F]
Ostsee[F]
Mar[M] Baltico

North Sea
Mar[M] del Norte
Mer[F] du Nord[M]
Nordsee[F]
Mare[F] del Nord[M]

Scandinavian Peninsula
Península[F] Escandinava
Péninsule[F] Scandinave
Skandinavische Halbinsel[F]
Penisola[F] Scandinava

Irish Sea
Mar[M] de Irlanda[F]
Mer[F] d'Irlande[F]
Irische See[F]
Mar[M] d'Irlanda[F]

Atlantic Ocean
Océano[M] Atlántico
Océan[M] Atlantique
Atlantischer Ozean[M]
Oceano[M] Atlantico

English Channel
Canal[M] de la Mancha[F]
Manche[F]
Ärmelkanal[M]
Canale[M] della Manica[F]

Vistula River
Río[M] Vístula
Vistule[F]
Weichsel[F]
Fiume[M] Vistola

Alps
Alpes[M]
Alpes[F]
Alpen
Alpi[F]

Black Sea
Mar[M] Negro
Mer[F] Noire
Schwarzes Meer[N]
Mar[M] Nero

Iberian Peninsula
Península[F] Ibérica
Péninsule[F] Ibérique
Iberische Halbinsel[F]
Penisola[F] Iberica

Strait of Gibraltar
Estrecho[M] de Gibraltar[M]
Détroit[M] de Gibraltar
Straße[F] von Gibraltar[N]
Stretto[M] di Gibilterra

Pyrenees
Pirineos[M]
Pyrénées[F]
Pyrenäen
Pirenei[M]

Danube River
Río[M] Danubio
Danube[M]
Donau[F]
Fiume[M] Danubio

Balkan Peninsula
Península[F] de los Balcanes[M]
Péninsule[F] des Balkans[M]
Balkanhalbinsel[F]
Penisola[F] Balcanica

Carpathian Mountains
Montes[M] Cárpatos[M]
Carpates[F]
Karpaten
Monti[M] Carpazi

Mediterranean Sea
Mar[M] Mediterráneo
Mer[F] Méditerranée[F]
Mittelmeer[N]
Mar[M] Mediterraneo

Adriatic Sea
Mar[M] Adriático
Mer[F] Adriatique
Adria[F]
Mar[M] Adriatico

Aegean Sea
Mar[M] Egeo
Mer[F] Égée
Ägäis[F]
Mare[M] Egeo

Asia
Asia^F
Asie^F
Asien^N
Asia^F

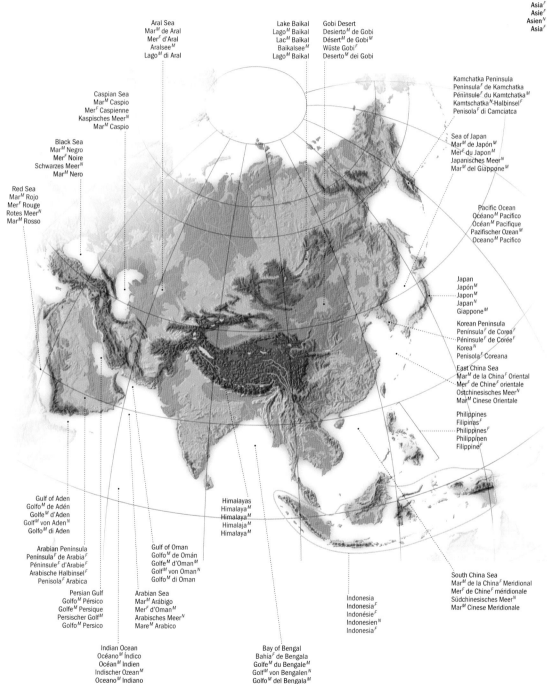

Aral Sea
Mar^M de Aral
Mer^F d'Aral
Aralsee^M
Lago^M di Aral

Lake Baikal
Lago^M Baikal
Lac^M Baikal
Baikalsee^M
Lago^M Baikal

Gobi Desert
Desierto^M de Gobi
Désert^M de Gobi^M
Wüste Gobi^F
Deserto^M dei Gobi

Kamchatka Peninsula
Península^F de Kamchatka
Péninsule^F du Kamtchatka^M
Kamtschatka^N-Halbinsel^F
Penisola^F di Camciatca

Caspian Sea
Mar^M Caspio
Mer^F Caspienne
Kaspisches Meer^N
Mar^M Caspio

Sea of Japan
Mar^M de Japón^M
Mer^E du Japon^M
Japanisches Meer^N
Mar^M del Giappone^M

Black Sea
Mar^M Negro
Mer^F Noire
Schwarzes Meer^N
Mar^M Nero

Pacific Ocean
Océano^M Pacifico
Océan^M Pacifique
Pazifischer Ozean^M
Oceano^M Pacifico

Red Sea
Mar^M Rojo
Mer^F Rouge
Rotes Meer^N
Mar^M Rosso

Japan
Japón^M
Japon^M
Japan^N
Giappone^M

Korean Peninsula
Península^F de Corea^F
Péninsule^F de Corée^F
Korea^N
Penisola^F Coreana

East China Sea
Mar^M de la China^F Oriental
Mer^F de Chine^F orientale
Ostchinesisches Meer^N
Mar^M Cinese Orientale

Philippines
Filipinas^F
Philippines^F
Philippinen
Filippine^F

Gulf of Aden
Golfo^M de Adén
Golfe^F d'Aden
Golf^M von Aden^N
Golfo^M di Aden

Himalayas
Himalaya^F
Himalaya^M
Himalaja^M
Himalaya^M

Arabian Peninsula
Península^F de Arabia^F
Péninsule^F d'Arabie^F
Arabische Halbinsel^F
Penisola^F Arabica

Gulf of Oman
Golfo^M de Omán
Golfe^M d'Oman^F
Golf^M von Oman^N
Golfo^M di Oman

South China Sea
Mar^M de la China^F Meridional
Mer^F de Chine^F méridionale
Südchinesisches Meer^N
Mar^M Cinese Meridionale

Persian Gulf
Golfo^M Pérsico
Golfe^M Persique
Persischer Golf^M
Golfo^M Persico

Arabian Sea
Mar^M Arábigo
Mer^F d'Oman^F
Arabisches Meer^N
Mare^M Arabico

Indonesia
Indonesia^F
Indonésie^F
Indonesien^N
Indonesia^F

Indian Ocean
Océano^M Índico
Océan^M Indien
Indischer Ozean^M
Oceano^M Indiano

Bay of Bengal
Bahía^F de Bengala
Golfe^M du Bengale^F
Golf^M von Bengalen^N
Golfo^M del Bengala^M

configuration of the continents

EARTH

Africa
África F
Afrique F
Afrika N
Africa F

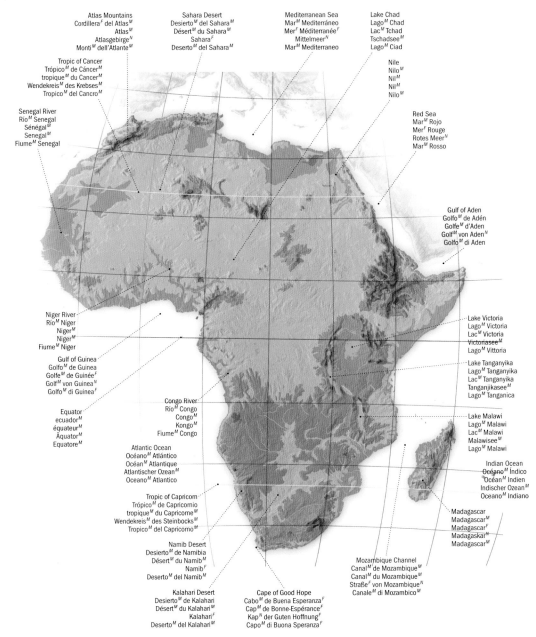

Atlas Mountains
Cordillera F del Atlas M
Atlas M
Atlasgebirge N
Monti M dell'Atlante M

Sahara Desert
Desierto M del Sahara M
Désert M du Sahara M
Sahara F
Deserto M del Sahara M

Mediterranean Sea
Mar M Mediterráneo
Mer F Méditerranée F
Mittelmeer N
Mar M Mediterraneo

Lake Chad
Lago M Chad
Lac M Tchad
Tschadsee M
Lago M Ciad

Tropic of Cancer
Trópico M de Cáncer M
tropique M du Cancer M
Wendekreis M des Krebses M
Tropico M del Cancro M

Nile
Nilo M
Nil M
Nil M
Nilo M

Senegal River
Río M Senegal
Sénégal M
Senegal M
Fiume M Senegal

Red Sea
Mar M Rojo
Mer F Rouge
Rotes Meer N
Mar M Rosso

Gulf of Aden
Golfo M de Adén
Golfe M d'Aden
Golf M von Aden N
Golfo M di Aden

Niger River
Río M Niger
Niger M
Niger M
Fiume M Niger

Lake Victoria
Lago M Victoria
Lac M Victoria
Victoriasee M
Lago M Vittoria

Gulf of Guinea
Golfo M de Guinea
Golfe M de Guinée F
Golf M von Guinea N
Golfo M di Guinea F

Lake Tanganyika
Lago M Tanganyika
Lac M Tanganyika
Tanganjikasee M
Lago M Tanganica

Equator
ecuador M
équateur M
Äquator M
Equatore M

Congo River
Río M Congo
Congo M
Kongo M
Fiume M Congo

Lake Malawi
Lago M Malawi
Lac M Malawi
Malawisee M
Lago M Malawi

Atlantic Ocean
Océano M Atlántico
Océan M Atlantique
Atlantischer Ozean M
Oceano M Atlantico

Indian Ocean
Océano M Índico
Océan M Indien
Indischer Ozean M
Oceano M Indiano

Tropic of Capricorn
Trópico M de Capricornio
tropique M du Capricorne M
Wendekreis M des Steinbocks M
Tropico M del Capricorno M

Madagascar
Madagascar M
Madagascar F
Madagaskar N
Madagascar M

Namib Desert
Desierto M de Namibia
Désert M du Namib F
Namib F
Deserto M del Namib M

Mozambique Channel
Canal M de Mozambique M
Canal M du Mozambique M
Straße F von Mozambique N
Canale M di Mozambico M

Kalahari Desert
Desierto M de Kalahari
Désert M du Kalahari
Kalahari F
Deserto M del Kalahari M

Cape of Good Hope
Cabo M de Buena Esperanza F
Cap M de Bonne-Espérance F
Kap N der Guten Hoffnung F
Capo M di Buona Speranza F

cartography

cartografía[F] | cartographie[F] | Kartographie[F] | cartografia[F]

Earth coordinate system
sistema[M] de coordenadas[F] terrestres
coordonnées[F] terrestres
Koordinatensystem[N] der Erdkugel[F]
sistema[M] di coordinate[F] terrestri

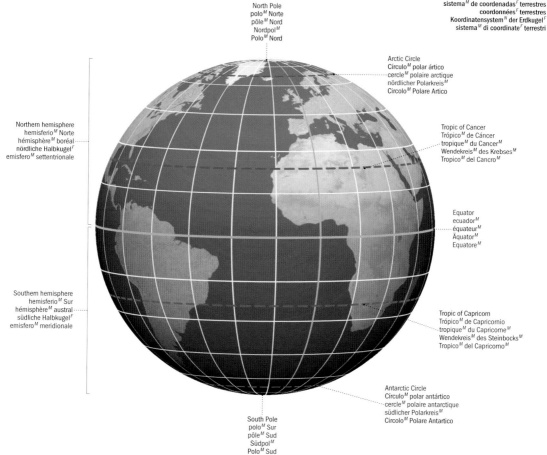

North Pole
polo[M] Norte
pôle[M] Nord
Nordpol[M]
Polo[M] Nord

Arctic Circle
Círculo[M] polar ártico
cercle[M] polaire arctique
nördlicher Polarkreis[M]
Circolo[M] Polare Artico

Northern hemisphere
hemisferio[M] Norte
hémisphère[M] boréal
nördliche Halbkugel[F]
emisfero[M] settentrionale

Tropic of Cancer
Trópico[M] de Cáncer
tropique[M] du Cancer[M]
Wendekreis[M] des Krebses[M]
Tropico[M] del Cancro[M]

Equator
ecuador[M]
équateur[M]
Äquator[M]
Equatore[M]

Southern hemisphere
hemisferio[M] Sur
hémisphère[M] austral
südliche Halbkugel[F]
emisfero[M] meridionale

Tropic of Capricorn
Trópico[M] de Capricornio
tropique[M] du Capricorne[M]
Wendekreis[M] des Steinbocks[M]
Tropico[M] del Capricorno[M]

Antarctic Circle
Círculo[M] polar antártico
cercle[M] polaire antarctique
südlicher Polarkreis[M]
Circolo[M] Polare Antartico

South Pole
polo[M] Sur
pôle[M] Sud
Südpol[M]
Polo[M] Sud

hemispheres
hemisferios[M]
hémisphères[M]
Hemisphären[F]
emisferi[M]

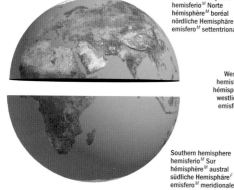

Northern hemisphere
hemisferio[M] Norte
hémisphère[M] boréal
nördliche Hemisphäre[F]
emisfero[M] settentrionale

Western hemisphere
hemisferio[M] occidental
hémisphère[M] occidental
westliche Hemisphäre[F]
emisfero[M] occidentale

Eastern hemisphere
hemisferio[M] oriental
hémisphère[M] oriental
östliche Hemisphäre[F]
emisfero[M] orientale

Southern hemisphere
hemisferio[M] Sur
hémisphère[M] austral
südliche Hemisphäre[F]
emisfero[M] meridionale

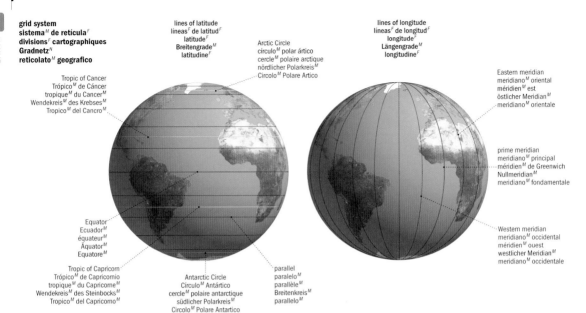

grid system
sistema^M **de retícula**^{F}
divisions^F **cartographiques**
Gradnetz^N
reticolato^M **geografico**

lines of latitude
lineas^F de latitud^F
latitude^F
Breitengrade^M
latitudine^F

Arctic Circle
círculo^M polar ártico
cercle^M polaire arctique
nördlicher Polarkreis^M
Circolo^M Polare Artico

Tropic of Cancer
Trópico^M de Cáncer
tropique^M du Cancer^M
Wendekreis^M des Krebses^M
Tropico^M del Cancro^M

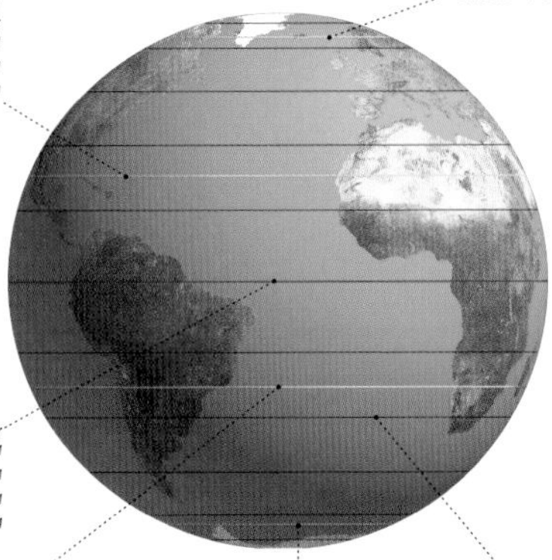

Equator
Ecuador^M
équateur^M
Äquator^M
Equatore^M

Tropic of Capricorn
Trópico^M de Capricornio
tropique^M du Capricorne^M
Wendekreis^M des Steinbocks^M
Tropico^M del Capricorno^M

Antarctic Circle
Círculo^M Antártico
cercle^M polaire antarctique
südlicher Polarkreis^M
Circolo^M Polare Antartico

parallel
paralelo^M
parallèle^M
Breitenkreis^M
parallelo^M

lines of longitude
lineas^F de longitud^F
longitude^F
Längengrade^M
longitudine^F

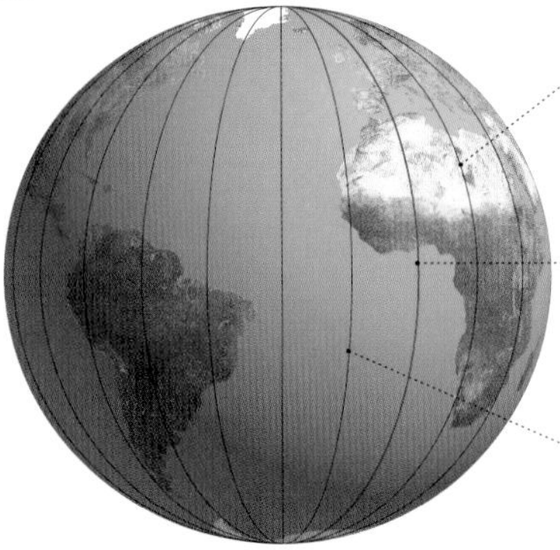

Eastern meridian
meridiano^M oriental
méridien^M est
östlicher Meridian^M
meridiano^M orientale

prime meridian
meridiano^M principal
méridien^M de Greenwich
Nullmeridian^M
meridiano^M fondamentale

Western meridian
meridiano^M occidental
méridien^M ouest
westlicher Meridian^M
meridiano^M occidentale

map projections
proyecciones^F **cartográficas**
projections^F **cartographiques**
Kartendarstellungen^F
proiezioni^F **cartografiche**

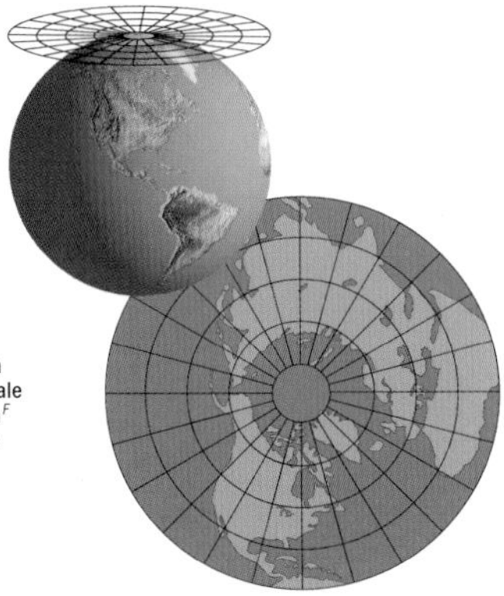

plane projection
proyección^F plana
projection^F horizontale
Azimutalprojektion^F
proiezione^F piana

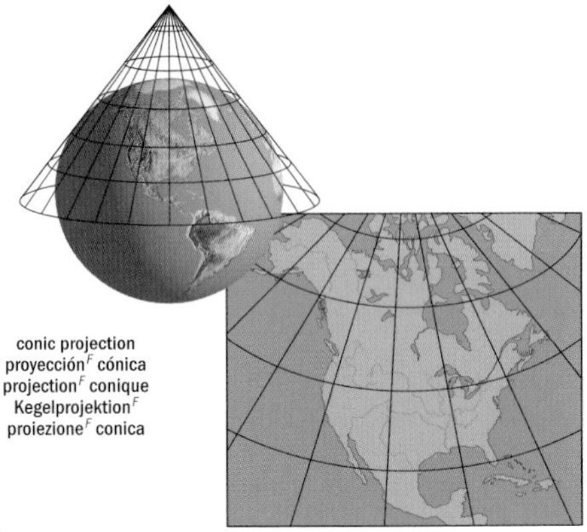

conic projection
proyección^F cónica
projection^F conique
Kegelprojektion^F
proiezione^F conica

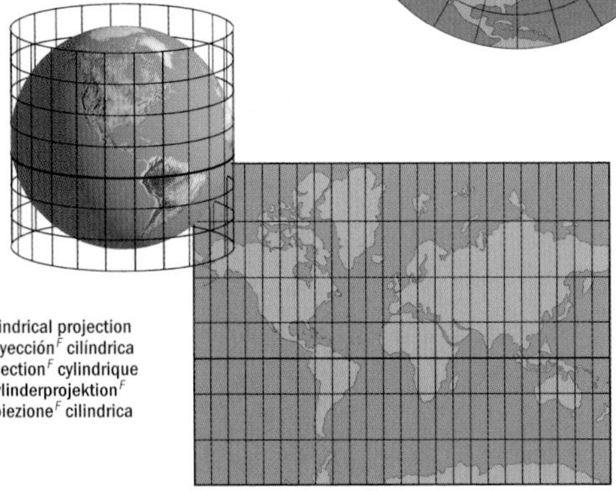

cylindrical projection
proyección^F cilíndrica
projection^F cylindrique
Zylinderprojektion^F
proiezione^F cilindrica

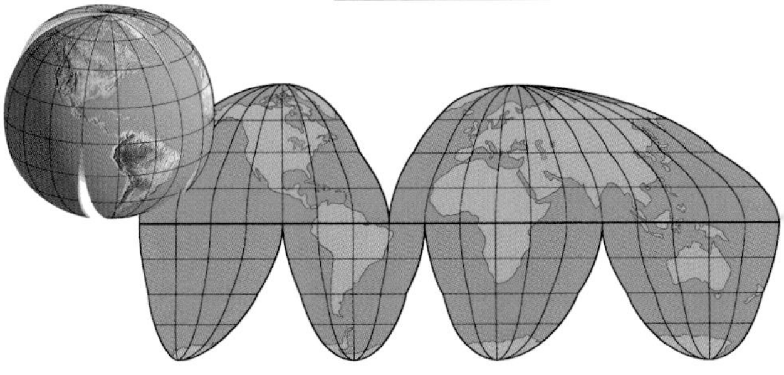

interrupted projection
proyección^F interrumpida
projection^F interrompue
zerlappte Projektion^F
proiezione^F interrotta

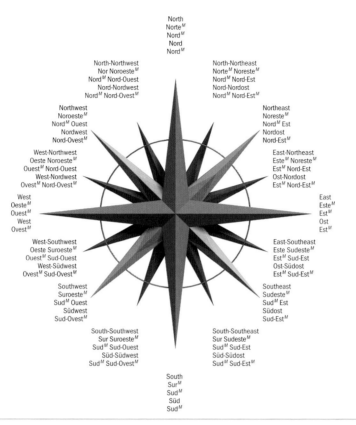

North
Norte^M
Nord^M
Nord
Nord^M

North-Northwest
Nor Noroeste^M
Nord^M Nord-Ouest
Nord-Nordwest
Nord^M Nord-Ovest^M

North-Northeast
Norte^M Noreste^M
Nord^M Nord-Est
Nord-Nordost
Nord^M Nord-Est^M

Northwest
Noroeste^M
Nord^M Ouest
Nordwest
Nord-Ovest^M

Northeast
Noreste^M
Nord^M Est
Nordost
Nord-Est^M

West-Northwest
Oeste Noroeste^M
Ouest^M Nord-Ouest
West-Nordwest
Ovest^M Nord-Ovest^M

East-Northeast
Este^M Noreste^M
Est^M Nord-Est
Ost-Nordost
Est^M Nord-Est^M

West
Oeste^M
Ouest^M
West
Ovest^M

East
Este^M
Est^M
Ost
Est^M

West-Southwest
Oeste Suroeste^M
Ouest^M Sud-Ouest
West-Südwest
Ovest^M Sud-Ovest^M

East-Southeast
Este Sudeste^M
Est^M Sud-Est
Ost-Südost
Est^M Sud-Est^M

Southwest
Suroeste^M
Sud^M Ouest
Südwest
Sud-Ovest^M

Southeast
Sudeste^M
Sud^M Est
Südost
Sud-Est^M

South-Southwest
Sur Suroeste^M
Sud^M Sud-Ouest
Süd-Südwest
Sud^M Sud-Ovest^M

South-Southeast
Sur Sudeste^M
Sud^M Sud-Est
Süd-Südost
Sud^M Sud-Est^M

South
Sur^M
Sud^M
Süd
Sud^M

compass rose
rosa^F de los vientos^M
rose^F des vents^M
Windrose^F
rosa^F dei venti^M

political map
mapa^M político
carte^F politique
politische Karte^F
carta^F politica

internal boundary
frontera^F interna
division^F territoriale
Provinzgrenze^F
confine^M interno

international boundary
frontera^F internacional
frontière^F
Staatsgrenze^F
confine^M internazionale

country
país^M
pays^M
Land^N
paese^M

province
provincia^F
province^F
Provinz^F
provincia^F

city
ciudad^F
grande ville^F
Stadt^F
città^F

capital
capital^F
capitale^F
Hauptstadt^F
capitale^F

state
estado^M
État^M
Bundesstaat^M
stato^M

CANADA

Edmonton
Vancouver
Calgary
Seattle
Winnipeg
Montréal
Toronto
Ottawa
New York
Detroit
Chicago
Washington

San Francisco
Denver
Atlanta

UNITED STATES

Los Angeles
San Diego
Dallas
Houston
Miami

Monterrey
Guadalajara

MEXICO

Ciudad de México

cartography

EARTH

physical map
mapa^M físico
carte^F physique
physische Karte^F
carta^F física

mountain range
cordillera^F
chaine^F de montagnes^F
Gebirgskette^F
catena^F montuosa

bay
bahia^F
baie^F
Bucht^F
baia^F

sea
mar^M
mer^F
Meer^N
mare^M

strait
estrecho^M
détroit^M
Meerenge^F
stretto^M

island
isla^F
ile^F
Insel^F
isola^F

ocean
océano^M
océan^M
Ozean^M
oceano^M

prairie
llanura^F
prairie^F
Prärie^F
prateria^F

mountain mass
macizo^M
massif^M montagneux
Gebirgsmassiv^N
massiccio montuoso^M

river estuary
estuario^M
estuaire^M
Flußmündung^F
estuario^M

lake
lago^M
lac^M
See^M
lago^M

river
rio^M
rivière^F
Fluß^M
fiume^M

archipelago
archipiélago^M
archipel^M
Archipel^M
arcipelago^M

plateau
meseta^F
plateau^M
Plateau^N, Hochebene^F
altopiano^M

gulf
golfo^M
golfe^M
Golf^M
golfo^M

peninsula
península^F
péninsule^F
Halbinsel^F
penisola^F

cape
cabo^M
cap^M
Kap^N
capo^M

plain
planicie^F
plaine^F
Ebene^F
pianura^F

river
rio^M
fleuve^M
Fluß^M
fiume^M

isthmus
istmo^M
isthme^M
Landenge^F
istmo^M

railroad line
vía^F férrea
chemin^M de fer^M
Eisenbahn^F
ferrovia^F

railroad station
estación^F del ferrocarril^M
gare^F
Bahnhof^M
stazione^F ferroviaria

bridge
puente^M
pont^M
Brücke^F
ponte^M

urban map
mapa^M urbano
plan^M urbain
Stadtplan^M
pianta^F di città^F

suburbs
zona^F residencial (de las afueras^F)
banlieue^F
Vororte^M
sobborghi^M

park
parque^M
parc^M
Park^M
parco^M

river
río^M
fleuve^M
Fluß^M
fiume^M

cemetery
cementerio^M
cimetière^F
Friedhof^M
cimitero^M

woods
bosques^M
bois^M
Wald^M
bosco^M

monument
monumento^M
monument^M
Denkmal^N
monumento^M

circular route
circunvalación^F
boulevard^M périphérique
Umgehungsstraße^F
circonvallazione^F

highway
autopista^F
autoroute^F
Autobahn^F
autostrada^F

traffic circle
rotonda^F
rond-point^M
Kreisverkehr^M
rotatoria^F

district
distrito^M
arrondissement^M
Stadtteil^M
quartiere^M

street
calle^F
rue^F
Straße^F
via^F

avenue
avenida^F
avenue^F
Allee^F
avenue^F

public building
edificio^M público
édifice^M public
öffentliches Gebäude^N
edificio^M pubblico

boulevard
bulevar^M
boulevard^M
Boulevard^M
boulevard^M

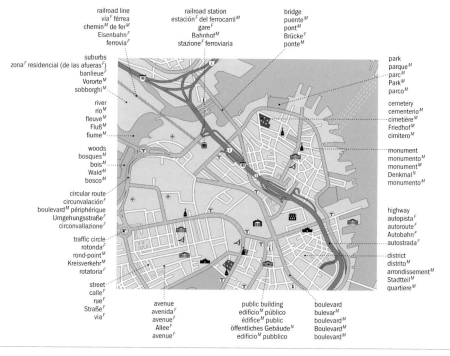

road map
mapa^M de carreteras^F
carte^F routière
Straßenkarte^F
carta^F stradale

highway number
número^M de la autopista^F
numéro^M d'autoroute^F
Autobahnnummer^F
numero^M di autostrada^F

road
carretera^F
route^F
Straße^F
strada^F

highway
autopista^F
autoroute^F
Autobahn^F
autostrada^F

road number
número^M de la carretera^F
numéro^M de route^F
Straßennummer^F
numero^M di strada^F

rest area
área^F de descanso^M
aire^F de repos^M
Rastplatz^M
area^F di sosta^F

airport
aeropuerto^M
aéroport^M
Flughafen^M
aeroporto^M

service area
área^F de servicio^M
aire^F de service^M
Raststätte^F
area^F di servizio^M

national park
parque^M nacional
parc^M national
Nationalpark^M
parco^M nazionale

belt highway
carretera^F de circunvalación^F
autoroute^F de ceinture^F
Umgehungsstraße^F
tangenziale^F

scenic route
ruta^F pintoresca
parcours^M pittoresque
landschaftlich schöne Strecke^F
strada^F panoramica

secondary road
carretera^F secundaria
route^F secondaire
Nebenstraße^F
strada^F secondaria

point of interest
punto^M de interés^M
curiosité^F
Sehenswürdigkeit^F
punto^M di interesse^M

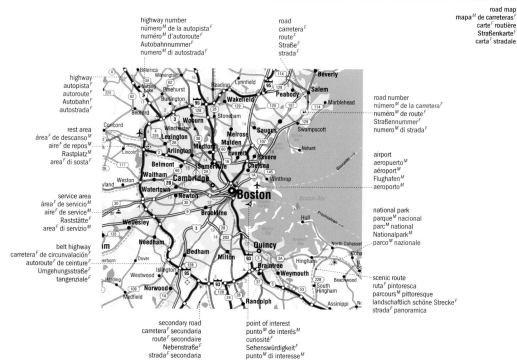

remote sensing

teledetección^M | télédétection^F | Fernerkundung^F | telerilevamento^M

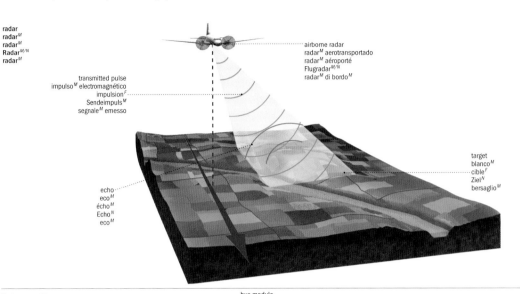

radar
radar^M
radar^M
Radar^{M/N}
radar^M

airborne radar
radar^M aerotransportado
radar^M aéroporté
Flugradar^{M/N}
radar^M di bordo^M

transmitted pulse
impulso^M electromagnético
impulsion^F
Sendeimpuls^M
segnale^M emesso

target
blanco^M
cible^F
Ziel^N
bersaglio^M

echo
eco^M
écho^M
Echo^N
eco^M

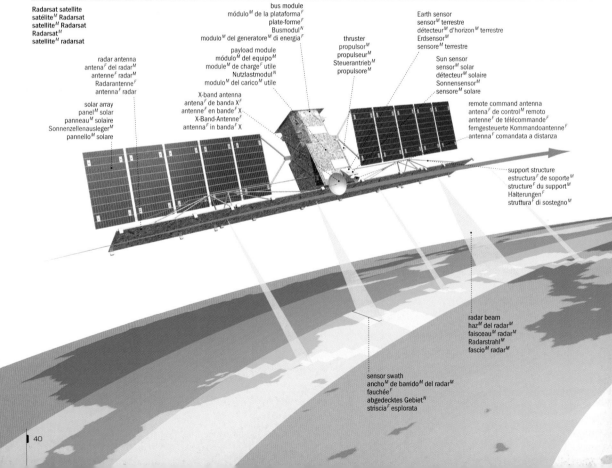

Radarsat satellite
satélite^M Radarsat
satellite^M Radarsat
Radarsat^M
satellite^M radarsat

bus module
módulo^M de la plataforma^F
plate-forme^F
Busmodul^N
modulo^M del generatore^M di energia^F

Earth sensor
sensor^M terrestre
détecteur^M d'horizon^M terrestre
Erdsensor^M
sensore^M terrestre

thruster
propulsor^M
propulseur^M
Steuerantrieb^M
propulsore^M

Sun sensor
sensor^M solar
détecteur^M solaire
Sonnensensor^M
sensore^M solare

payload module
módulo^M del equipo^M
module^F de charge^F utile
Nutzlastmodul^N
modulo^M del carico^M utile

radar antenna
antena^F del radar^M
antenne^F radar^M
Radarantenne^F
antenna^F radar

remote command antenna
antena^F de control^M remoto
antenne^F de télécommande^F
ferngesteuerte Kommandoantenne^F
antenna^F comandata a distanza

X-band antenna
antena^F de banda X^F
antenne^F en bande^F X
X-Band-Antenne^F
antenna^F in banda^F X

solar array
panel^M solar
panneau^M solaire
Sonnenzellenausleger^M
pannello^M solare

support structure
estructura^F de soporte^M
structure^F du support^M
Halterungen^F
struttura^F di sostegno^M

radar beam
haz^M del radar^M
faisceau^M radar^M
Radarstrahl^M
fascio^M radar^M

sensor swath
ancho^M de barrido^M del radar^M
fauchée^F
abgedecktes Gebiet^N
striscia^F esplorata

sonar
sonar^M
sonar^M
Sonar^N
sonar^M

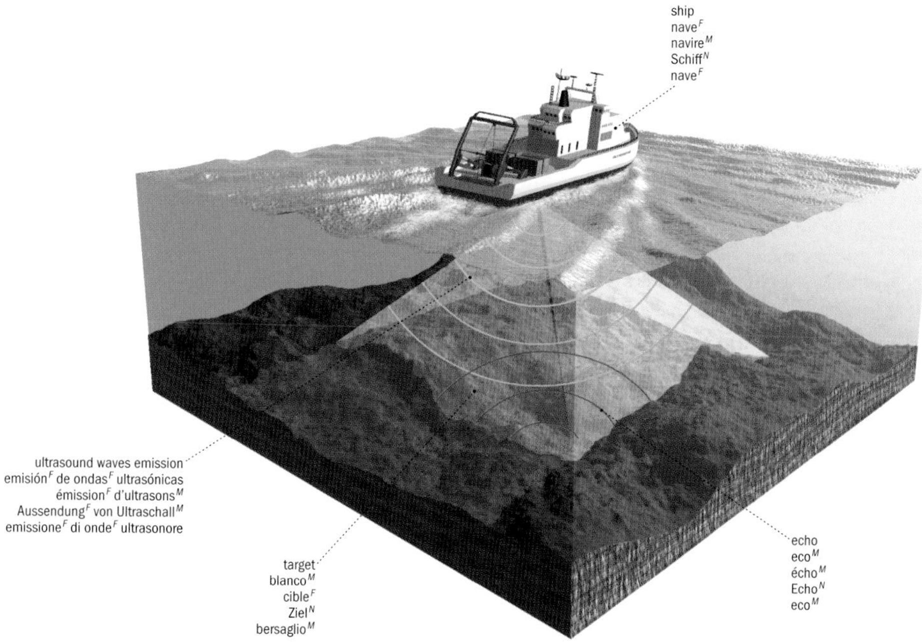

ship
nave^F
navire^M
Schiff^N
nave^F

ultrasound waves emission
emisión^F de ondas^F ultrasónicas
émission^F d'ultrasons^M
Aussendung^F von Ultraschall^M
emissione^F di onde^F ultrasonore

target
blanco^M
cible^F
Ziel^N
bersaglio^M

echo
eco^M
écho^M
Echo^N
eco^M

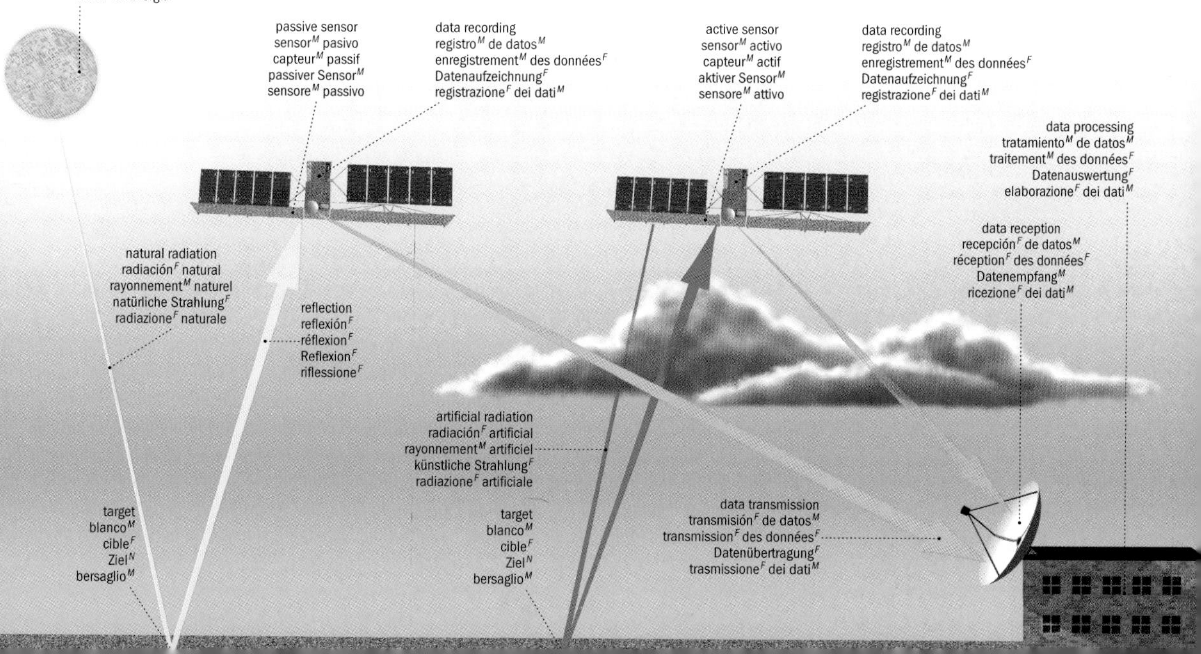

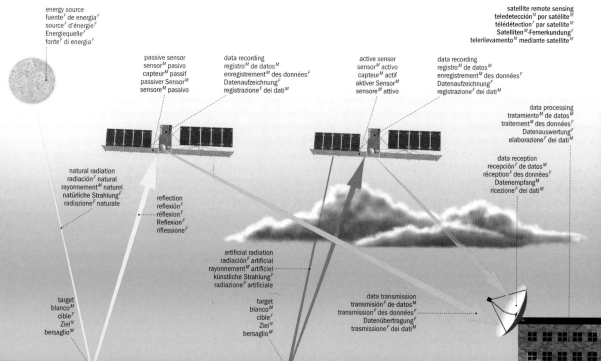

energy source
fuente^F de energía^F
source^F d'énergie^F
Energiequelle^F
fonte^F di energia^F

satellite remote sensing
teledetección^M por satélite^M
télédétection^F par satellite^M
Satelliten^M-Fernerkundung^F
telerilevamento^M mediante satellite^M

passive sensor
sensor^M pasivo
capteur^M passif
passiver Sensor^M
sensore^M passivo

data recording
registro^M de datos^M
enregistrement^M des données^F
Datenaufzeichnung^F
registrazione^F dei dati^M

active sensor
sensor^M activo
capteur^M actif
aktiver Sensor^M
sensore^M attivo

data recording
registro^M de datos^M
enregistrement^M des données^F
Datenaufzeichnung^F
registrazione^F dei dati^M

data processing
tratamiento^M de datos^M
traitement^M des données^F
Datenauswertung^F
elaborazione^F dei dati^M

natural radiation
radiación^F natural
rayonnement^M naturel
natürliche Strahlung^F
radiazione^F naturale

reflection
reflexión^F
réflexion^F
Reflexion^F
riflessione^F

data reception
recepción^F de datos^M
réception^F des données^F
Datenempfang^M
ricezione^F dei dati^M

artificial radiation
radiación^F artificial
rayonnement^M artificiel
künstliche Strahlung^F
radiazione^F artificiale

target
blanco^M
cible^F
Ziel^N
bersaglio^M

target
blanco^M
cible^F
Ziel^N
bersaglio^M

data transmission
transmisión^F de datos^M
transmission^F des données^F
Datenübertragung^F
trasmissione^F dei dati^M

EARTH

section of the Earth's crust

corte^M de la corteza^F terrestre | coupe^F de la croûte^F terrestre | Erdkruste^F im Querschnitt^M | sezione^F della crosta^F terrestre

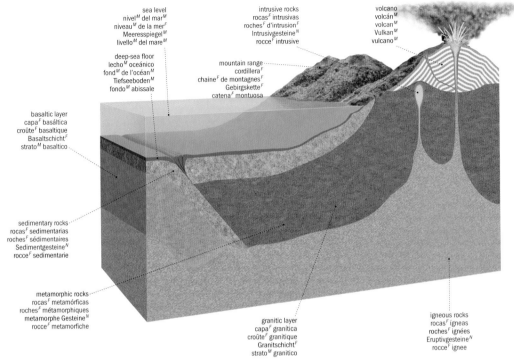

sea level
nivel^M del mar^M
niveau^F de la mer^F
Meeresspiegel^M
livello^M del mare^M

intrusive rocks
rocas^F intrusivas
roches^F d'intrusion^F
Intrusivgesteine^N
rocce^F intrusive

volcano
volcán^M
volcan^M
Vulkan^M
vulcano^M

deep-sea floor
lecho^M oceánico
fond^M de l'océan^M
Tiefseeboden^M
fondo^M abissale

mountain range
cordillera^F
chaîne^F de montagnes^F
Gebirgskette^F
catena^F montuosa

basaltic layer
capa^F basáltica
croûte^F basaltique
Basaltschicht^F
strato^M basaltico

sedimentary rocks
rocas^F sedimentarias
roches^F sédimentaires
Sedimentgesteine^N
rocce^F sedimentarie

metamorphic rocks
rocas^F metamórficas
roches^F métamorphiques
metamorphe Gesteine^N
rocce^F metamorfiche

granitic layer
capa^F granítica
croûte^F granitique
Granitschicht^F
strato^M granitico

igneous rocks
rocas^F ígneas
roches^F ignées
Eruptivgesteine^N
rocce^F ignee

structure of the Earth

estructura^F de la Tierra^F | structure^F de la Terre^F | Erdaufbau^M | struttura^F della Terra^F

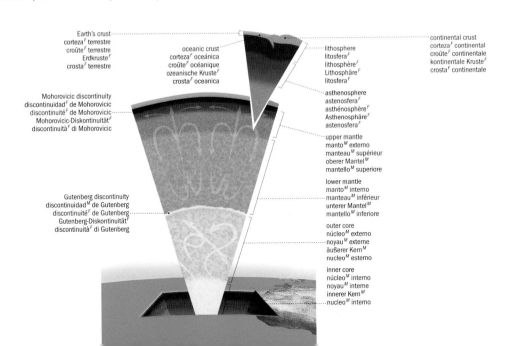

Earth's crust
corteza^F terrestre
croûte^F terrestre
Erdkruste^F
crosta^F terrestre

oceanic crust
corteza^F oceánica
croûte^F océanique
ozeanische Kruste^F
crosta^F oceanica

lithosphere
litosfera^F
lithosphère^F
Lithosphäre^F
litosfera^F

continental crust
corteza^F continental
croûte^F continentale
kontinentale Kruste^F
crosta^F continentale

Mohorovicic discontinuity
discontinuidad^F de Mohorovicic
discontinuité^F de Mohorovicic
Mohorovicic-Diskontinuität^F
discontinuità^F di Mohorovicic

asthenosphere
astenosfera^F
asthénosphère^F
Asthenosphäre^F
astenosfera^F

upper mantle
manto^M externo
manteau^M supérieur
oberer Mantel^M
mantello^M superiore

lower mantle
manto^M interno
manteau^M inférieur
unterer Mantel^M
mantello^M inferiore

Gutenberg discontinuity
discontinuidad^M de Gutenberg
discontinuité^F de Gutenberg
Gutenberg-Diskontinuität^F
discontinuità^F di Gutenberg

outer core
núcleo^M externo
noyau^M externe
äußerer Kern^M
nucleo^M esterno

inner core
núcleo^M interno
noyau^M interne
innerer Kern^M
nucleo^M interno

tectonic plates

placas^F tectónicas | plaques^F tectoniques | tektonische Platten^F | placche^F tettoniche

North American Plate
placa^F norteamericana
plaque^F nord-américaine
Nordamerikanische Platte^F
placca^F nordamericana

Cocos Plate
placa^F de Cocos
plaque^F des îles^F Cocos
Cocos-Platte^F
placca^F delle Cocos

Caribbean Plate
placa^F del Caribe
plaque^F des Caraïbes
Karibische Platte^F
placca^F caribica

Pacific Plate
placa^F del Pacifico
plaque^F pacifique
Pazifische Platte^F
placca^F del Pacifico^M

Nazca Plate
placa^F de Nazca
plaque^F Nazca
Nazca-Platte^F
placca^F di Nazca

Eurasian Plate
placa^F euroasiática
plaque^F eurasiatique
Eurasiatische Platte^F
placca^F euroasiatica

Philippine Plate
placa^F de Filipinas
plaque^F philippine
Philippinen-Platte^F
placca^F filippina

Australian-Indian Plate
placa^F indoaustraliana
plaque^F indo-australienne
Indisch-Australische Platte^F
placca^F indoaustraliana

Scotia Plate
placa^F de Escocia
plaque^F Scotia
Scotia-Platte^F
placca^F di Scozia

South American Plate
placa^F sudamericana
plaque^F sud-américaine
Südamerikanische Platte^F
placca^F sudamericana

African Plate
placa^F africana
plaque^F africaine
Afrikanische Platte^F
placca^F africana

Antarctic Plate
placa^F antártica
plaque^F antarctique
Antarktische Platte^F
placca^F antartica

subduction
subducción^M
subduction^F
Subduktionszone^F
subduzione^F

transform plate boundaries
fallas^F transformantes
plaques^F transformantes
Transformstörungen^F
placche^F trasformi

convergent plate boundaries
placas^F convergentes
plaques^F convergentes
konvergierende Plattengrenzen^F
placche^F convergenti

divergent plate boundaries
placas^F divergentes
plaques^F divergentes
divergierende Plattengrenzen^F
placche^F divergenti

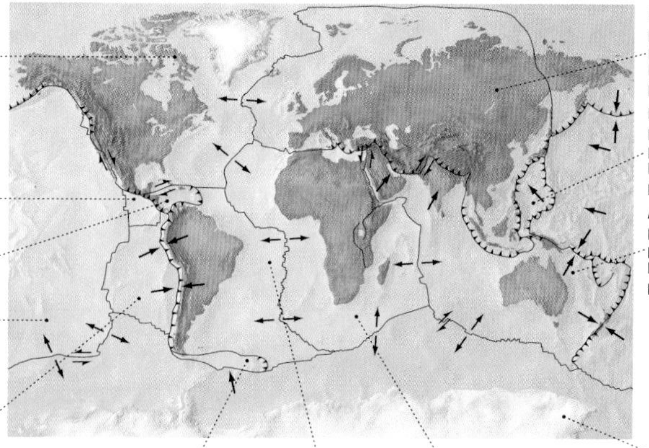

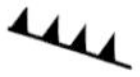

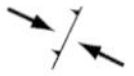

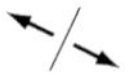

earthquake

terremoto^M | séisme^M | Erdbeben^N | terremoto^M

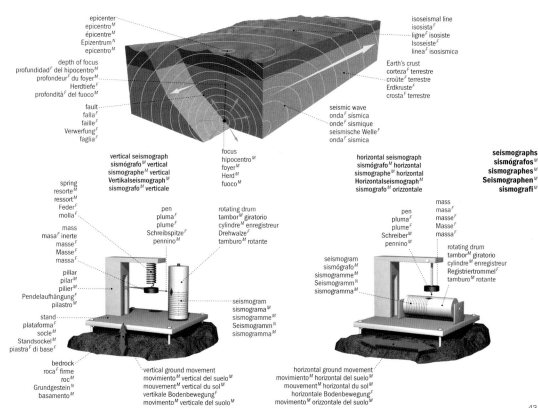

epicenter
epicentro^M
épicentre^M
Epizentrum^N
epicentro^M

depth of focus
profundidad^F del hipocentro^M
profondeur^F du foyer^M
Herdtiefe^F
profondità^F del fuoco^M

fault
falla^F
faille^F
Verwerfung^F
faglia^F

isoseismal line
isosista^F
ligne^F isosiste
Isoseiste^F
linea^F isosismica

Earth's crust
corteza^F terrestre
croûte^F terrestre
Erdkruste^F
crosta^F terrestre

seismic wave
onda^F sísmica
onde^F sismique
seismische Welle^F
onda^F sismica

focus
hipocentro^M
foyer^M
Herd^M
fuoco^M

vertical seismograph
sismógrafo^M vertical
sismographe^M vertical
Vertikalseismograph^M
sismografo^M verticale

horizontal seismograph
sismógrafo^M horizontal
sismographe^M horizontal
Horizontalseismograph^M
sismografo^M orizzontale

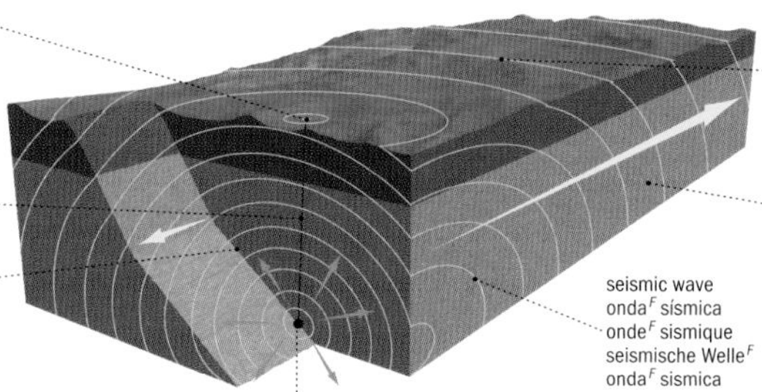

seismographs
sismógrafos^M
sismographes^M
Seismographen^M
sismografi^M

spring
resorte^M
ressort^M
Feder^F
molla^F

mass
masa^F inerte
masse^F
Masse^F
massa^F

pillar
pilar^M
pilier^M
Pendelaufhängung^F
pilastro^M

stand
plataforma^F
socle^M
Standsockel^M
piastra^F di base^M

bedrock
roca^F firme
roc^M
Grundgestein^N
basamento^M

pen
pluma^F
plume^F
Schreibspitze^F
pennino^M

rotating drum
tambor^M giratorio
cylindre^M enregistreur
Drehwalze^F
tamburo^M rotante

seismogram
sismograma^M
sismogramme^M
Seismogramm^N
sismogramma^M

vertical ground movement
movimiento^M vertical del suelo^M
mouvement^M vertical du sol^M
vertikale Bodenbewegung^F
movimento^M verticale del suolo^M

mass
masa^F
masse^F
Masse^F
massa^F

pen
pluma^F
plume^F
Schreiber^M
pennino^M

rotating drum
tambor^M giratorio
cylindre^M enregistreur
Registriertrommel^F
tamburo^M rotante

seismogram
sismógrafo^M
sismogramme^M
Seismogramm^N
sismogramma^M

horizontal ground movement
movimiento^M horizontal del suelo^M
mouvement^M horizontal du sol^M
horizontale Bodenbewegung^F
movimento^M orizzontale del suolo^M

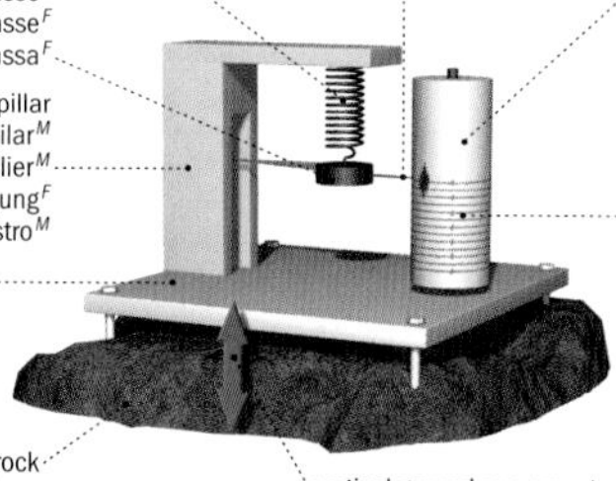

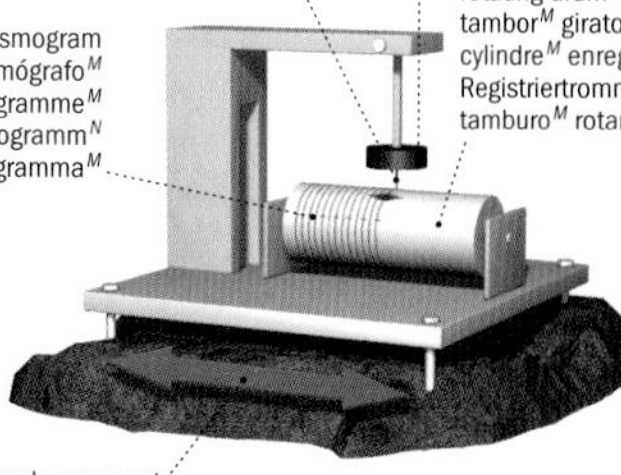

EARTH

volcano

volcán^M | volcan^M | Vulkan^M | vulcano^M

volcano during eruption
volcán^M en erupción^F
volcan^M en éruption^F
Vulkan^M mit Ausbruchstätigkeit^F
vulcano^M in eruzione^F

crater
cráter^M
cratère^M
Krater^M
cratere^M

cloud of volcanic ash
nube^F de cenizas^F
nuage^M de cendres^F
vulkanische Asche^F
nube^F di ceneri^F vulcaniche

volcanic bomb
bomba^F volcánica
bombe^F volcanique
vulkanische Bombe^F
bomba^F vulcanica

lava layer
estrato^M de lava^F
couche^F de laves^F
Lavaschicht^F
strato^M di lava^F

fumarole
fumarola^F
fumerolle^F
Fumarole^F
fumarola^F

lava flow
colada^F de lava^F
coulée^F de lave^F
Lavastrom^M
colata^F lavica

main vent
chimenea^F principal
cheminée^F
Hauptschlot^M
camino^M principale

geyser
géiser^M
geyser^M
Geysir^M
geyser^M

side vent
chimenea^F lateral
cône^M adventif
Seitenschlot^M
cono^M avventizio

ash layer
estrato^M de cenizas^F
couche^F de cendres^F
Ascheschicht^F
strato^M di ceneri^F

laccolith
lacolito^M
laccolite^F
Lakkolith^M
laccolite$^{M/F}$

magma chamber
cámara^F de magma^M
réservoir^M magmatique
Magmakammer^F
camera^F magmatica

dike
dique^M
dyke^M
Gang^M
dicco^M

magma
magma^M
magma^M
Magma^N
magma^M

sill
filón-capa^M
sill^M
Lagergang^M
filone strato^M

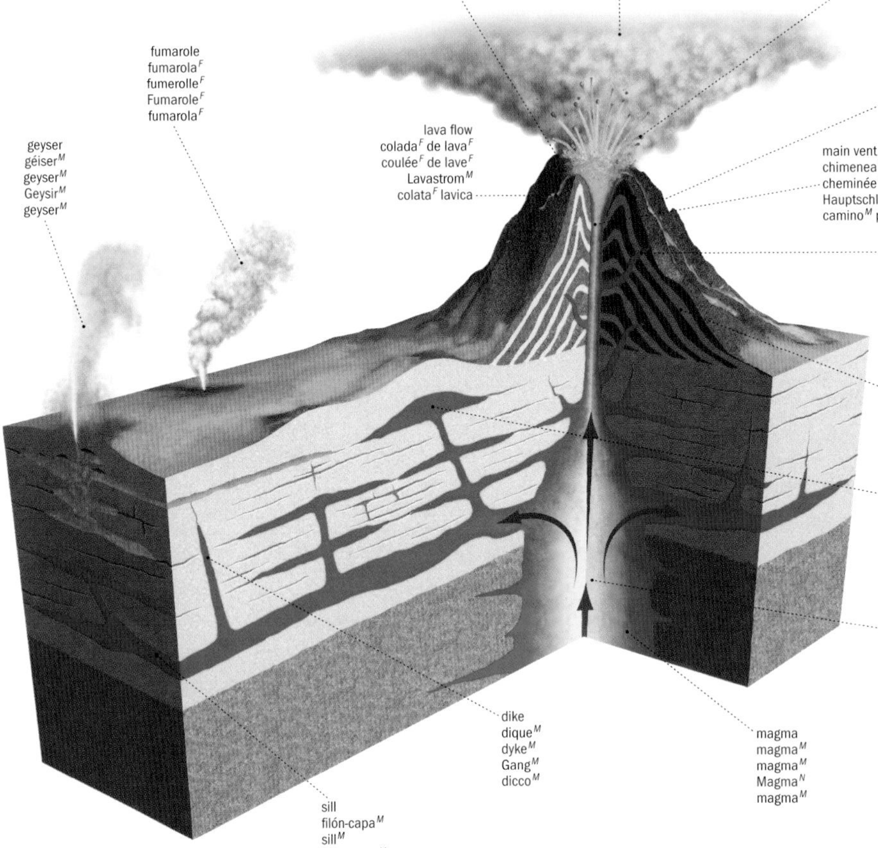

examples of volcanoes
ejemplos^M de volcanes^M
exemples^M de volcans^M
Vulkantypen^M
esempi^M di vulcani^M

explosive volcano
volcán^M explosivo
volcan^M explosif
explosiver Vulkan^M
vulcano^M esplosivo

effusive volcano
volcán^M efusivo
volcan^M effusif
effusiver Vulkan^M
vulcano^M effusivo

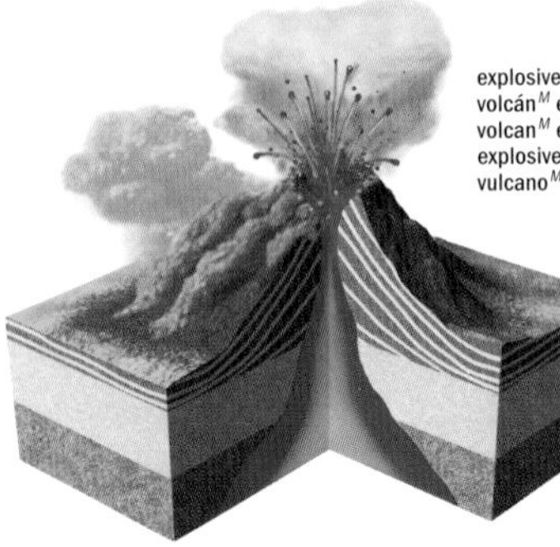

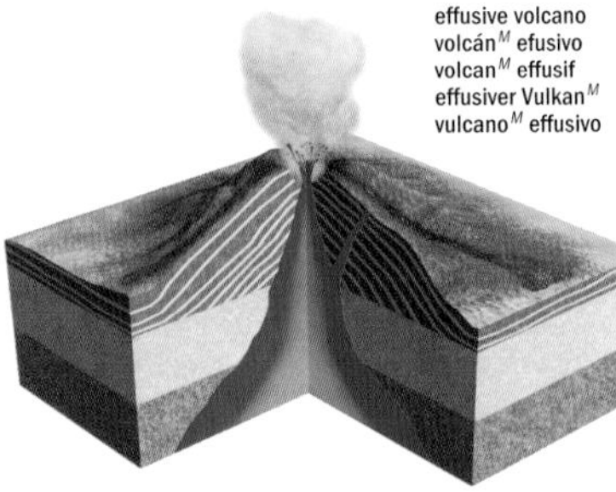

mountain

montaña[F] | montagne[F] | Berg[M] | montagna[F]

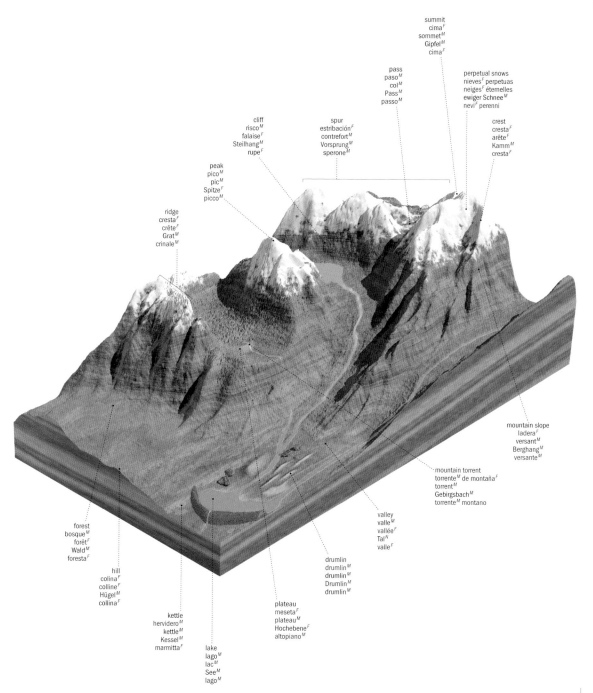

summit
cima[F]
sommet[M]
Gipfel[M]
cima[F]

pass
paso[M]
col[M]
Pass[M]
passo[M]

perpetual snows
nieves[F] perpetuas
neiges[F] éternelles
ewiger Schnee[M]
nevi[F] perenni

cliff
risco[M]
falaise[F]
Steilhang[M]
rupe[F]

spur
estribación[F]
contrefort[M]
Vorsprung[M]
sperone[M]

crest
cresta[F]
arête[F]
Kamm[M]
cresta[F]

peak
pico[M]
pic[M]
Spitze[F]
picco[M]

ridge
cresta[F]
crête[F]
Grat[M]
crinale[M]

mountain slope
ladera[F]
versant[M]
Berghang[M]
versante[M]

mountain torrent
torrente[M] de montaña[F]
torrent[M]
Gebirgsbach[M]
torrente[M] montano

forest
bosque[M]
forêt[F]
Wald[M]
foresta[F]

valley
valle[M]
vallée[F]
Tal[N]
valle[M]

hill
colina[F]
colline[F]
Hügel[M]
collina[F]

drumlin
drumlin[M]
drumlin[M]
Drumlin[M]
drumlin[M]

kettle
hervidero[M]
kettle[M]
Kessel[M]
marmitta[F]

plateau
meseta[F]
plateau[M]
Hochebene[F]
altopiano[M]

lake
lago[M]
lac[M]
See[M]
lago[M]

glacier

glaciar^M | glacier^M | Gletscher^M | ghiacciaio^M

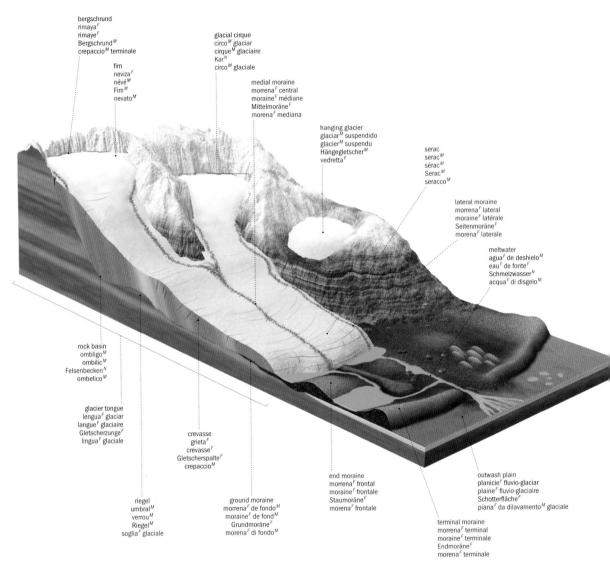

bergschrund
rimaya^F
rimaye^F
Bergschrund^M
crepaccio^M terminale

glacial cirque
circo^M glaciar
cirque^M glaciaire
Kar^N
circo^M glaciale

firn
neviza^F
névé^M
Firn^M
nevato^M

medial moraine
morrena^F central
moraine^F médiane
Mittelmoräne^F
morena^F mediana

hanging glacier
glaciar^M suspendido
glacier^M suspendu
Hängegletscher^M
vedretta^F

serac
serac^M
sérac^M
Serac^M
seracco^M

lateral moraine
morrena^F lateral
moraine^F latérale
Seitenmoräne^F
morena^F laterale

meltwater
agua^F de deshielo^M
eau^F de fonte^F
Schmelzwasser^N
acqua^F di disgelo^M

rock basin
ombligo^M
ombilic^M
Felsenbecken^N
ombelico^M

glacier tongue
lengua^F glaciar
langue^F glaciaire
Gletscherzunge^F
lingua^F glaciale

crevasse
grieta^F
crevasse^F
Gletscherspalte^F
crepaccio^M

riegel
umbral^M
verrou^M
Riegel^M
soglia^F glaciale

ground moraine
morrena^F de fondo^M
moraine^F de fond^M
Grundmoräne^F
morena^F di fondo^M

end moraine
morrena^F frontal
moraine^F frontale
Staumoräne^F
morena^F frontale

outwash plain
planicie^F fluvio-glaciar
plaine^F fluvio-glaciaire
Schotterfläche^F
piana^F da dilavamento^M glaciale

terminal moraine
morrena^F terminal
moraine^F terminale
Endmoräne^F
morena^F terminale

cave

gruta[F] | grotte[F] | Höhle[F] | grotta[F]

lapiaz
lapiaz[M]
lapiaz[M]
Schratten[M]
campi[M] solcati

stalactite
estalactita[F]
stalactite[F]
Stalaktit[M]
stalattite[F]

sinkhole
torca[F]
doline[F]
Doline[F]
dolina[F]

gorge
garganta[F]
gorge[F]
Schlucht[F]
gola[F]

pothole
hoyo[M]
aven[M]
Einstiegsloch[N]
pozzo[M]

waterfall
cascada[F]
chute[F]
Wasserfall[M]
cascata[F]

swallow hole
tragadero[M]
gouffre[M]
Schluckloch[N]
inghiottitoio[M]

gour
derrubios[M]
gour[M]
Kolk[M]
conca[F] di concrezione

water table
nivel[M] freático
nappe[F] phréatique
Grundwasserspiegel[M]
superficie[F] freatica

column
columna[F]
colonne[F]
Säule[F]
colonna[F]

subterranean stream
corriente[F] subterránea
rivière[F] souterraine
unterirdisches Gerinne[N]
corso[M] d'acqua[F] sotterraneo

stalagmite
estalagmita[F]
stalagmite[F]
Stalagmit[M]
stalagmite[F]

dry gallery
galería[F] seca
galerie[F] sèche
trocken liegender Höhlenraum[M]
galleria[F] secca

resurgence
resurgencia[F]
résurgence[F]
Wiederaustritt[M]
risorgiva[F]

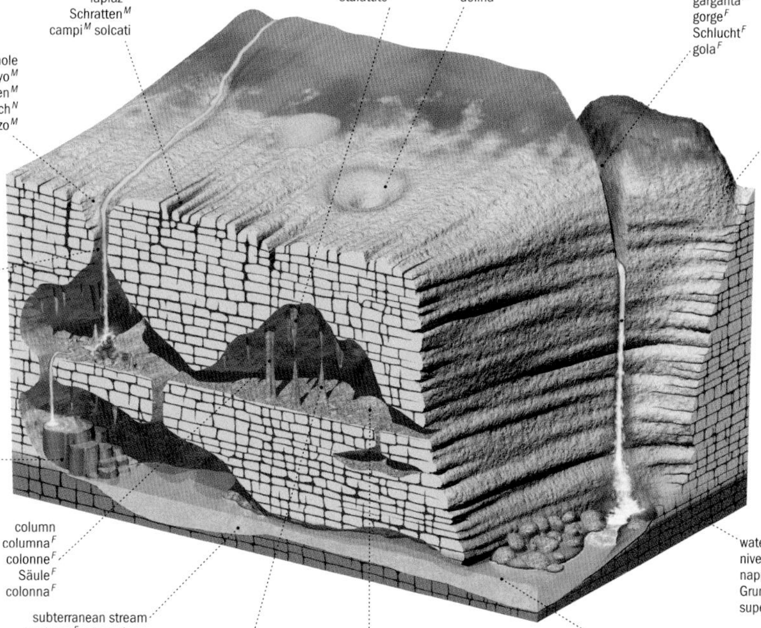

landslides

desprendimientos[M] de tierras[F] | mouvements[M] de terrain[M] | Bodenbewegungen[F] | movimenti del terreno[M]

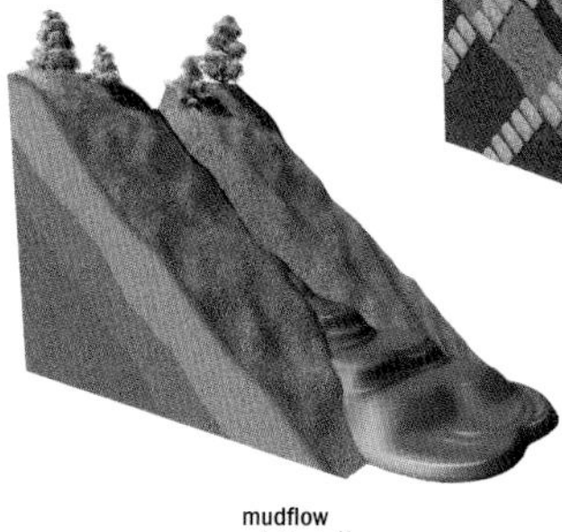

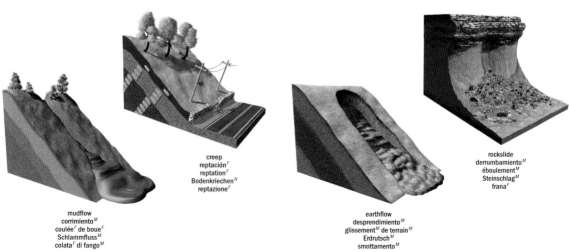

mudflow
corrimiento[M]
coulée[F] de boue[F]
Schlammfluss[M]
colata[F] di fango[M]

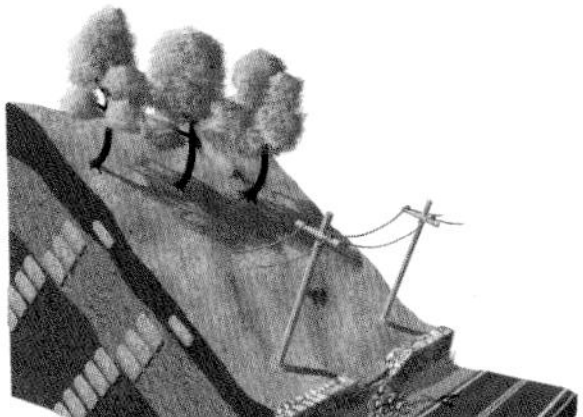

creep
reptación[F]
reptation[F]
Bodenkriechen[N]
reptazione[F]

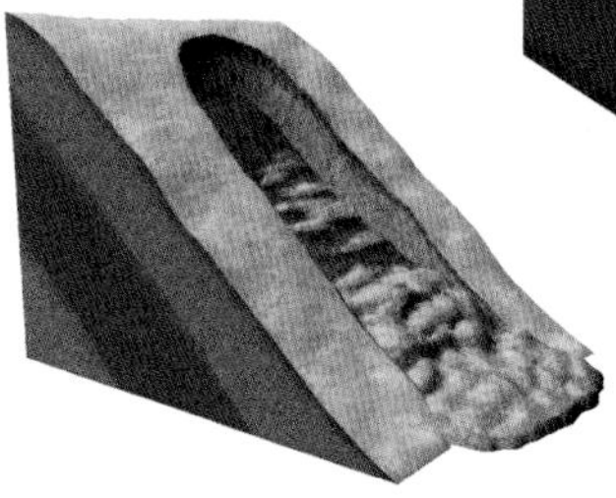

earthflow
desprendimiento[M]
glissement[M] de terrain[M]
Erdrutsch[M]
smottamento[M]

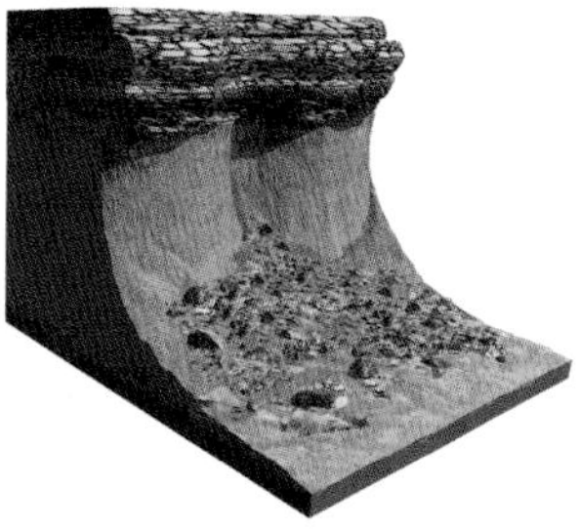

rockslide
derrumbamiento[M]
éboulement[M]
Steinschlag[M]
frana[F]

EARTH

watercourse

corriente^F de agua^F | cours^M d'eau^F | Flusslandschaft^F | corso^M d'acqua^F

spring
fuente^F
source^F
Quelle^F
sorgente^F

brook
arroyo^M
ruisseau^M
Bach^M
ruscello^M

glacier
glaciar^M
glacier^M
Gletscher^M
ghiacciaio^M

river
río^M
rivière^F
Fluss^M
fiume^M

valley
valle^M
vallée^F
Tal^N
valle^F

river
río^M
fleuve^M
Fluss^M
fiume^M

plain
llanura^F
plaine^F
Flachland^N
pianura^F

alluvial deposits
depósitos^M aluviales
alluvions^F
Alluvion^F
depositi^M alluvionali

oxbow
brazo^M muerto
bras^M mort
Altarm^M
meandro^M abbandonato

delta distributary
brazos^M del delta^M
bras^M de delta^M
Delta^N-Arm^M
canale^M deltizio

floodplain
llanura^F de inundación^F
plaine^F d'inondation^F
Überschwemmungsebene^F
piana^F inondabile

sea
mar^M
mer^F
See^F
mare^M

waterfall
cascada^F
chute^F d'eau^F
Wasserfall^M
cascata^F

lake
lago^M
lac^M
See^M
lago^M

gorge
garganta^F
gorge^F
Schlucht^F
gola^F

confluence
confluente^M
confluent^M
Zusammenfluss^M
confluente^M

effluent
efluente^M
effluent^M
Abfluss^M
emissario^M

affluent
afluente^M
affluent^M
Zufluss^M
affluente^M

meander
meandro^M
méandre^M
Mäander^M
meandro^M

delta
delta^M
delta^M
Delta^N
delta^M

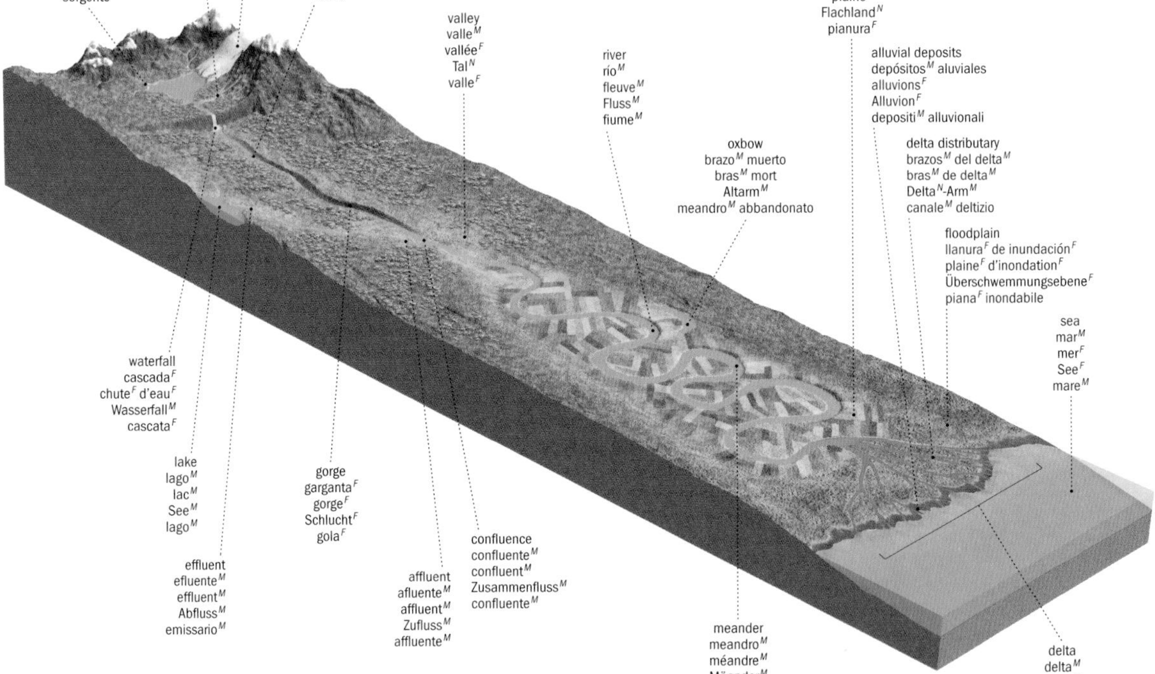

lakes

lagos^M | lacs^M | Seen^M | laghi^M

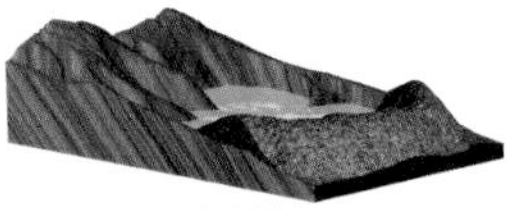

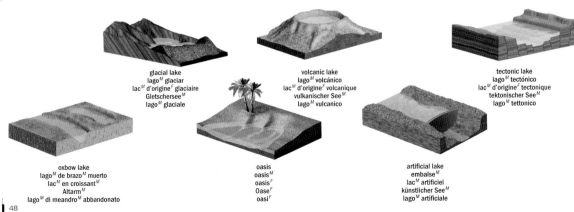

glacial lake
lago^M glaciar
lac^M d'origine^F glaciaire
Gletschersee^M
lago^M glaciale

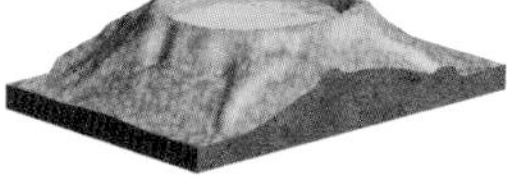

volcanic lake
lago^M volcánico
lac^M d'origine^F volcanique
vulkanischer See^M
lago^M vulcanico

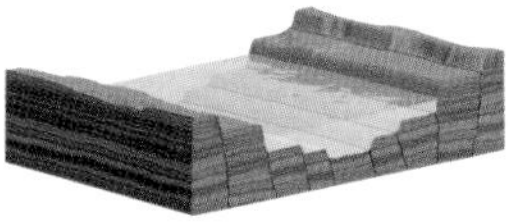

tectonic lake
lago^M tectónico
lac^M d'origine^F tectonique
tektonischer See^M
lago^M tettonico

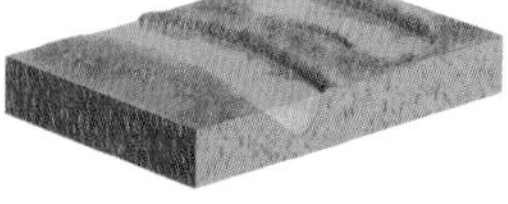

oxbow lake
lago^M de brazo^M muerto
lac^M en croissant^M
Altarm^M
lago^M di meandro^M abbandonato

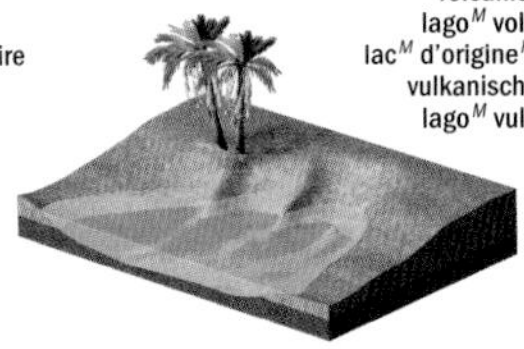

oasis
oasis^M
oasis^F
Oase^F
oasi^F

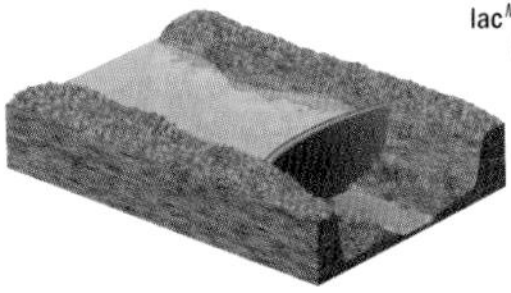

artificial lake
embalse^M
lac^M artificiel
künstlicher See^M
lago^M artificiale

wave

ola^F | vague^F | Welle^F | onda^F

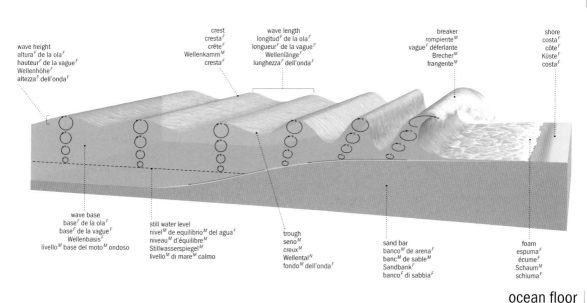

wave height
altura^F de la ola^F
hauteur^F de la vague^F
Wellenhöhe^F
altezza^F dell'onda^F

crest
cresta^F
crête^F
Wellenkamm^M
cresta^F

wave length
longitud^F de la ola^F
longueur^F de la vague^F
Wellenlänge^F
lunghezza^F dell'onda^F

breaker
rompiente^M
vague^F déferlante
Brecher^M
frangente^M

shore
costa^F
côte^F
Küste^F
costa^F

wave base
base^F de la ola^F
base^F de la vague^F
Wellenbasis^F
livello^M base del moto^M ondoso

still water level
nivel^M de equilibrio^M del agua^F
niveau^M d'équilibre^M
Stillwasserspiegel^M
livello^M di mare^M calmo

trough
seno^M
creux^M
Wellental^N
fondo^M dell'onda^F

sand bar
banco^M de arena^F
banc^M de sable^M
Sandbank^F
banco^M di sabbia^F

foam
espuma^F
écume^F
Schaum^M
schiuma^F

ocean floor

fondo^M oceánico | fond^M de l'océan^M | Meeresboden^M | fondale^M oceanico

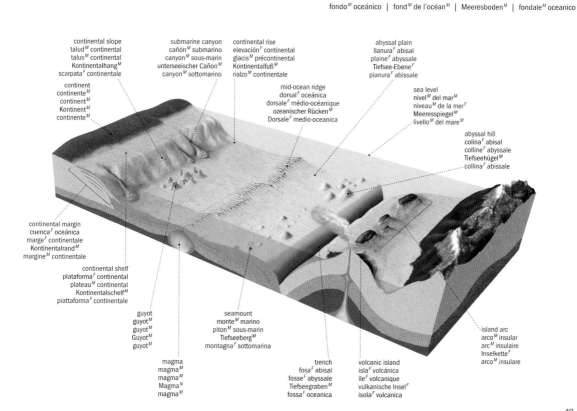

continental slope
talud^M continental
talus^M continental
Kontinentalhang^M
scarpata^F continentale

submarine canyon
cañón^M submarino
canyon^M sous-marin
unterseeischer Cañon^M
canyon^M sottomarino

continental rise
elevación^F continental
glacis^F précontinental
Kontinentalfuß^M
rialzo^M continentale

abyssal plain
llanura^F abisal
plaine^F abyssale
Tiefsee-Ebene^F
pianura^F abissale

continent
continente^M
continent^M
Kontinent^M
continente^M

mid-ocean ridge
dorsal^F oceánica
dorsale^F médio-océanique
ozeanischer Rücken^M
Dorsale^F medio-oceanica

sea level
nivel^M del mar^M
niveau^M de la mer^F
Meeresspiegel^M
livello^M del mare^M

abyssal hill
colina^F abisal
colline^F abyssale
Tiefseehügel^M
collina^F abissale

continental margin
cuenca^F oceánica
marge^F continentale
Kontinentalrand^M
margine^M continentale

continental shelf
plataforma^F continental
plateau^M continental
Kontinentalschelf^M
piattaforma^F continentale

guyot
guyot^M
guyot^M
Guyot^M
guyot^M

seamount
monte^M marino
piton^M sous-marin
Tiefseeberg^M
montagna^F sottomarina

island arc
arco^M insular
arc^M insulaire
Inselkette^F
arco^M insulare

magma
magma^M
magma^M
Magma^N
magma^M

trench
fosa^F abisal
fosse^F abyssale
Tiefseegraben^M
fossa^F oceanica

volcanic island
isla^F volcánica
île^F volcanique
vulkanische Insel^F
isola^F vulcanica

ocean trenches and ridges

fosas^F y dorsales^F oceánicas | fosses^F et dorsales^F océaniques | ozeanische Rücken^M und Gräben^M | fosse^F e dorsali^F oceaniche

EARTH

Aleutian Trench
Fosa^F de las Aleutianas^F
fosse^F des Aléoutiennes
Aleutengraben^M
Fossa^F delle Aleutine

North America
América^F del Norte
Amérique^F du Nord^M
Nordamerika^N
America^F Settentrionale

Mid-Atlantic Ridge
Dorsal^F del Atlántico^M medio
dorsale^F médio-atlantique
Mittelatlantischer Rücken^M
Dorsale^F Medio-Atlantica

Europe   Africa
Europa^F África^F
Europe^F Afrique^F
Europa^N Afrika^N
Europa^F Africa^F

Asia
Asia^F
Asie^F
Asien^N
Asia^F

Ryukyu Trench
Fosa^F Ryukyu
fosse^F des Ryukyu
Ryukyugraben^M
Fossa^F delle Ryukyu

Japan Trench
Fosa^F de Japón^M
fosse^F du Japon^M
Japangraben^M
Fossa^F del Giappone^M

Kuril Trench
Fosa^F de Kuril
fosse^F des Kouriles
Kurilengraben^M
Fossa^F delle Curili

Mariana Trench
Fosa^F de las Marianas^F
fosse^F des Mariannes
Marianengraben^M
Fossa^F delle Marianne

Philippine Trench
Fosa^F de las Filipinas^F
fosse^F des Philippines^F
Philippinengraben^M
Fossa^F delle Filippine

Java Trench
Fosa^F de Java
fosse^F de Java
Javagraben^M
Fossa^F di Giava^F

Kermadec-Tonga Trench
Fosa^F de Kermadec-Tonga^M
fosse^F des Tonga^F-Kermadec
Kermadec-Tonga^N-Graben^M
Fossa^F di Kermadec-Tonga

Australia
Australia^F
Australie^F
Australien^N
Australia^F

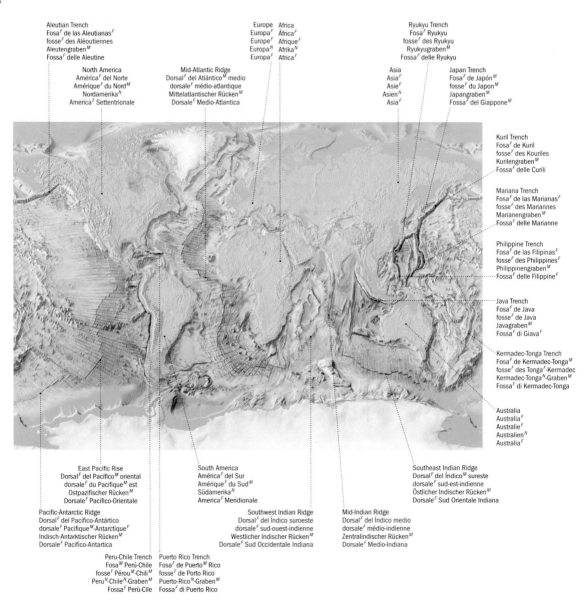

East Pacific Rise
Dorsal^F del Pacífico^M oriental
dorsale^F du Pacifique^M est
Ostpazifischer Rücken^M
Dorsale^F Pacifico-Orientale

Pacific-Antarctic Ridge
Dorsal^F del Pacífico-Antártico
dorsale^F Pacifique^M-Antarctique^F
Indisch-Antarktischer Rücken^M
Dorsale^F Pacifico-Antartica

South America
América^F del Sur
Amérique^F du Sud^M
Südamerika^N
America^F Meridionale

Southwest Indian Ridge
Dorsal^F del Índico suroeste
dorsale^F sud-ouest-indienne
Westlicher Indischer Rücken^M
Dorsale^F Sud Occidentale Indiana

Mid-Indian Ridge
Dorsal^F del Índico medio
dorsale^F médio-indienne
Zentralindischer Rücken^M
Dorsale^F Medio-Indiana

Southeast Indian Ridge
Dorsal^F del Índico^M sureste
dorsale^F sud-est-indienne
Östlicher Indischer Rücken^M
Dorsale^F Sud Orientale Indiana

Peru-Chile Trench
Fosa^M Perú-Chile
fosse^F Pérou^M-Chili^M
Peru^N-Chile^N-Graben^M
Fossa^F Perù-Cile

Puerto Rico Trench
Fosa^F de Puerto^M Rico
fosse^F de Porto Rico
Puerto-Rico^N-Graben^M
Fossa^F di Puerto Rico

common coastal features

configuración^F del litoral^M | configuration^F du littoral^M | typische Küstenformen^F | caratteristiche^F della costa^F

EARTH

stack
farallón^M
aiguille^F
Brandungspfeiler^M
faraglione^M

river estuary
estuario^M
estuaire^M
Flussmündung^F
estuario^M

dune
duna^F
dune^F
Düne^F
duna^F

lagoon
laguna^F
lagune^F
Lagune^F
laguna^F

cave
cueva^F
grotte^F
Höhle^F
grotta^F

natural arch
arco^M natural
arche^F naturelle
Brandungstor^N
arco^M naturale

beach
playa^F
plage^F
Strand^M
spiaggia^F

sand island
isla^F de arena^F
ile^F de sable^M
Sandinsel^F
isolotto^M sabbioso

rocky islet
islote^M rocoso
ilot^M rocheux
Felseninselchen^N
isolotto^M roccioso

tombolo
tómbolo^M
tombolo^M
Nehrung^F
tombolo^M

cliff
acantilado^M
falaise^F
Kliff^N, Klippe^F
falesia^F

skerry
escollo^M
écueil^M
Felssäule^F
scoglio^M

spit
barra^F
flèche^F littorale
Landzunge^F
lingua^F di terra^F

headland
promontorio^M
pointe^F
Landspitze^F
promontorio^M

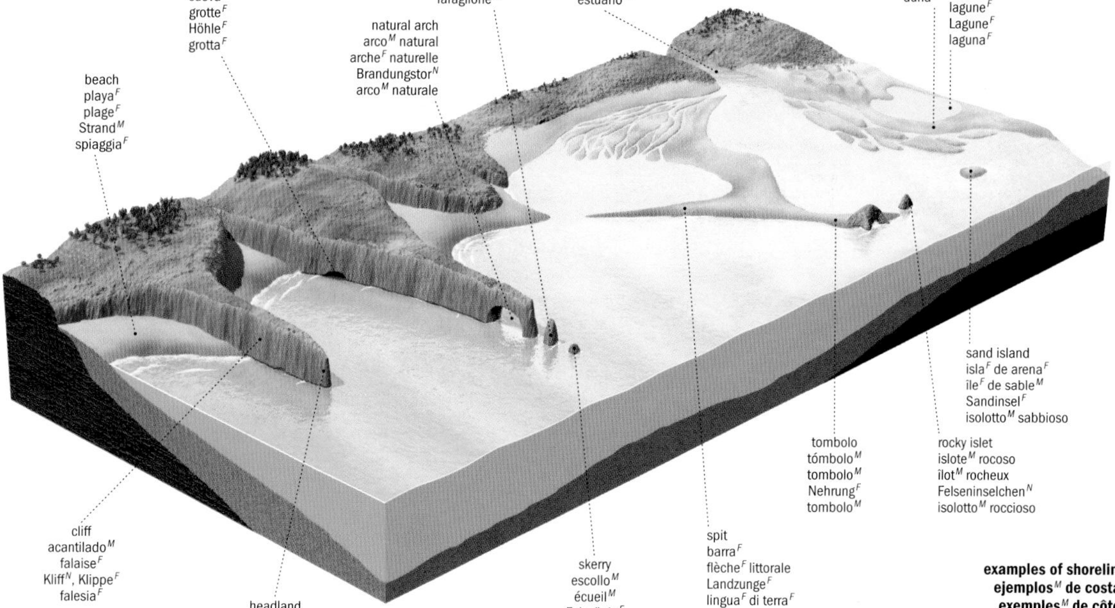

**examples of shorelines
ejemplos^M de costas^F
exemples^M de côtes^F
Küstenformen^F
esempi^M di linee^F di costa^F**

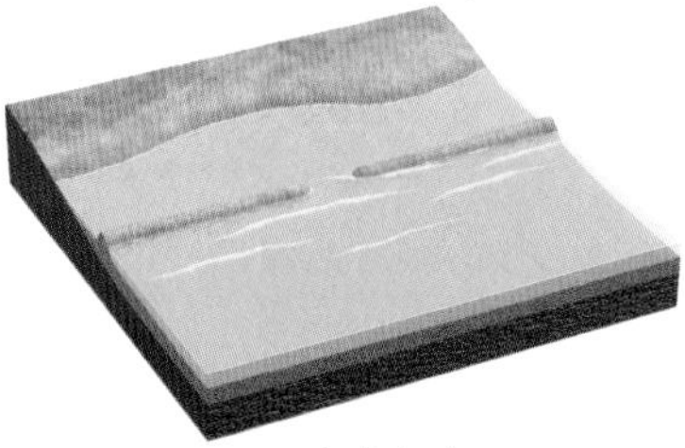

barrier beach
cordón^M litoral
cordon^M littoral
Riffküste^F
cordone^M litorale

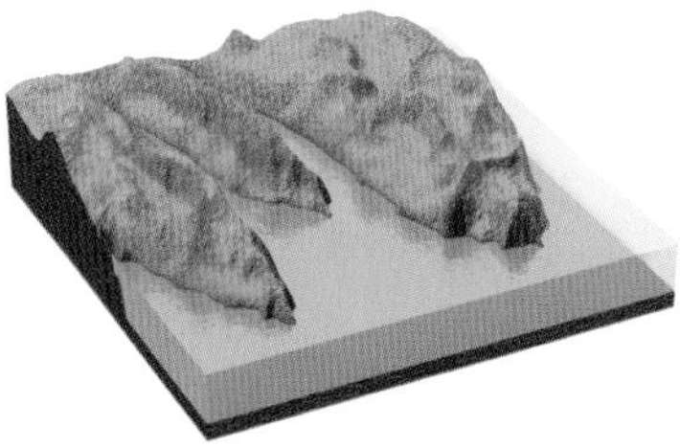

fjords
fiordo^M
fjords^F
Fjordküste^F
fiordi^M

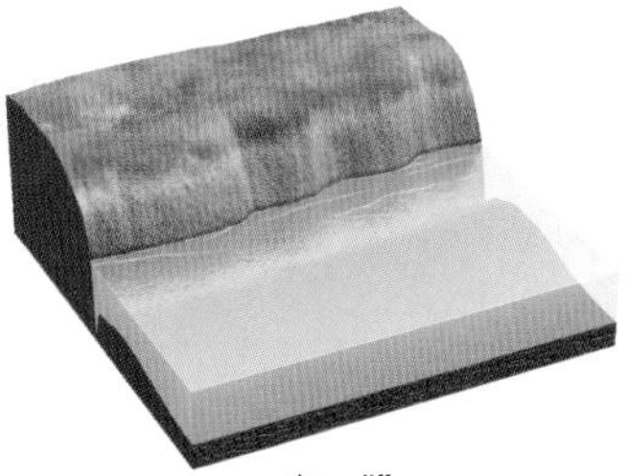

shore cliff
acantilado^M
falaise^F côtière
Steilküste^F
falesia^F costiera

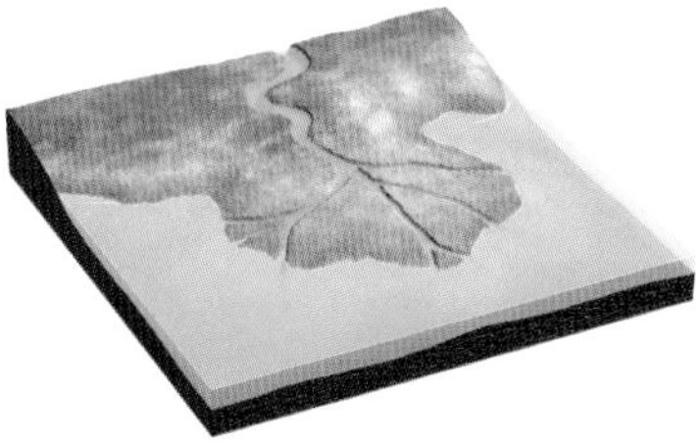

delta
delta^M
delta^M
Delta^N
delta^M

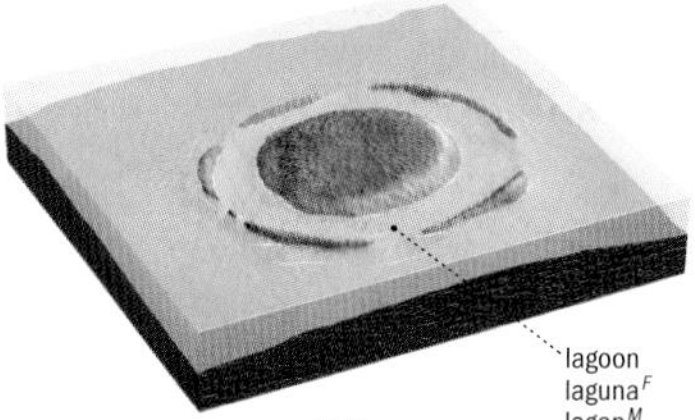

atoll
atolón^M
atoll^M
Atoll^N
atollo^M

lagoon
laguna^F
lagon^M
Lagune^F
laguna^F

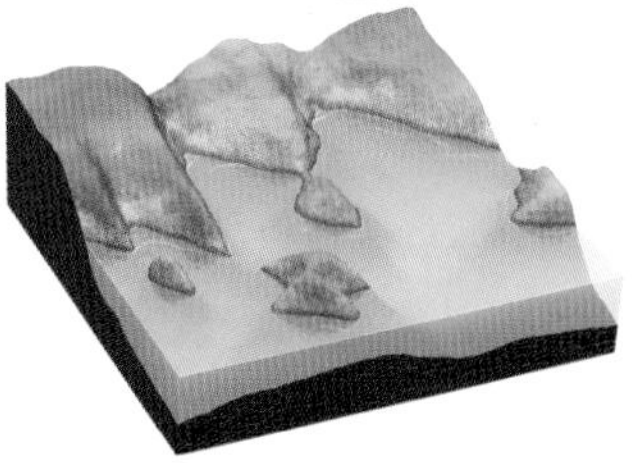

rias
rias^F
rias^F
Riasküste^F
costa^F a rias^F

desert

desierto^M | désert^M | Wüste^F | deserto^M

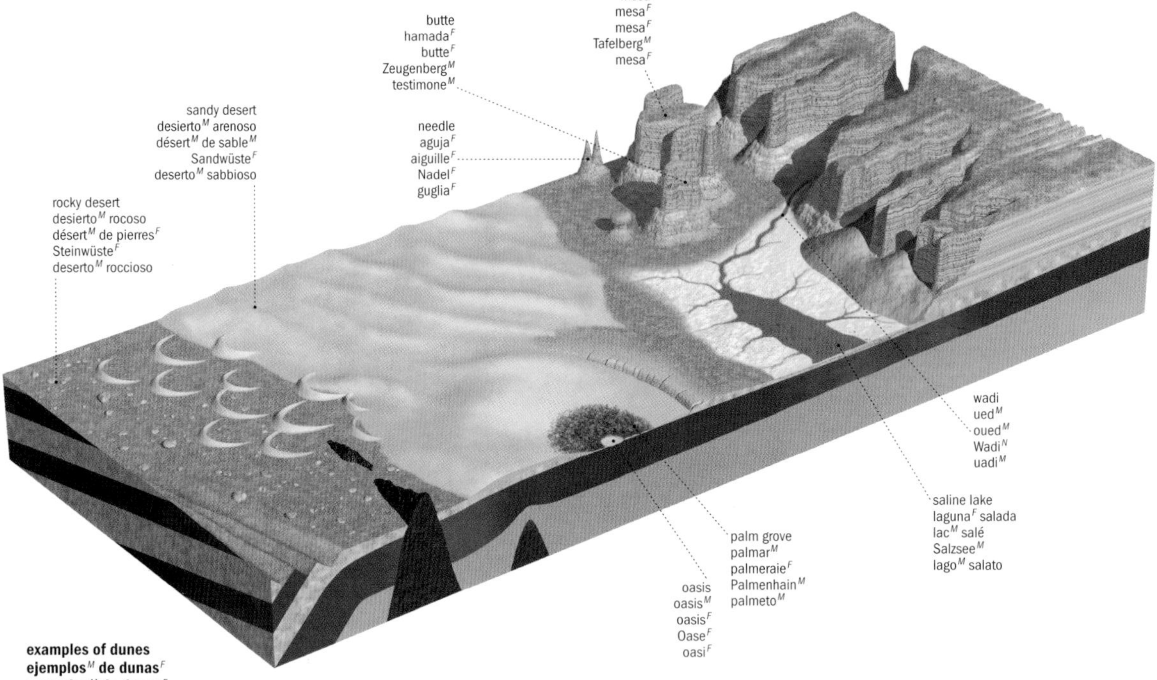

mesa
mesa^F
mesa^F
Tafelberg^M
mesa^F

butte
hamada^F
butte^F
Zeugenberg^M
testimone^M

sandy desert
desierto^M arenoso
désert^M de sable^M
Sandwüste^F
deserto^M sabbioso

needle
aguja^F
aiguille^F
Nadel^F
guglia^F

rocky desert
desierto^M rocoso
désert^M de pierres^F
Steinwüste^F
deserto^M roccioso

wadi
ued^M
oued^M
Wadi^N
uadi^M

saline lake
laguna^F salada
lac^M salé
Salzsee^M
lago^M salato

palm grove
palmar^M
palmeraie^F
Palmenhain^M
palmeto^M

oasis
oasis^M
oasis^F
Oase^F
oasi^F

examples of dunes
ejemplos^M de dunas^F
exemples^M de dunes^F
Dünenformen^F
esempi^M di dune^F

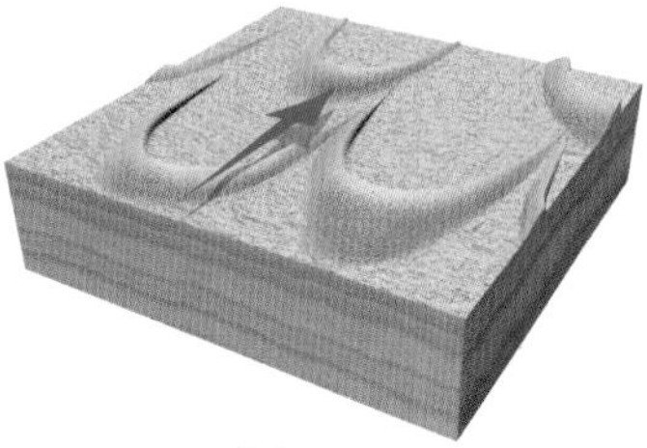

crescentic dune
barján^M
dune^F en croissant^M
Sicheldüne^F
barcana^F

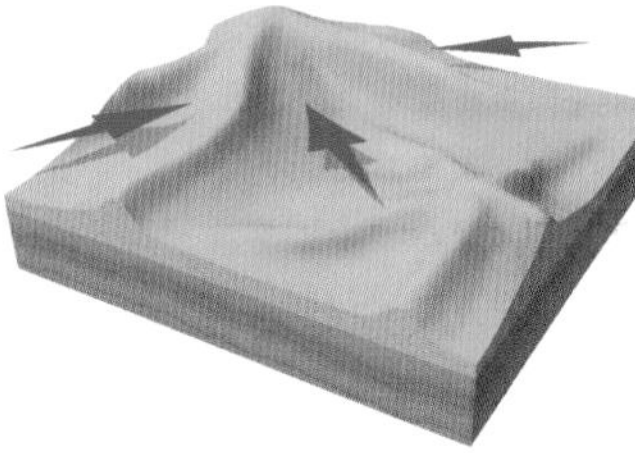

complex dune
duna^F compleja
dune^F complexe
komplexe Düne^F
duna^F complessa

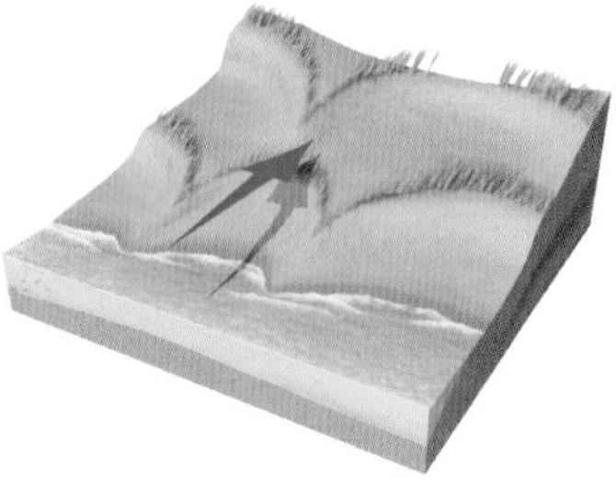

parabolic dune
duna^F parabólica
dune^F parabolique
Parabeldüne^F
duna^F parabolica

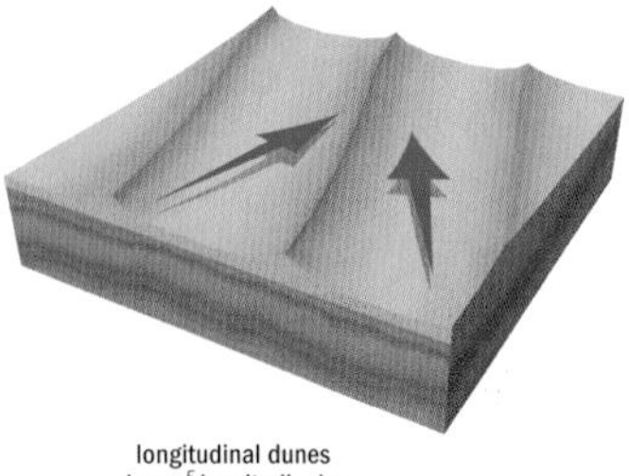

longitudinal dunes
dunas^F longitudinales
dunes^F longitudinales
Längsdünen^F
dune^F longitudinali

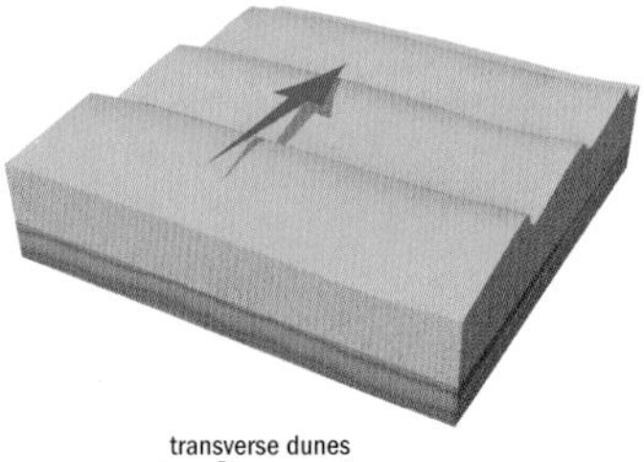

transverse dunes
dunas^F transversales
dunes^F transversales
Querdünen^F
dune^F trasversali

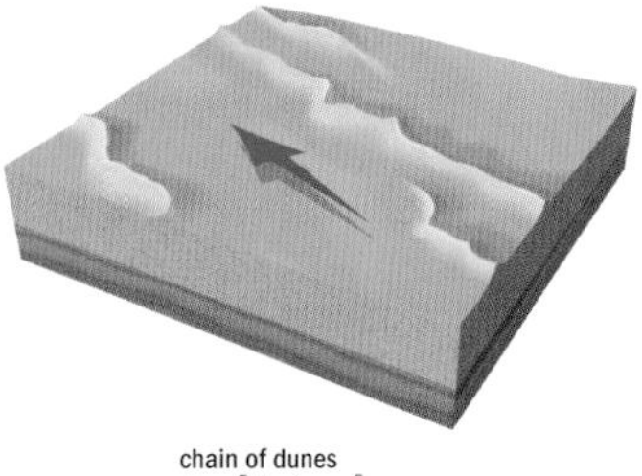

chain of dunes
cadena^F de dunas^F
cordon^M de dunes^F
Dünenzug^M
catena^F di dune^F

profile of the Earth's atmosphere

corte^M de la atmósfera^F terrestre | coupe^F de l'atmosphère^F terrestre | Erdatmosphäre^F im Querschnitt^M | profilo^M dell'atmosfera^F terrestre

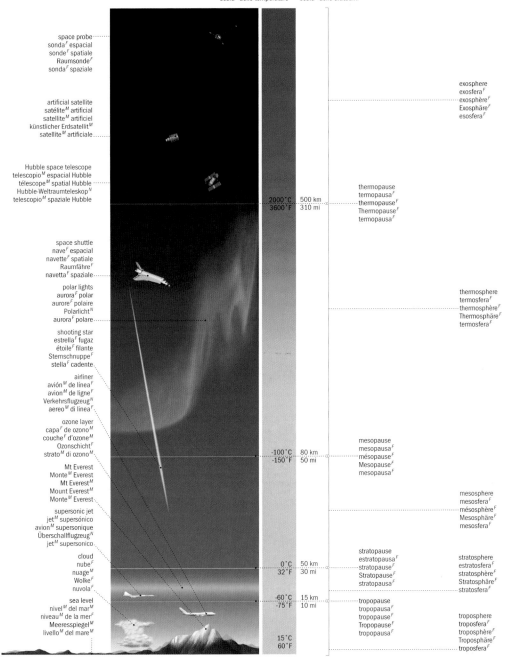

temperature scale
escala^F de temperaturas^F
échelle^F des températures^F
Temperaturskala^F
scala^F delle temperature^F

altitude scale
escala^F de altitud^F
échelle^F des altitudes^F
Höhenskala^F
scala^F delle altitudini^F

space probe
sonda^F espacial
sonde^F spatiale
Raumsonde^F
sonda^F spaziale

artificial satellite
satélite^M artificial
satellite^M artificiel
künstlicher Erdsatellit^M
satellite^M artificiale

Hubble space telescope
telescopio^M espacial Hubble
télescope^M spatial Hubble
Hubble-Weltraumteleskop^N
telescopio^M spaziale Hubble

space shuttle
nave^F espacial
navette^F spatiale
Raumfähre^F
navetta^F spaziale

polar lights
aurora^F polar
aurore^F polaire
Polarlicht^N
aurora^F polare

shooting star
estrella^F fugaz
étoile^F filante
Sternschnuppe^F
stella^F cadente

airliner
avión^M de línea^F
avion^M de ligne^F
Verkehrsflugzeug^N
aereo^M di linea^F

ozone layer
capa^F de ozono^M
couche^F d'ozone^M
Ozonschicht^F
strato^M di ozono^M

Mt Everest
Monte^M Everest
Mt Everest^M
Mount Everest^M
Monte^M Everest

supersonic jet
jet^M supersónico
avion^M supersonique
Überschallflugzeug^N
jet^M supersonico

cloud
nube^F
nuage^M
Wolke^F
nuvola^F

sea level
nivel^M del mar^M
niveau^M de la mer^F
Meeresspiegel^M
livello^M del mare^M

2000 °C | 500 km
3600 °F | 310 mi

-100 °C | 80 km
-150 °F | 50 mi

0 °C | 50 km
32 °F | 30 mi

-60 °C | 15 km
-75 °F | 10 mi

15 °C
60 °F

thermopause
termopausa^F
thermopause^F
Thermopause^F
termopausa^F

mesopause
mesopausa^F
mésopause^F
Mesopause^F
mesopausa^F

stratopause
estratopausa^F
stratopause^F
Stratopause^F
stratopausa^F

tropopause
tropopausa^F
tropopause^F
Tropopause^F
tropopausa^F

exosphere
exosfera^F
exosphère^F
Exosphäre^F
esosfera^F

thermosphere
termosfera^F
thermosphère^F
Thermosphäre^F
termosfera^F

mesosphere
mesosfera^F
mésosphère^F
Mesosphäre^F
mesosfera^F

stratosphere
estratosfera^F
stratosphère^F
Stratosphäre^F
stratosfera^F

troposphere
troposfera^F
troposphère^F
Troposphäre^F
troposfera^F

seasons of the year

estaciones^F del año^M | cycle^M des saisons^F | Jahreszeiten^F | stagioni^F dell'anno^M

EARTH

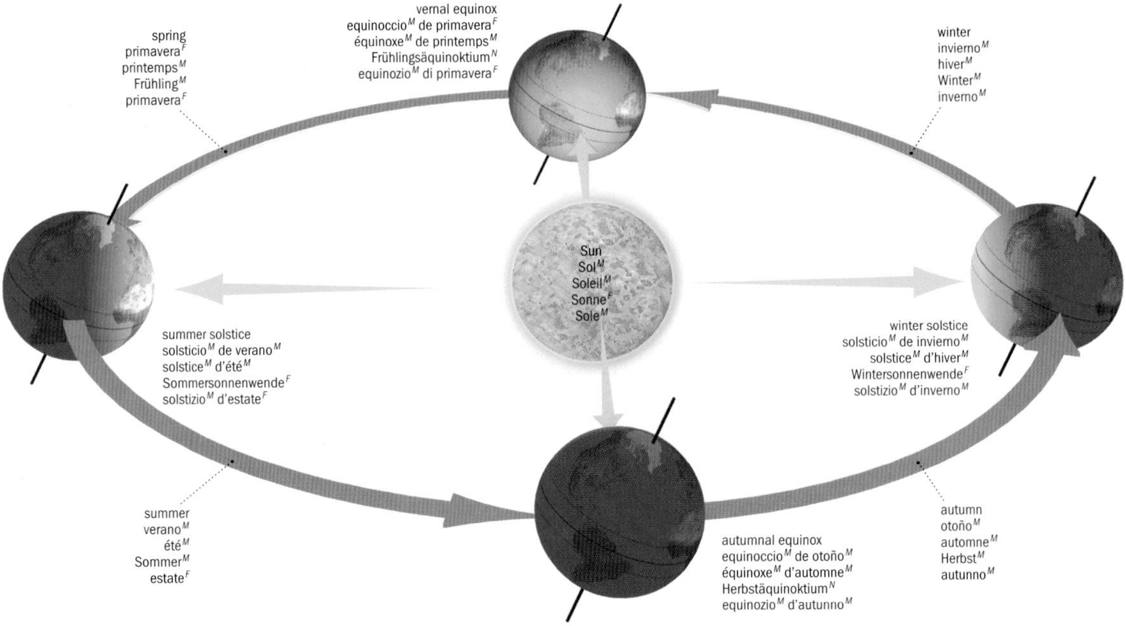

spring
primavera^F
printemps^M
Frühling^M
primavera^F

vernal equinox
equinoccio^M de primavera^F
équinoxe^M de printemps^M
Frühlingsäquinoktium^N
equinozio^M di primavera^F

winter
invierno^M
hiver^M
Winter^M
inverno^M

Sun
Sol^M
Soleil^M
Sonne^F
Sole^M

summer solstice
solsticio^M de verano^M
solstice^M d'été^M
Sommersonnenwende^F
solstizio^M d'estate^F

winter solstice
solsticio^M de invierno^M
solstice^M d'hiver^M
Wintersonnenwende^F
solstizio^M d'inverno^M

summer
verano^M
été^M
Sommer^M
estate^F

autumnal equinox
equinoccio^M de otoño^M
équinoxe^M d'automne^M
Herbstäquinoktium^N
equinozio^M d'autunno^M

autumn
otoño^M
automne^M
Herbst^M
autunno^M

meteorological forecast

previsión^F meteorológica | prévision^F météorologique | Wettervorhersage^F | previsioni^F meteorologiche

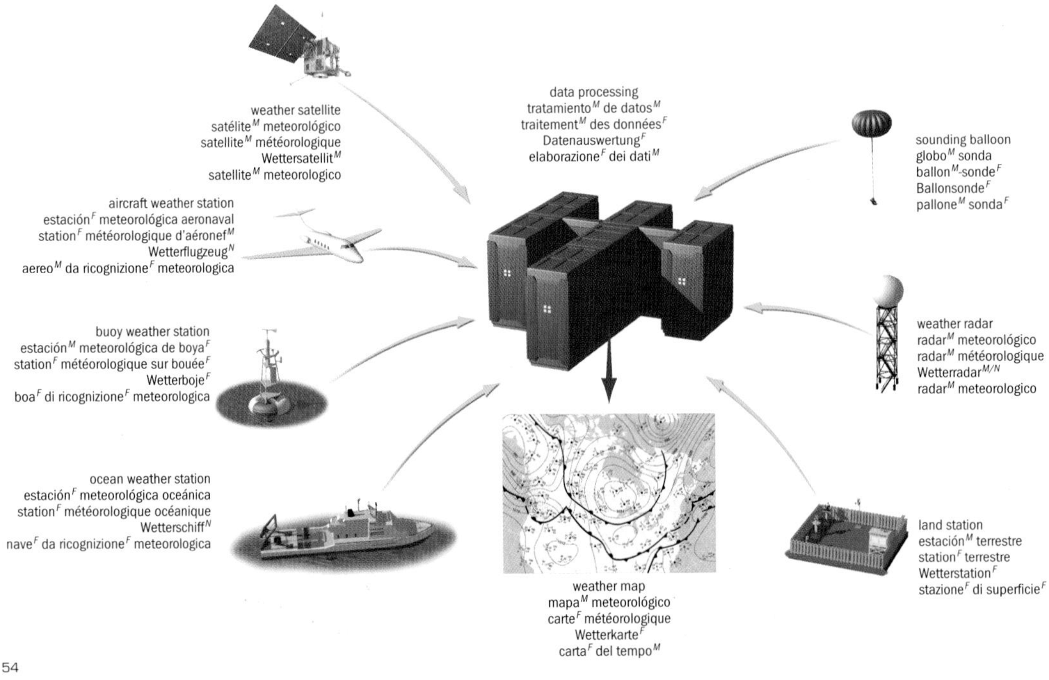

weather satellite
satélite^M meteorológico
satellite^M météorologique
Wettersatellit^M
satellite^M meteorologico

data processing
tratamiento^M de datos^M
traitement^M des données^F
Datenauswertung^F
elaborazione^F dei dati^M

sounding balloon
globo^M sonda
ballon^M-sonde^F
Ballonsonde^F
pallone^M sonda^F

aircraft weather station
estación^F meteorológica aeronaval
station^F météorologique d'aéronef^M
Wetterflugzeug^N
aereo^M da ricognizione^F meteorologica

buoy weather station
estación^M meteorológica de boya^F
station^F météorologique sur bouée^F
Wetterboje^F
boa^F di ricognizione^F meteorologica

weather radar
radar^M meteorológico
radar^M météorologique
Wetterradar$^{M/N}$
radar^M meteorologico

ocean weather station
estación^F meteorológica oceánica
station^F météorologique océanique
Wetterschiff^N
nave^F da ricognizione^F meteorologica

land station
estación^M terrestre
station^F terrestre
Wetterstation^F
stazione^F di superficie^F

weather map
mapa^M meteorológico
carte^F météorologique
Wetterkarte^F
carta^F del tempo^M

weather map

mapa ^{M} meteorológico | carte ^{F} météorologique | Wetterkarte ^{F} | carta ^{F} del tempo ^{M}

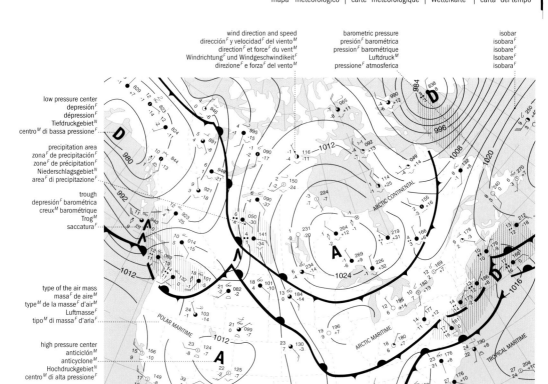

wind direction and speed
dirección ^{F} y velocidad ^{F} del viento ^{M}
direction ^{F} et force ^{F} du vent ^{M}
Windrichtung ^{F} und Windgeschwindigkeit ^{F}
direzione ^{F} e forza ^{F} del vento ^{M}

barometric pressure
presión ^{F} barométrica
pression ^{F} barométrique
Luftdruck ^{M}
pressione ^{F} atmosferica

isobar
isobara ^{F}
isobare ^{F}
Isobare ^{F}
isobara ^{F}

low pressure center
depresión ^{F}
dépression ^{F}
Tiefdruckgebiet ^{N}
centro ^{M} di bassa pressione ^{F}

precipitation area
zona ^{F} de precipitación ^{F}
zone ^{F} de précipitation ^{F}
Niederschlagsgebiet ^{N}
area ^{F} di precipitazione ^{F}

trough
depresión ^{F} barométrica
creux ^{M} barométrique
Trog ^{M}
saccatura ^{F}

type of the air mass
masa ^{F} de aire ^{M}
type ^{M} de la masse ^{F} d'air ^{M}
Luftmasse ^{F}
tipo ^{M} di massa ^{F} d'aria ^{F}

high pressure center
anticiclón ^{M}
anticyclone ^{M}
Hochdruckgebiet ^{N}
centro ^{M} di alta pressione ^{F}

station model

modelo ^{M} de estación ^{F} | disposition ^{F} des informations ^{F} d'une station ^{F} | Stationsmodell ^{N} | modello ^{M} di stazione ^{F}

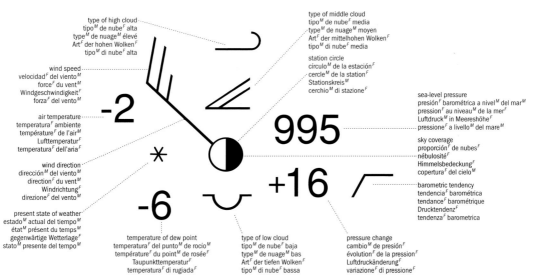

type of high cloud
tipo ^{M} de nube ^{F} alta
type ^{M} de nuage ^{M} élevé
Art ^{F} der hohen Wolken ^{F}
tipo ^{M} di nube ^{F} alta

type of middle cloud
tipo ^{M} de nube ^{F} media
type ^{M} de nuage ^{M} moyen
Art ^{F} der mittelhohen Wolken ^{F}
tipo ^{M} di nube ^{F} media

station circle
círculo ^{M} de la estación ^{F}
cercle ^{M} de la station ^{F}
Stationskreis ^{F}
cerchio ^{M} di stazione ^{F}

wind speed
velocidad ^{F} del viento ^{M}
force ^{F} du vent ^{M}
Windgeschwindigkeit ^{F}
forza ^{F} del vento ^{M}

air temperature
temperatura ^{F} ambiente
température ^{F} de l'air ^{M}
Lufttemperatur ^{F}
temperatura ^{F} dell'aria ^{F}

sea-level pressure
presión ^{F} barométrica a nivel ^{M} del mar ^{M}
pression ^{F} au niveau ^{M} de la mer ^{F}
Luftdruck ^{M} in Meereshöhe ^{F}
pressione ^{F} a livello ^{M} del mare ^{M}

sky coverage
proporción ^{F} de nubes ^{F}
nébulosité ^{F}
Himmelsbedeckung ^{F}
copertura ^{F} del cielo ^{M}

wind direction
dirección ^{M} del viento ^{M}
direction ^{F} du vent ^{M}
Windrichtung ^{F}
direzione ^{F} del vento ^{M}

barometric tendency
tendencia ^{F} barométrica
tendance ^{F} barométrique
Drucktendenz ^{F}
tendenza ^{F} barometrica

present state of weather
estado ^{M} actual del tiempo ^{M}
état ^{M} présent du temps ^{M}
gegenwärtige Wetterlage ^{F}
stato ^{M} presente del tempo ^{M}

temperature of dew point
temperatura ^{F} del punto ^{M} de rocío ^{M}
température ^{F} du point ^{M} de rosée ^{F}
Taupunkttemperatur ^{F}
temperatura ^{F} di rugiada ^{F}

type of low cloud
tipo ^{M} de nube ^{F} baja
type ^{M} de nuage ^{M} bas
Art ^{F} der tiefen Wolken ^{F}
tipo ^{M} di nube ^{F} bassa

pressure change
cambio ^{M} de presión ^{F}
évolution ^{F} de la pression ^{F}
Luftdruckänderung ^{F}
variazione ^{F} di pressione ^{F}

EARTH

international weather symbols

símbolos[M] meteorológicos internacionales | symboles[M] météorologiques internationaux | internationale Wettersymbole[N] | simboli[M] meteorologici internazionali

EARTH

wind
viento[M]
vent[M]
Wind[M]
vento[M]

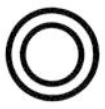

calm
sosegado[M]
air[M] calme
Windstille[F]
calma[F]

shaft
brisa[F] leve
hampe[F]
Pfeil[M]
segmento[M] orientato

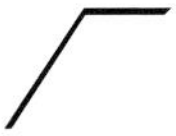

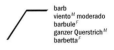

barb
viento[M] moderado
barbule[F]
ganzer Querstrich[M]
barbetta[F]

wind arrow
flecha[F] indicadora de la dirección[F] del viento[M]
flèche[F] du vent[M]
Windstärkefähnchen[N]
freccia[F] del vento[M]

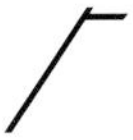

half barb
viento[M] suave
demi-barbule[F]
halber Querstrich[M]
mezza barbetta[F]

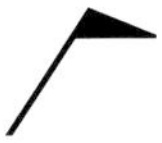

pennant
tempestad[F]
fanion[M]
Fähnchen[N]
banderuola[F]

fronts
frentes[M]
fronts[M]
Fronten[F]
fronti[M]

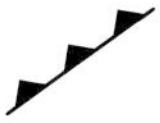

surface cold front
frente[M] frío de superficie[F]
front[M] froid en surface[F]
Kaltfront[F] am Boden[M]
fronte[M] freddo al suolo[M]

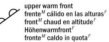

surface warm front
frente[M] cálido de superficie[F]
front[M] chaud en surface[F]
Warmfront[F] am Boden[M]
fronte[M] caldo al suolo[M]

occluded front
frente[M] ocluido
front[M] occlus
Okklusion[F]
fronte[M] occluso al suolo[M]

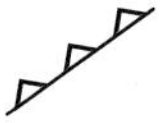

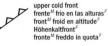

upper cold front
frente[M] frío en las alturas[F]
front[M] froid en altitude[F]
Höhenkaltfront[F]
fronte[M] freddo in quota[F]

upper warm front
frente[M] cálido en las alturas[F]
front[M] chaud en altitude[F]
Höhenwarmfront[F]
fronte[M] caldo in quota[F]

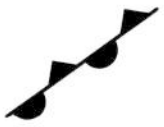

stationary front
frente[M] estacionario
front[M] stationnaire
stationäre Front[F]
fronte[M] stazionario

sky coverage
nubosidad[F]
nébulosité[F]
Bedeckungsgrad[M]
nuvolosità[F]

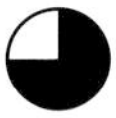

very cloudy sky
cielo[M] muy nuboso
ciel[M] très nuageux
stark bewölkter Himmel[M]
cielo[M] molto nuvoloso

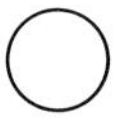

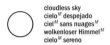

cloudless sky
cielo[M] despejado
ciel[M] sans nuages[M]
wolkenloser Himmel[M]
cielo[M] sereno

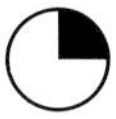

slightly covered sky
cielo[M] ligeramente nuboso
ciel[M] peu nuageux
heiterer Himmel[M]
cielo[M] poco nuvoloso

overcast sky
cielo[M] completamente nuboso
ciel[M] couvert
bedeckter Himmel[M]
cielo[M] coperto

clear sky
cielo[M] sereno
ciel[M] clair
klarer Himmel[M]
cielo[M] limpido

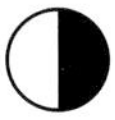

cloudy sky
cielo[M] medio nuboso
ciel[M] nuageux
bewölkter Himmel[M]
cielo[M] nuvoloso

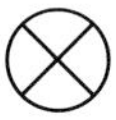

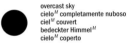

obscured sky
cielo[M] no observable
ciel[M] complètement obscurci
nicht angebbar (da nicht erkennbar)
cielo[M] invisibile

clouds
nubes[M]
nuages[M]
Wolken[F]
nuvole[F]

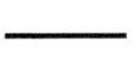

stratus
estrato[M]
stratus[M]
Stratus[M]
strato[M]

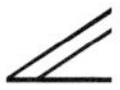

altostratus
altostrato[M]
alto-stratus[M]
Altostratus[M]
altostrato[M]

cirrus
cirro[M]
cirrus[M]
Zirrus[M]
cirro[M]

cumulonimbus
cumulonimbo[M]
cumulo-nimbus[M]
Kumulonimbus[M]
cumulonembo[M]

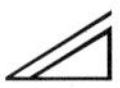

nimbostratus
nimbostrato[M]
nimbo-stratus[M]
Nimbostratus[M]
nembostrato[M]

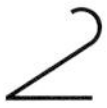

cirrostratus
cirrostrato[M]
cirro-stratus[M]
Zirrostratus[M]
cirrostrato[M]

cumulus
cúmulo[M]
cumulus[M]
Kumulus[M]
cumulo[M]

altocumulus
altocúmulo[M]
alto-cumulus[M]
Altokumulus[M]
altocumulo[M]

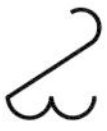

cirrocumulus
cirrocúmulo[M]
cirro-cumulus[M]
Zirrokumulus[M]
cirrocumulo[M]

stratocumulus
estratocúmulo[M]
strato-cumulus[M]
Stratokumulus[M]
stratocumulo[M]

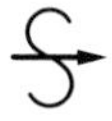

sandstorm or dust storm
tormenta[F] de polvo[M] y arena[F]
tempête[F] de sable[M] ou de poussière[F]
Sand- oder Staubsturm[M]
tempesta[F] di sabbia[F] o di polvere[F]

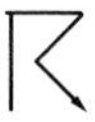

thunderstorm
tormenta[F]
orage[M]
Gewitter[N]
temporale[M]

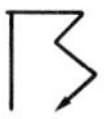

heavy thunderstorm
tormenta[F] eléctrica
orage[M] fort
starkes Gewitter[N]
temporale[M] forte

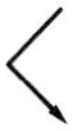

lightning
relámpago[M]
éclair[M]
Blitz[M]
fulmine[M]

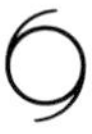

tropical storm
tormenta[F] tropical
tempête[F] tropicale
tropischer Sturm[M]
tempesta[F] tropicale

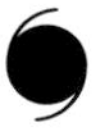

hurricane
huracán[M]
ouragan[M]
Orkan[M]
uragano[M]

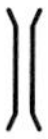

tornado
tornado[M]
tornade[F]
Tornado[M]
tornado[M]

light intermittent rain
lluvia[F] ligera intermitente
pluie[F] intermittente faible
zeitweise leichter Regen[M]
pioggia[F] leggera intermittente

light intermittent drizzle
llovizna[F] ligera intermitente
bruine[F] intermittente faible
zeitweise leichter Sprühregen[M]
pioviggine[F] leggera intermittente

light intermittent snow
nieve[F] ligera intermitente
neige[F] intermittente faible
zeitweise leichter Schneefall[M]
neve[F] leggera intermittente

moderate intermittent rain
lluvia[F] moderada intermitente
pluie[F] intermittente modérée
zeitweise mäßiger Regen[M]
pioggia[F] moderata intermittente

moderate intermittent drizzle
llovizna[F] moderada intermitente
bruine[F] intermittente modérée
zeitweise mäßiger Sprühregen[M]
pioviggine[F] moderata intermittente

moderate intermittent snow
nieve[F] moderada intermitente
neige[F] intermittente modérée
zeitweise mäßiger Schneefall[M]
neve[F] moderata intermittente

heavy intermittent rain
lluvia[F] intensa intermitente
pluie[F] intermittente forte
zeitweise starker Regen[M]
pioggia[F] forte intermittente

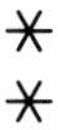

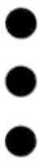

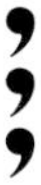

thick intermittent drizzle
llovizna[F] fuerte intermitente
bruine[F] intermittente forte
zeitweise dichter Sprühregen[M]
pioviggine[F] spessa intermittente

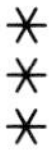

heavy intermittent snow
nieve[F] fuerte intermitente
neige[F] intermittente forte
zeitweise starker Schneefall[M]
neve[F] forte intermittente

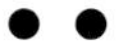

light continuous rain
lluvia[F] ligera continua
pluie[F] continue faible
anhaltend leichter Regen[M]
pioggia[F] leggera continua

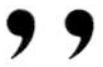

light continuous drizzle
llovizna[F] ligera continua
bruine[F] continue faible
anhaltend leichter Sprühregen[M]
pioviggine[F] leggera continua

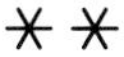

light continuous snow
nieve[F] ligera continua
neige[F] continue faible
anhaltend leichter Schneefall[M]
neve[F] leggera continua

moderate continuous rain
lluvia[F] moderada continua
pluie[F] continue modérée
anhaltend mäßiger Regen[M]
pioggia[F] moderata continua

moderate continuous drizzle
llovizna[F] moderada continua
bruine[F] continue modérée
anhaltend mäßiger Sprühregen[M]
pioviggine[F] moderata continua

moderate continuous snow
nieve[F] moderada continua
neige[F] continue modérée
anhaltend mäßiger Schneefall[M]
neve[F] moderata continua

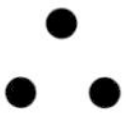

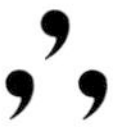

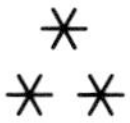

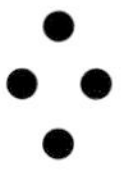

heavy continuous rain
lluvia[F] fuerte continua
pluie[F] continue forte
anhaltend starker Regen[M]
pioggia[F] forte continua

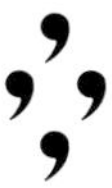

thick continuous drizzle
llovizna[F] fuerte continua
bruine[F] continue forte
anhaltend dichter Sprühregen[M]
pioviggine[F] spessa continua

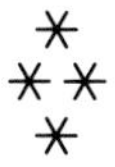

heavy continuous snow
nieve[F] fuerte continua
neige[F] continue forte
anhaltend starker Schneefall[M]
neve[F] forte continua

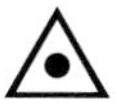

sleet
aguanieve[F]
grésil[M]
Schneeregen[M]
nevischio[M]

mist
neblina[F]
brume[F]
Dunst[M]
bruma[F] umida

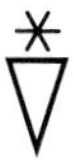

snow shower
chubasco[M] de nieve[F]
averse[F] de neige[F]
Schneeschauer[M]
rovesci[M] di neve[F]

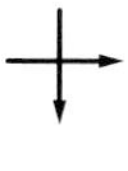

drifting snow low
viento[M] fuerte invernal alto
chasse-neige[F] basse ; poudrerie[F] basse
Schneefegen[N]
scacci019neve[M] basso

fog
niebla[F]
brouillard[M]
Nebel[M]
nebbia[F]

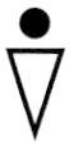

rain shower
chubasco[M]
averse[F] de pluie[F]
Regenschauer[M]
rovesci[M] di pioggia[F]

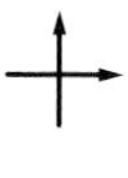

drifting snow high
viento[M] fuerte invernal bajo
chasse-neige[F] haute ; poudrerie[F] haute
Schneetreiben[N]
scacci019neve[M] alto

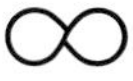

haze
neblina[F]
brume[F] sèche
Dunst[M]
foschia[F]

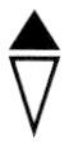

hail shower
granizada[F]
averse[F] de grêle[F]
Hagelschauer[M]
rovesci[M] di grandine[F]

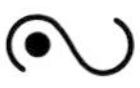

freezing rain
lluvia[F] helada
pluie[F] verglaçante
Eisregen[M]
pioggia[F] congelantesi

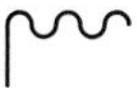

smoke
humo[M]
fumée[F]
Rauch[M]
fumo[M]

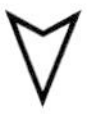

squall
chaparrón[M F]
grain[M]
Bö[F]
groppo[M]

EARTH

meteorological station

estación[F] meteorológica | station[F] météorologique | Wetterstation[F] | stazione[F] meteorologica

sunshine recorder
heliógrafo[M]
héliographe[M]
Sonnenscheinautograph[M]
eliografo[M]

wind vane
veleta[F]
girouette[F]
Windfahne[F]
banderuola[F]

pyranometer
piranómetro[M]
pyranomètre[M]
Pyranometer[N]
piranometro[M]

anemometer
anemómetro[M]
anémomètre[M]
Anemometer[N], Windgeschwindigkeitsmesser[M]
anemometro[M]

direct-reading rain gauge
pluviómetro[M] de lectura[F] directa
pluviomètre[M] à lecture[F] directe
Regenmesser[M] mit direkter Ablesung[F]
pluviometro[M] a lettura[F] diretta

instrument shelter
refugio[M] meteorológico
abri[M] météorologique
Wetterhütte[F]
capannina[F] meteorologica

snow gauge
nivómetro[M]
nivomètre[M]
Schneemesser[M]
nivometro[M]

rain gauge recorder
pluviómetro[M]
pluviomètre[M] enregistreur
Regenschreiber[M]
pluviografo[M]

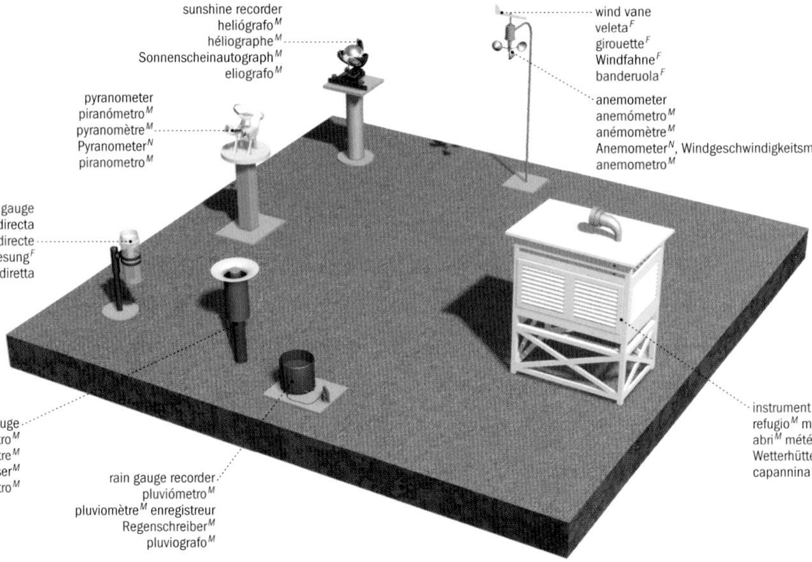

meteorological measuring instruments

instrumentos[M] de medición[F] meteorológica | instruments[M] de mesure[F] météorologique | meteorologische Messinstrumente[N] | strumenti[M] di misurazione[F] meteorologica

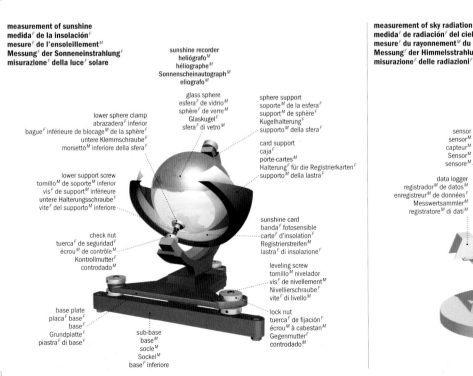

measurement of sunshine
medida[F] de la insolación[F]
mesure[F] de l'ensoleillement[M]
Messung[F] der Sonneneinstrahlung[F]
misurazione[F] della luce[F] solare

sunshine recorder
heliógrafo[M]
héliographe[M]
Sonnenscheinautograph[M]
eliografo[M]

glass sphere
esfera[F] de vidrio[M]
sphère[F] de verre[M]
Glaskugel[F]
sfera[F] di vetro[M]

sphere support
soporte[M] de la esfera[F]
support[M] de sphère[F]
Kugelhalterung[F]
supporto[M] della sfera[F]

lower sphere clamp
abrazadera[F] inferior
bague[F] inférieure de blocage[M] de la sphère[F]
untere Klemmschraube[F]
morsetto[M] inferiore della sfera[F]

card support
caja[F]
porte-cartes[M]
Halterung[F] für die Registrierkarten[F]
supporto[M] della lastra[F]

lower support screw
tornillo[M] de soporte[M] inferior
vis[F] de support[M] inférieure
untere Halterungsschraube[F]
vite[F] del supporto[M] inferiore

sunshine card
banda[F] fotosensible
carte[F] d'insolation[F]
Registrierstreifen[M]
lastra[F] di insolazione[F]

check nut
tuerca[F] de seguridad[F]
écrou[M] de contrôle[M]
Kontrollmutter[F]
controdado[M]

leveling screw
tornillo[M] nivelador
vis[F] de nivellement[M]
Nivellierschraube[F]
vite[F] di livello[M]

base plate
placa[F] base[F]
base[F]
Grundplatte[F]
piastra[F] di base[F]

sub-base
base[M]
socle[M]
Sockel[M]
base[F] inferiore

lock nut
tuerca[F] de fijación[F]
écrou[M] à cabestan[M]
Gegenmutter[F]
controdado[M]

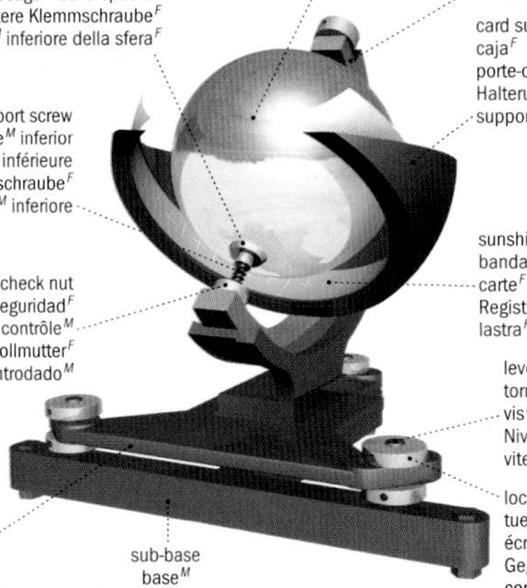

measurement of sky radiation
medida[F] de radiación[F] del cielo[M]
mesure[F] du rayonnement[M] du ciel[M]
Messung[F] der Himmelsstrahlung[F]
misurazione[F] delle radiazioni[F] solari

pyranometer
piranómetro[M]
pyranomètre[M]
Pyranometer[N]
piranometro[M]

shadow band
banda[F] parasol
bande[F] pare-soleil[M]
Schattenring[M]
anello[M] di schermo[M]

sensor
sensor[M]
capteur[M]
Sensor[M]
sensore[M]

data logger
registrador[M] de datos[M]
enregistreur[M] de données[F]
Messwertsammler[M]
registratore[M] di dati[M]

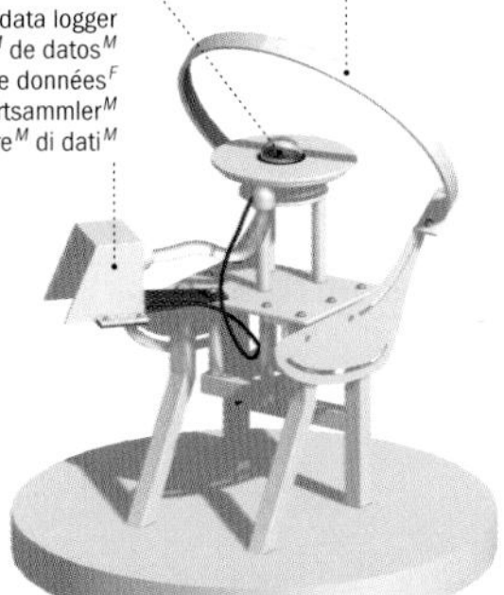

direct-reading rain gauge
pluviómetro ^{M} de lectura ^{F} directa
pluviomètre ^{M} à lecture ^{F} directe
selbst schreibender Regenmesser ^{M}
pluviometro ^{M} a lettura ^{F} diretta

collecting funnel
embudo ^{M} colector
entonnoir ^{M} collecteur
Sammeltrichter ^{M}
imbuto ^{M} collettore

tightening band
banda ^{F} de tensión ^{F}
collier ^{M} de serrage ^{M}
Schelle ^{F}
fascetta ^{F} di fissaggio ^{M}

measuring tube
probeta ^{F} graduada
éprouvette ^{F} graduée
Messrohr ^{N}
tubo ^{M} graduato

container
recipiente ^{M} de vertido ^{M}
récipient ^{M}
Behälter ^{M}
contenitore ^{M}

support
soporte ^{M}
support ^{M}
Ständer ^{M}
sostegno ^{M}

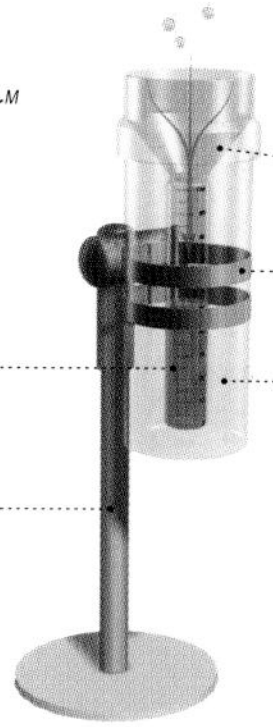

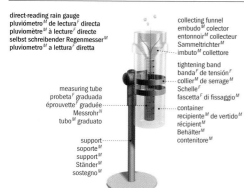

rain gauge recorder
pluviómetro ^{M}
pluviomètre ^{M} enregistreur
Niederschlagsschreiber ^{M}
pluviografo ^{M}

measurement of rainfall
medida ^{F} de la lluvia ^{F}
mesure ^{F} de la pluviosité ^{F}
Messung ^{F} der Regenmenge ^{F}
misurazione ^{F} delle precipitazioni ^{F}

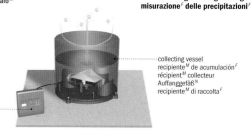

collecting vessel
recipiente ^{M} de acumulación ^{F}
récipient ^{M} collecteur
Auffanggefäß ^{N}
recipiente ^{M} di raccolta ^{F}

recording unit
unidad ^{F} de registro ^{M}
appareil ^{M} enregistreur
Aufzeichnungsgerät ^{N}
registratore ^{M}

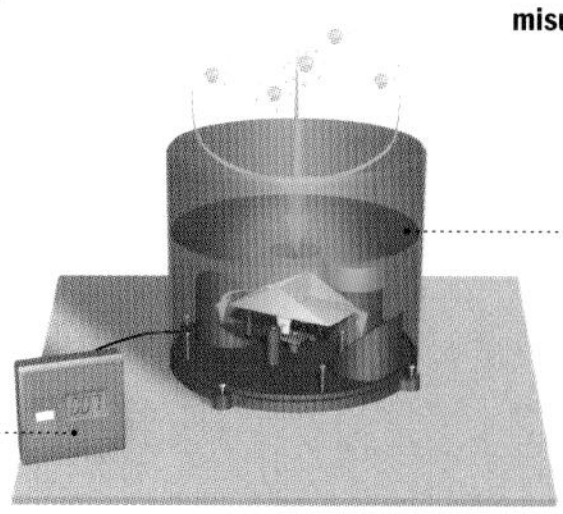

upper-air sounding
sondeo ^{M} en altitud ^{F}
sondage ^{M} en altitude ^{F}
Messung ^{F} in der oberen Atmosphäre ^{F}
scandagliamento ^{M} ad alta quota ^{F}

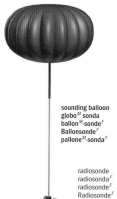

sounding balloon
globo ^{M} sonda
ballon ^{M}-sonde ^{F}
Ballonsonde ^{F}
pallone ^{M}-sonda ^{F}

radiosonde
radiosonda ^{F}
radiosonde ^{F}
Radiosonde ^{F}
radiosonda ^{F}

measurement of wind direction
medida ^{F} de la dirección ^{F} del viento ^{M}
mesure ^{F} de la direction ^{F} du vent ^{M}
Messung ^{F} der Windrichtung ^{F}
misurazione ^{F} della direzione ^{F} del vento ^{M}

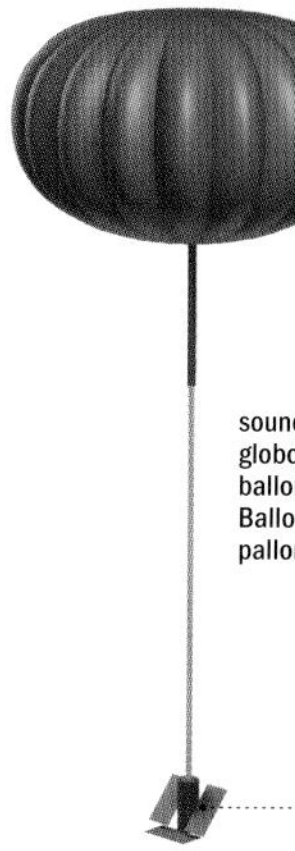

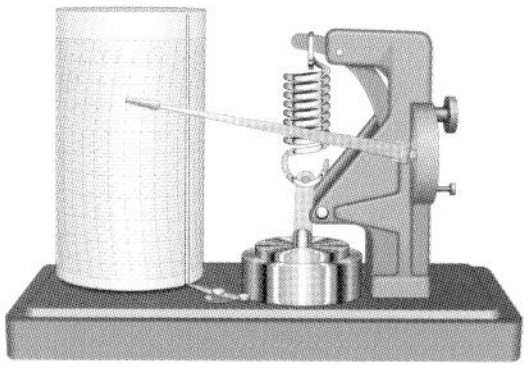

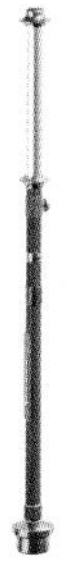

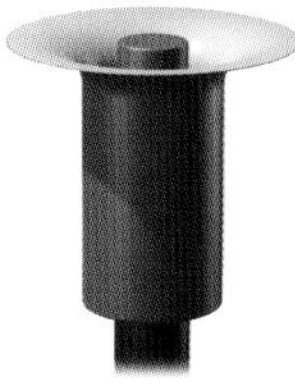

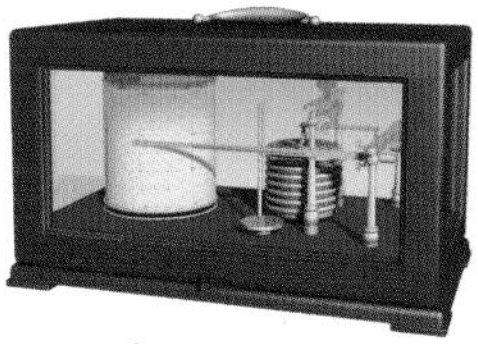

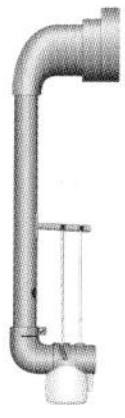

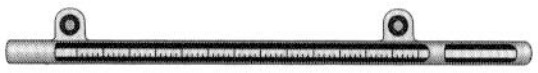

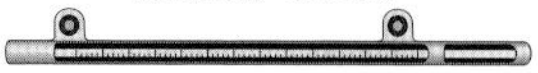

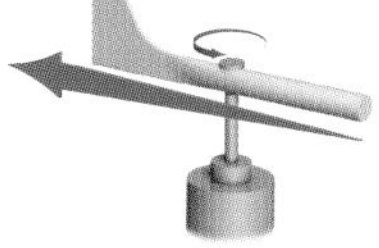

wind vane
veleta ^{F}
girouette ^{F}
Windfahne ^{F}
banderuola ^{F}

measurement of wind strength
medida ^{F} de la fuerza ^{F} del viento ^{M}
mesure ^{F} de la vitesse ^{F} du vent ^{M}
Messung ^{F} der Windstärke ^{F}
misurazione ^{F} della forza ^{F} del vento ^{M}

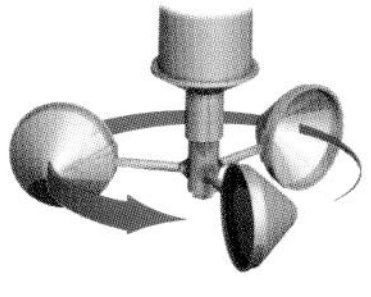

anemometer
anemómetro ^{M}
anémomètre ^{M}
Anemometer ^{N}
anemometro ^{M}

measurement of air pressure
medida ^{F} de la presión ^{F} del aire ^{M}
mesure ^{F} de la pression ^{F}
Messung ^{F} des Luftdrucks ^{M}
misurazione ^{F} della pressione ^{F} dell'aria ^{F}

barograph
barógrafo ^{M}
baromètre ^{M} enregistreur
Barograph ^{M}
barografo ^{M}

mercury barometer
barómetro ^{M} de mercurio ^{M}
baromètre ^{M} à mercure ^{M}
Quecksilberbarometer ^{N}
barometro ^{M} a mercurio ^{M}

measure of humidity
medida ^{F} de la humedad ^{F}
mesure ^{F} de l'humidité ^{F}
Messung ^{F} der Luftfeuchtigkeit ^{F}
misurazione ^{F} dell'umidità ^{F}

hygrograph
higrógrafo ^{M}
hygromètre ^{M} enregistreur
Hygrograph ^{M}
igrografo ^{M}

psychrometer
psicrómetro ^{M}
psychromètre ^{M}
Psychrometer ^{N}
psicrometro ^{M}

measurement of cloud ceiling
medida ^{F} de la altura ^{F} de las nubes ^{F}
mesure ^{F} de la hauteur ^{F} des nuages ^{M}
Messung ^{F} der Wolkenhöhe ^{F}
misurazione ^{F} dell'altezza ^{F} delle nubi ^{F}

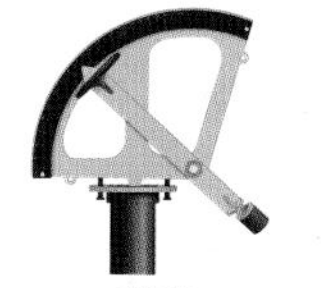

alidade
alidada ^{F}
alidada ^{F}
Alhidade ^{F}
alidada ^{F}

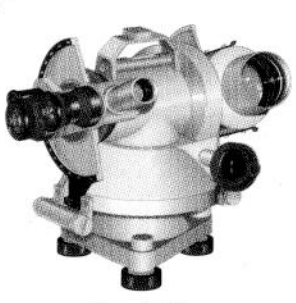

theodolite
teodolito ^{M}
théodolite ^{M}
Theodolit ^{M}
teodolite ^{M}

measurement of snowfall
medida ^{F} de nevadas ^{F}
mesure ^{F} de la chute ^{F} de neige ^{F}
Messung ^{F} des Schneefalls ^{M}
misurazione ^{F} delle precipitazioni ^{F} nevose

snow gauge
nivómetro ^{M}
nivomètre ^{M}
Schneemesser ^{M}
nivometro ^{M}

measurement of temperature
medida ^{F} de la temperatura ^{F}
mesure ^{F} de la température ^{F}
Messung ^{F} der Temperatur ^{F}
misurazione ^{F} della temperatura ^{F}

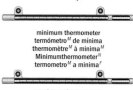

minimum thermometer
termómetro ^{M} de mínima
thermomètre ^{M} à minima ^{M}
Minimumthermometer ^{N}
termometro ^{M} a minima ^{F}

maximum thermometer
termómetro ^{M} de máxima
thermomètre ^{M} à maxima ^{M}
Maximumthermometer ^{N}
termometro ^{M} a massima ^{F}

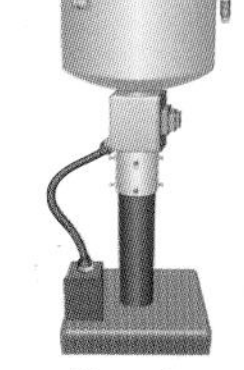

ceiling projector
proyector ^{M} de altura ^{F} máxima
projecteur ^{M} de plafond ^{M}
Wolkenhöhenmesser ^{M}
proiettore ^{M} per determinare l'altezza ^{F} delle nubi ^{F}

weather satellites

satélite^M meteorológico | satellites^M météorologiques | Wettersatellit^M | satelliti^M meteorologici

EARTH

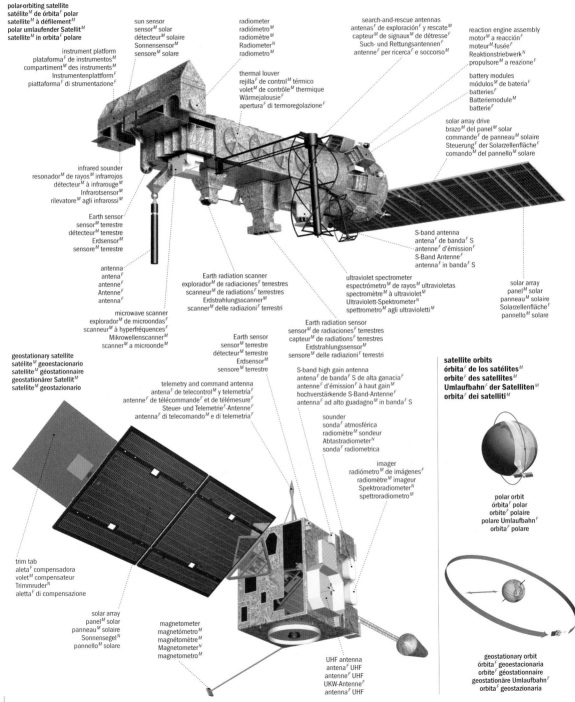

polar-orbiting satellite
satélite^M de órbita^F polar
satellite^M à défilement^M
polar umlaufender Satellit^M
satellite^M in orbita^F polare

sun sensor
sensor^M solar
détecteur^M solaire
Sonnensensor^M
sensore^M solare

radiometer
radiómetro^M
radiomètre^M
Radiometer^N
radiometro^M

search-and-rescue antennas
antenas^F de exploración^F y rescate^M
capteur^M de signaux^M de détresse^F
Such- und Rettungsantennen^M
antenne^F per ricerca^F e soccorso^M

reaction engine assembly
motor^M a reacción^F
moteur^M-fusée^F
Reaktionstriebwerk^N
propulsore^M a reazione^F

instrument platform
plataforma^F de instrumentos^M
compartiment^M des instruments^M
Instrumentenplattform^F
piattaforma^F di strumentazione^F

thermal louver
rejilla^F de control^M térmico
volet^M de contrôle^M thermique
Wärmejalousie^F
apertura^F di termoregolazione^F

battery modules
módulos^M de batería^F
batteries^F
Batteriemodule^M
batterie^F

solar array drive
brazo^M del panel^M solar
commande^F de panneau^M solaire
Steuerung^F der Solarzellenfläche^F
comando^M del pannello^M solare

infrared sounder
resonador^M de rayos^M infrarrojos
détecteur^M à infrarouge^M
Infrarotsensor^M
rilevatore^M agli infrarossi^M

Earth sensor
sensor^M terrestre
détecteur^M terrestre
Erdsensor^M
sensore^M terrestre

S-band antenna
antena^F de banda^F S
antenne^F d'émission^F
S-Band Antenne^F
antenna^F in banda^F S

antenna
antena^F
antenne^F
Antenne^F
antenna^F

Earth radiation scanner
explorador^M de radiaciones^F terrestres
scanneur^M de radiations^F terrestres
Erdstrahlungsscanner^M
scanner^M delle radiazioni^F terrestri

ultraviolet spectrometer
espectrómetro^M de rayos^M ultravioletas
spectromètre^M à ultraviolet^M
Ultraviolett-Spektrometer^N
spettrometro^M agli ultravioletti^M

solar array
panel^M solar
panneau^M solaire
Solarzellenfläche^F
pannello^M solare

microwave scanner
explorador^M de microondas^F
scanneur^M à hyperfréquences^F
Mikrowellenscanner^M
scanner^M a microonde^M

Earth radiation sensor
sensor^M de radiaciones^F terrestres
capteur^M de radiations^F terrestres
Erdstrahlungssensor^M
sensore^M delle radiazioni^F terrestri

Earth sensor
sensor^M terrestre
détecteur^M terrestre
Erdsensor^M
sensore^M terrestre

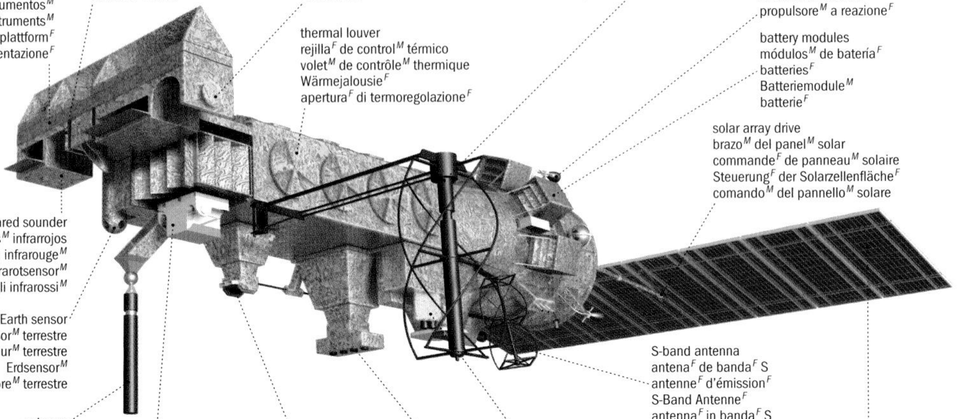

geostationary satellite
satélite^M geoestacionario
satellite^M géostationnaire
geostationärer Satellit^M
satellite^M geostazionario

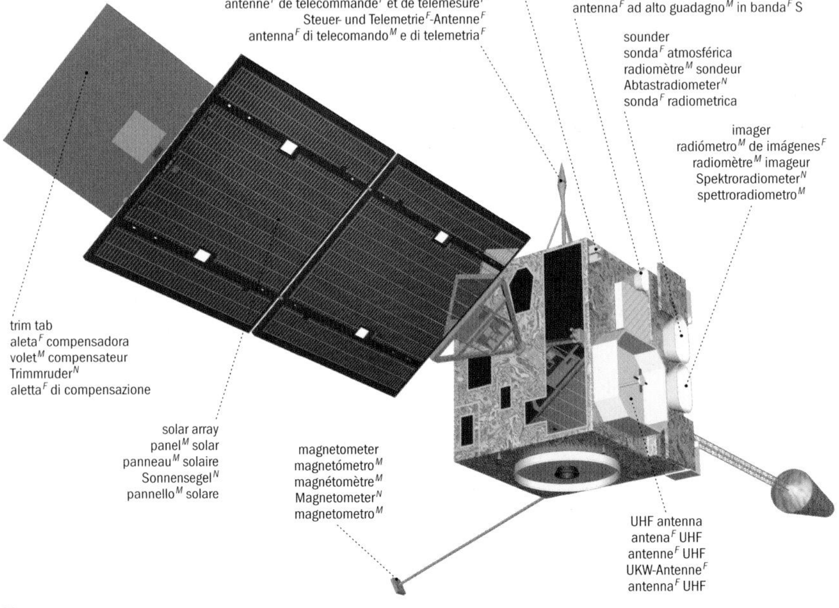

satellite orbits
órbita^F de los satélites^M
orbite^F des satellites^M
Umlaufbahn^F der Satelliten^M
orbita^F dei satelliti^M

telemetry and command antenna
antena^F de telecontrol^M y telemetría^F
antenne^F de télécommande^F et de télémesure^F
Steuer- und Telemetrie^F-Antenne^F
antenna^F di telecomando^M e di telemetria^F

S-band high gain antenna
antena^F de banda^F S de alta ganacia^F
antenne^F d'émission^F à haut gain^M
hochverstärkende S-Band-Antenne^F
antenna^F ad alto guadagno^M in banda^F S

sounder
sonda^F atmosférica
radiomètre^M sondeur
Abtastradiometer^N
sonda^F radiometrica

imager
radiómetro^M de imágenes^F
radiomètre^M imageur
Spektroradiometer^N
spettroradiometro^M

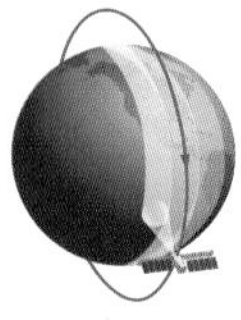

polar orbit
órbita^F polar
orbite^F polaire
polare Umlaufbahn^F
orbita^F polare

trim tab
aleta^F compensadora
volet^M compensateur
Trimmruder^N
aletta^F di compensazione

solar array
panel^M solar
panneau^M solaire
Sonnensegel^N
pannello^M solare

magnetometer
magnetómetro^M
magnétomètre^M
Magnetometer^N
magnetometro^M

UHF antenna
antena^F UHF
antenne^F UHF
UKW-Antenne^F
antenna^F UHF

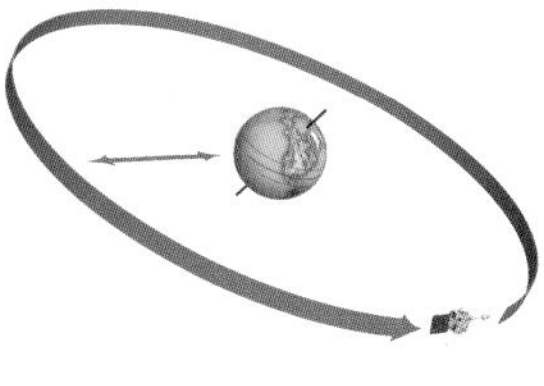

geostationary orbit
órbita^F geoestacionaria
orbite^F géostationnaire
geostationäre Umlaufbahn^F
orbita^F geostazionaria

climates of the world

climas^M del mundo^M | climats^M du monde^M | Klimate^N der Welt^F | climi^M del mondo^M

EARTH

tropical climates
climas^M tropicales
climats^M tropicaux
tropische Klimate^N
climi^M tropicali

tropical rain forest
tropical^M lluvioso
tropical humide
tropischer Regenwald^M
tropicale della foresta^F pluviale

tropical wet-and-dry (savanna)
tropical^M húmedo y seco (sabana^F)
tropical humide et sec (savane^F)
tropisch feucht und trocken (Savanne^F)
tropicale umido e secco (savana^F)

dry climates
climas^M áridos
climats^M arides
Trockenklimate^N
climi^M aridi

steppe
estepario
steppe^F
Steppe^F
steppico^M

desert
desértico
désert^M
Wüste^F
desertico^M

warm temperate climates
climas^M templados cálidos
climats^M tempérés chauds
warmgemäßigte Klimate^N.
climi^M temperati caldi

humid subtropical
subtropical húmedo
subtropical humide
feuchte Subtropen
subtropicale umido

Mediterranean subtropical
subtropical mediterráneo
méditerranéen
mediterrane Subtropen
subtropicale mediterraneo

marine
marítimo
océanique
maritim
marino

cold temperate climates
climas^M templados fríos
climats^M tempérés froids
kaltgemäßigte Klimate^N
climi^M temperati freddi

humid continental - hot summer
continental^M húmedo - verano^M tórrido
continental humide, à été^M chaud
feucht-kontinental - heißer Sommer^M
continentale umido - estate^F torrida

humid continental - warm summer
continental^M húmedo - verano^M fresco
continental humide, à été^M frais
feucht-kontinental - warmer Sommer^M
continentale umido - estate^F calda

subarctic
subártico^M
subarctique
subarktisch
subartico

polar climates
climas^M polares
climats^M polaires
Polarklimate^N
climi^M polari

polar tundra
tundra^F
toundra^F
Polartundra^F
della tundra^F polare

polar ice cap
hielos^M perpetuos
calotte^F glaciaire
Eiskappe^F
della calotta^F polare

highland climates
climas^M de alta montaña^F
climats^M de montagne^F
Hochlandklimate^N
climi^M di montagna^F

highland
climas^M de montaña^F
climats^M de montagne^F
Hochgebirge^N
di montagna^F

clouds

nubes^F | nuages^M | Wolken^F | nuvole^F

EARTH

high clouds
nubes^F altas
nuages^M de haute altitude^F
hohe Wolken^F
nubi^F alte

cirrostratus
cirrostratos^M
cirro-stratus^M
Zirrostratus^M
cirrostrato^M

cirrocumulus
cirrocúmulos^M
cirro-cumulus^M
Zirrokumulus^M
cirrocumulo^M

cirrus
cirros^M
cirrus^M
Zirrus^M
cirro^M

middle clouds
nubes^F medias
nuages^M de moyenne altitude^F
mittelhohe Wolken^F
nubi^F medie

altostratus
altostratos^M
alto-stratus^M
Altostratus^M
altostrato^M

altocumulus
altocúmulos^M
alto-cumulus^M
Altokumulus^M
altocumulo^M

low clouds
nubes^F bajas
nuages^M de basse altitude^F
tiefe Wolken^F
nubi^F basse

stratocumulus
estratocúmulos^M
strato-cumulus^M
Stratokumulus^M
stratocumulo^M

nimbostratus
nimbostratos^M
nimbo-stratus^M
Nimbostratus^M
nembostrato^M

cumulus
cúmulos^M
cumulus^M
Kumulus^M
cumulo^M

stratus
estratos^M
stratus^M
Stratus^M
strato^M

clouds of vertical development
nubes^F de desarrollo^M vertical
nuages^M à développement^M vertical
Quellwolken^F
nubi^F a sviluppo^M verticale

cumulonimbus
cumulonimbos^M
cumulo-nimbus^M
Kumulonimbus^M
cumulonembo^M

tornado and waterspout

tornado[M] y tromba[F] marina | tornade[F] et trombe[F] marine | Tornado[M] und Wasserhose[F] | tornado[M] e tromba[F] marina

EARTH

wall cloud
muro[M] de nubes[F]
mur[M] de nuages[M]
Gewitterwolken[F]
parete[F] di nuvole[F]

funnel cloud
nube[F] en forma[F] de embudo[M]
nuage[M] en entonnoir[M]
Wolkentrichter[M]
nube[F] a proboscide[F]

debris
detritos[M]
buisson[M]
aufgewirbelter Staub[M]
detriti[M]

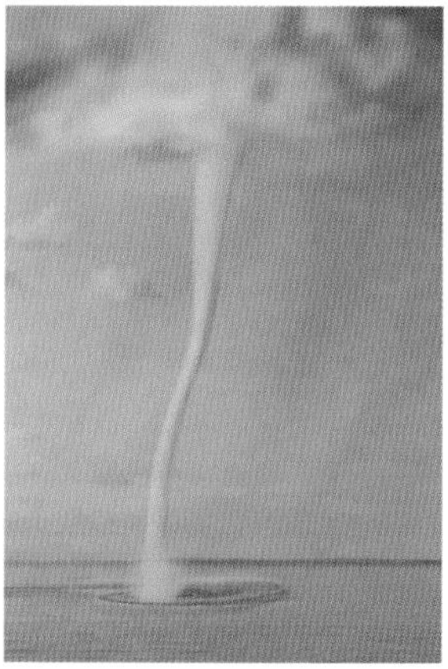

waterspout
tromba[F] marina
trombe[F] marine
Wasserhose[F]
tromba[F] marina

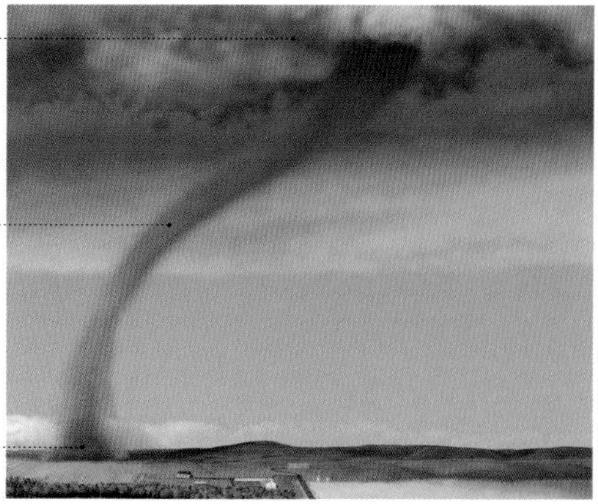

tornado
tornado[M]
tornade[F]
Tornado[M]
tornado[M]

tropical cyclone

ciclón[M] tropical | cyclone[M] tropical | tropischer Wirbelsturm[M] | ciclone[M] tropicale

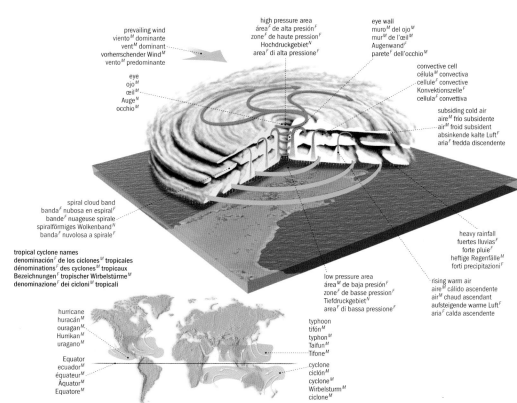

prevailing wind
viento[M] dominante
vent[M] dominant
vorherrschender Wind[M]
vento[M] predominante

high pressure area
área[F] de alta presión[F]
zone[F] de haute pression[F]
Hochdruckgebiet[N]
area[F] di alta pressione[F]

eye wall
muro[M] del ojo[M]
mur[M] de l'œil[M]
Augenwand[F]
parete[F] dell'occhio[M]

eye
ojo[M]
œil[M]
Auge[N]
occhio[M]

convective cell
célula[F] convectiva
cellule[F] convective
Konvektionszelle[F]
cellula[F] convettiva

subsiding cold air
aire[M] frío subsidente
air[M] froid subsident
absinkende kalte Luft[F]
aria[F] fredda discendente

spiral cloud band
banda[F] nubosa en espiral[F]
bande[F] nuageuse spirale
spiralförmiges Wolkenband[N]
banda[F] nuvolosa a spirale[F]

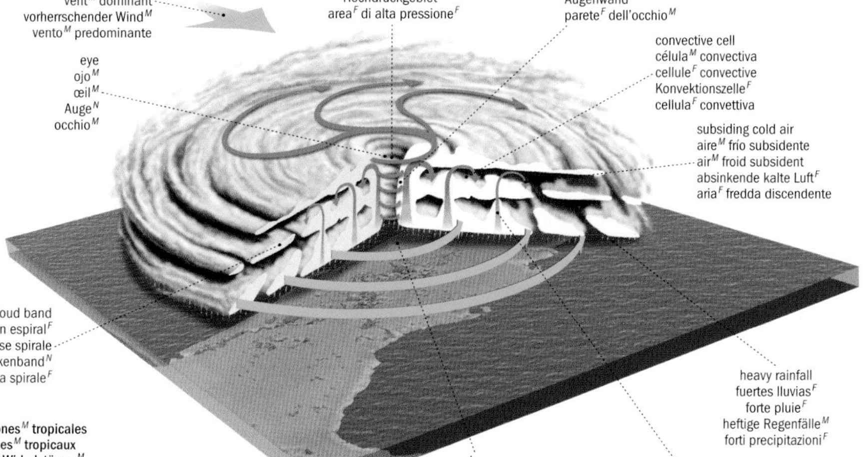

tropical cyclone names
denominación[F] de los ciclones[M] tropicales
dénominations[F] des cyclones[M] tropicaux
Bezeichnungen[F] tropischer Wirbelstürme[M]
denominazione[F] dei cicloni[M] tropicali

low pressure area
área[F] de baja presión[F]
zone[F] de basse pression[F]
Tiefdruckgebiet[N]
area[F] di bassa pressione[F]

heavy rainfall
fuertes lluvias[F]
forte pluie[F]
heftige Regenfälle[M]
forti precipitazioni[F]

rising warm air
aire[M] cálido ascendente
air[M] chaud ascendant
aufsteigende warme Luft[F]
aria[F] calda ascendente

hurricane
huracán[M]
ouragan[M]
Hurrikan[M]
uragano[M]

Equator
ecuador[M]
équateur[M]
Äquator[M]
Equatore[M]

typhoon
tifón[M]
typhon[M]
Taifun[M]
Tifone[M]

cyclone
ciclón[M]
cyclone[M]
Wirbelsturm[M]
ciclone[M]

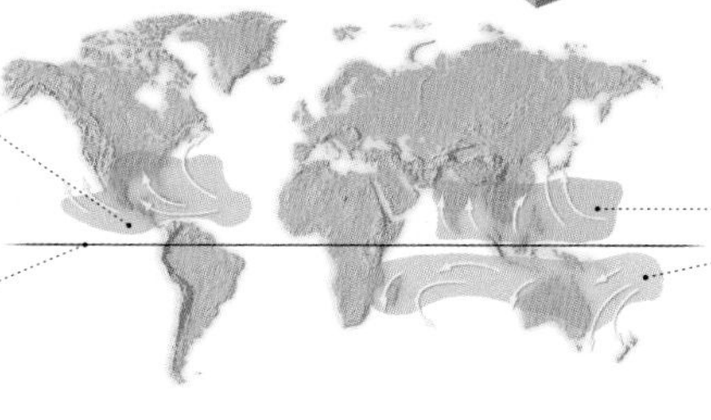

precipitation

precipitaciones[F] | précipitations[F] | Niederschläge[M] | precipitazioni[F]

EARTH

rain forms
formas[F] de lluvia[F]
formes[F] de pluie[F]
Regenarten[F]
tipologie[F] di pioggia[F]

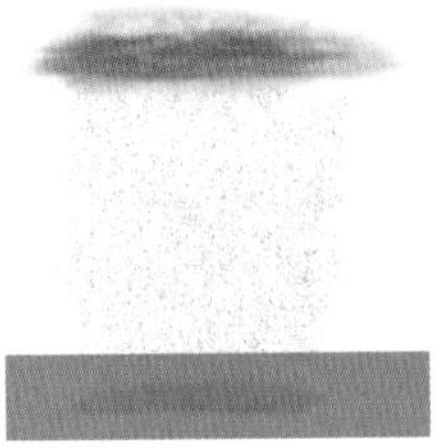

drizzle
llovizna[F]
bruine[F]
Sprühregen[M]
pioviggine[F]

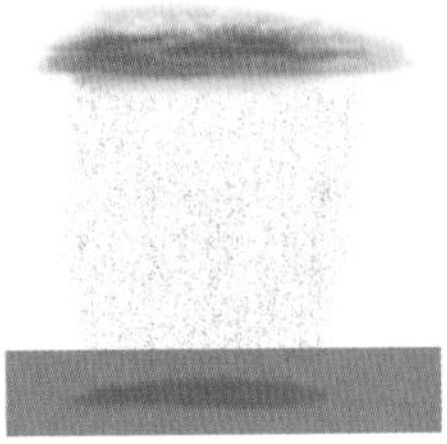

light rain
lluvia[F] ligera
pluie[F] faible
leichter Regen[M]
pioggia[F] leggera

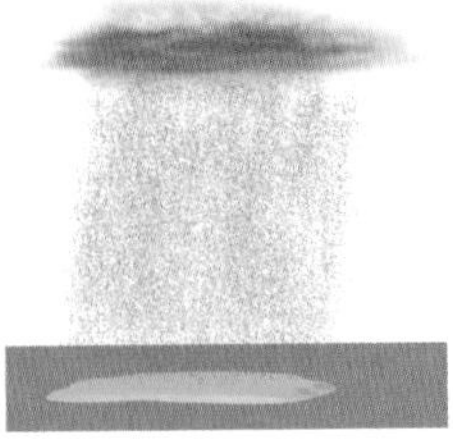

moderate rain
lluvia[F] moderada
pluie[F] modérée
mäßiger Regen[M]
pioggia[F] moderata

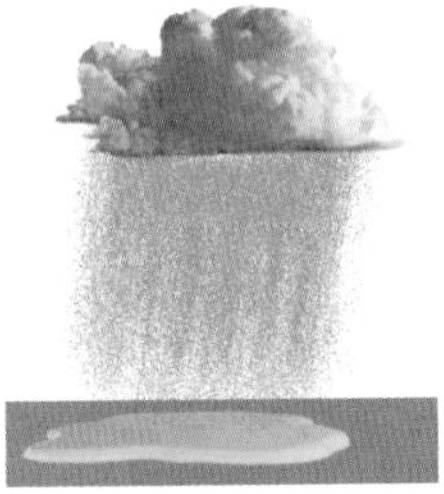

heavy rain
lluvia[F] intensa
pluie[F] forte
starker Regen[M]
pioggia[F] forte

winter precipitation
precipitaciones[F] invernales
précipitations[F] hivernales
Winterniederschläge[M]
precipitazioni[F] invernali

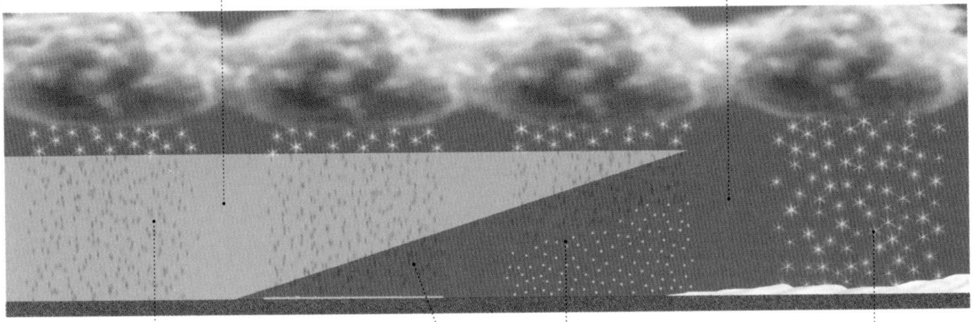

warm air
aire[M] caliente
air[M] chaud
warme Luft[F]
aria[F] calda

cold air
aire[M] frío
air[M] froid
kalte Luft[F]
aria[F] fredda

rain
lluvia[F]
pluie[F]
Regen[M]
pioggia[F]

freezing rain
lluvia[F] helada
pluie[F] verglaçante
gefrierender Regen[M]
pioggia[F] congelantesi

sleet
aguanieve[M]
grésil[M]
Schneeregen[M]
nevischio[M]

snow
nieve[M]
neige[F]
Schnee[M]
neve[F]

snow crystals
cristales[M] de nieve[F]
cristaux[M] de neige[F]
Schneekristalle[M]
cristalli[M] di neve[F]

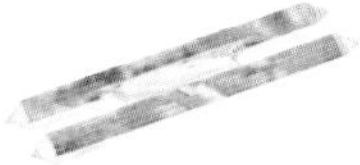

needle
aguja[F]
aiguille[F]
Nadel[F]
ago[M]

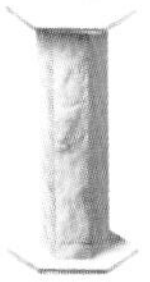

capped column
columna[F] con capuchón[M]
colonne[F] avec capuchon[M]
bedeckte Säule[F]
colonna[F] con lamelle terminali

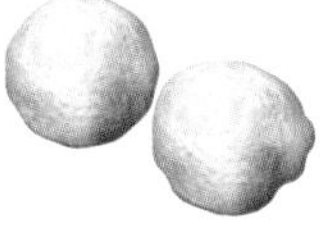

hail
granizo[M]
grêlon[M]
Hagel[M]
grandine[F]

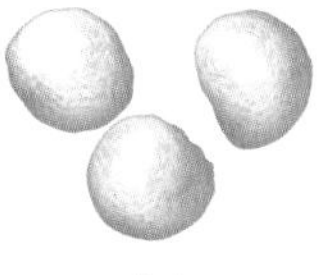

sleet
cellisca[F]
grésil[M]
Eiskörnchen[N]
nevischio[M]

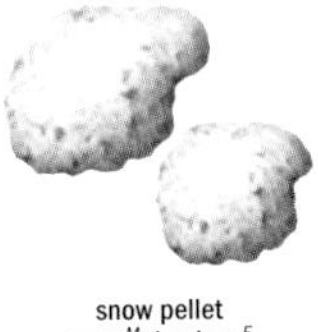

snow pellet
copo[M] de nieve[F]
neige[F] roulée
Reif- und Frostgraupel[F]
pallottoline[F] di neve[F]

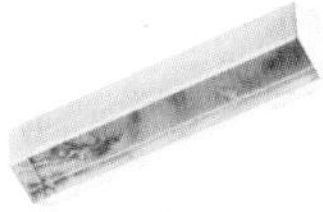

column
columna[F]
colonne[F]
Säule[F]
colonna[F]

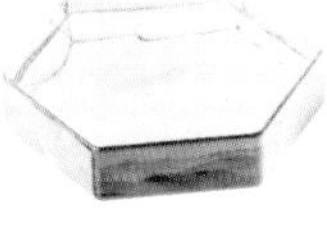

plate crystal
placa[F] de hielo[M]
plaquette[F]
Plättchen[N]
cristallo[M] lamellare

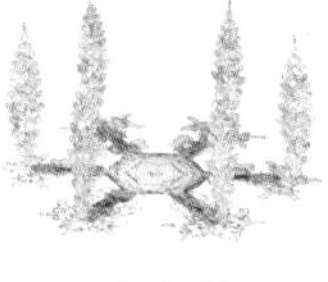

spatial dendrite
dendrita[F] espacial
dendrite[F] spatiale
räumlicher Dendrit[M]
cristallo[M] dendritico spaziale

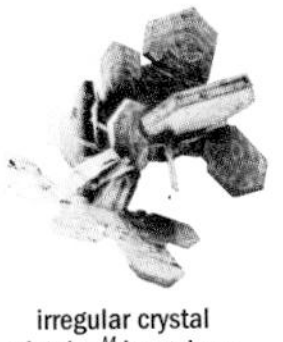

irregular crystal
cristales[M] irregulares
cristaux[M] irréguliers
irreguläres Aggregat[N]
cristallo[M] irregolare

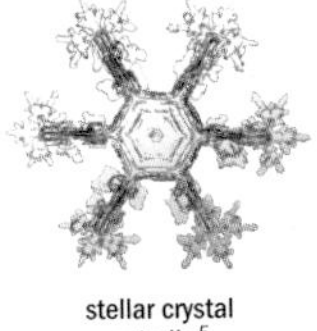

stellar crystal
estrella[F]
étoile[F]
Stern[M]
cristallo[M] stellare

stormy sky
cielo ^{M} turbulento
ciel ^{M} d'orage ^{M}
stürmischer Himmel ^{M}
cielo ^{M} tempestoso

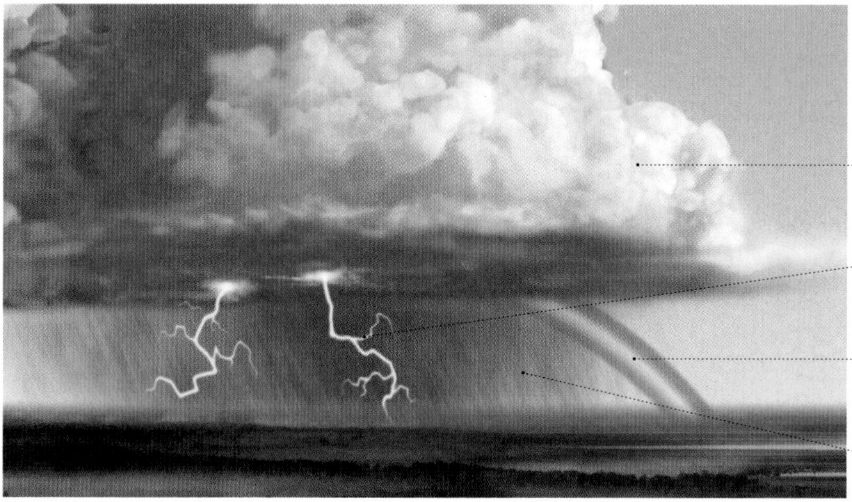

cloud
nube ^{F}
nuage ^{M}
Wolke ^{F}
nube ^{F}

lightning
rayo ^{M}
éclair ^{M}
Blitz ^{M}
fulmine ^{M}

rainbow
arco ^{M} iris
arc-en-ciel ^{M}
Regenbogen ^{M}
arcobaleno ^{M}

rain
lluvia ^{F}
pluie ^{F}
Regen ^{M}
pioggia ^{F}

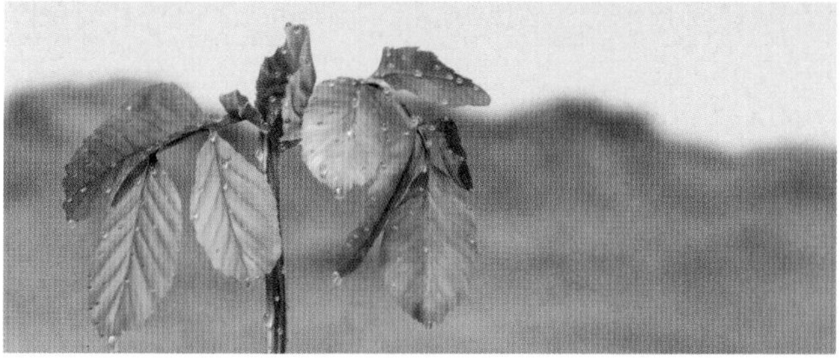

dew
rocío ^{M}
rosée ^{F}
Tau ^{M}
rugiada ^{F}

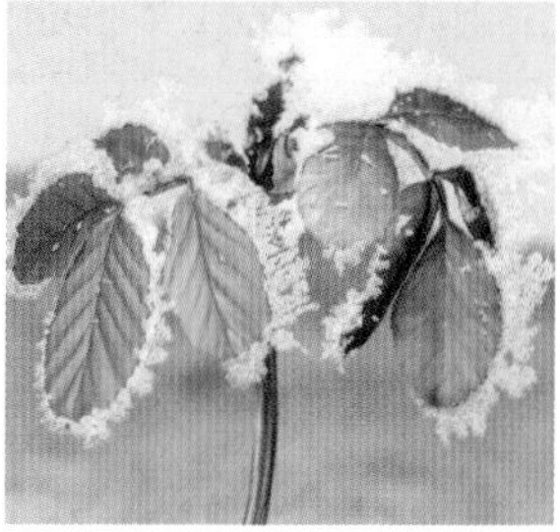

rime
escarcha ^{F}
givre ^{M}
Reif ^{M}
brina ^{F}

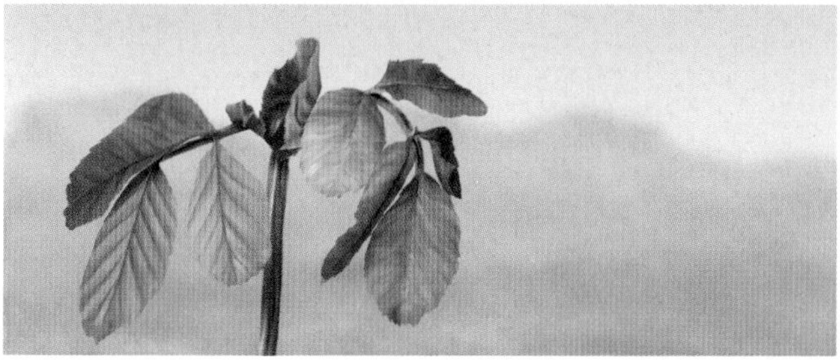

mist
neblina ^{F}
brume ^{F}
Dunst ^{M}
foschia ^{F}

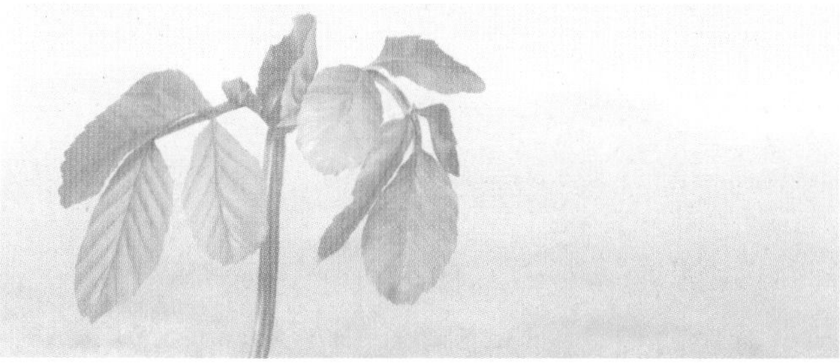

fog
niebla ^{F}
brouillard ^{M}
Nebel ^{M}
nebbia ^{F}

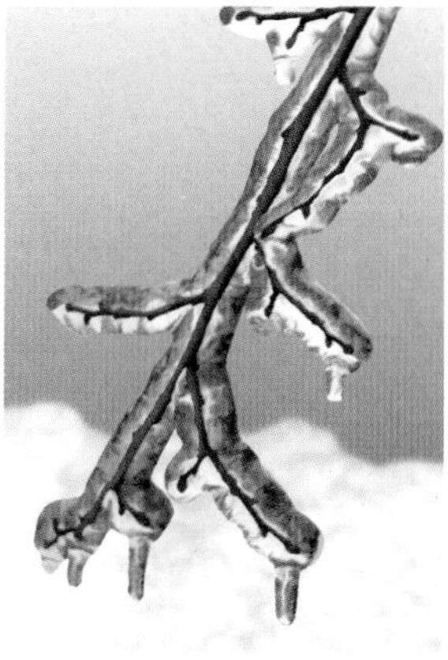

frost
hielo ^{M}
verglas ^{M}
Raureif ^{M}
vetrone ^{M}

EARTH

vegetation and biosphere

vegetación^F y biosfera^F | végétation^F et biosphère^F | Vegetation^F und Biosphäre^F | vegetazione^F e biosfera^F

vegetation regions
distribución^F de la vegetación^F
distribution^F de la végétation^F
Vegetationszonen^F
distribuzione^F della vegetazione^F

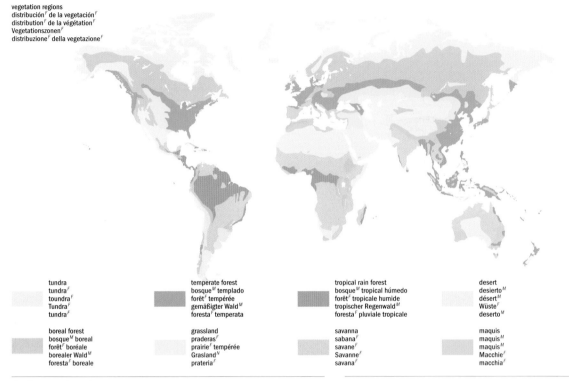

tundra
tundra^F
toundra^F
Tundra^F
tundra^F

boreal forest
bosque^M boreal
forêt^F boréale
borealer Wald^M
foresta^F boreale

temperate forest
bosque^M templado
forêt^F tempérée
gemäßigter Wald^M
foresta^F temperata

grassland
praderas^F
prairie^F tempérée
Grasland^N
prateria^F

tropical rain forest
bosque^M tropical húmedo
forêt^F tropicale humide
tropischer Regenwald^M
foresta^F pluviale tropicale

savanna
sabana^F
savane^F
Savanne^F
savana^F

desert
desierto^M
désert^M
Wüste^F
deserto^M

maquis
maquis^M
maquis^M
Macchie^F
macchia^F

elevation zones and vegetation
altitud^F y vegetación^F
paysage^M végétal selon l'altitude^F
Vegetationsbild^N nach Höhenlagen^F
altitudine^F e vegetazione^F

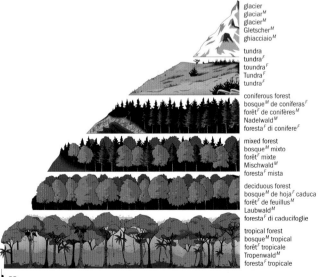

glacier
glaciar^M
glacier^M
Gletscher^M
ghiacciaio^M

tundra
tundra^F
toundra^F
Tundra^F
tundra^F

coniferous forest
bosque^M de coníferas^F
forêt^F de conifères^M
Nadelwald^M
foresta^F di conifere^F

mixed forest
bosque^M mixto
forêt^F mixte
Mischwald^M
foresta^F mista

deciduous forest
bosque^M de hoja^F caduca
forêt^F de feuillus^M
Laubwald^M
foresta^F di caducifoglie

tropical forest
bosque^M tropical
forêt^F tropicale
Tropenwald^M
foresta^F tropicale

structure of the biosphere
estructura^F de la biosfera^F
structure^F de la biosphère^F
Aufbau^M der Biosphäre^F
struttura^F della biosfera^F

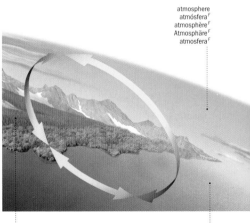

atmosphere
atmósfera^F
atmosphère^F
Atmosphäre^F
atmosfera^F

lithosphere
litosfera^F
lithosphère^F
Lithosphäre^F
litosfera^F

hydrosphere
hidrosfera^F
hydrosphère^F
Hydrosphäre^F
idrosfera^F

EARTH

food chain

cadena^F alimentaria | chaîne^F alimentaire | Nahrungskette^F | catena^F alimentare

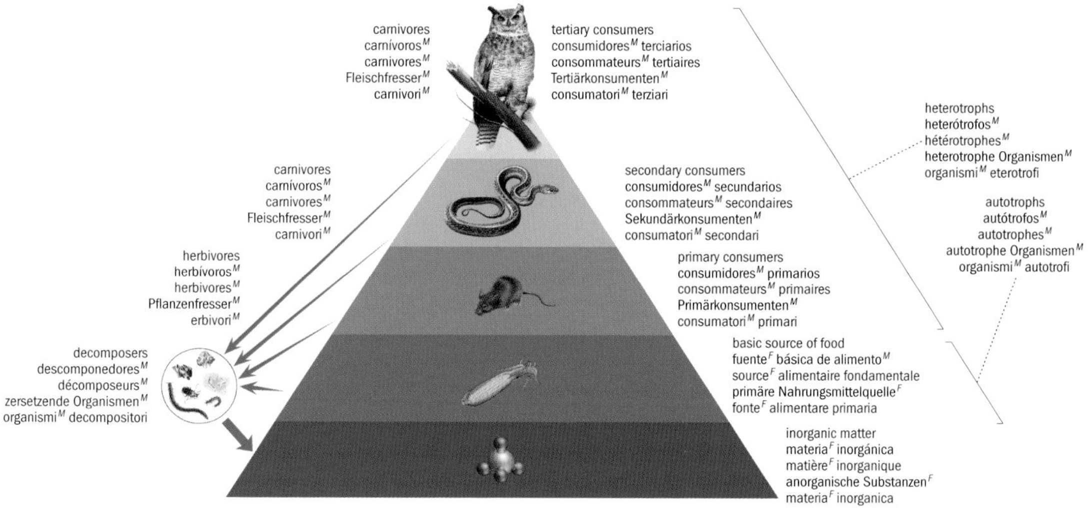

carnivores
carnívoros^M
carnivores^M
Fleischfresser^M
carnivori^M

tertiary consumers
consumidores^M terciarios
consommateurs^M tertiaires
Tertiärkonsumenten^M
consumatori^M terziari

heterotrophs
heterótrofos^M
hétérotrophes^M
heterotrophe Organismen^M
organismi^M eterotrofi

carnivores
carnívoros^M
carnivores^M
Fleischfresser^M
carnivori^M

secondary consumers
consumidores^M secundarios
consommateurs^M secondaires
Sekundärkonsumenten^M
consumatori^M secondari

autotrophs
autótrofos^M
autotrophes^M
autotrophe Organismen^M
organismi^M autotrofi

herbivores
herbívoros^M
herbivores^M
Pflanzenfresser^M
erbivori^M

primary consumers
consumidores^M primarios
consommateurs^M primaires
Primärkonsumenten^M
consumatori^M primari

decomposers
descomponedores^M
décomposeurs^M
zersetzende Organismen^M
organismi^M decompositori

basic source of food
fuente^F básica de alimento^M
source^F alimentaire fondamentale
primäre Nahrungsmittelquelle^F
fonte^F alimentare primaria

inorganic matter
materia^F inorgánica
matière^F inorganique
anorganische Substanzen^F
materia^F inorganica

hydrologic cycle

ciclo^M hidrológico | cycle^M de l'eau^F | Wasserkreislauf^M | ciclo^M idrologico

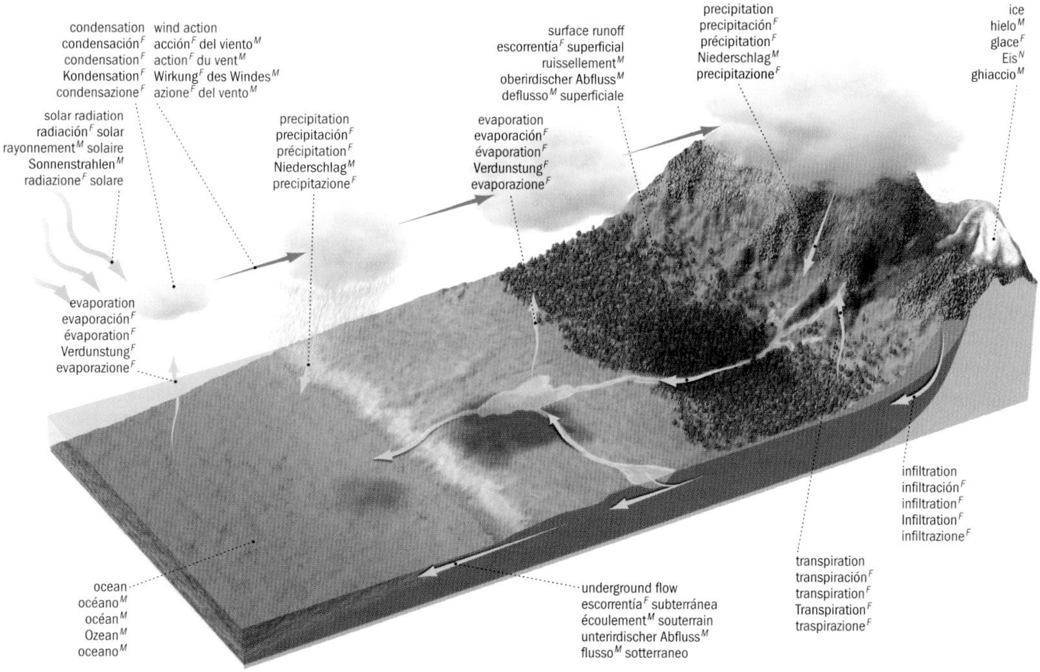

condensation
condensación^F
condensation^F
Kondensation^F
condensazione^F

wind action
acción^F del viento^M
action^F du vent^M
Wirkung^F des Windes^M
azione^F del vento^M

surface runoff
escorrentía^F superficial
ruissellement^M
oberirdischer Abfluss^M
deflusso^M superficiale

precipitation
precipitación^F
précipitation^F
Niederschlag^M
precipitazione^F

ice
hielo^M
glace^F
Eis^N
ghiaccio^M

solar radiation
radiación^F solar
rayonnement^M solaire
Sonnenstrahlen^M
radiazione^F solare

precipitation
precipitación^F
précipitation^F
Niederschlag^M
precipitazione^F

evaporation
evaporación^F
évaporation^F
Verdunstung^F
evaporazione^F

evaporation
evaporación^F
évaporation^F
Verdunstung^F
evaporazione^F

infiltration
infiltración^F
infiltration^F
Infiltration^F
infiltrazione^F

transpiration
transpiración^F
transpiration^F
Transpiration^F
traspirazione^F

ocean
océano^M
océan^M
Ozean^M
oceano^M

underground flow
escorrentía^F subterránea
écoulement^M souterrain
unterirdischer Abfluss^M
flusso^M sotterraneo

greenhouse effect

efecto^M invernadero | effet^M de serre^F | Treibhauseffekt^M | effetto^M serra^F

EARTH

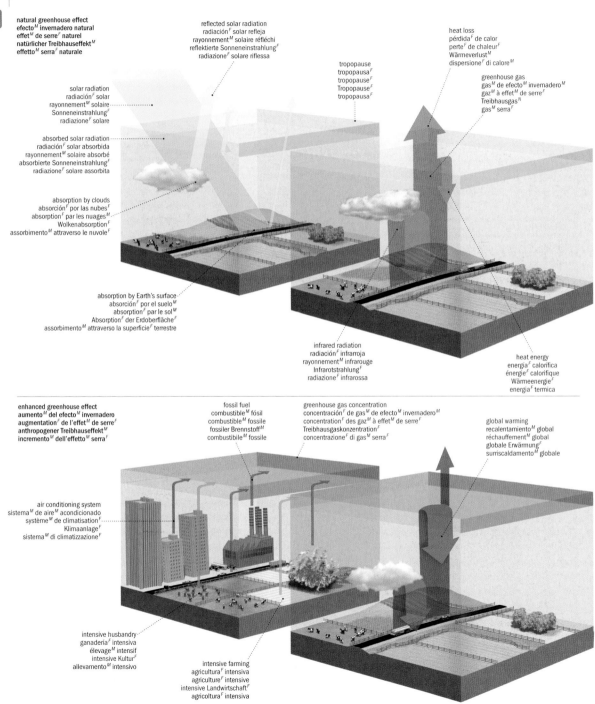

natural greenhouse effect
efecto^M invernadero natural
effet^M de serre^F naturel
natürlicher Treibhauseffekt^M
effetto^M serra^F naturale

reflected solar radiation
radiación^F solar refleja
rayonnement^M solaire réfléchi
reflektierte Sonneneinstrahlung^F
radiazione^F solare riflessa

heat loss
pérdida^F de calor
perte^F de chaleur^F
Wärmeverlust^M
dispersione^F di calore^M

tropopause
tropopausa^F
tropopause^F
Tropopause^F
tropopausa^F

greenhouse gas
gas^M de efecto^M invernadero^M
gaz^M à effet^M de serre^F
Treibhausgas^N
gas^M serra^F

solar radiation
radiación^F solar
rayonnement^M solaire
Sonneneinstrahlung^F
radiazione^F solare

absorbed solar radiation
radiación^F solar absorbida
rayonnement^M solaire absorbé
absorbierte Sonneneinstrahlung^F
radiazione^F solare assorbita

absorption by clouds
absorción^F por las nubes^F
absorption^F par les nuages^M
Wolkenabsorption^F
assorbimento^M attraverso le nuvole^F

absorption by Earth's surface
absorción^F por el suelo^M
absorption^F par le sol^M
Absorption^F der Erdoberfläche^F
assorbimento^M attraverso la superficie^F terrestre

infrared radiation
radiación^F infrarroja
rayonnement^M infrarouge
Infrarotstrahlung^F
radiazione^F infrarossa

heat energy
energía^F calorífica
énergie^F calorifique
Wärmeenergie^F
energia^F termica

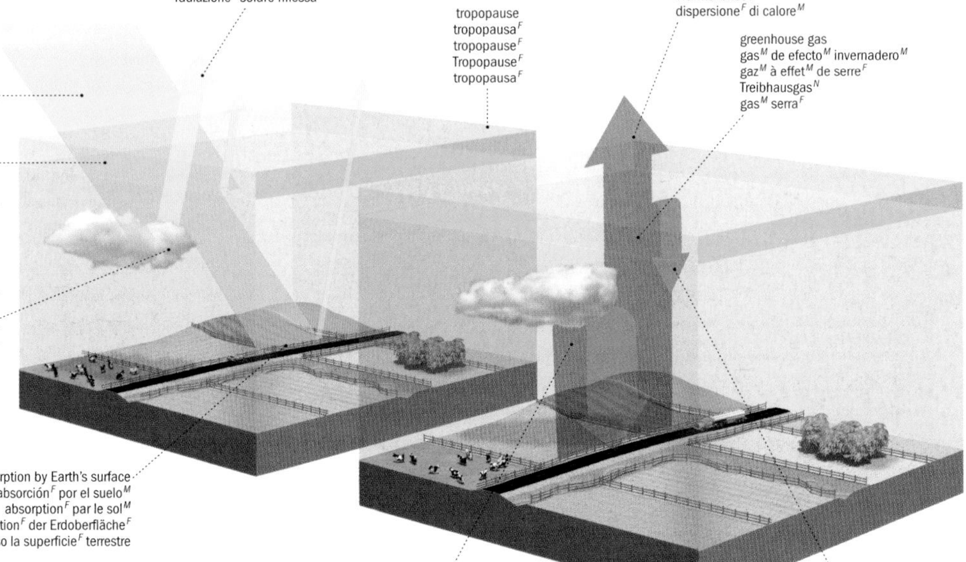

enhanced greenhouse effect
aumento^M del efecto^M invernadero
augmentation^F de l'effet^M de serre^F
anthropogener Treibhauseffekt^M
incremento^M dell'effetto^M serra^F

fossil fuel
combustible^M fósil
combustible^M fossile
fossiler Brennstoff^M
combustibile^M fossile

greenhouse gas concentration
concentración^F de gas^M de efecto^M invernadero^M
concentration^F des gaz^M à effet^M de serre^F
Treibhausgaskonzentration^F
concentrazione^F di gas^M serra^F

global warming
recalentamiento^M global
réchauffement^M global
globale Erwärmung^F
surriscaldamento^M globale

air conditioning system
sistema^M de aire^M acondicionado
système^M de climatisation^F
Klimaanlage^F
sistema^M di climatizzazione^F

intensive husbandry
ganadería^F intensiva
élevage^M intensif
intensive Kultur^F
allevamento^M intensivo

intensive farming
agricultura^F intensiva
agriculture^F intensive
intensive Landwirtschaft^F
agricoltura^F intensiva

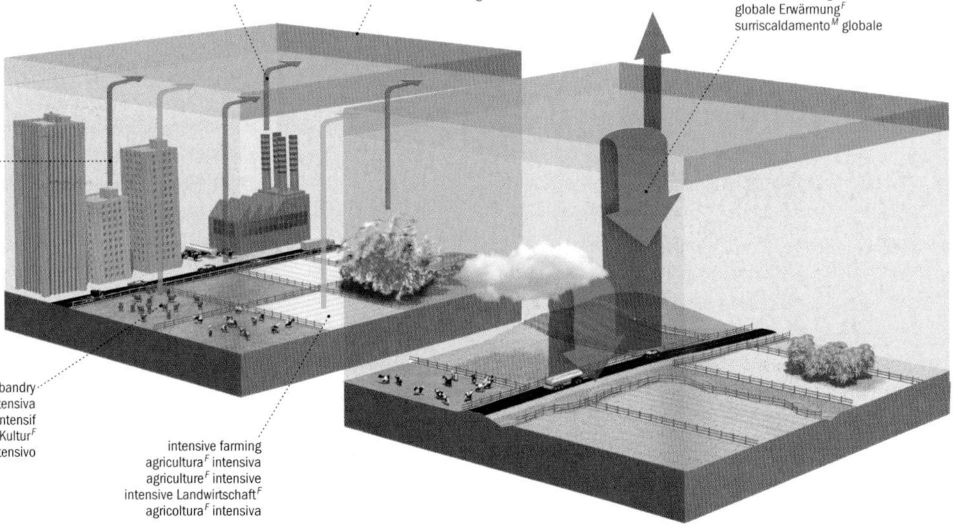

air pollution

contaminación^F del aire^M | pollution^F de l'air^M | Luftverschmutzung^F | inquinamento^M dell'aria^F

polluting gas emission
emisión^F de gases^M contaminantes
émission^F de gaz^M polluants
Emission^F schädlicher Gase^N
emissione^F di gas^M inquinanti

authorized landfill site
vertedero^M autorizado
site^M d'enfouissement^M
Mülldeponie^F
discarica^F autorizzata

air pollutants
contaminantes^M del aire^M
polluants^M atmosphériques
Luftschadstoffe^M
inquinanti^M atmosferici

smog
smog^M/niebla^F tóxica
smog^M
Smog^M
smog^M

wind
viento^M
vent^M
Wind^M
vento^M

acid rain
lluvia^F ácida
pluies^F acides
saurer Regen^M
piogge^F acide

forest fire
incendio^M forestal
incendie^M de forêt^F
Waldbrand^M
incendio^M delle foreste^F

industrial waste
residuos^{M F} industriales
rejets^M industriels
Industrieabfälle^M
rifiuti^M industriali

motor vehicle pollution
contaminación^F de automóviles^M
pollution^F automobile
Verschmutzung^F durch Autoabgase^N
inquinamento^M da gas^M di scarico^M delle automobili^F

deforestation
deforestación^F
déforestation^F
Entwaldung^F
deforestazione^F

paddy field
arrozal^M
rizière^F
Reisfeld^N
risaia^F

soil fertilization
fertilización^F del suelo^M
fertilisation^F des sols^M
Bodendüngung^F
fertilizzazione^F del suolo^M

intensive husbandry
ganadería^F intensiva
élevage^M intensif
intensive Kultur^F
allevamento^M intensivo

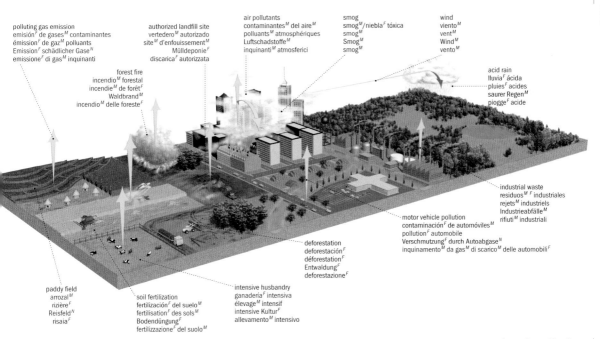

land pollution

contaminación^F del suelo^M | pollution^F du sol^M | Bodenverschmutzung^F | inquinamento^M del suolo^M

industrial pollution
contaminación^F industrial
pollution^F industrielle
industrielle Verschmutzung^F
inquinamento^M industriale

non-biodegradable pollutants
contaminantes^M no biodegradables
polluants^M non biodégradables
biologisch nicht abbaubare Schadstoffe^M
inquinanti^M non biodegradabili

intensive husbandry
ganadería^F intensiva
élevage^M intensif
intensive Kultur^F
allevamento^M intensivo

domestic pollution
contaminación^F doméstica
pollution^F domestique
Verschmutzung^F durch Haushalte^M
inquinamento^M domestico

agricultural pollution
contaminación^F agrícola
pollution^F agricole
landwirtschaftliche Verschmutzung^F
inquinamento^M agricolo

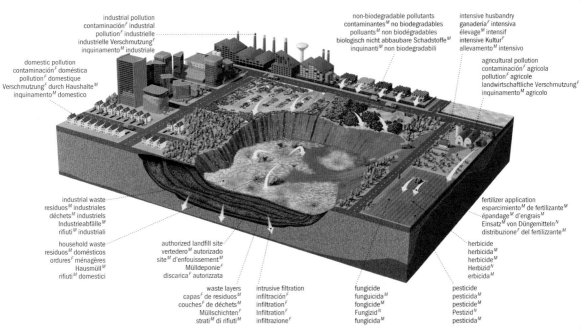

industrial waste
residuos^M industriales
déchets^M industriels
Industrieabfälle^M
rifiuti^M industriali

household waste
residuos^M domésticos
ordures^F ménagères
Hausmüll^M
rifiuti^M domestici

authorized landfill site
vertedero^M autorizado
site^M d'enfouissement^M
Mülldeponie^F
discarica^F autorizzata

fertilizer application
esparcimiento^M de fertilizante^M
épandage^M d'engrais^M
Einsatz^M von Düngemitteln^N
distribuzione^F del fertilizzante^M

herbicide
herbicida^M
herbicide^M
Herbizid^N
erbicida^M

waste layers
capas^F de residuos^M
couches^F de déchets^M
Müllschichten^F
strati^M di rifiuti^M

intrusive filtration
infiltración^F
infiltration^F
Infiltration^F
infiltrazione^F

fungicide
funguicida^M
fongicide^M
Fungizid^N
fungicida^M

pesticide
pesticida^M
pesticide^M
Pestizid^N
pesticida^M

water pollution

contaminación^F del agua^F | pollution^F de l'eau^F | Wasserverschmutzung^F | inquinamento^M dell'acqua^F

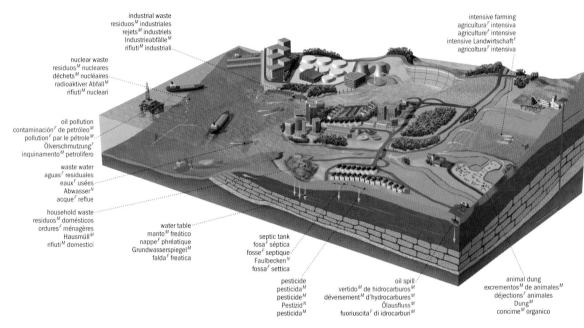

industrial waste
residuos^M industriales
rejets^M industriels
Industrieabfälle^M
rifiuti^M industriali

intensive farming
agricultura^F intensiva
agriculture^F intensive
intensive Landwirtschaft^F
agricoltura^F intensiva

nuclear waste
residuos^M nucleares
déchets^F nucléaires
radioaktiver Abfall^M
rifiuti^M nucleari

oil pollution
contaminación^F de petróleo^M
pollution^F par le pétrole^M
Ölverschmutzung^F
inquinamento^M petrolifero

waste water
aguas^F residuales
eaux^F usées
Abwasser^N
acque^F reflue

household waste
residuos^M domésticos
ordures^F ménagères
Hausmüll^M
rifiuti^M domestici

water table
manto^M freático
nappe^F phréatique
Grundwasserspiegel^M
falda^F freatica

septic tank
fosa^F séptica
fosse^F septique
Faulbecken^N
fossa^F settica

pesticide
pesticida^M
pesticide^M
Pestizid^N
pesticida^M

oil spill
vertido^M de hidrocarburos^M
déversement^M d'hydrocarbures^M
Ölausfluss^M
fuoriuscita^F di idrocarburi^M

animal dung
excrementos^M de animales^M
déjections^F animales
Dung^M
concime^M organico

acid rain

lluvia^F ácida | pluies^F acides | saurer Regen^M | piogge^F acide

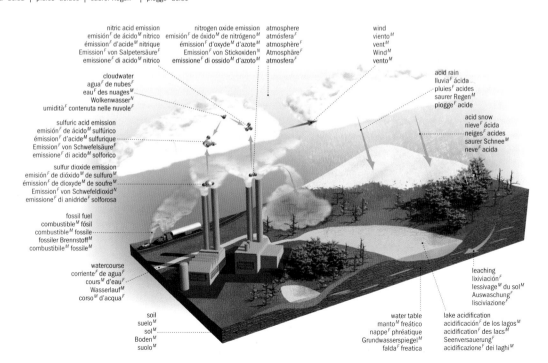

nitric acid emission
emisión^F de ácido^M nítrico
émission^F d'acide^M nitrique
Emission^F von Salpetersäure^F
emissione^F di acido^M nitrico

nitrogen oxide emission
emisión^F de óxido^M de nitrógeno^M
émission^F d'oxyde^M d'azote^M
Emission^F von Stickoxiden^N
emissione^F di ossido^M d'azoto^M

atmosphere
atmósfera^F
atmosphère^F
Atmosphäre^F
atmosfera^F

wind
viento^M
vent^M
Wind^M
vento^M

cloudwater
agua^F de nubes^F
eau^F des nuages^M
Wolkenwasser^N
umidità^F contenuta nelle nuvole^F

acid rain
lluvia^F ácida
pluies^F acides
saurer Regen^M
piogge^F acide

acid snow
nieve^F ácida
neiges^F acides
saurer Schnee^M
neve^F acida

sulfuric acid emission
emisión^F de ácido^M sulfúrico
émission^F d'acide^M sulfurique
Emission^F von Schwefelsäure^F
emissione^F di acido^M solforico

sulfur dioxide emission
emisión^F de dióxido^M de sulfuro^M
émission^F de dioxyde^M de soufre^M
Emission^F von Schwefeldioxid^N
emissione^F di anidride^F solforosa

fossil fuel
combustible^M fósil
combustible^M fossile
fossiler Brennstoff^M
combustibile^M fossile^M

watercourse
corriente^F de agua^F
cours^F d'eau^F
Wasserlauf^M
corso^M d'acqua^F

leaching
lixiviación^F
lessivage^M du sol^M
Auswaschung^F
lisciviazione^F

soil
suelo^M
sol^M
Boden^M
suolo^M

water table
manto^M freático
nappe^F phréatique
Grundwasserspiegel^M
falda^F freatica

lake acidification
acidificación^F de los lagos^M
acidification^F des lacs^M
Seenversauerung^F
acidificazione^F dei laghi^M

selective sorting of waste

separación^F selectiva de residuos^M | tri^M sélectif des déchets^M | Mülltrennung^F | smistamento^M selettivo dei rifiuti^M

crusher
trituradora^F
broyeur^M
Zerkleinerer^M
frantumatrice^F

paper/paperboard sorting
selección^F de papel^M/cartón^M
tri^M du papier^M/carton^M
Sortierung^F von Papier^N/Pappe^F
smistamento^M della carta^F/del cartone^M

sorting plant
planta^F de separación^F selectiva
centre^M de tri^M
Sortieranlage^F
impianto^M di smistamento^M

glass sorting
selección^F de vidrio^M
tri^M du verre^M
Sortierung^F von Glas^N
smistamento^M del vetro^M

non-reusable residue waste
residuos^M no reciclables
résidus^M non recyclables
nicht wieder verwertbarer Restmüll^M
rifiuti^M non riciclabili

burial
enterramiento^M
enfouissement^M
Endlagerung^F
interramento^M

incineration
incineración^F
incinération^F
Verbrennen^N
incenerimento^M

manual sorting
selección^F manual
tri^M manuel
Nachsortierung^F von Hand^F
smistamento^M manuale

plastics sorting
clasificación^F de plásticos^M
tri^M du plastique^M
Sortierung^F von Kunststoff^M
smistamento^M della plastica^F

conveyor belt
cinta^F transportadora
bande^F transporteuse
Förderband^N
nastro^M trasportatore

separate collection
recogida^F diferenciada
collecte^F sélective
getrennte Sammlung^F
raccolta^F differenziata

paper/paperboard separation
separación^F papel^M/cartón^M
séparation^F papier^M/carton^M
Sortierung^F von Papier^N/Pappe^F
separazione^F della carta^F/del cartone^M

baling
embalaje^M
mise^F en balles^F
Verpackung^F
imballaggio^M

metal sorting
selección^F de metal^M
tri^M des métaux^M
Sortierung^F von Metall^N
smistamento^M dei materiali^M metallici

recycling
reciclado^M
recyclage^M
Recycling^N
riciclaggio^M

magnetic separation
separación^F magnética
séparation^F magnétique
magnetische Trennung^F
separazione^M magnetica

compacting
compresión^F
compactage^M
Verdichtung^F
compattazione^F

optical sorting
selección^F óptica
tri^M optique
optische Sortierung^F
smistamento^M ottico

shredding
desmenuzamiento^M
déchiquetage^M
Zerkleinerung^F
sminuzzamento^M

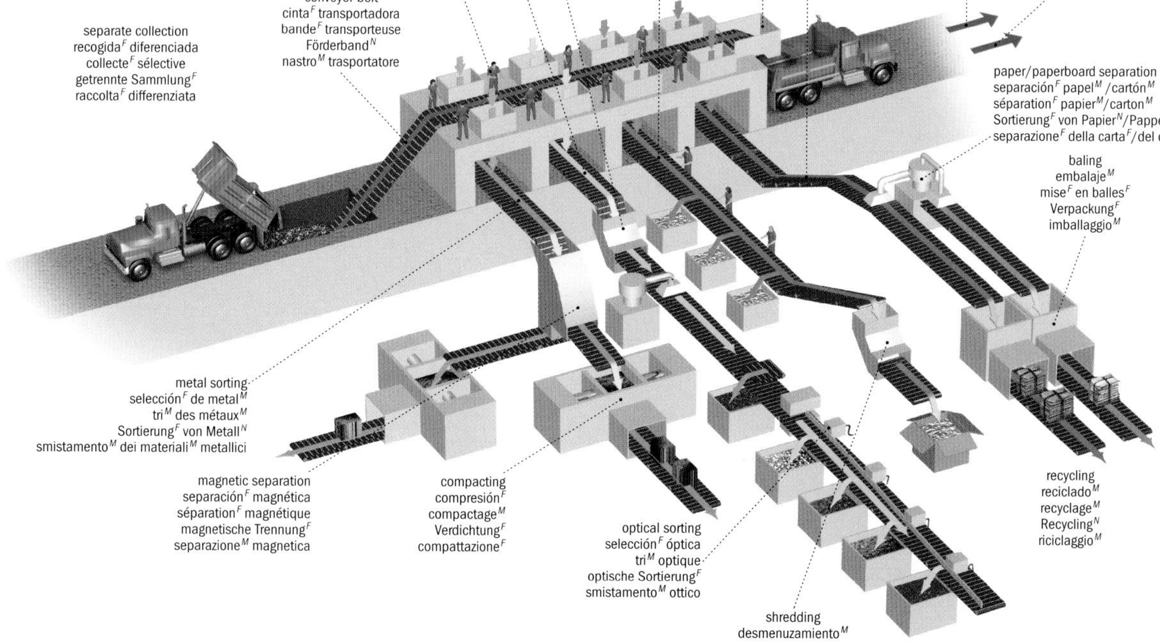

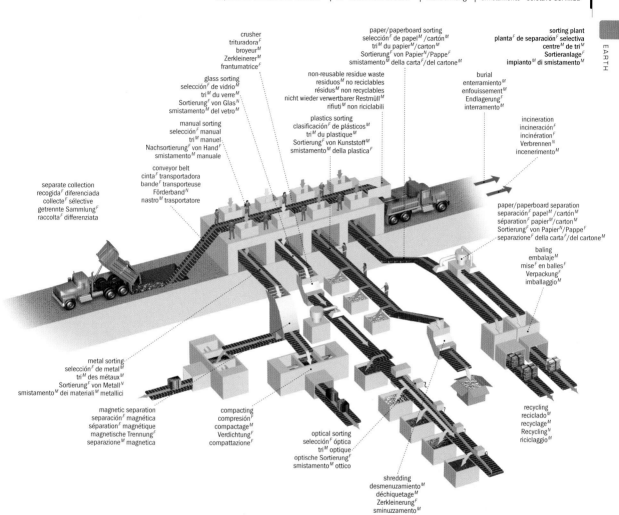

recycling containers
contenedores^M de reciclaje^M
conteneurs^M de collecte^F sélective
Wertstoff^M-Sammelbehälter^M
contenitori^M per la raccolta^F
differenziata

paper recycling container
contenedor^M de reciclado^M de papel^M
conteneur^M à papier^M
Altpapier^N-Sammelbehälter^M
bidone^M carrellato per il riciclaggio^M
della carta^F

glass recycling container
contenedor^M de reciclado^M de vidrio^M
conteneur^M à verre^M
Altglas^N-Sammelbehälter^M
bidone^M carrellato per il riciclaggio^M del vetro^M

aluminum recycling container
contenedor^M de reciclado^M de aluminio^M
conteneur^M à boîtes^F métalliques
Altaluminium^N-Sammelbehälter^M
bidone^M carrellato per il riciclaggio^M
dell'alluminio^M

paper collection unit
contenedor^M de recogida^F de papel^M
colonne^F de collecte^F du papier^M
Altpapier^N-Container^M
campana^F per la raccolta^F della carta^F

glass collection unit
contenedor^M de recogida^F de vidrio^M
colonne^F de collecte^F du verre^M
Altglas^N-Container^M
campana^F per la raccolta^F del vetro^M

recycling bin
cubo^M de basura^F reciclable
bac^M de recyclage^M
Bioabfallbehälter^M
contenitore^M per il riciclaggio^M

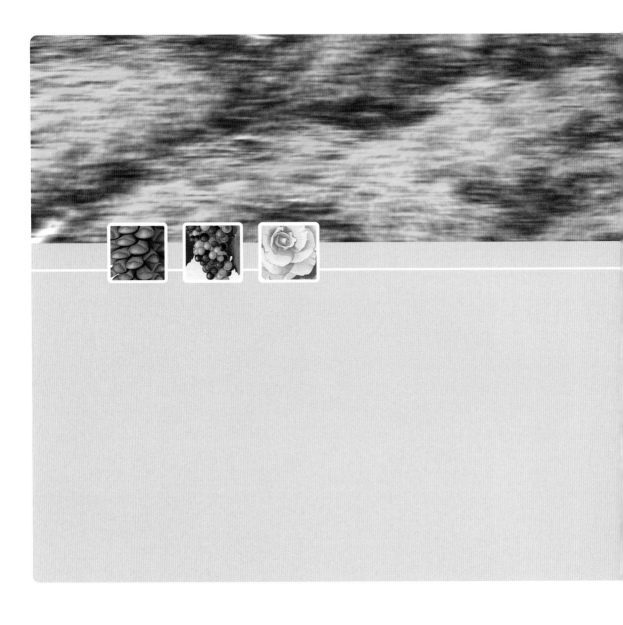

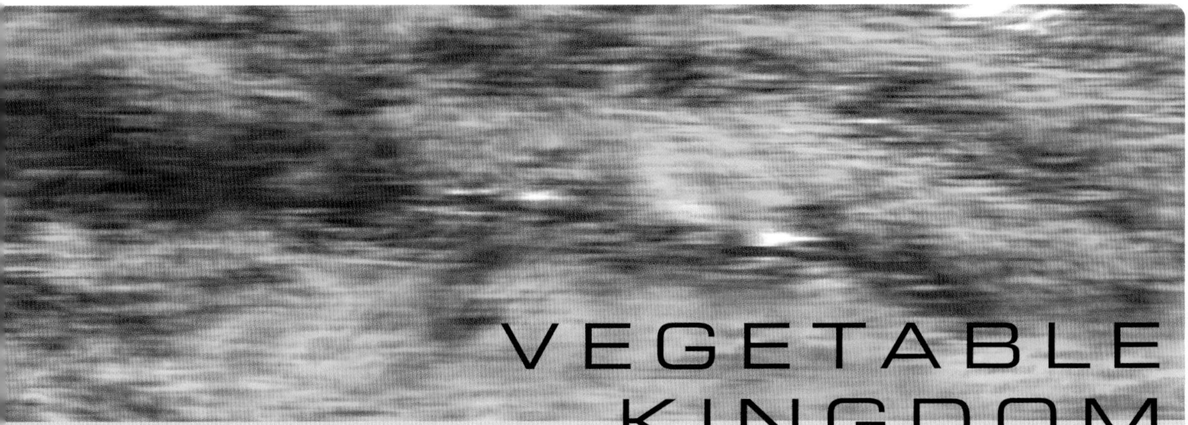

VEGETABLE KINGDOM

74

plant cell

célula^F vegetal | cellule^F végétale | Pflanzenzelle^F | cellula^F vegetale

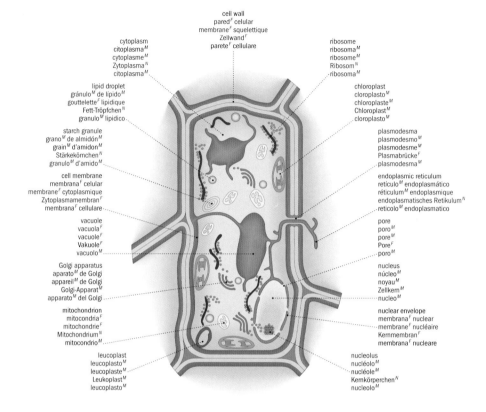

cell wall
pared^F celular
membrane^F squelettique
Zellwand^F
parete^F cellulare

cytoplasm
citoplasma^M
cytoplasme^M
Zytoplasma^N
citoplasma^M

ribosome
ribosoma^M
ribosome^M
Ribosom^N
ribosoma^M

lipid droplet
gránulo^M de lípido^M
gouttelette^F lipidique
Fett-Tröpfchen^N
granulo^M lipidico

chloroplast
cloroplasto^M
chloroplaste^M
Chloroplast^M
cloroplasto^M

starch granule
grano^M de almidón^M
grain^M d'amidon^M
Stärkekörnchen^N
granulo^M d'amido^M

plasmodesma
plasmodesmo^M
plasmodesme^M
Plasmabrücke^F
plasmodesma^M

cell membrane
membrana^F celular
membrane^F cytoplasmique
Zytoplasmamembran^F
membrana^F cellulare

endoplasmic reticulum
reticulo^M endoplasmático
réticulum^M endoplasmique
endoplasmatisches Retikulum^N
reticolo^M endoplasmatico

vacuole
vacuola^F
vacuole^F
Vakuole^F
vacuolo^M

pore
poro^M
pore^M
Pore^F
poro^M

Golgi apparatus
aparato^M de Golgi
appareil^M de Golgi
Golgi-Apparat^M
apparato^M del Golgi

nucleus
núcleo^M
noyau^M
Zellkern^M
nucleo^M

mitochondrion
mitocondria^F
mitochondrie^F
Mitochondrium^N
mitocondrio^M

nuclear envelope
membrana^F nuclear
membrane^F nucléaire
Kernmembran^F
membrana^F nucleare

leucoplast
leucoplasto^M
leucoplaste^M
Leukoplast^M
leucoplasto^M

nucleolus
nucléolo^M
nucléole^M
Kernkörperchen^N
nucleolo^M

lichen

liquen | lichen^M | Flechte^F | lichene^M

structure of a lichen
estructura^F de un liquen^M
structure^F d'un lichen^M
Aufbau^M einer Flechte^F
struttura^F di un lichene^M

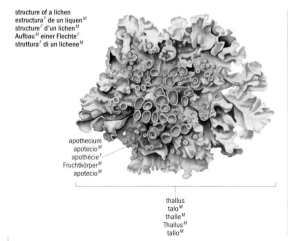

apothecium
apotecio^M
apothécie^F
Fruchtkörper^M
apotecio^M

thallus
talo^M
thalle^M
Thallus^M
tallo^M

examples of lichens
ejemplos^M de líquenes^M
exemples^M de lichens^M
Beispiele^N für Flechten^F
esempi^M di licheni^M

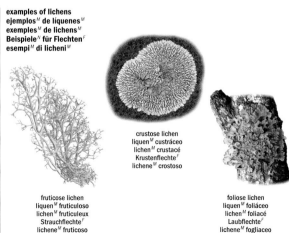

crustose lichen
liquen^M custráceo
lichen^M crustacé
Krustenflechte^F
lichene^M crostoso

fruticose lichen
liquen^M fruticuloso
lichen^M fruticuleux
Strauchflechte^F
lichene^M fruticoso

foliose lichen
liquen^M foliáceo
lichen^M foliacé
Laubflechte^F
lichene^M fogliaceo

musgo[M] | mousse[F] | Moos[N] | muschio[M]

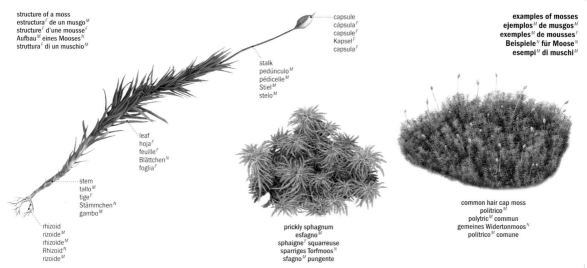

structure of a moss
estructura[F] de un musgo[M]
structure[F] d'une mousse[F]
Aufbau[M] eines Mooses[N]
struttura[F] di un muschio[M]

capsule
cápsula[F]
capsule[F]
Kapsel[F]
capsula[F]

stalk
pedúnculo[M]
pédicelle[M]
Stiel[M]
stelo[M]

leaf
hoja[F]
feuille[F]
Blättchen[N]
foglia[F]

stem
tallo[M]
tige[F]
Stämmchen[N]
gambo[M]

rhizoid
rizoide[M]
rhizoide[M]
Rhizoid[N]
rizoide[M]

examples of mosses
ejemplos[M] de musgos[M]
exemples[M] de mousses[F]
Beispiele[N] für Moose[F]
esempi[M] di muschi[M]

common hair cap moss
politrico[M]
polytric[M] commun
gemeines Widertonmoos[N]
politrico[M] comune

prickly sphagnum
esfagno[M]
sphaigne[F] squarreuse
sparriges Torfmoos[N]
sfagno[M] pungente

alga[F] | algues[F] | Algen[F] | alghe[F]

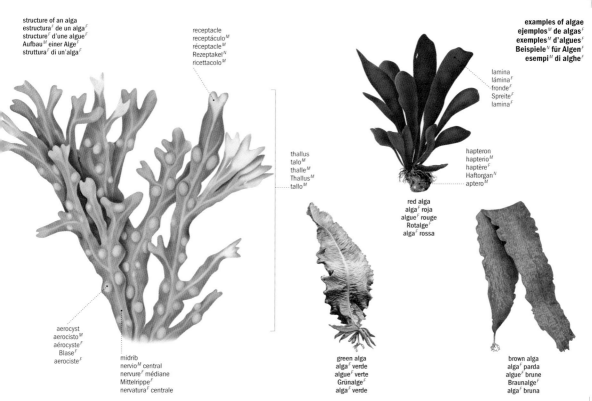

structure of an alga
estructura[F] de un alga[F]
structure[F] d'une algue[F]
Aufbau[M] einer Alge[F]
struttura[F] di un'alga[F]

receptacle
receptáculo[M]
réceptacle[M]
Rezeptakel[N]
ricettacolo[M]

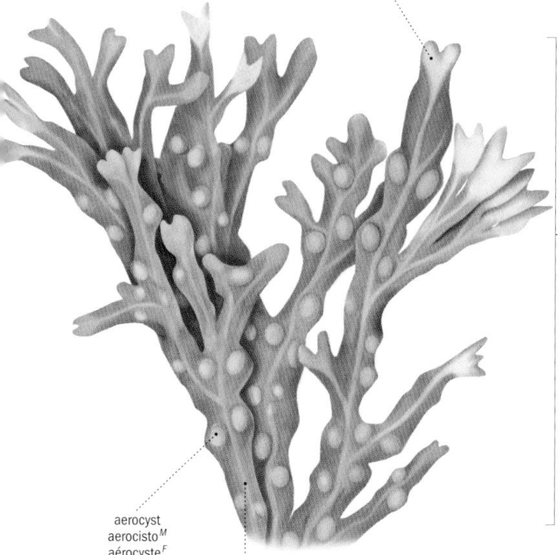

examples of algae
ejemplos[M] de algas[F]
exemples[M] d'algues[F]
Beispiele[N] für Algen[F]
esempi[M] di alghe[F]

lamina
lámina[F]
fronde[F]
Spreite[F]
lamina[F]

thallus
talo[M]
thalle[M]
Thallus[M]
tallo[M]

hapteron
hapterio[M]
haptère[F]
Haftorgan[N]
aptero[M]

red alga
alga[F] roja
algue[F] rouge
Rotalge[F]
alga[F] rossa

aerocyst
aerocisto[M]
aérocyste[F]
Blase[F]
aerociste[F]

midrib
nervio[M] central
nervure[F] médiane
Mittelrippe[F]
nervatura[F] centrale

green alga
alga[F] verde
algue[F] verte
Grünalge[F]
alga[F] verde

brown alga
alga[F] parda
algue[F] brune
Braunalge[F]
alga[F] bruna

mushroom

hongo^M | champignon^M | Pilz^M | fungo^M

structure of a mushroom
anatomía^F de un hongo^M
structure^F d'un champignon^M
Aufbau^M eines Pilzes^M
struttura^F di un fungo^M

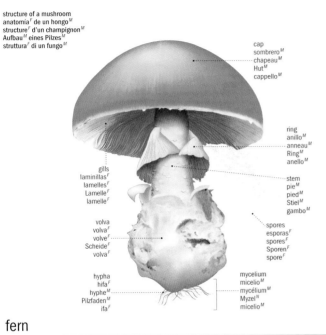

cap
sombrero^M
chapeau^M
Hut^M
cappello^M

ring
anillo^M
anneau^M
Ring^M
anello^M

gills
laminillas^F
lamelles^F
Lamelle^F
lamelle^F

stem
pie^M
pied^M
Stiel^M
gambo^M

volva
volva^F
volve^F
Scheide^F
volva^F

spores
esporas^F
spores^F
Sporen^F
spore^F

hypha
hifa^F
hyphe^M
Pilzfaden^M
ifa^F

mycelium
micelio^M
mycélium^M
Myzel^N
micelio^M

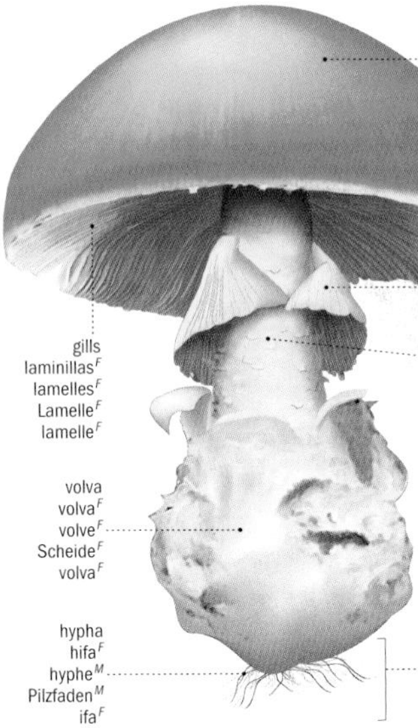

**deadly poisonous mushroom
hongo^M mortal
champignon^M mortel
tödlich giftiger Pilz^M
fungo^M velenoso e mortale**

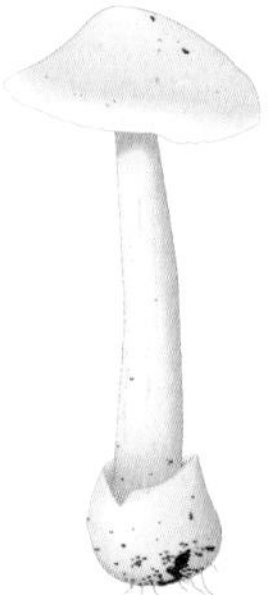

destroying angel
amanita^F virosa
amanite^F vireuse
Knollenblätterpilz^M
amanita^F virosa

**poisonous mushroom
hongo^M venenoso
champignon^M vénéneux
Giftpilz^M
fungo^M velenoso**

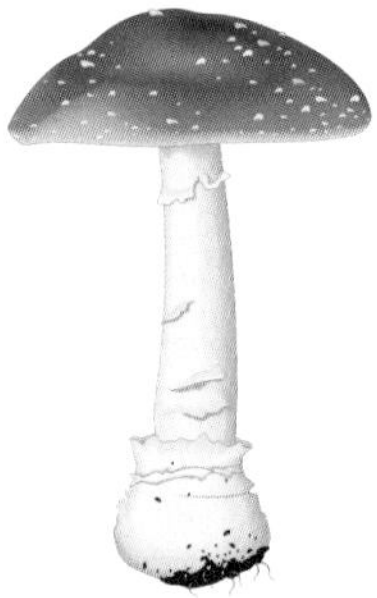

fly agaric
falsa oronja^F
fausse oronge^F
Fliegenpilz^M
amanita^F muscaria

fern

helecho^M | fougère^F | Farn^M | felce^F

structure of a fern
estructura^F de un helecho^M
structure^F d'une fougère^F
Aufbau^M eines Farns^M
struttura^F di una felce^F

sorus
soro^M
sore^M
Sorus^M
soro^M

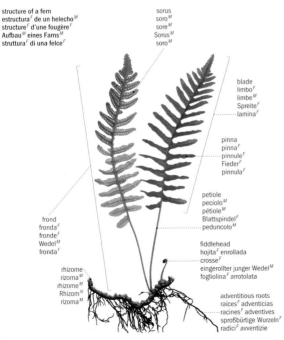

blade
limbo^F
limbe^M
Spreite^F
lamina^F

pinna
pinna^F
pinnule^F
Fieder^F
pinnula^F

petiole
peciolo^M
pétiole^M
Blattspindel^F
peduncolo^M

fiddlehead
hojita^F enrollada
crosse^F
eingerollter junger Wedel^M
fogliolina^F arrotolata

frond
fronda^F
fronde^F
Wedel^M
fronda^F

rhizome
rizoma^M
rhizome^M
Rhizom^N
rizoma^M

adventitious roots
raíces^F adventicias
racines^F adventives
sproßbürtige Wurzeln^F
radici^F avventizie

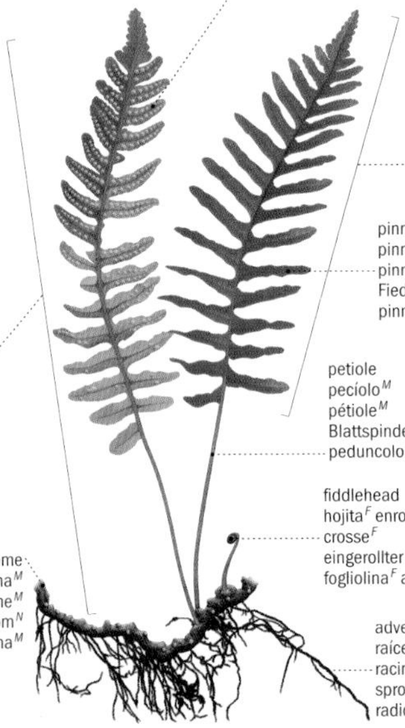

**examples of ferns
ejemplos^M de helechos^M
exemples^M de fougères^F
Beispiele^N für Farne^M
esempi^M di felci^F**

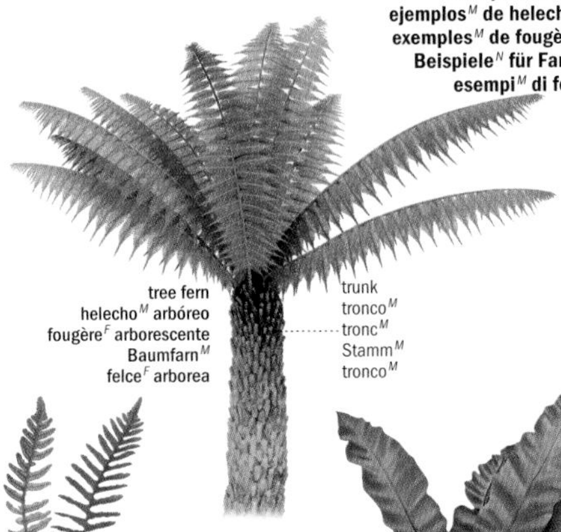

tree fern
helecho^M arbóreo
fougère^F arborescente
Baumfarn^M
felce^F arborea

trunk
tronco^M
tronc^M
Stamm^M
tronco^M

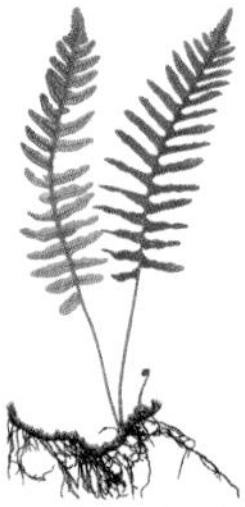

common polypody
polipodio^M común
polypode^M commun
gemeiner Tüpfelfarn^M
polipodio^M comune

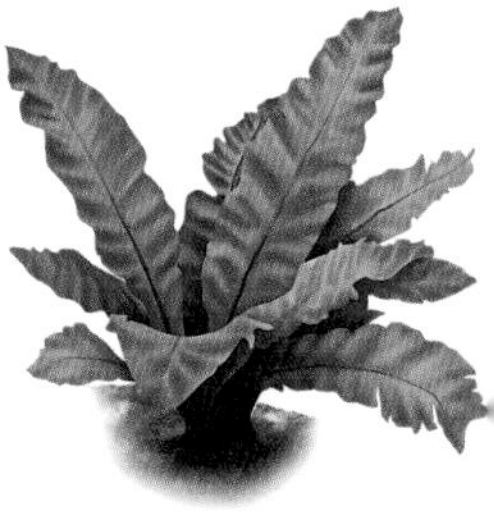

bird's nest fern
helecho^M nido^M de pájaro^M
fougère^F nid^M d'oiseau^M
Nestfarn^M
lingua^F di cervo^M

structure of a plant
anatomía^F de una planta^F
structure^F d'une plante^F
Aufbau^M einer Pflanze^F
struttura^F di una pianta^F

terminal bud
yema^F terminal
bourgeon^M terminal
Endknospe^F
gemma^F terminale

flower bud
capullo^M
bouton^M floral
Blütenknospe^F
gemma^F fiorale

flower
flor^F
fleur^F
Blüte^F
fiore^M

axillary bud
yema^F axilar
bourgeon^M axillaire
Achselknospe^F
gemma^F ascellare

shoot
brote^M
pousse^F
Schössling^M
germoglio^M

leaf node
nudo^M
nœud^M
Blattgrund^M
nodo^M

leaf
hoja^F
feuille^F
Blatt^N
foglia^F

twig
rama^F
rameau^M
Zweig^M
ramoscello^M

internode
entrenudo^M
entre-nœud^M
Stengelglied^N
internodo^M

stem
tallo^M
tige^F
Stengel^M
fusto^M

seed leaf
cotiledón^M
cotylédon^M
Keimblatt^N
cotiledone^M

collar
cuello^M
collet^M
Hals^M
colletto^M

secondary root
raíz^F secundaria
racine^F secondaire
Seitenwurzel^F
radice^F secondaria

radicle
radícula^F
radicelle^F
Faserwurzel^F
radichetta^F

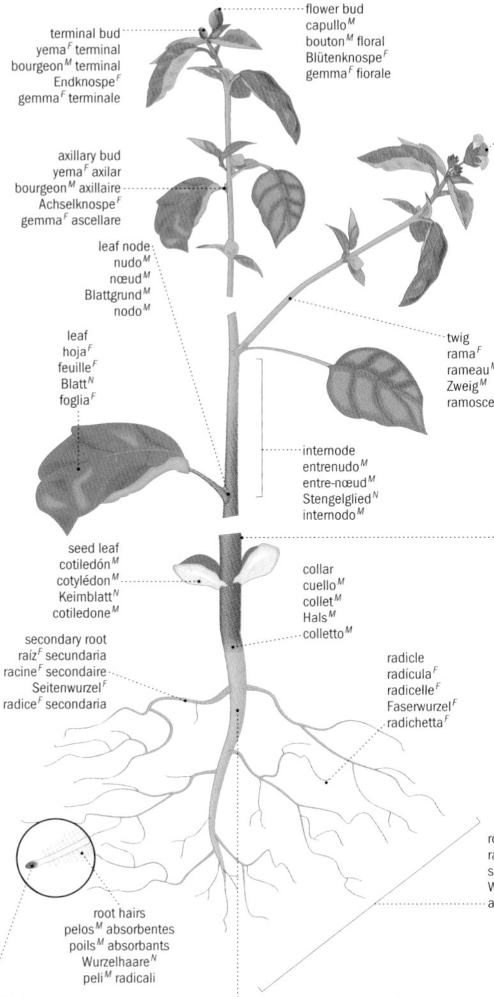

germination
germinación^F
germination^F
Keimung^F
germinazione^F

terminal bud
yema^F terminal
bourgeon^M terminal
Vegetationspunkt^M
gemma^F apicale

leaf
hoja^F
feuille^F
Blatt^N
foglia^F

cotyledon
cotiledón^M
cotylédon^M
verwelkendes Keimblatt^N
cotiledone^M

root system
raíces^F
système^M racinaire
Wurzelsystem^N
apparato^M radicale

root hairs
pelos^M absorbentes
poils^M absorbants
Wurzelhaare^N
peli^M radicali

first leaves
primeras hojas^F
premières feuilles^F
erste Laubblätter^N
prime foglie^F

root cap
caliptra^F
coiffe^F
Wurzelhaube^F
piloriza^F

secondary root
raíz^F secundaria
racine^F secondaire
Seitenwurzel^F
radice^F laterale

primary root
raíz^F principal
racine^F principale
Primärwurzel^F
radice^F principale

primary root
raíz^F primaria
racine^F principale
Hauptwurzel^F
radice^F principale

seed
semilla^F
graine^F
Samen^M
seme^M

radicle
radícula^F
radicule^F
Keimwurzel^F
radichetta^F

root hairs
pelos^M radicales
poils^M absorbants
Wurzelhaare^N
peli^M radicali

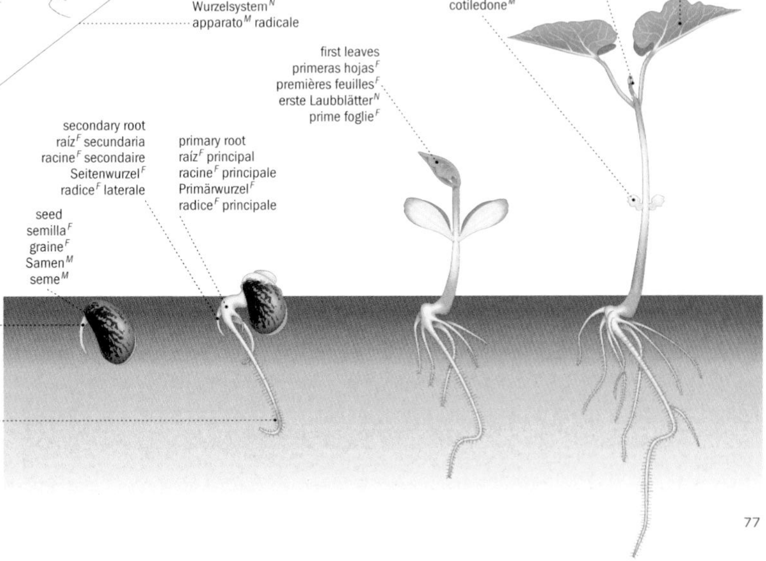

photosynthesis
fotosíntesis^F
photosynthèse^F
Photosynthese^F
fotosintesi^F

solar energy
energía^F solar
énergie^F solaire
Sonnenenergie^F
energia^F solare

leaf
hoja^F
feuille^F
Blatt^N
foglia^F

stem
tallo^M
tige^F
Stiel^M
stelo^M

glucose
glucosa^F
glucose^M
Glukose^F
glucosio^M

release of oxygen
producción^F de oxígeno^M
rejet^M d'oxygène^M
Abgabe^F von Sauerstoff^M
produzione^F di ossigeno^M

absorption of carbon dioxide
absorción^F de dióxido^M de carbono^M
absorption^F de dioxyde^M de carbone^M
Aufnahme^F von Kohlendioxid^N
assorbimento^M di anidride^F carbonica

absorption of water and mineral salts
absorción^F de agua^M y sales^F minerales
absorption^F d'eau^F et de sels^M minéraux
Aufnahme^F von Wasser^N und Mineralstoffen^M
assorbimento^M di acqua^F e sali^M minerali

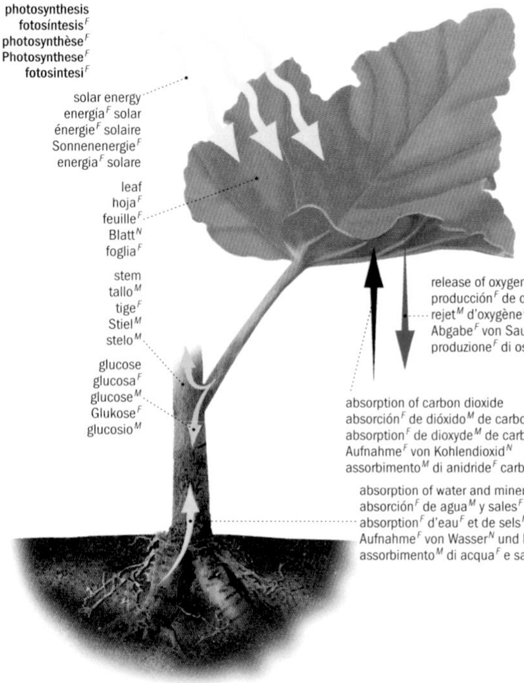

soil profile
perfil^M del suelo^M
profil^M du sol^M
Bodenprofil^N
profilo^M del suolo^M

plant litter
humus^M
litière^F
Auflagehumus^M
humus^M

topsoil
capa^F superficial del suelo^M
couche^F arable
Oberboden^M
strato^M superficiale del suolo^M

subsoil
subsuelo^M
sous-sol^M
Unterboden^M
sottosuolo^M

bedrock
roca^F madre
roche^F mère^F
Muttergestein^N
roccia^F in posto^M

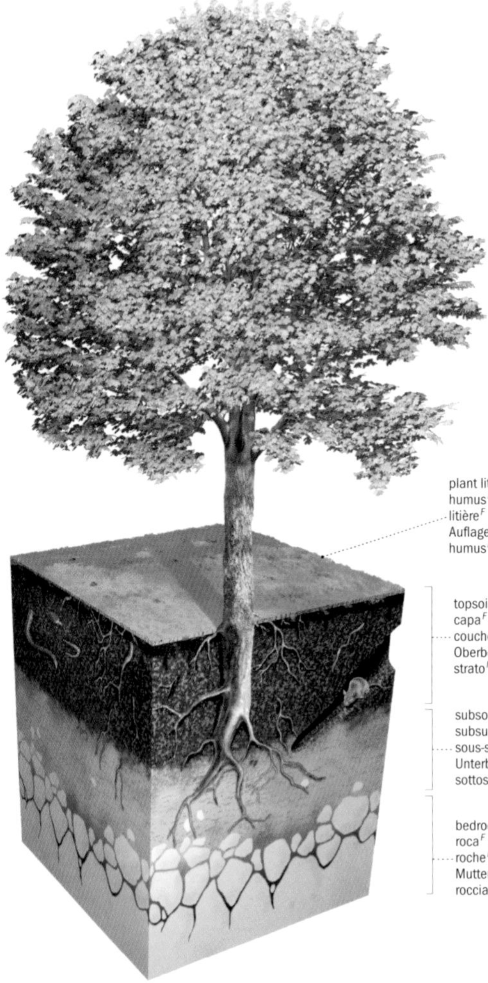

section of a bulb
corte de un bulbo^M
coupe^F d'un bulbe^M
Zwiebel^F im Querschnitt^M
sezione^F di un bulbo^M

scale leaf
hoja^F
tunique^F
Laubblatt^N
tunica^F

bud
yema^F
bourgeon^M
Knospe^F
gemma^F

fleshy leaf
hoja^F flexible
écaille^F
Schuppenblatt^N
foglia^F carnosa

bulbil
bulbillo^M
caïeu^M
Brutzwiebel^F
bulbillo^M

underground stem
tallo^M del bulbo^M
tige^F
Blütenstandstiel^M
fusto^M del bulbo^M

base
base^F del bulbo^M
plateau^M
Spross^M
base^F del bulbo^M

root
raíz^F
racine^F
Wurzel^F
radice^F

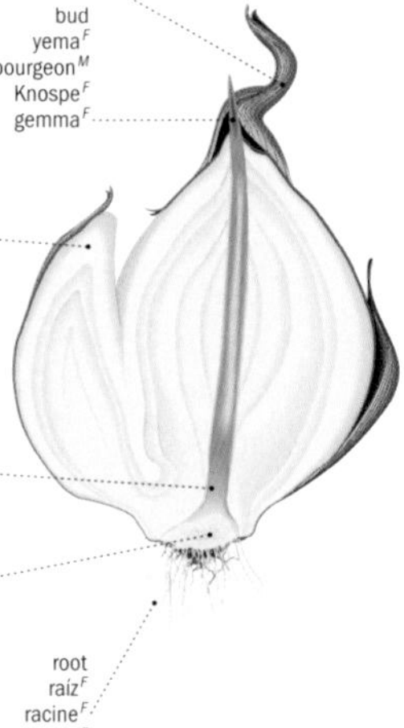

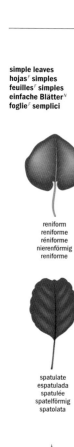

simple leaves
hojas^F simples
feuilles^F simples
einfache Blätter^N
foglie^F semplici

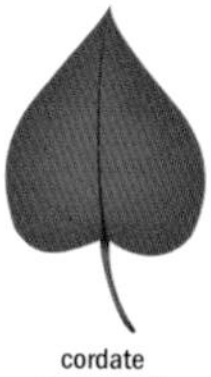

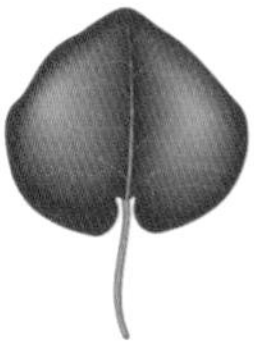

reniform
reniforme
réniforme
nierenförmig
reniforme

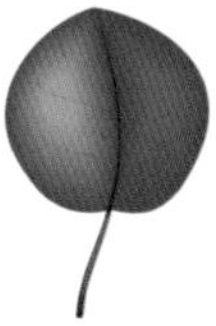

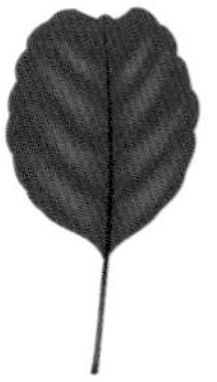

spatulate
espatulada
spatulée
spatelförmig
spatolata

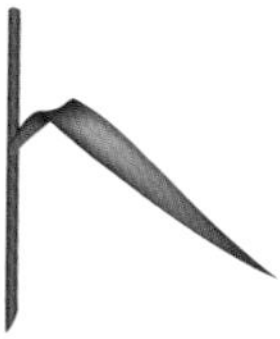

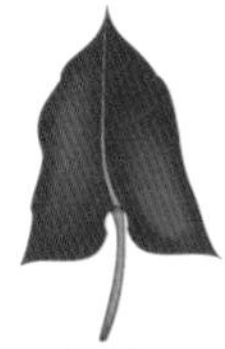

hastate
astada
hastée
Pfeilförmig
astata

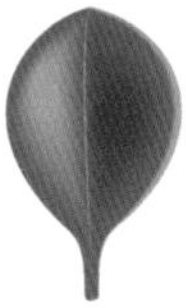

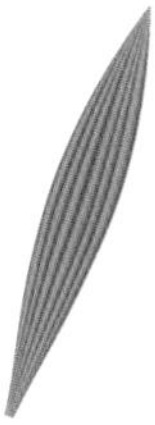

lanceolate
lanceolada
lancéolée
lanzettförmig
lanceolata

cordate
acorazonada
cordée
Herzförmig
cordata

orbiculate
orbicular
arrondie
rund
orbicolare

linear
acicular
linéaire
linealisch
lineare

ovate
aovada
ovoide
eiförmig
ovata

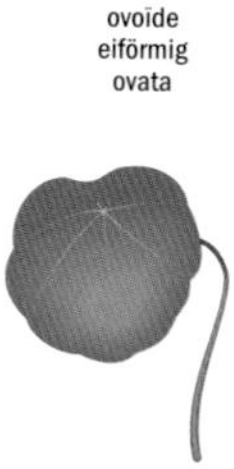

peltate
peltada
peltée
schildförmig
peltata

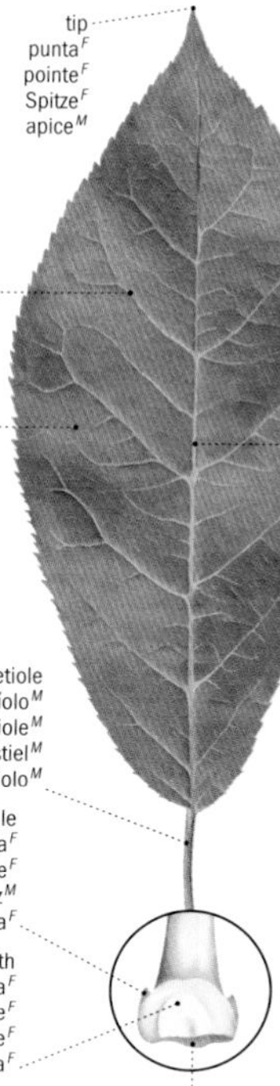

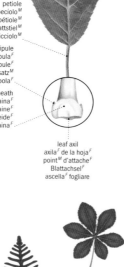

tip
punta^F
pointe^F
Spitze^F
apice^M

vein
nervadura^F secundaria
nervure^F secondaire
Blattader^F
nervatura^F

blade
hoja^F
limbe^M
Spreite^F
lamina^F

petiole
pecíolo^M
pétiole^M
Blattstiel^M
picciolo^M

stipule
estipula^F
stipule^F
Blattansatz^M
stipola^F

sheath
vaina^F
gaine^F
Blattscheide^F
guaina^F

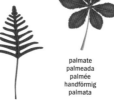

margin
borde^M
bord^M
Blattrand^M
margine^M

midrib
nervadura^F principal
nervure^F principale
Mittelrippe^F
nervatura^F centrale

structure of a leaf
estructura^F de una hoja^F
structure^F d'une feuille^F
Aufbau^M eines Blatts^N
struttura^F di una foglia^F

leaf axil
axila^F de la hoja^F
point^M d'attache^F
Blattachsel^F
ascella^F fogliare

compound leaves
hojas^F compuestas
feuilles^F composées
zusammengesetzte Blätter^N
foglie^F composte

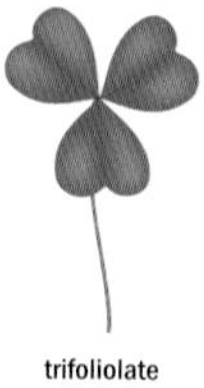

trifoliolate
trifoliada
trifoliée
dreizählig
trifogliata

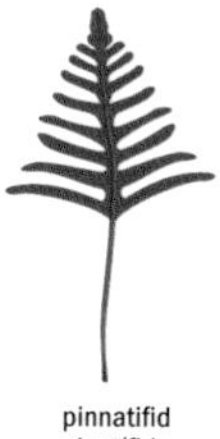

pinnatifid
pinnatifida
pennée
fiederteilig
pennatifida

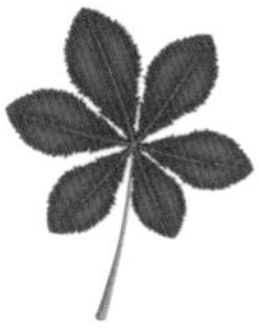

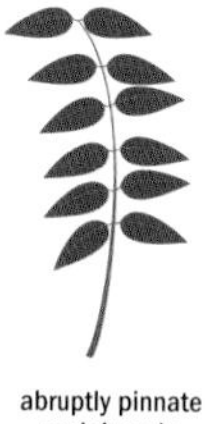

abruptly pinnate
paripinnada
paripennée
paarig gefiedert
paripennata

palmate
palmeada
palmée
handförmig
palmata

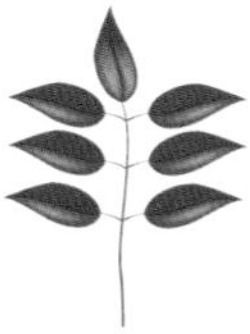

odd pinnate
imparipinnada
imparipennée
unpaarig gefiedert
imparipennata

leaf margins
la hoja^F según su borde^M
bord^M d'une feuille^F
Blattrand^M
margine^M fogliare

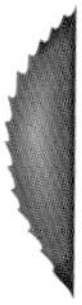

dentate
dentada
denté
gesägt
dentato

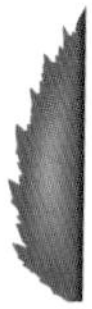

doubly dentate
doble dentada
doublement denté
doppelt gesägt
doppiamente dentato

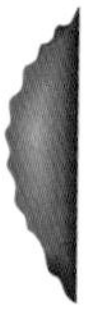

crenate
festoneada
crénelé
gekerbt
crenato

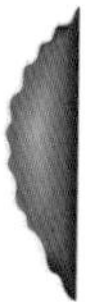

ciliate
ciliada
cilié
gewimpert
ciliato

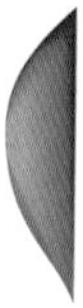

entire
entera
entier
ganzrandig
liscio

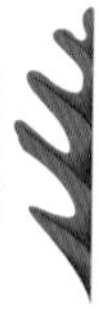

lobate
lobulada
lobé
gebuchtet
lobato

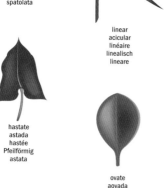

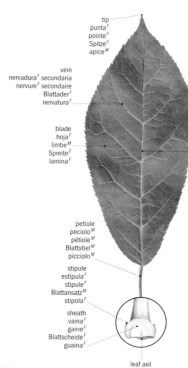

flower

flor^F | fleur^F | Blüte^F | fiore^M

structure of a flower
estructura^F de una flor^F
structure^F d'une fleur^F
Aufbau^M einer Blume^F
struttura^F di un fiore^M

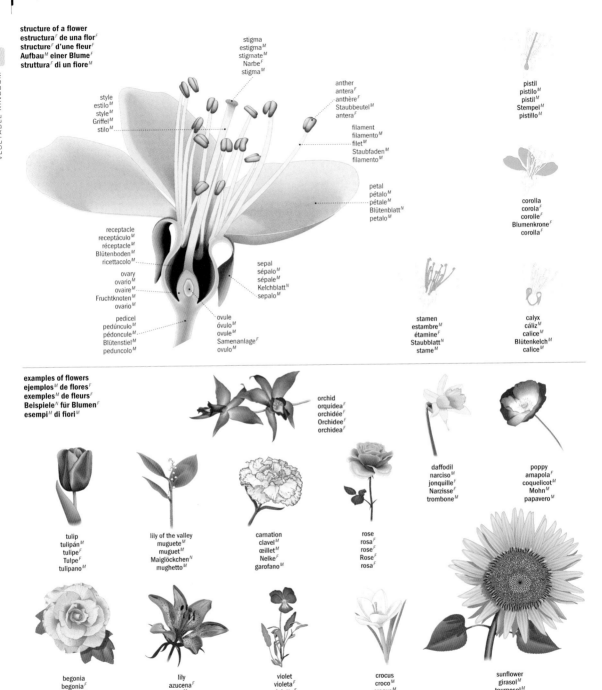

stigma
estigma^M
stigmate^M
Narbe^F
stigma^M

style
estilo^M
style^M
Griffel^M
stilo^M

anther
antera^F
anthère^F
Staubbeutel^M
antera^F

filament
filamento^M
filet^M
Staubfaden^M
filamento^M

petal
pétalo^M
pétale^F
Blütenblatt^N
petalo^M

receptacle
receptáculo^M
réceptacle^M
Blütenboden^M
ricettacolo^M

ovary
ovario^M
ovaire^M
Fruchtknoten^M
ovario^M

sepal
sépalo^M
sépale^M
Kelchblatt^N
sepalo^M

pedicel
pedúnculo^M
pédoncule^M
Blütenstiel^M
peduncolo^M

ovule
óvulo^M
ovule^M
Samenanlage^F
ovulo^M

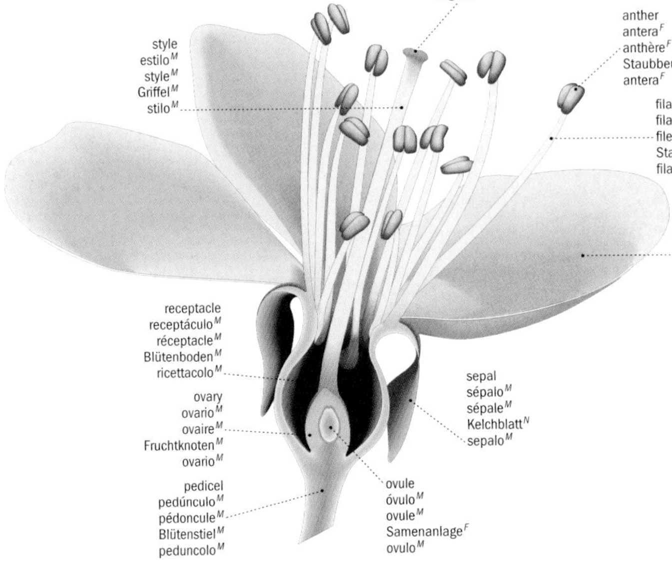

pistil
pistilo^M
pistil^M
Stempel^M
pistillo^M

corolla
corola^F
corolle^F
Blumenkrone^F
corolla^F

stamen
estambre^M
étamine^F
Staubblatt^N
stame^M

calyx
cáliz^M
calice^M
Blütenkelch^M
calice^M

examples of flowers
ejemplos^M de flores^F
exemples^M de fleurs^F
Beispiele^N für Blumen^F
esempi^M di fiori^M

orchid
orquídea^F
orchidée^F
Orchidee^F
orchidea^F

daffodil
narciso^M
jonquille^F
Narzisse^F
trombone^M

poppy
amapola^F
coquelicot^M
Mohn^M
papavero^M

tulip
tulipán^M
tulipe^F
Tulpe^F
tulipano^M

lily of the valley
muguete^M
muguet^M
Maiglöckchen^N
mughetto^M

carnation
clavel^M
œillet^M
Nelke^F
garofano^M

rose
rosa^F
rose^F
Rose^F
rosa^F

begonia
begonia^F
bégonia^M
Begonie^F
begonia^F

lily
azucena^F
lis^M
Lilie^F
giglio^M

violet
violeta^F
violette^F
Veilchen^N
viola^F

crocus
croco^M
crocus^M
Krokus^M
croco^M

sunflower
girasol^F
tournesol^M
Sonnenblume^F
girasole^M

VEGETABLE KINGDOM

types of inflorescences
variedades^F de inflorescencias^F
modes^M d'inflorescence^F
Arten^F von Blütenständen^M
tipi^M di inflorescenze^F

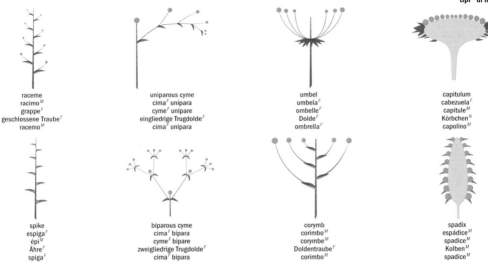

raceme
racimo^M
grappe^F
geschlossene Traube^F
racemo^M

uniparous cyme
cima^F unípara
cyme^F unipare
eingliedrige Trugdolde^F
cima^F unipara

umbel
umbela^F
ombelle^F
Dolde^F
ombrella^F

capitulum
cabezuela^F
capitule^M
Körbchen^N
capolino^M

spike
espiga^F
épi^M
Ähre^F
spiga^F

biparous cyme
cima^F bípara
cyme^F bipare
zweigliedrige Trugdolde^F
cima^F bipara

corymb
corimbo^M
corymbe^M
Doldentraube^F
corimbo^M

spadix
espádice^M
spadice^M
Kolben^M
spadice^M

fruit

fleshy fruit: stone fruit
drupa^F
fruit^M charnu à noyau^M
fleischige Steinfrucht^F
drupa^F

technical terms
términos^M técnicos
termes^M techniques
wissenschaftliche Bezeichnungen^F
termini^M tecnici

section of a peach
corte^M de un melocotón^M
coupe^F d'une pêche^F
Pfirsich^M im Querschnitt^M
sezione^F di una pesca^F

usual terms
términos^M familiares
termes^M familiers
gebräuchliche Bezeichnungen^F
termini^M comuni

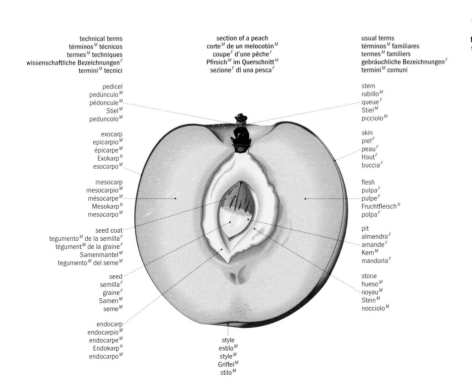

pedicel
pedúnculo^M
pédoncule^M
Stiel^M
peduncolo^M

stem
rabillo^M
queue^F
Stiel^M
picciolo^M

exocarp
epicarpio^M
épicarpe^M
Exokarp^N
esocarpo^M

skin
piel^F
peau^F
Haut^F
buccia^F

mesocarp
mesocarpio^M
mésocarpe^M
Mesokarp^N
mesocarpo^M

flesh
pulpa^F
pulpe^F
Fruchtfleisch^N
polpa^F

seed coat
tegumento^M de la semilla^F
tégument^M de la graine^F
Samenmantel^M
tegumento^M del seme^M

pit
almendra^F
amande^F
Kern^M
mandorla^F

seed
semilla^F
graine^F
Samen^M
seme^M

stone
hueso^M
noyau^M
Stein^M
nocciolo^M

endocarp
endocarpio^M
endocarpe^M
Endokarp^N
endocarpo^M

style
estilo^M
style^M
Griffel^M
stilo^M

fleshy fruit: pome fruit
pomo^M carnoso
fruit^M charnu à pépins^M
fleischige Apfelfrucht^F
frutto^M carnoso: mela

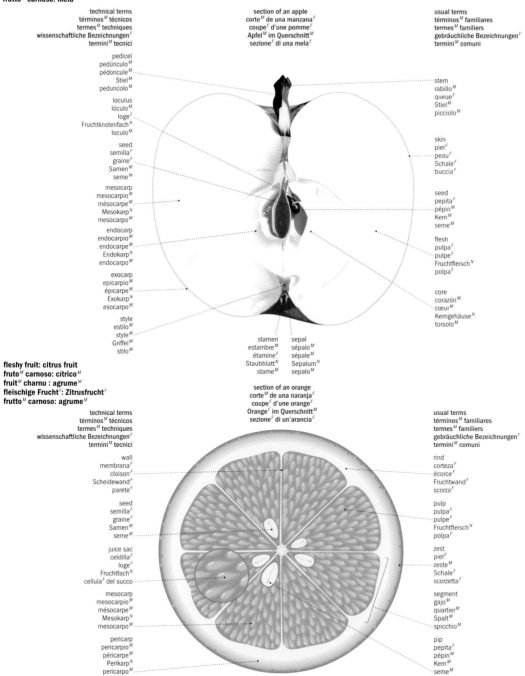

technical terms
términos^M técnicos
termes^M techniques
wissenschaftliche Bezeichnungen^F
termini^M tecnici

section of an apple
corte^M de una manzana^F
coupe^F d'une pomme^F
Apfel^M im Querschnitt^M
sezione^F di una mela^F

usual terms
términos^M familiares
termes^M familiers
gebräuchliche Bezeichnungen^F
termini^M comuni

pedicel
pedúnculo^M
pédoncule^M
Stiel^M
peduncolo^M

loculus
lóculo^M
loge^F
Fruchtknotenfach^N
loculo^M

seed
semilla^F
graine^F
Samen^M
seme^M

mesocarp
mesocarpio^M
mésocarpe^M
Mesokarp^N
mesocarpo^M

endocarp
endocarpio^M
endocarpe^M
Endokarp^N
endocarpo^M

exocarp
epicarpio^M
épicarpe^M
Exokarp^N
esocarpo^M

style
estilo^M
style^M
Griffel^M
stilo^M

stem
rabillo^M
queue^F
Stiel^M
picciolo^M

skin
piel^F
peau^F
Schale^F
buccia^F

seed
pepita^F
pépin^M
Kern^M
seme^M

flesh
pulpa^F
pulpe^F
Fruchtfleisch^N
polpa^F

core
corazón^M
cœur^M
Kerngehäuse^N
torsolo^M

stamen
estambre^M
étamine^F
Staubblatt^N
stame^M

sepal
sépalo^M
sépale^M
Sepalum^N
sepalo^M

fleshy fruit: citrus fruit
fruto^M carnoso: cítrico^M
fruit^M charnu : agrume^M
fleischige Frucht^F: Zitrusfrucht^F
frutto^M carnoso: agrume^M

technical terms
términos^M técnicos
termes^M techniques
wissenschaftliche Bezeichnungen^F
termini^M tecnici

section of an orange
corte^M de una naranja^F
coupe^F d'une orange^F
Orange^F im Querschnitt^M
sezione^F di un'arancia^F

usual terms
términos^M familiares
termes^M familiers
gebräuchliche Bezeichnungen^F
termini^M comuni

wall
membrana^F
cloison^F
Scheidewand^F
parete^F

seed
semilla^F
graine^F
Samen^M
seme^M

juice sac
celdilla^F
loge^F
Fruchtfach^N
cellula^F del succo

mesocarp
mesocarpio^M
mésocarpe^M
Mesokarp^N
mesocarpo^M

pericarp
pericarpio^M
péricarpe^M
Perikarp^N
pericarpo^M

rind
corteza^F
écorce^F
Fruchtwand^F
scorza^F

pulp
pulpa^F
pulpe^F
Fruchtfleisch^N
polpa^F

zest
piel^F
zeste^M
Schale^F
scorzetta^F

segment
gajo^M
quartier^M
Spalt^M
spicchio^M

pip
pepita^F
pépin^M
Kern^M
seme^M

fleshy fruit: berry fruit
fruto^{M} carnoso: baya^{F}
fruit^{M} charnu : baie^{F}
fleischige Frucht^{F}: Beere^{F}
frutto^{M} carnoso: bacca^{F}

technical terms
términos^{M} técnicos
termes^{M} techniques
wissenschaftliche Bezeichnungen^{F}
termini^{M} tecnici

section of a grape
corte^{M} de una uva^{F}
coupe^{F} d'un raisin^{M}
Weintraube^{F} im Querschnitt^{M}
sezione^{F} di un acino^{M}

usual terms
términos^{M} familiares
termes^{M} familiers
gebräuchliche Bezeichnungen^{F}
termini^{M} comuni

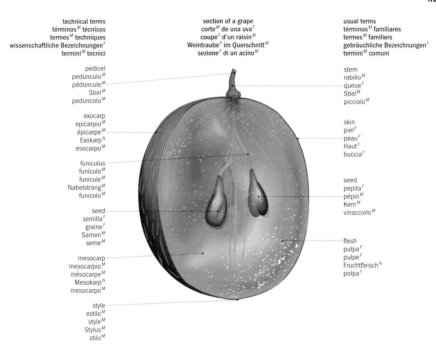

pedicel
pedúnculo^{M}
pédoncule^{M}
Stiel^{M}
peduncolo^{M}

exocarp
epicarpio^{M}
épicarpe^{M}
Exokarp^{N}
esocarpo^{M}

funiculus
funículo^{M}
funicule^{M}
Nabelstrang^{M}
funicolo^{M}

seed
semilla^{F}
graine^{F}
Samen^{M}
seme^{M}

mesocarp
mesocarpio^{M}
mésocarpe^{M}
Mesokarp^{N}
mesocarpo^{M}

style
estilo^{M}
style^{M}
Stylus^{M}
stilo^{M}

stem
rabillo^{M}
queue^{F}
Stiel^{M}
picciolo^{M}

skin
piel^{F}
peau^{F}
Haut^{F}
buccia^{F}

seed
pepita^{F}
pépin^{M}
Kern^{M}
vinacciolo^{M}

flesh
pulpa^{F}
pulpe^{F}
Fruchtfleisch^{N}
polpa^{F}

section of a strawberry
corte^{M} de una fresa^{F}
coupe^{F} d'une fraise^{F}
Erdbeere^{F} im Querschnitt^{M}
sezione^{F} di una fragola^{F}

section of a raspberry
corte^{M} de una frambuesa^{F}
coupe^{F} d'une framboise^{F}
Himbeere^{F} im Querschnitt^{M}
sezione^{F} di un lampone^{M}

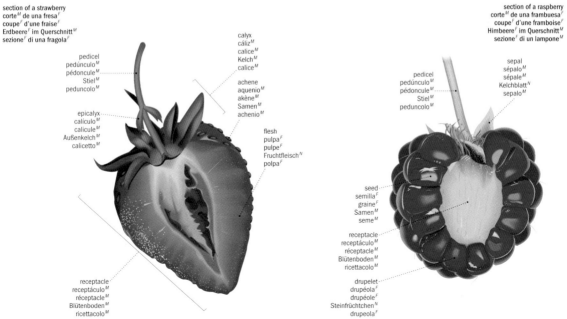

pedicel
pedúnculo^{M}
pédoncule^{M}
Stiel^{M}
peduncolo^{M}

epicalyx
calículo^{M}
calicule^{M}
Außenkelch^{M}
calicetto^{M}

receptacle
receptáculo^{M}
réceptacle^{M}
Blütenboden^{M}
ricettacolo^{M}

calyx
cáliz^{M}
calice^{M}
Kelch^{M}
calice^{M}

achene
aquenio^{M}
akène^{M}
Samen^{M}
achenio^{M}

flesh
pulpa^{F}
pulpe^{F}
Fruchtfleisch^{N}
polpa^{F}

pedicel
pedúnculo^{M}
pédoncule^{M}
Stiel^{M}
peduncolo^{M}

seed
semilla^{F}
graine^{F}
Samen^{M}
seme^{M}

receptacle
receptáculo^{M}
réceptacle^{M}
Blütenboden^{M}
ricettacolo^{M}

drupelet
drupéola^{F}
drupéole^{F}
Steinfrüchtchen^{N}
drupeola^{F}

sepal
sépalo^{M}
sépale^{M}
Kelchblatt^{N}
sepalo^{M}

VEGETABLE KINGDOM

dry fruits
frutos *M* **secos**
fruits *M* **secs**
Trockenfrüchte *F*
frutti *M* **secchi**

husk
cáscara *F*
brou *M*
Hülle *F*
mallo *M*

section of a follicle: star anise
corte *M* de un folículo *M* : anís *M* estrellado
coupe *F* d'un follicule *M* : anis *M* étoilé
Balg *M* im Querschnitt *M* : Sternanis *M*
sezione *F* di un follicolo *M* : anice *M* stellato

seed
semilla *F*
graine *F*
Samen *M*
seme *M*

follicle
folículo *M*
follicule *M*
Fruchtkapsel *F*
follicolo *M*

suture
sutura *F*
suture *F*
Naht *F*
sutura *F*

section of a silique: mustard
corte *M* de una silicua *F* : mostaza *F*
coupe *F* d'une silique *F* : moutarde *F*
Schote *F* im Querschnitt *M* : Senf *M*
sezione *F* di una siliqua *F* : senape *F* nera

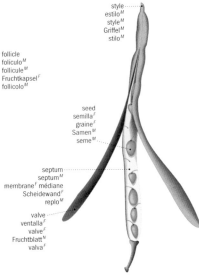

style
estilo *M*
style *M*
Griffel *M*
stilo *M*

seed
semilla *F*
graine *F*
Samen *M*
seme *M*

septum
septum *M*
membrane *F* médiane
Scheidewand *F*
replo *M*

valve
ventalla *F*
valve *F*
Fruchtblatt *N*
valva *F*

section of a hazelnut
corte *M* de una avellana *F*
coupe *F* d'une noisette *F*
Längsschnitt *M* durch eine Haselnuss *F*
sezione *F* di una nocciola *F*

cupule
cúpula *F*
cupule *F*
Fruchtbecher *M*
cupola *F*

bract
bráctea *F*
bractée *F*
Deckblatt *N*
brattea *F*

seed
semilla *F*
graine *F*
Samen *M*
seme *M*

pericarp
pericarpio *M*
péricarpe *M*
Fruchtwand *F*
pericarpo *M*

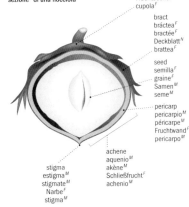

stigma
estigma *M*
stigmate *M*
Narbe *F*
stigma *M*

achene
aquenio *M*
akène *M*
Schließfrucht *F*
achenio *M*

section of a walnut
corte *M* de una nuez *F*
coupe *F* d'une noix *F*
Längsschnitt *M* durch eine Walnuss *F*
sezione *F* di una noce *F*

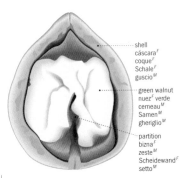

shell
cáscara *F*
coque *F*
Schale *F*
guscio *M*

green walnut
nuez *F* verde
cerneau *M*
Samen *M*
gheriglio *M*

partition
bizna *F*
zeste *M*
Scheidewand *F*
setto *M*

section of a legume: pea
corte *M* de una legumbre *F* : guisante *M*
coupe *F* d'une gousse *F* : pois *M*
Hülsenfrucht *F* im Querschnitt *M* : Erbse *F*
sezione *F* di un legume *M* : pisello *M*

calyx
cáliz *M*
calice *M*
Kelch *M*
calice *M*

midrib
nervadura *F* central
nervure *F* principale
Mittelrippe *F*
nervatura *F* centrale

pea
guisante *M*
pois *M*
Erbse *F*
pisello *M*

funiculus
funículo *M*
funicule *M*
Nabelstrang *M*
funicolo *M*

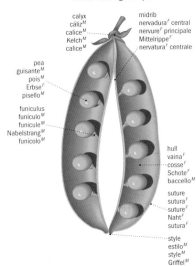

hull
vaina *F*
cosse *F*
Schote *F*
baccello *M*

suture
sutura *F*
suture *F*
Naht *F*
sutura *F*

style
estilo *M*
style *M*
Griffel *M*
stilo *M*

section of a capsule: poppy
corte *M* de una cápsula *F* : amapola *F*
coupe *F* d'une capsule *F* : pavot *M*
Fruchtkapsel *F* im Querschnitt *M* : Mohn *M*
sezione *F* di una capsula *F* : papavero *M*

pore
poro *M*
pore *F*
Pore *F*
poro *M*

seed
semilla *F*
graine *F*
Samen *M*
seme *M*

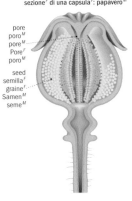

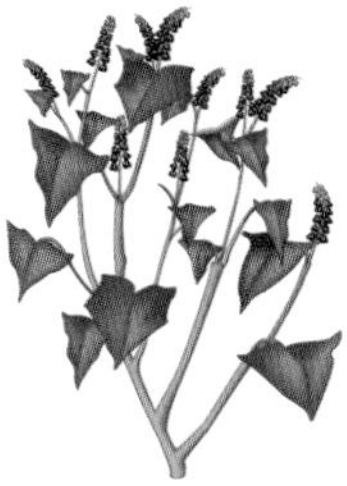

buckwheat
trigo M sarraceno
sarrasin M
Buchweizen M
grano M saraceno

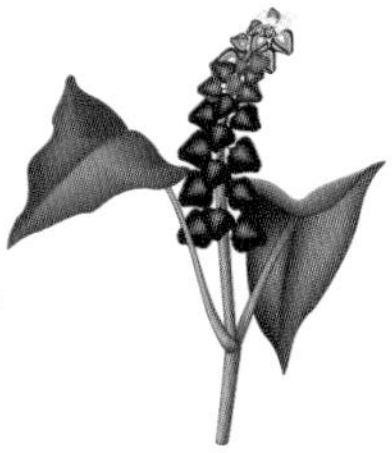

buckwheat: raceme
trigo M sarraceno: racimo M
sarrasin M : grappe F
Buchweizen M: Doldenrispe F
grano M saraceno: racemo M

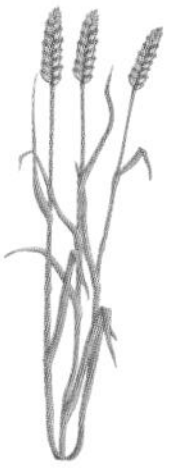

wheat
trigo M
blé M
Weizen M
grano M

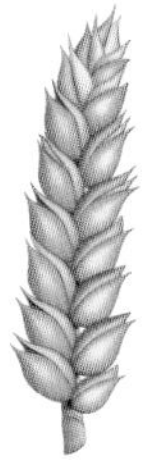

wheat: spike
trigo M : espiga F
blé M : épi M
Weizen M: Ähre F
grano M: spiga F

section of a grain of wheat
corte M de un grano M de trigo M
coupe F d'un grain M de blé M
Längsschnitt M durch ein Weizenkorn N
sezione F di un chicco M di grano M

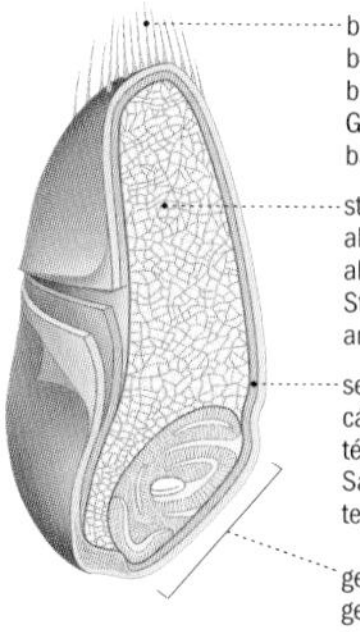

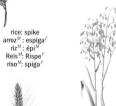

brush
brocha F
brosse F
Granne F
barbetta F

starch
almidón M
albumen M farineux
Stärke F
amido M

seed coat
cáscara F
tégument M
Samenschale F
tegumento M seminale

germ
germen M
germe M
Keim M
germe M

barley
cebada F
orge F
Gerste F
orzo M

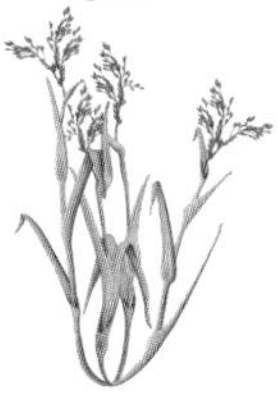

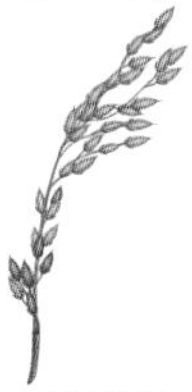

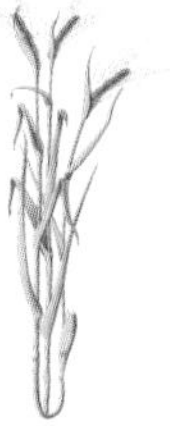

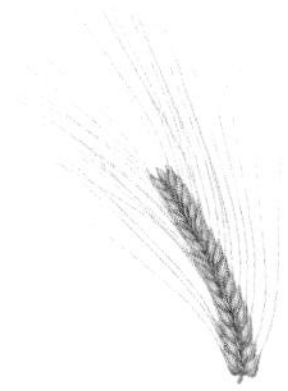

barley: spike
cebada F : espiga F
orge F : épi M
Gerste F: Ähre F
orzo M: spiga F

rice
arroz M
riz M
Reis M
riso M

rice: spike
arroz M : espiga F
riz M : épi M
Reis M: Rispe F
riso M: spiga F

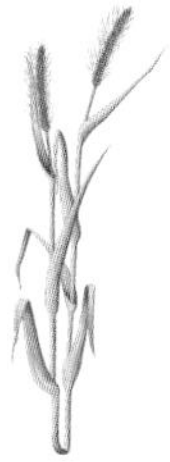

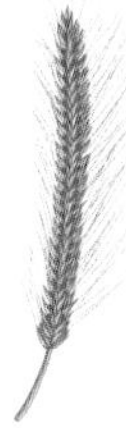

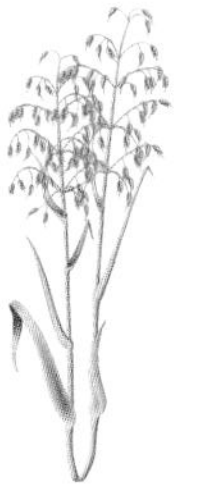

oats
avena F
avoine F
Hafer M
avena F

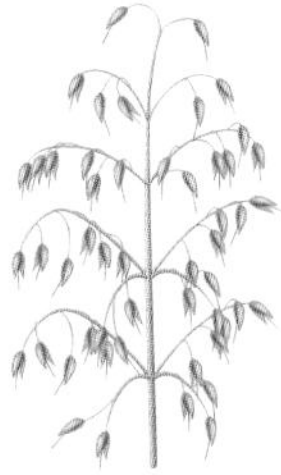

oats: panicle
avena F : panicula F
avoine F : panicule F
Hafer M: Ährchen N
avena F: pannocchia F

barley
cebada F
orge F
Gerste F
orzo M

rye
centeno M
seigle M
Roggen M
segale F

rye: spike
centeno M : espiga F
seigle M : épi M
Roggen M: Ähre F
segale F: spiga F

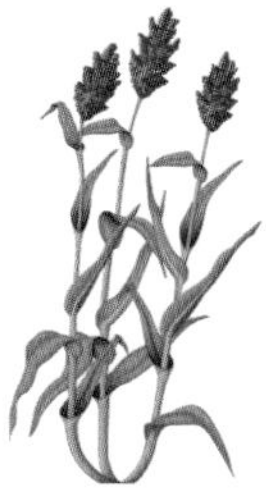

sorghum
sorgo M
sorgho M
Mohrenhirse F
sorgo M

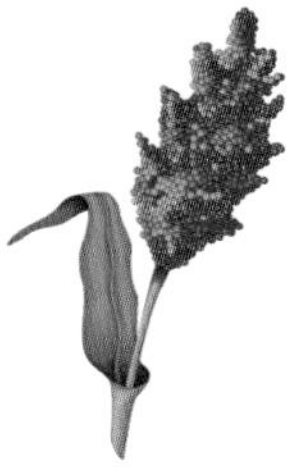

sorghum: panicle
sorgo M : panicula F
sorgho M : panicule F
Mohrenhirse F: Rispe F
sorgo M: pannocchia F

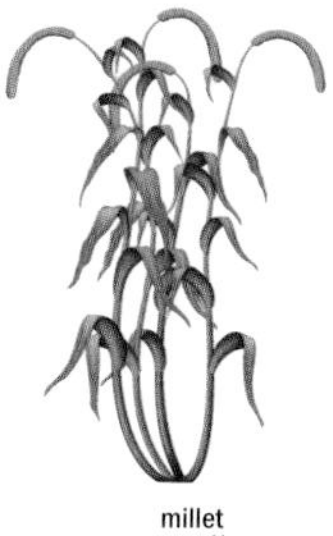

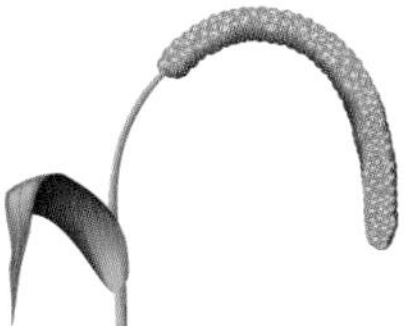

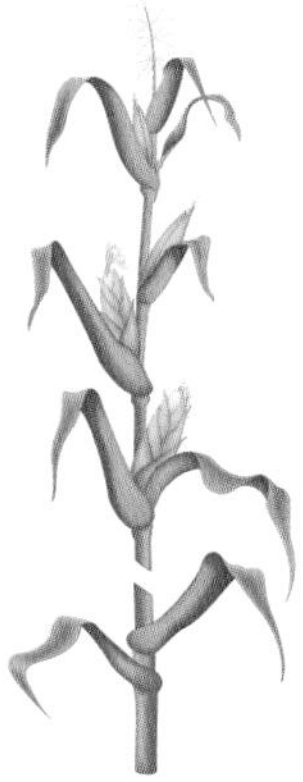

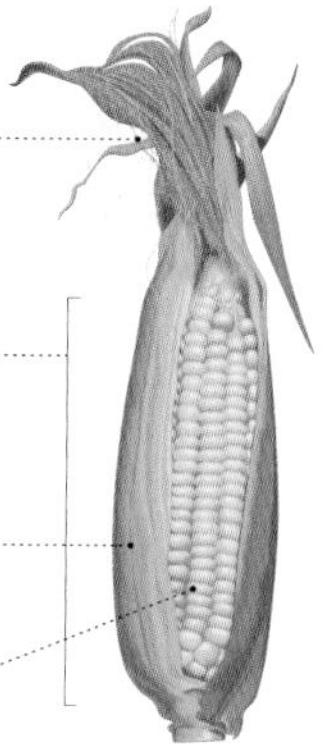

silk
pelo M de maíz M
barbe F
Bart M
barba F

cob
mazorca F
épi M
Kolben M
pannocchia F

husk
hoja F
feuille F
Hülse F
cartoccio M

kernel
grano M
grain M
Kern M
cariosside F

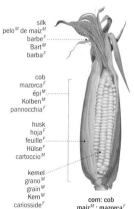

corn: cob
maíz M : mazorca F
maïs M : épi M
Mais M: Kolben M
mais M: pannocchia F

millet
mijo M
millet M
Hirse F
miglio M

millet: spike
mijo M : espiga F
millet M : épi M
Hirse F: Ährenrispe F
miglio M: spiga F

corn
maíz M
maïs M
Mais M
mais M

grape

uva^F | vigne^F | Rebe^F | vite^F

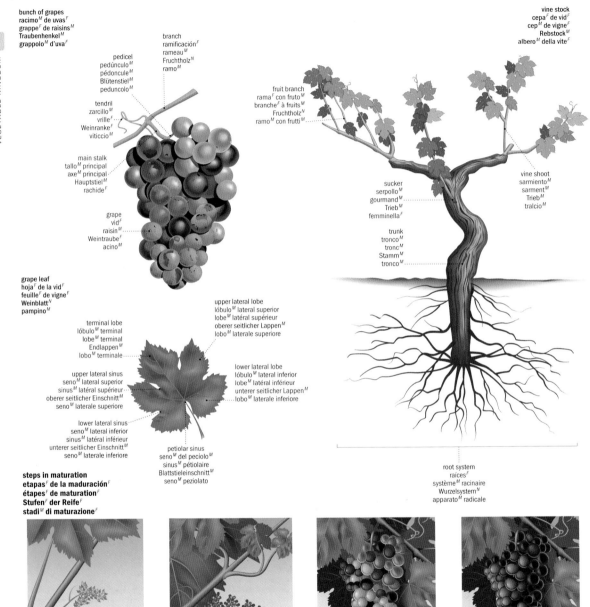

bunch of grapes
racimo^M de uvas^F
grappe^F de raisins^M
Traubenhenkel^M
grappolo^M d'uva^F

branch
ramificación^F
rameau^M
Fruchtholz^N
ramo^M

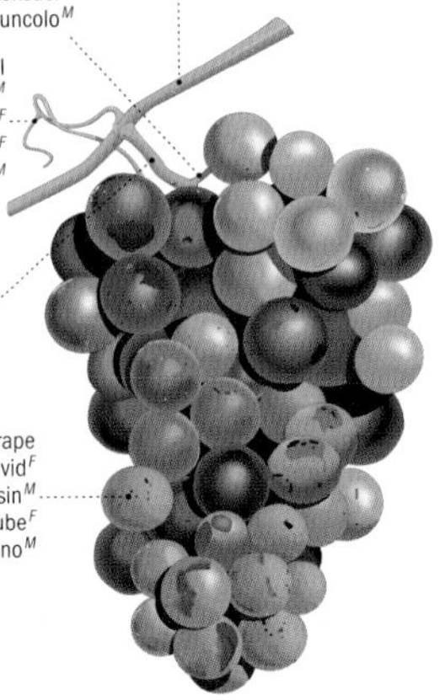

vine stock
cepa^F de vid^F
cep^M de vigne^F
Rebstock^M
albero^M della vite^F

pedicel
pedúnculo^M
pédoncule^M
Blütenstiel^M
peduncolo^M

fruit branch
rama^F con fruto^M
branche^F à fruits^M
Fruchtholz^N
ramo^M con frutti

tendril
zarcillo^M
vrille^F
Weinranke^F
viticcio^M

vine shoot
sarmiento^M
sarment^M
Trieb^M
tralcio^M

main stalk
tallo^M principal
axe^M principal
Hauptstiel^M
rachide^F

sucker
serpollo^M
gourmand^M
Trieb^M
femminella^F

grape
vid^F
raisin^M
Weintraube^F
acino^M

trunk
tronco^M
tronc^M
Stamm^M
tronco^M

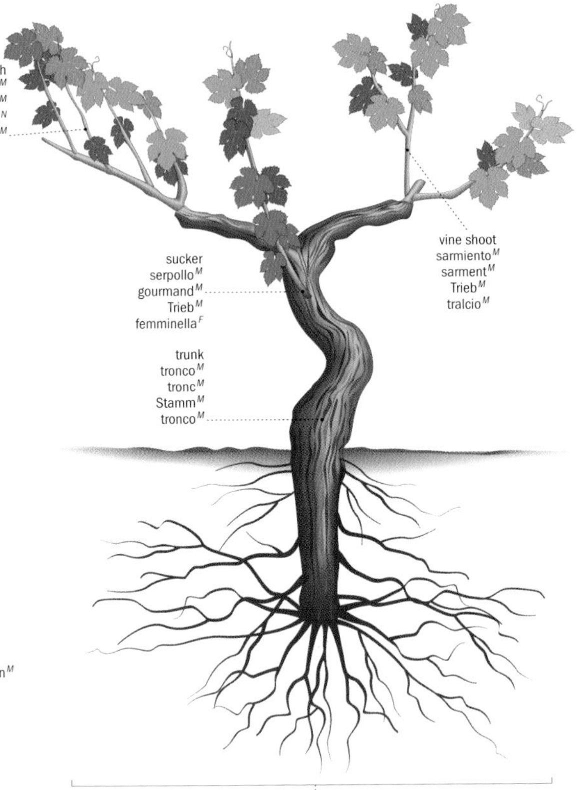

grape leaf
hoja^F de la vid^F
feuille^F de vigne^F
Weinblatt^N
pampino^M

upper lateral lobe
lóbulo^M lateral superior
lobe^M latéral supérieur
oberer seitlicher Lappen^M
lobo^M laterale superiore

terminal lobe
lóbulo^M terminal
lobe^M terminal
Endlappen^M
lobo^M terminale

lower lateral lobe
lóbulo^M lateral inferior
lobe^M latéral inférieur
unterer seitlicher Lappen^M
lobo^M laterale inferiore

upper lateral sinus
seno^M lateral superior
sinus^M latéral supérieur
oberer seitlicher Einschnitt^M
seno^M laterale superiore

lower lateral sinus
seno^M lateral inferior
sinus^M latéral inférieur
unterer seitlicher Einschnitt^M
seno^M laterale inferiore

petiolar sinus
seno^M del peciolo^M
sinus^M pétiolaire
Blattstieleinschnitt^M
seno^M peziolato

root system
raíces^F
système^M racinaire
Wurzelsystem^N
apparato^M radicale

steps in maturation
etapas^F de la maduración^F
étapes^F de maturation^F
Stufen^F der Reife^F
stadi^M di maturazione^F

flowering
floración^F
floraison^F
Blüte^F
fioritura^F

fruition
fructificación^F
nouaison^F
Fruchtbildung^F
fruttificazione^F

ripening
envero^M
véraison^F
Reifeprozess^M
maturazione^F

ripeness
madurez^F
maturité^F
Vollreife^F
maturità^F

VEGETABLE KINGDOM

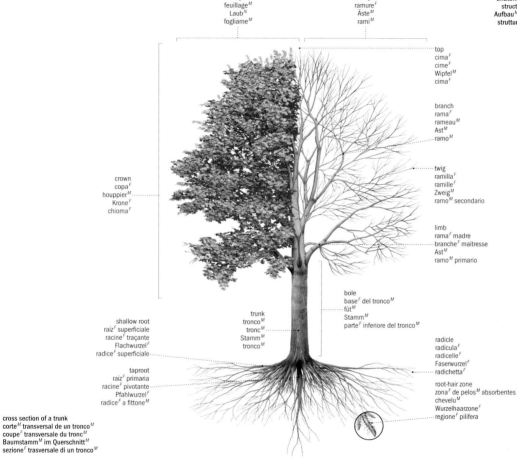

foliage
follaje^M
feuillage^M
Laub^N
fogliame^M

branches
ramaje^M
ramure^F
Äste^M
rami^M

structure of a tree
anatomía^F de un árbol^M
structure^F d'un arbre^M
Aufbau^M eines Baumes^M
struttura^F di un albero^M

top
cima^F
cime^F
Wipfel^M
cima^F

branch
rama^F
rameau^M
Ast^M
ramo^M

twig
ramilla^F
ramille^F
Zweig^M
ramo^M secondario

limb
rama^F madre
branche^F maitresse
Ast^M
ramo^M primario

crown
copa^F
houppier^M
Krone^F
chioma^F

bole
base^F del tronco^M
fût^M
Stamm^M
parte^F inferiore del tronco^M

trunk
tronco^M
tronc^M
Stamm^M
tronco^M

shallow root
raíz^F superficial
racine^F traçante
Flachwurzel^F
radice^F superficiale

taproot
raíz^F primaria
racine^F pivotante
Pfahlwurzel^F
radice^F a fittone^M

radicle
radicula^F
radicelle^F
Faserwurzel^F
radichetta^F

root-hair zone
zona^F de pelos^M absorbentes
chevelu^M
Wurzelhaarzone^F
regione^F pilifera

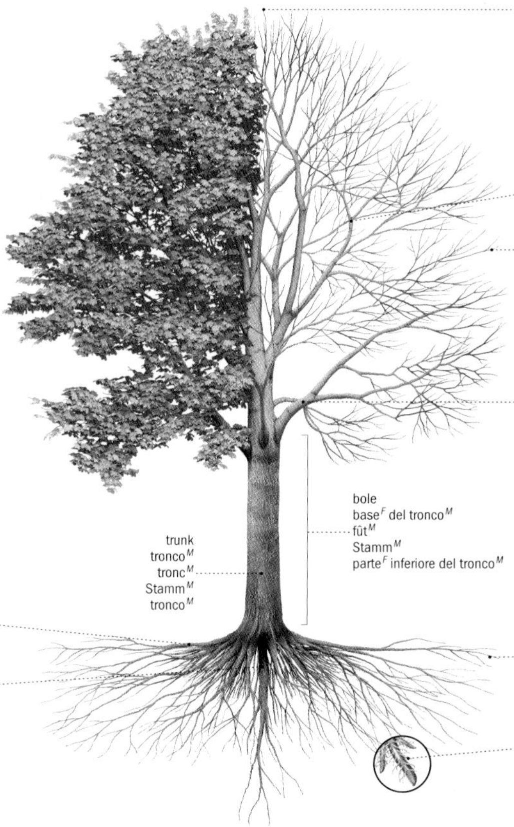

cross section of a trunk
corte^M transversal de un tronco^M
coupe^F transversale du tronc^M
Baumstamm^M im Querschnitt^M
sezione^F trasversale di un tronco^M

stump
tocón^M
souche^F
Stumpf^M
ceppo^M

wood ray
radio^M medular
rayon^M médullaire
Markstrahlen^M
raggio^M midollare

pith
médula^F
moelle^F
Mark^N
midollo^M

annual ring
anillo^M de crecimiento^M
cerne^M annuel
Jahresring^M
cerchia^F annuale

heartwood
duramen^M
bois^M de cœur^M
Kernholz^N
cuore^M del legno^M

cambium
cambium^M
cambium^M
Kambium^N
cambio^M

shoot
retoño^M
rejet^M
Schössling^M
pollone^M

phloem
liber^M
liber^M
Bast^M
floema^M

sapwood
albura^F
aubier^M
Splintholz^N
alburno^M

bark
corteza^M
écorce^F
Borke^F
corteccia^F

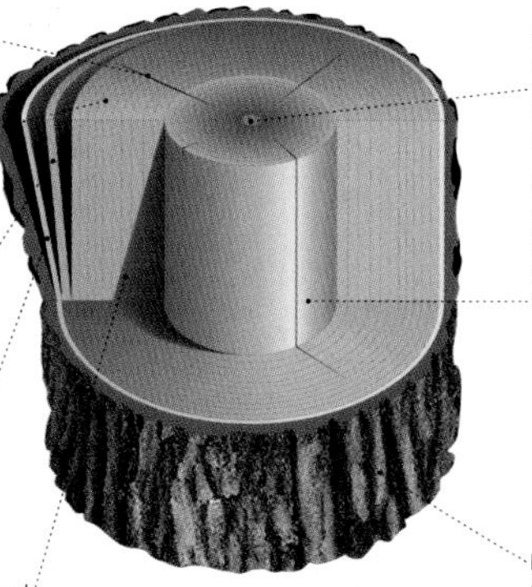

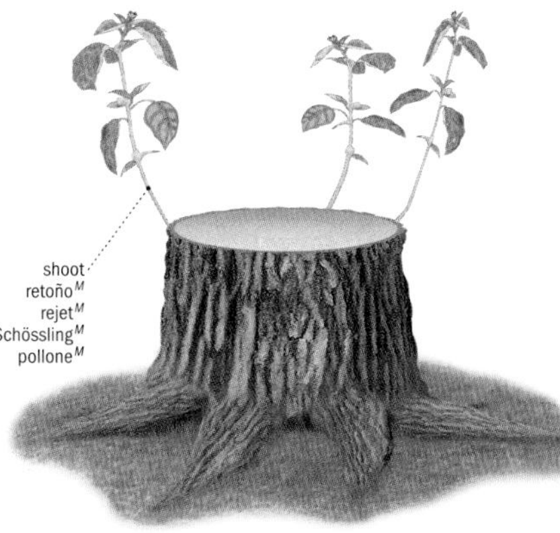

VEGETABLE KINGDOM

examples of broadleaved trees
ejemplos^M de latifolios^M
exemples^M d'arbres^M feuillus
Beispiele^N für Laubhölzer^N
esempi^M di latifoglie^F

oak
roble^M
chêne^M
Eiche^F
quercia^F

birch
abedul^M
bouleau^M
Birke^F
betulla^F

weeping willow
sauce^M llorón
saule^M pleureur
Trauerweide^F
salice^M piangente

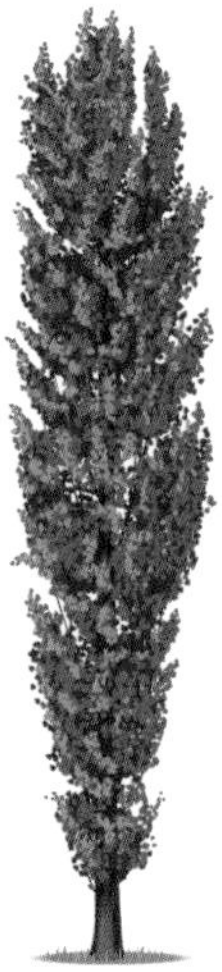

poplar
álamo^M
peuplier^M
Pappel^F
pioppo^M

palm tree
palmera^F
palmier^M
Palme^F
palma^F

maple
arce^M
érable^M
Ahorn^M
acero^M

beech
haya^F
hêtre^M
Buche^F
faggio^M

walnut
nogal^M
noyer^M
Walnuss^F
noce^M

conifera^F | conifère^M | Nadelbaum^M | conifera^F

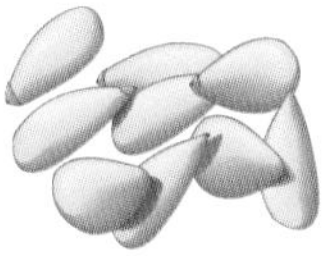

branch
rama^F
rameau^M
Ast^M
ramo^M

male cone
cono^M masculino
cône^M mâle
männliche Blütenstände^M
cono^M maschile

female cone
cono^M femenino
cône^M femelle
weibliche Blütenstände^M
cono^M femminile

cone
piña^F
cône^M
Zapfen^M
cono^M

pine seed
piñón^M
pignon^M
Pinienkern^M
pinolo^M

fir needles
agujas^F del abeto^M
aiguilles^F de sapin^M
Tannennadeln^F
aghi^M d'abete^M

pine needles
agujas^F del pino^M
aiguilles^F de pin^M
Kiefernnadeln^F
aghi^M di pino^M

examples of leaves
ejemplos^M de hojas^F
exemples^M de feuilles^F
Beispiele^N für Nadelblätter^N
esempi^M di foglie^F

cypress scalelike leaves
hojas^F escamadas del ciprés^M
écailles^F de cyprès^M
Zypressennadeln^F
foglie^F squamiformi del cipresso^M

examples of conifers
ejemplos^M de coníferas^F
exemples^M de conifères^M
Beispiele^N für Nadelhölzer^N
esempi^M di conifere^F

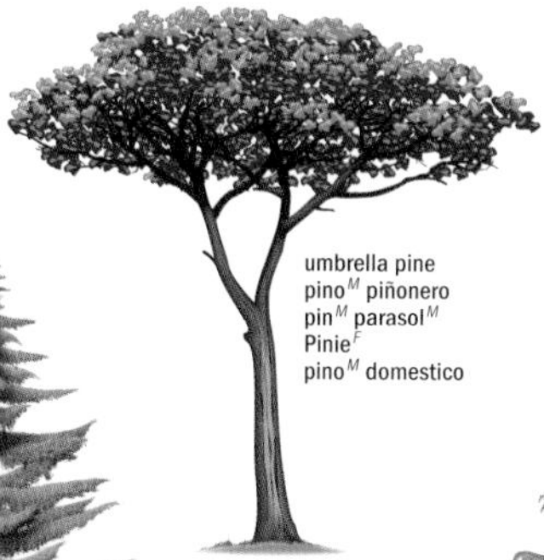

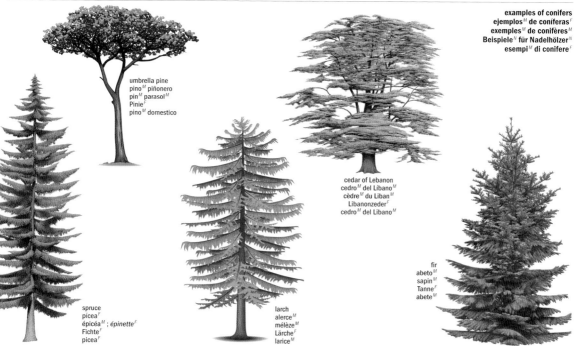

umbrella pine
pino^M piñonero
pin^M parasol^M
Pinie^F
pino^M domestico

cedar of Lebanon
cedro^M del Líbano^M
cèdre^M du Liban^M
Libanonzeder^F
cedro^M del Libano^M

fir
abeto^M
sapin^M
Tanne^F
abete^M

spruce
picea^F
épicéa^M ; épinette^F
Fichte^F
picea^F

larch
alerce^M
mélèze^M
Lärche^F
larice^M

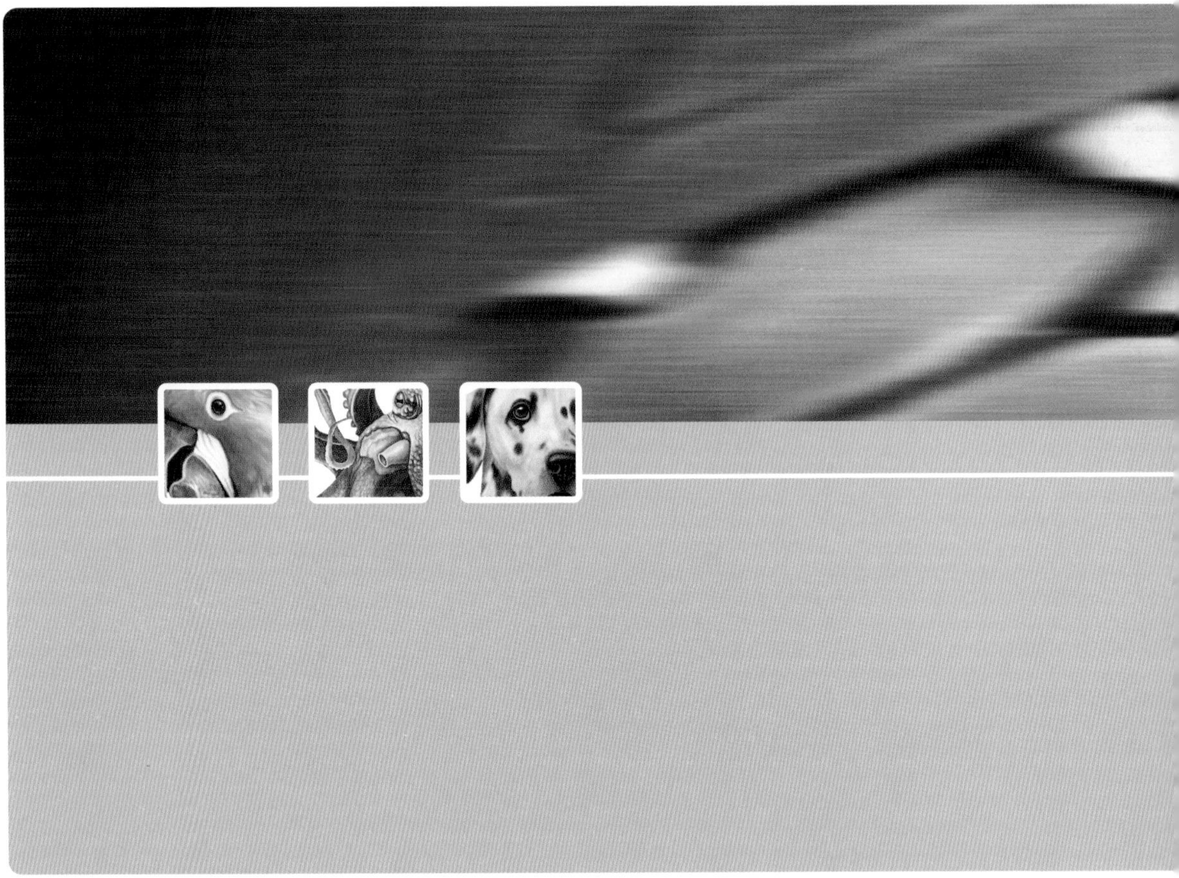

ANIMAL KINGDOM

REINO ANIMAL | RÈGNE ANIMAL | TIERREICH | REGNO ANIMALE

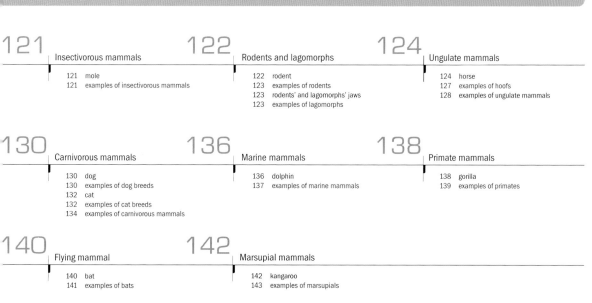

origin and evolution of species

origen^M y evolución^F de las especies^F | origine^F et évolution^F des espèces^F | Entstehung^F und Entwicklung^F der Arten^F | origine^F ed evoluzione^F delle specie^F

ANIMAL KINGDOM

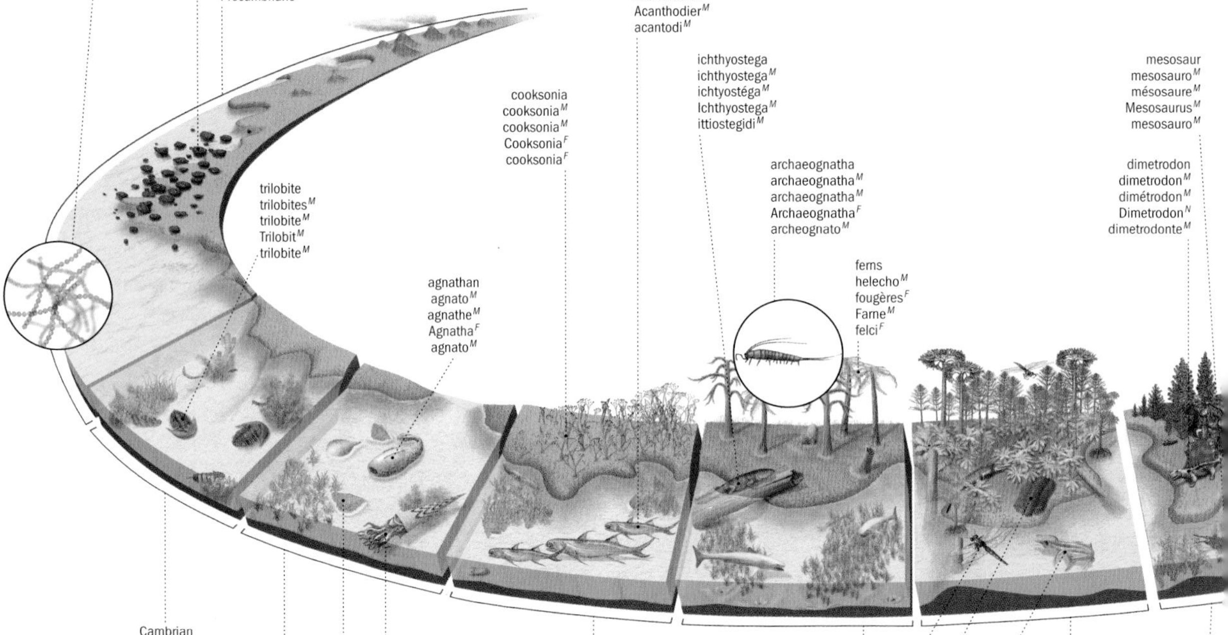

cyanobacteria
cianobacterias^F
cyanobactéries^F
Cyanobakterium^N
cianobatteri^M

stromatolite
estromatolito^M
stromatolite^M
Stromatolith^M
stromatolite^M

Precambrian
Precámbrico^M
Précambrien^M
Präkambrium^N
Precambriano^M

acanthodian
acantodio^M
acanthodien^M
Acanthodier^M
acantodi^M

mesosaur
mesosauro^M
mésosaure^M
Mesosaurus^M
mesosauro^M

ichthyostega
ichthyostega^M
ichtyostéga^M
Ichthyostega^M
ittiostegidi^M

cooksonia
cooksonia^M
cooksonia^M
Cooksonia^F
cooksonia^F

dimetrodon
dimetrodon^M
dimétrodon^M
Dimetrodon^N
dimetrodonte^M

archaeognatha
archaeognatha^M
archaeognatha^M
Archaeognatha^F
archeognato^M

trilobite
trilobites^M
trilobite^M
Trilobit^M
trilobite^M

ferns
helecho^M
fougères^F
Farne^M
felci^F

agnathan
agnato^M
agnathe^M
Agnatha^F
agnato^M

Cambrian
Cámbrico^M
Cambrien^M
Kambrium^N
Cambriano^M

Ordovician
Ordovícico^M
Ordovicien^M
Ordovizium^N
Ordoviciano^F

orthoceras
ortocerátido^M
orthocère^M
Orthoceras^M
ortocera^F

brachiopod
braquiópodo^M
brachiopode^M
Brachiopode^M
brachiopodo^M

Silurian
Silúrico^M
Silurien^M
Silur^N
Siluriano^M

Devonian
Devónico^M
Dévonien^M
Devon^N
Devoniano^M

meganeura
meganeura^F
meganeura^M
Meganeura^F
meganeura^F

arthropleura
artropleura^F
arthropleura^M
Arthropleura^F
artropleura^F

Carboniferous
Carbonífero^M
Carbonifère^M
Karbon^N
Carbonifero^M

Permian
Pérmico^M
Permien^M
Perm^N
Permiano^M

falcatus
falcatus^M
falcatus^M
Falcatus^M
falcatus^M

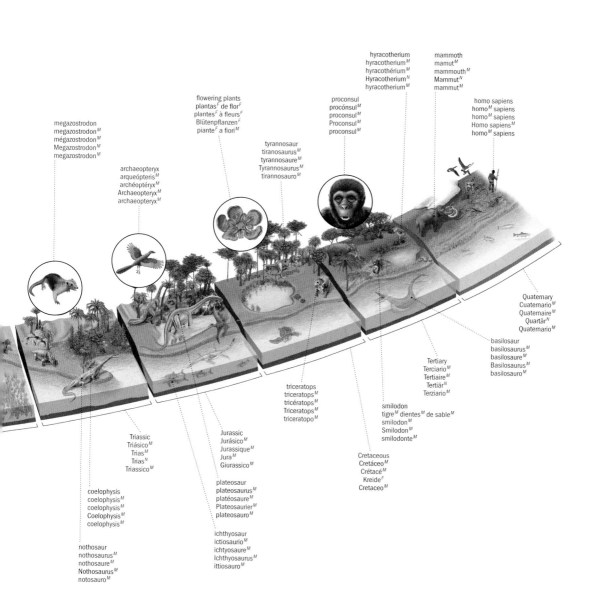

hyracotherium
hyracotherium^M
hyracothérium^M
Hyracotherium^N
hyracotherium^M

mammoth
mamut^M
mammouth^M
Mammut^N
mammut^M

flowering plants
plantas^F de flor^F
plantes^F à fleurs^F
Blütenpflanzen^F
piante^F a fiori^M

proconsul
procónsul^M
proconsul^M
Proconsul^M
proconsul^M

homo sapiens
homo^M sapiens
homo^M sapiens
Homo sapiens^M
homo^M sapiens

megazostrodon
megazostrodon^M
mégazostrodon^M
Megazostrodon^M
megazostrodon^M

archaeopteryx
arqueópteris^M
archéoptéryx^M
Archaeopteryx^M
archaeopteryx^M

tyrannosaur
tiranosaurus^M
tyrannosaure^M
Tyrannosaurus^M
tirannosauro^M

Quaternary
Cuaternario^M
Quaternaire^M
Quartär^N
Quaternario^M

basilosaur
basilosaurus^M
basilosaure^M
Basilosaurus^M
basilosauro^M

Tertiary
Terciario^M
Tertiaire^M
Tertiär^N
Terziario^M

triceratops
triceratops^M
tricératops^M
Triceratops^M
triceratopo^M

smilodon
tigre^M dientes^M de sable^M
smilodon^M
Smilodon^M
smilodonte^M

Triassic
Triásico^M
Trias^M
Trias^N
Triassico^M

Jurassic
Jurásico^M
Jurassique^M
Jura^M
Giurassico^M

Cretaceous
Cretáceo^M
Crétacé^M
Kreide^F
Cretaceo^M

coelophysis
coelophysis^M
coelophysis^M
Coelophysis^M
coelophysis^M

plateosaur
plateosaurus^M
platéosaure^M
Plateosaurier^M
plateosauro^M

nothosaur
nothosaurus^M
nothosaure^M
Nothosaurus^M
notosauro^M

ichthyosaur
ictiosaurio^M
ichtyosaure^M
Ichthyosaurus^M
ittiosauro^M

animal cell

célula^F animal | cellule^F animale | tierische Zelle^F | cellula^F animale

ANIMAL KINGDOM

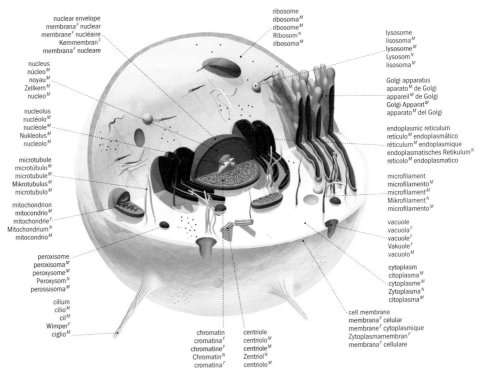

nuclear envelope
membrana^F nuclear
membrane^F nucléaire
Kernmembran^F
membrana^F nucleare

nucleus
núcleo^M
noyau^M
Zellkern^M
nucleo^M

nucleolus
nucléolo^M
nucléole^M
Nukleolus^M
nucleolo^M

microtubule
microtúbulo^M
microtubule^M
Mikrotubulus^M
microtubulo^M

mitochondrion
mitocondrio^M
mitochondrie^F
Mitochondrium^N
mitocondrio^M

peroxisome
peroxisoma^M
peroxysome^M
Peroxysom^N
perossisoma^M

cilium
cilio^M
cil^M
Wimper^F
ciglio^M

ribosome
ribosoma^M
ribosome^M
Ribosom^N
ribosoma^M

lysosome
lisosoma^M
lysosome^M
Lysosom^N
lisosoma^M

Golgi apparatus
aparato^M de Golgi
appareil^M de Golgi
Golgi-Apparat^M
apparato^M del Golgi

endoplasmic reticulum
retículo^M endoplasmático
réticulum^M endoplasmique
endoplasmatisches Retikulum^N
reticolo^M endoplasmatico

microfilament
microfilamento^M
microfilament^M
Mikrofilament^N
microfilamento^M

vacuole
vacuola^F
vacuole^F
Vakuole^F
vacuolo^M

cytoplasm
citoplasma^M
cytoplasme^M
Zytoplasma^N
citoplasma^M

cell membrane
membrana^F celular
membrane^F cytoplasmique
Zytoplasmamembran^F
membrana^F cellulare

chromatin
cromatina^F
chromatine^F
Chromatin^N
cromatina^F

centriole
centriolo^M
centriole^M
Zentriol^N
centriolo^M

unicellulars

unicelulares^M | unicellulaires^M | Einzeller^M | unicellulari^M

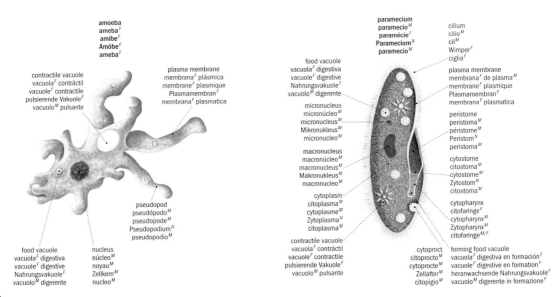

amoeba
ameba^F
amibe^F
Amöbe^F
ameba^F

contractile vacuole
vacuola^F contráctil
vacuole^F contractile
pulsierende Vakuole^F
vacuolo^M pulsante

plasma membrane
membrana^F plásmica
membrane^F plasmique
Plasmamembran^F
membrana^F plasmatica

pseudopod
pseudópodo^M
pseudopode^M
Pseudopodium^N
pseudopodio^M

food vacuole
vacuola^F digestiva
vacuole^F digestive
Nahrungsvakuole^F
vacuolo^M digerente

nucleus
núcleo^M
noyau^M
Zellkern^M
nucleo^M

paramecium
paramecio^M
paramécie^F
Paramecium^N
paramecio^M

food vacuole
vacuola^F digestiva
vacuole^F digestive
Nahrungsvakuole^F
vacuolo^M digerente

micronucleus
micronúcleo^M
micronucleus^M
Mikronukleus^M
micronucleo^M

macronucleus
macronúcleo^M
macronucleus^M
Makronukleus^M
macronucleo^M

cytoplasm
citoplasma^M
cytoplasme^M
Zytoplasma^M
citoplasma^M

contractile vacuole
vacuola^F contráctil
vacuole^F contractile
pulsierende Vakuole^F
vacuolo^M pulsante

cilium
cilio^M
cil^M
Wimper^F
ciglia^F

plasma membrane
membrana^F de plasma^M
membrane^F plasmique
Plasmamembran^F
membrana^F plasmatica

peristome
peristoma^M
péristome^M
Peristom^N
peristoma^M

cytostome
citostoma^M
cytostome^M
Zytostom^N
citostoma^M

cytopharynx
citofaringe^F
cytopharynx^M
Zytopharynx^M
citofaringe$^{M/F}$

cytoproct
citoprocto^M
cytoprocte^M
Zellafter^M
citopigio^M

forming food vacuole
vacuola^F digestiva en formación^F
vacuole^F digestive en formation^F
heranwachsende Nahrungsvakuole^F
vacuolo^M digerente in formazione^F

sponge

esponja^F | éponge^F | Schwamm^M | spugna^F

ANIMAL KINGDOM

calcareous sponge
esponja^F calcárea
éponge^F calcaire
Kalkschwamm^M
spugna^F calcarea

anatomy of a sponge
anatomía^F de una esponja^F
anatomie^F de l'éponge^F
Anatomie^F eines Schwamms^M
anatomia^F di una spugna^F

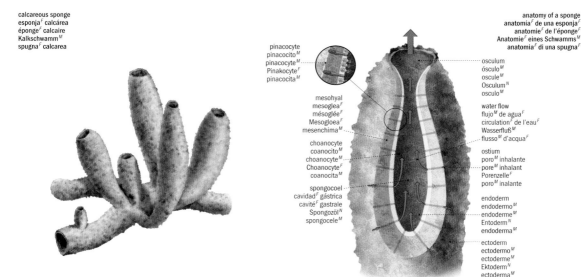

pinacocyte
pinacocito^M
pinacocyte^M
Pinakocyte^F
pinacocita^M

mesohyal
mesoglea^F
mésoglée^F
Mesogloea^F
mesenchima^M

choanocyte
coanocito^M
choanocyte^M
Choanocyte^F
coanocita^M

spongocoel
cavidad^F gástrica
cavité^F gastrale
Spongozöl^N
spongocele^M

osculum
ósculo^M
oscule^M
Osculum^N
osculo^M

water flow
flujo^M de agua^F
circulation^F de l'eau^F
Wasserfluß^M
flusso^M d'acqua^F

ostium
poro^M inhalante
pore^M inhalant
Porenzelle^F
poro^M inalante

endoderm
endodermo^M
endoderme^M
Entoderm^N
endoderma^M

ectoderm
ectodermo^M
ectoderme^M
Ektoderm^N
ectoderma^M

echinoderms

equinodermos^M | échinodermes^M | Echinodermen^M | echinodermi^M

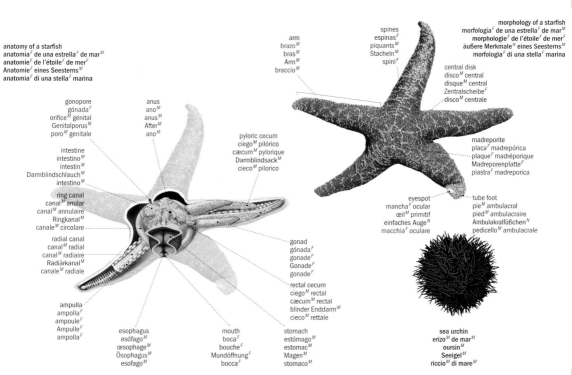

anatomy of a starfish
anatomía^F de una estrella^F de mar^M
anatomie^F de l'étoile^F de mer^M
Anatomie^F eines Seesterns^M
anatomia^F di una stella^F marina

gonopore
gónada^F
orifice^M génital
Genitalporus^M
poro^M genitale

anus
ano^M
anus^M
After^M
ano^M

intestine
intestino^M
intestin^M
Darmblindschlauch^M
intestino^M

pyloric cecum
ciego^M pilórico
cæcum^M pylorique
Darmblindsack^M
cieco^M pilorico

ring canal
canal^M anular
canal^M annulaire
Ringkanal^M
canale^M circolare

radial canal
canal^M radial
canal^M radiaire
Radiärkanal^M
canale^M radiale

ampulla
ampolla^F
ampoule^F
Ampulle^F
ampolla^F

esophagus
esófago^M
œsophage^M
Ösophagus^M
esofago^M

mouth
boca^F
bouche^F
Mundöffnung^F
bocca^F

stomach
estómago^M
estomac^M
Magen^M
stomaco^M

gonad
gónada^F
gonade^F
Gonade^F
gonade^F

rectal cecum
ciego^M rectal
cæcum^M rectal
blinder Enddarm^M
cieco^M rettale

arm
brazo^M
bras^M
Arm^M
braccio^M

spines
espinas^F
piquants^M
Stacheln^M
spini^F

morphology of a starfish
morfología^F de una estrella^F de mar^M
morphologie^F de l'étoile^F de mer^F
äußere Merkmale^N eines Seesterns^M
morfologia^F di una stella^F marina

central disk
disco^M central
disque^M central
Zentralscheibe^F
disco^M centrale

madreporite
placa^F madrepórica
plaque^F madréporique
Madreporenplatte^F
piastra^F madreporica

eyespot
mancha^F ocular
œil^M primitif
einfaches Auge^N
macchia^F oculare

tube foot
pie^M ambulacral
pied^M ambulacraire
Ambulakralfüßchen^N
pedicello^M ambulacrale

sea urchin
erizo^M de mar^M
oursin^M
Seeigel^M
riccio^M di mare^M

butterfly

mariposa[F] | papillon[M] | Schmetterling[M] | farfalla[F]

morphology of a butterfly
morfología[F] de una mariposa[F]
morphologie[F] du papillon[M]
äußere Merkmale[N] eines Schmetterlings[M]
morfologia[F] di una farfalla[F]

ANIMAL KINGDOM

cell
celda[F]
cellule[F]
Zelle[F]
cella[F]

head
cabeza[F]
tête[F]
Kopf[M]
capo[M]

compound eye
ojo[M] compuesto
œil[M] composé
Facettenauge[N]
occhio[M] composto

labial palp
palpo[M] labial
palpe[F] labial
Lippentaster[M]
palpo[M] labiale

antenna
antena[F]
antenne[F]
Antenne[F]
antenna[F]

proboscis
probóscide[M]
trompe[F]
Rüssel[M]
proboscide[F]

thorax
tórax[M]
thorax[M]
Thorax[M]
torace[M]

foreleg
pata[F] delantera
patte[F] antérieure
Vorderbein[N]
zampa[F] anteriore

middle leg
pata[F] media
patte[F] médiane
Mittelbein[N]
zampa[F] mediana

hind leg
pata[F] trasera
patte[F] postérieure
Hinterbein[N]
zampa[F] posteriore

abdomen
abdomen[M]
abdomen[M]
Hinterleib[M]
addome[M]

spiracle
estigma[M]
stigmate[M]
Stigma[N]
stigma[M]

forewing
ala[F] delantera
aile[F] antérieure
Vorderflügel[M]
ala[F] anteriore

wing vein
vena[F] alar
nervure[F]
Flügelader[F]
nervatura[F] alare

hind wing
ala[F] trasera
aile[F] postérieure
Hinterflügel[M]
ala[F] posteriore

hind leg
pata[F] trasera
patte[F] postérieure
Hinterbein[N]
zampa[F] posteriore

coxa
coxa[F]
hanche[F]
Hüfte[F]
coxa[F]

trochanter
trocánter[M]
trochanter[M]
Schenkelring[M]
trocantere[M]

femur
fémur[M]
fémur[M]
Schenkel[M]
femore[M]

tibia
tibia[F]
tibia[M]
Schiene[F]
tibia[F]

tarsus
tarso[M]
tarse[F]
Fuß[M]
tarso[M]

claw
pinza[F]
griffe[F]
Klaue[F]
unghia[F]

ANIMAL KINGDOM

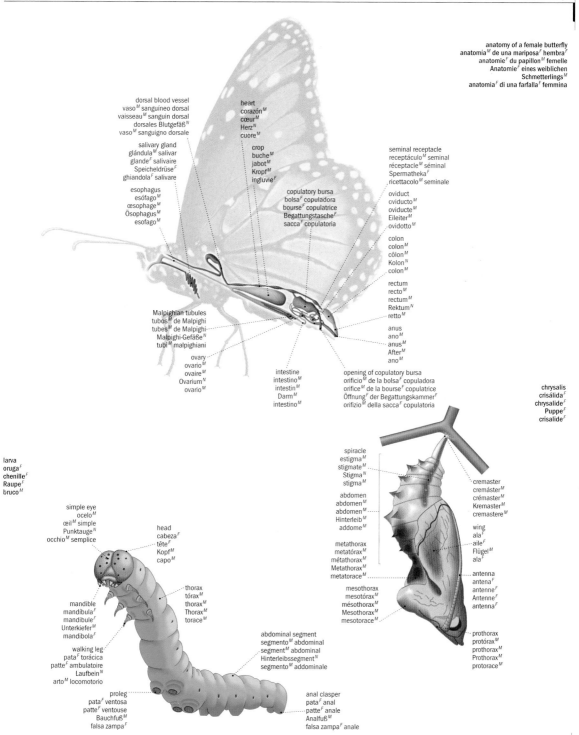

anatomy of a female butterfly
anatomía^M de una mariposa^M hembra^F
anatomie^F du papillon^M femelle
Anatomie^F eines weiblichen
Schmetterlings^M
anatomia^F di una farfalla^F femmina

dorsal blood vessel
vaso^M sanguíneo dorsal
vaisseau^M sanguin dorsal
dorsales Blutgefäß^N
vaso^M sanguigno dorsale

heart
corazón^M
cœur^M
Herz^N
cuore^M

salivary gland
glándula^M salivar
glande^F salivaire
Speicheldrüse^F
ghiandola^F salivare

crop
buche^F
jabot^M
Kropf^M
ingluvie^F

seminal receptacle
receptáculo^M seminal
réceptacle^M séminal
Spermatheka^F
ricettacolo^M seminale

esophagus
esófago^M
œsophage^M
Ösophagus^M
esofago^M

copulatory bursa
bolsa^F copuladora
bourse^F copulatrice
Begattungstasche^F
sacca^F copulatoria

oviduct
oviducto^M
oviducte^M
Eileiter^M
ovidotto^M

colon
colon^M
côlon^M
Kolon^N
colon^M

rectum
recto^M
rectum^M
Rektum^N
retto^M

Malpighian tubules
tubos^M de Malpighi
tubes^M de Malpighi
Malpighi-Gefäße^N
tubi^M malpighiani

anus
ano^M
anus^M
After^M
ano^M

ovary
ovario^M
ovaire^M
Ovarium^N
ovario^M

intestine
intestino^M
intestin^M
Darm^M
intestino^M

opening of copulatory bursa
orificio^M de la bolsa^F copuladora
orifice^M de la bourse^F copulatrice
Öffnung^F der Begattungskammer^F
orifizio^M della sacca^F copulatoria

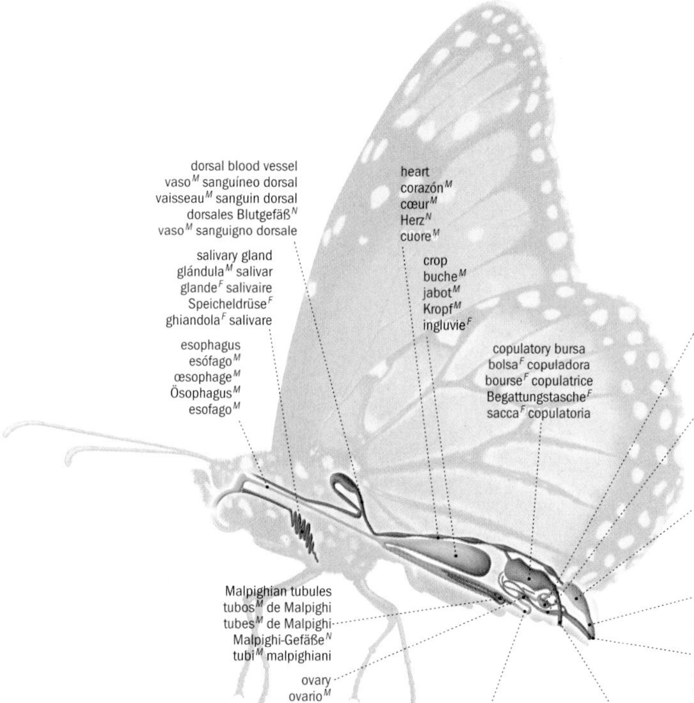

chrysalis
crisálida^F
chrysalide^F
Puppe^F
crisalide^F

larva
oruga^F
chenille^F
Raupe^F
bruco^M

spiracle
estigma^M
stigmate^M
Stigma^N
stigma^M

cremaster
cremáster^M
crémaster^M
Kremaster^M
cremastere^M

simple eye
ocelo^M
œil^M simple
Punktauge^N
occhio^M semplice

head
cabeza^F
tête^F
Kopf^M
capo^M

abdomen
abdomen^M
abdomen^M
Hinterleib^M
addome^M

wing
ala^F
aile^F
Flügel^M
ala^F

metathorax
metatórax^M
métathorax^M
Metathorax^M
metatorace^M

antenna
antena^F
antenne^F
Antenne^F
antenna^F

mandible
mandíbula^F
mandibule^F
Unterkiefer^M
mandibola^F

thorax
tórax^M
thorax^M
Thorax^M
torace^M

mesothorax
mesotórax^M
mésothorax^M
Mesothorax^M
mesotorace^M

walking leg
pata^F torácica
patte^F ambulatoire
Laufbein^N
arto^M locomotorio

abdominal segment
segmento^M abdominal
segment^M abdominal
Hinterleibssegment^N
segmento^M addominale

prothorax
protórax^M
prothorax^M
Prothorax^M
protorace^M

proleg
pata^F ventosa
patte^F ventouse
Bauchfuß^M
falsa zampa^F

anal clasper
pata^F anal
patte^F anale
Analfuß^M
falsa zampa^F anale

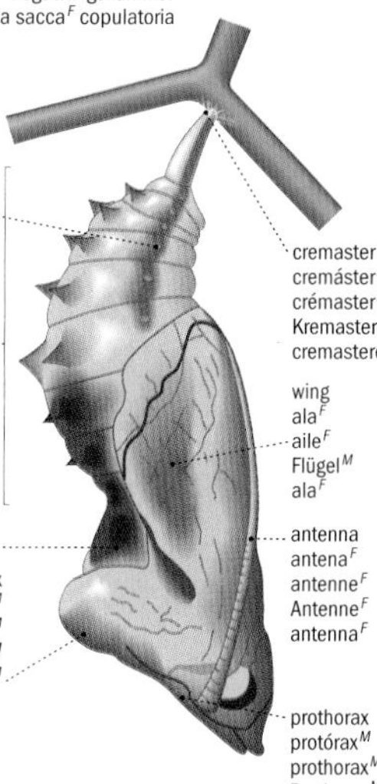

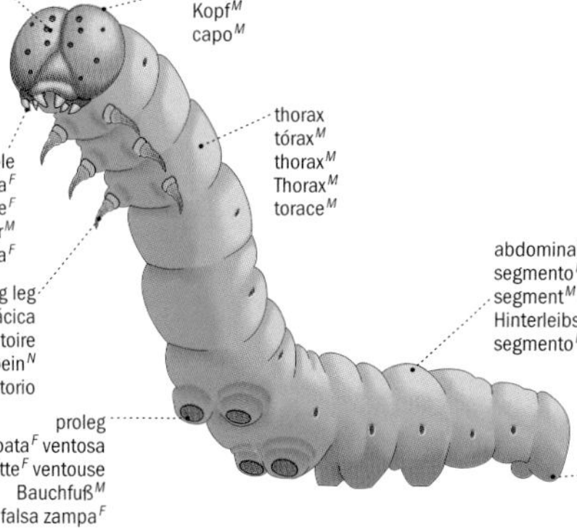

honeybee

abeja ^{F} | abeille ^{F} | Honigbiene ^{F} | ape ^{F}

morphology of a honeybee: worker
morfología ^{F} de una abeja ^{F} trabajadora ^{F}
morphologie ^{F} de l'abeille ^{F} : ouvrière ^{F}
äußere Merkmale ^{N} einer Honigbiene ^{F}: Arbeiterin ^{F}
morfologia ^{F} di un'ape ^{F}: operaia

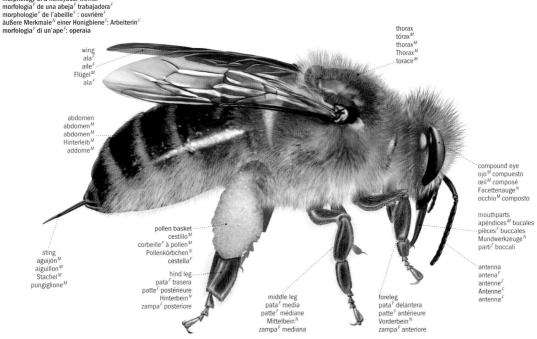

wing
ala ^{F}
aile ^{F}
Flügel ^{M}
ala ^{F}

thorax
tórax ^{M}
thorax ^{M}
Thorax ^{M}
torace ^{M}

abdomen
abdomen ^{M}
abdomen ^{M}
Hinterleib ^{M}
addome ^{M}

compound eye
ojo ^{M} compuesto
œil ^{M} composé
Facettenauge ^{N}
occhio ^{M} composto

mouthparts
apéndices ^{M} bucales
pièces ^{F} buccales
Mundwerkzeuge ^{N}
parti ^{F} boccali

sting
aguijón ^{M}
aiguillon ^{M}
Stachel ^{M}
pungiglione ^{M}

pollen basket
cestillo ^{M}
corbeille ^{F} à pollen ^{M}
Pollenkörbchen ^{N}
cestella ^{F}

hind leg
pata ^{F} trasera
patte ^{F} postérieure
Hinterbein ^{N}
zampa ^{F} posteriore

middle leg
pata ^{F} media
patte ^{F} médiane
Mittelbein ^{N}
zampa ^{F} mediana

foreleg
pata ^{F} delantera
patte ^{F} antérieure
Vorderbein ^{N}
zampa ^{F} anteriore

antenna
antena ^{F}
antenne ^{F}
Antenne ^{F}
antenna ^{F}

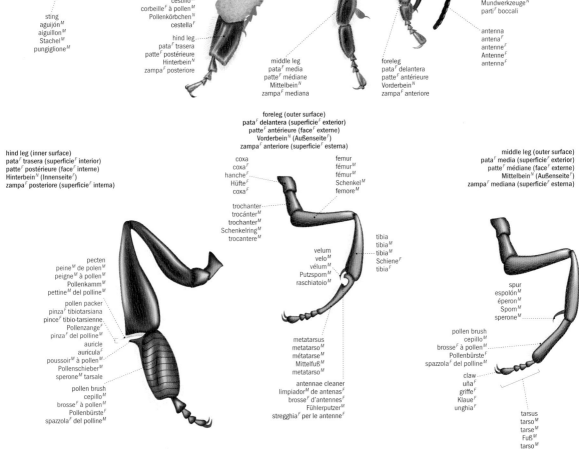

hind leg (inner surface)
pata ^{F} trasera (superficie ^{F} interior)
patte ^{F} postérieure (face ^{F} interne)
Hinterbein ^{N} (Innenseite ^{F})
zampa ^{F} posteriore (superficie ^{F} interna)

foreleg (outer surface)
pata ^{F} delantera (superficie ^{F} exterior)
patte ^{F} antérieure (face ^{F} externe)
Vorderbein ^{N} (Außenseite ^{F})
zampa ^{F} anteriore (superficie ^{F} esterna)

middle leg (outer surface)
pata ^{F} media (superficie ^{F} exterior)
patte ^{F} médiane (face ^{F} externe)
Mittelbein ^{N} (Außenseite ^{F})
zampa ^{F} mediana (superficie ^{F} esterna)

coxa
coxa ^{F}
hanche ^{F}
Hüfte ^{F}
coxa ^{F}

femur
fémur ^{M}
fémur ^{M}
Schenkel ^{M}
femore ^{M}

trochanter
trocánter ^{M}
trochanter ^{M}
Schenkelring ^{M}
trocantere ^{M}

pecten
peine ^{M} de polen ^{M}
peigne ^{M} à pollen ^{M}
Pollenkamm ^{M}
pettine ^{M} del polline ^{M}

pollen packer
pinza ^{F} tibiotarsiana
pince ^{F} tibio-tarsienne
Pollenzange ^{F}
pinza ^{F} del polline ^{M}

auricle
auricula ^{F}
poussoir ^{M} à pollen ^{M}
Pollenschieber ^{M}
sperone ^{M} tarsale

pollen brush
cepillo ^{M}
brosse ^{F} à pollen ^{M}
Pollenbürste ^{F}
spazzola ^{F} del polline ^{M}

velum
velo ^{M}
vélum ^{M}
Putzsporn ^{M}
raschiatoio ^{M}

tibia
tibia ^{M}
tibia ^{M}
Schiene ^{F}
tibia ^{F}

metatarsus
metatarso ^{M}
métatarse ^{M}
Mittelfuß ^{M}
metatarso ^{M}

antennae cleaner
limpiador ^{M} de antenas ^{F}
brosse ^{F} d'antennes ^{F}
Fühlerputzer ^{M}
stregghia ^{F} per le antenne ^{F}

spur
espolón ^{M}
éperon ^{M}
Sporn ^{M}
sperone ^{M}

pollen brush
cepillo ^{M}
brosse ^{F} à pollen ^{M}
Pollenbürste ^{F}
spazzola ^{F} del polline ^{M}

claw
uña ^{F}
griffe ^{F}
Klaue ^{F}
unghia ^{F}

tarsus
tarso ^{M}
tarse ^{F}
Fuß ^{M}
tarso ^{M}

INSECTS AND ARACHNIDS | INSECTOS Y ARÁCNIDOS
INSECTES ET ARACHNIDES | INSEKTEN UND SPINNENTIERE | INSETTI E ARACNIDI

honeybee

anatomy of a honeybee
anatomía^F de una abeja^F
anatomie^F de l'abeille^F
Anatomie^F einer Honigbiene^F
anatomia^F di un'ape^F

heart
corazón^M
cœur^M
Herz^N
cuore^M

dorsal aorta
aorta^F dorsal
aorte^F dorsale
Rückengefäß^N
aorta^F dorsale

Malpighian tubule
tubo^M de Malpighi
tubes^M de Malpighi
Malpighi-Gefäß^N
tubo^M malpighiano

nerve cord
cordón^M nervioso
chaine^F nerveuse
Nervensystem^N
cordone^M nervoso

rectum
recto^M
rectum^M
Rektum^N
retto^M

brain
cerebro^F
cerveau^M
Gehirn^N
cervello^M

pharynx
faringe^F
pharynx^M
Pharynx^M
faringe^F

venom sac
bolsa^F de veneno^M
poche^F à venin^M
Giftdrüse^F
ghiandola^F del veleno^M

ventriculus
intestino^M medio
intestin^M moyen
Mitteldarm^M
ileo^M

esophagus
esófago^M
œsophage^M
Ösophagus^M
esofago^M

salivary duct
canal^M salivar
canal^M salivaire
Speichelkanal^M
dotto^M salivare

honey stomach
buche^M
jabot^M
Kropf^M
borsa^F melaria

salivary gland
glándula^F salivar
glande^F salivaire
Speicheldrüse^F
ghiandola^F salivare

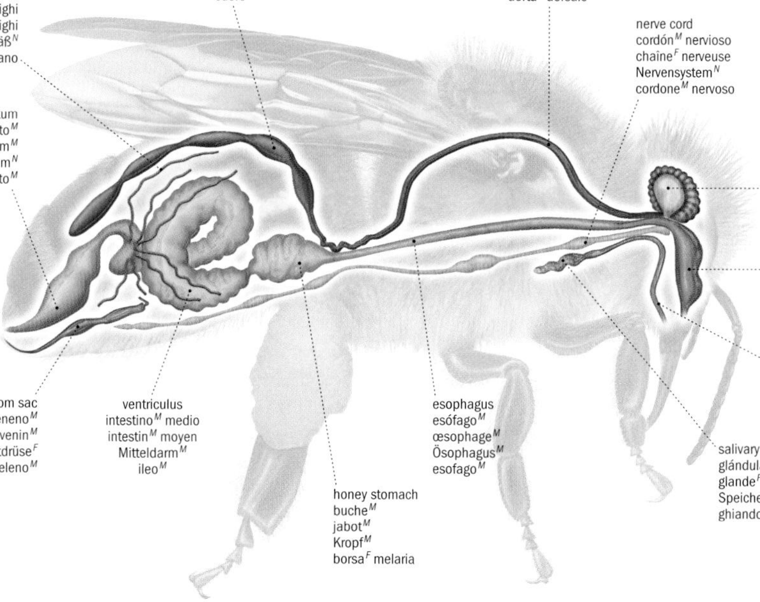

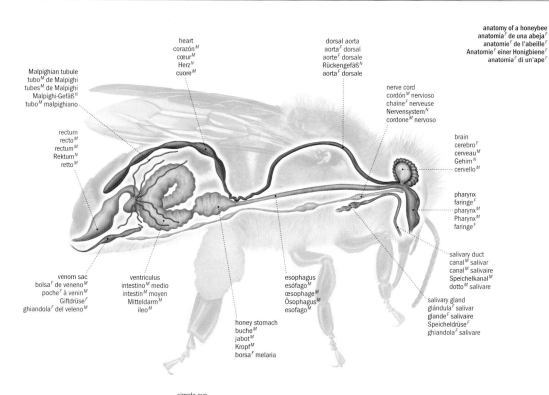

head
cabeza^F
tête^F
Kopf^M
capo^M

simple eye
ocelo^M
œil^M simple
Punktauge^N
occhio^M semplice

compound eye
ojo^M compuesto
œil^M composé
Facettenauge^N
occhio^M composto

antenna
antena^F
antenne^F
Antenne^F
antenna^F

labrum
labio^M superior
lèvre^F supérieure
Oberlippe^F
labbro^M superiore

maxilla
maxilar^M superior
mâchoire^F
Oberkiefer^M
mascella^F

mandible
mandibula^F
mandibule^F
Unterkiefer^M
mandibola^F

labial palp
palpo^M labial
palpe^M labial
Lippentaster^M
palpo^M labiale

glossae
lengua^F
langue^F
Zunge^F
lingua^F

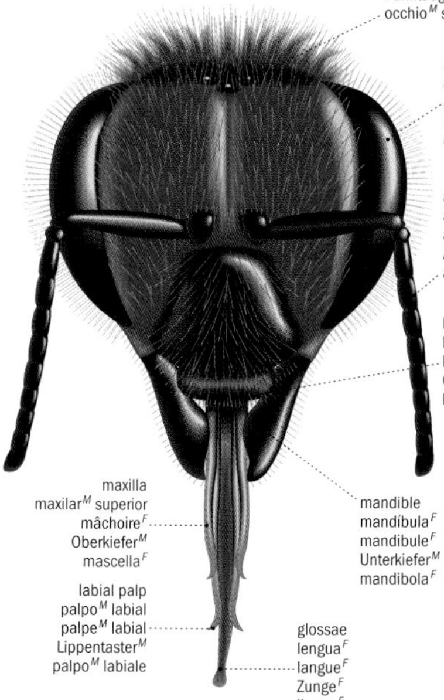

castes
castas^F
castes^F
Kasten^F
caste^F

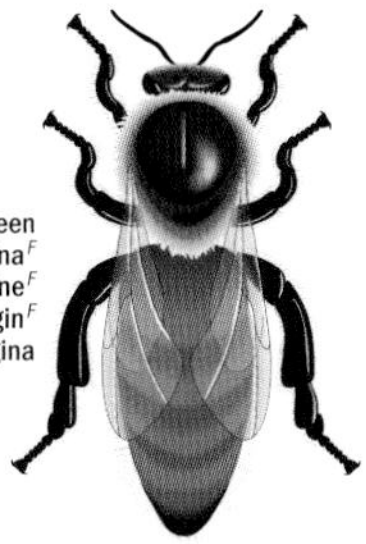

queen
reina^F
reine^F
Königin^F
ape^F regina

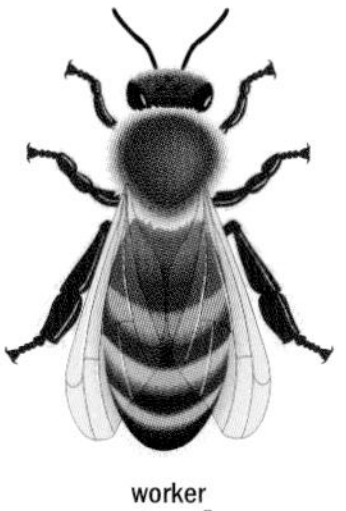

worker
obrera^F
ouvrière^F
Arbeiterin^F
ape^F operaia

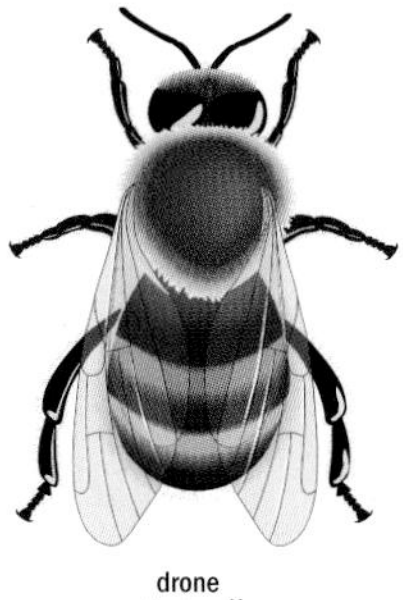

drone
zángano^M
faux bourdon^M
Drohne^F
fuco^M

INSECTS AND ARACHNIDS | INSECTOS Y ARÁCNIDOS
INSECTES ET ARACHNIDES | INSEKTEN UND SPINNENTIERE | INSETTI E ARACNIDI

honeybee

ANIMAL KINGDOM

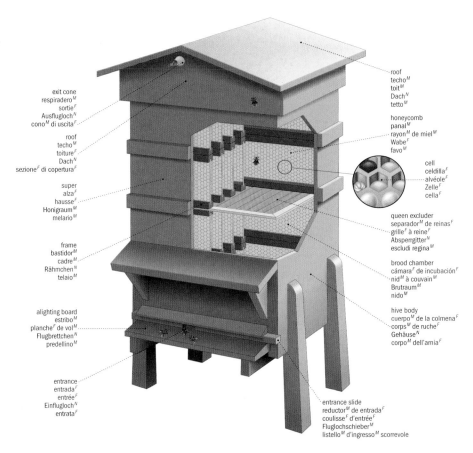

hive
colmena^F
ruche^F
Bienenstock^M
arnia^F

exit cone
respiradero^M
sortie^F
Ausflugloch^M
cono^M di uscita^F

roof
techo^M
toiture^F
Dach^N
sezione^F di copertura^F

super
alza^F
hausse^F
Honigraum^M
melario^M

frame
bastidor^M
cadre^M
Rähmchen^N
telaio^M

alighting board
estribo^M
planche^F de vol^M
Flugbrettchen^N
predellino^M

entrance
entrada^F
entrée^F
Einflugloch^N
entrata^F

roof
techo^M
toit^M
Dach^N
tetto^M

honeycomb
panal^M
rayon^M de miel^M
Wabe^F
favo^M

cell
celdilla^F
alvéole^F
Zelle^F
cella^F

queen excluder
separador^M de reinas^F
grille^F à reine^F
Absperrgitter^N
escludi regina^M

brood chamber
cámara^F de incubación^F
nid^M à couvain^M
Brutraum^M
nido^M

hive body
cuerpo^M de la colmena^F
corps^M de ruche^F
Gehäuse^N
corpo^M dell'arnia^F

entrance slide
reductor^M de entrada^F
coulisse^F d'entrée^F
Fluglochschieber^M
listello^M d'ingresso^M scorrevole

honeycomb section
corte^M de un panal^M
coupe^F d'un rayon^M de miel^M
Wabenausschnitt^M
sezione^F del favo^M

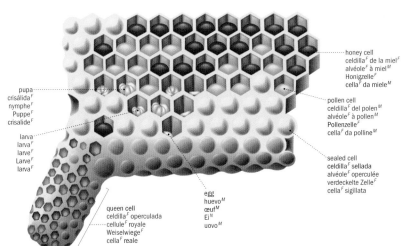

pupa
crisálida^F
nymphe^F
Puppe^F
crisalide^F

larva
larva^F
larve^F
Larve^F
larva^F

queen cell
celdilla^F operculada
cellule^F royale
Weiselwiege^F
cella^F reale

egg
huevo^M
œuf^M
Ei^N
uovo^M

honey cell
celdilla^F de la miel^F
alvéole^F à miel^M
Honigzelle^F
cella^F da miele^M

pollen cell
celdilla^F del polen^M
alvéole^F à pollen^M
Pollenzelle^F
cella^F da polline^M

sealed cell
celdilla^F sellada
alvéole^F operculée
verdeckelte Zelle^F
cella^F sigillata

examples of insects

ejemplos^M de insectos^M | exemples^M d'insectes^M | Beispiele^N für Insekten^N | esempi^M di insetti^M

ANIMAL KINGDOM

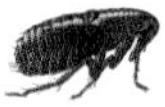

flea
pulga^F
puce^F
Floh^M
pulce^F

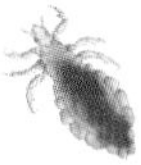

louse
piojo^M
pou^M
Laus^F
pidocchio^M

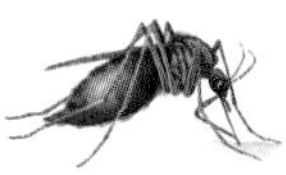

mosquito
mosquito^M
moustique^M
Moskito^M
zanzara^F

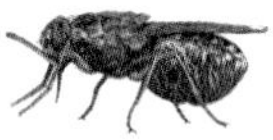

tsetse fly
mosca^F tsetsé
mouche^F tsé-tsé
Tsetsefliege^F
mosca^F tse-tse

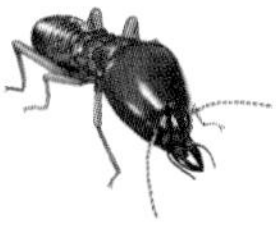

termite
termita^F
termite^M
Termite^F
termite^F

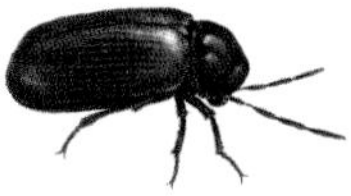

furniture beetle
carcoma^F
petite vrillette^F
Bockkäfer^M
tarlo^M

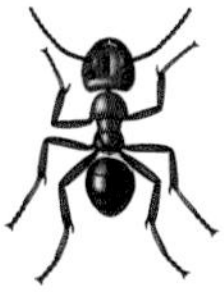

ant
hormiga^F
fourmi^F
Ameise^F
formica^F

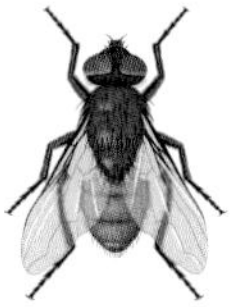

fly
mosca^F
mouche^F
Fliege^F
mosca^F

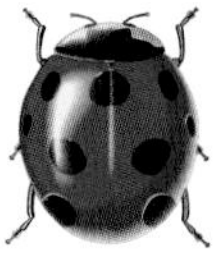

ladybird beetle
mariquita^F
coccinelle^F
Marienkäfer^M
coccinella^F

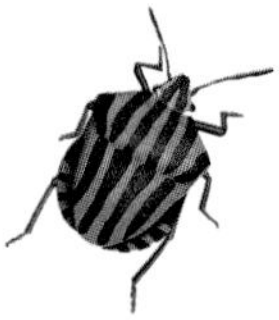

shield bug
chinche^F de campo^M
punaise^F rayée
Schildwanze^F
cimice^F rigata

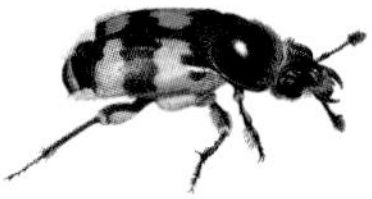

sexton beetle
escarabajo^M necrófaro
nécrophore^M
Totengräber^M
necroforo^M

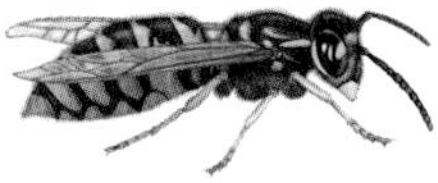

yellowjacket
avispa^F
guêpe^F
Wespe^F
vespa^F

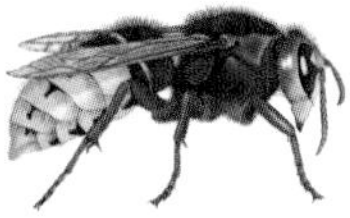

hornet
avispón^M
frelon^M
Hornisse^F
calabrone^M

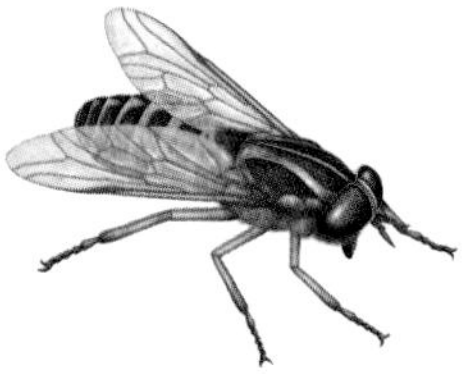

horsefly
tábano^M
taon^M
Bremse^F
tafano^M

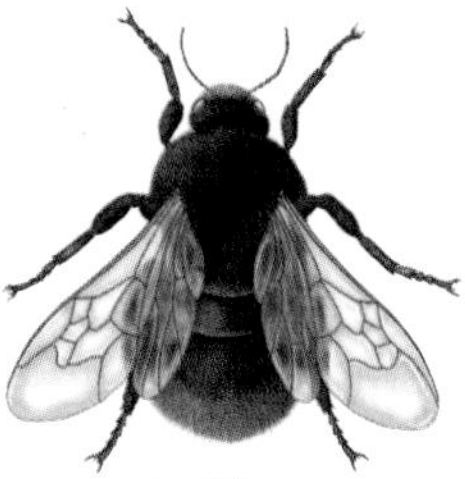

bumblebee
abejorro^M
bourdon^M
Hummel^F
bombo^M

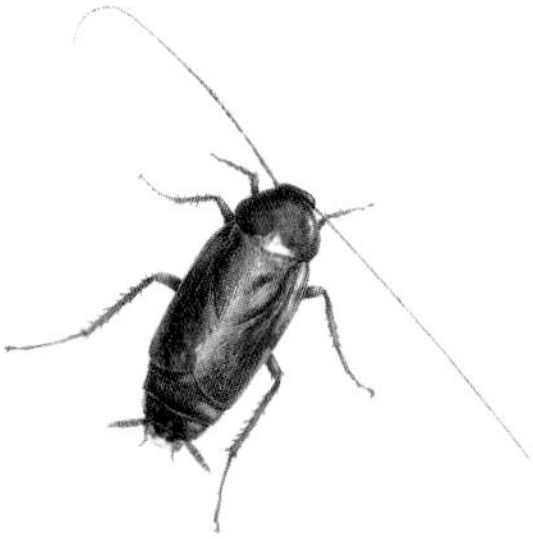

oriental cockroach
cucaracha^F oriental
blatte^F orientale
orientalische Schabe^F
blatta^F orientale

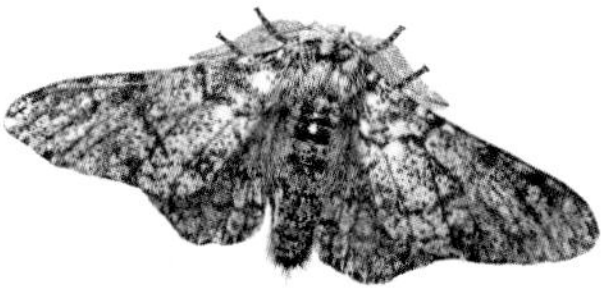

peppered moth
polilla^F de abedul^M
phalène^F du bouleau^M
Birkenspanner^M
falena^F della betulla^F

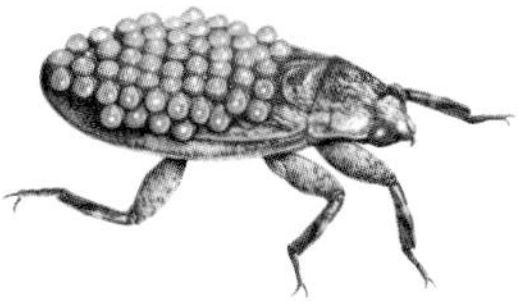

giant water bug (with eggs)
chinche^F acuática gigante (con huevos^M)
punaise^F d'eau^F géante (avec des oeufs^M)
Riesenwasserwanze^F (mit Eier^F)
cimice^F acquatica gigante (con uvi^M)

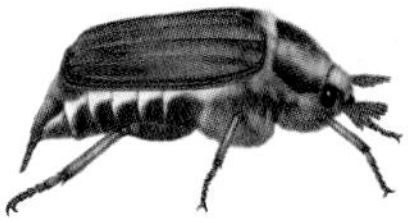

cockchafer
escarabajo^M
hanneton^M
Maikäfer^M
maggiolino^M

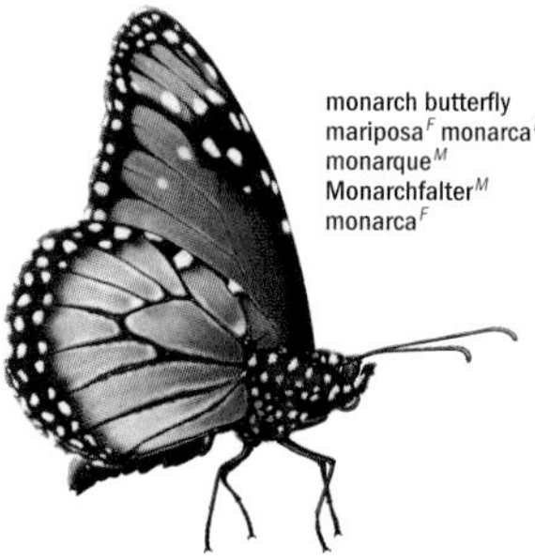

monarch butterfly
mariposa^F monarca^M
monarque^M
Monarchfalter^M
monarca^F

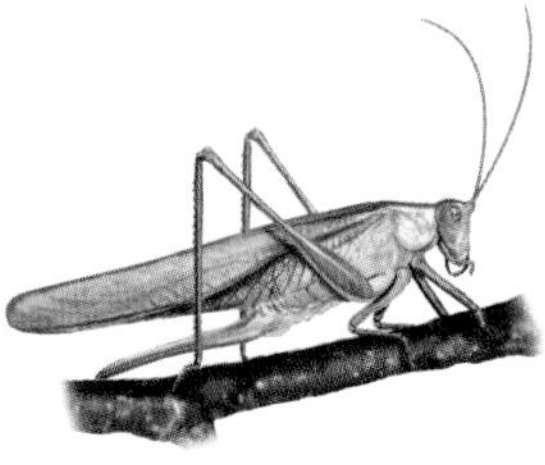

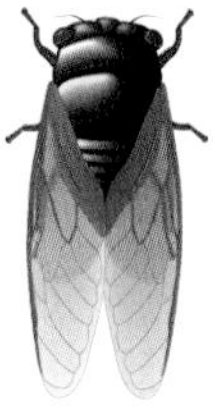

cicada
cigarra^F
cigale^F
Zikade^F
cicala^F

great green bush-cricket
saltamontes^M verde
grande sauterelle^F verte
Laubheuschrecke^F
cavalletta^F verde

examples of insects

ANIMAL KINGDOM

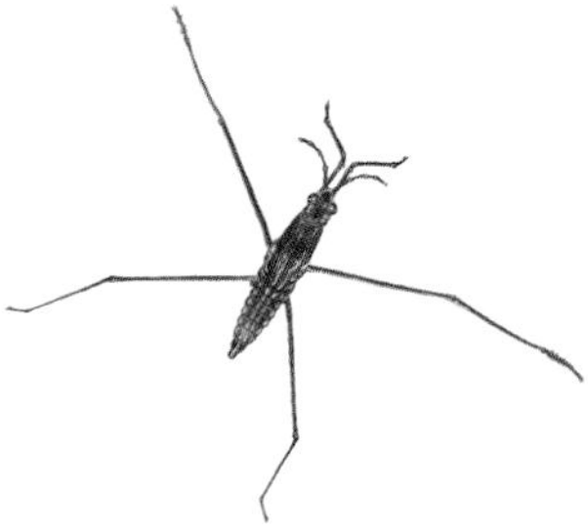

water strider
opilión[M]
patineur[M] d'eau[F]
Wasserläufer[M]
opilione[M]

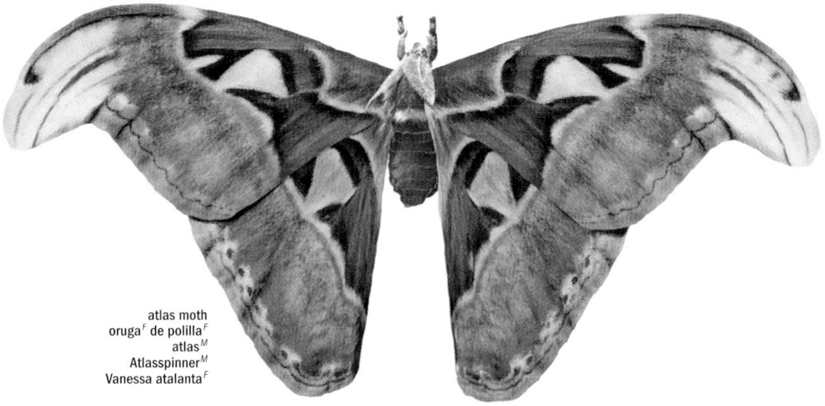

atlas moth
oruga[F] de polilla[F]
atlas[M]
Atlasspinner[M]
Vanessa atalanta[F]

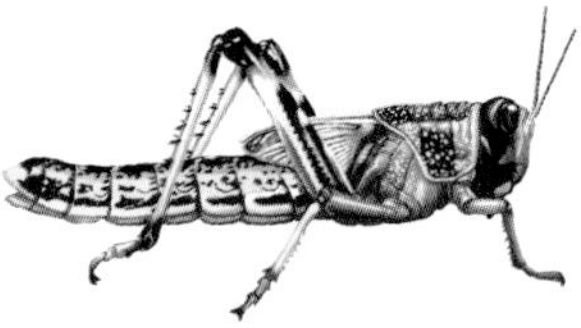

bow-winged grasshopper
grillo[M] campestre
criquet[M] mélodieux
Nachtigall[F]-Grashüpfer[M]
cavalletta[F]

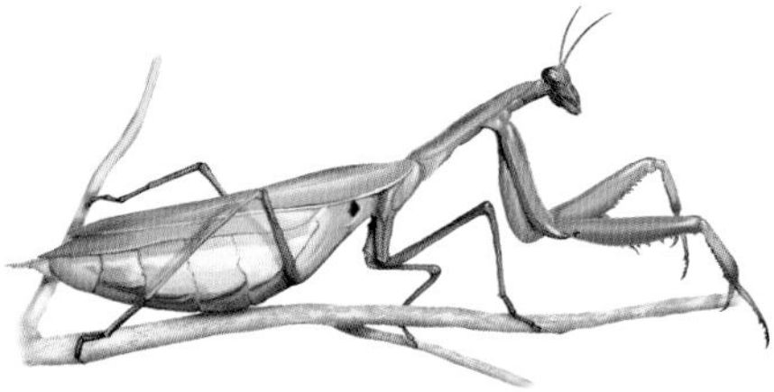

mantid
mantis[F] religiosa
mante[F] religieuse
Gottesanbeterin[F]
mantide[F] religiosa

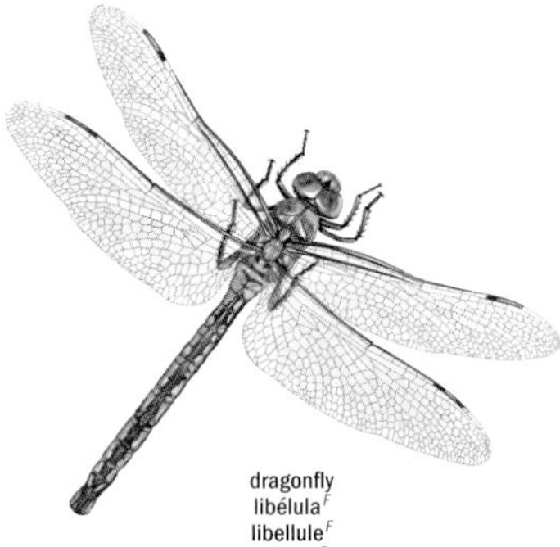

dragonfly
libélula[F]
libellule[F]
Libelle[F]
libellula[F]

examples of arachnids

ejemplos[M] de arácnidos[M] | exemples[M] d'arachnides[M] | Beispiele[N] für Spinnentiere[N] | esempi[M] di aracnidi[M]

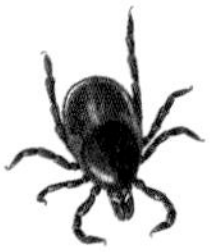

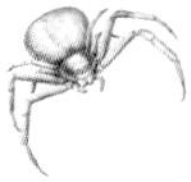

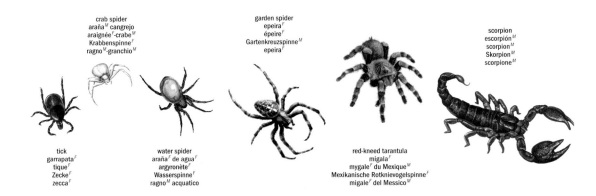

crab spider
araña[M] cangrejo
araignée[F]-crabe[M]
Krabbenspinne[F]
ragno[M]-granchio[M]

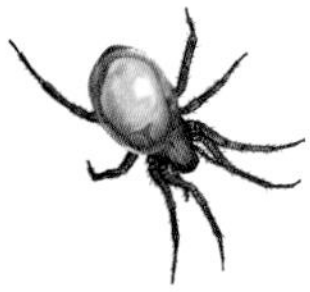

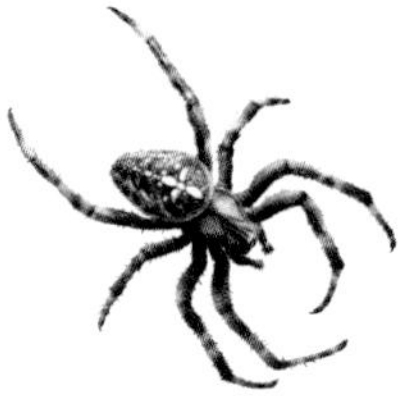

garden spider
epeira[F]
épeire[F]
Gartenkreuzspinne[M]
epeira[F]

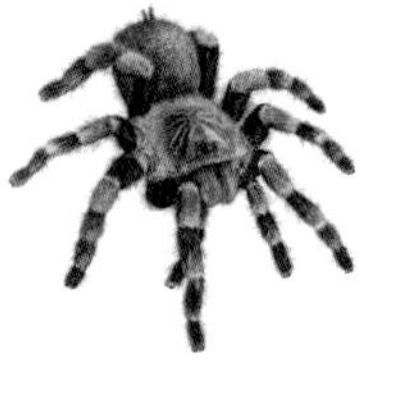

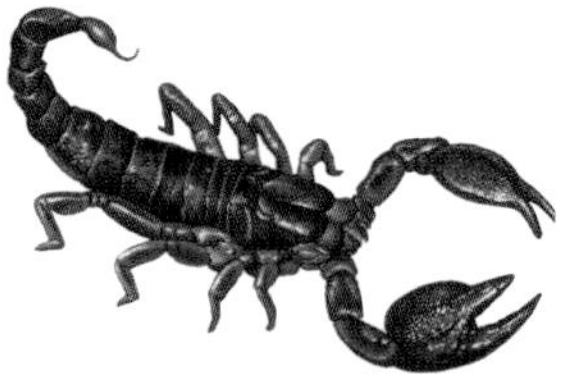

scorpion
escorpión[M]
scorpion[M]
Skorpion[M]
scorpione[M]

tick
garrapata[F]
tique[F]
Zecke[F]
zecca[F]

water spider
araña[F] de agua[F]
argyronète[F]
Wasserspinne[F]
ragno[M] acquatico

red-kneed tarantula
migala[F]
mygale[F] du Mexique[M]
Mexikanische Rotknievogelspinne[F]
migale[F] del Messico[M]

spider

araña[F] | araignée[F] | Spinne[F] | ragno[M]

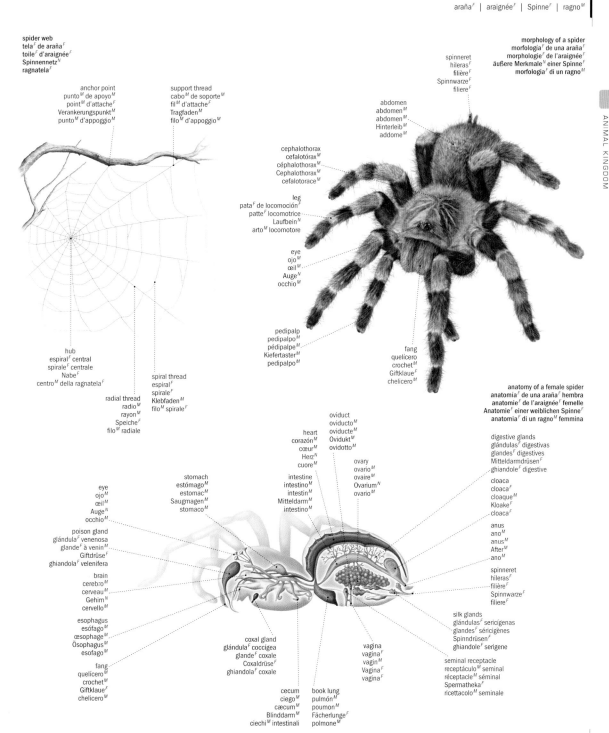

ANIMAL KINGDOM

spider web
tela[F] de araña[F]
toile[F] d'araignée[F]
Spinnennetz[N]
ragnatela[F]

morphology of a spider
morfología[F] de una araña[F]
morphologie[F] de l'araignée[F]
äußere Merkmale[N] einer Spinne[F]
morfologia[F] di un ragno[M]

anchor point
punto[M] de apoyo[M]
point[M] d'attache[F]
Verankerungspunkt[M]
punto[M] d'appoggio[M]

support thread
cabo[M] de soporte[M]
fil[M] d'attache[F]
Tragfaden[M]
filo[M] d'appoggio[M]

spinneret
hileras[F]
filière[F]
Spinnwarze[F]
filière[F]

abdomen
abdomen[M]
abdomen[M]
Hinterleib[M]
addome[M]

cephalothorax
cefalotórax[M]
céphalothorax[M]
Cephalothorax[M]
cefalotorace[M]

leg
pata[F] de locomoción[F]
patte[F] locomotrice
Laufbein[N]
arto[M] locomotore

eye
ojo[M]
œil[M]
Auge[N]
occhio[M]

pedipalp
pedipalpo[M]
pédipalpe[M]
Kiefertaster[M]
pedipalpo[M]

fang
quelícero[M]
crochet[M]
Giftklaue[F]
chelicero[M]

hub
espiral[F] central
spirale[F] centrale
Nabe[F]
centro[M] della ragnatela[F]

spiral thread
espiral[F]
spirale[F]
Klebfaden[M]
filo[M] spirale[F]

radial thread
radio[M]
rayon[M]
Speiche[F]
filo[M] radiale

anatomy of a female spider
anatomía[F] de una araña[F] hembra
anatomie[F] de l'araignée[F] femelle
Anatomie[F] einer weiblichen Spinne[F]
anatomia[F] di un ragno[M] femmina

oviduct
oviducto[M]
oviducte[M]
Ovidukt[M]
ovidotto[M]

heart
corazón[M]
cœur[M]
Herz[N]
cuore[M]

ovary
ovario[M]
ovaire[F]
Ovarium[N]
ovario[M]

digestive glands
glándulas[F] digestivas
glandes[F] digestives
Mitteldarmdrüsen[F]
ghiandole[F] digestive

stomach
estómago[M]
estomac[M]
Saugmagen[M]
stomaco[M]

intestine
intestino[M]
intestin[M]
Mitteldarm[M]
intestino[M]

cloaca
cloaca[F]
cloaque[M]
Kloake[F]
cloaca[F]

eye
ojo[M]
œil[M]
Auge[N]
occhio[M]

anus
ano[M]
anus[M]
After[M]
ano[M]

poison gland
glándula[F] venenosa
glande[F] à venin[M]
Giftdrüse[F]
ghiandola[F] velenifera

spinneret
hileras[F]
filière[F]
Spinnwarze[F]
filière[F]

brain
cerebro[M]
cerveau[M]
Gehirn[N]
cervello[M]

silk glands
glándulas[F] sericígenas
glandes[F] séricigènes
Spinndrüsen[F]
ghiandole[F] serigene

esophagus
esófago[M]
œsophage[M]
Ösophagus[M]
esofago[M]

seminal receptacle
receptáculo[M] seminal
réceptacle[M] séminal
Spermatheka[F]
ricettacolo[M] seminale

fang
quelícero[M]
crochet[M]
Giftklaue[F]
chelicero[M]

coxal gland
glándula[F] coccígea
glande[F] coxale
Coxaldrüse[F]
ghiandola[F] coxale

vagina
vagina[F]
vagin[M]
Vagina[F]
vagina[F]

cecum
ciego[M]
cæcum[M]
Blinddarm[M]
ciechi[M] intestinali

book lung
pulmón[M]
poumon[M]
Fächerlunge[F]
polmone[M]

snail

caracol^M | escargot^M | Schnecke^F | chiocciola^F

morphology of a snail
morfología^F de un caracol^M
morphologie^F de l'escargot^M
äußere Merkmale^N einer Schnecke^F
morfologia^F di una chiocciola^F

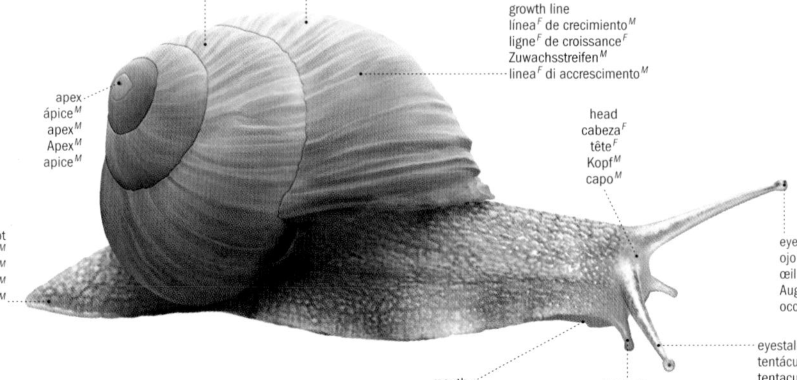

anatomy of a snail
anatomía^F de un caracol^M
anatomie^F de l'escargot^M
Anatomie^F einer Schnecke^F
anatomia^F di una chiocciola^F

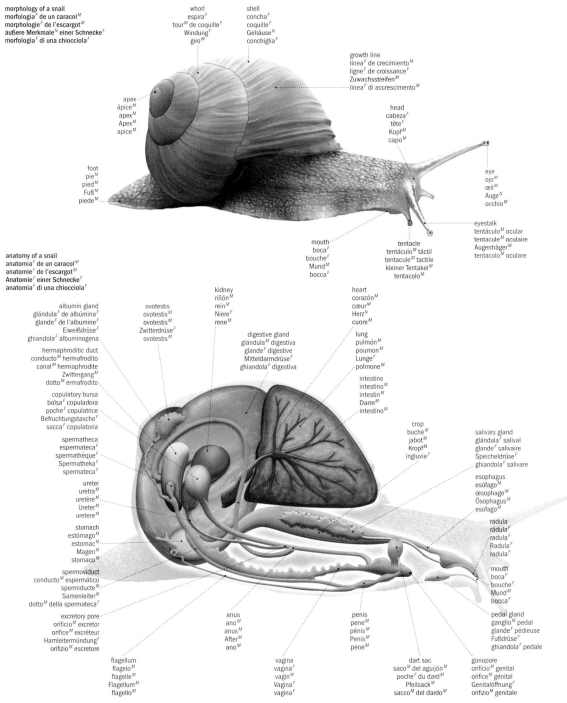

ANIMAL KINGDOM

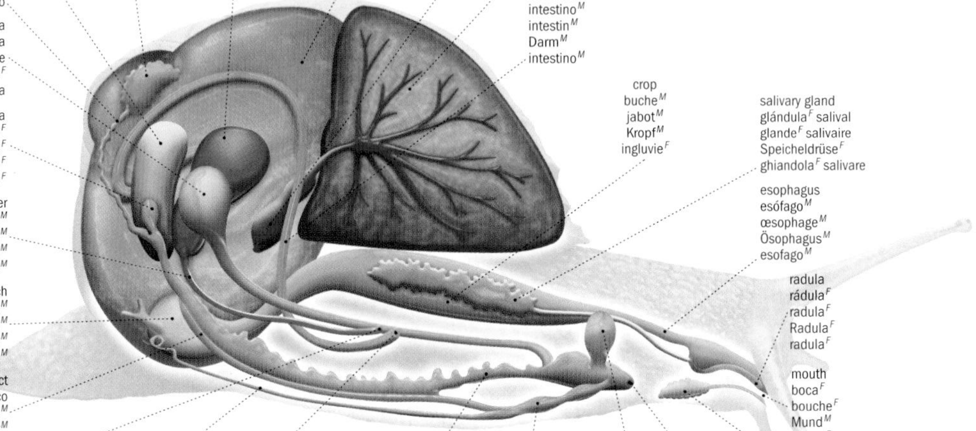

ANIMAL KINGDOM

univalve shell

concha^F univalva | coquillage^M univalve | einschalige Muschel^F | conchiglia^F univalve

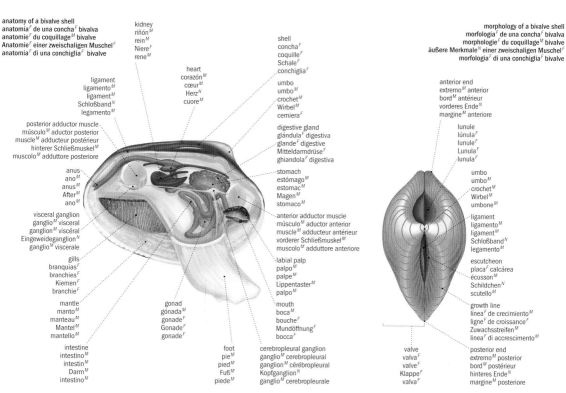

morphology of a univalve shell
morfología^F de una concha^F univalva
morphologie^F du coquillage^M univalve
äußere Merkmale^N einer einschaligen Muschel^F
morfologia^F di una conchiglia^F univalve

apex
ápice^M
apex^M
Apex^M
apice^M

nuclear whorl
espiral^F embrionaria
tour^M embryonnaire
Embryonalgewinde^N
giro^M embrionale

columella
columela^F
columelle^F
Spindel^F
columella^F

whorl
espiral^F
tour^M de spire^F
Windung^F
giro^M della spira^F

axial rib
costilla^F axial
côte^F axiale
Axialrippe^F
costa^F assiale

suture
sutura^F
ligne^F de suture^F
Naht^F
sutura^F

spiral rib
costilla^F espiral
côte^F spiralée
Spiralskulptur^F
costa^F spirale

aperture
apertura^F terminal
ouverture^F
Mündung^F
apertura^F

outer lip
labio^M externo
bord^M externe
Außenlippe^F
labbro^M esterno

columella fold
pliegue^M de la columela^F
pli^M de la columelle^F
Spindelfalte^F
piega^F della columella^F

inner lip
labio^M interno
bord^M interne
Innenlippe^F
labbro^M interno

siphonal canal
canal^M del sifón^M
canal^F siphonal
Siphonalkanal^M
canale^M del sifone^M

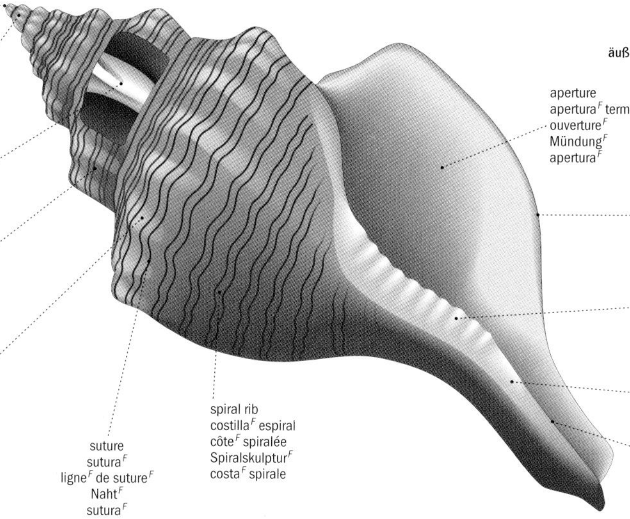

bivalve shell

concha^F bivalva | coquillage^M bivalve | zweischalige Muschel^F | conchiglia^F bivalve

anatomy of a bivalve shell
anatomía^F de una concha^F bivalva
anatomie^F du coquillage^M bivalve
Anatomie^F einer zweischaligen Muschel^F
anatomia^F di una conchiglia^F bivalve

kidney
riñón^M
rein^M
Niere^F
rene^M

heart
corazón^M
cœur^M
Herz^N
cuore^M

ligament
ligamento^M
ligament^M
Schloßband^N
legamento^M

posterior adductor muscle
músculo^M aductor posterior
muscle^M adducteur postérieur
hinterer Schließmuskel^M
muscolo^M adduttore posteriore

anus
ano^M
anus^M
After^M
ano^M

visceral ganglion
ganglio^M visceral
ganglion^M viscéral
Eingeweideganglion^N
ganglio^M viscerale

gills
branquias^F
branchies^F
Kiemen^F
branchie^F

mantle
manto^M
manteau^M
Mantel^M
mantello^M

intestine
intestino^M
intestin^M
Darm^M
intestino^M

gonad
gónada^M
gonade^F
Gonade^F
gonade^F

foot
pie^M
pied^M
Fuß^M
piede^M

cerebropleural ganglion
ganglio^M cerebropleural
ganglion^M cérébropleural
Kopfganglion^N
ganglio^M cerebropleurale

shell
concha^F
coquille^F
Schale^F
conchiglia^F

umbo
umbo^M
crochet^M
Wirbel^M
cerniera^F

digestive gland
glándula^F digestiva
glande^F digestive
Mitteldarmdrüse^F
ghiandola^F digestiva

stomach
estómago^M
estomac^M
Magen^M
stomaco^M

anterior adductor muscle
músculo^M aductor anterior
muscle^M adducteur antérieur
vorderer Schließmuskel^M
muscolo^M adduttore anteriore

labial palp
palpo^M
palpe^M
Lippentaster^M
palpo^M

mouth
boca^F
bouche^F
Mundöffnung^F
bocca^F

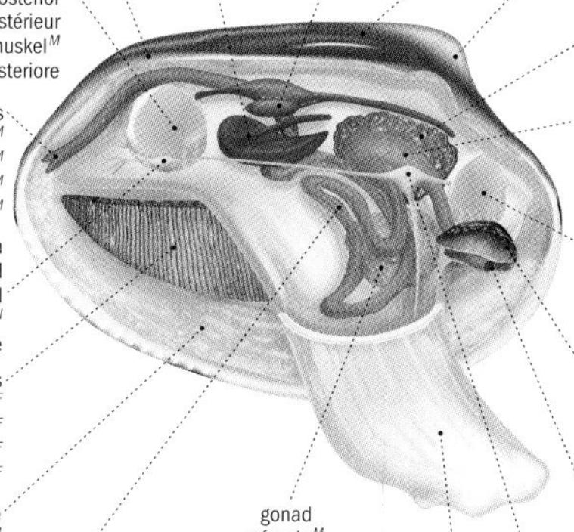

morphology of a bivalve shell
morfología^F de una concha^F bivalva
morphologie^F du coquillage^M bivalve
äußere Merkmale^N einer zweischaligen Muschel^F
morfologia^F di una conchiglia^F bivalve

anterior end
extremo^M anterior
bord^M antérieur
vorderes Ende^N
margine^M anteriore

lunule
lúnula^F
lunule^F
Lunula^F
lunula^F

umbo
umbo^M
crochet^M
Wirbel^M
umbone^M

ligament
ligamento^M
ligament^M
Schloßband^N
legamento^M

escutcheon
placa^F calcárea
écusson^M
Schildchen^N
scutello^M

growth line
línea^F de crecimiento^M
ligne^F de croissance^F
Zuwachsstreifen^M
linea^F di accrescimento^M

posterior end
extremo^M posterior
bord^M postérieur
hinteres Ende^N
margine^M posteriore

valve
valva^F
valve^F
Klappe^F
valva^F

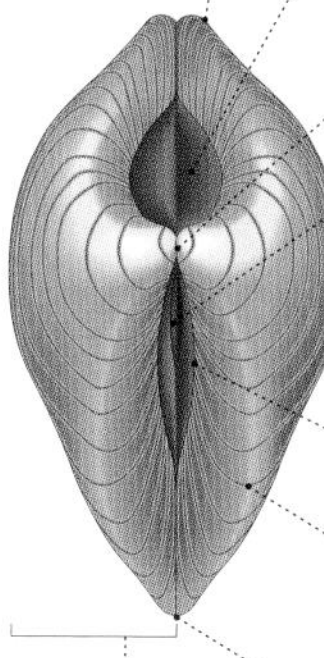

octopus

pulpo^M | pieuvre^F | Tintenfisch^M | polpo^M

morphology of an octopus
morfología^F de un pulpo^M
morphologie^F de la pieuvre^F
äußere Merkmale^N eines Tintenfischs^M
morfologia^F di un polpo^M

siphon
sifón^M
entonnoir^M
Trichter^M
sifone^M

eye
ojo^M
œil^F
Auge^N
occhio^M

tentacle
tentáculo^M
tentacule^M
Tentakel^M
tentacolo^M

mantle
manto^M
manteau^M
Mantel^M
mantello^M

sucker
ventosa^F
ventouse^F
Saugnapf^M
ventosa^F

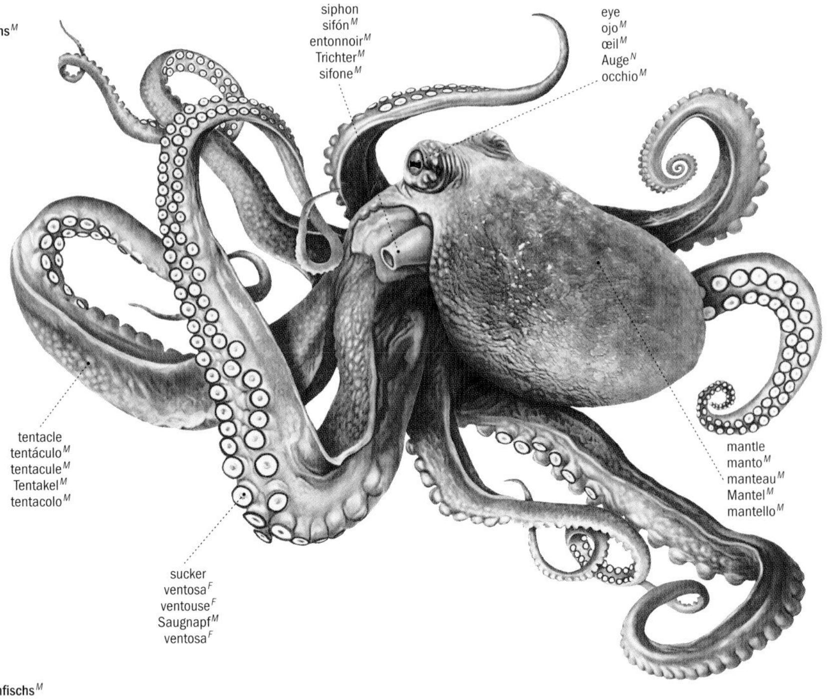

anatomy of a male octopus
anatomía^F de un pulpo^M macho
anatomie^F de la pieuvre^F mâle
Anatomie^F enies männliches Tintenfischs^M
anatomia^F di un polpo^M maschio

brain
cerebro^M
cerveau^M
Gehirn^N
cervello^M

skull
cráneo^M
crâne^M
Schädel^M
cranio^M

crop
buche^M
jabot^M
Kropf^M
ingluvie^F

mantle muscles
músculos^M del manto^M
muscles^M du manteau^M
Mantelmuskeln^M
muscoli^M del mantello^M

poison gland
glándula^M venenosa
glande^F à venin^M
Giftdrüse^F
ghiandola^F del veleno^M

dorsal mantle cavity
cavidad^F paleal
cavité^F palléale
Mantelhöhle^F
cavità^F palleale

shell rudiment
concha^F
coquille^F
Schale^F
conchiglia^F

beak
pico^M
bec^M
Kiefer^M
becco^M

digestive gland
glándula^F digestiva
glande^F digestive
Mitteldarmdrüse^F
ghiandola^F digestiva

stomach
estómago^M
estomac^M
Magen^M
stomaco^M

ink sac
bolsa^M de tinta^M
poche^F à encre^F
Tintenbeutel^M
sacca^F dell'inchiostro^M

heart
corazón^M
cœur^M
Herz^N
cuore^M

anus
ano^M
anus^M
After^M
ano^M

gill
branquia^F
branchie^F
Kieme^F
branchia^F

cecum
ciego^M
cæcum^M
Blinddarm^M
cieco^M intestinale

kidney
riñón^M
rein^M
Niere^N
rene^M

gonad
gónada^F
gonade^F
Gonade^F
gonade^F

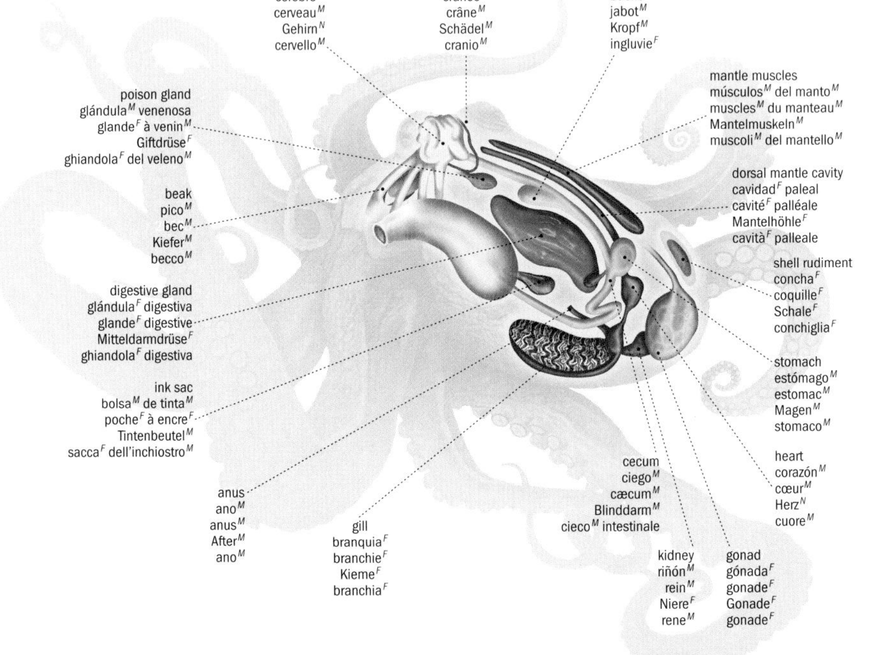

lobster

bogavante[M] | homard[M] | Hummer[M] | astice[M]

ANIMAL KINGDOM

thoracic legs
apéndices[M] torácicos
pattes[F] thoraciques
Brustbeine[N]
arti[M] toracici

cephalothorax
cefalotórax[M]
céphalothorax[M]
Kopfbruststück[N]
cefalotorace[M]

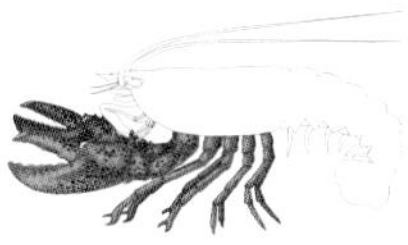

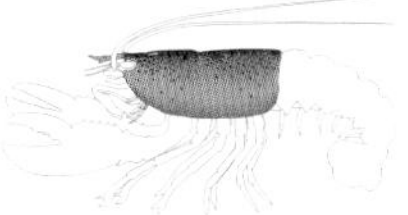

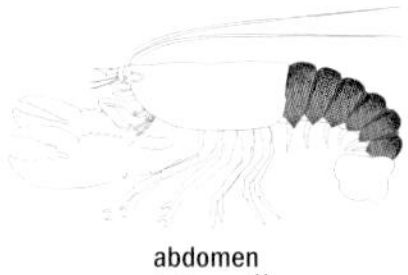

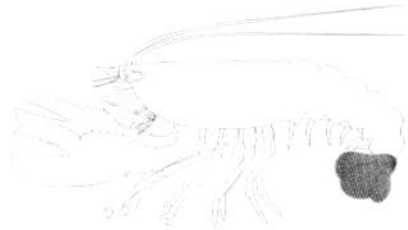

morphology of a lobster
morfología[F] de un bogavante[M]
morphologie[F] du homard[M]
äußere Merkmale[N] eines Hummers[M]
morfologia[F] di un astice[M]

antenna
antena[F]
antenne[F]
Antenne[F]
antenna[F]

antennule
anténula[F]
antennule[F]
Antennula[F]
antennula[F]

eye
ojo[M]
œil[M]
Auge[N]
occhio[M]

claw
pinza[F]
pince[F]
Schere[F]
chela[F]

abdomen
abdomen[M]
abdomen[M]
Hinterleib[N]
addome[M]

carapace
caparazón[M]
carapace[F]
Carapax[M]
carapace[M]

cheliped
pinza[F]
griffe[F]
Klaue[F]
unghia[F]

tail
cola[F]
nageoire[F] caudale
Schwanz[M]
coda[F]

telson
telson[M]
telson[M]
Telson[N]
telson[M]

uropod
urópodo[M]
uropode[M]
Schwanzfächer[M]
uropodio[M]

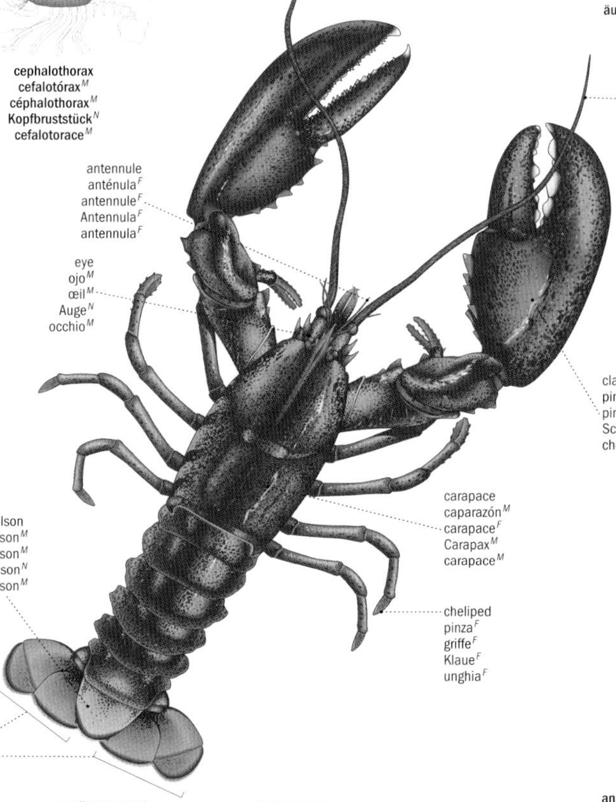

anatomy of a male lobster
anatomía[F] de un bogavante[M] macho
anatomie[F] du homard[M] mâle
Anatomie[F] enies männliches Hummers[M]
anatomia[F] di un astice[M] machio

brain
cerebro[M]
cerveau[M]
Gehirn[N]
cervello[M]

cardiac stomach
estómago[M] cardiaco
estomac[M] cardiaque
Magenmund[M]
stomaco[M] cardiaco

pyloric stomach
estómago[M] pilórico
estomac[M] pylorique
Magenpförtner[M]
stomaco[M] pilorico

dorsal abdominal artery
arteria[F] dorsoabdominal
artère[F] abdominale dorsale
Abdomenarterie[F]
arteria[F] addominale dorsale

heart
corazón[M]
cœur[M]
Herz[N]
cuore[M]

green gland
nefridio[M]
néphridie[F]
Nephridium[N]
nefridio[M]

intestine
intestino[M]
intestin[M]
Darm[M]
intestino[M]

mouth
boca[F]
bouche[F]
Mund[M]
bocca[F]

ventral nerve cord
cordón[F] nervioso ventral
chaine[F] nerveuse ventrale
ventraler Nervenstrang[M]
cordone[M] nervoso ventrale

digestive gland
glándula[F] digestiva
glande[F] digestive
Mitteldarmdrüse[F]
ghiandola[F] digestiva

sternal artery
arteria[F] esternal
artère[F] sternale
Sternalarterie[F]
arteria[F] sternale

ventral abdominal artery
arteria[F] ventral
artère[F] ventrale
Baucharterie[F]
arteria[F] ventrale

anus
ano[M]
anus[M]
After[M]
ano[M]

testis
testiculos[M]
testicules[M]
Hoden[M]
testicoli[M]

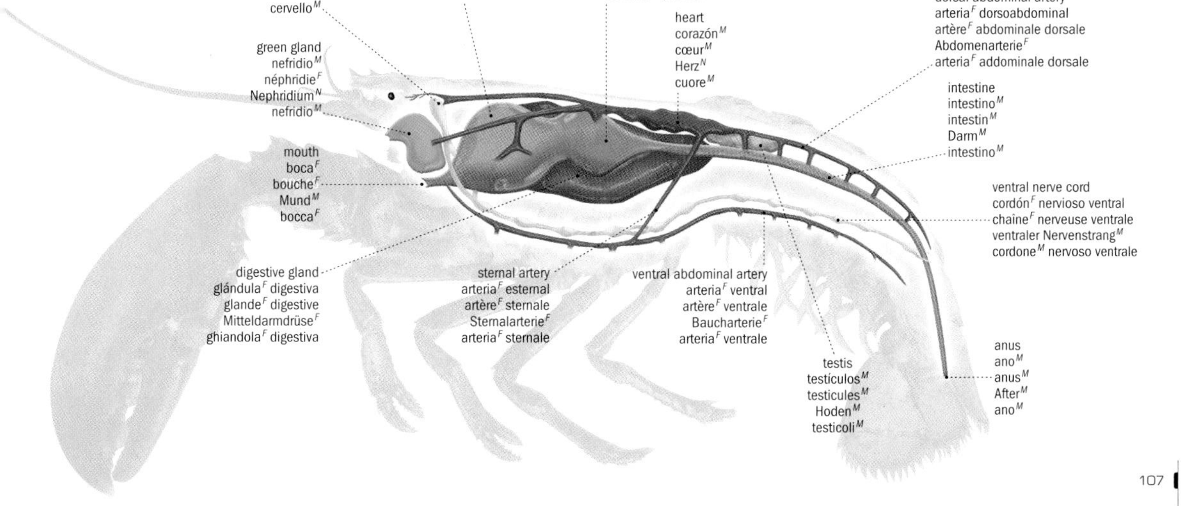

cartilaginous fish

pez^M cartilaginoso | poisson^M cartilagineux | Knorpelfisch^M | pesce^M cartilagineo

morphology of a female shark
morfología^F de un tiburón^M hembra
morphologie^F du requin^M femelle
äußere Merkmale^N eines weibliches Hais^M
morfologia^F di uno squalo^M femminile

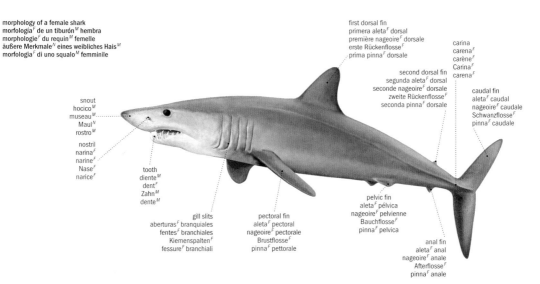

first dorsal fin
primera aleta^F dorsal
première nageoire^F dorsale
erste Rückenflosse^F
prima pinna^F dorsale

carina
carena^F
carène^F
Carina^F
carena^F

second dorsal fin
segunda aleta^F dorsal
seconde nageoire^F dorsale
zweite Rückenflosse^F
seconda pinna^F dorsale

caudal fin
aleta^F caudal
nageoire^F caudale
Schwanzflosse^F
pinna^F caudale

snout
hocico^M
museau^M
Maul^N
rostro^M

nostril
narina^F
narine^F
Nase^F
narice^F

tooth
diente^M
dent^F
Zahn^M
dente^M

gill slits
aberturas^F branquiales
fentes^F branchiales
Kiemenspalten^F
fessure^F branchiali

pectoral fin
aleta^F pectoral
nageoire^F pectorale
Brustflosse^F
pinna^F pettorale

pelvic fin
aleta^F pélvica
nageoire^F pelvienne
Bauchflosse^F
pinna^F pelvica

anal fin
aleta^F anal
nageoire^F anale
Afterflosse^F
pinna^F anale

bony fish

pez^M óseo | poisson^M osseux | Knochenfisch^M | pesce^M osseo

morphology of a perch
morfología^F de una perca^F
morphologie^F de la perche^F ; morphologie^F de la perchaude^F
äußere Merkmale^N eines Flußbarschs^M
morfologia^F di un persico^M

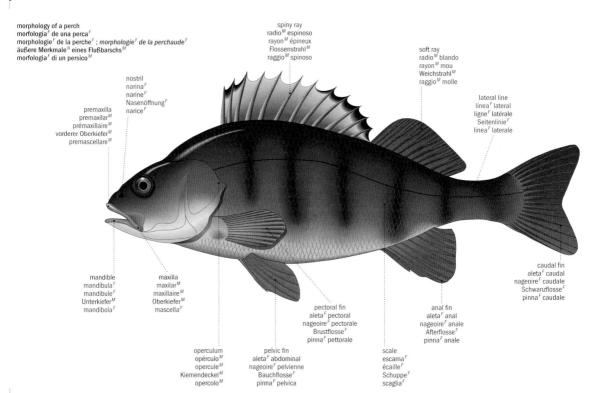

spiny ray
radio^M espinoso
rayon^M épineux
Flossenstrahl^M
raggio^M spinoso

soft ray
radio^M blando
rayon^M mou
Weichstrahl^M
raggio^M molle

lateral line
linea^F lateral
ligne^F latérale
Seitenlinie^F
linea^F laterale

nostril
narina^F
narine^F
Nasenöffnung^F
narice^F

premaxilla
premaxilar^M
prémaxillaire^M
vorderer Oberkiefer^M
premascellare^M

caudal fin
aleta^F caudal
nageoire^F caudale
Schwanzflosse^F
pinna^F caudale

mandible
mandibula^F
mandibule^F
Unterkiefer^M
mandibola^F

maxilla
maxilar^M
maxillaire^M
Oberkiefer^M
mascella^F

pectoral fin
aleta^F pectoral
nageoire^F pectorale
Brustflosse^F
pinna^F pettorale

anal fin
aleta^F anal
nageoire^F anale
Afterflosse^F
pinna^F anale

operculum
opérculo^M
opercule^M
Kiemendeckel^M
opercolo^M

pelvic fin
aleta^F abdominal
nageoire^F pelvienne
Bauchflosse^F
pinna^F pelvica

scale
escama^F
écaille^F
Schuppe^F
scaglia^F

anatomy of a female perch
anatomía^F de una perca^F hembra
anatomie^F de la perche^F femelle ; *anatomie de la perchaude*^F
Anatomie^F eines weibliches Flußbarschs^M
anatomia^F di un persico^M femminile

kidney
riñón^M
rein^M
Niere^F
rene^M

air bladder
vejiga^F natatoria
vessie^F natatoire
Schwimmblase^F
vescica^F natatoria

otolith
otolito^M
otolithe^F
Otolith^M
otolito^M

spinal cord
médula^F espinal
moelle^F épinière
Rückenmark^N
midollo^M spinale

urinary bladder
vejiga^F urinaria
vessie^F
Harnblase^F
vescica^F urinaria

brain
cerebro^M
cerveau^M
Gehirn^N
encefalo^M

skull
cráneo^M
crâne^M
Schädel^M
cranio^M

neural spine
espina^F neural
arête^F neurale
Neuralfortsatz^M
spina^F neurale

olfactory nerve
nervio^M olfativo
nerf^M olfactif
Riechnerv^M
nervo^M olfattorio

vertebral column
columna^F vertebral
colonne^F vertébrale
Wirbelsäule^F
colonna^F vertebrale

olfactory bulb
bulbo^M olfativo
bulbe^M olfactif
Riechkapsel^F
bulbo^M olfattorio

muscle segment
segmento^M muscular
myomère^M
Muskelblock^M
segmento^M muscolare

tongue
lengua^F
langue^F
Zunge^F
lingua^F

urogenital aperture
apertura^F urogenital
orifice^M uro-génital
Urogenital-Öffnung^F
seno^M urogenitale

ventral aorta
aorta^F ventral
aorte^F ventrale
ventrale Aorta^F
aorta^F ventrale

stomach
estómago^M
estomac^M
Magen^M
stomaco^M

anus
ano^M
anus^M
After^M
ano^M

gills
branquias^F
branchies^F
Kiemen^F
branchie^F

intestine
intestino^M
intestin^M
Darm^M
intestino^M

ovary
hueva^F
œufs^M
Eier^N
uova^M

heart
corazón^M
cœur^M
Herz^N
cuore^M

spleen
bazo^M
rate^F
Milz^F
milza^F

esophagus
esófago^M
œsophage^M
Speiseröhre^F
esofago^M

pyloric cecum
ciego^M pilórico
cæcum^M pylorique
pylorische Blindsäcke^M
cieco^M pilorico

liver
hígado^M
foie^M
Leber^F
fegato^M

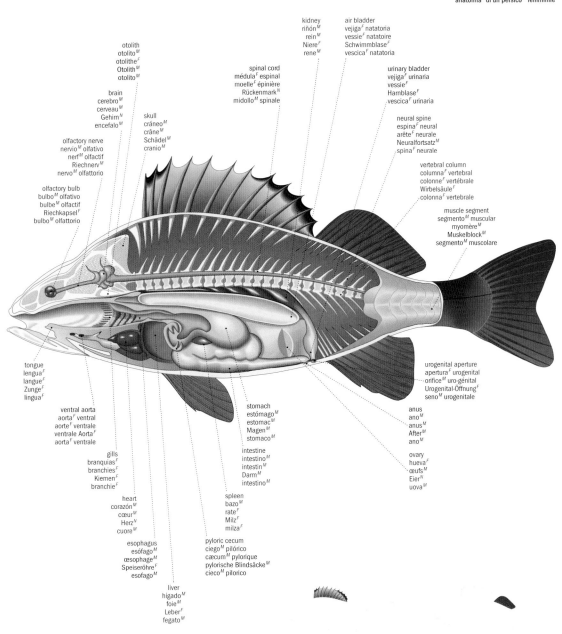

first dorsal fin
aleta^F dorsal anterior
première nageoire^F dorsale
erste Rückenflosse^F
prima pinna^F dorsale

second dorsal fin
aleta^F dorsal posterior
seconde nageoire^F dorsale
zweite Rückenflosse^F
seconda pinna^F dorsale

frog

rana^F | grenouille^F | Frosch^M | rana^F

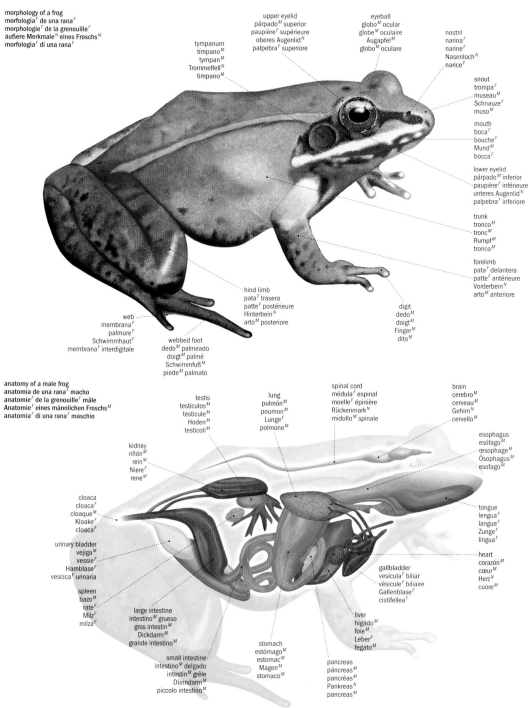

morphology of a frog
morfología^F de una rana^F
morphologie^F de la grenouille^F
äußere Merkmale^N eines Froschs^M
morfologia^F di una rana^F

tympanum
tímpano^M
tympan^M
Trommelfell^N
timpano^M

upper eyelid
párpado^M superior
paupière^F supérieure
oberes Augenlid^N
palpebra^F superiore

eyeball
globo^M ocular
globe^M oculaire
Augapfel^M
globo^M oculare

nostril
narina^F
narine^F
Nasenloch^N
narice^F

snout
trompa^F
museau^M
Schnauze^F
muso^M

mouth
boca^F
bouche^F
Mund^M
bocca^F

lower eyelid
párpado^M inferior
paupière^F inférieure
unteres Augenlid^N
palpebra^F inferiore

trunk
tronco^M
tronc^M
Rumpf^M
tronco^M

forelimb
pata^F delantera
patte^F antérieure
Vorderbein^N
arto^M anteriore

digit
dedo^M
doigt^M
Finger^M
dito^M

hind limb
pata^F trasera
patte^F postérieure
Hinterbein^N
arto^M posteriore

web
membrana^F
palmure^F
Schwimmhaut^F
membrana^F interdigitale

webbed foot
dedo^M palmeado
doigt^M palmé
Schwimmfuß^M
piede^M palmato

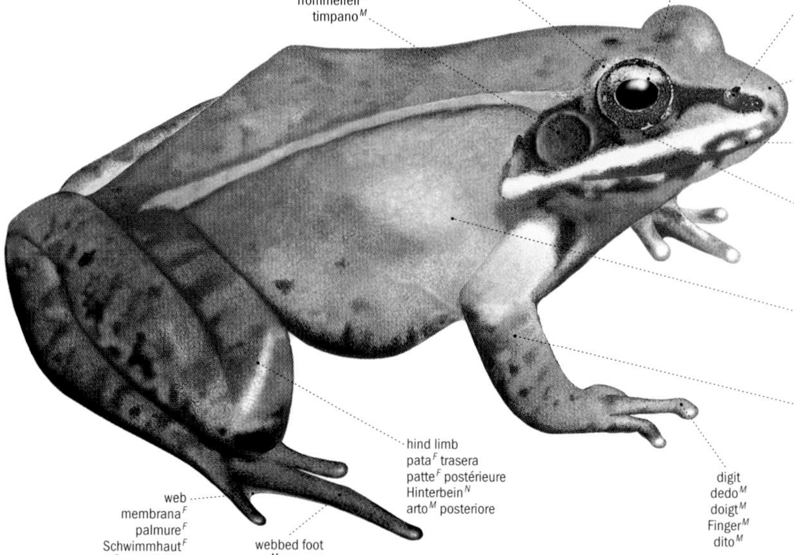

anatomy of a male frog
anatomía de una rana^F macho
anatomie^F de la grenouille^F mâle
Anatomie^F eines männlichen Froschs^M
anatomia^F di una rana^F maschio

testis
testículos^M
testicule^M
Hoden^M
testicoli^M

lung
pulmón^M
poumon^M
Lunge^F
polmone^M

spinal cord
médula^F espinal
moelle^F épinière
Rückenmark^N
midollo^M spinale

brain
cerebro^M
cerveau^M
Gehirn^N
cervello^M

esophagus
esófago^M
œsophage^M
Ösophagus^M
esofago^M

kidney
riñón^M
rein^M
Niere^F
rene^M

cloaca
cloaca^F
cloaque^M
Kloake^F
cloaca^F

tongue
lengua^F
langue^F
Zunge^F
lingua^F

urinary bladder
vejiga^M
vessie^F
Harnblase^F
vescica^F urinaria

heart
corazón^M
cœur^M
Herz^N
cuore^M

gallbladder
vesícula^F biliar
vésicule^F biliaire
Gallenblase^F
cistifellea^F

spleen
bazo^M
rate^F
Milz^F
milza^F

large intestine
intestino^M grueso
gros intestin^M
Dickdarm^M
grande intestino^M

liver
hígado^M
foie^M
Leber^F
fegato^M

small intestine
intestino^M delgado
intestin^M grêle
Dünndarm^M
piccolo intestino^M

stomach
estómago^M
estomac^M
Magen^M
stomaco^M

pancreas
páncreas^M
pancréas^M
Pankreas^N
pancreas^M

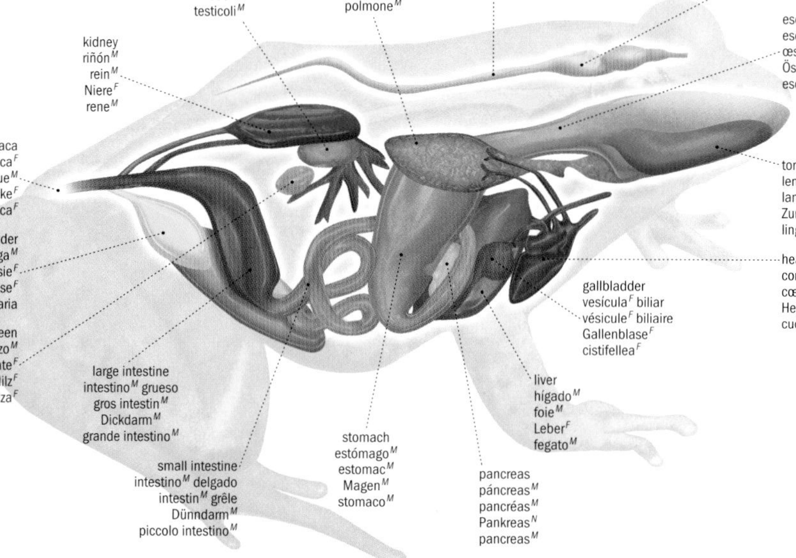

ANIMAL KINGDOM

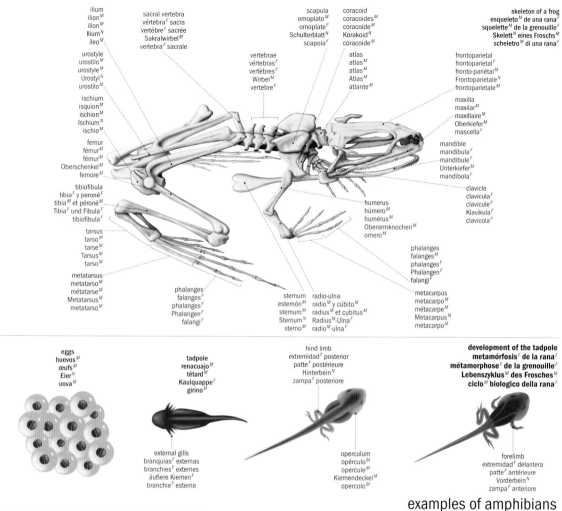

ilium
ilion ^{M}
ilion ^{M}
Ilium ^{N}
ileo ^{M}

sacral vertebra
vértebra ^{F} sacra
vertèbre ^{F} sacrée
Sakralwirbel ^{M}
vertebra ^{F} sacrale

scapula
omoplato ^{M}
omoplate ^{F}
Schulterblatt ^{M}
scapola ^{F}

coracoid
coracoides ^{M}
coracoïde ^{F}
Korakoid ^{N}
coracoide ^{N}

skeleton of a frog
esqueleto ^{M} de una rana ^{F}
squelette ^{M} de la grenouille ^{F}
Skelett ^{N} eines Froschs ^{M}
scheletro ^{M} di una rana ^{F}

urostyle
urostilo ^{M}
urostyle ^{M}
Urostyl ^{N}
urostilo ^{M}

vertebrae
vértebras ^{F}
vertèbres ^{F}
Wirbel ^{M}
vertebre ^{F}

atlas
atlas ^{M}
atlas ^{M}
Atlas ^{M}
atlante ^{M}

frontoparietal
frontoparietal ^{F}
fronto-pariétal ^{M}
Frontoparietale ^{N}
frontoparietale ^{M}

ischium
isquion ^{M}
ischion ^{M}
Ischium ^{N}
ischio ^{M}

maxilla
maxilar ^{M}
maxillaire ^{F}
Oberkiefer ^{M}
mascella ^{F}

femur
fémur ^{M}
fémur ^{M}
Oberschenkel ^{M}
femore ^{M}

mandible
mandibula ^{F}
mandibule ^{F}
Unterkiefer ^{M}
mandibola ^{F}

tibiofibula
tibia ^{F} y peroné ^{F}
tibia ^{M} et péroné ^{M}
Tibia ^{F} und Fibula ^{F}
tibiofibula ^{F}

clavicle
clavícula ^{F}
clavicule ^{F}
Klavikula ^{F}
clavicola ^{F}

humerus
húmero ^{M}
humérus ^{M}
Oberarmknochen ^{M}
omero ^{M}

tarsus
tarso ^{M}
tarse ^{M}
Tarsus ^{M}
tarso ^{M}

phalanges
falanges ^{M}
phalanges ^{F}
Phalangen ^{F}
falangi ^{F}

metatarsus
metatarso ^{M}
métatarse ^{M}
Metatarsus ^{M}
metatarso ^{M}

phalanges
falanges ^{F}
phalanges ^{F}
Phalangen ^{F}
falangi ^{F}

sternum
estemón ^{M}
sternum ^{M}
Sternum ^{N}
sterno ^{M}

radio-ulna
radio ^{M} y cúbito ^{M}
radius ^{M} et cubitus ^{M}
Radius ^{M}-Ulna ^{F}
radio ^{M}-ulna ^{F}

metacarpus
metacarpo ^{M}
métacarpe ^{M}
Metacarpus ^{M}
metacarpo ^{M}

---

eggs
huevos ^{M}
œufs ^{M}
Eier ^{N}
uova ^{M}

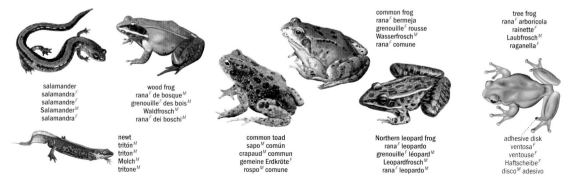

tadpole
renacuajo ^{M}
têtard ^{M}
Kaulquappe ^{F}
girino ^{M}

hind limb
extremidad ^{F} posterior
patte ^{F} postérieure
Hinterbein ^{N}
zampa ^{F} posteriore

development of the tadpole
metamórfosis ^{F} de la rana ^{F}
métamorphose ^{F} de la grenouille ^{F}
Lebenszyklus ^{M} des Frosches ^{M}
ciclo ^{M} biologico della rana ^{F}

external gills
branquias ^{F} externas
branchies ^{F} externes
äußere Kiemen ^{F}
branchie ^{F} esterne

operculum
opérculo ^{M}
opercule ^{M}
Kiemendeckel ^{M}
opercolo ^{M}

forelimb
extremidad ^{F} delantera
patte ^{F} antérieure
Vorderbein ^{N}
zampa ^{F} anteriore

examples of amphibians

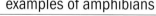

ejemplos ^{M} de anfibios ^{M} | exemples ^{M} d'amphibiens ^{M} | Beispiele ^{N} für Amphibien ^{F} | esempi ^{M} di anfibi ^{M}

common frog
rana ^{F} bermeja
grenouille ^{F} rousse
Wasserfrosch ^{M}
rana ^{F} comune

tree frog
rana ^{F} arborícola
rainette ^{F}
Laubfrosch ^{M}
raganella ^{F}

salamander
salamandra ^{F}
salamandre ^{F}
Salamander ^{M}
salamandra ^{F}

wood frog
rana ^{F} de bosque ^{M}
grenouille ^{F} des bois ^{M}
Waldfrosch ^{M}
rana ^{F} dei boschi ^{M}

newt
tritón ^{M}
triton ^{M}
Molch ^{M}
tritone ^{M}

common toad
sapo ^{M} común
crapaud ^{M} commun
gemeine Erdkröte ^{F}
rospo ^{M} comune

Northern leopard frog
rana ^{F} leopardo
grenouille ^{F} léopard ^{M}
Leopardfrosch ^{M}
rana ^{F} leopardo ^{M}

adhesive disk
ventosa ^{F}
ventouse ^{F}
Haftscheibe ^{F}
disco ^{M} adesivo

snake

serpiente[M] | serpent[M] | Schlange[F] | serpente[M]

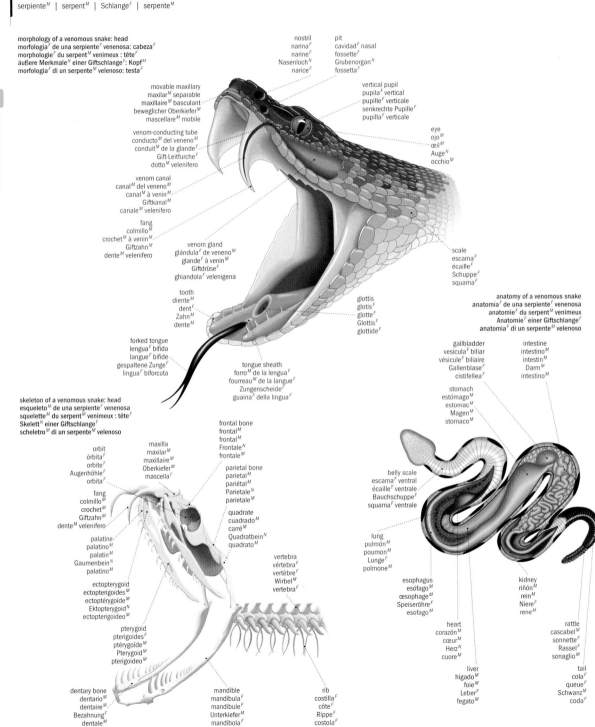

morphology of a venomous snake: head
morfología[F] de una serpiente[F] venenosa: cabeza[F]
morphologie[F] du serpent[M] venimeux : tête[F]
äußere Merkmale[N] einer Giftschlange[F]: Kopf[M]
morfologia[F] di un serpente[M] velenoso: testa[F]

nostril
narina[F]
narine[F]
Nasenloch[N]
narice[F]

pit
cavidad[F] nasal
fossette[F]
Grubenorgan[N]
fossetta[F]

movable maxillary
maxilar[M] separable
maxillaire[M] basculant
beweglicher Oberkiefer[M]
mascellare[M] mobile

vertical pupil
pupila[F] vertical
pupille[F] verticale
senkrechte Pupille[F]
pupilla[F] verticale

eye
ojo[M]
œil[M]
Auge[N]
occhio[M]

venom-conducting tube
conducto[M] del veneno[M]
conduit[M] de la glande[F]
Gift-Leitfurche[F]
dotto[M] velenifero

scale
escama[F]
écaille[F]
Schuppe[F]
squama[F]

venom canal
canal[M] del veneno[M]
canal[M] à venin[M]
Giftkanal[M]
canale[M] velenifero

fang
colmillo[M]
crochet[M] à venin[M]
Giftzahn[M]
dente[M] velenifero

venom gland
glándula[F] de veneno[M]
glande[F] à venin[M]
Giftdrüse[F]
ghiandola[F] velenigena

glottis
glotis[F]
glotte[F]
Glottis[F]
glottide[F]

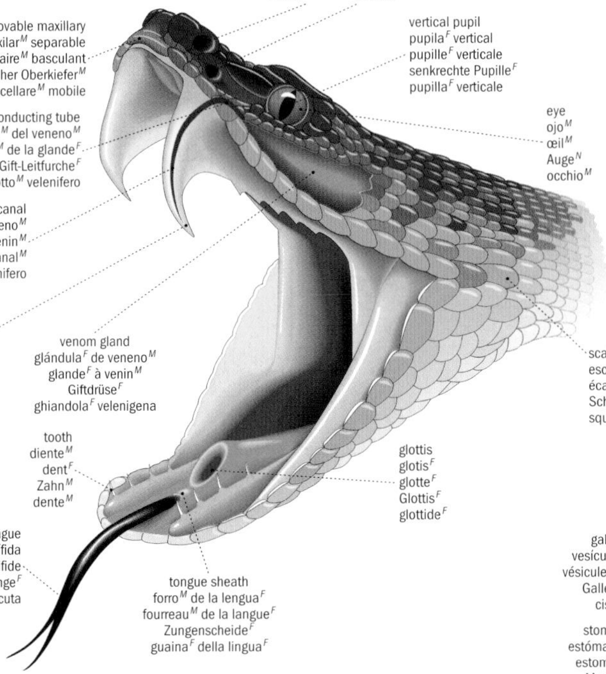

anatomy of a venomous snake
anatomía[F] de una serpiente[F] venenosa
anatomie[F] du serpent[M] venimeux
Anatomie[F] einer Giftschlange[F]
anatomia[F] di un serpente[M] velenoso

tooth
diente[M]
dent[F]
Zahn[M]
dente[M]

gallbladder
vesícula[F] biliar
vésicule[F] biliaire
Gallenblase[F]
cistifellea[F]

intestine
intestino[M]
intestin[M]
Darm[M]
intestino[M]

forked tongue
lengua[F] bífida
langue[F] bifide
gespaltene Zunge[F]
lingua[F] biforcuta

tongue sheath
forro[M] de la lengua[F]
fourreau[M] de la langue[F]
Zungenscheide[F]
guaina[F] della lingua[F]

stomach
estómago[M]
estomac[M]
Magen[M]
stomaco[M]

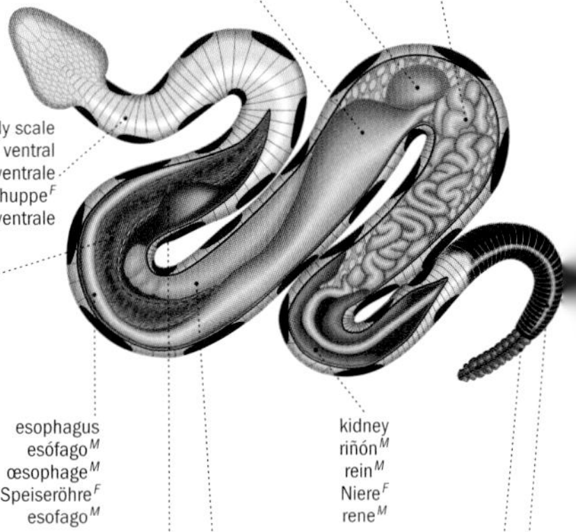

skeleton of a venomous snake: head
esqueleto[M] de una serpiente[F] venenosa
squelette[M] du serpent[M] venimeux : tête[F]
Skelett[N] einer Giftschlange[F]
scheletro[M] di un serpente[M] velenoso

frontal bone
frontal[M]
frontal[M]
Frontale[N]
frontale[M]

orbit
órbita[F]
orbite[F]
Augenhöhle[F]
orbita[F]

maxilla
maxilar[M]
maxillaire[M]
Oberkiefer[M]
mascella[F]

parietal bone
parietal[M]
pariétal[M]
Parietale[N]
parietale[M]

belly scale
escama[F] ventral
écaille[F] ventrale
Bauchschuppe[F]
squama[F] ventrale

fang
colmillo[M]
crochet[M]
Giftzahn[M]
dente[M] velenifero

quadrate
cuadrado[M]
carré[M]
Quadratbein[N]
quadrato[M]

lung
pulmón[M]
poumon[M]
Lunge[F]
polmone[M]

palatine
palatino[M]
palatin[M]
Gaumenbein[N]
palatino[M]

vertebra
vértebra[F]
vertèbre[F]
Wirbel[M]
vertebra[F]

esophagus
esófago[M]
œsophage[M]
Speiseröhre[F]
esofago[M]

kidney
riñón[M]
rein[M]
Niere[F]
rene[M]

ectopterygoid
ectopterigoides[M]
ectoptérygoïde[M]
Ektopterygoid[N]
ectopterigoideo[M]

pterygoid
pterigoides[F]
ptérygoïde[M]
Pterygoid[N]
pterigoideo[M]

heart
corazón[M]
cœur[M]
Herz[N]
cuore[M]

rattle
cascabel[M]
sonnette[F]
Rassel[F]
sonaglio[M]

dentary bone
dentario[M]
dentaire[F]
Bezahnung[F]
dentale[M]

mandible
mandíbula[F]
mandibule[F]
Unterkiefer[M]
mandibola[F]

rib
costilla[F]
côte[F]
Rippe[F]
costola[F]

liver
hígado[M]
foie[M]
Leber[F]
fegato[M]

tail
cola[F]
queue[F]
Schwanz[M]
coda[F]

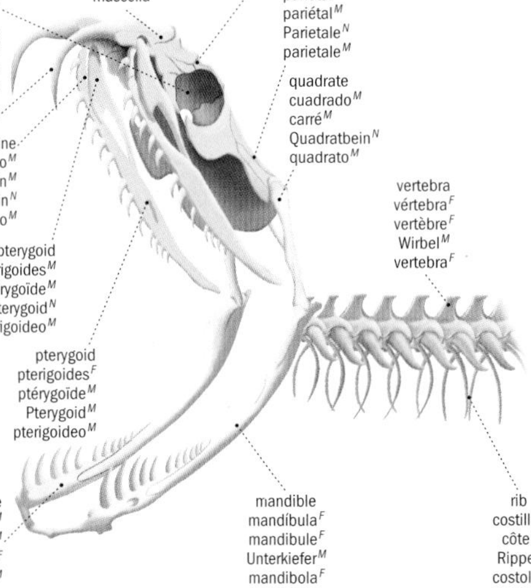

turtle

tortuga^F | tortue^F | Schildkröte^F | tartaruga^F

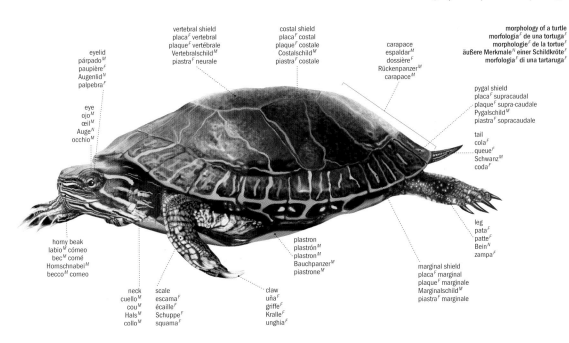

morphology of a turtle
morfología^F de una tortuga^F
morphologie^F de la tortue^F
äußere Merkmale^N einer Schildkröte^F
morfologia^F di una tartaruga^F

vertebral shield
placa^F vertebral
plaque^F vertébrale
Vertebralschild^M
piastra^F neurale

costal shield
placa^F costal
plaque^F costale
Costalschild^M
piastra^F costale

carapace
espaldar^M
dossière^F
Rückenpanzer^M
carapace^M

eyelid
párpado^M
paupière^F
Augenlid^N
palpebra^F

eye
ojo^M
œil^M
Auge^N
occhio^M

pygal shield
placa^F supracaudal
plaque^F supra-caudale
Pygalschild^M
piastra^F sopracaudale

tail
cola^F
queue^F
Schwanz^M
coda^F

leg
pata^F
patte^F
Bein^N
zampa^F

horny beak
labio^M córneo
bec^M corné
Hornschnabel^M
becco^M corneo

plastron
plastrón^M
plastron^M
Bauchpanzer^M
piastrone^M

marginal shield
placa^F marginal
plaque^F marginale
Marginalschild^M
piastra^F marginale

neck
cuello^M
cou^M
Hals^M
collo^M

scale
escama^F
écaille^F
Schuppe^F
squama^F

claw
uña^F
griffe^F
Kralle^F
unghia^F

ANIMAL KINGDOM

female turtle: digestive system
anatomía^F de una tortuga^F
anatomie^F de la tortue^F
Anatomie^F einer Schildkröte^F
anatomia^F di una tartaruga^F

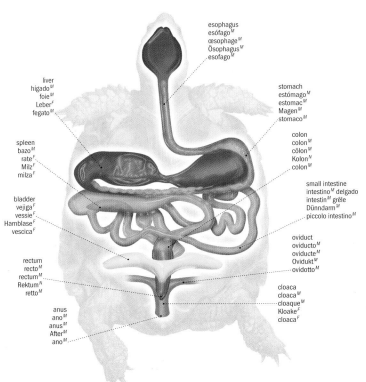

esophagus
esófago^M
œsophage^M
Ösophagus^M
esofago^M

liver
higado^M
foie^M
Leber^F
fegato^M

stomach
estómago^M
estomac^M
Magen^M
stomaco^M

spleen
bazo^M
rate^F
Milz^F
milza^F

colon
colon^M
côlon^M
Kolon^N
colon^M

bladder
vejiga^F
vessie^F
Harnblase^F
vescica^F

small intestine
intestino^M delgado
intestin^M grêle
Dünndarm^M
piccolo intestino^M

rectum
recto^M
rectum^M
Rektum^N
retto^M

oviduct
oviducto^M
oviducte^F
Ovidukt^M
ovidotto^M

cloaca
cloaca^F
cloaque^M
Kloake^F
cloaca^F

anus
ano^M
anus^M
After^M
ano^M

examples of reptiles

ejemplos^M de reptiles^M | exemples^M de reptiles^M | Beispiele^N für Reptilien^N | esempi^M di rettili^M

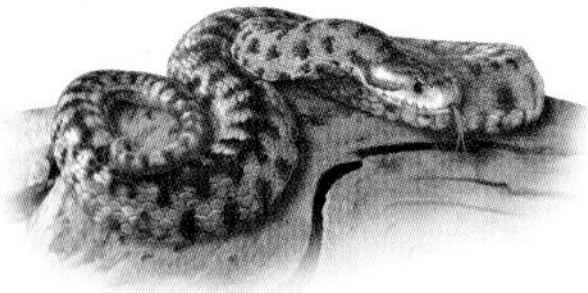

viper
vibora^F
vipère^F
Viper^F
vipera^F

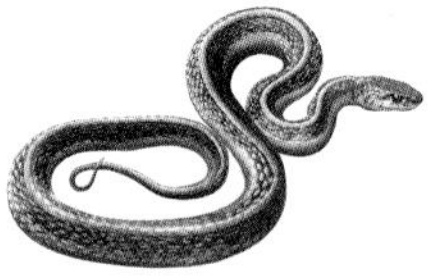

garter snake
serpiente^F de jarretera^F
couleuvre^F rayée
Ringelnatter^F
serpente^M giarrettiera^F

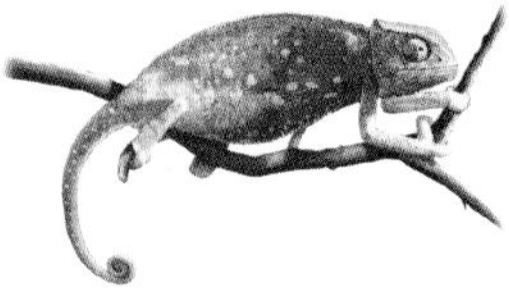

chameleon
camaleón^M
caméléon^M
Chamäleon^N
camaleonte^M

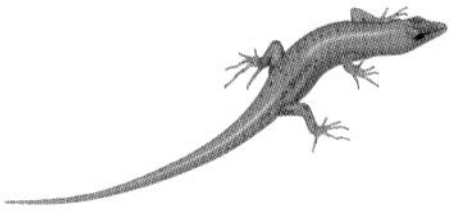

lizard
lagarto^M
lézard^M
Eidechse^F
lucertola^F

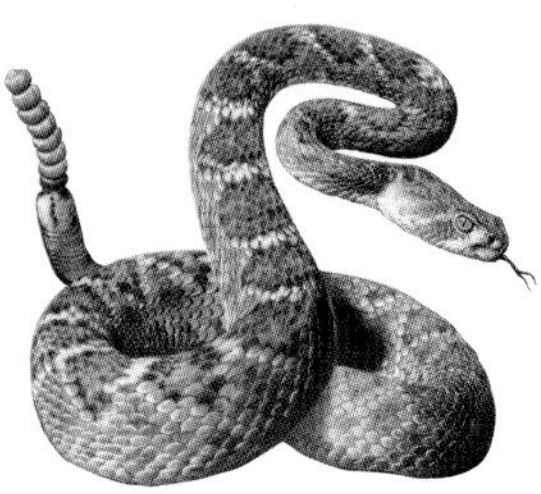

rattlesnake
serpiente^F de cascabel^M
serpent^M à sonnette^F
Klapperschlange^F
serpente^M a sonagli^M

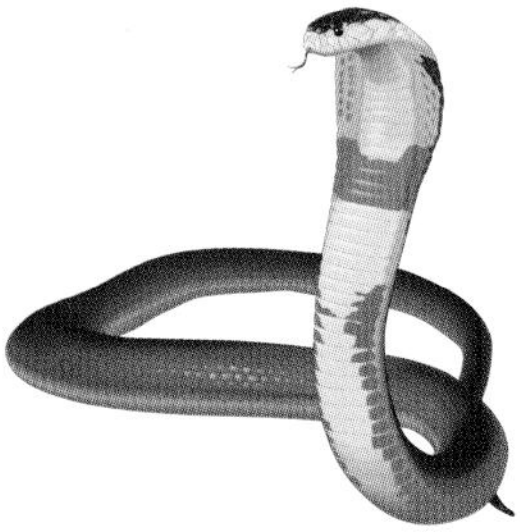

cobra
cobra^F
cobra^M
Kobra^F
cobra^M

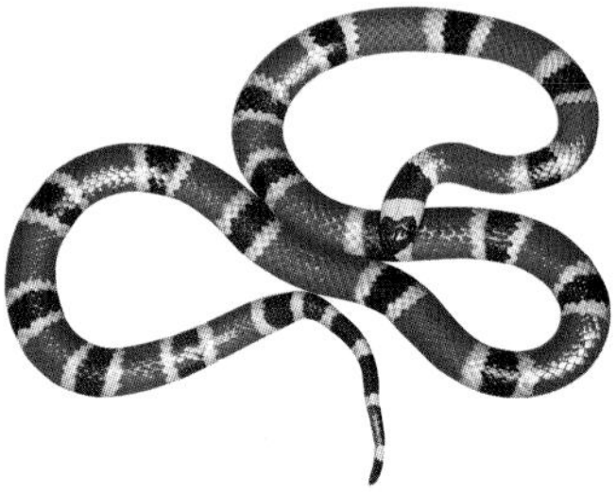

coral snake
serpiente^F coral
serpent^M corail^M
Korallennatter^F
serpente^M corallo^M

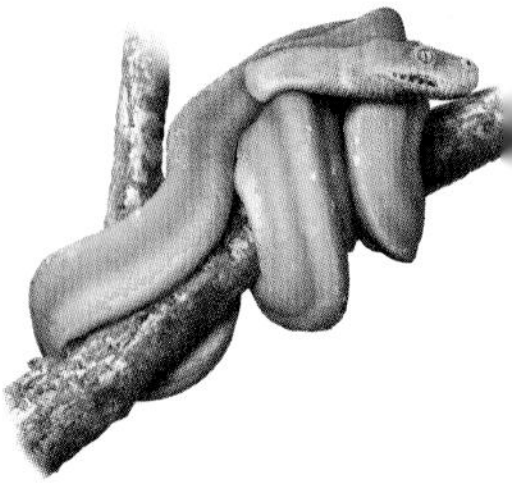

python
pitón^F
python^M
Python^M
pitone^M

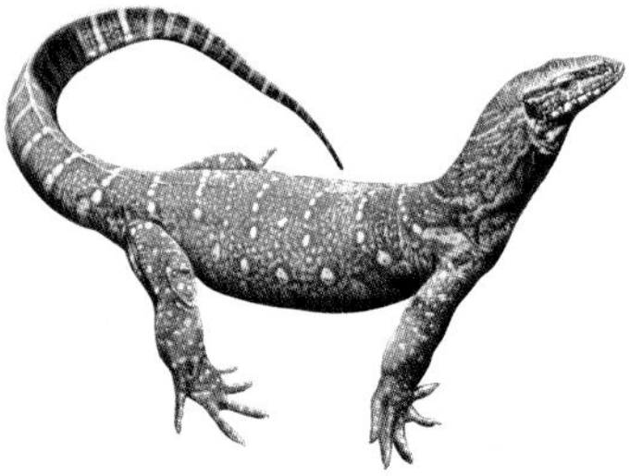

monitor lizard
varano^M
varan^M
Waran^M
varano^M

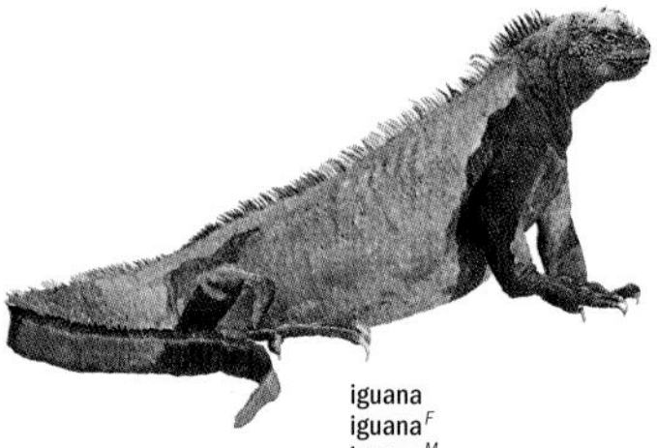

iguana
iguana^F
iguane^M
Leguan^M
iguana^F

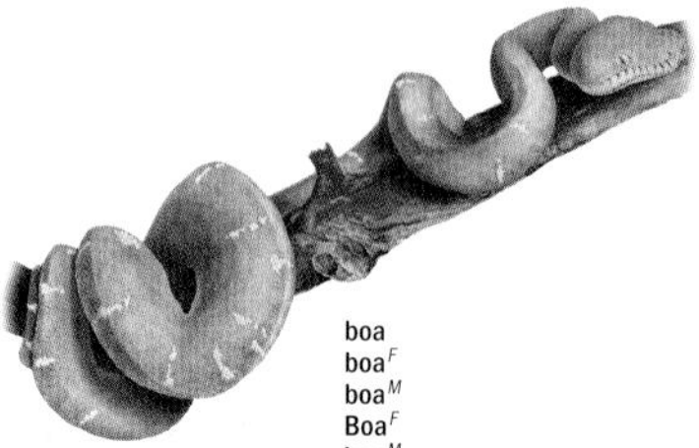

boa
boa^F
boa^M
Boa^F
boa^M

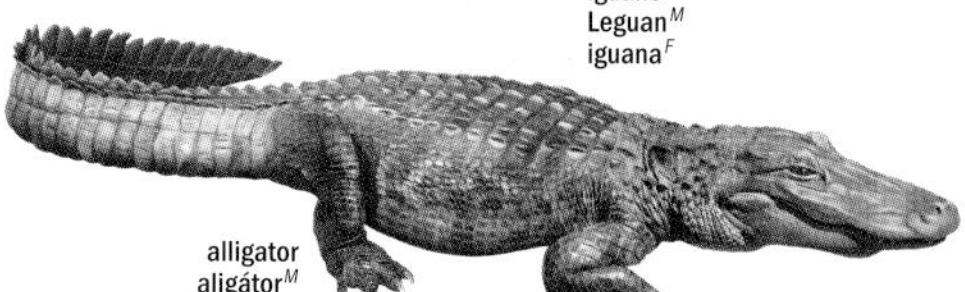

alligator
aligátor^M
alligator^M
Alligator^M
alligatore^M

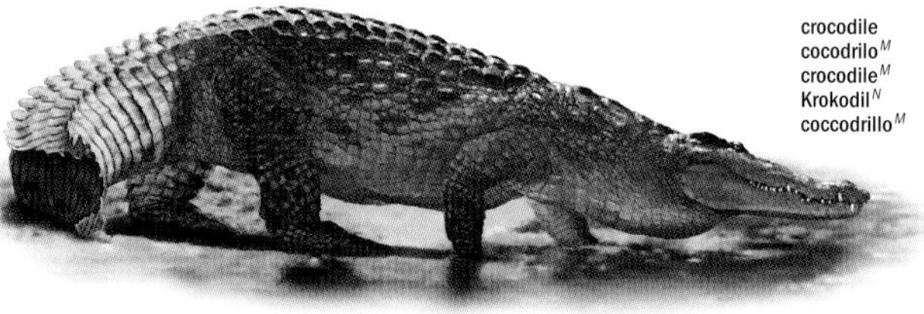

crocodile
cocodrilo^M
crocodile^M
Krokodil^N
coccodrillo^M

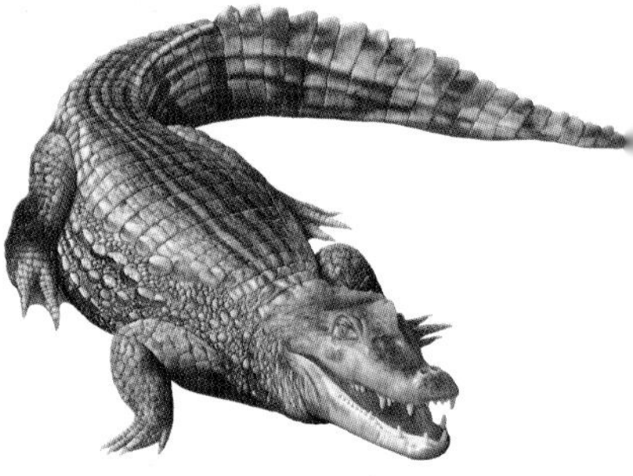

caiman
caimán^M
caïman^M
Kaiman^M
caimano^M

ANIMAL KINGDOM

morphology of a bird
morfología^F de un pájaro^M
morphologie^F de l'oiseau^M
äußere Merkmale^N eines Vogels^M
morfologia^F di un uccello^M

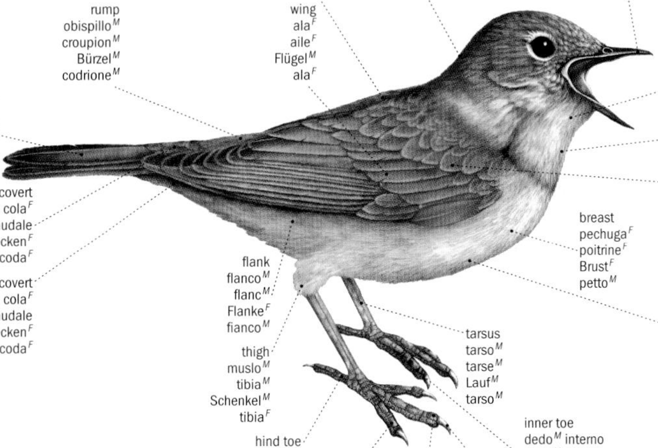

back
lomo^M
dos^M
Rücken^M
dorso^M

nape
cerviz^F
nuque^F
Nacken^M
nuca^F

bill
pico^M
bec^M
Schnabel^M
becco^M

rump
obispillo^M
croupion^M
Bürzel^M
codrione^M

wing
ala^F
aile^F
Flügel^M
ala^F

chin
mentón^M
menton^M
Kinn^N
mento^M

tail feather
plumas^F timoneras
rectrice^F
Schwanzfeder^F
penna^F timoniera

throat
garganta^F
gorge^F
Kehle^F
gola^F

upper tail covert
cobertera^F superior de la cola^F
tectrice^F sus-caudale
Oberschwanzdecken^F
penna^F copritrice superiore della coda^F

wing covert
coberteras^F
tectrice^F sus-alaire
Deckfeder^F
penna^F copritrice

under tail covert
cobertera^F inferior de la cola^F
tectrice^F sous-caudale
Unterschwanzdecken^F
penna^F copritrice inferiore della coda^F

flank
flanco^M
flanc^M
Flanke^F
fianco^M

breast
pechuga^F
poitrine^F
Brust^F
petto^M

abdomen
abdomen^M
abdomen^M
Bauch^M
addome^M

thigh
muslo^M
tibia^M
Schenkel^M
tibia^F

tarsus
tarso^M
tarse^F
Lauf^M
tarso^M

inner toe
dedo^M interno
doigt^M interne
zweite Zehe^F
dito^M interno

hind toe
dedo^M posterior
doigt^M postérieur
Hinterzehe^F
dito^M posteriore

contour feather
pluma^F
penne^F
Konturfeder^F
penna^F del contorno^M

outer toe
dedo^M externo
doigt^M externe
vierte Zehe^F
dito^M esterno

middle toe
dedo^M medio
doigt^M médian
dritte Zehe^F
dito^M medio

claw
uña^F
griffe^F
Kralle^F
unghia^F

head
cabeza^F
tête^F
Kopf^M
capo^M

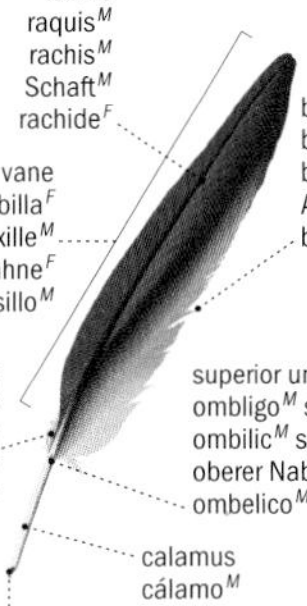

rachis
raquis^M
rachis^M
Schaft^M
rachide^F

barb
barba^F
barbe^F
Ast^M
barba^F

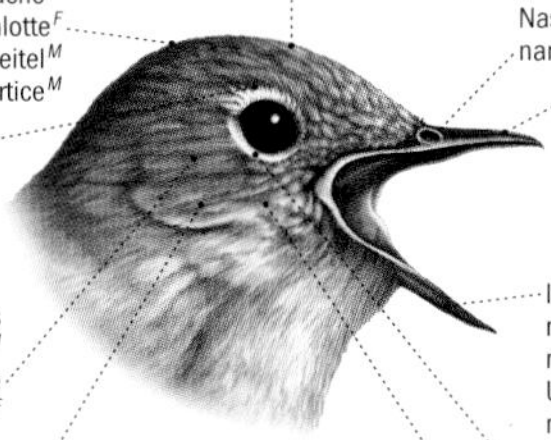

forehead
frente^F
front^M
Stirn^F
fronte^F

nostril
narina^F
narine^F
Nasenloch^N
narice^F

vane
barbilla^F
vexille^M
Fahne^F
vessillo^M

crown
penacho^M
calotte^F
Scheitel^M
vertice^M

upper mandible
mandíbula^F superior
maxillaire^M supérieur
Oberschnabel^M
mandibola^F superiore

eyebrow stripe
lista^F superciliar
raie^F sourcilière
Augenstreif^M
fascia^F sopracigliare

afterfeather
plumón^M
duvet^M
Afterfeder^F
iporachide^F

superior umbilicus
ombligo^M superior
ombilic^M supérieur
oberer Nabel^M
ombelico^M superiore

lower mandible
mandíbula^F inferior
mandibule^F
Unterschnabel^M
mandibola^F inferiore

auriculars
auriculares^M
région^F auriculaire
Ohrdecken^F
regione^F auricolare

calamus
cálamo^M
calamus^M
Spule^F
calamo^M

malar region
región^F malar
région^F malaire
Bartregion^F
regione^F malare

lore
puente^M
lorum^M
Zügel^M
redine^F

eye ring
anillo^M ocular
anneau^M oculaire
Augenring^M
anello^M oculare

inferior umbilicus
ombligo^M inferior
ombilic^M inférieur
unterer Nabel^M
ombelico^M inferiore

wing
ala^F
aile^F
Flügel^M
ala^F

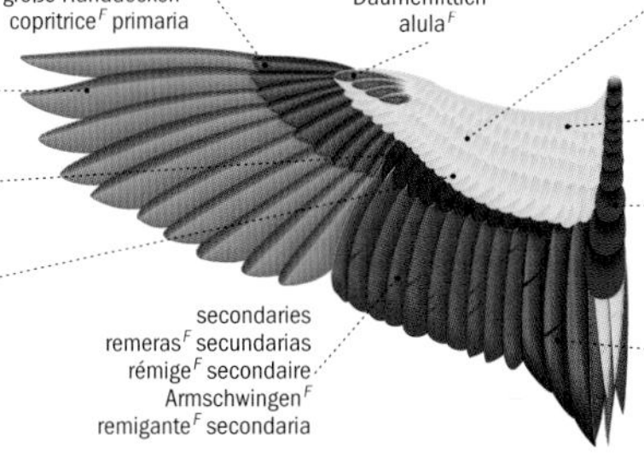

primary covert
coberteras^F primarias
tectrice^F primaire
große Handdecken^F
copritrice^F primaria

alula
álula^F
alule^F
Daumenfittich^M
alula^F

middle covert
coberteras^F medias
moyenne sus-alaire^F
mittlere Armdecken^F
copritrice^F secondaria mediana

primaries
remeras^F primarias
rémige^F primaire
Handschwingen^F
remigante^F primaria

lesser covert
coberteras^F menores
petite sus-alaire^F
kleine Armdecken^F
piccola copritrice^F secondaria

middle primary covert
coberteras^F primarias medias
moyenne tectrice^F primaire
mittlere Handdecken^F
copritrice^F primaria media

scapular
escapulares^M
scapulaire^F
Schulterfeder^F
scapolare^F

greater covert
coberteras^F mayores
grande sus-alaire^F
große Armdecken^F
grande copritrice^F secondaria

secondaries
remeras^F secundarias
rémige^F secondaire
Armschwingen^F
remigante^F secondaria

tertial
remeras^F terciarias
rémige^F tertiaire
Schirmfeder^F
remigante^F terziaria

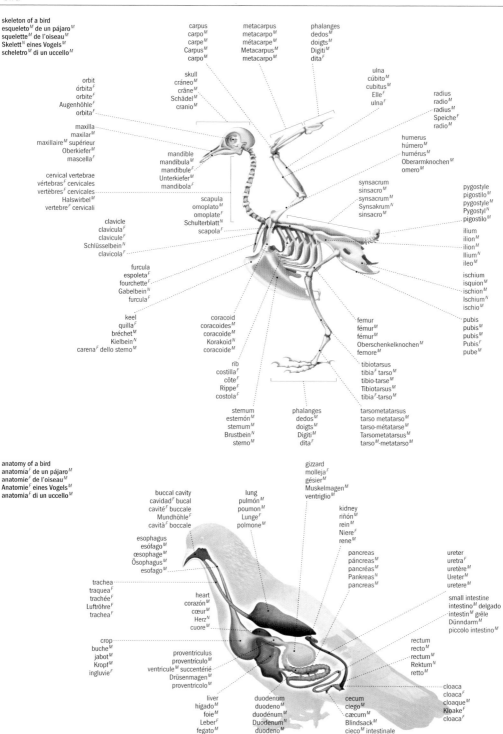

skeleton of a bird
esqueleto^M de un pájaro^M
squelette^M de l'oiseau^M
Skelett^N eines Vogels^M
scheletro^M di un uccello^M

carpus
carpo^M
carpe^F
Carpus^M
carpo^M

metacarpus
metacarpo^M
métacarpe^M
Metacarpus^M
metacarpo^M

phalanges
dedos^M
doigts^M
Digiti^M
dita^F

ulna
cúbito^M
cubitus^M
Elle^F
ulna^F

radius
radio^M
radius^M
Speiche^F
radio^M

orbit
órbita^F
orbite^F
Augenhöhle^F
orbita^F

skull
cráneo^M
crâne^M
Schädel^M
cranio^M

humerus
húmero^M
humérus^M
Oberarmknochen^M
omero^M

maxilla
maxilar^M
maxillaire^M supérieur
Oberkiefer^M
mascella^F

mandible
mandíbula^M
mandibule^F
Unterkiefer^M
mandibola^F

synsacrum
sinsacro^M
synsacrum^M
Synsakrum^N
sinsacro^M

pygostyle
pigostilo^M
pygostyle^M
Pygostyl^N
pigostilo^M

cervical vertebrae
vértebras^F cervicales
vertèbres^F cervicales
Halswirbel^M
vertebre^F cervicali

scapula
omóplato^M
omoplate^F
Schulterblatt^N
scapola^F

ilium
ilion^M
ilion^M
Ilium^N
ileo^M

clavicle
clavícula^F
clavicule^F
Schlüsselbein^N
clavicola^F

ischium
isquion^M
ischion^M
Ischium^N
ischio^M

furcula
espoleta^F
fourchette^F
Gabelbein^N
furcula^F

keel
quilla^F
bréchet^M
Kielbein^N
carena^F dello sterno^M

coracoid
coracoides^M
coracoïde^M
Korakoid^N
coracoide^M

femur
fémur^M
fémur^M
Oberschenkelknochen^M
femore^M

pubis
pubis^M
pubis^M
Pubis^F
pube^M

rib
costilla^F
côte^F
Rippe^F
costola^F

tibiotarsus
tibia^F tarso^M
tibio-tarse^M
Tibiotarsus^M
tibia^F-tarso^M

sternum
esternón^M
sternum^M
Brustbein^N
sterno^M

phalanges
dedos^M
doigts^M
Digiti^M
dita^F

tarsometatarsus
tarso metatarso^M
tarso-métatarse^M
Tarsometatarsus^M
tarso^M-metatarso^M

anatomy of a bird
anatomía^F de un pájaro^M
anatomie^F de l'oiseau^M
Anatomie^F eines Vogels^M
anatomia^F di un uccello^M

gizzard
molleja^F
gésier^M
Muskelmagen^M
ventriglio^M

buccal cavity
cavidad^F bucal
cavité^F buccale
Mundhöhle^F
cavità^F boccale

lung
pulmón^M
poumon^M
Lunge^F
polmone^M

kidney
riñón^M
rein^M
Niere^F
rene^M

esophagus
esófago^M
œsophage^M
Ösophagus^M
esofago^M

pancreas
páncreas^M
pancréas^M
Pankreas^N
pancreas^M

ureter
uretra^F
uretère^M
Ureter^M
uretere^M

trachea
tráquea^F
trachée^F
Luftröhre^F
trachea^F

heart
corazón^M
cœur^M
Herz^N
cuore^M

small intestine
intestino^M delgado
intestin^M grêle
Dünndarm^M
piccolo intestino^M

crop
buche^M
jabot^M
Kropf^M
ingluvie^F

proventriculus
proventrículo^M
ventricule^M succentérié
Drüsenmagen^M
proventricolo^M

rectum
recto^M
rectum^M
Rektum^N
retto^M

liver
hígado^M
foie^M
Leber^F
fegato^M

duodenum
duodeno^M
duodénum^M
Duodenum^N
duodeno^M

cecum
ciego^M
cæcum^M
Blindsack^M
cieco^M intestinale

cloaca
cloaca^F
cloaque^F
Kloake^F
cloaca^F

ANIMAL KINGDOM

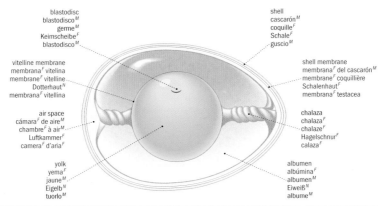

blastodisc
blastodisco[M]
germe[F]
Keimscheibe[F]
blastodisco[M]

shell
cascarón[M]
coquille[F]
Schale[F]
guscio[M]

egg
huevo[M]
œuf[M]
Ei[N]
uovo[M]

vitelline membrane
membrana[F] vitelina
membrane[F] vitelline
Dotterhaut[N]
membrana[F] vitellina

shell membrane
membrana[F] del cascarón[M]
membrane[F] coquillière
Schalenhaut[F]
membrana[F] testacea

air space
cámara[F] de aire[M]
chambre[F] à air[M]
Luftkammer[F]
camera[F] d'aria[F]

chalaza
chalaza[F]
chalaze[F]
Hagelschnur[F]
calaza[F]

yolk
yema[F]
jaune[M]
Eigelb[N]
tuorlo[M]

albumen
albúmina[F]
albumen[M]
Eiweiß[N]
albume[M]

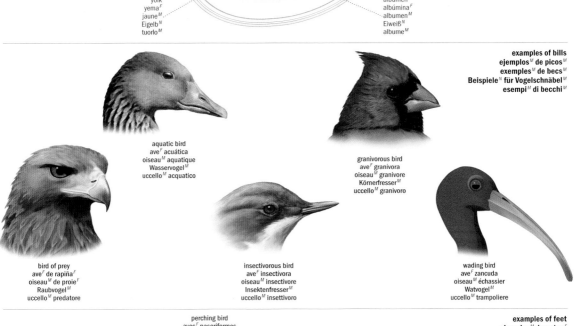

examples of bills
ejemplos[M] de picos[M]
exemples[M] de becs[M]
Beispiele[N] für Vogelschnäbel[M]
esempi[M] di becchi[M]

aquatic bird
ave[F] acuática
oiseau[M] aquatique
Wasservogel[M]
uccello[M] acquatico

granivorous bird
ave[F] granivora
oiseau[M] granivore
Körnerfresser[M]
uccello[M] granivoro

bird of prey
ave[F] de rapiña[F]
oiseau[M] de proie[F]
Raubvogel[M]
uccello[M] predatore

insectivorous bird
ave[F] insectivora
oiseau[M] insectivore
Insektenfresser[M]
uccello[M] insettivoro

wading bird
ave[F] zancuda
oiseau[M] échassier
Watvogel[M]
uccello[M] trampoliere

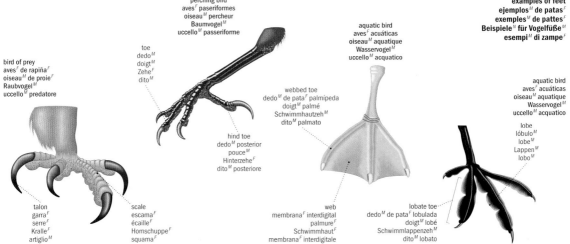

examples of feet
ejemplos[M] de patas[F]
exemples[M] de pattes[F]
Beispiele[N] für Vogelfüße[M]
esempi[M] di zampe[F]

perching bird
aves[F] paseriformes
oiseau[M] percheur
Baumvogel[M]
uccello[M] passeriforme

aquatic bird
aves[F] acuáticas
oiseau[M] aquatique
Wasservogel[M]
uccello[M] acquatico

bird of prey
aves[F] de rapiña[F]
oiseau[M] de proie[F]
Raubvogel[M]
uccello[M] predatore

aquatic bird
aves[F] acuáticas
oiseau[M] aquatique
Wasservogel[M]
uccello[M] acquatico

toe
dedo[M]
doigt[M]
Zehe[F]
dito[M]

webbed toe
dedo[M] de pata[F] palmípeda
doigt[M] palmé
Schwimmhautzeh[M]
dito[M] palmato

lobe
lóbulo[M]
lobe[M]
Lappen[M]
lobo[M]

hind toe
dedo[M] posterior
pouce[M]
Hinterzehe[F]
dito[M] posteriore

talon
garra[F]
serre[F]
Kralle[F]
artiglio[M]

scale
escama[F]
écaille[F]
Hornschuppe[F]
squama[F]

web
membrana[F] interdigital
palmure[F]
Schwimmhaut[F]
membrana[F] interdigitale

lobate toe
dedo[M] de pata[F] lobulada
doigt[M] lobé
Schwimmlappenzeh[M]
dito[M] lobato

examples of birds

ejemplos^M de pájaros^M | exemples^M d'oiseaux^M | unterschiedliche Vogeltypen^M | esempi^M di uccelli^M

ANIMAL KINGDOM

hummingbird
colibrí^M
colibri^M
Kolibri^M
colibri^M

European robin
petirrojo^M
rouge-gorge^M
Rotkehlchen^N
pettirosso^M

finch
pinzón^M
pinson^M
Fink^M
fringuello^M

goldfinch
jilguero^M
chardonneret^M
Stieglitz^M
cardellino^M

bullfinch
pardillo^M
bouvreuil^M
Gimpel^M
ciuffolotto^M

sparrow
gorrión^M
moineau^M
Sperling^M
passerotto^M

nightingale
ruiseñor^M
rossignol^M
Nachtigall^F
usignolo^M

swallow
golondrina^F
hirondelle^F
Schwalbe^F
rondine^F

kingfisher
martín^M pescador
martin-pêcheur^M
Eisvogel^M
martin pescatore^M

magpie
urraca^M
pie^F
Elster^F
gazza^F

cardinal
cardenal^M
cardinal^M
Kardinal^M
cardinale^M

jay
arrendajo^M
geai^M
Eichelhäher^M
ghiandaia^F

starling
estornino^M
étourneau^M
Star^M
stornello^M

swift
vencejo^M
martinet^M
Mauersegler^M
rondone^M

northern saw-whet owl
lechuza^F norteña
petite nyctale^F
Sägekauz^M
civetta^F acadica

partridge
perdiz^F
perdrix^F
Rebhuhn^N
pernice^F

lapwing
avefría^F
vanneau^M
Kiebitz^M
pavoncella^F

oystercatcher
ostrero^M
huitrier^M pie^F
Austernfischer^M
beccaccia^F di mare^M

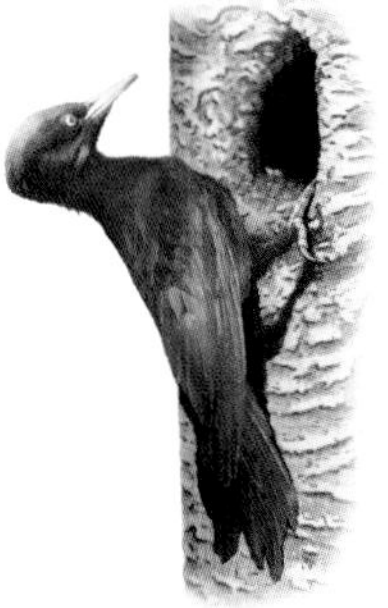

woodpecker
pájaro^M carpintero
pic^M
Specht^M
picchio^M

raven
cuervo^M
corbeau^M
Rabe^M
corvo^M

macaw
guacamayo^M
ara^M
Ara^M
macao^M

cockatoo
cacatúa^F
cacatoès^M
Kakadu^M
cacatua^M

tern
golondrina^F de mar
sterne^F
Seeschwalbe^F
rondine^F di mare^M

albatross
albatros^M
albatros^M
Albatros^M
albatros^M

toucan
tucán^M
toucan^M
Tukan^M
tucano^M

falcon
halcón^M
faucon^M
Falke^M
falco^M

great horned owl
búho^M real
grand duc^M d'Amérique^F
Uhu^M
gufo^M reale

heron
garza^F
héron^M
Reiher^M
airone^M

condor
cóndor^M
condor^M
Kondor^M
condor^M

eagle
águila^F
aigle^M
Adler^M
aquila^F

penguin
pingüino^M
manchot^M
Pinguin^M
pinguino^M

pelican
pelícano^M
pélican^M
Pelikan^M
pellicano^M

stork
cigüeña^F
cigogne^F
Storch^M
cicogna^F

vulture
buitre^M
vautour^M
Geier^M
avvoltoio^M

ostrich
avestruz^F
autruche^F
Strauß^M
struzzo^M

peacock
pavo^M real
paon^M
Pfau^M
pavone^M

flamingo
flamenco^M
flamant^M
Flamingo^M
fenicottero^M

examples of birds

chick
polluelo^M
poussin^M
Küken^N
pulcino^M

quail
codorniz^F
caille^F
Wachtel^F
quaglia^F

pigeon
paloma^F
pigeon^M
Taube^F
piccione^M

duck
pato^M
canard^M
Ente^F
anatra^F

hen
gallina^F
poule^F
Huhn^N
gallina^F

rooster
gallo^M
coq^M
Hahn^M
gallo^M

pheasant
faisán^M
faisan^M
Fasan^M
fagiano^M

guinea fowl
pintada^F
pintade^F
Perlhuhn^N
faraona^F

goose
oca^F
oie^F
Gans^F
oca^F

turkey
pavo^M
dindon^M
Truthahn^M
tacchino^M

mole

topo^M | taupe^F | Maulwurf^M | talpa^F

ANIMAL KINGDOM

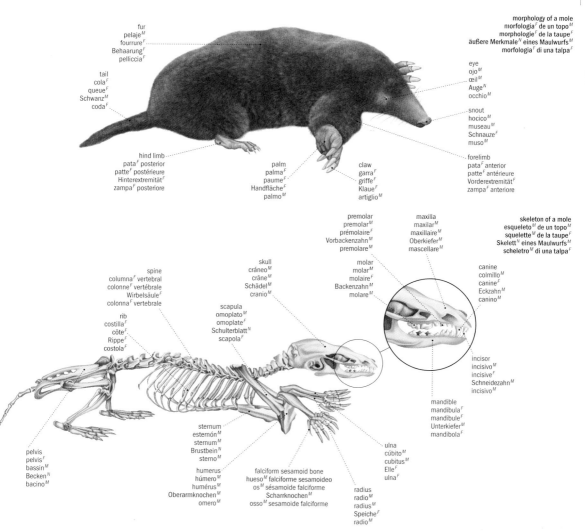

morphology of a mole
morfología^F de un topo^M
morphologie^F de la taupe^F
äußere Merkmale^N eines Maulwurfs^M
morfologia^F di una talpa^F

fur
pelaje^M
fourrure^F
Behaarung^F
pelliccia^F

eye
ojo^M
œil^M
Auge^N
occhio^M

tail
cola^F
queue^F
Schwanz^M
coda^F

snout
hocico^M
museau^M
Schnauze^F
muso^M

hind limb
pata^F posterior
patte^F postérieure
Hinterextremität^F
zampa^F posteriore

palm
palma^F
paume^F
Handfläche^F
palmo^M

claw
garra^F
griffe^F
Klaue^F
artiglio^M

forelimb
pata^F anterior
patte^F antérieure
Vorderextremität^F
zampa^F anteriore

premolar
premolar^M
prémolaire^F
Vorbackenzahn^M
premolare^M

maxilla
maxilar^M
maxillaire^M
Oberkiefer^M
mascellare^M

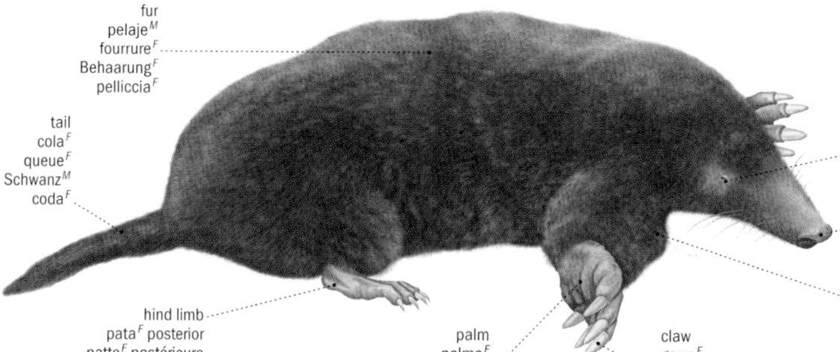

skeleton of a mole
esqueleto^M de un topo^M
squelette^M de la taupe^F
Skelett^N eines Maulwurfs^M
scheletro^M di una talpa^F

spine
columna^F vertebral
colonne^F vertébrale
Wirbelsäule^F
colonna^F vertebrale

skull
cráneo^M
crâne^M
Schädel^M
cranio^M

molar
molar^M
molaire^F
Backenzahn^M
molare^M

canine
colmillo^M
canine^F
Eckzahn^M
canino^M

scapula
omoplato^M
omoplate^F
Schulterblatt^N
scapola^F

rib
costilla^F
côte^F
Rippe^F
costola^F

incisor
incisivo^M
incisive^F
Schneidezahn^M
incisivo^M

mandible
mandíbula^F
mandibule^F
Unterkiefer^M
mandibola^F

pelvis
pelvis^F
bassin^M
Becken^N
bacino^M

sternum
esternón^M
sternum^M
Brustbein^N
sterno^M

ulna
cúbito^M
cubitus^M
Elle^F
ulna^F

humerus
húmero^M
humérus^M
Oberarmknochen^M
omero^M

falciform sesamoid bone
hueso^M falciforme sesamoideo
os^M sésamoïde falciforme
Scharrknochen^M
osso^M sesamoide falciforme

radius
radio^M
radius^M
Speiche^F
radio^M

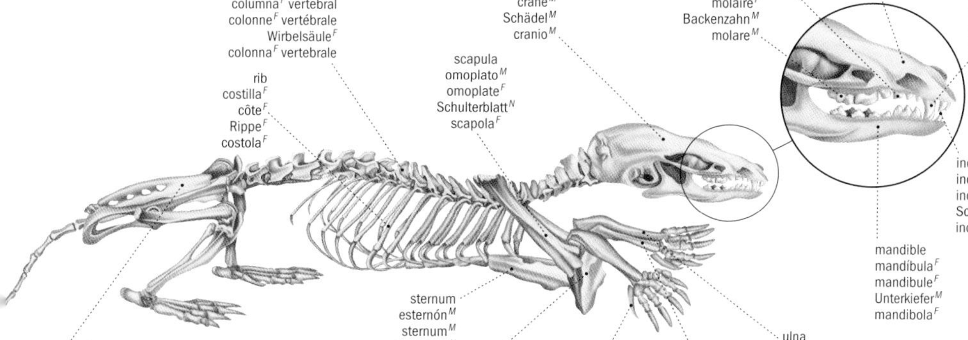

examples of insectivorous mammals

ejemplos^M de mamíferos ^{M} insectívoros | exemples^M de mammifères^M insectivores | Beispiele^N für Insektenfresser^M | esempi^M di mammiferi^M insettivori

mole
topo^M
taupe^F
Maulwurf^M
talpa^F

hedgehog
erizo^M
hérisson^M
Igel^M
riccio^M

shrew
musaraña^F
musaraigne^F
Spitzmaus^F
toporagno^M

rodent

roedor[M] | rongeur[M] | Nagetier[N] | roditore[M]

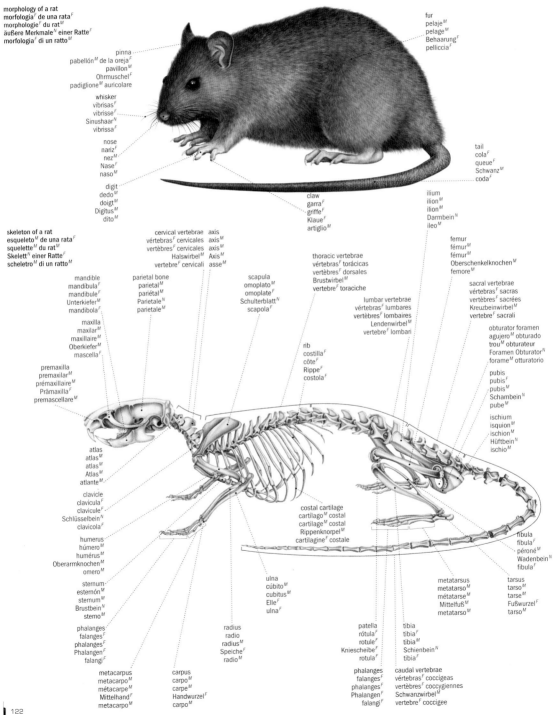

morphology of a rat
morfología[F] de una rata[F]
morphologie[F] du rat[M]
äußere Merkmale[N] einer Ratte[F]
morfologia[F] di un ratto[M]

pinna
pabellón[M] de la oreja[F]
pavillon[M]
Ohrmuschel[F]
padiglione[M] auricolare

whisker
vibrisas[F]
vibrisse[F]
Sinushaar[M]
vibrissa[F]

nose
nariz[F]
nez[M]
Nase[F]
naso[M]

digit
dedo[M]
doigt[M]
Digitus[M]
dito[M]

fur
pelaje[M]
pelage[M]
Behaarung[F]
pelliccia[F]

tail
cola[F]
queue[F]
Schwanz[M]
coda[F]

claw
garra[F]
griffe[F]
Klaue[F]
artiglio[M]

skeleton of a rat
esqueleto[M] de una rata[F]
squelette[M] du rat[M]
Skelett[N] einer Ratte[F]
scheletro[M] di un ratto[M]

cervical vertebrae
vértebras[F] cervicales
vertèbres[F] cervicales
Halswirbel[M]
vertebre[F] cervicali

axis
axis[M]
axis[M]
Axis[M]
asse[M]

thoracic vertebrae
vértebras[F] torácicas
vertèbres[F] dorsales
Brustwirbel[M]
vertebre[F] toraciche

ilium
ilion[M]
ilion[M]
Darmbein[N]
ileo[M]

femur
fémur[M]
fémur[M]
Oberschenkelknochen[M]
femore[M]

mandible
mandíbula[F]
mandibule[F]
Unterkiefer[M]
mandibola[F]

parietal bone
parietal[M]
pariétal[M]
Parietale[N]
parietale[M]

scapula
omóplato[M]
omoplate[F]
Schulterblatt[N]
scapola[F]

lumbar vertebrae
vértebras[F] lumbares
vertèbres[F] lombaires
Lendenwirbel[M]
vertebre[F] lombari

sacral vertebrae
vértebras[F] sacras
vertèbres[F] sacrées
Kreuzbeinwirbel[M]
vertebre[F] sacrali

obturator foramen
agujero[M] obturado
trou[M] obturateur
Foramen Obturator[N]
forame[M] otturatorio

maxilla
maxilar[M]
maxillaire[M]
Oberkiefer[M]
mascella[F]

rib
costilla[F]
côte[F]
Rippe[F]
costola[F]

pubis
pubis[F]
pubis[M]
Schambein[N]
pube[M]

premaxilla
premaxilar[M]
prémaxillaire[M]
Prämaxilla[F]
premascellare[M]

ischium
isquion[M]
ischion[M]
Hüftbein[N]
ischio[M]

atlas
atlas[M]
atlas[M]
Atlas[M]
atlante[M]

clavicle
clavícula[F]
clavicule[F]
Schlüsselbein[N]
clavicola[F]

costal cartilage
cartílago[M] costal
cartilage[M] costal
Rippenknorpel[M]
cartilagine[F] costale

fibula
fibula[F]
péroné[M]
Wadenbein[N]
fibula[F]

humerus
húmero[M]
humérus[M]
Oberarmknochen[M]
omero[M]

metatarsus
metatarso[M]
métatarse[M]
Mittelfuß[M]
metatarso[M]

tarsus
tarso[M]
tarse[M]
Fußwurzel[F]
tarso[M]

sternum
esternón[M]
sternum[M]
Brustbein[N]
sterno[M]

ulna
cúbito[M]
cubitus[M]
Elle[F]
ulna[F]

phalanges
falanges[F]
phalanges[F]
Phalangen[F]
falangi[F]

radius
radio[M]
radius[M]
Speiche[F]
radio[M]

patella
rótula[F]
rotule[F]
Kniescheibe[F]
rotula[F]

tibia
tibia[F]
tibia[F]
Schienbein[N]
tibia[F]

metacarpus
metacarpo[M]
métacarpe[F]
Mittelhand[F]
metacarpo[M]

carpus
carpo[M]
carpe[F]
Handwurzel[F]
carpo[M]

phalanges
falanges[F]
phalanges[F]
Phalangen[F]
falangi[F]

caudal vertebrae
vértebras[F] coccígeas
vertèbres[F] coccygiennes
Schwanzwirbel[M]
vertebre[F] coccigee

examples of rodents

ejemplos^M de roedores^M | exemples^M de mammifères^M rongeurs^M | Beispiele^N für Nagetiere^N | esempi^M di roditori^M

field mouse
ratón^M de campo^M
mulot^M
Feldmaus^F
topo^M campagnolo

chipmunk
ardilla^M listada
tamia^M
Backenhörnchen^N
tamia^M

jerboa
jerbo^M
gerboise^F
Wüstenspringmaus^F
gerboa^M

hamster
hámster^M
hamster^M
Hamster^M
criceto^M

squirrel
ardilla^F
écureuil^M
Eichhörnchen^N
scoiattolo^M

guinea pig
cobaya^F
cobaye^M
Meerschweinchen^N
cavia^F

rat
rata^F
rat^M
Ratte^F
ratto^M

groundhog
marmota^F
marmotte^F
Waldmurmeltier^N
marmotta^F

porcupine
puerco^M espín
porc-épic^M
Stachelschwein^N
porcospino^M

beaver
castor^M
castor^M
Biber^M
castoro^M

rodents' and lagomorphs' jaws

mandíbulas^F de roedores^M y lagomorfos^M | mâchoires^F de rongeur^M et de lagomorphe^M | Nagetierkiefer^M und Hasentierkiefer^M | fauci^F di roditori^M e lagomorfi^M

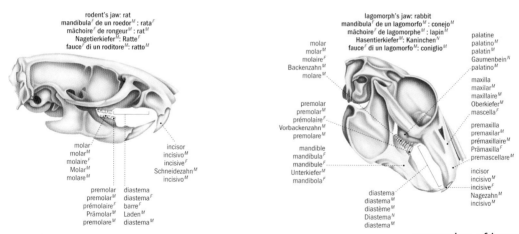

rodent's jaw: rat
mandíbula^F de un roedor^M : rata^F
mâchoire^F de rongeur^M : rat^M
Nagetierkiefer^M: Ratte^F
fauce^F di un roditore^M: ratto^M

molar
molar^M
molaire^F
Molar^M
molare^F

incisor
incisivo^M
incisive^F
Schneidezahn^M
incisivo^M

premolar
premolar^M
prémolaire^F
Prämolar^M
premolare^M

diastema
diastema^F
barre^F
Laden^M
diastema^M

lagomorph's jaw: rabbit
mandíbula^F de un lagomorfo^M : conejo^M
mâchoire^F de lagomorphe^M : lapin^M
Hasentierkiefer^M: Kaninchen^N
fauce^F di un lagomorfo^M: coniglio^M

molar
molar^M
molaire^F
Backenzahn^M
molare^M

premolar
premolar^M
prémolaire^F
Vorbackenzahn^M
premolare^M

mandible
mandíbula^F
mandibule^F
Unterkiefer^M
mandibola^F

diastema
diastema^M
diastème^M
Diastema^N
diastema^M

palatine
palatino^M
palatin^M
Gaumenbein^N
palatino^M

maxilla
maxilar^M
maxillaire^M
Oberkiefer^M
mascella^F

premaxilla
premaxilar^M
prémaxillaire^M
Prämaxilla^F
premascellare^M

incisor
incisivo^M
incisive^F
Nagezahn^M
incisivo^M

examples of lagomorphs

ejemplos^M de lagomorfos^M | exemples^M de mammifères^M lagomorphes^M | Beispiele^N für Hasentiere^N | esempi^M di lagomorfi^M

pika
pica^F
pika^M
Pfeifhase^M
lepre^F fischiante

rabbit
conejo^M
lapin^M
Kaninchen^N
coniglio^M

hare
liebre^F
lièvre^M
Hase^M
lepre^F

ANIMAL KINGDOM

123

ANIMAL KINGDOM

horse

caballo^M | cheval^M | Pferd^N | cavallo^M

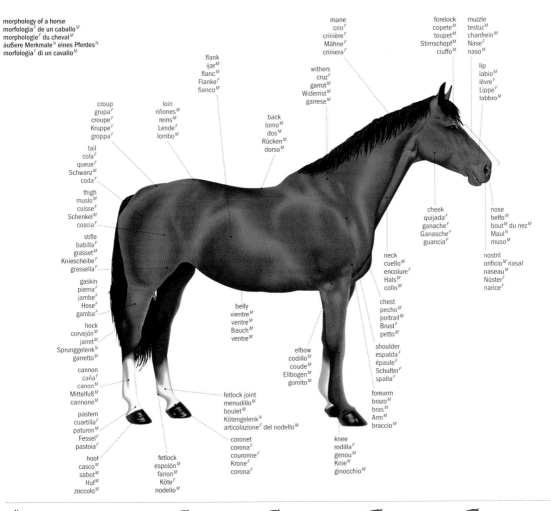

morphology of a horse
morfología^F de un caballo^M
morphologie^F du cheval^M
äußere Merkmale^N eines Pferdes^N
morfologia^F di un cavallo^M

flank
ijar^M
flanc^M
Flanke^F
fianco^M

withers
cruz^F
garrot^M
Widerrist^M
garrese^M

mane
crin^F
crinière^F
Mähne^F
criniera^F

forelock
copete^M
toupet^M
Stirnschopf^M
ciuffo^M

muzzle
testuz^M
chanfrein^M
Nase^F
naso^M

lip
labio^M
lèvre^F
Lippe^F
labbro^M

croup
grupa^F
croupe^F
Kruppe^F
groppa^F

loin
riñones^M
reins^M
Lende^F
lombo^M

back
lomo^M
dos^M
Rücken^M
dorso^M

tail
cola^F
queue^F
Schwanz^M
coda^F

thigh
muslo^M
cuisse^F
Schenkel^M
coscia^F

cheek
quijada^F
ganache^F
Ganasche^F
guancia^F

nose
belfo^M
bout^M du nez^M
Maul^N
muso^M

stifle
babilla^F
grasset^M
Kniescheibe^F
grassella^F

neck
cuello^M
encolure^F
Hals^M
collo^M

nostril
orificio^M nasal
naseau^M
Nüster^F
narice^F

gaskin
pierna^F
jambe^F
Hose^F
gamba^F

belly
vientre^M
ventre^M
Bauch^M
ventre^M

chest
pecho^M
poitrail^M
Brust^F
petto^M

hock
corvejón^M
jarret^M
Sprunggelenk^N
garretto^M

elbow
codillo^M
coude^M
Ellbogen^M
gomito^M

shoulder
espalda^F
épaule^F
Schulter^F
spalla^F

cannon
caña^F
canon^M
Mittelfuß^M
cannone^M

forearm
brazo^M
bras^M
Arm^M
braccio^M

pastern
cuartilla^F
paturon^M
Fessel^F
pastoia^F

fetlock joint
menudillo^M
boulet^M
Kötengelenk^N
articolazione^F del nodello^M

coronet
corona^F
couronne^F
Krone^F
corona^F

knee
rodilla^F
genou^M
Knie^N
ginocchio^M

hoof
casco^M
sabot^M
Huf^M
zoccolo^M

fetlock
espolón^M
fanon^M
Köte^F
nodello^M

gaits
andaduras^F
allures^F
Gangarten^F
andature^F

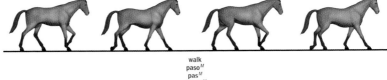

walk
paso^M
pas^M
Schritt^M
passo^M

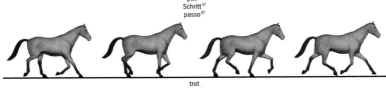

trot
trote^M
trot^M
Trab^M
trotto^M

ANIMAL KINGDOM

anatomy of a horse
anatomía^F de un caballo^M
anatomie^F du cheval^M
Anatomie^F eines Pferdes^N
anatomia^F di un cavallo^M

lung
pulmón^M
poumon^M
Lunge^F
polmone^M

kidney
riñón^M
rein^M
Niere^F
rene^M

cecum
intestino^M ciego
cæcum^M
Blinddarm^M
ciego^M

esophagus
esófago^M
œsophage^M
Ösophagus^M
esofago^M

rectum
recto^M
rectum^M
Rektum^N
retto^M

trachea
tráquea^F
trachée^F
Luftröhre^F
trachea^F

colon
colon^M
côlon^M
Kolon^N
colon^M

heart
corazón^M
cœur^M
Herz^N
cuore^M

spleen
bazo^M
rate^F
Milz^F
milza^F

small intestine
intestino^M delgado
intestin^M grêle
Dünndarm^M
intestino^M tenue

liver
hígado^M
foie^M
Leber^F
fegato^M

stomach
estómago^M
estomac^M
Magen^M
stomaco^M

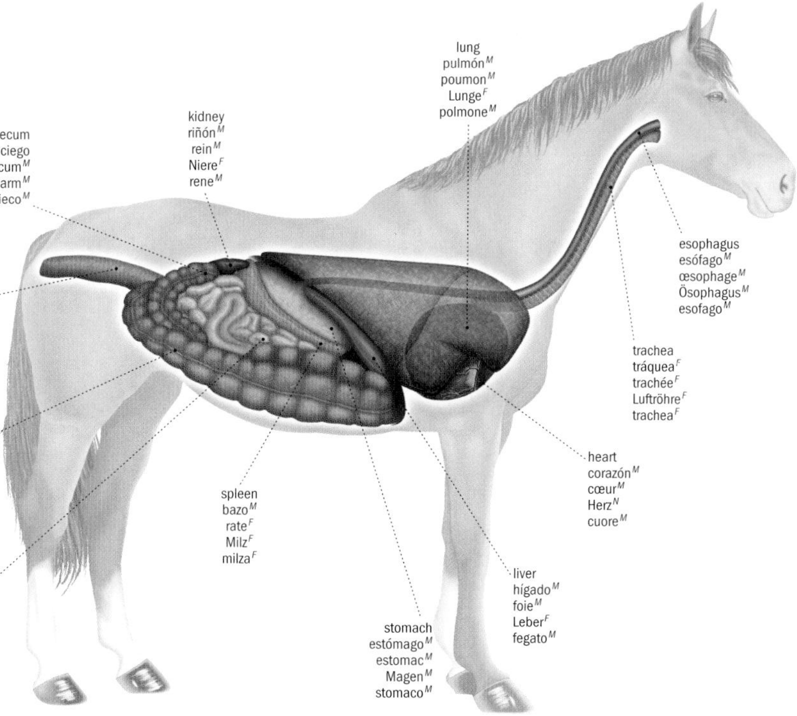

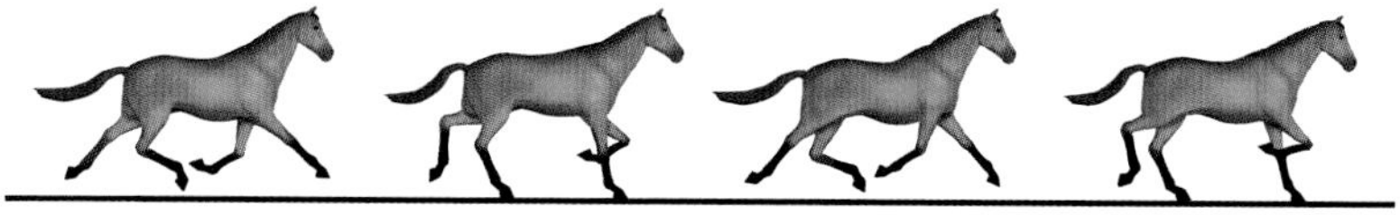

pace
portante^M
amble^M
Paßgang^M
ambio^M

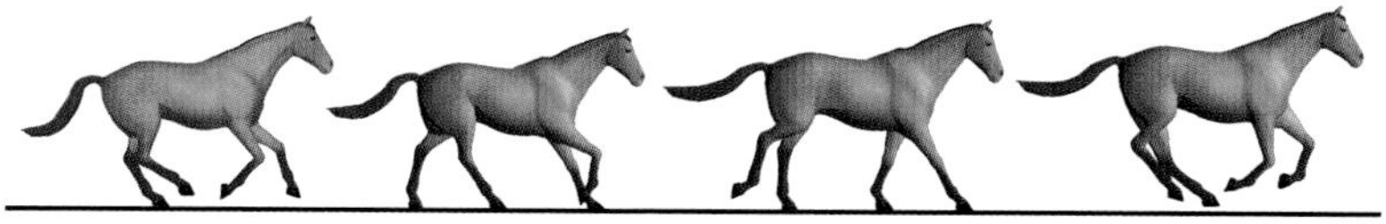

gallop
galope^M
galop^M
Galopp^M
galoppo^M

horse

ANIMAL KINGDOM

skeleton of a horse
esqueleto^M de un caballo^M
squelette^M du cheval^M
Skelett^N eines Pferdes^N
scheletro^M di un cavallo^M

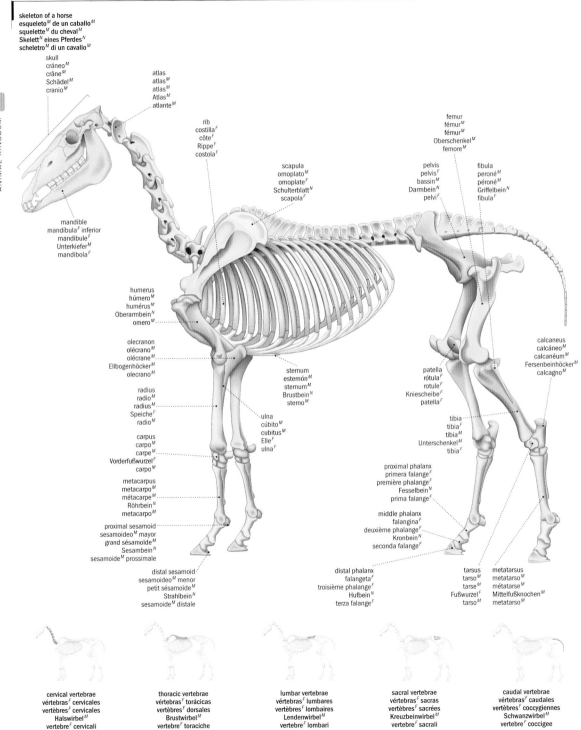

skull
cráneo^M
crâne^M
Schädel^M
cranio^M

atlas
atlas^M
atlas^M
Atlas^M
atlante^M

rib
costilla^F
côte^F
Rippe^F
costola^F

femur
fémur^M
fémur^M
Oberschenkel^M
femore^M

scapula
omoplato^M
omoplate^F
Schulterblatt^N
scapola^F

pelvis
pelvis^F
bassin^M
Darmbein^N
pelvi^F

fibula
peroné^M
péroné^M
Griffelbein^N
fibula^F

mandible
mandíbula^F inferior
mandibule^F
Unterkiefer^M
mandibola^F

humerus
húmero^M
humérus^M
Oberarmbein^N
omero^M

olecranon
olécrano^M
olécrane^M
Ellbogenhöcker^M
olecrano^M

sternum
esternón^M
sternum^M
Brustbein^N
sterno^M

patella
rótula^F
rotule^F
Kniescheibe^F
patella^F

calcaneus
calcáneo^M
calcanéum^M
Fersenbeinhöcker^M
calcagno^M

radius
radio^M
radius^M
Speiche^F
radio^M

ulna
cúbito^M
cubitus^M
Elle^F
ulna^F

tibia
tibia^F
tibia^M
Unterschenkel^M
tibia^F

carpus
carpo^M
carpe^F
Vorderfußwurzel^F
carpo^M

metacarpus
metacarpo^M
métacarpe^M
Röhrbein^N
metacarpo^M

proximal phalanx
primera falange^F
première phalange^F
Fesselbein^N
prima falange^F

proximal sesamoid
sesamoideo^M mayor
grand sésamoïde^M
Sesambein^N
sesamoide^M prossimale

middle phalanx
falangina^F
deuxième phalange^F
Kronbein^N
seconda falange^F

distal sesamoid
sesamoideo^M menor
petit sésamoïde^M
Strahlbein^N
sesamoide^M distale

distal phalanx
falangeta^F
troisième phalange^F
Hufbein^N
terza falange^F

tarsus
tarso^M
tarse^F
Fußwurzel^F
tarso^M

metatarsus
metatarso^M
métatarse^M
Mittelfußknochen^M
metatarso^M

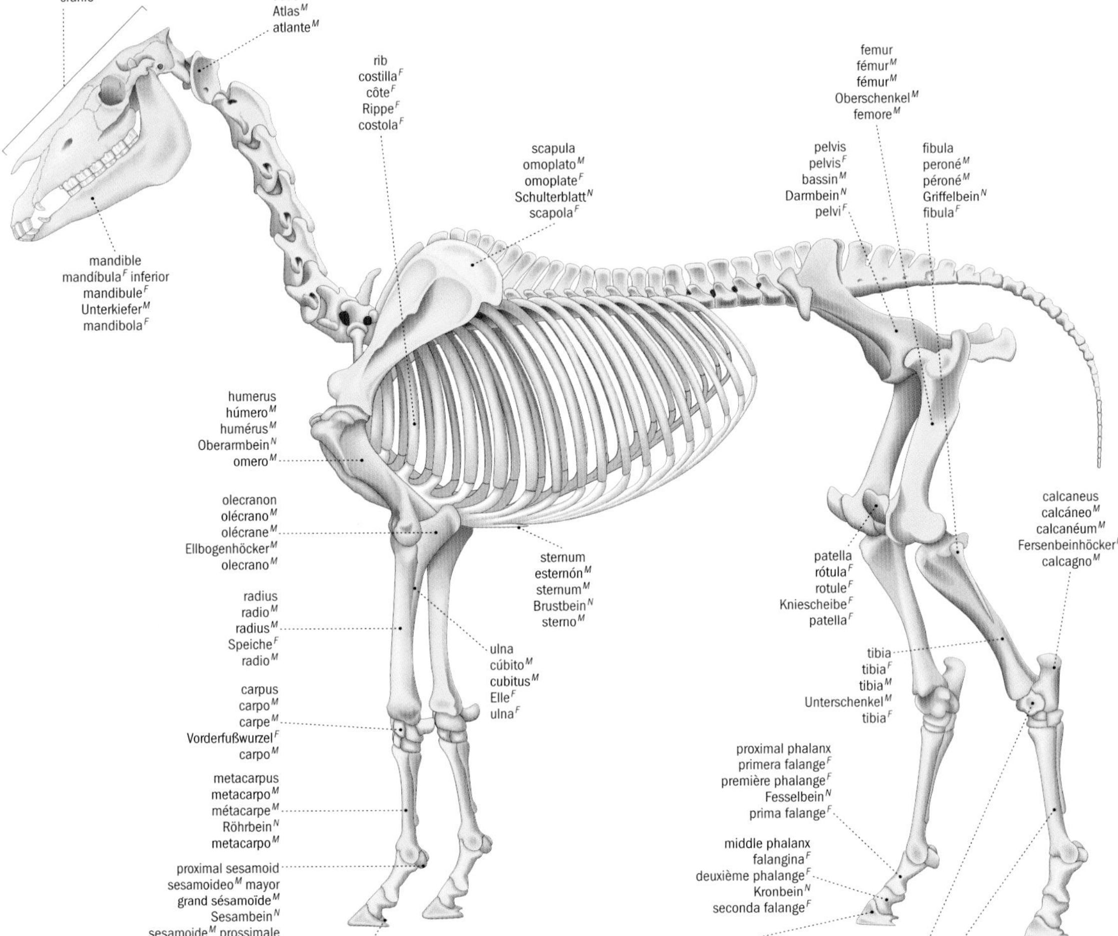

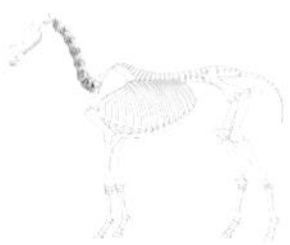

cervical vertebrae
vértebras^F cervicales
vertèbres^F cervicales
Halswirbel^M
vertebre^F cervicali

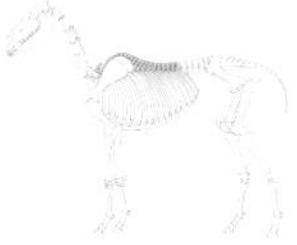

thoracic vertebrae
vértebras^F torácicas
vertèbres^F dorsales
Brustwirbel^M
vertebre^F toraciche

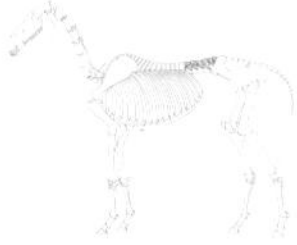

lumbar vertebrae
vértebras^F lumbares
vertèbres^F lombaires
Lendenwirbel^M
vertebre^F lombari

sacral vertebrae
vértebras^F sacras
vertèbres^F sacrées
Kreuzbeinwirbel^M
vertebre^F sacrali

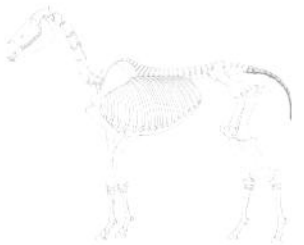

caudal vertebrae
vértebras^F caudales
vertèbres^F coccygiennes
Schwanzwirbel^M
vertebre^F coccigee

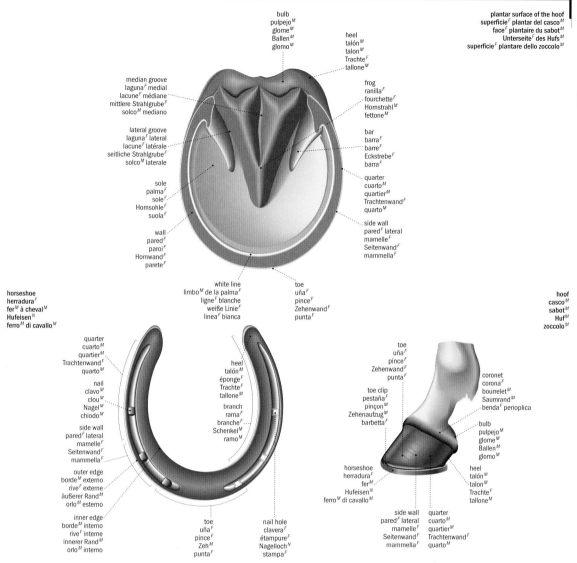

plantar surface of the hoof
superficie^F plantar del casco^M
face^F plantaire du sabot^M
Unterseite^F des Hufs^M
superficie^F plantare dello zoccolo^M

bulb
pulpejo^M
glome^M
Ballen^M
glomo^M

heel
talón^M
talon^M
Trachte^F
tallone^M

median groove
laguna^F medial
lacune^F médiane
mittlere Strahlgrube^F
solco^M mediano

frog
ranilla^F
fourchette^F
Hornstrahl^M
fettone^M

lateral groove
laguna^F lateral
lacune^F latérale
seitliche Strahlgrube^F
solco^M laterale

bar
barra^F
barre^F
Eckstrebe^F
barra^F

quarter
cuarto^M
quartier^M
Trachtenwand^F
quarto^M

sole
palma^F
sole^F
Hornsohle^F
suola^F

side wall
pared^F lateral
mamelle^F
Seitenwand^F
mammella^F

wall
pared^F
paroi^F
Hornwand^F
parete^F

white line
limbo^M de la palma^F
ligne^F blanche
weiße Linie^F
linea^F bianca

toe
uña^F
pince^F
Zehenwand^F
punta^F

hoof
casco^M
sabot^M
Huf^M
zoccolo^M

horseshoe
herradura^F
fer^M à cheval^M
Hufeisen^N
ferro^M di cavallo^M

quarter
cuarto^M
quartier^M
Trachtenwand^F
quarto^M

heel
talón^M
éponge^F
Trachte^F
tallone^M

nail
clavo^M
clou^M
Nagel^M
chiodo^M

branch
rama^F
branche^F
Schenkel^M
ramo^M

side wall
pared^F lateral
mamelle^F
Seitenwand^F
mammella^F

outer edge
borde^M externo
rive^F externe
äußerer Rand^M
orlo^M esterno

inner edge
borde^M interno
rive^F interne
innerer Rand^M
orlo^M interno

toe
uña^F
pince^F
Zeh^M
punta^F

nail hole
clavera^F
étampure^F
Nagelloch^N
stampa^F

toe
uña^F
pince^F
Zehenwand^F
punta^F

coronet
corona^F
bourrelet^M
Saumrand^M
benda^F perioplica

toe clip
pestaña^F
pinçon^M
Zehenaufzug^M
barbetta^F

bulb
pulpejo^M
glome^M
Ballen^M
glomo^M

horseshoe
herradura^F
fer^M
Hufeisen^N
ferro^M di cavallo^M

heel
talón^M
talon^M
Trachte^F
tallone^M

side wall
pared^F lateral
mamelle^F
Seitenwand^F
mammella^F

quarter
cuarto^M
quartier^M
Trachtenwand^F
quarto^M

examples of hoofs

ejemplos^M de pezuñas^F | exemples^M de sabots^M | Beispiele^N für Hufe^M | esempi^M di zoccoli^M

one-toe hoof
pezuña^F de un pesuño^M
sabot^M à un doigt^M
Ein-Zehenhuf^M
zoccolo^M monodattilo

two-toed hoof
pezuña^F de dos pesuños^M
sabot^M à deux doigts^M
Zwei-Zehenhuf^M
zoccolo^M bidattilo

three-toed hoof
pezuña^F de tres pesuños^M
sabot^M à trois doigts^M
Drei-Zehenhuf^M
zoccolo^M tridattilo

four-toed hoof
pezuña^F de cuatro pesuños^M
sabot^M à quatre doigts^M
Vier-Zehenhuf^M
zoccolo^M tetradattilo

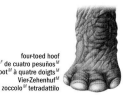

examples of ungulate mammals

ejemplos^M de mamíferos^M ungulados | exemples^M de mammifères^M ongulés | Beispiele^N für Huftiere^N | esempi^M di mammiferi^M ungulati

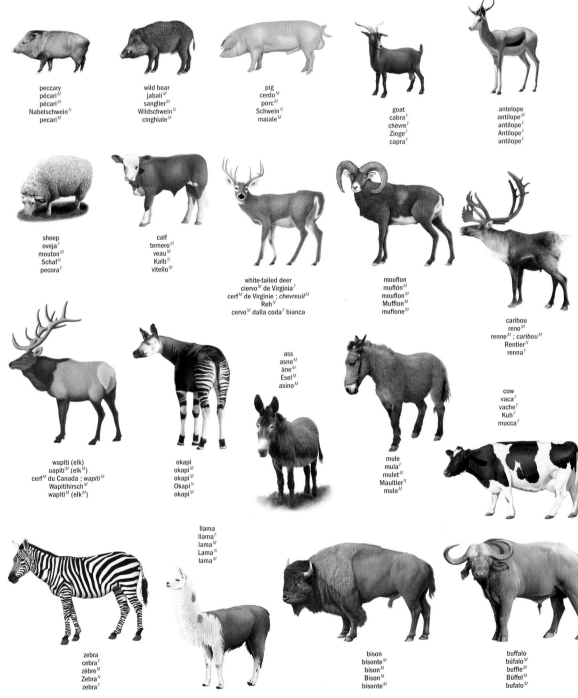

peccary
pécari^M
pécari^M
Nabelschwein^N
pecari^M

wild boar
jabalí^M
sanglier^M
Wildschwein^N
cinghiale^M

pig
cerdo^M
porc^M
Schwein^N
maiale^M

goat
cabra^F
chèvre^F
Ziege^F
capra^F

antelope
antílope^M
antilope^F
Antilope^F
antilope^F

sheep
oveja^F
mouton^M
Schaf^N
pecora^F

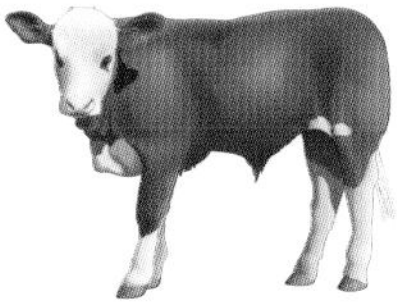

calf
ternero^M
veau^M
Kalb^N
vitello^M

white-tailed deer
ciervo^M de Virginia^F
cerf^M de Virginie ; chevreuil^M
Reh^N
cervo^M dalla coda^F bianca

mouflon
muflón^M
mouflon^M
Mufflon^M
muflone^M

caribou
reno^M
renne^M ; caribou^M
Rentier^N
renna^F

wapiti (elk)
uapití^M (elk^M)
cerf^M du Canada ; wapiti^M
Wapitihirsch^M
wapiti^M (elk^M)

okapi
okapi^M
okapi^M
Okapi^N
okapi^M

ass
asno^M
âne^M
Esel^M
asino^M

cow
vaca^F
vache^F
Kuh^F
mucca^F

mule
mula^F
mulet^M
Maultier^N
mulo^M

llama
llama^F
lama^M
Lama^N
lama^M

zebra
cebra^F
zèbre^M
Zebra^N
zebra^F

bison
bisonte^M
bison^M
Bison^N
bisonte^M

buffalo
búfalo^M
buffle^M
Büffel^M
bufalo^M

ox
buey[M]
bœuf[M]
Ochse[M]
bue[M]

yak
yak[M]
yack[M]
Yak[M]
yak[M]

horse
caballo[M]
cheval[M]
Pferd[N]
cavallo[M]

moose
alce[M]
élan[M] ; orignal[M]
Elch[M]
alce[F]

bactrian camel
camello[M]
chameau[M]
Kamel[N]
cammello[M]

dromedary camel
dromedario[M]
dromadaire[M]
Dromedar[N]
dromedario[M]

rhinoceros
rinoceronte[M]
rhinocéros[M]
Nashorn[N]
rinoceronte[M]

hippopotamus
hipopótamo[M]
hippopotame[M]
Nilpferd[N]
ippopotamo[M]

giraffe
jirafa[F]
girafe[F]
Giraffe[F]
giraffa[F]

elephant
elefante[M]
éléphant[M]
Elefant[M]
elefante[M]

dog

perro^M | chien^M | Hund^M | cane^M

ANIMAL KINGDOM

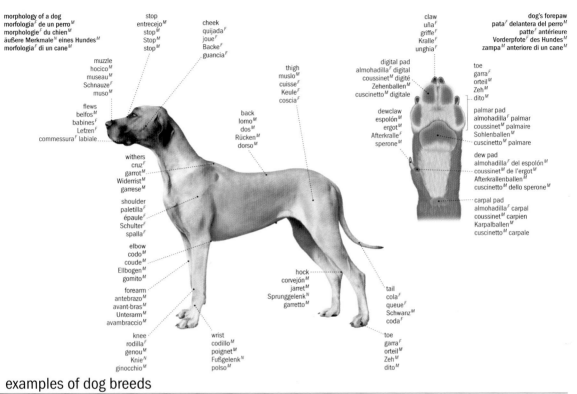

morphology of a dog
morfología^F de un perro^M
morphologie^F du chien^M
äußere Merkmale^N eines Hundes^M
morfologia^F di un cane^M

stop
entrecejo^M
stop^M
Stop^M
stop^M

cheek
quijada^F
joue^F
Backe^F
guancia^F

muzzle
hocico^M
museau^M
Schnauze^F
muso^M

flews
belfos^M
babines^F
Lefzen^F
commessura^F labiale

thigh
muslo^M
cuisse^F
Keule^F
coscia^F

back
lomo^M
dos^M
Rücken^M
dorso^M

claw
uña^F
griffe^F
Kralle^F
unghia^F

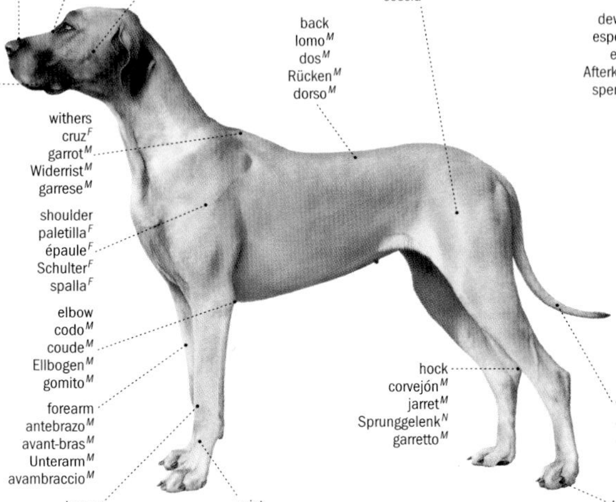

dog's forepaw
pata^F delantera del perro^M
patte^F antérieure
Vorderpfote^F des Hundes^M
zampa^F anteriore di un cane^M

digital pad
almohadilla^F digital
coussinet^M digité
Zehenballen^M
cuscinetto^M digitale

toe
garra^F
orteil^M
Zeh^M
dito^M

dewclaw
espolón^M
ergot^M
Afterkralle^F
sperone^M

palmar pad
almohadilla^F palmar
coussinet^M palmaire
Sohlenballen^M
cuscinetto^M palmare

dew pad
almohadilla^F del espolón^M
coussinet^M de l'ergot^M
Afterkrallenballen^M
cuscinetto^M dello sperone^M

carpal pad
almohadilla^F carpal
coussinet^M carpien
Karpalballen^M
cuscinetto^M carpale

withers
cruz^F
garrot^M
Widerrist^M
garrese^M

shoulder
paletilla^F
épaule^F
Schulter^F
spalla^F

elbow
codo^M
coude^M
Ellbogen^M
gomito^M

hock
corvejón^M
jarret^M
Sprunggelenk^N
garretto^M

tail
cola^F
queue^F
Schwanz^M
coda^F

forearm
antebrazo^M
avant-bras^M
Unterarm^M
avambraccio^M

knee
rodilla^F
genou^M
Knie^N
ginocchio^M

wrist
codillo^M
poignet^M
Fußgelenk^N
polso^M

toe
garra^F
orteil^M
Zeh^M
dito^M

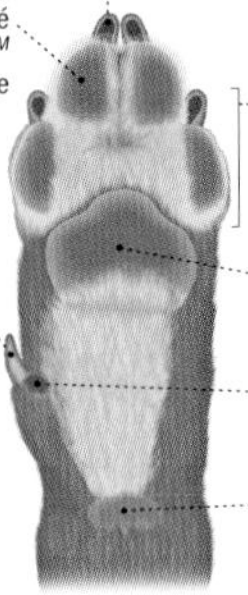

examples of dog breeds

razas^F de perros^M | races^F de chiens^M | Hunderassen^F | razze^F canine

bulldog
buldog^M
bouledogue^M
Bulldogge^F
bulldog^M

schnauzer
schnauzer^M
schnauzer^M
Schnauzer^M
schnauzer^M

poodle
caniche^M
caniche^M
Pudel^M
barbone^M

German shepherd
pastor^M alemán
berger^M allemand
Deutscher Schäferhund^M
pastore^M tedesco

chow chow
chow chow^M
chow-chow^M
Chow-Chow^M
chow-chow^M

collie
collie^M
colley^M
Collie^M
collie^M

skeleton of a dog
esqueleto^M de un perro^M
squelette^M du chien^M
Skelett^N eines Hunds^M
scheletro^M di un cane^M

atlas
atlas^M
atlas^M
Atlas^M
atlante^M

cervical vertebrae
vértebras^F cervicales
vertèbres^F cervicales
Halswirbel^M
vertebre^F cervicali

thoracic vertebrae
vértebras^F torácicas
vertèbres^F dorsales
Brustwirbel^M
vertebre^F toraciche

lumbar vertebrae
vértebras^F lumbares
vertèbres^F lombaires
Lendenwirbel^M
vertebre^F lombari

frontal bone
hueso^M frontal^M
frontal^M
Stirnbein^N
osso^M frontale

occipital bone
hueso^M occipital^M
occipital^M
Hinterhauptbein^N
osso^M occipitale

scapula
omoplato^M
omoplate^F
Schulterblatt^N
scapola^F

sacral vertebrae
vértebras^F sacras
vertèbres^F sacrées
Kreuzbeinwirbel^M
vertebre^F sacrali

parietal bone
hueso^M parietal^M
pariétal^M
Scheitelbein^N
osso^M parietale

femur
fémur^M
fémur^M
Oberschenkelknochen^M
femore^M

orbit
órbita^F
orbite^F
Augenhöhle^F
orbita^F

mandible
mandíbula^F
mandibule^F
Unterkiefer^M
mandibola^F

caudal vertebrae
vértebras^F caudales
vertèbres^F coccygiennes
Schwanzwirbel^M
vertebre^F coccigee

maxilla
maxilar^F
maxillaire^M supérieur
Oberkiefer^M
mascella^F

humerus
húmero^M
humérus^M
Oberarmknochen^M
omero^M

fibula
peroné^M
péroné^M
Wadenbein^N
fibula^F

radius
radio^M
radius^M
Speiche^F
radio^M

patella
rótula^F
rotule^F
Kniescheibe^F
rotula^F

tibia
tibia^M
tibia^M
Schienbein^N
tibia^F

ulna
cúbito^M
cubitus^M
Elle^F
ulna^F

carpus
carpo^M
carpe^M
Handwurzel^F
carpo^M

tarsus
tarso^M
tarse^M
Fußwurzel^F
tarso^M

metatarsus
metatarso^M
métatarse^M
Mittelfuß^M
metatarso^M

metacarpus
metacarpo^M
métacarpe^M
Mittelhand^F
metacarpo^M

phalanges
falanges^F
phalanges^F
Zehenglieder^N
falangi^F

sternum
esternón^M
sternum^M
Brustbein^N
sterno^M

rib
costilla^F
côte^F
Rippe^F
costola^F

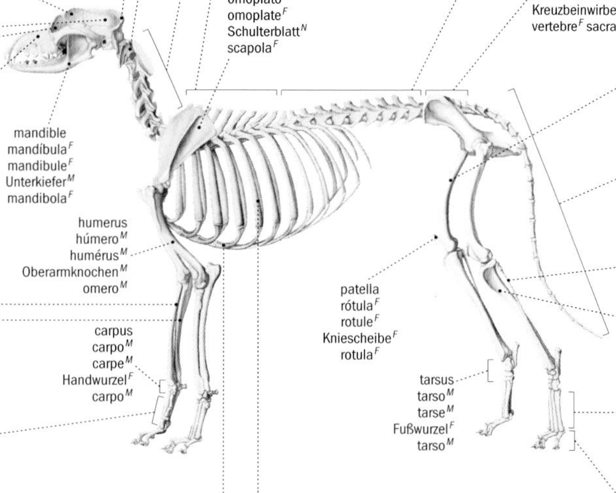

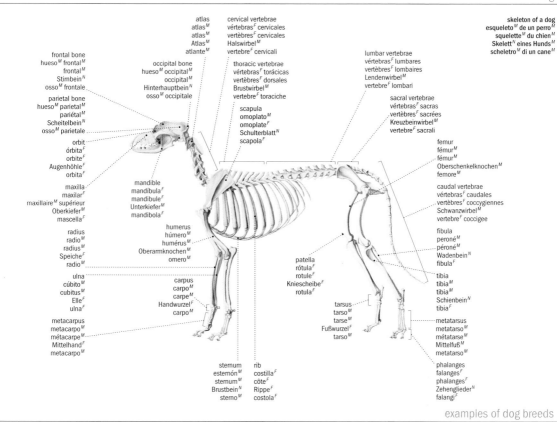

examples of dog breeds

Dalmatian
dálmata^M
dalmatien^M
Dalmatiner^M
dalmata^M

greyhound
lebrero^M
lévrier^M
Windhund^M
levriero^M

Saint Bernard
San Bernardo^M
saint-bernard^M
Bernhardiner^M
sanbernardo^M

Great Dane
gran danés^M
danois^M
Dänische Dogge^F
alano^M

ANIMAL KINGDOM

cat

gato^M doméstico | chat^M | Katze^F | gatto^M

cat's head
cabeza^F
tête^F
Kopf^M der Katze^F
testa^F di gatto^M

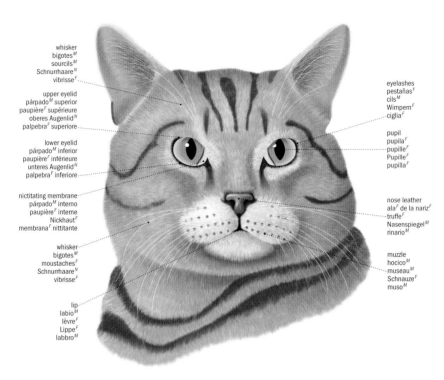

whisker
bigotes^M
sourcils^M
Schnurrhaare^N
vibrisse^F

upper eyelid
párpado^M superior
paupière^F supérieure
oberes Augenlid^N
palpebra^F superiore

lower eyelid
párpado^M inferior
paupière^F inférieure
unteres Augenlid^N
palpebra^F inferiore

nictitating membrane
párpado^M interno
paupière^F interne
Nickhaut^F
membrana^F nittitante

whisker
bigotes^M
moustaches^F
Schnurrhaare^N
vibrisse^F

lip
labio^M
lèvre^F
Lippe^F
labbro^M

eyelashes
pestañas^F
cils^M
Wimpern^F
ciglia^F

pupil
pupila^F
pupille^F
Pupille^F
pupilla^F

nose leather
ala^F de la nariz^F
truffe^F
Nasenspiegel^M
rinario^M

muzzle
hocico^M
museau^M
Schnauze^F
muso^M

examples of cat breeds

razas^F de gatos^M | races^F de chats^M | Katzenrassen^F | razze^F di gatti^M

American shorthair
pelo^M corto americano
américain^M à poil^M court
Amerikanische Kurzhaarkatze^F
gatto^M americano a pelo^M corto

Persian
persa^M
persan^M
Perserkatze^F
persiano^M

Maine coon
Maine coon^M
Maine coon^M
Maine Coon^M
gatto^M del Maine^M

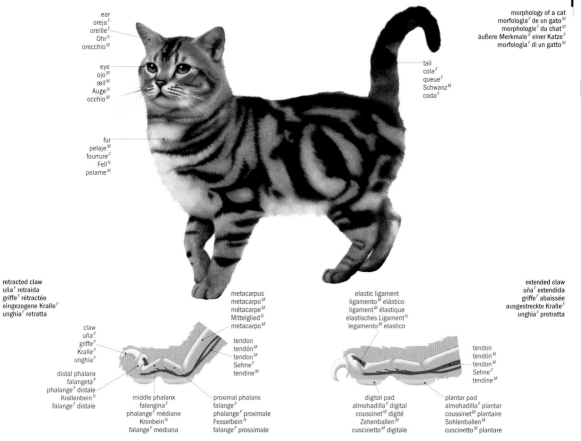

ear
oreja^F
oreille^F
Ohr^N
orecchio^M

eye
ojo^M
œil^M
Auge^N
occhio^M

fur
pelaje^M
fourrure^F
Fell^N
pelame^M

morphology of a cat
morfología^F de un gato^M
morphologie^F du chat^M
äußere Merkmale^N einer Katze^F
morfologia^F di un gatto^M

tail
cola^F
queue^F
Schwanz^M
coda^F

retracted claw
uña^F retraída
griffe^F rétractée
eingezogene Kralle^F
unghia^F retratta

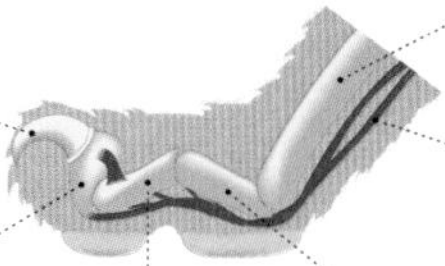

extended claw
uña^F extendida
griffe^F abaissée
ausgestreckte Kralle^F
unghia^F protratta

claw
uña^F
griffe^F
Kralle^F
unghia^F

distal phalanx
falangeta^F
phalange^F distale
Krallenbein^N
falange^F distale

metacarpus
metacarpo^M
métacarpe^M
Mittelglied^N
metacarpo^M

tendon
tendón^M
tendon^M
Sehne^F
tendine^M

elastic ligament
ligamento^M elástico
ligament^M élastique
elastisches Ligament^N
legamento^M elastico

tendon
tendón^M
tendon^M
Sehne^F
tendine^M

middle phalanx
falangina^F
phalange^F médiane
Kronbein^N
falange^F mediana

proximal phalanx
falange^F
phalange^F proximale
Fesselbein^N
falange^F prossimale

digital pad
almohadilla^F digital
coussinet^M digité
Zehenballen^N
cuscinetto^M digitale

plantar pad
almohadilla^F plantar
coussinet^M plantaire
Sohlenballen^M
cuscinetto^M plantare

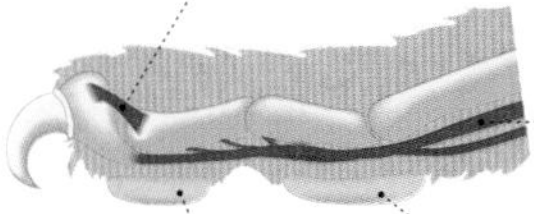

examples of cat breeds

Siamese
siamés^M
siamois^M
Siamkatze^F
siamese^M

Abyssinian
abisinio^M
abyssin^M
Abessinierkatze^F
abissino^M

Manx
Manx^M
chat^M de l'île^F de Man
Manxkatze^F
gatto^M dell'isola^F di Man

examples of carnivorous mammals

ejemplos^M de mamíferos^M carnívoros | exemples^M de mammifères^M carnivores | Beispiele^N für Raubtiere^N | esempi^M di mammiferi^M carnivori

ANIMAL KINGDOM

weasel
comadreja^F
belette^F
Wiesel^N
donnola^F

mink
visón^M
vison^M
Nerz^M
visone^M

stone marten
garduña^F
fouine^F
Steinmarder^M
faina^F

marten
marta^F
martre^F
Marder^M
martora^F

fox
zorro^M
renard^M
Fuchs^M
volpe^F

raccoon
mapache^M
raton^M laveur
Waschbär^M
procione^M

fennec
fenec^M
fennec^M
Wüstenfuchs^M
volpe^F del deserto^M

mongoose
mangosta^F
mangouste^F
Mungo^M
mangusta^F

river otter
nutria^F de rio^M
loutre^F de rivière^F
Seeotter^M
lontra^F comune

badger
tejón^M
blaireau^M
Dachs^M
tasso^M

skunk
mofeta^M
moufette^F
Stinktier^N
moffetta^F

hyena
hiena^F
hyène^F
Hyäne^F
iena^F

lynx
lince^M
lynx^M
Luchs^M
lince^F

wolf
lobo^M
loup^M
Wolf^M
lupo^M

cougar
puma^M
puma^M
Puma^M
puma^M

ANIMAL KINGDOM

cheetah
guepardo^M
guépard^M
Gepard^M
ghepardo^M

leopard
leopardo^M
léopard^M
Leopard^M
leopardo^M

lion
león^M
lion^M
Löwe^M
leone^M

jaguar
jaguar^M
jaguar^M
Jaguar^M
giaguaro^M

tiger
tigre^M
tigre^M
Tiger^M
tigre^F

polar bear
oso^M polar
ours^M polaire
Eisbär^M
orso^M polare

black bear
oso^M negro
ours^M noir
Schwarzbär^M
orso^M bruno

dolphin

delfín[M] | dauphin[M] | Delphin[M] | delfino[M]

ANIMAL KINGDOM

morphology of a dolphin
morfología[F] de un delfín[M]
morphologie[F] du dauphin[M]
äußere Merkmale[N] eines Delphins[M]
morfologia[F] di un delfino[M]

dorsal fin
aleta[F] dorsal
nageoire[F] dorsale
Rückenflosse[F]
pinna[F] dorsale

blowhole
espiráculo[M]
évent[M]
Spritzloch[N]
sfiatatoio[M]

beak
boca[F]
bouche[F]
Maul[N]
bocca[F]

tail
cola[F]
queue[F]
Schwanz[M]
coda[F]

eye
ojo[M]
œil[M]
Auge[N]
occhio[M]

pectoral fin
aleta[F] pectoral
nageoire[F] pectorale
Brustflosse[F]
pinna[F] pettorale

caudal fin
aleta[F] caudal
nageoire[F] caudale
Schwanzflosse[F]
pinna[F] caudale

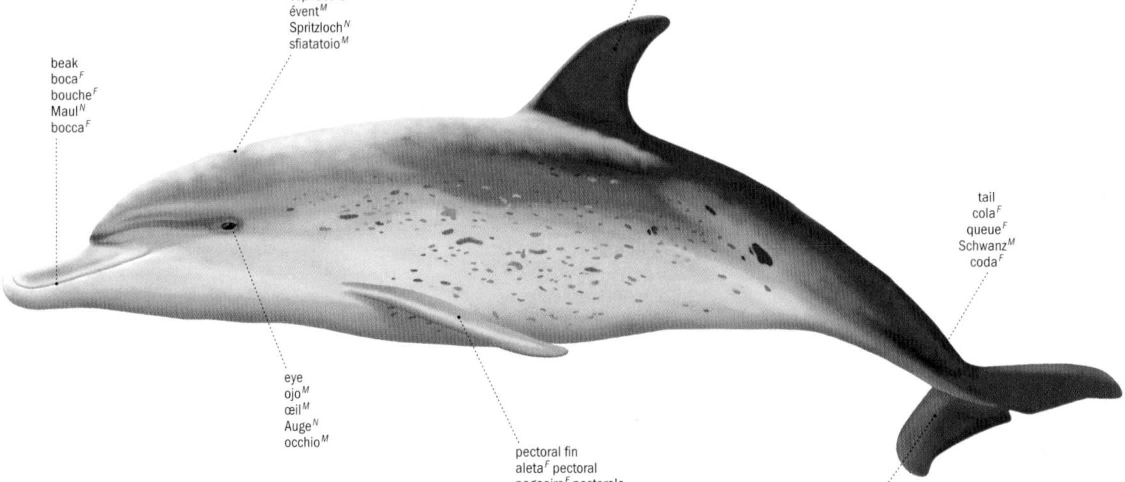

skeleton of a dolphin
esqueleto[M] de un delfín[M]
squelette[M] du dauphin[M]
Skelett[N] eines Delphins[M]
scheletro[M] di un delfino[M]

orbit
órbita[F]
orbite[F]
Augenhöhle[F]
orbita[F]

skull
cráneo[M]
crâne[M]
Schädel[M]
cranio[M]

maxilla
maxilar[M]
maxillaire[M]
Oberkiefer[M]
mascella[F]

scapula
omoplato[M]
omoplate[F]
Schulterblatt[N]
scapola[F]

vertebra
vértebra[F]
vertèbre[F]
Wirbel[M]
vertebra[F]

mandible
mandíbula[F]
mandibule[F]
Unterkiefer[M]
mandibola[F]

humerus
húmero[M]
humérus[M]
Oberarmknochen[M]
omero[M]

rib
costilla[F]
côte[F]
Rippe[F]
costola[F]

vestigial pelvis
pelvis[F] vestigial
pelvis[M] vestigial
rudimentäres Becken[N]
pelvi[F] vestigiale

radius
radio[M]
radius[M]
Speiche[F]
radio[M]

phalanges
falanges[F]
phalanges[F]
Phalangen[F]
falangi[F]

ulna
cúbito[M]
cubitus[M]
Elle[F]
ulna[F]

carpus
carpo[M]
carpe[M]
Handwurzel[F]
carpo[M]

metacarpus
metacarpo[M]
métacarpe[M]
Mittelhand[F]
metacarpo[M]

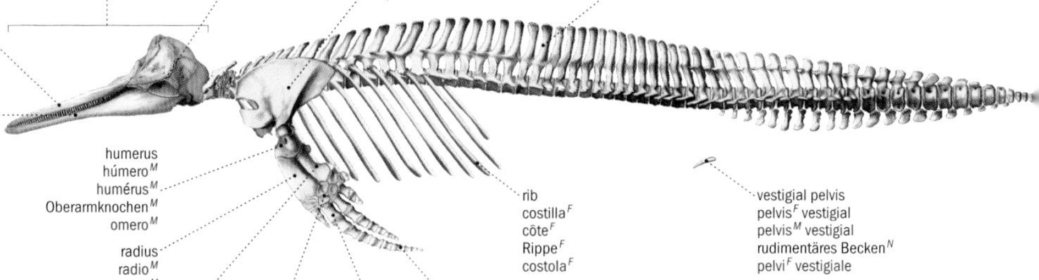

examples of marine mammals

ejemplos^M de mamíferos^M marinos | exemples^M de mammifères^M marins | Beispiele^N für Meeressäugetiere^N | esempi^M di mammiferi^M marini

ANIMAL KINGDOM

sea lion
otaria^F
otarie^F
Seelöwe^M
leone^M marino

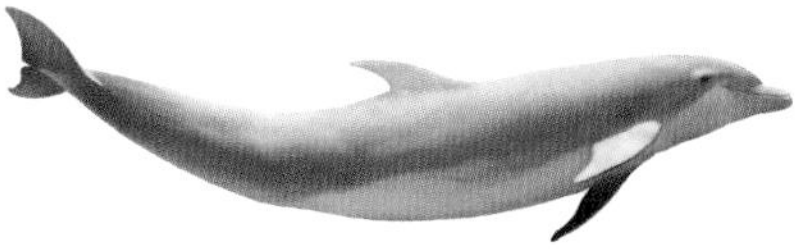

dolphin
delfín^F
dauphin^M
Delphin^M
delfino^M

seal
foca^F
phoque^M
Seehund^M
foca^F

porpoise
marsopa^F
marsouin^M
Tümmler^M
focena^F

narwhal
narval^M
narval^M
Narwal^M
narvalo^M

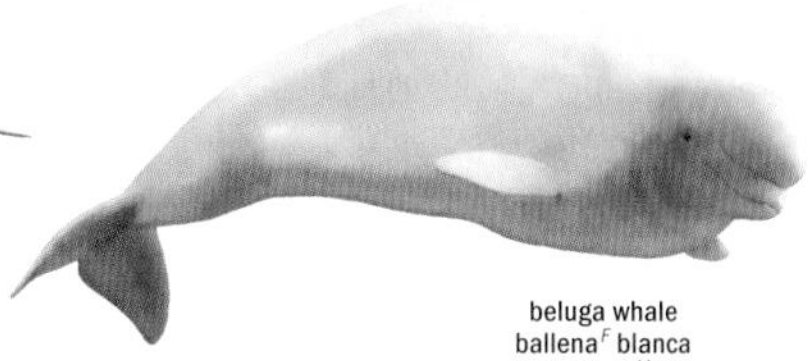

beluga whale
ballena^F blanca
béluga^M
Weißwal^M
balena^F bianca

walrus
morsa^F
morse^M
Walroß^N
tricheco^M

killer whale
orca^F
orque^F
Schwertwal^M
orca^F

humpback whale
rorcual^M
rorqual^M
Buckelwal^M
balenottera^F

northern right whale
ballena^F boréale
baleine^F franche
Nordkapper^M
balena^F franca

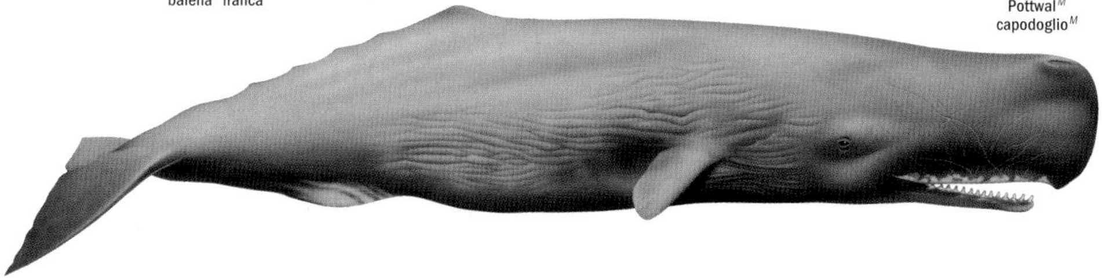

sperm whale
cachalote^M
cachalot^M
Pottwal^M
capodoglio^M

gorilla

gorila ^{M} | gorille ^{M} | Gorilla ^{M} | gorilla ^{M}

ANIMAL KINGDOM

skeleton of a gorilla
esqueleto ^{M} de un gorila ^{M}
squelette ^{M} du gorille ^{M}
Skelett ^{N} eines Gorillas ^{M}
scheletro ^{M} di un gorilla ^{M}

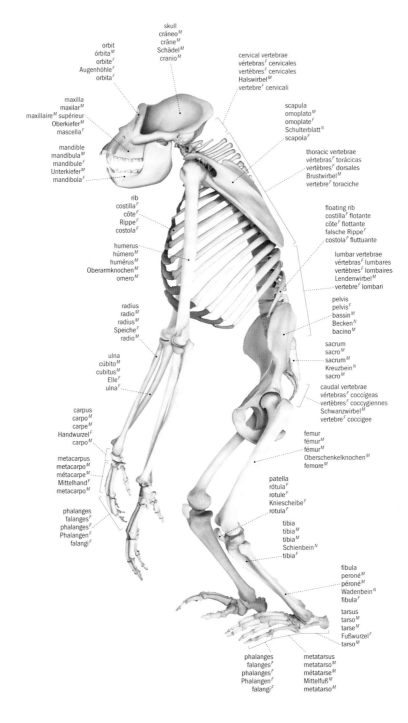

orbit
órbita ^{F}
orbite ^{F}
Augenhöhle ^{F}
orbita ^{F}

skull
cráneo ^{M}
crâne ^{M}
Schädel ^{M}
cranio ^{M}

cervical vertebrae
vértebras ^{F} cervicales
vertèbres ^{F} cervicales
Halswirbel ^{M}
vertebre ^{F} cervicali

maxilla
maxilar ^{M}
maxillaire ^{M} supérieur
Oberkiefer ^{M}
mascella ^{F}

scapula
omoplato ^{M}
omoplate ^{F}
Schulterblatt ^{N}
scapola ^{F}

mandible
mandíbula ^{M}
mandibule ^{F}
Unterkiefer ^{M}
mandibola ^{F}

thoracic vertebrae
vértebras ^{F} torácicas
vertèbres ^{F} dorsales
Brustwirbel ^{M}
vertebre ^{F} toraciche

rib
costilla ^{F}
côte ^{F}
Rippe ^{F}
costola ^{F}

floating rib
costilla ^{F} flotante
côte ^{F} flottante
falsche Rippe ^{F}
costola ^{F} fluttuante

humerus
húmero ^{M}
humérus ^{M}
Oberarmknochen ^{M}
omero ^{M}

lumbar vertebrae
vértebras ^{F} lumbares
vertèbres ^{F} lombaires
Lendenwirbel ^{M}
vertebre ^{F} lombari

radius
radio ^{M}
radius ^{M}
Speiche ^{F}
radio ^{F}

pelvis
pelvis ^{F}
bassin ^{M}
Becken ^{N}
bacino ^{M}

ulna
cúbito ^{M}
cubitus ^{M}
Elle ^{F}
ulna ^{F}

sacrum
sacro ^{M}
sacrum ^{M}
Kreuzbein ^{N}
sacro ^{M}

caudal vertebrae
vértebras ^{F} coccígeas
vertèbres ^{F} coccygiennes
Schwanzwirbel ^{M}
vertebre ^{F} coccigee

carpus
carpo ^{M}
carpe ^{F}
Handwurzel ^{F}
carpo ^{M}

femur
fémur ^{M}
fémur ^{M}
Oberschenkelknochen ^{M}
femore ^{M}

metacarpus
metacarpo ^{M}
métacarpe ^{F}
Mittelhand ^{F}
metacarpo ^{M}

patella
rótula ^{F}
rotule ^{F}
Kniescheibe ^{F}
rotula ^{F}

phalanges
falanges ^{F}
phalanges ^{F}
Phalangen ^{F}
falangi ^{F}

tibia
tibia ^{M}
tibia ^{M}
Schienbein ^{N}
tibia ^{F}

fibula
peroné ^{M}
péroné ^{M}
Wadenbein ^{N}
fibula ^{F}

tarsus
tarso ^{M}
tarse ^{M}
Fußwurzel ^{F}
tarso ^{M}

phalanges
falanges ^{F}
phalanges ^{F}
Phalangen ^{F}
falangi ^{F}

metatarsus
metatarso ^{M}
métatarse ^{M}
Mittelfuß ^{M}
metatarso ^{M}

gorilla

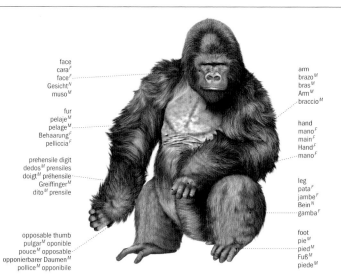

morphology of a gorilla
morfología^F de un gorila^M
morphologie^F du gorille^M
äußere Merkmale^N eines Gorillas^M
morfologia^F di un gorilla^M

face
cara^F
face^F
Gesicht^N
muso^M

arm
brazo^M
bras^M
Arm^M
braccio^M

fur
pelaje^M
pelage^M
Behaarung^F
pelliccia^F

hand
mano^F
main^F
Hand^F
mano^F

prehensile digit
dedos^M prensiles
doigt^M préhensile
Greiffinger^M
dito^M prensile

leg
pata^F
jambe^F
Bein^N
gamba^F

opposable thumb
pulgar^M oponible
pouce^M opposable
opponierbarer Daumen^M
pollice^M opponibile

foot
pie^M
pied^M
Fuß^M
piede^M

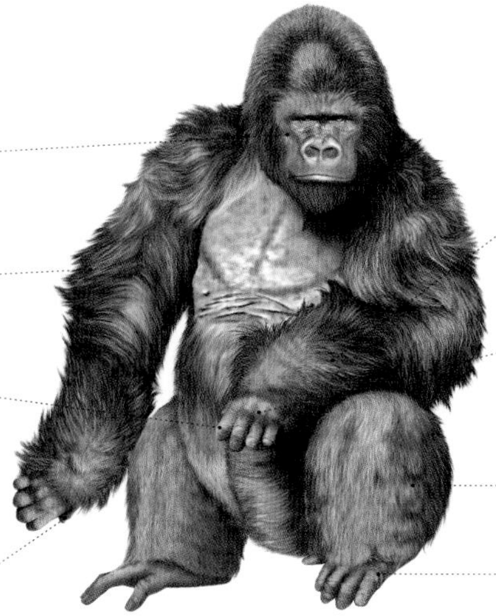

examples of primates

ejemplos^M de primates^M | exemples^M de mammifères^M primates | Beispiele^N für Primaten^M | esempi^M di primati^M

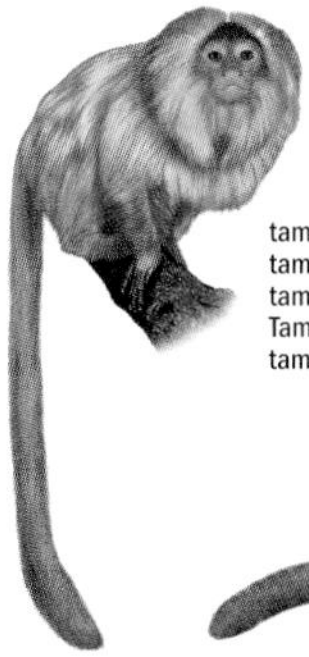

tamarin
tamarino^M
tamarin^M
Tamarin^M
tamarino^M

baboon
babuino^M
babouin^M
Pavian^M
babbuino^M

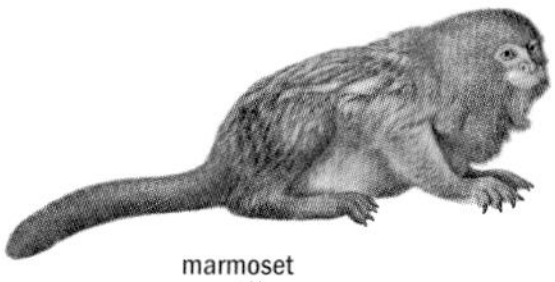

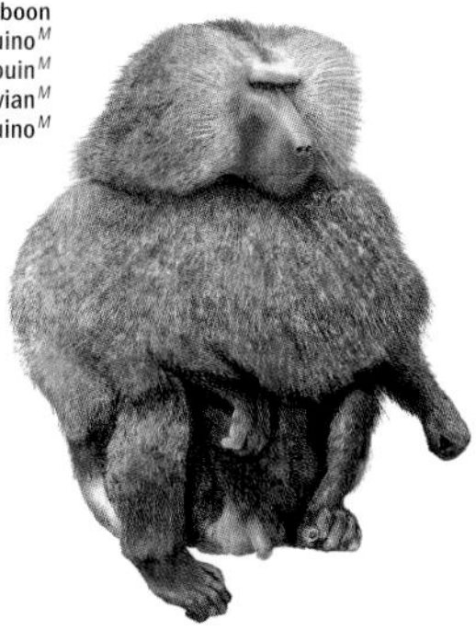

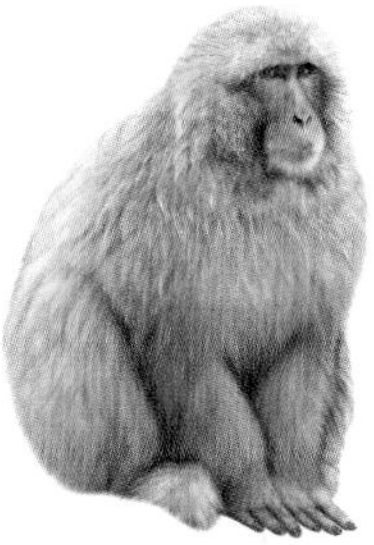

macaque
macaco^M
macaque^M
Makak^M
macaco^M

marmoset
tití^M
ouistiti^M
Pinseläffchen^N
uistiti^M

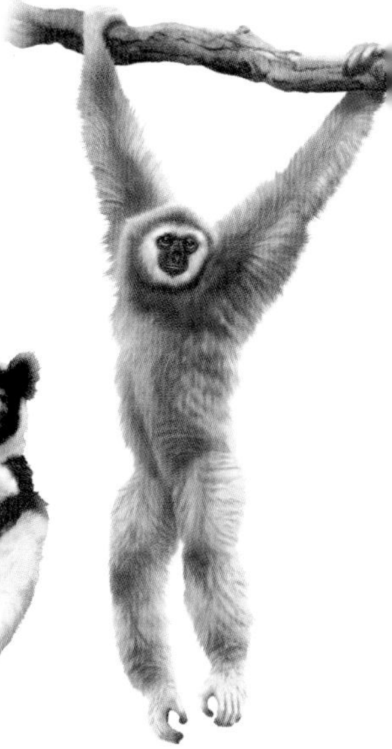

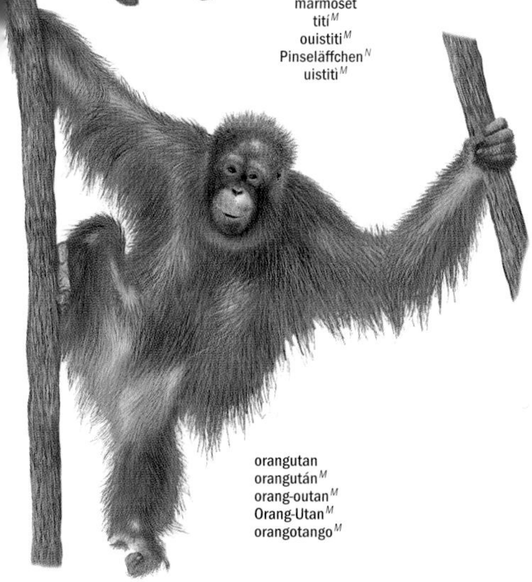

orangutan
orangután^M
orang-outan^M
Orang-Utan^M
orangotango^M

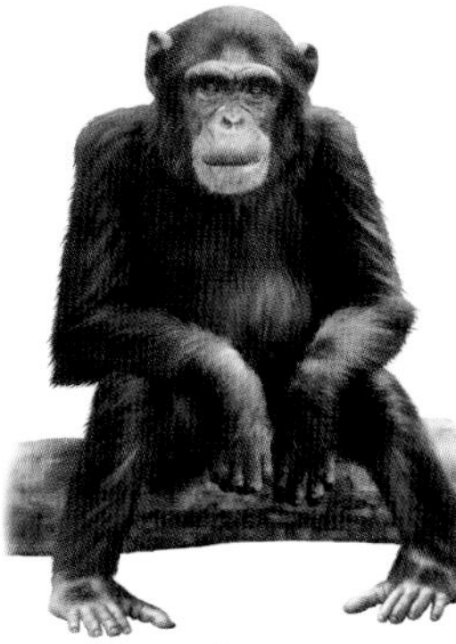

chimpanzee
chimpancé^M
chimpanzé^M
Schimpanse^M
scimpanzé^M

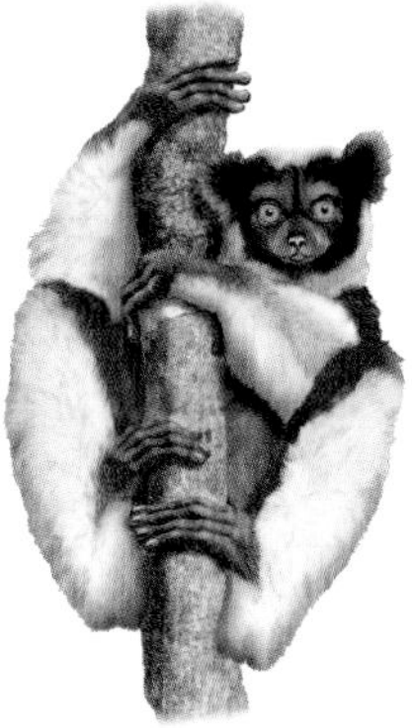

lemur
lémur^M
lémurien^M
Lemure^M
lemure^M

gibbon
gibón^M
gibbon^M
Gibbon^M
gibbone^M

bat

murciélago^M | chauve-souris^F | Fledermaus^F | pipistrello^M

morphology of a bat
morfología^F de un murciélago^M
morphologie^F de la chauve-souris^F
äußere Merkmale^N einer Fledermaus^F
morfologia^F di un pipistrello^M

wing membrane
membrana^F del ala^F
membrane^F alaire
Flughaut^F
membrana^F alare

blood vessels
vasos^M sanguíneos
vaisseaux^M sanguins
Blutgefäße^N
vasi^M sanguigni

2nd metacarpal
2° hueso^M metacarpiano
2e métacarpien^M
2. Finger^M
2° metacarpale^M

3rd metacarpal
3° hueso metacarpiano
3e métacarpien^M
3. Finger^M
3° metacarpale^M

4th metacarpal
4° hueso^M metacarpiano
4e métacarpien^M
4. Finger^M
4° metacarpale^M

thumb
pulgar^M
pouce^M
Daumen^M
pollice^M

claw
uña^F
griffe^F
Klaue^F
unghia^F

elbow
codo^M
coude^M
Ellbogen^M
gomito^M

wrist
muñeca^F
poignet^M
Handgelenk^N
polso^M

radius
radio^M
radius^M
Unterarm^M
radio^M

head
cabeza^F
tête^F
Kopf^M
testa^F

calcar
calcáneo^M
éperon^M calcanéen
Sporn^M
calcare^M

5th metacarpal
5° hueso^M metacarpiano
5e métacarpien^M
5. Finger^M
5° metacarpale^M

interfemoral membrane
membrana^F interfemoral
membrane^F interfémorale
Schwanzflughaut^F
membrana^F interfemorale

ear
oreja^F
oreille^F
Ohr^N
orecchio^M

tibia
tibia^F
tibia^M
Unterschenkel^M
tibia^F

foot
pie^M
pied^M
Fuß^M
piede^M

tail
cola^F
queue^F
Schwanz^M
coda^F

nose leaf
apéndice^M nasal
appendice^M nasal
Nasenblatt^N
foglia^F nasale

wings
alas^F
ailes^F
Flügel^M
ali^F

tragus
trago^M
tragus^M
Ohrklappe^F
trago^M

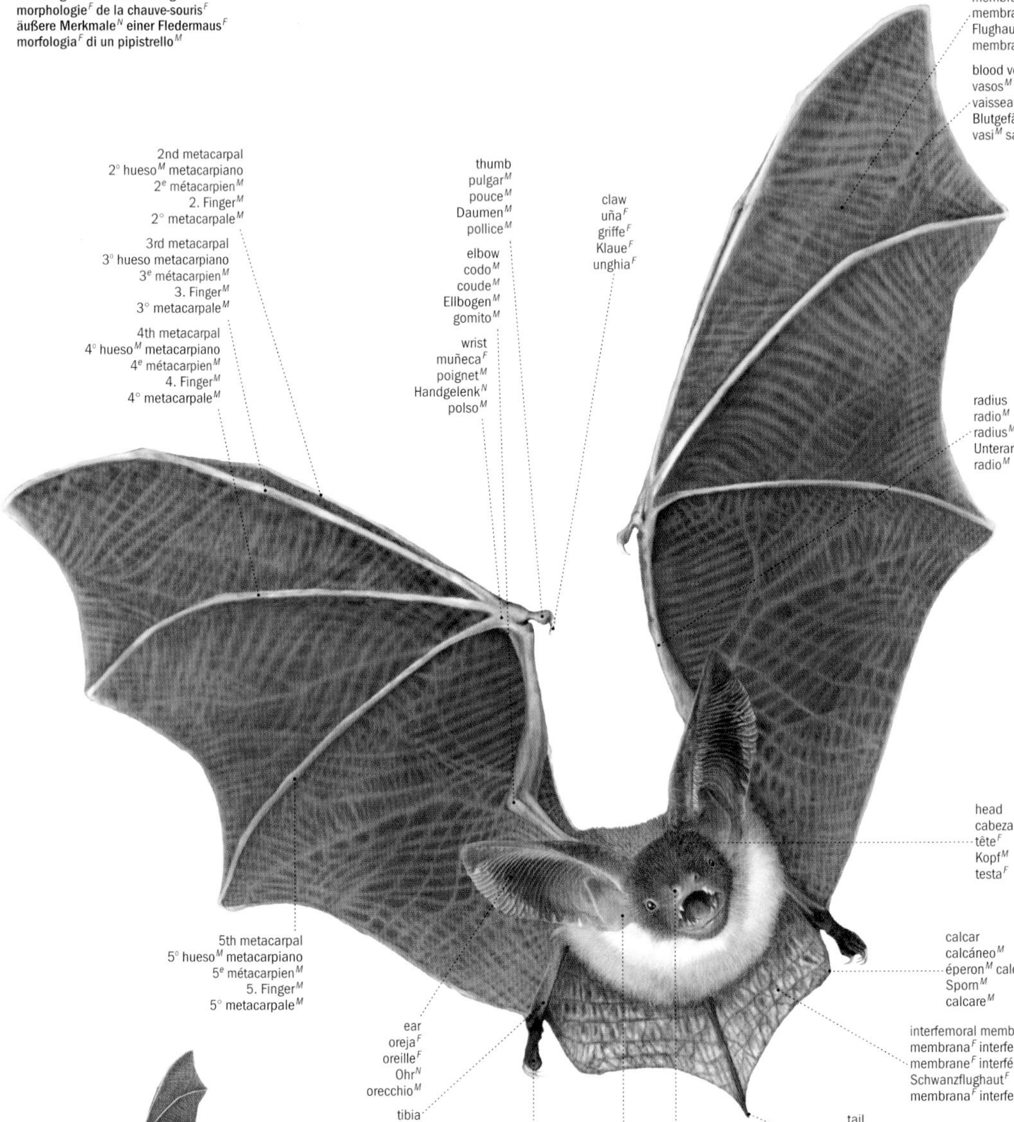

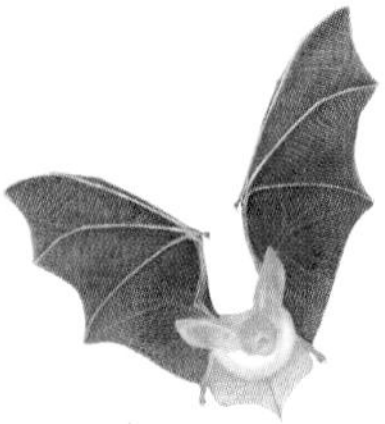

ANIMAL KINGDOM

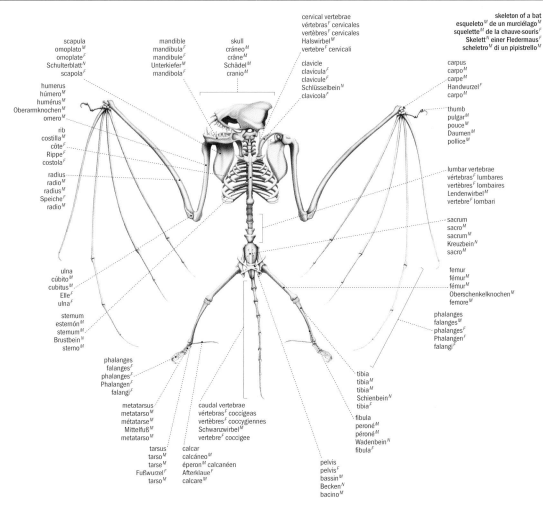

scapula
omoplato[M]
omoplate[F]
Schulterblatt[N]
scapola[F]

mandible
mandibula[F]
mandibule[F]
Unterkiefer[M]
mandibola[F]

skull
cráneo[M]
crâne[M]
Schädel[M]
cranio[M]

cervical vertebrae
vértebras[F] cervicales
vertèbres[F] cervicales
Halswirbel[M]
vertebre[F] cervicali

skeleton of a bat
esqueleto[M] de un murciélago[M]
squelette[M] de la chauve-souris[F]
Skelett[N] einer Fledermaus[F]
scheletro[M] di un pipistrello[M]

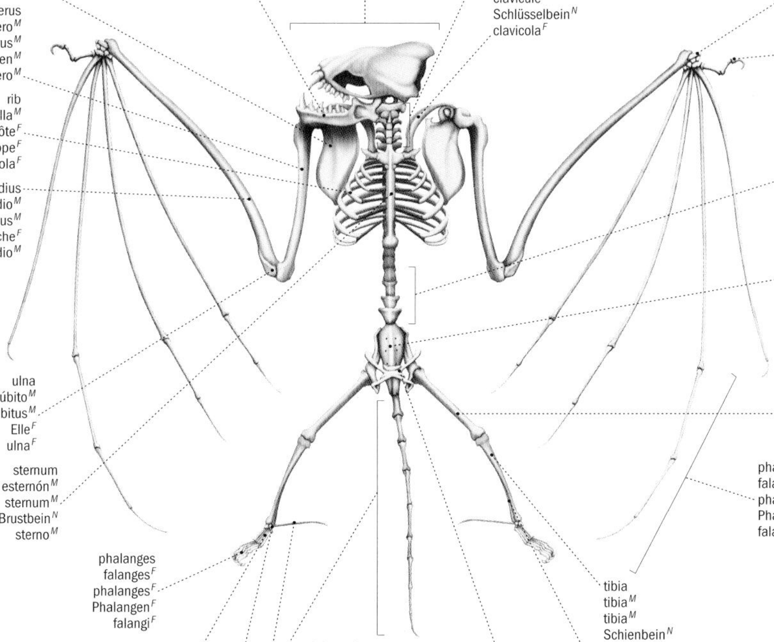

clavicle
clavícula[F]
clavicule[F]
Schlüsselbein[N]
clavicola[F]

carpus
carpo[M]
carpe[M]
Handwurzel[F]
carpo[M]

humerus
húmero[M]
humérus[M]
Oberarmknochen[M]
omero[M]

thumb
pulgar[M]
pouce[M]
Daumen[M]
pollice[M]

rib
costilla[M]
côte[F]
Rippe[F]
costola[F]

lumbar vertebrae
vértebras[F] lumbares
vertèbres[F] lombaires
Lendenwirbel[M]
vertebre[F] lombari

radius
radio[M]
radius[M]
Speiche[F]
radio[M]

sacrum
sacro[M]
sacrum[M]
Kreuzbein[N]
sacro[M]

ulna
cúbito[M]
cubitus[M]
Elle[F]
ulna[F]

femur
fémur[M]
fémur[M]
Oberschenkelknochen[M]
femore[M]

sternum
esternón[M]
sternum[M]
Brustbein[N]
sterno[M]

phalanges
falanges[M]
phalanges[F]
Phalangen[F]
falangi[F]

phalanges
falanges[F]
phalanges[F]
Phalangen[F]
falangi[F]

tibia
tibia[M]
tibia[M]
Schienbein[N]
tibia[F]

metatarsus
metatarso[M]
métatarse[M]
Mittelfuß[M]
metatarso[M]

caudal vertebrae
vértebras[F] coccígeas
vertèbres[F] coccygiennes
Schwanzwirbel[M]
vertebre[F] coccigee

fibula
peroné[M]
péroné[M]
Wadenbein[N]
fibula[F]

tarsus
tarso[M]
tarse[M]
Fußwurzel[F]
tarso[M]

calcar
calcáneo[M]
éperon[M] calcanéen
Afterklaue[F]
calcare[M]

pelvis
pelvis[F]
bassin[M]
Becken[N]
bacino[M]

examples of bats

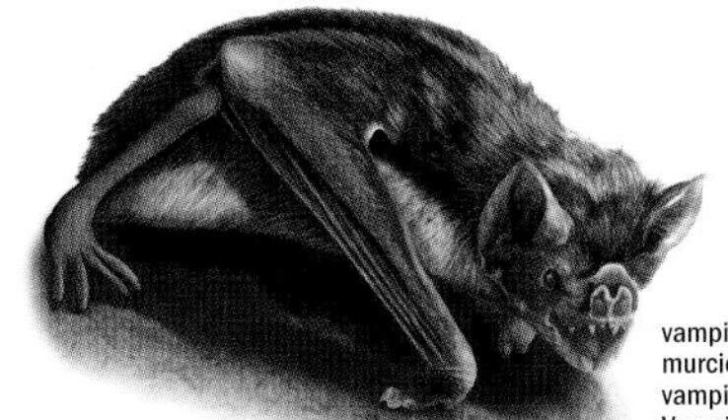

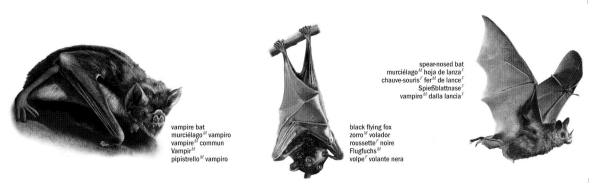

vampire bat
murciélago[M] vampiro
vampire[N] commun
Vampir[M]
pipistrello[M] vampiro

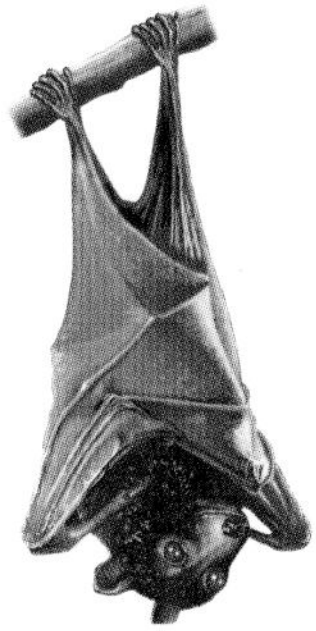

black flying fox
zorro[M] volador
roussette[F] noire
Flugfuchs[M]
volpe[F] volante nera

spear-nosed bat
murciélago[M] hoja de lanza[F]
chauve-souris[F] fer[M] de lance[F]
Spießblattnase[F]
vampiro[M] dalla lancia[F]

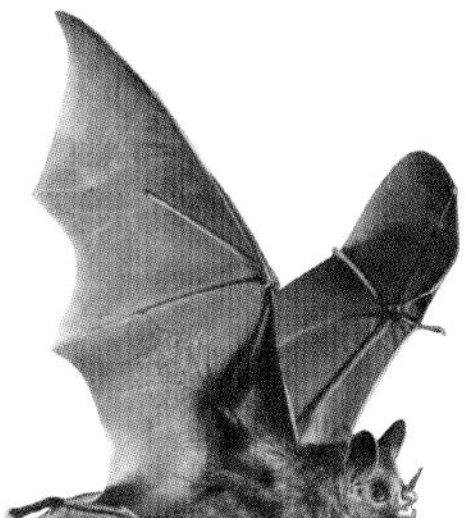

kangaroo

canguro[M] | kangourou[M] | Känguru[N] | canguro[M]

skeleton of a kangaroo
esqueleto[M] de un canguro[M]
squelette[M] du kangourou[M]
Skelett[N] eines Kängurus[N]
scheletro[M] di un canguro[M]

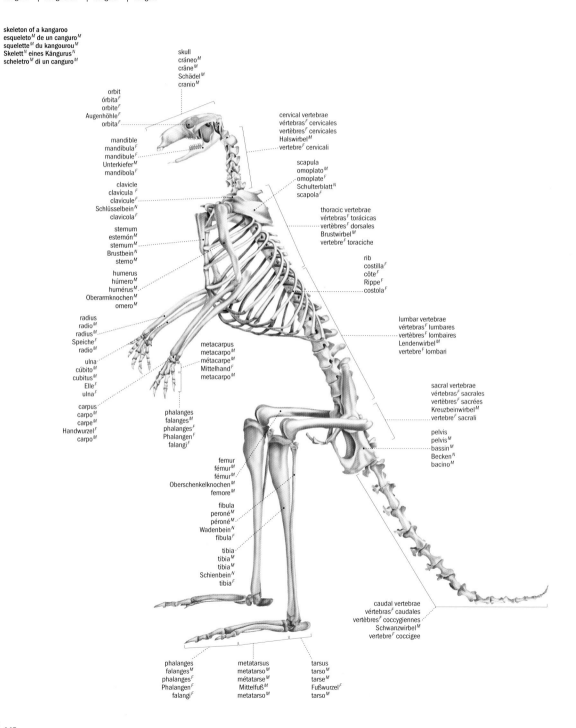

skull
cráneo[M]
crâne[M]
Schädel[M]
cranio[M]

orbit
órbita[F]
orbite[F]
Augenhöhle[F]
orbita[F]

mandible
mandíbula[F]
mandibule[F]
Unterkiefer[M]
mandíbola[F]

clavicle
clavícula[F]
clavicule[F]
Schlüsselbein[N]
clavicola[F]

sternum
esternón[M]
sternum[M]
Brustbein[N]
sterno[M]

humerus
húmero[M]
humérus[M]
Oberarmknochen[M]
omero[M]

radius
radio[M]
radius[M]
Speiche[F]
radio[M]

ulna
cúbito[M]
cubitus[M]
Elle[F]
ulna[F]

carpus
carpo[M]
carpe[M]
Handwurzel[F]
carpo[M]

cervical vertebrae
vértebras[F] cervicales
vertèbres[F] cervicales
Halswirbel[M]
vertebre[F] cervicali

scapula
omóplato[M]
omoplate[F]
Schulterblatt[N]
scapola[F]

thoracic vertebrae
vértebras[F] torácicas
vertèbres[F] dorsales
Brustwirbel[M]
vertebre[F] toraciche

rib
costilla[F]
côte[F]
Rippe[F]
costola[F]

lumbar vertebrae
vértebras[F] lumbares
vertèbres[F] lombaires
Lendenwirbel[M]
vertebre[F] lombari

metacarpus
metacarpo[M]
métacarpe[M]
Mittelhand[F]
metacarpo[M]

sacral vertebrae
vértebras[F] sacrales
vertèbres[F] sacrées
Kreuzbeinwirbel[M]
vertebre[F] sacrali

phalanges
falanges[M]
phalanges[F]
Phalangen[F]
falangi[F]

pelvis
pelvis[M]
bassin[M]
Becken[N]
bacino[M]

femur
fémur[M]
fémur[M]
Oberschenkelknochen[M]
femore[M]

fibula
peroné[M]
péroné[M]
Wadenbein[N]
fibula[F]

tibia
tibia[M]
tibia[M]
Schienbein[N]
tibia[F]

caudal vertebrae
vértebras[F] caudales
vertèbres[F] coccygiennes
Schwanzwirbel[M]
vertebre[F] coccigee

phalanges
falanges[M]
phalanges[F]
Phalangen[F]
falangi[F]

metatarsus
metatarso[M]
métatarse[M]
Mittelfuß[M]
metatarso[M]

tarsus
tarso[M]
tarse[M]
Fußwurzel[F]
tarso[M]

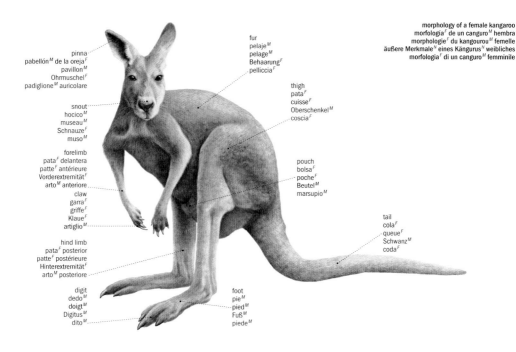

morphology of a female kangaroo
morfología[F] de un canguro[M] hembra
morphologie[F] du kangourou[M] femelle
äußere Merkmale[N] eines Kängurus[N] weibliches
morfologia[F] di un canguro[M] femminile

pinna
pabellón[M] de la oreja[F]
pavillon[M]
Ohrmuschel[F]
padiglione[M] auricolare

fur
pelaje[M]
pelage[M]
Behaarung[F]
pelliccia[F]

thigh
pata[F]
cuisse[F]
Oberschenkel[M]
coscia[F]

snout
hocico[M]
museau[M]
Schnauze[F]
muso[M]

forelimb
pata[F] delantera
patte[F] antérieure
Vorderextremität[F]
arto[M] anteriore

pouch
bolsa[F]
poche[F]
Beutel[M]
marsupio[M]

claw
garra[F]
griffe[F]
Klaue[F]
artiglio[M]

tail
cola[F]
queue[F]
Schwanz[M]
coda[F]

hind limb
pata[F] posterior
patte[F] postérieure
Hinterextremität[F]
arto[M] posteriore

digit
dedo[M]
doigt[M]
Digitus[M]
dito[M]

foot
pie[M]
pied[M]
Fuß[M]
piede[M]

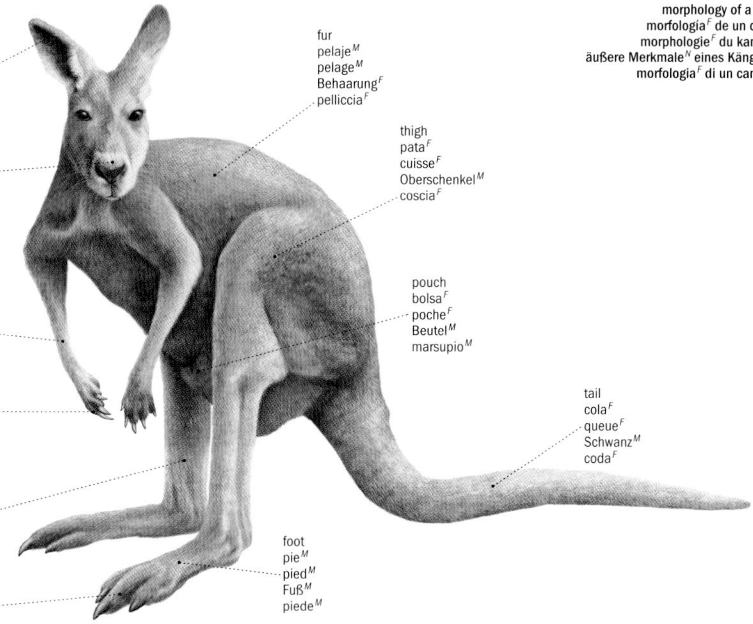

examples of marsupials

ejemplos[M] de marsupiales[M] | exemples[M] de marsupiaux[M] | Beispiele[N] für Beuteltiere[N] | esempi[M] di marsupiali[M]

Tasmanian devil
diablo[M] de Tasmania[F]
diable[M] de Tasmanie[F]
Tasmanischer Teufel[M]
diavolo[M] della Tasmania[F]

wallaby
walaby[M]
wallaby[M]
Wallaby[N]
wallaby[M]

koala
koala[F]
koala[M]
Koala[M]
koala[M]

opossum
oposum[M]
opossum[M]
Opossum[N]
opossum[M]

kangaroo
canguro[M]
kangourou[M]
Känguru[N]
canguro[M]

HUMAN BEING

SER HUMANO | ÊTRE HUMAIN | MENSCH | ESSERE UMANO

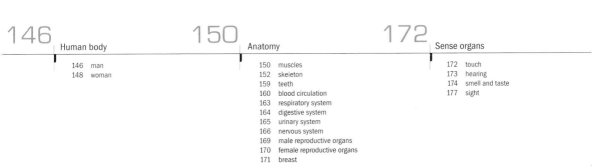

man

hombre^M | homme^M | Mann^M | uomo^M

anterior view
vista^F anterior
face^F antérieure
Vorderansicht^F
vista^F anteriore

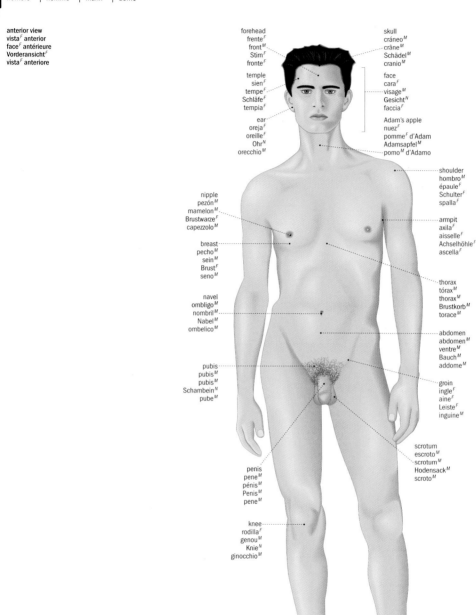

forehead
frente^F
front^M
Stirn^F
fronte^F

temple
sien^F
tempe^F
Schläfe^F
tempia^F

ear
oreja^F
oreille^F
Ohr^N
orecchio^M

skull
cráneo^M
crâne^M
Schädel^M
cranio^M

face
cara^F
visage^M
Gesicht^N
faccia^F

Adam's apple
nuez^F
pomme^F d'Adam
Adamsapfel^M
pomo^M d'Adamo

shoulder
hombro^M
épaule^F
Schulter^F
spalla^F

nipple
pezón^M
mamelon^M
Brustwarze^F
capezzolo^M

breast
pecho^M
sein^M
Brust^F
seno^M

navel
ombligo^M
nombril^M
Nabel^M
ombelico^M

pubis
pubis^M
pubis^M
Schambein^N
pube^M

penis
pene^M
pénis^M
Penis^M
pene^M

knee
rodilla^F
genou^M
Knie^N
ginocchio^M

armpit
axila^F
aisselle^F
Achselhöhle^F
ascella^F

thorax
tórax^M
thorax^M
Brustkorb^M
torace^M

abdomen
abdomen^M
ventre^M
Bauch^M
addome^M

groin
ingle^F
aine^F
Leiste^F
inguine^M

scrotum
escroto^M
scrotum^M
Hodensack^M
scroto^M

foot
pie^M
pied^M
Fuß^M
piede^M

toe
dedo^M del pie^M
orteil^M
Zeh^M
dito^M del piede^M

ankle
tobillo^M
cheville^F
Knöchel^M
caviglia^F

HUMAN BEING

posterior view
vista^F posterior
face^F postérieure
Rückenansicht^F
vista^F posteriore

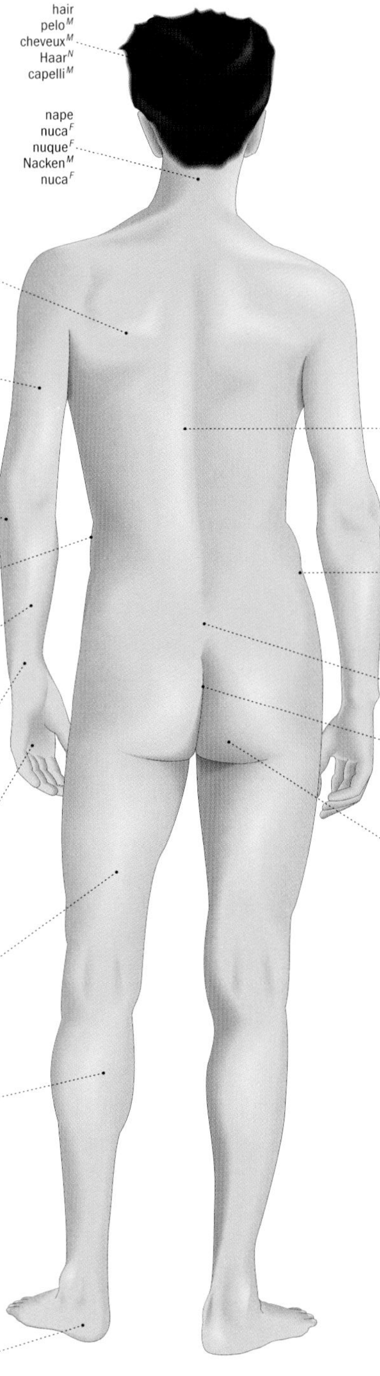

hair
pelo^M
cheveux^M
Haar^N
capelli^M

head
cabeza^F
tête^F
Kopf^M
testa^F

nape
nuca^F
nuque^F
Nacken^M
nuca^F

neck
cuello^M
cou^M
Hals^M
collo^M

shoulder blade
omoplato^M /escápula^F
omoplate^F
Schulterblatt^N
scapola^F

back
espalda^F
dos^M
Rücken^M
schiena^F

arm
brazo^M
bras^M
Arm^M
braccio^M

trunk
tronco^M
tronc^M
Rumpf^M
tronco^M

elbow
codo^M
coude^M
Ellbogen^M
gomito^M

hip
cadera^F
hanche^F
Hüfte^F
fianco^M

waist
cintura^F
taille^F
Taille^F
vita^F

loin
región^F lumbar
reins^M
Lende^F
lombo^M

forearm
antebrazo^M
avant-bras^M
Unterarm^M
avambraccio^M

posterior rugae
pliegue^M anal
raie^F des fesses^F
Afterfurche^F
fessura^F

wrist
muñeca^F
poignet^M
Handgelenk^N
polso^M

buttock
nalga^F
fesse^F
Gesäß^N
natica^F

hand
mano^F
main^F
Hand^F
mano^F

thigh
muslo^M
cuisse^F
Oberschenkel^M
coscia^F

leg
pierna^F
jambe^F
Bein^N
gamba^F

calf
pantorrilla^F
mollet^M
Wade^F
polpaccio^M

foot
pie^M
pied^M
Fuß^M
piede^M

heel
talón^M
talon^M
Ferse^F
tallone^M

147

woman

mujer^F | femme^F | Frau^F | donna^F

HUMAN BEING

anterior view
vista^F anterior
face^F antérieure
Vorderansicht^F
vista^F anteriore

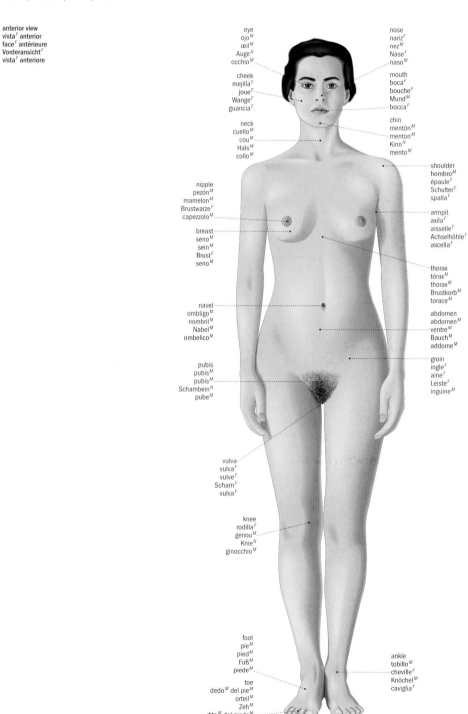

eye
ojo^M
œil^M
Auge^N
occhio^M

cheek
mejilla^F
joue^F
Wange^F
guancia^F

neck
cuello^M
cou^M
Hals^M
collo^M

nipple
pezón^M
mamelon^M
Brustwarze^F
capezzolo^M

breast
seno^M
sein^M
Brust^F
seno^M

navel
ombligo^M
nombril^M
Nabel^M
ombelico^M

pubis
pubis^M
pubis^M
Schambein^N
pube^M

vulva
vulva^F
vulve^F
Scham^F
vulva^F

knee
rodilla^F
genou^M
Knie^N
ginocchio^M

foot
pie^M
pied^M
Fuß^M
piede^M

toe
dedo^M del pie^M
orteil^M
Zeh^M
dito^M del piede^M

nose
nariz^F
nez^M
Nase^F
naso^M

mouth
boca^F
bouche^F
Mund^M
bocca^F

chin
mentón^M
menton^M
Kinn^N
mento^M

shoulder
hombro^M
épaule^F
Schulter^F
spalla^F

armpit
axila^F
aisselle^F
Achselhöhle^F
ascella^F

thorax
tórax^M
thorax^M
Brustkorb^M
torace^M

abdomen
abdomen^M
ventre^M
Bauch^M
addome^M

groin
ingle^F
aine^F
Leiste^F
inguine^M

ankle
tobillo^M
cheville^F
Knöchel^M
caviglia^F

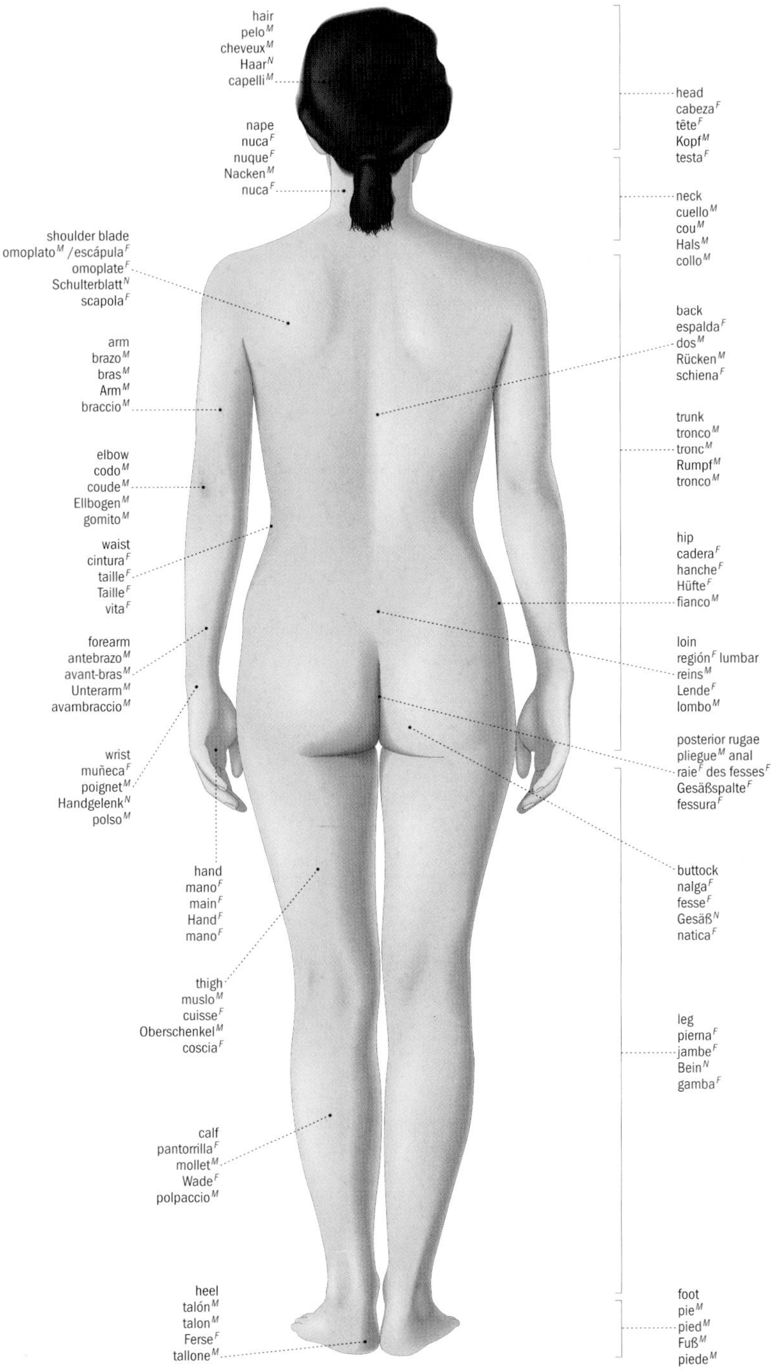

posterior view
vista^F posterior
face^F postérieure
Rückenansicht^F
vista^F posteriore

hair
pelo^M
cheveux^M
Haar^N
capelli^M

head
cabeza^F
tête^F
Kopf^M
testa^F

nape
nuca^F
nuque^F
Nacken^M
nuca^F

neck
cuello^M
cou^M
Hals^M
collo^M

shoulder blade
omoplato^M /escápula^F
omoplate^F
Schulterblatt^N
scapola^F

back
espalda^F
dos^M
Rücken^M
schiena^F

arm
brazo^M
bras^M
Arm^M
braccio^M

trunk
tronco^M
tronc^M
Rumpf^M
tronco^M

elbow
codo^M
coude^M
Ellbogen^M
gomito^M

hip
cadera^F
hanche^F
Hüfte^F
fianco^M

waist
cintura^F
taille^F
Taille^F
vita^F

loin
región^F lumbar
reins^M
Lende^F
lombo^M

forearm
antebrazo^M
avant-bras^M
Unterarm^M
avambraccio^M

posterior rugae
pliegue^M anal
raie^F des fesses^F
Gesäßspalte^F
fessura^F

wrist
muñeca^F
poignet^M
Handgelenk^N
polso^M

buttock
nalga^F
fesse^F
Gesäß^N
natica^F

hand
mano^F
main^F
Hand^F
mano^F

thigh
muslo^M
cuisse^F
Oberschenkel^M
coscia^F

leg
pierna^F
jambe^F
Bein^N
gamba^F

calf
pantorrilla^F
mollet^M
Wade^F
polpaccio^M

heel
talón^M
talon^M
Ferse^F
tallone^M

foot
pie^M
pied^M
Fuß^M
piede^M

HUMAN BEING

muscles

músculos^M | muscles^M | Muskeln^M | muscoli^M

anterior view
vista^F anterior
face^F antérieure
Vorderansicht^F
vista^F anteriore

orbicularis oculi
orbicular^M de los párpados^M
orbiculaire^M des paupières^F
Augenringmuskel^M
orbicolare^M dell'occhio^M

masseter
masetero^M
masséter^M
Kaumuskel^M
massetere^M

deltoid
deltoides^M
deltoïde^M
Deltamuskel^M
deltoide^M

external oblique
oblicuo^M mayor del abdomen^M
grand oblique^M de l'abdomen^M
äußerer schräger Bauchmuskel^M
obliquo^M esterno dell'addome^M

rectus abdominis
recto^M del abdomen^M
grand droit^M de l'abdomen^M
gerader Bauchmuskel^M
retto^M dell'addome^M

brachioradialis
supinador^M largo
huméro-stylo-radial^M
Oberarmspeichenmuskel^M
brachioradiale^M

tensor fasciae latae
tensor^M de la fascia lata^F
tenseur^M du fascia lata^M
Schenkelbindenspanner^M
tensore^M della fascia^F lata

adductor longus
aductor^M del muslo^M
moyen adducteur^M
langer Oberschenkelanzieher^M
adduttore^M lungo

sartorius
sartorio^M
couturier^M
Schneidermuskel^M
sartorio^M

rectus femoris
recto^M anterior
droit^M antérieur de la cuisse^F
gerader Schenkelmuskel^M
retto^M della coscia^F

vastus medialis
vasto^M externo
vaste^M interne du membre^M inférieur
innerer Schenkelmuskel^M
vasto^M mediale

peroneus longus
peroneo^M largo
long péronier^M latéral
langer Wadenbeinmuskel^M
peroneo^M lungo

tibialis anterior
tibial^M anterior
jambier^M antérieur
vorderer Schienbeinmuskel^M
tibiale^M anteriore

extensor digitorum brevis
extensor^M corto de los dedos^M del pie^M
pédieux^M
kurzer Zehenstrecker^M
estensore^M breve delle dita^F

frontalis
frontal^M
frontal^M
Stirn^F
frontale^M

sternomastoid
esternocleidomastoideo^M
sterno-cléido-mastoïdien^M
Kopfnicker^M
sternocleidomastoideo^M

trapezius
trapecio^M
trapèze^M
Kapuzenmuskel^M
trapezio^M

pectoralis major
pectoral^M mayor
grand pectoral^M
großer Brustmuskel^M
grande pettorale^M

biceps brachii
biceps^M braquial
biceps^M brachial
zweiköpfiger Armstrecker^M
bicipite^M brachiale

brachialis
braquial^M anterior
brachial^M antérieur
Armbeuger^M
brachiale^M

pronator teres
pronador^M redondo
rond pronateur^M
runder Einwärtsdreher^M
pronatore^M rotondo

palmaris longus
palmar^M mayor
grand palmaire^M
langer Hohlhandmuskel^M
palmare^M lungo

flexor carpi ulnaris
cubital^M anterior
cubital^M antérieur
Handbeuger^M der Ellenseite^F
flessore^M ulnare del carpo^M

palmaris brevis
palmar^M menor
petit palmaire^M
kurzer Hohlhandmuskel^M
palmare^M breve

vastus lateralis
vasto^M interno
vaste^M externe du membre^M inférieur
äußerer Schenkelmuskel^M
vasto^M laterale

gastrocnemius
gemelos^M
jumeau^M
Zwillingswadenmuskel^M
gastrocnemio^M

soleus
sóleo^M
soléaire^M
Schollenmuskel^M
soleo^M

extensor digitorum longus
extensor^M largo de los dedos^M del pie^M
extenseur^M commun des orteils^M
langer Zehenstrecker^M
estensore^M lungo delle dita^F

interosseus plantaris
interóseos^M del pie^M
interosseux^M
Zwischenknochenmuskel^M
interosseo^M plantare

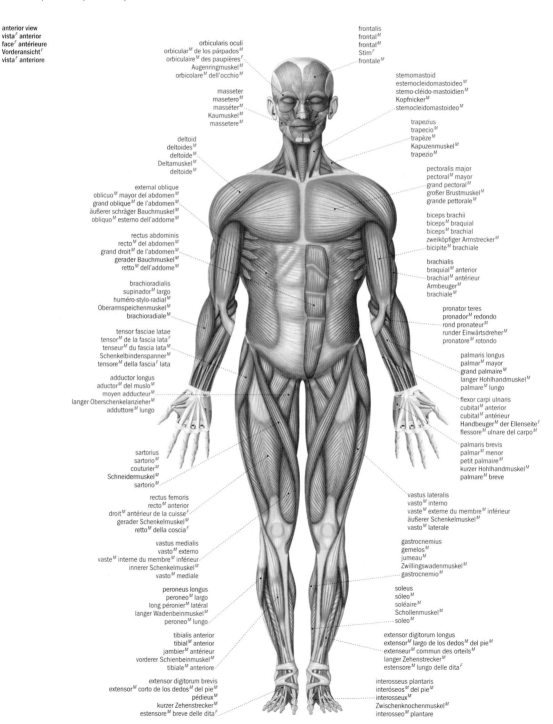

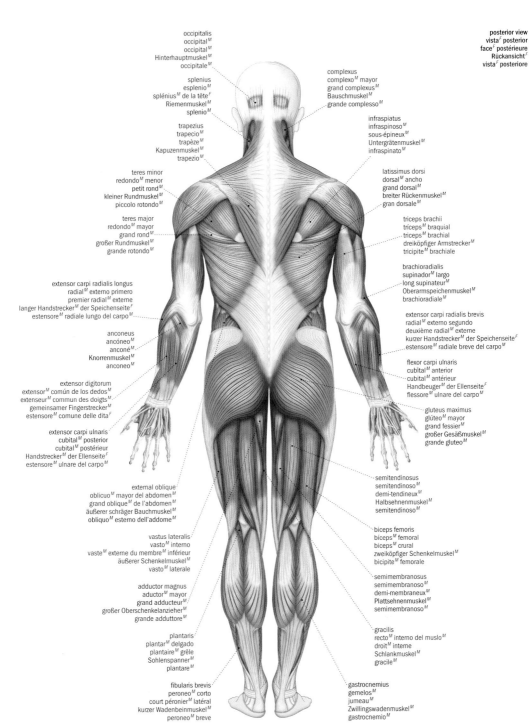

posterior view
vista[F] posterior
face[F] postérieure
Rückansicht[F]
vista[F] posteriore

occipitalis
occipital[M]
occipital[M]
Hinterhauptmuskel[M]
occipitale[M]

complexus
complexo[M] mayor
grand complexus[M]
Bauschmuskel[M]
grande complesso[M]

splenius
esplenio[M]
splénius[M] de la tête[F]
Riemenmuskel[M]
splenio[M]

infraspiatus
infraspinoso[M]
sous-épineux[M]
Untergrätenmuskel[M]
infraspinato[M]

trapezius
trapecio[M]
trapèze[M]
Kapuzenmuskel[M]
trapezio[M]

latissimus dorsi
dorsal[M] ancho
grand dorsal[M]
breiter Rückenmuskel[M]
gran dorsale[M]

teres minor
redondo[M] menor
petit rond[M]
kleiner Rundmuskel[M]
piccolo rotondo[M]

triceps brachii
triceps[M] braquial
triceps[M] brachial
dreiköpfiger Armstrecker[M]
tricipite[M] brachiale

teres major
redondo[M] mayor
grand rond[M]
großer Rundmuskel[M]
grande rotondo[M]

brachioradialis
supinador[M] largo
long supinateur[M]
Oberarmspeichenmuskel[M]
brachioradiale[M]

extensor carpi radialis longus
radial[M] externo primero
premier radial[M] externe
langer Handstrecker[M] der Speichenseite[F]
estensore[M] radiale lungo del carpo[M]

extensor carpi radialis brevis
radial[M] externo segundo
deuxième radial[M] externe
kurzer Handstrecker[M] der Speichenseite[F]
estensore[M] radiale breve del carpo[M]

anconeus
ancóneo[M]
anconé[M]
Knorrenmuskel[M]
anconeo[M]

flexor carpi ulnaris
cubital[M] anterior
cubital[M] antérieur
Handbeuger[M] der Ellenseite[F]
flessore[M] ulnare del carpo[M]

extensor digitorum
extensor[M] común de los dedos[M]
extenseur[M] commun des doigts[M]
gemeinsamer Fingerstrecker[M]
estensore[M] comune delle dita[F]

gluteus maximus
glúteo[M] mayor
grand fessier[M]
großer Gesäßmuskel[M]
grande gluteo[M]

extensor carpi ulnaris
cubital[M] posterior
cubital[M] postérieur
Handstrecker[M] der Ellenseite[F]
estensore[M] ulnare del carpo[M]

semitendinosus
semitendinoso[M]
demi-tendineux[M]
Halbsehnenmuskel[M]
semitendinoso[M]

external oblique
oblicuo[M] mayor del abdomen[M]
grand oblique[M] de l'abdomen[M]
äußerer schräger Bauchmuskel[M]
obliquo[M] esterno dell'addome[M]

biceps femoris
biceps[M] femoral
biceps[M] crural
zweiköpfiger Schenkelmuskel[M]
bicipite[M] femorale

vastus lateralis
vasto[M] interno
vaste[M] externe du membre[M] inférieur
äußerer Schenkelmuskel[M]
vasto[M] laterale

semimembranosus
semimembranoso[M]
demi-membraneux[M]
Plattsehnenmuskel[M]
semimembranoso[M]

adductor magnus
aductor[M] mayor
grand adducteur[M]
großer Oberschenkelanzieher[M]
grande adduttore[M]

gracilis
recto[M] interno del muslo[M]
droit[M] interne
Schlankmuskel[M]
gracile[M]

plantaris
plantar[M] delgado
plantaire[M] grêle
Sohlenspanner[M]
plantare[M]

fibularis brevis
peroneo[M] corto
court péronier[M] latéral
kurzer Wadenbeinmuskel[M]
peroneo[M] breve

gastrocnemius
gemelos[M]
jumeau[M]
Zwillingswadenmuskel[M]
gastrocnemio[M]

skeleton

esqueleto^M | squelette^M | Skelett^N | scheletro^M

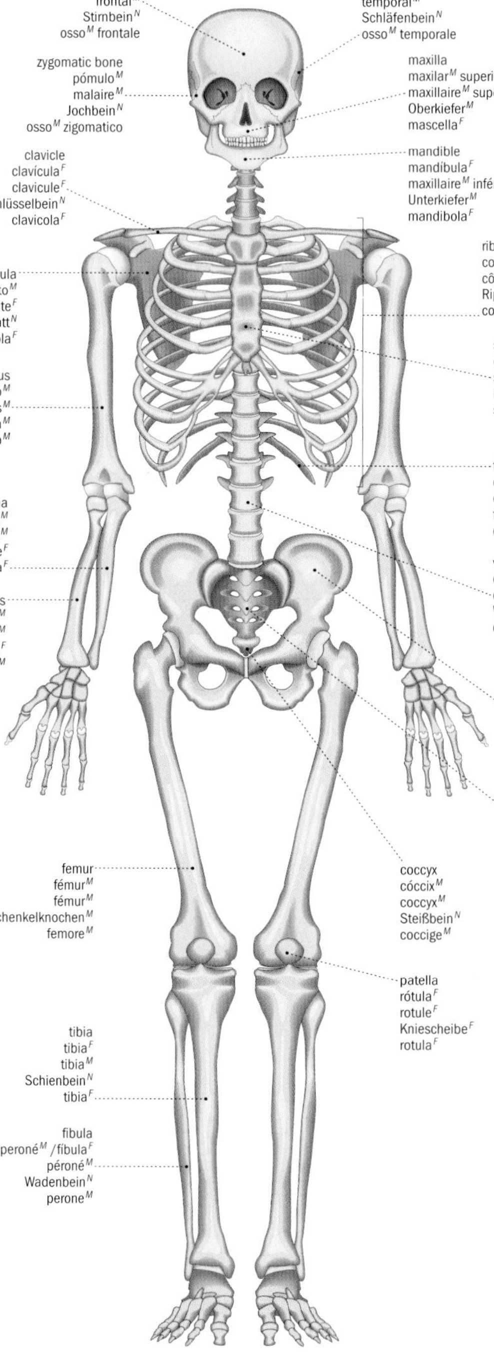

anterior view
vista^F anterior
vue^F antérieure
Vorderansicht^F
vista^F anteriore

frontal bone
hueso^M frontal
frontal^M
Stimbein^N
osso^M frontale

temporal bone
hueso^M temporal
temporal^M
Schläfenbein^N
osso^M temporale

zygomatic bone
pómulo^M
malaire^M
Jochbein^N
osso^M zigomatico

maxilla
maxilar^M superior
maxillaire^M supérieur
Oberkiefer^M
mascella^F

clavicle
clavícula^F
clavicule^F
Schlüsselbein^N
clavicola^F

mandible
mandíbula^F
maxillaire^M inférieur
Unterkiefer^M
mandibola^F

ribs
costillas^F
côtes^F
Rippen^F
costole^F

scapula
escápula^F /omóplato^M
omoplate^F
Schulterblatt^N
scapola^F

sternum
esternón^M
sternum^M
Brustbein^N
sterno^M

humerus
húmero^M
humérus^M
Oberarmknochen^M
omero^M

floating ribs (2)
costilla^F flotante (2)
côte^F flottante (2)
frei endende Rippe^F (2)
costole^F fluttuanti (2)

ulna
cúbito^M
cubitus^M
Elle^F
ulna^F

vertebral column
columna^F vertebral
colonne^F vertébrale
Wirbelsäule^F
colonna^F vertebrale

radius
radio^M
radius^M
Speiche^F
radio^M

ilium
hueso^M ilíaco^M
os^M iliaque
Darmbein^N
ileo^M

sacrum
sacro^M
sacrum^M
Kreuzbein^N
sacro^M

femur
fémur^M
fémur^M
Oberschenkelknochen^M
femore^M

coccyx
cóccix^M
coccyx^M
Steißbein^N
coccige^M

patella
rótula^F
rotule^F
Kniescheibe^F
rotula^F

tibia
tibia^F
tibia^M
Schienbein^N
tibia^F

fibula
peroné^M /fíbula^F
péroné^M
Wadenbein^N
perone^M

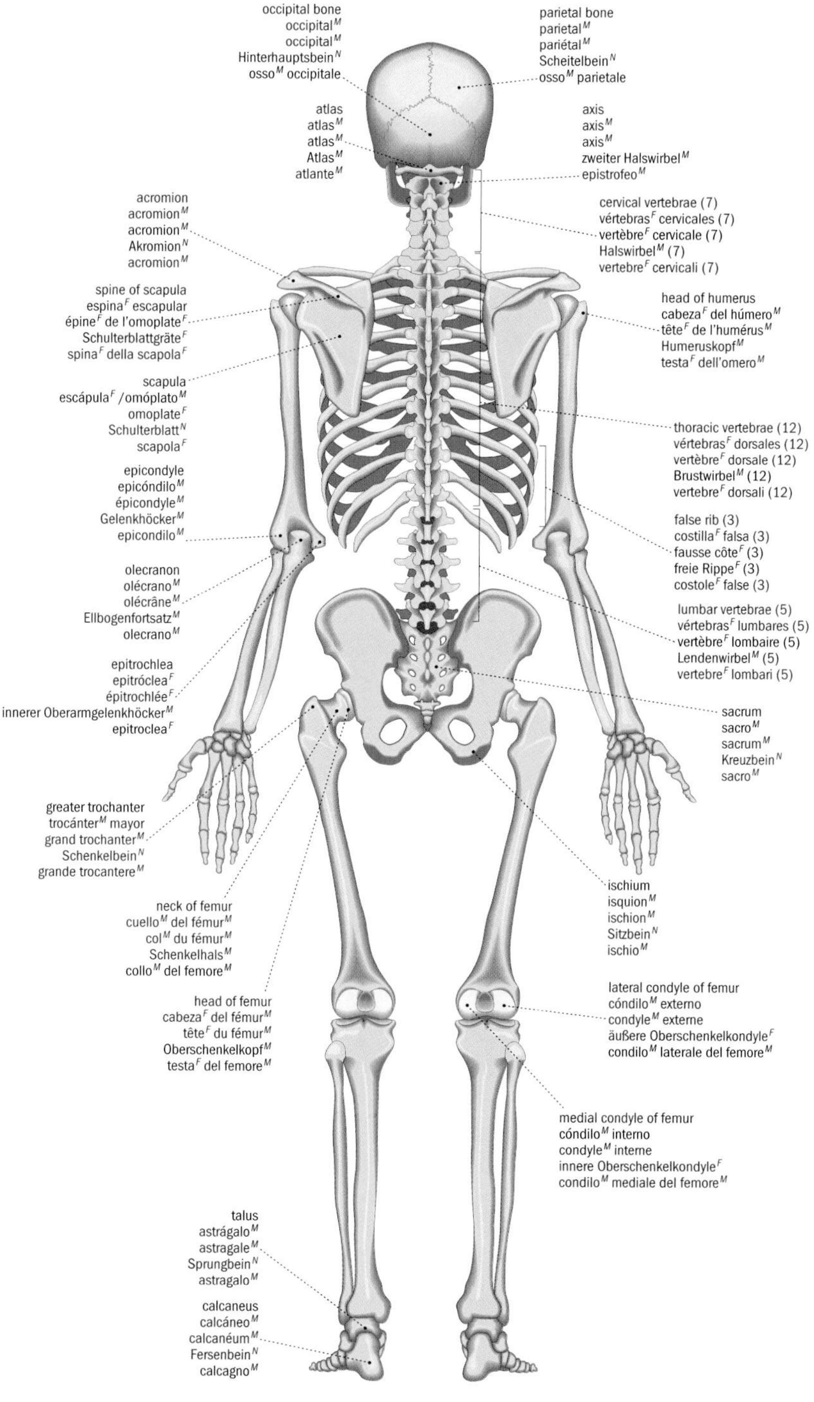

posterior view
vista^F posterior
vue^F postérieure
Rückansicht^F
vista^F posteriore

HUMAN BEING

occipital bone
occipital^M
occipital^M
Hinterhauptsbein^N
osso^M occipitale

parietal bone
parietal^M
pariétal^M
Scheitelbein^N
osso^M parietale

atlas
atlas^M
atlas^M
Atlas^M
atlante^M

axis
axis^M
axis^M
zweiter Halswirbel^M
epistrofeo^M

acromion
acromion^M
acromion^M
Akromion^M
acromion^M

cervical vertebrae (7)
vértebras^F cervicales (7)
vertèbre^F cervicale (7)
Halswirbel^M (7)
vertebre^F cervicali (7)

spine of scapula
espina^F escapular
épine^F de l'omoplate^F
Schulterblattgräte^F
spina^F della scapola^F

head of humerus
cabeza^F del húmero^M
tête^F de l'humérus^M
Humeruskopf^M
testa^F dell'omero^M

scapula
escápula^F /omóplato^M
omoplate^F
Schulterblatt^N
scapola^F

thoracic vertebrae (12)
vértebras^F dorsales (12)
vertèbre^F dorsale (12)
Brustwirbel^M (12)
vertebre^F dorsali (12)

epicondyle
epicóndilo^M
épicondyle^M
Gelenkhöcker^M
epicondilo^M

false rib (3)
costilla^F falsa (3)
fausse côte^F (3)
freie Rippe^F (3)
costole^F false (3)

olecranon
olécrano^M
olécrâne^M
Ellbogenfortsatz^M
olecrano^M

lumbar vertebrae (5)
vértebras^F lumbares (5)
vertèbre^F lombaire (5)
Lendenwirbel^M (5)
vertebre^F lombari (5)

epitrochlea
epitróclea^F
épitrochlée^F
innerer Oberarmgelenkhöcker^M
epitroclea^F

sacrum
sacro^M
sacrum^M
Kreuzbein^N
sacro^M

greater trochanter
trocánter^M mayor
grand trochanter^M
Schenkelbein^N
grande trocantere^M

ischium
isquion^M
ischion^M
Sitzbein^N
ischio^M

neck of femur
cuello^M del fémur^M
col^M du fémur^M
Schenkelhals^M
collo^M del femore^M

lateral condyle of femur
cóndilo^M externo
condyle^M externe
äußere Oberschenkelkondyle^F
condilo^M laterale del femore^M

head of femur
cabeza^F del fémur^M
tête^F du fémur^M
Oberschenkelkopf^M
testa^F del femore^M

medial condyle of femur
cóndilo^M interno
condyle^M interne
innere Oberschenkelkondyle^F
condilo^M mediale del femore^M

talus
astrágalo^M
astragale^M
Sprungbein^N
astragalo^M

calcaneus
calcáneo^M
calcanéum^M
Fersenbein^N
calcagno^M

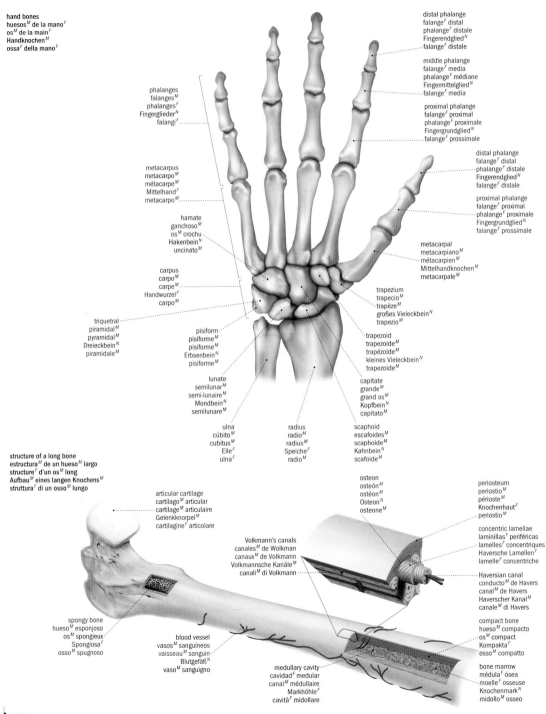

hand bones
huesos^M de la mano^F
os^M de la main^F
Handknochen^M
ossa^F della mano^F

phalanges
falanges^M
phalanges^F
Fingerglieder^N
falangi^F

metacarpus
metacarpo^M
métacarpe^M
Mittelhand^F
metacarpo^M

hamate
ganchoso^M
os^M crochu
Hakenbein^N
uncinato^M

carpus
carpo^M
carpe^M
Handwurzel^F
carpo^M

triquetral
piramidal^M
pyramidal^M
Dreieckbein^N
piramidale^M

pisiform
pisiforme^M
pisiforme^M
Erbsenbein^N
pisiforme^M

lunate
semilunar^M
semi-lunaire^M
Mondbein^N
semilunare^M

ulna
cúbito^M
cubitus^M
Elle^F
ulna^F

radius
radio^M
radius^M
Speiche^F
radio^M

scaphoid
escafoides^M
scaphoïde^M
Kahnbein^N
scafoide^M

capitate
grande^M
grand os^M
Kopfbein^N
capitato^M

trapezoid
trapecio^M
trapézoïde^M
kleines Vieleckbein^N
trapezoide^M

trapezium
trapecio^M
trapèze^M
großes Vieleckbein^N
trapezio^M

metacarpal
metacarpiano^M
métacarpien^M
Mittelhandknochen^M
metacarpale^M

proximal phalange
falange^F proximal
phalange^F proximale
Fingergrundglied^N
falange^F prossimale

distal phalange
falange^F distal
phalange^F distale
Fingerendglied^N
falange^F distale

proximal phalange
falange^F proximal
phalange^F proximale
Fingergrundglied^N
falange^F prossimale

middle phalange
falange^F media
phalange^F médiane
Fingermittelglied^N
falange^F media

distal phalange
falange^F distal
phalange^F distale
Fingerendglied^N
falange^F distale

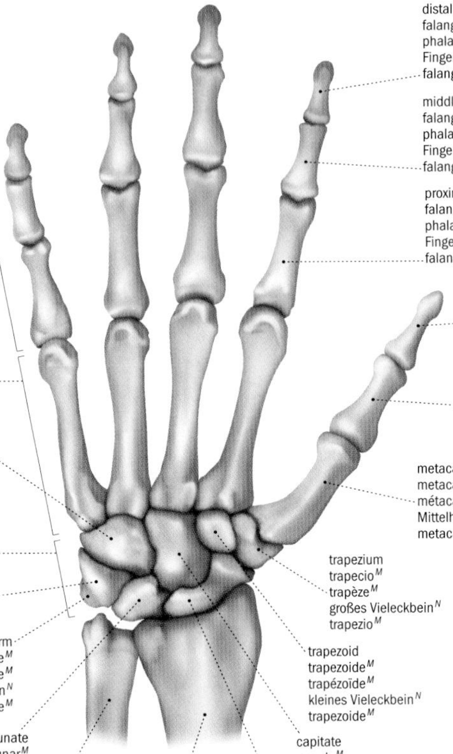

structure of a long bone
estructura^M de un hueso^M largo
structure^F d'un os^M long
Aufbau^M eines langen Knochens^M
struttura^F di un osso^M lungo

articular cartilage
cartilago^M articular
cartilage^M articulaire
Gelenkknorpel^M
cartilagine^F articolare

spongy bone
hueso^M esponjoso
os^M spongieux
Spongiosa^F
osso^M spugnoso

blood vessel
vasos^M sanguíneos
vaisseau^M sanguin
Blutgefäß^N
vaso^M sanguigno

Volkmann's canals
canales^M de Wolkman
canaux^M de Volkmann
Volkmannsche Kanäle
canali^M di Volkmann

medullary cavity
cavidad^F medular
canal^M médullaire
Markhöhle^F
cavità^F midollare

osteon
osteón^M
ostéon^M
Osteon^N
osteone^M

periosteum
periostio^M
périoste^M
Knochenhaut^F
periostio^M

concentric lamellae
laminillas^F periféricas
lamelles^F concentriques
Haversche Lamellen^F
lamelle^F concentriche

Haversian canal
conducto^M de Havers
canal^M de Havers
Haverscher Kanal^F
canale^M di Havers

compact bone
hueso^M compacto
os^M compact
Kompakta^F
osso^M compatto

bone marrow
médula^F ósea
moelle^F osseuse
Knochenmark^N
midollo^M osseo

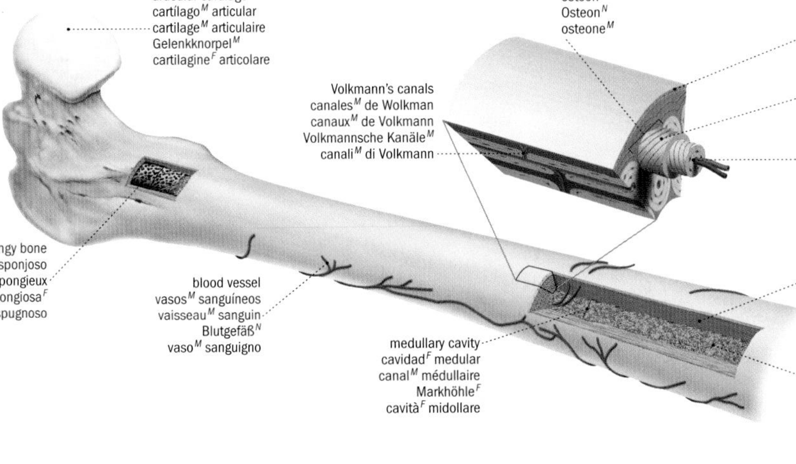

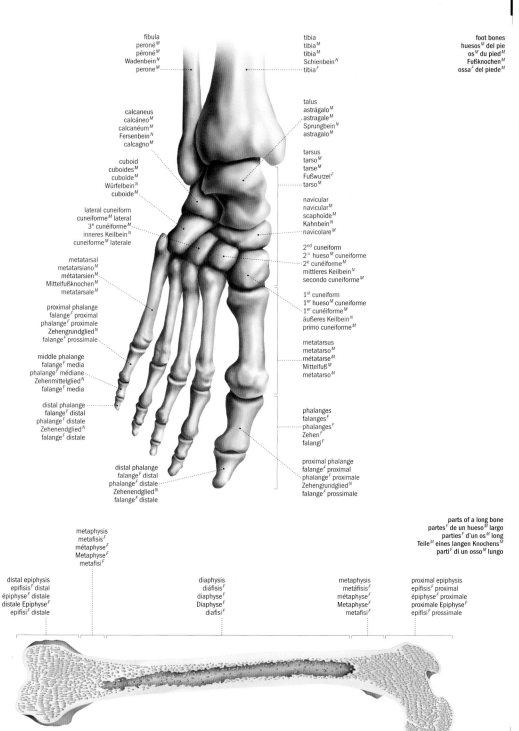

fibula
peroné ^{M}
péroné ^{M}
Wadenbein ^{N}
perone ^{M}

tibia
tibia ^{M}
tibia ^{M}
Schienbein ^{N}
tibia ^{F}

foot bones
huesos ^{M} del pie
os ^{M} du pied ^{M}
Fußknochen ^{M}
ossa ^{F} del piede ^{M}

calcaneus
calcáneo ^{M}
calcanéum ^{M}
Fersenbein ^{N}
calcagno ^{M}

talus
astrágalo ^{M}
astragale ^{M}
Sprungbein ^{N}
astragalo ^{M}

cuboid
cuboides ^{M}
cuboïde ^{M}
Würfelbein ^{N}
cuboide ^{M}

tarsus
tarso ^{M}
tarse ^{M}
Fußwurzel ^{F}
tarso ^{M}

navicular
navicular ^{M}
scaphoïde ^{M}
Kahnbein ^{N}
navicolare ^{M}

lateral cuneiform
cuneiforme ^{M} lateral
3 ^{e} cunéiforme ^{M}
inneres Keilbein ^{N}
cuneiforme ^{M} laterale

2 nd cuneiform
2° hueso ^{M} cuneiforme
2 ^{e} cunéiforme ^{M}
mittleres Keilbein ^{N}
secondo cuneiforme ^{M}

metatarsal
metatarsiano ^{M}
métatarsien ^{M}
Mittelfußknochen ^{M}
metatarsale ^{M}

1 st cuneiform
1 ^{er} hueso ^{M} cuneiforme
1 ^{er} cunéiforme ^{M}
äußeres Keilbein ^{N}
primo cuneiforme ^{M}

proximal phalange
falange ^{F} proximal
phalange ^{F} proximale
Zehengrundglied ^{N}
falange ^{F} prossimale

metatarsus
metatarso ^{M}
métatarse ^{M}
Mittelfuß ^{M}
metatarso ^{M}

middle phalange
falange ^{F} media
phalange ^{F} médiane
Zehenmittelglied ^{N}
falange ^{F} media

distal phalange
falange ^{F} distal
phalange ^{F} distale
Zehenendglied ^{N}
falange ^{F} distale

phalanges
falanges ^{F}
phalanges ^{F}
Zehen ^{F}
falangi ^{F}

distal phalange
falange ^{F} distal
phalange ^{F} distale
Zehenendglied ^{N}
falange ^{F} distale

proximal phalange
falange ^{F} proximal
phalange ^{F} proximale
Zehengrundglied ^{N}
falange ^{F} prossimale

parts of a long bone
partes ^{F} de un hueso ^{M} largo
parties ^{F} d'un os ^{M} long
Teile ^{M} eines langen Knochens ^{M}
parti ^{F} di un osso ^{M} lungo

metaphysis
metafisis ^{F}
métaphyse ^{F}
Metaphyse ^{F}
metafisi ^{F}

distal epiphysis
epífisis ^{F} distal
épiphyse ^{F} distale
distale Epiphyse ^{F}
epifisi ^{F} distale

diaphysis
diáfisis ^{F}
diaphyse ^{F}
Diaphyse ^{F}
diafisi ^{F}

metaphysis
metáfisis ^{F}
métaphyse ^{F}
Metaphyse ^{F}
metafisi ^{F}

proximal epiphysis
epifisis ^{F} proximal
épiphyse ^{F} proximale
proximale Epiphyse ^{F}
epifisi ^{F} prossimale

HUMAN BEING

types of synovial joints
tipos^M de articulaciones^F sinoviales
types^M d'articulations^F synoviales
Arten^F von echten Gelenken^N
tipi^M di articolazioni^F sinoviali

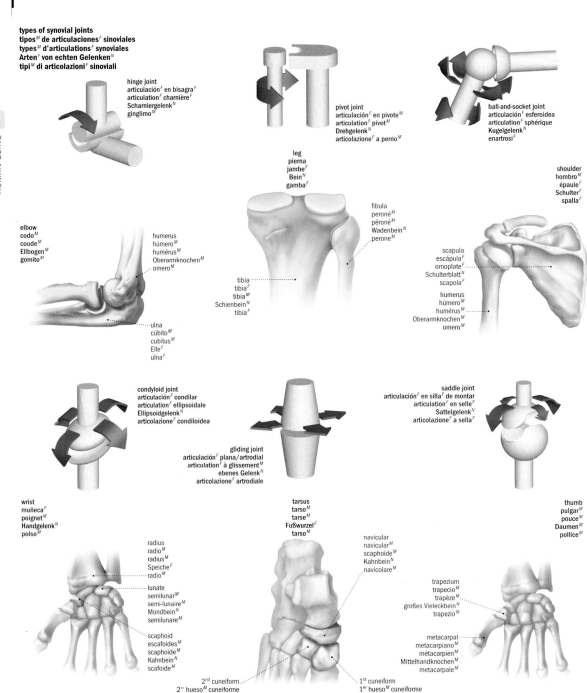

hinge joint
articulación^F en bisagra^F
articulation^F charnière^F
Scharniergelenk^N
ginglimo^M

pivot joint
articulación^F en pivote^M
articulation^F pivot^M
Drehgelenk^N
articolazione^F a perno^M

ball-and-socket joint
articulación^F esferoidea
articulation^F sphérique
Kugelgelenk^N
enartrosi^F

leg
pierna
jambe^F
Bein^N
gamba^F

shoulder
hombro^M
épaule^F
Schulter^F
spalla^F

elbow
codo^M
coude^M
Ellbogen^M
gomito^M

humerus
húmero^M
humérus^M
Oberarmknochen^M
omero^M

fibula
peroné^M
péroné^M
Wadenbein^N
perone^M

scapula
escápula^F
omoplate^F
Schulterblatt^N
scapola^F

tibia
tibia^F
tibia^M
Schienbein^N
tibia^F

humerus
húmero^M
humérus^M
Oberarmknochen^M
omero^M

ulna
cúbito^M
cubitus^M
Elle^F
ulna^F

condyloid joint
articulación^F condilar
articulation^F ellipsoidale
Ellipsoidgelenk^N
articolazione^F condiloidea

saddle joint
articulación^F en silla^F de montar
articulation^F en selle^F
Sattelgelenk^N
articolazione^F a sella^F

gliding joint
articulación^F plana/artrodial
articulation^F à glissement^M
ebenes Gelenk^N
articolazione^F artrodiale

wrist
muñeca^F
poignet^M
Handgelenk^N
polso^M

tarsus
tarso^M
tarse^M
Fußwurzel^F
tarso^M

thumb
pulgar^M
pouce^M
Daumen^M
pollice^M

radius
radio^M
radius^M
Speiche^F
radio^M

navicular
navicular^M
scaphoide^M
Kahnbein^N
navicolare^M

trapezium
trapecio^M
trapèze^M
großes Vieleckbein^N
trapezio^M

lunate
semilunar^M
semi-lunaire^M
Mondbein^N
semilunare^M

scaphoid
escafoides^M
scaphoide^M
Kahnbein^N
scafoide^M

metacarpal
metacarpiano^M
métacarpien^M
Mittelhandknochen^M
metacarpale^M

2nd cuneiform
2° hueso^M cuneiforme
2e cunéiforme^M
mittleres Keilbein^N
secondo cuneiforme^M

1st cuneiform
1er hueso^M cuneiforme
1er cunéiforme^M
äußeres Keilbein^N
primo cuneiforme^M

HUMAN BEING

vertebral column
columna^F vertebral
os^M de la colonne^F vertébrale
Wirbelsäule^F
colonna^F vertebrale

types of bones
tipos^M de huesos^M
types^M d'os^M
Knochenarten^F
tipi^M di ossa^F

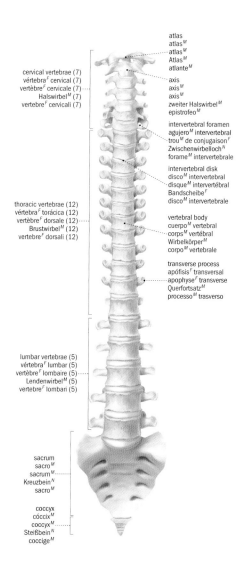

atlas
atlas^M
atlas^M
Atlas^M
atlante^M

cervical vertebrae (7)
vértebra^F cervical (7)
vertèbre^F cervicale (7)
Halswirbel^M (7)
vertebre^F cervicali (7)

axis
axis^M
axis^M
zweiter Halswirbel^M
epistrofeo^M

intervertebral foramen
agujero^M intervertebral
trou^M de conjugaison^F
Zwischenwirbelloch^N
forame^M intervertebrale

intervertebral disk
disco^M intervertebral
disque^M intervertébral
Bandscheibe^F
disco^M intervertebrale

thoracic vertebrae (12)
vértebra^F torácica (12)
vertèbre^F dorsale (12)
Brustwirbel^M (12)
vertebre^F dorsali (12)

vertebral body
cuerpo^M vertebral
corps^M vertébral
Wirbelkörper^M
corpo^M vertebrale

transverse process
apófisis^F transversal
apophyse^F transverse
Querfortsatz^M
processo^M trasverso

lumbar vertebrae (5)
vértebra^F lumbar (5)
vertèbre^F lombaire (5)
Lendenwirbel^M (5)
vertebre^F lombari (5)

sacrum
sacro^M
sacrum^M
Kreuzbein^N
sacro^M

coccyx
cóccix^M
coccyx^M
Steißbein^N
coccige^M

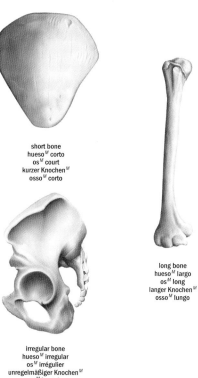

short bone
hueso^M corto
os^M court
kurzer Knochen^M
osso^M corto

long bone
hueso^M largo
os^M long
langer Knochen^M
osso^M lungo

irregular bone
hueso^M irregular
os^M irrégulier
unregelmäßiger Knochen^M
osso^M irregolare

flat bone
hueso^M plano
os^M plat
platter Knochen^M
osso^M piatto

HUMAN BEING

lateral view of adult skull
vista^F lateral del cráneo^M adulto
vue^F latérale du crâne^M adulte
Seitenansicht^F eines erwachser Schädels^M
vista^F laterale del cranio^M adulto

coronal suture
sutura^F coronal
suture^F coronale
Kranznaht^F
sutura^F coronale

temporal bone
hueso^M temporal
temporal^M
Schläfenbein^N
osso^M temporale

frontal bone
hueso^M frontal
frontal^M
Stimbein^N
osso^M frontale

squamous suture
sutura^F escamosa
suture^F squameuse
Schuppennaht^F
sutura^F squamosa

sphenoid bone
hueso^M esfenoides
sphénoïde^M
Keilbein^N
osso^M sfenoide

parietal bone
hueso^M parietal
pariétal^M
Scheitelbein^N
osso^M parietale

zygomatic bone
hueso^M cigomático
malaire^M
Jochbein^N
osso^M zigomatico

lambdoid suture
sutura^F lambdoidea
suture^F lambdoïde
Lambdanaht^F
sutura^F lambdoidea

nasal bone
hueso^M nasal
nasal^M
Nasenbein^N
osso^M nasale

occipital bone
hueso^M occipital
occipital^M
Hinterhauptsbein^N
osso^M occipitale

anterior nasal spine
espina^F nasal anterior
épine^F nasale antérieure
Nasenstachel^M
spina^F nasale anteriore

external auditory meatus
meato^M auditivo externo
conduit^M auditif externe
äußerer Gehörgang^M
meato^M uditivo esterno

maxilla
maxilar^M
maxillaire^M supérieur
Oberkieferknochen^M
mascella^F

mastoid process
apófisis^F mastoides
apophyse^F mastoïde
Warzenfortsatz^M
processo^M mastoideo

mandible
mandíbula^F
maxillaire^M inférieur
Unterkieferknochen^M
mandibola^F

styloid process
apófisis^F estiloides
apophyse^F styloïde
Griffelfortsatz^M
processo^M stiloideo

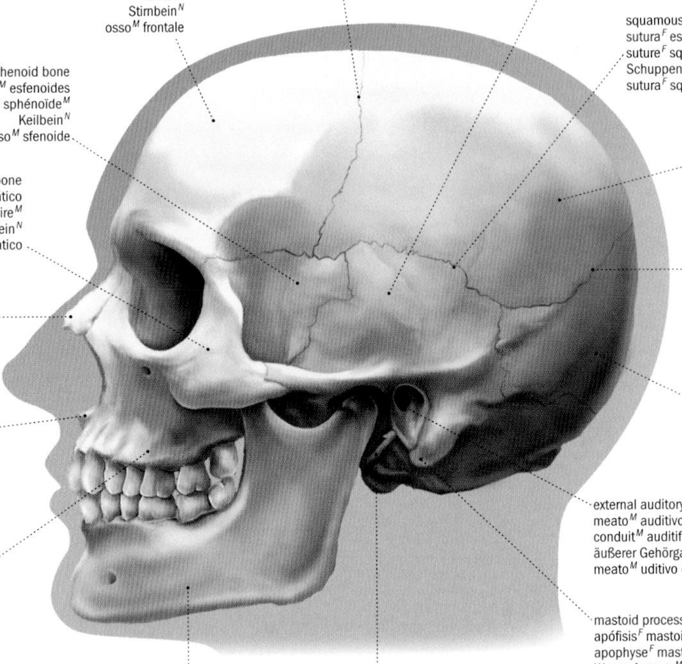

lateral view of child's skull
vista^F lateral del cráneo^M de un niño^M
vue^F latérale du crâne^M d'enfant^M
Seitenansicht^F der Schädel^M eines Kleinkindes^N
vista^F laterale del cranio^M di bambino^M

anterior fontanelle
fontanela^F anterior
fontanelle^F antérieure
Stimfontanelle^F
fontanella^F anteriore

parietal bone
hueso^M parietal
pariétal^M
Scheitelbein^N
osso^M parietale

coronal suture
sutura^F coronal
suture^F coronale
Kranznaht^F
sutura^F coronaria

posterior fontanelle
fontanela^F posterior
fontanelle^F postérieure
hintere Fontanelle^F
fontanella^F posteriore

frontal bone
hueso^M frontal
frontal^M
Stimbein^N
osso^M frontale

occipital bone
hueso^M occipital
occipital^M
Hinterhauptsbein^N
osso^M occipitale

sphenoidal fontanelle
fontanela^F esfenoidal
fontanelle^F sphénoïdale
vordere Seitenfontanelle^F
fontanella^F sfenoidale

mastoid fontanelle
fontanela^F mastoidea
fontanelle^F mastoïdienne
hintere Seitenfontanelle^F
fontanella^F mastoidea

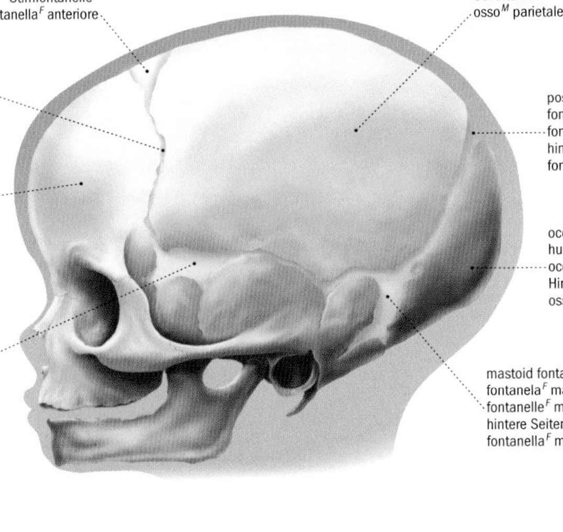

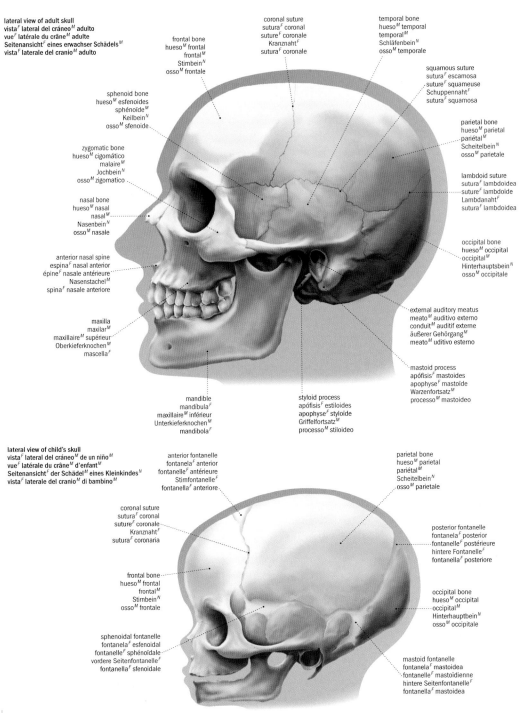

teeth

dientes^M | dents^F | Zähne^M | denti^M

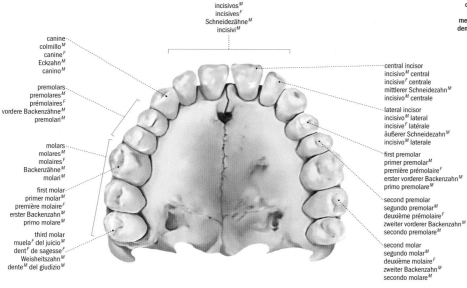

incisors
incisivos^M
incisives^F
Schneidezähne^M
incisivi^M

canine
colmillo^M
canine^F
Eckzahn^M
canino^M

premolars
premolares^M
prémolaires^F
vordere Backenzähne^M
premolari^M

molars
molares^M
molaires^F
Backenzähne^M
molari^M

first molar
primer molar^M
première molaire^F
erster Backenzahn^M
primo molare^M

third molar
muela^F del juicio^M
dent^F de sagesse^F
Weisheitszahn^M
dente^M del giudizio^M

human denture
dentadura^F humana
denture^F humaine
menschliches Gebiss^N
dentatura^F nell'uomo^M

central incisor
incisivo^M central
incisive^F centrale
mittlerer Schneidezahn^M
incisivo^M centrale

lateral incisor
incisivo^M lateral
incisive^F latérale
äußerer Schneidezahn^M
incisivo^M laterale

first premolar
primer premolar^M
première prémolaire^F
erster vorderer Backenzahn^M
primo premolare^M

second premolar
segundo premolar^M
deuxième prémolaire^F
zweiter vorderer Backenzahn^M
secondo premolare^M

second molar
segundo molar^M
deuxième molaire^F
zweiter Backenzahn^M
secondo molare^M

HUMAN BEING

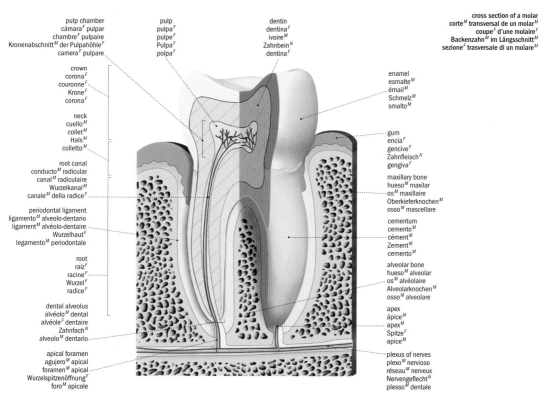

pulp chamber
cámara^F pulpar
chambre^F pulpaire
Kronenabschnitt^M der Pulpahöhle^F
camera^F pulpare

crown
corona^F
couronne^F
Krone^F
corona^F

neck
cuello^M
collet^M
Hals^M
colletto^M

root canal
conducto^M radicular
canal^M radiculaire
Wurzelkanal^M
canale^M della radice^F

periodontal ligament
ligamento^M alveolo-dentario
ligament^M alvéolo-dentaire
Wurzelhaut^F
legamento^M periodontale

root
raíz^F
racine^F
Wurzel^F
radice^F

dental alveolus
alvéolo^M dental
alvéole^F dentaire
Zahnfach^N
alveolo^M dentario

apical foramen
agujero^M apical
foramen^M apical
Wurzelspitzenöffnung^F
foro^M apicale

pulp
pulpa^F
pulpe^F
Pulpa^F
polpa^F

dentin
dentina^F
ivoire^M
Zahnbein^N
dentina^F

cross section of a molar
corte^M transversal de un molar^M
coupe^F d'une molaire^F
Backenzahn^M im Längsschnitt^M
sezione^F trasversale di un molare^M

enamel
esmalte^M
émail^M
Schmelz^M
smalto^M

gum
encía^F
gencive^F
Zahnfleisch^N
gengiva^F

maxillary bone
hueso^M maxilar
os^M maxillaire
Oberkieferknochen^M
osso^M mascellare

cementum
cemento^M
cément^M
Zement^M
cemento^M

alveolar bone
hueso^M alveolar
os^M alvéolaire
Alveolarknochen^M
osso^M alveolare

apex
ápice^M
apex^M
Spitze^F
apice^M

plexus of nerves
plexo^M nervioso
réseau^M nerveux
Nervengeflecht^N
plesso^M dentale

blood circulation

circulación^F sanguínea | circulation^F sanguine | Blutkreislauf^M | circolazione^F del sangue^M

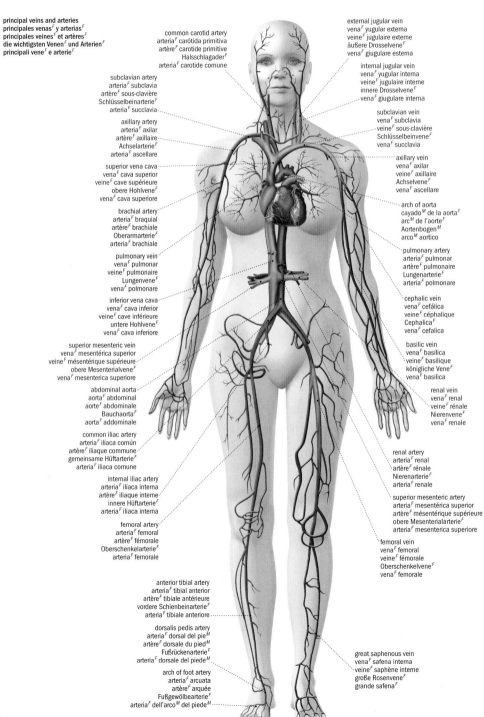

principal veins and arteries
principales venas^F y arterias^F
principales veines^F et artères^F
die wichtigsten Venen^F und Arterien^F
principali vene^F e arterie^F

common carotid artery
arteria^F carótida primitiva
artère^F carotide primitive
Halsschlagader^F
arteria^F carotide comune

subclavian artery
arteria^F subclavia
artère^F sous-clavière
Schlüsselbeinarterie^F
arteria^F succlavia

axillary artery
arteria^F axilar
artère^F axillaire
Achselarterie^F
arteria^F ascellare

superior vena cava
vena^F cava superior
veine^F cave supérieure
obere Hohlvene^F
vena^F cava superiore

brachial artery
arteria^F braquial
artère^F brachiale
Oberarmarterie^F
arteria^F brachiale

pulmonary vein
vena^F pulmonar
veine^F pulmonaire
Lungenvene^F
vena^F polmonare

inferior vena cava
vena^F cava inferior
veine^F cave inférieure
untere Hohlvene^F
vena^F cava inferiore

superior mesenteric vein
vena^F mesentérica superior
veine^F mésentérique supérieure
obere Mesenterialvene^F
vena^F mesenterica superiore

abdominal aorta
aorta^F abdominal
aorte^F abdominale
Bauchaorta^F
aorta^F addominale

common iliac artery
arteria^F ilíaca común
artère^F iliaque commune
gemeinsame Hüftarterie^F
arteria^F iliaca comune

internal iliac artery
arteria^F ilíaca interna
artère^F iliaque interne
innere Hüftarterie^F
arteria^F iliaca interna

femoral artery
arteria^F femoral
artère^F fémorale
Oberschenkelarterie^F
arteria^F femorale

anterior tibial artery
arteria^F tibial anterior
artère^F tibiale antérieure
vordere Schienbeinarterie^F
arteria^F tibiale anteriore

dorsalis pedis artery
arteria^F dorsal del pie^M
artère^F dorsale du pied^M
Fußrückenarterie^F
arteria^F dorsale del piede^M

arch of foot artery
arteria^F arcuata
artère^F arquée
Fußgewölbearterie^F
arteria^F dell'arco^M del piede^M

external jugular vein
vena^F yugular externa
veine^F jugulaire externe
äußere Drosselvene^F
vena^F giugulare esterna

internal jugular vein
vena^F yugular interna
veine^F jugulaire interne
innere Drosselvene^F
vena^F giugulare interna

subclavian vein
vena^F subclavia
veine^F sous-clavière
Schlüsselbeinvene^F
vena^F succlavia

axillary vein
vena^F axilar
veine^F axillaire
Achselvene^F
vena^F ascellare

arch of aorta
cayado^M de la aorta^F
arc^M de l'aorte^F
Aortenbogen^M
arco^M aortico

pulmonary artery
arteria^F pulmonar
artère^F pulmonaire
Lungenarterie^F
arteria^F polmonare

cephalic vein
vena^F cefálica
veine^F céphalique
Cephalica^F
vena^F cefalica

basilic vein
vena^F basílica
veine^F basilique
königliche Vene^F
vena^F basilica

renal vein
vena^F renal
veine^F rénale
Nierenvene^F
vena^F renale

renal artery
arteria^F renal
artère^F rénale
Nierenarterie^F
arteria^F renale

superior mesenteric artery
arteria^F mesentérica superior
artère^F mésentérique supérieure
obere Mesenterialarterie^F
arteria^F mesenterica superiore

femoral vein
vena^F femoral
veine^F fémorale
Oberschenkelvene^F
vena^F femorale

great saphenous vein
vena^F safena interna
veine^F saphène interne
große Rosenvene^F
grande safena^F

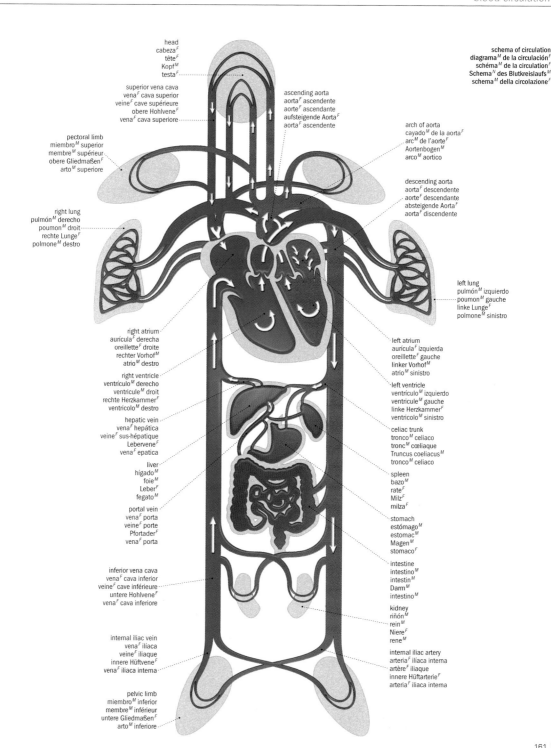

head
cabeza^F
tête^F
Kopf^M
testa^F

superior vena cava
vena^F cava superior
veine^F cave supérieure
obere Hohlvene^F
vena^F cava superiore

ascending aorta
aorta^F ascendente
aorte^F ascendante
aufsteigende Aorta^F
aorta^F ascendente

schema of circulation
diagrama^M de la circulación^F
schéma^M de la circulation^F
Schema^N des Blutkreislaufs^M
schema^M della circolazione^F

arch of aorta
cayado^M de la aorta^F
arc^M de l'aorte^F
Aortenbogen^M
arco^M aortico

pectoral limb
miembro^M superior
membre^M supérieur
obere Gliedmaßen^F
arto^M superiore

descending aorta
aorta^F descendente
aorte^F descendante
absteigende Aorta^F
aorta^F discendente

right lung
pulmón^M derecho
poumon^M droit
rechte Lunge^F
polmone^M destro

left lung
pulmón^M izquierdo
poumon^M gauche
linke Lunge^F
polmone^M sinistro

right atrium
aurícula^F derecha
oreillette^F droite
rechter Vorhof^M
atrio^M destro

left atrium
aurícula^F izquierda
oreillette^F gauche
linker Vorhof^M
atrio^M sinistro

right ventricle
ventrículo^M derecho
ventricule^M droit
rechte Herzkammer^F
ventricolo^M destro

left ventricle
ventrículo^M izquierdo
ventricule^M gauche
linke Herzkammer^F
ventricolo^M sinistro

hepatic vein
vena^F hepática
veine^F sus-hépatique
Lebervene^F
vena^F epatica

celiac trunk
tronco^M celiaco
tronc^M cœliaque
Truncus coeliacus^M
tronco^M celiaco

liver
hígado^M
foie^M
Leber^F
fegato^M

spleen
bazo^M
rate^F
Milz^F
milza^F

portal vein
vena^F porta
veine^F porte
Pfortader^F
vena^F porta

stomach
estómago^M
estomac^M
Magen^M
stomaco^F

intestine
intestino^M
intestin^M
Darm^M
intestino^M

inferior vena cava
vena^F cava inferior
veine^F cave inférieure
untere Hohlvene^F
vena^F cava inferiore

kidney
riñón^M
rein^M
Niere^F
rene^M

internal iliac vein
vena^F ilíaca
veine^F iliaque
innere Hüftvene^F
vena^F iliaca interna

internal iliac artery
arteria^F ilíaca interna
artère^F iliaque
innere Hüftarterie^F
arteria^F iliaca interna

pelvic limb
miembro^M inferior
membre^M inférieur
untere Gliedmaßen^F
arto^M inferiore

HUMAN BEING

blood circulation

HUMAN BEING

composition of the blood
composición^F de la sangre^F
composition^F du sang^M
Blutbestandteile^M
composizione^F del sangue^M

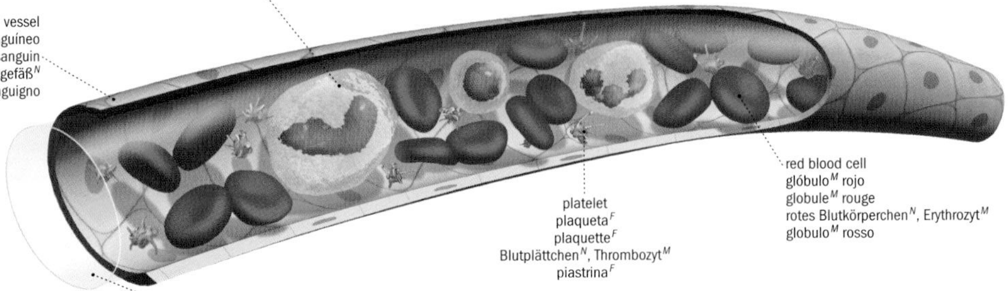

white blood cell
glóbulo^F blanco
globule^M blanc
weißes Blutkörperchen^N, Leukozyt^M
globulo^M bianco

blood vessel
vaso^M sanguíneo
vaisseau^M sanguin
Blutgefäß^N
vaso^M sanguigno

red blood cell
glóbulo^M rojo
globule^M rouge
rotes Blutkörperchen^N, Erythrozyt^M
globulo^M rosso

platelet
plaqueta^F
plaquette^F
Blutplättchen^N, Thrombozyt^M
piastrina^F

plasma
plasma^M
plasma^M
Blutplasma^N
plasma^M

heart
corazón^M
cœur^M
Herz^N
cuore^M

oxygenated blood
sangre^F oxigenada
sang^M oxygéné
sauerstoffreiches Blut^N
sangue^M ossigenato

deoxygenated blood
sangre^F desoxigenada
sang^M désoxygéné
sauerstoffarmes Blut^N
sangue^M deossigenato

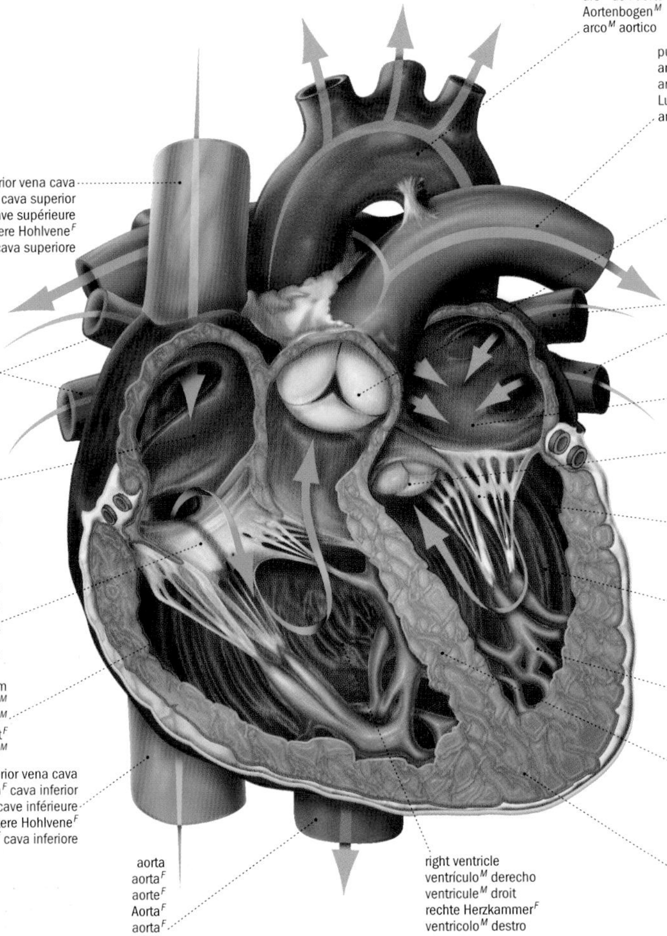

arch of aorta
cayado^M de la aorta^F
arc^M de l'aorte^F
Aortenbogen^M
arco^M aortico

pulmonary trunk
arteria^F pulmonar
artère^F pulmonaire
Lungenarterienstamm^M
arteria^M polmonare

superior vena cava
vena^F cava superior
veine^F cave supérieure
obere Hohlvene^F
vena^F cava superiore

pulmonary valve
válvula^F pulmonar
valvule^F pulmonaire
Pulmonalklappe^F
valvola^F polmonare

left pulmonary vein
vena^F pulmonar izquierda
veine^F pulmonaire gauche
linke Lungenvene^F
vena^F polmonare sinistra

right pulmonary vein
vena^F pulmonar derecha
veine^F pulmonaire droite
rechte Lungenvene^F
vena^F polmonare destra

left atrium
auricula^F izquierda
oreillette^F gauche
linker Vorhof^M
atrio^M sinistro

aortic valve
válvula^F aórtica
valvule^F aortique
Aortenklappe^F
valvola^F aortica

right atrium
auricula^F derecha
oreillette^F droite
rechter Vorhof^M
atrio^M destro

mitral valve
válvula^F mitral
valvule^F mitrale
Mitralklappe^F
valvola^F mitrale

tricuspid valve
válvula^F tricúspide
valvule^F tricuspide
Trikuspidalklappe^F
valvola^F tricuspide

left ventricle
ventrículo^M izquierdo
ventricule^M gauche
linke Herzkammer^F
ventricolo^M sinistro

papillary muscle
músculo^M papilar
muscle^M papillaire
Papillarmuskel^M
muscolo^M papillare

endocardium
endocardio^M
endocarde^F
Herzwandschicht^F
endocardio^M

inferior vena cava
vena^F cava inferior
veine^F cave inférieure
untere Hohlvene^F
vena^F cava inferiore

interventricular septum
tabique^M interventricular
septum^M interventriculaire
Kammerseptum^N
setto^M interventricolare

aorta
aorta^F
aorte^F
Aorta^F
aorta^F

right ventricle
ventrículo^M derecho
ventricule^M droit
rechte Herzkammer^F
ventricolo^M destro

myocardium
miocardio^M
myocarde^M
Herzmuskel^M
miocardio^M

respiratory system

aparato^M respiratorio | appareil^M respiratoire | Luftwege^M | apparato^M respiratorio

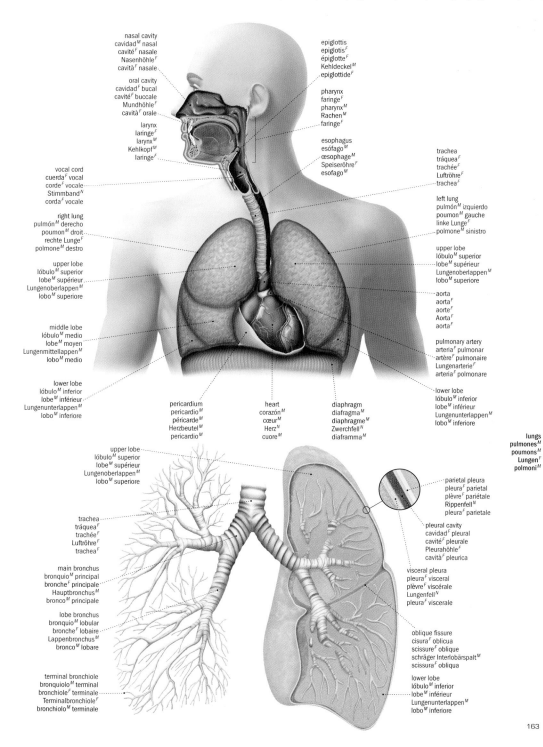

nasal cavity
cavidad^M nasal
cavité^F nasale
Nasenhöhle^F
cavità^F nasale

oral cavity
cavidad^F bucal
cavité^F buccale
Mundhöhle^F
cavità^F orale

larynx
laringe^F
larynx^M
Kehlkopf^M
laringe^F

vocal cord
cuerda^F vocal
corde^F vocale
Stimmband^N
corda^F vocale

right lung
pulmón^M derecho
poumon^M droit
rechte Lunge^F
polmone^M destro

upper lobe
lóbulo^M superior
lobe^M supérieur
Lungenoberlappen^M
lobo^M superiore

middle lobe
lóbulo^M medio
lobe^M moyen
Lungenmittellappen^M
lobo^M medio

lower lobe
lóbulo^M inferior
lobe^M inférieur
Lungenunterlappen^M
lobo^M inferiore

epiglottis
epiglotis^F
épiglotte^F
Kehldeckel^M
epiglottide^F

pharynx
faringe^F
pharynx^M
Rachen^M
faringe^F

esophagus
esófago^M
œsophage^M
Speiseröhre^F
esofago^M

trachea
tráquea^F
trachée^F
Luftröhre^F
trachea^F

left lung
pulmón^M izquierdo
poumon^M gauche
linke Lunge^F
polmone^M sinistro

upper lobe
lóbulo^M superior
lobe^M supérieur
Lungenoberlappen^M
lobo^M superiore

aorta
aorta^F
aorte^F
Aorta^F
aorta^F

pulmonary artery
arteria^F pulmonar
artère^F pulmonaire
Lungenarterie^F
arteria^F polmonare

lower lobe
lóbulo^M inferior
lobe^M inférieur
Lungenunterlappen^M
lobo^M inferiore

pericardium
pericardio^M
péricarde^M
Herzbeutel^M
pericardio^M

heart
corazón^M
cœur^M
Herz^N
cuore^M

diaphragm
diafragma^M
diaphragme^M
Zwerchfell^N
diaframma^M

lungs
pulmones^M
poumons^M
Lungen^F
polmoni^M

upper lobe
lóbulo^M superior
lobe^M supérieur
Lungenoberlappen^M
lobo^M superiore

trachea
tráquea^F
trachée^F
Luftröhre^F
trachea^F

main bronchus
bronquio^F principal
bronche^F principale
Hauptbronchus^M
bronco^M principale

lobe bronchus
bronquio^M lobular
bronche^F lobaire
Lappenbronchus^M
bronco^M lobare

terminal bronchiole
bronquiolo^M terminal
bronchiole^F terminale
Terminalbronchiole^F
bronchiolo^M terminale

parietal pleura
pleura^F parietal
plèvre^F pariétale
Rippenfell^N
pleura^F parietale

pleural cavity
cavidad^F pleural
cavité^F pleurale
Pleurahöhle^F
cavità^F pleurica

visceral pleura
pleura^F visceral
plèvre^F viscérale
Lungenfell^N
pleura^F viscerale

oblique fissure
cisura^F oblicua
scissure^F oblique
schräger Interlobärspalt^M
scissura^F obliqua

lower lobe
lóbulo^M inferior
lobe^M inférieur
Lungenunterlappen^M
lobo^M inferiore

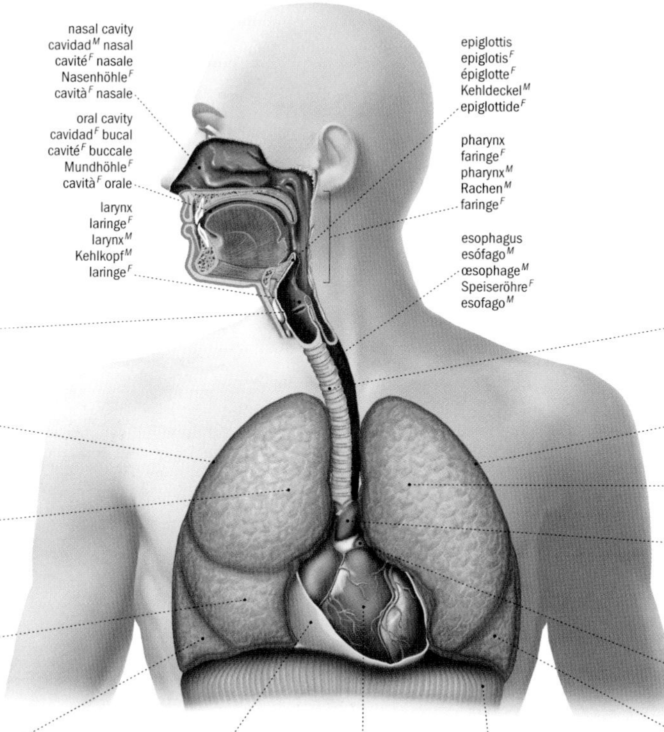

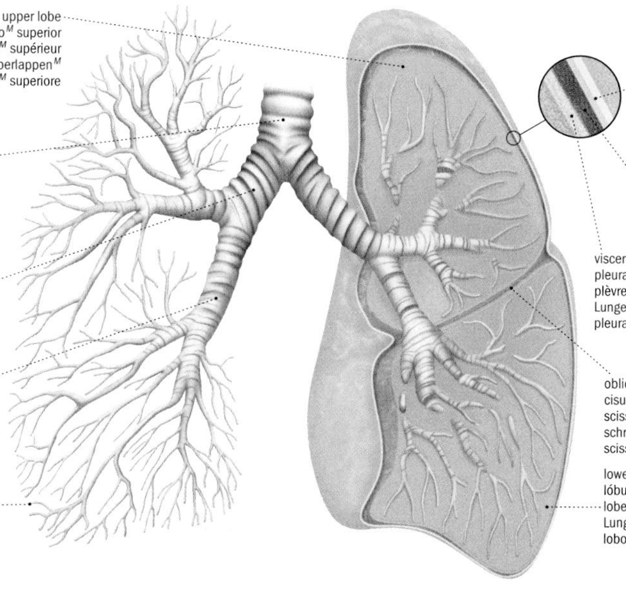

digestive system

aparato^M digestivo | appareil^M digestif | Verdauungsapparat^M | apparato^M digerente

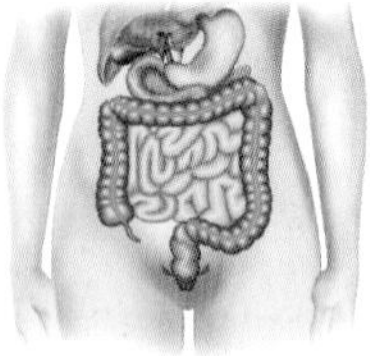

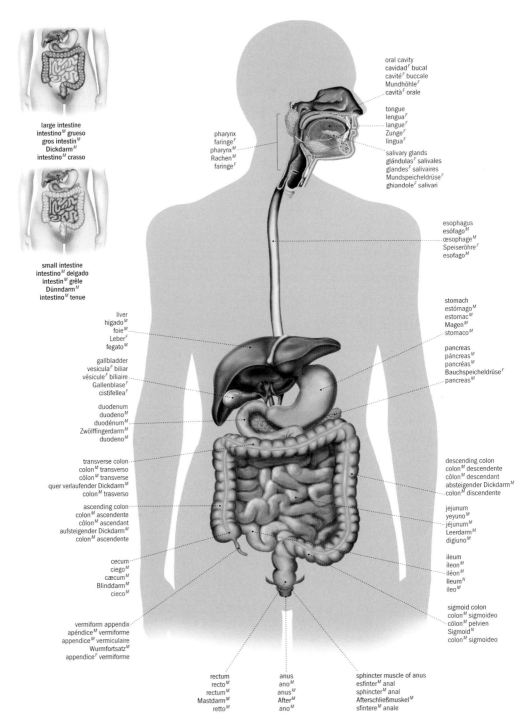

large intestine
intestino^M grueso
gros intestin^M
Dickdarm^M
intestino^M crasso

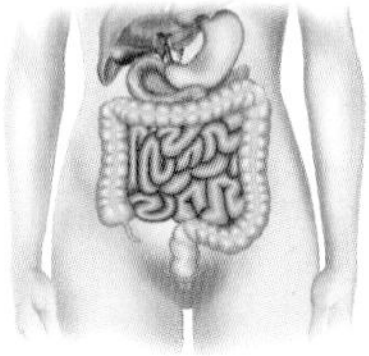

small intestine
intestino^M delgado
intestin^M grêle
Dünndarm^M
intestino^M tenue

oral cavity
cavidad^F bucal
cavité^F buccale
Mundhöhle^F
cavità^F orale

tongue
lengua^F
langue^F
Zunge^F
lingua^F

pharynx
faringe^F
pharynx^M
Rachen^M
faringe^F

salivary glands
glándulas^F salivales
glandes^F salivaires
Mundspeicheldrüse^F
ghiandole^F salivari

esophagus
esófago^M
œsophage^M
Speiseröhre^F
esofago^M

stomach
estómago^M
estomac^M
Magen^M
stomaco^M

pancreas
páncreas^M
pancréas^M
Bauchspeicheldrüse^F
pancreas^M

liver
higado^M
foie^M
Leber^F
fegato^M

gallbladder
vesicula^F biliar
vésicule^F biliaire
Gallenblase^F
cistifellea^F

duodenum
duodeno^M
duodénum^M
Zwölffingerdarm^M
duodeno^M

transverse colon
colon^M transverso
côlon^M transverse
quer verlaufender Dickdarm^M
colon^M trasverso

descending colon
colon^M descendente
côlon^M descendant
absteigender Dickdarm^M
colon^M discendente

jejunum
yeyuno^M
jéjunum^M
Leerdarm^M
digiuno^M

ascending colon
colon^M ascendente
côlon^M ascendant
aufsteigender Dickdarm^M
colon^M ascendente

ileum
ileon^M
iléon^M
Ileum^N
ileo^M

cecum
ciego^M
cæcum^M
Blinddarm^M
cieco^M

sigmoid colon
colon^M sigmoideo
côlon^M pelvien
Sigmoid^N
colon^M sigmoideo

vermiform appendix
apéndice^M vermiforme
appendice^M vermiculaire
Wurmfortsatz^M
appendice^F vermiforme

rectum
recto^M
rectum^M
Mastdarm^M
retto^M

anus
ano^M
anus^M
After^M
ano^M

sphincter muscle of anus
esfinter^M anal
sphincter^M anal
Afterschließmuskel^M
sfintere^M anale

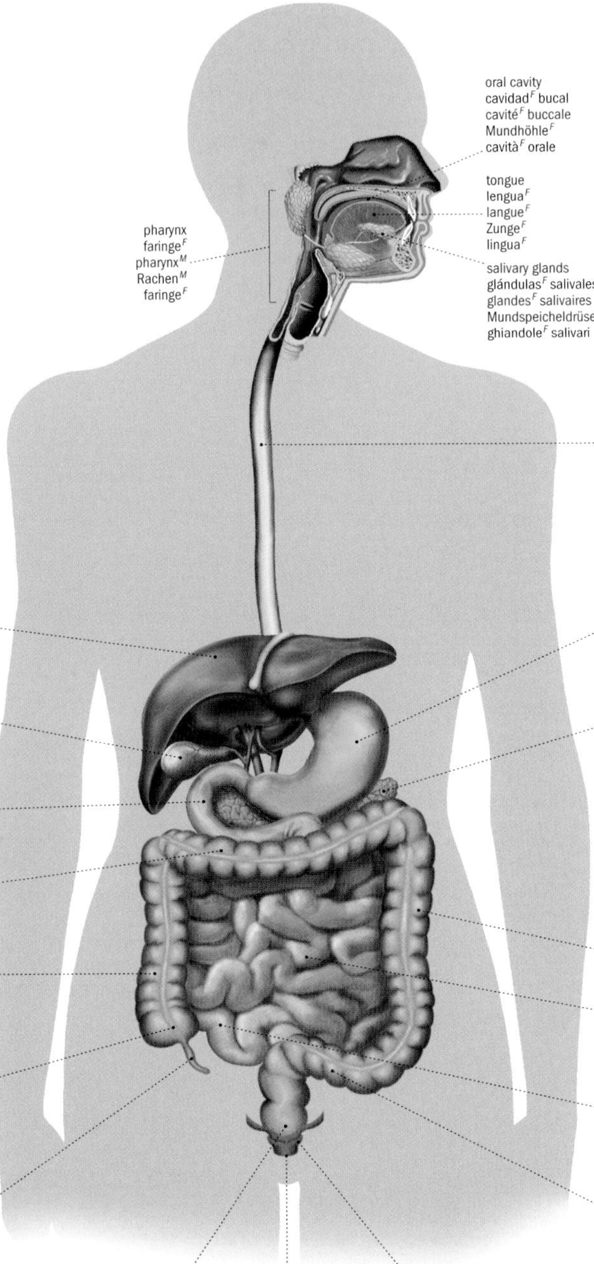

aparato ^{M} urinario | appareil ^{M} urinaire | Harnapparat ^{M} | apparato ^{M} urinario

abdominal aorta
aorta ^{F} abdominal
aorte ^{F} abdominale
Bauchaorta ^{F}
aorta ^{F} addominale

inferior vena cava
vena ^{F} cava inferior
veine ^{F} cave inférieure
untere Hohlvene ^{F}
vena ^{F} cava inferiore

suprarenal gland
glándula ^{F} suprarrenal
glande ^{F} surrénale
Nebenniere ^{F}
ghiandola ^{F} surrenale

right kidney
riñón ^{M} derecho
rein ^{M} droit
rechte Niere ^{F}
rene ^{M} destro

renal hilus
hilio ^{M} renal
hile ^{M} du rein ^{M}
Nierenhilus ^{M}
ilo ^{M} renale

inferior mesenteric artery
arteria ^{F} mesentérica inferior
artère ^{F} mésentérique inférieure
untere Mesenterialarterie ^{F}
arteria ^{F} mesenterica inferiore

ureter
uréter ^{M}
uretère ^{M}
Harnleiter ^{M}
uretere ^{M}

common iliac artery
arteria ^{F} ilíaca común
artère ^{F} iliaque commune
gemeinsame Hüftarterie ^{F}
arteria ^{F} iliaca comune

common iliac vein
vena ^{F} ilíaca común
veine ^{F} iliaque commune
gemeinsame Hüftvene ^{F}
vena ^{F} iliaca comune

urinary bladder
vejiga ^{F}
vessie ^{F}
Harnblase ^{F}
vescica ^{F} urinaria

celiac trunk
tronco ^{M} celiaco
tronc ^{M} cœliaque
Truncus coeliacus ^{M}
tronco ^{M} celiaco

left kidney
riñón ^{M} izquierdo
rein ^{M} gauche
linke Niere ^{F}
rene ^{M} sinistro

cortex
corteza ^{F} cortical
substance ^{F} corticale
Rinde ^{F}
sostanza ^{F} corticale

medulla
médula ^{F}
substance ^{F} médullaire
Mark ^{N}
sostanza ^{F} midollare

renal papilla
papila ^{F} renal
papille ^{F} rénale
Nierenpapille ^{F}
papilla ^{F} renale

calyx
cáliz ^{M}
calice ^{M}
Nierenkelch ^{M}
calice ^{M}

renal pelvis
pelvis ^{F} renal
bassinet ^{M}
Nierenbecken ^{N}
pelvi ^{F} renale

renal vein
vena ^{F} renal
veine ^{F} rénale
Nierenvene ^{F}
vena ^{F} renale

renal artery
arteria ^{F} renal
artère ^{F} rénale
Nierenarterie ^{F}
arteria ^{F} renale

superior mesenteric artery
arteria ^{F} mesentérica superior
artère ^{F} mésentérique supérieure
obere Mesenterialarterie ^{F}
arteria ^{F} mesenterica superiore

internal iliac artery
arteria ^{F} ilíaca interna
artère ^{F} iliaque interne
innere Hüftarterie ^{F}
arteria ^{F} iliaca interna

urethra
uretra ^{F}
urètre ^{M}
Harnröhre ^{F}
uretra ^{F}

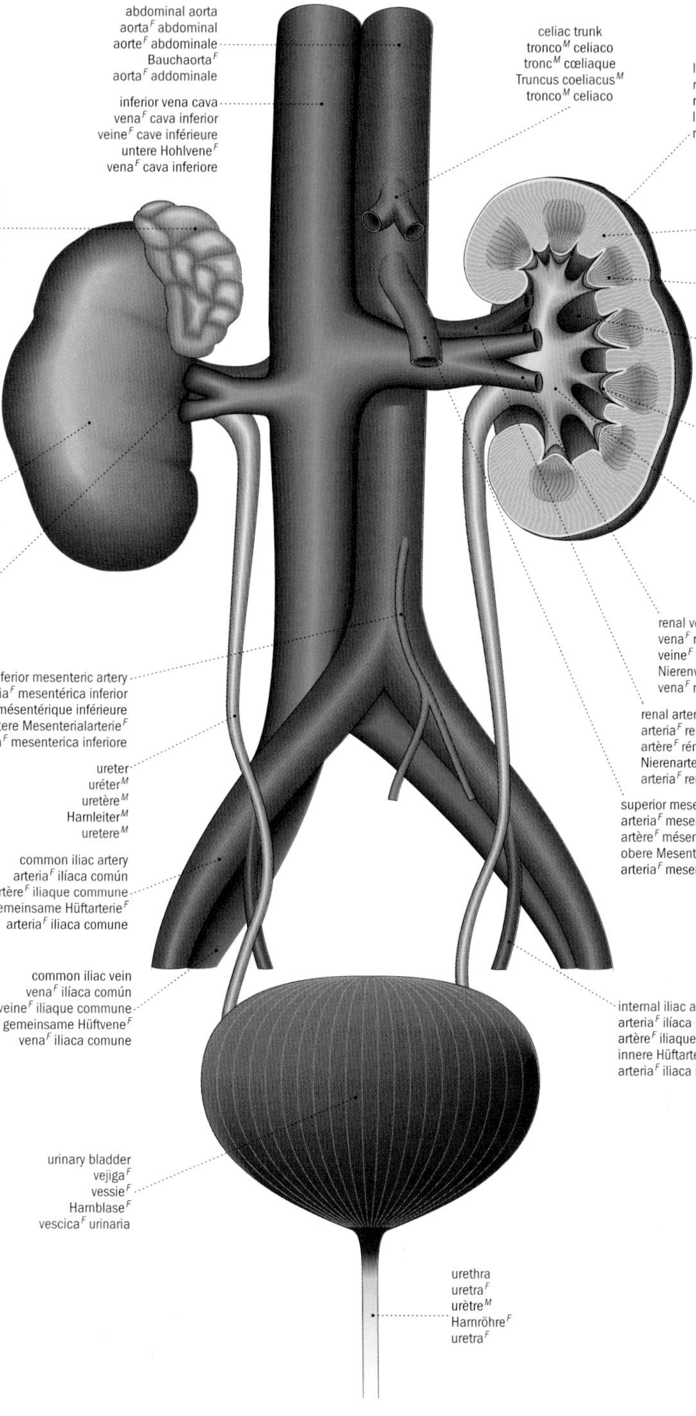

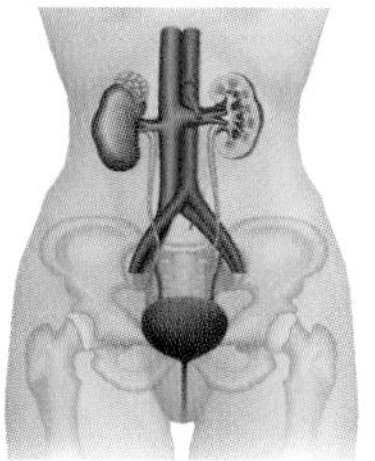

nervous system

sistema^M nervioso | système^M nerveux | Nervensystem^N | sistema^M nervoso

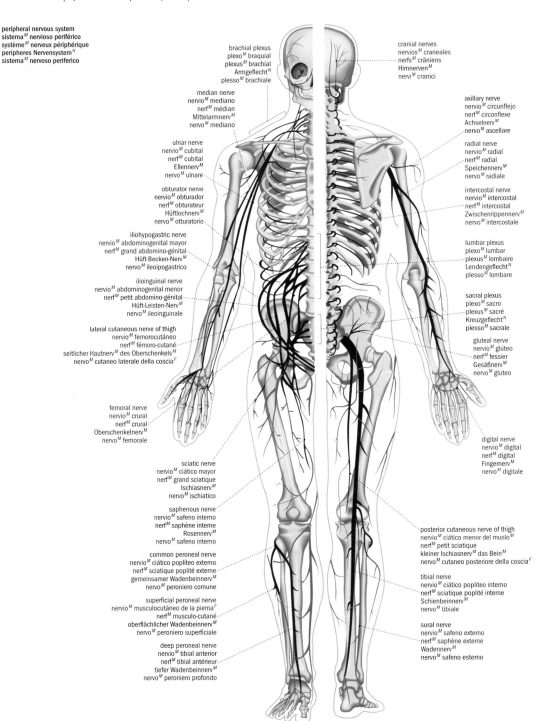

peripheral nervous system
sistema^M nervioso periférico
système^M nerveux périphérique
peripheres Nervensystem^N
sistema^M nervoso periferico

brachial plexus
plexo^M braquial
plexus^M brachial
Armgeflecht^N
plesso^M brachiale

median nerve
nervio^M mediano
nerf^M médian
Mittelarmnerv^M
nervo^M mediano

ulnar nerve
nervio^M cubital
nerf^M cubital
Ellennerv^M
nervo^M ulnare

obturator nerve
nervio^M obturador
nerf^M obturateur
Hüftlochnerv^M
nervo^M otturatorio

iliohypogastric nerve
nervio^M abdominogenital mayor
nerf^M grand abdomino-génital
Hüft-Becken-Nerv^M
nervo^M ileoipogastrico

ilioinguinal nerve
nervio^M abdominogenital menor
nerf^M petit abdomino-génital
Hüft-Leisten-Nerv^M
nervo^M ileoinguinale

lateral cutaneous nerve of thigh
nervio^M femorocutáneo
nerf^M fémoro-cutané
seitlicher Hautnerv^M des Oberschenkels^M
nervo^M cutaneo laterale della coscia^F

femoral nerve
nervio^M crural
nerf^M crural
Oberschenkelnerv^M
nervo^M femorale

sciatic nerve
nervio^M ciático mayor
nerf^M grand sciatique
Ischiasnerv^M
nervo^M ischiatico

saphenous nerve
nervio^M safeno interno
nerf^M saphène interne
Rosennerv^M
nervo^M safeno interno

common peroneal nerve
nervio^M ciático poplíteo externo
nerf^M sciatique poplité externe
gemeinsamer Wadenbeinnerv^M
nervo^M peroniero comune

superficial peroneal nerve
nervio^M musculocutáneo de la pierna^F
nerf^M musculo-cutané
oberflächlicher Wadenbeinnerv^M
nervo^M peroniero superficiale

deep peroneal nerve
nervio^M tibial anterior
nerf^M tibial antérieur
tiefer Wadenbeinnerv^M
nervo^M peroniero profondo

cranial nerves
nervios^M craneales
nerfs^M crâniens
Himnerven^M
nervi^M cranici

axillary nerve
nervio^M circunflejo
nerf^M circonflexe
Achselnerv^M
nervo^M ascellare

radial nerve
nervio^M radial
nerf^M radial
Speichennerv^M
nervo^M radiale

intercostal nerve
nervio^M intercostal
nerf^M intercostal
Zwischenrippennerv^M
nervo^M intercostale

lumbar plexus
plexo^M lumbar
plexus^M lombaire
Lendengeflecht^N
plesso^M lombare

sacral plexus
plexo^M sacro
plexus^M sacré
Kreuzgeflecht^N
plesso^M sacrale

gluteal nerve
nervio^M glúteo
nerf^M fessier
Gesäßnerv^M
nervo^M gluteo

digital nerve
nervio^M digital
nerf^M digital
Fingernerv^M
nervo^M digitale

posterior cutaneous nerve of thigh
nervio^M ciático menor del muslo^M
nerf^M petit sciatique
kleiner Ischiasnerv^M das Bein^M
nervo^M cutaneo posteriore della coscia^F

tibial nerve
nervio^M ciático poplíteo interno
nerf^M sciatique poplité interne
Schienbeinnerv^M
nervo^M tibiale

sural nerve
nervio^M safeno externo
nerf^M saphène externe
Wadennerv^M
nervo^M safeno esterno

HUMAN BEING

HUMAN BEING

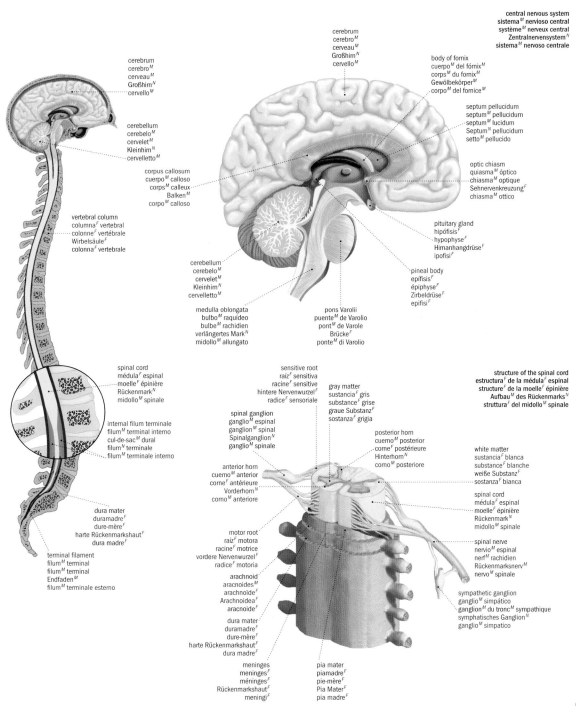

central nervous system
sistema^M nervioso central
système^M nerveux central
Zentralnervensystem^N
sistema^M nervoso centrale

cerebrum
cerebro^M
cerveau^M
Großhirn^N
cervello^M

body of fornix
cuerpo^M del fórnix^M
corps^M du fornix^M
Gewölbekörper^M
corpo^M del fornice

septum pellucidum
septum^M pellucidum
septum^M lucidum
Septum^N pellucidum
setto^M pellucido

optic chiasm
quiasma^M óptico
chiasma^M optique
Sehnervenkreuzung^F
chiasma^M ottico

pituitary gland
hipófisis^F
hypophyse^F
Hirnanhangdrüse^F
ipofisi^F

pineal body
epifisis^F
épiphyse^F
Zirbeldrüse^F
epifisi^F

cerebrum
cerebro^M
cerveau^M
Großhirn^N
cervello^M

cerebellum
cerebelo^M
cervelet^M
Kleinhirn^N
cervelletto^M

corpus callosum
cuerpo^M calloso
corps^M calleux
Balken^M
corpo^M calloso

vertebral column
columna^F vertebral
colonne^F vertébrale
Wirbelsäule^F
colonna^F vertebrale

cerebellum
cerebelo^M
cervelet^M
Kleinhirn^N
cervelletto^M

medulla oblongata
bulbo^M raquídeo
bulbe^M rachidien
verlängertes Mark^N
midollo^M allungato

pons Varolii
puente^M de Varolio
pont^M de Varole
Brücke^F
ponte^M di Varolio

spinal cord
médula^F espinal
moelle^F épinière
Rückenmark^N
midollo^M spinale

internal filum terminale
filum^M terminal interno
cul-de-sac^M dural
filum^N terminale
filum^M terminale interno

sensitive root
raíz^F sensitiva
racine^F sensitive
hintere Nervenwurzel^F
radice^F sensoriale

gray matter
sustancia^F gris
substance^F grise
graue Substanz^F
sostanza^F grigia

structure of the spinal cord
estructura^F de la médula^F espinal
structure^F de la moelle^F épinière
Aufbau^M des Rückenmarks^N
struttura^F del midollo^M spinale

spinal ganglion
ganglio^M espinal
ganglion^M spinal
Spinalganglion^N
ganglio^M spinale

posterior horn
cuerno^M posterior
corne^F postérieure
Hinterhorn^N
corno^M posteriore

white matter
sustancia^F blanca
substance^F blanche
weiße Substanz^F
sostanza^F bianca

anterior horn
cuerno^M anterior
corne^F antérieure
Vorderhorn^N
corno^M anteriore

spinal cord
médula^F espinal
moelle^F épinière
Rückenmark^N
midollo^M spinale

dura mater
duramadre^F
dure-mère^F
harte Rückenmarkshaut^F
dura madre^F

motor root
raíz^F motora
racine^F motrice
vordere Nervenwurzel^F
radice^F motoria

spinal nerve
nervio^M espinal
nerf^F rachidien
Rückenmarksnerv^M
nervo^M spinale

terminal filament
filum^M terminal
filum^M terminal
Endfaden^M
filum^M terminale esterno

arachnoid
aracnoides^M
arachnoïde^F
Arachnoidea^F
aracnoide^F

sympathetic ganglion
ganglio^M simpático
ganglion^M du tronc^M sympathique
sympathisches Ganglion^N
ganglio^M simpatico

dura mater
duramadre^F
dure-mère^F
harte Rückenmarkshaut^F
dura madre^F

meninges
meninges^F
méninges^F
Rückenmarkshaut^F
meningi^F

pia mater
piamadre^F
pie-mère^F
Pia Mater^F
pia madre^F

HUMAN BEING

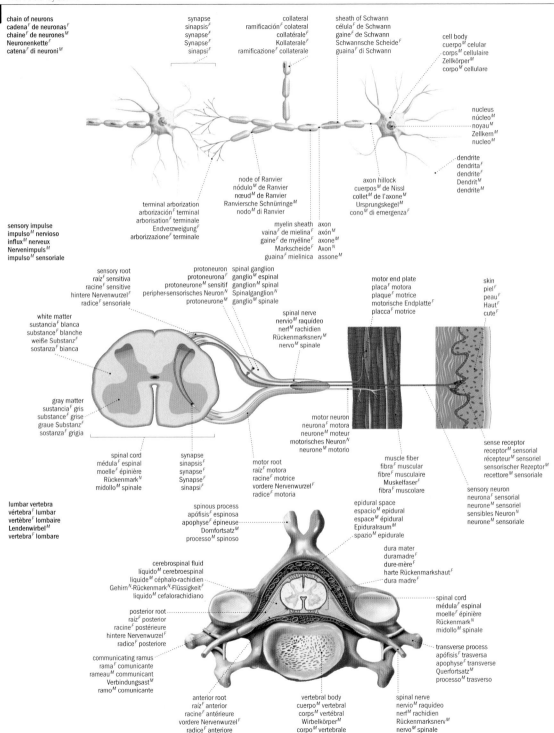

chain of neurons
cadena^F de neuronas^F
chaîne^F de neurones^M
Neuronenkette^F
catena^F di neuroni^M

synapse
sinapsis^F
synapse^F
Synapse^F
sinapsi^F

collateral
ramificación^F colateral
collatérale^F
Kollaterale^F
ramificazione^F collaterale

sheath of Schwann
célula^F de Schwann
gaine^F de Schwann
Schwannsche Scheide^F
guaina^F di Schwann

cell body
cuerpo^M celular
corps^M cellulaire
Zellkörper^M
corpo^M cellulare

nucleus
núcleo^M
noyau^M
Zellkern^M
nucleo^M

dendrite
dendrita^F
dendrite^F
Dendrit^M
dendrite^M

node of Ranvier
nódulo^M de Ranvier
nœud^M de Ranvier
Ranviersche Schnürringe^M
nodo^M di Ranvier

axon hillock
cuerpos^M de Nissl
collet^M de l'axone^M
Ursprungskegel^M
cono^M di emergenza^F

terminal arborization
arborización^F terminal
arborisation^F terminale
Endverzweigung^F
arborizzazione^F terminale

sensory impulse
impulso^M nervioso
influx^M nerveux
Nervenimpuls^M
impulso^M sensoriale

myelin sheath
vaina^F de mielina^F
gaine^F de myéline^F
Markscheide^F
guaina^F mielinica

axon
axón^M
axone^M
Axon^N
assone^M

sensory root
raíz^F sensitiva
racine^F sensitive
hintere Nervenwurzel^F
radice^F sensoriale

protoneuron
protoneurona^F
protoneurone^M sensitif
peripher-sensorisches Neuron^N
protoneurone^M

spinal ganglion
ganglio^M espinal
ganglion^M spinal
Spinalganglion^N
ganglio^M spinale

spinal nerve
nervio^M raquídeo
nerf^M rachidien
Rückenmarksnerv^M
nervo^M spinale

motor end plate
placa^F motora
plaque^F motrice
motorische Endplatte^F
placca^F motrice

skin
piel^F
peau^F
Haut^F
cute^F

white matter
sustancia^F blanca
substance^F blanche
weiße Substanz^F
sostanza^F bianca

gray matter
sustancia^F gris
substance^F grise
graue Substanz^F
sostanza^F grigia

motor neuron
neurona^F motora
neurone^M moteur
motorisches Neuron^N
neurone^M motorio

sense receptor
receptor^M sensorial
récepteur^M sensoriel
sensorischer Rezeptor^M
recettore^M sensoriale

spinal cord
médula^F espinal
moelle^F épinière
Rückenmark^N
midollo^M spinale

synapse
sinapsis^F
synapse^F
Synapse^F
sinapsi^F

motor root
raíz^F motora
racine^F motrice
vordere Nervenwurzel^F
radice^F motoria

muscle fiber
fibra^F muscular
fibre^F musculaire
Muskelfaser^F
fibra^F muscolare

sensory neuron
neurona^F sensorial
neurone^M sensoriel
sensibles Neuron^N
neurone^M sensoriale

lumbar vertebra
vértebra^F lumbar
vertèbre^F lombaire
Lendenwirbel^M
vertebra^F lombare

spinous process
apófisis^F espinosa
apophyse^F épineuse
Dornfortsatz^M
processo^M spinoso

epidural space
espacio^M epidural
espace^M épidural
Epiduralraum^M
spazio^M epidurale

dura mater
duramadre^F
dure-mère^F
harte Rückenmarkshaut^F
dura madre^F

cerebrospinal fluid
líquido^M cerebroespinal
liquide^M céphalo-rachidien
Gehirn^N-Rückenmark^N-Flüssigkeit^F
liquido^M cefalorachidiano

spinal cord
médula^F espinal
moelle^F épinière
Rückenmark^N
midollo^M spinale

posterior root
raíz^F posterior
racine^F postérieure
hintere Nervenwurzel^F
radice^F posteriore

transverse process
apófisis^F trasversa
apophyse^F transverse
Querfortsatz^M
processo^M trasverso

communicating ramus
rama^F comunicante
rameau^M communicant
Verbindungsast^M
ramo^M comunicante

anterior root
raíz^F anterior
racine^F antérieure
vordere Nervenwurzel^F
radice^F anteriore

vertebral body
cuerpo^M vertebral
corps^M vertébral
Wirbelkörper^M
corpo^M vertebrale

spinal nerve
nervio^M raquídeo
nerf^M rachidien
Rückenmarksnerv^M
nervo^M spinale

male reproductive organs

órganos^M genitales masculinos | organes^M génitaux masculins | männliche Geschlechtsorgane^N | organi^M genitali maschili

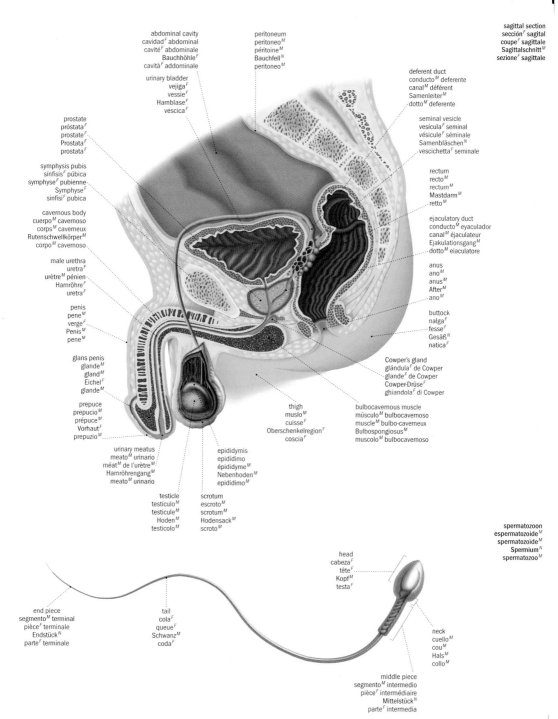

sagittal section
sección^F sagital
coupe^F sagittale
Sagittalschnitt^M
sezione^F sagittale

HUMAN BEING

abdominal cavity
cavidad^F abdominal
cavité^F abdominale
Bauchhöhle^F
cavità^F addominale

peritoneum
peritoneo^M
péritoine^M
Bauchfell^N
peritoneo^M

deferent duct
conducto^M deferente
canal^M déférent
Samenleiter^M
dotto^M deferente

urinary bladder
vejiga^F
vessie^F
Harnblase^F
vescica^F

seminal vesicle
vesícula^F seminal
vésicule^F séminale
Samenbläschen^N
vescichetta^F seminale

prostate
próstata^F
prostate^F
Prostata^F
prostata^F

rectum
recto^M
rectum^M
Mastdarm^M
retto^M

symphysis pubis
sínfisis^F púbica
symphyse^F pubienne
Symphyse^F
sinfisi^F pubica

ejaculatory duct
conducto^M eyaculador
canal^M éjaculateur
Ejakulationsgang^M
dotto^M eiaculatore

cavernous body
cuerpo^M cavernoso
corps^M caverneux
Rutenschwellkörper^M
corpo^M cavernoso

anus
ano^M
anus^M
After^M
ano^M

male urethra
uretra^F
urètre^M pénien
Harnröhre^F
uretra^F

buttock
nalga^F
fesse^F
Gesäß^N
natica^F

penis
pene^M
verge^F
Penis^M
pene^M

glans penis
glande^M
gland^M
Eichel^F
glande^M

Cowper's gland
glándula^F de Cowper
glande^F de Cowper
Cowper-Drüse^F
ghiandola^F di Cowper

prepuce
prepucio^M
prépuce^M
Vorhaut^F
prepuzio^M

thigh
muslo^M
cuisse^F
Oberschenkelregion^F
coscia^F

bulbocavernous muscle
músculo^M bulbocavernoso
muscle^M bulbo-caverneux
Bulbospongiosus^M
muscolo^M bulbocavernoso

urinary meatus
meato^M urinario
méat^M de l'urètre^M
Harnröhrengang^M
meato^M urinario

epididymis
epidídimo
épididyme^M
Nebenhoden^M
epididimo^M

testicle
testículo^M
testicule^M
Hoden^M
testicolo^M

scrotum
escroto^M
scrotum^M
Hodensack^M
scroto^M

spermatozoon
espermatozoide^M
spermatozoïde^M
Spermium^N
spermatozoo^M

head
cabeza^F
tête^F
Kopf^M
testa^F

end piece
segmento^M terminal
pièce^F terminale
Endstück^N
parte^F terminale

tail
cola^F
queue^F
Schwanz^M
coda^F

neck
cuello^M
cou^M
Hals^M
collo^M

middle piece
segmento^M intermedio
pièce^F intermédiaire
Mittelstück^N
parte^F intermedia

female reproductive organs

órganos^M genitales femeninos | organes^M génitaux féminins | weibliche Geschlechtsorgane^N | organi^M genitali femminili

sagittal section
sección^F sagital
coupe^F sagittale
Sagittalschnitt^M
sezione^F sagittale

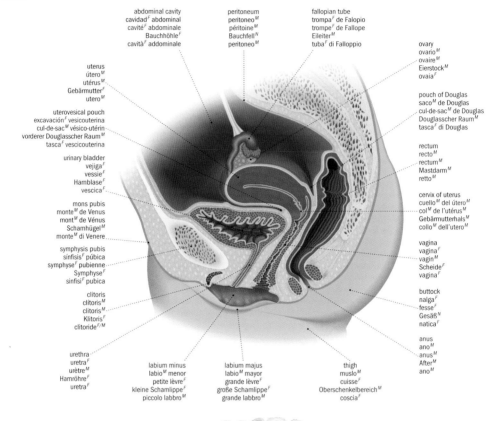

abdominal cavity
cavidad^F abdominal
cavité^F abdominale
Bauchhöhle^F
cavità^F addominale

peritoneum
peritoneo^M
péritoine^M
Bauchfell^N
peritoneo^M

fallopian tube
trompa^F de Falopio
trompe^F de Fallope
Eileiter^M
tuba^F di Falloppio

ovary
ovario^M
ovaire^M
Eierstock^M
ovaia^F

uterus
útero^M
utérus^M
Gebärmutter^F
utero^M

pouch of Douglas
saco^M de Douglas
cul-de-sac^M de Douglas
Douglasscher Raum^M
tasca^F di Douglas

uterovesical pouch
excavación^F vesicouterina
cul-de-sac^M vésico-utérin
vorderer Douglasscher Raum^M
tasca^F vescicouterina

rectum
recto^M
rectum^M
Mastdarm^M
retto^M

urinary bladder
vejiga^F
vessie^F
Harnblase^F
vescica^F

cervix of uterus
cuello^M del útero^M
col^M de l'utérus^M
Gebärmutterhals^M
collo^M dell'utero^M

mons pubis
monte^M de Venus
mont^M de Vénus
Schamhügel^M
monte^M di Venere

vagina
vagina^F
vagin^M
Scheide^F
vagina^F

symphysis pubis
sínfisis^F púbica
symphyse^F pubienne
Symphyse^F
sinfisi^F pubica

buttock
nalga^F
fesse^F
Gesäß^N
natica^F

clitoris
clítoris^M
clitoris^M
Klitoris^F
clitoride^{F/M}

anus
ano^M
anus^M
After^M
ano^M

urethra
uretra^F
urètre^M
Harnröhre^F
uretra^F

labium minus
labio^M menor
petite lèvre^F
kleine Schamlippe^F
piccolo labbro^M

labium majus
labio^M mayor
grande lèvre^F
große Schamlippe^F
grande labbro^M

thigh
muslo^M
cuisse^F
Oberschenkelbereich^M
coscia^F

egg
óvulo^M
ovule^M
Eizelle^F
ovulo^M

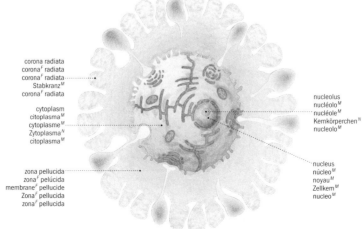

corona radiata
corona^F radiata
corona^F radiata
Stabkranz^M
corona^F radiata

nucleolus
nucléolo^M
nucléole^M
Kernkörperchen^N
nucleolo^M

cytoplasm
citoplasma^M
cytoplasme^M
Zytoplasma^N
citoplasma^M

nucleus
núcleo^M
noyau^M
Zellkern^M
nucleo^M

zona pellucida
zona^F pelúcida
membrane^F pellucide
Zona^F pellucida
zona^F pellucida

HUMAN BEING

HUMAN BEING

posterior view
vista^F posterior
vue^F postérieure
Rückansicht^F
vista^F posteriore

ampulla of fallopian tube
ampolla^F de la trompa^F uterina
ampoule^F de la trompe^F utérine
Eileiterampulle^F
ampolla^F della tuba^F di Falloppio

isthmus of fallopian tube
istmo^M de la trompa^F de Falopio
isthme^M de la trompe^F utérine
Eileiterenge^F
istmo^M della tuba^F di Falloppio

infundibulum of fallopian tube
pabellón^M de la trompa^F de Falopio
pavillon^M de la trompe^F utérine
Eileitertrichter^M
infundibolo^M della tuba^F di Falloppio

uterus
útero^M
utérus^M
Gebärmutter^F
utero^M

broad ligament of uterus
ligamento^M ancho del útero^M
ligament^M large de l'utérus^M
breites Mutterband^N
legamento^M largo dell'utero^M

vagina
vagina^F
vagin^M
Scheide^F
vagina^F

ovary
ovario^M
ovaire^M
Eierstock^M
ovaia^F

labium minus
labio^M menor
petite lèvre^F
kleine Schamlippe^F
piccolo labbro^M

labium majus
labio^M mayor
grande lèvre^F
große Schamlippe^F
grande labbro^M

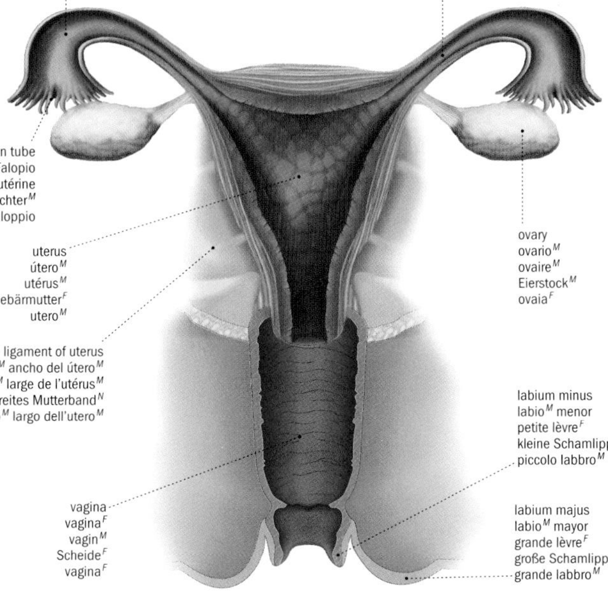

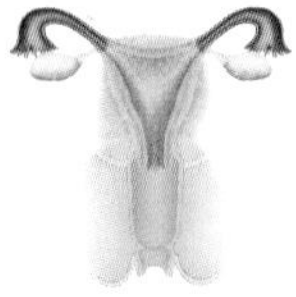

fallopian tubes
trompas^F de Falopio
trompes^F de Fallope
Eileiter^M
tube^F di Falloppio

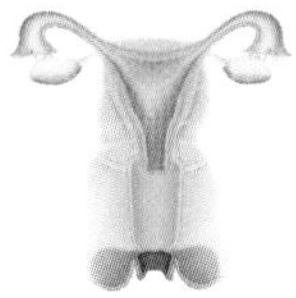

vulva
vulva^F
vulve^F
Scham^F
vulva^F

breast

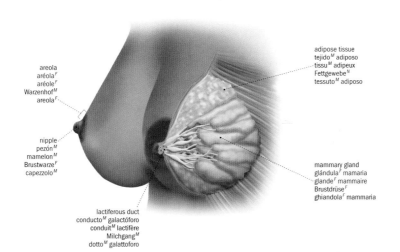

areola
aréola^F
aréole^F
Warzenhof^M
areola^F

nipple
pezón^M
mamelon^M
Brustwarze^F
capezzolo^M

lactiferous duct
conducto^M galactóforo
conduit^M lactifère
Milchgang^M
dotto^M galattoforo

adipose tissue
tejido^M adiposo
tissu^M adipeux
Fettgewebe^N
tessuto^M adiposo

mammary gland
glándula^F mamaria
glande^F mammaire
Brustdrüse^F
ghiandola^F mammaria

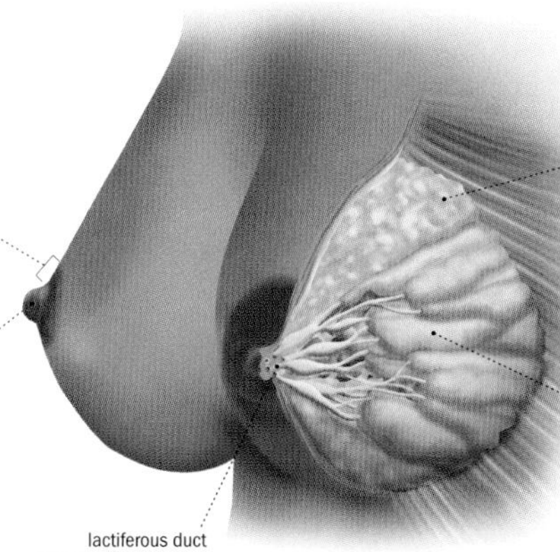

touch

tacto^M | toucher^M | Tastsinn^M | tatto^M

skin
piel^F
peau^F
Haut^F
cute^F

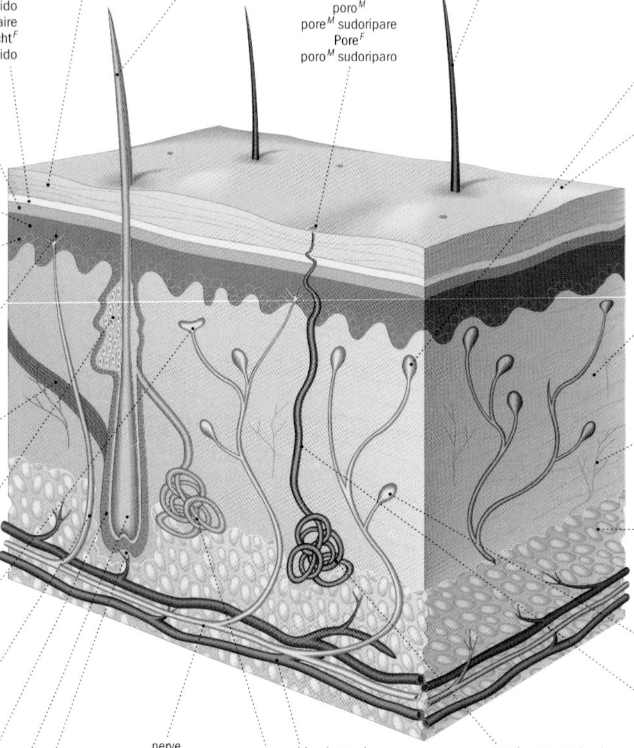

stratum corneum
estrato^M córneo
couche^F cornée
Hornschicht^F
strato^M corneo

hair shaft
tallo^M
tige^F du poil^M
Haarschaft^M
scapo^M

hair
pelo^M
poil^M
Haar^N
pelo^M

Meissner's corpuscle
corpúsculo^M de Meissner
corpuscule^M de Meissner
Meissnersches Tast-Körperchen^N
corpuscolo^M di Meissner

stratum lucidum
estrato^M lúcido
couche^F claire
Glanzschicht^F
strato^M lucido

pore
poro^M
pore^M sudoripare
Pore^F
poro^M sudoriparo

skin surface
superficie^F de la piel^F
surface^F de la peau^F
Hautoberfläche^F
superficie^F della cute^F

stratum granulosum
estrato^M granuloso
couche^F granuleuse
Körnerschicht^F
strato^M granulare

epidermis
epidermis^F
épiderme^M
Oberhaut^F
epidermide^F

stratum spinosum
estrato^M de Malpighi
couche^F de Malpighi
Stachelzellenschicht^F
strato^M spinoso

connective tissue
tejido^M conjuntivo
tissu^M conjonctif
Bindegewebe^N
tessuto^M connettivo

stratum basale
estrato^M basal
couche^F basale
Basalschicht^F
strato^M basale

dermis
dermis^F
derme^M
Lederhaut^F
derma^M

nerve termination
terminación^F nerviosa
terminaison^F nerveuse
Nervenendung^F
terminazione^F nervosa

capillary blood vessel
vaso^M capilar
vaisseau^M capillaire
Kapillargefäß^N
vaso^M capillare

arrector pili muscle
músculo^M erector del pelo^M
muscle^M arrecteur
Haaraufrichter^M
muscolo^M erettore del pelo^M

adipose tissue
tejido^M adiposo
tissu^M adipeux
Fettgewebe^N
tessuto^M adiposo

sebaceous gland
glándula^F sebácea
glande^F sébacée
Talgdrüse^F
ghiandola^F sebacea

subcutaneous tissue
tejido^M subcutáneo
hypoderme^M
Unterhautbindegewebe^N
tessuto^M sottocutaneo

Ruffini's corpuscle
corpúsculo^M de Ruffini
corpuscule^M de Ruffini
Ruffinisches Körperchen^N
corpuscolo^M di Ruffini

Pacinian corpuscle
corpúsculo^M de Pacini
corpuscule^M de Pacini
Vater-Pacinisches Körperchen^N
corpuscolo^M di Pacini

nerve fiber
fibra^F nerviosa
fibre^F nerveuse
Nervenfaser^F
fibra^F nervosa

nerve
nervio^M
nerf^M
Nerv^M
nervo^M

blood vessel
vaso^M sanguíneo
vaisseau^M sanguin
Blutgefäß^N
vaso^M sanguigno

eccrine sweat gland
glándula^F sudorípara ecrina
glande^F sudoripare eccrine
ekkrine Schweißdrüse^F
ghiandola^F sudoripara eccrina

sudoriferous duct
conducto^M sudorífero
canal^M sudoripare
Ausführungsgang^M der Schweißdrüse^F
dotto^M sudoriparo

hair follicle
folículo^M piloso
follicule^M
Haarbalg^M
follicolo^M pilifero

papilla
papila^F
papille^F
Papille^F
papilla^F

apocrine sweat gland
glándula^F sudorípara apocrina
glande^F sudoripare apocrine
apokrine Schweißdrüse^F
ghiandola^F sudoripara apocrina

hair bulb
bulbo^M piloso
bulbe^M
Haarzwiebel^F
bulbo^M del pelo^M

finger
dedo^M
doigt^M
Finger^M
dito^M

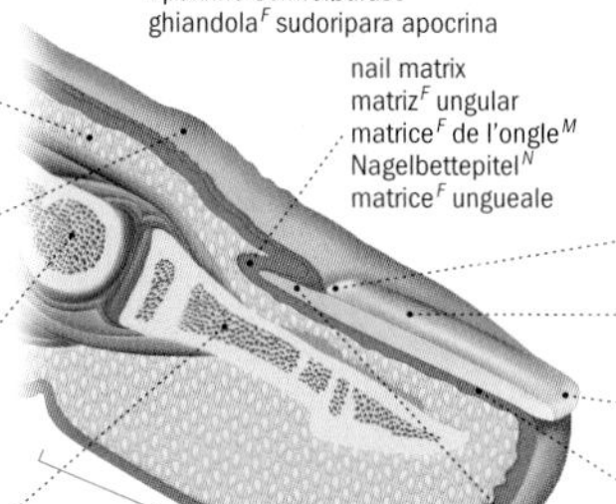

dermis
dermis^F
derme^M
Lederhaut^F
derma^M

nail matrix
matriz^F ungular
matrice^F de l'ongle^M
Nagelbettepitel^N
matrice^F ungueale

lunula
lúnula^F
lunule^F
Nagelhalbmond^M
lunula^F

epidermis
epidermis^F
épiderme^M
Oberhaut^F
epidermide^F

body of nail
cuerpo^M de la uña^F
corps^M de l'ongle^M
Nagelkörper^M
corpo^M dell'unghia^F

middle phalanx
falangina^F
phalange^F médiane
Fingermittelglied^N
seconda falange^F

free margin
extremo^M libre
bord^M libre
freier Nagelrand^M
margine^F libero

distal phalanx
falangeta^F
phalange^F distale
Fingerendglied^N
terza falange^F

digital pulp
yema^F
pulpe^F
Fingerbeere^F
polpastrello^M

root of nail
raíz^F de la uña^F
racine^F de l'ongle^M
Nagelwurzel^F
radice^F dell'unghia^F

nail bed
lecho^M ungular
lit^M de l'ongle^M
Nagelbett^N
letto^M ungueale

touch

hand
mano^F
main^F
Hand^F
mano^F

HUMAN BEING

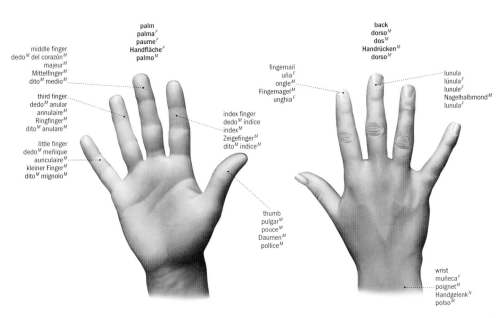

palm
palma^F
paume^F
Handfläche^F
palmo^M

back
dorso^M
dos^M
Handrücken^M
dorso^M

middle finger
dedo^M del corazón^M
majeur^M
Mittelfinger^M
dito^M medio^M

fingernail
uña^F
ongle^M
Fingernagel^M
unghia^F

lunula
lúnula^F
lunule^F
Nagelhalbmond^M
lunula^F

third finger
dedo^M anular
annulaire^M
Ringfinger^M
dito^M anulare^M

index finger
dedo^M índice
index^M
Zeigefinger^M
dito^M indice^M

little finger
dedo^M meñique
auriculaire^M
kleiner Finger^M
dito^M mignolo^M

thumb
pulgar^M
pouce^M
Daumen^M
pollice^M

wrist
muñeca^F
poignet^M
Handgelenk^N
polso^M

hearing

oído^M | ouïe^F | Gehör^N | udito^M

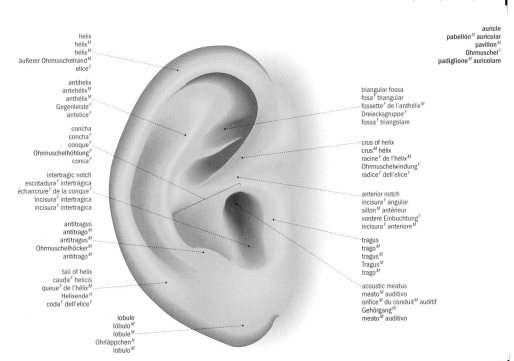

helix
hélix^M
hélix^M
äußerer Ohrmuschelrand^M
elice^F

auricle
pabellón^M auricular
pavillon^M
Ohrmuschel^F
padiglione^M auricolare

antihelix
antehélix^M
anthélix^M
Gegenleiste^F
antelice^F

triangular fossa
fosa^F triangular
fossette^F de l'anthélix^M
Dreiecksgruppe^F
fossa^F triangolare

concha
concha^F
conque^F
Ohrmuschelhöhlung^F
conca^F

crus of helix
crus^M hélix
racine^F de l'hélix^M
Ohrmuschelwindung^F
radice^F dell'elice^M

intertragic notch
escotadura^F intertrágica
échancrure^F de la conque^F
Incisura^F intertragica
incisura^F intertragica

anterior notch
incisura^F angular
sillon^M antérieur
vordere Einbuchtung^F
incisura^F anteriore^M

antitragus
antitrago^M
antitragus^M
Ohrmuschelhöcker^M
antitrago^M

tragus
trago^M
tragus^M
Tragus^M
trago^M

tail of helix
cauda^F helicis
queue^F de l'hélix^M
Helixende^N
coda^F dell'elice^F

acoustic meatus
meato^M auditivo
orifice^F du conduit^M auditif
Gehörgang^M
meato^M auditivo

lobule
lóbulo^M
lobule^M
Ohrläppchen^N
lobulo^M

hearing

structure of the ear
estructura^F del oído^M
structure^F de l'oreille^F
Aufbau^M des Ohres^N
struttura^F dell'orecchio^M

auricle
pabellón^M auricular
pavillon^M
Ohrmuschel^F
padiglione^M

auditory ossicles
huesillos^M auditivos
osselets^M
Gehörknöchelchen^N
ossicini^M dell'udito^M

posterior semicircular canal
conducto^M semicircular posterior
canal^M semi-circulaire postérieur
hinterer knöcherner Bogengang^M
canale^M semicircolare posteriore

superior semicircular canal
conducto^M semicircular superior
canal^M semi-circulaire antérieur
oberer knöcherner Bogengang^M
canale^M semicircolare superiore

lateral semicircular canal
conducto^M semicircular lateral
canal^M semi-circulaire externe
seitlicher knöcherner Bogengang^M
canale^M semicircolare laterale

vestibular nerve
nervio^M vestibular
nerf^M vestibulaire
Vestibularnerv^M
nervo^M vestibolare

external ear
oreja^F
oreille^F externe
äußeres Ohr^N
orecchio^M esterno

cochlear nerve
nervio^M auditivo
nerf^M cochléaire
Hörnerv^M
nervo^M cocleare

cochlea
cóclea^F
cochlée^F
Schnecke^F
coclea^F

middle ear
oído^M medio
oreille^F moyenne
Mittelohr^N
orecchio^M medio

Eustachian tube
trompa^F de Eustaquio
trompe^F d'Eustache
Ohrtrompete^F
tuba^F di Eustachio

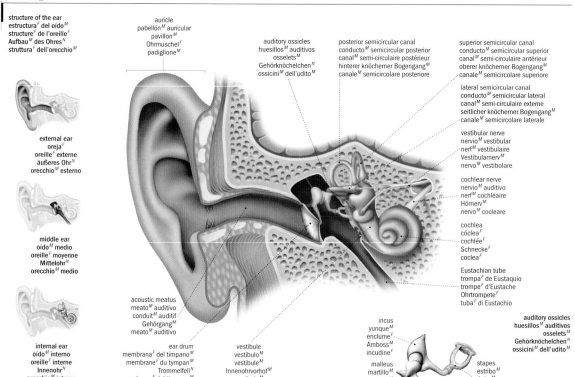

acoustic meatus
meato^M auditivo
conduit^M auditif
Gehörgang^M
meato^M auditivo

incus
yunque^M
enclume^F
Amboss^M
incudine^F

auditory ossicles
huesillos^M auditivos
osselets^M
Gehörknöchelchen^N
ossicini^M dell'udito^M

internal ear
oído^M interno
oreille^F interne
Innenohr^N
orecchio^M interno

ear drum
membrana^F del tímpano^M
membrane^F du tympan^M
Trommelfell^N
membrana^F del tímpano^M

vestibule
vestíbulo^M
vestibule^M
Innenohrvorhof^M
vestibolo^M

malleus
martillo^M
marteau^M
Hammer^M
martello^M

stapes
estribo^M
étrier^M
Steigbügel^M
staffa^F

smell and taste

olfato^M y gusto^M | odorat^M et goût^M | Geruchs-^{M} und Geschmackssinn^M | olfatto^M e gusto^M

mouth
boca^F
bouche^F
Mund^M
bocca^F

upper lip
labio^M superior
lèvre^F supérieure
Oberlippe^F
labbro^M superiore

gum
encía^F
gencive^F
Zahnfleisch^N
gengiva^F

superior dental arch
arco^M dentario superior
arcade^F dentaire supérieure
obere Zahnreihe^F
arcata^F dentale superiore

hard palate
bóveda^F palatina
voûte^F du palais^M
harter Gaumen^M
palato^M duro

isthmus of fauces
istmo^M de las fauces^F
isthme^M du gosier^M
Rachenenge^F
istmo^M delle fauci^F

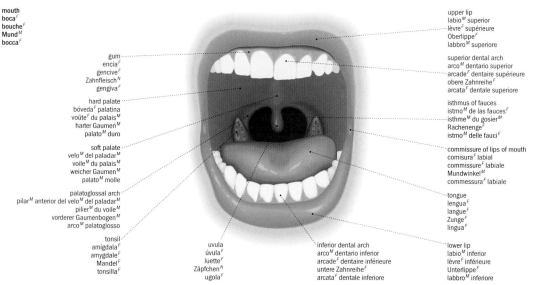

soft palate
velo^M del paladar^M
voile^M du palais^M
weicher Gaumen^M
palato^M molle

commissure of lips of mouth
comisura^F labial
commissure^F labiale
Mundwinkel^M
commessura^F labiale

palatoglossal arch
pilar^M anterior del velo^M del paladar^M
pilier^M du voile^M
vorderer Gaumenbogen^M
arco^M palatoglosso

tongue
lengua^F
langue^F
Zunge^F
lingua^F

tonsil
amígdala^F
amygdale^F
Mandel^F
tonsilla^F

uvula
úvula^F
luette^F
Zäpfchen^N
ugola^F

inferior dental arch
arco^M dentario inferior
arcade^F dentaire inférieure
untere Zahnreihe^F
arcata^F dentale inferiore

lower lip
labio^M inferior
lèvre^F inférieure
Unterlippe^F
labbro^M inferiore

HUMAN BEING

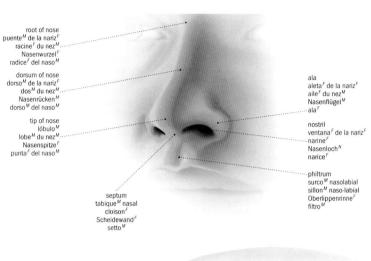

root of nose
puente^M de la nariz^F
racine^F du nez^M
Nasenwurzel^F
radice^F del naso^M

dorsum of nose
dorso^M de la nariz^F
dos^M du nez^M
Nasenrücken^M
dorso^M del naso^M

tip of nose
lóbulo^M
lobe^M du nez^M
Nasenspitze^F
punta^F del naso^M

septum
tabique^M nasal
cloison^F
Scheidewand^F
setto^M

external nose
nariz^F
parties^F externes du nez^M
äußere Nase^F
naso^M esterno

ala
aleta^F de la nariz^F
aile^F du nez^M
Nasenflügel^M
ala^F

nostril
ventana^F de la nariz^F
narine^F
Nasenloch^N
narice^F

philtrum
surco^M nasolabial
sillon^M naso-labial
Oberlippenrinne^F
filtro^M

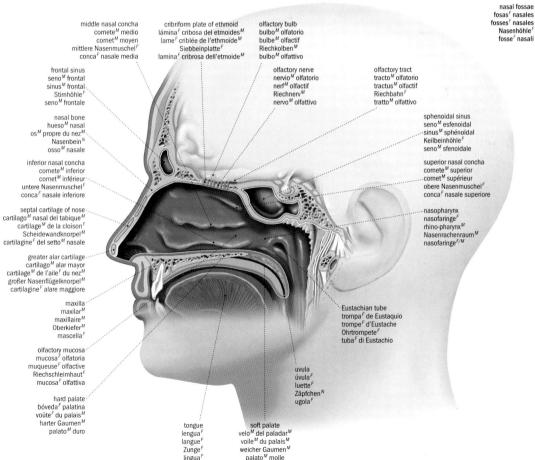

middle nasal concha
cornete^M medio
cornet^M moyen
mittlere Nasenmuschel^F
conca^F nasale media

cribriform plate of ethmoid
lámina^F cribosa del etmoides^M
lame^F criblée de l'ethmoïde^M
Siebbeinplatte^F
lamina^F cribrosa dell'etmoide^M

olfactory bulb
bulbo^M olfatorio
bulbe^M olfactif
Riechkolben^M
bulbo^M olfattivo

nasal fossae
fosas^F nasales
fosses^F nasales
Nasenhöhle^F
fosse^F nasali

frontal sinus
seno^M frontal
sinus^M frontal
Stirnhöhle^F
seno^M frontale

olfactory nerve
nervio^M olfatorio
nerf^M olfactif
Riechnerv^M
nervo^M olfattivo

olfactory tract
tracto^M olfatorio
tractus^M olfactif
Riechbahn^F
tratto^M olfattivo

nasal bone
hueso^M nasal
os^M propre du nez^M
Nasenbein^N
osso^M nasale

sphenoidal sinus
seno^M esfenoidal
sinus^M sphénoidal
Keilbeinhöhle^F
seno^M sfenoidale

inferior nasal concha
cornete^M inferior
cornet^M inférieur
untere Nasenmuschel^F
conca^F nasale inferiore

superior nasal concha
cornete^M superior
cornet^M supérieur
obere Nasenmuschel^F
conca^F nasale superiore

septal cartilage of nose
cartílago^M nasal del tabique^M
cartilage^M de la cloison^F
Scheidewandknorpel^M
cartilagine^F del setto^M nasale

nasopharynx
nasofaringe^F
rhino-pharynx^M
Nasenrachenraum^M
nasofaringe^{F/M}

greater alar cartilage
cartílago^M alar mayor
cartilage^M de l'aile^F du nez^M
großer Nasenflügelknorpel^M
cartilagine^F alare maggiore

maxilla
maxilar^M
maxillaire^M
Oberkiefer^M
mascella^F

Eustachian tube
trompa^F de Eustaquio
trompe^F d'Eustache
Ohrtrompete^F
tuba^F di Eustachio

olfactory mucosa
mucosa^F olfatoria
muqueuse^F olfactive
Riechschleimhaut^F
mucosa^F olfattiva

uvula
úvula^F
luette^F
Zäpfchen^N
ugola^F

hard palate
bóveda^F palatina
voûte^F du palais^M
harter Gaumen^M
palato^M duro

tongue
lengua^F
langue^F
Zunge^F
lingua^F

soft palate
velo^M del paladar^M
voile^M du palais^M
weicher Gaumen^M
palato^M molle

HUMAN BEING

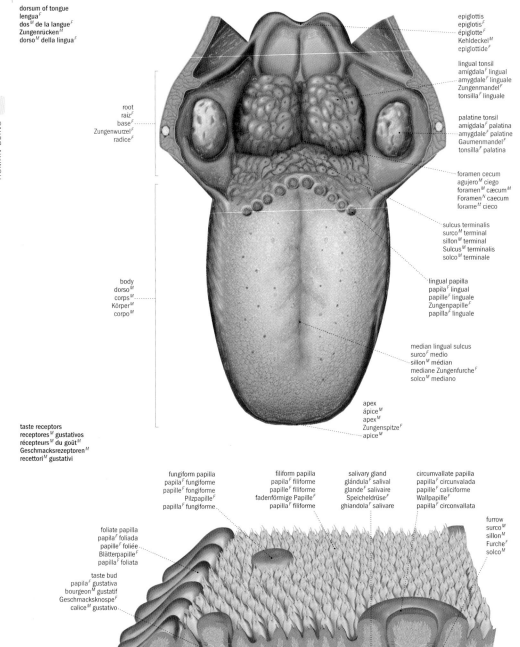

dorsum of tongue
lengua^F
dos^M de la langue^F
Zungenrücken^M
dorso^M della lingua^F

root
raíz^F
base^F
Zungenwurzel^F
radice^F

body
dorso^M
corps^M
Körper^M
corpo^M

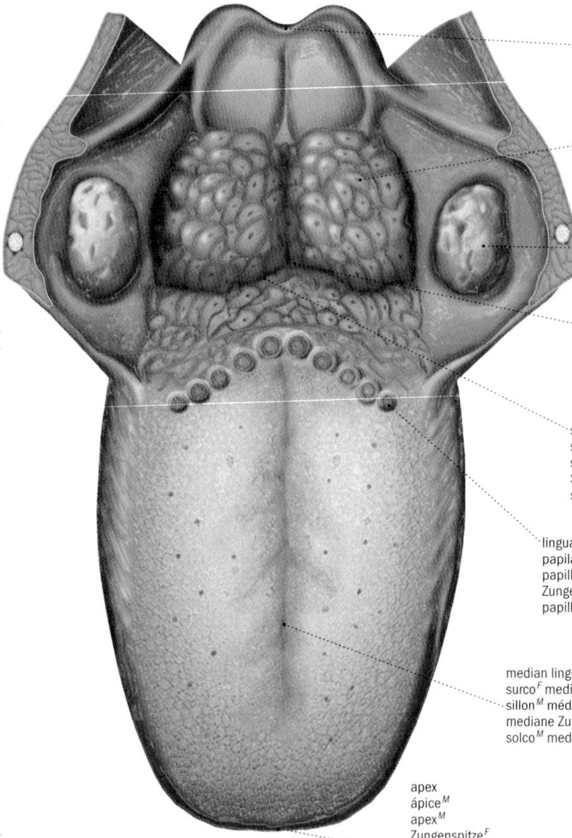

taste receptors
receptores^M gustativos
récepteurs^M du goût^M
Geschmacksrezeptoren^M
recettori^M gustativi

epiglottis
epiglotis^F
épiglotte^F
Kehldeckel^M
epiglottide^F

lingual tonsil
amigdala^F lingual
amygdale^F linguale
Zungenmandel^F
tonsilla^F linguale

palatine tonsil
amigdala^F palatina
amygdale^F palatine
Gaumenmandel^F
tonsilla^F palatina

foramen cecum
agujero^M ciego
foramen^M cæcum^M
Foramen^N caecum
forame^M cieco

sulcus terminalis
surco^M terminal
sillon^M terminal
Sulcus^M terminalis
solco^M terminale

lingual papilla
papila^F lingual
papille^F linguale
Zungenpapille^F
papilla^F linguale

median lingual sulcus
surco^F medio
sillon^M médian
mediane Zungenfurche^F
solco^M mediano

apex
ápice^M
apex^M
Zungenspitze^F
apice^M

fungiform papilla
papila^F fungiforme
papille^F fongiforme
Pilzpapille^F
papilla^F fungiforme

filiform papilla
papila^F filiforme
papille^F filiforme
fadenförmige Papille^F
papilla^F filiforme

salivary gland
glándula^F salival
glande^F salivaire
Speicheldrüse^F
ghiandola^F salivare

circumvallate papilla
papilla^F circunvalada
papille^F caliciforme
Wallpapille^F
papilla^F circonvallata

foliate papilla
papila^F foliada
papille^F foliée
Blätterpapille^F
papilla^F foliata

taste bud
papila^F gustativa
bourgeon^M gustatif
Geschmacksknospe^F
calice^M gustativo

furrow
surco^M
sillon^M
Furche^F
solco^M

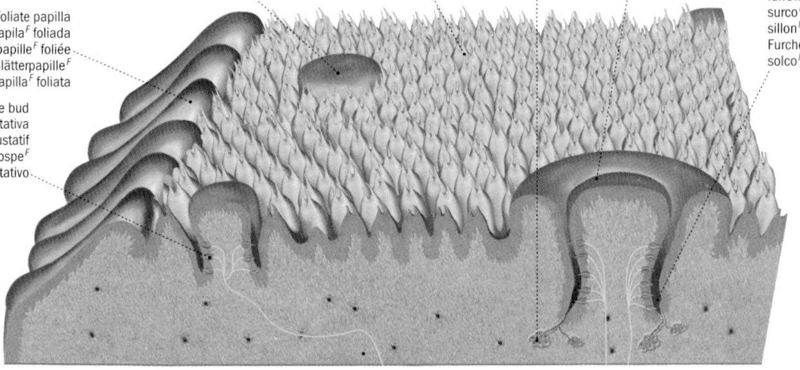

sight

vista^F | vue^F | Sehsinn^N | vista^F

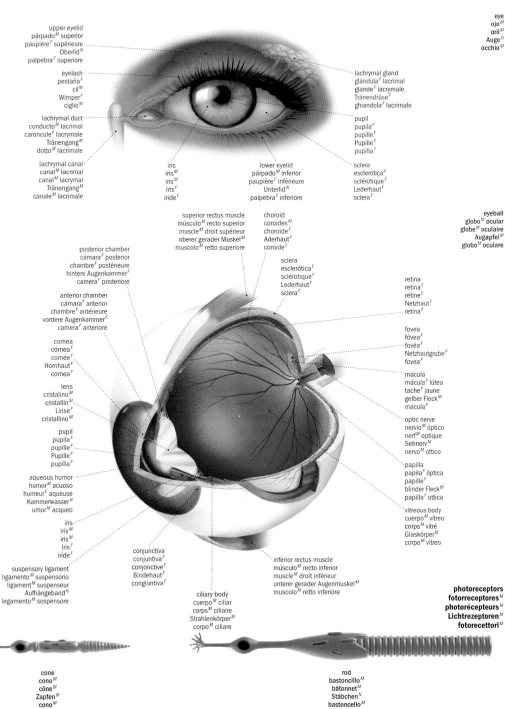

eye
ojo^M
œil^M
Auge^N
occhio^M

upper eyelid
párpado^M superior
paupière^F supérieure
Oberlid^N
palpebra^F superiore

eyelash
pestaña^F
cil^M
Wimper^F
ciglio^M

lachrymal duct
conducto^M lacrimal
caroncule^F lacrymale
Tränengang^M
dotto^M lacrimale

lachrymal canal
canal^M lacrimal
canal^M lacrymal
Tränengang^M
canale^M lacrimale

lachrymal gland
glándula^F lacrimal
glande^F lacrymale
Tränendrüse^F
ghiandola^F lacrimale

pupil
pupila^F
pupille^F
Pupille^F
pupilla^F

iris
iris^M
iris^M
Iris^F
iride^F

lower eyelid
párpado^M inferior
paupière^F inférieure
Unterlid^N
palpebra^F inferiore

sclera
esclerótica^F
sclérotique^F
Lederhaut^F
sclera^F

superior rectus muscle
músculo^M recto superior
muscle^M droit supérieur
oberer gerader Muskel^M
muscolo^M retto superiore

choroid
coroides^M
choroïde^F
Aderhaut^F
coroide^F

eyeball
globo^M ocular
globe^M oculaire
Augapfel^M
globo^M oculare

posterior chamber
cámara^F posterior
chambre^F postérieure
hintere Augenkammer^F
camera^F posteriore

sclera
esclerótica^F
sclérotique^F
Lederhaut^F
sclera^F

retina
retina^F
rétine^F
Netzhaut^F
retina^F

anterior chamber
cámara^F anterior
chambre^F antérieure
vordere Augenkammer^F
camera^F anteriore

fovea
fóvea^F
fovéa^F
Netzhautgrube^F
fovea^F

cornea
córnea^F
cornée^F
Hornhaut^F
cornea^F

macula
mácula^F lútea
tache^F jaune
gelber Fleck^M
macula^F

lens
cristalino^M
cristallin^M
Linse^F
cristallino^M

optic nerve
nervio^M óptico
nerf^M optique
Sehnerv^M
nervo^M ottico

pupil
pupila^F
pupille^F
Pupille^F
pupilla^F

papilla
papilla^F óptica
papille^F
blinder Fleck^M
papilla^F ottica

aqueous humor
humor^M acuoso
humeur^F aqueuse
Kammerwasser^N
umor^M acqueo

vitreous body
cuerpo^M vítreo
corps^M vitré
Glaskörper^M
corpo^M vitreo

iris
iris^M
iris^M
Iris^F
iride^F

conjunctiva
conjuntiva^F
conjonctive^F
Bindehaut^F
congiuntiva^F

inferior rectus muscle
músculo^M recto inferior
muscle^M droit inférieur
unterer gerader Augenmuskel^M
muscolo^M retto inferiore

suspensory ligament
ligamento^M suspensorio
ligament^M suspenseur
Aufhängeband^N
legamento^M sospensore

ciliary body
cuerpo^M ciliar
corps^M ciliaire
Strahlenkörper^M
corpo^M ciliare

photoreceptors
fotorreceptores^M
photorécepteurs^M
Lichtrezeptoren^M
fotorecettori^M

cone
cono^M
cône^M
Zapfen^M
cono^M

rod
bastoncillo^M
bâtonnet^M
Stäbchen^N
bastoncello^M

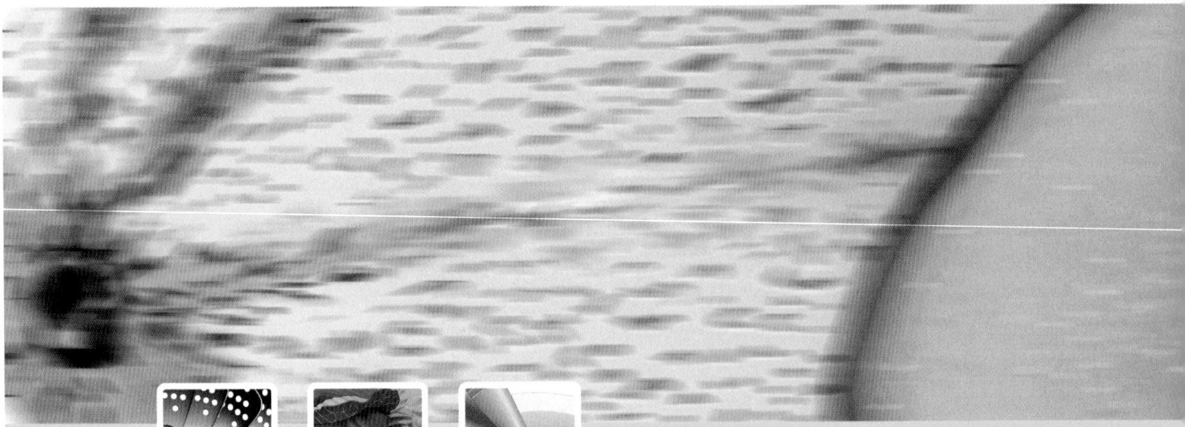

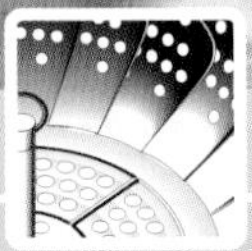

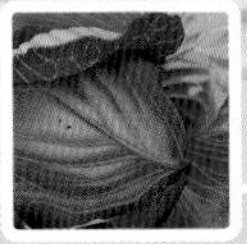

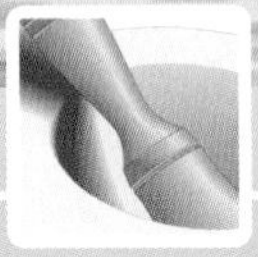

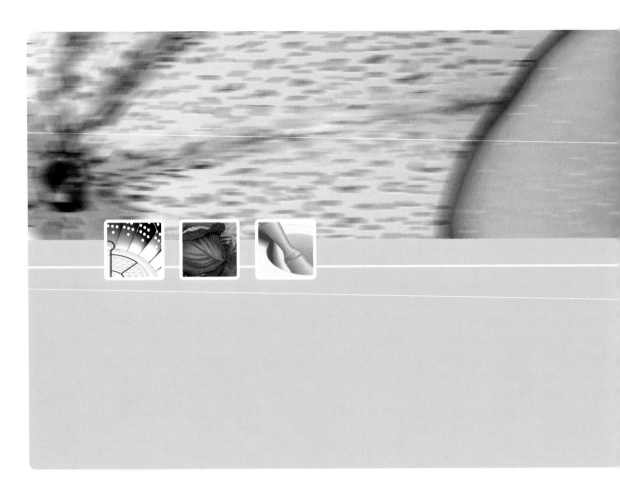

FOOD AND KITCHEN

PRODUCTOS ALIMENTICIOS Y DE COCINA | ALIMENTATION ET CUISINE | NAHRUNGSMITTEL UND KÜCHE | GENERI ALIMENTARI E CUCINA

supermarket

supermercado ^{M} | supermarché ^{M} | Supermarkt ^{M} | supermercato ^{M}

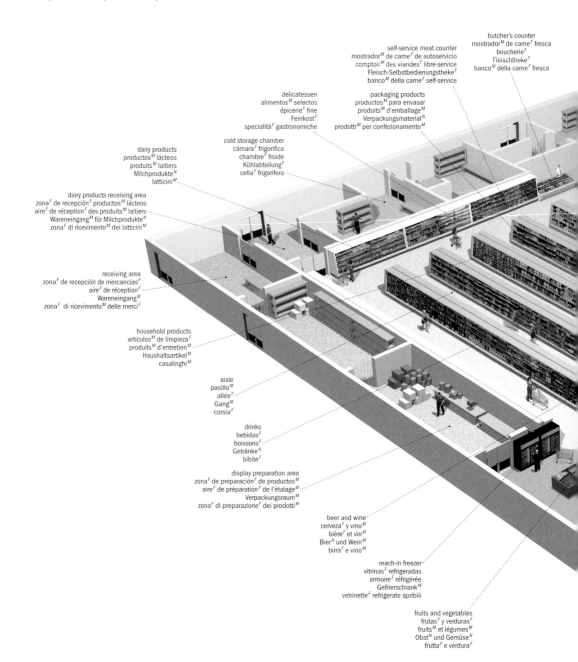

butcher's counter
mostrador ^{M} de carne ^{F} fresca
boucherie ^{F}
Fleischtheke ^{F}
banco ^{M} della carne ^{F} fresca

self-service meat counter
mostrador ^{M} de carne ^{F} de autoservicio
comptoir ^{M} des viandes ^{F} libre-service
Fleisch-Selbstbedienungstheke ^{F}
banco ^{M} della carne ^{F} self-service

delicatessen
alimentos ^{M} selectos
épicerie ^{F} fine
Feinkost ^{F}
specialità ^{F} gastronomiche

packaging products
productos ^{M} para envasar
produits ^{M} d'emballage ^{M}
Verpackungsmaterial ^{N}
prodotti ^{M} per confezionamento ^{M}

cold storage chamber
cámara ^{F} frigorifica
chambre ^{F} froide
Kühlabteilung ^{F}
cella ^{F} frigorifera

dairy products
productos ^{M} lácteos
produits ^{M} laitiers
Milchprodukte ^{N}
latticini ^{M}

dairy products receiving area
zona ^{F} de recepción ^{F} productos ^{M} lácteos
aire ^{F} de réception ^{F} des produits ^{M} laitiers
Wareneingang ^{M} für Milchprodukte ^{N}
zona ^{F} di ricevimento ^{M} dei latticini ^{M}

receiving area
zona ^{F} de recepción de mercancias ^{F}
aire ^{F} de réception ^{F}
Wareneingang ^{M}
zona ^{F} di ricevimento ^{M} delle merci ^{F}

household products
artículos ^{M} de limpieza ^{F}
produits ^{M} d'entretien ^{M}
Haushaltsartikel ^{M}
casalinghi ^{M}

aisle
pasillo ^{M}
allée ^{F}
Gang ^{M}
corsia ^{F}

drinks
bebidas ^{F}
boissons ^{F}
Getränke ^{N}
bibite ^{F}

display preparation area
zona ^{F} de preparación ^{F} de productos ^{M}
aire ^{F} de préparation ^{F} de l'étalage ^{M}
Verpackungsraum ^{M}
zona ^{F} di preparazione ^{F} dei prodotti ^{M}

beer and wine
cerveza ^{F} y vino ^{M}
bière ^{F} et vin ^{M}
Bier ^{N} und Wein ^{M}
birra ^{F} e vino ^{M}

reach-in freezer
vitrinas ^{F} refrigeradas
armoire ^{F} réfrigérée
Gefrierschrank ^{M}
vetrinette ^{F} refrigerate apribili

fruits and vegetables
frutas ^{F} y verduras ^{F}
fruits ^{M} et légumes ^{M}
Obst ^{N} und Gemüse ^{N}
frutta ^{F} e verdura ^{F}

FOOD AND KITCHEN

cold storage chamber
cámara^F frigorífica
chambre^F froide
Kühlabteilung^F
cella^F frigorifera

seafood
pescado^M
poissonnerie^F
Fisch^M
pesce^M

gondola
góndola^F
gondole^F
Regal^N
scaffale^M

convenience food
productos^M en oferta^F
aliments^M prêts-à-servir
Fertiggerichte^N
prodotti^M in offerta^F

frozen food storage
almacén^M de congelados^M
entreposage^M des produits^M congelés
Kühlraum^M
magazzino^M dei surgelati^M

frozen foods
congelados^M
aliments^M congelés
Tiefkühlprodukte^N
surgelati^M

cheese counter
mostrador^M de quesos^M
comptoir^M des fromages^M
Käsetheke^F
banco^M dei formaggi^M

prepared foods
precocinados^M
produits^M de traiteur^M
Fertiggerichte^N
cibi^M pronti

bakery
panadería^F
boulangerie^F
Backwaren^F
panetteria^F

pet food and supplies
alimentos^M y artículos^M para animales^M
produits^M pour animaux^M familiers
Heimtierbedarf^M
alimenti^M e prodotti^M per animali^M

health and beauty care
perfumería^F e higiene^F personal
parapharmacie^F et cosmétiques^M
Körperpflege^F
profumeria^F e igiene^F personale

checkouts
cajas^F
caisses^F
Kassen^F
casse^F

optical scanner
escáner^M óptico
lecteur^M optique
Scanner^M
scanner^M ottico

cash register
caja^F registradora
caisse^F enregistreuse
Registrierkasse^F
registratore^M di cassa^F

checkout
caja^F
caisse^F
Kasse^F
cassa^F

cashier
cajera^F
caissière^F
Kassiererin^F
cassiera^F

shopping carts
carritos^M del supermercado^M
chariots^M
Einkaufswagen^M
carrelli^M

end aisle display
expositor^M de final^M de pasillo^M
tête^F de gondole^F
Kopfregal^N
espositore^M di fine^F corsia^F

electronic payment terminal
terminal^M de pago^M electrónico
terminal^M de paiement^M électronique
elektronisches Zahlungsterminal^N
terminale^M per il pagamento^M elettronico

canned goods
conservas^M
conserves^F
Konserven^F
scatolame^M

grocery bags
bolsas^F
sacs^M à provisions^F
Einkaufstüten^F
sacchetti^M

bagger
ayudante^M
aide^M de caisse^F
Einpackhilfe^F
aiutante^M

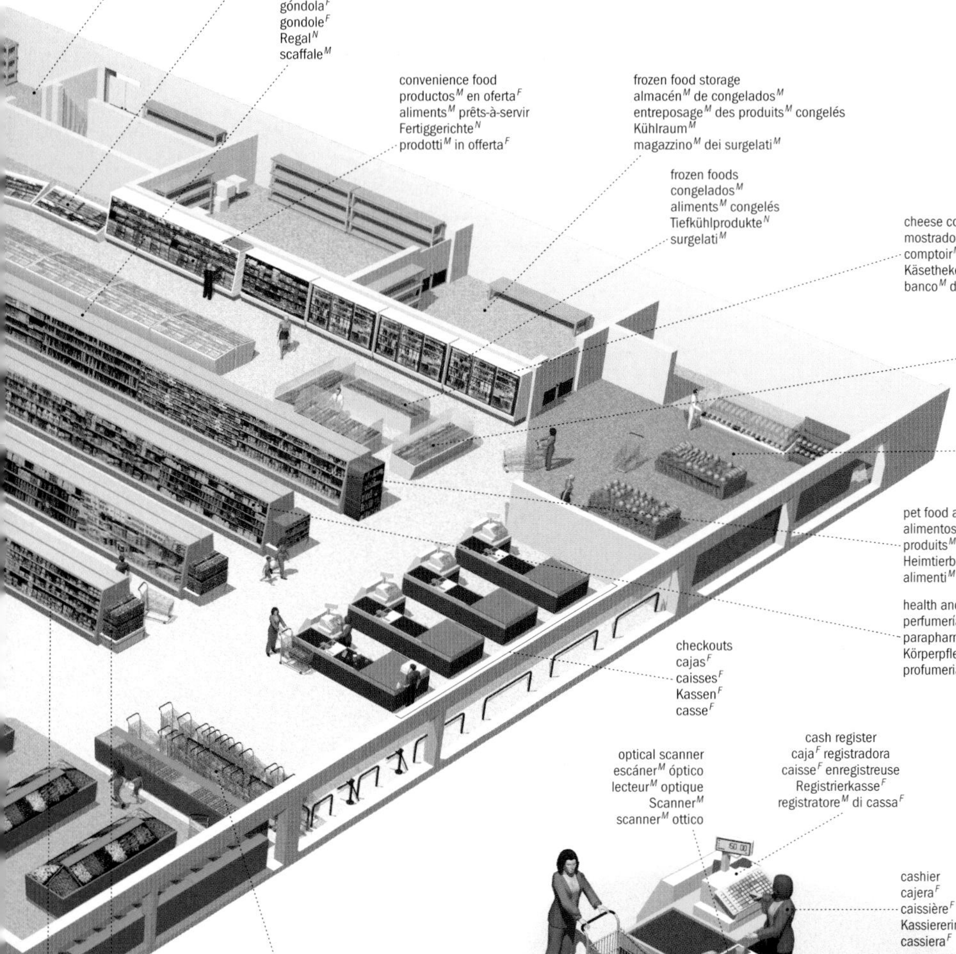

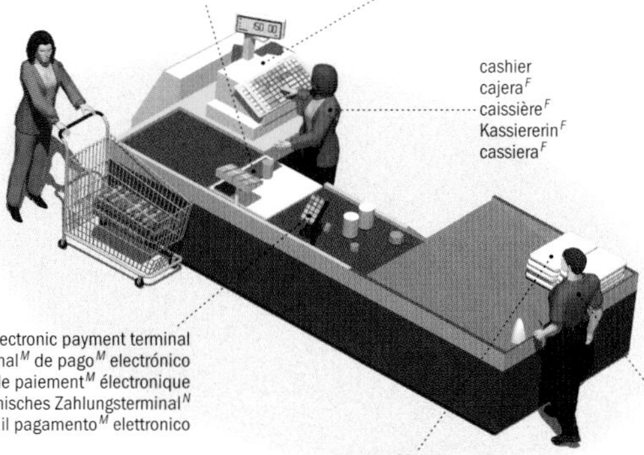

farmstead

granja[F] | ferme[F] | Bauernhof[M] | fattoria[F]

permanent pasture
prado[M]
pâturage[M]
Weideland[N]
pascolo[M]

fallow
barbecho[M]
jachère[F]
Brachacker[M]
maggese[M]

fodder corn
maíz[M] forrajero
maïs[M] fourrager
Futtergetreide[N]
mais[M] foraggero

dairy
vaquería[F]
laiterie[F]
Milchkammer[F]
latteria[F]

hayloft
henil[M]
fenil[M]
Heuboden[M]
fienile[M]

meadow
pradera[F]
prairie[F]
Wiese[F]
prato[M]

cowshed
establo[M]
étable[F]
Kuhstall[M]
stalla[F]

fence
cerca[F]
clôture[F]
Zaun[M]
recinzione[F]

tower silo
silo[M]
silo[M]-tour[F]
Hochsilo[M]
silo[M] verticale

barn
granero[M]
grange[F]
Scheune[F]
granaio[M]

bunker silo
troje[M]
silo[M]-couloir[M]
Flachsilo[M]
silo[M] orizzontale

machinery shed
cobertizo[M]
hangar[M]
Geräteschuppen[M]
rimessa[F]

pigsty
pocilga[F]
porcherie[F]
Schweinestall[M]
porcile[M]

hen house
gallinero[M]
poulailler[M]
Hühnerstall[M]
pollaio[M]

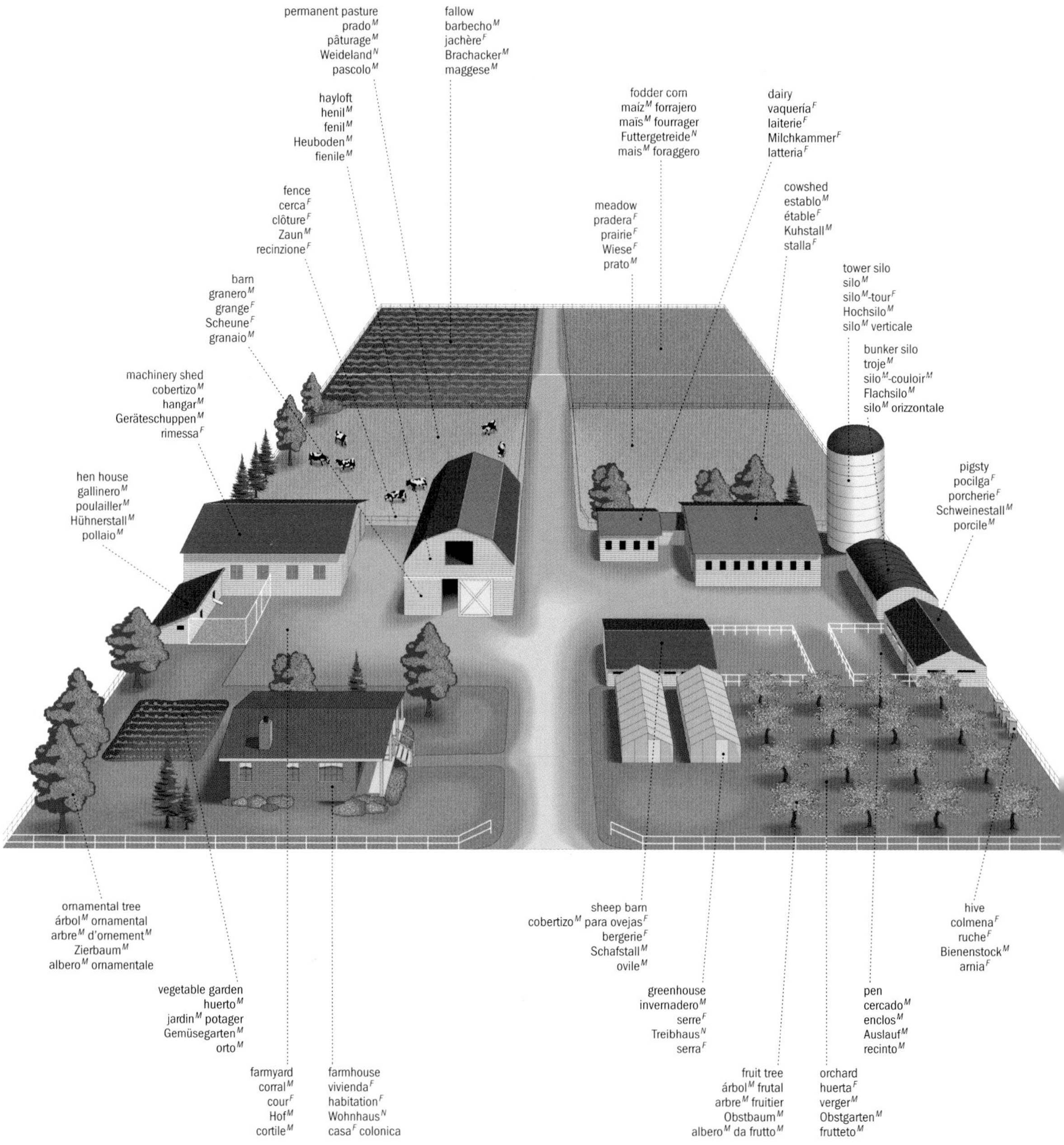

ornamental tree
árbol[M] ornamental
arbre[M] d'ornement[M]
Zierbaum[M]
albero[M] ornamentale

sheep barn
cobertizo[M] para ovejas[F]
bergerie[F]
Schafstall[M]
ovile[M]

hive
colmena[F]
ruche[F]
Bienenstock[M]
arnia[F]

vegetable garden
huerto[M]
jardin[M] potager
Gemüsegarten[M]
orto[M]

greenhouse
invernadero[M]
serre[F]
Treibhaus[N]
serra[F]

pen
cercado[M]
enclos[M]
Auslauf[M]
recinto[M]

farmyard
corral[M]
cour[F]
Hof[M]
cortile[M]

farmhouse
vivienda[F]
habitation[F]
Wohnhaus[N]
casa[F] colonica

fruit tree
árbol[M] frutal
arbre[M] fruitier
Obstbaum[M]
albero[M] da frutto[M]

orchard
huerta[F]
verger[M]
Obstgarten[M]
frutteto[M]

mushrooms

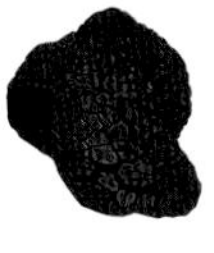

truffle
trufa^F
truffe^F
Trüffel^F
tartufo^M

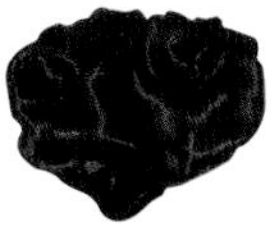

wood ear
oreja^F de Judas
oreille-de-Judas^F
Holzohr^N
orecchio^M di Giuda

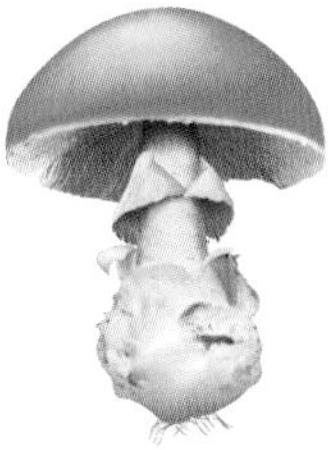

royal agaric
oronja^F
oronge^F vraie
Kaiserling^M
ovolo^M buono

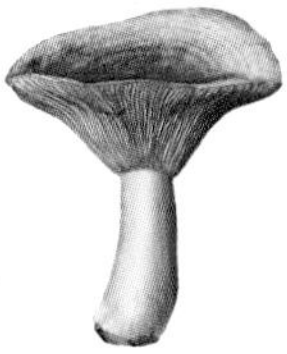

delicious lactarius
mízcalo^M
lactaire^M délicieux
echter Reizker^M
agarico^M delizioso

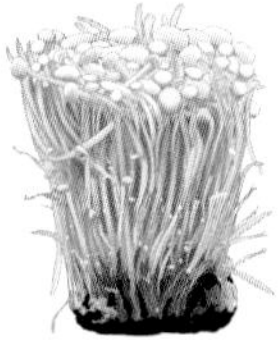

enoki
seta^F enoki
collybie^F à pied^M velouté
Enoki^M
collibia^F

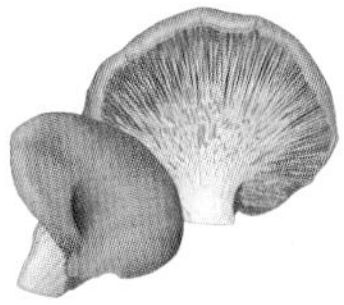

oyster
orellana^F
pleurote^M en forme^F d'huitre^F
Austernseitling^M
gelone^M

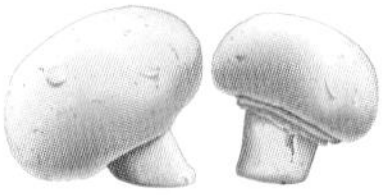

cultivated mushrooms
champiñón^M
champignon^M de couche^F
Zuchtchampignon^M
fungo^M coltivato

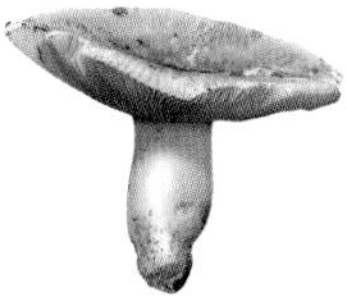

green russula
rusula^F verde
russule^F verdoyante
grasgrüner Täubling^M
verdone^M

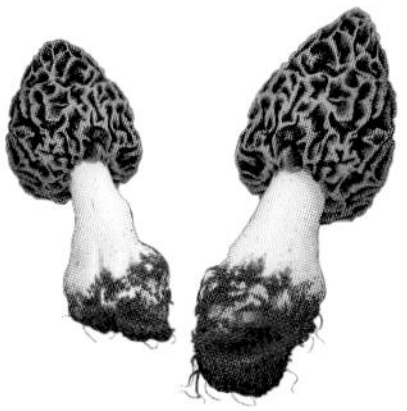

morels
morilla^F
morille^F
Morchel^F
spugnola^F

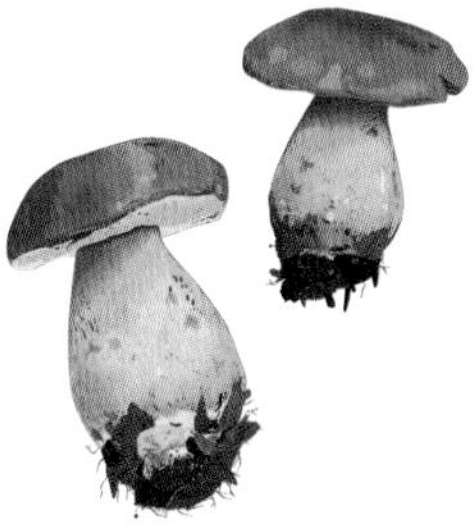

edible boletus
boleto^M comestible
cèpe^M
Steinpilz^M
porcino^M

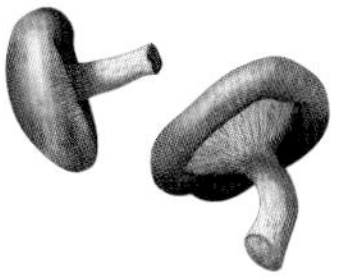

shitake
shiitake^M
shiitake^M
Schiitakepilz^M
shiitake^M

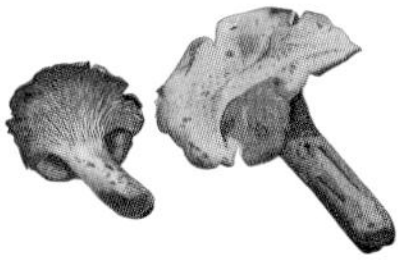

chanterelles
rebozuelo^M
chanterelle^F commune
Pfifferling^M
cantarello^M

seaweed

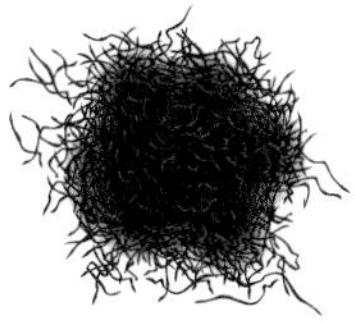

arame
arame^M
aramé^M
Arame^F
arame^F

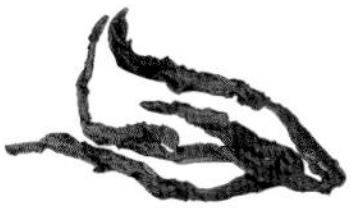

wakame
wakame^M
wakamé^M
Wakamé^F
wakame^F

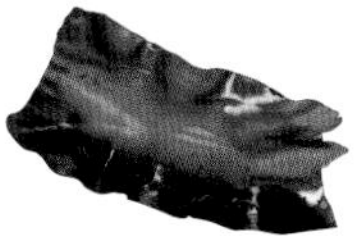

kombu
kombu^M
kombu^M
Kombu^F
kombu^M

spirulina
espirulina^F
spiruline^F
Spirulina^F
spirulina^F

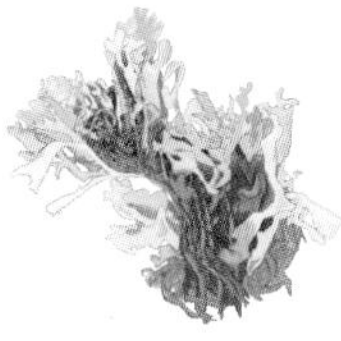

Irish moss
Irish moss^M
mousse^F d'Irlande^F
Irisch Moos^N
muschio^M d'Irlanda^M

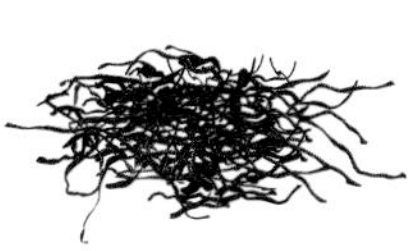

hijiki
hijiki^M
hijiki^M
Hijiki^F
hijiki^F

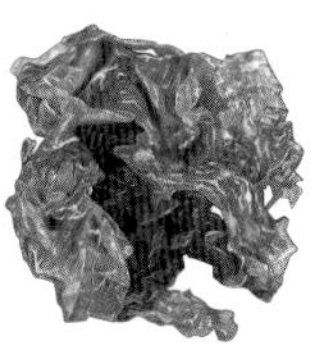

sea lettuce
lechuga^F marina
laitue^F de mer^F
Meersalat^M
lattuga^F marina

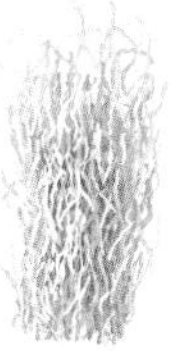

agar-agar
agar-agar^M
agar-agar^M
Agar-Agar^M/N
agar-agar^M

nori
nori^M
nori^M
Nori^N
nori^F

dulse
dulse^M
rhodyménie^F palmé
Dulse^F
dulse^F

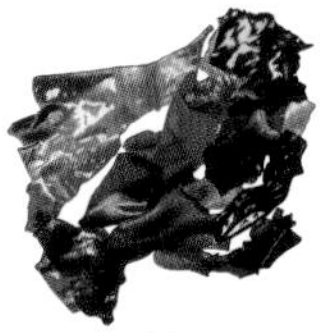

vegetables

hortalizas^F | légumes^M | Gemüse^N | ortaggi^M

bulb vegetables
bulbos^M
légumes^M **bulbes**^{M}
Zwiebelgemüse^N
ortaggi^M **da bulbo**^{M}

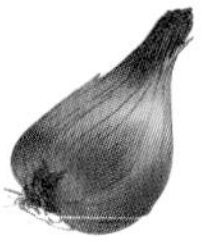

shallot
chalote^M
échalote^F
Schalotte^F
scalogno^M

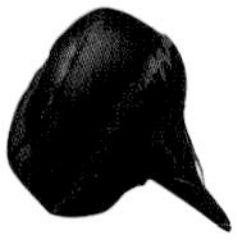

water chestnut
castaña^F de agua
châtaigne^F d'eau^F
Wassernuss^F
castagna^F d'acqua^F

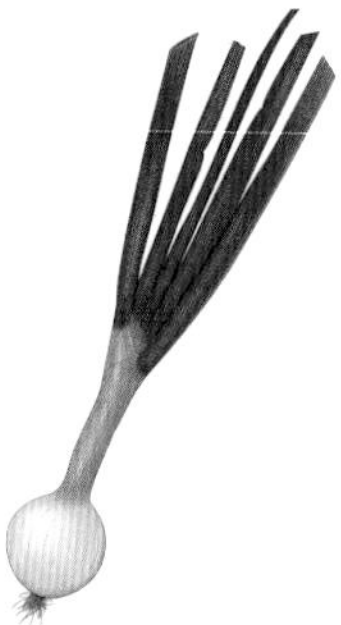

green onion
cebolla^F tierna
oignon^M vert
Frühlingszwiebel^F
cipolla^F verde

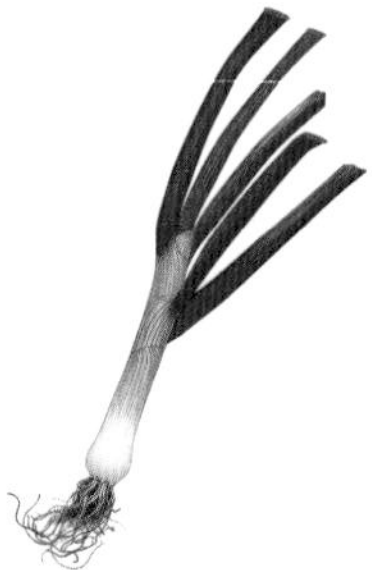

scallion
cebolla^F tierna
ciboule^F
Frühlingszwiebel^F
cipolla^F d'inverno^M

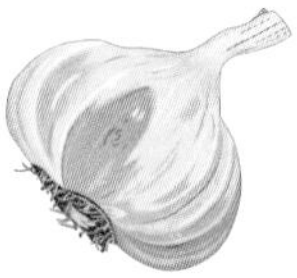

garlic
ajo^M
ail^M
Knoblauch^M
aglio^M

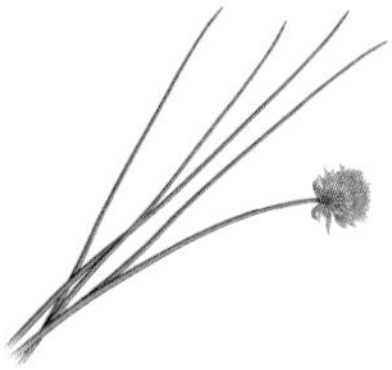

chives
cebollino^M
ciboulette^F
Schnittlauch^M
erba^F cipollina

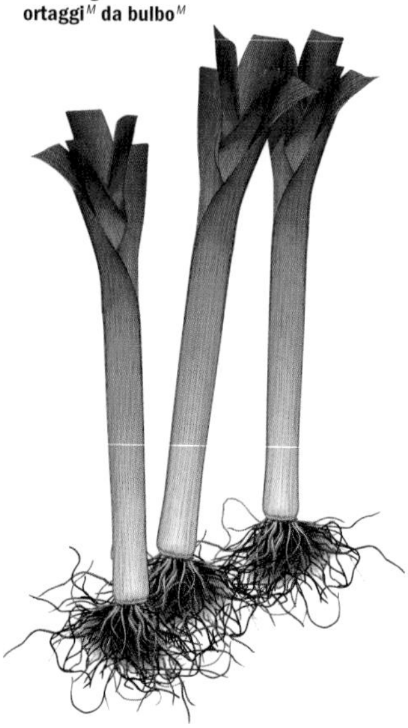

leeks
puerros^M
poireaux^M
Lauch^M
porri^M

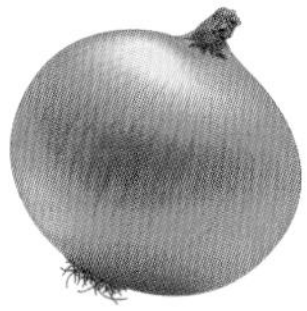

yellow onion
cebolla^F amarilla
oignon^M jaune
Gemüsezwiebel^F
cipolla^F di Spagna^F

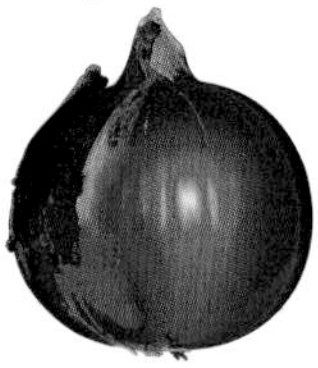

red onion
cebolla^F roja
oignon^M rouge
rote Zwiebel^F
cipolla^F rossa

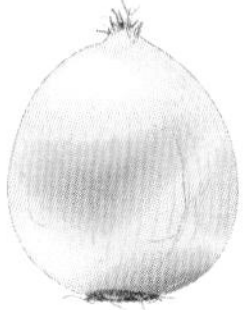

white onion
cebolla^F blanca
oignon^M blanc
weiße Zwiebel^F
cipolla^F bianca

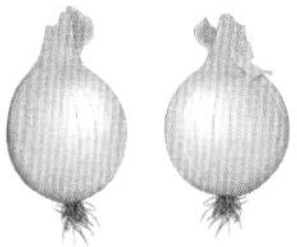

pickling onions
cebolletas^M
oignons^M à mariner
Perlzwiebeln^F
cipolline^F

tuber vegetables
tubérculos^M
légumes^M **tubercules**^{M}
Knollengemüse^N
ortaggi^M **da tubero**^{M}

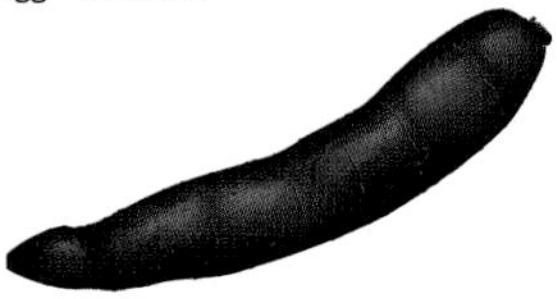

cassava
mandioca^F
manioc^M
Maniok^M
manioca^F

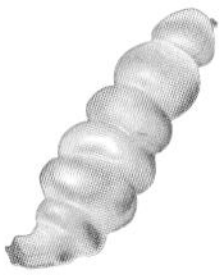

crosne
crosne^M
crosne^M
Knollenziest^M
crosne^M

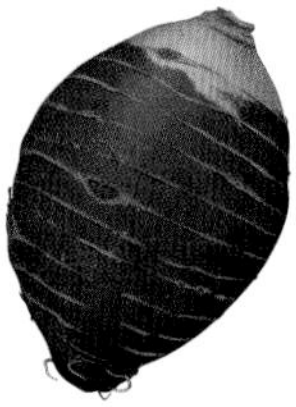

taro
taro^M
taro^M
Taro^M
taro^M

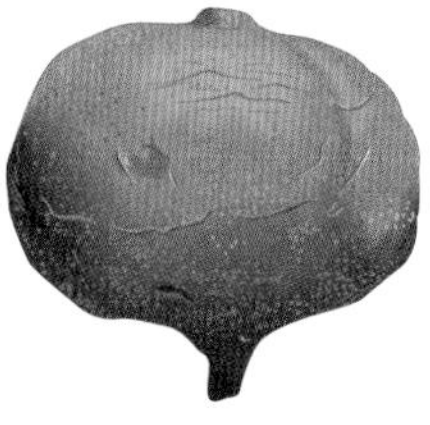

jicama
jicama^F
jicama^M
Jicama^F
jicama^F

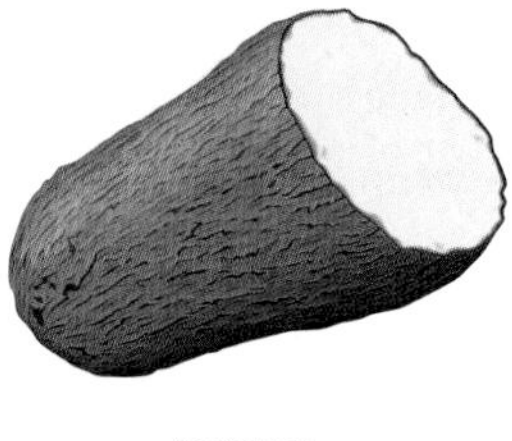

tropical yam
batata^F
igname^F
Süßkartoffel^F
patata^F americana

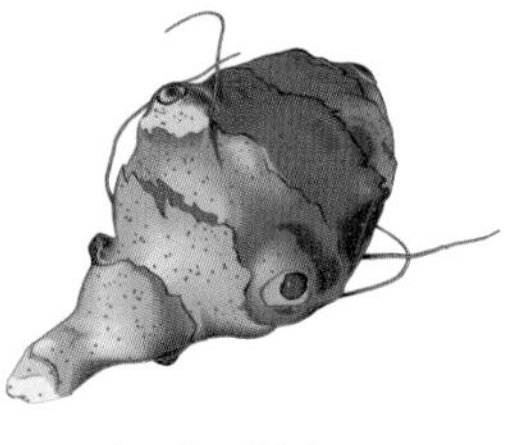

Jerusalem artichoke
aguaturma^F
topinambour^M
Topinambur$^{M/F}$
topinambur^M

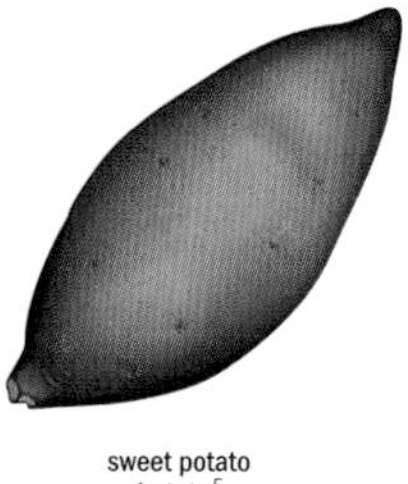

sweet potato
batata^F
patate^F
Süßkartoffel^F
patata^F americana

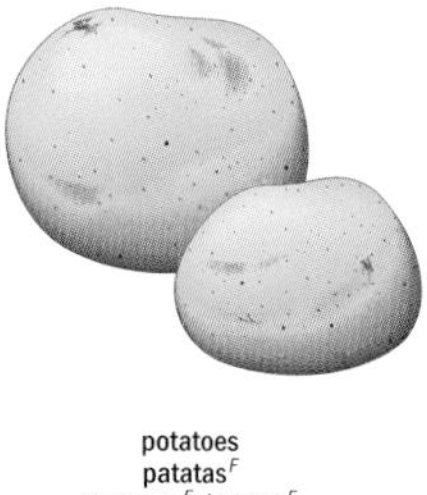

potatoes
patatas^F
pommes^F de terre^F
Kartoffeln^F
patate^F

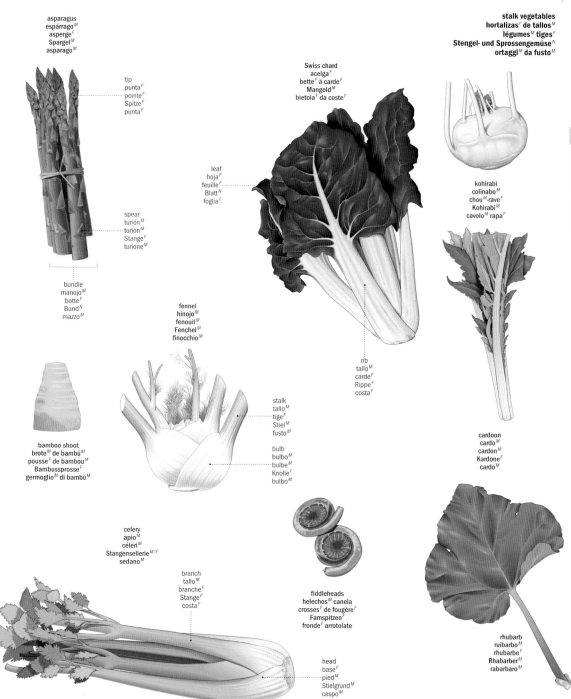

asparagus
espárrago ^{M}
asperge ^{F}
Spargel ^{M}
asparago ^{M}

tip
punta ^{F}
pointe ^{F}
Spitze ^{F}
punta ^{F}

spear
turión ^{M}
turion ^{M}
Stange ^{F}
turione ^{M}

bundle
manojo ^{M}
botte ^{F}
Bund ^{N}
mazzo ^{M}

stalk vegetables
hortalizas ^{F} de tallos ^{M}
légumes ^{M} tiges ^{F}
Stengel- und Sprossengemüse ^{N}
ortaggi ^{M} da fusto ^{M}

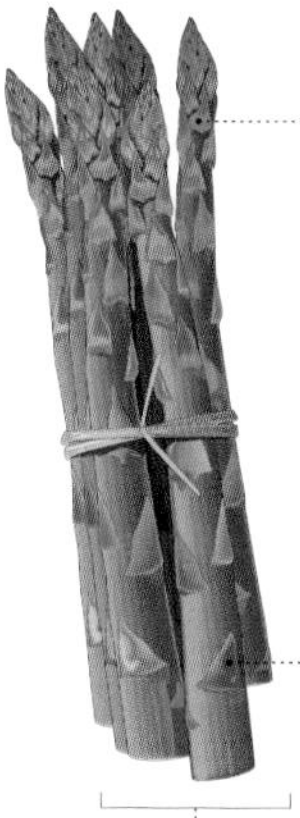

Swiss chard
acelga ^{F}
bette ^{F} à carde ^{F}
Mangold ^{M}
bietola ^{F} da coste ^{F}

leaf
hoja ^{F}
feuille ^{F}
Blatt ^{N}
foglia ^{F}

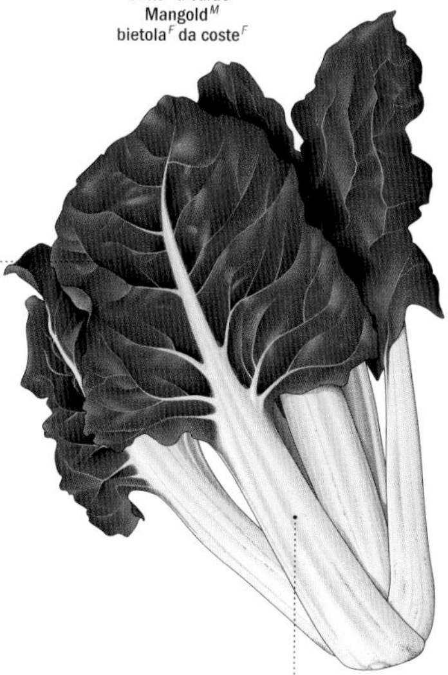

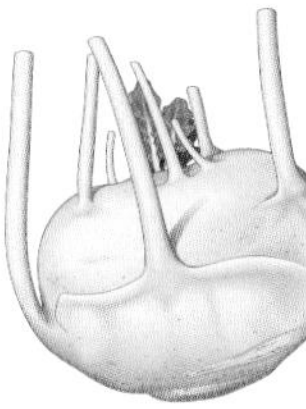

kohlrabi
colinabo ^{M}
chou ^{M}-rave ^{F}
Kohlrabi ^{M}
cavolo ^{M} rapa ^{F}

rib
tallo ^{M}
carde ^{F}
Rippe ^{F}
costa ^{F}

fennel
hinojo ^{M}
fenouil ^{M}
Fenchel ^{M}
finocchio ^{M}

stalk
tallo ^{M}
tige ^{F}
Stiel ^{M}
fusto ^{M}

bulb
bulbo ^{M}
bulbe ^{M}
Knolle ^{F}
bulbo ^{M}

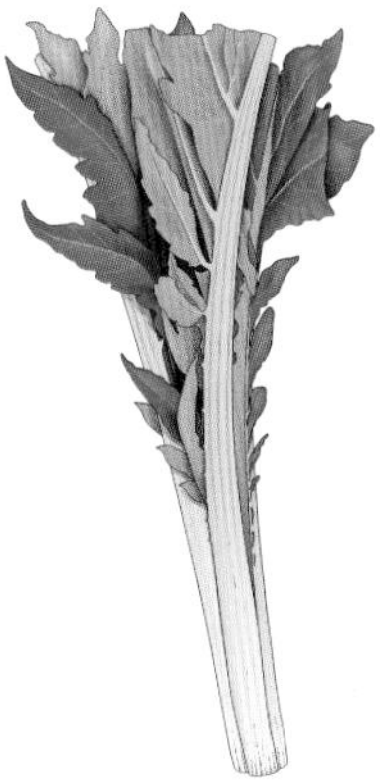

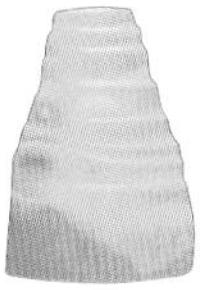

bamboo shoot
brote ^{M} de bambú ^{M}
pousse ^{F} de bambou ^{M}
Bambussprosse ^{F}
germoglio ^{M} di bambù ^{M}

cardoon
cardo ^{M}
cardon ^{M}
Kardone ^{F}
cardo ^{M}

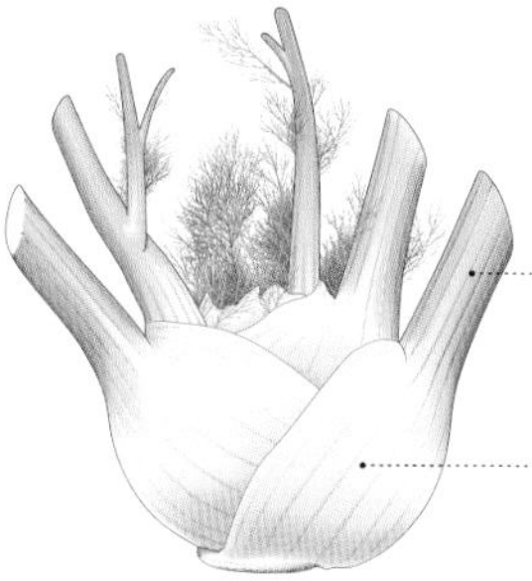

celery
apio ^{M}
céleri ^{M}
Stangensellerie $^{M/F}$
sedano ^{M}

branch
tallo ^{M}
branche ^{F}
Stange ^{F}
costa ^{F}

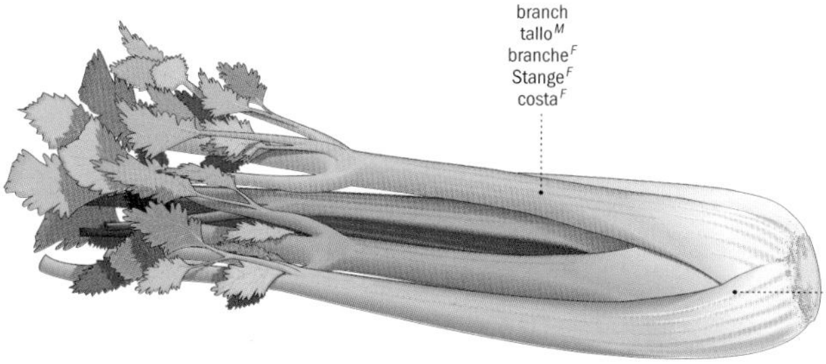

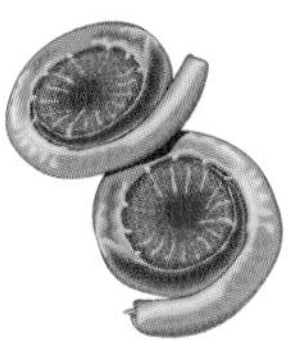

fiddleheads
helechos ^{M} canela
crosses ^{F} de fougère ^{F}
Farnspitzen ^{F}
fronde ^{F} arrotolate

head
base ^{F}
pied ^{M}
Stielgrund ^{M}
cespo ^{M}

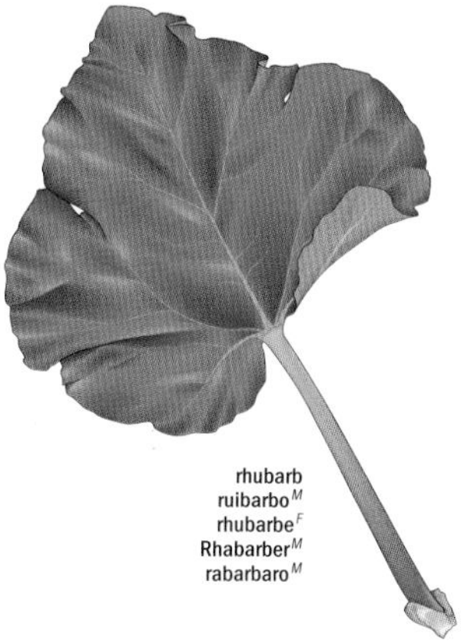

rhubarb
ruibarbo ^{M}
rhubarbe ^{F}
Rhabarber ^{M}
rabarbaro ^{M}

FOOD AND KITCHEN

vegetables

leaf vegetables
verduras^F de hojas^F
légumes^M feuilles^F
Blattgemüse^N
ortaggi^M da foglia^F

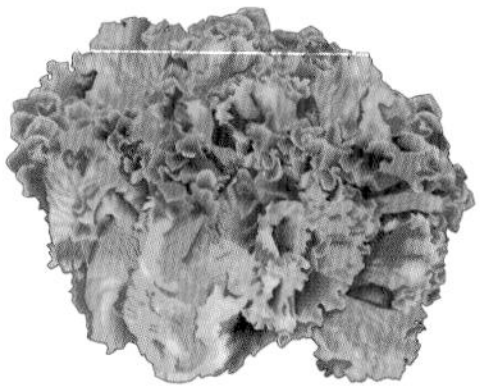

leaf lettuce
lechuga^F rizada
laitue^F frisée
Friséesalat^M
insalata^F riccia

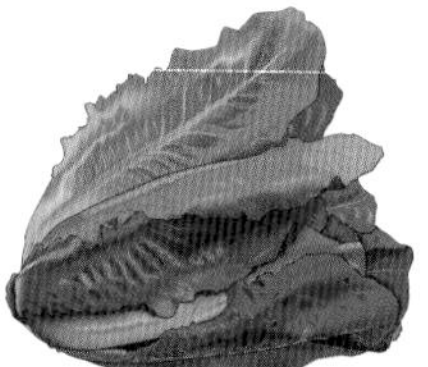

romaine lettuce
lechuga^F romana
romaine^F
Romagna-Salat^M
lattuga^F romana

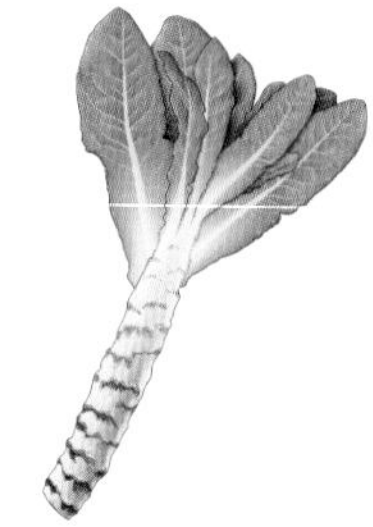

celtuce
lechuga^F de tallo^M
laitue^F asperge^F
Spargelsalat^M
lattuga^F asparago^M

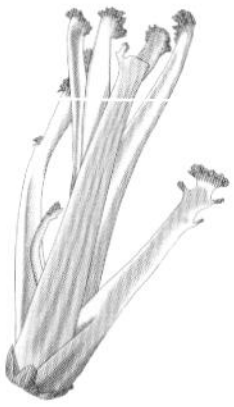

sea kale
col^F marina
chou^M marin
Meerkohl^M
cavolo^M marittimo

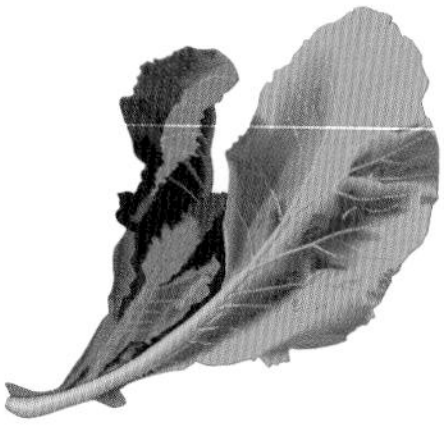

collards
berza^F
chou^M cavalier^M
Riesenkohl^M
gramigna^F crestata

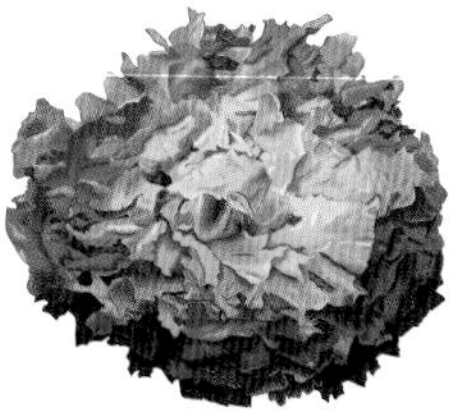

escarole
escarola^F
scarole^F
Eskariol^M
scarola^F

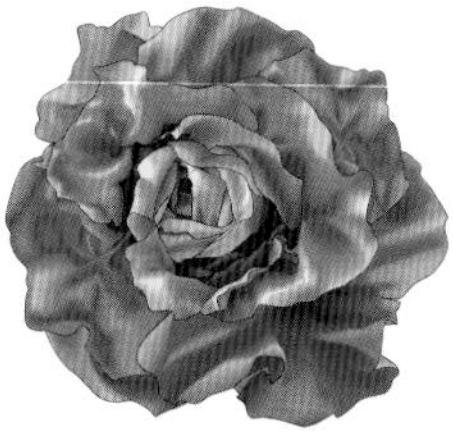

butter lettuce
lechuga^F de cogollo^M
laitue^F pommée
Kopfsalat^M
lattuga^F cappuccina

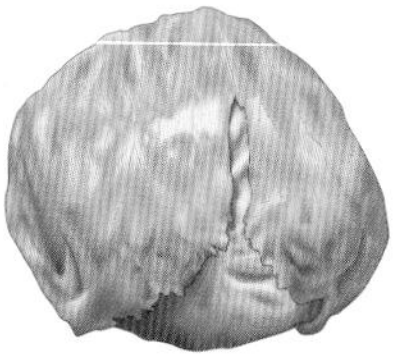

iceberg lettuce
lechuga^F iceberg
laitue^F iceberg^M
Eisbergsalat^M
lattuga^F iceberg^M

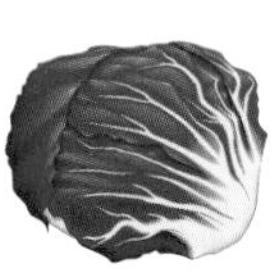

radicchio
achicoria^F de Treviso
chicorée^F de Trévise
Radicchio^M
radicchio^M

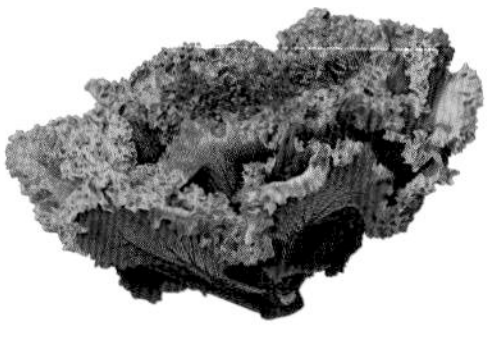

ornamental kale
col^F ornamental
chou^M laitue^F
Zierkohl^M
cavolo^M ornamentale

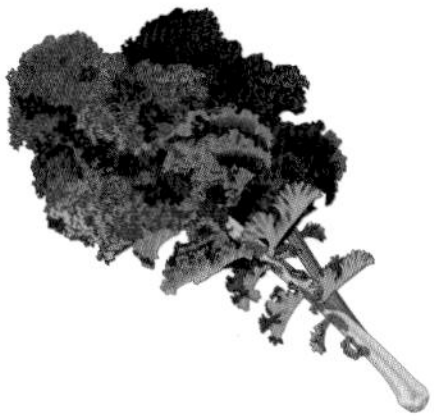

curly kale
col^F rizada
chou^M frisé
Grünkohl^M
cavolo^M riccio^M

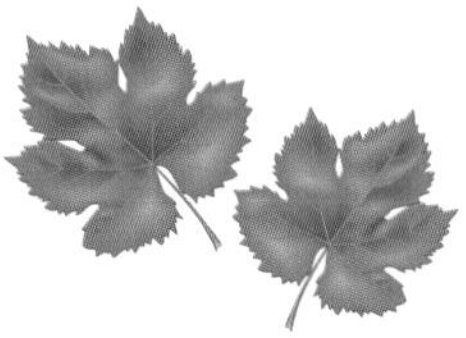

grape leaves
hoja^F de parra^F
feuille^F de vigne^F
Weinblatt^N
pampino^M

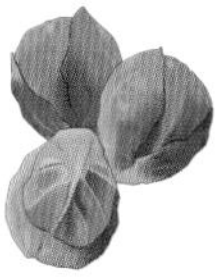

brussels sprouts
coles^F de Bruselas
choux^M de Bruxelles
Rosenkohl^M
cavolini^M di Bruxelles

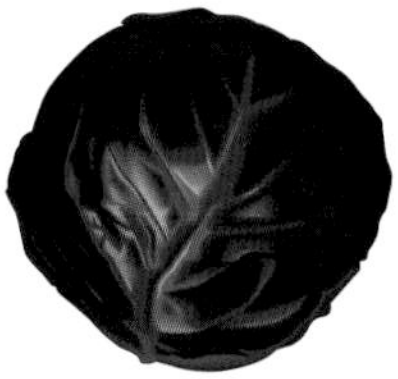

red cabbage
col^F lombarda
chou^M pommé rouge
Rotkohl^M
cavolo^M rosso

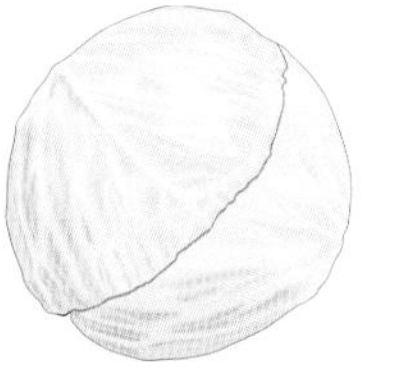

white cabbage
col^F/repollo^M
chou^M pommé blanc
Weißkohl^M
cavolo^M bianco

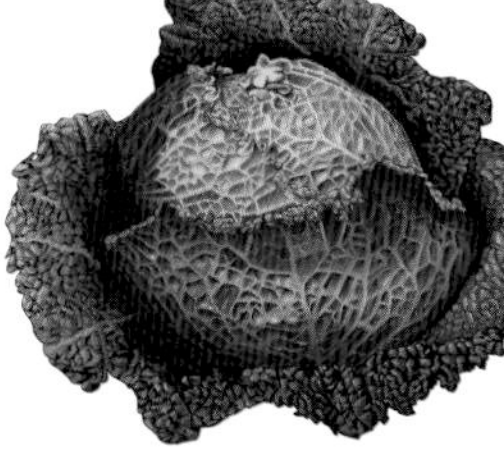

savoy cabbage
col^F rizada de otoño^M
chou^M de Milan
Wirsing^M
cavolo^M verzotto^M

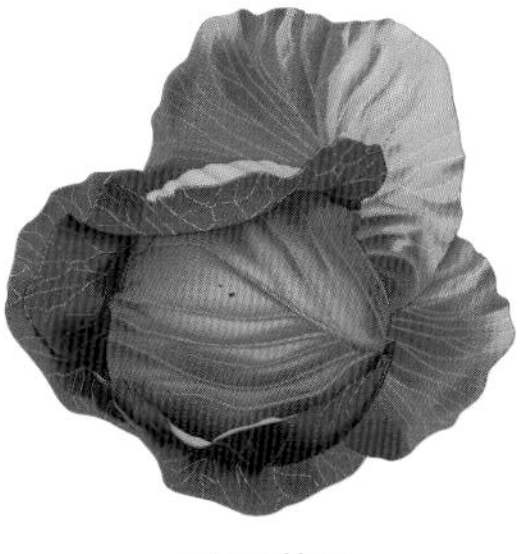

green cabbage
col^F verde/repollo^M verde
chou^M pommé vert
Kohl^M
cavolo^M verza^F

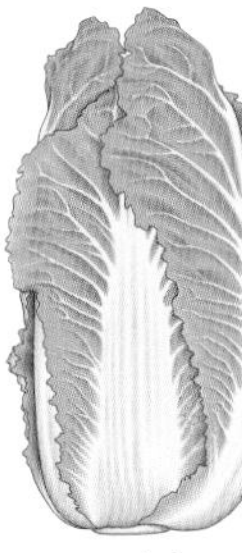

pe-tsai
col^M china
pe-tsaï^F
Chinakohl^M
pe-tsaï^M

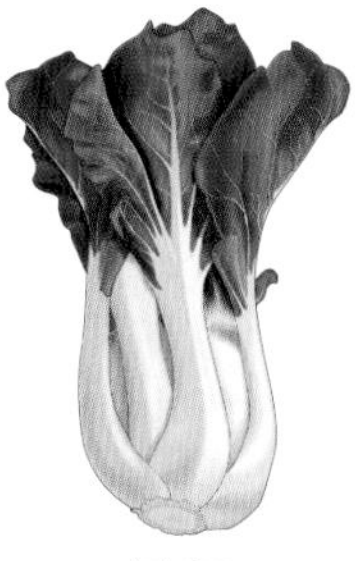

bok choy
pak-choi^M
pak-choï^M
Pak-Choi^M
pak-choi^M

vegetables

FOOD AND KITCHEN

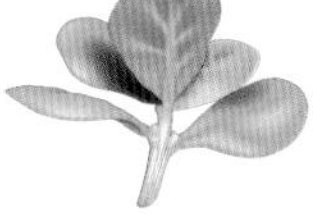

purslane
verdolaga^F
pourpier^M
Portulak^M
porcellana^F

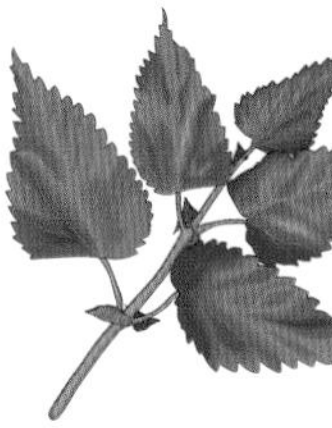

nettle
ortiga^F
ortie^F
Nessel^F
ortica^F

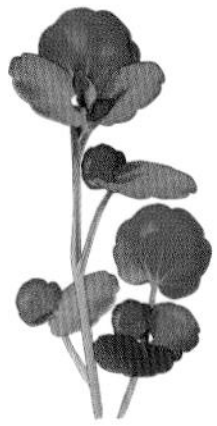

watercress
berro^M
cresson^M de fontaine^F
Brunnenkresse^F
crescione^M

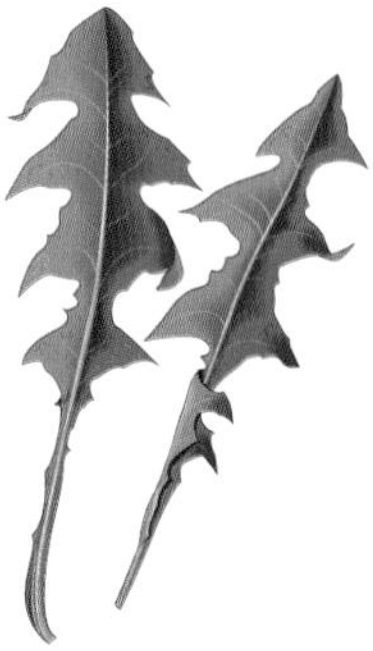

dandelion
diente^M de león
pissenlit^M
Löwenzahn^M
dente^M di leone^M

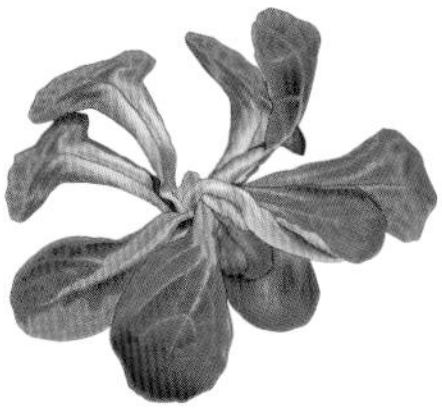

corn salad
colleja^F
mâche^F
Feldsalat^M
valerianella^F

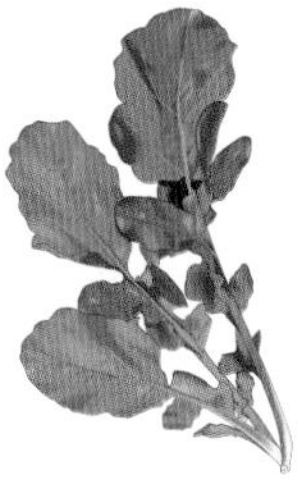

arugula
ruqueta^F
roquette^F
Rauke^F
rucola^F

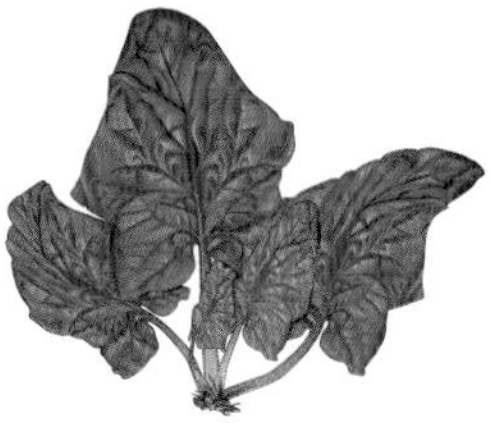

spinach
espinaca^F
épinard^M
Spinat^M
spinacio^M

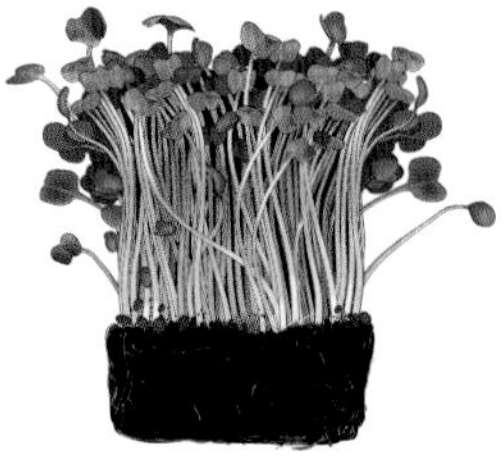

garden cress
berros^M de jardín
cresson^M alénois
Gartenkresse^F
crescione^M d'orto^M

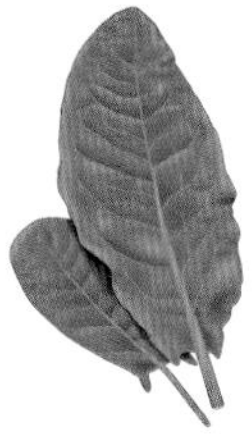

garden sorrel
acedera^F
oseille^F
Garten-Sauerampfer^M
acetosa^F

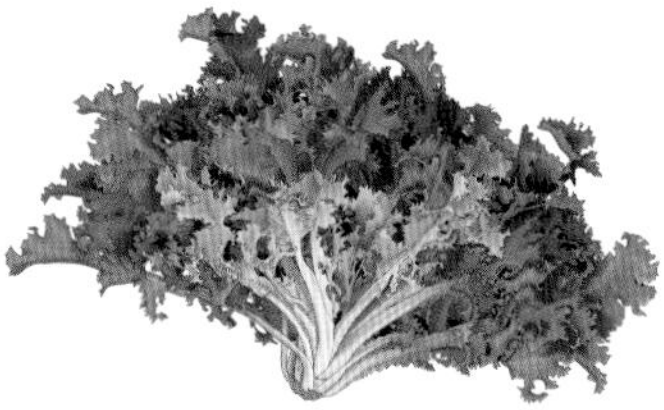

curly endive
escarola^F rizada
chicorée^F frisée
krause Endivie^F
indivia^F riccia

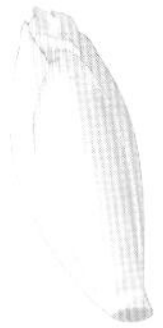

Belgian endive
endivia^F
endive^F
Chicorée^{M/F}
insalata^F belga

inflorescent vegetables
inflorescencias^F
légumes^M fleurs^F
Blütengemüse^N
ortaggi^M da inflorescenza^F

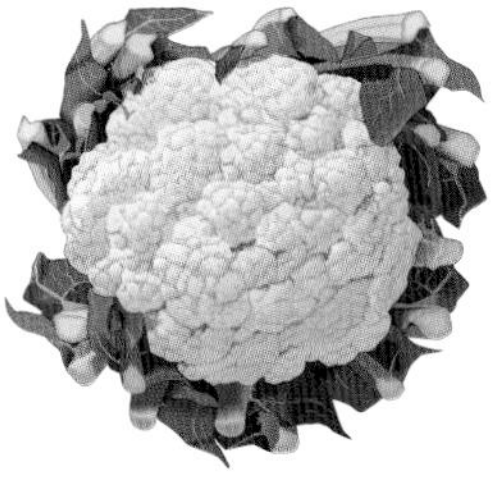

cauliflower
coliflor^F
chou^M-fleur^F
Blumenkohl^M
cavolfiore^M

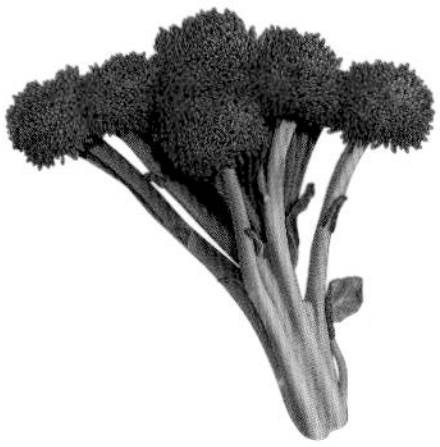

broccoli
brécol^M
brocoli^M
Broccoli^M
broccolo^M

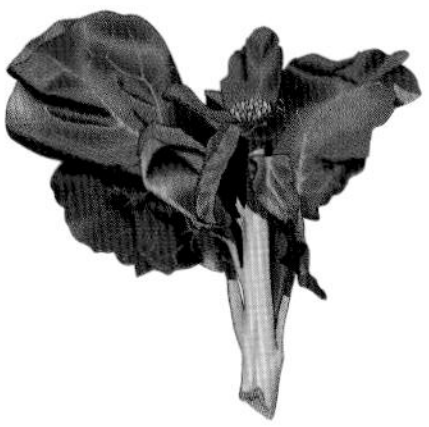

Gai-lohn
brécol^M chino
Gai Ion^M
China-Broccoli^M
Gai-lohn^M

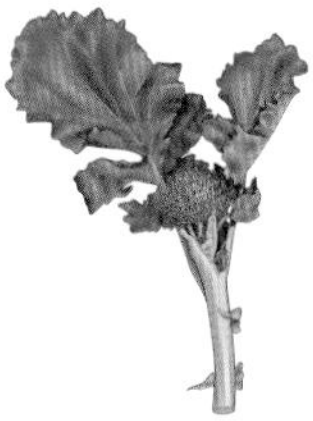

broccoli rabe
nabiza^F
brocoli^M italien
Rübenspross^M
cime^F di rapa^F

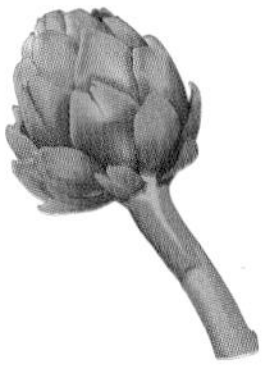

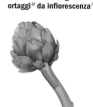

artichoke
alcachofa^F
artichaut^F
Artischocke^F
carciofo^M

vegetables

fruit vegetables
hortalizas^F **de fruto**^{M}
légumes^M **fruits**^{M}
Fruchtgemüse^N
ortaggi^M **da frutto**^{M}

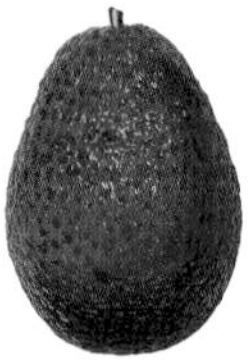

avocado
aguacate^M
avocat^M
Avocado^F
avocado^M

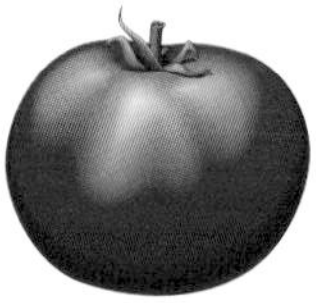

tomato
tomate^M
tomate^F
Tomate^F
pomodoro^M

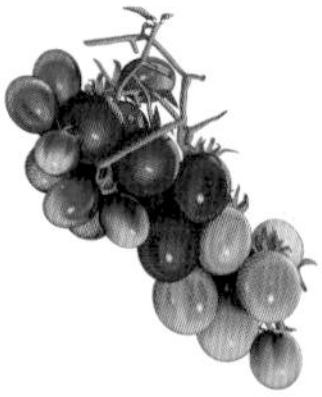

currant tomatoes
tomates^M en rama^F
tomates^F en grappe^F
Kirschtomaten^F
pomodorini^M a grappolo^M

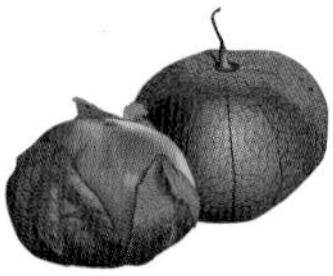

tomatillos
tomatillos^M
tomatilles^F
Tomatillo^F
tomatilli^M

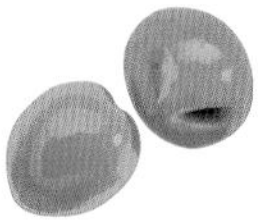

olives
aceitunas^M
olives^F
Oliven^F
olivi^F

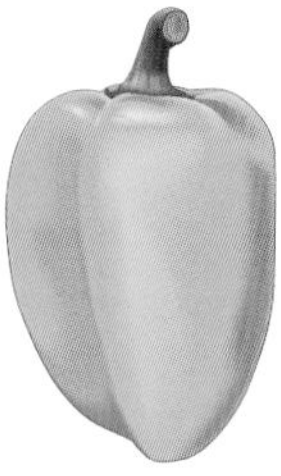

yellow sweet pepper
pimiento^M dulce amarillo
poivron^M jaune
gelber Paprika^M
peperone^M giallo

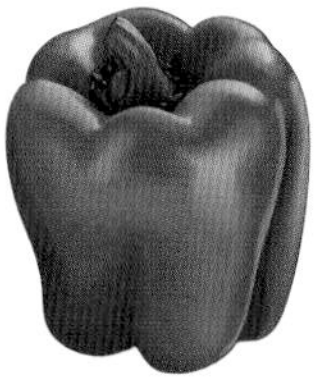

green sweet pepper
pimiento^M dulce verde
poivron^M vert
grüner Paprika^M
peperone^M verde

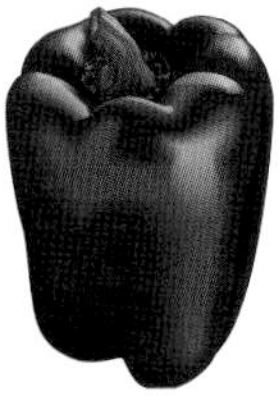

red sweet pepper
pimiento^M dulce rojo
poivron^M rouge
roter Paprika^M
peperone^M rosso

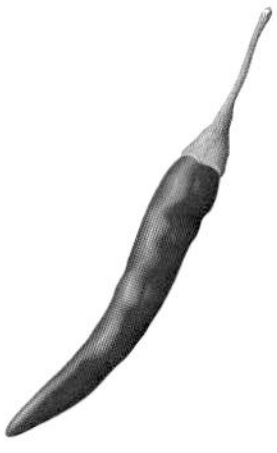

hot pepper
chile^M
piment^M
Pfefferschote^F
peperoncino^M

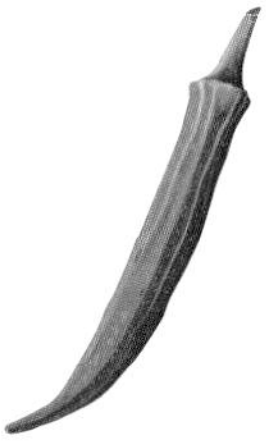

okra
gombo^M, quingombó^M
gombo^M
Okraschote^F
gombo^M

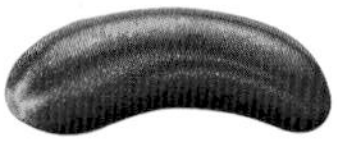

gherkin
pepinillo^M
cornichon^M
Einlegegurke^F
cetriolino^M

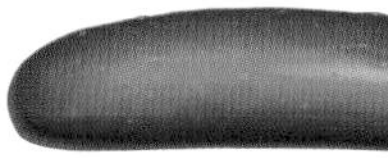

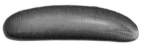

cucumber
pepino^M
concombre^M
Gurke^F
cetriolo^M

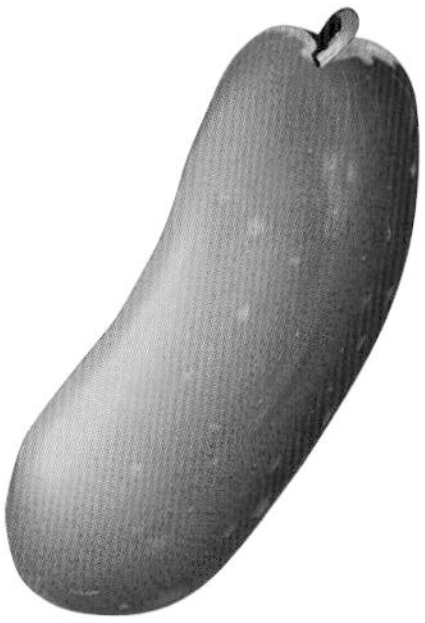

wax gourd (winter melon)
calabaza^F de China
melon^M d'hiver^M chinois
Wachskürbis^M
zucca^F bianca

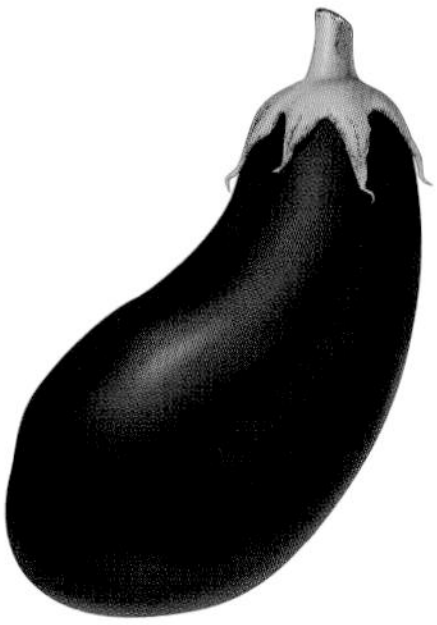

eggplant
berenjena^F
aubergine^F
Aubergine^F
melanzana^F

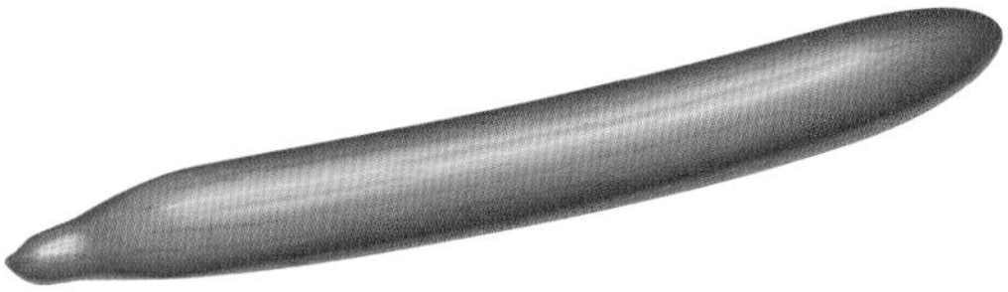

seedless cucumber
pepino^M sin pepitas^F
concombre^M sans pépins^M
kernlose Salatgurke^F
cetriolo^M senza semi^M

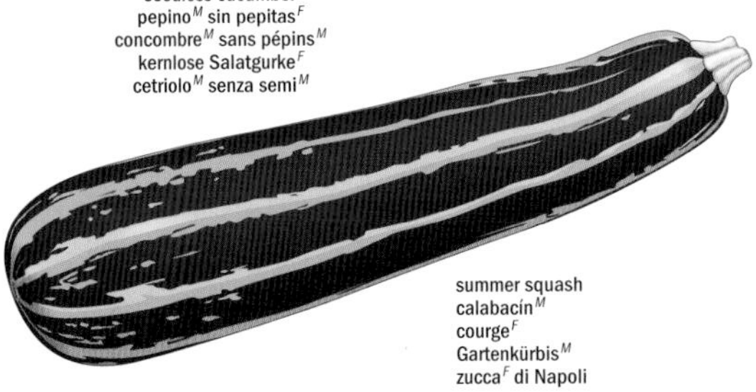

summer squash
calabacín^M
courge^F
Gartenkürbis^M
zucca^F di Napoli

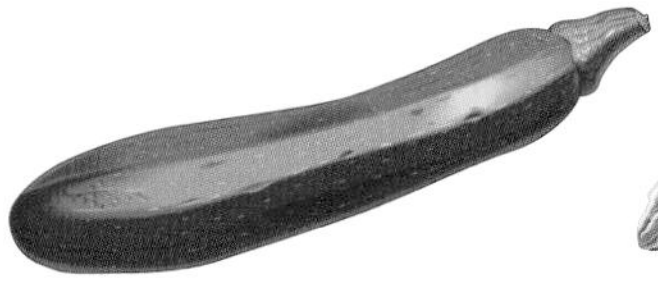

zucchini
calabacín^M
courgette^F
Zucchini^F
zucchina^F

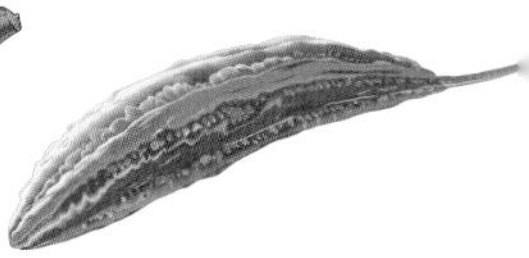

bitter melon
pepino^M amargo
margose^F
Bittermelone^F
melone^M amaro

vegetables

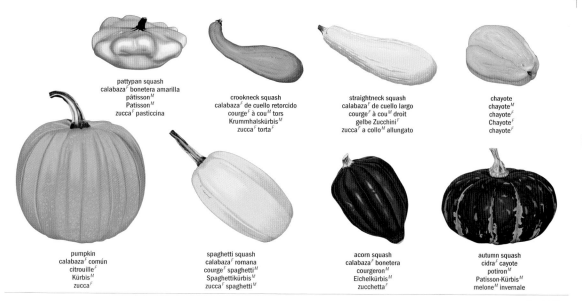

pattypan squash
calabaza^F bonetera amarilla
pâtisson^M
Patisson^M
zucca^F pasticcina

crookneck squash
calabaza^F de cuello retorcido
courge^F à cou^M tors
Krummhalskürbis^M
zucca^F torta^F

straightneck squash
calabaza^F de cuello largo
courge^F à cou^M droit
gelbe Zucchini^F
zucca^F a collo^M allungato

chayote
chayote^M
chayote^F
Chayote^F
chayote^F

pumpkin
calabaza^F común
citrouille^F
Kürbis^M
zucca^F

spaghetti squash
calabaza^F romana
courge^F spaghetti^M
Spaghettikürbis^M
zucca^F spaghetti^M

acorn squash
calabaza^F bonetera
courgeron^M
Eichelkürbis^M
zucchetta^F

autumn squash
cidra^F cayote
potiron^M
Patisson-Kürbis^M
melone^M invernale

root vegetables
raíces^F
légumes^M racines^F
Wurzelgemüse^N
ortaggi^M da radice^F

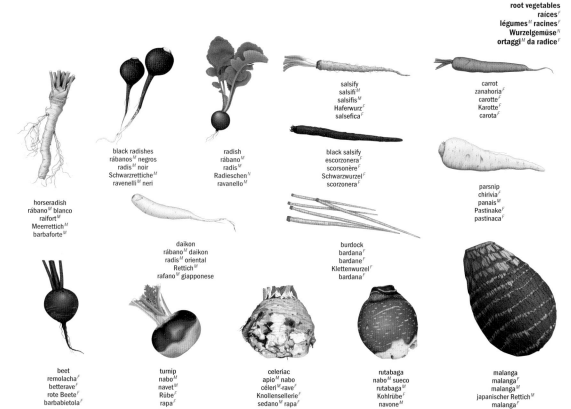

salsify
salsifí^M
salsifis^M
Haferwurz^F
salsefica^F

carrot
zanahoria^F
carotte^F
Karotte^F
carota^F

black radishes
rábanos^M negros
radis^M noir
Schwarzrettiche^M
ravenelli^M neri

radish
rábano^M
radis^M
Radieschen^N
ravanello^M

black salsify
escorzonera^F
scorsonère^F
Schwarzwurzel^F
scorzonera^F

parsnip
chirivía^F
panais^M
Pastinake^F
pastinaca^F

horseradish
rábano^M blanco
raifort^M
Meerrettich^M
barbaforte^M

daikon
rábano^M daikon
radis^M oriental
Rettich^M
rafano^M giapponese

burdock
bardana^F
bardane^F
Klettenwurzel^F
bardana^F

beet
remolacha^F
betterave^F
rote Beete^F
barbabietola^F

turnip
nabo^M
navet^M
Rübe^F
rapa^F

celeriac
apio^M nabo
céleri^M-rave^F
Knollensellerie^F
sedano^M rapa^F

rutabaga
nabo^M sueco
rutabaga^F
Kohlrübe^F
navone^M

malanga
malanga^F
malanga^F
japanischer Rettich^M
malanga^F

legumes

legumbres^F | légumineuses^F | Hülsenfrüchte^F | legumi^M

FOOD AND KITCHEN

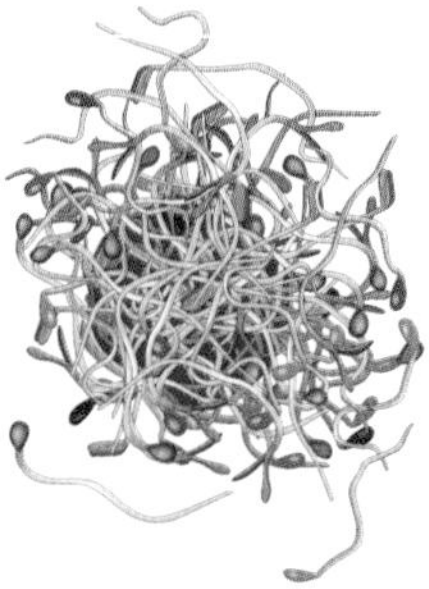

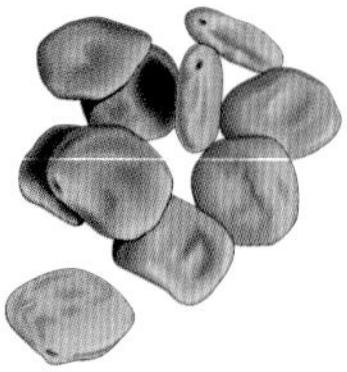

lupines
altramuz^M
lupin^M
Lupine^F
lupino^M

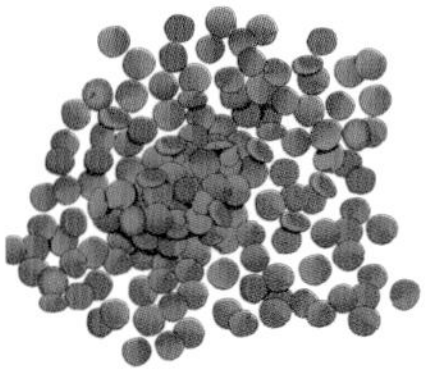

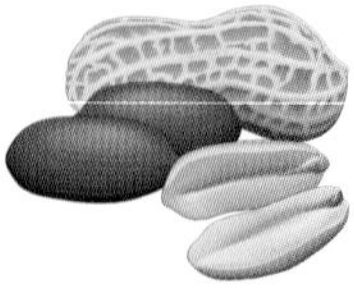

peanut
cacahuete^M
arachide^F
Erdnuss^F
arachide^F

alfalfa sprouts
alfalfa^F
luzerne^F
blaue Luzerne^F
erba^F medica

lentils
lentejas^F
lentilles^F
Linsen^F
lenticchie^F

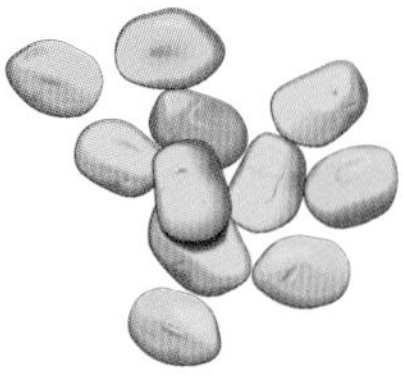

broad beans
habas^F
fèves^F
dicke Bohnen^F
fave^F

peas
guisantes^M
pois^M
Erbsen^F
piselli^M

dolichos beans
dolichos^M
doliques^M
Bohnen^F
dolichi^M

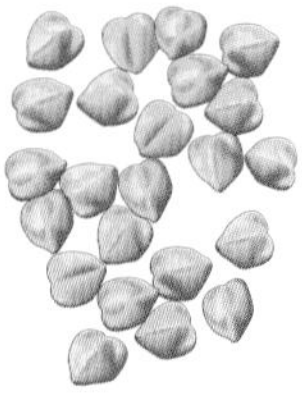

chick peas
garbanzos^M
pois^M chiches
Kichererbsen^F
ceci^M

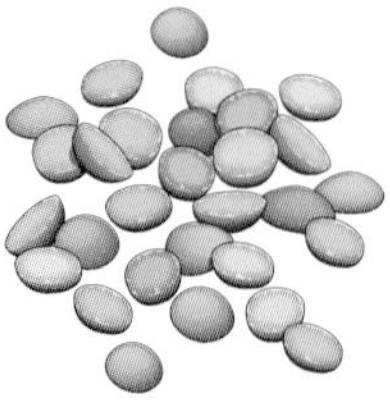

split peas
guisantes^M partidos
pois^M cassés
gespaltene Erbsen^F
piselli^M secchi spaccati

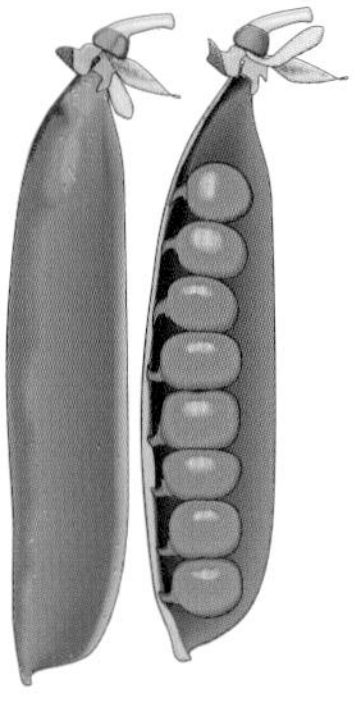

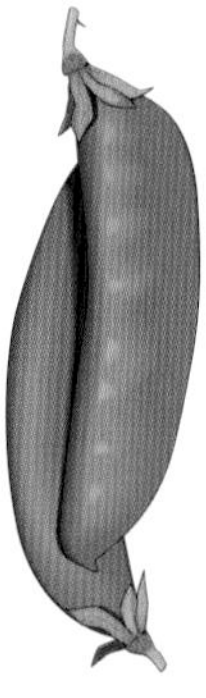

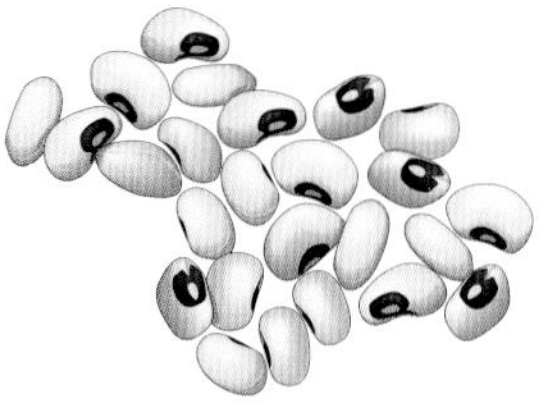

black-eyed peas
judías^F de ojo
dolique^M à œil^M noir
schwarzäugige Bohne^F
fagiolo^M dall'occhio^M nero

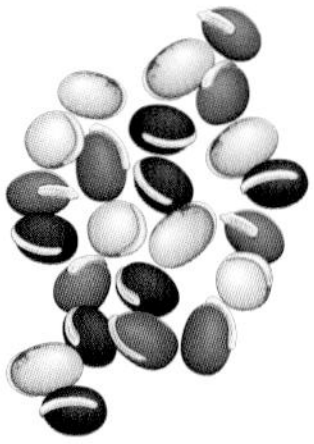

lablab beans
judía^F de Egipto
dolique^M d'Égypte^F
Helmbohne^F
fagiolo^M egiziano

green peas
guisantes^M
petits pois^M
grüne Erbsen^F
piselli^M

snow peas
guisantes^M mollares
pois^M mange-tout^M
Zuckererbsen^F
piselli^M mangiatutto

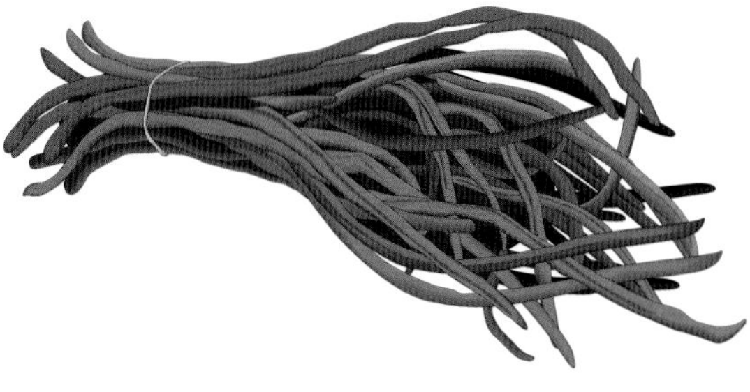

yard-long beans
judía^F china larga
dolique^M asperge^F
Spargelbohne^F
fagiolo^M asparagio^M

beans
judías^F
haricots^M
Bohnen^F
fagioli^M

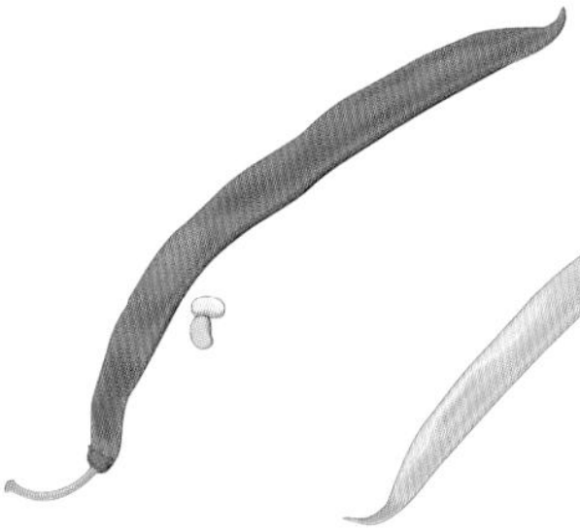

green bean
judía^F verde
haricot^M vert
grüne Bohne^F
fagiolino^M

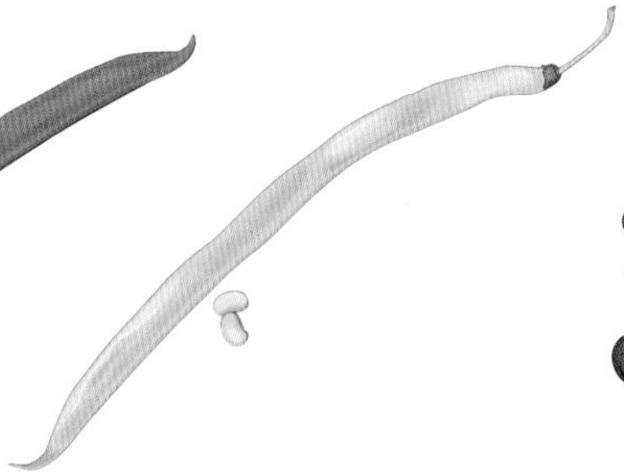

wax bean
judía^F amarilla
haricot^M jaune
Wachsbohne^F
fagiolino^M giallo

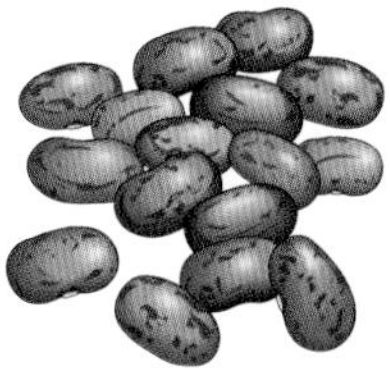

romano beans
judías^F romanas
haricots^M romains
römische Bohnen^F
fagioli^M romani

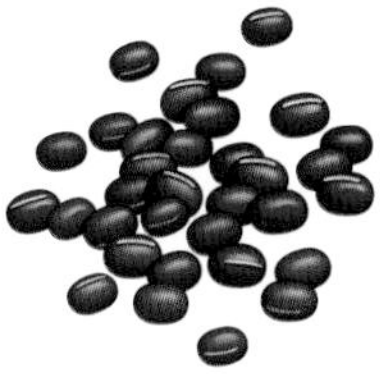

adzuki beans
judías^F adzuki
haricots^M adzuki
Asukibohnen^F
fagioli^M adzuki

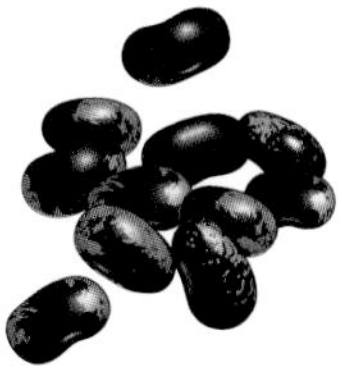

scarlet runner beans
judías^F pinta
haricots^M d'Espagne^F
Feuerbohnen^F
fagioli^M di Spagna^F

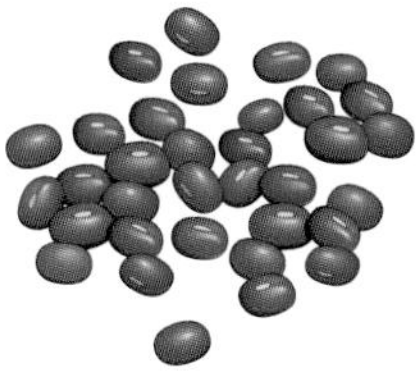

mung beans
judías^F mungo
haricots^M mungo
Mungobohnen^F
fagioli^M mungo

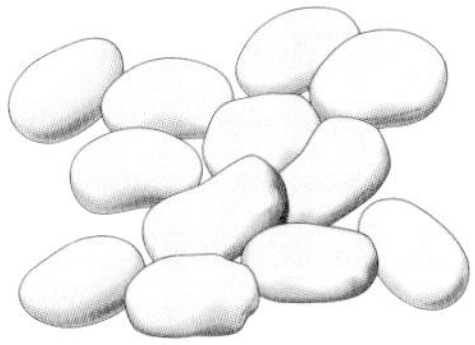

lima beans
judías^F de Limas
haricots^M de Lima
Limabohnen^F
fagioli^M di Lima

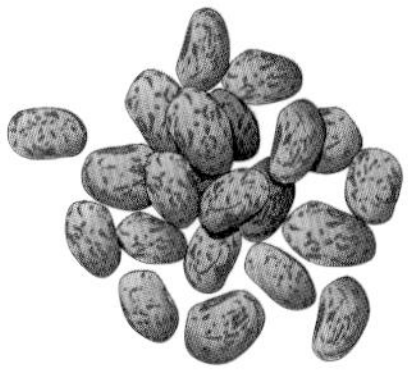

pinto beans
judías^F rojas
haricots^M pinto
Pintobohnen^F
fagioli^M pinti

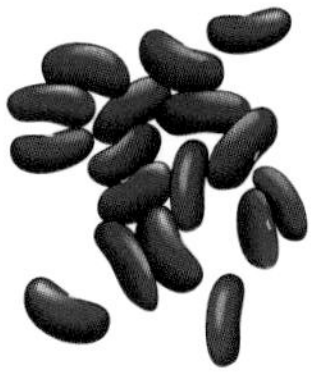

red kidney beans
judías^F rojas
haricots^M rouge
roten Kidneybohnen^F
fagioli^M borlotti

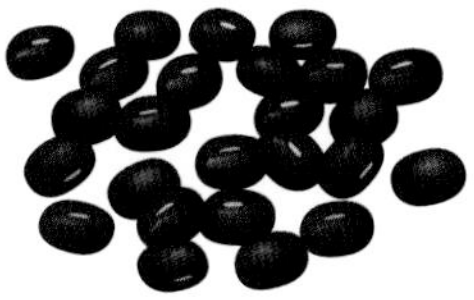

black gram beans
judías^F mungo negras
haricots^M mungo à grain^M noir
schwarzen Mungobohnen^F
fagioli^M mungo neri

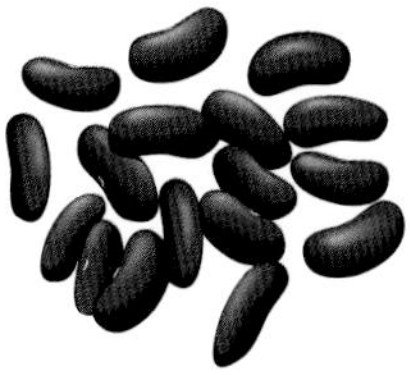

black beans
judías^F negras
haricots^M noir
schwarzen Bohnen^F
fagioli^M neri

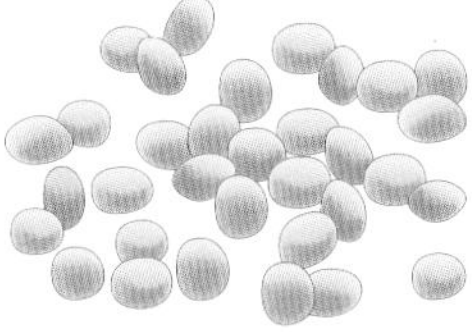

soybeans
semillas^F de soja^F
graine^F de soja^M ; graine^F de soya^M
Sojabohnen^F
semi^M di soia^F

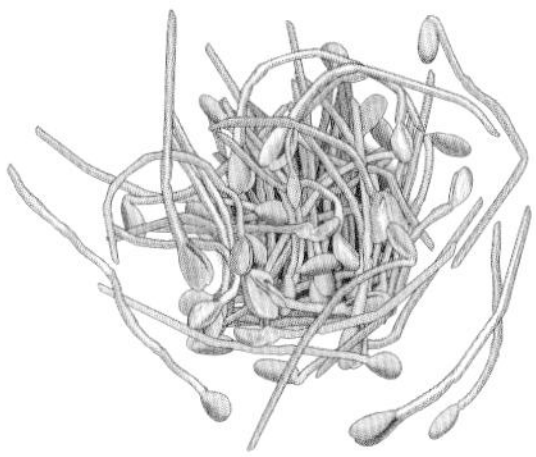

soybean sprouts
brotes^M de soja^F
germes^M de soja^M ; germes^M de soya^M
Sojasprossen^F
germogli^M di soia^F

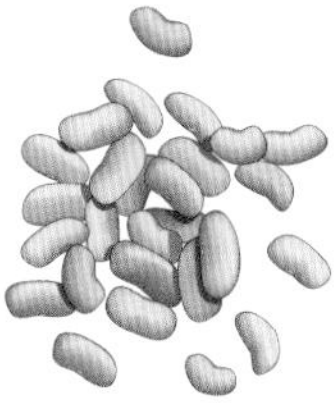

flageolets
frijoles^M
flageolets^M
Flageolet-Bohnen^F
fagioli^M cannellini^M

fruits

frutas^F | fruits^M | Obst^N | frutti^M

FOOD AND KITCHEN

berries
bayas^F
baies^F
Beeren^F
bacche^F

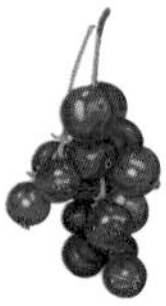

currants
grosellas^F
groseilles^F à grappes^F ; *gadelle*^{F}
Johannisbeeren^F
ribes^M

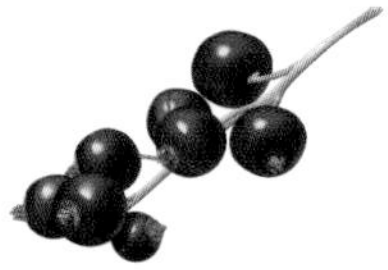

black currants
grosellas^F negras
cassis^M
schwarzen Johannisbeeren^F
ribes^M nero

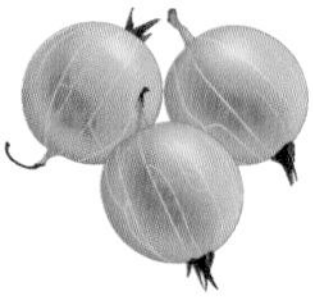

gooseberries
grosellas^F espinosas
groseilles^F à maquereau^M
Stachelbeeren^F
uvaspine^F

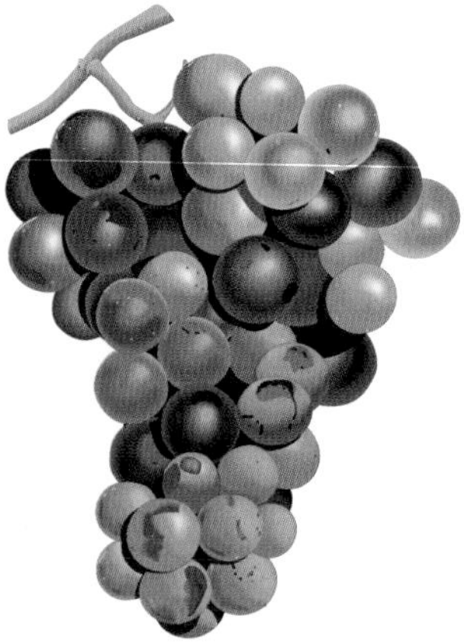

grapes
uvas^F
raisins^M
Weintrauben^F
uve^F

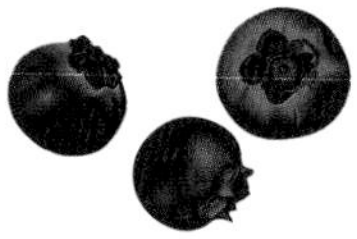

blueberries
arándanos^M
bleuets^M
Heidelbeeren^F
mirtilli^M

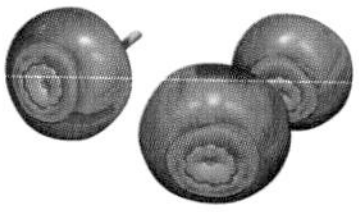

bilberries
arándanos^M negros
myrtilles^F
Heidelbeeren^F
mirtilli^M

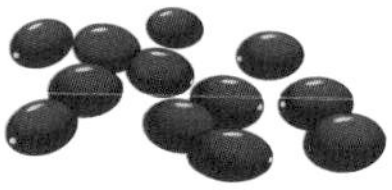

red whortleberries
arándanos^M rojos
airelles^F
rote Heidelbeeren^F
mirtilli^M rossi

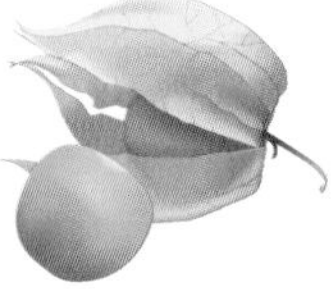

alkekengi
alquequenje^M
alkékenge^M
Physalis^F
alchechengi^M

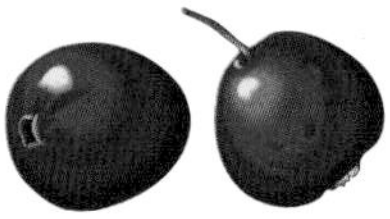

cranberries
arándanos^M agrios
canneberges^F ; *atoca*^{M}
Preiselbeeren^F
mirtilli^M palustri

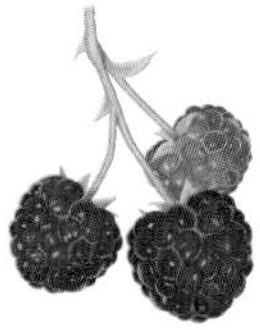

raspberries
frambuesas^F
framboises^F
Himbeeren^F
lampone^M

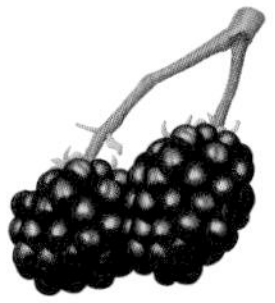

blackberries
moras^F
mûres^F
Brombeeren^F
more^F

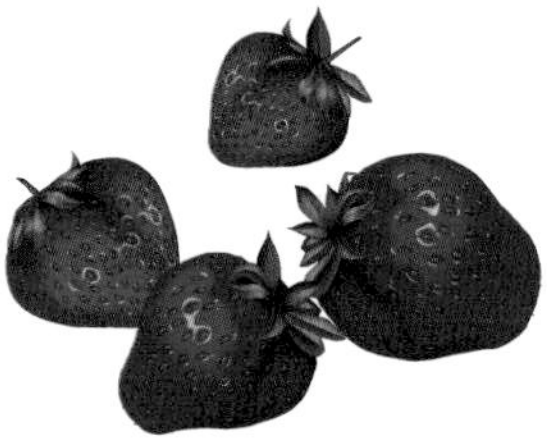

strawberries
fresas^F
fraises^F
Erdbeeren^F
fragole^F

---

stone fruits
drupas^F
fruits^M **à noyau**^{M}
Steinfrüchte^F
drupe^F

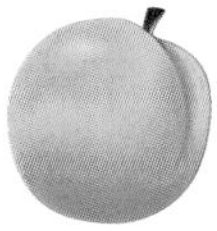

apricot
albaricoque^M
abricot^M
Aprikose^F
albicocca^F

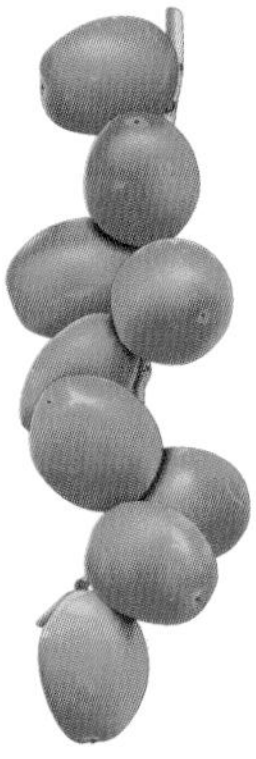

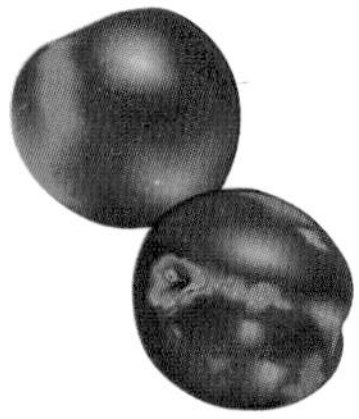

plums
ciruelas^F
prunes^F
Pflaumen^F
prugne^F

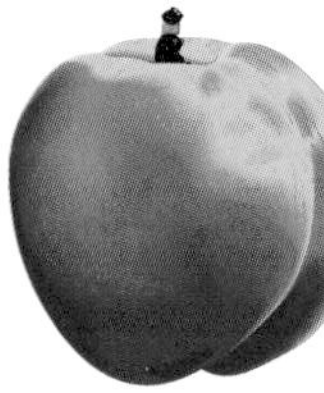

peach
melocotón^M
pêche^F
Pfirsich^M
pesca^F

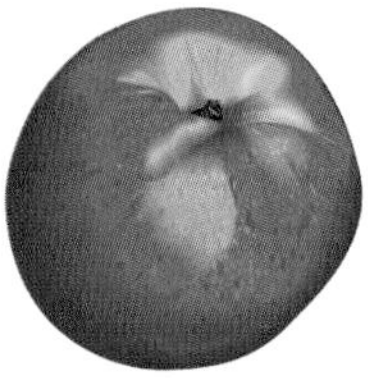

nectarine
nectarina^F
nectarine^F
Nektarine^F
nettarina^F

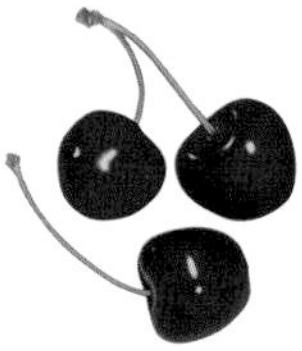

cherries
cerezas^F
cerises^F
Kirschen^F
ciliegie^F

dates
dátiles^M
dattes^F
Datteln^F
datteri^M

dry fruits
frutas^F secas
fruits^M secs
Trockenfrüchte^F
frutti^M secchi

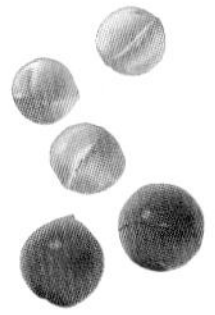

macadamia nuts
nuezes^F de macadamia^F
noix^F de macadamia^M
Macadamianussen^F
noce^F di macadamia^F

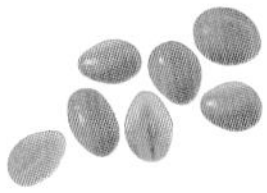

ginkgo nuts
nuezes^F de ginkgo
noix^F de ginkgo^M
Ginkgonussen^F
noce^F di ginco^M

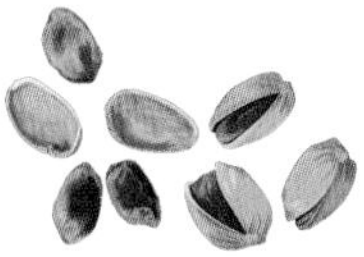

pistachio nuts
pistachos^M
pistaches^F
Pistazie^F
pistacchii^M

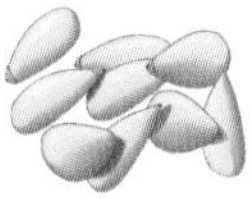

pine nuts
piñónes^M
pignons^M
Pinienkern^M
pinoli^M

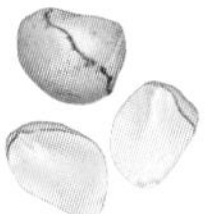

cola nuts
nuezes^F de cola
noix^F de cola^M
Kolanussen^F
noce^F di cola^F

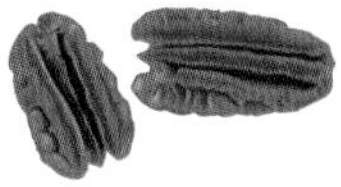

pecan nuts
pecanas^F
noix^F de pacane^F
Pecannuss^F
noce^F di pecan

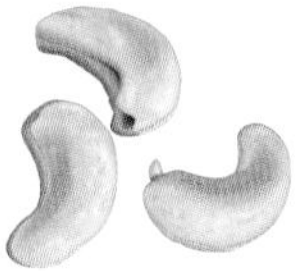

cashews
anacardos^M
noix^F de cajou^M
Cashewkern^M
noce^F di acagiù^M

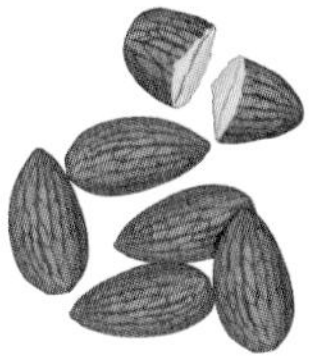

almonds
almendras^F
amandes^F
Mandeln^F
mandorle^F

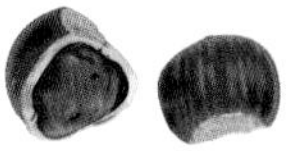

hazelnuts
avellanas^F
noisettes^F
Haselnuss^F
nocciole^F

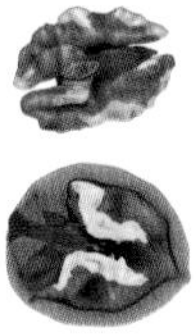

walnut
nuez^F
noix^F
Walnuss^F
noce^F

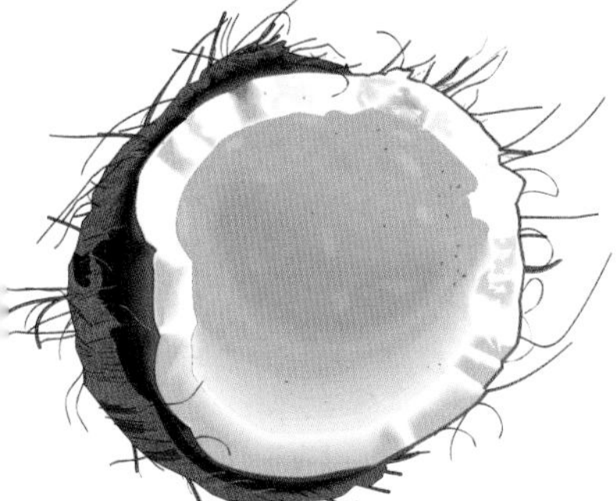

coconut
coco^M
noix^F de coco^M
Kokosnuss^F
noce^F di cocco^M

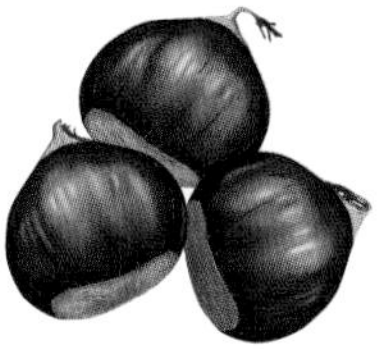

chestnuts
castañas^M
marrons^M
Esskastanin^F
castagne^F

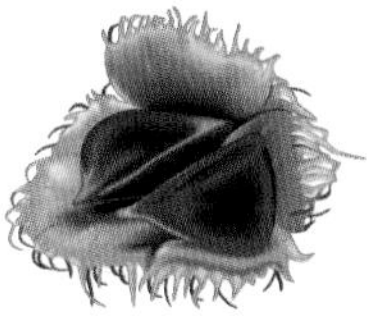

beechnut
hayuco^M
faine^F
Buchecker^F
faggiola^F

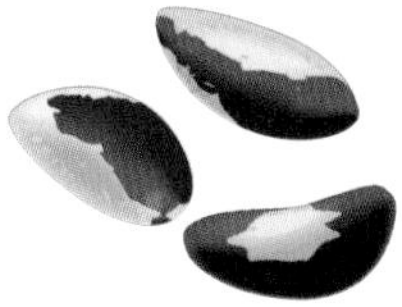

Brazil nuts
neuzes^F del Brasil^M
noix^F du Brésil^M
Paranussen^F
noce^F del Brasile^M

pome fruits
frutas^F pomo
fruits^M à pépins^M
Apfelfrüchte^F
pomi^M

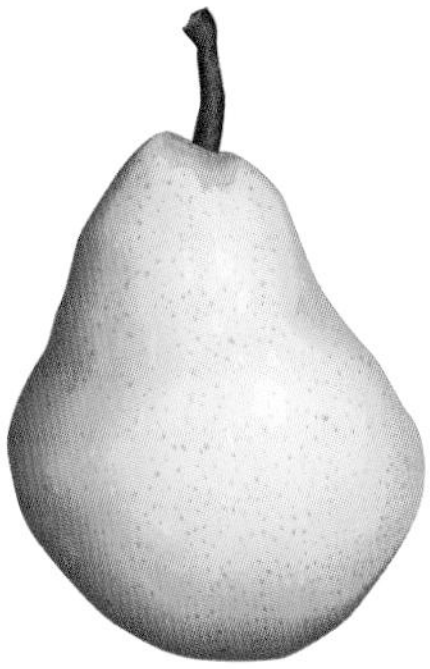

pear
pera^F
poire^F
Birne^F
pera^F

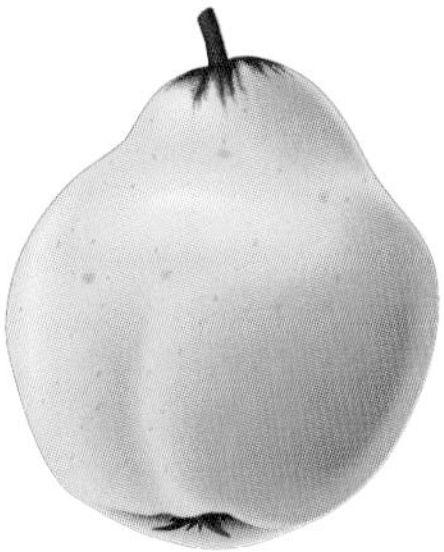

quince
membrillo^M
coing^M
Quitte^F
mela^F cotogna

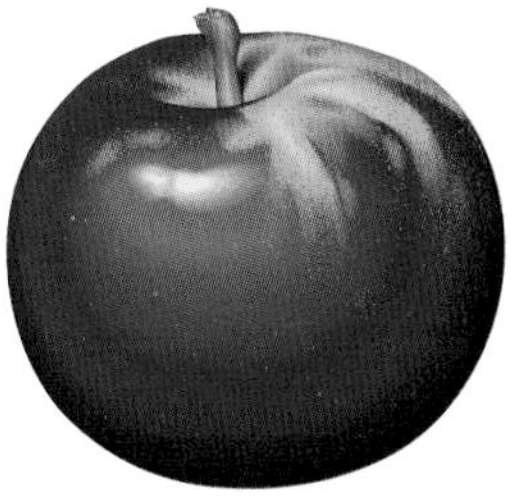

apple
manzana^F
pomme^F
Apfel^M
mela^F

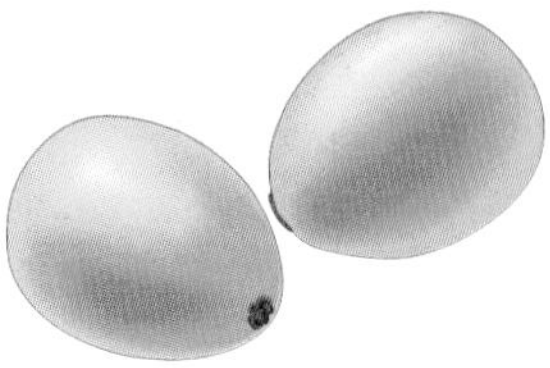

Japanese plums
nisperos^M
nèfles^F du Japon^M
Mispeln^F
nespole^F del Giappone^M

fruits

citrus fruits
cítricos^M
agrumes^M
Zitrusfrüchte^F
agrumi^M

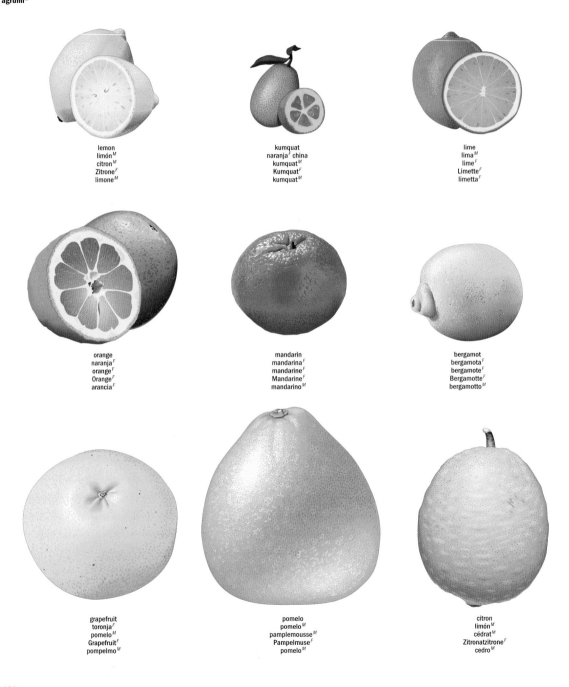

lemon
limón^M
citron^M
Zitrone^F
limone^M

kumquat
naranja^F china
kumquat^M
Kumquat^F
kumquat^M

lime
lima^M
lime^F
Limette^F
limetta^F

orange
naranja^F
orange^F
Orange^F
arancia^F

mandarin
mandarina^F
mandarine^F
Mandarine^F
mandarino^M

bergamot
bergamota^F
bergamote^F
Bergamotte^F
bergamotto^M

grapefruit
toronja^F
pomelo^M
Grapefruit^F
pompelmo^M

pomelo
pomelo^M
pamplemousse^M
Pampelmuse^F
pomelo^M

citron
limón^M
cédrat^M
Zitronatzitrone^F
cedro^M

FOOD AND KITCHEN

melons
melones^M
melons^M
Melonen^F
meloni^M

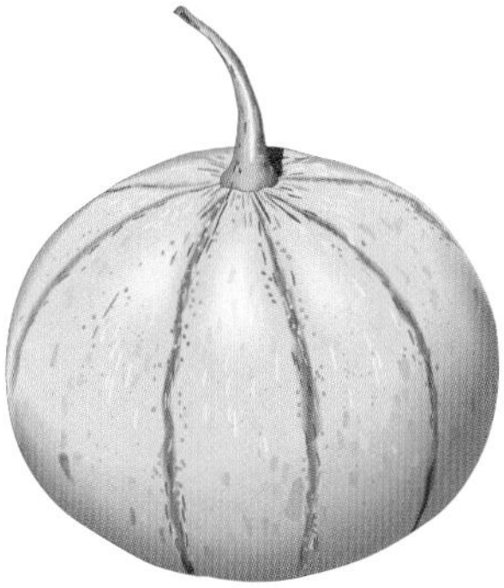
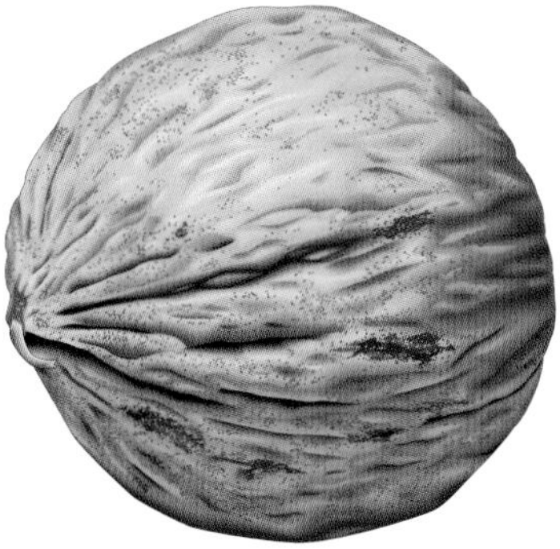
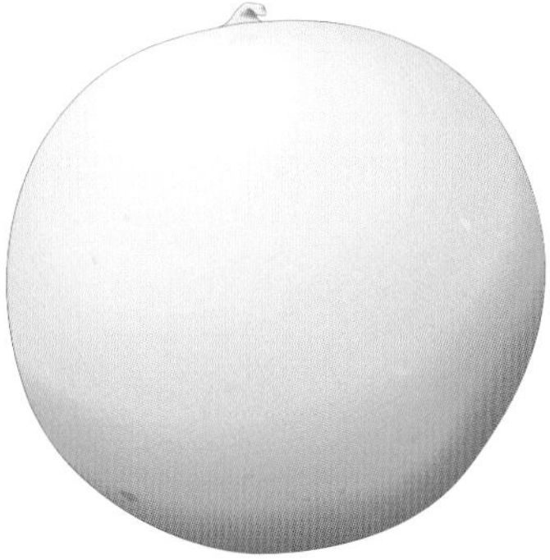

cantaloupe
melón^M cantalupo
cantaloup^M
Honigmelone^F
cantalupo^M

casaba melon
melón^M invernal
melon^M Casaba
Casabamelone^F
melone^M invernale

honeydew melon
melón^M de miel
melon^M miel^M
Honigmelone^F
melone^M mieloso

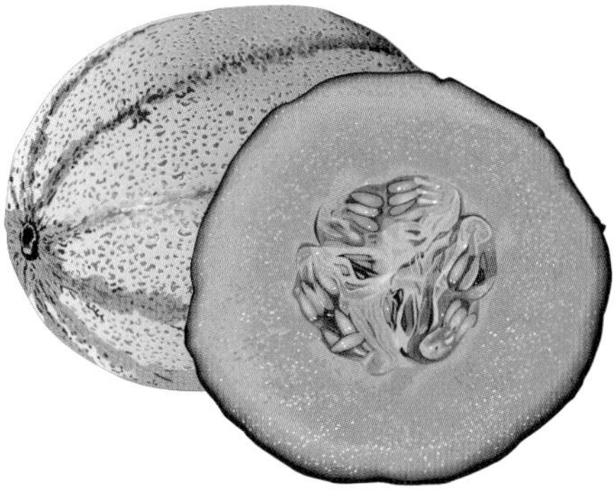
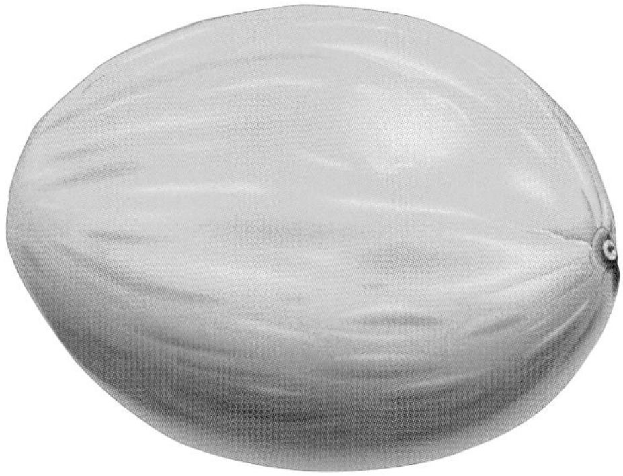

muskmelon
melón^M escrito
melon^M brodé
Zuckermelone^F
melone^M retato

canary melon
melón^M amarillo
melon^M brésilien
kanarische Melone^F
melone^M giallo canario

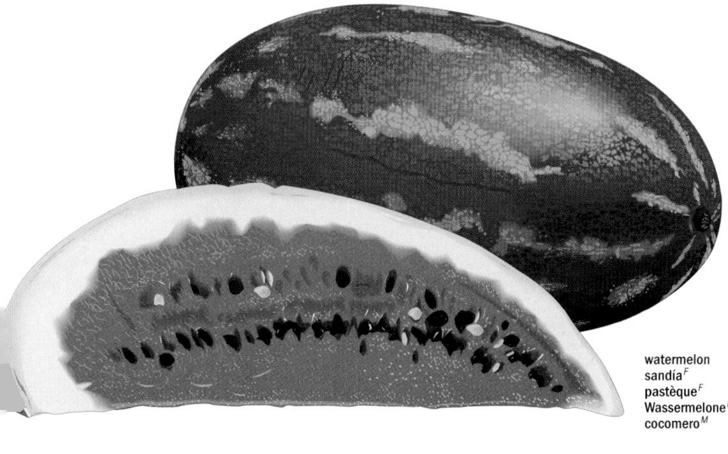
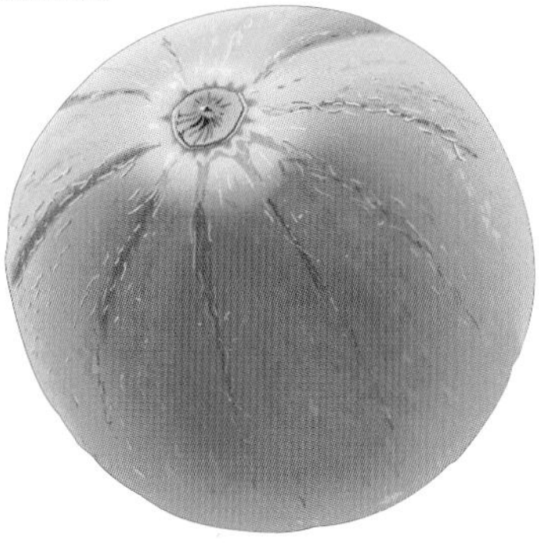

watermelon
sandía^F
pastèque^F
Wassermelone^F
cocomero^M

Ogen melon
melón^M de Ogen
melon^M d'Ogen
Ogenmelone^F
melone^M Ogen

fruits

tropical fruits
frutas **tropicales**
fruits^M **tropicaux**
Südfrüchte^F
frutti^M **tropicali**

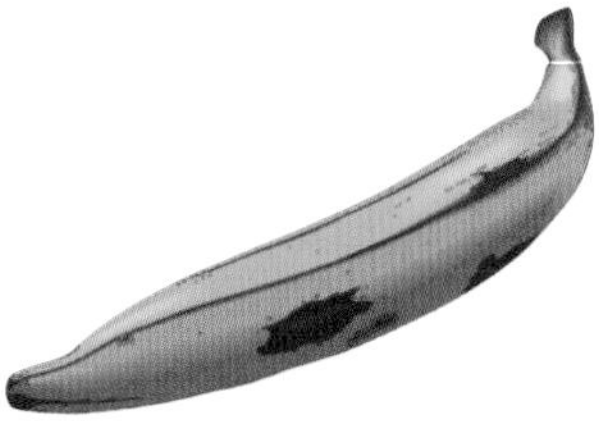

plantain
plátano^M
banane^F plantain^M
Plantainbanane^F
banana^F plantain

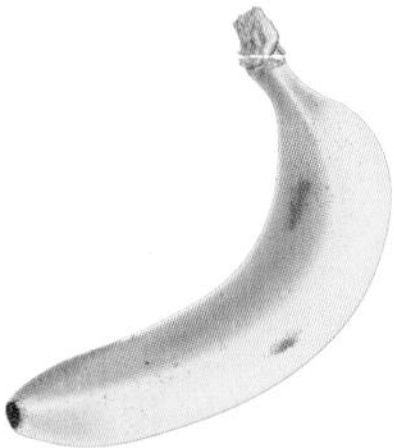

banana
banana^F
banane^F
Banane^F
banana^F

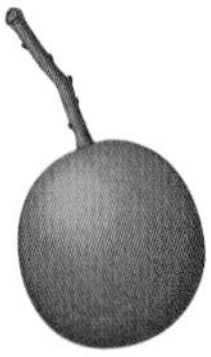

longan
longan^M
longane^M
Longanfrucht^F
longan^M

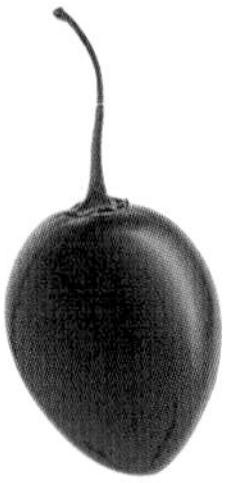

tamarillo
tamarillo^M
tamarillo^M
Baumtomate^F
tamarillo^M

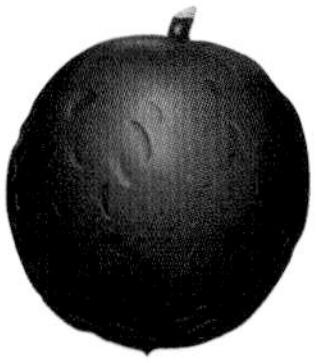

passion fruit
fruta^F de la pasión^F
fruit^M de la Passion^F
Passionsfrucht^F
maracuja^F

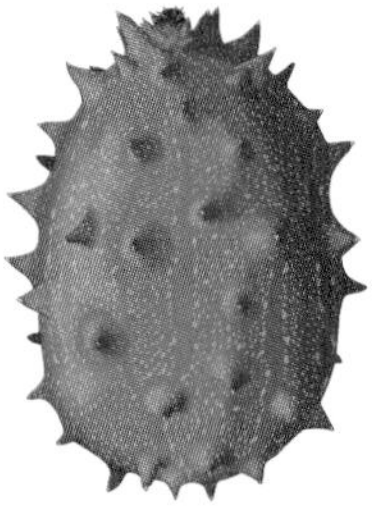

horned melon
kiwano^M
melon^M à cornes^F
Kiwano^F
kiwano^M

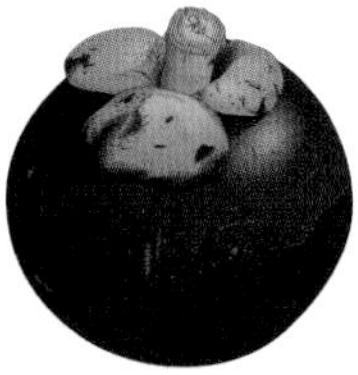

mangosteen
mangostán^M
mangoustan^M
Mangostane^F
mangostano^M

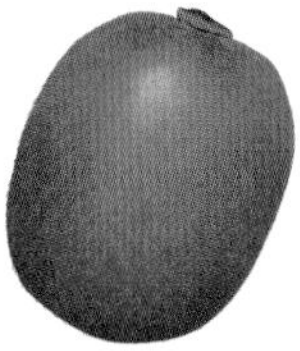

kiwi
kiwi^M
kiwi^M
Kiwi^F
kiwi^M

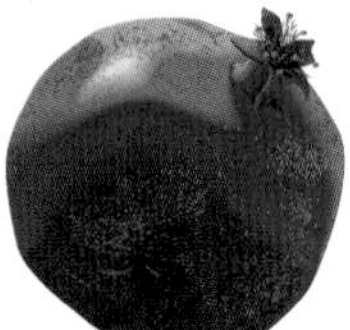

pomegranate
granada^F
grenade^F
Granatapfel^M
melograno^M

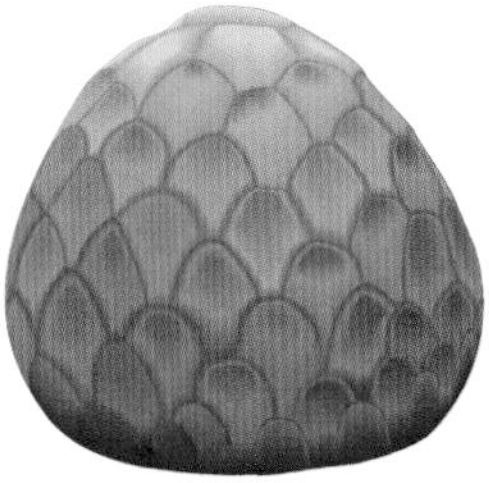

cherimoya
chirimoya^F
chérimole^F
Chirimoya^F
cerimolia^F

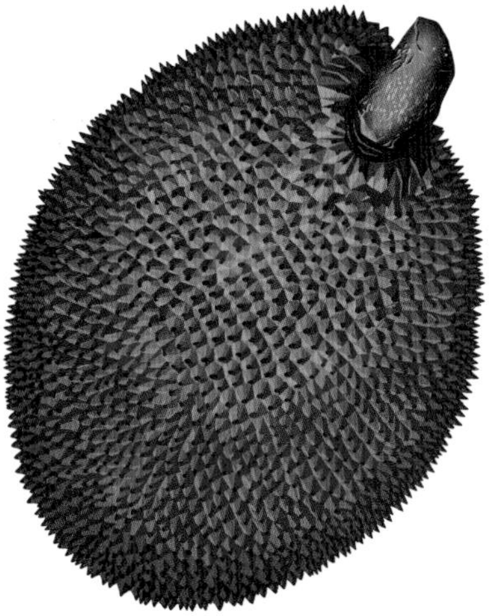

jackfruit
fruta^F de jack
jaque^M
Jackfrucht^F
frutto^M del jack

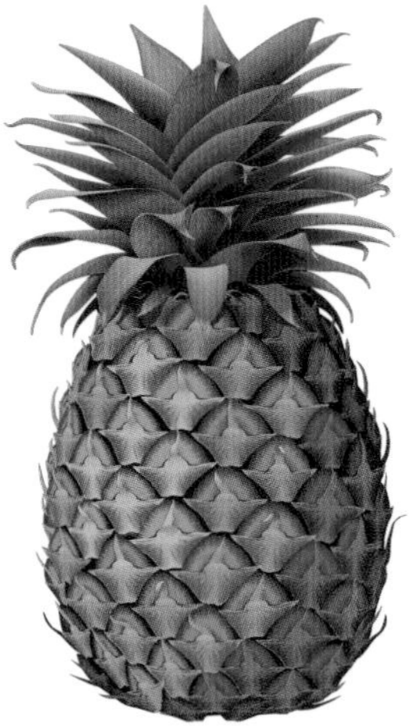

pineapple
piña^F
ananas^M
Ananas^F
ananas^M

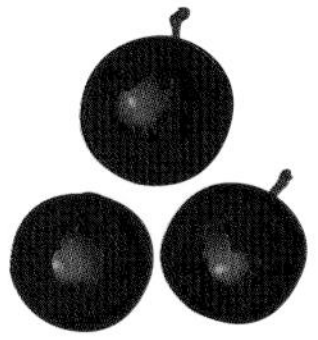

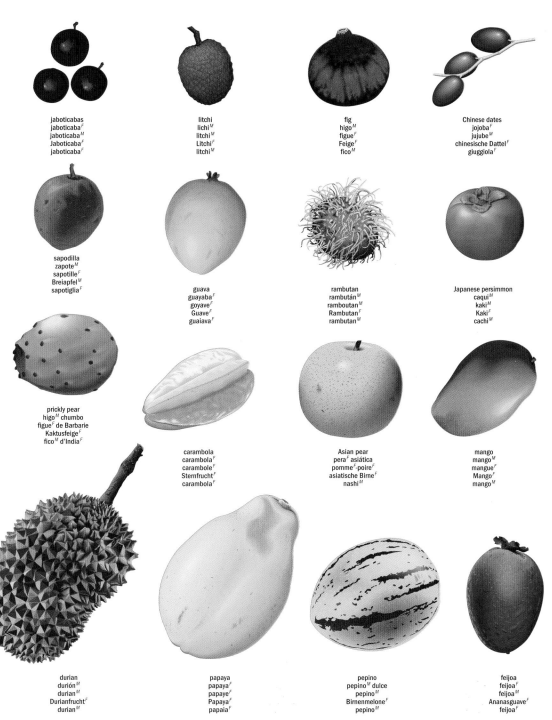

jaboticabas
jaboticaba^F
jaboticaba^M
Jaboticaba^F
jaboticaba^F

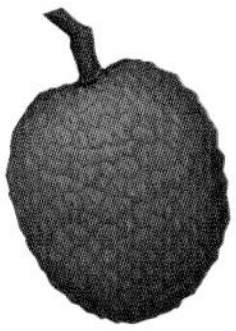

litchi
lichi^M
litchi^M
Litchi^F
litchi^M

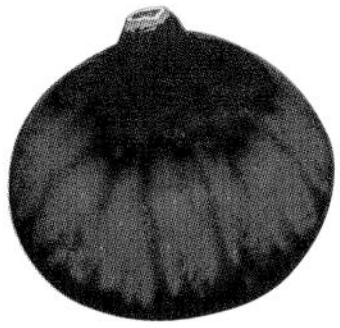

fig
higo^M
figue^F
Feige^F
fico^M

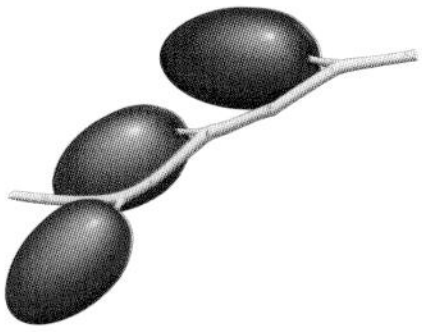

Chinese dates
jojoba^F
jujube^M
chinesische Dattel^F
giuggiola^F

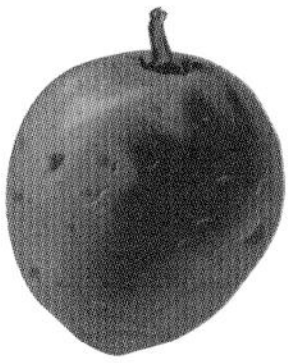

sapodilla
zapote^M
sapotille^F
Breiapfel^M
sapotiglia^F

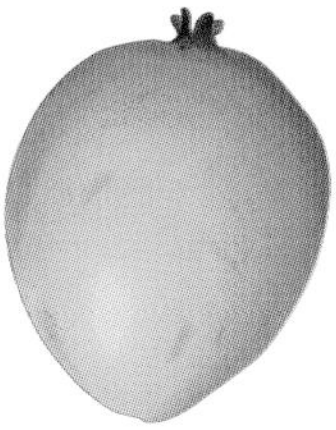

guava
guayaba^F
goyave^F
Guave^F
guaiava^F

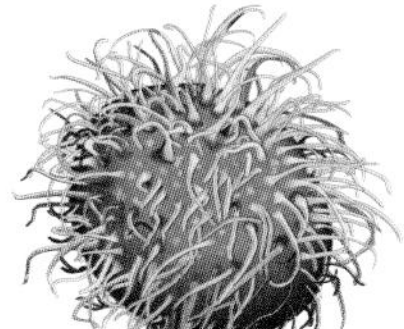

rambutan
rambután^M
rambutan^M
Rambutan^F
rambutan^M

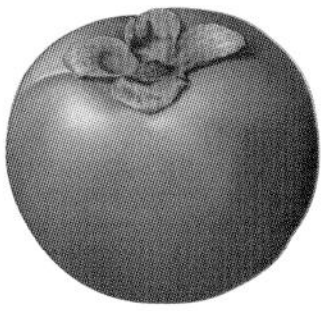

Japanese persimmon
caqui^M
kaki^M
Kaki^F
cachi^M

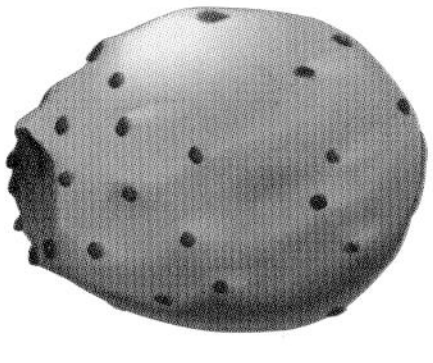

prickly pear
higo^M chumbo
figue^F de Barbarie
Kaktusfeige^F
fico^M d'India^F

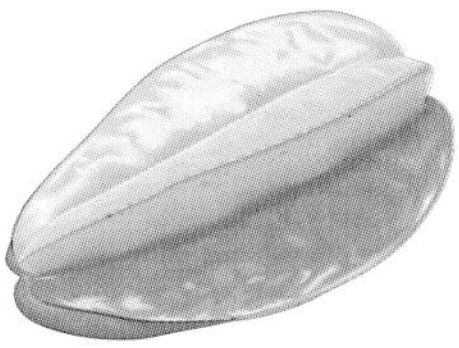

carambola
carambola^F
carambole^F
Sternfrucht^F
carambola^F

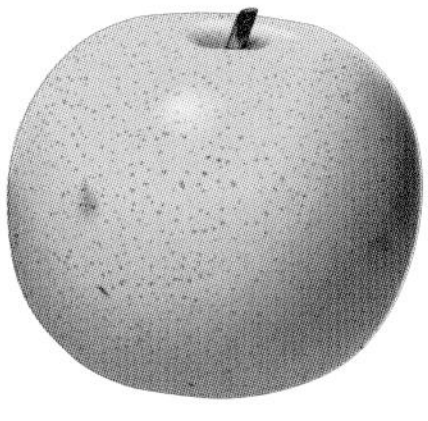

Asian pear
pera^F asiática
pomme^F-poire^F
asiatische Birne^F
nashi^M

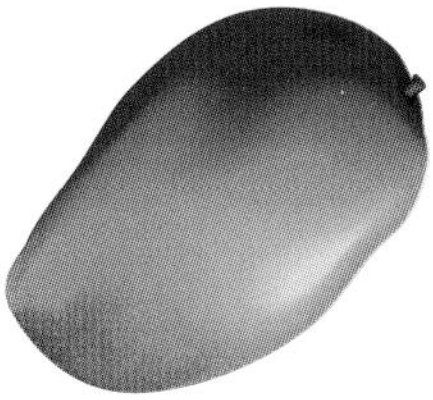

mango
mango^M
mangue^F
Mango^F
mango^M

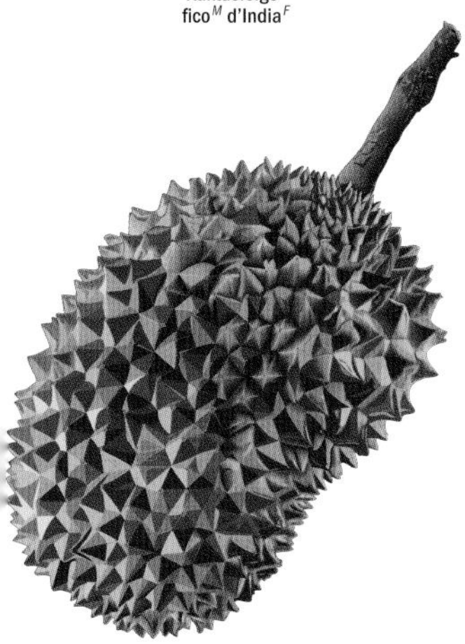

durian
durión^M
durian^M
Durianfrucht^F
durian^M

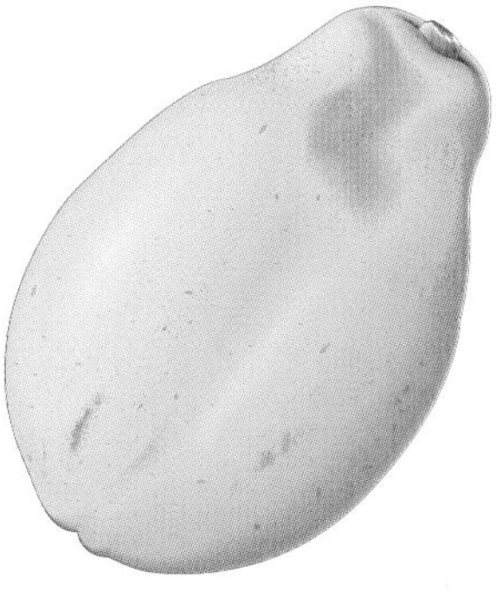

papaya
papaya^F
papaye^F
Papaya^F
papaia^F

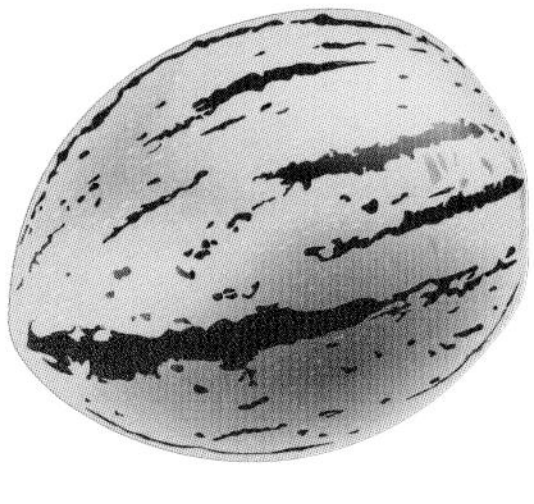

pepino
pepino^M dulce
pepino^M
Birnenmelone^F
pepino^M

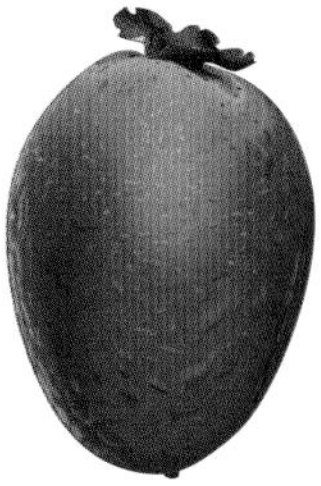

feijoa
feijoa^F
feijoa^M
Ananasguave^F
feijoa^F

spices

especias^F | épices^F | Gewürze^N | spezie^F

FOOD AND KITCHEN

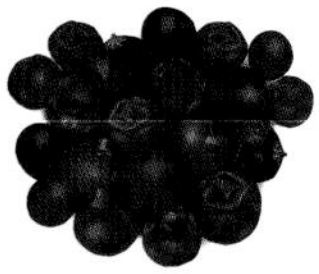

juniper berries
bayas^F de enebro^M
baies^F de genièvre^M
Wacholderbeeren^F
bacce^F di ginepro^M

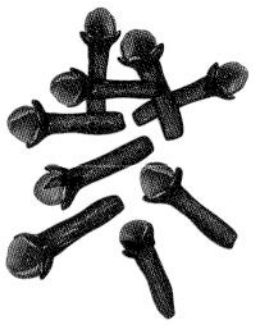

cloves
clavos^M
clou^M de girofle^M
Gewürznelke^F
chiodi^M di garofano^M

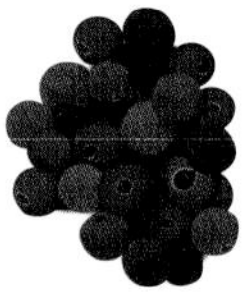

allspice
pimienta^F de Jamaica
piment^M de la Jamaique^F
Jamaikapfeffer^M
pepe^M della Giamaica^F

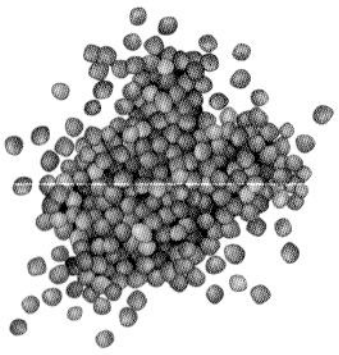

white mustard
mostaza^F blanca
moutarde^F blanche
weiße Senfkörner^N
senape^F bianca

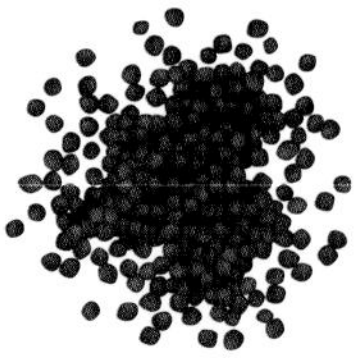

black mustard
mostaza^F negra
moutarde^F noire
schwarze Senfkörner^N
senape^F nera

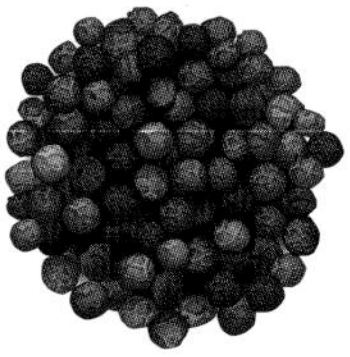

black pepper
pimienta^F negra
poivre^M noir
schwarzer Pfeffer^M
pepe^M nero

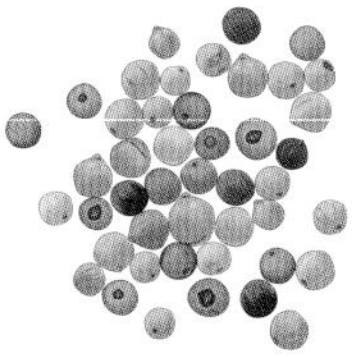

white pepper
pimienta^F blanca
poivre^M blanc
weißer Pfeffer^M
pepe^M bianco

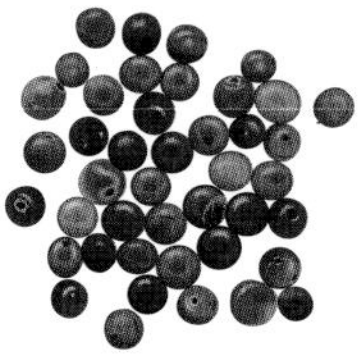

pink pepper
pimienta^F rosa
poivre^M rose
rosa Pfeffer^M
pepe^M rosa

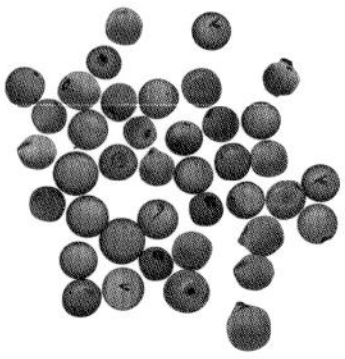

green pepper
pimienta^F verde
poivre^M vert
grüner Pfeffer^M
pepe^M verde

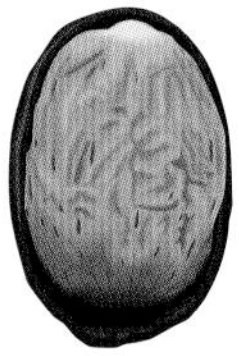

nutmeg
nuez^F moscada
noix^F de muscade^F
Muskatnuss^F
noce^F moscata

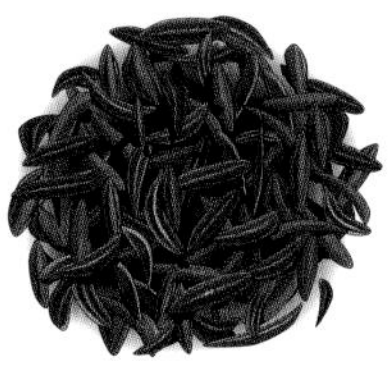

caraway
alcaravea^F
carvi^M
Kümmel^M
carvi^M

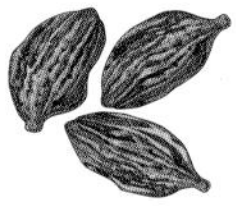

cardamom
cardamomo^M
cardamome^F
Kardamom$^{M/N}$
cardamomo^M

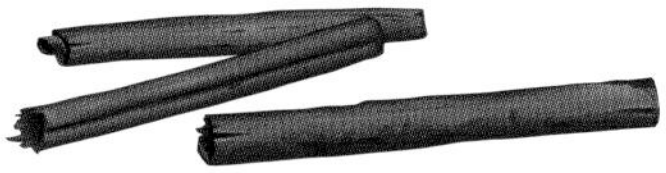

cinnamon
canela^F
cannelle^F
Zimtstangen^M
cannella^F

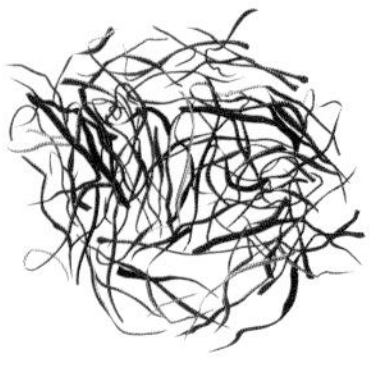

saffron
azafrán^M
safran^M
Safran^M
zafferano^M

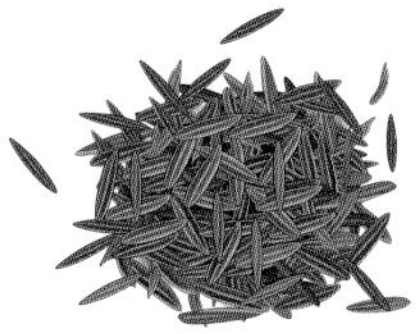

cumin
comino^M
cumin^M
Kreuzkümmel^M
cumino^M

curry
curry^M
curry^M
Curry^N
curry^M

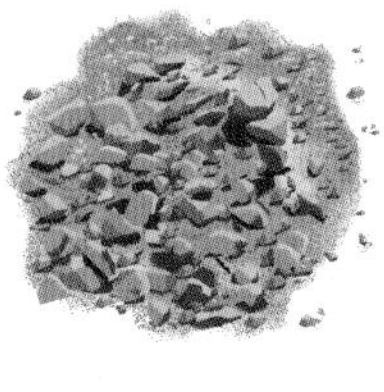

turmeric
cúrcuma^F
curcuma^M
Kurkuma^N
curcuma^F

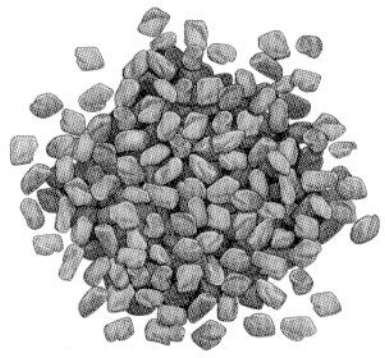

fenugreek
fenogreco^M
fenugrec^M
Bockshornkleesamen^M
fieno^M greco

jalapeño chile
chile^M jalapeño
piment^M Jalapeño
Jalapeño-Chili^M
peperoncino^M

bird's eye chile
guindilla^F
piment^M oiseau^M
Vogelaugenchili^M
peperoncino^M rosso

crushed chiles
guindilla^F triturada
piments^M broyés
zerstoßene Chilis^M
peperoncino^M tritato

dried chiles
guindilla^F seca^M
piments^M séchés
getrocknete Chilis^M
peperoncini^M secchi

cayenne pepper
pimienta^F de cayena^F
piment^M de Cayenne
Cayennepfeffer^M
pepe^M di Cayenna

paprika
pimentón^M
paprika^M
Paprika^M
paprika^F

ajowan
ajowán^M
ajowan^M
Ajowan^N
ajowan^M

asafetida
asafétida^F
asa-fœtida^F
Teufelsdreck^M
assafetida^F

garam masala
garam masala^M
garam masala^M
Garam Masala^N
garam masala^M

cajun spice seasoning
condimento^M de especias^F cajún
mélange^M d'épices^F cajun
Cajun-Gewürzmischung^F
condimento^M alle spezie^F cajun

marinade spices
especias^F para salmuera^F
épices^F à marinade^F
Mariniergewürze^N
spezie^F marinate

five spice powder
cinco especias^F chinas
cinq-épices^M chinois
Fünf-Kräuter^N-Gewürz^N
miscela^F di cinque spezie^F

chili powder
guindilla^F molida
assaisonnement^M au chili^M
Chilipulver^N
peperoncino^M in polvere^F

ground pepper
pimienta^F molida
poivre^M moulu
gemahlener Pfeffer^M
pepe^M macinato

ras el hanout
ras el hanout^M
ras-el-hanout^M
Ras-El-Hanout^N
ras el hanout^M

sumac
zumaque^M
sumac^M
Sumach^M
sumac^M

poppy seeds
semillas^F de adormidera^F
graines^F de pavot^M
Mohnsamen^M
semi^M di papavero^M

ginger
jengibre^M
gingembre^M
Ingwer^M
zenzero^M

condiments

condimentos ^{M} | condiments ^{M} | Würzen ^{F} | condimenti ^{M}

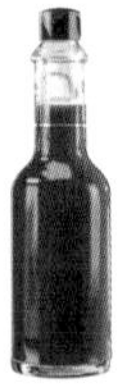

Tabasco® sauce
salsa ^{F} Tobasco® ^{M}
sauce ^{F} Tabasco®
Tabasco™-Soße ^{F}
salsa ^{F} Tobasco® ^{M}

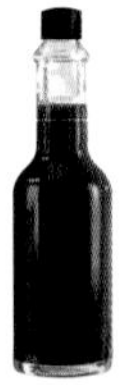

Worcestershire sauce
salsa ^{F} Worcertershire
sauce ^{F} Worcestershire
Worcestershire-Soße ^{F}
salsa ^{F} Worcestershire

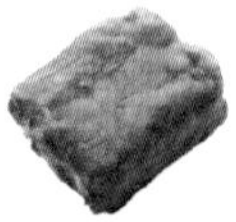

tamarind paste
salsa ^{F} de tamarindo ^{M}
pâte ^{F} de tamarin ^{M}
Tamarindenmark ^{N}
pasta ^{F} di tamarindo ^{M}

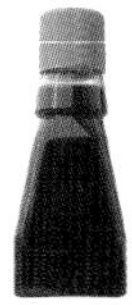

vanilla extract
extracto ^{M} de vainilla ^{F}
extrait ^{M} de vanille ^{F}
Vanille-Extrakt ^{M}
estratto ^{M} di vaniglia ^{F}

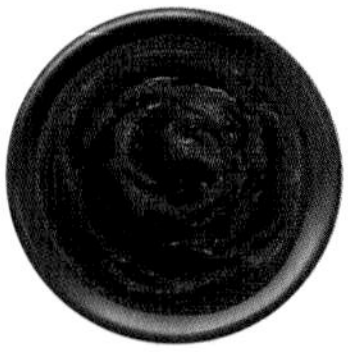

tomato paste
concentrado ^{M} de tomate ^{M}
concentré ^{M} de tomate ^{F}
Tomatenmark ^{N}
concentrato ^{F} di pomodoro ^{M}

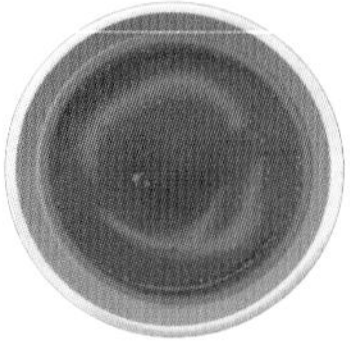

tomato sauce
salsa ^{F} de tomate ^{M}
coulis ^{M} de tomate ^{F}
Passierte Tomaten ^{F}
passata ^{F} di pomodoro ^{M}

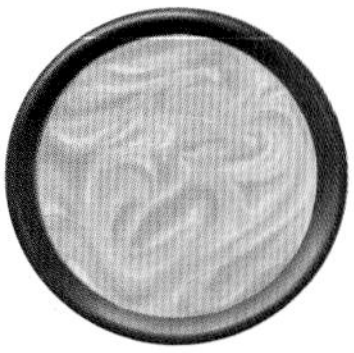

hummus
hummus ^{M}
hoummos ^{M}
Hummus ^{M}
hummus ^{M}

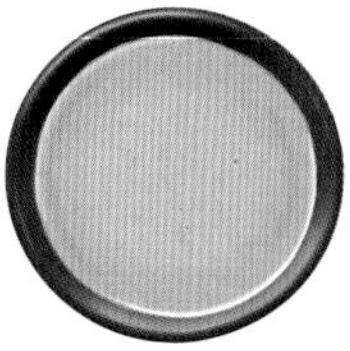

tahini
tajín ^{M}
tahini ^{M}
Tahinisoße ^{F}
tahini ^{M}

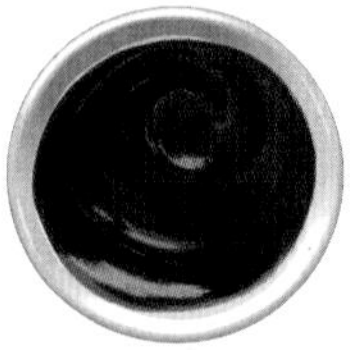

hoisin sauce
salsa ^{F} hoisin
sauce ^{F} hoisin
Hoisinsoße ^{F}
salsa ^{F} hoisin

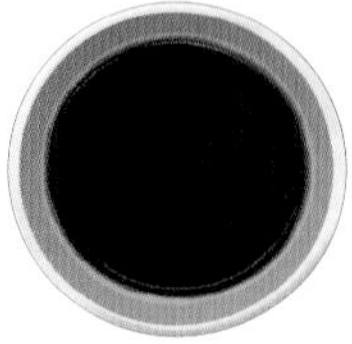

soy sauce
salsa ^{F} de soja ^{F}
sauce ^{F} soja ^{M} ; sauce ^{F} soya ^{M}
Sojasoße ^{F}
salsa ^{F} di soia ^{F}

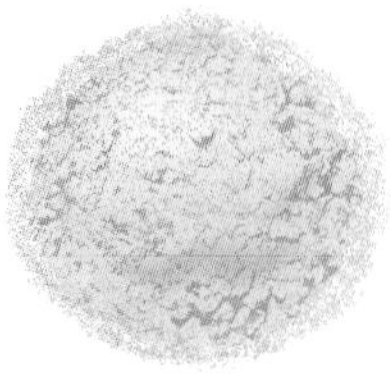

powdered mustard
mostaza ^{F} en polvo ^{M}
moutarde ^{F} en poudre ^{F}
Senfpulver ^{N}
senape ^{F} in polvere ^{F}

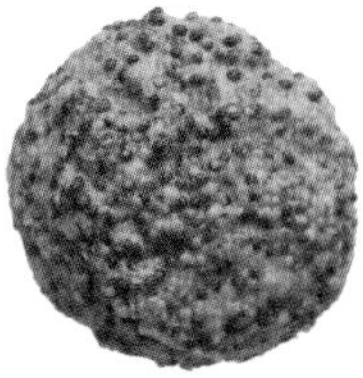

wholegrain mustard
mostaza ^{F} en grano ^{M}
moutarde ^{F} à l'ancienne ^{F}
Senfkörner ^{N}
senape ^{F} in granuli ^{M}

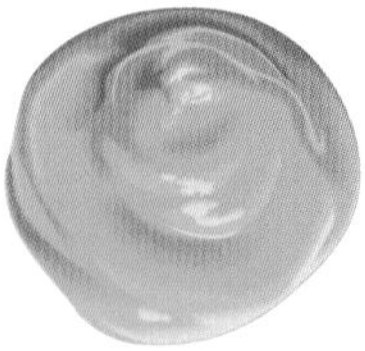

Dijon mustard
mostaza ^{F} de Dijon
moutarde ^{F} de Dijon
Dijon-Senf ^{M}
senape ^{F} di Digione

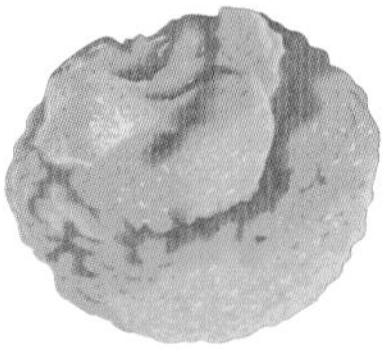

German mustard
mostaza ^{F} alemana
moutarde ^{F} allemande
deutscher Senf ^{M}
senape ^{F} tedesca

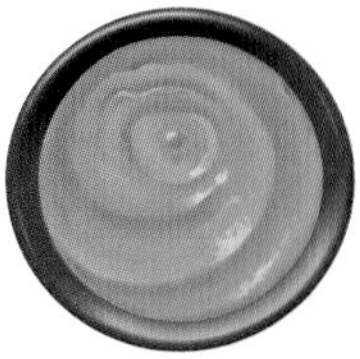

English mustard
mostaza ^{F} inglesa
moutarde ^{F} anglaise
englischer Senf ^{M}
senape ^{F} inglese

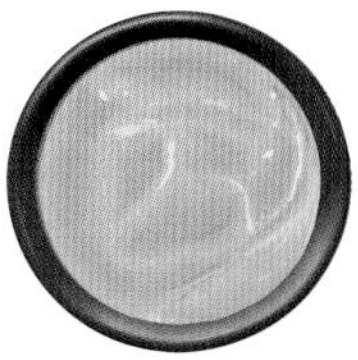

American mustard
mostaza ^{F} americana
moutarde ^{F} américaine
amerikanischer Senf ^{M}
senape ^{F} americana

FOOD AND KITCHEN

FOOD AND KITCHEN

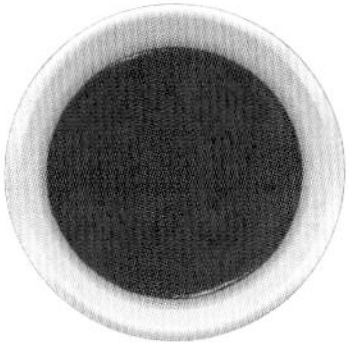

plum sauce
salsa^F de ciruelas^F
sauce^F aux prunes^F
Pflaumensoße^F
salsa^F di prugne^F

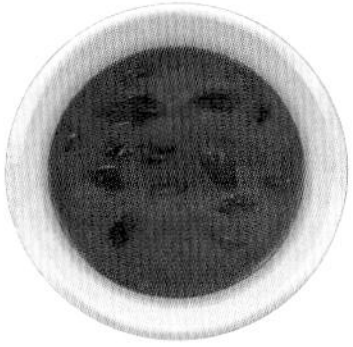

mango chutney
chutney^M de mango^M
chutney^M à la mangue^F
Mangochutney^N
chutney^M al mango^M

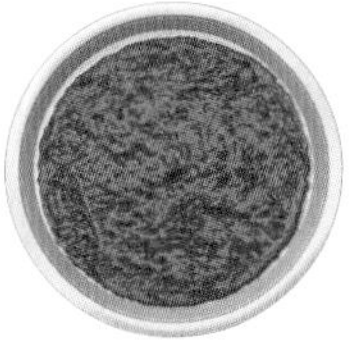

harissa
harissa^F
harissa^F
Harissasoße^F
harissa^F

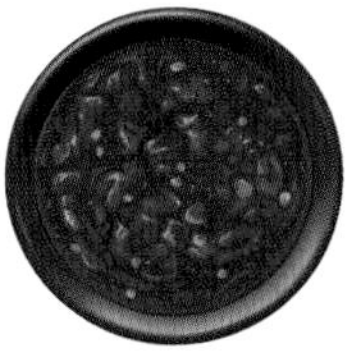

sambal oelek
sambal oelek^M
sambal oelek^M
Sambal Oelek^M
sambal oelek^M

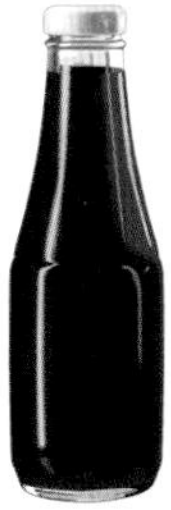

ketchup
ketchup^M
ketchup^M
Ketchup^M
ketchup^M

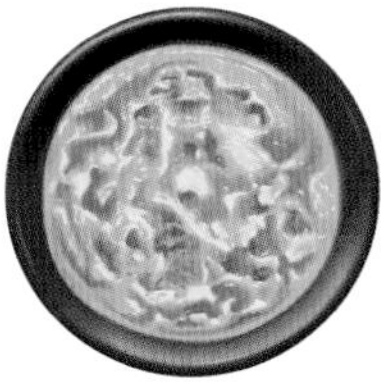

wasabi
wasabi^M
wasabi^M
Wasabipaste^F
wasabi^M

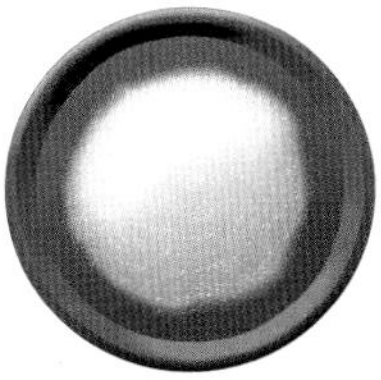

table salt
sal^F de mesa^F
sel^M fin
Tafelsalz^N
sale^M fino

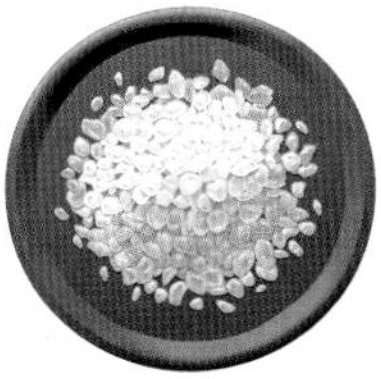

coarse salt
sal^F gorda
gros sel^M
grobes Salz^N
sale^M grosso

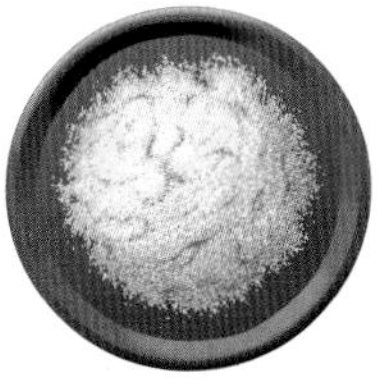

sea salt
sal^F marina
sel^M marin
Meersalz^N
sale^M marino

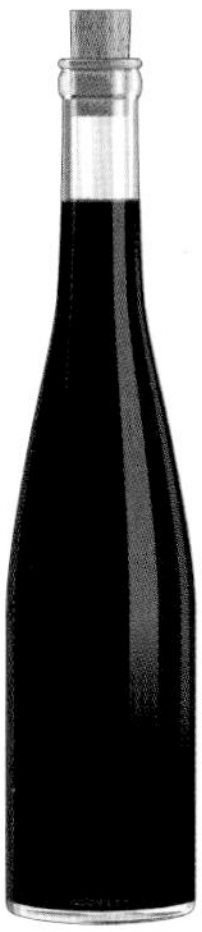

balsamic vinegar
vinagre^M balsámico
vinaigre^M balsamique
Balsamessig^M
aceto^M balsamico

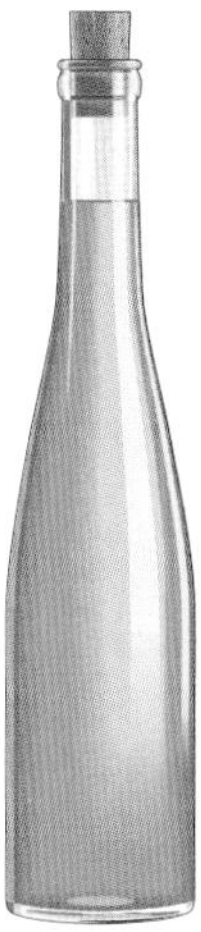

rice vinegar
vinagre^M de arroz^M
vinaigre^M de riz^M
Reisessig^M
aceto^M di riso^M

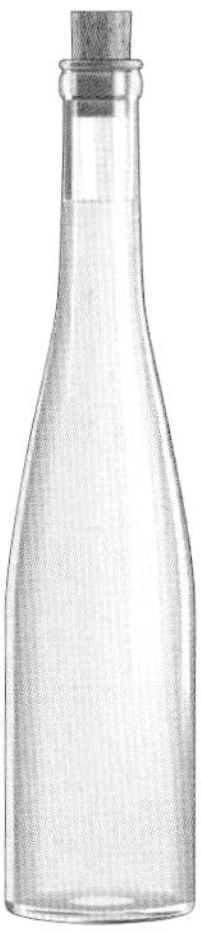

apple cider vinegar
vinagre^M de manzana^F
vinaigre^M de cidre^M
Apfelessig^M
aceto^M di mele^F

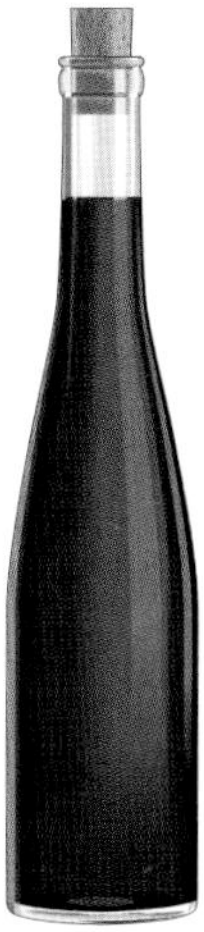

malt vinegar
vinagre^M de malta^F
vinaigre^M de malt^M
Malzessig^M
aceto^M di malto^M

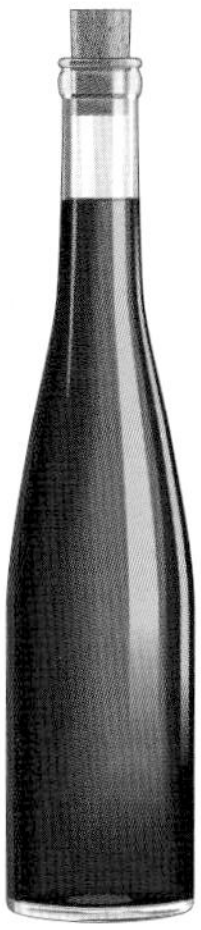

wine vinegar
vinagre^M de vino^M
vinaigre^M de vin^M
Weinessig^M
aceto^M di vino^M

herbs

hierbas^F aromáticas | fines herbes^F | Kräuter^N | piante^F aromatiche

dill
eneldo^M
aneth^M
Dill^M
aneto^M

anise
anis^M
anis^M
Anis^M
anice^M

sweet bay
laurel^M
laurier^M
Lorbeer^M
alloro^M

oregano
orégano^M
origan^M
Origano^N
origano^M

tarragon
estragón^M
estragon^M
Estragon^M
dragoncello^M

basil
albahaca^F
basilic^M
Basilikum^N
basilico^M

sage
salvia^F
sauge^F
Salbei^M
salvia^F

thyme
tomillo^M
thym^M
Thymian^M
timo^M

mint
hierbabuena^F
menthe^F
Minze^F
menta^F

parsley
perejil^M
persil^M
Petersilie^F
prezzemolo^M

chervil
perifollo^M
cerfeuil^M
Kerbel^M
cerfoglio^M

coriander
cilantro^M
coriandre^F
Koriander^M
coriandolo^M

rosemary
romero^M
romarin^M
Rosmarin^M
rosmarino^M

hyssop
hisopo^M
hysope^F
Ysop^M
issopo^M

borage
borraja^F
bourrache^F
Boretsch^M
borragine^F

lovage
alheña^F
livèche^F
Liebstöckel$^{M/N}$
sedano^M di monte^M

savory
ajedrea^F
sarriette^F
Bohnenkraut^N
santoreggia^F

lemon balm
melisa^F
mélisse^F
Zitronenmelisse^F
melissa^F

cereal

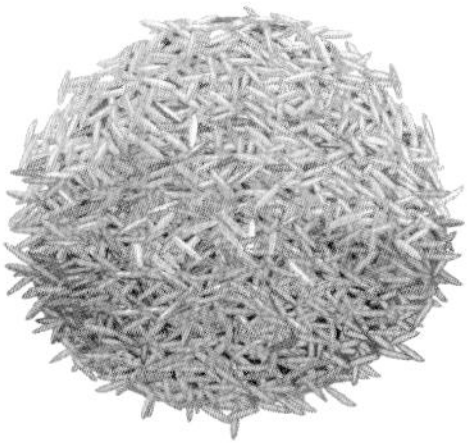

rice
arroz^M
riz^M
Reis^M
riso^M

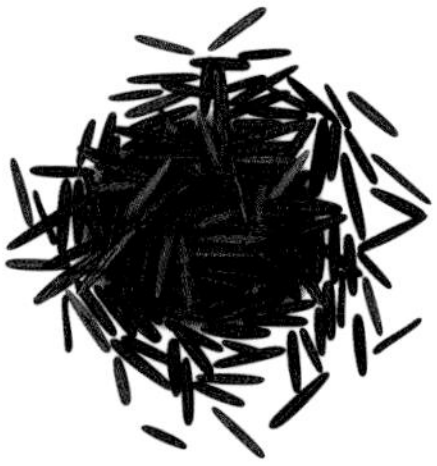

wild rice
arroz^M silvestre
riz^M sauvage
Wildreis^M
riso^M nero selvatico

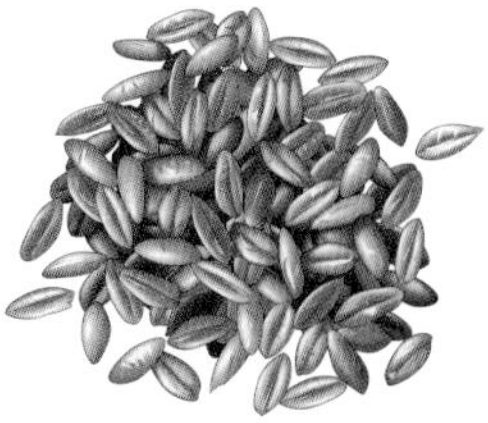

spelt wheat
escanda^F común
épeautre^M
Dinkel^M
farro^M

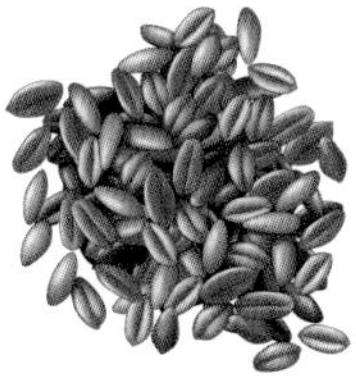

wheat
trigo^M
blé^M
Weizen^M
frumento^M

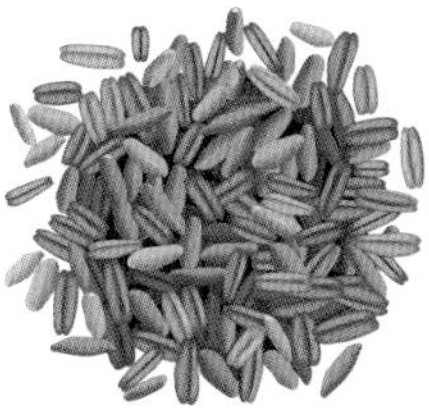

oats
avena^F
avoine^F
Hafer^M
avena^F

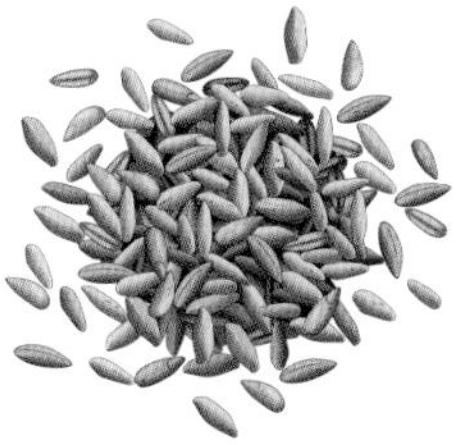

rye
centeno^M
seigle^M
Roggen^M
segale^F

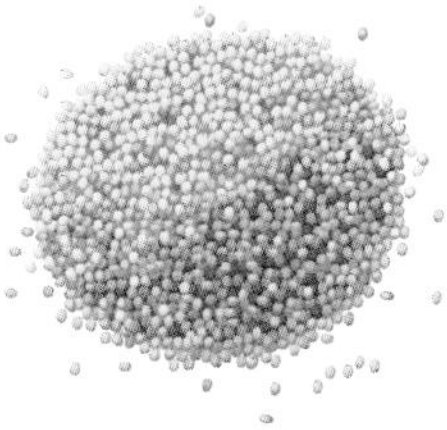

millet
mijo^M
millet^M
Hirse^F
miglio^M

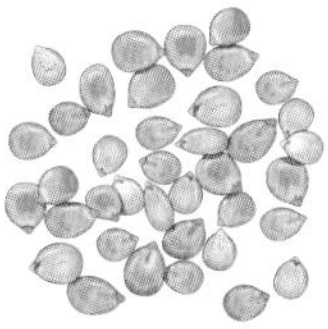

corn
maíz^M
mais^M
Mais^M
mais^M

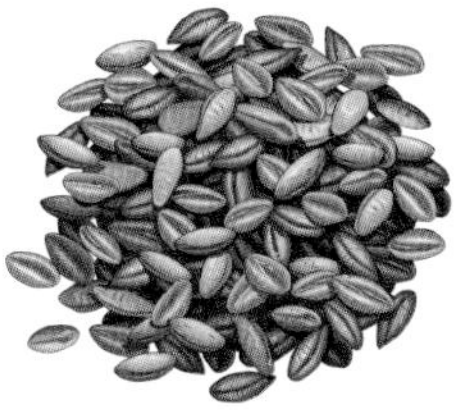

barley
cebada^F
orge^F
Gerste^F
orzo^M

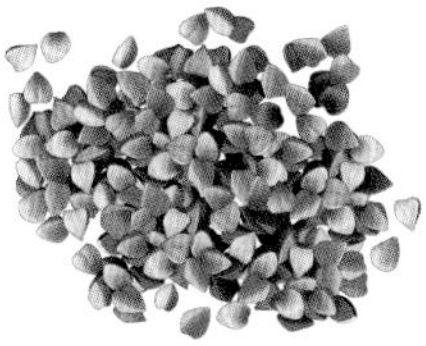

buckwheat
trigo^M sarraceno
sarrasin^M
Buchweizen^M
grano^M saraceno

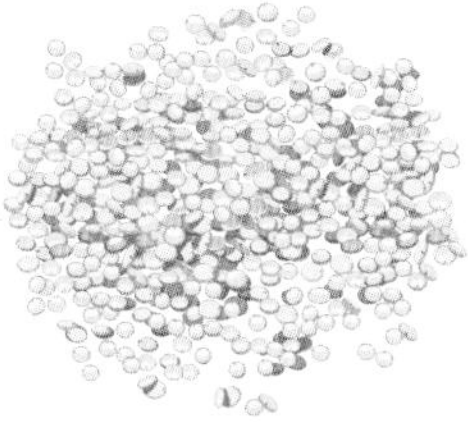

quinoa
quinua^F
quinoa^M
Reismelde^F
quinoa^M

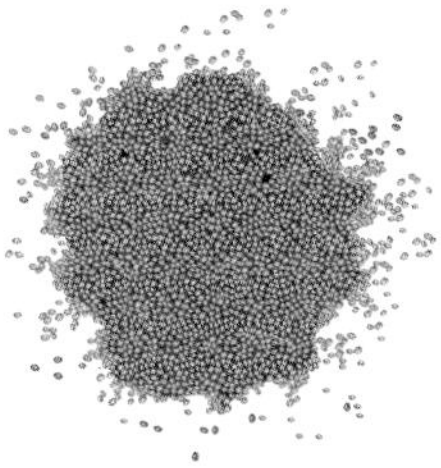

amaranth
amaranto^M
amarante^F
Amarant^M
amaranto^M

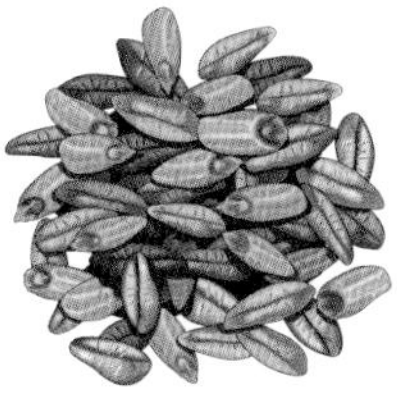

triticale
triticale^M
triticale^M
Triticale^M
triticale^M

FOOD AND KITCHEN

cereal products

cereales^M | produits^M céréaliers | Getreideprodukte^N | prodotti^M cerealicoli

flour and semolina
harina^F y sémola^F
farine^F et semoule^F
Mehl^N und Grieß^M
farina^F e semolino^M

semolina
sémola^F
semoule^F
Grieß^M
semolino^M

whole-wheat flour
harina^F integral
farine^F de blé^M complet ; *farine^F de blé^M entier*
Vollkornmehl^N
farina^F integrale

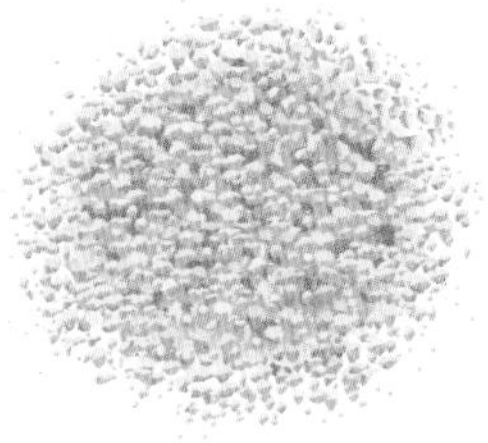

couscous
cuscús^M
couscous^M
Couscous^N
cuscus^M

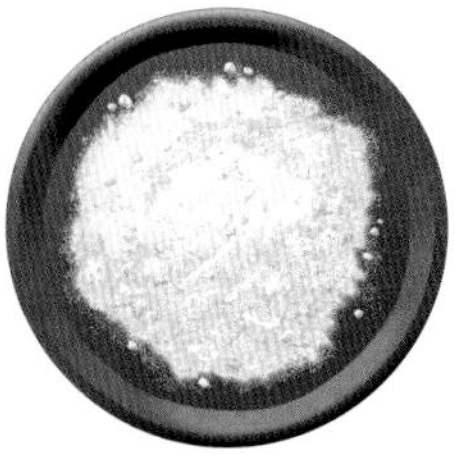

all-purpose flour
harina^F común
farine^F tout usage^M
Haushaltsmehl^N
farina^F semplice

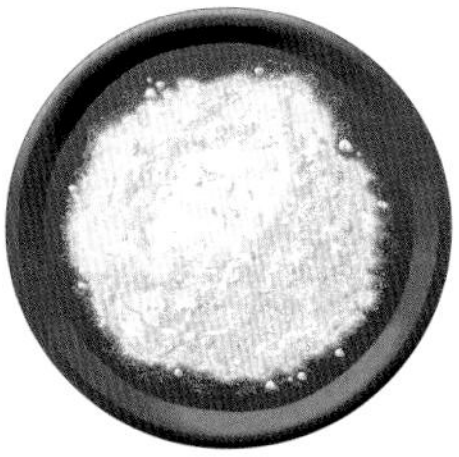

unbleached flour
harina^F sin blanquear
farine^F non blanchie
ungebleichtes Mehl^N
farina^F non trattata

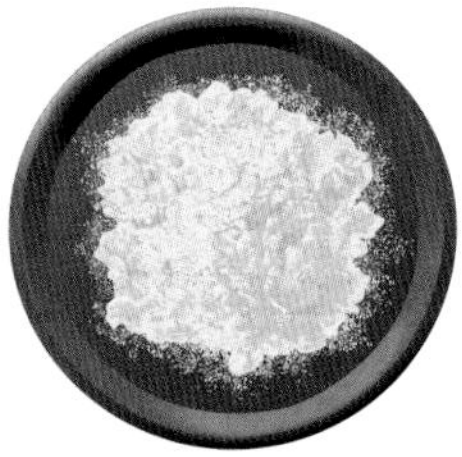

oat flour
harina^F de avena^F
farine^F d'avoine^F
Hafermehl^N
farina^F di avena^F

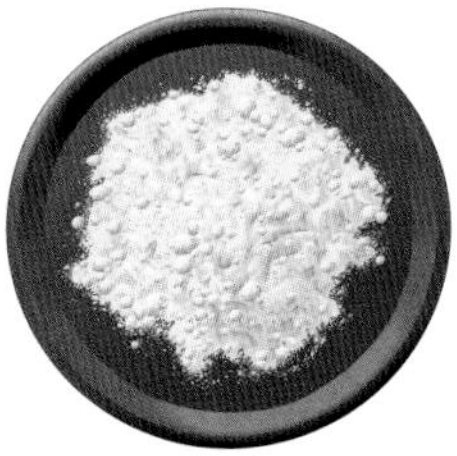

corn flour
harina^F de maíz^M
farine^F de maïs^M
Maismehl^N
farina^F di mais^M

bread
pan^M
pain^M
Brot^N
pane^M

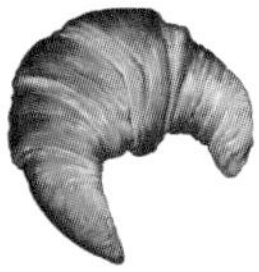

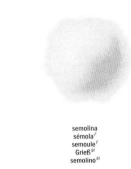

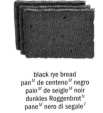

croissant
cruasán^M
croissant^M
Croissant^N
croissant^M

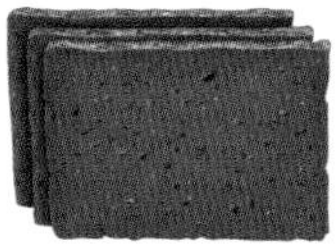

black rye bread
pan^M de centeno^M negro
pain^M de seigle^M noir
dunkles Roggenbrot^N
pane^M nero di segale^F

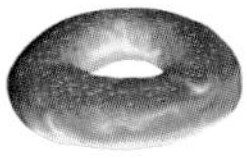

bagel
rosquilla^F
bagel^M
Kringel^M
ciambella^F

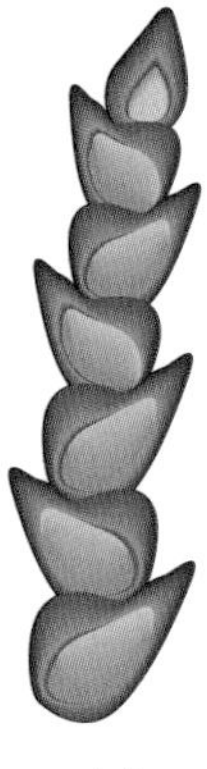

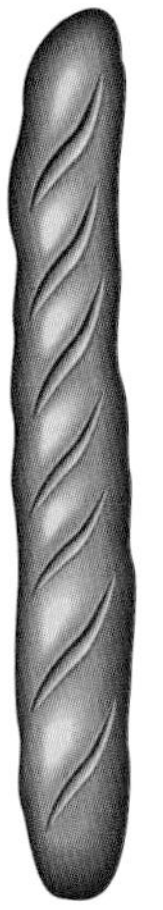

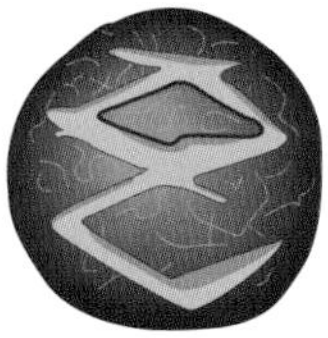

Greek bread
pan^M griego
pain^M grec
griechisches Brot^N
pane^F greco

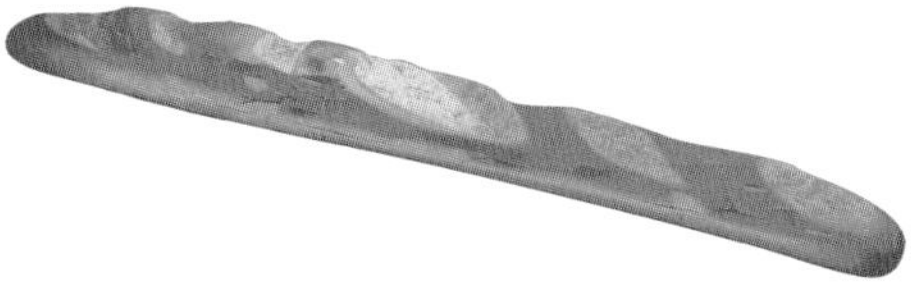

baguette
barra^F de pan^M
baguette^F parisienne
französisches Weißbrot^N
filone^M francese

ear loaf
pan^M espiga^F
baguette^F épi^M
Ährenbrot^N
spiga^F

French bread
baguette^F
pain^M parisien
Baguette^N
baguette^F

FOOD AND KITCHEN

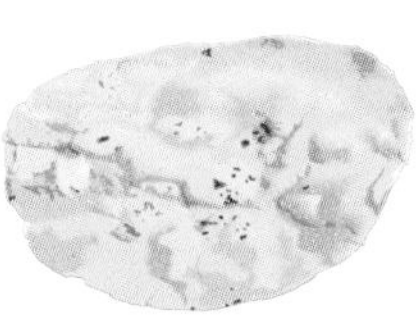

chapati
pan^M indio chapati
pain^M chapati indien
indisches Fladenbrot^N
pane^M chapati indiano

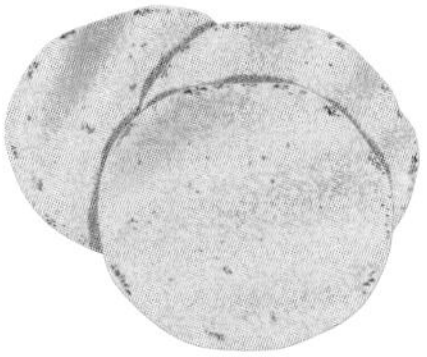

tortillas
tortillas^F
tortillas^F
Tortilla^F
tortilla^F

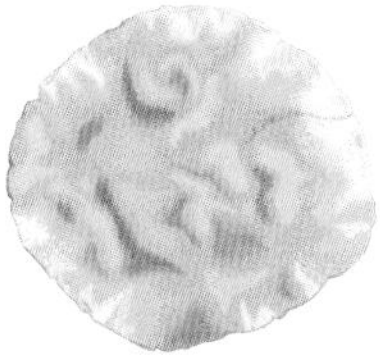

pita bread
pan^M de pita^F
pain^M pita
Pittabrot^N
pane^M pita

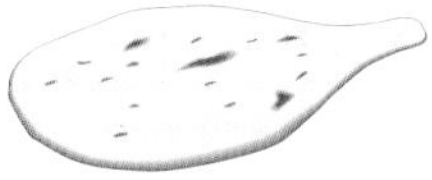

naan
pan^M indio naan
pain^M naan indien
indisches Naanbrot^N
pane^M naan indiano

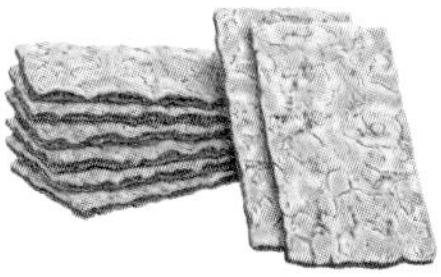

cracked rye bread
galleta^F de centeno^M
cracker^M de seigle^M
Roggenknäckebrot^N
galletta^F di segale^F

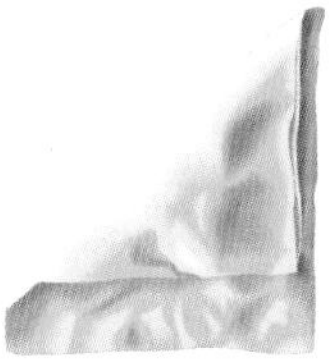

phyllo dough
pasta^F de hojaldre^M
pâte^F phyllo^F
Blätterteig^M
pasta^F sfoglia^F

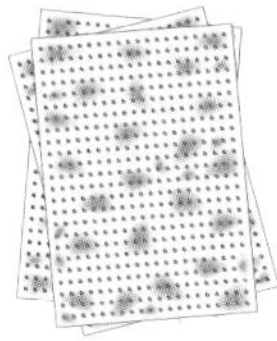

unleavened bread
pan^M ácimo
pain^M azyme
ungesäuertes Brot^N
pane^M azzimo

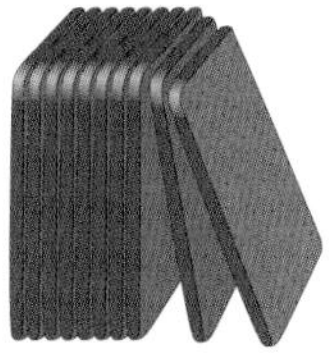

Danish rye bread
pan^M danés de centeno^M
pain^M de seigle^M danois
dänisches Roggenbrot^N
pane^M di segale^F danese

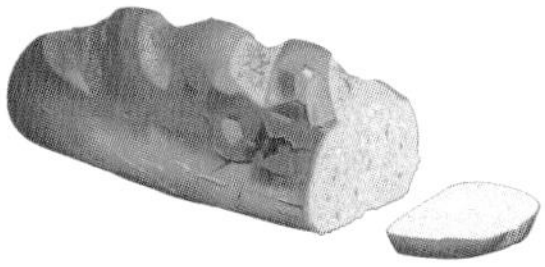

white bread
pan^M blanco
pain^M blanc
Weißbrot^N
pane^M bianco

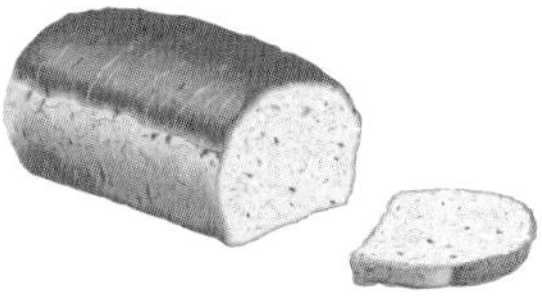

multigrain bread
pan^M multicereales
pain^M multicéréales
Mehrkornbrot^N
pane^M multicereali

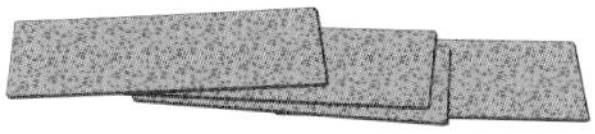

Scandinavian cracked bread
galleta^F escandinava
cracker^M scandinave
skandinavisches Knäckebrot^N
galletta^F scandinava

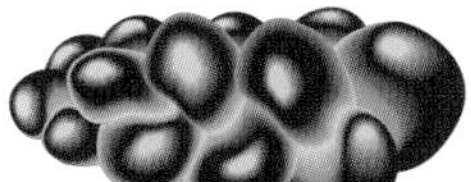

challah
pan^M judío hallah
pain^M tchallah juif
jüdisches Weißbrot^N
pane^M ebraico

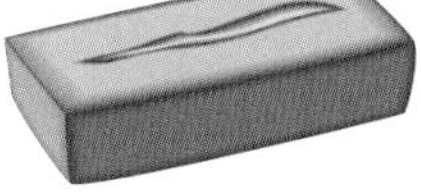

American corn bread
pan^M americano de maíz^M
pain^M de maïs^M américain
amerikanisches Maisbrot^N
pane^M di mais^M americano

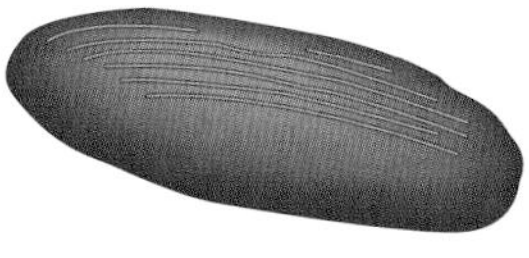

German rye bread
pan^M alemán de centeno^M
pain^M de seigle^M allemand
deutsches Roggenbrot^N
pane^M di segale^F tedesco

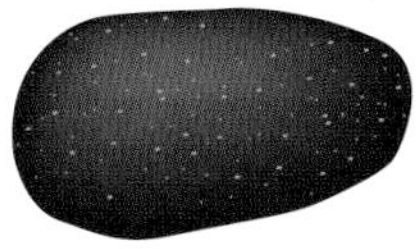

Russian pumpernickel
pan^M negro ruso
pain^M noir russe
russischer Pumpernickel^M
Pumpernickel^M russo

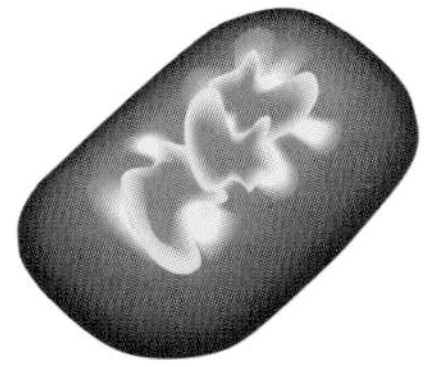

farmhouse bread
pan^M campesino
pain^M de campagne^F
Bauernbrot^N
pane^M casereccio

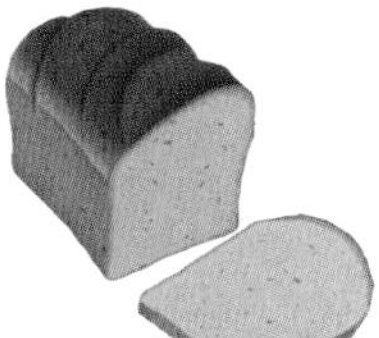

wholemeal bread
pan^M integral
pain^M complet
Vollkornbrot^N
pane^M integrale

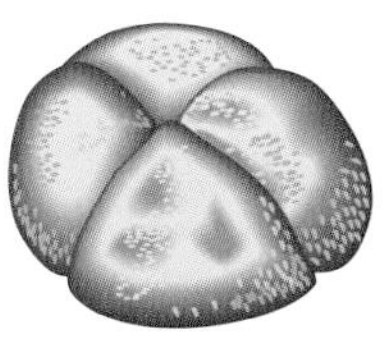

Irish soda bread
pan^M irlandés
pain^M irlandais
irisches Brot^N
pane^M irlandese

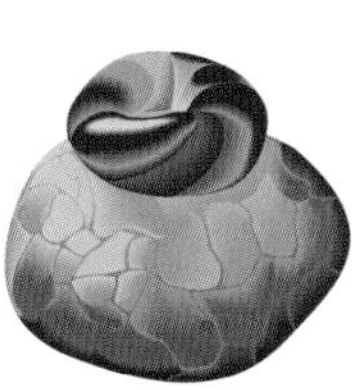

English loaf
pan^M de flor^F
pain^M de mie^F
englisches Weißbrot^N
pagnottella^F inglese

cereal products

pasta
pasta^F
pâtes^F **alimentaires**
Teigwaren^F
pasta^F

rigatoni
rigatoni^M
rigatoni^M
Rigatoni^M
rigatoni^M

rotini
sacacorchos^M
rotini^M
Rotini^M
eliche^F

conchiglie
conchitas^F
conchiglie^F
Conchiglie^F
conchiglie^F

fusilli
fusilli^M
fusilli^M
Fusilli^M
fusilli^M

spaghetti
espagueti^M
spaghetti^M
Spaghetti^M
spaghetti^M

ditali
dedalitos^M
ditali^M
Ditali^M
ditali^M

gnocchi
ñoquis^M
gnocchi^M
Gnocchi^M
gnocchi^M

tortellini
tortellini^M
tortellini^M
Tortellini^M
tortellini^M

elbows
tiburones^M
coudes^M
Hörnchennudeln^F
gomiti^M

penne
macarrones^M
penne^M
Penne^F
penne^F

cannelloni
canelones^M
cannelloni^M
Cannelloni^M
cannelloni^M

spaghettini
fideos^M
spaghettini^M
Spaghettini^M
spaghettini^M

lasagna
lasañas^F
lasagne^F
Lasagne^F
lasagne^F

ravioli
raviolis^M
ravioli^M
Ravioli^M
ravioli^M

spinach tagliatelle
tallarines^M de espinacas^F
tagliatelle^M aux épinards^M
grüne Tagliatelle^F
tagliatelle^F verdi

fettucine
fetuchinas^F
fettucine^M
Fettuccine^F
fettuccine^F

Asian noodles
fideos *M* **asiáticos**
nouilles *F* **asiatiques**
asiatische Teigwaren *F*
spaghetti *M* **asiatici**

soba noodles
fideos *M* de soba *F*
nouilles *F* soba
Sobanudeln *F*
spaghetti *M* soba

somen noodles
fideos *M* de somen *M*
nouilles *F* somen
Somennudeln *F*
spaghetti *M* somen

udon noodles
fideos *M* de udon *M*
nouilles *F* udon
Udonnudeln *F*
spaghetti *M* udon

rice paper
galletas *F* de arroz *M*
galettes *F* de riz *M*
Reispapier *N*
gallette *F* di riso *M*

rice noodles
fideos *M* de arroz *M*
nouilles *F* de riz *M*
Reisnudeln *F*
spaghetti *M* di riso *M*

bean thread cellophane noodles
fideos *M* de judias *F* mungo
nouilles *F* de haricots *M* mungo
Glasnudeln *F*
spaghetti *M* di fagioli *M* mungo

egg noodles
fideos *M* de huevo *M*
nouilles *F* aux œufs *M*
asiatische Eiernudeln *F*
spaghetti *M* all'uovo *M*

rice vermicelli
vermicelli *M* de arroz *M*
vermicelles *M* de riz *M*
Reisfadennudeln *F*
vermicelli *M* di riso *M*

won ton skins
pasta *F* won ton
pâtes *F* won-ton
Wan-tan-Teigblätter *N*
pasta *F* won ton

rice
arroz *M*
riz *M*
Reis *M*
riso *M*

white rice
arroz *M* blanco
riz *M* blanc
weißer Reis *M*
riso *M* bianco

brown rice
arroz *M* integral
riz *M* complet
Braunreis *M*
riso *M* integrale

parboiled rice
arroz *M* vaporizado
riz *M* étuvé
Parboiled Reis *M*
riso *M* parboiled

basmati rice
arroz *M* basmati
riz *M* basmati
Basmatireis *M*
riso *M* basmati

FOOD AND KITCHEN

coffee and infusions

café^M y infusionnes^F | café^M et infusions^F | Kaffee^M und Tee^M | caffè^M e infusi^M

coffee
café^M
café^M
Kaffee^M
caffè^M

herbal teas
tisanas^F
tisanes^F
Kräutertees^M
tisane^F

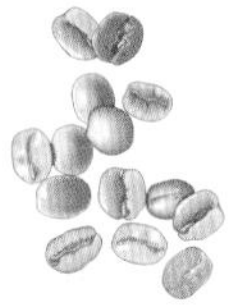

green coffee beans
granos^M verdes de café^M
grains^M de café^M verts
Rohkaffee^F
chicchi^M di caffè^M verdi

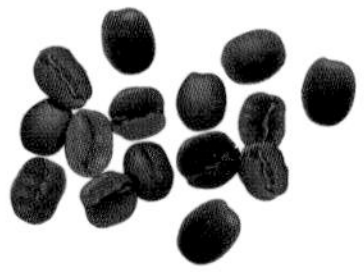

roasted coffee beans
granos^M torrefactos de café^M
grains^M de café^M torréfiés
geröstete Kaffeebohnen^F
chicchi^M di caffè^M tostati

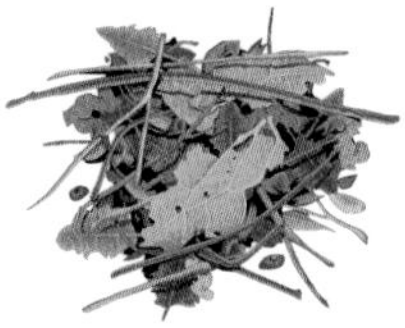

linden
tila^F
tilleul^M
Linde^F
tiglio^M

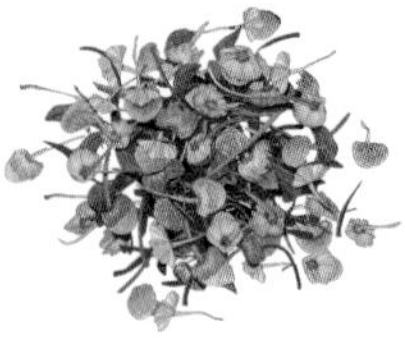

chamomile
manzanilla^F
camomille^F
Kamille^F
camomilla^F

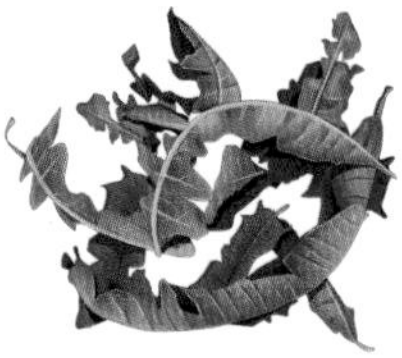

verbena
verbena^F
verveine^F
Verbene^F
verbena^F

tea
té^M
thé^M
Tee^M
tè^M

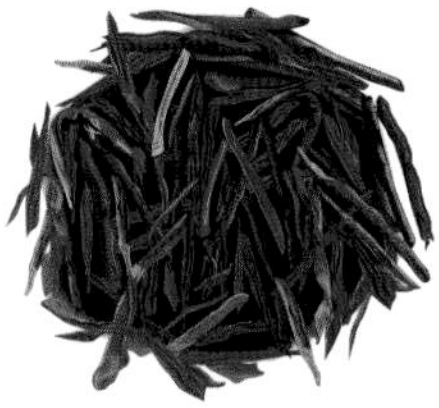

green tea
té^M verde
thé^M vert
grüner Tee^M
tè^M verde

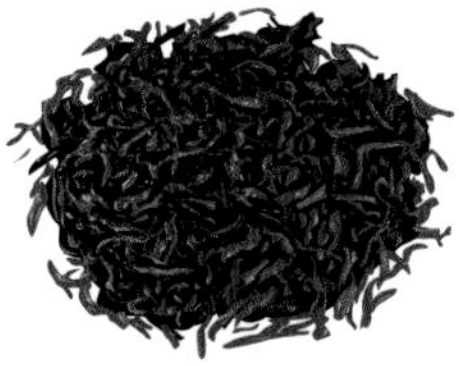

black tea
té^M negro
thé^M noir
schwarzer Tee^M
tè^M nero

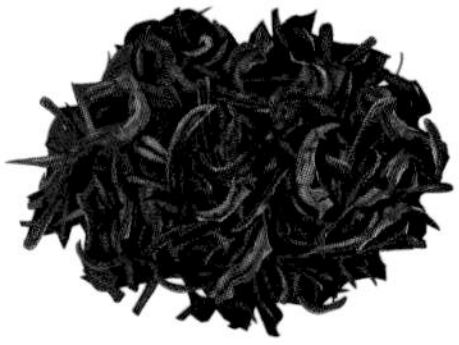

oolong tea
té^M oolong
thé^M oolong
Oolong-Tee^M
tè^M oolong

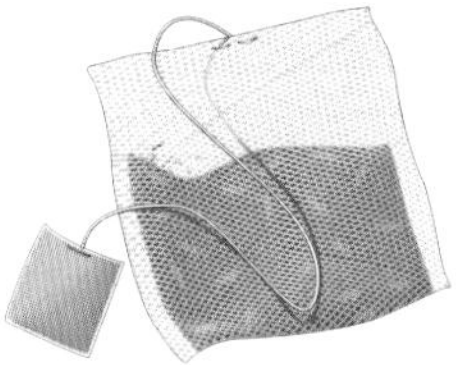

tea bag
bolsita^F de té^M
thé^M en sachet^M
Teebeutel^M
bustina^F di tè^M

chocolate

chocolate^M | chocolat^M | Schokolade^F | cioccolato^M

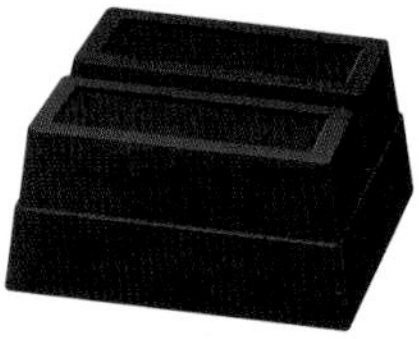

dark chocolate
chocolate^M amargo
chocolat^M noir
Bitterschokolade^F
cioccolato^M fondente

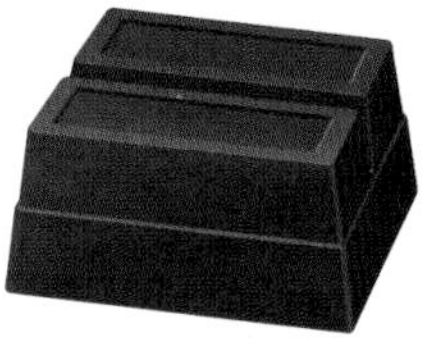

milk chocolate
chocolate^M con leche^F
chocolat^M au lait^M
Milchschokolade^F
cioccolato^M al latte^M

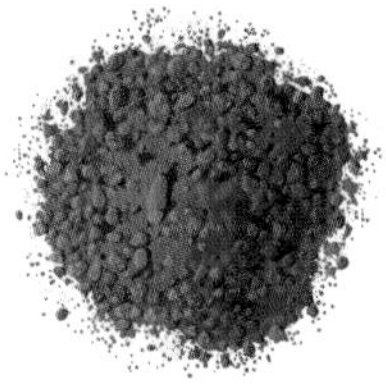

cocoa
cacao^M
cacao^M
Kakao^M
cacao^M

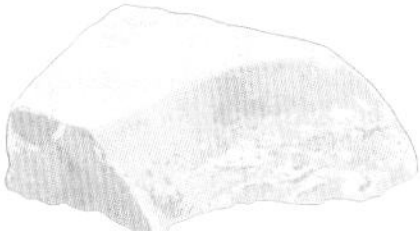

white chocolate
chocolate^M blanco
chocolat^M blanc
weiße Schokolade^F
cioccolato^M bianco

FOOD AND KITCHEN

sugar

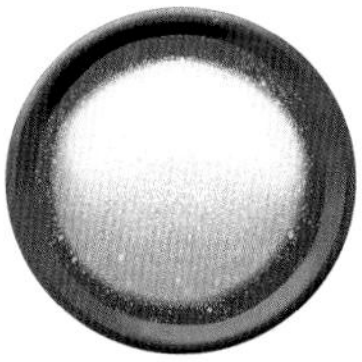

granulated sugar
azúcar^M granulado
sucre^M granulé
Kristallzucker^M
zucchero^M in grani^M

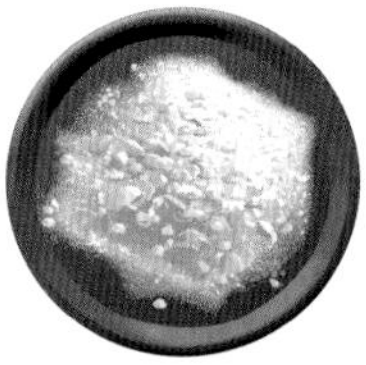

powdered sugar
azúcar^M glas
sucre^M glace^F
Puderzucker^M
zucchero^M a velo^M

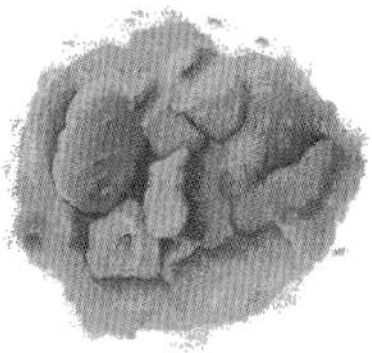

brown sugar
azúcar^M moreno
cassonade^F
brauner Zucker^M
zucchero^M di canna^F

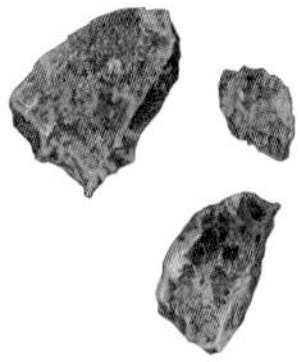

rock candy
azúcar^M candi
sucre^M candi
Kandiszucker^M
zucchero^M candito

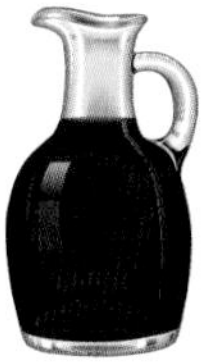

molasses
melazas^F
mélasse^F
Melasse^F
melassa^F

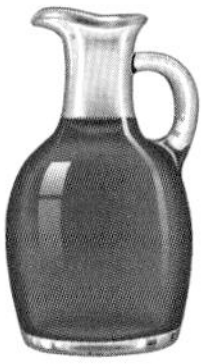

corn syrup
jarabe^M de maíz^M
sirop^M de mais^M
Maissirup^M
sciroppo^M di mais^M

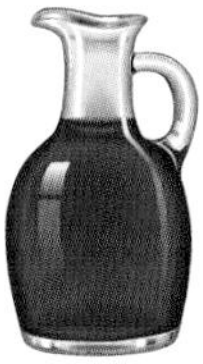

maple syrup
jarabe^M de arce^M
sirop^M d'érable^M
Ahornsirup^M
sciroppo^M d'acero^M

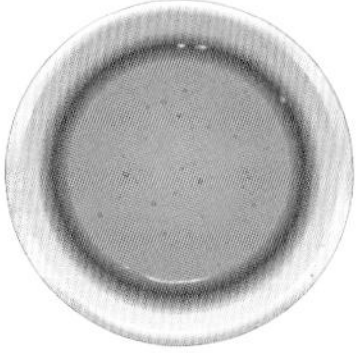

honey
miel^M
miel^M
Honig^M
miele^M

fats and oils

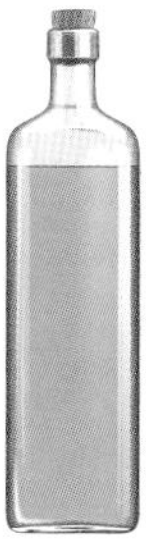

corn oil
aceite^M de maíz^M
huile^F de mais^M
Maisöl^N
olio^M di mais^M

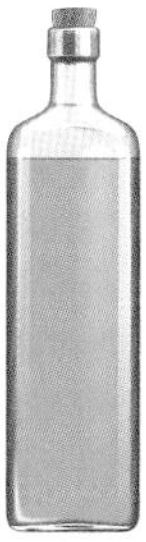

olive oil
aceite^M de oliva^F
huile^F d'olive^F
Olivenöl^N
olio^M d'oliva^F

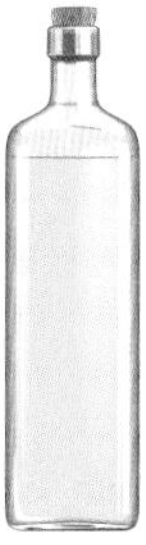

sunflower-seed oil
aceite^M de girasol^M
huile^F de tournesol^M
Sonnenblumenöl^N
olio^M di semi di girasole^M

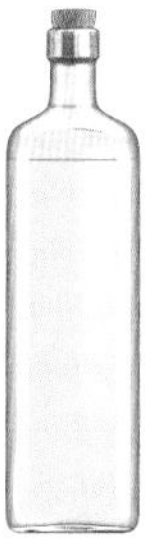

peanut oil
aceite^M de cacahuete^M
huile^F d'arachide^F
Erdnussöl^N
olio^M di arachidi^F

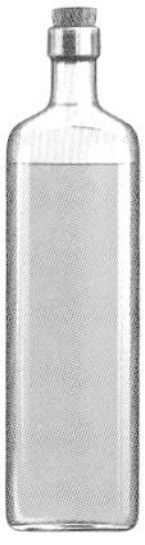

sesame oil
aceite^M de sésamo^M
huile^F de sésame^M
Sesamöl^N
olio^M di sesamo^M

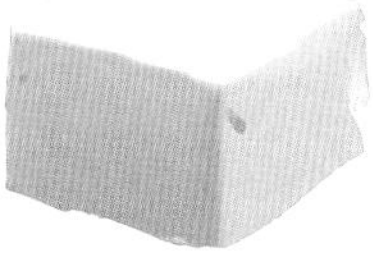

shortening
grasa^F para cocinar
saindoux^M
Backfett^N
grasso^M alimentare

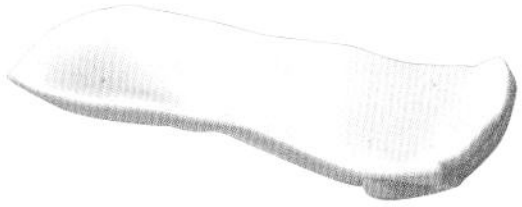

lard
manteca^F de cerdo^M
lard^M
Schweinespeck^M
lardo^M

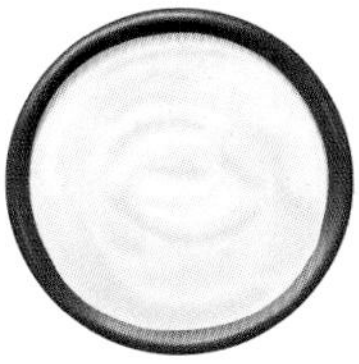

margarine
margarina^F
margarine^F
Margarine^F
margarina^F

dairy products

productos^M lácteos | produits^M laitiers | Milchprodukte^N | prodotti^M caseari

FOOD AND KITCHEN

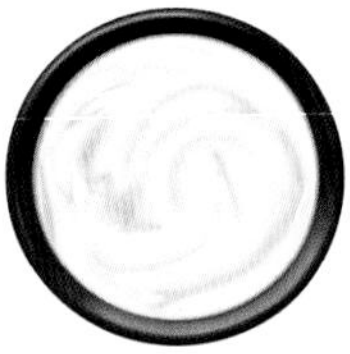

yogurt
yogur^M
yaourt^M ; yogourt^M
Joghurt^M
yogurt^M

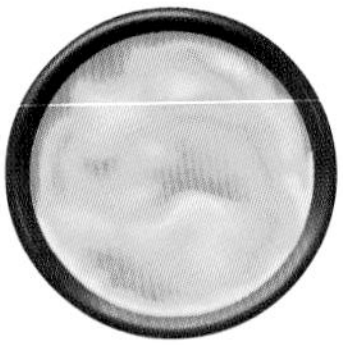

ghee
mantequilla^F clarificada
ghee^M
Ghee^N
ghi^M

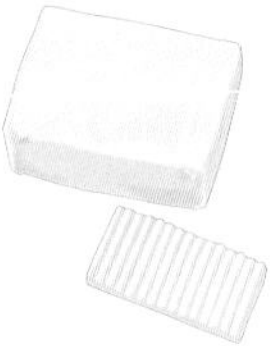

butter
mantequilla^M
beurre^M
Butter^F
burro^M

cream
nata^F
crème^F
Sahne^F
panna^F

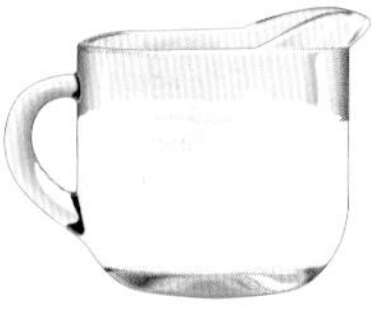

whipping cream
nata^F de montar
crème^F épaisse ; crème^F à fouetter
Schlagsahne^F
panna^F da montare

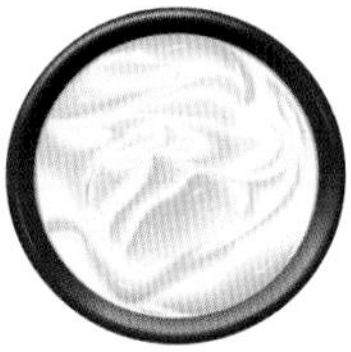

sour cream
nata^F agria
crème^F aigre ; crème^F sure
saure Sahne^F
panna^F acida

milk
leche^M
lait^M
Milch^F
latte^M

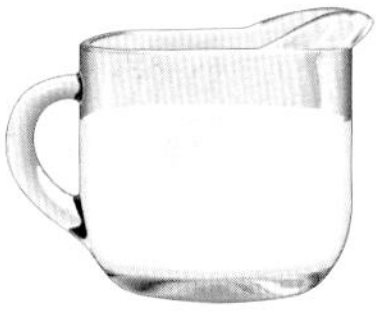

homogenized milk
leche^F homogeneizada
lait^M homogénéisé
homogenisierte Milch^F
latte^M omogeneizzato

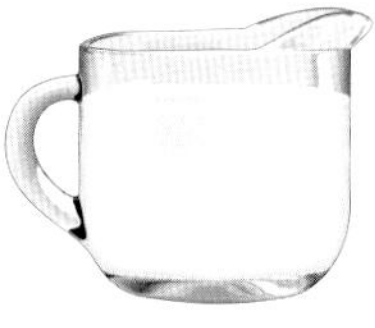

goat's milk
leche^F de cabra
lait^M de chèvre^F
Ziegenmilch^F
latte^M di capra^F

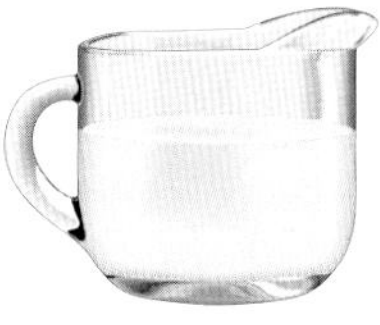

evaporated milk
leche^F evaporada
lait^M concentré
Kondensmilch^F
latte^M evaporato

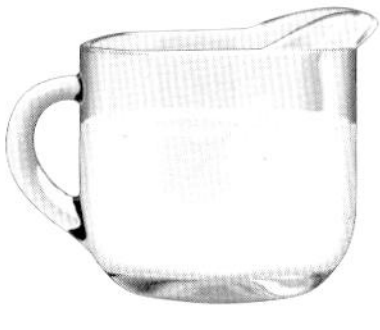

buttermilk
suero^M de la leche^F
babeurre^M
Buttermilch^F
latticello^M

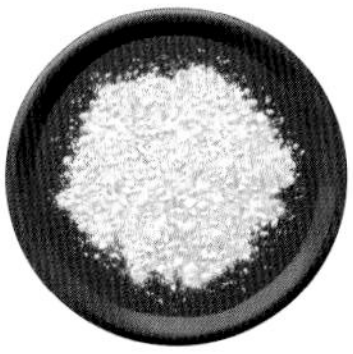

powdered milk
leche^F en polvo^M
lait^M en poudre^F
Milchpulver^N
latte^M in polvere^F

fresh cheeses
quesos^M **frescos**
fromages^M **frais**
Frischkäse^M
formaggi^M **freschi**

goat's-milk cheeses
quesos^M **de cabra**^F
fromages^M **de chèvre**^F
Ziegenkäse^M
formaggi^M **di capra**^F

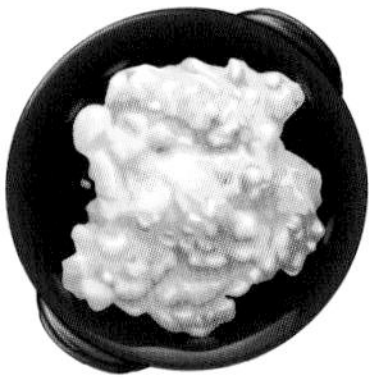

cottage cheese
queso^M cottage
cottage^M
Hüttenkäse^M
cottage cheese^M

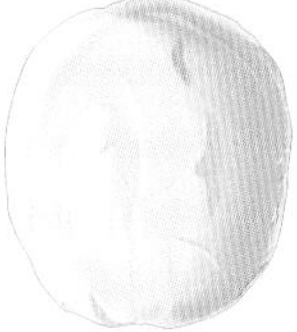

mozzarella
mozzarella^F
mozzarella^F
Mozzarella^M
mozzarella^F

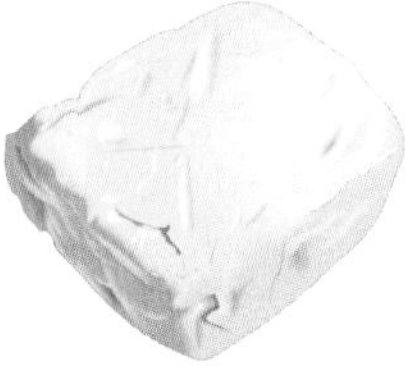

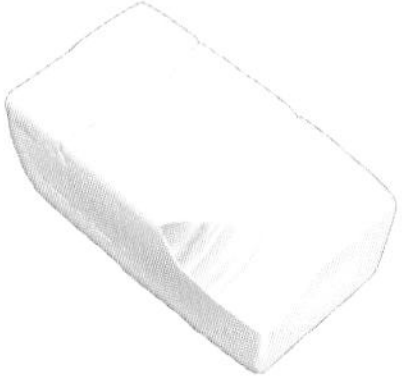

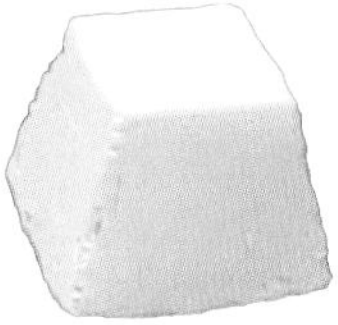

chèvre cheese
queso^M chèvre
chèvre^M frais
Ziegenfrischkäse^M
formaggio^M fresco di capra^F

ricotta
ricotta^F
ricotta^F
Ricotta^M
ricotta^F

cream cheese
queso^M cremoso
fromage^M à la crème^F
Streichkäse^M
formaggio^M cremoso

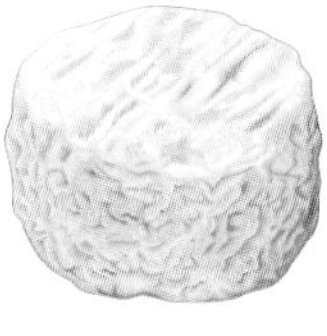

Crottin de Chavignol
Crottin^M de Chavignol
crottin^M de Chavignol
Crottin de Chavignol^M
crottin^M de chavignol

pressed cheeses
quesos[M] **prensados**
fromages[M] **à pâte**[F] **pressée**
Hartkäse[M]
formaggi[M] **a pasta**[F] **dura**

Jarlsberg
jarlsberg[M]
jarlsberg[M]
Jarlsberg[M]
jarlsberg[M]

Emmenthal
emmenthal[M]
emmenthal[M]
Emmentaler[M]
emmental[M]

raclette
raclette[F]
raclette[F]
Raclette[M]
raclette[F]

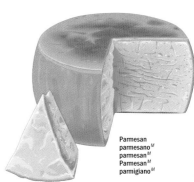

Parmesan
parmesano[M]
parmesan[M]
Parmesan[M]
parmigiano[M]

Gruyère
gruyère[M]
gruyère[M]
Gruyèrekäse[M]
groviera[M]

Romano
pecorino romano[M]
romano[M]
Pecorino Romano[M]
pecorino[M] romano

blue-veined cheeses
quesos[M] **azules**
fromages[M] **à pâte**[F] **persillée**
Edelpilzkäse[M]
formaggi[M] **erborinati**

Roquefort
roquefort[M]
roquefort[M]
Roquefort[M]
roquefort[M]

Stilton
stilton[M]
stilton[M]
Stilton[M]
stilton[M]

Gorgonzola
gorgonzola[M]
gorgonzola[M]
Gorgonzola[M]
gorgonzola[M]

Danish Blue
azul danés[M]
bleu[M] danois
Danish Blue[M]
danish blue[M]

soft cheeses
quesos[M] **blandos**
fromages[M] **à pâte**[F] **molle**
Weichkäse[M]
formaggi[M] **a pasta**[F] **molle**

Pont-l'Évêque
Pont-l'Éveque[M]
pont-l'évêque[M]
Pont-l'Évêque[M]
pont-l'évêque[M]

Coulommiers
coulommiers[M]
coulommiers[M]
Coulommiers[M]
coulommiers[M]

Munster
munster[M]
munster[M]
Munster[M]
munster[M]

Camembert
camembert[M]
camembert[M]
Camembert[M]
camembert[M]

Brie
brie[M]
brie[M]
Brie[M]
brie[M]

FOOD AND KITCHEN

organ meat

despojos^M | abats^M | Innereien^F | interiora^F

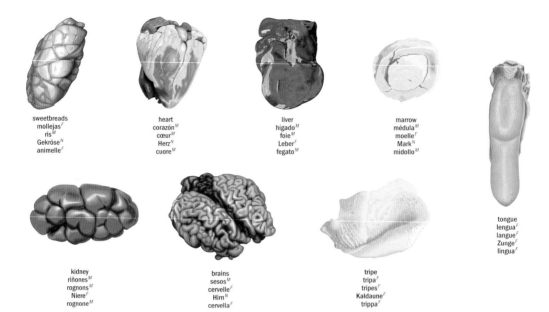

sweetbreads
mollejas^F
ris^M
Gekröse^N
animelle^F

heart
corazón^M
cœur^M
Herz^N
cuore^M

liver
hígado^M
foie^M
Leber^F
fegato^M

marrow
médula^M
moelle^F
Mark^N
midollo^M

tongue
lengua^F
langue^F
Zunge^F
lingua^F

kidney
riñones^M
rognons^M
Niere^F
rognone^M

brains
sesos^M
cervelle^F
Hirn^N
cervella^F

tripe
tripa^F
tripes^F
Kaldaune^F
trippa^F

game

caza^F | gibier^M | Wild^N | selvaggina^F

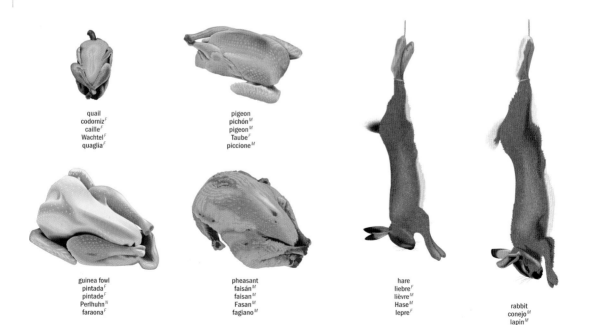

quail
codorniz^F
caille^F
Wachtel^F
quaglia^F

pigeon
pichón^M
pigeon^M
Taube^F
piccione^M

guinea fowl
pintada^F
pintade^F
Perlhuhn^N
faraona^F

pheasant
faisán^M
faisan^M
Fasan^M
fagiano^M

hare
liebre^F
lièvre^M
Hase^M
lepre^F

rabbit
conejo^M
lapin^M
Kaninchen^N
coniglio^M

FOOD AND KITCHEN

poultry

aves^F de corral^M | volaille^F | Geflügel^N | volatili^M

chicken
pollo^M
poulet^M
Huhn^N
pollo^M

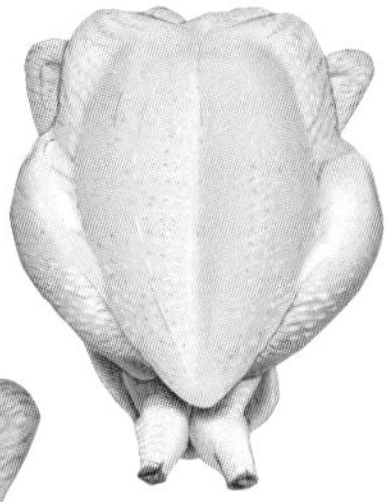

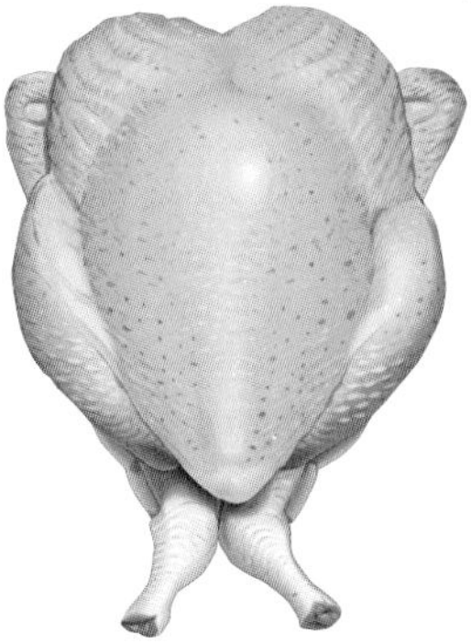

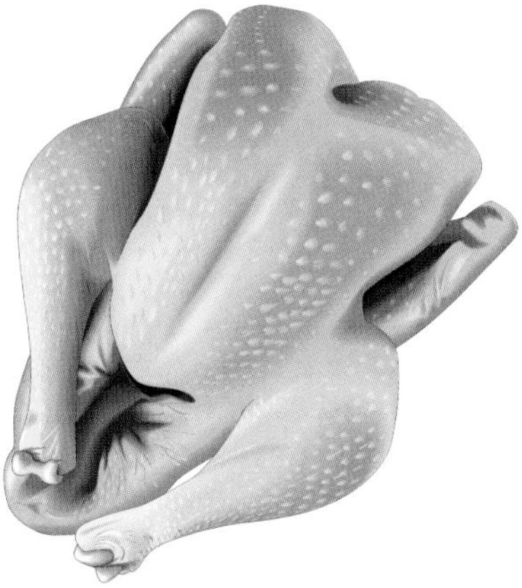

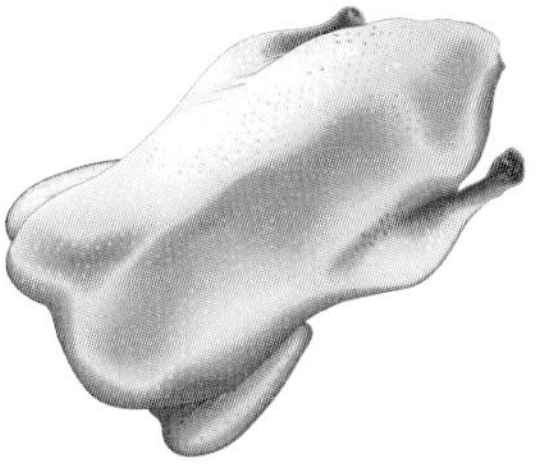

duck
pato^M
canard^M
Ente^F
anatra^F

capon
capón^M
chapon^M
Kapaun^M
cappone^M

turkey
pavo^M
dinde^F
Puter^M
tacchino^M

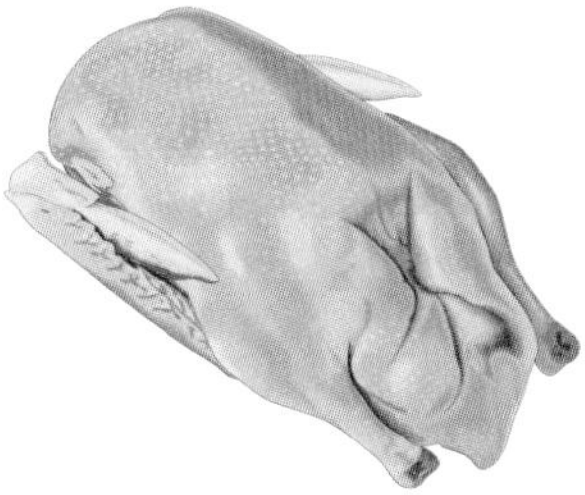

goose
oca^F
oie^F
Gans^F
oca^F

eggs

huevos^M | œufs^M | Eier^N | uova^F

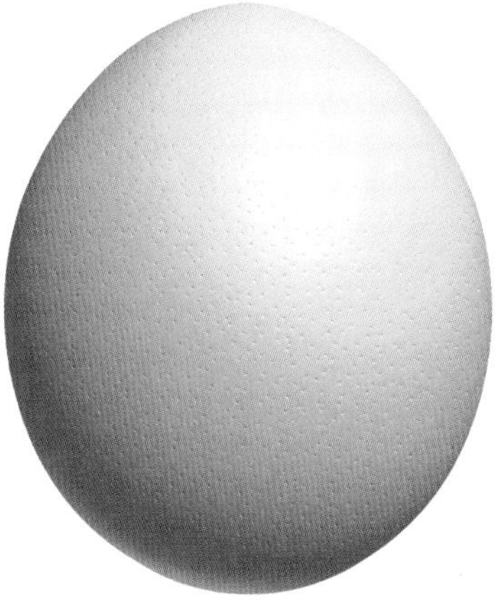

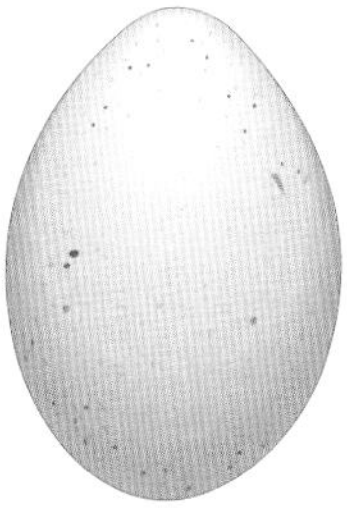

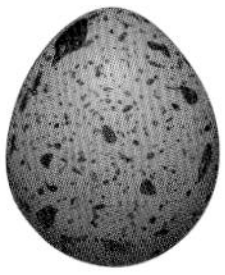

quail egg
huevo^F de codorniz^F
œuf^M de caille^F
Wachtelei^N
uovo^M di quaglia^F

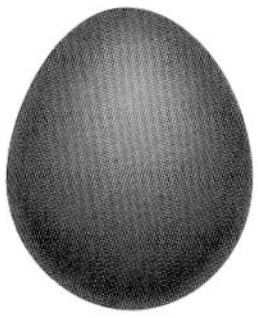

pheasant egg
huevo^M de faisán^M
œuf^M de faisane^F
Fasanenei^N
uovo^M di fagiano^M

goose egg
huevo^M de oca^F
œuf^M d'oie^F
Gänseei^N
uovo^M di oca^F

ostrich egg
huevo^M de avestruz^M
œuf^M d'autruche^F
Straußenei^N
uovo^M di struzzo^M

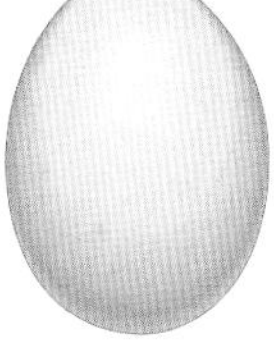

duck egg
huevo^M de pato^M
œuf^M de cane^F
Entenei^N
uovo^M di anatra^F

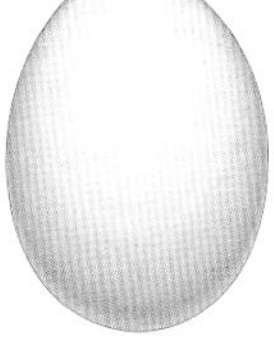

hen egg
huevo^M de gallina^F
œuf^M de poule^F
Hühnerei^N
uovo^M di gallina^F

meat

carne^F | viande^F | Fleisch^N | carne^F

cuts of beef
cortes^M de vacuno^M
découpes^F de bœuf^M
Rindfleisch^N
tagli^M di manzo^M

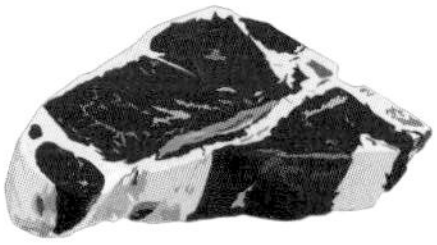

steak
bistec^M
bifteck^M
Steak^N
bistecca^F

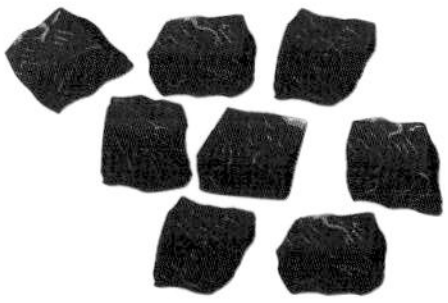

beef cubes
carne^F de vacuno^M troceada
cubes^M de bœuf^M
Rindfleischwürfel^M
spezzatino^M

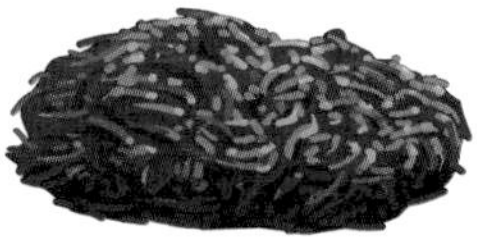

ground beef
carne^F picada
bœuf^M haché
Rinderhackfleisch^N
macinato^M

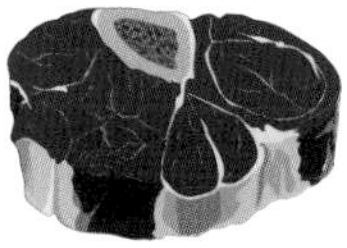

shank
morcillo^M
jarret^M
Hachse^F
ossobuco^M

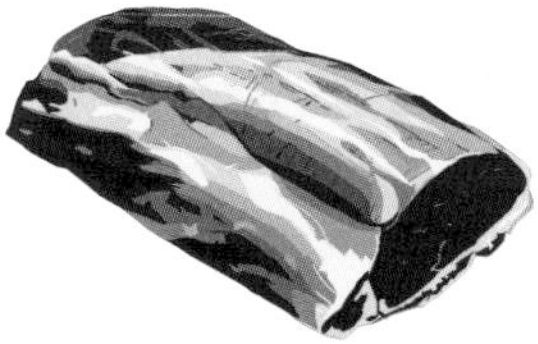

tenderloin roast
lomo^M
filet^M de bœuf^M
Rinderfilet^N
filetto^M

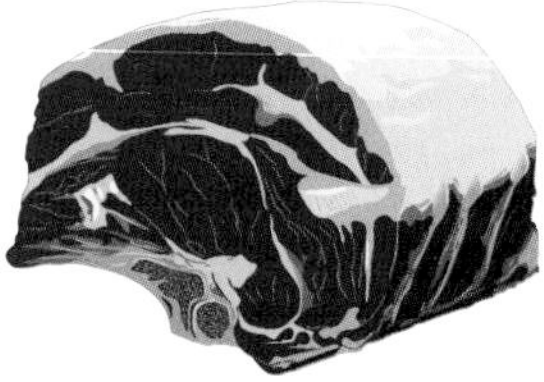

rib roast
chuletón^M
rôti^M de côtes^F
hohe Rippe^F
costate^F

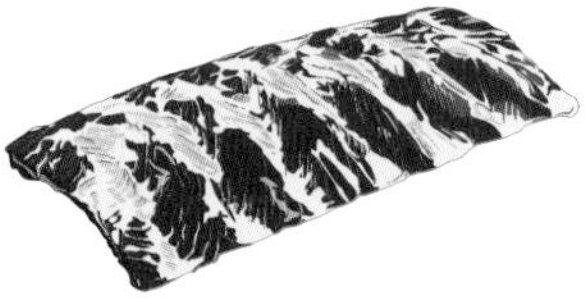

back ribs
costillar^M
côtes^F levées de dos^M
Querrippe^F
costine^F

cuts of veal
cortes^M de ternera^F
découpes^F de veau^M
Kalbfleisch^N
tagli^M di vitello^M

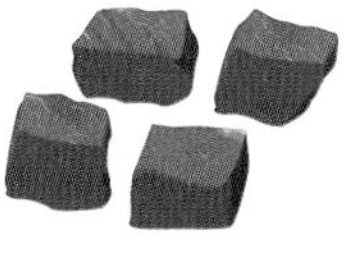

veal cubes
carne^F de ternera^F troceada
cubes^M de veau^M
Kalbfleischwürfel^M
spezzatino^M

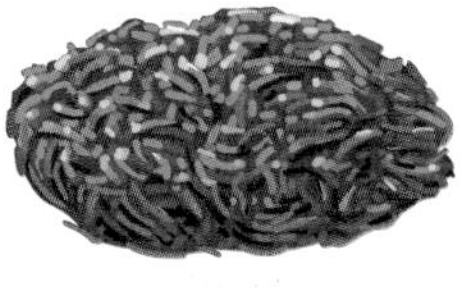

ground veal
carne^F picada de vacuno^M
veau^M haché
Kalbshackfleisch^N
macinato^M

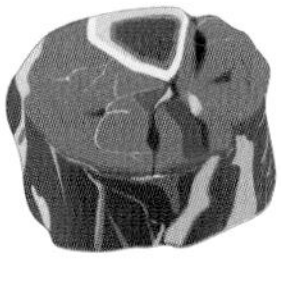

shank
paleta^F
jarret^M
Hachse^F
ossobuco^M

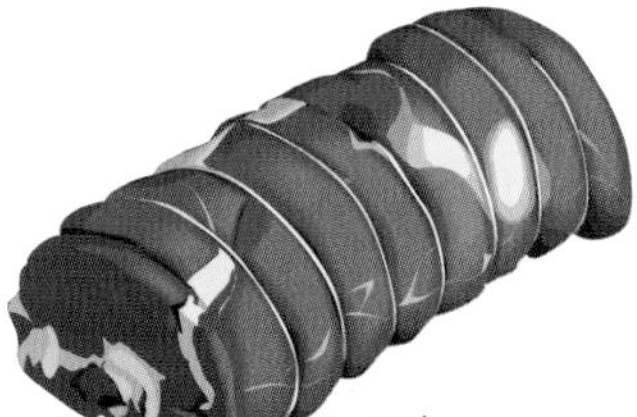

roast
asado^M
rôti^M
Rollbraten^M
arrotolato^M

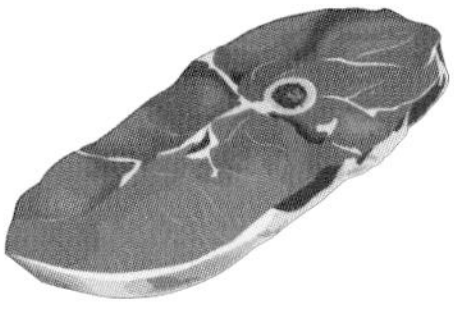

steak
bistec^M
bifteck^M
Schnitzel^N
bistecca^F

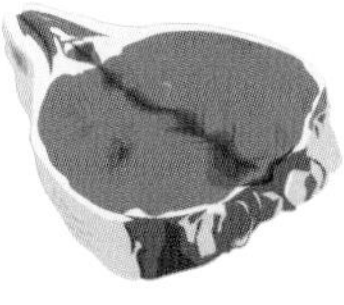

chop
chuleta^F
côte^F
Kotelett^N
braciola^F

cuts of lamb
cortes^M de cordero^M
découpes^F d'agneau^M
Lammfleisch^N
tagli^M di agnello^M

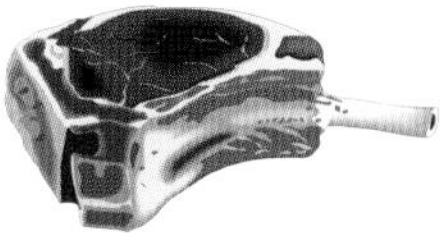

chop
chuleta^F
côte^F
Kotelett^N
braciola^F

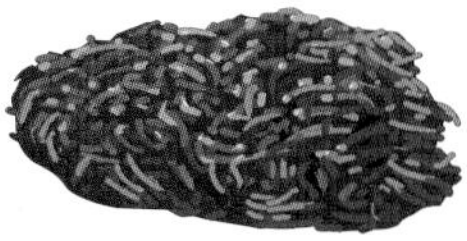

ground lamb
carne^F picada de cordero^M
agneau^M haché
Lammhackfleisch^N
macinato^M

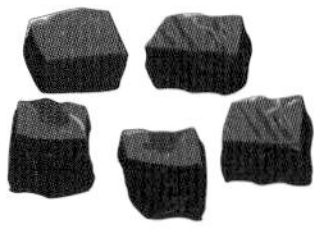

lamb cubes
carne^F de cordero^M troceada
cubes^M d'agneau^M
Lammfleischwürfel^M
spezzatino^M

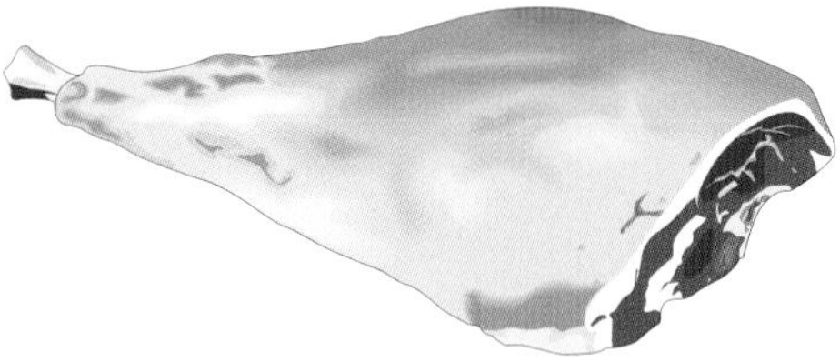

roast
pierna^F de cordero^M
rôti^M
Braten^M
arrosto^M

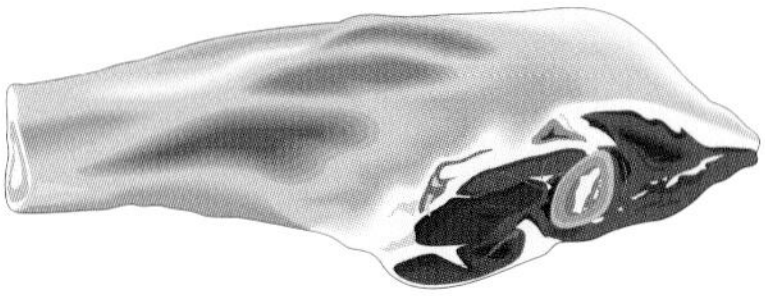

shank
paletilla^F
jarret^M
Hachse^F
stinco^M

cuts of pork
cortes^M de cerdo^M
découpes^F de porc^M
Schweinefleisch^N
tagli^M di maiale^M

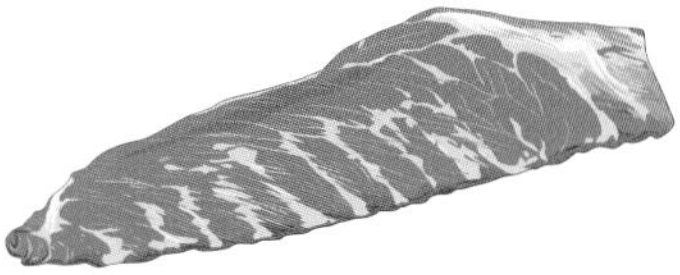

spareribs
costillar^M
travers^M ; côtes^F levées
Spareribs/Schälrippchen^N
costolette^F

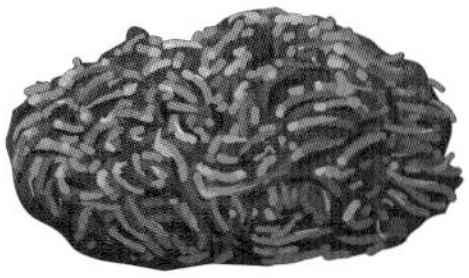

ground pork
carne^F picada de cerdo^M
porc^M haché
Schweinehackfleisch^N
macinato^M

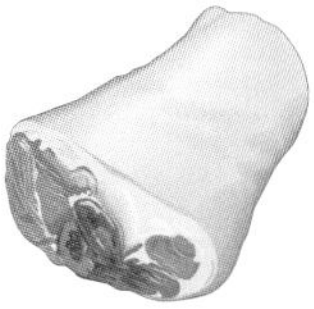

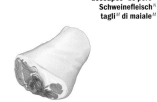

hock
codillo^M
jarret^M
Eisbein^N
piedino^M

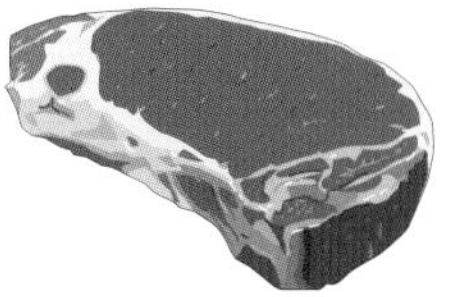

loin chop
chuleta^F
côtelette^F
Kotelett^N
lonza^F

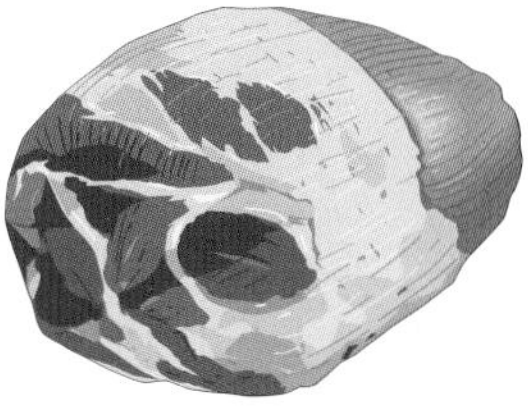

smoked ham
jamón^M ahumado
jambon^M fumé
Räucherschinken^M
prosciutto^M affumicato

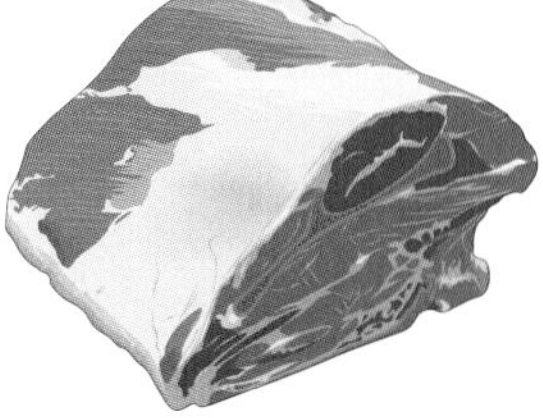

roast
asado^M de cerdo^M
rôti^M
Braten^M
arrosto^M

delicatessen

charcutería^F | charcuterie^F | Spezialitäten^F | gastronomia^F

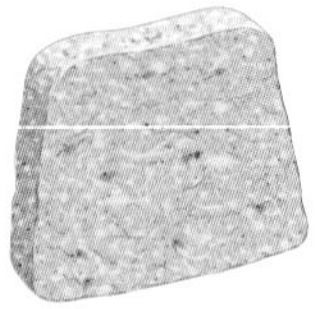

rillettes
rillettes^F
rillettes^F
Rillettes^F
ciccioli^M

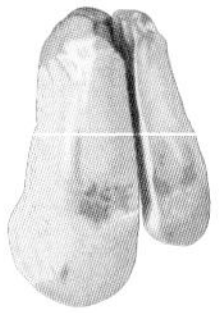

foie gras
foie-gras^M
foie^M gras
Stopfleber^F
foie-gras^M

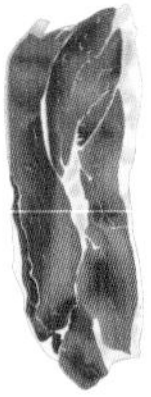

prosciutto
jamón^M serrano
prosciutto^M
roher Schinken^M
prosciutto^M

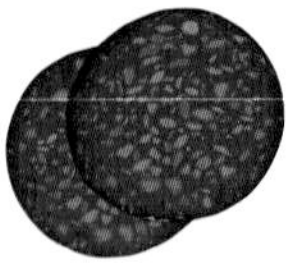

kielbasa sausage
salchicha^F kielbasa
saucisson^M kielbasa
Kielbasa-Wurst^F
salsiccia^F kielbasa

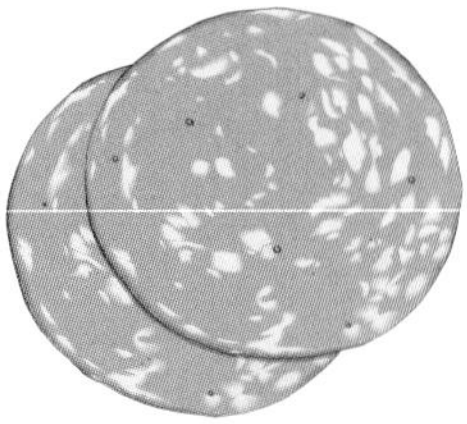

mortadella
mortadela^F
mortadelle^F
Mortadella^F
mortadella^F

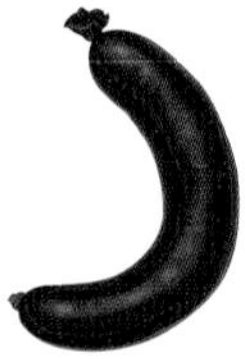

blood sausage
morcilla^F
boudin^M
Blutwurst^F
sanguinaccio^M

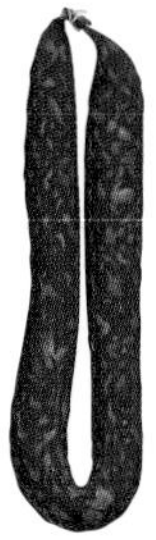

chorizo
chorizo^M
chorizo^M
Chorizo-Wurst^F
chorizo^M

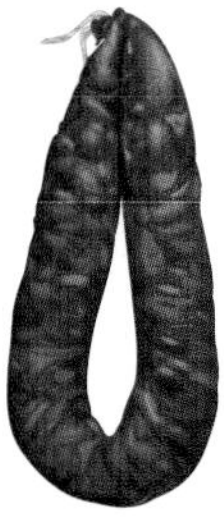

pepperoni
pepperoni^M
pepperoni^M
Pepperoniwurst^F
salsiccia^F piccante

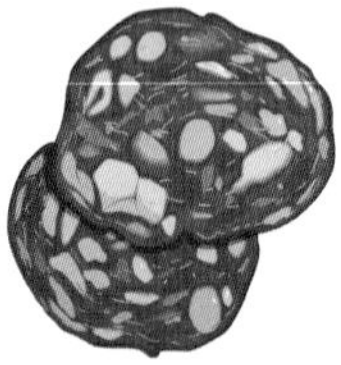

Genoa salami
salami^M de Génova
salami^M de Gênes
grobe Salami^F
salame^M di Genova

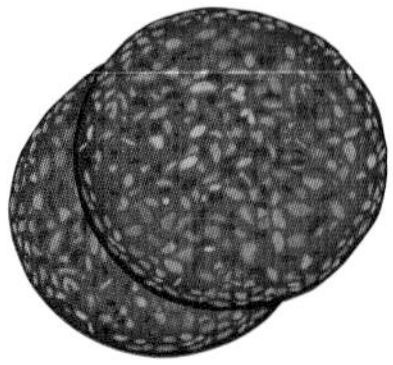

German salami
salami^M alemán
salami^M allemand
feine Salami^F
salame^M tedesco

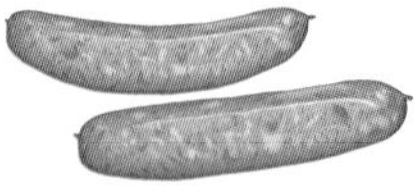

Toulouse sausages
salchicha^F de Toulouse
saucisse^F de Toulouse
Toulouser Wurst^F
salame^M di Tolosa

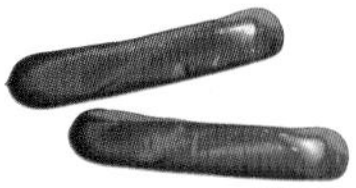

merguez sausages
salchicha^F merguez
merguez^F
Merguez-Wurst^F
merguez^F

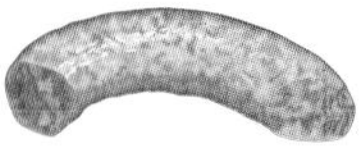

andouillette
andouillete^F
andouillette^F
Kuttelwurst^F
salsiccia^F di trippa^F

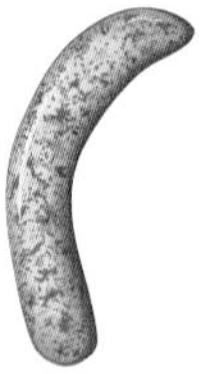

chipolata sausage
salchicha^F chipolata
chipolata^F
Bratwurst^F
salsiccia^F alle cipolle^F

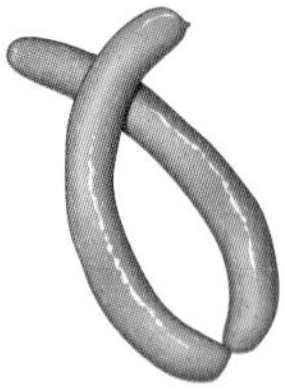

frankfurters
salchicha^F de Frankfurt
saucisse^F de Francfort
Frankfurter Würstchen^N
salsiccia^F di Francoforte

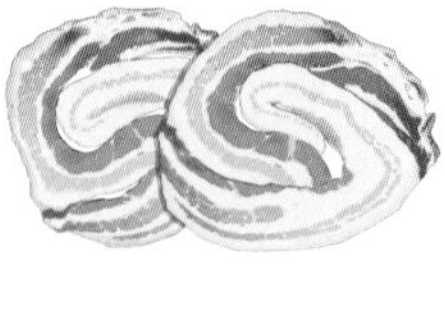

pancetta
panceta^F
pancetta^F
Bauchspeck^M
pancetta^F

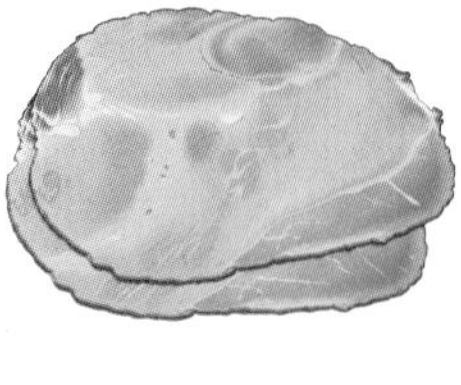

cooked ham
jamón^M de York
jambon^M cuit
gekochter Schinken^M
prosciutto^M cotto

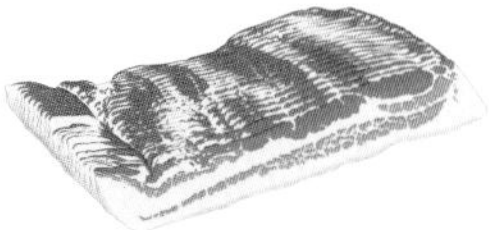

American bacon
bacón^M americano
bacon^M américain
amerikanischer Bacon^M
bacon^M americano

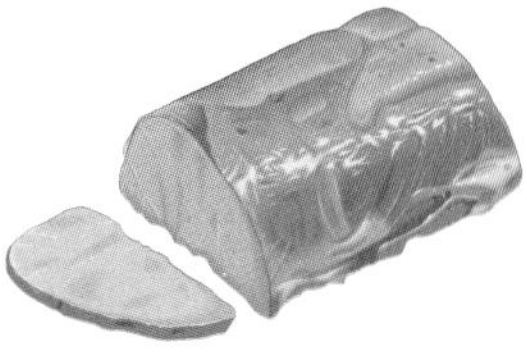

Canadian bacon
bacón^M canadiense
bacon^M canadien
kanadischer Bacon^M
bacon^M canadese

FOOD AND KITCHEN

mollusks

moluscos[M] | mollusques[M] | Mollusken[F] | molluschi[M]

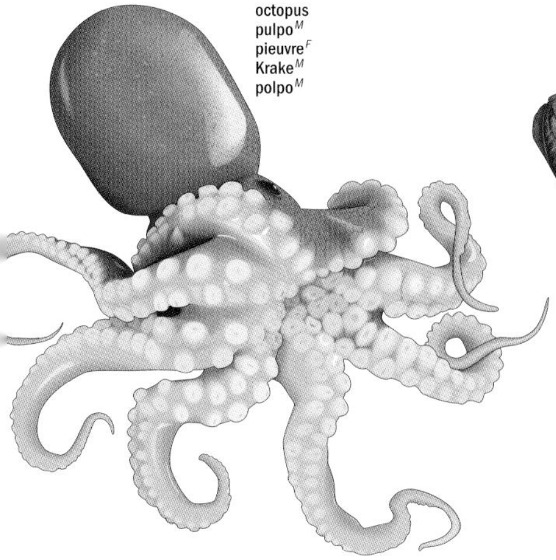

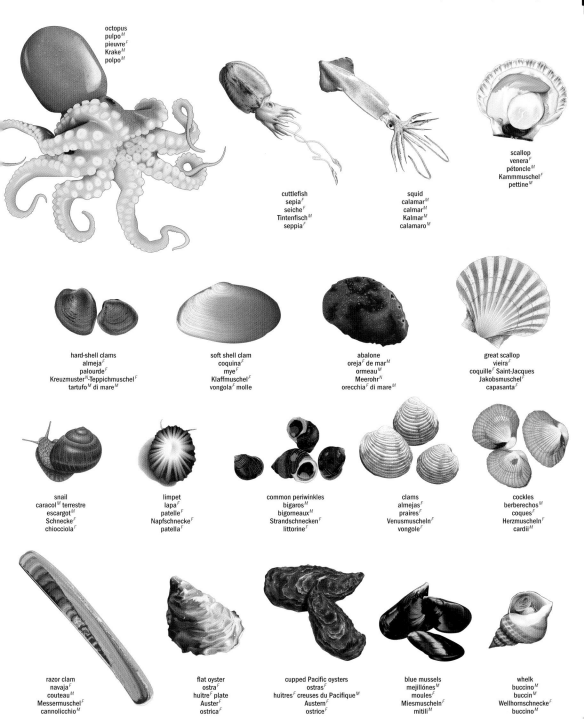

octopus
pulpo[M]
pieuvre[F]
Krake[M]
polpo[M]

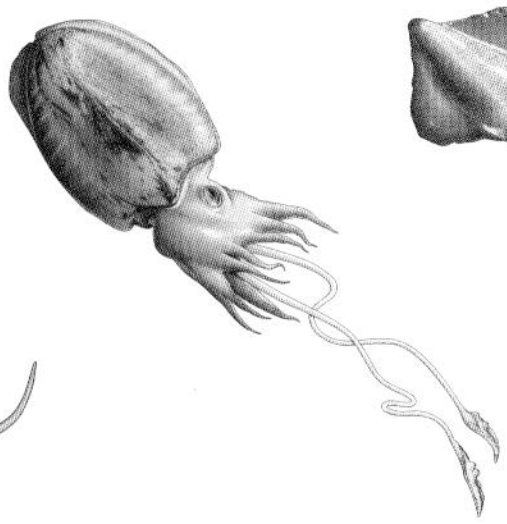

cuttlefish
sepia[F]
seiche[F]
Tintenfisch[M]
seppia[F]

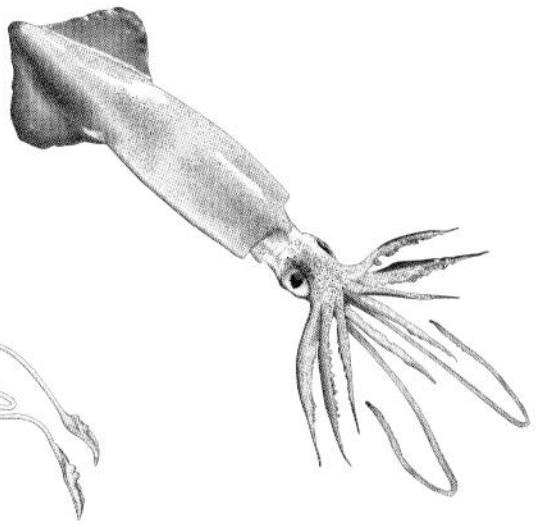

squid
calamar[M]
calmar[M]
Kalmar[M]
calamaro[M]

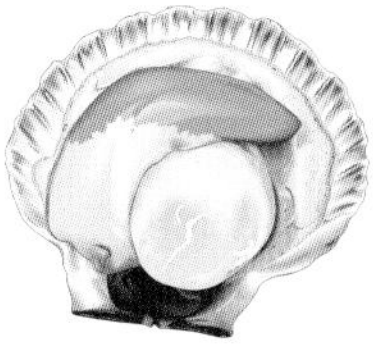

scallop
venera[F]
pétoncle[M]
Kammmuschel[F]
pettine[F]

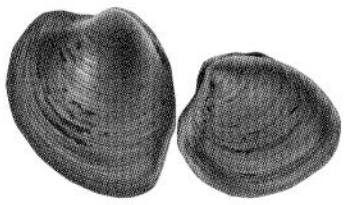

hard-shell clams
almeja[F]
palourde[F]
Kreuzmuster[N]-Teppichmuschel[F]
tartufo[M] di mare[M]

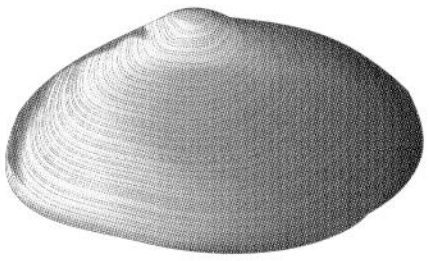

soft shell clam
coquina[F]
mye[F]
Klaffmuschel[F]
vongola[F] molle

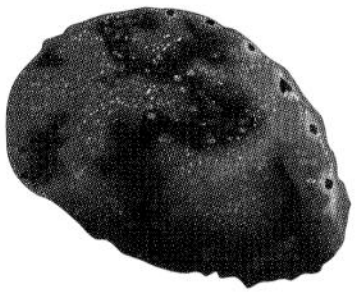

abalone
oreja[F] de mar[M]
ormeau[M]
Meerohr[N]
orecchia[F] di mare[M]

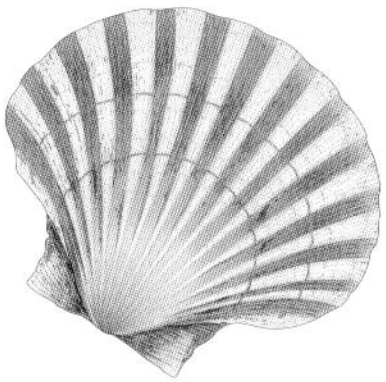

great scallop
vieira[F]
coquille[F] Saint-Jacques
Jakobsmuschel[F]
capasanta[F]

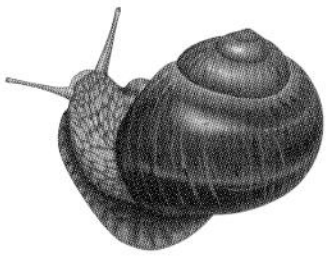

snail
caracol[M] terrestre
escargot[M]
Schnecke[F]
chiocciola[F]

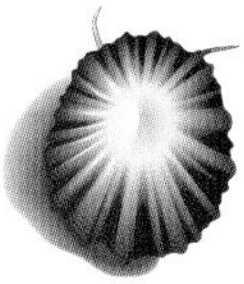

limpet
lapa[F]
patelle[F]
Napfschnecke[F]
patella[F]

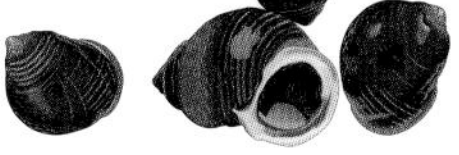

common periwinkles
bígaros[M]
bigorneaux[M]
Strandschnecken[F]
littorine[F]

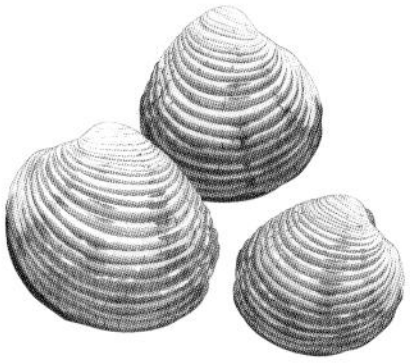

clams
almejas[F]
praires[F]
Venusmuscheln[F]
vongole[F]

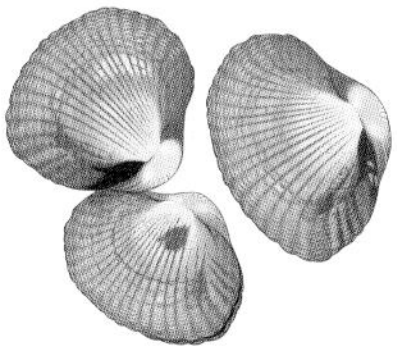

cockles
berberechos[M]
coques[F]
Herzmuscheln[F]
cardii[M]

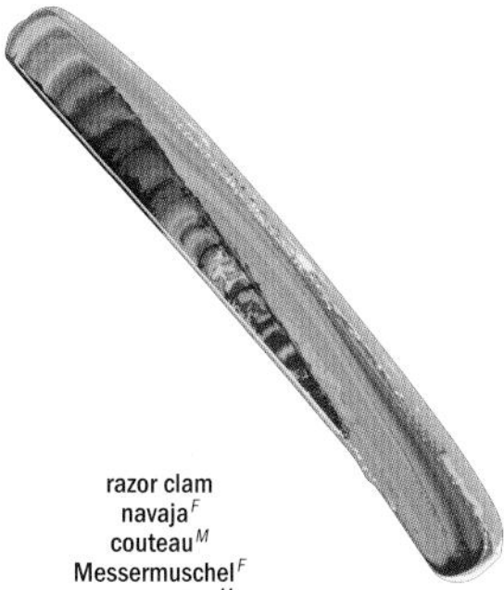

razor clam
navaja[F]
couteau[M]
Messermuschel[F]
cannolicchio[M]

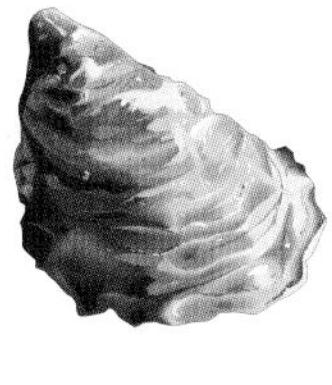

flat oyster
ostra[F]
huître[F] plate
Auster[F]
ostrica[F]

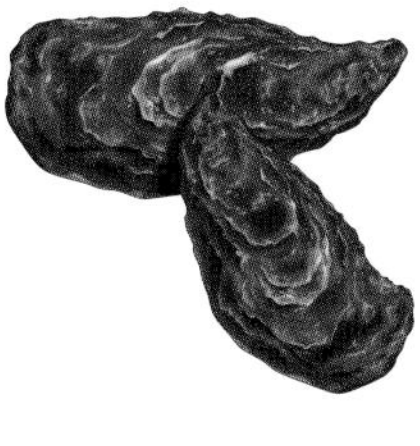

cupped Pacific oysters
ostras[F]
huîtres[F] creuses du Pacifique[M]
Austern[F]
ostrice[F]

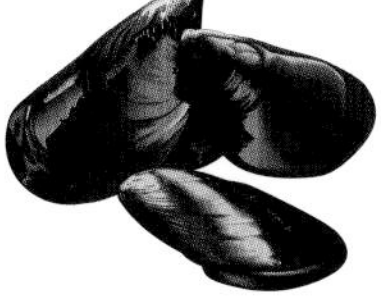

blue mussels
mejillónes[M]
moules[F]
Miesmuscheln[F]
mitili[M]

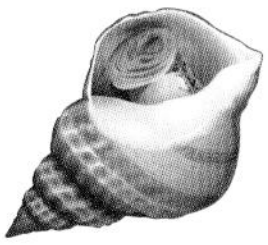

whelk
buccino[M]
buccin[M]
Wellhornschnecke[F]
buccino[M]

crustaceans

crustáceos ^{M} | crustacés ^{M} | Krebstiere ^{N} | crostacei ^{M}

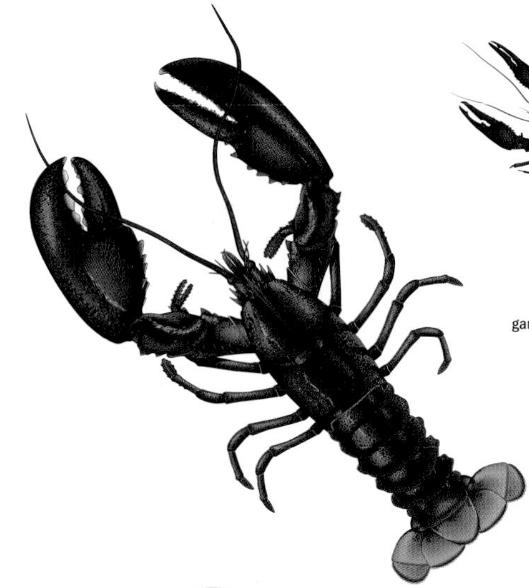

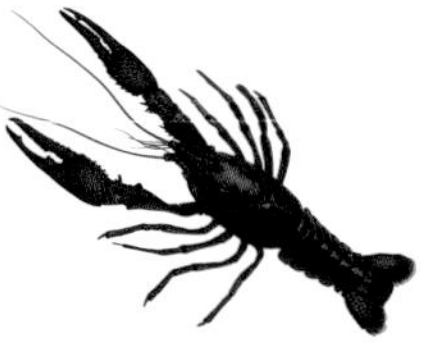

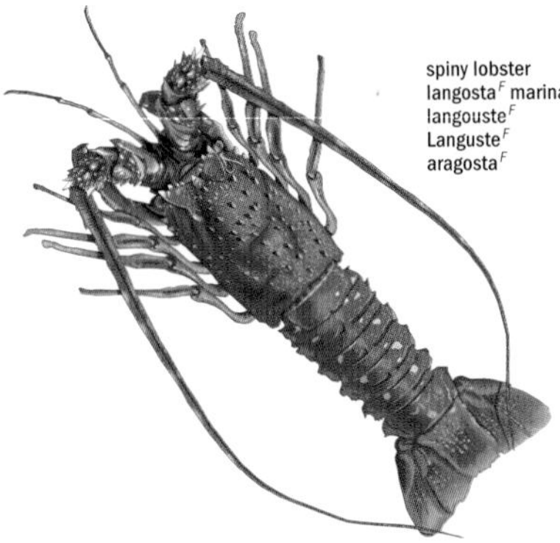

spiny lobster
langosta ^{F} marina
langouste ^{F}
Languste ^{F}
aragosta ^{F}

crayfish
cangrejo ^{M} de rio ^{M}
écrevisse ^{F}
Flusskrebs ^{M}
gambero ^{M} di acqua ^{F} dolce

lobster
bogavante ^{M}
homard ^{M}
Hummer ^{M}
astice ^{M}

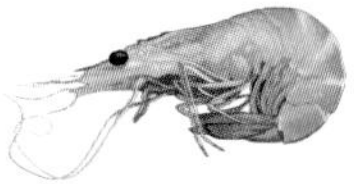

shrimp
gamba ^{F}
crevette ^{F}
Garnele ^{F}
gamberetto ^{M}

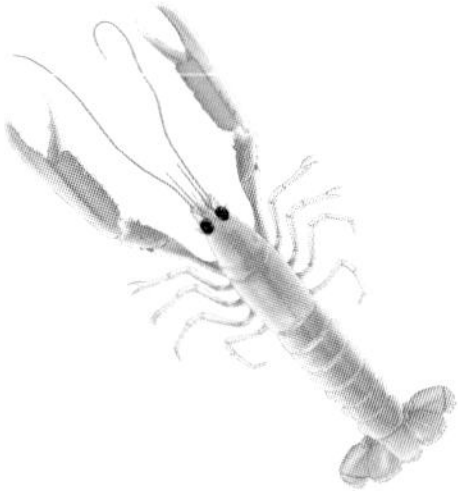

scampi
cigala ^{F}
langoustine ^{F}
Langustine ^{F}
scampo ^{M}

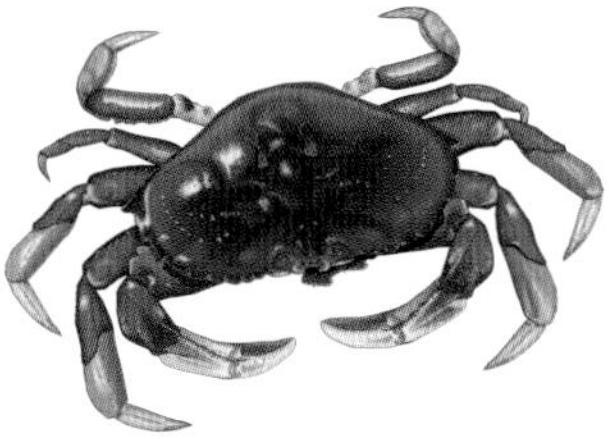

crab
cangrejo ^{M} de mar ^{M}
crabe ^{M}
Krabbe ^{F}
granchio ^{M}

cartilaginous fishes

peces ^{M} cartilaginosos | poissons ^{M} cartilagineux | Knorpelfische ^{M} | pesci ^{M} cartilaginei

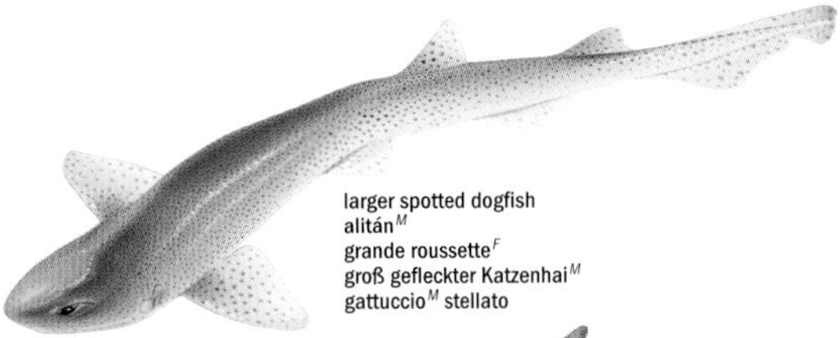

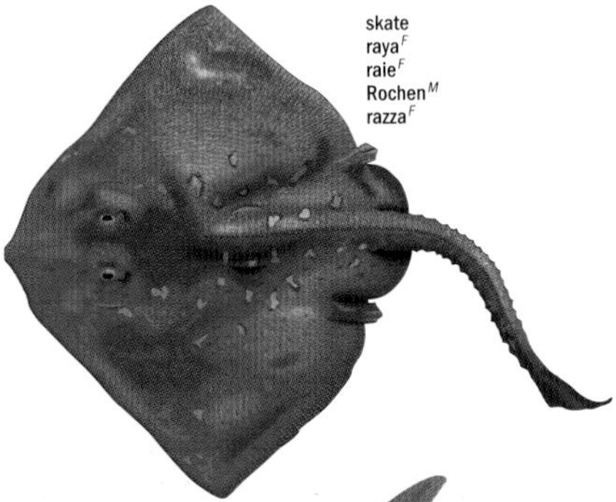

skate
raya ^{F}
raie ^{F}
Rochen ^{M}
razza ^{F}

larger spotted dogfish
alitán ^{M}
grande roussette ^{F}
groß gefleckter Katzenhai ^{M}
gattuccio ^{M} stellato

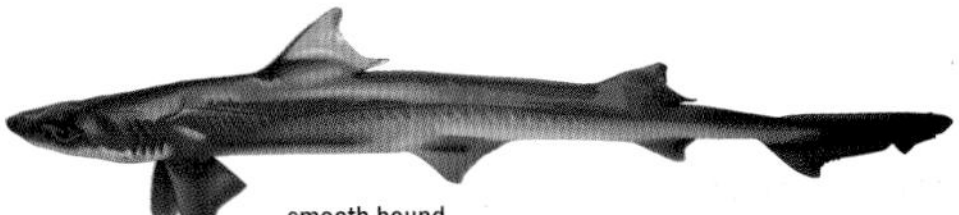

smooth hound
musola ^{F}
émissole ^{F}
Hundshai ^{M}
palombo ^{M} liscio

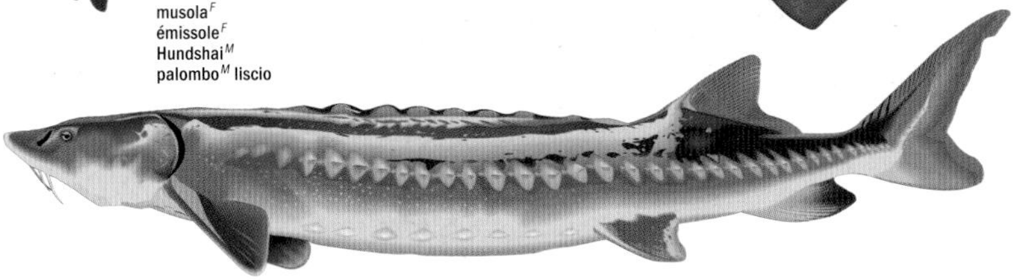

sturgeon
esturión ^{M}
esturgeon ^{M}
Stör ^{M}
storione ^{M}

bony fishes

peces^M óseos | poissons^M osseux | Knochenfische^M | pesci^M ossei

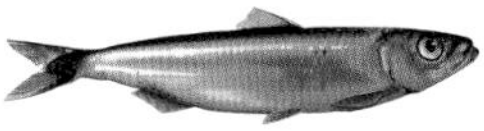

anchovy
boquerón^M
anchois^M
Sardelle^F
acciuga^F

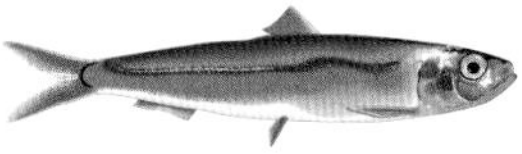

sardine
sardina^F
sardine^F
Sardine^F
sardina^F

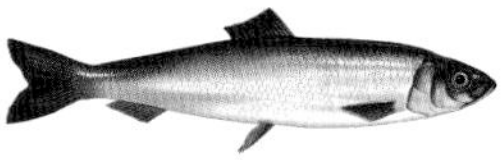

herring
arenque^M
hareng^M
Hering^M
aringa^F

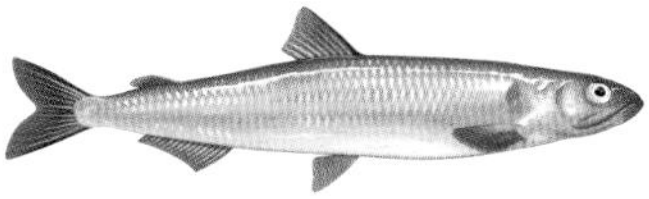

smelt
eperlano^M
éperlan^M
Stint^M
sperlano^M

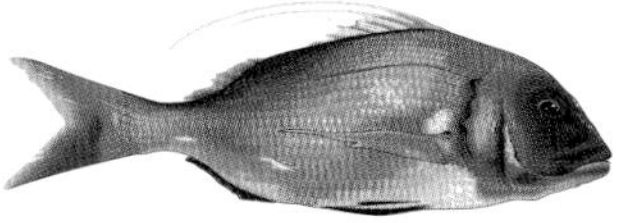

sea bream
dorada^F
dorade^F
Goldbrasse^F
orata^F

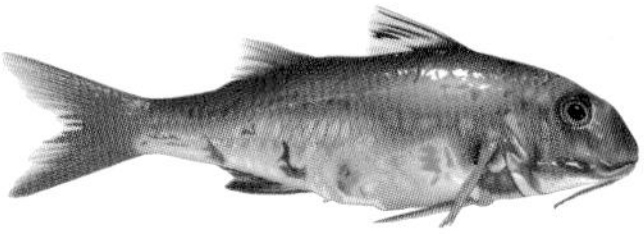

goatfish
salmonete^M
rouget^M barbet^M ; rouget^M
rote Meerbarbe^F
triglia^F

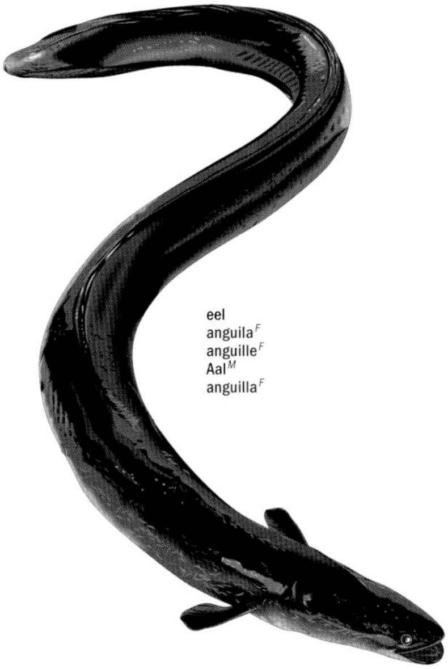

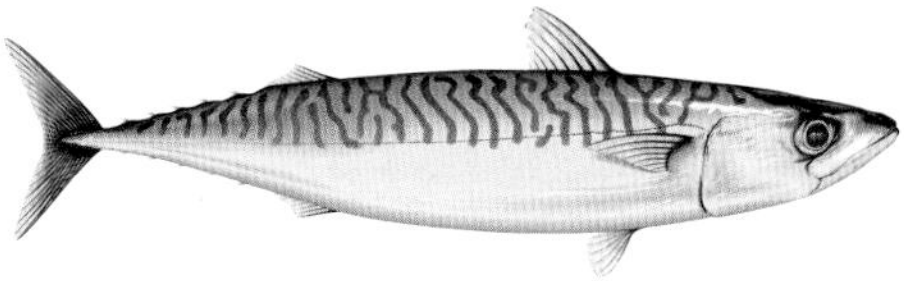

mackerel
caballa^F
maquereau^M
Makrele^F
sgombro^M

eel
anguila^F
anguille^F
Aal^M
anguilla^F

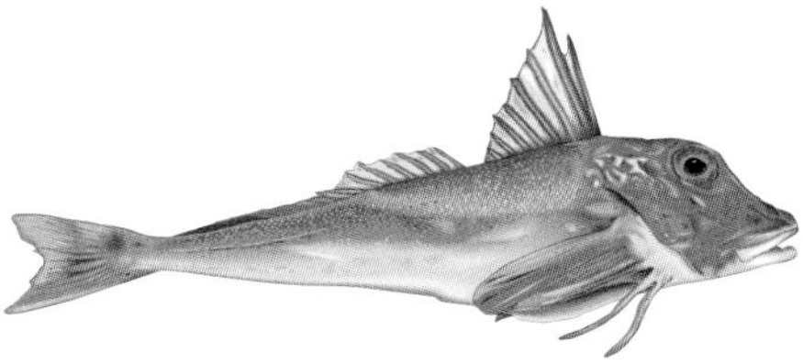

gurnard
rubio^M
grondin^M
Knurrhahn^M
pesce^M cappone^M

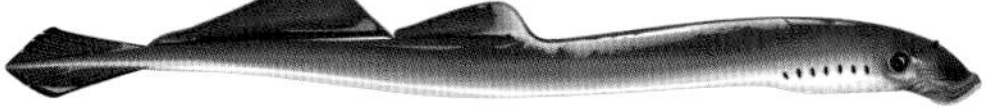

lamprey
lamprea^F
lamproie^F
Meerneunauge^N
lampreda^F

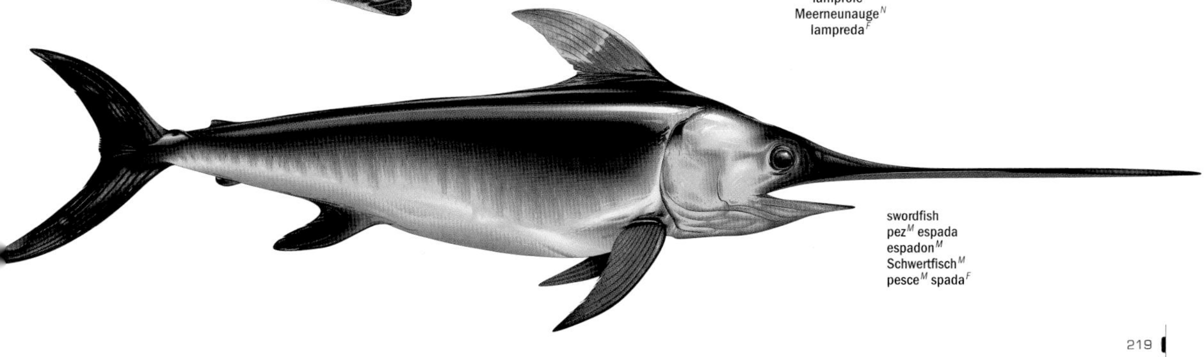

swordfish
pez^M espada
espadon^M
Schwertfisch^M
pesce^M spada^F

FOOD AND KITCHEN

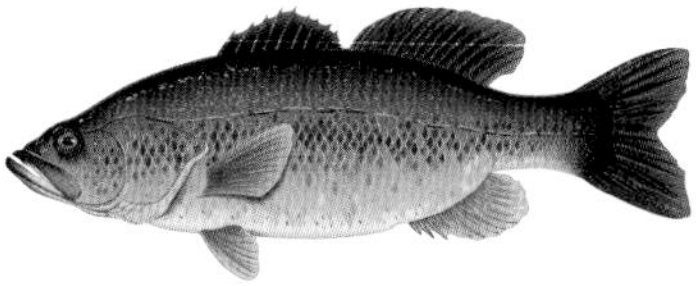

bass
róbalo[M]
perche[F] truitée ; achigan[M]
Barsch[M]
persico[M] trota[F]

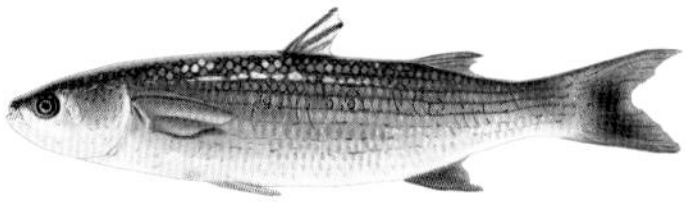

mullet
mújol[M]
mulet[M]
Meeräsche[F]
cefalo[M]

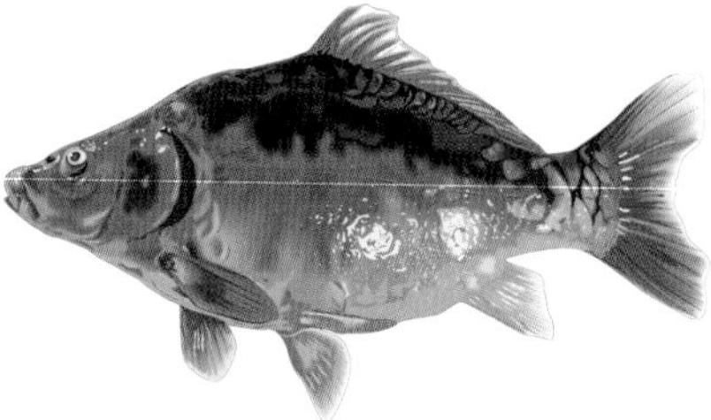

carp
carpa[F]
carpe[F]
Karpfen[M]
carpa[F]

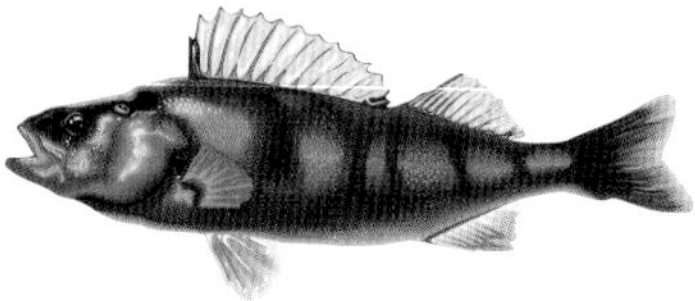

perch
perca[F]
perche[F] ; perchaude[F]
Flussbarsch[M]
persico[M]

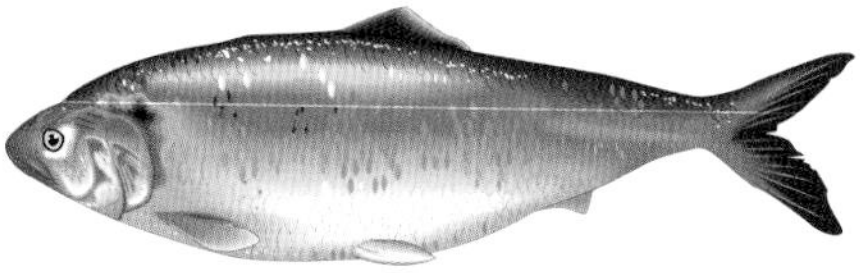

shad
sábalo[M]
alose[F]
Alse[F]
alosa[F]

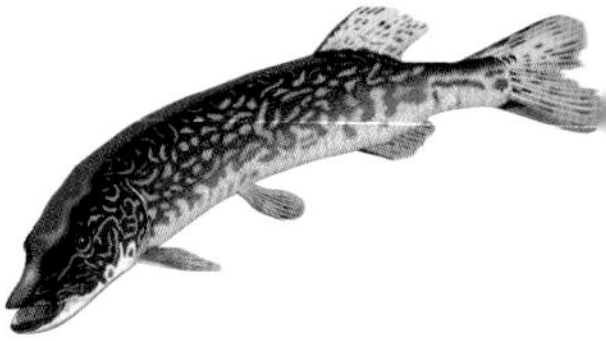

pike
lucio[M]
brochet[M]
Hecht[M]
luccio[M]

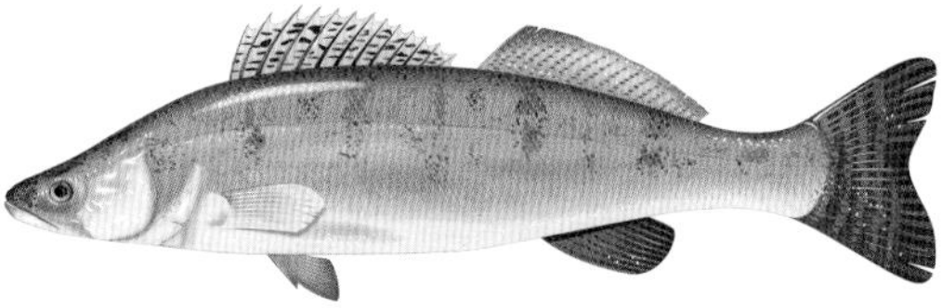

pike perch
lucioperca[M]
sandre[M] ; doré[M]
Zander[M]
lucioperca[M]

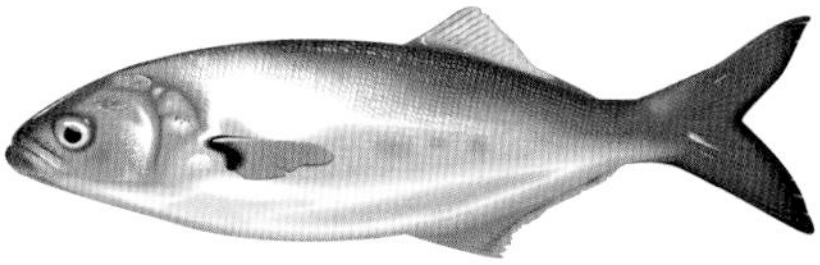

bluefish
anjova[F]
tassergal[M]
Blaufisch[M]
ballerino[M]

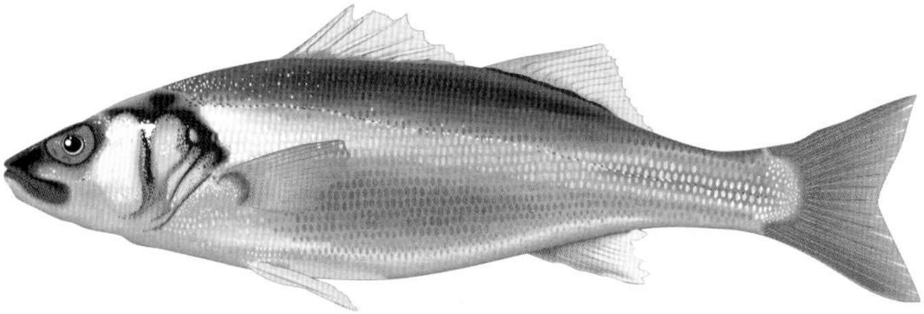

sea bass
lubina[F]
bar[M] commun
Seebarsch[M]
branzino[M]

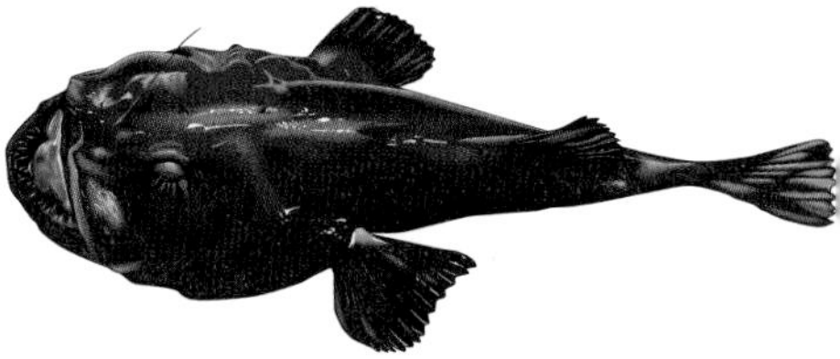

monkfish
rape[M]
baudroie[F]
Seeteufel[M]
pesce[M] rospo[M]

tuna
atún[M]
thon[M]
Thunfisch[M]
tonno[M]

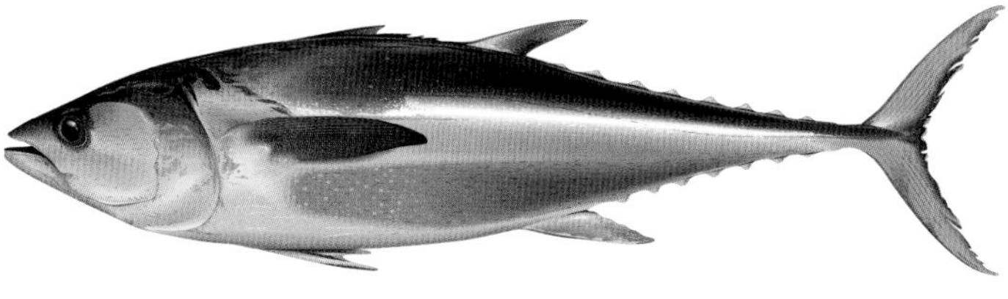

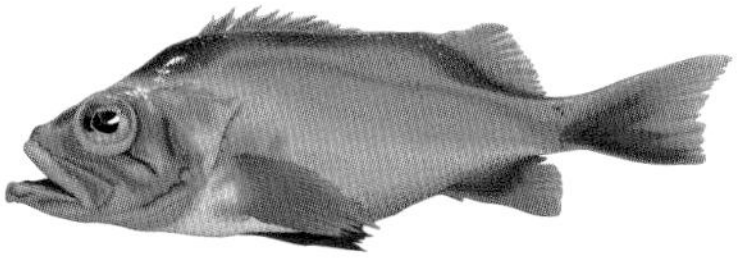

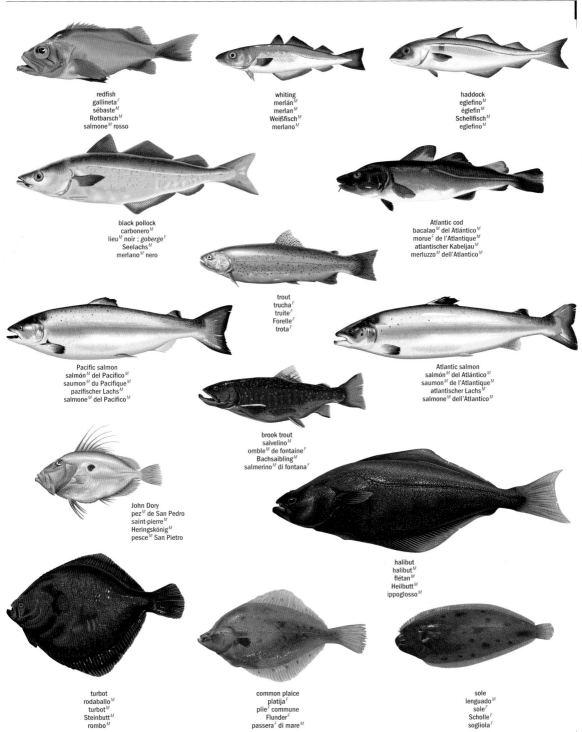

redfish
gallineta^F
sébaste^M
Rotbarsch^M
salmone^M rosso

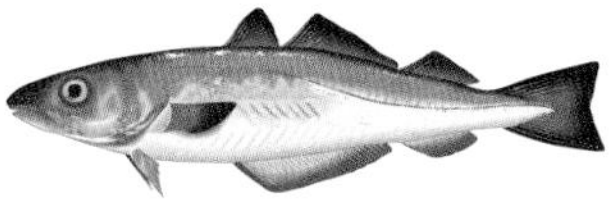

whiting
merlán^M
merlan^M
Weißfisch^M
merlano^M

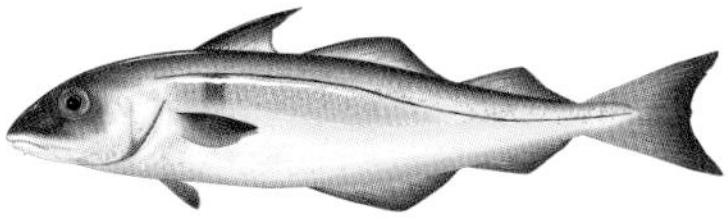

haddock
eglefino^M
églefin^M
Schellfisch^M
eglefino^M

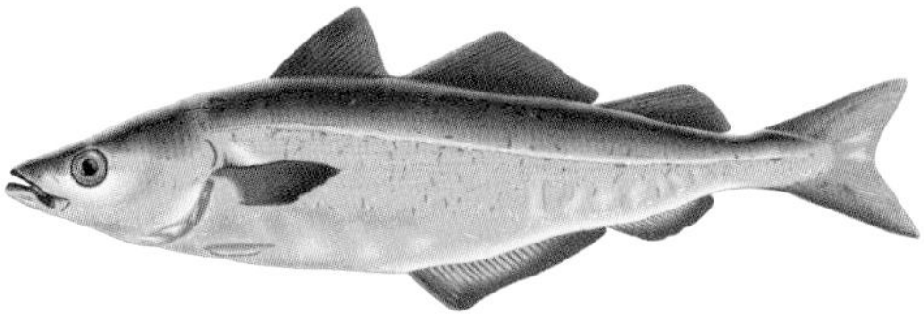

black pollock
carbonero^M
lieu^M noir ; goberge^F
Seelachs^M
merlano^M nero

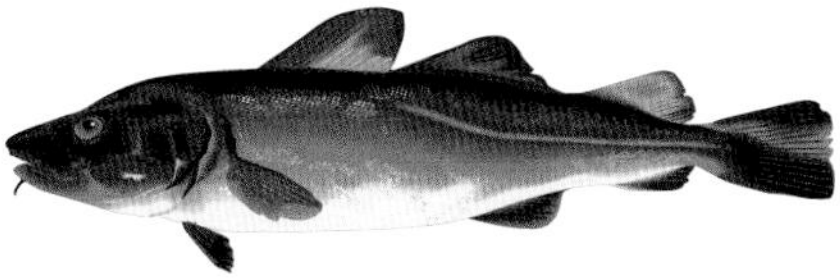

Atlantic cod
bacalao^M del Atlántico^M
morue^F de l'Atlantique^M
atlantischer Kabeljau^M
merluzzo^M dell'Atlantico^M

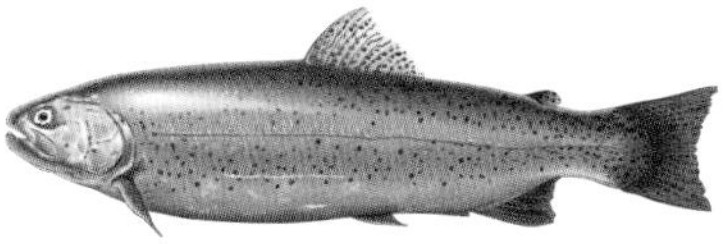

trout
trucha^F
truite^F
Forelle^F
trota^F

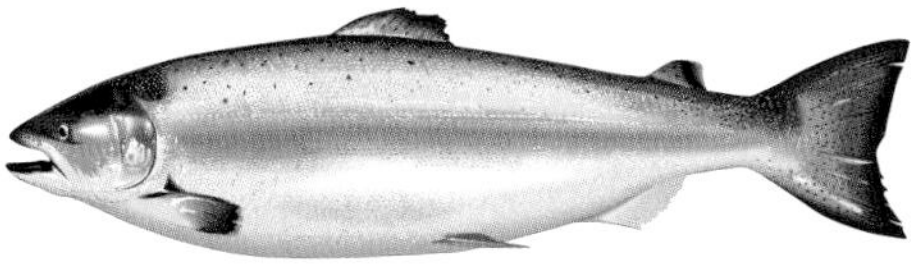

Pacific salmon
salmón^M del Pacífico^M
saumon^M du Pacifique^M
pazifischer Lachs^M
salmone^M del Pacífico^M

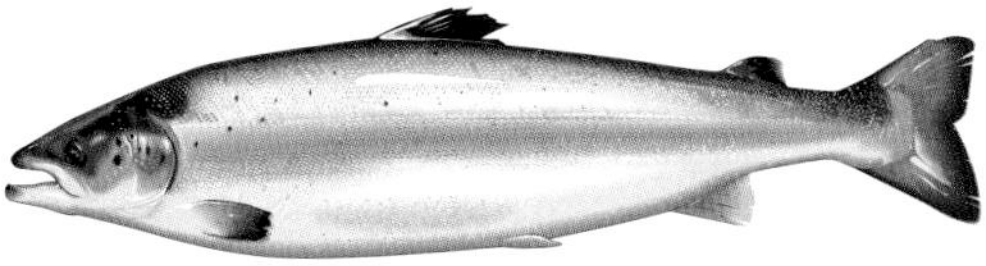

Atlantic salmon
salmón^M del Atlántico^M
saumon^M de l'Atlantique^M
atlantischer Lachs^M
salmone^M dell'Atlantico^M

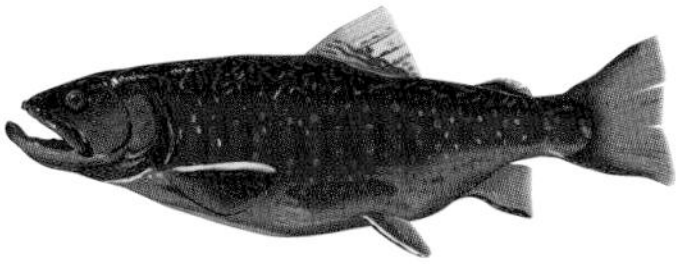

brook trout
salvelino^M
omble^M de fontaine^F
Bachsaibling^M
salmerino^M di fontana^F

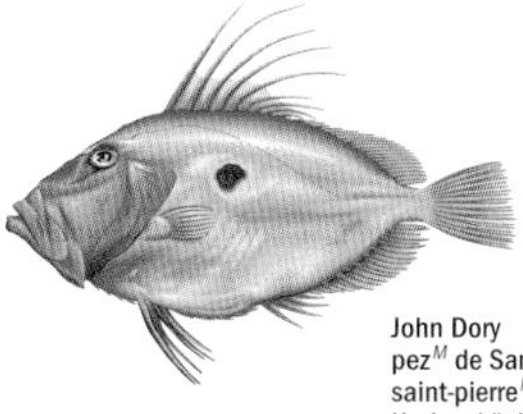

John Dory
pez^M de San Pedro
saint-pierre^M
Heringskönig^M
pesce^M San Pietro

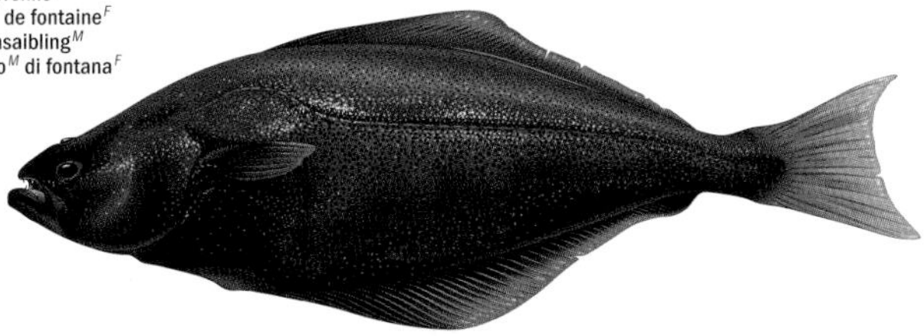

halibut
halibut^M
flétan^M
Heilbutt^M
ippoglosso^M

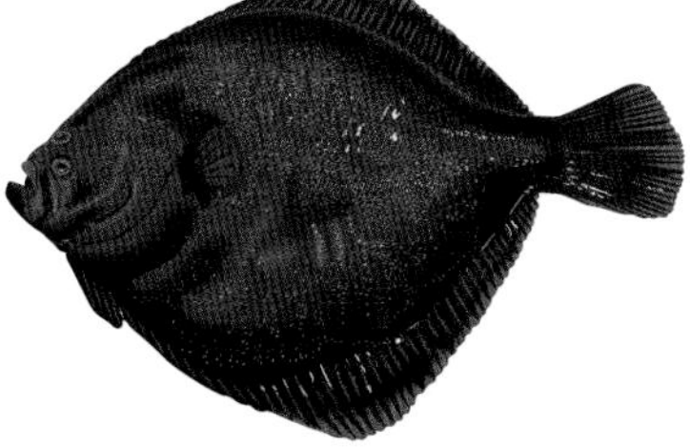

turbot
rodaballo^M
turbot^M
Steinbutt^M
rombo^M

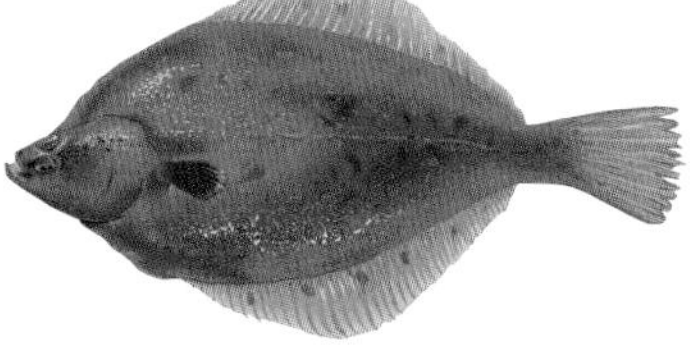

common plaice
platija^F
plie^F commune
Flunder^F
passera^F di mare^M

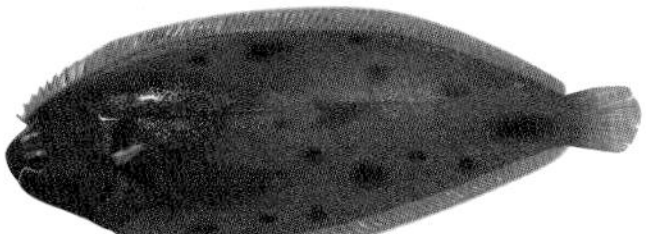

sole
lenguado^M
sole^F
Scholle^F
sogliola^F

packaging

envases^M | emballage^M | Verpackungen^F | confezioni^F

pouch
bolsa^F
sachet^M
Beutel^M
sacchetto^M

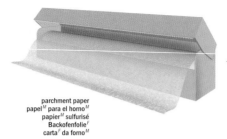

parchment paper
papel^M para el horno^M
papier^M sulfurisé
Backofenfolie^F
carta^F da forno^M

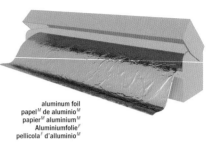

aluminum foil
papel^M de aluminio^M
papier^M aluminium^M
Aluminiumfolie^F
pellicola^F d'alluminio^M

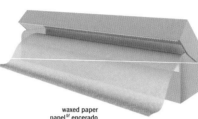

waxed paper
papel^M encerado
papier^M paraffiné ; papier^M ciré
Wachspapier^N
carta^F cerata

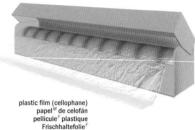

plastic film (cellophane)
papel^M de celofán
pellicule^F plastique
Frischhaltefolie^F
pellicola^F trasparente

freezer bag
bolsa^F para congelados^M
sac^M de congélation^F
Gefrierbeutel^M
sacchetto^M per freezer^M

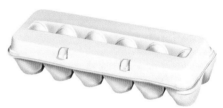

egg carton
cajas^F de cartón^M para huevos^M
boite^F à œufs^M
Eierkarton^M
confezione^F in cartone^M per uova^F

mesh bag
bolsa^F de malla^F
sac^M-filet^M
Netz^N
rete^F per alimenti^M

canisters
botes^M herméticos
boites^F alimentaires
Vorratsdosen^F
barattoli^M

food tray
barqueta^F
barquette^F
Schale^F
vaschetta^F per alimenti^M

small crate
caja^F pequeña
caissette^F
Kiste^F
cassetta^F piccola

small open crate
caja^F abierta
cageot^M
Holzkiste^F
cassetta^F aperta

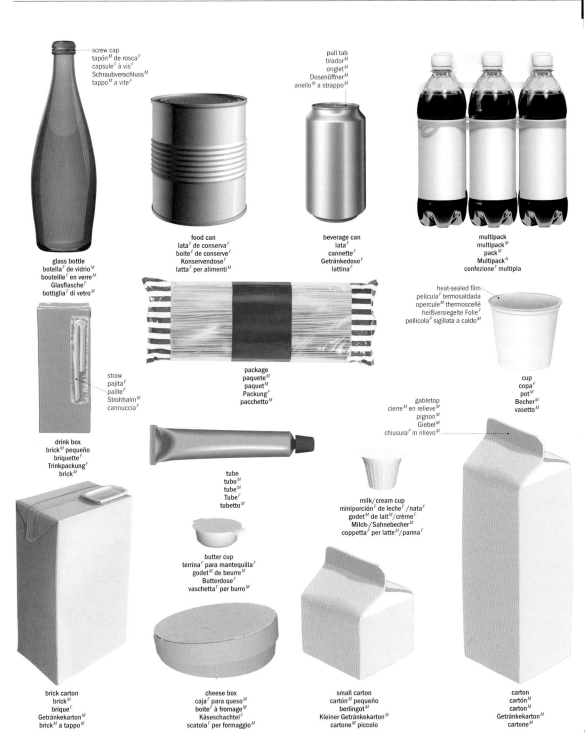

screw cap
tapón M de rosca F
capsule F à vis F
Schraubverschluss M
tappo M a vite F

pull tab
tirador M
onglet M
Dosenöffner M
anello M a strappo M

food can
lata F de conserva F
boite F de conserve F
Konservendose F
latta F per alimenti M

beverage can
lata F
cannette F
Getränkedose F
lattina F

multipack
multipack M
pack M
Multipack N
confezione F multipla

glass bottle
botella F de vidrio M
bouteille F en verre M
Glasflasche F
bottiglia F di vetro M

heat-sealed film
película F termosaldada
opercule M thermoscellé
heißversiegelte Folie F
pellicola F sigillata a caldo M

straw
pajita F
paille F
Strohhalm M
cannuccia F

package
paquete M
paquet M
Packung F
pacchetto M

cup
copa F
pot M
Becher M
vasetto M

drink box
brick M pequeño
briquette F
Trinkpackung F
brick M

gabletop
cierre M en relieve M
pignon M
Giebel M
chiusura F in rilievo M

tube
tubo M
tube M
Tube F
tubetto M

milk/cream cup
miniporción F de leche F /nata F
godet M de lait M/crème F
Milch-/Sahnebecher M
coppetta F per latte M/panna F

butter cup
terrina F para mantequilla F
godet M de beurre F
Butterdose F
vaschetta F per burro M

brick carton
brick M
brique F
Getränkekarton M
brick M a tappo M

cheese box
caja F para queso M
boite F à fromage M
Käseschachtel F
scatola F per formaggio M

small carton
cartón M pequeño
berlingot M
Kleiner Getränkekarton M
cartone M piccolo

carton
cartón M
carton M
Getränkekarton M
cartone M

FOOD AND KITCHEN

kitchen

cocina[F] | cuisine[F] | Küche[F] | cucina[F]

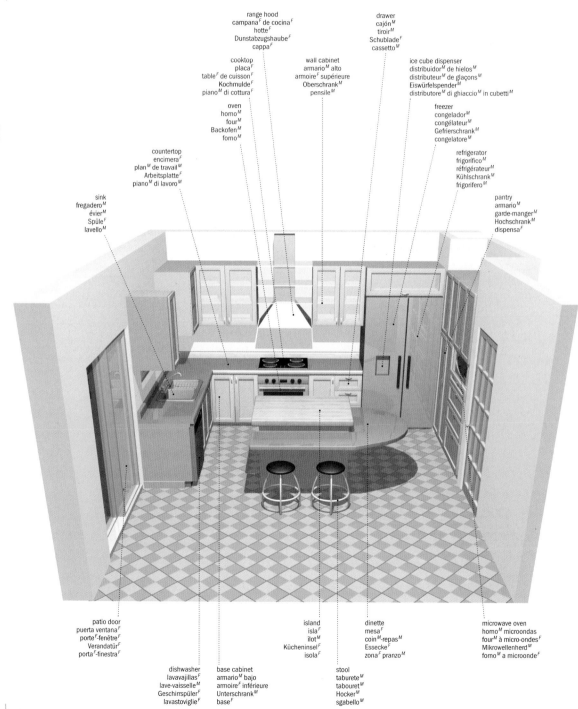

range hood
campana[F] de cocina[F]
hotte[F]
Dunstabzugshaube[F]
cappa[F]

drawer
cajón[M]
tiroir[M]
Schublade[F]
cassetto[M]

cooktop
placa[F]
table[F] de cuisson[F]
Kochmulde[F]
piano[M] di cottura[F]

wall cabinet
armario[M] alto
armoire[F] supérieure
Oberschrank[M]
pensile[M]

ice cube dispenser
distribuidor[M] de hielos[M]
distributeur[M] de glaçons[M]
Eiswürfelspender[M]
distributore[M] di ghiaccio[M] in cubetti[M]

oven
horno[M]
four[M]
Backofen[M]
forno[M]

freezer
congelador[M]
congélateur[M]
Gefrierschrank[M]
congelatore[M]

countertop
encimera[F]
plan[M] de travail[M]
Arbeitsplatte[F]
piano[M] di lavoro[M]

refrigerator
frigorifico[M]
réfrigérateur[M]
Kühlschrank[M]
frigorifero[M]

sink
fregadero[M]
évier[M]
Spüle[F]
lavello[M]

pantry
armario[M]
garde-manger[M]
Hochschrank[M]
dispensa[F]

patio door
puerta ventana[F]
porte[F]-fenêtre[F]
Verandatür[F]
porta[F]-finestra[F]

island
isla[F]
îlot[M]
Kücheninsel[F]
isola[F]

dinette
mesa[F]
coin[M]-repas[M]
Essecke[F]
zona[F] pranzo[M]

microwave oven
horno[M] microondas
four[M] à micro-ondes[F]
Mikrowellenherd[M]
forno[M] a microonde[F]

dishwasher
lavavajillas[F]
lave-vaisselle[M]
Geschirrspüler[M]
lavastoviglie[F]

base cabinet
armario[M] bajo
armoire[F] inférieure
Unterschrank[M]
base[F]

stool
taburete[M]
tabouret[M]
Hocker[M]
sgabello[M]

glassware

cristaleria ^{F} | verres ^{M} | Gläser ^{N} | cristalleria ^{F}

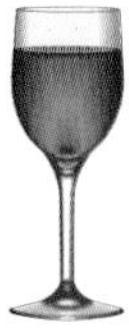

liqueur glass
copa ^{F} para licores ^{M}
verre ^{M} à liqueur ^{F}
Likörglas ^{N}
bicchierino ^{M} da liquore ^{M}

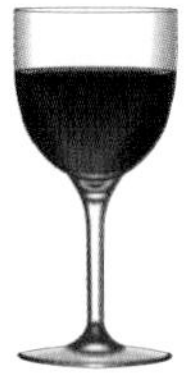

port glass
copa ^{F} para oporto ^{M}
verre ^{M} à porto ^{M}
Portweinglas ^{N}
bicchiere ^{M} da porto ^{M}

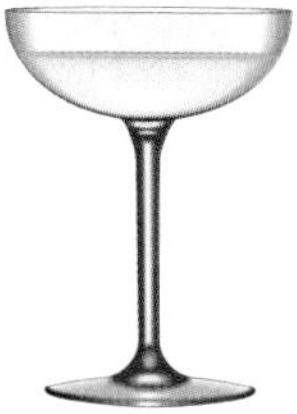

sparkling wine glass
copa ^{F} de champaña ^{F}
coupe ^{F} à mousseux ^{M}
Sektschale ^{F}
coppa ^{F} da spumante ^{M}

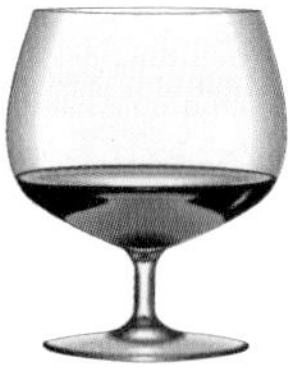

brandy snifter
copa ^{F} para brandy ^{M}
verre ^{M} à cognac ^{M}
Kognakschwenker ^{M}
bicchiere ^{M} da brandy ^{M}

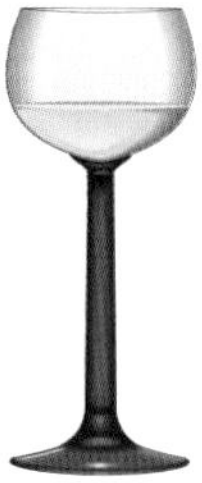

Alsace glass
copa ^{F} para vino ^{M} de Alsacia
verre ^{M} à vin ^{M} d'Alsace ^{F}
Elsassglas ^{N}
bicchiere ^{M} da vino ^{M} alsaziano

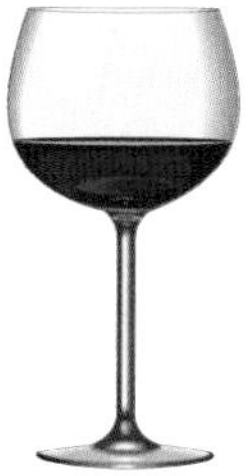

burgundy glass
copa ^{F} para vino ^{M} de Borgoña
verre ^{M} à bourgogne ^{M}
Rotweinglas ^{N}
bicchiere ^{M} da Borgogna ^{M}

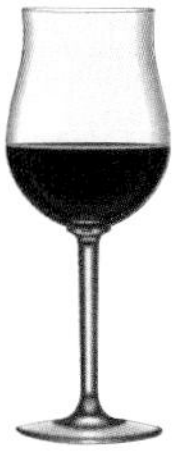

bordeaux glass
copa ^{F} para vino ^{M} de Burdeos
verre ^{M} à bordeaux ^{M}
Bordeauxglas ^{N}
bicchiere ^{M} da Bordeaux ^{M}

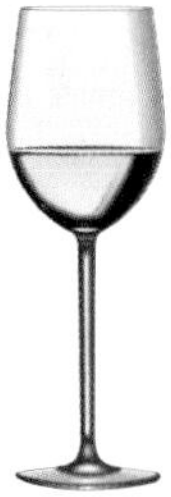

white wine glass
copa ^{F} para vino ^{M} blanco
verre ^{M} à vin ^{M} blanc
Weißweinglas ^{N}
bicchiere ^{M} da vino ^{M} bianco

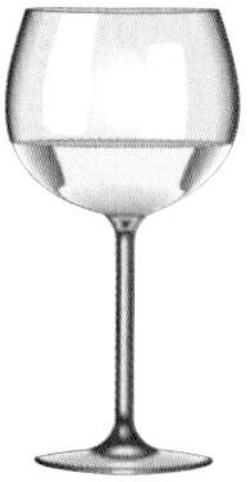

water goblet
copa ^{F} de agua ^{F}
verre ^{M} à eau ^{F}
Wasserglas ^{N}
bicchiere ^{M} da acqua ^{F}

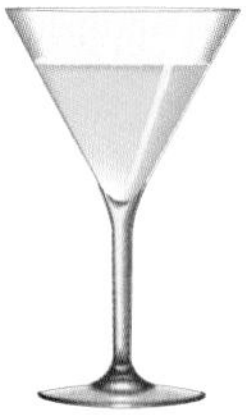

cocktail glass
copa ^{F} de cóctel ^{M}
verre ^{M} à cocktail ^{M}
Cocktailglas ^{N}
calice ^{M} da cocktail ^{M}

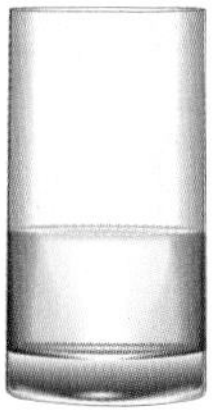

highball glass
vaso ^{M} largo
verre ^{M} à gin ^{M}
Longdrinkglas ^{N}
bicchiere ^{M} da bibita ^{F}

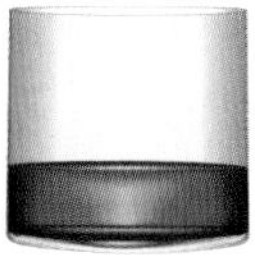

old-fashioned glass
vaso ^{M} corto
verre ^{M} à whisky ^{M}
Whiskyglas ^{M}
tumbler ^{M}

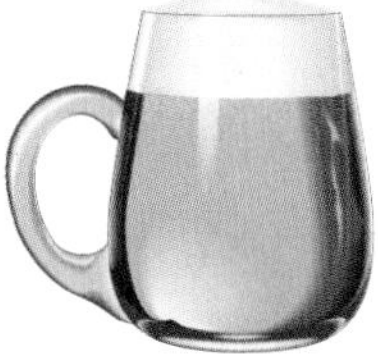

beer mug
jarra ^{M} de cerveza ^{F}
chope ^{F} à bière ^{F}
Bierkrug ^{M}
boccale ^{M} da birra ^{F}

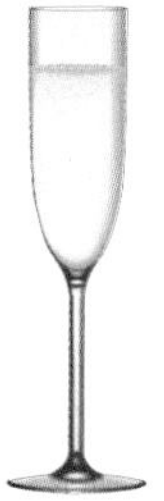

champagne flute
copa ^{F} de flauta ^{F}
flûte ^{F} à champagne ^{M}
Sektkelch ^{M}
flûte ^{M}

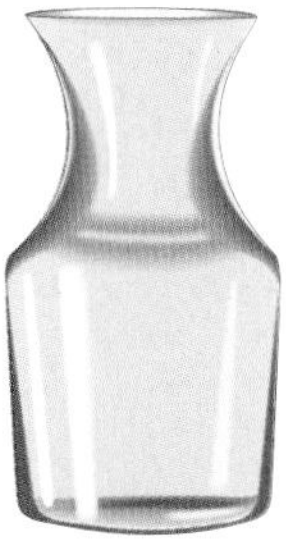

small decanter
decantador ^{M}
carafon ^{M}
kleine Karaffe ^{F}
caraffa ^{F}

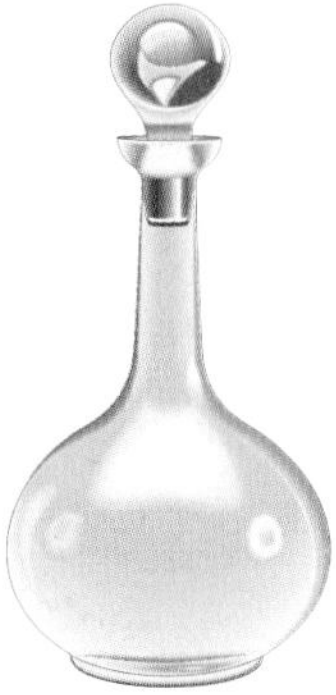

decanter
garrafa ^{F}
carafe ^{F}
Karaffe ^{F}
bottiglia ^{F} da tavola ^{F}

FOOD AND KITCHEN

dinnerware

vajilla^F y servicio^M de mesa^F | vaisselle^F | Geschirr^N | vasellame^M da tavola^F

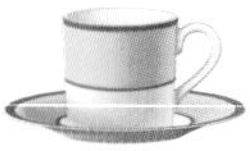

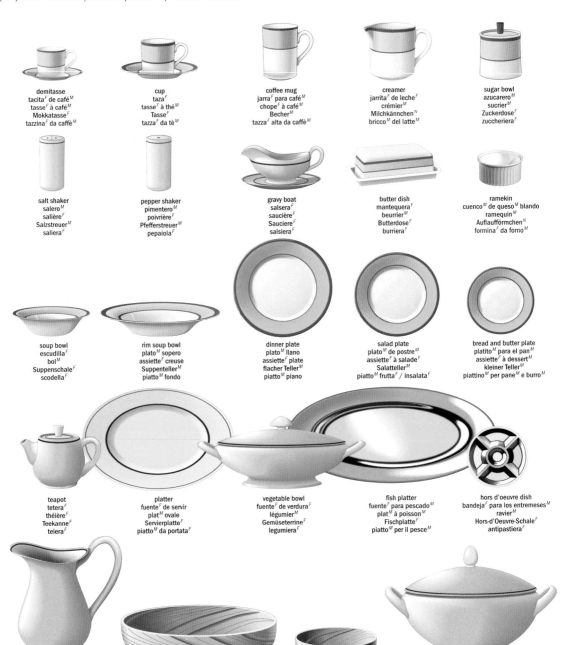

demitasse
tacita^F de café^M
tasse^F à café^M
Mokkatasse^F
tazzina^F da caffè^M

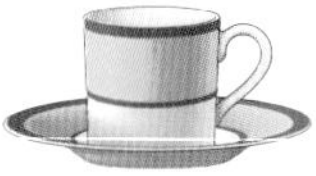

cup
taza^F
tasse^F à thé^M
Tasse^F
tazza^F da tè^M

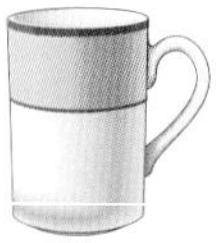

coffee mug
jarra^F para café^M
chope^F à café^M
Becher^M
tazza^F alta da caffè^M

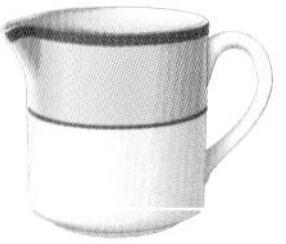

creamer
jarrita^F de leche^F
crémier^M
Milchkännchen^N
bricco^M del latte^M

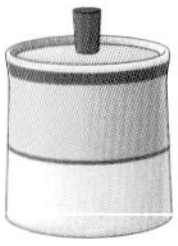

sugar bowl
azucarero^M
sucrier^M
Zuckerdose^F
zuccheriera^F

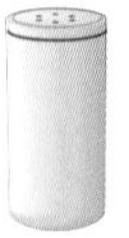

salt shaker
salero^M
salière^F
Salzstreuer^M
saliera^F

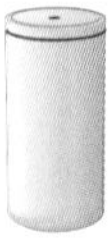

pepper shaker
pimentero^M
poivrière^F
Pfefferstreuer^M
pepaiola^F

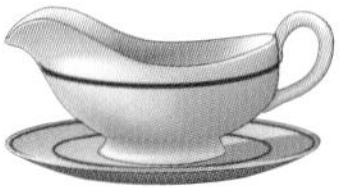

gravy boat
salsera^F
saucière^F
Sauciere^F
salsiera^F

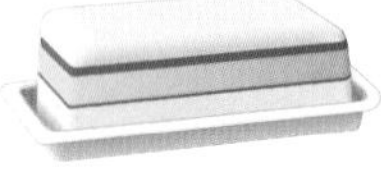

butter dish
mantequera^F
beurrier^M
Butterdose^F
burriera^F

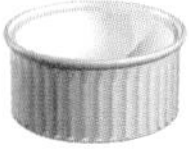

ramekin
cuenco^M de queso^M blando
ramequin^M
Auflaufförmchen^N
formina^F da forno^M

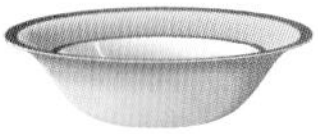

soup bowl
escudilla^F
bol^M
Suppenschale^F
scodella^F

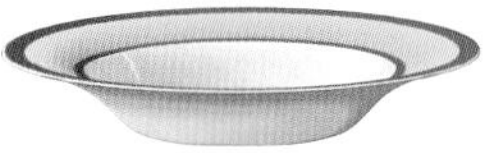

rim soup bowl
plato^M sopero
assiette^F creuse
Suppenteller^M
piatto^M fondo

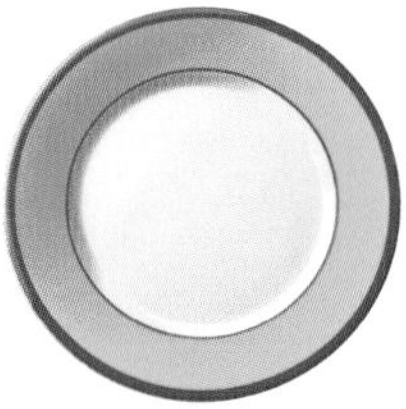

dinner plate
plato^M llano
assiette^F plate
flacher Teller^M
piatto^M piano

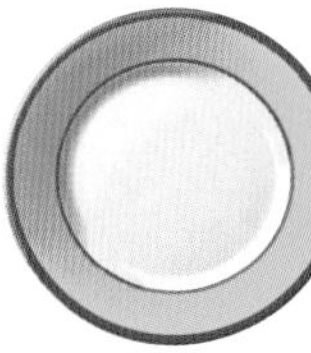

salad plate
plato^M de postre^M
assiette^F à salade^F
Salatteller^M
piatto^M frutta^F / insalata^F

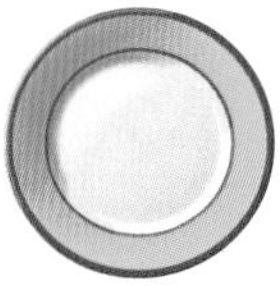

bread and butter plate
platito^M para el pan^M
assiette^F à dessert^M
kleiner Teller^M
piattino^M per pane^M e burro^M

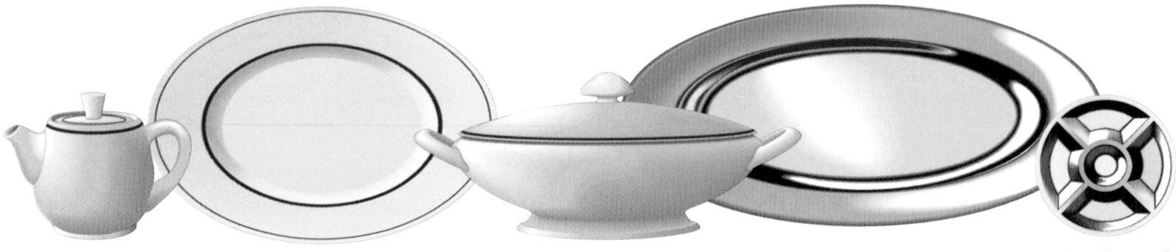

teapot
tetera^F
théière^F
Teekanne^F
teiera^F

platter
fuente^F de servir
plat^M ovale
Servierplatte^F
piatto^M da portata^F

vegetable bowl
fuente^F de verdura^F
légumier^M
Gemüseterrine^F
legumiera^F

fish platter
fuente^F para pescado^M
plat^M à poisson^M
Fischplatte^F
piatto^M per il pesce^M

hors d'oeuvre dish
bandeja^F para los entremeses^M
ravier^M
Hors-d'Oeuvre-Schale^F
antipastiera^F

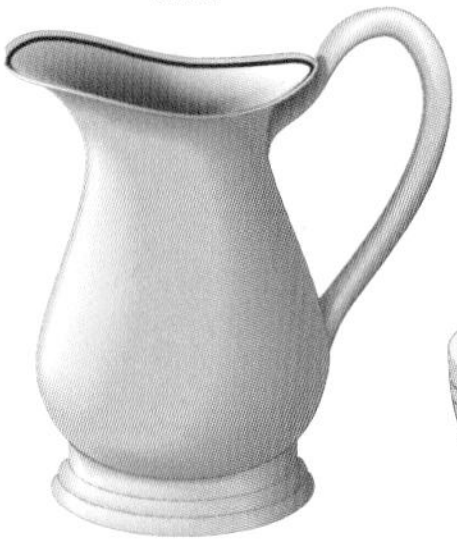

water pitcher
jarra^F de agua^F
pichet^M
Wasserkrug^M
caraffa^F

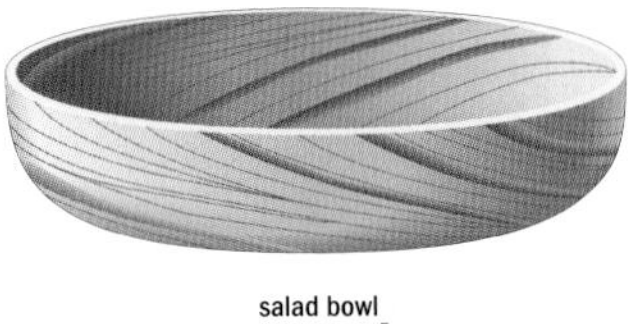

salad bowl
ensaladera^F
saladier^M
Salatschüssel^F
insalatiera^F

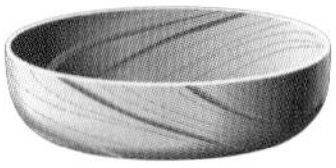

salad dish
bol^M para ensalada^F
bol^M à salade^F
Salatschale^F
coppetta^F per l'insalata^F

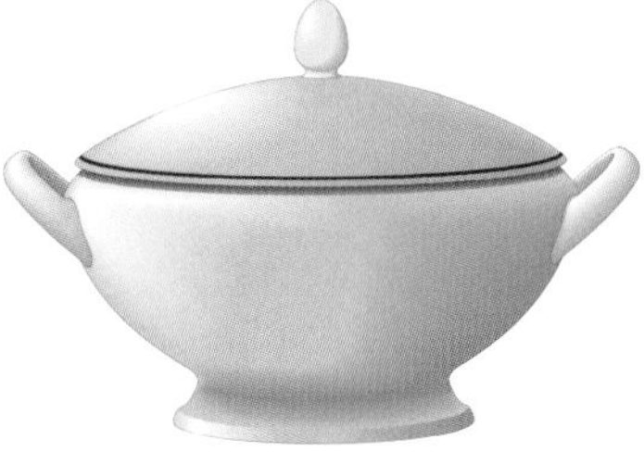

soup tureen
sopera^F
soupière^F
Suppenterrine^F
zuppiera^F

silverware

cubertería^F | couvert^M | Silberbesteck^N | posatería^F

knife
cuchillo^M
couteau^M
Messer^N
coltello^M

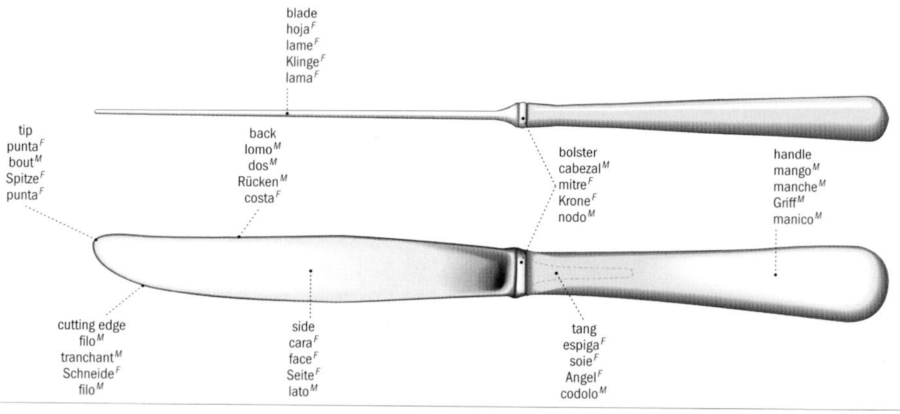

blade
hoja^F
lame^F
Klinge^F
lama^F

tip
punta^F
bout^M
Spitze^F
punta^F

back
lomo^M
dos^M
Rücken^M
costa^F

bolster
cabezal^M
mitre^F
Krone^F
nodo^M

handle
mango^M
manche^M
Griff^M
manico^M

cutting edge
filo^M
tranchant^M
Schneide^F
filo^M

side
cara^F
face^F
Seite^F
lato^M

tang
espiga^F
soie^F
Angel^F
codolo^M

fork
tenedor^M
fourchette^F
Gabel^F
forchetta^F

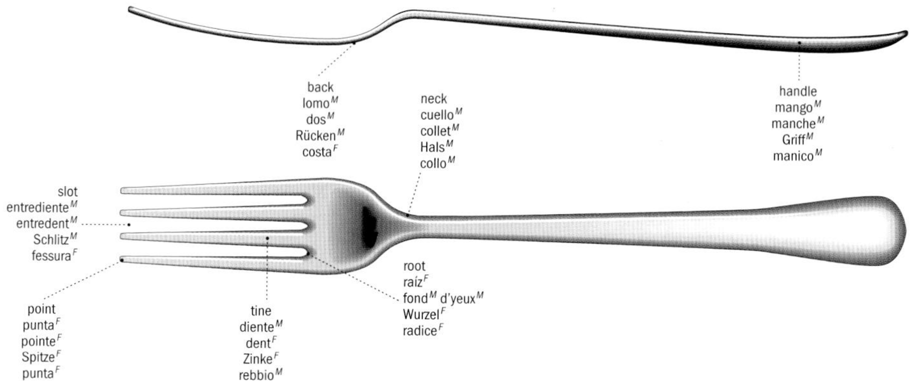

back
lomo^M
dos^M
Rücken^M
costa^F

neck
cuello^M
collet^M
Hals^M
collo^M

handle
mango^M
manche^M
Griff^M
manico^M

slot
entrediente^M
entredent^M
Schlitz^M
fessura^F

root
raíz^F
fond^M d'yeux^M
Wurzel^F
radice^F

point
punta^F
pointe^F
Spitze^F
punta^F

tine
diente^M
dent^F
Zinke^F
rebbio^M

spoon
cuchara^F
cuiller^F
Löffel^M
cucchiaio^M

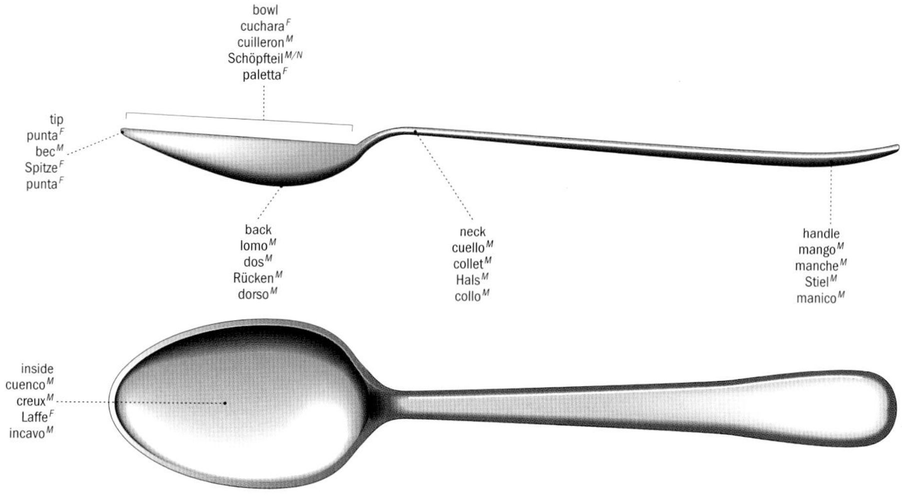

bowl
cuchara^F
cuilleron^M
Schöpfteil^{M/N}
paletta^F

tip
punta^F
bec^M
Spitze^F
punta^F

back
lomo^M
dos^M
Rücken^M
dorso^M

neck
cuello^M
collet^M
Hals^M
collo^M

handle
mango^M
manche^M
Stiel^M
manico^M

inside
cuenco^M
creux^M
Laffe^F
incavo^M

silverware

examples of forks
ejemplos^M de tenedores^F
exemples^M de fourchettes^F
Beispiele^N für Gabeln^F
esempi^M di forchette^F

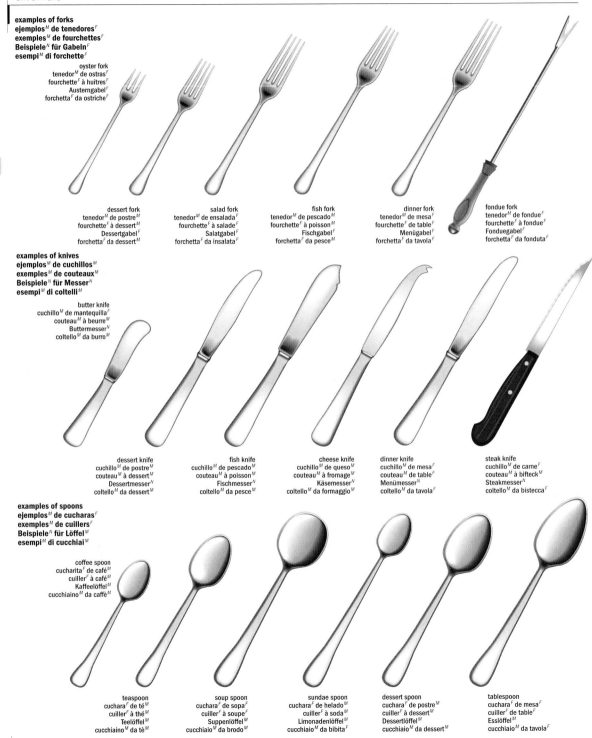

oyster fork
tenedor^M de ostras^F
fourchette^F à huîtres^F
Austerngabel^F
forchetta^F da ostriche^F

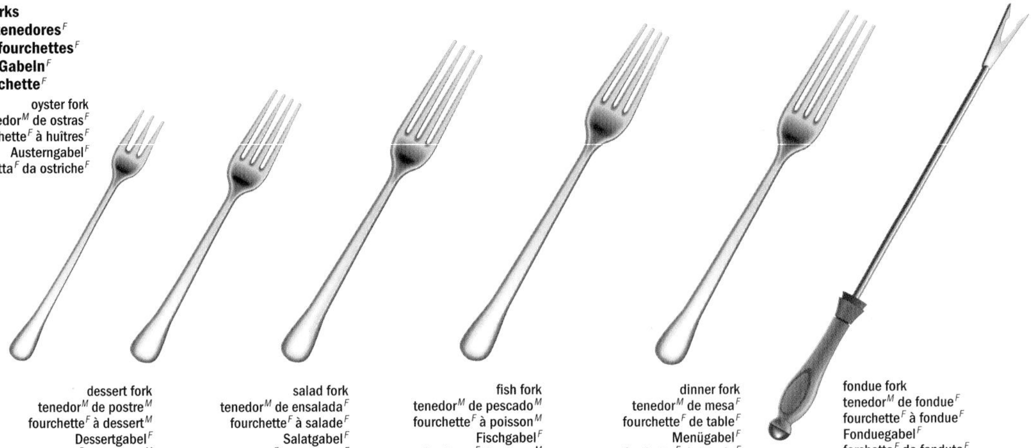

dessert fork
tenedor^M de postre^M
fourchette^F à dessert^M
Dessertgabel^F
forchetta^F da dessert^M

salad fork
tenedor^M de ensalada^F
fourchette^F à salade^F
Salatgabel^F
forchetta^F da insalata^F

fish fork
tenedor^M de pescado^M
fourchette^F à poisson^M
Fischgabel^F
forchetta^F da pesce^M

dinner fork
tenedor^M de mesa^F
fourchette^F de table^F
Menügabel^F
forchetta^F da tavola^F

fondue fork
tenedor^M de fondue^F
fourchette^F à fondue^F
Fonduegabel^F
forchetta^F da fonduta^F

examples of knives
ejemplos^M de cuchillos^M
exemples^M de couteaux^M
Beispiele^N für Messer^N
esempi^M di coltelli^M

butter knife
cuchillo^M de mantequilla^F
couteau^M à beurre^M
Buttermesser^N
coltello^M da burro^M

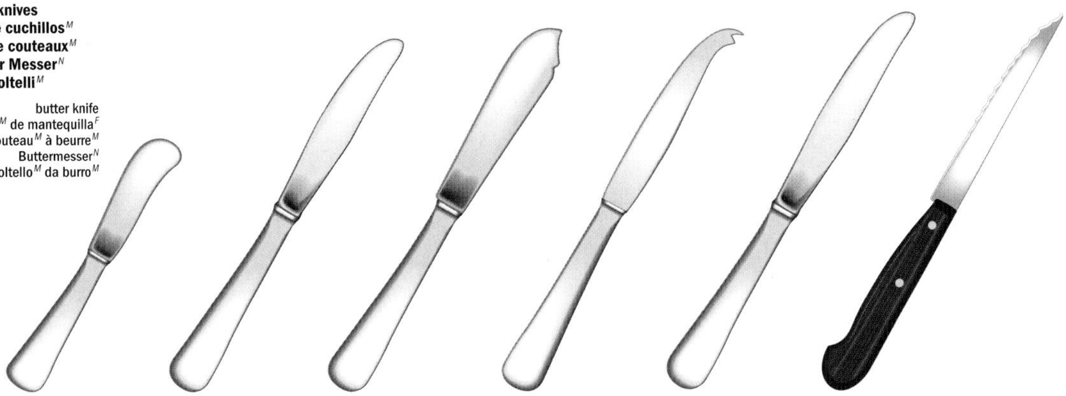

dessert knife
cuchillo^M de postre^M
couteau^M à dessert^M
Dessertmesser^N
coltello^M da dessert^M

fish knife
cuchillo^M de pescado^M
couteau^M à poisson^M
Fischmesser^N
coltello^M da pesce^M

cheese knife
cuchillo^M de queso^M
couteau^M à fromage^M
Käsemesser^N
coltello^M da formaggio^M

dinner knife
cuchillo^M de mesa^F
couteau^M de table^F
Menümesser^N
coltello^M da tavola^F

steak knife
cuchillo^M de carne^F
couteau^M à bifteck^M
Steakmesser^N
coltello^M da bistecca^F

examples of spoons
ejemplos^M de cucharas^F
exemples^M de cuillers^F
Beispiele^N für Löffel^M
esempi^M di cucchiai^M

coffee spoon
cucharita^F de café^M
cuiller^F à café^M
Kaffeelöffel^M
cucchiaino^M da caffè^M

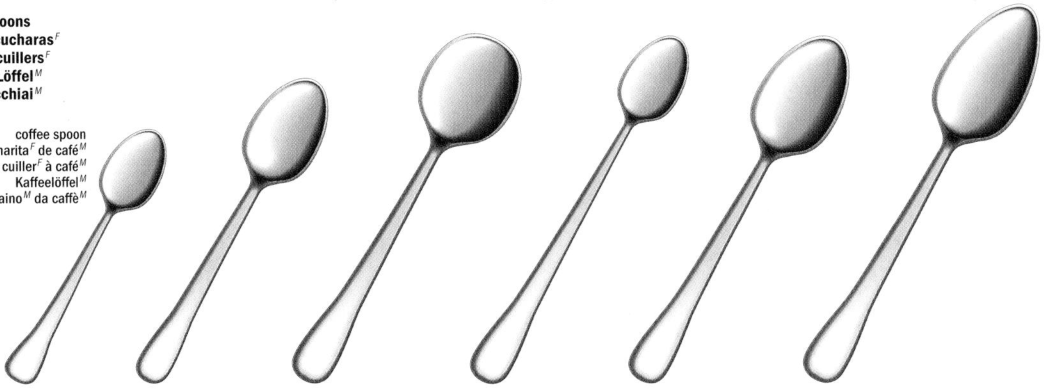

teaspoon
cuchara^F de té^M
cuiller^F à thé^M
Teelöffel^M
cucchiaino^M da tè^M

soup spoon
cuchara^F de sopa^F
cuiller^F à soupe^F
Suppenlöffel^M
cucchiaio^M da brodo^M

sundae spoon
cuchara^F de helado^M
cuiller^F à soda^M
Limonadenlöffel^M
cucchiaio^M da bibita^F

dessert spoon
cuchara^F de postre^M
cuiller^F à dessert^M
Dessertlöffel^M
cucchiaio^M da dessert^M

tablespoon
cuchara^F de mesa^F
cuiller^F de table^F
Esslöffel^M
cucchiaio^M da tavola^F

FOOD AND KITCHEN

228

kitchen utensils

utensilios^M de cocina^F | ustensiles^M de cuisine^F | Küchenutensilien^N | utensili^M da cucina^F

FOOD AND KITCHEN

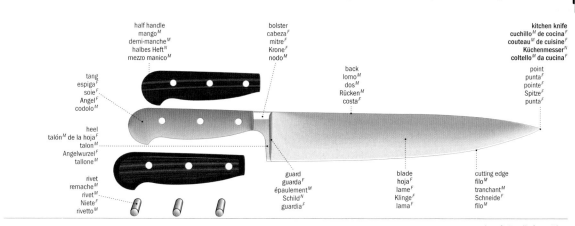

half handle
mango^M
demi-manche^M
halbes Heft^N
mezzo manico^M

bolster
cabeza^F
mitre^F
Krone^F
nodo^M

kitchen knife
cuchillo^M de cocina^F
couteau^M de cuisine^F
Küchenmesser^N
coltello^M da cucina^F

tang
espiga^F
soie^F
Angel^F
codolo^M

back
lomo^M
dos^M
Rücken^M
costa^F

point
punta^F
pointe^F
Spitze^F
punta^F

heel
talón^M de la hoja^F
talon^M
Angelwurzel^F
tallone^M

guard
guarda^F
épaulement^M
Schild^N
guardia^F

blade
hoja^F
lame^F
Klinge^F
lama^F

cutting edge
filo^M
tranchant^M
Schneide^F
filo^M

rivet
remache^M
rivet^M
Niete^F
rivetto^M

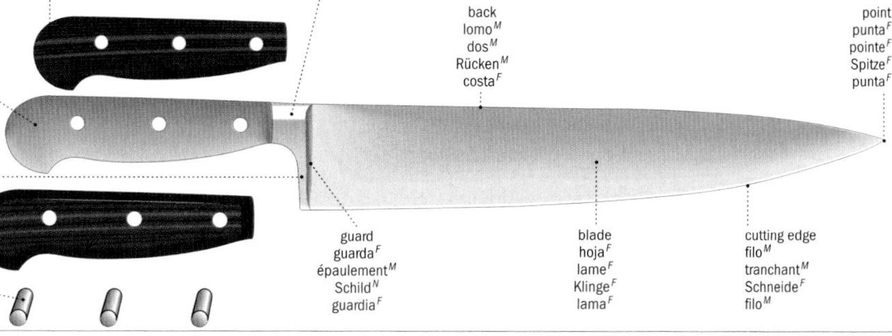

examples of utensils for cutting
ejemplos^M de cuchillos^M de cocina^F
exemples^M de couteaux^M de cuisine^F
Beispiele^N für Küchenmesser^N
esempi^M di coltelli^M da cucina^F

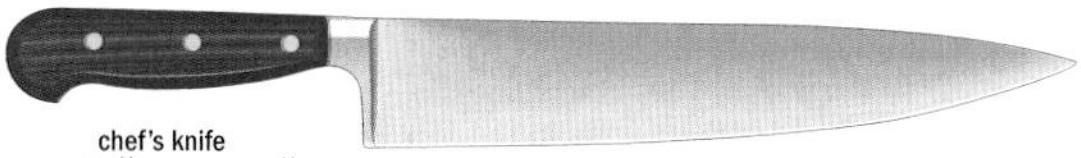

chef's knife
cuchillo^M de carnicero^M
couteau^M de chef^M
Kochmesser^N
coltello^M da cucina^F

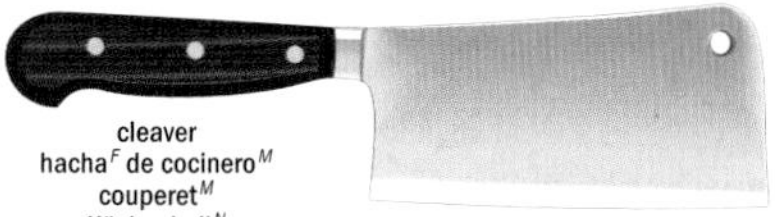

cleaver
hacha^F de cocinero^M
couperet^M
Küchenbeil^N
mannaia^F

bread knife
cuchillo^M de pan^M
couteau^M à pain^M
Brotmesser^N
coltello^M da pane^M

carving knife
cuchillo^M de trinchar
couteau^M à découper
Tranchiermesser^N
trinciante^M

ham knife
cuchillo^M para jamón^M
couteau^M à jambon^M
Schinkenmesser^N
coltello^M da prosciutto^M

filleting knife
cuchillo^M filetero
couteau^M à filets^M de sole^F
Filiermesser^N
coltello^M per affettare

paring knife
cuchillo^M de pelar
couteau^M d'office^M
Schälmesser^N
spelucchino^M

carving fork
tenedor^M de trinchar
fourchette^F à découper
Tranchiergabel^F
forchettone^M

boning knife
cuchillo^M para deshuesar
couteau^M à désosser
Ausbeinmesser^N
coltello^M per disossare

sharpening steel
afilador^M
fusil^M
Wetzstahl^M
acciaiolo^M

sharpening stone
piedra^F de afilar
pierre^F à affûter
Wetzstein^M
pietra^F affilacoltelli

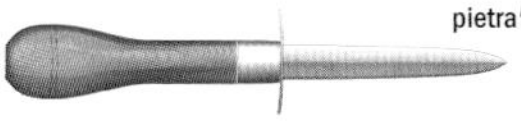

cutting board
tabla^F de cortar
planche^F à découper
Schneidbrett^N
tagliere^M

grapefruit knife
cuchillo^M para pomelos^M
couteau^M à pamplemousse^M
Grapefruitmesser^N
coltello^M da pompelmo^M

oyster knife
cuchillo^M para ostras^F
couteau^M à huitres^F
Austernmesser^N
coltello^M da ostriche^F

zester
rallador^M
couteau^M à zester
Zitronenschaber^M
sbuccialimoni^M

peeler
pelapatatas^M
éplucheur^M
Schäler^M
sbucciatore^M

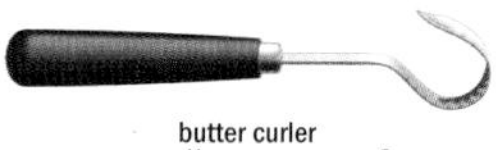

butter curler
rizador^M de mantequilla^F
coquilleur^M à beurre^M
Butterroller^M
arricciaburro^M

groove
ranura^F
rainure^F
Saftrinne^F
scanalatura^F

kitchen utensils

for opening
para abrir y descorchar
pour ouvrir
zum Öffnen^N
per aprire

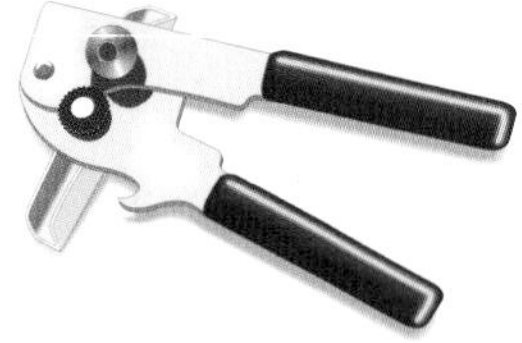

can opener
abrelatas^M
ouvre-boites^M
Büchsenöffner^M
apriscatole^M

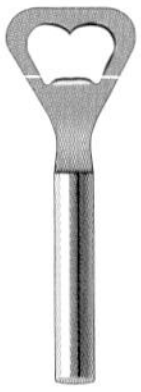

bottle opener
abrebotellas^M
décapsuleur^M
Flaschenöffner^M
apribottiglie^M

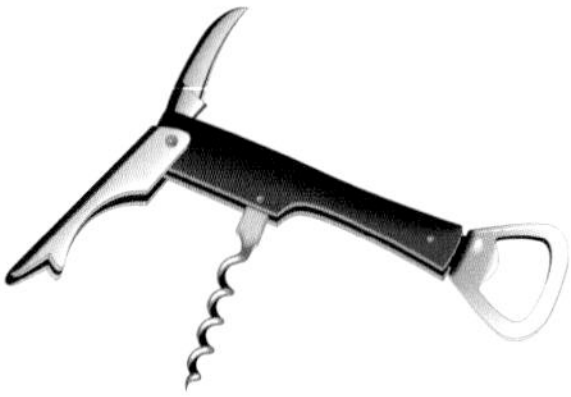

waiter's corkscrew
sacacorchos^M
tire-bouchon^M de sommelier^M
Kellnerbesteck^N
cavatappi^M da cameriere^M

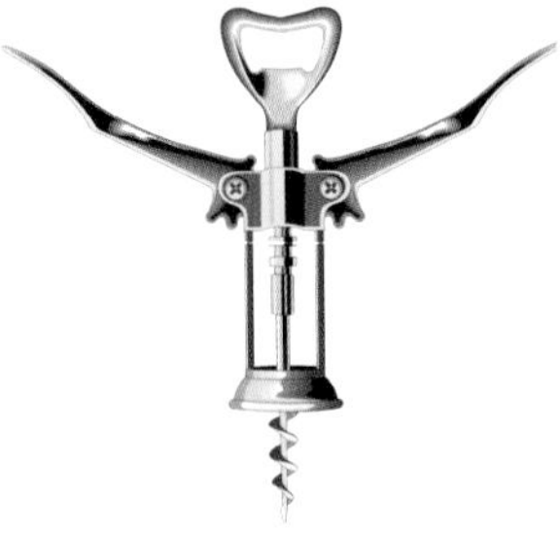

lever corkscrew
sacacorchos^M con brazos^M
tire-bouchon^M à levier^M
Hebel-Korkenzieher^M
cavatappi^M a leva^F

for grinding and grating
para moler y rallar
pour broyer et râper
zum Zerkleinern^N **und Zerreiben**^{N}
per macinare e grattugiare

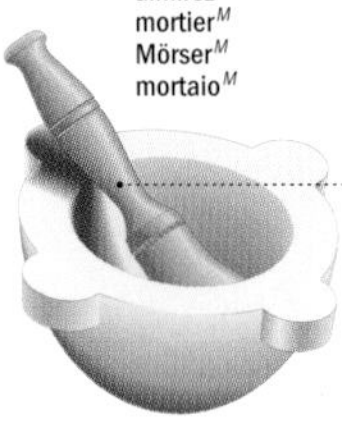

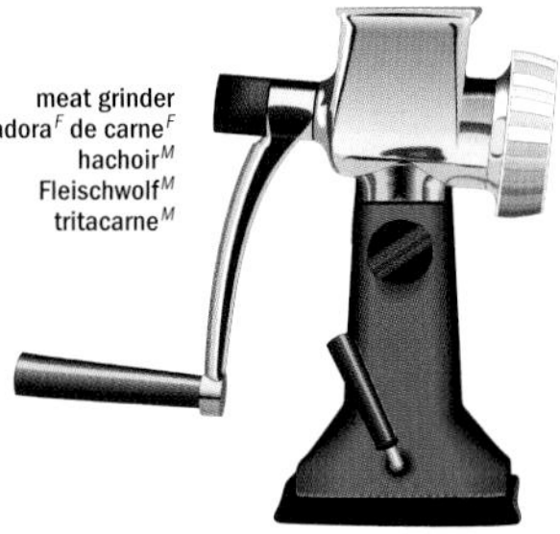

nutcracker
cascanueces^M
casse-noix^M
Nussknacker^M
schiaccianoci^M

mortar
almirez^M
mortier^M
Mörser^M
mortaio^M

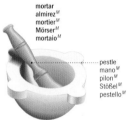

pestle
mano^M
pilon^M
Stößel^M
pestello^M

meat grinder
picadora^F de carne^F
hachoir^M
Fleischwolf^M
tritacarne^M

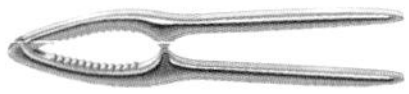

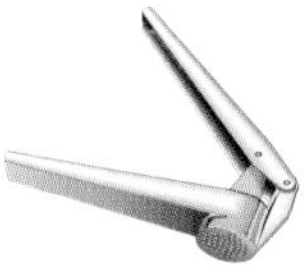

garlic press
triturador^M de ajos^M
presse-ail^M
Knoblauchpresse^F
spremiaglio^M

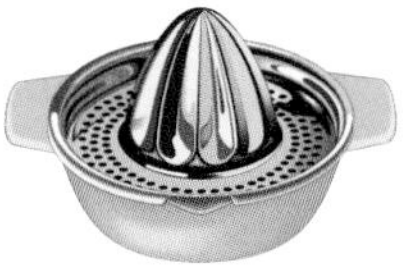

citrus juicer
exprimidor^M
presse-agrumes^M
Zitronenpresse^F
spremiagrumi^M

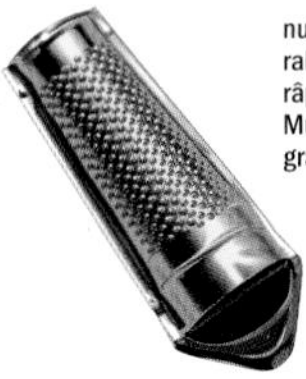

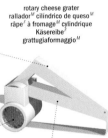

nutmeg grater
rallador^M de nuez^F moscada
râpe^F à muscade^F
Muskatnussreibe^F
grattugia^F per noce^F moscata

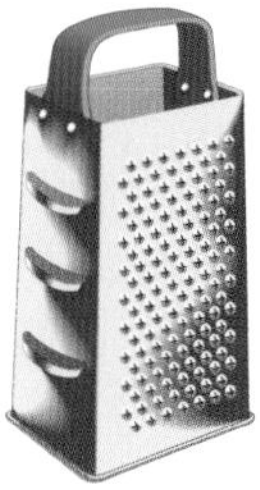

rotary cheese grater
rallador^M cilindrico de queso^M
râpe^F à fromage^M cylindrique
Käsereibe^F
grattugiaformaggio^M

pusher
empujador^M
poussoir^M
Presshebel^M
pigiatore^M

grater
rallador^M
râpe^F
Reibe^F
grattugia^F

crank
manivela^F
manivelle^F
Kurbel^F
levetta^F

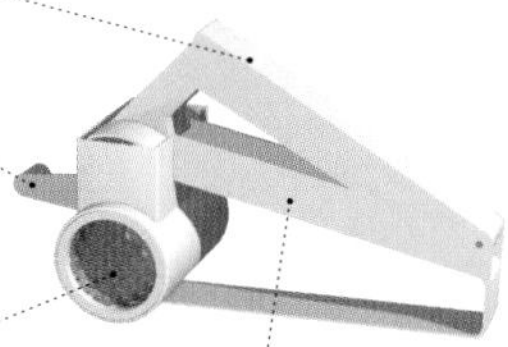

drum
tambor^M
tambour^M
Trommel^F
tamburo^M

handle
mango^M
poignée^F
Griff^M
impugnatura^F

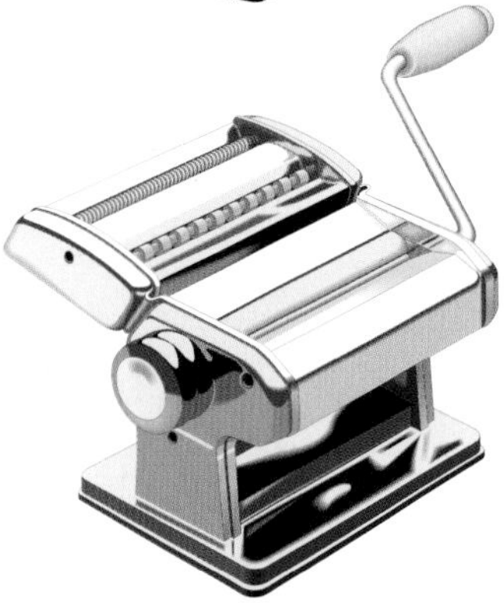

pasta maker
máquina^F para hacer pasta^F italiana
machine^F à faire les pâtes^F
Nudelmaschine^F
macchina^F per fare la pasta^F

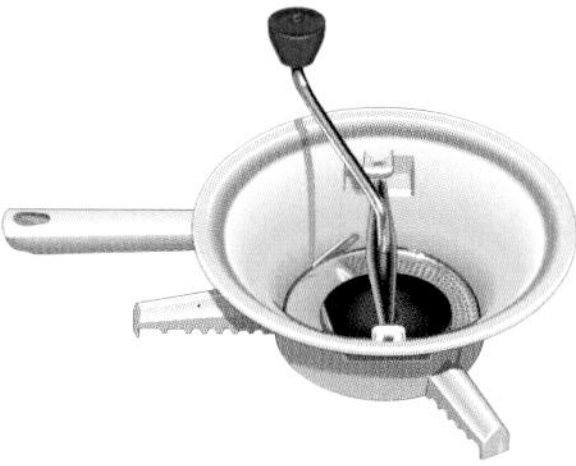

food mill
pasapurés^M
moulin^M à légumes^M
Passiergerät^N
passaverdure^M

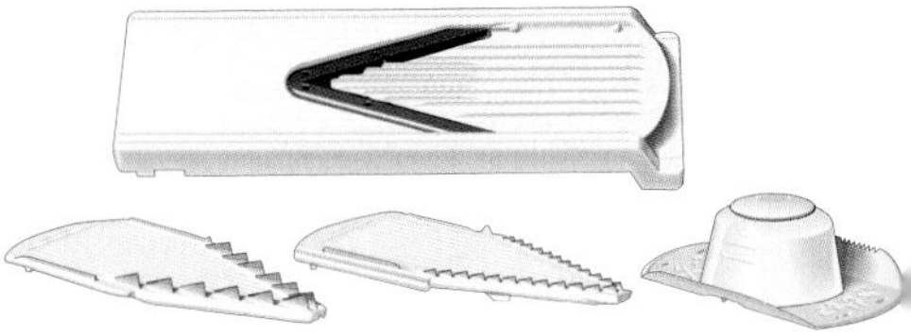

mandoline
mandolina^F
mandoline^F
Küchenreibe^F
affettaverdure^M

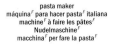

FOOD AND KITCHEN

for measuring
utensilios^M para medir
pour mesurer
zum Messen^N
per misurare

measuring spoons
cucharas^F dosificadoras
cuillers^F doseuses
Messlöffel^M
cucchiai^M dosatori

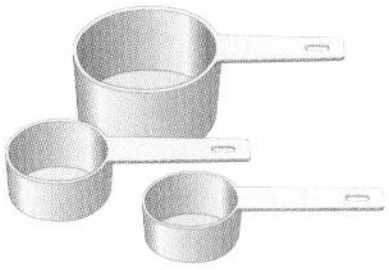

measuring cups
tazas^F medidoras
mesures^F
Messbecher^M
misurini^M

candy thermometer
termómetro^M de azúcar^M
thermomètre^M à sucre^M
Einmachthermometer^N
termometro^M per zucchero^M

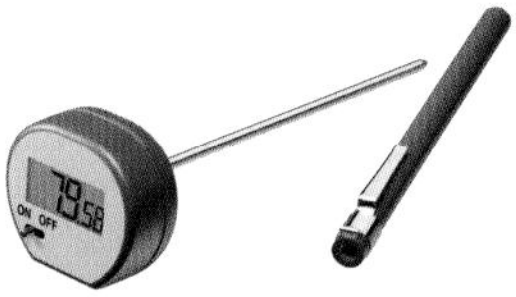

instant-read thermometer
termómetro^M de medida^F instantánea
thermomètre^M à mesure^F instantanée
digitales Bratenthermometer^N
termometro^M a lettura^F istantanea

measuring cup
jarra^F medidora
tasse^F à mesurer
Maß^N
tazza^F graduata

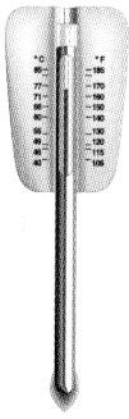

meat thermometer
termómetro^M para carne^F
thermomètre^M à viande^F
Fleischthermometer^N
termometro^M per carne^F

oven thermometer
termómetro^M de horno^M
thermomètre^M de four^M
Backofenthermometer^N
termometro^M del forno^M

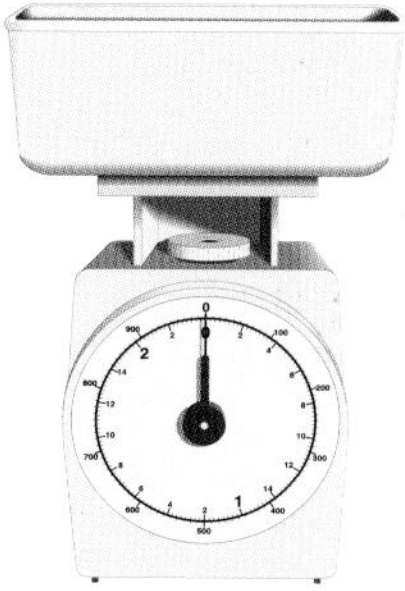

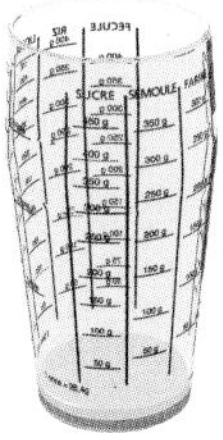

measuring beaker
vaso^M medidor
verre^M à mesurer
Messbecher^M
recipiente^M graduato

kitchen timer
minutero^M
minuteur^M
Küchenuhr^F
contaminuti^M

egg timer
reloj^M de arena^F
sablier^M
Eieruhr^F
clessidra^F per uova^F alla coque

kitchen scale
báscula^F de cocina^F
balance^F de cuisine^F
Küchenwaage^F
bilancia^F da cucina^F

---

for straining and draining
coladores^M y escurridores^M
pour passer et égoutter
zum Sieben^N und Abtropfen^N
per scolare e filtrare

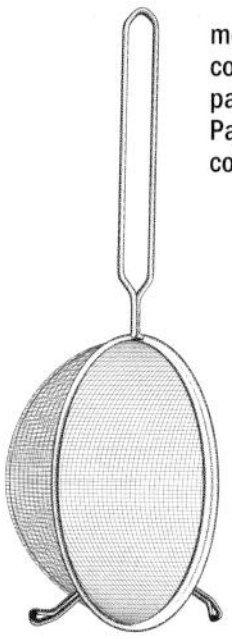

mesh strainer
colador^M fino
passoire^F fine
Passiersieb^N
colino^M

muslin
muselina^F
mousseline^F
Musselin^M
mussolina^F

chinois
chino^M
chinois^N
Spitzsieb^N
chinois^M

funnel
embudo^M
entonnoir^M
Trichter^M
imbuto^M

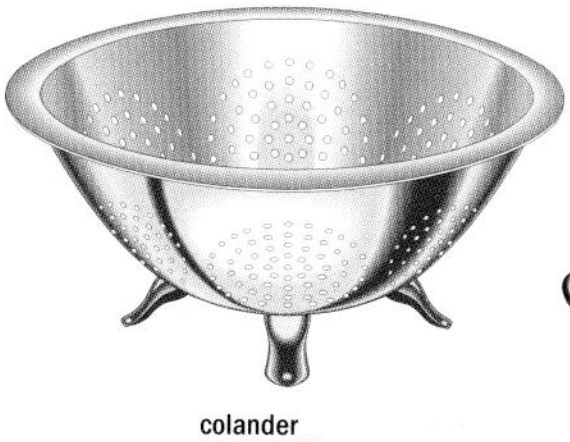

colander
escurridor^M
passoire^F
Seiher^M
colapasta^M

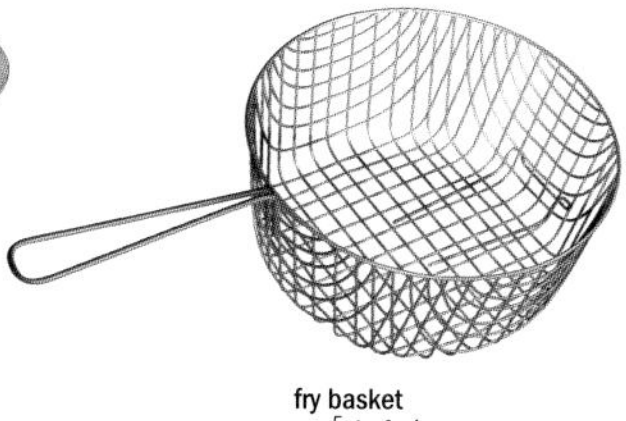

fry basket
cesta^F de freír
panier^M à friture^F
Frittierkorb^M
cestello^M per friggere

sieve
tamiz^M
tamis^M
Mehlsieb^N
setaccio^M

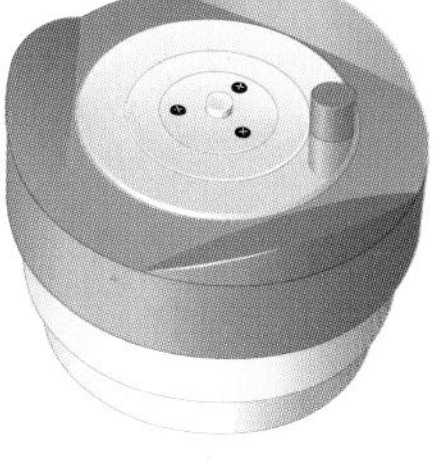

salad spinner
secadora^F de ensalada^F
essoreuse^F à salade^F
Salatschleuder^F
centrifuga^F scolainsalata

kitchen utensils

baking utensils
utensilios^M para repostería
pour la pâtisserie^F
Backgerät^N
utensili^M per dolci^M

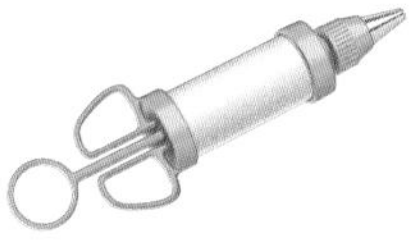

icing syringe
jeringa^F de decoración^F
piston^M à décorer
Garnierspritze^F
siringa^F per decorazioni

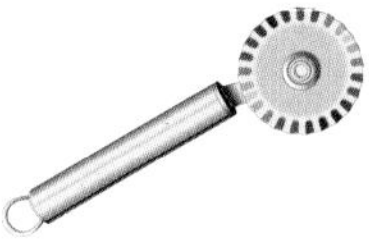

pastry cutting wheel
cortapastas^M
roulette^F de pâtissier^M
Kuchenrad^N
rotella^F tagliapasta

pastry brush
pincel^M de repostería^F
pinceau^M à pâtisserie^F
Kuchenpinsel^M
pennello^M per dolci^M

egg beater
batidor^M mecánico
batteur^M à œufs^M
Rad-Schneeschläger^M
frullino^M

whisk
batidor^M
fouet^M
Schneebesen^M
frusta^F

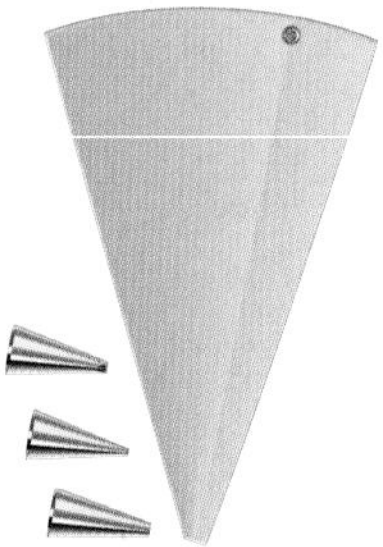

sifter
tamiz^M
tamis^M à farine^F
Mehlsieb^N
setaccio^M

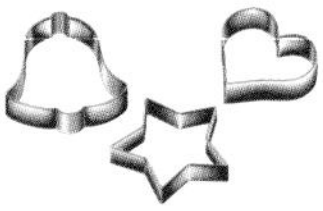

cookie cutters
moldes^M de pastas^F
emporte-pièces^M
Ausstechformen^F
tagliabiscotti^M

dredger
espolvoreador^M
saupoudreuse^F
Streuer^M
spolverino^M

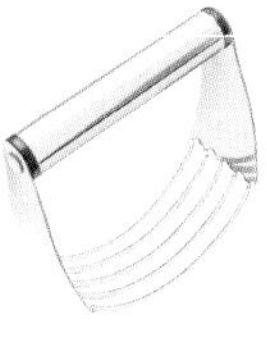

pastry blender
mezclador^M de pastelería^F
mélangeur^M à pâtisserie^F
Teigmischer^M
miscelatore^M per dolci^M

pastry bag and nozzles
manga^F y boquillas^F
poche^F à douilles^F
Spritzbeutel^M mit Tüllen^F
tasca^F e bocchette^F

mixing bowls
boles^M para batir
bols^M à mélanger
Rührschüsseln^F
ciotole^F per mescolare

rolling pin
rodillo^M
rouleau^M à pâtisserie^F
Nudelholz^N
matterello^M

baking sheet
bandeja^F de pastelería^F
plaque^F à pâtisserie^F
Backblech^N
teglia^F da forno^M

muffin pan
molde^M para magdalenas^F
moule^M à muffins^M
Muffinform^F
stampini^M per dolci^M

soufflé dish
molde^M de soufflé^M
moule^M à soufflé^M
Souffléform^F
tegamino^M per sufflè^M

charlotte mold
molde^M de carlota^F
moule^M à charlotte^F
Charlottenform^F
stampo^M per charlotte^F

spring-form pan
molde^M redondo con muelles^M
moule^M à fond^M amovible
Springform^F
teglia^F con fondo^M staccabile

pie pan
molde^M para tartas^F
moule^M à tarte^F
flache Kuchenform^F
teglia^F per torta^F

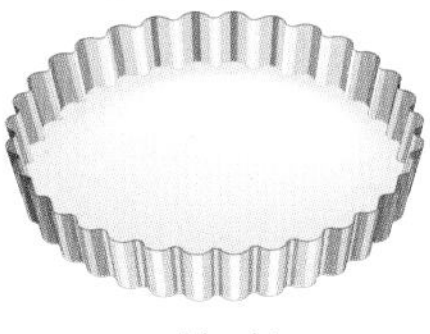

quiche plate
molde^M acanalado
moule^M à quiche^F
Quicheform^F
stampo^M per crostata^F

cake pan
molde^M para bizcocho^M
moule^M à gâteau^M
Kuchenform^F
tortiera^F

FOOD AND KITCHEN

set of utensils
juego^M **de utensilios**^{M}
jeu^M **d'ustensiles**^{M}
Küchenset^N
set^M **di utensili**^{M}

skimmer
espumadera^F
écumoire^F
Abseihkelle^F
schiumaiola^F

spatula
espátula^F
spatule^F
Palette^F
spatola^F

ladle
cazo^M
louche^F
Schöpflöffel^M
mestolo^M

draining spoon
escurridera^F
cuiller^F à égoutter
Abseihlöffel^M
cucchiaio^M forato

turner
paleta^F
pelle^F
Pfannenwender^M
paletta^F

potato masher
pasapuré^M
pilon^M
Kartoffelstampfer^M
schiacciapatate^M

miscellaneous utensils
utensilios^M **diversos**
ustensiles^M **divers**
verschiedene Utensilien^N
utensili^M **vari**

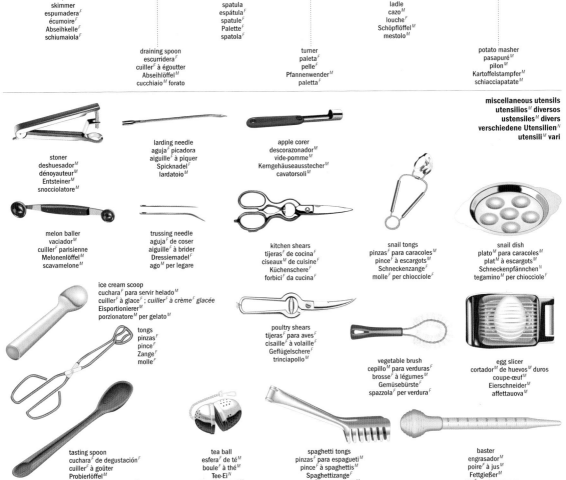

stoner
deshuesador^M
dénoyauteur^M
Entsteiner^M
snocciolatore^M

larding needle
aguja^F picadora
aiguille^F à piquer
Spicknadel^F
lardatoio^M

apple corer
descorazonador^M
vide-pomme^F
Kerngehäuseausstecher^M
cavatorsoli^M

melon baller
vaciador^M
cuiller^F parisienne
Melonenlöffel^M
scavamelone^M

trussing needle
aguja^F de coser
aiguille^F à brider
Dressiernadel^F
ago^M per legare

kitchen shears
tijeras^F de cocina^F
ciseaux^M de cuisine^F
Küchenschere^F
forbici^F da cucina^F

snail tongs
pinzas^F para caracoles^M
pince^F à escargots^M
Schneckenzange^F
molle^F per chiocciole^F

snail dish
plato^M para caracoles^M
plat^M à escargots^M
Schneckenpfännchen^N
tegamino^M per chiocciole^F

ice cream scoop
cuchara^F para servir helado^M
cuiller^F à glace^F ; cuiller^F à crème^F glacée
Eisportionierer^M
porzionatore^M per gelato^M

tongs
pinzas^F
pince^F
Zange^F
molle^F

poultry shears
tijeras^F para aves^F
cisaille^F à volaille^F
Geflügelschere^F
trinciapollo^M

vegetable brush
cepillo^M para verduras^F
brosse^F à légumes^M
Gemüsebürste^F
spazzola^F per verdura^F

egg slicer
cortador^M de huevos^M duros
coupe-œuf^M
Eierschneider^M
affettauova^M

tasting spoon
cuchara^F de degustación^F
cuiller^F à goûter
Probierlöffel^M
cucchiaio^M da assaggio^M

tea ball
esfera^F de té^M
boule^F à thé^M
Tee-Ei^N
filtro^M per il tè^M

spaghetti tongs
pinzas^F para espagueti^M
pince^F à spaghettis^M
Spaghettizange^F
molle^F per spaghetti^M

baster
engrasador^M
poire^F à jus^M
Fettgießer^M
peretta^F per ingrassare

cooking utensils

utensilios^M de cocina^F | batterie^F de cuisine^F | Kochgeräte^N | utensili^M per cucinare

wok set
wok^M
wok^M
Wok-Set^N
servizio^M da wok^M

tagine
tajina^F
tajine^M
Tajine^F
tajina^M

lid
tapa^F
couvercle^M
Deckel^M
coperchio^M

rack
rejilla^F
grille^F
Gittereinsatz^M
griglia^F

wok
wok^M
wok^M
Wok^M
wok^M

burner ring
quemador^M
collier^M
Aufsatz^M
bruciatore^M a corona^F

fondue set
servicio^M para fondue^F
service^M à fondue^F
Fondue-Set^N
servizio^M da fonduta^F

fish poacher
besuguera^F
poissonnière^F
Fischkochtopf^M
pesciera^F

rack
rejilla^F
grille^F
Gittereinsatz^M
griglia^F

fondue pot
cacerola^F para fondue^F
caquelon^M
Fonduetopf^M
tegame^M per fonduta^F

stand
soporte^M
support^M
Ständer^M
base^F

lid
tapa^F
couvercle^M
Deckel^M
coperchio^M

burner
quemador^M
réchaud^M
Brenner^M
fornellino^M

dripping pan
grasera^F
lèchefrite^F
Fettpfanne^F
leccarda^F

terrine
terrina^F
terrine^F
Terrine^F
terrina^F

roasting pans
asadores^M
plats^M à rôtir
Bräter^M
teglie^F da forno^M

pressure cooker
olla^F a presión^F
autocuiseur^M
Schnellkochtopf^M
pentola^F a pressione^F

pressure regulator
regulador^M de presión^F
régulateur^M de pression^F
Überdruckventil^N
regolatore^M di pressione^F

safety valve
válvula^F de seguridad^F
soupape^F
Sicherheitsventil^N
valvola^F di sicurezza^F

Dutch oven
cacerola^F refractaria
faitout^M
flacher Bratentopf^M
casseruola^F

stock pot
olla^F
marmite^F
Suppentopf^M
pentola^F

couscous kettle
olla^F para cuscús^M
couscoussier^M
Couscoustopf^M
pentola^F per cuscus^M

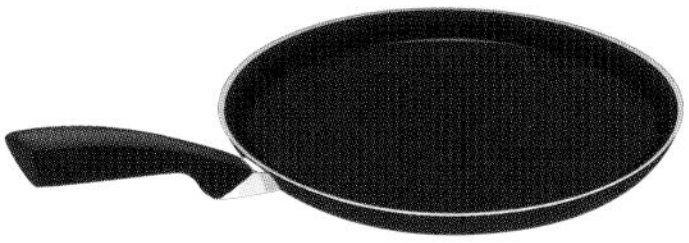

frying pan
sartén^F
poêle^F à frire
Bratpfanne^F
padella^F per friggere

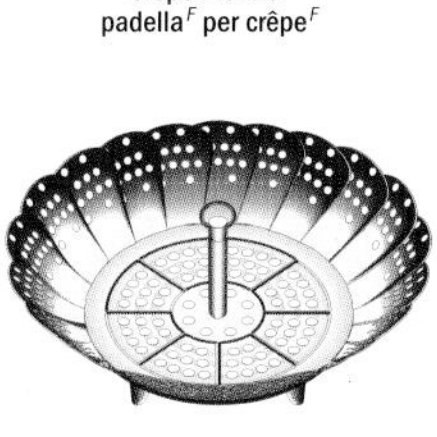

steamer
cazuela^F vaporera
cuit-vapeur^M
Dampfkochtopf^M
pentola^F a vapore^M

egg poacher
escalfador^M de huevos^M
pocheuse^F
Eipochierer^M
tegame^M per uova^F in camicia^F

sauté pan
sartén^F honda
sauteuse^F
Schmorpfanne^F
padella^F per rosolare

small saucepan
sartén^F pequeña
poêlon^M
Pfanne^F
piccolo tegame^M

diable
sartén^F doble
diable^M
Römertopf^M
padella^F doppia

crêpe pan
sartén^F para crepes^M
poêle^F à crêpes^F
Crêpe-Pfanne^F
padella^F per crêpe^F

steamer basket
cesto^M de cocción^M al vapor^M
panier^M cuit-vapeur^M
Dämpfeinsatz^M
cestello^M per la cottura^F a vapore^M

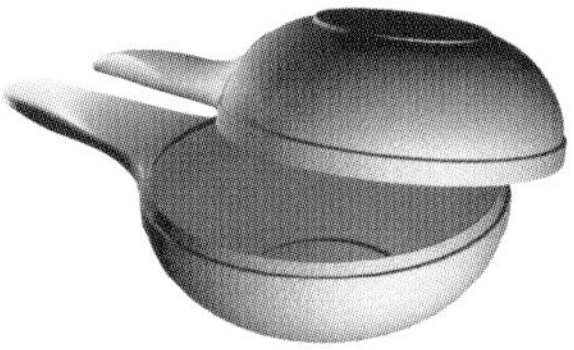

double boiler
cacerola^F para baño^M de Maria
bain-marie^M
Wasserbadtopf^M
pentola^F per cucinare a bagnomaria

saucepan
cacerola^F
casserole^F
Stielkasserolle^F
tegame^M

domestic appliances

aparatos^M electrodomésticos | appareils^M électroménagers | Haushaltsgeräte^N | elettrodomestici^M

FOOD AND KITCHEN

**for mixing and blending
para mezclar y batir
pour mélanger et battre
zum Mixen^N und Kneten^N
per frullare e miscelare**

blender
licuadora^F
mélangeur^M
Mixer^M
frullatore^M

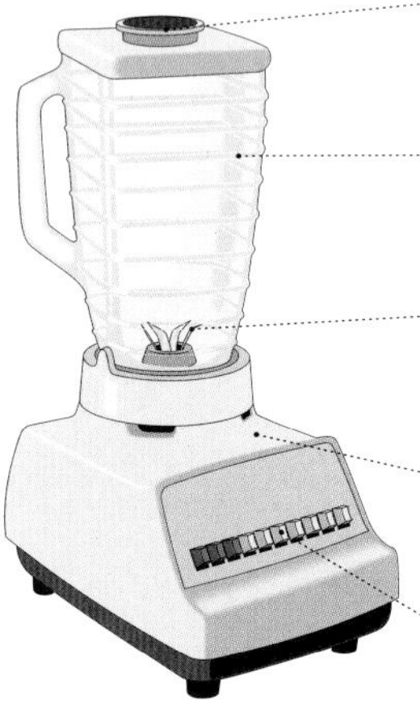

cap
tapa^F
bouchon^M
Deckelknopf^M
tappo^M

container
vaso^M mezclador
récipient^M
Behälter^M
bicchiere^M

cutting blade
cuchilla^F
couteau^M
Schneidmesser^N
coltello^M

motor unit
motor^M
bloc^M-moteur^M
Motorblock^M
blocco^M motore^M

push button
botón^M de velocidades^F
bouton^M-poussoir^M
Drucktaste^F
interruttore^M

hand blender
batidora^F de pie^M
mélangeur^M à main^F
Stabmixer^M
frullatore^M a immersione^F

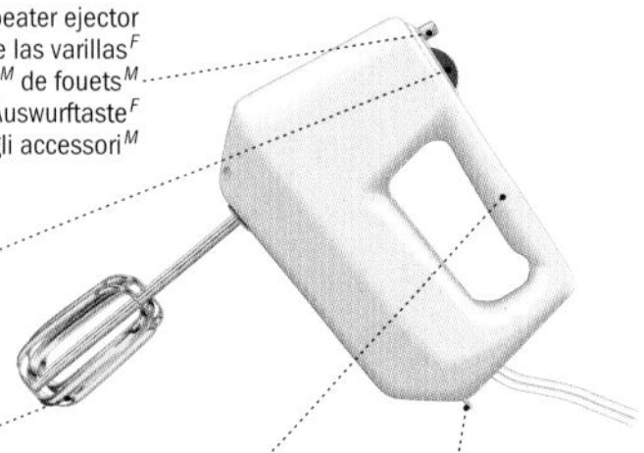

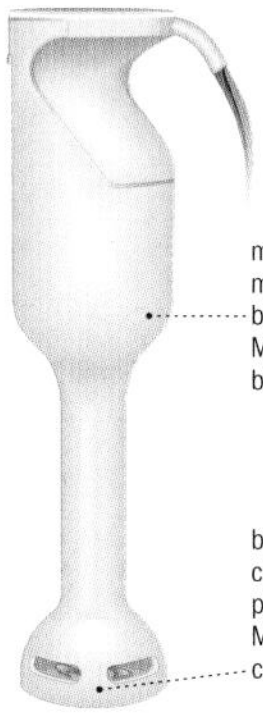

motor unit
motor^M
bloc^M-moteur^M
Motorblock^M
blocco^M motore^M

blending attachment
cuchillas^F para batir
pied^M-mélangeur^M
Messerschutz^M
coltello^M miscelatore

hand mixer
batidora^F de mano^F
batteur^M à main^F
Handrührgerät^N
frullatore^M elettrico a mano^F

beater ejector
eyector^M de las varillas^F
éjecteur^M de fouets^M
Auswurftaste^F
espulsore^M degli accessori^M

speed selector
selector^M de velocidad^F
sélecteur^M de vitesse^F
Geschwindigkeitswähler^M
selettore^M di velocità^F

beater
varilla^F de batir
fouet^M
Rührbesen^M
frusta^F

handle
asa^F
poignée^F
Griff^M
impugnatura^F

heel rest
talón^M de apoyo^M
talon^M d'appui^M
Heck^N
tallone^M d'appoggio^M

table mixer
batidora^F de mesa^F
batteur^M sur socle^M
Tischrührgerät^N
impastatrice^F

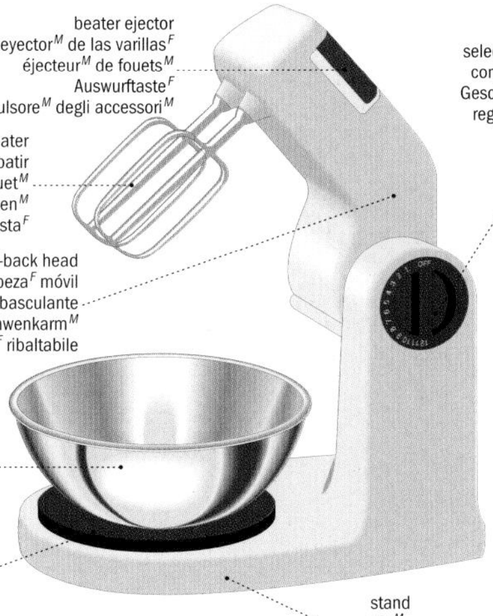

beater ejector
eyector^M de las varillas^F
éjecteur^M de fouets^M
Auswurftaste^F
espulsore^M degli accessori^M

beater
varilla^F de batir
fouet^M
Rührbesen^M
frusta^F

tilt-back head
cabeza^F móvil
tête^F basculante
Schwenkarm^M
testa^F ribaltabile

mixing bowl
bol^M mezclador
bol^M
Rührschüssel^F
ciotola^F

turntable
disco^M giratorio
plateau^M tournant
Drehscheibe^F
piattaforma^F girevole

speed control
selector^M de velocidades^F
commande^F de vitesse^F
Geschwindigkeitsregelung^F
regolatore^M di velocità^F

stand
pie^M
socle^M
Ständer^M
base^F

**beaters
tipos^M de varillas^F
fouets^M
Rührbesen^M
fruste^F**

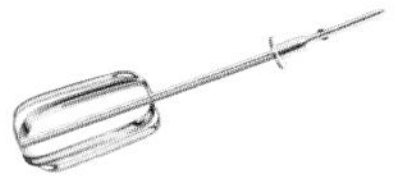

four blade beater
varilla de aspas^F
fouet^M quatre pales^F
Rührbesen^M
frusta^F a quattro bracci^M

spiral beater
varilla en espiral^F
fouet^M en spirale^F
Spiralkneter^M
frusta^F a spirale^F

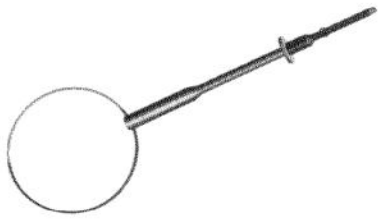

wire beater
varilla circular
fouet^M à fil^M
Drahtbesen^M
frusta^F ad anello^M

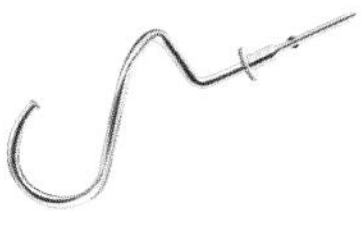

dough hook
varilla de gancho^M
crochet^M pétrisseur
Knethaken^M
gancio^M per l'impasto^M

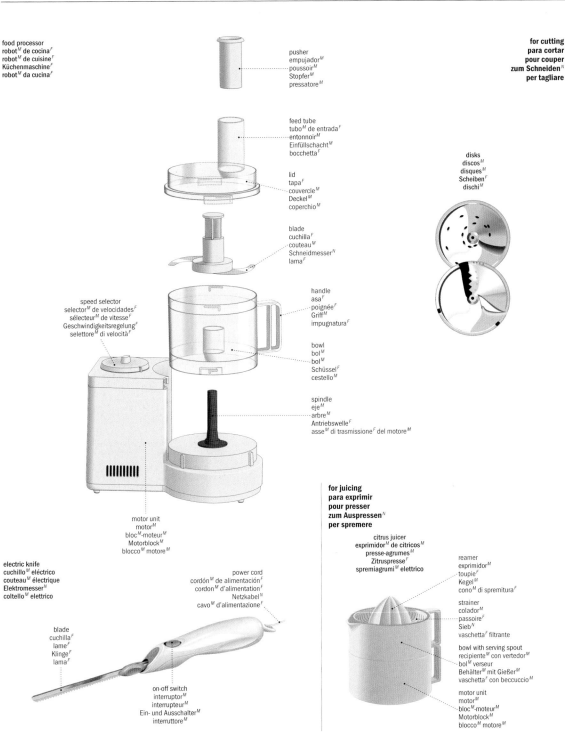

food processor
robot^M de cocina^F
robot^M de cuisine^F
Küchenmaschine^F
robot^M da cucina^F

pusher
empujador^M
poussoir^M
Stopfer^M
pressatore^M

for cutting
para cortar
pour couper
zum Schneiden^N
per tagliare

feed tube
tubo^M de entrada^F
entonnoir^M
Einfüllschacht^M
bocchetta^F

disks
discos^M
disques^M
Scheiben^F
dischi^M

lid
tapa^F
couvercle^M
Deckel^M
coperchio^M

blade
cuchilla^F
couteau^M
Schneidmesser^N
lama^F

speed selector
selector^M de velocidades^F
sélecteur^M de vitesse^F
Geschwindigkeitsregelung^F
selettore^M di velocità^F

handle
asa^F
poignée^F
Griff^M
impugnatura^F

bowl
bol^M
bol^M
Schüssel^F
cestello^M

spindle
eje^M
arbre^M
Antriebswelle^F
asse^M di trasmissione^F del motore^M

motor unit
motor^M
bloc^M-moteur^M
Motorblock^M
blocco^M motore^M

for juicing
para exprimir
pour presser
zum Auspressen^N
per spremere

citrus juicer
exprimidor^M de cítricos^M
presse-agrumes^M
Zitruspresse^F
spremiagrumi^M elettrico

reamer
exprimidor^M
toupie^F
Kegel^M
cono^M di spremitura^F

strainer
colador^M
passoire^F
Sieb^N
vaschetta^F filtrante

bowl with serving spout
recipiente^M con vertedor^M
bol^M verseur
Behälter^M mit Gießer^M
vaschetta^F con beccuccio^M

electric knife
cuchillo^M eléctrico
couteau^M électrique
Elektromesser^N
coltello^M elettrico

power cord
cordón^M de alimentación^F
cordon^M d'alimentation^F
Netzkabel^N
cavo^M d'alimentazione^F

motor unit
motor^M
bloc^M-moteur^M
Motorblock^M
blocco^M motore^M

blade
cuchilla^F
lame^F
Klinge^F
lama^F

on-off switch
interruptor^M
interrupteur^M
Ein- und Ausschalter^M
interruttore^M

domestic appliances

for cooking
para cocinar
pour cuire
zum Kochen[N]
per cucinare

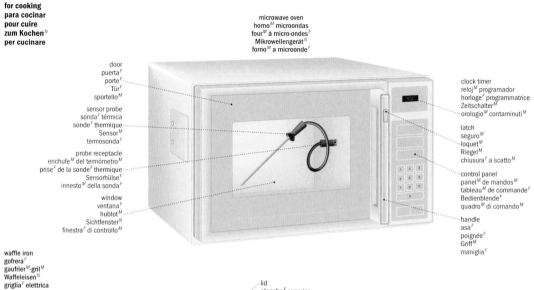

microwave oven
horno[M] microondas
four[M] à micro-ondes[F]
Mikrowellengerät[N]
forno[M] a microonde[F]

door
puerta[F]
porte[F]
Tür[F]
sportello[M]

sensor probe
sonda[F] térmica
sonde[F] thermique
Sensor[M]
termosonda[F]

probe receptacle
enchufe[M] del termómetro[M]
prise[F] de la sonde[F] thermique
Sensorhülse[F]
innesto[M] della sonda[F]

window
ventana[F]
hublot[M]
Sichtfenster[N]
finestra[F] di controllo[M]

clock timer
reloj[M] programador
horloge[F] programmatrice
Zeitschalter[M]
orologio[M] contaminuti[M]

latch
seguro[M]
loquet[M]
Riegel[M]
chiusura[F] a scatto[M]

control panel
panel[M] de mandos[M]
tableau[M] de commande[F]
Bedienblende[F]
quadro[M] di comando[M]

handle
asa[F]
poignée[F]
Griff[M]
maniglia[F]

waffle iron
gofrera[F]
gaufrier[M]-gril[M]
Waffeleisen[N]
griglia[F] elettrica

handle
asa[F]
poignée[F]
Griff[M]
maniglia[F]

plate
parrilla[F]
plaque[F]
Platte[F]
piastra[F]

temperature selector
selector[M] de temperatura[F]
sélecteur[M] de température[F]
Temperaturwähler[M]
selettore[M] della temperatura[F]

lid
plancha[F] superior
couvercle[M]
Deckel[M]
coperchio[M]

hinge
bisagra[F]
charnière[F]
Scharnier[N]
cerniera[F]

plate
parrilla[F]
plaque[F]
Platte[F]
piastra[F]

toaster
tostador[M]
grille-pain[M]
Toaster[M]
tostapane[M]

slot
ranura[F] para el pan[M]
fente[F]
Schlitz[M]
feritoia[F]

deep fryer
freidora[F]
friteuse[F]
Fritteuse[F]
friggitrice[F]

basket
canastilla[F]
panier[M]
Frittierkorb[M]
cestello[M]

rack
selector[M]
crémaillère[F]
Regler[M]
dispositivo[M] di espulsione[F] del cestello[M]

timer
reloj[M]
minuterie[F]
Zeituhr[F]
contaminuti[M]

thermostat
termostato[M]
thermostat[M]
Thermostat[M]
termostato[M]

signal lamp
piloto[M]
voyant[M] lumineux
Kontrollleuchte[F]
spia[F] luminosa

bread guide
rejilla[F]
guide[M]
Brothalter[M]
guida[F] per il pane[M]

lever
palanca[F]
manette[F]
Hebel[M]
leva[F]

temperature control
selector[M] de tostado[M]
thermostat[M]
Temperaturregler[M]
termostato[M]

handle
asa[F]
poignée[F]
Griff[M]
impugnatura[F]

filter
filtro[M]
filtre[M]
Filter[M]
filtro[M]

lid
tapa[F]
couvercle[M]
Deckel[M]
coperchio[M]

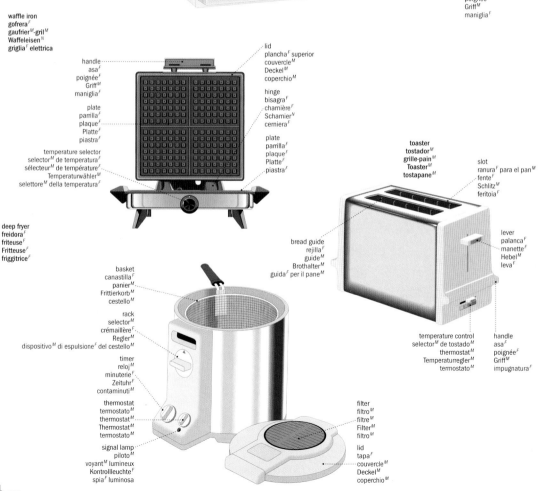

domestic appliances

FOOD AND KITCHEN

raclette with grill
raclette-grill^M
raclette^F-gril^M
Raclette^F-Grill^M
griglia^F per raclette^F

dish
bandeja^F
poêlon^M
Pfännchen^N
piatto^M

cooking plate
placa^F de cocción^F
surface^F de cuisson^F
Grillplatte^F
piastra^F di cottura^F

base
base^F
socle^M
Unterteil^M/N
base^F

electric steamer
vaporera^F eléctrica
cuit-vapeur^M électrique
elektrischer Schnellkocher^M
pentola^F a vapore^F elettrica

cooking dishes
platos^M de cocción^F
bols^M de cuisson^F
Einsätze^M
piatti^M di cottura^F

water level indicator
indicador^M del nivel^M del agua^F
indicateur^M de niveau^M d'eau^F
Wasserstandsanzeiger^M
indicatore^M del livello^M d'acqua^F

signal lamp
indicador^M luminoso
voyant^M lumineux
Kontrollleuchte^F
spia^F luminosa

timer
minutero^M
minuterie^F
Zeitschaltuhr^F
contaminuti^M

indoor electric grill
parrilla^F eléctrica
gril^M barbecue^M
Elektrischer Tischgrill^M
griglia^F elettrica per interni^M

insulated handle
asa^F aislante
poignée^F isolante
wärmeisolierter Griff^M
maniglia^F isolata

drip pan
grasera^F
bac^M ramasse-jus^M
Fettpfanne^F
leccarda^F

cooking surface
superficie^F de cocción^F
surface^F de cuisson^F
Grillfläche^F
piano^M di cottura^F

adjustable thermostat
termostato^M regulable
thermostat^M réglable
regelbarer Thermostat^M
termostato^M regolabile

bread machine
amasadora^F
robot^M boulanger^M
Brotbackautomat^M
impastatrice^F

lid
tapa^F
couvercle^M
Deckel^M
coperchio^M

control panel
panel^M de mandos^M
tableau^M de commande^F
Bedienungsfeld^N
quadro^M di comando^M

window
ventana^F
hublot^M
Sichtfenster^N
finestra^F di controllo^M

loaf pan
molde^M de pan^M
moule^M à pain^M
Backform^F
stampo^M per pane^M

electric griddle
plancha^F eléctrica
gril^M électrique
Grillplatte^F
piastra^F elettrica

cooking surface
plancha^F
surface^F de cuisson^F
Kochfeld^N
piano^M di cottura^F

handle
asa^F
poignée^F
Griff^M
maniglia^F

detachable control
enchufe^M y selector^M desmontables
commande^F amovible
abziehbarer Temperaturregler^M
regolatore^M staccabile

grease well
colector^M de grasa^F
collecteur^M de graisse^F
Fettauffangschale^F
bacinella^F raccogligrasso

miscellaneous domestic appliances

varios aparatos^M electrodomésticos | appareils^M électroménagers divers | verschiedene Haushaltsgeräte^N | elettrodomestici^M vari

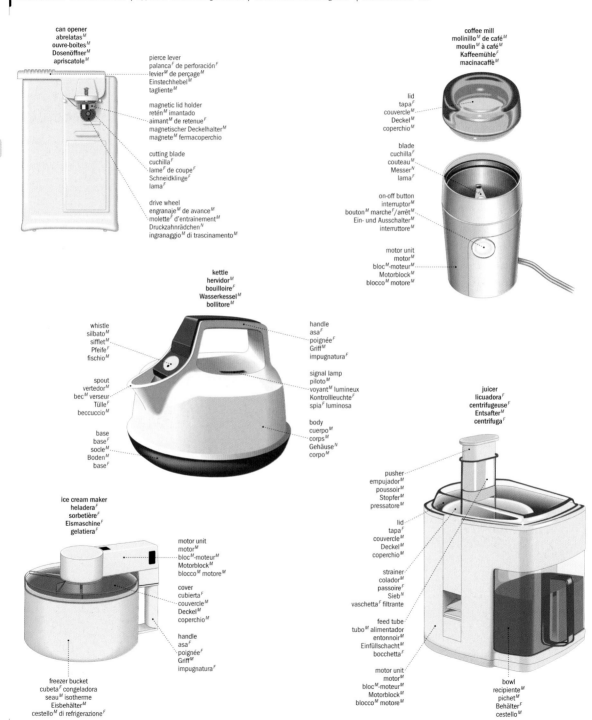

can opener
abrelatas^M
ouvre-boîtes^M
Dosenöffner^M
apriscatole^M

pierce lever
palanca^F de perforación^F
levier^M de perçage^M
Einstechhebel^M
tagliente^M

magnetic lid holder
retén^M imantado
aimant^M de retenue^F
magnetischer Deckelhalter^M
magnete^M fermacoperchio

cutting blade
cuchilla^F
lame^F de coupe^F
Schneidklinge^F
lama^F

drive wheel
engranaje^M de avance^M
molette^F d'entraînement^M
Druckzahnrädchen^N
ingranaggio^M di trascinamento^M

coffee mill
molinillo^M de café^M
moulin^M à café^M
Kaffeemühle^F
macinacaffè^M

lid
tapa^F
couvercle^M
Deckel^M
coperchio^M

blade
cuchilla^F
couteau^M
Messer^N
lama^F

on-off button
interruptor^M
bouton^M marche^F/arrêt^M
Ein- und Ausschalter^M
interruttore^M

motor unit
motor^M
bloc^M-moteur^M
Motorblock^M
blocco^M motore^M

kettle
hervidor^M
bouilloire^F
Wasserkessel^M
bollitore^M

whistle
silbato^M
sifflet^M
Pfeife^F
fischio^M

spout
vertedor^M
bec^M verseur^M
Tülle^F
beccuccio^M

base
base^F
socle^M
Boden^M
base^F

handle
asa^F
poignée^F
Griff^M
impugnatura^F

signal lamp
piloto^M
voyant^M lumineux
Kontrollleuchte^F
spia^F luminosa

body
cuerpo^M
corps^M
Gehäuse^N
corpo^M

juicer
licuadora^F
centrifugeuse^F
Entsafter^M
centrifuga^F

pusher
empujador^M
poussoir^M
Stopfer^M
pressatore^M

lid
tapa^F
couvercle^M
Deckel^M
coperchio^M

strainer
colador^M
passoire^F
Sieb^N
vaschetta^F filtrante

feed tube
tubo^M alimentador
entonnoir^M
Einfüllschacht^M
bocchetta^F

ice cream maker
heladera^F
sorbetière^F
Eismaschine^F
gelatiera^F

motor unit
motor^M
bloc^M-moteur^M
Motorblock^M
blocco^M motore^M

cover
cubierta^F
couvercle^M
Deckel^M
coperchio^M

handle
asa^F
poignée^F
Griff^M
impugnatura^F

freezer bucket
cubeta^F congeladora
seau^M isotherme
Eisbehälter^M
cestello^M di refrigerazione^F

motor unit
motor^M
bloc^M-moteur^M
Motorblock^M
blocco^M motore^M

bowl
recipiente^M
pichet^F
Behälter^F
cestello^M

FOOD AND KITCHEN

coffee makers

cafeteras^F | cafetières^F | Kaffeemaschinen^F | macchine^F da caffè^M

automatic drip coffee maker
cafetera^F de filtro^M automática
cafetière^F filtre^M
Kaffeemaschine^F
macchina^F da caffè^M a filtro^M

reservoir
depósito^M de agua^F
réservoir^M
Wasserbehälter^M
serbatoio^M

water level
nivel^M de agua^F
niveau^M d'eau^F
Wasserstand^M
livello^M dell'acqua^F

signal lamp
piloto^M
voyant^M lumineux
Kontrollleuchte^F
spia^F luminosa

on-off switch
interruptor^M
interrupteur^M
Ein- und Ausschalter^M
interruttore^M

lid
tapa^F
couvercle^M
Deckel^M
coperchio^M

basket
filtro^M
panier^M
Filterhalter^M
cassetta^F filtro^M

carafe
cafetera^F
verseuse^F
Kanne^F
caraffa^F

warming plate
placa^F térmica
plaque^F chauffante
Warmhalteplatte^F
piastra^F riscaldante

Neapolitan coffee maker
cafetera^F napolitana
cafetière^F napolitaine
Neapolitanische Tropfkanne^F
caffettiera^F napoletana

espresso machine
máquina^F de café^M exprés
machine^F à espresso^M
Espressomaschine^F
macchina^F per espresso^M

on-off switch
interruptor^M
interrupteur^M
Ein- und Ausschalter^M
interruttore^M

tamper
prensa-café^M
presse-café^M
Kaffeepresser^M
pressacaffè^M

drip tray
cubeta^F colectora de gotas^F
cuvette^F ramasse-gouttes^M
Auffangschale^F
vaschetta^F di raccolta^F

steam nozzle
tubo^M de vapor^M
buse^F vapeur^F
Aufschäumdüse^F
ugello^M vaporizzatore^M

steam control knob
manecilla^F de vapor^M
manette^F vapeur^F
Dampfregler^M
regolazione^F del vapore^M

filter holder
porta-filtro^M
porte-filtre^M
Filterhalter^M
portafiltro^M

water tank
depósito^M de agua^M
réservoir^M d'eau^F
Wassertank^M
serbatoio^M dell'acqua^F

vacuum coffee maker
cafetera^F de infusión^F
cafetière^F à infusion^F
Vakuum-Kaffeemaschine^F
caffettiera^F a infusione^F

upper bowl
recipiente^M superior
tulipe^F
oberer Glaskolben^M
coppa^F superiore

stem
tubo^M de subida^F del agua^F
tige^F
Röhre^F
gambo^M

lower bowl
recipiente^M inferior
ballon^M
unterer Glaskolben^M
coppa^F inferiore

percolator
percoladora^F
percolateur^M
Kaffee-Filterkanne^M
caffettiera^F a filtro^M

French press
cafetera^F de émbolo^M
cafetière^F à piston^M
Pressfilterkanne^F
caffettiera^F a pistone^M

espresso maker
cafetera^F italiana
cafetière^F espresso^M
Espresso-Maschine^F
caffettiera^F per espresso^M

spout
pitorro^M
bec^M verseur
Tülle^F
beccuccio^M

signal light
piloto^M
voyant^M lumineux
Kontrollleuchte^F
spia^F luminosa

FOOD AND KITCHEN

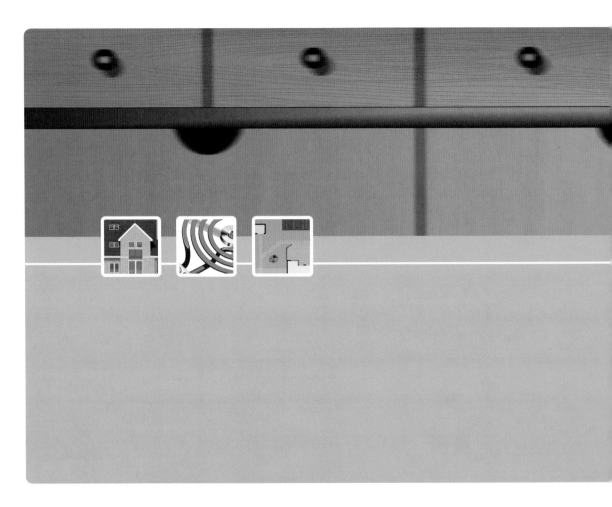

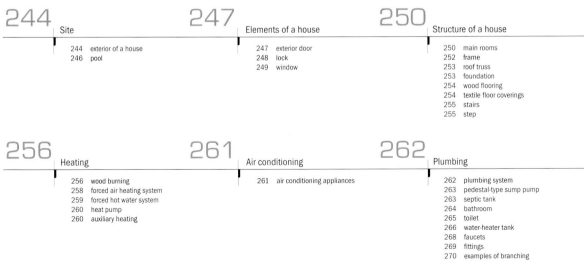

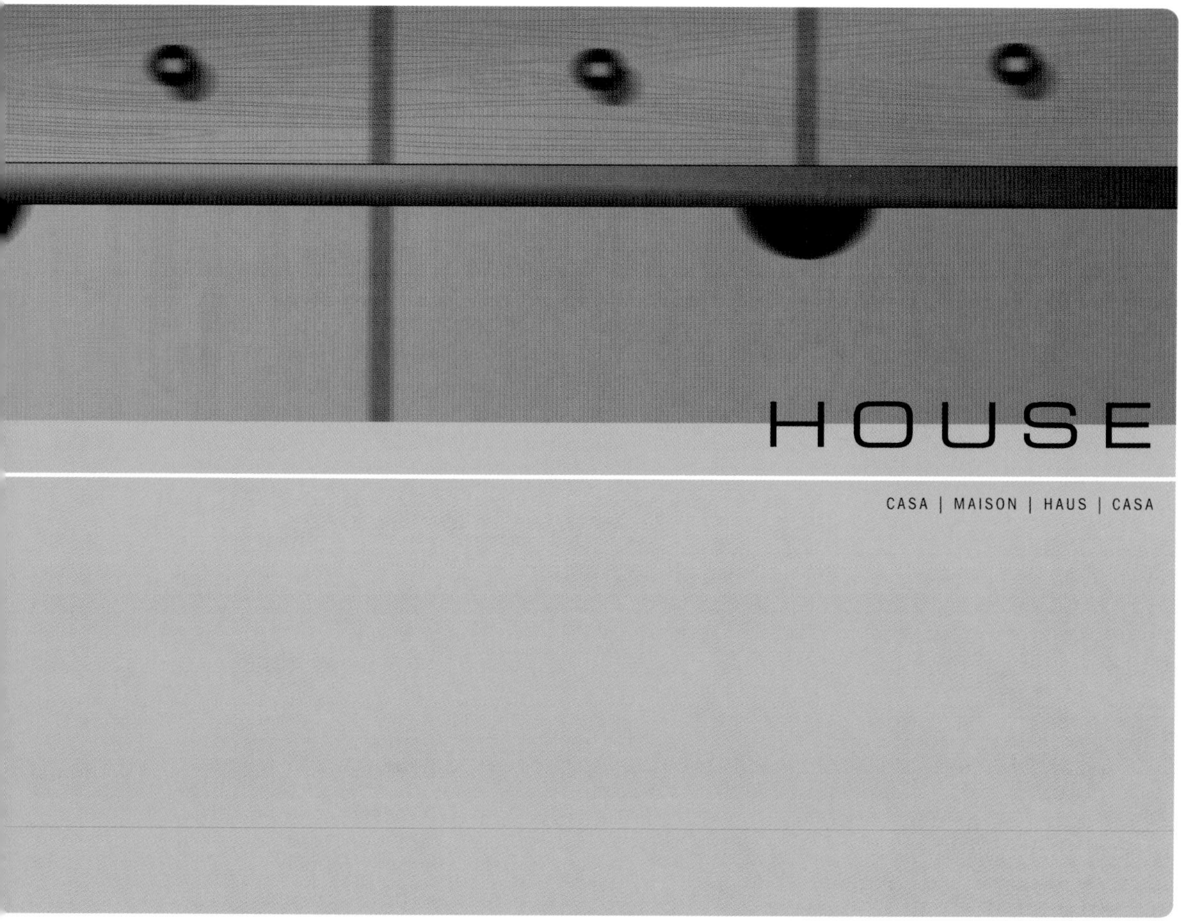

HOUSE

CASA | MAISON | HAUS | CASA

exterior of a house

exterior^M de una casa^F | extérieur^M d'une maison^F | Außenansicht^F eines Hauses^N | esterno^M di una casa^F

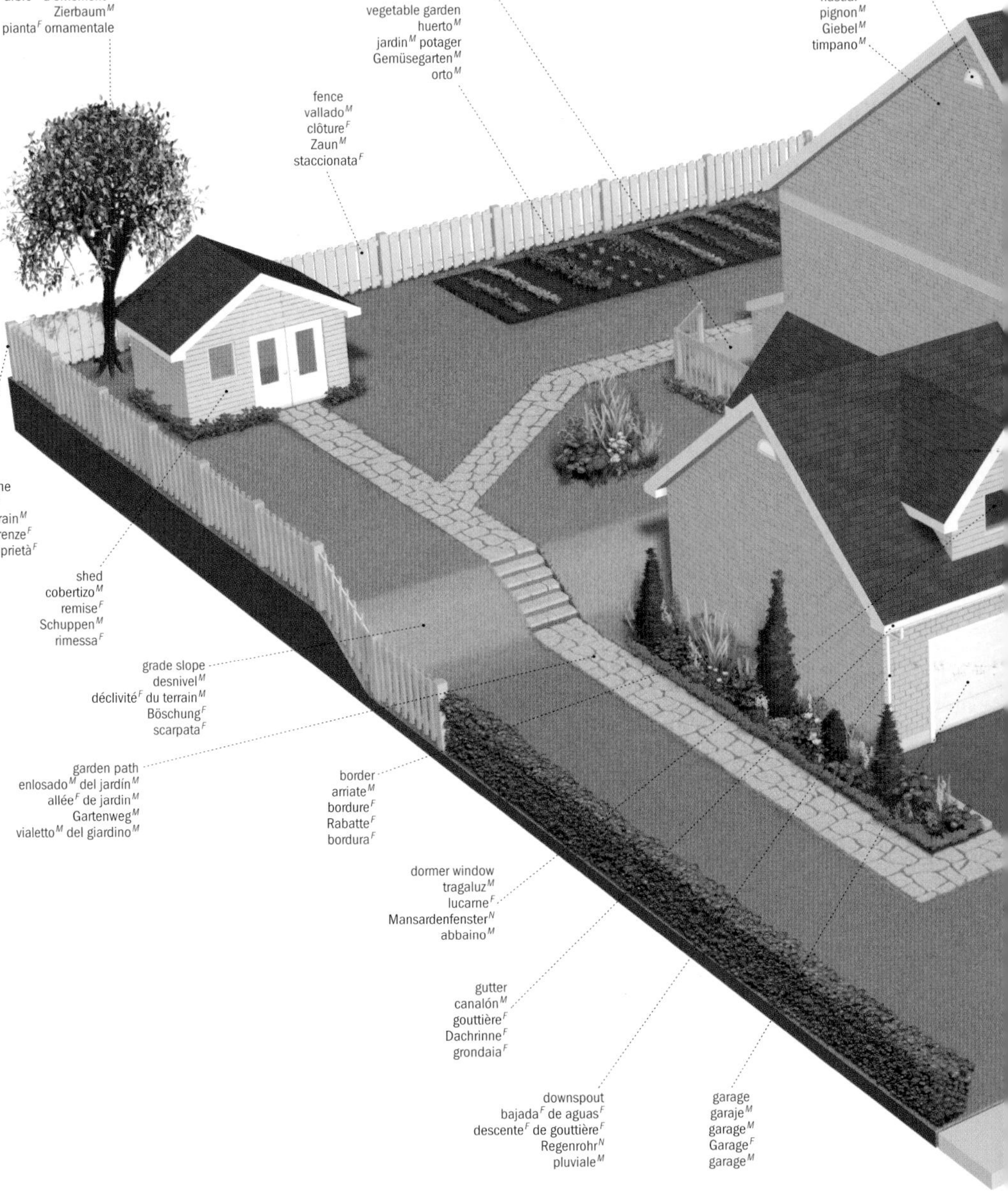

gable vent
respiradero^M
évent^M de pignon^M
Belüftungsfenster^N
griglia^F di aerazione^F

patio
terraza^F
terrasse^F
Terrasse^F
patio^M

gable
hastial^M
pignon^M
Giebel^M
timpano^M

ornamental tree
árbol^M ornamental
arbre^M d'ornement^M
Zierbaum^M
pianta^F ornamentale

vegetable garden
huerto^M
jardin^M potager
Gemüsegarten^M
orto^M

fence
vallado^M
clôture^F
Zaun^M
staccionata^F

property line
lindero^M
limite^F du terrain^M
Grundstücksgrenze^F
confine^M di proprietà^F

shed
cobertizo^M
remise^F
Schuppen^M
rimessa^F

grade slope
desnivel^M
déclivité^F du terrain^M
Böschung^F
scarpata^F

garden path
enlosado^M del jardín^M
allée^F de jardin^M
Gartenweg^M
vialetto^M del giardino^M

border
arriate^M
bordure^F
Rabatte^F
bordura^F

dormer window
tragaluz^M
lucarne^F
Mansardenfenster^N
abbaino^M

gutter
canalón^M
gouttière^F
Dachrinne^F
grondaia^F

downspout
bajada^F de aguas^F
descente^F de gouttière^F
Regenrohr^N
pluviale^M

garage
garaje^M
garage^M
Garage^F
garage^M

HOUSE

skylight
lucernario ^{M}
lanterneau ^{M}
Dachfenster ^{N}
lucernario ^{M}

lightning rod
pararrayos ^{M}
paratonnerre ^{M}
Blitzableiter ^{M}
parafulmine ^{M}

chimney pot
caperuza ^{M} de la chimenea ^{F}
mitron ^{M}
Kaminaufsatz ^{M}
comignolo ^{M}

chimney
chimenea ^{F}
cheminée ^{F}
Schornstein ^{M}
camino ^{M}

roof
tejado ^{M}
toit ^{M}
Dach ^{N}
tetto ^{M}

cornice
cornisa ^{F}
corniche ^{F}
Gesims ^{N}
cornicione ^{M}

steps
escalinata ^{F}
perron ^{M}
Treppenvorbau ^{M}
scala ^{F} esterna

basement window
ventana ^{F} del semisótano ^{M}
fenêtre ^{F} de sous-sol ^{M}
Kellerfenster ^{N}
finestra ^{F} del seminterrato ^{M}

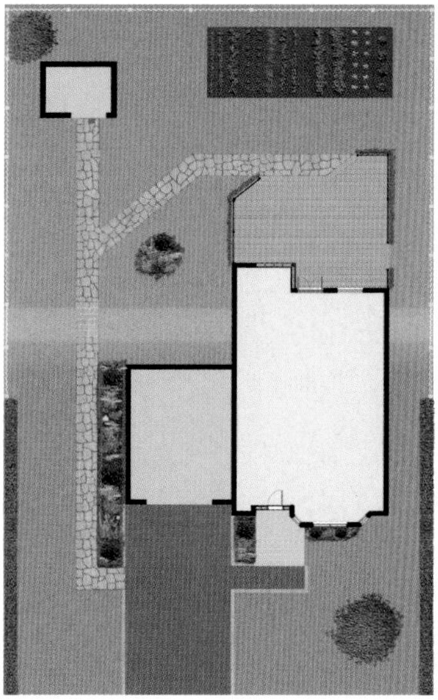

site plan
plano ^{M} del terreno ^{M}
plan ^{M} du terrain ^{M}
Lageplan ^{M}
pianta ^{F}

hedge
seto ^{M}
haie ^{F}
Hecke ^{F}
siepe ^{F}

lawn
césped ^{M}
pelouse ^{F}
Rasen ^{M}
prato ^{M}

flower bed
cuadro ^{M}
massif ^{M}
Beet ^{N}
aiuola ^{F}

sidewalk
acera ^{F}
trottoir ^{M}
Gehweg ^{M}
marciapiede ^{M}

porch
porche ^{M}
porche ^{M}
Vorbau ^{M}
portico ^{M}

driveway
entrada ^{F} del garaje ^{M}
entrée ^{F} de garage ^{M}
Zufahrtsweg ^{M}
vialetto ^{M} di accesso ^{M}

pool

piscina^F | piscine^F | Schwimmbecken^N | piscina^F

aboveground swimming pool
piscina^F elevada
piscine^F hors sol^M
freistehendes Schwimmbecken^N
piscina^F fuori terra^F

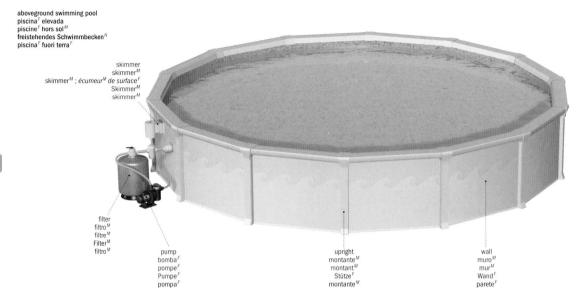

skimmer
skimmer^M
skimmer^M ; écumeur^M de surface^F
Skimmer^M
skimmer^M

filter
filtro^M
filtre^M
Filter^M
filtro^M

pump
bomba^F
pompe^F
Pumpe^F
pompa^F

upright
montante^M
montant^M
Stütze^F
montante^M

wall
muro^M
mur^M
Wand^F
parete^F

in-ground swimming pool
piscina^F enterrada
piscine^F enterrée ; piscine^F creusée
eingebautes Schwimmbecken^N
piscina^F interrata

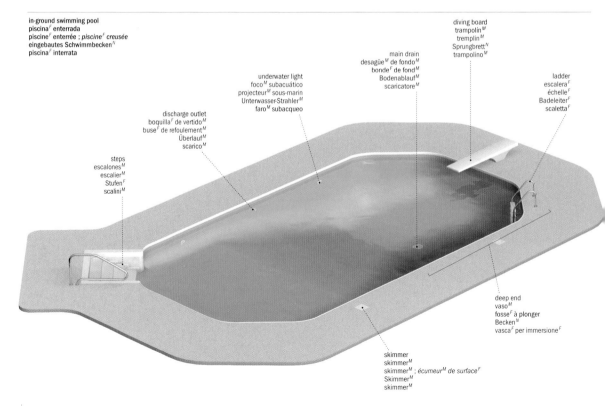

diving board
trampolín^M
tremplin^M
Sprungbrett^N
trampolino^M

main drain
desagüe^M de fondo^M
bonde^F de fond^M
Bodenablauf^M
scaricatore^M

underwater light
foco^M subacuático
projecteur^M sous-marin
Unterwasser-Strahler^M
faro^M subacqueo

ladder
escalera^F
échelle^F
Badeleiter^F
scaletta^F

discharge outlet
boquilla^F de vertido^M
buse^F de refoulement^M
Überlauf^M
scarico^M

steps
escalones^M
escalier^M
Stufen^F
scalini^M

deep end
vaso^M
fosse^F à plonger
Becken^N
vasca^F per immersione^F

skimmer
skimmer^M
skimmer^M ; écumeur^M de surface^F
Skimmer^M
skimmer^M

HOUSE

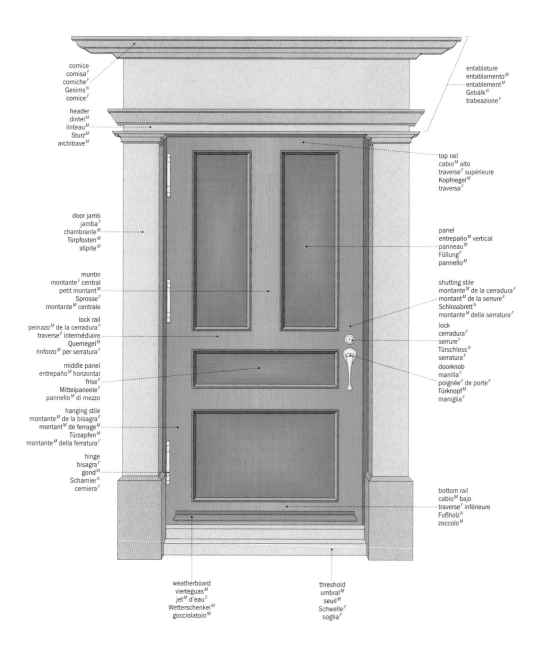

cornice
cornisa^F
corniche^F
Gesims^N
cornice^F

entablature
entablamento^M
entablement^M
Gebälk^N
trabeazione^F

header
dintel^M
linteau^M
Sturz^M
architrave^M

top rail
cabio^M alto
traverse^F supérieure
Kopfriegel^M
traversa^F

door jamb
jamba^F
chambranle^M
Türpfosten^M
stipite^M

panel
entrepaño^M vertical
panneau^M
Füllung^F
pannello^M

muntin
montante^F central
petit montant^M
Sprosse^F
montante^M centrale

shutting stile
montante^M de la cerradura^F
montant^M de la serrure^F
Schlossbrett^N
montante^M della serratura^F

lock rail
peinazo^M de la cerradura^F
traverse^F intermédiaire
Querriegel^M
rinforzo^M per serratura^F

lock
cerradura^F
serrure^F
Türschloss^N
serratura^F

middle panel
entrepaño^M horizontal
frise^F
Mittelpaneele^F
pannello^M di mezzo

doorknob
manilla^F
poignée^F de porte^F
Türknopf^M
maniglia^F

hanging stile
montante^M de la bisagra^F
montant^M de ferrage^M
Türzapfen^M
montante^M della ferratura^F

hinge
bisagra^F
gond^M
Scharnier^N
cerniera^F

bottom rail
cabio^M bajo
traverse^F inférieure
Fußholz^N
zoccolo^M

weatherboard
vierteguas^M
jet^M d'eau^F
Wetterschenkel^M
gocciolatoio^M

threshold
umbral^M
seuil^M
Schwelle^F
soglia^F

lock

cerrajería^F | serrure^F | Schloss^N | serratura^F

HOUSE

general view
vista^F general
vue^F d'ensemble^M
Gesamtansicht^F
visione^F di insieme^M

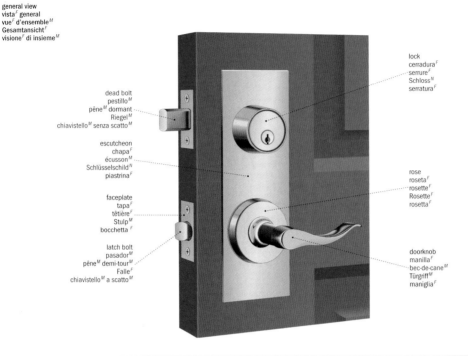

dead bolt
pestillo^M
pêne^M dormant
Riegel^M
chiavistello^M senza scatto^M

escutcheon
chapa^F
écusson^M
Schlüsselschild^N
piastrina^F

faceplate
tapa^F
têtière^F
Stulp^M
bocchetta^F

latch bolt
pasador^M
pêne^M demi-tour^M
Falle^F
chiavistello^M a scatto^M

lock
cerradura^F
serrure^F
Schloss^N
serratura^F

rose
roseta^F
rosette^F
Rosette^F
rosetta^F

doorknob
manilla^F
bec-de-cane^M
Türgriff^M
maniglia^F

tubular lock
cerradura^F tubular con seguro^M
serrure^F tubulaire
Einsteckschloss^N mit Dreh- und Verriegelungsmechanik^F
serratura^F premi-apri

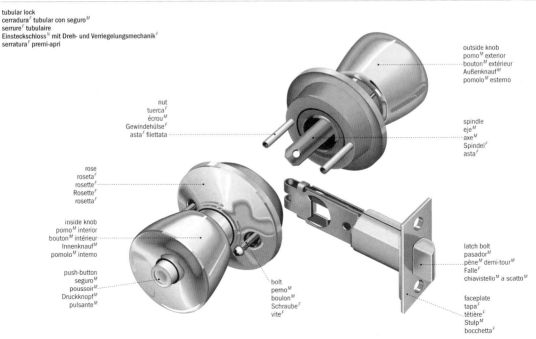

nut
tuerca^F
écrou^M
Gewindehülse^F
asta^F filettata

outside knob
pomo^M exterior
bouton^M extérieur
Außenknauf^M
pomolo^M esterno

spindle
eje^M
axe^M
Spindel^F
asta^F

rose
roseta^F
rosette^F
Rosette^F
rosetta^F

inside knob
pomo^M interior
bouton^M intérieur
Innenknauf^M
pomolo^M interno

push-button
seguro^M
poussoir^M
Druckknopf^M
pulsante^M

bolt
perno^M
boulon^M
Schraube^F
vite^F

latch bolt
pasador^M
pêne^M demi-tour^M
Falle^F
chiavistello^M a scatto^M

faceplate
tapa^F
têtière^F
Stulp^M
bocchetta^F

lock

mortise lock
cerradura^F embutida
serrure^F à mortaiser
Zylinderschloss^N
serratura^F a pomolo^M

HOUSE

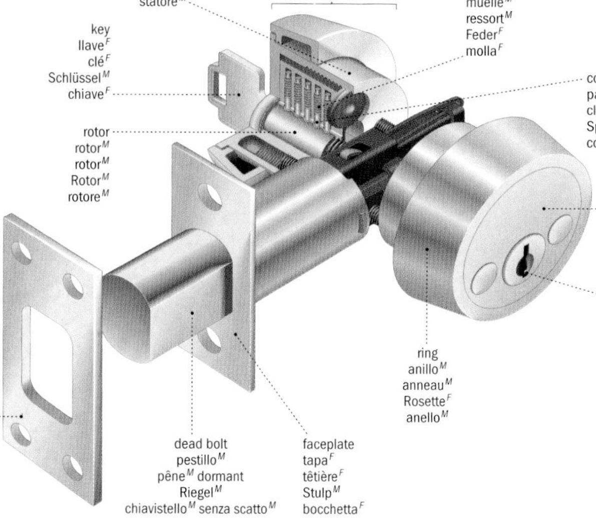

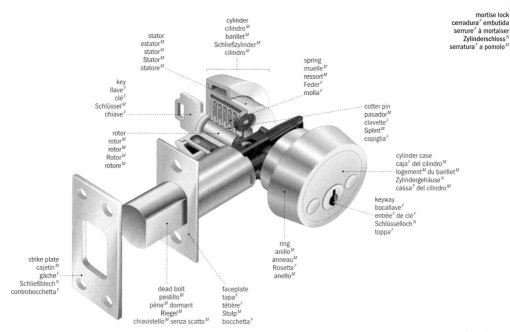

cylinder
cilindro^M
barillet^M
Schließzylinder^M
cilindro^M

stator
estator^M
stator^M
Stator^M
statore^M

spring
muelle^M
ressort^M
Feder^F
molla^F

key
llave^F
clé^F
Schlüssel^M
chiave^F

cotter pin
pasador^M
clavette^F
Splint^M
copiglia^F

rotor
rotor^M
rotor^M
Rotor^M
rotore^M

cylinder case
caja^F del cilindro^M
logement^M du barillet^M
Zylindergehäuse^N
cassa^F del cilindro^M

keyway
bocallave^F
entrée^F de clé^F
Schlüsselloch^N
toppa^F

strike plate
cajetín^M
gâche^F
Schließblech^N
controbocchetta^F

ring
anillo^M
anneau^M
Rosette^F
anello^M

dead bolt
pestillo^M
pêne^M dormant
Riegel^M
chiavistello^M senza scatto^M

faceplate
tapa^F
têtière^F
Stulp^M
bocchetta^F

window

ventana^F | fenêtre^F | Fenster^N | finestra^F

head of frame
travesaño^M superior
tête^F de dormant^M
Blendrahmen^M oben
parte^F superiore dell'intelaiatura^F

casing
marco^M
chambranle^M
Holzleibung^F
chiambrana^F

jalousie
celosía^F veneciana
persienne^F
Jalousie^F
persiana^F

structure
estructura^F
structure^F
Konstruktion^F
struttura^F

top rail of sash
travesaño^M superior de la vidriera^F
traverse^F supérieure d'ouvrant^M
Oberschenkel^M
traverso^M superiore del telaio^M

casement
batiente^M
battant^M
Flügel^M
telaio^M

muntin
parteluz^M
petit bois^M
Sprosse^F
listello^M rompitratta

hanging stile
larguero^M
montant^M de rive^F
Flügelrahmen^M
montante^M

pane
vidrio^M
carreau^M
Scheibe^F
vetro^M

sash frame
montante^M quicial
dormant^M
Blendrahmen^M
controtelaio^M

hook
pestillo^M
crochet^M
Hakenverriegelung^F
gancio^M

shutter
contraventana^F
contrevent^M
Fensterladen^M
imposta^F

weatherboard
vierteaguas^M
jet^M d'eau^F
Wetterschenkel^M
gocciolatoio^M

sill of frame
alféizar^M
base^F de dormant^M
Fensterbrett^N
base^F dell'intelaiatura^F

hinge
bisagra^F
paumelle^F
Scharnier^N
cerniera^F

stile tongue of sash
montante^M central
montant^M mouton^M
Deckleiste^F
giunzione^F a linguetta^F del telaio^M

stile groove of sash
montante^M embarbillado
montant^M embrevé
Falz^M
giunzione^F scanalata del telaio^M

main rooms

habitaciones^F principales | principales pièces^F d'une maison^F | Haupträume^M | stanze^F principali

HOUSE

elevation
alzado^M
élévation^F
Ansicht^F
prospetto^M

third floor
entresuelo^M
mezzanine^F
Zwischengeschoß^N
piano^M mansardato

second floor
planta^F alta
étage^M
erster Stock^M
primo piano^M

first floor
planta^F baja
rez-de-chaussée^M
Erdgeschoß^N
pianterreno^M

basement
semisótano^M
sous-sol^M
Keller^M
seminterrato^M

first floor
planta^F baja
rez-de-chaussée^M
Erdgeschoß^N
pianterreno^M

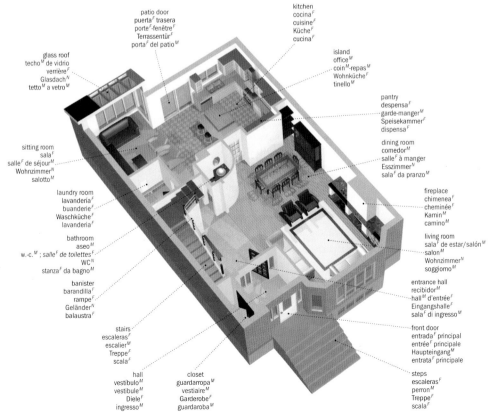

patio door
puerta^F trasera
porte^F-fenêtre^F
Terrassentür^F
porta^F del patio^M

kitchen
cocina^F
cuisine^F
Küche^F
cucina^F

glass roof
techo^M de vidrio
verrière^F
Glasdach^N
tetto^M a vetro^M

island
office^M
coin^M-repas^M
Wohnküche^F
tinello^M

pantry
despensa^F
garde-manger^M
Speisekammer^F
dispensa^F

sitting room
sala^F
salle^F de séjour^M
Wohnzimmer^N
salotto^M

dining room
comedor^M
salle^F à manger
Esszimmer^N
sala^F da pranzo^M

laundry room
lavanderia^F
buanderie^F
Waschküche^F
lavanderia^F

fireplace
chimenea^F
cheminée^F
Kamin^M
camino^M

bathroom
aseo^M
w.-c.^{M} ; salle^F de toilettes^F
WC^M
stanza^F da bagno^M

living room
sala^F de estar/salón^M
salon^M
Wohnzimmer^N
soggiorno^M

banister
barandilla^F
rampe^F
Geländer^N
balaustra^F

entrance hall
recibidor^M
hall^M d'entrée^F
Eingangshalle^F
sala^F di ingresso^M

stairs
escaleras^F
escalier^M
Treppe^F
scala^F

front door
entrada^F principal
entrée^F principale
Haupteingang^M
entrata^F principale

hall
vestíbulo^M
vestibule^M
Diele^F
ingresso^M

closet
guardaropa^M
vestiaire^M
Garderobe^F
guardaroba^M

steps
escaleras^F
perron^M
Treppe^F
scala^F

STRUCTURE OF A HOUSE | ESTRUCTURA DE UNA CASA
STRUCTURE D'UNE MAISON | KONSTRUKTION EINES HAUSES | STRUTTURA DI UNA CASA

main rooms

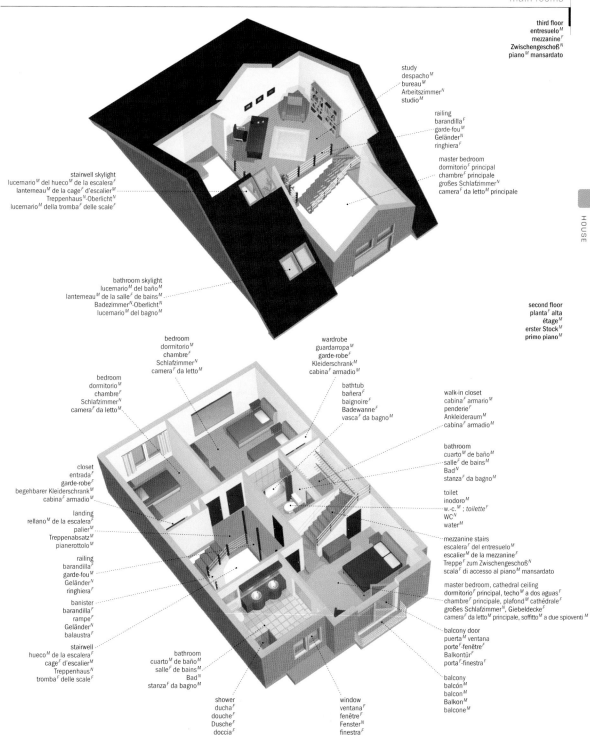

third floor
entresuelo ^{M}
mezzanine ^{F}
Zwischengeschoß ^{N}
piano ^{M} mansardato

study
despacho ^{M}
bureau ^{M}
Arbeitszimmer ^{N}
studio ^{M}

railing
barandilla ^{F}
garde-fou ^{M}
Geländer ^{N}
ringhiera ^{F}

master bedroom
dormitorio ^{F} principal
chambre ^{F} principale
großes Schlafzimmer ^{N}
camera ^{F} da letto ^{M} principale

stairwell skylight
lucernario ^{M} del hueco ^{M} de la escalera ^{F}
lanterneau ^{M} de la cage ^{F} d'escalier ^{M}
Treppenhaus ^{N}-Oberlicht ^{N}
lucernario ^{M} della tromba ^{F} delle scale ^{F}

bathroom skylight
lucernario ^{M} del baño ^{M}
lanterneau ^{M} de la salle ^{F} de bains ^{M}
Badezimmer ^{N}-Oberlicht ^{N}
lucernario ^{M} del bagno ^{M}

HOUSE

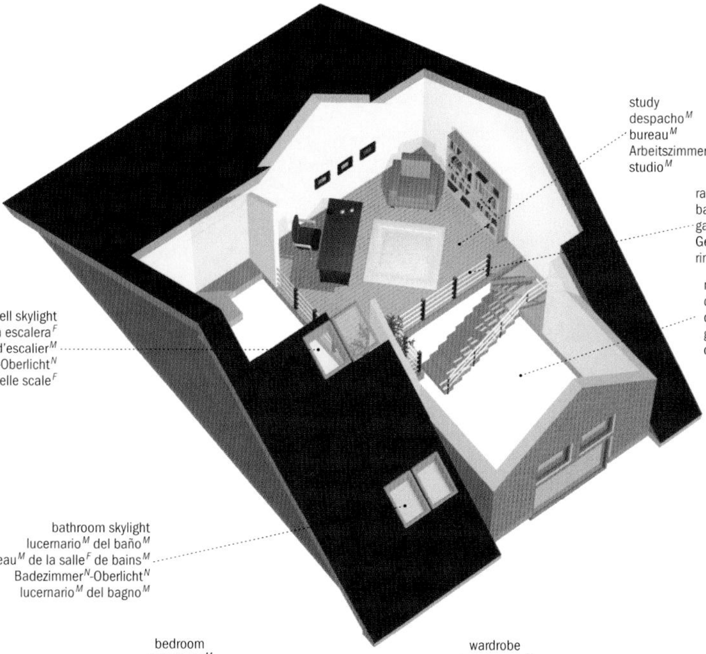

second floor
planta ^{F} alta
étage ^{M}
erster Stock ^{M}
primo piano ^{M}

bedroom
dormitorio ^{M}
chambre ^{F}
Schlafzimmer ^{N}
camera ^{F} da letto ^{M}

wardrobe
guardarropa ^{M}
garde-robe ^{F}
Kleiderschrank ^{M}
cabina ^{F} armadio ^{M}

bedroom
dormitorio ^{M}
chambre ^{F}
Schlafzimmer ^{N}
camera ^{F} da letto ^{M}

bathtub
bañera ^{F}
baignoire ^{F}
Badewanne ^{F}
vasca ^{F} da bagno ^{M}

walk-in closet
cabina ^{F} armario ^{M}
penderie ^{F}
Ankleideraum ^{M}
cabina ^{F} armadio ^{M}

closet
entrada ^{F}
garde-robe ^{F}
begehbarer Kleiderschrank ^{M}
cabina ^{F} armadio ^{M}

bathroom
cuarto ^{M} de baño ^{M}
salle ^{F} de bains ^{M}
Bad ^{N}
stanza ^{F} da bagno ^{M}

toilet
inodoro ^{M}
w.-c. ^{M} ; toilette ^{F}
WC ^{N}
water ^{M}

landing
rellano ^{M} de la escalera ^{F}
palier ^{M}
Treppenabsatz ^{M}
pianerottolo ^{M}

mezzanine stairs
escalera ^{F} del entresuelo ^{M}
escalier ^{M} de la mezzanine ^{F}
Treppe ^{F} zum Zwischengeschoß ^{N}
scala ^{F} di accesso al piano ^{M} mansardato

railing
barandilla ^{F}
garde-fou ^{M}
Geländer ^{N}
ringhiera ^{F}

master bedroom, cathedral ceiling
dormitorio ^{F} principal, techo ^{M} a dos aguas ^{F}
chambre ^{F} principale, plafond ^{M} cathédrale ^{F}
großes Schlafzimmer ^{N}, Giebeldecke ^{F}
camera ^{F} da letto ^{M} principale, soffitto ^{M} a due spioventi ^{M}

banister
barandilla ^{F}
rampe ^{F}
Geländer ^{N}
balaustra ^{F}

balcony door
puerta ^{M} ventana
porte ^{F}-fenêtre ^{F}
Balkontür ^{F}
porta ^{F}-finestra ^{F}

stairwell
hueco ^{M} de la escalera ^{F}
cage ^{F} d'escalier ^{M}
Treppenhaus ^{N}
tromba ^{F} delle scale ^{F}

bathroom
cuarto ^{M} de baño ^{M}
salle ^{F} de bains ^{M}
Bad ^{N}
stanza ^{F} da bagno ^{M}

balcony
balcón ^{M}
balcon ^{M}
Balkon ^{M}
balcone ^{M}

shower
ducha ^{F}
douche ^{F}
Dusche ^{F}
doccia ^{F}

window
ventana ^{F}
fenêtre ^{F}
Fenster ^{N}
finestra ^{F}

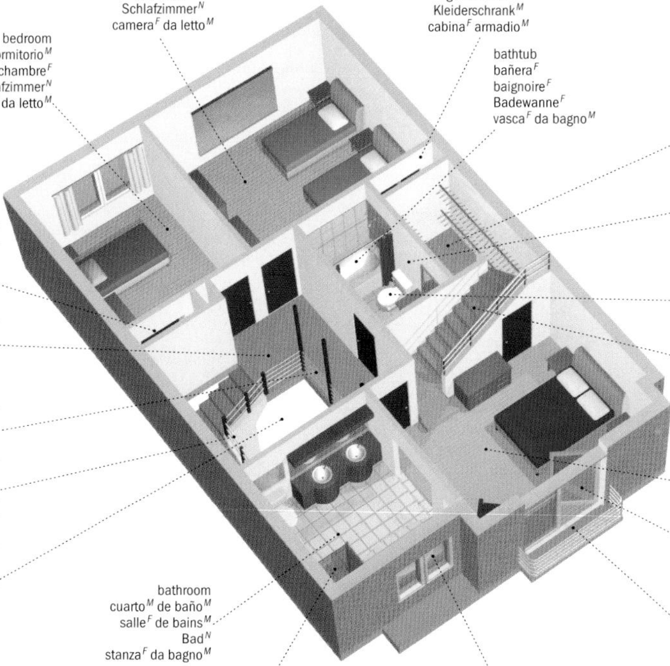

frame

armazón^M | charpente^F | Rahmen^M | struttura^F

HOUSE

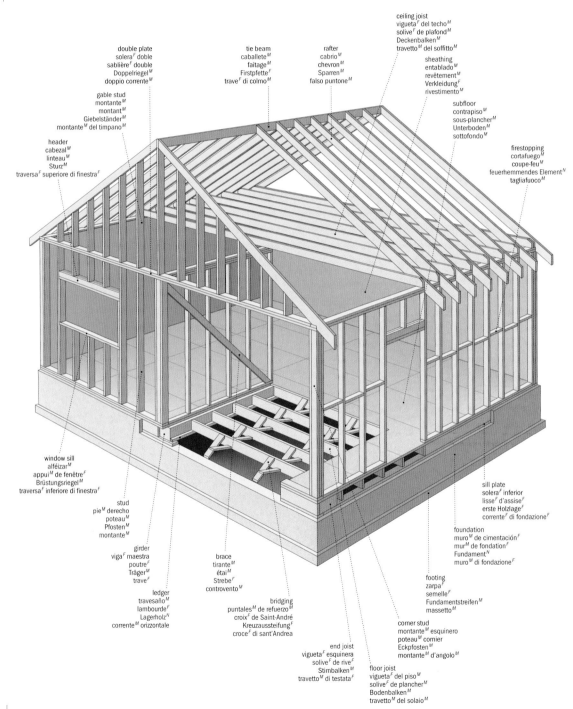

ceiling joist
vigueta^F del techo^M
solive^F de plafond^M
Deckenbalken^M
travetto^M del soffitto^M

sheathing
entablado^M
revêtement^M
Verkleidung^F
rivestimento^M

subfloor
contrapiso^M
sous-plancher^M
Unterboden^M
sottofondo^M

firestopping
cortafuego^M
coupe-feu^M
feuerhemmendes Element^N
tagliafuoco^M

double plate
solera^F doble
sablière^F double
Doppelriegel^M
doppio corrente^M

tie beam
caballete^M
faitage^M
Firstpfette^F
trave^F di colmo^M

rafter
cabrio^M
chevron^M
Sparren^M
falso puntone^M

gable stud
montante^M
montant^M
Giebelständer^M
montante^M del timpano^M

header
cabezal^M
linteau^M
Sturz^M
traversa^F superiore di finestra^F

window sill
alféizar^M
appui^M de fenêtre^F
Brüstungsriegel^M
traversa^F inferiore di finestra^F

stud
pie^M derecho
poteau^M
Pfosten^M
montante^M

girder
viga^F maestra
poutre^F
Träger^M
trave^F

brace
tirante^M
étai^M
Strebe^F
controvento^M

ledger
travesaño^M
lambourde^F
Lagerholz^N
corrente^M orizzontale

bridging
puntales^M de refuerzo^M
croix^F de Saint-André
Kreuzaussteifung^F
croce^F di sant'Andrea

sill plate
solera^F inferior
lisse^F d'assise^F
erste Holzlage^F
corrente^F di fondazione^F

foundation
muro^M de cimentación^F
mur^M de fondation^F
Fundament^N
muro^M di fondazione^F

footing
zarpa^F
semelle^F
Fundamentstreifen^M
massetto^M

corner stud
montante^M esquinero
poteau^M cornier
Eckpfosten^M
montante^M d'angolo^M

end joist
vigueta^F esquinera
solive^F de rive^F
Stirnbalken^M
travetto^M di testata^F

floor joist
vigueta^F del piso^M
solive^F de plancher^M
Bodenbalken^M
travetto^M del solaio^M

roof truss

armadura^F del techo^M | ferme^F de toit^M | Dachbinder^M | capriata^F

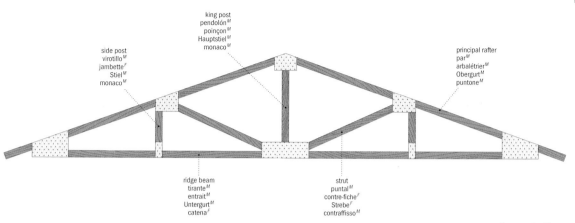

king post
pendolón^M
poinçon^M
Hauptstiel^M
monaco^M

side post
virotillo^M
jambette^F
Stiel^M
monaco^M

principal rafter
par^M
arbalétrier^M
Obergurt^M
puntone^M

ridge beam
tirante^M
entrait^M
Untergurt^M
catena^F

strut
puntal^M
contre-fiche^F
Strebe^F
contraffisso^M

foundation

cimientos^M | fondations^F | Fundament^N | fondazioni^F

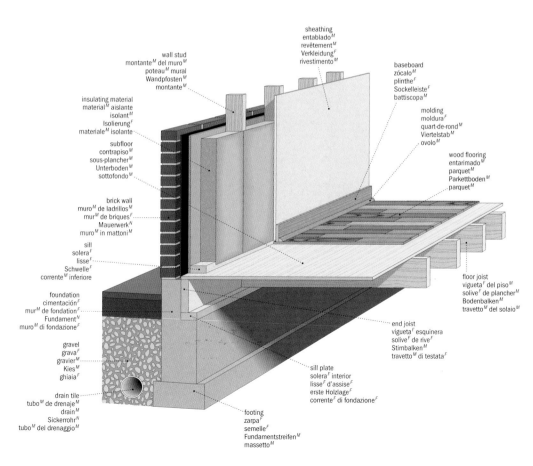

sheathing
entablado^M
revêtement^M
Verkleidung^F
rivestimento^M

wall stud
montante^M del muro^M
poteau^M mural
Wandpfosten^M
montante^M

baseboard
zócalo^M
plinthe^F
Sockelleiste^F
battiscopa^M

insulating material
material^M aislante
isolant^M
Isolierung^F
materiale^M isolante

molding
moldura^F
quart-de-rond^M
Viertelstab^M
ovolo^M

subfloor
contrapiso^M
sous-plancher^M
Unterboden^M
sottofondo^M

wood flooring
entarimado^M
parquet^M
Parkettboden^M
parquet^M

brick wall
muro^M de ladrillos^M
mur^M de briques^F
Mauerwerk^N
muro^M in mattoni^M

sill
solera^F
lisse^F
Schwelle^F
corrente^M inferiore

foundation
cimentación^F
mur^M de fondation^F
Fundament^N
muro^M di fondazione^F

floor joist
vigueta^F del piso^M
solive^F de plancher^M
Bodenbalken^M
travetto^M del solaio^M

end joist
vigueta^F esquinera
solive^F de rive^F
Stirnbalken^M
travetto^M di testata^F

gravel
grava^F
gravier^M
Kies^M
ghiaia^F

sill plate
solera^F interior
lisse^F d'assise^F
erste Holzlage^F
corrente^F di fondazione^F

drain tile
tubo^M de drenaje^M
drain^M
Sickerrohr^N
tubo^M del drenaggio^M

footing
zarpa^F
semelle^F
Fundamentstreifen^M
massetto^M

HOUSE

wood flooring

pisos^M de madera^F | parquet^M | Parkettboden^M | parquet^M

wood flooring on cement screed
parqué^M sobre base^F de cemento^M
parquet^M sur chape^F de ciment^M
Parkettboden^M auf Zementestrich^M
parquet^M su sottofondo^M di cemento^M

wood flooring on wooden structure
entarimado^M sobre estructura^F de madera^F
parquet^M sur ossature^F de bois^M
Parkettboden^M auf Holzunterbau^M
parquet^M su struttura^F lignea

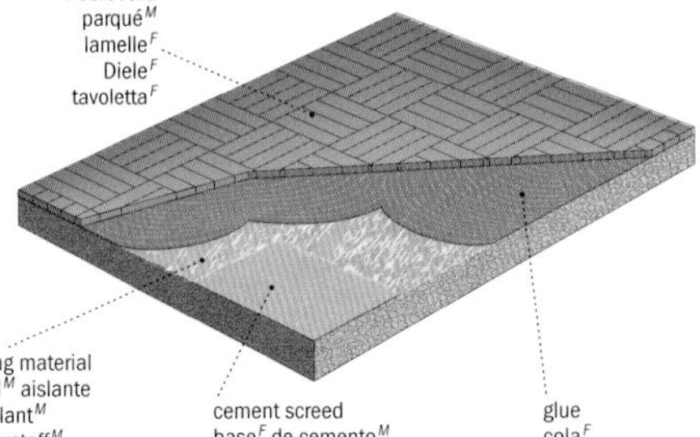

floorboard
parqué^M
lamelle^F
Diele^F
tavoletta^F

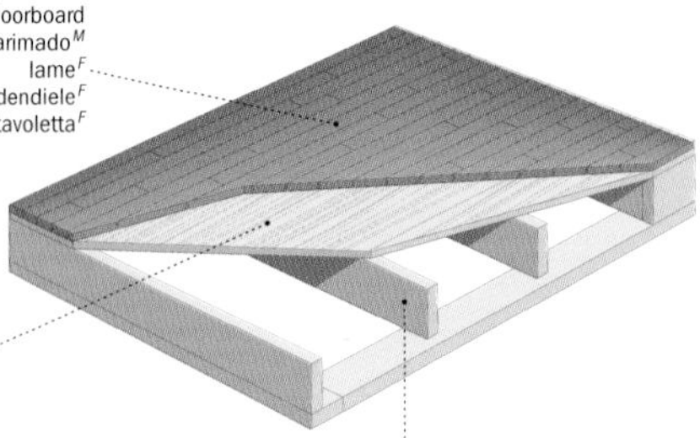

floorboard
entarimado^M
lame^F
Bodendiele^F
tavoletta^F

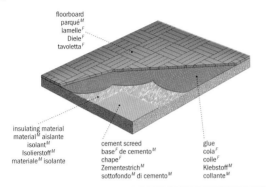

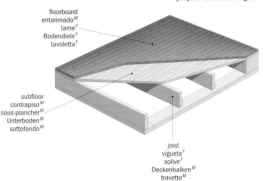

subfloor
contrapiso^M
sous-plancher^M
Unterboden^M
sottofondo^M

insulating material
material^M aislante
isolant^M
Isolierstoff^M
materiale^M isolante

cement screed
base^F de cemento^M
chape^F
Zementestrich^M
sottofondo^M di cemento^M

glue
cola^F
colle^F
Klebstoff^M
collante^M

joist
vigueta^F
solive^F
Deckenbalken^M
travetto^M

wood flooring arrangements
tipos^M de parqué^M
arrangements^M des parquets^M
Parkettmuster^N
tipi^M di parquet^M

overlay flooring
parqué^M sobrepuesto
parquet^M à coupe^F perdue
Stabparkett^N im Schiffsbodenverband^M
parquet^M a listoni^M

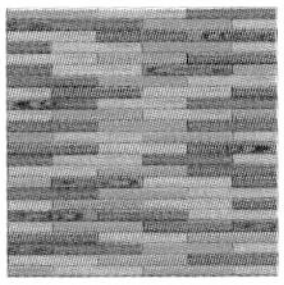

strip flooring with alternate joints
parqué^M alternado a la inglesa
parquet^M à coupe^F de pierre^F
Stabparkett^N
parquet^M a listelli^M

herringbone parquet
parqué^M espinapez^M
parquet^M à bâtons^M rompus
Fischgrätparkett^N
parquet^M a spina^F di pesce^M

herringbone pattern
parqué^M en punta^F de Hungria
parquet^M en chevrons^M
Fischgrätmuster^N
parquet^M a spina^F di pesce^M

inlaid parquet
parqué^M de mosaico
parquet^M mosaïque^F
Mosaikparkett^N
parquet^M a mosaico^M

basket weave pattern
parqué^M de cestería^F
parquet^M en vannerie^F
Würfelmusterparkett^N
parquet^M a tessitura^F di vimini^M

Arenberg parquet
parqué^M Arenberg
parquet^M d'Arenberg
Arenberg-Parkett^N
parquet^M Arenberg

Chantilly parquet
parqué^M Chantilly
parquet^M Chantilly
Chantilly-Parkett^N
parquet^M Chantilly

Versailles parquet
parqué^M Versalles
parquet^M Versailles
Versailles-Parkett^N
parquet^M Versailles

textile floor coverings

revestimientos^M textiles del suelo^M | revêtements^M de sol^M textiles | textile Bodenbeläge^M | rivestimenti^M in tessuto^M per pavimento^M

rug
alfombra^F
tapis^M
Teppich^M
tappeto^M

pile carpet
moqueta^F
moquette^F
Teppichboden^M
moquette^F

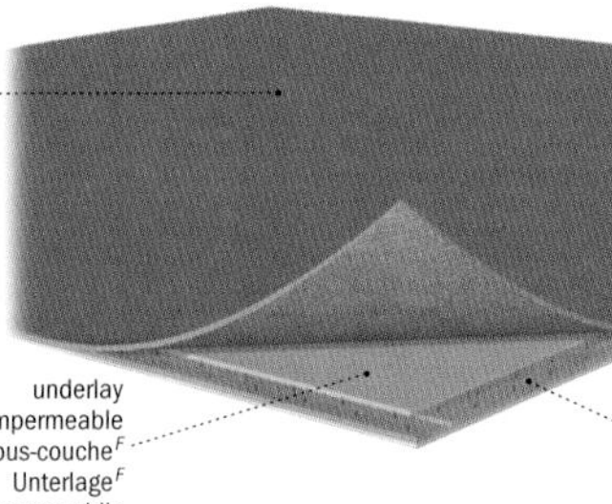

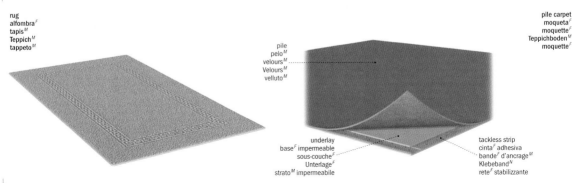

pile
pelo^M
velours^M
Velours^M
velluto^M

underlay
base^F impermeable
sous-couche^F
Unterlage^F
strato^M impermeabile

tackless strip
cinta^F adhesiva
bande^F d'ancrage^M
Klebeband^N
rete^F stabilizzante

HOUSE

stairs

escalera^F | escalier^M | Treppe^F | scale^F

HOUSE

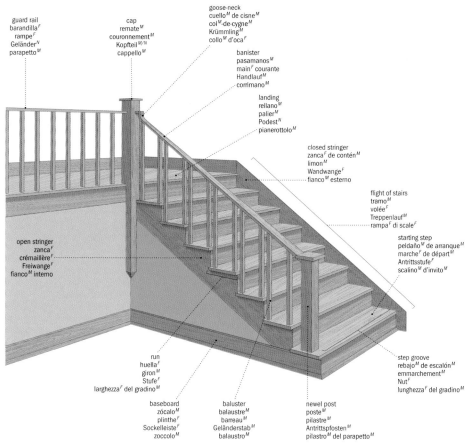

guard rail
barandilla^F
rampe^F
Geländer^N
parapetto^M

cap
remate^M
couronnement^M
Kopfteil$^{M/N}$
cappello^M

goose-neck
cuello^M de cisne^M
col^M-de-cygne^M
Krümmling^M
collo^M d'oca^F

banister
pasamanos^M
main^F courante
Handlauf^M
corrimano^M

landing
rellano^M
palier^M
Podest^N
pianerottolo^M

closed stringer
zanca^F de contén^M
limon^M
Wandwange^F
fianco^M esterno

flight of stairs
tramo^M
volée^F
Treppenlauf^M
rampa^F di scale^F

open stringer
zanca^F
crémaillère^F
Freiwange^F
fianco^M interno

starting step
peldaño^M de arranque^M
marche^F de départ^M
Antrittsstufe^F
scalino^M d'invito^M

run
huella^F
giron^M
Stufe^F
larghezza^F del gradino^M

step groove
rebajo^M de escalón^M
emmarchement^M
Nut^F
lunghezza^F del gradino^M

baseboard
zócalo^M
plinthe^F
Sockelleiste^F
zoccolo^M

baluster
balaustre^M
barreau^M
Geländerstab^M
balaustro^M

newel post
poste^M
pilastre^M
Antrittspfosten^M
pilastro^M del parapetto^M

step

peldaño^M | marche^F | Treppenstufe^F | gradino^M

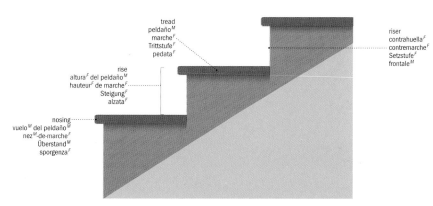

tread
peldaño^M
marche^F
Trittstufe^F
pedata^F

riser
contrahuella^F
contremarche^F
Setzstufe^F
frontale^M

rise
altura^F del peldaño^M
hauteur^F de marche^F
Steigung^F
alzata^F

nosing
vuelo^M del peldaño^M
nez^M-de-marche^F
Überstand^M
sporgenza^F

wood burning

calefacción^F de leña^F | chauffage^M au bois^M | Holzbeheizung^F | riscaldamento^M a legna^F

HOUSE

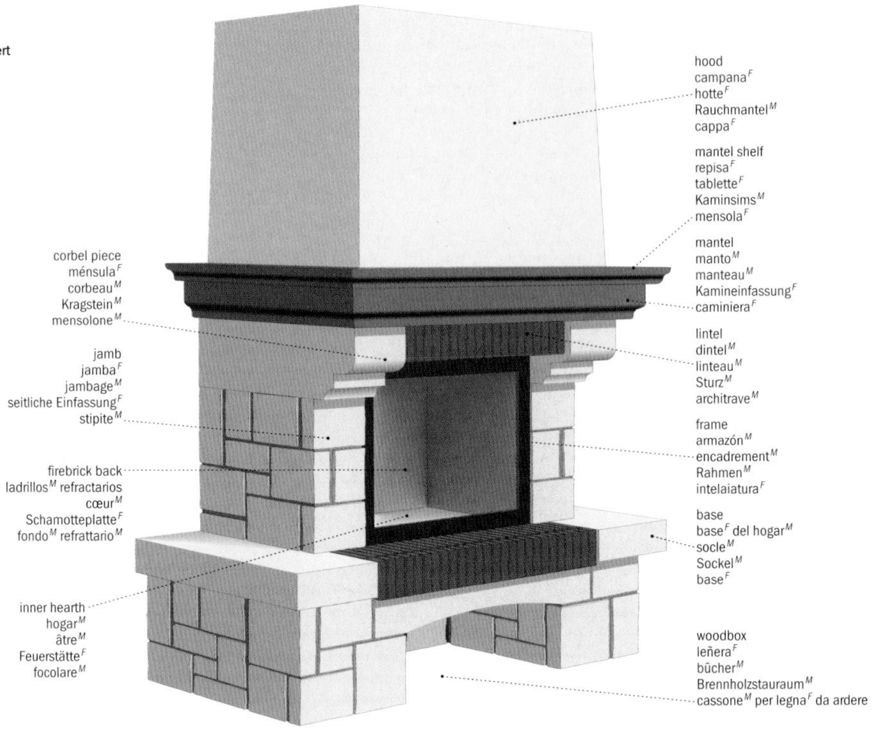

fireplace
chimenea^F
cheminée^F à foyer^M ouvert
Kamin^M
camino^M

hood
campana^F
hotte^F
Rauchmantel^M
cappa^F

mantel shelf
repisa^F
tablette^F
Kaminsims^M
mensola^F

mantel
manto^M
manteau^M
Kamineinfassung^F
caminiera^F

corbel piece
ménsula^F
corbeau^M
Kragstein^M
mensolone^M

lintel
dintel^M
linteau^M
Sturz^M
architrave^M

jamb
jamba^F
jambage^M
seitliche Einfassung^F
stipite^M

frame
armazón^M
encadrement^M
Rahmen^M
intelaiatura^F

firebrick back
ladrillos^M refractarios
cœur^M
Schamotteplatte^F
fondo^M refrattario^M

base
base^F del hogar^M
socle^M
Sockel^M
base^F

inner hearth
hogar^M
âtre^M
Feuerstätte^F
focolare^M

woodbox
leñera^F
bûcher^M
Brennholzstauraum^M
cassone^M per legna^F da ardere

slow-burning wood stove
estufa^F de leña^F a fuego^M lento
poêle^M à combustion^F lente
Dauerbrandofen^M
stufa^F a combustione^F lenta

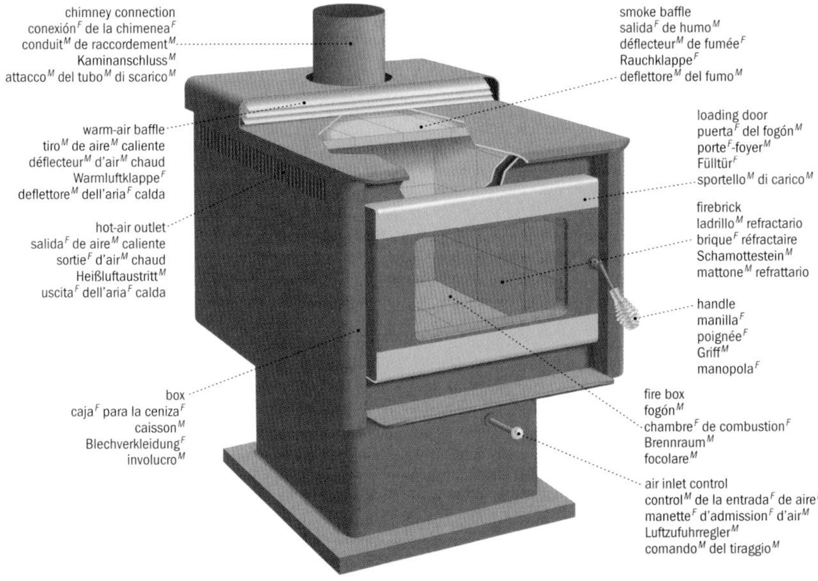

chimney connection
conexión^F de la chimenea^F
conduit^M de raccordement^M
Kaminanschluss^M
attacco^M del tubo^M di scarico^M

smoke baffle
salida^F de humo^M
déflecteur^M de fumée^F
Rauchklappe^F
deflettore^M del fumo^M

warm-air baffle
tiro^M de aire^M caliente
déflecteur^M d'air^M chaud
Warmluftklappe^F
deflettore^M dell'aria^F calda

loading door
puerta^F del fogón^M
porte^F-foyer^M
Fülltür^F
sportello^M di carico^M

firebrick
ladrillo^M refractario
brique^F réfractaire
Schamottestein^M
mattone^M refrattario

hot-air outlet
salida^F de aire^M caliente
sortie^F d'air^M chaud
Heißluftaustritt^M
uscita^F dell'aria^F calda

handle
manilla^F
poignée^F
Griff^M
manopola^F

box
caja^F para la ceniza^F
caisson^M
Blechverkleidung^F
involucro^M

fire box
fogón^M
chambre^F de combustion^F
Brennraum^M
focolare^M

air inlet control
control^M de la entrada^F de aire^M
manette^F d'admission^F d'air^M
Luftzufuhrregler^M
comando^M del tiraggio^M

HOUSE

chimney
chimenea^F
cheminée^F
Kamin^M
camino^M

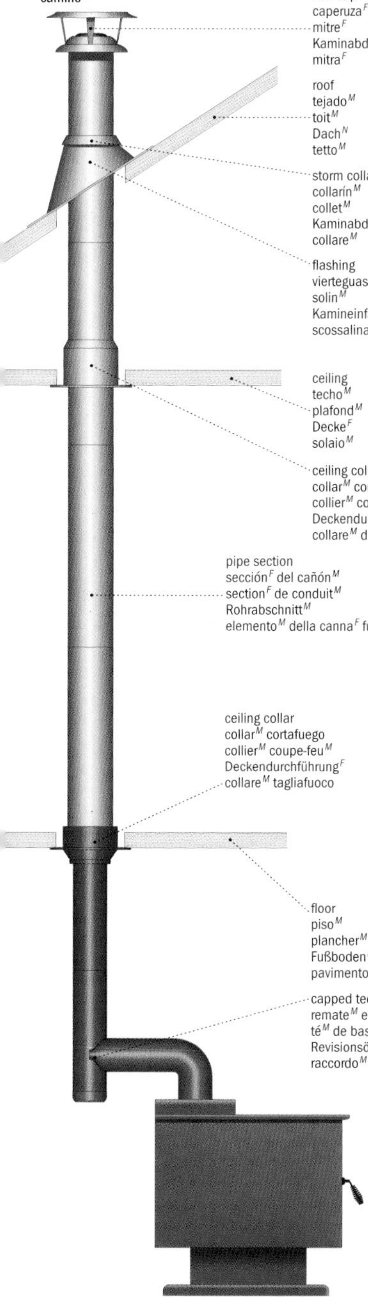

rain cap
caperuza^F
mitre^F
Kaminabdeckung^F
mitra^F

roof
tejado^M
toit^M
Dach^N
tetto^M

storm collar
collarín^M
collet^M
Kaminabdichtung^F
collare^M

flashing
vierteguas^M
solin^M
Kamineinfassung^F
scossalina^F

ceiling
techo^M
plafond^M
Decke^F
solaio^M

ceiling collar
collar^M cortafuego
collier^M coupe-feu^M
Deckendurchführung^F
collare^M del solaio^M

pipe section
sección^F del cañón^M
section^F de conduit^M
Rohrabschnitt^M
elemento^M della canna^F fumaria

ceiling collar
collar^M cortafuego
collier^M coupe-feu^M
Deckendurchführung^F
collare^M tagliafuoco

floor
piso^M
plancher^M
Fußboden^M
pavimento^M

capped tee
remate^M en T
té^M de base^F
Revisionsöffnung^F
raccordo^M a T

fire irons
utensilios^M para la chimenea^F
accessoires^M de foyer^M
Kaminbesteck^N
ferri^M per il camino^M

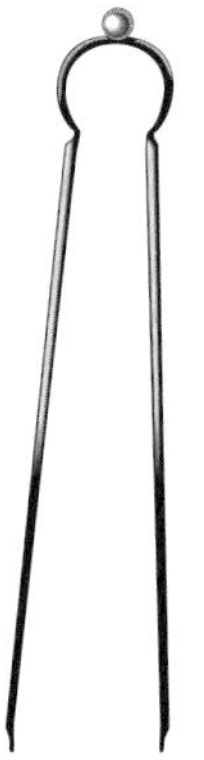

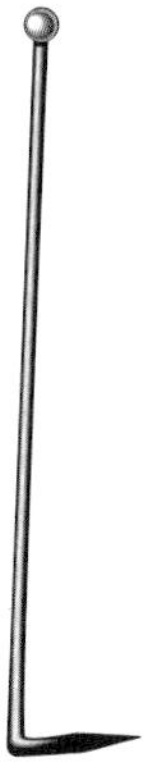

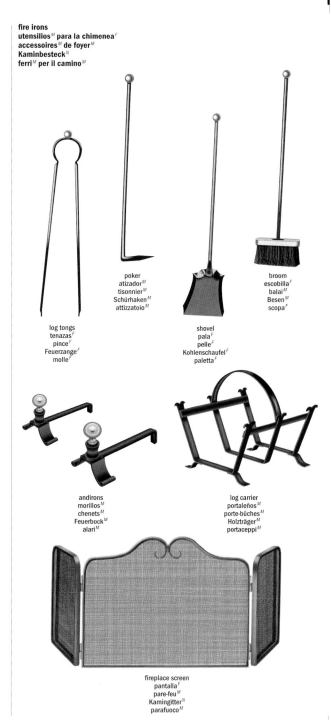

poker
atizador^M
tisonnier^M
Schürhaken^M
attizzatoio^M

log tongs
tenazas^F
pince^F
Feuerzange^F
molle^F

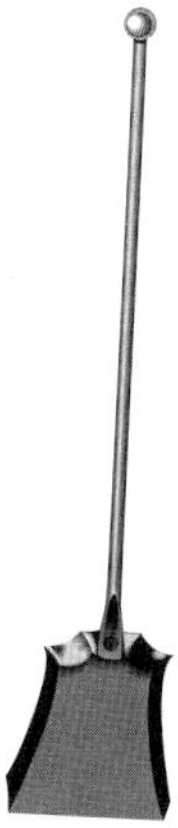

shovel
pala^F
pelle^F
Kohlenschaufel^F
paletta^F

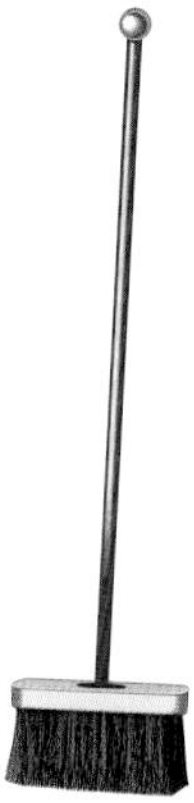

broom
escobilla^F
balai^M
Besen^M
scopa^F

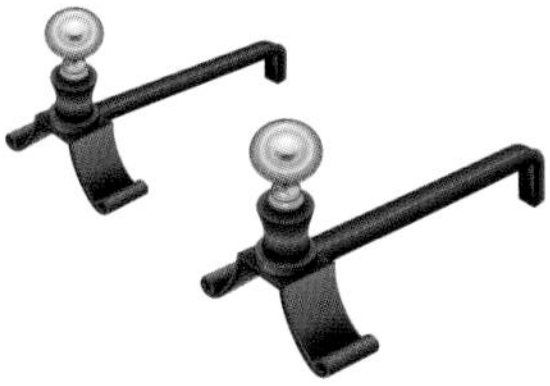

andirons
morillos^M
chenets^M
Feuerbock^M
alari^M

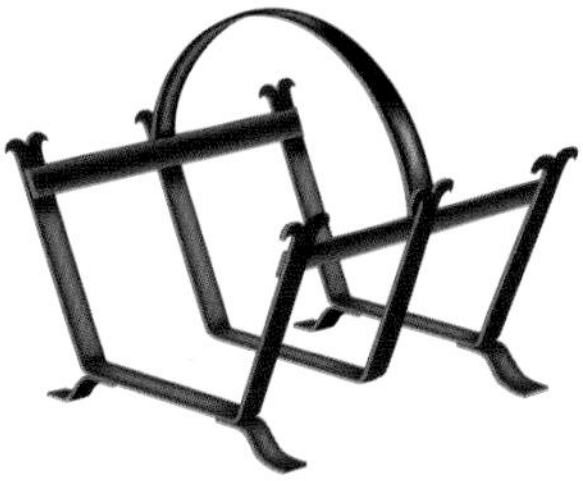

log carrier
portaleños^M
porte-bûches^M
Holzträger^M
portaceppi^M

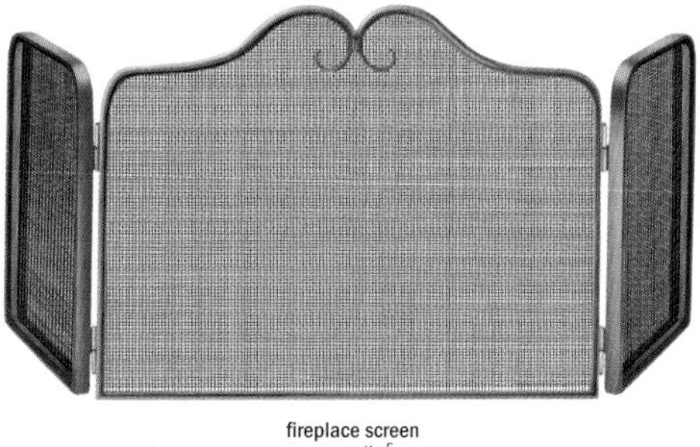

fireplace screen
pantalla^F
pare-feu^M
Kamingitter^N
parafuoco^M

257

forced air heating system

sistema^M de aire^M caliente a presión^F | installation^F à air^M chaud pulsé | Warmluftsystem^N mit Zwangsumlauf^M | impianto^M di riscaldamento^M ad aria^F calda

HOUSE

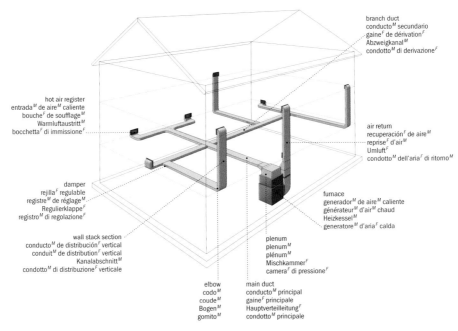

branch duct
conducto^M secundario
gaine^F de dérivation^F
Abzweigkanal^M
condotto^M di derivazione^F

hot air register
entrada^M de aire^M caliente
bouche^F de soufflage^M
Warmluftaustritt^M
bocchetta^F di immissione^F

air return
recuperación^F de aire^M
reprise^F d'air^M
Umluft^F
condotto^M dell'aria^F di ritorno^M

damper
rejilla^F regulable
registre^F de réglage^M
Regulierklappe^F
registro^M di regolazione^F

furnace
generador^M de aire^M caliente
générateur^M d'air^M chaud
Heizkessel^M
generatore^M d'aria^F calda

wall stack section
conducto^M de distribución^F vertical
conduit^M de distribution^F vertical
Kanalabschnitt^M
condotto^M di distribuzione^F verticale

plenum
plenum^M
plénum^M
Mischkammer^F
camera^F di pressione^F

elbow
codo^M
coude^M
Bogen^M
gomito^M

main duct
conducto^M principal
gaine^F principale
Hauptverteilleitung^F
condotto^M principale

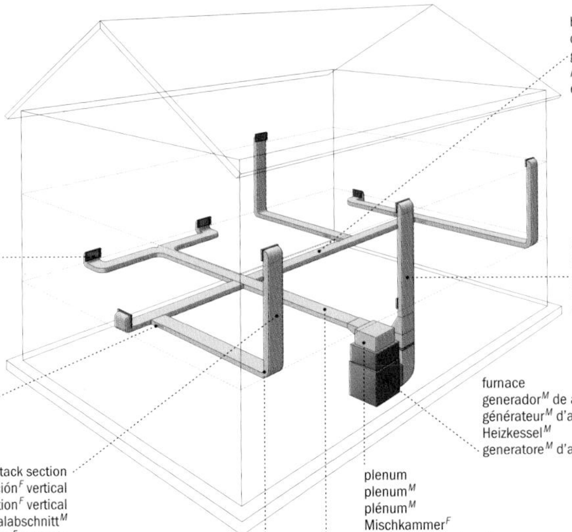

electric furnace
generador^M eléctrico de aire^M caliente
générateur^M d'air^M chaud électrique
elektrischer Heizkessel^M
generatore^M d'aria^F calda elettrico

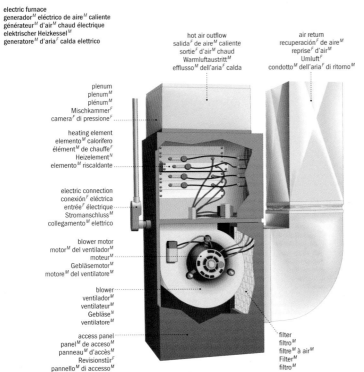

hot air outflow
salida^F de aire^M caliente
sortie^F d'air^M chaud
Warmluftaustritt^M
efflusso^M dell'aria^F calda

air return
recuperación^F de aire^M
reprise^F d'air^M
Umluft^F
condotto^M dell'aria^F di ritorno^M

plenum
plenum^M
plénum^M
Mischkammer^F
camera^F di pressione^F

heating element
elemento^M calorifero
élément^M de chauffe^F
Heizelement^N
elemento^M riscaldante

electric connection
conexión^F eléctrica
entrée^F électrique
Stromanschluss^M
collegamento^M elettrico

blower motor
motor^M del ventilador^M
moteur^M
Gebläsemotor^M
motore^M del ventilatore^M

blower
ventilador^M
ventilateur^M
Gebläse^N
ventilatore^M

access panel
panel^M de acceso^M
panneau^M d'accès^M
Revisionstür^F
pannello^M di accesso^M

filter
filtro^M
filtre^M à air^M
Filter^M
filtro^M

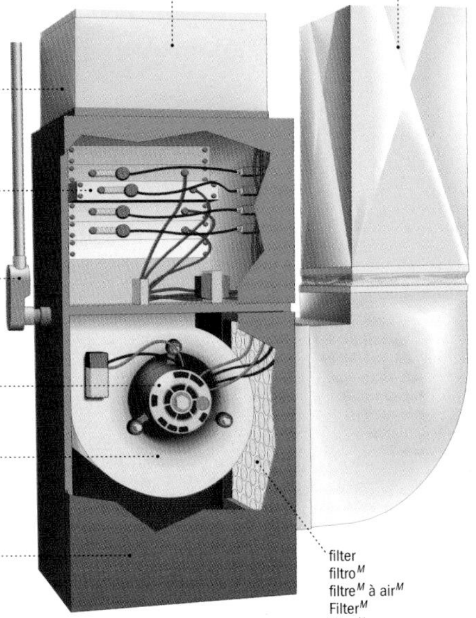

types of registers
tipos^M de rejillas^F
types^M de bouches^F
verschiedene Abzüge^M
tipi^M di bocchette^F

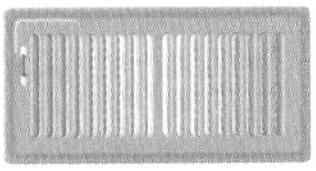

baseboard register
rejilla^F de piso^M
bouche^F de soufflage^M
Lüftungsgitter^N
bocchetta^F di immissione^F

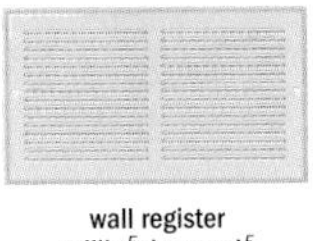

wall register
rejilla^F de pared^F
bouche^F d'extraction^F
Wandgitter^N
bocchetta^F di estrazione^F

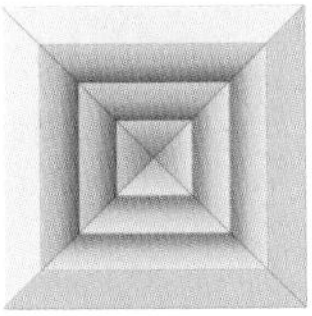

ceiling register
rejilla^F de techo^M
bouche^F à induction^F
Deckendurchlass^M
bocchetta^F a soffitto^M

forced hot water system

sistema^M de agua^F caliente a presión^F | installation^F à eau^F chaude | Warmwasserheizung^F mit Zwangsumlauf^M | impianto^M di riscaldamento^M ad acqua^F calda

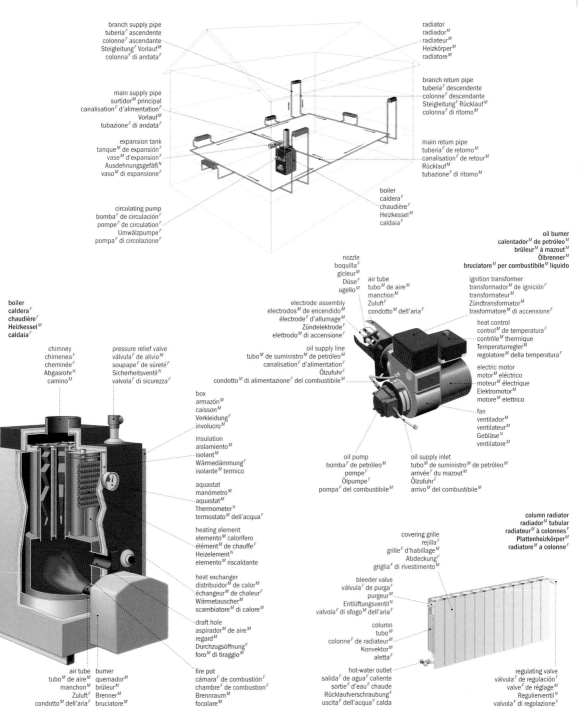

branch supply pipe
tubería^F ascendente
colonne^F ascendante
Steigleitung^F Vorlauf^M
colonna^F di andata^F

radiator
radiador^M
radiateur^M
Heizkörper^M
radiatore^M

main supply pipe
surtidor^M principal
canalisation^F d'alimentation^F
Vorlauf^M
tubazione^F di andata^F

branch return pipe
tubería^F descendente
colonne^F descendante
Steigleitung^F Rücklauf^M
colonna^F di ritorno^M

expansion tank
tanque^M de expansión^F
vase^M d'expansion^F
Ausdehnungsgefäß^N
vaso^M di espansione^F

main return pipe
tubería^F de retorno^M
canalisation^F de retour^M
Rücklauf^M
tubazione^F di ritorno^M

circulating pump
bomba^F de circulación^F
pompe^F de circulation^F
Umwälzpumpe^F
pompa^F di circolazione^F

boiler
caldera^F
chaudière^F
Heizkessel^M
caldaia^F

oil burner
calentador^M de petróleo^M
brûleur^M à mazout^M
Ölbrenner^M
bruciatore^M per combustibile^M liquido

nozzle
boquilla^F
gicleur^F
Düse^F
ugello^M

air tube
tubo^M de aire^M
manchon^M
Zuluft^M
condotto^M dell'aria^F

ignition transformer
transformador^M de ignición^F
transformateur^M
Zündtransformator^M
trasformatore^M di accensione^F

boiler
caldera^F
chaudière^F
Heizkessel^M
caldaia^F

electrode assembly
electrodos^M de encendido^M
électrode^F d'allumage^M
Zündelektrode^F
elettrodo^M di accensione^F

heat control
control^M de temperatura^F
contrôle^M thermique
Temperaturregler^M
regolatore^M della temperatura^F

oil supply line
tubo^M de suministro^M de petróleo^M
canalisation^F d'alimentation^F
Ölzufuhr^F
condotto^M di alimentazione^F del combustibile^M

electric motor
motor^M eléctrico
moteur^M électrique
Elektromotor^M
motore^M elettrico

chimney
chimenea^F
cheminée^F
Abgasrohr^N
camino^M

pressure relief valve
válvula^F de alivio^F
soupape^F de sûreté^F
Sicherheitsventil^N
valvola^F di sicurezza^F

box
armazón^M
caisson^M
Verkleidung^F
involucro^M

fan
ventilador^M
ventilateur^M
Gebläse^N
ventilatore^M

insulation
aislamiento^M
isolant^M
Wärmedämmung^F
isolante^M termico

oil pump
bomba^F de petróleo^M
pompe^F
Ölpumpe^F
pompa^F del combustibile^M

oil supply inlet
tubo^M de suministro^M de petróleo^M
arrivée^F du mazout^M
Ölzufuhr^F
arrivo^M del combustibile^M

aquastat
manómetro^M
aquastat^M
Thermometer^N
termostato^M dell'acqua^F

heating element
elemento^M calorífero
élément^M de chauffe^F
Heizelement^N
elemento^M riscaldante

column radiator
radiador^M tubular
radiateur^M à colonnes^F
Plattenheizkörper^M
radiatore^M a colonne^F

heat exchanger
distribuidor^M de calor^M
échangeur^M de chaleur^F
Wärmetauscher^M
scambiatore^M di calore^M

covering grille
rejilla^F
grille^F d'habillage^M
Abdeckung^F
griglia^F di rivestimento^M

draft hole
aspirador^M de aire^M
regard^M
Durchzugsöffnung^F
foro^M di tiraggio^M

bleeder valve
válvula^F de purga^F
purgeur^M
Entlüftungsventil^N
valvola^F di sfogo^M dell'aria^F

column
tubo^M
colonne^F de radiateur^M
Konvektor^M
aletta^F

air tube
tubo^M de aire^M
manchon^M
Zuluft^F
condotto^M dell'aria^F

burner
quemador^M
brûleur^M
Brenner^M
bruciatore^M

fire pot
cámara^F de combustión^F
chambre^F de combustion^F
Brennraum^M
focolare^M

hot-water outlet
salida^F de agua^F caliente
sortie^F d'eau^F chaude
Rücklaufverschraubung^F
uscita^F dell'acqua^F calda

regulating valve
válvula^F de regulación^F
valve^F de réglage^M
Regulierventil^N
valvola^F di regolazione^F

heat pump

sistema^M de bomba^F de calor^M | pompe^F à chaleur^F | Wärmepumpe^F | pompa^F di calore^M

circuit breaker
interruptor^M automático
disjoncteur^M
Sicherungsautomat^M
interruttore^M automatico

supply duct
manga^F de distribución^F
gaine^F de distribution^F
Zuluftkanal^M
condotto^M di alimentazione^F

fan
ventilador^M
ventilateur^M hélicoïde
Ventilator^M
ventilatore^M

indoor unit
unidad^F interior
module^M intérieur
Anlage^F für Innenaufstellung^F
impianto^M interno

outdoor unit
unidad^F exterior
module^M extérieur
Anlage^F für Außenaufstellung^F
impianto^M esterno

refrigerant tubing
tubería^F de refrigeración^F
liaison^F frigorifique
Kältemittelleitung^F
tubo^M del refrigerante^M

electric connection
conexión^F eléctrica
liaison^F électrique
Stromanschluss^M
collegamento^M elettrico

compressor
compresor^M
compresseur^M
Kompressor^M
compressore^M

refrigerant tubing
tubería^F de refrigeración^F
liaison^F frigorifique
Kältemittelleitung^F
tubo^M del refrigerante^M

auxiliary heating

calefacción^F auxillare | chauffage^M d'appoint^M | Zusatzheizung^F | mezzi^M integrativi di riscaldamento^M

electric baseboard radiator
radiador^M eléctrico
plinthe^F chauffante électrique
Elektrokonvektor^M
termoconvettore^M

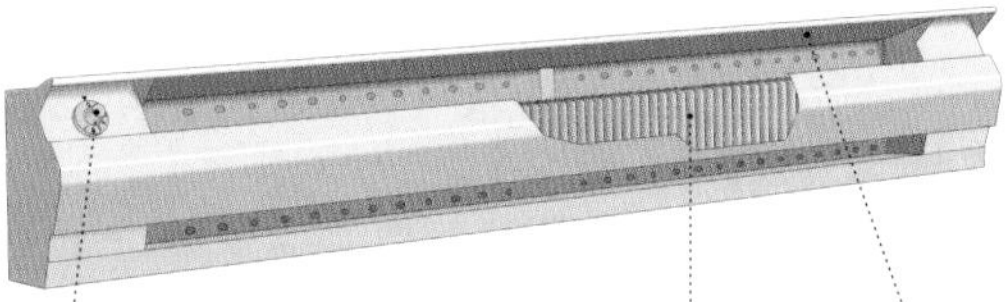

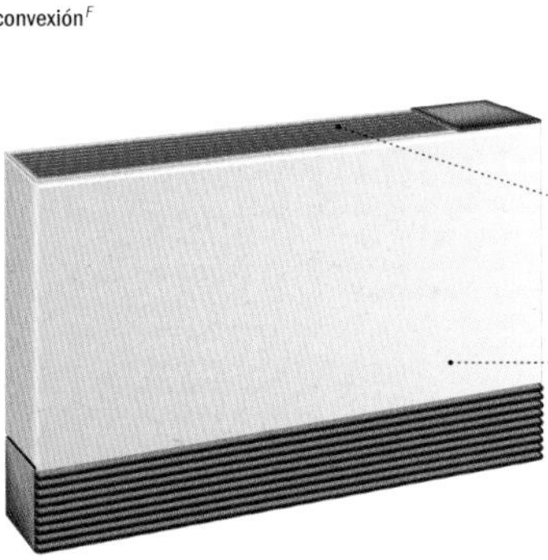

fan heater
ventilador^M de aire^M caliente
radiateur^M soufflant
Heizlüfter^M
termoventilatore^M

thermostat
termostato^M
thermostat^M
Thermostat^M
termostato^M

fin
aleta^F
ailette^F
Rippe^F
aletta^F radiante

deflector
deflector^M
déflecteur^M
Deflektor^M
deflettore^M

convector
radiador^M de convexión^F
convecteur^M
Konvektor^M
convettore^M

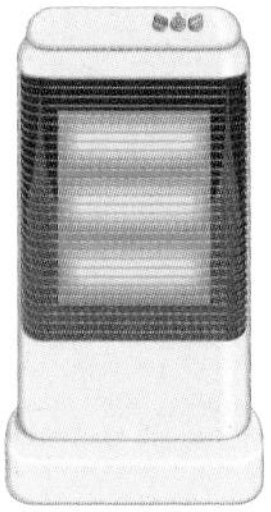

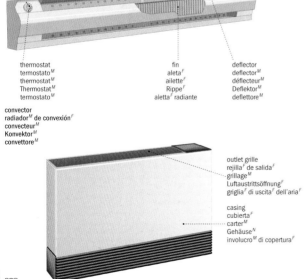

oil-filled heater
calefactor^M de aceite^M
radiateur^M bain^M d'huile^F
ölgefüllter Heizkörper^M
radiatore^M elettrico a olio^M

outlet grille
rejilla^F de salida^F
grillage^M
Luftaustrittsöffnung^F
griglia^F di uscita^F dell'aria^F

casing
cubierta^F
carter^M
Gehäuse^N
involucro^M di copertura^F

radiant heater
calefactor^M eléctrico a infrarrojos^M
radiateur^M rayonnant
Heizstrahler^M
stufa^F radiante

HOUSE

air conditioning appliances

aparatos^M acondicionadores^M | appareils^M de conditionnement^M de l'air^M | Klimageräte^N | apparecchi^M per il condizionamento^M dell'aria^F

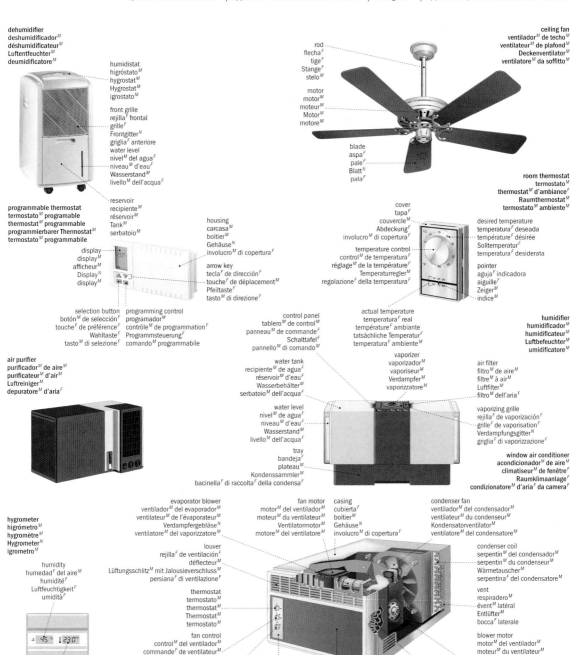

HOUSE

dehumidifier
deshumidificador^M
déshumidificateur^M
Luftentfeuchter^M
deumidificatore^M

humidistat
higróstato^M
hygrostat^M
Hygrostat^M
igrostato^M

front grille
rejilla^F frontal
grille^F
Frontgitter^N
griglia^F anteriore

water level
nivel^M del agua^F
niveau^M d'eau^F
Wasserstand^M
livello^M dell'acqua^F

reservoir
recipiente^M
réservoir^M
Tank^M
serbatoio^M

programmable thermostat
termostato^M programable
thermostat^M programmable
programmierbarer Thermostat^M
termostato^M programmabile

display
display^M
afficheur^M
Display^N
display^M

selection button
botón^M de selección^F
touche^F de préférence^F
Wahltaste^F
tasto^M di selezione^F

programming control
programador^M
contrôle^M de programmation^F
Programmsteuerung^F
comando^M programmabile

housing
carcasa^M
boitier^M
Gehäuse^N
involucro^M di copertura^F

arrow key
tecla^F de dirección^F
touche^F de déplacement^M
Pfeiltaste^F
tasto^M di direzione^F

air purifier
purificador^M de aire^M
purificateur^M d'air^M
Luftreiniger^M
depuratore^M d'aria^F

control panel
tablero^M de control^M
panneau^M de commande^F
Schalttafel^F
pannello^M di comando^M

water tank
recipiente^M de agua^F
réservoir^M d'eau^F
Wasserbehälter^M
serbatoio^M dell'acqua^F

water level
nivel^M de agua^F
niveau^M d'eau^F
Wasserstand^M
livello^M dell'acqua^F

tray
bandeja^F
plateau^M
Kondenssammler^M
bacinella^F di raccolta^F della condensa^F

rod
flecha^F
tige^F
Stange^F
stelo^M

motor
motor^M
moteur^M
Motor^M
motore^M

blade
aspa^F
pale^F
Blatt^N
pala^F

cover
tapa^F
couvercle^M
Abdeckung^F
involucro^M di copertura^F

temperature control
control^M de temperatura^F
réglage^M de la température^F
Temperaturregler^M
regolazione^F della temperatura^F

actual temperature
temperatura^F real
température^F ambiante
tatsächliche Temperatur^F
temperatura^F ambiente^F

vaporizer
vaporizador^M
vaporiseur^M
Verdampfer^M
vaporizzatore^M

ceiling fan
ventilador^M de techo^M
ventilateur^M de plafond^M
Deckenventilator^M
ventilatore^M da soffitto^M

room thermostat
termostato^M
thermostat^M d'ambiance^F
Raumthermostat^M
termostato^M ambiente^F

desired temperature
temperatura^F deseada
température^F désirée
Solltemperatur^F
temperatura^F desiderata

pointer
aguja^F indicadora
aiguille^F
Zeiger^M
indice^M

humidifier
humidificador^M
humidificateur^M
Luftbefeuchter^M
umidificatore^M

air filter
filtro^M de aire^M
filtre^M à air^M
Luftfilter^M
filtro^M dell'aria^F

vaporizing grille
rejilla^F de vaporización^F
grille^F de vaporisation^F
Verdampfungsgitter^N
griglia^F di vaporizzazione^F

window air conditioner
acondicionador^M de aire^M
climatiseur^M de fenêtre^F
Raumklimaanlage^F
condizionatore^M d'aria^F da camera^F

hygrometer
higrómetro^M
hygromètre^M
Hygrometer^N
igrometro^M

humidity
humedad^F del aire^M
humidité^F
Luftfeuchtigkeit^F
umidità^F

temperature
temperatura^F
température^F
Temperatur^F
temperatura^F

evaporator blower
ventilador^M del evaporador^M
ventilateur^M de l'évaporateur^M
Verdampfergebläse^N
ventilatore^M del vaporizzatore^M

louver
rejilla^F de ventilación^F
déflecteur^M
Lüftungsschlitz^M mit Jalousieverschluss^M
persiana^F di ventilazione^F

thermostat
termostato^M
thermostat^M
Thermostat^M
termostato^M

fan control
control^M del ventilador^M
commande^F du ventilateur^M
Ventilatorregler^M
comando^M del ventilatore^M

function selector
selector^M
sélecteur^M
Funktionswähler^M
selettore^M di funzione^F

control panel
tablero^M de control^M
tableau^M de commande^F
Schalttafel^F
pannello^M dei comandi^M

fan motor
motor^M del ventilador^M
moteur^M du ventilateur^M
Ventilatormotor^M
motore^M del ventilatore^M

casing
cubierta^F
boitier^M
Gehäuse^N
involucro^M di copertura^F

grille
rejilla^F
grillage^M
Gitter^N
griglia^F

condenser fan
ventilador^M del condensador^M
ventilateur^M du condenseur^M
Kondensatorventilator^M
ventilatore^M del condensatore^M

condenser coil
serpentín^M del condensador^M
serpentin^M du condenseur^M
Wärmetauscher^M
serpentina^F del condensatore^M

vent
respiradero^M
évent^M latéral
Entlüfter^M
bocca^F laterale

blower motor
motor^M del ventilador^M
moteur^M du ventilateur^M
Ventilatormotor^M
motore^M del ventilatore^M

evaporator coil
serpentín^M del evaporador^M
serpentin^M de l'évaporateur^M
Verdampferspirale^F
serpentina^F del vaporizzatore^M

plumbing system

cañerías^F | circuit^M de plomberie^F | Sanitärinstallationssystem^N | impianto^M idraulico

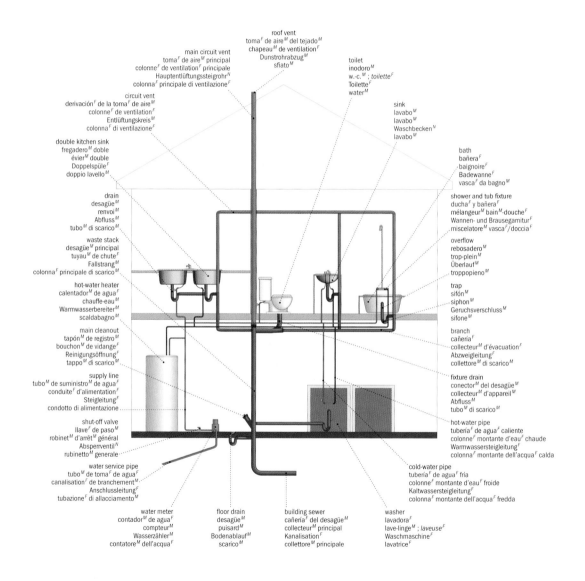

roof vent
toma^F de aire^M del tejado^M
chapeau^M de ventilation^F
Dunstrohrabzug^M
sfiato^M

main circuit vent
toma^F de aire^M principal
colonne^F de ventilation^F principale
Hauptentlüftungssteigrohr^N
colonna^F principale di ventilazione^F

toilet
inodoro^M
w.-c.^{M} ; toilette^F
Toilette^F
water^M

circuit vent
derivación^F de la toma^F de aire^M
colonne^F de ventilation^F
Entlüftungskreis^M
colonna^F di ventilazione^F

sink
lavabo^M
lavabo^M
Waschbecken^N
lavabo^M

double kitchen sink
fregadero^M doble
évier^M double
Doppelspüle^F
doppio lavello^M

bath
bañera^F
baignoire^F
Badewanne^F
vasca^F da bagno^M

drain
desagüe^M
renvoi^M
Abfluss^M
tubo^M di scarico^M

shower and tub fixture
ducha^F y bañera^F
mélangeur^M bain^M-douche^F
Wannen- und Brausegarnitur^F
miscelatore^M vasca^F/doccia^F

waste stack
desagüe^M principal
tuyau^M de chute^F
Fallstrang^M
colonna^F principale di scarico^M

overflow
rebosadero^M
trop-plein^M
Überlauf^M
troppopieno^M

hot-water heater
calentador^M de agua^F
chauffe-eau^M
Warmwasserbereiter^M
scaldabagno^M

trap
sifón^M
siphon^M
Geruchsverschluss^M
sifone^M

main cleanout
tapón^M de registro^M
bouchon^M de vidange^F
Reinigungsöffnung^F
tappo^M di scarico^M

branch
cañería^F
collecteur^M d'évacuation^F
Abzweigleitung^F
collettore^M di scarico^M

supply line
tubo^M de suministro^M de agua^F
conduite^F d'alimentation^F
Steigleitung^F
condotto di alimentazione

fixture drain
conector^M del desagüe^M
collecteur^M d'appareil^M
Abfluss^M
tubo^M di scarico^M

shut-off valve
llave^F de paso^M
robinet^M d'arrêt^M général
Absperrventil^N
rubinetto^M generale

hot-water pipe
tubería^F de agua^F caliente
colonne^F montante d'eau^F chaude
Warmwassersteigleitung^F
colonna^F montante dell'acqua^F calda

water service pipe
tubo^M de toma^F de agua^F
canalisation^F de branchement^M
Anschlussleitung^F
tubazione^F di allacciamento^M

cold-water pipe
tubería^F de agua^F fría
colonne^F montante d'eau^F froide
Kaltwassersteigleitung^F
colonna^F montante dell'acqua^F fredda

water meter
contador^M de agua^F
compteur^M
Wasserzähler^M
contatore^M dell'acqua^F

floor drain
desagüe^M
puisard^M
Bodenablauf^M
scarico^M

building sewer
cañería^F del desagüe^M
collecteur^M principal
Kanalisation^F
collettore^M principale

washer
lavadora^F
lave-linge^M ; laveuse^F
Waschmaschine^F
lavatrice^F

ventilating circuit
circuito^M de ventilación^F
circuit^M de ventilation^F
Entlüftungskreislauf^M
rete^F di ventilazione^F

draining circuit
circuito^M de desagüe^M
circuit^M d'évacuation^F
Abflusskreislauf^M
rete^F di scarico^M

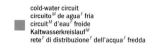

cold-water circuit
circuito^M de agua^F fría
circuit^M d'eau^F froide
Kaltwasserkreislauf^M
rete^F di distribuzione^F dell'acqua^F fredda

hot-water circuit
circuito^M de agua^F caliente
circuit^M d'eau^F chaude
Warmwasserkreislauf^M
rete^F di distribuzione^F dell'acqua^F calda

pedestal-type sump pump

bomba^F tipo^M pedestal^M para sumidero^M | pompe^F de puisard^M | Schmutzwasserhebeanlage^F | pompa^F di spurgo^M

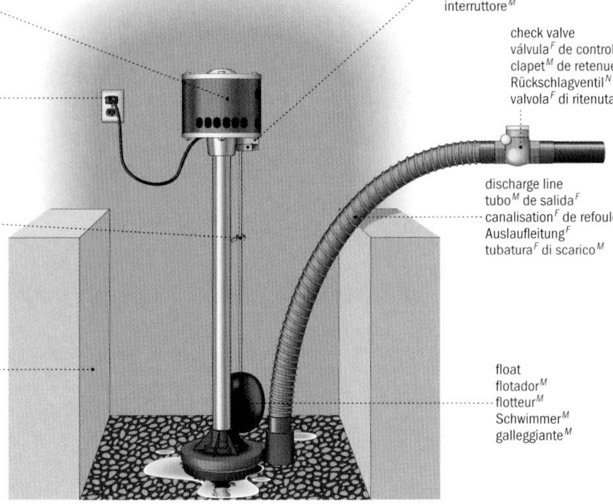

pump motor
motor^M de la bomba^F
moteur^M électrique
Pumpenmotor^M
motore^F della pompa^F

shut-off switch
interruptor^M de arranque^M automático
contacteur^M
Ein-/Ausschalter^M
interruttore^M

check valve
válvula^F de control^M
clapet^M de retenue^F
Rückschlagventil^N
valvola^F di ritenuta^F

grounded receptacle
contacto^M con conexión^F de tierra^F
prise^F avec borne^F de terre^F
wasserdichter Stromanschluss^M
impianto^M elettrico impermeabilizzato

float clamp
anillo^M de retención^F
étrier^M du flotteur^M
Schwimmerstange^F
asta^F del galleggiante^M

discharge line
tubo^M de salida^M
canalisation^F de refoulement^M
Auslaufleitung^F
tubatura^F di scarico^M

sump
sumidero^M
puisard^M
Pumpensumpf^M
pozzetto^M

float
flotador^M
flotteur^M
Schwimmer^M
galleggiante^M

septic tank

fosa^F séptica | fosse^F septique | Versitzgrube^F | fossa^F biologica

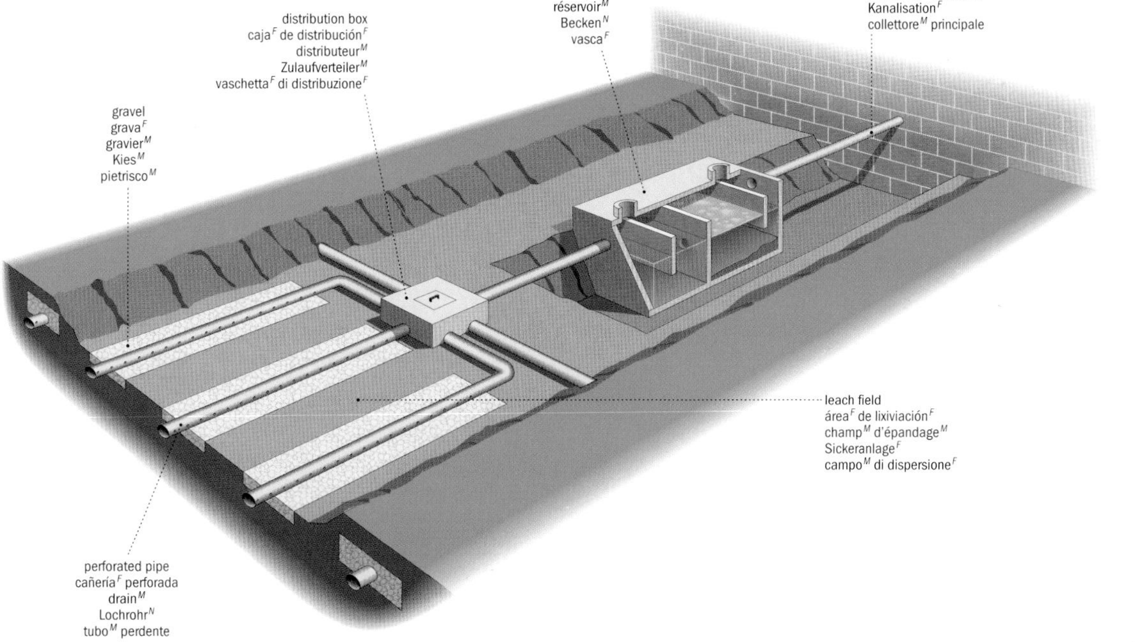

building sewer
cañería^F de desagüe^M
collecteur^M principal
Kanalisation^F
collettore^M principale

tank
tanque^M
réservoir^M
Becken^N
vasca^F

distribution box
caja^F de distribución^F
distributeur^M
Zulaufverteiler^M
vaschetta^F di distribuzione^F

gravel
grava^F
gravier^M
Kies^M
pietrisco^M

leach field
área^F de lixiviación^F
champ^M d'épandage^M
Sickeranlage^F
campo^M di dispersione^F

perforated pipe
cañería^F perforada
drain^M
Lochrohr^N
tubo^M perdente

bathroom

cuarto^M de baño^M | salle^F de bains^M | Badezimmer^N | stanza^F da bagno^M

HOUSE

sliding door
puerta^F plegable
porte^F coulissante
Schiebetür^F
porta^F scorrevole

spray hose
manguera^F
flexible^M
Brauseschlauch^M
tubo^M flessibile

shower head
alcachofa^F de la ducha^F
pomme^F de douche^F
Brausenkopf^M
doccia^F

shower stall
cabina^F de la ducha^F
cabine^F de douche^F
Duschkabine^F
box^M doccia^F

portable shower head
ducha^F de teléfono^M
douchette^F
Handbrause^F
doccia^F a telefono^M

faucet
grifo^M
robinet^M
Wasserhahn^M
rubinetto^M

overflow
desagüe^M
trop-plein^M
Überlauf^M
troppopieno^M

mirror
espejo^M
miroir^M
Spiegel^M
specchio^M

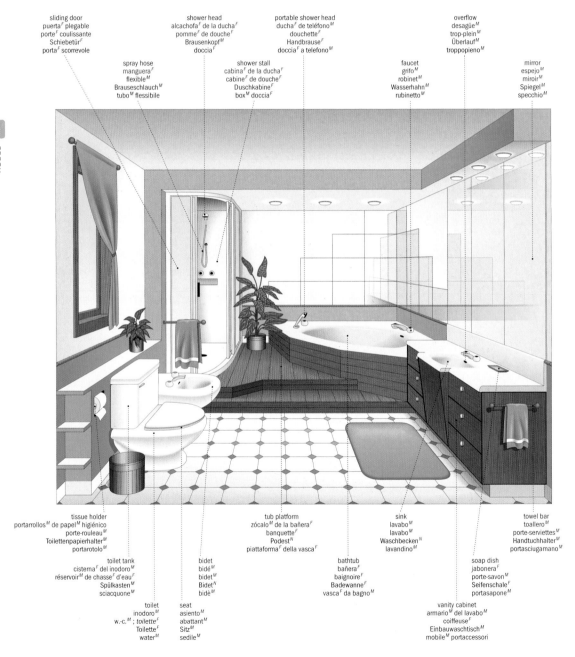

tissue holder
portarrollos^M de papel^M higiénico
porte-rouleau^M
Toilettenpapierhalter^M
portarotolo^M

tub platform
zócalo^M de la bañera^F
banquette^F
Podest^N
piattaforma^F della vasca^F

sink
lavabo^M
lavabo^M
Waschbecken^N
lavandino^M

towel bar
toallero^M
porte-serviettes^M
Handtuchhalter^M
portasciugamano^M

toilet tank
cisterna^F del inodoro^M
réservoir^M de chasse^F d'eau^F
Spülkasten^M
sciacquone^M

bidet
bidé^M
bidet^M
Bidet^N
bidè^M

bathtub
bañera^F
baignoire^F
Badewanne^F
vasca^F da bagno^M

soap dish
jabonera^F
porte-savon^M
Seifenschale^F
portasapone^M

toilet
inodoro^M
w.-c.^M ; *toilette*^F
Toilette^F
water^M

seat
asiento^M
abattant^M
Sitz^M
sedile^M

vanity cabinet
armario^M del lavabo^M
coiffeuse^F
Einbauwaschtisch^M
mobile^M portaccessori

toilet

inodoro[M] | w.-c.[M] ; *toilette*[F] | Toilette[F] | water[M]

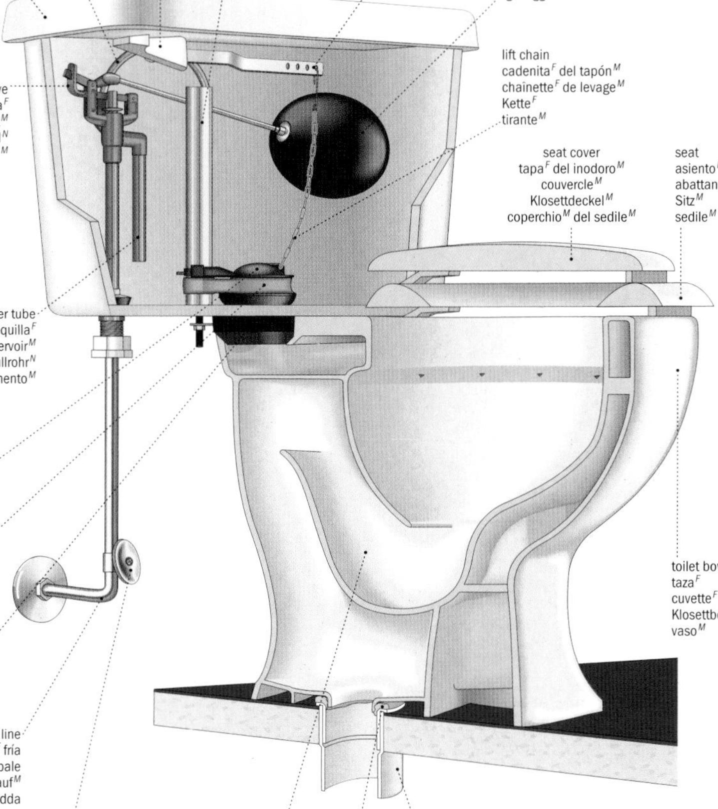

flush handle
palanca[F] de la cisterna[F]
manette[F] de chasse[F] d'eau[F]
Spülhebel[M]
levetta[F] dello sciacquone[M]

overflow tube
rebosadero[M]
trop-plein[M]
Überlauf[M]
tubo[M] del troppopieno[M]

trip lever
palanca[F] del tapón[M]
levier[M] de déclenchement[M]
Spülarm[M]
leva[F] di scatto[M]

refill tube
manguera[F] del rebosadero[M]
tube[M] de remplissage[M] de la cuvette[F]
Nachfüllrohr[N]
tubo[M] di carico[M]

float ball
flotador[M]
flotteur[M]
Schwimmer[M]
galleggiante[M]

tank lid
tapa[F] de la cisterna[F]
couvercle[M] de réservoir[M]
Spülkastendeckel[M]
coperchio[M] della cassetta[F]

lift chain
cadenita[F] del tapón[M]
chaînette[F] de levage[M]
Kette[F]
tirante[M]

ball-cock supply valve
válvula[F] de entrada[F]
robinet[M] flotteur à clapet[M]
Schwimmerventil[N]
valvola[F] del galleggiante[M]

seat cover
tapa[F] del inodoro[M]
couvercle[M]
Klosettdeckel[M]
coperchio[M] del sedile[M]

seat
asiento[M]
abattant[M]
Sitz[M]
sedile[M]

filler tube
boquilla[F]
tube[M] de remplissage[M] du réservoir[M]
Füllrohr[N]
tubo[M] di riempimento[M]

tank ball
tapón[M]
clapet[M]
Ventil[N]
valvola[F] di tenuta[F]

valve seat shaft
asiento[M] del tapón[M]
siège[M]
Ventilsitz[M]
sede[F] della valvola[F] di tenuta[F]

toilet bowl
taza[F]
cuvette[F]
Klosettbecken[N]
vaso[M]

conical washer
junta[F] cónica
rondelle[F] conique
Glockendichtung[F]
guarnizione[F] conica

cold-water supply line
tubería[F] de agua[F] fría
conduite[F] principale
Kaltwasserzulauf[M]
tubo[M] dell'acqua[F] fredda

shut-off valve
llave[F] de paso[M]
robinet[M] d'arrêt[M]
Absperrventil[N]
valvola[F] di chiusura[F]

trap
sifón[M]
siphon[M]
Geruchsverschluss[M]
sifone[M]

waste pipe
bajante[M]
tuyau[M] de chute[F]
Ablaufrohr[N]
tubo[M] di scarico[M]

wax seal
aislante[M] de cera[F]
anneau[M] d'étanchéité[F] en cire[F]
Rollring[M]
mastice[M] di tenuta[F]

HOUSE

water-heater tank

calentador^M de agua^F eléctrico | chauffe-eau^M | Wasserheizkessel^M | scaldabagno^M

**electric water-heater tank
calentador^M eléctrico
chauffe-eau^M électrique
elektrischer Heißwasserbereiter^M
scaldabagno^M elettrico**

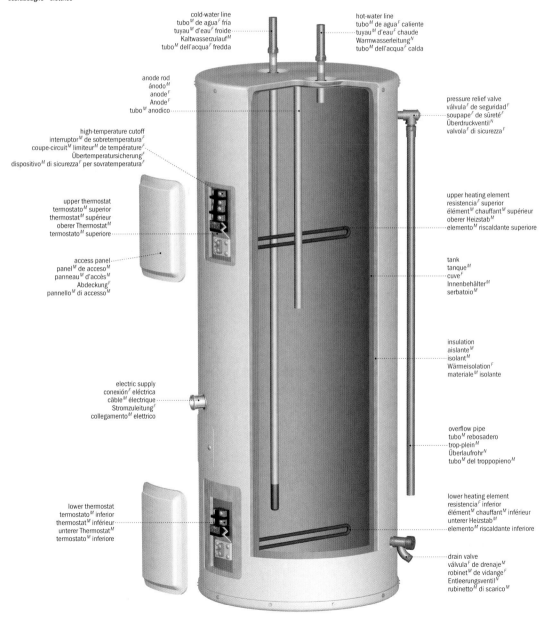

cold-water line
tubo^M de agua^F fría
tuyau^M d'eau^F froide
Kaltwasserzulauf^M
tubo^M dell'acqua^F fredda

hot-water line
tubo^M de agua^F caliente
tuyau^M d'eau^F chaude
Warmwasserleitung^N
tubo^M dell'acqua^F calda

anode rod
ánodo^M
anode^F
Anode^F
tubo^M anodico

pressure relief valve
válvula^F de seguridad^F
soupape^F de sûreté^F
Überdruckventil^N
valvola^F di sicurezza^F

high-temperature cutoff
interruptor^M de sobretemperatura^F
coupe-circuit^M limiteur^M de température^F
Übertemperatursicherung^F
dispositivo^M di sicurezza^F per sovratemperatura^F

upper heating element
resistencia^F superior
élément^M chauffant^M supérieur
oberer Heizstab^M
elemento^M riscaldante superiore

upper thermostat
termostato^M superior
thermostat^M supérieur
oberer Thermostat^M
termostato^M superiore

access panel
panel^M de acceso^M
panneau^M d'accès^M
Abdeckung^F
pannello^M di accesso^M

tank
tanque^M
cuve^F
Innenbehälter^M
serbatoio^M

insulation
aislante^M
isolant^M
Wärmeisolation^F
materiale^M isolante

electric supply
conexión^F eléctrica
câble^M électrique
Stromzuleitung^F
collegamento^M elettrico

overflow pipe
tubo^M rebosadero
trop-plein^M
Überlaufrohr^N
tubo^M del troppopieno^M

lower heating element
resistencia^F inferior
élément^M chauffant^M inférieur
unterer Heizstab^M
elemento^M riscaldante inferiore

lower thermostat
termostato^M inferior
thermostat^M inférieur
unterer Thermostat^M
termostato^M inferiore

drain valve
válvula^F de drenaje^M
robinet^M de vidange^F
Entleerungsventil^N
rubinetto^M di scarico^M

HOUSE

HOUSE

gas water-heater tank
caldera^F de gas^M
chauffe-eau^M au gaz^M
Gaswarmwasserbereiter^M
scaldabagno^M a gas^M

hot-water outlet
salida^F de agua^F caliente
tuyau^M d'eau^F chaude
Warmwasseraustritt^M
tubo^M di uscita^F dell'acqua^F calda

flue hat
caperuza^F
dériveur^M de tirage^M
Strömungssicherung^F
cappa^F di raccolta^F dei gas^M combusti

outer jacket
envoltura^F metálica
enveloppe^F extérieure
äußere Verkleidung^F
rivestimento^M esterno

pressure-relief valve
válvula^F de seguridad^F
soupape^F de sûreté^F
Sicherheitsventil^N
valvola^F di sicurezza^F

overflow pipe
tubo^M de desagüe^M
trop-plein^M
Überlauf^M
tubo^M del troppopieno^M

insulation
aislante^M
isolant^M
Isolierung^F
materiale^M isolante

cold-water supply line
entrada^F de agua^F fría
tuyau^M d'eau^F froide
Kaltwasserzulauf^M
ingresso^M dell'acqua^F fredda

flue
tubo^M
cheminée^F
Abgas^N
tubo^M di sfiato^M

glass-lined tank
revestimiento^M de fibra^F de vidrio^M
cuve^F vitrifiée
emaillierter Stahlbehälter^M
serbatoio^M vetrificato

reset button
botón^M de seguridad^F
allumage^M manuel
Zündknopf^M
pulsante^M di accensione^F

gas cock
llave^F de gas^M
régulateur^M
Gasventil^N
rubinetto^M del gas^M

control box
cajita^F reguladora
boîte^F de contrôle^M
Regelgerät^N
scatola^F di comando^M

temperature control
control^M de temperatura^F
contrôle^M de la température^F
Temperaturregler^M
regolazione^F della temperatura^F

drain valve
válvula^F de drenaje^M
robinet^M de vidange^F
Entleerungsventil^N
valvola^F di scarico^M

thermostat
termostato^M
thermostat^M
Thermostat^M
termostato^M

gas burner
quemador^M de gas^M
brûleur^M
Gasbrenner^M
bruciatore^M del gas^M

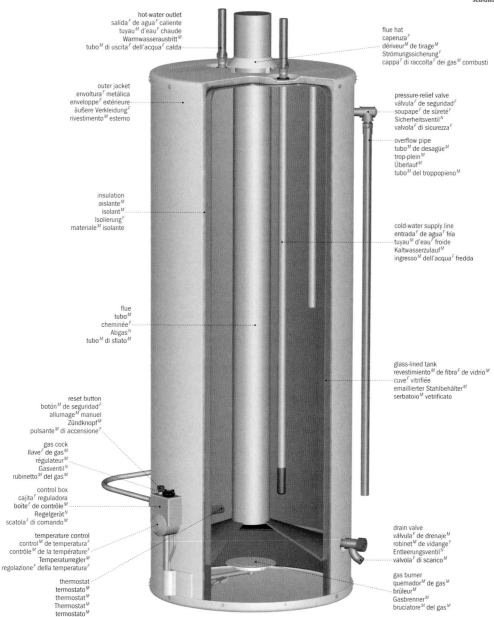

faucets

grifos^M y mezcladores^M | robinet^M et mitigeurs^M | Armaturen^F | rubinetto^M e miscelatore^M

stem faucet
grifo^M de plato^M
robinet^M
Wandauslaufventil^N
rubinetto^M a valvola^F

handle
cruceta^F
poignée^F
Hebel^M
manopola^F

disc faucet
mezclador^M de disco^M
mitigeur^M à disque^M
Mischbatterie^F mit Keramikdichtung^F
miscelatore^M a disco^M

packing nut
tuerca^F del prensaestopas^M
écrou^M du presse-étoupe^M
Dichtungsmutter^F
dado^M del premistoppa^M

handle
palanca^F
levier^M
Hebel^M
leva^F

packing
empaquetadura^F
presse-étoupe^M
Packung^F
premistoppa^M

washer
arandela^F
rondelle^F
Unterlegscheibe^F
rondella^F

bonnet
casquete^M
enjoliveur^M
Rosette^F
cappuccio^M

cylinder
cilindro^M
cylindre^M
Zylinder^M
cilindro^M

spindle
husillo^M
tige^F
Spindel^F
asta^F

stem holder
base^F de la espiga^F
cuvette^F porte-clapet^M
Ventilteller^M
piastra^F della valvola^F

spout
surtidor^M
bec^M
Auslauf^M
bocca^F di erogazione^F

seal
junta^F de estanquidad^F
anneau^M d'étanchéité^F
Dichtung^F
guarnizione^F

spout
surtidor^M
bec^M
Auslauf^M
bocca^F di erogazione^F

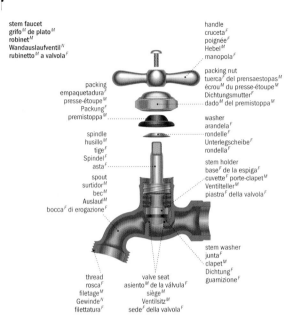

stem washer
junta^F
clapet^M
Dichtung^F
guarnizione^F

water inlet
entrada^F de agua^F
entrée^F d'eau^F
Wasserzulauf^M
entrata^F dell'acqua^F

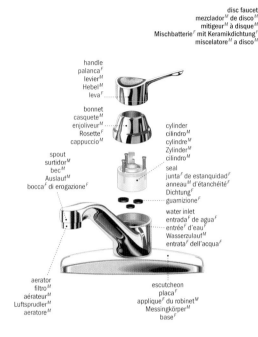

thread
rosca^F
filetage^M
Gewinde^N
filettatura^F

valve seat
asiento^M de la válvula^F
siège^M
Ventilsitz^M
sede^F della valvola^F

aerator
filtro^M
aérateur^M
Luftsprudler^M
aeratore^M

escutcheon
placa^F
applique^F du robinet^M
Messingkörper^M
base^F

ball-type faucet
grifo^M de bola^F
mitigeur^M à bille^F creuse
Mischbatterie^F mit Kugeldichtung^F
miscelatore^M a sfera^F

handle
palanca^F
levier^M
Hebel^M
leva^F

cartridge faucet
grifo^M de cartucho^M
mitigeur^M à cartouche^F
Mischbatterie^F mit Kartuschendichtung^F
miscelatore^M a cartuccia^F

spout
surtidor^M
bec^M
Auslauf^M
bocca^F di erogazione^F

lever
palanca^F
levier^M
Hebel^M
leva^F

bonnet
casquete^M
enjoliveur^M
Rosette^F
cappuccio^M

lever cover
casquete^M de la palanca^F
capuchon^M du levier^M
Deckel^M
cappuccio^M della leva^F

body
cuerpo^M
corps^M
Messingkörper^M
corpo^M

cartridge
cartucho^M
cartouche^F
Kartusche^F
cartuccia^F

aerator
filtro^M
aérateur^M
Luftsprudler^M
aeratore^M

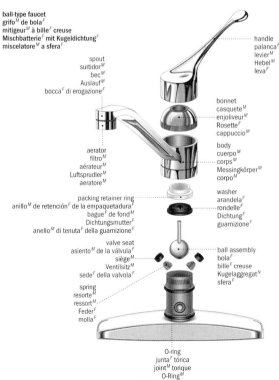

washer
arandela^F
rondelle^F
Dichtung^F
guarnizione^F

cartridge stem
espiga^F del cartucho^M
tige^F
Kartuschenkolben^M
perno^M della cartuccia^F

packing retainer ring
anillo^M de retención^F de la empaquetadura^F
bague^F de fond^M
Dichtungsmutter^F
anello^M di tenuta^F della guarnizione^F

spout
surtidor^M
bec^M
Auslauf^M
bocca^F di erogazione^F

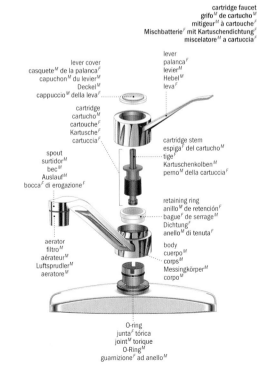

valve seat
asiento^M de la válvula^F
siège^M
Ventilsitz^M
sede^F della valvola^F

ball assembly
bola^F
bille^F creuse
Kugelaggregat^N
sfera^F

retaining ring
anillo^M de retención^F
bague^F de serrage^M
Dichtung^F
anello^M di tenuta^F

spring
resorte^M
ressort^M
Feder^F
molla^F

aerator
filtro^M
aérateur^M
Luftsprudler^M
aeratore^M

body
cuerpo^M
corps^M
Messingkörper^M
corpo^M

O-ring
junta^F tórica
joint^M torique
O-Ring^M
guarnizione^F ad anello^M

O-ring
junta^F tórica
joint^M torique
O-Ring^M
guarnizione^F ad anello^M

HOUSE

fittings

conexiones^F | adaptateurs^M et raccords^M | Fittings^N | adattatori^M e raccordi^M

steel to plastic
de acero^M a plástico^M
plastique^M et acier^M
Stahl^M auf Kunststoff^M
plastica^F-acciaio^M

copper to plastic
de cobre^M a plástico^M
plastique^M et cuivre^M
Kupfer^N auf Kunststoff^M
rame^M-plastica^F

copper to steel
de cobre^M a acero^M
cuivre^M et acier^M
Kupfer^N auf Stahl^M
rame^M-acciaio^M

examples of transition fittings
ejemplos^M de adaptadores^M
exemples^M d'adaptateurs^M
Beispiele^N für Übergangsfittings^N
esempi^M di adattatori^M

offset
codo^M de cambio^M de eje^M
coude^M de renvoi^M
Etagenbogen^M
deviatore^M

tee
derivación^F en T
té^M
Strömungs-T^N
raccordo^M a T

Y-branch
derivación^F en Y
culotte^M
Abzweig^M 45°
raccordo^M a Y

trap
sifón^M
siphon^M
Siphonwinkel^M
sifone^M

examples of fittings
ejemplos^M de racores^M
exemples^M de raccords^M
Beispiele^N für Fittings^N
esempi^M di raccordi^M

cap
tapón^M
bouchon^M femelle
Kappe^F
tappo^M femmina

U-bend
derivación^F en U
coude^M à 180°
Doppelbogen^M
raccordo^M a U

threaded cap
tapón^M hembra^F
bouchon^M femelle à visser
Gewindekappe^F
tappo^M femmina a vite^F

elbow
codo^M de 90 grados^M
coude^M
Winkel^M
raccordo^M a gomito^M

45° elbow
codo^M de 45 grados^M
coude^M à 45°
Winkel^M 45°
raccordo^M a gomito^M di 45°

pipe coupling
unión^F
manchon^M
Rohrverschraubung^F
manicotto^M

hexagon bushing
reductor^M con cabeza^F hexagonal
réduction^F mâle-femelle hexagonale
Sechskantreduzierhülse^F
riduzione^F esagonale

flush bushing
reductor^M
réduction^F mâle-femelle
Muffe^F
riduzione^F maschio/femmina

nipple
entrerrosca^F
mamelon^M double
Nippel^M
nipplo^M

reducing coupling
reductor^M de calibre^M
raccord^M de réduction^F
Reduziermuffennippel^M
manicotto^M di riduzione^F

square head plug
tapón^M macho^M
bouchon^M mâle sans bourrelet^M
Vierkantstopfen^M
tappo^M maschio a testa^F quadra

union
unión^F
raccord^M union^F
Verschraubung^F
raccordo^M per unione^F meccanica

mechanical connectors
racores^M mecánicas
raccords^M mécaniques
mechanische Verbindungen^F
raccordi^M meccanici

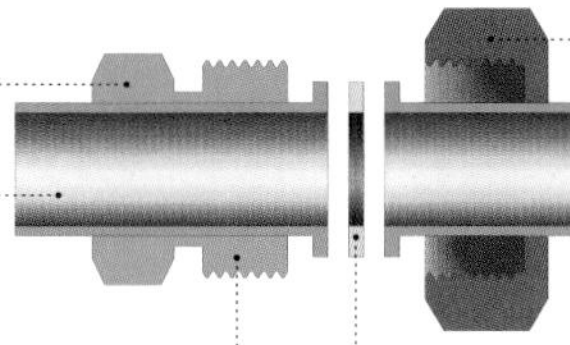

ring nut
anilla^F de la tuerca^F
écrou^M de serrage^M
Ringmutter^F
dado^M di serraggio^M

union nut
tuerca^F de ajuste^M
raccord^M femelle
Verschraubungsmutter^F
raccordo^M femmina

pipe A
tubo^M A
tube^M A
Rohr^N A
tubo^M A

pipe B
tubo^M B
tube^M B
Rohr^N B
tubo^M B

union nut
tuerca^F de ajuste^M
raccord^M mâle
Verschraubungsmutter^F
raccordo^M maschio

gasket
junta^F
rondelle^F de fibre^F
Dichtung^F
guarnizione^F

compression fitting
racor^M por compresión^F
raccord^M à compression^F
Quetschverschraubung^F
raccordo^M a compressione^F

flare joint
racor^M abocinado
raccord^M à collet^M repoussé
Bördelverbindung^F
raccordo^M a collarino^M pressato

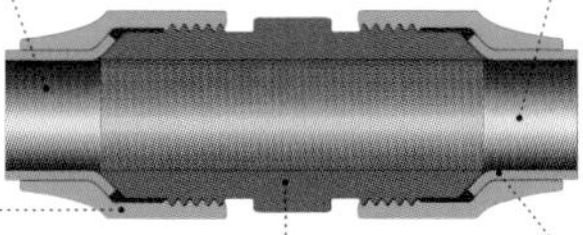

pipe A
tubo^M A
tube^M A
Rohr^N A
tubo^M A

pipe B
tubo^M B
tube^M B
Rohr^N B
tubo^M B

pipe A
tubo^M A
tube^M A
Rohr^N A
tubo^M A

pipe B
tubo^M B
tube^M B
Rohr^N B
tubo^M B

nut
tuerca^F
écrou^M
Mutter^F
ghiera^F

connector
conector^M
raccord^M
Verschraubung^F
manicotto^M

gasket
junta^F
garniture^F
Dichtung^F
guarnizione^F

nut
tuerca^F
écrou^M
Mutter^F
ghiera^F

connector
conector^M
raccord^M
Verschraubung^F
manicotto^M

tube end
extremo^M abocinado
collet^M repoussé
Rohrende^N
collarino^M

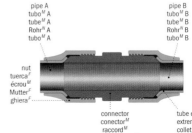

examples of branching

ejemplos^M de conexiones^F | exemples^M de branchement^M | Beispiele^N für Anschlüsse^M | esempi^M di allacciamento^M

garbage disposal sink
fregadero^M con triturador^M de basura^F
évier^M-broyeur^M
Spüle^F mit Müllschlucker^M
lavello^M con tritarifiuti^M

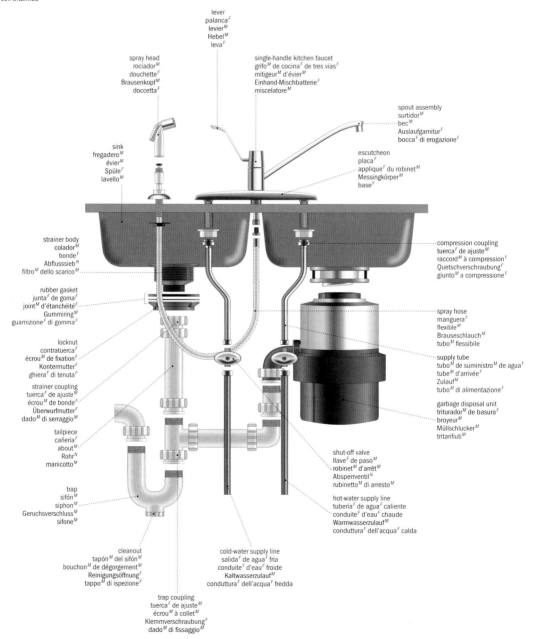

lever
palanca^F
levier^M
Hebel^M
leva^F

spray head
rociador^M
douchette^F
Brausenkopf^M
doccetta^F

single-handle kitchen faucet
grifo^M de cocina^F de tres vias^F
mitigeur^M d'évier^M
Einhand-Mischbatterie^F
miscelatore^M

spout assembly
surtidor^M
bec^M
Auslaufgarnitur^F
bocca^F di erogazione^F

sink
fregadero^M
évier^M
Spüle^F
lavello^M

escutcheon
placa^F
applique^F du robinet^M
Messingkörper^M
base^F

strainer body
colador^M
bonde^F
Abflusssieb^N
filtro^M dello scarico^M

compression coupling
tuerca^F de ajuste^F
raccord^M à compression^F
Quetschverschraubung^F
giunto^M a compressione^F

rubber gasket
junta^F de goma^F
joint^M d'étanchéité^F
Gummiring^M
guarnizione^F di gomma^F

spray hose
manguera^F
flexible^M
Brauseschlauch^M
tubo^M flessibile

locknut
contratuerca^F
écrou^M de fixation^F
Kontermutter^F
ghiera^F di tenuta^F

supply tube
tubo^M de suministro^M de agua^F
tube^M d'arrivée^F
Zulauf^M
tubo^M di alimentazione^F

strainer coupling
tuerca^F de ajuste^M
écrou^M de bonde^F
Überwurfmutter^F
dado^M di serraggio^M

garbage disposal unit
triturador^M de basura^F
broyeur^M
Müllschlucker^M
tritarifiuti^M

tailpiece
cañería^F
about^M
Rohr^N
manicotto^M

shut-off valve
llave^F de paso^M
robinet^M d'arrêt^M
Absperrventil^N
rubinetto^M di arresto^M

trap
sifón^M
siphon^M
Geruchsverschluss^M
sifone^M

hot-water supply line
tubería^F de agua^F caliente
conduite^F d'eau^F chaude
Warmwasserzulauf^M
conduttura^F dell'acqua^F calda

cleanout
tapón^M del sifón^M
bouchon^M de dégorgement^M
Reinigungsöffnung^F
tappo^M di ispezione^F

cold-water supply line
salida^F de agua^F fría
conduite^F d'eau^F froide
Kaltwasserzulauf^M
conduttura^F dell'acqua^F fredda

trap coupling
tuerca^F de ajuste^M
écrou^M à collet^M
Klemmverschraubung^F
dado^M di fissaggio^M

HOUSE

HOUSE

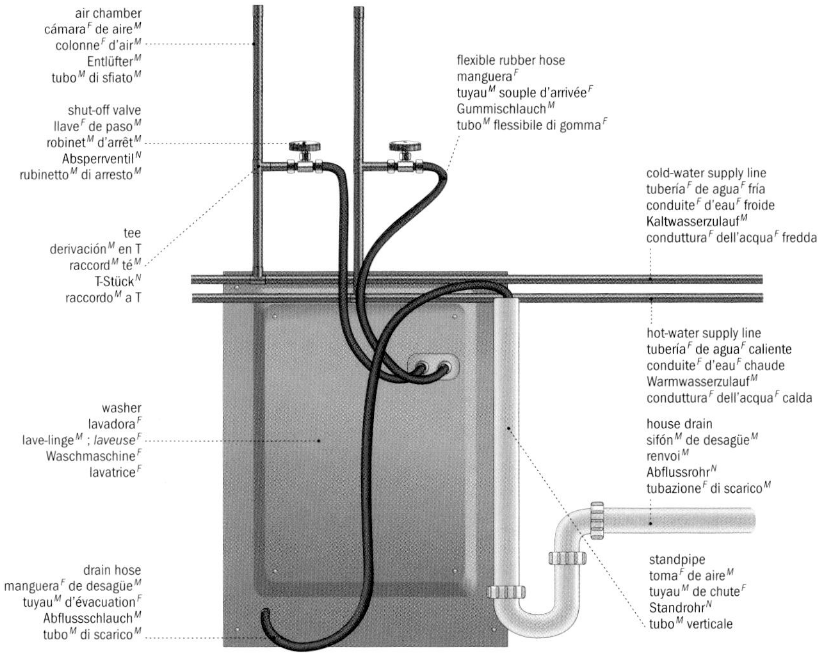

air chamber
cámara^F de aire^M
colonne^F d'air^M
Entlüfter^M
tubo^M di sfiato^M

flexible rubber hose
manguera^F
tuyau^M souple d'arrivée^F
Gummischlauch^M
tubo^M flessibile di gomma^F

shut-off valve
llave^F de paso^M
robinet^M d'arrêt^M
Absperrventil^N
rubinetto^M di arresto^M

cold-water supply line
tubería^F de agua^F fría
conduite^F d'eau^F froide
Kaltwasserzulauf^M
conduttura^F dell'acqua^F fredda

tee
derivación^M en T
raccord^M té^M
T-Stück^N
raccordo^M a T

hot-water supply line
tubería^F de agua^F caliente
conduite^F d'eau^F chaude
Warmwasserzulauf^M
conduttura^F dell'acqua^F calda

washer
lavadora^F
lave-linge^M ; *laveuse*^{F}
Waschmaschine^F
lavatrice^F

house drain
sifón^M de desagüe^M
renvoi^M
Abflussrohr^N
tubazione^F di scarico^M

standpipe
toma^F de aire^M
tuyau^M de chute^F
Standrohr^N
tubo^M verticale

drain hose
manguera^F de desagüe^M
tuyau^M d'évacuation^F
Abflussschlauch^M
tubo^M di scarico^M

washer
lavadora^F
lave-linge^M ; *laveuse*^{F}
Waschmaschine^F
lavatrice^F

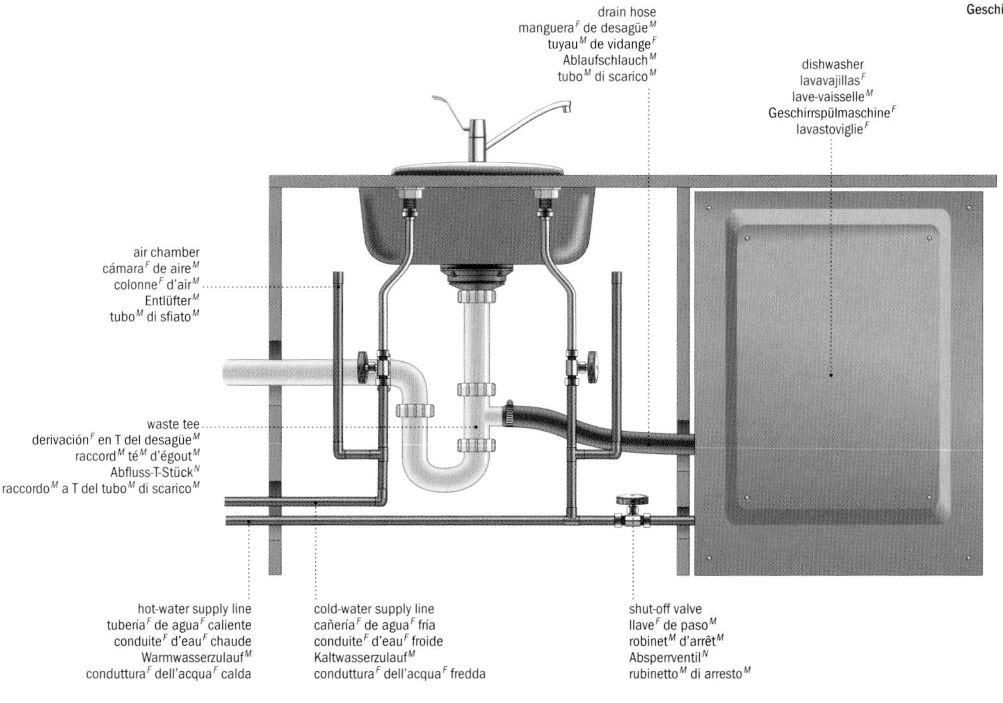

drain hose
manguera^F de desagüe^M
tuyau^M de vidange^F
Ablaufschlauch^M
tubo^M di scarico^M

dishwasher
lavavajillas^F
lave-vaisselle^M
Geschirrspülmaschine^F
lavastoviglie^F

dishwasher
lavavajillas^F
lave-vaisselle^M
Geschirrspülmaschine^F
lavastoviglie^F

air chamber
cámara^F de aire^M
colonne^F d'air^M
Entlüfter^M
tubo^M di sfiato^M

waste tee
derivación^F en T del desagüe^M
raccord^M té^M d'égout^M
Abfluss-T-Stück^N
raccordo^M a T del tubo^M di scarico^M

hot-water supply line
tubería^F de agua^F caliente
conduite^F d'eau^F chaude
Warmwasserzulauf^M
conduttura^F dell'acqua^F calda

cold-water supply line
cañería^F de agua^F fría
conduite^F d'eau^F froide
Kaltwasserzulauf^M
conduttura^F dell'acqua^F fredda

shut-off valve
llave^F de paso^M
robinet^M d'arrêt^M
Absperrventil^N
rubinetto^M di arresto^M

distribution panel

cuadro^M de distribución^F | panneau^M de distribution^F | Verteilerkasten^M | pannello^M di distribuzione^F

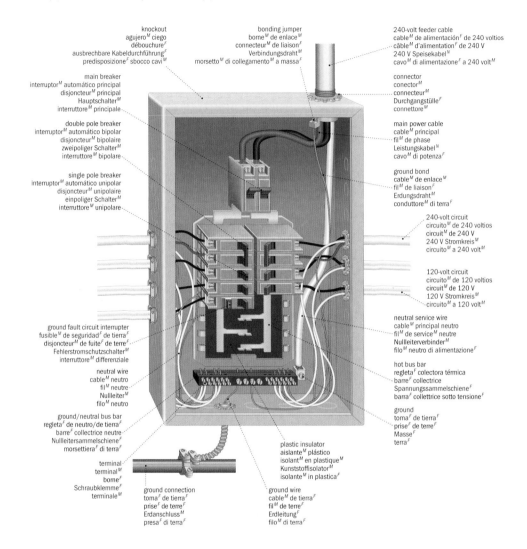

knockout
aguijero^M ciego
débouchure^F
ausbrechbare Kabeldurchführung^F
predisposizione^F sbocco cavi^M

bonding jumper
borne^M de enlace^F
connecteur^M de liaison^F
Verbindungsdraht^M
morsetto^M di collegamento^M a massa^F

240-volt feeder cable
cable^M de alimentación^F de 240 voltios
câble^M d'alimentation^F de 240 V
240 V Speisekabel^N
cavo^M di alimentazione^F a 240 volt^M

main breaker
interruptor^M automático principal
disjoncteur^M principal
Hauptschalter^M
interruttore^M principale

connector
conector^M
connecteur^M
Durchgangstülle^F
connettore^M

double pole breaker
interruptor^M automático bipolar
disjoncteur^M bipolaire
zweipoliger Schalter^M
interruttore^M bipolare

main power cable
cable^M principal
fil^M de phase
Leistungskabel^N
cavo^M di potenza^F

single pole breaker
interruptor^M automático unipolar
disjoncteur^M unipolaire
einpoliger Schalter^M
interruttore^M unipolare

ground bond
cable^M de enlace^M
fil^M de liaison^F
Erdungsdraht^M
conduttore^M di terra^F

240-volt circuit
circuito^M de 240 voltios
circuit^M de 240 V
240 V Stromkreis^M
circuito^M a 240 volt^M

120-volt circuit
circuito^M de 120 voltios
circuit^M de 120 V
120 V Stromkreis^M
circuito^M a 120 volt^M

ground fault circuit interrupter
fusible^M de seguridad^F de tierra^F
disjoncteur^M de fuite^F de terre^F
Fehlerstromschutzschalter^M
interruttore^M differenziale

neutral service wire
cable^M principal neutro
fil^M de service^M neutre
Nullleiterverbinder^M
filo^M neutro di alimentazione^F

neutral wire
cable^M neutro
fil^M neutre
Nullleiter^M
filo^M neutro

hot bus bar
regleta^F colectora térmica
barre^F collectrice
Spannungssammelschiene^F
barra^F collettrice sotto tensione^F

ground/neutral bus bar
regleta^F de neutro/de tierra^F
barre^F collectrice neutre
Nullleitersammelschiene^F
morsettiera^F di terra^F

ground
toma^F de tierra^F
prise^F de terre^F
Masse^F
terra^F

terminal
terminal^M
borne^F
Schraubklemme^F
terminale^M

plastic insulator
aislante^M plástico
isolant^M en plastique^M
Kunststoffisolator^M
isolante^M in plastica^F

ground connection
toma^F de tierra^F
prise^F de terre^F
Erdanschluss^M
presa^F di terra^F

ground wire
cable^M de tierra^F
fil^M de terre^F
Erdleitung^F
filo^M di terra^F

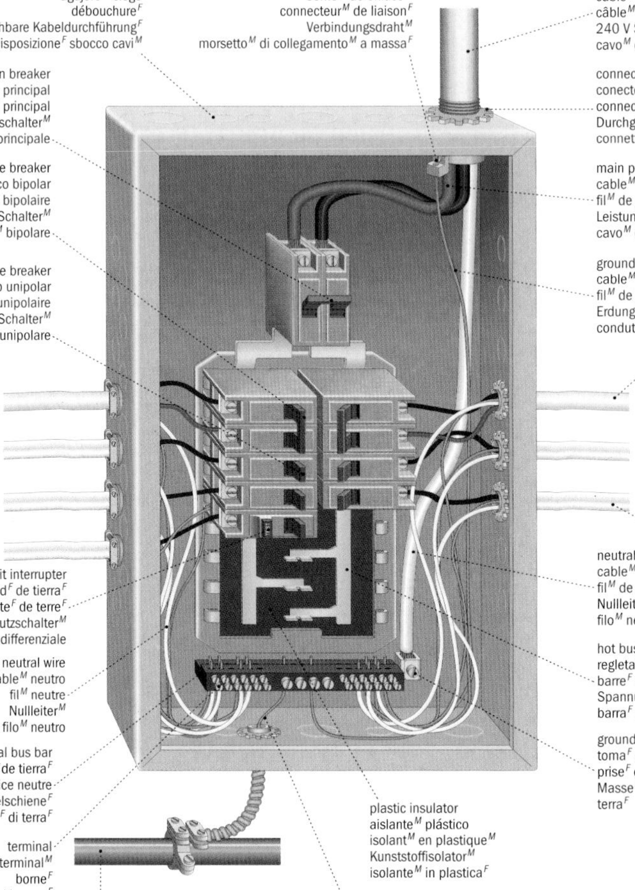

examples of fuses
ejemplos^M de fusibles
exemples^M de fusibles^M
Beispiele^N für Sicherungen^F
esempi^M di fusibili^M

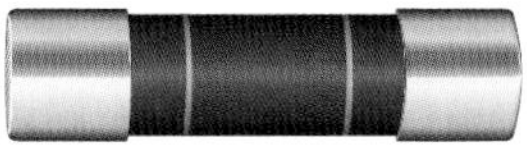

cartridge fuse
fusible^M de cartucho^M
fusible^M-cartouche^F
Patronensicherung^F
fusibile^M a cartuccia^F

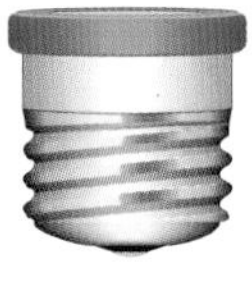

plug fuse
fusible^M de rosca^F
fusible^M à culot^M
Stöpselsicherung^F
fusibile^M a tappo^M

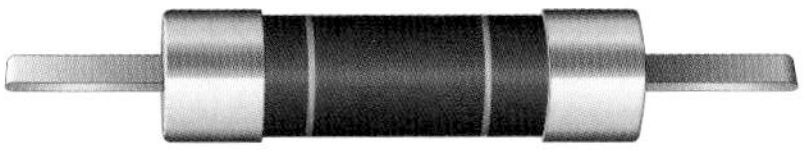

knife-blade cartridge fuse
fusible^M de bayoneta^F
fusible^M-cartouche^F à lames^F
Messersicherung^F
fusibile^M a cartuccia^F con terminali^M a coltello^M

HOUSE

network connection

conexión[F] a la red[F] | branchement[M] au réseau[M] | Hausanschluss[M] | allacciamento[M] alla rete[F]

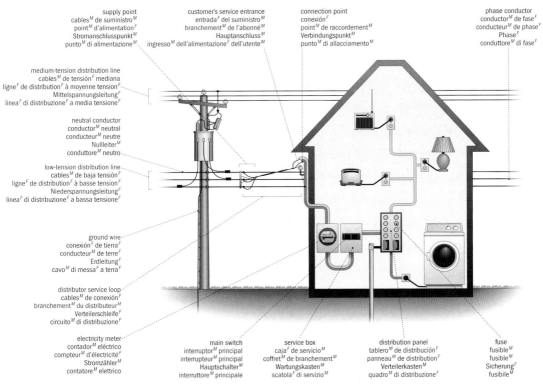

supply point
cables[M] de suministro[M]
point[F] d'alimentation[F]
Stromanschlusspunkt[M]
punto[M] di alimentazione[M]

customer's service entrance
entrada[F] del suministro[M]
branchement[M] de l'abonné[M]
Hauptanschluss[M]
ingresso[M] dell'alimentazione[F] dell'utente[M]

connection point
conexión[F]
point[M] de raccordement[M]
Verbindungspunkt[M]
punto[M] di allacciamento[M]

phase conductor
conductor[M] de fase[F]
conducteur[M] de phase[F]
Phase[F]
conduttore[M] di fase[F]

medium-tension distribution line
cables[M] de tensión[F] mediana
ligne[F] de distribution[F] à moyenne tension[F]
Mittelspannungsleitung[F]
linea[F] di distribuzione[F] a media tensione[F]

neutral conductor
conductor[M] neutral
conducteur[M] neutre
Nullleiter[M]
conduttore[M] neutro

low-tension distribution line
cables[M] de baja tensión[F]
ligne[F] de distribution[F] à basse tension[F]
Niederspannungsleitung[F]
linea[F] di distribuzione[F] a bassa tensione[F]

ground wire
conexión[F] de tierra[F]
conducteur[M] de terre[F]
Erdleitung[F]
cavo[M] di messa[F] a terra[F]

distributor service loop
cables[M] de conexión[F]
branchement[M] du distributeur[M]
Verteilerschleife[F]
circuito[M] di distribuzione[F]

electricity meter
contador[M] eléctrico
compteur[M] d'électricité[F]
Stromzähler[M]
contatore[M] elettrico

main switch
interruptor[M] principal
interrupteur[M] principal
Hauptschalter[M]
interruttore[M] principale

service box
caja[F] de servicio[M]
coffret[M] de branchement[M]
Wartungskasten[M]
scatola[F] di servizio[M]

distribution panel
tablero[M] de distribución[F]
panneau[M] de distribution[F]
Verteilerkasten[M]
quadro[M] di distribuzione[F]

fuse
fusible[M]
fusible[M]
Sicherung[F]
fusibile[M]

electricity meter

contador[M] de kilovatio-hora | compteur[M] d'électricité[F] | Kilowattstundenzähler[M] | contatore[M] di kilowattora[M]

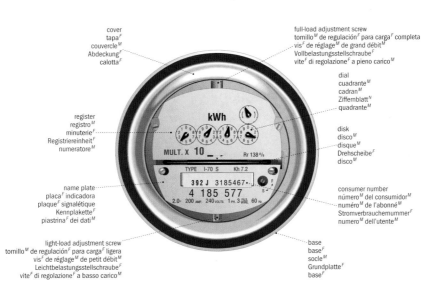

cover
tapa[F]
couvercle[M]
Abdeckung[F]
calotta[F]

full-load adjustment screw
tornillo[M] de regulación[F] para carga[F] completa
vis[F] de réglage[M] de grand débit[M]
Vollbelastungsstellschraube[F]
vite[F] di regolazione[F] a pieno carico[M]

dial
cuadrante[M]
cadran[M]
Ziffernblatt[N]
quadrante[M]

register
registro[M]
minuterie[F]
Registriereinheit[F]
numeratore[M]

disk
disco[M]
disque[M]
Drehscheibe[F]
disco[M]

name plate
placa[F] indicadora
plaque[F] signalétique
Kennplakette[F]
piastrina[F] dei dati[M]

consumer number
número[M] del consumidor[M]
numéro[M] de l'abonné[M]
Stromverbrauchernummer[F]
numero[M] dell'utente[M]

light-load adjustment screw
tornillo[M] de regulación[F] para carga[F] ligera
vis[F] de réglage[M] de petit débit[M]
Leichtbelastungsstellschraube[F]
vite[F] di regolazione[F] a basso carico[M]

base
base[F]
socle[M]
Grundplatte[F]
base[F]

contact devices

dispositivos^M de contacto^M | dispositifs^M de contact^M | Kontaktelemente^N | dispositivi^M di contatto^M

European plug
enchufe^M de tipo^M europeo
fiche^F européenne
Schukostecker^M
spina^F europea

clamp
abrazadera^F
étrier^M
Zugentlastungsklemme^F
morsetto^M

blade
contacto^M
broche^F
Stift^M
spinotto^M

grounding prong
terminal^M de tierra^F
contact^M de terre^F
Erdungsklemme^F
terminale^M di messa^F a terra^F

terminal
terminal^M
borne^F
Anschlussklemme^F
terminale^M

cover
tapa^F
couvercle^M
Kappe^F
coperchio^M

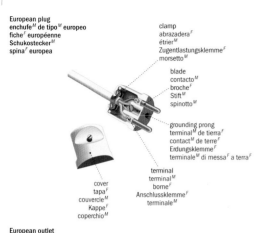

American plug
clavija^F de tipo^M americano
fiche^F américaine
dreipoliger, amerikanischer Stecker^M
spina^F americana

blade
contacto^M
lame^F
Spannungsstift^M
spinotto^M

grounding prong
contacto^M de conexión^F a tierra^F
contact^M de terre^F
Erdungsstift^M
spinotto^M di messa^F a terra^F

switch plate
placa^F del interruptor^M
plaque^F de commutateur^M
Schalterabdeckplatte^F
placca^F dell'interruttore^M

switch
interruptor^M
interrupteur^M
Schalter^M
interruttore^M

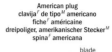

European outlet
clavija^F europea
prise^F de courant^M européenne
Schukosteckdose^F
presa^F europea

grounding prong
conector^M de tierra^F macho
contact^M de terre^F
Schutzkontaktbügel^M
maschio^M della messa^F a terra^F

socket-contact
alveolo^M
alvéole^F
Steckbuchse^F
alveolo^M della presa^F

plug adapter
adaptador^M de enchufes^M
adaptateur^M de fiche^F
Adapter^M
adattatore^M

American outlet
enchufe americano^M
prise^F de courant américaine^M
dreipolige, amerikanische Steckdose^F
presa^F per spina ^{F} americana

electrical box
caja^F de conexiones^F
boite^F d'encastrement^M
Buchsenhalter^M
scatola^F da incasso^M

dimmer switch
conmutador^M de intensidad^F
gradateur^F
Dimmerschalter^M
reostato^M

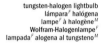

lighting

iluminación^F | éclairage^M | Beleuchtung^F | illuminazione^F

incandescent lightbulb
bombilla^F incandescente
lampe^F à incandescence^F
Glühlampe^F
lampadina^F a incandescenza^F

filament
filamento^M
filament^M
Glühfaden^M
filamento^M

support
soporte^M
support^M
Halter^M
supporto^M

stem
varilla^F
pied^M
Stab^M
asta^F

heat deflecting disc
disco^M desviador de calor^M
déflecteur^M de chaleur^F
Wärmedeflektorscheibe^F
disco^M deflettore^M del calore^M

exhaust tube
tubo^M de escape^M
queusot^M
Entladungsröhre^F
tubo^M di estrazione^F dell'aria^F

inert gas
gas^M inerte
gaz^M inerte
Edelgas^N
gas^M inerte

button
botón^M
bouton^M
Knopf^M
bottone^M

lead-in wire
entrada^F de corriente^F
entrée^F de courant^M
Zuleitungsdraht^M
filo^M conduttore

pinch
pie^M
pincement^M
Quetschfuß^M
codetta^F

base
casquillo^M
culot^M
Sockel^M
attacco^M

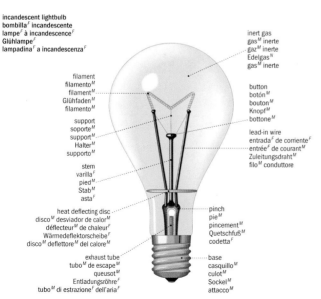

tungsten-halogen lightbulb
lámpara^F halógena
lampe^F à halogène
Wolfram-Halogenlampe^F
lampada^F alogena al tungsteno^M

filament support
filamento^M
support^M du filament^M
Wendelhalter^M
supporto^M del filamento^M

bulb
ampolla^F
ampoule^F
Kolben^M
bulbo^M

tungsten filament
filamento^M de tungsteno^M
filament^M de tungstène^M
Wolframwendel^F
filamento^M di tungsteno^M

electric circuit
circuito^M eléctrico
circuit^M électrique
elektrischer Kreislauf^M
circuito^M elettrico

inert gas
gas^M inerte
gaz^M inerte
Edelgas^N
gas^M inerte

contact
contacto^M
plot^M
Kontakt^M
contatto^M

base
casquillo^M
culot^M
Sockel^M
attacco^M

HOUSE

HOUSE

bayonet base
bombilla^F de bayoneta^F
culot^M à baïonnette^F
Bajonettfassung^F
attacco^M a baionetta^F

bulb
ampolla^F de vidrio^M
ampoule^F
Kolben^M
bulbo^M

parts of a lamp socket
componentes^F del portalámpara^M
éléments^M d'une douille^F de lampe^F
Teile$^{M/N}$ einer Lampenfassung^F
componenti^M del portalampada^M

lamp socket
portalámparas^M
douille^F de lampe^F
Lampenfassung^F
portalampada^M

screw base
bombilla^F de rosca^F
culot^M à vis^F
Schraubfassung^F
attacco^M a vite^F

cap
tapa^F
capuchon^M
Kappe^F
cappellotto^M

socket
casquillo^M
douille^F
Fassung^F
zoccolo^M

fluorescent tube
tubo^M fluorescente
tube^M fluorescent
Leuchtstoffröhre^F
tubo^M fluorescente

energy-saving bulb
bombilla^F de bajo consumo
lampe^F à économie^F d'énergie^F
Energiesparlampe^F
lampadina^F a risparmio^M di energia^F

insulating sleeve
manga^F de aislamiento^M
gaine^F isolante
Isolierhülse^F
manicotto^M isolante

bulb
ampolla^F
ampoule^F
Kolben^M
bulbo^M

tube retention clip
clip^M de ajuste^M
attache^F du tube^M
Cliphalterung^M
dispositivo^M di fissaggio^M del tubo^M

outer shell
cubierta^F
enveloppe^F
äußere Hülse^F
protezione^F esterna

mounting plate
placa^F de instalación^F
plaque^F de montage^M
Röhrenfassung^F
piastra^F di supporto^M

electronic ballast
electrodos^M
ballast^M électronique
elektronisches Vorschaltgerät^N
regolatore^M di corrente^M

housing
pantalla^F
boitier^M
Gehäuse^N
alloggiamento^M

base
casquillo^M
culot^M
Sockel^M
attacco^M

fluorescent tube
tubo^M fluorescente
tube^M fluorescent
Leuchtstoffröhre^F
tubo^M fluorescente

electrode
electrodo^M
électrode^F
Elektrode^F
elettrodo^M

phosphorescent coating
revestimiento^M de fósforo^M
couche^F fluorescente
Phosphorschicht^F
rivestimento^M fluorescente

pin base
base^F del tubo^M
culot^M à broches^F
Stiftsockel^M
attacco^M a spina^F

tungsten-halogen lamp
lámpara^F halógena
lampe^F à halogène^M
Wolfram-Halogenlampe^F
lampada^F alogena al tungsteno^M

lead-in wire
entrada^F de corriente^F
entrée^F de courant^M
Zuleitungsdraht^M
filo^M conduttore

bulb
tubo^M
tube^M
Kolben^M
tubo^M

exhaust tube
tubo^M de escape^M
queusot^M
Entladungsröhre^F
tubo^M di estrazione^F dell'aria^F

pin
pata^F
broche^F
Stift^M
spinotto^M

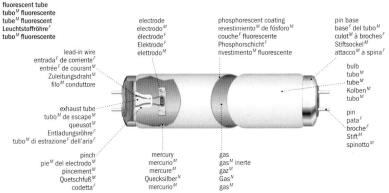

pinch
pie^M del electrodo^M
pincement^M
Quetschfuß^M
codetta^F

mercury
mercurio^M
mercure^M
Quecksilber^N
mercurio^M

gas
gas^M inerte
gaz^M
Gas^N
gas^M

pin
contacto^M
broche^F
Stift^M
spinotto^M

armchair

silla^F de brazos^M | fauteuil^M | Armlehnstuhl^M | poltrona^F

HOUSE

parts
partes^F
parties^F
Teile^{M/N}
parti^F

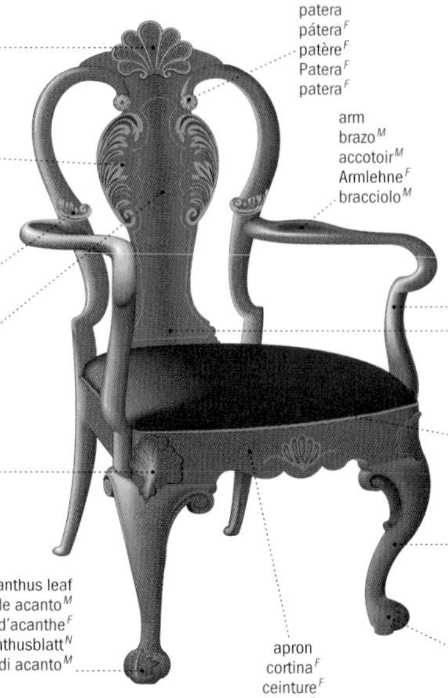

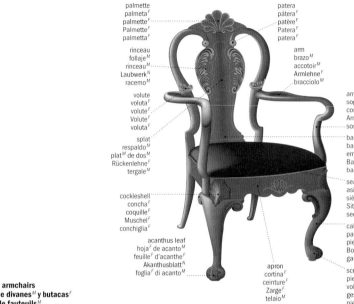

palmette
palmeta^F
palmette^F
Palmette^F
palmetta^F

patera
pátera^F
patère^F
Patera^F
patera^F

rinceau
follaje^M
rinceau^M
Laubwerk^N
racemo^M

arm
brazo^M
accotoir^M
Armlehne^F
bracciolo^M

volute
voluta^F
volute^F
Volute^F
voluta^F

arm stump
soporte^M del brazo^M
console^F d'accotoir^M
Armstütze^F
sostegno^M del bracciolo^M

splat
respaldo^M
plat^M de dos^M
Rückenlehne^F
tergale^M

base of splat
base^F del respaldo^M
embase^F de plat^M de dos^M
Basis^F der Rückenlehne^F
base^F del tergale^M

cockleshell
concha^F
coquille^F
Muschel^F
conchiglia^F

seat
asiento^M
siège^M
Sitz^M
sedile^M

acanthus leaf
hoja^F de acanto^M
feuille^F d'acanthe^F
Akanthusblatt^N
foglia^F di acanto^M

cabriole leg
pata^F curvada
pied^M cambré
Bocksfuß^M
gamba^F a capriolo^M

apron
cortina^F
ceinture^F
Zarge^F
telaio^M

scroll foot
pie^M de voluta^F
volute^F
geschwungener Fuß^M
piede^M a voluta^F

examples of armchairs
ejemplos^M de divanes^M y butacas^F
exemples^M de fauteuils^M
Beispiele^N für Armstühle^M
esempi^M di poltrone^F e divani^M

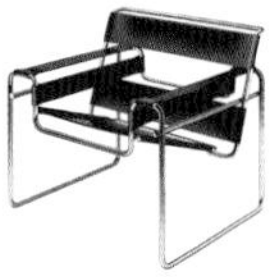

Wassily chair
silla^F Wassily
fauteuil^M Wassily
Wassily-Stuhl^M
poltrona^F Wassily

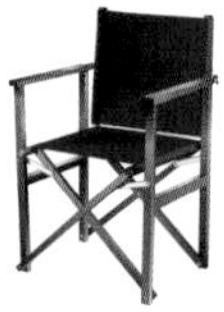

director's chair
silla^F plegable de lona^F
fauteuil^M metteur^M en scène^F
Regiestuhl^M
sedia^F da regista^M

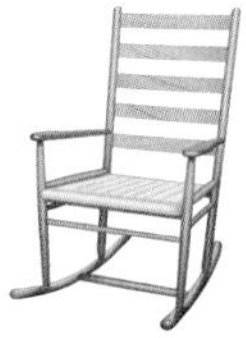

rocking chair
mecedora^F
berceuse^F
Schaukelstuhl^M
sedia^F a dondolo^M

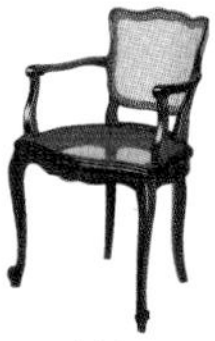

cabriolet
silla^F cabriolé
cabriolet^M
kleiner Lehnstuhl^M
cabriolet^F

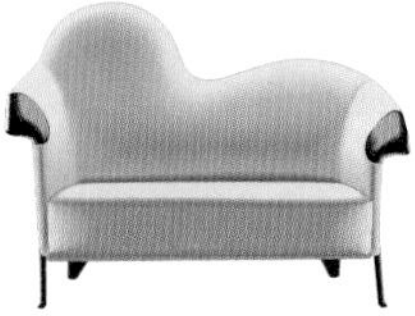

méridienne
meridiana^F
méridienne^F
Kanapee^N
méridienne^F

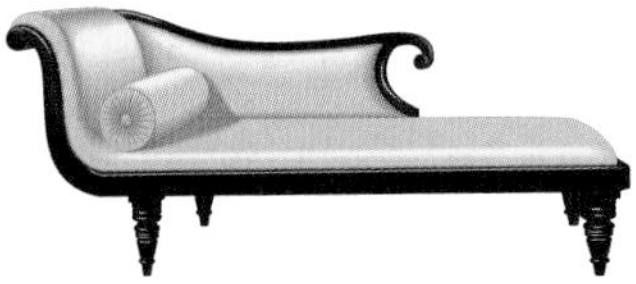

récamier
sofá^M tipo^M imperio
récamier^M
Chaiselongue^N
agrippina^F

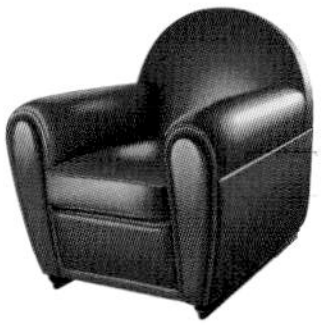

club chair
butaca^F
fauteuil^M club^M
Clubsessel^M
poltrona^F da salotto^M

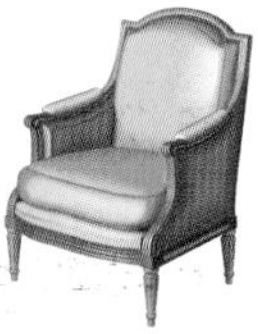

bergère
silla^F poltrona
bergère^F
Bergère^F
bergère^F

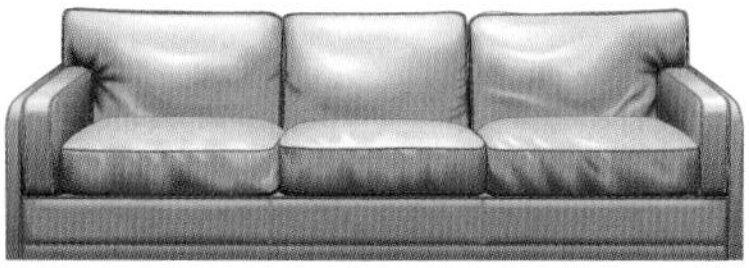

sofa
sofá^M
canapé^M
Sofa^N
divano^M

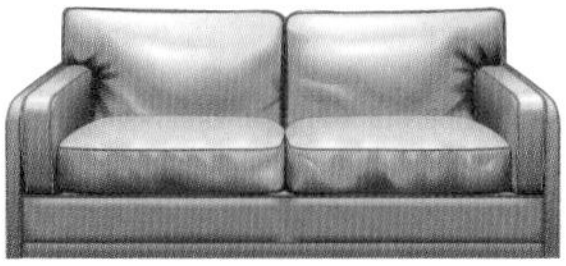

love seat
sofá^M de dos plazas^F
causeuse^F
Zweisitzer^M
divano^M a due posti^M

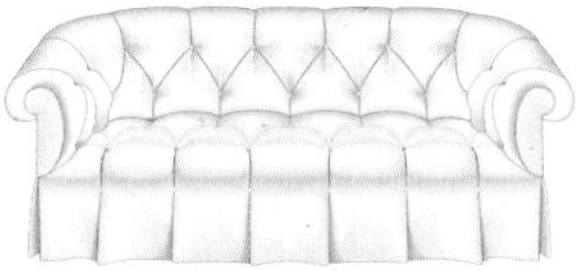

chesterfield
chesterfield^M
canapé^F capitonné
Chesterfieldsofa^N
divano^M Chesterfield

side chair

silla^F sin brazos^M | chaise^F | Stuhl^M | sedia^F

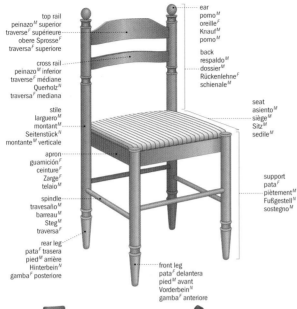

top rail
peinazo^M superior
traverse^F supérieure
obere Sprosse^F
traversa^F superiore

cross rail
peinazo^M inferior
traverse^F médiane
Querholz^N
traversa^F mediana

stile
larguero^M
montant^M
Seitenstück^N
montante^M verticale

apron
guarnición^F
ceinture^F
Zarge^F
telaio^M

spindle
travesaño^M
barreau^M
Steg^M
traversa^F

rear leg
pata^F trasera
pied^M arrière
Hinterbein^N
gamba^F posteriore

ear
pomo^M
oreille^F
Knauf^M
pomo^M

back
respaldo^M
dossier^M
Rückenlehne^F
schienale^M

seat
asiento^M
siège^M
Sitz^M
sedile^M

support
pata^F
piètement^M
Fußgestell^N
sostegno^M

front leg
pata^F delantera
pied^M avant
Vorderbein^N
gamba^F anteriore

parts
partes^F
parties^F
Teile^{M/N}
parti^F

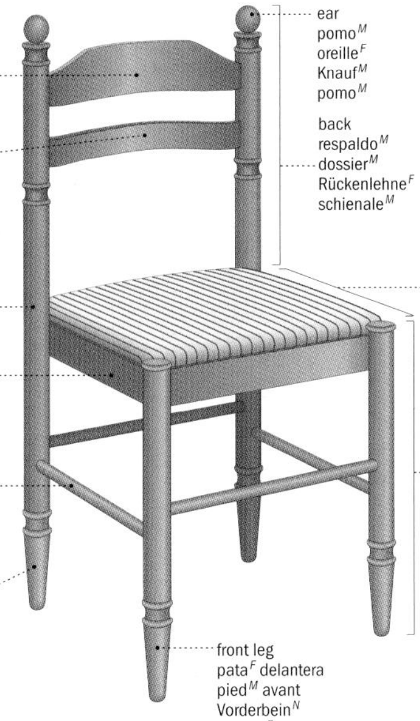

**examples of chairs
ejemplos^M de sillas^F
exemples^M de chaises^F
Beispiele^N für Stühle^M
esempi^M di sedie^F**

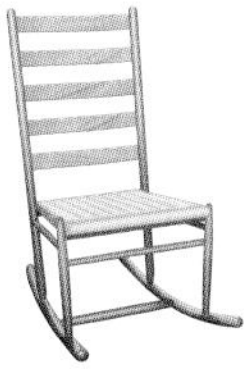

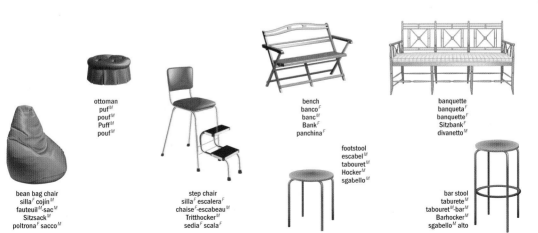

rocking chair
mecedora^F
chaise^F berçante
Schaukelstuhl^M
sedia^F a dondolo^M

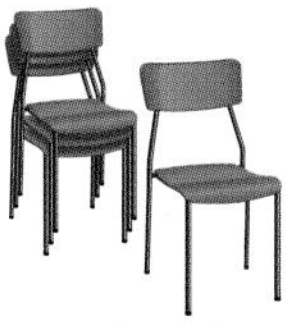

stacking chairs
sillas^F apilables
chaises^F empilables
Stapelstühle^M
sedie^F impilabili

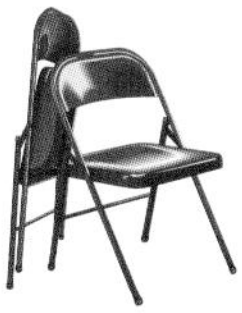

folding chairs
sillas^F plegables
chaises^F pliantes
Klappstühle^M
sedia^F pieghevole

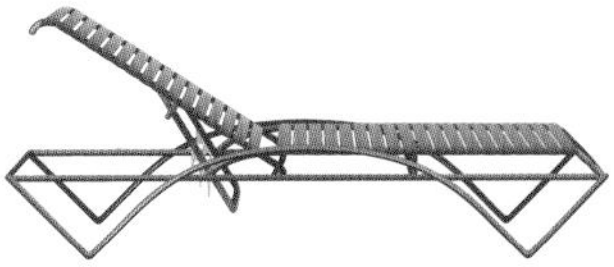

chaise longue
tumbona^F
chaise^F longue
Liegestuhl^M
sedia^F a sdraio^M

HOUSE

seats

asientos^M | sièges^M | Sitzmöbel^N | sedili^M

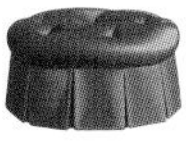

ottoman
puf^M
pouf^M
Puff^M
pouf^M

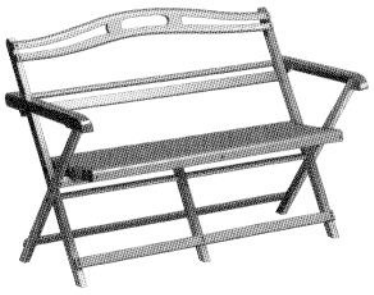

bench
banco^F
banc^M
Bank^F
panchina^F

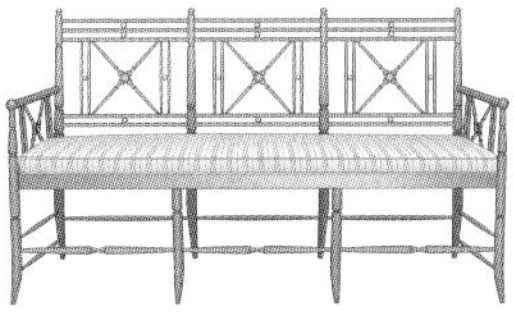

banquette
banqueta^F
banquette^F
Sitzbank^F
divanetto^M

footstool
escabel^M
tabouret^M
Hocker^M
sgabello^M

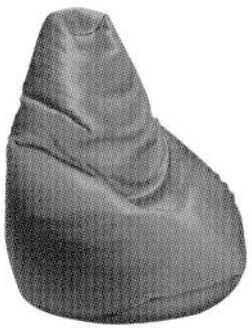

bean bag chair
silla^F cojín^M
fauteuil^M-sac^M
Sitzsack^M
poltrona^F sacco^M

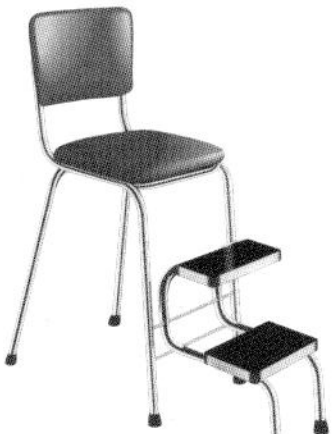

step chair
silla^F escalera^F
chaise^F-escabeau^M
Tritthocker^M
sedia^F scala^F

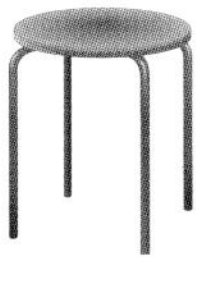

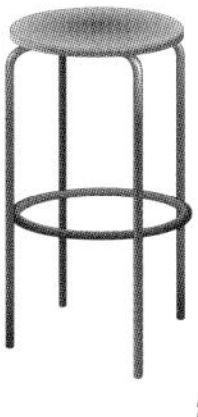

bar stool
taburete^M
tabouret^M-bar^M
Barhocker^M
sgabello^M alto

table

mesa^F | table^F | Tisch^M | tavolo^M

gate-leg table
mesa^F de hojas^F abatibles
table^F à abattants^M
Klapptisch^M
tavolo^M a cancello^M

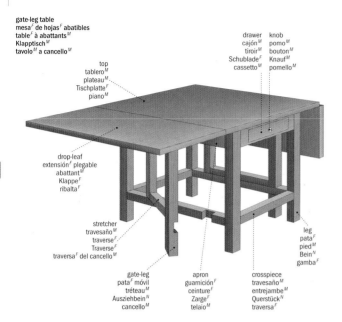

drawer
cajón^M
tiroir^M
Schublade^F
cassetto^M

knob
pomo^M
bouton^M
Knauf^M
pomello^M

top
tablero^M
plateau^M
Tischplatte^F
piano^M

drop-leaf
extensión^F plegable
abattant^M
Klappe^F
ribalta^F

stretcher
travesaño^M
traverse^F
Traverse^F
traversa^F del cancello^M

leg
pata^F
pied^M
Bein^N
gamba^F

gate-leg
pata^F móvil
tréteau^M
Ausziehbein^N
cancello^M

apron
guarnición^F
ceinture^F
Zarge^F
telaio^M

crosspiece
travesaño^M
entrejambe^M
Querstück^N
traversa^F

examples of tables
ejemplos^M de mesas^F
exemples^M de tables^F
Beispiele^N für Tische^M
esempi^M di tavoli^M

extension table
mesa^F plegable
table^F à rallonges^F
Ausziehtisch^M
tavolo^M allungabile

top
tablero^M
plateau^M
Tischplatte^F
piano^M

extension
extensión^F
rallonge^F
Auszug^M
prolunga^F

nest of tables
juego^M de mesas^F
tables^F gigognes
Satztische^M
tavolini^M sovrapponibili

serving cart
mesita^F de servicio^M
desserte^F
Servierwagen^M
carrello^M portavivande

storage furniture

muebles^M contenedores | meubles^M de rangement^M | Aufbewahrungsmöbel^N | mobili^M contenitori

armoire
armario^M
armoire^F
Kleiderschrank^M
armadio^M

frame
armazón^M
bâti^M
Rahmen^M
telaio^M

door
puerta^F
vantail^M
Tür^F
porta^F

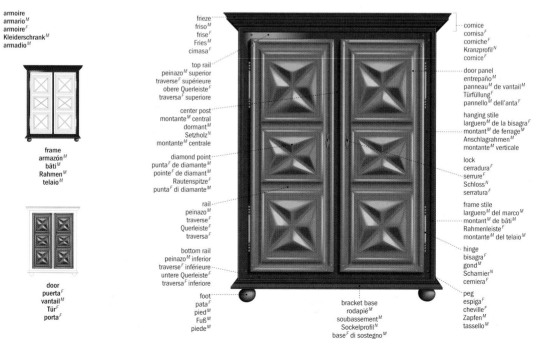

frieze
friso^M
frise^F
Fries^M
cimasa^F

top rail
peinazo^M superior
traverse^F supérieure
obere Querleiste^F
traversa^F superiore

center post
montante^M central
dormant^M
Setzholz^N
montante^M centrale

diamond point
punta^F de diamante^M
pointe^F de diamant^M
Rautenspitze^F
punta^F di diamante^M

rail
peinazo^M
traverse^F
Querleiste^F
traversa^F

bottom rail
peinazo^M inferior
traverse^F inférieure
untere Querleiste^F
traversa^F inferiore

foot
pata^F
pied^M
Fuß^M
piede^M

bracket base
rodapié^M
soubassement^M
Sockelprofil^N
base^F di sostegno^M

cornice
cornisa^F
corniche^F
Kranzprofil^N
cornice^F

door panel
entrepaño^M
panneau^M de vantail^M
Türfüllung^F
pannello^M dell'anta^F

hanging stile
larguero^M de la bisagra^F
montant^M de ferrage^M
Anschlagrahmen^M
montante^M verticale

lock
cerradura^F
serrure^F
Schloss^N
serratura^F

frame stile
larguero^M del marco^M
montant^M de bâti^M
Rahmenleiste^F
montante^M del telaio^M

hinge
bisagra^F
gond^M
Scharnier^N
cerniera^F

peg
espiga^F
cheville^F
Zapfen^M
tassello^M

HOUSE

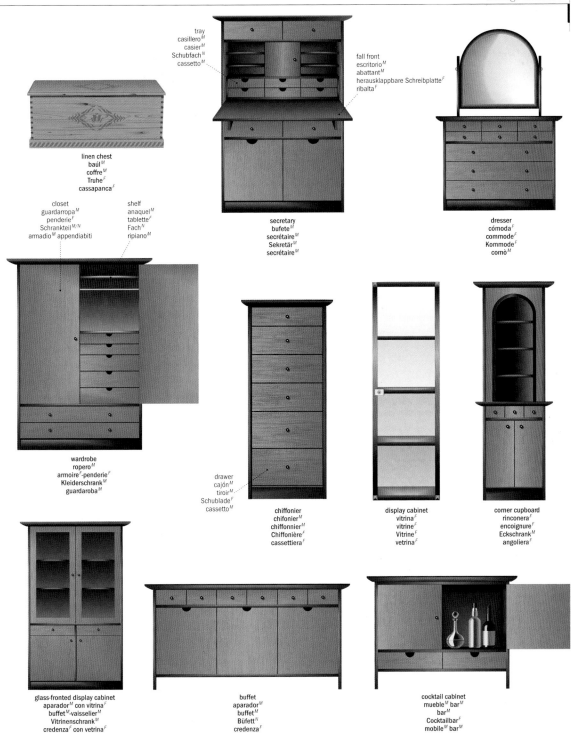

tray
casillero [M]
casier [M]
Schubfach [N]
cassetto [M]

fall front
escritorio [M]
abattant [M]
herausklappbare Schreibplatte [F]
ribalta [F]

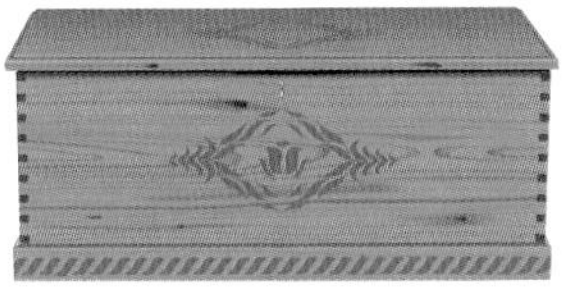

linen chest
baúl [M]
coffre [M]
Truhe [F]
cassapanca [F]

closet
guardarropa [M]
penderie [F]
Schrankteil [M/N]
armadio [M] appendiabiti

shelf
anaquel [M]
tablette [F]
Fach [N]
ripiano [M]

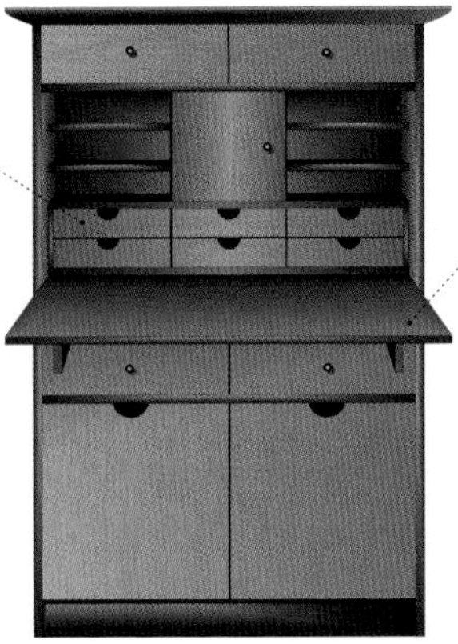

secretary
bufete [M]
secrétaire [M]
Sekretär [M]
secrétaire [M]

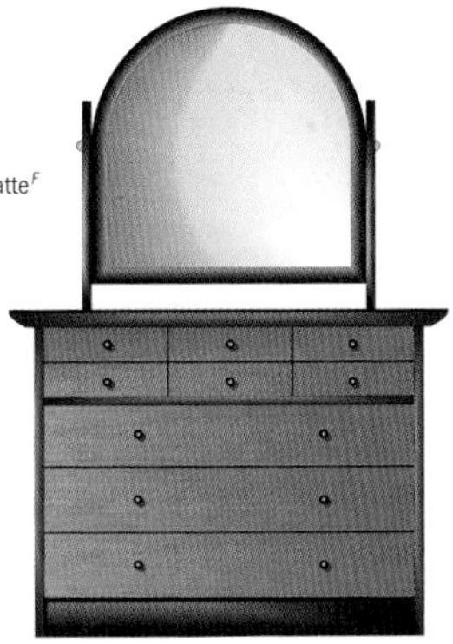

dresser
cómoda [F]
commode [F]
Kommode [F]
comò [M]

HOUSE

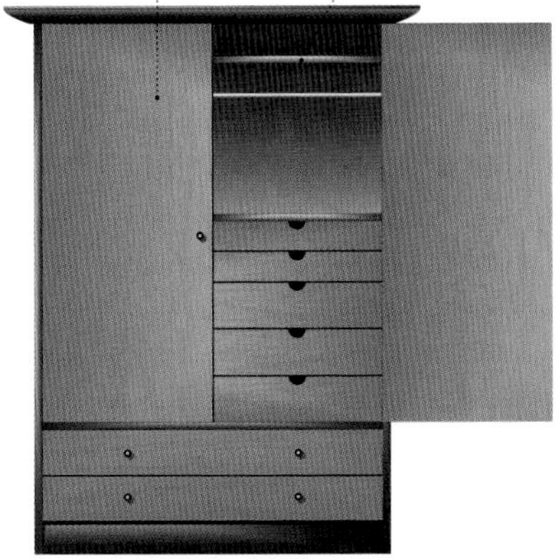

wardrobe
ropero [M]
armoire [F]-penderie [F]
Kleiderschrank [M]
guardaroba [M]

drawer
cajón [M]
tiroir [M]
Schublade [F]
cassetto [M]

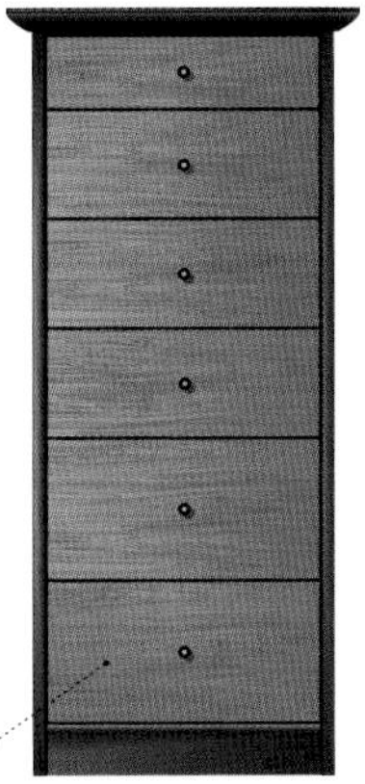

chiffonier
chifonier [M]
chiffonnier [M]
Chiffonière [F]
cassettiera [F]

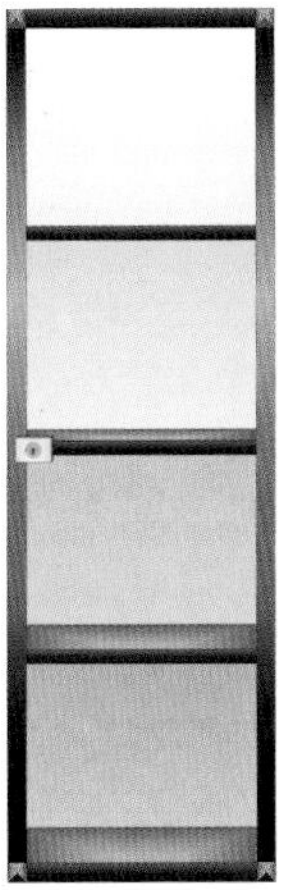

display cabinet
vitrina [F]
vitrine [F]
Vitrine [F]
vetrina [F]

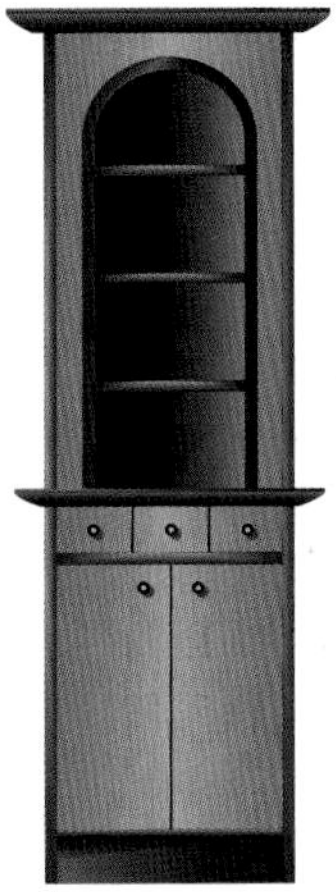

corner cupboard
rinconera [F]
encoignure [F]
Eckschrank [M]
angoliera [F]

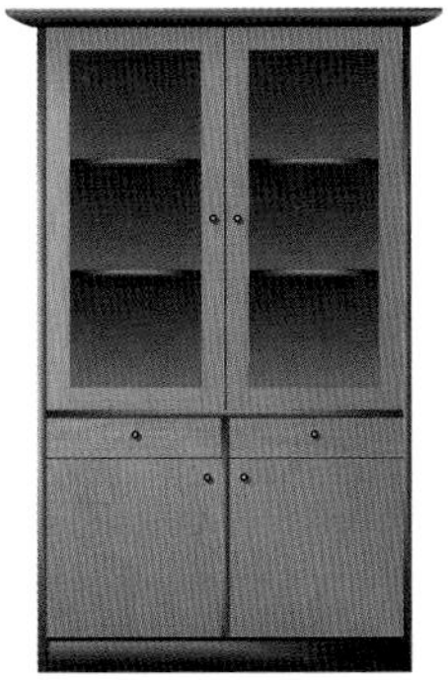

glass-fronted display cabinet
aparador [M] con vitrina [F]
buffet [M]-vaisselier [M]
Vitrinenschrank [M]
credenza [F] con vetrina [F]

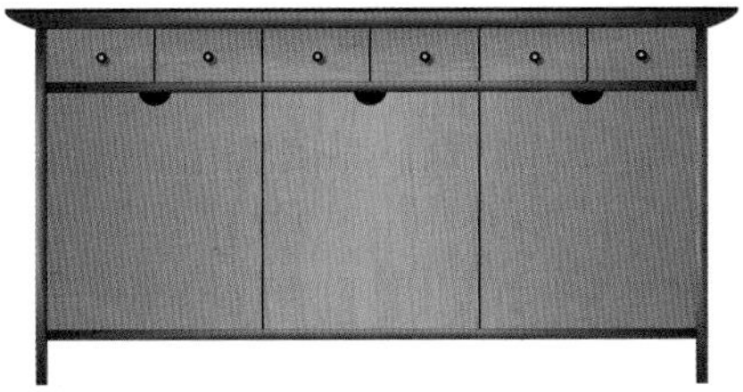

buffet
aparador [M]
buffet [M]
Büfett [N]
credenza [F]

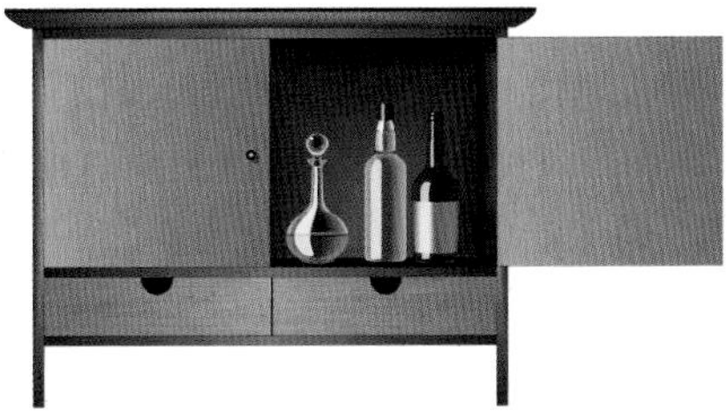

cocktail cabinet
mueble [M] bar [M]
bar [M]
Cocktailbar [F]
mobile [M] bar [M]

bed

cama^F | lit^M | Bett^N | letto^M

HOUSE

sofa bed
sofá cama^M
canapé^M convertible
Schlafcouch^F
divano-letto^M

futon
futón^M
futon^M
Auflage^F
futon^M

frame
armazón^M
cadre^M
Rahmen^M
telaio^M

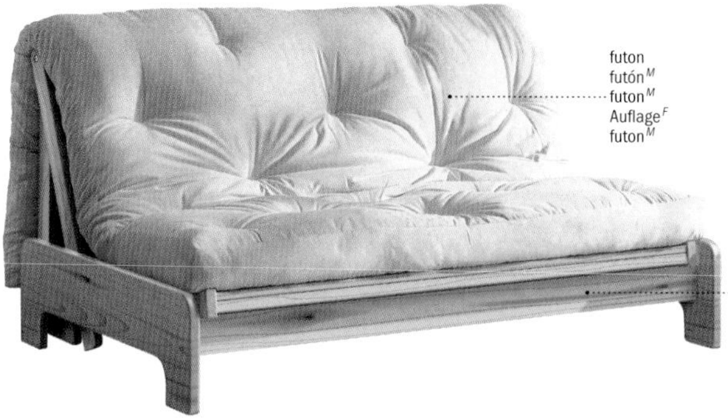

parts
partes^F
parties^F
Teile^{M/N}
parti^F

footboard
pie^M de la cama^F
pied^M de lit^M
Fußende^N
pediera^F

mattress cover
funda^F de colchón^M
protège-matelas^M
Matratzenauflage^F
coprimaterasso^M

pillow protector
funda^F de almohada^F
housse^F d'oreiller^M
Kopfkissenschonbezug^M
fodera^F del guanciale^M

elastic
elástico^M
élastique^M
Gummiband^N
elastico^M

mattress
colchón^M de muelles^M
matelas^M
Matratze^F
materasso^M

headboard
cabecera^F
tête^F de lit^M
Kopfende^N
testiera^F

bolster
cabezal^M
traversin^M
große Nackenrolle^F
capezzale^M

handle
asa^F
poignée^F
Griff^M
maniglia^F

box spring
somier^M
sommier^M tapissier^M
Sprungfederrahmen^M
rete^F a molle^F

pillow
almohada^F
oreiller^M
Kopfkissen^N
guanciale^M

leg
pata^F
pied^M
Fuß^M
gamba^F

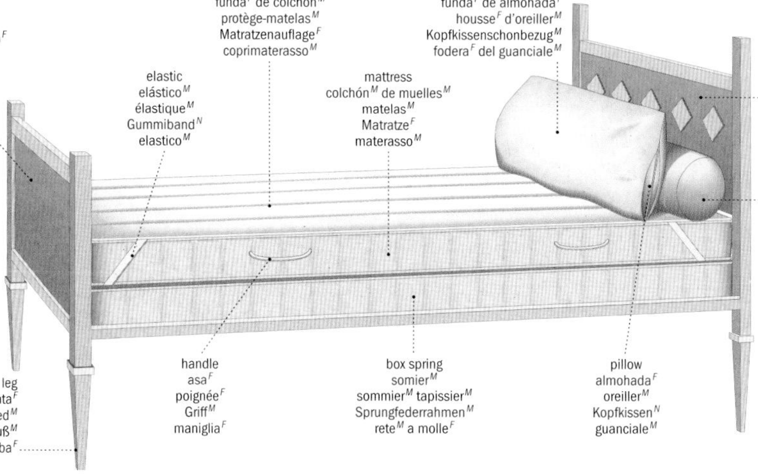

linen
ropa^F de cama^F
literie^F
Bettwäsche^F
biancheria^F da letto^M

comforter
edredón^M
édredon^M
Daunendecke^F
trapunta^F

scatter cushion
cojín^M
coussin^M carré
kleines Kissen^N
cuscino^M

sham
falso almohadón^M
couvre-oreiller^M
Schutzbezug^M
copriguanciale^M

pillowcase
funda^F de la almohada^F
taie^F d'oreiller^M
Kopfkissenbezug^M
federa^F

fitted sheet
sábana^F ajustable
drap^M-housse^F
Spannbetttuch^N
lenzuolo^M con angoli^M

flat sheet
sábana^F
drap^M
Betttuch^N
lenzuolo^M

blanket
manta^F
couverture^F
Decke^F
coperta^F

neck roll
cojín^M
polochon^M
Nackenrolle^F
cuscino^M a rullo^M

dust ruffle
faldón^M
volant^M
Volant^M
volant^M

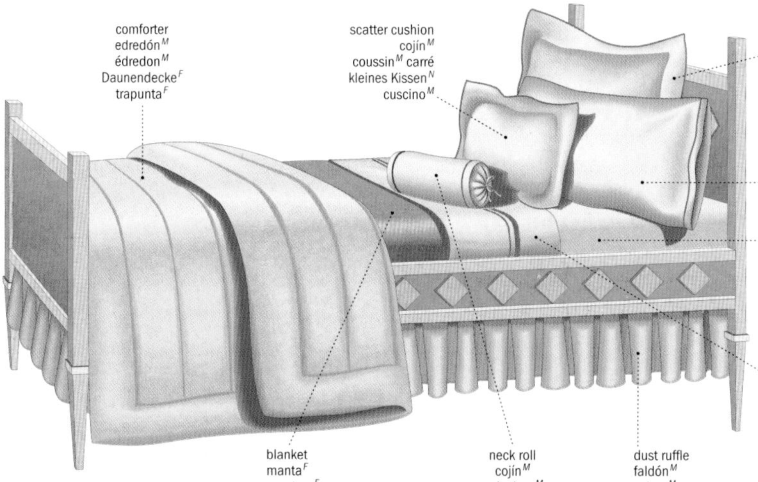

children's furniture

muebles^M infantiles | meubles^M d'enfants^M | Kindermöbel^N | mobili^M per bambini^M

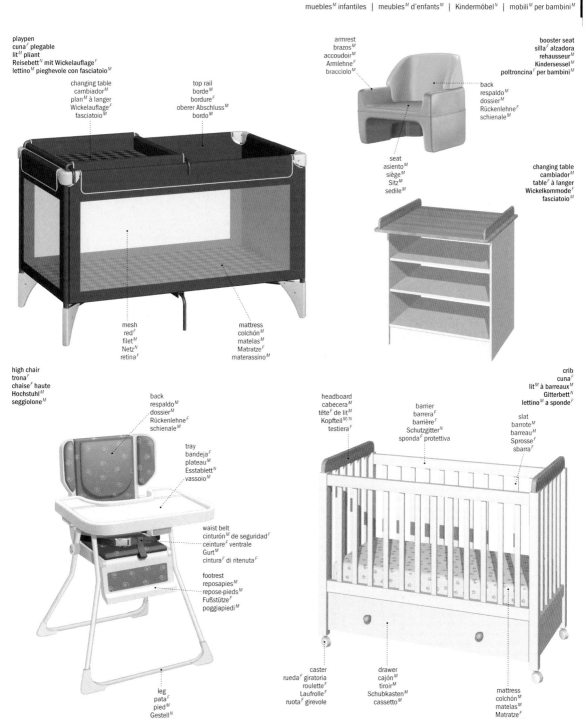

playpen
cuna^F plegable
lit^M pliant
Reisebett^N mit Wickelauflage^F
lettino^M pieghevole con fasciatoio^M

changing table
cambiador^M
plan^M à langer
Wickelauflage^F
fasciatoio^M

top rail
borde^M
bordure^F
oberer Abschluss^M
bordo^F

armrest
brazos^M
accoudoir^M
Armlehne^F
bracciolo^M

back
respaldo^M
dossier^M
Rückenlehne^F
schienale^M

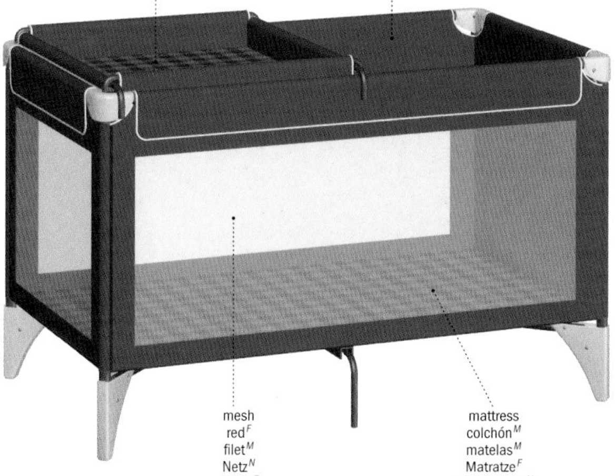

booster seat
silla^F alzadora
rehausseur^M
Kindersessel^M
poltroncina^F per bambini^M

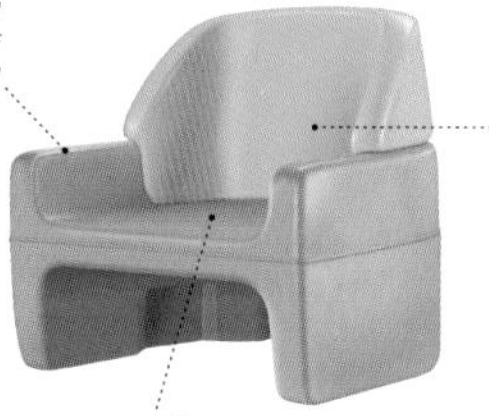

seat
asiento^M
siège^M
Sitz^M
sedile^M

changing table
cambiador^M
table^F à langer
Wickelkommode^F
fasciatoio^M

mesh
red^F
filet^M
Netz^N
retina^F

mattress
colchón^M
matelas^M
Matratze^F
materassino^M

HOUSE

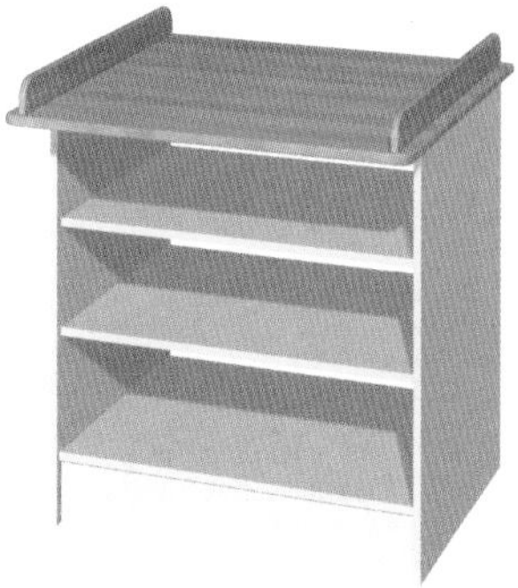

high chair
trona^F
chaise^F haute
Hochstuhl^M
seggiolone^M

back
respaldo^M
dossier^M
Rückenlehne^F
schienale^M

tray
bandeja^F
plateau^M
Esstablett^N
vassoio^M

waist belt
cinturón^M de seguridad^F
ceinture^F ventrale
Gurt^M
cintura^F di ritenuta^F

footrest
reposapies^M
repose-pieds^M
Fußstütze^F
poggiapiedi^M

leg
pata^F
pied^M
Gestell^N
gamba^F

headboard
cabecera^M
tête^F de lit^M
Kopfteil$^{M/N}$
testiera^F

barrier
barrera^F
barrière^F
Schutzgitter^N
sponda^F protettiva

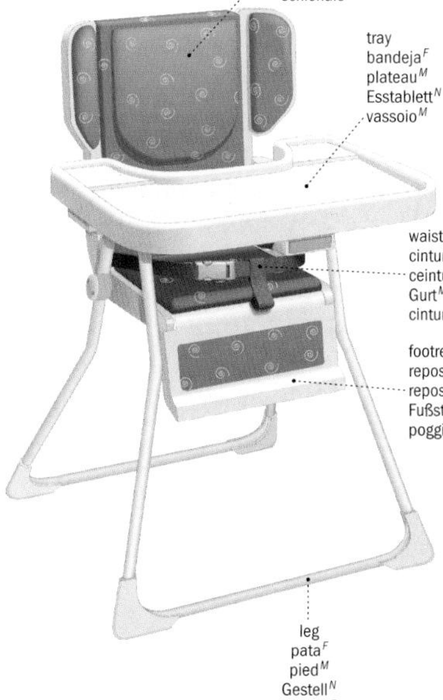

crib
cuna^F
lit^M à barreaux^M
Gitterbett^N
lettino^M a sponde^F

slat
barrote^M
barreau^M
Sprosse^F
sbarra^F

caster
rueda^F giratoria
roulette^F
Laufrolle^F
ruota^F girevole

drawer
cajón^M
tiroir^M
Schubkasten^M
cassetto^M

mattress
colchón^M
matelas^M
Matratze^F
materasso^M

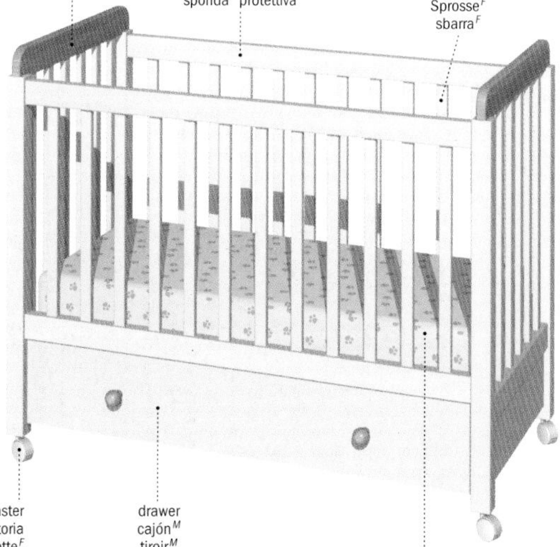

window accessories

accesorios^M para las ventanas^F | parures^F de fenêtre^F | Dekorationen^F | accessori^M per finestre^F

HOUSE

indoor shutters
postigos^M interiores
volets^M d'intérieur^M
Innenläden^M
imposte^F ripiegabili

window curtain
cortina^F de ventana^F
rideau^M de vitrage^M
Fenstergardine^F
tenda^F per finestra^F

valance
guardamalleta^F
cantonnière^F
Querbehang^M
mantovana^F

cottage curtain
cortinas^F recogidas
rideau^M bonne femme^F
Landhausgardine^F
tendina^F arricciata

tieback
alzapaños^M
embrasse^F
Raffhalter^M
bracciale^M

café curtain
visillo^M
rideau^M brise-bise^M
Kaffeehausgardine^F
tendina^F a mezzovetro^M

ruffle
volante^M
volant^M
Volant^M
volant^M

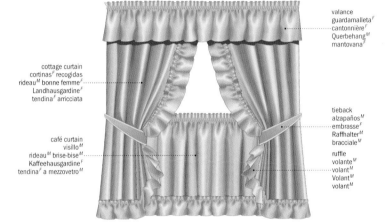

curtain
cortina^F
rideau^M
Vorhang^M
tenda^F

cornice
cenefa^F
bandeau^M
Schabracke^F
riloga^F sagomata

overdrapery
doble cortina^F
double rideau^M
Übergardine^F
soprattenda^F

draw drapery
cortinas^F corredera
rideau^M
Zugvorhang^M
tendone^M oscurante

holdback
anilla^F del cordón^M
patère^F à embrasse^F
Raffhalter^M
portabracciale^M

cord tieback
cordón^M
cordelière^F
Kordel^F
bracciale^M a cordoncino^M

tassel
borla^F
gland^M
Troddel^F
nappa^F

sheers
visillos^M
voilage^M
Store^M
tenda^F trasparente

window accessories

examples of pleats
ejemplos^M de fruncidos^M
exemples^M de plis^M
Beispiele^N für Kräuselfalten^F
esempi^M di arricciature^F

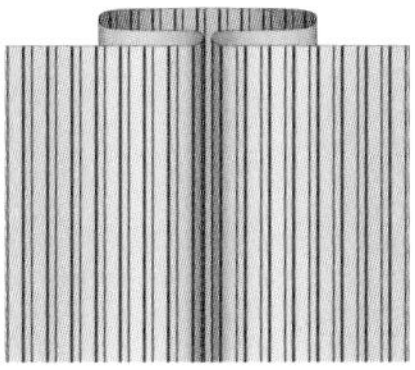

box pleat
pliegue^M de cajón^M
pli^M creux
Schachtelfalte^F
sfondo^M piega^F

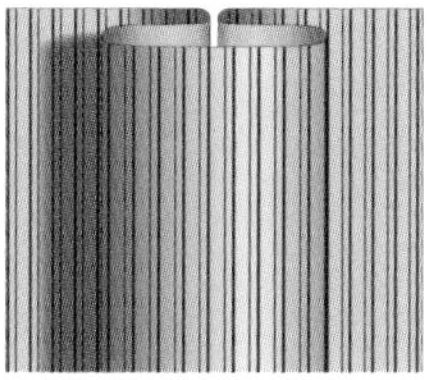

inverted pleat
pliegue^M de cajón^M invertido
pli^M rond
eingelegte Falte^F
cannone^M

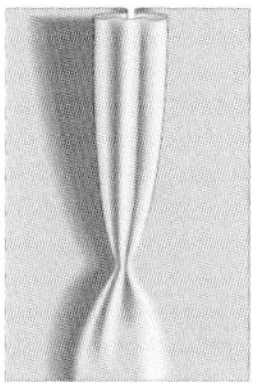

pinch pleat
pliegue^M de pinza^F
pli^M pincé
Kirsorfalte^F
arricciatura^F a pince^F

examples of headings
ejemplos^M de cenefas^F
exemples^F de têtes^F
Beispiele^N für Vorhangköpfe^M
esempi^M di fettucce^F

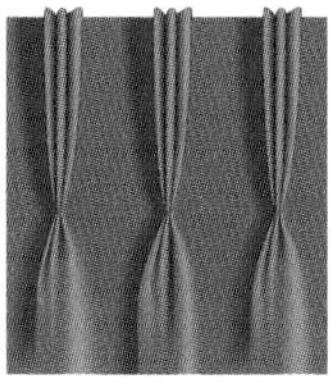

pleated heading
cenefa^F plisada
tête^F plissée
Kirschband^N
fettuccia^F plissettata

pencil pleat heading
cenefa^F plisada de canotillo^M
fronçage^M tuyauté
Bleistiftfaltenband^N
arricciatura^F a cannoncino^M

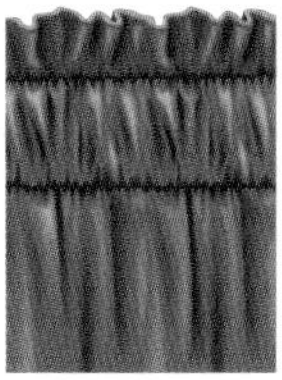

shirred heading
cenefa^F fruncida
tête^F froncée
Durchzug^M
fettuccia^F arricciata

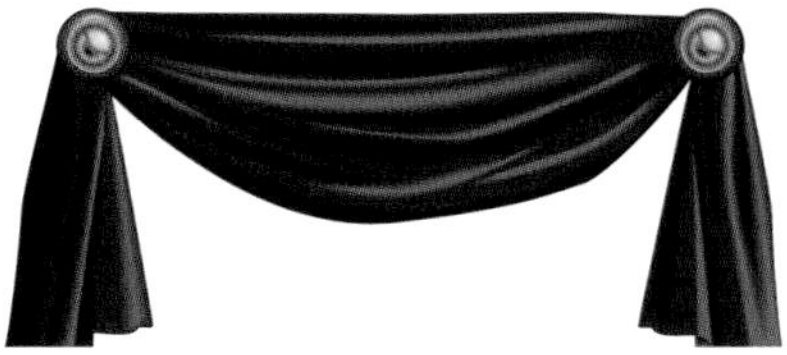

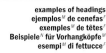

draped swag
cenefa^F drapeada
cantonnière^F drapée
Freihand-Dekoration^F
festone^M drappeggiato

examples of curtains
ejemplos^M de cortinas^F
exemples^M de rideaux^M
Beispiele^N für Vorhänge^M
esempi^M di tende^F

attached curtain
cortina^F sujeta de doble barra^F
rideau^M coulissé
Spanner^M
tenda^F a vetro^M

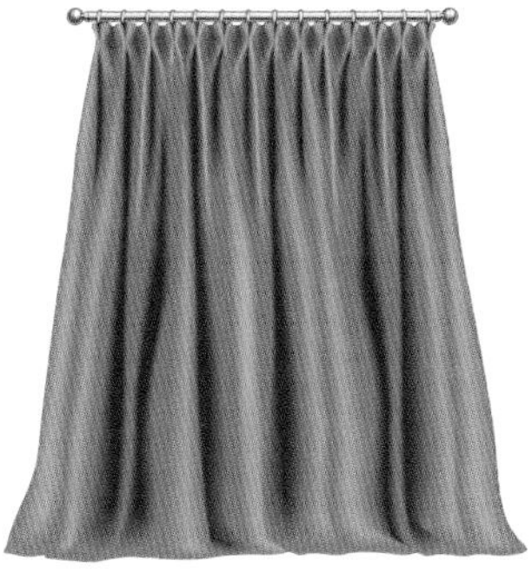

loose curtain
cortina^F suelta corrediza
rideau^M flottant
loser Vorhang^M
tenda^F a strappo^M

crisscross curtains
cortinas^F cruzadas
rideaux^M croisés
Raffgardine^F
tende^F con sormonto^M totale

balloon curtain
cortina^F abombada
rideau^M ballon^M
Wolkenstore^M
tenda^F a palloncino^M

HOUSE

window accessories

rods
varillas^F
tringles^F
Gardinenstangen^F
bastoni^M **da tenda**^{F}

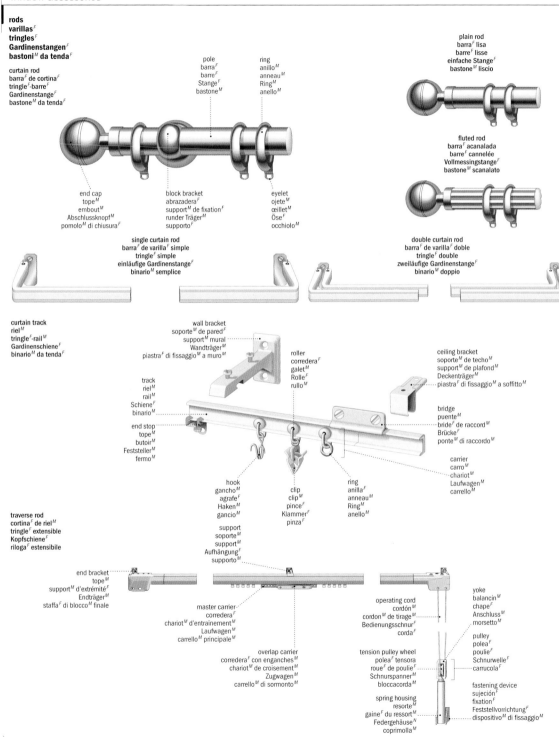

curtain rod
barra^F de cortina^F
tringle^F-barre^F
Gardinenstange^F
bastone^M da tenda^F

pole
barra^F
barre^F
Stange^F
bastone^M

ring
anillo^M
anneau^M
Ring^M
anello^M

plain rod
barra^F lisa
barre^F lisse
einfache Stange^F
bastone^M liscio

fluted rod
barra^F acanalada
barre^F cannelée
Vollmessingstange^F
bastone^M scanalato

end cap
tope^M
embout^M
Abschlussknopf^M
pomolo^M di chiusura^F

block bracket
abrazadera^F
support^M de fixation^F
runder Träger^M
supporto^F

eyelet
ojete^M
œillet^M
Öse^F
occhiolo^M

single curtain rod
barra^F de varilla^F simple
tringle^F simple
einläufige Gardinenstange^F
binario^M semplice

double curtain rod
barra^F de varilla^F doble
tringle^F double
zweiläufige Gardinenstange^F
binario^M doppio

curtain track
riel^M
tringle^F-rail^M
Gardinenschiene^F
binario^M da tenda^F

wall bracket
soporte^M de pared^F
support^M mural
Wandträger^M
piastra^F di fissaggio^M a muro^M

roller
corredera^F
galet^M
Rolle^F
rullo^M

ceiling bracket
soporte^M de techo^M
support^M de plafond^M
Deckenträger^M
piastra^F di fissaggio^M a soffitto^M

track
riel^M
rail^M
Schiene^F
binario^M

end stop
tope^M
butoir^M
Feststeller^M
fermo^M

bridge
puente^M
bride^F de raccord^M
Brücke^F
ponte^M di raccordo^M

carrier
carro^M
chariot^M
Laufwagen^M
carrello^M

hook
gancho^M
agrafe^F
Haken^M
gancio^M

clip
clip^M
pince^F
Klammer^F
pinza^F

ring
anilla^F
anneau^M
Ring^M
anello^M

traverse rod
cortina^F de riel^M
tringle^F extensible
Kopfschiene^F
riloga^F estensibile

support
soporte^M
support^M
Aufhängung^F
supporto^M

end bracket
tope^M
support^M d'extrémité^F
Endträger^M
staffa^F di blocco^M finale

master carrier
corredera^F
chariot^M d'entraînement^M
Laufwagen^M
carrello^M principale^M

operating cord
cordón^M
cordon^M de tirage^M
Bedienungsschnur^F
corda^F

yoke
balancin^M
chape^F
Anschluss^M
morsetto^M

pulley
polea^F
poulie^F
Schnurwelle^F
carrucola^M

overlap carrier
corredera^F con enganches^M
chariot^M de croisement^M
Zugwagen^M
carrello^M di sormonto^M

tension pulley wheel
polea^F tensora
roue^F de poulie^F
Schnurspanner^M
bloccacorda^M

fastening device
sujeción^F
fixation^F
Feststellvorrichtung^F
dispositivo^M di fissaggio^M

spring housing
resorte^M
gaine^F du ressort^M
Federgehäuse^N
coprimolla^M

HOUSE

blinds
persianas[F] **enrollables**
stores[M]
Rollo[N] **und Jalousie**[F]
tende[F] **avvolgibili**

roller shade
persiana[F] enrollable automática
store[M] à enroulement[M] automatique
Rollo[N]
tenda[F] avvolgibile

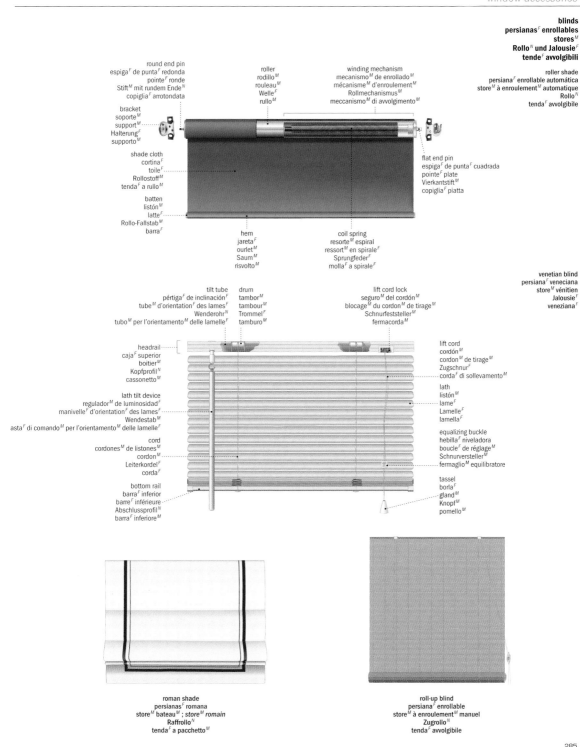

round end pin
espiga[F] de punta[F] redonda
pointe[F] ronde
Stift[M] mit rundem Ende[N]
copiglia[F] arrotondata

roller
rodillo[M]
rouleau[M]
Welle[F]
rullo[M]

winding mechanism
mecanismo[M] de enrollado[M]
mécanisme[M] d'enroulement[M]
Rollmechanismus[M]
meccanismo[M] di avvolgimento[M]

bracket
soporte[M]
support[M]
Halterung[F]
supporto[M]

shade cloth
cortina[F]
toile[F]
Rollostoff[M]
tenda[F] a rullo[M]

batten
listón[M]
latte[F]
Rollo-Fallstab[M]
barra[F]

flat end pin
espiga[F] de punta[F] cuadrada
pointe[F] plate
Vierkantstift[M]
copiglia[F] piatta

hem
jareta[F]
ourlet[M]
Saum[M]
risvolto[M]

coil spring
resorte[M] espiral
ressort[M] en spirale[F]
Sprungfeder[F]
molla[F] a spirale[F]

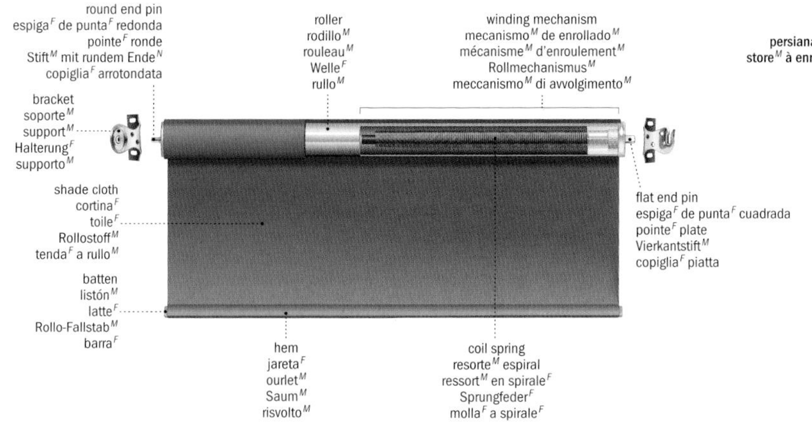

venetian blind
persiana[F] veneciana
store[M] vénitien
Jalousie[F]
veneziana[F]

tilt tube
pértiga[F] de inclinación[F]
tube[M] d'orientation[F] des lames[F]
Wenderohr[N]
tubo[M] per l'orientamento[M] delle lamelle[F]

drum
tambor[M]
tambour[M]
Trommel[F]
tamburo[M]

lift cord lock
seguro[M] del cordón[M]
blocage[M] du cordon[M] de tirage[M]
Schnurfeststeller[M]
fermacorda[F]

lift cord
cordón[M]
cordon[M] de tirage[M]
Zugschnur[F]
corda[F] di sollevamento[M]

headrail
caja[F] superior
boitier[M]
Kopfprofil[N]
cassonetto[M]

lath
listón[M]
lame[F]
Lamelle[F]
lamella[F]

lath tilt device
regulador[M] de luminosidad[F]
manivelle[F] d'orientation[F] des lames[F]
Wendestab[M]
asta[F] di comando[M] per l'orientamento[M] delle lamelle[F]

equalizing buckle
hebilla[F] niveladora
boucle[F] de réglage[M]
Schnurversteller[M]
fermaglio[M] equilibratore

cord
cordones[M] de listones[M]
cordon[M]
Leiterkordel[F]
corda[F]

tassel
borla[F]
gland[M]
Knopf[M]
pomello[M]

bottom rail
barra[F] inferior
barre[F] inférieure
Abschlussprofil[N]
barra[F] inferiore[M]

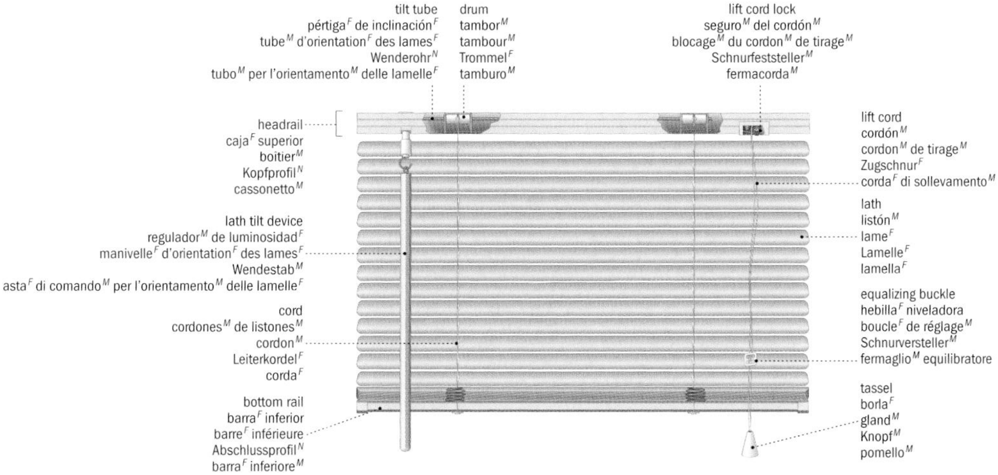

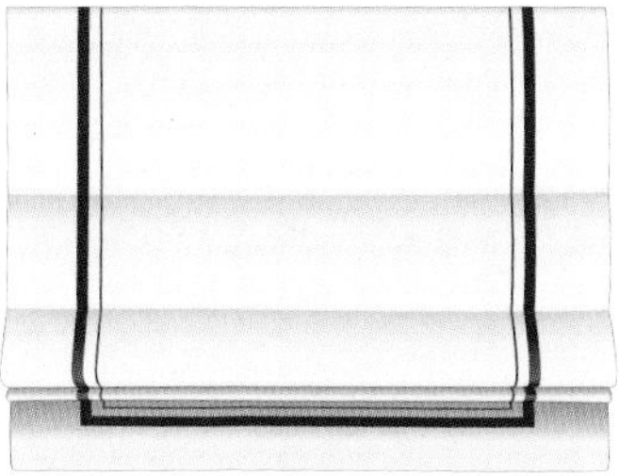

roman shade
persianas[F] romana
store[M] bateau[M] ; store[M] romain
Raffrollo[N]
tenda[F] a pacchetto[M]

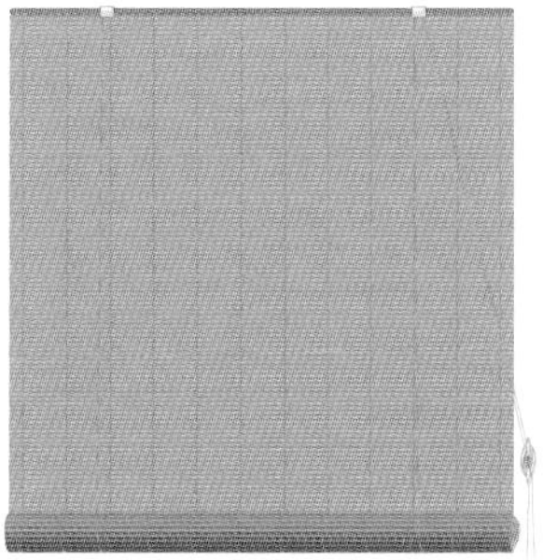

roll-up blind
persiana[F] enrollable
store[M] à enroulement[M] manuel
Zugrollo[N]
tenda[F] avvolgibile

HOUSE

285

lights

lámparas^F | luminaires^M | Lampen^F | luci^F

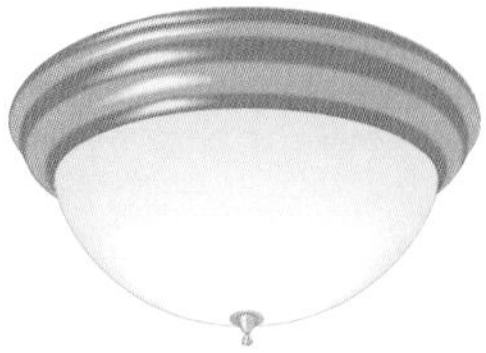

ceiling fixture
plafón^M
plafonnier^M
Deckenleuchte^F
plafoniera^F

hanging pendant
lámpara^F de techo^M
suspension^F
Hängeleuchte^F
lampada^F a sospensione^F

clamp spotlight
lámpara^F de pinza^F
spot^M à pince^F
Klemmspot^M
faretto^M a pinza^F

halogen desk lamp
lámpara^F de despacho^M halógena
lampe^F de bureau^M halogène
Halogen^N-Tischleuchte^F
lampada^F alogena da tavolo^M

arm
brazo^M
bras^M
Arm^M
braccio^M

base
base^M
socle^M
Fuß^M
base^F

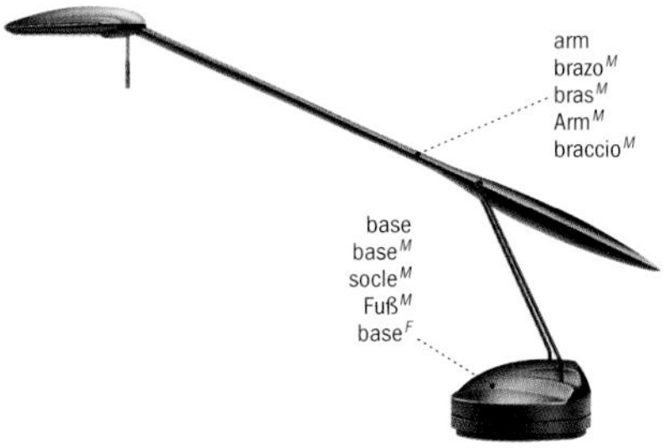

adjustable lamp
flexo^M
lampe^F d'architecte^M
Arbeitsleuchte^F
lampada^F a braccio^M regolabile

on-off switch
interruptor^M
interrupteur^M
Ein-/Ausschalter^M
interruttore^M

arm
brazo^M
bras^M
Arm^M
braccio^M

shade
pantalla^F
abat-jour^M
Schirm^M
paralume^M

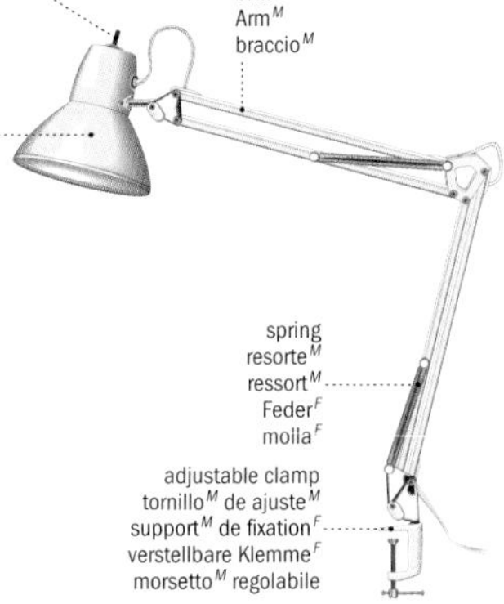

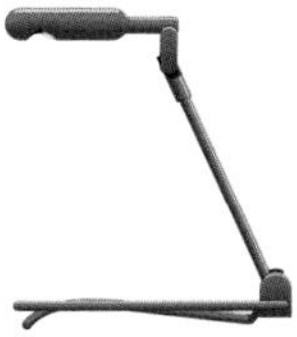

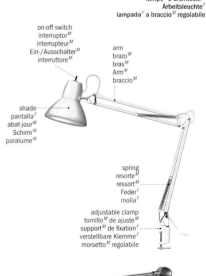

reading lamp
lámpara^F de cabecera^F
lampe^F liseuse
Leseleuchte^F
lampada^F da lettura^F

spring
resorte^M
ressort^M
Feder^F
molla^F

adjustable clamp
tornillo^M de ajuste^M
support^M de fixation^F
verstellbare Klemme^F
morsetto^M regolabile

shade
pantalla^F
abat-jour^M
Schirm^M
paralume^M

base
base^F
socle^M
Sockel^M
base^F

stand
pedestal^M
pied^M
Fuß^M
base^F

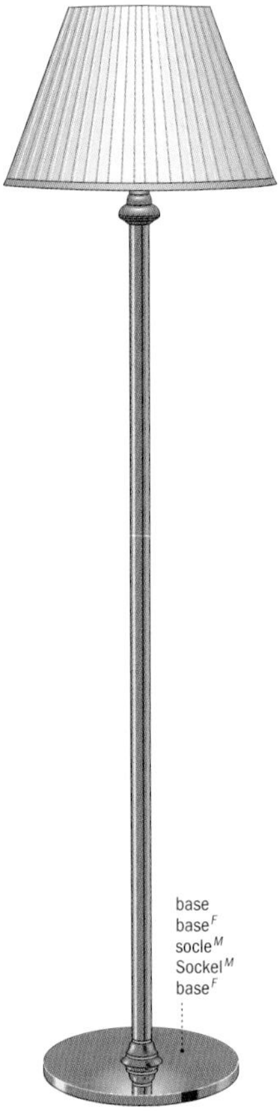

floor lamp
lámpara^F de pie^M
lampadaire^M
Standleuchte^F
lampada^F a stelo^M

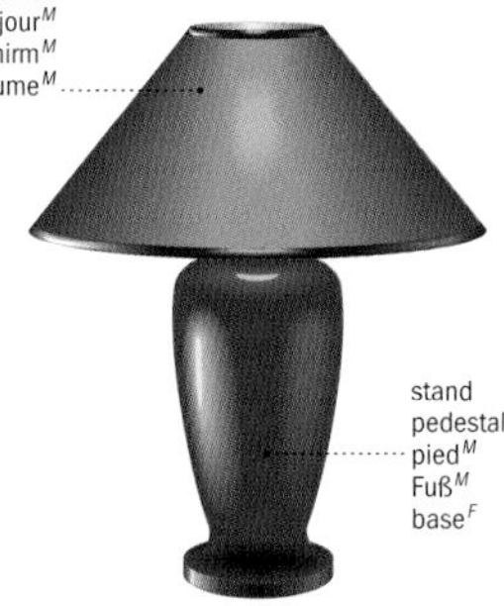

table lamp
lámpara^F de mesa^F
lampe^F de table^F
Tischleuchte^F
lampada^F da tavolo^M

desk lamp
lámpara^F de escritorio^M
lampe^F de bureau^M
Schreibtischleuchte^F
lampada^F da tavolo^M

HOUSE

chandelier
araña^F
lustre^M
Kronleuchter^M
lampadario^M

bobeche
arandela^F
coupelle^F
Teller^M
coppetta^F

crystal drop
colgante^M
pendeloque^F
Kristalltropfen^M
goccia^F di cristallo^M

crystal button
gota^F
pampille^F
Koppen^M
perlina^F di cristallo^M

column
columna^F
fût^M
Mittelsäule^F
colonna^F

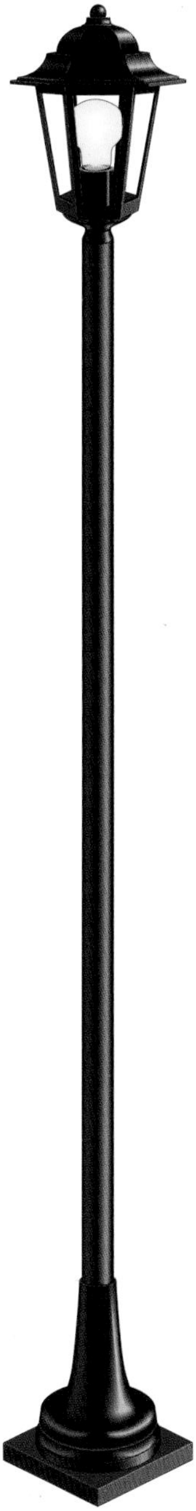

track lighting
riel^M de iluminación^F
rail^M d'éclairage^M
Beleuchtungsschiene^F
faretto^M da binario^M

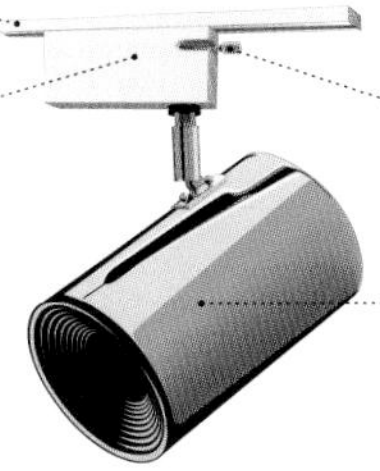

bar frame
armazón^M
gouttière^F
Schiene^F
binario^M

contact lever
interruptor^M
manette^F de contact^M
Befestigungshebel^M
leva^F di contatto^M

transformer
transformador^M
transformateur^M
Transformator^M
trasformatore^M

spot
foco^M
spot^M
Spot^M
faretto^M orientabile

wall lantern
farol^M
lanterne^F murale
Wandlaterne^F
lampione^M da parete^F

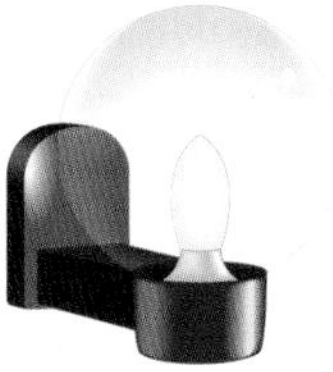

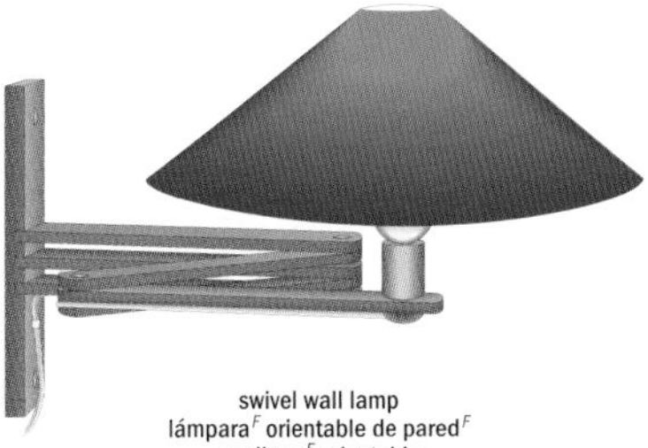

swivel wall lamp
lámpara^F orientable de pared^F
applique^F orientable
Scherenleuchte^F
lampada^F da parete^F con braccio^M estensibile

wall sconce
aplique^M
applique^F
Wandleuchte^F
lampada^F da parete^F

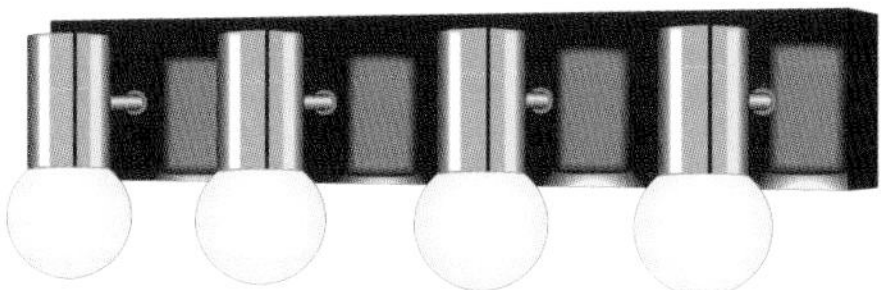

strip lights
lámparas^F en serie^F
rampe^F d'éclairage^M
Lampenreihe^F
lampade^F in serie^F

post lantern
farola^F
lanterne^F de pied^M
Straßenlaterne^F
lampione^M

HOUSE

domestic appliances

aparatos^M electrodomésticos | appareils^M électroménagers | Haushaltsgeräte^N | elettrodomestici^M

HOUSE

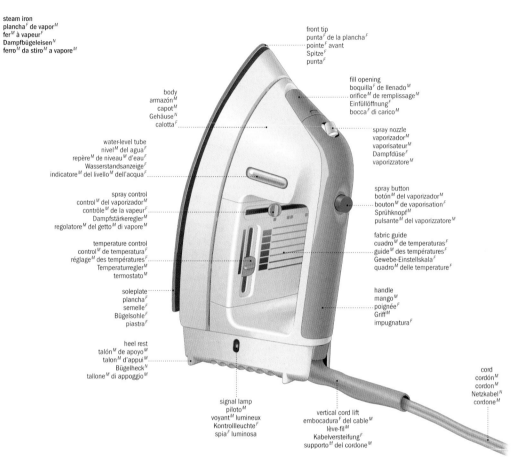

steam iron
plancha^F de vapor^M
fer^M à vapeur^F
Dampfbügeleisen^N
ferro^M da stiro^M a vapore^M

front tip
punta^F de la plancha^F
pointe^F avant
Spitze^F
punta^F

body
amazón^M
capot^M
Gehäuse^N
calotta^F

fill opening
boquilla^F de llenado^M
orifice^M de remplissage^M
Einfüllöffnung^F
bocca^F di carico^M

water-level tube
nivel^M del agua^F
repère^M de niveau^M d'eau^F
Wasserstandsanzeige^F
indicatore^M del livello^M dell'acqua^F

spray nozzle
vaporizador^M
vaporisateur^M
Dampfdüse^F
vaporizzatore^M

spray control
control^M del vaporizador^M
contrôle^M de la vapeur^F
Dampfstärkeregler^M
regolatore^M del getto^M di vapore^M

spray button
botón^M del vaporizador^M
bouton^M de vaporisation^F
Sprühknopf^M
pulsante^M del vaporizzatore^M

fabric guide
cuadro^M de temperaturas^F
guide^M des températures^F
Gewebe-Einstellskala^F
quadro^M delle temperature^F

temperature control
control^M de temperatura^F
réglage^M des températures^F
Temperaturregler^M
termostato^M

handle
mango^M
poignée^F
Griff^M
impugnatura^F

soleplate
plancha^F
semelle^F
Bügelsohle^F
piastra^F

heel rest
talón^M de apoyo^M
talon^M d'appui^M
Bügelheck^N
tallone^M di appoggio^M

cord
cordón^M
cordon^M
Netzkabel^N
cordone^M

signal lamp
piloto^M
voyant^M lumineux
Kontrollleuchte^F
spia^F luminosa

vertical cord lift
embocadura^F del cable^M
lève-fil^M
Kabelversteifung^F
supporto^M del cordone^M

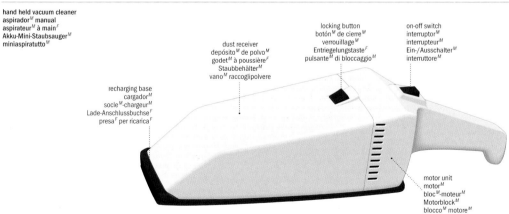

hand held vacuum cleaner
aspirador^M manual
aspirateur^M à main^F
Akku-Mini-Staubsauger^M
miniaspiratutto^M

locking button
botón^M de cierre^M
verrouillage^M
Entriegelungstaste^F
pulsante^M di bloccaggio^M

on-off switch
interruptor^M
interrupteur^M
Ein-/Ausschalter^M
interruttore^M

dust receiver
depósito^M de polvo^M
godet^M à poussière^F
Staubbehälter^M
vano^M raccoglipolvere

recharging base
cargador^M
socle^M-chargeur^M
Lade-Anschlussbuchse^F
presa^F per ricarica^F

motor unit
motor^M
bloc^M-moteur^M
Motorblock^M
blocco^M motore^M

HOUSE

upright vacuum cleaner
escoba^F eléctrica
aspirateur^M-balai^M
Handstaubsauger^M
aspirapolvere^F verticale

on/off switch
interruptor^M on/off
interrupteur^M
Ein-/Ausschalter^M
interruttore^M

cylinder vacuum cleaner
aspirador^M
aspirateur^M-traineau^M
Bodenstaubsauger^M
aspirapolvere^M

attachment storage area
cajetín^M de accesorios
compartiment^M d'accessoires^M
Zubehörfach^N
scomparto^M degli accessori^M

hose
tubo^M flexible
tuyau^M flexible
Schlauch^M
tubo^M flessibile

locking device
seguro^M
système^M de verrouillage^M
Verschluss^M
dispositivo^M di bloccaggio^M

bag compartment
cajetín^M portabolsa
compartiment^M de sac^M
Beutelfach^N
scomparto^M del sacchetto^M

pipe
tubo^M rígido
tube^M droit
Saugrohr^N
tubo^M rigido

cleaner height adjustment knob
palanca^F de regulación^F de altura^F
sélecteur^M de hauteur^F
Höhenverstellung^F
manopola^F di regolazione^F dell'altezza^F

flexible hose
tubo^M flexible
tuyau^M flexible
flexibler Schlauch^M
tubo^M flessibile

ventilating grille
rejilla^F del ventilador^M
grille^F de ventilation^F
Luftaustrittsschlitz^M
griglia^F di ventilazione^F

on-off switch
interruptor^M
interrupteur^M
Ein-/Ausschalter^M
interruttore^M

bumper
tope^M amortiguador
pare-chocs^M
Stoßleiste^F
protezione^F antiurto

caster
ruedecilla^F
roulette^F
Lenkrolle^F
ruota^F orientabile

brush
cepillo^M
brosse^F
Bürste^F
spazzola^F

attachments
accesorios^M
accessoires^M
Zubehör^N
accessori^M

extension pipe
tubo^M de extensión^F
rallonge^F
Ansatzrohr^N
tubo^M rigido di prolunga^F

handle
asa^F
poignée^F
Tragegriff^M
maniglia^F

cord
cordón^M
cordon^M
Kabel^M
cordone^M

hood
tapa^F
capot^M
Haube^F
calotta^F

rug and floor brush
boquilla^F para suelos^M y alfombras^F
suceur^M à tapis^M et planchers^M
Bodendüse^F
spazzola^F per tappeti^M e pavimenti^M

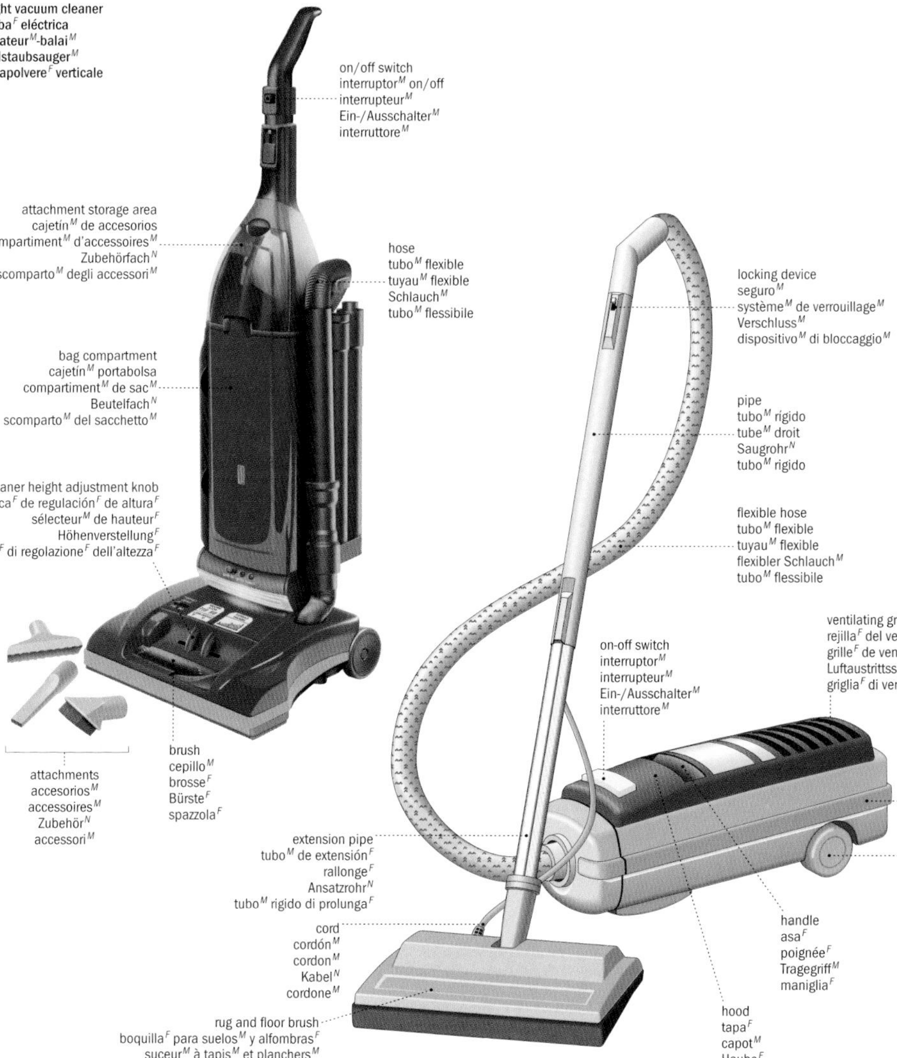

vacuum cleaner attachments
accesorios^M
accessoires^M
Saugzubehör^N
accessori^M di pulitura^F

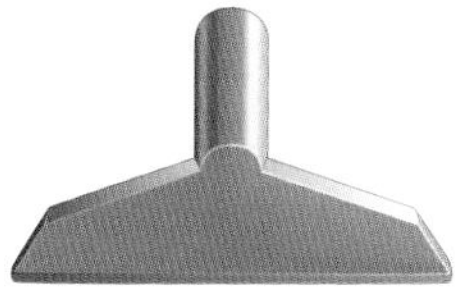

upholstery nozzle
boquilla^F para tapicería^F
suceur^M triangulaire à tissus^M
Polsterdüse^F
bocchetta^F per tappezzeria^F

dusting brush
cepillo^M-plumero^M
brosse^F à épousseter
Saugbürste^F
spazzola^F a pennello^M

crevice tool
boquilla^F rinconera
suceur^M plat
Fugendüse^F
bocchetta^F per fessure^F

floor brush
cepillo^M para suelos^M
brosse^F à planchers^M
Bürste^F
spazzola^F per pavimenti^M

domestic appliances

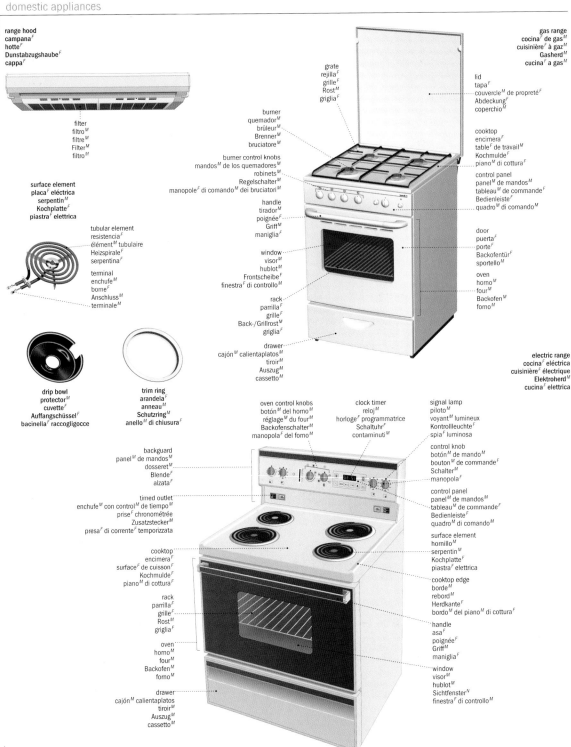

range hood
campana^F
hotte^F
Dunstabzugshaube^F
cappa^F

filter
filtro^M
filtre^M
Filter^M
filtro^M

surface element
placa^F eléctrica
serpentin^M
Kochplatte^F
piastra^F elettrica

tubular element
resistencia^F
élément^M tubulaire
Heizspirale^F
serpentina^F

terminal
enchufe^M
borne^F
Anschluss^M
terminale^M

drip bowl
protector^M
cuvette^F
Auffangschüssel^M
bacinella^F raccogligocce

trim ring
arandela^F
anneau^M
Schutzring^M
anello^M di chiusura^F

grate
rejilla^F
grille^F
Rost^M
griglia^F

burner
quemador^M
brûleur^M
Brenner^M
bruciatore^M

burner control knobs
mandos^M de los quemadores^M
robinets^M
Regelschalter^M
manopole^F di comando^M dei bruciatori^M

handle
tirador^M
poignée^F
Griff^M
maniglia^F

window
visor^M
hublot^M
Frontscheibe^F
finestra^F di controllo^M

rack
parrilla^F
grille^F
Back-/Grillrost^M
griglia^F

drawer
cajón^M calientaplatos^M
tiroir^M
Auszug^M
cassetto^M

gas range
cocina^F de gas^M
cuisinière^F à gaz^M
Gasherd^M
cucina^F a gas^M

lid
tapa^F
couvercle^M de propreté^F
Abdeckung^F
coperchio^M

cooktop
encimera^F
table^F de travail^M
Kochmulde^F
piano^M di cottura^F

control panel
panel^M de mandos^M
tableau^F de commande^F
Bedienleiste^F
quadro^M di comando^M

door
puerta^F
porte^F
Backofentür^F
sportello^M

oven
horno^M
four^M
Backofen^M
forno^M

electric range
cocina^F eléctrica
cuisinière^F électrique
Elektroherd^M
cucina^F elettrica

oven control knobs
botón^M del horno^M
réglage^M du four^M
Backofenschalter^M
manopola^F del forno^M

clock timer
reloj^M
horloge^F programmatrice
Schaltuhr^F
contaminuti^M

signal lamp
piloto^M
voyant^M lumineux
Kontrollleuchte^F
spia^F luminosa

backguard
panel^M de mandos^M
dosseret^M
Blende^F
alzata^F

timed outlet
enchufe^M con control^M de tiempo^M
prise^F chronométrée
Zusatzstecker^M
presa^F di corrente^F temporizzata

cooktop
encimera^F
surface^F de cuisson^F
Kochmulde^F
piano^M di cottura^F

rack
parrilla^F
grille^F
Rost^M
griglia^F

oven
horno^M
four^M
Backofen^M
forno^M

drawer
cajón^M calientaplatos
tiroir^M
Auszug^M
cassetto^M

control knob
botón^M de mando^M
bouton^M de commande^F
Schalter^M
manopola^F

control panel
panel^M de mandos^M
tableau^M de commande^F
Bedienleiste^F
quadro^M di comando^M

surface element
hornillo^M
serpentin^M
Kochplatte^F
piastra^F elettrica

cooktop edge
borde^M
rebord^M
Herdkante^F
bordo^M del piano^M di cottura^F

handle
asa^F
poignée^F
Griff^M
maniglia^F

window
visor^M
hublot^M
Sichtfenster^N
finestra^F di controllo^M

HOUSE

HOUSE

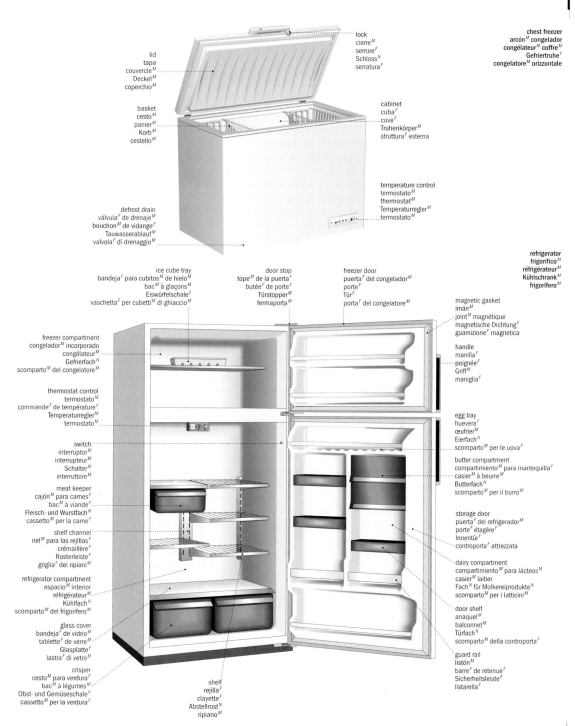

chest freezer
arcón^M congelador
congélateur^M coffre^M
Gefriertruhe^F
congelatore^M orizzontale

lock
cierre^M
serrure^F
Schloss^N
serratura^F

lid
tapa
couvercle^M
Deckel^M
coperchio^M

basket
cesto^M
panier^M
Korb^M
cestello^M

cabinet
cuba^F
cuve^F
Truhenkörper^M
struttura^F esterna

temperature control
termostato^M
thermostat^M
Temperaturregler^M
termostato^M

defrost drain
válvula^F de drenaje^M
bouchon^M de vidange^F
Tauwasserablauf^M
valvola^F di drenaggio^M

refrigerator
frigorífico^M
réfrigérateur^M
Kühlschrank^M
frigorifero^M

ice cube tray
bandeja^F para cubitos^M de hielo^M
bac^M à glaçons^M
Eiswürfelschale^F
vaschetta^F per cubetti^M di ghiaccio^M

door stop
tope^M de la puerta^F
butée^F de porte^F
Türstopper^M
fermaporta^M

freezer door
puerta^F del congelador^M
porte^F
Tür^F
porta^F del congelatore^M

magnetic gasket
imán^M
joint^M magnétique
magnetische Dichtung^F
guarnizione^F magnetica

freezer compartment
congelador^M incorporado
congélateur^M
Gefrierfach^N
scomparto^M del congelatore^M

handle
manilla^F
poignée^F
Griff^M
maniglia^F

thermostat control
termostato^M
commande^F de température^F
Temperaturregler^M
termostato^M

egg tray
huevera^F
œufrier^M
Eierfach^N
scomparto^M per le uova^F

switch
interruptor^M
interrupteur^M
Schalter^M
interruttore^M

butter compartment
compartimiento^M para mantequilla^F
casier^M à beurre^M
Butterfach^N
scomparto^M per il burro^M

meat keeper
cajón^M para cames^F
bac^M à viande^F
Fleisch- und Wurstfach^N
cassetto^M per la carne^F

storage door
puerta^F del refrigerador^M
porte^F étagère^F
Innentür^F
controporta^F attrezzata

shelf channel
riel^M para las rejillas^F
crémaillère^F
Rasterleiste^F
griglia^F dei ripiani^M

dairy compartment
compartimiento^M para lácteos^M
casier^M laitier
Fach^N für Molkereiprodukte^N
scomparto^M per i latticini^M

refrigerator compartment
espacio^M interior
réfrigérateur^M
Kühlfach^N
scomparto^M del frigorifero^M

door shelf
anaquel^M
balconnet^M
Türfach^N
scomparto^M della controporta^F

glass cover
bandeja^F de vidrio^M
tablette^F de verre^F
Glasplatte^F
lastra^F di vetro^M

guard rail
listón^M
barre^F de retenue^F
Sicherheitsleiste^F
listarella^F

crisper
cesto^M para verdura^F
bac^M à légumes^M
Obst- und Gemüseschale^F
cassetto^M per la verdura^F

shelf
rejilla^F
clayette^F
Abstellrost^N
ripiano^M

domestic appliances

HOUSE

washer
lavadora^F
lave-linge^M ; *laveuse*^F
Waschmaschine^F
lavatrice^F

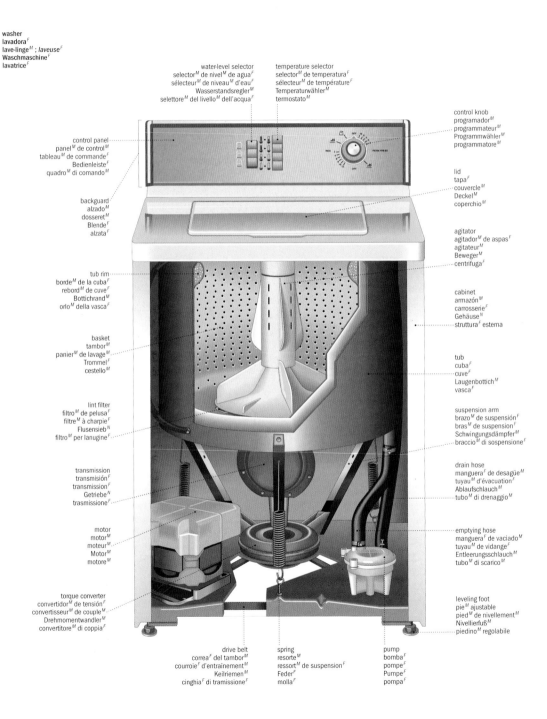

water-level selector
selector^M de nivel^M de agua^F
sélecteur^M de niveau^M d'eau^F
Wasserstandsregler^M
selettore^M del livello^M dell'acqua^F

temperature selector
selector^M de temperatura^F
sélecteur^M de température^F
Temperaturwähler^M
termostato^M

control knob
programador^M
programmateur^M
Programmwähler^M
programmatore^M

control panel
panel^M de control^M
tableau^M de commande^F
Bedienleiste^F
quadro^M di comando^M

lid
tapa^F
couvercle^M
Deckel^M
coperchio^M

backguard
alzado^M
dosseret^M
Blende^F
alzata^F

agitator
agitador^M de aspas^F
agitateur^M
Beweger^M
centrifuga^F

tub rim
borde^M de la cuba^F
rebord^M de cuve^F
Bottichrand^M
orlo^M della vasca^F

cabinet
armazón^M
carrosserie^F
Gehäuse^N
struttura^F esterna

basket
tambor^M
panier^M de lavage^M
Trommel^F
cestello^M

tub
cuba^F
cuve^F
Laugenbottich^M
vasca^F

lint filter
filtro^M de pelusa^F
filtre^M à charpie^F
Flusensieb^N
filtro^M per lanugine^F

suspension arm
brazo^M de suspensión^F
bras^M de suspension^F
Schwingungsdämpfer^M
braccio^M di sospensione^F

transmission
transmisión^F
transmission^F
Getriebe^N
trasmissione^F

drain hose
manguera^F de desagüe^M
tuyau^M d'évacuation^F
Ablaufschlauch^M
tubo^M di drenaggio^M

motor
motor^M
moteur^M
Motor^M
motore^M

emptying hose
manguera^F de vaciado^M
tuyau^M de vidange^F
Entleerungsschlauch^M
tubo^M di scarico^M

torque converter
convertidor^M de tensión^F
convertisseur^M de couple^M
Drehmomentwandler^M
convertitore^M di coppia^F

leveling foot
pie^M ajustable
pied^M de nivellement^M
Nivellierfuß^M
piedino^M regolabile

drive belt
correa^F del tambor^M
courroie^F d'entraînement^M
Keilriemen^M
cinghia^F di tramissione^F

spring
resorte^M
ressort^M de suspension^F
Feder^F
molla^F

pump
bomba^F
pompe^F
Pumpe^F
pompa^F

dryer
secadora^F de ropa^F
sèche-linge^M électrique ; sécheuse^F
Wäschetrockner^M
asciugatrice^F

temperature selector
selector^M de temperatura^F
sélecteur^M de température^F
Temperaturwähler^M
termostato^M

control panel
panel^M de control^M
tableau^M de commande^F
Bedienleiste^F
quadro^M di comando^M

control knob
programador^M
programmateur^M
Programmwähler^M
programmatore^M

start switch
interruptor^M
interrupteur^M de démarrage^M
Einschalter^M
pulsante^M di accensione^F

backguard
panel^M de mandos^M
dosseret^M
Blende^F
alzata^F

door switch
interruptor^M de la puerta^F
interrupteur^M de la porte^F
Türschloss^N
interruttore^M del portello^M

heating duct
conducto^M de aire^M caliente
conduit^M de chauffage^M
Warmluftzufuhr^F
condotto^M di riscaldamento^M

door
puerta^F
porte^F
Tür^F
portello^M

vane
aleta^F
ailette^F
Mitnehmerrippe^F
pala^F

drum
tambor^M
tambour^M
Trommel^F
tamburo^M

lint trap
filtro^M de pelusa^F
filtre^M à charpie^F
Fusselfilter^M
filtro^M per lanugine^F

fan
ventilador^M
ventilateur^M
Gebläse^N
ventilatore^M

cabinet
armazón^M
carrosserie^F
Gehäuse^N
armadio^M

leveling foot
pie^M ajustable
pied^M de nivellement^M
Nivellierfuß^M
piedino^M regolabile

motor
motor^M
moteur^M
Motor^M
motore^M

safety thermostat
termostato^M de seguridad^F
limiteur^M de surchauffe^F
Sicherheitsthermostat^M
termostato^M di sicurezza^F

heating element
resistencia^F
élément^M chauffant
Heizelement^N
elemento^M riscaldante

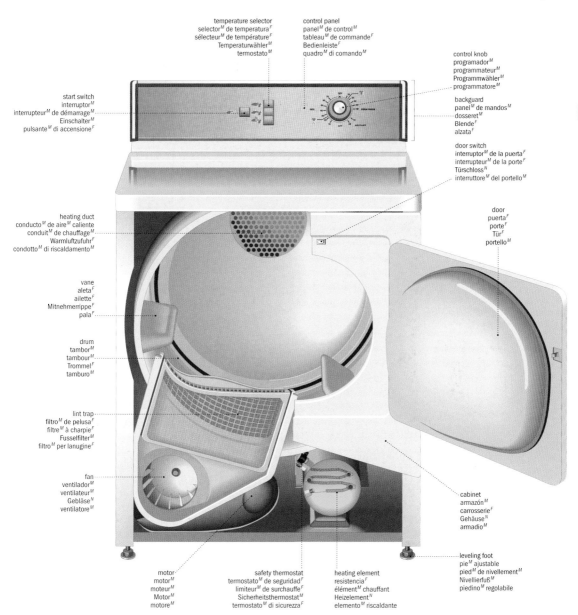

HOUSE

domestic appliances

HOUSE

control panel: dishwasher
panel^M de control^M
tableau^M de commande^F
Bedienleiste^F
quadro^M di comando^M

signal lamp
piloto^M
voyant^M lumineux
Kontrollleuchte^F
spia^F luminosa

control knob
programador^M
programmateur^M
Programmwähler^M
programmatore^M

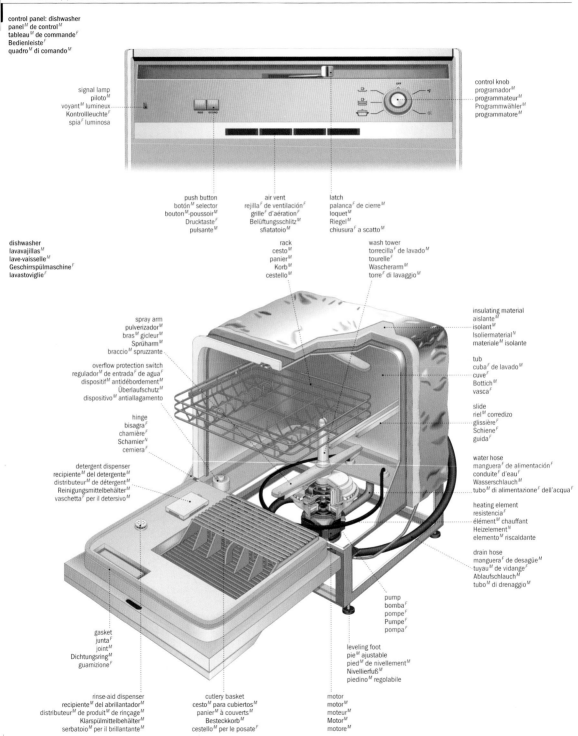

push button
botón^M selector
bouton^M-poussoir^M
Drucktaste^F
pulsante^M

air vent
rejilla^F de ventilación^F
grille^F d'aération^F
Belüftungsschlitz^M
sfiatatoio^M

latch
palanca^F de cierre^M
loquet^M
Riegel^M
chiusura^F a scatto^M

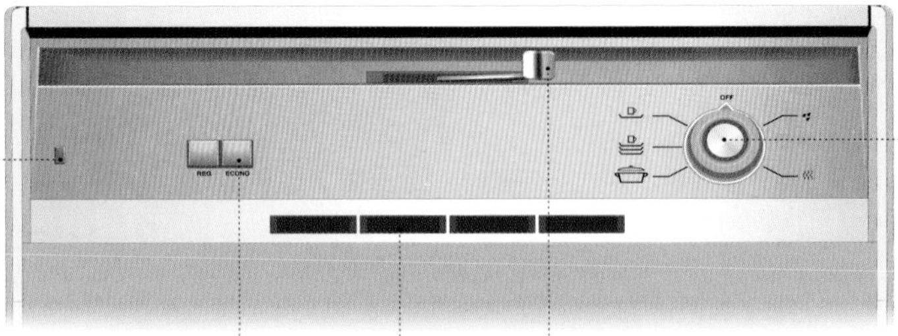

dishwasher
lavavajillas^M
lave-vaisselle^M
Geschirrspülmaschine^F
lavastoviglie^F

rack
cesto^M
panier^M
Korb^M
cestello^M

wash tower
torrecilla^F de lavado^M
tourelle^F
Wascherarm^M
torre^F di lavaggio^M

insulating material
aislante^M
isolant^M
Isoliermaterial^N
materiale^M isolante

spray arm
pulverizador^M
bras^M gicleur^F
Sprüharm^M
braccio^M spruzzante

overflow protection switch
regulador^M de entrada^F de agua^F
dispositif^M antidébordement^M
Überlaufschutz^M
dispositivo^M antiallagamento

tub
cuba^F de lavado^M
cuve^F
Bottich^M
vasca^F

slide
riel^M corredizo
glissière^F
Schiene^N
guida^F

hinge
bisagra^F
charnière^F
Scharnier^N
cerniera^F

water hose
manguera^F de alimentación^F
conduite^F d'eau^F
Wasserschlauch^M
tubo^M di alimentazione^F dell'acqua^F

detergent dispenser
recipiente^M del detergente^M
distributeur^M de détergent^M
Reinigungsmittelbehälter^M
vaschetta^F per il detersivo^M

heating element
resistencia^F
élément^M chauffant
Heizelement^N
elemento^M riscaldante

drain hose
manguera^F de desagüe^M
tuyau^M de vidange^F
Ablaufschlauch^M
tubo^M di drenaggio^M

pump
bomba^F
pompe^F
Pumpe^F
pompa^F

gasket
junta^F
joint^M
Dichtungsring^M
guarnizione^F

leveling foot
pie^M ajustable
pied^M de nivellement^M
Nivellierfuß^M
piedino^M regolabile

rinse-aid dispenser
recipiente^M del abrillantador^M
distributeur^M de produit^M de rinçage^M
Klarspülmittelbehälter^M
serbatoio^M per il brillante^M

cutlery basket
cesto^M para cubiertos^M
panier^M à couverts^M
Besteckkorb^M
cestello^M per le posate^F

motor
motor^M
moteur^M
Motor^M
motore^M

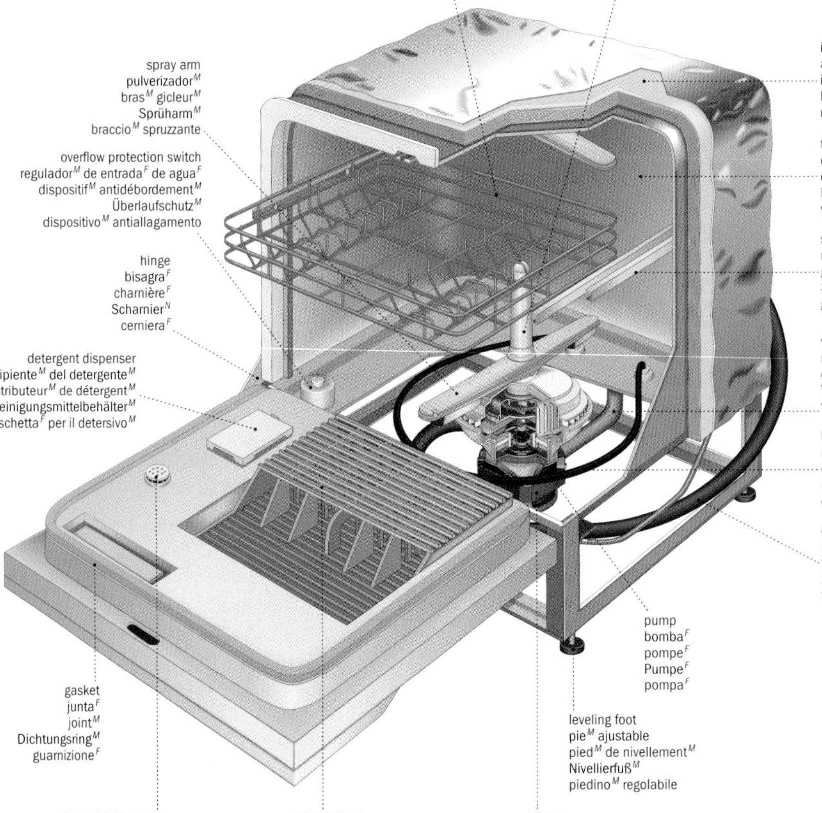

household equipment

articulos^M de limpieza^F | articles^M ménagers | Haushaltsgegenstände^M | attrezzi^M domestici

tea towel
bayeta^F de cocina^F
torchon^M
Geschirrtuch^N
strofinaccio^M da cucina^F

dustpan
recogedor^M
pelle^F à poussière^F ; *porte-poussière^M*
Kehrschaufel^F
paletta^F

broom
escoba^F
balai^M
Besen^M
scopa^F

mop
fregona^F
balai^M à franges^F ; *vadrouille^F*
Mop^M
scopa^F a frangia^F

scouring pad
estropajo^M con esponja^F
éponge^F à récurer
Putzschwamm^M
spugna^F abrasiva

brush
cepillo^M
brosse^F
Bürste^F
spazzola^F

block
lomo^M
monture^F
Bürstenkörper^M
dorso^M

handle
palo^M
manche^M
Stiel^M
manico^M

fibers
cerdas^F
fibres^F
Borsten^F
setole^F

garbage can
cubo^M de basura^F
poubelle^F
Abfalleimer^M
bidone^M dei rifiuti^M

lid
tapa^F
couvercle^M
Deckel^M
coperchio^M

fibers
cerdas^F
fibres^F
Borsten^F
setole^F

handle
asa^F
poignée^F
Griff^M
manico^M

pail
cubo^M
seau^M
Eimer^M
secchio^M

pouring spout
pitorro^M
bec^M verseur
Ausguss^M
beccuccio^M

handle
asa^F
anse^F
Henkel^M
manico^M

HOUSE

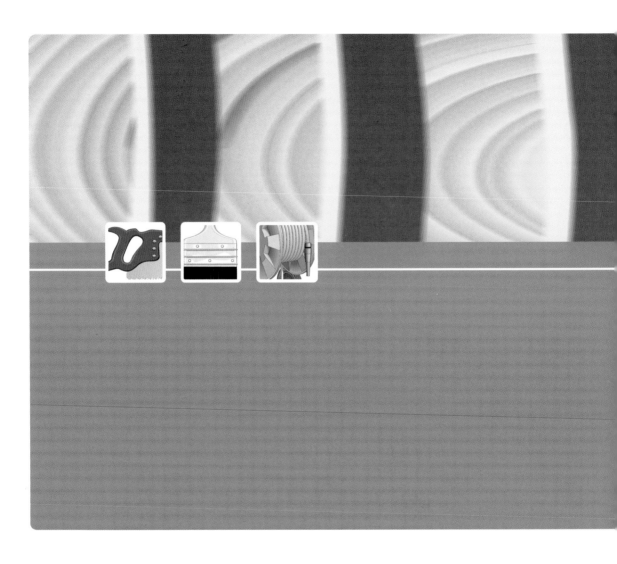

DO-IT-YOURSELF
AND GARDENING

BRICOLAJE Y JARDINERÍA | BRICOLAGE ET JARDINAGE | HEIMWERKEN UND GARTENARBEIT | FAI DA TE E GIARDINAGGIO

basic building materials

materiales^M básicos | matériaux^M de base^F | die wichtigsten Baumaterialien^N | materiali^M da costruzione^F di base^F

brick
ladrillo^M
brique^F
Ziegelstein^M
mattone^M

solid brick
ladrillo^M macizo
brique^F pleine
Vollziegel^M
mattone^M pieno

perforated brick
ladrillo^M perforado
brique^F perforée
Lochziegel^M
mattone^M perforato

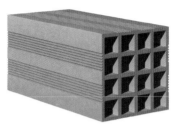

hollow brick
ladrillo^M hueco
brique^F creuse
Hohlziegel^M
mattone^M forato

partition tile
ladrillo^M tabiquero
brique^F plâtrière
Tonhohlplatte^M
mattone^M forato per tramezzo^M

brick wall
muro^M de ladrillos^M
mur^M de briques^F
Ziegelmauer^F
muro^M di mattoni^M

firebrick
ladrillo^M refractario
brique^F réfractaire
feuerfester Ziegel^M
mattone^M refrattario

mortar
mortero^M
mortier^M
Mörtel^M
malta^F

stone
piedra^F
pierre^F
Stein^M
pietra^F

flagstone
losa^F de piedra^F
dalle^F de pierre^F
Pflasterstein^M
pietra^F da lastrico^M

rubble
morrillo^M
moellon^M
Bruchstein^M
pietra^F da costruzione^F

cut stone
piedra^M tallada
pierre^F de taille^F
Haustein^M
pietra^F da taglio^M

stone wall
muro^M de piedras^F
mur^M de pierres^F
Steinmauer^F
muro^M di pietra^F

concrete
hormigón^M
béton^M
Beton^M
calcestruzzo^M

concrete block
bloque^M de hormigón^M
bloc^M de béton^M
Betonblock^M
blocco^M di calcestruzzo^M

prestressed concrete
hormigón^M pretensado
béton^M précontraint
Spannbeton^M
calcestruzzo^M precompresso

reinforced concrete
hormigón^M armado
béton^M armé
Stahlbeton^M
cemento^M armato

steel
acero^M
acier^M
Stahl^M
acciaio^M

covering materials

materiales ^{M} de revestimiento ^{M} | matériaux ^{M} de revêtement ^{M} | Verkleidungsmaterialien ^{N} | materiali ^{M} di rivestimento ^{M}

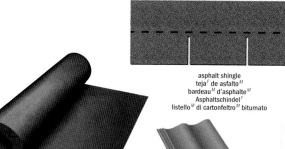

asphalt shingle
teja ^{F} de asfalto ^{M}
bardeau ^{M} d'asphalte ^{M}
Asphaltschindel ^{F}
listello ^{M} di cartonfeltro ^{M} bitumato

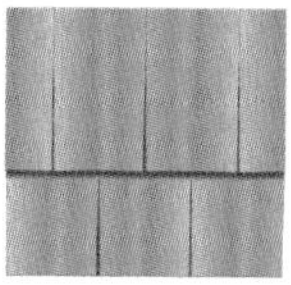

shingle
ripia ^{F}
bardeau ^{M}
Schindel ^{F}
scandola ^{F}

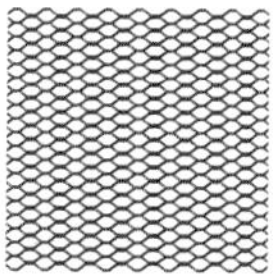

diamond-mesh metal lath
mallas ^{F} de metal ^{M} expandido
lattis ^{M} métallique à losanges ^{M}
Streckmetall ^{N}-Unterlage ^{F}
reticella ^{F} metallica a maglie ^{F} esagonali

tar paper
fieltro ^{M} asfáltico
papier ^{M} goudronné
Teerpappe ^{F}
carta ^{F} catramata

tile
teja ^{F}
tuile ^{F}
Dachziegel ^{M}
tegola ^{F}

gypsum tile
panel ^{M} de yeso ^{M}
carreau ^{M} de plâtre ^{M}
Gipskartonplatte ^{F}
piastrella ^{F} di gesso ^{M}

floor tile
baldosa ^{F}
carreau ^{M}
Fliese ^{F}
piastrella ^{F} per pavimenti ^{M}

gypsum board
tablero ^{M} de yeso ^{M}
plaque ^{F} de plâtre ^{M}
Gipskarton ^{M}-Bauplatte ^{F}
pannello ^{M} di gesso ^{M}

insulating materials

materiales ^{M} aislantes | isolants ^{M} | Isoliermaterialien ^{N} | materiali ^{M} isolanti

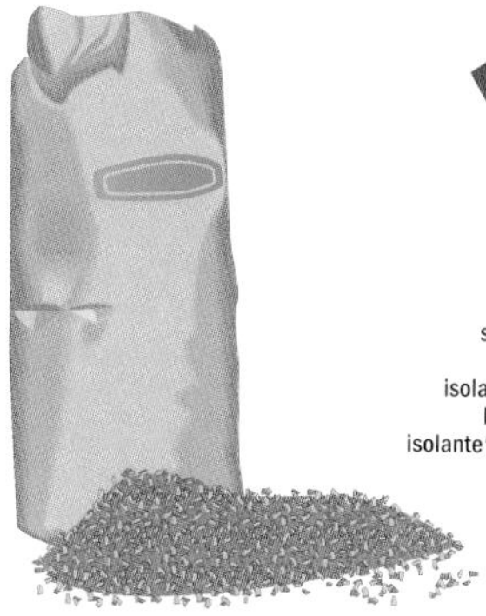

pipe-wrapping insulation
cinta ^{F} aislante para tubería ^{F}
isolant ^{M} en ruban ^{M}
Rohrummantelung ^{F}
rivestimento ^{M} isolante per tubi ^{M}

spring-metal insulation
cinta ^{F} metálica
isolant ^{M} en ruban ^{M} métallique
Metallbandisolierung ^{F}
isolante ^{M} a lamina ^{F} metallica elastica

vinyl insulation
aislante ^{M} vinílico
isolant ^{M} en vinyle ^{M}
Vinylisolierung ^{F}
isolante ^{M} vinilico

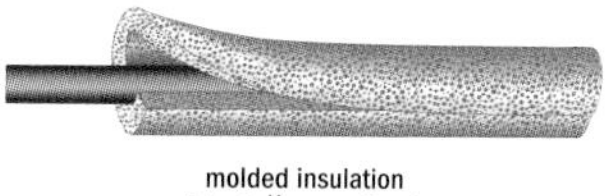

molded insulation
aislante ^{M} premoldeado
isolant ^{M} en coquille ^{F}
vorgeformte Rohrummantelung ^{F}
isolante ^{M} preformato

loose fill insulation
aislante ^{M} a granel ^{M}
isolant ^{M} en vrac ^{M}
Schüttungsisolierung ^{F}
isolante ^{M} sfuso granulare

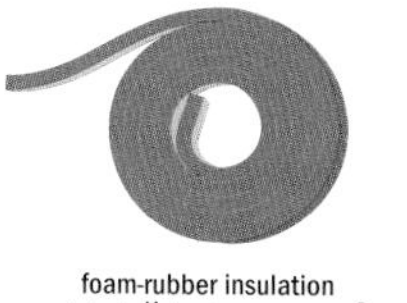

foam-rubber insulation
aislante ^{M} de gomaespuma ^{F}
isolant ^{M} en caoutchouc ^{M}-mousse ^{F}
Schaumgummiisolierung ^{F}
isolante ^{M} di gomma ^{F} espansa

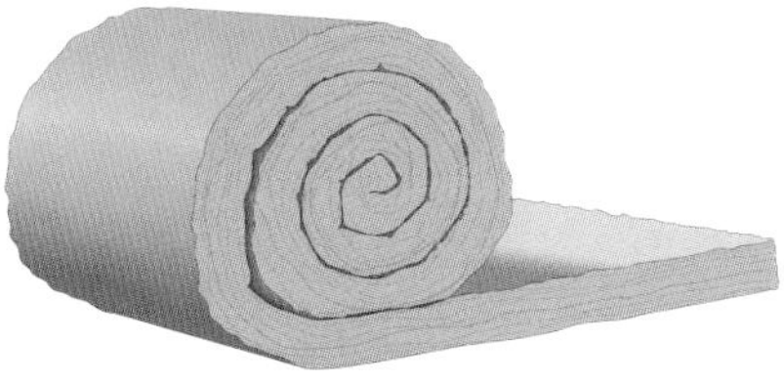

blanket insulation
lana ^{F} de vidrio ^{M} aislante
isolant ^{M} en rouleau ^{M}
Mattenisolierung ^{F}
isolante ^{M} in rotolo ^{M}

board insulation
tablero ^{M} rígido aislante
isolant ^{M} en panneau ^{M}
Plattenisolierung ^{F}
pannelli ^{M} isolanti

foam insulation
espuma ^{F} aislante ^{M}
isolant ^{M} moussé
Bauschaumisolierung ^{F}
schiuma ^{F} isolante ^{M}

wood

madera^F | bois^M | Holz^N | legno^M

section of a log
corte^M de un tronco^M
coupe^F d'une bille^F
Baumstamm^M im Querschnitt^M
sezione^F di un tronco^M

board
tabla^F
planche^F
Brett^N
asse^F

log
tronco^M
bille^F
Baumstamm^M
tronco^M

board
tabla^F
planche^F
Brett^N
asse^F

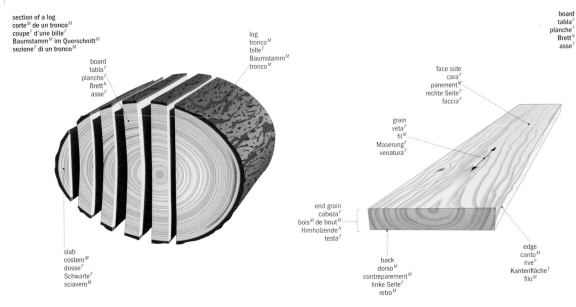

face side
cara^F
parement^M
rechte Seite^F
faccia^F

grain
veta^F
fil^M
Maserung^F
venatura^F

end grain
cabeza^F
bois^M de bout^M
Himholzende^N
testa^F

slab
costero^M
dosse^F
Schwarte^F
sciavero^M

back
dorso^M
contreparement^M
linke Seite^F
retro^M

edge
canto^M
rive^F
Kantenfläche^F
filo^M

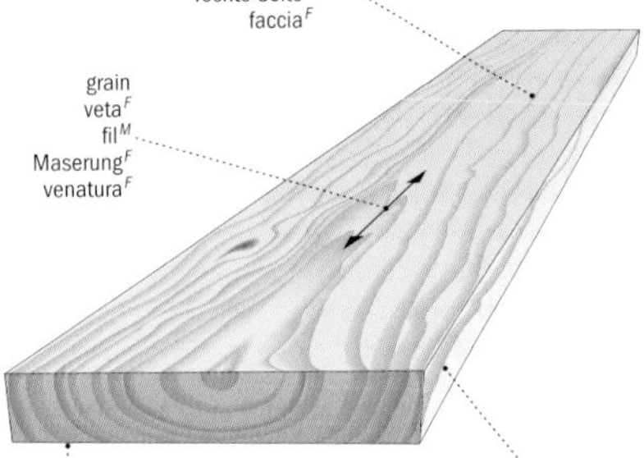

wood-based materials
láminas^F y tableros^M
dérivés^M du bois^M
Holzwerkstoffe^M
materiali^M derivati dal legno^M

ply
contrachapado^M
pli^M
Sperrholzschichten^F
strato^M

multi-ply plywood
contrachapado^M multiplex
contreplaqué^M multiplis
Mehrschichtsperrholz^N
pannello^M di compensato^M multistrato

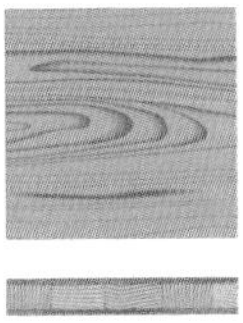

blockboard
tablero^M alistonado
panneau^M à âme^F lattée
Stabplatte^F
pannello^M di compensato^M impiallacciato

peeled veneer
chapa^F de madera^F de desenrollo^M
placage^M déroulé
Schälfurnier^N
impiallacciatura^F

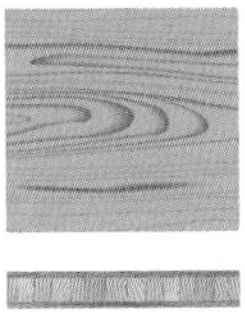

laminboard
tablero^M laminado
panneau^M à âme^F lamellée
Stäbchenplatte^F
pannello^M laminato in legno^M

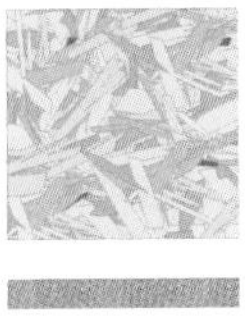

chip board
tablero^M de partículas^F waferboard
panneau^M de copeaux^M
Grobspanplatte^F
pannello^M di truciolato^M grezzo

hardboard
tablero^M de fibra^F de madera^F
panneau^M de fibres^F
Hartfaserplatte^F
pannello^M di truciolato^M

perforated hardboard
tablero^M de fibra^F de madera^F perforada
panneau^M de fibres^F perforé
gelochte Hartfaserplatte^F
pannello^M di truciolato^M forato

plastic-laminated particle board
tablero^M de aglomerado^M plastificado
panneau^M de particules^F lamifié
kunststoffbeschichtete Hartfaserplatte^F
pannello^M di truciolato^M laminato in plastica^F

particle board
tablero^M de aglomerado^M
panneau^M de particules^F
Spanplatte^F
pannello di masonite^F

carpentry: nailing tools

carpintería: herramientas^F para clavar | menuiserie^F : outils^M pour clouer | Bautischlerei^F: Nagelwerkzeuge^N | carpenteria^F: attrezzi^M per chiodare

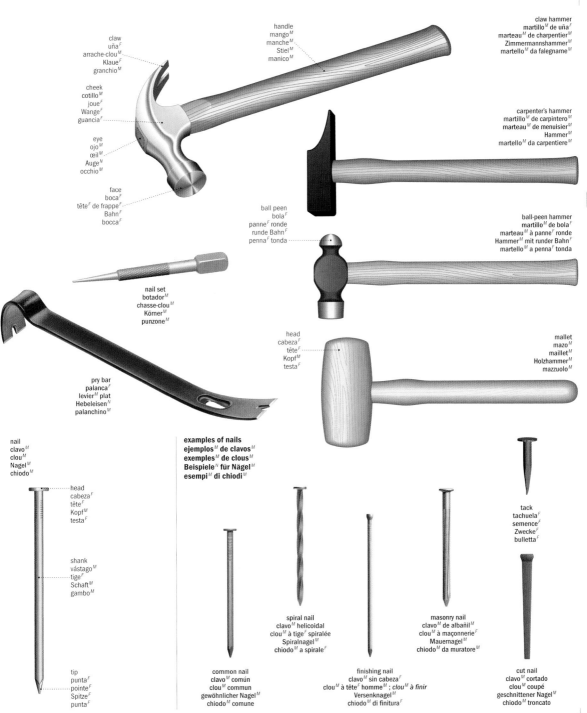

claw hammer
martillo^M de uña^F
marteau^M de charpentier^M
Zimmermannshammer^M
martello^M da falegname^M

handle
mango^M
manche^M
Stiel^M
manico^M

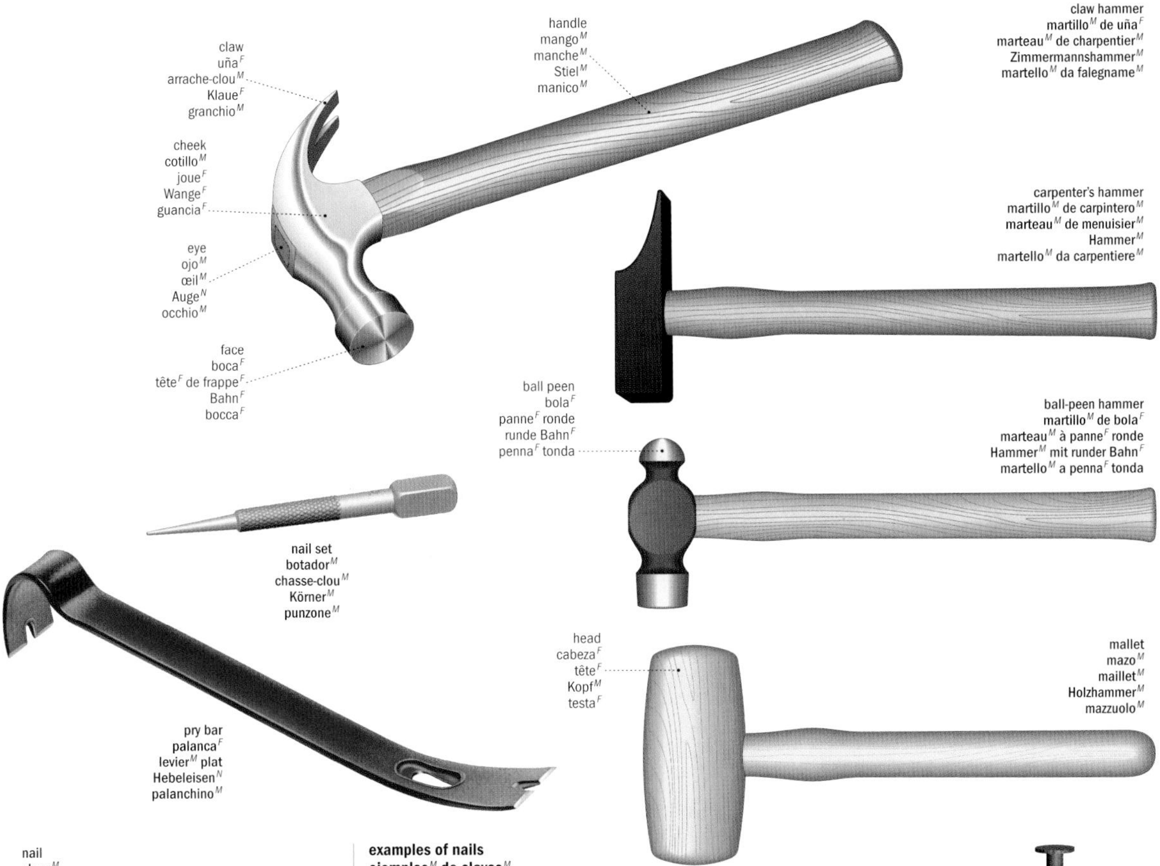

claw
uña^F
arrache-clou^M
Klaue^F
granchio^M

cheek
cotillo^M
joue^F
Wange^F
guancia^F

carpenter's hammer
martillo^M de carpintero^M
marteau^M de menuisier^M
Hammer^M
martello^M da carpentiere^M

eye
ojo^M
œil^M
Auge^N
occhio^M

ball-peen hammer
martillo^M de bola^F
marteau^M à panne^F ronde
Hammer^M mit runder Bahn^F
martello^M a penna^F tonda

face
boca^F
tête^F de frappe^F
Bahn^F
bocca^F

ball peen
bola^F
panne^F ronde
runde Bahn^F
penna^F tonda

nail set
botador^M
chasse-clou^M
Körner^M
punzone^M

head
cabeza^F
tête^F
Kopf^M
testa^F

mallet
mazo^M
maillet^M
Holzhammer^M
mazzuolo^M

pry bar
palanca^F
levier^M plat
Hebeleisen^N
palanchino^M

nail
clavo^M
clou^M
Nagel^M
chiodo^M

examples of nails
ejemplos^M de clavos^M
exemples^M de clous^M
Beispiele^N für Nägel^M
esempi^M di chiodi^M

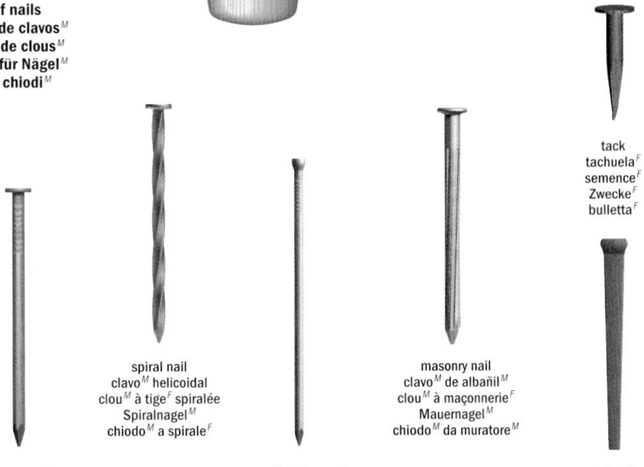

tack
tachuela^F
semence^F
Zwecke^F
bulletta^F

head
cabeza^F
tête^F
Kopf^M
testa^F

shank
vástago^M
tige^F
Schaft^M
gambo^M

spiral nail
clavo^M helicoidal
clou^M à tige^F spiralée
Spiralnagel^M
chiodo^M a spirale^F

masonry nail
clavo^M de albañil^M
clou^M à maçonnerie^F
Mauernagel^M
chiodo^M da muratore^M

tip
punta^F
pointe^F
Spitze^F
punta^F

common nail
clavo^M común
clou^M commun
gewöhnlicher Nagel^M
chiodo^M comune

finishing nail
clavo^M sin cabeza^F
clou^M à tête^F homme^M ; *clou^M à finir*
Versenknagel^M
chiodo^M di finitura^F

cut nail
clavo^M cortado
clou^M coupé
geschnittener Nagel^M
chiodo^M troncato

DO-IT-YOURSELF AND GARDENING

carpentry: screw-driving tools

carpintería^F : herramientas^F para atornillar | menuiserie^F : outils^M pour visser | Bautischlerei^F: Schraubwerkzeuge^N | carpenteria^F: utensili ^{M} per avvitare

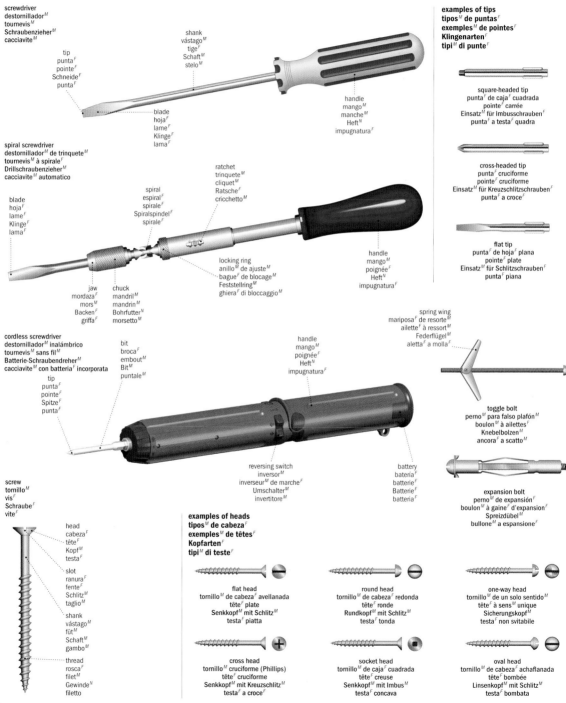

screwdriver
destornillador^M
tournevis^M
Schraubenzieher^M
cacciavite^F

tip
punta^F
pointe^F
Schneide^F
punta^F

shank
vástago^M
tige^F
Schaft^M
stelo^M

blade
hoja^F
lame^F
Klinge^F
lama^F

handle
mango^M
manche^M
Heft^N
impugnatura^F

spiral screwdriver
destornillador^M de trinquete^M
tournevis^M à spirale^F
Drillschraubenzieher^M
cacciavite^M automatico

blade
hoja^F
lame^F
Klinge^F
lama^F

spiral
espiral^F
spirale^F
Spiralspindel^F
spirale^F

ratchet
trinquete^M
cliquet^M
Ratsche^F
cricchetto^M

jaw
mordaza^F
mors^M
Backen^F
griffa^F

chuck
mandril^M
mandrin^M
Bohrfutter^N
morsetto^M

locking ring
anillo^M de ajuste^M
bague^F de blocage^M
Feststellring^M
ghiera^F di bloccaggio^M

handle
mango^M
poignée^F
Heft^N
impugnatura^F

cordless screwdriver
destornillador^M inalámbrico
tournevis^M sans fil^M
Batterie-Schraubendreher^M
cacciavite^M con batteria^F incorporata

tip
punta^F
pointe^F
Spitze^F
punta^F

bit
broca^F
embout^M
Bit^M
puntale^M

handle
mango^M
poignée^F
Heft^N
impugnatura^F

reversing switch
inversor^M
inverseur^M de marche^F
Umschalter^M
invertitore^M

battery
batería^F
batterie^F
Batterie^F
batteria^F

screw
tornillo^M
vis^F
Schraube^F
vite^F

head
cabeza^F
tête^F
Kopf^M
testa^F

slot
ranura^F
fente^F
Schlitz^M
taglio^M

shank
vástago^M
fût^M
Schaft^M
gambo^M

thread
rosca^F
filet^M
Gewinde^N
filetto^M

examples of tips
tipos^M de puntas^F
exemples^M de pointes^F
Klingenarten^F
tipi^M di punte^F

square-headed tip
punta^F de caja^F cuadrada
pointe^F carrée
Einsatz^M für Imbusschrauben^F
punta^F a testa^F quadra

cross-headed tip
punta^F cruciforme
pointe^F cruciforme
Einsatz^M für Kreuzschlitzschrauben^F
punta^F a croce^F

flat tip
punta^F de hoja^F plana
pointe^F plate
Einsatz^M für Schlitzschrauben^F
punta^F piana

spring wing
mariposa^F de resorte^M
ailette^F à ressort^M
Federflügel^M
aletta^F a molla^F

toggle bolt
perno^M para falso plafón^M
boulon^M à ailettes^F
Knebelbolzen^M
ancora^F a scatto^M

expansion bolt
perno^M de expansión^F
boulon^M à gaine^F d'expansion^F
Spreizdübel^M
bullone^M a espansione^F

examples of heads
tipos^M de cabeza^F
exemples^M de têtes^F
Kopfarten^F
tipi^M di teste^F

flat head
tornillo^M de cabeza^F avellanada
tête^F plate
Senkkopf^M mit Schlitz^M
testa^F piatta

round head
tornillo^M de cabeza^F redonda
tête^F ronde
Rundkopf^M mit Schlitz^M
testa^F tonda

one-way head
tornillo^M de un solo sentido^M
tête^F à sens^M unique
Sicherungskopf^M
testa^F non svitabile

cross head
tornillo^M cruciforme (Phillips)
tête^F cruciforme
Senkkopf^M mit Kreuzschlitz^M
testa^F a croce^F

socket head
tornillo^M de caja^F cuadrada
tête^F creuse
Senkkopf^M mit Imbus^M
testa^F concava

oval head
tornillo^M de cabeza^F achaflanada
tête^F bombée
Linsenkopf^M mit Schlitz^M
testa^F bombata

carpentry: sawing tools

carpinteria^F : herramientas^F para serrar | menuiserie^F : outils^M pour scier | Bautischlerei^F: Sägewerkzeuge^N | carpenteria^F: utensili^M per segare

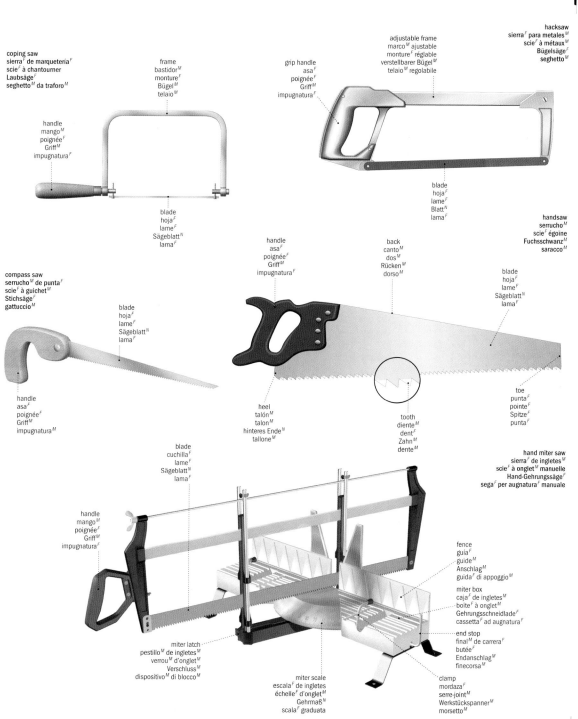

coping saw
sierra^F de marqueteria^F
scie^F à chantourner
Laubsäge^F
seghetto^M da traforo^M

frame
bastidor^M
monture^F
Bügel^M
telaio^M

grip handle
asa^F
poignée^F
Griff^M
impugnatura^F

adjustable frame
marco^M ajustable
monture^F réglable
verstellbarer Bügel^M
telaio^M regolabile

hacksaw
sierra^F para metales^M
scie^F à métaux^M
Bügelsäge^F
seghetto^M

handle
mango^M
poignée^F
Griff^M
impugnatura^F

blade
hoja^F
lame^F
Blatt^N
lama^F

blade
hoja^F
lame^F
Sägeblatt^N
lama^F

handle
asa^F
poignée^F
Griff^M
impugnatura^F

back
canto^M
dos^M
Rücken^M
dorso^M

handsaw
serrucho^M
scie^F égoïne
Fuchsschwanz^M
saracco^M

compass saw
serrucho^M de punta^F
scie^F à guichet^M
Stichsäge^F
gattuccio^M

blade
hoja^F
lame^F
Sägeblatt^N
lama^F

blade
hoja^F
lame^F
Sägeblatt^N
lama^F

handle
asa^F
poignée^F
Griff^M
impugnatura^M

heel
talón^M
talon^M
hinteres Ende^N
tallone^M

tooth
diente^M
dent^F
Zahn^M
dente^M

toe
punta^F
pointe^F
Spitze^F
punta^F

blade
cuchilla^F
lame^F
Sägeblatt^N
lama^F

hand miter saw
sierra^F de ingletes^M
scie^F à onglet^M manuelle
Hand-Gehrungssäge^F
sega^F per augnatura^F manuale

handle
mango^M
poignée^F
Griff^M
impugnatura^F

fence
guía^F
guide^F
Anschlag^M
guida^F di appoggio^M

miter box
caja^F de ingletes^M
boîte^F à onglet^M
Gehrungsschneidlade^F
cassetta^F ad augnatura^F

miter latch
pestillo^M de ingletes^M
verrou^M d'onglet^M
Verschluss^M
dispositivo^M di blocco^M

end stop
final^M de carrera^F
butée^F
Endanschlag^M
finecorsa^M

miter scale
escala^F de ingletes
échelle^F d'onglet^M
Gehrmaß^N
scala^F graduata

clamp
mordaza^F
serre-joint^M
Werkstückspanner^M
morsetto^M

carpentry: sawing tools

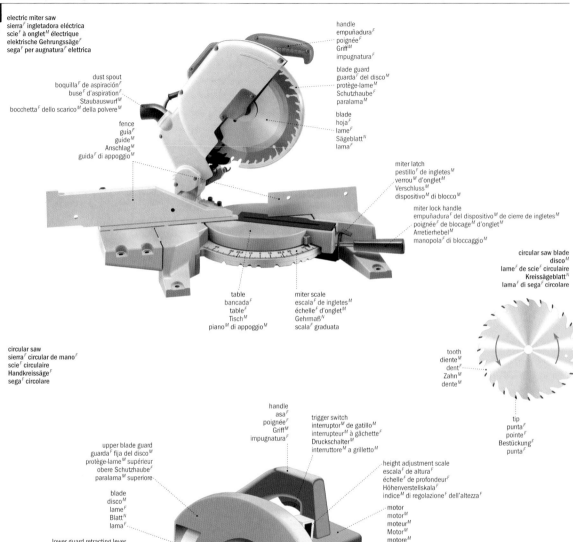

electric miter saw
sierra^F ingletadora eléctrica
scie^F à onglet^M électrique
elektrische Gehrungssäge^F
sega^F per augnatura^F elettrica

handle
empuñadura^F
poignée^F
Griff^M
impugnatura^F

blade guard
guarda^F del disco^M
protège-lame^M
Schutzhaube^F
paralama^F

dust spout
boquilla^F de aspiración^F
buse^F d'aspiration^F
Staubauswurf^M
bocchetta^F dello scarico^M della polvere^F

blade
hoja^F
lame^F
Sägeblatt^N
lama^F

fence
guía^F
guide^M
Anschlag^M
guida^F di appoggio^M

miter latch
pestillo^F de ingletes^M
verrou^M d'onglet^M
Verschluss^M
dispositivo^M di blocco^M

miter lock handle
empuñadura^F del dispositivo^M de cierre de ingletes^M
poignée^F de blocage^M d'onglet^M
Arretierhebel^M
manopola^F di bloccaggio^M

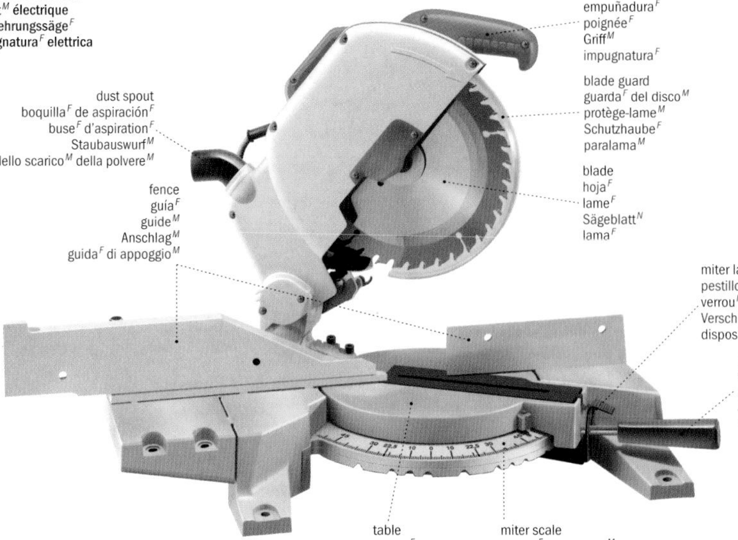

circular saw blade
disco^M
lame^F de scie^F circulaire
Kreissägeblatt^N
lama^F di sega^F circolare

table
bancada^F
table^F
Tisch^M
piano^M di appoggio^M

miter scale
escala^F de ingletes^M
échelle^F d'onglet^M
Gehrmaß^N
scala^F graduata

tooth
diente^M
dent^F
Zahn^M
dente^M

circular saw
sierra^F circular de mano^F
scie^F circulaire
Handkreissäge^F
sega^F circolare

tip
punta^F
pointe^F
Bestückung^F
punta^F

handle
asa^F
poignée^F
Griff^M
impugnatura^F

trigger switch
interruptor^M de gatillo^M
interrupteur^M à gâchette^F
Druckschalter^M
interruttore^M a grilletto^M

upper blade guard
guarda^F fija del disco^M
protège-lame^M supérieur
obere Schutzhaube^F
paralama^M superiore

height adjustment scale
escala^F de altura^F
échelle^F de profondeur^F
Höhenverstellskala^F
indice^M di regolazione^F dell'altezza^F

blade
disco^M
lame^F
Blatt^N
lama^F

motor
motor^M
moteur^M
Motor^M
motore^M

lower guard retracting lever
palanca^F retráctil de la guarda^F móvil
levier^M du protège-lame^M inférieur
Hebeleiste^F der unteren Schutzhaube^F
leva^F per togliere il paralama^M inferiore

blade tilting mechanism
escala^F de inclinación^F
inclinaison^F de la lame^F
Schrägstellungsvorrichtung^F
regolatore^M dell'inclinazione^F della lama^F

blade locking bolt
tornillo^M de sujeción^F
écrou^M de la lame^F
Feststellschraube^F für das Blatt^N
vite^F di blocco^M della lama^F

knob handle
perilla^F
bouton^M-guide^M
Führungsgriff^M
poggiamano^M

lower blade guard
guarda^F móvil del disco^M
protège-lame^M inférieur
untere Schutzhaube^F
paralama^M inferiore

blade tilting lock
seguro^M de inclinación^F del disco^M
blocage^M de l'inclinaison^F
Feststellschraube^F für Schrägstellung^F
dispositivo^M di blocco^M dell'inclinazione^F della lama^F

rip fence
guía^F de corte^M
guide^M de refend^M
Parallelanschlag^M
guida^F parallela

base plate
soporte^M
semelle^F
Gleitschuh^M
piastra^F di base^F

DO-IT-YOURSELF AND GARDENING

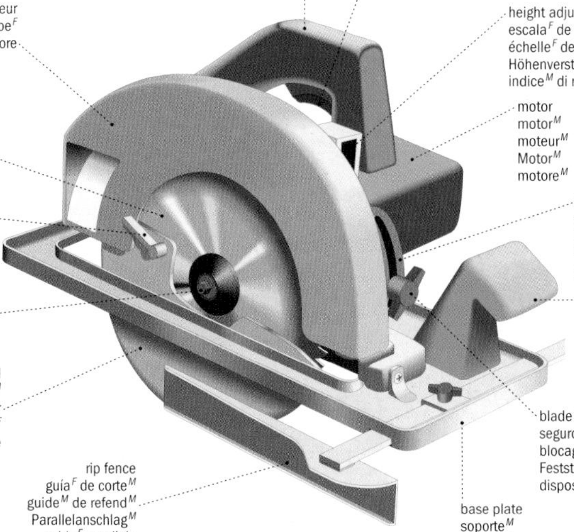

jig saw
sierra^F de calar
scie^F sauteuse
elektrische Stichsäge^F
seghetto^M alternativo

speed selector switch
interruptor^M selector^M de velocidad^F
sélecteur^M de vitesse^F
Hubzahlvorwahl^F
selettore^M di velocità^F

lock-on button
botón^M de bloqueo^M
bouton^M de verrouillage^M de l'interrupteur^M
Feststellknopf^M
pulsante^F di aggancio^M

trigger switch
interruptor^M de gatillo^M
interrupteur^M à gâchette^F
Druckschalter^M
interruttore^M a grilletto^M

handle
empuñadura^F
poignée^F
Griff^M
impugnatura^F

orbital-action selector
selector^M de movimiento^M orbital
sélecteur^M d'inclinaison^F de la lame^F
Pendelhub-Einstellung^F
selettore^M del movimento^M orbitale

chip cover
protector^M contra virutas^F
déflecteur^M de copeaux^M
Späneschutz^M
paratrucioli^M

power cord
cable^M de alimentación^F
cordon^M d'alimentation^F
Anschlusskabel^M
cavo^M di alimentazione^F

blade
hoja^F
lame^F
Sägeblatt^N
lama^F

base
base^F
semelle^F
Fußplatte^F
basamento^M

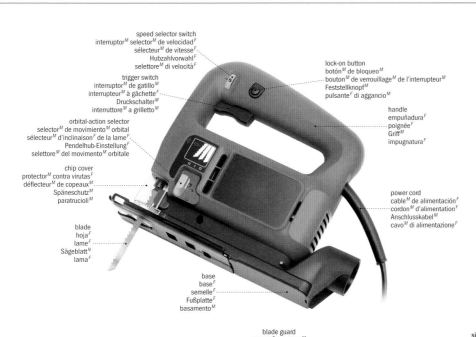

table saw
sierra^F circular de mesa^F
plateau^M de sciage^M
Tischkreissäge^F
sega^F da banco^M

blade guard
guarda^F del disco^M
protège-lame^M
Schutzhaube^F
paralama^M

table
mesa^F
plateau^M
Arbeitstisch^M
piano^M di lavoro^M

blade
disco^M
lame^F
Sägeblatt^N
lama^F

rip fence
guía^F de corte^M
guide^M de refend^M
Parallelanschlag^M
guida^F parallela

miter gauge slot
carril^M para el tope^M de ingletes^M
rainure^F du guide^M à onglet^M
Führungsnut^F für den Gehrungsanschlag^M
scanalatura^F della guida^F graduata

rip fence guide
corredera^F de la guía^F
glissière^F du guide^M
Anschlagführung^F
carrello^M della guida^F parallela

table extension
extensión^F de la mesa^F
rallonge^F du plateau^M
Tischverlängerung^F
piano^M aggiuntivo

miter gauge
tope^M de ingletes^M
guide^M à onglet^M
Gehrungsanschlag^M
guida^F graduata

rip fence lock
seguro^M de la guía^F
blocage^M du guide^M
Spannhebel^M
arresto^M della guida^F parallela

blade height adjustment
mecanismo^M elevador del disco^M
relèvement^M de la lame^F
Sägeblatthöhenverstellung^F
regolatore^M dell'altezza^F della lama^F

rip fence slot
ranura^F de corte^M
rainure^F du guide^M de refend^M
Führungsnut^F
scanalatura^F della guida^F parallela

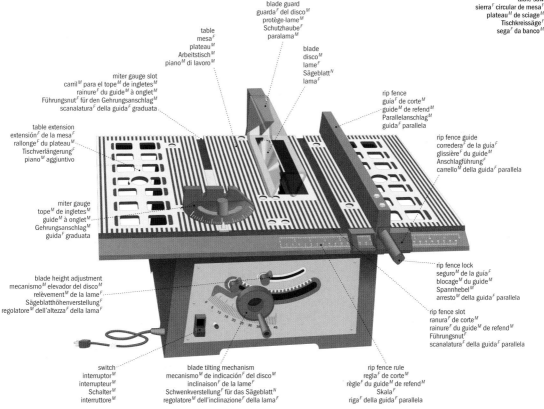

switch
interruptor^M
interrupteur^M
Schalter^M
interruttore^M

blade tilting mechanism
mecanismo^M de indicación^F del disco^M
inclinaison^F de la lame^F
Schwenkverstellung^F für das Sägeblatt^N
regolatore^M dell'inclinazione^F della lama^F

rip fence rule
regla^F de corte^M
règle^F du guide^M de refend^M
Skala^F
riga^F della guida^F parallela

DO-IT-YOURSELF AND GARDENING

carpentry: drilling tools

carpintería^F : herramientas^F percutoras | menuiserie^F : outils^M pour percer | Bautischlerei^F: Bohrwerkzeuge^N | carpenteria^F: attrezzi^M per trapanare

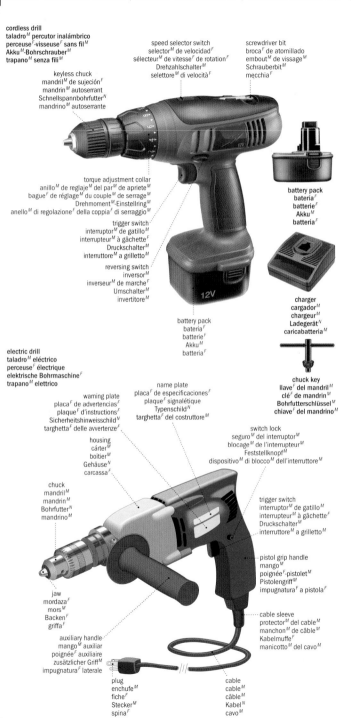

cordless drill
taladro^M percutor inalámbrico
perceuse^F-visseuse^F sans fil^M
Akku^M-Bohrschrauber^M
trapano^M senza fili^M

keyless chuck
mandril^M de sujeción^F
mandrin^M autoserrant
Schnellspannbohrfutter^N
mandrino^M autoserrante

speed selector switch
selector^M de velocidad^F
sélecteur^M de vitesse^F de rotation^F
Drehzahlschalter^M
selettore^M di velocità^F

screwdriver bit
broca^F de atornillado
embout^M de vissage^M
Schrauberbit^M
mecchia^F

torque adjustment collar
anillo^M de reglaje^M del par^M de apriete^M
bague^F de réglage^F du couple^M de serrage^M
Drehmoment^M-Einstellring^M
anello^M di regolazione^F della coppia^F di serraggio^M

trigger switch
interruptor^M de gatillo^M
interrupteur^M à gâchette^F
Druckschalter^M
interruttore^M a grilletto^M

reversing switch
inversor^M
inverseur^M de marche^F
Umschalter^M
invertitore^M

battery pack
batería^F
batterie^F
Akku^M
batteria^F

battery pack
batería^F
batterie^F
Akku^M
batteria^F

charger
cargador^M
chargeur^M
Ladegerät^N
caricabatteria^M

chuck key
llave^F del mandril^M
clé^F de mandrin^M
Bohrfutterschlüssel^M
chiave^F del mandrino^M

electric drill
taladro^M eléctrico
perceuse^F électrique
elektrische Bohrmaschine^F
trapano^M elettrico

warning plate
placa^F de advertencias^F
plaque^F d'instructions^F
Sicherheitshinweisschild^N
targhetta^F delle avvertenze^F

name plate
placa^F de especificaciones^F
plaque^F signalétique
Typenschild^N
targhetta^F del costruttore^M

switch lock
seguro^M del interruptor^M
blocage^M de l'interrupteur^M
Feststellknopf^M
dispositivo^M di blocco^M dell'interruttore^M

housing
cárter^M
boîtier^M
Gehäuse^N
carcassa^F

chuck
mandril^M
mandrin^M
Bohrfutter^N
mandrino^M

trigger switch
interruptor^M de gatillo^M
interrupteur^M à gâchette^F
Druckschalter^M
interruttore^M a grilletto^M

jaw
mordaza^F
mors^M
Backen^F
griffa^F

pistol grip handle
mango^M
poignée^F-pistolet^M
Pistolengriff^M
impugnatura^F a pistola^F

auxiliary handle
mango^M auxiliar
poignée^F auxiliaire
zusätzlicher Griff^M
impugnatura^F laterale

cable sleeve
protector^M del cable^M
manchon^M de câble^M
Kabelmuffe^F
manicotto^M del cavo^M

plug
enchufe^M
fiche^F
Stecker^M
spina^F

cable
cable^M
câble^M
Kabel^N
cavo^M

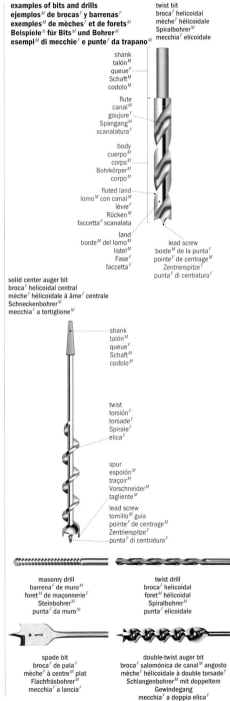

examples of bits and drills
ejemplos^M de brocas^F y barrenas^F
exemples^M de mèches^F et de forets^M
Beispiele^N für Bits^M und Bohrer^M
esempi^M di mecchie^F e punte^F da trapano^M

twist bit
broca^F helicoidal
mèche^F hélicoidale
Spiralbohrer^M
mecchia^F elicoidale

shank
talón^M
queue^F
Schaft^M
codolo^M

flute
canal^M
goujure^F
Spangang^M
scanalatura^F

body
cuerpo^M
corps^M
Bohrkörper^M
corpo^M

fluted land
lomo^M con canal^M
lèvre^F
Rücken^M
faccetta^F scanalata

land
borde^M del lomo^M
listel^M
Fase^F
faccetta^F

lead screw
borde^M de la punta^F
pointe^F de centrage^M
Zentrierspitze^F
punta^F di centratura^F

solid center auger bit
broca^F helicoidal central
mèche^F hélicoidale à âme^F centrale
Schneckenbohrer^M
mecchia^F a tortiglione^M

shank
talón^M
queue^F
Schaft^M
codolo^M

twist
torsión^F
torsade^F
Spirale^F
elica^F

spur
espolón^M
traçoir^M
Vorschneider^M
tagliente^M

lead screw
tornillo^M guía
pointe^F de centrage^M
Zentrierspitze^F
punta^F di centratura^F

masonry drill
barrena^F de muro^M
foret^M de maçonnerie^F
Steinbohrer^M
punta^F da muro^M

twist drill
broca^F helicoidal
foret^M hélicoidal
Spiralbohrer^M
punta^F elicoidale

spade bit
broca^F de pala^M
mèche^F à centre^M plat
Flachfräsbohrer^M
mecchia^F a lancia^F

double-twist auger bit
broca^F salomónica de canal^M angosto
mèche^F hélicoidale à double torsade^F
Schlangenbohrer^M mit doppeltem Gewindegang
mecchia^F a doppia elica^F

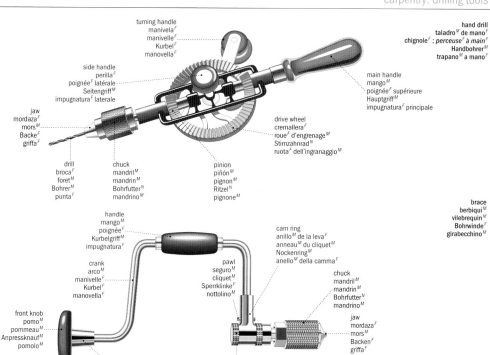

hand drill
taladro^M de mano^F
chignole^F ; *perceuse^F à main^F*
Handbohrer^M
trapano^M a mano^F

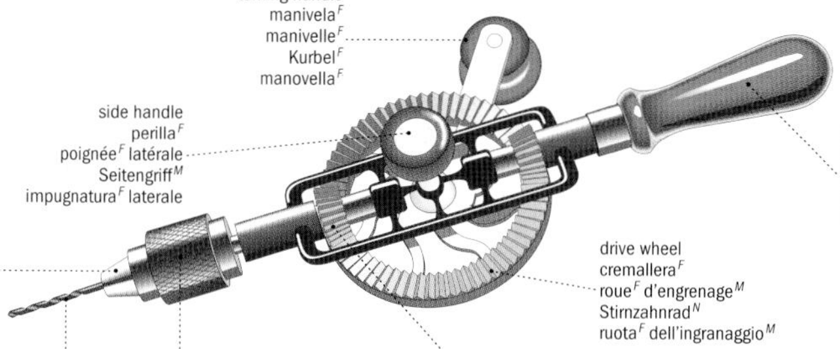

turning handle
manivela^F
manivelle^F
Kurbel^F
manovella^F

main handle
mango^M
poignée^F supérieure
Hauptgriff^M
impugnatura^F principale

side handle
perilla^F
poignée^F latérale
Seitengriff^M
impugnatura^F laterale

drive wheel
cremallera^F
roue^F d'engrenage^M
Stimzahnrad^N
ruota^F dell'ingranaggio^M

jaw
mordaza^F
mors^M
Backe^F
griffa^F

drill
broca^F
foret^M
Bohrer^M
punta^F

chuck
mandril^M
mandrin^M
Bohrfutter^N
mandrino^M

pinion
piñón^M
pignon^M
Ritzel^N
pignone^M

brace
berbiqui^M
vilebrequin^M
Bohrwinde^F
girabecchino^M

handle
mango^M
poignée^F
Kurbelgriff^M
impugnatura^F

cam ring
anillo^M de la leva^F
anneau^M du cliquet^M
Nockenring^M
anello^M della camma^F

crank
arco^M
manivelle^F
Kurbel^F
manovella^F

pawl
seguro^M
cliquet^M
Sperrklinke^F
nottolino^M

chuck
mandril^M
mandrin^M
Bohrfutter^N
mandrino^M

front knob
pomo^M
pommeau^M
Anpressknauf^M
pomolo^M

jaw
mordaza^F
mors^M
Backen^F
griffa^F

quill
manguito^M
fourreau^M
Scheide^F
manicotto^M cavo^M

ratchet
trinquete^M
rochet^M
Knarre^F
cricco^M

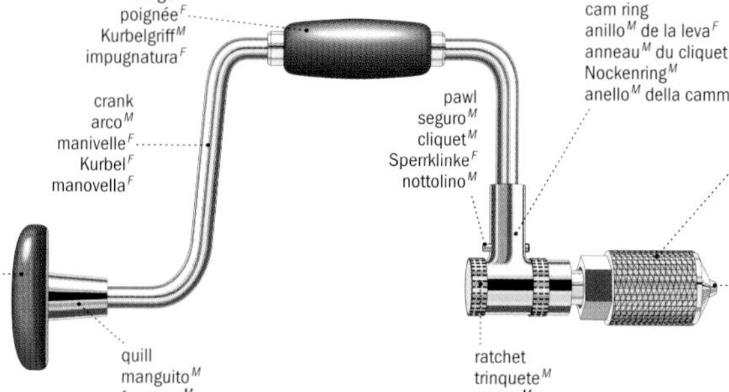

drill press
taladro^M vertical
perceuse^F à colonne^F
Ständerbohrmaschine^F
trapano^M a colonna^F

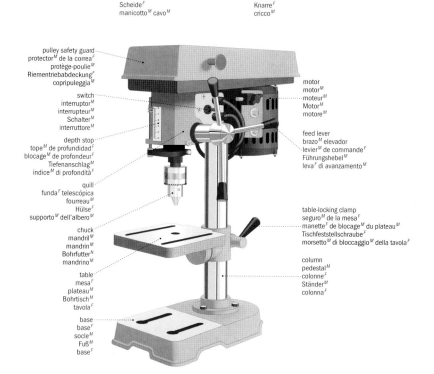

pulley safety guard
protector^M de la correa^F
protège-poulie^M
Riementriebabdeckung^F
copripuleggia^M

motor
motor^M
moteur^M
Motor^M
motore^M

switch
interruptor^M
interrupteur^M
Schalter^M
interruttore^M

feed lever
brazo^M elevador
levier^M de commande^F
Führungshebel^M
leva^F di avanzamento^M

depth stop
tope^M de profundidad^F
blocage^M de profondeur^F
Tiefenanschlag^M
indice^M di profondità^F

quill
funda^F telescópica
fourreau^M
Hülse^F
supporto^M dell'albero^M

table-locking clamp
seguro^M de la mesa^F
manette^F de blocage^M du plateau^M
Tischfeststellschraube^F
morsetto^M di bloccaggio^M della tavola^F

chuck
mandril^M
mandrin^M
Bohrfutter^N
mandrino^M

column
pedestal^M
colonne^F
Ständer^M
colonna^F

table
mesa^F
plateau^M
Bohrtisch^M
tavola^F

base
base^F
socle^M
Fuß^M
base^F

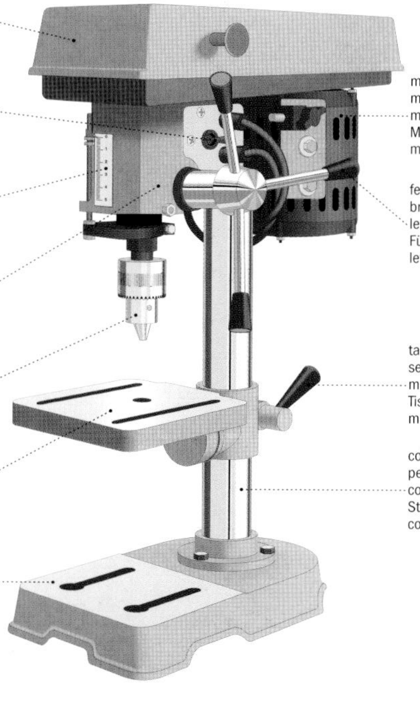

carpentry: shaping tools

carpintería^F : herramientas^F de perfilado^M | menuiserie^F : outils^M pour façonner | Bautischlerei^F: Formwerkzeuge^N | carpenteria^F: attrezzi^M per sagomare

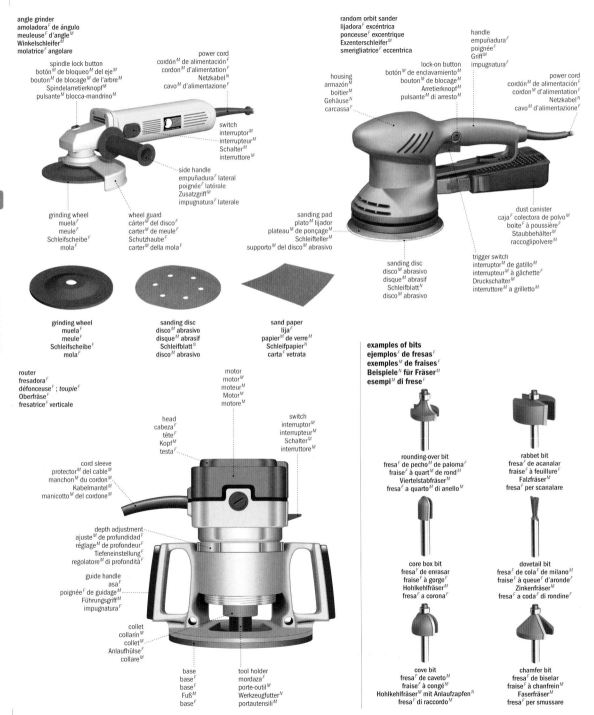

angle grinder
amoladora^F de ángulo
meuleuse^F d'angle^M
Winkelschleifer^M
molatrice^F angolare

spindle lock button
botón^M de bloqueo^M del eje^M
bouton^M de blocage^M de l'arbre^M
Spindelarretierknopf^M
pulsante^M blocca-mandrino^M

power cord
cordón^M de alimentación^F
cordon^M d'alimentation^F
Netzkabel^N
cavo^M d'alimentazione^F

switch
interruptor^M
interrupteur^M
Schalter^M
interruttore^M

side handle
empuñadura^F lateral
poignée^F latérale
Zusatzgriff^M
impugnatura^F laterale

grinding wheel
muela^F
meule^F
Schleifscheibe^F
mola^F

wheel guard
cárter^M del disco^F
carter^M de meule^F
Schutzhaube^F
carter^M della mola^F

grinding wheel
muela^F
meule^F
Schleifscheibe^F
mola^F

sanding disc
disco^M abrasivo
disque^M abrasif
Schleifblatt^N
disco^M abrasivo

sand paper
lija^F
papier^M de verre^M
Schleifpapier^N
carta^F vetrata

random orbit sander
lijadora^F excéntrica
ponceuse^F excentrique
Exzenterschleifer^M
smerigliatrice^F eccentrica

handle
empuñadura^F
poignée^F
Griff^M
impugnatura^F

lock-on button
botón^M de enclavamiento^M
bouton^M de blocage^M
Arretierknopf^M
pulsante^M di arresto^M

housing
armazón^M
boitier^M
Gehäuse^N
carcassa^F

power cord
cordón^M de alimentación^F
cordon^M d'alimentation^F
Netzkabel^N
cavo^M d'alimentazione^F

sanding pad
plato^M lijador
plateau^M de ponçage^M
Schleifteller^M
supporto^M del disco^M abrasivo

dust canister
caja^F colectora de polvo^M
boite^F à poussière^F
Staubbehälter^M
raccoglipolvere^M

trigger switch
interruptor^M de gatillo^M
interrupteur^M à gâchette^F
Druckschalter^M
interruttore^M a grilletto^M

sanding disc
disco^M abrasivo
disque^M abrasif
Schleifblatt^N
disco^M abrasivo

router
fresadora^F
défonceuse^F ; toupie^F
Oberfräse^F
fresatrice^F verticale

motor
motor^M
moteur^M
Motor^M
motore^M

head
cabeza^F
tête^F
Kopf^M
testa^F

switch
interruptor^M
interrupteur^M
Schalter^M
interruttore^M

cord sleeve
protector^M del cable^M
manchon^M du cordon^M
Kabelmantel^M
manicotto^M del cordone^M

depth adjustment
ajuste^M de profundidad^F
réglage^M de profondeur^F
Tiefeneinstellung^F
regolatore^M di profondità^F

guide handle
asa^F
poignée^F de guidage^M
Führungsgriff^M
impugnatura^F

collet
collarín^M
collet^M
Anlaufhülse^F
collare^M

base
base^F
base^F
Fuß^M
base^F

tool holder
mordaza^F
porte-outil^M
Werkzeugfutter^N
portautensili^M

examples of bits
ejemplos^F de fresas^F
exemples^M de fraises^F
Beispiele^N für Fräser^M
esempi^M di frese^F

rounding-over bit
fresa^F de pecho^M de paloma^F
fraise^F à quart^M de rond^M
Viertelstabfräser^M
fresa^F a quarto^M di anello^M

rabbet bit
fresa^F de acanalar
fraise^F à feuillure^F
Falzfräser^M
fresa^F per scanalare

core box bit
fresa^F de enrasar
fraise^F à gorge^F
Hohlkehlfräser^M
fresa^F a corona^M

dovetail bit
fresa^F de cola^F de milano^M
fraise^F à queue^F d'aronde^F
Zinkenfräser^M
fresa^F a coda^F di rondine^F

cove bit
fresa^F de caveto^M
fraise^F à congé^M
Hohlkehlfräser^M mit Anlaufzapfen^N
fresa^F di raccordo^M

chamfer bit
fresa^F de biselar
fraise^F à chanfrein^M
Faserfräser^M
fresa^F per smussare

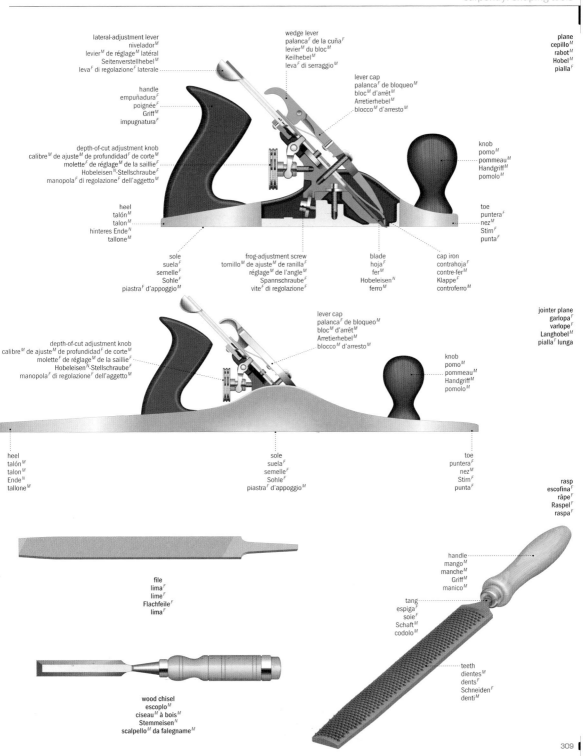

lateral-adjustment lever
nivelador^M
levier^M de réglage^M latéral
Seitenverstellhebel^M
leva^F di regolazione^F laterale

wedge lever
palanca^F de la cuña^F
levier^M du bloc^M
Keilhebel^M
leva^F di serraggio^M

plane
cepillo^M
rabot^M
Hobel^M
pialla^F

handle
empuñadura^F
poignée^F
Griff^M
impugnatura^F

lever cap
palanca^F de bloqueo^M
bloc^M d'arrêt^M
Arretierhebel^M
blocco^M d'arresto^M

knob
pomo^M
pommeau^M
Handgriff^M
pomolo^M

depth-of-cut adjustment knob
calibre^M de ajuste^M de profundidad^F de corte^M
molette^F de réglage^F de la saillie^F
Hobeleisen^N-Stellschraube^F
manopola^F di regolazione^F dell'aggetto^M

heel
talón^M
talon^M
hinteres Ende^N
tallone^M

toe
puntera^F
nez^M
Stirn^F
punta^F

sole
suela^F
semelle^F
Sohle^F
piastra^F d'appoggio^M

frog-adjustment screw
tornillo^M de ajuste^M de ranilla^F
réglage^M de l'angle^M
Spannschraube^F
vite^F di regolazione^F

blade
hoja^F
fer^M
Hobeleisen^N
ferro^M

cap iron
contrahoja^F
contre-fer^M
Klappe^F
controferro^M

jointer plane
garlopa^F
varlope^F
Langhobel^M
pialla^F lunga

lever cap
palanca^F de bloqueo^M
bloc^M d'arrêt^M
Arretierhebel^M
blocco^M d'arresto^M

depth-of-cut adjustment knob
calibre^M de ajuste^M de profundidad^F de corte^M
molette^F de réglage^F de la saillie^F
Hobeleisen^N-Stellschraube^F
manopola^F di regolazione^F dell'aggetto^M

knob
pomo^M
pommeau^M
Handgriff^M
pomolo^M

heel
talón^M
talon^M
Ende^N
tallone^M

sole
suela^F
semelle^F
Sohle^F
piastra^F d'appoggio^M

toe
puntera^F
nez^M
Stirn^F
punta^F

rasp
escofina^F
râpe^F
Raspel^F
raspa^F

handle
mango^M
manche^M
Griff^M
manico^M

tang
espiga^F
soie^F
Schaft^M
codolo^M

file
lima^F
lime^F
Flachfeile^F
lima^F

teeth
dientes^M
dents^F
Schneiden^F
denti^M

wood chisel
escoplo^M
ciseau^M à bois^M
Stemmeisen^N
scalpello^M da falegname^M

carpentry: gripping and tightening tools

carpintería^F : herramientas^F para apretar | menuiserie^F : outils^M pour serrer | Bautischlerei^F: Greif- und Spannwerkzeuge^N | carpenteria^F: attrezzi^M di serraggio^M

DO-IT-YOURSELF AND GARDENING

pliers
alicates^M
pinces^F
Zangen^F
pinze^F

slip joint pliers
pinzas^F universales
pince^F à joint^M coulissant
Kombizange^F
pinza^F a giunto^M scorrevole

curved jaw
mordaza^F curva
mâchoire^F incurvée
gekrümmte Greifbacke^F
ganascia^F curva

straight jaw
mordaza^F recta
mâchoire^F droite
gerade Greifbacke^F
ganascia^F diritta

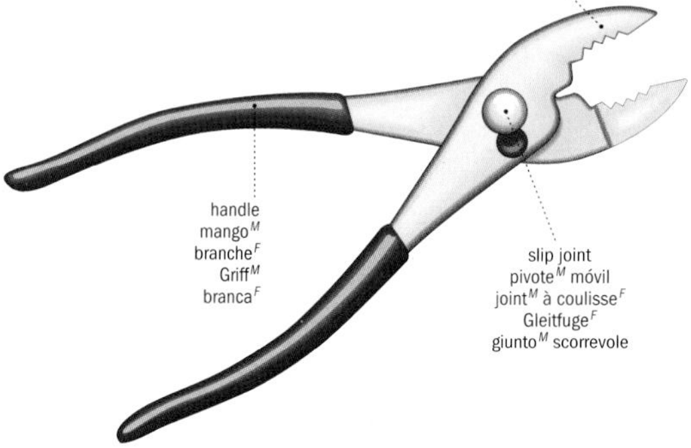

rib joint pliers
alicates^M pico^M de loro^M
pince^F multiprise
Wasserpumpen-Zange^F
pinza^F regolabile

bolt
perno^M
boulon^M
Bolzen^M
bullone^M

adjustable channel
canal^M de ajuste^M
cran^M de réglage^M
Verstellnut^F
cerniera^F regolabile

handle
mango^M
branche^F
Griff^M
branca^F

slip joint
pivote^M móvil
joint^M à coulisse^F
Gleitfuge^F
giunto^M scorrevole

nut
tuerca^F
écrou^M
Mutter^F
dado^M

handle
mango^M
branche^F
Griff^M
branca^F

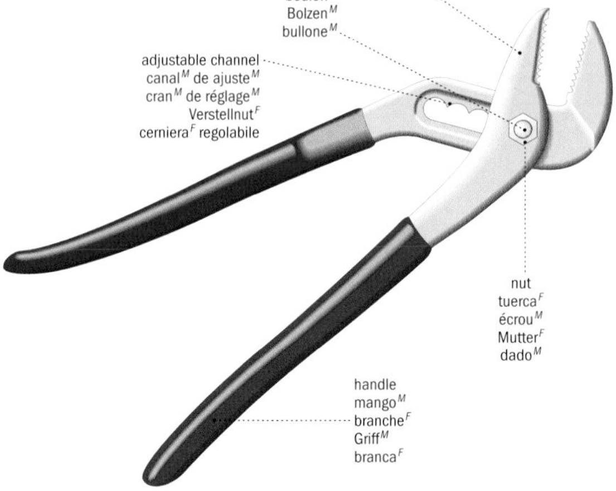

locking pliers
alicates^M de presión^F
pince^F-étau^M
Gripzange^F
pinza^F a scatto^M

spring
resorte^M
ressort^M
Feder^F
molla^F

lever
seguro^M
levier^M
Hebel^M
leva^F

adjusting screw
tornillo^M de ajuste^M
vis^F de réglage^M
Verstellung^F
vite^F di regolazione^F

toothed jaw
mordaza^F dentada
mâchoire^F dentée
gezahnte Greifbacke^F
ganascia^F dentata

rivet
remache^M
rivet^M
Niete^F
rivetto^M

release lever
liberador^M del seguro^M
levier^M de dégagement^M
Löshebel^M
leva^F di sbloccaggio^M

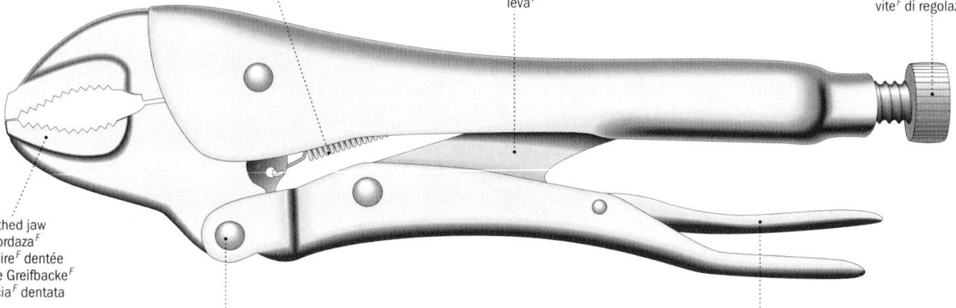

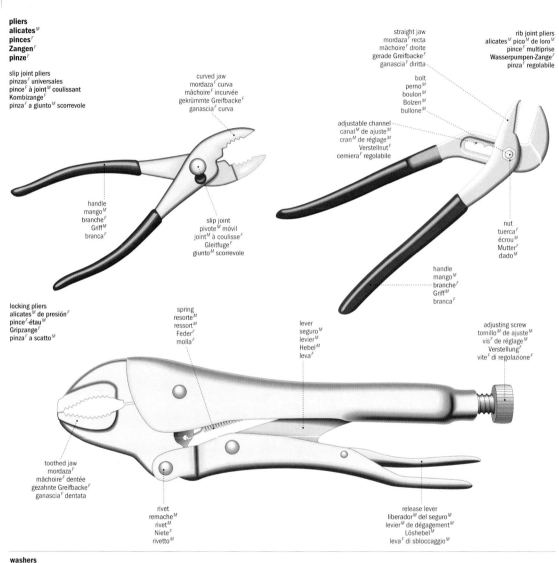

washers
arandelas^F
rondelles^F
Unterlegscheiben^F
rosette^F

flat washer
arandela^F plana
rondelle^F plate
Unterlegscheibe^F
rosetta^F piatta

lock washer
arandela^F de presión^F
rondelle^F à ressort^M
Federring^M
rosetta^F elastica

external tooth lock washer
arandela^F de presión^F de dientes^M externos
rondelle^F à denture^F extérieure
außengezahnte Fächerscheibe^F
rosetta^F a dentatura^F esterna

internal tooth lock washer
arandela^F de presión^F de dientes^M internos
rondelle^F à denture^F intérieure
innengezahnte Fächerscheibe^F
rosetta^F a dentatura^F interna

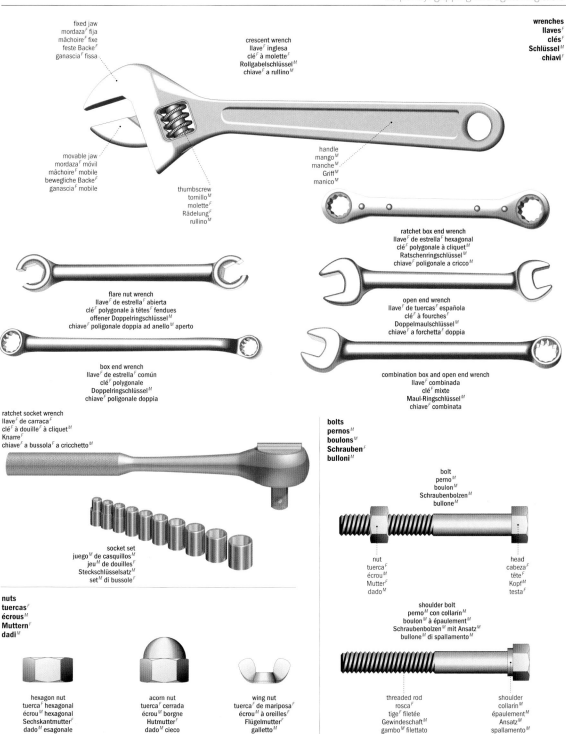

wrenches
llaves[F]
clés[F]
Schlüssel[M]
chiavi[F]

fixed jaw
mordaza[F] fija
mâchoire[F] fixe
feste Backe[F]
ganascia[F] fissa

crescent wrench
llave[F] inglesa
clé[F] à molette
Rollgabelschlüssel[M]
chiave[F] a rullino[M]

movable jaw
mordaza[F] móvil
mâchoire[F] mobile
bewegliche Backe[F]
ganascia[F] mobile

handle
mango[M]
manche[M]
Griff[M]
manico[M]

thumbscrew
tornillo[M]
molette[F]
Rädelung[F]
rullino[M]

ratchet box end wrench
llave[F] de estrella[F] hexagonal
clé[F] polygonale à cliquet[M]
Ratschenringschlüssel[M]
chiave[F] poligonale a cricco[M]

flare nut wrench
llave[F] de estrella[F] abierta
clé[F] polygonale à têtes[F] fendues
offener Doppelringschlüssel[M]
chiave[F] poligonale doppia ad anello[M] aperto

open end wrench
llave[F] de tuercas[F] española
clé[F] à fourches[F]
Doppelmaulschlüssel[M]
chiave[F] a forchetta[F] doppia

box end wrench
llave[F] de estrella[F] común
clé[F] polygonale
Doppelringschlüssel[M]
chiave[F] poligonale doppia

combination box and open end wrench
llave[F] combinada
clé[F] mixte
Maul-Ringschlüssel[M]
chiave[F] combinata

ratchet socket wrench
llave[F] de carraca[F]
clé[F] à douille[F] à cliquet[M]
Knarre[F]
chiave[F] a bussola[F] a cricchetto[M]

bolts
pernos[M]
boulons[M]
Schrauben[F]
bulloni[M]

bolt
perno[M]
boulon[M]
Schraubenbolzen[M]
bullone[M]

nut
tuerca[F]
écrou[M]
Mutter[F]
dado[M]

head
cabeza[F]
tête[F]
Kopf[M]
testa[F]

socket set
juego[M] de casquillos[M]
jeu[M] de douilles[F]
Steckschlüsselsatz[M]
set[M] di bussole[F]

shoulder bolt
perno[M] con collarin[M]
boulon[M] à épaulement[M]
Schraubenbolzen[M] mit Ansatz[M]
bullone[M] di spallamento[M]

nuts
tuercas[F]
écrous[M]
Muttern[F]
dadi[M]

hexagon nut
tuerca[F] hexagonal
écrou[M] hexagonal
Sechskantmutter[F]
dado[M] esagonale

acorn nut
tuerca[F] cerrada
écrou[M] borgne
Hutmutter[F]
dado[M] cieco

wing nut
tuerca[F] de mariposa[F]
écrou[M] à oreilles[F]
Flügelmutter[F]
galletto[M]

threaded rod
rosca[F]
tige[F] filetée
Gewindeschaft[M]
gambo[M] filettato

shoulder
collarin[M]
épaulement[M]
Ansatz[M]
spallamento[M]

carpentry: gripping and tightening tools

C-clamp
prensa^M en C
serre-joint^M
Zwinge^F
morsetto^M a C

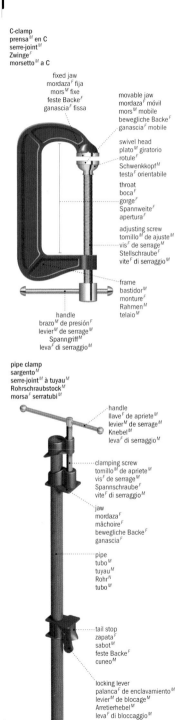

fixed jaw
mordaza^F fija
mors^M fixe
feste Backe^F
ganascia^F fissa

movable jaw
mordaza^F móvil
mors^M mobile
bewegliche Backe^F
ganascia^F mobile

swivel head
plato^M giratorio
rotule^F
Schwenkkopf^M
testa^F orientabile

throat
boca^F
gorge^F
Spannweite^F
apertura^F

adjusting screw
tornillo^M de ajuste^M
vis^F de serrage^M
Stellschraube^F
vite^F di serraggio^M

frame
bastidor^M
monture^F
Rahmen^M
telaio^M

handle
brazo^M de presión^F
levier^M de serrage^M
Spanngriff^M
leva^F di serraggio^M

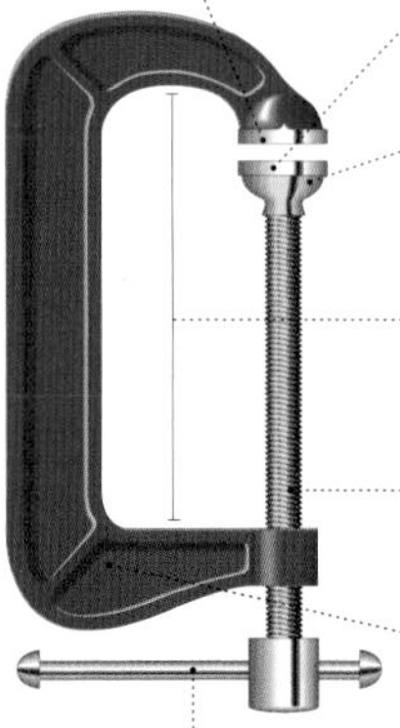

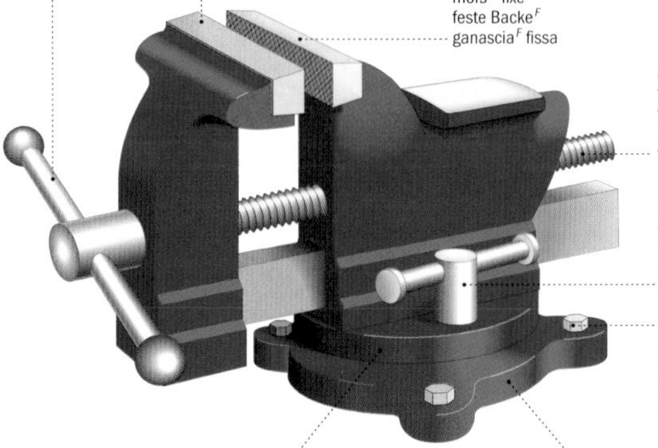

pipe clamp
sargento^M
serre-joint^M à tuyau^M
Rohrschraubstock^M
morsa^F serratubi^M

handle
llave^F de apriete^M
levier^M de serrage^M
Knebel^M
leva^F di serraggio^M

clamping screw
tornillo^M de apriete^M
vis^F de serrage^M
Spannschraube^F
vite^F di serraggio^M

jaw
mordaza^F
mâchoire^F
bewegliche Backe^F
ganascia^F

pipe
tubo^M
tuyau^M
Rohr^N
tubo^M

tail stop
zapata^F
sabot^M
feste Backe^F
cuneo^M

locking lever
palanca^F de enclavamiento^M
levier^M de blocage^M
Arretierhebel^M
leva^F di bloccaggio^M

handle
mango^M
levier^M de serrage^M
Spanngriff^M
leva^F di serraggio^M

movable jaw
mordaza^F móvil
mors^M mobile
bewegliche Backe^F
ganascia^F mobile

vise
torno^M de banco^M
étau^M
Schraubstock^M
morsa^F

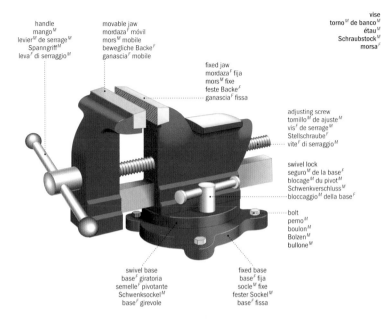

fixed jaw
mordaza^F fija
mors^M fixe
feste Backe^F
ganascia^F fissa

adjusting screw
tornillo^M de ajuste^M
vis^F de serrage^M
Stellschraube^F
vite^F di serraggio^M

swivel lock
seguro^M de la base^F
blocage^M du pivot^M
Schwenkverschluss^M
bloccaggio^M della base^F

bolt
perno^M
boulon^M
Bolzen^M
bullone^M

swivel base
base^F giratoria
semelle^F pivotante
Schwenksockel^M
base^F girevole

fixed base
base^F fija
socle^M fixe
fester Sockel^M
base^F fissa

peg
tope^M
cale^F
Spannpratze^F
spessore^M

crank
manivela^F
manivelle^F
Kurbel^F
manovella^F

jaws
mordazas^F
mâchoires^F
Backen^F
ganasce^F

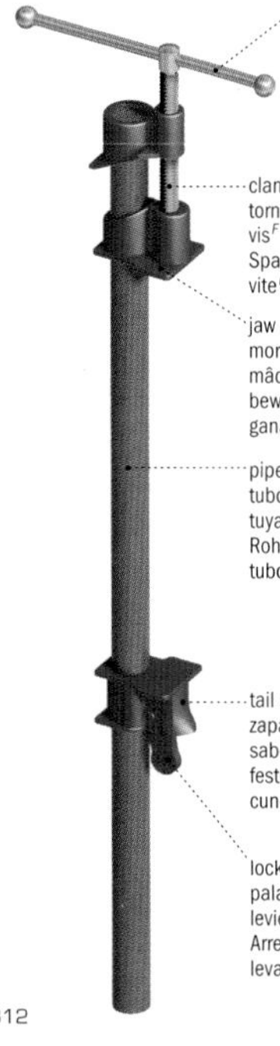

work bench and vise
banco^M de trabajo^M
établi^M étau^M
Werkbank^F und Schraubstock^M
piano^M di lavoro^M a morsa^F

work surface
tablero^M
plateau^M
Arbeitsplatte^F
piano^M di lavoro^M

footrest
reposapiés^M
appui-pieds^M
Fußstütze^F
appoggiapiedi^M

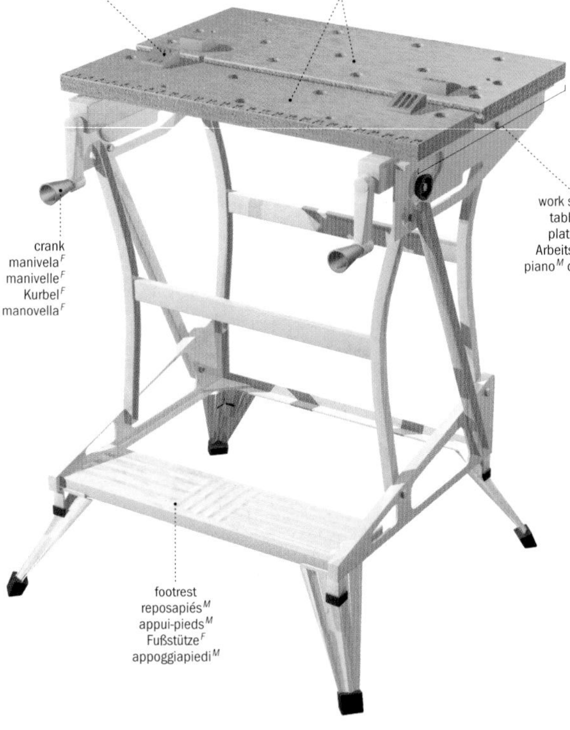

carpentry: measuring and marking tools

carpintería ^F : instrumentos ^M de trazado ^M y de medición ^F | menuiserie ^F : instruments ^M de traçage ^M et de mesure ^F | Bautischlerei ^F: Mess- und Markierinstrumente ^N |
carpentaria ^F: strumenti ^M di misurazione ^F e tracciamento ^M

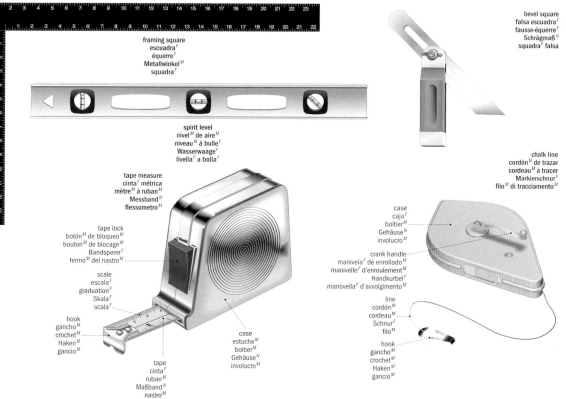

framing square
escuadra ^F
équerre ^F
Metallwinkel ^M
squadra ^F

bevel square
falsa escuadra ^F
fausse-équerre ^F
Schrägmaß ^N
squadra ^F falsa

spirit level
nivel ^M de aire ^M
niveau ^M à bulle ^F
Wasserwaage ^F
livella ^F a bolla ^F

chalk line
cordón ^M de trazar
cordeau ^M à tracer
Markierschnur ^F
filo ^M di tracciamento ^M

tape measure
cinta ^F métrica
mètre ^M à ruban ^M
Messband ^N
flessometro ^M

case
caja ^F
boîtier ^M
Gehäuse ^N
involucro ^M

tape lock
botón ^M de bloqueo ^M
bouton ^M de blocage ^M
Bandsperre ^F
fermo ^M del nastro ^M

crank handle
manivela ^F de enrollado ^M
manivelle ^F d'enroulement ^M
Handkurbel ^F
manovella ^F d'avvolgimento ^M

scale
escala ^F
graduation ^F
Skala ^F
scala ^F

line
cordón ^M
cordeau ^M
Schnur ^F
filo ^M

hook
gancho ^M
crochet ^M
Haken ^M
gancio ^M

case
estuche ^M
boîtier ^M
Gehäuse ^N
involucro ^M

hook
gancho ^M
crochet ^M
Haken ^M
gancio ^M

tape
cinta ^F
ruban ^M
Maßband ^N
nastro ^M

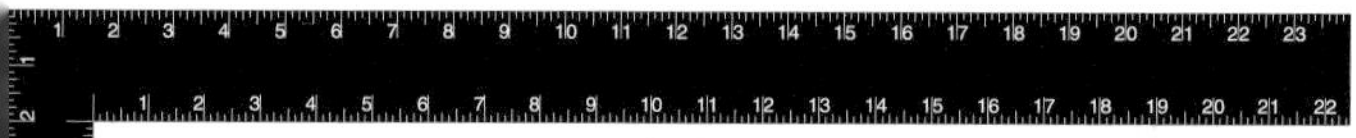

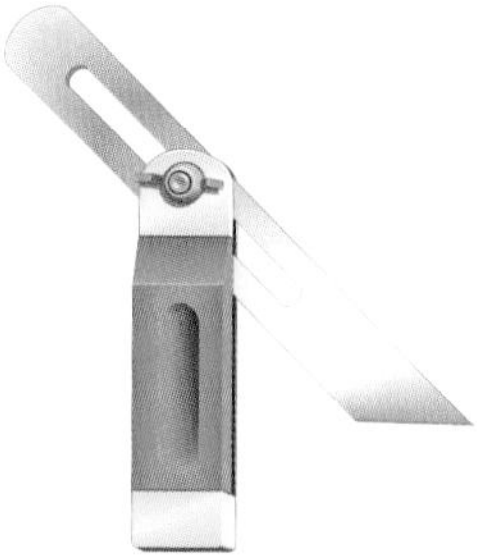

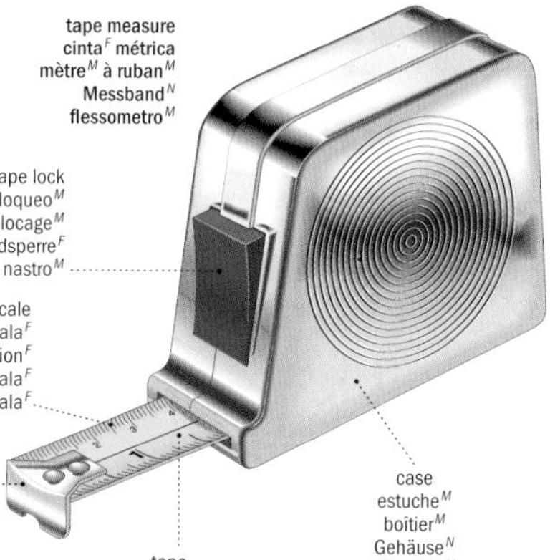

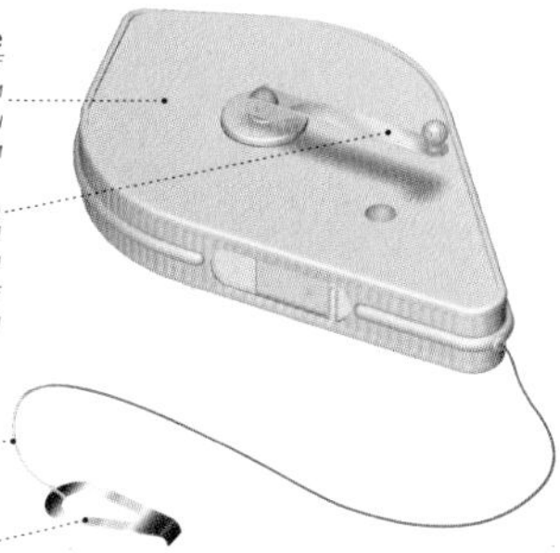

carpentry: miscellaneous material

carpintería ^F : materiales ^M varios | menuiserie ^F : matériel ^M divers | Bautischlerei ^F: verschiedenes Zubehör ^N | carpenteria ^F: materiale ^M vario

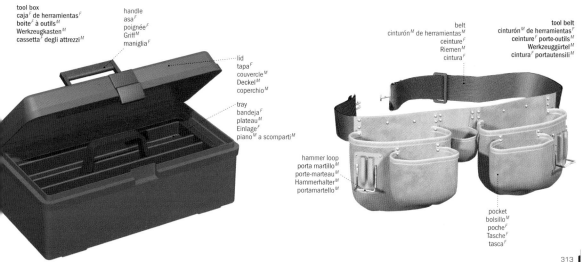

tool box
caja ^F de herramientas ^F
boite ^F à outils ^M
Werkzeugkasten ^M
cassetta ^F degli attrezzi ^M

handle
asa ^F
poignée ^F
Griff ^M
maniglia ^F

lid
tapa ^F
couvercle ^M
Deckel ^M
coperchio ^M

tray
bandeja ^F
plateau ^M
Einlage ^F
piano ^M a scomparti ^M

belt
cinturón ^M de herramientas ^M
ceinture ^F
Riemen ^M
cintura ^F

tool belt
cinturón ^M de herramientas ^F
ceinture ^F porte-outils ^M
Werkzeuggürtel ^M
cintura ^F portautensili ^M

hammer loop
porta martillo ^M
porte-marteau ^M
Hammerhalter ^M
portamartello ^M

pocket
bolsillo ^M
poche ^F
Tasche ^F
tasca ^F

DO-IT-YOURSELF AND GARDENING

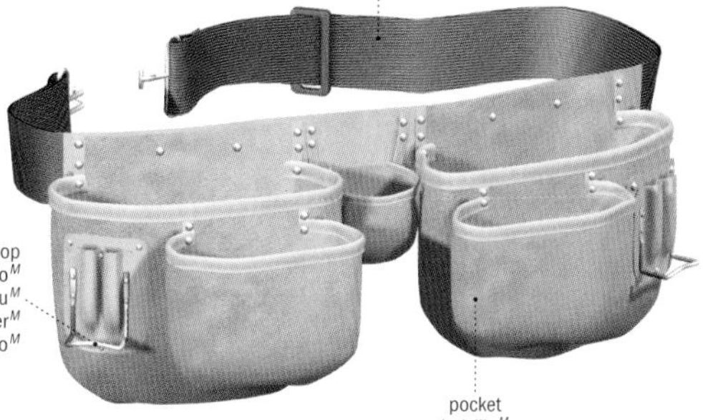

plumbing tools

fontanería^F : herramientas^F | plomberie^F : outils^M | Klempnerwerkzeuge^N | attrezzi^M idraulici

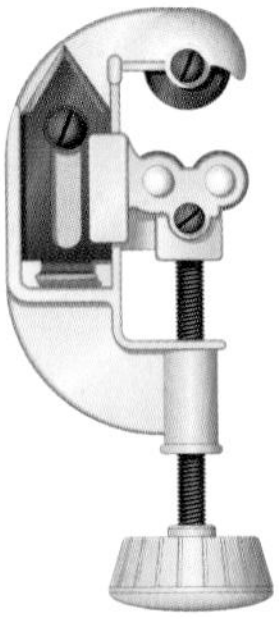

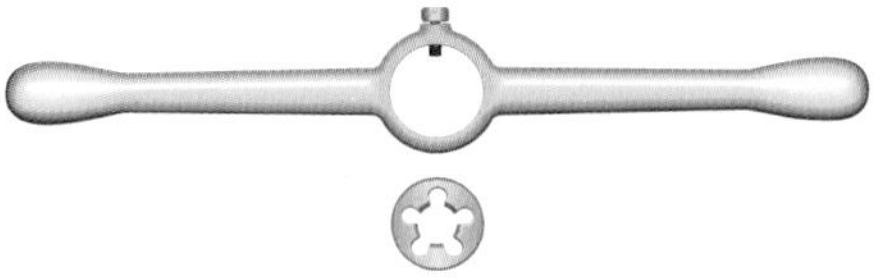

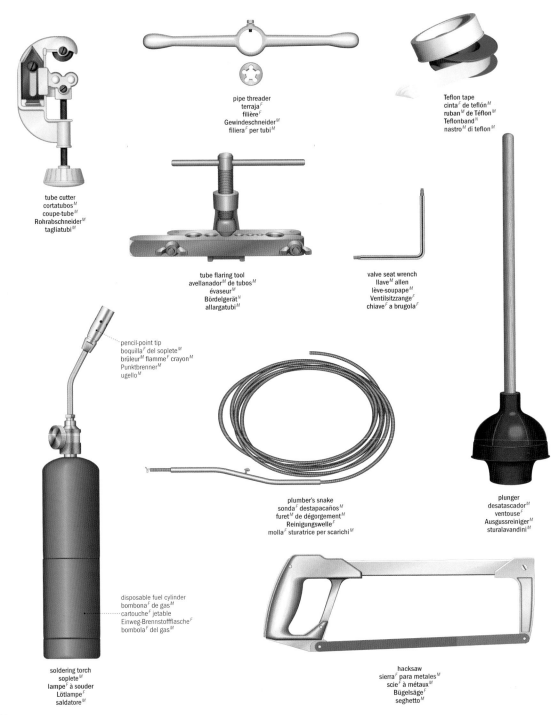

pipe threader
terraja^F
filière^F
Gewindeschneider^M
filiera^F per tubi^M

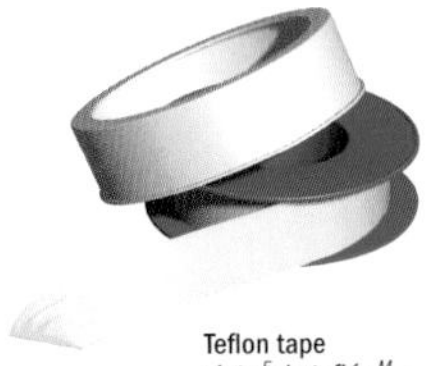

Teflon tape
cinta^F de teflón^M
ruban^M de Téflon^M
Teflonband^N
nastro^M di teflon^M

tube cutter
cortatubos^M
coupe-tube^M
Rohrabschneider^M
tagliatubi^M

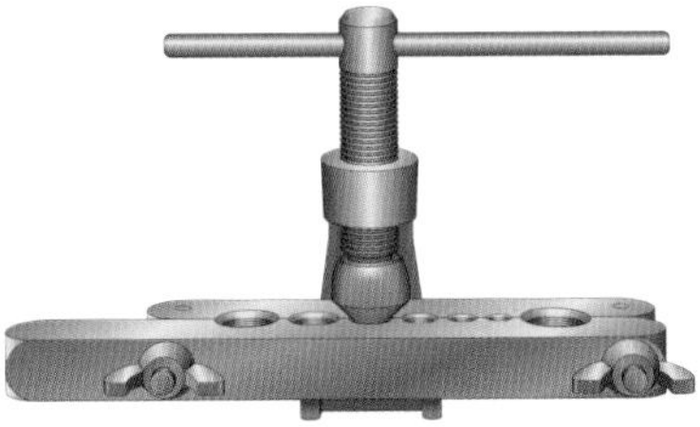

tube flaring tool
avellanador^M de tubos^M
évaseur^N
Bördelgerät^N
allargatubi^M

valve seat wrench
llave^M allen
lève-soupape^M
Ventilsitzzange^F
chiave^F a brugola^F

pencil-point tip
boquilla^F del soplete^M
brûleur^M flamme^F crayon^M
Punktbrenner^M
ugello^M

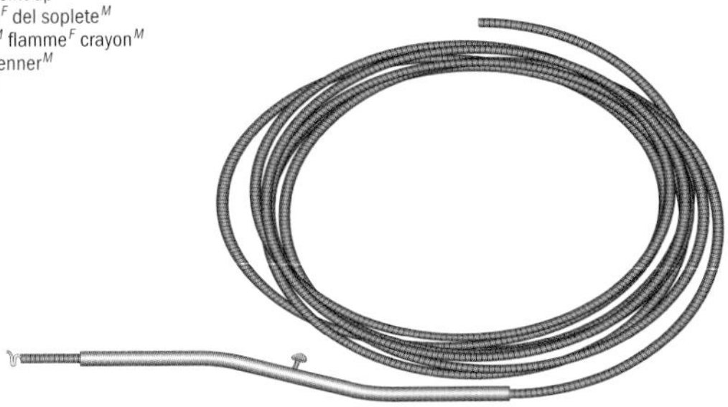

plumber's snake
sonda^F destapacaños^M
furet^M de dégorgement^M
Reinigungswelle^F
molla^F sturatrice per scarichi^M

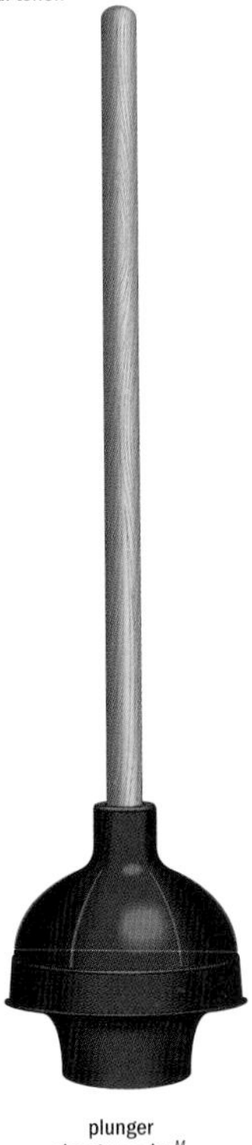

plunger
desatascador^M
ventouse^F
Ausgussreiniger^M
sturalavandini^M

disposable fuel cylinder
bombona^F de gas^M
cartouche^F jetable
Einweg-Brennstoffflasche^F
bombola^F del gas^M

soldering torch
soplete^M
lampe^F à souder
Lötlampe^F
saldatore^M

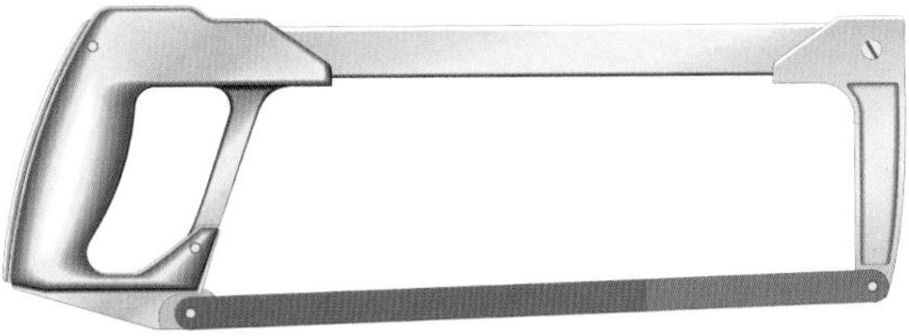

hacksaw
sierra^F para metales^M
scie^F à métaux^M
Bügelsäge^F
seghetto^M

DO-IT-YOURSELF AND GARDENING

plumbing tools

wrenches
llaves^F
clés^F
Rohrzangen^F
chiavi^F

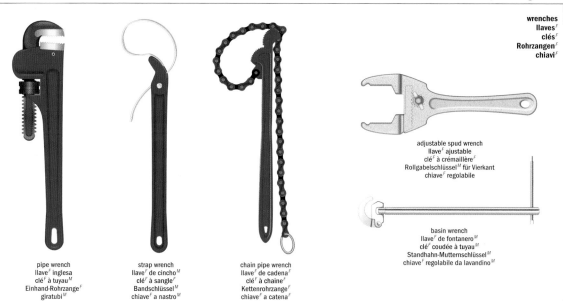

adjustable spud wrench
llave^F ajustable
clé^F à crémaillère^F
Rollgabelschlüssel^M für Vierkant
chiave^F regolabile

basin wrench
llave^F de fontanero^M
clé^F coudée à tuyau^M
Standhahn-Mutternschlüssel^M
chiave^F regolabile da lavandino^M

pipe wrench
llave^F inglesa
clé^F à tuyau^M
Einhand-Rohrzange^F
giratubi^M

strap wrench
llave^F de cincho^M
clé^F à sangle^F
Bandschlüssel^M
chiave^F a nastro^M

chain pipe wrench
llave^F de cadena^F
clé^F à chaine^F
Kettenrohrzange^F
chiave^F a catena^F

masonry tools

albañilería^F : herramientas^F | maçonnerie^F : outils^M | Maurerwerkzeuge^N | attrezzi^M da muratore^M

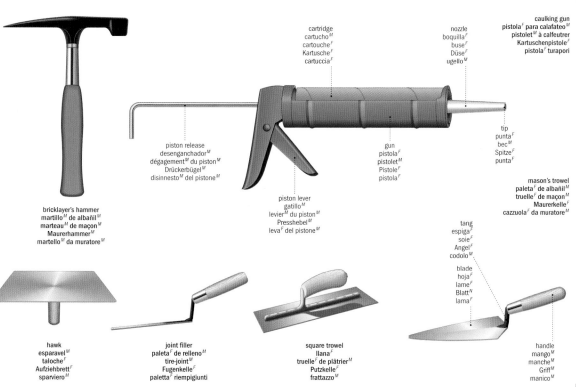

cartridge
cartucho^M
cartouche^F
Kartusche^F
cartuccia^F

nozzle
boquilla^F
buse^F
Düse^F
ugello^M

caulking gun
pistola^F para calafateo^M
pistolet^M à calfeutrer
Kartuschenpistole^F
pistola^F turapori

piston release
desenganchador^M
dégagement^M du piston^M
Drückerbügel^M
disinnesto^M del pistone^M

gun
pistola^F
pistolet^M
Pistole^F
pistola^F

tip
punta^F
bec^M
Spitze^F
punta^F

piston lever
gatillo^M
levier^M du piston^M
Presshebel^M
leva^F del pistone^M

mason's trowel
paleta^F de albañil^M
truelle^F de maçon^M
Maurerkelle^F
cazzuola^F da muratore^M

bricklayer's hammer
martillo^M de albañil^M
marteau^M de maçon^M
Maurerhammer^M
martello^M da muratore^M

tang
espiga^F
soie^F
Angel^F
codolo^M

blade
hoja^F
lame^F
Blatt^N
lama^F

hawk
esparavel^M
taloche^F
Aufziehbrett^F
sparviero^M

joint filler
paleta^F de relleno^M
tire-joint^M
Fugenkelle^F
paletta^F riempigiunti

square trowel
llana^F
truelle^F de plâtrier^M
Putzkelle^F
frattazzo^M

handle
mango^M
manche^F
Griff^M
manico^M

DO-IT-YOURSELF AND GARDENING

electricity tools

electricidad^F : herramientas^F | électricité^F : outils^M | Elektroinstallateurwerkzeuge^N | attrezzatura^F elettrica

multimeter
voltimetro^M
multimètre^M
Multimeter^N
multimetro^M

housing
caja^F
boitier^M
Gehäuse^N
cassa^F

digital display
registro^M digital
afficheur^M numérique
Digitalanzeige^F
visualizzatore^M digitale

data hold
retención^F de datos^M
mémorisation^F des données^F
Messdatenspeicher^M
memoria^F dati^M

selector switch
selector^M
commutateur^M
Bereichsumschalter^M
commutatore^M

input terminal
terminal^M de entrada^F
borne^F d'entrée^F
Eingangsbuchse^F
terminale^M di ingresso^M

probe
varilla^F de contacto^M
fiche^F
Messspitze^F
puntale^M

auto/manual range
selección^F auto/manual
lecture^F automatique/manuelle
Auto-Manualumschalter^M
selettore^M automatico/manuale

cord
cable^M
cordon^M
Messkabel^N
cordone^M

voltage tester
detector^M de tensión^F
vérificateur^M de tension^F
Spannungsprüfer^M
cercafase^M

insulated blade
vástago^M aislado
lame^F isolée
isolierte Klinge^F
lama^F isolata

insulated handle
mango^M aislado
manche^M isolé
isolierter Griff^M
manico^M isolato

neon lamp
lámpara^F de neón^M
lampe^F au néon^M
Glimmlampe^F
lampada^F al neon^M

drop light
linterna^F movible
baladeuse^F
Handlampe^F
lampada^F portatile a gabbia^F

continuity tester
detector^M de continuidad^F
vérificateur^M de continuité^F
Durchgangsprüfer^M
tester^M di continuità^F

hook
gancho^M
crochet^M
Haken^M
gancio^M

reflector
reflector^M
réflecteur^M
Reflektor^M
riflettore^M

bulb
bombilla^F
lampe^F
Glühbirne^F
lampadina^F

guard
reja^F
grillage^M de protection^F
Schutzgitter^N
gabbia^F di protezione^F

convenience outlet
enchufe^M
prise^F de courant^M
Zusatzsteckdose^F
presa^F di corrente^F

handle
mango^M
manche^M
Griff^M
impugnatura^F

cord
cable^M
cordon^M
Kabel^N
cordone^M

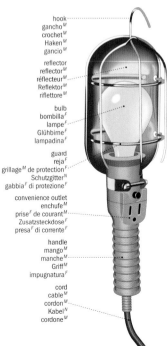

receptacle analyzer
probador^M de contactos^M con tierra^F
vérificateur^M de prise^F de courant^M
Steckdosenprüfer^M
tester^M di presa^F

neon tester
lámpara^F de prueba^F de neón^M
vérificateur^M de circuit^M
Prüflampe^F
lampada^F provacircuiti

high-voltage tester
detector^M de alta tensión^F
vérificateur^M de haute tension^F
Hochspannungsprüfer^M
tester^M dell'alta^F tensione^F

electricity tools

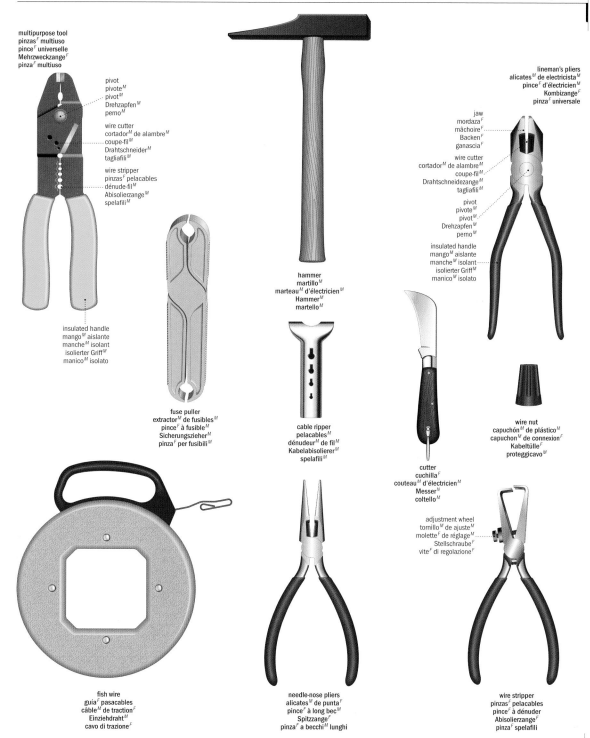

multipurpose tool
pinzas^F multiuso
pince^F universelle
Mehrzweckzange^F
pinza^F multiuso

pivot
pivote^M
pivot^M
Drehzapfen^M
perno^M

wire cutter
cortador^M de alambre^M
coupe-fil^M
Drahtschneider^M
tagliafili^M

wire stripper
pinzas^F pelacables
dénude-fil^M
Abisolierzange^M
spelafili^M

insulated handle
mango^M aislante
manche^M isolant
isolierter Griff^M
manico^M isolato

fuse puller
extractor^M de fusibles^M
pince^F à fusible^M
Sicherungszieher^M
pinza^F per fusibili^M

hammer
martillo^M
marteau^M d'électricien^M
Hammer^M
martello^M

cable ripper
pelacables^M
dénudeur^M de fil^M
Kabelabisolierer^M
spelafili^M

cutter
cuchilla^F
couteau^M d'électricien^M
Messer^N
coltello^M

lineman's pliers
alicates^M de electricista^M
pince^F d'électricien^M
Kombizange^F
pinza^F universale

jaw
mordaza^F
mâchoire^F
Backen^F
ganascia^F

wire cutter
cortador^M de alambre^M
coupe-fil^M
Drahtschneidezange^M
tagliafili^M

pivot
pivote^M
pivot^M
Drehzapfen^M
perno^M

insulated handle
mango^M aislante
manche^M isolant
isolierter Griff^M
manico^M isolato

wire nut
capuchón^M de plástico^M
capuchon^M de connexion^F
Kabeltülle^F
proteggicavo^M

fish wire
guía^F pasacables
câble^M de traction^F
Einziehdraht^M
cavo^M di trazione^F

needle-nose pliers
alicates^M de punta^F
pince^F à long bec^M
Spitzzange^F
pinza^F a becchi^M lunghi

adjustment wheel
tornillo^M de ajuste^M
molette^F de réglage^M
Stellschraube^F
vite^F di regolazione^F

wire stripper
pinzas^F pelacables
pince^F à dénuder
Abisolierzange^F
pinza^F spelafili

soldering and welding tools

herramientas^F de soldadura^F | soudage^M : outils^M | Löt- und Schweißwerkzeuge^N | attrezzi^M di brasatura^F e saldatura^F

soldering gun
pistola^F para soldar
pistolet^M à souder
Lötpistole^F
saldatore^M a pistola^F

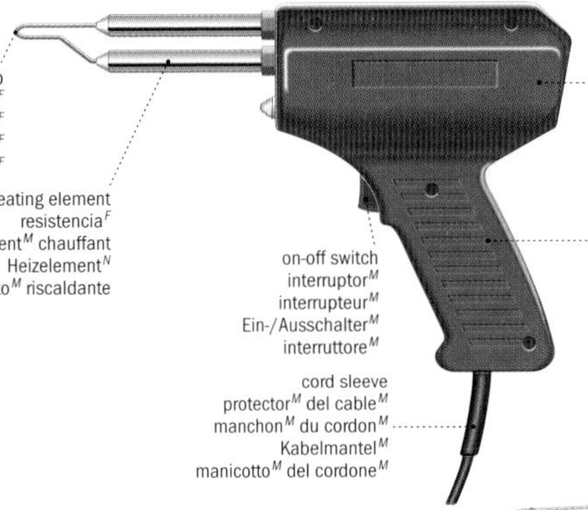

tip
punta^F
panne^F
Lötspitze^F
punta^F

heating element
resistencia^F
élément^M chauffant
Heizelement^N
elemento^M riscaldante

on-off switch
interruptor^M
interrupteur^M
Ein-/Ausschalter^M
interruttore^M

housing
caja^F
boîtier^M
Gehäuse^N
cassa^F

pistol grip handle
mango^M
poignée^F pistolet^M
Pistolengriff^M
impugnatura^F a pistola^F

cord sleeve
protector^M del cable^M
manchon^M du cordon^M
Kabelmantel^M
manicotto^M del cordone^M

soldering iron
soldador^M
fer^M à souder
Lötkolben^M
saldatore^M elettrico

solder
estaño^M de soldar
soudure^F
Lötzinn^M
filo^M per saldatura^F

tip cleaners
limpiador^M de boquillas^F
aiguilles^F de nettoyage^M
Düsenreiniger^M
alesatori^M per la pulizia^F degli ugelli^M

welding curtain
biombo^M para soldar
écran^M de soudeur^M
Schutzschirm^M
schermo^M di protezione^F

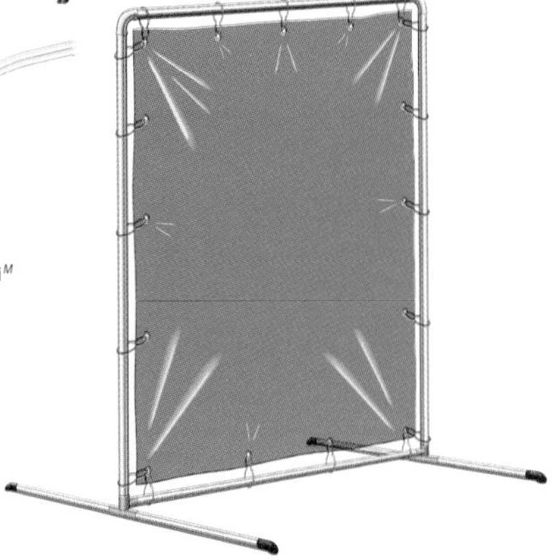

striker
encendedor^M
briquet^M
Anzünder^M
acciarino^M

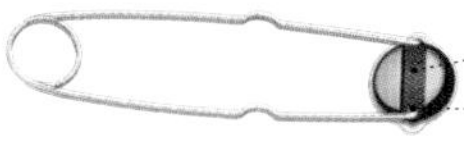

friction strip
frotador^M
frottoir^M
Reibfläche^F
striscia^F di sfregamento^M

flint
pedernal^M
pierre^F
Feuerstein^M
pietra^F focaia

arc welding
equipo^M de soldadura^F eléctrica
soudage^M à l'arc^M
Elektroschweißen^N
saldatura^F ad arco^M

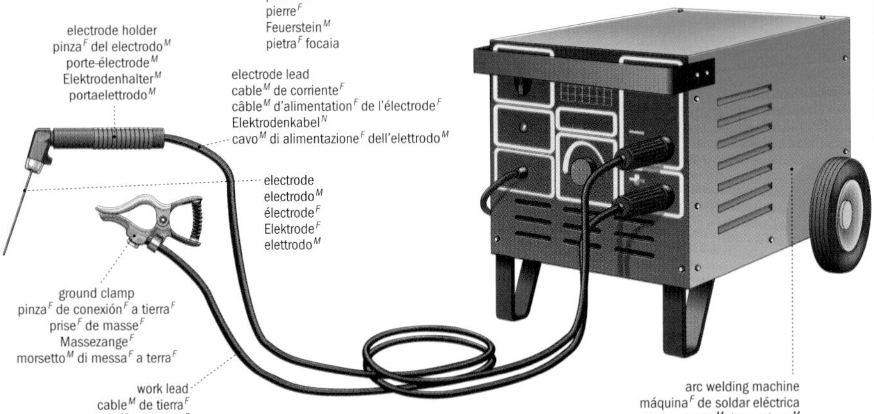

electrode holder
pinza^F del electrodo^M
porte-électrode^M
Elektrodenhalter^M
portaelettrodo^M

electrode lead
cable^M de corriente^F
câble^M d'alimentation^F de l'électrode^F
Elektrodenkabel^N
cavo^M di alimentazione^F dell'elettrodo^M

electrode
electrodo^M
électrode^F
Elektrode^F
elettrodo^M

ground clamp
pinza^F de conexión^F a tierra^F
prise^F de masse^F
Massezange^F
morsetto^M di messa^F a terra^F

work lead
cable^M de tierra^F
câble^M de masse^F
Massekabel^N
cavo^M di messa^F a terra^F

arc welding machine
máquina^F de soldar eléctrica
poste^M de soudage^M
Schweißtransformator^M
saldatrice^F ad arco^M

protective clothing
ropa^F de protección^M
équipement^M de protection^F
Schutzkleidung^F
abbigliamento^M antinfortunistico

goggles
gafas^F protectoras
lunettes^F
Schutzbrille^F
occhiali^M di protezione^F

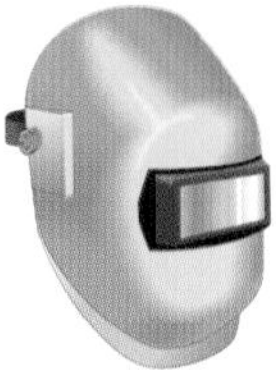

face shield
careta^F
casque^M
Gesichtsschutz^M
maschera^F da saldatore^M

hand shield
careta^F de mano^F
écran^M à main^F
Handschild^N
schermo^M a impugnatura^F

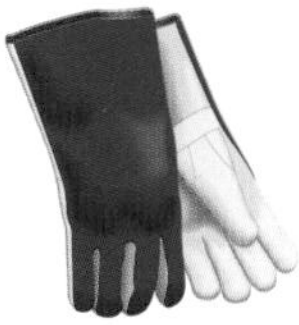

gauntlets
guantes^M
gant^M à crispin^M
fünffingriger Schweißerhandschuh^M
guanti^M di protezione^F

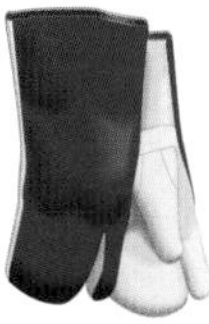

mittens
manoplas^F
moufle^F ; *mitaine^F*
Fausthandschuh^M
manopole^F

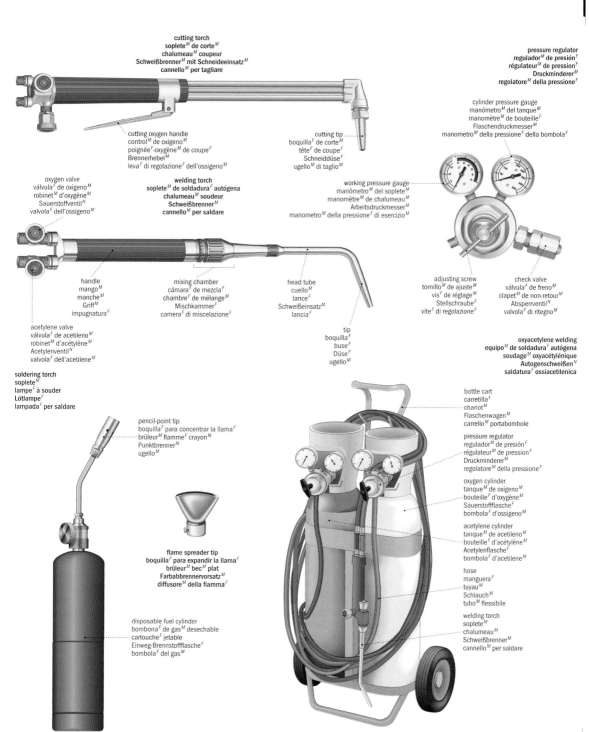

cutting torch
soplete^M de corte^M
chalumeau^M coupeur
Schweißbrenner^M mit Schneideeinsatz^M
cannello^M per tagliare

pressure regulator
regulador^F de presión^F
régulateur^M de pression^F
Druckminderer^M
regolatore^M della pressione^F

cutting oxygen handle
control^M de oxígeno^M
poignée^F-oxygène^M de coupe^F
Brennerhebel^M
leva^F di regolazione^F dell'ossigeno^M

cutting tip
boquilla^F de corte^M
tête^F de coupe^F
Schneiddüse^F
ugello^M di taglio^M

cylinder pressure gauge
manómetro^M del tanque^M
manomètre^M de bouteille^F
Flaschendruckmesser^M
manometro^M della pressione^F della bombola^F

oxygen valve
válvula^F de oxígeno^M
robinet^M d'oxygène^M
Sauerstoffventil^N
valvola^F dell'ossigeno^M

welding torch
soplete^M de soldadura^F autógena
chalumeau^M soudeur
Schweißbrenner^M
cannello^M per saldare

working pressure gauge
manómetro^M del soplete^M
manomètre^M de chalumeau^M
Arbeitsdruckmesser^M
manometro^M della pressione^F di esercizio^M

handle
mango^M
manche^M
Griff^M
impugnatura^F

mixing chamber
cámara^F de mezcla^F
chambre^F de mélange^M
Mischkammer^F
camera^F di miscelazione^F

head tube
cuello^M
lance^F
Schweißeinsatz^M
lancia^F

adjusting screw
tornillo^M de ajuste^M
vis^F de réglage^F
Stellschraube^F
vite^F di regolazione^F

check valve
válvula^F de freno^M
clapet^M de non-retour^M
Absperrventil^N
valvola^F di ritegno^M

acetylene valve
válvula^F de acetileno^M
robinet^M d'acétylène^M
Acetylenventil^N
valvola^F dell'acetilene^M

tip
boquilla^F
buse^F
Düse^F
ugello^M

oxyacetylene welding
equipo^M de soldadura^F autógena
soudage^M oxyacétylénique
Autogenschweißen^N
saldatura^F ossiacetilenica

soldering torch
soplete^M
lampe^F à souder
Lötlampe^F
lampada^F per saldare

pencil-point tip
boquilla^F para concentrar la llama^F
brûleur^F flamme^F crayon^M
Punktbrenner^M
ugello^M

bottle cart
carretilla^F
chariot^M
Flaschenwagen^M
carrello^M portabombole

pressure regulator
regulador^F de presión^F
régulateur^M de pression^F
Druckminderer^M
regolatore^M della pressione^F

oxygen cylinder
tanque^M de oxígeno^M
bouteille^F d'oxygène^M
Sauerstoffflasche^F
bombola^F d'ossigeno^M

acetylene cylinder
tanque^M de acetileno^M
bouteille^F d'acétylène^M
Acetylenflasche^F
bombola^F d'acetilene^M

flame spreader tip
boquilla^F para expandir la llama^F
brûleur^M bec^M plat
Farbabbrennervorsatz^M
diffusore^M della fiamma^F

hose
manguera^F
tuyau^M
Schlauch^M
tubo^M flessibile

welding torch
soplete^M
chalumeau^M
Schweißbrenner^M
cannello^M per saldare

disposable fuel cylinder
bombona^F de gas^M desechable
cartouche^F jetable
Einweg-Brennstoffflasche^F
bombola^F del gas^M

painting

mantenimiento^M de pinturas^F | peinture^F d'entretien^M | Anstreichen^N und Lackieren^N | verniciatura^F: manutenzione^F

spray paint gun
pistola^F de pintar
pistolet^M à peinture^F
Spritzpistole^F
pistola^F per verniciatura^F a spruzzo^M

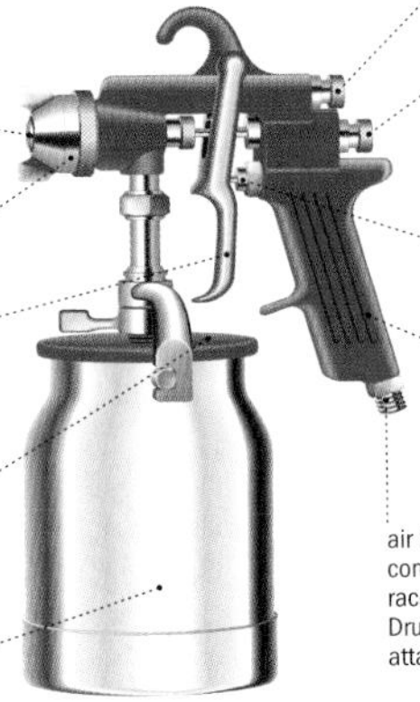

nozzle
boquilla^F
buse^F à fluide^M
Düse^F
ugello^M

air cap
anillo^M de ajuste^F
bouchon^M d'air^M
Lufteinlass^M
cappelletto^M dell'aria^F

trigger
gatillo^M
gâchette^F
Druckabzug^M
grilletto^M

vent hole
orificio^M de entrada^F de aire^M
orifice^M d'aération^F
Entlüftung^F
sfiatatoio^M

container
depósito^M de pintura^F
godet^M
Behälter^M
serbatoio^M

air compressor
compresor^M de aire^M
compresseur^M d'air^M
Kompressor^M
compressore^M d'aria^F

spreader adjustment screw
válvula^F de ajuste^M
soupape^F de réglage^M du fluide^M
Einstellventil^N für die Strahlbreite^F
vite^F di regolazione^F dello spruzzo^M

fluid adjustment screw
regulador^M de fluidos^M
réglage^M du pointeau^M du fluide^M
Einstellventil^N für die Flüssigkeitsmenge^F
vite^F di regolazione^F del fluido^M

air valve
válvula^F de aire^M
soupape^F à air^M
Luftventil^N
valvola^F dell'aria^F

gun body
empuñadura^F de pistola^F
corps^M du pistolet^M
Pistolengriff^M
impugnatura^F della pistola^F

air hose connection
conexión^F para la manguera^F de aire^M
raccord^M d'arrivée^F d'air^M
Druckluftanschluss^M
attacco^M del tubo^M dell'aria^F

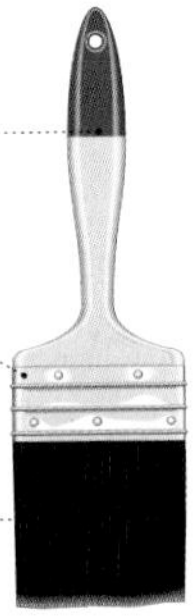

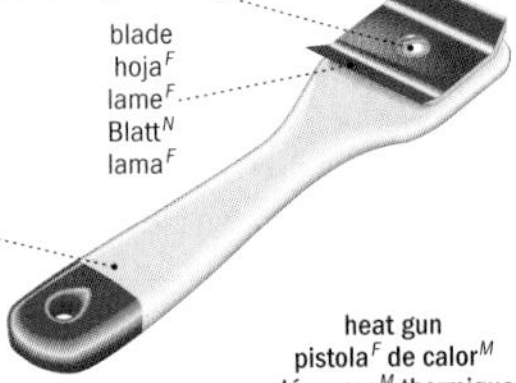

pump
bomba^F
pompe^F
Pumpe^F
pompa^F

motor
motor^M
moteur^M
Motor^M
motore^M

handle
empuñadura^F
poignée^F
Griff^M
impugnatura^F

air tank
tanque^M de aire^M
réservoir^M
Druckluftbehälter^M
serbatoio^M d'aria^F

wheel
rueda^F
roue^F
Rad^N
ruota^F

tray
bandeja^F de pintura^F
bac^M
Wanne^F
vaschetta^F

brush
brocha^F
pinceau^M
Malerpinsel^M
pennello^M

handle
mango^M
manche^M
Griff^M
manico^M

ferrule
collar^M
virole^F
Stock^M
ghiera^F

bristles
cerdas^F
soies^F
Borsten^F
setole^F

scraper
rasqueta^F
grattoir^M
Schaber^M
raschietto^M

knurled bolt
tornillo^M
bouton^M moleté
Rändelbolzen^M
bullone^M zigrinato

blade
hoja^F
lame^F
Blatt^N
lama^F

handle
mango^M
manche^M
Griff^M
manico^M

heat gun
pistola^F de calor^M
décapeur^M thermique
Heißluftpistole^F
pistola^F per sverniciatura^F

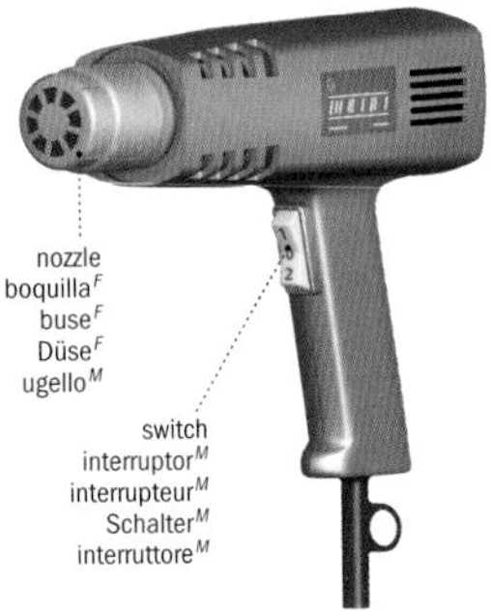

nozzle
boquilla^F
buse^F
Düse^F
ugello^M

switch
interruptor^M
interrupteur^M
Schalter^M
interruttore^M

paint roller
rodillo^M de pintor^M
rouleau^M
Farbroller^M
rullo^M

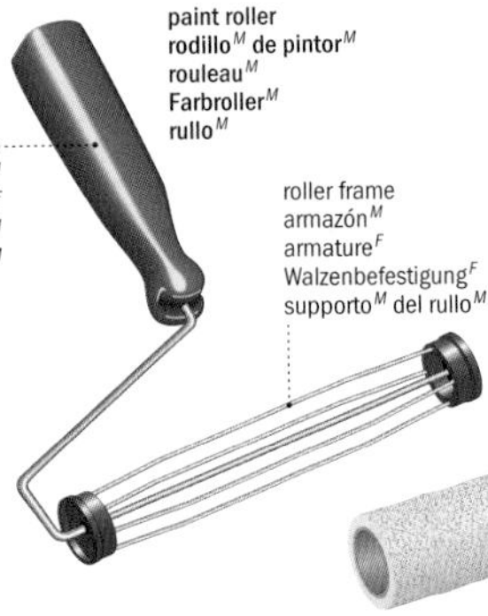

handle
mango^M
poignée^F
Griff^M
manico^M

roller frame
armazón^M
armature^F
Walzenbefestigung^F
supporto^M del rullo^M

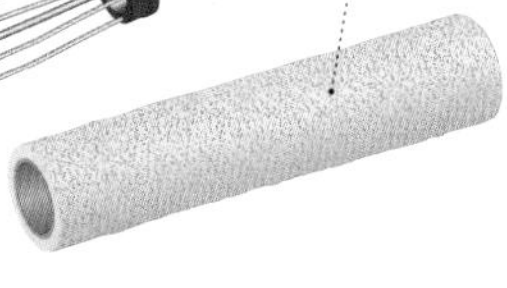

roller cover
rodillo^M
manchon^M
Walze^F
rullo^M

ladders and stepladders

escaleras^F de mano^F | échelles^F et escabeaux^M | Leitern^F und Stehleitern^F | scale^F e scale^F a libretto^M

foldaway ladder
escalera^F extensible de buhardilla^F
échelle^F escamotable
Dachbodenleiter^F
scala^F retrattile

straight ladder
escalera^F común
échelle^F droite
Anlegeleiter^F
scala^F a pioli^M

hook ladder
escalera^F de gancho^M
échelle^F à crochets^M
Einhängeleiter^F
scala^F a pioli^M con ganci^M

extension ladder
escalera^F extensible
échelle^F coulissante
Ausziehleiter^F
scala^F estensibile

rung
travesaño^M
échelon^M
Sprosse^F
piolo^M

side rail
larguero^M
montant^M
Holm^M
staggio^M

pulley
polea^F
poulie^F
Seilzug^M
puleggia^F

locking device
dispositivo^M de bloqueo^M
dispositif^M de blocage^M
Sprossenarretierung^F
dispositivo^M di blocco^M

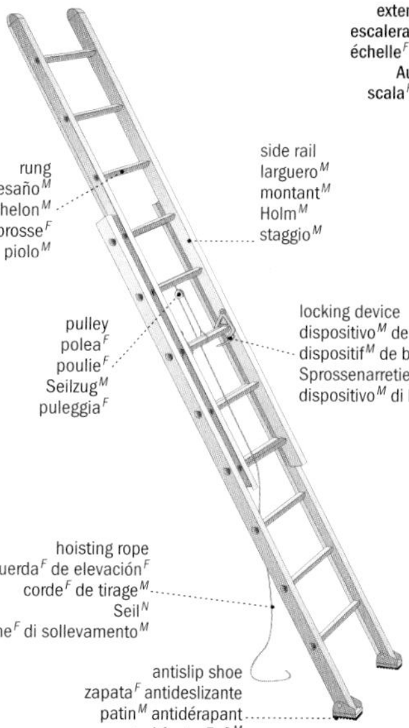

ladder scaffold
andamio^M sobre ruedas^F
échelle^F d'échafaudage^M
Leitergerüst^N
trabattello^M

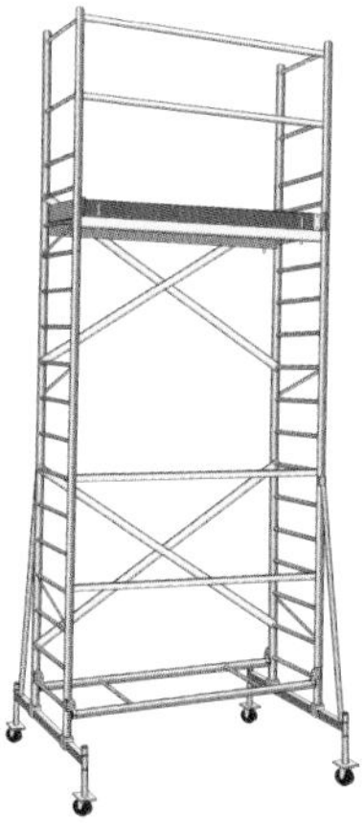

rope ladder
escalera^F de cuerda^F
échelle^F de corde^F
Strickleiter^F
biscaglina^F

fruit-picking ladder
escalera^F de recolección^F de fruta^F
échelle^F fruitière
landwirtschaftliche Nutzleiter^F
scala^F per agricoltura^F

hoisting rope
cuerda^F de elevación^F
corde^F de tirage^M
Seil^N
fune^F di sollevamento^M

antislip shoe
zapata^F antideslizante
patin^M antidérapant
rutschfester Fuß^M
piedino^M snodato antiscivolo

rolling ladder
escalera^F rodante
échelle^F roulante
Rollenleiter^F
scala^F a palchetto^M con ruote^F

multipurpose ladder
escalera^F multiuso
échelle^F transformable
Mehrzweckleiter^F
scala^F multiuso

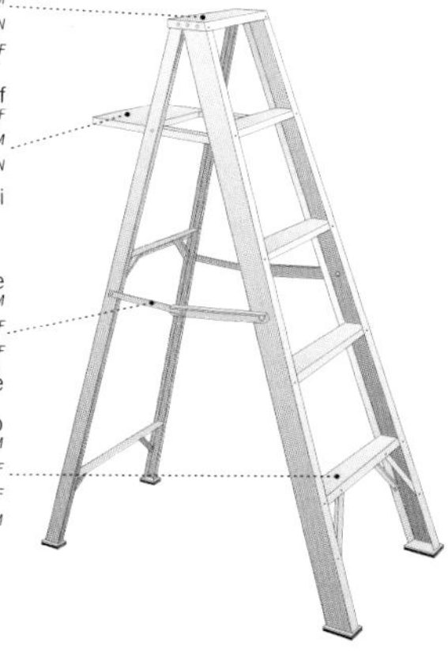

step stool
taburete^M escalera
tabouret^M-escabeau^M
Tritthocker^M
scala^F sgabello^M

stepladder
escalera^F de tijera^F
escabeau^M
Stehleiter^F
scala^F a libretto^M

platform ladder
escalera^F de plataforma^F
marchepied^M
Trittleiter^F
scala^F con piattaforma^F

top
parte^F superior
plateau^M
Podest^N
cima^F

tool shelf
bandeja^F para herramientas^F
tablette^F porte-outil^M
Arbeitsbrett^N
mensola^F portautensili

brace
tirante^M
entretoise^F
Ausklapparretierung^F
braccio^M distanziatore

step
peldaño^M
marche^F
Stufe^F
gradino^M

safety rail
barandilla^F
garde-corps^M
Sicherheitsholm^M
barra^F d'appoggio^M

frame
armazón^M
piètement^M
Gestell^N
montante^M

rubber tip
zapata^F de goma^F
embout^M
Gummistöpsel^M
piedino^M di gomma^F

shelf
entrepaño^M
tablette^F
Ablage^F
ripiano^M

platform
plataforma^F
plate-forme^F
Plattform^F
piattaforma^F

step
peldaño^M
marche^F
Tritt^M
gradino^M

DO-IT-YOURSELF AND GARDENING

321

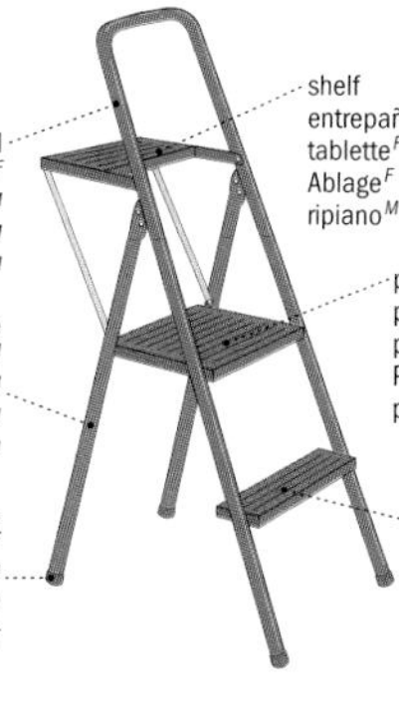

pleasure garden

jardín^M | jardin^M d'agrément^M | Ziergarten^M | giardino^M

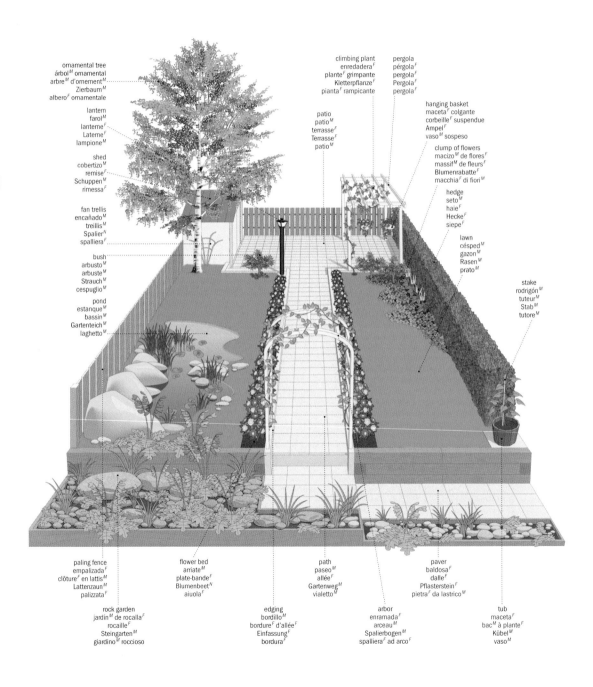

ornamental tree
árbol^M ornamental
arbre^M d'ornement^M
Zierbaum^M
albero^F ornamentale

lantern
farol^M
lanterne^F
Laterne^F
lampione^M

shed
cobertizo^M
remise^F
Schuppen^M
rimessa^F

fan trellis
encañado^M
treillis^M
Spalier^N
spalliera^F

bush
arbusto^M
arbuste^M
Strauch^M
cespuglio^M

pond
estanque^M
bassin^M
Gartenteich^M
laghetto^M

climbing plant
enredadera^F
plante^F grimpante
Kletterpflanze^F
pianta^F rampicante

pergola
pérgola^F
pergola^F
Pergola^F
pergola^F

patio
patio^M
terrasse^F
Terrasse^F
patio^M

hanging basket
maceta^F colgante
corbeille^F suspendue
Ampel^F
vaso^M sospeso

clump of flowers
macizo^M de flores^F
massif^M de fleurs^F
Blumenrabatte^F
macchia^F di fiori^M

hedge
seto^M
haie^F
Hecke^F
siepe^F

lawn
césped^M
gazon^M
Rasen^M
prato^M

stake
rodrigón^M
tuteur^M
Stab^M
tutore^M

paling fence
empalizada^F
clôture^F en lattis^M
Lattenzaun^M
palizzata^F

flower bed
arriate^M
plate-bande^F
Blumenbeet^N
aiuola^F

path
paseo^M
allée^F
Gartenweg^M
vialetto^M

paver
baldosa^F
dalle^F
Pflasterstein^F
pietra^F da lastrico^M

rock garden
jardín^M de rocalla^F
rocaille^F
Steingarten^M
giardino^M roccioso

edging
bordillo^M
bordure^F d'allée^F
Einfassung^F
bordura^F

arbor
enramada^F
arceau^M
Spalierbogen^M
spalliera^F ad arco^F

tub
maceta^F
bac^M à plante^F
Kübel^M
vaso^M

miscellaneous equipment

equipamiento^M vario | équipement^M divers | verschiedene Geräte^N | attrezzatura^F varia

motorized earth auger
taladro^M de motor^M
tarière^F motorisée
Erdbohrer^M
trivella^F a motore^M per terreno^M

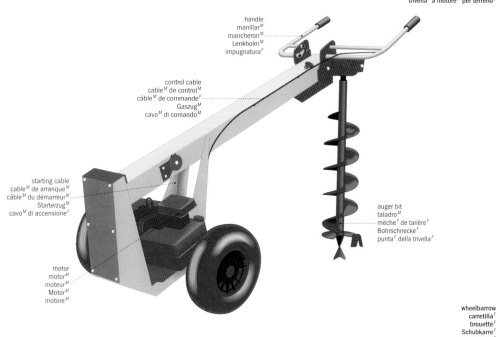

handle
manillar^M
mancheron^M
Lenkholm^M
impugnatura^F

control cable
cable^M de control^M
câble^M de commande^F
Gaszug^M
cavo^M di comando^M

starting cable
cable^M de arranque^M
câble^M du démarreur^M
Starterzug^M
cavo^M di accensione^F

auger bit
taladro^M
mèche^F de tarière^F
Bohrschnecke^F
punta^F della trivella^F

motor
motor^M
moteur^M
Motor^M
motore^M

wheelbarrow
carretilla^F
brouette^F
Schubkarre^F
carriola^F

compost bin
cajón^M de abono^M compuesto
bac^M à compost^M
Kompostkiste^F
contenitore^M della composta^F

tray
caja^F
caisse^F
Mulde^F
cassone^M

handle
brazo^M
brancard^M
Griff^M
stanga^F

leg
pata^F
pied^M
Stütze^F
piede^M

wheel
rueda^F
roue^F
Rad^N
ruota^F

seeding and planting tools

herramientas^F para sembrar y plantar | outils^M pour semer et planter | Werkzeuge^N zum Säen^N und Pflanzen^N | attrezzi^M per seminare e piantare

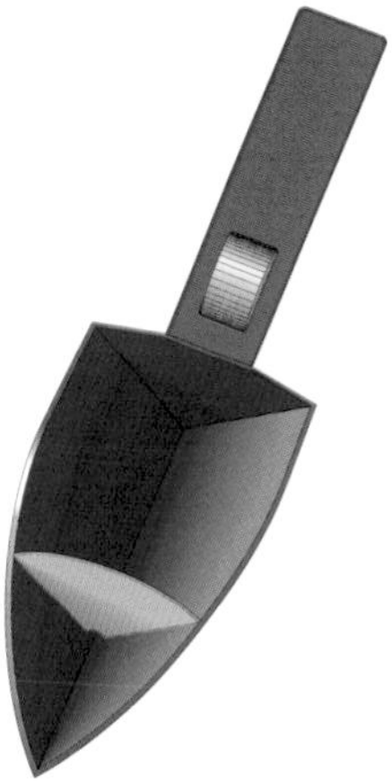

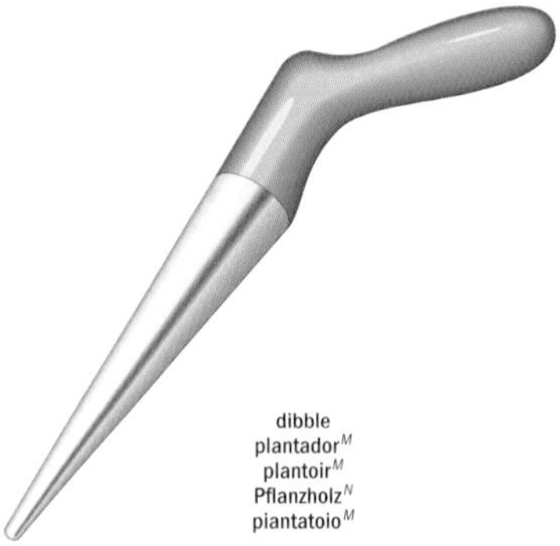

dibble
plantador^M
plantoir^M
Pflanzholz^N
piantatoio^M

seeder
sembradora^F de mano^F
semoir^M à main^F
Säkelle^F
seminatoio^M a mano^F

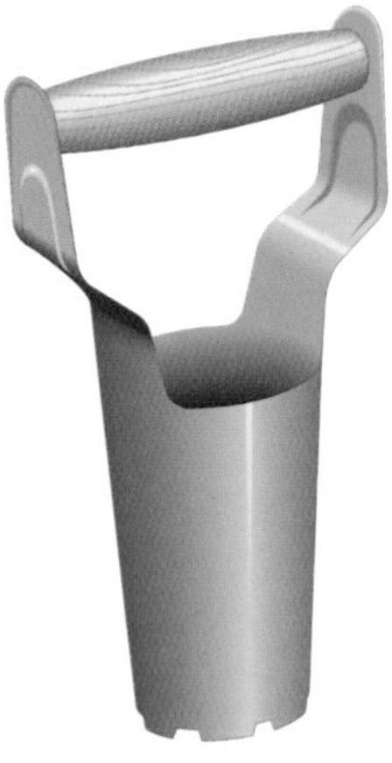

bulb dibble
plantador^M de bulbos^M
plantoir^M à bulbes^M
Pflanzlochstecher^M
piantabulbi^M

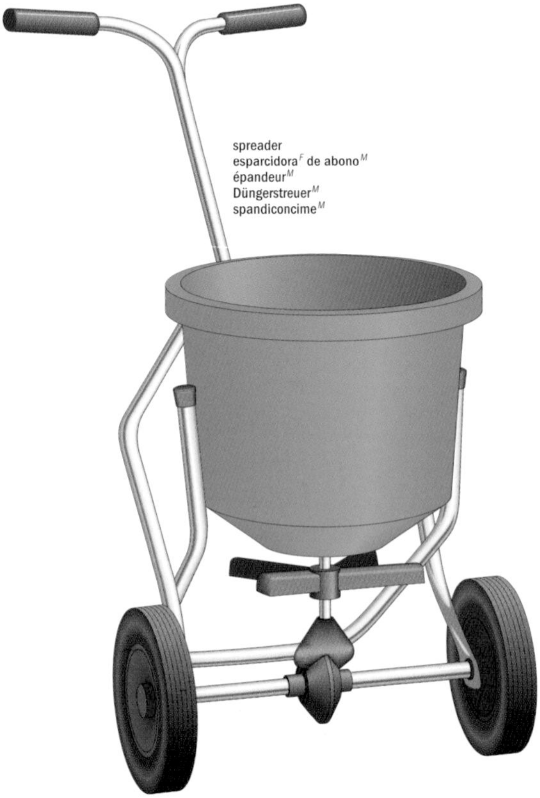

spreader
esparcidora^F de abono^M
épandeur^M
Düngerstreuer^M
spandiconcime^M

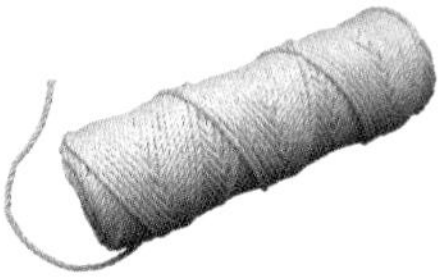

garden line
cuerda^F
cordeau^M
Pflanzschnur^F
filo^M da giardino^M

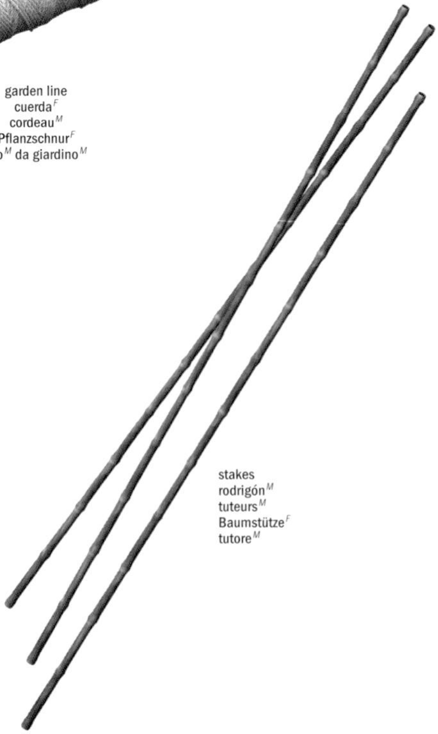

stakes
rodrigón^M
tuteurs^M
Baumstütze^F
tutore^M

hand tools

juego^M de pequeñas herramientas^F | jeu^M de petits outils^M | Handwerkzeuge^N | attrezzi^M per piccoli lavori^M di giardinaggio^M

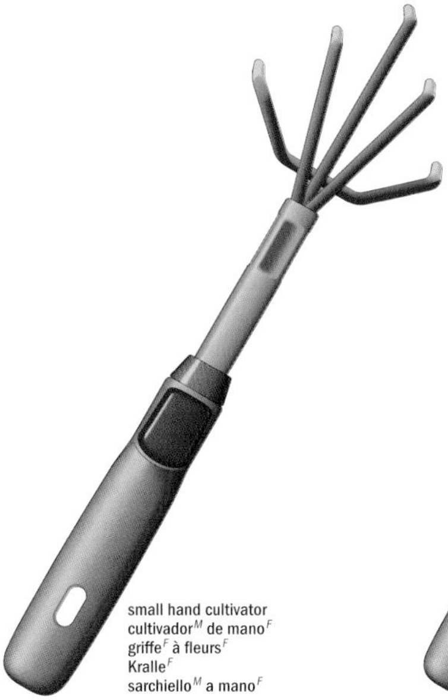

small hand cultivator
cultivador^M de mano^F
griffe^F à fleurs^F
Kralle^F
sarchiello^M a mano^F

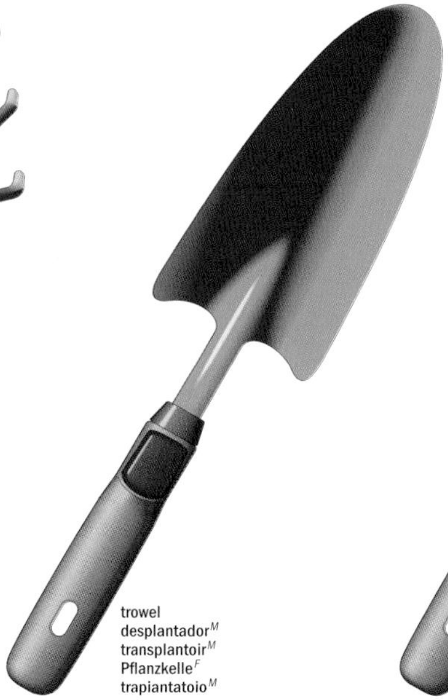

trowel
desplantador^M
transplantoir^M
Pflanzkelle^F
trapiantatoio^M

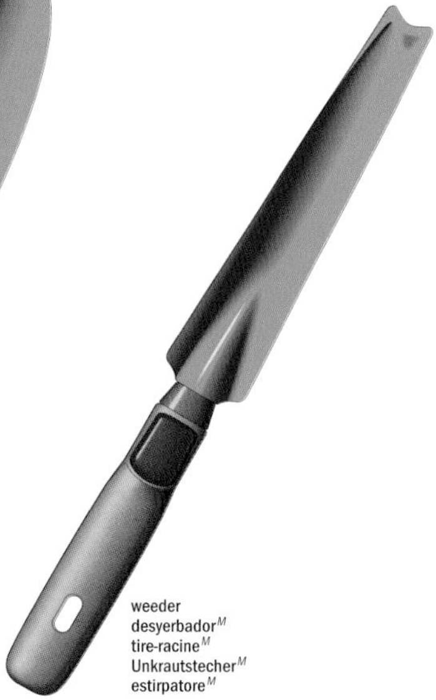

weeder
desyerbador^M
tire-racine^M
Unkrautstecher^M
estirpatore^M

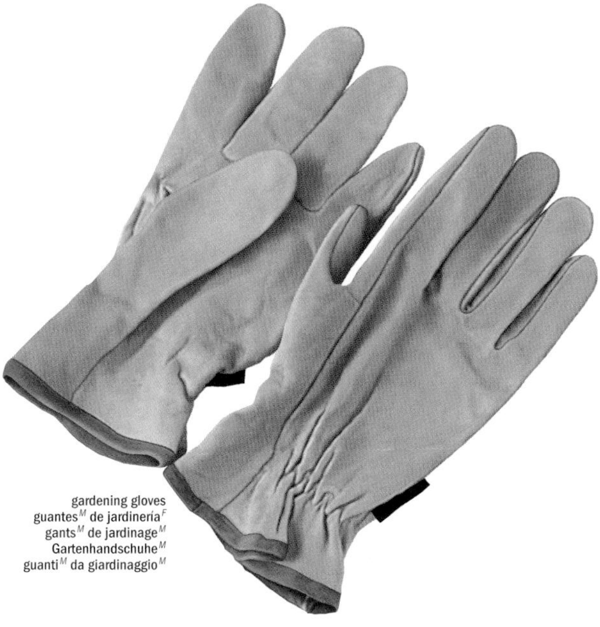

gardening gloves
guantes^M de jardineria^F
gants^M de jardinage^M
Gartenhandschuhe^M
guanti^M da giardinaggio^M

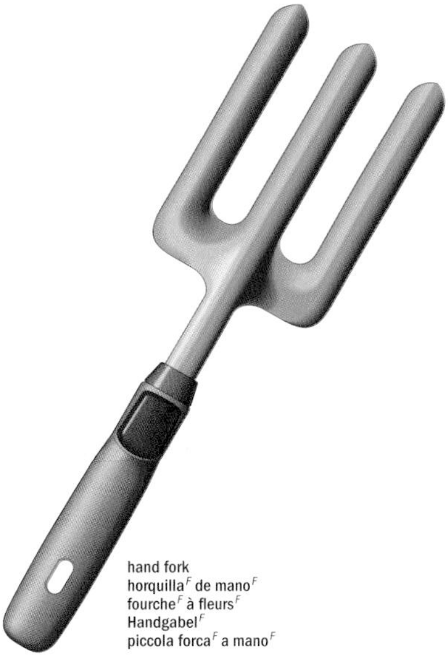

hand fork
horquilla^F de mano^F
fourche^F à fleurs^F
Handgabel^F
piccola forca^F a mano^F

DO-IT-YOURSELF AND GARDENING

tools for loosening the earth

herramientas^F para remover la tierra^F | outils^M pour remuer la terre^F | Geräte^N zur Erdbewegung^F | attrezzi^M per smuovere la terra^F

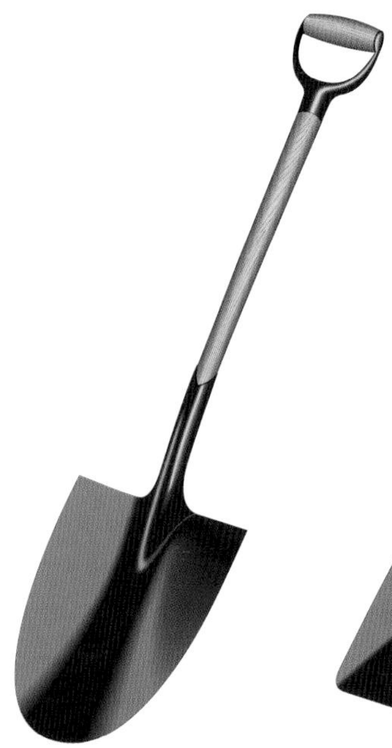

shovel
pala^F
pelle^F
Grabschaufel^F
badile^M

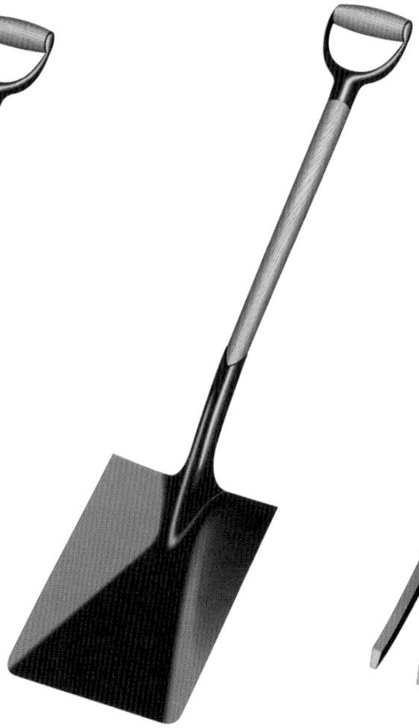

spade
laya^F
bêche^F
Spaten^M
vanga^F

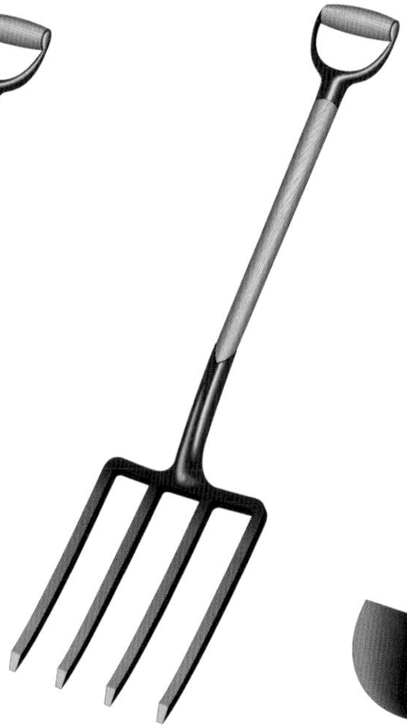

garden fork
horca^F
fourche^F à bêcher
Grabgabel^F
forcone^F

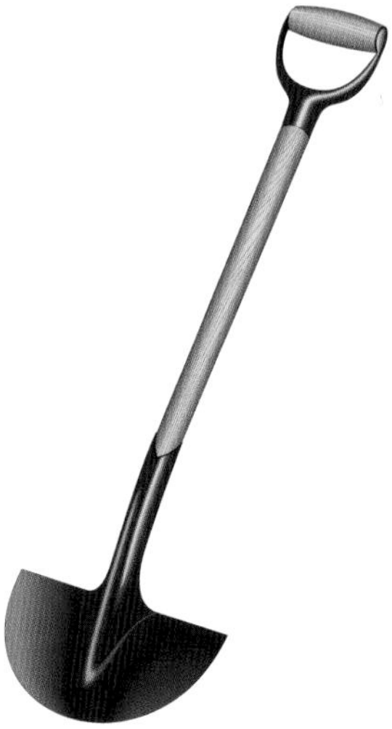

lawn edger
cuchilla^F para delimitar el césped^M
coupe-bordures^M
Kantenstecher^M
tagliabordi^M

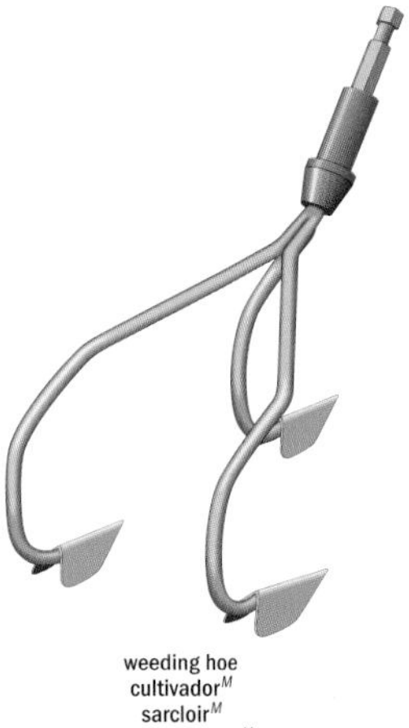

weeding hoe
cultivador^M
sarcloir^M
Handkultivator^M
coltivatore^M

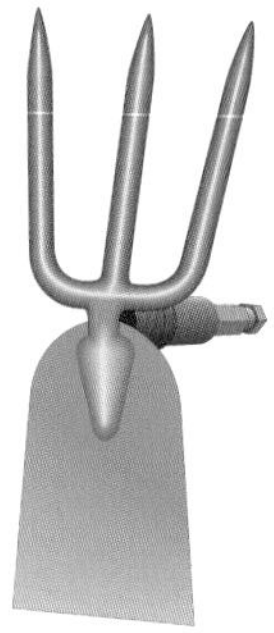

hoe-fork
azuela^F
serfouette^F
Kombihacke^F
zappetta^F tridente

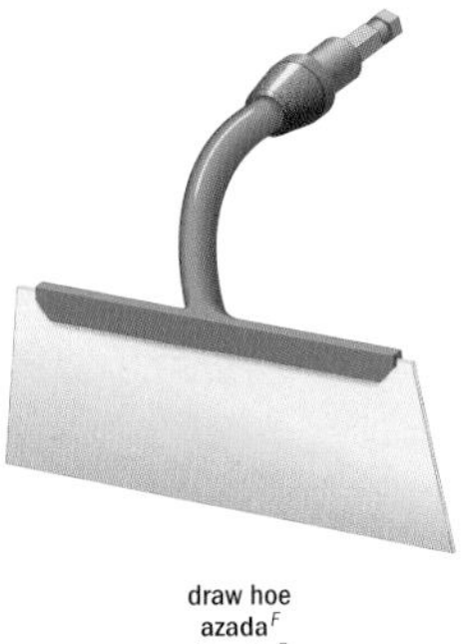

draw hoe
azada^F
binette^F
Rübenhacke^F
sarchiello^M

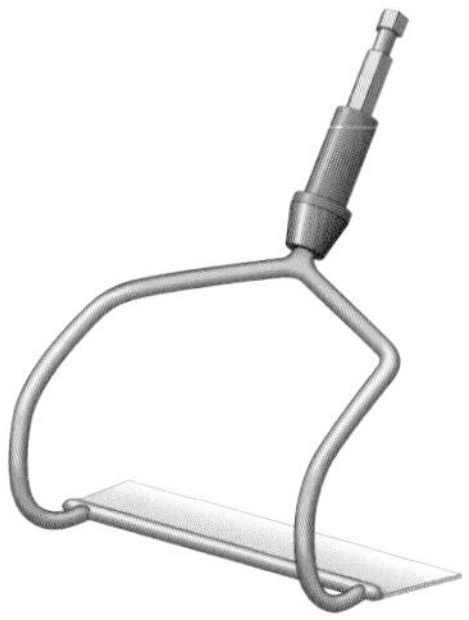

scuffle hoe
azada^F de doble filo^M
ratissoire^F
Ziehhacke^F
sarchio^M

DO-IT-YOURSELF AND GARDENING

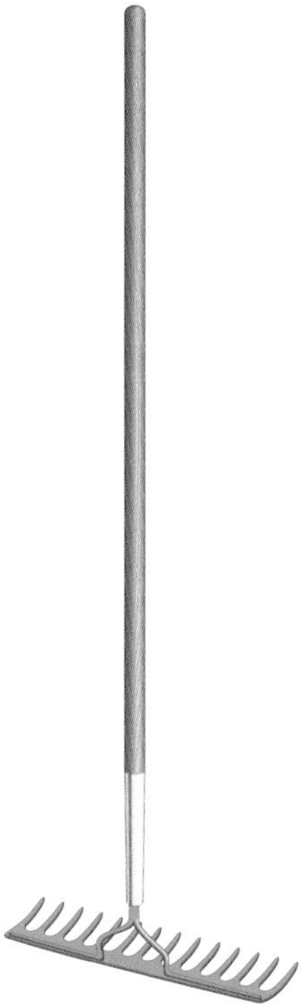

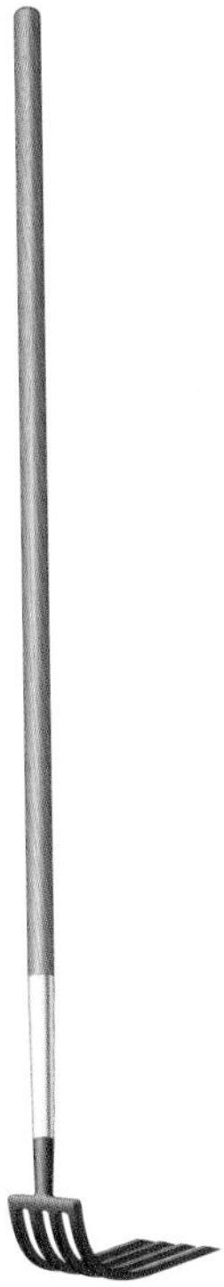

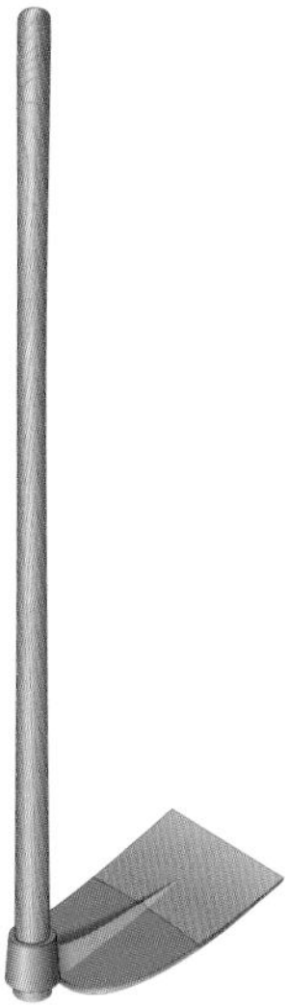

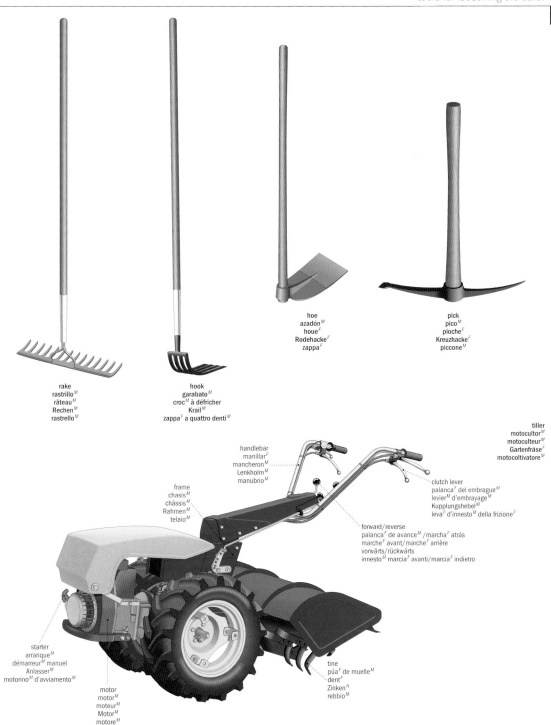

hoe
azadón^M
houe^F
Rodehacke^F
zappa^F

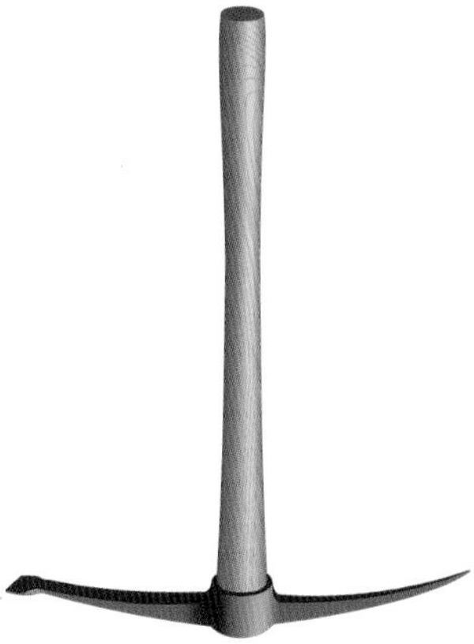

pick
pico^M
pioche^F
Kreuzhacke^F
piccone^M

rake
rastrillo^M
râteau^M
Rechen^M
rastrello^M

hook
garabato^M
croc^M à défricher
Krail^M
zappa^F a quattro denti^M

tiller
motocultor^M
motoculteur^M
Gartenfräse^F
motocoltivatore^M

handlebar
manillar^F
mancheron^M
Lenkholm^M
manubrio^M

frame
chasis^M
châssis^M
Rahmen^M
telaio^M

clutch lever
palanca^F del embrague^M
levier^M d'embrayage^M
Kupplungshebel^M
leva^F d'innesto^M della frizione^F

forward/reverse
palanca^F de avance^M /marcha^F atrás
marche^F avant/marche^F arrière
vorwärts/rückwärts
innesto^M marcia^F avanti/marcia^F indietro

starter
arranque^M
démarreur^M manuel
Anlasser^M
motorino^M d'avviamento^M

motor
motor^M
moteur^M
Motor^M
motore^M

tine
púa^F de muelle^M
dent^F
Zinken^N
rebbio^M

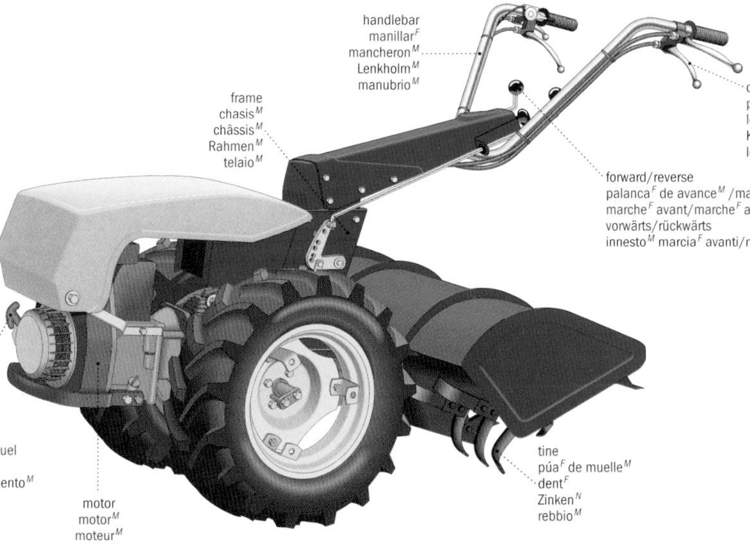

watering tools

herramientas^F para regar | outils^M pour arroser | Gießgeräte^N | attrezzi^M per annaffiare

hose trolley
carretilla^F para manguera^F
dévidoir^M sur roues^F
Schlauchwagen^M
carrello^M avvolgitubo

sprinkler hose
manguera^F de riego^M
tuyau^M perforé
Regnerschlauch^M
tubo^M per irrigazione^F

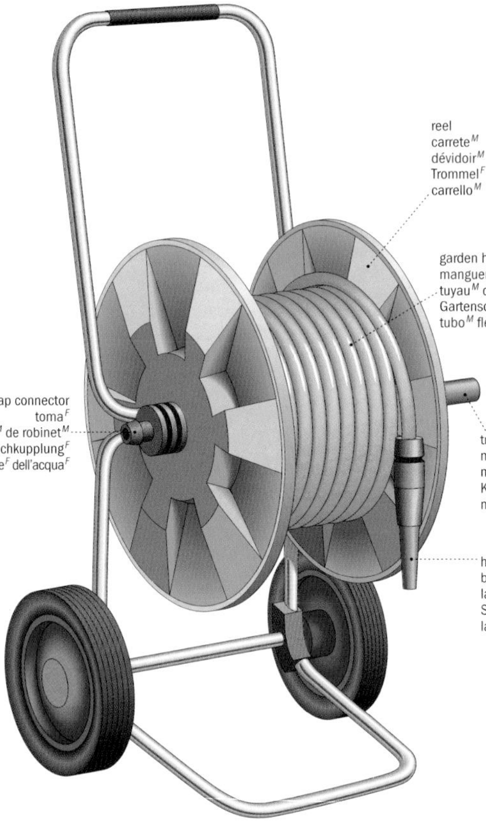

reel
carrete^M
dévidoir^M
Trommel^F
carrello^M

garden hose
manguera^F
tuyau^M d'arrosage^M
Gartenschlauch^M
tubo^M flessibile

tap connector
toma^F
raccord^M de robinet^M
Schlauchkupplung^F
attacco^M del tubo^M di alimentazione^F dell'acqua^F

trolley crank
manivela^F del carrete^M
manivelle^F
Kurbel^F
manovella^F

hose nozzle
boquilla^F
lance^F d'arrosage^M
Schlauchdüse^F
lancia^F

tank sprayer
pulverizador^M
pulvérisateur^M
Gartenspritze^F
atomizzatore^M

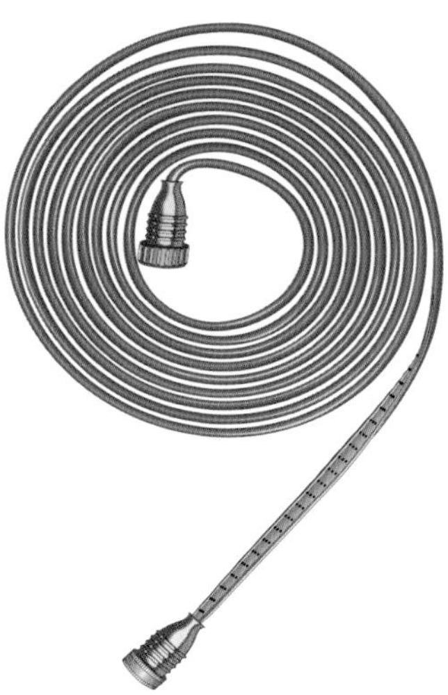

watering can
regadera^F
arrosoir^M
Gießkanne^F
annaffiatoio^M

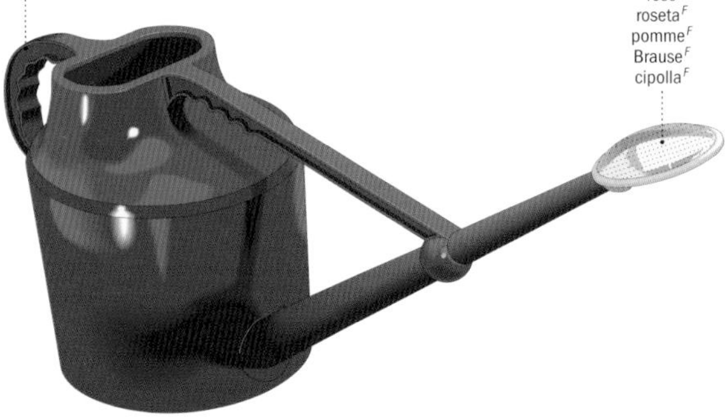

handle
asa^F
anse^F
Griff^M
manico^M

rose
roseta^F
pomme^F
Brause^F
cipolla^F

DO-IT-YOURSELF AND GARDENING

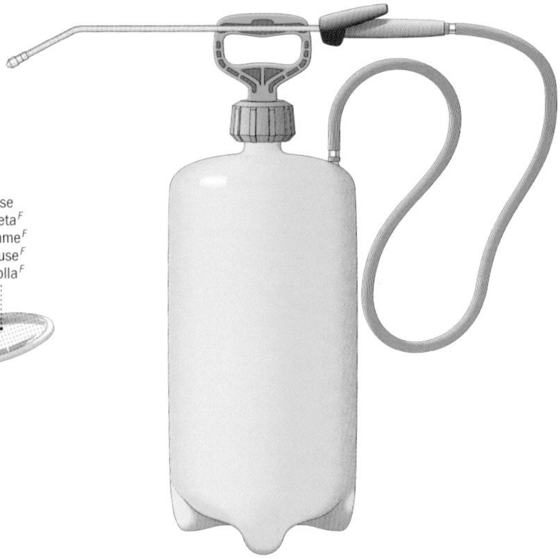

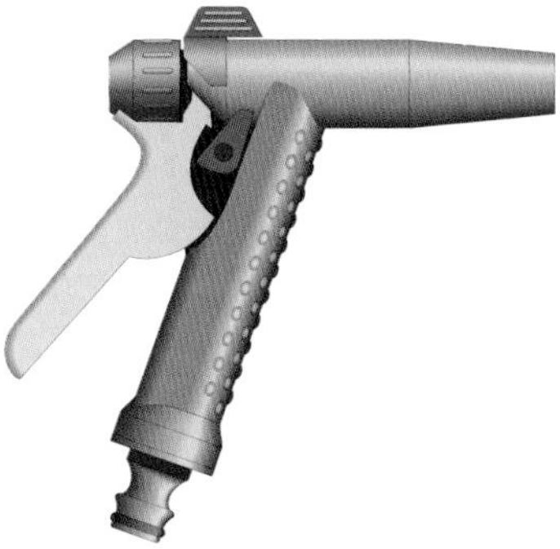

pistol nozzle
pistola^F pulverizadora
pistolet^M d'arrosage^M
Gießpistole^F
polverizzatore^M a pistola^F

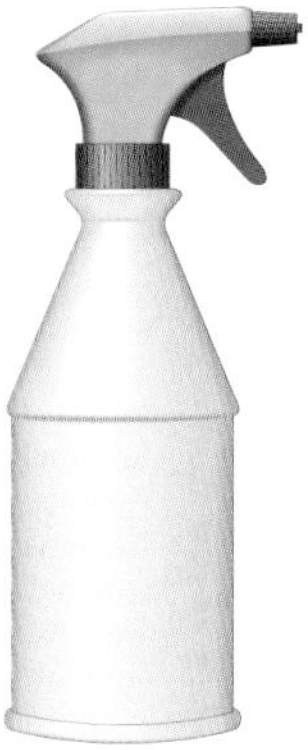

sprayer
pulverizador^M
vaporisateur^M
Sprühflasche^F
spruzzatore^M

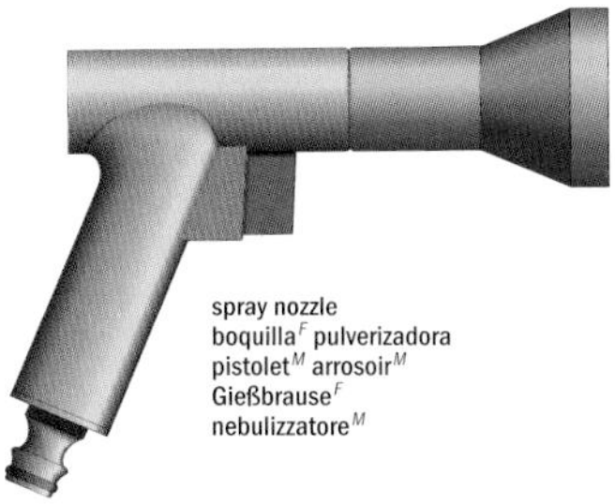

spray nozzle
boquilla^F pulverizadora
pistolet^M arrosoir^M
Gießbrause^F
nebulizzatore^M

arm
brazo^M
bras^M
Drehdüse^F
braccio^M

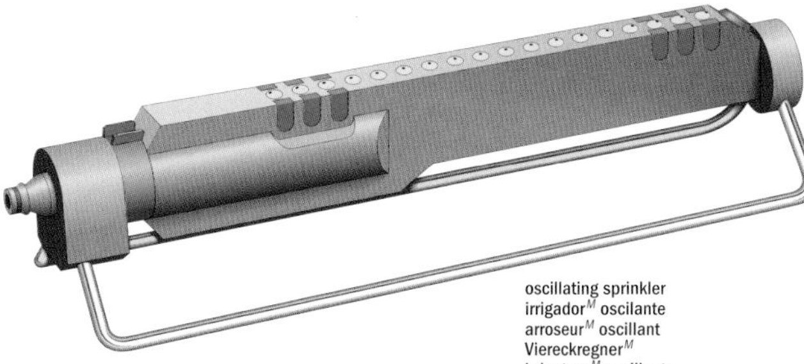

oscillating sprinkler
irrigador^M oscilante
arroseur^M oscillant
Vierecksregner^M
irrigatore^M oscillante

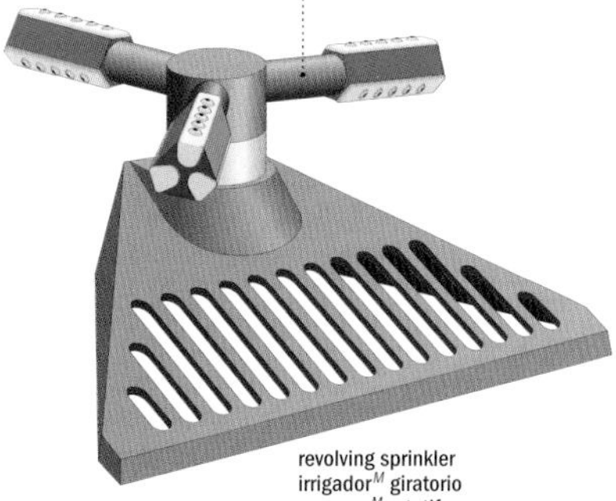

revolving sprinkler
irrigador^M giratorio
arroseur^M rotatif
Kreisregner^M
irrigatore^M rotativo a pioggia^F

metal arm
brazo^M metálico
balancier^M
Hammer^M
braccio^M metallico

nozzle
boquilla^F
buse^F
Düse^F
ugello^M

trip lever
disparador^M
bague^F de réglage^M
Stellring^M
anello^M di regolazione^F

diffuser pin
perno^M difusor
brise-jet^M
Zerstäuberstift^M
vite^F rompigetto

deflector
deflector^M
déflecteur^M
Strahlstörer^M
deflettore^M

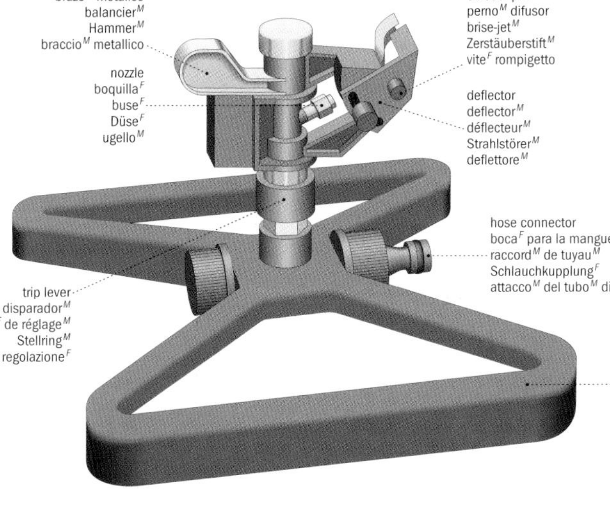

hose connector
boca^F para la manguera^F
raccord^M de tuyau^M
Schlauchkupplung^F
attacco^M del tubo^M di alimentazione^F dell'acqua^F

impulse sprinkler
irrigador^M de impulso^M
arroseur^M canon^M
Impulsregner^M
irrigatore^M a impulsi^M

sled
soporte^M
traineau^M
Fuß^M
slitta^F

pruning and cutting tools

herramientas^F para cortar | outils^M pour couper | Schneidwerkzeuge^N | attrezzi^M per potare e tagliare

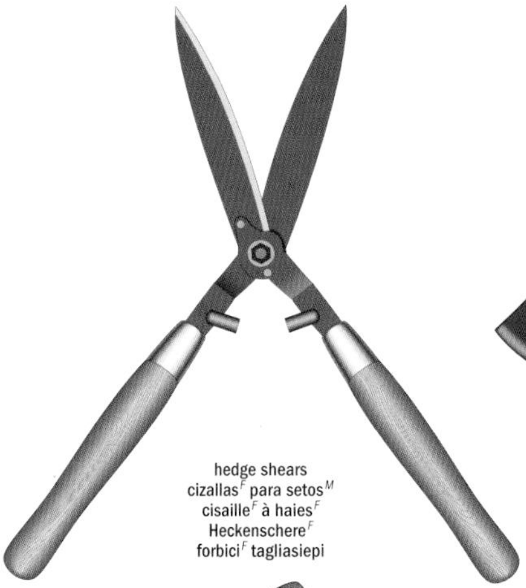

hedge shears
cizallas^F para setos^M
cisaille^F à haies^F
Heckenschere^F
forbici^F tagliasiepi

axe
hacha^F
hache^F
Axt^F
accetta^F

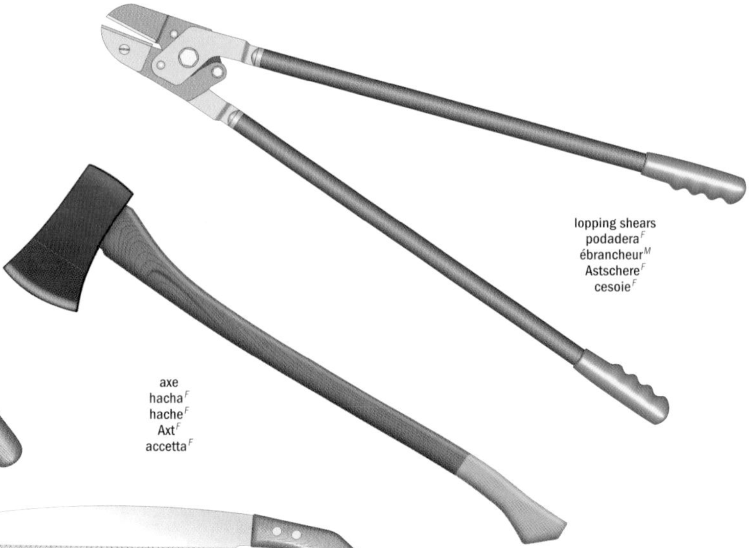

lopping shears
podadera^F
ébrancheur^M
Astschere^F
cesoie^F

pruning saw
sierra^F de podar
scie^F d'élagage^M
Baumsäge^F
sega^F da giardiniere^M

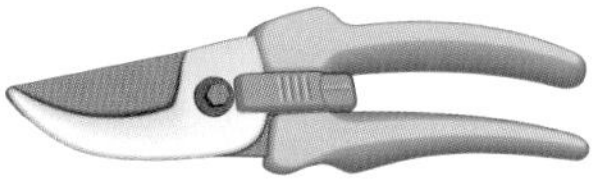

pruning shears
tijeras^F de podar
sécateur^M
Baumschere^F
cesoie^F da giardino^M

grafting knife
navaja^F de injertar
greffoir^M
Veredelungsmesser^N
innestatoio^M

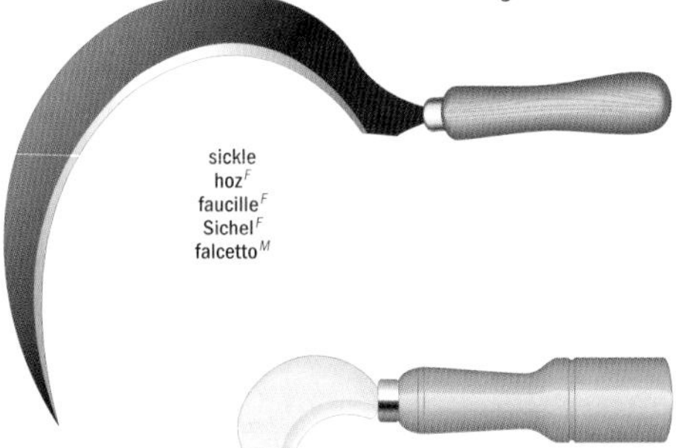

sickle
hoz^F
faucille^F
Sichel^F
falcetto^M

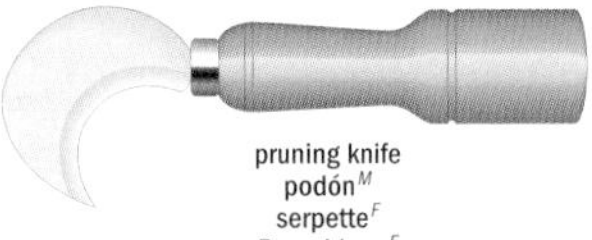

pruning knife
podón^M
serpette^F
Baumhippe^F
potatoio^M

tree pruner
podadera^F de árboles^M
échenilloir^M-élagueur^M
Raupenschere^F mit Teleskopstiel^M
svettatoio^M

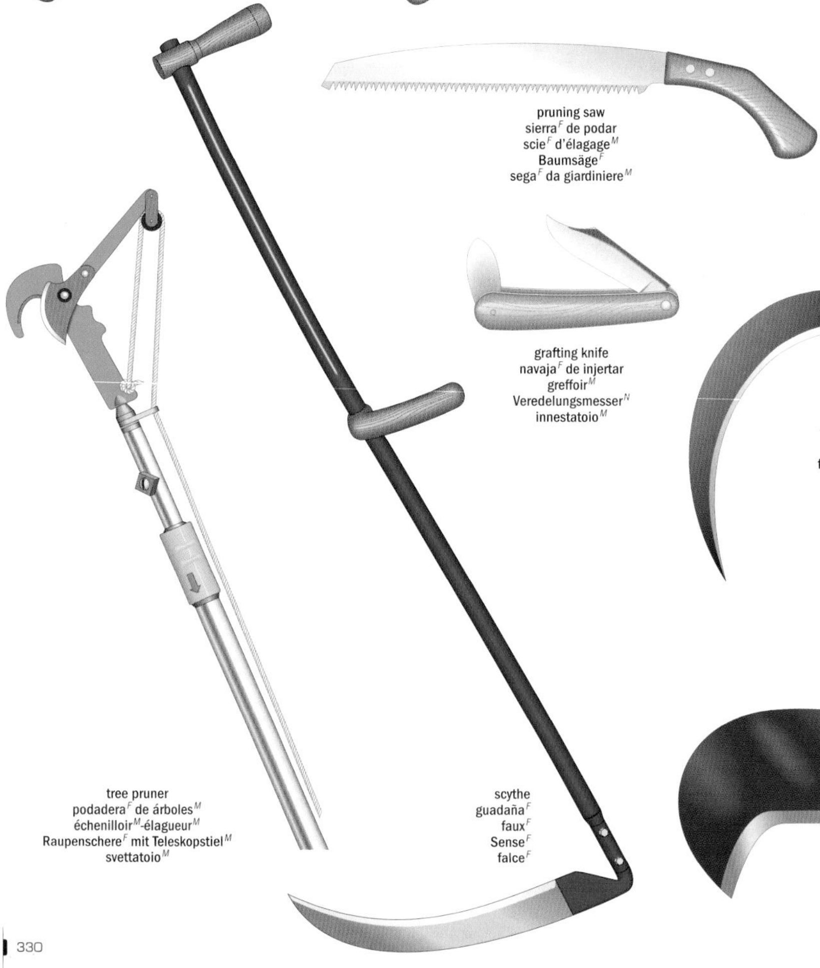

scythe
guadaña^F
faux^F
Sense^F
falce^F

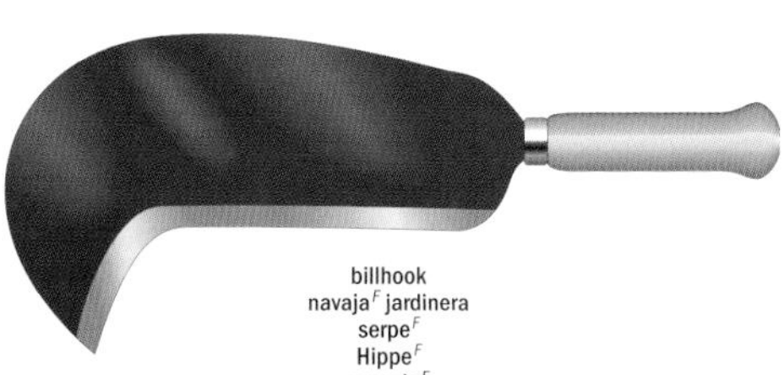

billhook
navaja^F jardinera
serpe^F
Hippe^F
roncola^F

DO-IT-YOURSELF AND GARDENING

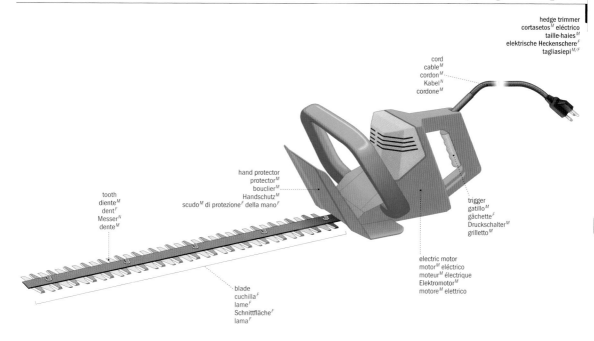

hedge trimmer
cortasetos^M eléctrico
taille-haies^M
elektrische Heckenschere^F
tagliasiepi^{M/F}

cord
cable^M
cordon^M
Kabel^N
cordone^M

hand protector
protector^M
bouclier^M
Handschutz^M
scudo^M di protezione^F della mano^F

trigger
gatillo^M
gâchette^F
Druckschalter^M
grilletto^M

tooth
diente^M
dent^F
Messer^N
dente^M

electric motor
motor^M eléctrico
moteur^M électrique
Elektromotor^M
motore^M elettrico

blade
cuchilla^F
lame^F
Schnittfläche^F
lama^F

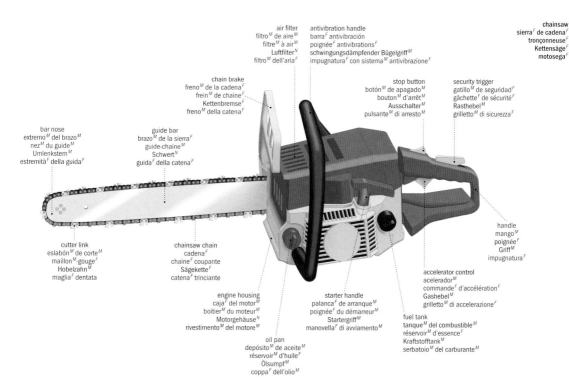

chainsaw
sierra^F de cadena^F
tronçonneuse^F
Kettensäge^F
motosega^F

air filter
filtro^M de aire^M
filtre^M à air^M
Luftfilter^N
filtro^M dell'aria^F

antivibration handle
barra^F antivibración
poignée^F antivibrations^F
schwingungsdämpfender Bügelgriff^M
impugnatura^F con sistema^M antivibrazione^F

stop button
botón^M de apagado^M
bouton^M d'arrêt^M
Ausschalter^M
pulsante^M di arresto^M

security trigger
gatillo^M de seguridad^F
gâchette^F de sécurité^F
Rasthebel^M
grilletto^M di sicurezza^F

chain brake
freno^M de la cadena^F
frein^M de chaine^F
Kettenbremse^F
freno^M della catena^F

bar nose
extremo^M del brazo^M
nez^M du guide^M
Umlenkstern^M
estremità^F della guida^F

guide bar
brazo^M de la sierra^F
guide-chaine^F
Schwert^N
guida^F della catena^F

handle
mango^M
poignée^F
Griff^M
impugnatura^F

cutter link
eslabón^M de corte^M
maillon^M-gouge^F
Hobelzahn^M
maglia^F dentata

chainsaw chain
cadena^F
chaine^F coupante
Sägekette^F
catena^F trinciante

accelerator control
acelerador^M
commande^F d'accélération^F
Gashebel^M
grilletto^M di accelerazione^F

engine housing
caja^F del motor^M
boitier^M du moteur^M
Motorgehäuse^N
rivestimento^M del motore^M

starter handle
palanca^F de arranque^M
poignée^F du démarreur^M
Startergriff^M
manovella^F di avviamento^M

fuel tank
tanque^M del combustible^M
réservoir^M d'essence^F
Kraftstofftank^M
serbatoio^M del carburante^M

oil pan
depósito^M de aceite^M
réservoir^M d'huile^F
Ölsumpf^M
coppa^F dell'olio^M

lawn care

cuidado^M del césped^M | soins^M de la pelouse^F | Rasenpflege^F | cura^F del prato^M

DO-IT-YOURSELF AND GARDENING

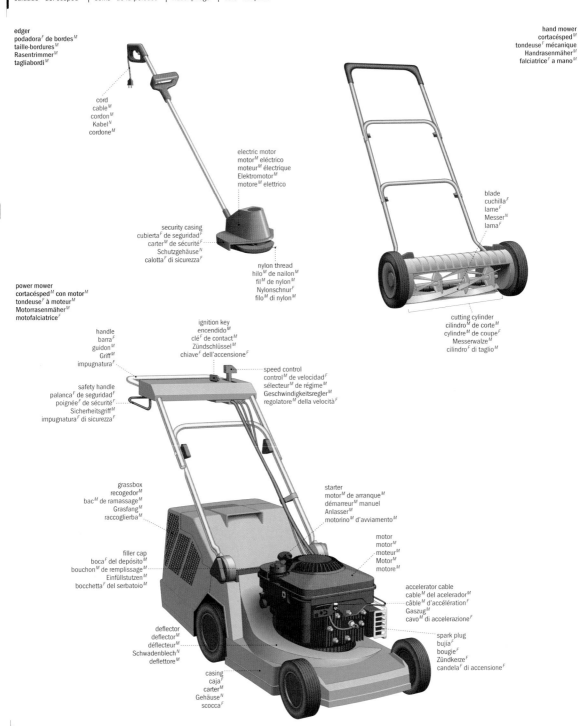

edger
podadora^F de bordes^M
taille-bordures^M
Rasentrimmer^M
tagliabordi^M

cord
cable^M
cordon^M
Kabel^N
cordone^M

electric motor
motor^M eléctrico
moteur^M électrique
Elektromotor^M
motore^M elettrico

security casing
cubierta^F de seguridad^F
carter^M de sécurité^F
Schutzgehäuse^N
calotta^F di sicurezza^F

nylon thread
hilo^M de nailon^M
fil^M de nylon^M
Nylonschnur^F
filo^M di nylon^M

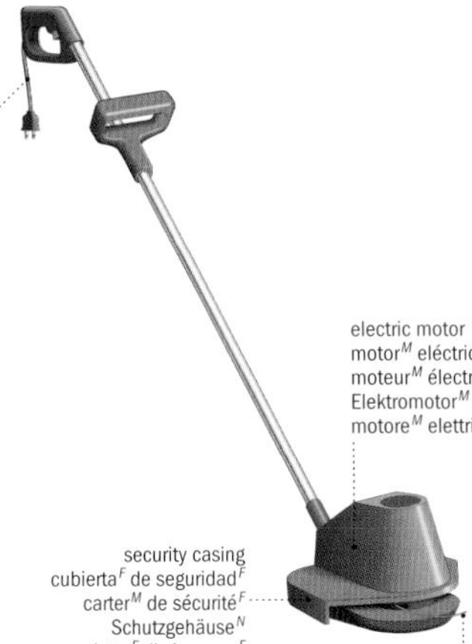

hand mower
cortacésped^M
tondeuse^F mécanique
Handrasenmäher^M
falciatrice^F a mano^M

blade
cuchilla^F
lame^F
Messer^N
lama^F

cutting cylinder
cilindro^M de corte^M
cylindre^M de coupe^F
Messerwalze^M
cilindro^F di taglio^M

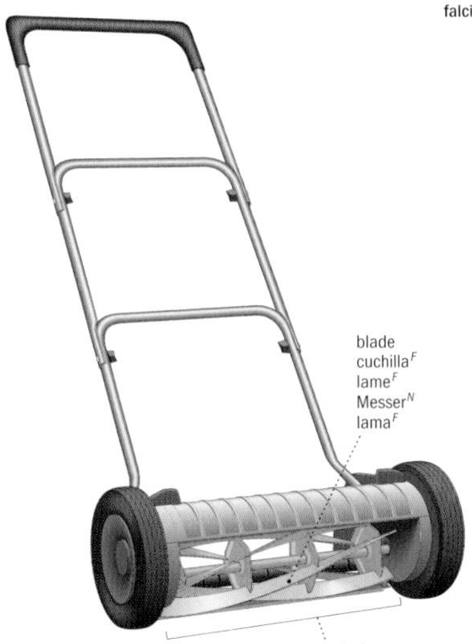

power mower
cortacésped^M con motor^M
tondeuse^F à moteur^M
Motorrasenmäher^M
motofalciatrice^F

handle
barra^F
guidon^M
Griff^M
impugnatura^F

ignition key
encendido^M
clé^F de contact^M
Zündschlüssel^M
chiave^F dell'accensione^F

speed control
control^M de velocidad^F
sélecteur^F de régime^M
Geschwindigkeitsregler^M
regolatore^M della velocità^F

safety handle
palanca^F de seguridad^F
poignée^F de sécurité^F
Sicherheitsgriff^M
impugnatura^F di sicurezza^F

grassbox
recogedor^M
bac^M de ramassage^M
Grasfang^M
raccoglierba^M

starter
motor^M de arranque^M
démarreur^M manuel
Anlasser^M
motorino^M d'avviamento^M

motor
motor^M
moteur^M
Motor^M
motore^M

filler cap
boca^F del depósito^M
bouchon^M de remplissage^M
Einfüllstutzen^M
bocchetta^F del serbatoio^M

accelerator cable
cable^M del acelerador^M
câble^M d'accélération^F
Gaszug^M
cavo^M di accelerazione^F

deflector
deflector^M
déflecteur^M
Schwadenblech^N
deflettore^M

spark plug
bujía^F
bougie^F
Zündkerze^F
candela^F di accensione^F

casing
caja^F
carter^M
Gehäuse^N
scocca^F

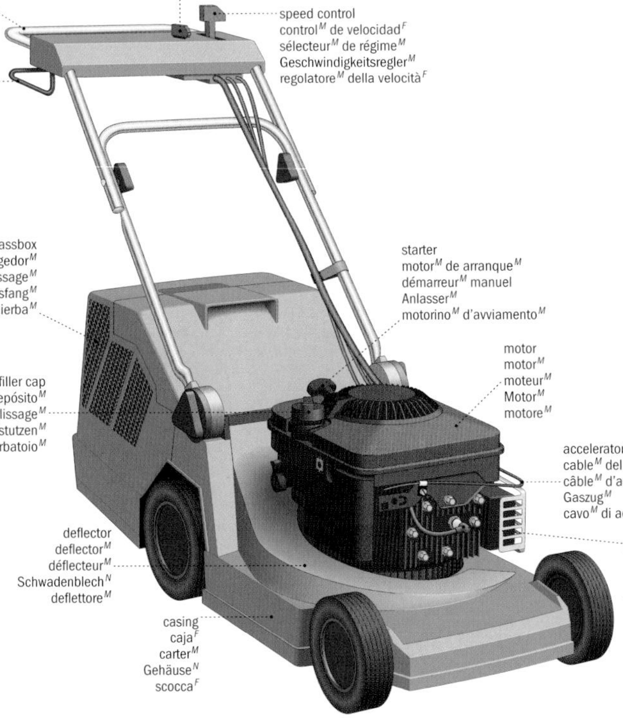

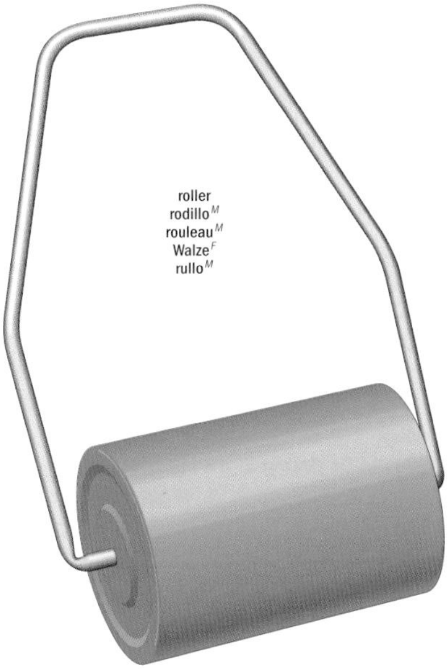

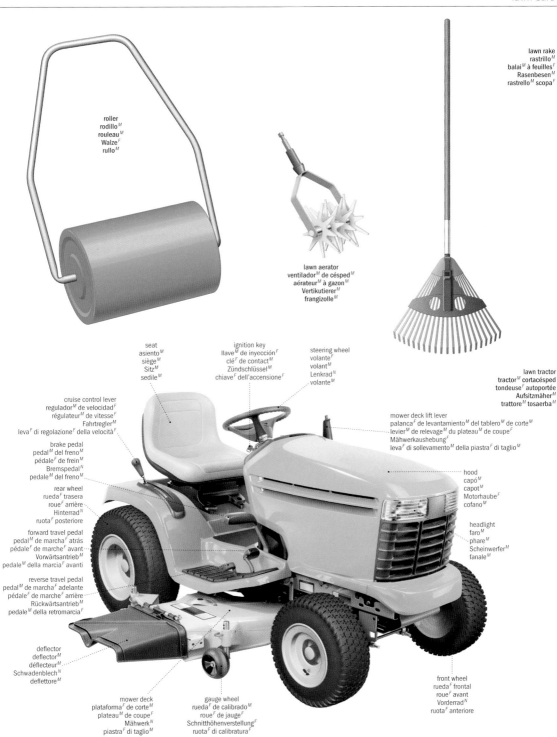

roller
rodillo ^{M}
rouleau ^{M}
Walze ^{F}
rullo ^{M}

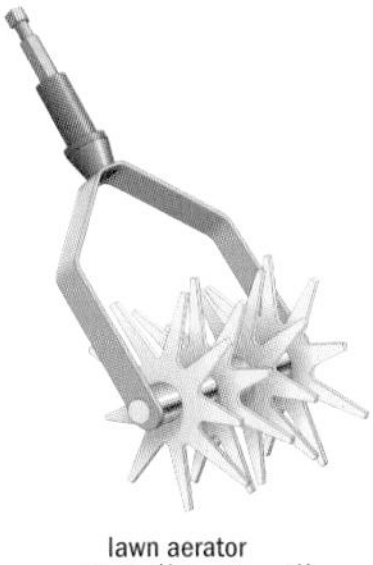

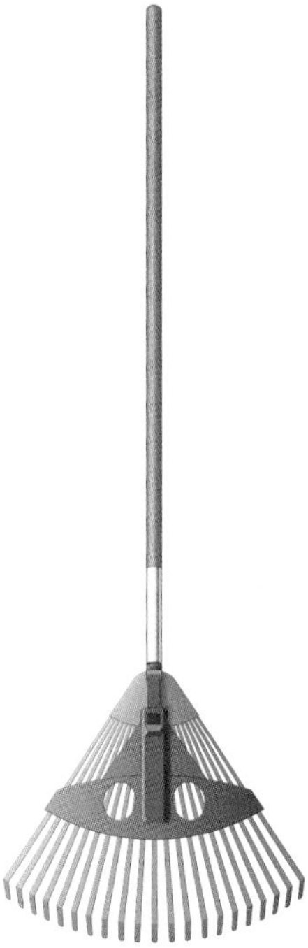

lawn rake
rastrillo ^{M}
balai ^{M} à feuilles ^{F}
Rasenbesen ^{M}
rastrello ^{M} scopa ^{F}

lawn aerator
ventilador ^{M} de césped ^{M}
aérateur ^{M} à gazon ^{M}
Vertikutierer ^{M}
frangizolle ^{M}

seat
asiento ^{M}
siège ^{M}
Sitz ^{M}
sedile ^{M}

ignition key
llave ^{M} de inyección ^{F}
clé ^{F} de contact ^{M}
Zündschlüssel ^{M}
chiave ^{F} dell'accensione ^{F}

steering wheel
volante ^{F}
volant ^{M}
Lenkrad ^{N}
volante ^{M}

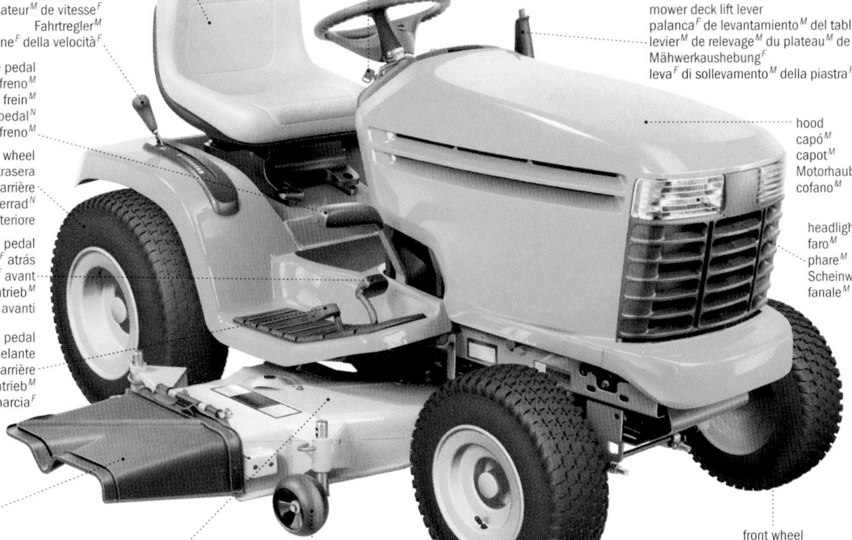

lawn tractor
tractor ^{M} cortacésped
tondeuse ^{F} autoportée
Aufsitzmäher ^{M}
trattore ^{M} tosaerba ^{M}

cruise control lever
regulador ^{M} de velocidad ^{F}
régulateur ^{M} de vitesse ^{F}
Fahrtregler ^{M}
leva ^{F} di regolazione ^{F} della velocità ^{F}

mower deck lift lever
palanca ^{F} de levantamiento ^{M} del tablero ^{M} de corte ^{M}
levier ^{M} de relevage ^{M} du plateau ^{M} de coupe ^{F}
Mähwerkaushebung ^{F}
leva ^{F} di sollevamento ^{M} della piastra ^{F} di taglio ^{M}

brake pedal
pedal ^{M} del freno ^{M}
pédale ^{F} de frein ^{M}
Bremspedal ^{N}
pedale ^{M} del freno ^{M}

hood
capó ^{M}
capot ^{M}
Motorhaube ^{F}
cofano ^{M}

rear wheel
rueda ^{F} trasera
roue ^{F} arrière
Hinterrad ^{N}
ruota ^{F} posteriore

headlight
faro ^{M}
phare ^{M}
Scheinwerfer ^{M}
fanale ^{M}

forward travel pedal
pedal ^{M} de marcha ^{F} atrás
pédale ^{F} de marche ^{F} avant
Vorwärtsantrieb ^{M}
pedale ^{M} della marcia ^{F} avanti

reverse travel pedal
pedal ^{M} de marcha ^{F} adelante
pédale ^{F} de marche ^{F} arrière
Rückwärtsantrieb ^{M}
pedale ^{M} della retromarcia ^{F}

deflector
deflector ^{M}
déflecteur ^{M}
Schwadenblech ^{N}
deflettore ^{M}

front wheel
rueda ^{F} frontal
roue ^{F} avant
Vorderrad ^{N}
ruota ^{F} anteriore

mower deck
plataforma ^{F} de corte ^{M}
plateau ^{M} de coupe ^{F}
Mähwerk ^{N}
piastra ^{F} di taglio ^{M}

gauge wheel
rueda ^{F} de calibrado ^{M}
roue ^{F} de jauge ^{F}
Schnitthöhenverstellung ^{F}
ruota ^{F} di calibratura ^{F}

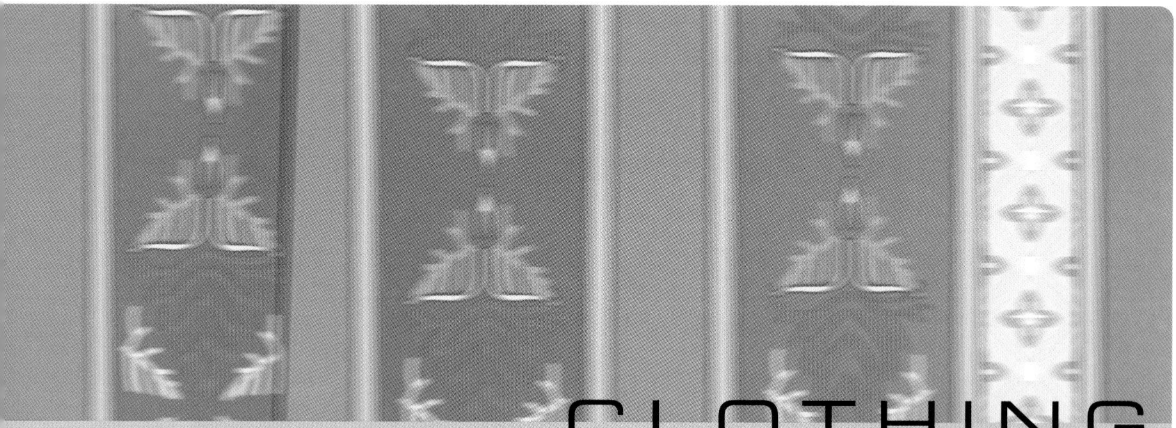

CLOTHING

VESTIDO | VÊTEMENTS | KLEIDUNG | ABBIGLIAMENTO

336

elements of historical clothing

indumentaria^F historica | éléments^M du costume^M ancien | Elemente^N historischer Kostüme^N | capi^M antichi

peplos
peplo^M
péplos^M
Peplos^M
peplo^M

fibula
fibula^F
fibule^F
Fibel^F
fibula^F

fold
pliegue^M
repli^M
Umschlag^M
piega^F

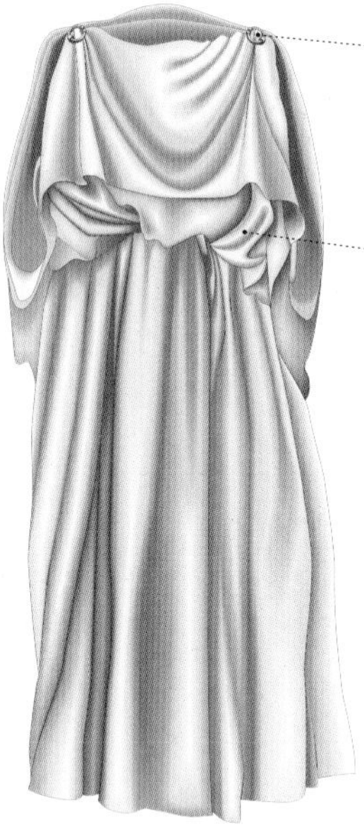

toga
toga^F
toge^F
Toga^F
toga^F

sinus
seno^M
sinus^M
Sinus^M
seno^M

purple border
orla^F de púrpura^F
bande^F de pourpre^F
Purpursaum^M
bordo^M di porpora^F

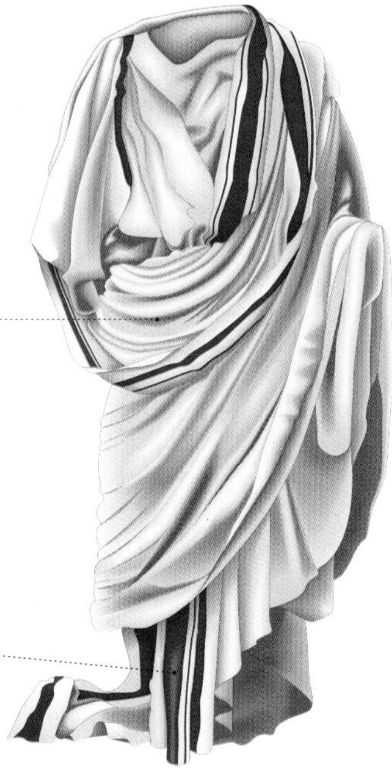

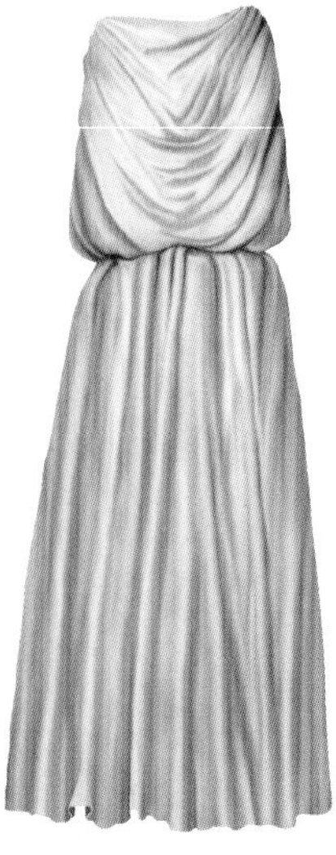

stola
stola^F
stola^F
Stola^F
stola^F

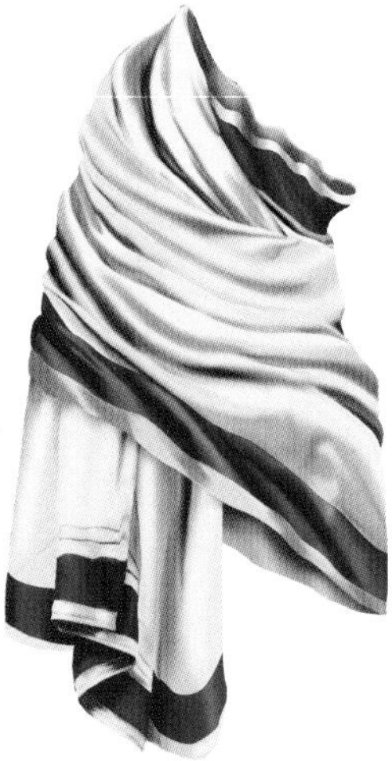

palla
palla^F
palla^F
Palla^F
palla^F

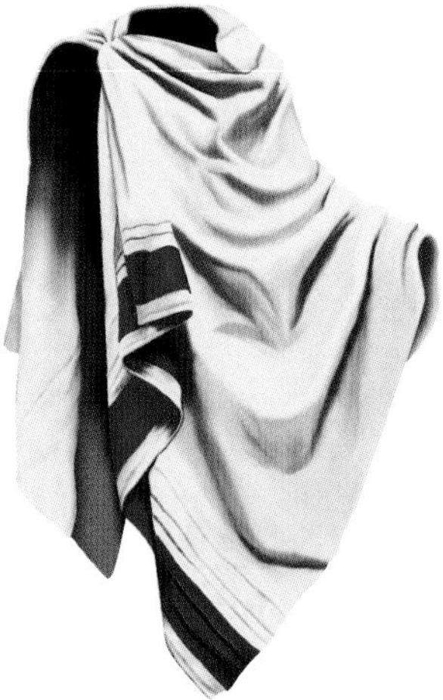

chlamys
clámide^F
chlamyde^F
Chlamys^F
clamide^F

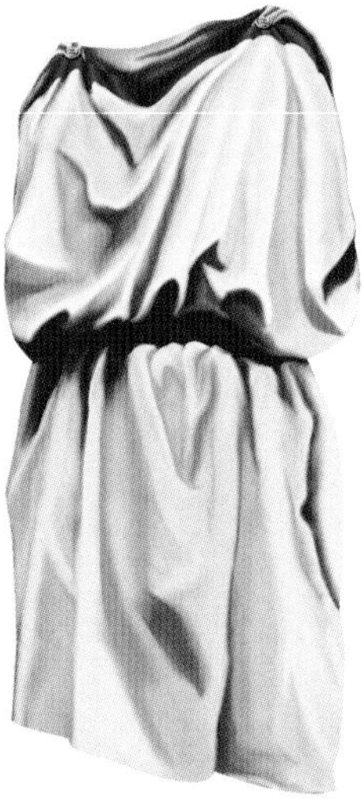

chiton
quitón^M
chiton^M
Chiton^M
chitone^M

CLOTHING

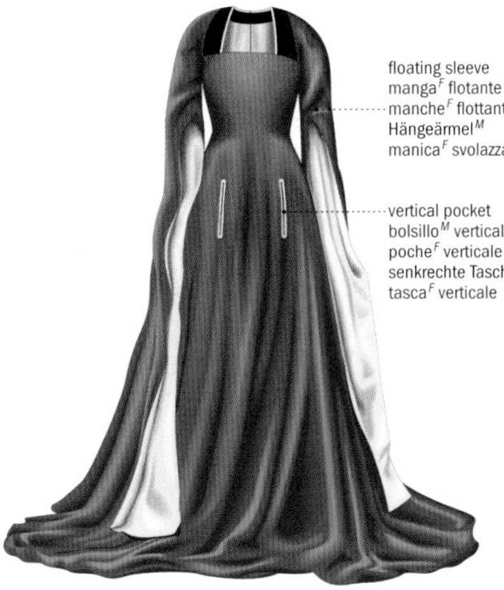

floating sleeve
manga^F flotante
manche^F flottante
Hängeärmel^M
manica^F svolazzante

vertical pocket
bolsillo^M vertical
poche^F verticale
senkrechte Tasche^F
tasca^F verticale

cotehardie
túnica^F de manga^F larga
cotardie^F
Cotardie^F
cottardita^F

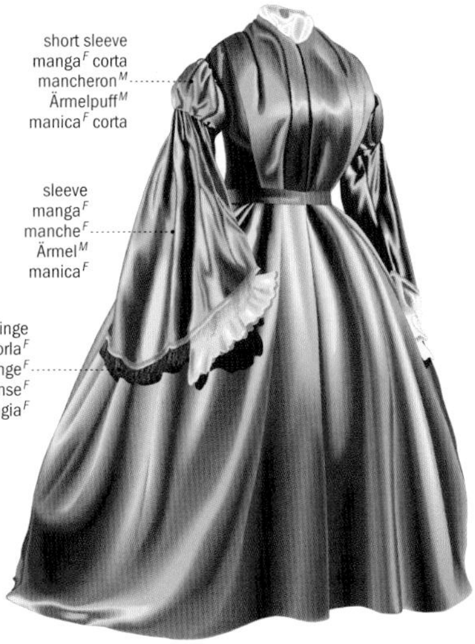

short sleeve
manga^F corta
mancheron^M
Ärmelpuff^M
manica^F corta

sleeve
manga^F
manche^F
Ärmel^M
manica^F

fringe
orla^F
frange^F
Franse^F
frangia^F

dress with crinoline
vestido^M con crinolina^F
robe^F à crinoline^F
Kleid^N mit Krinolinenrock^M
abito^M con crinolina^F

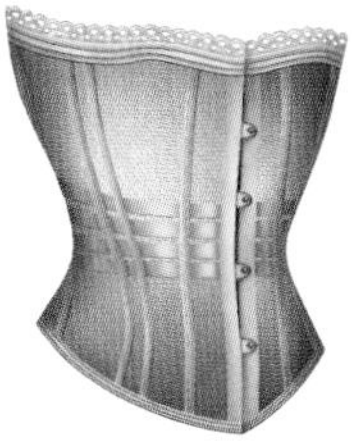

corset
corsé^M
corset^M
Korsett^N
corsetto^M

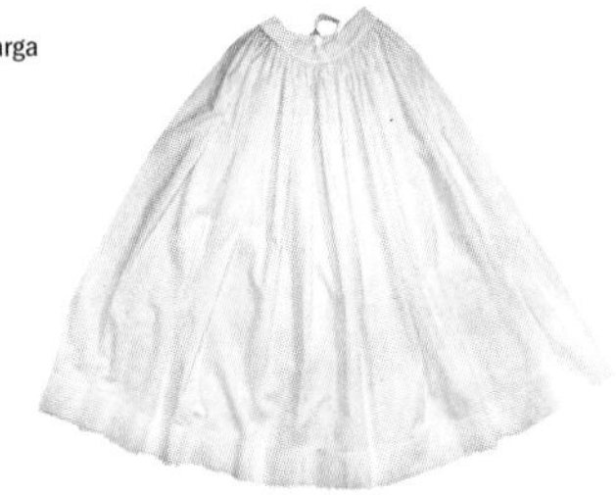

petticoat
enaguas^F
jupon^M
Unterrock^M
sottogonna^F

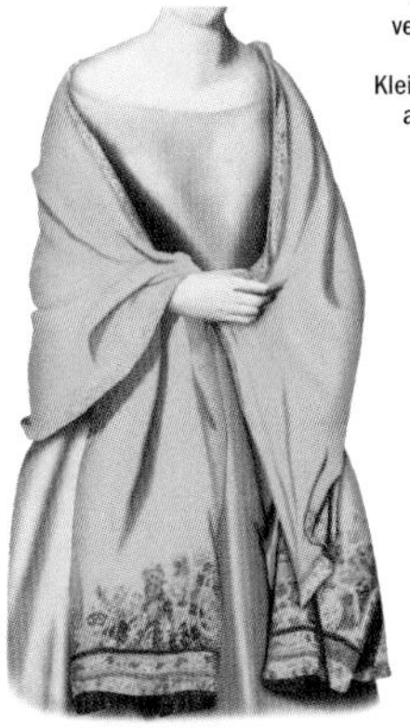

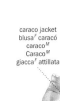

shawl
chal^M
châle^M
Schal^M
scialle^M

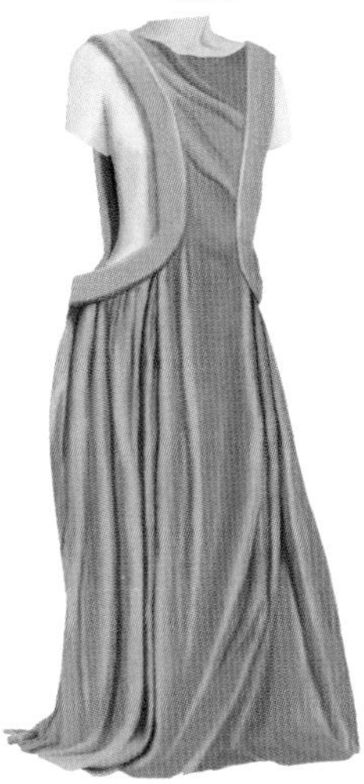

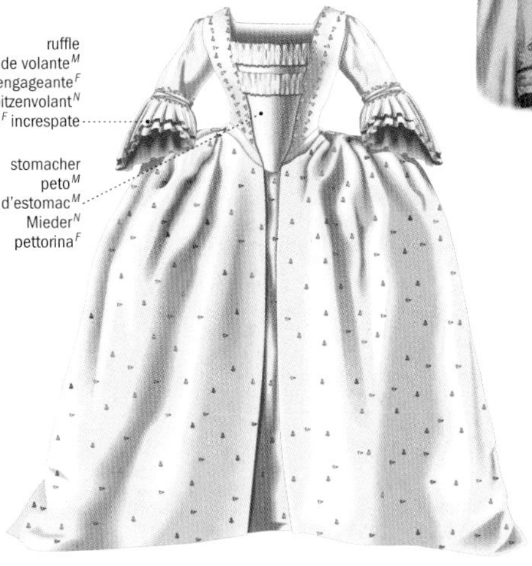

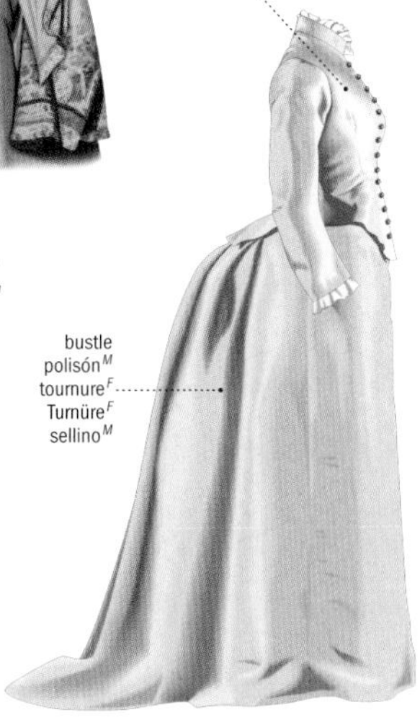

caraco jacket
blusa^F caracó
caraco^M
Caraco^M
giacca^F attillata

surcoat
sobreveste^M
surcot^M
Überkleid^N
sopravveste^F

ruffle
manga^F de volante^M
engageante^F
Spitzenvolant^N
balze^F increspate

stomacher
peto^M
pièce^F d'estomac^M
Mieder^N
pettorina^F

dress with panniers
vestido^M con miriñaque^M
robe^F à paniers^M
Kleid^N mit flachem Reifrock^M
abito^M con panieri^M

bustle
polisón^M
tournure^F
Turnüre^F
sellino^M

dress with bustle
vestido^M con polisón^M
robe^F à tournure^F
Kleid^N mit Turnüre^F
abito^M con sellino^M

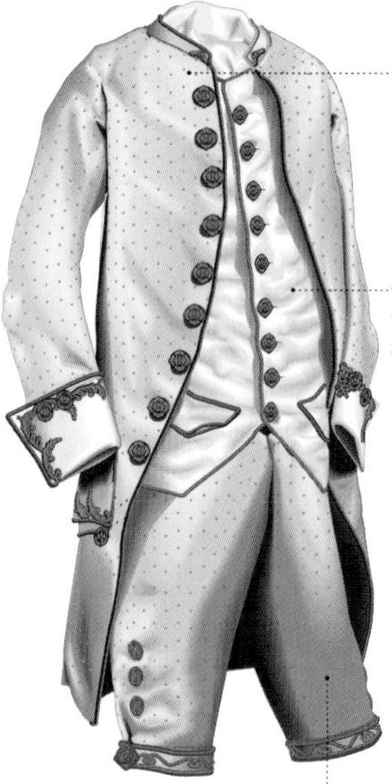

frock coat
levita^F
frac^M
Schoßrock^M
marsina^F

waistcoat
chaleco^M
gilet^M
Weste^F
panciotto^M

breeches
calzones^M
culotte^F
Kniehose^F
culottes^F

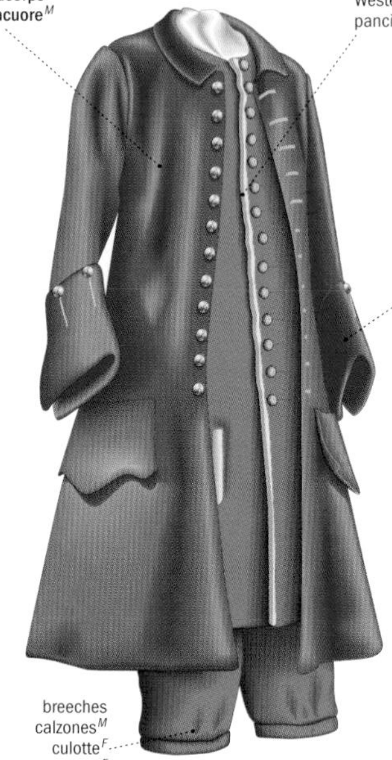

justaucorps
casaca^F
justaucorps^M
Justaucorps^N
giustacuore^M

vest
chaleco^M
veste^F
Weste^F
panciotto^M lungo

cuff
puño^M
parement^M
Aufschlag^M
polsino^M rivoltato

breeches
calzones^M
culotte^F
Kniehose^F
culottes^F

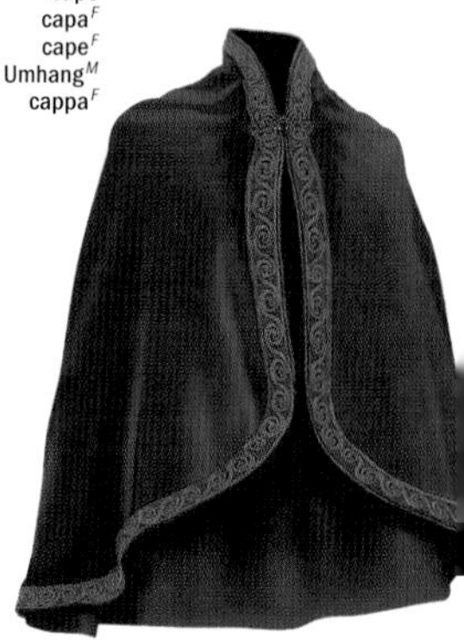

cape
capa^F
cape^F
Umhang^M
cappa^F

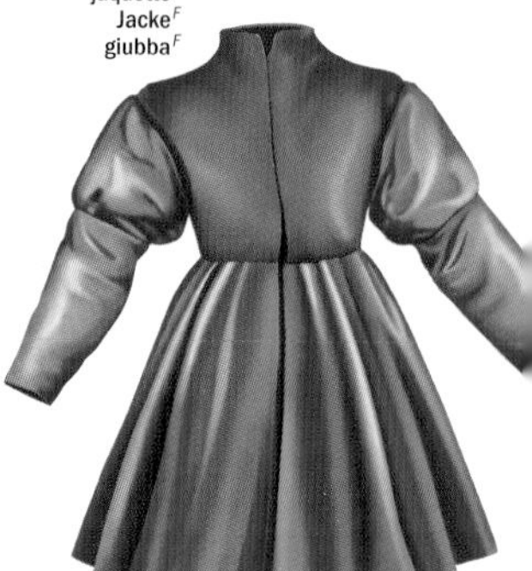

jacket
aljuba^F
jaquette^F
Jacke^F
giubba^F

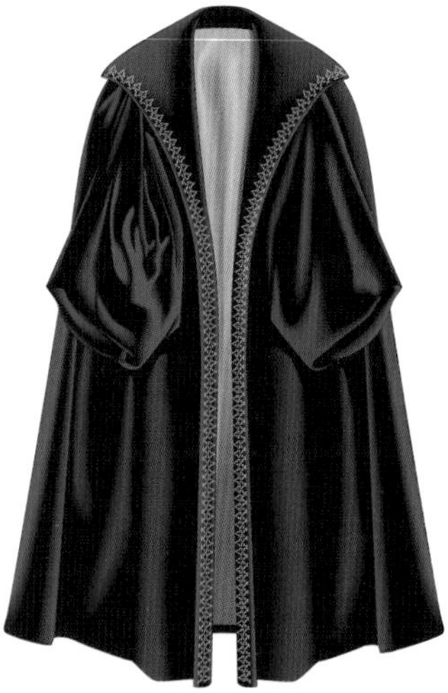

houppelande
hopa^F
houppelande^F
Houppelande^F
pelanda^F

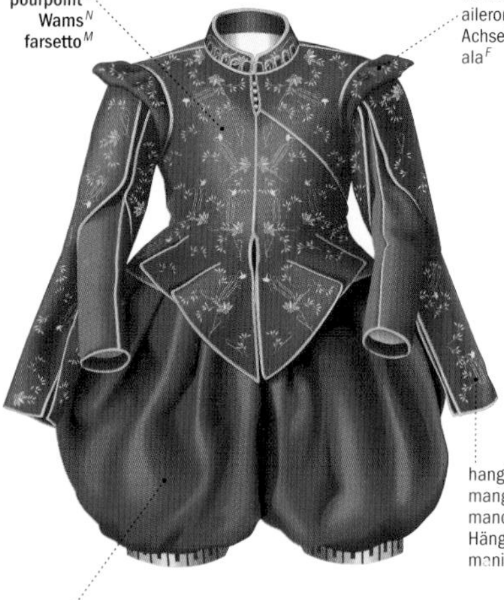

doublet
jubón^M
pourpoint^M
Wams^N
farsetto^M

wing
hombrera^F
aileron^M
Achselstück^N
ala^F

hanging sleeve
manga^F colgante
manche^F pendante
Hängeärmel^M
manica^F pendente

trunk hose
gregüescos^M
haut-de-chausse^M
Pluderhose^F
calzoni^M a palloncino^M

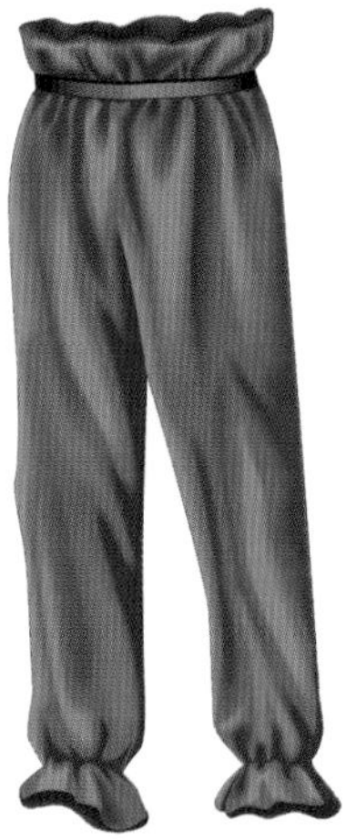

braies
calzas^F
braies^F
Beinlinge^M
brache^F

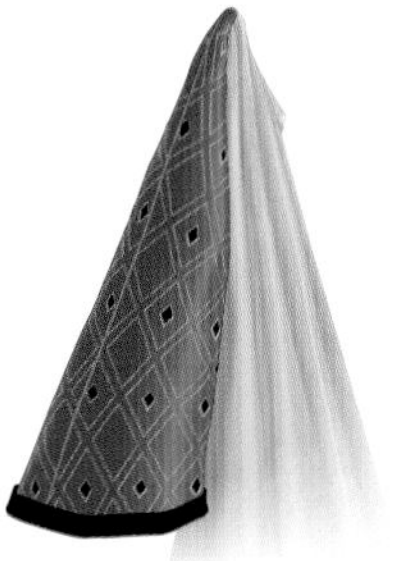

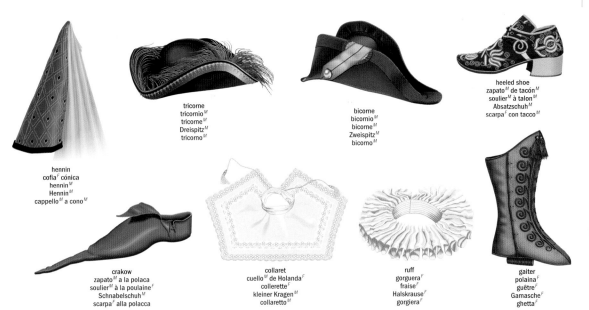

hennin
cofia^F cónica
hennin^M
Hennin^M
cappello^M a cono^M

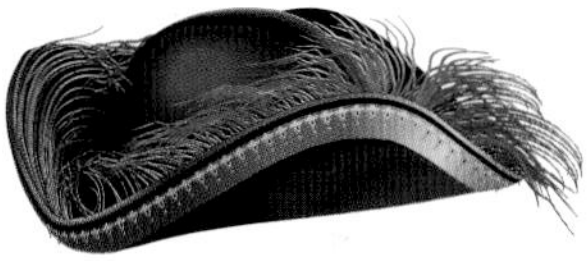

tricorne
tricornio^M
tricorne^M
Dreispitz^M
tricorno^M

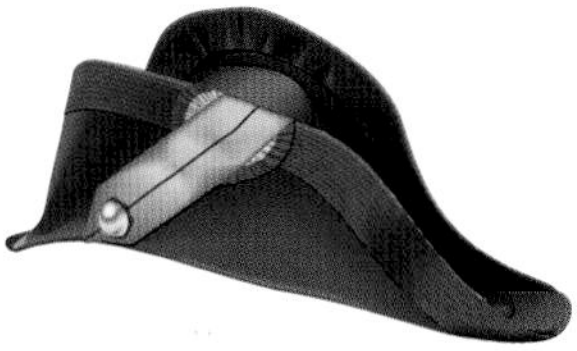

bicorne
bicornio^M
bicorne^M
Zweispitz^M
bicorno^M

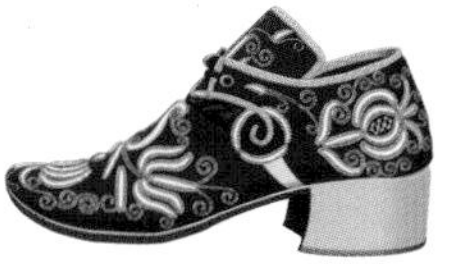

heeled shoe
zapato^M de tacón^M
soulier^M à talon^M
Absatzschuh^M
scarpa^F con tacco^M

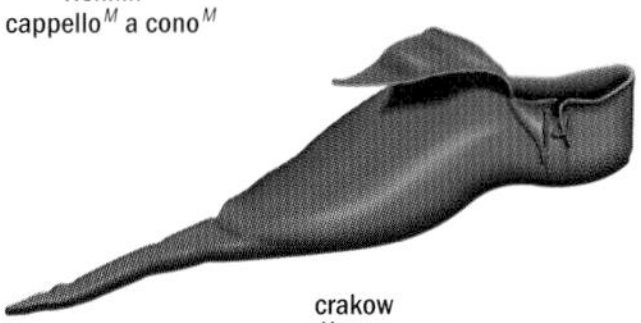

crakow
zapato^M a la polaca
soulier^M à la poulaine^F
Schnabelschuh^M
scarpa^F alla polacca

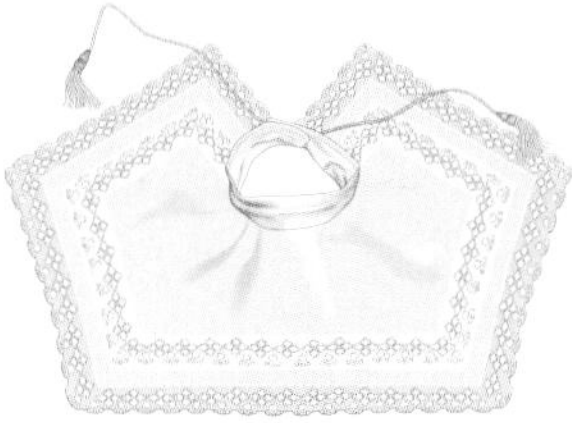

collaret
cuello^M de Holanda^F
collerette^F
kleiner Kragen^M
collaretto^M

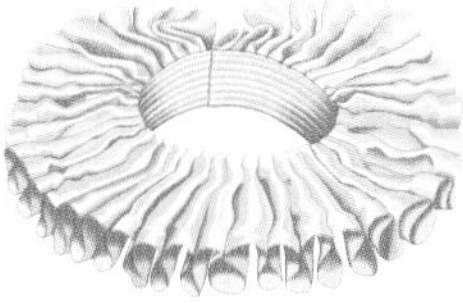

ruff
gorguera^F
fraise^F
Halskrause^F
gorgiera^F

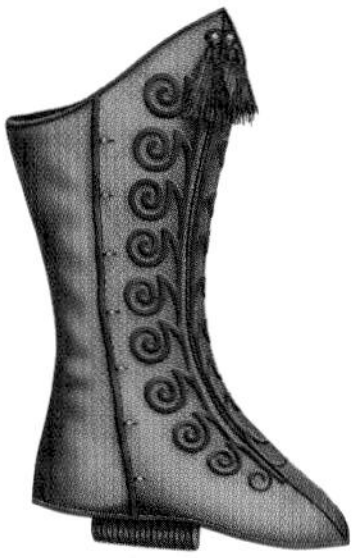

gaiter
polaina^F
guêtre^F
Gamasche^F
ghetta^F

CLOTHING

traditional clothing

indumentaria^F tradicional | vêtements^M traditionnels | traditionelle Kleidung^F | abiti^M tradizionali

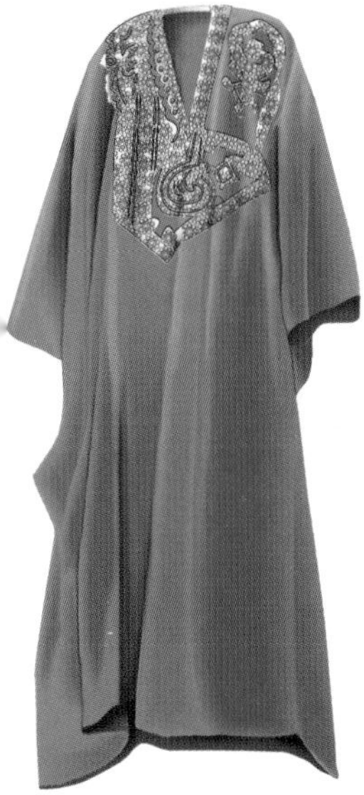

boubou
boubou^M
boubou^M
Boubou^M
boubou^M

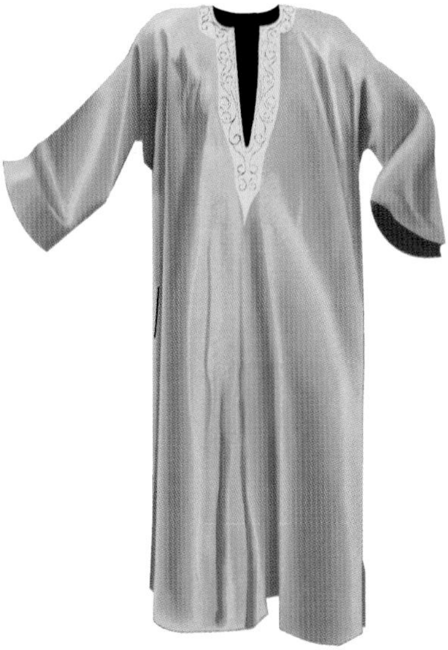

caftan
caftán^M
cafetan^M
Kaftan^M
caffettano^M

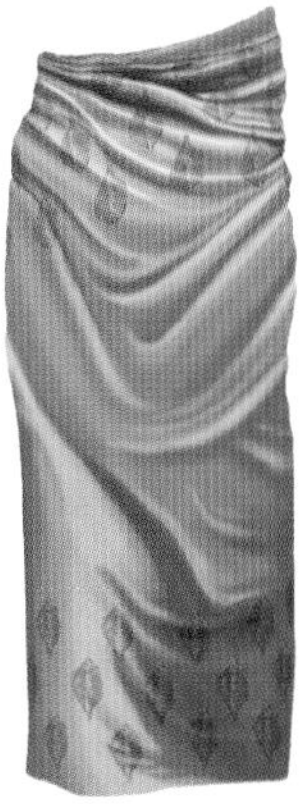

loincloth
pareo^M
pagne^M
Wickelrock^M
pareo^M

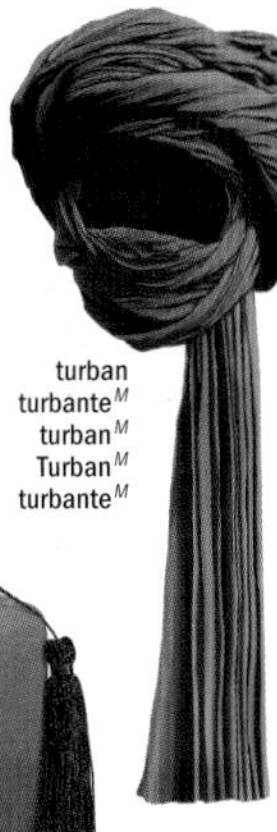

turban
turbante^M
turban^M
Turban^M
turbante^M

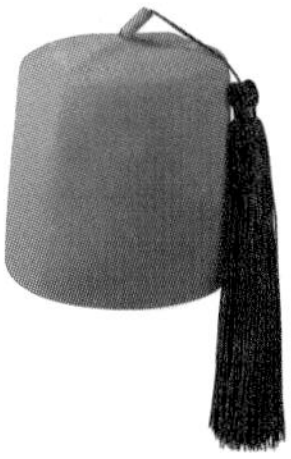

fez
fez^M
fez^M
Fes^M
fez^M

headgear

sombreros^M | coiffure^F | Kopfbedeckungen^F | copricapi^M

men's headgear
sombreros^M de hombre^M
coiffures^F d'homme^M
Herrenkopfbedeckungen^F
copricapi^M maschili

felt hat
sombrero^M de fieltro^M
chapeau^M de feutre^M
Filzhut^M
cappello^M di feltro^M

hatband
cinta^F
bourdalou^M
Hutband^N
nastro^M

crown
copa^F
calotte^F
Kopfteil^{M/N}
calotta^F

binding
ribete^M
galon^M
Einfassband^N
orlo^M

brim
ala^F
bord^M
Krempe^F
tesa^F

bow
lazo^M
nœud^M plat
Schleife^F
fiocco^M

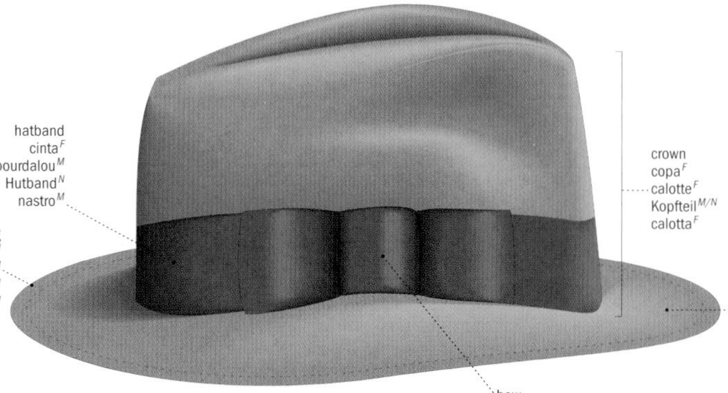

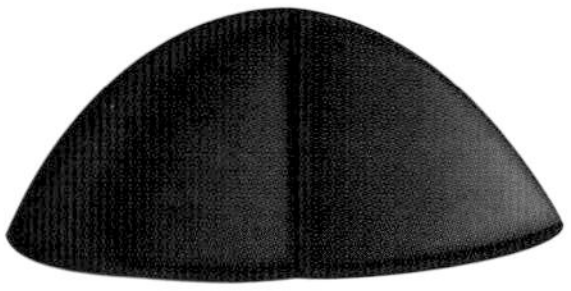

derby
sombrero^M de hongo^M
melon^M
Melone^F
bombetta^F

boater
canotier^M
canotier^M
Strohhut^M
paglietta^F

skullcap
solideo^M
calotte^F
Käppchen^N
papalina^F

garrison cap
gorra^F de cuartel^M
calot^M
Fellmütze^F
bustina^F

top hat
chistera^F
haut-de-forme^M
Zylinder^M
cilindro^M

shapka
chapka^F
chapka^M
Kosakenmütze^F
colbacco^M

hunting cap
gorra^F noruega
casquette^F norvégienne
Jagdkappe^F
berretto^M da cacciatore^M

ear flap
orejera^F
cache-oreilles^M abattant
Ohrenschützer^M
paraorecchi^M

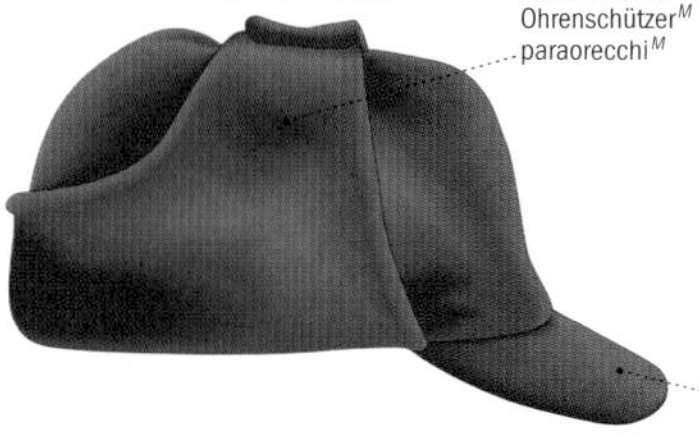

cap
gorra^F
casquette^F
Schirmmütze^F
berretto^M

panama
panamá^M
panama^M
Panamahut^M
panama^M

peak
visera^F
visière^F
Mützenschirm^M
visiera^F

CLOTHING

pillbox hat
sombrero ^{M} sin alas ^{F}
tambourin ^{M}
Pillbox ^{F}
tocco ^{M}

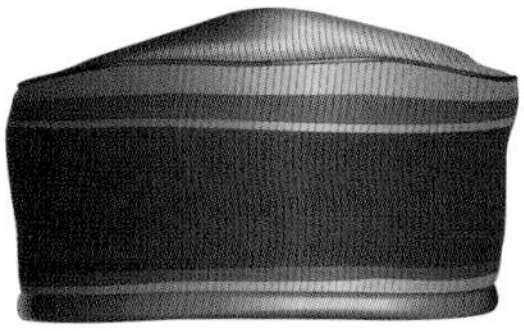

cartwheel hat
pamela ^{F}
capeline ^{F}
Wagenradhut ^{M}
cappello ^{M} a falda ^{F} larga

women's headgear
sombreros ^{M} de mujer ^{F}
coiffures ^{F} de femme ^{F}
Damenkopfbedeckungen ^{F}
copricapi ^{M} femminili

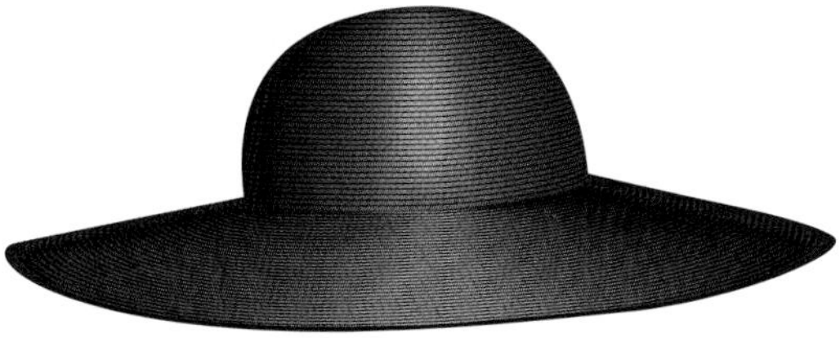

cloche
sombrero ^{M} de campana ^{F}
cloche ^{F}
Topfhut ^{M}
cloche ^{F}

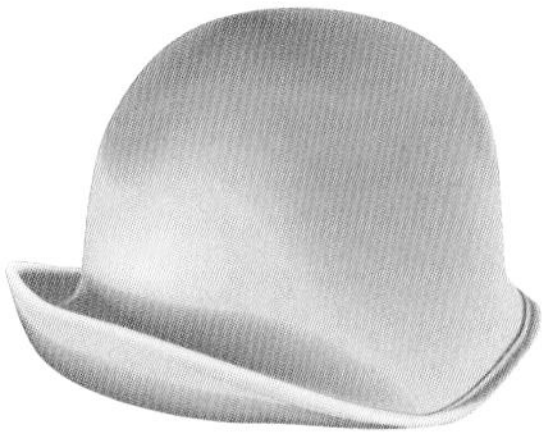

toque
toca ^{F}
toque ^{F}
Toque ^{F}
toque ^{F}

gob hat
gorro ^{M} de marinero ^{M}
bob ^{M}
Regenhut ^{M}
cappello ^{M} da marinaio ^{M}

crown
copa ^{F}
calotte ^{F}
Kopfteil $^{M/N}$
calotta ^{F}

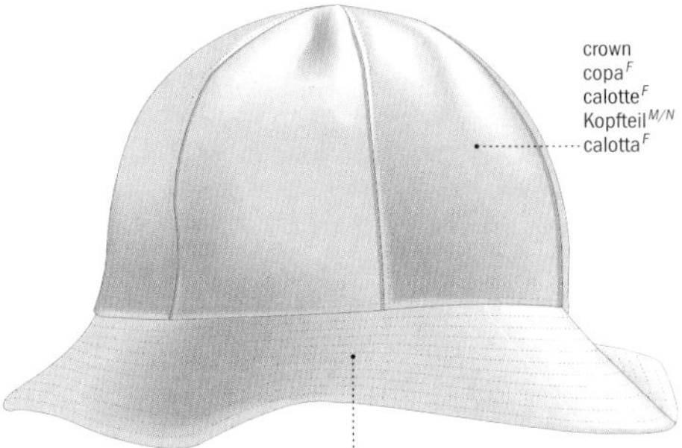

turban
turbante ^{M}
turban ^{M}
Turban ^{M}
turbante ^{M}

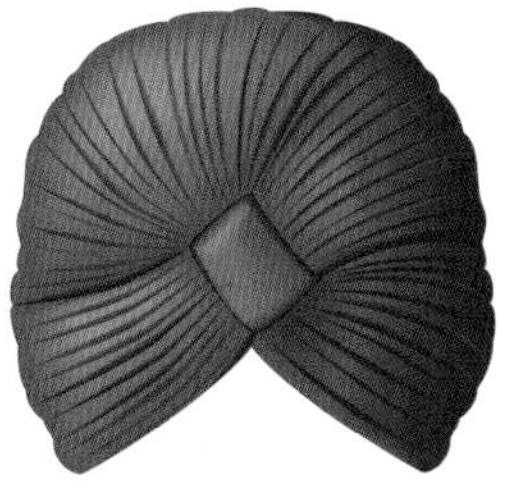

sou'wester
sueste ^{M}
suroit ^{M}
Südwester ^{M}
berretto ^{M} impermeabile

brim
ala ^{F}
bord ^{M}
Krempe ^{F}
tesa ^{F}

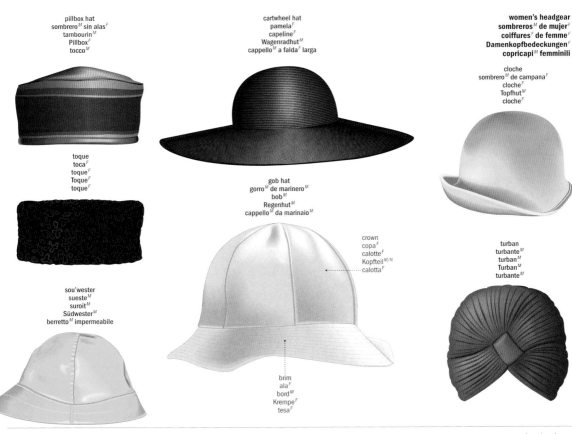

CLOTHING

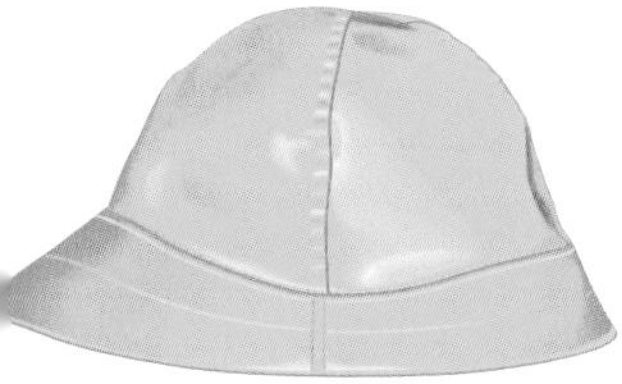

unisex headgear
sombreros ^{M} unisex
coiffures ^{F} unisexes
Unisex-Kopfbedeckungen ^{F}
copricapi ^{M} unisex

balaclava
pasamontañas ^{M}
cagoule ^{F}
Kapuzenmütze ^{F}
passamontagna ^{M}

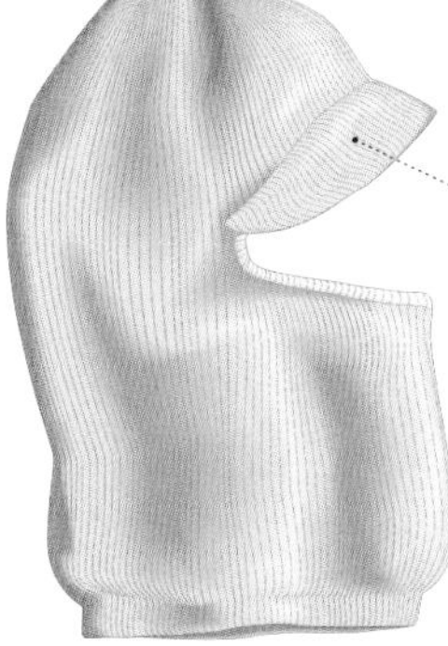

beret
boina ^{F}
béret ^{M}
Baskenmütze ^{F}
basco ^{M}

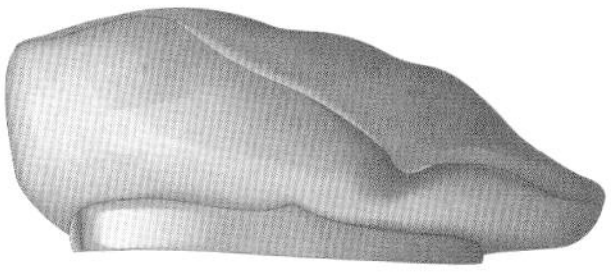

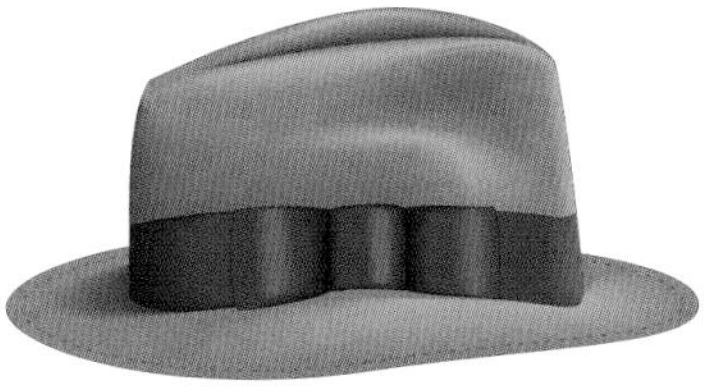

stocking cap
gorro ^{M} de punto ^{M} con borla ^{F}
bonnet ^{M} pompon ^{M} ; tuque ^{F}
Pudelmütze ^{F}
berretto ^{M} con pompon ^{M}

peak
visera ^{F}
visière ^{F}
Mützenschirm ^{M}
visiera ^{F}

felt hat
sombrero ^{M} de fieltro ^{M}
feutre ^{M}
Filzhut ^{M}
cappello ^{M} di feltro ^{M}

341

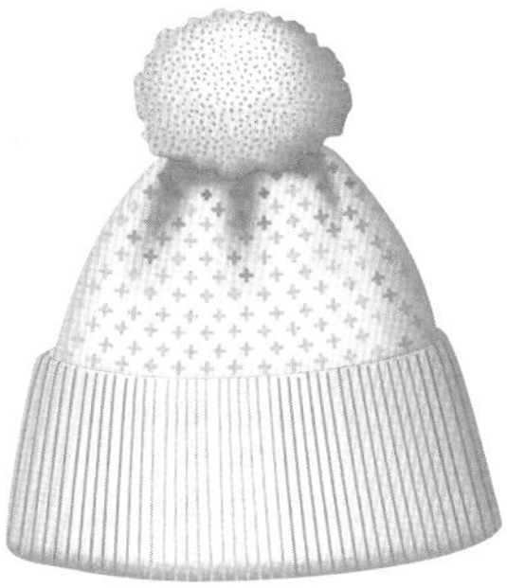

shoes

calzados^M | chaussures^F | Schuhe^M | scarpe^F

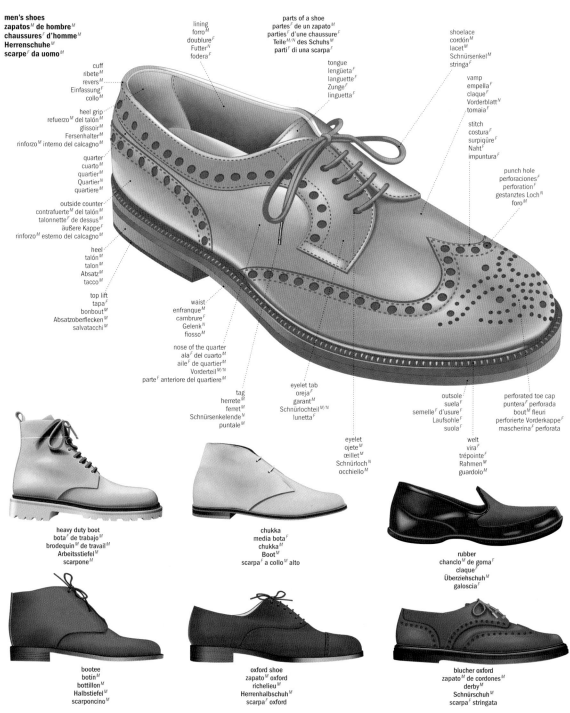

men's shoes
zapatos^M de hombre^M
chaussures^F d'homme^M
Herrenschuhe^M
scarpe^F da uomo^M

lining
forro^M
doublure^F
Futter^N
fodera^F

parts of a shoe
partes^F de un zapato^M
parties^F d'une chaussure^F
Teile^M/N des Schuhs^M
parti^F di una scarpa^F

shoelace
cordón^M
lacet^M
Schnürsenkel^M
stringa^F

cuff
ribete^M
revers^M
Einfassung^F
collo^M

tongue
lengüeta^F
languette^F
Zunge^F
linguetta^F

vamp
empella^F
claque^F
Vorderblatt^N
tomaia^F

heel grip
refuerzo^M del talón^M
glissoir^M
Fersenhalter^M
rinforzo^M interno del calcagno^M

stitch
costura^F
surpiqûre^F
Naht^F
impuntura^F

quarter
cuarto^M
quartier^M
Quartier^M
quartiere^M

punch hole
perforaciones^F
perforation^F
gestanztes Loch^N
foro^M

outside counter
contrafuerte^M del talón^M
talonnette^F de dessus^M
äußere Kappe^F
rinforzo^M esterno del calcagno^M

heel
talón^M
talon^M
Absatz^M
tacco^M

top lift
tapa^F
bonbout^M
Absatzoberflecken^M
salvatacchi^M

waist
enfranque^M
cambrure^F
Gelenk^N
fiosso^M

nose of the quarter
ala^F del cuarto^M
aile^F de quartier^M
Vorderteil^M/N
parte^F anteriore del quartiere^M

tag
herrete^M
ferret^M
Schnürsenkelende^N
puntale^M

eyelet tab
oreja^F
garant^M
Schnürlochteil^M/N
lunetta^F

outsole
suela^F
semelle^F d'usure^F
Laufsohle^F
suola^F

perforated toe cap
puntera^F perforada
bout^M fleuri
perforierte Vorderkappe^F
mascherina^F perforata

eyelet
ojete^M
œillet^M
Schnürloch^N
occhiello^M

welt
vira^F
trépointe^F
Rahmen^M
guardolo^M

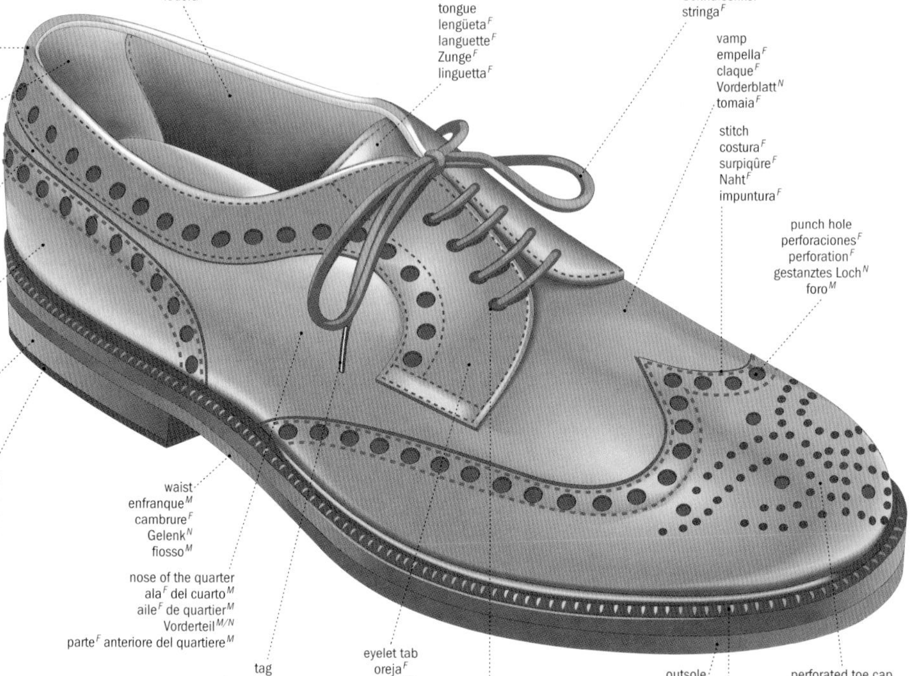

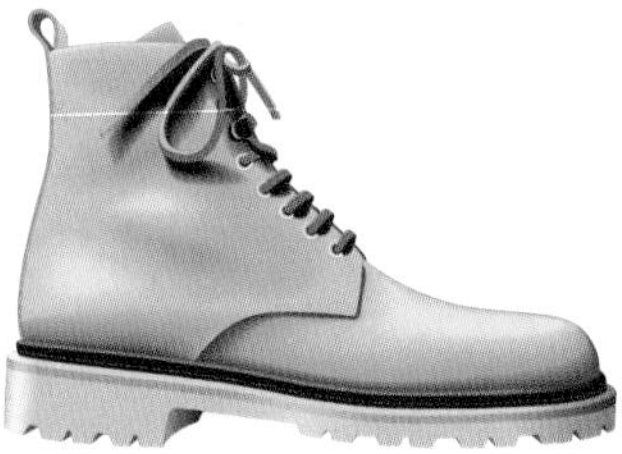

heavy duty boot
bota^F de trabajo^M
brodequin^M de travail^M
Arbeitsstiefel^M
scarpone^M

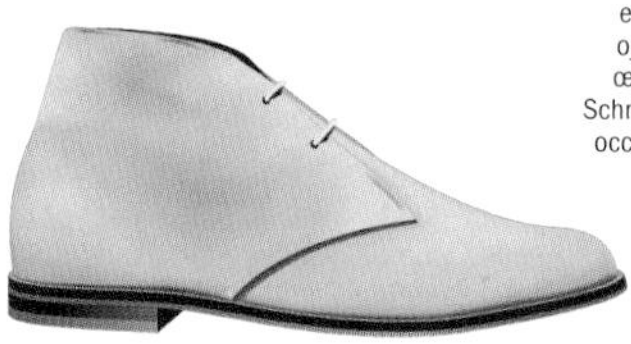

chukka
media bota^F
chukka^M
Boot^M
scarpa^F a collo^M alto

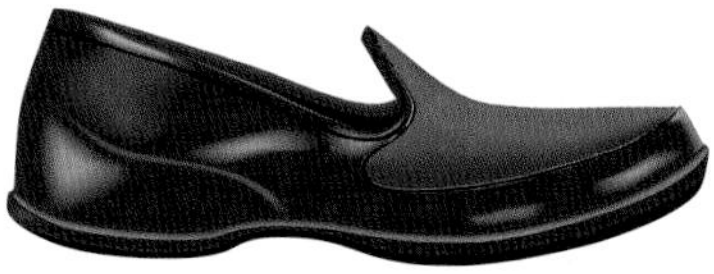

rubber
chanclo^M de goma^F
claque^F
Überziehschuh^M
galoscia^F

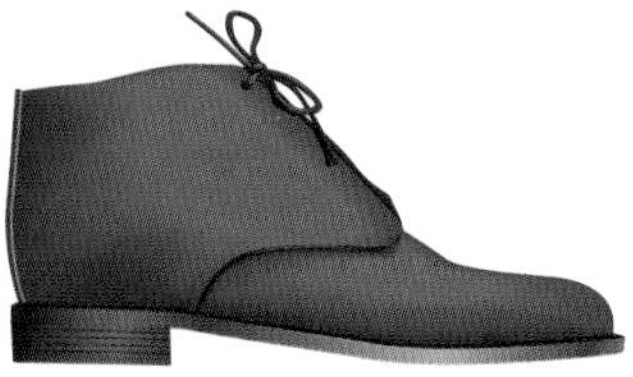

bootee
botín^M
bottillon^M
Halbstiefel^M
scarponcino^M

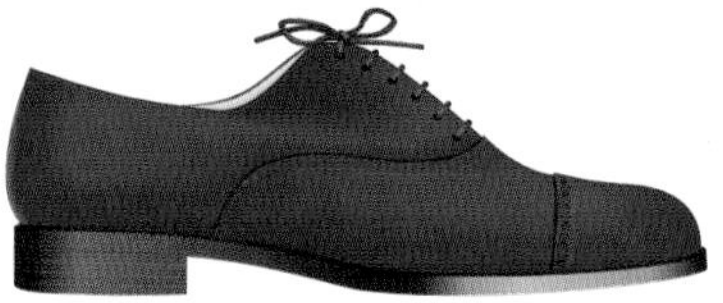

oxford shoe
zapato^M oxford
richelieu^M
Herrenhalbschuh^M
scarpa^F oxford

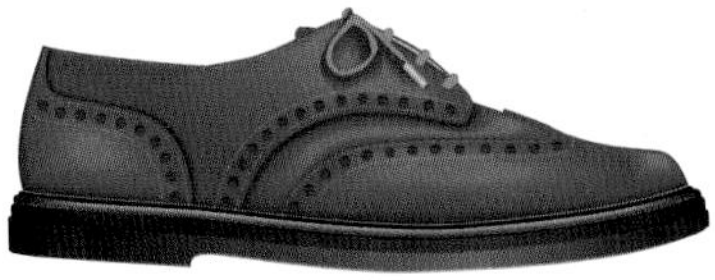

blucher oxford
zapato^M de cordones^M
derby^M
Schnürschuh^M
scarpa^F stringata

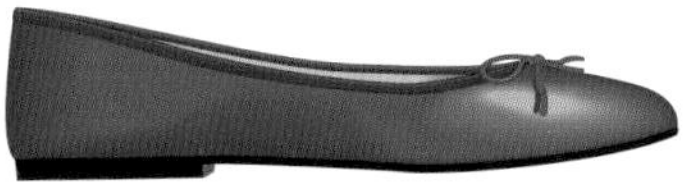

ballerina slipper
bailarina[F]
ballerine[F]
Ballerinaschuh[M]
ballerina[F]

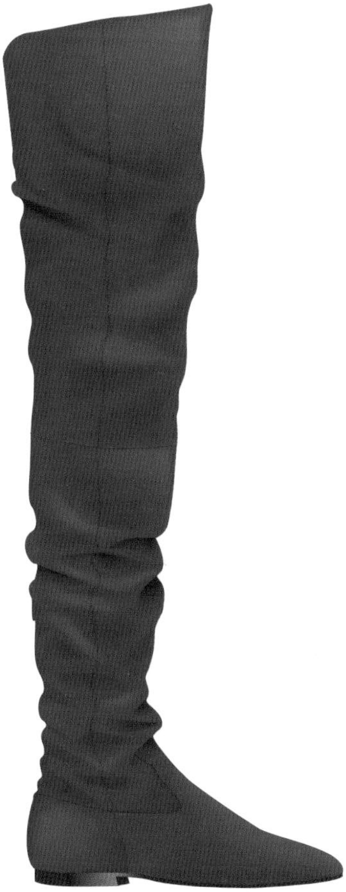

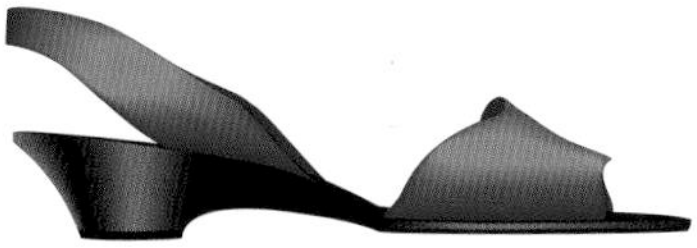

sandal
sandalia[F]
sandale[F]
Sandalette[F] mit Fersenriemen[M]
sandalo[M]

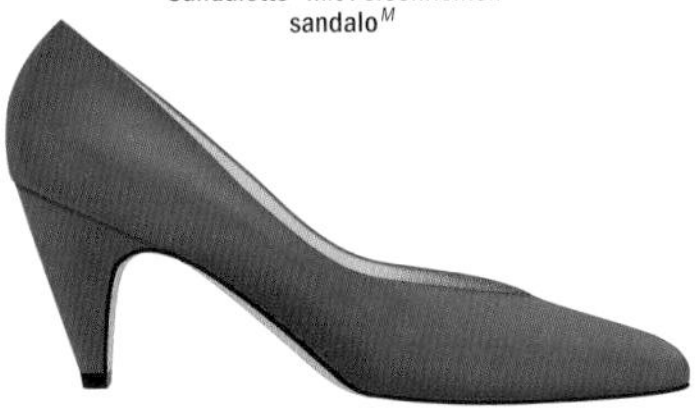

pump
zapato[M] de salón[M]
escarpin[M]
Pumps[M]
scarpa[F] décolleté[M]

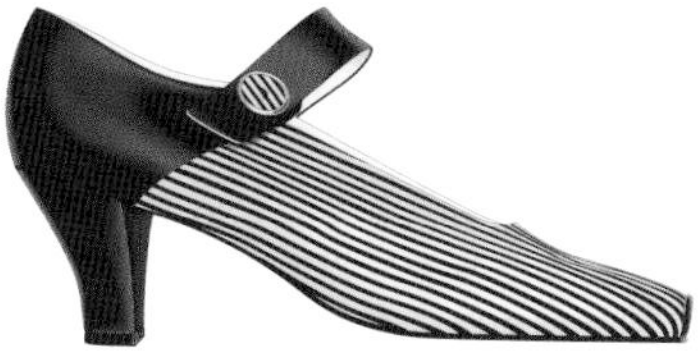

one-bar shoe
zapato[M] de tacón[M] con correa[F]
Charles IX[M]
Einspangenschuh[M]
scarpa[F] con cinturino[M]

women's shoes
zapatos[M] de mujer[F]
chaussures[F] de femme[F]
Damenschuhe[M]
scarpe[F] da donna[F]

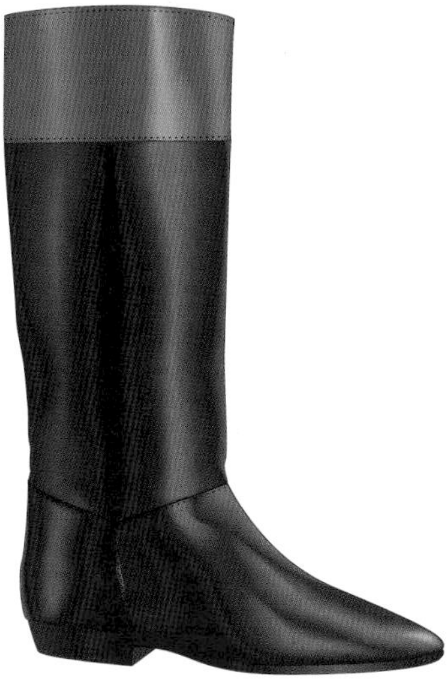

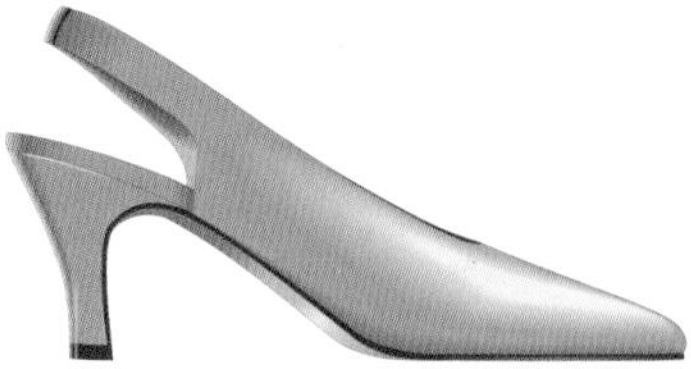

sling back shoe
zapato[M] de talón abierto
escarpin[M]-sandale[F]
Slingpumps[M]
scarpa[F] chanel

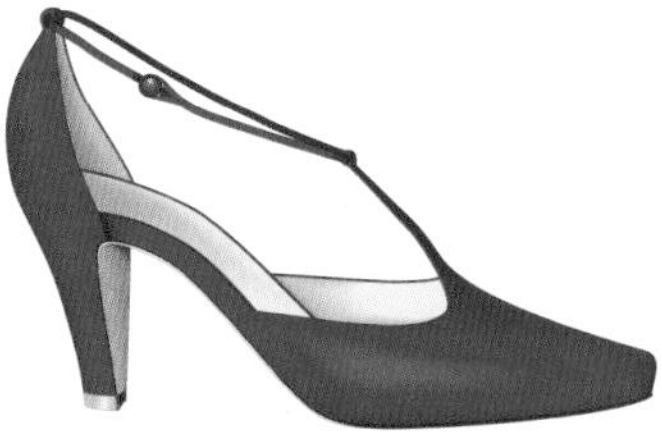

T-strap shoe
zapato[M] de correa[F]
salomé[M]
Stegspangenschuh[M]
scarpa[F] con cinturino[M] a T

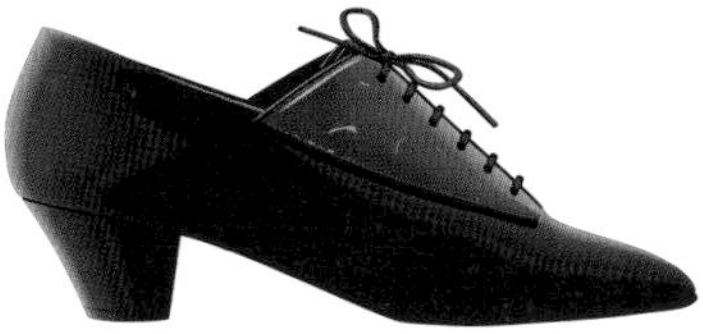

casual shoe
zapato[M] con cordones[M]
trotteur[M]
Straßenschuh[M]
francesina[F]

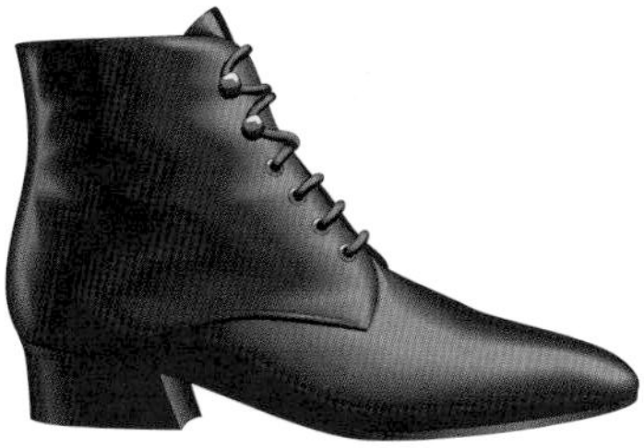

ankle boot
botín[M]
bottine[F]
knöchelhohe Stiefelette[F]
polacchina[F]

thigh-boot
bota[F] de medio muslo[M]
cuissarde[F]
Schaftstiefel[M]
stivale[M] alla moschettiera

boot
bota[F]
botte[F]
Stiefel[M]
stivale[M]

unisex shoes
calzados^M **unisex**
chaussures^F **unisexes**
Unisex-Schuhe^M
scarpe^F **unisex**

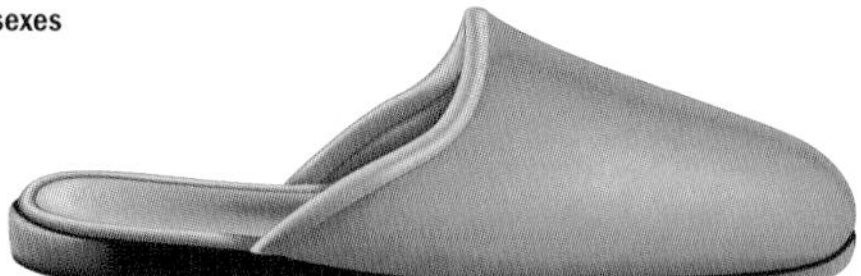

mule
pantufla^F
mule^F
Pantoffel^M
pianella^F

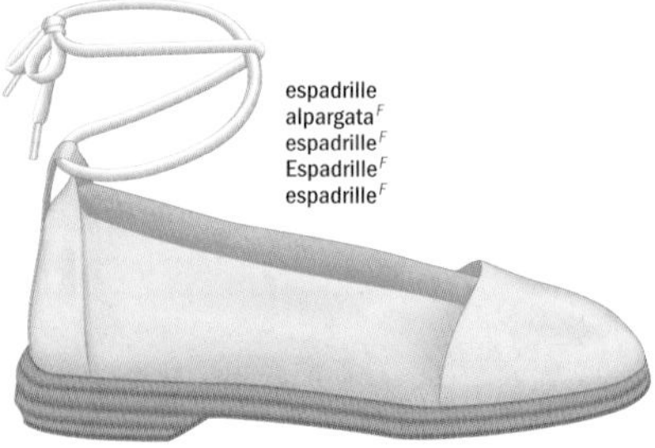

espadrille
alpargata^F
espadrille^F
Espadrille^F
espadrille^F

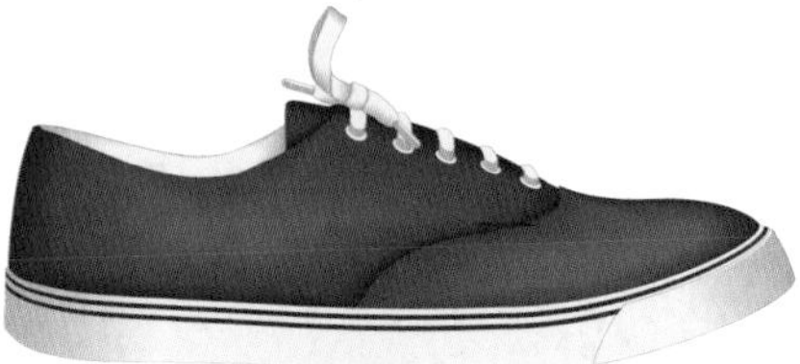

tennis shoe
zapatilla^F de tenis^M
tennis^M
Tennisschuh^M
scarpa^F da tennis^M

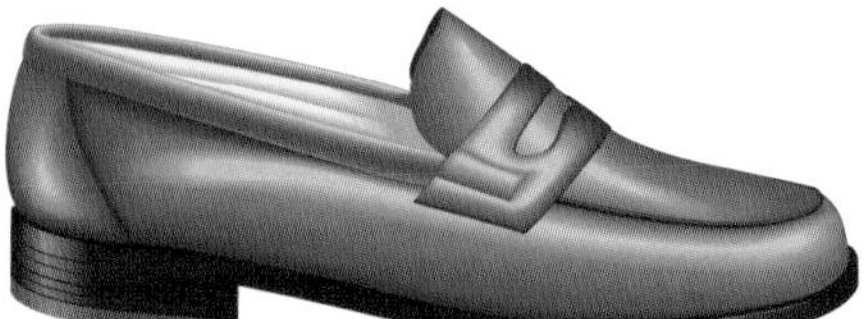

loafer
mocasín^M
loafer^M ; flâneur^M
Slipper^M
mocassino^M classico

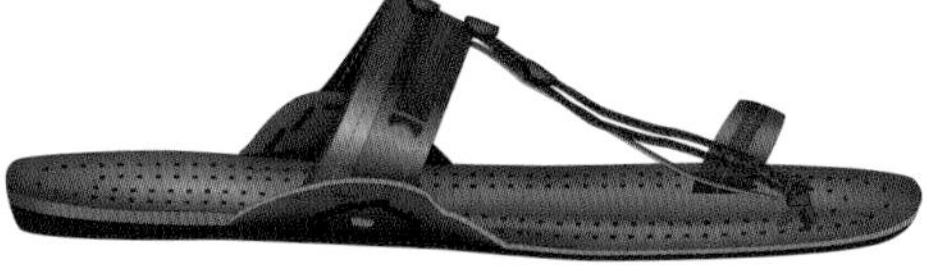

sandal
sandalia^F
nu-pied^M
Sandale^F mit Zehenriemchen^N
sandalo^M indiano

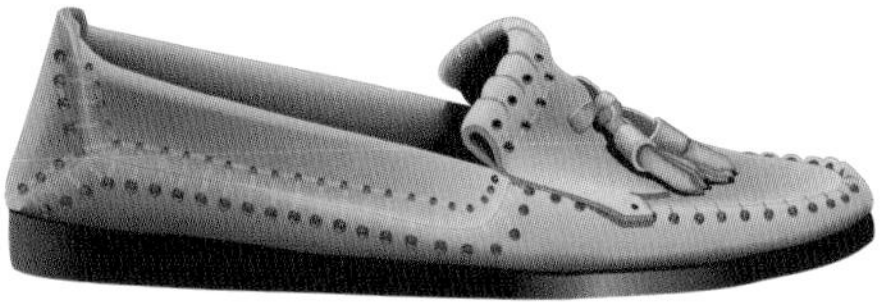

moccasin
mocasín^M
mocassin^M
Mokassin^M
mocassino^M

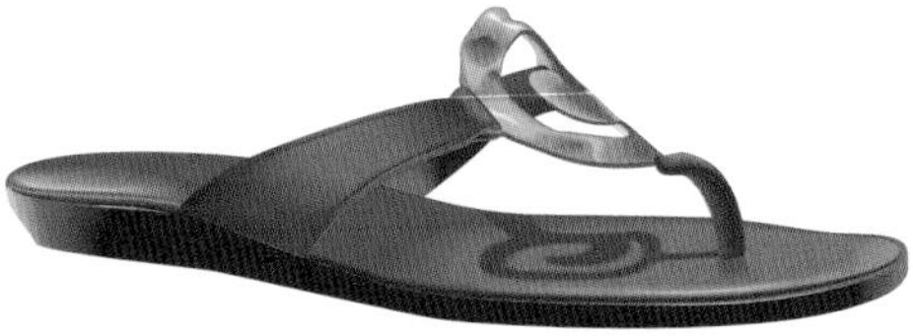

thong
chancleta^F playera
tong^M
Römerpantolette^F
infradito^M

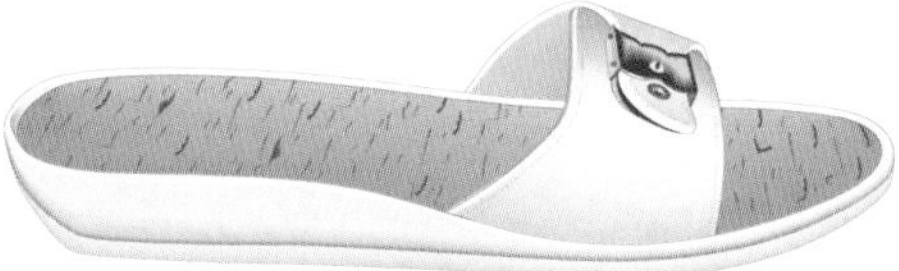

clog
chancleta^F
socque^M
Pantolette^F
zoccolo^M

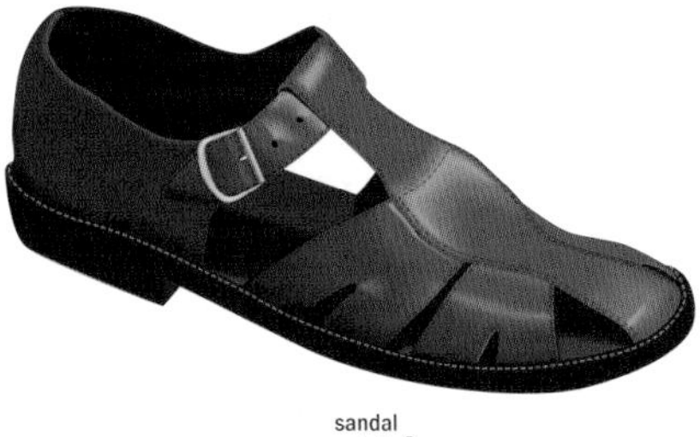

sandal
sandalia^F
sandalette^F
Sandale^F
sandalo^M

hiking boot
bota^F de montaña
brodequin^M de randonnée^F
Wanderschuh^M
pedula^F

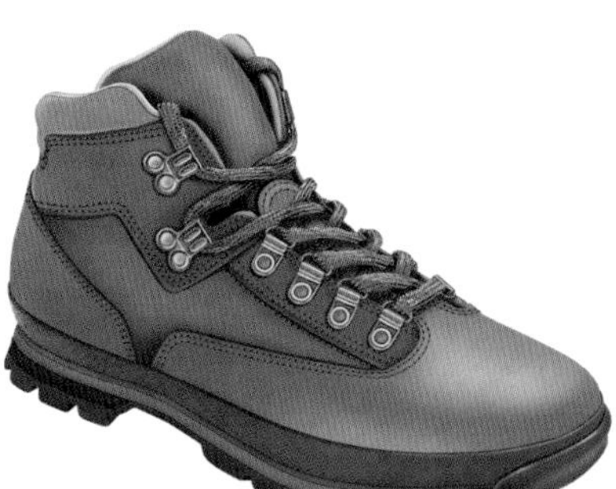

CLOTHING

shoeshine kit
juego^M limpiabotas^M
nécessaire^M à chaussures^F
Schuhputzzeug^N
kit^M per la pulizia^F delle scarpe^F

chamois leather
gamuza^F
peau^F de chamois^M
Ledertuch^N
pelle^F di camoscio^M

case
estuche^M
étui^M
Tasche^F
astuccio^M

shoebrush
cepillo^M
brosse^F à chaussure^F
Schuhbürste^F
spazzola^F

shoe polish
betún^M
boîte^F de cirage^M
Schuhcreme^F
lucido^M

shoe rack
zapatero^M de alambre^M
porte-chaussures^M
Schuhständer^M
scarpiera^F

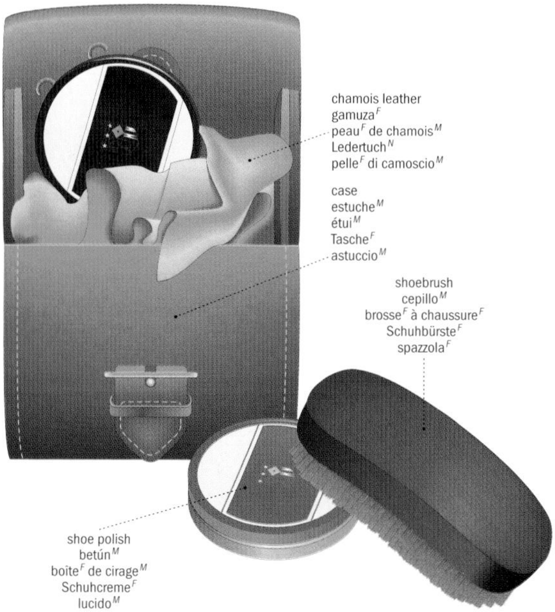

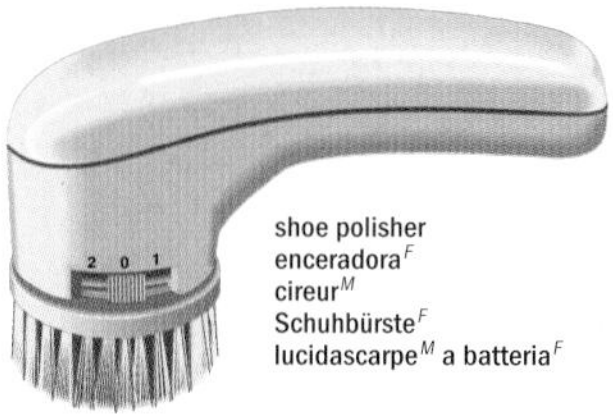

shoe polisher
enceradora^F
cireur^M
Schuhbürste^F
lucidascarpe^M a batteria^F

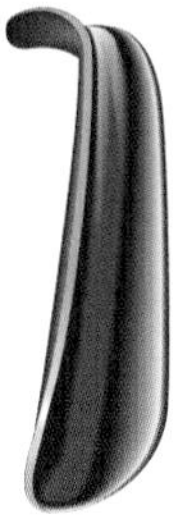

shoehorn
calzador^M
chausse-pied^M
Schuhlöffel^M
calzascarpe^M

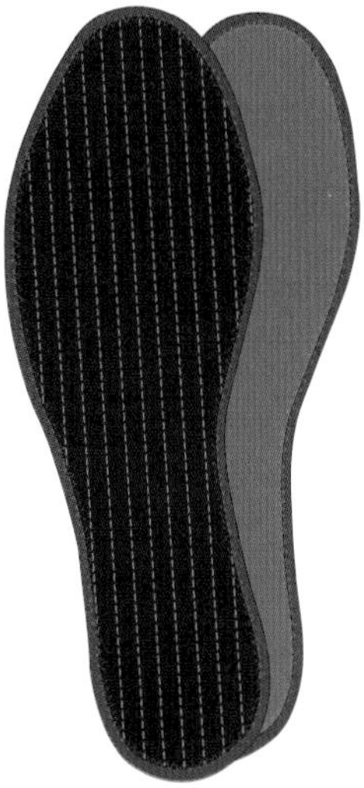

insole
plantilla^F
semelle^F
Einlegesohle^F
soletta^F

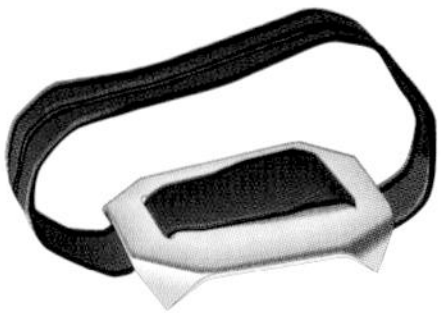

crampon
trepadora^F
crampon^M
Steigeisen^N
rampone^M

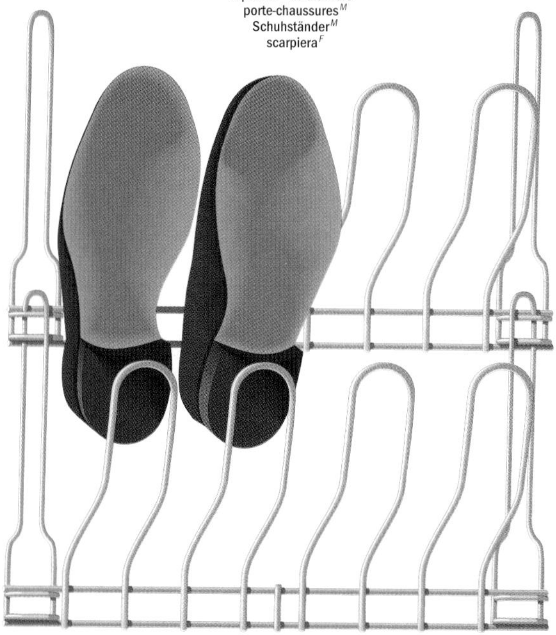

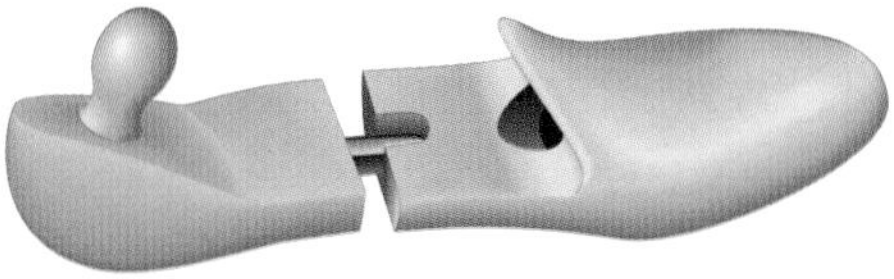

shoetree
horma^F
embauchoir^M
Schuhspanner^M
forma^F

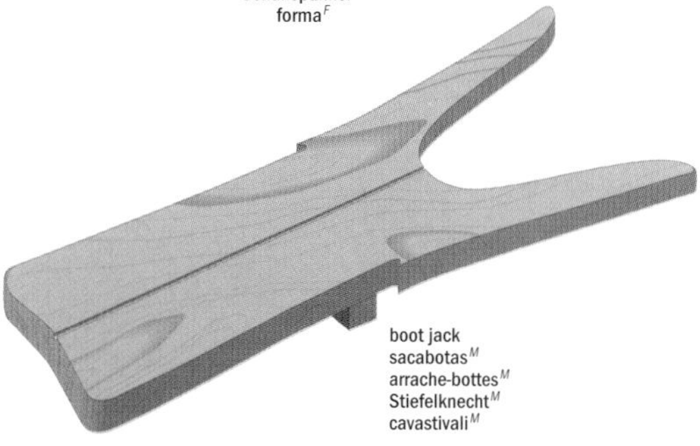

boot jack
sacabotas^M
arrache-bottes^M
Stiefelknecht^M
cavastivali^M

gloves

guantes^M | gants^M | Handschuhe^M | guanti^M

men's gloves
guantes^M de hombre^M
gants^M d'homme^M
Herrenhandschuhe^M
guanti^M da uomo^M

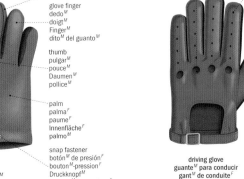

back of a glove
dorso^M de un guante^M
dos^M d'un gant^M
Handschuh^M-Außenseite^F
dorso^M del guanto^M

palm of a glove
palma^F de un guante^M
paume^F d'un gant^M
Handschuh^M-Innenseite^F
palmo^M del guanto^M

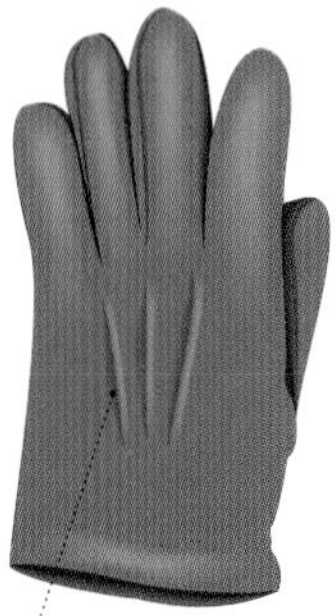

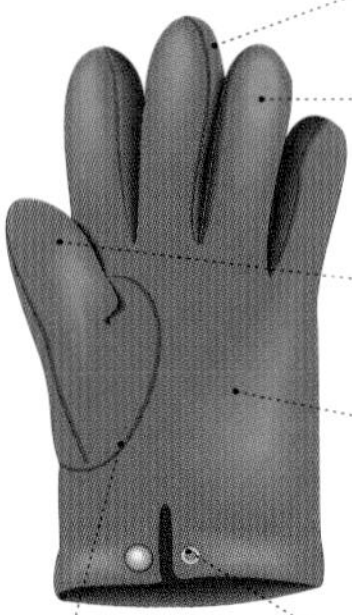

fourchette
horquilla^F
fourchette^F
Keil^M
linguella^F

glove finger
dedo^M
doigt^M
Finger^M
dito^M del guanto^M

thumb
pulgar^M
pouce^M
Daumen^M
pollice^M

palm
palma^F
paume^F
Innenfläche^F
palmo^M

snap fastener
botón^M de presión^F
bouton^M-pression^F
Druckknopf^M
bottone^M a pressione^F

stitching
pespunte^M
baguette^F
Ziernaht^F
impuntura^F

seam
costura^F
couture^F d'assemblage^M
Naht^F
cucitura^F

opening
aberturas^F para los nudillos^M
fenêtre^F
Öffnung^F
apertura^F

perforation
perforaciones^F
perforation^F
Perforierung^F
foro^M

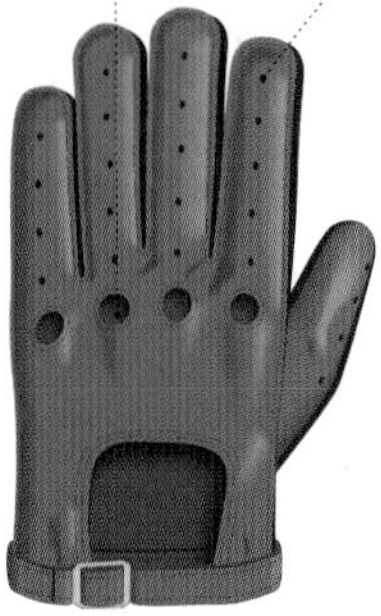

driving glove
guante^M para conducir
gant^M de conduite^F
Autohandschuh^M
guanto^M da guida^F

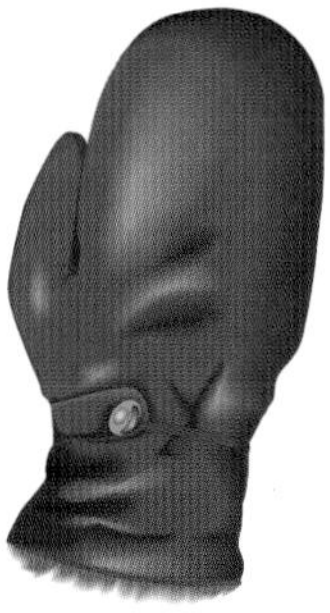

mitten
manopla^F
moufle^F ; mitaine^F
Fäustling^M
muffola^F

women's gloves
guantes^M de mujer^F
gants^M de femme^F
Damenhandschuhe^M
guanti^M da donna^F

gauntlet
manopla^F
gant^M à crispin^M
Stulpenhandschuh^M
guanto^M alla scudiera^F

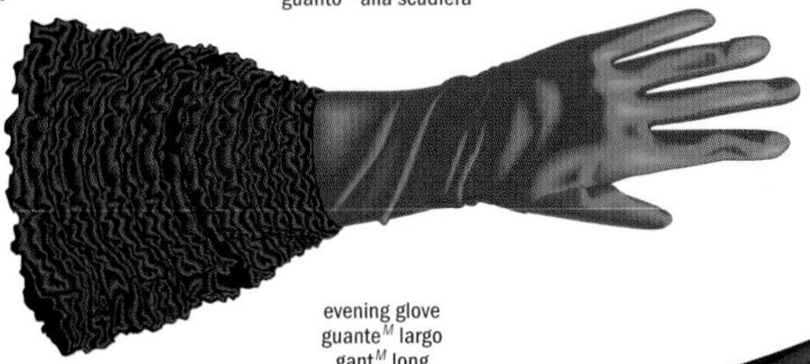

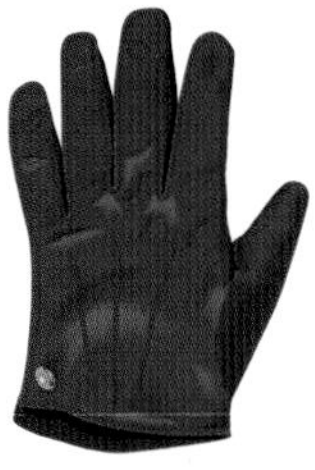

short glove
guante^M corto
gant^M court
Kurzhandschuh^M
guanto^M corto

evening glove
guante^M largo
gant^M long
langer Abendhandschuh^M
guanto^M da sera^F

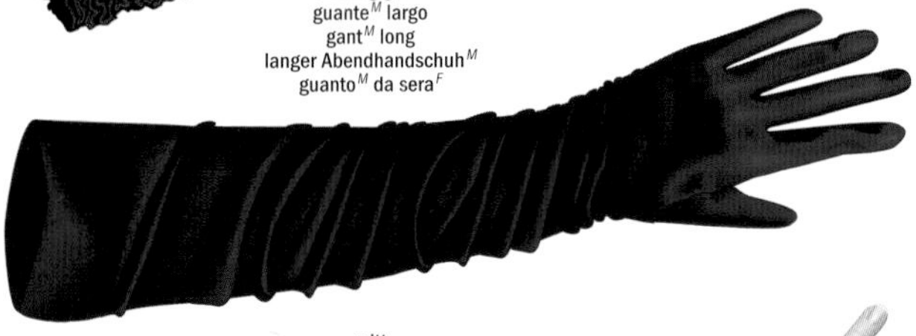

mitt
mitón^M largo
mitaine^F
fingerloser Spitzenhandschuh^M
mezzoguanto^M

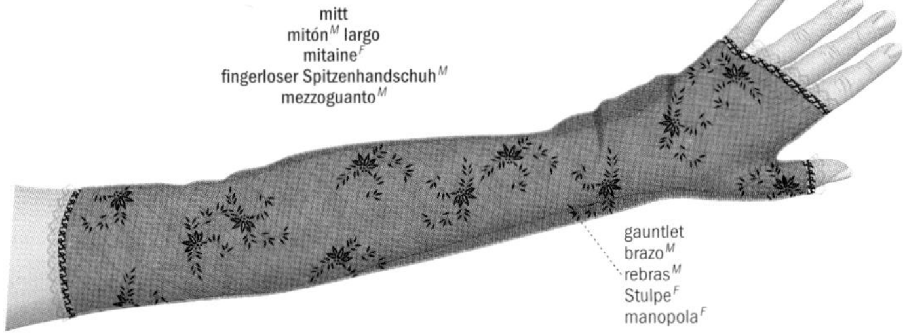

gauntlet
brazo^M
rebras^M
Stulpe^F
manopola^F

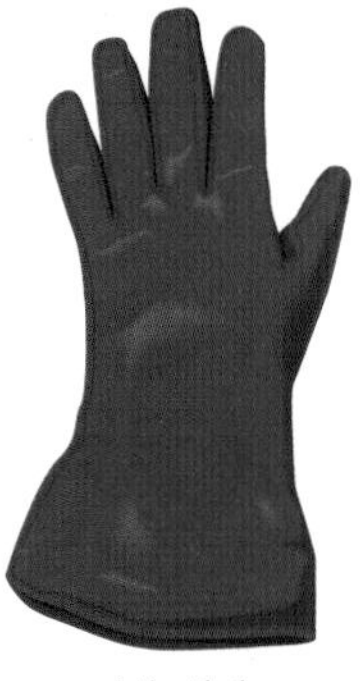

wrist-length glove
guante^M a la muñeca^F
gant^M saxe
Langhandschuh^M
guanto^M lungo

CLOTHING

fabric care symbols

símbolos^M del cuidado^M de los tejidos^M | symboles^M d'entretien^M des tissus^M | Wasch- und Pflegesymbole^N | simboli^M delle istruzioni^F sui tessuti^M

washing
lavado^M
lavage^M
Waschen^N
lavaggio^M

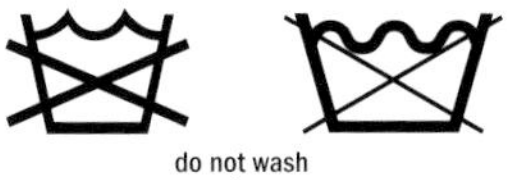

do not wash
no lavar
ne pas laver
nicht waschen
non lavare

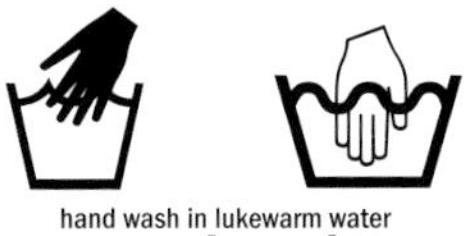

hand wash in lukewarm water
lavar a mano^M con agua^F tibia
laver à la main^F à l'eau^F tiède
Handwäsche^F, handwarme
lavare a mano^F in acqua^F tiepida

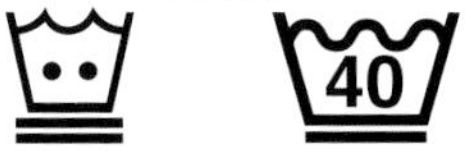

machine wash in lukewarm water at a gentle setting/reduced agitation
lavar a máquina^F con agua^F tibia en el ciclo^M para ropa^F delicada
laver à la machine^F à l'eau^F tiède avec agitation^F réduite
Maschinenwäsche^F, Schonwaschgang^M, 40 Grad
lavare in lavatrice^F in acqua^F tiepida e velocità^F ridotta

machine wash in warm water at a gentle setting/reduced agitation
lavar a máquina^F con agua^F caliente en el ciclo^M para ropa^F delicada
laver à la machine^F à l'eau^F chaude avec agitation^F réduite
Maschinenwäsche^F, Schonwaschgang^M, 60 Grad
lavare in lavatrice^F in acqua^F calda e velocità^F ridotta

machine wash in warm water at a normal setting
lavar a máquina^F con agua^F caliente, en el ciclo^M normal
laver à la machine^F à l'eau^F chaude avec agitation^F normale
Maschinenwäsche^F, Normalwaschgang^M, 60 Grad
lavare in lavatrice^F in acqua^F calda e velocità^F normale

machine wash in hot water at a normal setting
lavar en lavadora^F con agua^F muy caliente, en el ciclo^M normal
laver à la machine^F à l'eau^F très chaude avec agitation^F normale
Maschinenwäsche^F, Normalwaschgang^M, 90 Grad
lavare in lavatrice^F in acqua^F molto calda e velocità^F normale

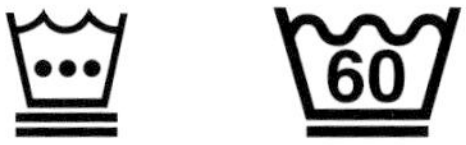

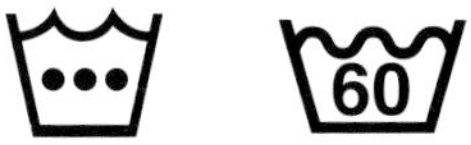

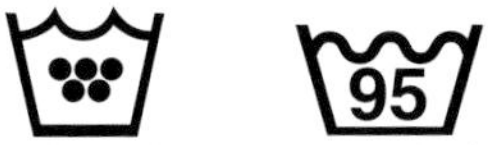

do not use chlorine bleach
no blanquear con cloro
ne pas utiliser de chlorure^M décolorant
Chlorbleiche nicht möglich
non candeggiare

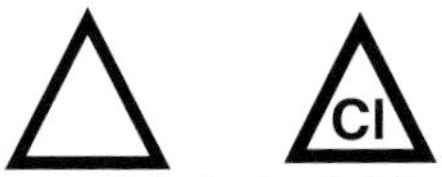

use chlorine bleach as directed
blanquear con cloro^M, siguiendo las indicaciones^F
utiliser un chlorure^M décolorant suivant les indications^F
Chlorbleiche möglich
usare il candeggiante^M secondo le istruzioni^F

drying
secado^M
séchage^M
Trocknen^N
asciugatura^F

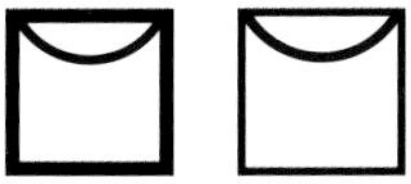

hang to dry
colgar al aire^M libre después de escurrir
suspendre pour sécher
zum Trocknen^N hängen
appendere per asciugare

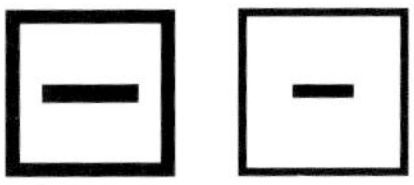

dry flat
secar extendido sobre una toalla^F después de escurrir
sécher à plat
zum Trocknen^N legen
distendere per asciugare

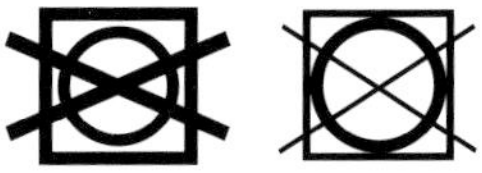

do not tumble dry
no secar en secadora^F mecánica
ne pas sécher par culbutage^M
Nicht in die Trockenmaschine^F geben
non centrifugare

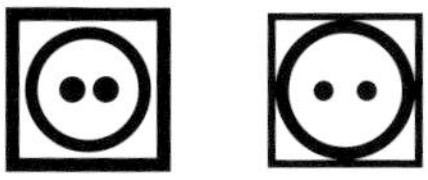

tumble dry at medium temperature
secar en secadora^F a temperatura^F media
sécher par culbutage^M à moyenne température^F
Bei mittlerer Temperatur^F in den Wäschetrockner^M geben
centrifugare a temperatura^F media

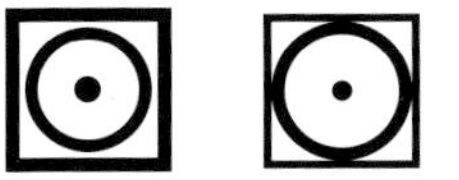

tumble dry at low temperature
secar en secadora^F a baja temperatura^F
sécher par culbutage^M à basse température^F
Bei niedriger Temperatur^F in den Wäschetrockner^M geben
centrifugare a bassa temperatura^F

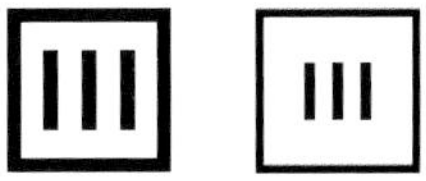

drip dry
secar sin escurrir
suspendre pour sécher sans essorer
tropfnass hängen
appendere senza strizzare

ironing
planchado^M
repassage^M
Bügeln^N
stiratura^F

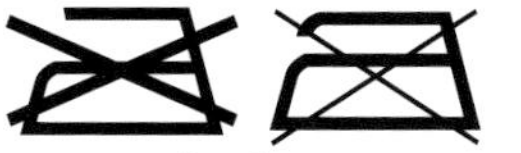

do not iron
no planchar
ne pas repasser
nicht bügeln
non stirare

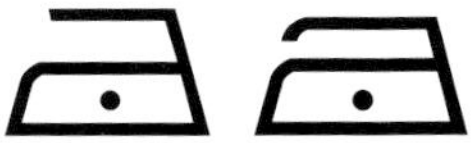

iron at low setting
usar plancha^F tibia
repasser à basse température^F
bei niedriger Temperatur^F bügeln
stirare a bassa temperatura^F

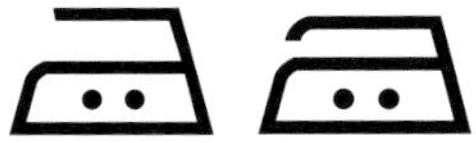

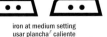

iron at medium setting
usar plancha^F caliente
repasser à moyenne température^F
bei mittlerer Temperatur^F bügeln
stirare a media temperatura^F

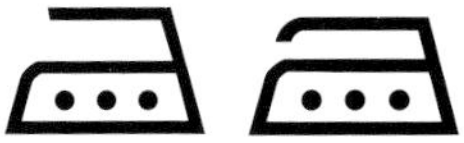

iron at high setting
usar plancha^F muy caliente
repasser à haute température^F
bei hoher Temperatur^F bügeln
stirare ad alta temperatura^F

left: American symbols
izquierda: símbolos^M americanos
gauche^F : symboles^M américains
links: amerikanische Symbole^N
sinistra^F: simboli^M americani

right: European symbols
derecha: símbolos^M europeos
droite^F : symboles^M européens
rechts: europäische Symbole^N
destra^F: simboli^M europei

CLOTHING

jackets
chaquetas^F y chalecos^M
veston^M et veste^F
Jackett^N und Weste^F
giacche^F e gilè^M

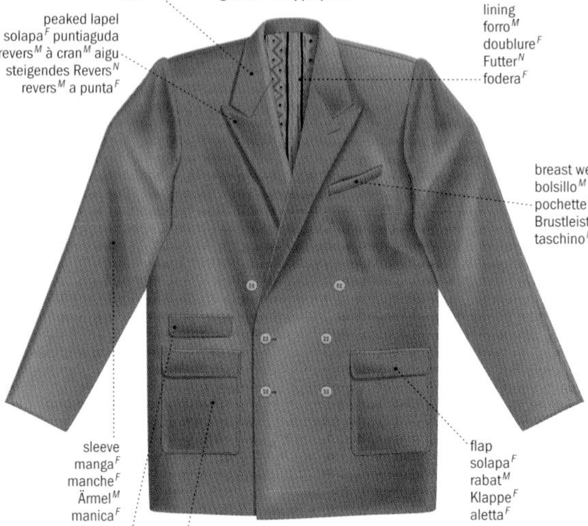

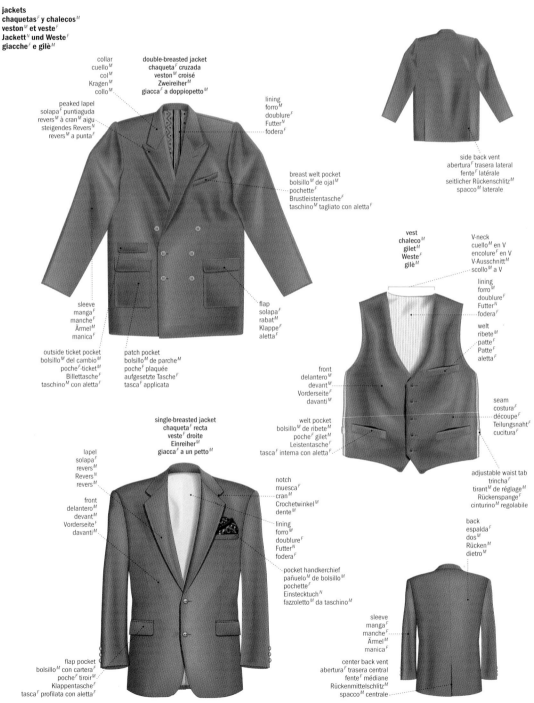

collar
cuello^M
col^M
Kragen^M
collo^M

double-breasted jacket
chaqueta^F cruzada
veston^M croisé
Zweireiher^M
giacca^F a doppiopetto^M

peaked lapel
solapa^F puntiaguda
revers^M à cran^M aigu
steigendes Revers^N
revers^M a punta^F

lining
forro^M
doublure^F
Futter^N
fodera^F

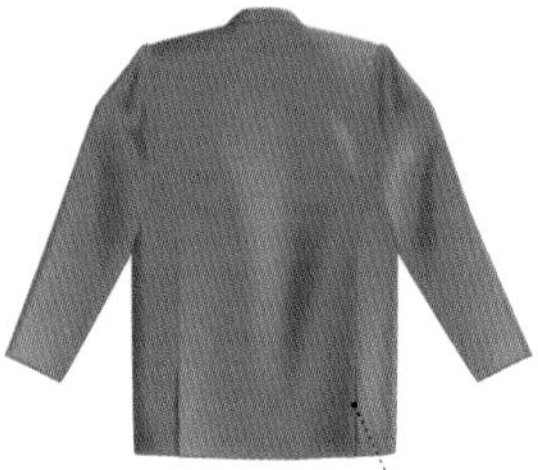

side back vent
abertura^F trasera lateral
fente^F latérale
seitlicher Rückenschlitz^M
spacco^M laterale

breast welt pocket
bolsillo^M de ojal^M
pochette^F
Brustleistentasche^F
taschino^M tagliato con aletta^F

vest
chaleco^M
gilet^M
Weste^F
gilè^M

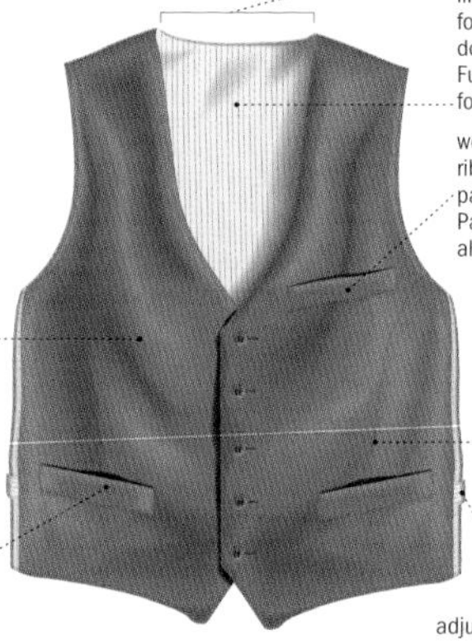

V-neck
cuello^M en V
encolure^F en V
V-Ausschnitt^M
scollo^M a V

lining
forro^M
doublure^F
Futter^N
fodera^F

welt
ribete^M
patte^F
Patte^F
aletta^F

sleeve
manga^F
manche^F
Ärmel^M
manica^F

flap
solapa^F
rabat^M
Klappe^F
aletta^F

outside ticket pocket
bolsillo^M del cambio^M
poche^F-ticket^M
Billettasche^F
taschino^M con aletta^F

patch pocket
bolsillo^M de parche^M
poche^F plaquée
aufgesetzte Tasche^F
tasca^F applicata

front
delantero^M
devant^M
Vorderseite^F
davanti^M

seam
costura^F
découpe^F
Teilungsnaht^F
cucitura^F

single-breasted jacket
chaqueta^F recta
veste^F droite
Einreiher^M
giacca^F a un petto^M

welt pocket
bolsillo^M de ribete^M
poche^F gilet^M
Leistentasche^F
tasca^F interna con aletta^F

adjustable waist tab
trincha^F
tirant^M de réglage^M
Rückenspange^F
cinturino^M regolabile

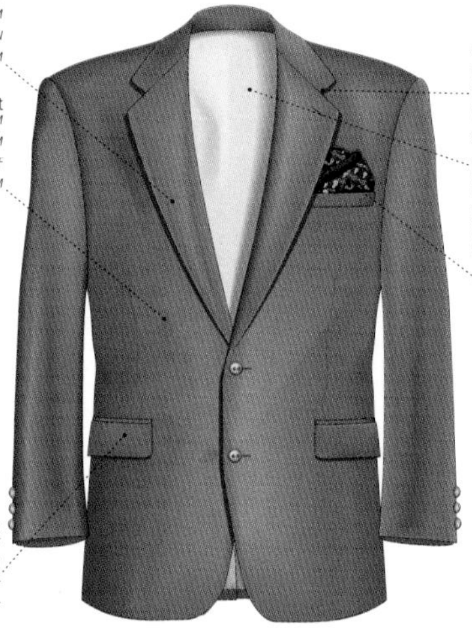

lapel
solapa^F
revers^M
Revers^N
revers^M

notch
muesca^F
cran^M
Crochetwinkel^M
dente^M

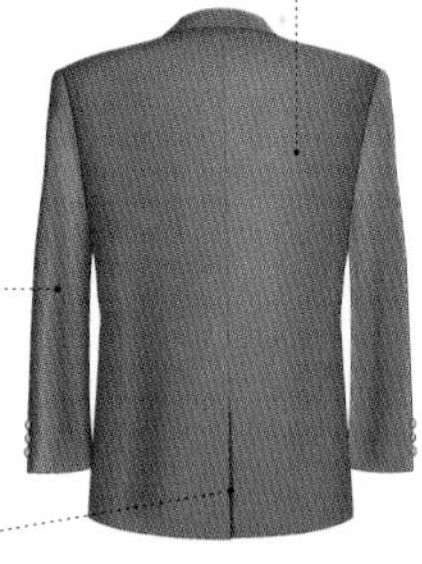

back
espalda^F
dos^M
Rücken^M
dietro^M

front
delantero^M
devant^M
Vorderseite^F
davanti^M

lining
forro^M
doublure^F
Futter^N
fodera^F

pocket handkerchief
pañuelo^M de bolsillo^M
pochette^F
Einstecktuch^N
fazzoletto^M da taschino^M

sleeve
manga^F
manche^F
Ärmel^M
manica^F

flap pocket
bolsillo^M con cartera^F
poche^F tiroir^M
Klappentasche^F
tasca^F profilata con aletta^F

center back vent
abertura^F trasera central
fente^F médiane
Rückenmittelschlitz^M
spacco^M centrale

CLOTHING

collar
cuello^M
col^M
Kragen^M
colletto^M

set-in sleeve
manga^F empotrada
manche^F montée
eingesetzter Ärmel^M
manica^F a giro^M

breast pocket
bolsillo^M superior
poche^F poitrine^F
Brusttasche^F
tasca^F applicata con aletta^F

buttoned placket
tirilla^F
patte^F de boutonnage^M
Knopfleiste^F
cannoncino^M

pointed tab end
abertura^F con tirilla^F
patte^F capucin^M
Ärmelschlitz^M
profilo^M dello spacco^M

cuff
puño^M
poignet^M
Manschette^F
polsino^M

yoke
canesú^M
empiècement^M
Sattel^M
sprone^M

collar point
punta^F del cuello^M
pointe^F de col^M
Kragenspitze^F
punta^F del colletto^M

front
delantero^M
devant^M
Vorderseite^F
davanti^M

button
botón^M
bouton^M
Knopf^M
bottone^M

shirttail
faldón^M de la camisa^F
pan^M
Schoß^M
lembo^M della camicia^F

shirt
camisa^F
chemise^F
Hemd^N
camicia^F

CLOTHING

collar stay
ballena^F
baleine^F de col^M
Kragenstäbchen^N
tendicollo^M

buttondown collar
cuello^M con botones^M
col^M pointes^F boutonnées
Button-Down-Kragen^M
collo^M button-down

ascot tie
corbata^F inglesa
lavallière^F
Krawattenschal^M
lavallière^F

bow tie
pajarita^F
nœud^M papillon^M
Fliege^F
papillon^M

spread collar
cuello^M italiano
col^M italien
gespreizter Kragen^M
collo^M a camicia^F

necktie
corbata^F
cravate^F
Krawatte^F
cravatta^F

front apron
faldón^M delantero
pan^M avant
Vorderteil^{M/N}
lembo^M anteriore

neck end
contorno^M del cuello^M
tour^M de cou^M
Bindeteil^{M/N}
annodatura^F

rear apron
faldón^M trasero
pan^M arrière
Endteil^{M/N}
lembo^M posteriore

lining
forro^M
doublure^F
Futter^N
fodera^F

loop
presilla^F
passant^M
Schlaufe^F
passante^M

slip-stitched seam
costura^F invisible
couture^F médiane
Verziehnaht^F
cucitura^F a sottopunto^M

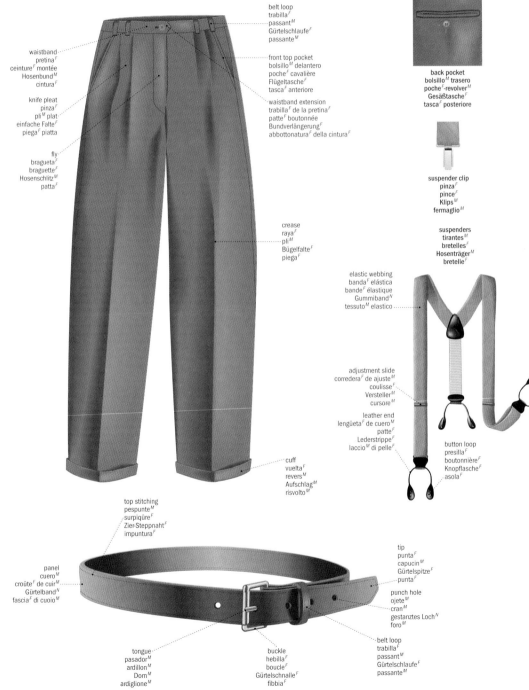

pants
pantalones^M
pantalon^M
Hose^F
pantaloni^M

belt loop
trabilla^F
passant^M
Gürtelschlaufe^F
passante^M

waistband
pretina^F
ceinture^F montée
Hosenbund^M
cintura^F

front top pocket
bolsillo^M delantero
poche^F cavalière
Flügeltasche^F
tasca^F anteriore

knife pleat
pinza^F
pli^M plat
einfache Falte^F
piega^F piatta

waistband extension
trabilla^F de la pretina^F
patte^F boutonnée
Bundverlängerung^F
abbottonatura^F della cintura^F

fly
bragueta^F
braguette^F
Hosenschlitz^M
patta^F

crease
raya^F
pli^M
Bügelfalte^F
piega^F

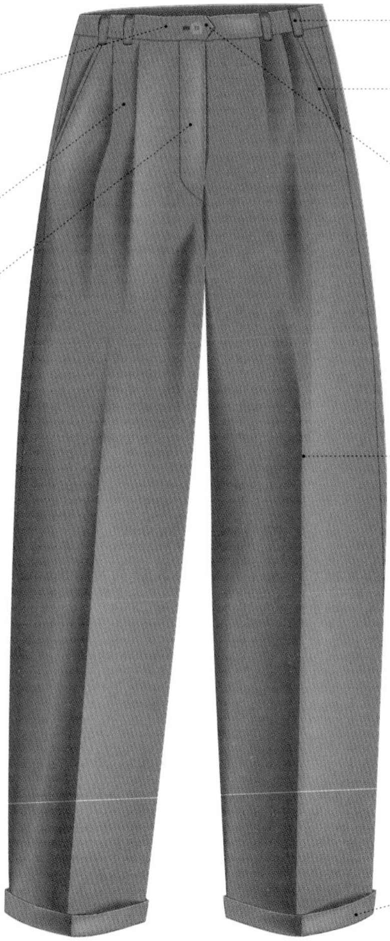

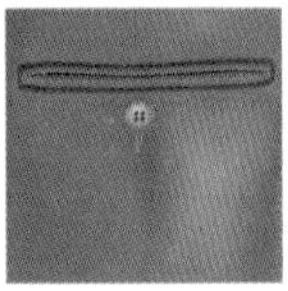

back pocket
bolsillo^M trasero
poche^F-revolver^M
Gesäßtasche^F
tasca^F posteriore

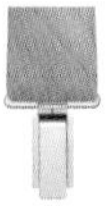

suspender clip
pinza^F
pince^F
Klips^M
fermaglio^M

suspenders
tirantes^M
bretelles^F
Hosenträger^M
bretelle^F

elastic webbing
banda^F elástica
bande^F élastique
Gummiband^N
tessuto^M elastico

adjustment slide
corredera^F de ajuste^M
coulisse^F
Versteller^M
cursore^M

leather end
lengüeta^F de cuero^M
patte^F
Lederstrippe^F
laccio^M di pelle^F

button loop
presilla^F
boutonnière^F
Knopflasche^F
asola^F

cuff
vuelta^F
revers^M
Aufschlag^M
risvolto^M

belt
cinturón^M
ceinture^F
Gürtel^M
cintura^F

top stitching
pespunte^M
surpiqûre^F
Zier-Steppnaht^F
impuntura^F

tip
punta^F
capucin^M
Gürtelspitze^F
punta^F

panel
cuero^M
croûte^F de cuir^M
Gürtelband^N
fascia^F di cuoio^M

punch hole
ojete^M
cran^M
gestanztes Loch^N
foro^M

tongue
pasador^M
ardillon^M
Dorn^M
ardiglione^M

buckle
hebilla^F
boucle^F
Gürtelschnalle^F
fibbia^F

belt loop
trabilla^F
passant^M
Gürtelschlaufe^F
passante^M

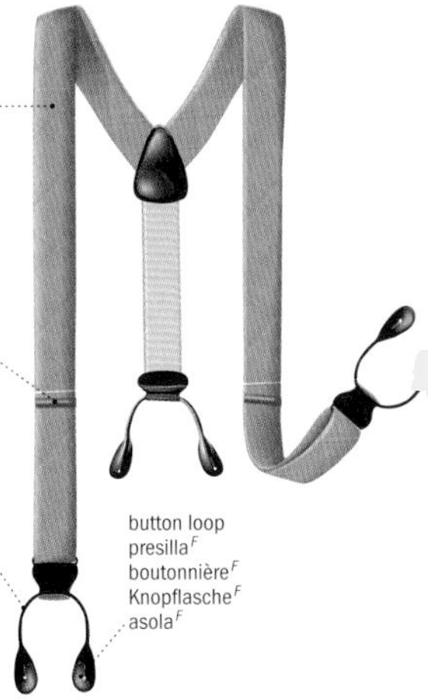

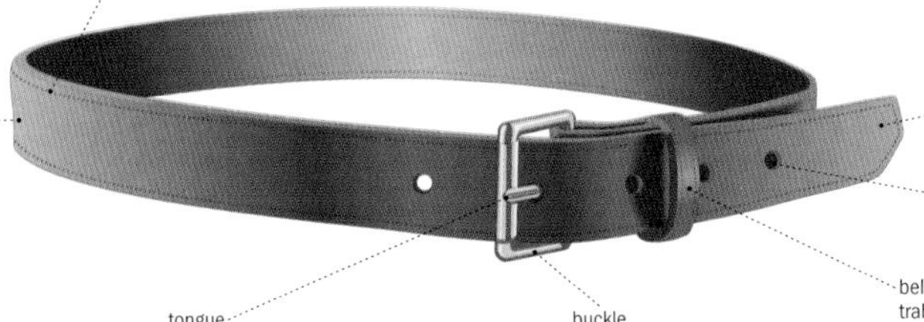

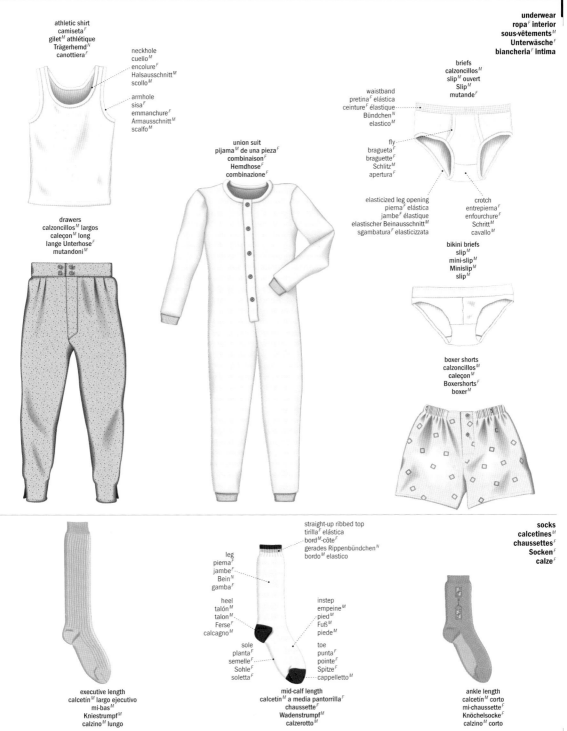

athletic shirt
camiseta^F
gilet^M athlétique
Trägerhemd^N
canottiera^F

neckhole
cuello^M
encolure^F
Halsausschnitt^M
scollo^M

armhole
sisa^F
emmanchure^F
Armausschnitt^M
scalfo^M

drawers
calzoncillos^M largos
caleçon^M long
lange Unterhose^F
mutandoni^M

union suit
pijama^M de una pieza^F
combinaison^F
Hemdhose^F
combinazione^F

underwear
ropa^F interior
sous-vêtements^M
Unterwäsche^F
biancheria^F intima

briefs
calzoncillos^M
slip^M ouvert
Slip^M
mutande^F

waistband
pretina^F elástica
ceinture^F élastique
Bündchen^N
elastico^M

fly
bragueta^F
braguette^F
Schlitz^M
apertura^F

elasticized leg opening
pierna^F elástica
jambe^F élastique
elastischer Beinausschnitt^M
sgambatura^F elasticizzata

crotch
entrepierna^F
enfourchure^F
Schritt^M
cavallo^M

bikini briefs
slip^M
mini-slip^M
Minislip^M
slip^M

boxer shorts
calzoncillos^M
caleçon^M
Boxershorts^F
boxer^M

CLOTHING

socks
calcetines^M
chaussettes^F
Socken^F
calze^F

straight-up ribbed top
tirilla^F elástica
bord^M-côte^F
gerades Rippenbündchen^N
bordo^M elastico

leg
pierna^F
jambe^F
Bein^N
gamba^F

heel
talón^M
talon^M
Ferse^F
calcagno^M

instep
empeine^M
pied^M
Fuß^M
piede^M

sole
planta^F
semelle^F
Sohle^F
soletta^F

toe
punta^F
pointe^F
Spitze^F
cappelletto^M

executive length
calcetín^M largo ejecutivo
mi-bas^M
Kniestrumpf^M
calzino^M lungo

mid-calf length
calcetín^M a media pantorrilla^F
chaussette^F
Wadenstrumpf^M
calzerotto^M

ankle length
calcetín^M corto
mi-chaussette^F
Knöchelsocke^F
calzino^M corto

coats
abrigos^M **e impermeables**^{F}
manteaux^M **et blousons**^{M}
Mäntel^M **und Jacken**^{F}
esempi^M **di giacconi e cappotti**^{M}

raincoat
impermeable^M
imperméable^M
Regenmantel^M
impermeabile^M

overcoat
abrigo^M
pardessus^M
Mantel^M
cappotto^M

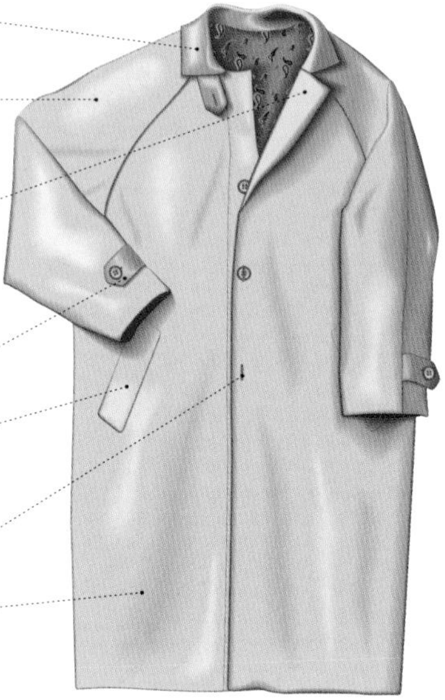

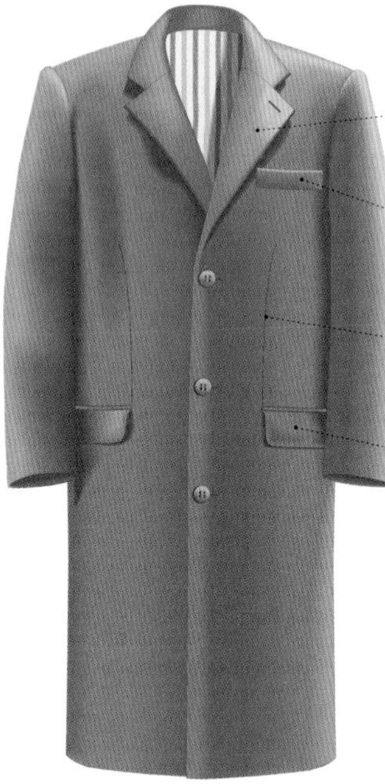

collar
cuello^M
col^M
Kragen^M
collo^M

raglan sleeve
manga^F raglán
manche^F raglan
Raglanärmel^M
manica^F alla raglan^M

notched lapel
solapa^F con ojal^M
revers^M cranté
abfallendes Revers^N
revers^M

tab
lengüeta^F
patte^F
Spange^F
linguetta^F

broad-welt side pocket
bolsillo^M de ribete^M ancho
poche^F raglan
schräge Pattentasche^F
tasca^F interna con aletta^F

buttonhole
ojal^M
boutonnière^F
Knopfloch^N
occhiello^M

side panel
paño^M lateral
pan^M
Seitenteil$^{M/N}$
falda^F

notched lapel
solapa^F con ojal^M
revers^M cranté
abfallendes Revers^N
revers^M

breast pocket
bolsillo^M superior
poche^F poitrine^F
Brusttasche^F
taschino^M

breast dart
pinza^F
pince^F de taille^F
Taillenabnäher^M
ripresa^F

flap pocket
bolsillo^M con cartera^F
poche^F à rabat^F
Klappentasche^F
tasca^F profilata con aletta^F

trench coat
trinchera^F
trench^M
Trenchcoat^M
trench^M

two-way collar
cuello^M de doble vista^F
col^M transformable
Wendekragen^M
collo^M

gun flap
protector^M
bavolet^M
Koller^N
aletta^F staccata

double-breasted buttoning
botonadura^F cruzada
double boutonnage^M
zweireihig
abbottonatura^F a doppiopetto^M

belt
cinturón^M
ceinture^F
Gürtel^M
cintura^F

belt loop
presilla^F del cinturón^M
passant^M
Gürtelschlaufe^F
passante^M della cintura^F

frame
hebilla^F
boucle^F de ceinture^F
Schnalle^F
fibbia^F

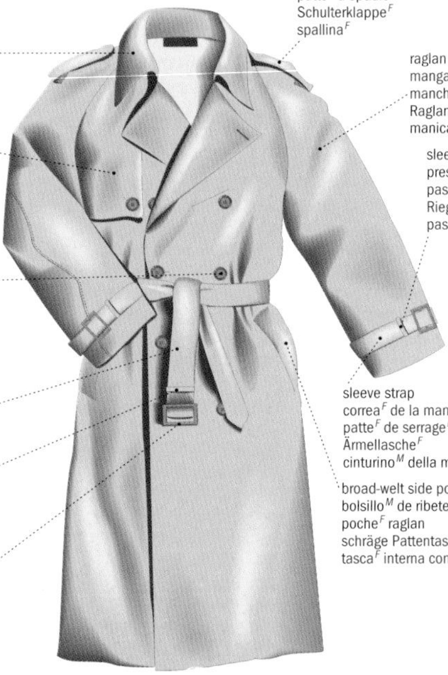

epaulet
hombrera^F
patte^F d'épaule^F
Schulterklappe^F
spallina^F

raglan sleeve
manga^F raglán
manche^F raglan
Raglanärmel^M
manica^F alla raglan^M

sleeve strap loop
presilla^F de la manga^F
passant^M
Riegel^M
passante^M del cinturino^M

sleeve strap
correa^F de la manga^F
patte^F de serrage^M
Ärmellasche^F
cinturino^M della manica^F

broad-welt side pocket
bolsillo^M de ribete^M ancho
poche^F raglan
schräge Pattentasche^F
tasca^F interna con aletta^F

three-quarter coat
abrigo^M de tres cuartos
paletot^M
dreiviertellange Jacke^F
trequarti^M

CLOTHING

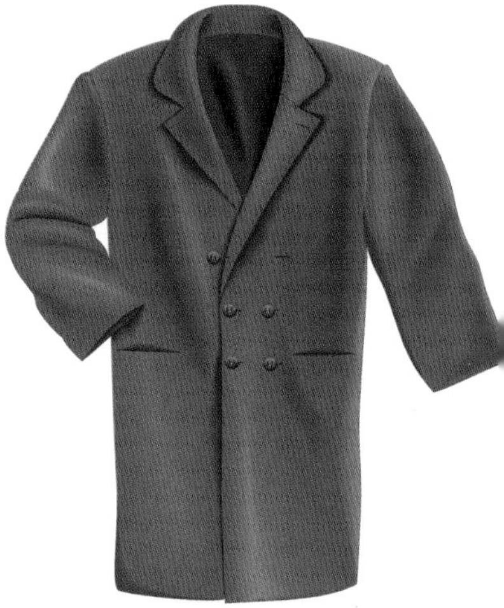

CLOTHING

parka
parka^F
parka^F ; *parka*^M
Parka^M
parka^M

sheepskin jacket
zamarra^F
canadienne^F
Lammfelljacke^F
montone^M

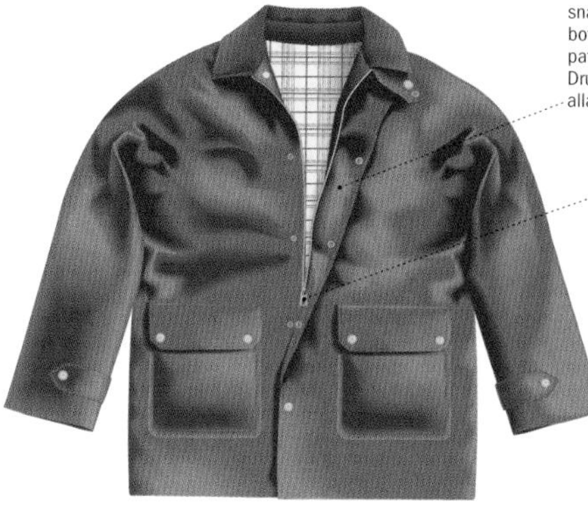

snap-fastening tab
botón^M de presión^F
patte^F à boutons^M-pression^F
Druckknopfleiste^F
allacciatura^F con bottoni^M a pressione^F

zipper
cremallera^F
fermeture^F à glissière^F
Reißverschluss^M
chiusura^F lampo

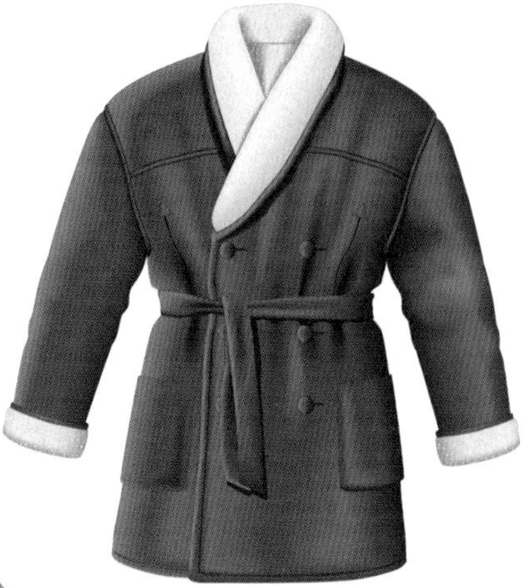

duffle coat
trenca^F
duffle-coat^M ; *corvette*^F
Dufflecoat^M
montgomery^M

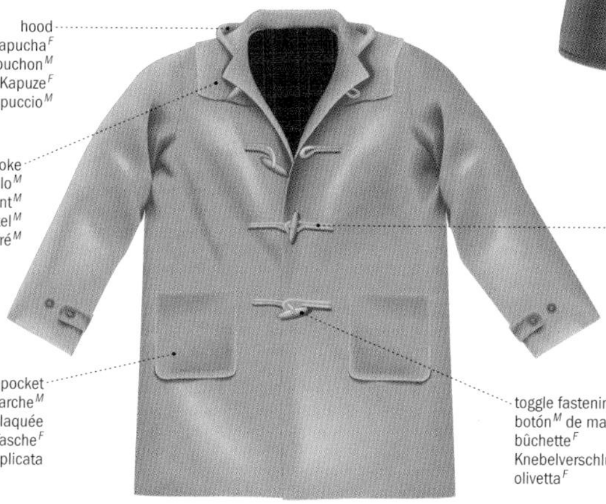

hood
capucha^F
capuchon^M
Kapuze^F
cappuccio^M

frog
alamar^M
brandebourg^M
Lasche^F
alamaro^M

yoke
hombrillo^M
empiècement^M
Sattel^M
carré^M

patch pocket
bolsillo^M de parche^M
poche^F plaquée
aufgesetzte Tasche^F
tasca^F applicata

toggle fastening
botón^M de madera^F
büchette^F
Knebelverschluss^M
olivetta^F

jacket
cazadora^F
blouson^M court
Blouson^M
giacca^F a vento^M

windbreaker
cazadora^F
blouson^M long
Windjacke^F
giacca^F a vento^M

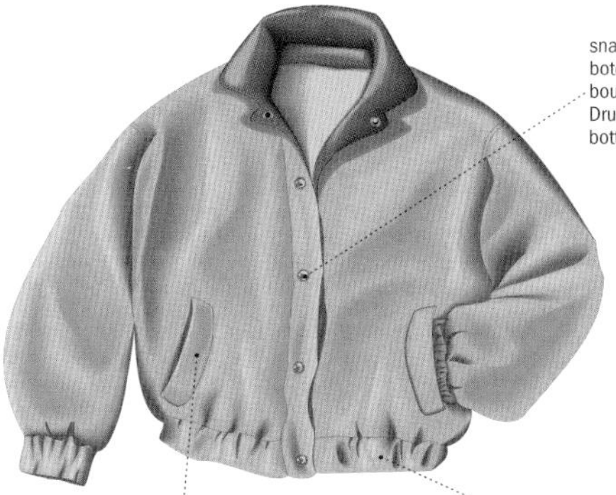

snap fastener
botón^M de presión^M
bouton^M-pression^F
Druckknopf^M
bottone^M a pressione^F

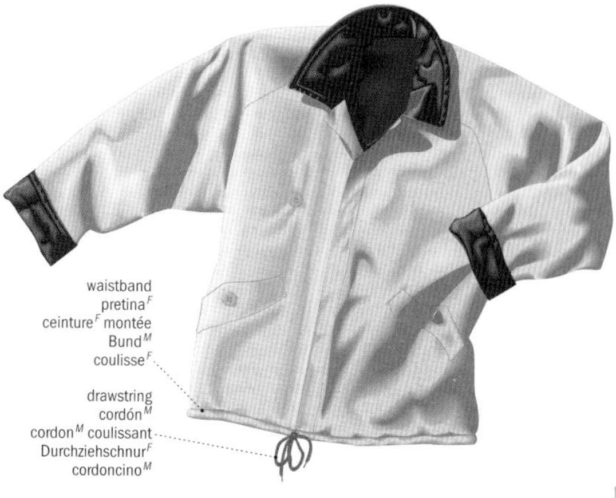

waistband
pretina^F
ceinture^F montée
Bund^M
coulisse^F

drawstring
cordón^M
cordon^M coulissant
Durchziehschnur^F
cordoncino^M

hand-warmer pocket
bolsillo^M de ojal^M
poche^F repose-bras^M
Mufftasche^F
tasca^F interna con aletta^F

elastic waistband
pretina^F elástica
ceinture^F élastique
elastischer Bund^M
fascia^F elastica

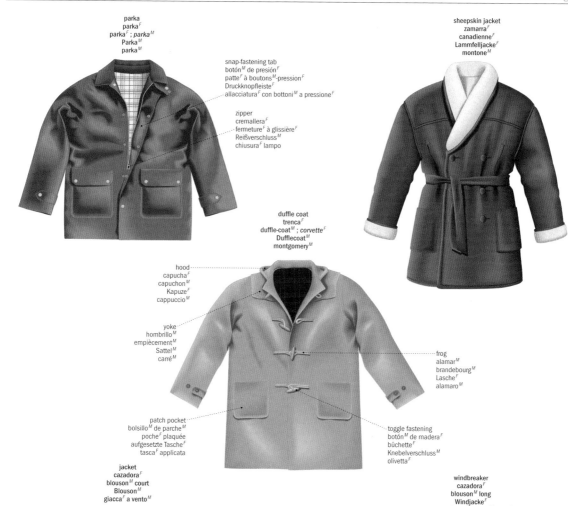

CLOTHING

V-neck cardigan
cárdigan
gilet[M] de laine[F]
Strickjacke[F] mit V-Ausschnitt[M]
cardigan[M] con scollo[M] a V

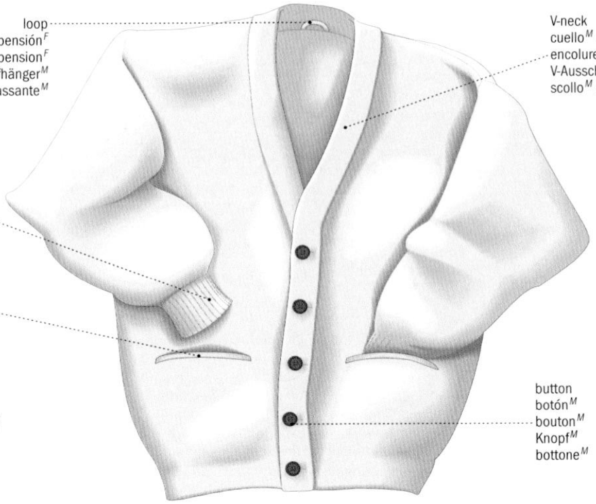

loop
trabilla[F] de suspensión[F]
bride[F] de suspension[F]
Aufhänger[M]
passante[M]

V-neck
cuello[M] de pico[M]
encolure[F] en V
V-Ausschnitt[M]
scollo[M] a V

ribbing
tirilla[F] elástica
bord[M]-côte[F]
Patent-Strickbündchen[N]
bordo[M] a coste[F]

welt pocket
bolsillo[M]
poche[F] passepoilée
Paspeltasche[F]
tasca[F] profilata

button
botón[M]
bouton[M]
Knopf[M]
bottone[M]

sweater vest
chaleco[M] de punto[M]
débardeur[M]
Pullunder[M]
gilè[M]

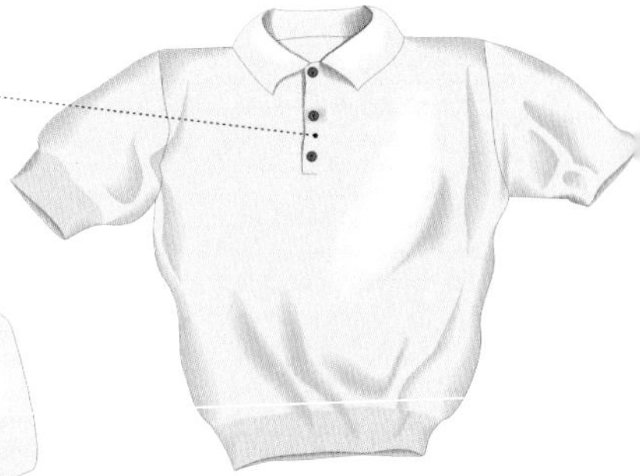

buttoned placket
tirilla[F]
patte[F] polo[M]
Knopfleiste[F]
abbottonatura[F] a polo[F]

knit shirt
polo[M]
polo[M]
Poloshirt[N]
polo[F]

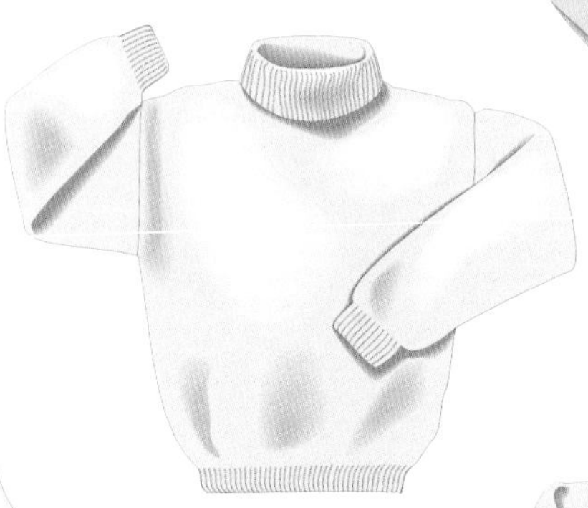

turtleneck
jersey[M] de cuello[M] de tortuga[F]
col[M] roulé
Rollkragenpullover[M]
maglione[M] dolcevita[M]

crew neck sweater
jersey[M] de cuello[M] redondo
ras-de-cou[M]
Pullover[M] mit halsnahem Ausschnitt[M]
maglione[M] girocollo[M]

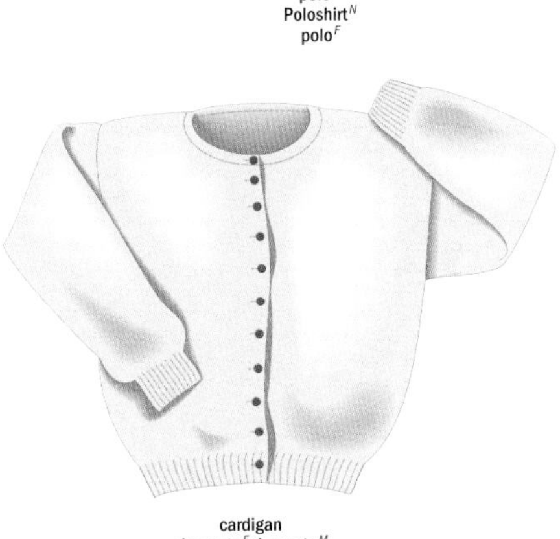

cardigan
chaqueta[F] de punto[M]
cardigan[M]
Strickjacke[F]
cardigan[M]

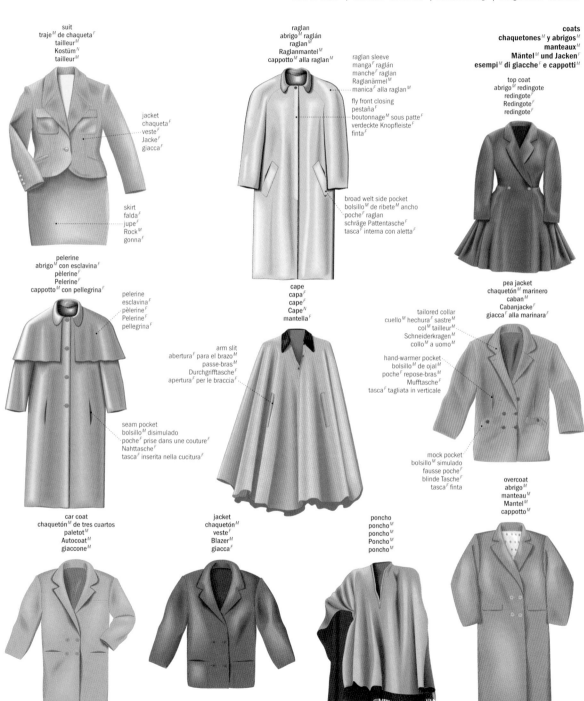

suit
traje^M de chaqueta^F
tailleur^M
Kostüm^N
tailleur^M

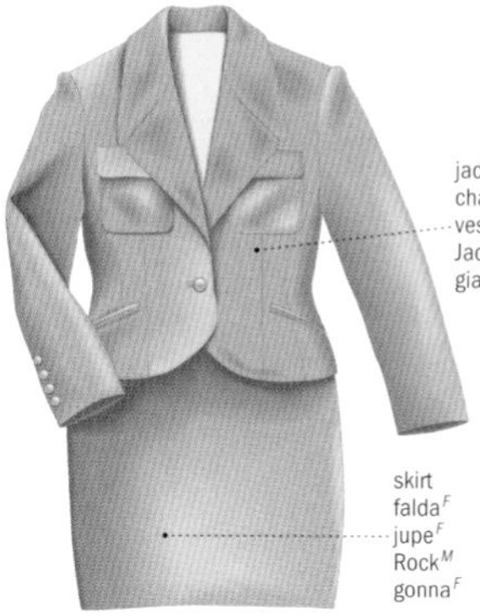

jacket
chaqueta^F
veste^F
Jacke^F
giacca^F

skirt
falda^F
jupe^F
Rock^M
gonna^F

raglan
abrigo^M raglán
raglan^F
Raglanmantel^M
cappotto^M alla raglan^M

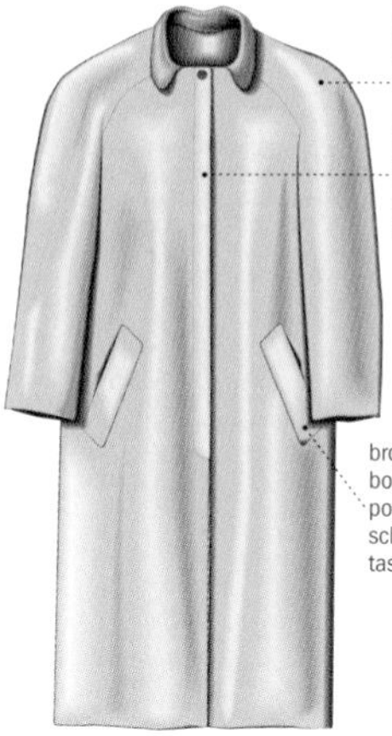

raglan sleeve
manga^F raglán
manche^F raglan
Raglanärmel^M
manica^F alla raglan^M

fly front closing
pestaña^F
boutonnage^M sous patte^F
verdeckte Knopfleiste^F
finta^F

broad welt side pocket
bolsillo^M de ribete^M ancho
poche^F raglan
schräge Pattentasche^F
tasca^F interna con aletta^F

coats
chaquetones^M y abrigos^M
manteaux^M
Mäntel^M und Jacken^F
esempi^M di giacche^F e cappotti^M

top coat
abrigo^M redingote
redingote^F
Redingote^F
redingote^F

CLOTHING

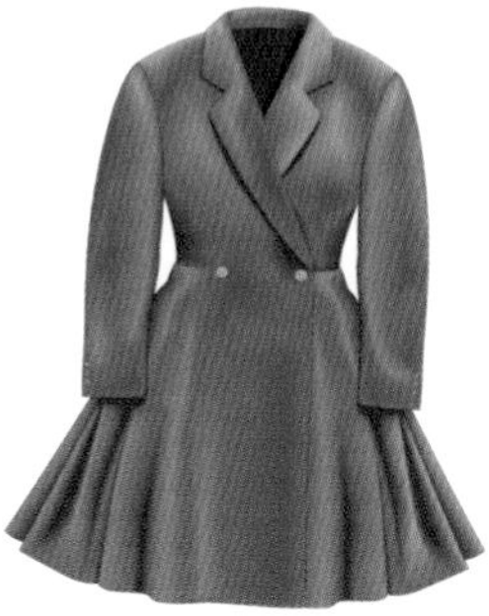

pelerine
abrigo^M con esclavina^F
pèlerine^F
Pelerine^F
cappotto^M con pellegrina^F

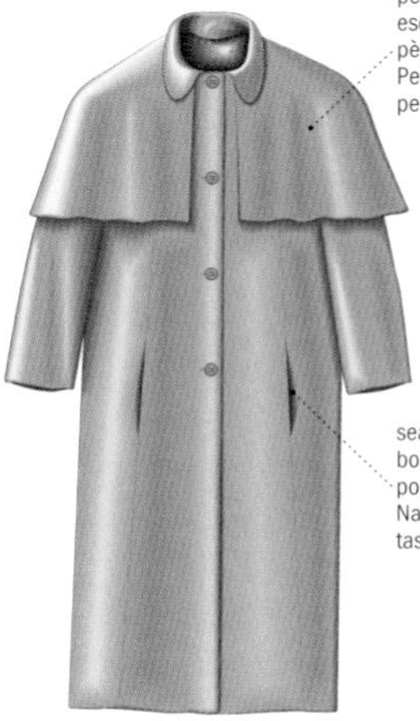

pelerine
esclavina^F
pèlerine^F
Pelerine^F
pellegrina^F

seam pocket
bolsillo^M disimulado
poche^F prise dans une couture^F
Nahttasche^F
tasca^F inserita nella cucitura^F

cape
capa^F
cape^F
Cape^N
mantella^F

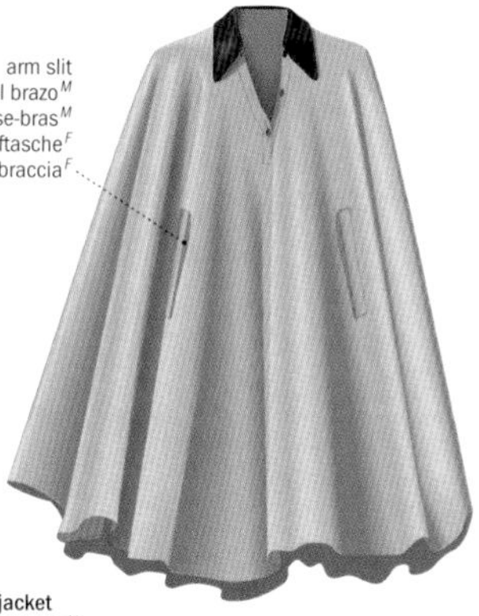

arm slit
abertura^F para el brazo^M
passe-bras^M
Durchgrifftasche^F
apertura^F per le braccia^F

pea jacket
chaquetón^M marinero
caban^M
Cabanjacke^F
giacca^F alla marinara^F

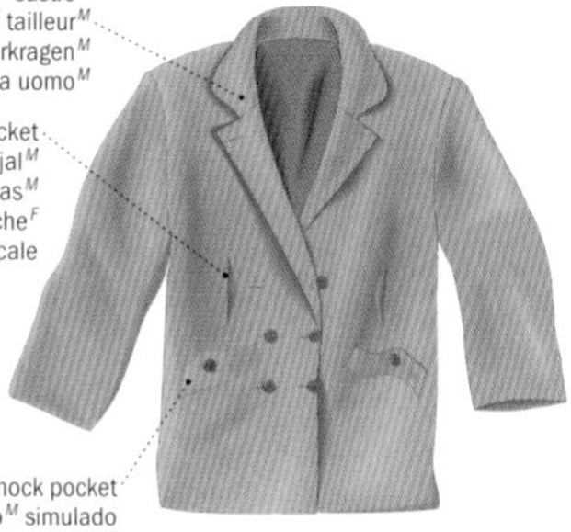

tailored collar
cuello^M hechura^F sastre^M
col^M tailleur^M
Schneiderkragen^M
collo^M a uomo^M

hand-warmer pocket
bolsillo^M de ojal^M
poche^F repose-bras^M
Mufftasche^F
tasca^F tagliata in verticale

mock pocket
bolsillo^M simulado
fausse poche^F
blinde Tasche^F
tasca^F finta

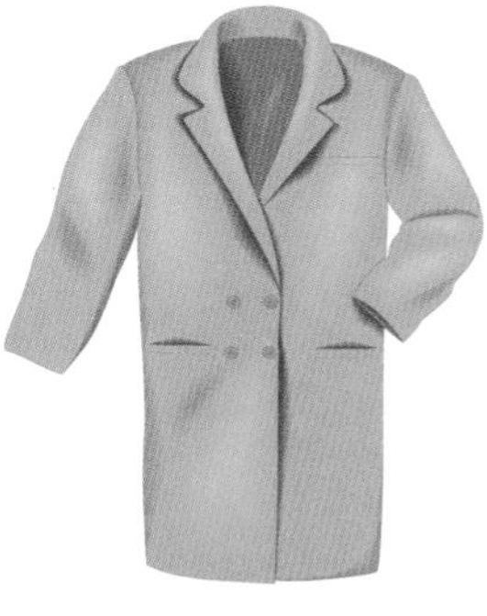

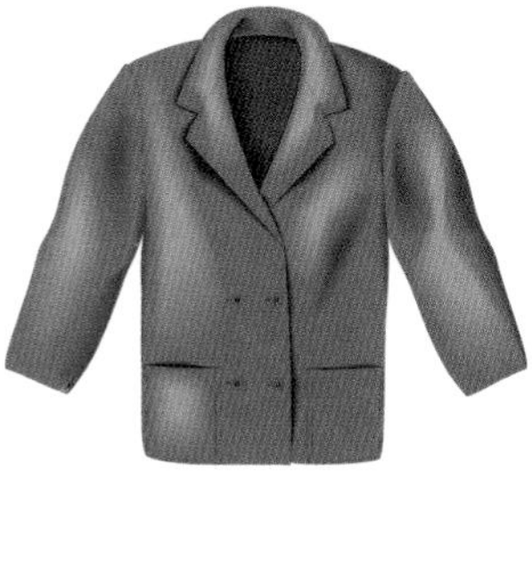

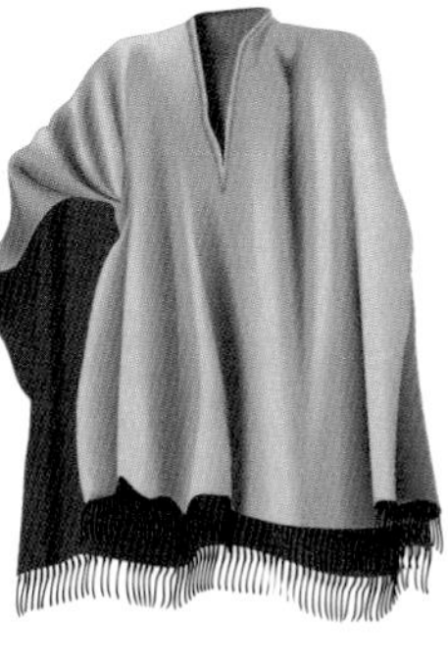

overcoat
abrigo^M
manteau^M
Mantel^M
cappotto^M

car coat
chaquetón^M de tres cuartos
paletot^M
Autocoat^M
giaccone^M

jacket
chaquetón^M
veste^F
Blazer^M
giacca^F

poncho
poncho^M
poncho^M
Poncho^M
poncho^M

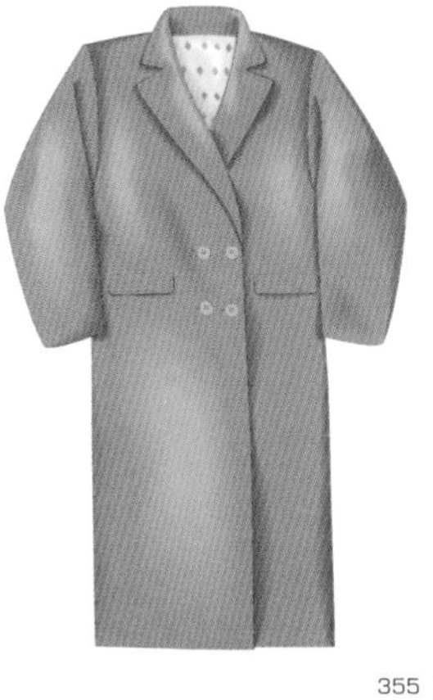

examples of dresses
ejemplos^M **de vestidos**^{M}
exemples^M **de robes**^{F}
Beispiele^N **für Kleider**^{N}
esempi^M **di abiti**^{M}

sheath dress
recto^M entallado
robe^F fourreau^M
Schlauchkleid^N
tubino^M

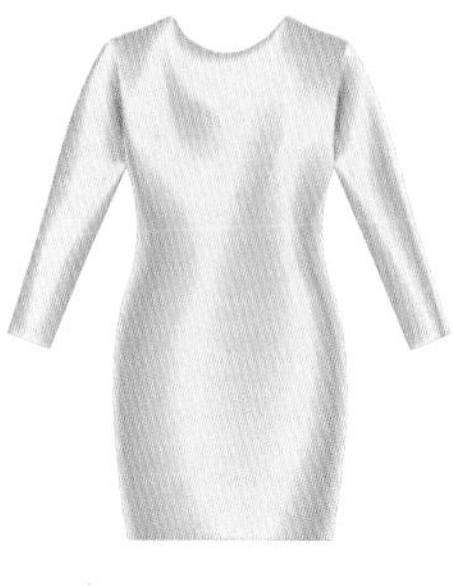

princess-seamed dress
corte^M princesa^F
robe^F princesse^F
Prinzesskleid^N
princesse^F

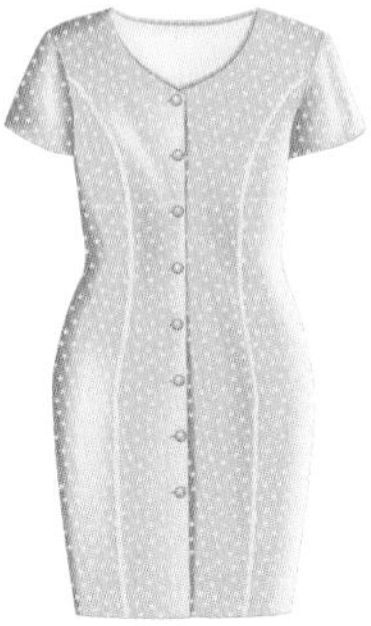

coat dress
traje^M cruzado
robe^F-manteau^M
Mantelkleid^N
robe-manteau$^{F/M}$

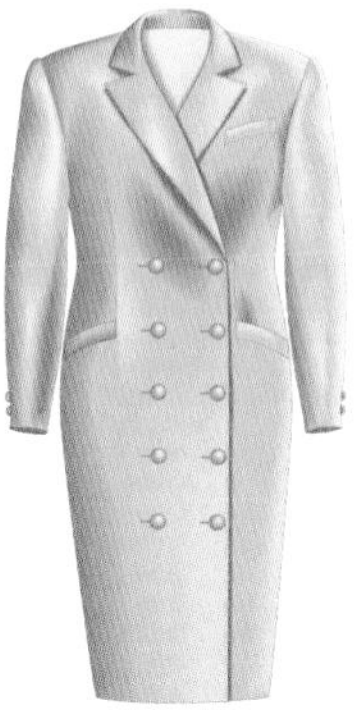

polo dress
vestido^M de camiseta^F
robe^F-polo^M
Polokleid^N
abito^M a polo^F

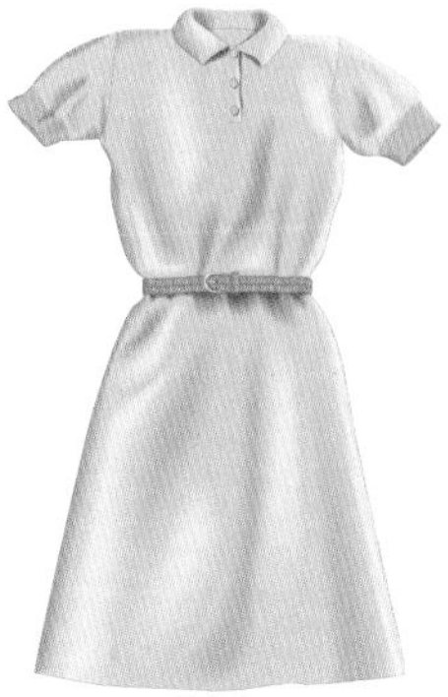

housedress
vestido^M camisero sin mangas
robe^F de maison^F
Hauskleid^N
abito^M da casa^F

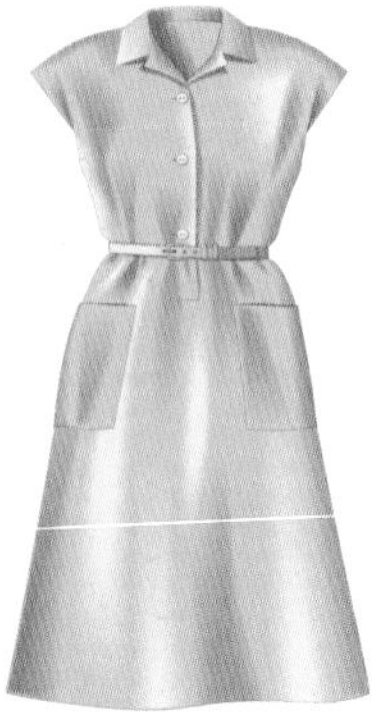

shirtwaist dress
vestido^M camisero
robe^F chemisier^M
Hemdblusenkleid^N
chemisier^M

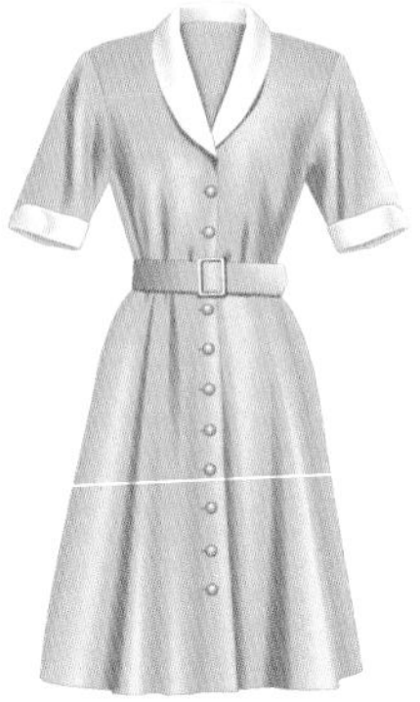

drop-waist dress
vestido^M de talle^M bajo
robe^F taille^F basse
Kleid^N mit angesetztem Schoß^M
abito^M a vita^F bassa

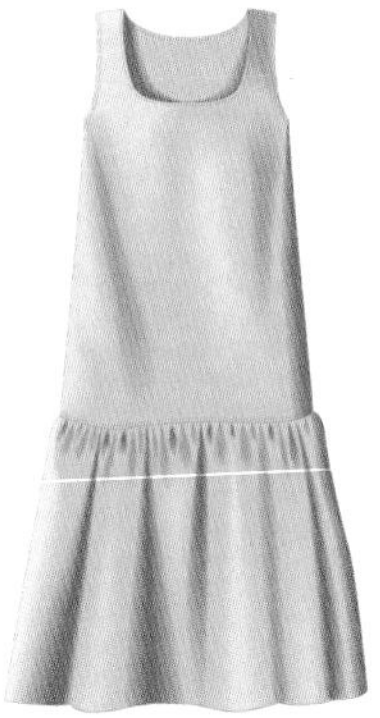

trapeze dress
vestido^M acampanado
robe^F trapèze^M
Kleid^N in Trapez-Form^F
abito^M a trapezio^M

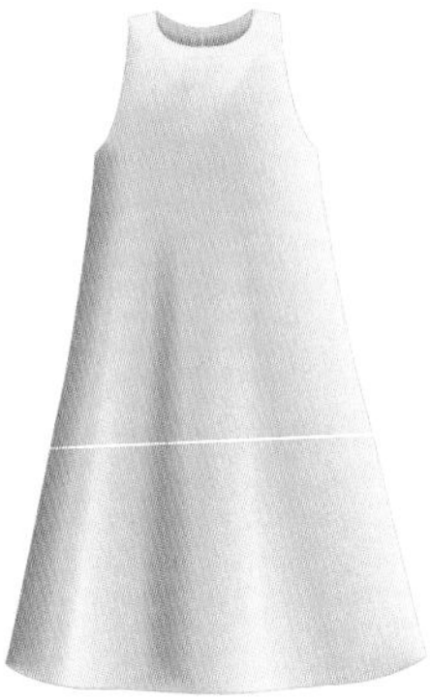

sundress
vestido^M de tirantes^M
robe^F bain^M-de-soleil^M
leichtes Sonnenkleid^N
prendisole^M

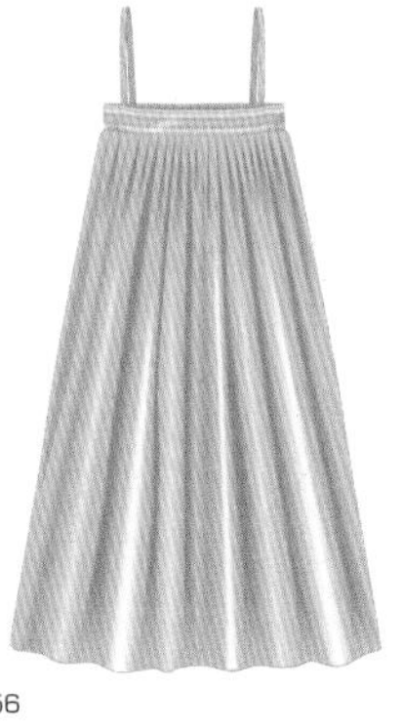

wraparound dress
vestido^M cruzado
robe^F enveloppe^F
Wickelkleid^N
abito^M a vestaglia^F

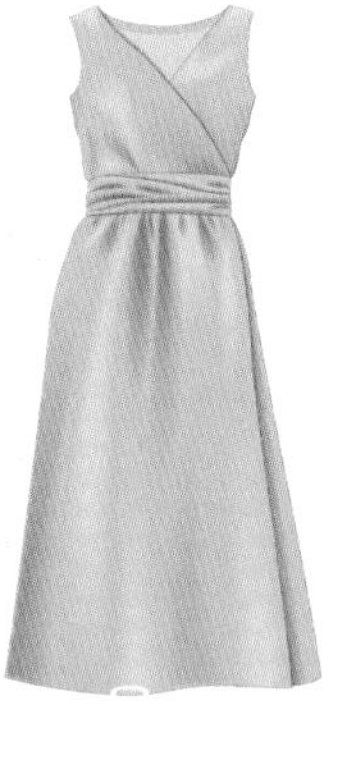

tunic dress
túnica^F
robe^F tunique^F
Tunikakleid^N
abito^M a tunica^F

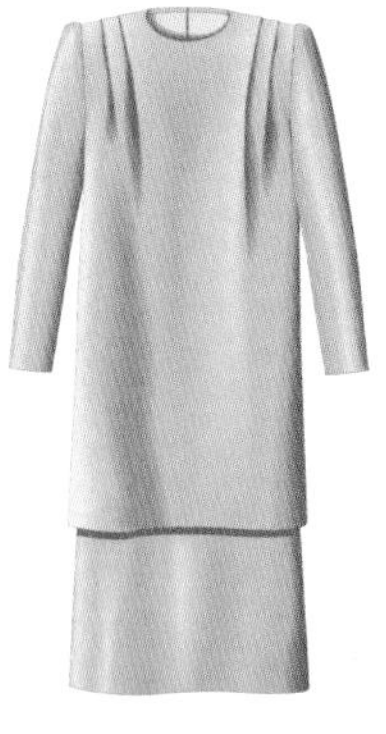

jumper
pichi^M
chasuble^F
Trägerrock^M
scamiciato^M

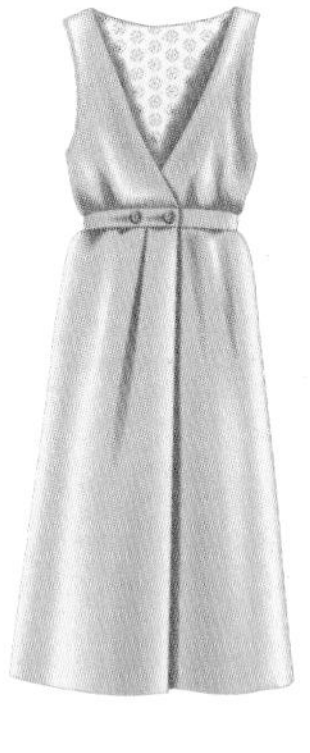

examples of skirts
ejemplos^M de faldas^F
exemples^M de jupes^F
Beispiele^N für Röcke^M
esempi^M di gonne^F

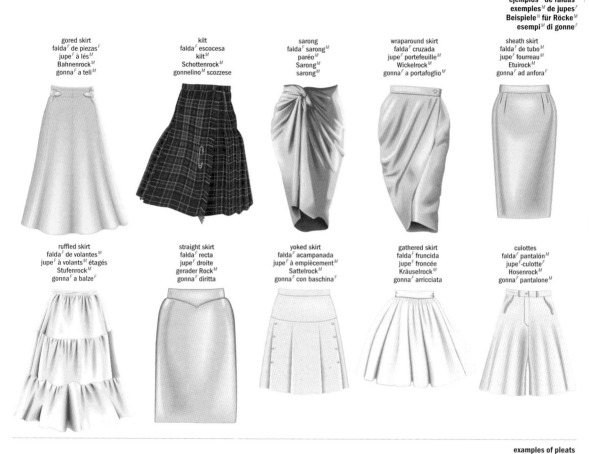

gored skirt
falda^F de piezas^F
jupe^F à lés^M
Bahnenrock^M
gonna^F a teli^M

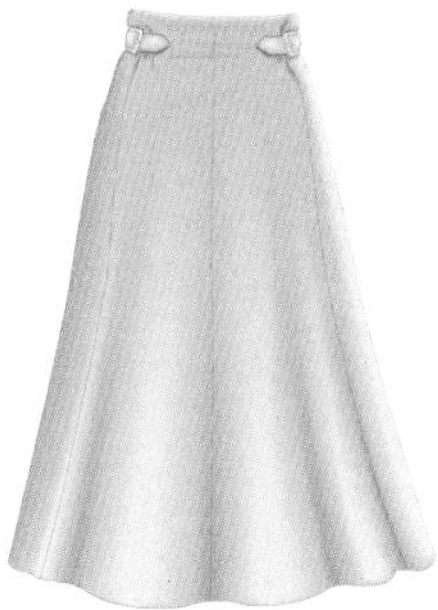

kilt
falda^F escocesa
kilt^M
Schottenrock^M
gonnelino^M scozzese

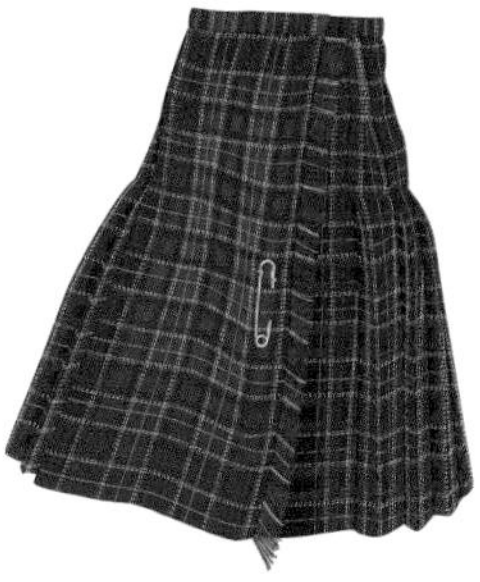

sarong
falda^F sarong^M
paréo^M
Sarong^M
sarong^M

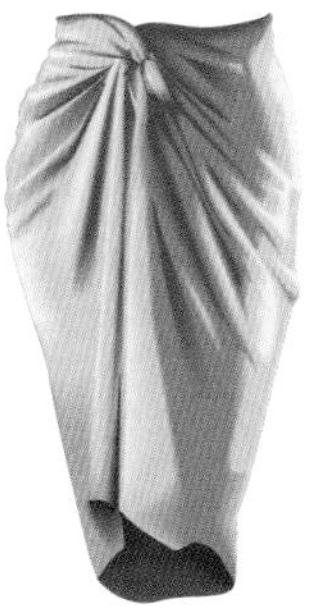

wraparound skirt
falda^F cruzada
jupe^F portefeuille^M
Wickelrock^M
gonna^F a portafoglio^M

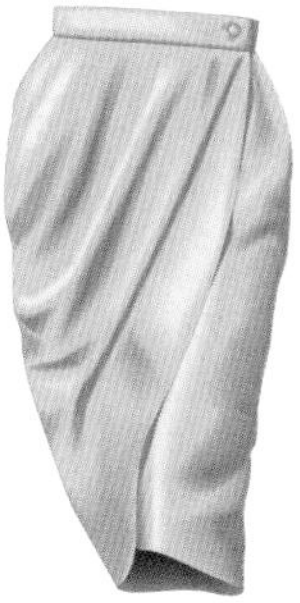

sheath skirt
falda^F de tubo^M
jupe^F fourreau^M
Etuirock^M
gonna^F ad anfora^F

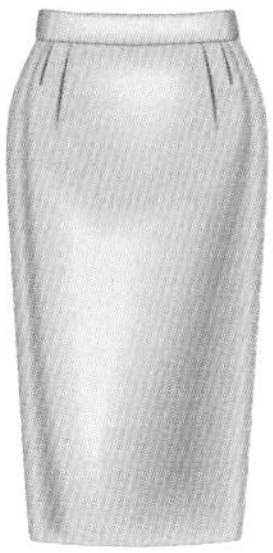

ruffled skirt
falda^F de volantes^M
jupe^F à volants^M étagés
Stufenrock^M
gonna^F a balze^F

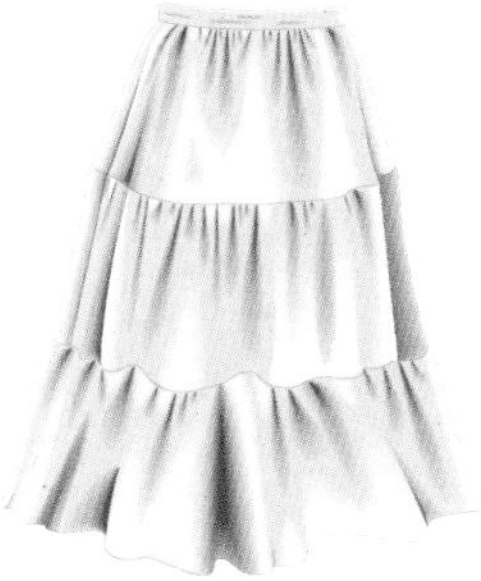

straight skirt
falda^F recta
jupe^F droite
gerader Rock^M
gonna^F diritta

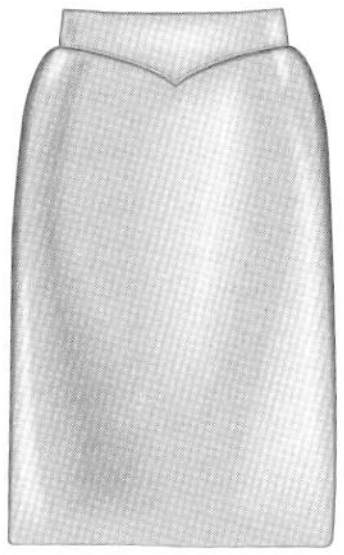

yoked skirt
falda^F acampanada
jupe^F à empiècement^M
Sattelrock^M
gonna^F con baschina^F

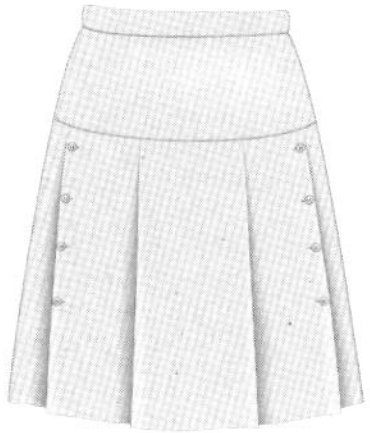

gathered skirt
falda^F fruncida
jupe^F froncée
Kräuselrock^M
gonna^F arricciata

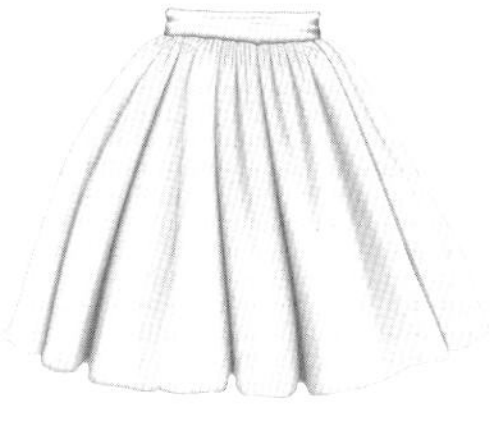

culottes
falda^F pantalón^M
jupe^F-culotte^F
Hosenrock^M
gonna^F pantalone^M

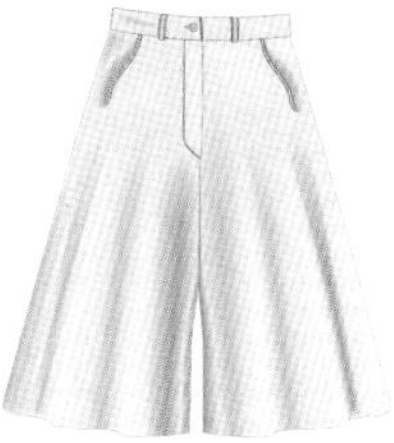

examples of pleats
ejemplos^M de tablas^F
exemples^M de plis^M
Beispiele^N für Falten^F
esempi^M di pieghe^F

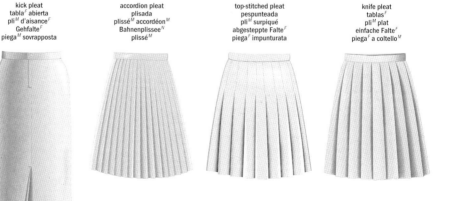

inverted pleat
tabla^F delantera
pli^M creux
Kellerfalte^F
piega^F invertita

kick pleat
tabla^F abierta
pli^M d'aisance^F
Gehfalte^F
piega^M sovrapposta

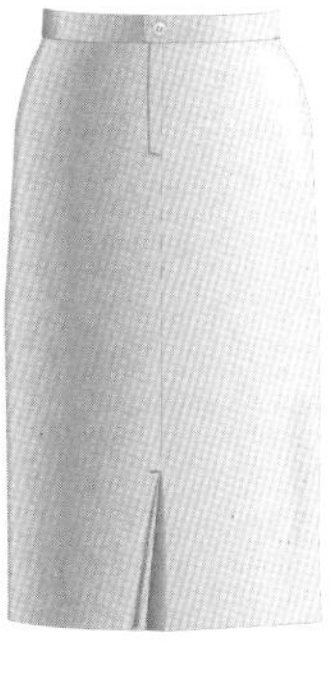

accordion pleat
plisada
plissé^M accordéon^M
Bahnenplissee^N
plissé^M

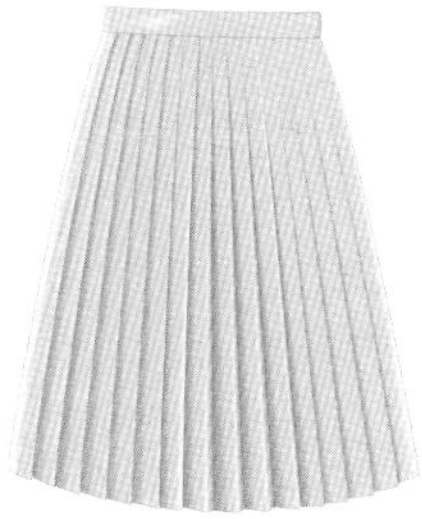

top-stitched pleat
pespunteada
pli^M surpiqué
abgesteppte Falte^F
piega^F impunturata

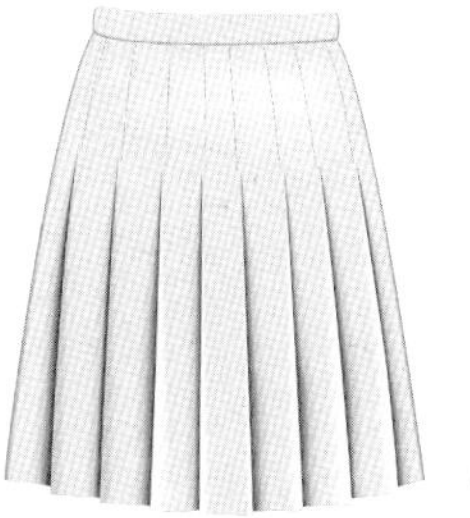

knife pleat
tablas^F
pli^M plat
einfache Falte^F
piega^F a coltello^M

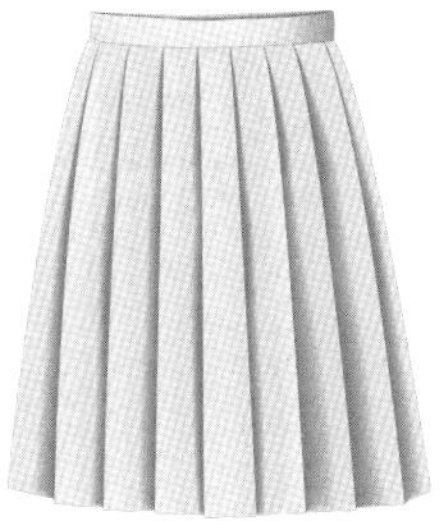

examples of pants
ejemplos^M de pantalones^M
exemples^M de pantalons^M
Beispiele^N **für Hosen**^{F}
esempi^M di pantaloni^M

shorts
pantalóns^M cortos
short^M
Shorts^F
shorts^M

Bermuda shorts
bermudas^M
bermuda^M
Bermudashorts^F
bermuda^M

knickers
bombachos^M
knicker^M
Kniebundhose^F
pantaloni^M alla zuava^F

pedal pushers
pirata^M
corsaire^M
Caprihose^F
pantaloni^M alla pescatora^F

jeans
vaqueros^M
jean^M
Jeans^F
jeans^M

ski pants
pantalones^M de tubo^M
fuseau^M
Steghose^F
fuseau^M

footstrap
trabilla^F
sous-pied^M
Steg^M
staffa^F

jumpsuit
buzo^M
combinaison^F-pantalon^M
Overall^M
tuta^F

overalls
pantalón^M peto^M
salopette^F
Latzhose^F
salopette^F

bell bottoms
pantalones^M acampanados
pantalon^M pattes^F d'éléphant^M
Schlaghose^F
pantaloni^M a zampa^F di elefante^M

jackets, vest and sweaters
chaleco^M, jerseys^M y chaquetas^F
vestes^F et pulls^M
Westen^N **und Jacken**^{F}
esempi^M di giacche^F e pullover^M

bolero
bolero^M
boléro^M
Bolero^M
bolero^M

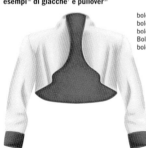

spencer
bolero^M con botones^M
spencer^M
Spenzer^M
spencer^M

blazer
americana^F
blazer^M
Blazer^M
blazer^M

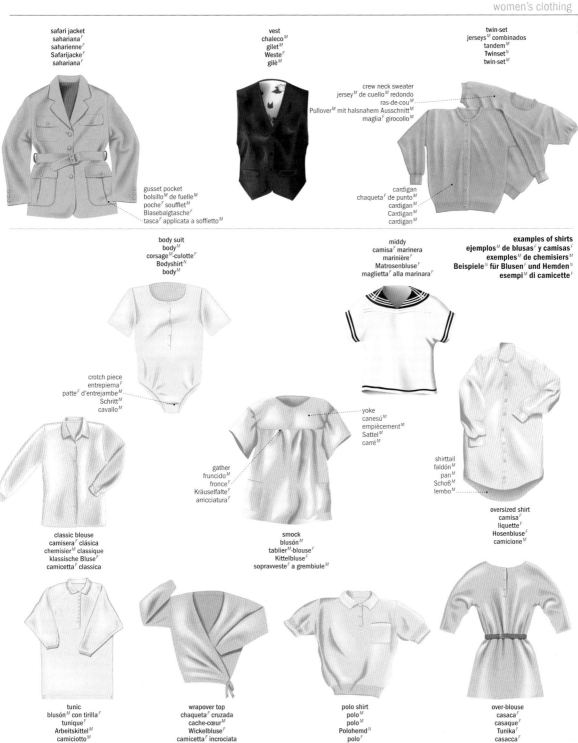

safari jacket
sahariana^F
saharienne^F
Safarijacke^F
sahariana^F

vest
chaleco^M
gilet^M
Weste^F
gilè^M

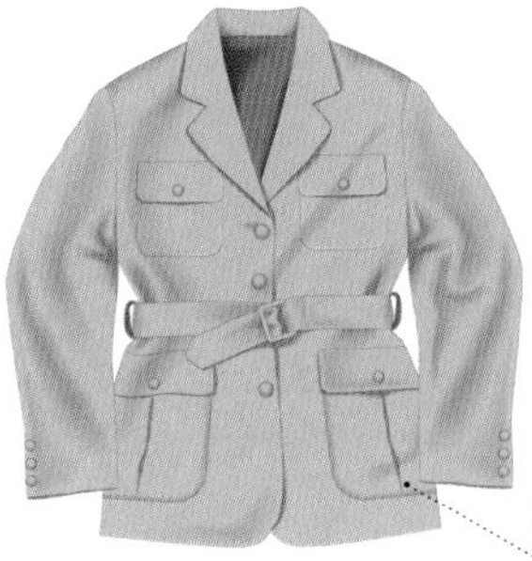

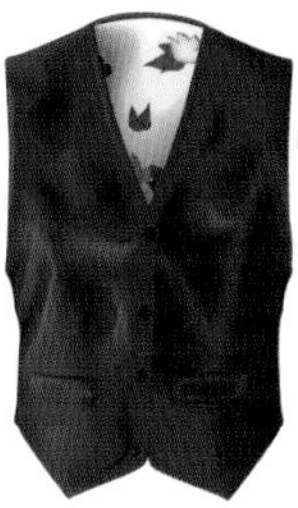

twin-set
jerseys^M combinados
tandem^M
Twinset^N
twin-set^M

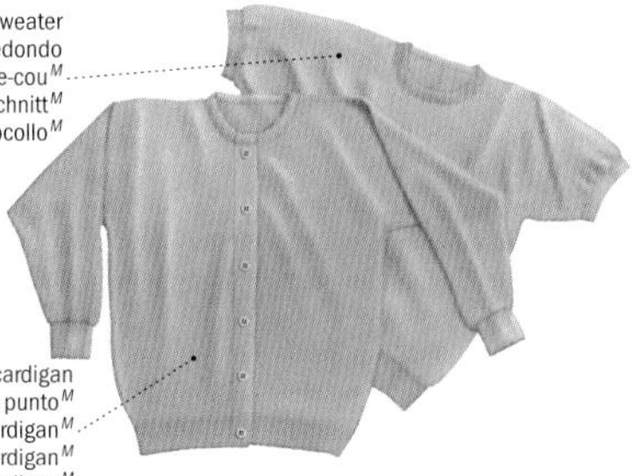

crew neck sweater
jersey^M de cuello^M redondo
ras-de-cou^M
Pullover^M mit halsnahem Ausschnitt^M
maglia^F girocollo^M

cardigan
chaqueta^F de punto^M
cardigan^M
Cardigan^M
cardigan^M

gusset pocket
bolsillo^M de fuelle^M
poche^F soufflet^M
Blasebalgtasche^F
tasca^F applicata a soffietto^M

body suit
body^M
corsage^M-culotte^F
Bodyshirt^N
body^M

middy
camisa^F marinera
marinière^F
Matrosenbluse^F
maglietta^F alla marinara^F

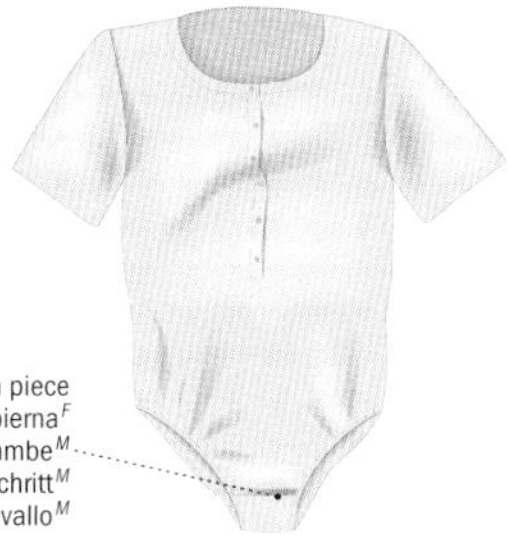

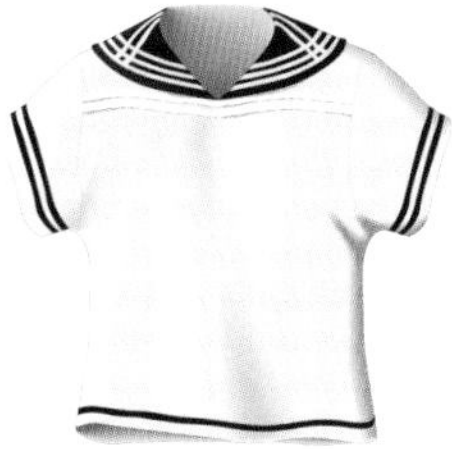

examples of shirts
ejemplos^M de blusas^F y camisas^F
exemples^M de chemisiers^M
Beispiele^N für Blusen^F und Hemden^N
esempi^M di camicette^F

CLOTHING

crotch piece
entrepierna^F
patte^F d'entrejambe^M
Schritt^M
cavallo^M

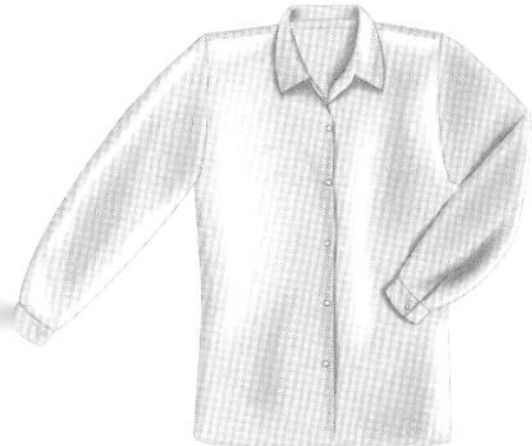

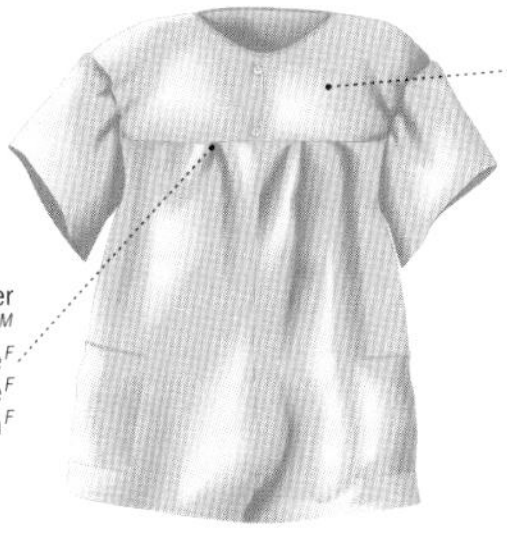

yoke
canesú^M
empiècement^M
Sattel^M
carré^M

gather
fruncido^M
fronce^F
Kräuselfalte^F
arricciatura^F

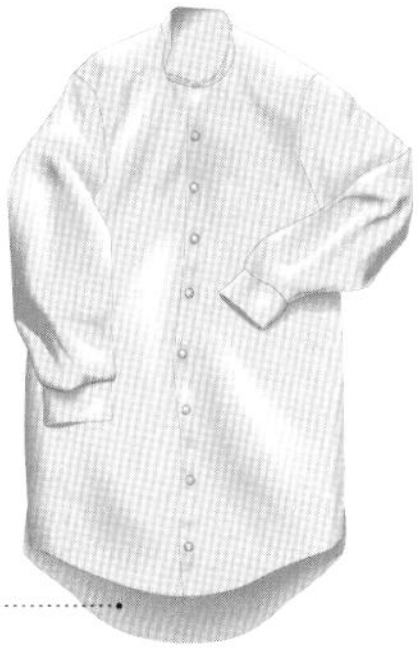

shirttail
faldón^M
pan^M
Schoß^M
lembo^M

oversized shirt
camisa^F
liquette^F
Hosenbluse^F
camicione^M

classic blouse
camisera^F clásica
chemisier^M classique
klassische Bluse^F
camicetta^F classica

smock
blusón^M
tablier^M-blouse^F
Kittelbluse^F
sopravveste^F a grembiule^M

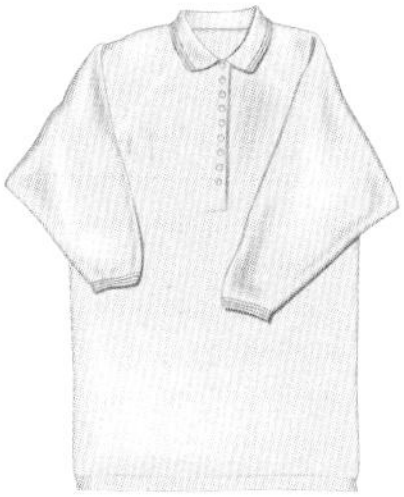

tunic
blusón^M con tirilla^F
tunique^F
Arbeitskittel^M
camiciotto^M

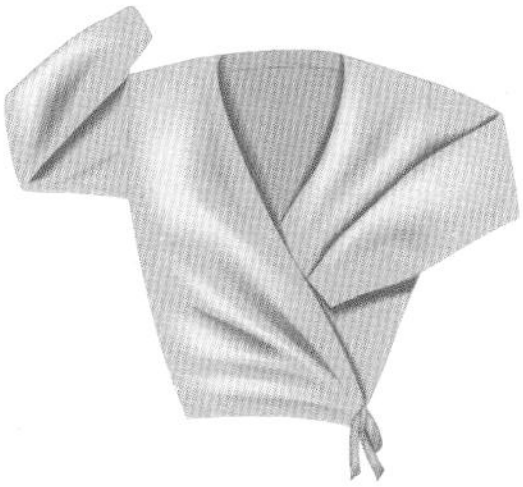

wrapover top
chaqueta^F cruzada
cache-cœur^M
Wickelbluse^F
camicetta^F incrociata

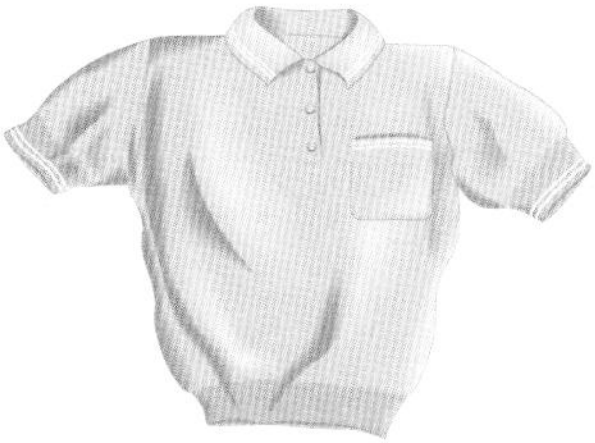

polo shirt
polo^M
polo^M
Polohemd^N
polo^F

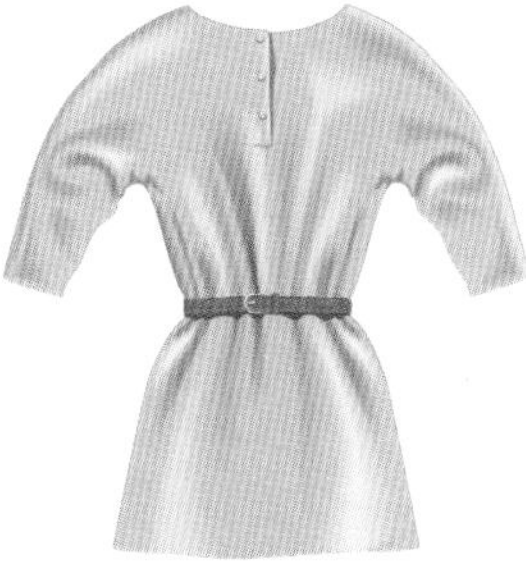

over-blouse
casaca^F
casaque^F
Tunika^F
casacca^F

CLOTHING

examples of pockets
ejemplos^M de bolsillos^M
exemples^M de poches^F
Beispiele^N für Taschen^F
esempi^M di tasche^F

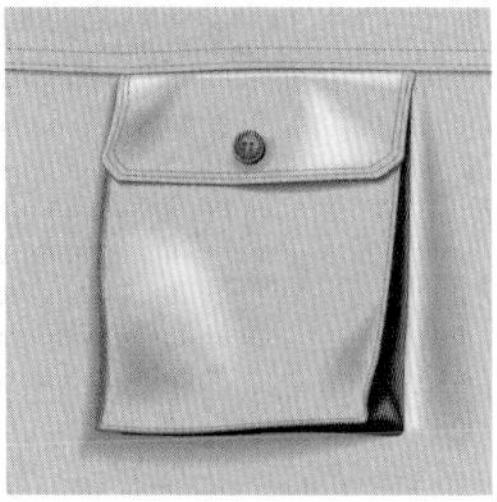

gusset pocket
bolsillo^M de fuelle^M
poche^F soufflet^M
Blasebalgtasche^F
tasca^F applicata a soffietto^M

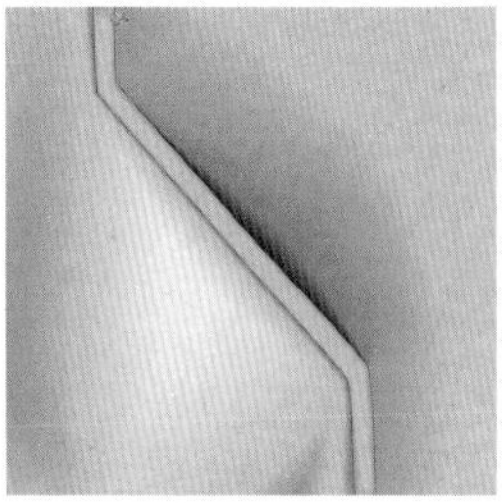

inset pocket
bolsillo^M simulado
poche^F prise dans une découpe^F
eingesetzte Tasche^F
tasca^F sagomata

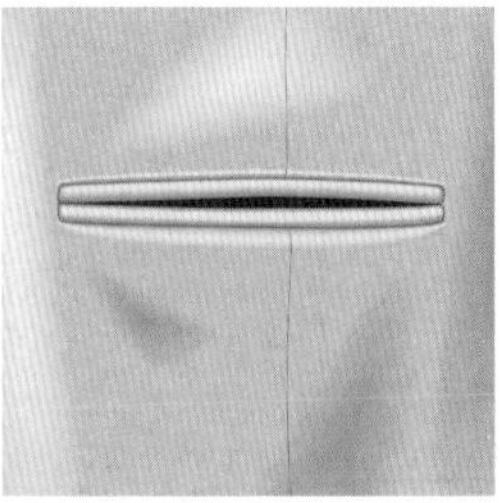

welt pocket
bolsillo^M de ojal^M de sastre^M
poche^F passepoilée
Paspeltasche^F
tasca^F profilata

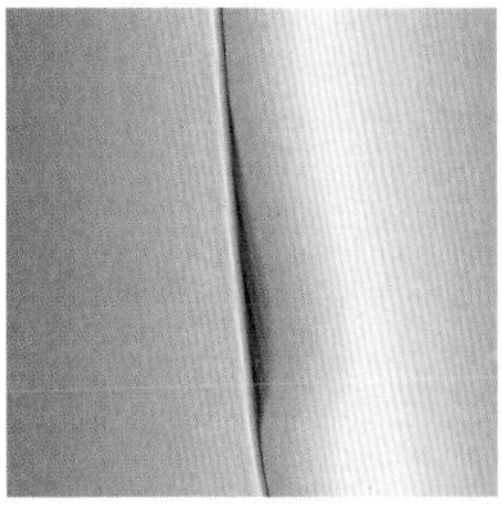

seam pocket
bolsillo^M disimulado
poche^F prise dans une couture^F
Nahttasche^F
tasca^F inserita nella cucitura^F

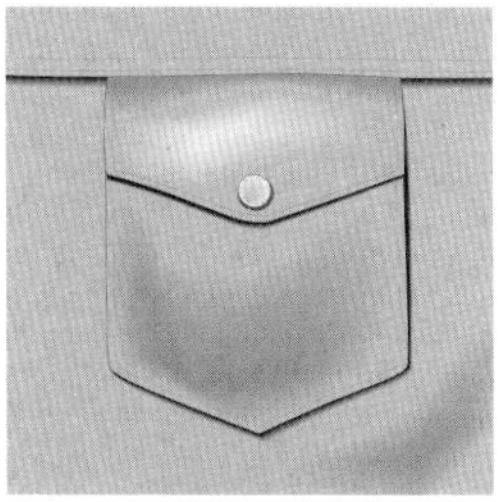

flap pocket
bolsillo^M de parche^M con cartera^F
poche^F à rabat^M
Klappentasche^F
tasca^F applicata con aletta^F

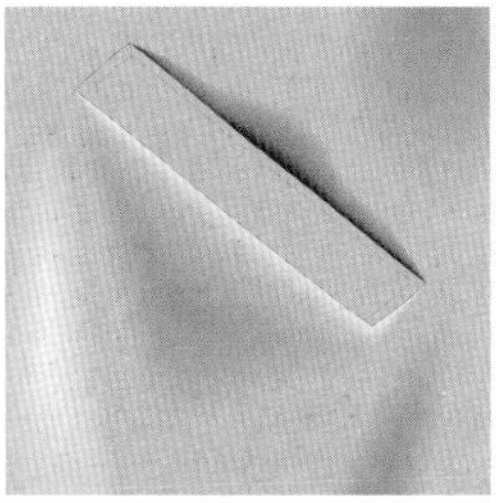

broad-welt side pocket
bolsillo^M de ojal^M con ribete^M
poche^F raglan
schräge Pattentasche^F
tasca^F interna con aletta^F

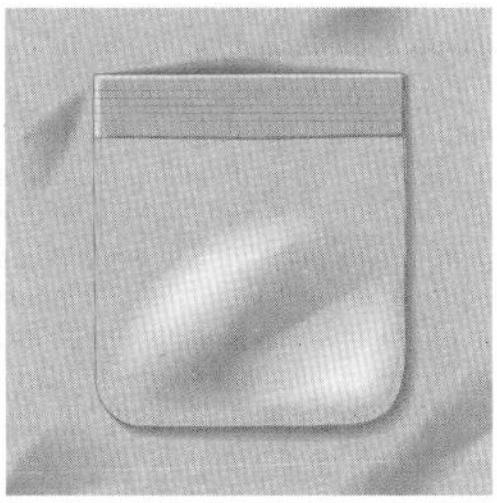

patch pocket
bolsillo^M de parche^M
poche^F plaquée
aufgesetzte Tasche^F
tasca^F applicata

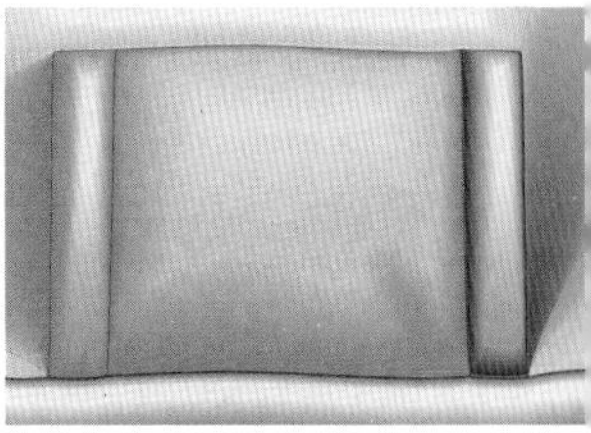

hand-warmer pouch
bolsillo^M de manguito^M
poche^F manchon^M
Mufftasche^F
manicotto^M

examples of sleeves
ejemplos^M de mangas^F
exemples^M de manches^F
Beispiele^N für Ärmel^M
esempi^M di maniche^F

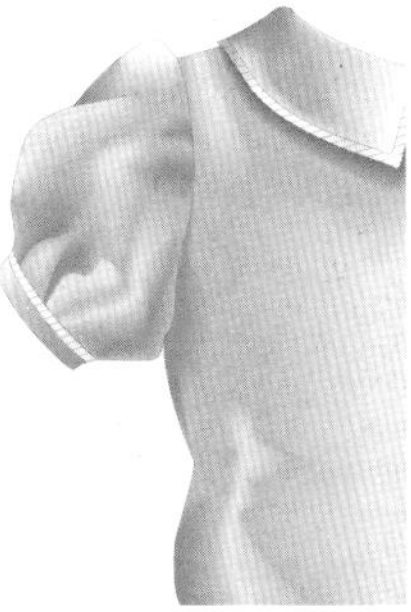

puffed sleeve
manga^F farol
manche^F ballon^M
Puffärmel^M
manica^F a palloncino^M

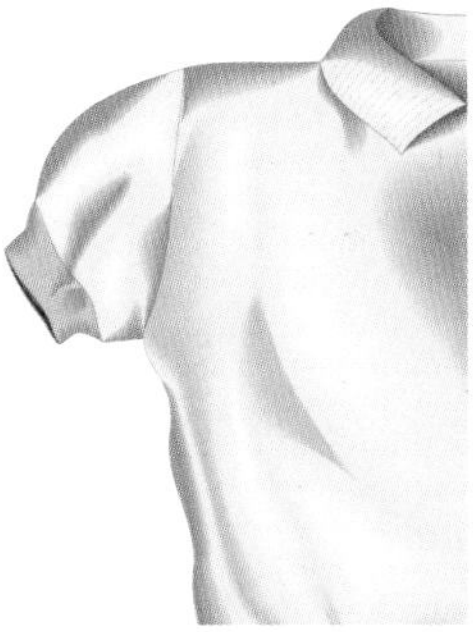

cap sleeve
manga^F corta sencilla
mancheron^M
angeschnittener Ärmel^M
manica^F ad aletta^F

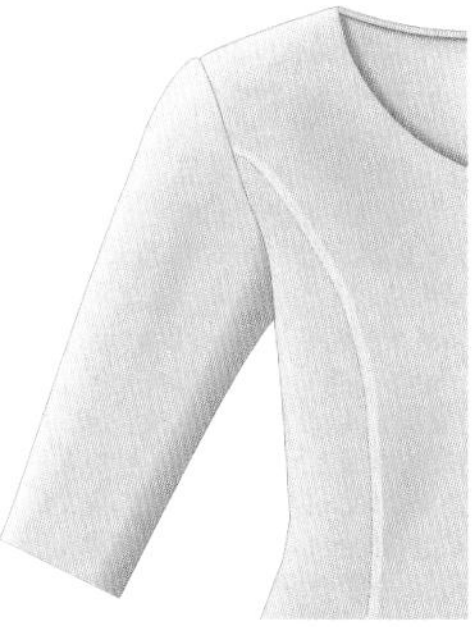

three-quarter sleeve
manga^F recta de tres cuartos^M
manche^F trois-quarts
Dreiviertelarm^M
manica^F a tre quarti^M

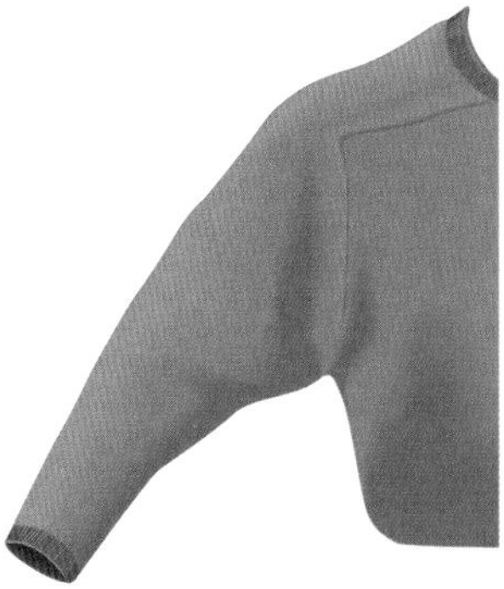

epaulet sleeve
manga^F con hombrera^F
manche^F marteau^M
Zungenraglan^M
manica^F con spallina^F

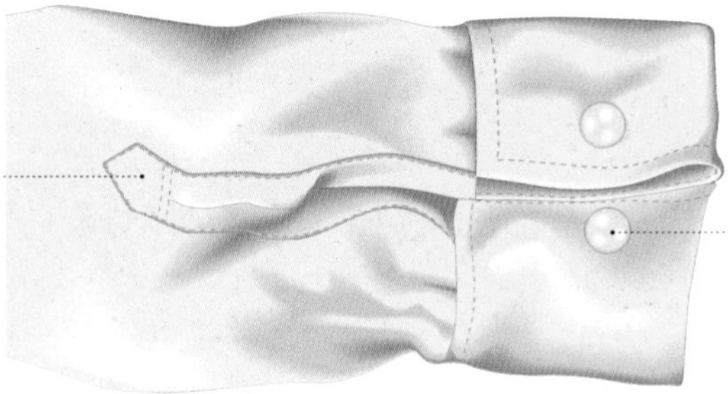

French cuff
puño^M para gemelos^M
poignet^M mousquetaire^M
Doppelmanschette^F
polsino^M doppio

pointed tab end
tirilla^F
patte^F capucin^M
Ärmelschlitz^M
profilo^M dello spacco^M

cuff link
gemelos^M
bouton^M de manchette^F
Manschettenknopf^M
gemello^M

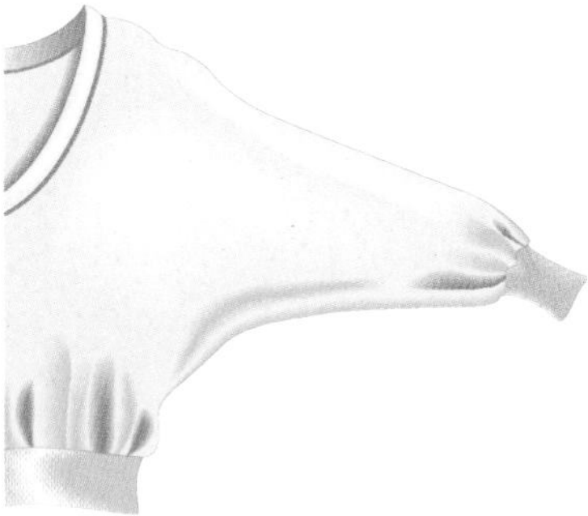

batwing sleeve
manga^F de murciélago^M
manche^F chauve-souris^F
Fledermausärmel^M
manica^F a pipistrello^M

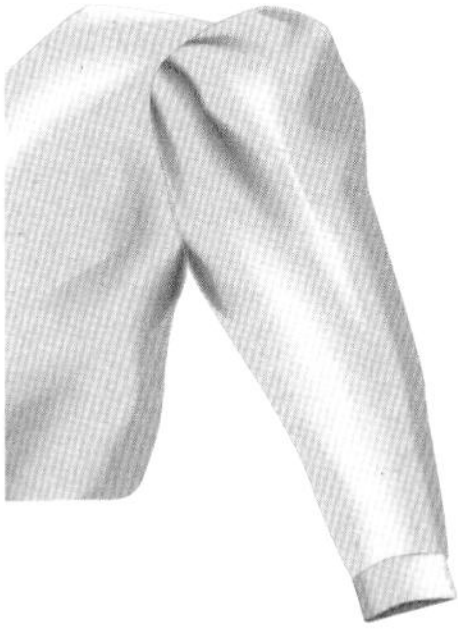

leg-of-mutton sleeve
manga^F de jamón^M
manche^F gigot^M
Keulenärmel^M
manica^F a prosciutto^M

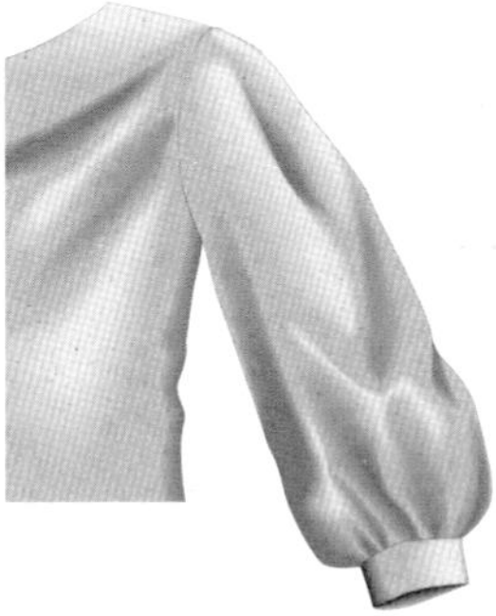

bishop sleeve
manga^F común fruncida
manche^F bouffante
Bauschärmel^M
manica^F da vescovo^M

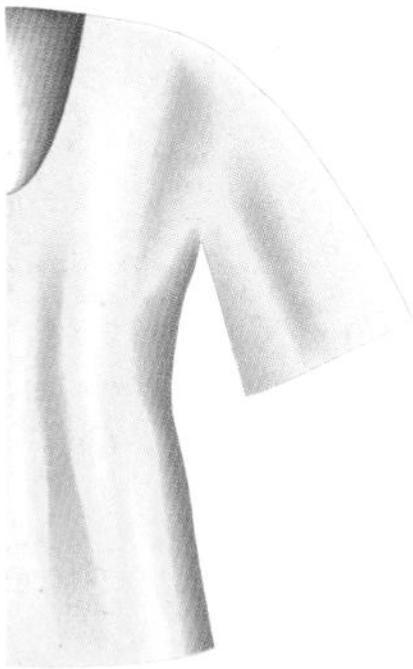

kimono sleeve
manga^F kimono^M
manche^F kimono^M
Kimonoärmel^M
manica^F a kimono^M

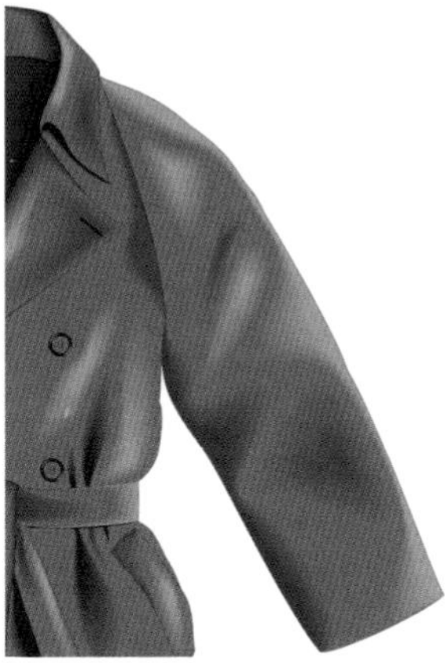

raglan sleeve
manga^F raglán
manche^F raglan
Raglanärmel^M
manica^F alla raglan^M

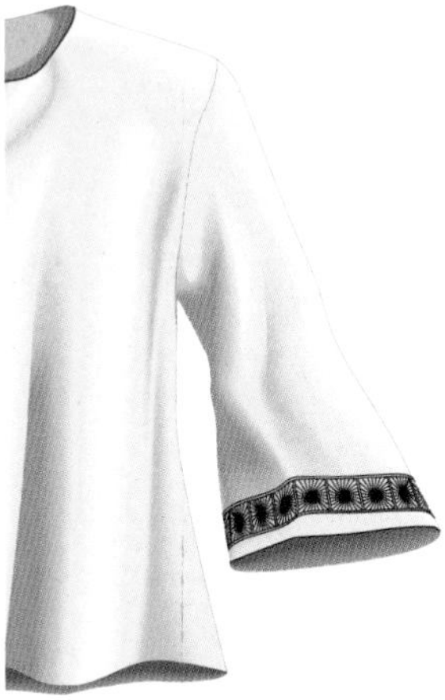

pagoda sleeve
manga^F de pagoda^F
manche^F pagode^F
Pagodenärmel^M
manica^F a pagoda^F

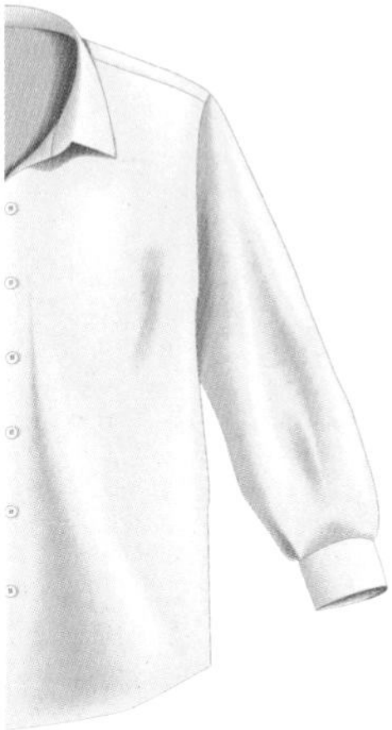

shirt sleeve
manga^F camisera^F
manche^F chemisier^M
Hemdblusenärmel^M
manica^F di camicia^F

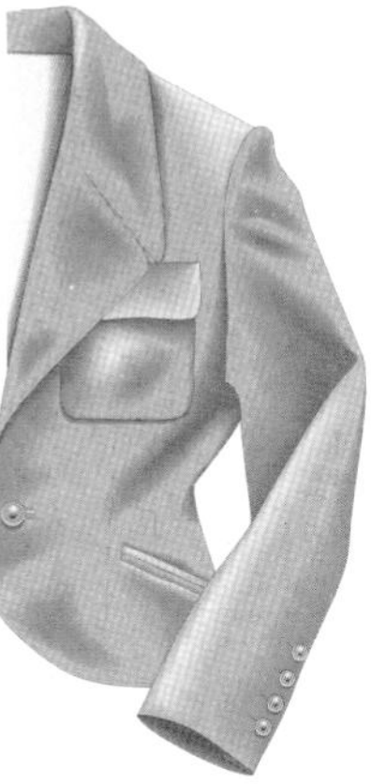

tailored sleeve
manga^F de hechura^F sastre^M
manche^F tailleur^M
Schneiderärmel^M
manica^F a giro^M

CLOTHING

examples of collars
ejemplos^M **de cuellos**^M
exemples^M **de cols**^M
Beispiele^N **für Kragen**^M
esempi^M **di colli**^M

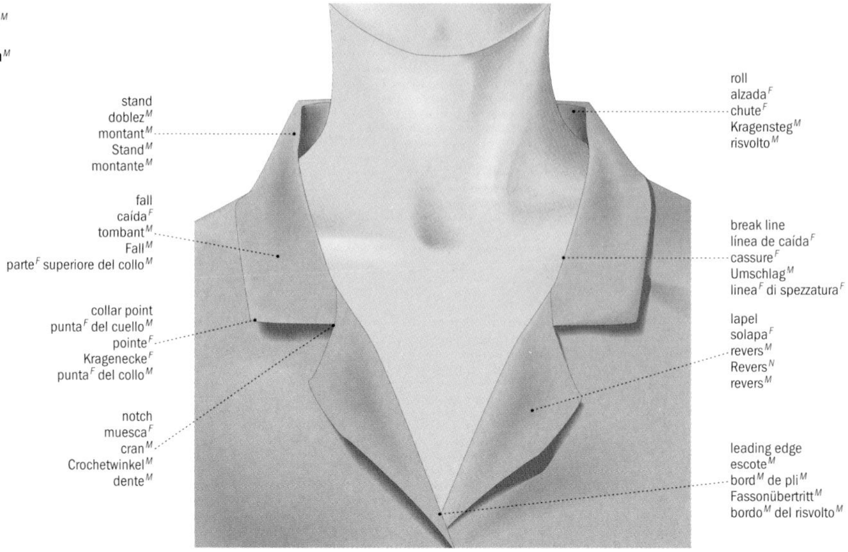

stand
doblez^M
montant^M
Stand^M
montante^M

fall
caida^F
tombant^M
Fall^M
parte^F superiore del collo^M

collar point
punta^F del cuello^M
pointe^F
Kragenecke^F
punta^F del collo^M

notch
muesca^F
cran^M
Crochetwinkel^M
dente^M

roll
alzada^F
chute^F
Kragensteg^M
risvolto^M

break line
linea de caída^F
cassure^F
Umschlag^M
linea^F di spezzatura^F

lapel
solapa^F
revers^M
Revers^N
revers^M

leading edge
escote^M
bord^M de pli^M
Fassonübertritt^M
bordo^M del risvolto^M

collar
cuello^M
col^M
Kragen^M
collo^M

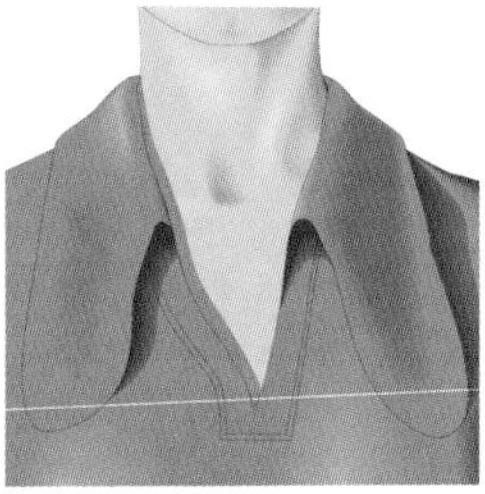

dog ear collar
cuello^M plano con orejas^F
col^M banane^F
Dackelohrkragen^M
collo^M a orecchie^F di cane^M

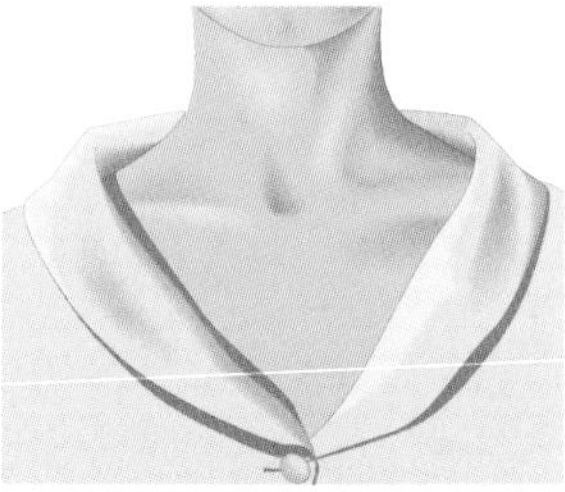

shawl collar
cuello^M de chal^M
col^M châle^M
Schalkragen^M
collo^M a scialle^M

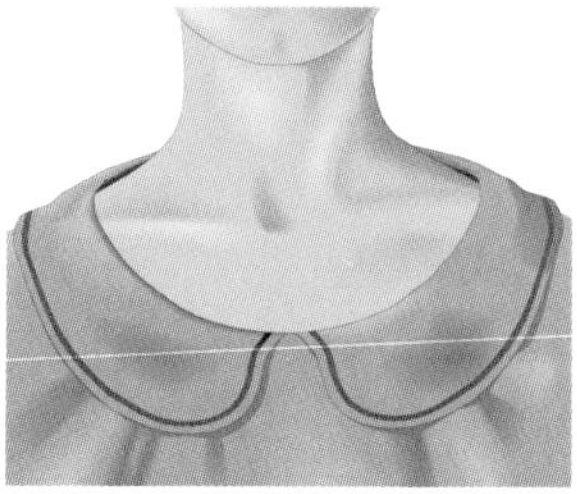

Peter Pan collar
cuello^M plano tipo^M Peter Pan
col^M Claudine
Bubikragen^M
collo^M alla Peter Pan

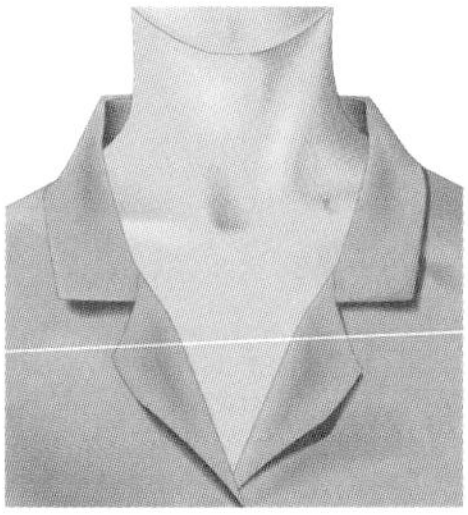

shirt collar
cuello^M camisero
col^M chemisier^M
Hemdblusenkragen^M
collo^M a camicia^F

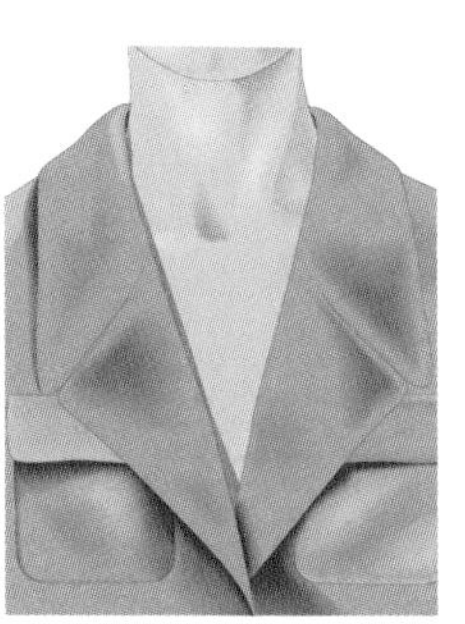

tailored collar
cuello^M de hechura^F de sastre^M
col^M tailleur^M
Schneiderkragen^M
collo^M a uomo^M

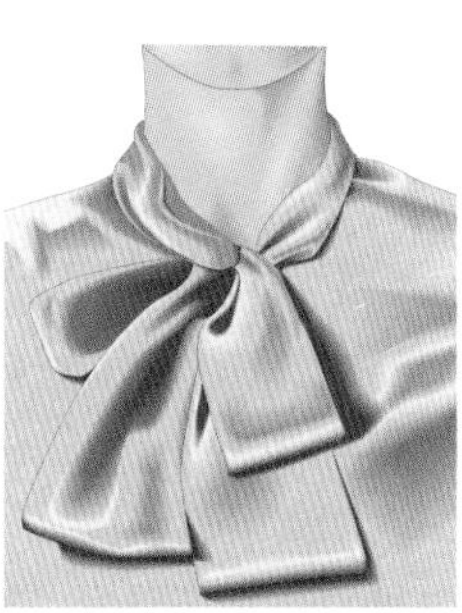

bow collar
cuello^M de lazo^M
col^M cravate^M
Schleifenkragen^M
collo^M con sciarpa^F

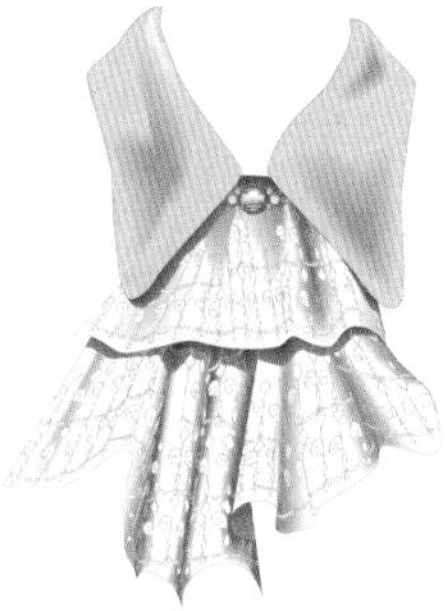

jabot
chorrera^F
jabot^M
Jabot^N
jabot^M

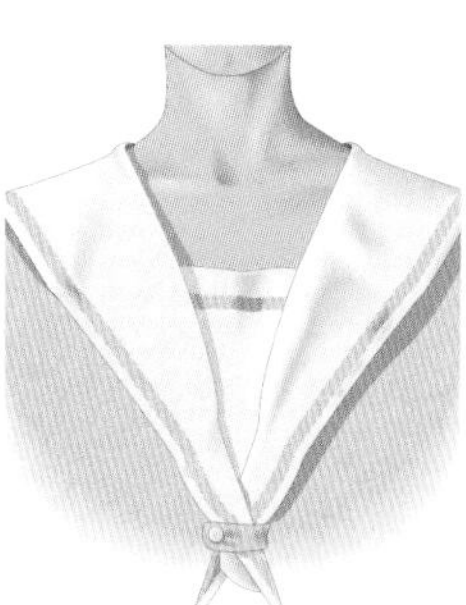

sailor collar
cuello^M marinero
col^M marin^M
Matrosenkragen^M
collo^M alla marinara^F

mandarin collar
cuello M chino
col M chinois
Chinesenkragen M
collo M alla coreana F

collaret
cuello M de volantes M
collerette F
Halskrause F
collaretto F

bertha collar
cuello M Berta
col M berthe F
Berthe F
berta F

turtleneck
cuello M de tortuga F
col M roulé
Rollkragen M
dolcevita F

cowl neck
cuello M tipo cogulla F
col M cagoule F
Kuttenkragen M
collo M a cappuccio M

polo collar
cuello M de polo M
col M polo M
Polokragen M
collo M a polo F

stand-up collar
cuello M Mao
col M officier M
Stehbundkragen M
collo M a listino M

necklines and necks
escotes M
décolletés M et encolures F
Dekolletés N und Ausschnitte M
scollature F

plunging neckline
escote M bajo
décolleté M plongeant
spitzes Dekolleté N
scollatura F profonda a V

sweetheart neckline
escote M de corazón M
décolleté M en cœur M
Cœur-Dekolleté N
scollatura F a cuore M

V-shaped neck
escote M de pico M
décolleté M en V
V-Ausschnitt M
scollatura F a V

square neck
escote M cuadrado
décolleté M carré
viereckiger Ausschnitt M
scollatura F quadrata

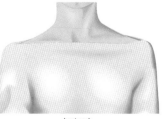

boat neck
escote M de barco M
encolure F bateau M
Bateau-Kragen M
scollatura F a barchetta F

draped neck
cuello M drapeado
encolure F drapée
drapierter Kragen M
girocollo M drappeggiato

draped neckline
descote M rapeado
décolleté M drapé
drapierter Ausschnitt M
scollatura F drappeggiata

crew neck
cuello M redondo
encolure F ras-de-cou M
runder Ausschnitt M
girocollo M

nightwear
lencería^F
vêtements^M **de nuit**^F
Nachtwäsche^F
biancheria^F **da notte**^F

nightgown
camisón^M
chemise^F de nuit^F
Nachthemd^N
camicia^F da notte^F

baby doll
picardía^M
nuisette^F
Baby-Doll^N
baby-doll^M

kimono
kimono^M
kimono^M
Kimono^M
kimono^M

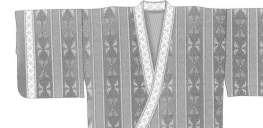

pajamas
pijama^M
pyjama^M
Schlafanzug^M
pigiama^M

negligee
bata^F
déshabillé^M
Negligé^N
vestaglia^F

bathrobe
albornoz^M
peignoir^M
Bademantel^M
accappatoio^M

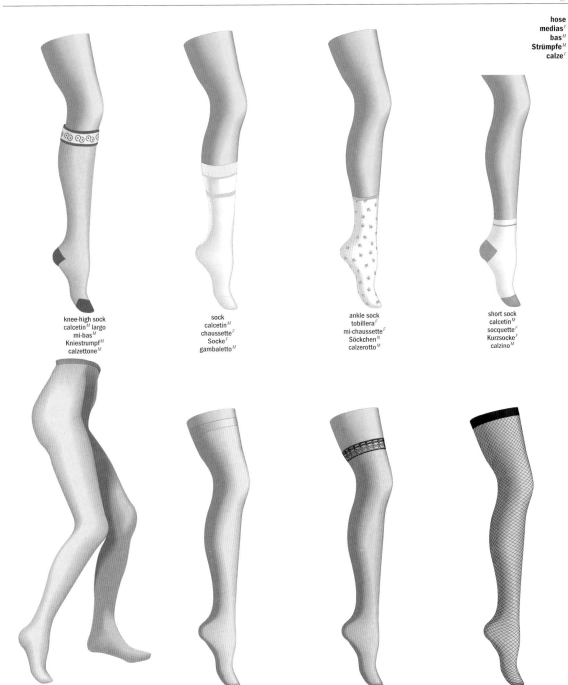

CLOTHING

knee-high sock
calcetín^M largo
mi-bas^M
Kniestrumpf^M
calzettone^M

sock
calcetín^M
chaussette^F
Socke^F
gambaletto^M

ankle sock
tobillera^F
mi-chaussette^F
Söckchen^N
calzerotto^M

short sock
calcetín^M
socquette^F
Kurzsocke^F
calzino^M

panty hose
pantis^M/medias^F
collant^M
Strumpfhose^F
collant^M

stocking
media^F
bas^M
Strumpf^M
calza^F

thigh-high stocking
media^F antideslizante
bas^M-cuissarde^F
Overknee-Strumpf^M
calza^F autoreggente

fish net stocking
media^F de malla^F
bas^M résille^F
Netzstrumpf^M
calza^F a rete^F

underwear
ropa^F **interior**
sous-vêtements^M
Unterwäsche^F
biancheria^F **intima**

camisole
camisola^F
caraco^M ; *camisole*^{F}
Camisol^N
top^M

teddy
canesú^M
teddy^M ; *combinaison*^{F}*-culotte*^{F}
Teddy^N
pagliaccetto^M

body suit
body^M
body^M ; *combiné-slip*^{M}
Bodysuit^M
body^M

corselette
faja^F con sostén^M
combiné^M
Korselett^N
modellatore^M aperto

panty corselette
faja^F corsé^M
combiné^M-culotte^F
Panty-Korselett^N
modellatore^M sgambato

princess seams
costura^F de corte^M princesa^F
découpe^F princesse^F
Prinzessnaht^F
cucitura^F a princesse^F

half-slip
falda^F combinación^F
jupon^M
Unterrock^M
sottogonna^F

foundation slip
combinación^F
fond^M de robe^F
Vollachsel-Unterkleid^N
sottoveste^F

slip
combinación^F con sujetador^M
combinaison^F-jupon^M
Unterkleid^N
sottoveste^F con reggiseno^M

CLOTHING

underwire
varilla[F]
armature[F]
Unterbruststäbchen[N]
ferretto[M]

bikini
braga[F]
slip[M]
Slip[M]
slip[M]

garter
liga[F]
jarretelle[F]
Strumpfhalter[M]
giarrettiera[F]

hose
medias[F]
bas[M]
Strumpf[M]
calza[F]

wasp-waisted corset
corsé[M] de cintura[F] de avispa[F]
guêpière[F]
Torselett[N]
guepière[F]

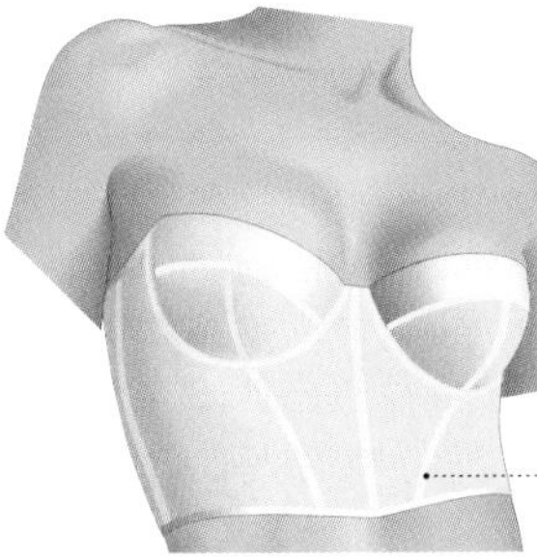

strapless bra
sujetador[M] sin tirantes[M]
bustier[M]
trägerloser Büstenhalter[M]
reggiseno[M] a bustino[M]

steel
varilla[F]
baleine[F]
Stab[M]
stecca[F]

push-up bra
sujetador[M] de aros[M]
soutien-gorge[F] balconnet[M]
Dirndl-BH[M]
reggiseno[M] a balconcino[M]

girdle
faja[F]
gaine[F]
Mieder[N]
panciera[F]

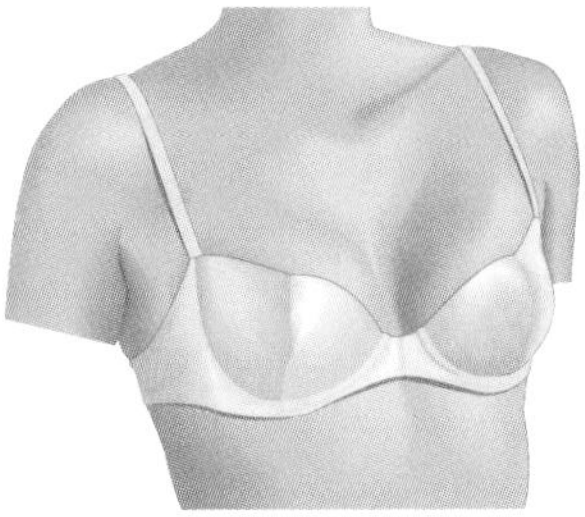

décolleté bra
sujetador[M] de escote[M] bajo
soutien-gorge[F] corbeille[F]
Halbschale[F]
reggiseno[M] décolleté[M]

panel
refuerzo[M]
plastron[M]
Magenstütze[F]
pannello[M]

shoulder strap
tirante[M]
bretelle[F]
Träger[M]
spallina[F]

cup
copa[F]
bonnet[M]
Büstenschale[F]
coppa[F] del reggiseno[M]

midriff band
talle[M] corto
basque[F]
Mittelsteg[M]
triangolo[M] divisorio

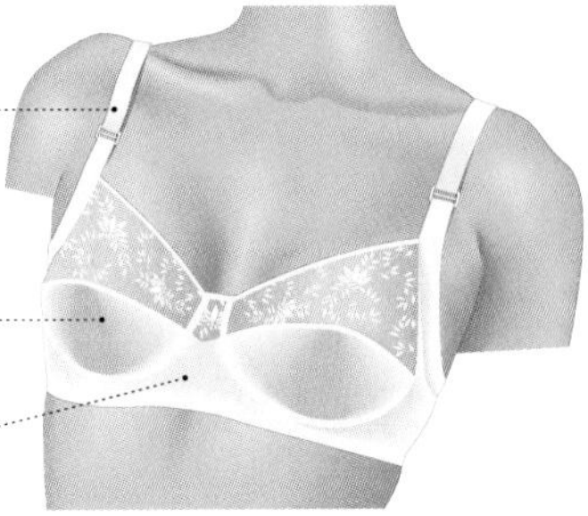

bra
sujetador[M]
soutien-gorge[M]
BH[M]
reggiseno[M]

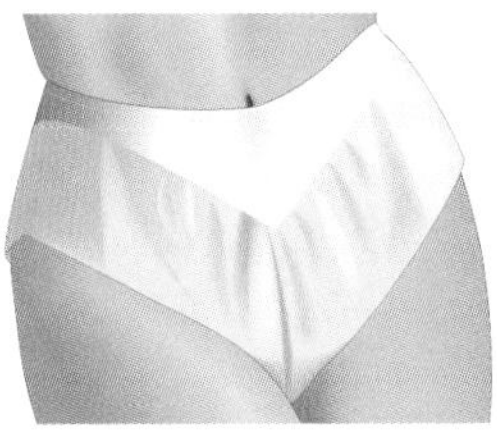

briefs
braga[F]
culotte[F]
Slip[M]
mutandina[F]

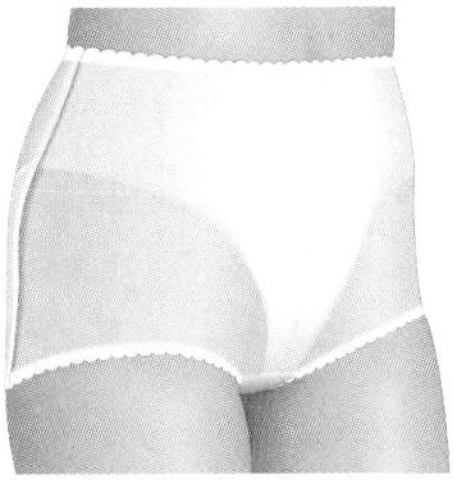

panty girdle
faja[M] braga
gaine[F]-culotte[F]
Miederhose[F]
mutandina[F] elastica

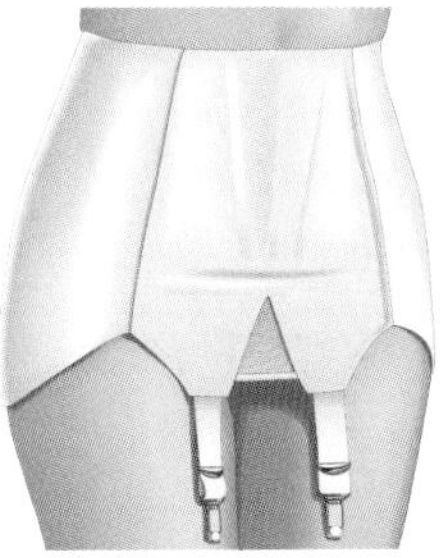

corset
faja[F] con liguero[M]
corset[M]
Korsett[N]
corsetto[M]

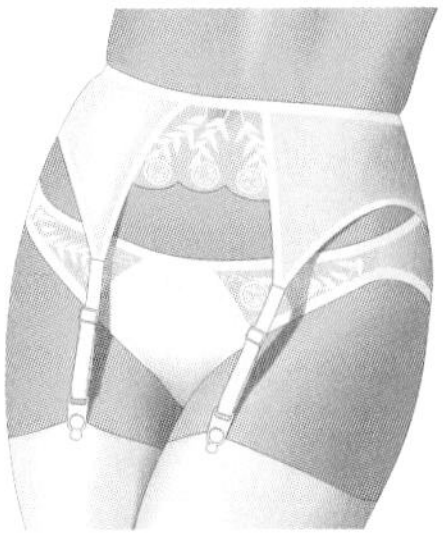

garter belt
liguero[M]
porte-jarretelles[M]
Strumpfhaltergürtel[M]
reggicalze[M]

CLOTHING

CLOTHING

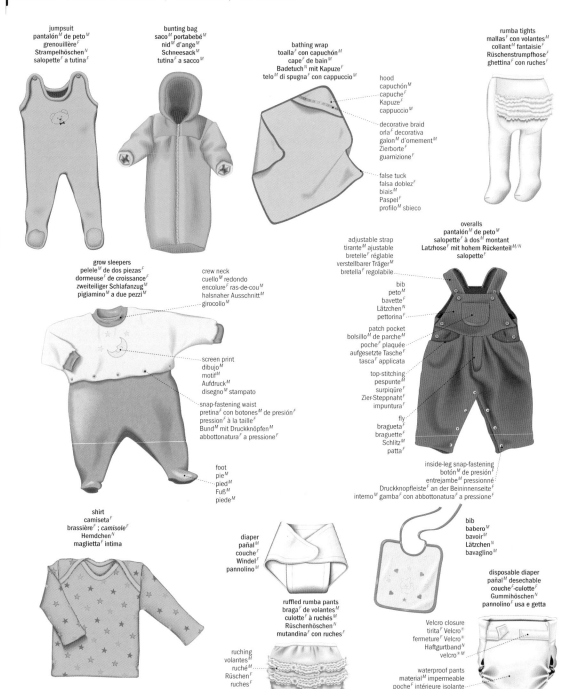

jumpsuit
pantalón^M de peto^M
grenouillère^F
Strampelhöschen^N
salopette^F a tutina^F

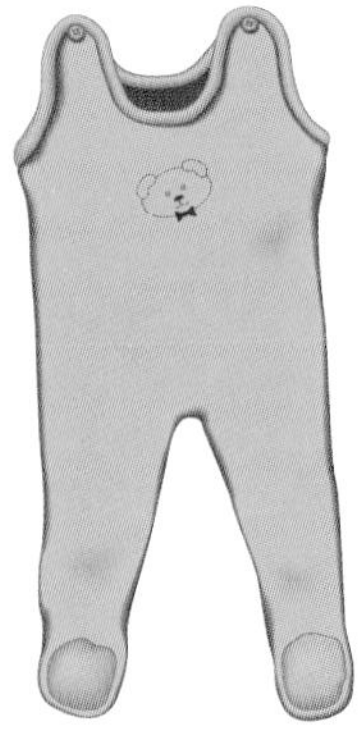

bunting bag
saco^M portabebé^M
nid^M d'ange^M
Schneesack^M
tutina^F a sacco^M

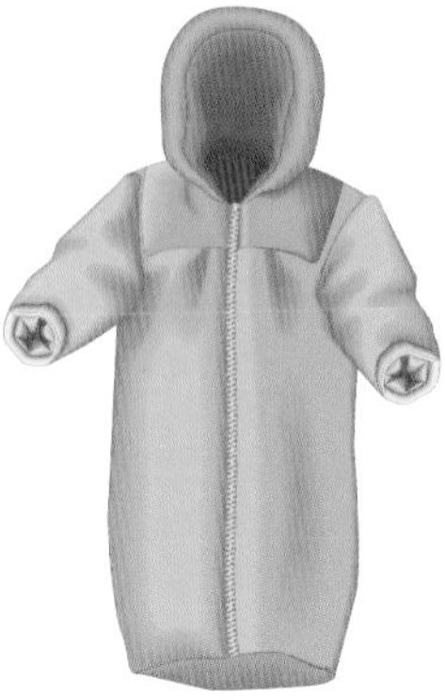

bathing wrap
toalla^F con capuchón^M
cape^F de bain^M
Badetuch^N mit Kapuze^F
telo^M di spugna^F con cappuccio^M

rumba tights
mallas^F con volantes^M
collant^M fantaisie^F
Rüschenstrumpfhose^F
ghettina^F con ruches^F

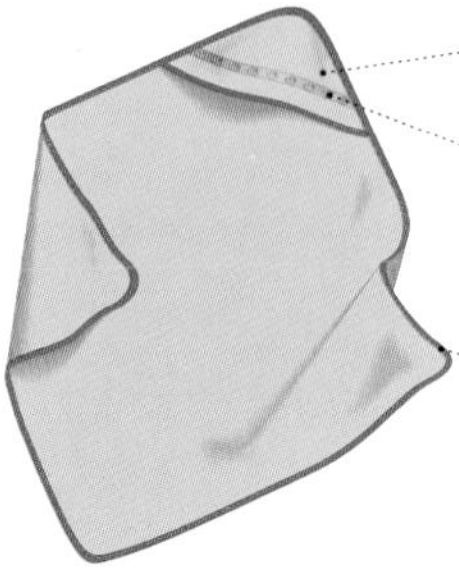

hood
capuchón^M
capuche^F
Kapuze^F
cappuccio^M

decorative braid
orla^F decorativa
galon^M d'ornement^M
Zierborte^F
guarnizione^F

false tuck
falsa doblez^F
biais^M
Paspel^F
profilo^M sbieco

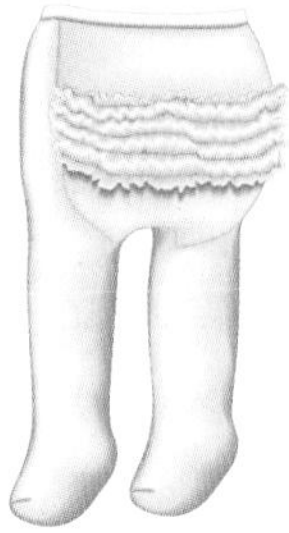

grow sleepers
pelele^M de dos piezas^F
dormeuse^F de croissance^F
zweiteiliger Schlafanzug^M
pigiamino^M a due pezzi^M

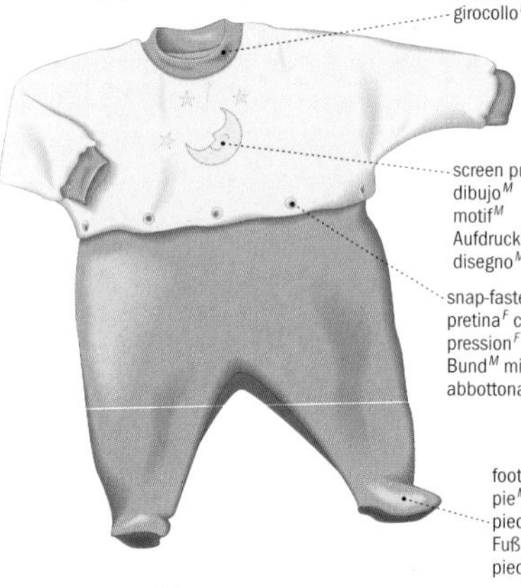

crew neck
cuello^M redondo
encolure^F ras-de-cou^M
halsnaher Ausschnitt^M
girocollo^M

screen print
dibujo^M
motif^M
Aufdruck^M
disegno^M stampato

snap-fastening waist
pretina^F con botones^M de presión^F
pression^F à la taille^F
Bund^M mit Druckknöpfen^M
abbottonatura^F a pressione^F

foot
pie^M
pied^M
Fuß^M
piede^M

overalls
pantalón^M de peto^M
salopette^F à dos^M montant
Latzhose^F mit hohem Rückenteil^{M/N}
salopette^F

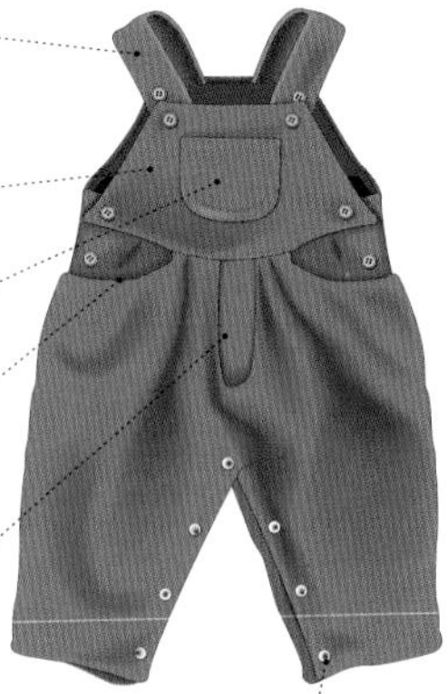

adjustable strap
tirante^M ajustable
bretelle^F réglable
verstellbarer Träger^M
bretella^F regolabile

bib
peto^M
bavette^F
Lätzchen^N
pettorina^F

patch pocket
bolsillo^M de parche^M
poche^F plaquée
aufgesetzte Tasche^F
tasca^F applicata

top-stitching
pespunte^M
surpiqûre^F
Zier-Steppnaht^F
impuntura^F

fly
bragueta^F
braguette^F
Schlitz^M
patta^F

inside-leg snap-fastening
botón^M de presión^F
entrejambe^M pressionné
Druckknopfleiste^F an der Beininnenseite^F
interno^M gamba^F con abbottonatura^F a pressione^F

shirt
camiseta^F
brassière^F ; camisole^F
Hemdchen^N
maglietta^F intima

diaper
pañal^M
couche^F
Windel^F
pannolino^M

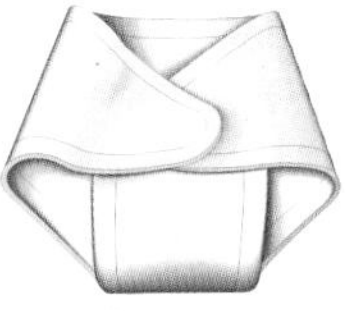

bib
babero^M
bavoir^M
Lätzchen^N
bavaglino^M

disposable diaper
pañal^M desechable
couche^F-culotte^F
Gummihöschen^N
pannolino^M usa e getta

ruffled rumba pants
braga^F de volantes^M
culotte^F à ruchés^M
Rüschenhöschen^N
mutandina^F con ruches^F

ruching
volantes^M
ruché^M
Rüschen^F
ruches^F

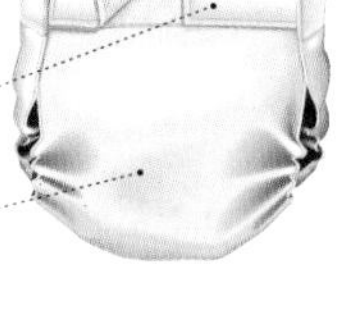

Velcro closure
tirita^F Velcro®
fermeture^F Velcro®
Haftgurtband^N
velcro^{®M}

waterproof pants
material^M impermeable
poche^F intérieure isolante
dichtes Windelhöschen^N
mutandina^F impermeabile

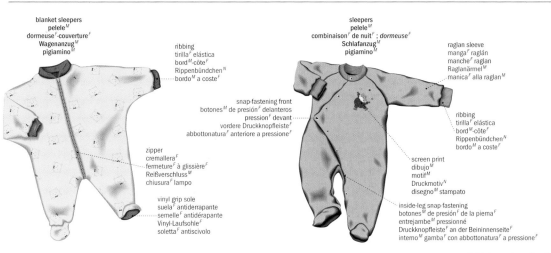

blanket sleepers
pelele[M]
dormeuse[F]-couverture[F]
Wagenanzug[M]
pigiamino[M]

sleepers
pelele[M]
combinaison[F] de nuit[F] ; dormeuse[F]
Schlafanzug[M]
pigiamino[M]

ribbing
tirilla[F] elástica
bord[M]-côte[F]
Rippenbündchen[N]
bordo[M] a coste[F]

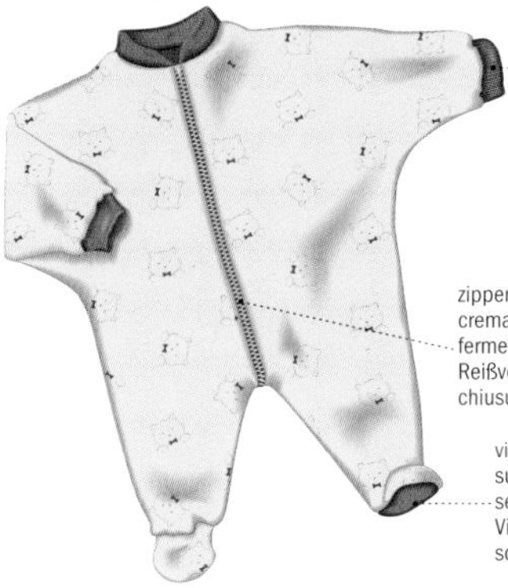

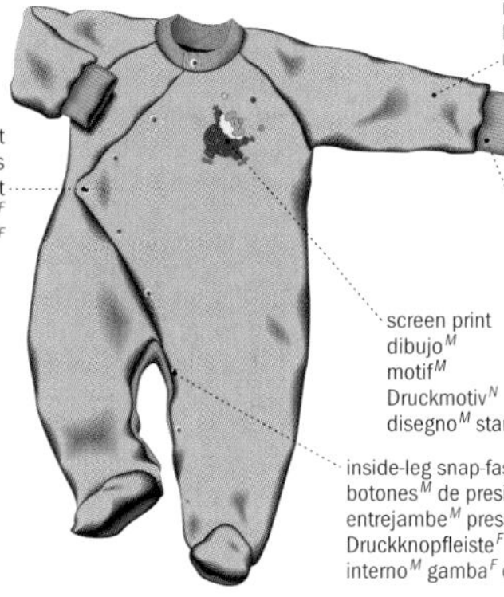

raglan sleeve
manga[F] raglán
manche[F] raglan
Raglanärmel[M]
manica[F] alla raglan[M]

snap-fastening front
botones[M] de presión[F] delanteros
pression[F] devant
vordere Druckknopfleiste[F]
abbottonatura[F] anteriore a pressione[F]

ribbing
tirilla[F] elástica
bord[M]-côte[F]
Rippenbündchen[N]
bordo[M] a coste[F]

zipper
cremallera[F]
fermeture[F] à glissière[F]
Reißverschluss[M]
chiusura[F] lampo

screen print
dibujo[M]
motif[M]
Druckmotiv[N]
disegno[M] stampato

vinyl grip sole
suela[F] antiderrapante
semelle[F] antidérapante
Vinyl-Laufsohle[F]
soletta[F] antiscivolo

inside-leg snap-fastening
botones[M] de presión[F] de la pierna[F]
entrejambe[M] pressionné
Druckknopfleiste[F] an der Beininnenseite[F]
interno[M] gamba[F] con abbottonatura[F] a pressione[F]

children's clothing

ropa[F] de niños[M] | vêtements[M] d'enfant[M] | Kinderbekleidung[F] | vestiti[M] per bambini[M]

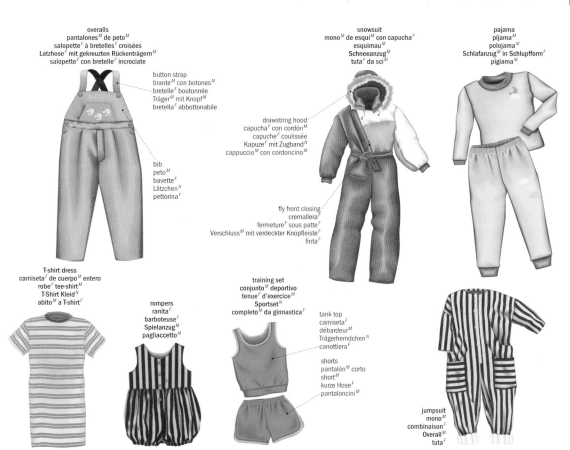

overalls
pantalones[M] de peto[M]
salopette[F] à bretelles[F] croisées
Latzhose[F] mit gekreuzten Rückenträgern[M]
salopette[F] con bretelle[F] incrociate

snowsuit
mono[M] de esquí con capucha[F]
esquimau[M]
Schneeanzug[M]
tuta[F] da sci[M]

pajama
pijama[M]
polojama[M]
Schlafanzug[M] in Schlupfform[F]
pigiama[M]

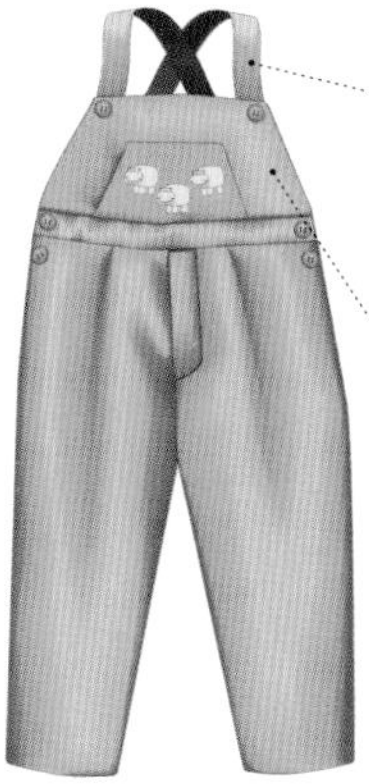

button strap
tirante[M] con botones[M]
bretelle[F] boutonnée
Träger[M] mit Knopf[M]
bretella[F] abbottonabile

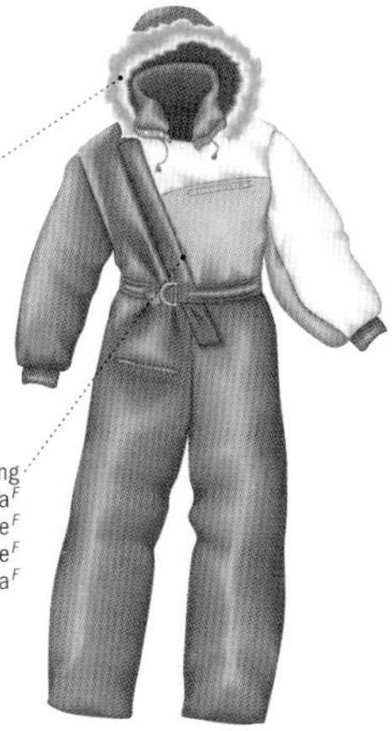

drawstring hood
capucha[F] con cordón[M]
capuche[F] coulissée
Kapuze[F] mit Zugband[N]
cappuccio[M] con cordoncino[M]

bib
peto[M]
bavette[F]
Lätzchen[N]
pettorina[F]

fly front closing
cremallera[F]
fermeture[F] sous patte[F]
Verschluss[M] mit verdeckter Knopfleiste[F]
finta[F]

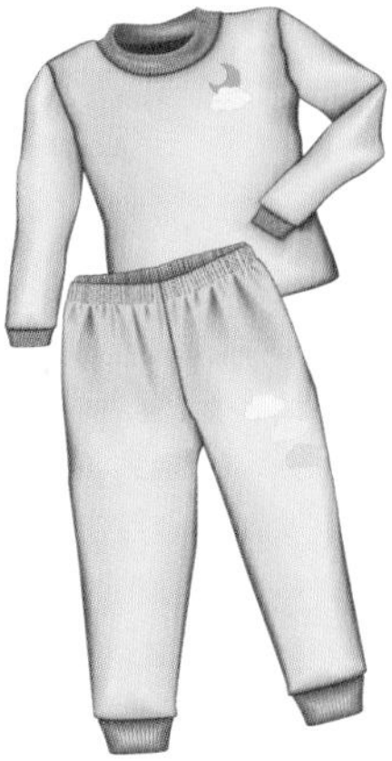

T-shirt dress
camiseta[F] de cuerpo[M] entero
robe[F] tee-shirt[M]
T-Shirt Kleid[N]
abito[M] a T-shirt[F]

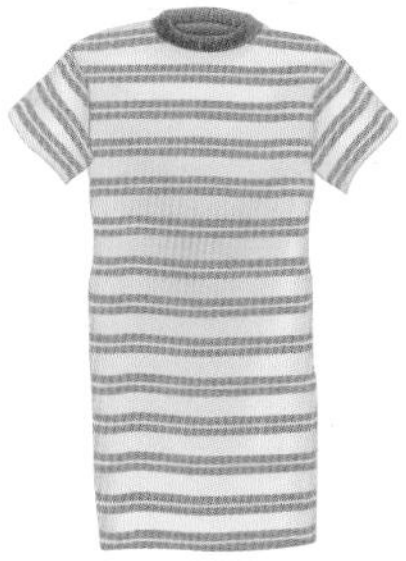

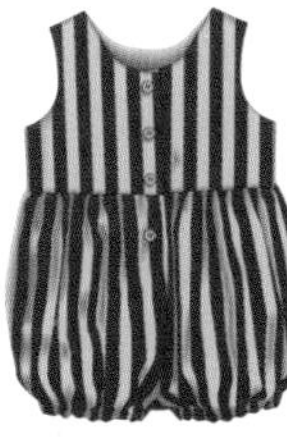

training set
conjunto[M] deportivo
tenue[F] d'exercice[M]
Sportset[N]
completo[M] da ginnastica[F]

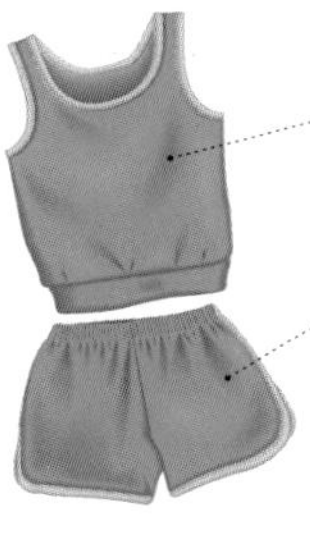

tank top
camiseta[F]
débardeur[F]
Trägerhemdchen[N]
canottiera[F]

rompers
ranita[F]
barboteuse[F]
Spielanzug[M]
pagliaccetto[M]

shorts
pantalón[M] corto
short[M]
kurze Hose[F]
pantaloncini[M]

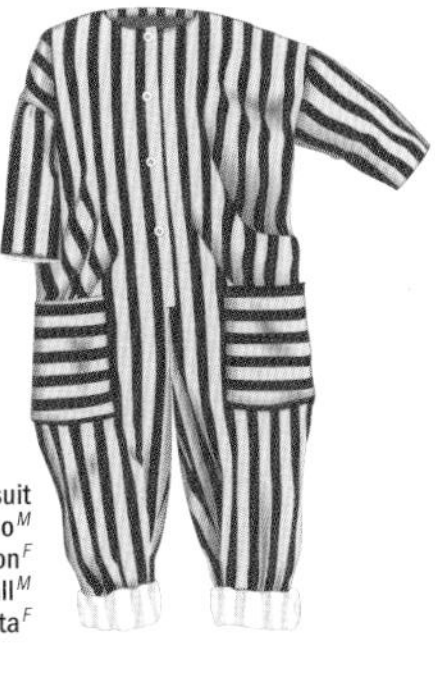

jumpsuit
mono[M]
combinaison[F]
Overall[M]
tuta[F]

running shoe
zapatilla^F deportiva
chaussure^F de sport^M
Joggingschuh^M
scarpa^F da corsa^F

lining
forro^M
doublure^F
Futter^N
fodera^F

tongue
lengüeta^F
languette^F
Zunge^F
linguetta^F

nose of the quarter
ala^F del cuarto^M
aile^F de quartier^M
Vorderteil^{M/N}
parte^F anteriore del quartiere^M

collar
ribete^M
col^M
Fersenrand^M
collo^M

counter
contrafuerte^M
contrefort^M
Hinterkappe^F
rinforzo^M del calcagno^M

quarter
cuarto^M
quartier^M
Quartier^N
quartiere^M

stitch
pespunteado^M
surpiqûre^F
Naht^F
impuntura^F

heel
talón^M
talon^M
Absatz^M
tallone^M

middle sole
cambrillón^M
semelle^F intercalaire
Zwischensohle^F
intersuola^F

air unit
cámara^F de aire^M
coussin^M d'air^M
Luftpolster^N
cuscinetto^M ad aria^F

tag
herrete^M
ferret^M
Schnürsenkelende^N
puntale^M

shoelace
cordón^M
lacet^M
Schnürsenkel^M
laccio^M

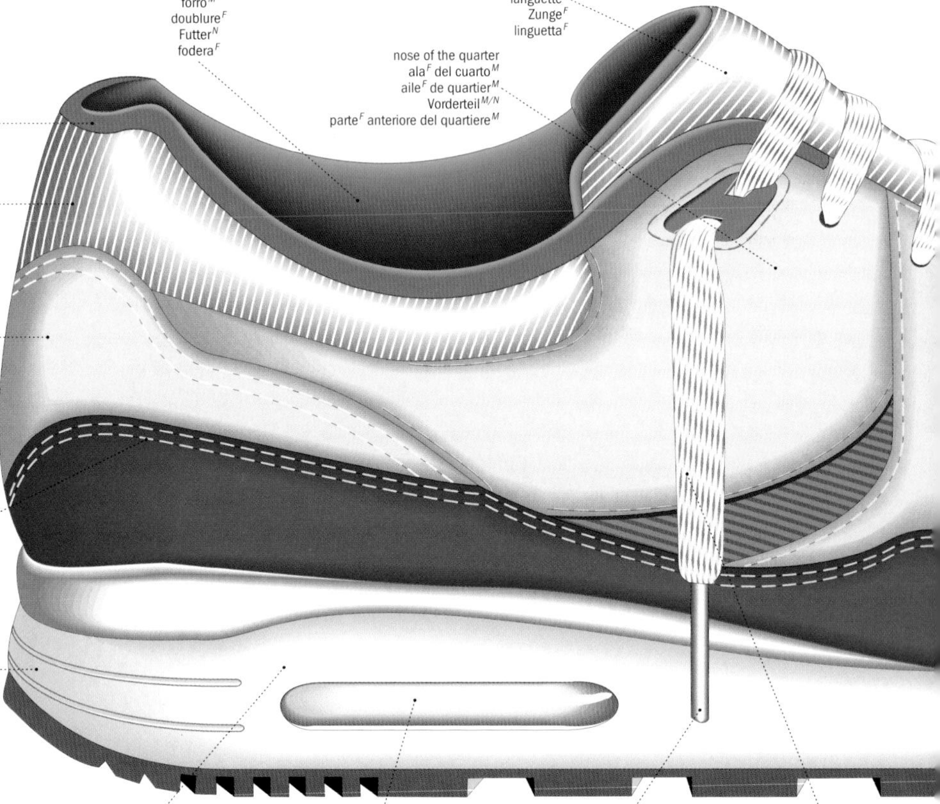

sweat suit
traje^M de entrenamiento^M
survêtement^M
Trainingsanzug^M
tuta^F sportiva

hooded sweat shirt
sudadera^F con capucha^F
pull^M à capuche^F
Sweatshirt^N mit Kapuze^F
felpa^F con cappuccio^M

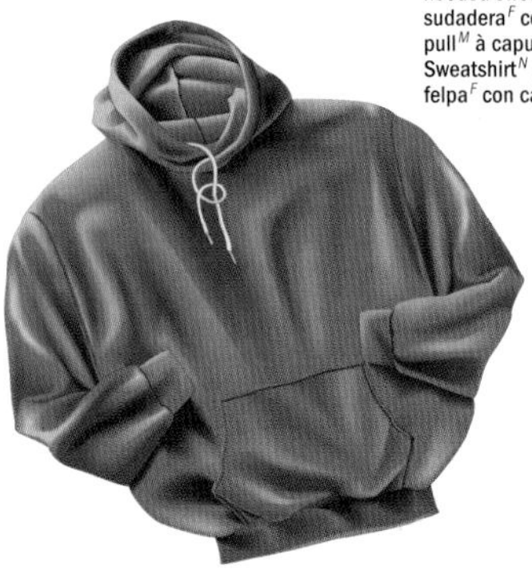

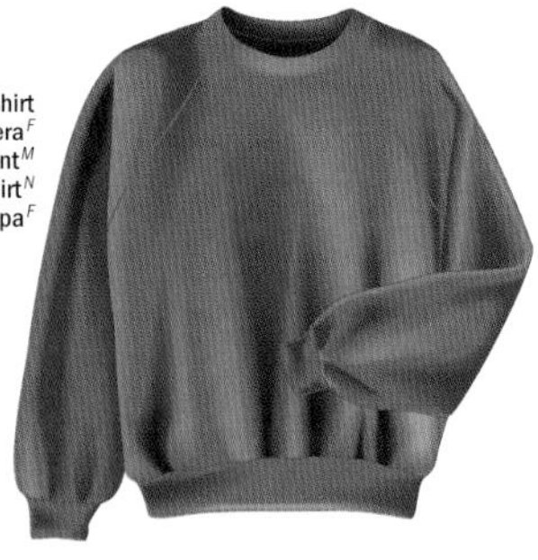

sweat pants
pantalones^M de chándal^M
pantalon^M molleton^M
Trainingshose^F
pantaloni^M felpati

sweat shirt
sudadera^F
pull^M d'entrainement^M
Sweatshirt^N
felpa^F

CLOTHING

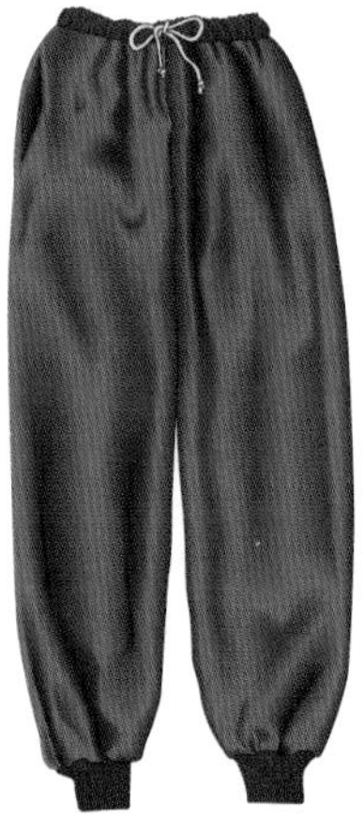

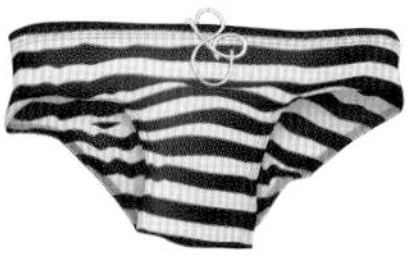

swimming trunks
traje^M de baño^M
slip^M de bain^M
Badehose^F
slip^M da bagno^M

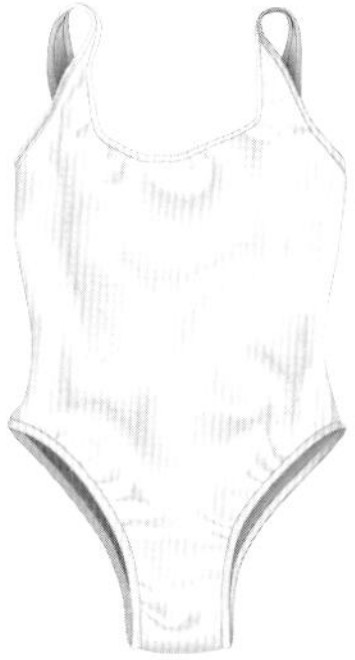

swimsuit
traje^M de baño^M
maillot^M de bain^M
Badeanzug^M
costume^M da bagno^M

exercise wear
ropa^F para ejercicio^M
vêtements^M d'exercice^M
Sportkleidung^F
abbigliamento^M da ginnastica^F

eyelet
ojete^M
œillet^M
Öse^F
occhiello^M

vamp
empella^F
claque^F
Vorderblatt^N
tomaia^F

punch hole
perforación^F
perforation^F
gestanztes Loch^N
foro^M

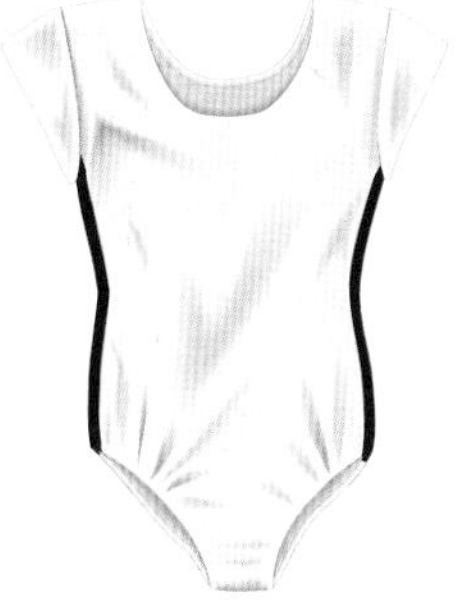

leotard
body^M
justaucorps^M
Trikot^N
body^M

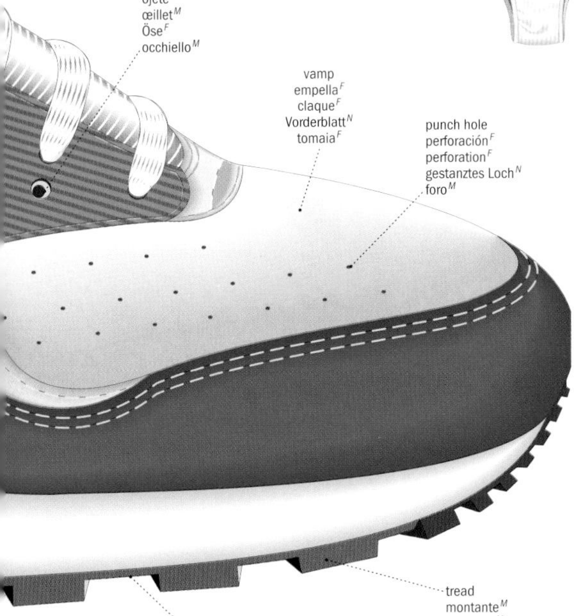

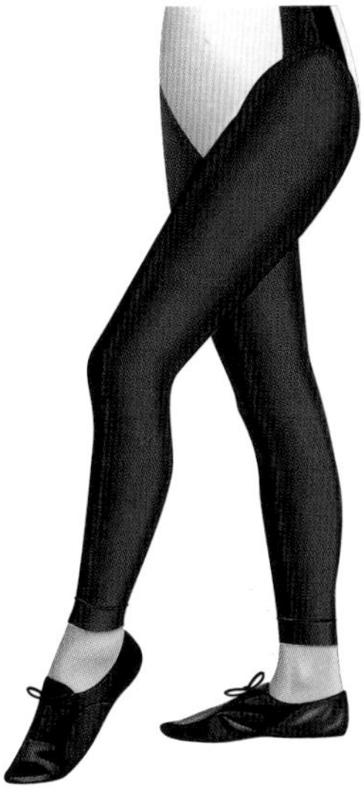

footless tights
mallas^F
collant^M sans pied^M
Leggins^F
pantacollant^M

tread
montante^M
crampon^M
Stollen^M
tacchetto^M

outsole
suela^F
semelle^F d'usure^F
Laufsohle^F
suola^F

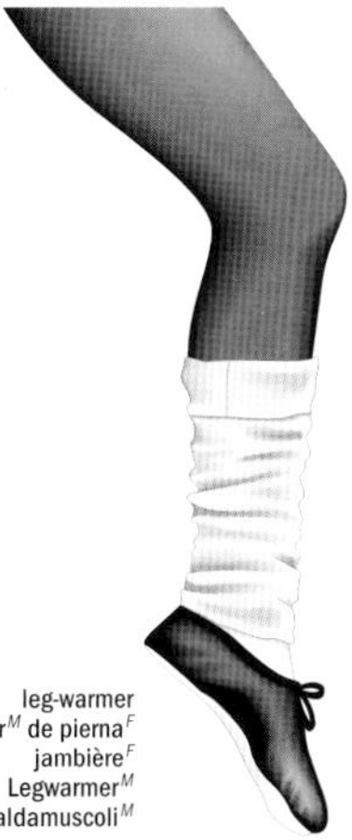

leg-warmer
calentador^M de pierna^F
jambière^F
Legwarmer^M
scaldamuscoli^M

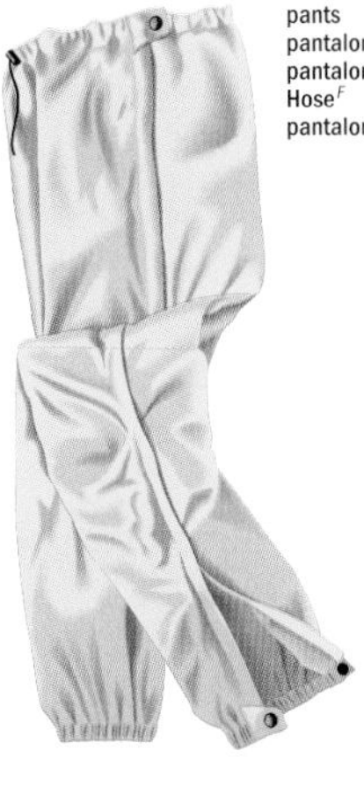

pants
pantalones^M
pantalon^M
Hose^F
pantaloni^M

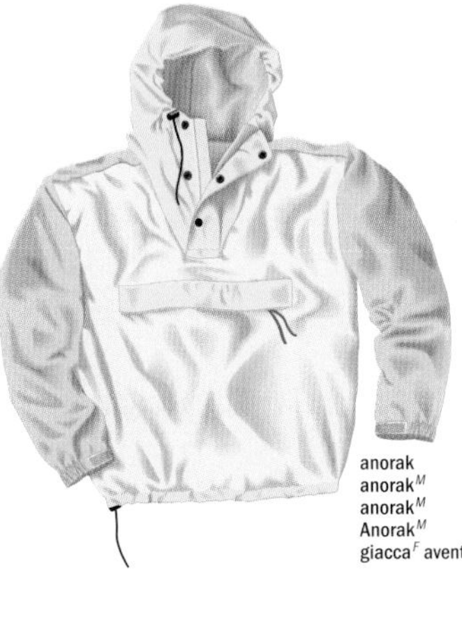

anorak
anorak^M
anorak^M
Anorak^M
giacca^F avento^M

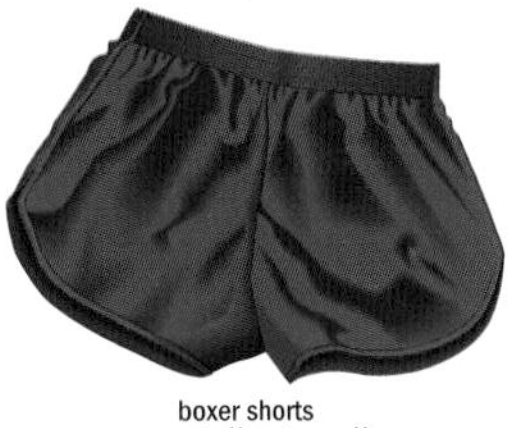

boxer shorts
pantalón^M de boxeo^M
short^M boxeur^M
Shorts^F
pantaloncini^M da corsa^F

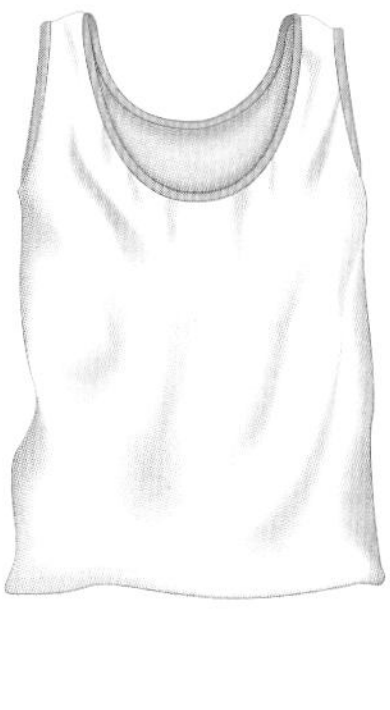

tank top
camiseta^F
débardeur^M
Trägerhemd^N
canottiera^F

CLOTHING

371

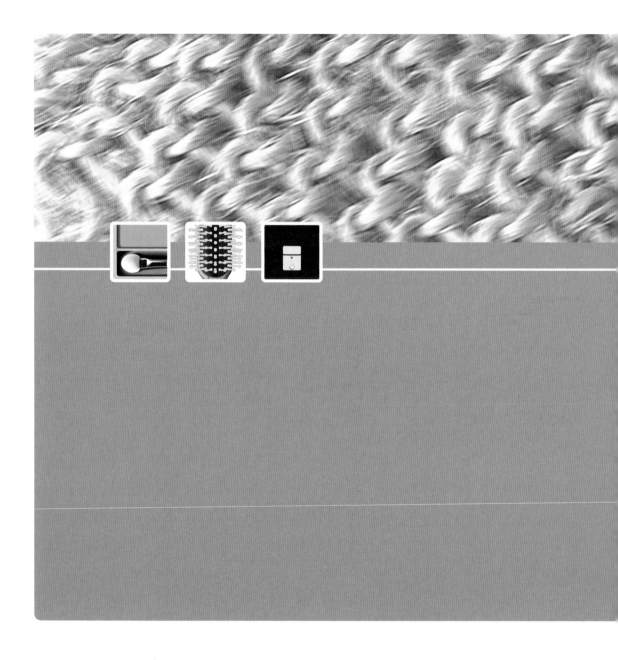

PERSONAL ADORNMENT AND ARTICLES

ACCESORIOS Y ARTÍCULOS PERSONALES | PARURE ET OBJETS PERSONNELS | PERSÖNLICHE AUSSTATTUNG | ACCESSORI E ARTICOLI PERSONALI

jewelry

joyería^F | bijouterie^F | Schmuck^M | gioielli^M

earrings
pendientes^M
boucles^F d'oreille^F
Ohrringe^M
orecchini^M

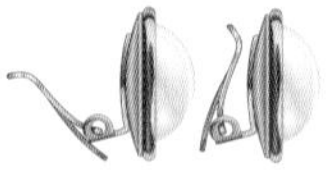

clip earrings
pendientes^M de clip^M
boucles^F d'oreille^F à pince^F
Klips^M
orecchini^M a clip^F

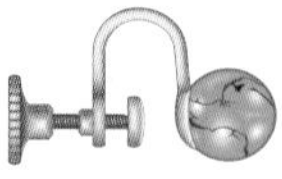

screw earring
pendientes^M de tornillo^M
boucles^F d'oreille^F à vis^F
Ohrringe^M mit Schraubverschluss^M
orecchini^M a vite^F

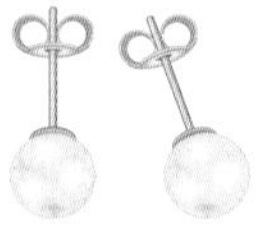

pierced earrings
pendientes^M de espiga^F
boucles^F d'oreille^F à tige^F
Ohrstecker^M
orecchini^M a perno^M

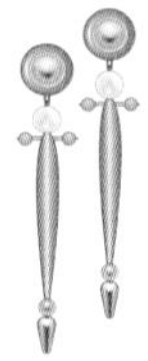

drop earrings
pendientes^M
pendants^M d'oreille^F
Ohrgehänge^N
orecchini^M pendenti

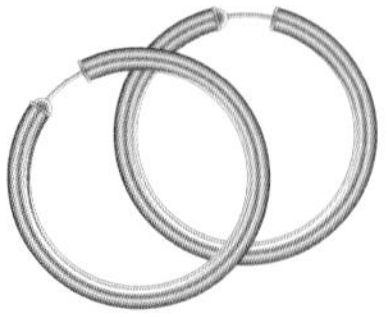

hoop earrings
pendientes^M de aro^M
anneaux^M
Kreolen^F
orecchini^M ad anello^M

necklaces
collares^M
colliers^M
Halsketten^F
collane^F

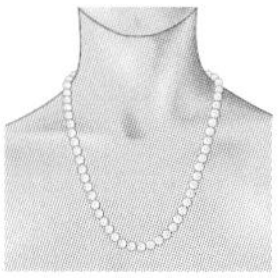

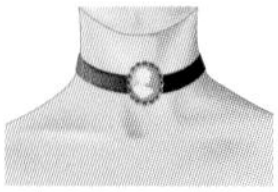

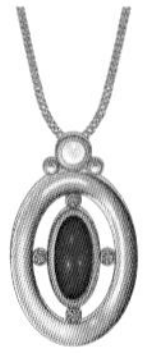

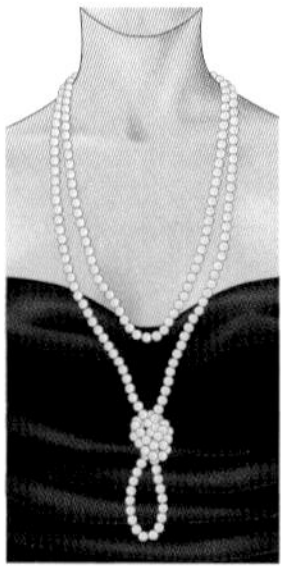

rope necklace
lazo^M
sautoir^M
Endlosperlenkette^F
collana^F lunga alla vita^F

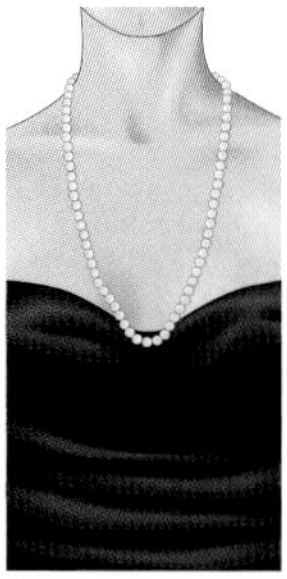

opera-length necklace
collar^M de una vuelta^F, ópera^F
sautoir^M, longueur^F opéra^M
Halskette^F in Opernlänge^F
collana^F lunga

matinee-length necklace
collar^M de una vuelta^F, matinée^F
collier^M de perles^F, longueur^F matinée^F
Halskette^F in Matineelänge^F
collana^F

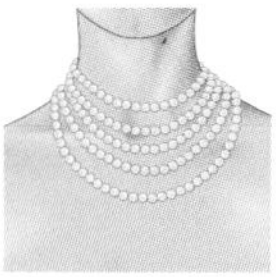

bib necklace
collar^M de 5 vueltas^M, peto^M
collier^M de soirée^F
mehrreihige Halskette^F
collana^F a cinque giri^M

velvet-band choker
gargantilla^F de terciopelo^M
collier^M-de-chien^M
Samtkropfband^N
collarino^M di velluto^M

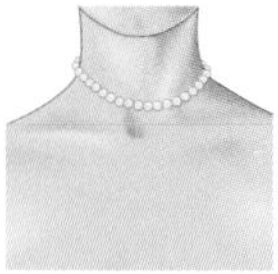

choker
gargantilla^F
ras-de-cou^M
Chokerkette^F
girocollo^M

pendant
pendiente^M
pendentif^M
Anhänger^M
pendenti^M

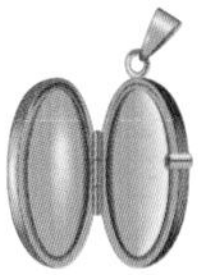

locket
medallón^M
médaillon^M
Medaillon^N
medaglione^M

brilliant cut facets
talla^F brillante de un diamante^M
taille^F d'un diamant^M
Facetten^F des Brillantschliffs^M
sfaccettature^F del taglio^M a brillante^M

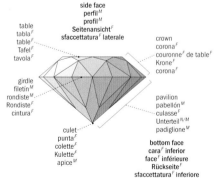

table
tabla^F
table^F
Tafel^F
tavola^F

side face
perfil^M
profil^M
Seitenansicht^F
sfaccettatura^F laterale

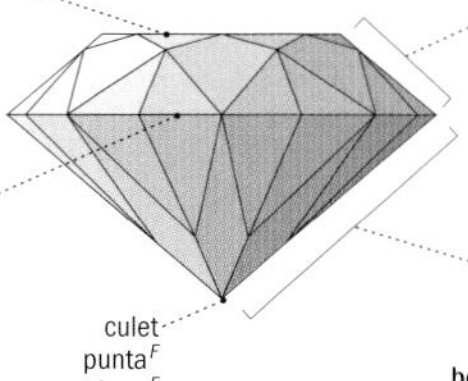

crown
corona^F
couronne^F de table^F
Krone^F
corona^F

girdle
filetín^M
rondiste^M
Rondiste^F
cintura^F

pavilion
pabellón^M
culasse^F
Unterteil^{N/M}
padiglione^M

culet
punta^F
colette^F
Kulette^F
apice^M

top face
cara^F superior
face^F supérieure
Vorderseite^F
sfaccettatura^F superiore

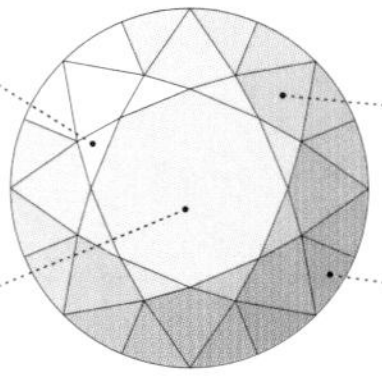

star facet (8)
faceta^F estrella^F (8)
étoile^F (8)
Tafelfacette^F (8)
faccia^F della stella^F (8)

table
tabla^F
table^F
Tafel^F
tavola^F

bezel facet (8)
faceta^F fundamental exterior (8)
bezel^M (8)
Oberteilhauptfacette^F (8)
faccia^F principale della corona^F (8)

upper girdle facet (16)
media faceta^F superior (16)
halefis^M de table^F (16)
obere Rondistenfacette^F (16)
faccia^F superiore della cintura^F (16)

bottom face
cara^F inferior
face^F inférieure
Rückseite^F
sfaccettatura^F inferiore

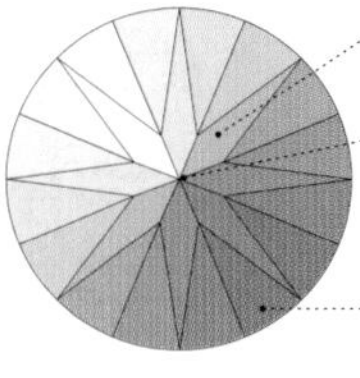

pavilion facet (8)
faceta^F de pabellón^M (8)
pavillon^M (8)
Unterteilhauptfacette^F (8)
faccia^F del padiglione^M (8)

culet
culata^F
colette^F
Kulette^F
apice^M

lower girdle facet (16)
faceta^F inferior del contorno^M (16)
halefis^M de culasse^F (16)
untere Rondistenfacette^F (16)
faccia^F inferiore della cintura^F (16)

cuts for gemstones
tallas^F de piedras^F preciosas
taille^F des pierres^F
Schliffformen^F für Edelsteine^M
tagli^M di pietre^F preziose

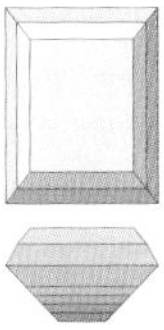

step cut
talla^F escalonada
taille^F en escalier^M
Treppenschliff^M
taglio^M a gradini^M

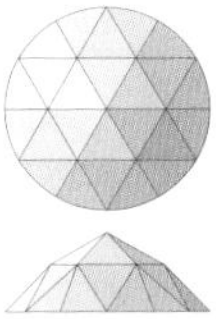

rose cut
talla^F en rosa^F holandesa
taille^F en rose^F
Rosenschliff^M
taglio^M a rosetta^F

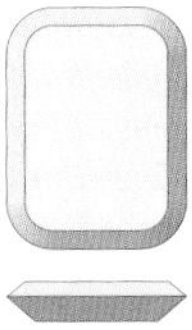

table cut
talla^F en tabla^F
taille^F en table^F
Tafelschliff^M
taglio^M a tavola^F

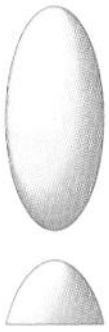

cabochon cut
talla^F en cabujón^M
taille^F cabochon^M
Cabochonschliff^M
taglio^M a cabochon^M

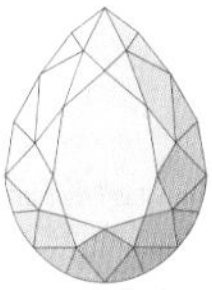

pear-shaped cut
talla^F en pera^F
taille^F en poire^F
Pendeloque-Schliff^M
taglio^M a pera^F

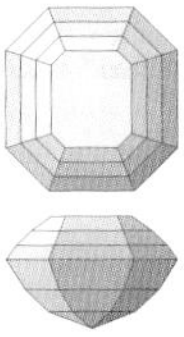

emerald cut
talla^F esmeralda^F
taille^F émeraude^F
Emeraldcut^M
taglio^M a smeraldo^M

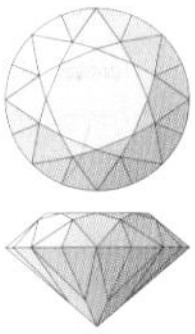

brilliant full cut
talla^F brillante^M
taille^F brillant^M
Vollbrillantschliff^M
taglio^M a brillante^F

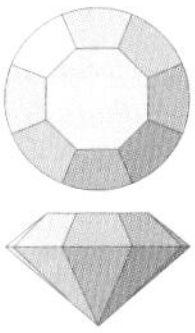

eight cut
talla^F octógono
taille^F huit facettes^F
Achtkantschliff^M
taglio^M ottagonale

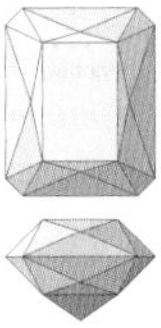

scissors cut
talla^F en tijera^F
taille^F en ciseaux^M
Scherenschliff^M
taglio^M a forbice^M

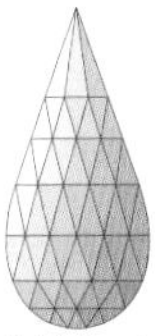

briolette cut
talla^F en briolette^F
taille^F en goutte^F
Briolettschliff^M
taglio^M a briolette

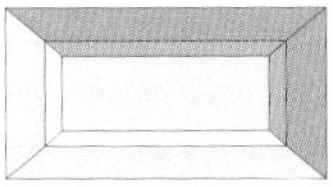

baguette cut
talla^F en baguette^F
taille^F baguette^F
Baguetteform^F
taglio^M a baguette^F

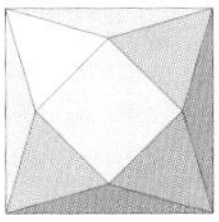

French cut
talla^F francesa
taille^F française
Frenchcut^M
taglio^M francese

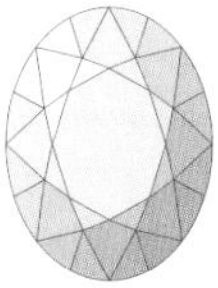

oval cut
talla^F oval
taille^F ovale
ovale Form^F
taglio^M ovale

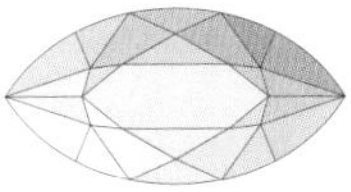

navette cut
talla^F marquesa^F
taille^F marquise^F
Navette^F
taglio^M a marquise^F

semiprecious stones
piedras^F semipreciosas
pierres^F fines
Halbedelsteine^M
pietre^F semipreziose

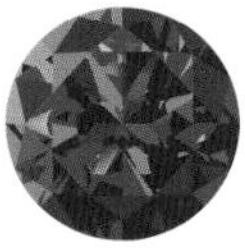

amethyst
amatista^F
améthyste^F
Amethyst^M
ametista^F

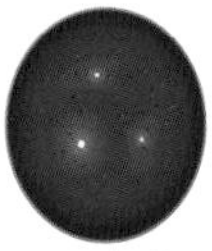

lapis lazuli
lapislázuli^M
lapis-lazuli^M
Lapislazuli^M
lapislazzuli^M

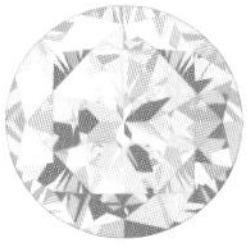

aquamarine
aguamarina^F
aigue-marine^F
Aquamarin^M
acquamarina^F

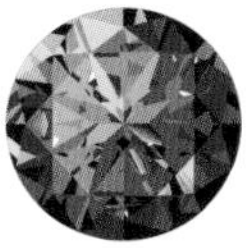

topaz
topacio^M
topaze^F
Topas^M
topazio^M

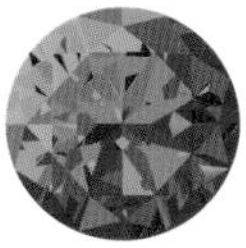

tourmaline
turmalina^F
tourmaline^F
Turmalin^M
tormalina^F

opal
ópalo^M
opale^F
Opal^M
opale^M

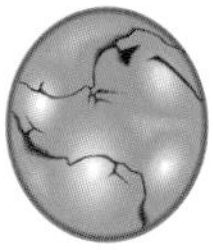

turquoise
turquesa^F
turquoise^F
Türkis^M
turchese^M

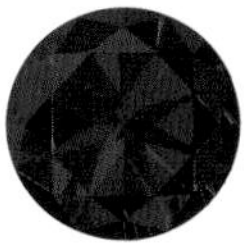

garnet
granate^M
grenat^M
Granat^M
granato^M

precious stones
piedras^F preciosas
pierres^F précieuses
Edelsteine^M
pietre^F preziose

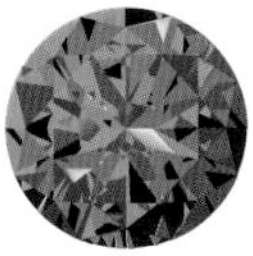

emerald
esmeralda^F
émeraude^F
Smaragd^M
smeraldo^M

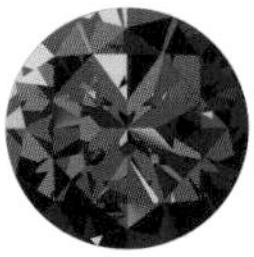

sapphire
zafiro^M
saphir^M
Saphir^M
zaffiro^M

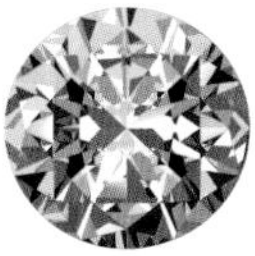

diamond
diamante^M
diamant^M
Diamant^M
diamante^M

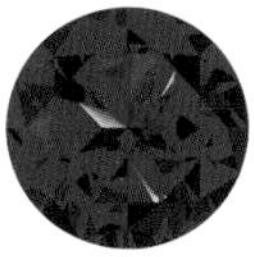

ruby
rubí^M
rubis^M
Rubin^M
rubino^M

jewelry

rings
anillos^M
bagues^F
Ringe^M
anelli^M

parts of a ring
partes^M de un anillo^M
parties^F d'une bague^F
Teile$^{M/N}$ eines Rings^M
componenti^M di un anello^M

setting
engaste^M
sertissure^F
Fassung^F
incastonatura^F

claw
garra^F
griffe^F
Krappe^F
montatura^F

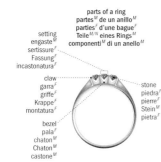

stone
piedra^F
pierre^F
Stein^M
pietra^F

bezel
pala^F
chaton^M
Chaton^M
castone^M

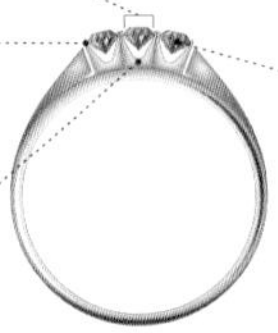

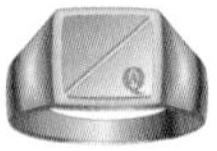

signet ring
sortija^F de sello^M
chevalière^F
Herrenring^M
anello^M con sigillo^M

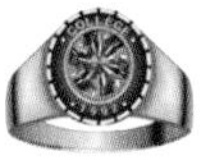

class ring
anillo^M de graduación^F
bague^F de finissant^M
Collegering^M
anello^M studentesco

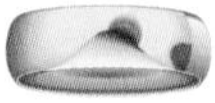

band ring
alianza^F
jonc^M
Bandring^M
anello^M a fascia^F

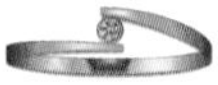

engagement ring
anillo^M de compromiso^M
bague^F de fiançailles^F
Verlobungsring^M
anello^M di fidanzamento^M

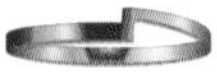

wedding ring
alianza^F
alliance^F
Ehering^M
fede^F nuziale

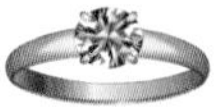

solitaire ring
solitario^M
bague^F solitaire^M
Solitärring^M
solitario^M

bracelets
brazaletes^M
bracelets^M
Armbänder^N
bracciali^M

charms
dijes^M
breloques^F
Anhänger^M
ciondoli^M

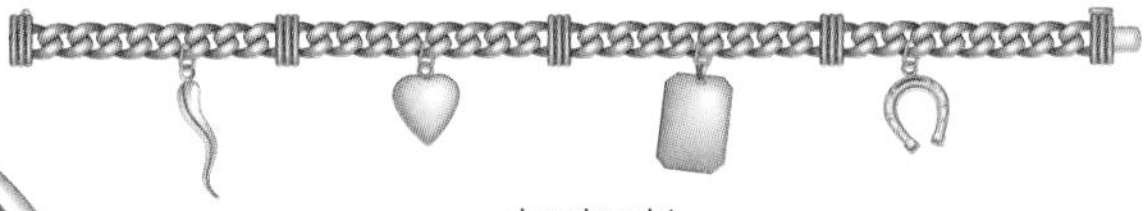

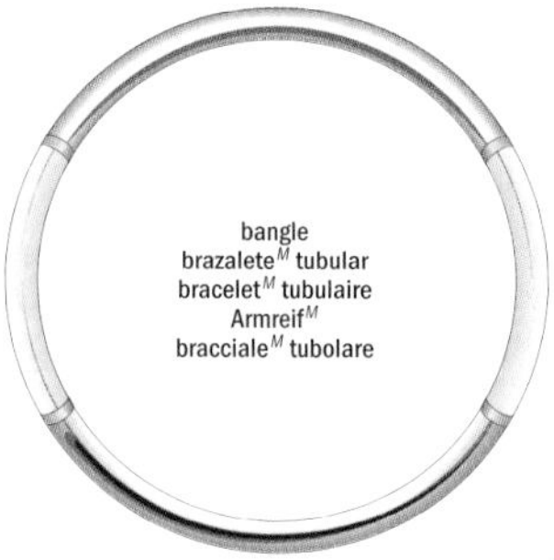

bangle
brazalete^M tubular
bracelet^M tubulaire
Armreif^M
bracciale^M tubolare

charm bracelet
pulsera^F de dijes^M
gourmette^F
Armband^N
bracciale^M con ciondoli^M

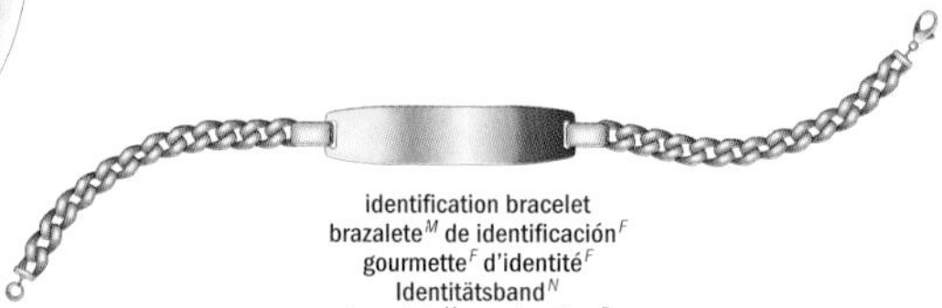

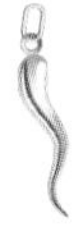

horn
cuerno^M
corne^F
Horn^N
corno^M

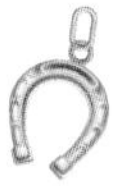

horseshoe
herradura^F
fer^F à cheval^M
Hufeisen^N
ferro^F di cavallo^M

identification bracelet
brazalete^M de identificación^F
gourmette^F d'identité^F
Identitätsband^N
bracciale^M con piastrina^F

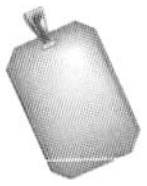

nameplate
placa^F de identificación^F
plaque^F d'identité^F
Gravurplatte^F
piastrina^F d'identità^F

pins
alfileres^M
épingles^F
Anstecknadeln^F
spille^F

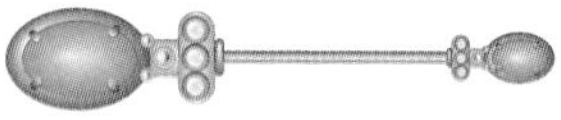

stickpin
alfiler^M de corbata^F
broche^F épingle^F
Sticker^M
spillone^M

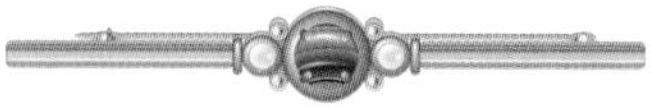

brooch
broche^F
broche^F
Brosche^F
spilla^F

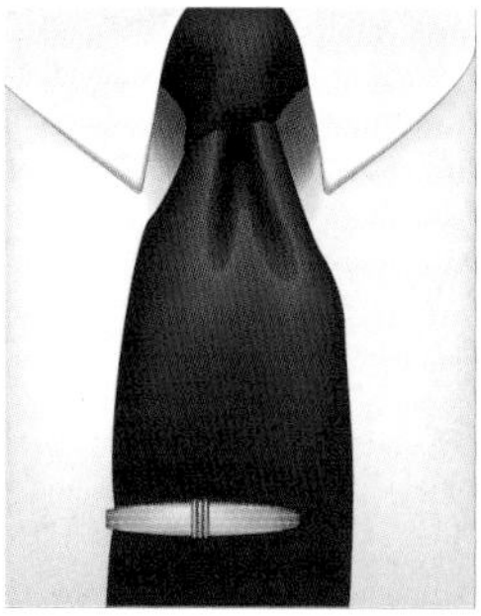

tie bar
pisacorbatas^M
pince^F à cravate^F
Krawattenklemme^F
fermacravatta^M

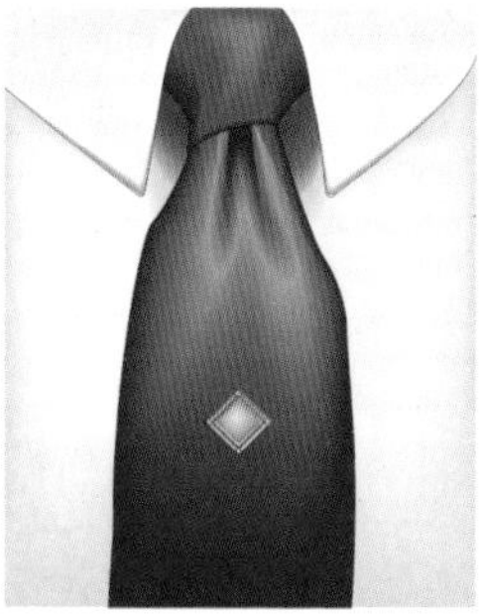

tiepin
alfiler^M de corbata^F
épingle^F à cravate^F
Krawattennadel^F
spillo^M fermacravatta^M

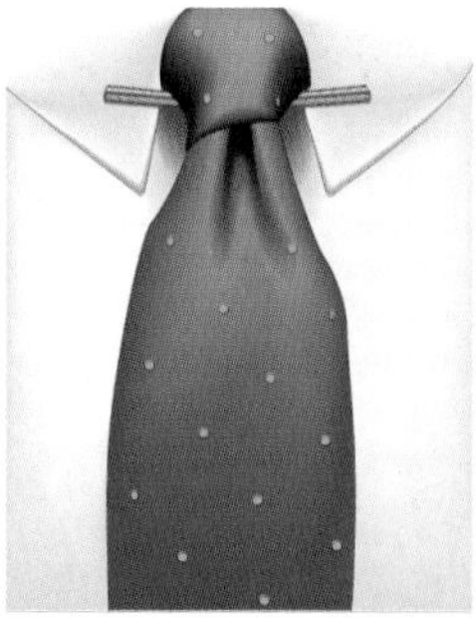

collar bar
yugo^M
tige^F pour col^M
Kragenklammer^F
fermacolletto^M

nail care

manicura[F] | manucure[F] | Maniküre[F] | manicure[F]

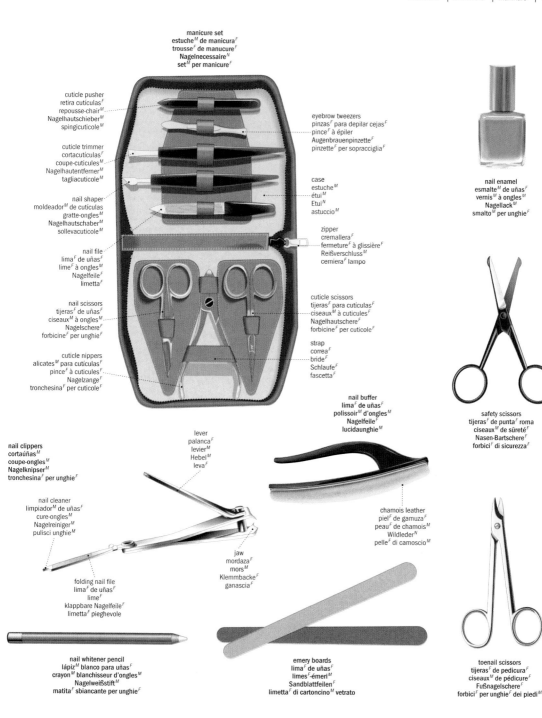

manicure set
estuche[M] de manicura[F]
trousse[F] de manucure[F]
Nagelnecessaire[N]
set[M] per manicure[F]

cuticle pusher
retira cutículas[F]
repousse-chair[M]
Nagelhautschieber[M]
spingicuticole[M]

cuticle trimmer
cortacuticulas[F]
coupe-cuticules[F]
Nagelhautentferner[M]
tagliacuticole[M]

nail shaper
moldeador[M] de cuticulas[F]
gratte-ongles[F]
Nagelhautschaber[M]
sollevacuticole[M]

nail file
lima[F] de uñas[F]
lime[F] à ongles[M]
Nagelfeile[F]
limetta[F]

nail scissors
tijeras[F] de uñas[F]
ciseaux[M] à ongles[F]
Nagelschere[F]
forbicine[F] per unghie[F]

cuticle nippers
alicates[M] para cuticulas[F]
pince[F] à cuticules[F]
Nagelzange[F]
tronchesina[F] per cuticole[F]

eyebrow tweezers
pinzas[F] para depilar cejas[F]
pince[F] à épiler
Augenbrauenpinzette[F]
pinzette[F] per sopracciglia[F]

case
estuche[M]
étui[M]
Etui[N]
astuccio[M]

zipper
cremallera[F]
fermeture[F] à glissière[F]
Reißverschluss[M]
cerniera[F] lampo

cuticle scissors
tijeras[F] para cuticulas[F]
ciseaux[M] à cuticules[F]
Nagelhautschere[F]
forbicine[F] per cuticole[F]

strap
correa[F]
bride[F]
Schlaufe[F]
fascetta[F]

nail enamel
esmalte[M] de uñas[F]
vernis[F] à ongles[M]
Nagellack[M]
smalto[M] per unghie[F]

safety scissors
tijeras[F] de punta[F] roma
ciseaux[M] de sûreté[F]
Nasen-Bartschere[F]
forbici[F] di sicurezza[F]

nail buffer
lima[F] de uñas[F]
polissoir[M] d'ongles[M]
Nagelfeile[F]
lucidaunghie[M]

lever
palanca[F]
levier[M]
Hebel[M]
leva[F]

nail clippers
cortaúñas[M]
coupe-ongles[M]
Nagelknipser[M]
tronchesina[F] per unghie[F]

nail cleaner
limpiador[M] de uñas[F]
cure-ongles[M]
Nagelreiniger[M]
pulisci unghie[M]

folding nail file
lima[F] de uñas[F]
lime[F]
klappbare Nagelfeile[F]
limetta[F] pieghevole

chamois leather
piel[F] de gamuza[F]
peau[F] de chamois[M]
Wildleder[N]
pelle[F] di camoscio[M]

jaw
mordaza[F]
mors[M]
Klemmbacke[F]
ganascia[F]

nail whitener pencil
lápiz[M] blanco para uñas[F]
crayon[M] blanchisseur d'ongles[M]
Nagelweißstift[M]
matita[F] sbiancante per unghie[F]

emery boards
lima[F] de uñas[F]
limes[F]-émeri[M]
Sandblattfeilen[F]
limetta[F] di cartoncino[F] vetrato

toenail scissors
tijeras[F] de pedicura[F]
ciseaux[M] de pédicure[F]
Fußnagelschere[F]
forbici[F] per unghie[F] dei piedi[M]

makeup

maquillaje^M | maquillage^M | Make-up^N | trucco^M

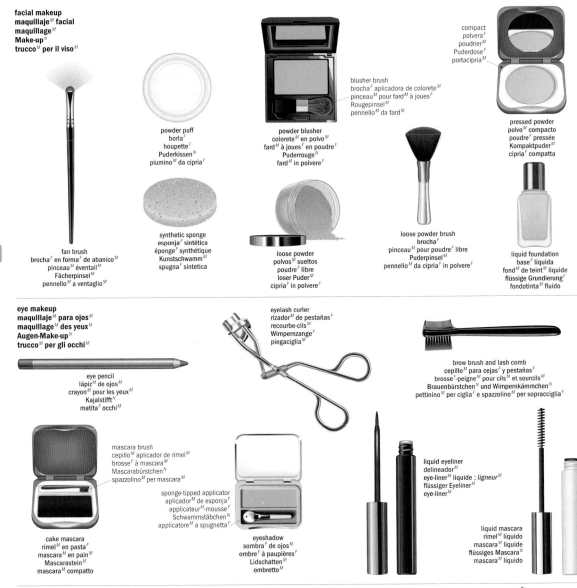

facial makeup
maquillaje^M facial
maquillage^M
Make-up^N
trucco^M per il viso^M

compact
polvera^F
poudrier^M
Puderdose^F
portacipria^M

blusher brush
brocha^F aplicadora de colorete^M
pinceau^M pour fard^M à joues^F
Rougepinsel^M
pennello^M da fard^M

powder puff
borla^F
houpette^F
Puderkissen^N
piumino^M da cipria^F

powder blusher
colorete^M en polvo^M
fard^M à joues^F en poudre^F
Puderrouge^M
fard^M in polvere^F

pressed powder
polvo^M compacto
poudre^F pressée
Kompaktpuder^M
cipria^F compatta

synthetic sponge
esponja^F sintética
éponge^F synthétique
Kunstschwamm^M
spugna^F sintetica

loose powder
polvos^M sueltos
poudre^F libre
loser Puder^M
cipria^F in polvere^F

loose powder brush
brocha^F
pinceau^M pour poudre^F libre
Puderpinsel^M
pennello^M da cipria^F in polvere^F

liquid foundation
base^F líquida
fond^M de teint^M liquide
flüssige Grundierung^F
fondotinta^M fluido

fan brush
brocha^F en forma^F de abanico^M
pinceau^M éventail^M
Fächerpinsel^M
pennello^M a ventaglio^M

eye makeup
maquillaje^M para ojos^M
maquillage^M des yeux^M
Augen-Make-up^N
trucco^M per gli occhi^M

eyelash curler
rizador^M de pestañas^F
recourbe-cils^M
Wimpernzange^F
piegaciglia^M

brow brush and lash comb
cepillo^M para cejas^F y pestañas^F
brosse^F-peigne^M pour cils^M et sourcils^M
Brauenbürstchen^N und Wimpernkämmchen^N
pettinino^M per ciglia^F e spazzolino^M per sopracciglia^F

eye pencil
lápiz^M de ojos^M
crayon^M pour les yeux^M
Kajalstift^N
matita^F occhi^M

mascara brush
cepillo^M aplicador de rímel^M
brosse^F à mascara^M
Mascarabürstchen^N
spazzolino^M per mascara^M

liquid eyeliner
delineador^M
eye-liner^M liquide ; ligneur^M
flüssiger Eyeliner^M
eye-liner^M

sponge-tipped applicator
aplicador^M de esponja^F
applicateur^M-mousse^F
Schwammstäbchen^N
applicatore^M a spugnetta^F

cake mascara
rímel^M en pasta^F
mascara^M en pain^M
Mascarastein^M
mascara^M compatto

eyeshadow
sombra^F de ojos^M
ombre^F à paupières^F
Lidschatten^M
ombretto^M

liquid mascara
rímel^M líquido
mascara^M liquide
flüssiges Mascara^N
mascara^M liquido

lip makeup
maquillaje^M labial
maquillage^M des lèvres^F
Lippen-Make-up^N
trucco^M per le labbra^F

lip brush
pincel^M para labios^M
pinceau^M à lèvres^F
Lippenpinsel^M
pennellino^M per labbra^F

lipliner
delineador^M de labios^M
crayon^M contour^M des lèvres^F
Lippenkonturenstift^M
matite^F per il contour^M delle labbra^F

lipstick
pintalabios^M
rouge^M à lèvres^F
Lippenstift^M
rossetto^M

PERSONAL ADORNMENT AND ARTICLES

body care

cuidado^M personal | soins^M du corps^M | Körperpflege^F | cura^F del corpo^M

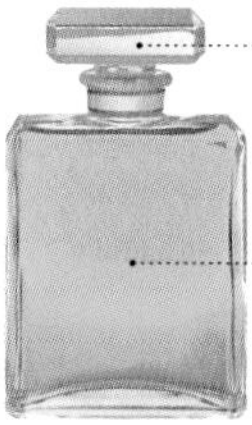

stopper
tapón^M
bouchon^M
Stopfen^M
tappo^M

bottle
botella^F
flacon^M
Flasche^F
bottiglia^F

eau de parfum
agua^F de perfume^M
eau^F de parfum^M
Eau de parfum^N
profumo^M

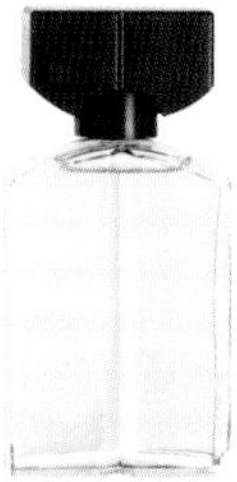

eau de toilette
agua^F de colonia^F
eau^F de toilette^F
Eau de toilette^N
eau de toilette^F

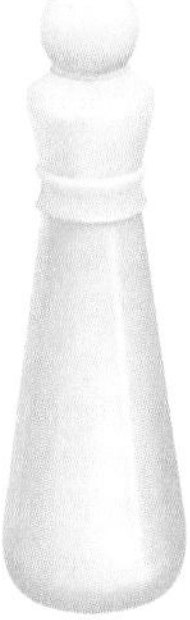

bubble bath
gel^M de baño^M
bain^M moussant
Schaumbad^N
bagnoschiuma^M

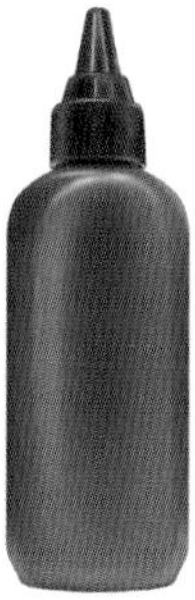

haircolor
tinte^M para el cabello^M
colorant^M capillaire
Haarfärbemittel^N
tintura^F per capelli^M

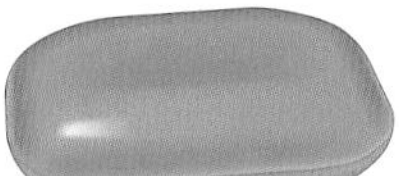

toilet soap
jabón^M de tocador^M
savon^M de toilette^F
Toilettenseife^F
saponetta^F

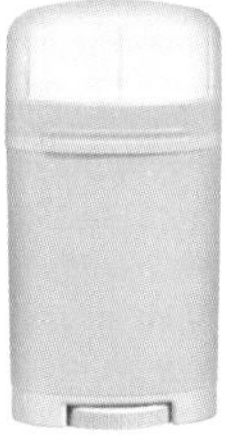

deodorant
desodorante^M
déodorant^M
Deodorant^N
deodorante^M

hair conditioner
acondicionador^M
revitalisant^M capillaire
Haarspülung^F
balsamo^M per capelli^M

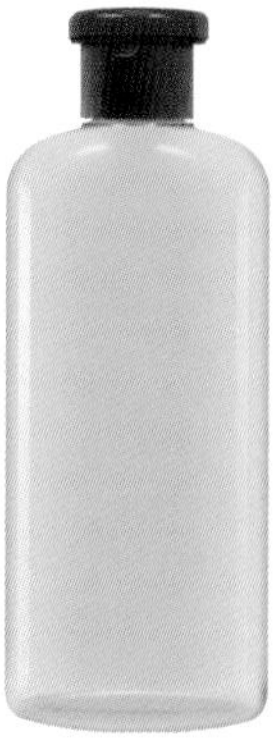

shampoo
champú^M
shampooing^M
Shampoo^N
shampoo^M

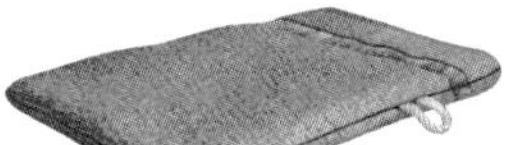

washcloth
manopla^F de baño^M
gant^M de toilette^F
Waschhandschuh^M
manopola^F

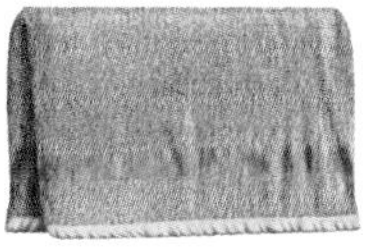

washcloth
toalla^F para la cara^F
débarbouillette^F
Waschlappen^M
ospite^M

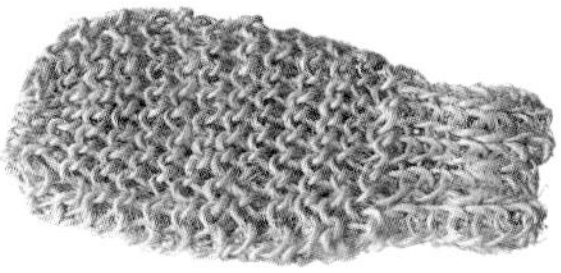

massage glove
guante^M de crin^M
gant^M de crin^M
Massagehandschuh^M
guanto^M di crine^M

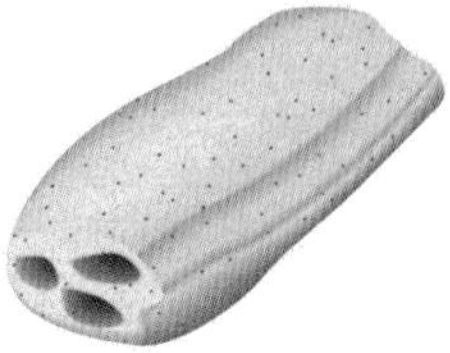

vegetable sponge
esponja^F vegetal
éponge^F végétale
Luffaschwamm^M
spugna^F vegetale

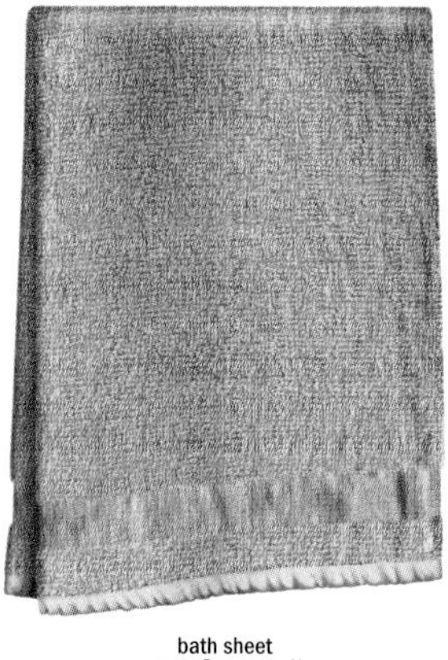

bath sheet
toalla^F de baño^M
drap^M de bain^M
Badetuch^N
asciugamano^M da bagno^M

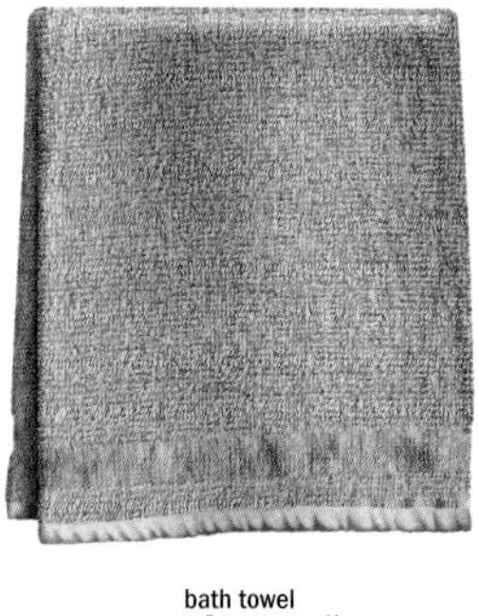

bath towel
toalla^F de lavabo^M
serviette^F de toilette^F
Handtuch^N
asciugamano^M

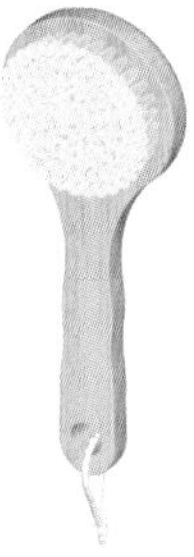

bath brush
cepillo^M de baño^M
brosse^F pour le bain^M
Badebürste^F
spazzola^F da bagno^M

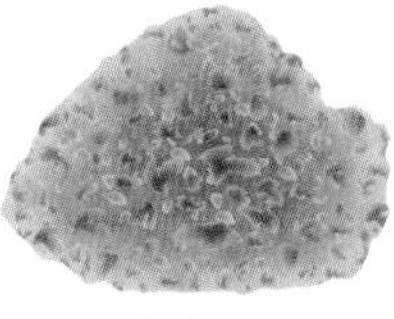

natural sponge
esponja^F natural
éponge^F de mer^F
Naturschwamm^M
spugna^F naturale

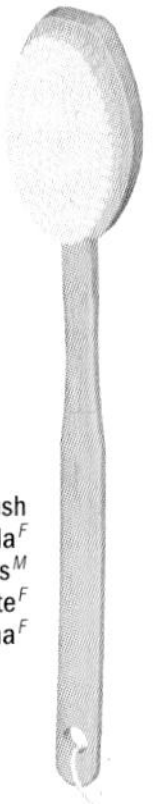

back brush
cepillo^M de espalda^F
brosse^F pour le dos^M
Massagebürste^F
spazzola^F per la schiena^F

hairdressing

peinado^M | coiffure^F | Haarpflege^F | articoli^M per acconciatura^F

hairbrushes
cepillos^M
brosses^F **à cheveux**^M
Haarbürsten^F
spazzole^F **per capelli**^M

flat-back brush
cepillo^M con base^F de goma^F
brosse^F pneumatique
flache Frisierbürste^F
spazzola^F a dorso^M piatto

round brush
cepillo^M redondo
brosse^F ronde
Rundbürste^F
spazzola^F rotonda

quill brush
cepillo^M de púas^F
brosse^F anglaise
Drahtbürste^F
spazzola^F antistatica

vent brush
cepillo^M de esqueleto^M
brosse^F-araignée^F
Skelettbürste^F
spazzola^F ragno

combs
peines^M
peignes^M
Kämme^M
pettini^M

teaser comb
peine^M de cardar
peigne^M à crêper
Toupierkamm^M
pettine^M per cotonare

barber comb
peine^M de peluquero^M
peigne^M de coiffeur^M
Haarschneidekamm^M
pettine^M da barbiere^M

rake comb
peine^M para desenredar
démêloir^M
Griffkamm^M
pettine^M rado

Afro pick
peine^M afro
peigne^M afro
Strähnenkamm^M
pettine^M afro

tail comb
peine^M de mango^M
peigne^M à tige^F
Stielkamm^M
pettine^M a coda^F

pitchfork comb
peine^M combinado
combiné^M 2 dans 1
Haarliftkamm^M
pettine^M a forchetta^F

hair roller
rulo^M para el cabello^M
bigoudi^M
Lockenwickler^M
bigodino^M

roller
rulo^M
rouleau^M
Wickler^M
rullo

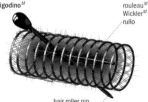

hair roller pin
alfiler^M
épingle^F à bigoudi^M
Haarstecker^M
spillone^M

wave clip
pinza^F para rizar
pince^F à boucles^F de cheveux^M
Abteilklammer^F
pinza^F per capelli^M

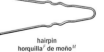

hairpin
horquilla^F de moño^M
épingle^F à cheveux^M
Lockennadel^F
forcina^F

bobby pin
horquilla^F
pince^F à cheveux^M
Haarklemme^F
molletta^F

hair clip
pinza^F para el cabello^M
pince^F de mise^F en plis^M
Haarclip^M
beccuccio^M

barrette
pasador^M
barrette^F
Haarspange^F
fermacapelli^M

lighted mirror
espejo^M luminoso
miroir^M lumineux
beleuchteter Spiegel^M
specchio^M luminoso

lighting
iluminación^F
éclairage^M
Beleuchtung^F
luce^F

dual swivel mirror
espejo^M doble giratorio
miroir^M double pivotant
Drehspiegel^M
specchio^M doppio girevole

side mirror
espejo^M lateral
miroir^M latéral
Seitenspiegel^M
specchio^M laterale

base
base^F
base^F
Sockel^M
base^F

on-off switch
interruptor^M
interrupteur^M d'éclairage^M
Schalter^M
interruttore^M

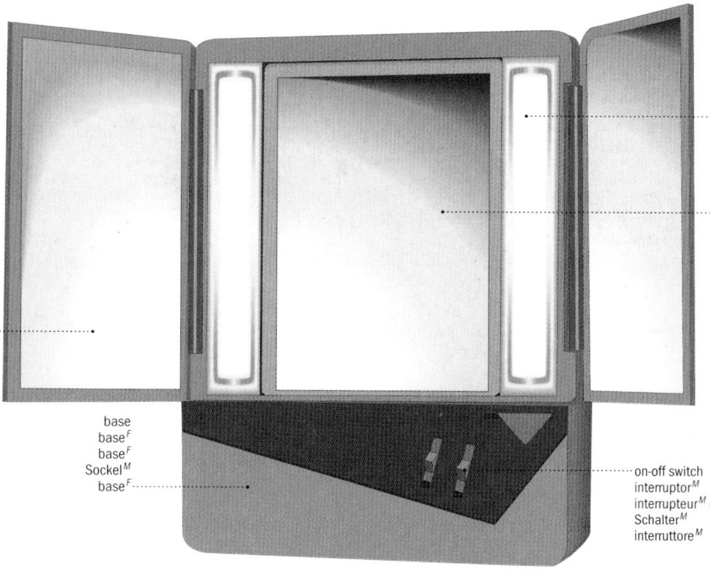

straightening iron
plancha^F de pelo
pince^F à défriser
Haarglätter^M
piastra^F stiracapelli

handle
mango^M
poignée^F
Griff^M
impugnatura^F

plate
plancha^F
plaque^F
Platte^F
piastra^F

power cord
cordón^M de alimentación^F
cordon^M d'alimentation^F
Netzkabel^N
cavo^M di alimentazione^F

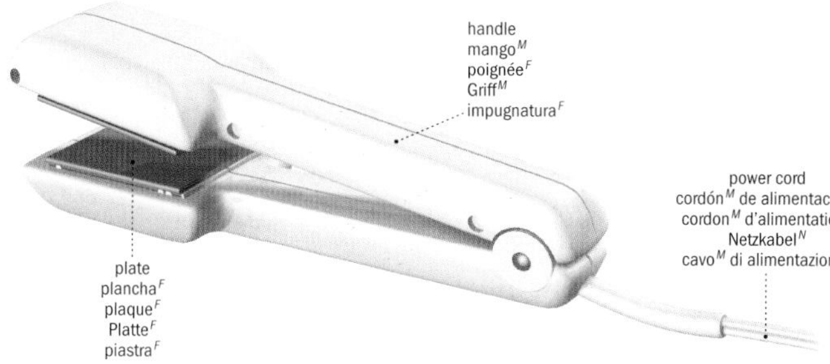

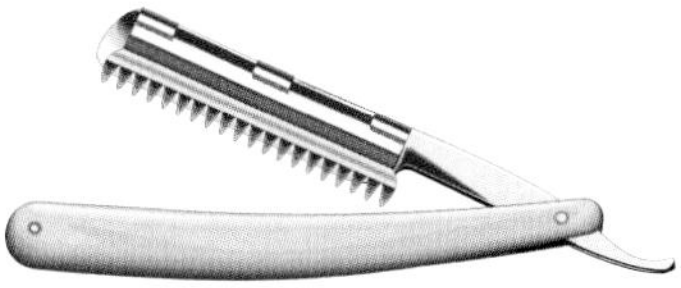

thinning razor
navaja^F para entresacar
rasoir^M effileur
Effiliermesser^N
rasoio^M sfoltitore

handle
mango^M
poignée^F profilée
Griff^M
impugnatura^F sagomata

curling iron
tenacillas^F
fer^M à friser
Lockenstab^M
arricciacapelli^M

on-off switch
interruptor^M
interrupteur^M
Schalter^M
interruttore^M

clamp lever
palanca^F
levier^M
Hebel^M für den Klemmbügel^M
leva^F della pinza^F

swivel cord
cable^M de alimentación^M
cordon^M d'alimentation^F pivotant
Knickschutztülle^F
cavo^M di alimentazione^F

heat ready indicator
indicador^M de temperatura^F
point^M indicateur^M de température^F
Bereitschaftsanzeige^F
indicatore^M di temperatura^F

on-off indicator
luz^F piloto^M
voyant^M lumineux
Kontrolllampe^F
spia^F

clamp
pinza^F
pince^F
Klemmbügel^M
pinza^F

stand
soporte^M
support^M
Ständer^M
supporto^M

barrel
varilla^F rizadora
tube^M
Zylinder^M
rullo^M

cool tip
punta^F de plástico^M
embout^M isolant
nicht wärmeleitende Spitze^F
punta^F fredda

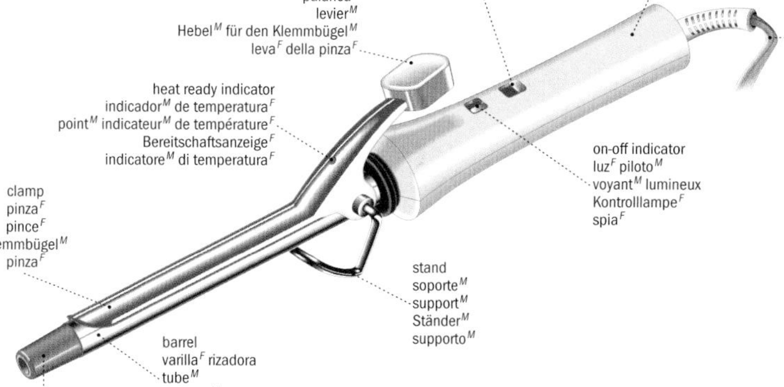

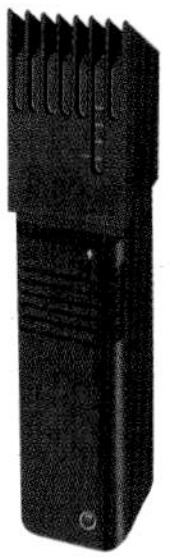

clippers
maquinilla^F para cortar el cabello^M
tondeuse^F
Haarschneider^M
macchinetta^F

PERSONAL ADORNMENT AND ARTICLES

hairdressing

haircutting scissors
tijeras^F de peluquero^M
ciseaux^M de coiffeur^M
Haarschneideschere^F
forbici^F da parrucchiere^M

pivot
pivote^M
pivot^M
Bolzen^M
perno^M

ringhandle
ojo^M
anneau^M
Auge^N
anello^M

cutting edge
filo^M
tranchant^M
Schneide^F
filo^M della lama^F

blade close stop
tope^M
amortisseur^M
Klingenstopper^M
fermo^M della lama^F

blade
hoja^F
lame^F
Blatt^N
lama^F

shank
brazo^M
branche^F
Halm^M
braccio^M

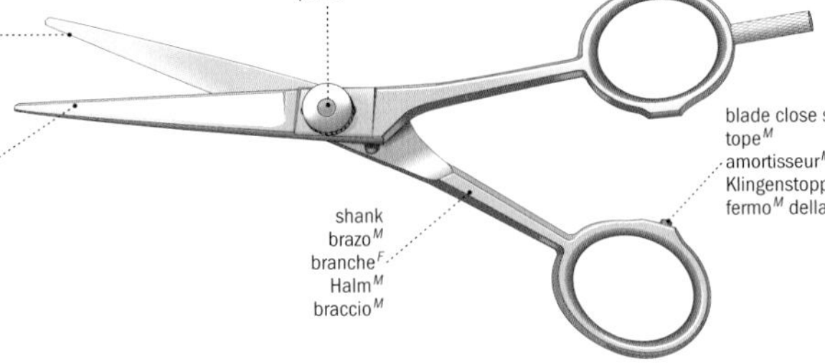

notched single-edged thinning scissors
tijeras^F con filo^M simple para entresacar
ciseaux^M sculpteurs
einseitig gezahnte Effilierschere^F
forbice^F sfoltitrice a lama^F singola dentellata

notched edge
hoja^F dentada
lame^F dentée
gekerbtes Scherenblatt^N
lama^F dentellata

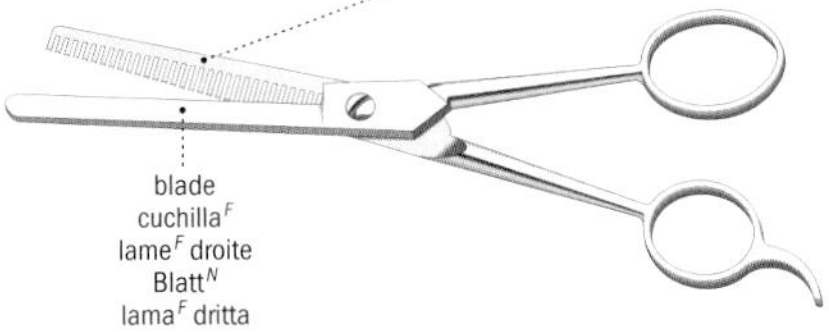

notched double-edged thinning scissors
tijeras^F con doble filo^M para entresacar
ciseaux^M à effiler
zweiseitig gezahnte Effilierschere^F
forbice^F sfoltitrice a doppia lama^F dentellata

blade
cuchilla^F
lame^F droite
Blatt^N
lama^F dritta

tooth
diente^M
dent^F
Zahn^M
dente^M

fan housing
caja^F del ventilador^M
boitier^M du ventilateur^M
Föngehäuse^N
alloggiamento^M del ventilatore^M

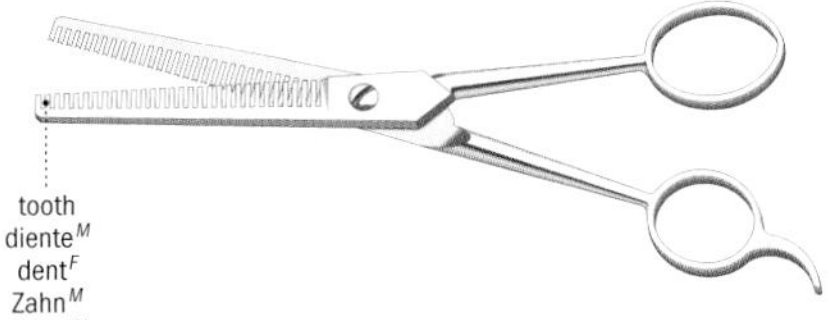

hair dryer
secador^M de mano^F
sèche-cheveux^M
Fön^M
asciugacapelli^M

barrel
tubo^M de aire^M
corps^M
Zylinder^M
corpo^M

air-inlet grille
rejilla^F de entrada^F de aire^M
grille^F d'aspiration^F
Ansauggitter^N
presa^F d'aria^F posteriore

air-outlet grille
rejilla^F de salida^F de aire^M
grille^F de sortie^F d'air^M
Luftaustrittsöffnung^F
griglia^F di uscita^F dell'aria^F

speed selector switch
botón^M selector de velocidad^F
sélecteur^M de vitesse^F
Luftstromschalter^M
selettore^M della velocità^F

on-off switch
interruptor^M
interrupteur^M
Schalter^M
interruttore^M

heat air
heat selector switch
botón^M selector de temperatura^F
sélecteur^M de température^F
Temperaturschalter^M
selettore^M della temperatura^F

hang-up ring
anilla^F para colgar
anneau^M de suspension^F
Aufhängeöse^F
anello^M di sospensione^F

air concentrator
concentrador^M de aire^M
buse^F
Luftstromrichtdüse^F
riduttore^M

handle
mango^M
poignée^F
Griff^M
manico^M

power supply cord
cable^M de alimentación^F
cordon^M d'alimentation^F
Netzkabel^N
cavo^M di alimentazione^F

shaving

afeitado[M] | rasage[M] | Rasur[F] | rasatura[F]

electric razor
máquina[F] de afeitar eléctrica
rasoir[M] électrique
Elektrorasierer[M]
rasoio[M] elettrico

floating head
cabezal[M] flotante
tête[F] flottante
Scherkopf[M]
testina[F] rotante

screen
peine[M] y cuchilla[F]
grille[F]
Scherkopfhalter[M]
griglia[F]

trimmer
cortapatillas[M]
tondeuse[F]
Langhaarschneider[M]
tagliabasette[M]

closeness setting
selector[M] de corte[M]
sélecteur[M] de coupe[F]
Justierring[M]
regolatore[M] delle testine[F]

housing
caja[F]
boitier[M]
Gehäuse[N]
cassa[F]

cleaning brush
escobilla[F] limpiadora
brosse[F] de nettoyage[M]
Reinigungsbürste[F]
spazzolino[M] di pulizia[F]

charge indicator
indicador[M] de recarga[F]
indicateur[M] de charge[F]
Ladeanzeige[F]
indicatore[M] di carica[F]

charging light
luz[F] de encendido[M]
voyant[M] de charge[F]
Ladekontrolllampe[F]
spia[F] luminosa di carica[F]

charging plug
enchufe[M] de recarga[F]
prise[F] de charge[F]
Geräteanschluss[M]
presa[F] di ricarica[F]

on-off switch
interruptor[M]
interrupteur[M]
Schalter[M]
interruttore[M]

shaving foam
espuma[F] de afeitar
mousse[F] à raser
Rasierschaum[M]
schiuma[F] da barba[F]

power cord
cable[M] de alimentación[F]
cordon[M] d'alimentation[F]
Netzkabel[N]
cordone[M] dell'alimentazione[F]

shaving brush
brocha[F] de afeitar
blaireau[M]
Rasierpinsel[M]
pennello[M] da barba[F]

plug adapter
adaptador[M]
adaptateur[M] de fiche[F]
Adapter[M]
adattatore[M]

bristle
cerdas[F]
soie[F]
Borste[F]
setola[F]

aftershave
loción[F] para después del afeitado[M]
après-rasage[M]
Rasierwasser[N]
dopobarba[M]

straight razor
navaja[F] de barbero[M]
rasoir[M] à manche[M]
Rasiermesser[N]
rasoio[M] a mano[F] libera

blade
hoja[F]
lame[F]
Klinge[F]
lama[F]

handle
mango[M]
manche[M]
Griff[M]
impugnatura[F]

pivot
eje[M]
pivot[M]
Bolzen[M]
perno[M]

double-edged razor
maquinilla[F] de afeitar
rasoir[M] à double tranchant[M]
zweischneidiger Rasierer[M]
rasoio[M] di sicurezza[F]

disposable razor
maquinilla[F] desechable
rasoir[M] jetable
Einwegrasierer[M]
rasoio[M] usa e getta

head
cabeza[F]
tête[F]
Kopf[M]
testina[F]

collar
anillo[M]
anneau[M]
Ring[M]
colletto[M]

blade injector
distribuidor[M] de hojas[F] de afeitar
distributeur[M] de lames[F]
Klingendose[F]
caricatore[M] di lamette[F]

shaving mug
jabonera[F]
bol[M] à raser
Seifenbecher[M]
tazza[F] per sapone[M] da barba[F]

double-edged blade
hoja[F] de afeitar
lame[F] à double tranchant[M]
zweischneidige Klinge[F]
lametta[F] a due tagli[M]

handle
mango[M]
manche[M]
Griff[M]
manico[M]

PERSONAL ADORNMENT AND ARTICLES

PERSONAL ADORNMENT AND ARTICLES

dental care

higiene^F dental | hygiène^F dentaire | Zahnpflege^F | igiene^F orale

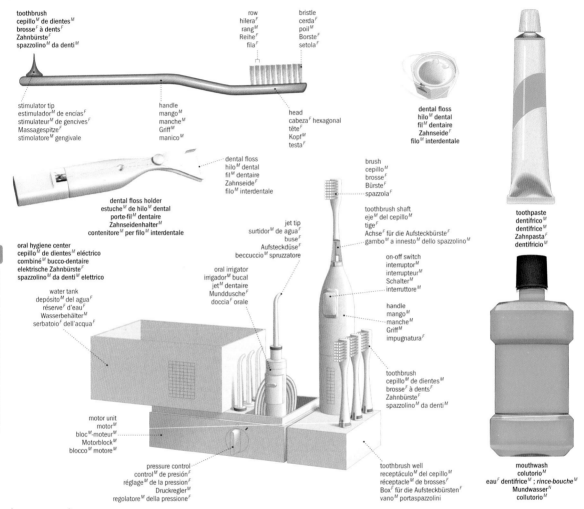

toothbrush
cepillo^M de dientes^M
brosse^F à dents^F
Zahnbürste^F
spazzolino^M da denti^M

row
hilera^F
rang^M
Reihe^F
fila^F

bristle
cerda^F
poil^M
Borste^F
setola^F

stimulator tip
estimulador^M de encías^F
stimulateur^M de gencives^F
Massagespitze^F
stimolatore^M gengivale

handle
mango^M
manche^M
Griff^M
manico^M

head
cabeza^F hexagonal
tête^F
Kopf^M
testa^F

dental floss
hilo^M dental
fil^M dentaire
Zahnseide^F
filo^M interdentale

dental floss
hilo^M dental
fil^M dentaire
Zahnseide^F
filo^M interdentale

brush
cepillo^M
brosse^F
Bürste^F
spazzola^F

dental floss holder
estuche^M de hilo^M dental
porte-fil^M dentaire
Zahnseidenhalter^M
contenitore^M per filo^M interdentale

jet tip
surtidor^M de agua^F
buse^F
Aufsteckdüse^F
beccuccio^M spruzzatore

toothbrush shaft
eje^M del cepillo^M
tige^F
Achse^F für die Aufsteckbürste^F
gambo^M a innesto^M dello spazzolino^M

oral hygiene center
cepillo^M de dientes^M eléctrico
combiné^M bucco-dentaire
elektrische Zahnbürste^F
spazzolino^M da denti^M elettrico

oral irrigator
irrigador^M bucal
jet^M dentaire
Munddusche^F
doccia^F orale

on-off switch
interruptor^M
interrupteur^M
Schalter^M
interruttore^M

water tank
depósito^M del agua^F
réserve^F d'eau^F
Wasserbehälter^M
serbatoio^M dell'acqua^F

handle
mango^M
manche^M
Griff^M
impugnatura^F

toothbrush
cepillo^M de dientes^M
brosse^F à dents^F
Zahnbürste^F
spazzolino^M da denti^M

motor unit
motor^M
bloc^M-moteur^M
Motorblock^M
blocco^M motore^M

pressure control
control^M de presión^F
réglage^M de la pression^F
Druckregler^M
regolatore^M della pressione^F

toothbrush well
receptáculo^M del cepillo^M
réceptacle^M de brosses^F
Box^F für die Aufsteckbürsten^F
vano^M portaspazzolini

dental floss
hilo^M dental
fil^M dentaire
Zahnseide^F
filo^M interdentale

toothpaste
dentífrico^M
dentifrice^M
Zahnpasta^F
dentifricio^M

mouthwash
colutorio^M
eau^F dentifrice^M ; *rince-bouche*^M
Mundwasser^N
collutorio^M

contact lenses

lentes^F de contacto^M | lentilles^F de contact^M | Kontaktlinsen^F | lenti^F a contatto^M

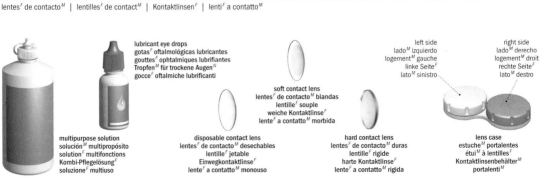

lubricant eye drops
gotas^F oftalmológicas lubricantes
gouttes^F ophtalmiques lubrifiantes
Tropfen^M für trockene Augen^N
gocce^F oftalmiche lubrificanti

left side
lado^M izquierdo
logement^M gauche
linke Seite^F
lato^M sinistro

right side
lado^M derecho
logement^M droit
rechte Seite^F
lato^M destro

soft contact lens
lentes^F de contacto^M blandas
lentille^F souple
weiche Kontaktlinse^F
lente^F a contatto^M morbida

multipurpose solution
solución^M multipropósito
solution^F multifonctions
Kombi-Pflegelösung^F
soluzione^F multiuso

disposable contact lens
lentes^F de contacto^M desechables
lentille^F jetable
Einwegkontaktlinse^F
lente^F a contatto^M monouso

hard contact lens
lentes^F de contacto^M duras
lentille^F rigide
harte Kontaktlinse^F
lente^F a contatto^M rigida

lens case
estuche^M portalentes
étui^M à lentilles^F
Kontaktlinsenbehälter^M
portalenti^M

eyeglasses

gafas^F | lunettes^F | Brille^F | occhiali^M

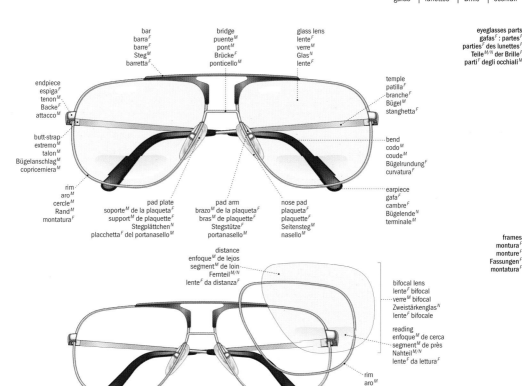

eyeglasses parts
gafas^F : partes^F
parties^F des lunettes^F
Teile^{M/N} der Brille^F
parti^F degli occhiali^M

bar
barra^F
barre^F
Steg^M
barretta^F

bridge
puente^M
pont^M
Brücke^F
ponticello^M

glass lens
lente^F
verre^M
Glas^N
lente^F

endpiece
espiga^F
tenon^M
Backe^F
attacco^M

temple
patilla^F
branche^F
Bügel^M
stanghetta^F

butt-strap
extremo^M
talon^M
Bügelanschlag^M
copricerniera^M

bend
codo^M
coude^M
Bügelrundung^F
curvatura^F

rim
aro^M
cercle^M
Rand^M
montatura^F

pad plate
soporte^M de la plaqueta^F
support^M de plaquette^F
Stegplättchen^N
placchetta^F del portanasello^M

pad arm
brazo^M de la plaqueta^F
bras^M de plaquette^F
Stegstütze^F
portanasello^M

nose pad
plaqueta^F
plaquette^F
Seitensteg^M
nasello^M

earpiece
gafa^F
cambre^M
Bügelende^N
terminale^M

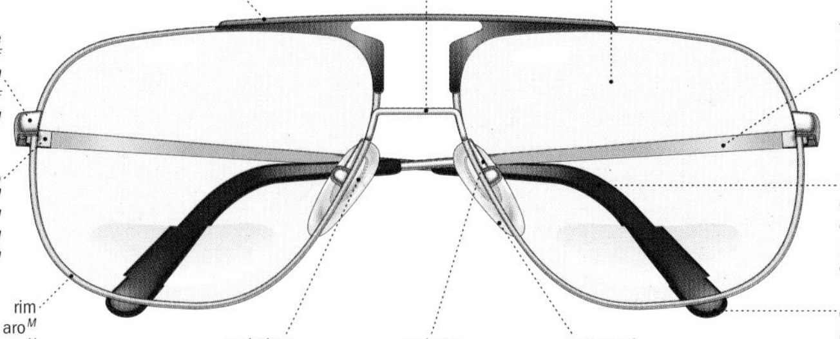

frames
montura^F
monture^F
Fassungen^F
montatura^F

distance
enfoque^M de lejos
segment^M de loin
Fernteil^{M/N}
lente^F da distanza^F

bifocal lens
lente^F bifocal
verre^M bifocal
Zweistärkenglas^N
lente^F bifocale

reading
enfoque^M de cerca
segment^M de près
Nahteil^{M/N}
lente^F da lettura^F

rim
aro^M
cercle^M
Rand^M
montatura^F

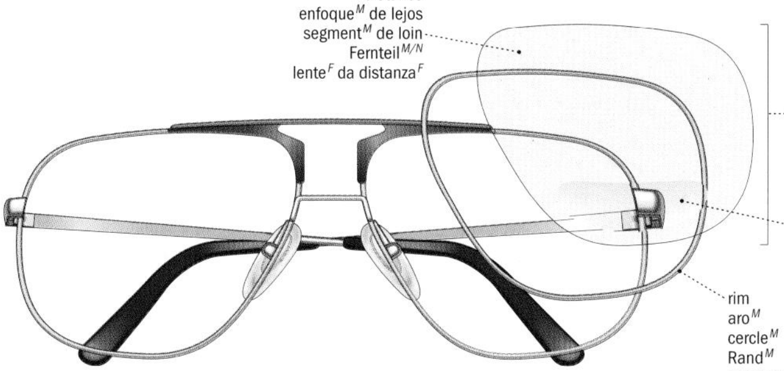

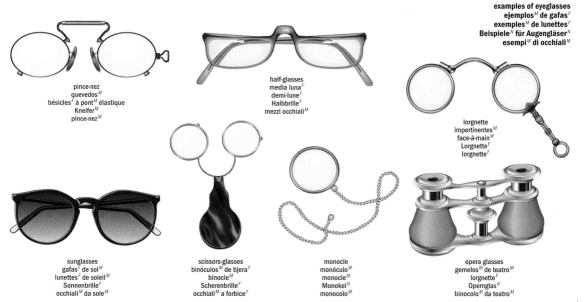

examples of eyeglasses
ejemplos^M de gafas^F
exemples^M de lunettes^F
Beispiele^N für Augengläser^N
esempi^M di occhiali^M

pince-nez
quevedos^M
bésicles^F à pont^M élastique
Kneifer^M
pince-nez^M

half-glasses
media luna^F
demi-lune^F
Halbbrille^F
mezzi occhiali^M

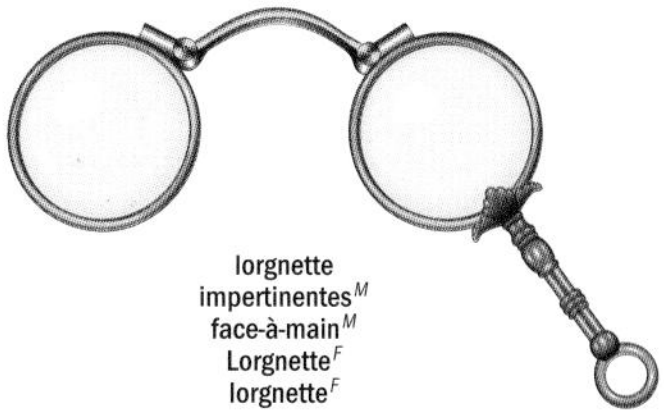

lorgnette
impertinentes^M
face-à-main^M
Lorgnette^F
lorgnette^F

sunglasses
gafas^F de sol^M
lunettes^F de soleil^M
Sonnenbrille^F
occhiali^M da sole^M

scissors-glasses
binóculos^M de tijera^F
binocle^M
Scherenbrille^F
occhiali^M a forbice^F

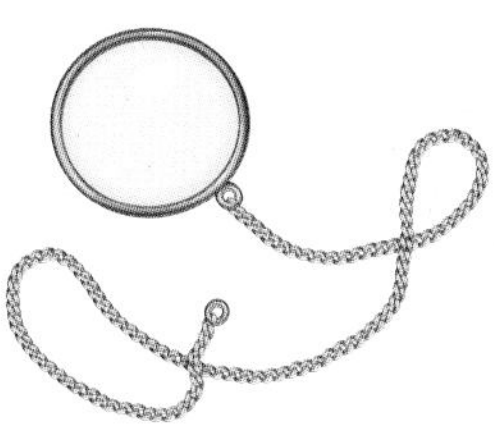

monocle
monóculo^M
monocle^M
Monokel^N
monocolo^M

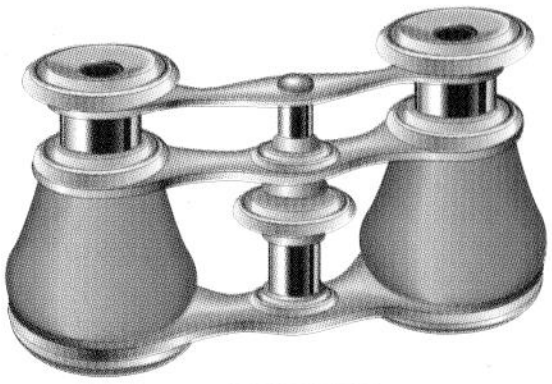

opera glasses
gemelos^M de teatro^M
lorgnette^F
Opernglas^N
binocolo^M da teatro^M

PERSONAL ADORNMENT AND ARTICLES

leather goods

articulos^M de marroquinería | articles^M de maroquinerie^F | Lederwaren^F | articoli^M di pelletteria^F

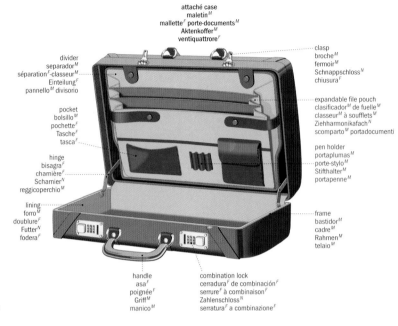

attaché case
maletín^M
mallette^F porte-documents^M
Aktenkoffer^M
ventiquattrore^F

divider
separador^M
séparation^F-classeur^M
Einteilung^F
pannello^M divisorio

pocket
bolsillo^M
pochette^F
Tasche^F
tasca^F

hinge
bisagra^F
charnière^F
Scharnier^N
reggicoperchio^M

lining
forro^M
doublure^F
Futter^N
fodera^F

clasp
broche^M
fermoir^M
Schnappschloss^N
chiusura^F

expandable file pouch
clasificador^M de fuelle^M
classeur^M à soufflets^M
Ziehharmonikafach^N
scomparto^M portadocumenti

pen holder
portaplumas^M
porte-stylo^M
Stifthalter^M
portapenne^M

frame
bastidor^M
cadre^M
Rahmen^M
telaio^M

handle
asa^F
poignée^F
Griff^M
manico^M

combination lock
cerradura^F de combinación^F
serrure^F à combinaison^F
Zahlenschloss^N
serratura^F a combinazione^F

bottom-fold portfolio
cartera^F de fondo^M plegable
porte-documents^M à soufflet^M
Kollegmappe^F mit Griff^M
portacarte^M a soffietto^M

briefcase
cartera^F
serviette^F
Aktentasche^F
borsa^F a soffietto^M

retractable handle
asa^F extensible
poignée^F rentrante
ausziehbarer Griff^M
manico^M a scomparsa^F

exterior pocket
bolsillo^M delantero
poche^F extérieure
Außentasche^F
tasca^F esterna

tab
lengüeta^F
patte^F
Lasche^F
linguetta^F

key lock
cerradura^F
serrure^F à clé^F
Schlüsselschloss^N
serratura^F a chiave^F

gusset
fuelle^M
soufflet^M
Keil^M
soffietto^M

checkbook/secretary clutch
chequera^F con calculadora^F
portefeuille^M chéquier^M
Etui^N für Taschenrechner^M und Scheckheft^N
portassegni^M/portacalcolatrice^M

card case
tarjetero^M
porte-cartes^M
Kreditkartenetui^N
portafoglio^M per carte^F di credito^M

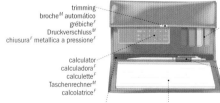

trimming
broche^M automático
grébiche^F
Druckverschluss^M
chiusura^F metallica a pressione^F

card case
tarjetero^M
porte-cartes^M
Kreditkartenfach^N
scomparto^M per carte^F di credito^M

calculator
calculadora^F
calculette^F
Taschenrechner^M
calcolatrice^F

pen holder
portaplumas^M
porte-stylo^M
Stifthalter^M
portapenne^M

hidden pocket
bolsillo^M secreto
poche^F secrète
Unterfach^N
tasca^F nascosta

checkbook
talonario^M de cheques^M
chéquier^M
Scheckheft^N
libretto^M degli assegni^M

bill compartment
billetera^F
poche^F américaine
Geldscheinfach^N
scomparto^M per banconote^F

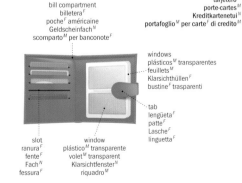

windows
plásticos^M transparentes
feuillets^F
Klarsichthüllen^F
bustine^F trasparenti

tab
lengüeta^F
patte^F
Lasche^F
linguetta^F

slot
ranura^F
fente^F
Fach^N
fessura^F

window
plástico^M transparente
volet^M transparent
Klarsichtfenster^N
riquadro^M

leather goods

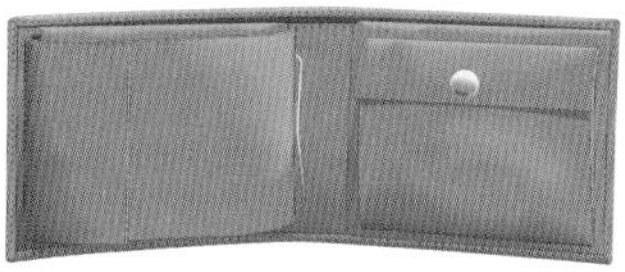

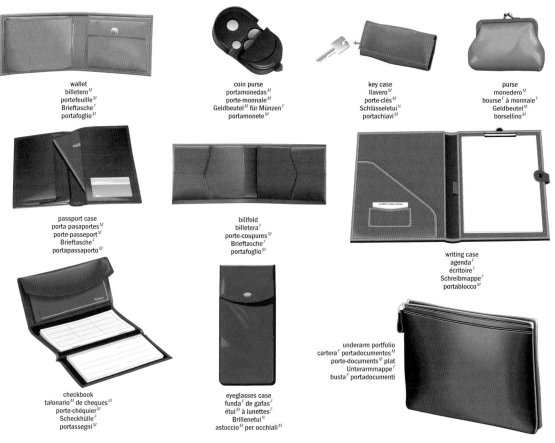

wallet
billetero[M]
portefeuille[M]
Brieftasche[F]
portafoglio[M]

coin purse
portamonedas[M]
porte-monnaie[M]
Geldbeutel[M] für Münzen[F]
portamonete[M]

key case
llavero[M]
porte-clés[M]
Schlüsseletui[N]
portachiavi[M]

purse
monedero[M]
bourse[F] à monnaie[F]
Geldbeutel[M]
borsellino[M]

passport case
porta pasaportes[M]
porte-passeport[M]
Brieftasche[F]
portapassaporto[M]

billfold
billetera[F]
porte-coupures[M]
Brieftasche[F]
portafoglio[M]

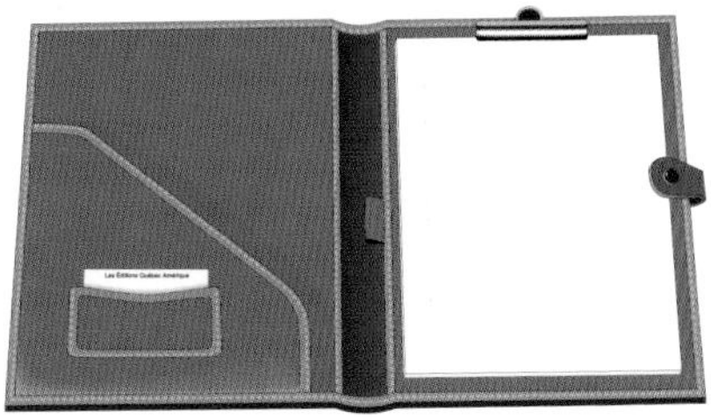

writing case
agenda[F]
écritoire[F]
Schreibmappe[F]
portablocco[M]

checkbook
talonario[M] de cheques[M]
porte-chéquier[M]
Scheckhülle[F]
portassegni[M]

eyeglasses case
funda[F] de gafas[F]
étui[M] à lunettes[F]
Brillenetui[N]
astuccio[M] per occhiali[M]

underarm portfolio
cartera[F] portadocumentos[M]
porte-documents[M] plat
Unterarmmappe[F]
busta[F] portadocumenti

handbags

bolsos[M] | sacs[M] à main[F] | Handtaschen[F] | borse[F]

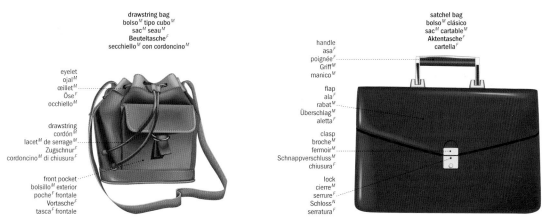

drawstring bag
bolso[M] tipo cubo[M]
sac[M] seau[M]
Beuteltasche[F]
secchiello[M] con cordoncino[M]

satchel bag
bolso[M] clásico
sac[M] cartable[M]
Aktentasche[F]
cartella[F]

eyelet
ojal[M]
œillet[M]
Öse[F]
occhiello[M]

handle
asa[F]
poignée[F]
Griff[M]
manico[M]

drawstring
cordón[M]
lacet[M] de serrage[M]
Zugschnur[F]
cordoncino[M] di chiusura[F]

flap
ala[F]
rabat[M]
Überschlag[M]
aletta[F]

clasp
broche[M]
fermoir[M]
Schnappverschluss[M]
chiusura[F]

front pocket
bolsillo[M] exterior
poche[F] frontale
Vortasche[F]
tasca[F] frontale

lock
cierre[M]
serrure[F]
Schloss[N]
serratura[F]

387

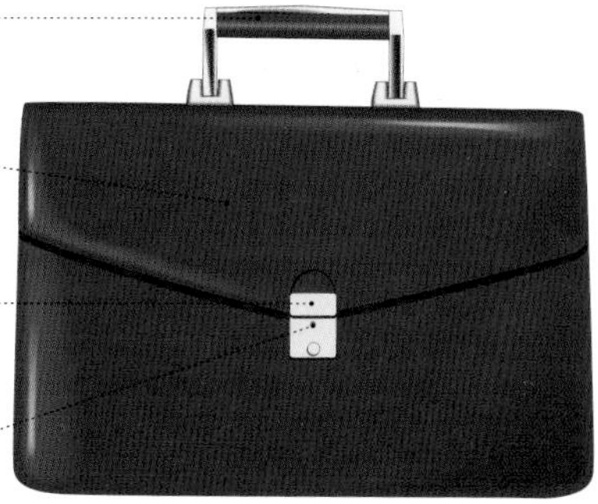

handbags

box bag
bolso^M de vestir
sac^M boîte^F
Boxtasche^F
borsa^F a telaio^M rigido

shoulder bag
bolso^M de bandolera^F
sac^M à bandoulière^F
Schultertasche^F
borsa^F a tracolla^F

buckle
hebilla^F
boucle^F
Schnalle^F
fibbia^F

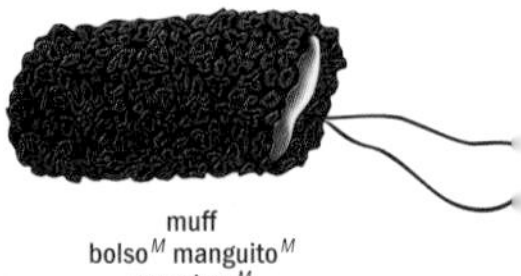

muff
bolso^M manguito^M
manchon^M
Mufftasche^F
borsa^F a manicotto^M

drawstring bag
bolso^M saco
balluchon^F
kleine Beuteltasche^F
secchiello^M piccolo con cordoncino^M

shoulder strap
bandolera^F
bandoulière^F
Schulterriemen^M
tracolla^F

accordion bag
bolso^M de fuelle^M
sac^M accordéon^F
Umhängetasche^F mit Dehnfalte^F
borsa^F da postino^M

hobo bag
morral^M
sac^M besace^F
Umhängetasche^F mit Reißverschluss^M
sacca^F a tracolla^F

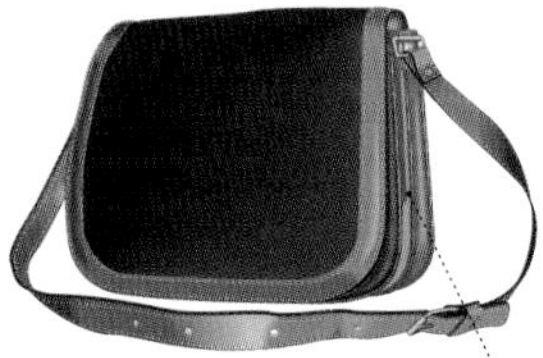

gusset
fuelle^M
soufflet^M
Keil^M
soffietto^M

tote bag
bolsa^F de lona^F
sac^M fourre-tout^M
Einkaufstasche^F
sporta^F

men's bag
bolso^M de hombre
pochette^F d'homme^M
Herrentasche^F
borsello^M

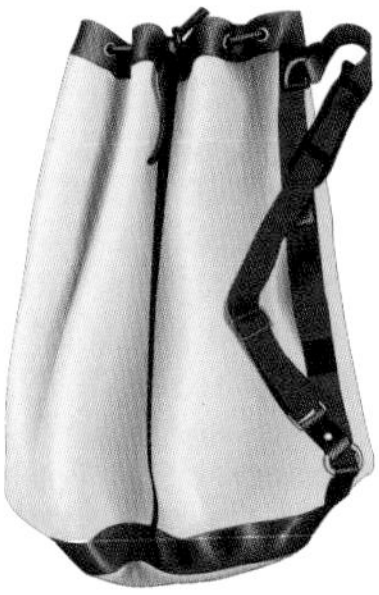

sea bag
saco^M de marinero^M
sac^M marin^M
Matchbeutel^M
sacca^F da marinaio^M

duffel bag
bolso^M de viaje^M
sac^M polochon^M
geräumige Tasche^F
borsone^M da viaggio^M

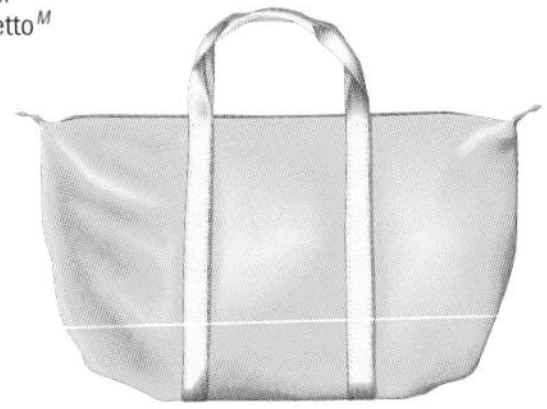

carrier bag
bolso^M de la compra^F
sac^M à provisions^F
Einkaufstasche^F
borsa^F della spesa^F

shopping bag
capazo^M
cabas^M
große Einkaufstasche^F
borsa^F della spesa^F

luggage

equipaje^M | bagages^M | Gepäck^N | bagagli^M

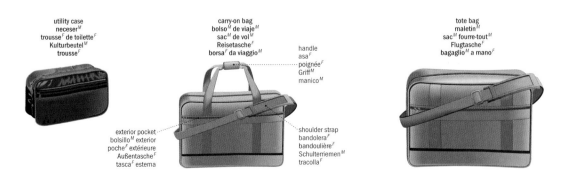

utility case
neceser^M
trousse^F de toilette^F
Kulturbeutel^M
trousse^F

carry-on bag
bolso^M de viaje^M
sac^M de vol^F
Reisetasche^F
borsa^F da viaggio^M

handle
asa^F
poignée^F
Griff^M
manico^M

tote bag
maletín^M
sac^M fourre-tout^M
Flugtasche^F
bagaglio^M a mano^F

exterior pocket
bolsillo^M exterior
poche^F extérieure
Außentasche^F
tasca^F esterna

shoulder strap
bandolera^F
bandoulière^F
Schulterriemen^M
tracolla^F

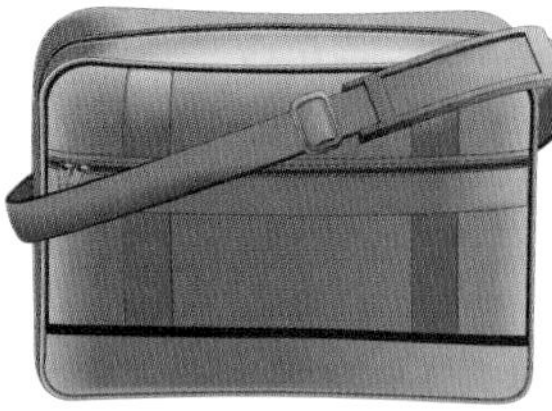

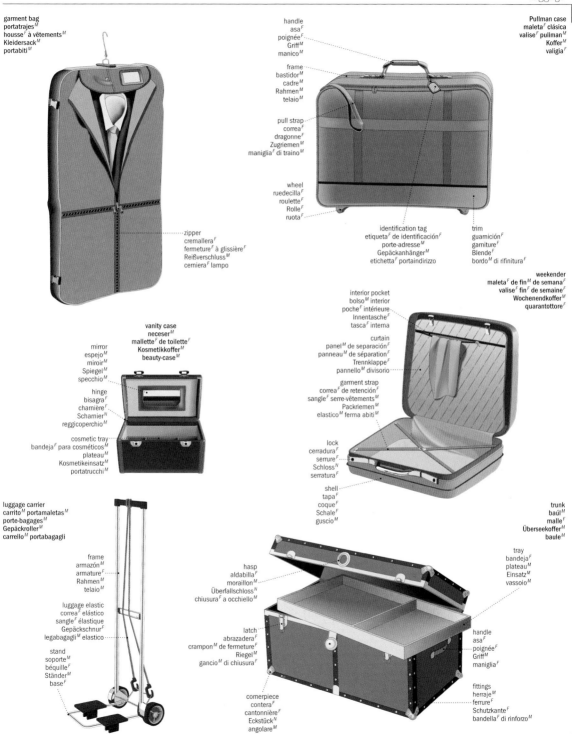

garment bag
portatrajes^M
housse^F à vêtements^M
Kleidersack^M
portabiti^M

zipper
cremallera^F
fermeture^F à glissière^F
Reißverschluss^M
cerniera^F lampo

handle
asa^F
poignée^F
Griff^M
manico^M

frame
bastidor^M
cadre^M
Rahmen^M
telaio^M

pull strap
correa^F
dragonne^F
Zugriemen^M
maniglia^F di traino^M

wheel
ruedecilla^F
roulette^F
Rolle^F
ruota^F

identification tag
etiqueta^F de identificación^F
porte-adresse^M
Gepäckanhänger^M
etichetta^F portaindirizzo

trim
guamición^F
garniture^F
Blende^F
bordo^M di rifinitura^F

Pullman case
maleta^F clásica
valise^F pullman^M
Koffer^M
valigia^F

vanity case
neceser^M
mallette^F de toilette^F
Kosmetikkoffer^M
beauty-case^M

mirror
espejo^M
miroir^M
Spiegel^M
specchio^M

hinge
bisagra^F
charnière^F
Scharnier^N
reggicoperchio^M

cosmetic tray
bandeja^F para cosméticos^M
plateau^M
Kosmetikeinsatz^M
portatrucchi^M

interior pocket
bolso^M interior
poche^F intérieure
Innentasche^F
tasca^F interna

curtain
panel^M de separación^F
panneau^M de séparation^F
Trennklappe^F
pannello^M divisorio

garment strap
correa^F de retención^F
sangle^F serre-vêtements^M
Packriemen^M
elastico^M ferma abiti^M

lock
cerradura^F
serrure^F
Schloss^N
serratura^F

shell
tapa^F
coque^F
Schale^F
guscio^M

weekender
maleta^F de fin^M de semana^F
valise^F fin^F de semaine^F
Wochenendkoffer^M
quarantottore^F

luggage carrier
carrito^M portamaletas^M
porte-bagages^M
Gepäckroller^M
carrello^M portabagagli

frame
armazón^M
armature^F
Rahmen^M
telaio^M

luggage elastic
correa^F elástico
sangle^F élastique
Gepäckschnur^F
legabagagli^M elastico

stand
soporte^M
béquille^F
Ständer^M
base^F

hasp
aldabilla^F
moraillon^M
Überfallschloss^N
chiusura^F a occhiello^M

latch
abrazadera^F
crampon^M de fermeture^F
Riegel^M
gancio^M di chiusura^F

cornerpiece
contera^F
cantonnière^F
Eckstück^N
angolare^M

trunk
baúl^M
malle^F
Überseekoffer^M
baule^M

tray
bandeja^F
plateau^M
Einsatz^M
vassoio^M

handle
asa^F
poignée^F
Griff^M
maniglia^F

fittings
herraje^M
ferrure^F
Schutzkante^F
bandella^F di rinforzo^M

smoking accessories

articulos^M de fumador^M | articles^M de fumeur^M | Raucherbedarf^M | accessori^M per fumatori^M

pipe
pipa^F
pipe^F
Pfeife^F
pipa^F

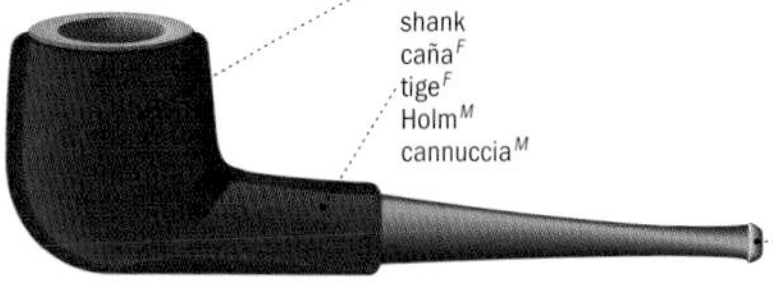

bowl
cazoleta^F
talon^M
Pfeifenkopf^M
fornello^M

shank
caña^F
tige^F
Holm^M
cannuccia^F

bit
boquilla^F
lentille^F
Biss^M
dente^M

stummel
barba^F
tête^F
Pfeifenstummel^M
testa^F

stem
cañón^M
tuyau^M
Pfeifenmundstück^N
bocchino^M

pipe tools
accesorios^M para la pipa^F
bourre-pipe^M
Pfeifenbesteck^N
curapipe^M

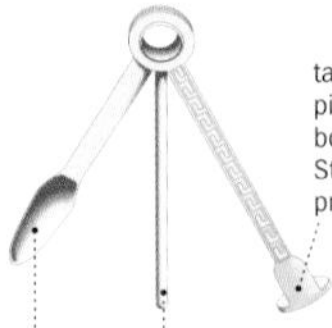

tamper
pisón^M
bourre-pipe^M
Stopfer^M
premitabacco^M

scoop
raspador^M
curette^F
Auskratzer^M
cucchiaino^M

pick
palillo^M
pointe^F
Dorn^M
stilo^M

pipe cleaners
escobillas^F
nettoie-pipes^M
Pfeifenputzer^M
scovolini^M

cross section of a pipe
corte^M transversal de una pipa^F
coupe^F d'une pipe^F
Pfeife^F im Querschnitt^M
sezione^F di una pipa^F

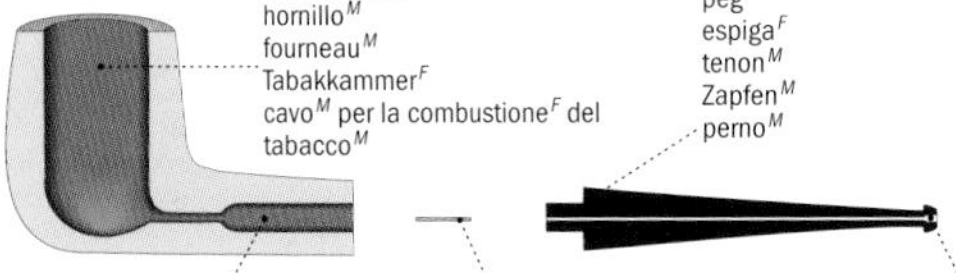

tobacco hole
hornillo^M
fourneau^M
Tabakkammer^F
cavo^M per la combustione^F del tabacco^M

peg
espiga^F
tenon^M
Zapfen^M
perno^M

mortise
tiro^F
mortaise^F
Zapfenloch^N
mortasa^F

filter
filtro^M
système^M filtre^M
Filter^M
filtro^M

air hole
tiraje^M
trou^M de l'embout^M
Luftloch^N
foro^M per l'aria^F

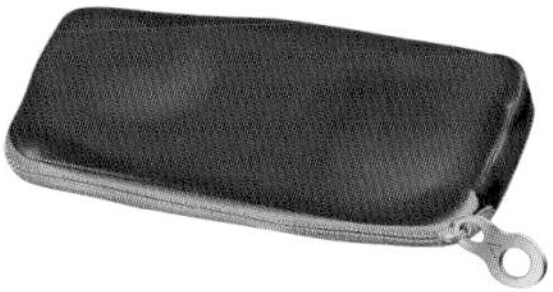

tobacco pouch
tabaquera^F
blague^F à tabac^M
Tabaksbeutel^M
borsa^F del tabacco^M

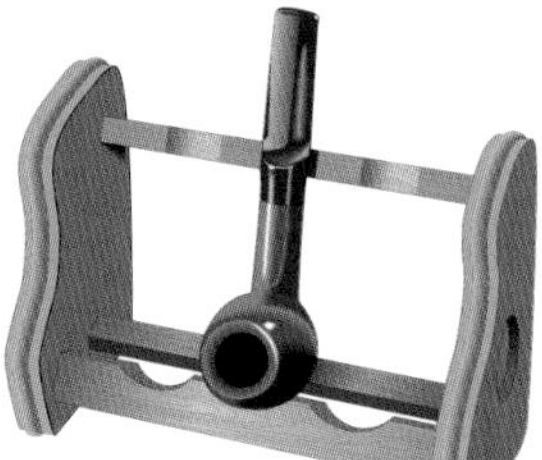

pipe rack
porta pipas^M
porte-pipes^M
Pfeifenständer^M
portapipe^M

cigar
puro^M
cigare^M
Zigarre^F
sigaro^M

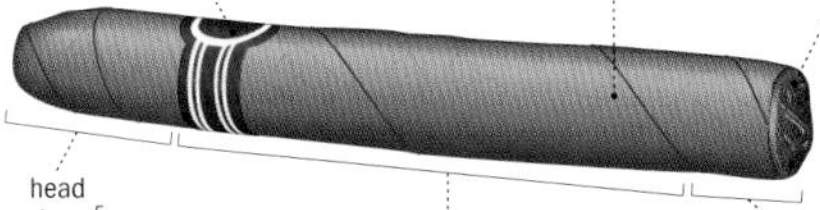

cigar band
vitola^F
bague^F
Banderole^F
fascetta^F del sigaro^M

wrapper
capa^F
cape^F
Deckblatt^N
fascia^F

tobacco
tabaco^M
tabac^M
Tabak^M
tabacco^M

head
cabeza^F
tête^F
Spitze^F
testa^F

bunch
cuerpo^M
corps^M
Mittelstück^N
corpo^M

filler
tripa^F
tripe^F
Einlage^F
ripieno^M

tuck
punta^F
pied^M
Endstück^N
piede^M

cigar cutter
cortapuros^M
coupe-cigare^M
Zigarrenschneider^M
tagliasigari^M

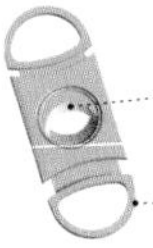

blade
cuchilla^F
lame^F
Klinge^F
lama^F

ring handle
anillo^M
anneau^M
Ring^M
impugnatura^F a anello^M

cigarette papers
papel^M de fumar
papier^M à cigarettes^F
Zigarettenpapier^N
cartine^F per sigarette^F

carton
cartón^M de cigarrillos^M
cartouche^F
Stange^F
stecca^F

cigarette
cigarrillo^M
cigarette^F
Zigarette^F
sigaretta^F

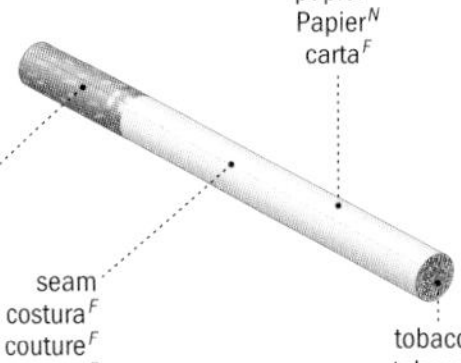

paper
papel^M
papier^M
Papier^N
carta^F

filter tip
filtro^M
bout^M-filtre^M
Filterspitze^F
filtro^M

seam
costura^F
couture^F
Naht^F
giuntura^F

tobacco
tabaco^M
tabac^M
Tabak^M
tabacco^M

cigarette pack
paquete^M de cigarrillos^M
paquet^M de cigarettes^F
Zigarettenschachtel^F
pacchetto^M di sigarette^F

stamp
timbre^M
timbre^M
Steuermarke^F
bollo^M del monopolio^M

tear tape
tira^F para rasgar la envoltura^F
bandelette^F d'arrachage^M
Aufreißband^N
linguetta^F a strappo^M

trade name
marca^F registrada
marque^F déposée
Markenname^M
marca^F

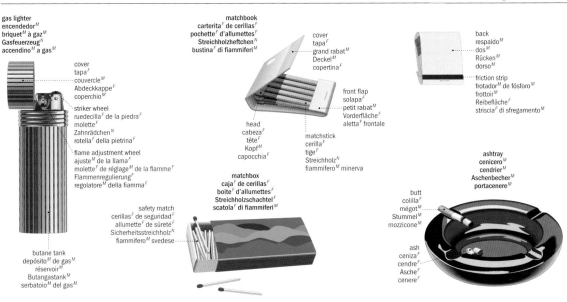

gas lighter
encendedor^M
briquet^M à gaz^M
Gasfeuerzeug^N
accendino^M a gas^M

cover
tapa^F
couvercle^M
Abdeckkappe^F
coperchio^M

striker wheel
ruedecilla^F de la piedra^F
molette^F
Zahnrädchen^N
rotella^F della pietrina^F

flame adjustment wheel
ajuste^M de la llama^F
molette^F de réglage^M de la flamme^F
Flammenregulierung^F
regolatore^M della fiamma^F

butane tank
depósito^M de gas^M
réservoir^M
Butangastank^M
serbatoio^M del gas^M

matchbook
carterita^F de cerillas^F
pochette^F d'allumettes^F
Streichholzheftchen^N
bustina^F di fiammiferi^M

cover
tapa^F
grand rabat^M
Deckel^M
copertina^F

head
cabeza^F
tête^F
Kopf^M
capocchia^F

front flap
solapa^F
petit rabat^M
Vorderfläche^F
aletta^F frontale

matchstick
cerilla^F
tige^F
Streichholz^N
fiammifero^M minerva

matchbox
caja^F de cerillas^F
boîte^F d'allumettes^F
Streichholzschachtel^F
scatola^F di fiammiferi^M

safety match
cerillas^F de seguridad^F
allumette^F de sûreté^F
Sicherheitsstreichholz^N
fiammifero^M svedese

back
respaldo^M
dos^M
Rücken^M
dorso^M

friction strip
frotador^M de fósforo^M
frottoir^M
Reibefläche^F
striscia^F di sfregamento^M

ashtray
cenicero^M
cendrier^M
Aschenbecher^M
portacenere^M

butt
colilla^F
mégot^M
Stummel^M
mozzicone^M

ash
ceniza^F
cendre^F
Asche^F
cenere^F

---

umbrellas and stick

paraguas^M y bastones^M | parapluies^M et canne^F | Schirme^F und Stock^M | ombrelli^M e bastone^M

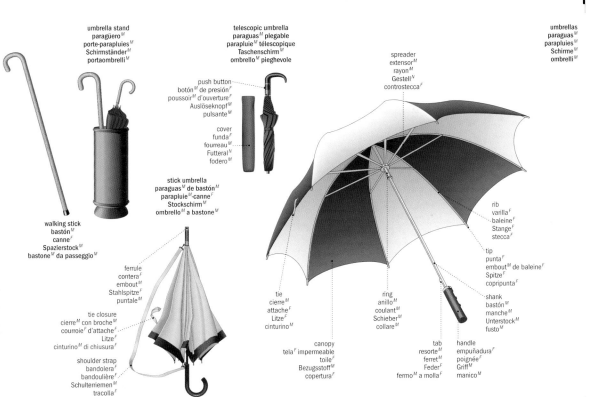

umbrella stand
paragüero^M
porte-parapluies^M
Schirmständer^M
portaombrelli^M

telescopic umbrella
paraguas^M plegable
parapluie^M télescopique
Taschenschirm^M
ombrello^M pieghevole

push button
botón^M de presión^F
poussoir^M d'ouverture^F
Auslöseknopf^M
pulsante^M

cover
funda^F
fourreau^M
Futteral^N
fodero^M

stick umbrella
paraguas^M de bastón^M
parapluie^M-canne^F
Stockschirm^M
ombrello^M a bastone^M

walking stick
bastón^M
canne^F
Spazierstock^M
bastone^M da passeggio^M

ferrule
contera^F
embout^M
Stahlspitze^F
puntale^M

tie closure
cierre^M con broche^M
courroie^F d'attache^F
Litze^F
cinturino^M di chiusura^F

shoulder strap
bandolera^F
bandoulière^F
Schulterriemen^M
tracolla^F

spreader
extensor^M
rayon^M
Gestell^N
controstecca^F

umbrellas
paraguas^M
parapluies^M
Schirme^M
ombrelli^M

tie
cierre^M
attache^F
Litze^F
cinturino^M

canopy
tela^F impermeable
toile^F
Bezugsstoff^M
copertura^F

ring
anillo^M
coulant^M
Schieber^M
collare^M

tab
resorte^M
ferret^M
Feder^F
fermo^M a molla^F

rib
varilla^F
baleine^F
Stange^F
stecca^F

tip
punta^F
embout^M de baleine^F
Spitze^F
copripunta^F

shank
bastón^M
manche^M
Unterstock^M
fusto^M

handle
empuñadura^F
poignée^F
Griff^M
manico^M

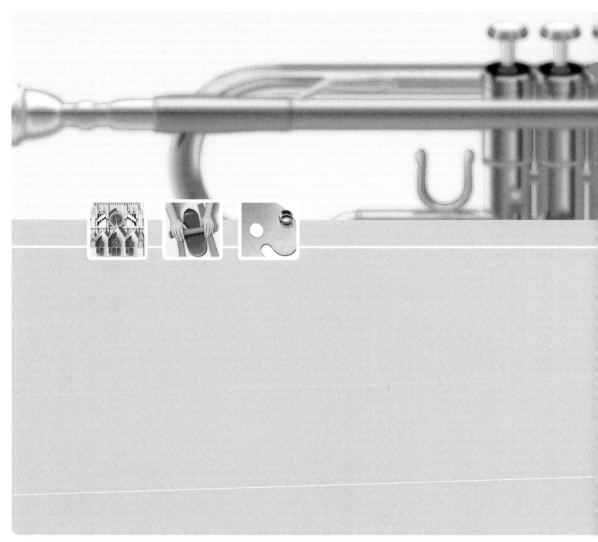

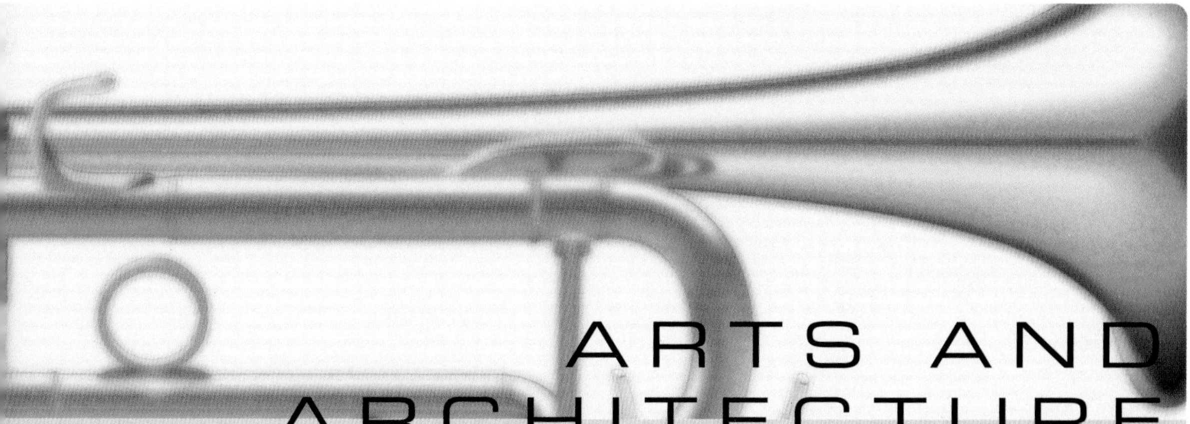

ARTS AND ARCHITECTURE

ARTE Y ARQUITECTURA | ARTS ET ARCHITECTURE | KUNST UND ARCHITEKTUR | ARTE E ARCHITETTURA

museum

museo^M | musée^M | Museum^N | museo^M

auditorium
auditorio^M
auditorium^M
Hörsaal^M
auditorium^M

storage
depósito^M
réserve^F
Lagerraum^M
deposito^M

ticket clerk
controlador^M de entradas^F
préposé^M au contrôle^M des billets^M
Kartenkontrolleur^M
addetto^M al controllo^M biglietti^M

archives
archivos^M
archives^F
Archiv^N
archivi^M

curator's office
despacho^F del conservador^M
bureau^M du conservateur^M
Büro^N des Konservators^M
ufficio^M del conservatore^M

superintendent's office
despacho^F del director^M
bureau^M du directeur^M
Büro^N des Direktors^M
ufficio^M del direttore^M

coatroom
guardarropa^F
vestiaire^M
Garderobe^F
guardaroba^M

administration
administración^F
administration^F
Verwaltung^F
amministrazione^F

control center
puesto^M de control^M
poste^M de surveillance^F
Überwachungsraum^M
postazione^F di sorveglianza^F

meeting room
sala^F de reuniones^F
salle^F de réunion^F
Sitzungssaal^M
sala^F riunioni^F

exhibition billboard
cartelera^F de las exposiciones^F
tableau^M d'affichage^M des expositions^F
Anschlagtafel^F der Ausstellungen^F
tabellone^M d'affissione^F delle mostre^F

banner for the coming exhibition
banderola^F de la exposición^F futura
banderole^F d'exposition^F à venir
Banner^N der kommenden Ausstellung^F
manifesto^M della mostra^F successiva

entrance hall
vestíbulo^M de entrada^F
hall^M d'entrée^F
Eingangshalle^F
ingresso^M

ticket office
taquilla^F
billetterie^F
Kasse^F
biglietteria^F

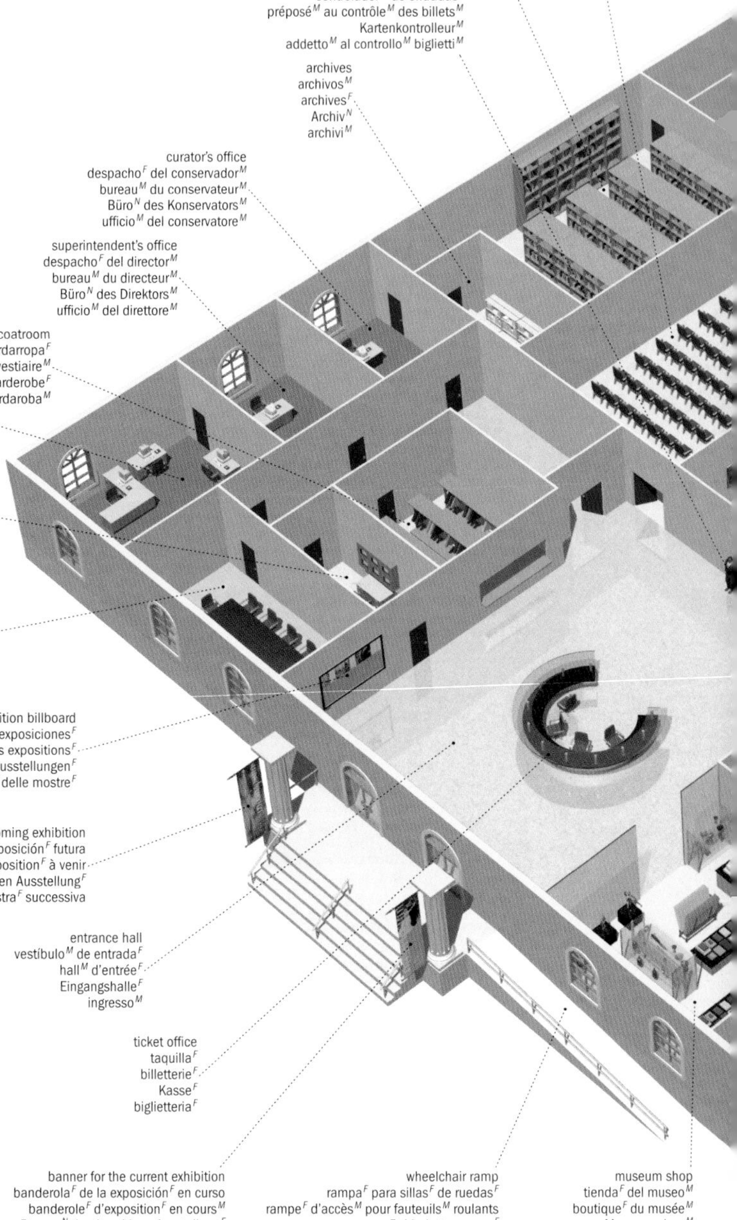

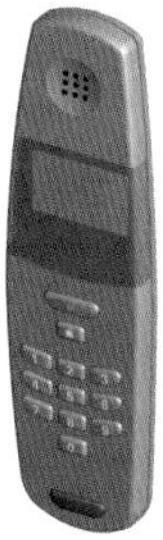

audioguide
audioguía^F
audioguide^M
Audioführer^M
audioguida^F

banner for the current exhibition
banderola^F de la exposición^F en curso
banderole^F d'exposition^F en cours^M
Banner^N der derzeitigen Ausstellung^F
manifesto^M della mostra^F in corso^M

wheelchair ramp
rampa^F para sillas^F de ruedas^F
rampe^F d'accès^M pour fauteuils^M roulants
Behindertenrampe^F
rampa^F per sedie^F a rotelle^F

museum shop
tienda^F del museo^M
boutique^F du musée^M
Museumsshop^M
negozio^M del museo^M

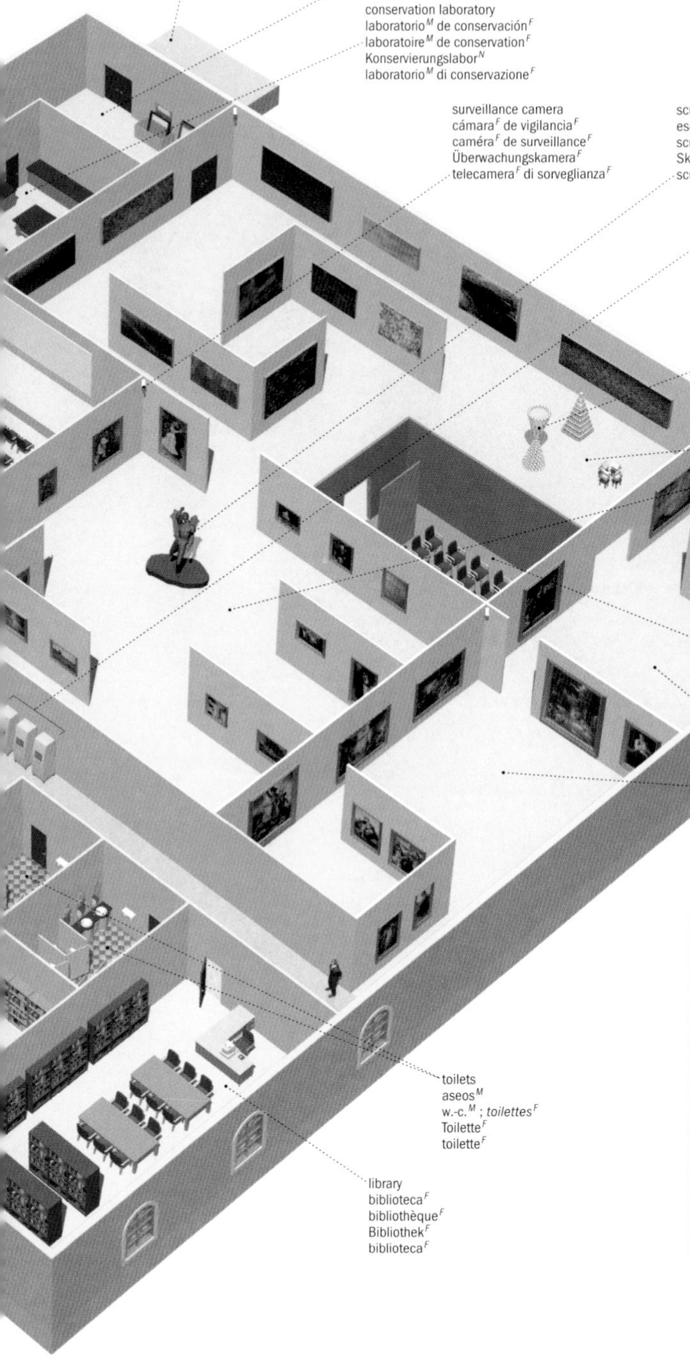

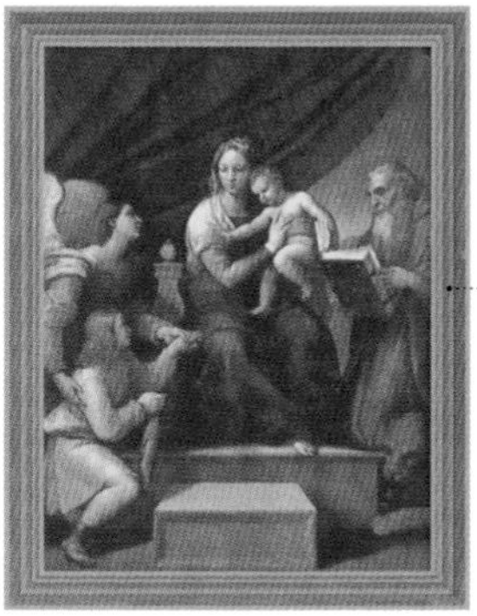

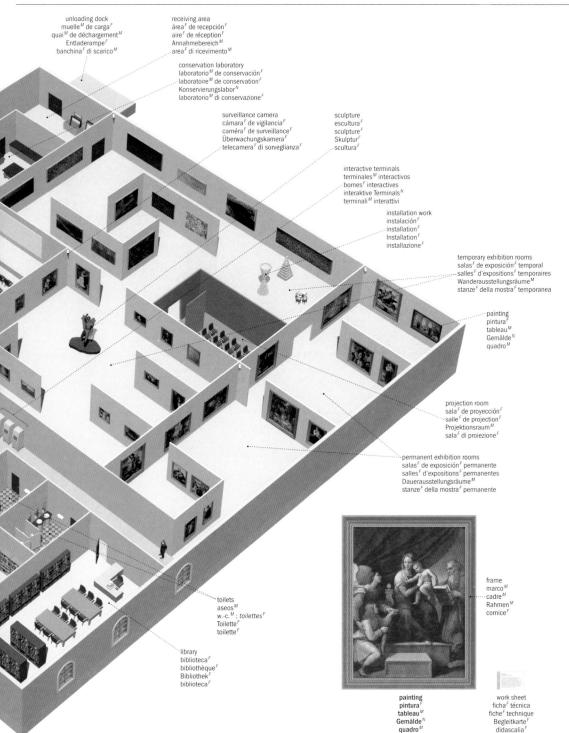

unloading dock
muelle^M de carga^F
quai^M de déchargement^M
Entladerampe^F
banchina^F di scarico^M

receiving area
área^F de recepción^F
aire^F de réception^F
Annahmebereich^M
area^F di ricevimento^M

conservation laboratory
laboratorio^M de conservación^F
laboratoire^M de conservation^F
Konservierungslabor^N
laboratorio^M di conservazione^F

surveillance camera
cámara^F de vigilancia^F
caméra^F de surveillance^F
Überwachungskamera^F
telecamera^F di sorveglianza^F

sculpture
escultura^F
sculpture^F
Skulptur^F
scultura^F

interactive terminals
terminales^M interactivos
bornes^F interactives
interaktive Terminals^N
terminali^M interattivi

installation work
instalación^F
installation^F
Installation^F
installazione^F

temporary exhibition rooms
salas^F de exposición^F temporal
salles^F d'expositions temporaires
Wanderausstellungsräume^M
stanze^F della mostra^F temporanea

painting
pintura^F
tableau^M
Gemälde^N
quadro^M

projection room
sala^F de proyección^F
salle^F de projection^F
Projektionsraum^M
sala^F di proiezione^F

permanent exhibition rooms
salas^F de exposición^F permanente
salles^F d'expositions^F permanentes
Dauerausstellungsräume^M
stanze^F della mostra^F permanente

toilets
aseos^M
w.-c.^{M} ; toilettes^F
Toilette^F
toilette^F

library
biblioteca^F
bibliothèque^F
Bibliothek^F
biblioteca^F

frame
marco^M
cadre^M
Rahmen^M
cornice^F

painting
pintura^F
tableau^M
Gemälde^N
quadro^M

work sheet
ficha^F técnica
fiche^F technique
Begleitkarte^F
didascalia^F

ARTS AND ARCHITECTURE

painting and drawing

pintura^F y dibujo^M | peinture^F et dessin^M | Malen^N und Zeichnen^N | disegno^M e pittura^F

major techniques
técnicas^F principales
principales techniques^F
die wichtigsten Techniken^F
tecniche^F principali

ink drawing
dibujo^M de tinta^F china
dessin^M à l'encre^F
Tuschezeichnung^F
disegno^M a inchiostro^M

charcoal drawing
dibujo^M al carboncillo^M
dessin^M au fusain^M
Kohlezeichnung^F
disegno^M a carboncino^M

oil painting
pintura^F al óleo^M
peinture^F à l'huile^F
Ölmalerei^F
pittura^F a olio^M

watercolor
acuarela^F
aquarelle^F
Aquarell^N
acquerello^M

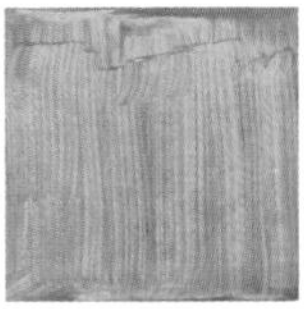

gouache
guache^M
gouache^F
Gouache^F
pittura^F a guazzo^M

felt tip pen drawing
pintura^F con rotuladores^M
dessin^M au feutre^M
Filzstiftzeichnung^F
disegno^M a pennarelli^M

dry pastel drawing
pintura^F al pastel^M blando
dessin^M au pastel^M sec
Trockenpastell^N
disegno^M a pastelli^M secchi

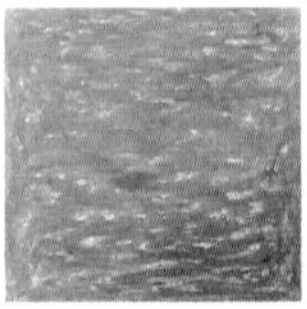

oil pastel drawing
pintura^F al pastel^M al óleo^M
dessin^M au pastel^M gras
Ölpastell^N
disegno^M a pastelli^M a olio^M

colored pencil drawing
dibujo^M de lápices^M de colores^M
dessin^M au crayon^M de couleur^F
Buntstiftzeichnung^F
disegno^M a matite^F colorate

wax crayon drawing
dibujo^M a la cera^F
dessin^M au crayon^M de cire^F
Wachsmalerei^F
disegno^M a pastelli^M a cera^F

equipment
equipo^M
matériel^M
Ausstattung^F
attrezzatura^F

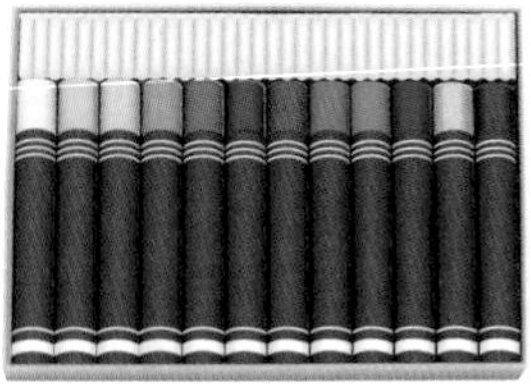

oil pastels
pastels^M al óleo^M
pastels^M gras
Ölpastelle^N
pastelli^M a olio^M

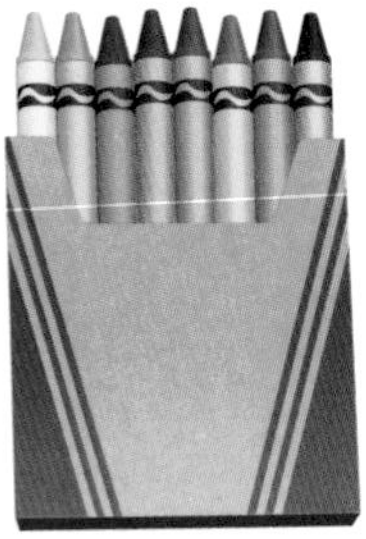

wax crayons
ceras^F
crayons^M de cire^F
Wachsfarbstifte^M
pastelli^M a cera^F

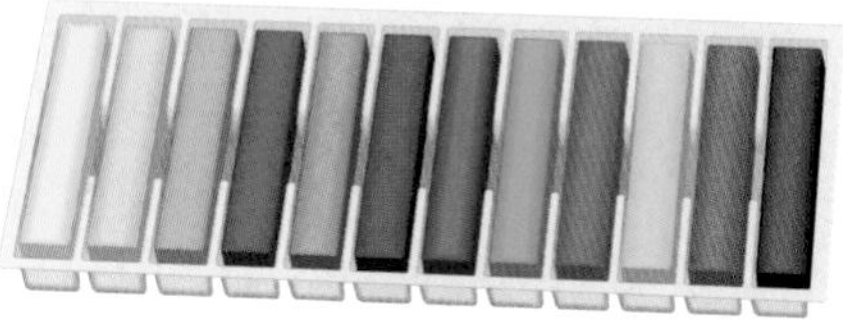

soft pastels
pastels^M
pastels^M secs
Pastelle^N
pastelli^M morbidi

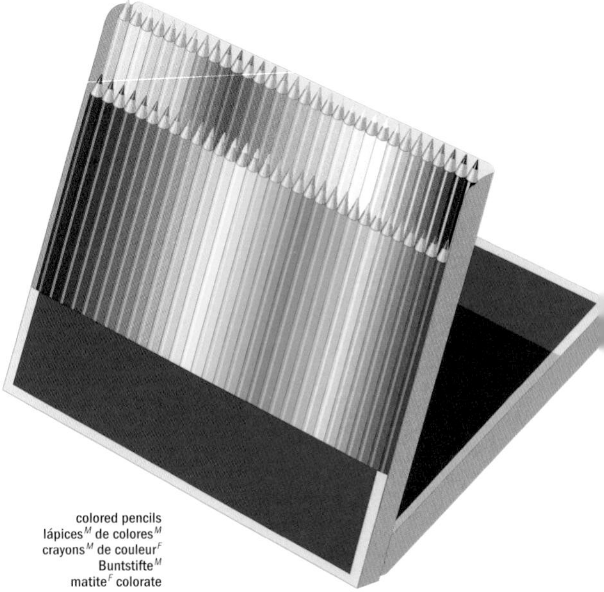

colored pencils
lápices^M de colores^M
crayons^M de couleur^F
Buntstifte^M
matite^F colorate

ARTS AND ARCHITECTURE

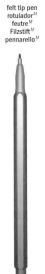

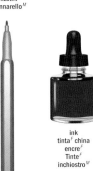

felt tip pen
rotulador[M]
feutre[M]
Filzstift[M]
pennarello[M]

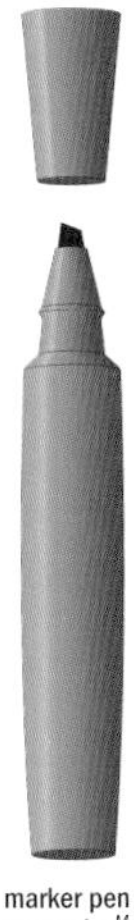

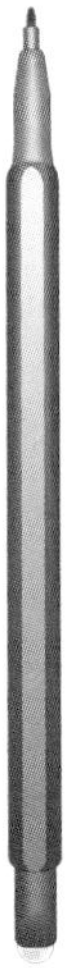

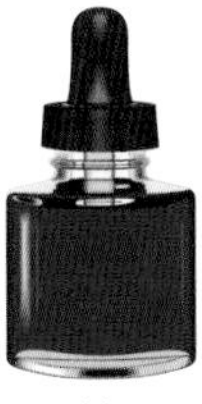

ink
tinta[F] china
encre[F]
Tinte[F]
inchiostro[M]

oil paint
óleo[M]
couleur[F] à l'huile[F]
Ölfarbe[F]
colore[M] a olio[M]

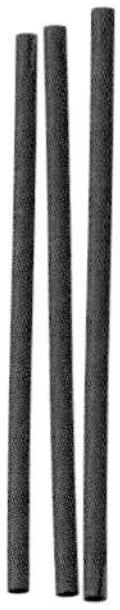

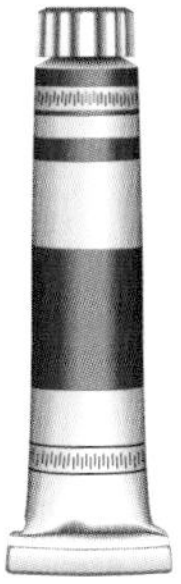

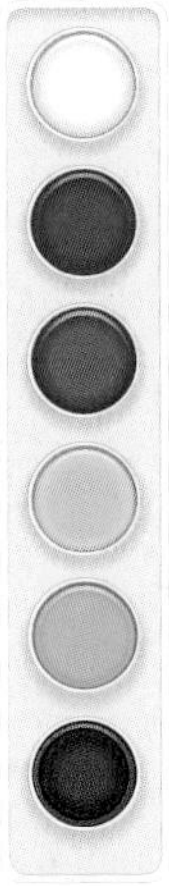

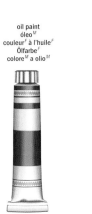

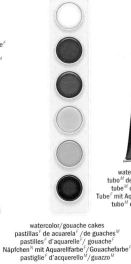

watercolor/gouache tube
tubo[M] de acuarela[F] /de guache[M]
tube[M] d'aquarelle[F] / gouache[F]
Tube[F] mit Aquarellfarbe[F]/Gouachefarbe[F]
tubo[M] d'acquerello[M]/guazzo[M]

marker pen
marcador[M]
marqueur[M]
Marker[M]
evidenziatore[M]

charcoal
carboncillo[M]
fusain[M]
Kohle[F]
carboncino[M]

watercolor/gouache cakes
pastillas[F] de acuarela[F] /de guaches[M]
pastilles[F] d'aquarelle[F] / gouache[F]
Näpfchen[N] mit Aquarellfarbe[F]/Gouachefarbe[F]
pastiglie[F] d'acquerello[M]/guazzo[M]

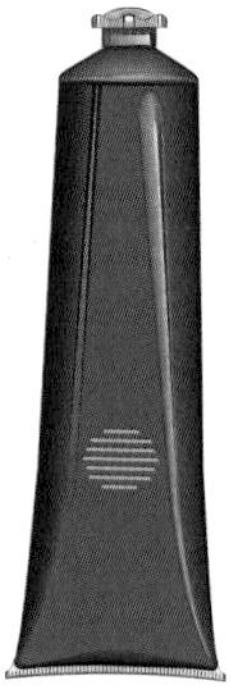

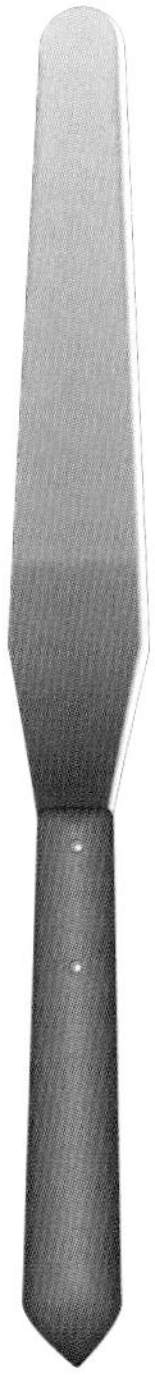

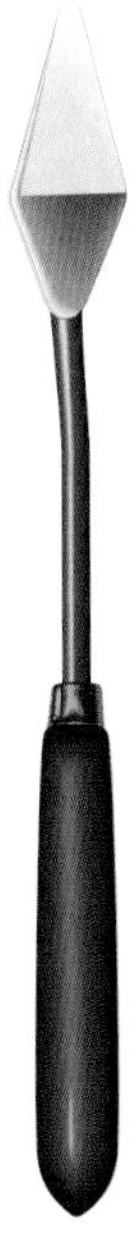

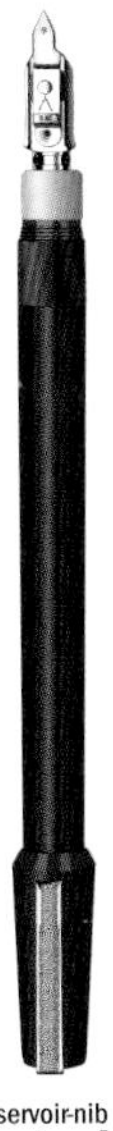

reservoir-nib pen
pluma[F]
plume[F]
Graphosfeder[F]
pennino[M]

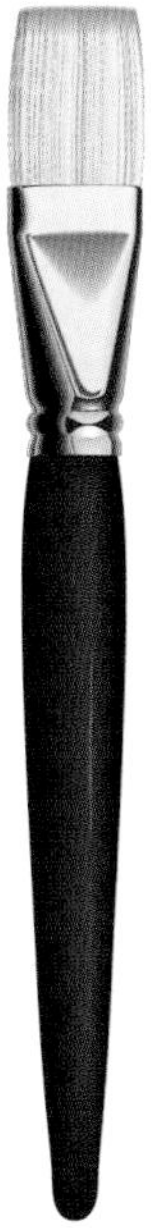

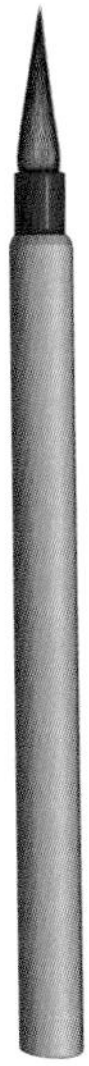

sumi-e brush
sumie[M]
pinceau[M] à sumie[M]
Japanpinsel[M]
penna[F] sumi

spatula
espátula[F]
spatule[F]
Palettmesser[N]
spatola[F]

painting knife
cuchillo[M] paleta[F]
couteau[M] à peindre
Malspachtel[M]
mestichino[M]

flat brush
pincel[M] plano
brosse[F]
Flachpinsel[M]
pennello[M] piatto[M]

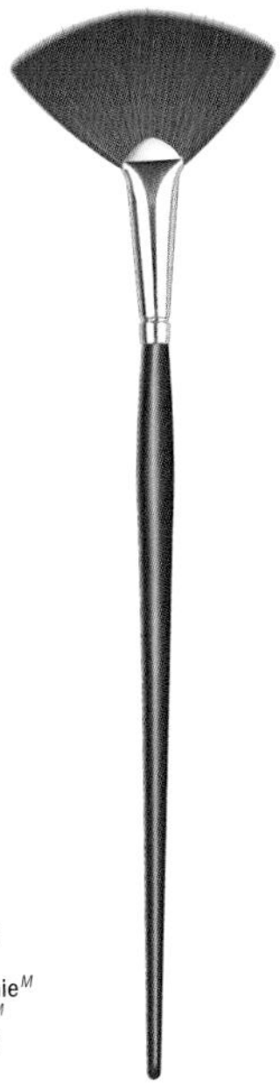

fan brush
brocha[F]
brosse[F] éventail[M]
Fächerpinsel[M]
pennello[M] a ventaglio[M]

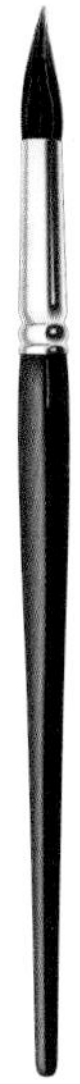

brush
pincel[M]
pinceau[M]
Pinsel[M]
pennello[M]

painting and drawing

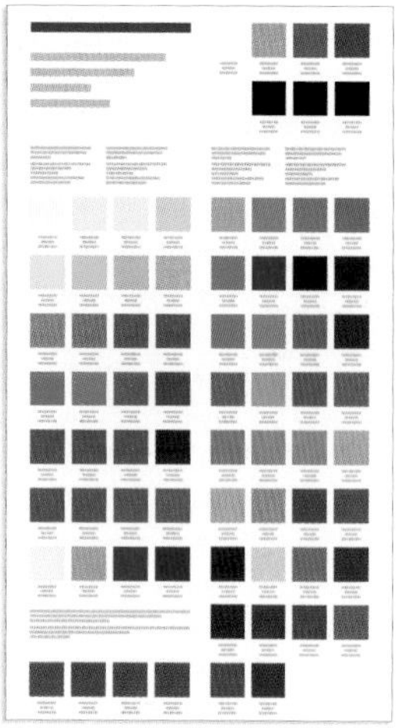

color chart
gama[F] de colores[M]
nuancier[M]
Farbtafel[F]
tabella[F] dei colori[M]

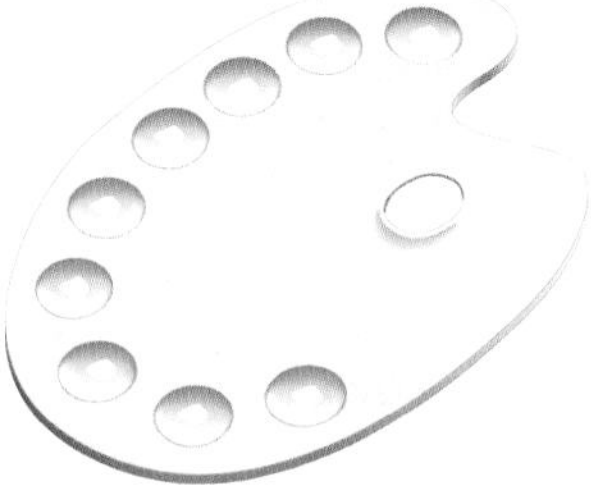

palette with hollows
paleta[F] con huecos[M] para pintura[F]
palette[F] à alvéoles[F]
Palette[F] mit Vertiefungen[F]
tavolozza[F] con vaschette[F]

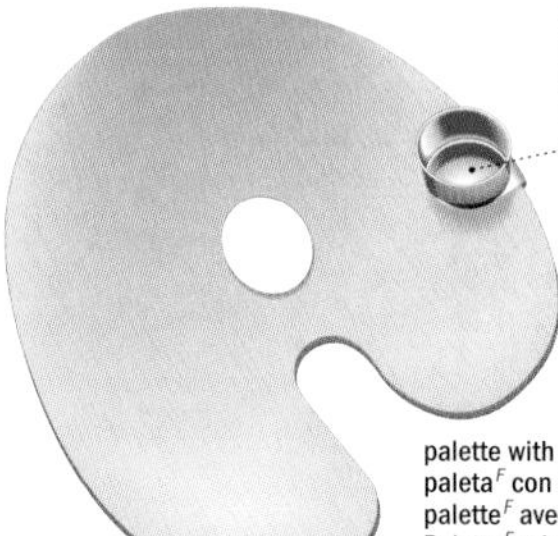

palette with dipper
paleta[F] con tarrito[M]
palette[F] avec godet[M]
Palette[F] mit Palettstecker[M]
tavolozza[F] con vasetto[M]

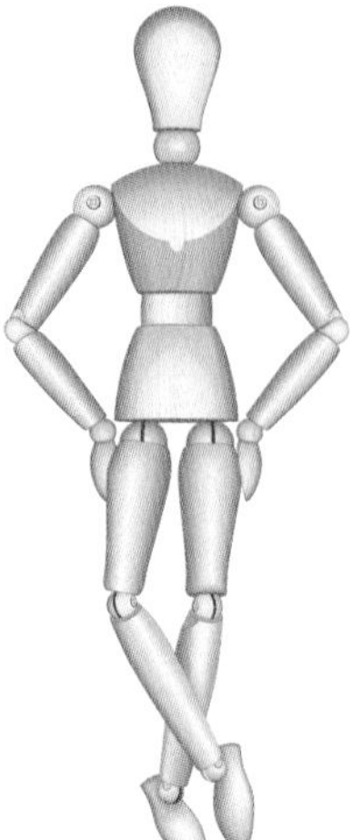

articulated mannequin
maniquí[M]
mannequin[M] articulé
Gliederpuppe[F]
manichino[M] snodabile

airbrush
aerógrafo[M]
aérographe[M]
Spritzpistole[F]
aerografo[M]

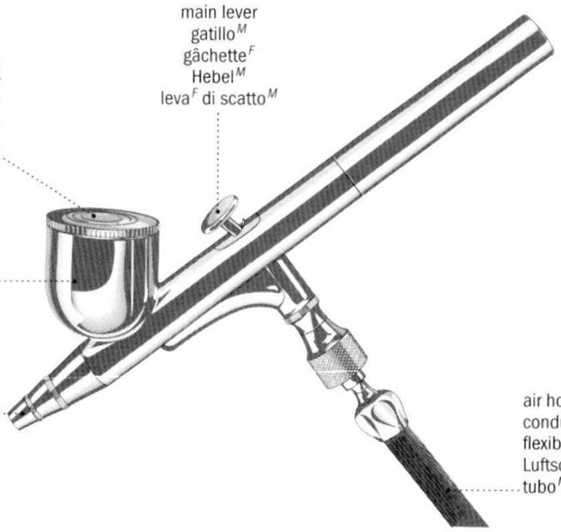

cross section of an airbrush
sección[M] transversal de un aerógrafo[M]
coupe[F] d'un aérographe[M]
Spritzpistole[F] im Querschnitt[M]
sezione[F] trasversale di un aerografo[M]

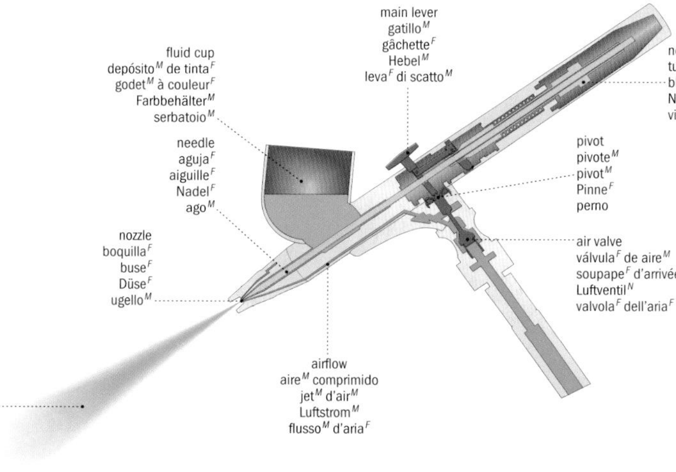

ARTS AND ARCHITECTURE

accessories
accesorios^M
accessoires^M
Zubehör^N
accessori^M

drafting table
tablero^M de dibujo^M
table^F à dessin^M
Reißbrett^N
tavolo^M da disegno^M

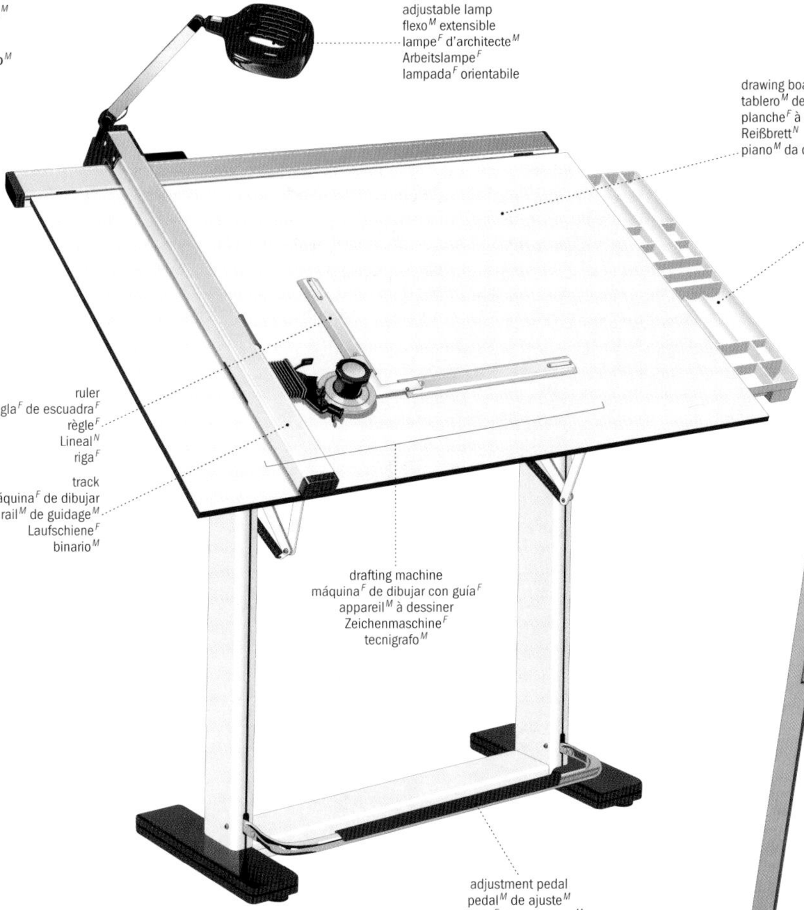

adjustable lamp
flexo^M extensible
lampe^F d'architecte^M
Arbeitslampe^F
lampada^F orientabile

drawing board
tablero^M de dibujo^M
planche^F à dessin^M
Reißbrett^N
piano^M da disegno^M

storage tray
bandeja^F de accesorios^M
plateau^M de rangement^M
Ablagebrett^N
vaschette^F portaaccessori

ruler
regla^F de escuadra^F
règle^F
Lineal^N
riga^F

track
guía^F de la máquina^F de dibujar
rail^M de guidage^M
Laufschiene^F
binario^M

drafting machine
máquina^F de dibujar con guía^F
appareil^M à dessiner
Zeichenmaschine^F
tecnigrafo^M

adjustment pedal
pedal^M de ajuste^M
pédale^F d'ajustement^M
Pedal^N zur Verstellung^F
pedale^M di regolazione^F

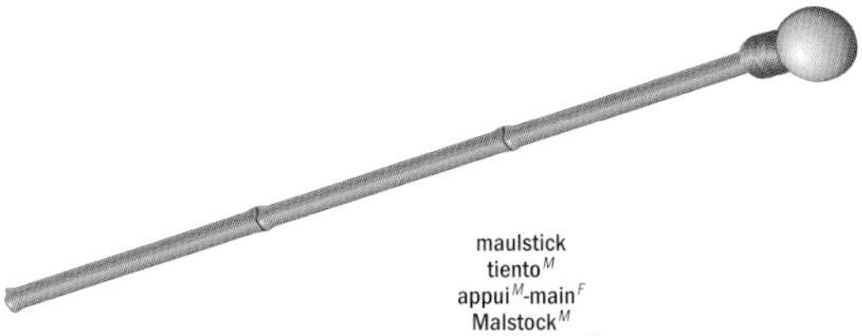

maulstick
tiento^M
appui^M-main^F
Malstock^M
appoggiamano^M

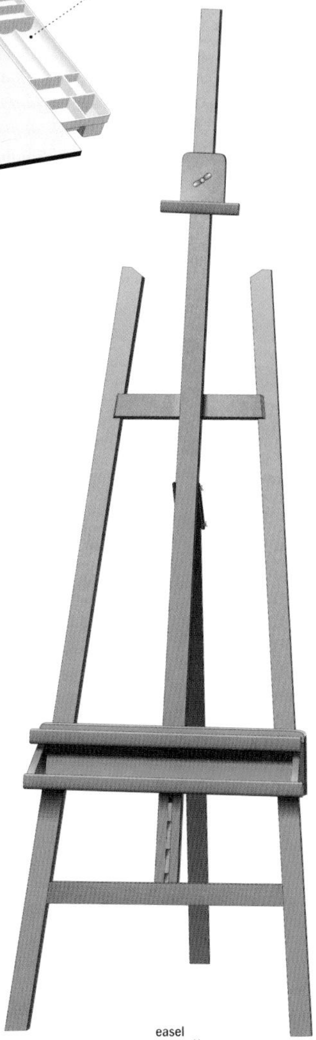

easel
caballete^M
chevalet^M
Staffelei^F
cavalletto^M

ARTS AND ARCHITECTURE

painting and drawing

color circle
círculo^M **de los colores**^{M}
cercle^M **des couleurs**^{F}
Farbkreis^M
cerchio^M **dei colori**^{M}

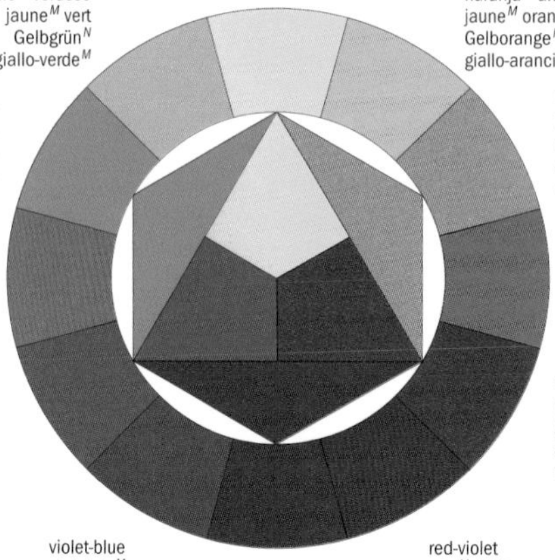

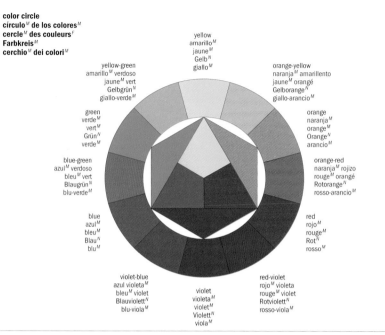

yellow
amarillo^M
jaune^M
Gelb^N
giallo^M

yellow-green
amarillo^M verdoso
jaune^M vert
Gelbgrün^N
giallo-verde^M

orange-yellow
naranja^M amarillento
jaune^M orangé
Gelborange^N
giallo-arancio^M

green
verde^M
vert^M
Grün^N
verde^M

orange
naranja^M
orange^M
Orange^N
arancio^M

blue-green
azul^M verdoso
bleu^M vert
Blaugrün^N
blu-verde^M

orange-red
naranja^M rojizo
rouge^M orangé
Rotorange^N
rosso-arancio^M

blue
azul^M
bleu^M
Blau^N
blu^M

red
rojo^M
rouge^M
Rot^N
rosso^M

violet-blue
azul violeta^M
bleu^M violet
Blauviolett^N
blu-viola^M

violet
violeta^M
violet^M
Violett^N
viola^M

red-violet
rojo^M violeta
rouge^M violet
Rotviolett^N
rosso-viola^M

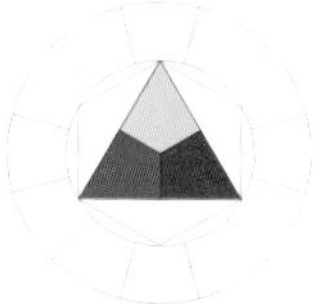

primary colors
colores^M primarios
couleurs^F primaires
Farben^F erster Ordnung^F
colori^M primari

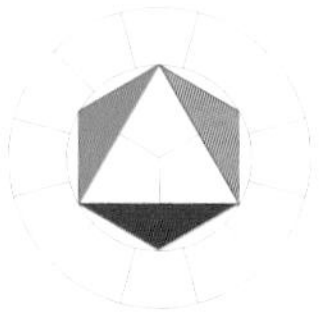

secondary colors
colores^M secundarios
couleurs^F secondaires
Farben^F zweiter Ordnung^F
colori^M secondari

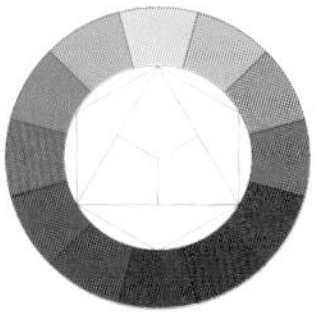

tertiary colors
colores^M terciarios
couleurs^F tertiaires
Farben^F dritter Ordnung^F
colori^M terziari

utility liquids
líquidos^M **accesorios**
liquides^M **d'appoint**^{M}
Hilfsmittel^N
liquidi^M **utilizzabili**

linseed oil
aceite^M de linaza^F
huile^F de lin^M
Leinöl^N
olio^M di semi^M di lino^M

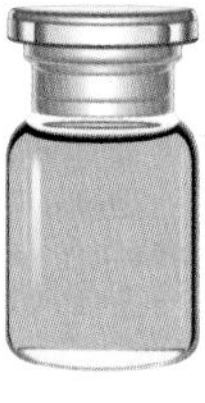

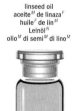

varnish
barniz^M
vernis^M
Firnis^M
lacca^F

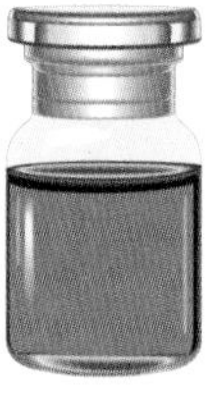

fixative
fijador^M
fixatif^M
Fixativ^N
fissativo^M

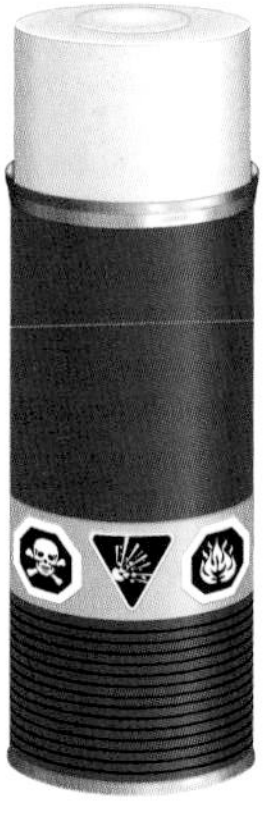

turpentine
aguarrás^M
térébenthine^F
Terpentin^N
acquaragia^F

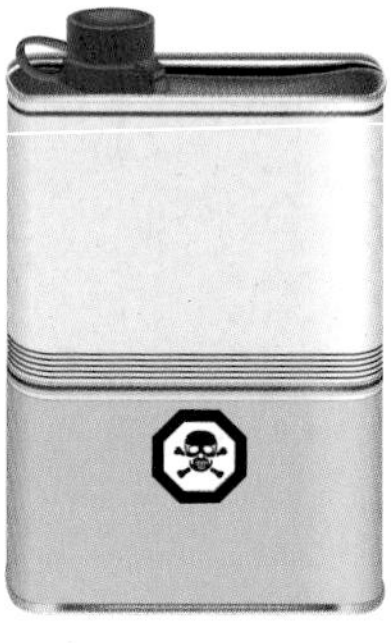

supports
soportes^M
supports^M
Bildträger^M
supporti^M

paper
papel^M
papier^M
Papier^N
carta^F

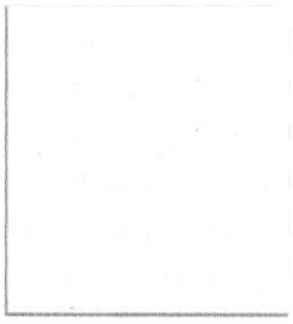

cardboard
cartón^M
carton^M
Malpappe^F
cartoncino^M

canvas
lienzo^M
toile^F
Leinwand^F
tela^F

panel
tabla^F
panneau^M
Platte^F
pannello^M

ARTS AND ARCHITECTURE

wood carving

talla^F en madera^F | sculpture^F sur bois^M | Holzschnitzerei^F | scultura^F in legno^M

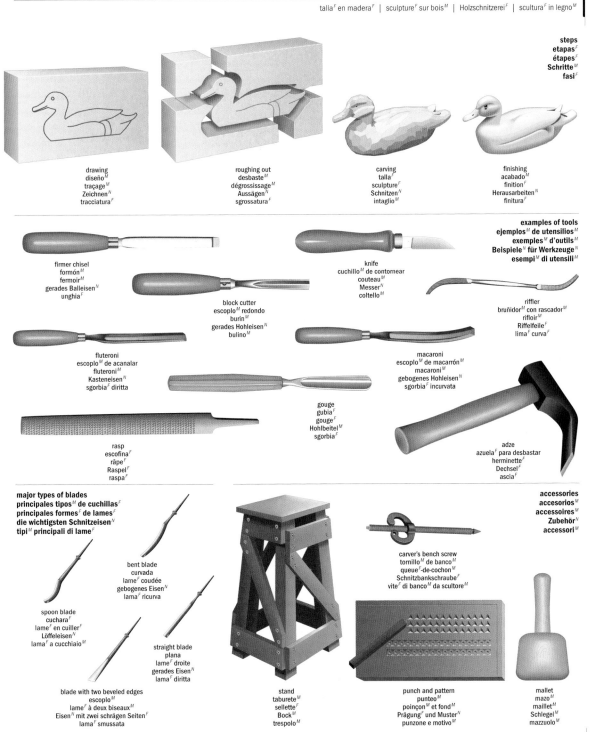

steps
etapas^F
étapes^F
Schritte^M
fasi^F

drawing
diseño^M
traçage^M
Zeichnen^N
tracciatura^F

roughing out
desbaste^M
dégrossissage^M
Aussägen^N
sgrossatura^F

carving
talla^F
sculpture^F
Schnitzen^N
intaglio^M

finishing
acabado^M
finition^F
Herausarbeiten^N
finitura^F

examples of tools
ejemplos^M **de utensilios**^{M}
exemples^M **d'outils**^{M}
Beispiele^N **für Werkzeuge**^{N}
esempi di utensili^M

firmer chisel
formón^M
fermoir^M
gerades Balleisen^N
unghia^F

knife
cuchillo^M de contornear
couteau^M
Messer^N
coltello^M

block cutter
escoplo^M redondo
burin^M
gerades Hohleisen^N
bulino^M

riffler
bruñidor^M con rascador^M
rifloir^M
Riffelfeile^F
lima^F curva^F

fluteroni
escoplo^M de acanalar
fluteroni^M
Kasteneisen^N
sgorbia^F diritta

macaroni
escoplo^M de macarrón^M
macaroni^M
gebogenes Hohleisen^N
sgorbia^F incurvata

gouge
gubia^F
gouge^F
Hohlbeitel^M
sgorbia^F

rasp
escofina^F
râpe^F
Raspel^F
raspa^F

adze
azuela^F para desbastar
herminette^F
Dechsel^F
ascia^F

major types of blades
principales tipos^M **de cuchillas**^{F}
principales formes^F **de lames**^{F}
die wichtigsten Schnitzeisen^N
tipi^M **principali di lame**^{F}

accessories
accesorios^M
accessoires^M
Zubehör^N
accessori^M

bent blade
curvada
lame^F coudée
gebogenes Eisen^N
lama^F ricurva

carver's bench screw
tornillo^M de banco^M
queue^F-de-cochon^M
Schnitzbankschraube^F
vite^F di banco^M da scultore^M

spoon blade
cuchara^F
lame^F en cuiller^F
Löffeleisen^N
lama^F a cucchiaio^M

straight blade
plana
lame^F droite
gerades Eisen^N
lama^F diritta

blade with two beveled edges
escoplo^M
lame^F à deux biseaux^M
Eisen^N mit zwei schrägen Seiten^F
lama^F smussata

stand
taburete^M
sellette^F
Bock^M
trespolo^M

punch and pattern
punteo^M
poinçon^M et fond^M
Prägung^F und Muster^N
punzone e motivo^M

mallet
mazo^M
maillet^M
Schlegel^M
mazzuolo^M

ARTS AND ARCHITECTURE

pyramid

pirámide^F | pyramide^F | Pyramide^F | piramide^F

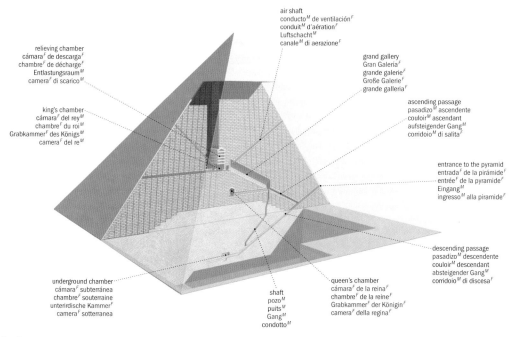

air shaft
conducto^M de ventilación^F
conduit^M d'aération^F
Luftschacht^M
canale^M di aerazione^F

relieving chamber
cámara^F de descarga^F
chambre^F de décharge^F
Entlastungsraum^M
camera^F di scarico^M

grand gallery
Gran Galeria^F
grande galerie^F
Große Galerie^F
grande galleria^F

king's chamber
cámara^F del rey^M
chambre^F du roi^M
Grabkammer^F des Königs^M
camera^F del re^M

ascending passage
pasadizo^M ascendente
couloir^M ascendant
aufsteigender Gang^M
corridoio^M di salita^F

entrance to the pyramid
entrada^F de la pirámide^F
entrée^F de la pyramide^F
Eingang^M
ingresso^M alla piramide^F

descending passage
pasadizo^M descendente
couloir^M descendant
absteigender Gang^M
corridoio^M di discesa^F

underground chamber
cámara^F subterránea
chambre^F souterraine
unterirdische Kammer^F
camera^F sotterranea

shaft
pozo^M
puits^M
Gang^M
condotto^M

queen's chamber
cámara^F de la reina^F
chambre^F de la reine^F
Grabkammer^F der Königin^F
camera^F della regina^F

Greek theater

teatro^M griego | théâtre^M grec | griechisches Theater^N | teatro^M greco

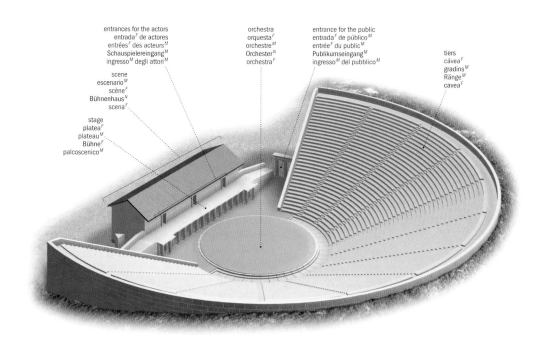

entrances for the actors
entrada^F de actores
entrées^F des acteurs^M
Schauspielereingang^M
ingresso^M degli attori^M

orchestra
orquesta^F
orchestre^M
Orchester^N
orchestra^F

entrance for the public
entrada^F de público^M
entrée^F du public^M
Publikumseingang^M
ingresso^M del pubblico^M

tiers
cávea^F
gradins^M
Ränge^M
cavea^F

scene
escenario^M
scène^F
Bühnenhaus^N
scena^F

stage
platea^F
plateau^M
Bühne^F
palcoscenico^M

ARTS AND ARCHITECTURE

Greek temple

templo^M griego | temple^M grec | griechischer Tempel^M | tempio^M greco

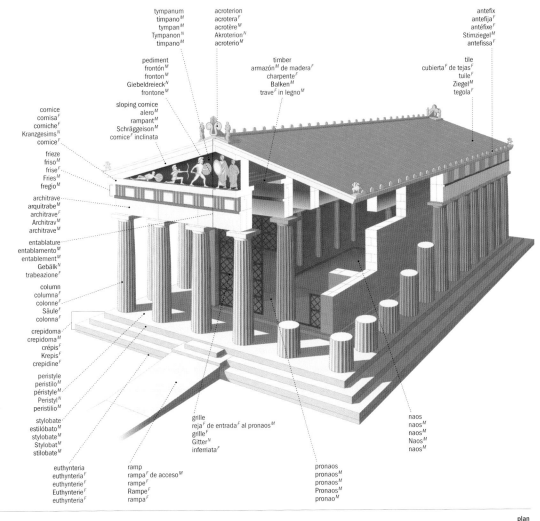

tympanum
timpano^M
tympan^M
Tympanon^N
timpano^M

acroterion
acrotera^F
acrotère^F
Akroterion^N
acroterio^M

antefix
antefija^F
antéfixe^F
Stirnziegel^M
antefissa^F

pediment
frontón^M
fronton^M
Giebeldreieck^N
frontone^M

timber
armazón^M de madera^F
charpente^F
Balken^M
trave^F in legno^M

tile
cubierta^F de tejas^F
tuile^F
Ziegel^M
tegola^F

cornice
cornisa^F
corniche^F
Kranzgesims^N
cornice^F

sloping cornice
alero^M
rampant^M
Schräggeison^M
cornice^F inclinata

frieze
friso^M
frise^F
Fries^M
fregio^M

architrave
arquitrabe^M
architrave^F
Architrav^M
architrave^M

entablature
entablamento^M
entablement^M
Gebälk^N
trabeazione^F

column
columna^F
colonne^F
Säule^F
colonna^F

crepidoma
crepidoma^M
crépis^F
Krepis^F
crepidine^F

peristyle
peristilo^M
péristyle^M
Peristyl^N
peristilio^M

stylobate
estilóbato^M
stylobate^F
Stylobat^M
stilobate^M

grille
reja^F de entrada^F al pronaos^M
grille^F
Gitter^N
inferriata^F

naos
naos^M
naos^M
Naos^M
naos^M

euthynteria
euthynteria^F
euthynterie^F
Euthynterie^F
euthynteria^F

ramp
rampa^F de acceso^M
rampe^F
Rampe^F
rampa^F

pronaos
pronaos^M
pronaos^M
Pronaos^M
pronao^M

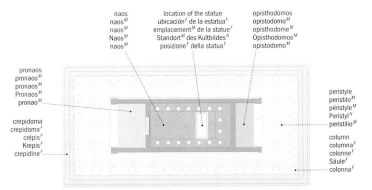

naos
naos^M
naos^M
Naos^M
naos^M

location of the statue
ubicación^F de la estatua^F
emplacement^M de la statue^F
Standort^M des Kultbildes^N
posizione^F della statua^F

opisthodomos
opistodomo^M
opisthodome^M
Opisthodomos^M
opistodomo^M

plan
plano^M
plan^M
Grundriss^M
pianta^F

pronaos
pronaos^M
pronaos^M
Pronaos^M
pronao^M

peristyle
peristilo^M
péristyle^M
Peristyl^N
peristilio^M

crepidoma
crepidoma^F
crépis^F
Krepis^F
crepidine^F

column
columna^F
colonne^F
Säule^F
colonna^F

architectural styles

estilos^M arquitectónicos | styles^M d'architecture^F | Baustile^M | stili^M architettonici

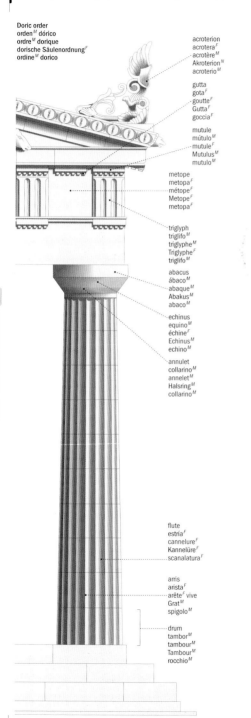

Doric order
orden^M dórico
ordre^M dorique
dorische Säulenordnung^F
ordine^M dorico

acroterion
acrotera^F
acrotère^M
Akroterion^N
acroterio^M

gutta
gota^F
goutte^F
Gutta^F
goccia^F

mutule
mútulo^M
mutule^F
Mutulus^M
mutulo^M

metope
metopa^F
métope^F
Metope^F
metopa^F

triglyph
triglifo^M
triglyphe^M
Triglyphe^F
triglifo^M

abacus
ábaco^M
abaque^M
Abakus^M
abaco^M

echinus
equino^M
échine^F
Echinus^M
echino^M

annulet
collarino^M
annelet^M
Halsring^M
collarino^M

flute
estria^F
cannelure^F
Kannelüre^F
scanalatura^F

arris
arista^F
arête^F vive
Grat^M
spigolo^M

drum
tambor^M
tambour^M
Tambour^M
rocchio^M

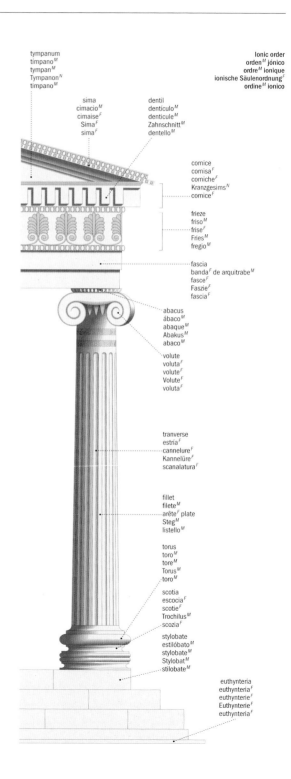

tympanum
tímpano^M
tympan^M
Tympanon^N
timpano^M

Ionic order
orden^M jónico
ordre^M ionique
ionische Säulenordnung^F
ordine^M ionico

sima
cimacio^M
cimaise^F
Sima^F
sima^F

dentil
denticulo^M
denticule^F
Zahnschnitt^M
dentello^M

cornice
cornisa^F
corniche^F
Kranzgesims^N
cornice^F

frieze
friso^M
frise^F
Fries^M
fregio^M

fascia
banda^F de arquitrabe^M
fasce^F
Faszie^F
fascia^F

abacus
ábaco^M
abaque^M
Abakus^M
abaco^M

volute
voluta^F
volute^F
Volute^F
voluta^F

tranverse
estria^F
cannelure^F
Kannelüre^F
scanalatura^F

fillet
filete^M
arête^F plate
Steg^M
listello^M

torus
toro^M
tore^M
Torus^M
toro^M

scotia
escocia^F
scotie^F
Trochilus^M
scozia^F

stylobate
estilóbato^M
stylobate^F
Stylobat^M
stilobate^M

euthynteria
euthynteria^F
euthynterie^F
Euthynterie^F
euthynteria^F

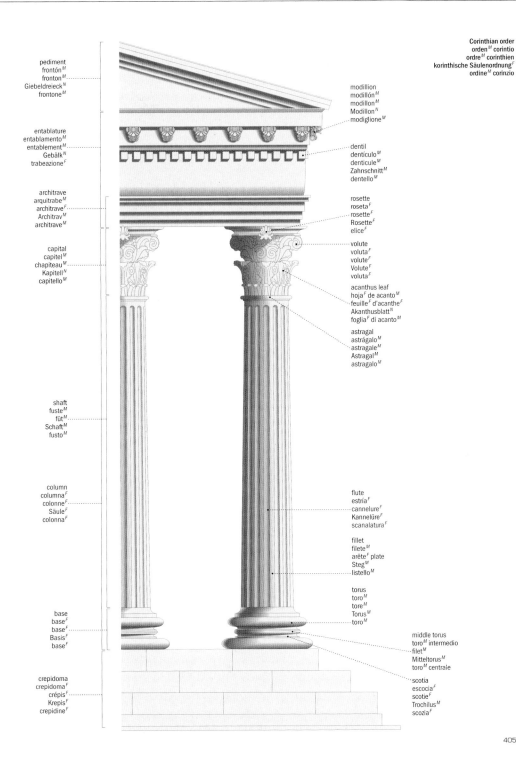

Corinthian order
orden ^{M} corintio
ordre ^{M} corinthien
korinthische Säulenordnung ^{F}
ordine ^{M} corinzio

pediment
frontón ^{M}
fronton ^{M}
Giebeldreieck ^{N}
frontone ^{M}

entablature
entablamento ^{M}
entablement ^{M}
Gebälk ^{N}
trabeazione ^{F}

architrave
arquitrabe ^{M}
architrave ^{F}
Architrav ^{M}
architrave ^{M}

capital
capitel ^{M}
chapiteau ^{M}
Kapitell ^{N}
capitello ^{M}

shaft
fuste ^{M}
fût ^{M}
Schaft ^{M}
fusto ^{M}

column
columna ^{F}
colonne ^{F}
Säule ^{F}
colonna ^{F}

base
base ^{F}
base ^{F}
Basis ^{F}
base ^{F}

crepidoma
crepidoma ^{F}
crépis ^{F}
Krepis ^{F}
crepidine ^{F}

modillion
modillón ^{M}
modillon ^{M}
Modillon ^{N}
modiglione ^{M}

dentil
dentículo ^{M}
denticule ^{M}
Zahnschnitt ^{M}
dentello ^{M}

rosette
roseta ^{F}
rosette ^{F}
Rosette ^{F}
elice ^{F}

volute
voluta ^{F}
volute ^{F}
Volute ^{F}
voluta ^{F}

acanthus leaf
hoja ^{F} de acanto ^{M}
feuille ^{F} d'acanthe ^{F}
Akanthusblatt ^{N}
foglia ^{F} di acanto ^{M}

astragal
astrágalo ^{M}
astragale ^{M}
Astragal ^{M}
astragalo ^{M}

flute
estria ^{F}
cannelure ^{F}
Kannelüre ^{F}
scanalatura ^{F}

fillet
filete ^{M}
arête ^{F} plate
Steg ^{M}
listello ^{M}

torus
toro ^{M}
tore ^{M}
Torus ^{M}
toro ^{M}

middle torus
toro ^{M} intermedio
filet ^{M}
Mitteltorus ^{M}
toro ^{M} centrale

scotia
escocia ^{F}
scotie ^{F}
Trochilus ^{M}
scozia ^{F}

Roman house

casa^F romana | maison^F romaine | römisches Wohnhaus^N | casa^F romana

tablinum
tablinum^M
tablinum^M
Tablinum^N
tablino^M

compluvium
compluvio^M
compluvium^M
Compluvium^N
compluvio^M

timber
viga^F
charpente^F
Balken^M
trave^F in legno^M

peristyle
peristilo^M
péristyle^M
Peristyl^N
peristilio^M

garden
jardín^M
jardin^M
Garten^M
giardino^M

fresco
fresco^M
fresque^F
Fresko^N
affresco^M

tile
teja^F
tuile^F
Ziegel^M
tegola^F

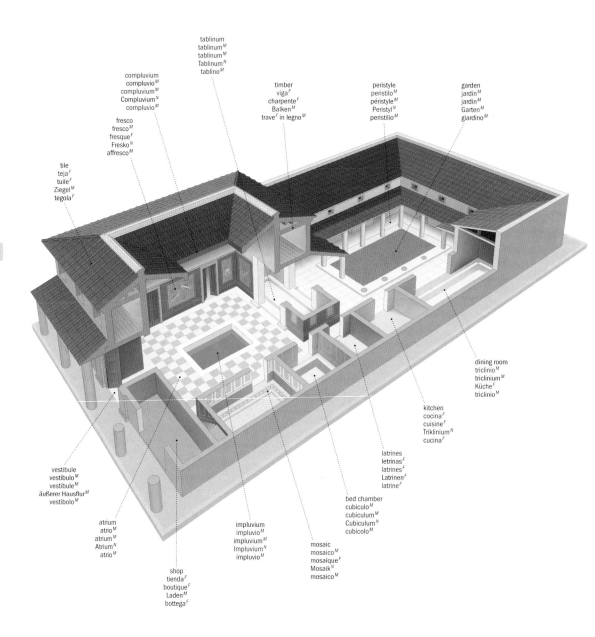

dining room
triclinio^M
triclinium^M
Küche^F
triclinio^M

kitchen
cocina^F
cuisine^F
Triklinium^N
cucina^F

latrines
letrinas^F
latrines^F
Latrinen^F
latrine^F

vestibule
vestibulo^M
vestibule^M
äußerer Hausflur^M
vestibolo^M

bed chamber
cubículo^M
cubiculum^M
Cubiculum^N
cubicolo^M

atrium
atrio^M
atrium^M
Atrium^N
atrio^M

impluvium
impluvio^M
impluvium^M
Impluvium^N
impluvio^M

mosaic
mosaico^M
mosaïque^F
Mosaik^N
mosaico^M

shop
tienda^F
boutique^F
Laden^M
bottega^F

Roman amphitheater

anfiteatro ^{M} romano | amphithéâtre ^{M} romain | römisches Amphitheater ^{N} | anfiteatro ^{M} romano

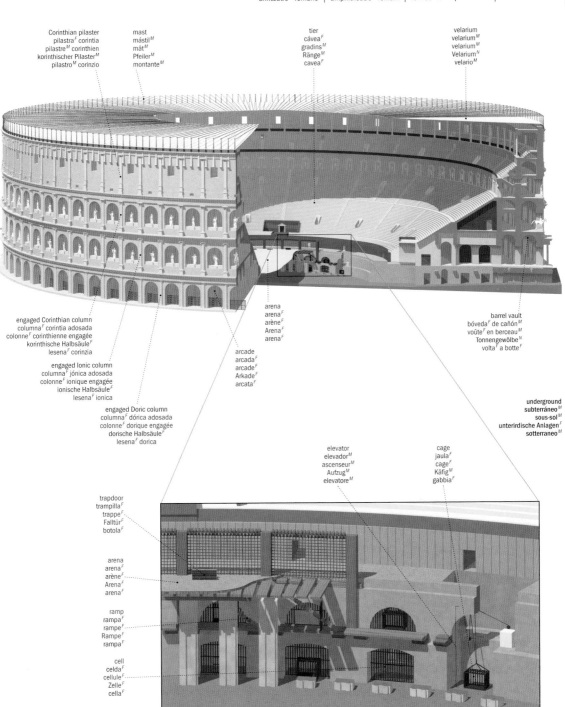

Corinthian pilaster
pilastra ^{F} corintia
pilastre ^{M} corinthien
korinthischer Pilaster ^{M}
pilastro ^{M} corinzio

mast
mástil ^{M}
mât ^{M}
Pfeiler ^{M}
montante ^{M}

tier
cávea ^{F}
gradins ^{M}
Ränge ^{M}
cavea ^{F}

velarium
velarium ^{M}
velarium ^{M}
Velarium ^{N}
velario ^{M}

engaged Corinthian column
columna ^{F} corintia adosada
colonne ^{F} corinthienne engagée
korinthische Halbsäule ^{F}
lesena ^{F} corinzia

engaged Ionic column
columna ^{F} jónica adosada
colonne ^{F} ionique engagée
ionische Halbsäule ^{F}
lesena ^{F} ionica

engaged Doric column
columna ^{F} dórica adosada
colonne ^{F} dorique engagée
dorische Halbsäule ^{F}
lesena ^{F} dorica

arena
arena ^{F}
arène ^{F}
Arena ^{F}
arena ^{F}

arcade
arcada ^{F}
arcade ^{F}
Arkade ^{F}
arcata ^{F}

barrel vault
bóveda ^{F} de cañón ^{M}
voûte ^{F} en berceau ^{M}
Tonnengewölbe ^{N}
volta ^{F} a botte ^{F}

underground
subterráneo ^{M}
sous-sol ^{M}
unterirdische Anlagen ^{F}
sotterraneo ^{M}

elevator
elevador ^{M}
ascenseur ^{M}
Aufzug ^{M}
elevatore ^{M}

cage
jaula ^{F}
cage ^{F}
Käfig ^{M}
gabbia ^{F}

trapdoor
trampilla ^{F}
trappe ^{F}
Falltür ^{F}
botola ^{F}

arena
arena ^{F}
arène ^{F}
Arena ^{F}
arena ^{F}

ramp
rampa ^{F}
rampe ^{F}
Rampe ^{F}
rampa ^{F}

cell
celda ^{F}
cellule ^{F}
Zelle ^{F}
cella ^{F}

ARTS AND ARCHITECTURE

.407

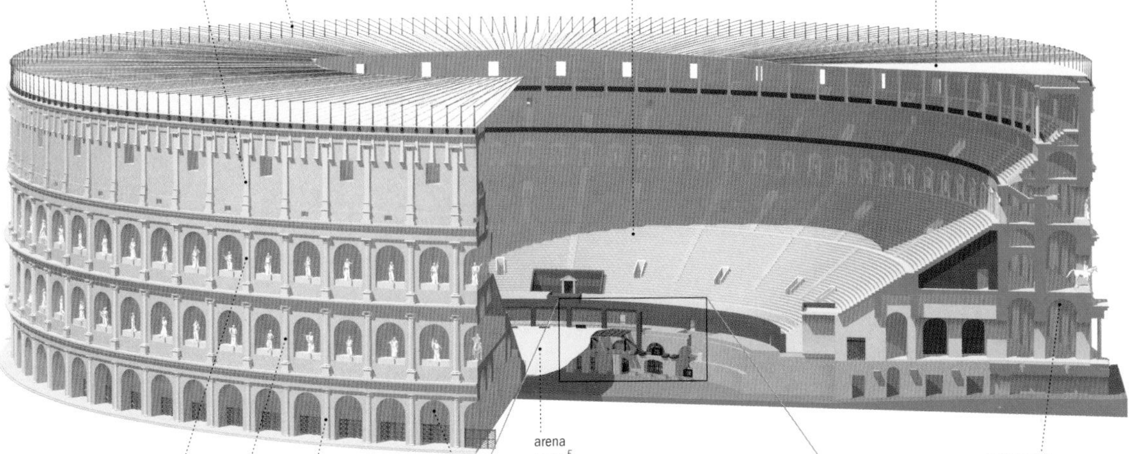

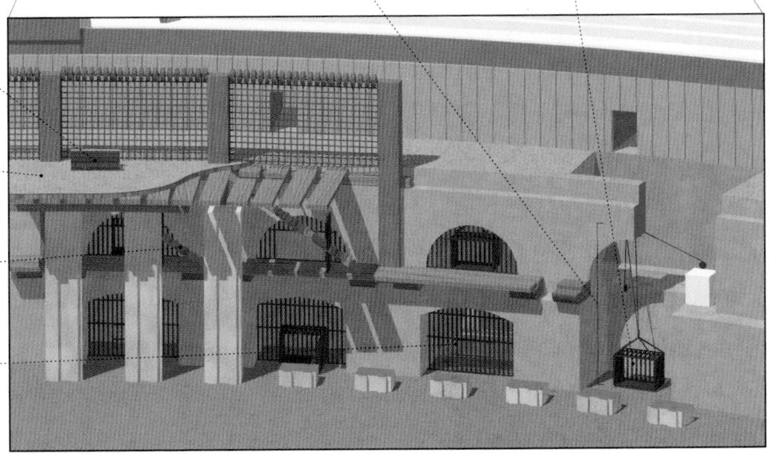

castle

castillo^M | château^M fort | Burg^F | castello^M

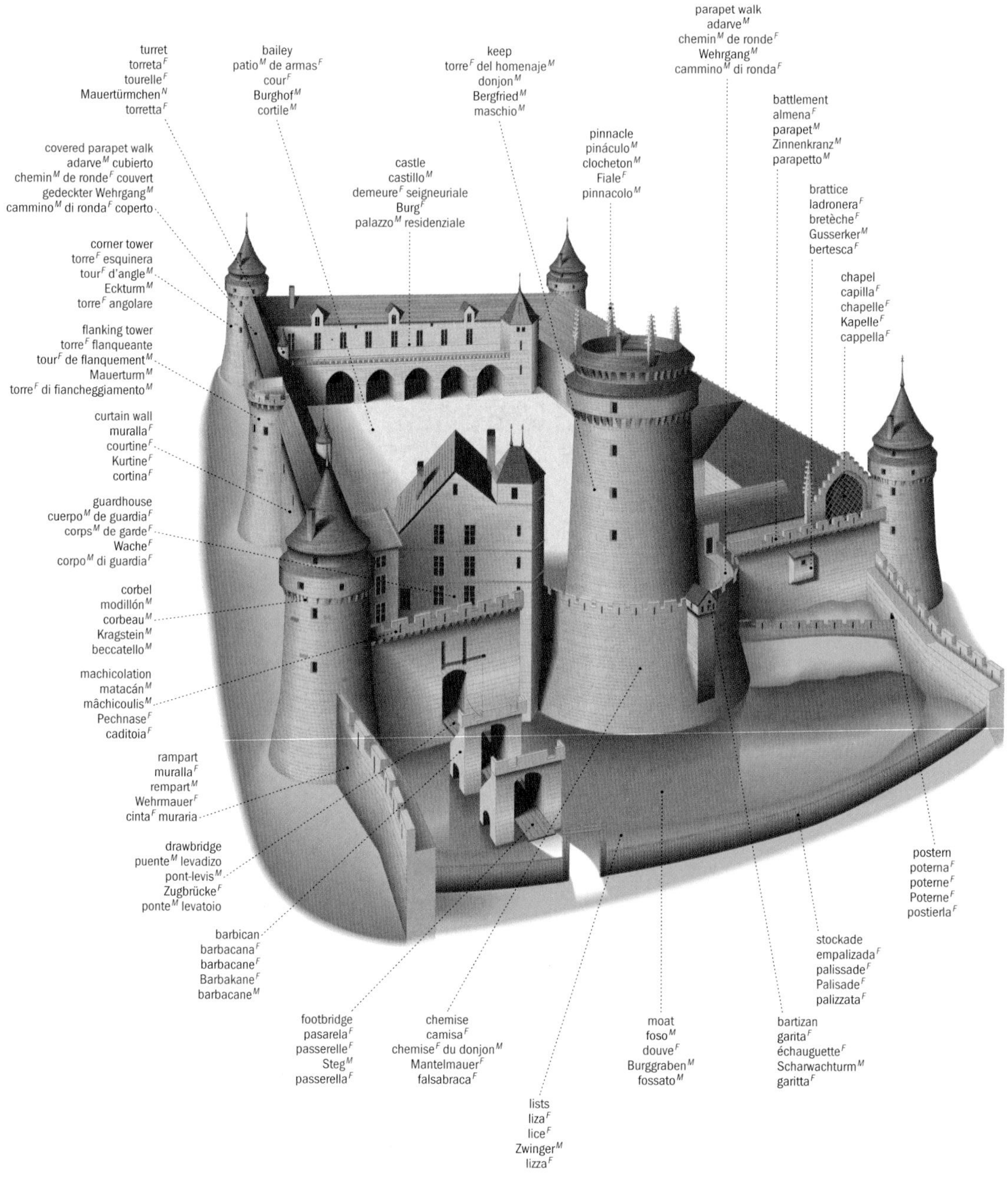

parapet walk
adarve^M
chemin^M de ronde^F
Wehrgang^M
cammino^M di ronda^F

turret
torreta^F
tourelle^F
Mauertürmchen^N
torretta^F

bailey
patio^M de armas^F
cour^F
Burghof^M
cortile^M

keep
torre^F del homenaje^M
donjon^M
Bergfried^M
maschio^M

battlement
almena^F
parapet^M
Zinnenkranz^M
parapetto^M

covered parapet walk
adarve^M cubierto
chemin^M de ronde^F couvert
gedeckter Wehrgang^M
cammino^M di ronda^F coperto

pinnacle
pináculo^M
clocheton^M
Fiale^F
pinnacolo^M

castle
castillo^M
demeure^F seigneuriale
Burg^F
palazzo^M residenziale

brattice
ladronera^F
bretèche^F
Gusserker^M
bertesca^F

corner tower
torre^F esquinera
tour^F d'angle^M
Eckturm^M
torre^F angolare

chapel
capilla^F
chapelle^F
Kapelle^F
cappella^F

flanking tower
torre^F flanqueante
tour^F de flanquement^M
Mauerturm^M
torre^F di fiancheggiamento^M

curtain wall
muralla^F
courtine^F
Kurtine^F
cortina^F

guardhouse
cuerpo^M de guardia^F
corps^M de garde^F
Wache^F
corpo^M di guardia^F

corbel
modillón^M
corbeau^M
Kragstein^M
beccatello^M

machicolation
matacán^M
mâchicoulis^M
Pechnase^F
caditoia^F

rampart
muralla^F
rempart^M
Wehrmauer^F
cinta^F muraria

drawbridge
puente^M levadizo
pont-levis^M
Zugbrücke^F
ponte^M levatoio

postern
poterna^F
poterne^F
Poterne^F
postierla^F

barbican
barbacana^F
barbacane^F
Barbakane^F
barbacane^M

stockade
empalizada^F
palissade^F
Palisade^F
palizzata^F

footbridge
pasarela^F
passerelle^F
Steg^M
passerella^F

chemise
camisa^F
chemise^F du donjon^M
Mantelmauer^F
falsabraca^F

moat
foso^M
douve^F
Burggraben^M
fossato^M

bartizan
garita^F
échauguette^F
Scharwachturm^M
garitta^F

lists
liza^F
lice^F
Zwinger^M
lizza^F

ARTS AND ARCHITECTURE

Vauban fortification

fortificación[F] de Vauban | fortification[F] à la Vauban | Festung[F] | fortificazione[F] alla Vauban

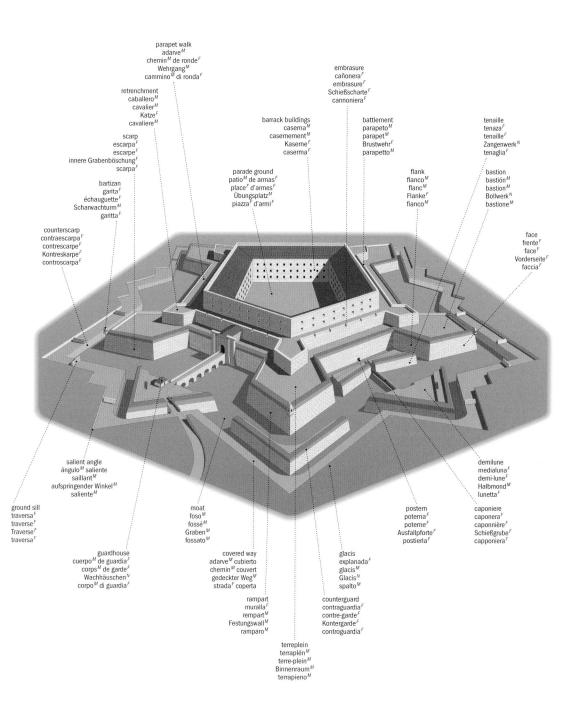

parapet walk
adarve[M]
chemin[M] de ronde[F]
Wehrgang[M]
cammino[M] di ronda[F]

retrenchment
caballero[M]
cavalier[M]
Katze[F]
cavaliere[M]

scarp
escarpa[F]
escarpe[F]
innere Grabenböschung[F]
scarpa[F]

bartizan
garita[F]
échauguette[F]
Scharwachtturm[M]
garitta[F]

counterscarp
contraescarpa[F]
contrescarpe[F]
Kontreskarpe[F]
controscarpa[F]

embrasure
cañonera[F]
embrasure[F]
Schießscharte[F]
cannoniera[F]

barrack buildings
caserna[M]
casernement[M]
Kaserne[F]
caserma[F]

battlement
parapeto[M]
parapet[M]
Brustwehr[F]
parapetto[M]

tenaille
tenaza[F]
tenaille[F]
Zangenwerk[N]
tenaglia[F]

parade ground
patio[M] de armas[F]
place[F] d'armes[F]
Übungsplatz[M]
piazza[F] d'armi[F]

flank
flanco[M]
flanc[M]
Flanke[F]
fianco[M]

bastion
bastión[M]
bastion[M]
Bollwerk[N]
bastione[M]

face
frente[F]
face[F]
Vorderseite[F]
faccia[F]

salient angle
ángulo[M] saliente
saillant[M]
aufspringender Winkel[M]
saliente[M]

demilune
medialuna[F]
demi-lune[F]
Halbmond[M]
lunetta[F]

ground sill
traversa[F]
traverse[F]
Traverse[F]
traversa[F]

moat
foso[M]
fossé[M]
Graben[M]
fossato[M]

postern
poterna[F]
poterne[F]
Ausfallpforte[F]
postierla[F]

caponiere
caponera[F]
caponnière[F]
Schießgrube[F]
capponiera[F]

guardhouse
cuerpo[M] de guardia[F]
corps[M] de garde[F]
Wachhäuschen[N]
corpo[M] di guardia[F]

covered way
adarve[M] cubierto
chemin[M] couvert
gedeckter Weg[M]
strada[F] coperta

glacis
explanada[F]
glacis[M]
Glacis[N]
spalto[M]

rampart
muralla[F]
rempart[M]
Festungswall[M]
ramparo[M]

counterguard
contraguardia[F]
contre-garde[F]
Kontergarde[F]
controguardia[F]

terreplein
terraplén[M]
terre-plein[M]
Binnenraum[M]
terrapieno[M]

ARTS AND ARCHITECTURE

cathedral

catedral^F | cathédrale^F | Dom^M | cattedrale^F

Gothic cathedral
catedral^F gótica
cathédrale^F gothique
gotischer Dom^M
cattedrale^F gotica

vault
bóveda^F
voûte^F
Gewölbe^N
volta^F

keystone
clave^F
clé^F de voûte^F
Schlussstein^M
chiave^F di volta^F

traverse arch
nervio^M transversal
arc^M-doubleau^M
Schildbogen^M
arco^M trasversale

lierne
nervio^M secundario
lierne^F
Scheitelrippe^F
costolone^M dorsale

tierceron
tercelete^F
tierceron^M
Tierceron^M
costolone^M intermedio

formeret
arco^M formero
arc^M-formeret^M
Gurtbogen^M
arco^M longitudinale

diagonal buttress
nervio^M diagonal
arc^M diagonal
Kreuzrippe^F
arco^M diagonale

tower
torre^F
tour^F
Turm^M
torre^F

pinnacle
pináculo^M
pinacle^M
Fiale^F
pinnacolo^M

abutment
estribo^M
culée^F
Widerlager^M
spalla^F

transept spire
aguja^F del transepto^M
flèche^F de transept^M
Vierungsturm^M
guglia^F

flying buttress
arbotante^M
arc^M-boutant
Strebebogen^M
arco^M rampante

Lady chapel
capilla^F axial
chapelle^F axiale
Chorscheitelkapelle^F
cappella^F assiale

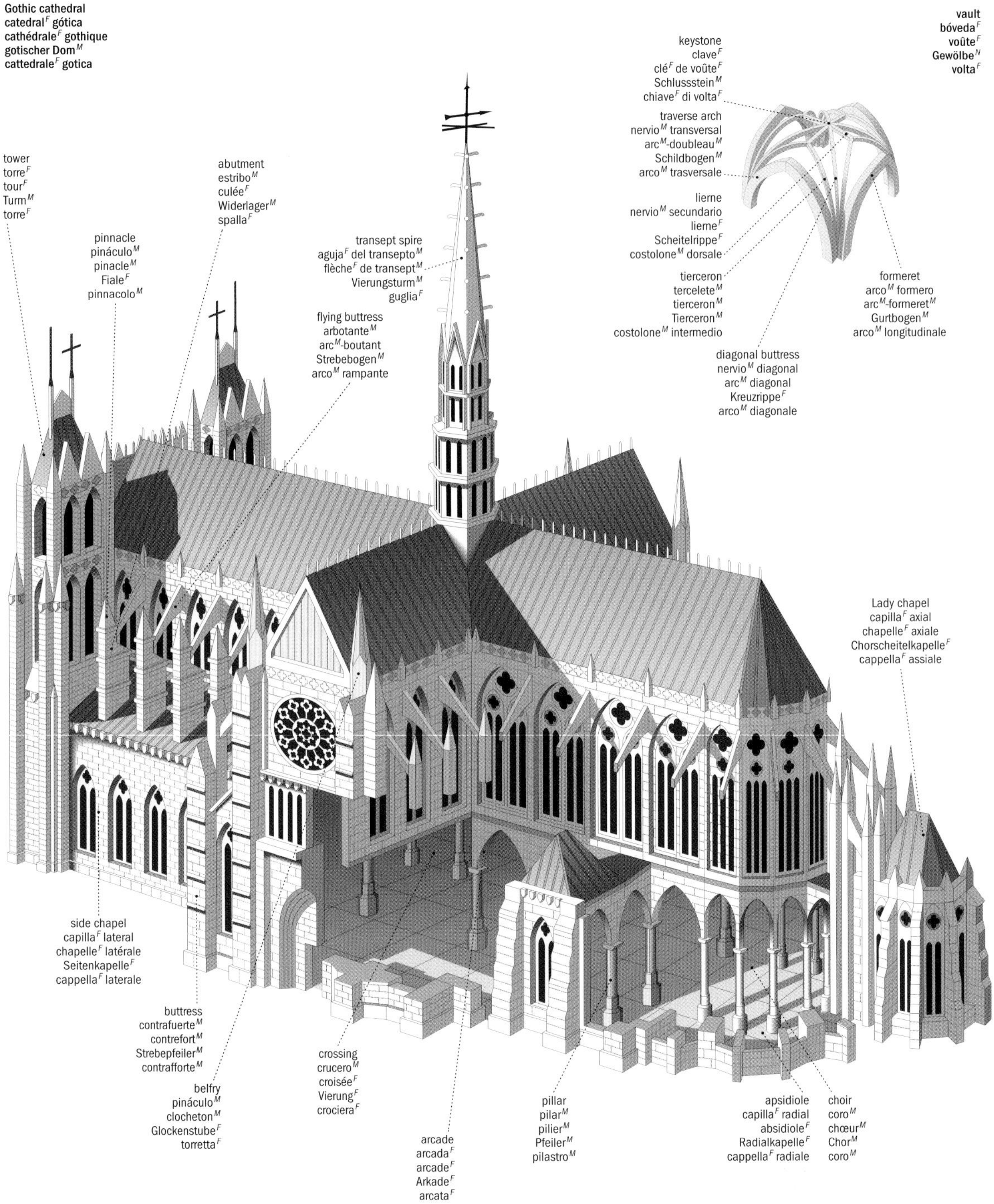

side chapel
capilla^F lateral
chapelle^F latérale
Seitenkapelle^F
cappella^F laterale

buttress
contrafuerte^M
contrefort^M
Strebepfeiler^M
contrafforte^M

belfry
pináculo^M
clocheton^M
Glockenstube^F
torretta^F

crossing
crucero^M
croisée^F
Vierung^F
crociera^F

arcade
arcada^F
arcade^F
Arkade^F
arcata^F

pillar
pilar^M
pilier^M
Pfeiler^M
pilastro^M

apsidiole
capilla^F radial
absidiole^F
Radialkapelle^F
cappella^F radiale

choir
coro^M
chœur^M
Chor^M
coro^M

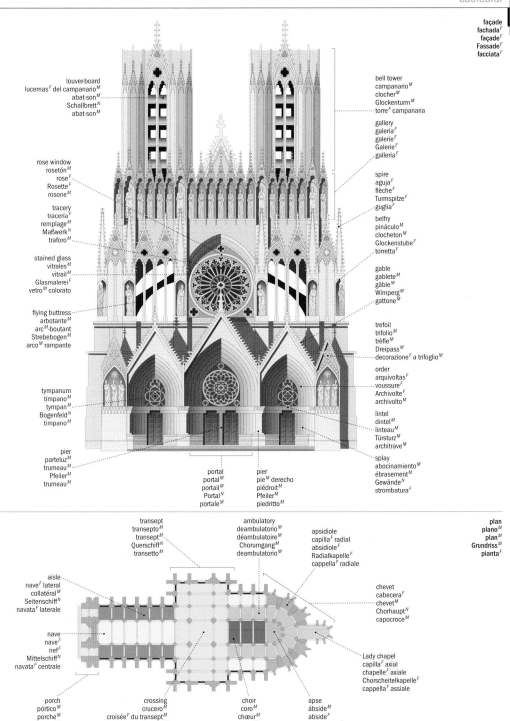

façade
fachada[F]
façade[F]
Fassade[F]
facciata[F]

louver-board
lucernas[F] del campanario[M]
abat-son[M]
Schallbrett[N]
abat-son[M]

bell tower
campanario[M]
clocher[M]
Glockenturm[M]
torre[F] campanaria

gallery
galería[F]
galerie[F]
Galerie[F]
galleria[F]

rose window
rosetón[M]
rose[F]
Rosette[F]
rosone[M]

spire
aguja[F]
flèche[F]
Turmspitze[F]
guglia[F]

tracery
tracería[F]
remplage[M]
Maßwerk[N]
traforo[M]

belfry
pináculo[M]
clocheton[M]
Glockenstube[F]
torretta[F]

stained glass
vitrales[M]
vitrail[M]
Glasmalerei[F]
vetro[M] colorato

gable
gablete[M]
gâble[M]
Wimperg[M]
gattone[M]

flying buttress
arbotante[M]
arc[M]-boutant
Strebebogen[M]
arco[M] rampante

trefoil
trifolio[M]
trèfle[M]
Dreipass[M]
decorazione[F] a trifoglio[M]

order
arquivoltas[F]
voussure[F]
Archivolte[F]
archivolto[M]

tympanum
tímpano[M]
tympan[M]
Bogenfeld[N]
timpano[M]

lintel
dintel[M]
linteau[M]
Türsturz[M]
architrave[M]

pier
parteluz[M]
trumeau[M]
Pfeiler[M]
trumeau[M]

portal
portal[M]
portail[M]
Portal[N]
portale[M]

pier
pie[M] derecho
piédroit[M]
Pfeiler[M]
piedritto[M]

splay
abocinamiento[M]
ébrasement[M]
Gewände[N]
strombatura[F]

plan
plano[M]
plan[M]
Grundriss[M]
pianta[F]

transept
transepto[M]
transept[M]
Querschiff[N]
transetto[M]

ambulatory
deambulatorio[M]
déambulatoire[M]
Chorumgang[M]
deambulatorio[M]

apsidiole
capilla[F] radial
absidiole[F]
Radialkapelle[F]
cappella[F] radiale

aisle
nave[F] lateral
collatéral[M]
Seitenschiff[N]
navata[F] laterale

chevet
cabecera[F]
chevet[M]
Chorhaupt[N]
capocroce[M]

nave
nave[F]
nef[F]
Mittelschiff[N]
navata[F] centrale

Lady chapel
capilla[F] axial
chapelle[F] axiale
Chorscheitelkapelle[F]
cappella[F] assiale

porch
pórtico[M]
porche[M]
Portal[N]
portico[M]

crossing
crucero[M]
croisée[F] du transept
Vierung[F]
crociera[F]

choir
coro[M]
chœur[M]
Chor[M]
coro[M]

apse
ábside[M]
abside[F]
Hauptapsis[F]
abside[F]

pagoda

pagoda^F | pagode^F | Pagode^F | pagoda^F

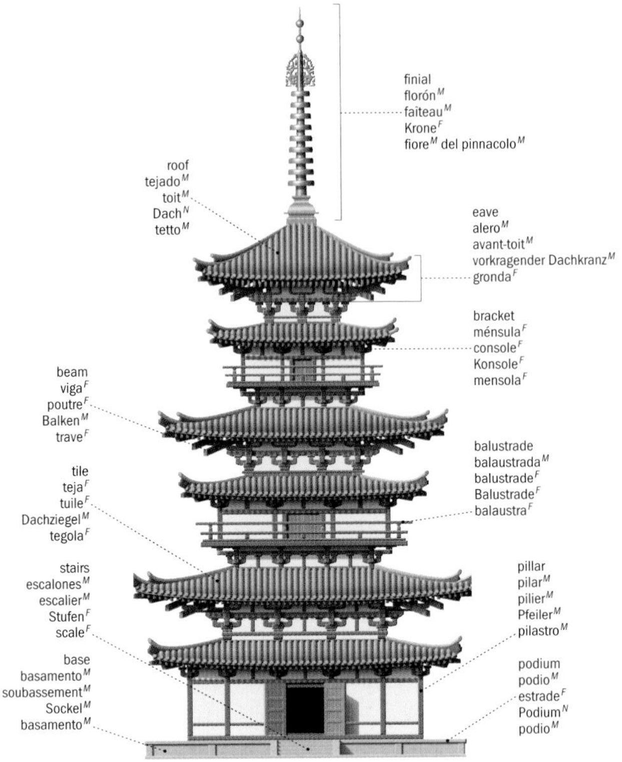

finial
florón^M
faiteau^M
Krone^F
fiore^M del pinnacolo^M

roof
tejado^M
toit^M
Dach^N
tetto^M

eave
alero^M
avant-toit^M
vorkragender Dachkranz^M
gronda^F

bracket
ménsula^F
console^F
Konsole^F
mensola^F

beam
viga^F
poutre^F
Balken^M
trave^F

balustrade
balaustrada^M
balustrade^F
Balustrade^F
balaustra^F

tile
teja^F
tuile^F
Dachziegel^M
tegola^F

stairs
escalones^M
escalier^M
Stufen^F
scale^F

pillar
pilar^M
pilier^M
Pfeiler^M
pilastro^M

base
basamento^M
soubassement^M
Sockel^M
basamento^M

podium
podio^M
estrade^F
Podium^N
podio^M

Aztec temple

templo^M azteca | temple^M aztèque | aztekischer Tempel^M | tempio^M azteco

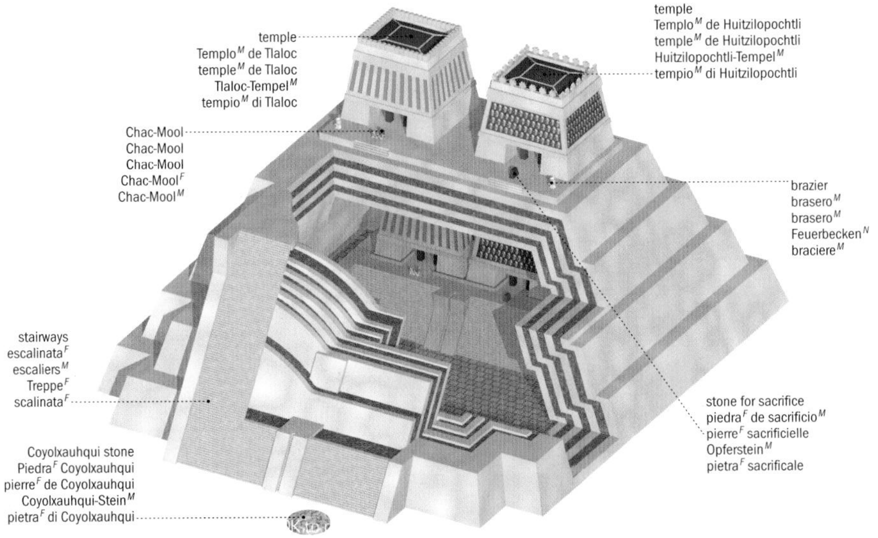

temple
Templo^M de Tlaloc
temple^M de Tlaloc
Tlaloc-Tempel^M
tempio^M di Tlaloc

temple
Templo^M de Huitzilopochtli
temple^M de Huitzilopochtli
Huitzilopochtli-Tempel^M
tempio^M di Huitzilopochtli

Chac-Mool
Chac-Mool
Chac-Mool
Chac-Mool^F
Chac-Mool^M

brazier
brasero^M
brasero^M
Feuerbecken^N
braciere^M

stairways
escalinata^F
escaliers^M
Treppe^F
scalinata^F

stone for sacrifice
piedra^F de sacrificio^M
pierre^F sacrificielle
Opferstein^M
pietra^F sacrificale

Coyolxauhqui stone
Piedra^F Coyolxauhqui
pierre de Coyolxauhqui
Coyolxauhqui-Stein^M
pietra^F di Coyolxauhqui

elements of architecture

elementos*M* arquitectónicos | éléments*M* d'architecture*F* | Architekturelemente*N* | elementi*M* architettonici

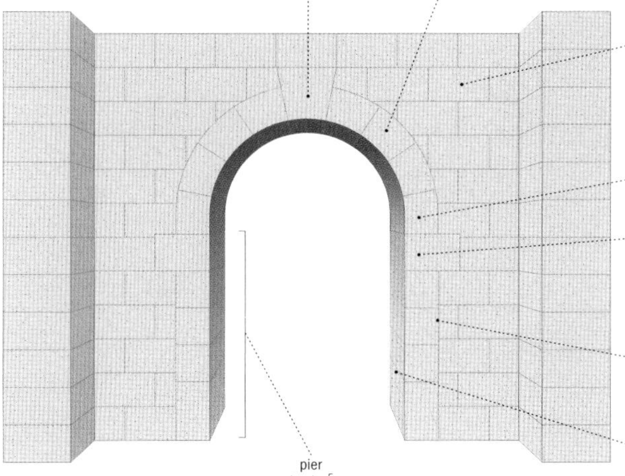

keystone
clave*F*
clé*F* de voûte*F*
Schlussstein*M*
chiave*F*

voussoir
dovela*F*
claveau*M*
Keilstein*M*
fianco*M*

semicircular arch
arco*M* de medio punto*M*
arc*M* en plein cintre*M*
Rundbogen*M*
arco*M* a tutto sesto

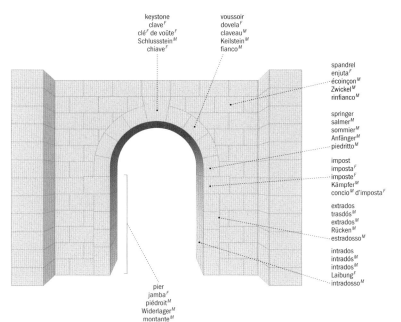

spandrel
enjuta*F*
écoinçon*M*
Zwickel*M*
rinfianco*M*

springer
salmer*M*
sommier*M*
Anfänger*M*
piedritto*M*

impost
imposta*F*
imposte*F*
Kämpfer*M*
concio*M* d'imposta*F*

extrados
trasdós*M*
extrados*M*
Rücken*M*
estradosso*M*

intrados
intradós*M*
intrados*M*
Laibung*F*
intradosso*M*

pier
jamba*F*
piédroit*M*
Widerlager*M*
montante*M*

examples of arches
ejemplos*M* de arcos*M*
exemples*M* d'arcs*M*
Beispiele*N* für Bögen*M*
esempi*M* di archi*M*

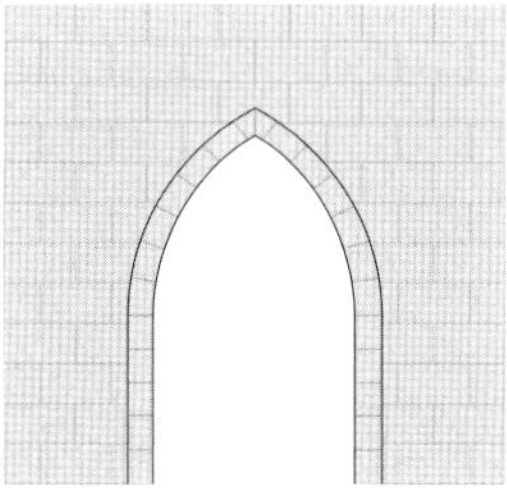

equilateral
ojival*M*
en ogive*F*
Spitzbogen*M*
ogivale

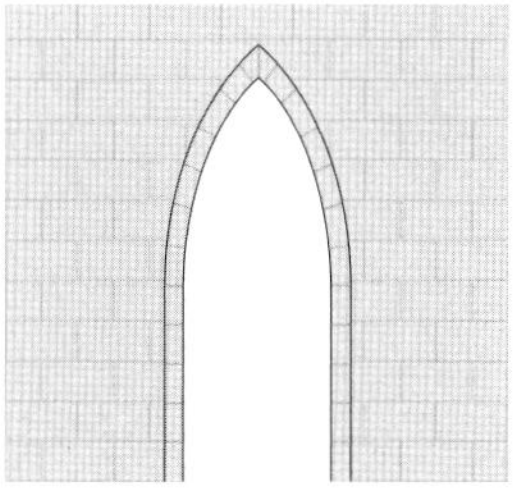

lancet
de ojiva*F* lanceolada
en lancette*F*
Lanzettbogen*M*
lanceolato

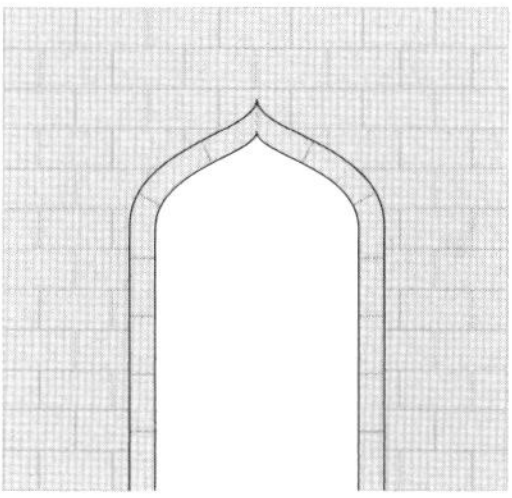

ogee
conopial*M*
en accolade*F*
Kielbogen*M*
inflesso

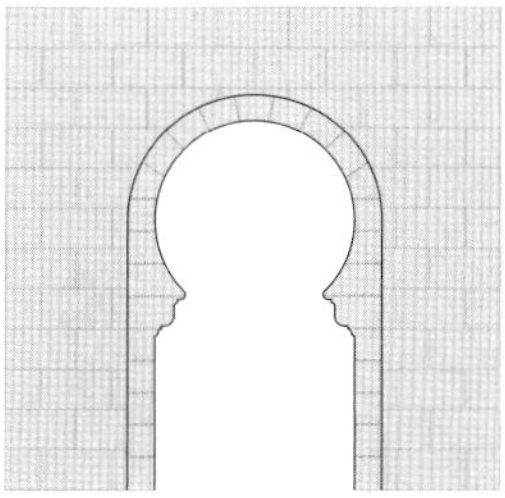

horseshoe
de herradura*F*
en fer*M* à cheval*M*
Hufeisenbogen*M*
a ferro*M* di cavallo*M*

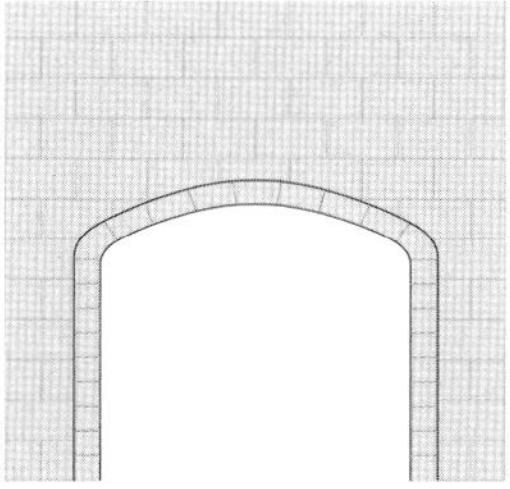

basket handle
rebajado*M*
surbaissé
Flachbogen*M*
ribassato policentrico

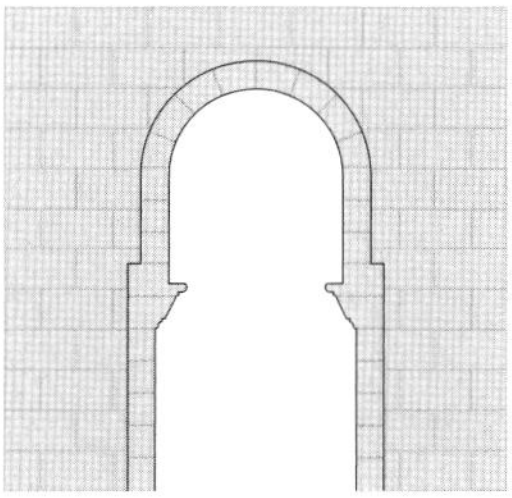

stilted
peraltado*M*
surhaussé
gestelzter Bogen*M*
rialzato

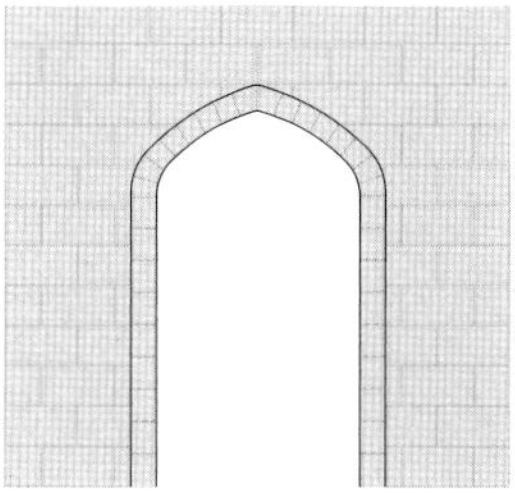

Tudor
Tudor
Tudor
Tudorbogen*M*
Tudor

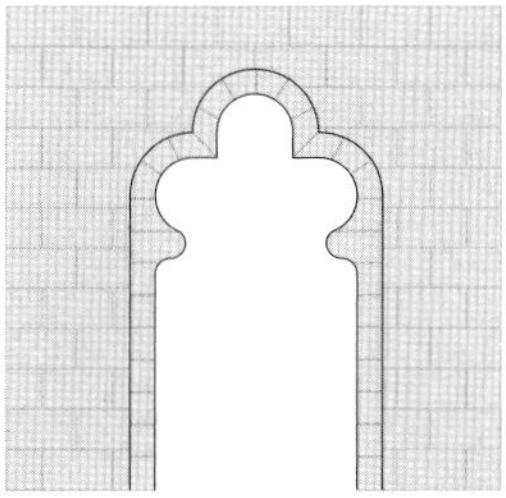

trefoil
trebolado
trilobé
Kleeblattbogen*M*
trilobato

elements of architecture

examples of roofs
ejemplos^M **de cubiertas**^F
exemples^M **de toits**^M
Beispiele^N **für Dächer**^N
esempi^M **di tetti**^M

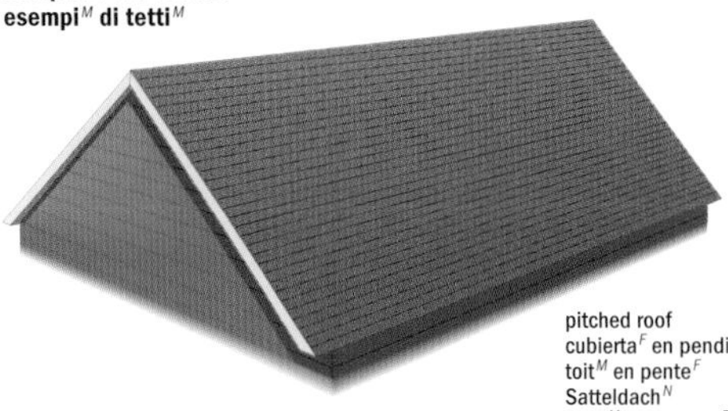

pitched roof
cubierta^F en pendiente^F
toit^M en pente^F
Satteldach^N
tetto^M a capanna^F

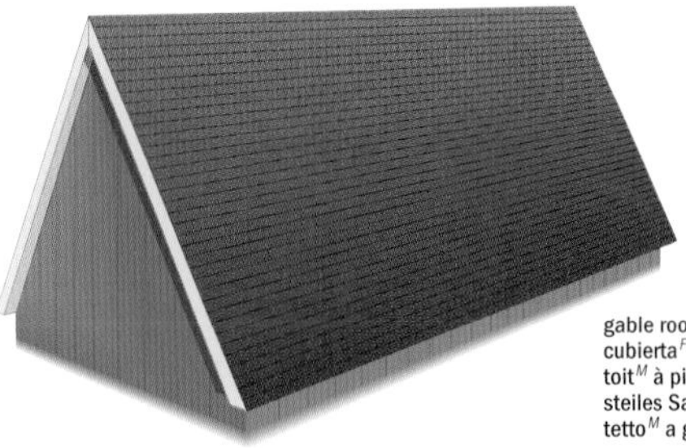

gable roof
cubierta^F de dos aguas^F
toit^M à pignon^M
steiles Satteldach^N
tetto^M a ghimberga^F

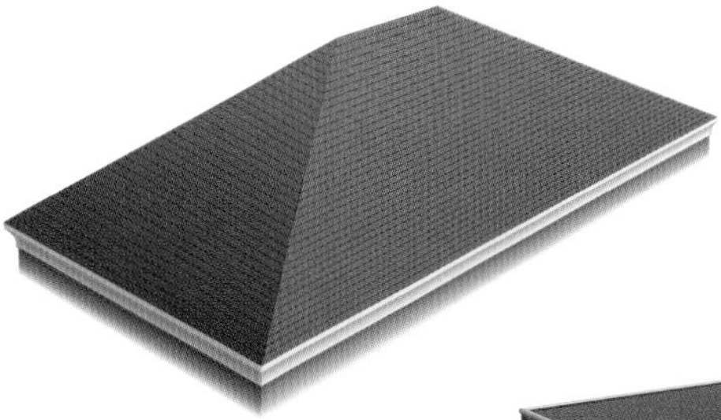

hip roof
cubierta^F de cuatro aguas^F
toit^M à deux croupes^F
Walmdach^N
tetto^M a padiglione^M

flat roof
plano^M
toit^M plat
Flachdach^N
tetto^M piano

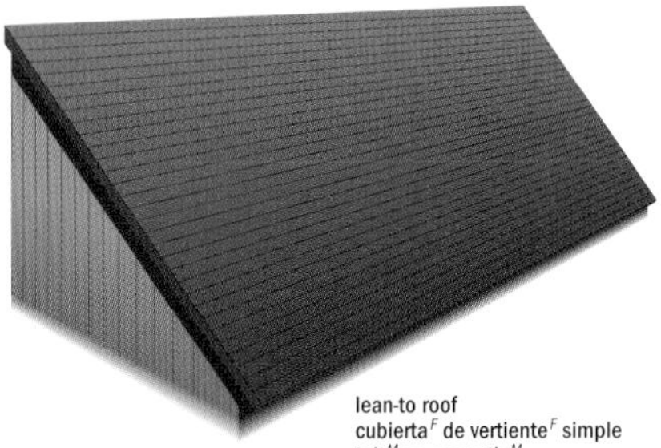

lean-to roof
cubierta^F de vertiente^F simple
toit^M en appentis^M
Pultdach^N
tetto^M a falda^F unica

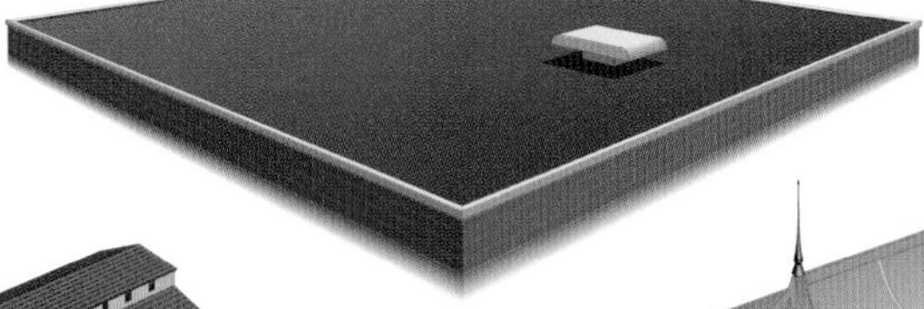

monitor roof
cubierta^F de linternilla^F
toit^M avec lanterneau^M
Dach^N mit Firstlaterne^F
tetto^M con lucernario^M

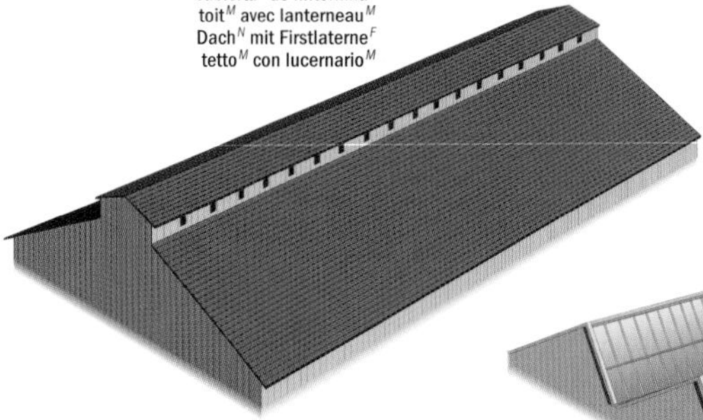

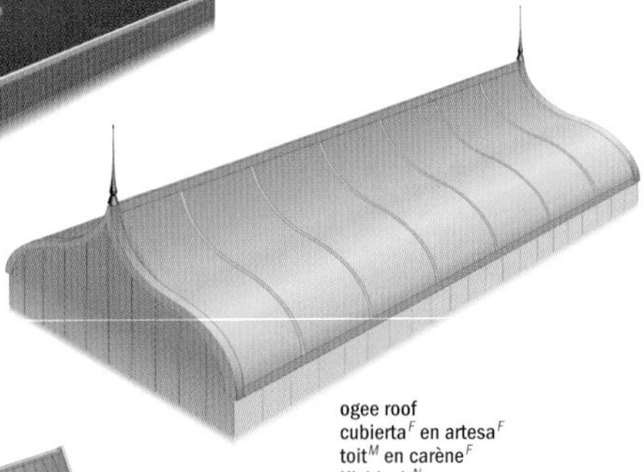

ogee roof
cubierta^F en artesa^F
toit^M en carène^F
Kieldach^N
tetto^M a carena^F

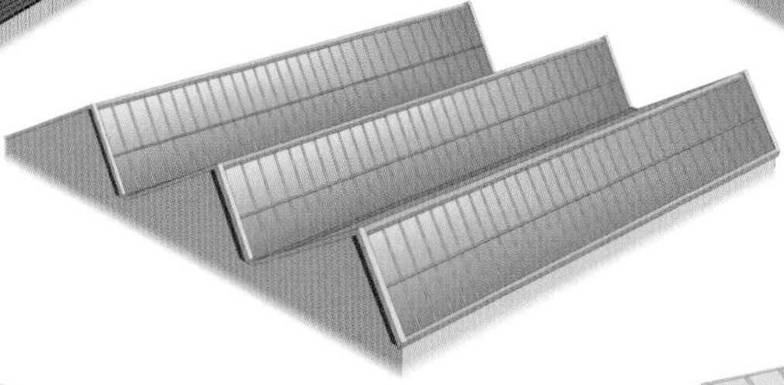

sawtooth roof
cubierta^F en diente^M de sierra^F
toit^M en shed^M
Sheddach^N
tetto^M a shed^M

mansard roof
cubierta^F mansarda
toit^M à la Mansard
Mansardendach^N
tetto^M a mansarda^F

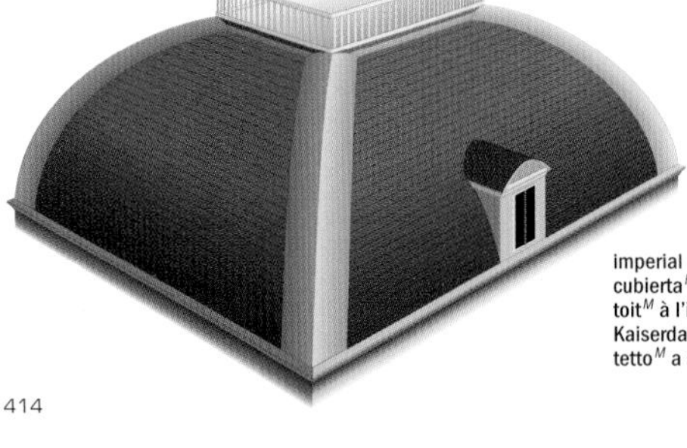

imperial roof
cubierta^F imperial
toit^M à l'impériale^F
Kaiserdach^N
tetto^M a schifo^M

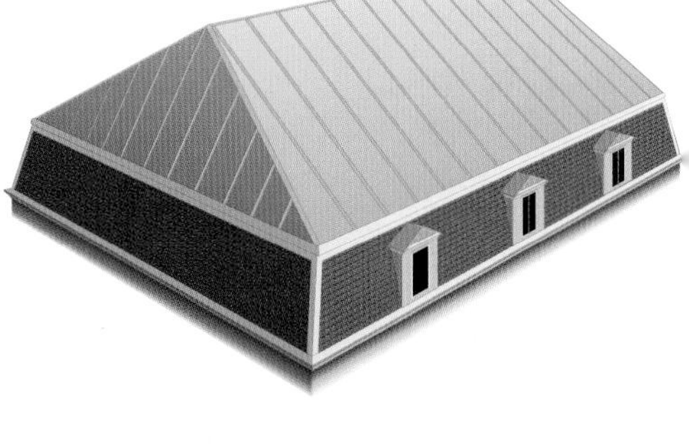

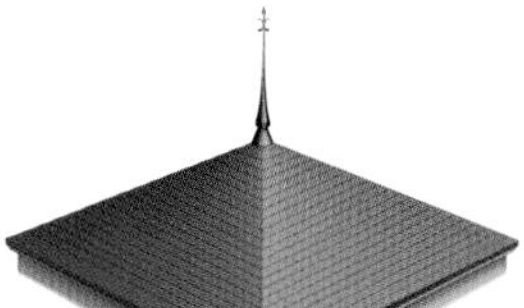

pavilion roof
cubierta^F de pabellón^M
toit^M en pavillon^M
Pavillondach^N
tetto^M a piramide^F

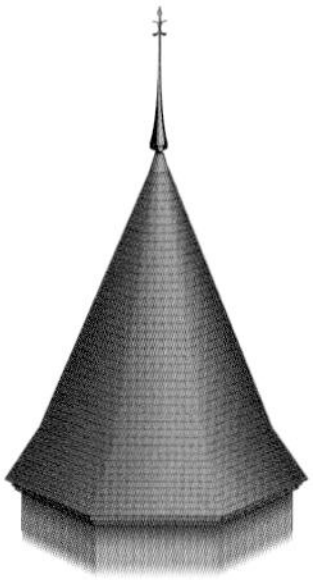

sloped turret
cubierta^F de torrecilla^F
toit^M à tourelle^F à pans^M
Faltkegeldach^N
torretta^F spiovente

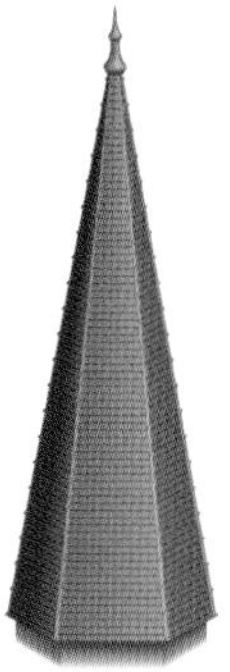

helm roof
cubierta^F piramidal
toit^M en flèche^F
Helmdach^N
tetto^M a padiglione^F da torre^F

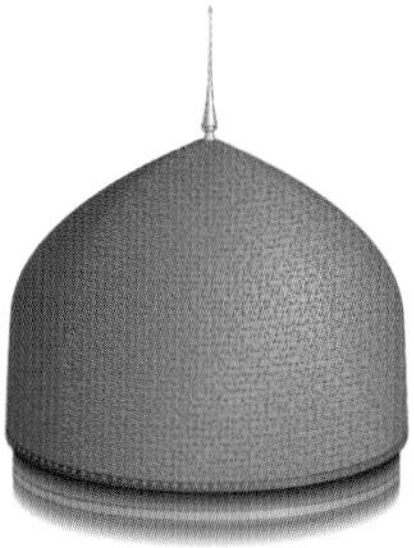

bell roof
cubierta^F de cúpula^F peraltada
toit^M en coupole^F
Glockendach^N
cupola^F ovoide rialzata

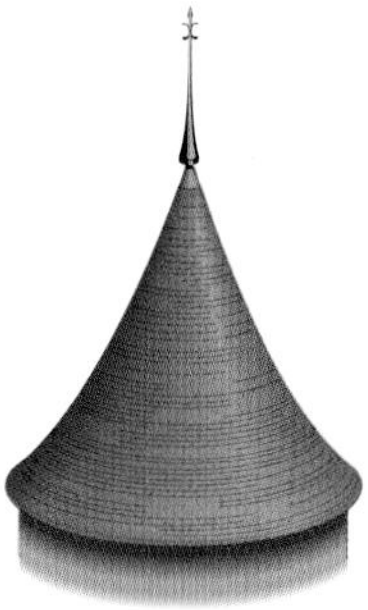

conical broach roof
cubierta^F cónica
toit^M en poivrière^F
Kegeldach^N
tetto^M a cono^M

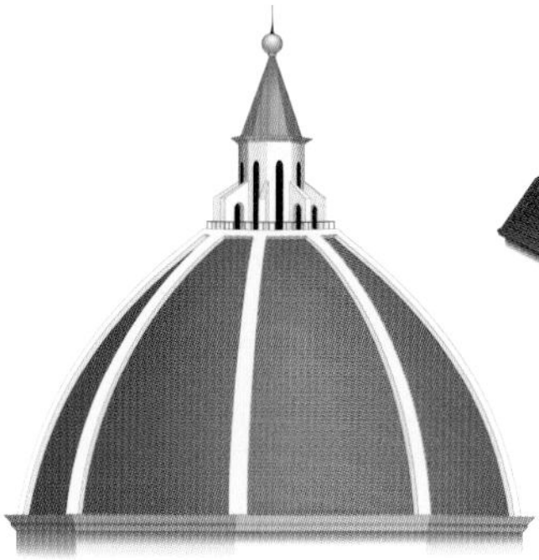

dome roof
cúpula^F
toit^M en dôme^M
Kuppeldach^N
cupola^F

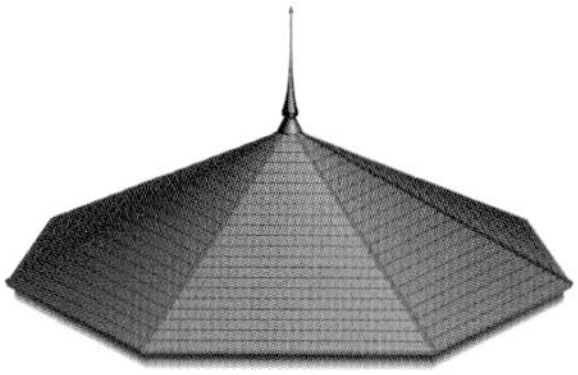

rotunda roof
cubierta^F de rotonda^F
toit^M en rotonde^F
Pyramidendach^N
tetto^M a ombrello^M

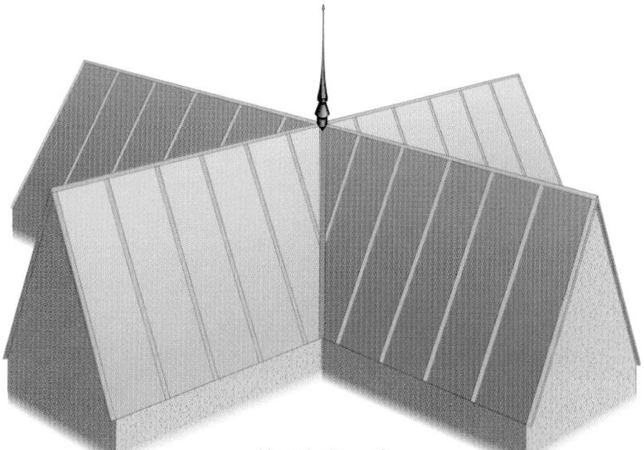

hip-and-valley roof
cubierta^F de cuatro aguas^F con canalera^F
toit^M à quatre versants^M
eingeschnittenes Satteldach^N
tetto^M a bracci^M

ARTS AND ARCHITECTURE

examples of windows
ejemplos^M de ventanas^F
exemples^M de fenêtres^F
Beispiele^N für Fenster^N
esempi^M di finestre^F

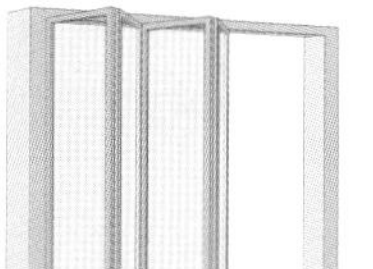

sliding folding window
ventana^F de librillo^M
fenêtre^F en accordéon^M
Faltfenster^N
finestra^F a libro^M

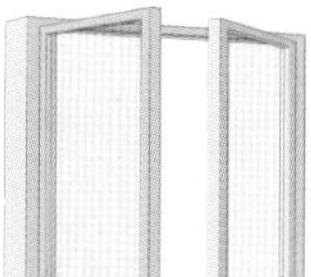

French window
ventana^F a la francesa^F
fenêtre^F à la française^F
Drehflügel^M nach innen
finestra^F a battenti^M con apertura^F all'interno^M

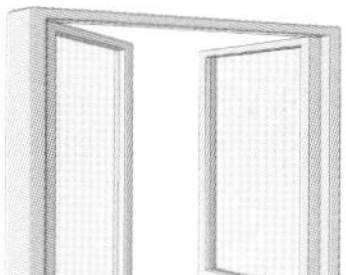

casement window
ventana^F a la inglesa^F
fenêtre^F à l'anglaise^F
Drehflügel^M nach außen
finestra^F a battenti^M

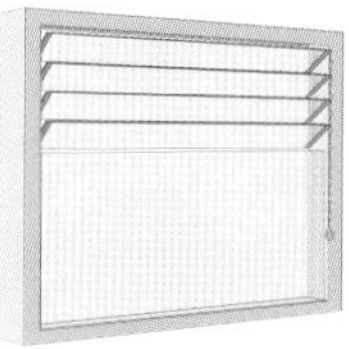

louvered window
ventana^F de celosia^F
fenêtre^F à jalousies^F
Jalousiefenster^N
finestra^F a gelosia^F

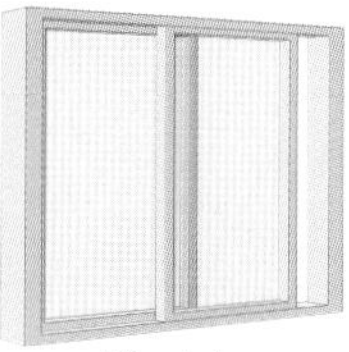

sliding window
ventana^F corredera
fenêtre^F coulissante
horizontales Schiebefenster^N
finestra^F scorrevole

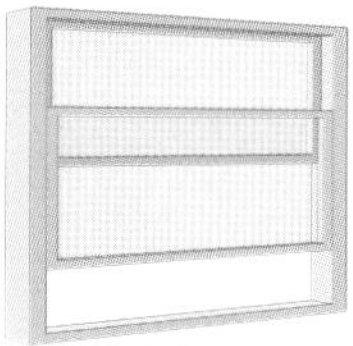

sash window
ventana^F de guillotina^F
fenêtre^F à guillotine^F
vertikales Schiebefenster^N
finestra^F a ghigliottina^F

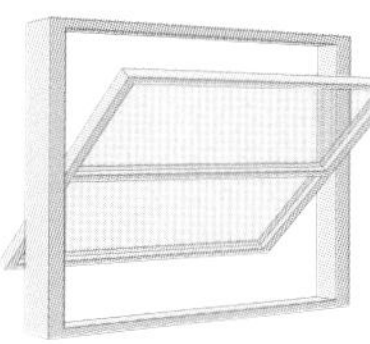

horizontal pivoting window
ventana^F basculante
fenêtre^F basculante
Schwingflügel^M
finestra^F a bilico^M orizzontale

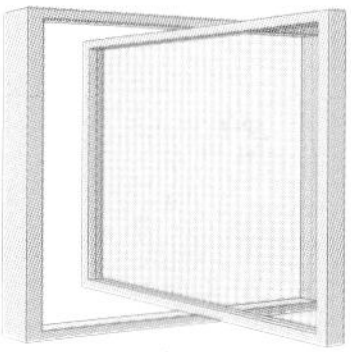

vertical pivoting window
ventana^F pivotante
fenêtre^F pivotante
Wendeflügel^M
finestra^F a bilico^M verticale

elements of architecture

examples of doors
ejemplos^M **de puertas**^{F}
exemples^M **de portes**^{F}
Beispiele^N **für Türen**^{F}
esempi^M **di porte**^{F}

manual revolving door
puerta^F giratoria manual
porte^F à tambour^M manuelle
Drehtür^F
porta^F girevole manuale

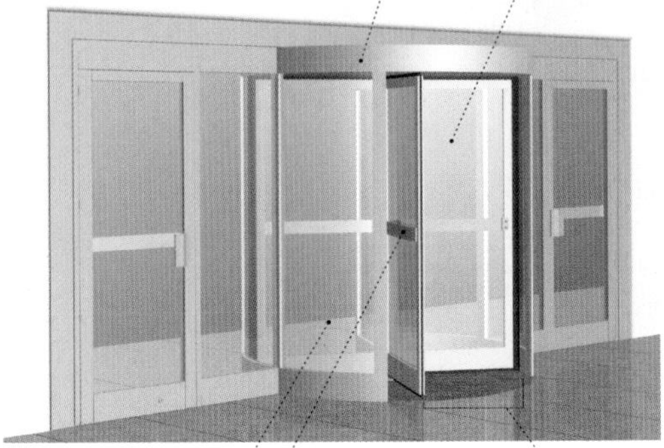

canopy
tambor^M
couronne^F
Gehäusedach^N
cappello^M

wing
hoja^F
vantail^M
Flügel^M
battente^M

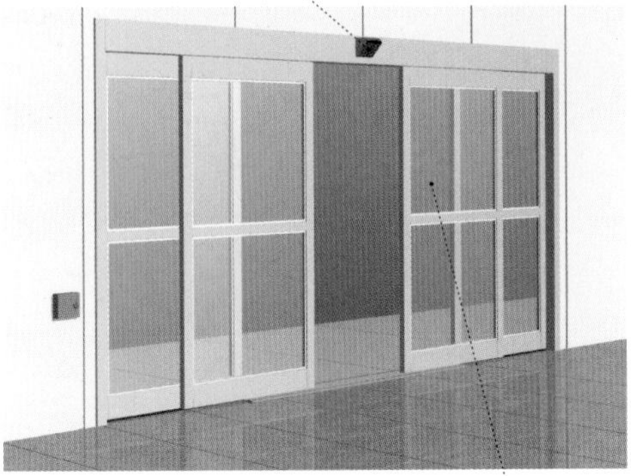

motion detector
sensor^M de movimiento
détecteur^M de mouvement^M
Bewegungsmelder^M
rilevatore^M di movimento^M

automatic sliding door
puerta^F corredera automática
porte^F coulissante automatique
automatische Schiebetür^F
porta^F scorrevole automatica

enclosure
estructura^F interior
sas^M
Drehgehäuse^N
alloggiamento

push bar
tirador^M
barre^F de poussée^F
Handgriff^M
maniglia^F di spinta^F

compartment
compartimiento^M
compartiment^M
Zelle^F
vano^M

wing
hoja^F
vantail^M
Flügel^M
battente^M

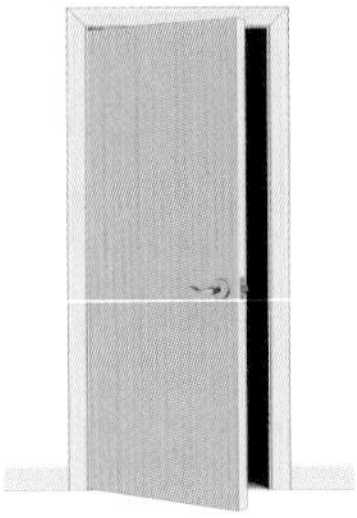

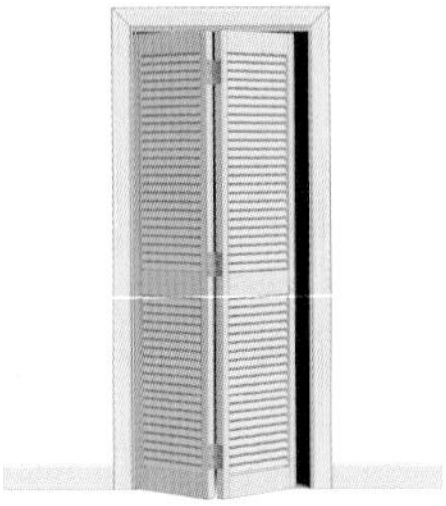

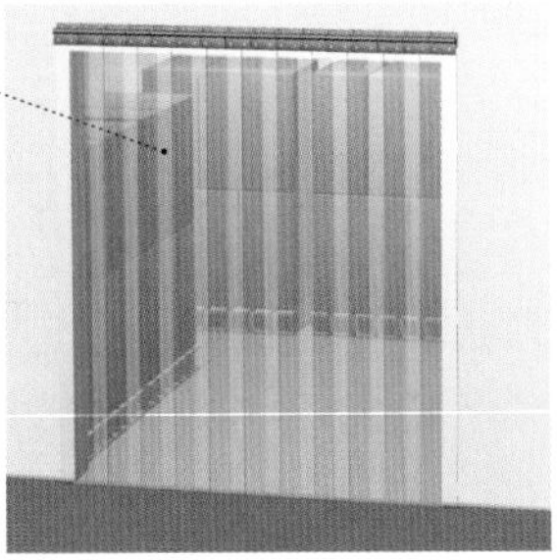

strip
tira^F
lanière^F
Streifen^M
banda^F

conventional door
puerta^F convencional
porte^F classique
Drehflügeltür^F
porta^F a un battente^M

folding door
puerta^F plegable
porte^F pliante
Falttür^F
porta^F a libro^M

strip door
puerta^F de tiras^F
porte^F à lanières^F
Streifenvorhang^M
porta^F a bande^F verticali

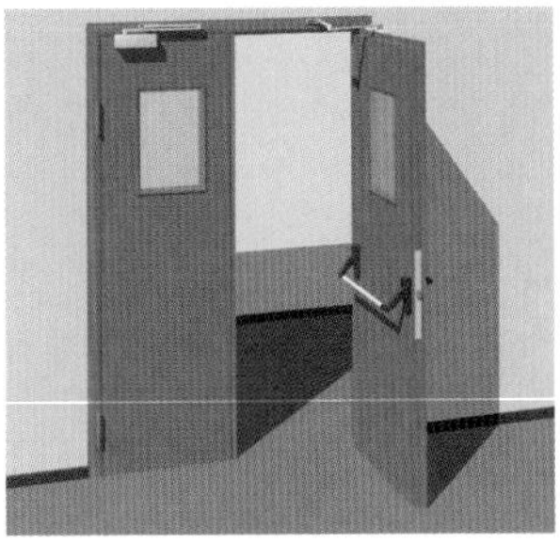

fire door
puerta^F cortafuego
porte^F coupe-feu
Feuerschutztür^F
porta^F antincendio

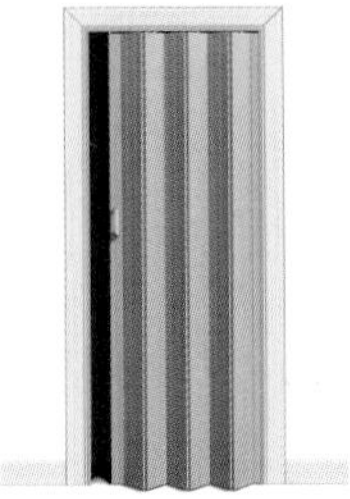

sliding folding door
puerta^F de librillo^M
porte^F accordéon^M
Harmonikatür^F
porta^F a fisarmonica^F

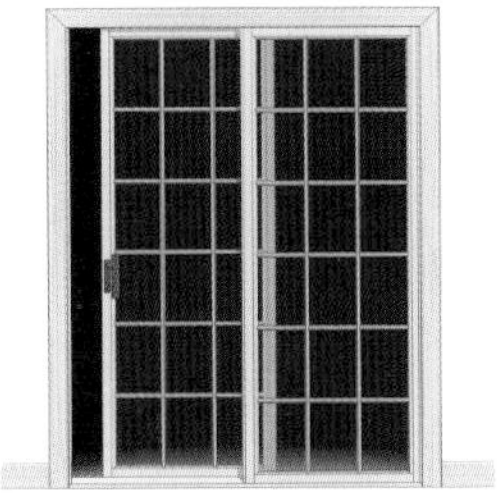

sliding door
puerta^F corredera
porte^F coulissante
Schiebetür^F
porta^F scorrevole

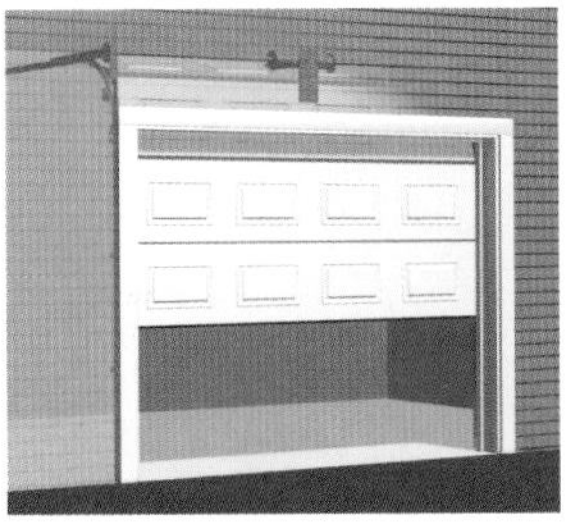

sectional garage door
puerta^F de garaje^M seccional
porte^F de garage^M sectionnelle
Sektionalgaragentor^N
porta^F sezionale del garage^M

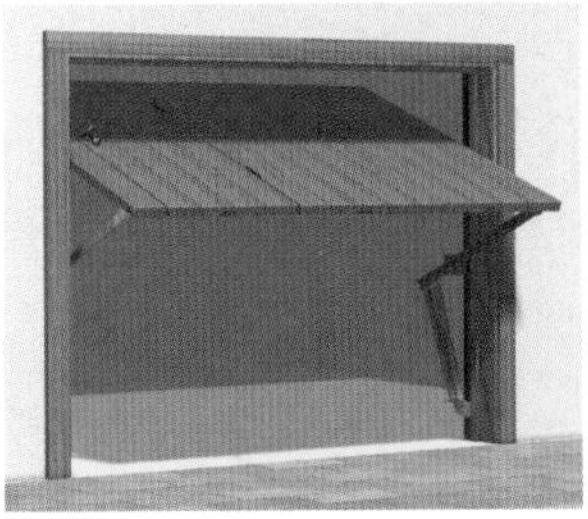

up and over garage door
puerta^F basculante de garaje^M
porte^F de garage^M basculante
Schwinggaragentor^N
porta^F basculante del garage^M

ARTS AND ARCHITECTURE

escalator

escalera^F mecánica | escalier^M mécanique | Rolltreppe^F | scala^F mobile

handrail
pasamanos^M
main^F courante
Handlauf^M
corrimano^M

balustrade
barandilla^F
balustrade^F
Balustrade^F
balaustra^F

newel
cabeza^F
crosse^F
Gerüstprofil^N
profilo^M di sostegno^M

comb
peine^M
peigne^M
Kamm^M
zigrinatura^F

lower landing
rellano^M inferior
palier^M inférieur
unterer Absatz^M
piattaforma^F inferiore

upper landing
rellano^M superior
palier^M supérieur
oberer Absatz^M
piattaforma^F superiore

step
peldaño^M
marche^F
Trittstufe^F
gradino^M

skirt
rodapié^M
plinthe^F
Sockelleiste^F
zoccolo^M

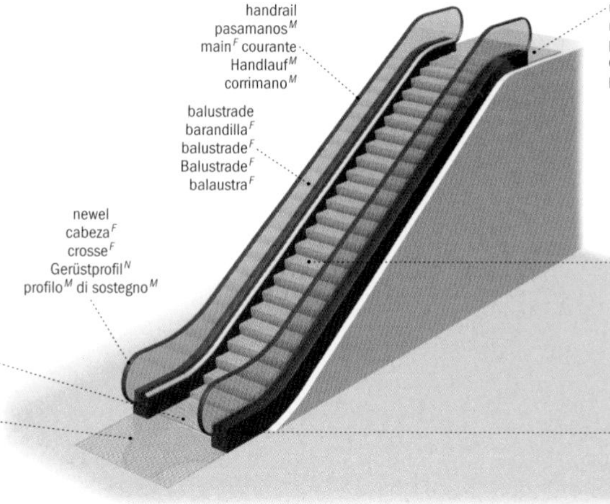

elevator

ascensor^M | ascenseur^M | Aufzug^M | ascensore^M

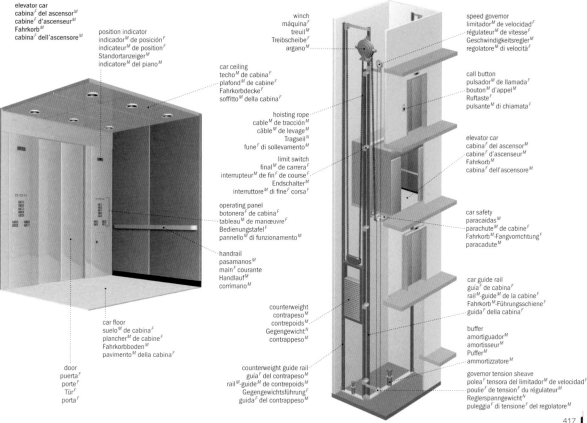

elevator car
cabina^F del ascensor^M
cabine^F d'ascenseur^M
Fahrkorb^M
cabina^F dell'ascensore^M

position indicator
indicador^M de posición^F
indicateur^M de position^F
Standortanzeiger^M
indicatore^M del piano^M

car ceiling
techo^M de cabina^F
plafond^M de cabine^F
Fahrkorbdecke^F
soffitto^M della cabina^F

hoisting rope
cable^M de tracción^F
câble^M de levage^M
Tragseil^N
fune^F di sollevamento^M

limit switch
final^M de carrera^F
interrupteur^M de fin^F de course^F
Endschalter^M
interruttore^M di fine^F corsa^F

operating panel
botonera^F de cabina^F
tableau^M de manœuvre^F
Bedienungstafel^F
pannello^M di funzionamento^M

handrail
pasamanos^M
main^F courante
Handlauf^M
corrimano^M

winch
máquina^F
treuil^M
Treibscheibe^F
argano^M

counterweight
contrapeso^M
contrepoids^M
Gegengewicht^N
contrappeso^M

counterweight guide rail
guía^F del contrapeso^M
rail^M-guide^M de contrepoids^M
Gegengewichtsführung^F
guida^F del contrappeso^M

car floor
suelo^M de cabina^F
plancher^M de cabine^F
Fahrkorbboden^M
pavimento^M della cabina^F

door
puerta^F
porte^F
Tür^F
porta^F

speed governor
limitador^M de velocidad^F
régulateur^M de vitesse^F
Geschwindigkeitsregler^M
regolatore^M di velocità^F

call button
pulsador^M de llamada^F
bouton^M d'appel^M
Ruftaste^F
pulsante^M di chiamata^F

elevator car
cabina^F del ascensor^M
cabine^F d'ascenseur^M
Fahrkorb^M
cabina^F dell'ascensore^M

car safety
paracaídas^M
parachute^M de cabine^F
Fahrkorb^M-Fangvorrichtung^F
paracadute^M

car guide rail
guía^F de cabina^F
rail^M-guide^M de la cabine^F
Fahrkorb^M-Führungsschiene^F
guida^F della cabina^F

buffer
amortiguador^M
amortisseur^M
Puffer^M
ammortizzatore^M

governor tension sheave
polea^F tensora del limitador^M de velocidad^F
poulie^F de tension^F du régulateur^M
Reglerspanngewicht^N
puleggia^F di tensione^F del regolatore^M

417

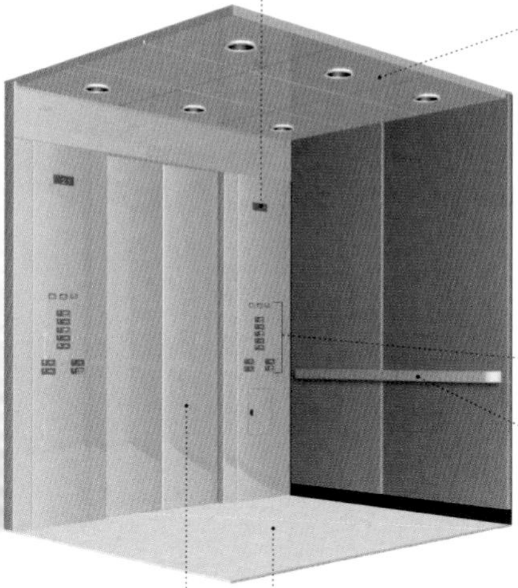

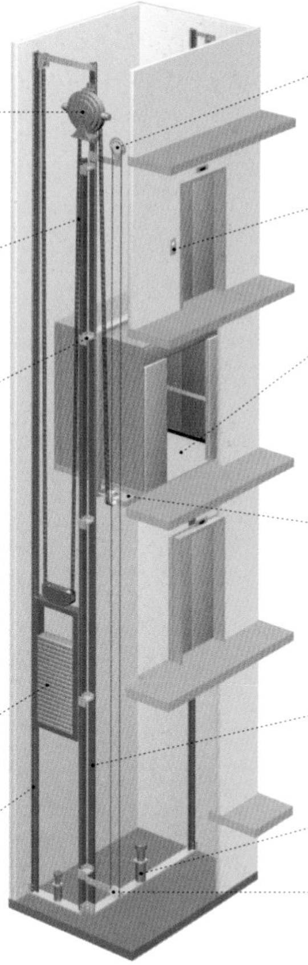

traditional houses

viviendas^F tradicionales | maisons^F traditionnelles | traditionelle Wohnhäuser^N | case^F tradizionali

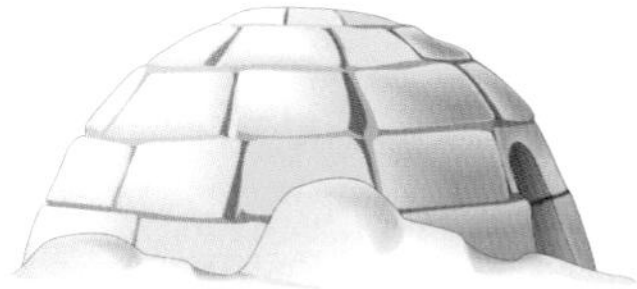

igloo
iglú^M
igloo^M
Iglu^M
igloo^M

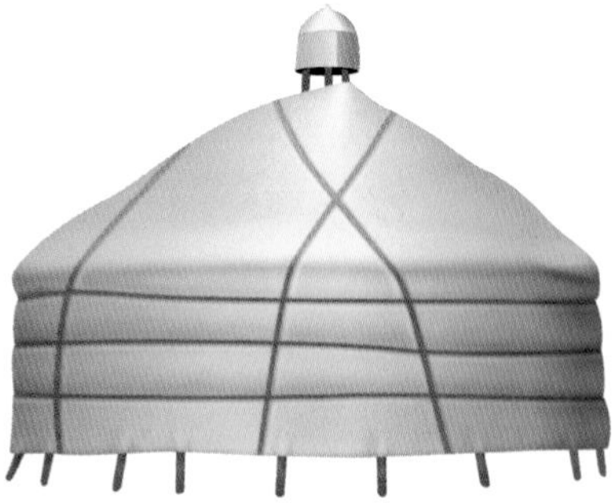

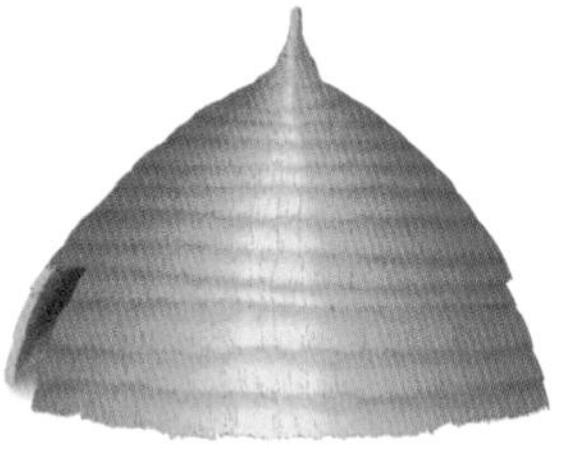

hut
choza^F indígena
hutte^F
Strohhütte^F
capanna^F di paglia^F

yurt
yurta^F
yourte^F
Jurte^F
iurta^F

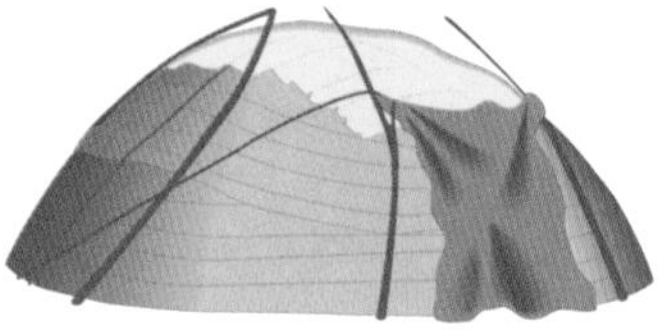

wigwam
wigwam^M
wigwam^M
Wigwam^M
wigwam^M

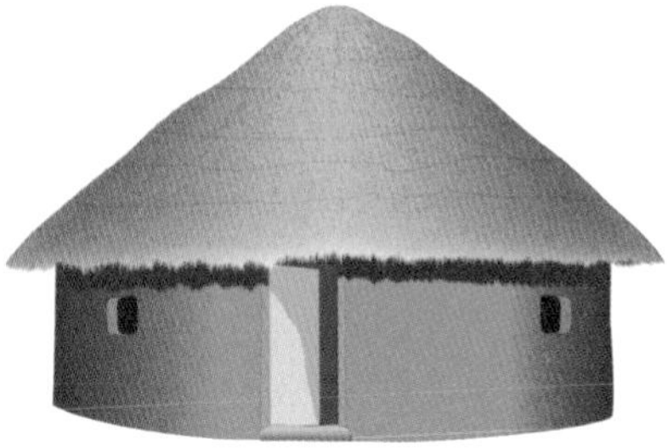

hut
choza^F
case^F
Lehmhütte^F
capanna^F di fango^M

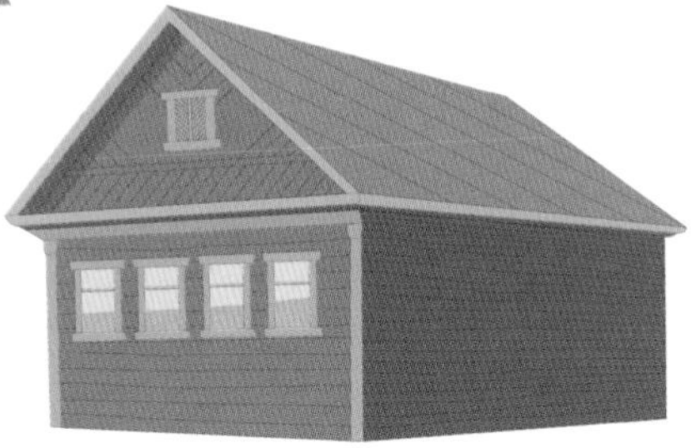

isba
isba^F
isba^F
Isba^F
isba^F

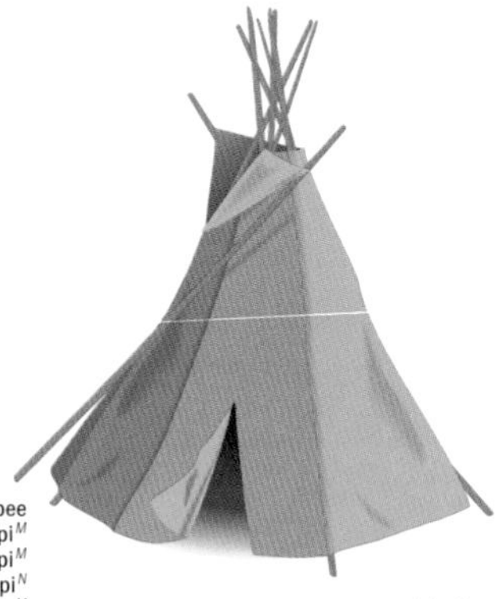

tepee
tipi^M
tipi^M
Tipi^N
tepee^M

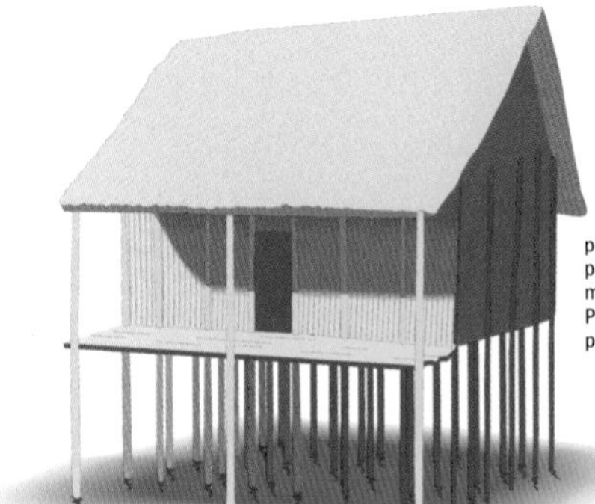

pile dwelling
palafito^M
maison^F sur pilotis^M
Pfahlbau^M
palafitta^F

beam
viga^F
poutre^F
Balken^M
trave^F

adobe house
casa^F de adobes^M
maison^F en adobe^M
Backsteinhaus^N
casa^F in mattoni^M cotti

ladder
escalera^F
échelle^F
Leiter^F
scala^F

ARTS AND ARCHITECTURE

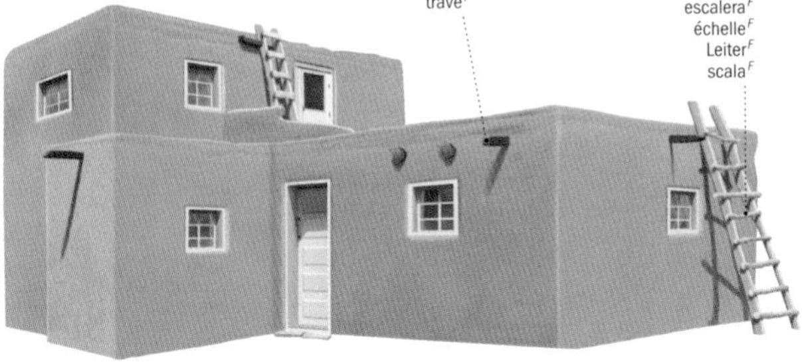

city houses

viviendas^F urbanas | maisons^F de ville^F | Häuserformen^F in der Stadt^F | abitazioni^F urbane

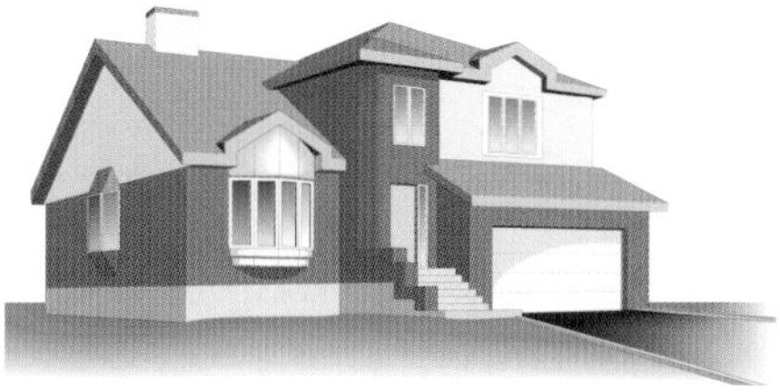

two-storey house
casa^F de dos plantas^M
maison^F à deux étages^M
zweistöckiges Haus^N
casa^F a due piani^M

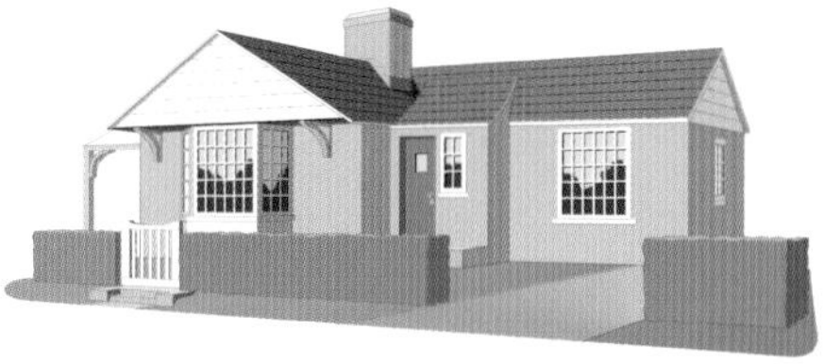

one-storey house
casa^F de una planta^F
maison^F de plain-pied^M
einstöckiges Haus^N
casa^F a un piano^M

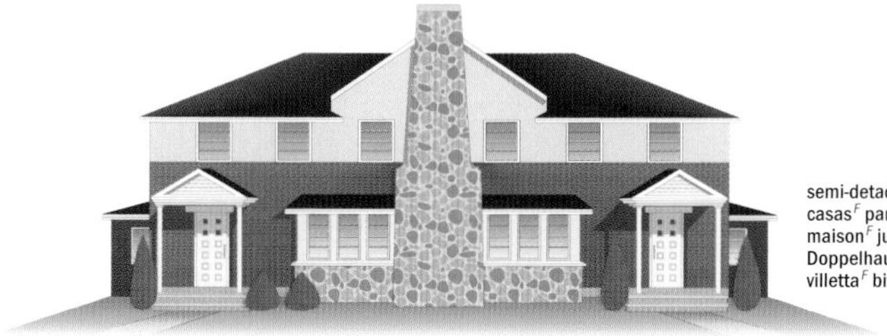

semi-detached cottage
casas^F pareadas
maison^F jumelée
Doppelhaus^N
villetta^F bifamiliare

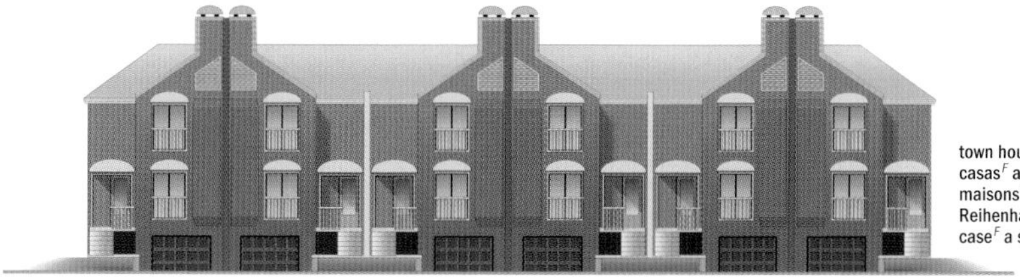

town houses
casas^F adosadas
maisons^F en rangée^F
Reihenhaus^N
case^F a schiera^F

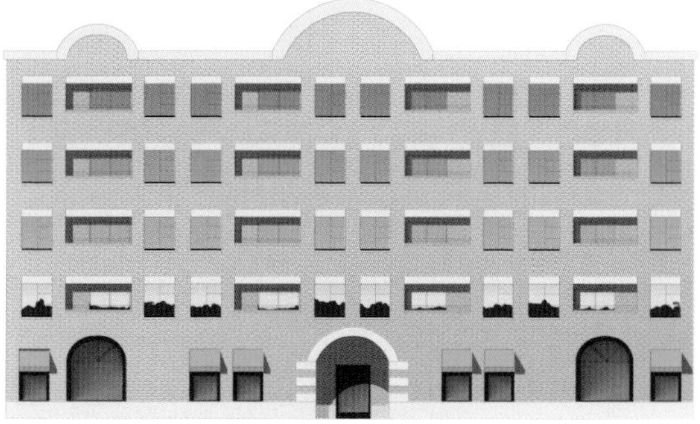

condominiums
viviendas^F plurifamiliares
appartements^M en copropriété^F
Eigentumswohnungen^F
palazzo^M in condominio^M

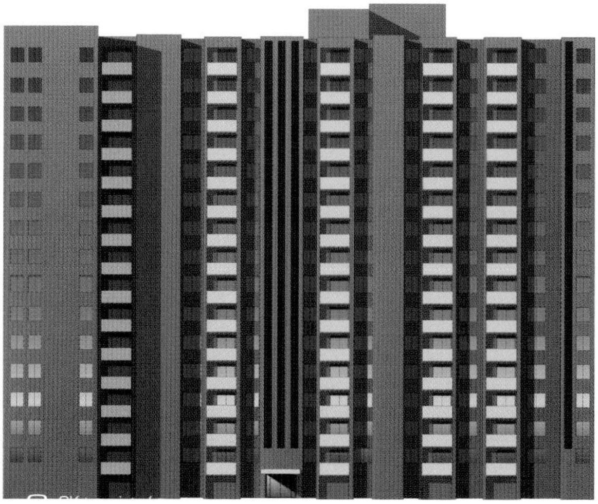

high-rise apartment
bloque^M de apartamentos^M
tour^F d'habitation^F
Wohnblock^M
casatorre^F

printing

impresión[F] | impression[F] | Drucken[N] | stampa[F]

relief printing
impresión[F] en relieve[M]
impression[F] en relief[M]
Hochdruck[M]
stampa[F] in rilievo[M]

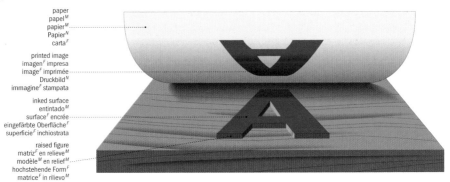

paper
papel[M]
papier[M]
Papier[N]
carta[F]

printed image
imagen[F] impresa
image[F] imprimée
Druckbild[N]
immagine[F] stampata

inked surface
entintado[M]
surface[F] encrée
eingefärbte Oberfläche[F]
superficie[F] inchiostrata

raised figure
matriz[F] en relieve[M]
modèle[M] en relief[M]
hochstehende Form[F]
matrice[F] in rilievo[M]

intaglio printing
huecograbado[M]
impression[F] en creux[M]
Tiefdruck[M]
stampa[F] in cavo[M]

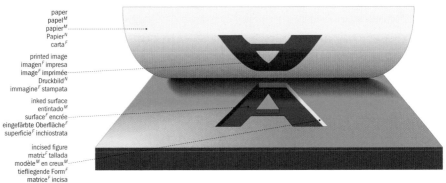

paper
papel[M]
papier[M]
Papier[N]
carta[F]

printed image
imagen[F] impresa
image[F] imprimée
Druckbild[N]
immagine[F] stampata

inked surface
entintado[M]
surface[F] encrée
eingefärbte Oberfläche[F]
superficie[F] inchiostrata

incised figure
matriz[F] tallada
modèle[M] en creux[M]
tiefliegende Form[F]
matrice[F] incisa

lithographic printing
impresión[F] litográfica
impression[F] à plat[M]
Lithografie[F]
litografia[F]

printed image
imagen[F] impresa
image[F] imprimée
Druckbild[N]
immagine[F] stampata

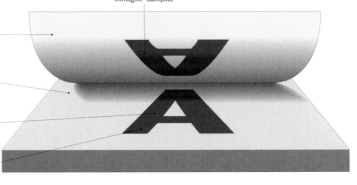

paper
papel[M]
papier[M]
Papier[N]
carta[F]

moist surface
superficie[F] humedecida
surface[F] mouillée
befeuchtete Oberfläche[F]
superficie[F] inumidita

inked surface
entintado[M]
surface[F] encrée
eingefärbte Oberfläche[F]
superficie[F] inchiostrata

plane figure
matriz[F] plana
modèle[M] à plat[M]
Flachform[F]
matrice[F] piana

relief printing process

impresión^F en relieve^M | gravure^F en relief^M | Hochdruckverfahren^N | metodo^M di stampa^F in rilievo^M

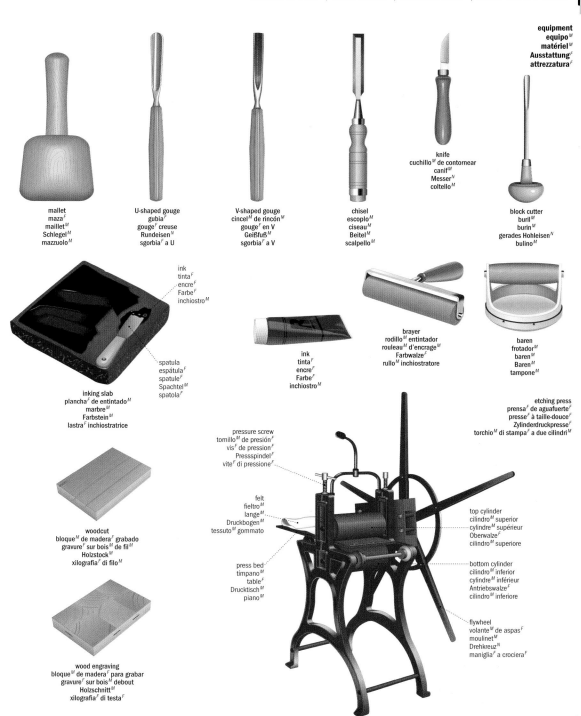

equipment
equipo^M
matériel^M
Ausstattung^F
attrezzatura^F

knife
cuchillo^M de contornear
canif^M
Messer^N
coltello^M

mallet
maza^F
maillet^M
Schlegel^M
mazzuolo^M

U-shaped gouge
gubia^F
gouge^F creuse
Rundeisen^N
sgorbia^F a U

V-shaped gouge
cincel^M de rincón^M
gouge^F en V
Geißfuß^M
sgorbia^F a V

chisel
escoplo^M
ciseau^M
Beitel^M
scalpello^M

block cutter
buril^M
burin^M
gerades Hohleisen^N
bulino^M

ink
tinta^F
encre^F
Farbe^F
inchiostro^M

spatula
espátula^F
spatule^F
Spachtel^M
spatola^F

inking slab
plancha^F de entintado^M
marbre^M
Farbstein^M
lastra^F inchiostratrice

ink
tinta^F
encre^F
Farbe^F
inchiostro^M

brayer
rodillo^M entintador
rouleau^M d'encrage^M
Farbwalze^F
rullo^M inchiostratore

baren
frotador^M
baren^M
Baren^M
tampone^M

etching press
prensa^F de aguafuerte^F
presse^F à taille-douce^F
Zylinderdruckpresse^F
torchio^M di stampa^F a due cilindri^M

woodcut
bloque^M de madera^F grabado
gravure^F sur bois^M de fil^M
Holzstock^M
xilografia^F di filo^M

pressure screw
tornillo^M de presión^F
vis^F de pression^F
Pressspindel^M
vite^F di pressione^F

felt
fieltro^M
lange^M
Druckbogen^M
tessuto^M gommato

press bed
tímpano^M
table^F
Drucktisch^M
piano^M

top cylinder
cilindro^M superior
cylindre^M supérieur
Oberwalze^F
cilindro^M superiore

bottom cylinder
cilindro^M inferior
cylindre^M inférieur
Antriebswalze^F
cilindro^M inferiore

flywheel
volante^M de aspas^F
moulinet^M
Drehkreuz^N
maniglia^F a crociera^F

wood engraving
bloque^M de madera^F para grabar
gravure^F sur bois^M debout
Holzschnitt^M
xilografia^F di testa^F

ARTS AND ARCHITECTURE

intaglio printing process

impresión^F en huecograbado^M | gravure^F en creux^M | Tiefdruckverfahren^N | metodo^M di stampa^F in cavo^M

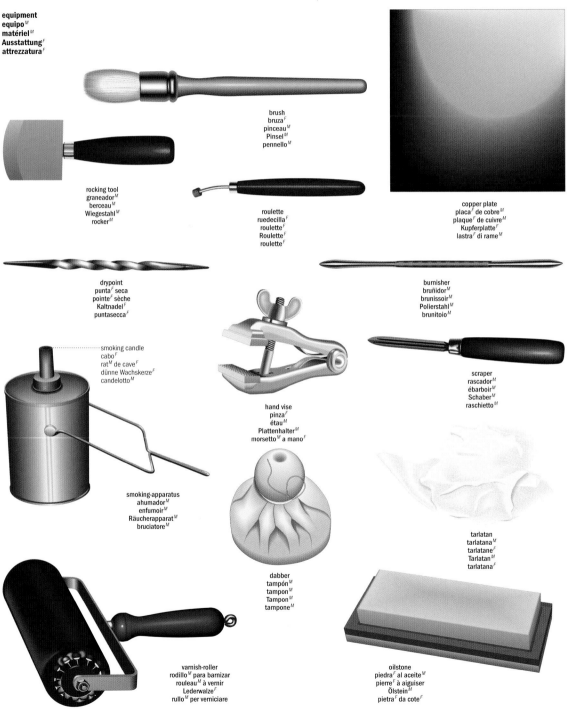

equipment
equipo^M
matériel^M
Ausstattung^F
attrezzatura^F

brush
bruza^F
pinceau^M
Pinsel^M
pennello^M

rocking tool
graneador^M
berceau^M
Wiegestahl^M
rocker^M

roulette
ruedecilla^F
roulette^F
Roulette^F
roulette^F

copper plate
placa^F de cobre^M
plaque^F de cuivre^M
Kupferplatte^F
lastra^F di rame^M

drypoint
punta^F seca
pointe^F sèche
Kaltnadel^F
puntasecca^F

burnisher
bruñidor^M
brunissoir^M
Polierstahl^M
brunitoio^M

smoking candle
cabo^F
rat^M de cave^F
dünne Wachskerze^F
candelotto^M

scraper
rascador^M
ébarboir^M
Schaber^M
raschietto^M

hand vise
pinza^F
étau^M
Plattenhalter^M
morsetto^M a mano^F

smoking-apparatus
ahumador^M
enfumoir^M
Räucherapparat^M
bruciatore^M

tarlatan
tarlatana^M
tarlatane^F
Tarlatan^M
tarlatana^F

dabber
tampón^M
tampon^M
Tampon^M
tampone^M

varnish-roller
rodillo^M para barnizar
rouleau^M à vernir
Lederwalze^F
rullo^M per verniciare

oilstone
piedra^F al aceite^M
pierre^F à aiguiser
Ölstein^M
pietra^F da cote^F

ARTS AND ARCHITECTURE

lithography

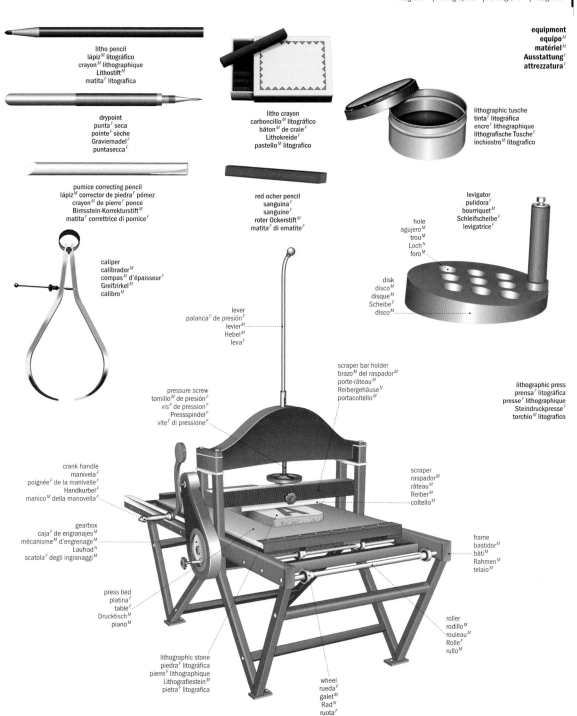

equipment
equipo[M]
matériel[M]
Ausstattung[F]
attrezzatura[F]

litho pencil
lápiz[M] litográfico
crayon[M] lithographique
Lithostift[M]
matita[F] litografica

drypoint
punta[F] seca
pointe[F] sèche
Graviernadel[F]
puntasecca[F]

litho crayon
carboncillo[M] litográfico
bâton[M] de craie[F]
Lithokreide[F]
pastello[M] litografico

lithographic tusche
tinta[F] litográfica
encre[F] lithographique
lithografische Tusche[F]
inchiostro[M] litografico

pumice correcting pencil
lápiz[M] corrector de piedra[F] pómez
crayon[M] de pierre[F] ponce
Bimsstein-Korrekturstift[M]
matita[F] correttrice di pomice[F]

red ocher pencil
sanguina[F]
sanguine[F]
roter Ockerstift[M]
matita[F] di ematite[F]

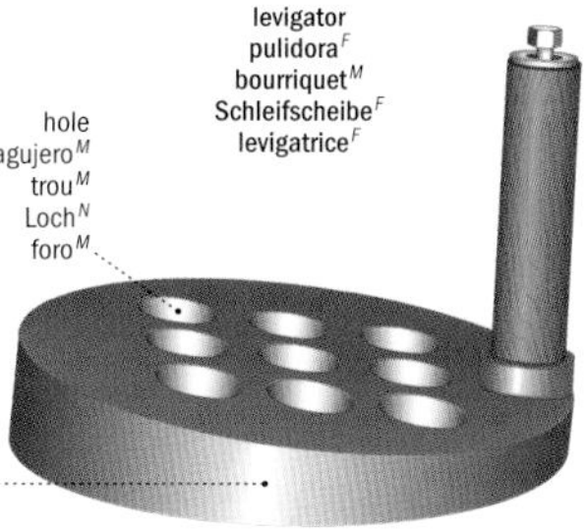

levigator
pulidora[F]
bourriquet[M]
Schleifscheibe[F]
levigatrice[F]

hole
agujero[M]
trou[M]
Loch[N]
foro[M]

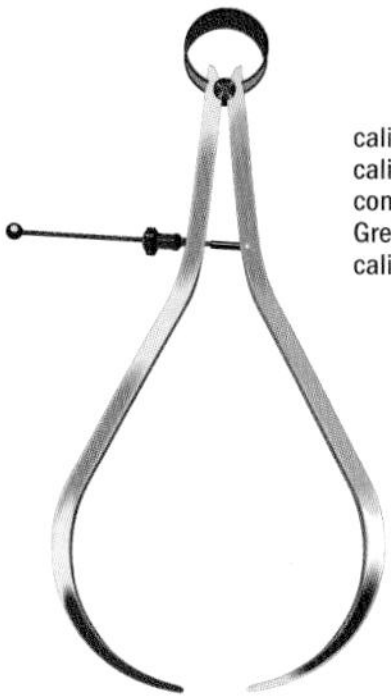

caliper
calibrador[M]
compas[M] d'épaisseur[F]
Greifzirkel[M]
calibro[M]

disk
disco[M]
disque[M]
Scheibe[F]
disco[M]

lever
palanca[F] de presión[F]
levier[M]
Hebel[M]
leva[F]

scraper bar holder
brazo[M] del raspador[M]
porte-râteau[M]
Reibergehäuse[N]
portacoltello[M]

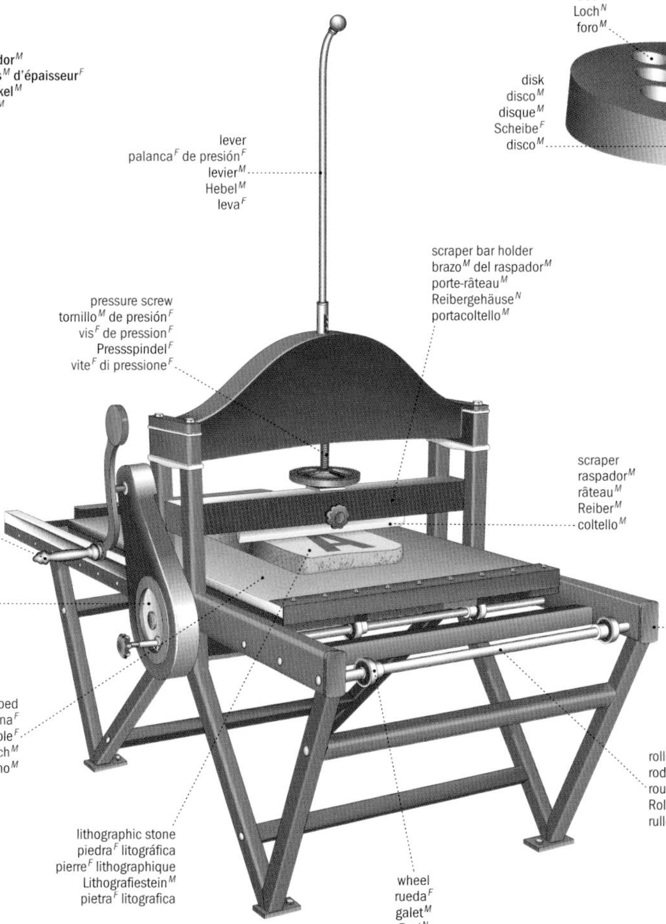

lithographic press
prensa[F] litográfica
presse[F] lithographique
Steindruckpresse[F]
torchio[M] litografico

pressure screw
tornillo[M] de presión[F]
vis[F] de pression[F]
Pressspindel[F]
vite[F] di pressione[F]

scraper
raspador[M]
râteau[M]
Reiber[M]
coltello[M]

crank handle
manivela[F]
poignée[F] de la manivelle[F]
Handkurbel[F]
manico[M] della manovella[F]

gearbox
caja[F] de engranajes[M]
mécanisme[M] d'engrenage[M]
Laufrad[N]
scatola[F] degli ingranaggi[M]

frame
bastidor[M]
bâti[M]
Rahmen[M]
telaio[M]

press bed
platina[F]
table[F]
Drucktisch[M]
piano[M]

roller
rodillo[M]
rouleau[M]
Rolle[F]
rullo[M]

lithographic stone
piedra[F] litográfica
pierre[F] lithographique
Lithografiestein[M]
pietra[F] litografica

wheel
rueda[F]
galet[M]
Rad[N]
ruota[F]

fine bookbinding

encuadernación^F a mano^F | reliure^F d'art^M | Handbuchbinderei^F | rilegatura^F a mano^F

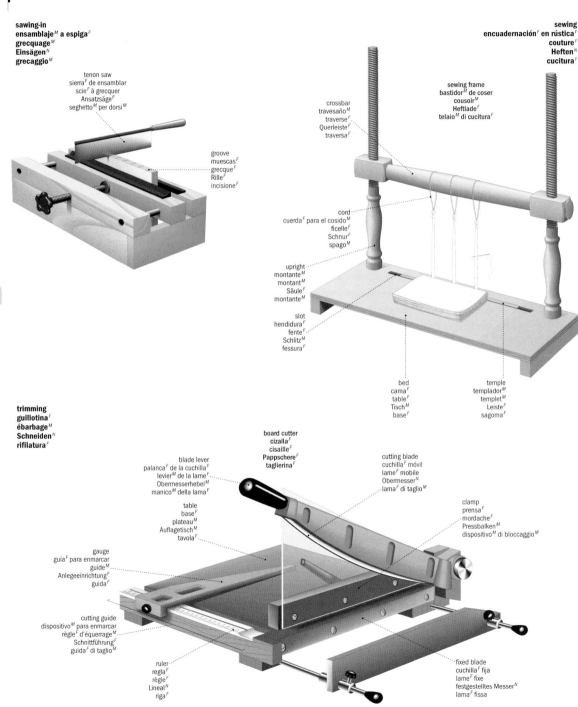

sawing-in
ensamblaje^M a espiga^F
grecquage^M
Einsägen^N
grecaggio^M

tenon saw
sierra^F de ensamblar
scie^F à grecquer
Ansatzsäge^F
seghetto^M per dorsi^M

groove
muescas^F
grecque^F
Rille^F
incisione^F

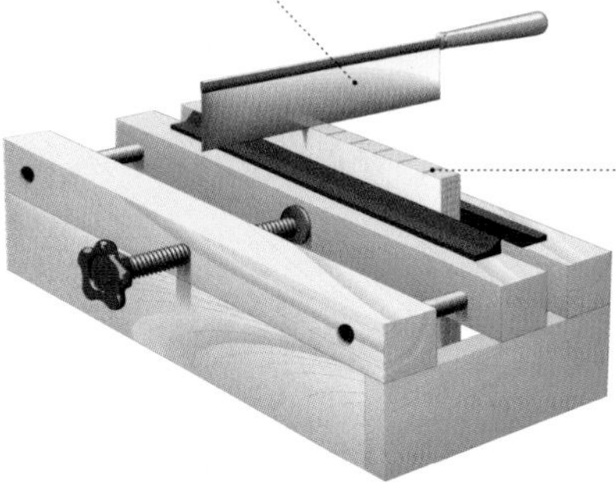

sewing
encuadernación^F en rústica^F
couture^F
Heften^N
cucitura^F

sewing frame
bastidor^M de coser
cousoir^M
Heftlade^F
telaio^M di cucitura^F

crossbar
travesaño^M
traverse^F
Querleiste^F
traversa^F

cord
cuerda^F para el cosido^M
ficelle^F
Schnur^F
spago^M

upright
montante^M
montant^M
Säule^F
montante^M

slot
hendidura^F
fente^F
Schlitz^M
fessura^F

bed
cama^F
table^F
Tisch^M
base^F

temple
templador^M
templet^M
Leiste^F
sagoma^F

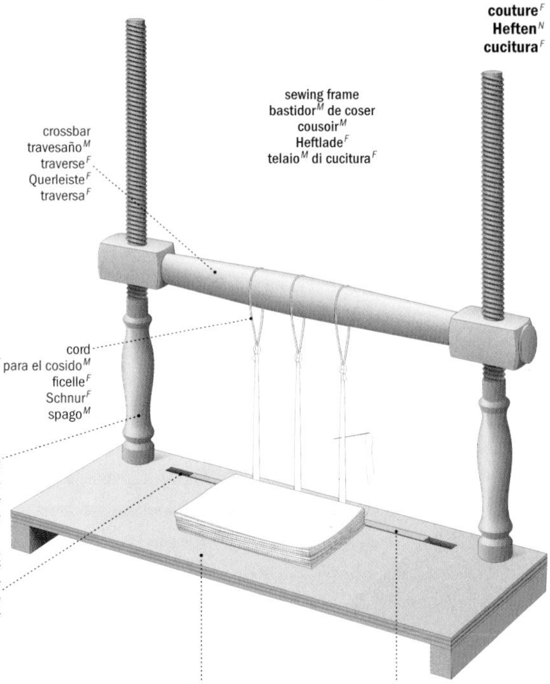

trimming
guillotina^F
ébarbage^M
Schneiden^N
rifilatura^F

board cutter
cizalla^F
cisaille^F
Pappschere^F
taglierina^F

blade lever
palanca^F de la cuchilla^F
levier^M de la lame^F
Obermesserhebel^M
manico^M della lama^F

table
base^F
plateau^M
Auflagetisch^M
tavola^F

gauge
guía^F para enmarcar
guide^M
Anlegeeinrichtung^F
guida^F

cutting blade
cuchilla^F móvil
lame^F mobile
Obermesser^N
lama^F di taglio^M

clamp
prensa^F
mordache^F
Pressbalken^M
dispositivo^M di bloccaggio^M

cutting guide
dispositivo^M para enmarcar
règle^F d'équerrage^M
Schnittführung^F
guida^F di taglio^M

ruler
regla^F
règle^F
Lineal^N
riga^F

fixed blade
cuchilla^F fija
lame^F fixe
festgestelltes Messer^N
lama^F fissa

ARTS AND ARCHITECTURE

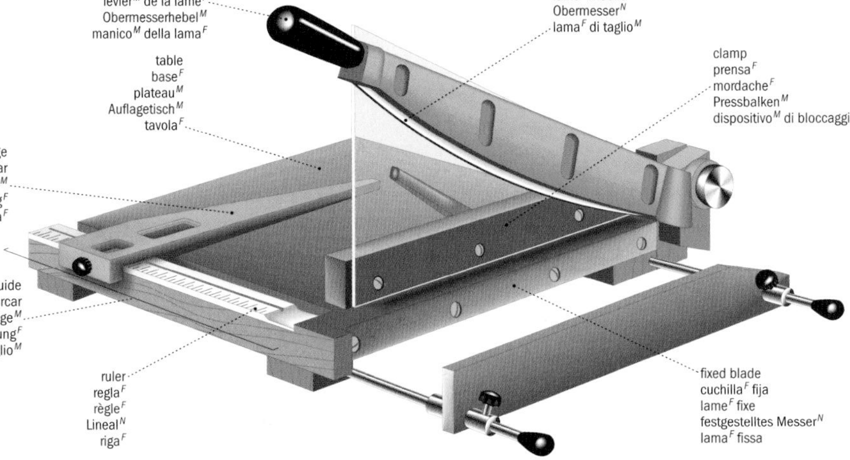

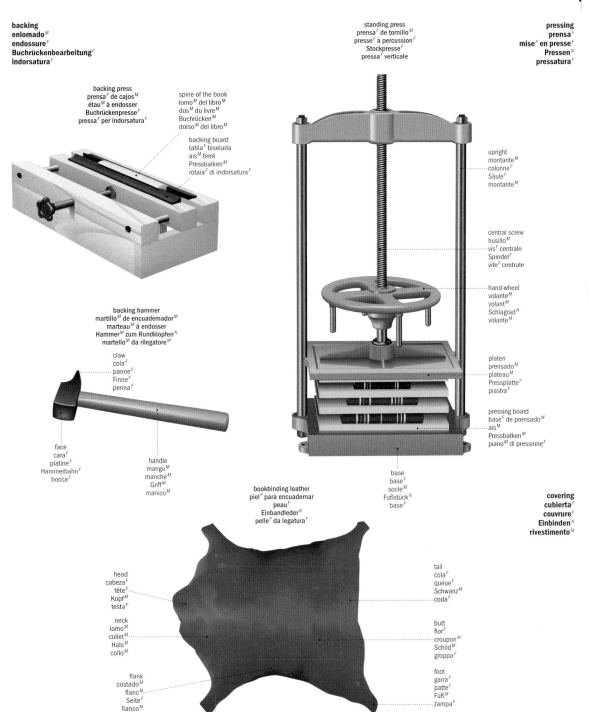

backing
enlomado[M]
endossure[F]
Buchrückenbearbeitung[F]
indorsatura[F]

standing press
prensa[F] de tornillo[M]
presse[F] à percussion[F]
Stockpresse[F]
pressa[F] verticale

pressing
prensa[F]
mise[F] en presse[F]
Pressen[N]
pressatura[F]

backing press
prensa[F] de cajos[M]
étau[M] à endosser
Buchrückenpresse[F]
pressa[F] per indorsatura[F]

spine of the book
lomo[M] del libro[M]
dos[M] du livre[M]
Buchrücken[M]
dorso[M] del libro[M]

backing board
tabla[F] biselada
ais[M] ferré
Pressbalken[M]
rotaia[F] di indorsatura[F]

upright
montante[M]
colonne[F]
Säule[F]
montante[M]

central screw
husillo[M]
vis[F] centrale
Spindel[F]
vite[F] centrale

hand-wheel
volante[M]
volant[M]
Schlagrad[N]
volante[M]

backing hammer
martillo[M] de encuadernador[M]
marteau[M] à endosser
Hammer[M] zum Rundklopfen[N]
martello[M] da rilegatore[M]

claw
cola[F]
panne[F]
Finne[F]
penna[F]

platen
prensado[M]
plateau[M]
Pressplatte[F]
piastra[F]

pressing board
base[F] de prensado[M]
ais[M]
Pressbalken[M]
piano[M] di pressione[F]

face
cara[F]
platine[F]
Hammerbahn[F]
bocca[F]

handle
mango[M]
manche[M]
Griff[M]
manico[M]

base
base[F]
socle[M]
Fußstück[N]
base[F]

bookbinding leather
piel[F] para encuadernar
peau[F]
Einbandleder[N]
pelle[F] da legatura[F]

covering
cubierta[F]
couvrure[F]
Einbinden[N]
rivestimento[M]

head
cabeza[F]
tête[F]
Kopf[M]
testa[F]

tail
cola[F]
queue[F]
Schwanz[M]
coda[F]

neck
lomo[M]
collet[M]
Hals[M]
collo[M]

butt
flor[F]
croupon[M]
Schild[M]
groppa[F]

flank
costado[M]
flanc[M]
Seite[F]
fianco[M]

foot
garra[F]
patte[F]
Fuß[M]
zampa[F]

fine bookbinding

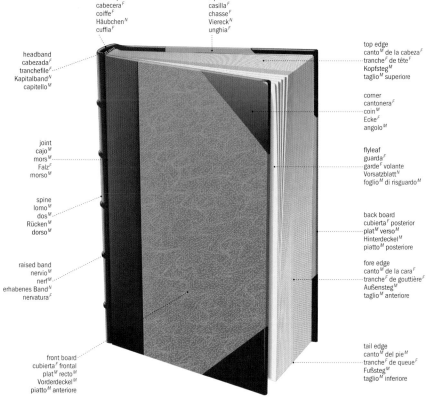

bound book
libro^M encuadernado
livre^M relié
gebundenes Buch^N
libro^M rilegato

headcap
cabecera^F
coiffe^F
Häubchen^N
cuffia^F

square
casilla^F
chasse^F
Viereck^N
unghia^F

headband
cabezada^F
tranchefile^F
Kapitalband^N
capitello^M

top edge
canto^M de la cabeza^F
tranche^F de tête^F
Kopfsteg^M
taglio^M superiore

corner
cantonera^F
coin^M
Ecke^F
angolo^M

joint
cajo^M
mors^M
Falz^F
morso^M

flyleaf
guarda^F
garde^F volante
Vorsatzblatt^N
foglio^M di risguardo^M

spine
lomo^M
dos^M
Rücken^M
dorso^M

back board
cubierta^F posterior
plat^M verso^M
Hinterdeckel^M
piatto^M posteriore

raised band
nervio^M
nerf^M
erhabenes Band^N
nervatura^F

fore edge
canto^M de la cara^F
tranche^F de gouttière^F
Außensteg^M
taglio^M anteriore

front board
cubierta^F frontal
plat^M recto^M
Vorderdeckel^M
piatto^M anteriore

tail edge
canto^M del pie^M
tranche^F de queue^F
Fußsteg^M
taglio^M inferiore

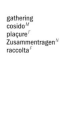

gathering
cosido^M
plaçure^F
Zusammentragen^N
raccolta^F

signature
cuadernillo^M
cahier^M
Signatur^F
segnatura^F

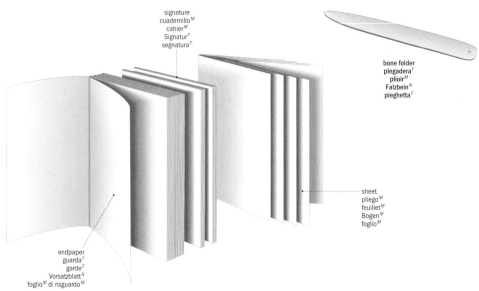

bone folder
plegadera^F
plioir^M
Falzbein^N
pieghetta^F

sheet
pliego^M
feuillet^M
Bogen^M
foglio^M

endpaper
guarda^F
garde^F
Vorsatzblatt^N
foglio^M di risguardo^M

movie theater

cine^M | cinéma^M | Kino^N | cinema^M

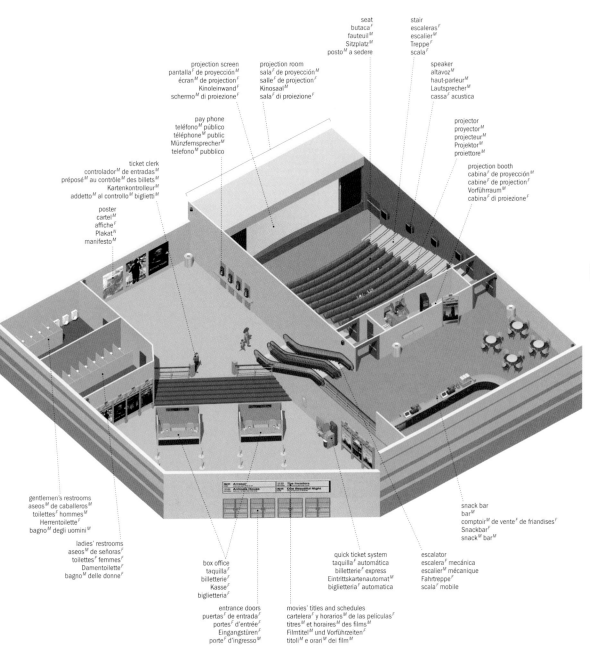

seat
butaca^F
fauteuil^M
Sitzplatz^M
posto^M a sedere

stair
escaleras^F
escalier^M
Treppe^F
scala^F

projection screen
pantalla^F de proyección^M
écran^M de projection^F
Kinoleinwand^F
schermo^M di proiezione^F

projection room
sala^F de proyección^M
salle^F de projection^F
Kinosaal^M
sala^F di proiezione^F

speaker
altavoz^M
haut-parleur^M
Lautsprecher^M
cassa^F acustica

projector
proyector^M
projecteur^M
Projektor^M
proiettore^M

pay phone
teléfono^M público
téléphone^M public
Münzfernsprecher^M
telefono^M pubblico

ticket clerk
controlador^M de entradas^M
préposé^M au contrôle^M des billets^M
Kartenkontrolleur^M
addetto^M al controllo^M biglietti^M

projection booth
cabina^F de proyección^M
cabine^F de projection^F
Vorführraum^M
cabina^F di proiezione^F

poster
cartel^M
affiche^F
Plakat^N
manifesto^M

gentlemen's restrooms
aseos^M de caballeros^M
toilettes^F hommes^M
Herrentoilette^F
bagno^M degli uomini^M

snack bar
bar^M
comptoir^M de vente^F de friandises^F
Snackbar^F
snack^M bar^M

ladies' restrooms
aseos^M de señoras^F
toilettes^F femmes^F
Damentoilette^F
bagno^M delle donne^F

box office
taquilla^F
billetterie^F
Kasse^F
biglietteria^F

quick ticket system
taquilla^F automática
billetterie^F express
Eintrittskartenautomat^M
biglietteria^F automatica

escalator
escalera^F mecánica
escalier^M mécanique
Fahrtreppe^F
scala^F mobile

entrance doors
puertas^F de entrada^F
portes^F d'entrée^F
Eingangstüren^F
porte^F d'ingresso^M

movies' titles and schedules
cartelera^F y horarios^M de las películas^F
titres^M et horaires^M des films^M
Filmtitel^M und Vorführzeiten^F
titoli^M e orari^M dei film^M

sound stage

plató^M de rodaje^M | plateau^M de tournage^M | Aufnahmebühne^F | set^M delle riprese^F

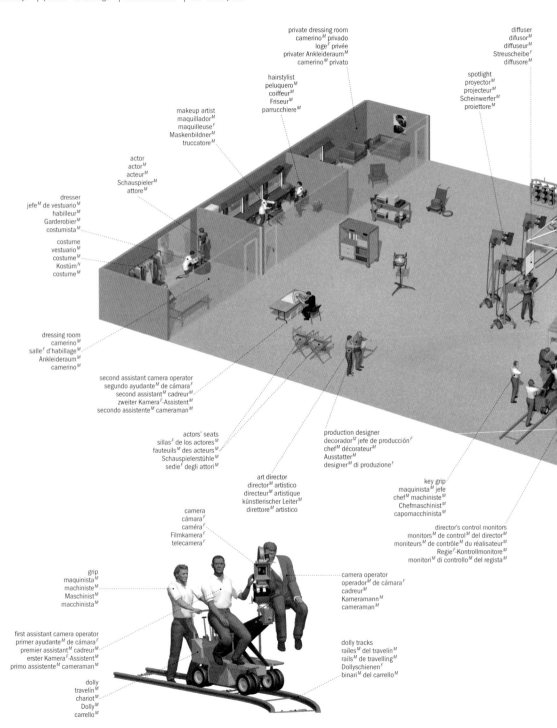

private dressing room
camerino^M privado
loge^F privée
privater Ankleideraum^M
camerino^M privato

diffuser
difusor^M
diffuseur^M
Streuscheibe^F
diffusore^M

hairstylist
peluquero^M
coiffeur^M
Friseur^M
parrucchiere^M

spotlight
proyector^M
projecteur^M
Scheinwerfer^M
proiettore^M

makeup artist
maquillador^M
maquilleuse^F
Maskenbildner^M
truccatore^M

actor
actor^M
acteur^M
Schauspieler^M
attore^M

dresser
jefe^M de vestuario^M
habilleur^M
Garderobier^M
costumista^M

costume
vestuario^M
costume^M
Kostüm^N
costume^M

dressing room
camerino^M
salle^F d'habillage^M
Ankleideraum^M
camerino^M

second assistant camera operator
segundo ayudante^M de cámara^F
second assistant^M cadreur^M
zweiter Kamera^F-Assistent^M
secondo assistente^M cameraman^M

actors' seats
sillas^F de los actores^M
fauteuils^M des acteurs^M
Schauspielerstühle^M
sedie^F degli attori^M

production designer
decorador^M jefe de producción^F
chef^M décorateur^M
Ausstatter^M
designer^M di produzione^F

art director
director^M artístico
directeur^M artistique
künstlerischer Leiter^M
direttore^M artistico

key grip
maquinista^M jefe
chef^M machiniste^M
Chefmaschinist^M
capomacchinista^M

camera
cámara^F
caméra^F
Filmkamera^F
telecamera^F

director's control monitors
monitors^M de control^M del director^M
moniteurs^M de contrôle^M du réalisateur^M
Regie^F-Kontrollmonitore^M
monitori^M di controllo^M del regista^M

grip
maquinista^M
machiniste^M
Maschinist^M
macchinista^M

camera operator
operador^M de cámara^F
cadreur^M
Kameramann^M
cameraman^M

first assistant camera operator
primer ayudante^M de cámara^F
premier assistant^M cadreur^M
erster Kamera^F-Assistent^M
primo assistente^M cameraman^M

dolly tracks
railes^M del travelín^M
rails^M de travelling^M
Dollyschienen^F
binari^M del carrello^M

dolly
travelín^M
chariot^M
Dolly^M
carrello^M

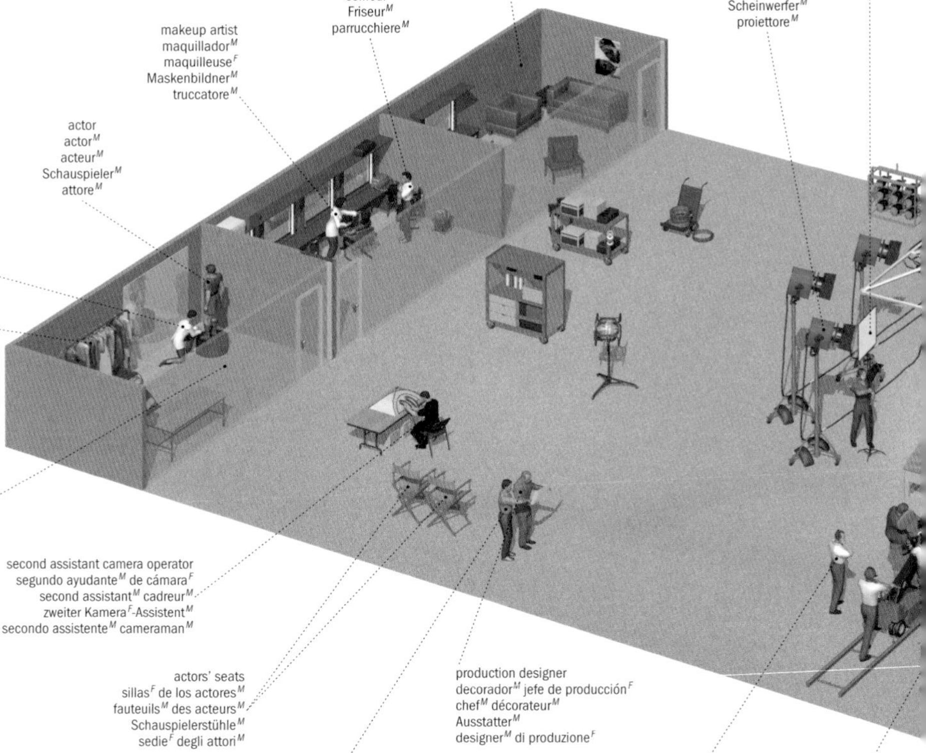

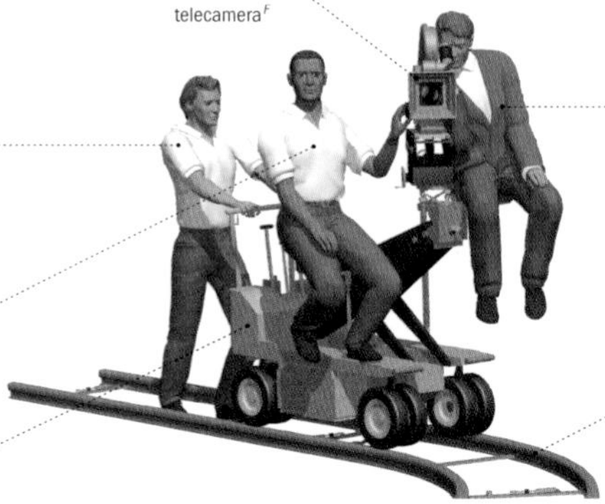

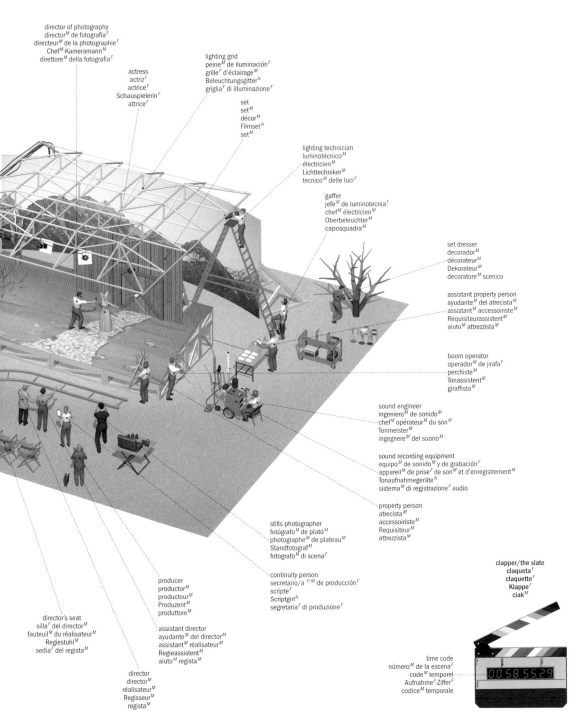

director of photography
director^M de fotografía^F
directeur^M de la photographie^F
Chef^M-Kameramann^M
direttore^M della fotografia^F

actress
actriz^F
actrice^F
Schauspielerin^F
attrice^F

lighting grid
peine^M de iluminación^F
grille^F d'éclairage^M
Beleuchtungsgitter^N
griglia^F di illuminazione^F

set
set^M
décor^M
Filmset^N
set^M

lighting technician
luminotécnico^M
électricien^M
Lichttechniker^M
tecnico^M delle luci^F

gaffer
jefe^M de luminotecnia^F
chef^M électricien^M
Oberbeleuchter^M
caposquadra^M

set dresser
decorador^M
décorateur^M
Dekorateur^M
decoratore^M scenico

assistant property person
ayudante^M del atrecista^M
assistant^M accessoiriste^M
Requisiteurassistent^M
aiuto^M attrezzista^M

boom operator
operador^M de jirafa^F
perchiste^M
Tonassistent^M
giraffista^M

sound engineer
ingeniero^M de sonido^M
chef^M opérateur du son^M
Tonmeister^M
ingegnere^M del suono^M

sound recording equipment
equipo^M de sonido^M y de grabación^F
appareil^M de prise^F de son^M et d'enregistrement^M
Tonaufnahmegeräte^N
sistema^M di registrazione^F audio

property person
atrecista^M
accessoiriste^M
Requisiteur^M
attrezzista^M

stills photographer
fotógrafo^M de plató^M
photographe^M de plateau^M
Standfotograf^M
fotografo^M di scena^F

continuity person
secretario/a^{F/M} de producción^F
scripte^F
Scriptgirl^N
segretaria^F di produzione^F

producer
productor^M
producteur^M
Produzent^M
produttore^M

assistant director
ayudante^M del director^M
assistant^M réalisateur^M
Regieassistent^M
aiuto^M regista^M

director's seat
silla^F del director^M
fauteuil^M du réalisateur^M
Regiestuhl^M
sedia^F del regista^M

director
director^M
réalisateur^M
Regisseur^M
regista^M

clapper/the slate
claqueta^F
claquette^F
Klappe^F
ciak^M

time code
número^M de la escena^F
code^M temporel
Aufnahme^F-Ziffer^F
codice^M temporale

00:58:55:29

theater

teatro^M | salle^F de spectacle^M | Theater^N | teatro^M

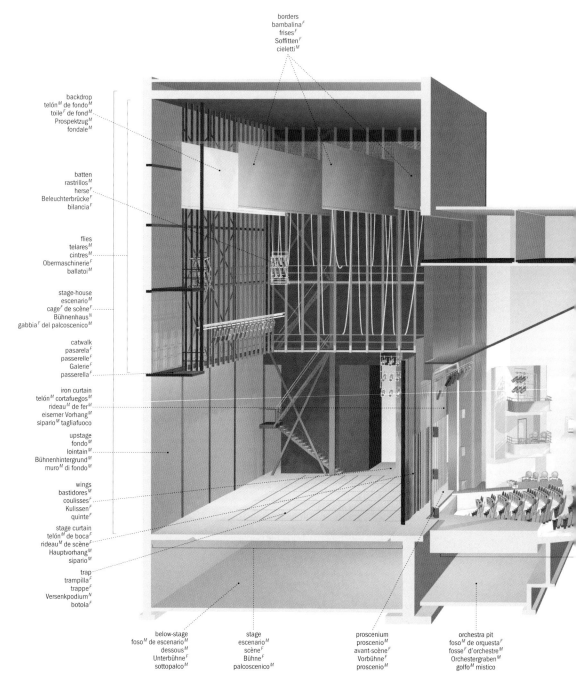

borders
bambalina^F
frises^F
Soffitten^F
cieletti^M

backdrop
telón^M de fondo^M
toile^F de fond^F
Prospektzug^M
fondale^M

batten
rastrillos^M
herse^F
Beleuchterbrücke^F
bilancia^F

flies
telares^M
cintres^M
Obermaschinerie^F
ballatoi^M

stage-house
escenario^M
cage^F de scène^F
Bühnenhaus^N
gabbia^F del palcoscenico^M

catwalk
pasarela^F
passerelle^F
Galerie^F
passerella^F

iron curtain
telón^M cortafuegos^M
rideau^M de fer^F
eisemer Vorhang^M
sipario^M tagliafuoco

upstage
fondo^M
lointain^M
Bühnenhintergrund^M
muro^M di fondo^M

wings
bastidores^M
coulisses^F
Kulissen^F
quinte^F

stage curtain
telón^M de boca^F
rideau^M de scène^F
Hauptvorhang^M
sipario^M

trap
trampilla^F
trappe^F
Versenkpodium^N
botola^F

below-stage
foso^M de escenario^M
dessous^M
Unterbühne^F
sottopalco^M

stage
escenario^M
scène^F
Bühne^F
palcoscenico^M

proscenium
proscenio^M
avant-scène^F
Vorbühne^F
proscenio^M

orchestra pit
foso^M de orquesta^F
fosse^F d'orchestre^M
Orchestergraben^M
golfo^M mistico

ARTS AND ARCHITECTURE

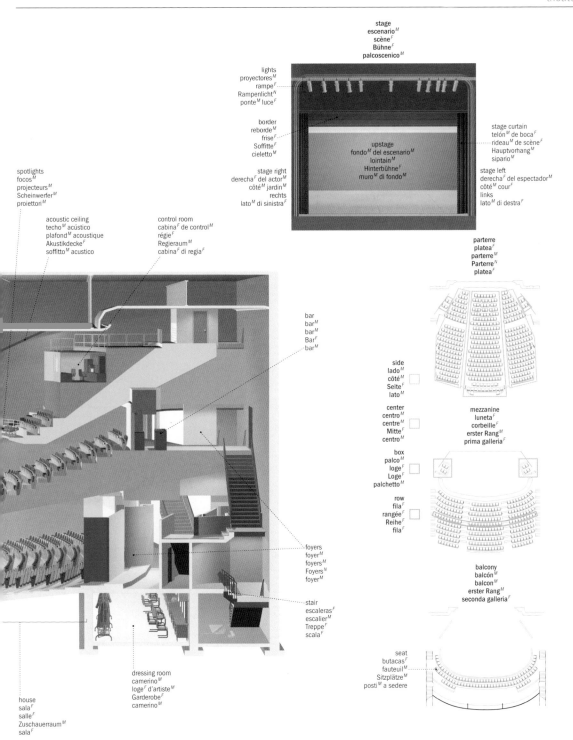

stage
escenario^M
scène^F
Bühne^F
palcoscenico^M

lights
proyectores^M
rampe^F
Rampenlicht^N
ponte^M luce^F

border
reborde^M
frise^F
Soffitte^F
cieletto^M

stage curtain
telón^M de boca^F
rideau^M de scène^F
Hauptvorhang^M
sipario^M

upstage
fondo^M del escenario^M
lointain^M
Hinterbühne^F
muro^M di fondo^M

stage right
derecha^F del actor^M
côté^F jardin^M
rechts
lato^M di sinistra^F

stage left
derecha^F del espectador^M
côté^F cour^F
links
lato^M di destra^F

spotlights
focos^M
projecteurs^M
Scheinwerfer^M
proiettori^M

acoustic ceiling
techo^M acústico
plafond^M acoustique
Akustikdecke^F
soffitto^M acustico

control room
cabina^F de control^M
régie^F
Regieraum^M
cabina^F di regia^F

parterre
platea^F
parterre^M
Parterre^N
platea^F

bar
bar^M
bar^M
Bar^F
bar^M

side
lado^M
côté^F
Seite^F
lato^M

center
centro^M
centre^M
Mitte^F
centro^M

mezzanine
luneta^F
corbeille^F
erster Rang^M
prima galleria^F

box
palco^M
loge^F
Loge^F
palchetto^M

row
fila^F
rangée^F
Reihe^F
fila^F

foyers
foyer^M
foyers^M
Foyers^N
foyer^M

balcony
balcón^M
balcon^M
erster Rang^M
seconda galleria^F

stair
escaleras^F
escalier^M
Treppe^F
scala^F

seat
butacas^F
fauteuil^M
Sitzplätze^M
posti^M a sedere

dressing room
camerino^M
loge^F d'artiste^M
Garderobe^F
camerino^M

house
sala^F
salle^F
Zuschauerraum^M
sala^F

traditional musical instruments

instrumentos^M musicales tradicionales | instruments^M traditionnels | traditionelle Musikinstrumente^N | strumenti^M musicali tradizionali

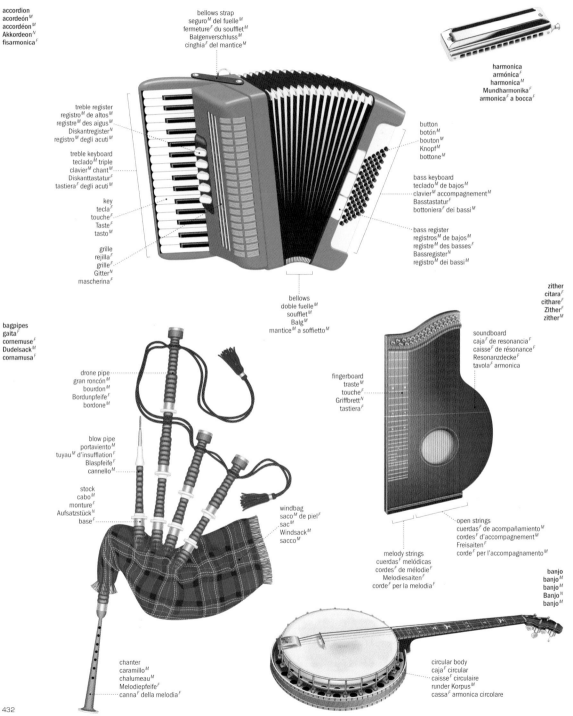

accordion
acordeón^M
accordéon^M
Akkordeon^N
fisarmonica^F

bellows strap
seguro^M del fuelle^M
fermeture^F du soufflet^M
Balgenverschluss^M
cinghia^F del mantice^M

harmonica
armónica^F
harmonica^M
Mundharmonika^F
armonica^F a bocca^F

treble register
registro^M de altos^M
registre^M des aigus^M
Diskantregister^N
registro^M degli acuti^M

button
botón^M
bouton^M
Knopf^M
bottone^M

treble keyboard
teclado^M triple
clavier^M chant^M
Diskanttastatur^F
tastiera^F degli acuti^M

bass keyboard
teclado^M de bajos^M
clavier^M accompagnement^M
Basstastatur^F
bottoniera^F dei bassi^M

key
tecla^F
touche^F
Taste^F
tasto^M

bass register
registros^M de bajos^M
registre^M des basses^F
Bassregister^N
registro^M dei bassi^M

grille
rejilla^F
grille^F
Gitter^N
mascherina^F

bellows
doble fuelle^M
soufflet^M
Balg^M
mantice^M a soffietto^M

zither
citara^F
cithare^F
Zither^F
zither^M

bagpipes
gaita^F
cornemuse^F
Dudelsack^M
cornamusa^F

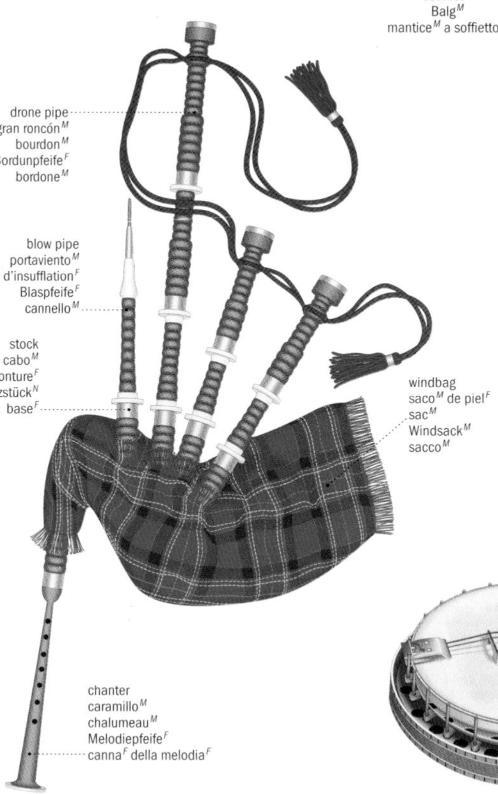

soundboard
caja^F de resonancia^F
caisse^F de résonance^F
Resonanzdecke^F
tavola^F armonica

drone pipe
gran roncón^M
bourdon^M
Bordunpfeife^F
bordone^M

fingerboard
traste^M
touche^F
Griffbrett^N
tastiera^F

blow pipe
portaviento^M
tuyau^M d'insufflation^F
Blaspfeife^F
cannello^M

stock
cabo^M
monture^F
Aufsatzstück^N
base^F

windbag
saco^F de piel^F
sac^M
Windsack^M
sacco^M

open strings
cuerdas^F de acompañamiento^M
cordes^F d'accompagnement^M
Freisaiten^F
corde^F per l'accompagnamento^M

melody strings
cuerdas^F melódicas
cordes^F de mélodie^F
Melodiesaiten^F
corde^F per la melodia^F

banjo
banjo^M
banjo^M
Banjo^N
banjo^M

chanter
caramillo^M
chalumeau^M
Melodiepfeife^F
canna^F della melodia^F

circular body
caja^F circular
caisse^F circulaire
runder Korpus^M
cassa^F armonica circolare

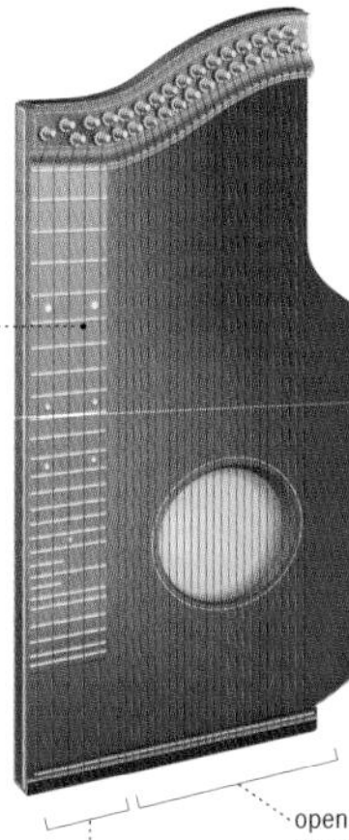

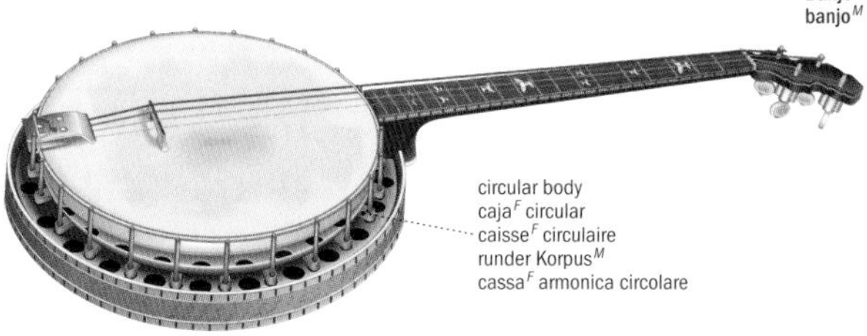

kora
kora^M
kora^M
Kora^F
kora^F

mandolin
mandolina^F
mandoline^F
Mandoline^F
mandolino^M

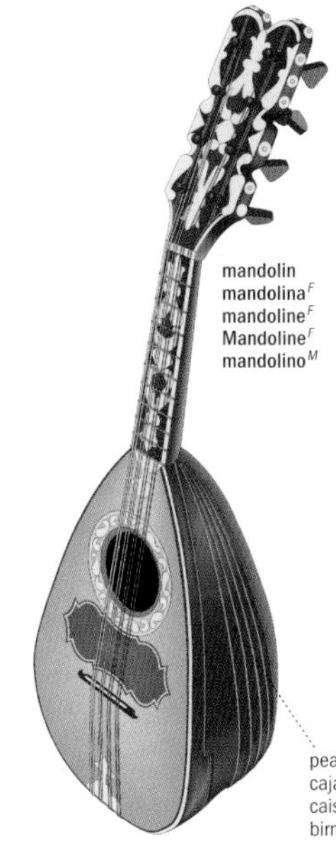

balalaika
balalaika^F
balalaïka^F
Balalaika^F
balalaica^F

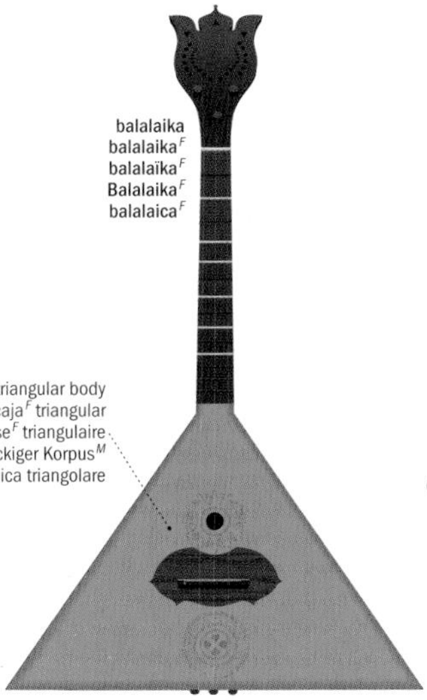

neck
mástil^M
manche^M
Hals^M
manico^M

strings
cuerdas^F
cordes^F
Saiten^F
corde^F

triangular body
caja^F triangular
caisse^F triangulaire
dreieckiger Korpus^M
cassa^F armonica triangolare

hand post
soporte^M de la mano^M
support^M de main^F
Handgriff^M
poggiamano^M

tuning ring
anillo^M de sonido^M
attache^F d'accordage^M
Stimmring^M
anello^M d'accordatura^F

sound box
caja^F de resonancia^F
caisse^F de résonance^F
Resonanzkörper^M
cassa^F di risonanza^F

snare head
piel^F armónica
peau^F de timbre^M
Klangfell^N
pelle^F armonica

pear-shaped body
caja^F media pera^F
caisse^F bombée
birnenförmiger Korpus^M
cassa^F armonica piriforme

bridge
puente^M
chevalet^M
Steg^M
ponticello^M

tailpiece
cordal^M
cordier^M
Saitenhalterung^F
cordiera^F

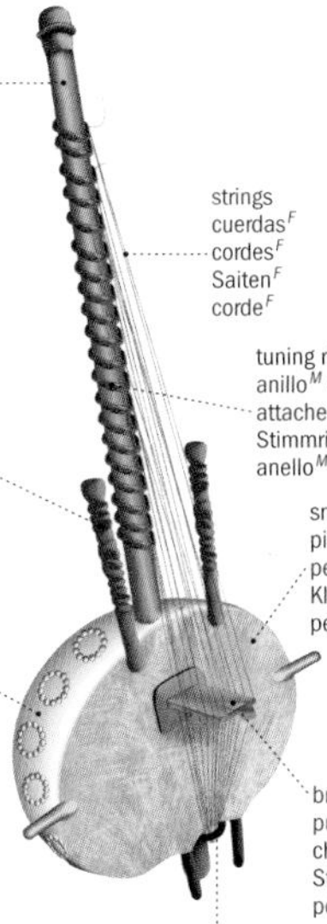

lyre
lira^F
lyre^F
Lyra^F
lira^F

frame
estructura^F
cadre^M
Rahmen^M
telaio^M

tongue
lengüeta^F de la caña^F
lame^F
Zunge^F
linguetta^F

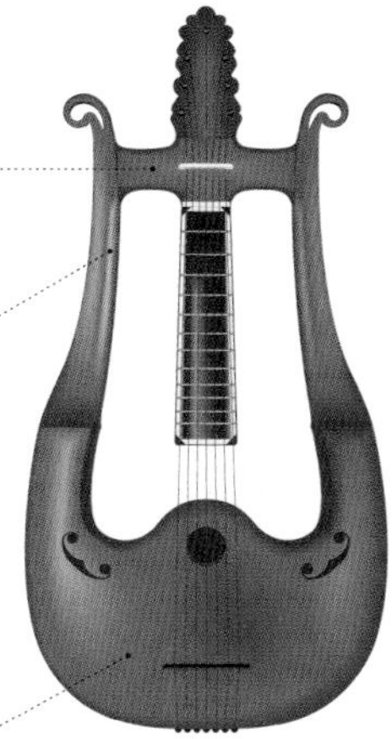

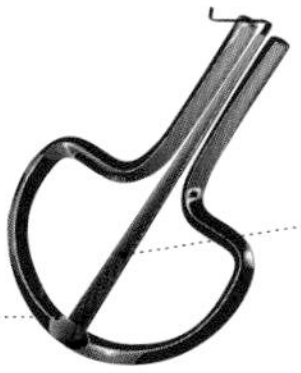

drumstick
baqueta^F
mailloche^F
Trommelschlegel^M
mazzuolo^M

crossbar
travesaño^M
traverse^F
Querjoch^N
traversa^F

plectrum
púa^F
médiator^M
Plektron^N
plettro^M

Jew's harp
birimbao^M
guimbarde^F
Maultrommel^F
scacciapensieri^M

arm
brazo^M
montant^M
Jocharm^M
braccio^M

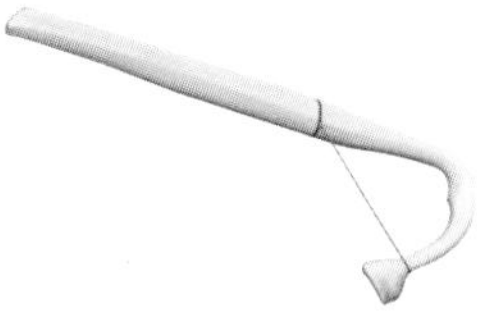

djembe
yembé^M
djembé^M
Djembe^F
djembè^M

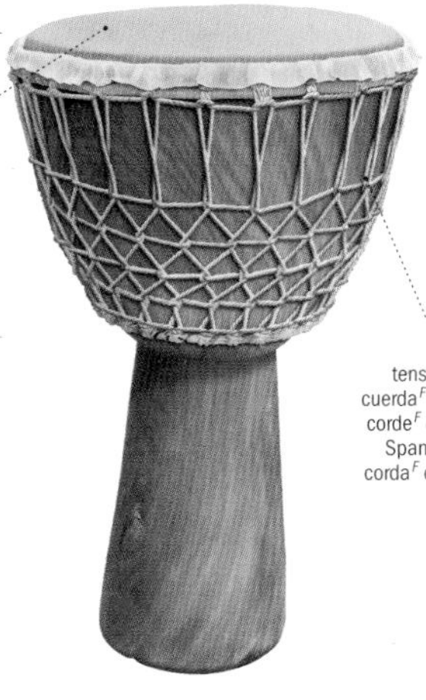

talking drum
tambor^M hablante
tambour^M d'aisselle^F
Sprechtrommel^F
tamburo^M parlante

soundboard
caja^F de resonancia^F
caisse^F de résonance^F
Resonanzdecke^F
tavola^F armonica

batter skin
piel^F
peau^F de batterie^F
Trommelfell^N
battitoia^F

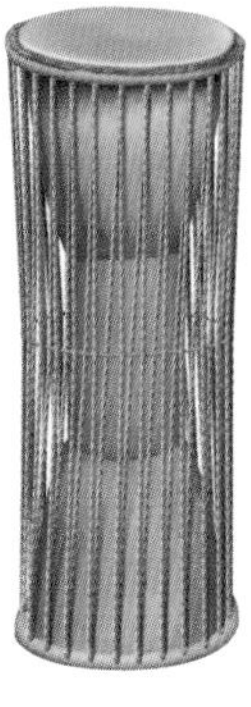

panpipe
zampoña^F
flûte^F de Pan
Panflöte^F
flauto^M di Pan

sound box
caja^F de resonancia^F
caisse^F de résonance^F
Resonanzkörper^M
cassa^F di risonanza^F

tension rope
cuerda^F de tensión^F
corde^F de tension^F
Spannschnur^F
corda^F di tensione^F

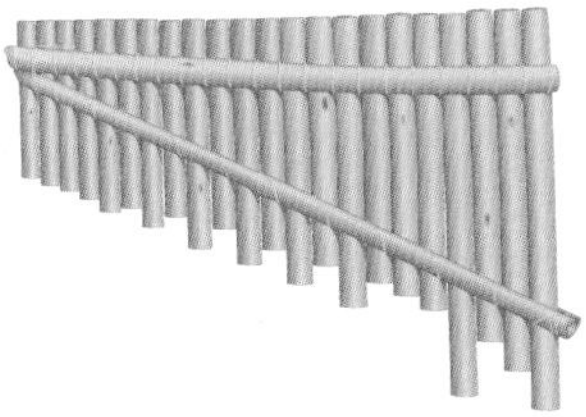

musical notation

notación^F musical | notation^F musicale | Musiknotation^F | notazione^F musicale

staff
pentagrama^F
portée^F
Liniensystem^N
pentagramma^M

space
espacio^M
interligne^M
Zwischenraum^M
spazio^M

line
linea^F
ligne^F
Notenlinie^F
linea^F

ledger line
linea^F suplementaria
ligne^F supplémentaire
Hilfslinie^F
taglio^M addizionale

clefs
claves^F
clés^F
Notenschlüssel^M
chiavi^F

treble clef
clave^F de sol
clé^F de sol^M
Violinschlüssel^M
chiave^F di violino^M

bass clef
clave^F de fa
clé^F de fa^M
Bassschlüssel^M
chiave^F di basso^M

C clef
clave^F de do
clé^F d'ut^M
Altschlüssel^M
chiave^F di contralto^M

time signatures
compás^M
mesures^F
Taktarten^F
indicazioni^F di tempo^M

two-two time
de dos mitades^F
mesure^F à deux temps^M
Zweihalbetakt^M
tempo^M di due metà^F

four-four time
de cuatro cuartos^M
mesure^F à quatre temps^M
Viervierteltakt^M
tempo^M di quattro quarti^M

repeat mark
barra^F de repetición^F
barre^F de reprise^F
Wiederholungszeichen^N
ritornello^M

three-four time
de tres cuartos^M
mesure^F à trois temps^M
Dreivierteltakt^M
tempo^M di tre quarti^M

bar line
barra^F de compás^M
barre^F de mesure^F
Taktstrich^M
stanghetta^F

intervals
intervalos^M
intervalles^M
Intervalle^N
intervalli^M

unison
unisono^M
unisson^M
Prime^F
unisono^M

third
tercera^F
tierce^F
Terz^F
terza^F

fifth
quinta^F
quinte^F
Quinte^F
quinta^F

seventh
séptima^F
septième^F
Septime^F
settima^F

second
segunda^F
seconde^F
Sekunde^F
seconda^F

fourth
cuarta^F
quarte^F
Quarte^F
quarta^F

sixth
sexta^F
sixte^F
Sexte^F
sesta^F

octave
octava^F
octave^F
Oktave^F
ottava^F

scale
escala^F
gamme^F
Tonleiter^F
scala^F

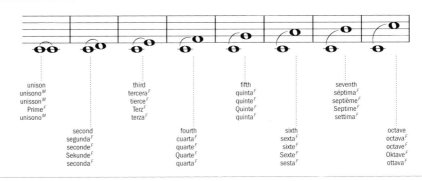

C	D	E	F	G	A	B	C
do (C)	re (D)	mi (E)	fa (F)	sol (G)	la (A)	si (B)	do (C)
do^M	ré^M	mi^M	fa^M	sol^M	la^M	si^M	do^M
C	D	E	F	G	A	H	C
do^M	re^M	mi^M	fa^M	sol^M	la^M	si^M	do^M

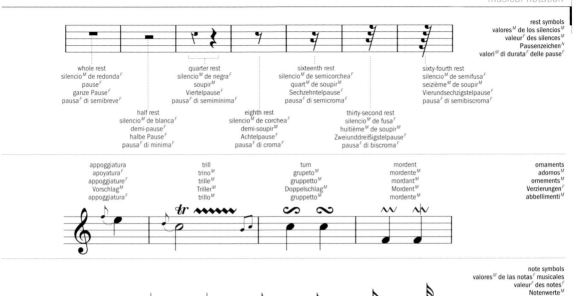

rest symbols
valores[M] de los silencios[M]
valeur[F] des silences[M]
Pausenzeichen[N]
valori[M] di durata[F] delle pause[F]

whole rest
silencio[M] de redonda[F]
pause[F]
ganze Pause[F]
pausa[F] di semibreve[F]

quarter rest
silencio[M] de negra[F]
soupir[M]
Viertelpause[F]
pausa[F] di semiminima[F]

sixteenth rest
silencio[M] de semicorchea[F]
quart[M] de soupir[M]
Sechzehntelpause[F]
pausa[F] di semicroma[F]

sixty-fourth rest
silencio[M] de semifusa[F]
seizième[M] de soupir[M]
Vierundsechzigstelpause[F]
pausa[F] di semibiscroma[F]

half rest
silencio[M] de blanca[F]
demi-pause[F]
halbe Pause[F]
pausa[F] di minima[F]

eighth rest
silencio[M] de corchea[F]
demi-soupir[M]
Achtelpause[F]
pausa[F] di croma[F]

thirty-second rest
silencio[M] de fusa[F]
huitième[M] de soupir[M]
Zweiunddreißigstelpause[F]
pausa[F] di biscroma[F]

appoggiatura
apoyatura[F]
appoggiature[F]
Vorschlag[M]
appoggiatura[F]

trill
trino[M]
trille[M]
Triller[M]
trillo[M]

turn
grupeto[M]
gruppetto[M]
Doppelschlag[M]
gruppetto[M]

mordent
mordente[M]
mordant[M]
Mordent[M]
mordente[M]

ornaments
adornos[M]
ornements[M]
Verzierungen[F]
abbellimenti[M]

note symbols
valores[M] de las notas[F] musicales
valeur[F] des notes[F]
Notenwerte[M]
valori[M] di durata[F] delle note[F]

whole note
redonda[F]
ronde[F]
ganze Note[F]
semibreve[F]

quarter note
negra[F]
noire[F]
Viertelnote[F]
semiminima[F]

sixteenth note
semicorchea[F]
double croche[F]
Sechzehntelnote[F]
semicroma[F]

sixty-fourth note
semifusa[F]
quadruple croche[F]
Vierundsechzigstelnote[F]
semibiscroma[F]

half note
blanca[M]
blanche[F]
halbe Note[F]
minima[F]

eighth note
corchea[F]
croche[F]
Achtelnote[F]
croma[F]

thirty-second note
fusa[F]
triple croche[F]
Zweiunddreißigstelnote[F]
biscroma[F]

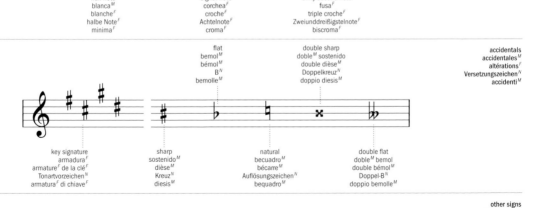

flat
bemol[M] sostenido
bémol[M]
B[N]
bemolle[M]

double sharp
doble[M] sostenido
double dièse[M]
Doppelkreuz[N]
doppio diesis[M]

accidentals
accidentales[M]
altérations[F]
Versetzungszeichen[N]
accidenti[M]

key signature
armadura[F]
armature[F] de la clé[F]
Tonartvorzeichen[N]
armatura[F] di chiave[F]

sharp
sostenido[M]
dièse[M]
Kreuz[N]
diesis[M]

natural
becuadro[M]
bécarre[M]
Auflösungszeichen[N]
bequadro[M]

double flat
doble[M] bemol
double bémol[M]
Doppel-B[N]
doppio bemolle[M]

other signs
otros signos[M]
autres signes[M]
andere Zeichen[N]
altri segni[M]

accent mark
acento[M]
accent[M]
Marcato-Zeichen[N]
accento[M]

arpeggio
arpegio[M]
arpège[M]
Arpeggio[N]
arpeggio[M]

fermata
calderón[M]
point[M] d'orgue[M]
Pause[F]
punto[M] coronato

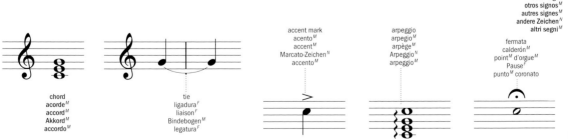

chord
acorde[M]
accord[M]
Akkord[M]
accordo[M]

tie
ligadura[F]
liaison[F]
Bindebogen[M]
legatura[F]

musical accessories

accesorios^M musicales | accessoires^M | Musikzubehör^N | accessori^M musicali

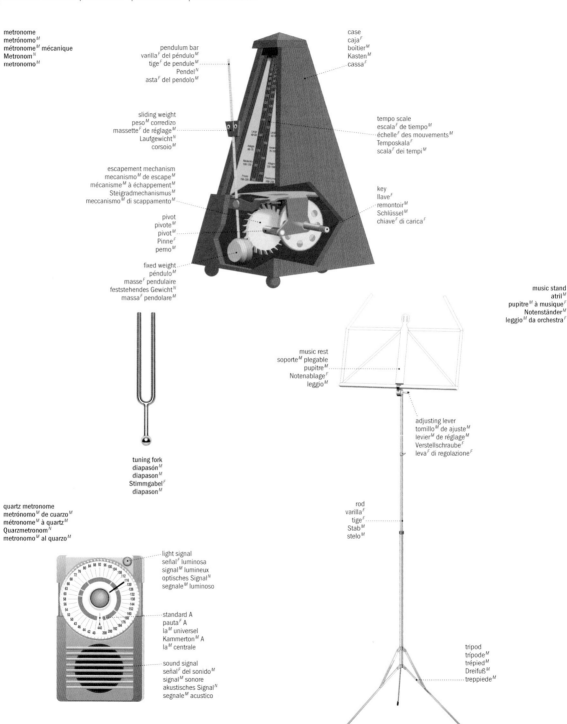

metronome
metrónomo^M
métronome^M mécanique
Metronom^N
metronomo^M

pendulum bar
varilla^F del péndulo^M
tige^F de pendule^M
Pendel^N
asta^F del pendolo^M

case
caja^F
boîtier^M
Kasten^M
cassa^F

sliding weight
peso^M corredizo
massette^F de réglage^M
Laufgewicht^N
corsoio^M

tempo scale
escala^F de tiempo^M
échelle^F des mouvements^M
Temposkala^F
scala^F dei tempi^M

escapement mechanism
mecanismo^M de escape^M
mécanisme^M à échappement^M
Steigradmechanismus^M
meccanismo^M di scappamento^M

key
llave^F
remontoir^M
Schlüssel^M
chiave^F di carica^F

pivot
pivote^M
pivot^M
Pinne^F
perno^M

fixed weight
péndulo^M
masse^F pendulaire
feststehendes Gewicht^N
massa^F pendolare^M

music stand
atril^M
pupitre^M à musique^F
Notenständer^M
leggio^M da orchestra^F

music rest
soporte^M plegable
pupitre^M
Notenablage^F
leggio^M

adjusting lever
tornillo^M de ajuste^M
levier^M de réglage^M
Verstellschraube^F
leva^F di regolazione^F

tuning fork
diapasón^M
diapason^M
Stimmgabel^F
diapason^M

quartz metronome
metrónomo^M de cuarzo^M
métronome^M à quartz^M
Quarzmetronom^N
metronomo^M al quarzo^M

rod
varilla^F
tige^F
Stab^M
stelo^M

light signal
señal^F luminosa
signal^M lumineux
optisches Signal^N
segnale^M luminoso

standard A
pauta^F A
la^M universel
Kammerton^M A
la^M centrale

sound signal
señal^F del sonido^M
signal^M sonore
akustisches Signal^N
segnale^M acustico

tripod
trípode^M
trépied^M
Dreifuß^M
treppiede^M

ARTS AND ARCHITECTURE

symphony orchestra

orquesta^F sinfónica | orchestre^M symphonique | Sinfonieorchester^N | orchestra^F sinfonica

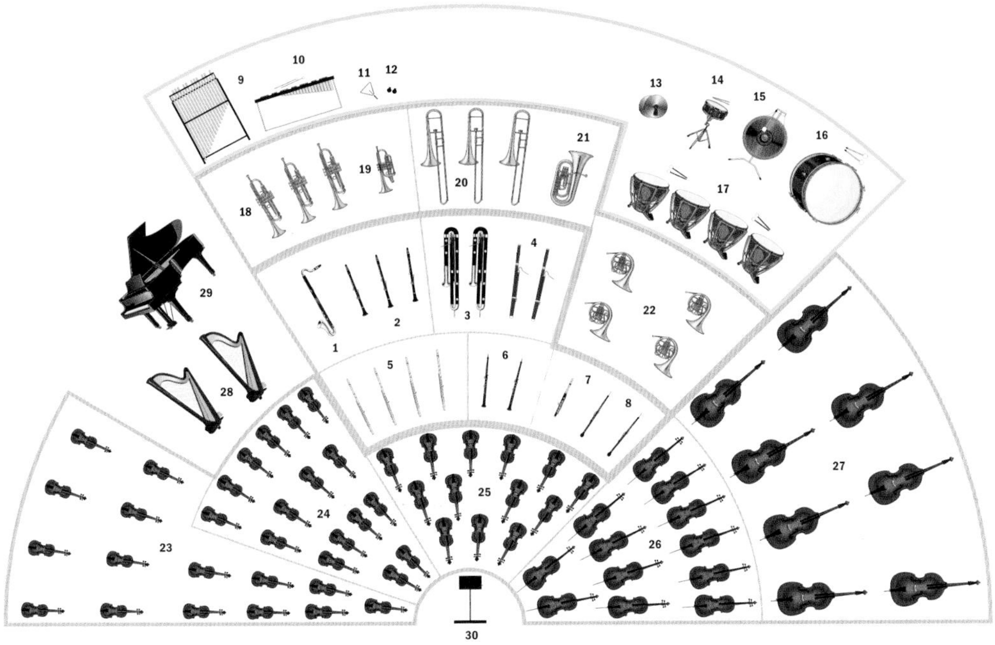

woodwind section
familia^F de viento^M
famille^F des bois^M
Familie^F der Holzblasinstrumente^N
sezione^F dei legni^M

bass clarinet
clarinete^M bajo
1 clarinette^F basse
Bassklarinette^F
clarinetto^M basso

clarinets
clarinetes^M
2 clarinettes^F
Klarinetten^F
clarinetti^M

contrabassoons
contrafagotes^M
3 contrabassons^M
Kontrafagott^N
controfagotti^M

bassoons
fagotes^M
4 bassons^M
Fagotte^N
fagotti^M

flutes
flautas^F traverseras
5 flûtes^F
Querflöten^F
flauti^M

oboes
oboes^M
6 hautbois^M
Oboen^F
oboi^M

piccolo
píccolo^M
7 piccolo^M
Pikkoloflöte^F
ottavino^M

English horns
cornos^M ingleses
8 cors^M anglais
Englischhörner^N
corni^M inglesi

percussion section
sección de percusión^F
instruments^M à percussion^F
Schlaginstrumente^N
strumenti^M a percussione^F

tubular bells
campanas^F tubulares
9 carillon^M tubulaire
Röhrenglocken^F
campane^F tubolari

xylophone
xilófono^M
10 xylophone^F
Xylophon^N
xilofono^M

triangle
triángulo^M
11 triangle^F
Triangel^M
triangolo^M

castanets
castañuelas^F
12 castagnettes^F
Kastagnetten^F
nacchere^F

cymbals
platillos^M
13 cymbales^F
Becken^N
piatti^M

snare drum
caja^F clara
14 caisse^F claire
kleine Trommel^F
cassa^F chiara

gong
gong^M
15 gong^M
Gong^M
gong^M

bass drum
bombo^M
16 grosse caisse^F
Basstrommel^F
grancassa^F

timpani
timbales^M
17 timbales^F
Pauken^F
timpani^M

harps
arpas^F
28 harpes^F
Harfen^F
arpe^F

brass section
familia^F de viento^M metal
famille^F des cuivres^M
Familie^F der Blechbläser^M
sezione^F degli ottoni^M

trumpets
trompetas^F
18 trompettes^F
Trompeten^F
trombe^F

cornet
cornetín^M
19 cornet^M à pistons^M
Kornett^N
cornetta^F

trombones
trombones^M
20 trombones^M
Posaunen^F
tromboni^M

tuba
tuba^F
21 tuba^M
Tuba^F
tuba^F

French horns
cornos^M franceses/trompas^F
22 cors^M d'harmonie^F
Waldhörner^M
corni^M

piano
piano^M
29 piano^M
Flügel^M
pianoforte^M

string section
familia^F de cuerdas^F
famille^F du violon^M
Geigenfamilie^F
sezione^F degli archi^M

first violins
primeros violines^M
23 premiers violons^M
erste Violinen^F
primi violini^M

second violins
segundos violines^M
24 seconds violons^M
zweite Violinen^F
secondi violini^M

violas
violas^F
25 altos^M
Bratschen^F
viole^F

cellos
violoncelos^M
26 violoncelles^M
Celli^N
violoncelli^M

double basses
contrabajos^M
27 contrebasses^F
Kontrabasse^M
contrabbassi^M

conductor's podium
estrado^M del director^M
30 pupitre^M du chef^M d'orchestre^M
Dirigentenpult^N
podio^M del direttore^M d'orchestra^F

examples of instrumental groups

ejemplos^M de conjuntos^M instrumentales | exemples^M de groupes^M instrumentaux | Beispiele^N für Instrumentalgruppierungen^F | esempi^M di gruppi^M strumentali

duo
dúo^M
duo^M
Duo^N
duo^M

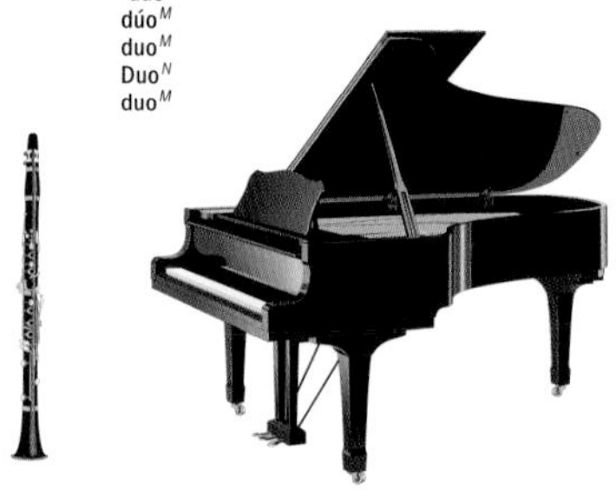

trio
trio^M
trio^M
Trio^N
trio^M

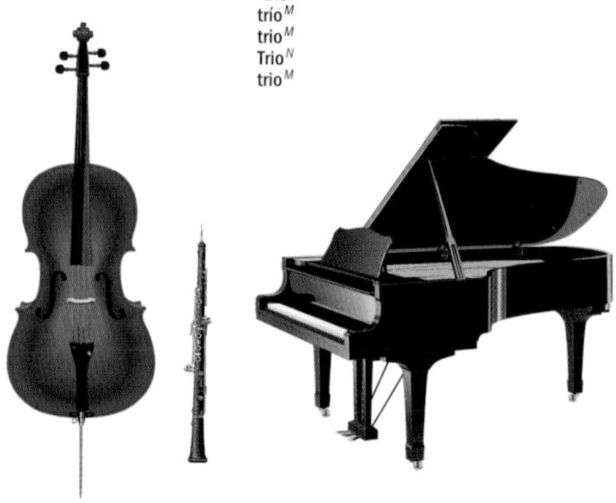

quartet
cuarteto^M
quatuor^M
Quartett^N
quartetto^M

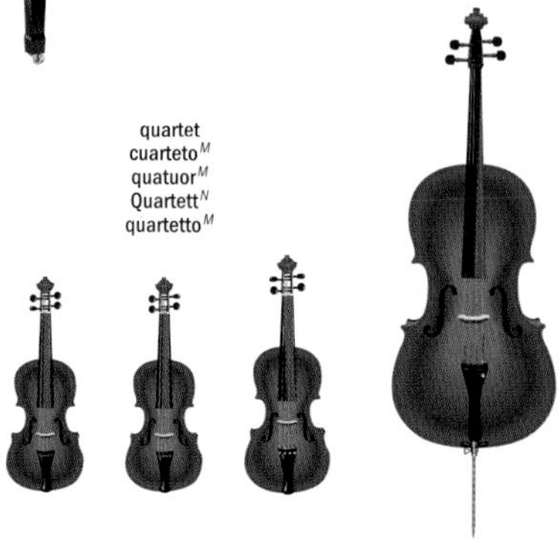

quintet
quinteto^M
quintette^M
Quintett^N
quintetto^M

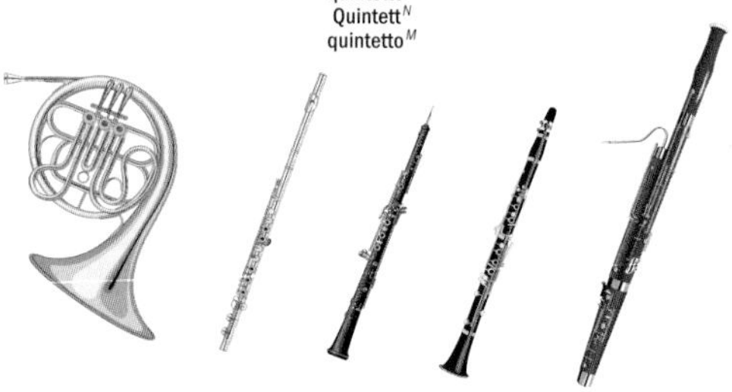

sextet
sexteto^M
sextuor^M
Sextett^N
sestetto^M

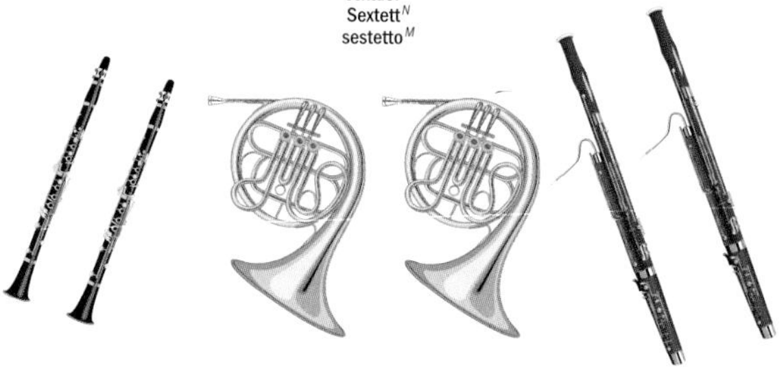

jazz band
banda^F de jazz^M
formation^F de jazz^M
Jazzband^F
jazz-band^F

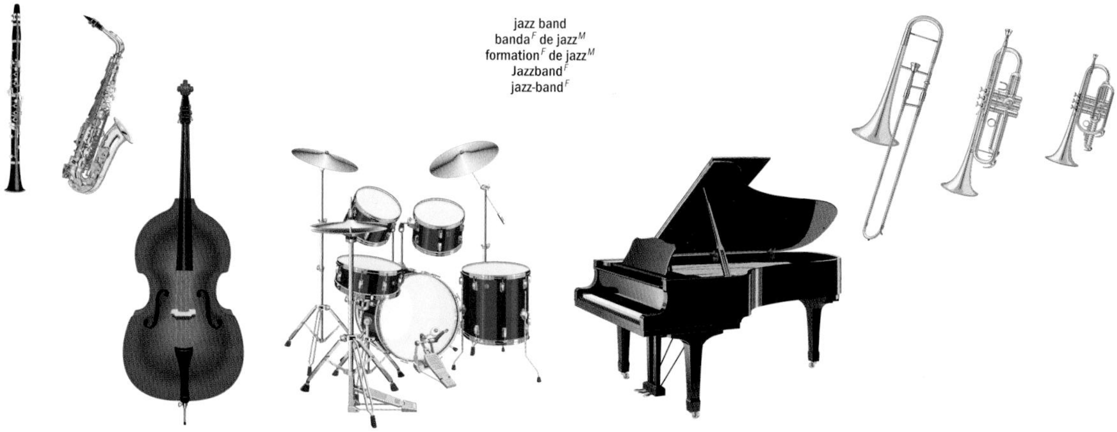

stringed instruments

instrumentos^M de cuerda^F | instruments^M à cordes^F | Saiteninstrumente^N | strumenti^M a corde^F

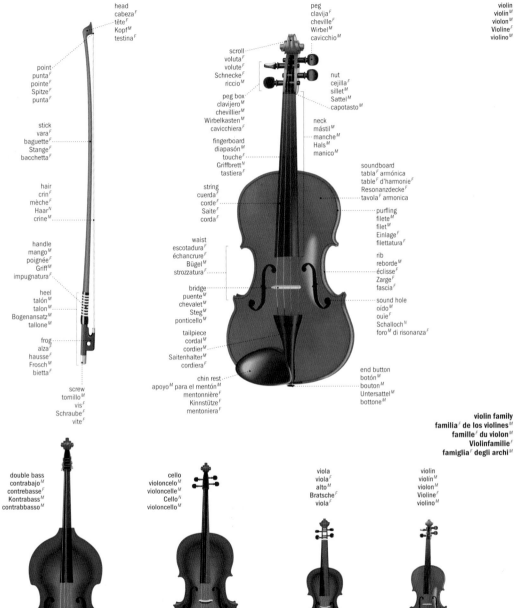

bow
arco^M
archet^M
Bogen^M
archetto^M

head
cabeza^F
tête^F
Kopf^M
testina^F

peg
clavija^F
cheville^F
Wirbel^M
cavicchio^M

violin
violín^M
violon^M
Violine^F
violino^M

point
punta^F
pointe^F
Spitze^F
punta^F

scroll
voluta^F
volute^F
Schnecke^F
riccio^M

nut
cejilla^F
sillet^M
Sattel^M
capotasto^M

peg box
clavijero^M
chevillier^M
Wirbelkasten^M
cavicchiera^F

stick
vara^F
baguette^F
Stange^F
bacchetta^F

neck
mástil^M
manche^M
Hals^M
manico^M

fingerboard
diapasón^M
touche^F
Griffbrett^N
tastiera^F

soundboard
tabla^F armónica
table^F d'harmonie^F
Resonanzdecke^F
tavola^F armonica

hair
crin^F
mèche^F
Haar^N
crine^M

string
cuerda^F
corde^F
Saite^F
corda^F

purfling
filete^M
filet^M
Einlage^F
filettatura^F

handle
mango^M
poignée^F
Griff^M
impugnatura^F

waist
escotadura^F
échancrure^F
Bügel^M
strozzatura^F

rib
reborde^M
éclisse^F
Zarge^F
fascia^F

heel
talón^M
talon^M
Bogenansatz^M
tallone^M

bridge
puente^M
chevalet^M
Steg^M
ponticello^M

sound hole
oído^M
ouïe^F
Schalloch^N
foro^M di risonanza^F

frog
alza^F
hausse^F
Frosch^M
bietta^F

tailpiece
cordal^M
cordier^M
Saitenhalter^M
cordiera^F

end button
botón^M
bouton^M
Untersattel^M
bottone^M

screw
tornillo^M
vis^F
Schraube^F
vite^F

chin rest
apoyo^M para el mentón^M
mentonnière^F
Kinnstütze^F
mentoniera^F

violin family
familia^F de los violines^M
famille^F du violon^M
Violinfamilie^F
famiglia^F degli archi^M

double bass
contrabajo^M
contrebasse^F
Kontrabass^M
contrabbasso^M

cello
violoncelo^M
violoncelle^F
Cello^N
violoncello^M

viola
viola^F
alto^M
Bratsche^F
viola^F

violin
violín^M
violon^M
Violine^F
violino^M

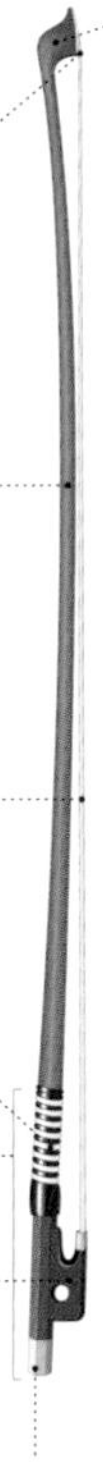

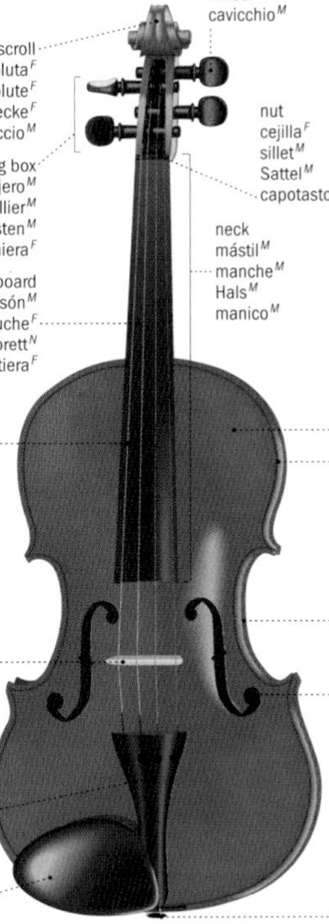

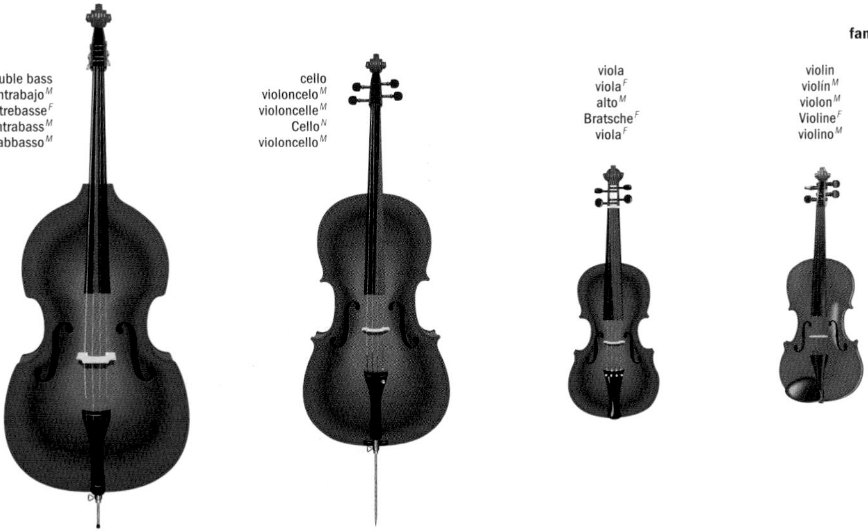

stringed instruments

harp
arpa^F
harpe^F
Harfe^F
arpa^F

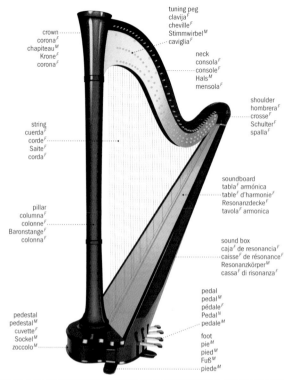

crown
corona^F
chapiteau^M
Krone^F
corona^F

tuning peg
clavija^F
cheville^F
Stimmwirbel^M
caviglia^F

neck
consola^F
console^F
Hals^M
mensola^F

shoulder
hombrera^F
crosse^F
Schulter^F
spalla^F

string
cuerda^F
corde^F
Saite^F
corda^F

soundboard
tabla^F armónica
table^F d'harmonie^F
Resonanzdecke^F
tavola^F armonica

pillar
columna^F
colonne^F
Baronstange^F
colonna^F

sound box
caja^F de resonancia^F
caisse^F de résonance^F
Resonanzkörper^M
cassa^F di risonanza^F

pedal
pedal^M
pédale^F
Pedal^N
pedale^M

pedestal
pedestal^M
cuvette^F
Sockel^M
zoccolo^M

foot
pie^M
pied^M
Fuß^M
piede^M

acoustic guitar
guitarra^F clásica
guitare^F acoustique
akustische Gitarre^F
chitarra^F acustica

soundboard
tabla^F armónica
table^F d'harmonie^F
Resonanzdecke^F
tavola^F armonica

body
caja^F
caisse^F
Korpus^M
cassa^F

neck
mástil^M
manche^M
Hals^M
manico^M

head
cabeza^F
tête^F
Kragen^M
paletta^F

peg
clavija^F
cheville^F
Wirbel^M
cavicchio^M

position marker
marcador^M de posición^F
repère^M de touche^F
Orientierungseinlage^F
tasto^M di posizione^F

nut
cejilla^F
sillet^M
Sattel^M
capotasto^M

heel
talón^M
talon^M
Bodenplättchen^N
tallone^M

fret
traste^M
frette^F
Bund^M
traversina^F

bridge
puente^M
chevalet^M
Steg^M
ponticello^M

rose
roseta^F
rosace^F
Schallrose^F
rosa^F

rib
reborde^M
éclisse^F
Zarge^F
fascia^F

purfling
filete^M
filet^M
Einlage^F
filettatura^F

ARTS AND ARCHITECTURE

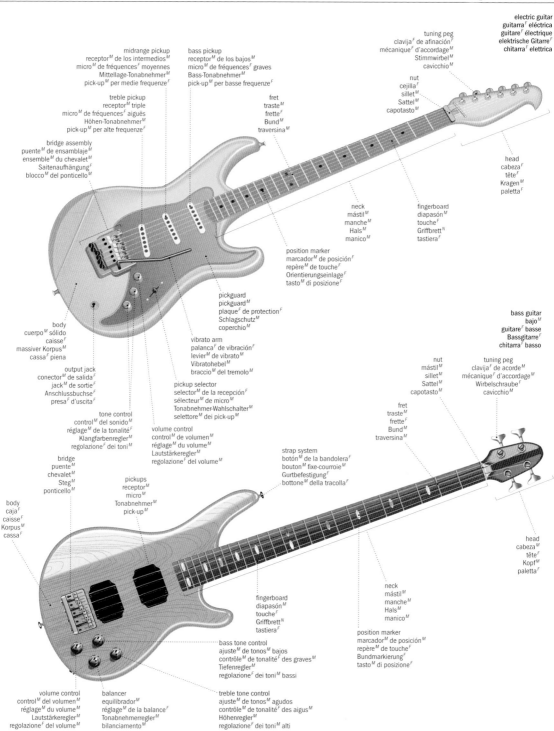

electric guitar
guitarra^F eléctrica
guitare^F électrique
elektrische Gitarre^F
chitarra^F elettrica

tuning peg
clavija^F de afinación^F
mécanique^F d'accordage^M
Stimmwirbel^M
cavicchio^M

midrange pickup
receptor^M de los intermedios^M
micro^M de fréquences^F moyennes
Mittellage-Tonabnehmer^M
pick-up^M per medie frequenze^F

bass pickup
receptor^M de los bajos^M
micro^M de fréquences^F graves
Bass-Tonabnehmer^M
pick-up^M per basse frequenze^F

nut
cejilla^F
sillet^M
Sattel^M
capotasto^M

treble pickup
receptor^M triple
micro^M de fréquences^F aiguës
Höhen-Tonabnehmer^M
pick-up^M per alte frequenze^F

fret
traste^M
frette^F
Bund^M
traversina^M

head
cabeza^F
tête^F
Kragen^M
paletta^F

bridge assembly
puente^M de ensamblaje^M
ensemble^M du chevalet^M
Saitenaufhängung^F
blocco^M del ponticello^M

neck
mástil^M
manche^M
Hals^M
manico^M

fingerboard
diapasón^M
touche^F
Griffbrett^N
tastiera^F

position marker
marcador^M de posición^F
repère^M de touche^F
Orientierungseinlage^F
tasto^M di posizione^F

pickguard
pickguard^M
plaque^F de protection^F
Schlagschutz^M
coperchio^M

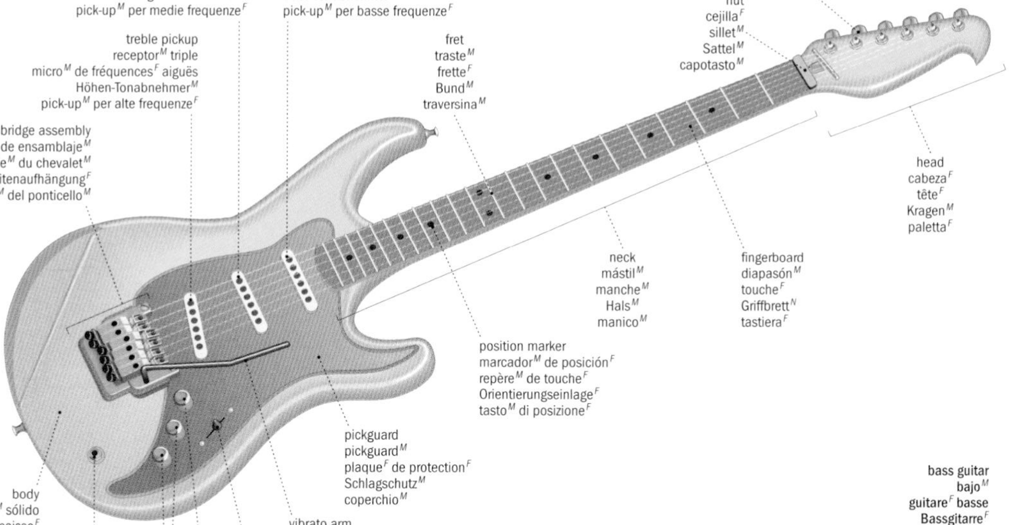

bass guitar
bajo^M
guitare^F basse
Bassgitarre^F
chitarra^F basso

body
cuerpo^M sólido
caisse^F
massiver Korpus^M
cassa^F piena

vibrato arm
palanca^F de vibración^F
levier^M de vibrato^M
Vibratohebel^M
braccio^M del tremolo^M

nut
mástil^M
sillet^M
Sattel^M
capotasto^M

tuning peg
clavija^F de acorde^M
mécanique^F d'accordage^M
Wirbelschraube^F
cavicchio^M

output jack
conector^M de salida^F
jack^M de sortie^F
Anschlussbuchse^F
presa^F d'uscita^F

pickup selector
selector^M de la recepción^F
sélecteur^M de micro^M
Tonabnehmer-Wahlschalter^M
selettore^M dei pick-up^M

fret
traste^M
frette^F
Bund^M
traversina^M

tone control
control^M del sonido^M
réglage^M de la tonalité^F
Klangfarbenregler^M
regolazione^F dei toni^M

volume control
control^M de volumen^M
réglage^M du volume^M
Lautstärkeregler^M
regolazione^F del volume^M

strap system
botón^M de la bandolera^F
bouton^M fixe-courroie^M
Gurtbefestigung^F
bottone^M della tracolla^F

bridge
puente^M
chevalet^M
Steg^M
ponticello^M

pickups
receptor^M
micro^M
Tonabnehmer^M
pick-up^M

head
cabeza^M
tête^F
Kopf^M
paletta^F

body
caja^F
caisse^F
Korpus^M
cassa^F

fingerboard
diapasón^M
touche^F
Griffbrett^N
tastiera^F

neck
mástil^M
manche^M
Hals^M
manico^M

position marker
marcador^M de posición^F
repère^M de touche^F
Bundmarkierung^F
tasto^M di posizione^F

bass tone control
ajuste^M de tonos^M bajos
contrôle^M de tonalité^F des graves
Tiefenregler^M
regolazione^F dei toni^M bassi

volume control
control^M del volumen^M
réglage^M du volume^M
Lautstärkeregler^M
regolazione^F del volume^M

balancer
equilibrador^M
réglage^M de la balance^F
Tonabnehmerregler^M
bilanciamento^M

treble tone control
ajuste^M de tonos^M agudos
contrôle^M de tonalité^F des aigus^M
Höhenregler^M
regolazione^F dei toni^M alti

ARTS AND ARCHITECTURE

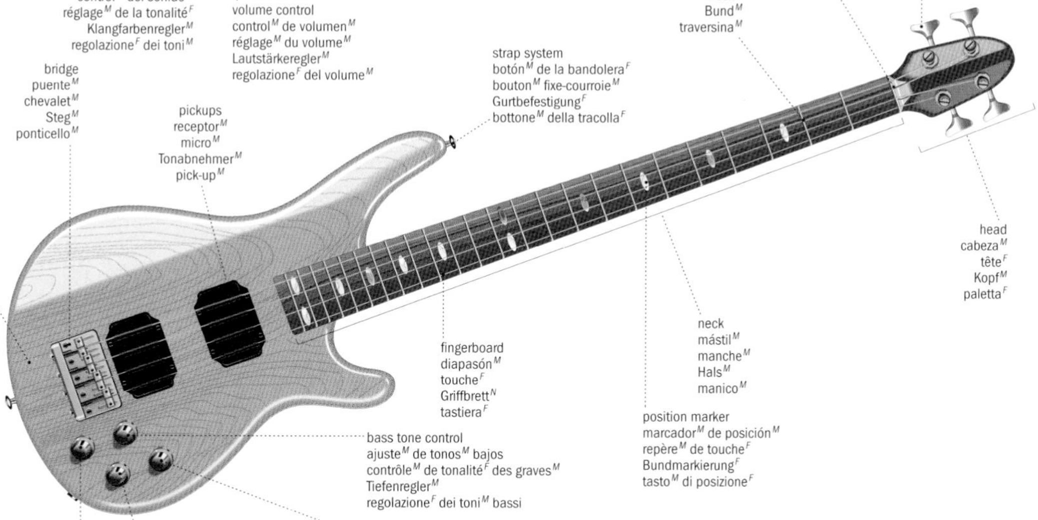

keyboard instruments

instrumentos^M de teclado^M | instruments^M à clavier^M | Tasteninstrumente^N | strumenti^M a tastiera^F

upright piano
piano^M vertical
piano^M droit
Klavier^N
pianoforte^M verticale

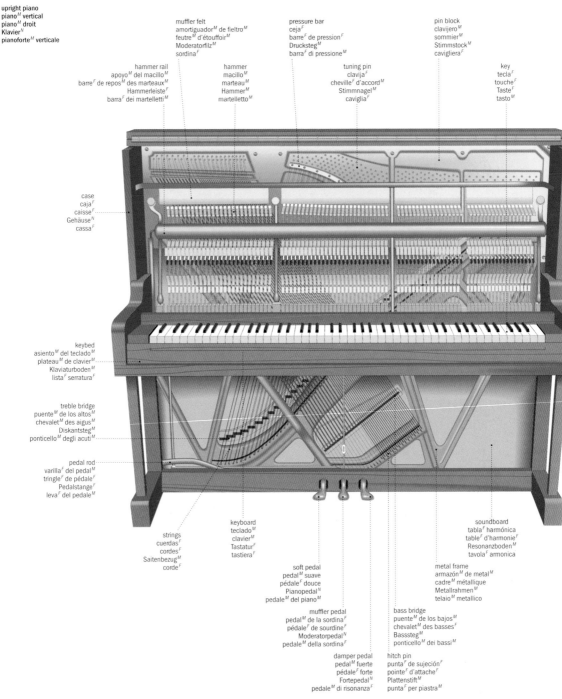

muffler felt
amortiguador^M de fieltro^M
feutre^M d'étouffoir^M
Moderatorfilz^M
sordina^F

pressure bar
ceja^F
barre^F de pression^F
Drucksteg^M
barra^F di pressione^M

pin block
clavijero^M
sommier^M
Stimmstock^M
cavigliera^F

hammer rail
apoyo^M del macillo^M
barre^F de repos^M des marteaux^F
Hammerleiste^F
barra^F dei martelletti^M

hammer
macillo^M
marteau^M
Hammer^M
martelletto^M

tuning pin
clavija^F
cheville^F d'accord^M
Stimmnagel^M
caviglia^F

key
tecla^F
touche^F
Taste^F
tasto^M

case
caja^F
caisse^F
Gehäuse^N
cassa^F

keybed
asiento^M del teclado^M
plateau^M de clavier^M
Klaviaturboden^M
lista^F serratura^F

treble bridge
puente^M de los altos^M
chevalet^M des aigus^M
Diskantsteg^M
ponticello^M degli acuti^M

pedal rod
varilla^F del pedal^M
tringle^F de pédale^F
Pedalstange^F
leva^F del pedale^M

strings
cuerdas^F
cordes^F
Saitenbezug^M
corde^F

keyboard
teclado^M
clavier^M
Tastatur^F
tastiera^F

soundboard
tabla^F harmónica
table^F d'harmonie^F
Resonanzboden^M
tavola^F armonica

soft pedal
pedal^M suave
pédale^F douce
Pianopedal^N
pedale^M del piano^M

metal frame
armazón^M de metal^M
cadre^M métallique
Metallrahmen^M
telaio^M metallico

muffler pedal
pedal^M de la sordina^F
pédale^F de sourdine^F
Moderatorpedal^N
pedale^M della sordina^F

bass bridge
puente^M de los bajos^M
chevalet^M des basses^F
Basssteg^M
ponticello^M dei bassi^M

damper pedal
pedal^M fuerte
pédale^F forte
Fortepedal^N
pedale^M di risonanza^F

hitch pin
punta^F de sujeción^F
pointe^F d'attache^F
Plattenstift^M
punta^F per piastra^M

ARTS AND ARCHITECTURE

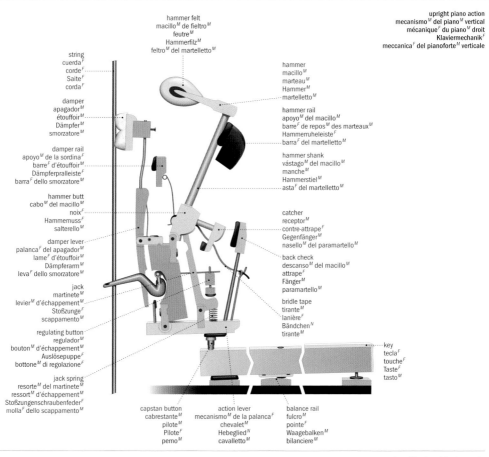

string
cuerda^F
corde^F
Saite^F
corda^F

hammer felt
macillo^M de fieltro^M
feutre^M
Hammerfilz^M
feltro^M del martelletto^M

upright piano action
mecanismo^M del piano^M vertical
mécanique^F du piano^M droit
Klaviermechanik^F
meccanica^F del pianoforte^M verticale

hammer
macillo^M
marteau^M
Hammer^M
martelletto^M

damper
apagador^M
étouffoir^M
Dämpfer^M
smorzatore^M

hammer rail
apoyo^M del macillo^M
barre^F de repos^M des marteaux^M
Hammerruheleiste^F
barra^F del martelletto^M

damper rail
apoyo^M de la sordina^F
barre^F d'étouffoir^M
Dämpferpralleiste^F
barra^F dello smorzatore^M

hammer shank
vástago^M del macillo^M
manche^M
Hammerstiel^M
asta^F del martelletto^M

hammer butt
cabo^M del macillo^M
noix^F
Hammemuss^F
salterello^M

catcher
receptor^M
contre-attrape^F
Gegenfänger^M
nasello^F del paramartello^M

back check
descanso^M del macillo^M
attrape^F
Fänger^M
paramartello^M

damper lever
palanca^F del apagador^M
lame^F d'étouffoir^M
Dämpferarm^M
leva^F dello smorzatore^M

jack
martinete^M
levier^M d'échappement^M
Stoßzunge^F
scappamento^M

bridle tape
tirante^M
lanière^F
Bändchen^N
tirante^M

regulating button
regulador^M
bouton^M d'échappement^M
Auslösepuppe^F
bottone^M di regolazione^F

key
tecla^F
touche^F
Taste^F
tasto^M

jack spring
resorte^M del martinete^M
ressort^M d'échappement^M
Stoßzungenschraubenfeder^F
molla^F dello scappamento^M

capstan button
cabrestante^M
pilote^M
Pilote^F
perno^M

action lever
mecanismo^M de la palanca^F
chevalet^M
Hebeglied^N
cavalletto^M

balance rail
fulcro^M
pointe^F
Waagebalken^M
bilanciere^M

ARTS AND ARCHITECTURE

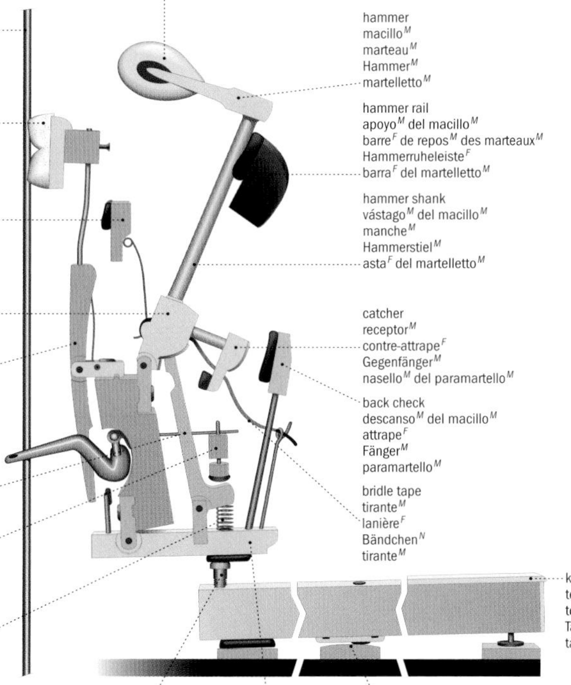

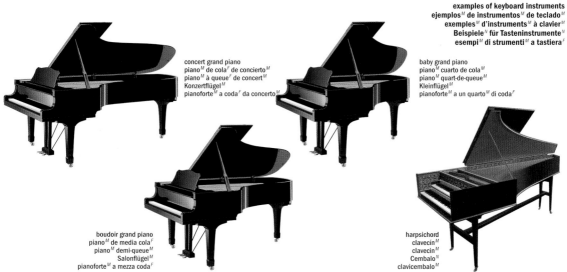

examples of keyboard instruments
ejemplos^M de instrumentos^M de teclado^M
exemples^M d'instruments^M à clavier^M
Beispiele^N für Tasteninstrumente^N
esempi^M di strumenti^M a tastiera^F

concert grand piano
piano^M de cola^F de concierto^M
piano^M à queue^F de concert^M
Konzertflügel^M
pianoforte^M a coda^F da concerto^M

baby grand piano
piano^M cuarto de cola^M
piano^M quart-de-queue^M
Kleinflügel^M
pianoforte^M a un quarto^M di coda^F

boudoir grand piano
piano^M de media cola^F
piano^M demi-queue^M
Salonflügel^M
pianoforte^M a mezza coda^F

harpsichord
clavecín^M
clavecin^M
Cembalo^N
clavicembalo^M

organ
órgano^M
orgue^M
Orgel^F
organo^M

organ console
consola^F
console^F d'orgue^M
Orgelspieltisch^M
console^F dell'organo^M

stop knob
botón^M de registro^M
bouton^M de registre^M
Registerzug^M
tasto^M di registro^M

music stand
atril^M
pupitre^M
Notenablage^F
leggio^N

swell organ manual
teclado^M del órgano^M de expresión^F
clavier^M de récit^M
Manual^N für das Oberwerk^N
manuale^M dell'organo^M espressivo

coupler-tilt tablet
tableta^F de resonancia^F
domino^M d'accouplement^M
Koppel-Kipptaste^F
placchetta^F a bilanciere^M

choir organ manual
teclado^M del órgano^M positivo
clavier^M de positif^M
Manual^N für das Rückpositiv^N
manuale^M dell'organo^M positivo

manuals
teclados^M manuales
claviers^M manuels
Manuale^N
manuali^M

great organ manual
teclado^M del órgano^M mayor
clavier^M de grand orgue^M
Manual^N für das Hauptwerk^N
manuale^M del grand'organo^M

thumb piston
botón^M de acoplamiento^M
bouton^M de combinaisons^F
Druckknopf^M
pistoncino^M del manuale^M

crescendo pedal
pedal^M crescendo
pédale^F crescendo^M
Rollschweller^M
pedale^M del crescendo^M

pedal key
tecla^F de pedal^M
touche^F de pédalier^M
Pedaltaste^F
pedale^M

toe piston
acoplamiento^M de pedal^M
pédale^F de combinaisons^F
Fußtritt^M
pistoncino^M del pedale^M

swell pedals
pedal^M de expresión^F
pédales^F d'expression^F
Jalousieschweller^M
pedali^M d'espressione^F

pedal keyboard
pedalero^M
clavier^M à pédales^F
Pedalklaviatur^F
pedaliera^F

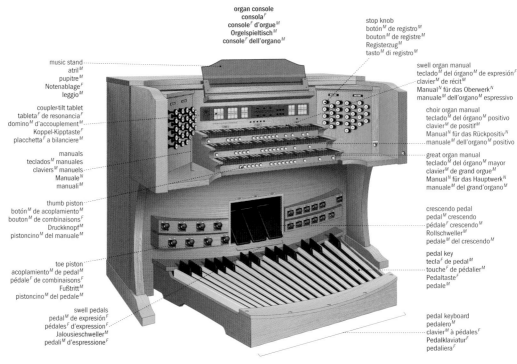

reed pipe
tubo^M de lengüeta^F
tuyau^M à anche^F
Zungenpfeife^F
canna^F ad ancia^F

flue pipe
tubo^M de embocadura^F
tuyau^M à bouche^F
Lippenpfeife^F
canna^F ad anima^F

resonator
resonador^M
pavillon^M
Schallbecher^M
padiglione^M

tuning wire
afinador^M
rasette^F
Stimmkrücke^F
asta^F d'accordo^M

body
tapa^F
corps^M
Körper^M
corpo^M

block
bloque^M
noyau^M
Bleikopf^M
blocco^F

upper lip
labio^M superior
lèvre^F supérieure
Oberlippe^F
labbro^M superiore

mouth
boca^F
bouche^F
Aufschnitt^M
bocca^F

wedge
cuña^F
coin^M
Keil^M
cuneo^M

languid
alma^F
biseau^M
Kern^M
anima^F

shallot
caña^F
anche^F
Kehle^F
gola^F

tongue
lengüeta^F
languette^F
Zunge^F
ancia^F

flue
caño^M
lumière^F
Kernspalte^F
fessura^F

lower lip
labio^M inferior
lèvre^F inférieure
Unterlippe^F
labbro^M inferiore

foot
pie^M
pied^M
Stiefel^M
stivale^M

foot
pie^M
pied^M
Fuß^M
piede^M

foot hole
orificio^M del pie^M
orifice^M du pied^M
Fußbohrung^F
foro^M del piede^M

foot hole
orificio^M del pie^M
orifice^M du pied^M
Fußbohrung^F
foro^M del piede^M

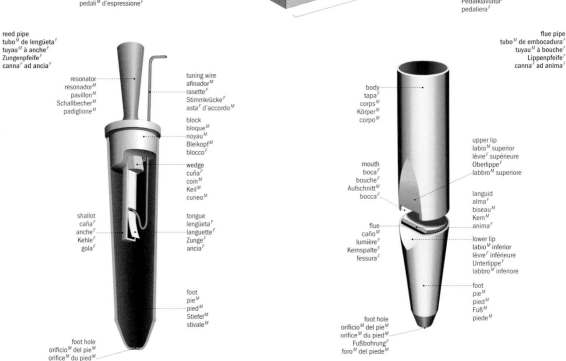

ARTS AND ARCHITECTURE

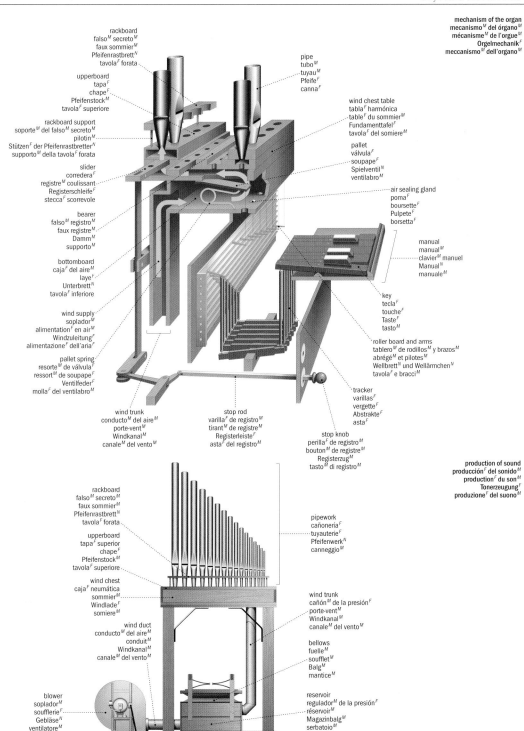

mechanism of the organ
mecanismo^M del órgano^M
mécanisme^M de l'orgue^M
Orgelmechanik^F
meccanismo^M dell'organo^M

rackboard
falso^M secreto^M
faux sommier^M
Pfeifenrastbrett^N
tavola^F forata

upperboard
tapa^F
chape^F
Pfeifenstock^M
tavola^F superiore

rackboard support
soporte^M del falso^M secreto^M
pilotin^M
Stützen^F der Pfeifenrastbretter^N
supporto^M della tavola^F forata

slider
corredera^F
registre^M coulissant
Registerschleife^F
stecca^F scorrevole

bearer
falso^M registro^M
faux registre^M
Damm^M
supporto^M

bottomboard
caja^F del aire^M
laye^F
Unterbrett^N
tavola^F inferiore

wind supply
soplador^M
alimentation^F en air^M
Windzuleitung^F
alimentazione^F dell'aria^F

pallet spring
resorte^M de válvula^F
ressort^M de soupape^F
Ventilfeder^F
molla^F del ventilabro^M

pipe
tubo^M
tuyau^M
Pfeife^F
canna^F

wind chest table
tabla^F harmónica
table^F du sommier^M
Fundamenttafel^F
tavola^F del somiere^M

pallet
válvula^F
soupape^F
Spielventil^N
ventilabro^M

air sealing gland
poma^M
boursette^F
Pulpete^F
borsetta^F

manual
manual^M
clavier^M manuel
Manual^N
manuale^M

key
tecla^F
touche^F
Taste^F
tasto^M

roller board and arms
tablero^M de rodillos^M y brazos^M
abrégé^M et pilotes^M
Wellbrett^N und Wellärmchen^N
tavola^F e bracci^M

tracker
varillas^F
vergette^F
Abstrakte^F
asta^F

wind trunk
conducto^M del aire^M
porte-vent^M
Windkanal^M
canale^M del vento^M

stop rod
varilla^F de registro^M
tirant^M de registre^M
Registerleiste^F
asta^F del registro^M

stop knob
perilla^F de registro^M
bouton^M de registre^M
Registerzug^M
tasto^M di registro^M

production of sound
producción^F del sonido^M
production^F du son^M
Tonerzeugung^F
produzione^F del suono^M

rackboard
falso^M secreto^M
faux sommier^M
Pfeifenrastbrett^N
tavola^F forata

upperboard
tapa^F superior
chape^F
Pfeifenstock^M
tavola^F superiore

wind chest
caja^F neumática
sommier^M
Windlade^F
somiere^M

wind duct
conducto^M del aire^M
conduit^M
Windkanal^M
canale^M del vento^M

pipework
cañonería^F
tuyauterie^F
Pfeifenwerk^N
canneggio^M

wind trunk
cañón^M de la presión^F
porte-vent^M
Windkanal^M
canale^M del vento^M

bellows
fuelle^M
soufflet^M
Balg^M
mantice^M

blower
soplador^M
soufflerie^F
Gebläse^N
ventilatore^M

reservoir
regulador^M de la presión^F
réservoir^M
Magazinbalg^M
serbatoio^M

wind instruments

instrumentos ^{M} de viento ^{M} | instruments ^{M} à vent ^{M} | Blasinstrumente ^{N} | strumenti ^{M} a fiato ^{M}

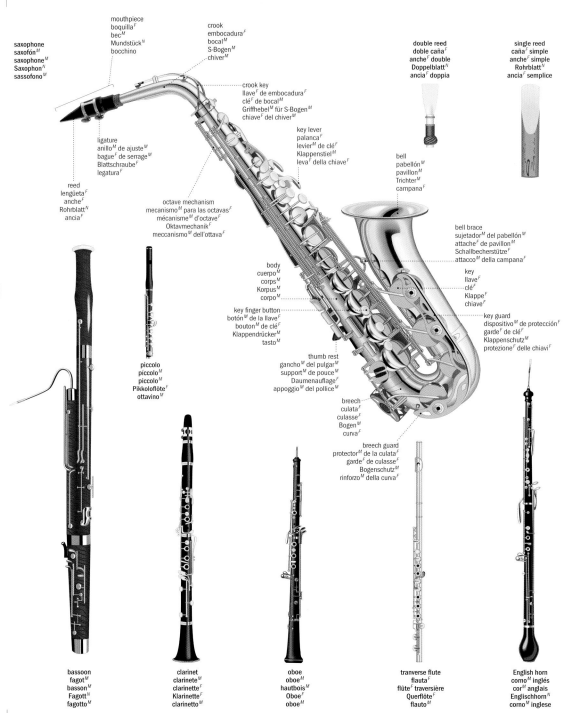

saxophone
saxofón ^{M}
saxophone ^{M}
Saxophon ^{N}
sassofono ^{M}

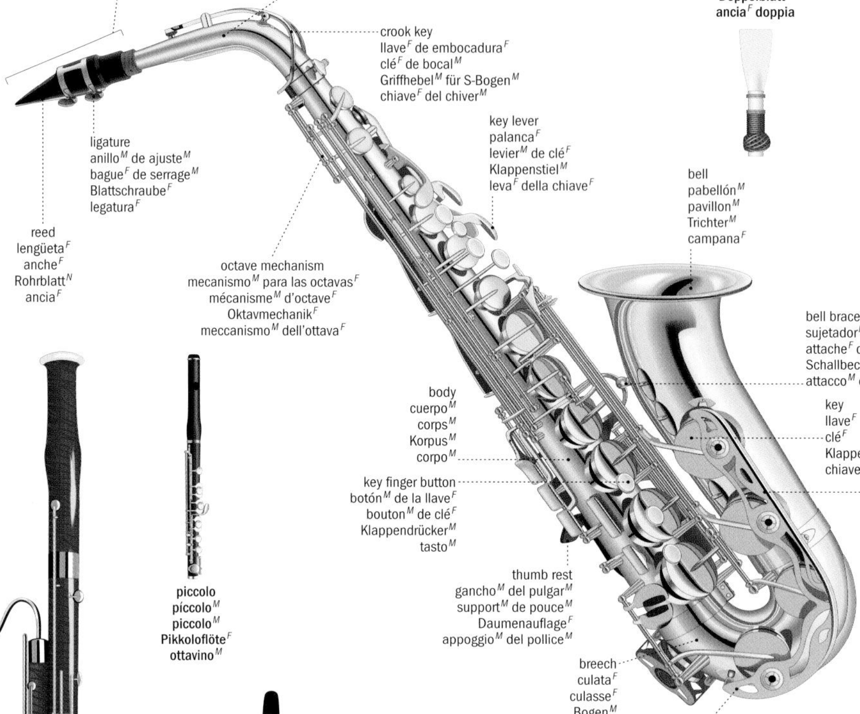

mouthpiece
boquilla ^{F}
bec ^{M}
Mundstück ^{N}
bocchino

crook
embocadura ^{F}
bocal ^{M}
S-Bogen ^{M}
chiver ^{M}

crook key
llave ^{F} de embocadura ^{F}
clé ^{F} de bocal ^{M}
Griffhebel ^{M} für S-Bogen ^{M}
chiave ^{F} del chiver ^{M}

key lever
palanca ^{F}
levier ^{M} de clé ^{F}
Klappenstiel ^{M}
leva ^{F} della chiave ^{F}

double reed
doble caña ^{F}
anche ^{F} double
Doppelblatt ^{N}
ancia ^{F} doppia

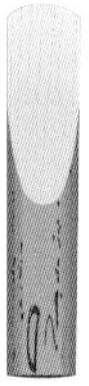

single reed
caña ^{F} simple
anche ^{F} simple
Rohrblatt ^{N}
ancia ^{F} semplice

ligature
anillo ^{M} de ajuste ^{M}
bague ^{F} de serrage ^{M}
Blattschraube ^{F}
legatura ^{F}

bell
pabellón ^{M}
pavillon ^{M}
Trichter ^{M}
campana ^{F}

reed
lengüeta ^{F}
anche ^{F}
Rohrblatt ^{N}
ancia ^{F}

octave mechanism
mecanismo ^{M} para las octavas ^{F}
mécanisme ^{M} d'octave ^{F}
Oktavmechanik ^{F}
meccanismo ^{M} dell'ottava ^{F}

bell brace
sujetador ^{M} del pabellón ^{M}
attache ^{F} de pavillon ^{M}
Schallbecherstütze ^{F}
attacco ^{M} della campana ^{F}

key
llave ^{F}
clé ^{F}
Klappe ^{F}
chiave ^{F}

body
cuerpo ^{M}
corps ^{M}
Korpus ^{M}
corpo ^{M}

key finger button
botón ^{M} de la llave ^{F}
bouton ^{M} de clé ^{F}
Klappendrücker ^{M}
tasto ^{M}

key guard
dispositivo ^{M} de protección ^{F}
garde ^{F} de clé ^{F}
Klappenschutz ^{M}
protezione ^{F} delle chiavi ^{F}

piccolo
píccolo ^{M}
piccolo ^{M}
Pikkoloflöte ^{F}
ottavino ^{M}

thumb rest
gancho ^{M} del pulgar ^{M}
support ^{M} de pouce ^{M}
Daumenauflage ^{F}
appoggio ^{M} del pollice ^{M}

breech
culata ^{F}
culasse ^{F}
Bogen ^{M}
curva ^{F}

breech guard
protector ^{M} de la culata ^{F}
garde ^{F} de culasse ^{F}
Bogenschutz ^{M}
rinforzo ^{M} della curva ^{F}

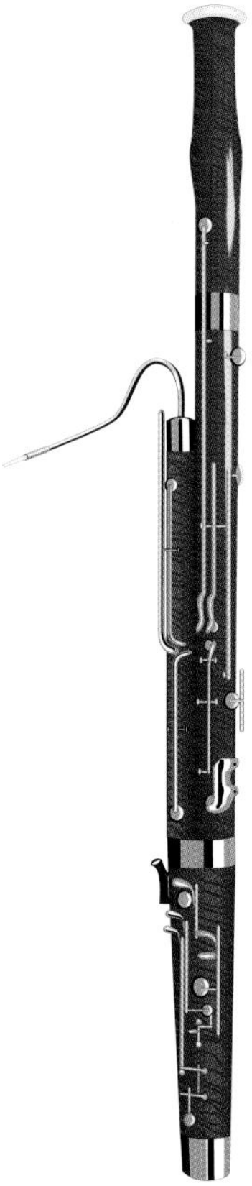

bassoon
fagot ^{M}
basson ^{M}
Fagott ^{N}
fagotto ^{M}

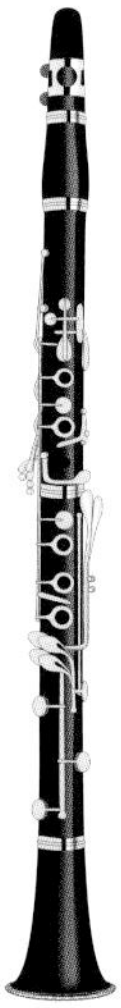

clarinet
clarinete ^{M}
clarinette ^{F}
Klarinette ^{F}
clarinetto ^{M}

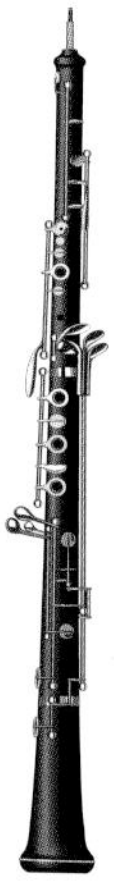

oboe
oboe ^{M}
hautbois ^{M}
Oboe ^{F}
oboe ^{M}

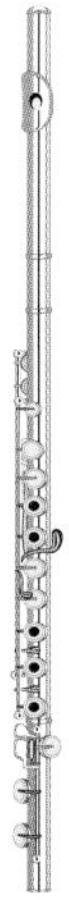

tranverse flute
flauta ^{F}
flûte ^{F} traversière
Querflöte ^{F}
flauto ^{M}

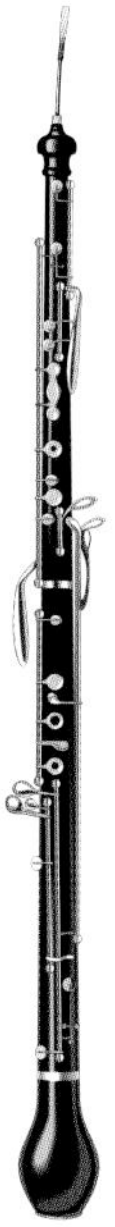

English horn
corno ^{M} inglés
cor ^{M} anglais
Englischhorn ^{N}
corno ^{M} inglese

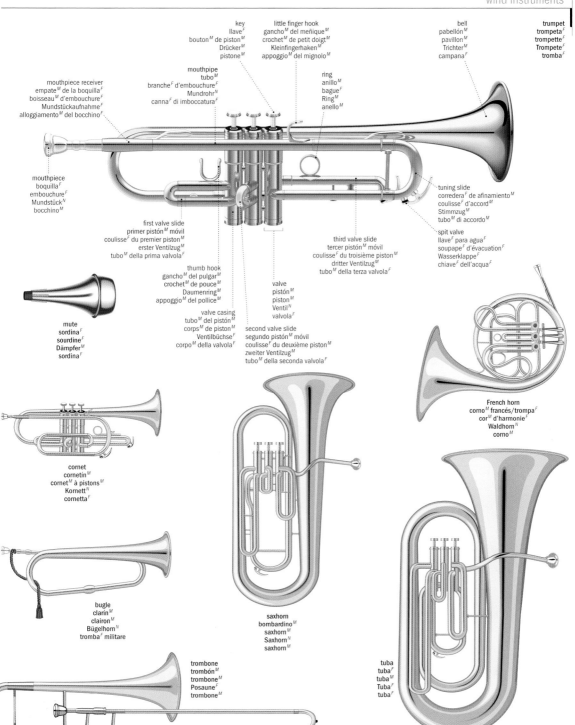

key
llave^F
bouton^M de piston^M
Drücker^M
pistone^M

little finger hook
gancho^M del meñique^M
crochet^M de petit doigt^M
Kleinfingerhaken^M
appoggio^M del mignolo^M

bell
pabellón^M
pavillon^M
Trichter^M
campana^F

trumpet
trompeta^F
trompette^F
Trompete^F
tromba^F

mouthpiece receiver
empate^M de la boquilla^F
boisseau^M d'embouchure^F
Mundstückaufnahme^F
alloggiamento^M del bocchino^F

mouthpipe
tubo^M
branche^F d'embouchure^F
Mundrohr^N
canna^F di imboccatura^F

ring
anillo^M
bague^F
Ring^M
anello^M

mouthpiece
boquilla^F
embouchure^F
Mundstück^N
bocchino^M

tuning slide
corredera^F de afinamiento^M
coulisse^F d'accord^M
Stimmzug^M
tubo^M di accordo^M

first valve slide
primer pistón^M móvil
coulisse^F du premier piston^M
erster Ventilzug^M
tubo^M della prima valvola^F

third valve slide
tercer pistón^M móvil
coulisse^F du troisième piston^M
dritter Ventilzug^M
tubo^M della terza valvola^F

spit valve
llave^F para agua^F
soupape^F d'évacuation^F
Wasserklappe^F
chiave^F dell'acqua^F

thumb hook
gancho^M del pulgar^M
crochet^M de pouce^M
Daumenring^M
appoggio^M del pollice^M

valve
pistón^M
piston^M
Ventil^N
valvola^F

valve casing
tubo^M del pistón^M
corps^M de piston^M
Ventilbüchse^F
corpo^M della valvola^F

second valve slide
segundo pistón^M móvil
coulisse^F du deuxième piston^M
zweiter Ventilzug^M
tubo^M della seconda valvola^F

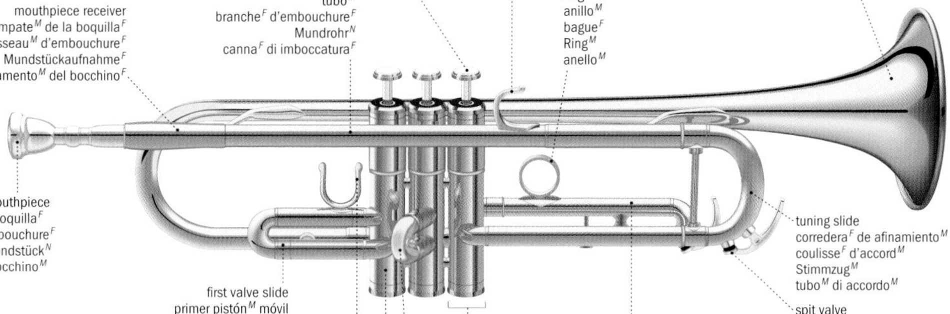

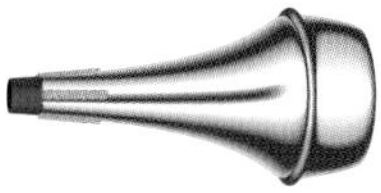

mute
sordina^F
sourdine^F
Dämpfer^M
sordina^F

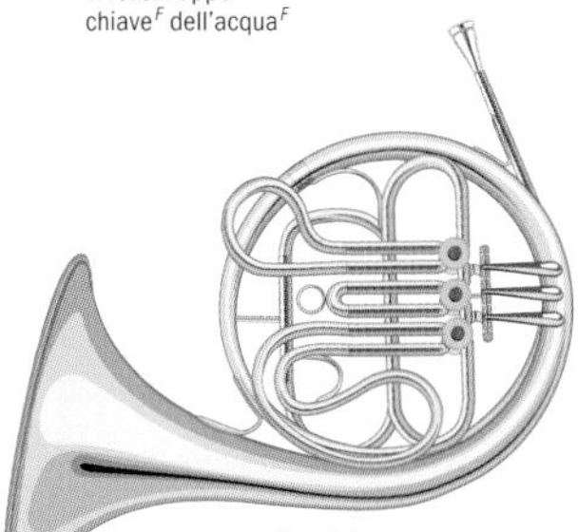

French horn
corno^M francés/trompa^F
cor^M d'harmonie^F
Waldhorn^N
corno^M

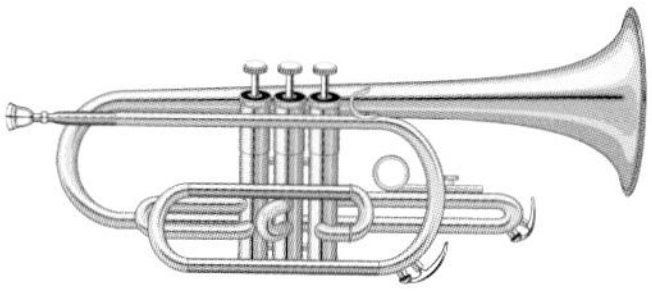

cornet
cornetín^M
cornet^M à pistons^M
Kornett^N
cornetta^F

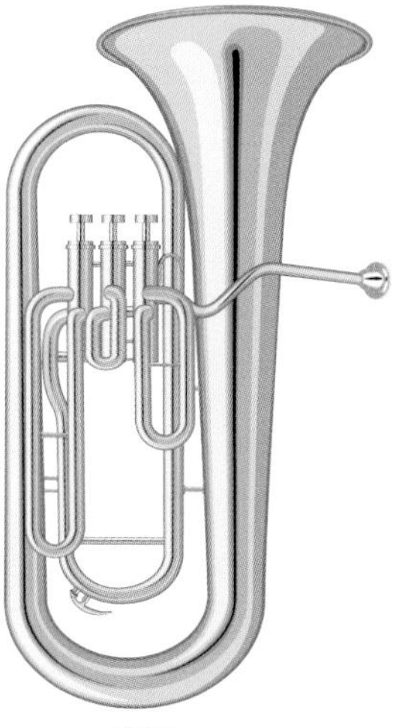

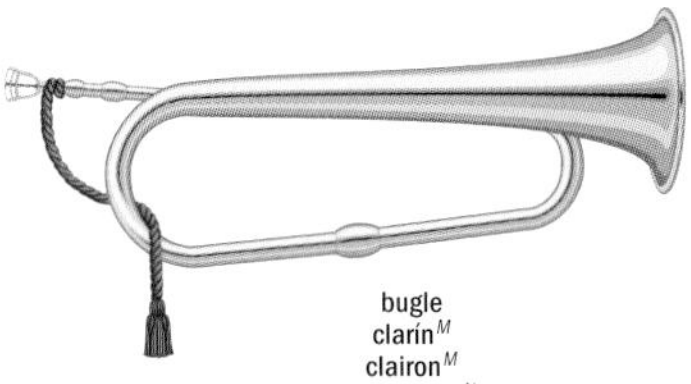

bugle
clarín^M
clairon^M
Bügelhorn^N
tromba^F militare

saxhorn
bombardino^M
saxhorn^M
Saxhorn^N
saxhorn^M

tuba
tuba^F
tuba^M
Tuba^F
tuba^F

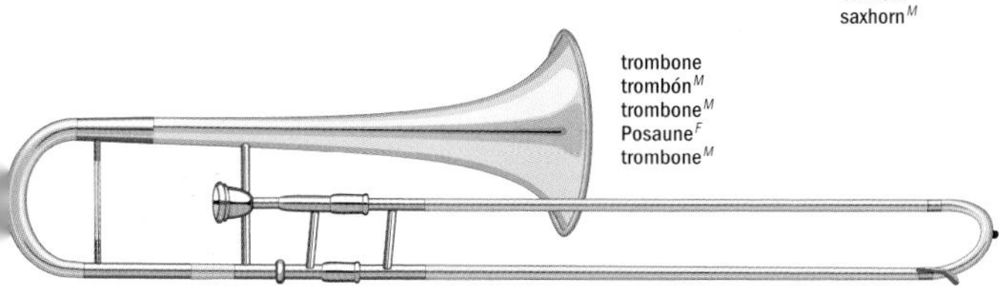

trombone
trombón^M
trombone^M
Posaune^F
trombone^M

ARTS AND ARCHITECTURE

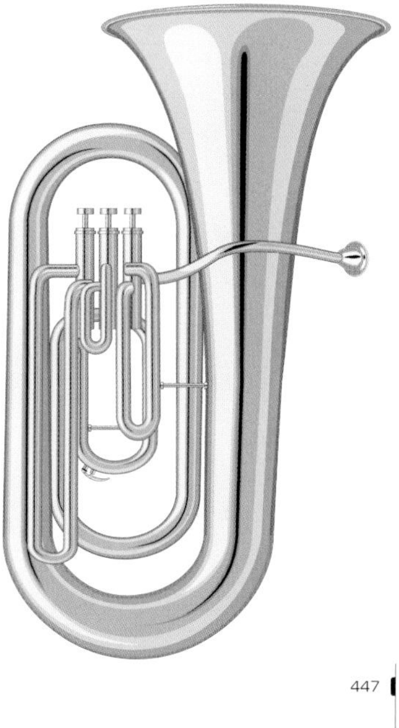

percussion instruments

instrumentos^M de percusión^F | instruments^M à percussion^F | Schlaginstrumente^N | strumenti^M a percussione^F

drums
bateria^F
batterie^F
Trommeln^F
batteria^F

tom-tom
tam-tam^M
tam-tam^M
Tomtom^N
tom tom^M

cymbal
platillo^M suspendido
cymbale^F suspendue
Becken^N
piatto^M

mallet
palillo^M
mailloche^F
Schlegel^M
mazza^F

high-hat cymbal
platillo^M high hat
cymbale^F charleston
Charlestonmaschine^F
charleston^M

tenor drum
tamboril^M
caisse^F roulante
Standtom^N
tamburo^M tenore^M

superior cymbal
platillo^M superior
cymbale^F supérieure
oberes Becken^N
piatto^M superiore

spur
espolón^M
éperon^M
Feststellspitze^F
piedino^M

inferior cymbal
platillo^M inferior
cymbale^F inférieure
unteres Becken^N
piatto^M inferiore

pedal
pedal^M
pédale^F
Pedal^N
pedale^M

batter head
parche^M superior
peau^F de batterie^F
Trommelfell^N
battitoia^F

leg
pata^F
pied^M
Bein^N
piedino^M

snare drum
caja^F clara
caisse^F claire
kleine Trommel^F
cassa^F chiara

tripod stand
trípode^M
trépied^M
Dreifußständer^M
treppiede^M

stand
soporte^M
support^M
Ständer^M
supporto^M

kettledrum
timbal^M
timbale^F
Kesselpauke^F
timpano^M

bass drum
bombo^M
grosse caisse^F
Basstrommel^F
grancassa^F

tension screw
clavija^F de tensión^F
vis^F de tension^F
Stellschraube^F
tirante^M a vite^F

snare drum
caja^F clara
caisse^F claire
kleine Trommel^F
cassa^F chiara

lug
sujetador^M
attache^F
Böckchen^N
blocchetto^M

tie rod
barra^F sujetadora
tirant^M
Spannschraube^F
tirante^M a vite^F

batter head
parche^M superior
peau^F de batterie^F
Trommelfell^N
battitoia^F

metal counterhoop
arco^M tensor
cercle^M de serrage^M
Metallspannreifen^M
cerchio^M di serraggio^M

tuning gauge
afinación^F
manomètre^M d'accord^M
Stimmanzeiger^M
chiavi^F di tensione^F

tension rod
varilla^F de tensión^F
tringle^F de tension^F
Stimmeinrichtung^F
tirante^M

shell
concha^F
fût^M
Kessel^M
caldaia^F

snare strainer
tensor^M de las cuerdas^F
tendeur^M de timbre^M
Schnarrsaitenspanner^M
tirante^M della cordiera^F

strut
puntal^M
châssis^M
Strebe^F
gabbia^F

snare
cuerdas^F
cordes^F de timbre^M
Schnarrsaite^F
cordiera^F

tension rod
varilla^F de tensión^F
tringle^F de tension^F
Stimmeinrichtung^F
tirante^M

crown
corona^F
couronne^F
Aufhängung^F
corona^F

snare head
parche^M inferior
peau^F de timbre^M
Resonanzfell^N
bordoniera^F

caster
ruedecilla^F
roulette^F
Rolle^F
rotella^F orientabile

foot
pata^F
pied^M
Bodenplatte^F
base^F

pedal
pedal^M
pédale^F
Pedal^N
pedale^M

ARTS AND ARCHITECTURE

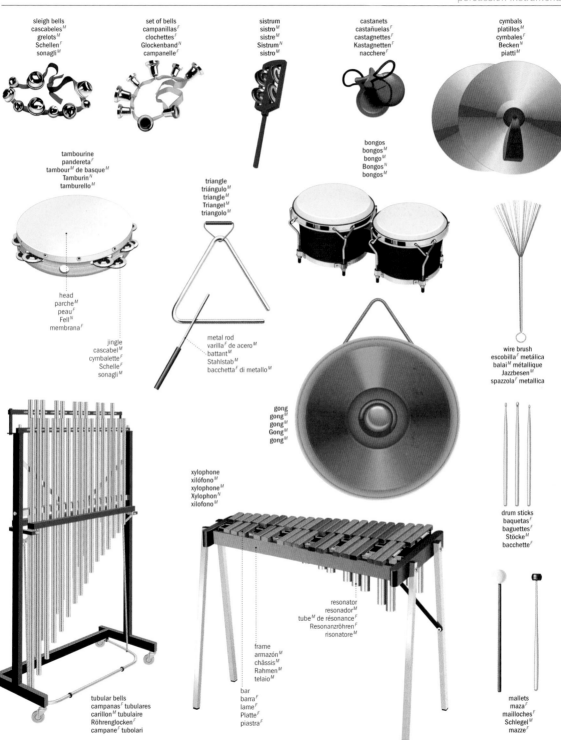

sleigh bells
cascabeles[M]
grelots[M]
Schellen[F]
sonagli[M]

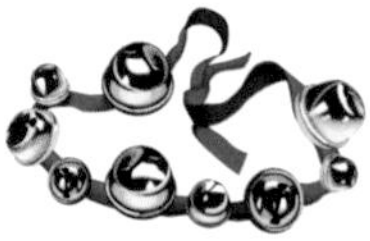

set of bells
campanillas[F]
clochettes[F]
Glockenband[N]
campanelle[F]

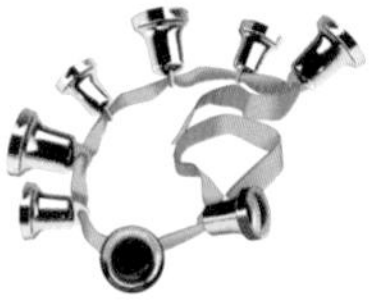

sistrum
sistro[M]
sistre[M]
Sistrum[N]
sistro[M]

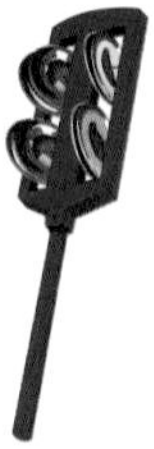

castanets
castañuelas[F]
castagnettes[F]
Kastagnetten[F]
nacchere[F]

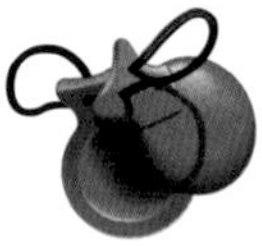

cymbals
platillos[M]
cymbales[F]
Becken[N]
piatti[M]

bongos
bongos[M]
bongo[M]
Bongos[N]
bongos[M]

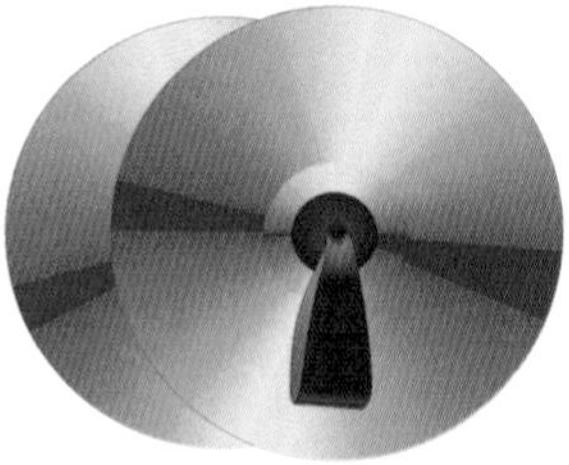

tambourine
pandereta[F]
tambour[M] de basque[M]
Tamburin[N]
tamburello[M]

triangle
triángulo[M]
triangle[M]
Triangel[M]
triangolo[M]

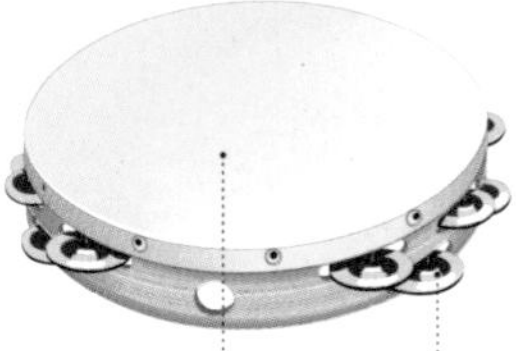

head
parche[M]
peau[F]
Fell[N]
membrana[F]

jingle
cascabel[M]
cymbalette[F]
Schelle[F]
sonagli[M]

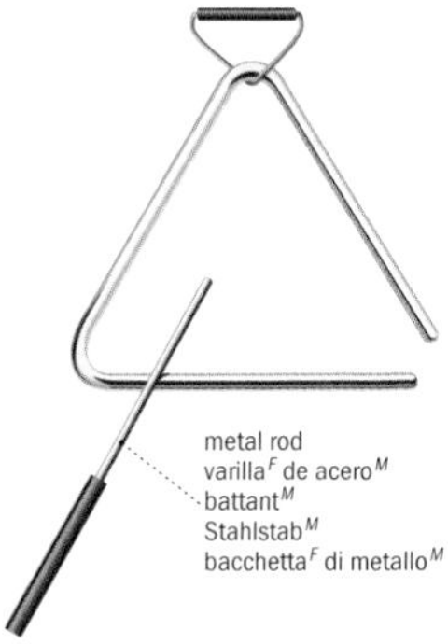

metal rod
varilla[F] de acero[M]
battant[M]
Stahlstab[M]
bacchetta[F] di metallo[M]

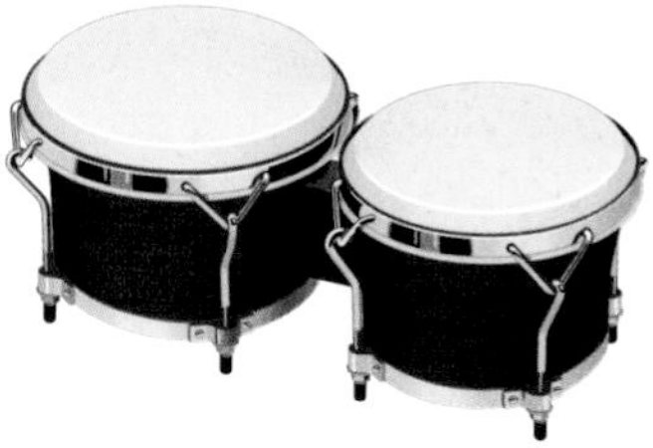

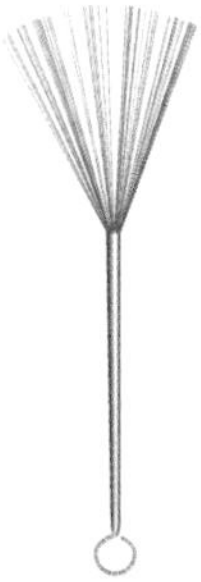

wire brush
escobilla[F] metálica
balai[M] métallique
Jazzbesen[M]
spazzola[F] metallica

gong
gong[M]
gong[M]
Gong[M]
gong[M]

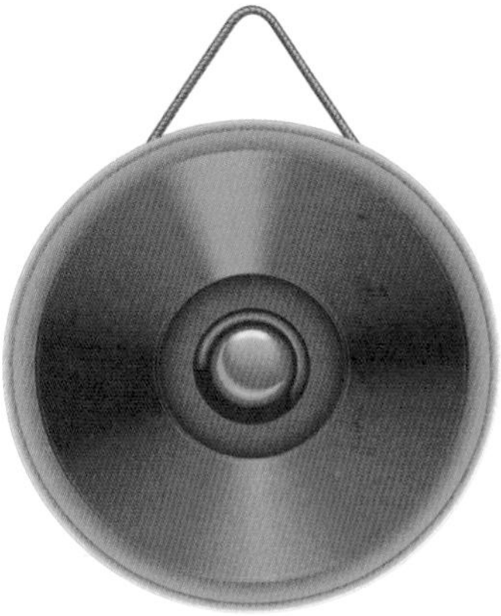

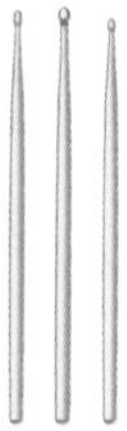

drum sticks
baquetas[F]
baguettes[F]
Stöcke[M]
bacchette[F]

xylophone
xilófono[M]
xylophone[M]
Xylophon[N]
xilofono[M]

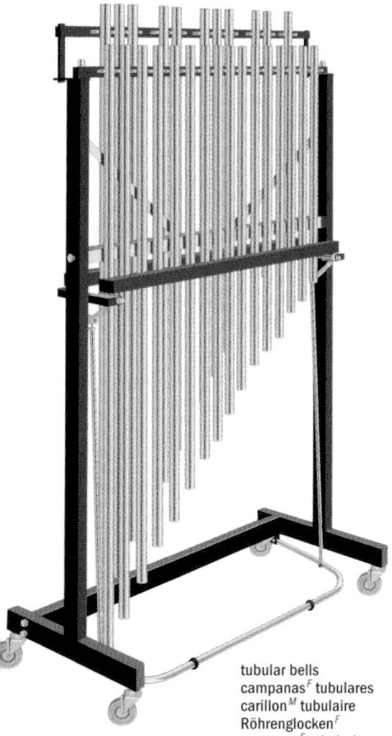

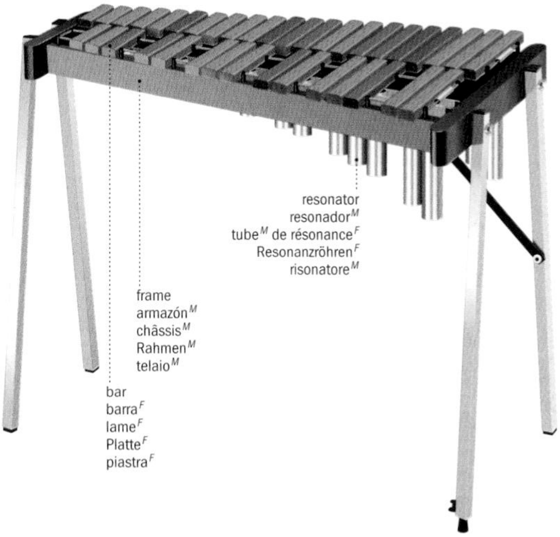

resonator
resonador[M]
tube[M] de résonance[F]
Resonanzröhren[F]
risonatore[M]

frame
armazón[M]
châssis[M]
Rahmen[M]
telaio[M]

tubular bells
campanas[F] tubulares
carillon[M] tubulaire
Röhrenglocken[F]
campane[F] tubolari

bar
barra[F]
lame[F]
Platte[F]
piastra[F]

mallets
maza[F]
mailloches[F]
Schlegel[M]
mazze[F]

ARTS AND ARCHITECTURE

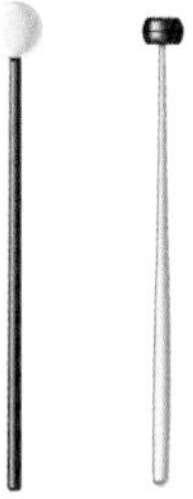

electronic instruments

instrumentos^M electrónicos | instruments^M électroniques | elektronische Instrumente^N | strumenti^M elettronici

sequencer
secuenciador^M
séquenceur^M
Sequencer^M
sequencer^M

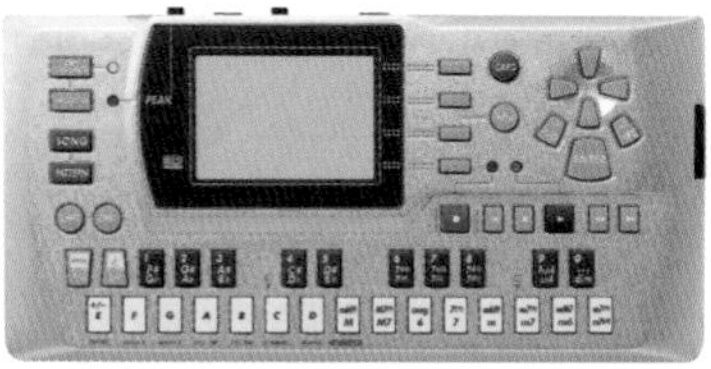

sampler
muestreador^M
échantillonneur^M
Sampler^M
campionatore^M

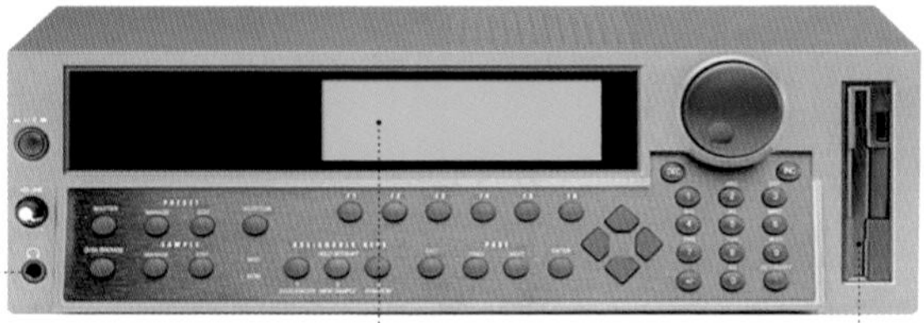

headphone jack
toma^F para auriculares^M
prise^F casque^M
Kopfhöreranschlussbuchse^F
presa^F per cuffia^F

function display
display^M de las funciones^M
affichage^M des fonctions^F
Funktionsdisplay^N
display^M delle funzioni^F

disk drive
lector^M de discos^M
lecteur^M de disquette^F
Diskettenlaufwerk^N
unità^F a disco^M

expander
amplificador^M
expandeur^M
Expander^M
expander^M

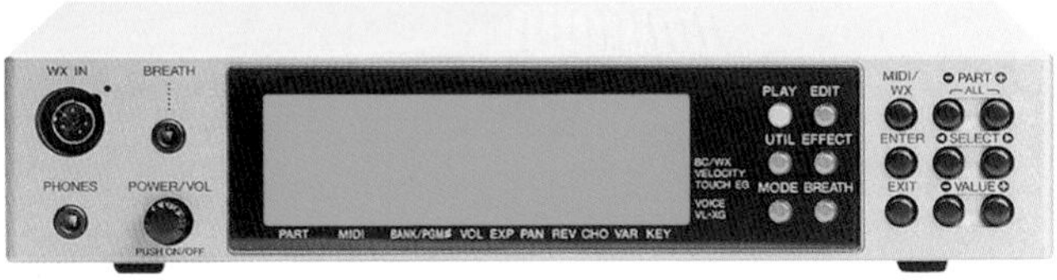

synthesizer
sintetizador^M
synthétiseur^M
Synthesizer^M
sintetizzatore^M

volume control
control^M de volumen^M
contrôle^M du volume^M
Lautstärkeregler^M
controllo^M del volume^M

fine data-entry control
control^M de entrada^F de información^F fina
modification^F fine des variables^F
Feinregler^M für Dateneingabe^F
controllo^M fine dei dati^M

disk drive
unidad^F de discos^M
lecteur^M de disquette^F
Diskettenlaufwerk^N
unità^F a disco^M

system buttons
sistema^M de botones^M
fonctions^F système^M
Systemschalter^M
tasti^M di sistema^M

function display
display^M de funciones^F
affichage^M des fonctions^F
Funktionsanzeige^F
display^M delle funzioni^F

sequencer control
control^M de secuencias^F
contrôle^M du séquenceur^M
Sequenzerregler^M
controllo^M del sequencer^M

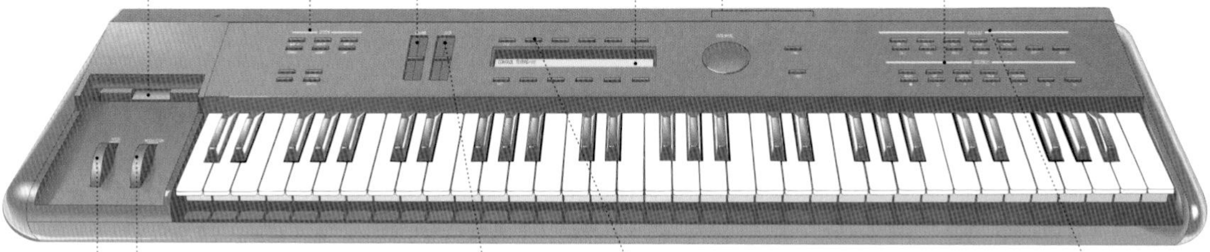

fast data-entry control
control^M de entrada^F de información^F rápida
modification^F rapide des variables^F
Grobregler^M für Dateneingabe^F
controllo^M veloce dei dati^M

program selector
selector^M de programa^M
sélecteur^M de programme^M
Programmwahlschalter^M
selettore^M di programma^M

keyboard
teclado^M
clavier^M
Tastatur^F
tastiera^F

modulation wheel
rueda^F de modulación^F
modulation^F du timbre^M du son^M
Modulationsrad^N
rotella^F di modulazione^F

voice edit buttons
botones^M para editar la voz^F
programmation^F des voix^F
Stimmenwahlschalter^M
tasti^M per l'editing^M del suono^M

pitch wheel
rueda^F para ajustar el tono^M
modulation^F de la hauteur^F du son^M
Tonhöhenrad^N
rotella^F di intonazione^F

ARTS AND ARCHITECTURE

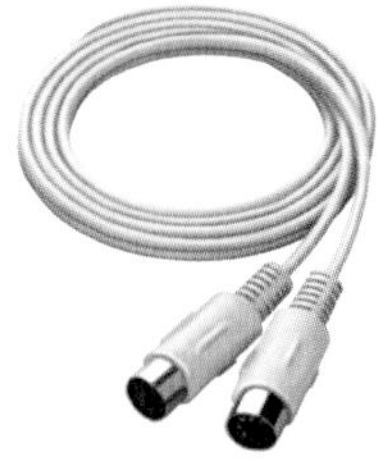

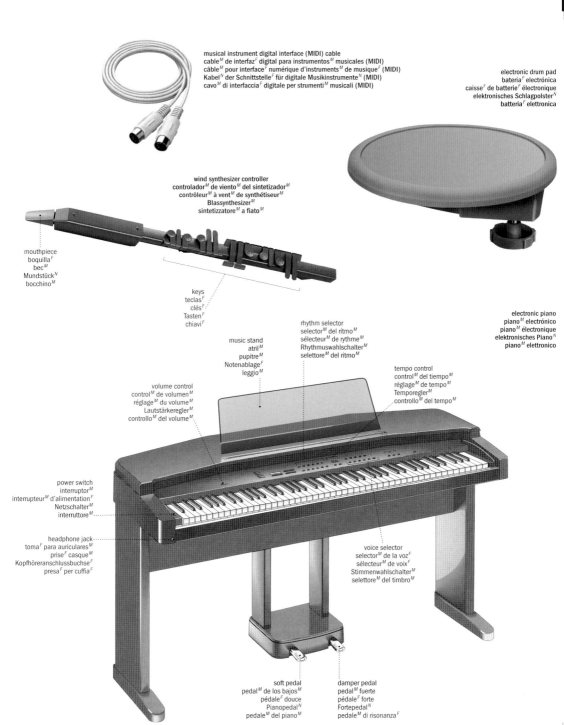

musical instrument digital interface (MIDI) cable
cable^M de interfaz^F digital para instrumentos^M musicales (MIDI)
câble^M pour interface^F numérique d'instruments^M de musique^F (MIDI)
Kabel^N der Schnittstelle^F für digitale Musikinstrumente^N (MIDI)
cavo^M di interfaccia^F digitale per strumenti^M musicali (MIDI)

electronic drum pad
batería^F electrónica
caisse^F de batterie^F électronique
elektronisches Schlagpolster^N
batteria^F elettronica

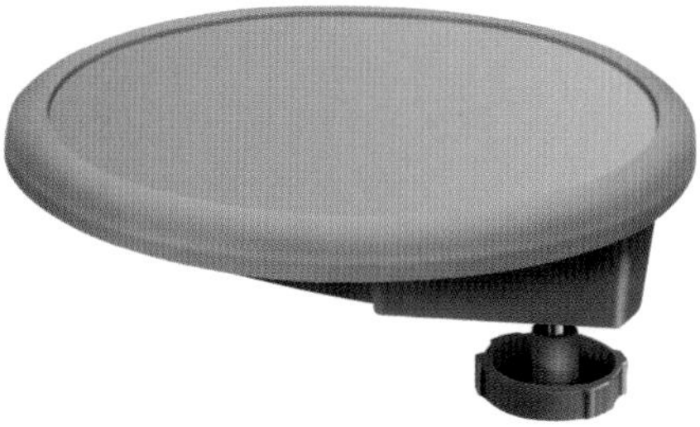

wind synthesizer controller
controlador^M de viento^M del sintetizador^M
contrôleur^M à vent^M de synthétiseur^M
Blassynthesizer^M
sintetizzatore^M a fiato^M

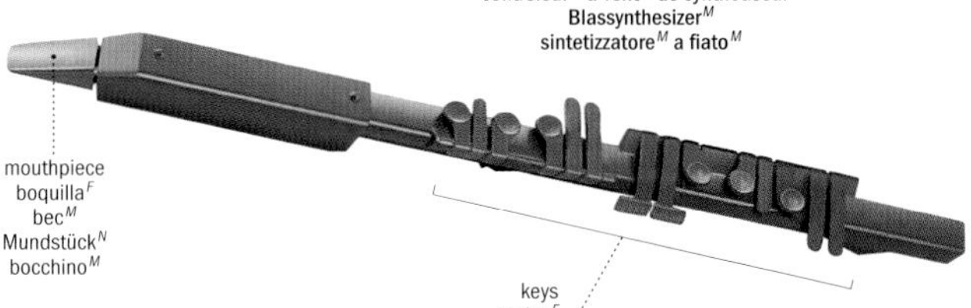

mouthpiece
boquilla^F
bec^M
Mundstück^N
bocchino^M

keys
teclas^F
clés^F
Tasten^F
chiavi^F

electronic piano
piano^M electrónico
piano^M électronique
elektronisches Piano^N
piano^M elettronico

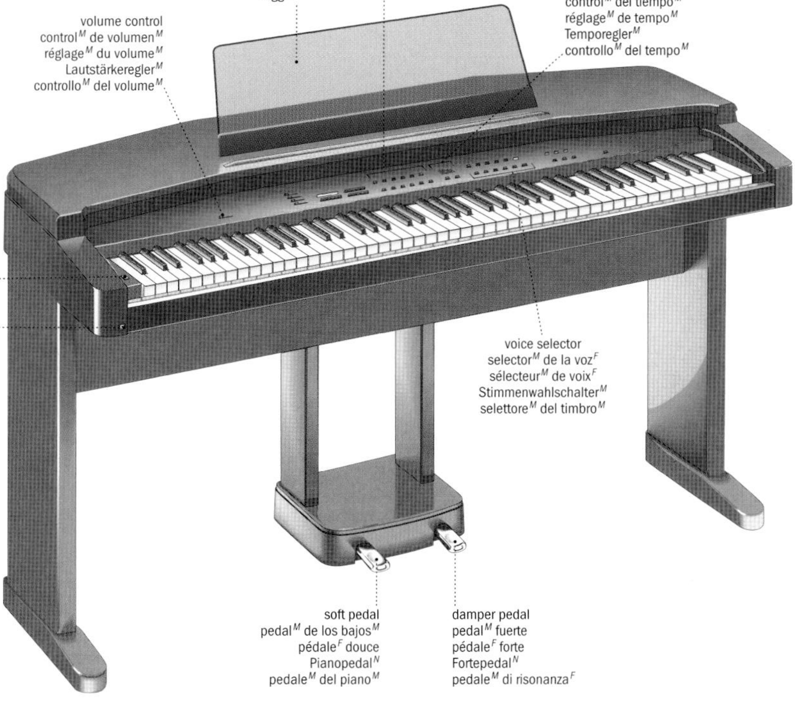

rhythm selector
selector^M del ritmo^M
sélecteur^M de rythme^M
Rhythmuswahlschalter^M
selettore^M del ritmo^M

music stand
atril^M
pupitre^M
Notenablage^F
leggio^M

tempo control
control^M del tiempo^M
réglage^M de tempo^M
Temporegler^M
controllo^M del tempo^M

volume control
control^M de volumen^M
réglage^M du volume^M
Lautstärkeregler^M
controllo^M del volume^M

power switch
interruptor^M
interrupteur^M d'alimentation^F
Netzschalter^M
interruttore^M

headphone jack
toma^F para auriculares^M
prise^F casque^M
Kopfhöreranschlussbuchse^F
presa^F per cuffia^F

voice selector
selector^M de la voz^F
sélecteur^M de voix^F
Stimmenwahlschalter^M
selettore^M del timbro^M

soft pedal
pedal^M de los bajos^M
pédale^F douce
Pianopedal^N
pedale^M del piano^M

damper pedal
pedal^M fuerte
pédale^F forte
Fortepedal^N
pedale^M di risonanza^F

ARTS AND ARCHITECTURE

sewing

costura^F | couture^F | Nähen^N | cucito^M

sewing machine
máquina^F de coser
machine^F à coudre
Nähmaschine^F
macchina^F da cucire

thread guide
guía del hilo^M
guide-fil^M
Fadenleitöse^F
guidafilo^M

arm
brazo^M
bras^M
Arm^M
braccio^M

spool pin
portabobina^M
broche^F porte-bobine^M
Garnrollenstift^M
portarocchetto^M

thread take-up lever
palanca^F tensora
releveur^M de fil^M
Fadenhebel^M
leva^F tirafilo

stitch width selector
regulador^M de ancho^M de puntada^F
réglage^M de largeur^F de point^M
Stichbreitenwähler^M
selettore^M dell'ampiezza^F dei punti^M

bobbin winder
rebobinador^M
bobineur^M
Spuler^M
avvolgitore^M della bobina^F

pressure dial
regulador^M de presión^F
réglage^M de pression^F
Druckeinsteller^M
regolatore^M di pressione^F

hand wheel
volante^M
volant^M
Handrad^N
volantino^M

needle position selector
selector^M de posición^F de aguja^F
positionneur^M
Nadelpositionswähler^M
selettore^M della posizione^F dell'ago^M

head
cabeza^F
tête^F
Kopf^M
testa^F

stitch length regulator
regulador^M de largo^M de puntada^F
règle-point^M
Stichlängenwähler^M
regolatore^M della lunghezza^F dei punti^M

needle
aguja^F
aiguille^F
Nadel^F
ago^M

reverse stitch button
botón^M de puntada^F
bouton^M de point^M arrière
Nährichtungseinsteller^M
bottone^M di marcia^F indietro

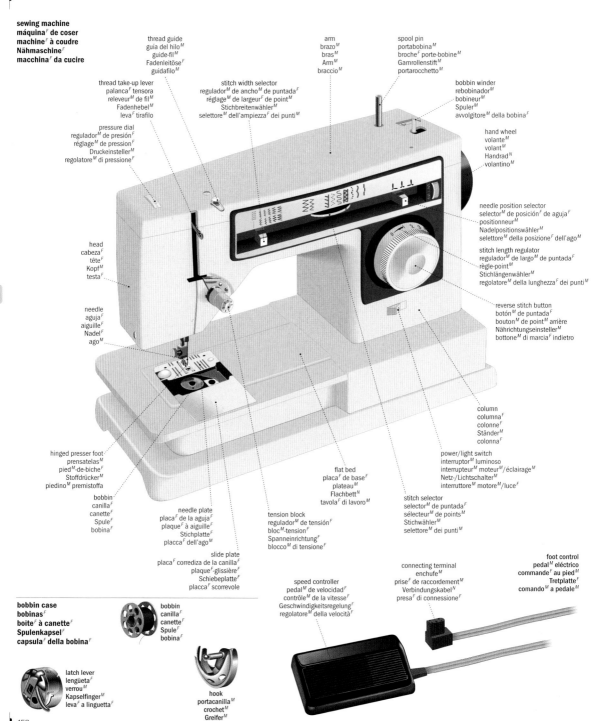

column
columna^F
colonne^F
Ständer^M
colonna^F

hinged presser foot
prensatelas^M
pied^M-de-biche^F
Stoffdrücker^M
piedino^M premistoffa

power/light switch
interruptor^M luminoso
interrupteur^M moteur^M/éclairage^M
Netz-/Lichtschalter^M
interruttore^M motore^M/luce^F

bobbin^F
canilla^F
canette^F
Spule^F
bobina^F

needle plate
placa^F de la aguja^F
plaque^F à aiguille^F
Stichplatte^F
placca^F dell'ago^M

flat bed
placa^F de base^F
plateau^M
Flachbett^N
tavola^F di lavoro^M

stitch selector
selector^M de puntada^F
sélecteur^M de points^M
Stichwähler^M
selettore^M dei punti^M

tension block
regulador^M de tensión^F
bloc^M-tension^F
Spanneinrichtung^F
blocco^M di tensione^F

slide plate
placa^F corrediza de la canilla^F
plaque^F-glissière^F
Schiebeplatte^F
placca^F scorrevole

connecting terminal
enchufe^M
prise^F de raccordement^M
Verbindungskabel^N
presa^F di connessione^F

foot control
pedal^M eléctrico
commande^F au pied^M
Tretplatte^F
comando^M a pedale^F

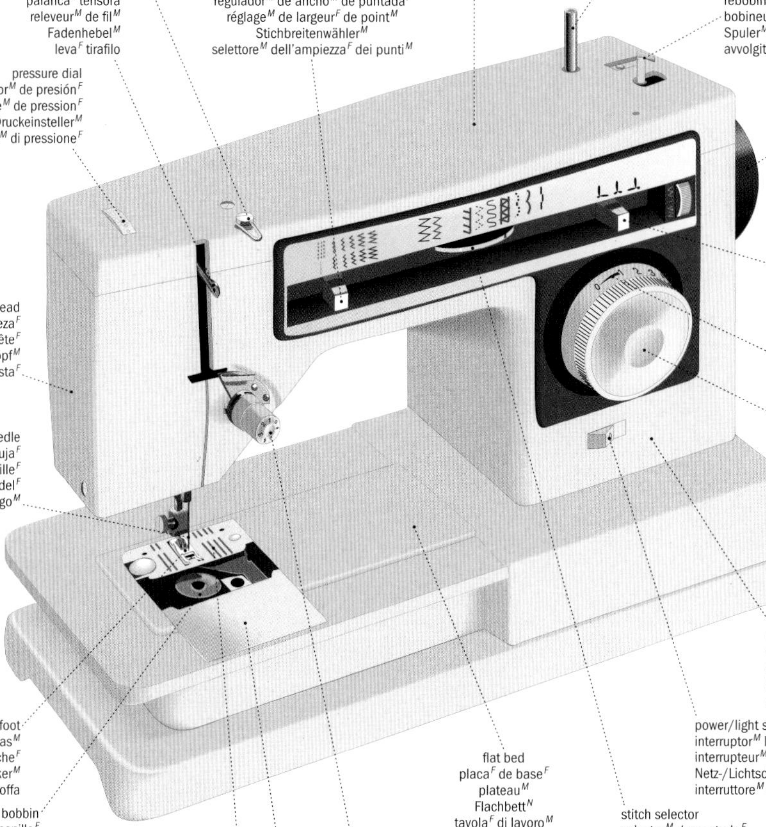

bobbin case
bobinas^F
boîte^F à canette^F
Spulenkapsel^F
capsula^F della bobina^F

bobbin
canilla^F
canette^F
Spule^F
bobina^F

speed controller
pedal^M de velocidad^F
contrôle^M de la vitesse^F
Geschwindigkeitsregelung^F
regolatore^M della velocità^F

latch lever
lengüeta^F
verrou^M
Kapselfinger^M
leva^F a linguetta^F

hook
portacanilla^M
crochet^M
Greifer^M
crochet^M

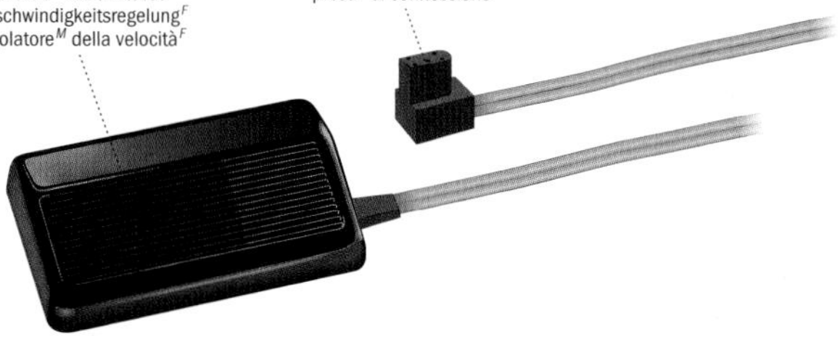

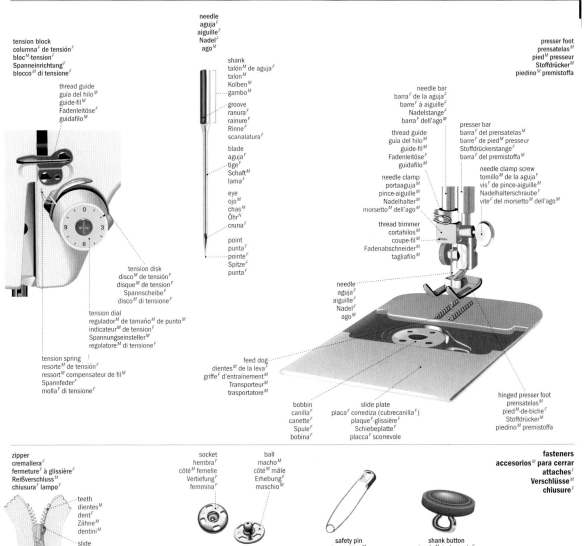

needle
aguja^F
aiguille^F
Nadel^F
ago^M

tension block
columna^F de tensión^F
bloc^M-tension^F
Spanneinrichtung^F
blocco^M di tensione^F

thread guide
guía del hilo^M
guide-fil^M
Fadenleitöse^F
guidafilo^M

eye
ojo^M
chas^M
Öhr^N
cruna^F

tension disk
disco^M de tensión^F
disque^M de tension^F
Spannscheibe^F
disco^M di tensione^F

tension dial
regulador^M de tamaño^M de punto^M
indicateur^M de tension^F
Spannungseinsteller^M
regolatore^M di tensione^F

tension spring
resorte^M de tensión^F
ressort^M compensateur de fil^M
Spannfeder^F
molla^F di tensione^F

shank
talón^M de aguja^F
talon^M
Kolben^M
gambo^M

groove
ranura^F
rainure^F
Rinne^F
scanalatura^F

blade
aguja^F
tige^F
Schaft^M
lama^F

point
punta^F
pointe^F
Spitze^F
punta^F

feed dog
dientes^M de la leva^F
griffe^F d'entrainement^M
Transporteur^M
trasportatore^M

presser foot
prensatelas^M
pied^M presseur
Stoffdrücker^M
piedino^M premistoffa

needle bar
barra^F de la aguja^F
barre^F à aiguille^F
Nadelstange^F
barra^F dell'ago^M

presser bar
barra^F del prensatelas^M
barre^F de pied^M presseur
Stoffdrückerstange^F
barra^F del premistoffa^M

thread guide
guía del hilo^M
guide-fil^M
Fadenleitöse^F
guidafilo^M

needle clamp screw
tornillo^M de la aguja^F
vis^F de pince-aiguille^M
Nadelhalterschraube^F
vite^F del morsetto dell'ago^M

needle clamp
portaaguja^M
pince-aiguille^M
Nadelhalter^M
morsetto^M dell'ago^M

thread trimmer
cortahilos^M
coupe-fil^M
Fadenabschneider^M
tagliafilo^M

needle
aguja^F
aiguille^F
Nadel^F
ago^M

hinged presser foot
prensatelas^M
pied^M-de-biche^F
Stoffdrücker^M
piedino^M premistoffa

bobbin
canilla^F
canette^F
Spule^F
bobina^F

slide plate
placa^F corrediza (cubrecanilla^F)
plaque^F-glissière^F
Schiebeplatte^F
placca^F scorrevole

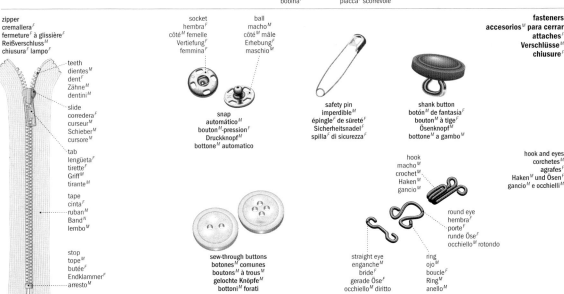

zipper
cremallera^F
fermeture^F à glissière^F
Reißverschluss^M
chiusura^F lampo^M

teeth
dientes^M
dent^F
Zähne^M
dentini^M

slide
corredera^F
curseur^M
Schieber^M
cursore^M

tab
lengüeta^F
tirette^F
Griff^M
tirante^M

tape
cinta^F
ruban^M
Band^N
lembo^M

stop
tope^M
butée^F
Endklammer^F
arresto^M

socket
hembra^F
côté^M femelle
Vertiefung^F
femmina^F

ball
macho^M
côté^M mâle
Erhebung^F
maschio^M

snap
automático^M
bouton^N-pression^F
Druckknopf^M
bottone^M automatico

safety pin
imperdible^M
épingle^F de sûreté^F
Sicherheitsnadel^F
spilla^F di sicurezza^F

sew-through buttons
botones^M comunes
boutons^M à trous^M
gelochte Knöpfe^M
bottoni^M forati

shank button
botón^M de fantasía^F
bouton^M à tige^F
Ösenknopf^M
bottone^M a gambo^M

fasteners
accesorios^M para cerrar
attaches^F
Verschlüsse^M
chiusure^F

hook
macho^M
crochet^M
Haken^M
gancio^M

round eye
hembra^F
porte^F
runde Öse^F
occhiello^M rotondo

hook and eyes
corchetes^M
agrafes^F
Haken^M und Ösen^F
gancio^M e occhielli^M

ring
ojo^M
boucle^F
Ring^M
anello^M

straight eye
enganche^M
bride^F
gerade Öse^F
occhiello^M diritto

sewing

accessories
accesorios
accessoires[M]
Zubehör[N]
accessori[M]

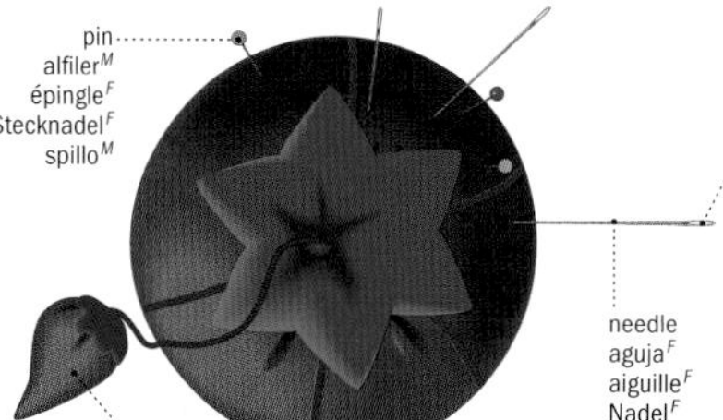

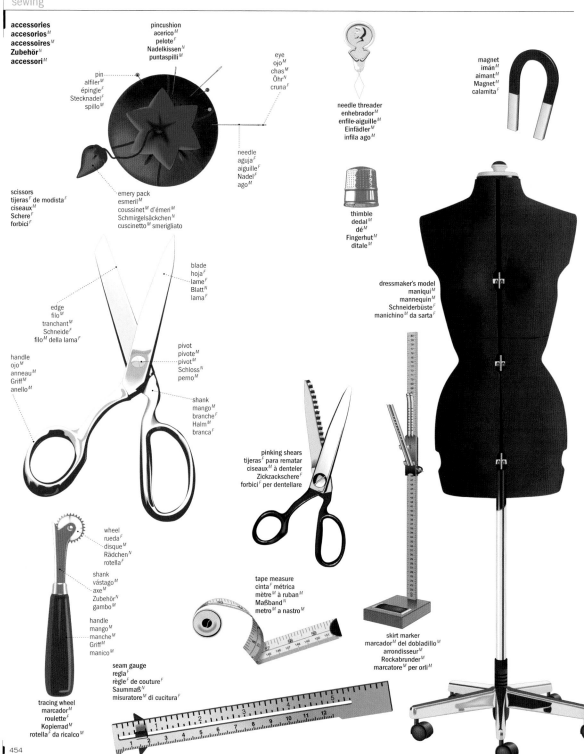

pincushion
acerico[M]
pelote[F]
Nadelkissen[N]
puntaspilli[M]

eye
ojo[M]
chas[M]
Öhr[N]
cruna[F]

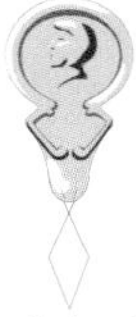

magnet
imán[M]
aimant[M]
Magnet[M]
calamita[F]

pin
alfiler[M]
épingle[F]
Stecknadel[F]
spillo[M]

needle threader
enhebrador[M]
enfile-aiguille[M]
Einfädler[M]
infila ago[M]

needle
aguja[F]
aiguille[F]
Nadel[F]
ago[M]

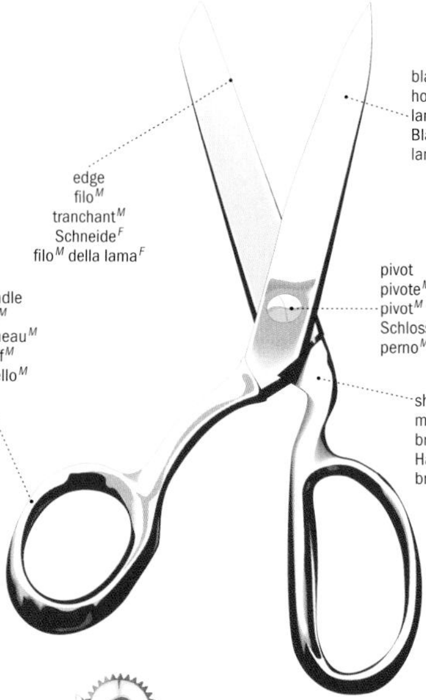

scissors
tijeras[F] de modista[F]
ciseaux[M]
Schere[F]
forbici[F]

emery pack
esmeril[M]
coussinet[M] d'émeri[M]
Schmirgelsäckchen[N]
cuscinetto[M] smerigliato

thimble
dedal[M]
dé[M]
Fingerhut[M]
ditale[M]

blade
hoja[F]
lame[F]
Blatt[N]
lama[F]

dressmaker's model
maniquí[M]
mannequin[M]
Schneiderbüste[F]
manichino[M] da sarta[F]

edge
filo[M]
tranchant[M]
Schneide[F]
filo[M] della lama[F]

pivot
pivote[M]
pivot[M]
Schloss[N]
perno[M]

handle
ojo[M]
anneau[M]
Griff[M]
anello[M]

shank
mango[M]
branche[F]
Halm[M]
branca[F]

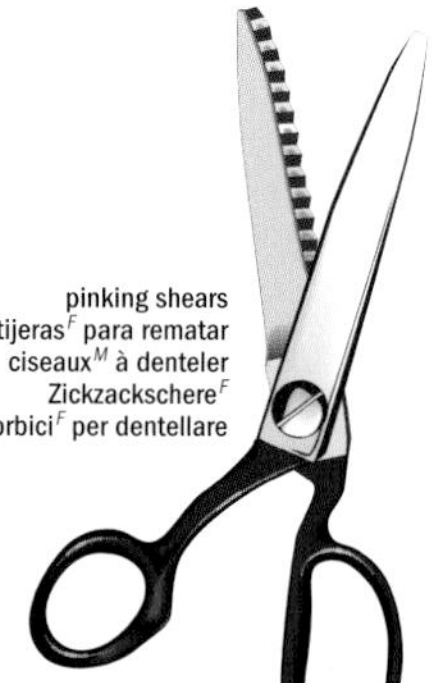

pinking shears
tijeras[F] para rematar
ciseaux[M] à denteler
Zickzackschere[F]
forbici[F] per dentellare

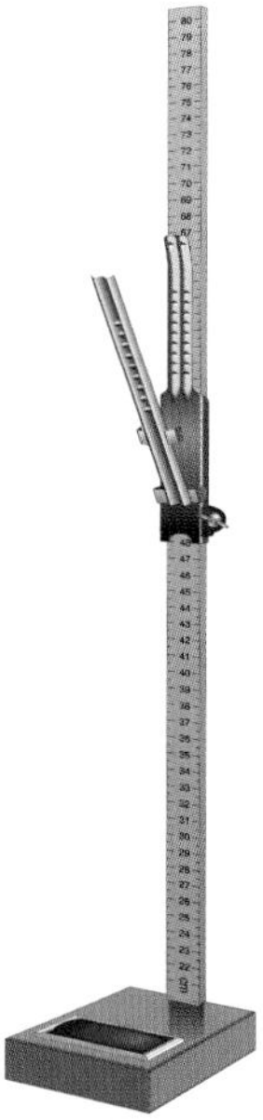

wheel
rueda[F]
disque[M]
Rädchen[N]
rotella[F]

shank
vástago[M]
axe[M]
Zubehör[N]
gambo[M]

tape measure
cinta[F] métrica
mètre[M] à ruban[M]
Maßband[N]
metro[M] a nastro[M]

handle
mango[M]
manche[M]
Griff[M]
manico[M]

skirt marker
marcador[M] del dobladillo[M]
arrondisseur[M]
Rockabrunder[M]
marcatore[M] per orli[M]

seam gauge
regla[F]
règle[F] de couture[F]
Saummaß[N]
misuratore[M] di cucitura[F]

tracing wheel
marcador[M]
roulette[F]
Kopierrad[M]
rotella[F] da ricalco[M]

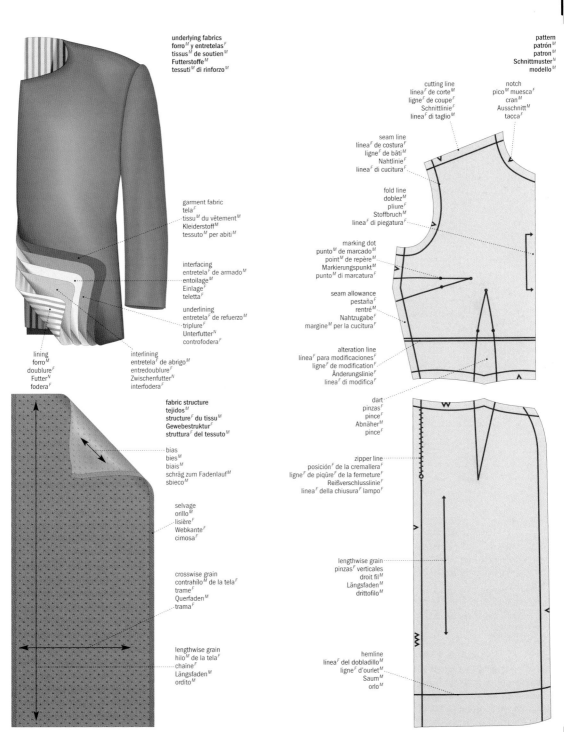

underlying fabrics
forro^M y entretelas^F
tissus^M de soutien^M
Futterstoffe^M
tessuti^M di rinforzo^M

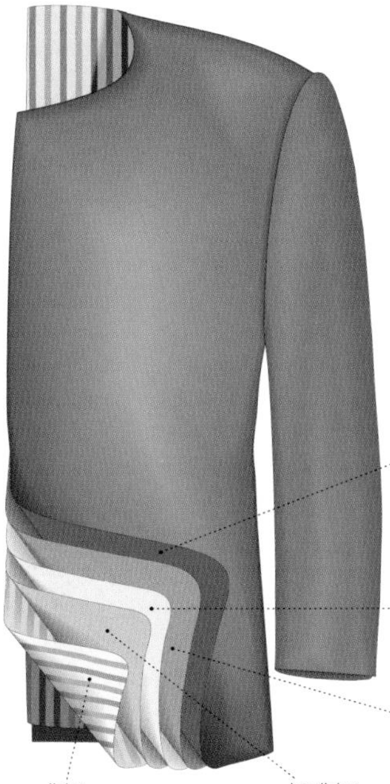

garment fabric
tela^F
tissu^M du vêtement^M
Kleiderstoff^M
tessuto^M per abiti^M

interfacing
entretela^F de armado^M
entoilage^M
Einlage^F
teletta^F

underlining
entretela^F de refuerzo^M
triplure^F
Unterfutter^N
controfodera^F

lining
forro^M
doublure^F
Futter^N
fodera^F

interlining
entretela^F de abrigo^M
entredoublure^F
Zwischenfutter^N
interfodera^F

fabric structure
tejidos^M
structure^F du tissu^M
Gewebestruktur^F
struttura^F del tessuto^M

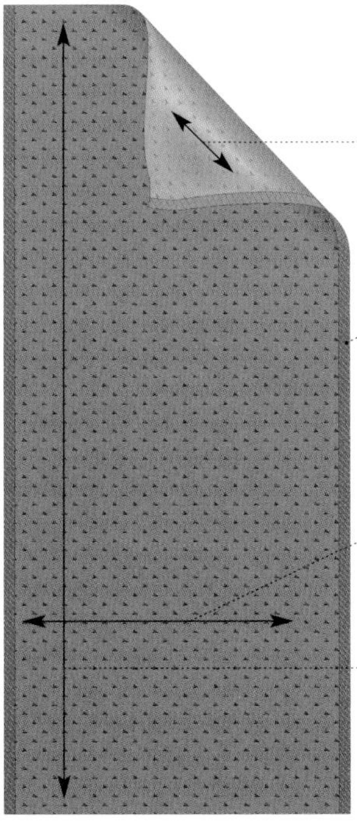

bias
bies^M
biais^M
schräg zum Fadenlauf^M
sbieco^M

selvage
orillo^M
lisière^F
Webkante^F
cimosa^F

crosswise grain
contrahilo^M de la tela^F
trame^F
Querfaden^M
trama^F

lengthwise grain
hilo^M de la tela^F
chaîne^F
Längsfaden^M
ordito^M

pattern
patrón^M
patron^M
Schnittmuster^N
modello^M

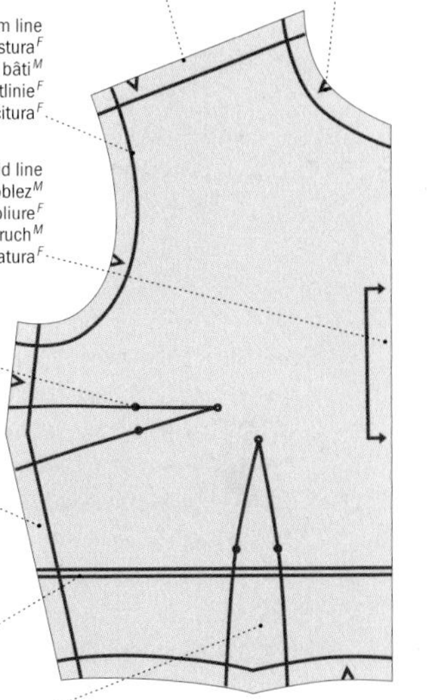

cutting line
línea^F de corte^M
ligne^F de coupe^F
Schnittlinie^F
linea^F di taglio^M

notch
pico^M muesca^F
cran^M
Ausschnitt^M
tacca^F

seam line
línea^F de costura^F
ligne^F de bâti^M
Nahtlinie^F
linea^F di cucitura^F

fold line
doblez^M
pliure^F
Stoffbruch^M
linea^F di piegatura^F

marking dot
punto^M de marcado^M
point^M de repère^M
Markierungspunkt^M
punto^M di marcatura^F

seam allowance
pestaña^F
rentré^M
Nahtzugabe^F
margine^M per la cucitura^F

alteration line
línea^F para modificaciones^F
ligne^F de modification^F
Änderungslinie^F
linea^F di modifica^F

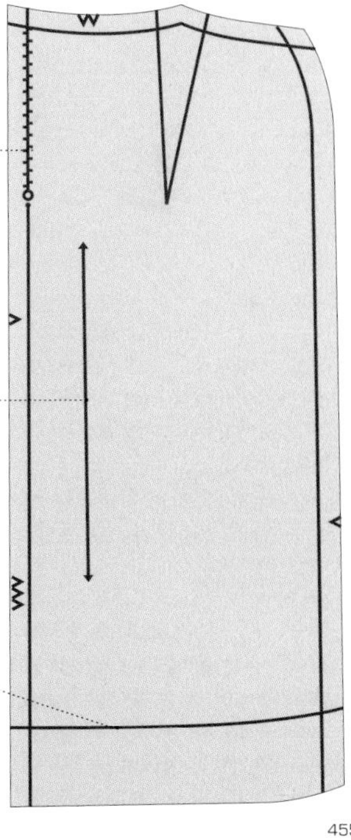

dart
pinzas^F
pince^F
Abnäher^M
pince^F

zipper line
posición^F de la cremallera^F
ligne^F de piqûre^F de la fermeture^F
Reißverschlusslinie^F
linea^F della chiusura^F lampo^F

lengthwise grain
pinzas^F verticales
droit fil^M
Längsfaden^M
drittofilo^M

hemline
línea^F del dobladillo^M
ligne^F d'ourlet^M
Saum^M
orlo^M

ARTS AND ARCHITECTURE

knitting machine

máquina^F tricotar | machine^F à tricoter | Strickmaschine^F | macchina^F da maglieria^F

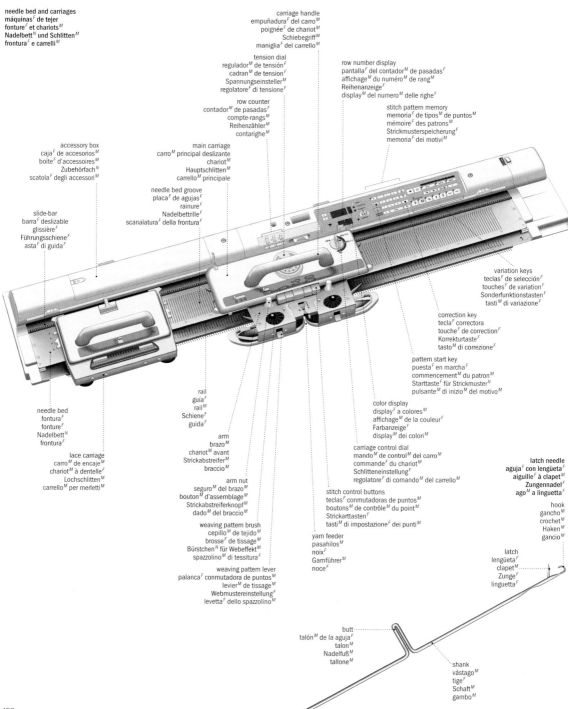

needle bed and carriages
máquinas^F de tejer
fonture^F et chariots^M
Nadelbett^N und Schlitten^M
frontura^F e carrelli^M

carriage handle
empuñadura^F del carro^M
poignée^F de chariot^M
Schiebegriff^M
maniglia^F del carrello^M

row number display
pantalla^F del contador^M de pasadas^F
affichage^M du numéro^M de rang^M
Reihenanzeige^F
display^M del numero^M delle righe^F

tension dial
regulador^M de tensión^F
cadran^M de tension^F
Spannungseinsteller^M
regolatore^F di tensione^F

stitch pattern memory
memoria^F de tipos^M de puntos^M
mémoire^F des patrons^M
Strickmusterspeicherung^F
memoria^F dei motivi^M

row counter
contador^M de pasadas^F
compte-rangs^M
Reihenzähler^M
contarighe^M

accessory box
caja^F de accesorios^M
boîte^F d'accessoires^M
Zubehörfach^N
scatola^F degli accessori^M

main carriage
carro^M principal deslizante
chariot^M
Hauptschlitten^M
carrello^M principale

needle bed groove
placa^F de agujas^F
rainure^F
Nadelbettrille^F
scanalatura^F della frontura^F

slide-bar
barra^F deslizable
glissière^F
Führungsschiene^F
asta^F di guida^F

variation keys
teclas^F de selección^F
touches^F de variation^F
Sonderfunktionstasten^F
tasti^M di variazione^F

correction key
tecla^F correctora
touche^F de correction^F
Korrekturtaste^F
tasto^M di correzione^F

pattern start key
puesta^F en marcha^F
commencement^M du patron^M
Starttaste^F für Strickmuster^N
pulsante^M di inizio^M del motivo^M

needle bed
fontura^F
fonture^F
Nadelbett^N
frontura^F

rail
guía^F
rail^M
Schiene^F
guida^F

color display
display^F a colores^M
affichage^M de la couleur^F
Farbanzeige^F
display^M dei colori^M

lace carriage
carro^M de encaje^M
chariot^M à dentelle^F
Lochschlitten^M
carrello^M per merletti^M

arm
brazo^M
chariot^M avant
Strickabstreifer^M
braccio^M

carriage control dial
mando^M de control^M del carro^M
commande^F du chariot^M
Schlitteneinstellung^F
regolatore^F di comando^M del carrello^M

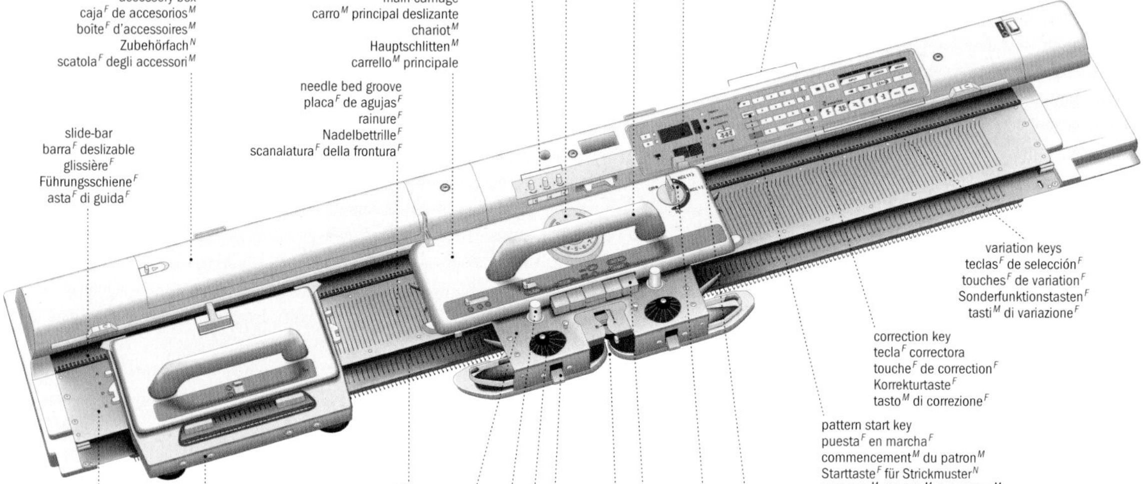

latch needle
aguja^F con lengüeta^F
aiguille^F à clapet^M
Zungennadel^F
ago^M a linguetta^F

arm nut
seguro^M del brazo^M
bouton^M d'assemblage^M
Strickabstreiferknopf^M
dado^M del braccio^M

stitch control buttons
teclas^F conmutadoras de puntos^M
boutons^M de contrôle^M du point^M
Strickarttasten^F
tasti^M di impostazione^F dei punti^M

hook
gancho^M
crochet^M
Haken^M
gancio^M

weaving pattern brush
cepillo^M de tejido^M
brosse^F de tissage^M
Bürstchen^N für Webeffekt^M
spazzolino^M di tessitura^F

yarn feeder
pasahilos^M
noix^F
Garnführer^M
noce^F

latch
lengüeta^F
clapet^M
Zunge^F
linguetta^F

weaving pattern lever
palanca^F conmutadora de puntos^M
levier^M de tissage^M
Webmustereinstellung^F
levetta^F dello spazzolino^M

butt
talón^M de la aguja^F
talon^M
Nadelfuß^M
tallone^M

shank
vástago^M
tige^F
Schaft^M
gambo^M

ARTS AND ARCHITECTURE

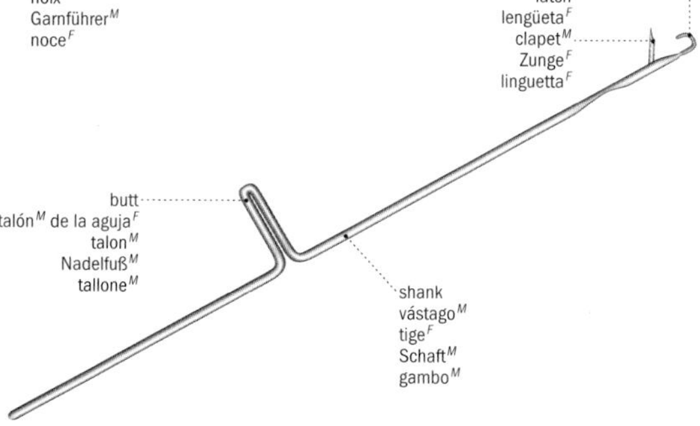

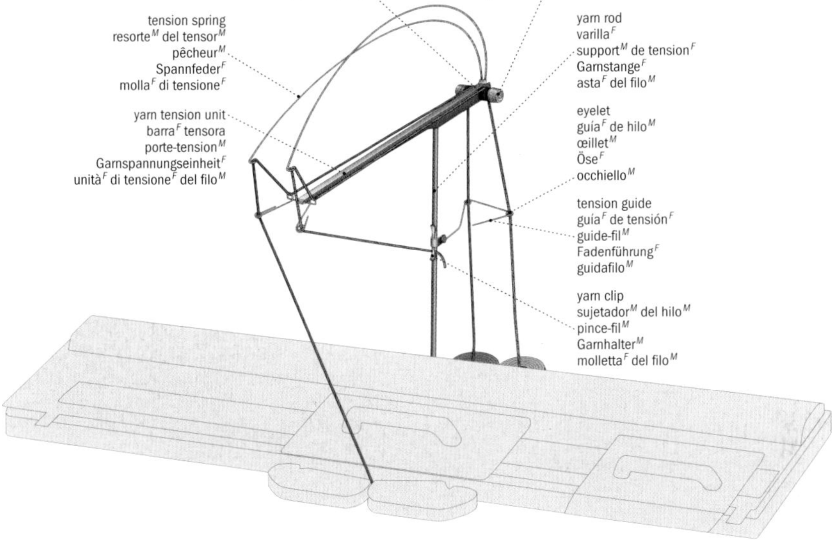

tension disk
disco^M de tensión^F
disque^M de tension^F
Spannscheibe^F
disco^M di tensione^F

tension dial
regulador^M de tensión^F
bouton^M de tension^F
Spannungseinsteller^M
regolatore^M di tensione^F

tension block
sistema^M de tensión^F
bloc^M-tension^F
Spanneinrichtung^F
blocco^M di tensione^F

tension spring
resorte^M del tensor^M
pêcheur^M
Spannfeder^F
molla^F di tensione^F

yarn rod
varilla^F
support^M de tension^F
Garnstange^F
asta^F del filo^M

yarn tension unit
barra^F tensora
porte-tension^M
Garnspannungseinheit^F
unità^F di tensione^F del filo^M

eyelet
guía^F de hilo^M
œillet^M
Öse^F
occhiello^M

tension guide
guía^F de tensión^F
guide-fil^M
Fadenführung^F
guidafilo^M

yarn clip
sujetador^M del hilo^M
pince-fil^M
Garnhalter^M
molletta^F del filo^M

knitting

tejido^M de punto^M | tricot^M | Stricken^N | lavoro^M a maglia^F

knitting needle
aguja^F de punto^M
aiguille^F à tricoter
Stricknadel^F
ferro^M da maglia^F

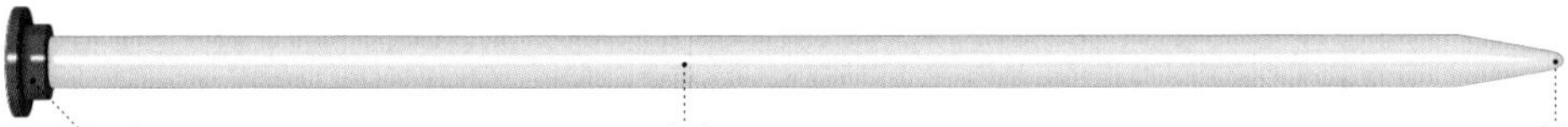

head
cabeza^F
tête^F
Kopf^M
testa^F

shank
varilla^F
tige^F
Schaft^M
gambo^M

point
punta^F
pointe^F
Spitze^F
punta^F

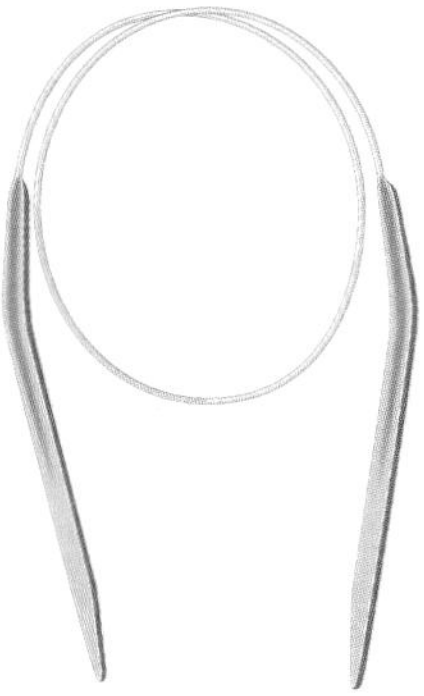

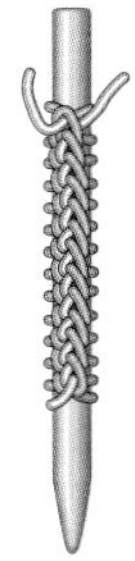

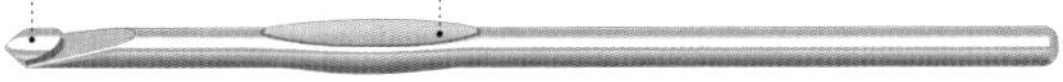

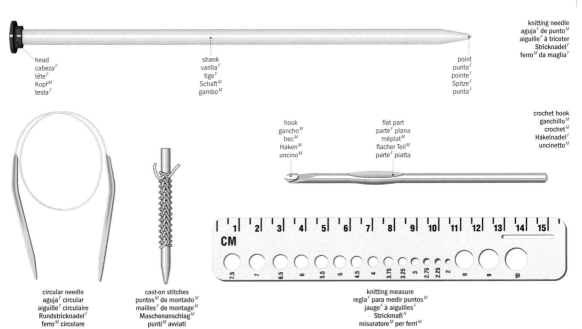

hook
gancho^M
bec^M
Haken^M
uncino^M

flat part
parte^F plana
méplat^M
flacher Teil^M
parte^F piatta

crochet hook
ganchillo^M
crochet^M
Häkelnadel^F
uncinetto^M

circular needle
aguja^F circular
aiguille^F circulaire
Rundstricknadel^F
ferro^M circolare

cast-on stitches
puntos^M de montado^M
mailles^F de montage^M
Maschenanschlag^M
punti^M avviati

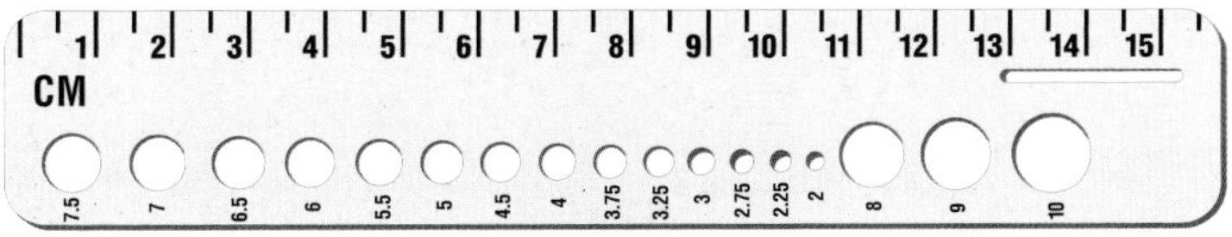

knitting measure
regla^F para medir puntos^M
jauge^F à aiguilles^F
Strickmaß^N
misuratore^M per ferri^M

ARTS AND ARCHITECTURE

stitch patterns
tipos^M **de punto**^{M}
points^M **de tricot**^{M}
Strickmuster^N
motivi^M

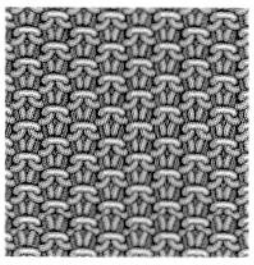

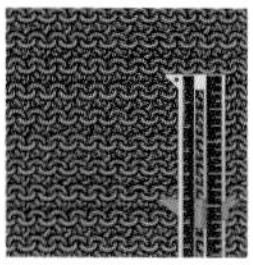

sample
muestra^F
échantillon^M
Maschenprobe^F
campione^M

moss stitch
punto^M de arroz^M
point^M de riz^M
Gerstenkornmuster^N
punto^M riso^M

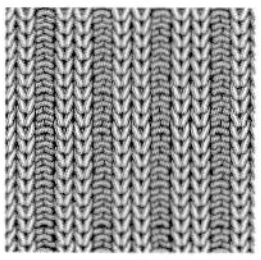

rib stitch
punto^M de respiguilla^F
point^M de côtes^F
Perlrippen^F
maglia^F a coste^F

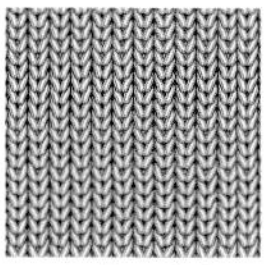

stocking stitch
punto^M del derecho^M
point^M de jersey^M
Glattstrick^M
maglia^F diritta

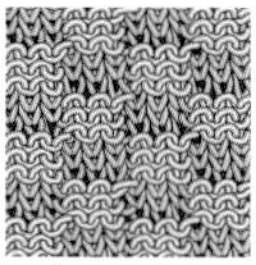

basket stitch
punto^M de malla^F
point^M de damier^M
Wabenstrick^M
scacchi^M

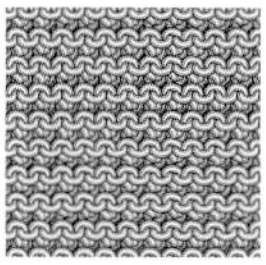

garter stitch
punto^M del revés^M
point^M mousse^F
Krausstrick^M
maglia^F rovescia

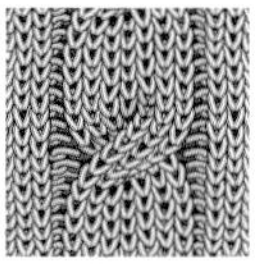

cable stitch
punto^M de ochos^M
point^M de torsades^F
Zopfmuster^N
treccia^F

bobbin lace

encaje^M de bolillos^M | dentelle^F aux fuseaux^M | Klöppelspitze^F | pizzo^M al tombolo^M

pillow
bolillos^M
carreau^M
Klöppelkissen^N
tombolo^M

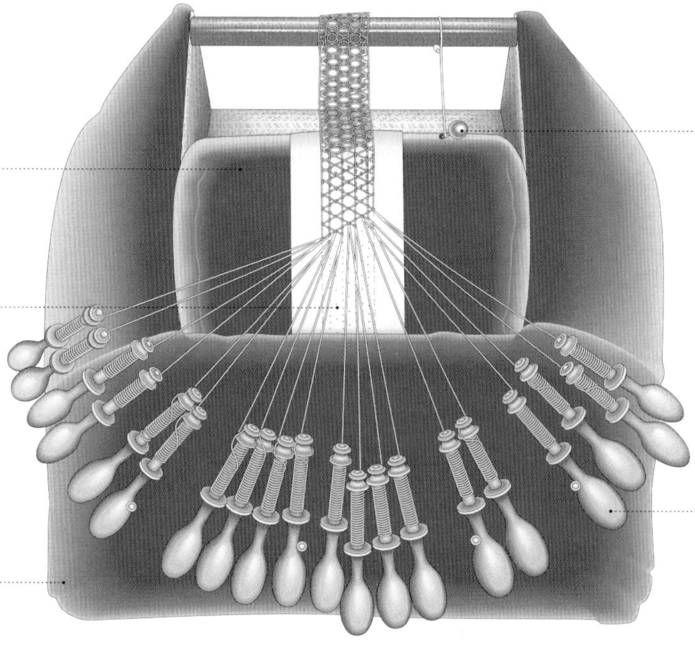

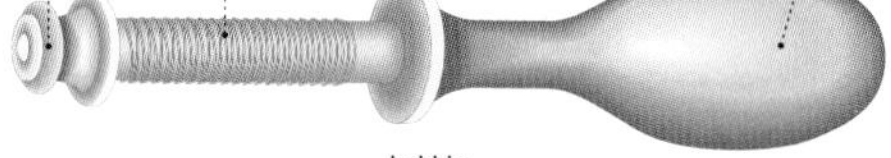

revolving cylinder
cilindro^M de rotación^F
cylindre^M rotatif
drehbare Walze^F
cilindro^M rotante

pattern
dibujo^M
patron^M
Klöppelbrief^M
motivo^M

pillow
cojín^M
coussin^M
Kissen^N
tombolo^M

stop
amarre^M
frein^M
Stop^M
dispositivo^M di arresto^M

bobbin
bolillo^M
fuseau^M
Klöppel^M
fusello^M

head
cabeza^F
tête^F
Kopf^M
testa^F

spool
carrete^M
bobine^F
Hals^M
rocchetto^M

handle
bolillo^M
manche^M
Griff^M
manico^M

bobbin
bolillo^M
fuseau^M
Klöppel^M
fusello^M

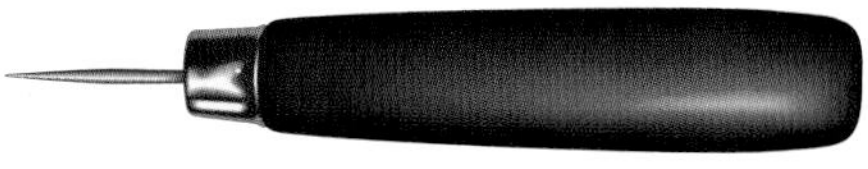

pricker
punzón^M
piquoir^M
Stecher^M
punteruolo^M

embroidery

bordado^M | broderie^F | Stickerei^F | ricamo^M

hoops
aro^M
tambour^M
runder Stickrahmen^M
telaio^M circolare

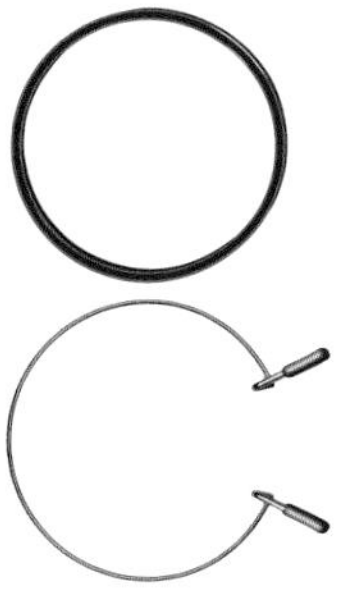

frame
bastidor^M
métier^M à broder
Rahmen^M
telaio^M

embroidered fabric
tela^F bordada
tissu^M brodé
bestickter Stoff^M
tessuto^M ricamato

peg
espiga^F
cheville^F
Zapfen^M
piolo^M

tape
cinta^F
tirette^F
Band^N
nastro^M

slat
listón^M de madera^F
latte^F
Latte^F
assicella^F

webbing
tira^F de tela^F
coutisse^F
Stoffstreifen^M
canovaccio^M

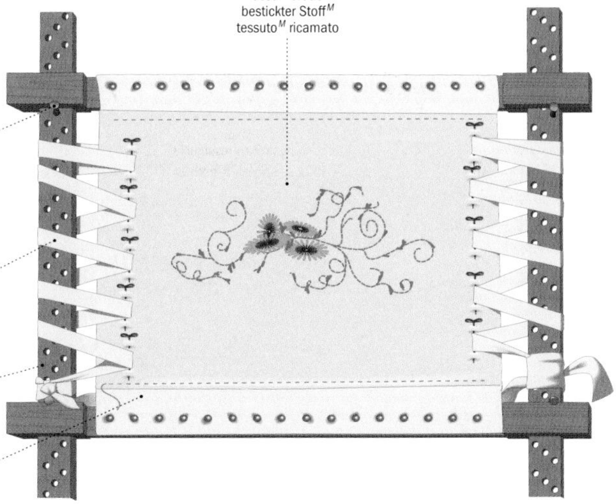

stitches
tipos^M de puntos^M
catégories^F de points^M
Stickstiche^M
punti^M

cross stitches
puntos^M de cruz^F
points^M croisés
Kreuzstiche^M
punti^M incrociati

loop stitches
puntos^M de malla^F
points^M bouclés
Schlingstiche^M
gruppo^M di punti^M a cappio^M

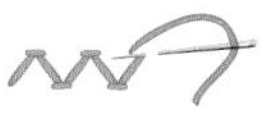

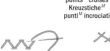

herringbone stitch
punto^M de escapulario^M
point^M de chausson^M
Smokstich^M
punto^M gallone^M

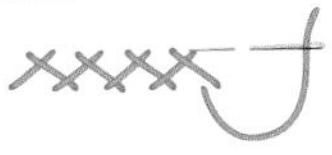

chevron stitch
punto^M de cruz^F
point^M de chevron^M
Hexenstich^M
punto^M strega^F

knot stitches
puntos^M de relleno^M sueltos
points^M noués
Knötchenstiche^M
punti^M annodati

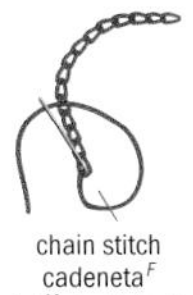

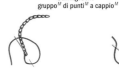

chain stitch
cadeneta^F
point^M de chainette^F
Kettenstich^M
punto^M catenella^F

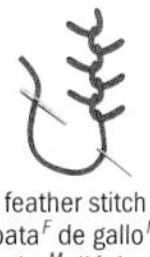

feather stitch
pata^F de gallo^M
point^M d'épine^F
Krähenfußstich^M
punto^M spina^F

flat stitches
puntos^M de relleno^M
points^M plats
Plattstiche^M
punti^M piatti

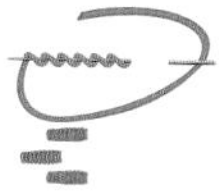

bullion stitch
pespunte^M
point^M de poste^F
Tressenstich^M
punto^M vapore^M

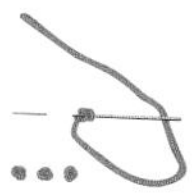

French knot stitch
punto^M de nudos^M
point^M de nœud^M
französischer Knötchenstich^M
punto^M nodi^M

couched stitches
bordados^M planos
points^M couchés
Überfangstiche^M
punti^M stuoia

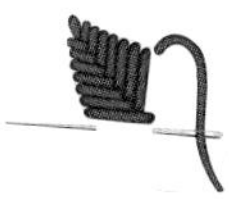

fishbone stitch
punto^M de espiga^F
point^M d'arête^F
Zopfstich^M
punto^M spina^F di pesce^F

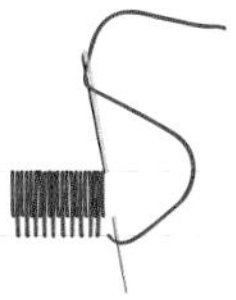

long and short stitch
lanzado^M desigual
point^M passé empiétant
langer und kurzer Spannstich^M
punto^M piatto intercalato

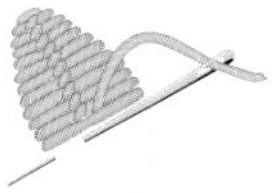

Romanian couching stitch
bordado^M plano
point^M roumain
rumänischer Überfangstich^M
punto^M rumeno

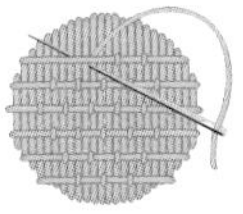

Oriental couching stitch
relleno^M alternado
point^M d'Orient^M
orientalischer Überfangstich^M
punto^M d'Oriente^M

ARTS AND ARCHITECTURE

weaving

tejido^M | tissage^M | Weben^N | tessitura^F

low-warp loom
telar^M de cuatro marcos^M
métier^M de basse lisse^F
Flachwebstuhl^M
telaio^M a ordito^M basso

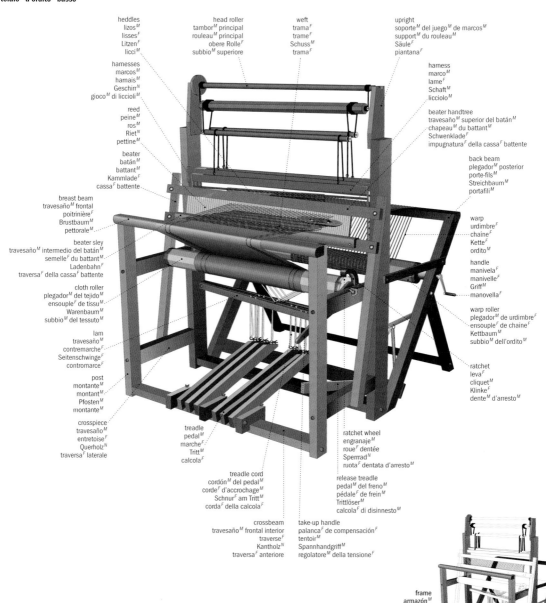

heddles
lizos^M
lisses^F
Litzen^F
licci^M

head roller
tambor^M principal
rouleau^M principal
obere Rolle^F
subbio^M superiore

weft
trama^F
trame^F
Schuss^M
trama^F

upright
soporte^M del juego^M de marcos^M
support^M du rouleau^M
Säule^F
piantana^F

harnesses
marcos^M
harnais^M
Geschirr^N
gioco^M di liccioli^M

harness
marco^M
lame^F
Schaft^M
licciolo^M

reed
peine^M
ros^M
Riet^N
pettine^M

beater handtree
travesaño^M superior del batán^M
chapeau^M du battant^M
Schwenklade^F
impugnatura^F della cassa^F battente

beater
batán^M
battant^M
Kammlade^F
cassa^F battente

back beam
plegador^M posterior
porte-fils^M
Streichbaum^M
portafili^M

breast beam
travesaño^M frontal
poitrinière^F
Brustbaum^M
pettorale^M

warp
urdimbre^F
chaine^F
Kette^F
ordito^M

beater sley
travesaño^M intermedio del batán^M
semelle^F du battant^M
Ladenbahn^F
traversa^F della cassa^F battente

handle
manivela^F
manivelle^F
Griff^M
manovella^F

cloth roller
plegador^M del tejido^M
ensouple^F de tissu^M
Warenbaum^M
subbio^M del tessuto^M

warp roller
plegador^M de urdimbre^F
ensouple^F de chaine^F
Kettbaum^M
subbio^M dell'ordito^M

lam
travesaño^M
contremarche^F
Seitenschwinge^F
contromarce^M

ratchet
leva^F
cliquet^M
Klinke^F
dente^M d'arresto^M

post
montante^M
montant^M
Pfosten^M
montante^M

crosspiece
travesaño^M
entretoise^F
Querholz^N
traversa^F laterale

treadle
pedal^M
marche^F
Tritt^M
calcola^F

ratchet wheel
engranaje^M
roue^F dentée
Sperrrad^N
ruota^F dentata d'arresto^M

treadle cord
cordón^M del pedal^M
corde^F d'accrochage^M
Schnur^F am Tritt^M
corda^F della calcola^F

release treadle
pedal^M del freno^M
pédale^F de frein^M
Trittlöser^M
calcola^F di disinnesto^M

crossbeam
travesaño^M frontal interior
traverse^F
Kantholz^N
traversa^F anteriore

take-up handle
palanca^F de compensación^F
tentoir^M
Spannhandgriff^M
regolatore^M della tensione^F

frame
armazón^M
bâti^M
Rahmen^M
incastellatura^F

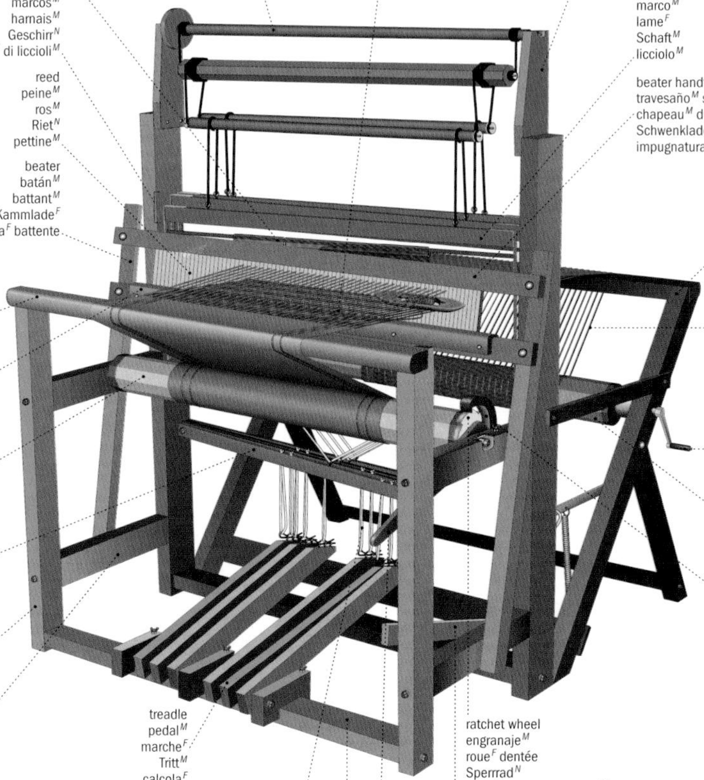

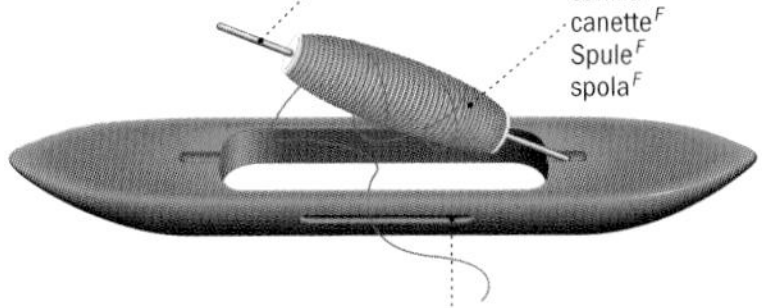

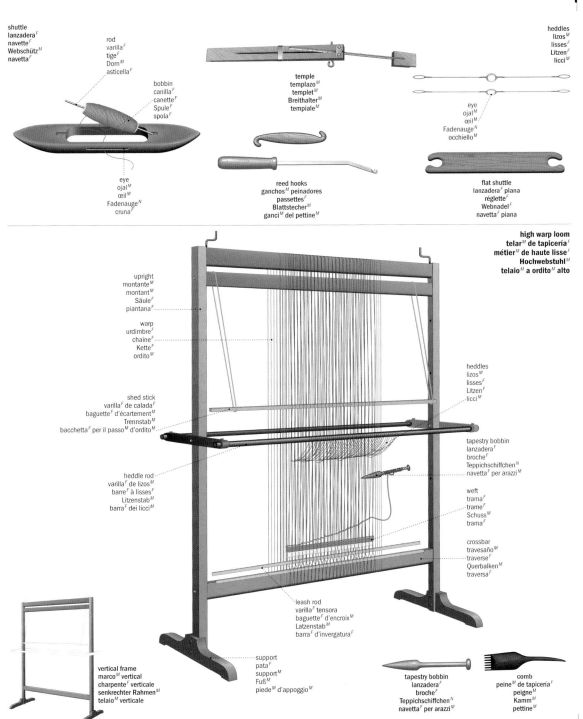

shuttle
lanzadera[F]
navette[F]
Webschütz[M]
navetta[F]

rod
varilla[F]
tige[F]
Dorn[M]
asticella[F]

bobbin
canilla[F]
canette[F]
Spule[F]
spola[F]

eye
ojal[M]
œil[M]
Fadenauge[N]
cruna[F]

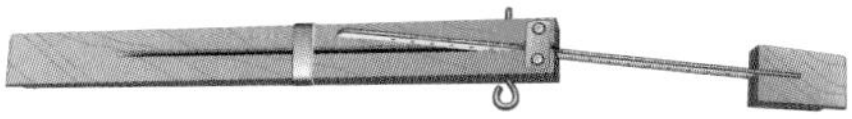

temple
templazo[M]
templet[M]
Breithalter[M]
tempiale[M]

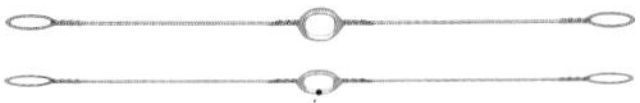

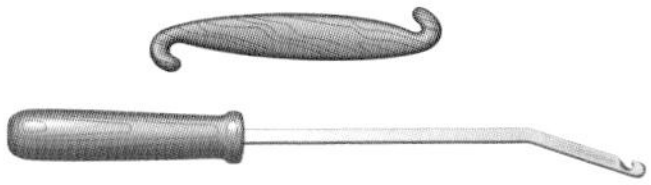

reed hooks
ganchos[M] peinadores[M]
passettes[F]
Blattstecher[M]
ganci[M] del pettine[M]

heddles
lizos[M]
lisses[F]
Litzen[F]
licci[M]

eye
ojal[M]
œil[M]
Fadenauge[N]
occhiello[M]

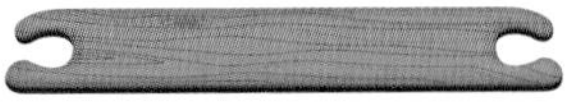

flat shuttle
lanzadera[F] plana
réglette[F]
Webnadel[F]
navetta[F] piana

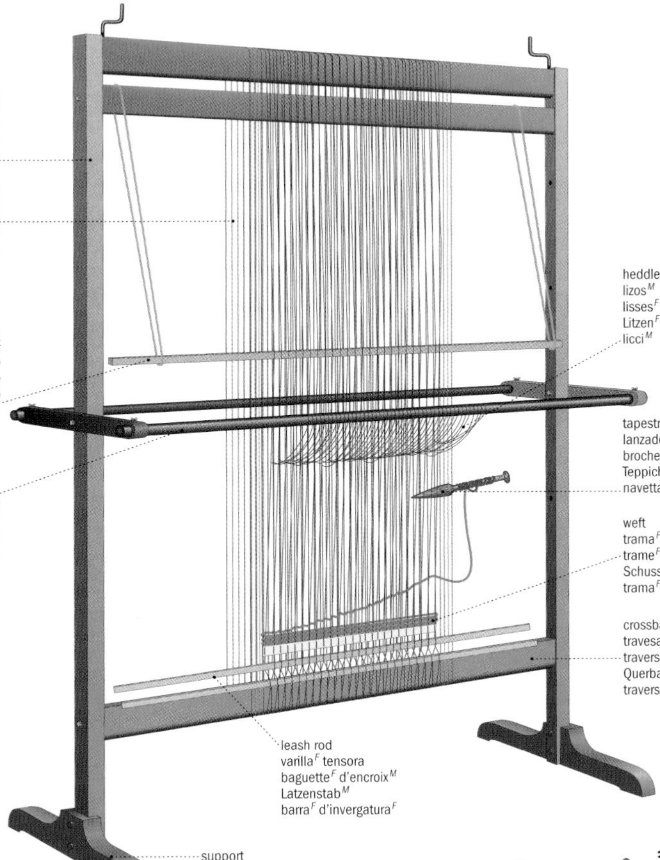

high warp loom
telar[M] de tapicería[F]
métier[M] de haute lisse[F]
Hochwebstuhl[M]
telaio[M] a ordito[M] alto

upright
montante[M]
montant[M]
Säule[F]
piantana[F]

warp
urdimbre[F]
chaîne[F]
Kette[F]
ordito[M]

shed stick
varilla[F] de calada[F]
baguette[F] d'écartement[M]
Trennstab[M]
bacchetta[F] per il passo[M] d'ordito[M]

heddle rod
varilla[F] de lizos[M]
barre[F] à lisses[F]
Litzenstab[M]
barra[F] dei licci[M]

heddles
lizos[M]
lisses[F]
Litzen[F]
licci[M]

tapestry bobbin
lanzadera[F]
broche[F]
Teppichschiffchen[N]
navetta[F] per arazzi[M]

weft
trama[F]
trame[F]
Schuss[M]
trama[F]

crossbar
travesaño[M]
traverse[F]
Querbalken[M]
traversa[F]

leash rod
varilla[F] tensora
baguette[F] d'encroix[M]
Latzenstab[M]
barra[F] d'invergatura[F]

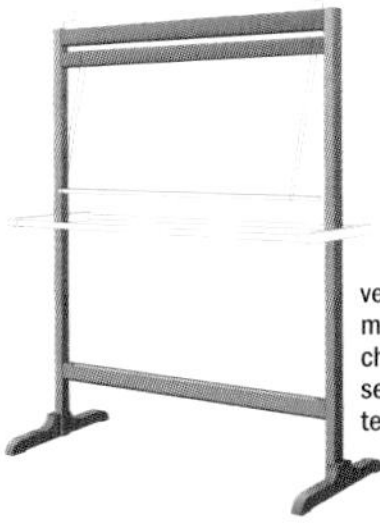

vertical frame
marco[M] vertical
charpente[F] verticale
senkrechter Rahmen[M]
telaio[M] verticale

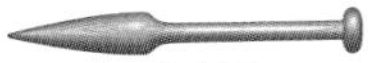

support
pata[F]
support[M]
Fuß[M]
piede[M] d'appoggio[M]

tapestry bobbin
lanzadera[F]
broche[F]
Teppichschiffchen[N]
navetta[F] per arazzi[M]

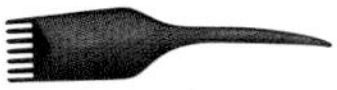

comb
peine[M] de tapicería[F]
peigne[M]
Kamm[M]
pettine[M]

ARTS AND ARCHITECTURE

461

accessories
accesorios^M
accessoires^M
Zubehör^N
accessori^M

bobbin winder
devanador^M de bobinas^F
canetière^F
Handspulgerät^N
roccatrice^F

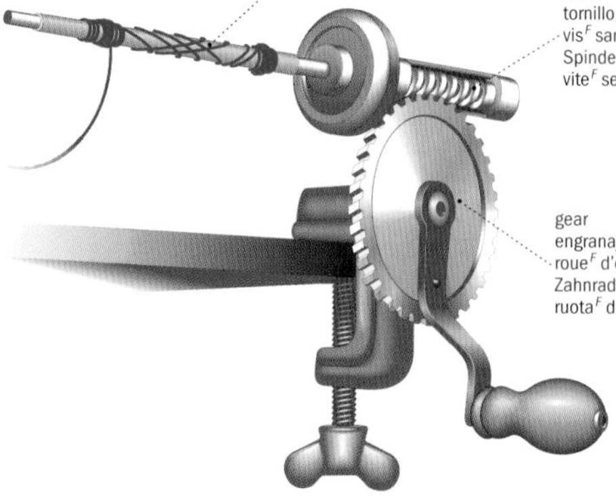

shaft
eje^M
fuseau^M
Dorn^M
fuso^M

worm
tornillo^M sinfín
vis^F sans fin^F
Spindel^F
vite^F senza fine

gear
engranaje^M
roue^F d'engrenage^M
Zahnrad^N
ruota^F dentata

ball winder
devanador^M
bobinoir^M
elektrisches Spulgerät^N
aggomitolatore^M

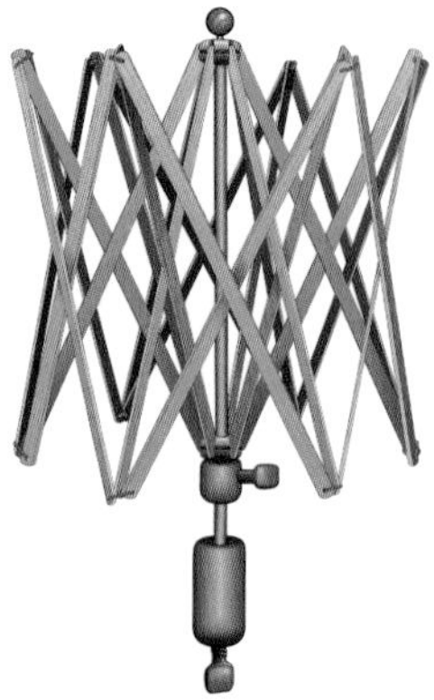

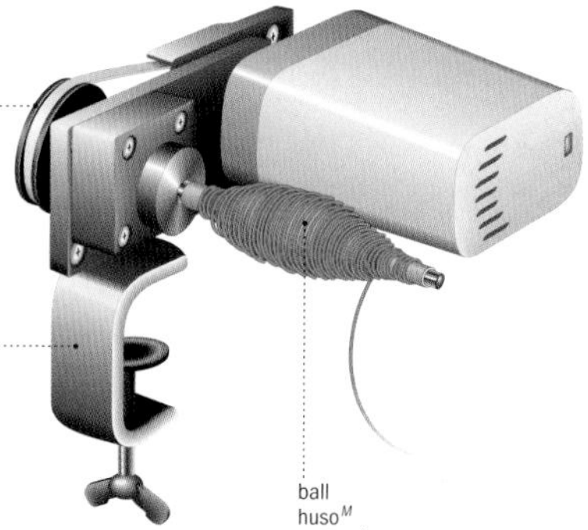

driving wheel
polea^F de transmisión^F
roue^F d'entrainement^M
Spulrad^N
ruota^F motrice

clamp
tornillo^M
serre-joint^M
Zwinge^F
morsetto^M

ball
huso^M
bobine^F
Knäuel^N
gomitolo^M

swift
devanadera^F
dévidoir^M
Schirmwinde^F
aspo^M

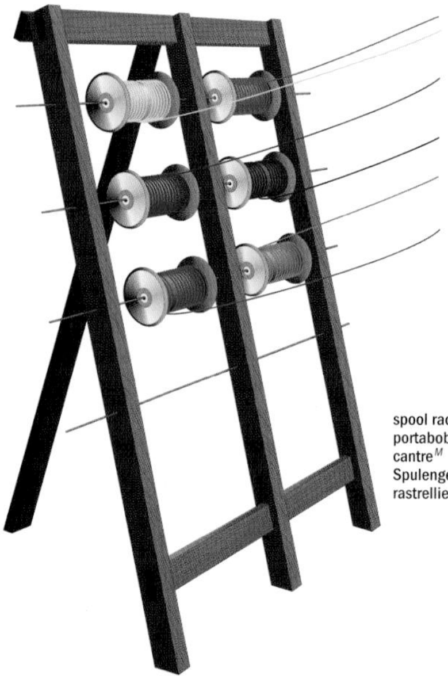

spool rack
portabobinas^M
cantre^M
Spulengestell^N
rastrelliera^F dei rocchetti^M

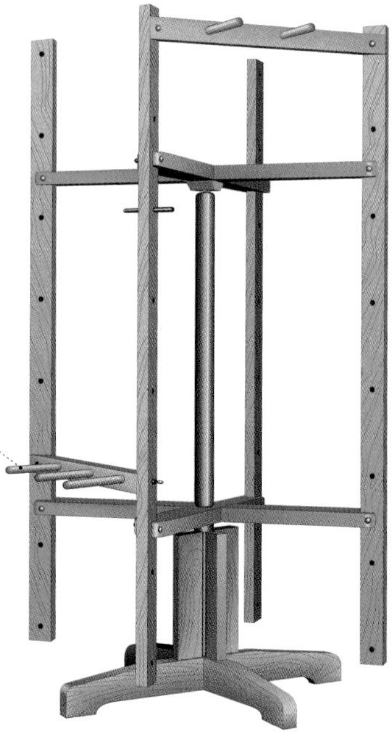

peg
espiga^F
cheville^F
Zapfen^M
piolo^M

warping frame
urdidor^M
ourdissoir^M
Schärbaum^M
orditoio^M

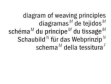

diagram of weaving principles
diagramas^M de tejidos^M
schéma^M du principe^M du tissage^M
Schaubild^N für das Webprinzip^N
schema^M della tessitura^F

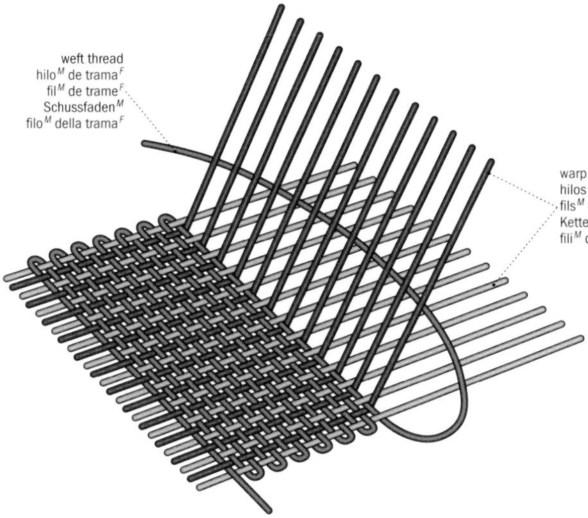

weft thread
hilo^M de trama^F
fil^M de trame^F
Schussfaden^M
filo^M della trama^F

warp threads
hilos^M de urdimbre^M
fils^M de chaine^F
Kettenfäden^M
fili^M dell'ordito^M

basic weaves
ligamentos^M textiles básicos
armures^F de base^F
Grundbindungen^F
armature^F di base^F

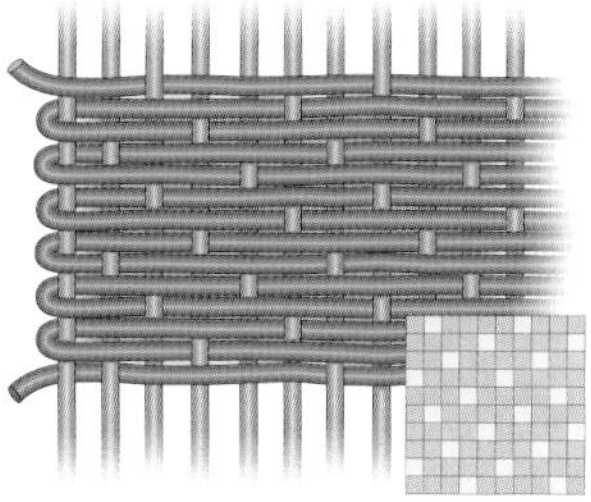

satin weave
satén^M
satin^M
Atlasbindung^F
raso^M

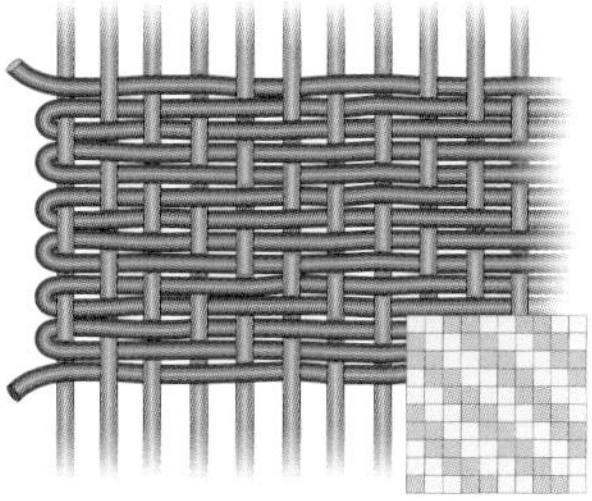

twill weave
sarga^F
sergé^M
Köperbindung^F
saia^F

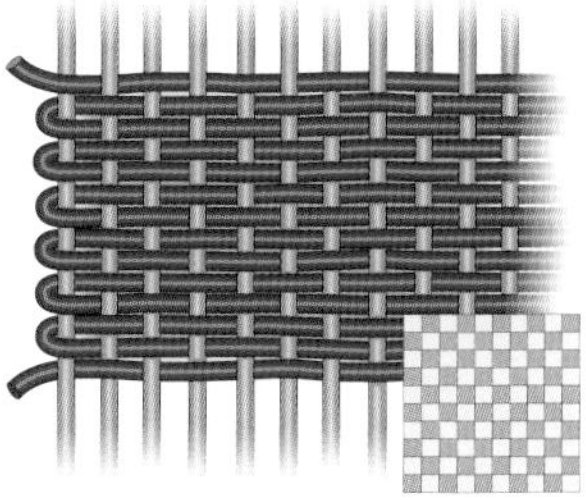

tabby
tafetán^M
toile^F
Leinwandbindung^F
tela^F

other weaving techniques
otros ligamentos^M textiles
autres techniques^F du tissage^M
andere Textilen^F Techniken^F
altre techniche^F della tessitura^F

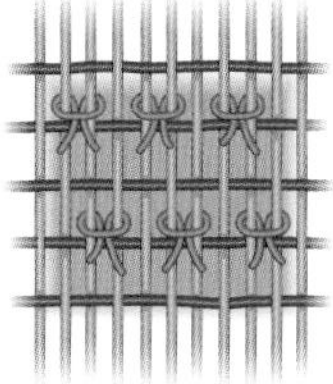

knot
anudado
nœud^M
Knoten^M
annodatura^F

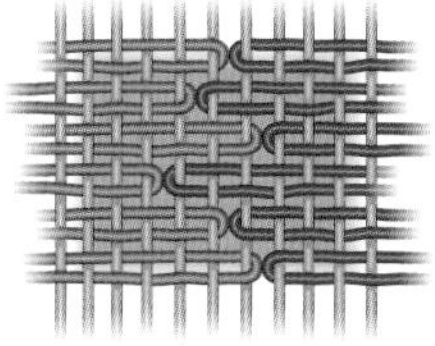

hatching
punteado
hachure^F
Kelimbindung^F mit wechselnden Wenden^F
ombreggiatura^F

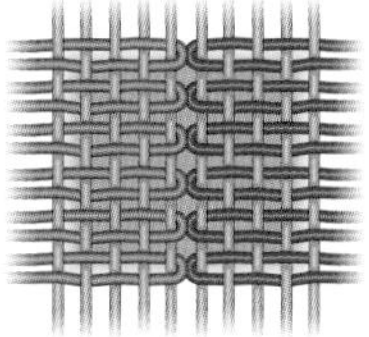

slit
vertical
fente^F
senkrechte Kelimbindung^F
fessura^F

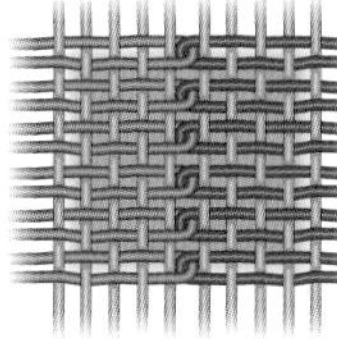

interlock
entrecruzado
croisement^M
Gobelinbindung^F
incrocio^M

pottery

cerámica^F | poterie^F | Töpferei^F | ceramica^F

ARTS AND ARCHITECTURE

turning
torno^M
tournage^M
Drehen^N
tornitura^F

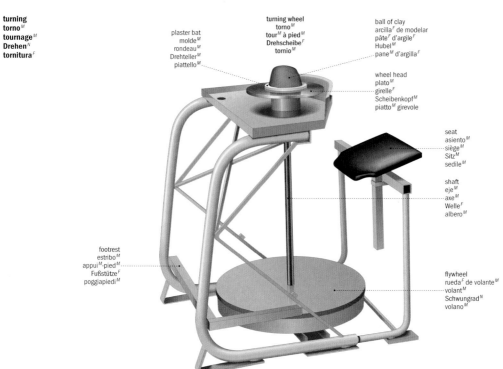

turning wheel
torno^M
tour^M à pied^M
Drehscheibe^F
tornio^M

plaster bat
molde^M
rondeau^M
Drehteller^M
piattello^M

ball of clay
arcilla^F de modelar
pâte^F d'argile^F
Hubel^M
pane^M d'argilla^F

wheel head
plato^M
girelle^F
Scheibenkopf^M
piatto^M girevole

seat
asiento^M
siège^M
Sitz^M
sedile^M

shaft
eje^M
axe^M
Welle^F
albero^M

footrest
estribo^M
appui^M-pied^M
Fußstütze^F
poggiapiedi^M

flywheel
rueda^F de volante^M
volant^M
Schwungrad^N
volano^M

tools
herramientas^F
outils^M
Werkzeug^N
utensili^M

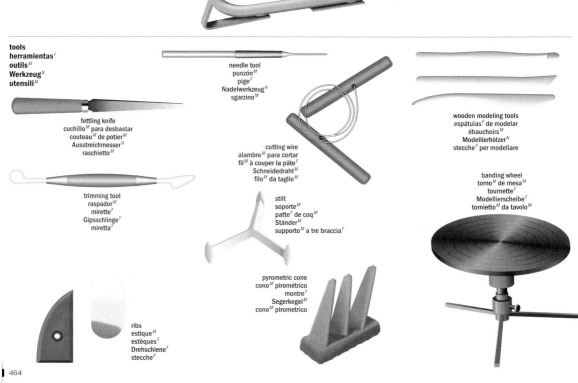

needle tool
punzón^M
pige^F
Nadelwerkzeug^N
sgarzino^M

fettling knife
cuchillo^M para desbastar
couteau^M de potier^M
Ausstreichmesser^N
raschietto^M

wooden modeling tools
espátulas^F de modelar
ébauchoirs^M
Modellierhölzer^N
stecche^F per modellare

cutting wire
alambre^M para cortar
fil^M à couper la pâte^F
Schneidedraht^M
filo^M da taglio^M

trimming tool
raspador^M
mirette^F
Gipsschlinge^F
miretta^F

banding wheel
torno^M de mesa^M
tournette^F
Modellierscheibe^F
tornietto^M da tavolo^M

stilt
soporte^M
patte^F de coq^M
Ständer^M
supporto^M a tre braccia^F

pyrometric cone
cono^M pirométrico
montre^F
Segerkegel^M
cono^M pirometrico

ribs
estique^M
estèques^F
Drehschiene^F
stecche^F

slab building
rodillo^M
galettage^M
Platten^F ausrollen
tecnica^F a nastro^M

coiling
cordón^M para espirales^F
colombin^M
Spiralwülste^F rollen
tecnica^F a colombino^M

firing
cocción^F
cuisson^F
Brennen^N
cottura^F

electric kiln
horno^M eléctrico
four^M électrique
elektrischer Brennofen^M
forno^M elettrico

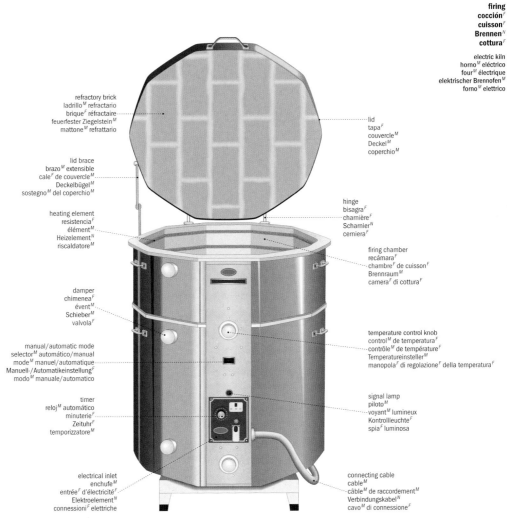

refractory brick
ladrillo^M refractario
brique^F réfractaire
feuerfester Ziegelstein^M
mattone^M refrattario

lid
tapa^F
couvercle^M
Deckel^M
coperchio^M

lid brace
brazo^M extensible
cale^F de couvercle^M
Deckelbügel^M
sostegno^M del coperchio^M

hinge
bisagra^F
charnière^F
Scharnier^N
cerniera^F

heating element
resistencia^F
élément^M
Heizelement^N
riscaldatore^M

firing chamber
recámara^F
chambre^F de cuisson^F
Brennraum^M
camera^F di cottura^F

damper
chimenea^F
évent^M
Schieber^M
valvola^F

temperature control knob
control^M de temperatura^F
contrôle^M de température^F
Temperatureinsteller^M
manopola^F di regolazione^F della temperatura^F

manual/automatic mode
selector^M automático/manual
mode^M manuel/automatique
Manuell-/Automatikeinstellung^F
modo^M manuale/automatico

timer
reloj^M automático
minuterie^F
Zeituhr^F
temporizzatore^M

signal lamp
piloto^M
voyant^M lumineux
Kontrollleuchte^F
spia^F luminosa

electrical inlet
enchufe^M
entrée^F d'électricité^F
Elektroelement^N
connessioni^F elettriche

connecting cable
cable^M
câble^M de raccordement^M
Verbindungskabel^N
cavo^M di connessione^F

ARTS AND ARCHITECTURE

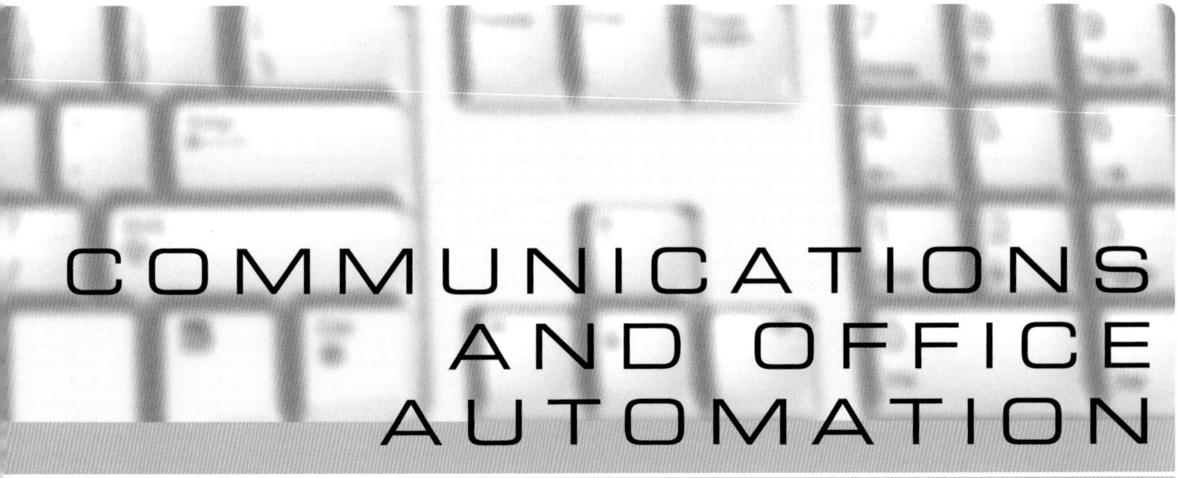

COMMUNICATIONS AND OFFICE AUTOMATION

COMUNICACIONES Y OFIMÁTICA | COMMUNICATIONS ET BUREAUTIQUE | KOMMUNIKATION UND BÜROTECHNIK | COMUNICAZIONI E BUROTICA

languages of the world

lenguas^F del mundo | langues^F du monde^M | Sprachen^F der Erde^F | lingue^F del mondo^M

major language families
grandes familias^F linguisticas
grandes familles^F de langues^F
wichtigste Sprachgruppen^F
principali famiglie^F linguistiche

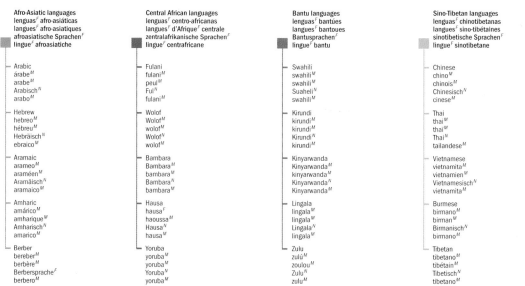

Afro-Asiatic languages	Central African languages	Bantu languages	Sino-Tibetan languages
lenguas^F afro-asiáticas	lenguas^F centro-africanas	lenguas^F bantúes	lenguas^F chinotibetanas
langues^F afro-asiatiques	langues^F d'Afrique^F centrale	langues^F bantoues	langues^F sino-tibétaines
afroasiatische Sprachen^F	zentralafrikanische Sprachen^F	Bantusprachen^F	sinotibetische Sprachen^F
lingue^F afroasiatiche	lingue^F centrafricane	lingue^F bantu	lingue^F sinotibetane

— Arabic	— Fulani	— Swahili	— Chinese
árabe^M	fulani^M	swahili^M	chino^M
arabe^M	peul^M	swahili^M	chinois^M
Arabisch^N	Ful^N	Suaheli^N	Chinesisch^N
arabo^M	fulani^M	swahili^M	cinese^M
— Hebrew	— Wolof	— Kirundi	— Thai
hebreo^M	Wolof^M	kirundi^M	thai^M
hébreu^M	wolof^M	kirundi^M	thai^M
Hebräisch^N	Wolof^N	Kirundi^N	Thai^N
ebraico^M	wolof^M	kirundi^M	tailandese^M
— Aramaic	— Bambara	— Kinyarwanda	— Vietnamese
arameo^M	Bambara^M	Kinyarwanda^M	vietnamita^M
araméen^M	bambara^M	kinyarwanda^M	vietnamien^M
Aramäisch^N	Bambara^N	Kinyarwanda^N	Vietnamesisch^N
aramaico^M	bambara^M	Kinyarwanda^M	vietnamita^M
— Amharic	— Hausa	— Lingala	— Burmese
amárico^M	hausa^F	lingala^M	birmano^M
amharique^M	haoussa^M	lingala^M	birman^M
Amharisch^N	Hausa^N	Lingala^N	Birmanisch^N
amarico^M	hausa^M	lingala^M	birmano^M
— Berber	— Yoruba	— Zulu	— Tibetan
bereber^M	yoruba^M	zulú^M	tibetano^M
berbère^M	yoruba^M	zoulou^M	tibétain^M
Berbersprache^F	Yoruba^N	Zulu^N	Tibetisch^N
berbero^M	yoruba^M	zulu^M	tibetano^M

Indo-European languages
lenguas[F] indoeuropeas
langues[F] indo-européennes
indoeuropäische Sprachen[F]
lingue[F] indoeuropee

Romance languages
lenguas[F] romances
langues[F] romanes
romanische Sprachen[F]
lingue[F] romanze

- French
  francés[M]
  français[M]
  Französisch[N]
  francese[M]

- Spanish
  español[M]
  espagnol[M]
  Spanisch[N]
  spagnolo[M]

- Catalan
  catalán[M]
  catalan[M]
  Katalanisch[N]
  catalano[M]

- Portuguese
  português[M]
  portugais[M]
  Portugiesisch[N]
  portoghese[M]

- Italian
  italiano[M]
  italien[M]
  Italienisch[N]
  italiano[M]

- Romanian
  rumano[M]
  roumain[M]
  Rumänisch[N]
  rumeno[M]

Germanic languages
lenguas[F] germánicas
langues[F] germaniques
germanische Sprachen[F]
lingue[F] germaniche

- English
  inglés[M]
  anglais[M]
  Englisch[N]
  inglese[M]

- German
  alemán[M]
  allemand[M]
  Deutsch[N]
  tedesco[M]

- Dutch
  holandés[M]
  néerlandais[M]
  Niederländisch[N]
  olandese[M]

- Danish
  danés[M]
  danois[M]
  Dänisch[N]
  danese[M]

- Swedish
  sueco[M]
  suédois[M]
  Schwedisch[N]
  svedese[M]

- Norwegian
  noruego[M]
  norvégien[M]
  Norwegisch[N]
  norvegese[M]

- Icelandic
  islandés[M]
  islandais[M]
  Isländisch[N]
  islandese[M]

- Yiddish
  yidish[M]
  yiddish[M]
  Jiddisch[N]
  yiddish[M]

Celtic languages
lenguas[F] célticas
langues[F] celtiques
keltische Sprachen[F]
lingue[F] celtiche

- Breton
  bretón[M]
  breton[M]
  Bretonisch[N]
  bretone[M]

- Welsh
  galés[M]
  gallois[M]
  Walisisch[N]
  gallese[M]

- Scottish
  escocés[M]
  écossais[M]
  Schottisch-Gälisch[N]
  scozzese[M]

- Irish
  irlandés[M]
  irlandais[M]
  Irisch[N]
  irlandese[M]

isolated languages
lenguas[F] aisladas
langues[F] isolées
isolierte Sprachen[F]
lingue[F] isolate

- Greek
  griego[M]
  grec[M]
  Griechisch[N]
  greco[M]

- Albanian
  albanés[M]
  albanais[M]
  Albanisch[N]
  albanese[M]

- Armenian
  armeno[M]
  arménien[M]
  Armenisch[N]
  armeno[M]

Slavic languages
lenguas[F] eslavas
langues[F] slaves
slawische Sprachen[F]
lingue[F] slave

- Czech
  checo[M]
  tchèque[M]
  Tschechisch[N]
  ceco[M]

- Slovak
  eslovaco[M]
  slovaque[M]
  Slowakisch[N]
  slovacco[M]

- Polish
  polaco[M]
  polonais[M]
  Polnisch[N]
  polacco[M]

- Russian
  ruso[M]
  russe[M]
  Russisch[N]
  russo[M]

- Ukrainian
  ucranio[M]
  ukrainien[M]
  Ukrainisch[N]
  ucraino[M]

- Bulgarian
  búlgaro[M]
  bulgare[M]
  Bulgarisch[N]
  bulgaro[M]

- Slovene
  esloveno[M]
  slovène[M]
  Slowenisch[N]
  sloveno[M]

- Serbo-Croatian
  serbocroata[M]
  serbo-croate[M]
  Serbokroatisch[N]
  serbo-croato[M]

Indo-Iranian languages
lenguas[F] indoiranias
langues[F] indo-iraniennes
indoarische Sprachen[F]
lingue[F] indoiraniche

- Persian
  persa[M]
  persan[M]
  Persisch[N]
  persiano[M]

- Urdu
  urdu[M]
  ourdou[M]
  Urdu[N]
  urdu[M]

- Hindi
  Hindi[M]
  hindi[M]
  Hindi[N]
  hindi[M]

Amerindian languages
lenguas[F] amerindias
langues[F] amérindiennes
Indianersprachen[F]
lingue[F] amerindie

- Inuktitut
  inuktitut[M]
  inuktitut[N]
  Inuktikut[N]
  inuktitut[M]

- Cree
  cree[M]
  cri[M]
  Cree[N]
  cree[M]

- Montagnais
  montagnais[M]
  montagnais[N]
  Montagnais[N]
  montagnais[N]

- Navajo
  navajo[M]
  navaho[M]
  Navajo[N]
  navajo[M]

- Nahuatl
  nahualt[M]
  nahuatl[M]
  Nahuatl[N]
  nahuatl[M]

- Maya
  maya[M]
  maya[M]
  Maya[N]
  maya[M]

- Quechua
  quechua[M]
  quechua[M]
  Ketschua[N]
  quechua[M]

- Aymara
  aymara[M]
  aymara[M]
  Aimara[N]
  aymara[M]

- Guarani
  guaraní[M]
  guarani[M]
  Guarani[N]
  guarani[M]

Ural-Altaic languages
lenguas[F] uraloaltaicas
langues[F] ouralo-altaiques
altaische Sprachen[F]
lingue[F] uralo-altaiche

- Japanese
  japonés[M]
  japonais[M]
  Japanisch[N]
  giapponese[M]

- Korean
  coreano[M]
  coréen[M]
  Koreanisch[N]
  coreano[M]

- Mongolian
  mogol[M]
  mongol[M]
  Mongolisch[N]
  mongolo[M]

- Turkish
  turco[M]
  turc[M]
  Türkisch[N]
  turco[M]

Malayo-Polynesian languages
lenguas[F] malayo-polinesias
langues[F] malayo-polynésiennes
malaiopolynesische Sprachen[F]
lingue[F] maleopolinesiane

- Indonesian
  indonesio[M]
  indonésien[M]
  Indonesisch[N]
  indonesiano[M]

- Tagalog
  tagalo[M]
  tagalog[M]
  Tagalog[N]
  tagalog[M]

- Malagasy
  malgache[M]
  malgache[M]
  Malagasy[N]
  malgascio[M]

- Samoan
  samoano[M]
  samoan[M]
  Samoanisch[N]
  samoano[M]

- Tahitian
  tahitiano[M]
  tahitien[M]
  Tahitianisch[N]
  tahitiano[M]

- Hawaiian
  hawaiano[M]
  hawaïen[M]
  Hawaiianisch[N]
  hawaiano[M]

- Maori
  maori[M]
  maori[M]
  Maori[N]
  maori[M]

Oceanian languages
lenguas[F] oceánicas
langues[F] d'Océanie[F]
ozeanische Sprachen[F]
lingue[F] dell'Oceania[F]

- Melanesian
  melanesia
  mélanésien[M]
  Melanesisch[N]
  melanesiano[M]

- Papuan languages
  lenguas[F] papúas
  langues[F] papoues
  Papuasprachen[F]
  lingue[F] papuane

- Australian aboriginal languages
  lenguas[F] australianas aborígenas
  langues[F] aborigènes d'Australie[F]
  australische Sprachen[F]
  lingue[F] aborigene dell'Australia[F]

writing instruments

instrumentos^M para escribir | instruments^M d'écriture^F | Schreibgeräte^N | strumenti^M scrittori

quill
pluma^F de ave^F
plume^F d'oie^F
Federkiel^F
penna^F d'oca^F

Roman metal pen
pluma^F metálica romana
plume^F métallique romaine
römische Metallfeder^F
stilo^M metallico romano

cane pen
pluma^F de caña^F
plume^F creuse de roseau^M
Rohrfeder^F
calamo^M vegetale

lead pencil
lápiz^M de grafito^M
crayon^M en plomb^M
Graphitstift^M
stilo^M di piombo^M

writing brush
pincel^M
pinceau^M
Schreibpinsel^M
pennello^M per scrivere

stylus
estilo^M
stylet^M
Stilus^M
stilo^M

steel pen
pluma^F metálica
plume^F métallique
Stahlschreibfeder^F
penna^F con pennino^M metallico

Egyptian reed pens
cálamos^M egípcios
calames^M
Binsenstängeln^M
stili^M di canna^F

marker
marcador^M
marqueur^M
Marker^M
evidenziatore^M

fountain pen
pluma^F estilográfica
stylo^M-plume^F
Füllfederhalter^M
penna^F stilografica

nib
punta^F
plume^F
Feder^F
pennino^M

cap
tapa^F
capuchon^M
Kappe^F
cappuccio^M

mechanical pencil
portaminas^F
porte-mine^M
Druckbleistift^M
portamine^M

air hole
orificio^M
évent^M
Luftloch^N
occhio^M

barrel
caña^F
corps^M
Tintenraum^M
corpo^M

pencil
lápiz^M
crayon^M
Bleistift^M
matita^F

ballpoint pen
bolígrafo^M
stylo^M-bille^F
Kugelschreiber^M
penna^F a sfera^F

cartridge
carga^F
cartouche^F
Mine^F
cartuccia^F

joint
unión^F
joint^M
Verbindung^F
raccordo^M

clip
pinza^F
agrafe^F
Clip^M
fermaglio^M

point
punta^F
pointe^F
Spitze^F
punta^F

spring
resorte^M
ressort^M
Feder^F
molla^F

thrust device
mecanismo^M de empuje^M
dispositif^M de poussée^F
Druckmechanik^F
meccanismo^M a scatto^M

thrust tube
tubo^M de empuje^M
tube^M de poussée^F
Druckrohr^N
asta^F del meccanismo^M a scatto^M

push-button
botón^M de presión^F
bouton^M-poussoir^M
Druckknopf^M
pulsante^M

ball bearing
bola^F de rodamiento^M
bille^F
Kugel^F
sfera^F

ink
tinta^F
encre^F
Farbmasse^F
inchiostro^M

refill
repuesto^M
recharge^F
Nachfüllmine^F
refill^M

newspaper

periódico[M] | journal[M] | Zeitung[F] | giornale[M]

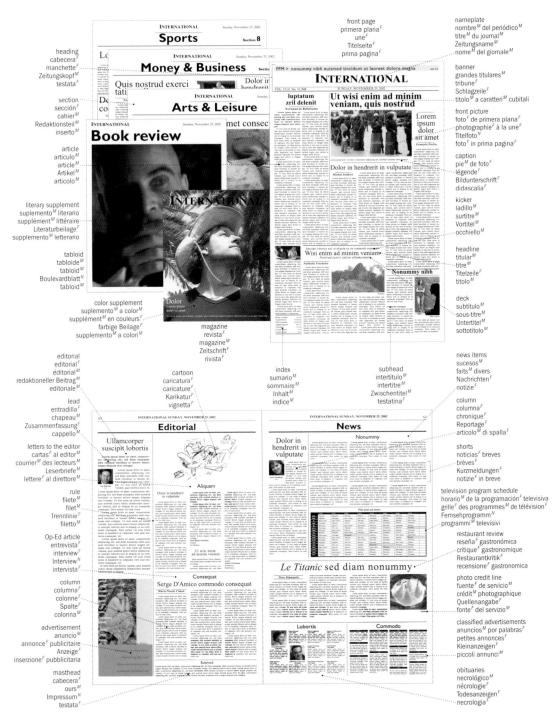

heading
cabecera[F]
manchette[F]
Zeitungskopf[M]
testata[F]

section
sección[F]
cahier[M]
Redaktionsteil[M]
inserto[M]

article
artículo[M]
article[M]
Artikel[M]
articolo[M]

literary supplement
suplemento[M] literario
supplément[M] littéraire
Literaturbeilage[F]
supplemento[M] letterario

tabloid
tabloide[M]
tabloid[M]
Boulevardblatt[N]
tabloid[M]

color supplement
suplemento[M] a color[M]
supplément[M] en couleurs[M]
farbige Beilage[F]
supplemento[M] a colori[M]

magazine
revista[F]
magazine[M]
Zeitschrift[F]
rivista[F]

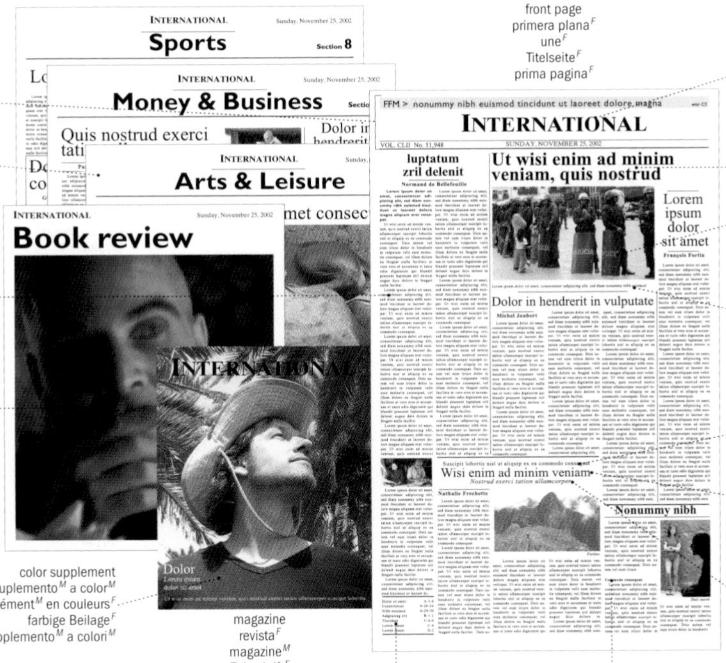

front page
primera plana[F]
une[F]
Titelseite[F]
prima pagina[F]

nameplate
nombre[M] del periódico[M]
titre[M] du journal[M]
Zeitungsname[M]
nome[M] del giornale[M]

banner
grandes titulares[M]
tribune[F]
Schlagzeile[F]
titolo[M] a caratteri[M] cubitali

front picture
foto[F] de primera plana[F]
photographie[F] à la une[F]
Titelfoto[N]
foto[F] in prima pagina[F]

caption
pie[M] de foto[F]
légende[F]
Bildunterschrift[F]
didascalia[F]

kicker
ladillo[M]
surtitre[M]
Vortitel[M]
occhiello[M]

headline
titular[M]
titre[M]
Titelzeile[F]
titolo[M]

deck
subtítulo[M]
sous-titre[M]
Untertitel[M]
sottotitolo[M]

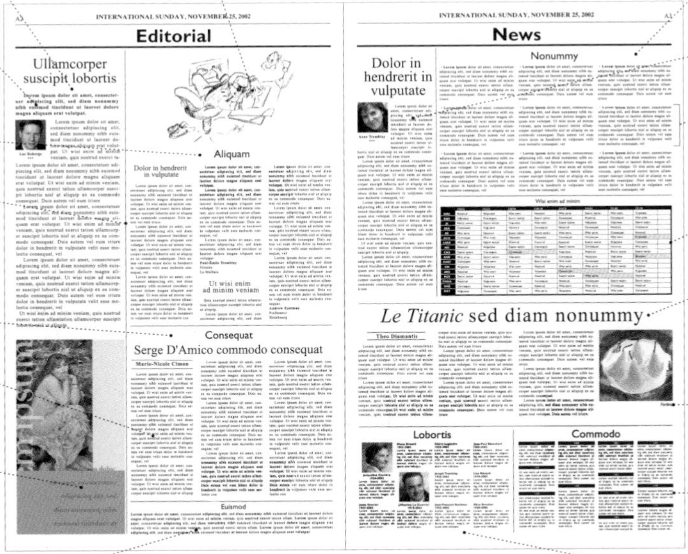

editorial
editorial[F]
éditorial[M]
redaktioneller Beitrag[M]
editoriale[M]

lead
entradilla[F]
chapeau[M]
Zusammenfassung[F]
cappello[M]

letters to the editor
cartas[F] al editor[M]
courrier[M] des lecteurs[M]
Leserbriefe[F]
lettere[F] al direttore[M]

rule
filete[M]
filet[M]
Trennlinie[F]
filetto[M]

Op-Ed article
entrevista[F]
interview[F]
Interview[N]
intervista[F]

column
columna[F]
colonne[F]
Spalte[F]
colonna[M]

advertisement
anuncio[M]
annonce[F] publicitaire
Anzeige[F]
inserzione[F] pubblicitaria

masthead
cabecera[F]
ours[M]
Impressum[N]
testata[F]

index
sumario[M]
sommaire[M]
Inhalt[M]
indice[M]

cartoon
caricatura[F]
caricature[F]
Karikatur[F]
vignetta[F]

subhead
intertítulo[M]
intertitre[M]
Zwischentitel[M]
testatina[F]

news items
sucesos[M]
faits[M] divers
Nachrichten[F]
notizie[F]

column
columna[F]
chronique[F]
Reportage[F]
articolo[M] di spalla[F]

shorts
noticias[F] breves
brèves[F]
Kurzmeldungen[F]
notizie[F] in breve

television program schedule
horario[M] de la programación[F] televisiva
grille[F] des programmes[M] de télévision[F]
Fernsehprogramm[N]
programmi[M] televisivi

restaurant review
reseña[F] gastronómica
critique[F] gastronomique
Restaurantkritik[F]
recensione[F] gastronomica

photo credit line
fuente[F] de servicio[M]
crédit[M] photographique
Quellenangabe[F]
fonte[F] del servizio[M]

classified advertisements
anuncios[M] por palabras[F]
petites annonces[F]
Kleinanzeigen[F]
piccoli annunci[M]

obituaries
necrológico[M]
nécrologie[F]
Todesanzeigen[F]
necrologia[F]

typography

tipografía^F | typographie^F | Typografie^F | tipografia^F

characters of a font
caracteres^M de una fundición^F
caractères^M d'une police^F
Schriftarten^F
caratteri^M di un font^M

sans serif type
tipo^M sans serif
caractère^M sans empattement^M
Groteskschrift^F
carattere senza grazie

serif type
tipo^M serif
caractère^M avec empattements^M
Serifenschrift^F
carattere con grazie

abcdefghijklmnopqrstuvwxyz 0123456789 abcdefghijklmnopqrstuvwxyz 0123456789

letters
letras^F
lettres^F
Buchstaben^M
lettere^F

figures
cifras^F
chiffres^M
Ziffern^F
cifre^F

shape of characters
forma^F de los caracteres^M
forme^F des caractères^M
Zeichenform^F
forma^F dei caratteri^M

ABCDEF ABCDEF abcdef *abcdef*

uppper case
mayúscula
capitale^F
Majuskel^F
maiuscolo^M

small capital
versalita
petite capitale^F
Kapitälchen^N
maiuscoletto^M

lower case
minúscula
bas^M de casse^F
Minuskel^F
minuscolo^M

italic
cursiva
italique^M
kursiv
corsivo^M

weight
tamaño^M
graisse^F
Schriftstärke^F
spessore^M

light
fina
maigre
mager
sottile

semi-bold
semi-negrita
demi-gras
halbfett
semi-grassetto

black
negro
noir
doppelfett
nero

extra-light
extra-fina
extra-maigre
extra mager
molto sottile

medium
media
normal
normal
medio

bold
negrita
gras
fett
grassetto

extra-bold
extra-negrita
extra-gras
extra fett
extra-nero

set width
espacio^M
chasse^F
Dickte^F
spaziatura^F

condensed
condensada
serré
extra schmal
ridotta

narrow
estrecha
étroit
schmal
piccola

normal
normal
normal
normal
normale

wide
ancha
large
breit
intera

extended
alargada
étendu
extra breit
espansa

leading
interlineado^M
interlignage^M
Durchschuss^M
interlinea^F

position of a character
posición^F de un carácter^M
position^F d'un caractère^M
Zeichenstellung^F
posizione^F di un carattere^M

Lorem ipsum dolor sit amet, consectetuer adipiscing elit, sed

Lorem ipsum dolor sit amet, consectetuer adipiscing elit, sed

Lorem ipsum dolor sit amet, consectetuer adipiscing elit, sed

H_2SO_4

XXe

simple spacing
interlineado^M sencillo
interligne^M simple
einfacher Zeilenabstand^M
interlinea^F singola

1.5 spacing
interlineado^M 1.5
interligne^M 1,5
Zeilenabstand^M 1,5 Zeilen^F
interlinea^F 1,5

double spacing
interlineado^M doble
interligne^M double
doppelter Zeilenabstand^M
interlinea^F doppia

inferior (sub-script)
subindice
indice^M
tiefgestellt
pedice^M

superior (super-script)
superindice
exposant^M
hochgestellt
apice^M

diacritic symbols

signos^M diacríticos | signes^M diacritiques | diakritische Zeichen^N | simboli^M diacritici

grave accent
acento^M grave
accent^M grave
Accent^M grave
accento^M grave

acute accent
acento^M agudo
accent^M aigu
Accent^M aigu
accento^M acuto

cedilla
cedilla^F
cédille^F
Cedille^F
cediglia^F

umlaut (dieresis)
diéresis^F
tréma^M
Umlaut^M
dieresi^F

circumflex accent
acento^M circunflejo
accent^M circonflexe
Circumflex^M
accento^M circonflesso

tilde
tilde^F
tilde^M
Tilde^F
tilde^{M/F}

miscellaneous symbols

varios | symboles^M divers | Weitere Symbole^N | varie^F

registered trademark
marca^F registrada
marque^F déposée
eingetragenes Warenzeichen^N
marchio^M registrato

copyright
copyright (derechos^M de autor^M)
copyright^M
Copyright^N
copyright^M

ampersand
y
esperluette^F
Et-Zeichen^N
e^F commerciale

apostrophe
apóstrofe^M
apostrophe^F
Apostroph^M
apostrofo^M

punctuation marks

signos^M de puntuación^F | signes^M de ponctuation^F | Satzzeichen^N | segni^M di interpunzione^F

period
punto^M
point^M
Punkt^M
punto^M

semicolon
punto^M y coma^F
point^M-virgule^F
Strichpunkt^M
punto^M e virgola^F

comma
coma^F
virgule^F
Komma^N
virgola^F

ellipses
puntos^M suspensivos
points^M de suspension^F
Fortführungspunkte^M
puntini^M di sospensione^F

colon
dos puntos^M
deux-points^M
Doppelpunkt^M
due punti^M

asterisk
asterisco^M
astérisque^M
Sternchen^N
asterisco^M

dash
guión^M largo
tiret^M
Gedankenstrich^M
trattino^M

parentheses
paréntesis^M
parenthèses^F
runde Klammern^F
parentesi^F

square brackets
corchetes^M
crochets^M
eckige Klammern^F
parentesi^F quadre

virgule
diagonal^F
barre^F oblique
Schrägstrich^M
barra^F obliqua

exclamation point
exlamación^F
point^M d'exclamation^F
Ausrufezeichen^N
punto^M esclamativo

question mark
interrogación^F
point^M d'interrogation^F
Fragezeichen^N
punto^M interrogativo

single quotation marks
comillas^F sencillas
guillemets^M
halbe Anführungszeichen^N
virgolette^F semplici

quotation marks
comillas^F
guillemets^M
Anführungszeichen^N
virgolette^F doppie

quotation marks (French)
comillas^F
guillemets^M
Anführungszeichen^N (französisch)
caporali^F

public postal network

red^F de correos^M pública | réseau^M public postal | öffentliches Postnetz^N | rete^F pubblica postale

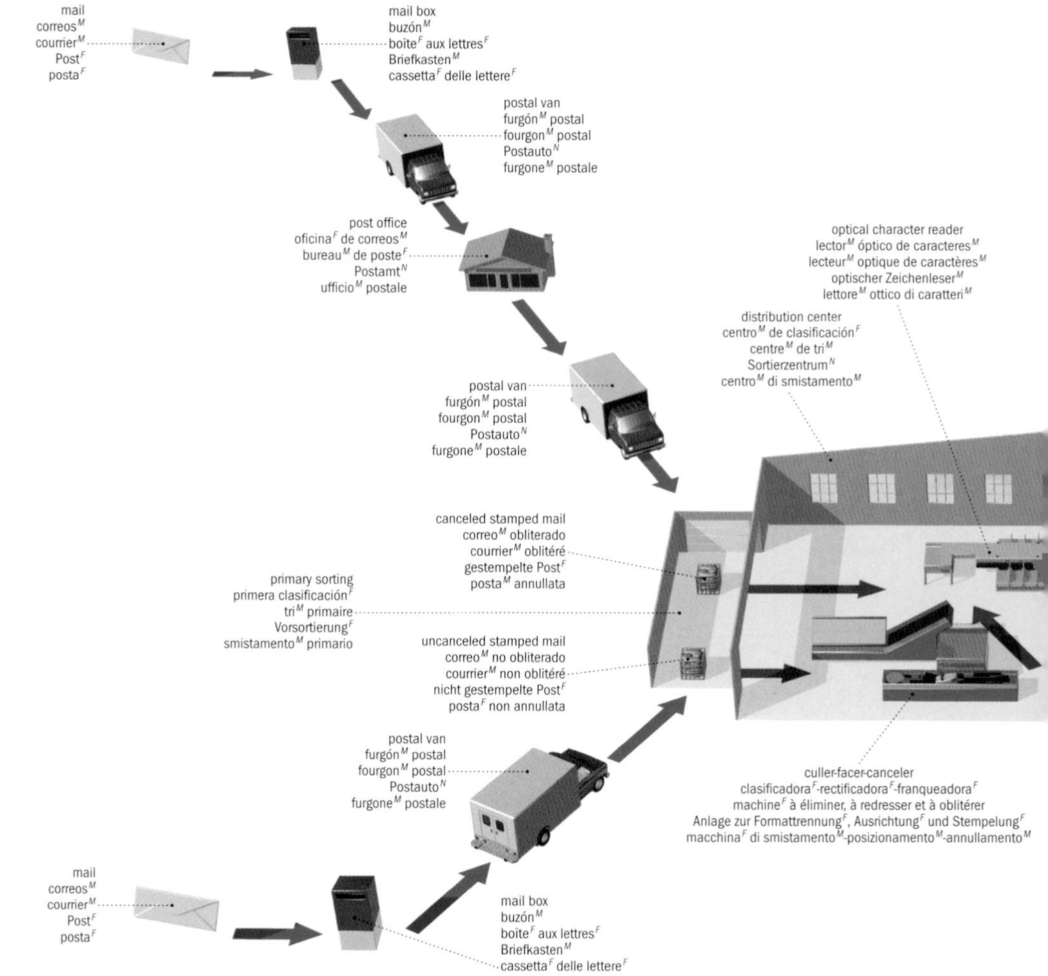

mail
correos^M
courrier^M
Post^F
posta^F

mail box
buzón^M
boîte^F aux lettres^F
Briefkasten^M
cassetta^F delle lettere^F

postal van
furgón^M postal
fourgon^M postal
Postauto^N
furgone^M postale

post office
oficina^F de correos^M
bureau^M de poste^F
Postamt^N
ufficio^M postale

optical character reader
lector^M óptico de caracteres^M
lecteur^M optique de caractères^M
optischer Zeichenleser^M
lettore^M ottico di caratteri^M

distribution center
centro^M de clasificación^F
centre^M de tri^M
Sortierzentrum^N
centro^M di smistamento^M

postal van
furgón^M postal
fourgon^M postal
Postauto^N
furgone^M postale

canceled stamped mail
correo^M obliterado
courrier^M oblitéré
gestempelte Post^F
posta^M annullata

primary sorting
primera clasificación^F
tri^M primaire
Vorsortierung^F
smistamento^M primario

uncanceled stamped mail
correo^M no obliterado
courrier^M non oblitéré
nicht gestempelte Post^F
posta^F non annullata

postal van
furgón^M postal
fourgon^M postal
Postauto^N
furgone^M postale

culler-facer-canceler
clasificadora^F-rectificadora^F-franqueadora^F
machine^F à éliminer, à redresser et à oblitérer
Anlage zur Formattrennung^F, Ausrichtung^F und Stempelung^F
macchina^F di smistamento^M-posizionamento^M-annullamento^M

mail
correos^M
courrier^M
Post^F
posta^F

mail box
buzón^M
boîte^F aux lettres^F
Briefkasten^M
cassetta^F delle lettere^F

mail
correo^M
courrier^M
Post^F
posta^F

postage stamp
sello^M de correos^M
timbre^M-poste^F
Briefmarke^F/Postwertzeichen^N
francobollo^M

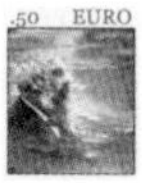

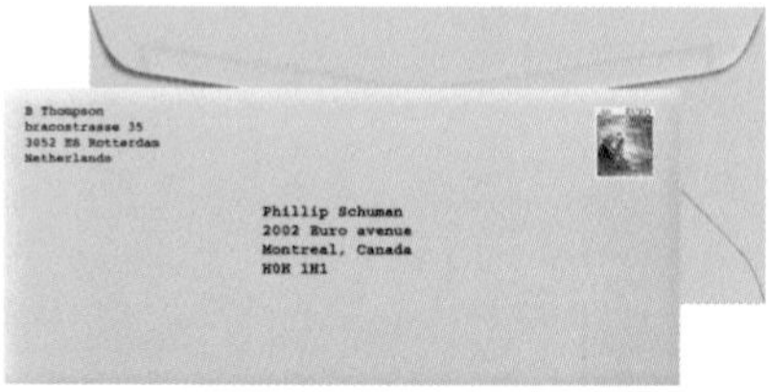

letter
carta^F
lettre^F
Brief^M
lettera^F

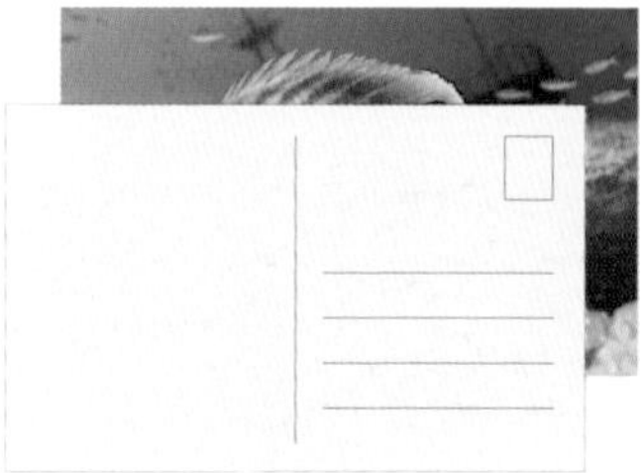

postcard
postal^F
carte^F postale
Postkarte^F
cartolina^F

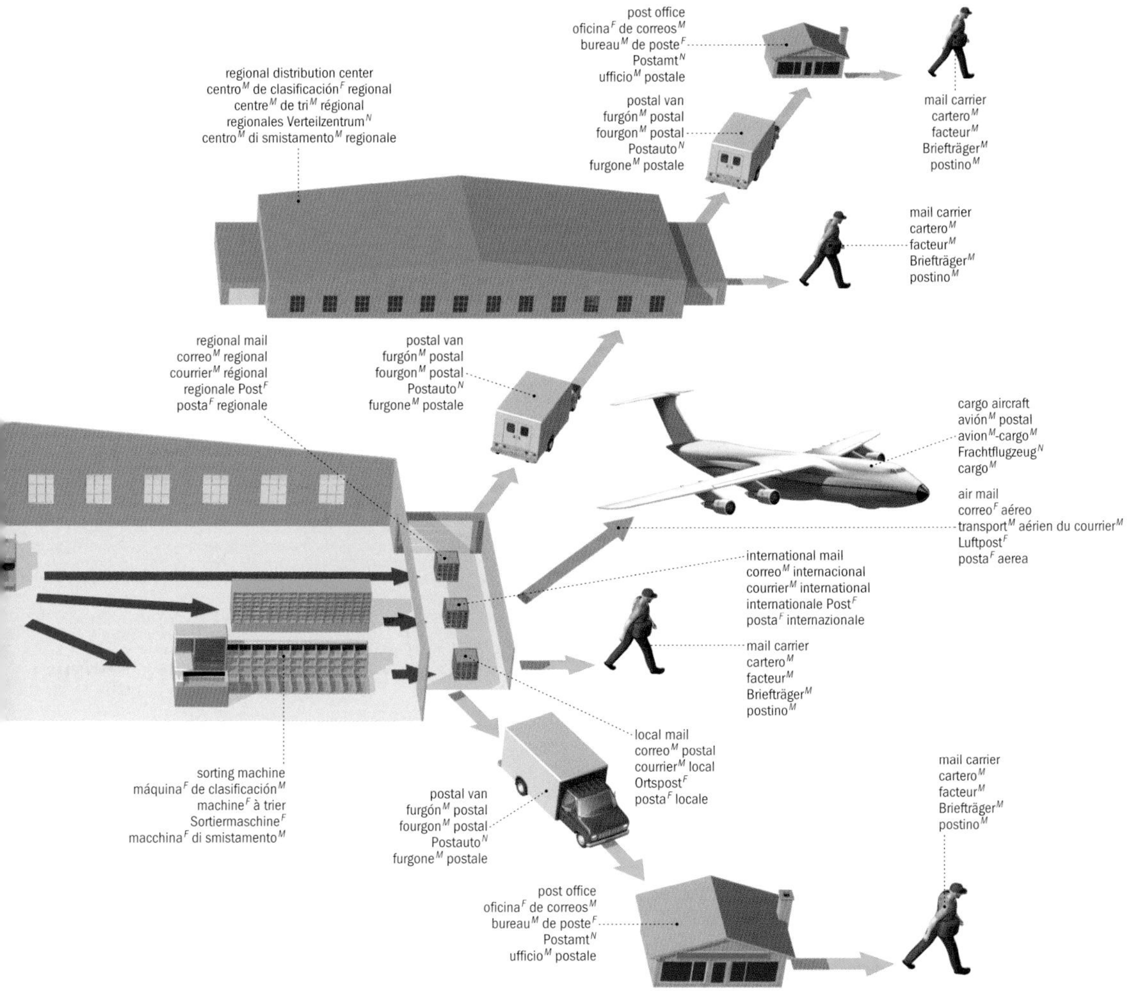

post office
oficina^F de correos^M
bureau^M de poste^F
Postamt^N
ufficio^M postale

regional distribution center
centro^M de clasificación^F regional
centre^M de tri^M régional
regionales Verteilzentrum^N
centro^M di smistamento^M regionale

postal van
furgón^M postal
fourgon^M postal
Postauto^N
furgone^M postale

mail carrier
cartero^M
facteur^M
Briefträger^M
postino^M

mail carrier
cartero^M
facteur^M
Briefträger^M
postino^M

regional mail
correo^M regional
courrier^M régional
regionale Post^F
posta^F regionale

postal van
furgón^M postal
fourgon^M postal
Postauto^N
furgone^M postale

cargo aircraft
avión^M postal
avion^M-cargo^M
Frachtflugzeug^N
cargo^M

air mail
correo^F aéreo
transport^M aérien du courrier^M
Luftpost^F
posta^F aerea

international mail
correo^M internacional
courrier^M international
internationale Post^F
posta^F internazionale

mail carrier
cartero^M
facteur^M
Briefträger^M
postino^M

sorting machine
máquina^F de clasificación^F
machine^F à trier
Sortiermaschine^F
macchina^F di smistamento^M

local mail
correo^M postal
courrier^M local
Ortspost^F
posta^F locale

postal van
furgón^M postal
fourgon^M postal
Postauto^N
furgone^M postale

mail carrier
cartero^M
facteur^M
Briefträger^M
postino^M

post office
oficina^F de correos^M
bureau^M de poste^F
Postamt^N
ufficio^M postale

mail carrier
cartero^M
facteur^M
Briefträger^M
postino^M

COMMUNICATIONS AND OFFICE AUTOMATION

bulk mail letter
correo^M de masa^F
envoi^M en nombre^M
Massenversand^M
posta^F a tariffa ridotta^F

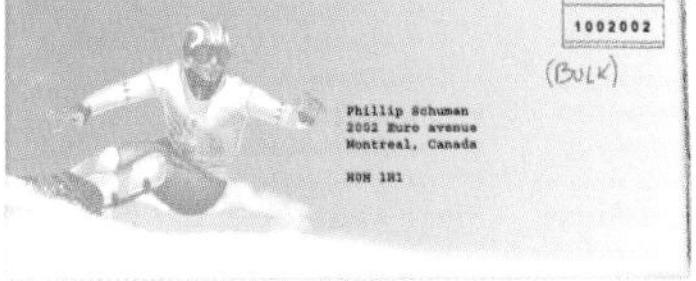

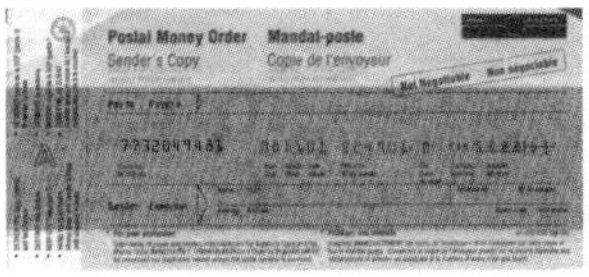

postal money order
giro^M postal
mandat^M-poste^F
Postanweisung^F
vaglia^M postale

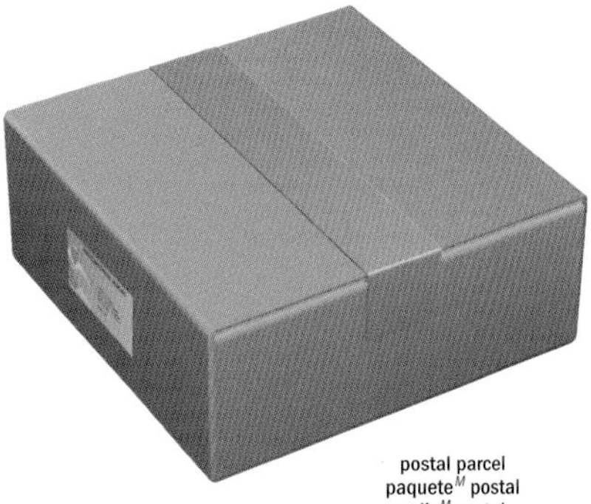

postal parcel
paquete^M postal
colis^M postal
Postpaket^N
pacco^M postale

photography

fotografía^F | photographie^F | Fotografie^F | fotografia^F

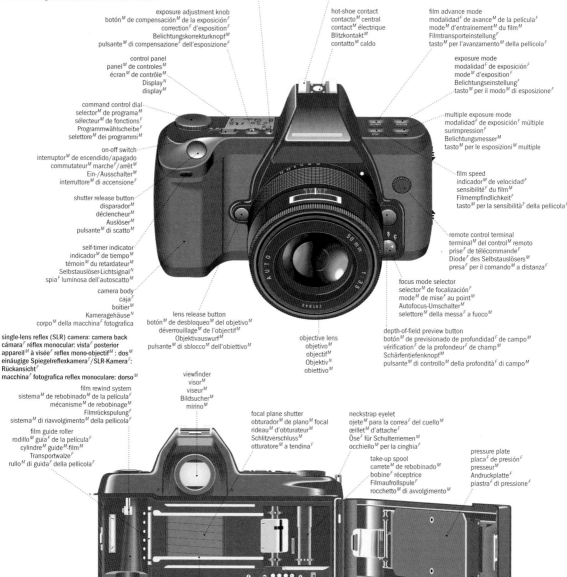

single-lens reflex (SLR) camera: front view
cámara^F réflex monocular: vista^F frontal
appareil^M à visée^F reflex mono-objectif^M : vue^F avant
einäugige Spiegelreflexkamera^F/SLR-Kamera: Vorderansicht^F
macchina^F fotografica reflex monoculare: vista^F frontale

film rewind knob
botón^M de rebobinado^M de la película^F
rebobinage^M
Rückspulknopf^M
pulsante^M di riavvolgimento^M della pellicola^F

accessory shoe
patín^M de los accesorios^M
griffe^F porte-accessoires^M
Zubehörschuh^M
slitta^F per accessori^M

exposure adjustment knob
botón^M de compensación^M de la exposición^F
correction^F d'exposition^F
Belichtungskorrekturknopf^M
pulsante^M di compensazione^F dell'esposizione^F

hot-shoe contact
contacto^M central
contact^M électrique
Blitzkontakt^M
contatto^M caldo

film advance mode
modalidad^F de avance^M de la película^F
mode^M d'entrainement^M du film^M
Filmtransporteinstellung^F
tasto^M per l'avanzamento^M della pellicola^F

control panel
panel^M de controles^M
écran^M de contrôle^M
Display^N
display^M

exposure mode
modalidad^F de exposición^F
mode^M d'exposition^F
Belichtungseinstellung^F
tasto^M per il modo^M di esposizione^F

command control dial
selector^M de programa^M
sélecteur^M de fonctions^F
Programmwählscheibe^F
selettore^M dei programmi^M

multiple exposure mode
modalidad^F de exposición^F múltiple
surimpression^F
Belichtungsmesser^M
tasto^M per le esposizioni^M multiple

on-off switch
interruptor^M de encendido/apagado^M
commutateur^M marche^F/arrêt^M
Ein-/Ausschalter^M
interruttore^M di accensione^F

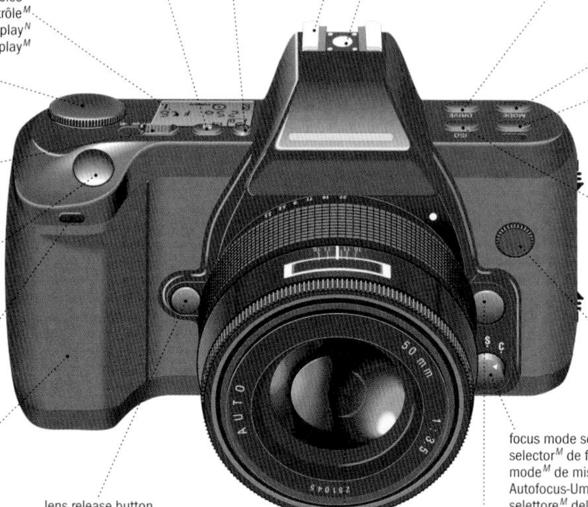

film speed
indicador^M de velocidad^F
sensibilité^F du film^M
Filmempfindlichkeit^F
tasto^M per la sensibilità^F della pellicola^F

shutter release button
disparador^M
déclencheur^M
Auslöser^M
pulsante^M di scatto^M

remote control terminal
terminal^M del control^M remoto
prise^F de télécommande^F
Diode^F des Selbstauslösers^M
presa^F per il comando^M a distanza^F

self-timer indicator
indicador^M de tiempo^M
témoin^M du retardateur^M
Selbstauslöser-Lichtsignal^N
spia^F luminosa dell'autoscatto^M

focus mode selector
selector^M de focalización^F
mode^M de mise^F au point^M
Autofocus-Umschalter^M
selettore^M della messa^F a fuoco^M

camera body
caja^F
boîtier^M
Kameragehäuse^N
corpo^M della macchina^F fotografica

lens release button
botón^M de desbloqueo^M del objetivo^M
déverrouillage^M de l'objectif^M
Objektivauswurf^M
pulsante^M di sblocco^M dell'obiettivo^M

objective lens
objetivo^M
objectif^M
Objektiv^N
obiettivo^M

depth-of-field preview button
botón^M de previsionado de profundidad^F de campo^M
vérification^F de la profondeur^F de champ^M
Schärfentiefenknopf^M
pulsante^M di controllo^M della profondità^F di campo^M

single-lens reflex (SLR) camera: camera back
cámara^F réflex monocular: vista^F posterior
appareil^M à visée^F reflex mono-objectif^M : dos^M
einäugige Spiegelreflexkamera^F/SLR-Kamera:
Rückansicht^F
macchina^F fotografica reflex monoculare: dorso^M

viewfinder
visor^M
viseur^M
Bildsucher^M
mirino^M

film rewind system
sistema^M de rebobinado^M de la película^F
mécanisme^M de rebobinage^M
Filmrückspulung^F
sistema^M di riavvolgimento^M della pellicola^F

focal plane shutter
obturador^M de plano^M focal
rideau^M d'obturateur^M
Schlitzverschluss^M
otturatore^M a tendina^F

neckstrap eyelet
ojete^M para la correa^F del cuello^M
œillet^M d'attache^F
Öse^F für Schulterriemen^M
occhiello^M per la cinghia^F

pressure plate
placa^F de presión^F
presseur^M
Andruckplatte^F
piastra^F di pressione^F

film guide roller
rodillo^M guía^F de la película^F
cylindre^M guide^M-film^M
Transportwalze^F
rullo^M di guida^F della pellicola^F

take-up spool
carrete^M de rebobinado^M
bobine^F réceptrice
Filmaufrollspule^F
rocchetto^M di avvolgimento^M

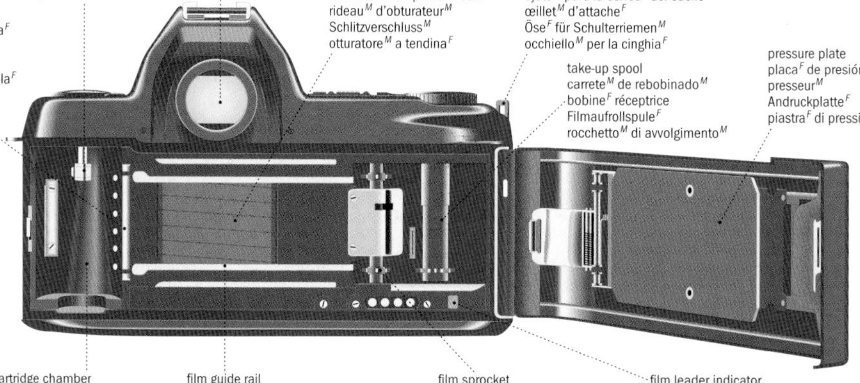

film cartridge chamber
cámara^F para el carrete^M de la película^F
logement^M de la bobine^F
Patronenkammer^F
alloggiamento^M del caricatore^M

film guide rail
carril^M guía^F de la película^F
rail^M guide^M-film^M
Transportschiene^F
guida^F della pellicola^F

film sprocket
piñón^M la rueda^F de la película^F
tambour^M d'entraînement^M
Transporträdchen^N
rocchetto^M di trascinamento^M della pellicola^F

film leader indicator
indicador^M de inicio^M de la película^F
témoin^M de l'amorce^F du film^M
Markierung^F für Filmanfang^M
spia^F della coda^F della pellicola^F

photography

cross section of a reflex camera
sección^F transversal de una cámara^F reflex
coupe^F d'un appareil^M reflex
Spiegelreflexkamera^F im Querschnitt^M
macchina^F fotografica reflex monoculare: sezione^F

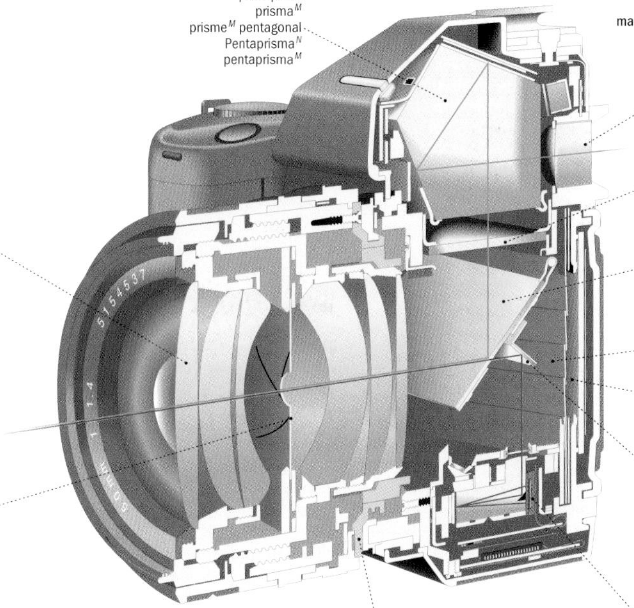

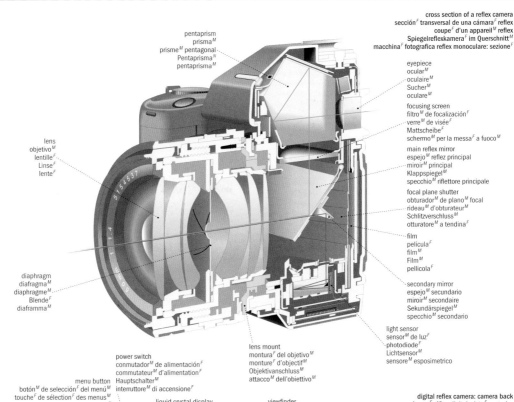

pentaprism
prisma^M
prisme^M pentagonal
Pentaprisma^N
pentaprisma^M

eyepiece
ocular^M
oculaire^F
Sucher^M
oculare^M

focusing screen
filtro^M de focalización^F
verre^M de visée^F
Mattscheibe^F
schermo^M per la messa^F a fuoco^M

lens
objetivo^M
lentille^F
Linse^F
lente^F

main reflex mirror
espejo^M reflex principal
miroir^M principal
Klappspiegel^M
specchio^M riflettore principale

focal plane shutter
obturador^M de plano^M focal
rideau^M d'obturateur^M
Schlitzverschluss^M
otturatore^M a tendina^F

film
película^F
film^M
Film^M
pellicola^F

diaphragm
diafragma^M
diaphragme^M
Blende^F
diaframma^M

secondary mirror
espejo^M secundario
miroir^M secondaire
Sekundärspiegel^M
specchio^M secondario

light sensor
sensor^M de luz^F
photodiode^F
Lichtsensor^M
sensore^M esposimetrico

power switch
conmutador^M de alimentación^F
commutateur^M d'alimentation^F
Hauptschalter^M
interruttore^M di accensione^F

lens mount
montura^F del objetivo^M
monture^F d'objectif^M
Objektivanschluss^M
attacco^M dell'obiettivo^M

menu button
botón^M de selección^F del menú^M
touche^F de sélection^F des menus^M
Menütaste^F
pulsante^M del menu^M

liquid crystal display
pantalla^F de cristal^M líquido
écran^M à cristaux^M liquides
Flüssigkristallanzeige^F
display^M a cristalli^M liquidi

viewfinder
visor^M
viseur^M
Sucherokular^N
mirino^M

digital reflex camera: camera back
cámara^F reflex digital: vista^F posterior
appareil^M à visée^F reflex numérique : dos^M
digitale Spiegelreflexkamera^F: Rückansicht^F
macchina^F fotografica reflex digitale: dorso^M

settings display button
botón^M de visualización^F de ajustes^M
touche^F d'affichage^M des réglages^M
Einstellungsanzeige^F
pulsante^M di visualizzazione^F delle impostazioni^F

compact memory card
tarjeta^F de memoria^F
carte^F de mémoire^F
Speicherkarte^F
scheda^F di memoria^F

cover
tapa^F
couvercle^M
Abdeckung^F
coperchio^M

strap eyelet
ojete^M para la correa^F
œillet^M d'attache^F
Öse^F für Tragriemen^M
occhiello^M per la tracolla^F

multi-image jump button
botón^M de salto^M de imágenes^F
touche^F de saut^M d'images^F
Bildvorlauf^M
pulsante^M per il salto^M di immagini^F

video and digital terminals
tomas^F vídeo y digital
prises^F vidéo et numérique
Anschlussbuchsen^F für Video- und Digitalübertragung^F
prese^F video e digitali

image review button
botón^M de visualización^F de imágenes^F
touche^F de visualisation^F des images^F
Bildanzeige^F
pulsante^M di visualizzazione^F delle immagini^F

remote control terminal
botón^M de control^M remoto
prise^F de télécommande^F
Fernsteuerungsanschlussbuchse^F
presa^F per il comando^M a distanza^F

index/enlarge button
botón^M de índice^M/ampliación^F
touche^F d'index^M/agrandissement^M
Indexanzeige^F-/Zoomregler^M
pulsante^M per l'indice^M e per l'ingrandimento^M

erase button
botón^M de cancelación^F
touche^F d'effacement^M
Löschtaste^F
pulsante^M di cancellazione^F

four-way selector
selector^M cuadro-direccional
sélecteur^M quadridirectionnel
Vierwegeregler^M
selettore^M quadridirezionale

eject button
botón^M de expulsión^M
bouton^M d'éjection^F
Auswurftaste^F
pulsante^M di espulsione^F

photography

lenses
objetivos[M]
objectifs[M]
Objektive[N]
obiettivi[M]

standard lens
objetivo[M] normal
objectif[M] normal
Standardobjektiv[N]
obiettivo[M] normale

lens
objetivo[M]
lentille[F]
Linse[F]
lente[F]

distance scale
escala[F] de distancia[F]
échelle[F] des distances[F]
Entfernungsskala[F]
scala[F] delle distanze[F]

focus setting ring
anillo[M] de ajuste[M] del enfoque[M]
bague[F] de mise[F] au point[M]
Scharfstellring[M]
ghiera[F] di messa[F] a fuoco[M]

depth-of-field scale
escala[F] de profundidad[F] de campo[M] de visión[F]
échelle[F] de profondeur[F] de champ[M]
Schärfentiefenskala[F]
scala[F] delle profondità[F] di campo[M]

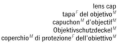

lens aperture scale
escala[F] de abertura[F] del diafragma[M]
échelle[F] d'ouverture[F] de diaphragme[M]
Blendenskala[F]
scala[F] dell'apertura[F] di diaframma[M]

zoom lens
objetivo[M] zoom[M]
objectif[M] zoom[M]
Zoomobjektiv[N]
obiettivo[M] zoom

bayonet mount
montura[F] de bayoneta[F]
monture[F] baionnette[F]
Bajonettanschluss[M]
attacco[M] a baionetta[F]

lens accessories
accesorios[M] **para el objetivo**[M]
accessoires[M] **de l'objectif**[M]
Objektivzubehör[N]
accessori dell'obiettivo[M]

lens cap
tapa[F] del objetivo[M]
capuchon[M] d'objectif[M]
Objektivschutzdeckel[M]
coperchio[M] di protezione[F] dell'obiettivo[M]

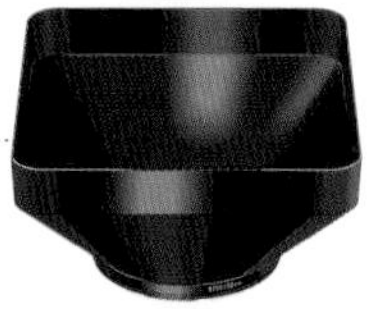

lens hood
capuchón[M]
parasoleil[M]
Gegenlichtblende[F]
paraluce[M]

color filter
filtro[M] de color[M]
filtre[M] de couleur[F]
Farbfilter[M]
filtro[M] colorato

close-up lens
lente[F] de acercamiento[M]
lentille[F] de macrophotographie[F]
Nahlinse[F]
lente[F] addizionale per macrofotografie[F]

wide-angle lens
objetivo[M] gran angular[M]
objectif[M] grand-angulaire
Weitwinkelobjektiv[N]
obiettivo[M] grandangolare

macro lens
objetivo[M] macro
objectif[M] macro
Makroobjektiv[N]
obiettivo[M] macro

telephoto lens
teleobjetivo[M]
téléobjectif[M]
Teleobjektiv[N]
teleobiettivo[M]

polarizing filter
filtro[M] de polarización[F]
filtre[M] de polarisation[F]
Polarisationsfilter[M]
filtro[M] polarizzatore

objective lens
objetivo[M]
objectif[M]
Objektiv[N]
obiettivo[M]

fisheye lens
lente[F] de 180 grados[M]
hypergone[M]
Fischauge[N]
fish-eye[M]

semi-fisheye lens
objetivo[M] ojo[M] de pez[M]
objectif[M] super-grand-angle[M]
Super-Weitwinkelobjektiv[N]
obiettivo[M] supergrandangolare

tele-converter
teleconvertidor[M]
multiplicateur[M] de focale[F]
Telekonverter[M]
moltiplicatore[M] di focale[F]

exposure meter
fotómetro^M
posemètre^M photoélectrique
Belichtungsmesser^M
esposimetro^M

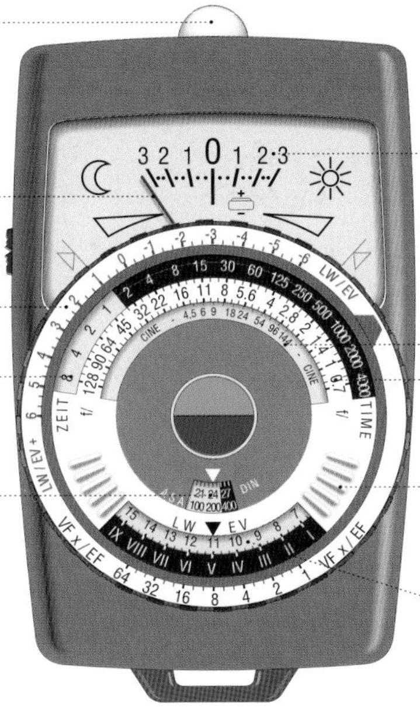

diffuser
difusor^M
tête^F diffusante
Diffusionskalotte^F
diffusore^M

indicator needle
aguja^F indicadora
aiguille^F
Anzeigenadel^F
indice^M

light-reading scale
escala^F de lectura^F
échelle^F de lecture^F de la luminosité^F
Lichtwertskala^F
scala^F della luminosità^F

exposure value
índices^M de exposición^F
indice^M d'exposition^F
Belichtungswert^M
indice^M di esposizione^F

cine scale
escala^F de imágenes^F por segundo^M
cadence^F images^F/seconde^F
Cine-Skala^F
scala^F cine

exposure-time scale
escala^F de duración^F de la exposición^F
échelle^F des temps^M d'exposition^F
Belichtungszeitskala^F
scala^F dei tempi^M di esposizione^F

aperture scale
escala^F de abertura^F
échelle^F d'ouverture^F
Blendenskala^F
scala^F dell'apertura^F del diaframma^M

film speed
velocidad^F de la película^F
sensibilité^F du film^M
Filmempfindlichkeit^F
sensibilità^F della pellicola^F

calculator dial
cuadrante^M calculador
disque^M de réglage^M
Rechenscheibe^F
ghiera^F di calcolo^M

transfer scale
escala^F de transferencia^F
report^M de lecture^F
Umrechnungsskala^F
scala^F di conversione^F

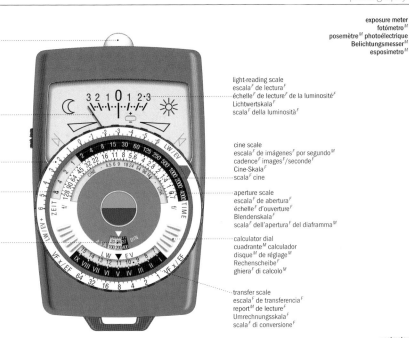

spotmeter
fotómetro^M spot
posemètre^M à visée^F reflex
Spotmeter^M
esposimetro^M spot

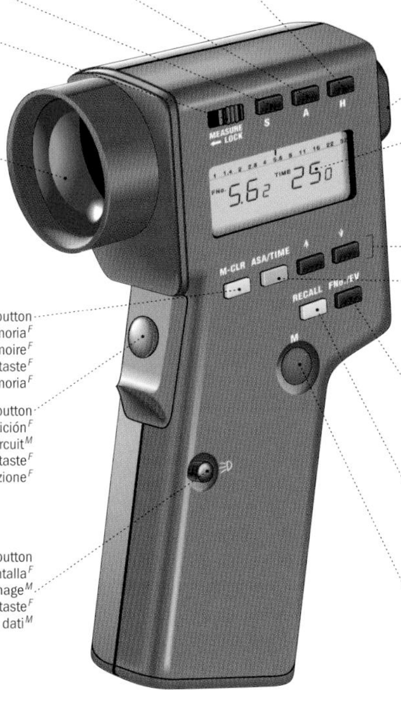

shadow key
botón^M de sombra^F
réglage^M sur ombre^F
Taste^F für schattiges Licht^N
regolazione^F sulle basse luci^F

average key
botón^M de luminosidad^F media
réglage^F sur demi-teinte^F
Taste^F für Normallicht^N
regolazione^F sulle medie luci^F

highlight key
botón^M de fuerte luminosidad^F
réglage^M sur haute lumière^F
Taste^F für helles Licht^N
regolazione^F sulle alte luci^F

eyepiece
ocular^M
oculaire^M
Sucher^M
oculare^M

lock switch
seguro^M
fixe-lecture^M
Ein-/Ausschalter^M
interruttore^M di blocco^M

data display
display^M de la información^F
écran^M d'affichage^M
Display^N
display^M dei dati^M

objective lens
objetivo^M
objectif^M
Objektiv^N
obiettivo^M

shutter speed setting
ajuste^M de la velocidad^F del obturador^M
réglage^M de la vitesse^F d'obturation^F
Tasten^F für Erhöhen^N/Absenken^N
impostazione^F del tempo^M di esposizione^F

film speed
sensibilidad^F de la película^F
sensibilité^F du film^M
Filmempfindlichkeit^F
tasto^M per la sensibilità^F della pellicola^F

memory cancel button
botón^M para cancelar la memoria^F
effacement^M de mémoire^F
Speicherlöschtaste^F
tasto^M di cancellazione^F della memoria^F

aperture/exposure value display
visualización^F de valores^M de abertura^F y de exposición^F
affichage^M ouverture^F/indice^M d'exposition^F
Anzeige^F für Blende^F/Belichtungswert^M
tasto^M per il valore^M di apertura^F e di esposizione^F

measuring button
botón^M de medición^F
bouton^M de mise^F en circuit^M
Messtaste^F
pulsante^M di avvio^M della misurazione^F

memory recall key
botón^M de llamada^F de memoria^F
rappel^M de mémoire^F
Rückruftaste^F
tasto^M di richiamo^M della memoria^F

data display illumination button
botón^M de iluminación^F de la pantalla^F
éclairage^M de l'écran^M d'affichage^M
Displaybeleuchtungstaste^F
pulsante^M di illuminazione^F del display^M dei dati^M

memory key
botón^M de memoria^F
commande^F de mémoire^F
Speichertaste^F
tasto^M di memoria^F

photography

still cameras
cámaras^F fijas
appareils^M photographiques
Fotoapparate^M
macchine^F fotografiche

rangefinder
telémetro^M
appareil^M à télémètre^M couplé
Sucherkamera^F
macchina^F fotografica autofocus

Polaroid® camera
cámara^F Polaroid Land
Polaroid®^{M}
Sofortbildkamera^F
Polaroid^F

underwater camera
cámara^F submarina
appareil^M de plongée^F
Unterwasserkamera^F
macchina^F fotografica subacquea

single-lens reflex (SLR) camera
cámara^F reflex de un solo objetivo^M
appareil^M à visée^F reflex mono-objectif^M
einäugige Spiegelreflexkamera^F
macchina^F fotografica reflex

disposable camera
cámara^F desechable
appareil^M jetable
Einwegkamera^F
macchina^F fotografica usa e getta

pocket camera
cámara^F de bolsillo^M
appareil^M petit-format^M
Pocket-Instamatic-Kamera^F
macchina^F fotografica tascabile

twin-lens reflex camera
cámara^F réflex con dos objetivos^M
appareil^M reflex à deux objectifs^M
Zweiäugige Spiegelreflexkamera^F
macchina^F fotografica reflex biottica

view camera
cámara^F de fuelle^M
chambre^F photographique
Großformatkamera^F
macchina^F fotografica a banco^M ottico

stereo camera
cámara^F estereoscópica
appareil^M stéréoscopique
Stereokamera^F
macchina^F fotografica stereoscopica

medium-format SLR (6 x 6)
cámara^F reflex de formato^M medio SLR (6x6)
appareil^M reflex 6 X 6 mono-objectif^M
Mittelformatkamera^F SLR (6 x 6)
macchina^F fotografica reflex (6x6)

digital camera
cámara^F digital
appareil^M numérique
Digitalkamera^F
macchina fotografica digitale

disk camera
cámara^F de disco^M
appareil^M pour photodisque^M
Disc-Kamera^F
macchina^F fotografica a disco^M

film and digital storage
películas^F y almacenamiento^M digital
pellicules^F et stockage^M numérique
Filme^M und digitale Speicher^M
pellicole^F e supporti^M digitali

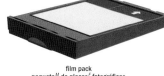

film pack
paquete^M de placas^F fotográficas
film^M-pack^M
Filmkassette^F
filmpack^M

compact flash memory card
tarjeta^F de memoria^F compact flash^M
carte^F de mémoire^F flash compacte
Compact-Flash-Speicherkarte^F
scheda^F di memoria^F compact flash

sheet film
hoja^F de la película^F
pellicule^F en feuille^F
Planfilm^M
pellicola^F piana

roll film
rollo^M de película^F
rouleau^M de pellicule^F
Rollfilm^M
pellicola^F in rotolo^M

film disk
película^F de disco^M
film^M-disque^M
Filmdiskette^F
pellicola^F a disco^M

still video film disk
disquete^M para video^M fijo
disque^M vidéophoto^F
Videofilmdiskette^F
disco^M per macchina^F fotografica digitale

cartridge film
cartucho^M de la película^F
cassette^F de pellicule^F
Kassettenfilm^M
caricatore^M

photographic accessories
accesorios^M **fotográficos**
accessoires^M **photographiques**
fotografisches Zubehör^N
accessori^M **fotografici**

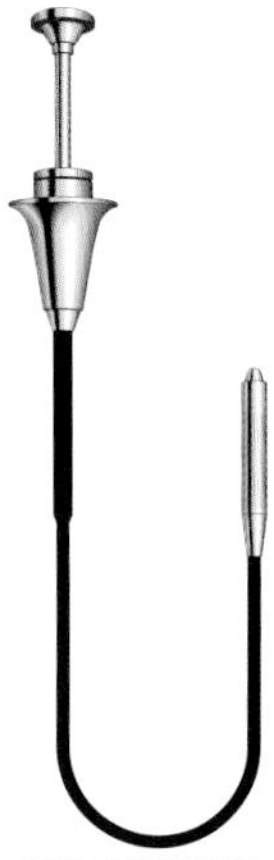

air bulb shutter release
disparador^M neumático
déclencheur^M pneumatique
pneumatischer Auslöser^M
flessibile^M pneumatico

electronic flash
flash^M electrónico
flash^M électronique
Elektronenblitz^M
flash^M elettronico

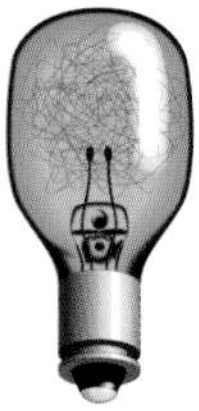

flashtube
tubo^M de flash^M
réflecteur^M
Blitzröhre^F
lampada^F a tubo^M per flash^M

battery
pila^F
pile^F
Batterie^F
batteria^F

photoelectric cell
celda^F fotoeléctrica
cellule^F photoélectrique
Fotozelle^F
cellula^F fotoelettrica

flash lamp
bombilla^F de flash^M
lampe^F-éclair^M
Blitzbirne^F
lampada^F per flash^M

flashcube
cubo^M de flash^M
flash^M-cube^M
Blitzwürfel^M
cuboflash^M

mounting foot
pie^M de montura^F
pied^F de fixation^F
Aufsteckschuh^M
piedino^M di montaggio^M

cable shutter release
disparador^M de cable^M
déclencheur^M souple
Drahtauslöser^M
flessibile^M

tripod
trípode^M
trépied^M
Stativ^N
treppiede^M

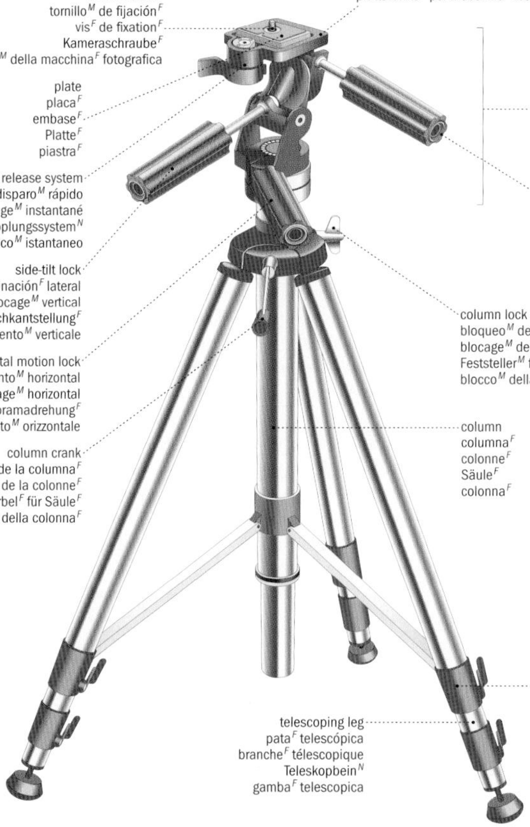

camera platform
plataforma^F
plate-forme^F
Kameraplattform^F
piattaforma^F per macchina^F fotografica

camera screw
tornillo^M de fijación^F
vis^F de fixation^F
Kameraschraube^F
vite^F di fissaggio^M della macchina^F fotografica

plate
placa^F
embase^F
Platte^F
piastra^F

panoramic head
cabeza^F panorámica
tête^F panoramique
Panoramakopf^M
testa^F panoramica

quick release system
sistema^M de disparo^M rápido
déblocage^M instantané
Schnellkupplungssystem^N
sblocco^M istantaneo

side-tilt lock
bloqueo^M de inclinación^F lateral
blocage^M vertical
Feststellgriff^M für Hochkantstellung^F
blocco^M del movimento^M verticale

camera platform lock
bloqueo^M de la plataforma^F
blocage^M de la plate-forme^F
Feststellgriff^M für Kameraplattform^F
blocco^M della piattaforma^F

column lock
bloqueo^M de la columna^F
blocage^M de la colonne^F
Feststeller^M für Säule^F
blocco^M della colonna^F

horizontal motion lock
bloqueo^M de movimiento^M horizontal
blocage^M horizontal
Feststellgriff^M für Panoramadrehung^F
blocco^M del movimento^M orizzontale

column
columna^F
colonne^F
Säule^F
colonna^F

column crank
manivela^F de la columna^F
manivelle^F de la colonne^F
Kurbel^F für Säule^F
manovella^F della colonna^F

collet
anillo^M
bague^F de serrage^M
Beinklemme^F
manicotto^M di bloccaggio^M

telescoping leg
pata^F telescópica
branche^F télescopique
Teleskopbein^N
gamba^F telescopica

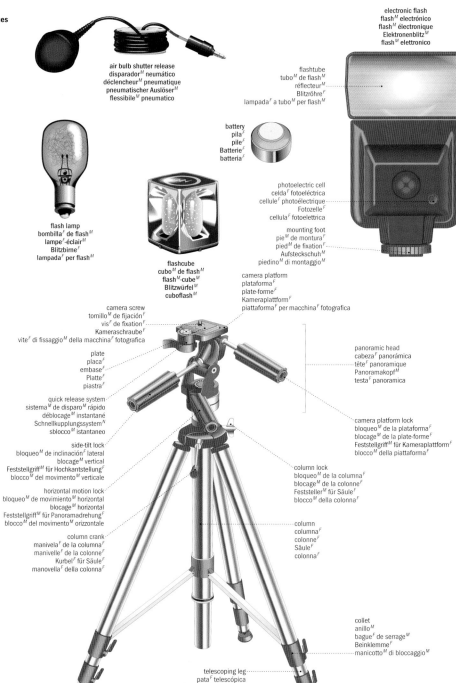

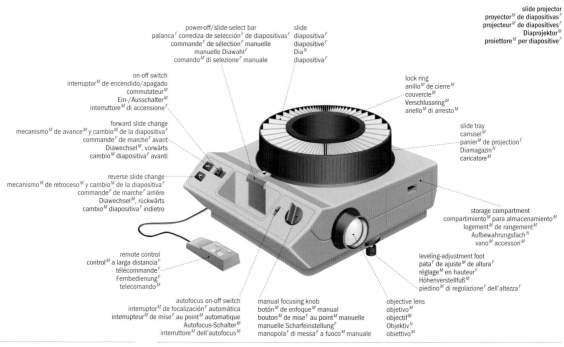

slide projector
proyector^M de diapositivas^F
projecteur^M de diapositives^F
Diaprojektor^M
proiettore^M per diapositive^F

power-off/slide-select bar
palanca^F corrediza de selección^F de diapositivas^F
commande^F de sélection^F manuelle
manuelle Diawahl^F
comando^M di selezione^F manuale

slide
diapositiva^F
diapositive^F
Dia^N
diapositiva^F

on-off switch
interruptor^M de encendido/apagado
commutateur^M
Ein-/Ausschalter^M
interruttore^M di accensione^F

lock ring
anillo^M de cierre^M
couvercle^M
Verschlussring^M
anello^M di arresto^M

forward slide change
mecanismo^M de avance^M y cambio^M de la diapositiva^F
commande^F de marche^F avant
Diawechsel^M, vorwärts
cambio^M diapositiva^F avanti

slide tray
carrusel^M
panier^M de projection^F
Diamagazin^N
caricatore^M

reverse slide change
mecanismo^M de retroceso^M y cambio^M de la diapositiva^F
commande^F de marche^F arrière
Diawechsel^M, rückwärts
cambio^M diapositiva^F indietro

storage compartment
compartimiento^M para almacenamiento^M
logement^M de rangement^M
Aufbewahrungsfach^N
vano^M accessori^M

remote control
control^M a larga distancia^F
télécommande^F
Fernbedienung^F
telecomando^M

leveling-adjustment foot
pata^F de ajuste^M de altura^F
réglage^M en hauteur^F
Höhenverstellfuß^M
piedino^M di regolazione^F dell'altezza^F

autofocus on-off switch
interruptor^M de focalización^F automática
interrupteur^M de mise^F au point^M automatique
Autofocus-Schalter^M
interruttore^M dell'autofocus^M

manual focusing knob
botón^M de enfoque^M manual
bouton^M de mise^F au point^M manuelle
manuelle Scharfeinstellung^F
manopola^M di messa^F a fuoco^M manuale

objective lens
objetivo^M
objectif^M
Objektiv^N
obiettivo^M

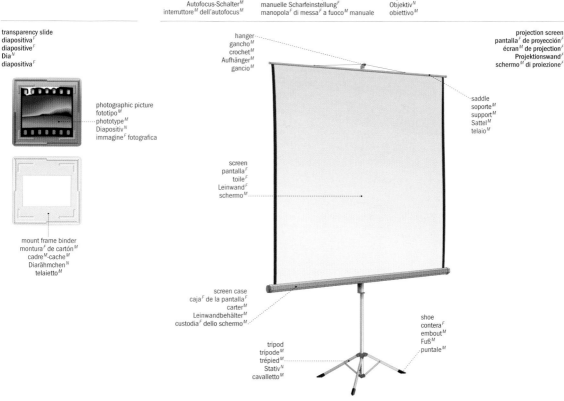

transparency slide
diapositiva^F
diapositive^F
Dia^N
diapositiva^F

hanger
gancho^M
crochet^M
Aufhänger^M
gancio^M

projection screen
pantalla^F de proyección^F
écran^M de projection^F
Projektionswand^F
schermo^M di proiezione^F

photographic picture
fototipo^M
phototype^M
Diapositiv^N
immagine^F fotografica

saddle
soporte^M
support^M
Sattel^M
telaio^M

screen
pantalla^F
toile^F
Leinwand^F
schermo^M

mount frame binder
montura^F de cartón^M
cadre^M-cache^M
Diarähmchen^N
telaietto^M

screen case
caja^F de la pantalla^F
carter^M
Leinwandbehälter^M
custodia^F dello schermo^M

shoe
contera^F
embout^M
Fuß^M
puntale^M

tripod
trípode^M
trépied^M
Stativ^N
cavalletto^M

photography

darkroom
cámara^F **oscura**
chambre^F **noire**
Dunkelkammer^F
camera^F **oscura**

developing tank
tanque^M de revelado
cuve^F de développement^M
Entwicklungstrommel^F
sviluppatrice^F

cap
capuchón^M
capuchon^M
Kappe^F
tappo^M

lid
tapa^F
couvercle^M
Deckel^M
coperchio^M

reel
espiral^F
spirale^F
Spirale^F
spirale^F

tank
cubeta^F
cuve^F
Dose^F
vaschetta^F

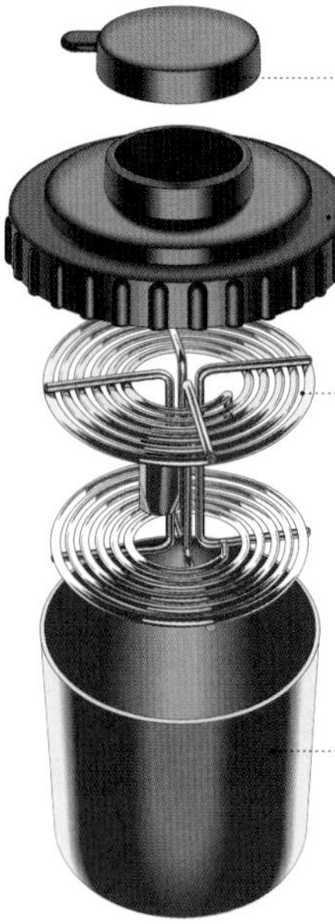

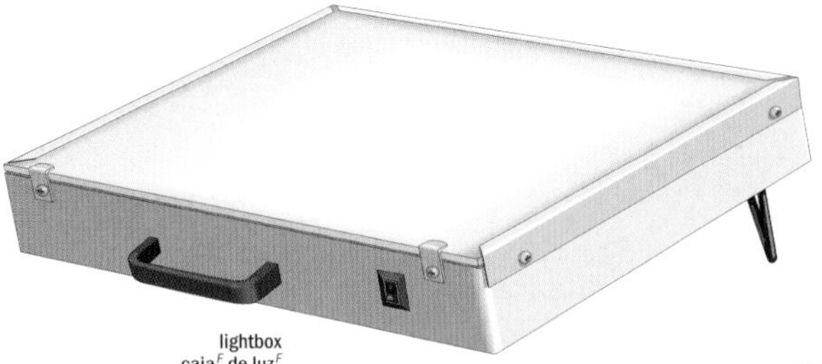

lightbox
caja^F de luz^F
négatoscope^M
Leuchtpult^N
visore^M

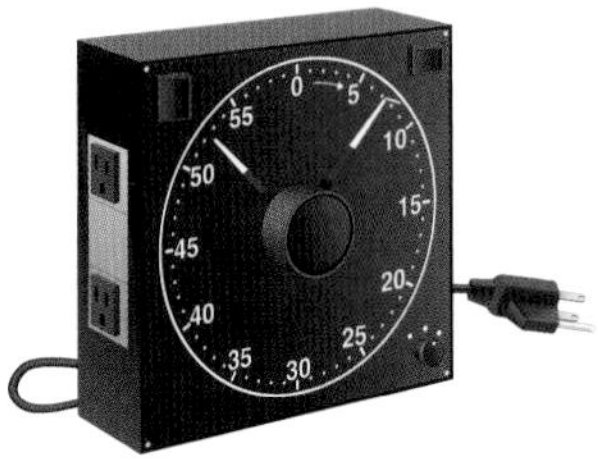

timer
reloj^M
minuterie^F
Laboruhr^F
temporizzatore^M

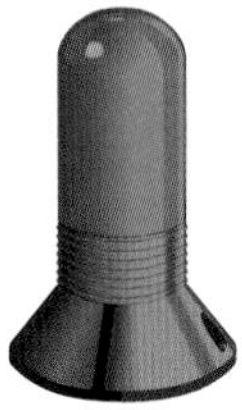

safelight
luz^F de seguridad^F
éclairage^M inactinique
Laborleuchte^F
luce^F inattinica

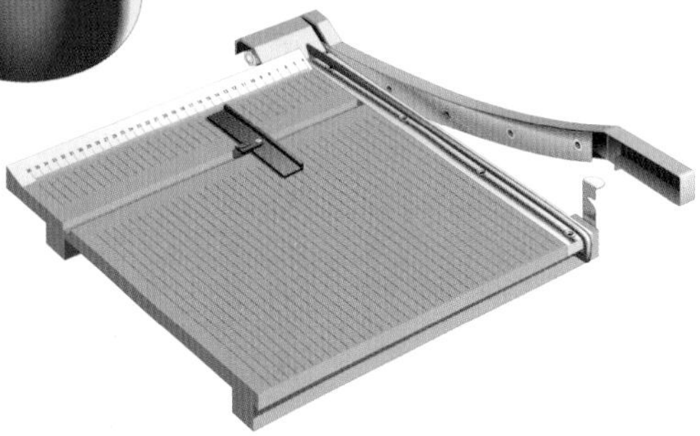

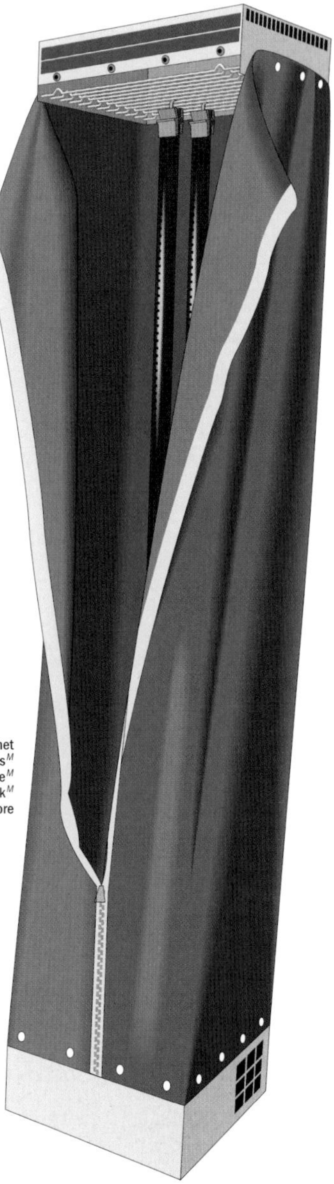

film drying cabinet
armario^M de secado^M de negativos^M
armoire^F de séchage^M
Trockenschrank^M
armadio^M essiccatore

guillotine trimmer
guillotina^F
cisaille^F
Schneidegerät^N
taglierina^F

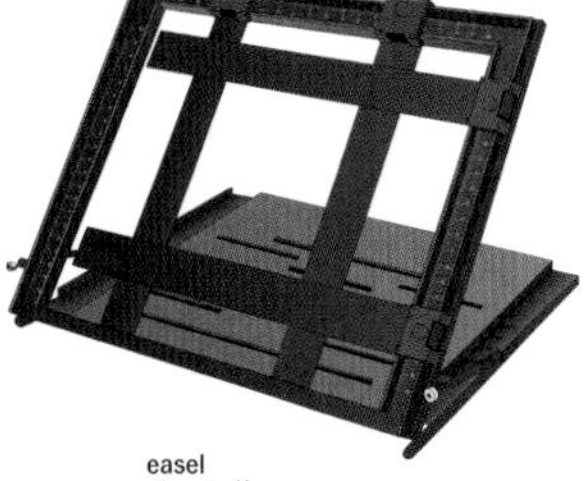

easel
marginador^M
margeur^M
Vergrößerungsrahmen^M
marginatore^M

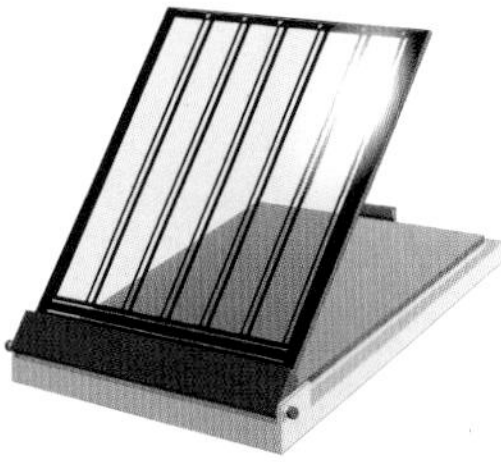

contact printer
prensa^F de contactos^M
châssis^M-presse^F
Kontaktkopiergerät^N
bromografo^M

enlarger
ampliadora^F
agrandisseur^M
Vergrößerer^M
ingranditore^M

window
ventana^F
fenêtre^F
Sichtfenster^N
finestra^F

negative
negativo^M
négatif^M
Negativ^N
negativo^M

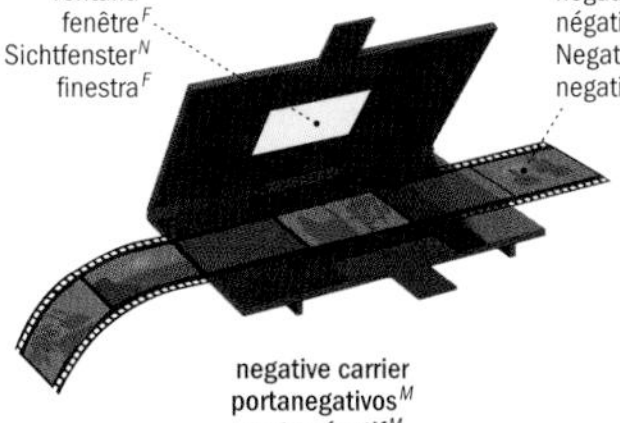

column
columna^F
colonne^F
Säule^F
colonna^F

lamphouse head
cabeza^F de la caja^F de iluminación^F
boîte^F à lumière^F
Beleuchtungskopf^M
testa^F portalampada

negative carrier
portanegativos^M
porte-négatif^M
Negativhalter^M
portanegativi^M

lamphouse elevation control
control^M de elevación^F de la caja^F de iluminación^F
ouverture^F de la boîte^F à lumière^F
Scharfeinsteller^M
regolatore^M dell'altezza^F della testa^F

height control
control^M de altura^F
réglage^M en hauteur^F
Höhenkontrolle^F
manopola^F della messa^F a fuoco^M

bellows
fuelle^M
soufflet^M
Balgen^M
soffietto^M

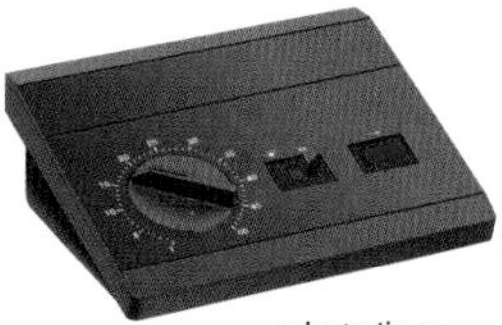

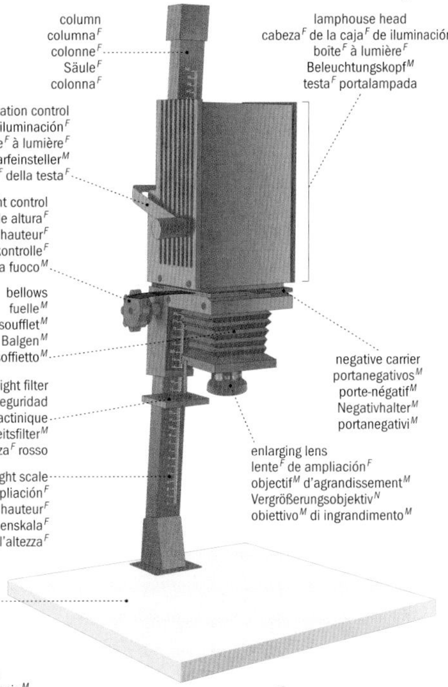

negative carrier
portanegativos^M
porte-négatif^M
Negativhalter^M
portanegativi^M

red safelight filter
filtro^M rojo^M de seguridad
filtre^M rouge inactinique
roter Sicherheitsfilter^M
filtro^M di sicurezza^F rosso

enlarger timer
reloj^M de la ampliadora^F
compte-pose^F
Belichtungs-Schaltuhr^F
temporizzatore^M dell'ingranditore^M

enlarging lens
lente^F de ampliación^F
objectif^M d'agrandissement^M
Vergrößerungsobjektiv^N
obiettivo^M di ingrandimento^M

height scale
escala^F de ampliación^F
échelle^F de hauteur^F
Höhenskala^F
scala^F dell'altezza^F

baseboard
tablero^M de base^F
plateau^M
Grundplatte^F
piano^M di stampa^F

print washer
cubeta^F para lavar impresiones^F
laveuse^F pour épreuves^F
Bilderwascher^M
vasca^F di lavaggio^M delle stampe^F

overflow tube
tubo^M de drenaje^M
trop-plein^M
Überlaufstutzen^M
tubo^M di troppopieno^M

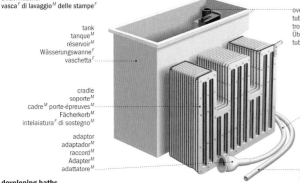

tank
tanque^M
réservoir^M
Wässerungswanne^F
vaschetta^F

inlet hose
manguera^F de llenado
flexible^M de branchement^M
Schlauch^M für Wasserzufluss^M
tubo^M di entrata^F

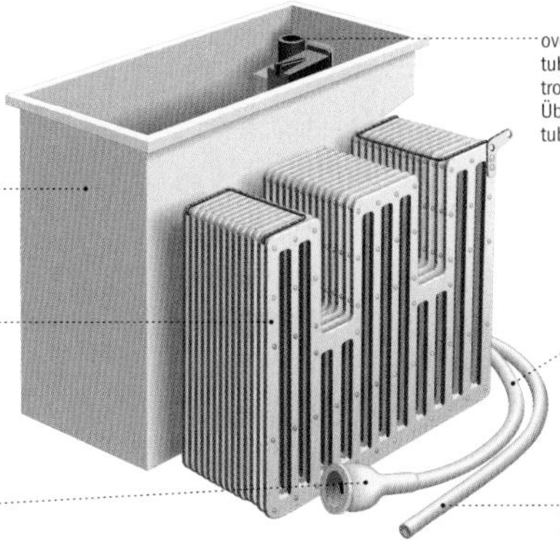

cradle
soporte^M
cadre^M porte-épreuves^M
Fächerkorb^M
intelaiatura^F di sostegno^M

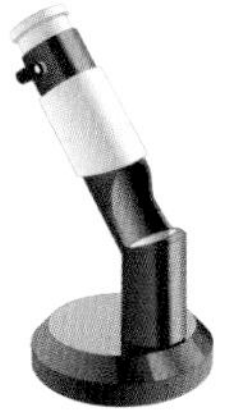

focusing magnifier
lupa^F de focalización^F
loupe^F de mise^F au point^M
Scharfsteller^M
lente^F di ingrandimento^M per la messa^F a fuoco^M

adaptor
adaptador^M
raccord^M
Adapter^M
adattatore^M

outlet hose
manguera^F de vaciado
renvoi^M d'eau^F
Schlauch^M für Wasserablauf^M
tubo^M di uscita^F

developing baths
baños^M de revelado^M
bains^M de développement^M
Entwicklungsbäder^N
bagni^M di sviluppo^M

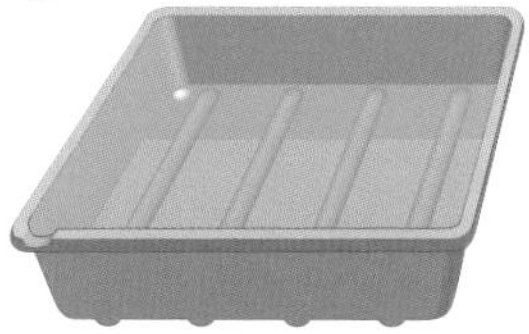

developer bath
baño^M de revelado^M
bain^M de révélateur^M
Entwickler^M
bagno^M di sviluppo^M

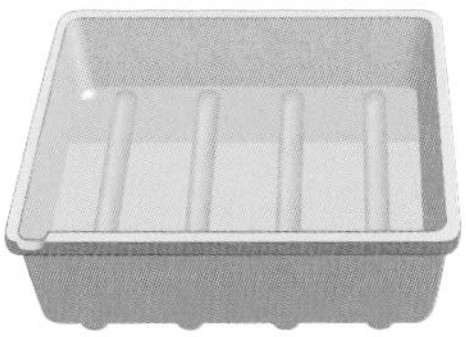

stop bath
baño^M de stop^M
bain^M d'arrêt^M
Stoppbad^N
bagno^M di arresto^M

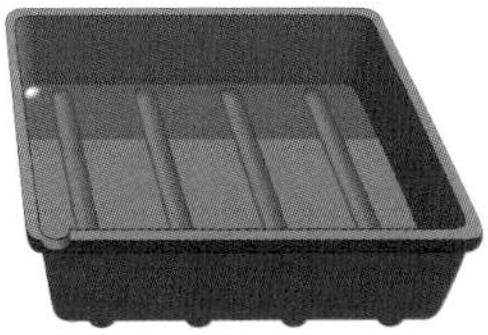

fixing bath
baño^M de fijación^F
bain^M de fixation^F
Fixierbad^N
bagno^M di fissaggio^M

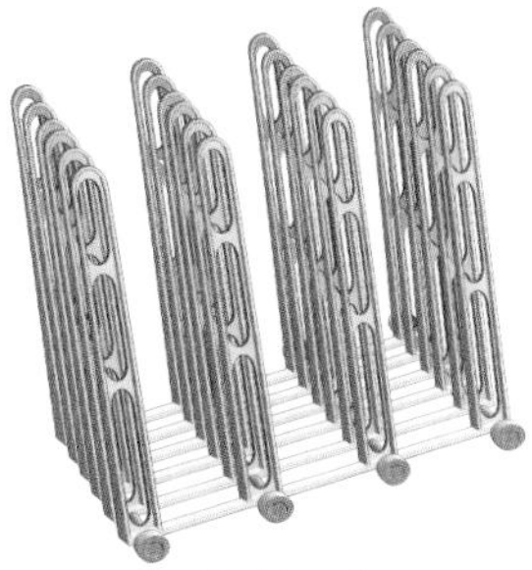

print drying rack
secadora^F de pruebas^F
séchoir^M d'épreuves^F
Trockenständer^M
rastrelliera^F

broadcast satellite communication

comunicación[F] vía satélite | télédiffusion[F] par satellite[M] | Satellitenübertragungstechnik[F] | trasmissione[F] via satellite[M]

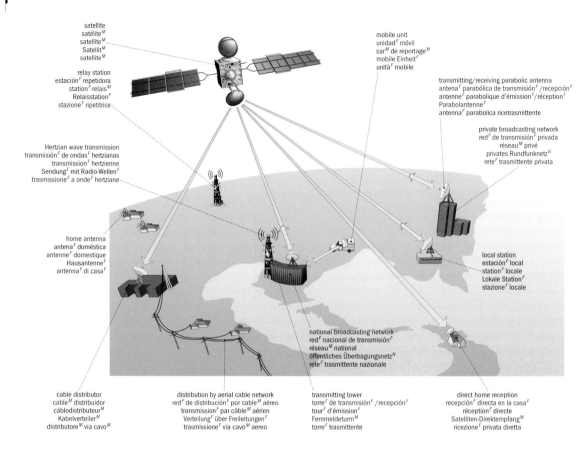

satellite
satélite[M]
satellite[M]
Satellit[M]
satellite[M]

relay station
estación[F] repetidora
station[F]-relais[M]
Relaisstation[F]
stazione[F] ripetitrice

Hertzian wave transmission
transmisión[F] de ondas[F] hertzianas
transmission[F] hertzienne
Sendung[F] mit Radio-Wellen[F]
trasmissione[F] a onde[F] hertziane

home antenna
antena[F] doméstica
antenne[F] domestique
Hausantenne[F]
antenna[F] di casa[F]

mobile unit
unidad[F] móvil
car[M] de reportage[M]
mobile Einheit[F]
unità[F] mobile

transmitting/receiving parabolic antenna
antena[F] parabólica de transmisión[F]/recepción[F]
antenne[F] parabolique d'émission[F]/réception[F]
Parabolantenne[F]
antenna[F] parabolica ricetrasmittente

private broadcasting network
red[F] de transmisión[F] privada
réseau[M] privé
privates Rundfunknetz[N]
rete[F] trasmittente privata

local station
estación[F] local
station[F] locale
Lokale Station[F]
stazione[F] locale

national broadcasting network
red[F] nacional de transmisión[F]
réseau[M] national
öffentliches Übertragungsnetz[N]
rete[F] trasmittente nazionale

cable distributor
cable[M] distribuidor
câblodistributeur[M]
Kabelverteiler[M]
distributore[M] via cavo[M]

distribution by aerial cable network
red[F] de distribución[F] por cable[M] aéreo
transmission[F] par câble[M] aérien
Verteilung[F] über Freileitungen[F]
trasmissione[F] via cavo[M] aereo

transmitting tower
torre[F] de transmisión[F]/recepción[F]
tour[F] d'émission[F]
Fernmeldeturm[M]
torre[F] trasmittente

direct home reception
recepción[F] directa en la casa[F]
réception[F] directe
Satelliten-Direktempfang[M]
ricezione[F] privata diretta

telecommunication satellites

satélites[M] de telecomunicaciones[F] | satellites[M] de télécommunications[F] | Fernmeldesatelliten[M] | satelliti[M] per telecomunicazioni[F]

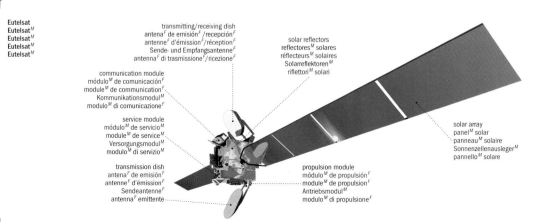

Eutelsat
Eutelsat[M]
Eutelsat[M]
Eutelsat[M]
Eutelsat[M]

transmitting/receiving dish
antena[F] de emisión[F]/recepción[F]
antenne[F] d'émission[F]/réception[F]
Sende- und Empfangsantenne[F]
antenna[F] di trasmissione[F]/ricezione[F]

communication module
módulo[M] de comunicación[F]
module[M] de communication[F]
Kommunikationsmodul[M]
modulo[M] di comunicazione[F]

service module
módulo[M] de servicio[M]
module[M] de service[M]
Versorgungsmodul[M]
modulo[M] di servizio[M]

transmission dish
antena[F] de emisión[F]
antenne[F] d'émission[F]
Sendeantenne[F]
antenna[F] emittente

solar reflectors
reflectores[M] solares
réflecteurs[M] solaires
Solarreflektoren[M]
riflettori[M] solari

solar array
panel[M] solar
panneau[M] solaire
Sonnenzellenausleger[M]
pannello[M] solare

propulsion module
módulo[M] de propulsión[F]
module[M] de propulsion[F]
Antriebsmodul[M]
modulo[M] di propulsione[F]

telecommunications by satellite

telecomunicaciones^F via satélite^M | télécommunications^F par satellite^M | Telekommunikation^F über Nachrichtensatellit^M | telecomunicazioni^F via satellite^M

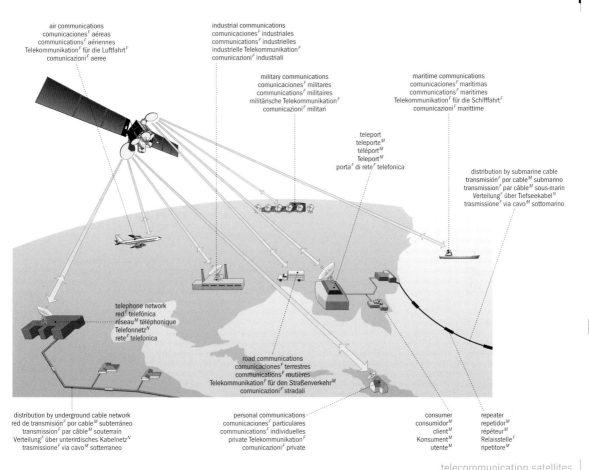

air communications
comunicaciones^F aéreas
communications^F aériennes
Telekommunikation^F für die Luftfahrt^F
comunicazioni^F aeree

industrial communications
comunicaciones^F industriales
communications^F industrielles
industrielle Telekommunikation^F
comunicazioni^F industriali

military communications
comunicaciones^F militares
communications^F militaires
militärische Telekommunikation^F
comunicazioni^F militari

maritime communications
comunicaciones^F maritimas
communications^F maritimes
Telekommunikation^F für die Schifffahrt^F
comunicazioni^F marittime

teleport
teleporte^M
téléport^M
Teleport^M
porta^F di rete^F telefonica

distribution by submarine cable
transmisión^F por cable^M submarino
transmission^F par câble^M sous-marin
Verteilung^F über Tiefseekabel^N
trasmissione^F via cavo^M sottomarino

telephone network
red^F telefónica
réseau^M téléphonique
Telefonnetz^N
rete^F telefonica

road communications
comunicaciones^F terrestres
communications^F routières
Telekommunikation^F für den Straßenverkehr^M
comunicazioni^F stradali

distribution by underground cable network
red de transmisión^F por cable^M subterráneo
transmission^F par câble^M souterrain
Verteilung^F über unterirdisches Kabelnetz^N
trasmissione^F via cavo^M sotterraneo

personal communications
comunicaciones^F particulares
communications^F individuelles
private Telekommunikation^F
comunicazioni^F private

consumer
consumidor^M
client^M
Konsument^M
utente^M

repeater
repetidor^M
répéteur^M
Relaisstelle^F
ripetitore^M

telecommunication satellites

Anik
Anik^M
Anik^M
Anik^M
Anik^M

Intelsat
Intelsat^M
Intelsat^M
Intelsat^M
Intelsat^M

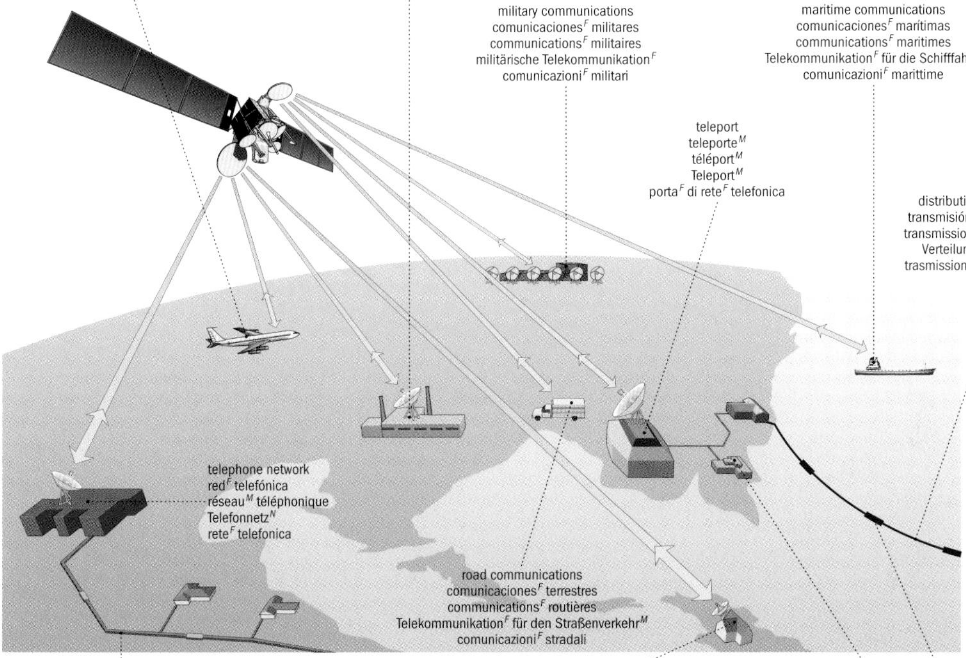

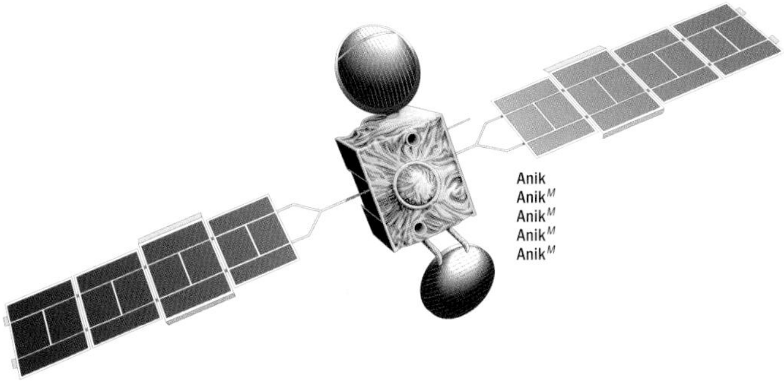

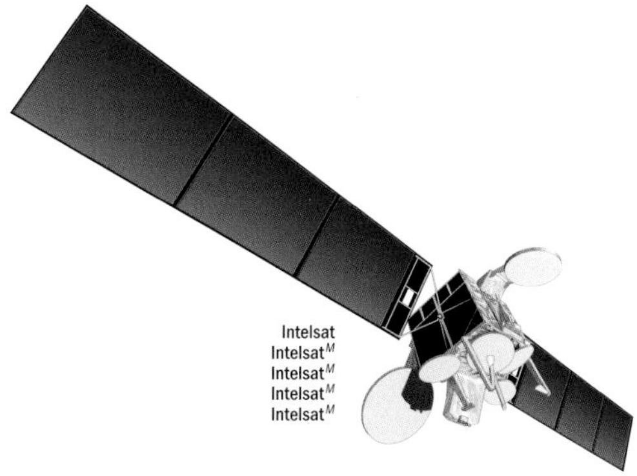

dynamic microphone

micrófono^M electrodinámico | microphone^M dynamique | elektrodynamisches Mikrofon^N | microfono^M dinamico

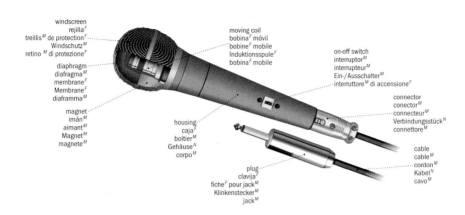

windscreen
rejilla^F
treillis^M de protection^F
Windschutz^M
retino^M di protezione^F

diaphragm
diafragma^M
membrane^F
Membrane^F
diaframma^M

magnet
imán^M
aimant^M
Magnet^M
magnete^M

moving coil
bobina^F móvil
bobine^F mobile
Induktionsspule^F
bobina^F mobile

on-off switch
interruptor^M
interrupteur^M
Ein-/Ausschalter^M
interruttore^M di accensione^F

connector
conector^M
connecteur^M
Verbindungsstück^N
connettore^M

housing
caja^F
boîtier^M
Gehäuse^N
corpo^M

cable
cable^M
cordon^M
Kabel^N
cavo^M

plug
clavija^F
fiche^F pour jack^M
Klinkenstecker^M
jack^M

radio: studio and control room

radio^M : estudio^M y sala^F de control^M | radio^F : studio^M et régie^F | Rundfunk^M: Sprecherraum^M und Regieraum^M | radio^F: studio^M e cabina^F di regia^F

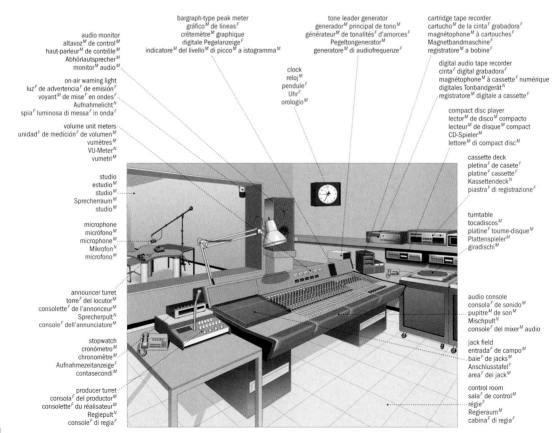

bargraph-type peak meter
gráfico^M de líneas^F
crêtemètre^M graphique
digitale Pegelanzeige^F
indicatore^M del livello^M di picco^M a istogramma^M

tone leader generator
generador^M principal de tono^M
générateur^M de tonalités^F d'amorces^F
Pegeltongenerator^M
generatore^M di audiofrequenze^F

cartridge tape recorder
cartucho^M de la cinta^F grabadora^F
magnétophone^M à cartouches^F
Magnetbandmaschine^F
registratore^M a bobine^F

audio monitor
altavoz^M de control^M
haut-parleur^M de contrôle^M
Abhörlautsprecher^M
monitor^M audio^M

digital audio tape recorder
cinta^F digital grabadora^F
magnétophone^M à cassette^F numérique
digitales Tonbandgerät^N
registratore^M digitale a cassette^F

on-air warning light
luz^F de advertencia^F de emisión^F
voyant^M de mise^F en ondes^F
Aufnahmelicht^N
spia^F luminosa di messa^F in onda^F

clock
reloj^M
pendule^F
Uhr^F
orologio^M

compact disc player
lector^M de disco^M compacto
lecteur^M de disque^M compact
CD-Spieler^M
lettore^M di compact disc^M

volume unit meters
unidad^F de medición^F de volumen^M
vumètres^M
VU-Meter^N
vumetri^M

cassette deck
pletina^F de casete^F
platine^F cassette^F
Kassettendeck^N
piastra^F di registrazione^F

studio
estudio^M
studio^M
Sprecherraum^M
studio^M

turntable
tocadiscos^M
platine^F tourne-disque^M
Plattenspieler^M
giradischi^M

microphone
micrófono^M
microphone^M
Mikrofon^N
microfono^M

announcer turret
torre^F del locutor^M
consolette^F de l'annonceur^M
Sprecherpult^N
console^F dell'annunciatore^M

audio console
consola^F de sonido^M
pupitre^M de son^M
Mischpult^N
console^F del mixer^M audio

stopwatch
cronómetro^M
chronomètre^M
Aufnahmezeitanzeige^F
contasecondi^M

jack field
entrada^F de campo^M
baie^F de jacks^M
Anschlusstafel^F
area^F dei jack^M

producer turret
consola^F del productor^M
consolette^F du réalisateur^M
Regiepult^N
console^F di regia^F

control room
sala^F de control^M
régie^F
Regieraum^M
cabina^F di regia^F

COMMUNICATIONS AND OFFICE AUTOMATION

television

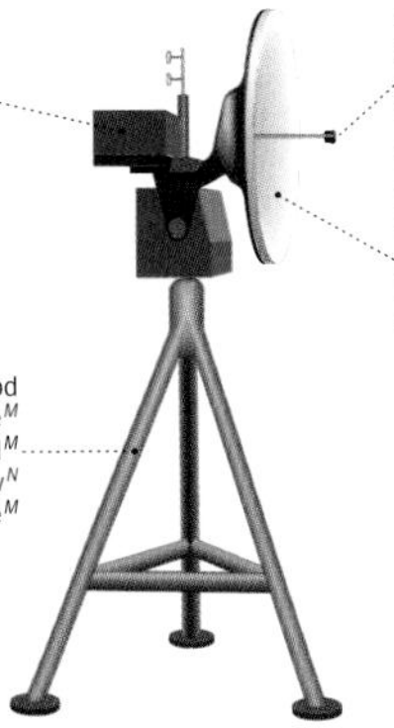

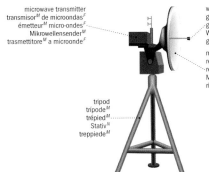

microwave transmitter
transmisor^M de microondas^F
émetteur^M micro-ondes^F
Mikrowellensender^M
trasmettitore^M a microonde^F

wave guide
guía^F de la onda^F
guide^M d'ondes^F
Wellenleiter^M
guida^F di onda^F

parabolic antenna
antena^F parabólica
antenne^F parabolique
Parabolantenne^F
antenna^F parabolica

microwave dish
reflector^M parabólico de microondas^F
réflecteur^M parabolique
Mikrowellenschüssel^F
riflettore^M parabolico a microonde^F

equipment rack
equipo^M de soporte^M
bâti^M d'équipement^M
Ausrüstungsspind^M
rack^M per apparecchiature^F

tripod
trípode^M
trépied^M
Stativ^N
treppiede^M

mobile unit
unidad^F móvil
car^M de reportage^M
Übertragungswagen^M
unità^F mobile

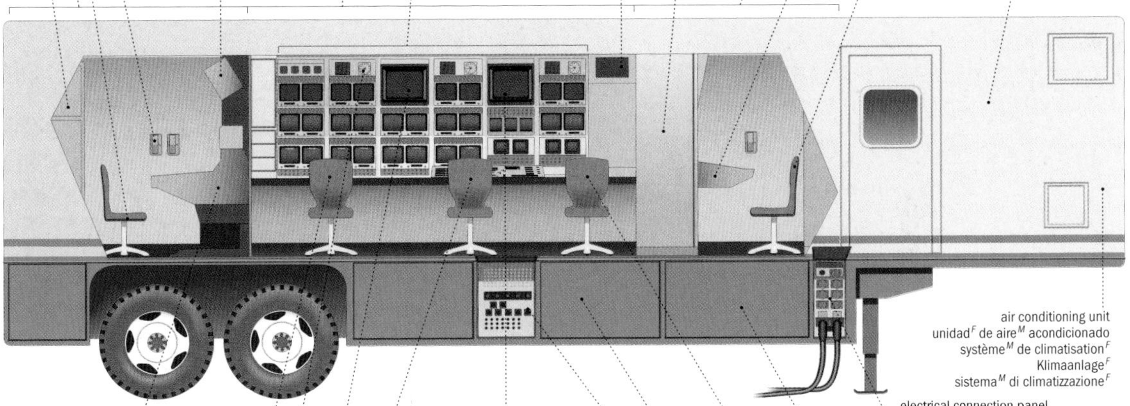

audio control room
sala^F de control^M de sonido^M
régie^F du son^M
Tonregieraum^M
cabina^F di controllo^M audio^M

camera control area
área^M de control^M de la cámara^F
régie^F image^F
Bereich^M der Bildkontrolle^F
area^F di controllo^M delle telecamere^F

audio technician
técnico^M de sonido^M
preneur^M de son^M
Tontechniker^M
tecnico^M audio^M

production control room
sala^F de control^M de la producción^F
régie^F de production^F
Regieraum^M
cabina^F di regia^F

equipment rack
equipo^M de soporte^M
bâti^M d'équipement^M
Geräteschrank^M
rack^M per apparecchiature^F

camera control unit
unidad^F de control^M de la cámara^F
bloc^M de commande^F des caméras^F
Bildkontrolle^F
unità^F di controllo^M delle telecamere^F

telephone set
teléfono^M
poste^M téléphonique
Telefonapparat^M
apparecchio^M telefonico

monitor wall
panel^M de control^M
baie^F de contrôle^M
Kontrollmonitore^M
parete^M dei monitor^M

camera control technician
técnico^M de control^M de la cámara^F
contrôleur^M d'images^F
Bildtechniker^M
tecnico^M di controllo^M delle immagini^F

audio monitor
monitor^M de sonido^M
haut-parleur^M de contrôle^M
Abhörlautsprecher^M
monitor^M audio^M

audio monitor
monitor^M de sonido^M
haut-parleur^M de contrôle^M
Abhörlautsprecher^M
monitor^M audio^M

maintenance area
área^M de mantenimiento^M
secteur^M maintenance^F
Eingangsbereich^M
area^F di servizio^M

air conditioning unit
unidad^F de aire^M acondicionado
système^M de climatisation^F
Klimaanlage^F
sistema^M di climatizzazione^F

electrical connection panel
panel^M de conexiones^F eléctricas
panneau^M de raccordement^M électrique
Stromverteiler^M
pannello^M dei collegamenti^M elettrici

technical equipment compartment
compartimiento^M del equipo^M técnico
soute^F d'équipement^M technique
Fach^N für technische Ausrüstung^F
scomparto^M delle attrezzature^F tecniche

audio console
consola^F de sonido^M
pupitre^M de son^M
Tonregiepult^N
mixer^M audio^M

preview monitor
monitor^M de visualización^F previa
écran^M de précontrôle^M
Vorschaumonitor^M
monitor^M di anteprima^F

technical producer
productor^M técnico
directeur^M technique
Aufsichtsingenieur^M
direttore^M tecnico

producer
productor^M
réalisateur^M
Sendeleiter^M
responsabile^M di regia^F

video switcher technician
operador^M técnico de video^M
technicien^M aiguilleur^M
Video-Switcher^M
tecnico^M di commutazione^F video^M

clock
reloj^M
pendule^F
Kontrolluhr^F
orologio^M

output monitor
monitor^M de producción^F
écran^M de sortie^F
Ausgangsmonitor^M
monitor^M di uscita^F

video connection panel
panel^M de conexión^F del video^M
panneau^M de raccordement^M vidéo
Videoschalttafel^F
pannello^M dei collegamenti^M video^M

cable drum compartment
compartimiento^M del cable^M de la batería^F
soute^F des bobines^F de câbles^M
Fach^N für Kabeltrommel^F
scomparto^M delle bobine^F dei cavi^M

studio and control rooms
estudio^M de televisión^F y cabinas^F de control^M
plateau^M et régies^F
Sprecher- und Regieräume^M
studio^M e cabine^F di regia^F

auxiliary facilities room
sala^F de instalaciones^F auxiliares
salle^F polyvalente
allgemeiner Geräteraum^M
sala^F delle strutture^F ausiliarie

lighting technician
técnico^M de luces^F
éclairagiste^M
Beleuchtungstechniker^M
tecnico^M delle luci^F

dimmer room
sala^F de regulación^F de luces
salle^F des gradateurs^M
Dimmerraum^M
sala^F di regolazione^F delle luci^F

lighting grid access
puerta^F de acceso^M a la rejilla^F de las luces^F
accès^M à la grille^F d'éclairage^F
Zugang^M zur Beleuchtungsanlage^F
accesso^M alla griglia^F di illuminazione^F

camera control technician
técnico^M de control^M de cámaras^F
contrôleur^M d'images^F
Bildtechniker^M
tecnico^M video^M

additional production personnel
personal^M suplementario de producción^F
personnel^M additionnel de production^F
zusätzliches Studiopersonal^N
personale^M ausiliario di produzione^F

lighting board operator
operador^M del tablero^M de luces^F
opérateur^M de régie^F d'éclairage^M
Oberbeleuchtungstechniker^M
operatore^M del pannello^M delle luci^F

connection box
caja^F de conexiones^F
boîte^F de raccordement^M
Kamera-Steckfeld^N
scatola^F dei collegamenti^M

lighting board
tablero^M de luces^F
pupitre^M d'éclairage^M
Lichtregelanlage^F
pannello^M delle luci^F

camera control unit
unidad^F de control^M de cámaras^F
bloc^M de commande^F des caméras^F
Bildkontrolle^F
unità^F di controllo^M video^M

camera
cámara^F
caméra^F
Kamera^F
telecamera^F

technical producer
productor^M técnico
directeur^M technique
Aufsichtsingenieur^M
direttore^M tecnico

monitor wall
panel^M de monitores^M
baie^F de contrôle^M
Kontrollmonitore
parete^F dei monitor^M

microphone boom
jirafa^F del micrófono^M
perche^F
Mikrofonausleger^M
giraffa^F

video switcher technician
operador^M técnico de video^M
technicien^M aiguilleur^M
Video-Switch-Techniker^M
tecnico^M di commutazione^F video^M

producer
productor^M
réalisateur^M
Sendeleiter^M
regista^M

script assistant
asistente^M del guionista^M
assistant^M à la réalisation^F
Skript-Assistent^M
segretario^M di edizione^F

production adviser
consejero^M de producción^F
conseiller^M de production^F
Regieassistent^M
assistente^M alla regia^F

audio console
consola^F de sonido^M
pupitre^M de son^M
Tonregiepult^N
console^F del mixer^M audio^M

musical advisers
consejeros^M musicales
conseillers^M musicaux
Musikregie^F
consulenti^M musicali

equipment rack
soporte^M para el equipo^M
bâti^M d'équipement^M
Ausrüstungsspind^M
rack^M per apparecchiature^F

bass trap
panel^M absorbente de frecuencias^F bajas
trappe^F acoustique
Bassfalle^F
pannello^M di assorbimento^F dei bassi^M

audio technician
técnico^M de sonido^M
preneur^M de son^M
Tontechniker^M
tecnico^M audio^M

audio monitor
monitor^M del sonido^M
haut-parleur^M de contrôle^M
Lautsprecher^M
monitor^M audio^M

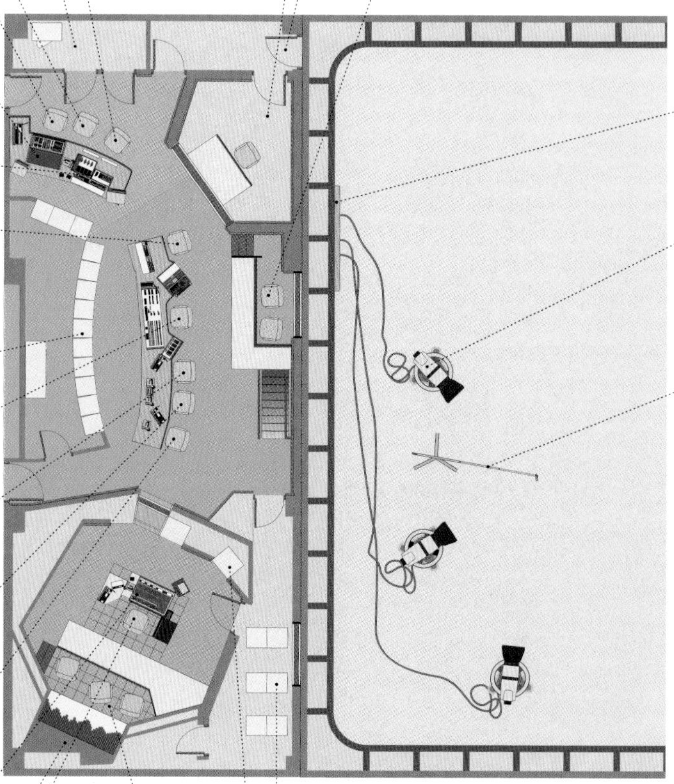

studio floor
estudio^M
plateau^M
Studioebene^F
studio^M televisivo

lighting/camera control area
sala^F de control^M de luces^F/de cámara^F
régie^F image^F/éclairage^M
Beleuchtung^F/Bildregie^F
area^F di controllo^M luci^F/video^M

audio control room
control^M de sonido^M
régie^F du son^M
Tonregieraum^M
cabina^F di controllo^M audio^M

production control room
sala^F de producción^F y control^M
régie^F de production^F
Regieraum^M
cabina^F di regia^F

production control room
sala^F de control^M de producción^F
régie^F de production^F
Regieraum^M
cabina^F di regia^F

audio/video preview unit
unidad de visualización de imagen^F/sonido^M
poste^M de contrôle^M audio/vidéo
Ton-/Bild-Vorschaueinheit^F
console^F di anteprima^F audio^M/video^M

stereo phase monitor
control^M del sonido^M estereofónico
oscilloscope^M de phase^F audio
Lautsprecher^M zum Prüfen^N von Zweikanalton^M
monitor^M di fase^F stereo

preview monitors
monitores^M de visualización^F previa
écrans^M de précontrôle^M
Vorschaumonitore^M
serie^F dei monitor^M di anteprima^F

vector/waveform monitor
osciloscopio^M de control^M de las formas^F de onda^F
oscilloscope^M/vectoscope^M
Oszillograph-/Oszilloskopmonitor^M
monitor^M per il controllo^M della forma^F d'onda^F

input monitors
monitores^M de entrada^F
écrans^F d'entrée^F
Eingangsmonitore^M
serie^F dei monitor^M di ingresso^M

monitor wall
panel^M de monitores^M
baie^F de contrôle^M
Kontrollmonitore^M
parete^F dei monitor^M

digital video effects monitor
monitor^M de efectos^M video/digitales
écran^M du truqueur^M numérique
Trickmischer^M
monitor^M degli effetti^M video^M digitali

technical producer's monitor
monitor^M de la producción^F técnica
écran^M du directeur^M technique
Kontrollmonitor^M des Aufsichtsingenieurs^M
monitor^M del direttore^M tecnico

audio monitor
monitor^M de sonido^M
haut-parleur^M de contrôle^M
Lautsprecher^M
monitor^M audio^M

output monitor
monitor^M de salida^F
écran^M de sortie^F
Ausgangsmonitor^M
monitor^M di uscita^F

clock
reloj^M
pendule^F
Kontrolluhr^F
orologio^M

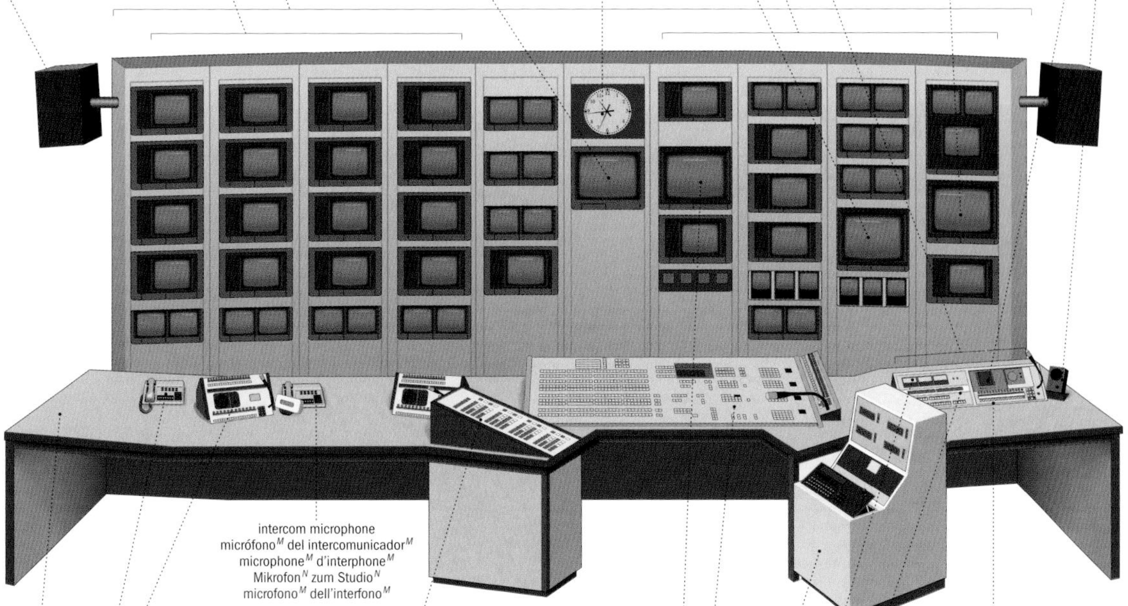

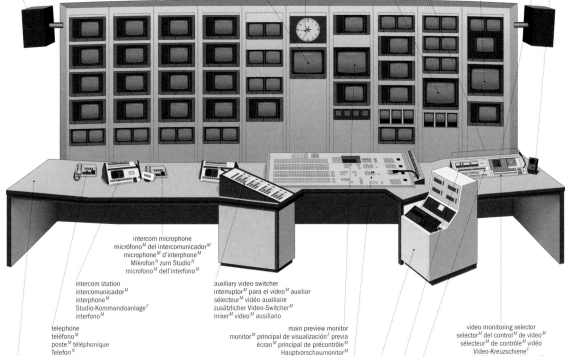

intercom microphone
micrófono^M del intercomunicador^M
microphone^M d'interphone^M
Mikrofon^N zum Studio^N
microfono^M dell'interfono^M

intercom station
intercomunicador^M
interphone^M
Studio-Kommandoanlage^F
interfono^M

auxiliary video switcher
interruptor^M para el vídeo^M auxiliar
sélecteur^M vidéo auxiliaire
zusätzlicher Video-Switcher^M
mixer^M video^M ausiliario

video monitoring selector
selector^M del control^M de vídeo^M
sélecteur^M de contrôle^M vidéo
Video-Kreuzschiene^F
selettore^M di controllo^M video^M

telephone
teléfono^M
poste^M téléphonique
Telefon^N
telefono^M

main preview monitor
monitor^M principal de visualización^F previa
écran^M principal de précontrôle^M
Hauptvorschaumonitor^M
monitor^M principale di anteprima^F

audio monitoring selector
selector^M del control^M de volumen^M
sélecteur^M de contrôle^M audio
Tonvormischung^F
selettore^M di controllo^M audio^M

production desk
mesa^F de producción^F
table^F de production^F
Regiepult^N
console^F di regia^F

production video switcher
interruptor^M para la producción^F de video^M
aiguilleur^M vidéo de production^F
Video-Switcher^M
commutatore^M video^M di regia^F

digital video special effects
efectos^M especiales video/digitales
truqueur^M numérique
Trickmischer^M
effetti^M speciali video^M digitali

audio volume unit meters
vúmetro^M
vumètres^M audio
VU-Meter^N
vumetri^M

television

studio floor
estudio ^{M}
plateau ^{M}
Studioebene ^{F}
studio ^{M} televisivo

floodlight
proyector ^{M} de luz ^{F} difusa
projecteur ^{M} d'ambiance ^{F}
Flächenleuchte ^{F}
riflettore ^{M}

test pattern
patrón ^{M} de prueba ^{F}
mire ^{F} de réglage ^{M}
Testbild ^{N}
monoscopio ^{M}

floodlight on pantograph
proyector ^{M} sobre el pantógrafo ^{M}
projecteur ^{M} d'ambiance ^{F} sur pantographe ^{M}
Flächenleuchte ^{F} an Scherenaufhängung ^{F}
riflettore ^{M} con presa ^{F} a pantografo ^{M}

lighting grid
rejilla ^{F} de iluminación ^{F}
grille ^{F} d'éclairage ^{M}
Beleuchtungsanlage ^{F}
griglia ^{F} di illuminazione ^{F}

spotlight
reflector ^{M} orientable
projecteur ^{M} à faisceau ^{M} concentré
Spotlight ^{N}
riflettore ^{M} orientabile

curtain
cortina ^{F}
rideau ^{M}
Vorhang ^{M}
sipario ^{M}

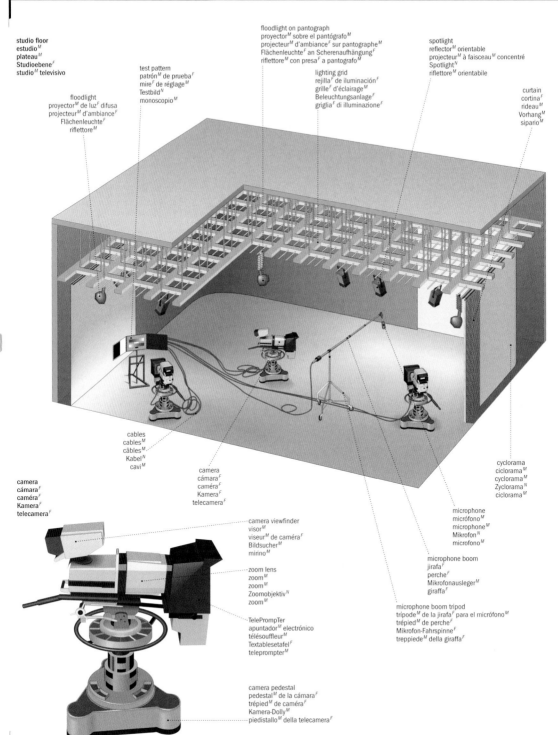

cables
cables ^{M}
câbles ^{M}
Kabel ^{N}
cavi ^{M}

camera
cámara ^{F}
caméra ^{F}
Kamera ^{F}
telecamera ^{F}

cyclorama
ciclorama ^{M}
cyclorama ^{M}
Zyclorama ^{N}
ciclorama ^{M}

camera
cámara ^{F}
caméra ^{F}
Kamera ^{F}
telecamera ^{F}

microphone
micrófono ^{M}
microphone ^{M}
Mikrofon ^{N}
microfono ^{M}

camera viewfinder
visor ^{M}
viseur ^{M} de caméra ^{F}
Bildsucher ^{M}
mirino ^{M}

zoom lens
zoom ^{M}
zoom ^{M}
Zoomobjektiv ^{N}
zoom ^{M}

TelePrompTer
apuntador ^{M} electrónico
télésouffleur ^{M}
Textablesetafel ^{F}
teleprompter ^{M}

microphone boom
jirafa ^{F}
perche ^{F}
Mikrofonausleger ^{M}
giraffa ^{F}

microphone boom tripod
trípode ^{M} de la jirafa ^{F} para el micrófono ^{M}
trépied ^{M} de perche ^{F}
Mikrofon-Fahrspinne ^{F}
treppiede ^{M} della giraffa ^{F}

camera pedestal
pedestal ^{M} de la cámara ^{F}
trépied ^{M} de caméra ^{F}
Kamera-Dolly ^{M}
piedistallo ^{M} della telecamera ^{F}

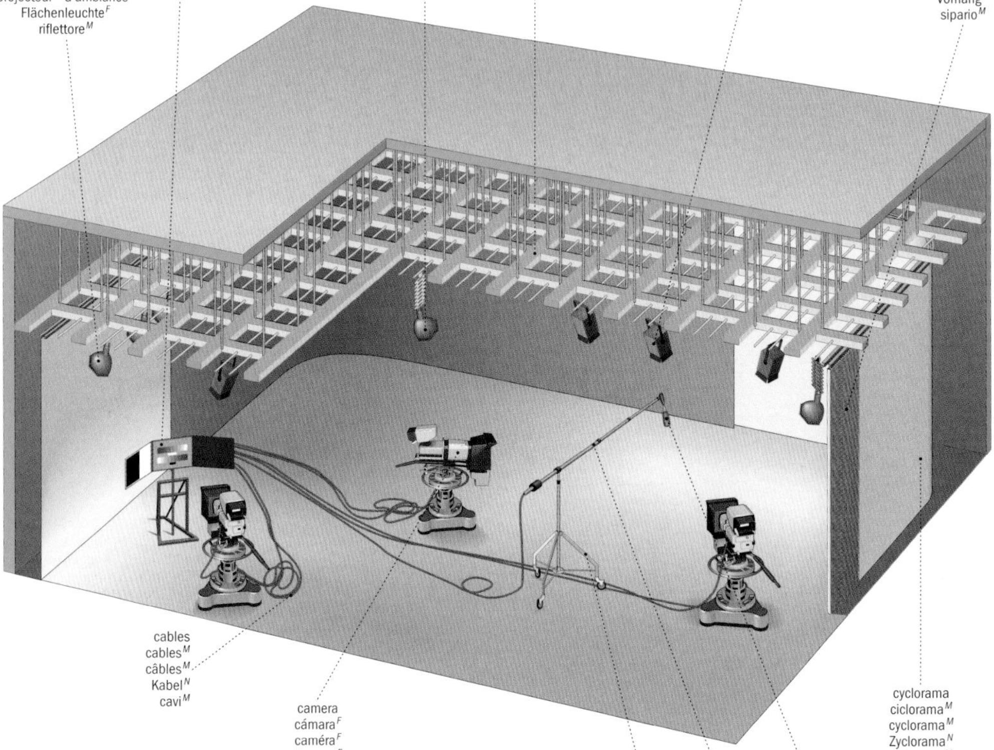

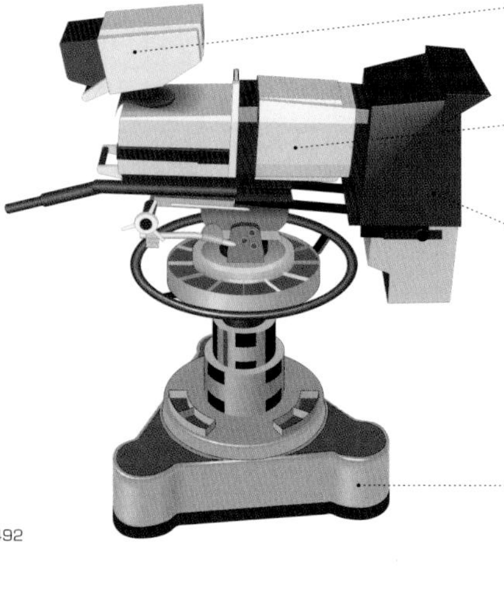

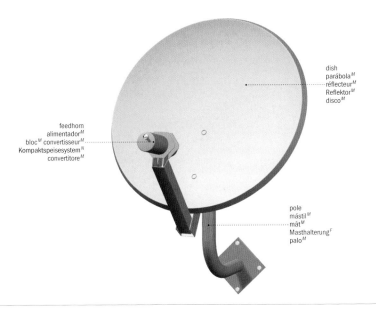

dish antenna
antena^F parabólica
antenne^F parabolique
Parabolantenne^F
antenna^F parabolica

dish
parábola^M
réflecteur^M
Reflektor^M
disco^M

feedhorn
alimentador^M
bloc^M convertisseur^M
Kompaktspeisesystem^N
convertitore^M

pole
mástil^M
mât^M
Masthalterung^F
palo^M

receiver
receptor^M
terminal^M numérique
Receiver^M
ricevitore^M

card reader
lector^M de tarjeta^F
lecteur^M de carte^F
Kartenleser^M
lettore^M di schede^F

remote control
mando^M a distancia^F
télécommande^F
Fernbedienung^F
telecomando^M

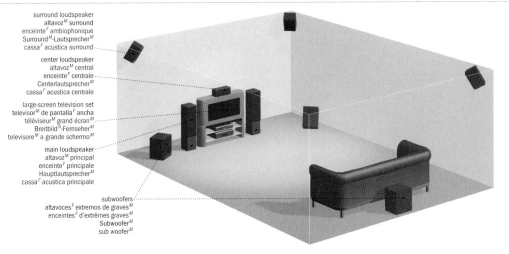

surround loudspeaker
altavoz^M surround
enceinte^F ambiophonique
Surround^M-Lautsprecher^M
cassa^F acustica surround

home theater
home^M theatre
cinéma^M maison^F
Heimkino^N
home theatre^M

center loudspeaker
altavoz^M central
enceinte^F centrale
Centerlautsprecher^M
cassa^F acustica centrale

large-screen television set
televisor^M de pantalla^F ancha
téléviseur^M grand écran^M
Breitbild^N-Fernseher^M
televisore^M a grande schermo^M

main loudspeaker
altavoz^M principal
enceinte^F principale
Hauptlautsprecher^M
cassa^F acustica principale

subwoofers
altavoces^F extremos de graves^M
enceintes^F d'extrêmes graves^M
Subwoofer^M
sub woofer^M

television

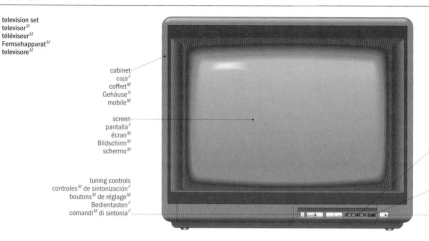

television set
televisor[M]
téléviseur[M]
Fernsehapparat[M]
televisore[M]

cabinet
caja[F]
coffret[M]
Gehäuse[N]
mobile[M]

screen
pantalla[F]
écran[M]
Bildschirm[M]
schermo[M]

tuning controls
controles[M] de sintonización[F]
boutons[M] de réglage[M]
Bedientasten[F]
comandi[M] di sintonia[F]

indicators
indicadores[M]
lampes[F] témoins[M]
Betriebsanzeigen[F]
spie[F] luminose

remote control sensor
sensor[M] del mando[M] a distancia[F]
capteur[M] de télécommande[F]
Sensor[M] für Fernbedienung[F]
sensore[M] del telecomando[M]

power button
botón[M] de encendido
interrupteur[M] d'alimentation[F]
Netzschalter[M]
interruttore[M] di accensione[F]

picture tube
tubo[M] de pantalla[F]
tube[M]-image[F]
Bildröhre[F]
cinescopio[M]

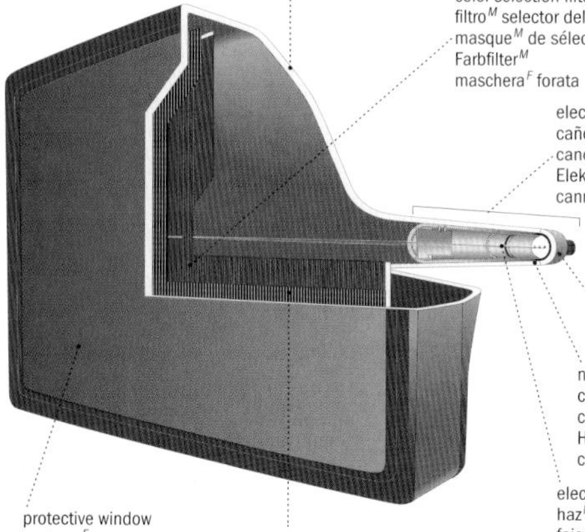

funnel
cono[M]
cône[M]
Trichter[M]
imbuto[M]

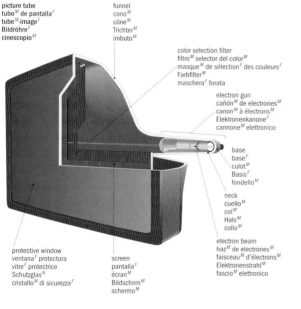

color selection filter
filtro[M] selector del color[M]
masque[M] de sélection[F] des couleurs[F]
Farbfilter[M]
maschera[F] forata

electron gun
cañón[M] de electrones[M]
canon[M] à électrons[M]
Elektronenkanone[F]
cannone[M] elettronico

base
base[F]
culot[M]
Basis[F]
fondello[M]

neck
cuello[M]
col[M]
Hals[M]
collo[M]

electron beam
haz[M] de electrones[M]
faisceau[M] d'électrons[M]
Elektronenstrahl[M]
fascio[M] elettronico

protective window
ventana[F] protectora
vitre[F] protectrice
Schutzglas[N]
cristallo[M] di sicurezza[F]

screen
pantalla[F]
écran[M]
Bildschirm[M]
schermo[M]

electron gun
cañón[M] de electrones[M]
canon[M] à électrons[M]
Elektronenkanone[F]
cannone[M] elettronico

red beam
haz[M] rojo
faisceau[M] rouge
Rotstrahl[M]
fascio[M] rosso

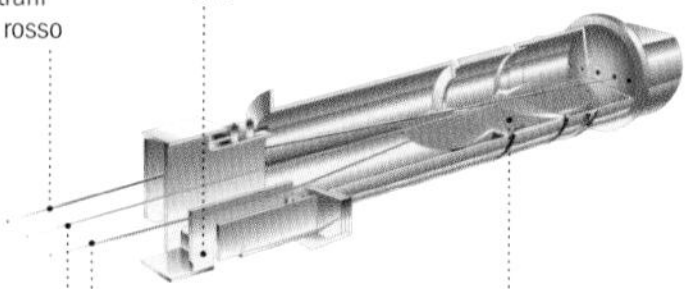

grid
rejilla[F]
grille[F]
Gitter[N]
griglia[F]

green beam
haz[M] verde
faisceau[M] vert
Grünstrahl[M]
fascio[M] verde

magnetic field
campo[M] magnético
champ[M] magnétique
magnetisches Feld[N]
campo[M] magnetico

blue beam
haz[M] azul
faisceau[M] bleu
Blaustrahl[M]
fascio[M] blu

DVD player
reproductor[M] DVD
lecteur[M] de DVD[M] vidéo
DVD[F]-Spieler[M]
lettore[M] DVD[M]

power button
interruptor[M] de alimentación[F]
interrupteur[M] d'alimentation[F]
Ein-/Ausschalter[M]
pulsante[M] di alimentazione[F]

disc tray
bandeja[F] del disco
plateau[M] de chargement[M]
DVD[F]-Lade[F]
vassoio[M] portadischi

display
pantalla[F]
afficheur[M]
Display[N]
display[M]

digital versatile disc (DVD)
disco[M] versátil digital (DVD)
disque[M] numérique polyvalent (DVD)
DVD[F]
disco[M] versatile digitale (DVD)

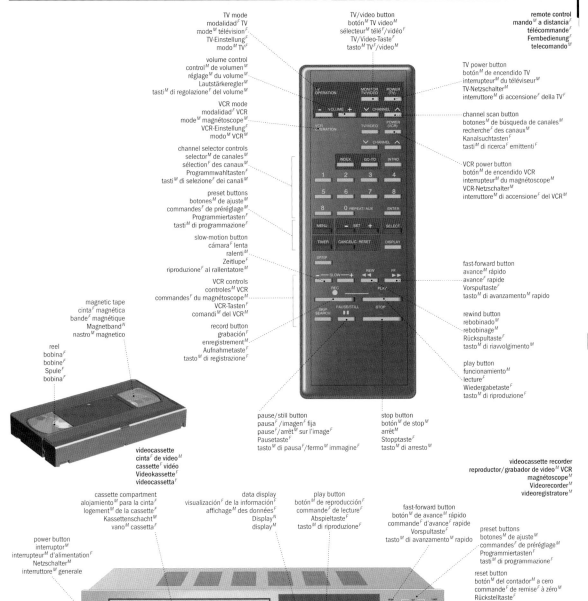

TV mode
modalidad^F TV
mode^M télévision^F
TV-Einstellung^F
modo^M TV^F

volume control
control^M de volumen^M
réglage^M du volume^M
Lautstärkeregler^M
tasti^M di regolazione^F del volume^M

VCR mode
modalidad^F VCR
mode^M magnétoscope^M
VCR-Einstellung^F
modo^M VCR^M

channel selector controls
selector^M de canales^M
sélection^F des canaux^M
Programmwahltasten^F
tasti^M di selezione^F dei canali^M

preset buttons
botones^M de ajuste^M
commandes^F de préréglage^M
Programmiertasten^F
tasti^M di programmazione^F

slow-motion button
cámara^F lenta
ralenti^M
Zeitlupe^F
riproduzione^F al rallentatore^M

VCR controls
controles^M VCR
commandes^F du magnétoscope^M
VCR-Tasten^F
comandi^M del VCR^M

magnetic tape
cinta^F magnética
bande^F magnétique
Magnetband^N
nastro^M magnetico

reel
bobina^F
bobine^F
Spule^F
bobina^F

record button
grabación^F
enregistrement^M
Aufnahmetaste^F
tasto^M di registrazione^F

videocassette
cinta^F de video^M
cassette^F vidéo
Videokassette^F
videocassetta^F

TV/video button
botón^M TV video^M
sélecteur^M télé^F/vidéo^F
TV/Video-Taste^F
tasto^M TV^F/video^M

remote control
mando^M a distancia^F
télécommande^F
Fernbedienung^F
telecomando^M

TV power button
botón^M de encendido TV
interrupteur^F du téléviseur^M
TV-Netzschalter^M
interruttore^M di accensione^F della TV^F

channel scan button
botones^M de búsqueda de canales^M
recherche^F des canaux^M
Kanalsuchtasten^F
tasti^M di ricerca^F emittenti^F

VCR power button
botón^M de encendido VCR
interrupteur^M du magnétoscope^M
VCR-Netzschalter^M
interruttore^M di accensione^F del VCR^M

fast-forward button
avance^M rápido
avance^M rapide
Vorspultaste^F
tasto^M di avanzamento^M rapido

rewind button
rebobinado^M
rebobinage^M
Rückspultaste^F
tasto^M di riavvolgimento^M

play button
funcionamiento^M
lecture^F
Wiedergabetaste^F
tasto^M di riproduzione^F

pause/still button
pausa^F/imagen^F fija
pause^F/arrêt^M sur l'image^F
Pausetaste^F
tasto^M di pausa^F/fermo^M immagine^F

stop button
botón^M de stop^M
arrêt^M
Stopptaste^F
tasto^M di arresto^M

videocassette recorder
reproductor/grabador de video^M VCR
magnétoscope^M
Videorecorder^M
videoregistratore^M

cassette compartment
alojamiento^M para la cinta^F
logement^M de la cassette^F
Kassettenschacht^M
vano^M cassetta^F

data display
visualización^F de la información^F
affichage^M des données^F
Display^N
display^M

play button
botón^M de reproducción^F
commande^F de lecture^F
Abspieltaste^F
tasto^M di riproduzione^F

fast-forward button
botón^M de avance^M rápido
commande^F d'avance^F rapide
Vorspultaste^F
tasto^M di avanzamento^M rapido

preset buttons
botones^M de ajuste^M
commandes^F de préréglage^M
Programmiertasten^F
tasti^M di programmazione^F

reset button
botón^M del contador^M a cero
commande^F de remise^F à zéro^M
Rückstelltaste^F
tasto^M di azzeramento^M

record button
botón^M de grabación^F
commande^F d'enregistrement^M
Aufnahmetaste^F
tasto^M di registrazione^F

channel scan buttons
botones^M para búsqueda^F de canales^M
recherche^F des canaux^M
Kanalsuchtasten^F
tasti^M di ricerca delle emittenti^F

power button
interruptor^M
interrupteur^M d'alimentation^F
Netzschalter^M
interruttore^M generale

cassette eject switch
botón^M de expulsión^F
commande^F d'éjection^F de la cassette^F
Kassettenauswurfschalter^M
tasto^M di espulsione^F

stop button
botón^M de stop^M
commande^F d'arrêt^M
Stopptaste^F
tasto^M di arresto^M

rewind button
botón^M de rebobinado^M
commande^F de rebobinage^M
Rückspultaste^F
tasto^M di riavvolgimento^M

pause/still button
pausa^F/imagen^F fija
pause^F/arrêt^M sur l'image^F
Pausetaste^F
tasto^M di pausa^F/fermo^M immagine^F

television

analog camcorder: front view
videocámara^F analógica: vista^F frontal
caméscope^M analogique : vue^F avant
Analog-Camcorder^M: Vorderansicht^F
videocamera^F portatile: vista^F frontale

edit search button
botón^M de selección^F y montaje^M
touche^F de raccord^M d'enregistrement^M
Editier-Such-Taste^F
tasto^M di selezione^F e montaggio^M

zoom lens
objetivo^M zoom
objectif^M zoom^M
Zoomobjektiv^N
zoom^M

microphone
micrófono^M
microphone^M
Mikrofon^N
microfono^M

near/far dial
ruleta^F de enfoque^M lejos/cerca
molette^F de réglage^M près/loin
Zoomer^M
rotella^F regolatrice vicino/lontano

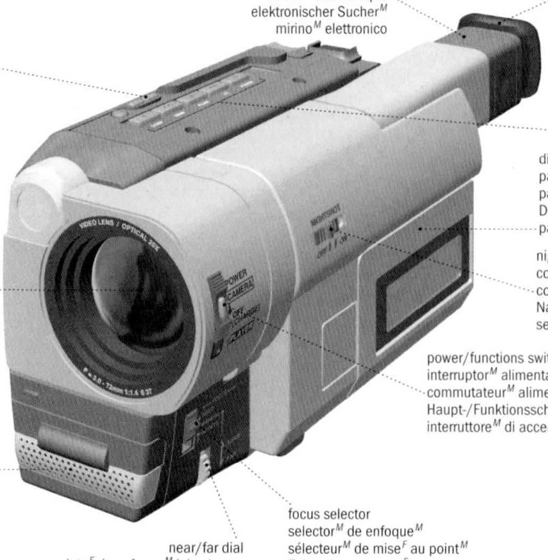

electronic viewfinder
visor^M electrónico
viseur^M électronique
elektronischer Sucher^M
mirino^M elettronico

eyecup
ojera^F
œilleton^M
Sonnenschutzblende^F
adattatore^M per oculare^M

videotape operation controls
mandos^M de la cinta^F de video^M
commandes^F de la bande^F vidéo
Videobandsteuerungen^F
comandi^M della videocassetta^F

display panel
panel^M del display^M
panneau^M de l'écran^M
Display^N-Panel^N
pannello^M del display^M

nightshot switch
conmutador^M de grabación^F nocturna
commutateur^M de prise^F de vues^F nocturne
Nachtaufnahmeschalter^M
selettore^M di registrazione^F notturna

power/functions switch
interruptor^M alimentación^F/funciones^F
commutateur^M alimentation^F/fonctions^F
Haupt-/Funktionsschalter^M
interruttore^M di accensione^F/funzioni^F

cassette compartment
alojamiento^M de la cinta^F
logement^M de la cassette^F
Videokassettenschacht^M
vano^M della videocassetta^F

focus selector
selector^M de enfoque^M
sélecteur^M de mise^F au point^M
Fokussiersteuerung^F
selettore^M della messa^F a fuoco^M

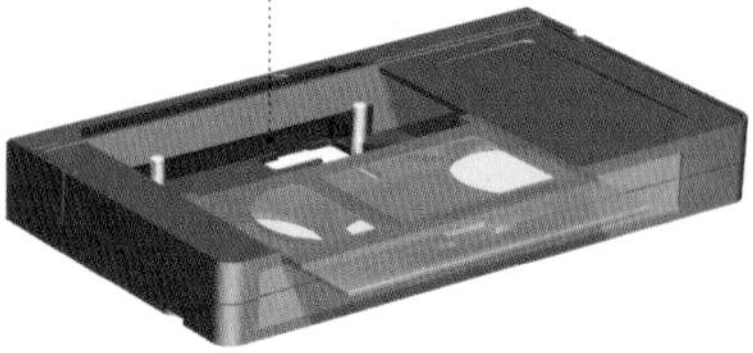

compact videocassette adapter
adaptador^M de cinta^F de vídeo^M compacto
adaptateur^M de cassette^F vidéo compacte
Videokassettenadapter^M
adattatore^M per videocassette^F compatte

analog camcorder: back view
videocámara^F analógica: vista^F posterior
caméscope^M analogique : vue^F arrière
Analog-Camcorder^M: Rückansicht^F
videocamera^F portatile: dorso^M

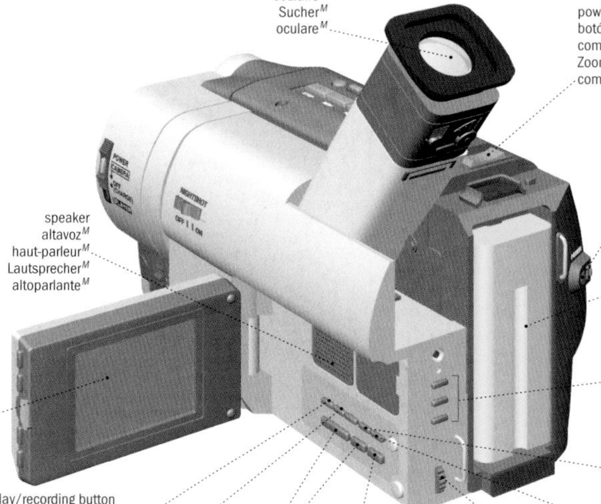

eyepiece
ocular^M
oculaire^M
Sucher^M
oculare^M

power zoom button
botón^M del zoom^M eléctrico
commande^F électrique du zoom^M
Zoomwippe^F
comando^M dello zoom^M elettrico

recording start/stop button
tecla^F de inicio/stop de grabación^F
touche^F d'enregistrement^M
Aufnahme^F-Start^M-/Stopptaste^F
tasto^M di avvio^M/arresto^M registrazione^F

rechargeable battery pack
pila^F recargable
pile^F rechargeable
Akku^M
batteria^F ricaricabile

image adjustment buttons
botones^M de ajuste^M de imagen^F
touches^F de réglage^M de l'image^F
Bildeinstelltasten^F
tasti^M di regolazione^F dell'immagine^F

indicators display button
tecla^F de fijación^F de pantalla^F
touche^F d'affichage^M des indicateurs^M
Anzeigetaste^F
tasto^M di visualizzazione^F degli indicatori^M

end search button
tecla^F de final^M de búsqueda^F
touche^F de raccord^M d'enregistrement^M
End-Suchtaste^F
tasto^M di ricerca^F della fine^F

speaker
altavoz^M
haut-parleur^M
Lautsprecher^M
altoparlante^M

liquid crystal display
pantalla^F táctil LCD
écran^M à cristaux^M liquides
Flüssigkristallanzeige^F
display^M a cristalli^M liquidi

date display/recording button
botón^M grabación^F/visualización^F fecha^F
touche^F de la date^F
Datumeinblende-/Aufnahmetaste^F
tasto^M di registrazione^F e di visualizzazione^F della data^M

time display/recording button
botón^M grabación^F/visualización^F hora^F
touche^F de l'heure^F
Zeiteinblende-/Aufnahmetaste^F
tasto^M di registrazione^F e di visualizzazione^F dell'ora^F

special effects buttons
botones^M de efectos^M especiales
touches^F d'effets^M spéciaux
Trickeffektetasten^F
tasti^M degli effetti^M speciali

title display button
tecla^F de visualización^F del título^M
touche^F d'affichage^M de titre^M
Titeleinblendetaste^F
tasto^M di visualizzazione^F dei titoli^M

special effects selection dial
ruleta^F de selección^F de efectos^M especiales
molette^F de sélection^F des effets^M spéciaux
Trickeffektewähler^M
rotella^F di selezione^F degli effetti^M speciali

sound reproducing system

equipo^M de alta fidelidad^F | chaine^F stéréo | Tonwiedergabesystem^N | impianto^M hi-fi di riproduzione^F del suono^M

ampli-tuner: front view
amplificador^M /sintonizador^M : vista^F frontal
ampli^M-syntoniseur^M : vue^F avant
Receiver^M: Vorderansicht^F
sintoamplificatore^M: vista^F frontale

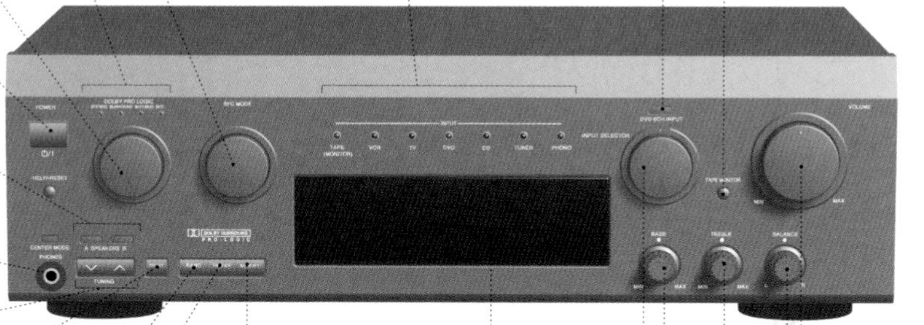

sound mode lights
indicadores^M del modo^M audio
voyants^M d'indication^F du mode^M sonore
Klangwahlanzeige^F
spie^F della modalità^F audio

sound field control
control^M del campo^M audio
contrôle^M du champ^M sonore
Feldstärkeregler^M
controllo^M del campo^M audio

sound mode selector
selector^M del modo^M audio
sélecteur^M de mode^M sonore
Klangwahlschalter^M
selettore^M della modalità^F audio

input lights
indicadores^M de entrada^F
voyants^M d'entrée^F
Kontrollleuchten^F für Tonsignalquellen^F
luci^F delle sorgenti^F

input select button
tecla^F de selección^F de entrada^F
touche^F de sélection^F d'entrée^F
Tonsignalquellen^F-Wahltaster^M
tasto^M di selezione^F delle sorgenti^F

tape recorder select button
tecla^F de selección^F del grabador^M
touche^F de sélection^F du magnétophone^M
Kassettenrekorder^M-Wahltaste^F
tasto^M di selezione^F del registratore^M

power button
botón^M de encendido
interrupteur^M d'alimentation^F
Netzschalter^M
interruttore^M di accensione^F

loudspeaker system select buttons
teclas^F de selección^F de los altavoces^M
touches^F de sélection^F des enceintes^F
Kanalwahltasten^F für Lautsprecher^M
tasti^M di selezione^F delle casse^F acustiche

headphone jack
toma^F para los auriculares^M
prise^F casque^M
Kopfhörerbuchse^F
presa^F per cuffia^F

tuning buttons
teclas^F de selección^F de la sintonía^F
touches^F de sélection^F des stations^F
Sendersuchlauftasten^F
tasti^M di selezione^F della sintonia^F

preset tuning button
tecla^F de selección^F sintonía^F
touche^F de présélection^F
Vorwahlsender^M-Wahltaste^F
tasto^M di preselezione^F della sintonia^F

memory button
tecla^M memoria
touche^F mémoire^F
Speichertaste^F
tasto^M di memorizzazione^F

band select button
tecla^F de selección^F de banda
touche^F de modulation^F
Bandwahltaste^F
tasto^M di selezione^F della banda^F

FM mode select button
tecla^F de selección^F de modalidad^F FM
touche^F de sélection^F du mode^M FM
UKW^F-Wahltaste^F
tasto^M di selezione^F della modalità^F FM

display
display^M
afficheur^M
Display^N
display^M

input selector
selector^M de entrada^F
sélecteur^M d'entrée^F
Eingangsschalter^M
selettore^M di ingresso^M

bass tone control
control^M de graves^M
contrôle^M de tonalité^F des graves^M
Bassregler^M
regolatore^M dei bassi^M

volume control
control^M del volumen^M
réglage^M du volume^M
Lautstärkeregler^M
regolatore^M di volume^M

balance control
control^M de balance^M
équilibrage^M des haut-parleurs^M
Balanceregler^M
bilanciamento^M degli altoparlanti^M

treble tone control
control^M de agudos^M
contrôle^M de tonalité^F des aigus^M
Höhenregler^M
regolatore^M degli alti^M

ampli-tuner: back view
amplificador^M /sintonizador^M : vista^F posterior
ampli^M-syntoniseur^M : vue^F arrière
Amplituner^M: Rückansicht^F
sintoamplificatore^M: dorso^M

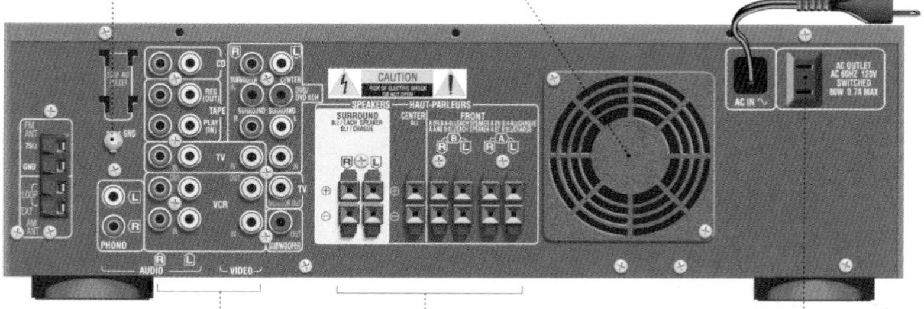

ground terminal
conector^M de puesta^F de tierra^F
borne^F de mise^F à la terre^F
Massekontakt^M
terminale^M della messa^F a terra^F

cooling fan
ventilador^M
ventilateur^M
Lüfter^M
ventola^F

power cord
cable^M de alimentación^F
cordon^M d'alimentation^F
Netzkabel^N
cavo^M di alimentazione^F

antenna terminals
conectores^M de antenas^F
bornes^F de raccordement^M des antennes^F
Antennenbuchsen^F
terminali^M di collegamento^M delle antenne^F

input/output audio/video jacks
tomas^F entrada^F /salida^F video^M
prises^F d'entrée^F/de sortie^F audio/vidéo
Video-Ein- und -Ausgänge^M
ingressi^M uscite^F audio^M/video^M

loudspeaker terminals
conector^F de altavoces^M
bornes^F de raccordement^M des enceintes^F
Lautsprecherbuchsen^F
terminali^M di collegamento^M delle casse^F acustiche

switched outlet
conmutador^M de corriente^F
prise^F de courant^M commutée
geschaltete Steckdose^F
presa^F di corrente^F commutata

sound reproducing system

tuner
sintonizador^M
syntoniseur^M
Rundfunkempfänger^M
sintonizzatore^M

power button
botón^M de encendido
interrupteur^M d'alimentation^F
Netzschalter^M
interruttore^M di accensione^F

memory button
botón^M de memoria^F
touche^F mémoire^F
Speichertaste^F
tasto^M di memorizzazione^F

mode selector
selector^M mono/estéreo
commutateur^M mono^F/stéréo^F
Mono-Stereo-Taste^F
commutatore^M mono/stereo

active tracking
búsqueda^F automática de canales^M
balayage^M automatique des stations^F
automatischer Sendersuchlauf^M
ricerca^F automatica

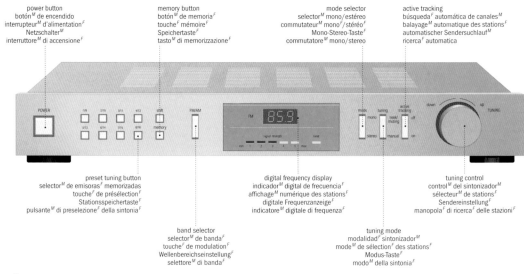

preset tuning button
selector^M de emisoras^F memorizadas
touche^F de présélection^F
Stationsspeichertaste^F
pulsante^M di preselezione^F della sintonia^F

band selector
selector^M de banda^F
touche^F de modulation^F
Wellenbereichseinstellung^F
selettore^M di banda^F

digital frequency display
indicador^M digital de frecuencia^F
affichage^M numérique des stations^F
digitale Frequenzanzeige^F
indicatore^M digitale di frequenza^F

tuning mode
modalidad^F sintonizador^M
mode^M de sélection^F des stations^F
Modus-Taste^F
modo^M della sintonia^F

tuning control
control^M del sintonizador^M
sélecteur^F de stations^F
Sendereinstellung^F
manopola^F di ricerca^F delle stazioni^F

graphic equalizer
compensador^M gráfico de sintonización^F
égalisateur^M graphique
Equalizer^M
equalizzatore^M grafico

frequency bands
bandas^F de frecuencia^F
bandes^F de fréquences^F
Frequenzbänder^N
bande^F di frequenza^F

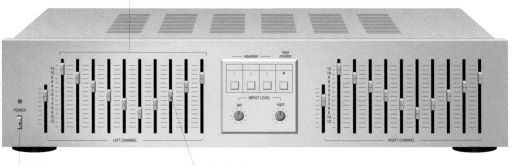

power button
interruptor^M de alimentación^F
interrupteur^M d'alimentation^F
Ein-/Ausschalter^M
interruttore^M di accensione^F

frequency-setting slide control
cursor^M de ajuste^M de la frecuencia^F
curseur^M de réglage^M de la fréquence^F
Frequenzregler^M
cursore^M di regolazione^F della frequenza^F

COMMUNICATIONS AND OFFICE AUTOMATION

sound reproducing system

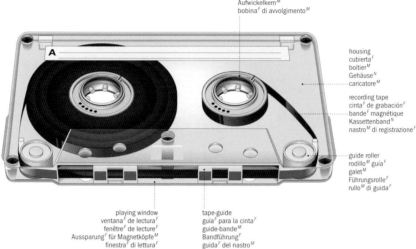

cassette
casete^F
cassette^F
Kassette^F
cassetta^F

take-up reel
carrete^M receptor de la cinta^F
bobine^F réceptrice
Aufwickelkern^M
bobina^F di avvolgimento^M

housing
cubierta^F
boitier^M
Gehäuse^N
caricatore^M

recording tape
cinta^F de grabación^F
bande^F magnétique
Kassettenband^N
nastro^M di registrazione^F

guide roller
rodillo^M guía^F
galet^M
Führungsrolle^F
rullo^M di guida^F

playing window
ventana^F de lectura^F
fenêtre^F de lecture^F
Aussparung^F für Magnetköpfe^M
finestra^F di lettura^F

tape-guide
guía^F para la cinta^F
guide-bande^M
Bandführung^F
guida^F del nastro^M

cassette tape deck
pletina^F de casete^F
platine^F cassette^F
Kassettendeck^N
piastra^F di registrazione^F

counter reset button
botón^M de ajuste^M a cero^M del contador^M
bouton^M de remise^F à zéro^M
Rückstelltaste^F
tasto^M di azzeramento^M del contatore^M

tape selector
selector^M de tipo^M de cinta^F
sélecteur^M de bandes^F
Bandsortenschalter^M
selettore^M del nastro^M

fast-forward button
botón^M de avance^M rápido
avance^F rapide
Schnellvorlauf-Taste^F
tasto^M di avanzamento^M rapido

eject button
botón^M de expulsión^F
bouton^M d'éjection^F
Auswurf-Taste^F
tasto^M di espulsione^F

tape counter
contador^M
compteur^M
Zählwerk^N
contatore^M

play button
botón^M de reproducción^F
lecture^F
Play-Taste^F
tasto^M di riproduzione^F

peak-level meter
medidor^M de altos niveles^M de frecuencia^F
indicateur^M de niveau^M
LED-Pegelanzeige^F
LED^M indicatore^M del livello^M di picco^M

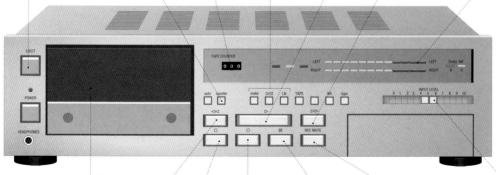

cassette holder
alojamiento^M de la casete^M
logement^M de cassette^F
Kassettenfach^N
vano^M della cassetta^F

pause button
botón^M de pausa^F
pause^F
Pause-Taste^F
tasto^M di pausa^F

record muting button
botón^M de grabación^F silenciosa
interrupteur^M d'accord^M
Stummaufnahme-Taste^F
muting^M

rewind button
botón^M de rebobinado^M
rebobinage^M
Rücklauf-Taste^F
tasto^M di riavvolgimento^M

stop button
botón^M de stop^M
arrêt^M
Stopp-Taste^F
tasto^M di arresto^M

record button
botón^M de inicio^M de grabación^F
enregistrement^M
Aufnahme-Taste^F
tasto^M di registrazione^F

recording level control
botón^M de nivel^M de grabación^F
réglage^M de niveau^M d'enregistrement^M
manuelle Aussteuerung^F
selettore^M del livello^M di registrazione^M

COMMUNICATIONS AND OFFICE AUTOMATION

sound reproducing system

record
disco^M
disque^M
Schallplatte^F
disco^M

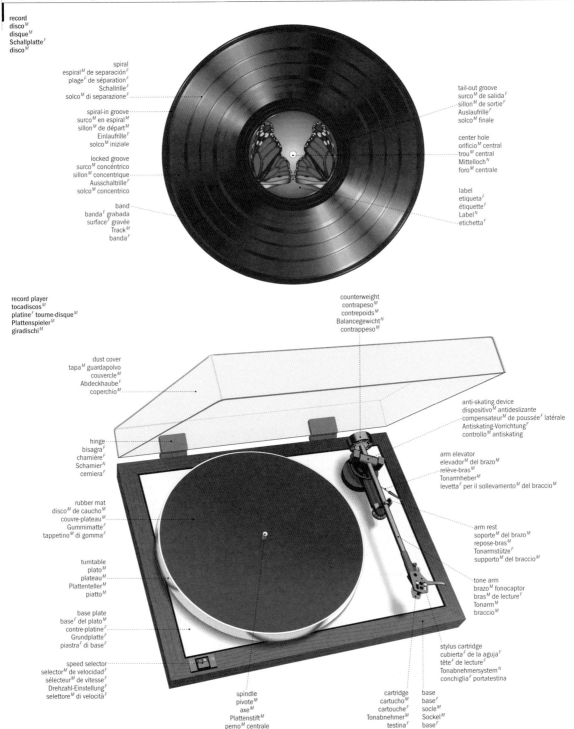

spiral
espiral^M de separación^F
plage^F de séparation^F
Schallrille^F
solco^M di separazione^F

spiral-in groove
surco^M en espiral^M
sillon^M de départ^M
Einlaufrille^F
solco^M iniziale

locked groove
surco^M concéntrico
sillon^M concentrique
Ausschaltrille^F
solco^M concentrico

band
banda^F grabada
surface^F gravée
Track^M
banda^F

tail-out groove
surco^M de salida^F
sillon^M de sortie^F
Auslaufrille^F
solco^M finale

center hole
orificio^M central
trou^M central
Mittelloch^N
foro^M centrale

label
etiqueta^F
étiquette^F
Label^N
etichetta^F

record player
tocadiscos^M
platine^F tourne-disque^M
Plattenspieler^M
giradischi^M

counterweight
contrapeso^M
contrepoids^M
Balancegewicht^N
contrappeso^M

dust cover
tapa^M guardapolvo
couvercle^M
Abdeckhaube^F
coperchio^M

anti-skating device
dispositivo^M antideslizante
compensateur^M de poussée^F latérale
Antiskating-Vorrichtung^F
controllo^M antiskating

hinge
bisagra^F
charnière^F
Scharnier^N
cerniera^F

arm elevator
elevador^M del brazo^M
relève-bras^M
Tonarmheber^M
levetta^F per il sollevamento^M del braccio^M

rubber mat
disco^M de caucho^M
couvre-plateau^M
Gummimatte^F
tappetino^M di gomma^F

arm rest
soporte^M del brazo^M
repose-bras^M
Tonarmstütze^F
supporto^M del braccio^M

turntable
plato^M
plateau^M
Plattenteller^M
piatto^M

tone arm
brazo^M fonocaptor
bras^M de lecture^F
Tonarm^M
braccio^M

base plate
base^F del plato^M
contre-platine^F
Grundplatte^F
piastra^F di base^F

stylus cartridge
cubierta^F de la aguja^F
tête^F de lecture^F
Tonabnehmersystem^N
conchiglia^F portatestina

speed selector
selector^M de velocidad^F
sélecteur^M de vitesse^F
Drehzahl-Einstellung^F
selettore^M di velocità^F

spindle
pivote^M
axe^M
Plattenstift^M
perno^M centrale

cartridge
cartucho^M
cartouche^F
Tonabnehmer^M
testina^F

base
base^F
socle^M
Sockel^M
base^F

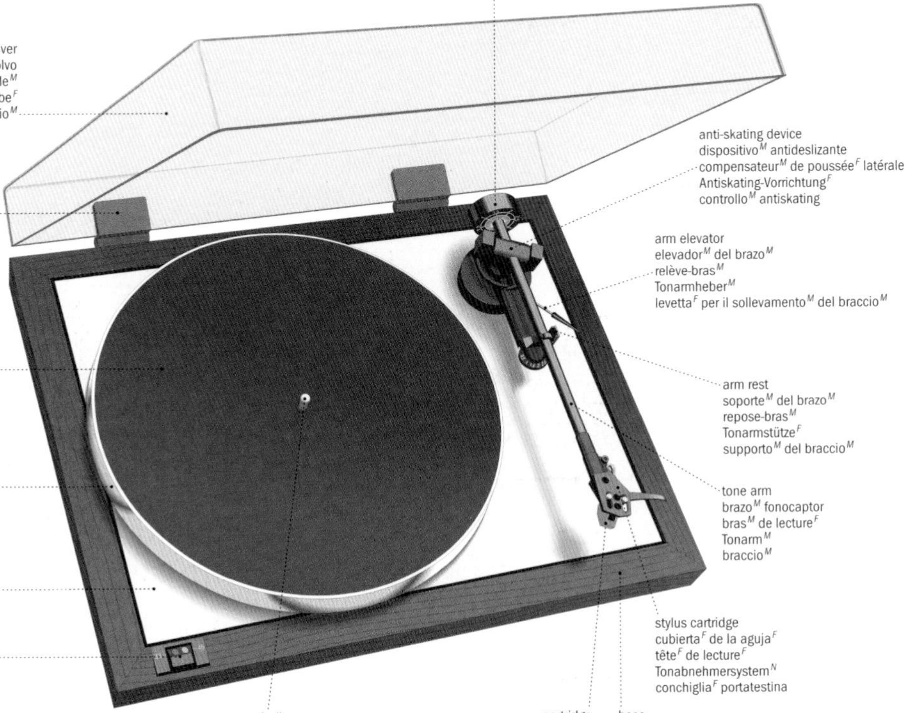

sound reproducing system

compact disc
disco^M compacto
disque^M compact
CD^F
compact disc^M

technical identification band
banda^F de identificación^F técnica
bande^F d'identification^F technique
technische Identifikationsnummer^F
banda^F di identificazione^F tecnica

compact disc reading
lectura^F de disco^M compacto
lecture^F du disque^M compact
Lesen^N von Compact Discs^F
lettura^F di compact disc^M

objective lens
objetivo^M
objectif^M
Objektivlinse^F
lente^F

pit
pit^M
aspérité^F
Pit^N
pit^M

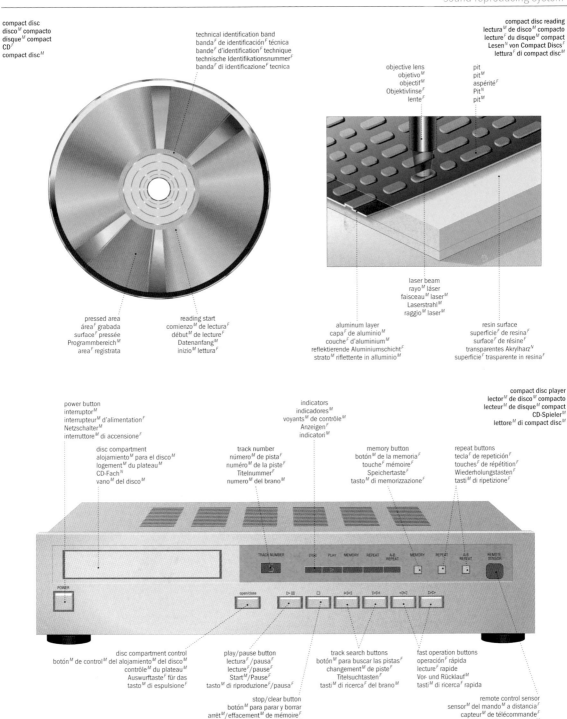

laser beam
rayo^M láser
faisceau^M laser^M
Laserstrahl^M
raggio^M laser^M

pressed area
área^F grabada
surface^F pressée
Programmbereich^M
area^F registrata

reading start
comienzo^M de lectura^F
début^M de lecture^F
Datenanfang^M
inizio^M lettura^F

aluminum layer
capa^F de aluminio^M
couche^F d'aluminium^M
reflektierende Aluminiumschicht^F
strato^M riflettente in alluminio^M

resin surface
superficie^F de resina^F
surface^F de résine^F
transparentes Akrylharz^N
superficie^F trasparente in resina^F

power button
interruptor^M
interrupteur^M d'alimentation^F
Netzschalter^M
interruttore^M di accensione^F

indicators
indicadores^M
voyants^M de contrôle^M
Anzeigen^F
indicatori^M

compact disc player
lector^M de disco^M compacto
lecteur^M de disque^M compact
CD-Spieler^M
lettore^M di compact disc^M

disc compartment
alojamiento^M para el disco^M
logement^M du plateau^M
CD-Fach^N
vano^M del disco^M

track number
número^M de pista^F
numéro^M de la piste^F
Titelnummer^F
numero^M del brano^M

memory button
botón^M de la memoria^F
touche^F mémoire^F
Speichertaste^F
tasto^M di memorizzazione^F

repeat buttons
tecla^F de repetición^F
touches^F de répétition^F
Wiederholungstasten^F
tasti^M di ripetizione^F

disc compartment control
botón^M de control^M del alojamiento^M del disco^M
contrôle^M du plateau^M
Auswurftaste^F für das
tasto^M di espulsione^F

play/pause button
lectura^F/pausa^F
lecture^F/pause^F
Start^M/Pause^F
tasto^M di riproduzione^F/pausa^F

track search buttons
botón^M para buscar las pistas^F
changement^M de piste^F
Titelsuchtasten^F
tasti^M di ricerca^F del brano^M

fast operation buttons
operación^F rápida
lecture^F rapide
Vor- und Rücklauf^M
tasti^M di ricerca^F rapida

stop/clear button
botón^M para parar y borrar
arrêt^M/effacement^M de mémoire^F
Stopp-/Löschtaste^F
tasto^M di arresto^M/cancellazione^F

remote control sensor
sensor^M del mando^M a distancia^F
capteur^M de télécommande^F
Fembedienungssensor^M
sensore^M del telecomando^M

sound reproducing system

headphones
auriculares^M
casque^M d'écoute^F
Kopfhörer^M
cuffia^F

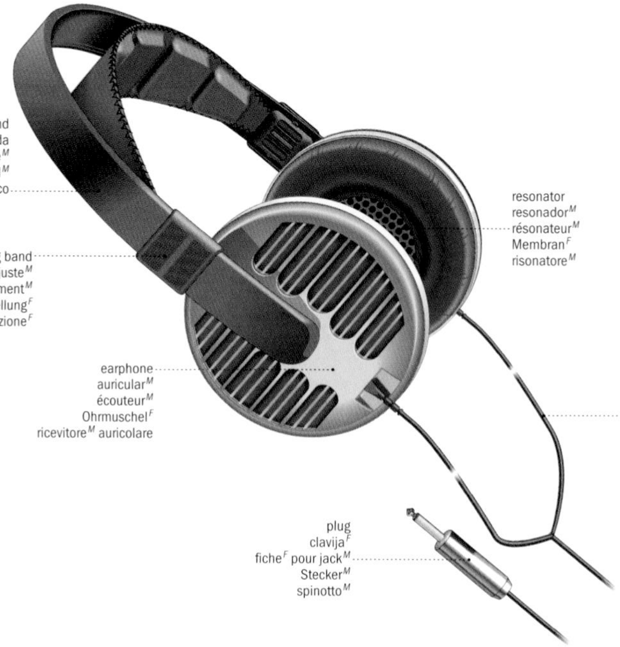

headband
banda^F acolchada
serre-tête^M
Bügel^M
supporto^M elastico

resonator
resonador^M
résonateur^M
Membran^F
risonatore^M

adjusting band
banda^F de ajuste^M
glissière^F d'ajustement^M
Einstellung^F
fascia^F di regolazione^F

earphone
auricular^M
écouteur^M
Ohrmuschel^F
ricevitore^M auricolare

connecting cable
cable^M de conexión^F
câble^M de raccordement^M
Anschlusskabel^N
cavo^M di collegamento^M

plug
clavija^F
fiche^F pour jack^M
Stecker^M
spinotto^M

loudspeakers
altavoz^M
enceinte^F acoustique
Lautsprecherbox^F
cassa^F acustica

right channel
canal^M derecho
canal^M droit
rechter Kanal^M
canale^M destro

left channel
canal^M izquierdo
canal^M gauche
linker Kanal^M
canale^M sinistro

tweeter
altavoz^M defrecuencias^F altas
haut-parleur^M d'aigus^M
Hochtöner^M
tweeter^M

midrange
altavoz^M de frecuenciasde medias^M
haut-parleur^M de médium^M
Mitteltöner^M
midrange^M

speaker cover
rejilla^F protectora
treillis^M
Abdeckung^F
griglia^F

woofer
altavoz^M de frecuencias^F de graves^M
haut-parleur^M de graves^M
Tieftöner^M
woofer^M

diaphragm
diafragma^M
membrane^F
Membran^F
diaframma^M

mini stereo sound system

mini-cadena^F estéreo | minichaine^F stéréo | Mini-HiFi^F-System^N | mini impianto^M hi-fi

compact disc player
lector de disco^M compacto
lecteur^M de disque^M compact
CD^F-Spieler^M
lettore^M di compact disc^M

ampli-tuner
amplificador^M-sintonizador^M
ampli^M-syntoniseur^M
Receiver^M
sintoamplificatore^M

loudspeaker
altavoz^M
enceinte^F acoustique
Lautsprecher^M
cassa^F acustica

compact disc recorder
reproductor^M de disco^M compacto
graveur^M de disque^M compact
CD^F-Rekorder^M
registratore^M di compact disc^M

dual cassette deck
doble pletina^F de casete^F
double platine^F cassette^F
Doppel-Kassettendeck^N
doppia piastra^F di registrazione^F

portable sound systems

sistemas^M de sonido^M portátiles | appareils^M de son^M portatifs | tragbare Tonwiedergabesysteme^N | riproduttori^M portatili

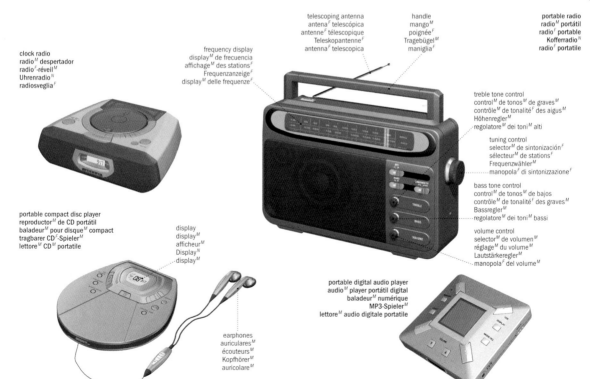

clock radio
radio^M despertador
radio^F-réveil^M
Uhrenradio^N
radiosveglia^F

frequency display
display^M de frecuencia
affichage^M des stations^F
Frequenzanzeige^F
display^M delle frequenze^F

telescoping antenna
antena^F telescópica
antenne^F télescopique
Teleskopantenne^F
antenna^F telescopica

handle
mango^M
poignée^F
Tragebügel^M
maniglia^F

portable radio
radio^M portátil
radio^F portable
Kofferradio^N
radio^F portatile

treble tone control
control^M de tonos^M de graves^M
contrôle^M de tonalité^F des aigus^M
Höhenregler^M
regolatore^M dei toni^M alti

tuning control
selector^M de sintonización^F
sélecteur^M de stations^F
Frequenzwähler^M
manopola^F di sintonizzazione^F

bass tone control
control^M de tonos^M de bajos^M
contrôle^M de tonalité^F des graves^M
Bassregler^M
regolatore^M dei toni^M bassi

volume control
selector^M de volumen^M
réglage^M du volume^M
Lautstärkeregler^M
manopola^F del volume^M

portable compact disc player
reproductor^M de CD portátil
baladeur^M pour disque^M compact
tragbarer CD^F-Spieler^M
lettore^M CD^M portatile

display
display^M
afficheur^M
Display^N
display^M

portable digital audio player
audio^M player portátil digital
baladeur^M numérique
MP3-Spieler^M
lettore^M audio digitale portatile

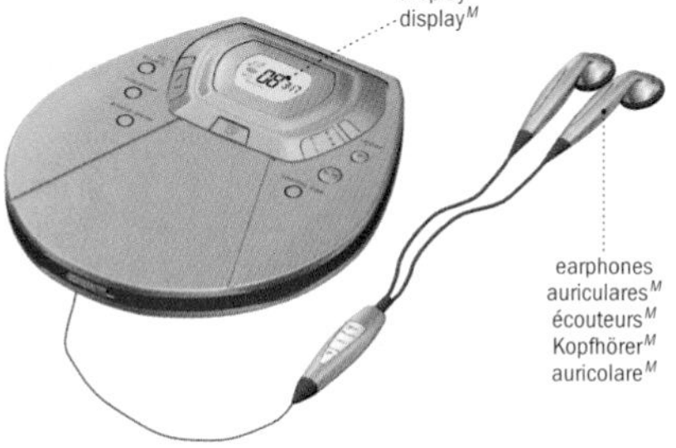

earphones
auriculares^M
écouteurs^M
Kopfhörer^M
auricolare^M

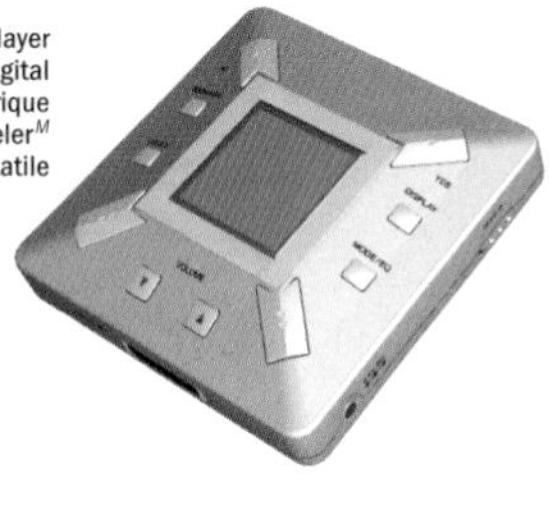

COMMUNICATIONS AND OFFICE AUTOMATION

portable sound systems

personal radio cassette player
radiocasete^M porttil personal (Walkman®)
baladeur^M
Walkman^{® M} mit Radioteil^N
Walkman^{® M}

cable
cable^M
cordon^M
Kabel^N
cavo^M

headphone plug
enchufe^M para auriculares^M
prise^F casque^M
Kopfhörerstecker^M
spinotto^M della cuffia^F

tuning dial
botón^M de sintonización^F
sélecteur^M de stations^F
Sendereinstellung^F
manopola^F della sintonia^F

on-off button
encendido/apagado
marche^F/arrêt^M
Ein/Aus
interruttore^M di accensione^F

rewind button
botón^M de rebobinado^M
rebobinage^M
Rücklauftaste^F
tasto^M di riavvolgimento^M

play button
botón^M de funcionamiento^M
avance^F
Wiedergabetaste^F
tasto^M di riproduzione^F

fast-forward button
botón^M de rebobinado^M rápido
avance^F rapide
Schnellvorlauftaste^F
tasto^M di avanzamento^M rapido

auto-reverse button
botón^M de rebobinado^M automático
auto-inversion^F
Autoreverse-Taste^F
tasto^M dell'auto-reverse^M

headband
banda^F de ajuste^M
serre-tête^F
Kopfbügel^M
supporto^M elastico

volume control
control^M de volumen^M
réglage^M du volume^M
Lautstärkeregler^M
manopola^F del volume^M

headphones
auriculares^M
casque^M d'écoute^F
Kopfhörer^M
cuffia^F

cassette
casete^F
cassette^F
Kassette^F
cassetta^F

cassette player
lector^M de casetes^F
lecteur^M de cassette^F
Kassettenteil^N
riproduttore^M a cassette^F

tuner
sintonizador^M
radio^F
Empfangsteil^N
sintonizzatore^M

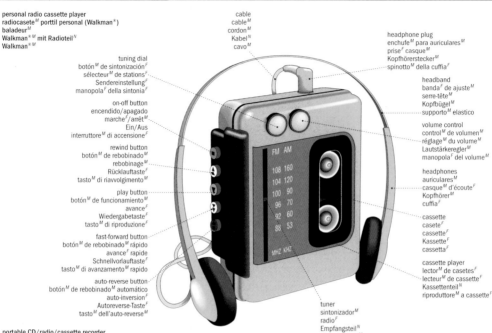

portable CD/radio/cassette recorder
radiocasete^M con lector^M de disco^M compacto
radiocassette^F laser^M
Radiorecorder^M mit CD-Spieler^M
radioregistratore^M con compact disc^M

antenna
antena^F
antenne^F
Antenne^F
antenna^F

handle
asa^F
poignée^F
Tragebügel^M
maniglia^F

mode selectors
selectores^M de modalidad^F
sélecteurs^M de mode^M
Betriebseinstellung^F
selettori^M di modo^M

on-off/volume
encendido/apagado/volumen^M
marche^F/arrêt^M/volume^M
Ein/Aus/Lautstärke^F
interruttore^M di accensione^F e del volume^M

stereo control
control^M estéreo
contrôle^M de la stéréophonie^F
Stereotaste^F
selettore^M stereo/mono

headphone jack
toma^F para auriculares^M
prise^F casque^M
Kopfhörerbuchse^F
presa^F per cuffia^F

compact disc player
lector^M de discos^M compactos
lecteur^M de disque^M compact
CD-Spieler^M
lettore^M di compact disc^M

compact disc
disco^M compacto
disque^M compact
CD^F
compact disc^M

speaker
altavoz^M
haut-parleur^M
Lautsprecher^M
altoparlante^M

power plug
enchufe^M
alimentation^F sur secteur^M
Netzanschluss^M
presa^F di alimentazione^F

tuning control
control^M de sintonización^F
sélecteur^M de stations^F
Sendereinstellung^F
manopola^F della sintonia^F

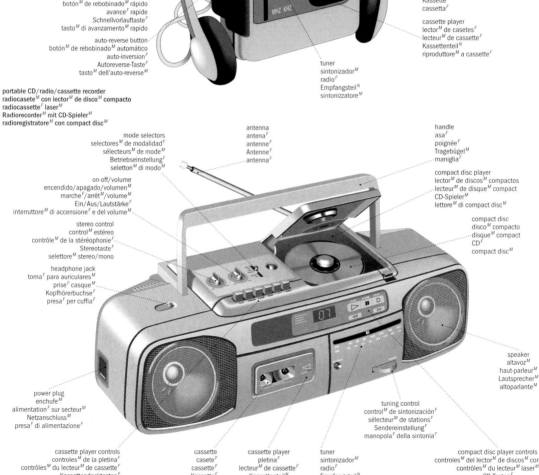

cassette player controls
controles^M de la pletina^F
contrôles^M du lecteur^M de cassette^F
Kassettendecktasten^F
tasti^M del riproduttore^M a cassette^F

cassette
casete^F
cassette^F
Kassette^F
cassetta^F

cassette player
pletina^F
lecteur^M de cassette^F
Kassettenteil^N
riproduttore^M a cassette^F

tuner
sintonizador^M
radio^F
Empfangsteil^N
sintonizzatore^M

compact disc player controls
controles^M del lector^M de discos^M compactos
contrôles^M du lecteur^M laser^M
CD-Tasten^F
tasti^M del lettore^M di compact disc^M

wireless communication

comunicación^M sin hilos^M | communication^F sans fil^M | drahtlose Kommunikation^F | comunicazione^F senza fili^M

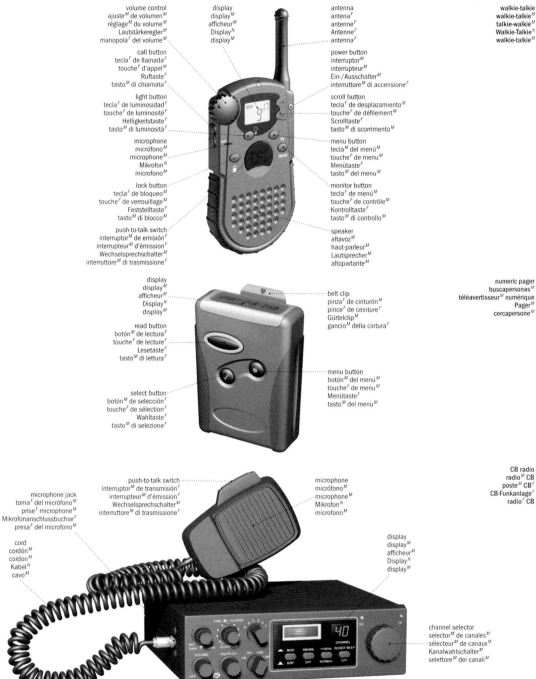

volume control
ajuste^M de volumen^M
réglage^M du volume^M
Lautstärkeregler^M
manopola^F del volume^M

display
display^M
afficheur^M
Display^N
display^M

antenna
antena^F
antenne^F
Antenne^F
antenna^F

walkie-talkie
walkie-talkie^M
talkie-walkie^M
Walkie-Talkie^N
walkie-talkie^M

call button
tecla^F de llamada^F
touche^F d'appel^M
Ruftaste^F
tasto^M di chiamata^F

power button
interruptor^M
interrupteur^M
Ein-/Ausschalter^M
interruttore^M di accensione^F

light button
tecla^F de luminosidad^F
touche^F de luminosité^F
Helligkeitstaste^F
tasto^M di luminosità^F

scroll button
tecla^F de desplazamiento^M
touche^F de défilement^M
Scrolltaste^F
tasto^M di scorrimento^M

microphone
micrófono^M
microphone^M
Mikrofon^N
microfono^M

menu button
tecla^M del menú^M
touche^F de menu^M
Menütaste^F
tasto^M del menu^M

lock button
tecla^F de bloqueo^M
touche^F de verrouillage^M
Feststelltaste^F
tasto^M di blocco^M

monitor button
tecla^F de menú^M
touche^F de contrôle^M
Kontrolltaste^F
tasto^M di controllo^M

push-to-talk switch
interruptor^M de emisión^F
interrupteur^M d'émission^F
Wechselsprechschalter^M
interruttore^M di trasmissione^F

speaker
altavoz^M
haut-parleur^M
Lautsprecher^M
altoparlante^M

display
display^M
afficheur^M
Display^N
display^M

belt clip
pinza^F de cinturón^M
pince^F de ceinture^F
Gürtelclip^M
gancio^M della cintura^F

numeric pager
buscapersonas^M
téléavertisseur^M numérique
Pager^M
cercapersone^M

read button
botón^M de lectura^F
touche^F de lecture^F
Lesetaste^F
tasto^M di lettura^F

menu button
botón^M del menú^M
touche^F de menu^M
Menütaste^F
tasto^M del menu^M

select button
botón^M de selección^F
touche^F de sélection^F
Wahltaste^F
tasto^M di selezione^F

push-to-talk switch
interruptor^M de transmisión^F
interrupteur^M d'émission^F
Wechselsprechschalter^M
interruttore^M di trasmissione^F

microphone
micrófono^M
microphone^M
Mikrofon^N
microfono^M

CB radio
radio^M CB
poste^M CB^F
CB-Funkanlage^F
radio^F CB

microphone jack
toma^F del micrófono^M
prise^F microphone^M
Mikrofonanschlussbuchse^F
presa^F del microfono^M

cord
cordón^M
cordon^M
Kabel^N
cavo^M

display
display^M
afficheur^M
Display^N
display^M

channel selector
selector^M de canales^M
sélecteur^M de canaux^M
Kanalwahlschalter^M
selettore^M dei canali^M

COMMUNICATIONS AND OFFICE AUTOMATION

communication by telephone

comunicación^F por teléfono^M | communication^F par téléphone^M | Telefonieren^N | comunicazione^F via telefono^M

portable cellular telephone
teléfono^M móvil
téléphone^M portable
Handy^N
telefono^M cellulare

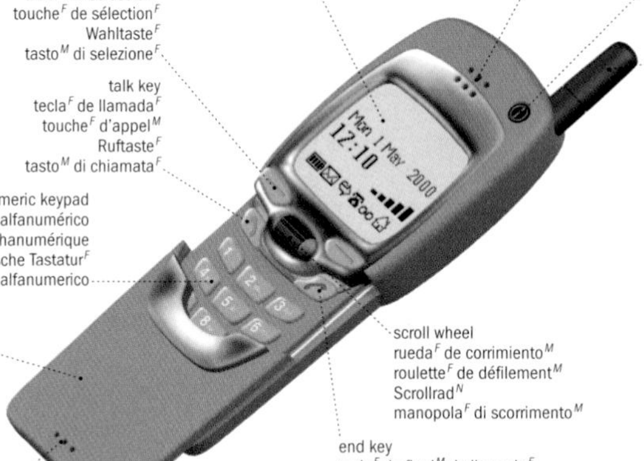

display
display^M
afficheur^M
Display^N
display^M

receiver
receptor^M
récepteur^M
Lautsprecher^M
ricevitore^M

power button
interruptor^M
interrupteur^M
Ein-/Ausschalter^M
interruttore^M

selection key
tecla^F de selección^F
touche^F de sélection^F
Wahltaste^F
tasto^M di selezione^F

talk key
tecla^F de llamada^F
touche^F d'appel^M
Ruftaste^F
tasto^M di chiamata^F

alphanumeric keypad
teclado^M alfanumérico
clavier^M alphanumérique
alphanumerische Tastatur^F
tastierino^M alfanumerico

sliding cover
tapa^F deslizante
clapet^M
verschiebbarer Tastaturschutz^M
coperchio^M scorrevole

microphone
micrófono^M
microphone^M
Mikrofon^N
microfono^M

antenna
antena^F
antenne^F
Antenne^F
antenna^F

headset kit
equipo^M de auricular^M /micrófono^M
ensemble^M oreillette^F/microphone^M
Freisprechanlage^F
kit^M con cuffia^F dotata di microfono^M

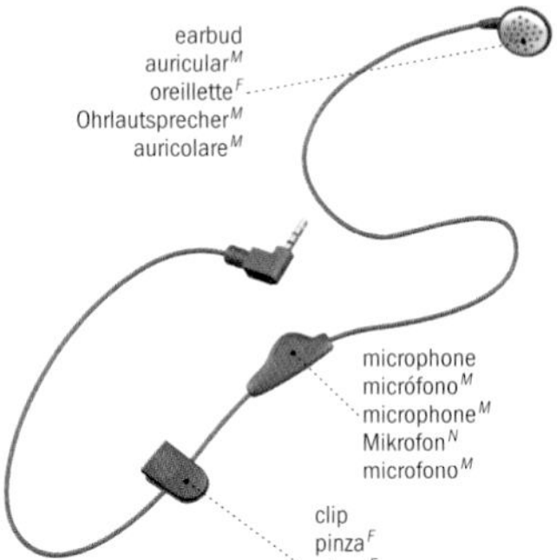

earbud
auricular^M
oreillette^F
Ohrlautsprecher^M
auricolare^M

scroll wheel
rueda^F de corrimiento^M
roulette^F de défilement^M
Scrollrad^N
manopola^F di scorrimento^M

end key
tecla^F de final^M de llamada^F
touche^F de fin^F d'appel^M
Ruf^M-beenden-Taste^F
tasto^M di fine^F chiamata^F

microphone
micrófono^M
microphone^M
Mikrofon^N
microfono^M

clip
pinza^F
pince^F
Clip^M
clip^F

telephone set
teléfono^M
poste^M téléphonique
Telefonapparat^M
apparecchio^M telefonico

receiver
receptor^M
récepteur^M
Hörmuschel^F
ricevitore^M

display
display^M
afficheur^M
Display^N
display^M

handset
auricular^M
combiné^M
Hörer^M
microtelefono^M

receiver volume control
control^M de volumen^M del auricular^M
commande^F de volume^M du récepteur^M
Lautstärkeregler^M für den Hörer^M
regolatore^M del volume^M di ricezione^F

transmitter
transmisor^M
microphone^M
Sprechmuschel^F
microfono^M

on-off light
luz^F de encendido/apagado
voyant^M de mise^F en circuit^M
An-/Aus-Kontrolllampe^F
spia^F luminosa di accensione^F/spegnimento^M

display setting
ajuste^M del display^M
réglage^M de l'afficheur^M
Displayeinstellung^F
regolatore^M del display^M

ringing volume control
control^M de volumen^M del timbre^M
commande^F de volume^M de la sonnerie^F
Lautstärkeregler^M für den Rufton^M
regolatore^M del volume^M e della suoneria^F

function selectors
selectores^M de funciones^F
sélecteurs^M de fonctions^F
Funktionswahltaste^F
selettori^M di funzione^F

handset cord
cable^M del auricular^M
cordon^M de combiné^M
Schnur^F
cordone^M del microtelefono^M

push buttons
teclado^M
clavier^M
Tasten^F
tastiera^F

telephone index
agenda^F telefónica
répertoire^M téléphonique
Rufnummernregister^N
rubrica^F telefonica

automatic dialer index
marcador^M automático
index^M de composition^F automatique
Rufnummernregister^N für automatische Wahl^F
tasti^M di chiamata^F automatica

memory button
botón^M de memoria^F
commande^F mémoire^F
Speichertaste^F
tasto^M di memorizzazione^F

COMMUNICATIONS AND OFFICE AUTOMATION

pay phone
teléfono[M] público
téléphone[M] public
öffentlicher Fernsprecher[M]
apparecchio[M] telefonico a gettoni[M]

examples of telephones
ejemplos[M] de teléfonos[M]
exemples[M] de postes[M] téléphoniques
Beispiele[N] für Telefone[N]
esempi[M] di telefoni[M]

coin slot
ranura[F] para monedas[F]
fente[F] à monnaie[F]
Münzeinwurf[M]
fessura[F] per gettoni[M]

volume control
control[M] de volumen[M]
contrôle[M] du volume[M]
Lautstärkeregler[M]
regolatore[M] del volume[M]

display
visualización[F]
écran[M]
Display[N]
display[M]

next call
próxima llamada[F]
appel[M] suivant
nächster Ruf[M]
tasto[M] di chiamata[F] successiva

language display button
botón[M] de selección[F] de idioma[M]
choix[M] de la langue[F] d'affichage[M]
Sprachanzeigetaste[F]
tasto[M] di selezione[F] della lingua[F] del display[M]

handset
auricular[M]
combiné[M]
Hörer[M]
microtelefono[M]

push button
teclado[M]
clavier[M]
Taste[F]
tastiera[F]

card reader
lector[M] de tarjetas[F]
lecteur[M] de carte[F]
Kartenschlitz[M]
lettore[M] di schede[F]

coin return slot
devolución[F] de monedas[F]
sébile[F] de remboursement[M]
Geldrückgabefach[N]
finestrella[F] per la restituzione[F] dei gettoni[M]

armored cord
cable[M] con funda[F] metálica
cordon[M] à gaine[F] métallique
Panzerschnur[F]
cavo[M] armato

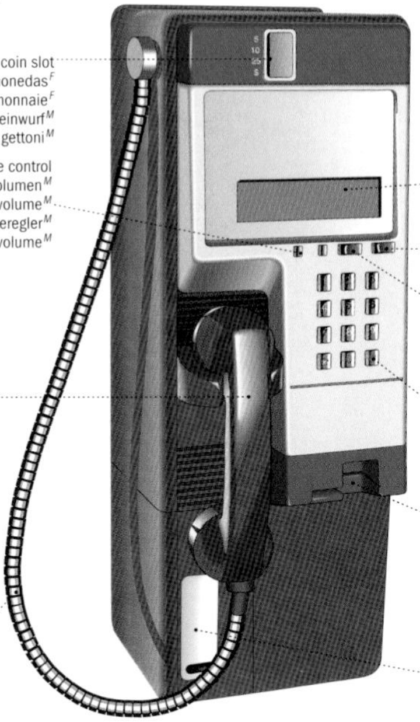

cordless telephone
teléfono[M] inalámbrico
poste[M] sans cordon[M]
schnurloses Telefon[N]
telefono[M] senza fili[M]

telecommunication terminal
terminal[M] de comunicaciones[F]
terminal[M] de télécommunication[F]
Kommunikationsterminal[N]
videoterminale[M]

housing
caja[F]
boîtier[M]
Gehäuse[N]
monitor[M]

visual display unit
monitor[M]
écran[M]
Bildschirm[N]
schermo[M]

function keys
teclas[F] de función[F]
touches[F] de fonctions[F]
Funktionstasten[F]
tasti[M] funzione[F]

numeric keyboard
teclado[M] numérico
clavier[M] numérique
numerische Tastatur[F]
tastiera[F] numerica

alphanumeric keyboard
teclado[M] alfanumérico
clavier[M] alphanumérique
alphanumerische Tastatur[F]
tastiera[F] alfanumerica

operation keys
teclas[F] de operación[F]
touches[F] de commande[F]
Bedienungstasten[F]
tasti[M] di comando[M]

keyboard
teclado[M]
clavier[M]
Tastatur[F]
tastiera[F]

push-button telephone
teléfono[M] de teclado[M]
poste[M] à clavier[M]
Tastentelefon[N]
telefono[M] a tastiera[F]

call director telephone
centralita[F]
pupitre[M] dirigeur
Telefonzentrale[F]
centralina[F]

communication by telephone

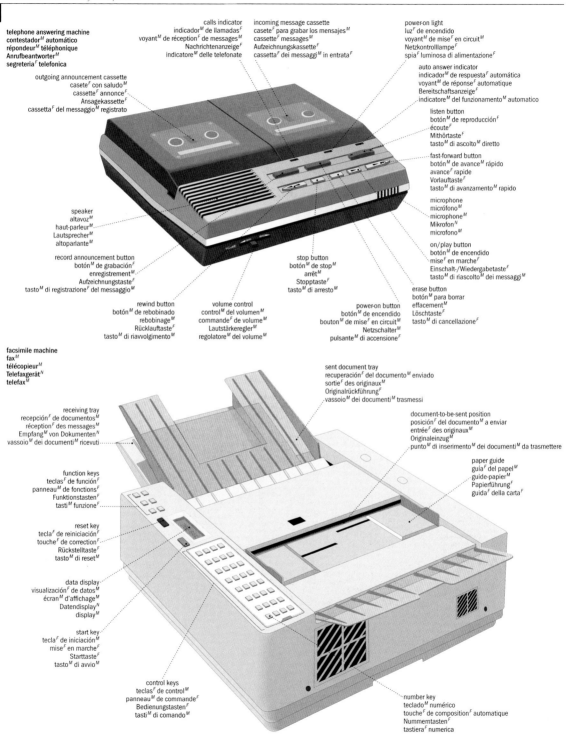

telephone answering machine
contestador^M automático
répondeur^M téléphonique
Anrufbeantworter^M
segreteria^F telefonica

calls indicator
indicador^M de llamadas^F
voyant^M de réception^F de messages^M
Nachrichtenanzeige^F
indicatore^M delle telefonate

incoming message cassette
casete^F para grabar los mensajes^M
cassette^F messages^M
Aufzeichnungskassette^F
cassetta^F dei messaggi^M in entrata^F

power-on light
luz^F de encendido
voyant^M de mise^F en circuit^M
Netzkontrolllampe^F
spia^F luminosa di alimentazione^F

auto answer indicator
indicador^M de respuesta^F automática
voyant^M de réponse^F automatique
Bereitschaftsanzeige^F
indicatore^M del funzionamento^M automatico

outgoing announcement cassette
casete^F con saludo^M
cassette^F annonce^F
Ansagekassette^F
cassetta^F del messaggio^M registrato

listen button
botón^M de reproducción^F
écoute^F
Mithörtaste^F
tasto^M di ascolto^M diretto

fast-forward button
botón^M de avance^F rápido
avance^F rapide
Vorlauftaste^F
tasto^M di avanzamento^M rapido

microphone
micrófono^M
microphone^M
Mikrofon^N
microfono^M

speaker
altavoz^M
haut-parleur^M
Lautsprecher^M
altoparlante^M

stop button
botón^M de stop^M
arrêt^M
Stopptaste^F
tasto^M di arresto^M

on/play button
botón^M de encendido
mise^F en marche^F
Einschalt-/Wiedergabetaste^F
tasto^M di riascolto^M dei messaggi^M

record announcement button
botón^M de grabación^F
enregistrement^M
Aufzeichnungstaste^F
tasto^M di registrazione^F del messaggio^M

erase button
botón^M para borrar
effacement^M
Löschtaste^F
tasto^M di cancellazione^F

rewind button
botón^M de rebobinado
rebobinage^M
Rücklauftaste^F
tasto^M di riavvolgimento^M

volume control
control^M del volumen^M
commande^F de volume^M
Lautstärkeregler^M
regolatore^M del volume^M

power-on button
botón^M de encendido
bouton^M de mise^F en circuit^M
Netzschalter^M
pulsante^M di accensione^F

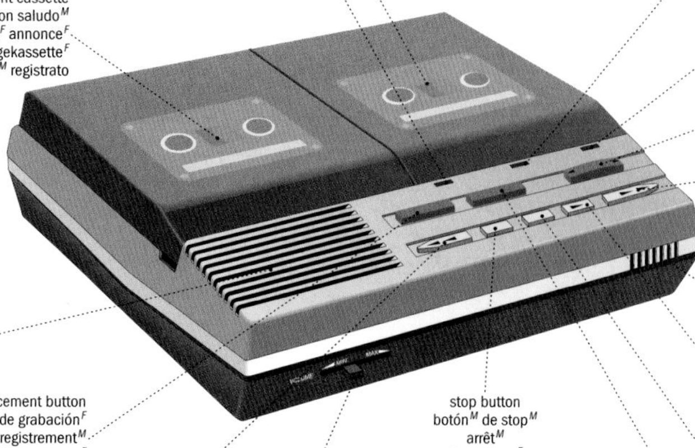

facsimile machine
fax^M
télécopieur^M
Telefaxgerät^N
telefax^M

sent document tray
recuperación^F del documento^M enviado
sortie^F des originaux^M
Originalrückführung^F
vassoio^M dei documenti^M trasmessi

receiving tray
recepción^F de documentos^M
réception^F des messages^M
Empfang^M von Dokumenten^N
vassoio^M dei documenti^M ricevuti

document-to-be-sent position
posición^F del documento^M a enviar
entrée^F des originaux^M
Originaleinzug^M
punto^M di inserimento^M dei documenti^M da trasmettere

function keys
teclas^F de función^F
panneau^M de fonctions^F
Funktionstasten^F
tasti^M funzione^F

paper guide
guía^F del papel^M
guide-papier^M
Papierführung^F
guida^F della carta^F

reset key
tecla^F de reiniciación^F
touche^F de correction^F
Rückstelltaste^F
tasto^M di reset^M

data display
visualización^F de datos^M
écran^M d'affichage^M
Datendisplay^N
display^M

start key
tecla^F de iniciación^M
mise^F en marche^F
Starttaste^F
tasto^M di avvio^M

control keys
teclas^F de control^M
panneau^M de commande^F
Bedienungstasten^F
tasti^M di comando^M

number key
teclado^M numérico
touche^F de composition^F automatique
Nummerntasten^F
tastiera^F numerica

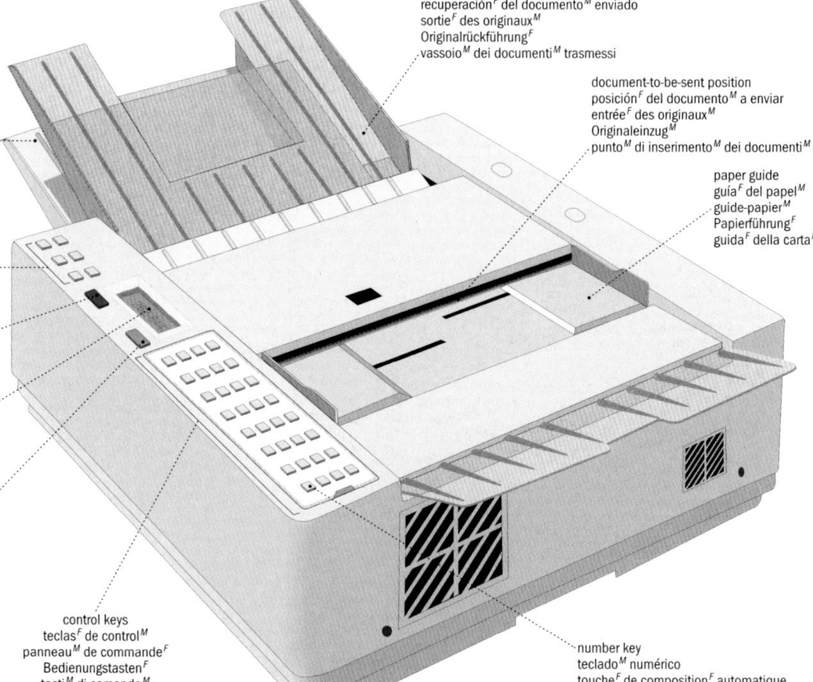

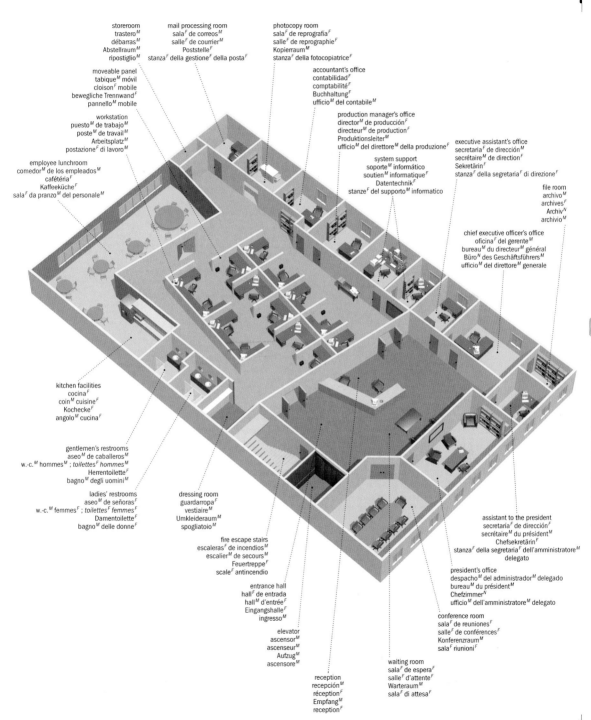

storeroom
trastero^M
débarras^M
Abstellraum^M
ripostiglio^M

mail processing room
sala^F de correos^M
salle^F de courrier^M
Poststelle^F
stanza^F della gestione^F della posta^F

photocopy room
sala^F de reprografía^F
salle^F de reprographie^F
Kopierraum^M
stanza^F della fotocopiatrice^F

accountant's office
contabilidad^F
comptabilité^F
Buchhaltung^F
ufficio^M del contabile^M

moveable panel
tabique^M móvil
cloison^F mobile
bewegliche Trennwand^F
pannello^M mobile

production manager's office
director^M de producción
directeur^M de production
Produktionsleiter^M
ufficio^M del direttore^M della produzione^F

workstation
puesto^M de trabajo^M
poste^M de travail^M
Arbeitsplatz^M
postazione^F di lavoro^M

executive assistant's office
secretaria^F de dirección
secrétaire^M de direction^F
Sekretärin^F
stanza^F della segretaria^F di direzione^F

system support
soporte^M informático
soutien^M informatique^F
Datentechnik^F
stanze^F del supporto^M informatico

employee lunchroom
comedor^M de los empleados^M
cafétéria^F
Kaffeeküche^F
sala^F da pranzo^M del personale^M

file room
archivo^M
archives^F
Archiv^N
archivio^M

chief executive officer's office
oficina^F del gerente
bureau^M du directeur^M général
Büro^N des Geschäftsführers^M
ufficio^M del direttore^M generale

kitchen facilities
cocina^F
coin^M cuisine^F
Kochecke^F
angolo^M cucina^F

gentlemen's restrooms
aseo^M de caballeros^M
w.-c.^M hommes^M ; toilettes^F hommes^M
Herrentoilette^F
bagno^M degli uomini^M

ladies' restrooms
aseo^M de señoras^F
w.-c.^M femmes^F ; toilettes^F femmes^F
Damentoilette^F
bagno^M delle donne^F

dressing room
guardarropa^F
vestiaire^M
Umkleideraum^M
spogliatoio^M

assistant to the president
secretaria^F de dirección^F
secrétaire^M du président^M
Chefsekretärin^F
stanza^F della segretaria^F dell'amministratore^M delegato

fire escape stairs
escaleras^F de incendios^M
escalier^M de secours^M
Feuertreppe^F
scale^F antincendio

president's office
despacho^M del administrador^M delegado
bureau^M du président^M
Chefzimmer^N
ufficio^M dell'amministratore^M delegato

entrance hall
hall^M de entrada
hall^M d'entrée^F
Eingangshalle^F
ingresso^M

conference room
sala^F de reuniones^F
salle^F de conférences^F
Konferenzraum^M
sala^F riunioni^F

elevator
ascensor^M
ascenseur^M
Aufzug^M
ascensore^M

reception
recepción^M
réception^F
Empfang^M
reception^F

waiting room
sala^F de espera^F
salle^F d'attente^F
Warteraum^M
sala^F di attesa^F

office furniture

muebles^M de oficina^F | mobilier^M de bureau^M | Büromöbel^N | mobili^M per ufficio^M

filing furniture
archivadores^M
meubles^M **de classement**^{M}
Archivmöbel^N
mobili^M **di archivio**^{M}

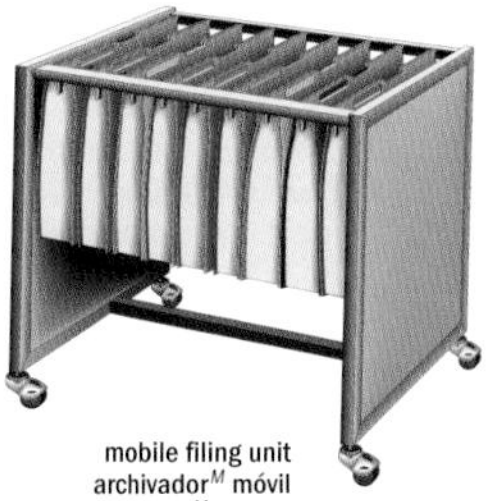

mobile filing unit
archivador^M móvil
classeur^M mobile
fahrbare Aktenablage^F
schedario^M mobile

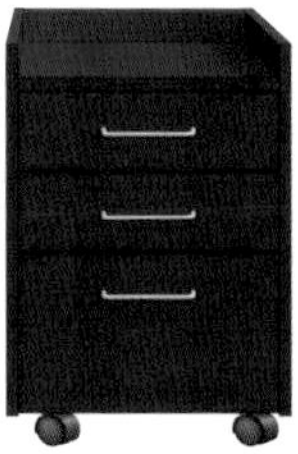

mobile drawer unit
cajonera^F móvil
caisson^M
fahrbares Schubladenelement^N
cassettiera^F mobile

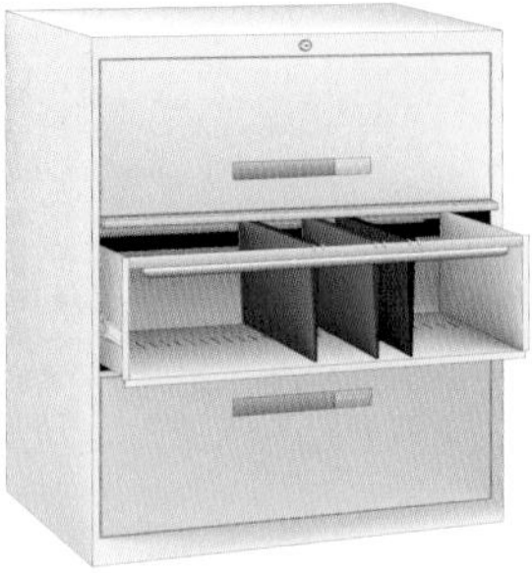

lateral filing cabinet
archivador^M lateral
classeur^M à clapets^M
Hängekartei^F
schedario^M a visibilità^F laterale

storage furniture
muebles^M **contenedores**
meubles^M **de rangement**^{M}
Aufbewahrungsmöbel^N
mobili^M **contenitori**^{M}

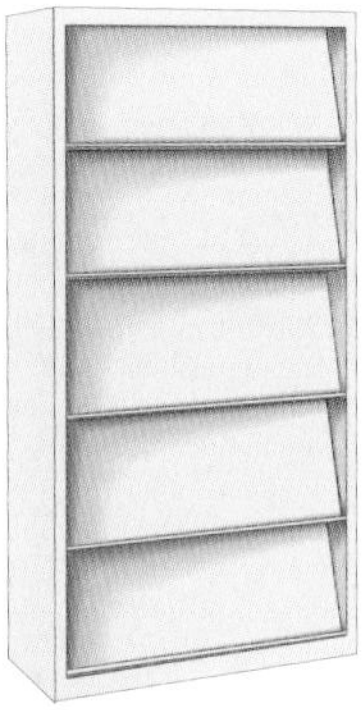

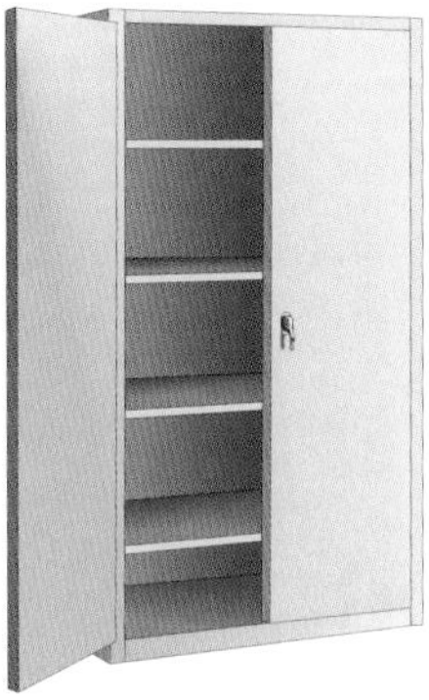

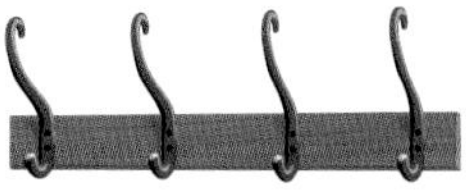

coat hooks
perchero^M de pared^F
patère^F
Kleiderhaken^M
attaccapanni^M a muro^M

display cabinet
estante^M para revistas^F
présentoir^M à revues^F
Ausstellungsregal^N
espositore^M

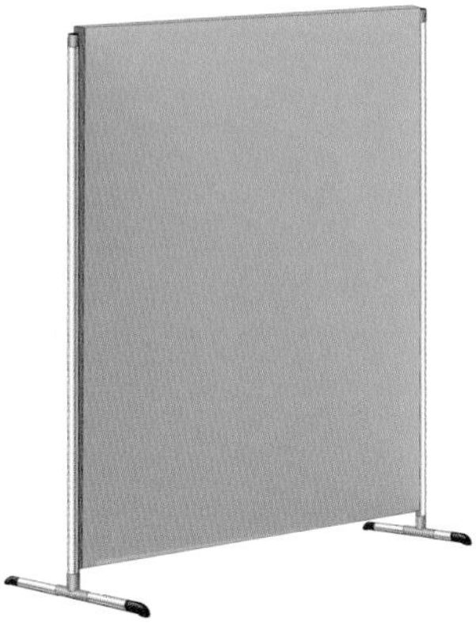

movable panel
tabique^M móvil
cloison^F mobile
flexible Trennwand^F
pannello^M mobile

stationery cabinet
armario^M para papelería^F
armoire^F à papeterie^F
Schrank^M
armadietto^M per cancelleria^F

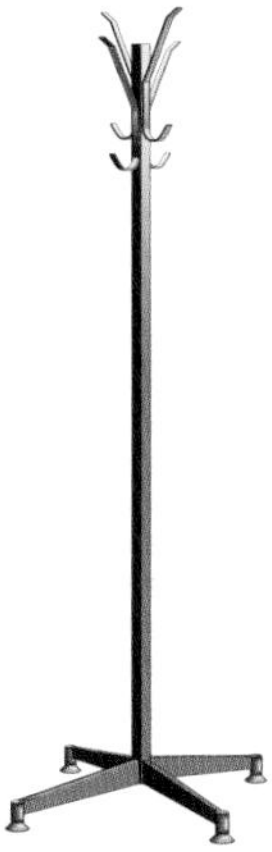

coat tree
perchero^M de pie^M
porte-manteau^M
Garderobenständer^M
attaccapanni^M a stelo^M

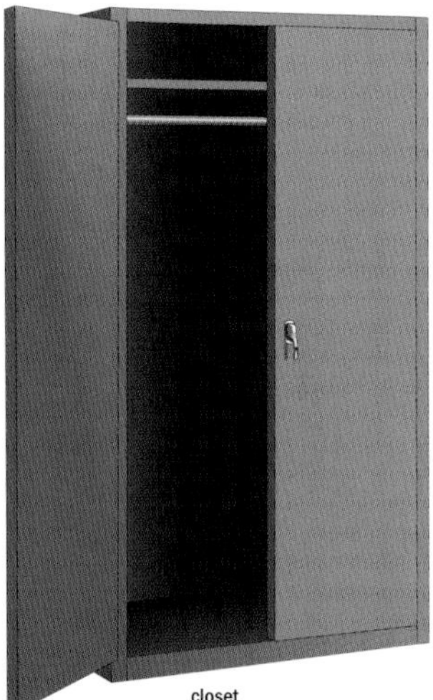

closet
guardarropa^M
armoire^F-vestiaire^M
Kleiderschrank^M
armadietto^M

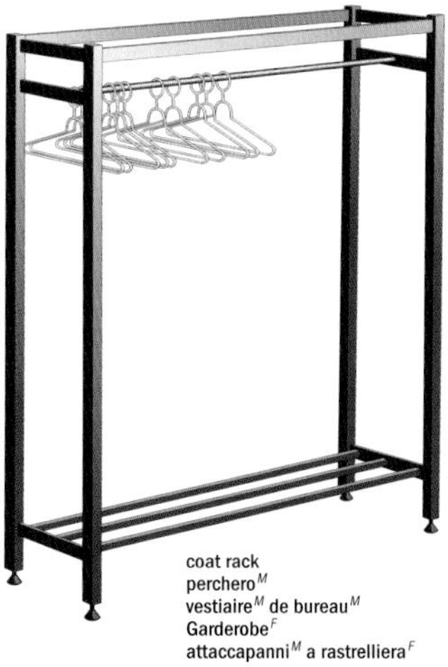

coat rack
perchero^M
vestiaire^M de bureau^M
Garderobe^F
attaccapanni^M a rastrelliera^F

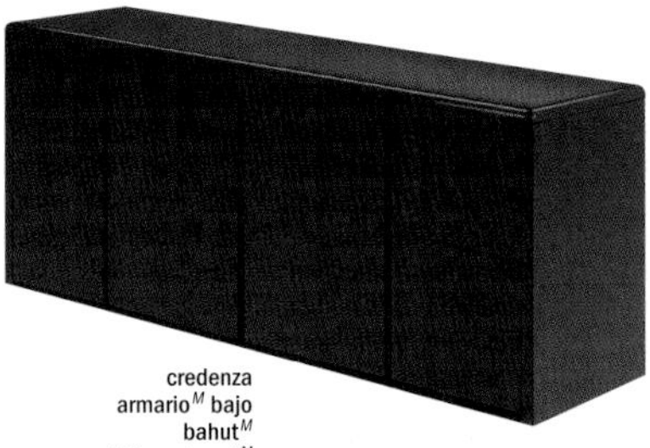

credenza
armario^M bajo
bahut^M
Aktenschrank^M
mobile^M contenitore

office furniture

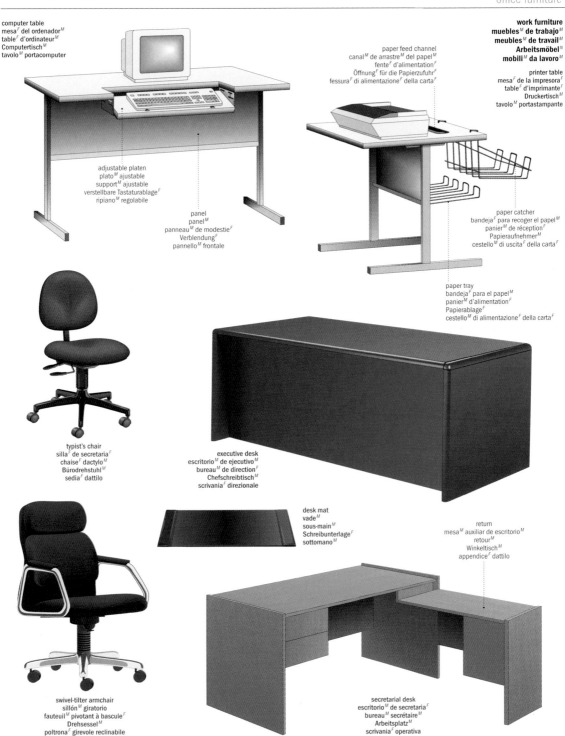

computer table
mesa^F del ordenador^M
table^F d'ordinateur^M
Computertisch^M
tavolo^M portacomputer

work furniture
muebles^M de trabajo^M
meubles^M de travail^M
Arbeitsmöbel^N
mobili^M da lavoro^M

paper feed channel
canal^M de arrastre^M del papel^M
fente^F d'alimentation^F
Öffnung^F für die Papierzufuhr^F
fessura^F di alimentazione^F della carta^F

printer table
mesa^F de la impresora^F
table^F d'imprimante^F
Druckertisch^M
tavolo^M portastampante

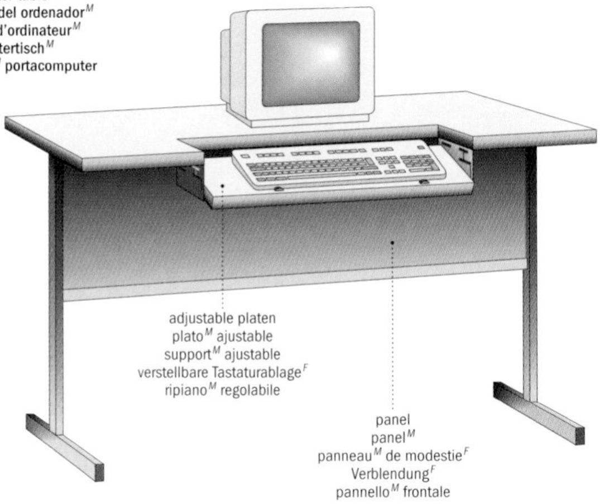

adjustable platen
plato^M ajustable
support^M ajustable
verstellbare Tastaturablage^F
ripiano^M regolabile

panel
panel^M
panneau^M de modestie^F
Verblendung^F
pannello^M frontale

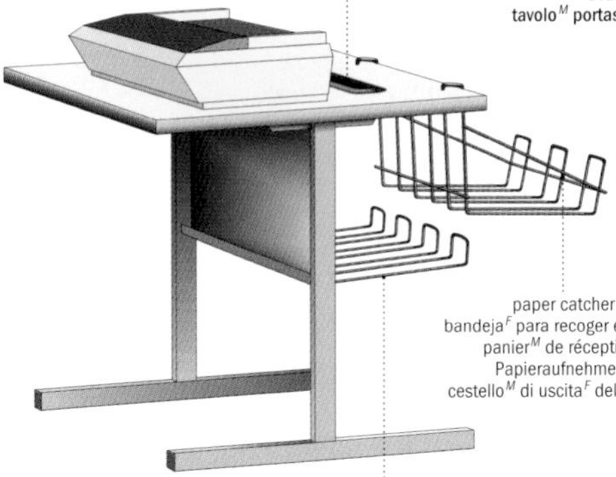

paper catcher
bandeja^F para recoger el papel^M
panier^M de réception^F
Papieraufnehmer^M
cestello^M di uscita^F della carta^F

paper tray
bandeja^F para el papel^M
panier^M d'alimentation^F
Papierablage^F
cestello^M di alimentazione^F della carta^F

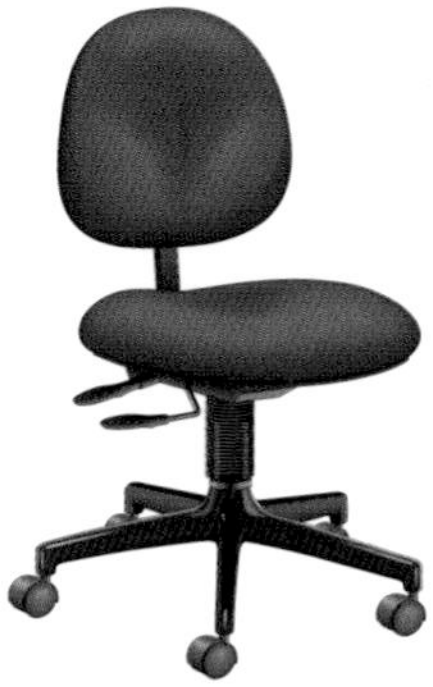

typist's chair
silla^F de secretaria^F
chaise^F dactylo^M
Bürodrehstuhl^M
sedia^F dattilo

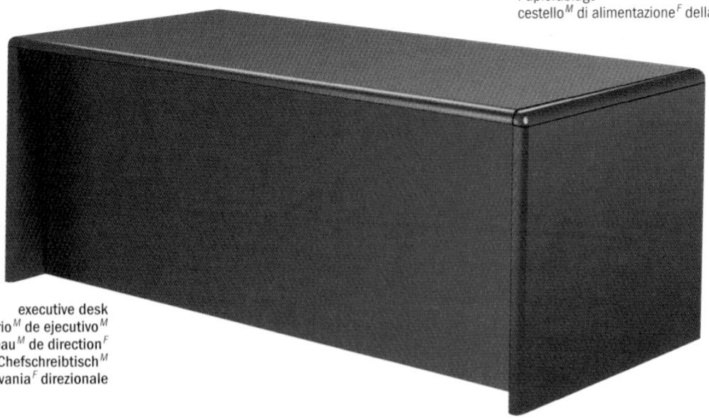

executive desk
escritorio^M de ejecutivo^M
bureau^M de direction^F
Chefschreibtisch^M
scrivania^F direzionale

desk mat
vade^M
sous-main^M
Schreibunterlage^F
sottomano^M

return
mesa^M auxiliar de escritorio^M
retour^M
Winkeltisch^M
appendice^F dattilo

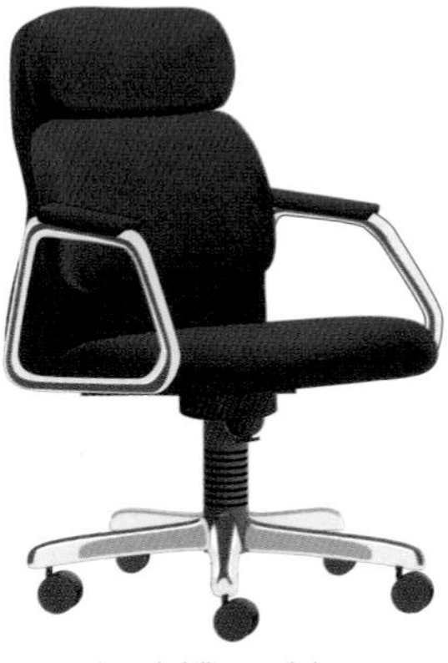

swivel-tilter armchair
sillón^M giratorio
fauteuil^M pivotant à bascule^F
Drehsessel^M
poltrona^F girevole reclinabile

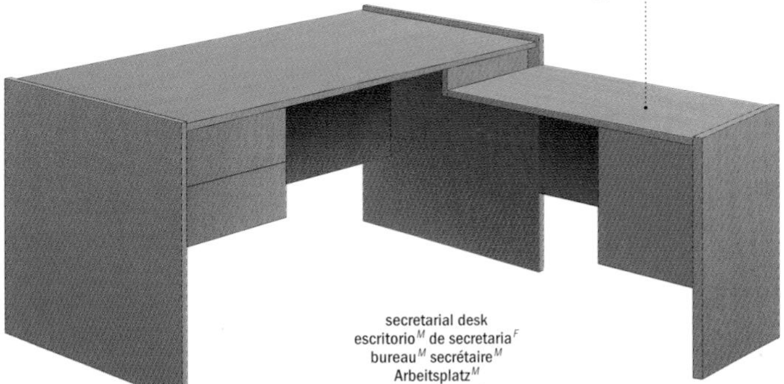

secretarial desk
escritorio^M de secretaria^F
bureau^M secrétaire^M
Arbeitsplatz^M
scrivania^F operativa

COMMUNICATIONS AND OFFICE AUTOMATION

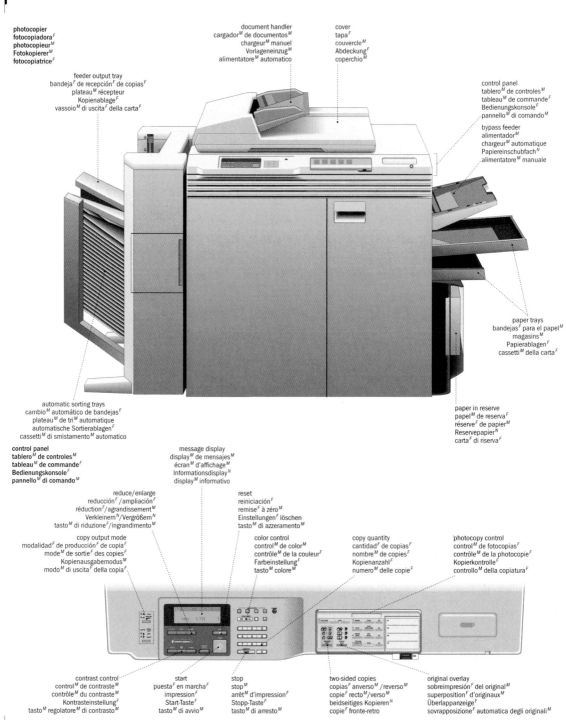

photocopier
fotocopiadora^F
photocopieur^M
Fotokopierer^M
fotocopiatrice^F

document handler
cargador^M de documentos^M
chargeur^M manuel
Vorlageneinzug^M
alimentatore^M automatico

cover
tapa^F
couvercle^M
Abdeckung^F
coperchio^M

feeder output tray
bandeja^F de recepción^F de copias^F
plateau^M récepteur
Kopienablage^F
vassoio^M di uscita^F della carta^F

control panel
tablero^M de controles^M
tableau^M de commande^F
Bedienungskonsole^F
pannello^M di comando^M

bypass feeder
alimentador^M
chargeur^M automatique
Papiereinschubfach^N
alimentatore^M manuale

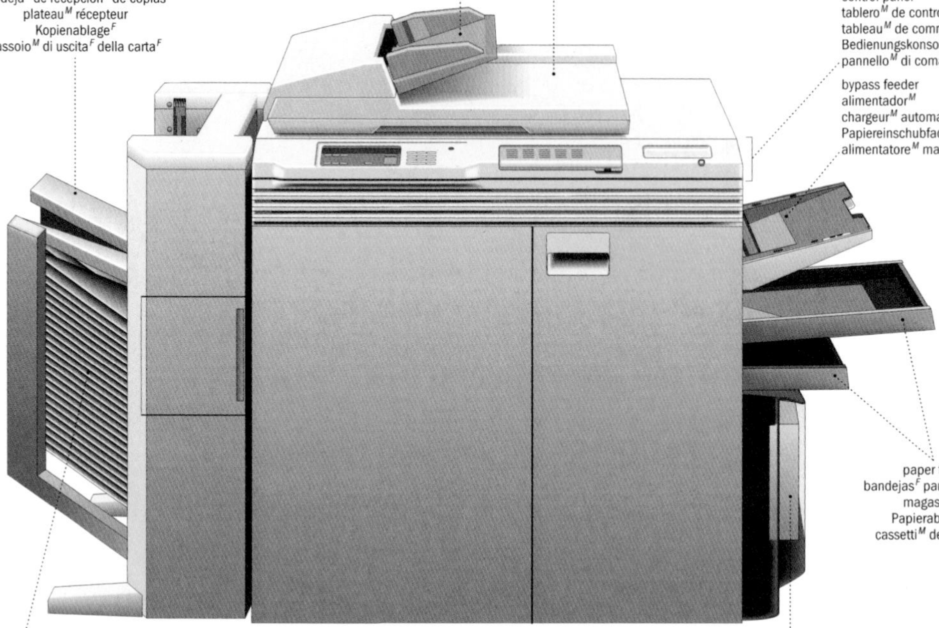

paper trays
bandejas^F para el papel^M
magasins^M
Papierablagen^F
cassetti^M della carta^F

paper in reserve
papel^M de reserva^F
réserve^F de papier^M
Reservepapier^N
carta^F di riserva^F

automatic sorting trays
cambio^M automático de bandejas^F
plateau^M de tri^M automatique
automatische Sortierablagen^F
cassetti^M di smistamento^M automatico

control panel
tablero^M de controles^M
tableau^M de commande^F
Bedienungskonsole^F
pannello^M di comando^M

message display
display^M de mensajes^M
écran^M d'affichage^M
Informationsdisplay^N
display^M informativo

reduce/enlarge
reducción^F/ampliación^F
réduction^F/agrandissement^M
Verkleinern^N/Vergrößern^N
tasto^M di riduzione^F/ingrandimento^M

reset
reiniciación^F
remise^F à zéro^M
Einstellungen^F löschen
tasto^M di azzeramento^M

copy output mode
modalidad^F de producción^F de copia^F
mode^M de sortie^F des copies^F
Kopienausgabemodus^M
modo^M di uscita^F della copia^F

color control
control^M de color^M
contrôle^M de la couleur^F
Farbeinstellung^F
tasto^M colore^M

copy quantity
cantidad^F de copias^F
nombre^M de copies^F
Kopienanzahl^F
numero^M delle copie^F

photocopy control
control^M de fotocopias^F
contrôle^M de la photocopie^F
Kopierkontrolle^F
controllo^M della copiatura^F

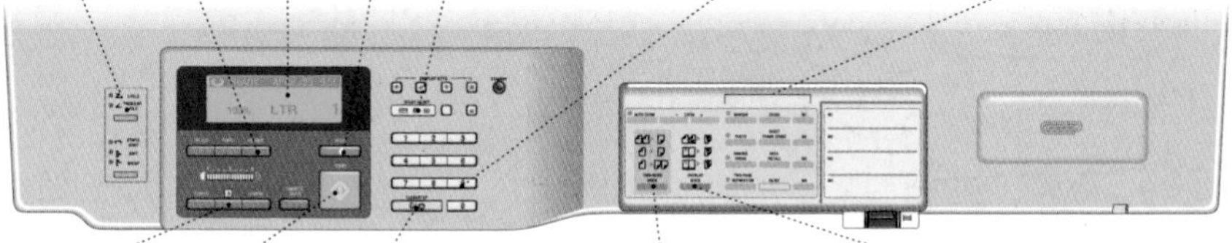

contrast control
control^M de contraste^M
contrôle^M du contraste^M
Kontrasteinstellung^F
tasto^M regolatore^M di contrasto^M

start
puesta^F en marcha^F
impression^F
Start-Taste^F
tasto^M di avvio^M

stop
stop^M
arrêt^M d'impression^F
Stopp-Taste^F
tasto^M di arresto^M

two-sided copies
copias^F anverso^F/reverso^M
copie^F recto^M/verso^M
beidseitiges Kopieren^N
copie^F fronte-retro

original overlay
sobreimpresión^F del original^M
superposition^F d'originaux^M
Überlappanzeige^F
sovrapposizione^F automatica degli originali^M

COMMUNICATIONS AND OFFICE AUTOMATION

personal computer

ordenador^M personal | micro-ordinateur^M | Personalcomputer^M | personal computer^M

tower case: back view
ordenador^M : vista^F posterior
boîtier^M tour^F : vue^F arrière
Towergehäuse^N: Rückansicht^F
châssis^M: dorso^M

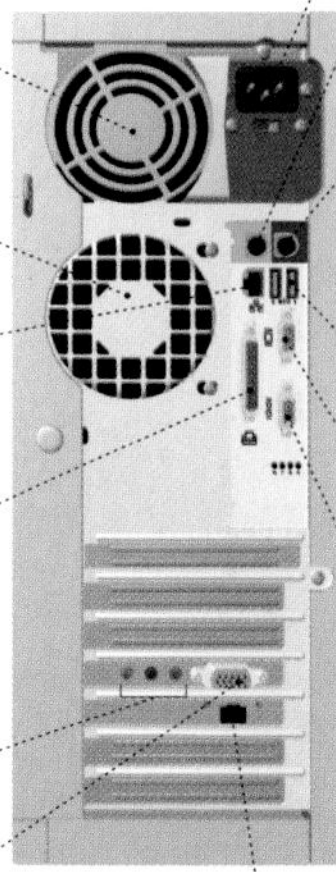

power supply fan
ventilador^M del equipo^M de alimentación^F
ventilateur^M du bloc^M d'alimentation^F
Netzteillüfter^M
ventola^F dell'alimentatore^M

case fan
ventilador^M de la carcasa^F
ventilateur^M du boîtier^M
Gehäuselüfter^M
ventola^F dello châssis^M

network port
puerto^M de red^F
port^M réseau^M
Netzwerkschnittstelle^F
porta^F di rete^F

parallel port
puerto^M paralelo
port^M parallèle
Parallelschnittstelle^F
porta^F parallela

audio jack
toma^F audio
prise^F audio
Audiobuchse^F
presa^F audio

game/MIDI port
puerto^M juego^M/puerto^M MIDI
port^M jeux^M/MIDI
Spiele^N-/MIDI-Schnittstelle^F
porta^F giochi^M/ porta^F MIDI

power cable plug
toma^F de alimentación^F
prise^F d'alimentation^F
Netzanschlussbuchse^F
presa^F di alimentazione^F

mouse port
puerto^M ratón
port^M souris^F
Mausschnittstelle^F
porta^F del mouse^M

keyboard port
puerto^M teclado
port^M clavier^M
Tastaturschnittstelle^F
porta^F della tastiera^F

earphone jack
toma^F de auriculares^M
prise^F pour écouteurs^M
Kopfhöreranschlussbuchse^F
presa^F per cuffie^F

bay filler panel
panel^M de cierre^M
obturateur^M de baie^F
Schutzdeckel^M
otturatore^M

USB port
puerto^M USB
port^M USB
USB-Schnittstelle^F
porta^F USB

video port
puerto^M de vídeo^M
port^M vidéo
Videoschnittstelle^F
porta^F video^M

serial port
puerto^M serial
port^M série
serielle Schnittstelle^F
porta^F seriale

internal modem port
puerto^M de módem^M interno
port^M modem^M interne
interne Modemschnittstelle^F
porta^F del modem^M interno

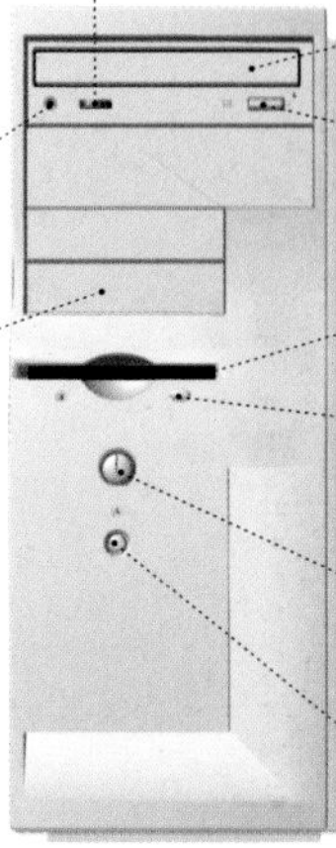

volume control
control^M de volumen^M
réglage^M du volume^M
Lautstärkeregler^M
rotella^F del volume^M

tower case: front view
ordenador^M : vista^F frontal
boîtier^M tour^F : vue^F avant
Towergehäuse^N: Vorderansicht^F
châssis^M: vista^F frontale

CD/DVD-ROM drive
unidad^F de CD/DVD-ROM
lecteur^M de CD/DVD-ROM
CD^F-/DVD^F-Laufwerk^N
lettore^M CD^M/DVD-ROM^M

CD/DVD-ROM eject button
botón^M de expulsión de CD/DVD-ROM
bouton^M d'éjection^F du CD/DVD-ROM^M
CD^F-/DVD^F-Auswurftaste^F
pulsante^M di espulsione^F del CD^M/DVD-ROM^M

floppy disk drive
unidad^F de disquete^M
lecteur^M de disquette^F
Diskettenlaufwerk^N
unità^F floppy disk^M

floppy disk eject button
botón^M de expulsión de disquete^M
bouton^M d'éjection^F de la disquette^F
Disketten-Auswurftaste^F
pulsante^M di espulsione^F del floppy disk^M

power button
interruptor^M de encendido
bouton^M de démarrage^M
Ein-/Ausschalter^M
interruttore^M di accensione^F

reset button
botón^M de reiniciación^F
bouton^M de réinitialisation^F
Resettaste^F
pulsante^M di reset^M

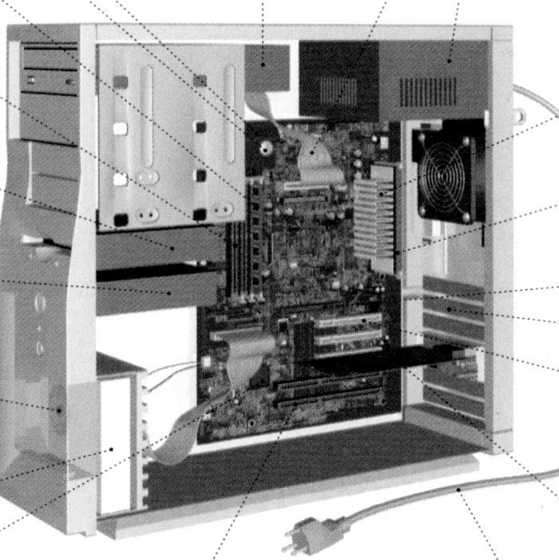

battery
batería^F
pile^F
Akku^M
pila^F

motherboard
tarjeta^F madre
carte^F mère^F
Motherboard^N
scheda^F madre^F

bus
bus^M
bus^M
Bus^M
bus^M

tower case: interior view
ordenador^M : vista^F interna
boîtier^M tour^F : vue^F intérieure
Towergehäuse^N: Innenansicht^F
châssis^M: interno^M

random access memory (RAM) module
unidad^F de memoria^F de acceso^M aleatorio (RAM)
barrette^F de mémoire^F vive (RAM)
Schreib-Lese-Speicher^M (RAM^M)
modulo^M RAM^F

RAM connector
conector^M de RAM
connecteur^M de mémoire^F vive
RAM^M-Anschluss^M
connettore^M RAM^F

floppy disk drive
unidad^F de disquetes^M
lecteur^M de disquette^F
Diskettenlaufwerk^N
unità^F floppy disk^M

secondary hard disk drive
unidad^F secundaria de disco^M duro
lecteur^M de disque^M dur secondaire
zusätzliches Festplattenlaufwerk^N
unità^F hard disk^M secondaria

speaker
altavoz^M
haut-parleur^M
Lautsprecher^M
altoparlante^M

primary hard disk drive
unidad^F de disco^M duro primario
lecteur^M de disque^M dur primaire
Hauptfestplattenlaufwerk^N
unità^F hard disk^M principale

chipset
chipset^M
jeu^M de puces^F
Chipset^N
chipset^M

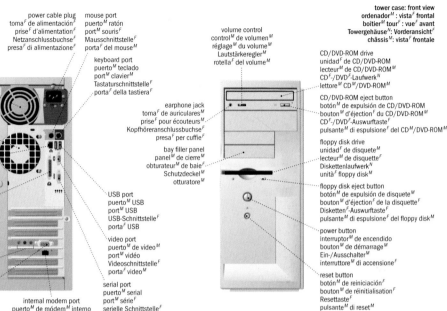

CD/DVD-ROM drive
unidad^F CD/DVD-ROM
lecteur^M de CD/DVD-ROM^M
CD^F-/DVD^F-Laufwerk^N
lettore^M CD^M/DVD-ROM^M

power supply unit
unidad^F de grupo^M de la alimentación^F
bloc^M d'alimentation^F
Netzteil^N
alimentatore^M

heat sink
disipador^M térmico
dissipateur^M thermique
Wärmesenke^F
dissipatore^M termico

processor
procesador^M
processeur^M
Prozessor^M
processore^M

AGP expansion connector
conector^M de expansión^F AGP
connecteur^M d'extension^F AGP
AGP-Erweiterungsport^M
connettore^M per espansioni^F AGP

filler plate
obturador^M
obturateur^M
Schutzdeckel^M
otturatore^M

PCI expansion connector
conector^M de expansión^F PCI
connecteur^M d'extension^F PCI
PCI-Erweiterungsport^M
connettore^M per espansioni^F PCI

PCI expansion card
tarjeta^F de expansión^F PCI
carte^F d'extension^F PCI
PCI-Erweiterungskarte^F
scheda^F di espansione^F PCI

ISA expansion connector
conector^M de extensión^F ISA
connecteur^M d'extension^F ISA
ISA-Erweiterungsport^M
connettore^M per espansioni^F ISA

power cable
cable^M de alimentación^F
câble^M d'alimentation^F
Netzkabel^N
cavo^M di alimentazione^F

COMMUNICATIONS AND OFFICE AUTOMATION

input devices

unidades^F de entrada^F de información^F | périphériques^M d'entrée^F | Eingabegeräte^N | dispositivi^M di entrata^F

keyboard and pictograms
teclado^M y pictogramas^M
clavier^M et pictogrammes^M
Tastatur^F und Piktogramme^N
tastiera^F e pittogrammi^M

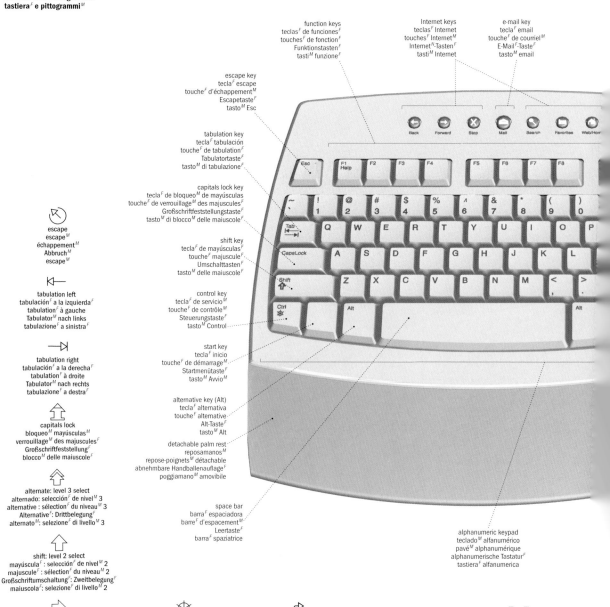

function keys
teclas^F de funciones^F
touches^F de fonction^F
Funktionstasten^F
tasti^M funzione^F

Internet keys
teclas^F Internet
touches^F Internet^M
Internet^N-Tasten^F
tasti^M Internet

e-mail key
tecla^F email
touche^F de courriel^M
E-Mail^F-Taste^F
tasto^M email

escape key
tecla^F escape
touche^F d'échappement^M
Escapetaste^F
tasto^M Esc

tabulation key
tecla^F tabulación
touche^F de tabulation^F
Tabulatortaste^F
tasto^M di tabulazione^F

capitals lock key
tecla^F de bloqueo^M de mayúsculas
touche^F de verrouillage^M des majuscules
Großschriftfeststellungstaste^F
tasto^M di blocco^M delle maiuscole^F

escape
escape^M
échappement^M
Abbruch^M
escape^M

shift key
tecla^F de mayúsculas^F
touche^F majuscule^F
Umschalttasten^F
tasto^M delle maiuscole^F

tabulation left
tabulación^F a la izquierda^F
tabulation^F à gauche
Tabulator^M nach links
tabulazione^F a sinistra^F

control key
tecla^F de servicio^M
touche^F de contrôle^M
Steuerungstaste^F
tasto^M Control

tabulation right
tabulación^F a la derecha^F
tabulation^F à droite
Tabulator^M nach rechts
tabulazione^F a destra^F

start key
tecla^F inicio
touche^F de démarrage^M
Startmenütaste^F
tasto^M Avvio^M

capitals lock
bloqueo^M mayúsculas^M
verrouillage^M des majuscules^F
Großschriftfeststellung^F
blocco^M delle maiuscole^F

alternative key (Alt)
tecla^F alternativa
touche^F alternative^F
Alt-Taste^F
tasto^M Alt

detachable palm rest
reposamanos^M
repose-poignets^M détachable
abnehmbare Handballenauflage^F
poggiamano^M amovibile

alternate: level 3 select
alternado: selección^F de nivel^M 3
alternative : sélection^F du niveau^M 3
Alternative^F: Drittbelegung^F
alternato^M: selezione^F di livello^M 3

space bar
barra^F espaciadora
barre^F d'espacement^M
Leertaste^F
barra^F spaziatrice

alphanumeric keypad
teclado^M alfanumérico
pavé^M alphanumérique
alphanumerische Tastatur^F
tastiera^F alfanumerica

shift: level 2 select
mayúscula^F : selección^F de nivel^M 2
majuscule^F : sélection^F du niveau^M 2
Großschriftumschaltung^F: Zweitbelegung^F
maiuscola^F: selezione^F di livello^M 2

control: group select
control^M : selección^F de grupo^M
contrôle^M : sélection^F de groupe^M
Steuerung^F: Gruppenwahl^F
controllo^M: selezione^F di gruppo^M

control
control^M
contrôle^M
Steuerung^F
controllo^M

alternate
alternativa^F
alternative
Alternative^F
alternato^M

space
espacio^M
espace^F
Leerzeichen^N
spazio^M

nonbreaking space
espacio^M sin pausa^F
espace^F insécable
geschütztes Leerzeichen^N
spazio^M unificatore

print screen/system request key
tecla^F de impresión^M pantalla/petición^F del sistema^F
touche^F d'impression^F de l'écran^M/d'appel^M système^M
Taste^F Druck^M/Systemabfrage^F
tasto^M di stampa^F/chiamata^F sistema^M

backspace key
tecla^F de retroceso^M
touche^F d'effacement^M
Taste^F löschender Rückschritt^M
tasto^M backspace

indicator lights
luces^F de estado^M
voyants^M
Kontrollleuchten^F
spie^F luminose

scrolling lock key
bloqueo^M corrimiento^M
touche^F d'arrêt^M du défilement^M
Scrollen^N-Feststelltaste^F
tasto^M di arresto^M e di scorrimento^M

insert key
insert^M
touche^F d'insertion^F
Einfügetaste^F
tasto^M Ins

pause/break key
tecla^F pausa
touche^F de pause^F/d'interruption^F
Taste^F Pause^F/Unterbrechung^F
tasto^M di pausa^F/interruzione^F

home key
inicio^M
touche^F début^M
Taste^F Cursor^M an Zeilenanfang^M
tasto^M Home

numeric lock key
tecla^F bloqueo^M numérico
touche^F de verrouillage^M numérique
Taste^F numerischer Block^M
tasto^M di blocco^M numerico

page up key
página^F atrás
touche^F page^F précédente
Taste^F vorherige Seite^F
tasto^M di pagina^F su

page down key
página^F adelante
touche^F page^F suivante
Taste^F nächste Seite^F
tasto^M di pagina^F giù

enter key
tecla^F de enter
touche^F de retour^M
Eingabetaste^F
tasto^M Invio^M

end key
fin^M
touche^F fin^F
Taste^F Ende^F
tasto^M Fine^F

numeric keypad
teclado^M numérico
pavé^M numérique
numerisches Tastenfeld^N
tastierino^M numerico

enter key
tecla^F de enter
touche^F de retour^M
Eingabetaste^F
tasto^M Invio^M

cursor movement keys
teclas^F de cursor
touches^F de déplacement^M du curseur^M
Richtungstasten^F
tasti^M del cursore^M

delete key
suprimir
touche^F de suppression^F
Löschtaste^F
tasto^M di cancellazione^F

pause
pausa^F
pause^F
Pause^F
pausa^F

break
pausa^F
interruption^F
Unterbrechung^F
interruzione^F

numeric lock
bloqueo^M numérico
verrouillage^M numérique
numerischer Block^M
blocco^M numerico

scrolling
desplazamiento^M
défilement^M
Scrollen^N
scorrimento^M

insert
insertar
insertion^F
Einfügen^N
inserimento^M

delete
borrar
suppression^F
Löschen^N
cancellazione^F

home
inicio^M
début^M
Cursor^M an Zeilenanfang^M
home^F

end
fin^M
fin^F
Cursor^M an Zeilenende^N
fine^F

page up
ventana^F arriba
page^F précédente
vorherige Seite^F
pagina^F precedente

page down
ventana^F abajo
page^F suivante
nächste Seite^F
pagina^F successiva

backspace
retroceso^M
effacement^M arrière : effacement^M
löschender Rückschritt^M
backspace^M

print screen
impresión^F pantalla^F
impression^F de l'écran^M
Bildschirminhalt^M drucken
stampa^F

cursor left
cursor^M hacia la izquierda^F
curseur^M vers la gauche^F
Cursor^M nach links
cursore^M a sinistra^F

cursor right
cursor^M hacia la derecha^F
curseur^M vers la droite^F
Cursor^M nach rechts
cursore^M a destra^F

cursor up
cursor^M arriba
curseur^M vers le haut^M
Cursor^M nach oben
cursore^M in alto^M

cursor down
cursor^M abajo
curseur^M vers le bas^M
Cursor^M nach unten
cursore^M in basso^M

return
retorno^M
retour^M
Eingabe^F
invio^M

input devices

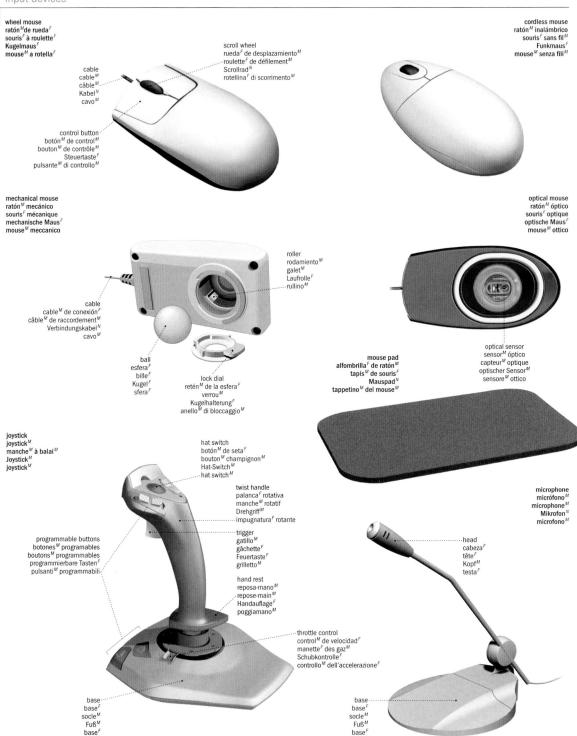

wheel mouse
ratón^M de rueda^F
souris^F à roulette^F
Kugelmaus^F
mouse^M a rotella^F

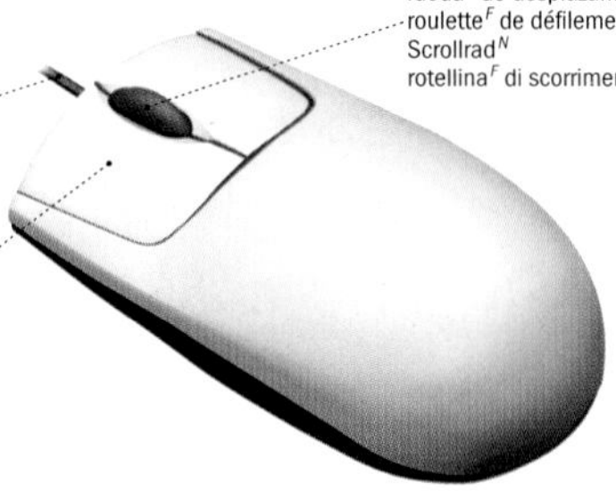

cordless mouse
ratón^M inalámbrico
souris^F sans fil^M
Funkmaus^F
mouse^M senza fili^M

scroll wheel
rueda^F de desplazamiento^M
roulette^F de défilement^M
Scrollrad^N
rotellina^F di scorrimento^M

cable
cable^M
câble^M
Kabel^N
cavo^M

control button
botón^M de control^M
bouton^M de contrôle^M
Steuertaste^F
pulsante^M di controllo^M

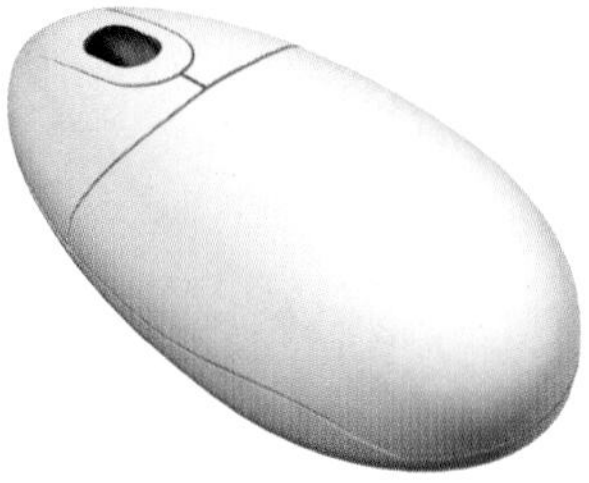

mechanical mouse
ratón^M mecánico
souris^F mécanique
mechanische Maus^F
mouse^M meccanico

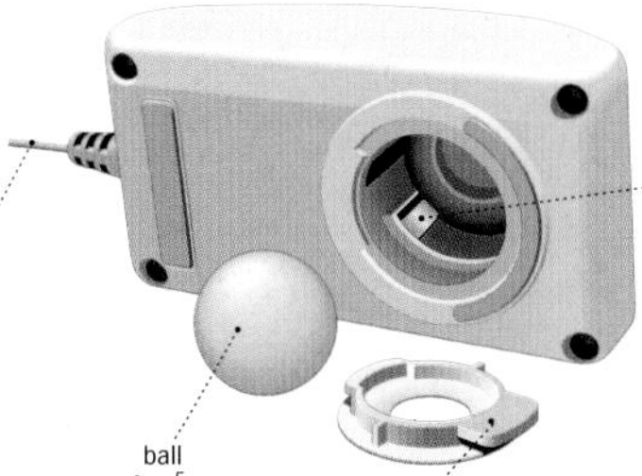

optical mouse
ratón^M óptico
souris^F optique
optische Maus^F
mouse^M ottico

roller
rodamiento^M
galet^M
Laufrolle^F
rullino^M

cable
cable^M de conexión^F
câble^M de raccordement^M
Verbindungskabel^N
cavo^M

ball
esfera^F
bille^F
Kugel^F
sfera^F

lock dial
retén^M de la esfera^F
verrou^M
Kugelhalterung^F
anello^M di bloccaggio^M

optical sensor
sensor^M óptico
capteur^M optique
optischer Sensor^M
sensore^M ottico

mouse pad
alfombrilla^F de ratón^M
tapis^M de souris^F
Mauspad^N
tappetino^M del mouse^M

joystick
joystick^M
manche^M à balai^M
Joystick^M
joystick^M

hat switch
botón^M de seta^F
bouton^M champignon^M
Hat-Switch^M
hat switch^M

twist handle
palanca^F rotativa
manche^M rotatif
Drehgriff^M
impugnatura^F rotante

programmable buttons
botones^M programables
boutons^M programmables
programmierbare Tasten^F
pulsanti^M programmabili

trigger
gatillo^M
gâchette^F
Feuertaste^F
grilletto^M

hand rest
reposa-mano^M
repose-main^M
Handauflage^F
poggiamano^M

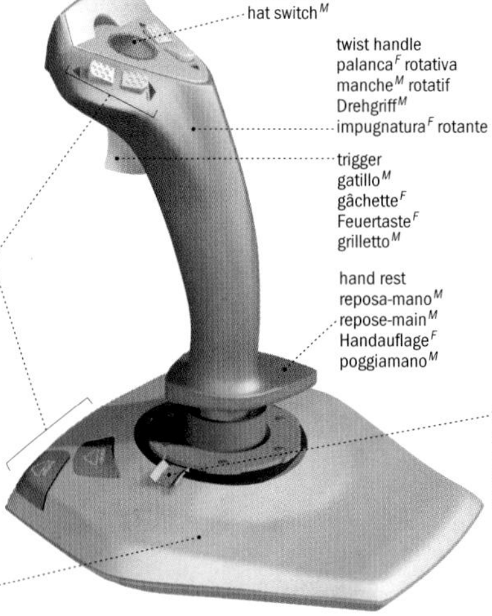

microphone
micrófono^M
microphone^M
Mikrofon^N
microfono^M

head
cabeza^F
tête^F
Kopf^M
testa^F

throttle control
control^M de velocidad^F
manette^F des gaz^M
Schubkontrolle^F
controllo^M dell'accelerazione^F

base
base^F
socle^M
Fuß^M
base^F

base
base^F
socle^M
Fuß^M
base^F

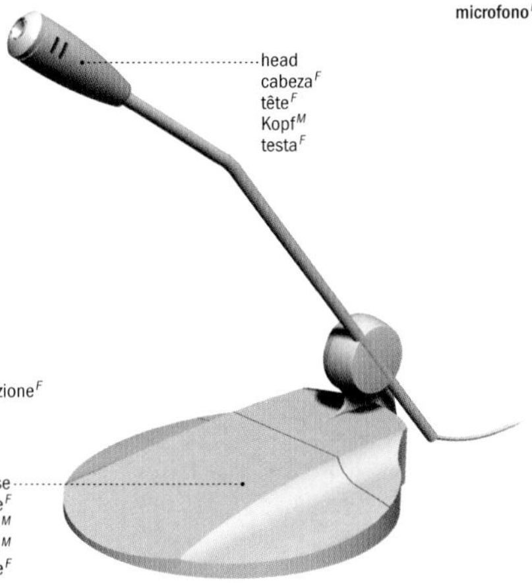

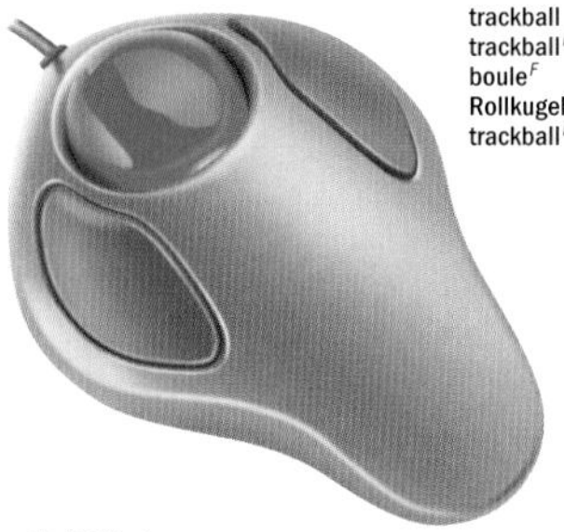

trackball
trackball[M]
boule[F]
Rollkugel[F]
trackball[M]

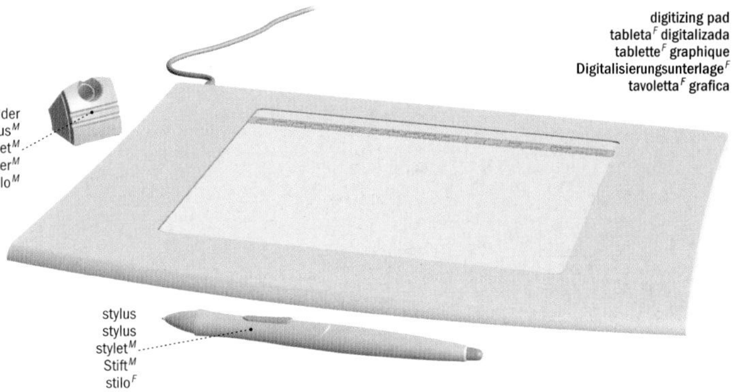

digitizing pad
tableta[F] digitalizada
tablette[F] graphique
Digitalisierungsunterlage[F]
tavoletta[F] grafica

stylus holder
porta stilus[M]
porte-stylet[M]
Stifthalter[M]
portastilo[M]

CD/ROM player
lector[M] de CD-ROM
lecteur[M] de disque[M] compact
CD-ROM-Laufwerk[N]
lettore[M] di compact disc[M]

stylus
stylus
stylet[M]
Stift[M]
stilo[F]

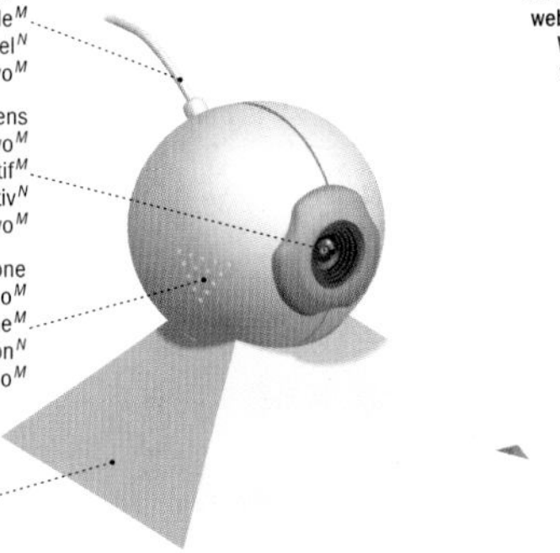

cable
cable[M]
câble[M]
Kabel[N]
cavo[M]

Webcam
cámara[F] web
webcaméra[F]
Webcam[F]
webcam[F]

lens
objetivo[M]
objectif[M]
Objektiv[N]
obiettivo[M]

microphone
micrófono[M]
microphone[M]
Mikrofon[N]
microfono[M]

base
base[F]
socle[M]
Fuß[M]
base[F]

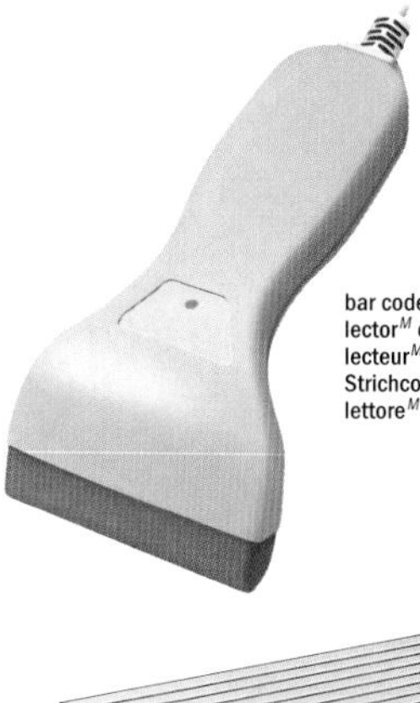

bar code reader
lector[M] de código[M] de barras[M]
lecteur[M] de code-barres[M]
Strichcodeleser[M]
lettore[M] dei codici[M] a barre[F]

digital camera
cámara[F] digital
appareil[M] numérique
Digitalkamera[F]
macchina[F] fotografica digitale

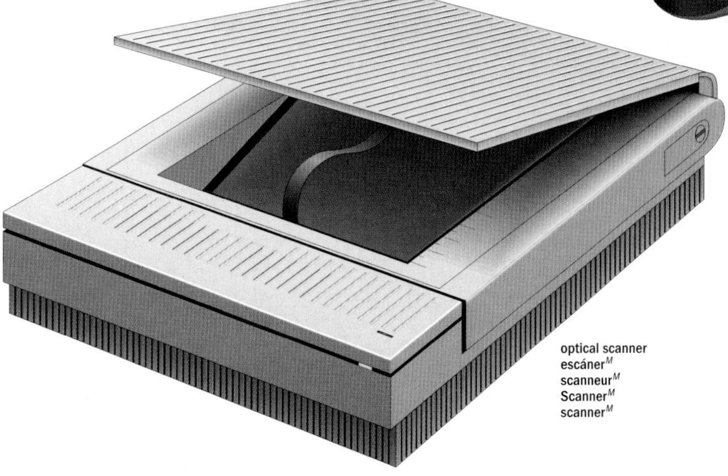

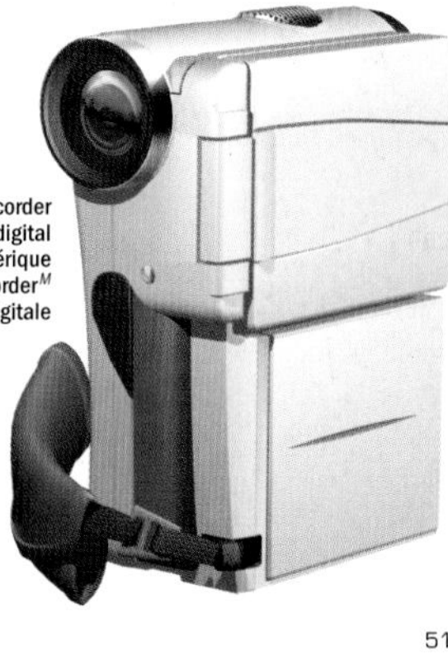

digital camcorder
camcorder[F] digital
caméscope[M] numérique
Digital-Camcorder[M]
videocamera[F] digitale

optical scanner
escáner[M]
scanneur[M]
Scanner[M]
scanner[M]

output devices

unidades^F de salida^F de información^F | périphériques^M de sortie^F | Ausgabegeräte^N | dispositivi^M di uscita^F

flat screen monitor
pantalla^F plana
écran^M plat
Flachbildschirm^M
monitor^M a schermo^M piatto

video monitor
monitor^M de video^M
écran^M
Bildschirm^M
monitor^M

vertical control
control^M vertical
réglage^M vertical
vertikale Einstellung^F
regolazione^F verticale

horizontal control
control^M horizontal
réglage^M horizontal
horizontale Einstellung^F
regolazione^F orizzontale

centering control
control^M de centrado^M
réglage^M de centrage^M
Zentriereinstellung^F
regolatore^M di centratura^F

contrast control
control^M de contraste^M
réglage^M du contraste^M
Kontrastregler^M
regolatore^M di contrasto^M

power indicator
indicador^M de encendido
témoin^M d'alimentation^F
Leuchtanzeige^F
spia^F di alimentazione^F

power switch
interruptor^M
interrupteur^M
Netzschalter^M
interruttore^M di accensione^F

brightness control
control^M de brillo^M
réglage^M de la luminosité^F
Helligkeitsregler^M
regolatore^M di luminosità^F

projector
digital proyector^M
vidéoprojecteur^M
Projektor^M
proiettore^M

control panel
panel^M de control^M
panneau^M de contrôle^M
Bedienfeld^N
pannello^M di controllo^M

lens
objetivo^M
objectif^M
Objektiv^N
obiettivo^M

remote sensor
sensor infrarrojos
capteur^M infrarouge^M
Infrarotsensor^M
telesensore^M

power switch
interruptor^M de encendido
interrupteur^M d'alimentation^F
Ein-/Ausschalter^M
interruttore^M di accensione^F

connector panel
panel^M de conexión^F
panneau^M de connexions^F
Anschlussfeld^N
pannello^M di connessione^F

computer connector
conector^M del ordenador^M
entrée^F informatique
Computeranschlussbuchse^F
ingresso^M per il computer^M

mouse port
conector^M del ratón^M
port^M souris^F
Mausschnittstelle^F
porta^F del mouse^M

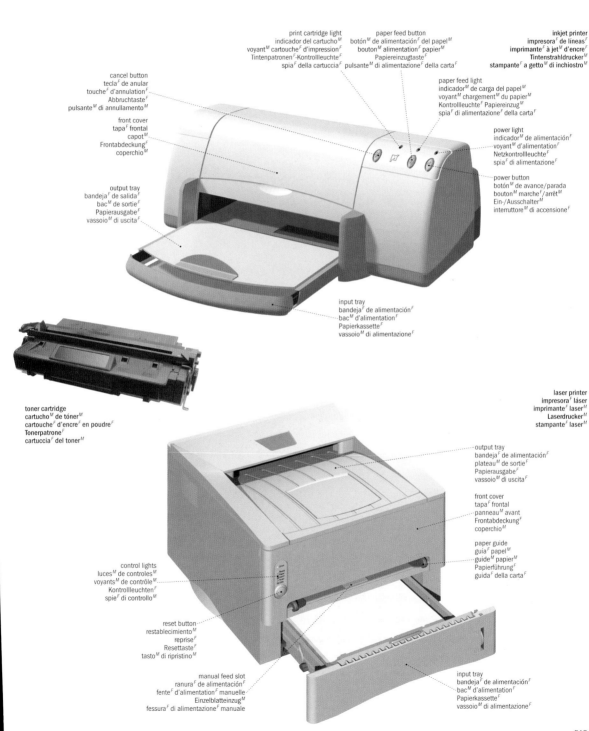

print cartridge light
indicador del cartucho^M
voyant^M cartouche^F d'impression^F
Tintenpatronen^F-Kontrollleuchte^F
spia^F della cartuccia^F

paper feed button
botón^M de alimentación^F del papel^M
bouton^M alimentation^F papier^M
Papiereinzugtaste^F
pulsante^M di alimentazione^F della carta^F

inkjet printer
impresora^F de líneas^F
imprimante^F à jet^M d'encre^F
Tintenstrahldrucker^M
stampante^F a getto^M di inchiostro^M

cancel button
tecla^F de anular
touche^F d'annulation^F
Abbruchtaste^F
pulsante^M di annullamento^M

paper feed light
indicador^M de carga del papel^M
voyant^M chargement^M du papier^M
Kontrollleuchte^F Papiereinzug^M
spia^F di alimentazione^F della carta^F

front cover
tapa^F frontal
capot^M
Frontabdeckung^F
coperchio^M

power light
indicador^M de alimentación^F
voyant^M d'alimentation^F
Netzkontrollleuchte^F
spia^F di alimentazione^F

output tray
bandeja^F de salida^F
bac^M de sortie^F
Papierausgabe^F
vassoio^F di uscita^F

power button
botón^M de avance/parada
bouton^M marche^F/arrêt^M
Ein-/Ausschalter^M
interruttore^M di accensione^F

input tray
bandeja^F de alimentación^F
bac^M d'alimentation^F
Papierkassette^F
vassoio^M di alimentazione^F

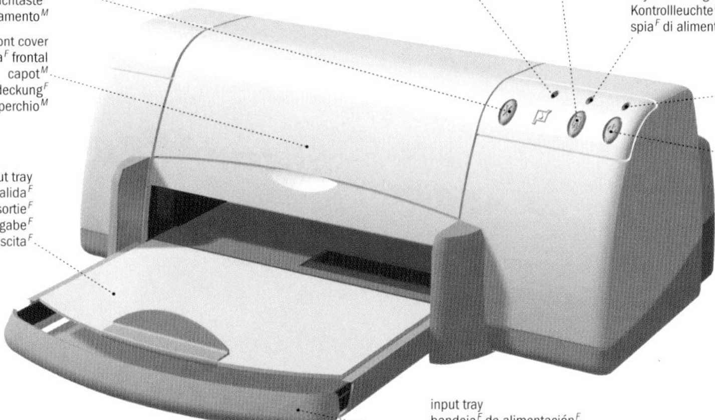

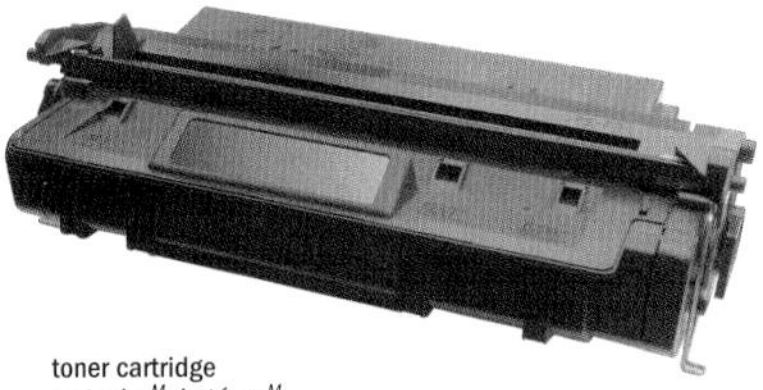

toner cartridge
cartucho^M de tóner^M
cartouche^F d'encre^F en poudre^F
Tonerpatrone^F
cartuccia^F del toner^M

laser printer
impresora^F láser
imprimante^F laser^M
Laserdrucker^M
stampante^F laser^M

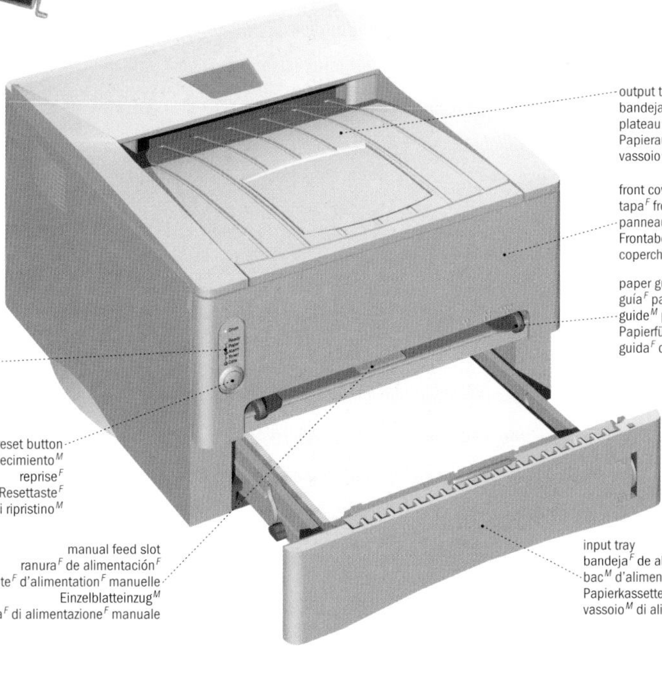

output tray
bandeja^F de alimentación^F
plateau^M de sortie^F
Papierausgabe^F
vassoio^M di uscita^F

front cover
tapa^F frontal
panneau^M avant
Frontabdeckung^F
coperchio^M

paper guide
guía^F papel^M
guide^M papier^M
Papierführung^F
guida^F della carta^F

control lights
luces^M de controles^M
voyants^M de contrôle^M
Kontrollleuchten^F
spie^F di controllo^M

reset button
restablecimiento^M
reprise^F
Resettaste^F
tasto^M di ripristino^M

manual feed slot
ranura^F de alimentación^F
fente^F d'alimentation^F manuelle
Einzelblatteinzug^M
fessura^F di alimentazione^F manuale

input tray
bandeja^F de alimentación^F
bac^M d'alimentation^F
Papierkassette^F
vassoio^M di alimentazione^F

output devices

COMMUNICATIONS AND OFFICE AUTOMATION

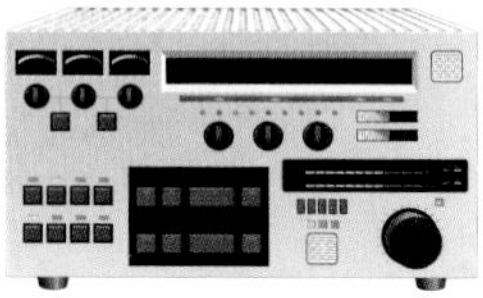

desktop video unit
consola^F de la unidad^F de video^M
unité^F vidéo
Schreibtisch-Videogerät^N
unità^F video^M da tavolo^M

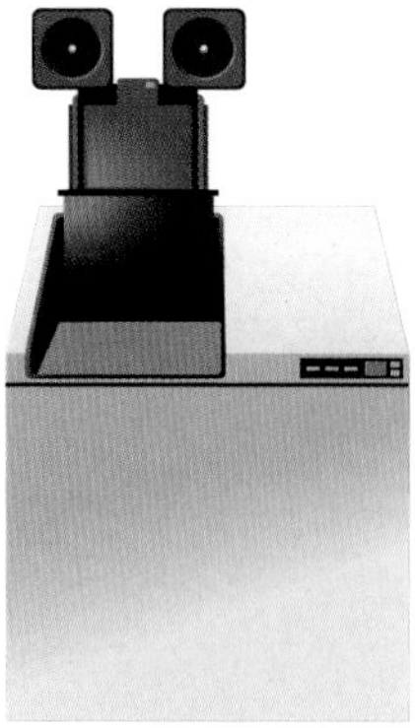

film recorder
filmadora^F
enregistreur^M de film^M
Filmaufnahmegerät^N
registratore^M di microfilm^M

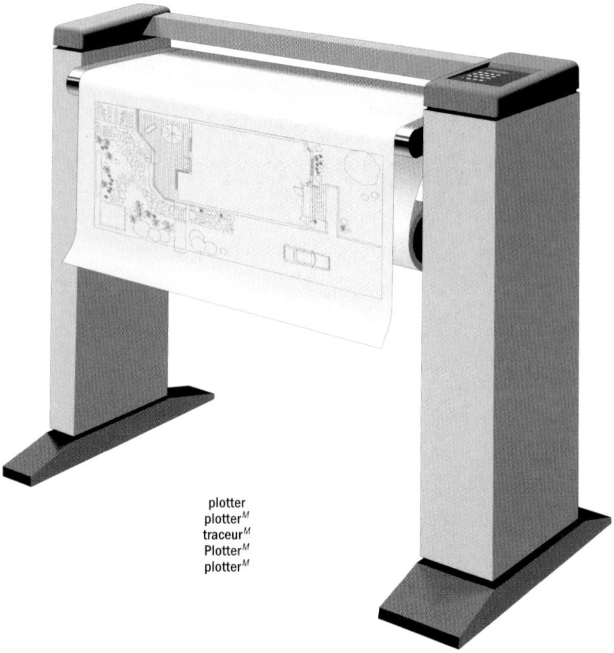

plotter
plotter^M
traceur^M
Plotter^M
plotter^M

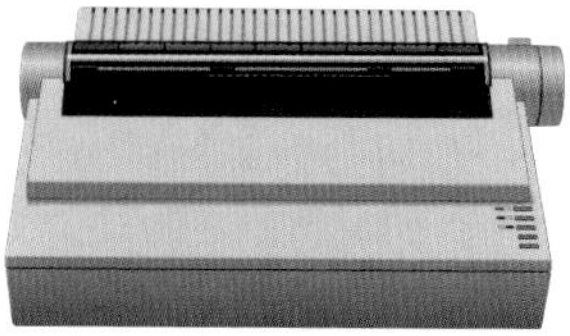

dot matrix printer
impresora^F matriz
imprimante^F matricielle
Nadeldrucker^M
stampante^F ad aghi^M

uninterruptible power supply (UPS)

sistema^F de alimentación ininterrumpida (SAI/UPS) | onduleur^M | unterbrechungsfreie Stromversorgung^F (USV) | gruppo^M di continuità^F

telephone surge protection jacks
tomas^F telefónicas contra sobretensiones^F
prises^F téléphoniques antisurtension
Telefonsteckdose^F zur Stoßspannungsunterdrückung^F
prese^F telefoniche antisovratensione

computer interface port
puerto^M de interfaz^F de ordenador^M
port^M d'interface^F ordinateur^M
Computer^M-Schnittstellenport^M
porta^F di interfaccia^F del computer^M

control lights
indicadores^M de control^M
voyants^M de contrôle^M
Kontrollleuchten^F
spie^F di controllo^M

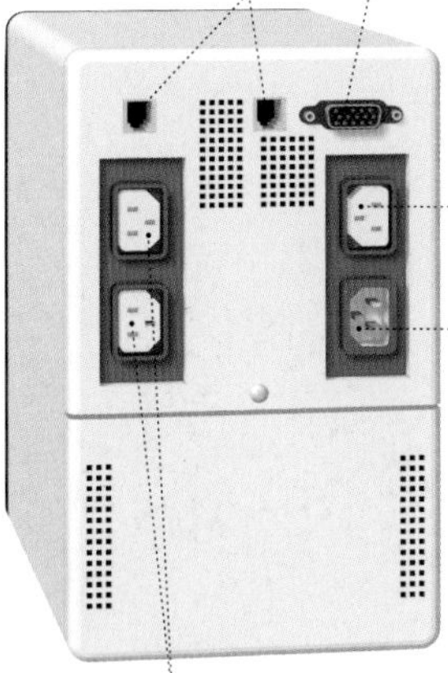

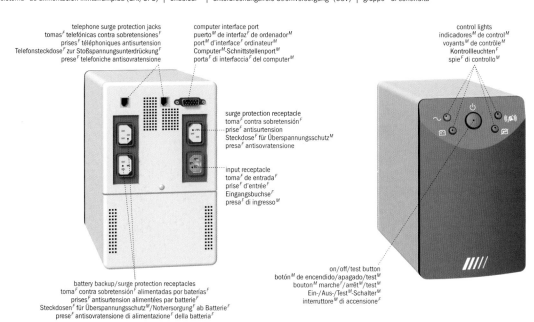

surge protection receptacle
toma^F contra sobretensión^F
prise^F antisurtension
Steckdose^F für Überspannungsschutz^M
presa^F antisovratensione

input receptacle
toma^F de entrada^F
prise^F d'entrée^F
Eingangsbuchse^F
presa^F di ingresso^M

battery backup/surge protection receptacles
toma^F contra sobretensión^F alimentadas por baterías^F
prises^F antisurtension alimentées par batterie^F
Steckdosen^F für Überspannungsschutz^M/Notversorgung^F ab Batterie^F
prese^F antisovratensione di alimentazione^F della batteria^F

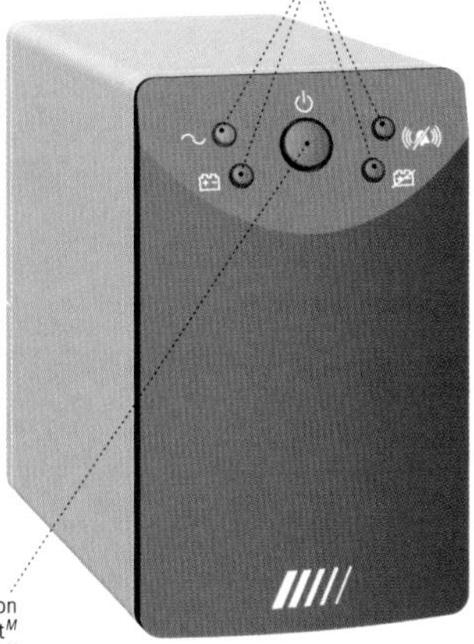

on/off/test button
botón^M de encendido/apagado/test^M
bouton^M marche^F/arrêt^M/test^M
Ein-/Aus-/Test^M-Schalter^M
interruttore^M di accensione^F

data storage devices

unidades^F de almacenamiento^F de información^F | périphériques^M de stockage^M | Speichergeräte^N | dispositivi^M di memorizzazione^F dei dati^M

removable hard disk drive
unidad^F de disco^M duro extraible
lecteur^M de disque^M dur amovible
externes Festplattenlaufwerk^N
unità^F hard disk^M estraibile

hard disk drive
unidad^F del disco^M duro
lecteur^M de disque^M dur
Festplattenlaufwerk^N
unità^F hard disk^M

disk
disco^M
disque^M
Platte^F
disco^M

disk motor
motor^M del disco^M
moteur^M de disques^M
Laufwerksantrieb^M
motore^M del disco^M

actuator arm
brazo^M actuador
guide^M
Sucharm^M
braccio^M

disk eject button
botón^M de expulsión^F del disco^F
bouton^M d'éjection^F du disque^M
Diskettenauswurftaste^F
pulsante^M di espulsione^F del disco^M

actuator arm motor
motor^M del brazo^M actuador
moteur^M de guides^M
Führungsschienenantrieb^M
motore^M del braccio^M

removable hard disk
disco^M duro extraible
disque^M dur amovible
herausnehmbare Festplatte^F
hard disk^M estraibile

read/write head
cabeza^F de lectura^F/escritura^F
tête^F de lecture^F/écriture^F
Schreib-/Lesekopf^M
testina^F di lettura^F/scrittura^F

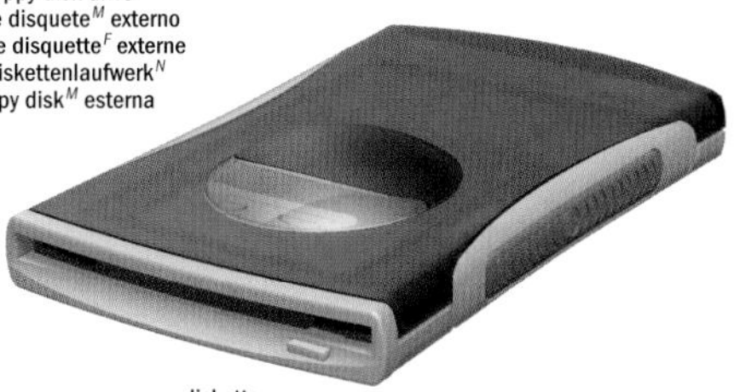

DVD recorder
reproductor^M de DVD
graveur^M de DVD^M
DVD^F-Rekorder^M
registratore^M DVD^M

external floppy disk drive
unidad^F de disquete^M externo
lecteur^M de disquette^F externe
externes Diskettenlaufwerk^N
unità^F floppy disk^M esterna

diskette
disquete^M
disquette^F
Diskette^F
floppy disk^M

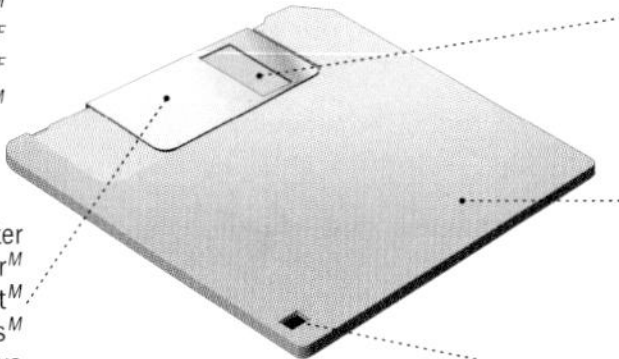

access window
ventana^F de acceso^M
fenêtre^F de lecture^F
Zugriffsöffnung^F
finestra^F di accesso^M

jacket
carcasa^F
enveloppe^F
Hülle^F
involucro^M

shutter
obturador^M
volet^M
Verschluss^M
coperchio^M protettivo

compact disc rewritable recorder
grabador^M de disco^M compacto regrabable
graveur^M de disque^M compact réinscriptible
Rewritable-Rekorder^M
registratore^M di compact disc^M riscrivibili

protect tab
lengüeta^F protectora
taquet^M de verrouillage^M
Schreibschutz^M
linguetta^F di protezione^F

cassette drive
unidad^F de casetes^F
lecteur^M de cassette^F
Kassettenlaufwerk^N
drive^M per cassette^F

cassette
casete^F
cassette^F
Kassette^F
cassetta^F

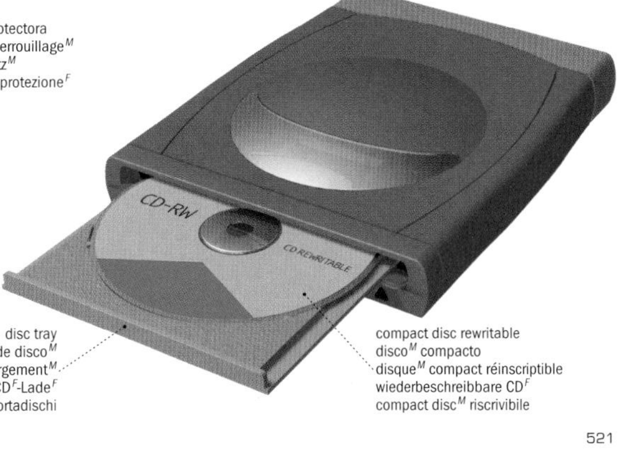

disc tray
alojamiento^F de disco^M
plateau^M de chargement^M
CD^F-Lade^F
vassoio^M portadischi

compact disc rewritable
disco^M compacto
disque^M compact réinscriptible
wiederbeschreibbare CD^F
compact disc^M riscrivibile

communication devices

unidades^F de comunicación^F | périphériques^M de communication^F | Übertragungsgeräte^N | dispositivi^M di comunicazione^F

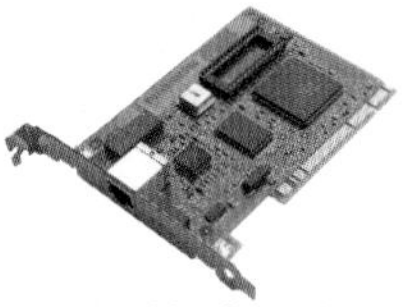

network interface card
tarjeta^F de interfaz^F de red^F
carte^F réseau^M
Netzwerkkarte^F, LAN-Karte^F
scheda^F di rete^F

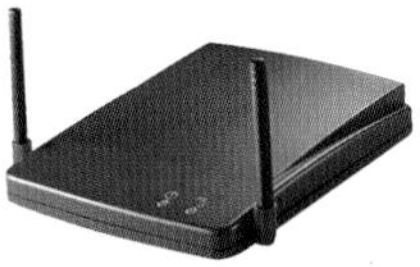

network access point transceiver
emisor^M-receptor^M de acceso^M a la red^F
émetteur^M-récepteur^M d'accès^M réseau^M
Basisstation^F für Funknetzwerk^N
ricetrasmittente^F di accesso^M alla rete^F

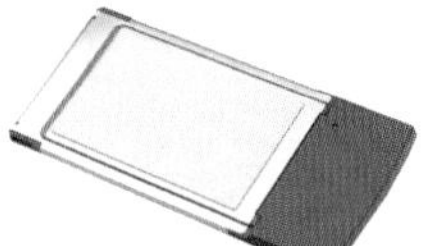

wireless network interface card
tarjeta^F de interfaz^F de red^F sin hilos^M
carte^F réseau^M sans fil^M
Funknetzwerkkarte^F, wireless-LAN-Karte^F
scheda^F di rete^F senza fili^M

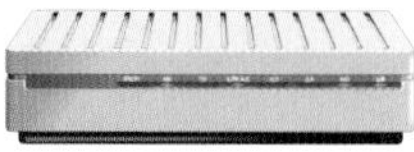

modem
módem^M
modem^M
Modem^N
modem^M

examples of networks

ejemplos^M de redes^F | exemples^M de réseaux^M | Beispiele^N für Netzwerke^N | esempi^M di reti^F

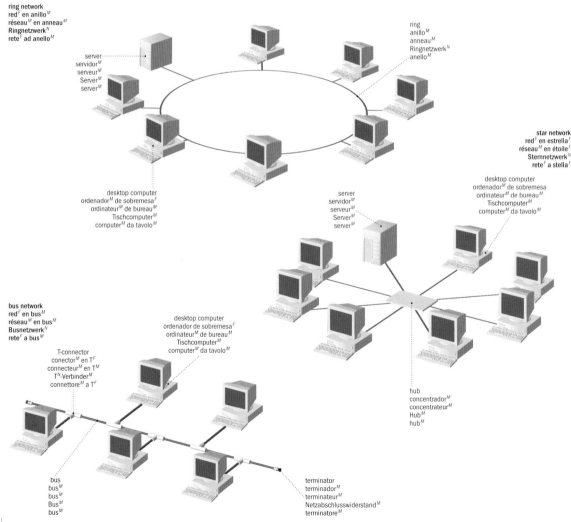

ring network
red^F en anillo^M
réseau^M en anneau^M
Ringnetzwerk^N
rete^F ad anello^M

server
servidor^M
serveur^M
Server^M
server^M

ring
anillo^M
anneau^M
Ringnetzwerk^N
anello^M

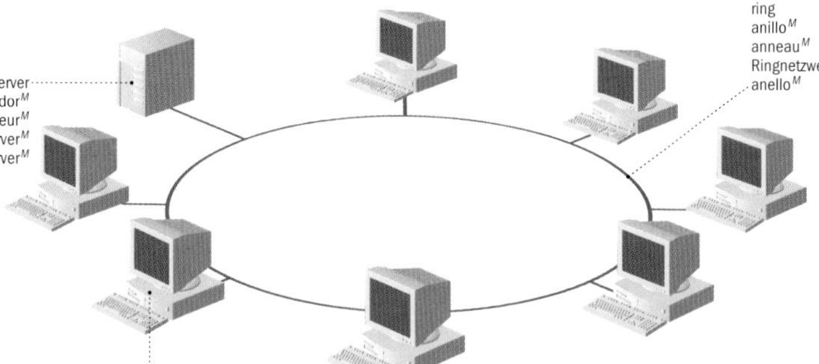

star network
red^F en estrella^F
réseau^M en étoile^F
Sternnetzwerk^N
rete^F a stella^F

desktop computer
ordenador^M de sobremesa^F
ordinateur^M de bureau^M
Tischcomputer^M
computer^M da tavolo^M

server
servidor^M
serveur^M
Server^M
server^M

desktop computer
ordenador^M de sobremesa
ordinateur^M de bureau^M
Tischcomputer^M
computer^M da tavolo^M

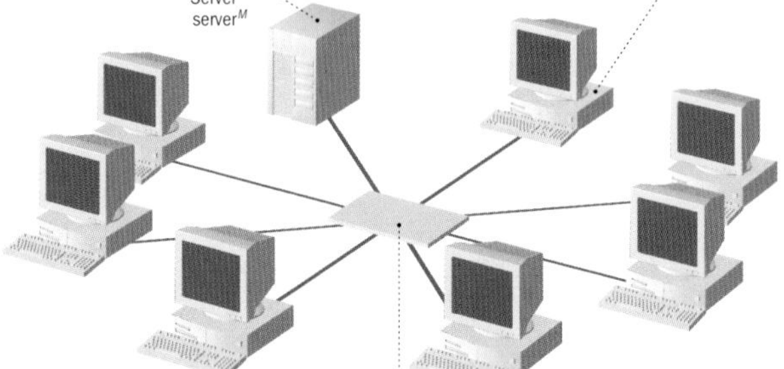

bus network
red^F en bus^M
réseau^M en bus^M
Busnetzwerk^N
rete^F a bus^M

desktop computer
ordenador de sobremesa^F
ordinateur^M de bureau^M
Tischcomputer^M
computer^M da tavolo^M

T-connector
conector^M en T^F
connecteur^M en T^M
T^N-Verbinder^M
connettore^M a T^F

hub
concentrador^M
concentrateur^M
Hub^M
hub^M

bus
bus^M
bus^M
Bus^M
bus^M

terminator
terminador^M
terminateur^M
Netzabschlusswiderstand^M
terminatore^M

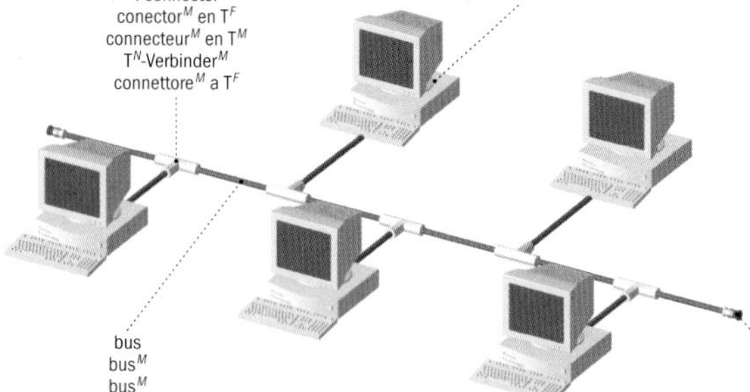

computer network

red^F informática | réseau^M informatique | Rechnernetzwerk^N | rete^F informatica

desktop computer
ordenador^M de sobremesa^F
ordinateur^M de bureau^M
Tischcomputer^M
computer^M da tavolo^M

server
servidor^M
serveur^M
Server^M
server^M

wide area network
red^F de área^F amplia
réseau^M étendu
Weitverkehrsnetzwerk^N
rete^F estesa

hub
concentrador^M
concentrateur^M
Hub^M
hub^M

uninterruptible power supply
sistema^F de alimentación ininterrumpida
onduleur^M
unterbrechungsfreie Stromversorgung^F
gruppo^M di continuità^F

routers
routers^M
routeurs^M
Router^M
router^M

telephone/cable/satellite line
línea^F telefónica/cableada/satélite
ligne^F téléphonique/câblée/satellite^M
Telefon^N-/Kabel^N-/Satellitenleitung^F
linea^F telefonica/cablata/satellitare

switch
conmutador^M
commutateur^M
Umschalter^M
commutatore^M

dedicated line
línea^F reservada
ligne^F dédiée
Standleitung^F
linea^F dedicata

laptop computer
ordenador^M portátil
ordinateur^M portable
Laptop^M
computer^M portatile

modem
módem^M
modem^M
Modem^N
modem^M

Internet
Internet^M
Internet^M
Internet^N
Internet

gateway
pasarela^F
passerelle^F
Gateway^N
gateway^M

firewall
cortafuego^M
pare-feu^M
Firewall^F
firewall^M

backbone
dorsal^M
dorsale^F
Backbone^M
rete^F dorsale

file server
servidor^M de archivos^M
serveur^M de fichiers^M
Fileserver^M
file^M server^M

printer
impresora^F
imprimante^F
Drucker^M
stampante^F

bridge
puente^M
pont^M
Bridge^F
adattatore^M

hub
concentrador^M
concentrateur^M
Hub^M
hub^M

backup storage unit
unidad^F de copia^F de seguridad^F
unité^F de sauvegarde^F
Backup^M-Speichereinheit^F
unità^F di backup^M

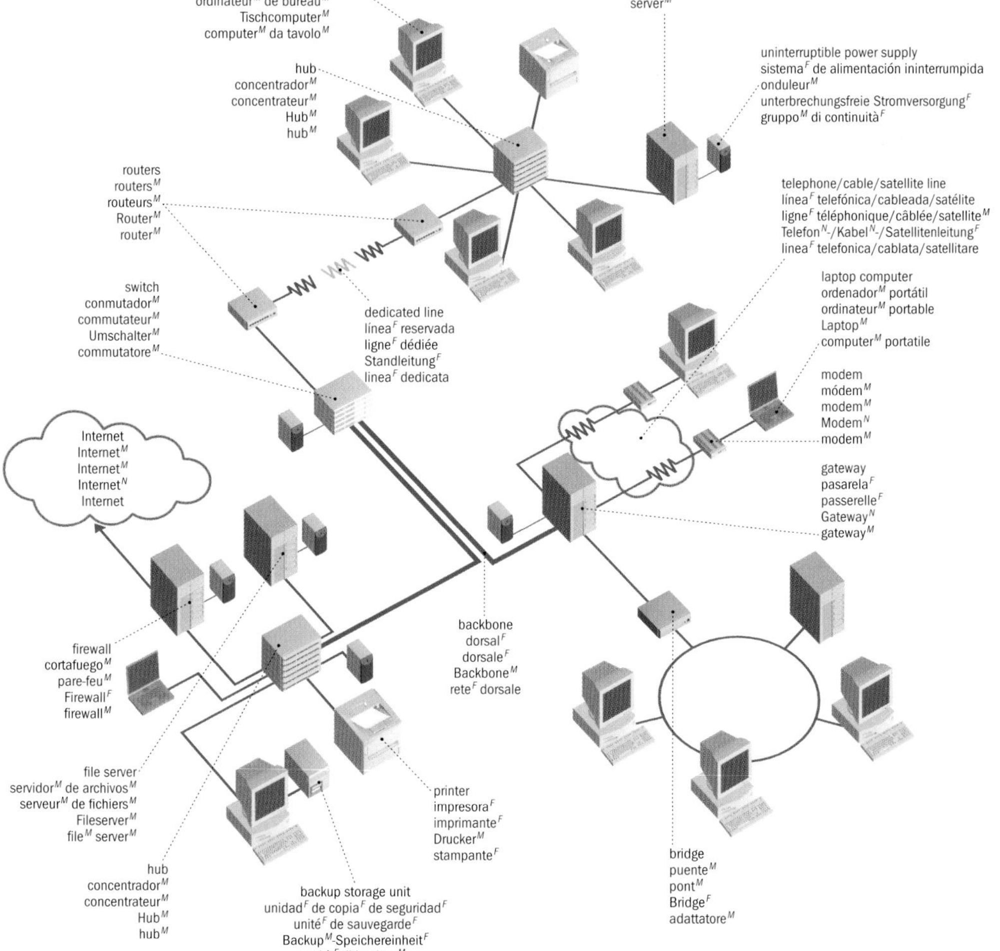

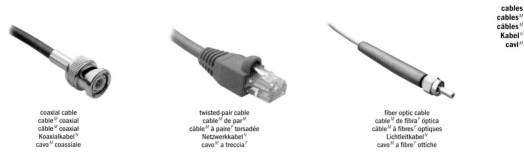

cables
cables^M
câbles^M
Kabel^N
cavi^M

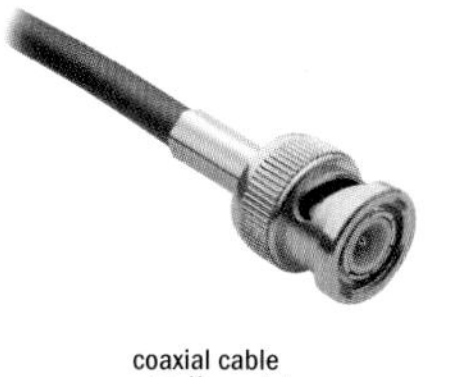

coaxial cable
cable^M coaxial
câble^M coaxial
Koaxialkabel^N
cavo^M coassiale

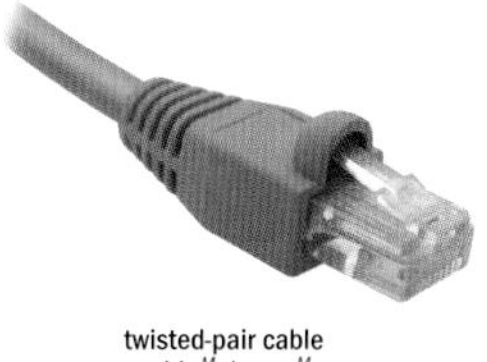

twisted-pair cable
cable^M de par^M
câble^M à paire^F torsadée
Netzwerkkabel^N
cavo^M a treccia^F

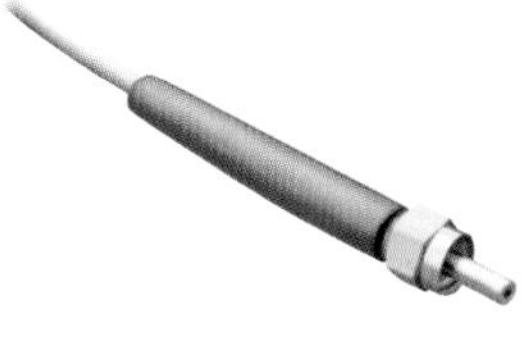

fiber optic cable
cable^M de fibra^F óptica
câble^M à fibres^F optiques
Lichtleitkabel^N
cavo^M a fibre^F ottiche

Internet

Internet[M] | Internet[M] | Internet[N] | Internet

URL (uniform resource locator)
URL localizador universal de recursos
adresse[F] URL[F] (localisateur[M] universel de ressources[F])
URL-Adresse[F] (vereinheitlichter Ressourcenzugriff[M])
URL (localizzatore[M] universale di risorse[F])

communication protocol
protocolo[M] de comunicación[F]
protocole[M] de communication[F]
Kommunikationsprotokoll[N]
protocollo[M] di comunicazione[F]

domain name
nombre[M] del dominio[M]
nom[M] de domaine[M]
Domainname[M]
nome[M] del dominio[M]

file format
formato[M] del archivo[M]
format[M] du fichier[M]
Dateiformat[N]
formato[M] del file[M]

http://www.un.org/aboutun/index.htm

double virgule
doble barra[F] oblicua
double barre[F] oblique
Doppelschrägstrich[M]
doppio slash[M]

second-level domain
dominio[M] de segundo nivel[M]
domaine[M] de second niveau[M]
Domain[F] zweiten Grades[M]
dominio[M] di secondo livello[M]

file
archivo[M]
fichier[M]
Datei[F]
file[M]

server
servidor[M]
serveur[M]
Server[M]
server[M]

top-level domain
dominio[M] de primer nivel[M]
domaine[M] de premier niveau[M]
Toplevel[N]-Domain[F]
dominio[M] di livello[M] superiore

directory
directorio[M]
répertoire[M]
Ordner[M], Verzeichnis[N]
directory[F]

browser
navegador
navigateur[M]
Browser[M]
browser[M]

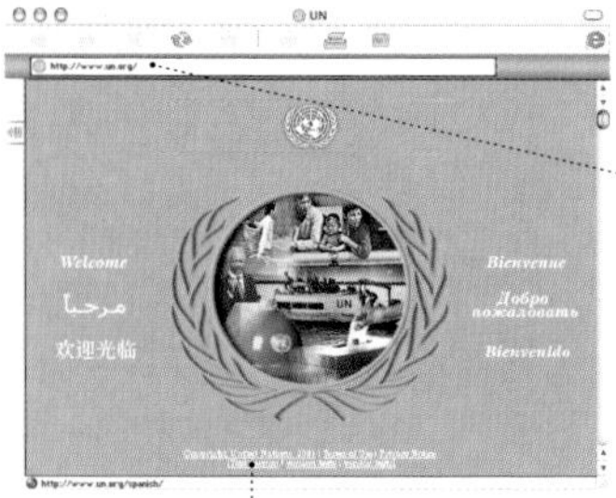

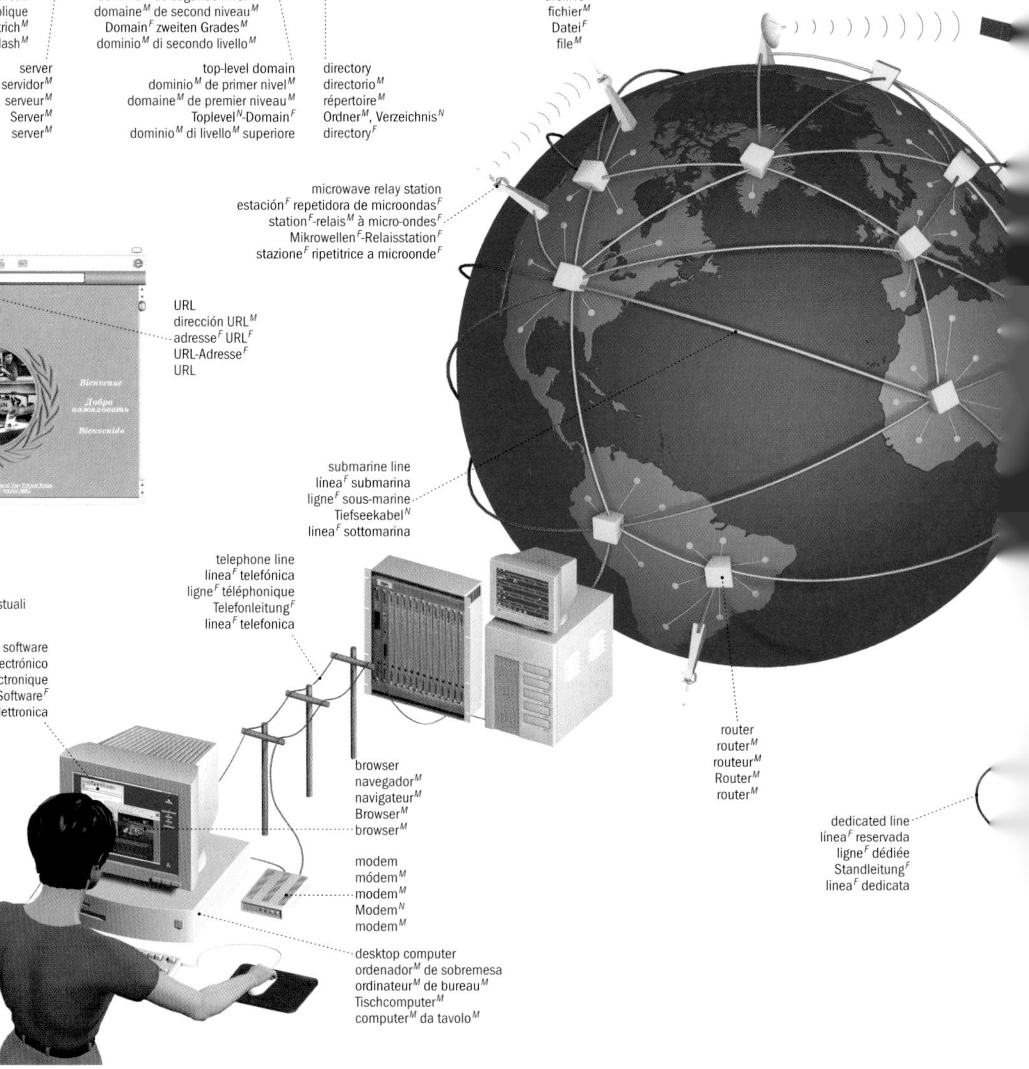

microwave relay station
estación[F] repetidora de microondas[F]
station[F]-relais à micro-ondes[F]
Mikrowellen[F]-Relaisstation[F]
stazione[F] ripetitrice a microonde[F]

URL
dirección URL[M]
adresse[F] URL[F]
URL-Adresse[F]
URL

submarine line
linea[F] submarina
ligne[F] sous-marine
Tiefseekabel[N]
linea[F] sottomarina

hyperlinks
hipervínculos[M]
hyperliens[M]
Hyperlinks[M]
collegamenti[M] ipertestuali

telephone line
linea[F] telefónica
ligne[F] téléphonique
Telefonleitung[F]
linea[F] telefonica

e-mail software
programa[M] de correo[M] electrónico
logiciel[M] de courrier[M] électronique
E-Mail[F]-Software[F]
software[M] di posta[F] elettronica

Internet user
internauta[M]
internaute[F]
Internet[N]-Nutzer[M]
utente[M] di Internet

browser
navegador[M]
navigateur[M]
Browser[M]
browser[M]

router
router[M]
routeur[M]
Router[M]
router[M]

modem
módem[M]
modem[M]
Modem[M]
modem[M]

dedicated line
linea[F] reservada
ligne[F] dédiée
Standleitung[F]
linea[F] dedicata

desktop computer
ordenador[M] de sobremesa
ordinateur[M] de bureau[M]
Tischcomputer[M]
computer[M] da tavolo[M]

Internet uses

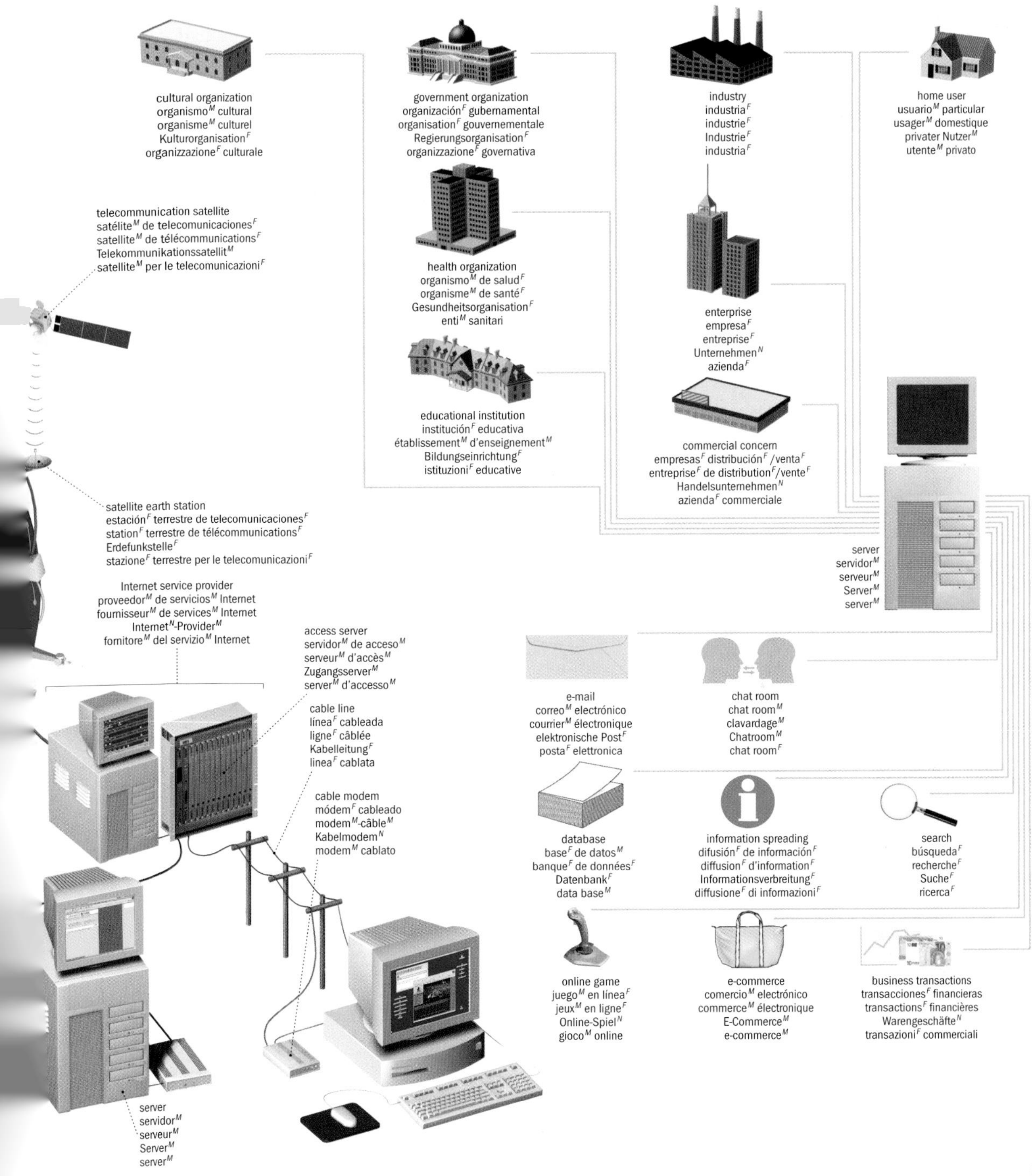

cultural organization
organismo^M cultural
organisme^M culturel
Kulturorganisation^F
organizzazione^F culturale

government organization
organización^F gubernamental
organisation^F gouvernementale
Regierungsorganisation^F
organizzazione^F governativa

industry
industria^F
industrie^F
Industrie^F
industria^F

home user
usuario^M particular
usager^M domestique
privater Nutzer^M
utente^M privato

telecommunication satellite
satélite^M de telecomunicaciones^F
satellite^M de télécommunications^F
Telekommunikationssatellit^M
satellite^M per le telecomunicazioni^F

health organization
organismo^M de salud^F
organisme^M de santé^F
Gesundheitsorganisation^F
enti^M sanitari

enterprise
empresa^F
entreprise^F
Unternehmen^N
azienda^F

educational institution
institución^F educativa
établissement^M d'enseignement^M
Bildungseinrichtung^F
istituzioni^F educative

commercial concern
empresas^F distribución^F/venta^F
entreprise^F de distribution^F/vente^F
Handelsunternehmen^N
azienda^F commerciale

satellite earth station
estación^F terrestre de telecomunicaciones^F
station^F terrestre de télécommunications^F
Erdefunkstelle^F
stazione^F terrestre per le telecomunicazioni^F

server
servidor^M
serveur^M
Server^M
server^M

Internet service provider
proveedor^M de servicios^M Internet
fournisseur^M de services^M Internet
Internet^N-Provider^M
fornitore^M del servizio^M Internet

access server
servidor^M de acceso^M
serveur^M d'accès^M
Zugangsserver^M
server^M d'accesso^M

e-mail
correo^M electrónico
courrier^M électronique
elektronische Post^F
posta^F elettronica

chat room
chat room
clavardage^M
Chatroom^M
chat room^F

cable line
línea^F cableada
ligne^F câblée
Kabelleitung^F
linea^F cablata

cable modem
módem^M cableado
modem^M-câble^M
Kabelmodem^N
modem^M cablato

database
base^F de datos^M
banque^F de données^F
Datenbank^F
data base^M

information spreading
difusión^F de información^F
diffusion^F d'information^F
Informationsverbreitung^F
diffusione^F di informazioni^F

search
búsqueda^F
recherche^F
Suche^F
ricerca^F

online game
juego^M en línea^F
jeux^M en ligne^F
Online-Spiel^N
gioco^M online

e-commerce
comercio^M electrónico
commerce^M électronique
E-Commerce^M
e-commerce^M

business transactions
transacciones^F financieras
transactions^F financières
Warengeschäfte^N
transazioni^F commerciali

server
servidor^M
serveur^M
Server^M
server^M

laptop computer

ordenador^M portátil | ordinateur^M portable | Laptop^M | computer^M portatile

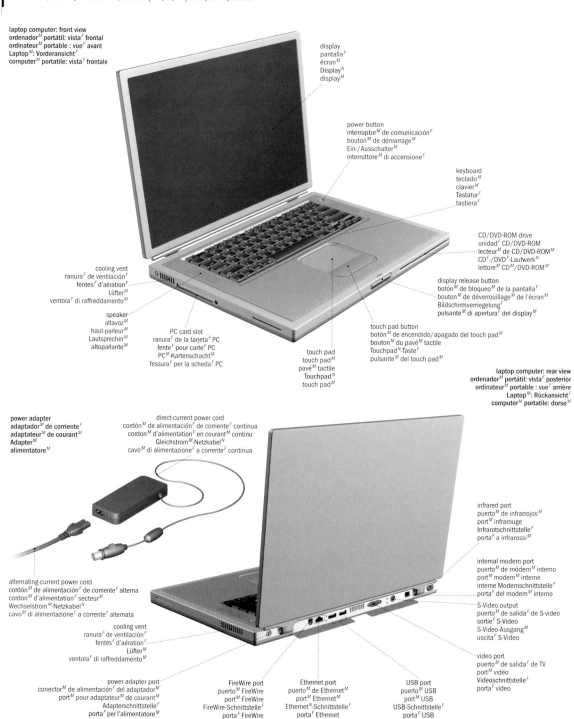

laptop computer: front view
ordenador^M portátil: vista^F frontal
ordinateur^M portable: vue^F avant
Laptop^M: Vorderansicht^F
computer^M portatile: vista^F frontale

display
pantalla^F
écran^M
Display^N
display^M

power button
interruptor^M de comunicación^F
bouton^M de démarrage^M
Ein-/Ausschalter^M
interruttore^M di accensione^F

keyboard
teclado^M
clavier^M
Tastatur^F
tastiera^F

CD/DVD-ROM drive
unidad^F CD/DVD-ROM
lecteur^M de CD/DVD-ROM^M
CD^F-/DVD^F-Laufwerk^N
lettore^M CD^M/DVD-ROM^M

display release button
botón^M de bloqueo^M de la pantalla^F
bouton^M de déverrouillage^M de l'écran^M
Bildschirmverriegelung^F
pulsante^M di apertura^F del display^M

cooling vent
ranura^F de ventilación^F
fentes^F d'aération^F
Lüfter^M
ventola^F di raffreddamento^M

speaker
altavoz^M
haut-parleur^M
Lautsprecher^M
altoparlante^M

PC card slot
ranura^F de la tarjeta^F PC
fente^F pour carte^F PC
PC^M-Kartenschacht^M
fessura^F per la scheda^F PC

touch pad button
botón^M de encendido/apagado del touch pad^M
bouton^M du pavé^M tactile
Touchpad^N-Taste^F
pulsante^M del touch pad^M

touch pad
touch pad^M
pavé^M tactile
Touchpad^N
touch pad^M

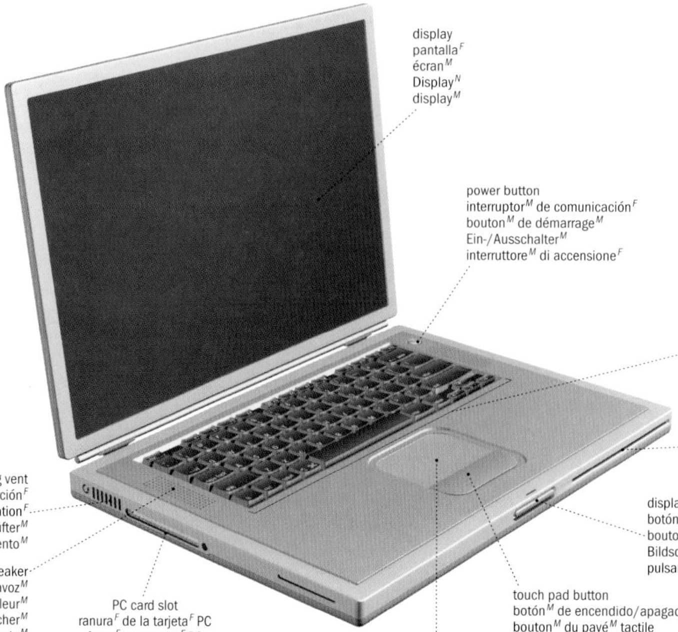

laptop computer: rear view
ordenador^M portátil: vista^F posterior
ordinateur^M portable : vue^F arrière
Laptop^M: Rückansicht^F
computer^M portatile: dorso^M

power adapter
adaptador^M de corriente^F
adaptateur^M de courant^M
Adapter^M
alimentatore^M

direct-current power cord
cordón^M de alimentación^F de corriente^F continua
cordon^M d'alimentation^F en courant^M continu
Gleichstrom^M-Netzkabel^N
cavo^M di alimentazione^F a corrente^F continua

infrared port
puerto^M de infrarrojos^M
port^M infrarouge
Infrarotschnittstelle^F
porta^F a infrarossi^M

internal modem port
puerto^M de módem^M interno
port^M modem^M interne
interne Modemschnittstelle^F
porta^F del modem^M interno

S-Video output
puerto^M de salida^F de S-video
sortie^F S-Video
S-Video-Ausgang^M
uscita^F S-Video

alternating-current power cord
cordón^M de alimentación^F de corriente^F alterna
cordon^M d'alimentation^F secteur^M
Wechselstrom^M-Netzkabel^N
cavo^M di alimentazione^F a corrente^F alternata

cooling vent
ranura^F de ventilación^F
fentes^F d'aération^F
Lüfter^M
ventola^F di raffreddamento^M

video port
puerto^M de salida^F de TV
port^M vidéo
Videoschnittstelle^F
porta^F video

power adapter port
conector^M de alimentación^F del adaptador^M
port^M pour adaptateur^M de courant^M
Adapterschnittstelle^F
porta^F per l'alimentatore^M

FireWire port
puerto^M FireWire
port^M FireWire
FireWire-Schnittstelle^F
porta^F FireWire

Ethernet port
puerto^M de Ethernet^M
port^M Ethernet^M
Ethernet^N-Schnittstelle^F
porta^F Ethernet

USB port
puerto^M USB
port^M USB
USB-Schnittstelle^F
porta^F USB

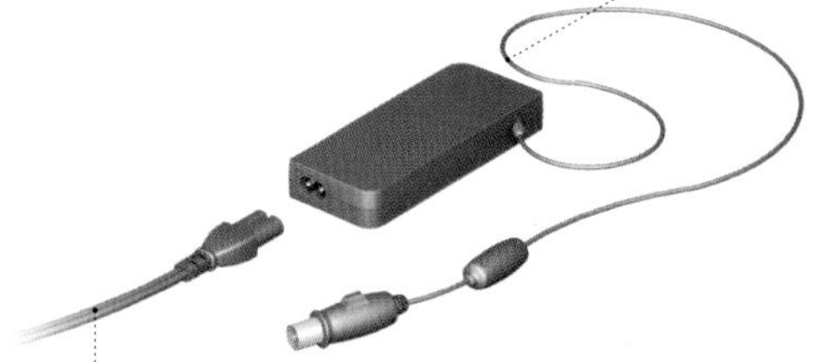

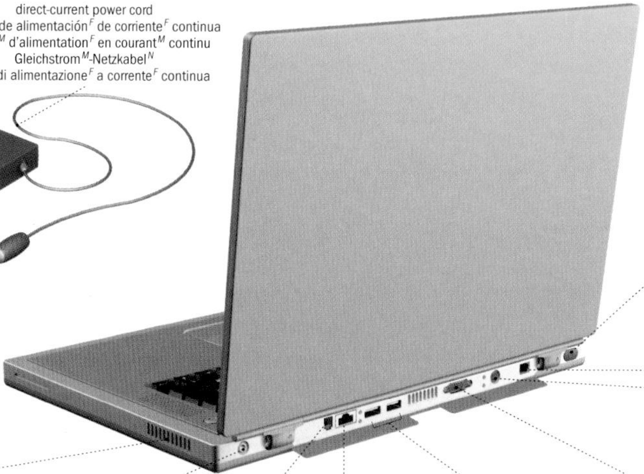

laptop computer

laptop computer briefcase
maletin^M para ordenador^M portátil
mallette^F d'ordinateur^M portable
Laptop^M-Tasche^F
valigetta^F per il computer^M portatile

computer compartment
compartimiento^M para ordenador^M
compartiment^M pour ordinateur^M
Computerfach^N
scomparto^M per il computer^M

document compartment
compartimiento^M de documentos^M
compartiment^M pour documents^M
Dokumentenfach^N
scomparto^M per i documenti^M

shoulder strap
bandolera^F
bandoulière^F
Schulterriemen^M
tracolla^F

electronic book

libro^M electrónico | livre^M électronique | elektronisches Buch^N | libro^M elettronico

page forward button
botón^M página^F siguiente
page^F suivante
Taste^F nächste Seite^F
tasto^M di pagina^F successiva

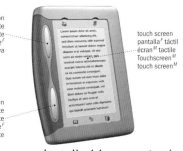

touch screen
pantalla^F táctil
écran^M tactile
Touchscreen^M
touch screen^M

page backward button
botón^M página^F precedente
page^F précédente
Taste^F vorherige Seite^F
tasto^M di pagina^F precedente

handheld computer/personal digital assistant (PDA)

ordenador^M de bolsillo^M | ordinateur^M de poche^F | Handheld-Computer^M | computer^M tascabile

audio input/output jack
toma^F de entrada^F/salida^F audio
prise^F d'entrée^F/sortie^F audio
Audio-Ein- und -Ausgänge^M
ingresso^M/uscita^F audio

microphone
micrófono
microphone^M
Mikrofon^N
microfono^M

infrared port
puerto^M infrarrojos
port^M infrarouge
Infrarotschnittstelle^F
porta^F a infrarossi^M

voice recorder button
botón^M de grabador^M vocal
bouton^M d'enregistreur^M vocal
Sprachaufnahmetaste^F
pulsante^M del registratore^M vocale

alarm/charge indicator light
luz^F indicadora de cargado/alarma^F
voyant^M d'alarme^F/de mise^F en charge^F
Kontrollleuchte^F Alarm^M/Aufladen^N
spia^F di allarme^M e di messa^F in carica^F

dial/action button
rueda^F de mando^M
roulette^F de commande^F
Wahlrad^N
rotella^F di comando^M

touch screen
pantalla^F táctil
écran^M tactile
Touchscreen^M
touch screen^M

exit button
botón^M de salida^M
bouton^M de sortie^F
Abbruchtaste^F
pulsante^M di uscita^F

application launch buttons
botones^M de lanzamiento^M de las aplicaciones^M
boutons^M de lancement^M d'applications^F
Anwendungsstarttasten^F
pulsanti^M di avvio^M delle applicazioni^F

sync cable
cable^M de sincronización^F
câble^M de synchronisation^F
Synchronisationskabel^N
cavo^M di sincronizzazione^F

power and backlight button
botón^M de inicio^M y de retroiluminación^F
bouton^M de démarrage^M et de rétroéclairage^M
Betriebsschalter^M und Hintergrundbeleuchtung^F
pulsante^M di alimentazione^F e di controluce^F

power plug
clavija^F de alimentación^F
fiche^F d'alimentation^F
Netzstecker^M
spina^F di alimentazione^F

docking cradle
soporte^M de acoplamiento^M
station^F d'accueil^M
Docking-Station^F
alloggiamento^M

stylus
stylus^M
stylet^M
Stift^M
stilo^F

stationery

artículos^M de escritorio^M | articles^M de bureau^M | Schreibwaren^F | articoli^M di cancelleria^F

electronic typewriter
máquina^F de escribir electrónica
machine^F à écrire électronique
elektrische Schreibmaschine^F
macchina^F da scrivere elettronica

top plate
tapa^F
capot^M
Gehäuseabdeckung^F
coperchio^M

paper support
soporte^M del papel^M
support^M-papier^M
Papierstütze^F
piano^M reggifoglio

paper bail release lever
palanca^F para liberar el sujetapapel^M
levier^M de dégagement^M du presse-papier^M
Papierfreigabehebel^M
leva^F di svincolo^M del premicarta^M

printing unit
unidad^F de impresión^F
tête^F d'impression^F
Schreibkopf^M
testina^F di stampa^F

paper bail
sujetapapel^M
presse-papier^M
Papierhalter^M
premicarta^M

paper release lever
palanca^F de aflojar el papel^M
levier^M de dégagement^M du papier^M
Papierlösehebel^M
leva^F liberacarta

pitch scale
escala^F de ajuste^M
échelle^F d'espacement^M
Schriftgrößenskala^F
scala^M dei passi^M di scrittura^F

platen
rodillo^M
cylindre^M
Walze^F
rullo^M

variable spacer
tambor^M distanciador
bouton^F d'interligne^M variable
Walzendrehknopf^M
manopola^F distanziatrice

margin release
liberador^M del margen^M
dégagement^M du margeur^M
Randlösetaste^F
tasto^M liberamargine

tabulator
tabulador^M
tabulateur^M
Tabulatortaste^F
tasto^M tabulatore^M

indent
tecla^F de sangrado^M
retrait^M
Einzugtaste^F
tasto^M del paragrafo^M rientrato

character correction
corrección^F de caracteres^M
correction^F de caractères^M
Zeichenkorrekturtaste^F
tasto^M di correzione^F del carattere^M

half indexing
indicador^M de la mitad^F
positionnement^M du papier^M
Hoch-/Tiefstelltaste^F
tasto^M di movimento^M di mezza interlinea^F

decimal tab
tabulador^M decimal
tabulateur^M décimal
Dezimal-Tabuliertaste^F
tasto^M di tabulazione^F decimale

margin control
control^M del margen^M
commande^F de marge^F
Randkontrolltaste^F
tasto^M marginatore^M

EXEGI MONUMENTUM AERE PERENIUS

tab setting
ajuste^M del tabulador^M
contrôle^F de tabulation^F
Tabulatoreinstelltaste^F
tasto^M di impostazione^F degli arresti^M
di tabulazione^F

centering
tecla^F de centrado^M
centrage^M
Zentriertaste^F
tasto^M di centratura^F

set
ajuste^M
validation^F
Tabulatorsetztaste^F
tasto^M di conferma^F della tabulazione^M

spelling corrector
corrector^M de ortografía^F
correcteur^M orthographique
Rechtschreibkorrekturtaste^F
tasto^M di correzione^F ortografica

text display
pantalla^F
affichage^M du texte^M
Textanzeige^F
display^M

relocation
reposicionamiento^M
repositionnement^M
Fixiertaste^F
tasto^M di riposizionamento^M

text
texto^M
texte^M
Texttaste^F
tasto^M di memorizzazione^F del testo^M

code
código^M
code^M
Code-Taste^F
tasto^M selezionatore^F di comandi^M

carriage return
tecla^F de regreso^M del carro^M
retour^M de chariot^M
Wagenrücklauftaste^F
tasto^M di ritorno^M del carrello^M

shift lock key
tecla^F de seguro^M para las mayúsculas^F
touche^F fixe-majuscules^F
Umschaltfeststelltaste^F
tasto^M del blocco delle maiuscole

shift key
tecla^F de mayúsculas^F
touche^F-majuscules^F
Umschalttaste^F
tasto^M delle maiuscole

space bar
barra^F espaciadora
barre^F d'espacement^M
Leertaste^F
barra^F spaziatrice

word correction
corrección^F de palabras^F
correction^F de mots^F
Wortkorrekturtaste^F
tasto^M di correzione^F della parola^F

mode
modalidad^F
mode^M
Mode-Taste^F
tasto^M di selezione^F dello stato^M di stampa^F

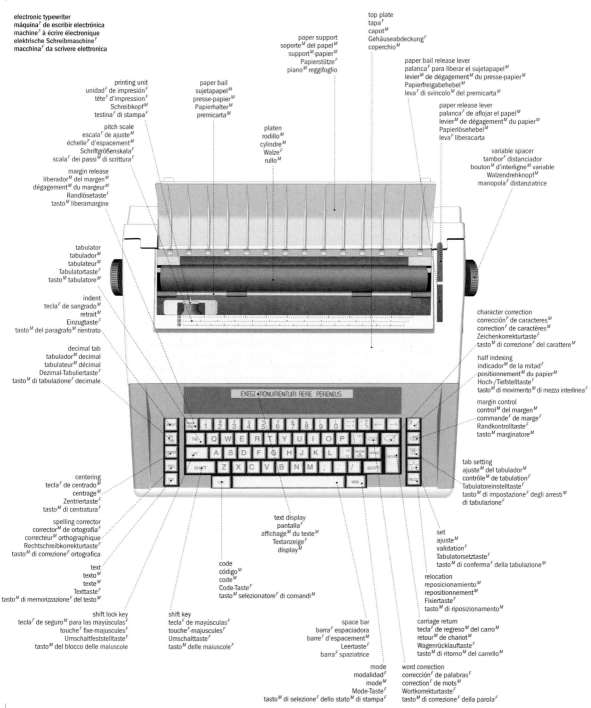

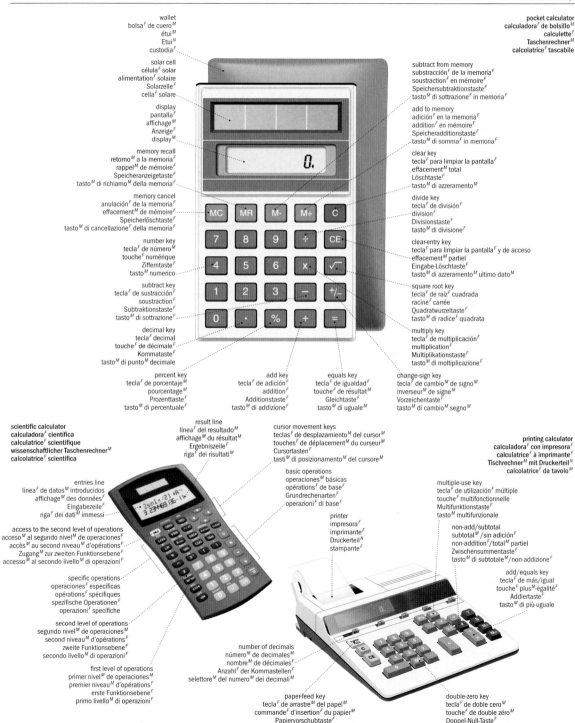

wallet
bolsa^F de cuero^M
étui^M
Etui^N
custodia^F

pocket calculator
calculadora^F de bolsillo^M
calculette^F
Taschenrechner^M
calcolatrice^F tascabile

solar cell
célula^F solar
alimentation^F solaire
Solarzelle^F
cella^F solare

display
pantalla^F
affichage^M
Anzeige^F
display^M

memory recall
retorno^M a la memoria^F
rappel^M de mémoire^F
Speicheranzeigetaste^F
tasto^M di richiamo^M della memoria^F

memory cancel
anulación^F de la memoria^F
effacement^M de mémoire^F
Speicherlöschtaste^F
tasto^M di cancellazione^F della memoria^F

number key
tecla^F de número^M
touche^F numérique
Zifferntaste^F
tasto^M numerico

subtract key
tecla^F de sustracción^F
soustraction^F
Subtraktionstaste^F
tasto^M di sottrazione^F

decimal key
tecla^F decimal
touche^F de décimale^F
Kommataste^F
tasto^M di punto^M decimale

subtract from memory
substracción^F de la memoria^F
soustraction^F en mémoire^F
Speichersubtraktionstaste^F
tasto^M di sottrazione^F in memoria^F

add to memory
adición^F en la memoria^F
addition^F en mémoire^F
Speicheradditionstaste^F
tasto^M di somma^F in memoria^F

clear key
tecla^F para limpiar la pantalla^F
effacement^M total
Löschtaste^F
tasto^M di azzeramento^M

divide key
tecla^F de división^F
division^F
Divisionstaste^F
tasto^M di divisione^F

clear-entry key
tecla^F para limpiar la pantalla^F y de acceso
effacement^M partiel
Eingabe-Löschtaste^F
tasto^M di azzeramento^M ultimo dato^M

square root key
tecla^F de raíz^F cuadrada
racine^F carrée
Quadratwurzeltaste^F
tasto^M di radice^F quadrata

multiply key
tecla^F de multiplicación^F
multiplication^F
Multiplikationstaste^F
tasto^M di moltiplicazione^F

percent key
tecla^F de porcentaje^M
pourcentage^M
Prozenttaste^F
tasto^M di percentuale^F

add key
tecla^F de adición^F
addition^F
Additionstaste^F
tasto^M di addizione^F

equals key
tecla^F de igualdad^F
touche^F de résultat^M
Gleichtaste^F
tasto^M di uguale^M

change-sign key
tecla^F de cambio^M de signo^M
inverseur^M de signe^M
Vorzeichentaste^F
tasto^M di cambio^M segno^M

scientific calculator
calculadora^F científica
calculatrice^F scientifique
wissenschaftlicher Taschenrechner^M
calcolatrice^F scientifica

result line
línea^F del resultado^M
affichage^M du résultat^M
Ergebniszeile^F
riga^F dei risultati^M

entries line
línea^F de datos^M introducidos
affichage^M des données^F
Eingabezeile^F
riga^F dei dati^M immessi

cursor movement keys
teclas^F de desplazamiento^M del cursor^M
touches^F de déplacement^M du curseur^M
Cursortasten^F
tasti^M di posizionamento^M del cursore^M

basic operations
operaciones^M básicas
opérations^F de base^F
Grundrechenarten^F
operazioni^F di base^F

printer
impresora^F
imprimante^F
Druckerteil^N
stampante^F

printing calculator
calculadora^F con impresora^F
calculatrice^F à imprimante^F
Tischrechner^M mit Druckerteil^M
calcolatrice^F da tavolo^M

multiple-use key
tecla^F de utilización^F múltiple
touche^F multifonctionnelle
Multifunktionstaste^F
tasto^M multifunzionale

access to the second level of operations
acceso^M al segundo nivel^M de operaciones^F
accès^M au second niveau^M d'opérations^F
Zugang^M zur zweiten Funktionsebene^F
accesso^M al secondo livello^M di operazioni^F

non-add/subtotal
subtotal^M/sin adición^F
non-addition^F/total^M partiel
Zwischensummentaste^F
tasto^M di subtotale^M/non-addizione^F

add/equals key
tecla^F de más/igual
touche^F plus^M-égalité^F
Addiertaste^F
tasto^M di più-uguale

specific operations
operaciones^F específicas
opérations^F spécifiques
spezifische Operationen^F
operazioni^F specifiche

second level of operations
segundo nivel^M de operaciones^M
second niveau^M d'opérations^F
zweite Funktionsebene^F
secondo livello^M di operazioni^F

first level of operations
primer nivel^M de operaciones^M
premier niveau^M d'opérations^F
erste Funktionsebene^F
primo livello^M di operazioni^F

number of decimals
número^M de decimales^M
nombre^M de décimales^F
Anzahl^F der Kommastellen^F
selettore^M del numero^M dei decimali^M

paper-feed key
tecla^F de arrastre^M del papel^M
commande^F d'insertion^F du papier^M
Papiervorschubtaste^F
tasto^M di alimentazione^F della carta^F

double-zero key
tecla^F de doble cero^M
touche^F de double zéro^M
Doppel-Null-Taste^F
tasto^M di doppio zero^M

stationery

for time management
para el empleo^M **del tiempo**^{M}
pour l'emploi^M **du temps**^{M}
für die Terminplanung^F
per la gestione^F **del tempo**^{M}

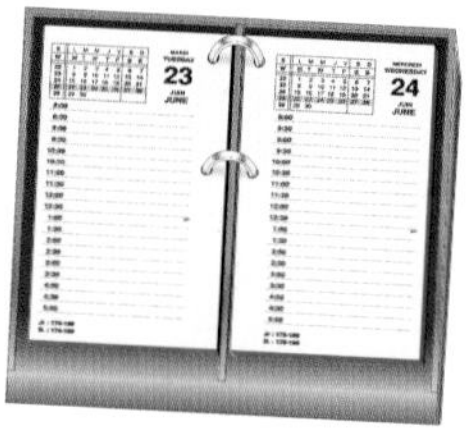

calendar pad
calendario^M de sobremesa
bloc^M-éphéméride^F
Ringbuchkalender^M
calendario^M da tavolo^M

electronic organizer
agenda^F electrónica
organiseur^M
Organizer^M
organizer^M

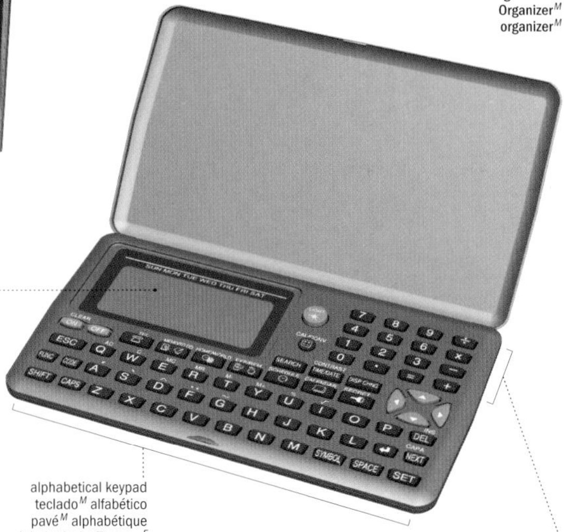

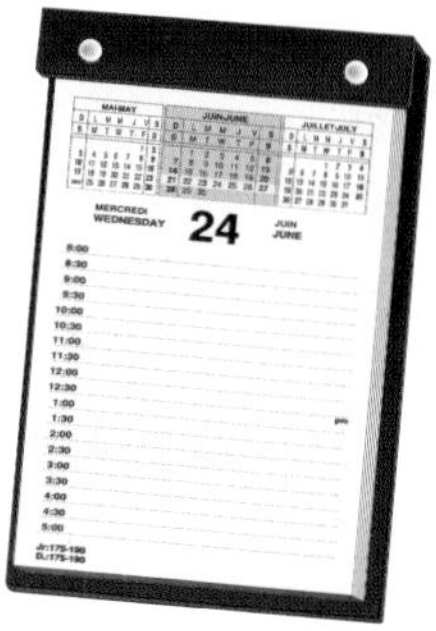

tear-off calendar
calendario^M de sobremesa
calendrier^M-mémorandum^M
Abreißkalender^M
calendario^M a fogli^M staccabili

display
pantalla^F
écran^M
Display^N
display^M

alphabetical keypad
teclado^M alfabético
pavé^M alphabétique
alphabetische Tastatur^F
tastierino^M alfabetico

numeric keypad
teclado^M numérico
pavé^M numérique
numerische Tastatur^F
tastierino^M numerico

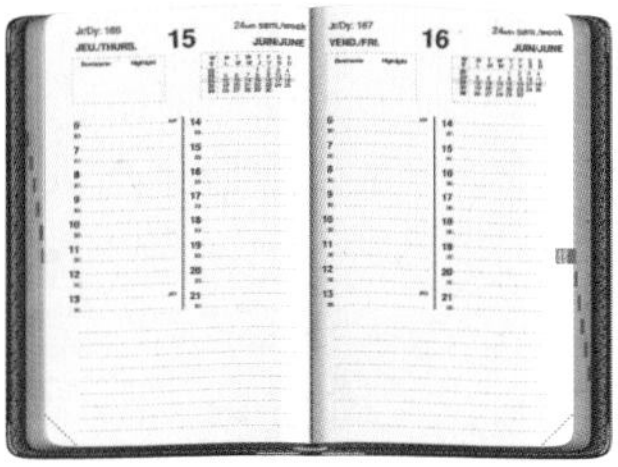

appointment book
agenda^F
agenda^M
Terminkalender^M
agenda^F

display
pantalla^F
écran^M
Display^N
display^M

time clock
timbradora^F
pointeuse^F
Stempeluhr^F
orologio^M per la timbratura^F dei cartellini^M

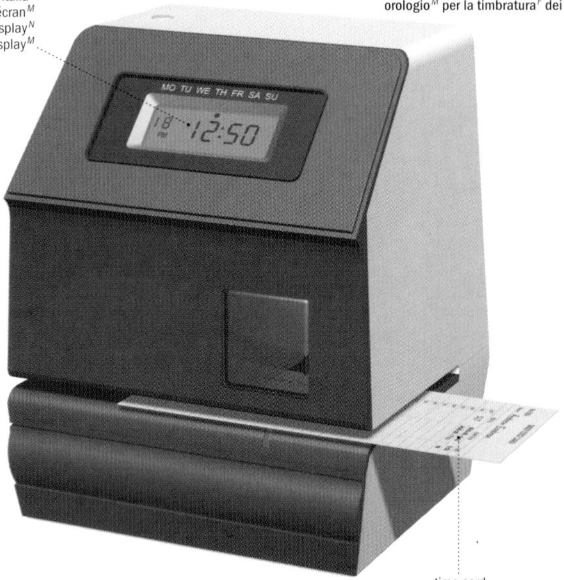

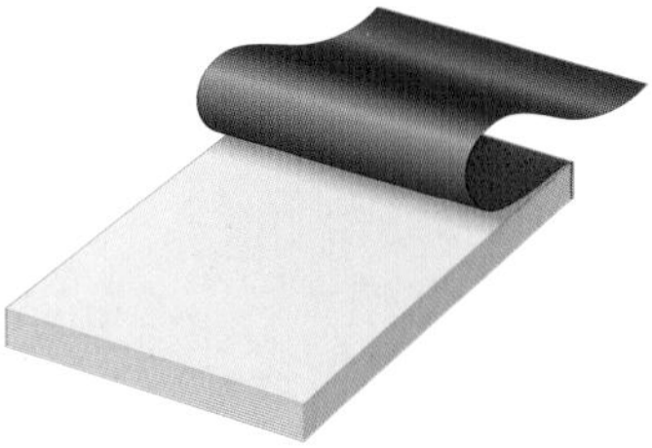

memo pad
libreta^F
bloc^M-notes^F
Notizblock^M
bloc-notes^M

time card
calendario^M
carte^F de pointage^M
Stempelkarte^F
cartellino^M orario

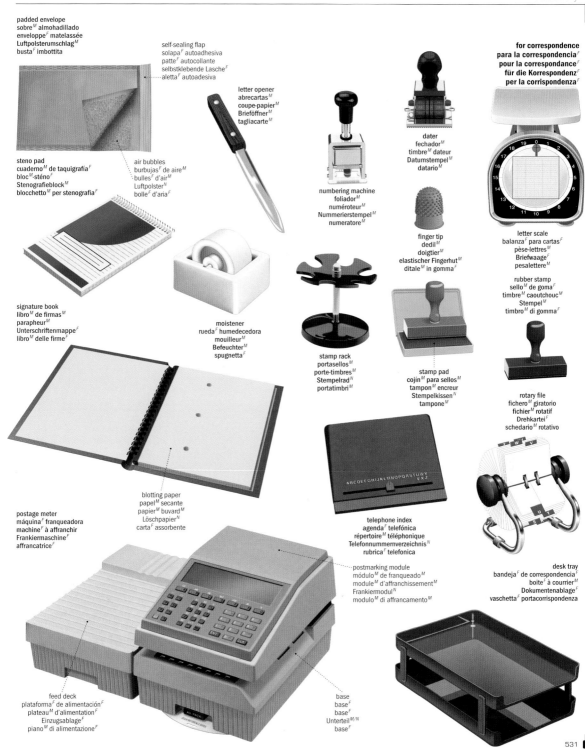

padded envelope
sobre^M almohadillado
enveloppe^F matelassée
Luftpolsterumschlag^M
busta^F imbottita

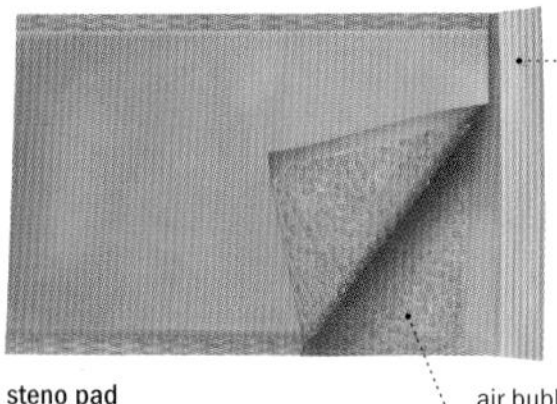

self-sealing flap
solapa^F autoadhesiva
patte^F autocollante
selbstklebende Lasche^F
aletta^F autoadesiva

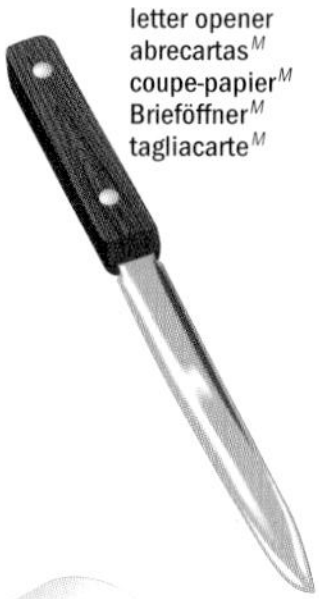

letter opener
abrecartas^M
coupe-papier^M
Brieföffner^M
tagliacarte^M

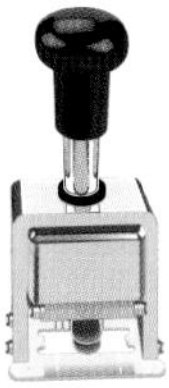

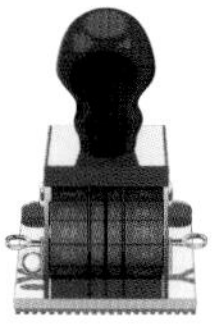

dater
fechador^M
timbre^M dateur
Datumstempel^M
datario^M

for correspondence
para la correspondencia^F
pour la correspondance^F
für die Korrespondenz^F
per la corrispondenza^F

steno pad
cuaderno^M de taquigrafía^F
bloc^M-sténo^F
Stenografieblock^M
blocchetto^M per stenografia^F

air bubbles
burbujas^F de aire^M
bulles^F d'air^M
Luftpolster^N
bolle^F d'aria^F

numbering machine
foliador^M
numéroteur^M
Nummerierstempel^M
numeratore^M

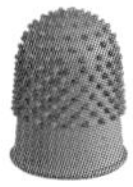

finger tip
dedil^M
doigtier^M
elastischer Fingerhut^M
ditale^M in gomma^F

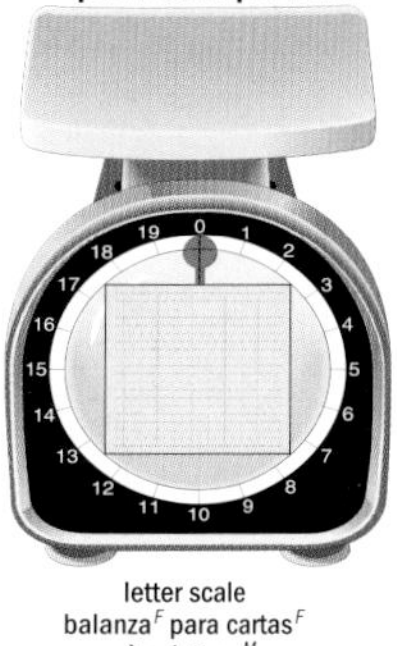

letter scale
balanza^F para cartas^F
pèse-lettres^M
Briefwaage^F
pesalettere^M

rubber stamp
sello^M de goma^F
timbre^M caoutchouc^M
Stempel^M
timbro^M di gomma^F

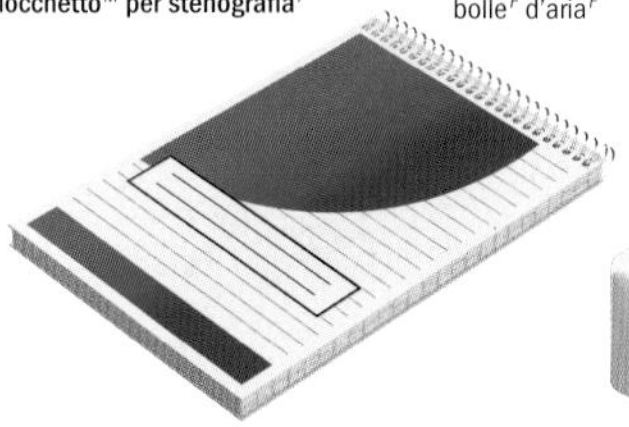

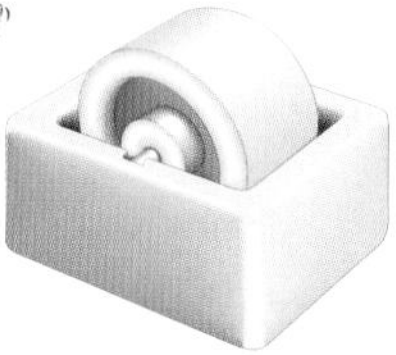

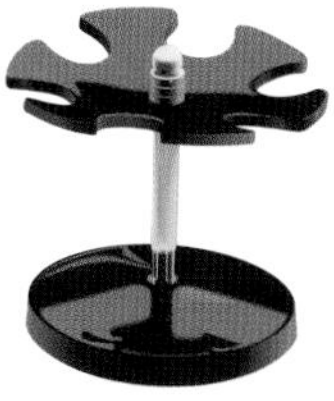

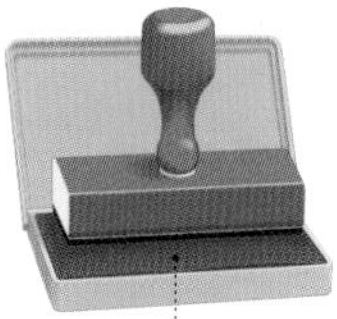

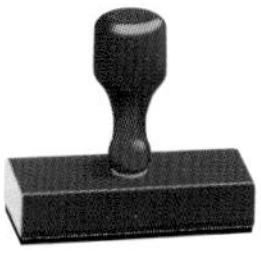

signature book
libro^M de firmas^M
parapheur^M
Unterschriftenmappe^F
libro^M delle firme^F

moistener
rueda^F humedecedora
mouilleur^M
Befeuchter^M
spugnetta^F

stamp rack
portasellos^M
porte-timbres^M
Stempelrad^N
portatimbri^M

stamp pad
cojín^M para sellos^M
tampon^M encreur
Stempelkissen^N
tampone^M

rotary file
fichero^M giratorio
fichier^M rotatif
Drehkartei^F
schedario^M rotativo

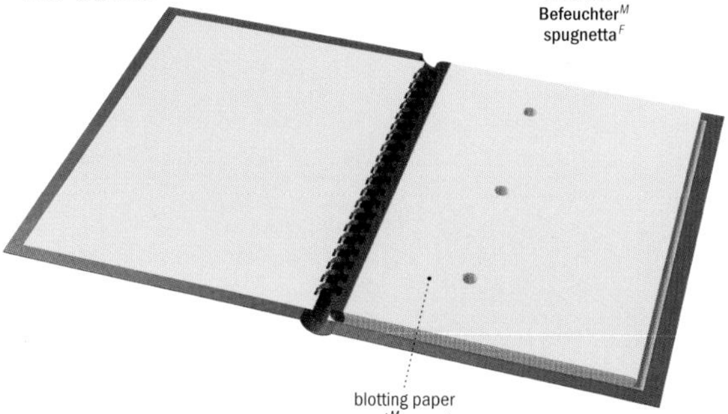

blotting paper
papel^M secante
papier^M buvard^M
Löschpapier^N
carta^F assorbente

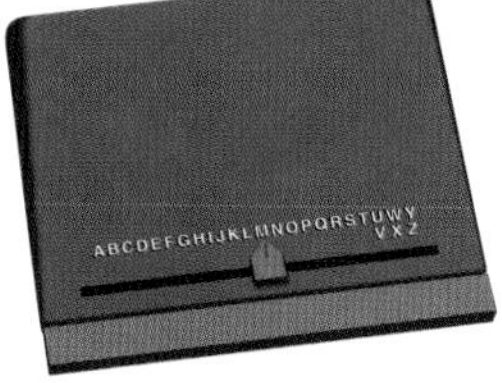

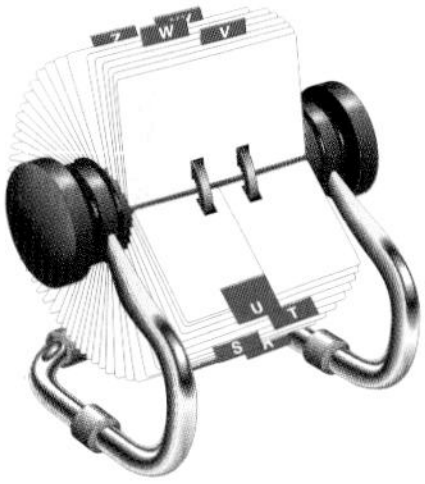

postage meter
máquina^F franqueadora
machine^F à affranchir
Frankiermaschine^F
affrancatrice^F

telephone index
agenda^F telefónica
répertoire^M téléphonique
Telefonnummernverzeichnis^N
rubrica^F telefonica

ABCDEFGHIJKLMNOPQRSTUVWXYZ

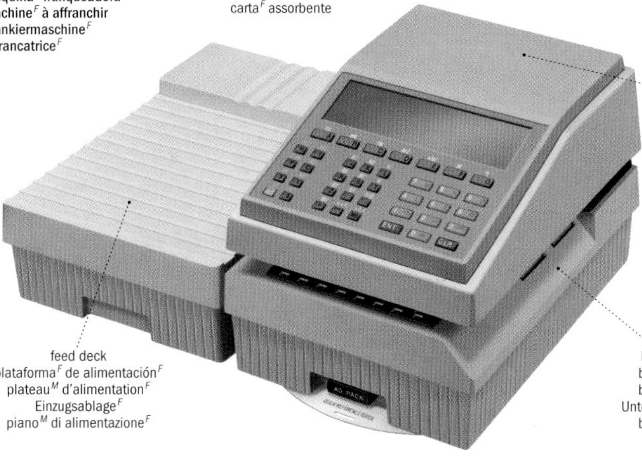

postmarking module
módulo^M de franqueado^M
module^M d'affranchissement^M
Frankiermodul^N
modulo^M di affrancamento^M

desk tray
bandeja^F de correspondencia^F
boîte^F à courrier^M
Dokumentenablage^F
vaschetta^F portacorrispondenza

feed deck
plataforma^F de alimentación^F
plateau^M d'alimentation^F
Einzugsablage^F
piano^M di alimentazione^F

base
base^F
base^F
Unterteil$^{M/N}$
base^F

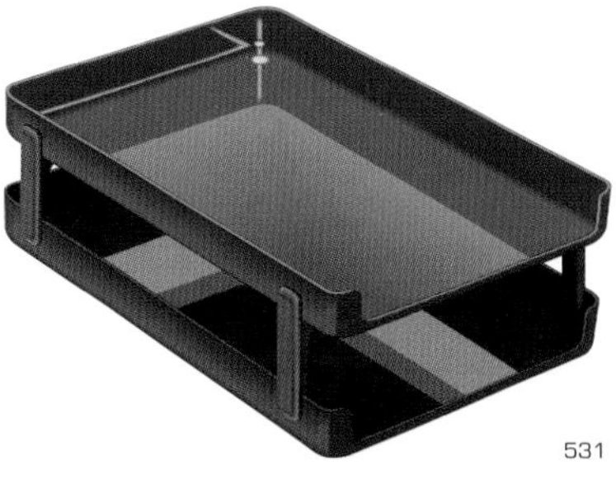

stationery

for filing
para archivar
pour le classement[M]
für die Ablage[F]
per l'archiviazione[F]

self-adhesive labels
etiquetas[F] adhesivas
étiquettes[F] autocollantes
Selbstklebeetiketten[N]
etichette[F] autoadesive

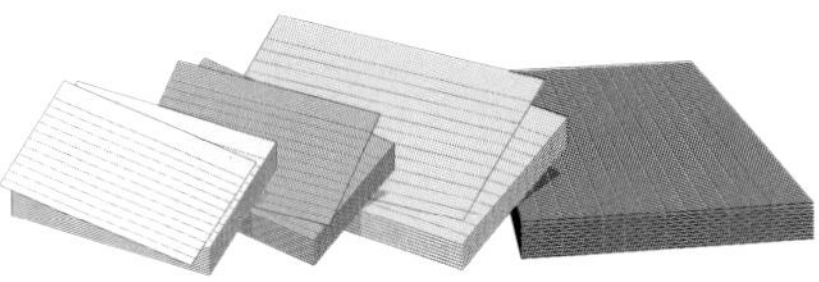

index cards
fichas[F]
fiches[F]
Karteikarten[F]
schede[F]

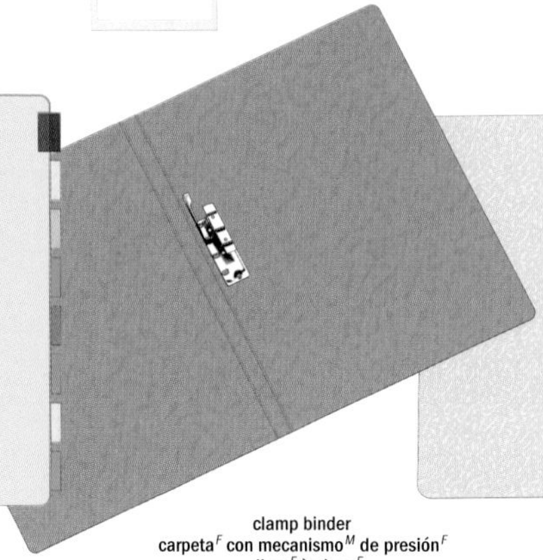

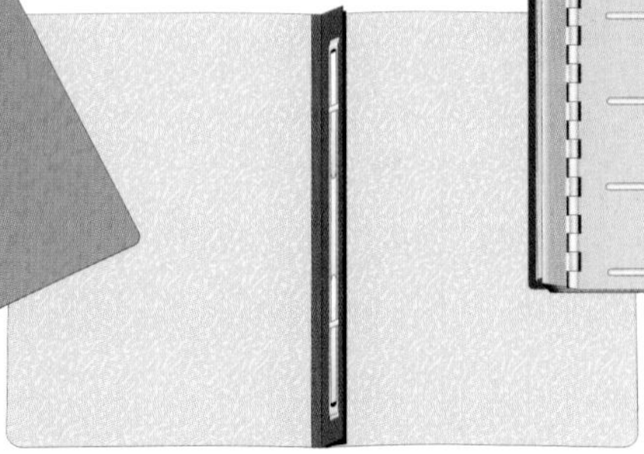

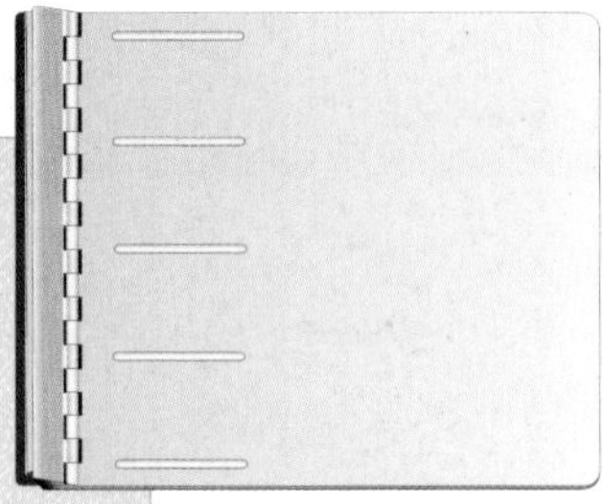

spring binder
carpeta[F] de costilla[F] de resorte[M]
reliure[F] à ressort[M]
Klemmhefter[M]
raccoglitore[M] a molla[F]

dividers
divisores[M]
feuillets[M] intercalaires
Registriereinlagen[F]
divisori[M]

clamp binder
carpeta[F] con mecanismo[M] de presión[F]
reliure[F] à pince[F]
Aktenordner[M]
cartella[F] con pressino[M]

fastener binder
carpeta[F] de broches[M]
reliure[F] à glissière[F]
Schnellhefter[M]
cartella[F] con linguetta[F]

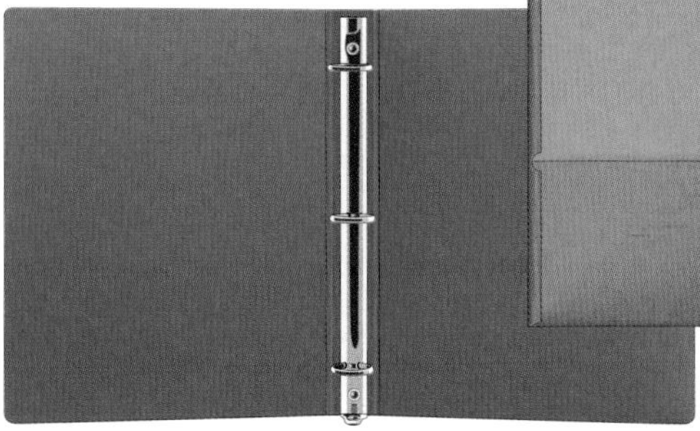

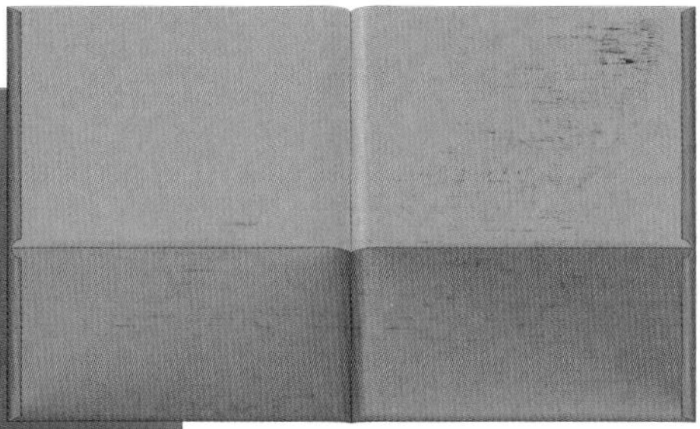

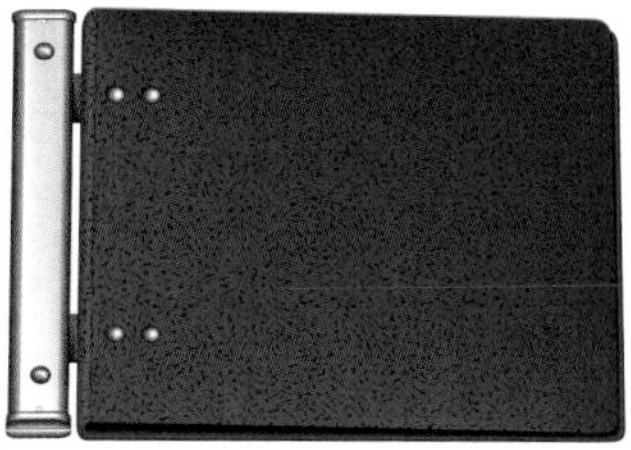

post binder
carpeta[F] de tornillos[M]
reliure[F] à vis[F]
Hefter[M]
portatabulati[M]

ring binder
carpeta[F] de argollas[F]
classeur[M] ; reliure[F] à anneaux[M]
Ringbuch[N]
raccoglitore[M] ad anelli[M]

document folder
carpeta[F] con guardas[F]
pochette[F] d'information[F]
Dokumentenmappe[F]
cartella[F] per documenti[M]

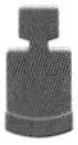

tab
indicador[M]
onglet[M]
Reiter[M]
linguetta[F]

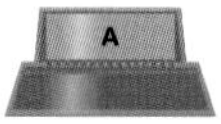

window tab
indicador[M] transparente
onglet[M] à fenêtre[F]
durchsichtiger Reiter[M]
linguetta[F] con finestra[F]

folder
carpeta[F] de archivo[M]
chemise[F]
Aktenmappe[F]
cartelletta[F]

file guides
guías[F] de archivo[M]
guides[M] de classement[M]
Karteiregister[N]
divisori[M] alfabetici per schedario[M]

hanging file
archivador[M] colgante
dossier[M] suspendu
Hängemappe[F]
cartella[F] sospesa

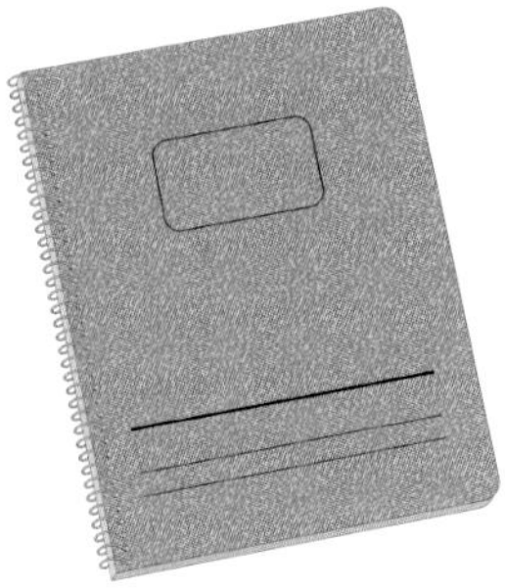

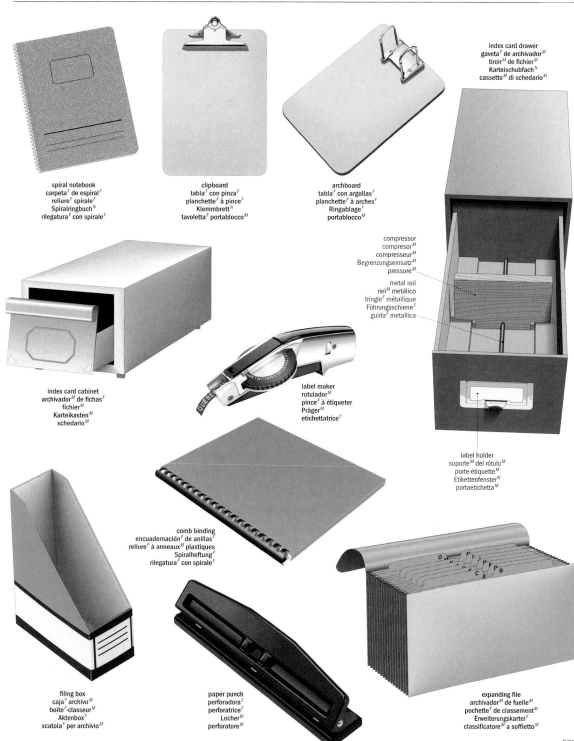

spiral notebook
carpeta^F de espiral^F
reliure^F spirale^F
Spiralringbuch^N
rilegatura^F con spirale^F

clipboard
tabla^F con pinza^F
planchette^F à pince^F
Klemmbrett^N
tavoletta^F portablocco^M

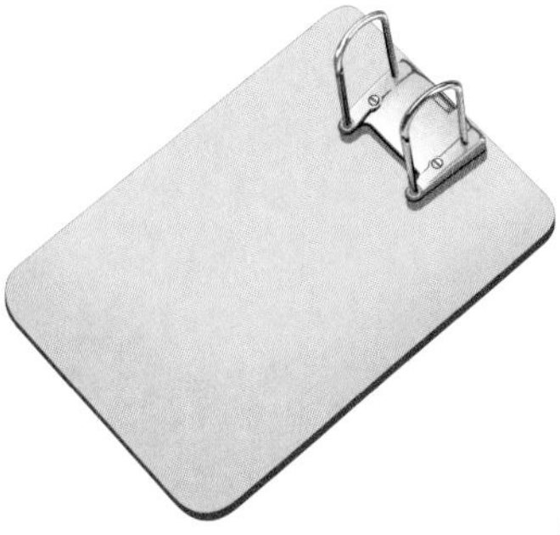

archboard
tabla^F con argollas^F
planchette^F à arches^F
Ringablage^F
portablocco^M

index card drawer
gaveta^F de archivador^M
tiroir^M de fichier^M
Karteischubfach^N
cassetto^M di schedario^M

compressor
compresor^M
compresseur^M
Begrenzungseinsatz^M
pressore^M

metal rail
riel^M metálico
tringle^F métallique
Führungsschiene^F
guida^F metallica

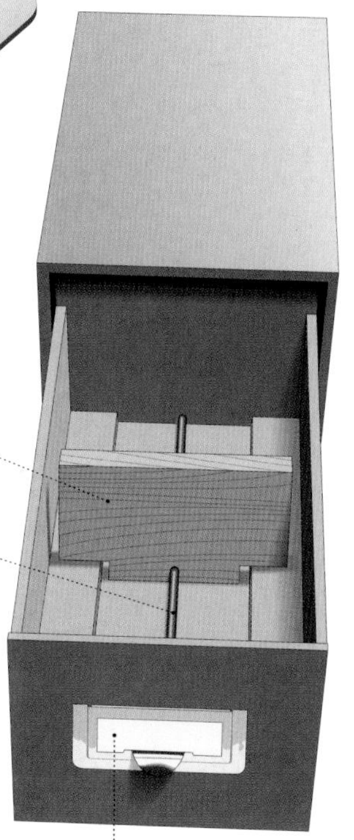

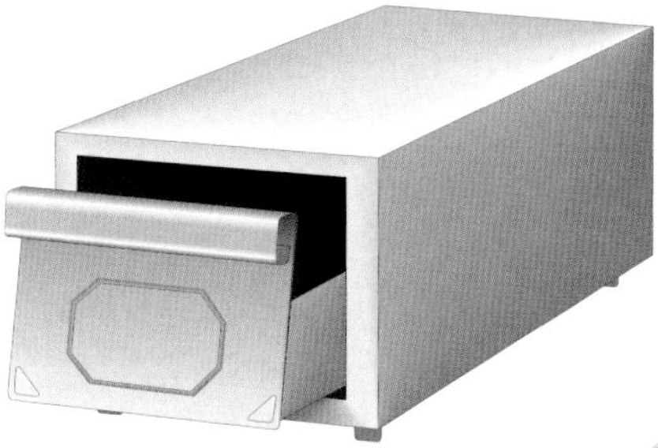

index card cabinet
archivador^M de fichas^F
fichier^M
Karteikasten^M
schedario^M

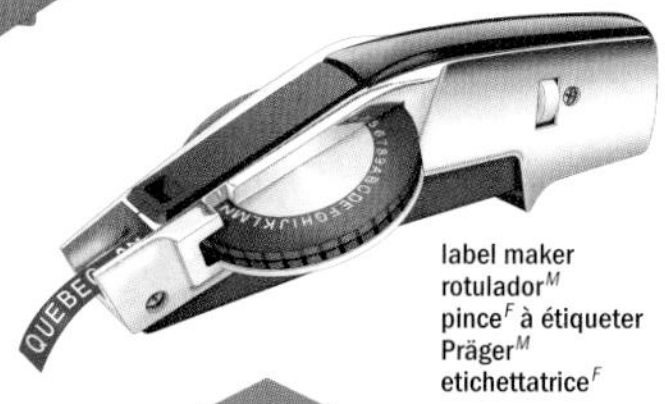

label maker
rotulador^M
pince^F à étiqueter
Präger^M
etichettatrice^F

label holder
soporte^M del rótulo^M
porte-étiquette^M
Etikettenfenster^N
portaetichetta^M

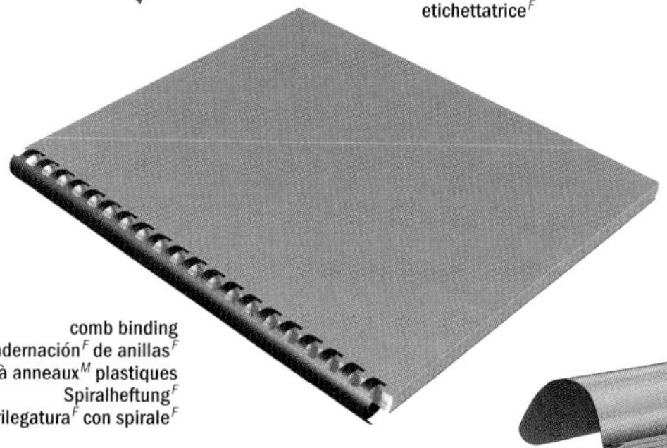

comb binding
encuadernación^F de anillas^F
reliure^F à anneaux^M plastiques
Spiralheftung^F
rilegatura^F con spirale^F

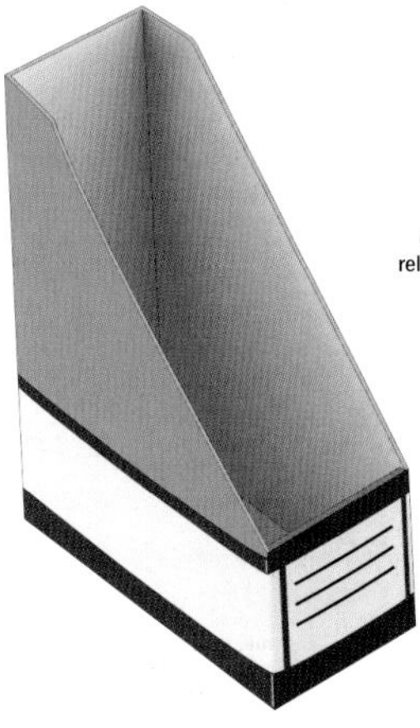

filing box
caja^F archivo^M
boîte^F-classeur^M
Aktenbox^F
scatola^F per archivio^M

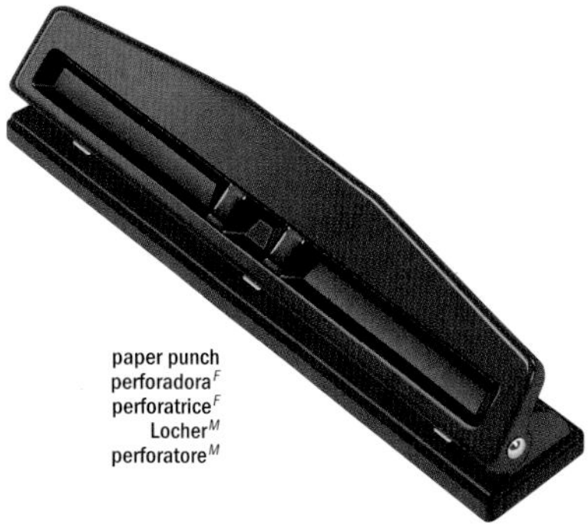

paper punch
perforadora^F
perforatrice^F
Locher^M
perforatore^M

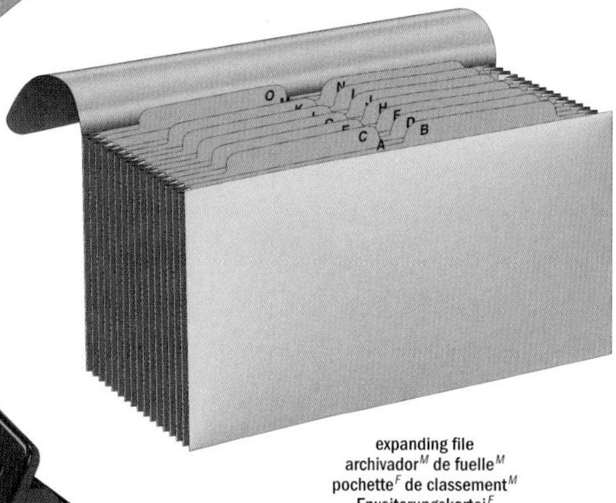

expanding file
archivador^M de fuelle^M
pochette^F de classement^M
Erweiterungskartei^F
classificatore^M a soffietto^M

stationery

miscellaneous articles
artículos^M **varios**
articles^M **divers**
Verschiedenes^N
articoli^M **vari**

packing tape dispenser
porta-cinta^M adhesiva
dévidoir^M pistolet^M
Klebebandabroller^M
nastratrice^F

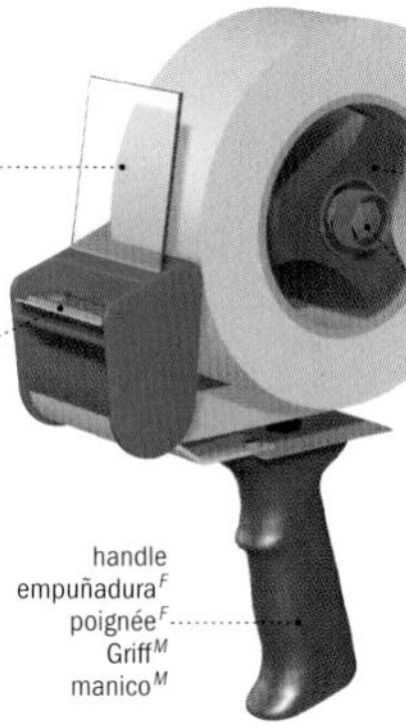

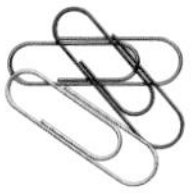

paper clips
clip^M
trombones^F
Büroklammern^F
fermagli^M

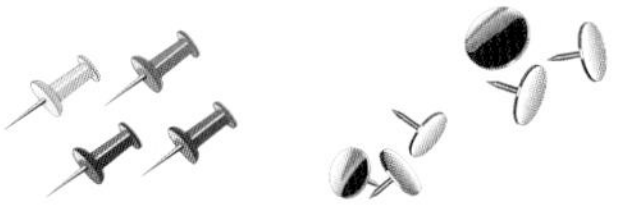

thumb tacks
chinchetas^F
punaises^F
Reißnägel^M
puntine^F da disegno^M

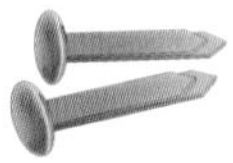

paper fasteners
tachuelas^F para papel^M
attaches^F parisiennes
Beutelklammern^F
fermacampioni^M

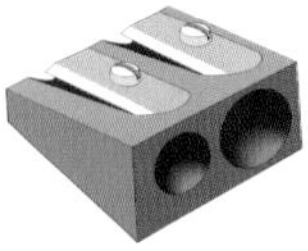

tape guide
guía^F de cinta^F
guide-bande^M
Bandführung^F
guida^F del nastro^M

hub
cubo^M
moyeu^M
Nabe^F
mozzo^M

cutting blade
cuchilla^F
lame^F
Messer^N
lama^F

tension-adjusting screw
tornillo^M de ajuste^M de tensión^F
vis^F de réglage^M de tension^F
Feststellschraube^F
vite^F di regolazione^F della tensione^F

pencil sharpener
sacapuntas^M
taille-crayon^M
Bleistiftspitzer^M
temperamatite^M

handle
empuñadura^F
poignée^F
Griff^M
manico^M

paper clip holder
distribuidor^M de clips^M
distributeur^M de trombones^M
Büroklammerhalter^M
portafermagli^M

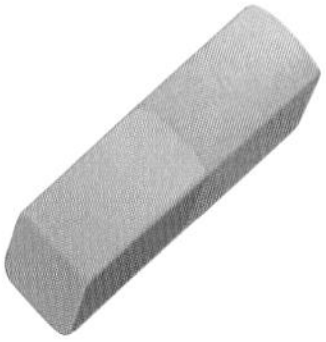

eraser
goma^F
gomme^F
Radiergummi^M
gomma^F

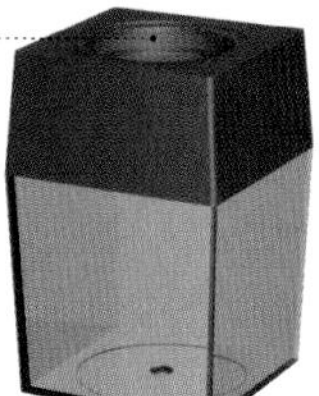

magnet
imán^M
aimant^M
Magnet^M
calamita^F

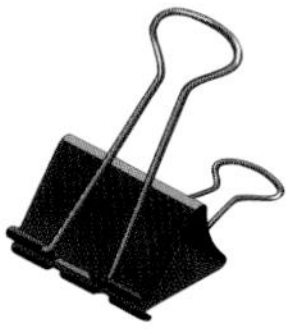

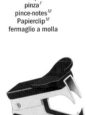

clip
pinza^F
pince-notes^M
Papierclip^M
fermaglio a molla

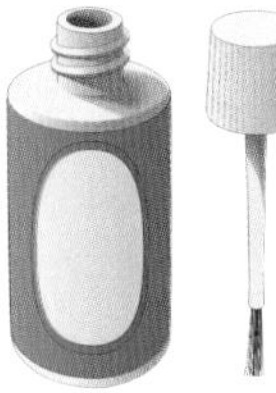

correction fluid
líquido^M corrector
correcteur^M liquide
Korrekturflüssigkeit^F
correttore^M líquido

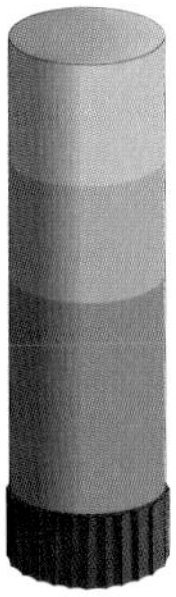

glue stick
lápiz^M adhesivo
bâtonnet^M de colle^F
Klebestift^M
colla^F in stick^M

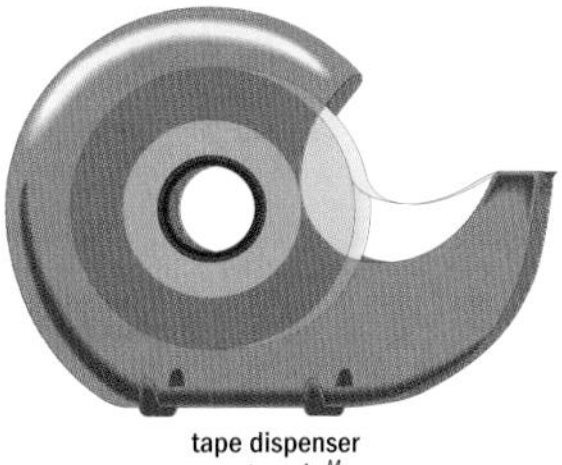

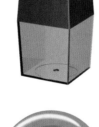

tape dispenser
porta-celo^M
dévidoir^M de ruban^M adhésif
Klebefilmspender^M
chiocciola^F per nastro^M adesivo

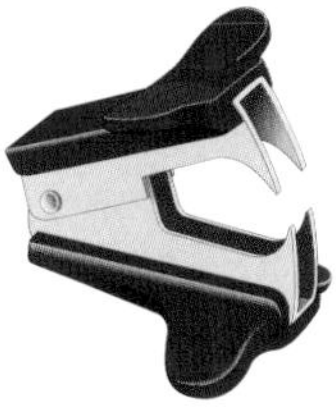

staple remover
quitagrapas^M
dégrafeuse^F
Entklammerer^M
levapunti^M

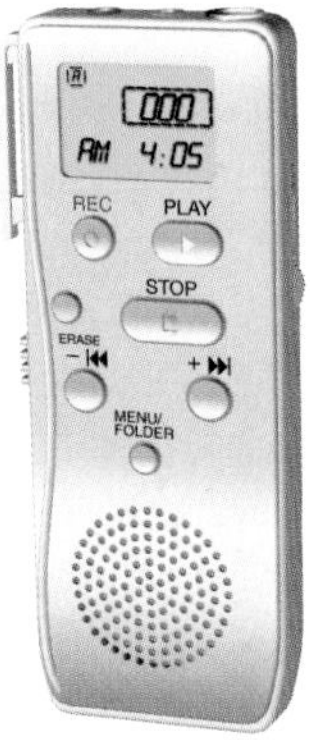

digital voice recorder
grabadora^F digital
enregistreur^M numérique
Diktiergerät^N
registratore^M digitale

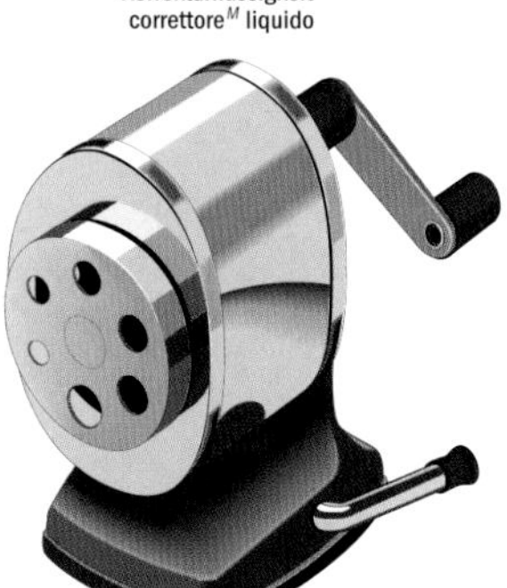

pencil sharpener
sacapuntas^M
taille-crayon^M
Bleistiftspitzer^M
temperamatite^M

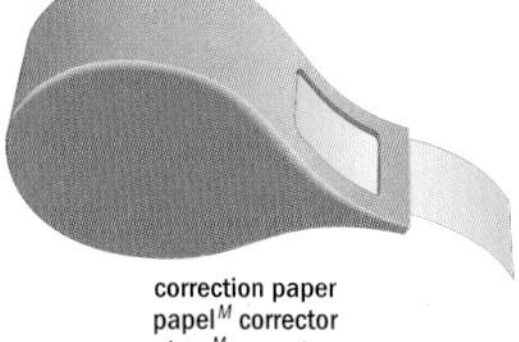

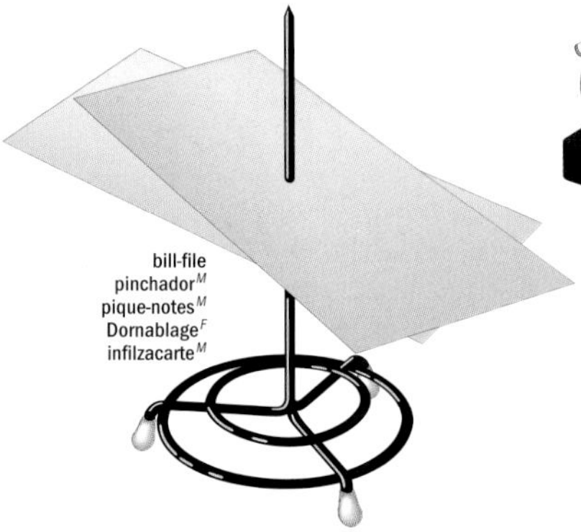

bill-file
pinchador^M
pique-notes^M
Dornablage^F
infilzacarte^M

correction paper
papel^M corrector
ruban^M correcteur
Korrekturstreifen^M
nastro^M per correzioni^F

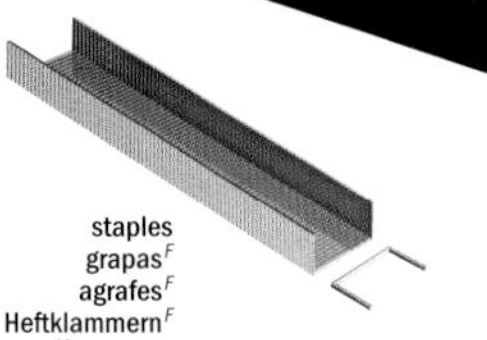

staples
grapas^F
agrafes^F
Heftklammern^F
punti^M metallici

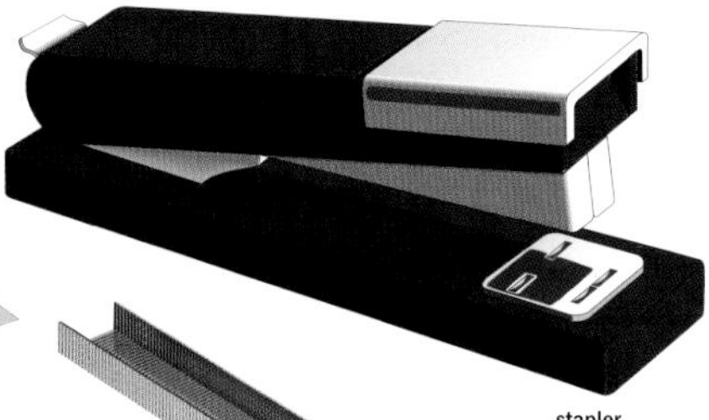

stapler
grapadora^F
agrafeuse^F
Hefter^M
cucitrice^F

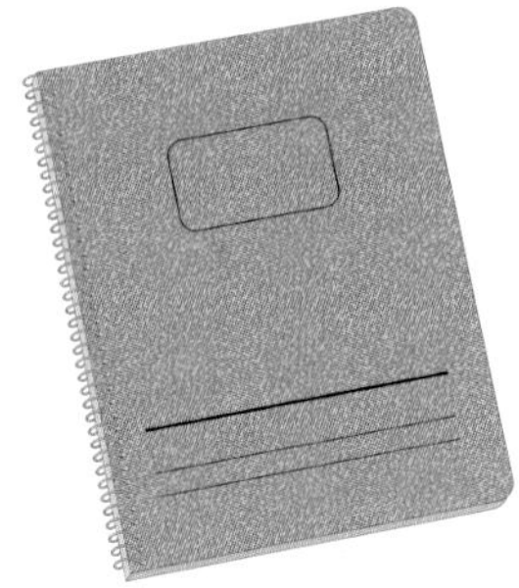

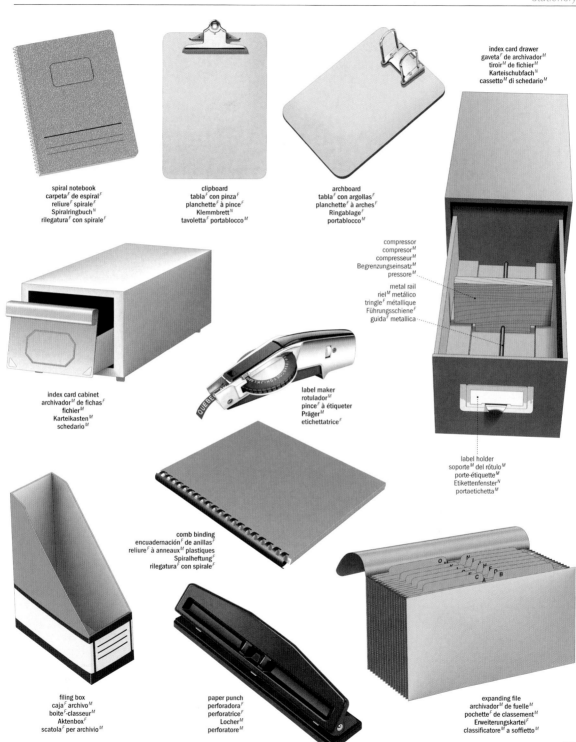

spiral notebook
carpeta^F de espiral^F
reliure^F spirale^F
Spiralringbuch^N
rilegatura^F con spirale^F

clipboard
tabla^F con pinza^F
planchette^F à pince^F
Klemmbrett^N
tavoletta^F portablocco^M

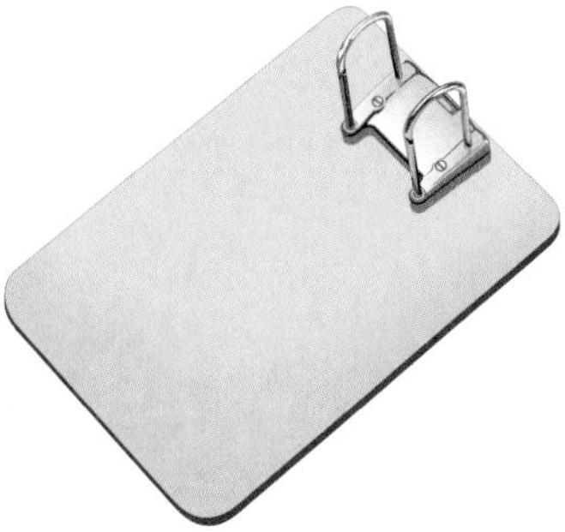

archboard
tabla^F con argollas^F
planchette^F à arches^F
Ringablage^F
portablocco^M

index card drawer
gaveta^F de archivador^M
tiroir^M de fichier^M
Karteischubfach^N
cassetto^M di schedario^M

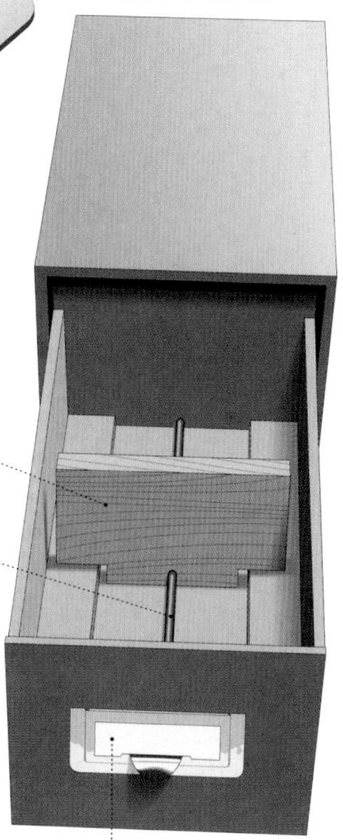

compressor
compresor^M
compresseur^M
Begrenzungseinsatz^M
pressore^M

metal rail
riel^M metálico
tringle^F métallique
Führungsschiene^F
guida^F metallica

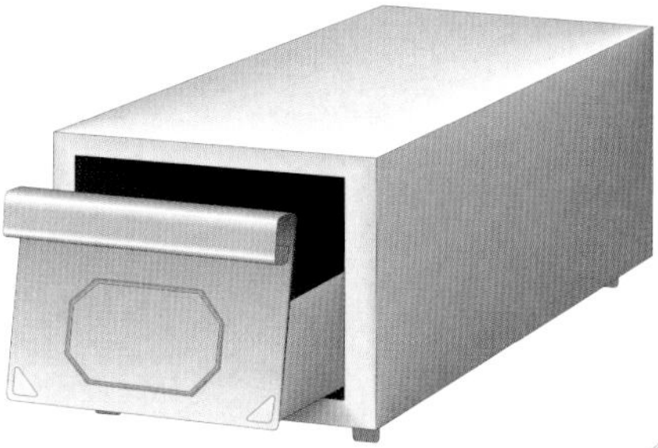

index card cabinet
archivador^M de fichas^F
fichier^M
Karteikasten^M
schedario^M

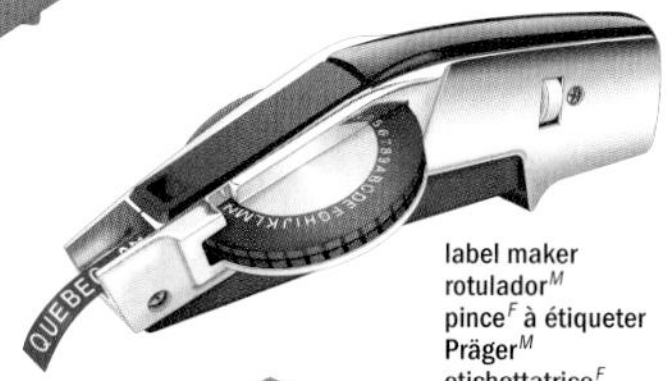

label maker
rotulador^M
pince^F à étiqueter
Präger^M
etichettatrice^F

label holder
soporte^M del rótulo^M
porte-étiquette^M
Etikettenfenster^N
portaetichetta^M

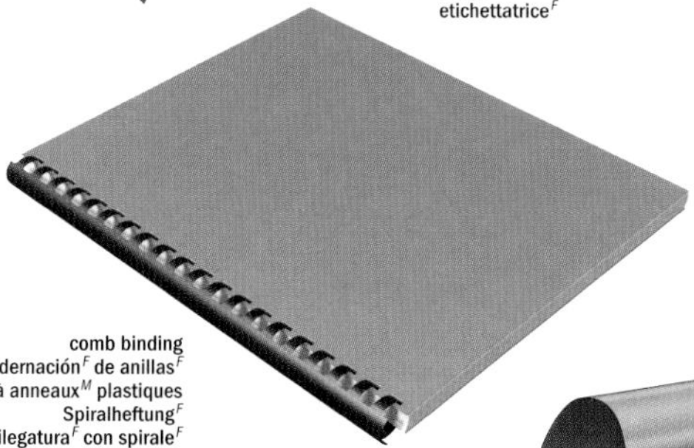

comb binding
encuadernación^F de anillas^F
reliure^F à anneaux^M plastiques
Spiralheftung^F
rilegatura^F con spirale^F

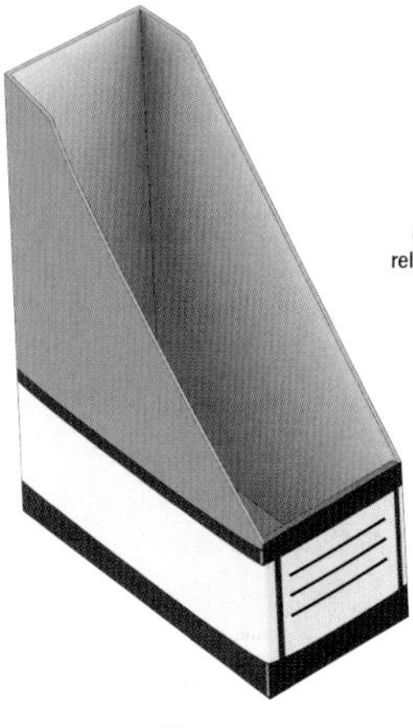

filing box
caja^F archivo^M
boîte^F-classeur^M
Aktenbox^F
scatola^F per archivio^M

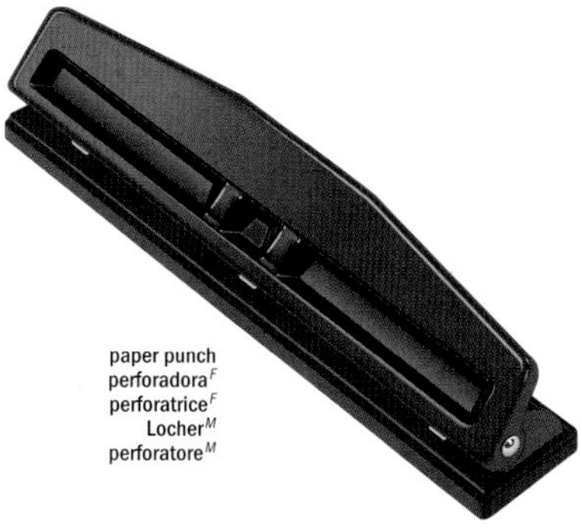

paper punch
perforadora^F
perforatrice^F
Locher^M
perforatore^M

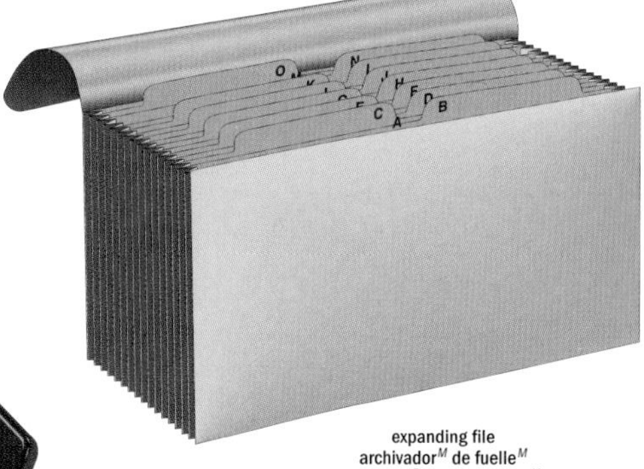

expanding file
archivador^M de fuelle^M
pochette^F de classement^M
Erweiterungskartei^F
classificatore^M a soffietto^M

stationery

miscellaneous articles
artículos[M] **varios**
articles[M] **divers**
Verschiedenes[N]
articoli[M] **vari**

packing tape dispenser
porta-cinta[M] adhesiva
dévidoir[M] pistolet[M]
Klebebandabroller[M]
nastratrice[F]

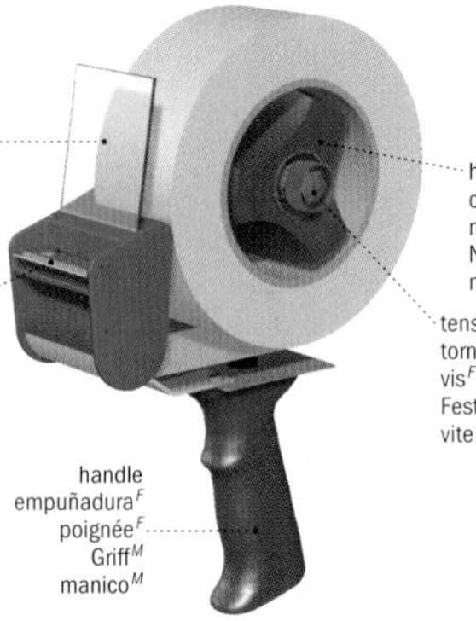

tape guide
guía[F] de cinta[F]
guide-bande[M]
Bandführung[F]
guida[F] del nastro[M]

cutting blade
cuchilla[F]
lame[F]
Messer[N]
lama[F]

handle
empuñadura[F]
poignée[F]
Griff[M]
manico[M]

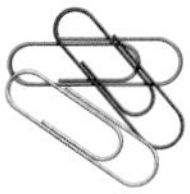

paper clips
clip[M]
trombones[M]
Büroklammern[F]
fermagli[M]

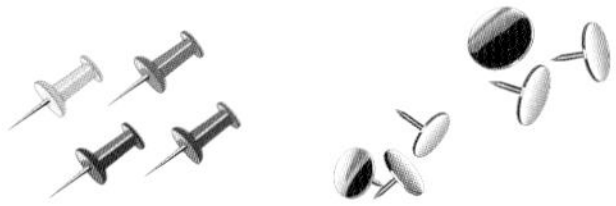

thumb tacks
chinchetas[F]
punaises[F]
Reißnägel[M]
puntine[F] da disegno[M]

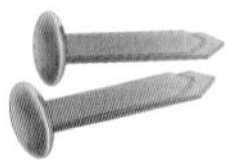

paper fasteners
tachuelas[F] para papel[M]
attaches[F] parisiennes
Beutelklammern[F]
fermacampioni[M]

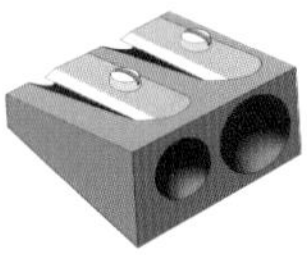

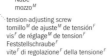

hub
cubo[M]
moyeu[M]
Nabe[F]
mozzo[M]

tension-adjusting screw
tornillo[M] de ajuste[M] de tensión[F]
vis[F] de réglage[M] de tension[F]
Feststellschraube[F]
vite[F] di regolazione[F] della tensione[F]

pencil sharpener
sacapuntas[M]
taille-crayon[M]
Bleistiftspitzer[M]
temperamatite[M]

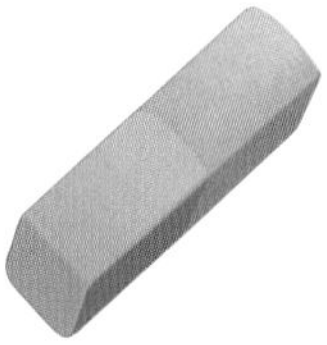

eraser
goma[F]
gomme[F]
Radiergummi[M]
gomma[F]

paper clip holder
distribuidor[M] de clips[M]
distribuiteur[M] de trombones[M]
Büroklammerhalter[M]
portafermagli[M]

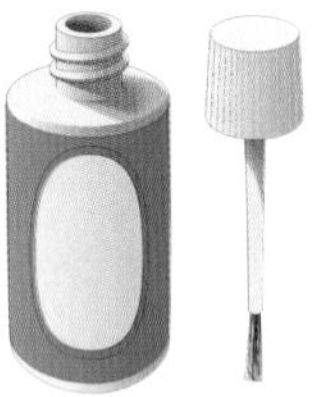

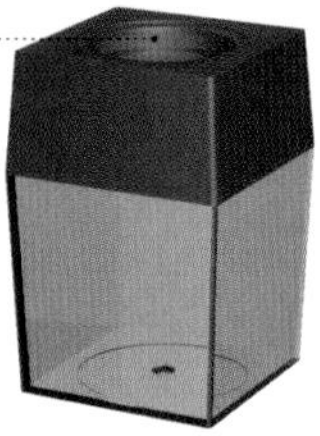

magnet
imán[M]
aimant[M]
Magnet[M]
calamita[F]

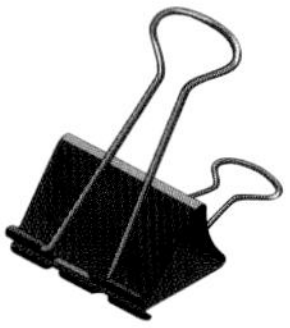

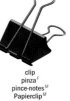

clip
pinza[F]
pince-notes[M]
Papierclip[M]
fermaglio a molla

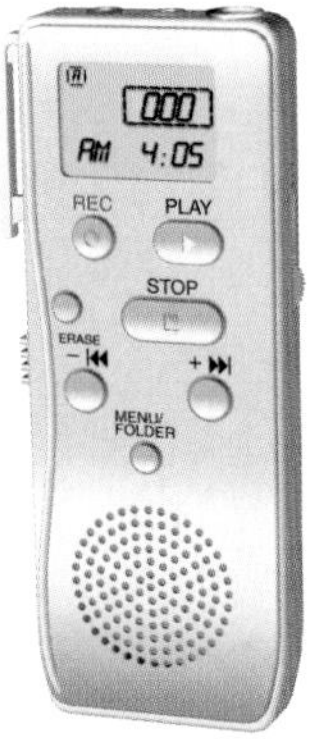

correction fluid
líquido[M] corrector
correcteur[M] liquide
Korrekturflüssigkeit[F]
correttore[M] liquido

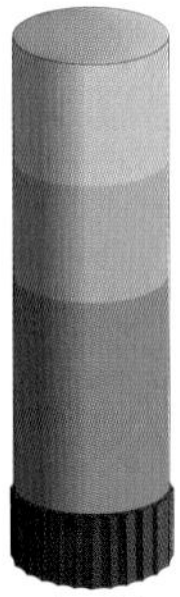

glue stick
lápiz[M] adhesivo
bâtonnet[M] de colle[F]
Klebestift[M]
colla[F] in stick[M]

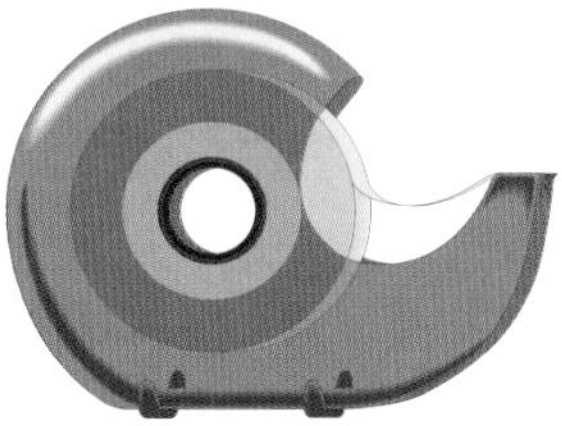

tape dispenser
porta-celo[M]
dévidoir[M] de ruban[M] adhésif
Klebefilmspender[M]
chiocciola[F] per nastro[M] adesivo

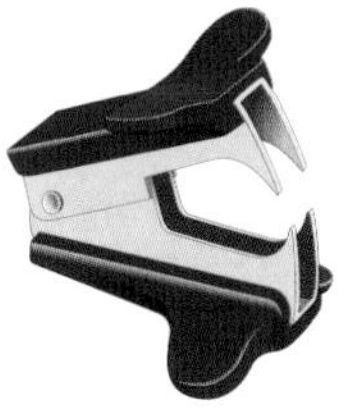

staple remover
quitagrapas[M]
dégrafeuse[F]
Entklammerer[M]
levapunti[M]

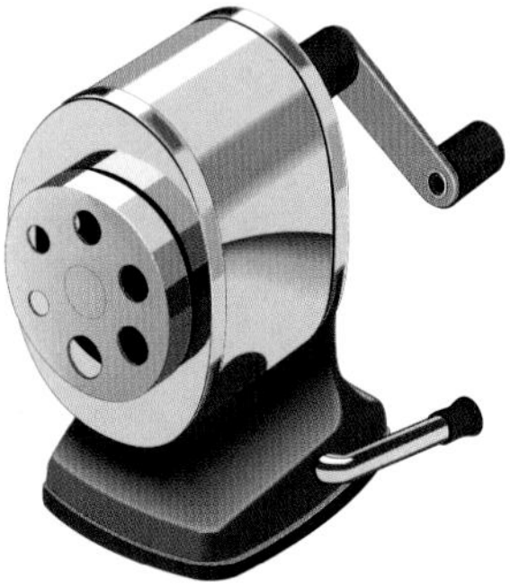

digital voice recorder
grabadora[F] digital
enregistreur[M] numérique
Diktiergerät[N]
registratore[M] digitale

pencil sharpener
sacapuntas[M]
taille-crayon[M]
Bleistiftspitzer[M]
temperamatite[M]

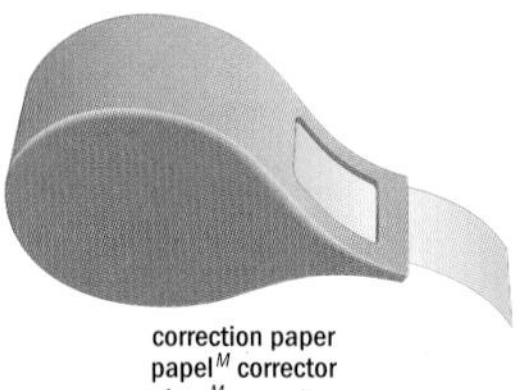

correction paper
papel[M] corrector
ruban[M] correcteur
Korrekturstreifen[M]
nastro[M] per correzioni[F]

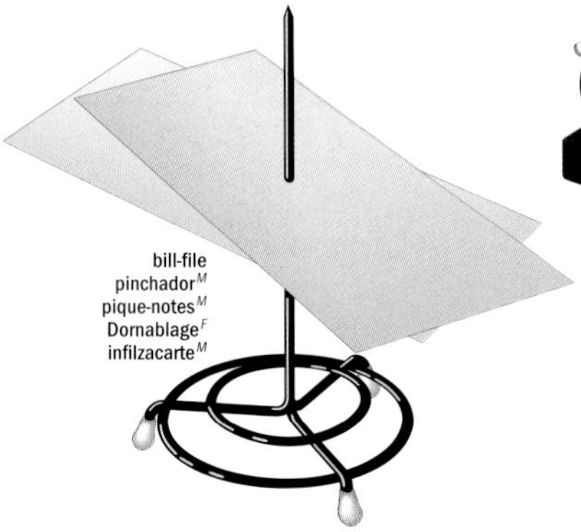

bill-file
pinchador[M]
pique-notes[M]
Dornablage[F]
infilzacarte[M]

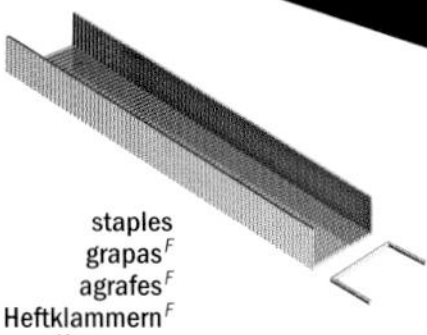

staples
grapas[F]
agrafes[F]
Heftklammern[F]
punti[M] metallici

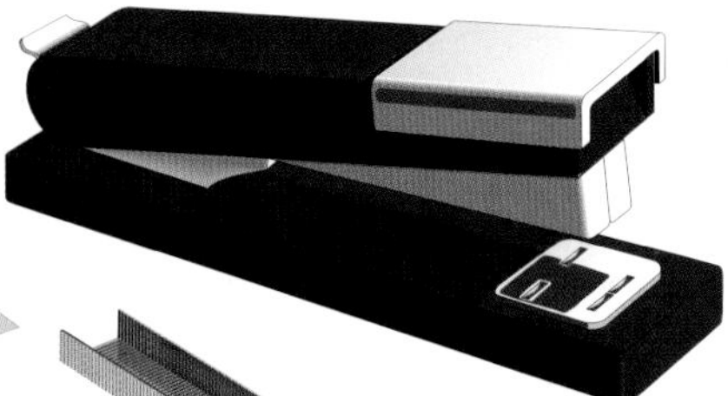

stapler
grapadora[F]
agrafeuse[F]
Hefter[M]
cucitrice[F]

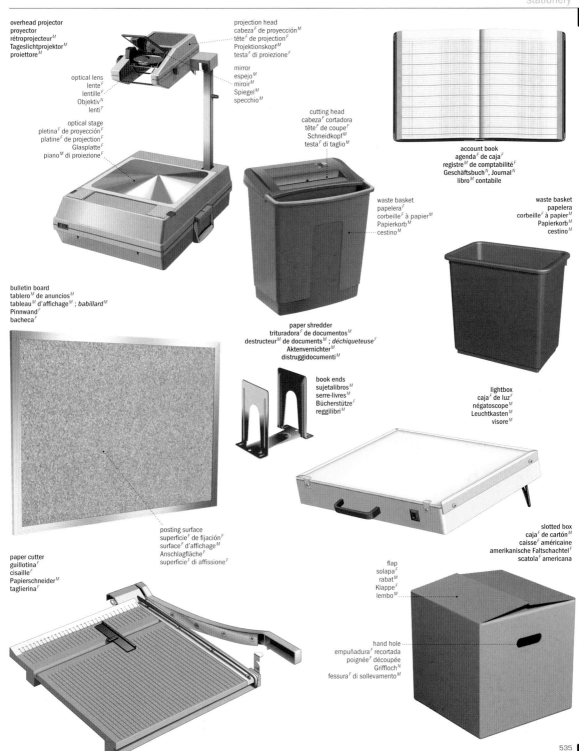

overhead projector
proyector
rétroprojecteur^M
Tageslichtprojektor^M
proiettore^M

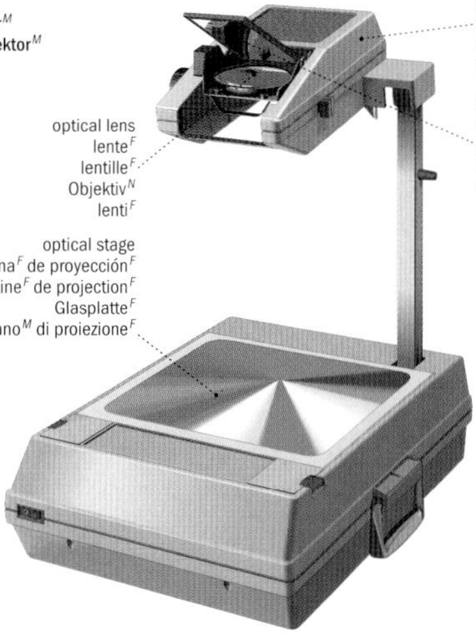

projection head
cabeza^F de proyección^M
tête^F de projection^F
Projektionskopf^M
testa^F di proiezione^F

optical lens
lente^F
lentille^F
Objektiv^N
lenti^F

mirror
espejo^M
miroir^M
Spiegel^M
specchio^M

optical stage
pletina^F de proyección^F
platine^F de projection^F
Glasplatte^F
piano^M di proiezione^F

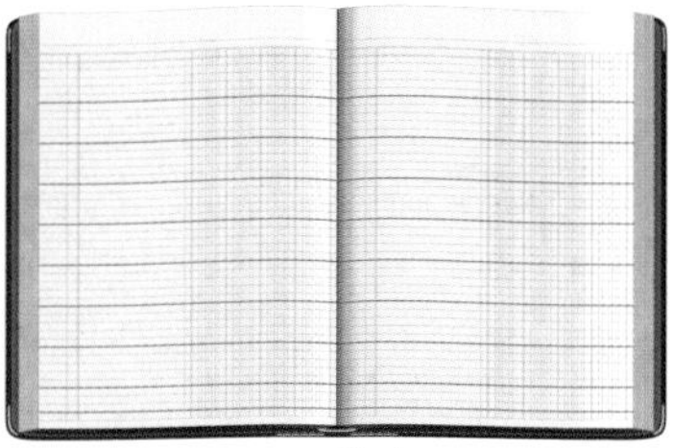

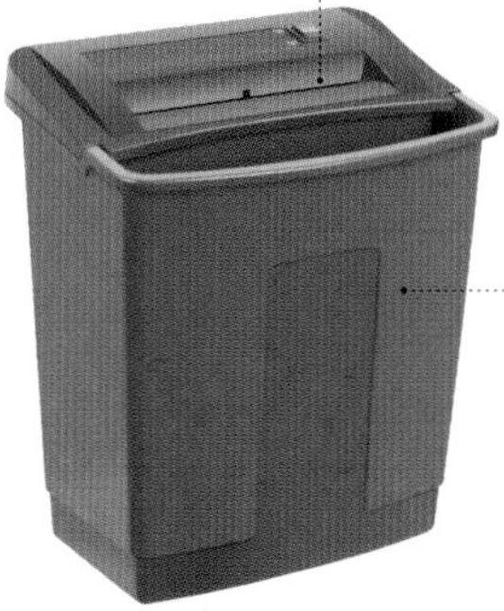

cutting head
cabeza^F cortadora
tête^F de coupe^F
Schneidkopf^M
testa^F di taglio^M

account book
agenda^F de caja^F
registre^M de comptabilité^F
Geschäftsbuch^N, Journal^N
libro^M contabile

waste basket
papelera^F
corbeille^F à papier^M
Papierkorb^M
cestino^M

waste basket
papelera
corbeille^F à papier^M
Papierkorb^M
cestino^M

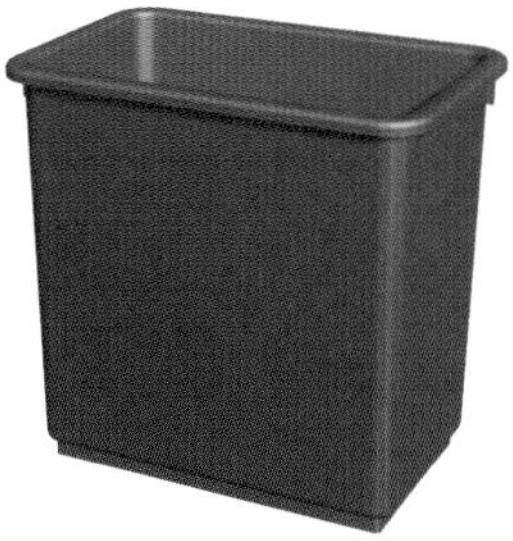

bulletin board
tablero^M de anuncios^M
tableau^M d'affichage^M ; babillard^M
Pinnwand^F
bacheca^F

paper shredder
trituradora^F de documentos^M
destructeur^M de documents^M ; déchiqueteuse^F
Aktenvernichter^M
distruggidocumenti^M

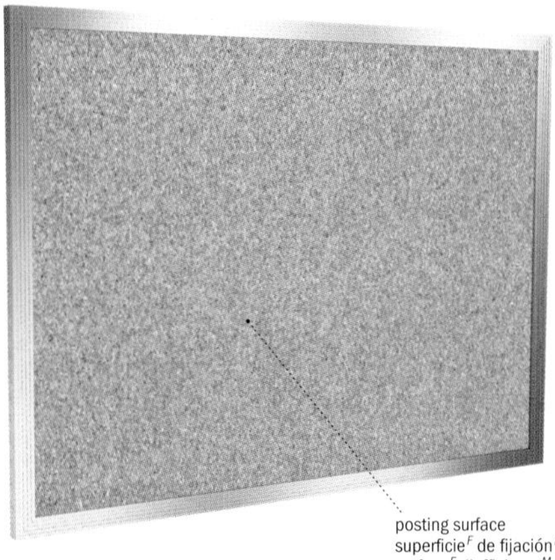

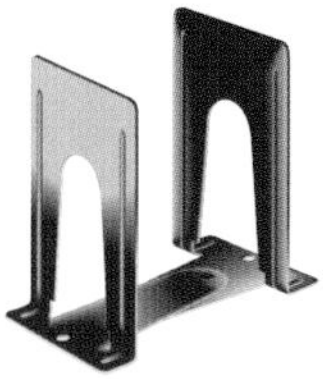

book ends
sujetalibros^M
serre-livres^M
Bücherstütze^F
reggilibri^M

lightbox
caja^F de luz^F
négatoscope^M
Leuchtkasten^M
visore^M

posting surface
superficie^F de fijación^F
surface^F d'affichage^M
Anschlagfläche^F
superficie^F di affissione^F

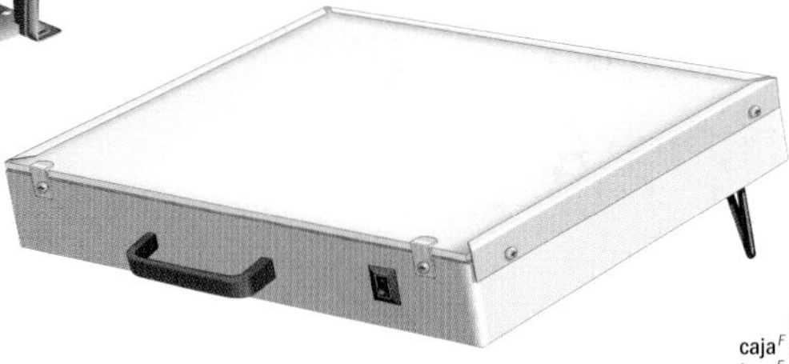

paper cutter
guillotina^F
cisaille^F
Papierschneider^M
taglierina^F

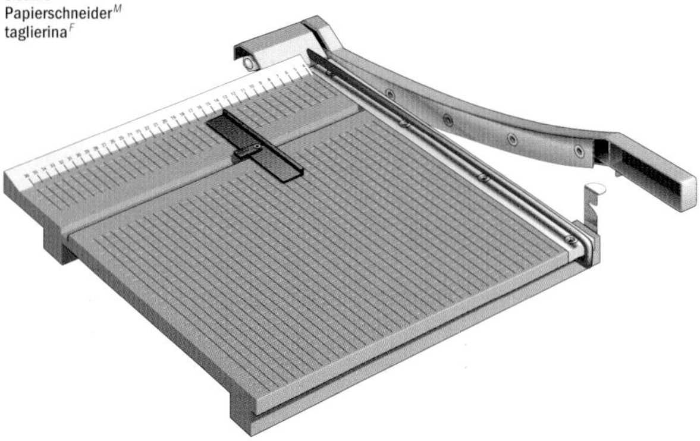

slotted box
caja^F de cartón^M
caisse^F américaine
amerikanische Faltschachtel^F
scatola^F americana

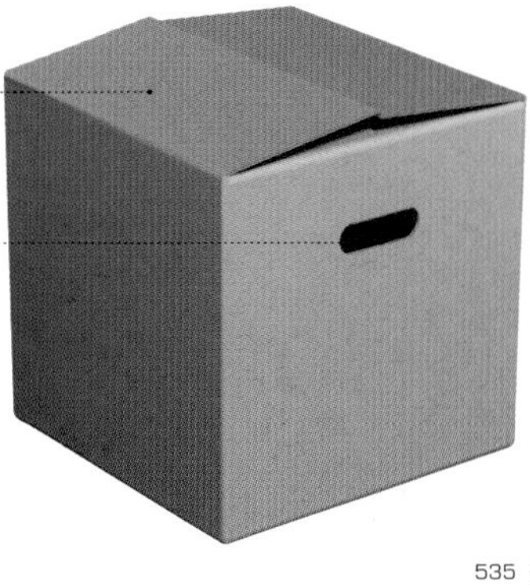

flap
solapa^F
rabat^M
Klappe^F
lembo^M

hand hole
empuñadura^F recortada
poignée^F découpée
Griffloch^N
fessura^F di sollevamento^M

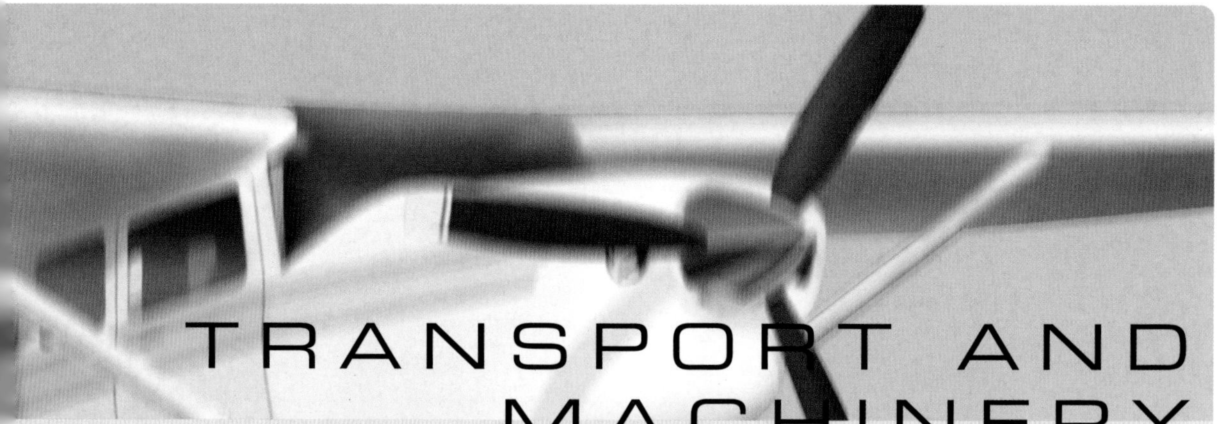

TRANSPORT AND MACHINERY

TRANSPORTE Y VEHÍCULOS | TRANSPORT ET MACHINERIE | TRANSPORT UND FAHRZEUGE | TRASPORTI E VEICOLI

road system

sistema^M de carreteras^F | système^M routier | Straßenbau^M | sistema^M stradale

cross section of a road
sección^F transversal de una carretera^F
coupe^F d'une route^F
Straße^F im Querschnitt^M
sezione^F trasversale di una strada^F

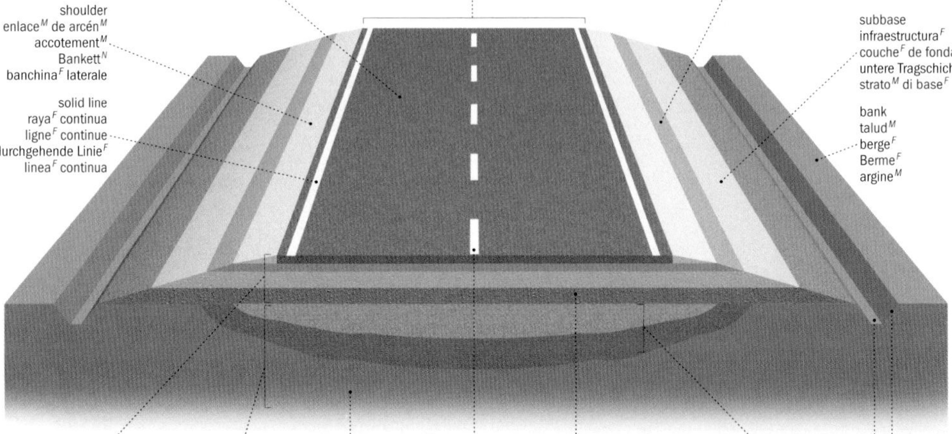

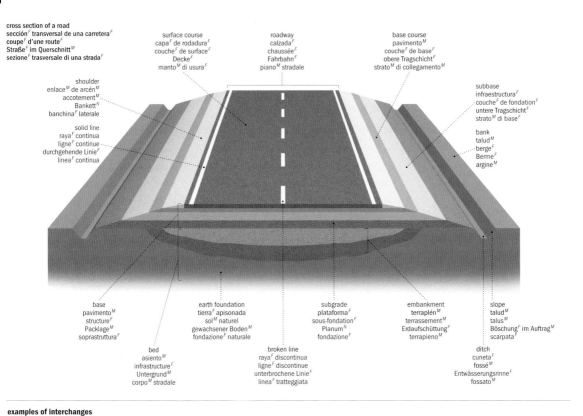

surface course
capa^F de rodadura^F
couche^F de surface^F
Decke^F
manto^M di usura^F

roadway
calzada^F
chaussée^F
Fahrbahn^F
piano^M stradale

base course
pavimento^M
couche^F de base^F
obere Tragschicht^F
strato^M di collegamento^M

shoulder
enlace^F de arcén^M
accotement^M
Bankett^N
banchina^F laterale

subbase
infraestructura^F
couche^F de fondation^F
untere Tragschicht^F
strato^M di base^F

solid line
raya^F continua
ligne^F continue
durchgehende Linie^F
linea^F continua

bank
talud^M
berge^F
Berme^F
argine^M

base
pavimento^M
structure^F
Packlage^M
soprastruttura^F

earth foundation
tierra^F apisonada
sol^M naturel
gewachsener Boden^M
fondazione^F naturale

subgrade
plataforma^F
sous-fondation^F
Planum^N
fondazione^F

embankment
terraplén^M
terrassement^M
Erdaufschüttung^F
terrapieno^M

slope
talud^M
talus^M
Böschung^F im Auftrag^M
scarpata^F

bed
asiento^M
infrastructure^F
Untergrund^M
corpo^M stradale

broken line
raya^F discontinua
ligne^F discontinue
unterbrochene Linie^F
linea^F tratteggiata

ditch
cuneta^F
fossé^M
Entwässerungsrinne^F
fossato^M

examples of interchanges
ejemplos^M de enlaces^M de carreteras^F
exemples^M d'échangeurs^M
Beispiele^N für Anschlussstellen^F
esempi^M di raccordo^M

cloverleaf
enlace^M de trébol^M
échangeur^M en trèfle^M
Kleeblatt^N
raccordo^M a quadrifoglio^M

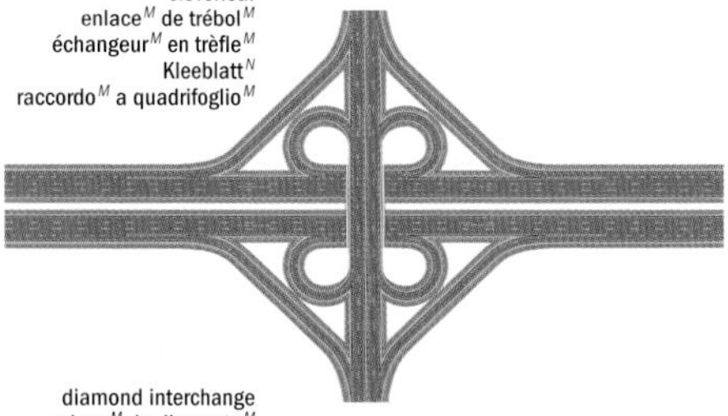

traffic circle
enlace^M de glorieta^F
carrefour^M giratoire
Verteiler^M
raccordo^M a rotatoria^F

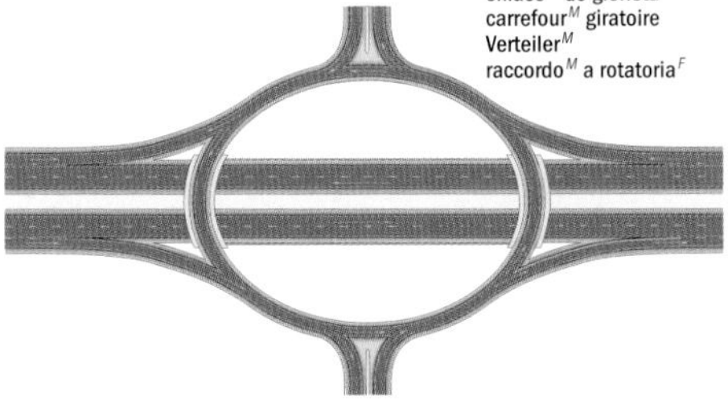

diamond interchange
enlace^M de diamante^M
échangeur^M en losange^M
Raute^F
raccordo^M a losanga^F

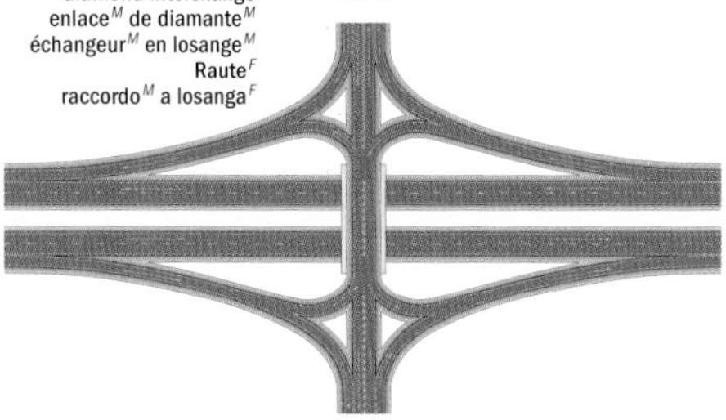

trumpet interchange
trompeta^F
échangeur^M en trompette^F
Trompete^F
raccordo^M a tromba^F

TRANSPORT AND MACHINERY

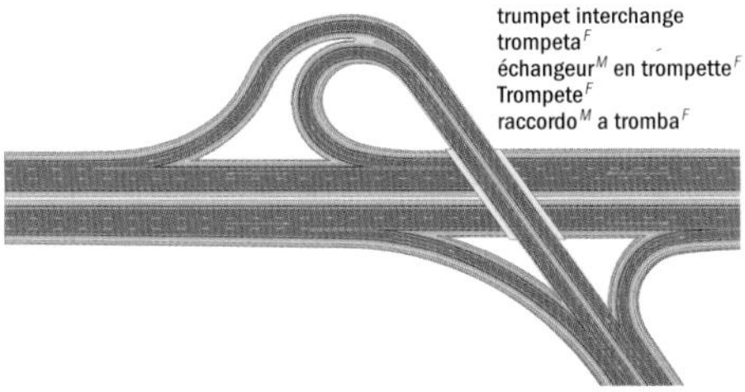

cloverleaf
enlace^M de trébol^M
échangeur^M en trèfle^M
Kleeblatt^N
raccordo^M a quadrifoglio^M

deceleration lane
carril^M de desaceleración^F
voie^F de décélération^F
Ausfahrtspur^F
corsia^F di decelerazione^F

acceleration lane
carril^M de aceleración^F
voie^F d'accélération^F
Beschleunigungsspur^F
corsia^F di accelerazione^F

exit
salida^F
sortie^F
Ausfahrt^F
corsia^F di uscita^F

entrance
entrada^F
entrée^F
Einfahrt^F
corsia^F di entrata^F

broken line
raya^F discontinua
ligne^F discontinue
unterbrochene Linie^F
linea^F tratteggiata

transfer ramp
ramal^M de enlace^M
bretelle^F de raccordement^M
Auffahrt^F
bretella^F di raccordo^M

median
mediana^M
terre-plein^M central
Mittelstreifen^M
spartitraffico^M

island
isla^F
îlot^M
Insel^F
isola^F

side lane
línea^F lateral
voie^F latérale
Seitenspur^F
corsia^F laterale

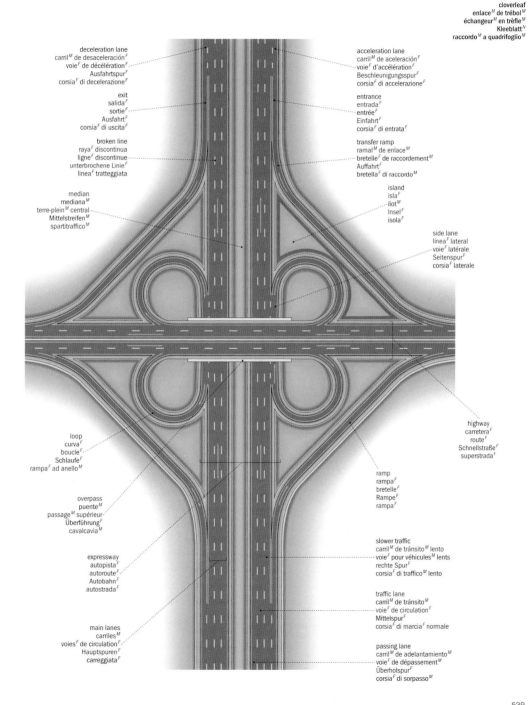

loop
curva^F
boucle^F
Schlaufe^F
rampa^F ad anello^M

highway
carretera^F
route^F
Schnellstraße^F
superstrada^F

ramp
rampa^F
bretelle^F
Rampe^F
rampa^F

overpass
puente^M
passage^M supérieur
Überführung^F
cavalcavia^M

slower traffic
carril^M de tránsito^M lento
voie^F pour véhicules^M lents
rechte Spur^F
corsia^F di traffico^M lento

expressway
autopista^F
autoroute^F
Autobahn^F
autostrada^F

traffic lane
carril^M de tránsito^M
voie^F de circulation^F
Mittelspur^F
corsia^F di marcia^F normale

main lanes
carriles^M
voies^F de circulation^F
Hauptspuren^F
carreggiata^F

passing lane
carril^M de adelantamiento^M
voie^F de dépassement^M
Überholspur^F
corsia^F di sorpasso^M

fixed bridges

puentes^M fijos | ponts^M fixes | starre Brücken^F | ponti^M fissi

beam bridge
puente^M de viga^F
pont^M à poutre^F
Balkenbrücke^F
ponte^M a travata^F

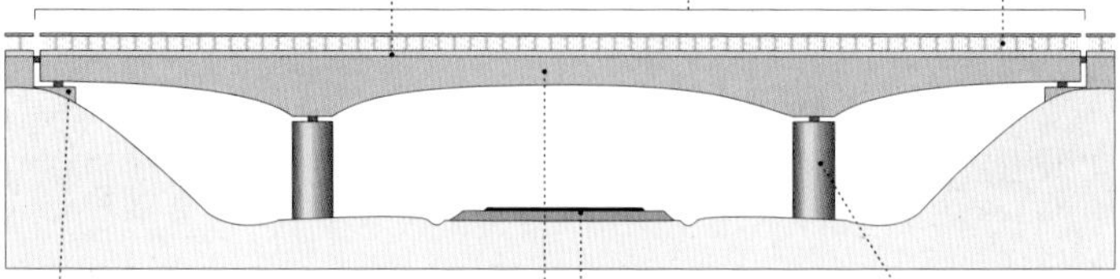

overpass
paso^M elevado
passage^M supérieur
Überführung^F
cavalcavia^M

continuous beam
viga^F continua
poutre^F continue
Durchlaufträger^M
travata^F continua

parapet
parapeto^M
garde-corps^M
Geländer^N
parapetto^M

abutment
contrafuerte^M
culée^F
Widerlager^N
spalla^F

deck
tablero^M
tablier^M
Fahrbahn^F
impalcato^M

underpass
paso^M inferior
passage^M inférieur
Unterführung^F
sottovia^M

pier
pilar^M
pile^F
Pfeiler^M
pila^F

arch bridge
puente^M de arco^M
pont^M en arc^M
Bogenbrücke^F
ponte^M ad arco^M

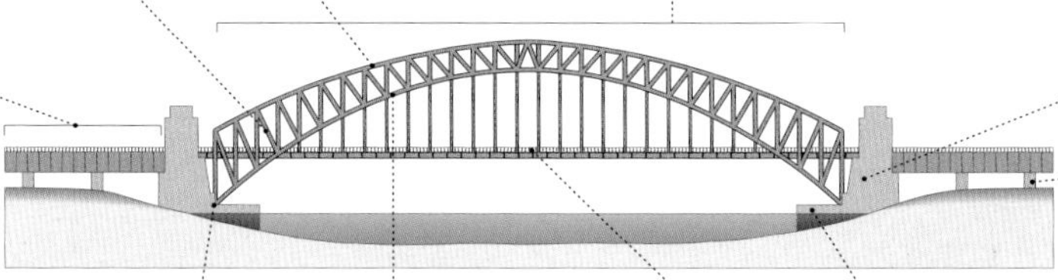

trussed arch
arco^M de entramado^M
arc^M métallique à treillis^M
Fachwerkbogen^M
arco^M reticolare

upper chord
cuerda^F superior
membrure^F supérieure
Obergurt^M
briglia^F superiore

arch
arco^M
arche^F
Bogen^M
arco^M

portal frame
portal^M
portique^M
Portalrahmen^M
travata^F a portale^M

pier
pilar^M
pile^F
Pfeiler^M
pila^F

column
columna^F
poteau^M
Säule^F
pilastro^M

thrust
empuje^M
butée^F
Landfeste^F
imposta^F

lower chord
cuerda^F inferior
membrure^F inférieure
Untergurt^M
briglia^F inferiore

deck
tablero^M
tablier^M
Fahrbahn^F
impalcato^M

abutment
contrafuerte^M
culée^F
Widerlager^N
spalla^F

suspension bridge
puente^M colgante
pont^M suspendu à câble^M porteur
Hängebrücke^F
ponte^M sospeso

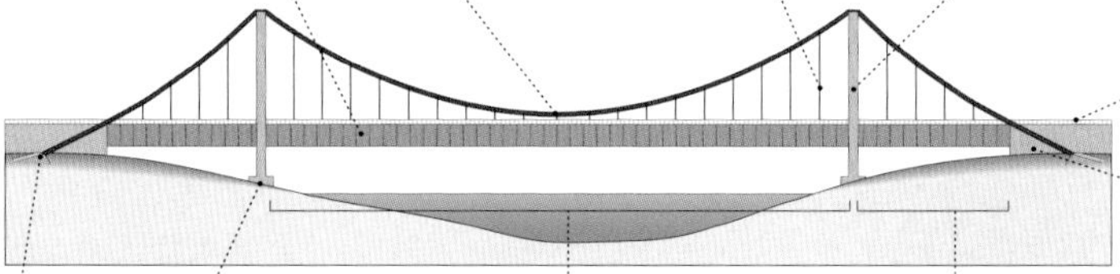

deck
tablero^M
tablier^M
Fahrbahn^F
impalcato^M

suspension cable
cable^M portante
câble^M porteur
Tragkabel^N
cavo^M di sospensione^F

suspender
tirante^M
suspente^F
Hänger^M
tirante^M

tower
pilón^M
pylône^M
Pylon^M
pilone^M

approach ramp
rampa^F de acceso^M
rampe^F d'accès^M
Auffahrt^F
rampa^F

abutment
contrafuerte^M
culée^F
Widerlager^N
spalla^F

anchorage block
anclaje^M
massif^M d'ancrage^M des câbles^M
Verankerung^F
blocco^M di ancoraggio^M dei cavi^M

foundation of tower
cimiento^M del pilón^M
fondation^F de pylône^M
Pfeilerfundament^N
fondazione^F del pilone^M

center span
tramo^M central
travée^F centrale
Jochweite^F
campata^F centrale

side span
tramo^M lateral
travée^F latérale
Seitenöffnung^F
campata^F laterale

cantilever bridge
puente^M cantilever
pont^M cantilever
Auslegerbrücke^F
ponte^M a cantilever^M

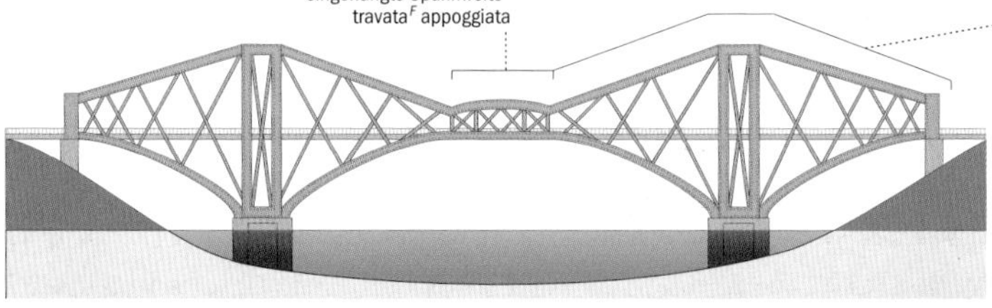

suspended span
tramo^M suspendido
poutre^F suspendue
eingehängte Spannweite^F
travata^F appoggiata

cantilever span
viga^F cantilever^M
poutre^F cantilever
Kragträger^M
travata^F a cantilever^M

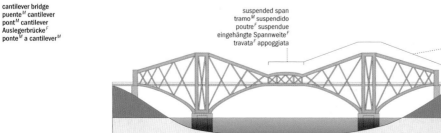

fixed bridges

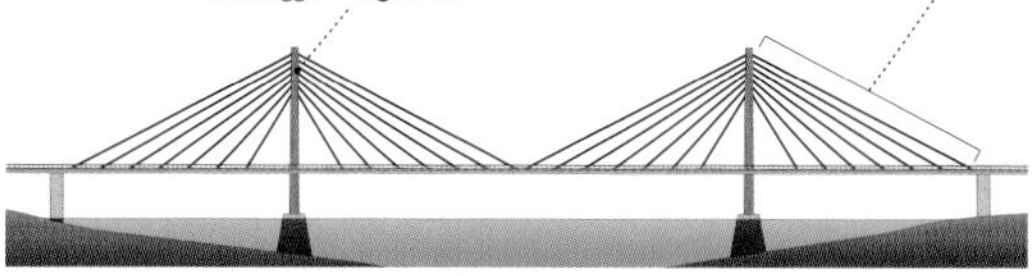

cable stay anchorage
pilón^M de los tirantes^M
ancrage^M des haubans^M
Schrägseilverankerung^F
ancoraggio^M degli stralli^M

stays
tirantes^M
haubans^M
Abspannseile^N
stralli^M

cable-stayed bridges
puentes^M de tirantes^M
ponts^M suspendus à haubans^M
Schrägseilbrücke^F
ponti^M strallati

fan cable stays
tirantes^M en abanico^M
haubans^M en éventail^M
Zügelgurte^M
stralli^M a ventaglio^M

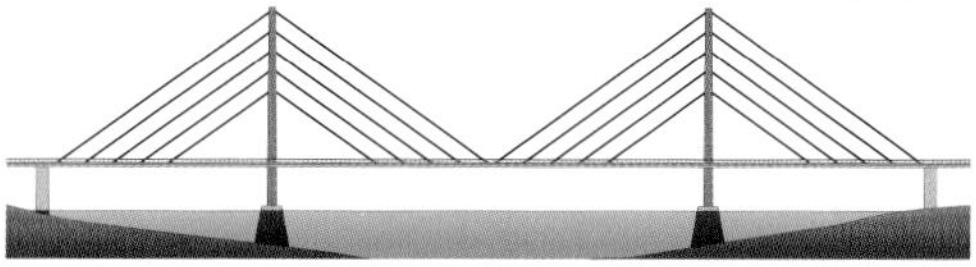

harp cable stays
tirantes^M en forma^F de arpa^F
haubans^M en harpe^F
parallele Zügelgurte^M
stralli^M ad arpa^F

examples of arch bridges
ejemplos^M de puentes^M en arco^M
exemples^M de ponts^M en arc^M
Beispiele^N für Bogenbrücken^F
esempi^M di ponti^M ad arco^M

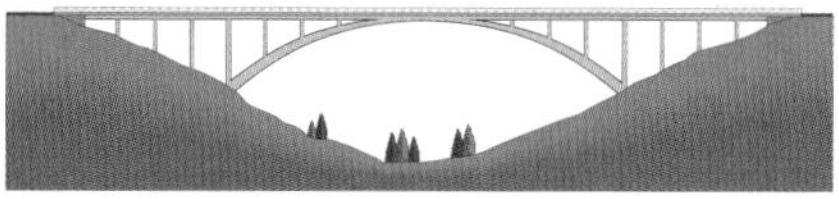

deck arch bridge
puente^M de tablero^M superior
pont^M à tablier^M supérieur
aufgeständerte Bogenbrücke^F
ponte^M a via^F superiore

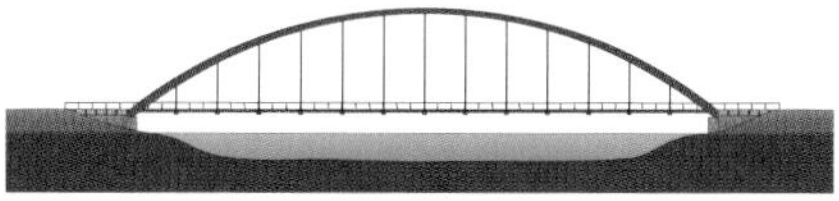

through arch bridge
puente^M de tablero^M inferior
pont^M à tablier^M inférieur
Brücke^F mit untenliegender Fahrbahn^F
ponte^M a via^F inferiore

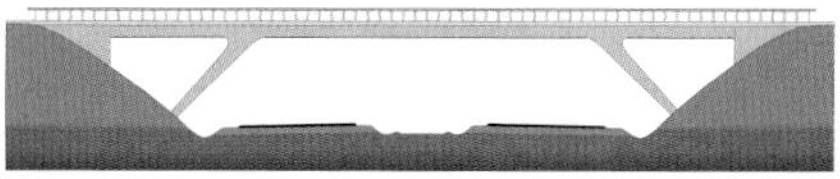

portal bridge
puente^M de portal^M
pont^M à béquilles^F
Portalbrücke^F
ponte^M a portale^M

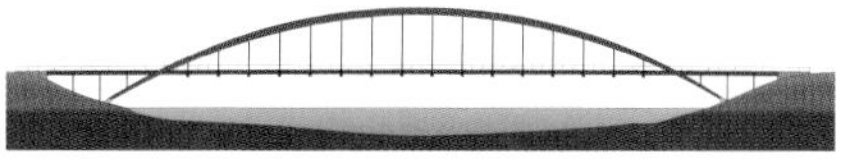

half-through arch bridge
puente^M de tablero^M intermedio
pont^M à tablier^M intermédiaire
Halbtrogbrücke^F
ponte^M a via^F intermedia

examples of arches
ejemplos^M de arcos^M
exemples^M d'arcs^M
Beispiele^N für Bögen^M
esempi^M di archi^M

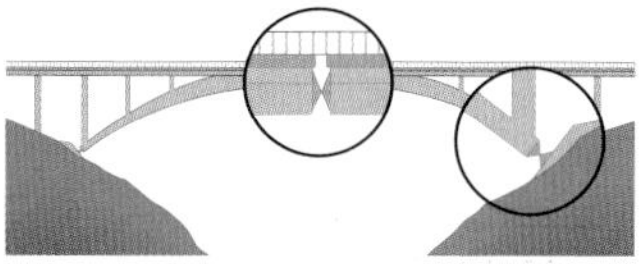

three-hinged arch
arco^M de tres articulaciones^F
arc^M à trois articulations^F
Dreigelenkbogen^M
arco^M a tre cerniere^F

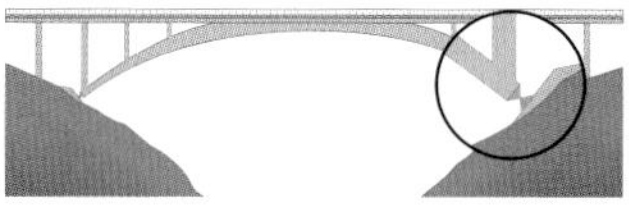

two-hinged arch
arco^M de dos articulaciones^F
arc^M à deux articulations^F
Zweigelenkbogen^M
arco^M a due cerniere^F

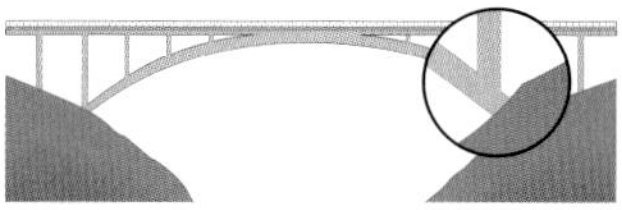

fixed arch
arco^M fijo
arc^M encastré
gelenkloser Bogen^M
arco^M senza cerniere^F

examples of beam bridges
ejemplos^M de puentes^M de vigas^F
exemples^M de ponts^M à poutre^F
Beispiele^N für Balkenbrücken^F
esempi^M di ponti^M a travata^F

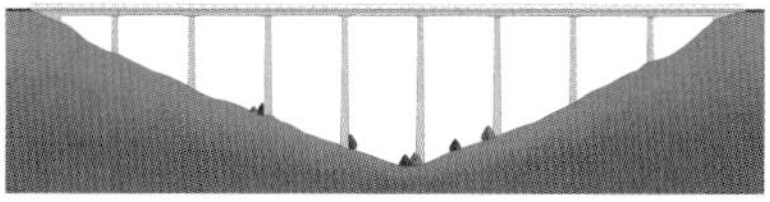

viaduct
viaducto^M
viaduc^M
Viadukt^M
viadotto^M

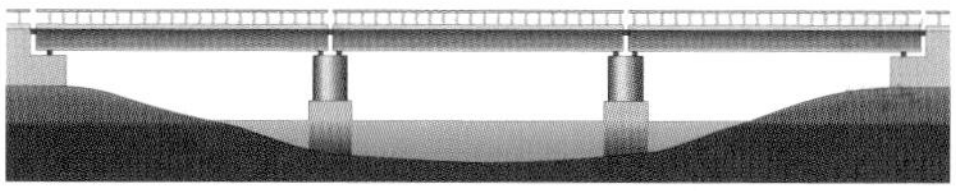

multiple-span beam bridge
puente^M de viga^F de varios tramos^M
pont^M à poutres^F indépendantes
Mehrfeldbrücke^F
ponte^M a travi^F semplici indipendenti

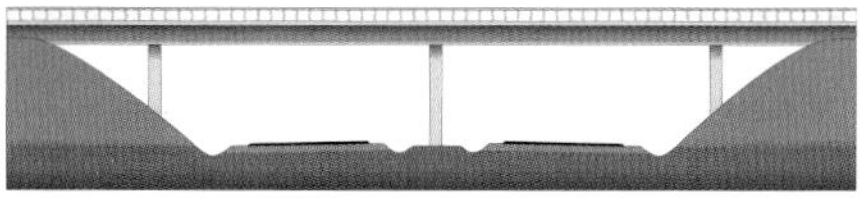

simple-span beam bridge
puente^M de viga^F de un tramo^M
pont^M à poutre^F simple
Einfeldbrücke^F
ponte^M a trave^M continua

movable bridges

puentes^M móviles | ponts^M mobiles | bewegliche Brücken^F | ponti^M mobili

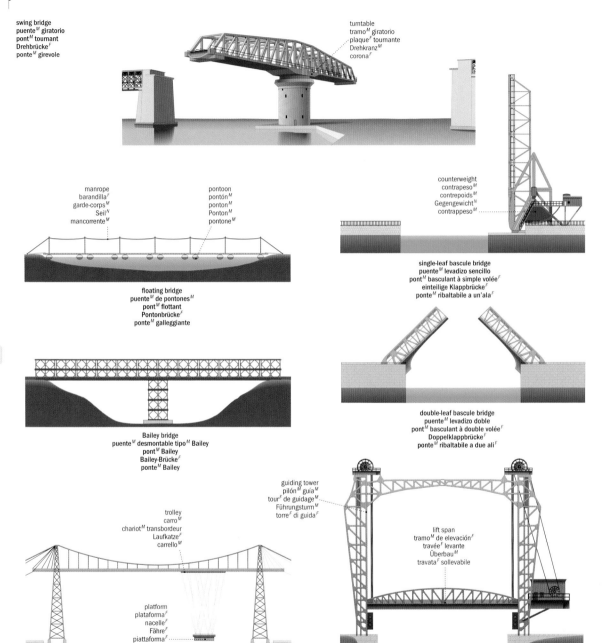

swing bridge
puente^M giratorio
pont^M tournant
Drehbrücke^F
ponte^M girevole

turntable
tramo^M giratorio
plaque^F tournante
Drehkranz^M
corona^F

manrope
barandilla^F
garde-corps^M
Seil^N
mancorrente^M

pontoon
pontón^M
ponton^M
Ponton^N
pontone^M

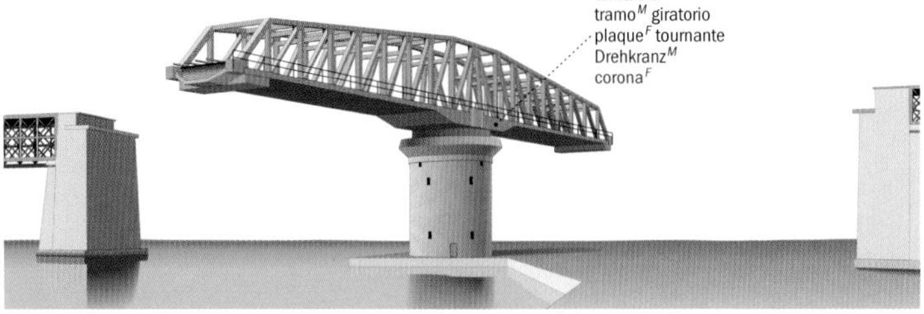

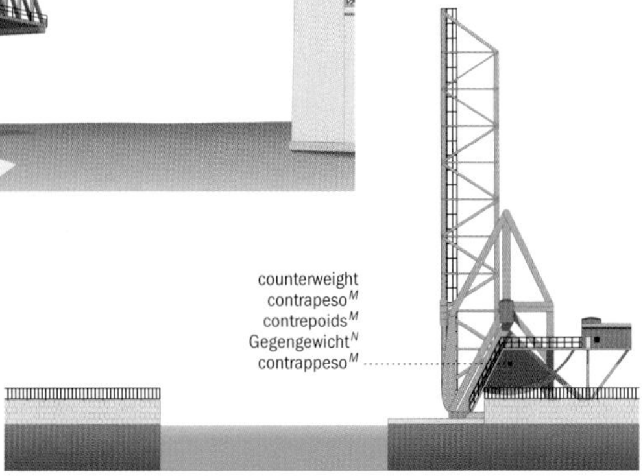

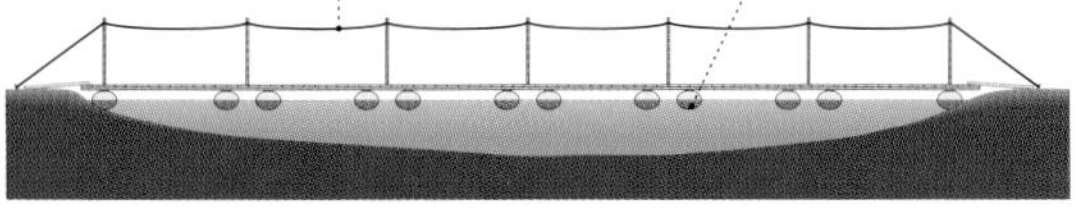

floating bridge
puente^M de pontones^M
pont^M flottant
Pontonbrücke^F
ponte^M galleggiante

counterweight
contrapeso^M
contrepoids^M
Gegengewicht^N
contrappeso^M

single-leaf bascule bridge
puente^M levadizo sencillo
pont^M basculant à simple volée^F
einteilige Klappbrücke^F
ponte^M ribaltabile a un'ala^F

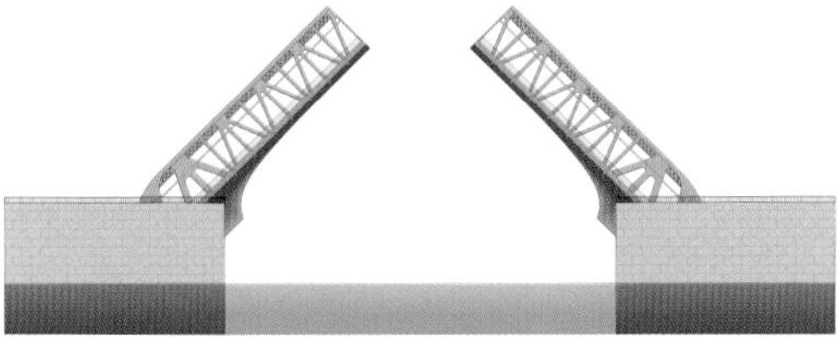

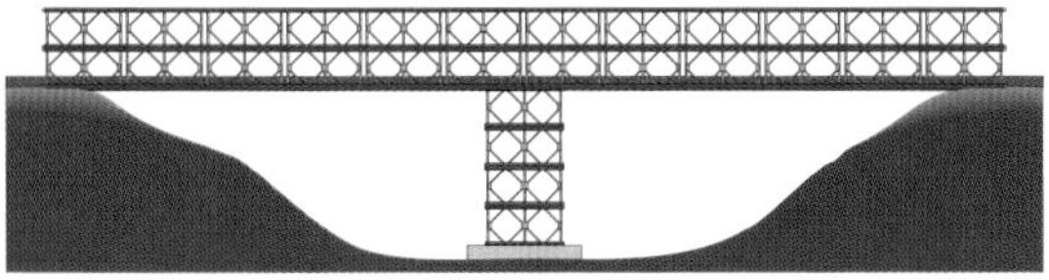

Bailey bridge
puente^M desmontable tipo^M Bailey
pont^M Bailey
Bailey-Brücke^F
ponte^M Bailey

double-leaf bascule bridge
puente^M levadizo doble
pont^M basculant à double volée^F
Doppelklappbrücke^F
ponte^M ribaltabile a due ali^F

trolley
carro^M
chariot^M transbordeur
Laufkatze^F
carrello^M

guiding tower
pilón^M guía^M
tour^F de guidage^M
Führungsturm^M
torre^F di guida^F

lift span
tramo^M de elevación^F
travée^F levante
Überbau^M
travata^F sollevabile

platform
plataforma^F
nacelle^F
Fähre^F
piattaforma^F

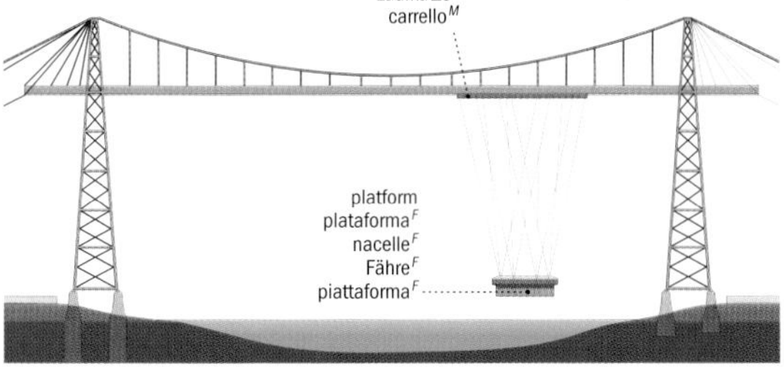

transporter bridge
puente^M transbordador
pont^M transbordeur
Fährbrücke^F
ponte^M trasportatore

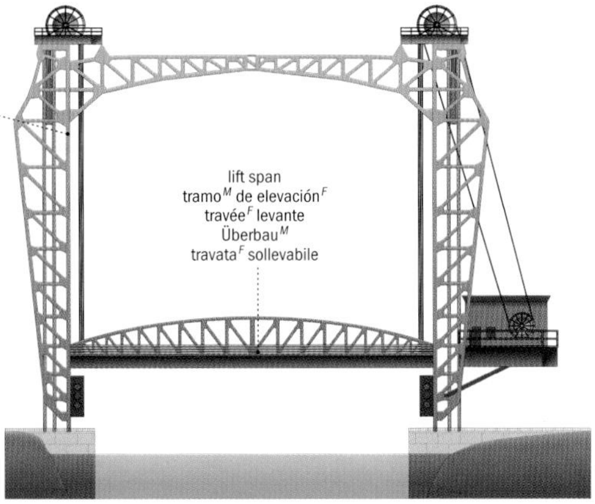

lift bridge
puente^M elevador
pont^M levant
Hubbrücke^F
ponte^M sollevabile

TRANSPORT AND MACHINERY

road tunnel

túnel^M de carretera^F | tunnel^M routier | Straßentunnel^M | galleria^F

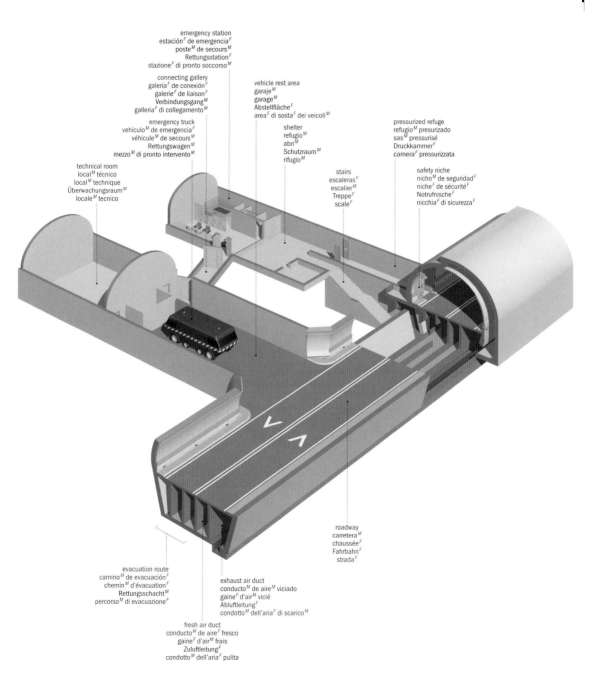

emergency station
estación^F de emergencia^F
poste^M de secours^M
Rettungsstation^F
stazione^F di pronto soccorso^M

connecting gallery
galeria^F de conexión^F
galerie^F de liaison^F
Verbindungsgang^M
galleria^F di collegamento^M

vehicle rest area
garaje^M
garage^M
Abstellfläche^F
area^F di sosta^F dei veicoli^M

pressurized refuge
refugio^M presurizado
sas^M pressurisé
Druckkammer^F
camera^F pressurizzata

emergency truck
vehículo^M de emergencia^F
véhicule^M de secours^M
Rettungswagen^M
mezzo^M di pronto intervento^M

shelter
refugio^M
abri^M
Schutzraum^M
rifugio^M

technical room
local^M técnico
local^M technique
Überwachungsraum^M
locale^M tecnico

stairs
escaleras^F
escalier^M
Treppe^F
scale^F

safety niche
nicho^M de seguridad^F
niche^F de sécurité^F
Notrufnische^F
nicchia^F di sicurezza^F

roadway
carretera^M
chaussée^F
Fahrbahn^F
strada^F

evacuation route
camino^M de evacuación^F
chemin^M d'évacuation^F
Rettungsschacht^M
percorso^M di evacuazione^F

exhaust air duct
conducto^M de aire^M viciado
gaine^F d'air^M vicié
Abluftleitung^F
condotto^M dell'aria^F di scarico^M

fresh air duct
conducto^M de aire^F fresco
gaine^F d'air^M frais
Zuluftleitung^F
condotto^M dell'aria^F pulita

TRANSPORT AND MACHINERY

road signs

señales^F de circulación^F | signalisation^F routière | Verkehrszeichen^N | segnali^M stradali

major international road signs
principales señales^F de circulación^F internacionales
principaux panneaux^M internationaux
die wichtigsten internationalen Verkehrszeichen^N
principali segnali^M stradali internazionali

right bend
curva^F a la derecha^F
virage^M à droite^F
Rechtskurve^F
curva^F a destra

double bend
doble curva^F
double virage^M
Doppelkurve^F
doppia curva^F, la prima a destra

roadway narrows
estrechamiento^M de la calzada^F
chaussée^F rétrécie
verengte Fahrbahn^F
strettoia^F simmetrica

stop at intersection
stop^M
arrêt^M à l'intersection^F
Halt! Vorfahrt^F gewähren
fermarsi e dare precedenza^F

no entry
prohibido el paso^M
accès^M interdit
Verbot^N der Einfahrt^F
senso^M vietato

no U-turn
media vuelta^F prohibida
interdiction^F de faire demi-tour^M
Wenden^N verboten
divieto^M di inversione^F di marcia^F

passing prohibited
prohibido adelantar
interdiction^F de dépasser
Überholverbot^N
divieto^M di sorpasso^M

direction to be followed
dirección^F obligatoria
direction^F obligatoire
vorgeschriebene Fahrtrichtung^F
preaviso^M di direzione^F obbligatoria a sinistra

direction to be followed
dirección^F obligatoria
direction^F obligatoire
vorgeschriebene Fahrtrichtung^F
direzione^F obbligatoria a sinistra

direction to be followed
dirección^F obligatoria
direction^F obligatoire
vorgeschriebene Fahrtrichtung^F
direzione^F obbligatoria diritto

direction to be followed
dirección^F obligatoria
direction^F obligatoire
vorgeschriebene Fahrtrichtung^F
direzioni^F consentite diritto e a sinistra

one-way traffic
una vía^F
voie^F à sens^M unique
Einbahnstraße^F
strada^F a senso^M unico

two-way traffic
doble vía^F
circulation^F dans les deux sens^M
Gegenverkehr^M
doppio senso^M di circolazione^F

yield
ceda el paso^M
cédez le passage^M
Vorfahrt^F gewähren
dare precedenza^F

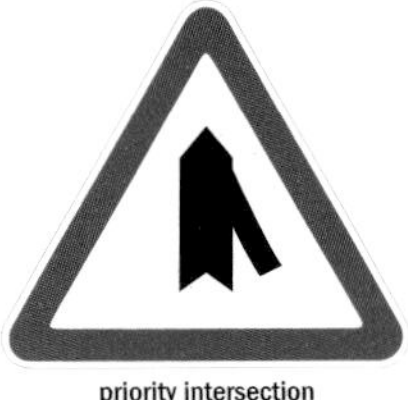

priority intersection
cruce^M con preferencia^F
intersection^F avec priorité^F
Vorfahrt^F an nächster Einmündung^F
confluenza^F a destra

TRANSPORT AND MACHINERY

falling rocks
desprendimientos[M]
chutes[F] de pierres[F]
Steinschlag[M]
caduta[F] massi[M]

overhead clearance
altura[F] máxima
limitation[F] de hauteur[F]
Verbot[N] für Fahrzeuge[N] mit mehr als der angegebenen Höhe[F]
transito[M] vietato ai veicoli[M] con altezza[F] superiore a

signal ahead
semáforo[M]
signalisation[F] lumineuse
Ampelanlage[F]
semaforo[M]

school zone
zona[F] escolar
zone[F] scolaire
Kinder[N]
bambini[M]

pedestrian crossing
paso[M] de peatones[M]
passage[M] pour piétons[M]
Fußgängerüberweg[M]
attraversamento[M] pedonale

road works ahead
obras[F]
travaux[M]
Baustelle[F]
lavori[M]

slippery road
pavimento[M] deslizante
chaussée[F] glissante
Schleudergefahr[F]
strada[F] sdrucciolevole

railroad crossing
paso[M] a nivel[M]
passage[M] à niveau[M]
Bahnübergang[M]
passaggio[M] a livello[M] con barriere[F]

deer crossing
cruce[M] de animales[M] en libertad[F]
passage[M] d'animaux[M] sauvages
Wildwechsel[M]
animali[M] selvatici vaganti

steep hill
bajada[F] peligrosa
descente[F] dangereuse
Gefälle[N]
discesa[F] pericolosa

bumps
badén[M]
chaussée[F] cahoteuse
unebene Fahrbahn[F]
strada[F] deformata

closed to bicycles
prohibido el paso[M] de bicicletas[F]
accès[M] interdit aux bicyclettes[F]
Verbot[N] für Radfahrer[M]
transito[M] vietato alle biciclette[F]

closed to motorcycles
prohibido el paso[M] de motocicletas[F]
accès[M] interdit aux motocycles[M]
Verbot[N] für Krafträder[N]
transito[M] vietato ai motocicli[M]

closed to trucks
prohibido el paso[M] de camiones[M]
accès[M] interdit aux camions[M]
Verbot[N] für Lkws[M] über einem zulässigen Gesamtgewicht[N]
transito[M] vietato agli autocarri[M]

closed to pedestrians
prohibido el paso[M] de peatones[M]
accès[M] interdit aux piétons[M]
Verbot[N] für Fußgänger[M]
transito[M] vietato ai pedoni[M]

TRANSPORT AND MACHINERY

road signs

major North American road signs
principales señales^F de circulación^F norteamericanas
principaux panneaux^M nord-américains
die wichtigsten nordamerikanischen Verkehrszeichen^N
principali segnali^M stradali nordamericani

stop at intersection
alto
arrêt^M à l'intersection^F
Halt! Vorfahrt^F gewähren
fermarsi e dare precedenza^F

no entry
prohibido el paso^M
accès^M interdit
Verbot^N der Einfahrt^F
senso^M vietato

yield
ceda el paso^M
cédez le passage^M
Vorfahrt^F gewähren
dare precedenza^F

closed to motorcycles
prohibido el paso^M de motocicletas^F
accès^M interdit aux motocycles^M
Verbot^N für Krafträder^N
transito^M vietato ai motocicli^M

closed to pedestrians
prohibido el paso^M de peatones^M
accès^M interdit aux piétons^M
Verbot^N für Fußgänger^M
transito^M vietato ai pedoni^M

closed to bicycles
prohibido el paso^M de bicicletas^F
accès^M interdit aux bicyclettes^F
Verbot^N für Radfahrer^M
transito^M vietato alle biciclette^F

closed to trucks
prohibido el paso^M de camiones^M
accès^M interdit aux camions^M
Verbot^N für Lkws^M über einem zulässigen Gesamtgewicht^N
transito^M vietato agli autocarri^M

direction to be followed
dirección^F obligatoria
direction^F obligatoire
vorgeschriebene Fahrtrichtung^F
direzioni^F consentite diritto e a destra

direction to be followed
dirección^F obligatoria
direction^F obligatoire
vorgeschriebene Fahrtrichtung^F
direzione^F obbligatoria a sinistra

direction to be followed
dirección^F obligatoria
direction^F obligatoire
vorgeschriebene Fahrtrichtung^F
direzione^F obbligatoria a destra

direction to be followed
dirección^F obligatoria
direction^F obligatoire
vorgeschriebene Fahrtrichtung^F
direzione^F obbligatoria diritto

no U-turn
prohibido^M el cambio^M de sentido^M
interdiction^F de faire demi-tour^M
Wenden^N verboten
divieto^M di inversione^F di marcia^F

passing prohibited
prohibido adelantar
interdiction^F de dépasser
Überholverbot^N
divieto^M di sorpasso^M

one-way traffic
una vía^F
voie^F à sens^M unique
Einbahnstraße^F
strada^F a senso^M unico

two-way traffic
doble vía^F
circulation^F dans les deux sens^M
Gegenverkehr^M
doppio senso^M di circolazione^F

double bend
curva^F doble
double virage^M
Doppelkurve^F
doppia curva^F, la prima a destra

merging traffic
señal^F de unión^M
intersection^F avec priorité^F
Vorfahrt^F an nächster Einmündung^F
confluenza^F a destra

right bend
curva^F a la derecha^F
virage^M à droite^F
Rechtskurve^F
curva^F a destra

roadway narrows
estrechamiento^M de la calzada^F
chaussée^F rétrécie
verengte Fahrbahn^F
strettoia^F simmetrica

slippery road
pavimento^M deslizante
chaussée^F glissante
Schleudergefahr^F
strada^F sdrucciolevole

deer crossing
cruce^M de animales^M en libertad
passage^M d'animaux^M sauvages
Wildwechsel^M
animali^M selvatici vaganti

road works ahead
obras^F
travaux^M
Baustelle^F
lavori^M

bumps
superficie^F irregular
chaussée^F cahoteuse
unebene Fahrbahn^F
strada^F deformata

steep hill
bajada^F pronunciada
descente^F dangereuse
Gefälle^N
discesa^F pericolosa

falling rocks
desprendimientos^M
chutes^F de pierres^F
Steinschlag^M
caduta^F massi^M

railroad crossing
paso^M a nivel^M
passage^M à niveau^M
Bahnübergang^M
passaggio^M a livello^M

overhead clearance
altura^F máxima
limitation^F de hauteur^F
Verbot^N für Fahrzeuge^N mit mehr als der angegebenen Höhe^F
transito^M vietato ai veicoli^M con altezza^F superiore a

signal ahead
semáforo^M
signalisation^F lumineuse
Ampelanlage^F
semaforo^M

school zone
zona^F escolar
zone^F scolaire
Schule^F
bambini^M

pedestrian crossing
paso^M de peatones^M
passage^M pour piétons^M
Fußgängerüberweg^M
attraversamento^M pedonale

TRANSPORT AND MACHINERY

service station

estación^F de servicio^M | station^F-service^M | Tankstelle^F | stazione^F di servizio^M

gasoline pump
surtidor^M de gasolina^F
distributeur^M d'essence^F
Zapfsäule^F
pompa^F della benzina^F

display
display^M
écran^M
Anzeige^F
display^M

total sale display
indicador^M del importe^M total^M
afficheur^M totaliseur
Zahlungsbetragsanzeige^F
importo^M da pagare

card-reader slot
ranura^F de lectura^F de tarjeta^F
fente^F du lecteur^M de carte^F
Kartenleserschlitz^M
lettore^M di carte^F

volume display
cuentalitros^M
afficheur^M volume^M
Füllmengenanzeige^F
litri^M erogati

alphanumeric keyboard
teclado^M alfanumérico
clavier^M alphanumérique
alphanumerische Tastatur^F
tastiera^F alfanumerica

price per gallon/liter
indicador^M del precio^M por litro^M /galón^M
afficheur^M prix^M
Preis^M pro Liter^M/Gallone^F
prezzo^M per litro^M/gallone^M

slip presenter
expedidor^M de recibo^M
sortie^F des tickets^M
Belegausgabe^F
emissione^F dello scontrino^M

pump number
número^M del surtidor^M
numéro^M de la pompe^F
Zapfsäulennummer^F
numero^M della pompa^F

type of fuel
tipo^M de combustible^M
type^M de carburant^M
Treibstoffart^F
tipo^M di carburante^M

pump nozzle
pistola^F del surtidor^M
pistolet^M de distribution^F
Zapfhahn^M
pistola^F di erogazione^F

operating instructions
instrucciones^F operativas
mode^M d'emploi^M
Bedienungsanleitung^F
istruzioni^F per l'uso^M

gasoline pump hose
manguera^F de servicio^M
flexible^M de distribution^F
Zapfschlauch^M
tubo^M della pompa^F

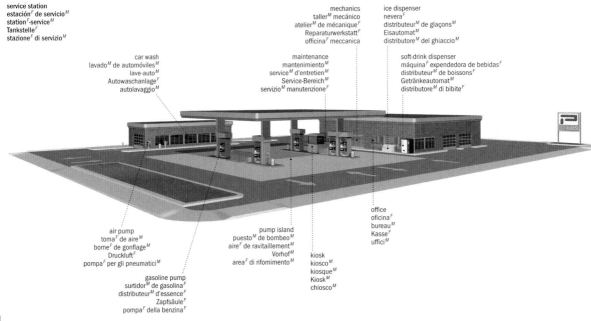

service station
estación^F de servicio^M
station^F-service^M
Tankstelle^F
stazione^F di servizio^M

mechanics
taller^M mecánico
atelier^M de mécanique^F
Reparaturwerkstatt^F
officina^F meccanica

ice dispenser
nevera^F
distributeur^M de glaçons^M
Eisautomat^M
distributore^M del ghiaccio^M

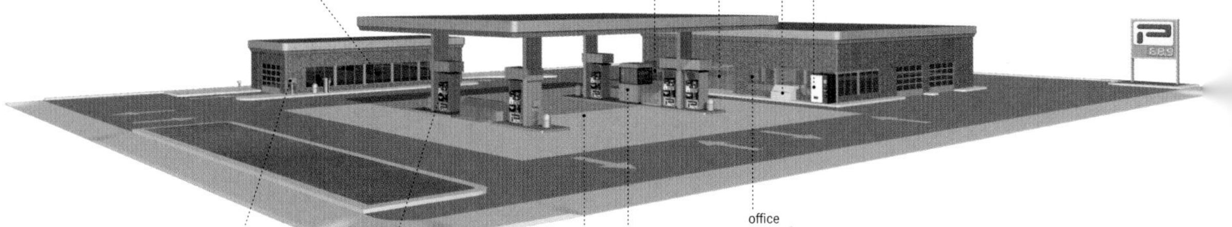

car wash
lavado^M de automóviles^M
lave-auto^M
Autowaschanlage^F
autolavaggio^M

maintenance
mantenimiento^M
service^M d'entretien^M
Service-Bereich^M
servizio^M manutenzione^F

soft-drink dispenser
máquina^F expendedora de bebidas^F
distributeur^M de boissons^F
Getränkeautomat^M
distributore^M di bibite^F

air pump
toma^F de aire^M
borne^F de gonflage^M
Druckluft^F
pompa^F per gli pneumatici^M

pump island
puesto^M de bombeo^M
aire^F de ravitaillement^M
Vorhof^M
area^F di rifornimento^M

office
oficina^F
bureau^M
Kasse^F
uffici^M

kiosk
kiosco^M
kiosque^M
Kiosk^M
chiosco^M

gasoline pump
surtidor^M de gasolina^F
distributeur^M d'essence^F
Zapfsäule^F
pompa^F della benzina^F

automobile

automóvil[M] | automobile[F] | Auto[N] | automobile[F]

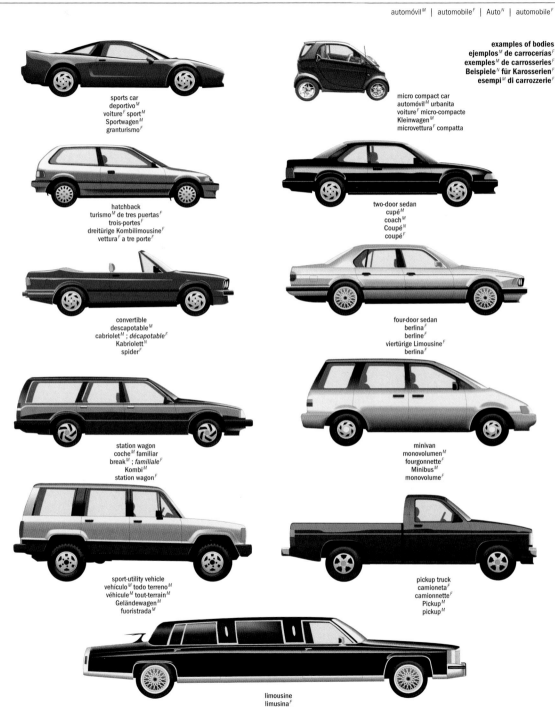

examples of bodies
ejemplos[M] de carrocerías[F]
exemples[M] de carrosseries[F]
Beispiele[N] für Karosserien[F]
esempi[M] di carrozzerie[F]

sports car
deportivo[M]
voiture[F] sport[M]
Sportwagen[M]
granturismo[F]

micro compact car
automóvil[M] urbanita
voiture[F] micro-compacte
Kleinwagen[M]
microvettura[F] compatta

hatchback
turismo[M] de tres puertas[F]
trois-portes[F]
dreitürige Kombilimousine[F]
vettura[F] a tre porte[F]

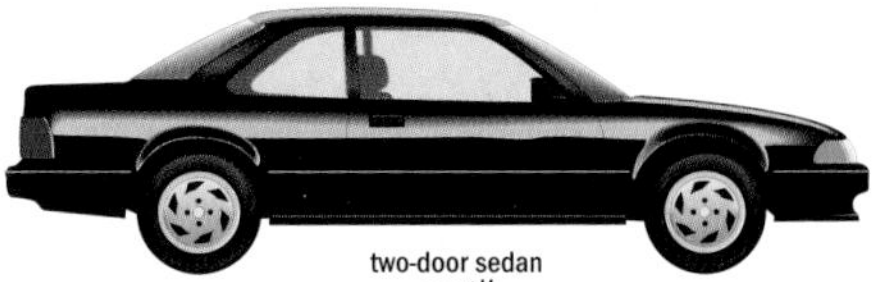

two-door sedan
cupé[M]
coach[M]
Coupé[N]
coupé[F]

convertible
descapotable[M]
cabriolet[M] ; décapotable[F]
Kabriolett[N]
spider[F]

four-door sedan
berlina[F]
berline[F]
viertürige Limousine[F]
berlina[F]

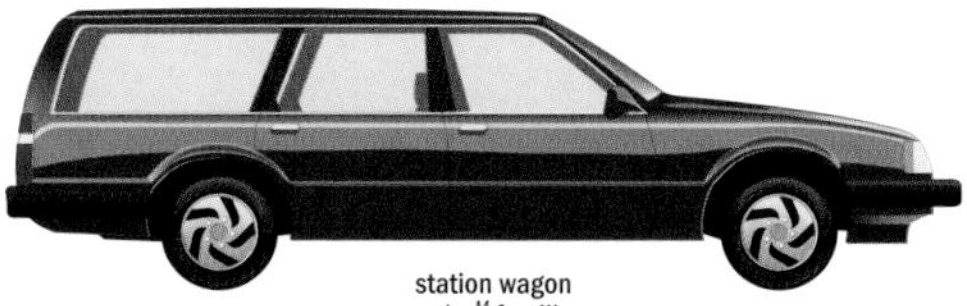

station wagon
coche[M] familiar
break[M] ; familiale[F]
Kombi[M]
station wagon[F]

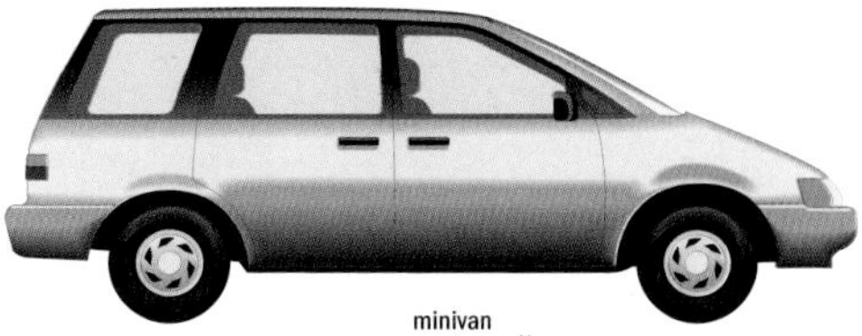

minivan
monovolumen[M]
fourgonnette[F]
Minibus[M]
monovolume[F]

sport-utility vehicle
vehículo[M] todo terreno[M]
véhicule[M] tout-terrain[M]
Geländewagen[M]
fuoristrada[M]

pickup truck
camioneta[F]
camionnette[F]
Pickup[M]
pickup[M]

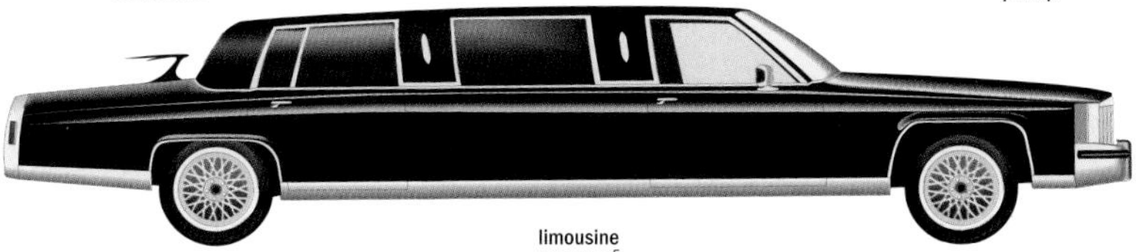

limousine
limusina[F]
limousine[F]
Pullman Limousine[F]
limousine[F]

TRANSPORT AND MACHINERY

automobile

body
carroceria[F]
carrosserie[F]
Karosserie[F]
carrozzeria[F]

windshield
parabrisas[M]
pare-brise[M]
Windschutzscheibe[F]
parabrezza[M]

outside mirror
espejo[M] lateral
rétroviseur[M] extérieur
Seitenspiegel[M]
specchietto[M] retrovisore[M] esterno

windshield wiper
limpiaparabrisas[M]
essuie-glace[M]
Scheibenwischer[M]
tergicristallo[M]

cowl
bóveda[F] del salpicadero[M]
auvent[M]
Windlaufquerteil[N]
pannello[M] di copertura[F]

washer nozzle
pulverizador[M] de agua[F]
gicleur[M] de lave-glace[M]
Scheibenwaschdüse[F]
ugello[M] del lavaparabrezza[M]

hood
capó[M]
capot[M]
Motorhaube[F]
cofano[M] anteriore

grille
calandra[F]
calandre[F]
Kühlergrill[M]
mascherina[F]

bumper molding
resguardo[M] del parachoques[M]
moulure[F] de pare-chocs[M]
kunststoffummantelter Stoßfänger[M]
modanatura[F]

headlight
faro[M] delantero
phare[M]
Scheinwerfer[M]
proiettore[M]

front fascia
banda[F] frontal
carénage[M] avant
Frontstoßfänger[M]
fascione[M] anteriore

fender
guardabarros[M]
aile[F]
Kotflügel[M]
parafango[M]

automobile

automóvil[M] | automobile[F] | Auto[N] | automobile[F]

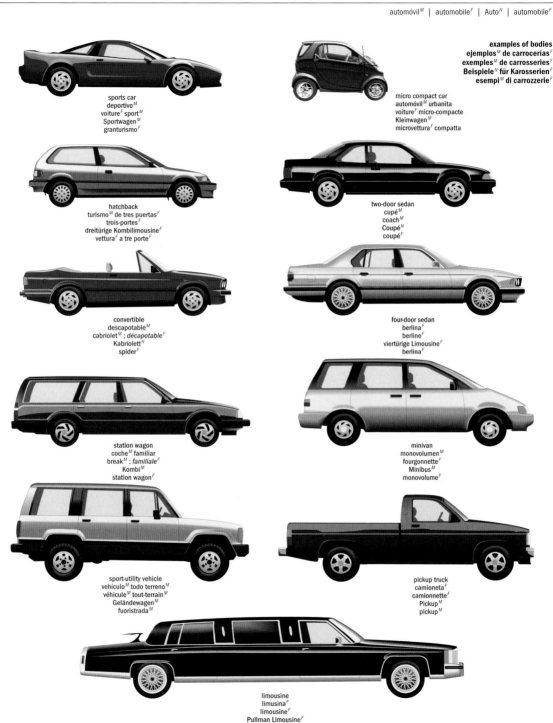

examples of bodies
ejemplos[M] de carrocerías[F]
exemples[M] de carrosseries[F]
Beispiele[N] für Karosserien[F]
esempi[M] di carrozzerie[F]

sports car
deportivo[M]
voiture[F] sport[M]
Sportwagen[M]
granturismo[F]

micro compact car
automóvil[M] urbanita
voiture[F] micro-compacte
Kleinwagen[M]
microvettura[F] compatta

hatchback
turismo[M] de tres puertas[F]
trois-portes[F]
dreitürige Kombilimousine[F]
vettura[F] a tre porte[F]

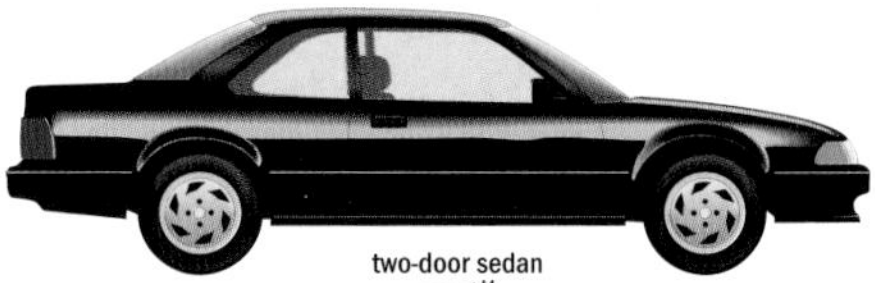

two-door sedan
cupé[M]
coach[M]
Coupé[N]
coupé[F]

convertible
descapotable[M]
cabriolet[M]; décapotable[F]
Kabriolett[N]
spider[F]

four-door sedan
berlina[F]
berline[F]
viertürige Limousine[F]
berlina[F]

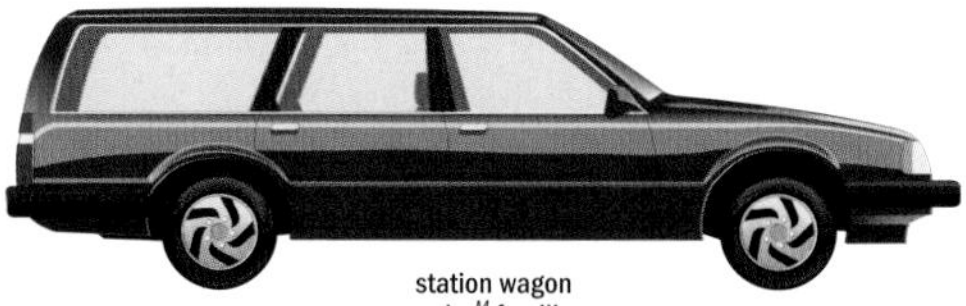

station wagon
coche[M] familiar
break[M]; familiale[F]
Kombi[M]
station wagon[F]

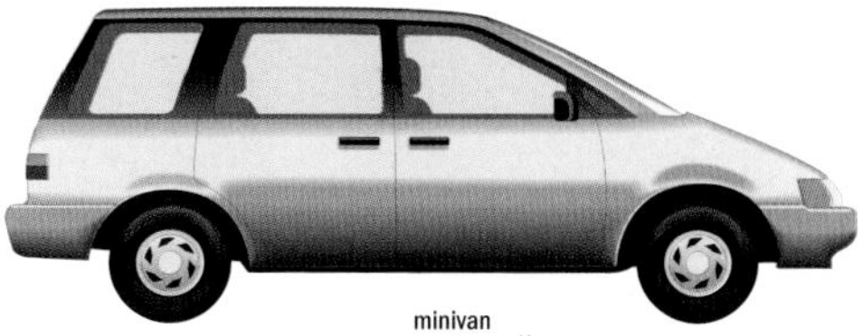

minivan
monovolumen[M]
fourgonnette[F]
Minibus[M]
monovolume[F]

sport-utility vehicle
vehículo[M] todo terreno[M]
véhicule[M] tout-terrain[M]
Geländewagen[M]
fuoristrada[M]

pickup truck
camioneta[F]
camionnette[F]
Pickup[M]
pickup[M]

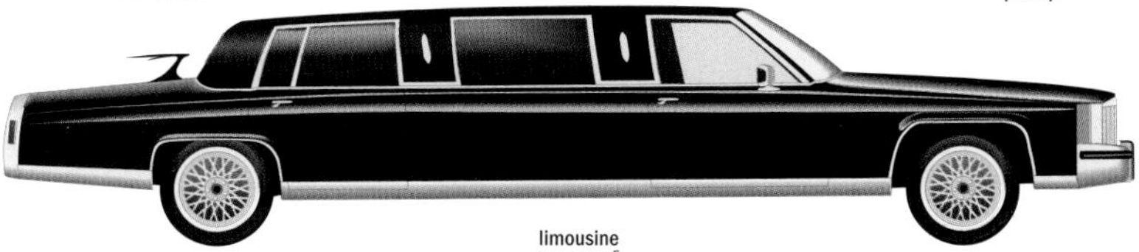

limousine
limusina[F]
limousine[F]
Pullman Limousine[F]
limousine[F]

automobile

body
carroceria[F]
carrosserie[F]
Karosserie[F]
carrozzeria[F]

windshield
parabrisas[M]
pare-brise[M]
Windschutzscheibe[F]
parabrezza[M]

outside mirror
espejo[M] lateral
rétroviseur[M] extérieur
Seitenspiegel[M]
specchietto[M] retrovisore[M] esterno

windshield wiper
limpiaparabrisas[M]
essuie-glace[M]
Scheibenwischer[M]
tergicristallo[M]

cowl
bóveda[F] del salpicadero[M]
auvent[M]
Windlaufquerteil[N]
pannello[M] di copertura[F]

hood
capó[M]
capot[M]
Motorhaube[F]
cofano[M] anteriore

washer nozzle
pulverizador[M] de agua[F]
gicleur[M] de lave-glace[M]
Scheibenwaschdüse[F]
ugello[M] del lavaparabrezza[M]

grille
calandra[F]
calandre[F]
Kühlergrill[M]
mascherina[F]

bumper molding
resguardo[M] del parachoques[M]
moulure[F] de pare-chocs[M]
kunststoffummantelter Stoßfänger[M]
modanatura[F]

headlight
faro[M] delantero
phare[M]
Scheinwerfer[M]
proiettore[M]

front fascia
banda[F] frontal
carénage[M] avant
Frontstoßfänger[M]
fascione[M] anteriore

fender
guardabarros[M]
aile[F]
Kotflügel[M]
parafango[M]

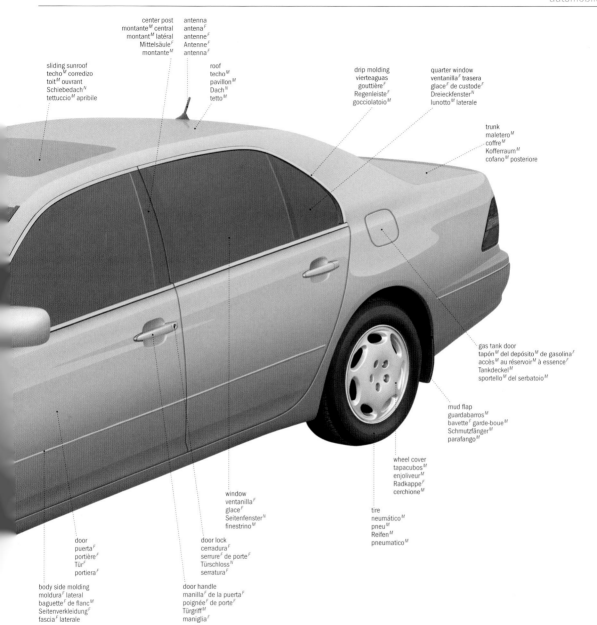

center post
montante^M central
montant^M latéral
Mittelsäule^F
montante^M

antenna
antena^F
antenne^F
Antenne^F
antenna^F

roof
techo^M
pavillon^M
Dach^N
tetto^M

drip molding
vierteaguas
gouttière^F
Regenleiste^F
gocciolatoio^M

quarter window
ventanilla^F trasera
glace^F de custode^F
Dreieckfenster^N
lunotto^M laterale

trunk
maletero^M
coffre^M
Kofferraum^M
cofano^M posteriore

sliding sunroof
techo^M corredizo
toit^M ouvrant
Schiebedach^N
tettuccio^M apribile

gas tank door
tapón^M del depósito^M de gasolina^F
accès^M au réservoir^M à essence^F
Tankdeckel^M
sportello^M del serbatoio^M

mud flap
guardabarros^M
bavette^F garde-boue^M
Schmutzfänger^M
parafango^M

wheel cover
tapacubos^M
enjoliveur^M
Radkappe^F
cerchione^M

window
ventanilla^F
glace^F
Seitenfenster^N
finestrino^M

tire
neumático^M
pneu^M
Reifen^M
pneumatico^M

door
puerta^F
portière^F
Tür^F
portiera^F

door lock
cerradura^F
serrure^F de porte^F
Türschloss^N
serratura^F

body side molding
moldura^F lateral
baguette^F de flanc^M
Seitenverkleidung^F
fascia^F laterale

door handle
manilla^F de la puerta^F
poignée^F de porte^F
Türgriff^M
maniglia^F

TRANSPORT AND MACHINERY

automobile systems: main parts
automóviles^M: componentes^M principales
principaux organes^M des systèmes^M automobiles
Kraftfahrzeuge^N: Hauptbauteile^N
sistemi^M dell'automobile^F: componenti^M principali

clutch
embrague^M
embrayage^M
Kupplung^F
frizione^F

distributor cap
delco^M
allumeur^M
Zündverteiler^M
spinterogeno^M

spark plug cable
cable^M de las bujías^F
câble^M de bougie^F
Zündkerzenkabel^N
cavo^M della candela^F

cylinder head cover
tapa^F de la culata^F
couvercle^M de culasse^F
Zylinderkopfabdeckung^F
coperchio^M delle punterie^F

air filter
filtro^M del aire^M
filtre^M à air^M
Luftfilter^M
filtro^M dell'aria^F

battery
batería^F
batterie^F d'accumulateurs^M
Batterie^F
batteria^F

radiator
radiador^M
radiateur^M
Kühler^M
radiatore^M

cooling fan
ventilador^M
ventilateur^M
Lüfter^M
ventola^F di raffreddamento^M

alternator/fan belt
correa^F del ventilador^M
courroie^F de ventilateur^M
Keilriemen^M
cinghia^F della ventola^F

alternator
alternador^M
alternateur^M
Lichtmaschine^F
alternatore^M

exhaust manifold
colector^M de escape^M
collecteur^M d'échappement^M
Auspuffkrümmer^M
collettore^M di scarico^M

front hydraulic brake line
circuito^M de frenado^M
circuit^M de freinage^M
Bremsleitung^F
circuito^M frenante

disc brake
freno^M de disco^M
frein^M à disque^M
Scheibenbremse^F
freno^M a disco^M

brake booster
servofreno^M
servofrein^M
Bremskraftverstärker^M
servofreno^M

gearbox
caja^F de cambios^M
boîte^F de vitesses^F
Getriebe^N
scatola^F del cambio^M

exhaust pipe
tubo^M de escape^M
tuyau^M d'échappement^M
vorderes Auspuffrohr^N
tubo^M di scarico^M

brake pedal
pedal^M del freno^M
pédale^F de frein^M
Bremspedal^N
pedale^M del freno^M

steering wheel
volante^M
volant^M
Lenkrad^N
volante^M

steering column
barra^F de dirección^F
colonne^F de direction^F
Lenksäule^F
piantone^M del volante^M

gearshift lever
palanca^F de cambio^M
levier^M de vitesses^F
Schalthebel^M
leva^F del cambio^M

hand brake
freno^M de mano^F
frein^M à main^F
Handbremse^F
freno^M a mano^F

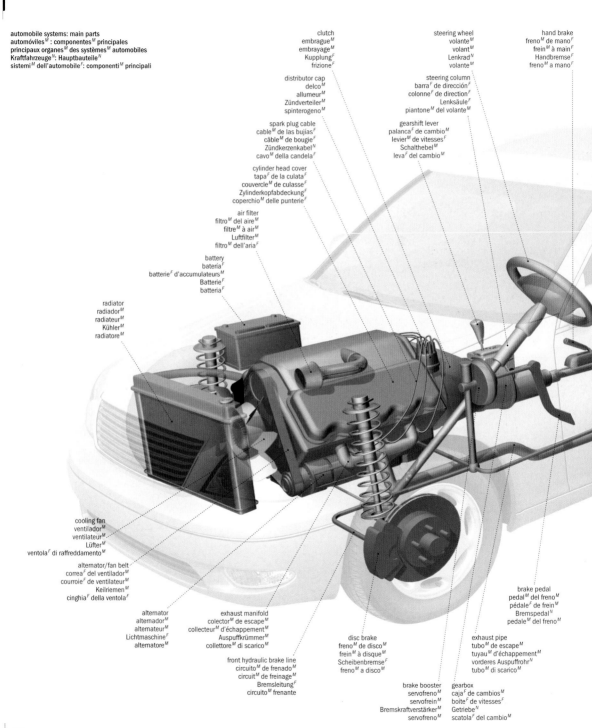

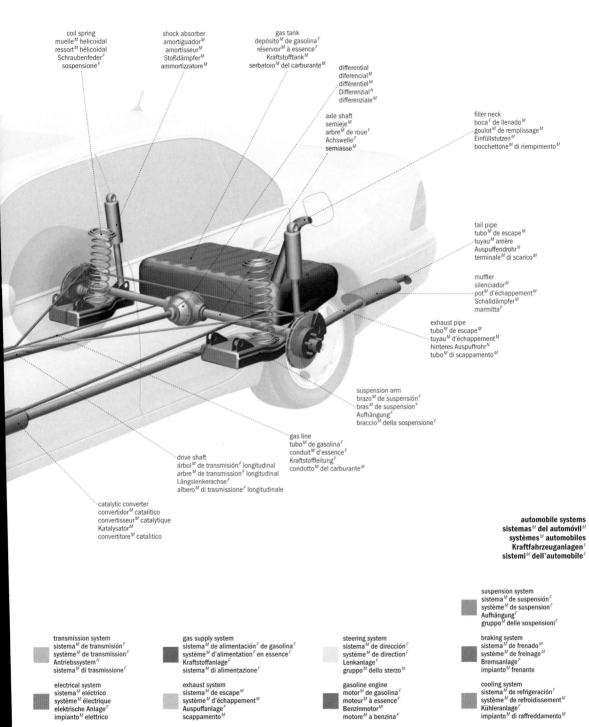

coil spring
muelle[M] helicoidal
ressort[M] hélicoïdal
Schraubenfeder[F]
sospensione[F]

shock absorber
amortiguador[M]
amortisseur[M]
Stoßdämpfer[M]
ammortizzatore[M]

gas tank
depósito[M] de gasolina[F]
réservoir[M] à essence[F]
Kraftstofftank[M]
serbatoio[M] del carburante[M]

differential
diferencial[M]
différentiel[M]
Differenzial[N]
differenziale[M]

axle shaft
semieje[M]
arbre[M] de roue[F]
Achswelle[F]
semiasse[M]

filler neck
boca[F] de llenado[M]
goulot[M] de remplissage[M]
Einfüllstutzen[M]
bocchettone[M] di riempimento[M]

tail pipe
tubo[M] de escape[M]
tuyau[M] arrière
Auspuffendrohr[N]
terminale[M] di scarico[M]

muffler
silenciador[M]
pot[M] d'échappement[M]
Schalldämpfer[M]
marmitta[F]

exhaust pipe
tubo[M] de escape[M]
tuyau[M] d'échappement[M]
hinteres Auspuffrohr[N]
tubo[M] di scappamento[M]

suspension arm
brazo[M] de suspensión[F]
bras[M] de suspension[F]
Aufhängung[F]
braccio[M] della sospensione[F]

gas line
tubo[M] de gasolina[F]
conduit[M] d'essence[F]
Kraftstoffleitung[F]
condotto[M] del carburante[M]

drive shaft
árbol[M] de transmisión[F] longitudinal
arbre[M] de transmission[F] longitudinal
Längslenkerachse[F]
albero[M] di trasmissione[F] longitudinale

catalytic converter
convertidor[M] catalítico
convertisseur[M] catalytique
Katalysator[M]
convertitore[M] catalítico

**automobile systems
sistemas[M] del automóvil[M]
systèmes[M] automobiles
Kraftfahrzeuganlagen[F]
sistemi[M] dell'automobile[F]**

suspension system
sistema[M] de suspensión[F]
système[M] de suspension[F]
Aufhängung[F]
gruppo[M] delle sospensioni[F]

transmission system
sistema[M] de transmisión[F]
système[M] de transmission[F]
Antriebssystem[N]
sistema[M] di trasmissione[F]

gas supply system
sistema[M] de alimentación[F] de gasolina[F]
système[M] d'alimentation[F] en essence[F]
Kraftstoffanlage[F]
sistema[M] di alimentazione[F]

steering system
sistema[M] de dirección[F]
système[M] de direction[F]
Lenkanlage[F]
gruppo[M] dello sterzo[M]

braking system
sistema[M] de frenado[M]
système[M] de freinage[M]
Bremsanlage[F]
impianto[M] frenante

electrical system
sistema[M] eléctrico
système[M] électrique
elektrische Anlage[F]
impianto[M] elettrico

exhaust system
sistema[M] de escape[M]
système[M] d'échappement[M]
Auspuffanlage[F]
scappamento[M]

gasoline engine
motor[M] de gasolina[F]
moteur[M] à essence[F]
Benzinmotor[M]
motore[M] a benzina[F]

cooling system
sistema[M] de refrigeración[F]
système[M] de refroidissement[M]
Kühleranlage[F]
impianto[M] di raffreddamento[M]

TRANSPORT AND MACHINERY

automobile

headlights
faros^M delanteros
feux^M avant
Frontscheinwerfer^F
luci^F anteriori

high beam
luz^F larga
feu^M de route^F
Fernlicht^N
proiettore^M abbagliante e anabbagliante

low beam
luz^F de cruce^M
feu^M de croisement^M
Abblendlicht^N
luce^F di posizione^F

fog light
luz^F antiniebla
feu^M antibrouillard
Nebelleuchte^F
faro^M fendinebbia

turn signal
intermitente^M
feu^M clignotant
Blinkleuchte^F
indicatore^M di direzione^F

side-marker light
luz^M de posición^F
feu^M de gabarit^M
Begrenzungsleuchte^F
luce^F di ingombro^M laterale

taillights
luces^F traseras
feux^M arrière
Heckleuchten^F
luci^F posteriori

turn signal
intermitente^M
feu^M clignotant
Blinkleuchte^F
indicatore^M di direzione^F

brake light
luz^F de freno^M
feu^M stop^M
Bremsleuchte^F
luce^F di arresto^M

license plate light
iluminación^F de la placa^F de matrícula^F
feu^M de plaque^F
Nummernschildbeleuchtung^F
luce^F della targa^F

brake light
luz^F de freno^M
feu^M stop^M
Bremsleuchte^F
luce^F di arresto^M

reverse light
luz^F de marcha^F atrás
feu^M de recul^M
Rückfahrscheinwerfer^M
luce^F di retromarcia^F

taillight
luz^F trasera
feu^M rouge arrière
Schlussleuchte^F
luce^F di posizione^F posteriore

side-marker light
luz^F de posición^F
feu^M de gabarit^M
Begrenzungsleuchte^F
luce^F di ingombro^M laterale

door
puerta^F
portière^F
Wagentür^F
portiera^F

interior door handle
tirador^M de la puerta^F
poignée^F intérieure
Türöffnungshebel^M
maniglia^F interna

assist grip
asidero^M
poignée^F de maintien^M
Seitengriff^M
maniglia^F fissa

outside mirror control
control^M del espejo^M retrovisor exterior
commande^F du rétroviseur^M
Seitenspiegelverstellhebel^M
regolazione^F dello specchietto^M retrovisore^M esterno

window regulator handle
manivela^F de la ventanilla^F
manivelle^F de lève-glace^M
Fensterheber^M
manopola^F alzacristalli^M

hinge
bisagra^F
charnière^F
Scharnier^N
cardine^M

accessory pocket
bolsillo^M lateral
vide-poches^M
Seitenfach^N
tasca^F portaoggetti^M

window
ventanilla^F
glace^F
Fenster^N
finestrino^M

interior door lock button
botón^M del seguro^M
bouton^M de verrouillage^M
Sicherungsknopf^M
pomello^M della sicura^F

armrest
soporte^M para el brazo^M
appui^M-bras^M
Armstütze^F
bracciolo^M

lock
cerradura^F
serrure^F
Türschloss^N
serratura^F

trim panel
panel^M de la puerta^F
panneau^M de garnissage^M
Türverkleidung^F
pannello^M

inner door shell
revestimiento^M interior
caisson^M de porte^F
Türinnenverschalung^F
telaio^M interno della portiera^F

bucket seat: front view
asiento^M : vista^F frontal
siège^M-baquet^M : vue^F de face^F
Schalensitz^M: Vorderansicht^F
sedile^M: vista^F anteriore

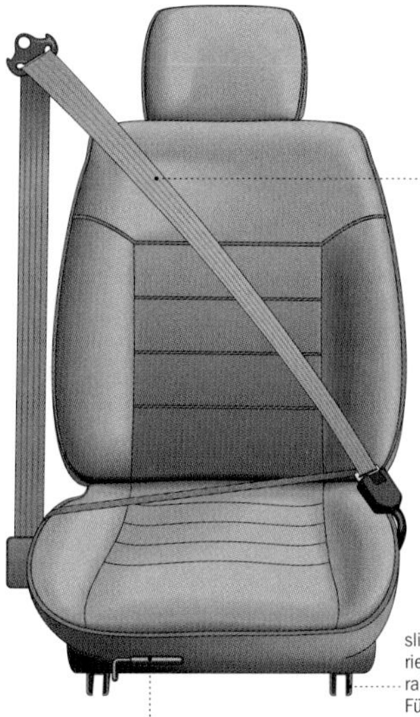

bucket seat: side view
asiento^M : vista^F lateral
siège^M-baquet^M : vue^F de profil^M
Schalensitz^M: Seitenansicht^F
sedile^M: vista^F laterale

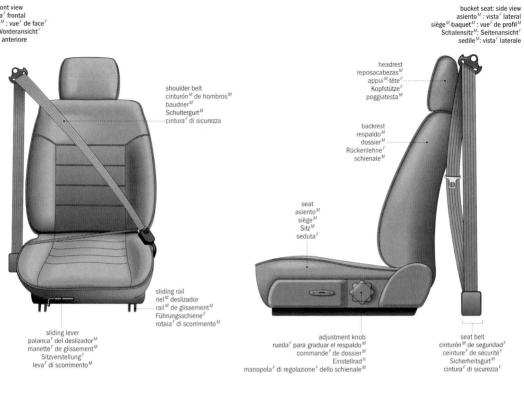

shoulder belt
cinturón^M de hombros^M
baudrier^M
Schultergurt^M
cintura^F di sicurezza

headrest
reposacabezas^M
appui^M-tête^F
Kopfstütze^F
poggiatesta^M

backrest
respaldo^M
dossier^M
Rückenlehne^F
schienale^M

seat
asiento^M
siège^M
Sitz^M
seduta^F

sliding rail
riel^M deslizador
rail^M de glissement^M
Führungsschiene^F
rotaia^F di scorrimento^M

sliding lever
palanca^F del deslizador^M
manette^F de glissement^M
Sitzverstellung^F
leva^F di scorrimento^M

adjustment knob
rueda^F para graduar el respaldo^M
commande^F de dossier^M
Einstellrad^N
manopola^F di regolazione^F dello schienale^M

seat belt
cinturón^M de seguridad^F
ceinture^F de sécurité^F
Sicherheitsgurt^M
cintura^F di sicurezza^F

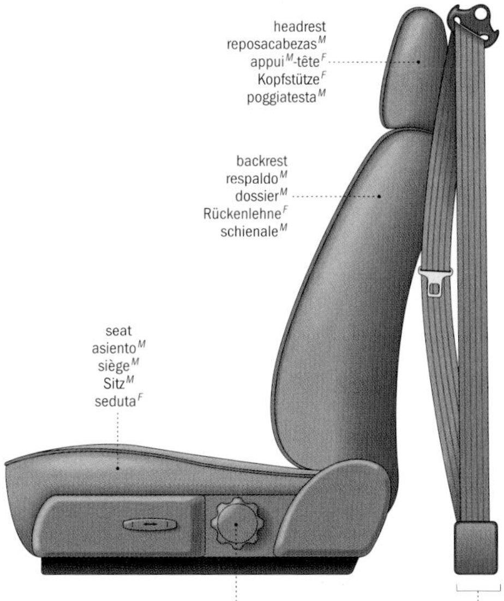

rear seat
asiento^M trasero
banquette^F arrière
Rückbank^F
divano^M posteriore

armrest
reposabrazo^M
appui^M-bras^M
Armstütze^F
bracciolo^M

webbing
cinturón^M subabdominal
sangle^F
Beckengurt^M
cintura^F ventrale

buckle
enganche^M
boucle^F
Gurtschließe^F
fibbia^F

bench seat
asiento^M
banquette^F
Sitzbank^F
seduta^F del divano^M posteriore

automobile

dashboard
salpicadero[M]
tableau[M] de bord[M]
Armaturenbrett[N]
plancia[F]

rearview mirror
espejo[M] retrovisor
rétroviseur[M]
Rückspiegel[M]
specchietto[M] retrovisore[M]

vanity mirror
espejo[M] de cortesía[F]
miroir[M] de courtoisie[F]
Spiegel[M]
specchietto[M] di cortesia[F]

wiper switch
interruptor[M] del limpiaparabrisas[M]
commande[F] d'essuie-glace[M]
Scheibenwischerhebel[M]
comando[M] del tergicristallo[M]

on-board computer
ordenador[M] de a bordo[M]
ordinateur[M] de bord[M]
Bordcomputer[M]
computer[M] di bordo[M]

sun visor
parasol[M]
pare-soleil[M]
Sonnenblende[F]
aletta[F] parasole

cruise control
regulador[M] de velocidad[F]
régulateur[M] de vitesse[F]
Tempomat[M]
controllo[M] della velocità[F] di crociera[F]

glove compartment
guantera[F]
boîte[F] à gants[M]
Handschuhfach[N]
vano[M] portaoggetti[M]

ignition switch
interruptor[M] de encendido[M]
commutateur[M] d'allumage[M]
Zündschloss[N]
blocchetto[M] di accensione[F]

vent
ventilación[F]
bouche[F] d'air[M]
Luftdüse[F]
bocchetta[F] di ventilazione[F]

horn
claxón[M]
avertisseur[M]
Hupe[F]
clacson[M]

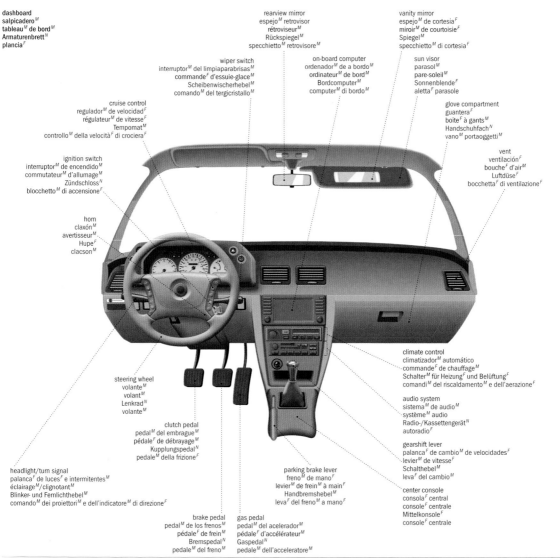

steering wheel
volante[M]
volant[M]
Lenkrad[N]
volante[M]

clutch pedal
pedal[M] del embrague[M]
pédale[F] de débrayage[M]
Kupplungspedal[N]
pedale[M] della frizione[F]

climate control
climatizador[M] automático
commande[F] de chauffage[M]
Schalter[M] für Heizung[F] und Belüftung[F]
comandi[M] del riscaldamento[M] e dell'aerazione[F]

audio system
sistema[M] de audio[M]
système[M] audio
Radio-/Kassettengerät[N]
autoradio[F]

gearshift lever
palanca[F] de cambio[M] de velocidades[F]
levier[M] de vitesse[F]
Schalthebel[M]
leva[F] del cambio[M]

center console
consola[F] central
console[F] centrale
Mittelkonsole[F]
console[F] centrale

headlight/turn signal
palanca[F] de luces[F] e intermitentes[M]
éclairage[M]/clignotant[M]
Blinker- und Fernlichthebel[M]
comando[M] dei proiettori[M] e dell'indicatore[M] di direzione[F]

parking brake lever
freno[M] de mano[F]
levier[M] de frein[M] à main[F]
Handbremshebel[M]
leva[F] del freno[M] a mano[F]

brake pedal
pedal[M] de los frenos[M]
pédale[F] de frein[M]
Bremspedal[N]
pedale[M] del freno[M]

gas pedal
pedal[M] del acelerador[M]
pédale[F] d'accélérateur[M]
Gaspedal[N]
pedale[M] dell'acceleratore[M]

air bag restraint system
sistema[M] de restricción[F] del airbag[M]
système[M] de retenue[F] à sacs[M] gonflables
Airbag[M]-Rückhaltesystem[N]
sistema[M] di ritenuta[F] degli air bag[M]

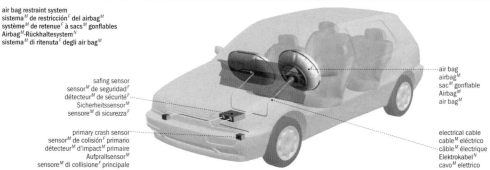

safing sensor
sensor[M] de seguridad[F]
détecteur[M] de sécurité[F]
Sicherheitssensor[M]
sensore[M] di sicurezza[F]

air bag
airbag[M]
sac[M] gonflable
Airbag[M]
air bag[M]

primary crash sensor
sensor[M] de colisión[F] primario
détecteur[M] d'impact[M] primaire
Aufprallsensor[M]
sensore[M] di collisione[F] principale

electrical cable
cable[M] eléctrico
câble[M] électrique
Elektrokabel[N]
cavo[M] elettrico

instrument panel
instrumentos^M del salpicadero^M
instruments^M de bord^M
Instrumententafel^F
quadro^M degli strumenti^M di controllo^M

alternator warning light
luz^F de advertencia^F del alternador^M
témoin^M de charge^F
Batterieladekontrollleuchte^F
spia^F della batteria^F

oil warning light
luz^F de advertencia^F del aceite^M
témoin^M de niveau^M d'huile^F
Öldruckwarnleuchte^F
spia^F della pressione^F dell'olio^M

temperature indicator
indicador^M de temperatura^F
indicateur^M de température^F
Temperaturanzeige^F
indicatore^M della temperatura^F del liquido^M di raffreddamento^M

high beam indicator light
luz^F indicadora de luz^F larga
témoin^M des feux^M de route^F
Fernlichtanzeige^F
spia^F dei proiettori^M abbaglianti

low fuel warning light
luz^F de advertencia^F de la gasolina^F
témoin^M de bas niveau^M de carburant^M
Kraftstoffreserveanzeige^F
spia^F della riserva^F di carburante^M

fuel indicator
indicador^M de nivel^M de gasolina^F
indicateur^M de niveau^M de carburant^M
Kraftstoffanzeige^F
indicatore^M del livello^M di carburante^M

warning lights
luces^F de advertencia^F
lampes^F témoins^M
Warnleuchten^F
spie^F

turn signal indicator
intermitente^M
témoin^M de clignotants^M
Blinklichtkontrolle^F
spia^F dell'indicatore^M di direzione^F

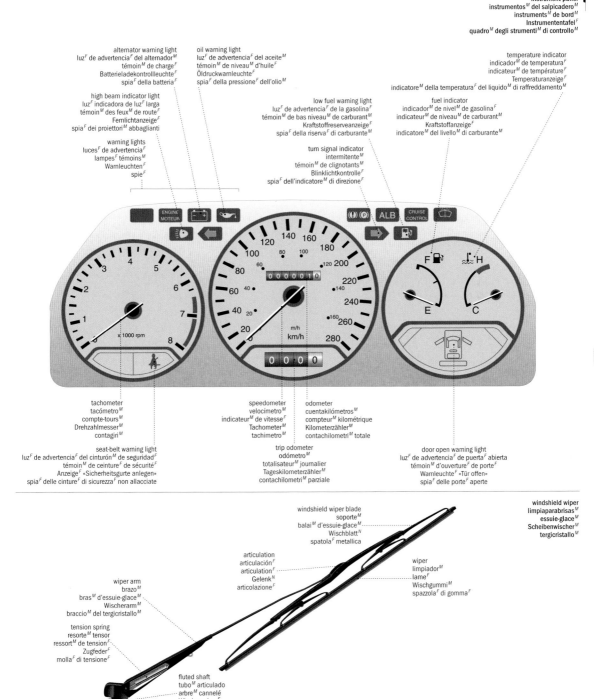

tachometer
tacómetro^M
compte-tours^M
Drehzahlmesser^M
contagiri^M

speedometer
velocímetro^M
indicateur^M de vitesse^F
Tachometer^M
tachimetro^M

odometer
cuentakilómetros^M
compteur^M kilométrique
Kilometerzähler^M
contachilometri^M totale

temperature indicator
(see above)

seat-belt warning light
luz^F de advertencia^F del cinturón^M de seguridad^F
témoin^M de ceinture^F de sécurité^F
Anzeige^F «Sicherheitsgurte anlegen»
spia^F delle cinture^F di sicurezza^F non allacciate

trip odometer
odómetro^M
totalisateur^M journalier
Tageskilometerzähler^M
contachilometri^M parziale

door open warning light
luz^F de advertencia^F de puerta^F abierta
témoin^M d'ouverture^F de porte^F
Warnleuchte^F «Tür offen»
spia^F delle porte^F aperte

windshield wiper
limpiaparabrisas^M
essuie-glace^M
Scheibenwischer^M
tergicristallo^M

windshield wiper blade
soporte^M
balai^M d'essuie-glace^M
Wischblatt^N
spatola^F metallica

articulation
articulación^F
articulation^F
Gelenk^N
articolazione^F

wiper
limpiador^M
lame^F
Wischgummi^M
spazzola^F di gomma^F

wiper arm
brazo^M
bras^M d'essuie-glace^M
Wischerarm^M
braccio^M del tergicristallo^M

tension spring
resorte^M tensor
ressort^M de tension^F
Zugfeder^F
molla^F di tensione^F

fluted shaft
tubo^M articulado
arbre^M cannelé
Wischerachse^F
perno^M oscillante

automobile

accessories
accesorios^M
accessoires^M
Zubehör^N
accessori^M

jumper cables
cables^M de emergencia^F
câbles^M de démarrage^M
Starthilfekabel^N
cavi^M di accoppiamento^M

floor mat
alfombrilla^F
tapis^M de plancher^M
Fußraummatte^F
tappetino^M

black clamp
pinza^F negra
pince^F noire
schwarze Klemme^F
morsetto^M nero

roller shade
cortina^F de enrollamiento automático
store^M à enroulement^M automatique
Sonnenrollo^N
tendina^F parasole avvolgibile

red clamp
pinza^F roja
pince^F rouge
rote Klemme^F
morsetto^M rosso

cable
cable^M
câble^M
Kabel^N
cavo^M

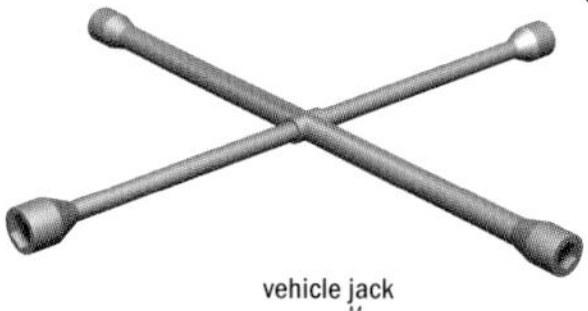

snow brush with scraper
escoba^F de nieve^F con rascador^M
balai^M à neige^F à grattoir^M
Schneefeger^M mit Eiskratzer^M
spazzola^F da neve^F con raschietto^M

ball mount
enganche^M de bola^F
ferrure^F d'attelage^M
Unterteil^N
supporto^M della sfera^F

four-way lug wrench
llave^F en cruz^M
clé^F en croix^M
Kreuzschlüssel^M
chiave^F a croce^F

hitch ball
gancho^M de arrastre^M
boule^F d'attelage^M
Anhängerkupplung^F
occhione^M di traino^M

ski rack
porta-esqui^M
porte-skis^M
Skiträger^M
portasci^M

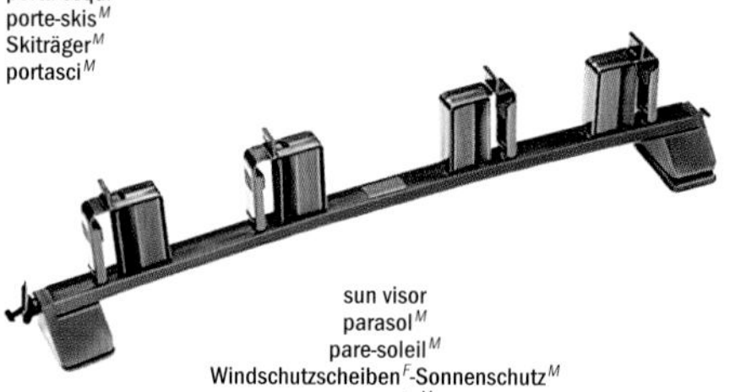

vehicle jack
gato^M
cric^M
Wagenheber^M
cric^M

bike carrier
portabicicletas^M
porte-vélos^M
Fahrradträger^M
portabici^M

sun visor
parasol^M
pare-soleil^M
Windschutzscheiben^F-Sonnenschutz^M
parasole^M

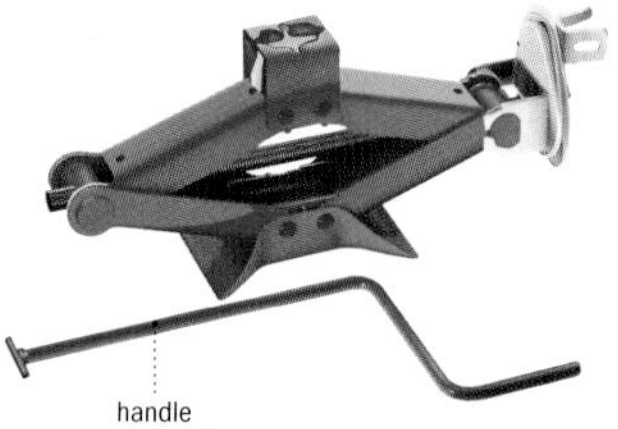

handle
manivela^F
manivelle^F
Kurbel^F
manovella^F

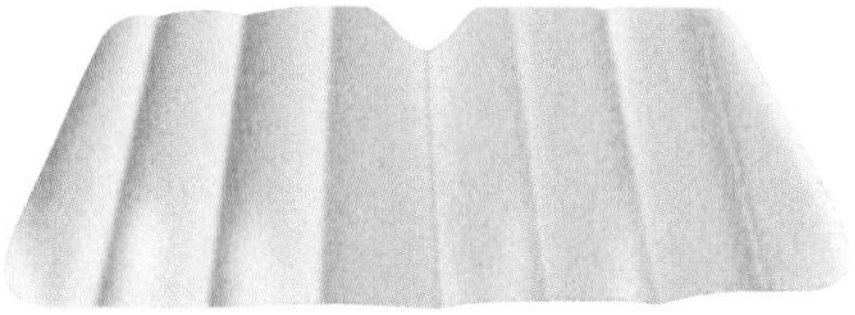

car cover
funda^F de automóvil^M
housse^F pour automobile^F
Autoplane^F
telone^M proteggiauto

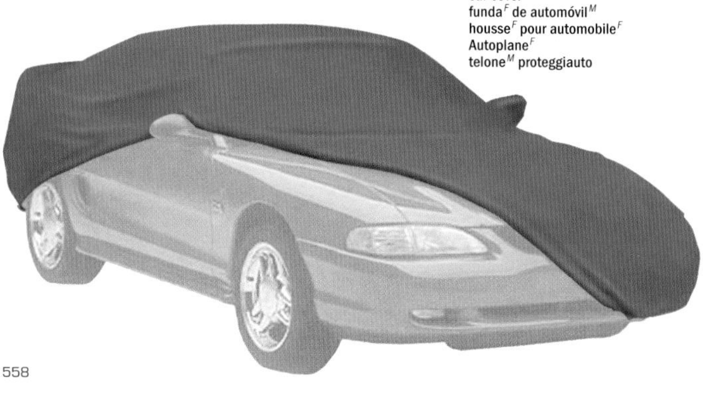

child safety seat
silla^F de seguridad^F para niños^M
siège^M de sécurité^F pour enfant^M
Kindersitz^M
seggiolino^M per bambini^M

TRANSPORT AND MACHINERY

brakes

frenos[M] | freins[M] | Bremsen[F] | freni[M]

disc brake
freno[M] de disco[M]
frein[M] à disque[M]
Scheibenbremse[F]
freno[M] a disco[M]

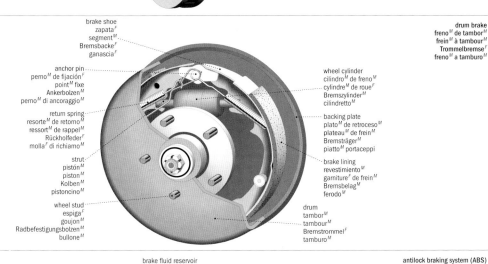

caliper
calibrador[M]
étrier[M]
Bremssattel[M]
pinza[F]

brake line
manguera[F] de liquido[M] para frenos[M]
canalisation[F]
Bremsschlauch[M]
tubazione[F] del freno[M]

piston
pistón[M]
piston[M]
Kolben[M]
pistoncino[M]

brake pad
pastilla[F] de fricción[F]
plaquette[F]
Bremsbelag[M]
pastiglia[F]

disc
disco[M]
disque[M]
Bremsscheibe[F]
disco[M]

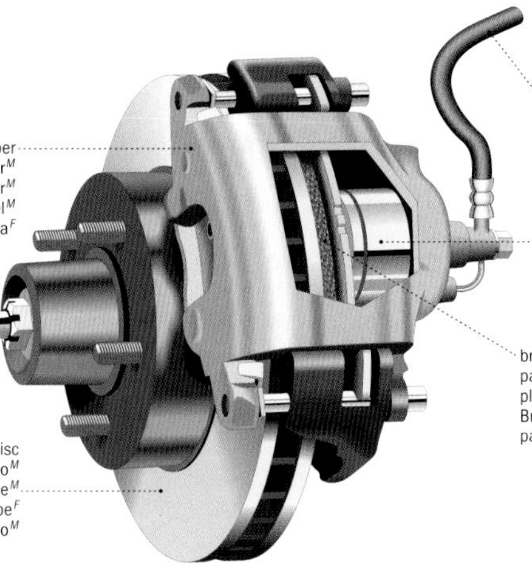

drum brake
freno[M] de tambor[M]
frein[M] à tambour[M]
Trommelbremse[F]
freno[M] a tamburo[M]

brake shoe
zapata[F]
segment[M]
Bremsbacke[F]
ganascia[F]

anchor pin
perno[M] de fijación[F]
point[M] fixe
Ankerbolzen[M]
perno[M] di ancoraggio[M]

return spring
resorte[M] de retorno[M]
ressort[M] de rappel[M]
Rückholfeder[F]
molla[F] di richiamo[M]

strut
pistón[M]
piston[M]
Kolben[M]
pistoncino[M]

wheel stud
espiga[F]
goujon[M]
Radbefestigungsbolzen[M]
bullone[M]

wheel cylinder
cilindro[M] de freno[M]
cylindre[M] de roue[F]
Bremszylinder[M]
cilindretto[M]

backing plate
plato[M] de retroceso[M]
plateau[M] de frein[M]
Bremsträger[M]
piatto[M] portaceppi

brake lining
revestimiento[M]
garniture[F] de frein[M]
Bremsbelag[M]
ferodo[M]

drum
tambor[M]
tambour[M]
Bremstrommel[F]
tamburo[M]

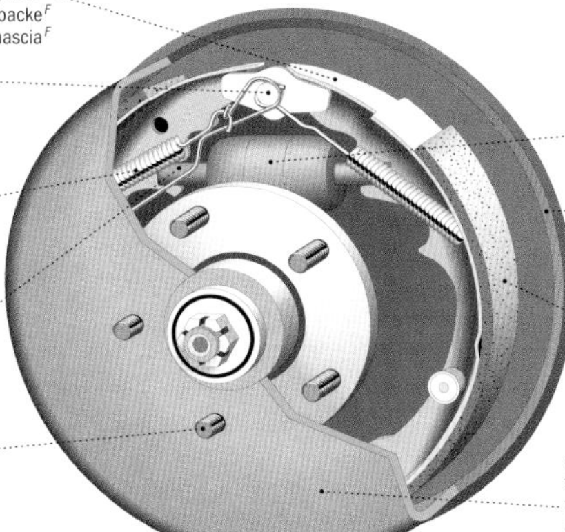

antilock braking system (ABS)
sistema[M] antibloqueo de frenos[M]
système[M] de freinage[M] antiblocage
Antiblockiersystem[N] (ABS)
ABS, sistema[M] frenante antibloccaggio

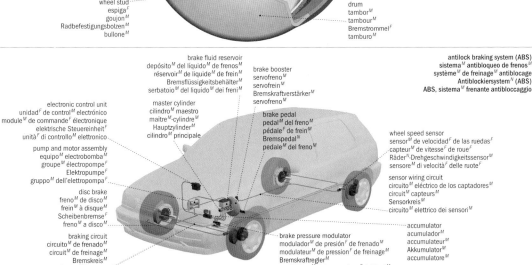

brake fluid reservoir
depósito[M] del liquido[M] de frenos[M]
réservoir[M] de liquide[M] de frein[M]
Bremsflüssigkeitsbehälter[M]
serbatoio[M] del liquido[M] dei freni[M]

brake booster
servofreno[M]
servofrein[M]
Bremskraftverstärker[M]
servofreno[M]

electronic control unit
unidad[F] de control[M] electrónico
module[M] de commande[F] électronique
elektrische Steuereinheit[F]
unità[F] di controllo[M] elettronico

master cylinder
cilindro[M] maestro
maitre[M]-cylindre[M]
Hauptzylinder[M]
cilindro[M] principale

brake pedal
pedal[M] del freno[M]
pédale[F] de frein[M]
Bremspedal[N]
pedale[M] del freno[M]

wheel speed sensor
sensor[M] de velocidad[F] de las ruedas[F]
capteur[M] de vitesse[F] de roue[F]
Räder[N]-Drehgeschwindigkeitssensor[M]
sensore[M] di velocità[F] delle ruote[F]

pump and motor assembly
equipo[M] electrobomba[M]
groupe[M] électropompe[F]
Elektropumpe[F]
gruppo[M] dell'elettropompa[F]

sensor wiring circuit
circuito[M] eléctrico de los captadores[M]
circuit[M] capteurs[M]
Sensorkreis[M]
circuito[M] elettrico dei sensori[M]

disc brake
freno[M] de disco[M]
frein[M] à disque[M]
Scheibenbremse[F]
freno[M] a disco[M]

accumulator
acumulador[M]
accumulateur[M]
Akkumulator[M]
accumulatore[M]

braking circuit
circuito[M] de frenado[M]
circuit[M] de freinage[M]
Bremskreis[M]
circuito[M] frenante

brake pressure modulator
modulador[M] de presión[F] de frenado[M]
modulateur[M] de pression[F] de freinage[M]
Bremskraftregler[M]
modulatore[M] della pressione[F] dei freni[M]

TRANSPORT AND MACHINERY

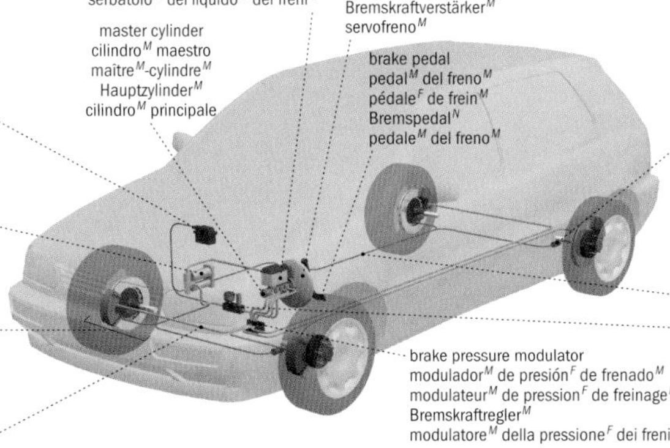

tire

neumático^M | pneu^M | Reifen^M | pneumatico^M

technical specifications
especificaciones^F técnicas^F
spécifications^F techniques
Kennzeichnung^F
dati^M tecnici

tread design
dibujo^M de la superficie^F de rodadura^F
sculptures^F
Profil^N
scolpitura^F del battistrada^M

rubbing strip
banda^F protectora
bourrelet^M
Scheuerleiste^F
striscia^F antiabrasiva

rubber wall
costado^M
flanc^M
Reifenflanke^F
fianco^M

bead
moldura^F
talon^M
Wulst^M
tallone^M

disk
disco^M
voile^M
Radschüssel^F
disco^M

wheel
rueda^F
roue^F
Rad^N
ruota^F

rim
llanta^F
jante^F
Felge^F
cerchio^M

rim flange
pestaña^F de la llanta^F
joue^F de jante^F
Felgenhorn^N
bordo^M del cerchio^M

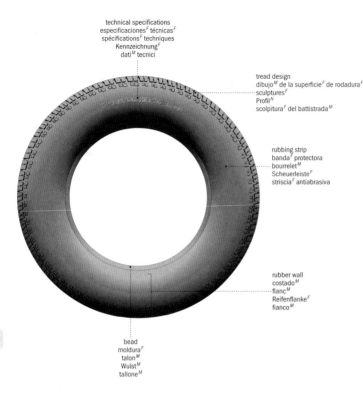

examples of tires
ejemplos^M de neumáticos^M
exemples^M de pneus^M
Reifenarten^F
esempi^M di pneumatici^M

performance tire	all-season tire	winter tire	touring tire	studded tire
neumático^M de rendimiento^M	neumático^M de todas las estaciones^F	neumático^M de invierno^M	neumático^M de turismo^M	neumático^M de tacos^M
pneu^M de performance^F	pneu^M toutes saisons^F	pneu^M d'hiver^M	pneu^M autoroutier	pneu^M à crampons^M
Sportreifen^M	Ganzjahresreifen^M	Winterreifen^M	Touringreifen^M	Spikereifen^M
pneumatico^M sportivo	pneumatico^M per tutte le stagioni^F	pneumatico^M invernale	pneumatico^M granturismo	pneumatico^M chiodato

TRANSPORT AND MACHINERY

bias-ply tire
neumático^M de capas^F al sesgo^M
pneu^M à carcasse^F diagonale
Diagonalreifen^M
pneumatico^M con carcassa^F a struttura^F diagonale

radial tire
neumático^M radial
pneu^M à carcasse^F radiale
Radialreifen^M
pneumatico^M con carcassa^F a struttura^F radiale

steel belted radial tire
neumático^M radial con cinturones^M
pneu^M à carcasse^F radiale ceinturée
Radialgürtelreifen^M
pneumatico^M a carcassa^F radiale cinturata

tread
superficie^F de rodadura^F
bande^F de roulement^M
Lauffläche^F
battistrada^M

tread design
dibujo^M de la superficie^F de rodadura^F
sculptures^F
Profil^N
scolpitura^F del battistrada^M

rubbing strip
banda^F protectora
bourrelet^M
Scheuerrippe^F
striscia^F antiabrasiva

belt
cinturón^M
ceinture^F
Gürtellage^F
cintura^F

radial ply
capa^F del casco^M
pli^M
Radialkarkasse^F
tela^F radiale

inner lining
revestimiento^M interior
revêtement^M intérieur
Innenisolierung^F
rivestimento^M interno

bead wire
alambre^M del reborde^M
tringle^F
Wulstkern^M
cerchietto^M

rubber wall
costado^M
flanc^M
Seitenwand^F
fianco^M

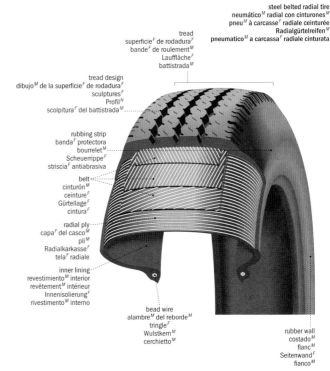

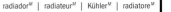

radiator

radiador^M | radiateur^M | Kühler^M | radiatore^M

filler cap
tapa^F
bouchon^M de remplissage^M
Kühlerverschlussdeckel^M
tappo^M

cooling fan
ventilador^M
ventilateur^M
Lüfter^M
ventilatore^M

temperature sensor
sensor^M de temperatura^F
thermocontact^M
Temperaturfühler^M
sensore^M di temperatura^F

lower radiator hose
manguito^M inferior del radiador^M
durite^F de radiateur^M
unterer Kühleranschluss^M
manicotto^M inferiore del radiatore^M

grille
rejilla^F
grille^F
Kühlerblock^M
griglia^F

electric fan motor
motor^M eléctrico
moteur^M électrique
Elektromotor^M
motore^M elettrico

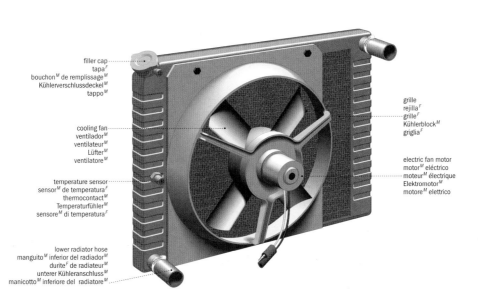

TRANSPORT AND MACHINERY

spark plug

bujía^F | bougie^F d'allumage^M | Zündkerze^F | candela^F

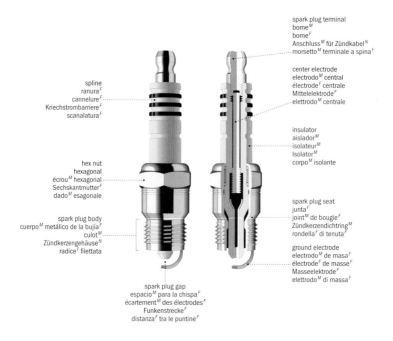

spark plug terminal
borne^M
borne^F
Anschluss^M für Zündkabel^N
morsetto^M terminale a spina^F

center electrode
electrodo^M central
électrode^F centrale
Mittelelektrode^F
elettrodo^M centrale

spline
ranura^F
cannelure^F
Kriechstrombarriere^F
scanalatura^F

insulator
aislador^M
isolateur^M
Isolator^M
corpo^M isolante

hex nut
hexagonal
écrou^M hexagonal
Sechskantmutter^F
dado^M esagonale

spark plug seat
junta^F
joint^F de bougie^F
Zündkerzendichtring^M
rondella^F di tenuta^F

spark plug body
cuerpo^M metálico de la bujía^F
culot^M
Zündkerzengehäuse^N
radice^F filettata

ground electrode
electrodo^M de masa^F
électrode^F de masse^F
Masseelektrode^F
elettrodo^M di massa^F

spark plug gap
espacio^M para la chispa^F
écartement^M des électrodes^F
Funkenstrecke^F
distanza^F tra le puntine^F

battery

batería^F | batterie^F d'accumulateurs^M | Batterie^F | batteria^F

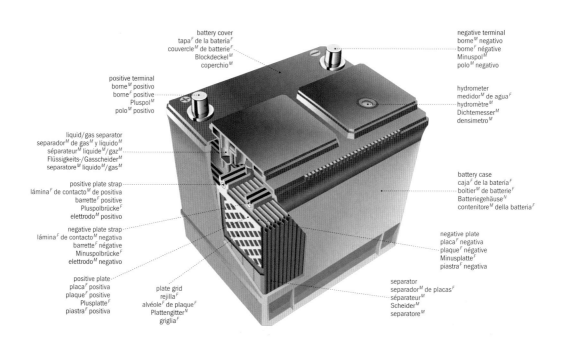

battery cover
tapa^F de la batería^F
couvercle^M de batterie^F
Blockdeckel^M
coperchio^M

negative terminal
borne^M negativo
borne^F négative
Minuspol^M
polo^M negativo

positive terminal
borne^M positivo
borne^F positive
Pluspol^M
polo^M positivo

hydrometer
medidor^M de agua^F
hydromètre^M
Dichtemesser^M
densimetro^M

liquid/gas separator
separador^M de gas^M y líquido^M
séparateur^M liquide^M/gaz^M
Flüssigkeits-/Gasscheider^M
separatore^M liquido^M/gas^M

battery case
caja^F de la batería^F
boîtier^M de batterie^F
Batteriegehäuse^N
contenitore^M della batteria^F

positive plate strap
lámina^F de contacto^M de positiva
barrette^F positive
Pluspolbrücke^F
elettrodo^M positivo

negative plate strap
lámina^F de contacto^M negativa
barrette^F négative
Minuspolbrücke^F
elettrodo^M negativo

negative plate
placa^F negativa
plaque^F négative
Minusplatte^F
piastra^F negativa

positive plate
placa^F positiva
plaque^F positive
Plusplatte^F
piastra^F positiva

plate grid
rejilla^F
alvéole^F de plaque^F
Plattengitter^N
griglia^F

separator
separador^M de placas^F
séparateur^M
Scheider^M
separatore^M

electric automobile

automóvil ^{M} eléctrico | automobile ^{F} électrique | Elektrofahrzeug ^{N} | automobile ^{F} elettrica

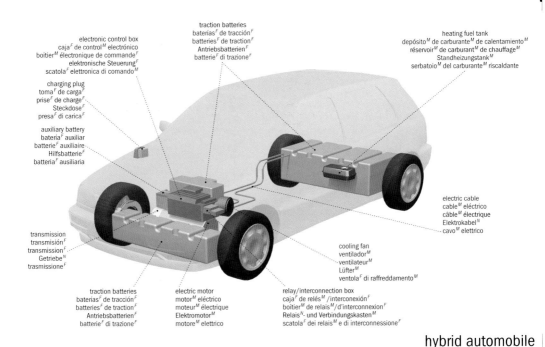

electronic control box
caja ^{F} de control ^{M} electrónico
boitier ^{M} électronique de commande ^{F}
elektronische Steuerung ^{F}
scatola ^{F} elettronica di comando ^{M}

traction batteries
baterías ^{F} de tracción ^{F}
batteries ^{F} de traction ^{F}
Antriebsbatterien ^{F}
batterie ^{F} di trazione ^{F}

heating fuel tank
depósito ^{M} de carburante ^{M} de calentamiento ^{M}
réservoir ^{M} de carburant ^{M} de chauffage ^{M}
Standheizungstank ^{M}
serbatoio ^{M} del carburante ^{M} riscaldante

charging plug
toma ^{F} de carga ^{F}
prise ^{F} de charge ^{F}
Steckdose ^{F}
presa ^{F} di carica ^{F}

auxiliary battery
batería ^{F} auxiliar
batterie ^{F} auxiliaire
Hilfsbatterie ^{F}
batteria ^{F} ausiliaria

electric cable
cable ^{M} eléctrico
câble ^{M} électrique
Elektrokabel ^{N}
cavo ^{M} elettrico

transmission
transmisión ^{F}
transmission ^{F}
Getriebe ^{N}
trasmissione ^{F}

cooling fan
ventilador ^{M}
ventilateur ^{M}
Lüfter ^{M}
ventola ^{F} di raffreddamento ^{M}

traction batteries
baterías ^{F} de tracción ^{F}
batteries ^{F} de traction ^{F}
Antriebsbatterien ^{F}
batterie ^{F} di trazione ^{F}

electric motor
motor ^{M} eléctrico
moteur ^{M} électrique
Elektromotor ^{M}
motore ^{M} elettrico

relay/interconnection box
caja ^{F} de relés ^{F} /interconexión ^{F}
boitier ^{M} de relais ^{F}/d'interconnexion ^{F}
Relais ^{N}- und Verbindungskasten ^{M}
scatola ^{F} dei relais ^{M} e di interconnessione ^{F}

hybrid automobile

automóvil ^{M} híbrido | automobile ^{F} hybride | Hybridfahrzeug ^{N} | automobile ^{F} ibrida

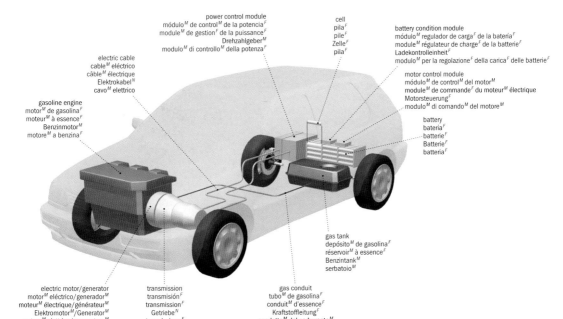

power control module
módulo ^{M} de control ^{M} de la potencia ^{F}
module ^{M} de gestion ^{F} de la puissance ^{F}
Drehzahlgeber ^{M}
modulo ^{M} di controllo ^{M} della potenza ^{F}

cell
pila ^{F}
pile ^{F}
Zelle ^{F}
pila ^{F}

battery condition module
módulo ^{M} regulador de carga ^{F} de la batería ^{F}
module ^{M} régulateur de charge ^{F} de la batterie ^{F}
Ladekontrolleinheit ^{F}
modulo ^{M} per la regolazione ^{F} della carica ^{F} delle batterie ^{F}

electric cable
cable ^{M} eléctrico
câble ^{M} électrique
Elektrokabel ^{N}
cavo ^{M} elettrico

motor control module
módulo ^{M} de control ^{M} del motor ^{M}
module ^{M} de commande ^{F} du moteur ^{M} électrique
Motorsteuerung ^{F}
modulo ^{M} di comando ^{M} del motore ^{M}

gasoline engine
motor ^{M} de gasolina ^{F}
moteur ^{M} à essence ^{F}
Benzinmotor ^{M}
motore ^{M} a benzina ^{F}

battery
batería ^{F}
batterie ^{F}
Batterie ^{F}
batteria ^{F}

gas tank
depósito ^{M} de gasolina ^{F}
réservoir ^{M} à essence ^{F}
Benzintank ^{M}
serbatoio ^{M}

electric motor/generator
motor ^{M} eléctrico/generador ^{M}
moteur ^{M} électrique/générateur ^{M}
Elektromotor ^{M}/Generator ^{M}
motore ^{M} elettrico/ generatore ^{M}

transmission
transmisión ^{F}
transmission ^{F}
Getriebe ^{N}
trasmissione ^{F}

gas conduit
tubo ^{M} de gasolina ^{F}
conduit ^{M} d'essence ^{F}
Kraftstoffleitung ^{F}
condotto ^{M} del carburante ^{M}

types of engines

tipos^M de motores^M | types^M de moteurs^M | Motortypen^M | tipi^M di motori^M

turbo-compressor engine
motor^M turbocompresor
moteur^M à turbocompression^F
Motor^M mit Abgasturbolader^M
motore^M turbocompresso

exhaust gas admission
toma^F de gases^M de combustión^F
entrée^F des gaz^M d'échappement^M
Abgaseintritt^M
immissione^F dei gas^M di scarico^M

intake manifold
conducto^M de admisión^F
admisión^F d'air^M refroidi
Ansaugkrümmer^M
collettore^M di aspirazione^F

charge air cooler warm air outlet
salida^F de aire^M caliente
sortie^F d'air^M chaud
Warmluftauslass^M
condotto^M di scarico^M dell'aria^F calda

exhaust manifold
colector^M de escape^M
collecteur^M d'échappement^M
Auspuffkrümmer^M
collettore^M di scarico^M

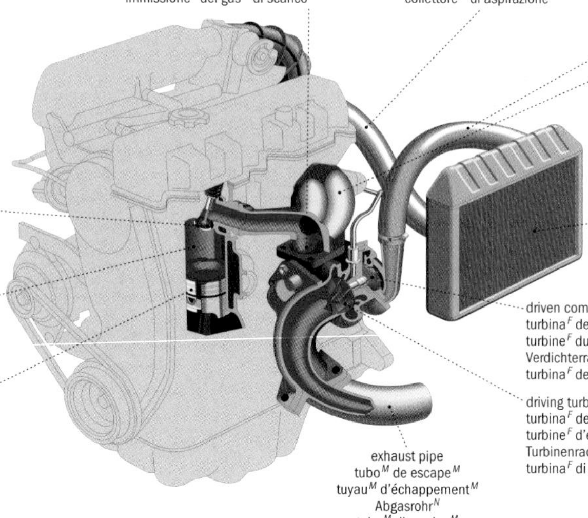

exhaust valve
válvula^F de escape^M
soupape^F d'échappement^M
Auslassventil^N
valvola^F di scarico^M

charge air cooler
refrigerador^M de aire^M
refroidisseur^M d'air^M
Luftkühler^M
raffreddatore^M d'aria^F

combustion chamber
cámara^F de combustión^F
chambre^F de combustion^F
Verbrennungsraum^M
camera^F di scoppio^M

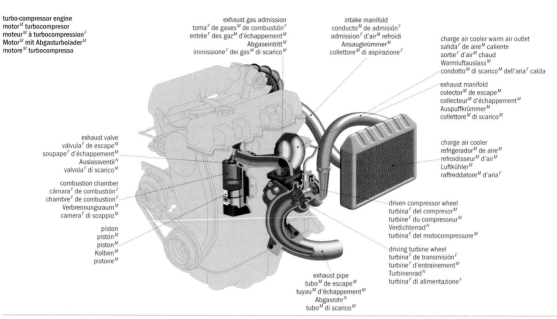

driven compressor wheel
turbina^F del compresor^M
turbine^F du compresseur^M
Verdichterrad^N
turbina^F del motocompressore^M

piston
pistón^M
piston^M
Kolben^M
pistone^M

driving turbine wheel
turbina^F de transmisión^F
turbine^F d'entrainement^M
Turbinenrad^N
turbina^F di alimentazione^F

exhaust pipe
tubo^M de escape^M
tuyau^M d'échappement^M
Abgasrohr^M
tubo^M di scarico^M

four-stroke-cycle engine
motor^M de cuatro tiempos^M
moteur^M à quatre temps^M
Viertaktmotor^M
motore^M a quattro tempi^M

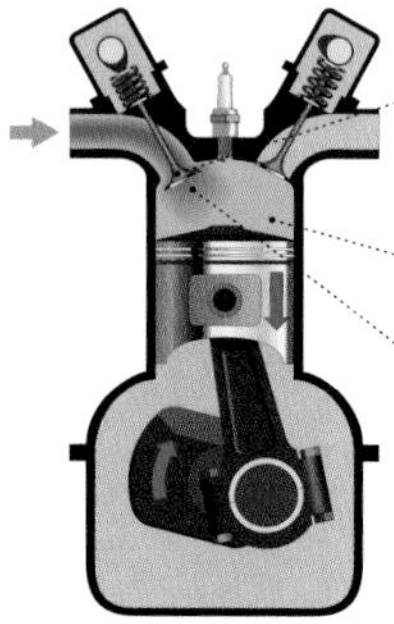

intake valve
válvula^F de admisión^F
soupape^F d'admission^F
Einlassventil^N
valvola^F di aspirazione^F

cylinder
cilindro^M
cylindre^M
Zylinder^M
cilindro^M

air/fuel mixture
mezcla^F de aire^M y combustible^M
mélange^M air^M/carburant^M
Kraftstoff-Luft-Gemisch^N
miscela^F aria^F/carburante^M

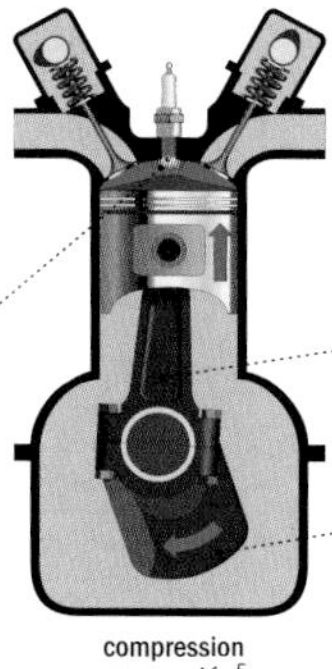

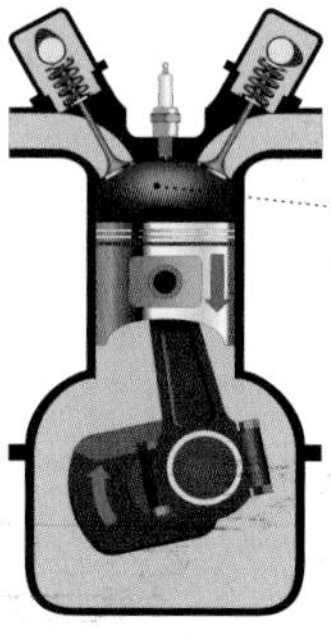

explosion
explosión^F
explosion^F
Zündung^F
esplosione^F

exhaust valve
válvula^F de escape^M
soupape^F d'échappement^M
Auslassventil^N
valvola^F di scarico^M

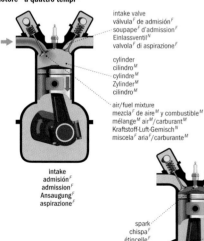

intake
admisión^F
admission^F
Ansaugung^F
aspirazione^F

spark
chispa^F
étincelle^F
Funken^M
scintilla^F

connecting rod
biela^F
bielle^F
Pleuelstange^F
biella^F

crankshaft
cigüeñal^M
vilebrequin^M
Kurbelwelle^F
albero^M a gomiti^M

combustion
combustión^F
combustion^F
Verbrennung^F
scoppio^M

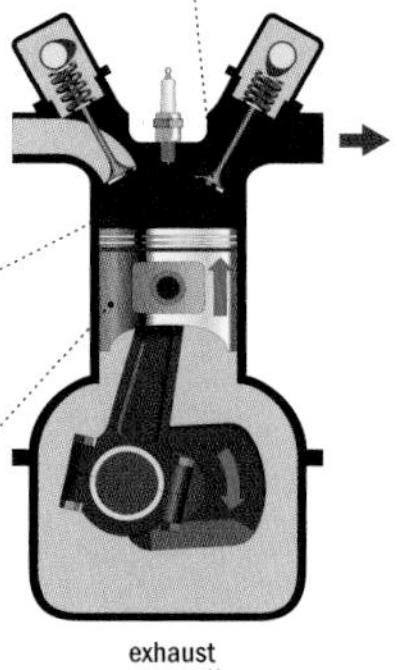

burned gases
gases^M quemados
gaz^M brûlés
Abgase^N
gas^M combusti

piston
pistón^M
piston^M
Kolben^M
pistone^M

compression
compresión^F
compression^F
Verdichtung^F
compressione^F

exhaust
escape^M
échappement^M
Ausstoß^F
scarico^M

types of engines

two-stroke-cycle engine cycle
ciclo^M de un motor^M de dos tiempos^M
cycle^M d'un moteur^M à deux temps^M
Arbeitsprozess^M des Zweitaktmotors^M
ciclo^M del motore^M a due tempi^M

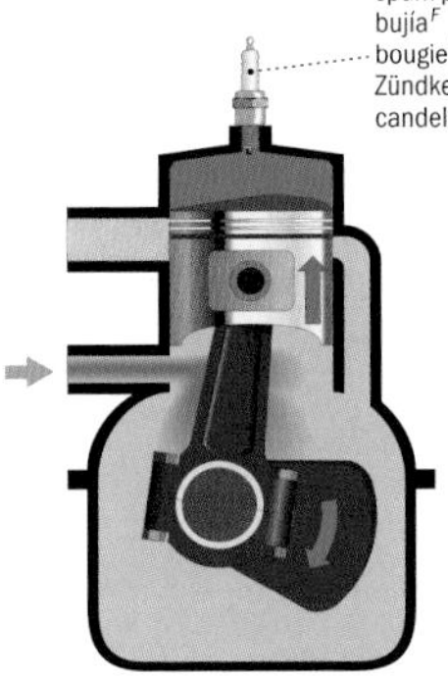

spark plug
bujía^F
bougie^F d'allumage^M
Zündkerze^F
candela^F

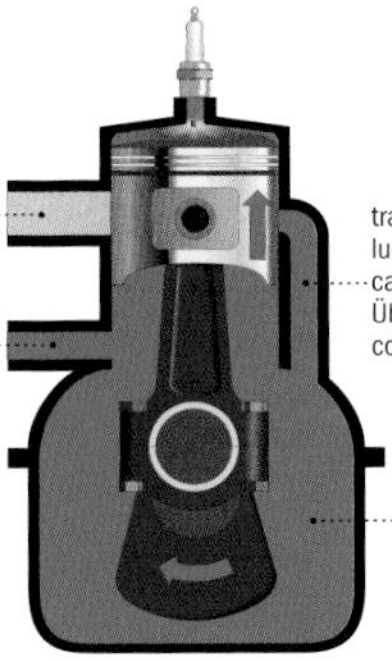

exhaust port
lumbrera^F de escape^M
canal^M d'échappement^M
Auspuffkanal^M
luce^F di scarico^M

transfer port
lumbrera^F de transferencia^F
canal^M de transfert^M
Überströmkanal^M
condotto^M di passaggio^M della miscela^F

intake port
lumbrera^F de admisión^F
canal^M d'admission^F
Ansaugkanal^M
luce^F di aspirazione^F

air/fuel/oil mixture
cárter^M
carter^M
Kurbelgehäuse^N
carter^M

compression/intake
compresión^F/admisión^F
compression^F/admission^F
Verdichtung^F/Ansaugung^F
compressione^F/aspirazione^F

combustion
combustión^F
combustion^F
Verbrennung^F
scoppio^M

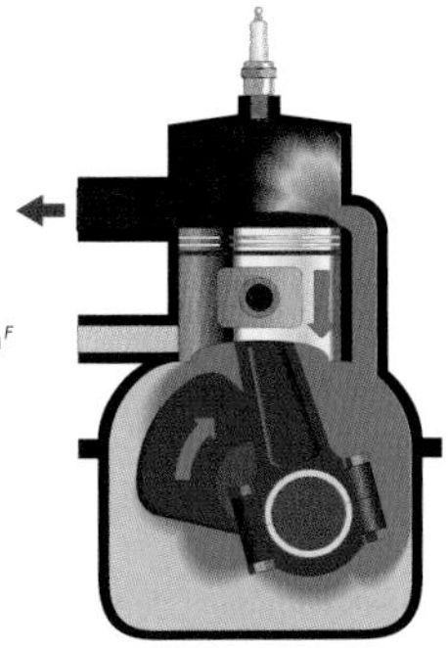

exhaust/scavaging
escape^M
échappement^M
Ausstoß^M
scarico^M

rotary engine cycle
ciclo^M de un motor^M rotatorio
cycle^M d'un moteur^M rotatif
Arbeitsprozess^M des Kreiskolbenmotors^M
ciclo^M del motore^M rotativo

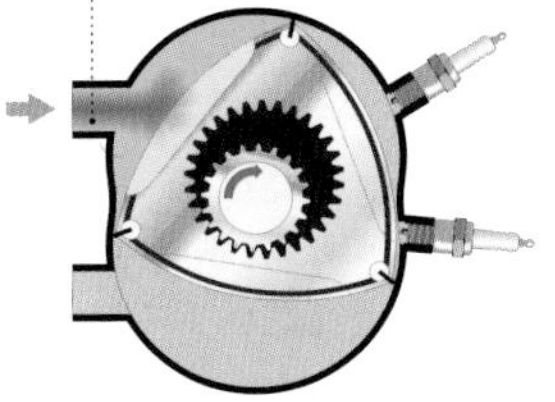

intake manifold
colector^M de admisión^F
tubulure^F d'admission^F
Einlasskanal^M
collettore^M di aspirazione^F

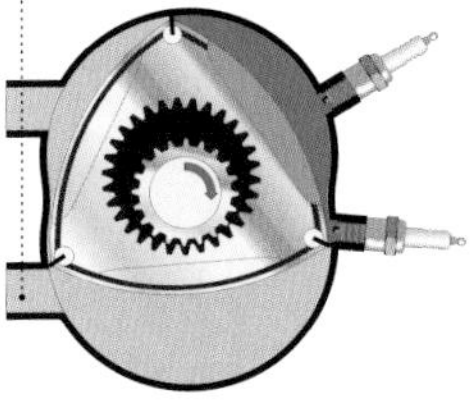

exhaust manifold
colector^M de escape^M
tubulure^F d'échappement^M
Auslasskanal^M
collettore^M di scarico^M

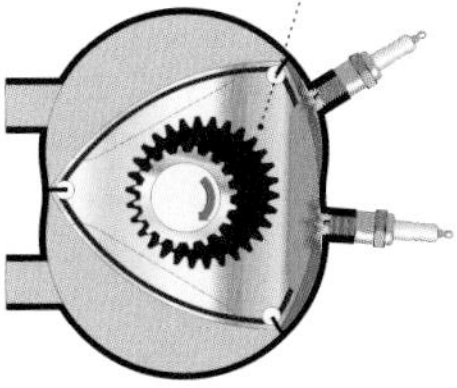

rotor
rotor^M
rotor^M
Kolben^M
rotore^M

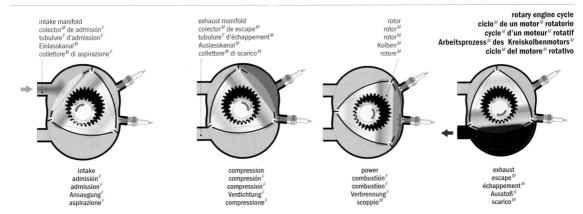

intake
admisión^F
admission^F
Ansaugung^F
aspirazione^F

compression
compresión^F
compression^F
Verdichtung^F
compressione^F

power
combustión^F
combustion^F
Verbrennung^F
scoppio^M

exhaust
escape^M
échappement^M
Ausstoß^G
scarico^M

diesel engine cycle
ciclo^M de un motor^M diesel
cycle^M d'un moteur^M diesel
Arbeitsprozess^M des Dieselmotors^M
ciclo^M del motore^M diesel

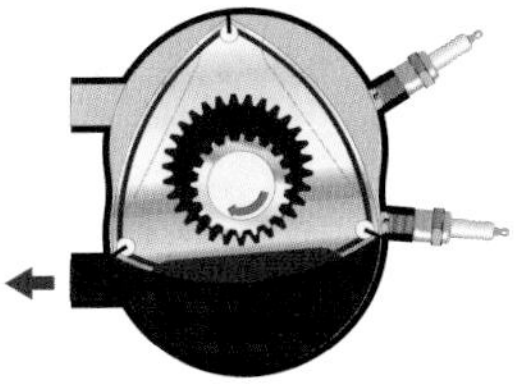

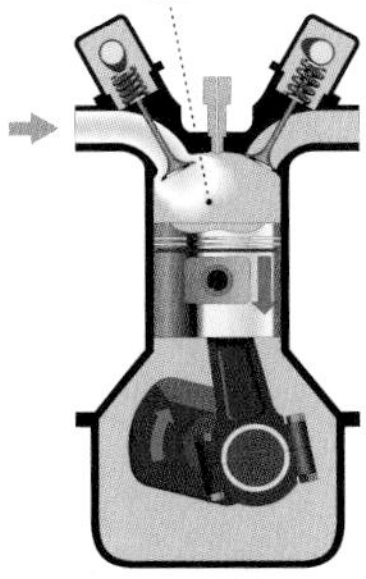

air
aire^M
air^M
Luft^F
aria^F

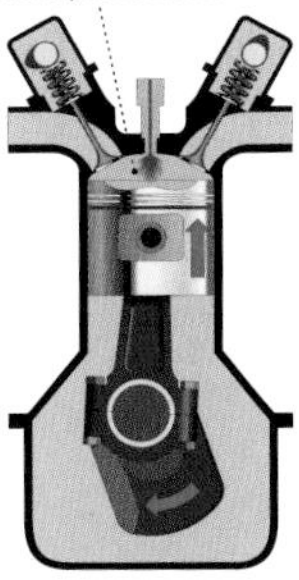

injection/combustion
inyección^F/combustión^F
injection^F/explosion^F
Einspritzung^F/Verbrennung^F
iniezione^F/combustione^F

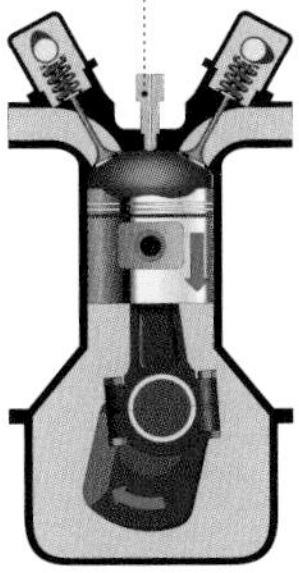

fuel injector
inyector^M de combustible^M
injecteur^M
Einspritzdüse^F
iniettore^M

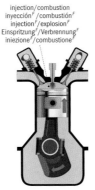

intake
admisión^F
admission^F
Ansaugung^F
aspirazione^F

compression
compresión^F
compression^F
Verdichten^N
compressione^F

power
combustión^M
combustion^F
Verbrennung^F
combustione^F

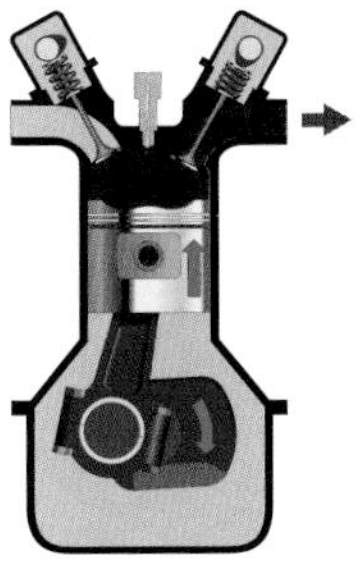

exhaust
escape^M
échappement^M
Ausstoß^F
scarico^M

TRANSPORT AND MACHINERY

types of engines

gasoline engine
motor^M de gasolina^F
moteur^M à essence^F
Ottomotor^M
motore^M a benzina^F

TRANSPORT AND MACHINERY

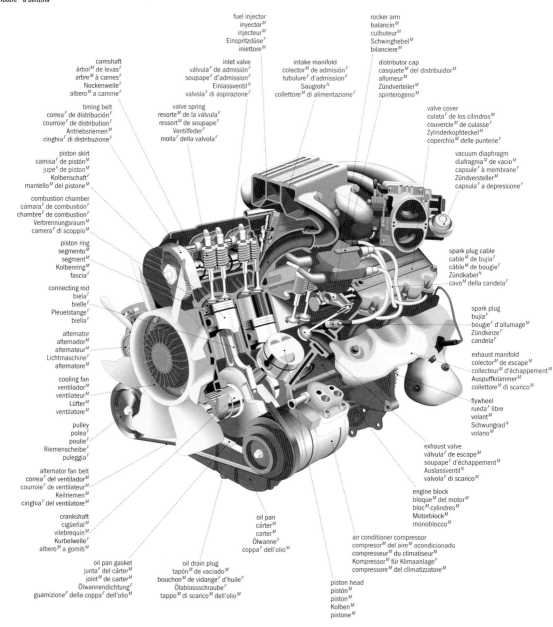

fuel injector
inyector^M
injecteur^M
Einspritzdüse^F
iniettore^M

rocker arm
balancín^M
culbuteur^M
Schwinghebel^M
bilanciere^M

camshaft
árbol^M de levas^F
arbre^M à cames^F
Nockenwelle^F
albero^M a camme^F

inlet valve
válvula^F de admisión^F
soupape^F d'admission^F
Einlassventil^N
valvola^F di aspirazione^F

intake manifold
colector^M de admisión^F
tubulure^F d'admission^F
Saugrohr^N
collettore^M di alimentazione^F

distributor cap
casquete^M del distribuidor^M
allumeur^M
Zündverteiler^M
spinterogeno^M

timing belt
correa^F de distribución^F
courroie^F de distribution^F
Antriebsriemen^M
cinghia^F di distribuzione^F

valve spring
resorte^M de la válvula^F
ressort^M de soupape^F
Ventilfeder^F
molla^F della valvola^F

valve cover
culata^F de los cilindros^M
couvercle^M de culasse^F
Zylinderkopfdeckel^M
coperchio^M delle punterie^F

piston skirt
camisa^F de pistón^M
jupe^F de piston^M
Kolbenschaft^F
mantello^M del pistone^M

vacuum diaphragm
diafragma^M de vacío^M
capsule^F à membrane^F
Zündversteller^M
capsula^F a depressione^F

combustion chamber
cámara^F de combustión^F
chambre^F de combustion^F
Verbrennungsraum^M
camera^F di scoppio^M

piston ring
segmento^M
segment^M
Kolbenring^M
fascia^F

spark plug cable
cable^M de bujía^F
câble^M de bougie^F
Zündkabel^N
cavo^M della candela^F

connecting rod
biela^F
bielle^F
Pleuelstange^F
biella^F

spark plug
bujía^F
bougie^F d'allumage^M
Zündkerze^F
candela^F

alternator
alternador^M
alternateur^M
Lichtmaschine^F
alternatore^M

exhaust manifold
colector^M de escape^M
collecteur^M d'échappement^M
Auspuffkrümmer^M
collettore^M di scarico^M

cooling fan
ventilador^M
ventilateur^M
Lüfter^M
ventilatore^M

flywheel
rueda^F libre
volant^M
Schwungrad^N
volano^M

pulley
polea^F
poulie^F
Riemenscheibe^F
puleggia^F

exhaust valve
válvula^F de escape^M
soupape^F d'échappement^M
Auslassventil^N
valvola^F di scarico^M

alternator fan belt
correa^F del ventilador^M
courroie^F de ventilateur^M
Keilriemen^M
cinghia^F del ventilatore^M

engine block
bloque^M del motor^M
bloc^M-cylindres^M
Motorblock^M
monoblocco^M

crankshaft
cigüeñal^M
vilebrequin^M
Kurbelwelle^F
albero^M a gomiti^F

oil pan
cárter^M
carter^M
Ölwanne^F
coppa^F dell'olio^M

air conditioner compressor
compresor^M del aire^M acondicionado
compresseur^M du climatiseur^M
Kompressor^M für Klimaanlage^F
compressore^M del climatizzatore^M

oil pan gasket
junta^F del cárter^M
joint^M de carter^M
Ölwannendichtung^F
guarnizione^F della coppa^F dell'olio^M

oil drain plug
tapón^M de vaciado^M
bouchon^M de vidange^F d'huile^F
Ölablassschraube^F
tappo^M di scarico^M dell'olio^M

piston head
pistón^M
piston^M
Kolben^M
pistone^M

camping trailers

caravana^F | caravane^F | Wohnwagen^M | rimorchi^M e autocaravan^M

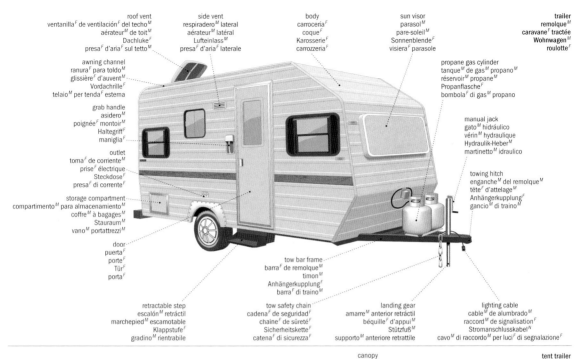

roof vent
ventanilla^F de ventilación^F del techo^M
aérateur^M de toit^M
Dachluke^F
presa^F d'aria^F sul tetto^M

side vent
respiradero^M lateral
aérateur^M latéral
Lufteinlass^M
presa^F d'aria^F laterale

body
carrocería^F
coque^F
Karosserie^F
carrozzeria^F

sun visor
parasol^M
pare-soleil^M
Sonnenblende^F
visiera^F parasole

trailer
remolque^M
caravane^F tractée
Wohnwagen^M
roulotte^F

awning channel
ranura^F para toldo^M
glissière^F d'auvent^M
Vordachrille^F
telaio^M per tenda^F esterna

propane gas cylinder
tanque^M de gas^M propano^M
réservoir^M propane^M
Propanflasche^F
bombola^F di gas^M propano

grab handle
asidero^M
poignée^F montoir^M
Haltegriff^M
maniglia^F

manual jack
gato^M hidráulico
vérin^M hydraulique
Hydraulik-Heber^M
martinetto^M idraulico

outlet
toma^F de corriente^M
prise^F électrique
Steckdose^F
presa^F di corrente^F

towing hitch
enganche^M del remolque^M
tête^F d'attelage^M
Anhängerkupplung^F
gancio^M di traino^M

storage compartment
compartimento^M para almacenamiento^M
coffre^M à bagages^M
Stauraum^M
vano^M portattrezzi^M

door
puerta^F
porte^F
Tür^F
porta^F

tow bar frame
barra^F de remolque^M
timon^M
Anhängerkupplung^F
barra^F di traino^M

retractable step
escalón^M retráctil
marchepied^M escamotable
Klappstufe^F
gradino^M rientrabile

tow safety chain
cadena^F de seguridad^F
chaîne^F de sûreté^F
Sicherheitskette^F
catena^F di sicurezza^F

landing gear
amarre^M anterior retráctil
béquille^F d'appui^M
Stützfuß^M
supporto^M anteriore retrattile

lighting cable
cable^M de alumbrado^M
raccord^M de signalisation^F
Stromanschlusskabel^N
cavo^M di raccordo^M per luci^F di segnalazione^F

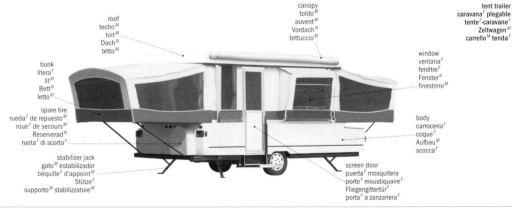

canopy
toldo^M
auvent^M
Vordach^N
tettuccio^M

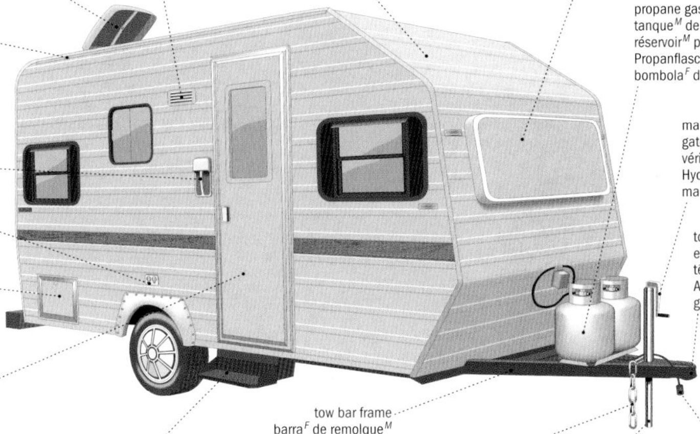

tent trailer
caravana^F plegable
tente^F-caravane^F
Zeltwagen^M
carrello^M tenda^F

roof
techo^M
toit^M
Dach^N
tetto^M

window
ventana^F
fenêtre^F
Fenster^N
finestrino^M

bunk
litera^F
lit^M
Bett^N
letto^M

spare tire
rueda^F de repuesto^M
roue^F de secours^M
Reserverad^N
ruota^F di scorta^F

body
carrocería^F
coque^F
Aufbau^M
scocca^F

stabilizer jack
gato^M estabilizador
béquille^F d'appoint^M
Stütze^F
supporto^M stabilizzatore^M

screen door
puerta^F mosquitera
porte^F moustiquaire^F
Fliegengittertür^F
porta^F a zanzariera^F

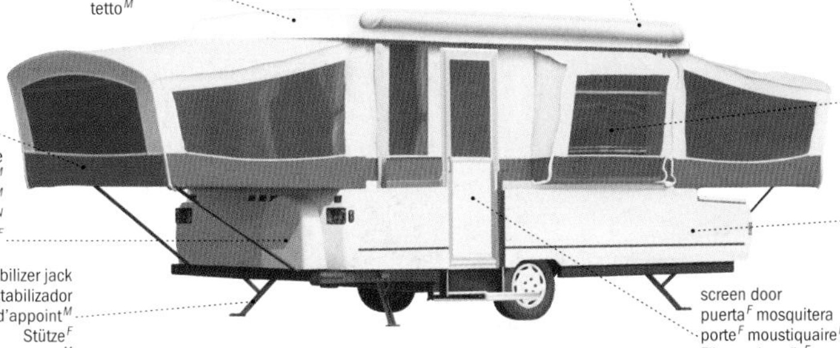

motor home
autocaravana^M
auto^F-caravane^F
Wohnmobil^N
autocaravan^M

air conditioner
aire^M acondicionado
climatiseur^M
Klimaanlage^F
condizionatore^M

luggage rack
portaequipajes^M
porte-bagages^M
Gepäckträger^M
portabagagli^M

ladder
escalerilla^F
échelle^F
Leiter^F
scala^F

TRANSPORT AND MACHINERY

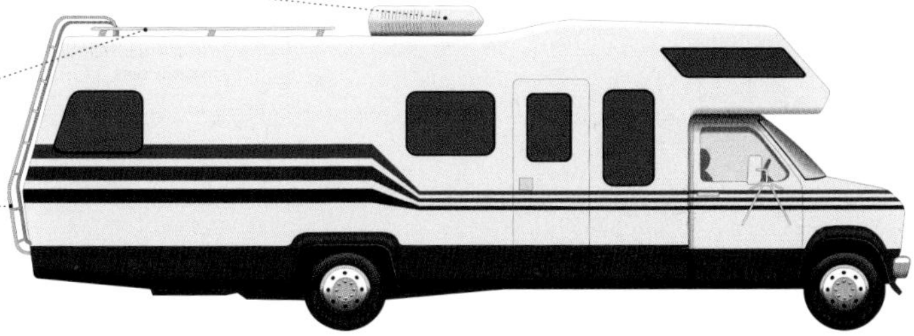

buses

autobúses^M | autobus^M | Buse^M | autobus^M

TRANSPORT AND MACHINERY

school bus
autobús^M escolar
autobus^M scolaire
Schulbus^M
scuolabus^M

outside mirror
espejo^M retrovisor exterior
rétroviseur^M extérieur
Außenspiegel^M
specchietto^M retrovisore^M esterno

blind spot mirror
retrovisor^M de gran angular^M
rétroviseur^M grand angle^M
Weitwinkelspiegel^M
specchietto^M per il punto^M cieco

blinking lights
faros^M intermitentes
feux^M intermittents
Blinklichter^N
luci^F intermittenti

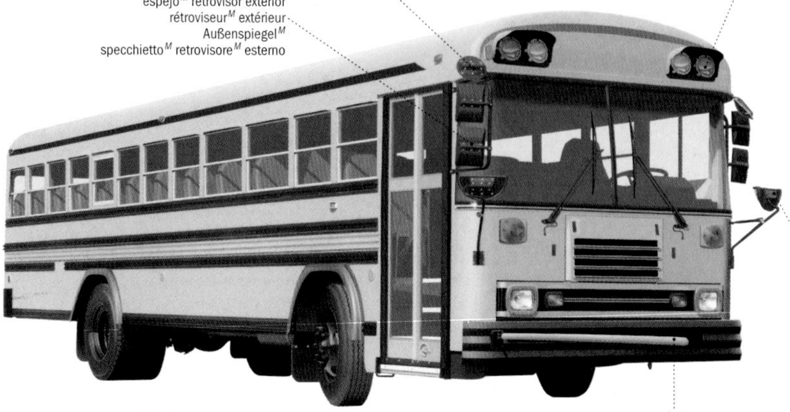

crossover mirror
espejo^M de cercanías^F
miroir^M de traversée^F avant
Sicherheitsspiegel^M
specchietto^M anteriore di accostamento^M

city bus
autobús^M urbano
autobus^M
Linienbus^M
autobus^M urbano

air intake
toma^F de aire^M
prise^F d'air^M
Lufteinlass^M
presa^F d'aria^F

two-leaf door
puerta^F de dos hojas^F
porte^F à deux vantaux^M
zweiflügelige Ausgangstür^F
porta^F a due battenti^M

crossing arm
barra^F distanciadora
bras^M d'éloignement^M
Absperrarm^M
barra^F distanziatrice

route sign
indicador^M de línea^F
indicateur^M de ligne^F
Linienanzeige^F
indicatore^M di linea^F

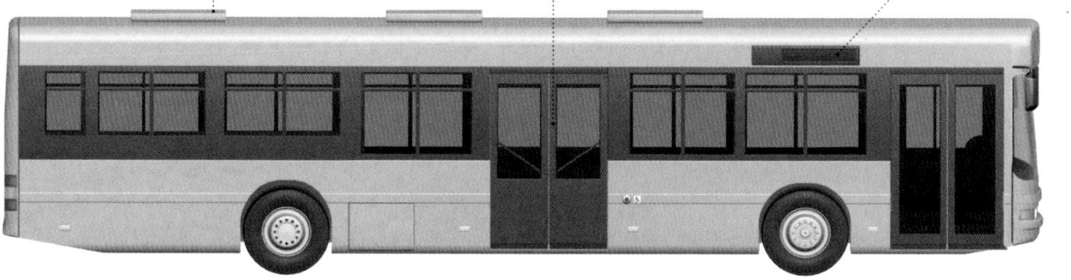

coach
autocar^M
autocar^M
Reisebus^M
pullman^M

engine air intake
toma^F de aire^M del motor^M
prise^F d'air^M du moteur^M
Motorlufteinlass^M
presa^F d'aria^F del motore^M

entrance door
puerta^F de entrada^F
porte^F d'entrée^F
Einstiegstür^F
porta^F di entrata^F

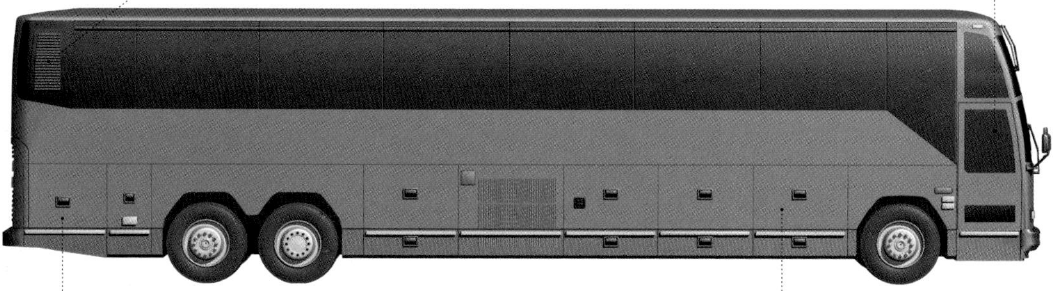

engine compartment
compartimiento^M motor
compartiment^M moteur^M
Motorraum^M
vano^M motore^M

baggage compartment
maletero^M
soute^F à bagages^M
Gepäckraum^M
bagagliaio^M

double-decker bus
autocar^M de dos pisos^M
autobus^M à impériale^F
Doppeldeckerbus^M
autobus^M a due piani^M

route sign
indicador^M de línea^F
indicateur^M de ligne^F
Linienanzeige^F
indicatore^M di linea^F

upper deck
piso^M superior
impériale^F
Oberdeck^N
piano^M superiore

minibus
minibús^M
minibus^M
Kleinbus^M
minibus^M

lift door
puerta^F de la plataforma^F elevadora
porte^F de l'élévateur^M
elektrische Schiebetür^F
porta^F dell'elevatore^M

blind spot mirror
retrovisor^M gran angular
rétroviseur^M grand angle^M
Weitwinkelspiegel^M
specchietto^M per il punto^M cieco

West Coast mirror
espejo^M retrovisor
rétroviseur^M
Außenspiegel^M
specchietto^M retrovisore^M

handrail
pasamano^M
barre^F de maintien^M
Haltegriff^M
corrimano^M

wheelchair lift
plataforma^F elevadora para silla^F de ruedas^F
élévateur^M pour fauteuils^M roulants
Rollstuhllift^M
elevatore^M per sedie^F a rotelle^F

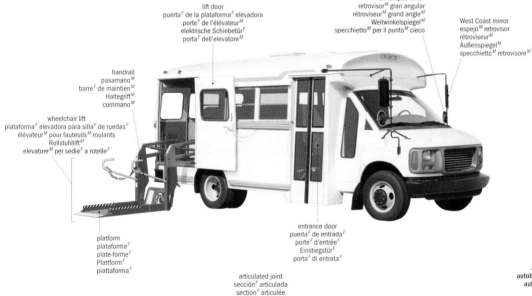

platform
plataforma^F
plate-forme^F
Plattform^F
piattaforma^F

entrance door
puerta^F de entrada^F
porte^F d'entrée^F
Einstiegstür^F
porta^F di entrata^F

articulated bus
autobús^M articulado
autobus^M articulé
Gelenkbus^M
autobus^M articolato

articulated joint
sección^F articulada
section^F articulée
Gelenk^N
passaggio^M a soffietto^M

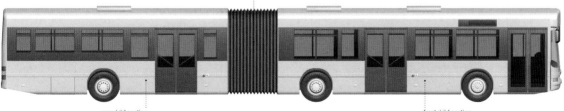

rear rigid section
remolque^M rígido trasero
tronçon^M rigide arrière
steifer Nachläufer^M
sezione^F rigida posteriore

front rigid section
sección^F rígida de tracción^F delantera
tronçon^M rigide avant
steifes Vorderteil^N
sezione^F rigida anteriore

TRANSPORT AND MACHINERY

trucking

camiones^M | camionnage^M | Lastkraftfahrzeuge^N | autoveicoli^M industriali

truck tractor
camión^M tractor^M
tracteur^M routier
Sattelschlepper^M
motrice^F

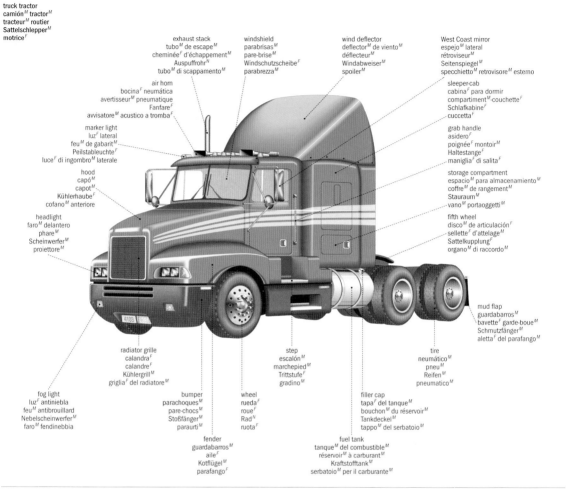

exhaust stack
tubo^M de escape^M
cheminée^F d'échappement^M
Auspuffrohr^N
tubo^M di scappamento^M

windshield
parabrisas^M
pare-brise^M
Windschutzscheibe^F
parabrezza^F

wind deflector
deflector^M de viento^M
déflecteur^M
Windabweiser^M
spoiler^M

West Coast mirror
espejo^M lateral
rétroviseur^M
Seitenspiegel^M
specchietto retrovisore^M esterno

air horn
bocina^F neumática
avertisseur^M pneumatique
Fanfare^F
avvisatore^M acustico a tromba^F

sleeper-cab
cabina^F para dormir
compartiment^M-couchette^F
Schlafkabine^F
cuccetta^F

marker light
luz^F lateral
feu^M de gabarit^M
Peilstableuchte^F
luce^F di ingombro^M laterale

grab handle
asidero^F
poignée^F montoir^M
Haltestange^F
maniglia^F di salita^F

hood
capó^M
capot^M
Kühlerhaube^F
cofano^M anteriore

storage compartment
espacio^M para almacenamiento^M
coffre^M de rangement^M
Stauraum^M
vano^M portaoggetti^M

headlight
faro^M delantero
phare^M
Scheinwerfer^M
proiettore^M

fifth wheel
disco^M de articulación^F
sellette^F d'attelage^M
Sattelkupplung^F
organo^M di raccordo^M

mud flap
guardabarros^M
bavette^F garde-boue^M
Schmutzfänger^M
aletta^F del parafango^M

radiator grille
calandra^F
calandre^F
Kühlergrill^M
griglia^F del radiatore^M

step
escalón^M
marchepied^M
Trittstufe^F
gradino^M

tire
neumático^M
pneu^M
Reifen^M
pneumatico^M

fog light
luz^F antiniebla
feu^M antibrouillard
Nebelscheinwerfer^M
faro^M fendinebbia

bumper
parachoques^M
pare-chocs^M
Stoßfänger^M
paraurti^M

wheel
rueda^F
roue^F
Rad^N
ruota^F

filler cap
tapa^F del tanque^M
bouchon^M du réservoir^M
Tankdeckel^M
tappo^M del serbatoio^M

fender
guardabarros^M
aile^F
Kotflügel^M
parafango^F

fuel tank
tanque^M del combustible^M
réservoir^M à carburant^M
Kraftstofftank^M
serbatoio^M per il carburante^M

tandem tractor trailer
camión^M articulado
train^M routier
Sattelzug^M
autoarticolato^M

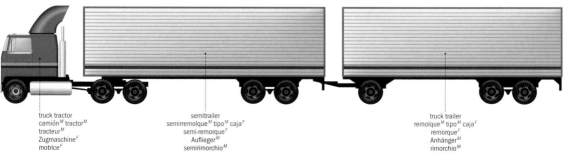

truck tractor
camión^M tractor^M
tracteur^M
Zugmaschine^F
motrice^F

semitrailer
semirremolque^M tipo^M caja^F
semi-remorque^F
Auflieger^M
semirimorchio^M

truck trailer
remolque^M tipo^M caja^F
remorque^F
Anhänger^M
rimorchio^M

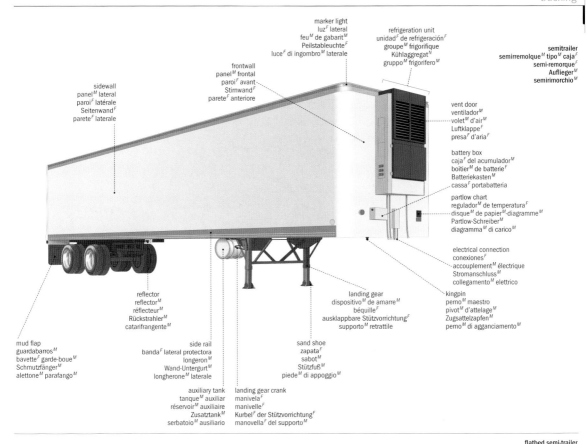

marker light
luz^F lateral
feu^M de gabarit^M
Peilstableuchte^F
luce^F di ingombro^M laterale

refrigeration unit
unidad^F de refrigeración^F
groupe^M frigorifique
Kühlaggregat^N
gruppo^M frigorifero^M

semitrailer
semirremolque^M tipo^M caja^F
semi-remorque^F
Auflieger^M
semirimorchio^M

frontwall
panel^M frontal
paroi^F avant
Stirnwand^F
parete^F anteriore

sidewall
panel^M lateral
paroi^F latérale
Seitenwand^F
parete^F laterale

vent door
ventilador^M
volet^M d'air^M
Luftklappe^F
presa^F d'aria^F

battery box
caja^F del acumulador^M
boîtier^M de batterie^F
Batteriekasten^M
cassa^F portabatteria

partlow chart
regulador^M de temperatura^F
disque^M de papier^M-diagramme^M
Partlow-Schreiber^M
diagramma^M di carico^M

electrical connection
conexiones^F
accouplement^M électrique
Stromanschluss^M
collegamento^M elettrico

reflector
reflector^M
réflecteur^M
Rückstrahler^M
catarifrangente^M

landing gear
dispositivo^M de amarre^M
béquille^F
ausklappbare Stützvorrichtung^F
supporto^M retrattile

kingpin
perno^M maestro
pivot^M d'attelage^M
Zugsattelzapfen^M
perno^M di agganciamento^M

mud flap
guardabarros^M
bavette^F garde-boue^M
Schmutzfänger^M
alettone^M parafango^M

side rail
banda^F lateral protectora
longeron^M
Wand-Untergurt^M
longherone^M laterale

sand shoe
zapata^F
sabot^M
Stützfuß^M
piede^M di appoggio^M

auxiliary tank
tanque^M auxiliar
réservoir^M auxiliaire
Zusatztank^M
serbatoio^M ausiliario

landing gear crank
manivela^F
manivelle^F
Kurbel^F der Stützvorrichtung^F
manovella^F del supporto^M

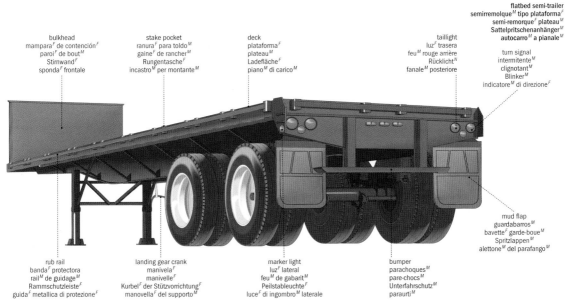

flatbed semi-trailer
semirremolque^M tipo plataforma^F
semi-remorque^F plateau^M
Sattelpritschenanhänger^M
autocarro^M a pianale^M

bulkhead
mampara^F de contención^F
paroi^F de bout^M
Stirnwand^F
sponda^F frontale

stake pocket
ranura^F para toldo^M
gaine^F de rancher^M
Rungentasche^F
incastro^M per montante^M

deck
plataforma^F
plateau^M
Ladefläche^F
piano^M di carico^M

taillight
luz^F trasera
feu^M rouge arrière
Rücklicht^N
fanale^M posteriore

turn signal
intermitente^M
clignotant^M
Blinker^M
indicatore^M di direzione^F

rub rail
banda^F protectora
rail^M de guidage^M
Rammschutzleiste^F
guida^F metallica di protezione^F

landing gear crank
manivela^F
manivelle^F
Kurbel^F der Stützvorrichtung^F
manovella^F del supporto^M

marker light
luz^F lateral
feu^M de gabarit^M
Peilstableuchte^F
luce^F di ingombro^M laterale

bumper
parachoques^M
pare-chocs^M
Unterfahrschutz^M
paraurti^M

mud flap
guardabarros^M
bavette^F garde-boue^M
Spritzlappen^M
alettone^M del parafango^M

trucking

examples of semitrailers
ejemplos[M] **de camiones**[M] **articulados**
exemples[M] **de semi-remorques**[F]
Beispiele[N] **für Sattelkraftfahrzeuge**[N]
esempi[M] **di autoarticolati**[M]

tank trailer
camión[M] cisterna[F]
semi-remorque[F] citerne[F]
Tanklastzug[M]
autocisterna[F]

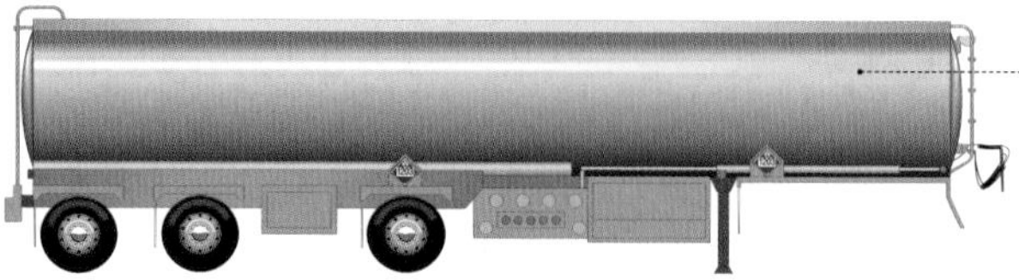

tank body
cisterna[F]
citerne[F]
Tankauflieger[M]
cisterna[F]

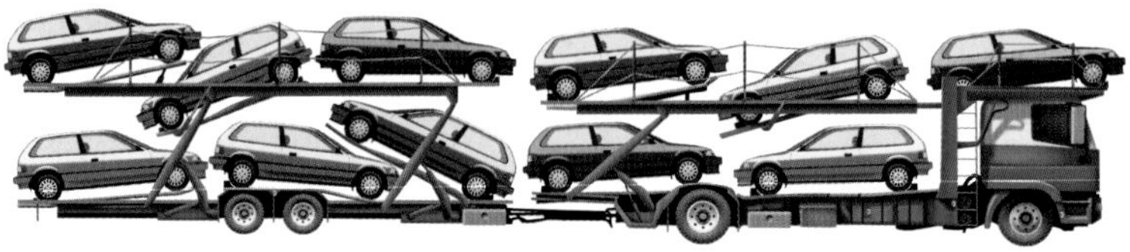

automobile transport semitrailer
trailer[M] para transporte[M] de vehiculos[M]
semi-remorque[F] porte-véhicules[M]
Autotransporter[M]
bisarca[F]

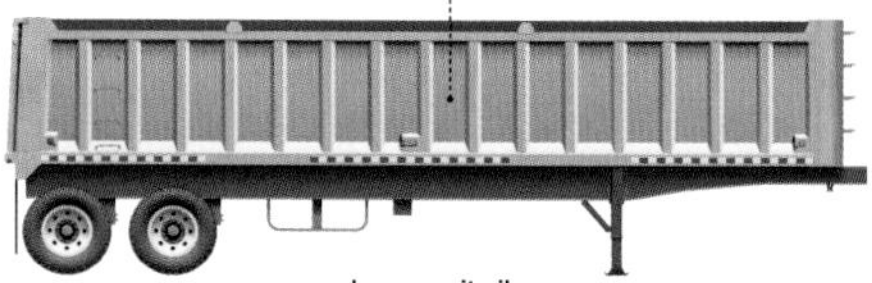

dump body
volquete[M] basculante
benne[F] basculante
aufgesattelter Kippanhänger[M]
cassone[M] ribaltabile

dump semitrailer
camión[M] volquete
semi-remorque[F] benne[F]
Kipplader[M]
ribaltabile[M]

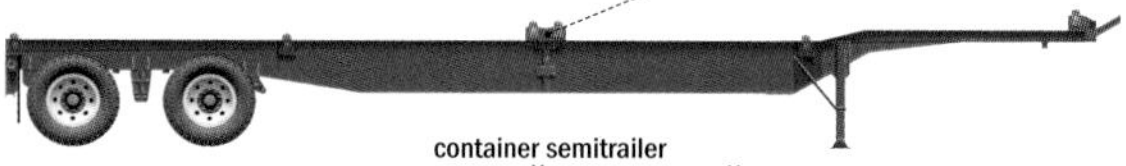

twist lock
bloqueo[M] giratorio
verrou[M] tournant
Drehfeststeller[M]
fermo[M] girevole

container semitrailer
semirremolque[M] porta container[M]
semi-remorque[F] porte-conteneur[M]
Containerauflieger[M]
semirimorchio[M] portacontainer[M]

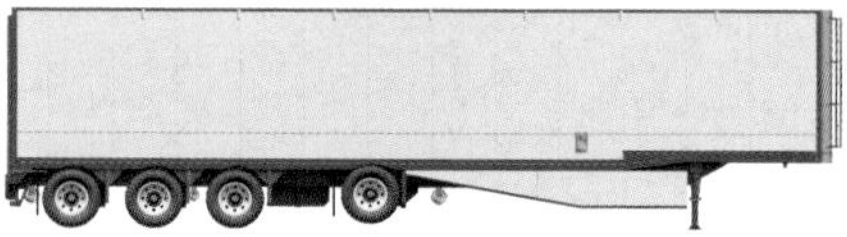

chip van
semirremolque[M] con lona[F]
semi-remorque[F] à copeaux[M]
Sattelanhänger[M] für den Spantransport[M]
autocarro[M] per trucioli[M]

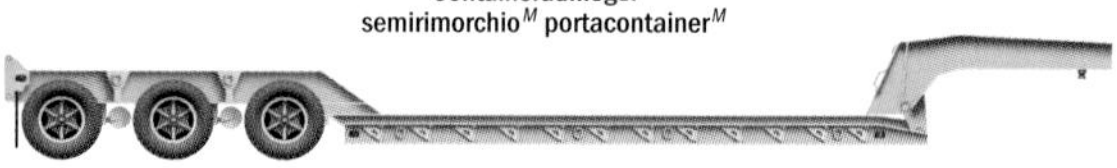

double-drop lowbed semitrailer
semirremolque[M] bajo portamáquinas[M]
semi-remorque[F] porte-engins[M] surbaissée
Satteltiefladeanhänger[M] für den Transport[M] von Panzerfahrzeugen[N]
semirimorchio[M] ribassato per il trasporto[M] di mezzi[M] corazzati

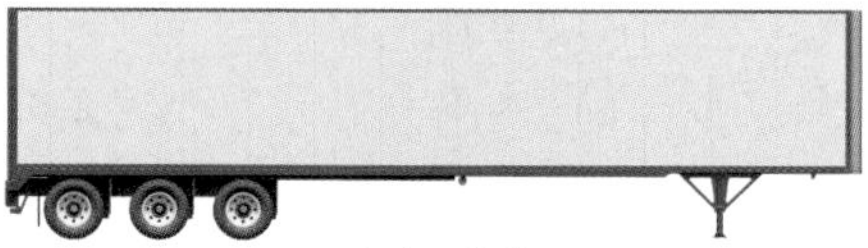

van body semitrailer
semirremolque[M] furgón
semi-remorque[F] fourgon[M]
Kofferauflieger[M]
semirimorchio[M] furgonato

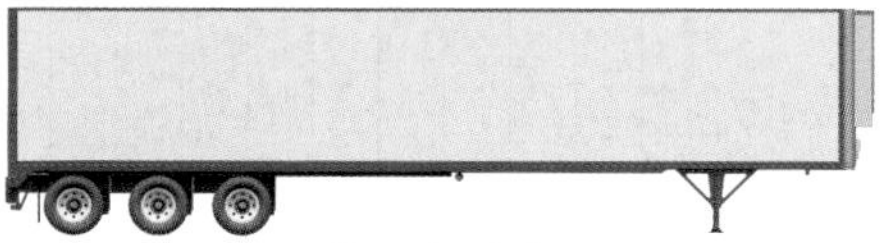

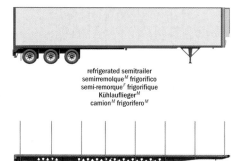

refrigerated semitrailer
semirremolque[M] frigorifico
semi-remorque[F] frigorifique
Kühlauflieger[M]
camion[M] frigorifero[M]

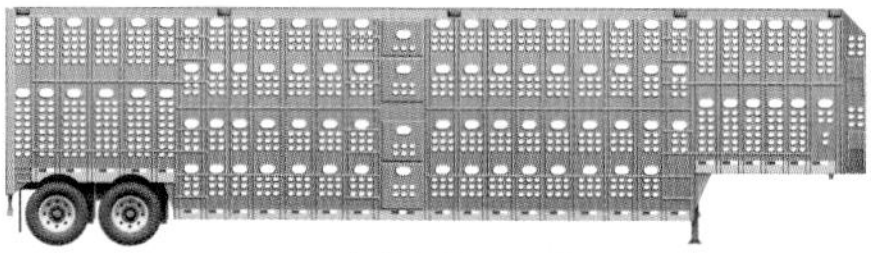

possum-belly body semitrailer
semirremolque[M] jaula[F] bajo para transporte[M] ganadero
semi-remorque[F] bétaillère surbaissée
Satteltiefladeanhänger[M] für den Tiertransport[M]
semirimorchio[M] ribassato per il trasporto[M] del bestiame[M]

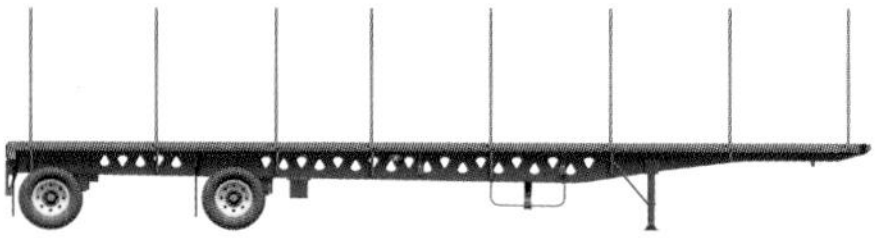

log semitrailer
semirremolque[M] para el transporte[M] de troncos[M]
semi-remorque[F] à grumes[F]
Sattelanhänger[M] für den Baumstammtransport[M]
autocarro[M] per il trasporto[M] dei tronchi[M]

TRANSPORT AND MACHINERY

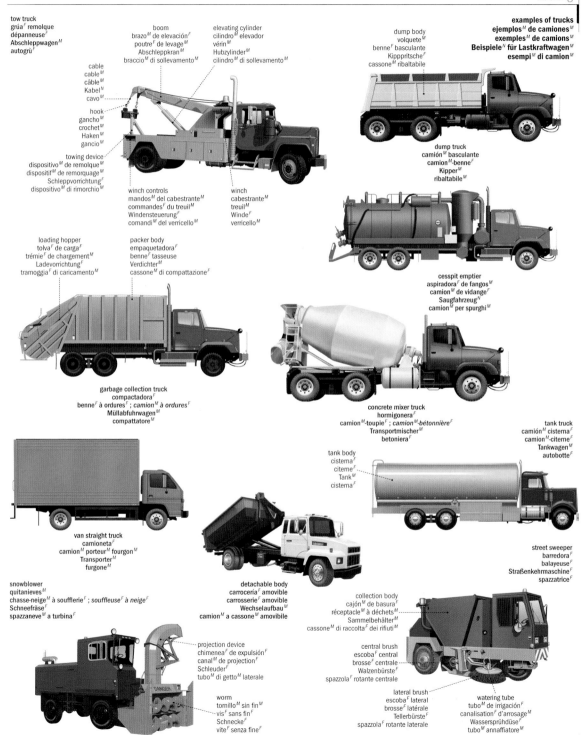

tow truck
grúa^F remolque
dépanneuse^F
Abschleppwagen^M
autogrù^F

boom
brazo^M de elevación^F
poutre^F de levage^M
Abschleppkran^M
braccio^M di sollevamento^M

elevating cylinder
cilindro^M elevador
vérin^M
Hubzylinder^M
cilindro^M di sollevamento^M

dump body
volquete^M
benne^F basculante
Kipppritsche^F
cassone^M ribaltabile

examples of trucks
ejemplos^M de camiones^M
exemples^M de camions^M
Beispiele^N für Lastkraftwagen^M
esempi^M di camion^M

cable
cable^M
câble^M
Kabel^N
cavo^M

hook
gancho^M
crochet^M
Haken^M
gancio^M

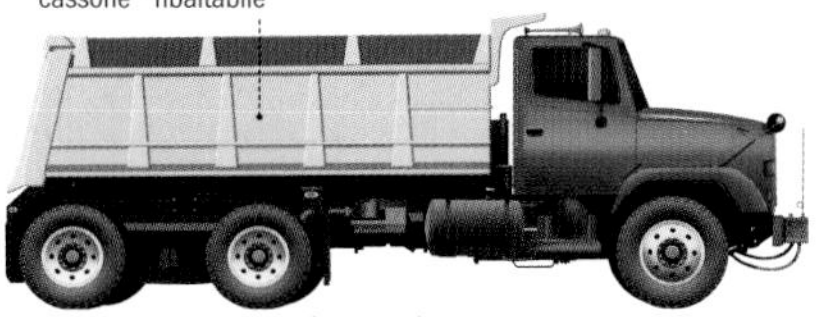

dump truck
camión^M basculante
camion^M-benne^F
Kipper^M
ribaltabile^M

towing device
dispositivo^M de remolque^M
dispositif^M de remorquage^M
Schleppvorrichtung^F
dispositivo^M di rimorchio^M

winch controls
mandos^M del cabestrante^M
commandes^F du treuil^M
Windensteuerung^F
comandi^M del verricello^M

winch
cabestrante^M
treuil^M
Winde^F
verricello^M

cesspit emptier
aspiradora^F de fangos^M
camion^M de vidange^F
Saugfahrzeug^N
camion^M per spurghi^M

loading hopper
tolva^F de carga^F
trémie^F de chargement^M
Ladevorrichtung^F
tramoggia^F di caricamento^M

packer body
empaquetadora^F
benne^F tasseuse
Verdichter^M
cassone^M di compattazione^F

garbage collection truck
compactadora^F
benne^F à ordures^F ; camion^M à ordures^F
Müllabfuhrwagen^M
compattatore^M

concrete mixer truck
hormigonera^F
camion^M-toupie^F ; camion^M-bétonnière^F
Transportmischer^M
betoniera^F

tank truck
camión^M cisterna^F
camion^M-citerne^F
Tankwagen^M
autobotte^F

tank body
cisterna^F
citerne^F
Tank^M
cisterna^F

van straight truck
camioneta^F
camion^M porteur^M fourgon^M
Transporter^M
furgone^M

street sweeper
barredora^F
balayeuse^F
Straßenkehrmaschine^F
spazzatrice^F

snowblower
quitanieves^M
chasse-neige^M à soufflerie^F ; souffleuse^F à neige^F
Schneefräse^F
spazzaneve^M a turbina^F

detachable body
carrocería^F amovible
carrosserie^F amovible
Wechselaufbau^M
camion^M a cassone^M amovibile

collection body
cajón^M de basura^F
réceptacle^M à déchets^M
Sammelbehälter^M
cassone^M di raccolta^F dei rifiuti^M

projection device
chimenea^F de expulsión^F
canal^M de projection^F
Schleuder^F
tubo^M di getto^M laterale

central brush
escoba^F central
brosse^F centrale
Walzenbürste^F
spazzola^F rotante centrale

worm
tornillo^M sin fin^M
vis^F sans fin^M
Schnecke^F
vite^F senza fine^F

lateral brush
escoba^F lateral
brosse^F latérale
Tellerbürste^F
spazzola^F rotante laterale

watering tube
tubo^M de irrigación^F
canalisation^F d'arrosage^M
Wassersprühdüse^F
tubo^M annaffiatore^M

TRANSPORT AND MACHINERY

motorcycle

motocicleta^F | moto^F | Motorrad^N | motocicletta^F

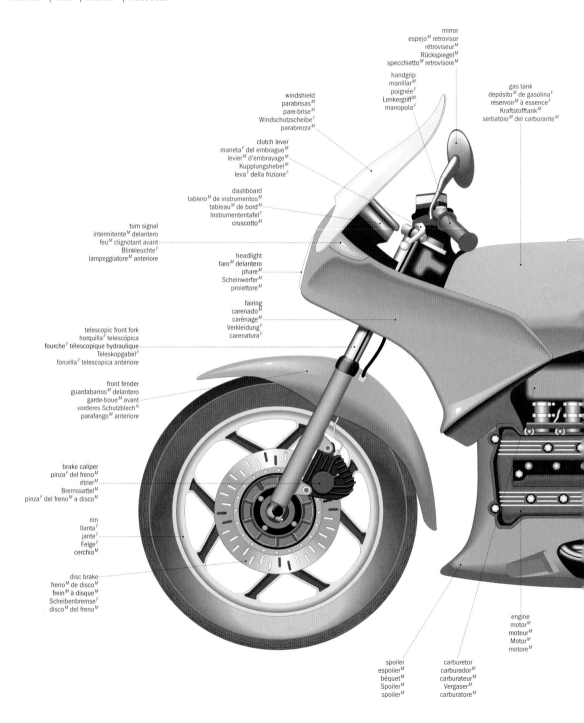

mirror
espejo^M retrovisor
rétroviseur^M
Rückspiegel^M
specchietto^M retrovisore^M

handgrip
manillar^M
poignée^F
Lenkergriff^M
manopola^F

gas tank
depósito^M de gasolina^F
réservoir^M à essence^F
Kraftstofftank^M
serbatoio^M del carburante^M

windshield
parabrisas^M
pare-brise^M
Windschutzscheibe^F
parabrezza^M

clutch lever
maneta^F del embrague^M
levier^M d'embrayage^M
Kupplungshebel^M
leva^F della frizione^F

dashboard
tablero^M de instrumentos^M
tableau^M de bord^M
Instrumententafel^F
cruscotto^M

turn signal
intermitente^M delantero
feu^M clignotant avant
Blinkleuchte^F
lampeggiatore^M anteriore

headlight
faro^M delantero
phare^M
Scheinwerfer^M
proiettore^M

fairing
carenado^M
carénage^M
Verkleidung^F
carenatura^F

telescopic front fork
horquilla^F telescópica
fourche^F télescopique hydraulique
Teleskopgabel^F
forcella^F telescopica anteriore

front fender
guardabarros^M delantero
garde-boue^M avant
vorderes Schutzblech^N
parafango^M anteriore

brake caliper
pinza^F del freno^M
étrier^M
Bremssattel^M
pinza^F del freno^M a disco^M

rim
llanta^F
jante^F
Felge^F
cerchio^M

disc brake
freno^M de disco^M
frein^M à disque^M
Scheibenbremse^F
disco^M del freno^M

spoiler
espoiler^M
béquet^M
Spoiler^M
spoiler^M

carburetor
carburador^M
carburateur^M
Vergaser^M
carburatore^M

engine
motor^M
moteur^M
Motor^M
motore^M

TRANSPORT AND MACHINERY

574

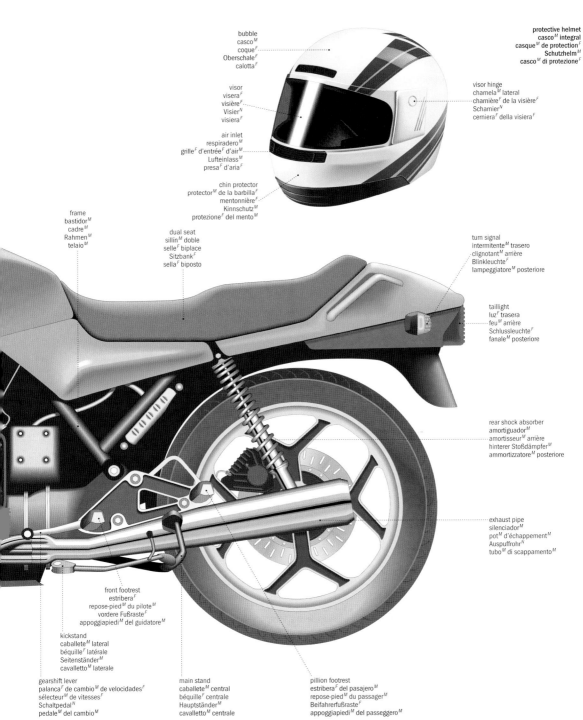

bubble
casco^M
coque^F
Oberschale^F
calotta^F

protective helmet
casco^M integral
casque^M de protection^F
Schutzhelm^M
casco^M di protezione^F

visor
visera^F
visière^F
Visier^N
visiera^F

visor hinge
charnela^M lateral
charnière^F de la visière^F
Scharnier^N
cerniera^F della visiera^F

air inlet
respiradero^M
grille^F d'entrée^F d'air^M
Lufteinlass^M
presa^F d'aria^F

chin protector
protector^M de la barbilla^F
mentonnière^F
Kinnschutz^M
protezione^F del mento^M

frame
bastidor^M
cadre^M
Rahmen^M
telaio^M

dual seat
sillín^M doble
selle^F biplace
Sitzbank^F
sella^F biposto

turn signal
intermitente^M trasero
clignotant^M arrière
Blinkleuchte^F
lampeggiatore^M posteriore

taillight
luz^F trasera
feu^M arrière
Schlussleuchte^F
fanale^M posteriore

rear shock absorber
amortiguador^M
amortisseur^M arrière
hinterer Stoßdämpfer^M
ammortizzatore^M posteriore

exhaust pipe
silenciador^M
pot^M d'échappement^M
Auspuffrohr^N
tubo^M di scappamento^M

front footrest
estribera^F
repose-pied^M du pilote^M
vordere Fußraste^F
appoggiapiedi^M del guidatore^M

kickstand
caballete^M lateral
béquille^F latérale
Seitenständer^M
cavalletto^M laterale

gearshift lever
palanca^F de cambio^M de velocidades^F
sélecteur^M de vitesses^F
Schaltpedal^N
pedale^M del cambio^M

main stand
caballete^M central
béquille^F centrale
Hauptständer^M
cavalletto^M centrale

pillion footrest
estribera^F del pasajero^M
repose-pied^M du passager^M
Beifahrerfußraste^F
appoggiapiedi^M del passeggero^M

TRANSPORT AND MACHINERY

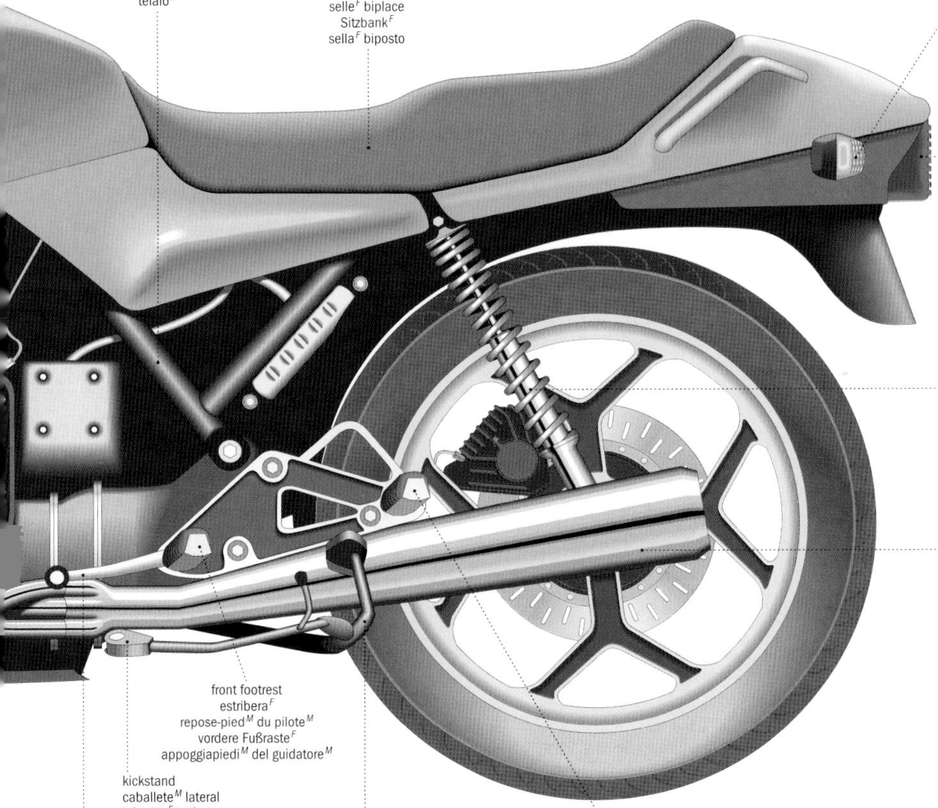

motorcycle

motorcycle dashboard
tablero^M de instrumentos^M
tableau^M de bord^M
Instrumententafel^F
cruscotto^M

speedometer
velocímetro^M
indicateur^F de vitesse^F
Tachometer^M
tachimetro^M

tachometer
tacómetro^M
tachymètre^M
Drehzahlmesser^M
contagiri^M

oil pressure warning indicator
luz^F indicadora de la presión^F del aceite^M
témoin^M de pression^F d'huile^F
Öldruckkontrollleuchte^F
spia^F della pressione^F dell'olio^M

high beam warning indicator
indicador^M de luz^F larga
témoin^M de phare^M
Fernlichtkontrollleuchte^F
spia^F delle luci^F abbaglianti

neutral indicator
indicador^M de punto^M muerto
témoin^M de position^F neutre
Leerlaufanzeige^N
spia^F della posizione^F di folle

turn signal indicator
indicador^M del intermitente^M
témoin^M de clignotants^M
Blinkerkontrollleuchte^F
spia^F dell'indicatore^M di direzione^F

ignition switch
interruptor^M de encendido^M
démarreur^M électrique
Zündschalter^M
blocchetto^M di avviamento^M

motorcycle: view from above
motocicleta^F : vista^F desde lo alto^M
moto^F : vue^F en plongée^F
Motorrad^N: Draufsicht^F
motocicletta^F: vista^F dall'alto^M

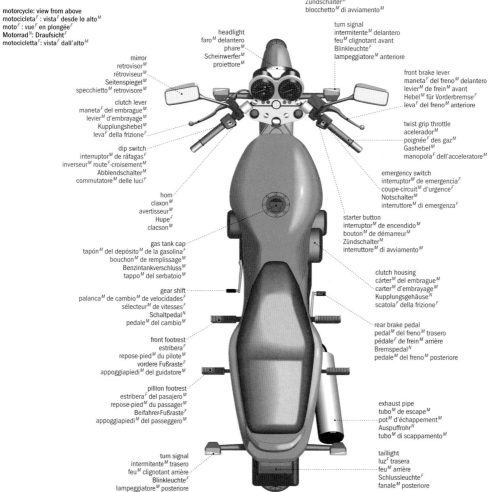

turn signal
intermitente^M delantero
feu^M clignotant avant
Blinkleuchte^F
lampeggiatore^M anteriore

headlight
faro^M delantero
phare^M
Scheinwerfer^M
proiettore^M

mirror
retrovisor^M
rétroviseur^M
Seitenspiegel^M
specchietto^M retrovisore^M

front brake lever
maneta^F del freno^M delantero
levier^M de frein^M avant
Hebel^M für Vorderbremse^F
leva^F del freno^M anteriore

clutch lever
maneta^F del embrague^M
levier^M d'embrayage^M
Kupplungshebel^M
leva^F della frizione^F

twist grip throttle
acelerador^M
poignée^F des gaz^M
Gashebel^M
manopola^F dell'acceleratore^M

dip switch
interruptor^M de ráfagas^F
inverseur^M route^F-croisement^M
Abblendschalter^M
commutatore^M delle luci^F

emergency switch
interruptor^M de emergencia^F
coupe-circuit^M d'urgence^F
Notschalter^M
interruttore^M di emergenza^F

horn
claxon^M
avertisseur^M
Hupe^F
clacson^M

starter button
interruptor^M de encendido^M
bouton^M de démarreur^M
Zündschalter^M
interruttore^M di avviamento^M

gas tank cap
tapón^M del depósito^M de la gasolina^F
bouchon^M de remplissage^M
Benzintankverschluss^M
tappo^M del serbatoio^M

clutch housing
cárter^M del embrague^M
carter^M d'embrayage^M
Kupplungsgehäuse^N
scatola^F della frizione^F

gear shift
palanca^F de cambio^M de velocidades^F
sélecteur^M de vitesses^F
Schaltpedal^N
pedale^M del cambio^M

rear brake pedal
pedal^M del freno^M trasero
pédale^F de frein^M arrière
Bremspedal^N
pedale^M del freno^M posteriore

front footrest
estribera^F
repose-pied^M du pilote^M
vordere Fußraste^F
appoggiapiedi^M del guidatore^M

pillion footrest
estribera^F del pasajero^M
repose-pied^M du passager^M
Beifahrer-Fußraste^F
appoggiapiedi^M del passeggero^M

exhaust pipe
tubo^M de escape^M
pot^M d'échappement^M
Auspuffrohr^N
tubo^M di scappamento^M

turn signal
intermitente^M trasero
feu^M clignotant arrière
Blinkleuchte^F
lampeggiatore^M posteriore

taillight
luz^F trasera
feu^M arrière
Schlussleuchte^F
fanale^M posteriore

motor scooter
escúter[M]
scooter[M]
Motorroller[M]
scooter[M]

seat
sillín[M]
selle[F]
Sitz[M]
sella[F]

mirror
espejo[M] retrovisor
rétroviseur[M]
Spiegel[M]
specchietto[M] retrovisore[M]

apron
salpicadero[M]
tablier[M]
Frontblech[M]
pannello[M] di protezione[F]

luggage rack
portaequipajes[M]
porte-bagages[M]
Gepäckträger[M]
portapacchi[M]

floorboard
reposapies[M]
plancher[M]
Fußstütze[F]
appoggiapiedi[M]

moped
ciclomotor[M]
cyclomoteur[M]
Mofa[N]
ciclomotore[M]

carrier
portaequipajes[M]
porte-bagages[M]
Gepäckträger[M]
portapacchi[M]

kickstand
soporte[M]
béquille[F] latérale
Raststütze[F]
cavalletto[M] laterale

seat
asiento[M]
selle[F]
Sitz[M]
sella[F]

examples of motorcycles
ejemplos[M] de motocicletas[F]
exemples[M] de motos[F]
Beispiele[N] für Motorräder[N]
esempi[M] di motociclette[F] e ciclomotore[M]

off-road motorcycle (dirtbike)
motocicleta[F] todo terreno[M]
moto[F] tout-terrain
Geländemotorrad[N]
motocicletta[F] da cross[M]

telescopic front fork
horquilla[F] telescópica
fourche[F] télescopique
Teleskopgabel[F]
forcella[F] telescopica anteriore

knobby tread tire
neumático[M] de tacos[M]
pneu[M] à crampons[M]
Stollenreifen[M]
pneumatico[M] scolpito

touring motorcycle
motocicleta[F] de turismo[M]
moto[F] de tourisme[M]
Touring[N]-Motorrad[N]
motocicletta[F] da turismo[M]

antenna
antena[F]
antenne[F]
Antenne[F]
antenna[F]

backrest
respaldo[M]
dossier[M]
Rückenlehne[F]
schienale[M]

top box
cofre[M]
coffre[M]
Topcase[N]
bauletto[M]

saddlebag
maleta[F]
sacoche[F]
Seitenkoffer[M]
borsa[F] laterale

windshield
parabrisas[M]
pare-brise[M]
Windschutzscheibe[F]
parabrezza[M]

passenger seat
sillín[M] del pasajero[M]
selle[F] passager[M]
Soziussitz[M]
sella[F] del passeggero[M]

driver's seat
sillín[M] del conductor[M]
selle[F] conducteur[M]
Fahrersitz[M]
sella[F] del guidatore[M]

4 X 4 all-terrain vehicle

quad[M] | quad[M] | 4x4-Geländemotorrad[N] | veicolo[M] a trazione[F] integrale 4x4

rear cargo rack
portaequipajes[M] posterior
porte-bagages[M] arrière
Gepäckträger[M]
portapacchi[M] posteriore

rear fender
parachoques[M] posterior
garde-boue[M] arrière
hinterer Kotflügel[M]
paraurti[M] posteriore

muffler
silenciador[M]
pot[M] d'échappement[M]
Auspuffrohr[N]
tubo[M] di scappamento[M]

seat
sillín[M]
selle[F]
Sitz[M]
sella[F]

gas tank
depósito[M] de gasolina[F]
réservoir[M] à essence[F]
Kraftstofftank[M]
serbatoio[M] del carburante[M]

handgrip
manillar[M]
poignée[F]
Lenkergriff[M]
manopola[F]

bumper
parachoques[M]
pare-chocs[M]
Stoßfänger[M]
paraurti[M]

front shock absorber
amortiguador[M] delantero
amortisseur[M] avant
Frontstoßdämpfer[M]
ammortizzatore[M] anteriore

gearshift lever
palanca[F] de cambio[M] de velocidades[F]
sélecteur[M] de vitesses[F]
Schalthebel[M]
pedale[M] del cambio[M]

bicycle

bicicleta^F | bicyclette^F | Fahrrad^N | bicicletta^F

parts of a bicycle
partes^F de una bicicleta^F
parties^F d'une bicyclette^F
Teile^N eines Fahrrads^N
componenti^M di una bicicletta^F

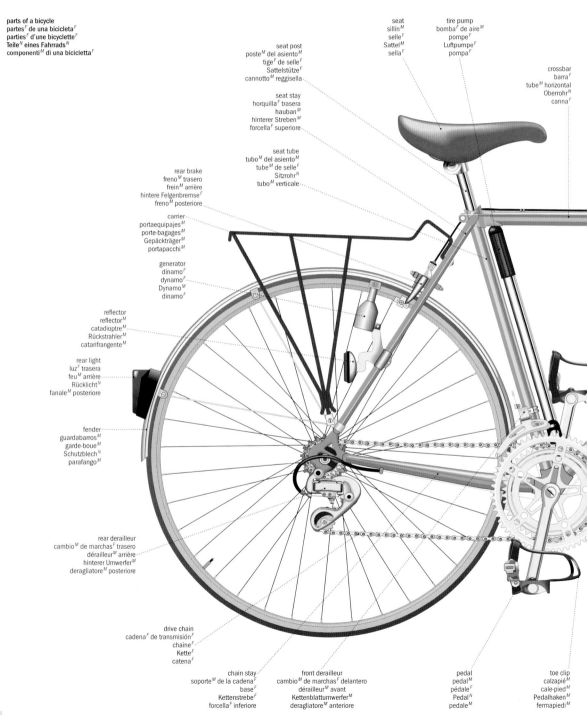

seat post
poste^M del asiento^M
tige^F de selle^F
Sattelstütze^F
cannotto^M reggisella

seat stay
horquilla^F trasera
hauban^M
hinterer Streben^M
forcella^F superiore

seat tube
tubo^M del asiento^M
tube^M de selle^F
Sitzrohr^N
tubo^M verticale

seat
sillín^M
selle^F
Sattel^M
sella^F

tire pump
bomba^F de aire^M
pompe^F
Luftpumpe^F
pompa^F

crossbar
barra^F
tube^M horizontal
Oberrohr^N
canna^F

rear brake
freno^M trasero
frein^M arrière
hintere Felgenbremse^F
freno^M posteriore

carrier
portaequipajes^M
porte-bagages^M
Gepäckträger^M
portapacchi^M

generator
dínamo^F
dynamo^F
Dynamo^M
dinamo^F

reflector
reflector^M
catadioptre^M
Rückstrahler^M
catarifrangente^M

rear light
luz^F trasera
feu^M arrière
Rücklicht^N
fanale^M posteriore

fender
guardabarros^M
garde-boue^M
Schutzblech^N
parafango^M

rear derailleur
cambio^M de marchas^F trasero
dérailleur^M arrière
hinterer Umwerfer^M
deragliatore^M posteriore

drive chain
cadena^F de transmisión^F
chaîne^F
Kette^F
catena^F

chain stay
soporte^M de la cadena^F
base^F
Kettenstrebe^F
forcella^F inferiore

front derailleur
cambio^M de marchas^F delantero
dérailleur^M avant
Kettenblattumwerfer^M
deragliatore^M anteriore

pedal
pedal^M
pédale^F
Pedal^N
pedale^M

toe clip
calzapié^M
cale-pied^M
Pedalhaken^M
fermapiedi^M

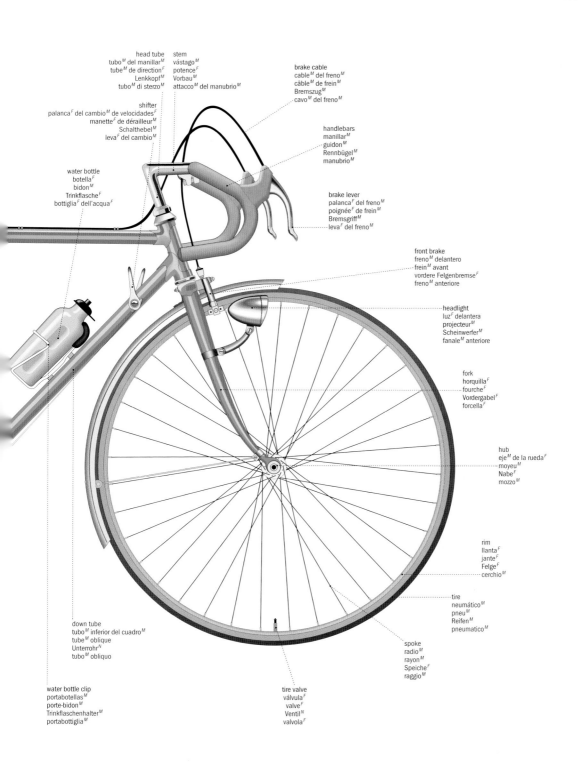

head tube
tubo^M del manillar^M
tube^M de direction^F
Lenkkopf^M
tubo^M di sterzo^M

stem
vástago^M
potence^F
Vorbau^M
attacco^M del manubrio^M

brake cable
cable^M del freno^M
câble^M de frein^M
Bremszug^M
cavo^M del freno^M

shifter
palanca^F del cambio^M de velocidades^F
manette^F de dérailleur^M
Schalthebel^M
leva^F del cambio^M

handlebars
manillar^M
guidon^M
Rennbügel^M
manubrio^M

water bottle
botella^F
bidon^M
Trinkflasche^F
bottiglia^F dell'acqua^F

brake lever
palanca^F del freno^M
poignée^F de frein^M
Bremsgriff^M
leva^F del freno^M

front brake
freno^M delantero
frein^M avant
vordere Felgenbremse^F
freno^M anteriore

headlight
luz^F delantera
projecteur^M
Scheinwerfer^M
fanale^M anteriore

fork
horquilla^F
fourche^F
Vordergabel^F
forcella^F

hub
eje^M de la rueda^F
moyeu^M
Nabe^F
mozzo^M

rim
llanta^F
jante^F
Felge^F
cerchio^M

tire
neumático^M
pneu^M
Reifen^M
pneumatico^M

down tube
tubo^M inferior del cuadro^M
tube^M oblique
Unterrohr^N
tubo^M obliquo

spoke
radio^M
rayon^M
Speiche^F
raggio^M

water bottle clip
portabotellas^M
porte-bidon^M
Trinkflaschenhalter^M
portabottiglia^M

tire valve
válvula^F
valve^F
Ventil^N
valvola^F

bicycle

power train
transmisión^F de cadena^F
mécanisme^M de propulsion^F
Kraftübertragung^F
organi^M di trasmissione^F

front derailleur
cambio^M de marchas^F delantero
dérailleur^M avant
Kettenblattumwerfer^M
deragliatore^M anteriore

chain guide
guía^F de la cadena^F
guide-chaîne^M
Kettenführung^F
guida^F della catena^F

shifter
palanca^F del cambio^M de velocidades^F
manette^F de dérailleur^M
Schalthebel^M
leva^F del cambio^M

toe clip
calapié^M
cale-pied^M
Pedalhaken^M
fermapiedi^M

freewheel
piñón^M libre
roue^F libre
Freilauf^M
ruota^F libera

chain
cadena^F
chaîne^F
Kette^F
catena^F

control cable
cable^M del cambio^M
câble^M de commande^M
Schaltzug^M
cavo^M del cambio^M

chain wheel A
corona^F externa de la cadena^F
plateau^M A
großes Kettenblatt^N
ruota^F dentata A

bottom bracket axle
eje^M del pedal^M
axe^M du pédalier^M
Tretlager^N
albero^M delle pedivelle^F

rear derailleur
cambio^M de marchas^F trasero
dérailleur^M arrière
hinterer Umwerfer^M
deragliatore^M posteriore

chain wheel B
corona^F interna de la cadena^F
plateau^M B
kleines Kettenblatt^N
ruota^F dentata B

jockey rollers
poleas^F de tensión^F
galets^M tendeurs
Abhalter^M
rullini^M tenditori^M

pedal
pedal^M
pédale^F
Pedal^N
pedale^M

crank
manivela^F
manivelle^F
Kurbel^F
pedivella^F

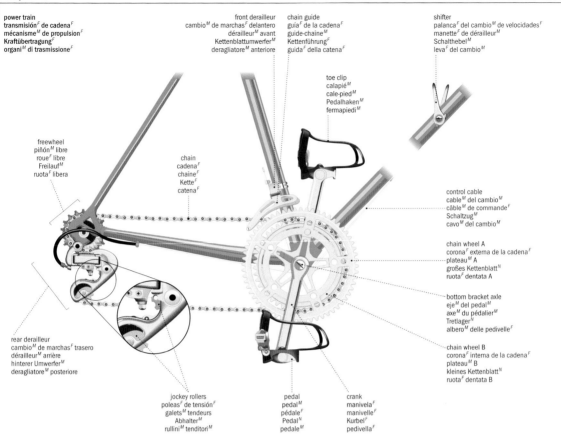

accessories
accesorios^M
accessoires^M
Zubehör^N
accessori^M

lock
candado^M para bicicleta^F
cadenas^M
Schloss^N
lucchetto^M

protective helmet
casco^M protector
casque^M de protection^F
Fahrradhelm^M
casco^M di protezione^F

tool kit
herramientas^F
trousse^F de dépannage^M
Werkzeugsatz^M
kit^M di attrezzi^M

bicycle bag (pannier)
cartera^F
sacoche^F
Satteltasche^F
zaino^M

child carrier
silla^F porta-niño^M
siège^F de vélo^M pour enfant^M
Kindersitz^M
seggiolino^M per bambini^M

child's tricycle
triciclo[M]
tricycle[M] d'enfant[M]
Dreirad[N]
triciclo[M]

examples of bicycles
ejemplos[M] de bicicletas[F]
exemples[M] de bicyclettes[F]
Beispiele[N] für Fahrräder[N]
esempi[M] di biciclette[F]

BMX bike
bicicleta[F] BMX
vélo[M] cross[M]
BMX-Rad[N], Mountainbike[N]
mountain bike[F] da cross[M]

mountain bike
bicicleta[F] todo terreno[M]
bicyclette[F] tout-terrain
Mountain Bike[N]
mountain bike[F]

Dutch bicycle
bicicleta[F] holandesa
bicyclette[F] hollandaise
Hollandrad[N]
bicicletta[F] olandese

road bicycle
bicicleta[F] de carretera[F]
bicyclette[F] de course[F]
Rennrad[N]
bicicletta[F] da corsa[F]

city bicycle
bicicleta[F] de ciudad[F]
bicyclette[F] de ville[F]
Stadtrad[N]
city bike[F]

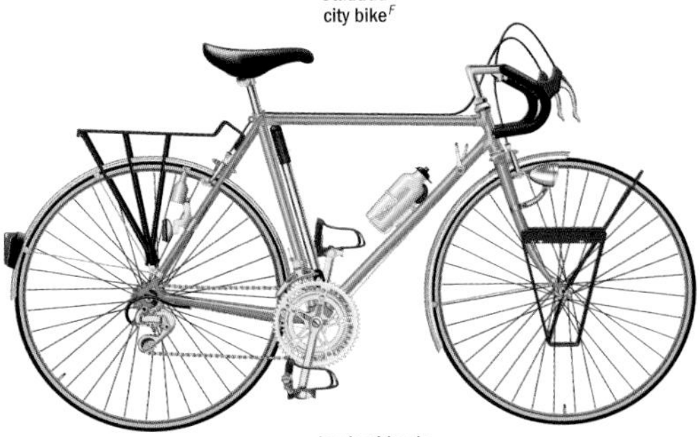

touring bicycle
bicicleta[F] de turismo[M]
bicyclette[F] de tourisme[M]
Tourenrad[N]
bicicletta[F] da turismo[M]

tandem bicycle
tándem[M]
tandem[M]
Tandem[N]
tandem[M]

TRANSPORT AND MACHINERY

581

passenger station

estación^F de ferrocarril^M | gare^F de voyageurs^M | Bahnhof^M | stazione^F dei viaggiatori^M

office
oficina^F
locaux^M administratifs
Büro^N
uffici^M

indicator board
tablero^M de información^F
panneau^M indicateur
Fahrplan^M
tabellone^M degli orari^M

baggage cart
carro^M portaequipaje
chariot^M à bagages^M
Förderwagen^M
carrello^M portabagagli

baggage lockers
taquillas^F de consigna^F automática
consigne^F automatique
Gepäckschließfächer^N
cassette^F di deposito^M per bagagli^M

glassed roof
techo^M de vidrio^M
verrière^F
Glasüberdachung^F
tettoia^F vetrata

metal structure
estructura^F de metal^M
structure^F métallique
Eisenträger^M
struttura^F metallica

platform number
indicador^M de número^M de andén^M
numéro^M de quai^M
Gleisnummer^F
numero^M del binario^M

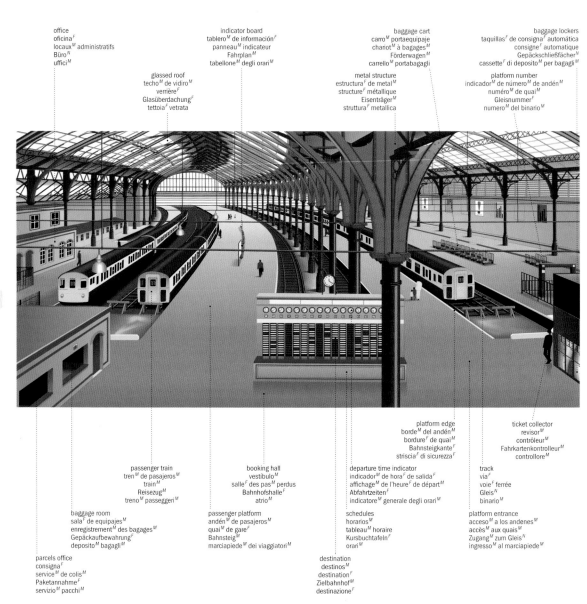

platform edge
borde^M del andén^M
bordure^F de quai^M
Bahnsteigkante^F
striscia^F di sicurezza^F

ticket collector
revisor^M
contrôleur^M
Fahrkartenkontrolleur^M
controllore^M

passenger train
tren^M de pasajeros^M
train^M
Reisezug^M
treno^M passeggeri^M

booking hall
vestíbulo^M
salle^F des pas^M perdus
Bahnhofshalle^F
atrio^M

departure time indicator
indicador^M de hora^F de salida^F
affichage^M de l'heure^F de départ^M
Abfahrtzeiten^F
indicatore^M generale degli orari^M

track
vía^F
voie^F ferrée
Gleis^N
binario^M

baggage room
sala^F de equipajes^M
enregistrement^M des bagages^M
Gepäckaufbewahrung^F
deposito^M bagagli^M

passenger platform
andén^M de pasajeros^M
quai^M de gare^F
Bahnsteig^M
marciapiede^M dei viaggiatori^M

schedules
horarios^M
tableau^M horaire
Kursbuchtafeln^F
orari^M

platform entrance
acceso^M a los andenes^M
accès^M aux quais^M
Zugang^M zum Gleis^N
ingresso^M al marciapiede^M

parcels office
consigna^F
service^M de colis^M
Paketannahme^F
servizio^M pacchi^M

destination
destinos^M
destination^F
Zielbahnhof^M
destinazione^F

582

railroad station

estación^F de ferrocarril^M | gare^F | Bahnhof^M | stazione^F ferroviaria

passenger station
estación^F de ferrocarril^M
gare^F de voyageurs^M
Personenbahnhof^M
stazione^F dei viaggiatori^M

station platform
andén^M
quai^M
Bahnsteig^M
marciapiede^M

commuter train
tren^M suburbano
train^M de banlieue^F
Nahverkehrszug^M
treno^M locale

main line
vía^F principal
grandes lignes^F
Hauptgleis^N
linea^F ferroviaria principale

suburban commuter railroad
vía^F de tren^M suburbano
voie^F de banlieue^F
S-Bahn-Strecke^F
linea^F ferroviaria locale

subsidiary track
vía^F subsidiaria
voie^F de service^M
Nebengleis^N
binario^M morto

bumper
tope^M
butoir^M
Prellbock^M
respingente^M

level crossing
paso^F a nivel^M
passage^F à niveau^M
Bahnübergang^M
passaggio^M a livello^M

parking
estacionamiento^M
parking^M ; stationnement^M
Parkplatz^M
parcheggio^M

platform shelter
marquesina^F del andén^M
abri^M
Bahnsteigüberdachung^F
pensilina^F

footbridge
pasarela^F
passerelle^F
Fußgängerbrücke^F
ponte^M pedonale

signal
semáforo^M
sémaphore^M
Signal^N
semaforo^M

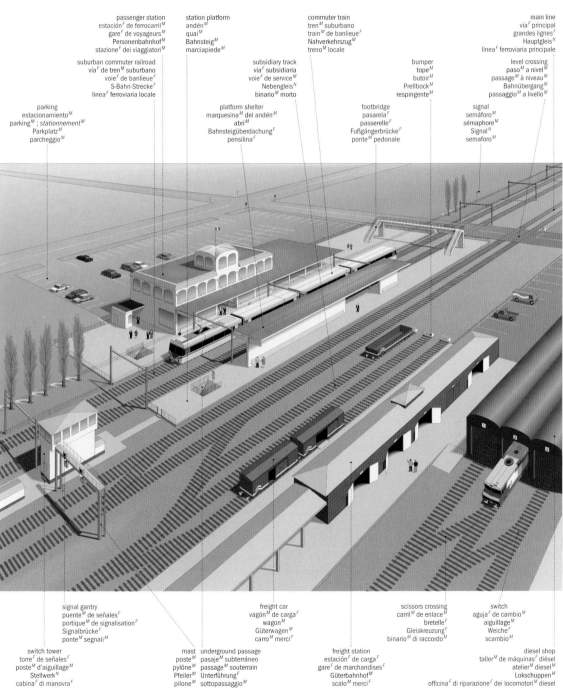

signal gantry
puente^M de señales^F
portique^M de signalisation^F
Signalbrücke^F
ponte^M segnali^M

freight car
vagón^M de carga^F
wagon^M
Güterwagen^M
carro^M merci^F

scissors crossing
carril^M de enlace^M
bretelle^F
Gleiskreuzung^F
binario^M di raccordo^M

switch
aguja^F de cambio^M
aiguillage^M
Weiche^F
scambio^M

switch tower
torre^F de señales^F
poste^M d'aiguillage^M
Stellwerk^N
cabina^F di manovra^F

mast
poste^M
pylône^M
Pfeiler^M
pilone^M

underground passage
pasaje^M subterráneo
passage^M souterrain
Unterführung^F
sottopassaggio^M

freight station
estación^F de carga^F
gare^F de marchandises^F
Güterbahnhof^M
scalo^M merci^F

diesel shop
taller^M de máquinas^F diésel
atelier^M diesel^M
Lokschuppen^M
officina^F di riparazione^F dei locomotori^M diesel

types of passenger cars

vagones^M de pasajeros^M | types^M de voitures^F | Personenzüge^M: Wagentypen^M | tipi^M di vagoni^M passeggeri^M

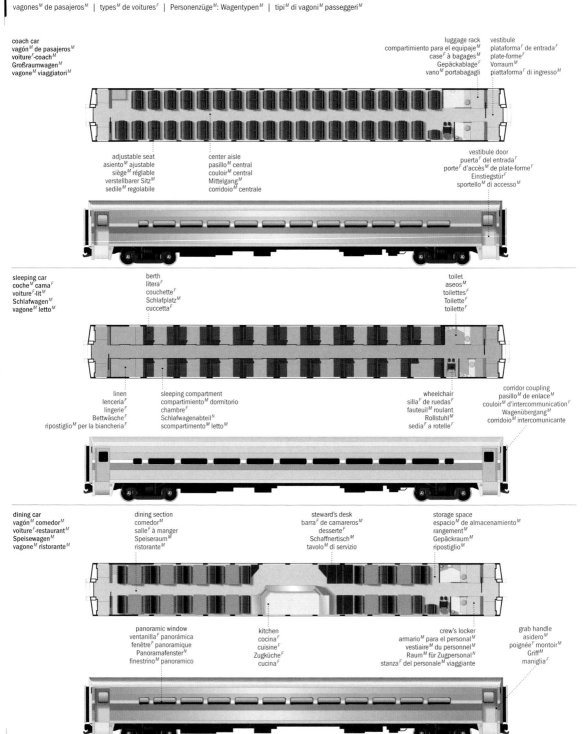

coach car
vagón^M de pasajeros^M
voiture^F-coach^M
Großraumwagen^M
vagone^M viaggiatori^M

luggage rack
compartimiento para el equipaje^M
case^F à bagages^M
Gepäckablage^F
vano^M portabagagli

vestibule
plataforma^F de entrada^F
plate-forme^F
Vorraum^M
piattaforma^F di ingresso^M

adjustable seat
asiento^M ajustable
siège^M réglable
verstellbarer Sitz^M
sedile^M regolabile

center aisle
pasillo^M central
couloir^M central
Mittelgang^M
corridoio^M centrale

vestibule door
puerta^F del entrada^F
porte^F d'accès^M de plate-forme^F
Einstiegstür^F
sportello^M di accesso^M

sleeping car
coche^M cama^F
voiture^F-lit^M
Schlafwagen^M
vagone^M letto^M

berth
litera^F
couchette^F
Schlafplatz^M
cuccetta^F

toilet
aseos^M
toilettes^F
Toilette^F
toilette^F

linen
lencería^F
lingerie^F
Bettwäsche^F
ripostiglio^M per la biancheria^F

sleeping compartment
compartimiento^M dormitorio
chambre^F
Schlafwagenabteil^N
scompartimento^M letto^M

wheelchair
silla^F de ruedas^F
fauteuil^M roulant
Rollstuhl^M
sedia^F a rotelle^F

corridor coupling
pasillo^M de enlace^M
couloir^M d'intercommunication^F
Wagenübergang^M
corridoio^M intercomunicante

dining car
vagón^M comedor^M
voiture^F-restaurant^M
Speisewagen^M
vagone^M ristorante^M

dining section
comedor^M
salle^F à manger
Speiseraum^M
ristorante^M

steward's desk
barra^F de camareros^M
desserte^F
Schaffnertisch^M
tavolo^M di servizio

storage space
espacio^M de almacenamiento^M
rangement^M
Gepäckraum^M
ripostiglio^M

panoramic window
ventanilla^F panorámica
fenêtre^F panoramique
Panoramafenster^N
finestrino^M panoramico

kitchen
cocina^F
cuisine^F
Zugküche^F
cucina^F

crew's locker
armario^M para el personal^M
vestiaire^M du personnel^M
Raum^M für Zugpersonal^N
stanza^F del personale^M viaggiante

grab handle
asidero^M
poignée^F montoir^M
Griff^M
maniglia^F

TRANSPORT AND MACHINERY

high-speed train

tren^M de alta velocidad^F | train^M à grande vitesse^F (T.G.V.) | Hochgeschwindigkeitszug^M | treno^M ad alta velocità^F

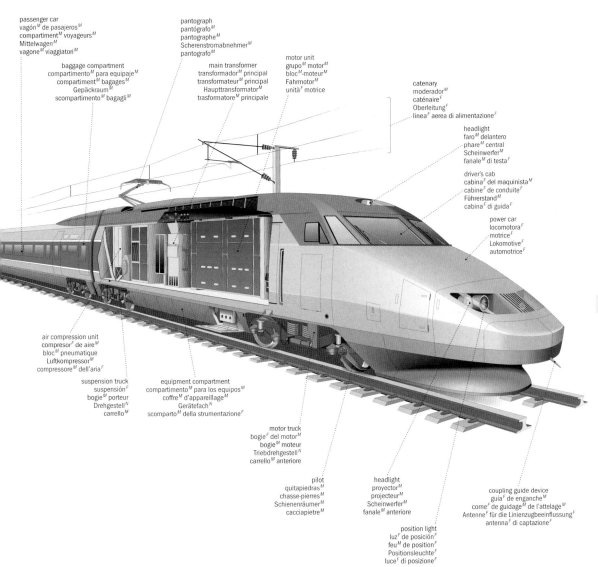

passenger car
vagón^M de pasajeros^M
compartiment^M voyageurs^M
Mittelwagen^M
vagone^M viaggiatori^M

baggage compartment
compartimento^M para equipaje^M
compartiment^M bagages^M
Gepäckraum^M
scompartimento^M bagagli^M

pantograph
pantógrafo^M
pantographe^M
Scherenstromabnehmer^M
pantografo^M

main transformer
transformador^M principal
transformateur^M principal
Haupttransformator^M
trasformatore^M principale

motor unit
grupo^M motor^M
bloc^M-moteur^M
Fahrmotor^M
unità^F motrice

catenary
moderador^M
caténaire^F
Oberleitung^F
linea^F aerea di alimentazione^F

headlight
faro^M delantero
phare^M central
Scheinwerfer^M
fanale^M di testa^F

driver's cab
cabina^F del maquinista^M
cabine^F de conduite^F
Führerstand^M
cabina^F di guida^F

power car
locomotora^F
motrice^F
Lokomotive^F
automotrice^F

air compression unit
compresor^F de aire^M
bloc^M pneumatique
Luftkompressor^M
compressore^M dell'aria^F

suspension truck
suspensión^F
bogie^M porteur
Drehgestell^N
carrello^M

equipment compartment
compartimento^M para los equipos^M
coffre^M d'appareillage^M
Gerätefach^N
scomparto^M della strumentazione^F

motor truck
bogie^F del motor^M
bogie^M moteur
Triebdrehgestell^N
carrello^M anteriore

pilot
quitapiedras^M
chasse-pierres^M
Schienenräumer^M
cacciapietre^M

headlight
proyector^M
projecteur^M
Scheinwerfer^M
fanale^M anteriore

coupling guide device
guia^F de enganche^M
corne^F de guidage^M de l'attelage^M
Antenne^F für die Linienzugbeeinflussung^F
antenna^F di captazione^F

position light
luz^F de posición^F
feu^M de position^F
Positionsleuchte^F
luce^F di posizione^F

diesel-electric locomotive

locomotora^F diésel eléctrica | locomotive^F diesel-électrique | dieselelektrische Lokomotive^F | locomotiva^F diesel-elettrica

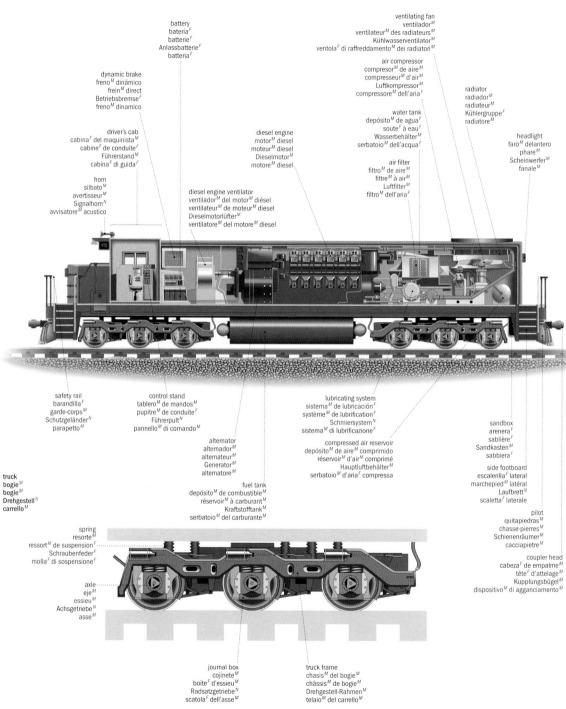

battery
batería^F
batterie^F
Anlassbatterie^F
batteria^F

ventilating fan
ventilador^M
ventilateur^M des radiateurs^M
Kühlwasserventilator^M
ventola^F di raffreddamento^M dei radiatori^M

air compressor
compresor^M de aire^M
compresseur^M d'air^M
Luftkompressor^M
compressore^M dell'aria^M

radiator
radiador^M
radiateur^M
Kühlergruppe^F
radiatore^M

dynamic brake
freno^M dinámico
frein^M direct
Betriebsbremse^F
freno^M dinamico

driver's cab
cabina^F del maquinista^M
cabine^F de conduite^F
Führerstand^M
cabina^F di guida^F

water tank
depósito^M de agua^F
soute^F à eau^F
Wasserbehälter^M
serbatoio^M dell'acqua^F

headlight
faro^M delantero
phare^M
Scheinwerfer^M
fanale^M

diesel engine
motor^M diesel
moteur^M diesel
Dieselmotor^M
motore^M diesel

air filter
filtro^M de aire^M
filtre^M à air^M
Luftfilter^M
filtro^M dell'aria^M

horn
silbato^M
avertisseur^M
Signalhorn^N
avvisatore^M acustico

diesel engine ventilator
ventilador^M del motor^M diésel
ventilateur^M de moteur^M diesel
Dieselmotorlüfter^M
ventilatore^M del motore^M diesel

safety rail
barandilla^F
garde-corps^M
Schutzgeländer^N
parapetto^M

control stand
tablero^M de mandos^M
pupitre^M de conduite^F
Führerpult^N
pannello^M di comando^M

lubricating system
sistema^M de lubricación^F
système^M de lubrification^F
Schmiersystem^N
sistema^M di lubrificazione^F

sandbox
arenera^F
sablière^F
Sandkasten^M
sabbiera^F

alternator
alternador^M
alternateur^M
Generator^M
alternatore^M

compressed air reservoir
depósito^M de aire^M comprimido
réservoir^M d'air^M comprimé
Hauptluftbehälter^M
serbatoio^M d'aria^F compressa

side footboard
escalerilla^F lateral
marchepied^M latéral
Laufbrett^N
scaletta^F laterale

truck
bogie^M
bogie^M
Drehgestell^N
carrello^M

fuel tank
depósito^M de combustible^M
réservoir^M à carburant^M
Kraftstofftank^M
serbatoio^M del carburante^M

pilot
quitapiedras^M
chasse-pierres^M
Schienenräumer^M
cacciapietre^M

spring
resorte^M
ressort^M de suspension^F
Schraubenfeder^F
molla^F di sospensione^F

coupler head
cabeza^F de empalme^M
tête^F d'attelage^M
Kupplungsbügel^M
dispositivo^M di agganciamento^M

axle
eje^M
essieu^M
Achsgetriebe^N
asse^M

journal box
cojinete^M
boîte^F d'essieu^M
Radsatzgetriebe^N
scatola^F dell'asse^M

truck frame
chasis^M del bogie^M
châssis^M de bogie^M
Drehgestell-Rahmen^M
telaio^M del carrello^M

car

vagón^M | wagon^M | Waggon^M | carro^M merci^M

box car
furgón^M
wagon^M couvert
Drehgestellkastenwagen^M
carro^M chiuso

hand brake wheel
volante^M del freno^M manual
volant^M de frein^M à main^F
Handbremsrad^N
ruota^F del freno^M a mano^F

horizontal end handhold
asidero^M horizontal
main^F courante
Handstange^F
corrimano^M

corner cap
esquinera^F
chapeau^M d'angle^M
Eckbeschlag^M
testa^F d'angolo^M

routing cardboard
tarjeta^F de ruta^F
porte-étiquette^F d'acheminement^M
Wagenlaufschild^N
cartellino^M indicatore^M di destinazione^F

placard board
tablero^M de rótulo^M
porte-étiquette^M
Anschriftentafel^F
cartellino^M segnaletico

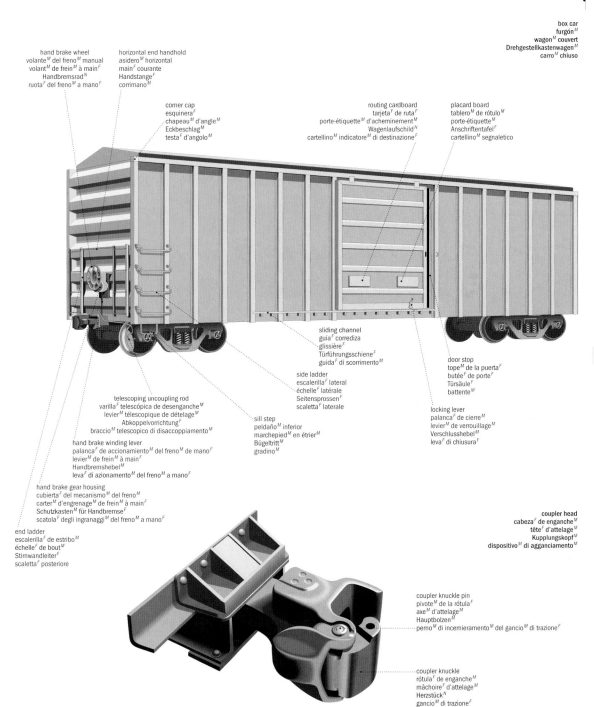

sliding channel
guía^F corrediza
glissière^F
Türführungsschiene^F
guida^F di scorrimento^M

door stop
tope^M de la puerta^F
butée^F de porte^F
Türsäule^F
battente^M

side ladder
escalerilla^F lateral
échelle^F latérale
Seitensprossen^F
scaletta^F laterale

telescoping uncoupling rod
varilla^F telescópica de desenganche^M
levier^M télescopique de dételage^M
Abkoppelvorrichtung^F
braccio^M telescopico di disaccoppiamento^M

sill step
peldaño^M inferior
marchepied^M en étrier^M
Bügeltritt^M
gradino^M

locking lever
palanca^F de cierre^M
levier^M de verrouillage^M
Verschlusshebel^M
leva^F di chiusura^F

hand brake winding lever
palanca^F de accionamiento^M del freno^M de mano^F
levier^M de frein^M à main^F
Handbremshebel^M
leva^F di azionamento^M del freno^M a mano^F

hand brake gear housing
cubierta^F del mecanismo^M del freno^M
carter^M d'engrenage^M de frein^M à main^F
Schutzkasten^M für Handbremse^F
scatola^F degli ingranaggi^M del freno^M a mano^F

end ladder
escalerilla^F de estribo^M
échelle^F de bout^M
Stirnwandleiter^F
scaletta^F posteriore

coupler head
cabeza^F de enganche^M
tête^F d'attelage^M
Kupplungskopf^M
dispositivo^M di agganciamento^M

coupler knuckle pin
pivote^M de la rótula^F
axe^M d'attelage^M
Hauptbolzen^M
perno^M di incernieramento^M del gancio^M di trazione^F

coupler knuckle
rótula^F de enganche^M
mâchoire^F d'attelage^M
Herzstück^N
gancio^M di trazione^F

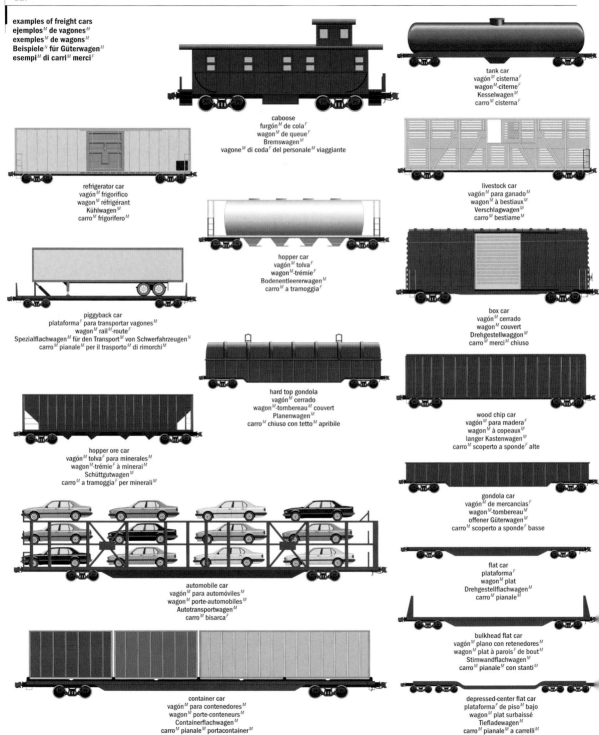

examples of freight cars
ejemplos[M] de vagones[M]
exemples[M] de wagons[M]
Beispiele[N] für Güterwagen[M]
esempi[M] di carri[M] merci[F]

caboose
furgón[M] de cola[F]
wagon[M] de queue[F]
Bremswagen[M]
vagone[M] di coda[F] del personale[M] viaggiante

tank car
vagón[M] cisterna[F]
wagon[M]-citerne[F]
Kesselwagen[M]
carro[M] cisterna[F]

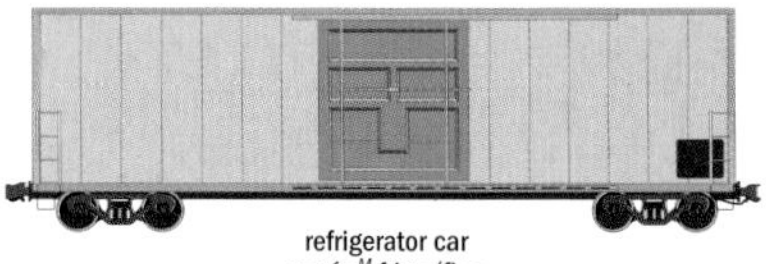

refrigerator car
vagón[M] frigorífico
wagon[M] réfrigérant
Kühlwagen[M]
carro[F] frigorifero[M]

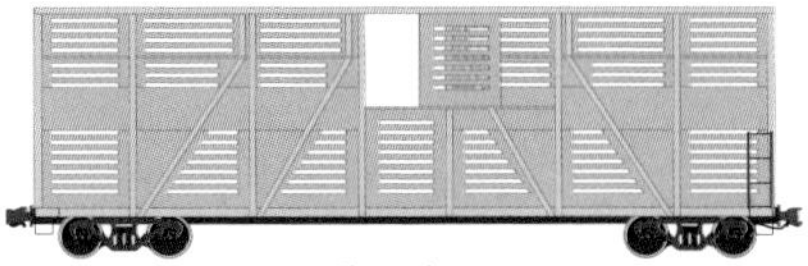

livestock car
vagón[M] para ganado[M]
wagon[M] à bestiaux[M]
Verschlagwagen[M]
carro[M] bestiame[M]

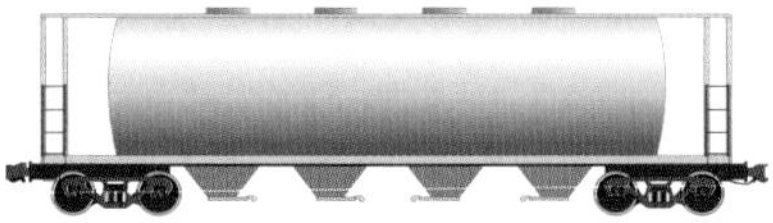

hopper car
vagón[M] tolva[F]
wagon[M]-trémie[F]
Bodenentleererwagen[M]
carro[M] a tramoggia[F]

piggyback car
plataforma[F] para transportar vagones[M]
wagon[M] rail[M]-route[F]
Spezialflachwagen[M] für den Transport[M] von Schwerfahrzeugen[N]
carro[M] pianale[M] per il trasporto[M] di rimorchi[M]

box car
vagón[M] cerrado
wagon[M] couvert
Drehgestellwaggon[M]
carro[M] merci[M] chiuso

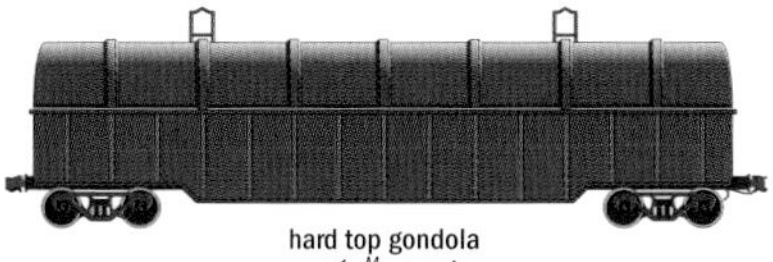

hard top gondola
vagón[M] cerrado
wagon[M]-tombereau[M] couvert
Planenwagen[M]
carro[M] chiuso con tetto[M] apribile

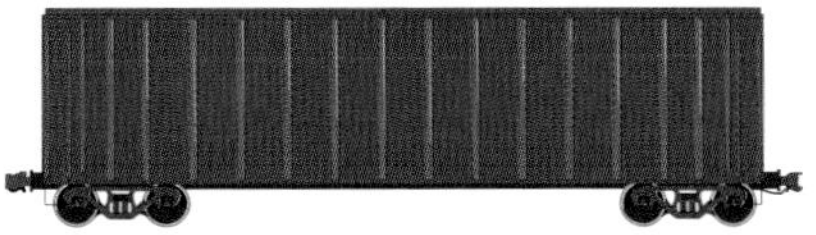

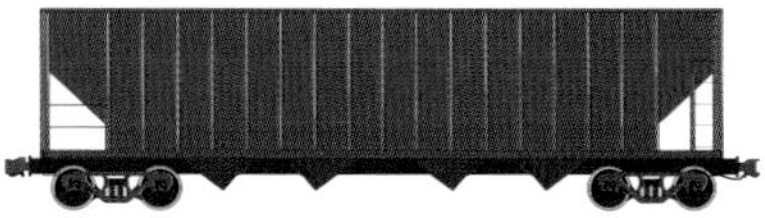

hopper ore car
vagón[M] tolva[F] para minerales[M]
wagon[M]-trémie[F] à minerai[M]
Schüttgutwagen[M]
carro[M] a tramoggia[F] per minerali[M]

wood chip car
vagón[M] para madera[F]
wagon[M] à copeaux[M]
langer Kastenwagen[M]
carro[M] scoperto a sponde[F] alte

gondola car
vagón[M] de mercancías[F]
wagon[M]-tombereau[M]
offener Güterwagen[M]
carro[M] scoperto a sponde[F] basse

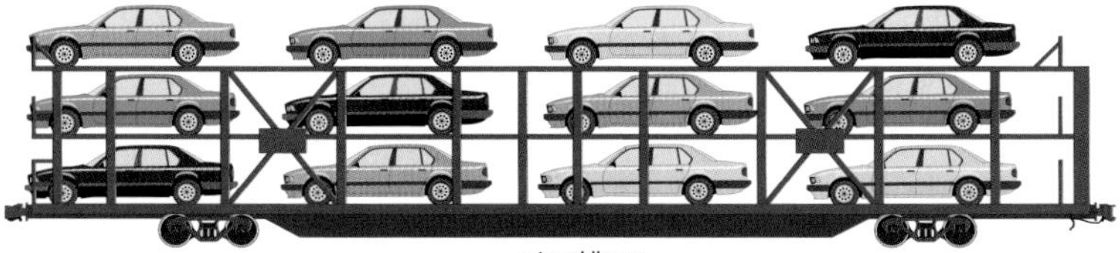

automobile car
vagón[M] para automóviles[M]
wagon[M] porte-automobiles[M]
Autotransportwagen[M]
carro[M] bisarca[F]

flat car
plataforma[F]
wagon[M] plat
Drehgestellflachwagen[M]
carro[M] pianale[M]

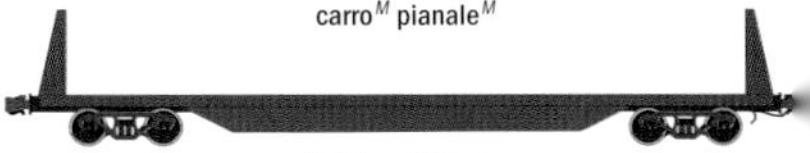

bulkhead flat car
vagón[M] plano con retenedores[M]
wagon[M] plat à parois[F] de bout[M]
Stirnwandflachwagen[M]
carro[M] pianale[M] con stanti[M]

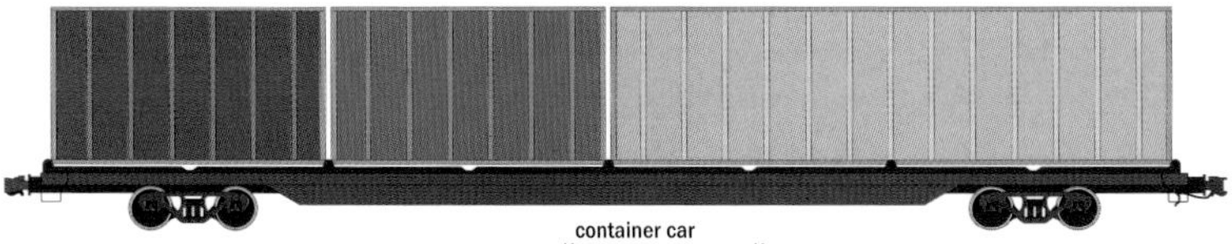

container car
vagón[M] para contenedores[M]
wagon[M] porte-conteneurs[M]
Containerflachwagen[M]
carro[M] pianale[M] portacontainer[M]

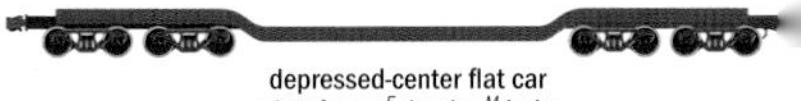

depressed-center flat car
plataforma[F] de piso[M] bajo
wagon[M] plat surbaissé
Tiefladewagen[M]
carro[M] pianale[M] a carrelli[M]

TRANSPORT AND MACHINERY

yard

estación^M de clasificación^M | gare^F de triage^M | Rangierbahnhof^M | stazione^F di smistamento^M

second classification track
segunda vía^F de clasificación^F
voie^F de tri^M secondaire
Richtungsgleis^N
binario^M di secondo smistamento^M

car cleaning yard
zona^F de lavado^M de vagones^M
zone^F de lavage^M des wagons^M
Waschplatte^F
area^F di lavaggio^M delle carrozze^F

receiving yard
zona^M de recepción^F
zone^F de réception^F
Empfangsgleise^N
area^F ricevitrice

classification yard
zona^F de clasificación^F
zone^F de triage^M
Ordnungsgleis^N
area^F di smistamento^M

water tower
tanque^M de agua^F
château^F d'eau^F
Wasserturm^M
serbatoio^M dell'acqua^F

outbound track
vía^F de salida^F
voie^F de sortie^F
Ausfahrgleis^N
binario^M di uscita^F

car repair shop
taller^M de reparación^F de vagones^M
atelier^M de réparation^F des wagons^M
Wagenausbesserungshalle^F
officina^F di manutenzione^F dei vagoni^M

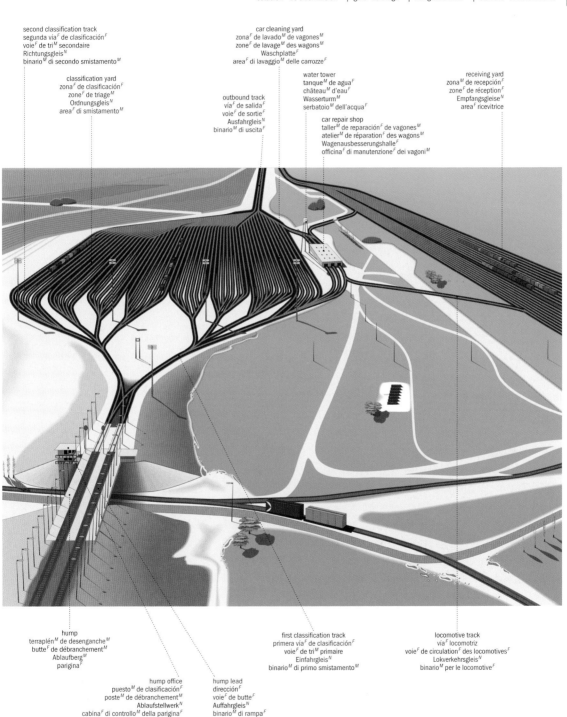

hump
terraplén^M de desenganche^M
butte^F de débranchement^M
Ablaufberg^M
parigina^F

hump office
puesto^M de clasificación^F
poste^M de débranchement^M
Ablaufstellwerk^N
cabina^F di controllo^M della parigina^F

hump lead
dirección^F
voie^F de butte^F
Auffahrgleis^N
binario^M di rampa^F

first classification track
primera vía^F de clasificación^F
voie^F de tri^M primaire
Einfahrgleis^N
binario^M di primo smistamento^M

locomotive track
vía^F locomotriz
voie^F de circulation^F des locomotives^F
Lokverkehrsgleis^N
binario^M per le locomotive^F

TRANSPORT AND MACHINERY

railroad track

vía^F férrea | voie^F ferrée | Eisenbahn-Oberbau^M | strada^F ferrata

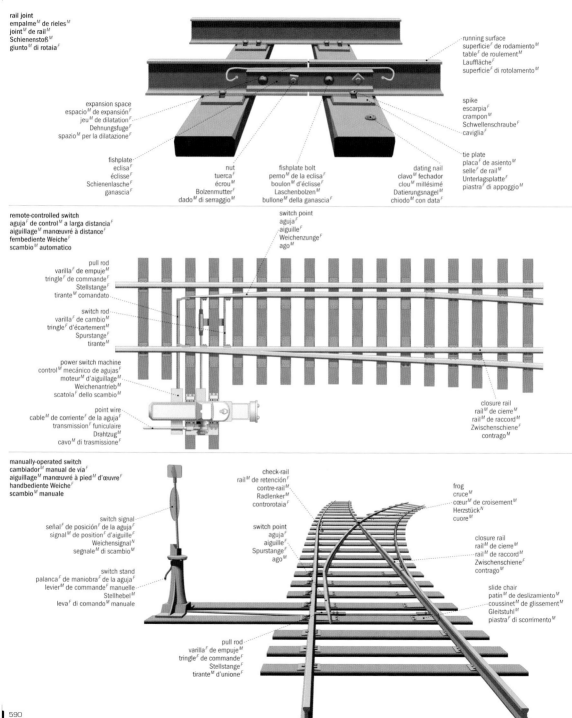

rail joint
empalme^M de rieles^M
joint^M de rail^M
Schienenstoß^M
giunto^M di rotaia^F

running surface
superficie^F de rodamiento^M
table^F de roulement^M
Lauffläche^F
superficie^F di rotolamento^M

expansion space
espacio^M de expansión^F
jeu^M de dilatation^F
Dehnungsfuge^F
spazio^M per la dilatazione^F

spike
escarpia^F
crampon^M
Schwellenschraube^F
caviglia^F

fishplate
eclisa^F
éclisse^F
Schienenlasche^F
ganascia^F

nut
tuerca^F
écrou^M
Bolzenmutter^F
dado^M di serraggio^M

fishplate bolt
perno^M de la eclisa^F
boulon^M d'éclisse^F
Laschenbolzen^M
bullone^M della ganascia^F

dating nail
clavo^M fechador
clou^M millésimé
Datierungsnagel^M
chiodo^M con data^F

tie plate
placa^F de asiento^M
selle^F de rail^M
Unterlagsplatte^F
piastra^F di appoggio^M

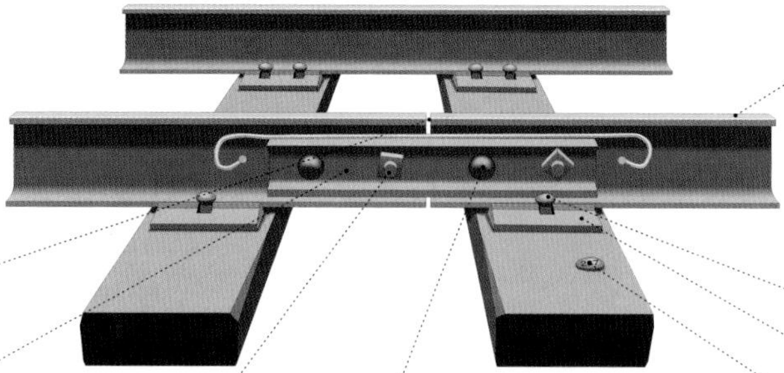

remote-controlled switch
aguja^F de control^M a larga distancia^F
aiguillage^M manœuvré à distance^F
fernbediente Weiche^F
scambio^M automatico

switch point
aguja^F
aiguille^F
Weichenzunge^F
ago^M

pull rod
varilla^F de empuje^M
tringle^F de commande^F
Stellstange^F
tirante^M comandato

switch rod
varilla^F de cambio^M
tringle^F d'écartement^M
Spurstange^F
tirante^M

power switch machine
control^M mecánico de agujas^F
moteur^M d'aiguillage^M
Weichenantrieb^M
scatola^F dello scambio^M

closure rail
rail^M de cierre^M
rail^M de raccord^M
Zwischenschiene^F
contrago^M

point wire
cable^M de corriente^F de la aguja^F
transmission^F funiculaire
Drahtzug^M
cavo^M di trasmissione^F

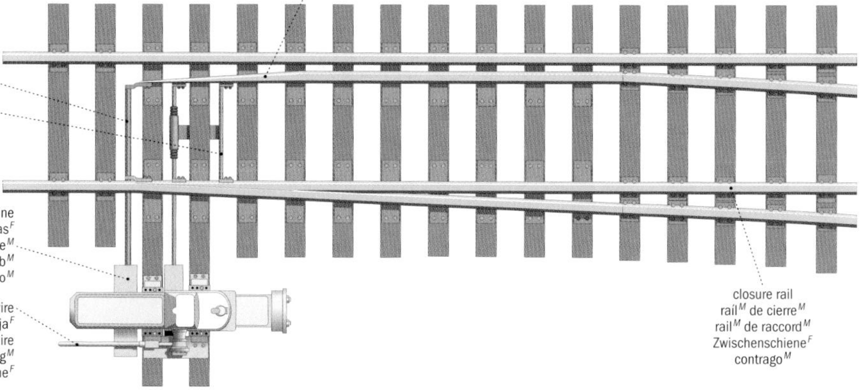

manually-operated switch
cambiador^M manual de vía^F
aiguillage^M manœuvré à pied^M d'œuvre^F
handbediente Weiche^F
scambio^M manuale

check-rail
rail^M de retención^F
contre-rail^M
Radlenker^M
controrotaia^F

frog
cruce^M
cœur^M de croisement^M
Herzstück^N
cuore^M

switch signal
señal^F de posición^F de la aguja^F
signal^M de position^F d'aiguille^F
Weichensignal^N
segnale^M di scambio^M

switch point
aguja^F
aiguille^F
Spurstange^F
ago^M

closure rail
rail^M de cierre^M
rail^M de raccord^M
Zwischenschiene^F
contrago^M

switch stand
palanca^F de maniobra^F de la aguja^F
levier^M de commande^F manuelle
Stellhebel^M
leva^F di comando^M manuale

slide chair
patín^M de deslizamiento^M
coussinet^M de glissement^M
Gleitstuhl^M
piastra^F di scorrimento^M

pull rod
varilla^F de empuje^M
tringle^F de commande^F
Stellstange^F
tirante^M d'unione^F

TRANSPORT AND MACHINERY

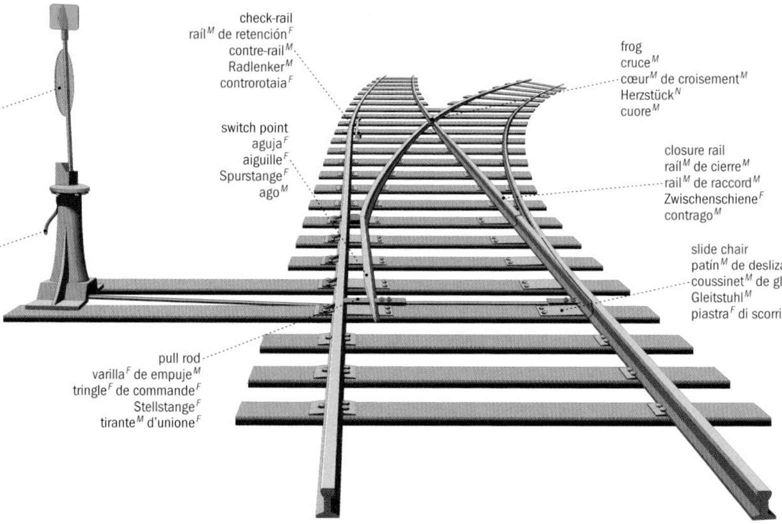

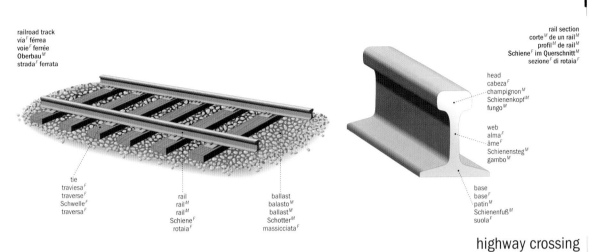

railroad track
via^F férrea
voie^F ferrée
Oberbau^M
strada^F ferrata

rail section
corte^M de un rail^M
profil^M de rail^M
Schiene^F im Querschnitt^M
sezione^F di rotaia^F

head
cabeza^F
champignon^M
Schienenkopf^M
fungo^M

web
alma^F
âme^F
Schienensteg^M
gambo^M

base
base^F
patin^M
Schienenfuß^M
suola^F

tie
traviesa^F
traverse^F
Schwelle^F
traversa^F

rail
rail^M
rail^M
Schiene^F
rotaia^F

ballast
balasto^M
ballast^M
Schotter^M
massicciata^F

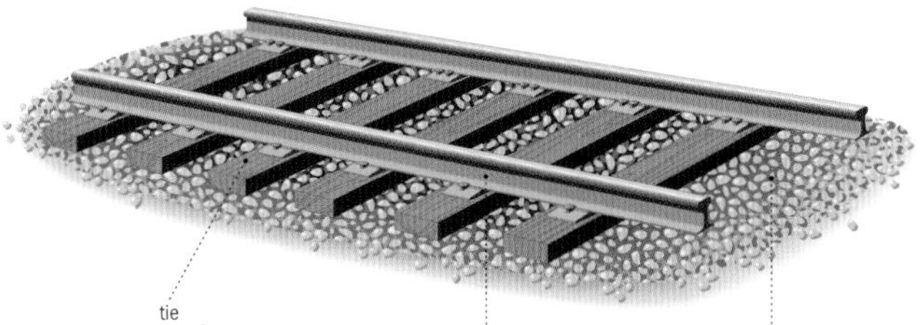

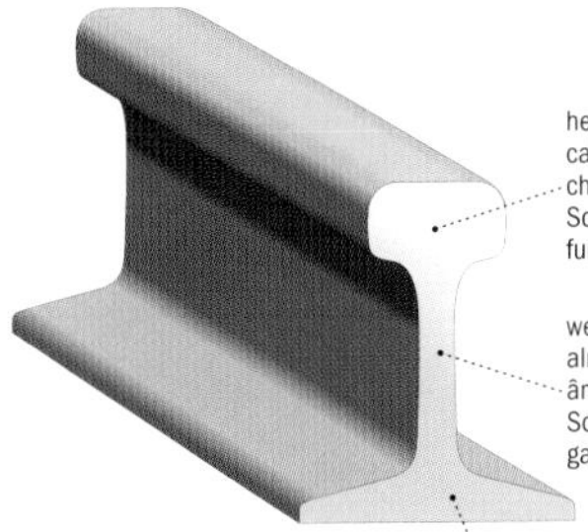

highway crossing
paso^M a nivel^M | passage^M à niveau^M | schienengleicher, gesicherter Bahnübergang^M | passaggio^M a livello^M

highway crossing bell
campana^F de aviso^M de cruce^M
sonnerie^F de passage^M à niveau^M
Vorläutewerk^N
avvisatore^M acustico

crossbuck sign
cruz^F de San Andrés
croix^F de Saint-André
Warnkreuz^N
segnale^M di passaggio^M a livello^M

mast
poste^M
mât^M
Mast^M
palo^M

junction box
caja^F de empalmes^M
boîte^F de jonction^F
Verteilerdose^F
scatola^F di collegamento^M

visor
visera^F
visière^F
Schirm^M
visiera^F

signal background plate
fondo^M de la señal^F
écran^M de visibilité^F
Signalschirm^M
schermo^M di aiuto^M della visibilità^F

peep hole
mirilla^F
œil^M témoin^M
Guckloch^N
occhio^M di controllo^M

number of tracks sign
letrero^M de número^M de vías^F
panneau^M nombre^M de voies^F
Anzahl^F der Gleise^N
cartello^M del numero^M di binari^M

flashing light
luz^F intermitente
feu^M clignotant
Blinklicht^N
semaforo^M a luce^F intermittente

gate arm lamp
luz^F de la barrera^F
feu^M de lisse^F
Lampe^F
luce^F della sbarra^F

gate arm support
soporte^M de la barrera^F
support^M de lisse^F
Stütze^F
sostegno^M della sbarra^F

counterweight
contrapeso^M
contrepoids^M
Gegengewicht^N
contrappeso^M

gate arm
barrera^F del paso^M a nivel^M
lisse^F
Schranke^F
sbarra^F

base
base^F
base^F
Sockel^M
base^F

crossing gate mechanism
mecanismo^M de la barrera^F
commande^F de barrières^F
Antrieb^M
scatola^F di comando^M della sbarra^F

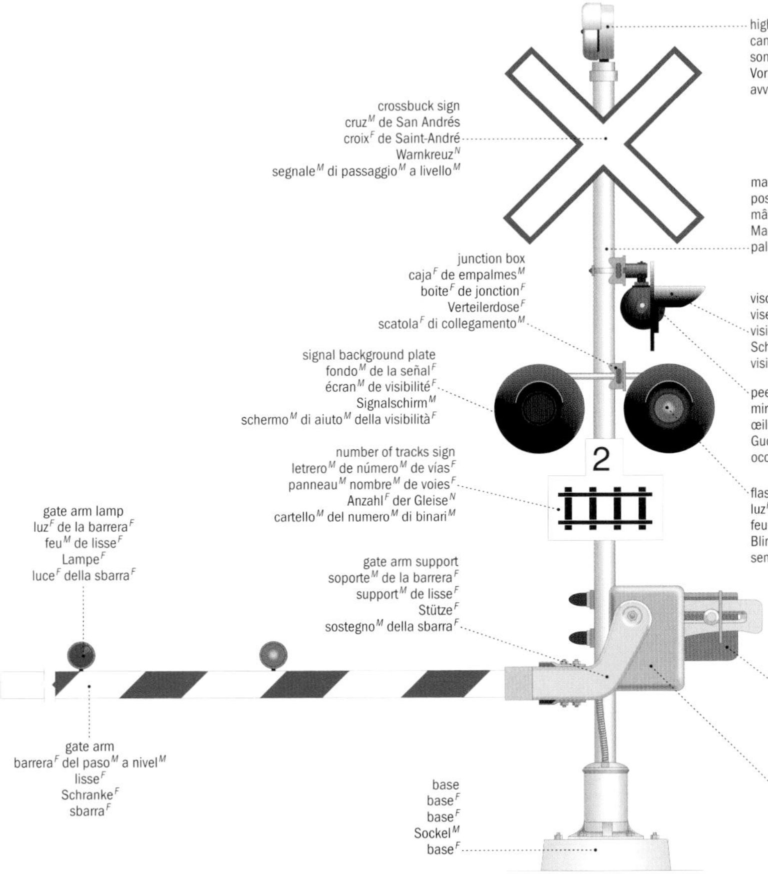

subway

metro^M | chemin^M de fer^M métropolitain | U-Bahn^F | metropolitana^F

subway station
estación^F de metro^M
station^F de métro^M
U-Bahn-Station^F
stazione^F della metropolitana^F

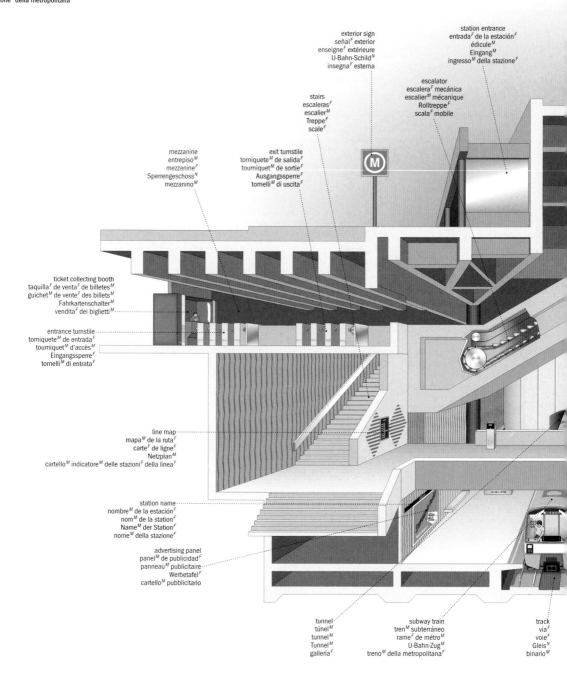

exterior sign
señal^F exterior
enseigne^F extérieure
U-Bahn-Schild^N
insegna^F esterna

station entrance
entrada^F de la estación^F
édicule^M
Eingang^M
ingresso^M della stazione^F

stairs
escaleras^F
escalier^M
Treppe^F
scale^F

escalator
escalera^F mecánica
escalier^M mécanique
Rolltreppe^F
scala^F mobile

mezzanine
entrepiso^M
mezzanine^F
Sperrengeschoss^N
mezzanino^M

exit turnstile
torniquete^M de salida^F
tourniquet^M de sortie^F
Ausgangssperre^F
tornelli^M di uscita^F

ticket collecting booth
taquilla^F de venta^F de billetes^M
guichet^M de vente^F des billets^M
Fahrkartenschalter^M
vendita^F dei biglietti^M

entrance turnstile
torniquete^M de entrada^F
tourniquet^M d'accès^M
Eingangssperre^F
tornelli^M di entrata^F

line map
mapa^M de la ruta^F
carte^F de ligne^F
Netzplan^M
cartello^M indicatore^M delle stazioni^F della linea^F

station name
nombre^M de la estación^F
nom^M de la station^F
Name^M der Station^F
nome^M della stazione^F

advertising panel
panel^M de publicidad^F
panneau^M publicitaire
Werbetafel^F
cartello^M pubblicitario

tunnel
túnel^M
tunnel^M
Tunnel^M
galleria^F

subway train
tren^M subterráneo
rame^F de métro^M
U-Bahn-Zug^M
treno^M della metropolitana^F

track
vía^F
voie^F
Gleis^N
binario^N

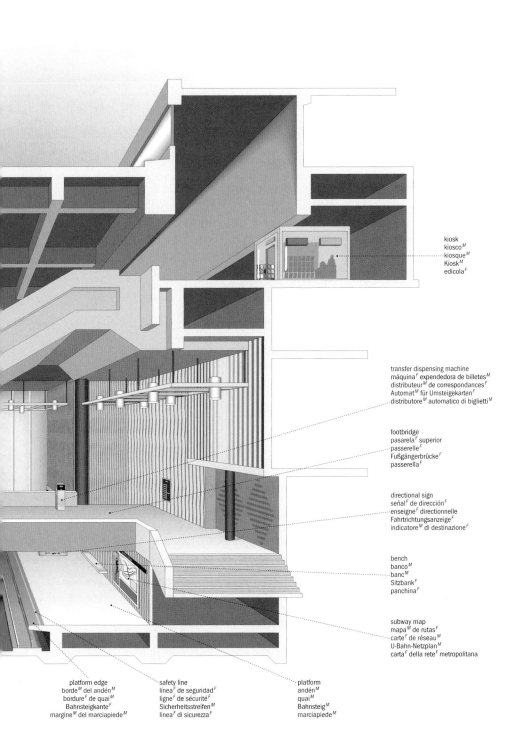

kiosk
kiosco^M
kiosque^M
Kiosk^M
edicola^F

transfer dispensing machine
máquina^F expendedora de billetes^M
distributeur^M de correspondances^F
Automat^M für Umsteigekarten^F
distributore^M automatico di biglietti^M

footbridge
pasarela^F superior
passerelle^F
Fußgängerbrücke^F
passerella^F

directional sign
señal^F de dirección^F
enseigne^F directionnelle
Fahrtrichtungsanzeige^F
indicatore^M di destinazione^F

bench
banco^M
banc^M
Sitzbank^F
panchina^F

subway map
mapa^M de rutas^F
carte^F de réseau^M
U-Bahn-Netzplan^M
carta^F della rete^F metropolitana

platform edge
borde^M del andén^M
bordure^F de quai^M
Bahnsteigkante^F
margine^M del marciapiede^M

safety line
línea^F de seguridad^F
ligne^F de sécurité^F
Sicherheitsstreifen^M
linea^F di sicurezza^F

platform
andén^M
quai^M
Bahnsteig^M
marciapiede^M

subway

passenger car
vagón^M de pasajeros^M
voiture^F
Mittelwagen^M
carrozza^F passeggeri^M

communication set
altavoz^M de comunicación^F
poste^M de communication^F
Gegensprechanlage^F
altoparlante^M

emergency brake
freno^M de emergencia^F
frein^M d'urgence^F
Notbremse^F
freno^M di emergenza^F

side door
puerta^F lateral
porte^F latérale
Einstiegstür^F
porta^F

ventilator
ventilador^M
grille^F d'aération^F
Lüftung^F
griglia^F di aerazione^F

side handrail
asidero^M lateral
poignée^F
Einsteigegriff^M
maniglia^F laterale

light
lámpara^F
éclairage^M
Innenbeleuchtung^F
luce^F

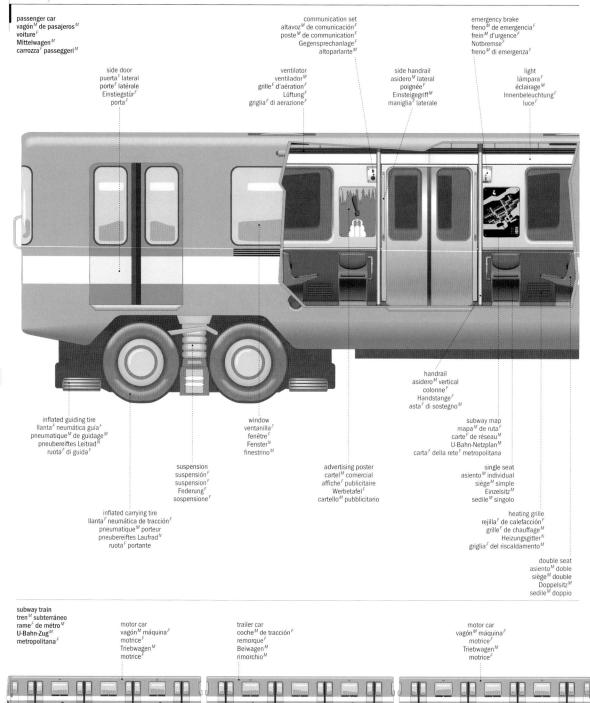

inflated guiding tire
llanta^F neumática guía^F
pneumatique^M de guidage^M
pneubereiftes Leitrad^N
ruota^F di guida^F

window
ventanilla^F
fenêtre^F
Fenster^N
finestrino^M

handrail
asidero^M vertical
colonne^F
Handstange^F
asta^F di sostegno^M

subway map
mapa^M de ruta^F
carte^F de réseau^M
U-Bahn-Netzplan^M
carta^F della rete^F metropolitana

suspension
suspensión^F
suspension^F
Federung^F
sospensione^F

advertising poster
cartel^M comercial
affiche^F publicitaire
Werbetafel^F
cartello^M pubblicitario

single seat
asiento^M individual
siège^M simple
Einzelsitz^M
sedile^M singolo

inflated carrying tire
llanta^F neumática de tracción^F
pneumatique^M porteur
pneubereiftes Laufrad^N
ruota^F portante

heating grille
rejilla^F de calefacción^F
grille^F de chauffage^M
Heizungsgitter^N
griglia^F del riscaldamento^M

double seat
asiento^M doble
siège^M double
Doppelsitz^M
sedile^M doppio

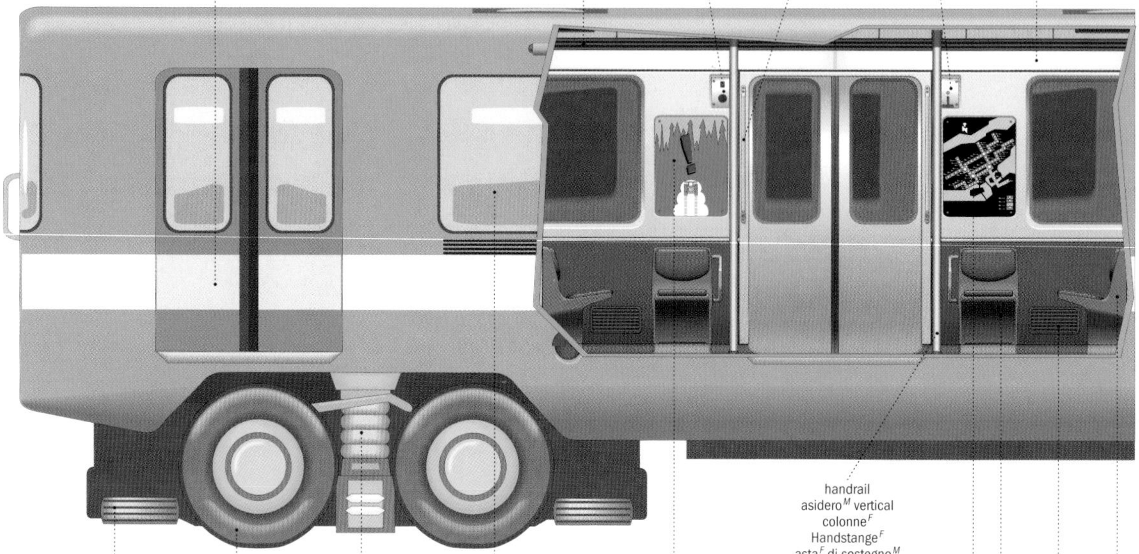

subway train
tren^M subterráneo
rame^F de métro^M
U-Bahn-Zug^M
metropolitana^F

motor car
vagón^M máquina^F
motrice^F
Triebwagen^M
motrice^F

trailer car
coche^M de tracción^F
remorque^F
Beiwagen^M
rimorchio^M

motor car
vagón^M máquina^F
motrice^F
Triebwagen^M
motrice^F

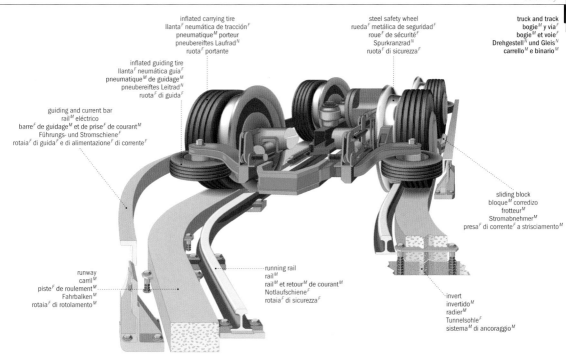

inflated carrying tire
llanta^F neumática de tracción^F
pneumatique^M porteur
pneubereiftes Laufrad^N
ruota^F portante

steel safety wheel
rueda^F metálica de seguridad^F
roue^F de sécurité^F
Spurkranzrad^N
ruota^F di sicurezza^F

truck and track
bogie^M y vía^F
bogie^M et voie^F
Drehgestell^N und Gleis^N
carrello^M e binario^M

inflated guiding tire
llanta^F neumática guía^F
pneumatique^M de guidage^M
pneubereiftes Leitrad^N
ruota^F di guida^F

guiding and current bar
rail^M eléctrico
barre^F de guidage^M et de prise^F de courant^M
Führungs- und Stromschiene^F
rotaia^F di guida^F e di alimentazione^F di corrente^F

sliding block
bloque^M corredizo
frotteur^M
Stromabnehmer^M
presa^F di corrente^F a strisciamento^M

runway
carril^M
piste^F de roulement^M
Fahrbalken^M
rotaia^F di rotolamento^M

running rail
rail^M
rail^M et retour^M de courant^M
Notlaufschiene^F
rotaia^F di sicurezza^F

invert
invertido^M
radier^M
Tunnelsohle^F
sistema^M di ancoraggio^M

streetcar

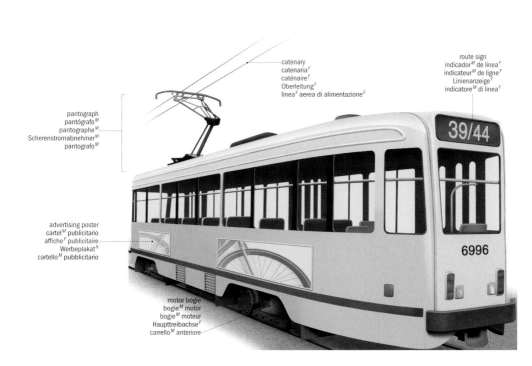

catenary
catenaria^F
caténaire^F
Oberleitung^F
linea^F aerea di alimentazione^F

route sign
indicador^M de línea^F
indicateur^M de ligne^F
Linienanzeige^F
indicatore^M di línea^F

pantograph
pantógrafo^M
pantographe^M
Scherenstromabnehmer^M
pantografo^M

advertising poster
cartel^M publicitario
affiche^F publicitaire
Werbeplakat^N
cartello^M pubblicitario

motor bogie
bogie^M motor
bogie^M moteur
Haupttreibachse^F
carrello^M anteriore

39/44

6996

harbor

puerto^M | port^M maritime | Hafen^M | porto^M marittimo

canal lock
esclusa^F de canal^M
écluse^F
Kanalschleuse^F
chiusa^F di un canale^M

container-loading bridge
puente^M de carga^F para contenedores^M
portique^M de chargement^M de conteneurs^M
Containerbrücke^F
ponte^M di caricamento^M per containers^M

oil terminal
terminal^F de petróleo^M
terminal^M pétrolier
Öllöschbrücke^F
deposito^M del petrolio^M

dry dock
dique^M seco
bassin^M de radoub^M
Trockendock^N
bacino^M di carenaggio^M

transit shed
depósito^M de mercancía^F en tránsito^M
hangar^M de transit^M
Transitlagerschuppen^M
capannoni^M delle merci^F in transito^M

tanker
petrolero^M
pétrolier^M
Tanker^M
petroliera^F

quayside crane
grúa^F de muelle^M
grue^F à flèche^F
Werftkran^M
gru^F mobile a braccio^M

bulk terminal
terminal^F de carga^F
terminal^M de vrac^M
Massengut-Terminal^M
deposito^M delle rinfuse^F

cold shed
cámara^F frigorífica
entrepôt^M frigorifique
Kühlhaus^N
magazzino^M frigorifero^M

ferryboat
transbordador^M
transbordeur^M
Hafenfähre^F
traghetto^M

gate
compuerta^F
porte^F
Tor^N
porta^F del bacino^M

quay
muelle^M
quai^M
Kai^M
banchina^F

lighthouse
faro^M
phare^M
Leuchtturm^M
faro^M

passenger terminal
terminal^F de pasajeros^M
gare^F maritime
Fahrgastanlage^F
stazione^F dei viaggiatori^M

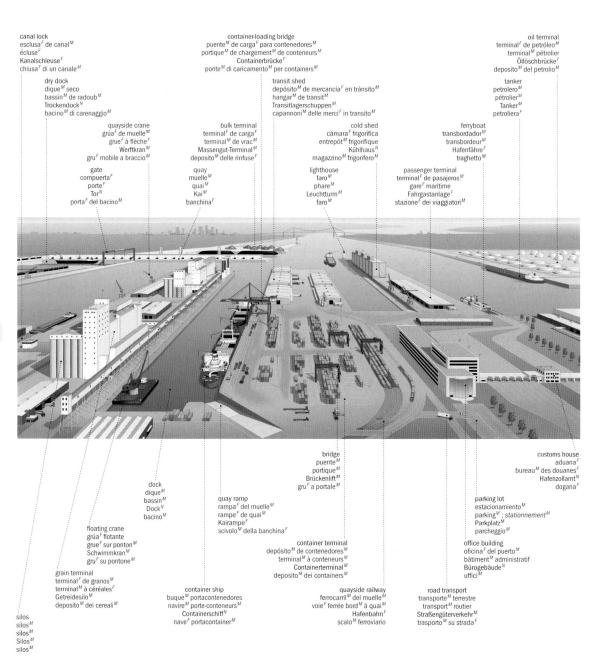

bridge
puente^M
portique^M
Brückenlift^M
gru^F a portale^M

customs house
aduana^F
bureau^M des douanes^F
Hafenzollamt^N
dogana^F

dock
dique^M
bassin^M
Dock^N
bacino^M

quay ramp
rampa^F del muelle^M
rampe^F de quai^M
Kairampe^F
scivolo^M della banchina^F

parking lot
estacionamiento^M
parking^M ; stationnement^M
Parkplatz^M
parcheggio^M

floating crane
grúa^F flotante
grue^F sur ponton^M
Schwimmkran^M
gru^F su pontone^M

container terminal
depósito^M de contenedores^M
terminal^M à conteneurs^M
Containerterminal^M
deposito^M dei containers^M

office building
oficina^F del puerto^M
bâtiment^M administratif
Bürogebäude^N
uffici^M

grain terminal
terminal^F de granos^M
terminal^M à céréales^F
Getreidesilo^M
deposito^M dei cereali^M

container ship
buque^M portacontenedores
navire^M porte-conteneurs^M
Containerschiff^N
nave^F portacontainer^M

quayside railway
ferrocarril^M del muelle^M
voie^F ferrée bord^M à quai^M
Hafenbahn^F
scalo^M ferroviario

road transport
transporte^M terrestre
transport^M routier
Straßengüterverkehr^M
trasporto^M su strada^F

silos
silos^M
silos^M
Silos^M
silos^M

canal lock

esclusa^F de canal^M | écluse^F | Kanalschleuse^F | chiusa^F di un canale^M

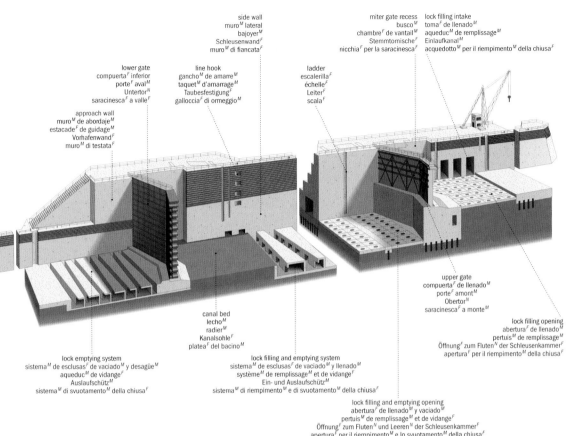

side wall
muro^M lateral
bajoyer^M
Schleusenwand^F
muro^M di fiancata^F

miter gate recess
busco^M
chambre^F de vantail^M
Stemmtornische^F
nicchia^F per la saracinesca^F

lock filling intake
toma^F de llenado^M
aqueduc^M de remplissage^M
Einlaufkanal^M
acquedotto^M per il riempimento^M della chiusa^F

lower gate
compuerta^F inferior
porte^F aval^M
Untertor^N
saracinesca^F a valle^F

line hook
gancho^M de amarre^M
taquet^M d'amarrage^M
Taubesfestigung^F
galloccia^F di ormeggio^M

ladder
escalerilla^F
échelle^F
Leiter^F
scala^F

approach wall
muro^M de abordaje^M
estacade^F de guidage^M
Vorhafenwand^F
muro^M di testata^F

upper gate
compuerta^F de llenado^M
porte^F amont^M
Obertor^N
saracinesca^F a monte^M

canal bed
lecho^M
radier^M
Kanalsohle^F
platea^F del bacino^M

lock filling opening
abertura^F de llenado^M
pertuis^M de remplissage^M
Öffnung^F zum Fluten^N der Schleusenkammer^F
apertura^F per il riempimento^M della chiusa^F

lock emptying system
sistema^M de esclusas^F de vaciado^M y desagüe^M
aqueduc^M de vidange^F
Auslaufschütz^M
sistema^M di svuotamento^M della chiusa^F

lock filling and emptying system
sistema^M de esclusas^F de vaciado^M y llenado^M
système^M de remplissage^M et de vidange^F
Ein- und Auslaufschütz^M
sistema^M di riempimento^M e di svuotamento^M della chiusa^F

lock filling and emptying opening
abertura^F de llenado^M y vaciado^M
pertuis^M de remplissage^M et de vidange^F
Öffnung^F zum Fluten^N und Leeren^N der Schleusenkammer^F
apertura^F per il riempimento^M e lo svuotamento^M della chiusa^F

canal lock: side view
esclusa^F : vista^F lateral
écluse^F : vue^F latérale
Schleuse^F: Seitenansicht^F
chiusa^F di un canale^M: vista^F laterale

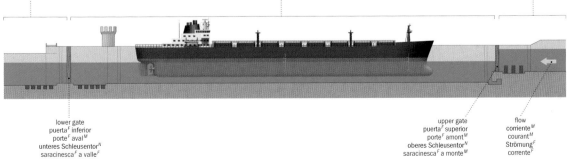

lower level
nivel^M inferior
tête^F aval^M
niedrigerer Wasserstand^M
livello^M inferiore

lock-chamber
cámara^F de la esclusa^F
sas^M
Schleusenkammer^F
bacino^M

upper level
nivel^M superior
tête^F amont^M
höherer Wasserstand^M
livello^M superiore

lower gate
puerta^F inferior
porte^F aval^M
unteres Schleusentor^N
saracinesca^F a valle^F

upper gate
puerta^F superior
porte^F amont^M
oberes Schleusentor^N
saracinesca^F a monte^M

flow
corriente^M
courant^M
Strömung^F
corrente^F

historical ships

embarcaciones^F antiguas | embarcations^F anciennes | historische Schiffe^N | imbarcazioni^F antiche

longship
dragón^M vikingo
drakkar^M
Wikingerschiff^N
drakar^M

stern
popa^F
poupe^F
Achtersteven^M
poppa^F

steering oar
remo^M de dirección^F
aviron^M de queue^F
Steuerruder^N
remo^M-timone^M

stay
estay^M
étai^M
Fall^N
strallo^M

stempost
estrave^F
étrave^F
Vordersteven^M
dritto^M di prua^F

oar
remo^M
aviron^M
Ruder^N
remo^M

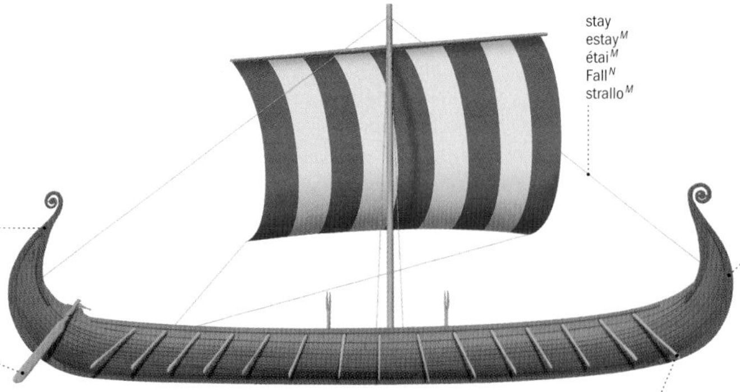

galley
galera^F
galère^F
Galeere^F
galea^F

oar
remo^M
aviron^M
Ruder^N
remo^M

ram
espolón^M
éperon^M
Rammsporn^M
rostro^M

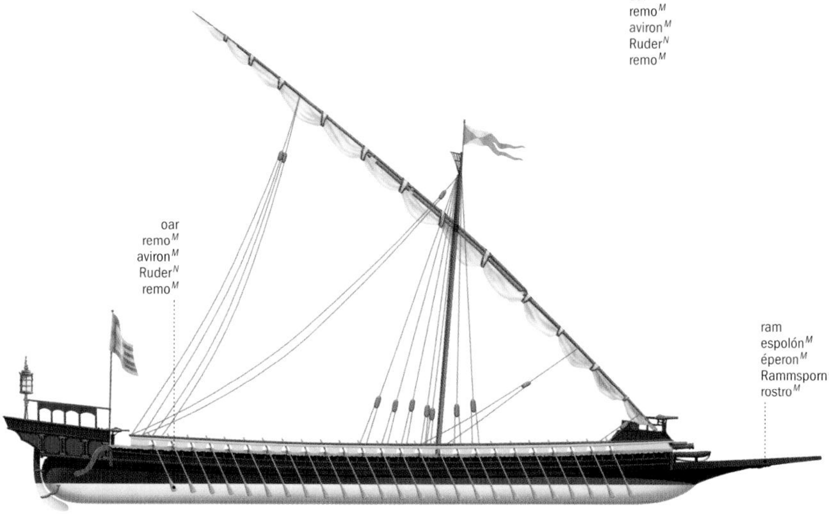

trireme
trirreme^M
trirème^F
Trireme^F
trireme^F

carved prow
proa^F tallada
proue^F sculptée
geschnitzter Bug^M
prua^F scolpita

steering oar
remo^M de dirección^F
aviron^M de queue^F
Steuerruder^N
remo^M-timone^M

oar
remo^M
aviron^M
Ruder^N
remo^M

ram
espolón^M
éperon^M
Rammsporn^M
rostro^M

TRANSPORT AND MACHINERY

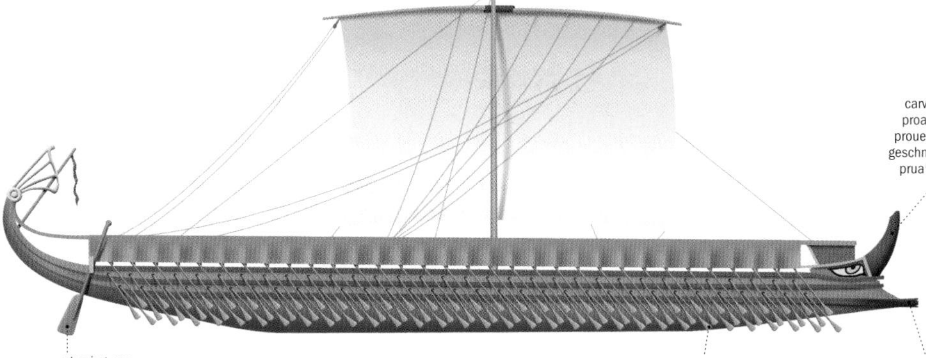

funnel
chimenea[F]
cheminée[F]
Schornstein[M]
fumaiolo[M]

side-wheeler
barco[M] de vapor[M] de ruedas[F]
bateau[M] à vapeur[F] à roues[F] latérales
Schaufelraddampfer[M]
battello[M] a vapore[M] a ruote[F] laterali

paddle wheel
rueda[F] de aspas[F]
roue[F] à aubes[F]
Schaufelrad[N]
ruota[F] a pale[F]

galleon
galeón[M]
galion[M]
Galeone[F]
galeone[M]

caravel
carabela[F]
caravelle[F]
Karavelle[F]
caravella[F]

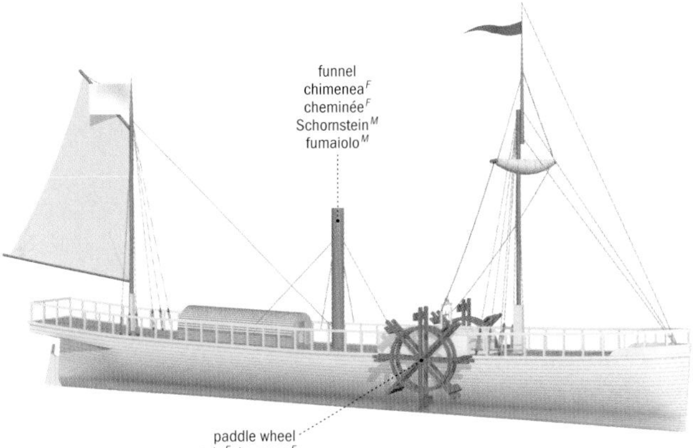

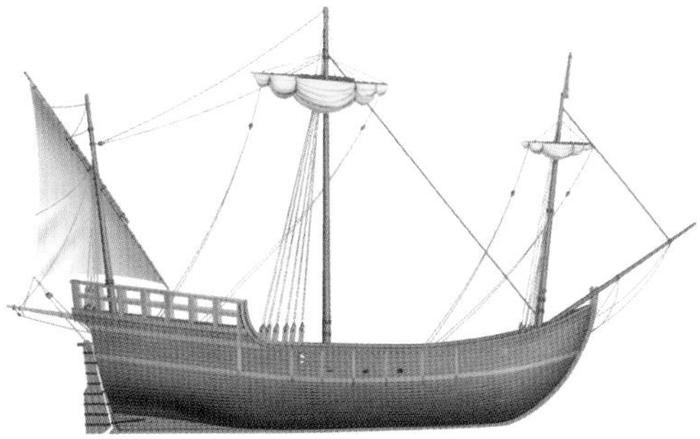

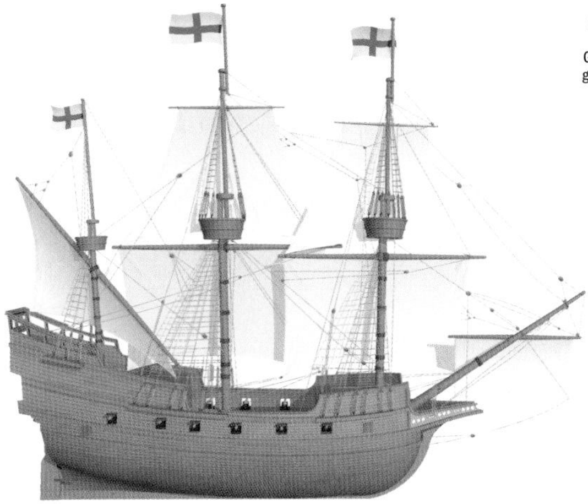

traditional watercraft

embarcaciones[F] tradicionales | embarcations[F] traditionnelles | traditionelle Boote[N] | imbarcazioni[F] tradizionali

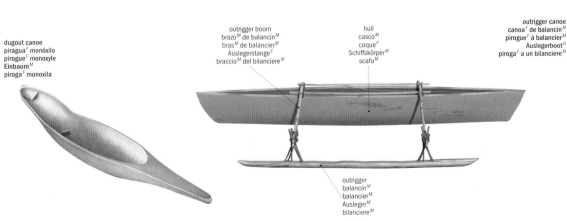

outrigger boom
brazo[M] de balancín[M]
bras[M] de balancier[M]
Auslegerstange[F]
braccio[M] del bilanciere[M]

hull
casco[M]
coque[F]
Schiffskörper[M]
scafo[M]

outrigger canoe
canoa[F] de balancín[M]
pirogue[F] à balancier[M]
Auslegerboot[N]
piroga[F] a un bilanciere[M]

dugout canoe
piragua[F] monóxilo
pirogue[F] monoxyle
Einbaum[M]
piroga[F] monoxila

outrigger
balancín[M]
balancier[M]
Ausleger[M]
bilanciere[M]

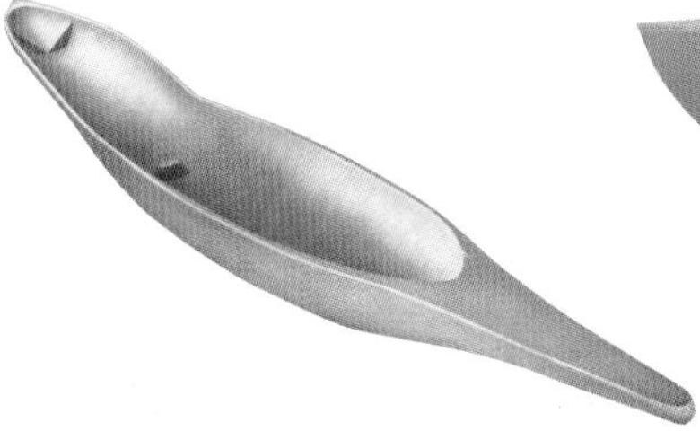

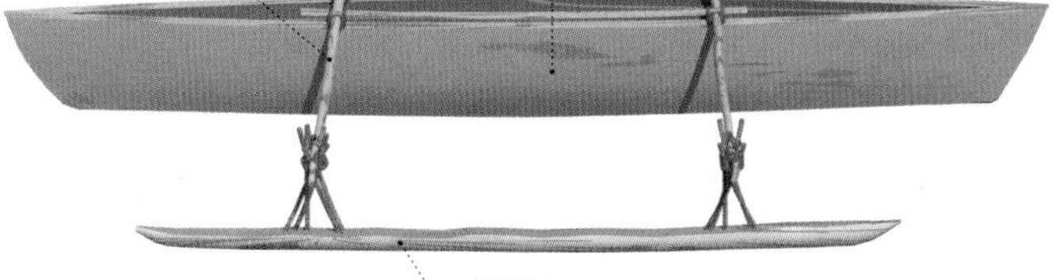

traditional watercraft

junk
junco[M]
jonque[F]
Dschunke[F]
giunca[F]

mizzenmast
palo[M] de mesana[F]
mât[M] d'artimon[M]
Besanmast[M]
albero[M] di mezzana[F]

mainmast
palo[M] mayor
grand mât[M]
Großmast[M]
albero[M] di maestra[F]

foremast
palo[M] de trinquete[M]
mât[M] de misaine[F]
Fockmast[M]
albero[M] di trinchetto[M]

batten
quilla[F]
latte[F]
Segellatte[F]
canna[F]

rudder
timón[M]
gouvernail[M]
Ruder[N]
timone[M]

mast
mástil[M]
mât[M]
Mast[M]
albero[M]

oar
remo[M]
aviron[M]
Ruder[N]
remo[M]

prow ornament
ornamento[M] de proa[F]
ornement[M] de proue[F]
Bugverzierung[F]
ornamento[M] di prua[F]

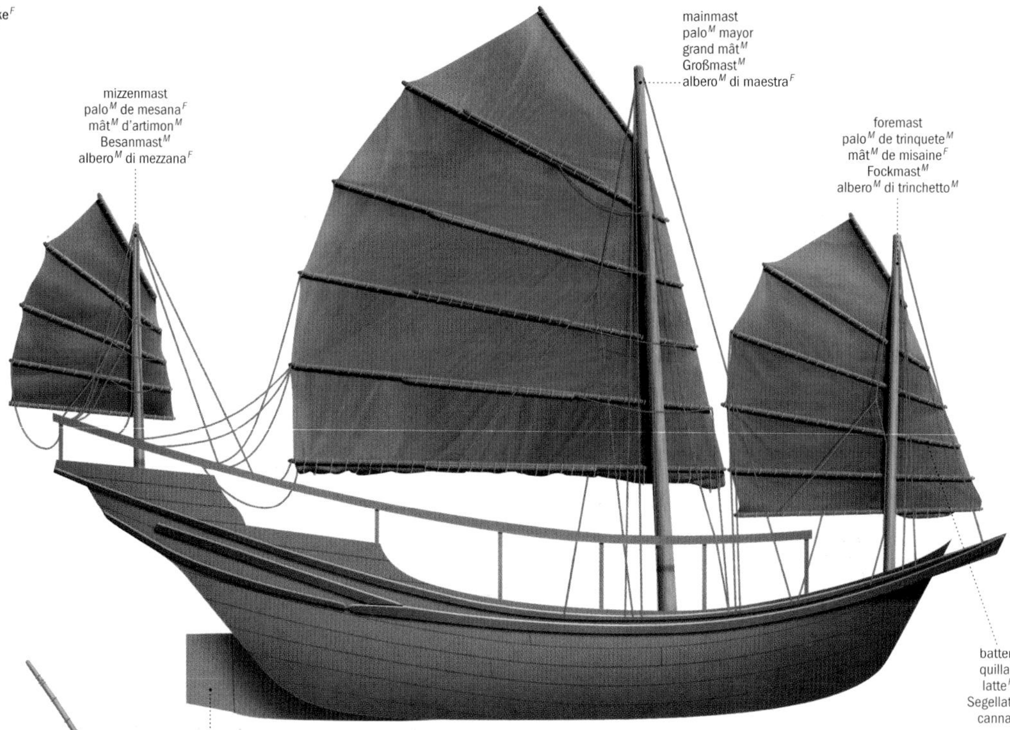

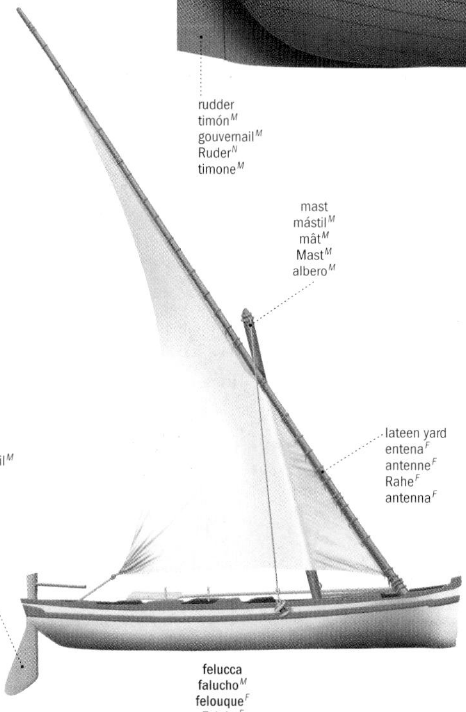

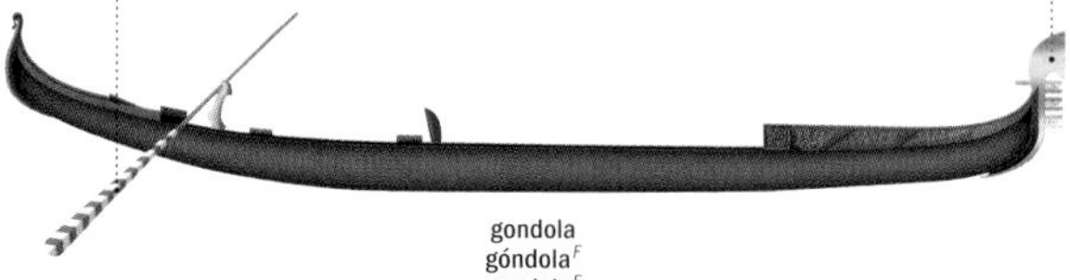

gondola
góndola[F]
gondole[F]
Gondel[F]
gondola[F]

rudder
timón[M]
gouvernail[M]
Ruder[N]
timone[M]

lateen yard
entena[F]
antenne[F]
Rahe[F]
antenna[F]

felucca
falucho[M]
felouque[F]
Feluke[F]
feluca[F]

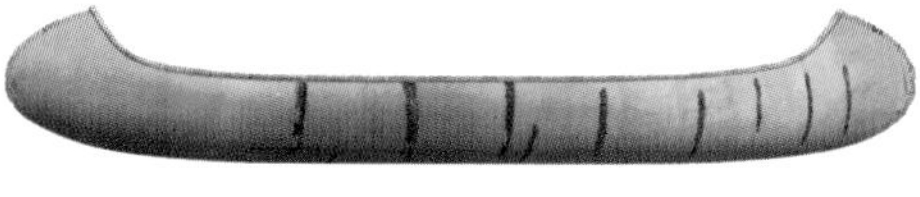

canoe
canoa[F]
canoë[M] ; canot[M]
Kanu[N]
canoa[F]

examples of sails

ejemplos^M de velas^F | exemples^M de voiles^F | Beispiele^N für Segel^N | esempi^M di vele^F

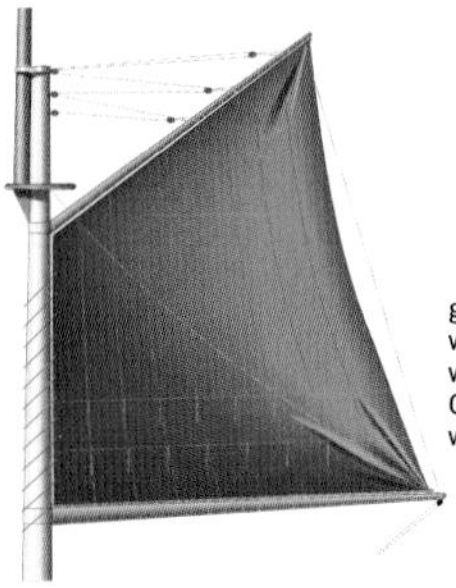

gaff sail
vela^F áurica
voile^F aurique
Gaffelsegel^N
vela^F aurica

Bermuda sail
vela^F Bermuda
voile^F bermudienne
Spitzsegel^N
vela^F Marconi

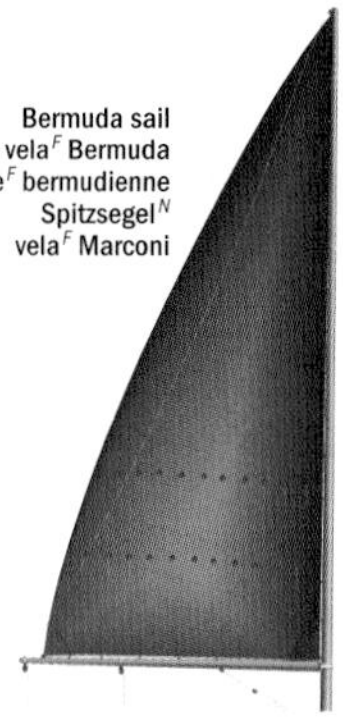

lug sail
vela^F al tercio^M
voile^F au tiers^M
Luggersegel^N
vela^F al terzo^M

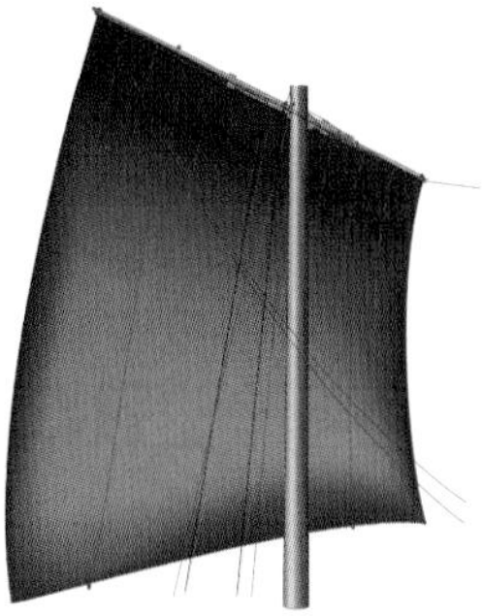

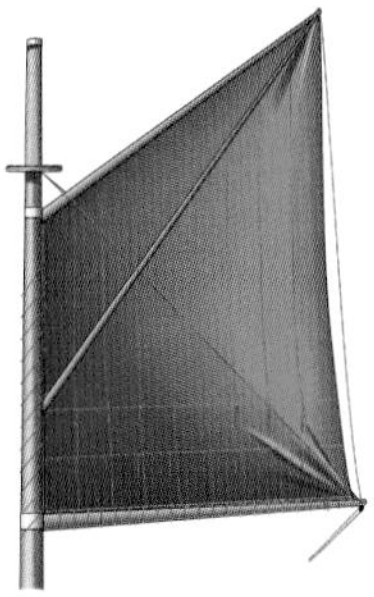

spritsail
vela^F tarquina
voile^F à livarde^F
Sprietsegel^N
vela^F a tarchia^F

lateen sail
vela^F latina
voile^F latine
Lateinersegel^N
vela^F latina

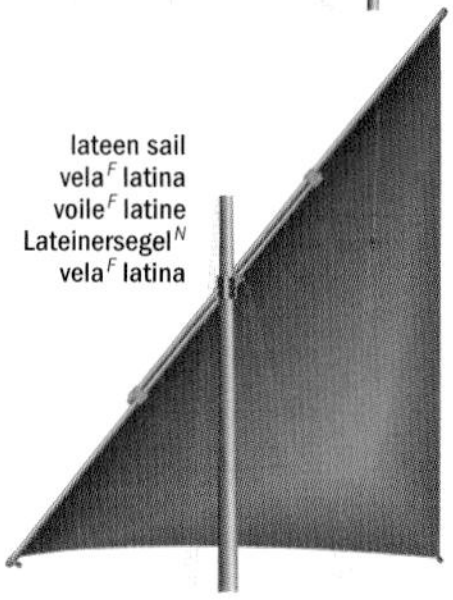

square sail
vela^F cuadrada
voile^F carrée
Rahsegel^N
vela^F quadra

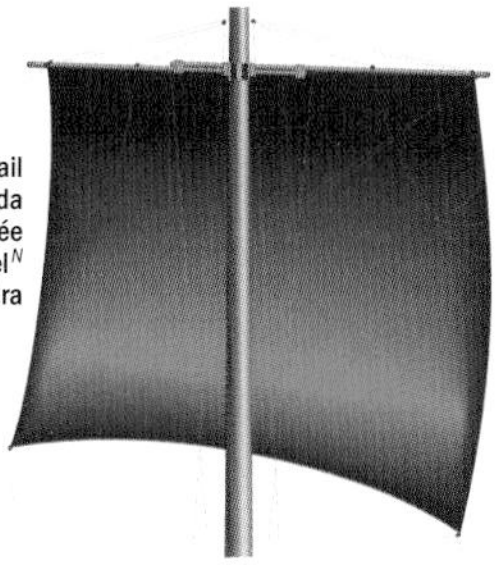

examples of rigs

ejemplos^M de aparejos^M | exemples^M de gréements^M | Beispiele^N für Riggs^N | esempi^M di attrezzature^F

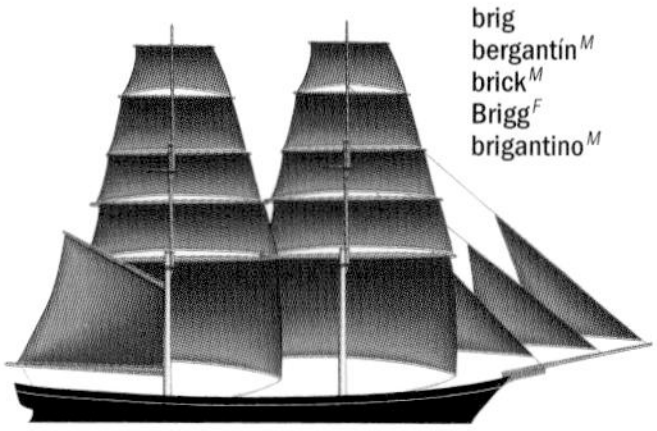

brig
bergantín^M
brick^M
Brigg^F
brigantino^M

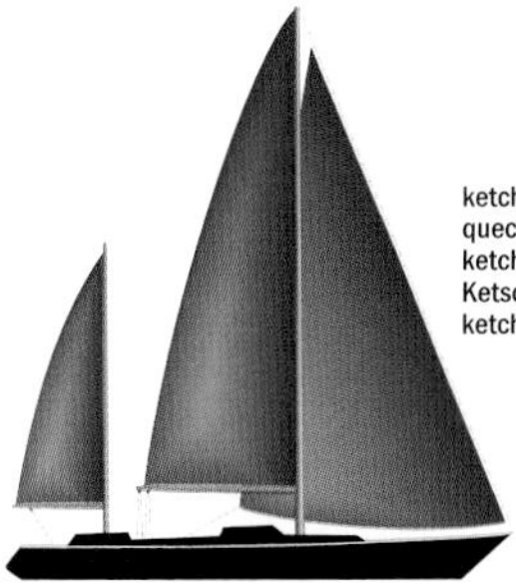

ketch
queche^M
ketch^M
Ketsch^F
ketch^M

brigantine
bergantín^M goleta^F
brigantin^M
Brigantine^F
brigantino^M goletta^F

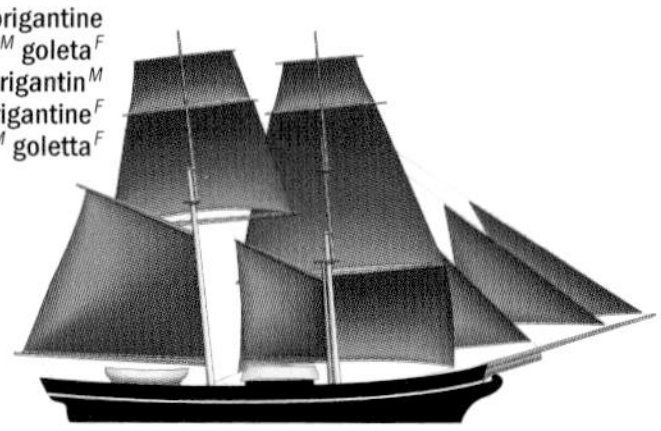

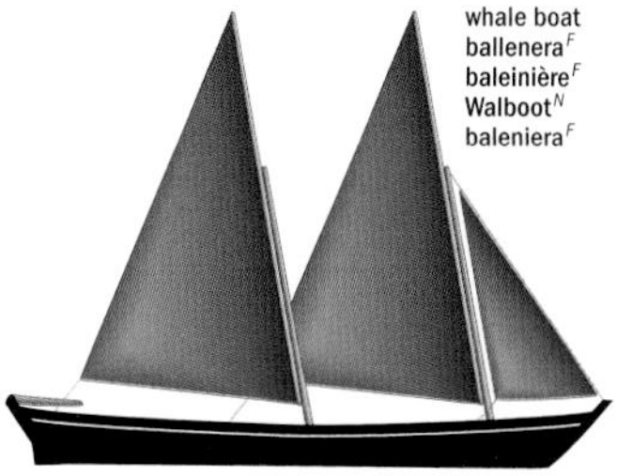

whale boat
ballenera^F
baleinière^F
Walboot^N
baleniera^F

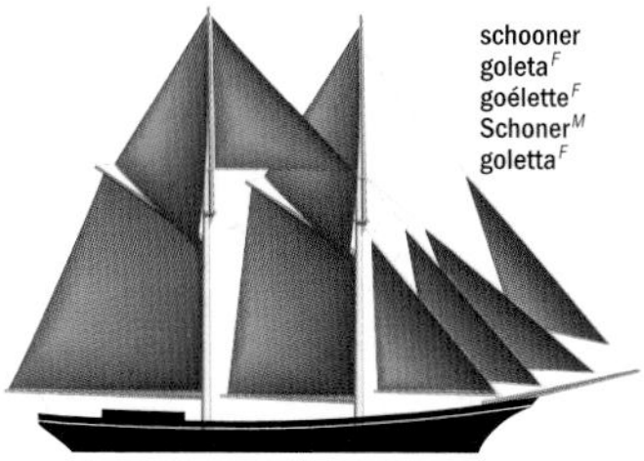

schooner
goleta^F
goélette^F
Schoner^M
goletta^F

Marconi cutter
cúter^M Marconi
cotre^M Marconi
Marconikutter^M
ketch^M Marconi

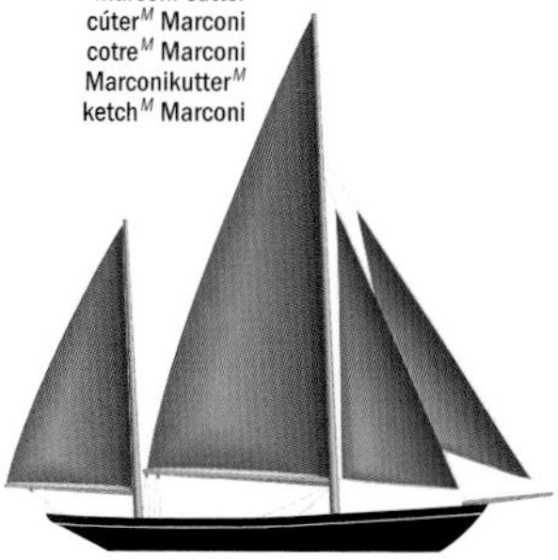

four-masted bark

barco^M de vela^F de cuatro palos^M | quatre-mâts^M barque^F | Viermastbark^F | veliero^M a quattro alberi^M

masting and rigging
arboladura^F y aparejos^M
mâture^F et gréement^M
Takelage^F
alberatura^F e velatura^F

fore-royal mast
mastelero^M de sobrejuanete^M
mât^M de cacatois^M
Royalstenge^F
albero^M di controvelaccino^M

fore-topgallant mast
mastelero^M de juanete^M
mât^M de perroquet^M
Bramstenge^F
albero^M di velaccino^M

masthead
cabeza^F del mastil^M
ton^M de mât^M
Vorbramsaling^F
testa^F d'albero^M

fore-topmast
mastelero^M
mât^M de hune^F
Marsstenge^F
albero^M di parrocchetto^M

top
tope^M
hune^F
Saling^F
coffa^F

lower mast
palo^M macho
bas-mât^M
Untermast^M
tronco^M di mezzana^F

pole
estaca^F
fusée^F
Spitze^F
spigone^M

yard
verga^F
vergue^F
Rah^F
pennone^M

footrope
marchapié^M
marchepied^M
Fußpferd^N
marciapiede^M

mainmast
palo^M mayor
grand mât^M avant
Großmast^M
albero^M di maestra^F

mizzenmast
palo^M de mesana^F
grand mât^M arrière
Kreuzmast^M
albero^M di mezzana^F

foremast
palo^M de trinquete^M
mât^M de misaine^F
Fockmast^M
albero^M di trinchetto^M

jiggermast
contramesana^F
mât^M d'artimon^M
Besanmast^M
albero^M di contromezzana^F

topping lift
amantillo^M de botavara^F
martinet^M
Hanger^M
drizza^F di picco^M

gaff
botavara^F
corne^F
Gaffel^F
picco^M

lift
amantillo^M
balancine^F
Toppnant^F
amantiglio^M

gaff sail boom
botavara^F de cangreja^F
gui^M
Besanbaum^M
boma^M

poop
popa^F
dunette^F
Poop^F
poppa^F

backstay
burda^F
galhauban^M
Pardune^F
paterazzo^M

shroud
obenque^M
hauban^M
Want^M
sartia^F

side
banda^F
bord^M
Seite^F
fianco^M

stay
estay^M
étai^M
Stag^N
strallo^M

staysail-stay
nervio^M de vela^F estay^M
draille^F
Stagsegel-Stag^N
draglia^F

lifeboat
bote^M salvavidas
canot^M de sauvetage^M
Rettungsboot^N
scialuppa^F di salvataggio^M

davit
pescante^M
bossoir^M
Davit^M
gru^F

stem
roda^F
étrave^F
Steven^M
prua^F

bulwark
amurada^F
pavois^M
Schanzkleid^N
murata^F

bowsprit
bauprés^M
mât^M de beaupré^F
Bugspriet^M
bompresso^M

bobstay
barbiquejo^M
martingale^F
Stampfstag^N
briglia^F del bompresso^M

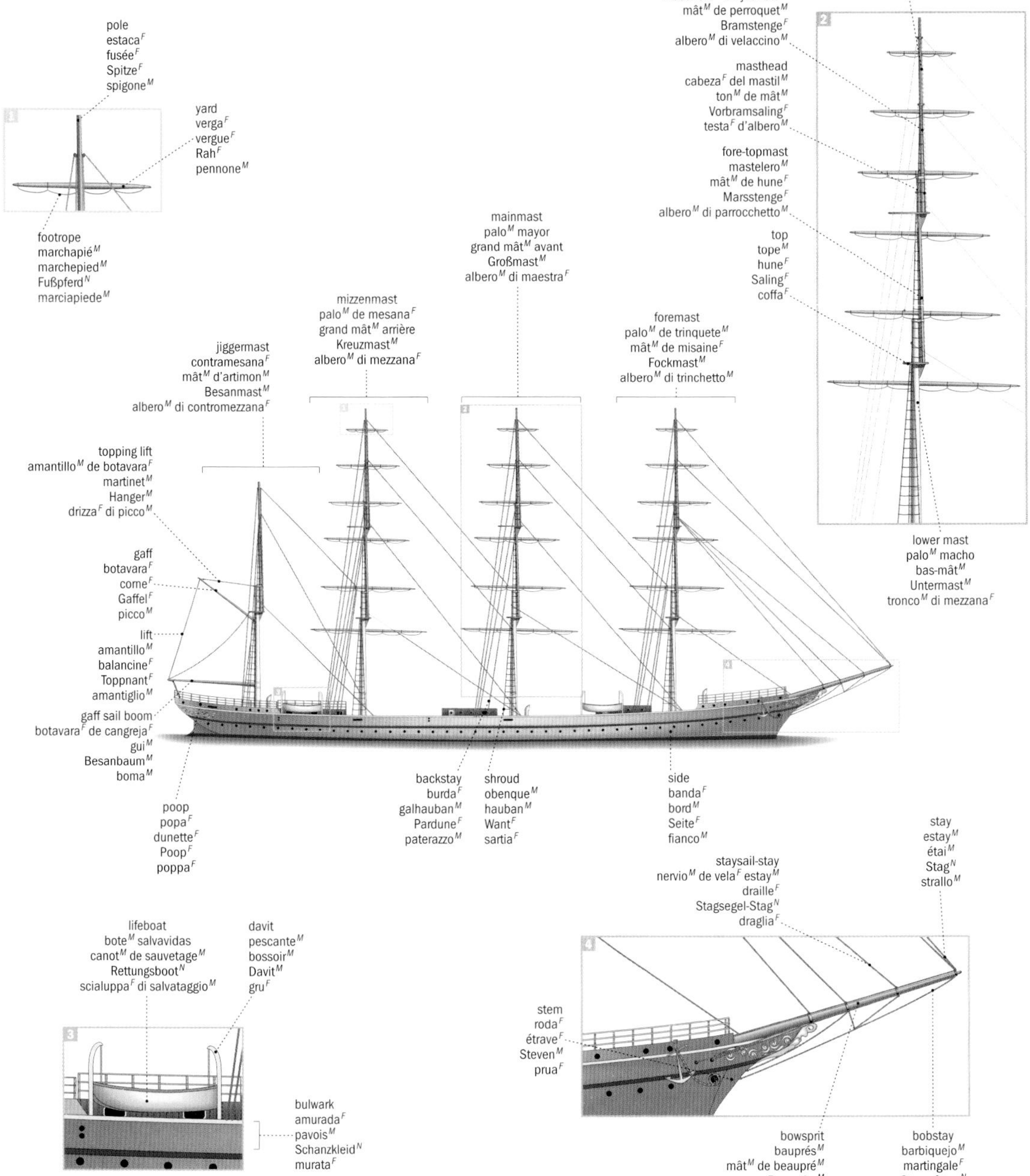

sails
velamen^M
voilure^F
Segel^N
vele^F

mizzen royal staysail
sobrejuanete^M de mesana^F de estay^M
voile^F d'étai^M de grand perroquet^M arrière
Kreuz-Royalstagsegel^N
vela^F di strallo^M di controvelaccio^M

mizzen topgallant staysail
juanete^M de mesana^F de estay^M
voile^F d'étai^M de hune^F arrière
Kreuz-Bramstagsegel^N
vela^F di strallo^M di velaccio^M

mizzen topmast staysail
mastelero^M de mesana^F de estay^M
grand-voile^F d'étai^M arrière
Kreuz-Stengestagsegel^N
vela^F di strallo^M di gabbia^F

jigger topgallant staysail
aparejo^M de juanete^M de estay^M
voile^F d'étai^M de flèche^F
Besan-Bramstagsegel^N
vela^F di strallo^M di belvedere^M

jigger topmast staysail
aparejo^M de mastelero^M de estay^M
marquise^F
Besan-Stengestagsegel^N
vela^F di strallo^M di mezzana^F

mizzen royal brace
brazas^F de sobrejuanete^M de mesana^F
bras^M de grand cacatois^M arrière
Kreuz-Royalbrasse^F
braccio^M del pennone^M di controbelvedere^M

gaff topsail
escandalosa^F
voile^F de flèche^F
Besantoppsegel^N
controroranda^F

spanker
cangreja^F de popa^F
brigantine^F
Besan^M
randa^F

main royal sail
sobrejuanete^M mayor
grand cacatois^M avant
Groß-Royalsegel^N
controvelaccio^M

main upper topgallant sail
juanete^M mayor proel alto
grand perroquet^M volant avant
Groß-Oberbramsegel^N
velaccio^M volante

main lower topgallant sail
juanete^M mayor bajo
grand perroquet^M fixe avant
Groß-Unterbramsegel^N
velaccio^M fisso

main upper topsail
gavia^F mayor alta
grand hunier^M volant avant
Groß-Obermarssegel^N
gabbia^F volante

fore royal sail
sobrejuanete^M de proa^F
petit cacatois^M
Vor-Royalsegel^N
controvelaccino^M

upper fore topgallant sail
juanete^M de proa^F alto
petit perroquet^M volant
Vor-Oberbramsegel^N
velaccino^M volante

lower fore topgallant sail
juanete^M de proa^F bajo
petit perroquet^M fixe
Vor-Unterbramsegel^N
velaccino^M fisso

upper fore topsail
gavia^F proel alta
petit hunier^M volant
Vor-Obermarssegel^N
parrocchetto^M volante

flying jib
petifoque^M
clinfoc^M
Flieger^M
controfiocco^M

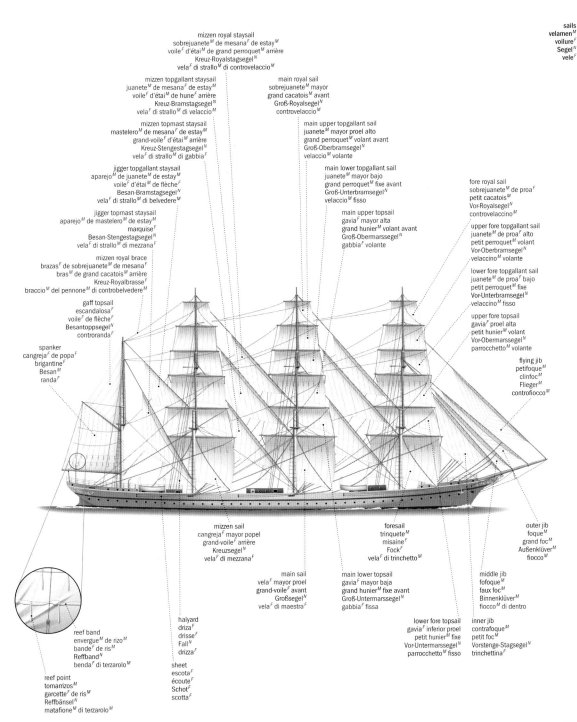

mizzen sail
cangreja^F mayor popel
grand-voile^F arrière
Kreuzsegel^N
vela^F di mezzana^F

foresail
trinquete^M
misaine^F
Fock^F
vela^F di trinchetto^M

outer jib
foque^M
grand foc^M
Außenklüver^M
fiocco^M

main sail
vela^F mayor proel
grand-voile^F avant
Großsegel^N
vela^F di maestra^F

main lower topsail
gavia^F mayor baja
grand hunier^M fixe avant
Groß-Untermarssegel^N
gabbia^F fissa

middle jib
fofoque^M
faux foc^M
Binnenklüver^M
fiocco^M di dentro

halyard
driza^F
drisse^F
Fall^N
drizza^F

reef band
envergue^M de rizo^M
bande^F de ris^M
Reffband^N
benda^F di terzarolo^M

sheet
escota^F
écoute^F
Schot^F
scotta^F

lower fore topsail
gavia^F inferior proel
petit hunier^M fixe
Vor-Untermarssegel^N
parrocchetto^M fisso

inner jib
contrafoque^M
petit foc^M
Vorstenge-Stagsegel^N
trinchettina^F

reef point
tomarrizos^M
garcette^F de ris^M
Reffbänsel^N
matafione^F di terzarolo^M

examples of boats and ships

ejemplos^M de barcos^M y embarcaciones^F | exemples^M de bateaux^M et d'embarcations^F | Beispiele^N für Boote^N und Schiffe^N | esempi^M di barche^F e navi^F

drill ship
barco^M perforador
navire^M de forage^M
Bohrschiff^N
nave^F da perforazione^F

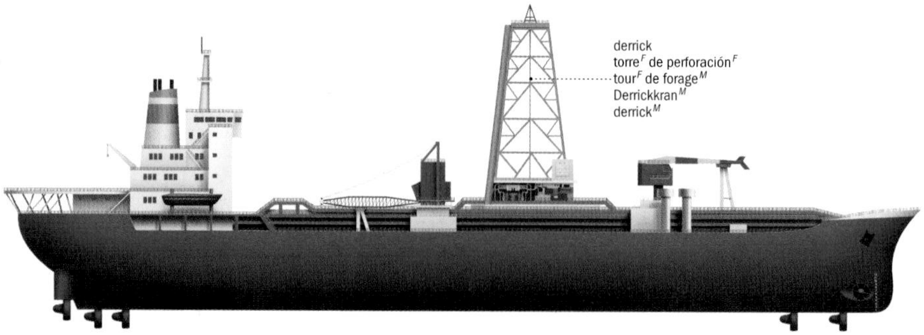

derrick
torre^F de perforación^F
tour^F de forage^M
Derrickkran^M
derrick^M

bulk carrier
buque^M de carga^F
vraquier^M
Frachtschiff^N
nave^F per il trasporto^M delle merci^F

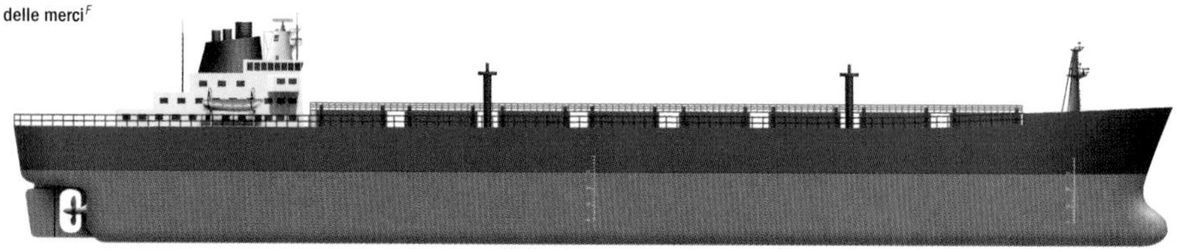

container ship
carguero^M portacontenedores
navire^M porte-conteneurs^M
Containerschiff^N
nave^F portacontainer^M

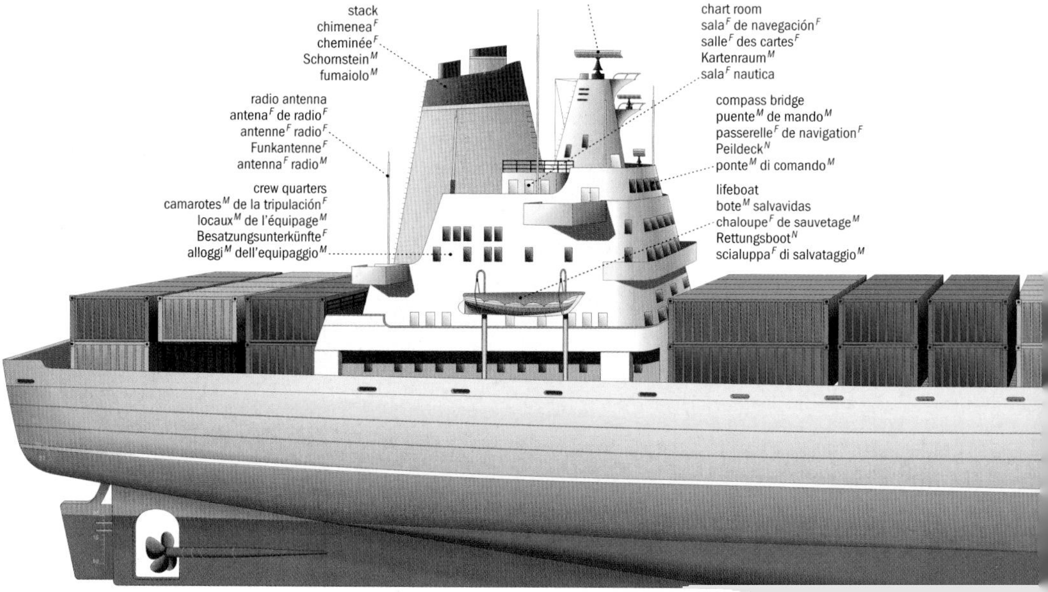

radar
radar^M
radar^M
Radar^N
radar^M

stack
chimenea^F
cheminée^F
Schornstein^M
fumaiolo^M

chart room
sala^F de navegación^F
salle^F des cartes^F
Kartenraum^M
sala^F nautica

radio antenna
antena^F de radio^F
antenne^F radio^F
Funkantenne^F
antenna^F radio^M

compass bridge
puente^M de mando^M
passerelle^F de navigation^F
Peildeck^N
ponte^M di comando^M

crew quarters
camarotes^M de la tripulación^F
locaux^M de l'équipage^M
Besatzungsunterkünfte^F
alloggi^M dell'equipaggio^M

lifeboat
bote^M salvavidas
chaloupe^F de sauvetage^M
Rettungsboot^N
scialuppa^F di salvataggio^M

examples of boats and ships

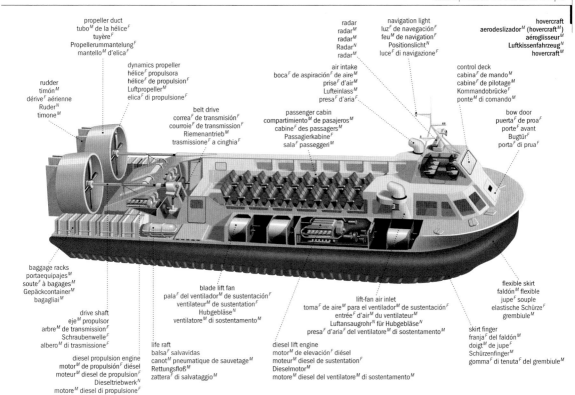

propeller duct
tubo^M de la hélice^F
tuyère^F
Propellerummantelung^F
mantello^M d'elica^F

dynamics propeller
hélice^F propulsora
hélice^F de propulsion^F
Luftpropeller^M
elica^F di propulsione^F

rudder
timón^M
dérive^F aérienne
Ruder^N
timone^M

belt drive
correa^F de transmisión^F
courroie^F de transmission^F
Riemenantrieb^M
trasmissione^F a cinghia^F

radar
radar^M
radar^M
Radar^N
radar^M

navigation light
luz^F de navegación^F
feu^M de navigation^F
Positionslicht^N
luce^F di navigazione^F

hovercraft
aerodeslizador^M (hovercraft^M)
aéroglisseur^M
Luftkissenfahrzeug^N
hovercraft^M

air intake
boca^F de aspiración^F de aire^M
prise^F d'air^M
Lufteinlass^M
presa^F d'aria^F

control deck
cabina^F de mando^M
cabine^F de pilotage^M
Kommandobrücke^F
ponte^M di comando^M

passenger cabin
compartimiento^M de pasajeros^M
cabine^F des passagers^M
Passagierkabine^F
sala^F passeggeri^M

bow door
puerta^F de proa^F
porte^F avant
Bugtür^F
porta^F di prua^F

baggage racks
portaequipajes^M
soute^F à bagages^M
Gepäckcontainer^M
bagagliai^M

blade lift fan
pala^F del ventilador^M de sustentación^F
ventilateur^M de sustentation^F
Hubgebläse^N
ventilatore^M di sostentamento^M

lift-fan air inlet
toma^F de aire^M para el ventilador^M de sustentación^F
entrée^F d'air^M du ventilateur^M
Luftansaugrohr^N für Hubgebläse^N
presa^F d'aria^F del ventilatore^M di sostentamento^M

flexible skirt
faldón^M flexible
jupe^F souple
elastische Schürze^F
grembiule^M

skirt finger
franja^F del faldón^M
doigt^M de jupe^F
Schürzenfinger^M
gomma^F di tenuta^F del grembiule^M

drive shaft
eje^M propulsor
arbre^M de transmission^F
Schraubenwelle^F
albero^M di trasmissione^F

life raft
balsa^F salvavidas
canot^M pneumatique de sauvetage^M
Rettungsfloß^N
zattera^F di salvataggio^M

diesel lift engine
motor^M de elevación^F diésel
moteur^M diesel de sustentation^F
Dieselmotor^M
motore^M diesel del ventilatore^M di sostentamento^M

diesel propulsion engine
motor^M de propulsión^F diésel
moteur^M diesel de propulsion^F
Dieseltriebwerk^M
motore^M diesel di propulsione^F

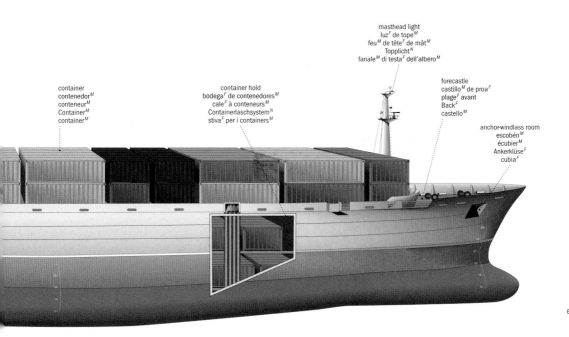

masthead light
luz^F de tope^M
feu^M de tête^F de mât^M
Topplicht^N
fanale^M di testa^F dell'albero^M

container
contenedor^M
conteneur^M
Container^M
container^M

container hold
bodega^F de contenedores^M
cale^F à conteneurs^M
Containerlaschsystem^N
stiva^F per i containers^M

forecastle
castillo^M de proa^F
plage^F avant
Back^M
castello^M

anchor-windlass room
escobén^M
écubier^M
Ankerklüse^F
cubia^F

examples of boats and ships

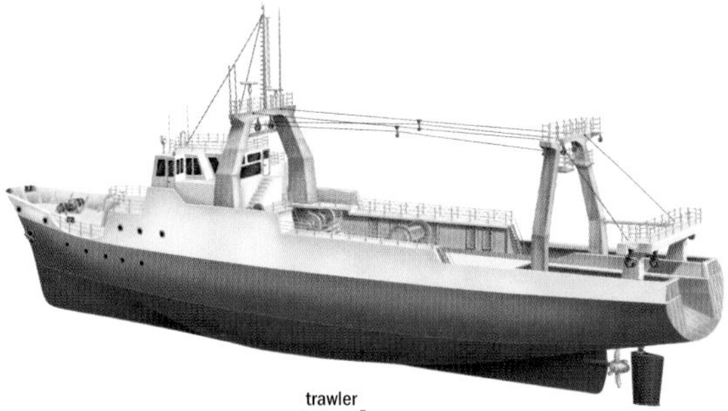

trawler
trainera^F
chalutier^M
Trawler^M
peschereccio^M

wheelhouse
cámara^F del timón^M
timonerie^F
Ruderhaus^N
timoneria^F

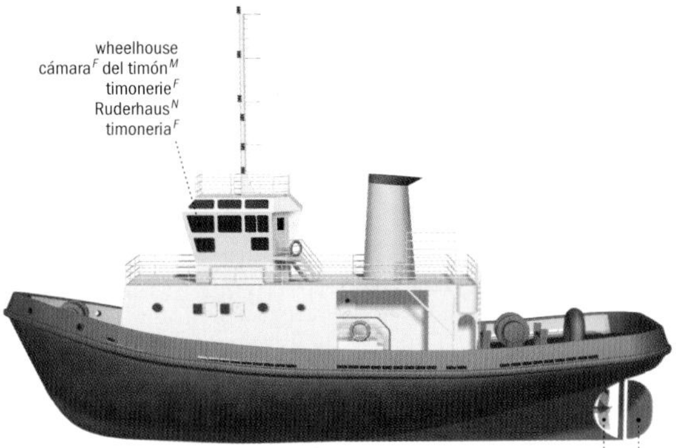

tug
remolcador^M
remorqueur^M
Schlepper^M
rimorchiatore^M

propeller
hélice^F
hélice^F
Schraube^F
elica^F

rudder blade
pala^F de timón^M
safran^M
Ruderblatt^N
pala^F del timone^M

stem
proa^F
étrave^F
Bug^M
prua^F

stem propeller
hélice^F de proa^F
hélice^F d'étrave^F
Bugpropeller^M
elica^F di prua^F

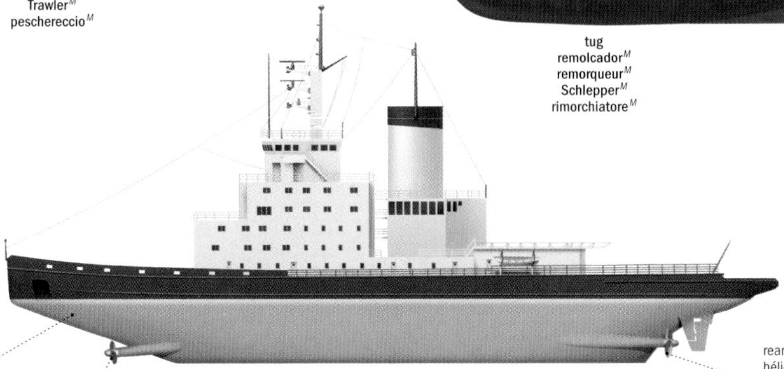

ice breaker
rompehielos^M
brise-glace^M
Eisbrecher^M
rompighiaccio^M

rear propeller
hélice^F posterior
hélice^F arrière
Heckpropeller^M
elica^F posteriore

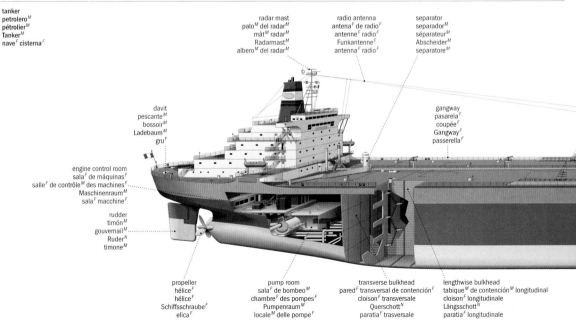

tanker
petrolero^M
pétrolier^M
Tanker^M
nave^F cisterna^F

radar mast
palo^M del radar^M
mât^M radar^M
Radarmast^M
albero^M del radar^M

radio antenna
antena^F de radio^F
antenne^F radio^F
Funkantenne^F
antenna^F radio^F

separator
separador^M
séparateur^M
Abscheider^M
separatore^M

davit
pescante^M
bossoir^M
Ladebaum^M
gru^F

gangway
pasarela^F
coupée^F
Gangway^F
passerella^F

engine control room
sala^F de máquinas^F
salle^F de contrôle^M des machines^F
Maschinenraum^M
sala^F macchine^F

rudder
timón^M
gouvernail^M
Ruder^N
timone^M

propeller
hélice^F
hélice^F
Schiffsschraube^F
elica^F

pump room
sala^F de bombeo^M
chambre^F des pompes^F
Pumpenraum^M
locale^M delle pompe^F

transverse bulkhead
pared^F transversal de contención^F
cloison^F transversale
Querschott^N
paratia^F trasversale

lengthwise bulkhead
tabique^M de contención^M longitudinal
cloison^F longitudinale
Längsschott^N
paratia^F longitudinale

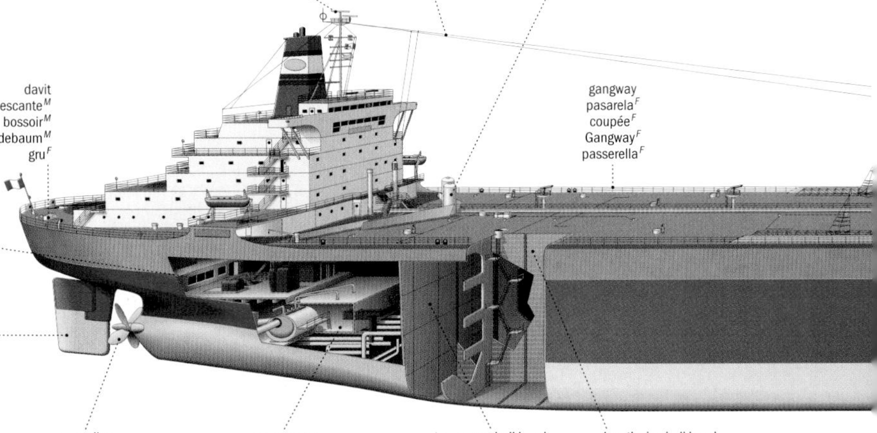

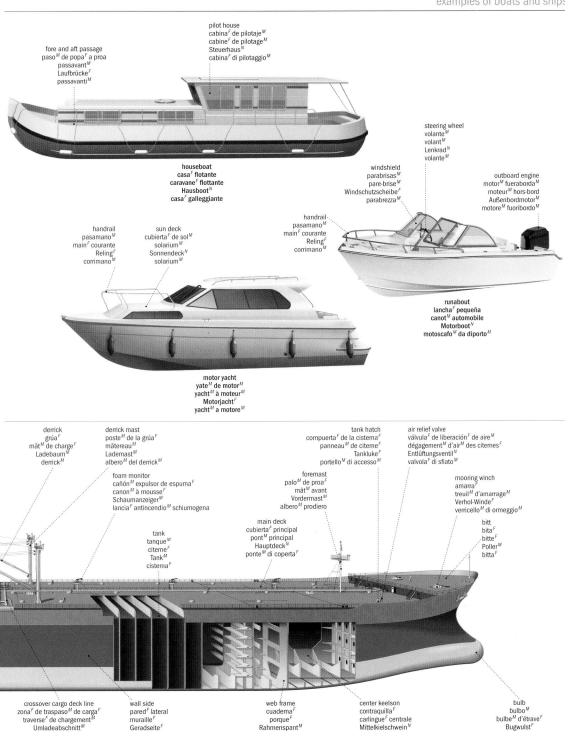

pilot house
cabina^F de pilotaje^M
cabine^F de pilotage^M
Steuerhaus^N
cabina^F di pilotaggio^M

fore and aft passage
paso^M de popa^F a proa
passavant^M
Laufbrücke^F
passavanti^M

steering wheel
volante^M
volant^M
Lenkrad^N
volante^M

windshield
parabrisas^M
pare-brise^M
Windschutzscheibe^F
parabrezza^F

outboard engine
motor^M fueraborda^M
moteur^M hors-bord
Außenbordmotor^M
motore^M fuoribordo^M

houseboat
casa^F flotante
caravane^F flottante
Hausboot^N
casa^F galleggiante

handrail
pasamano^M
main^F courante
Reling^F
corrimano^M

sun deck
cubierta^F de sol^M
solarium^M
Sonnendeck^N
solarium^M

handrail
pasamano^M
main^F courante
Reling^F
corrimano^M

runabout
lancha^F pequeña
canot^M automobile
Motorboot^N
motoscafo^M da diporto^M

motor yacht
yate^M de motor^M
yacht^M à moteur^M
Motorjacht^F
yacht^M a motore^M

derrick
grúa^F
mât^M de charge^F
Ladebaum^M
derrick^M

derrick mast
poste^M de la grúa^F
mâtereau^M
Lademast^M
albero^M del derrick^M

tank hatch
compuerta^F de la cisterna^F
panneau^M de citerne^F
Tankluke^F
portello^M di accesso^M

air relief valve
válvula^F de liberación^F de aire^M
dégagement^M d'air^M des citernes^F
Entlüftungsventil^N
valvola^F di sfiato^M

foam monitor
cañón^M expulsor de espuma^F
canon^M à mousse^F
Schaumanzeiger^M
lancia^F antincendio^M schiumogena

foremast
palo^M de proa^F
mât^M avant
Vordermast^M
albero^M prodiero^M

mooring winch
amarra^F
treuil^M d'amarrage^M
Verhol-Winde^F
verricello^M di ormeggio^M

tank
tanque^M
citerne^F
Tank^M
cisterna^F

main deck
cubierta^F principal
pont^M principal
Hauptdeck^N
ponte^M di coperta^F

bitt
bita^F
bitte^F
Poller^M
bitta^F

crossover cargo deck line
zona^F de traspaso^M de carga^F
traverse^F de chargement^M
Umladeabschnitt^M
tubolatura^F di carico^M trasversale

wall side
pared^F lateral
muraille^F
Geradseite^F
murata^F

web frame
cuaderna^F
porque^F
Rahmenspant^M
ordinata^F rinforzata

center keelson
contraquilla^F
carlingue^F centrale
Mittelkielschwein^N
paramezzale^M centrale

bulb
bulbo^M
bulbe^M d'étrave^F
Bugwulst^F
bulbo^M

examples of boats and ships

ferry
transbordador[M]
transbordeur[M] ; traversier[M]
Fähre[F]
nave[F] traghetto[M]

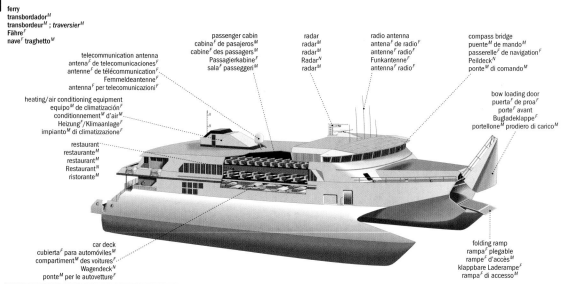

passenger cabin
cabina[F] de pasajeros[M]
cabine[F] des passagers[M]
Passagierkabine[F]
sala[F] passeggeri[M]

radar
radar[M]
radar[M]
Radar[N]
radar[M]

radio antenna
antena[F] de radio[F]
antenne[F] radio[F]
Funkantenne[F]
antenna[F] radio[F]

compass bridge
puente[M] de mando[M]
passerelle[F] de navigation[F]
Peildeck[N]
ponte[M] di comando[M]

telecommunication antenna
antena[F] de telecomunicaciones[F]
antenne[F] de télécommunication[F]
Femmeldeantenne[F]
antenna[F] per telecomunicazioni[F]

heating/air conditioning equipment
equipo[M] de climatización[F]
conditionnement[M] d'air[M]
Heizung[F]/Klimaanlage[F]
impianto[M] di climatizzazione[F]

bow loading door
puerta[F] de proa[F]
porte[F] avant
Bugladeklappe[F]
portellone[M] prodiero di carico[M]

restaurant
restaurante[M]
restaurant[M]
Restaurant[N]
ristorante[M]

car deck
cubierta[F] para automóviles[M]
compartiment[M] des voitures[F]
Wagendeck[N]
ponte[M] per le autovetture[F]

folding ramp
rampa[F] plegable
rampe[F] d'accès[M]
klappbare Laderampe[F]
rampa[F] di accesso[M]

passenger liner
buque[M] trasatlántico
paquebot[M]
Passagierdampfer[M]
transatlantico[M]

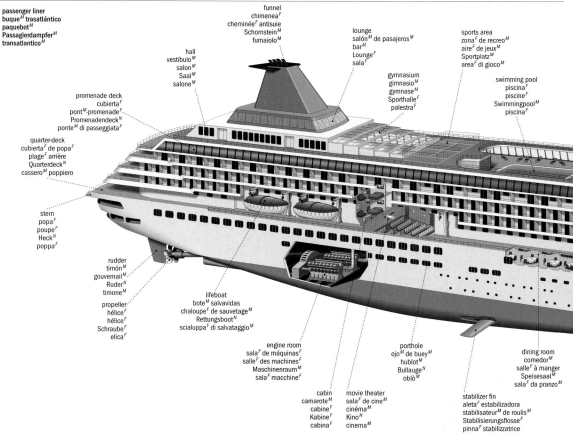

funnel
chimenea[F]
cheminée[F] antisuie
Schornstein[M]
fumaiolo[M]

lounge
salón[M] de pasajeros[M]
bar[M]
Lounge[F]
sala[F]

sports area
zona[F] de recreo[M]
aire[F] de jeux[M]
Sportplatz[M]
area[F] di gioco[M]

hall
vestíbulo[M]
salon[M]
Saal[M]
salone[M]

gymnasium
gimnasio[M]
gymnase[M]
Sporthalle[F]
palestra[F]

swimming pool
piscina[F]
piscine[F]
Swimmingpool[M]
piscina[F]

promenade deck
cubierta[F]
pont[M]-promenade[F]
Promenadendeck[N]
ponte[M] di passeggiata[F]

quarter-deck
cubierta[F] de popa[F]
plage[F] arrière
Quarterdeck[N]
cassero[M] poppiero

stern
popa[F]
poupe[F]
Heck[N]
poppa[F]

rudder
timón[M]
gouvernail[M]
Ruder[N]
timone[M]

propeller
hélice[F]
hélice[F]
Schraube[F]
elica[F]

lifeboat
bote[M] salvavidas
chaloupe[F] de sauvetage[M]
Rettungsboot[N]
scialuppa[F] di salvataggio[M]

engine room
sala[F] de máquinas[F]
salle[F] des machines[F]
Maschinenraum[M]
sala[F] macchine[F]

cabin
camarote[M]
cabine[F]
Kabine[F]
cabina[F]

movie theater
sala[F] de cine[M]
cinéma[M]
Kino[N]
cinema[M]

porthole
ojo[M] de buey[M]
hublot[M]
Bullauge[N]
oblò[M]

dining room
comedor[M]
salle[F] à manger
Speisesaal[M]
sala[F] da pranzo[M]

stabilizer fin
aleta[F] estabilizadora
stabilisateur[M] de roulis[M]
Stabilisierungsflosse[F]
pinna[F] stabilizzatrice

TRANSPORT AND MACHINERY

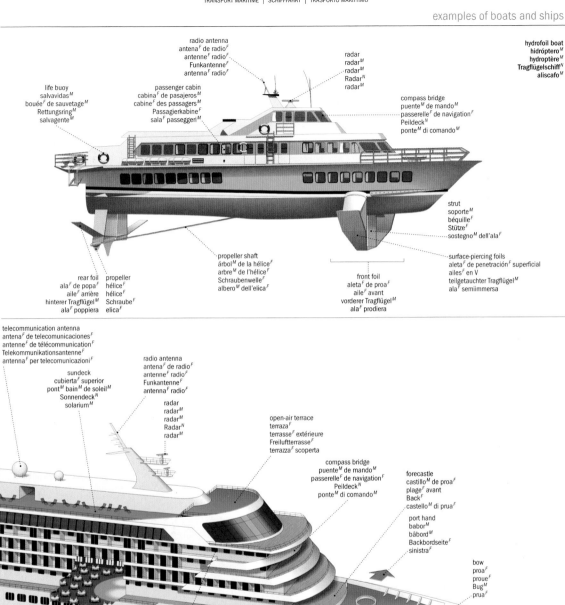

hydrofoil boat
hidróptero[M]
hydroptère[M]
Tragflügelschiff[N]
aliscafo[M]

radio antenna
antena[F] de radio[F]
antenne[F] radio[F]
Funkantenne[F]
antenna[F] radio[F]

radar
radar[M]
radar[M]
Radar[N]
radar[M]

passenger cabin
cabina[F] de pasajeros[M]
cabine[F] des passagers[M]
Passagierkabine[F]
sala[F] passeggeri

compass bridge
puente[M] de mando[M]
passerelle[F] de navigation[F]
Peildeck[N]
ponte[M] di comando[M]

life buoy
salvavidas[M]
bouée[F] de sauvetage[M]
Rettungsring[M]
salvagente[M]

strut
soporte[M]
béquille[F]
Stütze[F]
sostegno[M] dell'ala[F]

propeller shaft
árbol[M] de la hélice[F]
arbre[M] de l'hélice[F]
Schraubenwelle[F]
albero[M] dell'elica[F]

surface-piercing foils
aleta[F] de penetración[F] superficial
ailes[F] en V
teilgetauchter Tragflügel[M]
ala[F] semiimmersa

front foil
aleta[F] de proa[F]
aile[F] avant
vorderer Tragflügel[M]
ala[F] prodiera

rear foil
ala[F] de popa[F]
aile[F] arrière
hinterer Tragflügel[M]
ala[F] poppiera

propeller
hélice[F]
hélice[F]
Schraube[F]
elica[F]

telecommunication antenna
antena[F] de telecomunicaciones[F]
antenne[F] de télécommunication[F]
Telekommunikationsantenne[F]
antenna[F] per telecomunicazioni[F]

radio antenna
antena[F] de radio[F]
antenne[F] radio[F]
Funkantenne[F]
antenna[F] radio[F]

sundeck
cubierta[F] superior
pont[M] bain[M] de soleil[M]
Sonnendeck[N]
solarium[M]

radar
radar[M]
radar[M]
Radar[N]
radar[M]

open-air terrace
terraza[F]
terrasse[F] extérieure
Freilufterrasse[F]
terrazza[F] scoperta

compass bridge
puente[M] de mando[M]
passerelle[F] de navigation[F]
Peildeck[N]
ponte[M] di comando[M]

forecastle
castillo[M] de proa[F]
plage[F] avant
Back[F]
castello[M] di prua[F]

port hand
babor[M]
bâbord[M]
Backbordseite[F]
sinistra[F]

bow
proa[F]
proue[F]
Bug[M]
prua[F]

anchor-windlass room
escobén[M]
écubier[M]
Ankerklüse[F]
cubia[F]

stem bulb
bulbo[M]
bulbe[F] d'étrave[F]
Bugwulst[M]
bulbo[M]

ballroom
salón[M] de baile[M]
salle[F] de bal[M]
Tanzsaal[M]
sala[F] da ballo[M]

captain's quarters
camarote[M] del capitán[M]
appartement[M] du commandant[M]
Offizierskabine[F]
alloggio[M] del comandante[M]

bow thruster
propulsor[M] de proa[F]
propulseur[M] d'étrave[F]
Bugstrahler[M]
propulsore[M] di prua[F]

starboard hand
estribor[M]
tribord[M]
Steuerbordseite[F]
dritta[F]

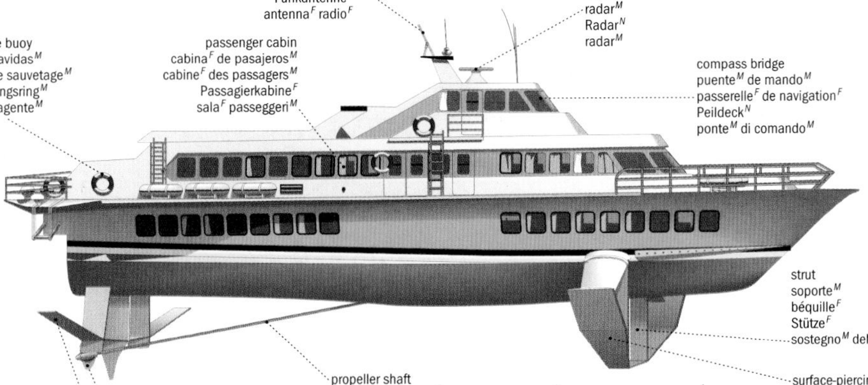

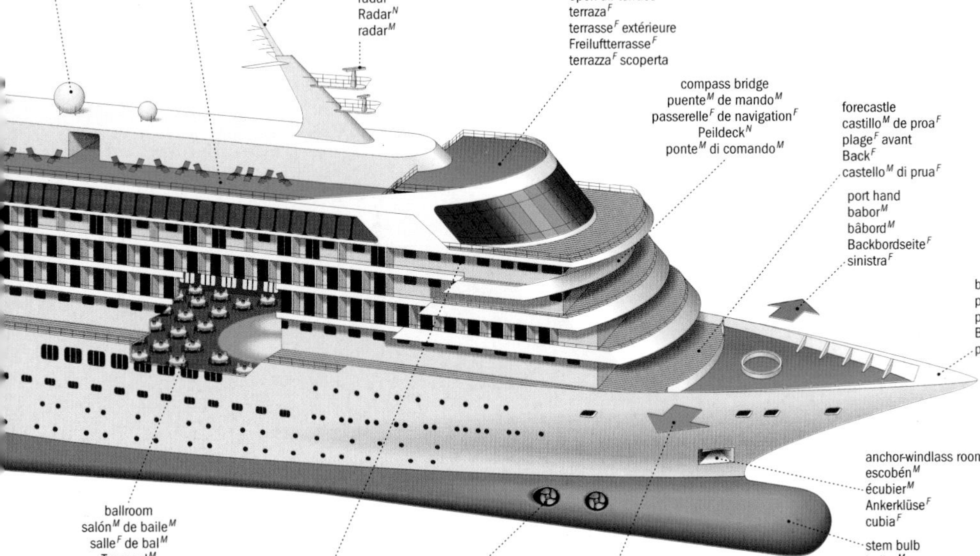

anchor

ancla^F | ancre^F | Anker^M | ancora^F

ship's anchor
ancla^F de buque^M
ancre^F de marine^F
Schiffsanker^M
ancora^F della nave^F

arm
brazo^M
bras^M
Arm^M
braccio^M

crown
cruz^F
diamant^M
Kreuz^N
diamante^M

throat
unión^F de caña^F y brazos^M
collet^M
Hals^M
collo^M

gravity band
anillo^M de gravedad^F
centre^M de gravité^F
Schäkelband^N
fascia^F di gravità^F

shank
caña^F
verge^F
Schaft^M
fuso^M

ring
arganeo^M
organeau^M
Ring^M
cicala^F

palm
mapa^F
patte^F
Flunke^F
marra^F

fluke
uña^F
oreille^F
Ankerhand^F
orecchio^M

hoisting ring
argolla^F de izar
organeau^M de hissage^M
Heißring^M
anello^M di sollevamento^M

bill
pico^M de loro^M
bec^M
Ankerspitze^F
unghia^F

stock
cepo^M
jas^M
Stock^M
ceppo^M

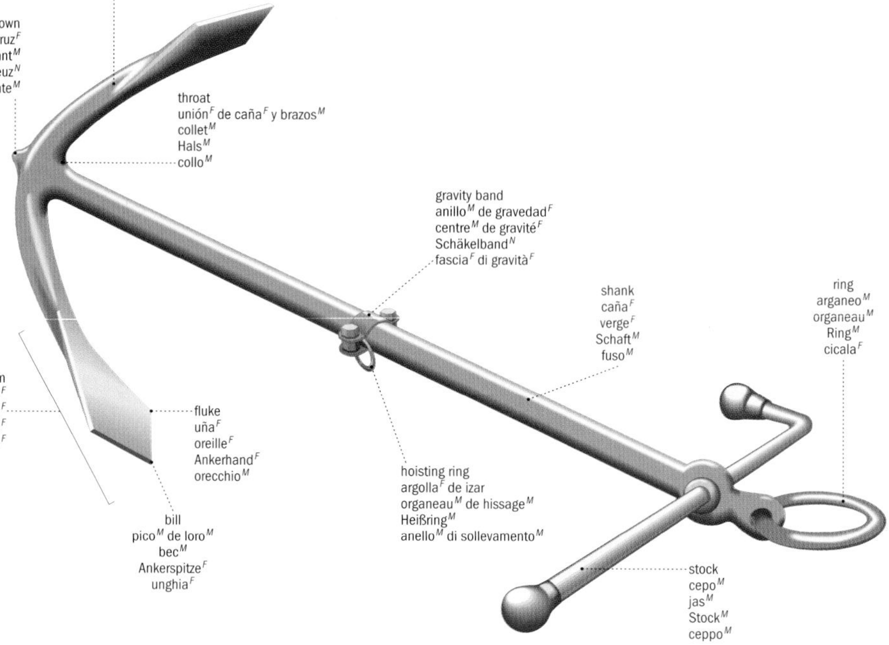

examples of anchors
ejemplos^M de anclas^F
exemples^M d'ancres^F
Beispiele^N für Anker^M
esempi^M di ancore^F

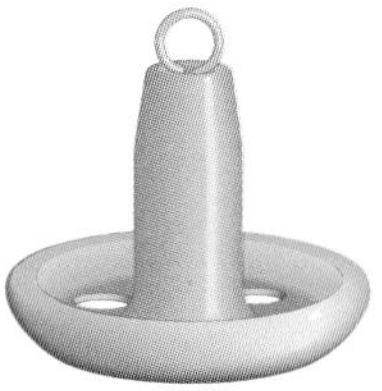

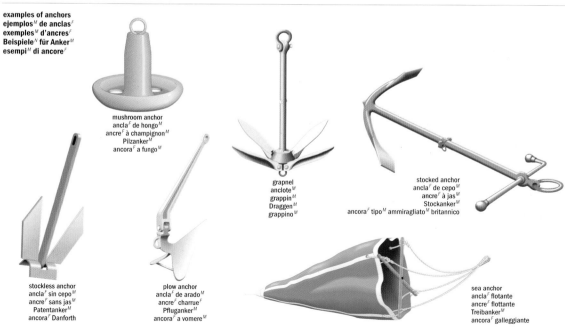

mushroom anchor
ancla^F de hongo^M
ancre^F à champignon^M
Pilzanker^M
ancora^F a fungo^M

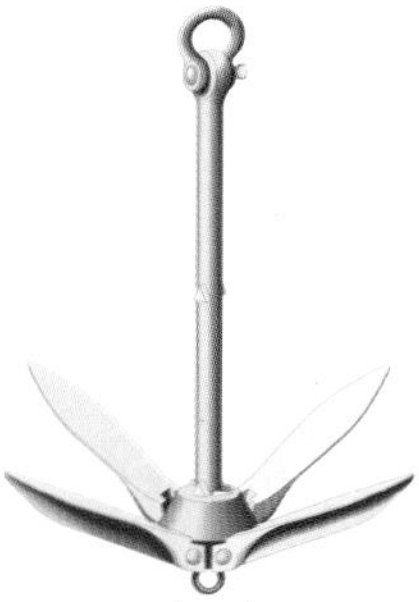

grapnel
anclote^M
grappin^M
Draggen^M
grappino^M

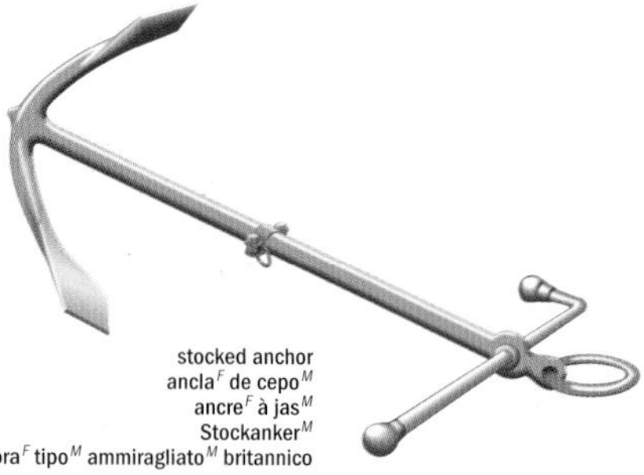

stocked anchor
ancla^F de cepo^M
ancre^F à jas^M
Stockanker^M
ancora^F tipo^M ammiragliato^M britannico

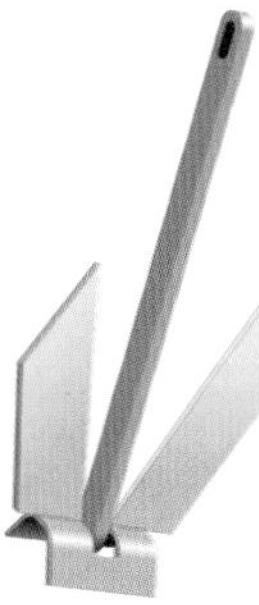

stockless anchor
ancla^F sin cepo^M
ancre^F sans jas^M
Patentanker^M
ancora^F Danforth

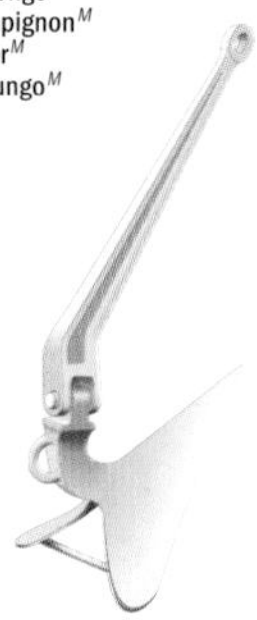

plow anchor
ancla^F de arado^M
ancre^F charrue^F
Pfluganker^M
ancora^F a vomere^M

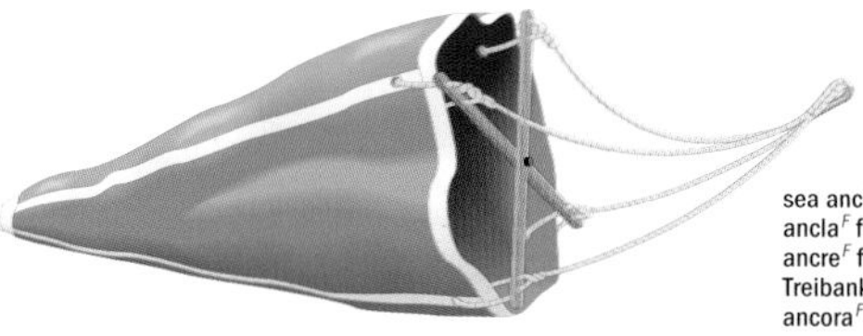

sea anchor
ancla^F flotante
ancre^F flottante
Treibanker^M
ancora^F galleggiante

life-saving equipment

equipo^M salvavidas | équipement^M de sauvetage^M | Rettungsgeräte^N | equipaggiamento^M di salvataggio^M

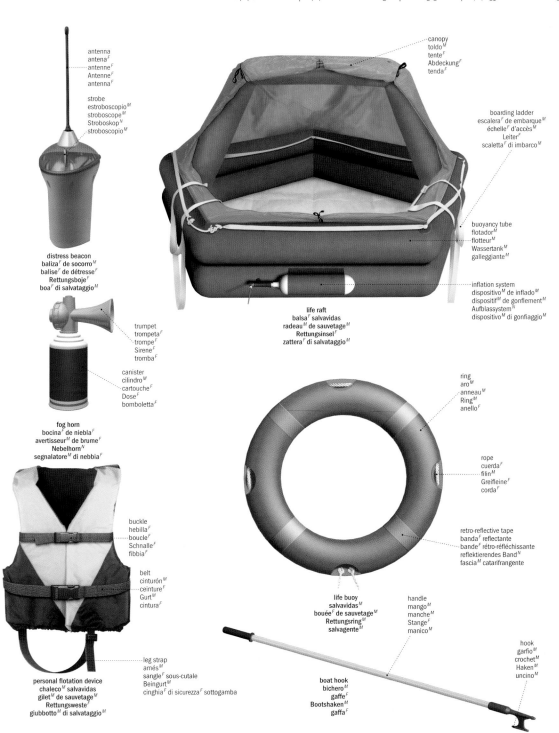

antenna
antena^F
antenne^F
Antenne^F
antenna^F

strobe
estroboscopio^M
stroboscope^M
Stroboskop^N
stroboscopio^M

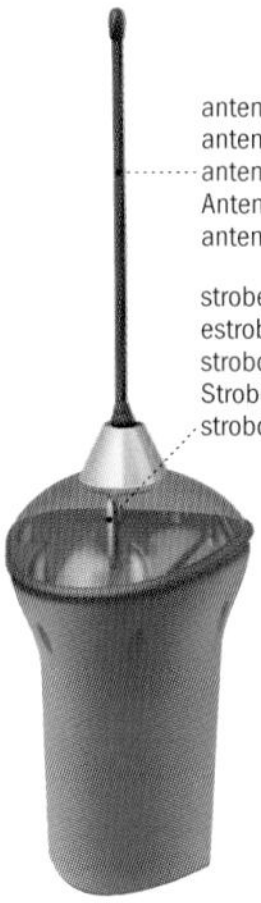

distress beacon
baliza^F de socorro^M
balise^F de détresse^F
Rettungsboje^F
boa^F di salvataggio^M

trumpet
trompeta^F
trompe^F
Sirene^F
tromba^F

canister
cilindro^M
cartouche^F
Dose^F
bomboletta^F

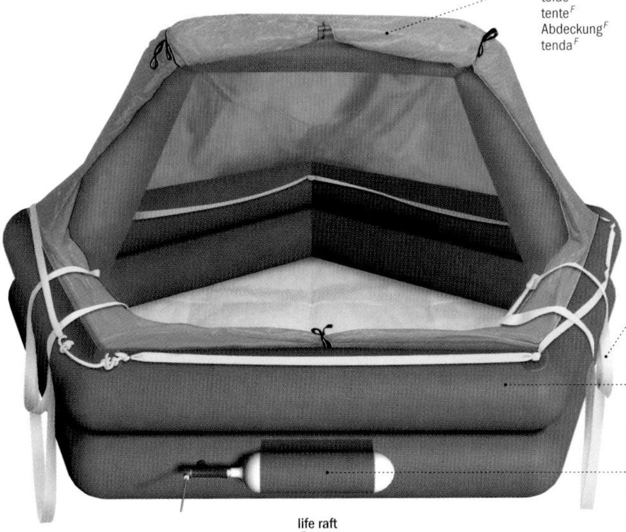

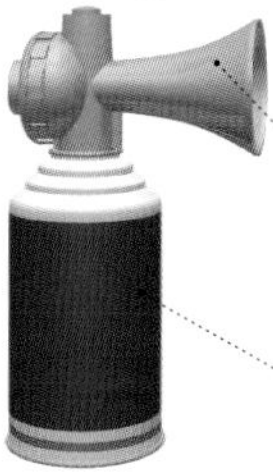

fog horn
bocina^F de niebla^F
avertisseur^M de brume^F
Nebelhorn^N
segnalatore^M di nebbia^F

buckle
hebilla^F
boucle^F
Schnalle^F
fibbia^F

belt
cinturón^M
ceinture^F
Gurt^M
cintura^F

leg strap
arnés^M
sangle^F sous-cutale
Beingurt^M
cinghia^F di sicurezza^F sottogamba

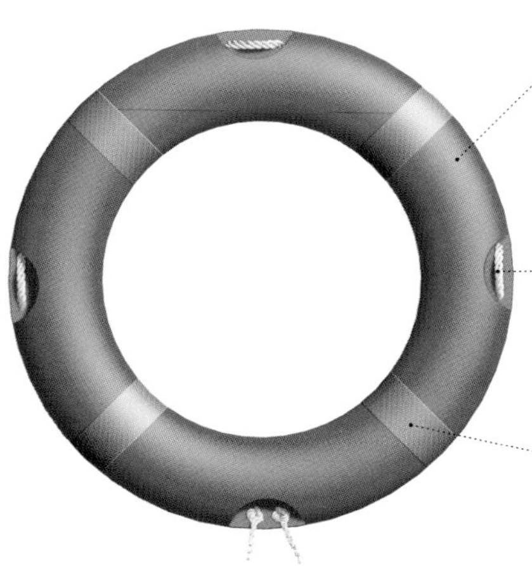

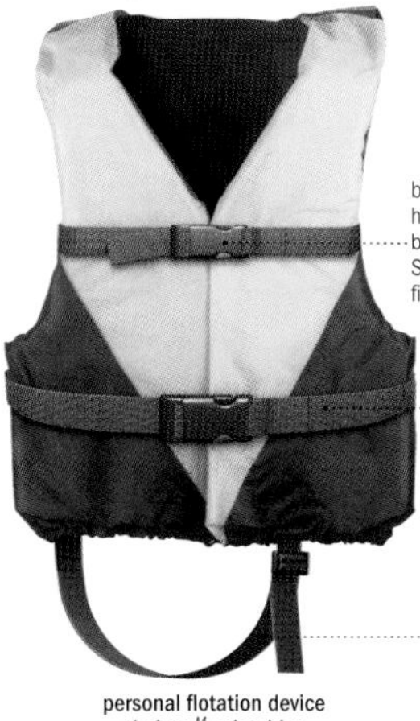

personal flotation device
chaleco^M salvavidas
gilet^M de sauvetage^M
Rettungsweste^F
giubbotto^M di salvataggio^M

canopy
toldo^M
tente^F
Abdeckung^F
tenda^F

boarding ladder
escalera^F de embarque^M
échelle^F d'accès^M
Leiter^F
scaletta^F di imbarco^M

buoyancy tube
flotador^M
flotteur^M
Wassertank^M
galleggiante^M

inflation system
dispositivo^M de inflado^M
dispositif^M de gonflement^M
Aufblassystem^N
dispositivo^M di gonfiaggio^M

life raft
balsa^F salvavidas
radeau^M de sauvetage^M
Rettungsinsel^F
zattera^F di salvataggio^M

ring
aro^M
anneau^M
Ring^M
anello^F

rope
cuerda^F
filin^M
Greifleine^F
corda^F

retro-reflective tape
banda^F reflectante
bande^F rétro-réfléchissante
reflektierendes Band^N
fascia^M catarifrangente

life buoy
salvavidas^M
bouée^F de sauvetage^M
Rettungsring^M
salvagente^M

handle
mango^M
manche^M
Stange^F
manico^M

hook
garfio^M
crochet^M
Haken^M
uncino^M

boat hook
bichero^M
gaffe^F
Bootshaken^M
gaffa^F

TRANSPORT AND MACHINERY

611

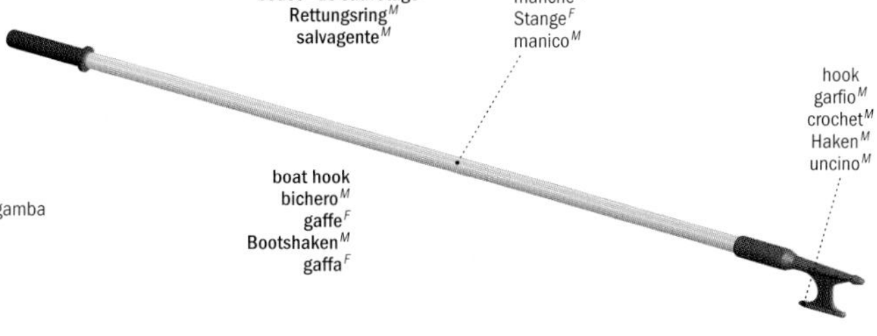

navigation devices

instrumentos^M de navegación^F | appareils^M de navigation^F | Navigationsinstrumente^N | strumenti^M per la navigazione^F

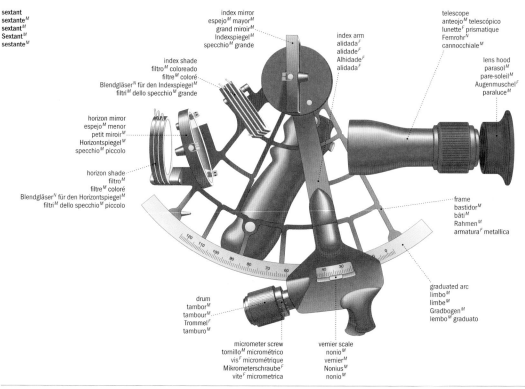

sextant
sextante^M
sextant^M
Sextant^M
sestante^M

index mirror
espejo^M mayor^M
grand miroir^M
Indexspiegel^M
specchio^M grande

index arm
alidada^F
alidade^F
Alhidade^F
alidada^F

telescope
anteojo^M telescópico
lunette^F prismatique
Fernrohr^N
cannocchiale^M

index shade
filtro^M coloreado
filtre^M coloré
Blendgläser^N für den Indexspiegel^M
filtri^M dello specchio^M grande

lens hood
parasol^M
pare-soleil^M
Augenmuschel^F
paraluce^M

horizon mirror
espejo^M menor
petit miroir^M
Horizontspiegel^M
specchio^M piccolo

horizon shade
filtro^M
filtre^M coloré
Blendgläser^N für den Horizontspiegel^M
filtri^M dello specchio^M piccolo

frame
bastidor^M
bâti^M
Rahmen^M
armatura^F metallica

drum
tambor^M
tambour^M
Trommel^F
tamburo^M

graduated arc
limbo^M
limbe^M
Gradbogen^M
lembo^M graduato

micrometer screw
tornillo^M micrométrico
vis^F micrométrique
Mikrometerschraube^F
vite^F micrometrica

vernier scale
nonio^M
vernier^M
Nonius^M
nonio^M

liquid compass
brújula^F líquida
compas^M magnétique liquide
Flüssigkeitskompass^M
bussola^F a liquido^M

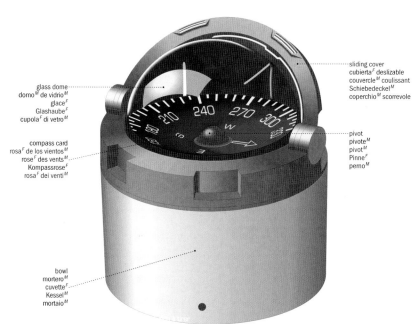

glass dome
domo^M de vidrio^M
glace^F
Glashaube^F
cupola^F di vetro^M

sliding cover
cubierta^F deslizable
couvercle^M coulissant
Schiebedeckel^M
coperchio^M scorrevole

compass card
rosa^F de los vientos^M
rose^F des vents^M
Kompassrose^F
rosa^F dei venti^M

pivot
pivote^M
pivot^M
Pinne^F
perno^M

bowl
mortero^M
cuvette^F
Kessel^M
mortaio^M

TRANSPORT AND MACHINERY

echo sounder
sonar^M
sondeur^M à éclats^M
Echolot^N
ecoscandaglio^M

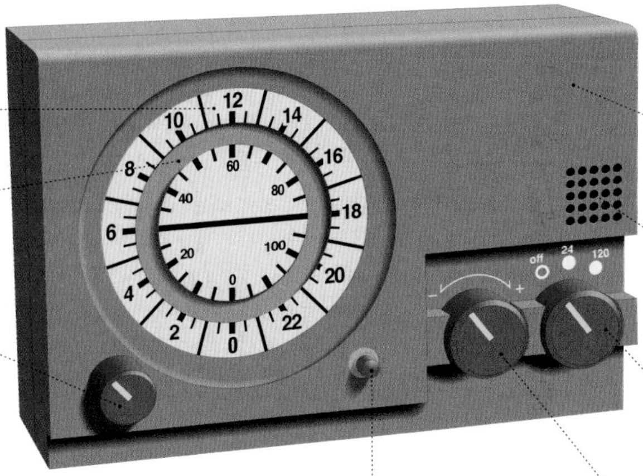

depth scale
escala^F de profundidad
échelle^F de profondeur^F
Tiefenskala^F in m
scala^F di profondità^F in metri^M

housing
caja^F
boîtier^M
Gehäuse^N
contenitore^M

dial-type display
indicador^M del cuadrante^M
écran^M
Anzeigeskala^F
quadrante^M indicatore^M

sound alarm
alarma^F sonora
alarme^F sonore
Lautsprecher^M
allarme^M acustico

alarm threshold setting
control^M del nivel^M de alarma^F
réglage^M du seuil^M d'alarme^F
Alarmschwellenwert-Einstellung^F
regolazione^F della soglia^F di allarme^M

on-off switch
interruptor^M
interrupteur^M
Ein-/Ausschalter^M
interruttore^M

echo sounder probe
sonda^F
sonde^F
Schwinger^M
sonda^F dell'ecoscandaglio^M

alarm threshold display button
botón^M de visualización^F del nivel^M de alarma^F
visualisation^F du seuil^M d'alarme^F
Knopf^M für Alarmschwellenwert-Anzeige^F
pulsante^M per la visualizzazione^F della soglia^F di allarme^M

gain control
control^M de ganancia^F
contrôle^M du gain^M
Verstärkerregler^M
regolatore^M di amplificazione^F

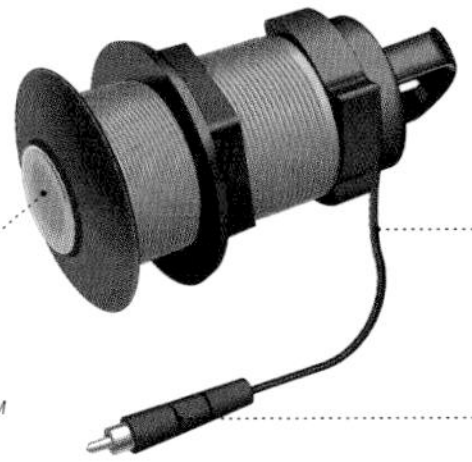

transmission cable
cable^M de transmisión^F
câble^M de transmission^F
Übertragungskabel^N
cavo^M di trasmissione^F

transducer
transductor^M
émetteur^M/récepteur^M
Messwandler^M
trasduttore^M

plug
clavija^F
fiche^F
Stecker^M
spinotto^M

satellite navigation system
sistema^M de navegación^F por satélite^M
traceur^M de route^F
Satelliten^M-Navigationssystem^N
sistema^M di navigazione^F satellitare

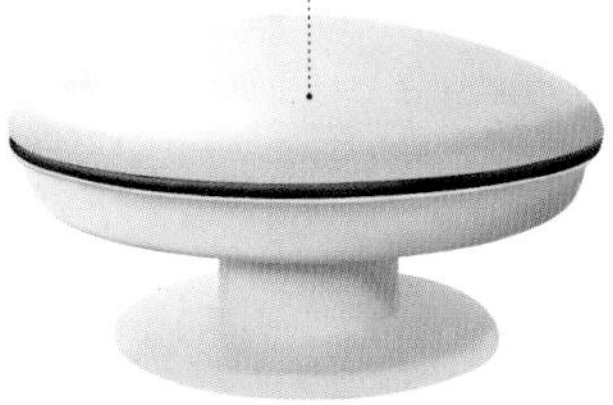

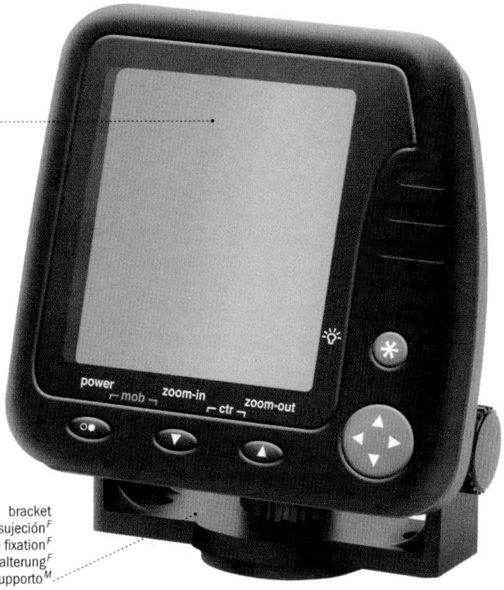

display
pantalla^F
écran^M
Bildschirm^M
display^M

GPS receiver-antenna
antena^F-receptor^M GPS
antenne^F-récepteur^M GPS
GPS-Empfangsantenne^F
antenna^F ricevente GPS

bracket
brida^F de sujeción^F
étrier^M de fixation^F
schwenkbare Halterung^F
base^F di supporto^M

maritime signals

señales^F marítimas | signalisation^F maritime | Seezeichen^N | segnali^M marittimi

lighthouse lantern
linterna^F del faro^M
lanterne^F de phare^M
Leuchtturmlampe^F
lanterna^F del faro^M

cupola
cúpula^F
coupole^F
Kuppel^F
cupola^F

lantern
linterna^F
lanterne^F
Laterne^F
lanterna^F

lantern pane
vidriera^F
vitrage^M
Fenster^N des Scheinwerferraumes^M
pannelli^M di vetro^M

gallery
balcón^M
balcon^M de veille^F
Galerie^F
ballatoio^M

tower
torre^F
tour^F
Turm^M
torre^F

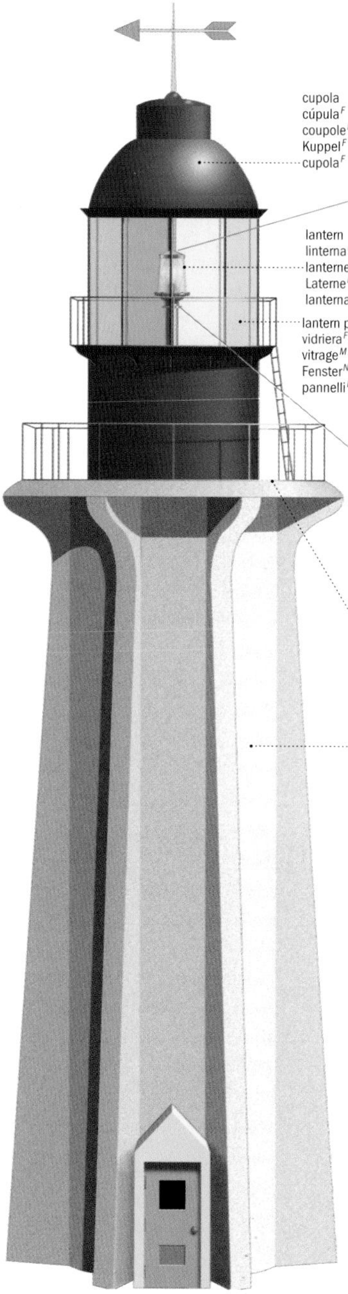

lighthouse
faro^M marítimo
phare^M
Leuchtturm^M
faro^M

ventilation hood
capucha^F de ventilación^F
capuchon^M de ventilation^F
Lüfterkopf^M
cappa^F di ventilazione^F

incandescent lamp
lámpara^F incandescente
lampe^F à incandescence^F
Glühlampe^F
lampada^F ad incandescenza^F

dioptric ring
anillo^M dióptrico
anneau^M dioptrique
dioptrischer Ring^M
anello^M diottrico

lamp base
base^F de la lámpara^F
culot^M
Boden^M
base^F della lampada^F

housing
caja^F
boitier^M
Gehäuse^N
alloggiamento^M

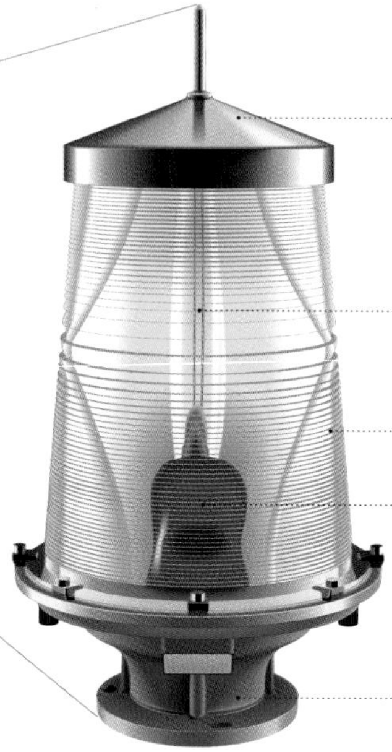

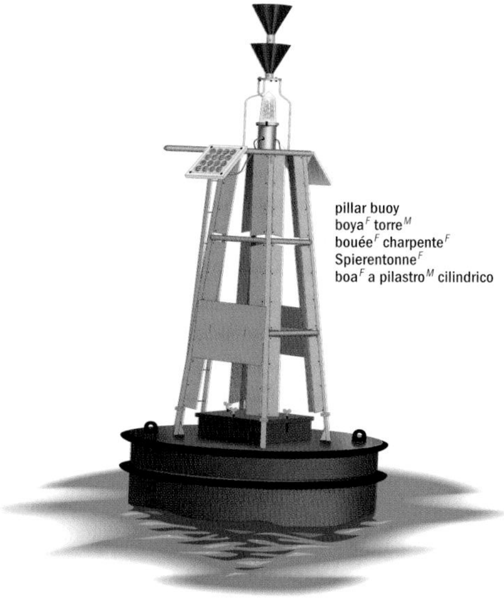

pillar buoy
boya^F torre^M
bouée^F charpente^F
Spierentonne^F
boa^F a pilastro^M cilindrico

TRANSPORT AND MACHINERY

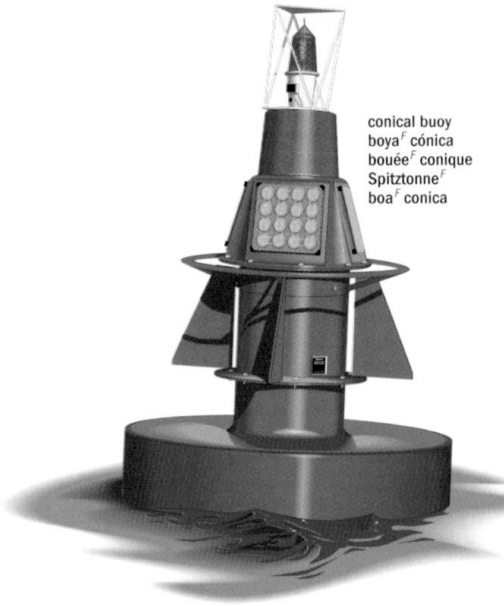

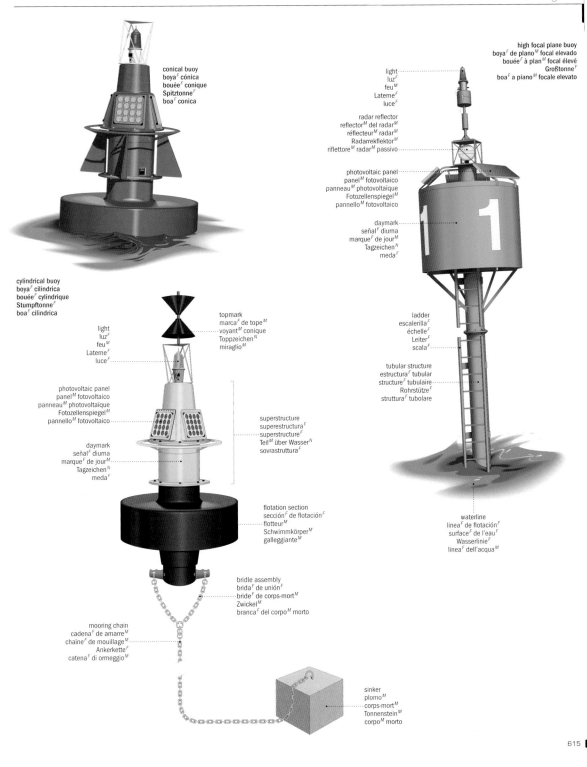

conical buoy
boya^F cónica
bouée^F conique
Spitztonne^F
boa^F conica

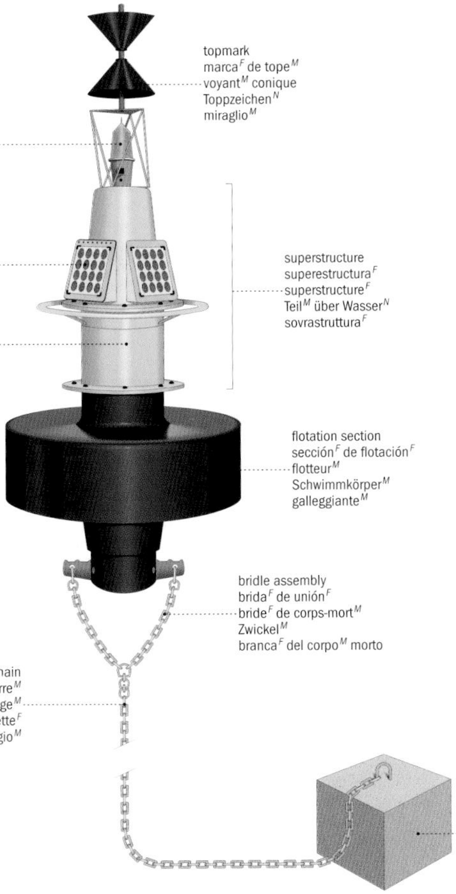

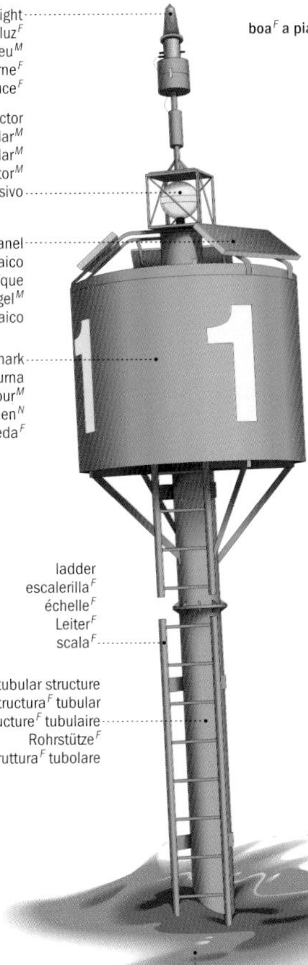

high focal plane buoy
boya^F de plano^M focal elevado
bouée^F à plan^M focal élevé
Großtonne^F
boa^F a piano^M focale elevato

light
luz^F
feu^M
Laterne^F
luce^F

radar reflector
reflector^M del radar^M
réflecteur^M radar^M
Radarreflektor^M
riflettore^M radar^M passivo

photovoltaic panel
panel^M fotovoltaico
panneau^M photovoltaïque
Fotozellenspiegel^M
pannello^M fotovoltaico

daymark
señal^F diurna
marque^F de jour^M
Tagzeichen^N
meda^F

ladder
escalerilla^F
échelle^F
Leiter^F
scala^F

tubular structure
estructura^F tubular
structure^F tubulaire
Rohrstütze^F
struttura^F tubolare

cylindrical buoy
boya^F cilindrica
bouée^F cylindrique
Stumpftonne^F
boa^F cilindrica

light
luz^F
feu^M
Laterne^F
luce^F

topmark
marca^F de tope^M
voyant^M conique
Toppzeichen^N
miraglio^M

photovoltaic panel
panel^M fotovoltaico
panneau^M photovoltaïque
Fotozellenspiegel^M
pannello^M fotovoltaico

superstructure
superestructura^F
superstructure^F
Teil^M über Wasser^N
sovrastruttura^F

daymark
señal^F diurna
marque^F de jour^M
Tagzeichen^N
meda^F

flotation section
sección^F de flotación^F
flotteur^M
Schwimmkörper^M
galleggiante^M

bridle assembly
brida^F de unión^F
bride^F de corps-mort^M
Zwickel^M
branca^F del corpo^M morto

mooring chain
cadena^F de amarre^M
chaîne^F de mouillage^M
Ankerkette^F
catena^F di ormeggio^M

waterline
línea^F de flotación^F
surface^F de l'eau^F
Wasserlinie^F
linea^F dell'acqua^M

sinker
plomo^M
corps-mort^M
Tonnenstein^M
corpo^M morto

maritime buoyage system

sistema^M de boyas^F maritimas | système^M de balisage^M maritime | Betonnungssystem^N | sistema^M di segnalamento^M marittimo per mezzo di boe^F

cardinal marks
señales^F de los puntos^M cardinales
marques^F cardinales
Kardinalseezeichen^N
segnalamento^M dei punti^M cardinali

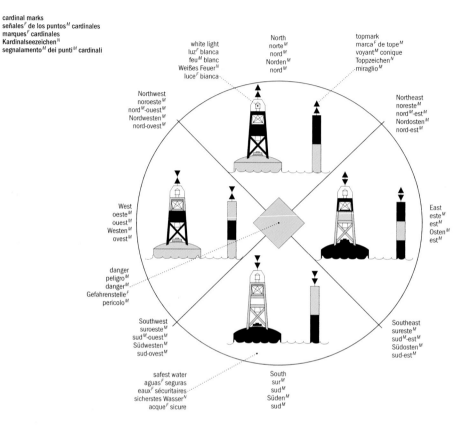

white light
luz^F blanca
feu^M blanc
Weißes Feuer^N
luce^F bianca

North
norte^M
nord^M
Norden^M
nord^M

topmark
marca^F de tope^M
voyant^M conique
Toppzeichen^N
miraglio^M

Northwest
noroeste^M
nord^M-ouest^M
Nordwesten^M
nord-ovest^M

Northeast
noreste^M
nord^M-est^M
Nordosten^M
nord-est^M

West
oeste^M
ouest^M
Westen^M
ovest^M

East
este^M
est^M
Osten^M
est^M

danger
peligro^M
danger^M
Gefahrenstelle^F
pericolo^M

Southwest
suroeste^M
sud^M-ouest^M
Südwesten^M
sud-ovest^M

Southeast
sureste^M
sud^M-est^M
Südosten^M
sud-est^M

safest water
aguas^F seguras
eaux^F sécuritaires
sicherstes Wasser^N
acque^F sicure

South
sur^M
sud^M
Süden^M
sud^M

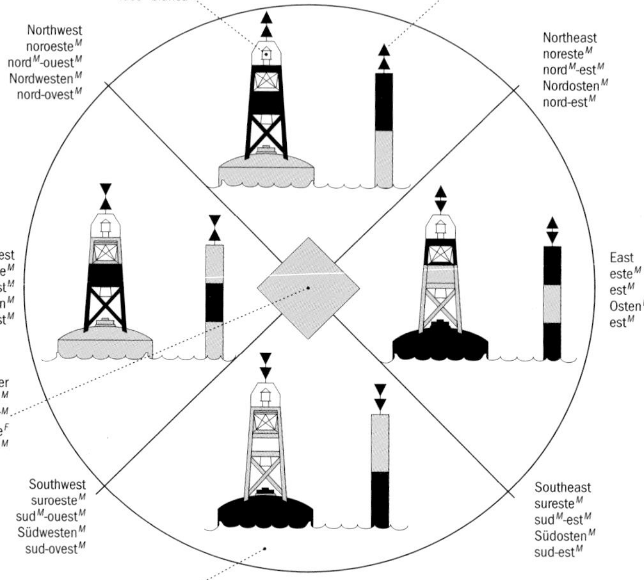

buoyage regions
regiones^F de boyas^F
régions^F de balisage^M
Betonnte Fahrwasser^N
regioni^F con segnalamento^M mediante boe^F

port hand
babor^M
bâbord^M
Backbordseite^F
sinistra^F

starboard hand
estribor^M
tribord^M
Steuerbordseite^F
dritta^F

TRANSPORT AND MACHINERY

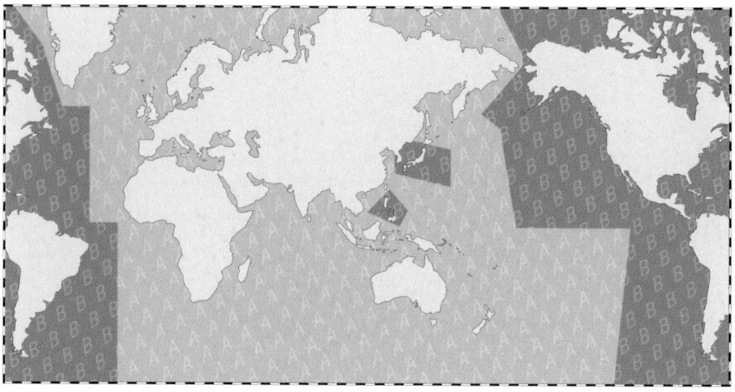

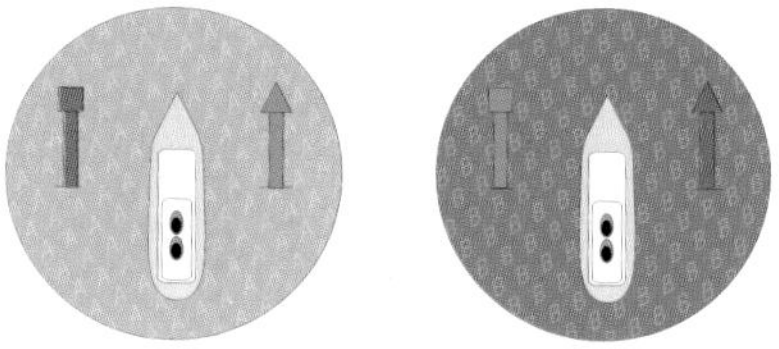

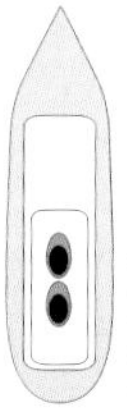

light
luz ^{F}
lumière ^{F}
Lichterscheinung ^{F}
luce ^{F}

darkness
oscuridad ^{F}
obscurité ^{F}
Verdunkelung ^{F}
oscurità ^{F}

rhythm of marks by night
ritmo ^{M} de las señales ^{F} nocturnas
rythme ^{M} des marques ^{F} de nuit ^{F}
Leuchtfeuerkennung ^{F}
ritmo ^{M} dei segnalamenti ^{M} notturni

period
periodo ^{M}
période ^{F}
Taktkennung ^{F}
periodo ^{M}

period
periodo ^{M}
période ^{F}
Taktkennung ^{F}
periodo ^{M}

period
periodo ^{M}
période ^{F}
Taktkennung ^{F}
periodo ^{M}

interval
intervalo ^{M}
intervalle ^{M}
Unterbrechung ^{F}
intervallo ^{M}

interval
intervalo ^{M}
intervalle ^{M}
Unterbrechung ^{F}
intervallo ^{M}

daymarks (region B)
señales ^{F} diurnas (región ^{F} B)
marques ^{F} de jour ^{M} (région ^{F} B)
Tagzeichen ^{N} (Region ^{F} B)
mede ^{F} (regione ^{F} B)

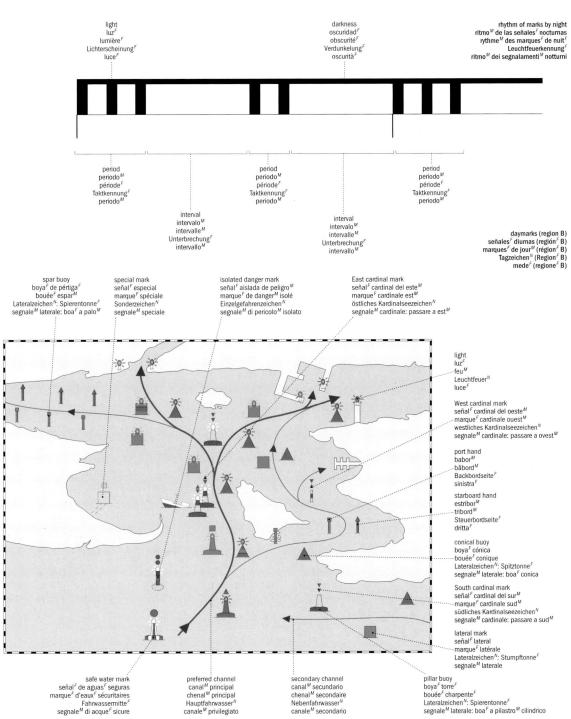

spar buoy
boya ^{F} de pértiga ^{F}
bouée ^{F} espar ^{M}
Lateralzeichen ^{N}: Spierentonne ^{F}
segnale ^{M} laterale: boa ^{F} a palo ^{M}

special mark
señal ^{F} especial
marque ^{F} spéciale
Sonderzeichen ^{N}
segnale ^{M} speciale

isolated danger mark
señal ^{F} aislada de peligro ^{M}
marque ^{F} de danger ^{M} isolé
Einzelgefahrenzeichen ^{N}
segnale ^{M} di pericolo ^{N} isolato

East cardinal mark
señal ^{F} cardinal del este ^{M}
marque ^{F} cardinale est ^{M}
östliches Kardinalseezeichen ^{N}
segnale ^{M} cardinale: passare a est ^{M}

light
luz ^{F}
feu ^{M}
Leuchtfeuer ^{N}
luce ^{F}

West cardinal mark
señal ^{F} cardinal del oeste ^{M}
marque ^{F} cardinale ouest ^{M}
westliches Kardinalseezeichen ^{N}
segnale ^{M} cardinale: passare a ovest ^{M}

port hand
babor ^{M}
bâbord ^{M}
Backbordseite ^{F}
sinistra ^{F}

starboard hand
estribor ^{M}
tribord ^{M}
Steuerbordseite ^{F}
dritta ^{F}

conical buoy
boya ^{F} cónica
bouée ^{F} conique
Lateralzeichen ^{N}: Spitztonne ^{F}
segnale ^{M} laterale: boa ^{F} conica

South cardinal mark
señal ^{F} cardinal del sur ^{M}
marque ^{F} cardinale sud ^{M}
südliches Kardinalseezeichen ^{N}
segnale ^{M} cardinale: passare a sud ^{M}

lateral mark
señal ^{F} lateral
marque ^{F} latérale
Lateralzeichen ^{N}: Stumpftonne ^{F}
segnale ^{M} laterale

safe water mark
señal ^{F} de aguas ^{F} seguras
marque ^{F} d'eaux ^{F} sécuritaires
Fahrwassermitte ^{F}
segnale ^{M} di acque ^{F} sicure

preferred channel
canal ^{M} principal
chenal ^{M} principal
Hauptfahrwasser ^{N}
canale ^{M} privilegiato

secondary channel
canal ^{M} secundario
chenal ^{M} secondaire
Nebenfahrwasser ^{N}
canale ^{M} secondario

pillar buoy
boya ^{F} torre ^{F}
bouée ^{F} charpente ^{F}
Lateralzeichen ^{N}: Spierentonne ^{F}
segnale ^{M} laterale: boa ^{F} a pilastro ^{M} cilindrico

TRANSPORT AND MACHINERY

airport

aeropuerto^M | aéroport^M | Flughafen^M | aeroporto^M

high-speed exit taxiway
salida^F de la pista^F de alta velocidad^F
sortie^F de piste^F à grande vitesse^F
Schnellabrollbahn^F
bretella^F di uscita^F della pista^F ad alta velocità^F

control tower cab
cabina^F de la torre^F de control^M
vigie^F
Kontrollraum^M
cabina^F della torre^F di controllo^M

control tower
torre^F de control^M
tour^F de contrôle^M
Kontrolltower^M
torre^F di controllo^M

access road
carretera^F de acceso^M
route^F d'accès^M
Zufahrtsstraße^F
strada^F di accesso^M

taxiway
pista^F de rodaje^M
voie^F de circulation^F
Rollbahn^F
pista^F di rullaggio^M

by-pass taxiway
pista^F de enlace^M
bretelle^F
Überholrollbahn^F
pista^F di accesso^M

taxiway
pista^F de rodaje^M
voie^F de circulation^F
Rollbahn^F
pista^F di rullaggio^M

apron
pista^F de estacionamiento^M
aire^F de trafic^M
Vorfeld^N
piazzale^M

service road
ruta^F de servicio^M
voie^F de service^M
Versorgungsstraße^M
strada^F di servizio^M

apron
pista^F de estacionamiento^M
aire^F de manœuvre^F
Vorfeld^N
piazzale^M

passenger terminal
terminal^F de pasajeros^M
aérogare^F de passagers^M
Passagierterminal^M
terminal^M dei passeggeri^M

maintenance hangar
hangar^M de mantenimiento^M
hangar^M
Flugzeugwartungshalle^F
aviorimessa^F

parking area
parque^M de estacionamiento^M
aire^F de stationnement^M
Abstellplatz^M
area^F di parcheggio^M

telescopic corridor
pasarela^F telescópico
passerelle^F télescopique
ausziehbare Fluggastbrücke^F
corridoio^M telescopico

service area
zona^F de servicio^M
aire^F de service^M
Versorgungsbereich^M
area^F di servizio^M

boarding walkway
túnel^M de embarque^M
quai^M d'embarquement^M
Fluggastbrücke^F
passerella^F di imbarco^M

taxiway line
línea^F de pista^F
marques^F de circulation^F
Rollbahnmarkierung^F
linea^F di rullaggio^M

radial passenger-loading area
terminal^F satélite de pasajeros^M
aérogare^F satellite^M
radiale Einsteigestation^F
terminal^M satellite^M dei passeggeri^M

TRANSPORT AND MACHINERY

airport

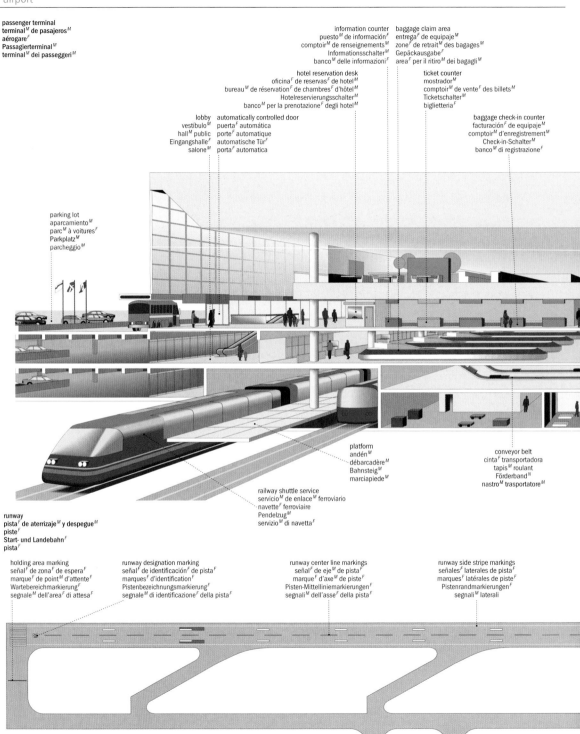

passenger terminal
terminal^M de pasajeros^M
aérogare^F
Passagierterminal^M
terminal^M dei passeggeri^M

information counter
puesto^M de información^F
comptoir^M de renseignements^M
Informationsschalter^M
banco^M delle informazioni^F

baggage claim area
entrega^F de equipaje^M
zone^F de retrait^M des bagages^M
Gepäckausgabe^F
area^F per il ritiro^M dei bagagli^M

hotel reservation desk
oficina^F de reservas^F de hotel^M
bureau^M de réservation^F de chambres^F d'hôtel^M
Hotelreservierungsschalter^M
banco^M per la prenotazione^F degli hotel^M

ticket counter
mostrador^M
comptoir^M de vente^F des billets^M
Ticketschalter^M
biglietteria^F

lobby
vestíbulo^M
hall^M public
Eingangshalle^F
salone^M

automatically controlled door
puerta^F automática
porte^F automatique
automatische Tür^F
porta^F automatica

baggage check-in counter
facturación^F de equipaje^M
comptoir^M d'enregistrement^M
Check-in-Schalter^M
banco^M di registrazione^F

parking lot
aparcamiento^M
parc^M à voitures^F
Parkplatz^M
parcheggio^M

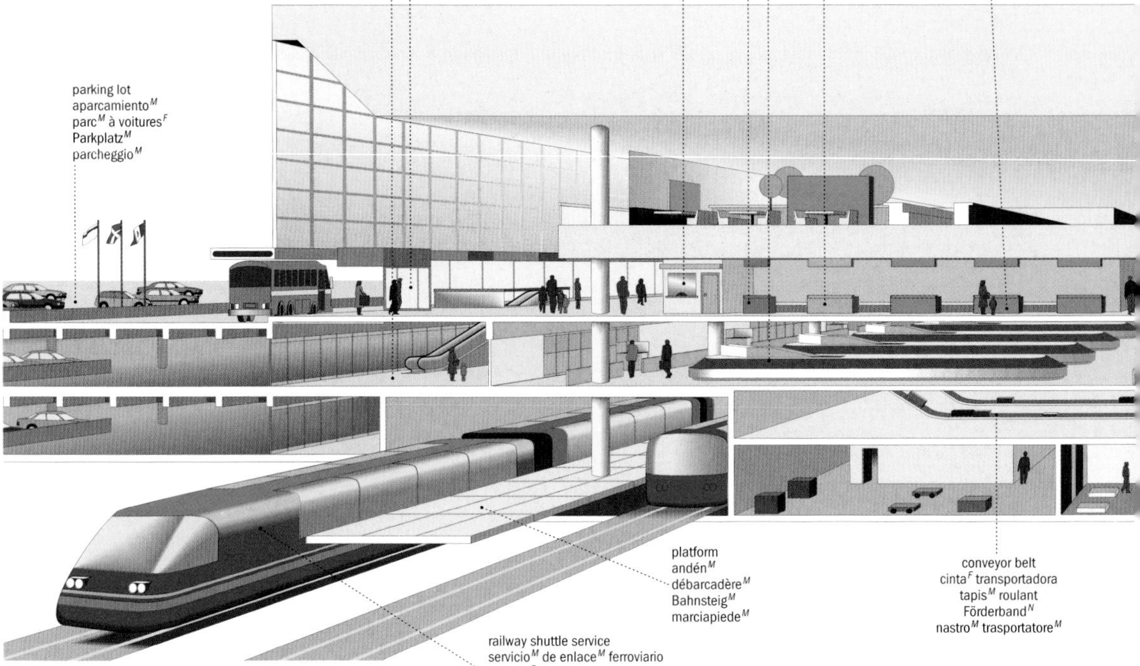

platform
andén^M
débarcadère^M
Bahnsteig^M
marciapiede^M

conveyor belt
cinta^F transportadora
tapis^M roulant
Förderband^N
nastro^M trasportatore^M

railway shuttle service
servicio^M de enlace^M ferroviario
navette^F ferroviaire
Pendelzug^M
servizio^M di navetta^F

runway
pista^F de aterrizaje^M y despegue^M
piste^F
Start- und Landebahn^F
pista^F

holding area marking
señal^F de zona^F de espera^F
marque^F de point^M d'attente^F
Wartebereichmarkierung^F
segnale^M dell'area^F di attesa^F

runway designation marking
señal^F de identificación^F de pista^F
marques^F d'identification^F
Pistenbezeichnungsmarkierung^F
segnale^M di identificazione^F della pista^F

runway center line markings
señal^F de eje^M de pista^F
marque^F d'axe^M de piste^F
Pisten-Mittellliniemarkierungen^F
segnali^M dell'asse^F della pista^F

runway side stripe markings
señales^F laterales de pista^F
marques^F latérales de piste^F
Pistenrandmarkierungen^F
segnali^M laterali

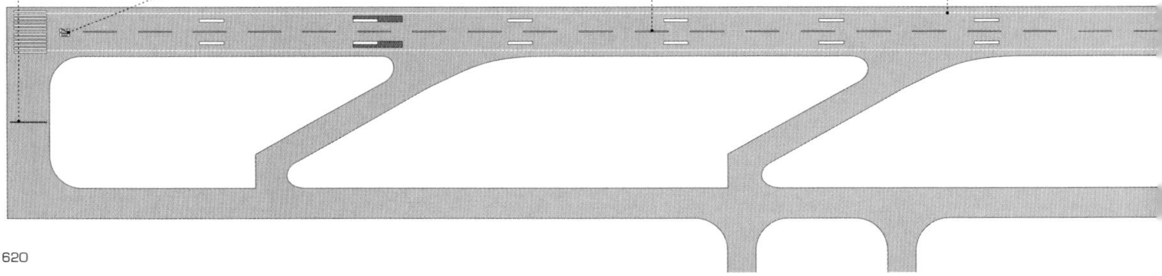

security check
control^M de seguridad^F
contrôle^M de sécurité^F
Sicherheitskontrolle^F
controllo^M di sicurezza^F

duty-free shop
tienda^F libre de impuestos^M
boutique^F hors taxe^F
Duty-free-Shop^M
duty free^M

observation deck
mirador^M
terrasse^F
Besucherterrasse^F
terrazza^F

flight information board
tablero^M de llegadas^F y salidas^F
tableau^M d'affichage^M des vols^M
Fluginformationsanzeige^F
tabellone^M degli arrivi^M e delle partenze^F

freight expedition
expedición^F de carga^F
expédition^F du fret^M
Frachtversand^M
spedizione^F merci^F

passport control
control^M de pasaportes^M
contrôle^M des passeports^M
Passkontrolle^F
controllo^M dei passaporti^M

boarding room
sala^F de espera^F de embarque^M
salle^F d'embarquement^M
Abflugwartehalle^F
sala^F di imbarco^M

passenger transfer vehicle
transbordador^M
transbordeur^M
Passagiertransferfahrzeug^N
navetta^F per il trasbordo^M dei passeggeri^M

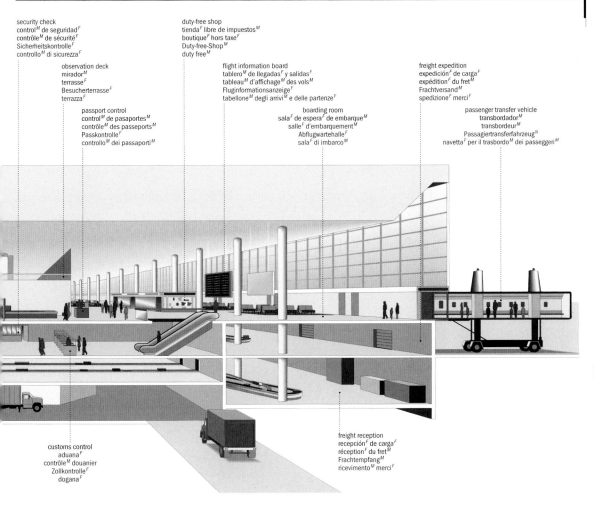

customs control
aduana^F
contrôle^M douanier
Zollkontrolle^F
dogana^F

freight reception
recepción^F de carga^F
réception^F du fret^M
Frachtempfang^M
ricevimento^M merci^F

exit taxiway
salida^F de la pista^F
sortie^F de piste^F
Abrollbahn^F
bretella^F di uscita^F

runway touchdown zone marking
señal^F de zona^F de contacto^M de pista^F
marque^F d'aire^F de prise^F de contact^M
Aufsetzzonenmarkierungen^F
segnale^M di zona^F di contatto^M

runway threshold markings
señales^F de límite^M de la pista^F
marques^F de seuil^M de piste^F
Schwellenmarkierungen^F
segnali^M della soglia^F della pista^F

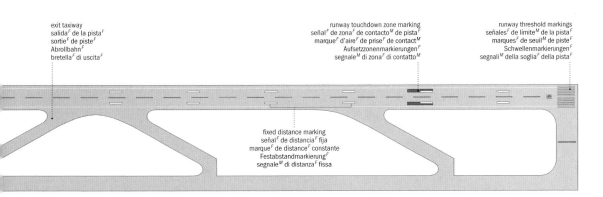

fixed distance marking
señal^F de distancia^F fija
marque^F de distance^F constante
Festabstandmarkierung^F
segnale^M di distanza^F fissa

airport

ground airport equipment
equipo^M **de tierra**^{F}
équipements^M **aéroportuaires**
Bodenausrüstung^F
attrezzature^F **di terra**^{F}

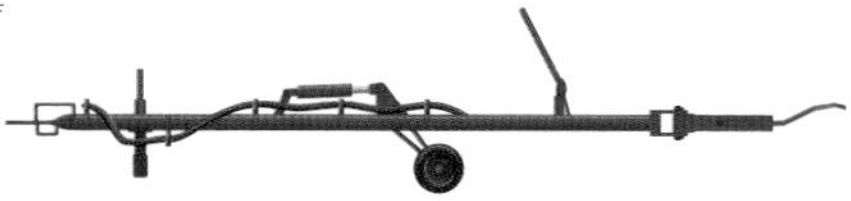

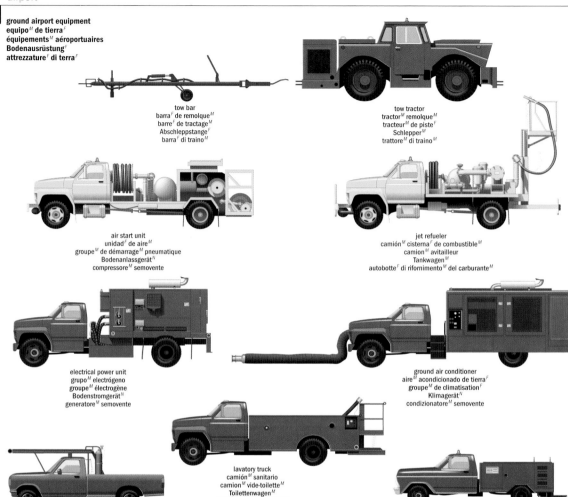

tow bar
barra^F de remolque^M
barre^F de tractage^M
Abschleppstange^F
barra^F di traino^M

tow tractor
tractor^M remolque^M
tracteur^M de piste^F
Schlepper^M
trattore^M di traino^M

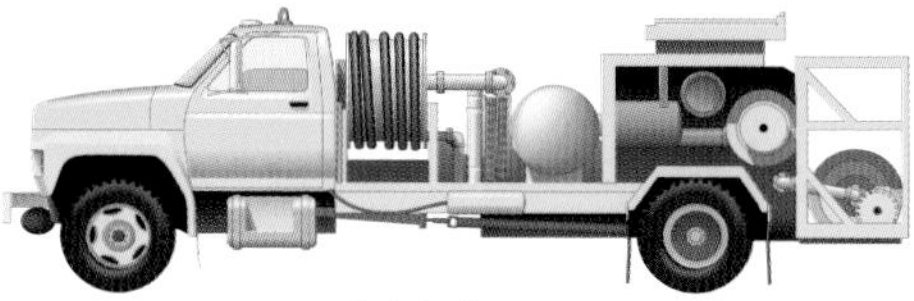

air start unit
unidad^F de aire^M
groupe^M de démarrage^M pneumatique
Bodenanlassgerät^N
compressore^M semovente

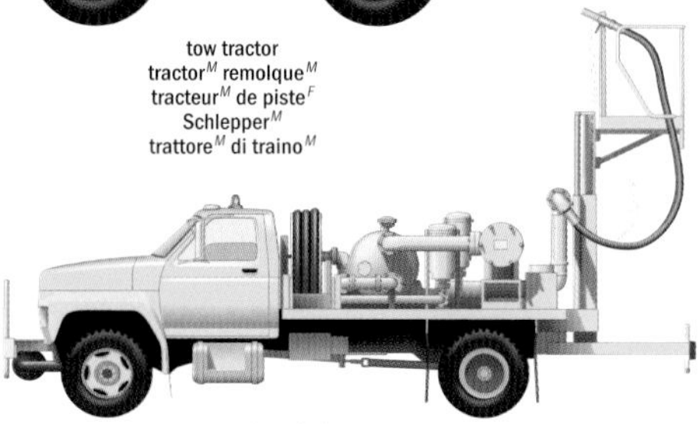

jet refueler
camión^M cisterna^F de combustible^M
camion^M avitailleur
Tankwagen^M
autobotte^F di rifornimento^M del carburante^M

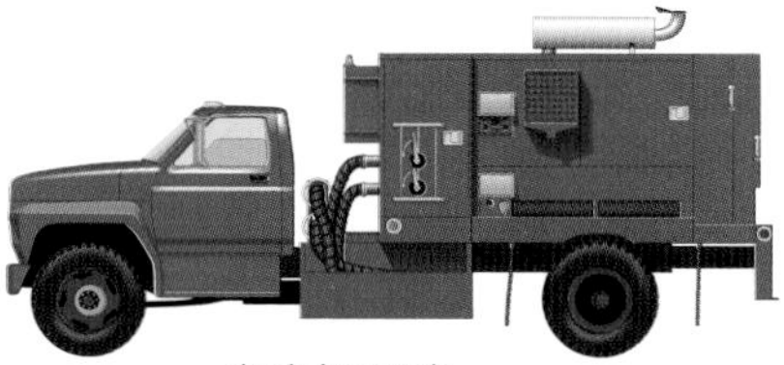

electrical power unit
grupo^M electrógeno
groupe^M électrogène
Bodenstromgerät^N
generatore^M semovente

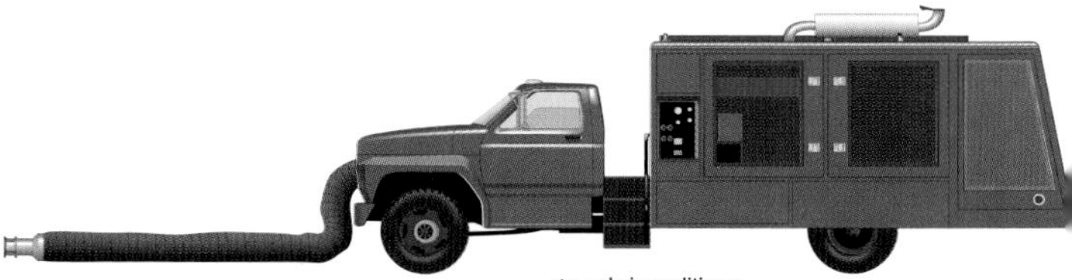

ground air conditioner
aire^M acondicionado de tierra^F
groupe^M de climatisation^F
Klimagerät^N
condizionatore^M semovente

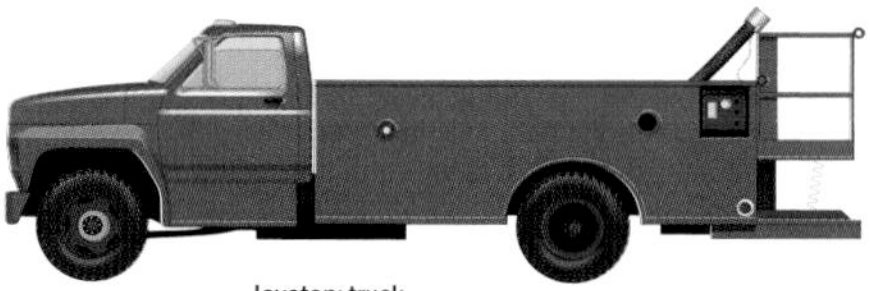

aircraft maintenance truck
camioneta^F de mantenimiento^M de aviones^M
véhicule^M de service^M technique
Wartungsfahrzeug^N
automezzo^M per l'assistenza^F tecnica

lavatory truck
camión^M sanitario
camion^M vide-toilette^M
Toilettenwagen^M
botte^F igienica semovente

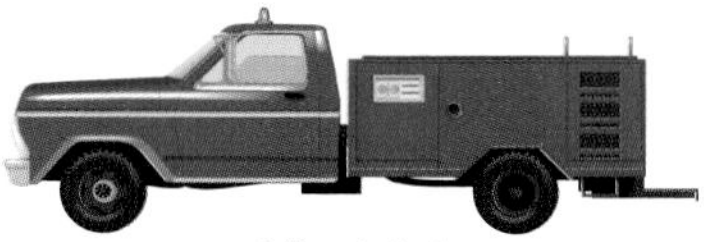

potable water truck
camión^M cisterna^F de agua^F potable
camion^M-citerne^F d'eau^F potable
Frischwasserwagen^M
autobotte^F per il rifornimento^M dell'acqua^F potabile

wheel chock
calzo^M de la rueda^F
cale^F
Bremsklotz^M
tacco^M

boom truck
camioneta^F con canastilla^F telescópica
nacelle^F élévatrice
Tankwagen^M mit beweglichem Ausleger^M
automezzo^M con braccio^M mobile

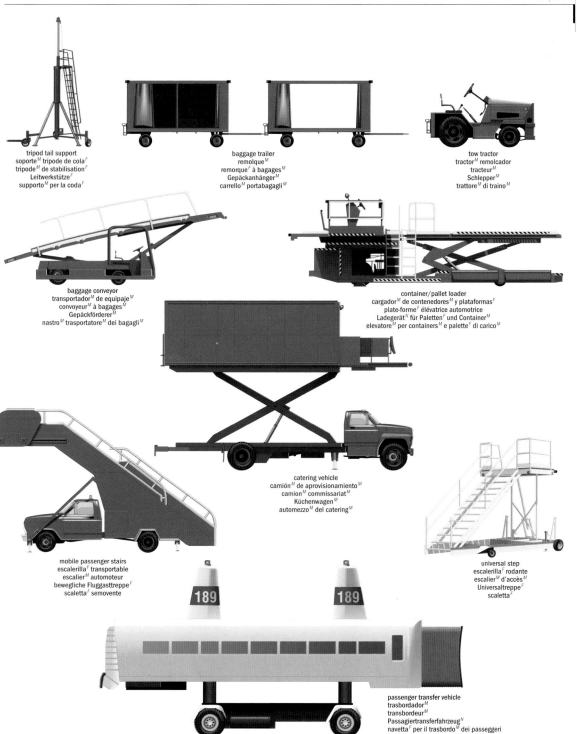

tripod tail support
soporte^M tripode de cola^F
tripode^M de stabilisation^F
Leitwerkstütze^F
supporto^M per la coda^F

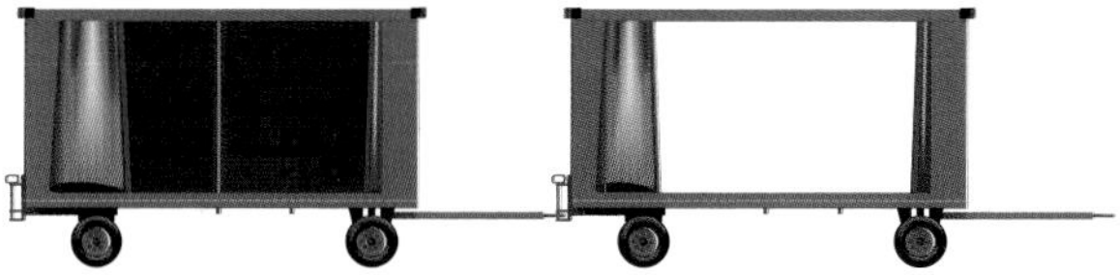

baggage trailer
remolque^M
remorque^F à bagages^M
Gepäckanhänger^M
carrello^M portabagagli^M

tow tractor
tractor^M remolcador
tracteur^M
Schlepper^M
trattore^M di traino^M

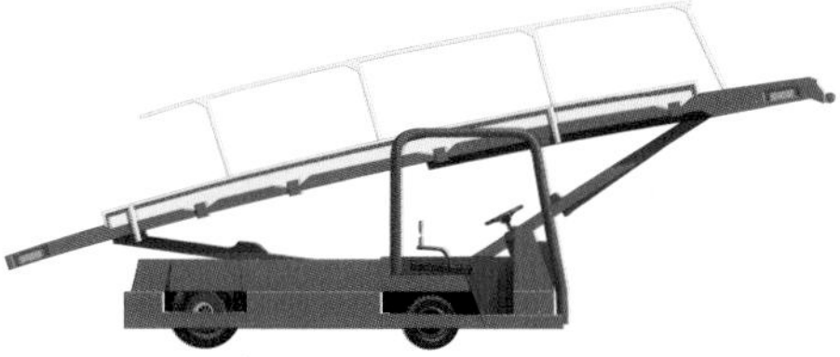

baggage conveyor
transportador^M de equipaje^M
convoyeur^M à bagages^M
Gepäckförderer^M
nastro^M trasportatore dei bagagli^M

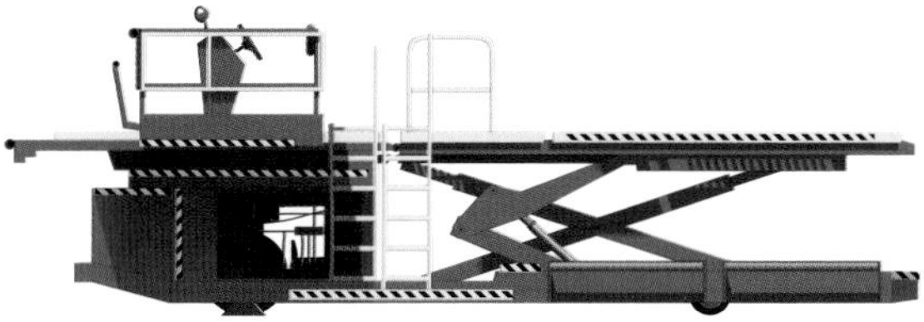

container/pallet loader
cargador^M de contenedores^M y plataformas^F
plate-forme^F élévatrice automotrice
Ladegerät^N für Paletten^F und Container^M
elevatore^M per containers^M e palette^F di carico^M

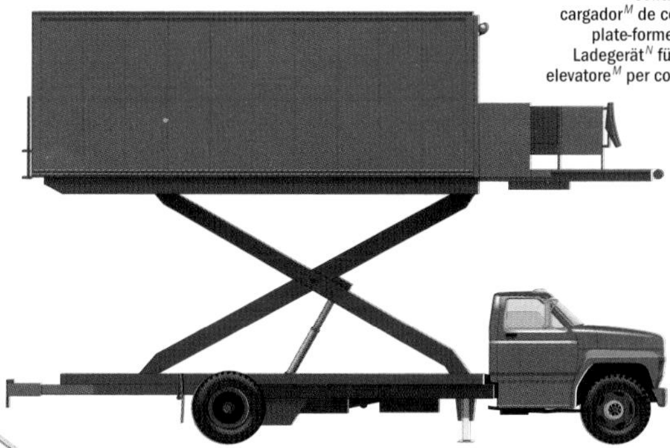

catering vehicle
camión^M de aprovisionamiento^M
camion^M commissariat^M
Küchenwagen^M
automezzo^M del catering^M

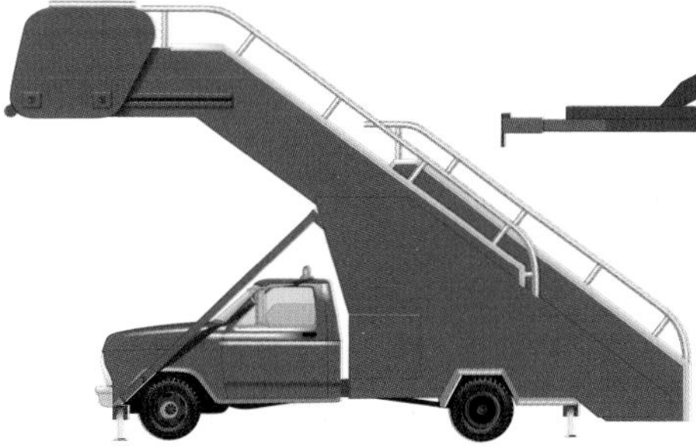

mobile passenger stairs
escalerilla^F transportable
escalier^M automoteur
bewegliche Fluggasttreppe^F
scaletta^F semovente

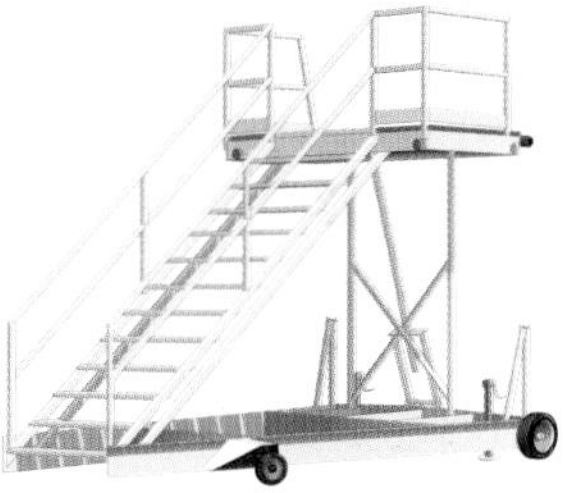

universal step
escalerilla^F rodante
escalier^M d'accès^M
Universaltreppe^F
scaletta^F

189   189

passenger transfer vehicle
trasbordador^M
transbordeur^M
Passagiertransferfahrzeug^N
navetta^F per il trasbordo^M dei passeggeri

TRANSPORT AND MACHINERY

long-range jet

avión^M turborreactor de pasajeros^M | avion^M long-courrier^M | Langstrecken-Düsenflugzeug^N | aviogetto^M a lungo raggio^M

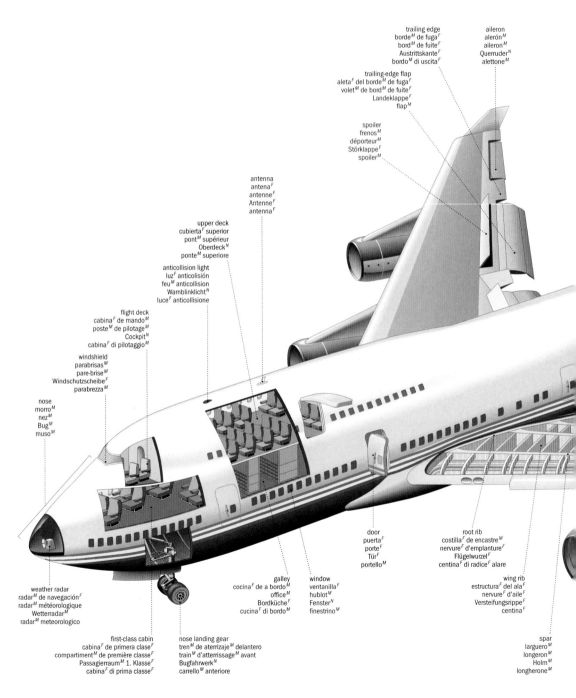

trailing edge
borde^M de fuga^F
bord^M de fuite^F
Austrittskante^F
bordo^M di uscita^F

aileron
alerón^M
aileron^M
Querruder^N
alettone^M

trailing-edge flap
aleta^F del borde^M de fuga^F
volet^M de bord^M de fuite^F
Landeklappe^F
flap^M

spoiler
frenos^M
déporteur^M
Störklappe^F
spoiler^M

antenna
antena^F
antenne^F
Antenne^F
antenna^F

upper deck
cubierta^F superior
pont^M supérieur
Oberdeck^N
ponte^M superiore

anticollision light
luz^F anticolisión
feu^M anticollision
Warnblinklicht^N
luce^F anticollisione

flight deck
cabina^F de mando^M
poste^M de pilotage^M
Cockpit^N
cabina^F di pilotaggio^M

windshield
parabrisas^M
pare-brise^M
Windschutzscheibe^F
parabrezza^M

nose
morro^M
nez^M
Bug^M
muso^M

weather radar
radar^M de navegación^F
radar^M météorologique
Wetterradar^M
radar^M meteorologico

first-class cabin
cabina^F de primera clase^F
compartiment^M de première classe^F
Passagierraum^M 1. Klasse^F
cabina^F di prima classe^F

nose landing gear
tren^M de aterrizaje^M delantero
train^M d'atterrissage^M avant
Bugfahrwerk^N
carrello^M anteriore

galley
cocina^F de a bordo^M
office^M
Bordküche^F
cucina^F di bordo^M

window
ventanilla^F
hublot^M
Fenster^N
finestrino^M

door
puerta^F
porte^F
Tür^F
portello^M

root rib
costilla^F de encastre^M
nervure^F d'emplanture^F
Flügelwurzel^F
centina^F di radice^F alare

wing rib
estructura^F del ala^F
nervure^F d'aile^F
Versteifungsrippe^F
centina^F

spar
larguero^M
longeron^M
Holm^M
longherone^M

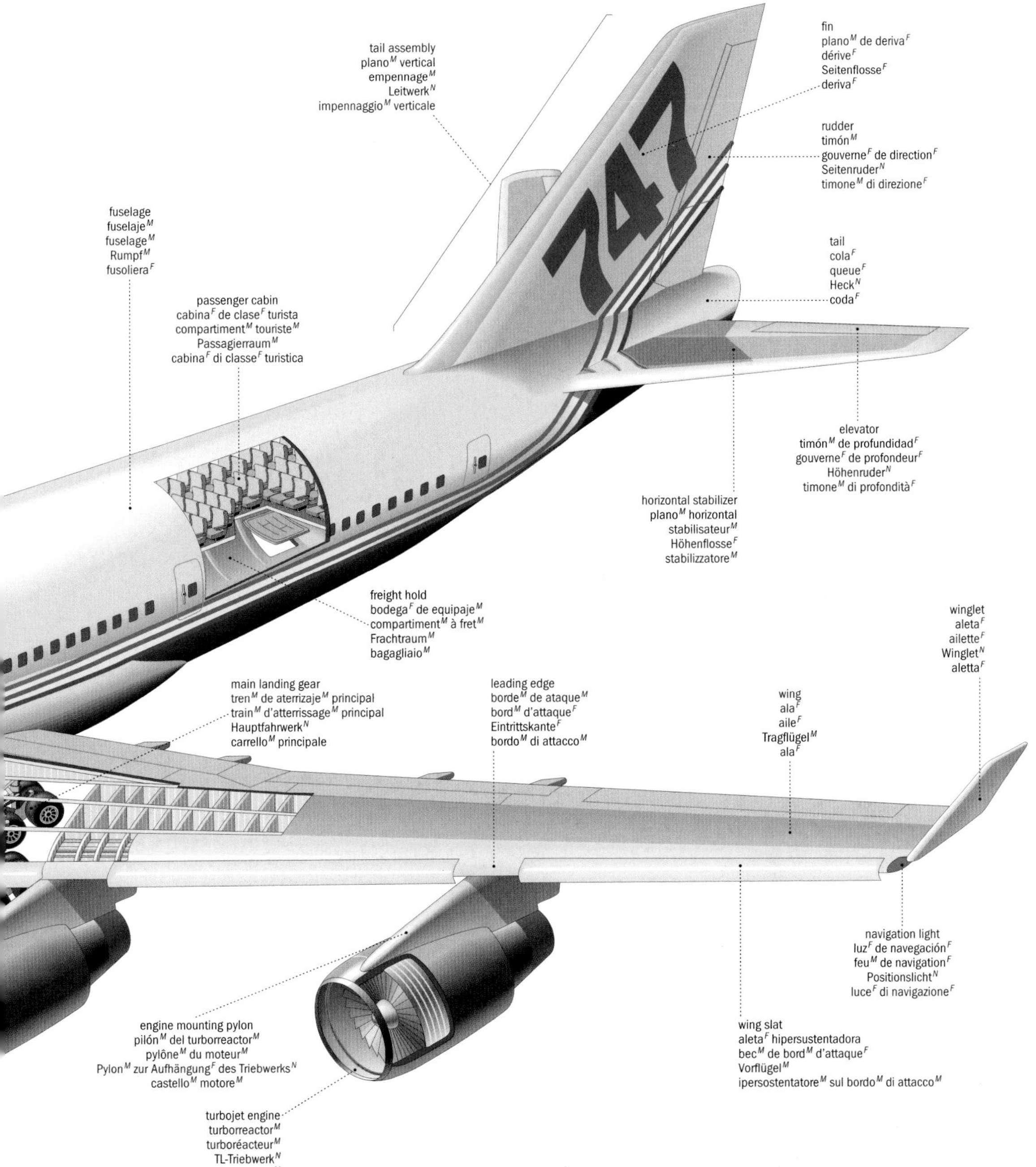

tail assembly
plano^M vertical
empennage^M
Leitwerk^N
impennaggio^M verticale

fin
plano^M de deriva^F
dérive^F
Seitenflosse^F
deriva^F

rudder
timón^M
gouverne^F de direction^F
Seitenruder^N
timone^F di direzione^F

fuselage
fuselaje^M
fuselage^M
Rumpf^M
fusoliera^F

tail
cola^F
queue^F
Heck^N
coda^F

passenger cabin
cabina^F de clase^F turista
compartiment^M touriste^M
Passagierraum^M
cabina^F di classe^F turistica

elevator
timón^M de profundidad^F
gouverne^F de profondeur^F
Höhenruder^N
timone^M di profondità^F

horizontal stabilizer
plano^M horizontal
stabilisateur^M
Höhenflosse^F
stabilizzatore^M

freight hold
bodega^F de equipaje^M
compartiment^M à fret^M
Frachtraum^M
bagagliaio^M

winglet
aleta^F
ailette^F
Winglet^N
aletta^F

main landing gear
tren^M de aterrizaje^M principal
train^M d'atterrissage^M principal
Hauptfahrwerk^N
carrello^M principale

leading edge
borde^M de ataque^M
bord^M d'attaque^F
Eintrittskante^F
bordo^M di attacco^M

wing
ala^F
aile^F
Tragflügel^M
ala^F

navigation light
luz^F de navegación^F
feu^M de navigation^F
Positionslicht^N
luce^F di navigazione^F

engine mounting pylon
pilón^M del turborreactor^M
pylône^M du moteur^M
Pylon^M zur Aufhängung^F des Triebwerks^N
castello^M motore^M

wing slat
aleta^F hipersustentadora
bec^M de bord^M d'attaque^F
Vorflügel^M
ipersostentatore^M sul bordo^M di attacco^M

turbojet engine
turborreactor^M
turboréacteur^M
TL-Triebwerk^N
turboreattore^M

TRANSPORT AND MACHINERY

flight deck

puente^M de mando^M | poste^M de pilotage^M | Cockpit^N | cabina^F di pilotaggio^M

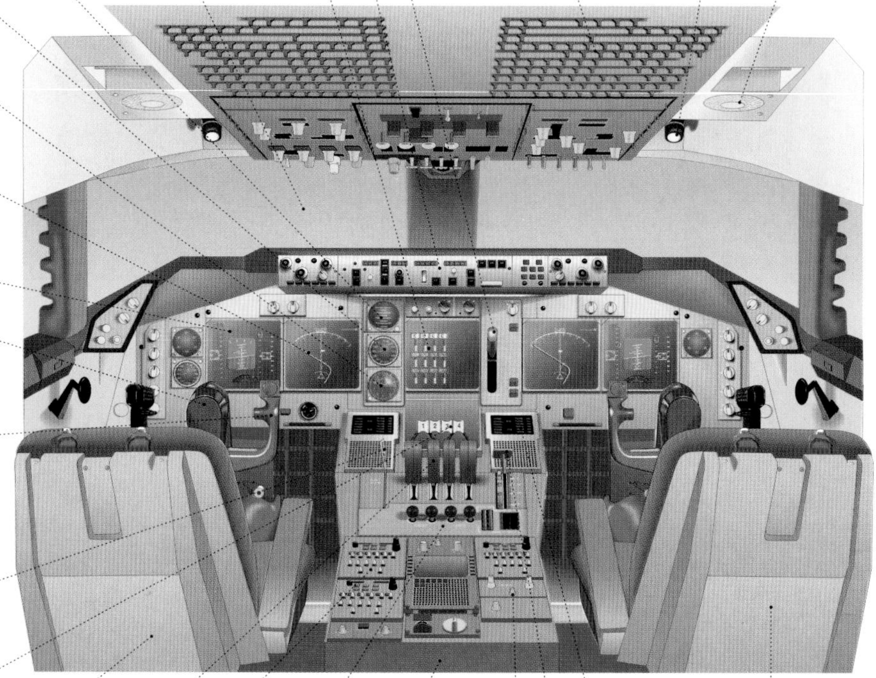

autopilot controls
controles^M del piloto^M automático
commandes^F du pilote^M automatique
Steueranlage^F für den Autopiloten^M
comandi^M del pilota^M automatico

landing gear lever
palanca^F del tren^M de aterrizaje delantero
levier^M du train^M d'atterrissage^M
Fahrwerkhebel^M
leva^F del carrello^M

speaker
altavoz^M
haut-parleur^M
Lautsprecher^M
altoparlante^M

engine and crew alarm display
pantalla^F de alarma^F de motor y tripulación^F
paramètres^M moteurs^M/alarmes^F
Warnanzeige^F Besatzung^F und Triebwerke^N
display^M dei parametri^M del motore^M e delle avarie^F

lighting
luz^F
éclairage^M
Beleuchtung^F
luce^F

standby attitude indicator
indicador^M de emergencia^F de inclinación^F
horizon^M de secours^M
Reserve-Fluglageanzeige^F
girorizzonte^M di riserva^F

windshield
parabrisas^M
pare-brise^M
Windschutzscheibe^F
parabrezza^M

overhead switch panel
tablero^M de conmutadores^M
panneau^M de disjoncteurs^M
Überkopfschaltbrett^N
pannello^M superiore degli interruttori^M

standby airspeed indicator
anemómetro^M de emergencia^F
anémomètre^M de secours^M
Reserve-Fahrtmesser^M
anemometro^M di riserva^F

standby altimeter
altímetro^M de emergencia^F
altimètre^M de secours^M
Reserve-Höhenmesser^M
altimetro^M di riserva^F

navigation display
pantalla^F de navegación^F
informations^F-navigation^F
Navigationsanzeige^F
display^M di navigazione^F

primary flight display
pantalla^F principal de vuelo^M
informations^F-pilotage^M
Hauptanzeige^F der Flugdaten^N
display^M di pilotaggio^M

control column
columna^F de control^M
manche^F de commande^F
Steuerknüppel^M
barra^F di comando^M

control wheel
timón^M de control^M
volant^M de manche^M
Steuerrad^N
volantino^M

speedbrake lever
palanca^F de freno^M
levier^M des aérofreins^M
Flugbremshebel^M
leva^F degli aerofreni^M

systems display
pantalla^F de los sistemas^M
informations^F-systèmes^M de bord^M
Displayanzeige^F
display^M dei controlli^M di bordo^M

captain's seat
asiento^M del capitán^M
siège^M du commandant^M
Kapitänssitz^M
sedile^M del comandante^M

first officer's seat
asiento^M del copiloto^M
siège^M du copilote^M
Kopilotensitz^M
sedile^M del copilota^M

throttles
válvulas^F de control^M de combustible^M
manettes^F de poussée^F
Gashebel^M
manette^F di accelerazione^F dei motori^M

flight management computer
ordenador^M de gestión^F de vuelo^M
ordinateur^M de gestion^F de vol^M
Flugrechner^M
elaboratore^M di gestione^F del volo^M

communication panels
paneles^M de comunicación^F
panneaux^M de commandes^F radio^F
Kommunikationsschaltbrett^N
comandi^M radio^F

flap lever
palanca^F de los alerones^M de hipersustentación^F
levier^M des volets^M
Klappenhebel^M
leva^F dei flap^M

engine fuel valves
válvulas^F de combustible^M del motor^M
robinets^M de carburant^M
Brennstoffventile^N
valvole^F di controllo^M del flusso^M di carburante^M

control console
consola^F de control^M
pupitre^M de commande^F
Steuerpult^N
console^F di comando^M

air data computer
ordenador^M de vuelo^M
ordinateur^M des données^F aérodynamiques
Luftdatenrechner^M
elaboratore^M dei dati^M aerodinamici

turbofan engine

turborreactor ^{M} | turboréacteur ^{M} à double flux ^{M} | Zweistromtriebwerk ^{N} | turboreattore ^{M} a doppio flusso ^{M}

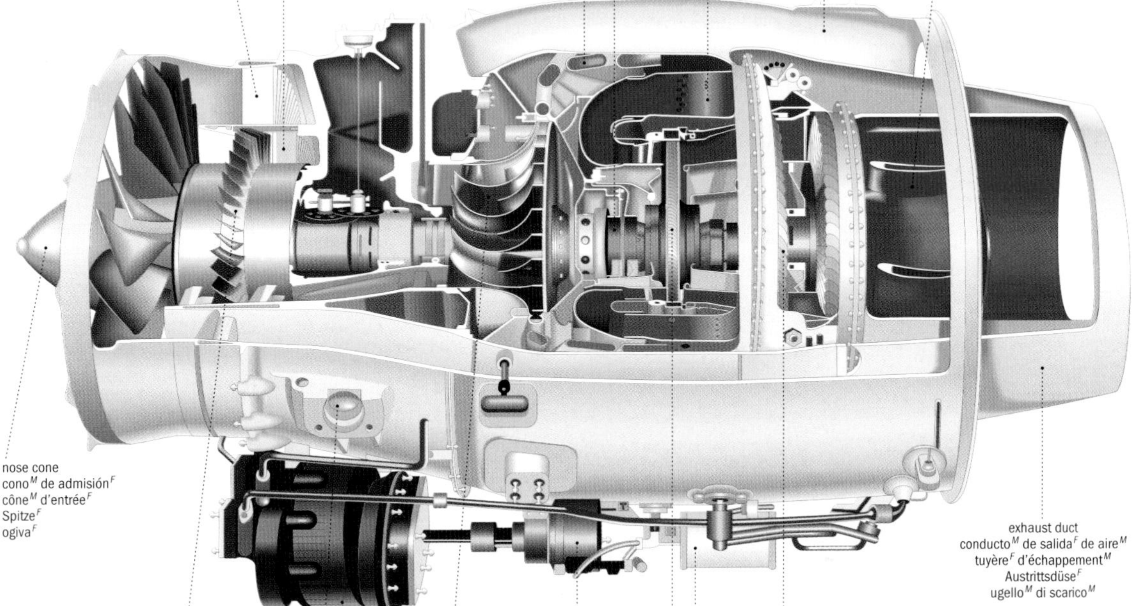

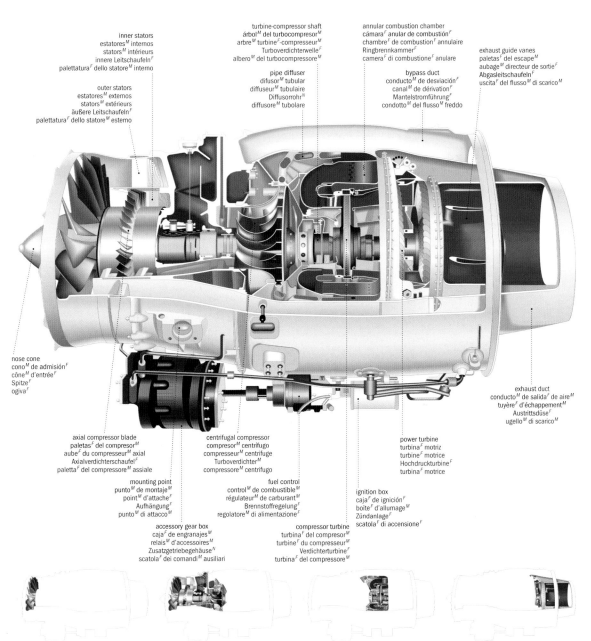

inner stators
estatores ^{M} internos
stators ^{M} intérieurs
innere Leitschaufeln ^{F}
palettatura ^{F} dello statore ^{M} interno

turbine-compressor shaft
árbol ^{M} del turbocompresor ^{M}
arbre ^{M} turbine ^{F}-compresseur ^{F}
Turboverdichterwelle ^{F}
albero ^{M} del turbocompressore ^{M}

annular combustion chamber
cámara ^{F} anular de combustión ^{F}
chambre ^{F} de combustion ^{F} annulaire
Ringbrennkammer ^{F}
camera ^{F} di combustione ^{F} anulare

exhaust guide vanes
paletas ^{F} del escape ^{M}
aubage ^{M} directeur de sortie ^{F}
Abgasleitschaufeln ^{F}
uscita ^{F} del flusso ^{M} di scarico ^{M}

outer stators
estatores ^{M} externos
stators ^{M} extérieurs
äußere Leitschaufeln ^{F}
palettatura ^{F} dello statore ^{M} esterno

pipe diffuser
difusor ^{M} tubular
diffuseur ^{M} tubulaire
Diffusorrohr ^{N}
diffusore ^{M} tubolare

bypass duct
conducto ^{M} de desviación ^{F}
canal ^{M} de dérivation ^{F}
Mantelstromführung ^{F}
condotto ^{M} del flusso ^{M} freddo

nose cone
cono ^{M} de admisión ^{F}
cône ^{M} d'entrée ^{F}
Spitze ^{F}
ogiva ^{F}

exhaust duct
conducto ^{M} de salida ^{F} de aire ^{M}
tuyère ^{F} d'échappement ^{M}
Austrittsdüse ^{F}
ugello ^{M} di scarico ^{M}

axial compressor blade
paletas ^{F} del compresor ^{M}
aube ^{M} du compresseur ^{M} axial
Axialverdichterschaufel ^{F}
paletta ^{F} del compressore ^{M} assiale

centrifugal compressor
compresor ^{M} centrífugo
compresseur ^{M} centrifuge
Turboverdichter ^{M}
compressore ^{M} centrifugo

power turbine
turbina ^{F} motriz
turbine ^{F} motrice
Hochdruckturbine ^{F}
turbina ^{F} motrice

mounting point
punto ^{M} de montaje ^{M}
point ^{M} d'attache ^{F}
Aufhängung ^{F}
punto ^{M} di attacco ^{F}

fuel control
control ^{M} de combustible ^{M}
régulateur ^{M} de carburant ^{M}
Brennstoffregelung ^{F}
regolatore ^{M} di alimentazione ^{F}

ignition box
caja ^{F} de ignición ^{F}
boîte ^{F} d'allumage ^{M}
Zündanlage ^{F}
scatola ^{F} di accensione ^{F}

accessory gear box
caja ^{F} de engranajes ^{M}
relais ^{M} d'accessoires ^{M}
Zusatzgetriebegehäuse ^{N}
scatola ^{F} dei comandi ^{M} ausiliari

compressor turbine
turbina ^{F} del compresor ^{M}
turbine ^{F} du compresseur ^{M}
Verdichterturbine ^{F}
turbina ^{F} del compressore ^{M}

fan
ventilador ^{M}
soufflante ^{F}
Niederdruckverdichtung ^{F}
soffiante ^{M}

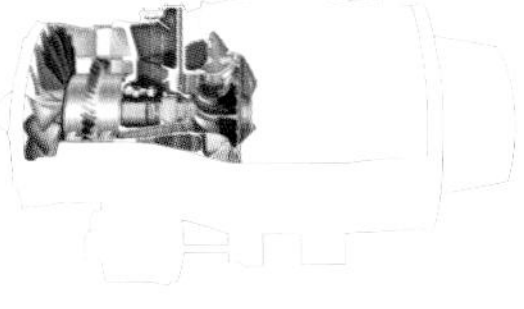

compression
compresión ^{F}
compression ^{F}
Verdichtung ^{F}
compressione ^{F}

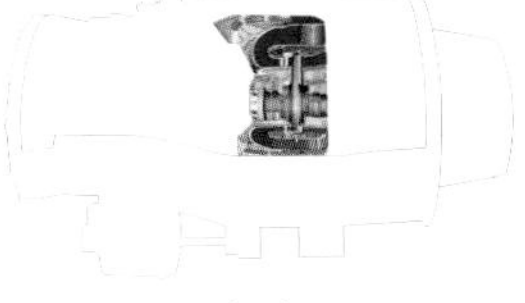

combustion
combustión ^{F}
combustion ^{F}
Verbrennung ^{F}
combustione ^{F}

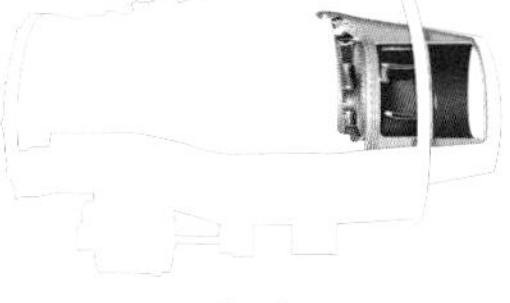

exhaust
escape ^{M}
échappement ^{M}
Abgas ^{N}
scarico ^{M}

examples of airplanes

ejemplos^M de aviones^M | exemples^M d'avions^M | Beispiele^N für Flugzeuge^N | esempi^M di aeroplani^M

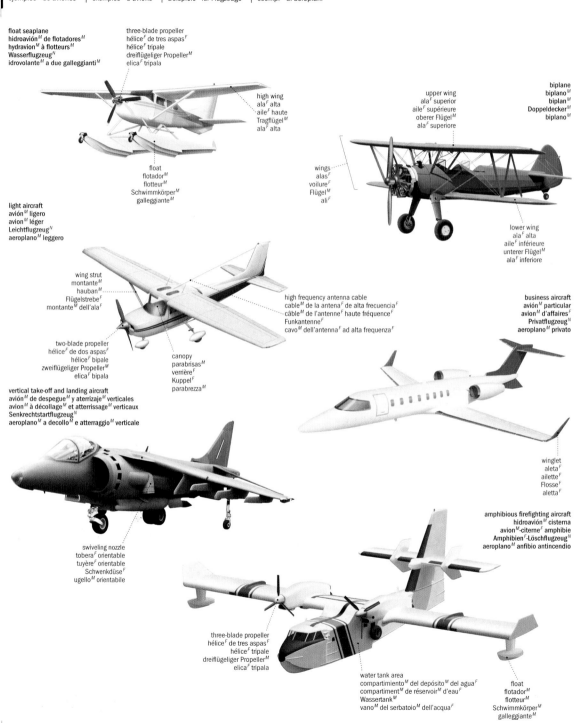

float seaplane
hidroavión^M de flotadores^M
hydravion^M à flotteurs^M
Wasserflugzeug^N
idrovolante^M a due galleggianti^M

three-blade propeller
hélice^F de tres aspas^F
hélice^F tripala
dreiflügeliger Propeller^M
elica^F tripala

high wing
ala^F alta
aile^F haute
Tragflügel^M
ala^F alta

float
flotador^M
flotteur^M
Schwimmkörper^M
galleggiante^M

biplane
biplano^M
biplan^M
Doppeldecker^M
biplano^M

upper wing
ala^F superior
aile^F supérieure
oberer Flügel^M
ala^F superiore

wings
alas^F
voilure^F
Flügel^M
ali^F

lower wing
ala^F alta
aile^F inférieure
unterer Flügel^M
ala^F inferiore

light aircraft
avión^M ligero
avion^M léger
Leichtflugzeug^N
aeroplano^M leggero

wing strut
montante^M
hauban^M
Flügelstrebe^F
montante^M dell'ala^F

high frequency antenna cable
cable^M de la antena^F de alta frecuencia^F
câble^M de l'antenne^F haute fréquence^F
Funkantenne^F
cavo^M dell'antenna^F ad alta frequenza^F

business aircraft
avión^M particular
avion^M d'affaires^F
Privatflugzeug^N
aeroplano^M privato

two-blade propeller
hélice^F de dos aspas^F
hélice^F bipale
zweiflügeliger Propeller^M
elica^F bipala

canopy
parabrisas^M
verrière^F
Kuppel^F
parabrezza^M

vertical take-off and landing aircraft
avión^M de despegue^M y aterrizaje^M verticales
avion^M à décollage^M et atterrissage^M verticaux
Senkrechtstartflugzeug^N
aeroplano^M a decollo^M e atterraggio^M verticale

winglet
aleta^F
ailette^F
Flosse^F
aletta^F

amphibious firefighting aircraft
hidroavión^M cisterna
avion^M-citerne^F amphibie
Amphibien^F-Löschflugzeug^N
aeroplano^M anfibio antincendio

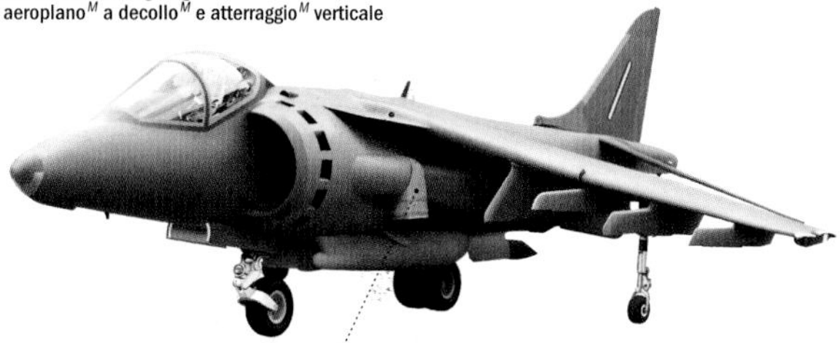

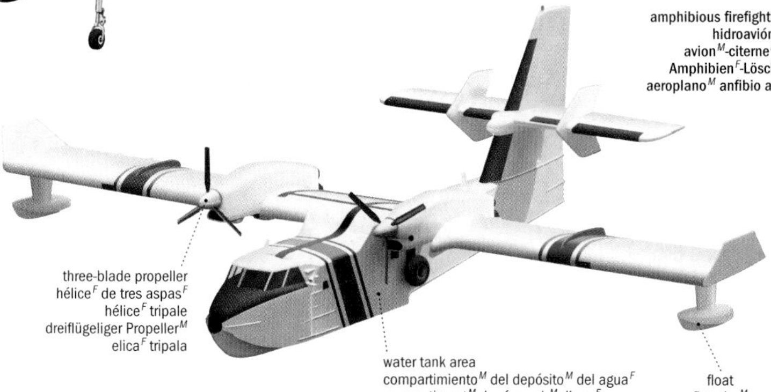

swiveling nozzle
tobera^F orientable
tuyère^F orientable
Schwenkdüse^F
ugello^M orientabile

three-blade propeller
hélice^F de tres aspas^F
hélice^F tripala
dreiflügeliger Propeller^M
elica^F tripala

water tank area
compartimiento^M del depósito^M del agua^M
compartiment^M de réservoir^M d'eau^F
Wassertank^M
vano^M del serbatoio^M dell'acqua^F

float
flotador^M
flotteur^M
Schwimmkörper^M
galleggiante^M

TRANSPORT AND MACHINERY

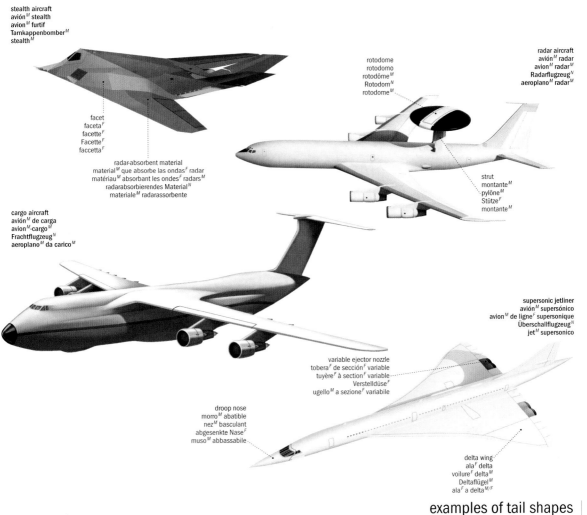

stealth aircraft
avión^M stealth
avion^M furtif
Tarnkappenbomber^M
stealth^M

facet
faceta^F
facette^F
Facette^F
faccetta^F

radar-absorbent material
material^M que absorbe las ondas^F radar
matériau^M absorbant les ondes^F radars^M
radarabsorbierendes Material^N
materiale^M radarassorbente

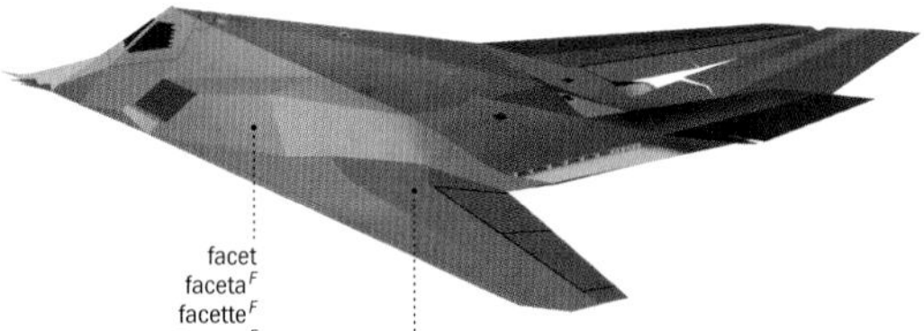

radar aircraft
avión^M radar
avion^M radar^M
Radarflugzeug^N
aeroplano^M radar^M

rotodome
rotodomo
rotodôme^M
Rotodom^N
rotodome^M

strut
montante^M
pylône^M
Stütze^F
montante^M

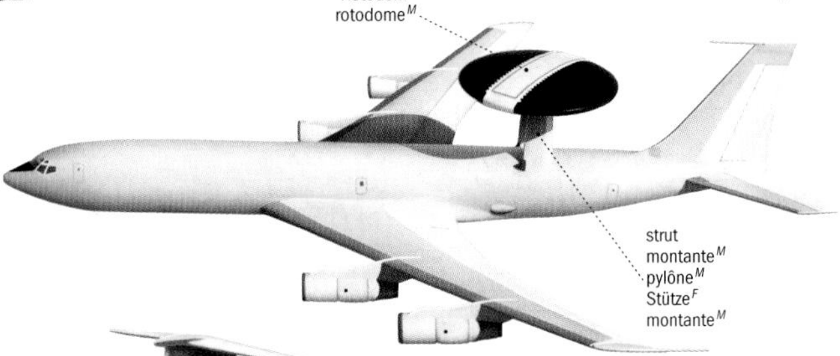

cargo aircraft
avión^M de carga
avion^M-cargo^M
Frachtflugzeug^N
aeroplano^M da carico^M

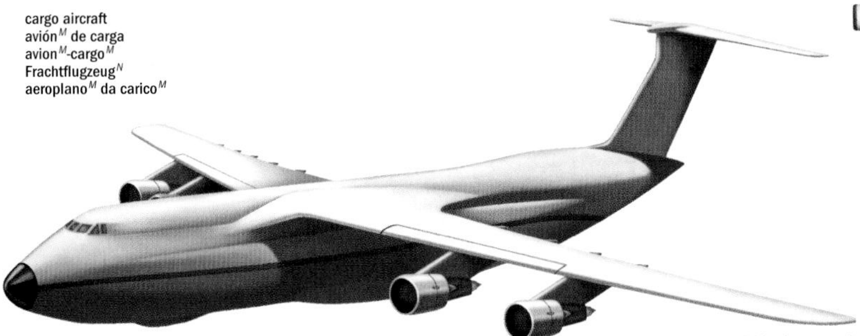

supersonic jetliner
avión^M supersónico
avion^M de ligne^F supersonique
Überschallflugzeug^N
jet^M supersonico

variable ejector nozzle
tobera^F de sección^F variable
tuyère^F à section^F variable
Verstelldüse^F
ugello^M a sezione^F variabile

droop nose
morro^M abatible
nez^M basculant
abgesenkte Nase^F
muso^M abbassabile

delta wing
ala^F delta
voilure^F delta^M
Deltaflügel^M
ala^F a delta$^{M/F}$

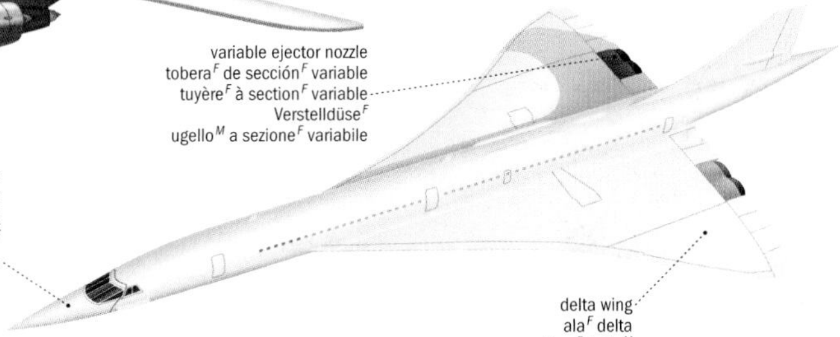

examples of tail shapes

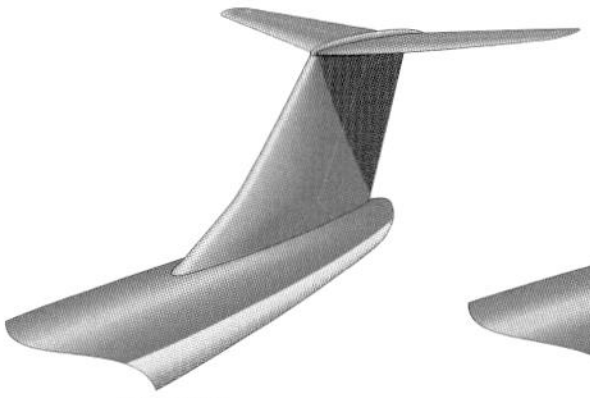

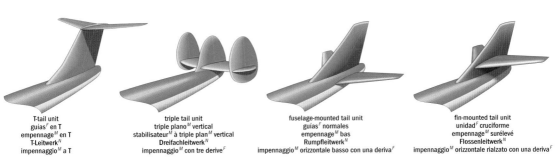

T-tail unit
guías^F en T
empennage^M en T
T-Leitwerk^N
impennaggio^M a T

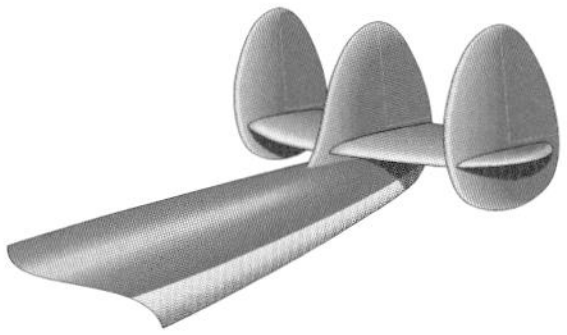

triple tail unit
triple plano^M vertical
stabilisateur^M à triple plan^M vertical
Dreifachleitwerk^N
impennaggio^M con tre derive^F

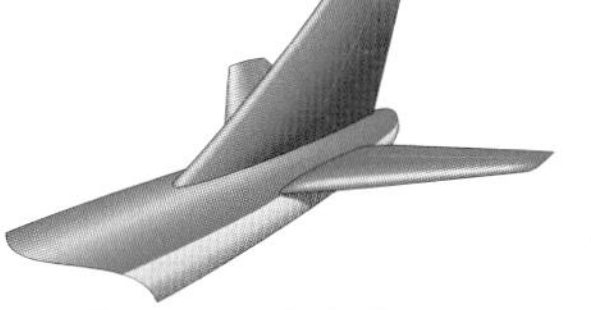

fuselage-mounted tail unit
guías^F normales
empennage^M bas
Rumpfleitwerk^N
impennaggio^M orizzontale basso con una deriva^F

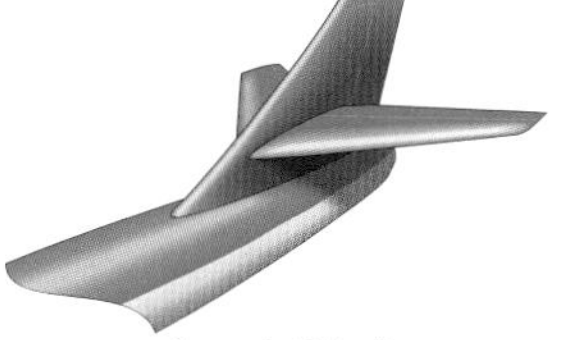

fin-mounted tail unit
unidad^F cruciforme
empennage^M surélevé
Flossenleitwerk^N
impennaggio^M orizzontale rialzato con una deriva^F

TRANSPORT AND MACHINERY

examples of wing shapes

diferentes formas^F de alas^F | exemples^M de voilures^F | Tragflügelformen^F | tipi^M di ali^F

straight wing
ala^F recta
voilure^F droite
Rechteckflügel^M
ala^F rettangolare

variable geometry wing
ala^F variable
aile^F à géométrie^F variable
Schwenkflügel^M
ala^F a geometria^F variabile

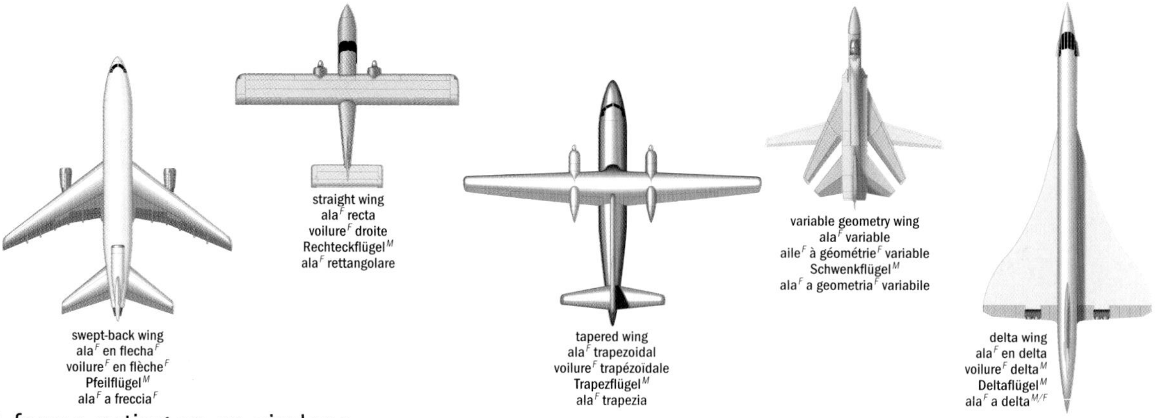

swept-back wing
ala^F en flecha^F
voilure^F en flèche^F
Pfeilflügel^M
ala^F a freccia^F

tapered wing
ala^F trapezoidal
voilure^F trapézoidale
Trapezflügel^M
ala^F trapezia

delta wing
ala^F en delta
voilure^F delta^M
Deltaflügel^M
ala^F a delta$^{M/F}$

forces acting on an airplane

fuerzas^F que actúan sobre un avión^M | forces^F agissant sur un avion^M | auf Flugzeuge^N wirkende Kräfte^F | forze^F che agiscono su un aeroplano^M

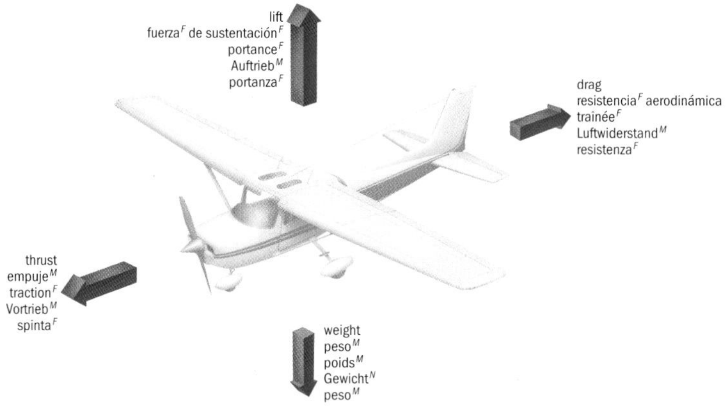

lift
fuerza^F de sustentación^F
portance^F
Auftrieb^M
portanza^F

drag
resistencia^F aerodinámica
trainée^F
Luftwiderstand^M
resistenza^F

thrust
empuje^M
traction^F
Vortrieb^M
spinta^F

weight
peso^M
poids^M
Gewicht^N
peso^M

movements of an airplane

movimientos^M de un avión^M | mouvements^M de l'avion^M | Bewegungen^F eines Flugzeugs^N | movimenti^M di un aeroplano^M

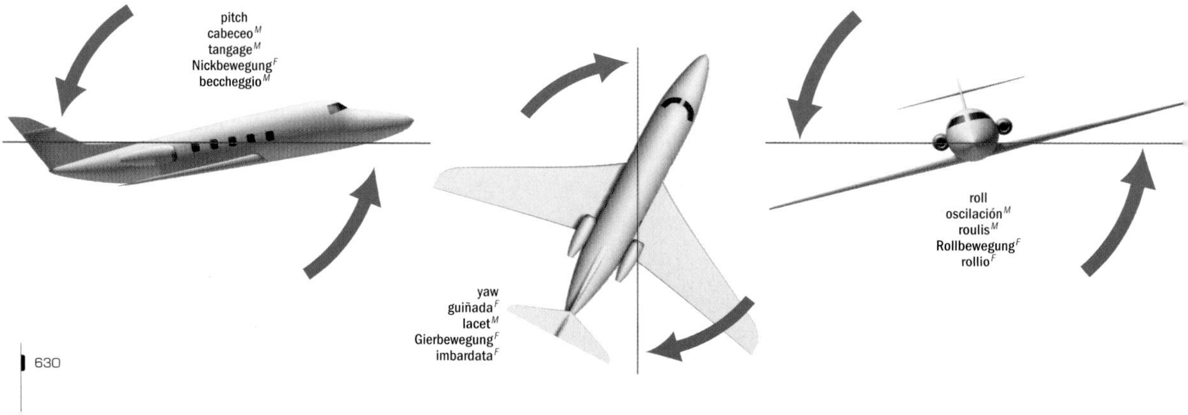

pitch
cabeceo^M
tangage^M
Nickbewegung^F
beccheggio^M

yaw
guiñada^F
lacet^M
Gierbewegung^F
imbardata^F

roll
oscilación^M
roulis^M
Rollbewegung^F
rollio^F

helicopter

helicóptero^M | hélicoptère^M | Hubschrauber^M | elicottero^M

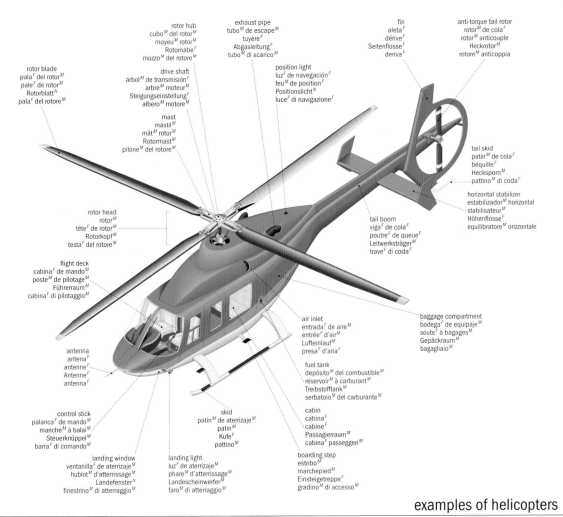

rotor hub
cubo^M del rotor^M
moyeu^M rotor^M
Rotornabe^F
mozzo^M del rotore^M

exhaust pipe
tubo^M de escape^M
tuyère^F
Abgasleitung^F
tubo^M di scarico^M

fin
aleta^F
dérive^F
Seitenflosse^F
deriva^F

anti-torque tail rotor
rotor^M de cola^F
rotor^M anticouple
Heckrotor^M
rotore^M anticoppia

rotor blade
pala^F del rotor^M
pale^F de rotor^M
Rotorblatt^N
pala^F del rotore^M

drive shaft
árbol^M de transmisión^F
arbre^M moteur^M
Steigungseinstellung^F
albero^M motore^M

position light
luz^F de navegación^F
feu^M de position^F
Positionslicht^N
luce^F di navigazione^F

tail skid
patín^M de cola^F
béquille^F
Hecksporn^M
pattino^M di coda^F

mast
mástil^M
mât^M rotor^M
Rotormast^M
pilone^M del rotore^M

horizontal stabilizer
estabilizador^M horizontal
stabilisateur^M
Höhenflosse^F
equilibratore^M orizzontale

rotor head
rotor^M
tête^F de rotor^M
Rotorkopf^M
testa^F del rotore^M

tail boom
viga^F de cola^F
poutre^F de queue^F
Leitwerksträger^M
trave^F di coda^F

flight deck
cabina^F de mando^M
poste^M de pilotage^M
Führerraum^M
cabina^F di pilotaggio^M

air inlet
entrada^F de aire^M
entrée^F d'air^M
Lufteinlauf^M
presa^F d'aria^F

baggage compartment
bodega^F de equipaje^M
soute^F à bagages^M
Gepäckraum^M
bagagliaio^M

antenna
antena^F
antenne^F
Antenne^F
antenna^F

fuel tank
depósito^M del combustible^M
réservoir^M à carburant^M
Treibstofftank^M
serbatoio^M del carburante^M

control stick
palanca^F de mando^M
manche^M à balai^M
Steuerknüppel^M
barra^F di comando^M

skid
patín^M de aterrizaje^M
patin^M
Kufe^F
pattino^M

cabin
cabina^F
cabine^F
Passagierraum^M
cabina^F passeggeri^M

landing window
ventanilla^F de aterrizaje^M
hublot^M d'atterrissage^M
Landefenster^N
finestrino^M di atterraggio^M

landing light
luz^F de aterrizaje^M
phare^M d'atterrissage^M
Landescheinwerfer^M
faro^M di atterraggio^M

boarding step
estribo^M
marchepied^M
Einsteigetreppe^F
gradino^M di accesso^M

TRANSPORT AND MACHINERY

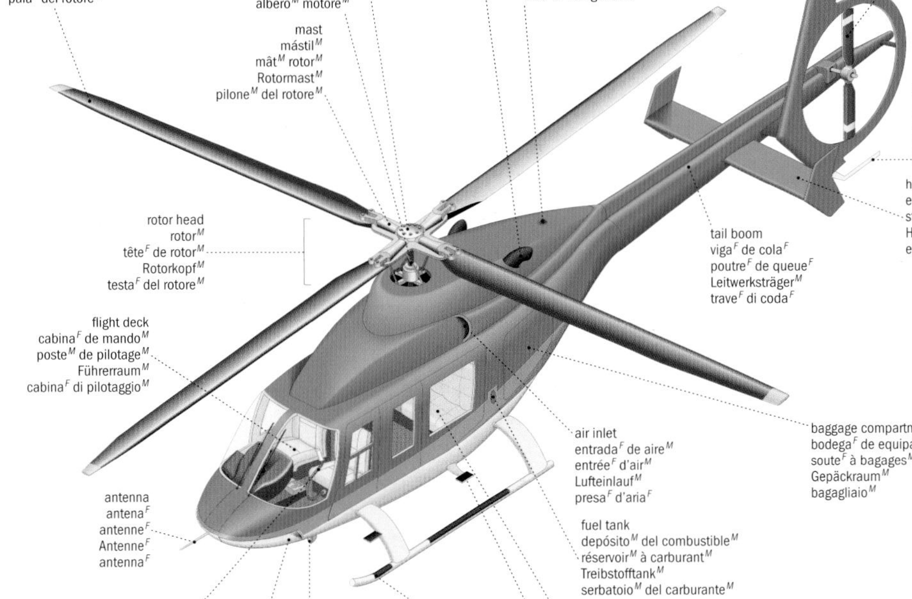

examples of helicopters

ejemplos^M de helicópteros^M | exemples^M d'hélicoptères^M | Beispiele^N für Hubschrauber^M | esempi^M di elicotteri^M

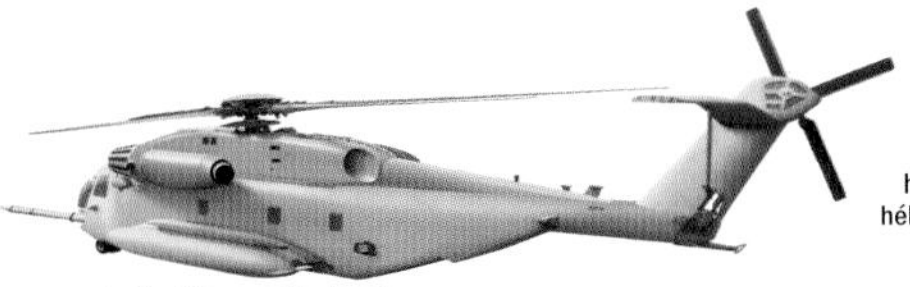

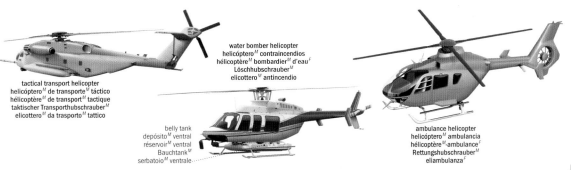

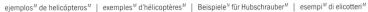

tactical transport helicopter
helicóptero^M de transporte^M táctico
hélicoptère^M de transport^M tactique
taktischer Transporthubschrauber^M
elicottero^M da trasporto^M tattico

water bomber helicopter
helicóptero^M contraincendios
hélicoptère^M bombardier^M d'eau^F
Löschhubschrauber^M
elicottero^M antincendio

belly tank
depósito^M ventral
réservoir^M ventral
Bauchtank^M
serbatoio^M ventrale

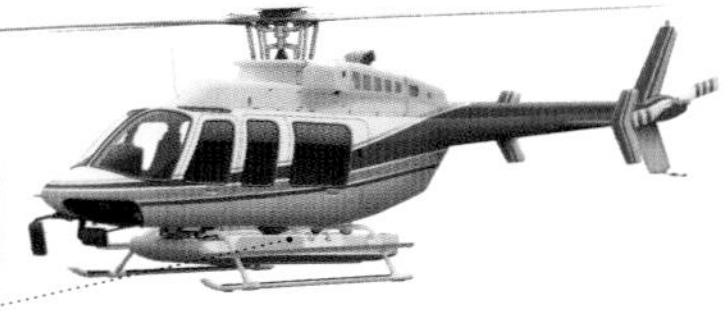

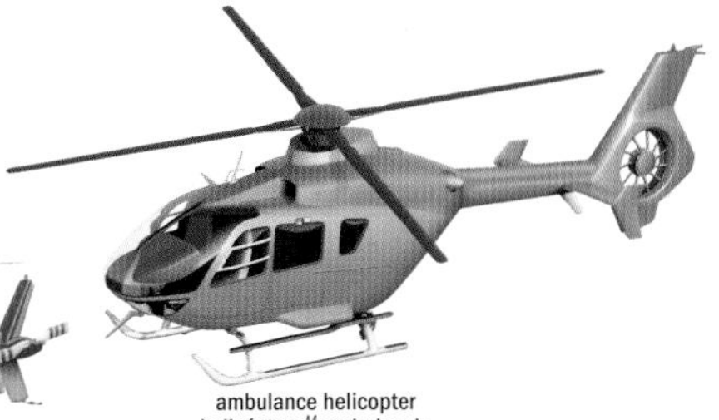

ambulance helicopter
helicóptero^M ambulancia
hélicoptère^M-ambulance^F
Rettungshubschrauber^M
eliambulanza^F

material handling

manejo^M de materiales^M | manutention^F | Lastenfortbewegung^F | movimentazione^F dei materiali^M

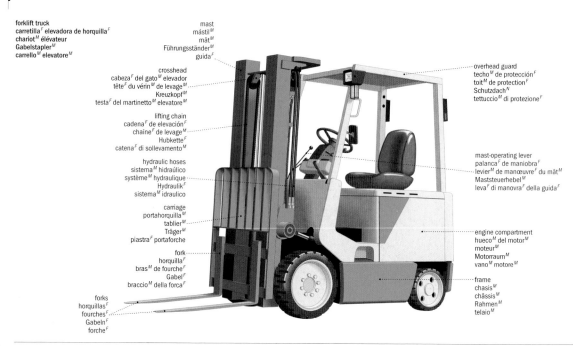

forklift truck
carretilla^F elevadora de horquilla^F
chariot^M élévateur
Gabelstapler^M
carrello^M elevatore^M

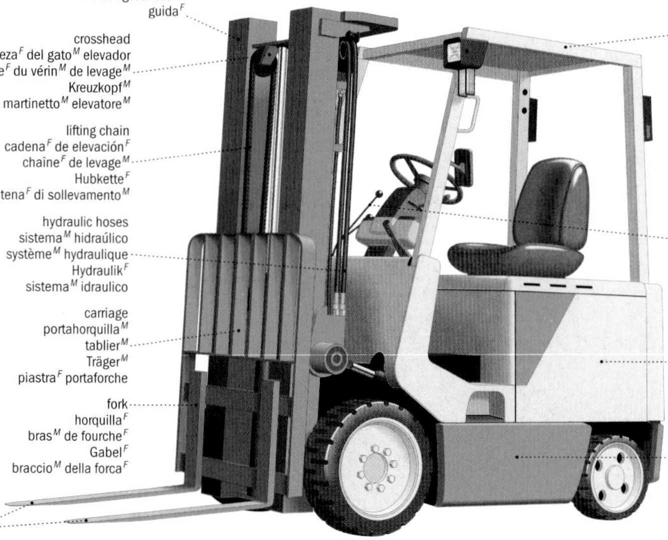

mast
mástil^M
mât^M
Führungsständer^M
guida^F

crosshead
cabeza^F del gato^M elevador
tête^F du vérin^M de levage^M
Kreuzkopf^M
testa^F del martinetto^M elevatore^M

lifting chain
cadena^F de elevación^F
chaîne^F de levage^M
Hubkette^F
catena^F di sollevamento^M

hydraulic hoses
sistema^M hidraúlico
système^M hydraulique
Hydraulik^F
sistema^M idraulico

carriage
portahorquilla^M
tablier^M
Träger^M
piastra^F portaforche

fork
horquilla^F
bras^M de fourche^F
Gabel^F
braccio^M della forca^F

forks
horquillas^F
fourches^F
Gabeln^F
forche^F

overhead guard
techo^M de protección^F
toit^M de protection^F
Schutzdach^N
tettuccio^M di protezione^F

mast-operating lever
palanca^F de maniobra^F
levier^M de manœuvre^F du mât^M
Maststeuerhebel^M
leva^F di manovra^F della guida^F

engine compartment
hueco^M del motor^M
moteur^M
Motorraum^M
vano^M motore^M

frame
chasis^M
châssis^M
Rahmen^M
telaio^M

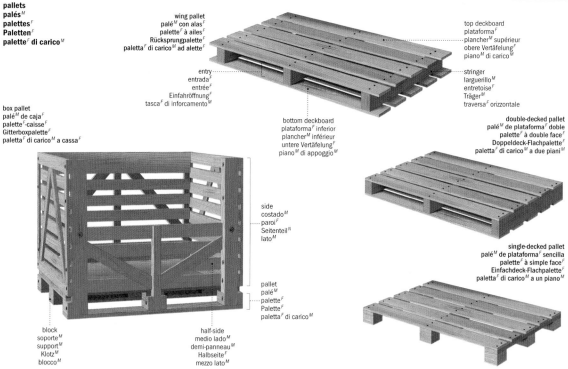

pallets
palés^M
palettes^F
Paletten^F
palette^F di carico^M

wing pallet
palé^M con alas^F
palette^F à ailes^F
Rücksprungpalette^F
paletta^F di carico^M ad alette^F

entry
entrada^F
entrée^F
Einfahröffnung^F
tasca^F di inforcamento^M

box pallet
palé^M de caja^F
palette^F-caisse^F
Gitterboxpalette^F
paletta^F di carico^M a cassa^F

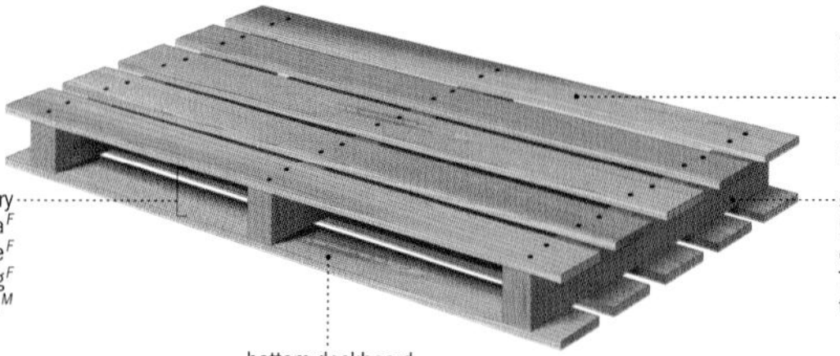

top deckboard
plataforma^F
plancher^M supérieur
obere Vertäfelung^F
piano^M di carico^M

stringer
larguerillo^M
entretoise^F
Träger^M
traversa^F orizzontale

bottom deckboard
plataforma^F inferior
plancher^M inférieur
untere Vertäfelung^F
piano^M di appoggio^M

double-decked pallet
palé^M de plataforma^F doble
palette^F à double face^F
Doppeldeck-Flachpalette^F
paletta^F di carico^M a due piani^M

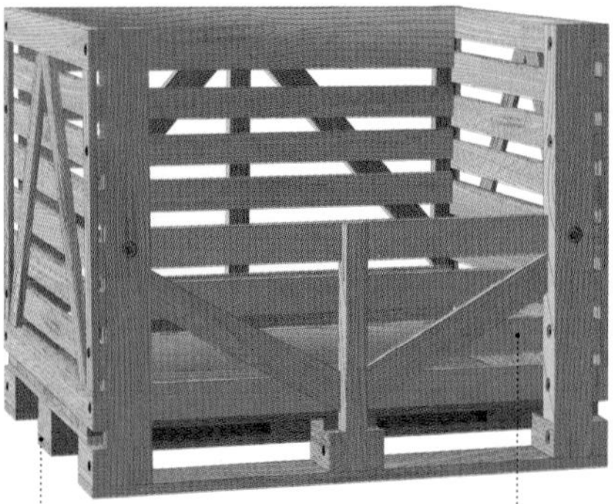

side
costado^M
paroi^F
Seitenteil^N
lato^M

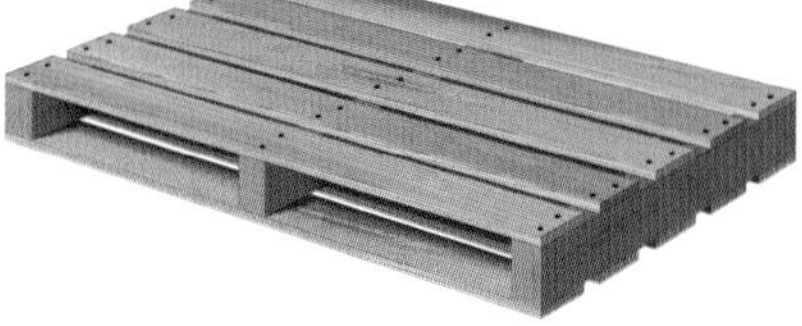

single-decked pallet
palé^M de plataforma^F sencilla
palette^F à simple face^F
Einfachdeck-Flachpalette^F
paletta^F di carico^M a un piano^M

pallet
palé^M
palette^F
Palette^F
paletta^F di carico^M

block
soporte^M
support^M
Klotz^M
blocco^M

half-side
medio lado^M
demi-panneau^M
Halbseite^F
mezzo lato^M

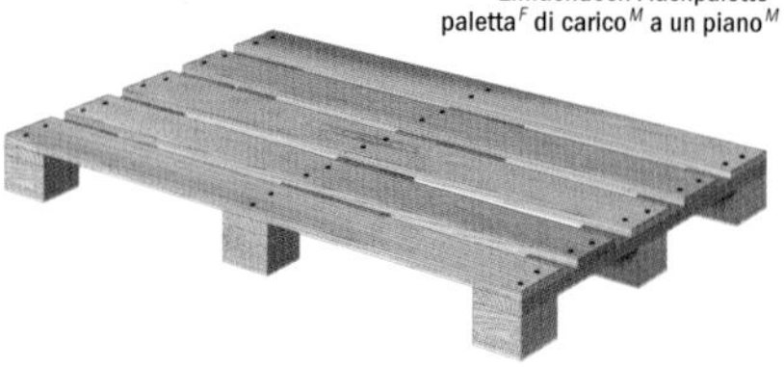

hydraulic pallet truck
apilador hidráulico
gerbeur^M
hydraulischer Palettenhubwagen^M
carrello^M idraulico per palette^F di carico^M

mast
mástil^M
mât^M
Führungsständer^M
guida^F

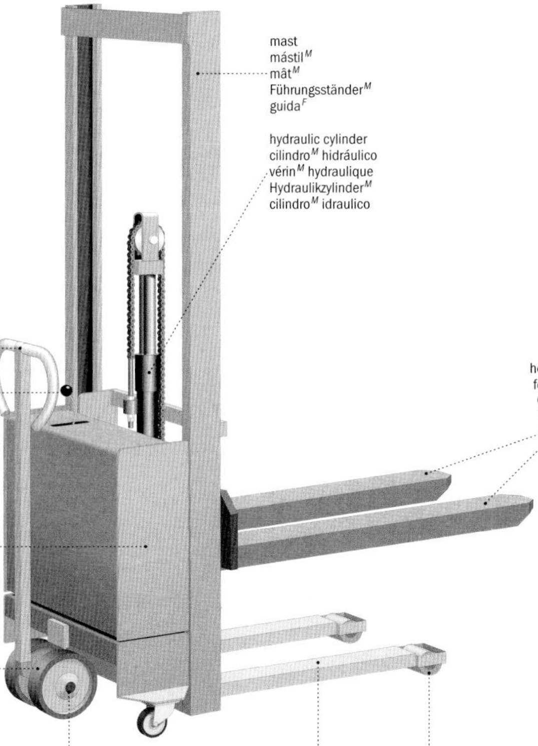

hand truck
carretilla^F
diable^M
Sackkarren^M
carrello^M

hydraulic cylinder
cilindro^M hidráulico
vérin^M hydraulique
Hydraulikzylinder^M
cilindro^M idraulico

steering lever
palanca^F de dirección^F
levier^M de conduite^F
Lenkhebel^M
leva^F direzionale

forks
horquillas^F
fourches^F
Gabeln^F
forche^F

mast-control lever
palanca^F de maniobra^F
levier^M de manœuvre^F du mât^M
Maststeuerhebel^M
leva^F di manovra^F della guida^F

frame
chasis^M
châssis^M
Rahmen^M
telaio^M

solid rubber tire
llanta^F maciza
bandage^M de roue^F caoutchoutée
Vollgummirad^N
gomma^F piena

steering axle
eje^M de dirección^F
essieu^M directeur
Lenkachse^F
asse^M sterzante

stabilizing frame
barra^F estabilizadora
longeron^M stabilisateur
Stabilisator^M
barra^F di stabilizzazione^F

roller
rueda^F
roulette^F
Rolle^F
rotella^F

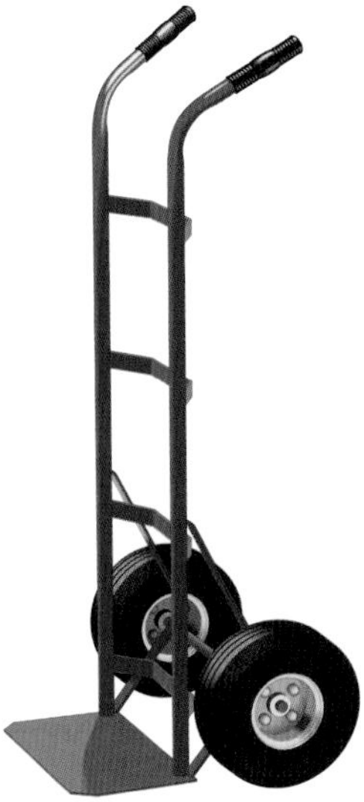

pallet truck
transpaleta^F
transpalette^F manuelle
Palettenhubwagen^M
carrello^M a forca^F per palette^F di carico^M

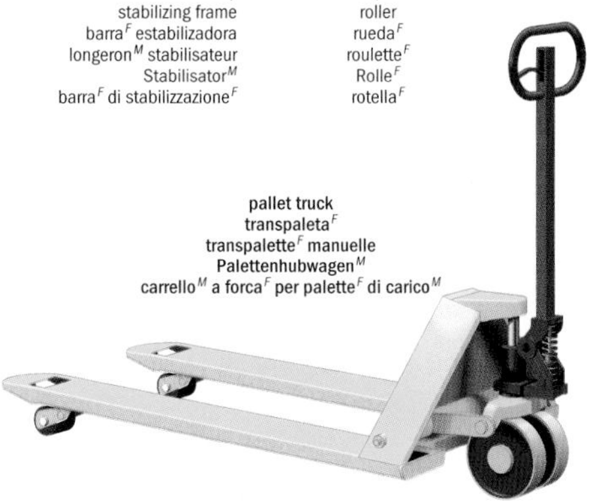

platform pallet truck
carretilla^F transportadora
chariot^M à palette^F
Flachpalettenwagen^M
carrello^M a piattaforma^F per palette^F di carico^M

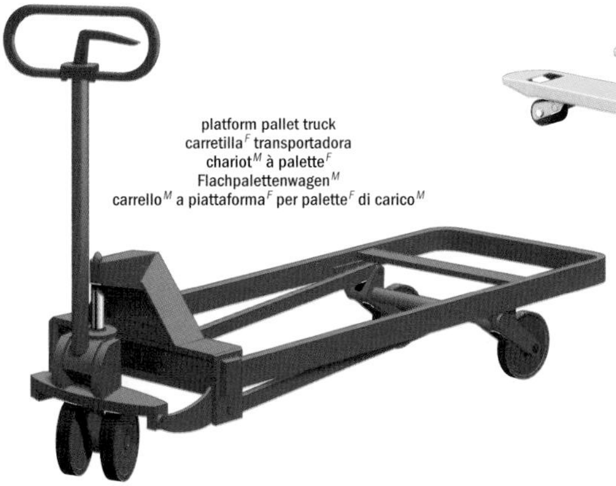

flatbed pushcart
plataforma^F móvil
chariot^M à plateau^M
Handwagen^M
carrello^M a piattaforma^F

TRANSPORT AND MACHINERY

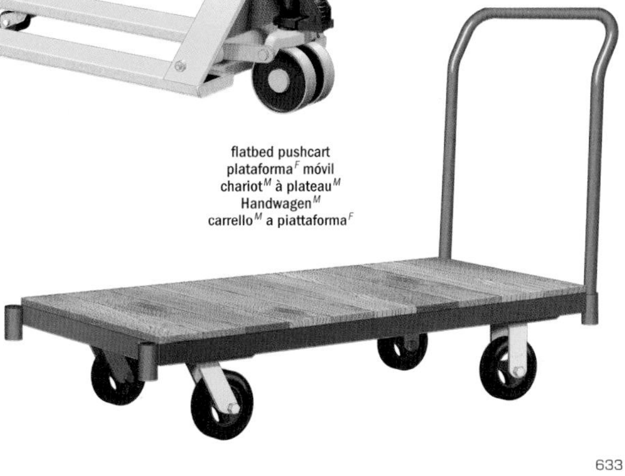

cranes

grúas^F | grues^F et portique^M | Kräne^M | gru^F

tower crane
grúa^F torre^F
grue^F à tour^F
Turmkran^M
gru^F a torre^F

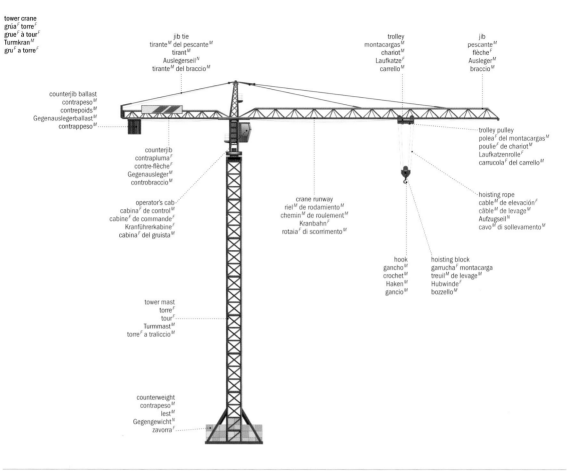

jib tie
tirante^M del pescante^M
tirant^M
Auslegerseil^N
tirante^M del braccio^M

trolley
montacargas^M
chariot^M
Laufkatze^F
carrello^M

jib
pescante^M
flèche^F
Ausleger^M
braccio^M

counterjib ballast
contrapeso^M
contrepoids^M
Gegenauslegerballast^M
contrappeso^M

trolley pulley
polea^F del montacargas^M
poulie^F de chariot^M
Laufkatzenrolle^F
carrucola^F del carrello^M

counterjib
contrapluma^F
contre-flèche^F
Gegenausleger^M
controbraccio^M

operator's cab
cabina^F de control^M
cabine^F de commande^F
Kranführerkabine^F
cabina^F del gruista^M

crane runway
riel^M de rodamiento^M
chemin^M de roulement^M
Kranbahn^F
rotaia^F di scorrimento^M

hoisting rope
cable^M de elevación^F
câble^M de levage^M
Aufzugseil^N
cavo^M di sollevamento^M

hook
gancho^M
crochet^M
Haken^M
gancio^M

hoisting block
garrucha^F montacarga
treuil^M de levage^M
Hubwinde^F
bozzello^M

tower mast
torre^F
tour^F
Turmmast^M
torre^F a traliccio^M

counterweight
contrapeso^M
lest^M
Gegengewicht^N
zavorra^F

truck crane
grúa^F móvil
grue^F sur porteur^M
Fahrkran^M
autogrù^F

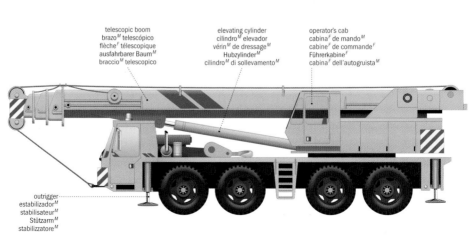

telescopic boom
brazo^M telescópico
flèche^F télescopique
ausfahrbarer Baum^M
braccio^M telescopico

elevating cylinder
cilindro^M elevador
vérin^M de dressage^M
Hubzylinder^M
cilindro^M di sollevamento^M

operator's cab
cabina^F de mando^M
cabine^F de commande^F
Führerkabine^F
cabina^F dell'autogruista^M

outrigger
estabilizador^M
stabilisateur^M
Stützarm^M
stabilizzatore^M

TRANSPORT AND MACHINERY

cranes

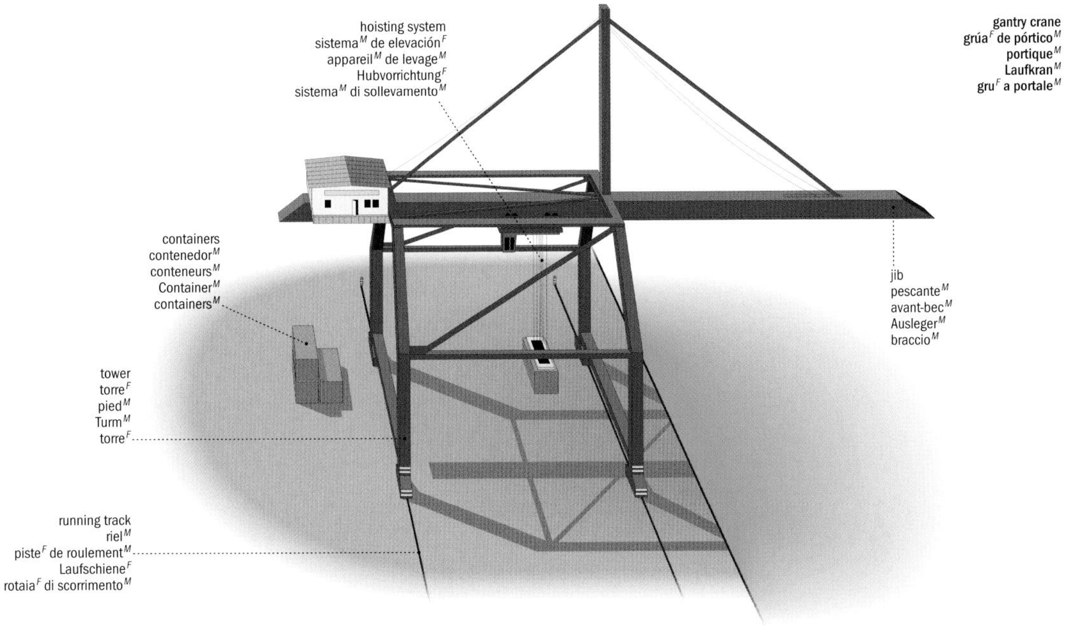

hoisting system
sistema^M de elevación^F
appareil^M de levage^M
Hubvorrichtung^F
sistema^M di sollevamento^M

gantry crane
grúa^F de pórtico^M
portique^M
Laufkran^M
gru^F a portale^M

containers
contenedor^M
conteneurs^M
Container^M
containers^M

jib
pescante^M
avant-bec^M
Ausleger^M
braccio^M

tower
torre^F
pied^M
Turm^M
torre^F

running track
riel^M
piste^F de roulement^M
Laufschiene^F
rotaia^F di scorrimento^M

container

contenedor^M | conteneur^M | Container^M | container^M

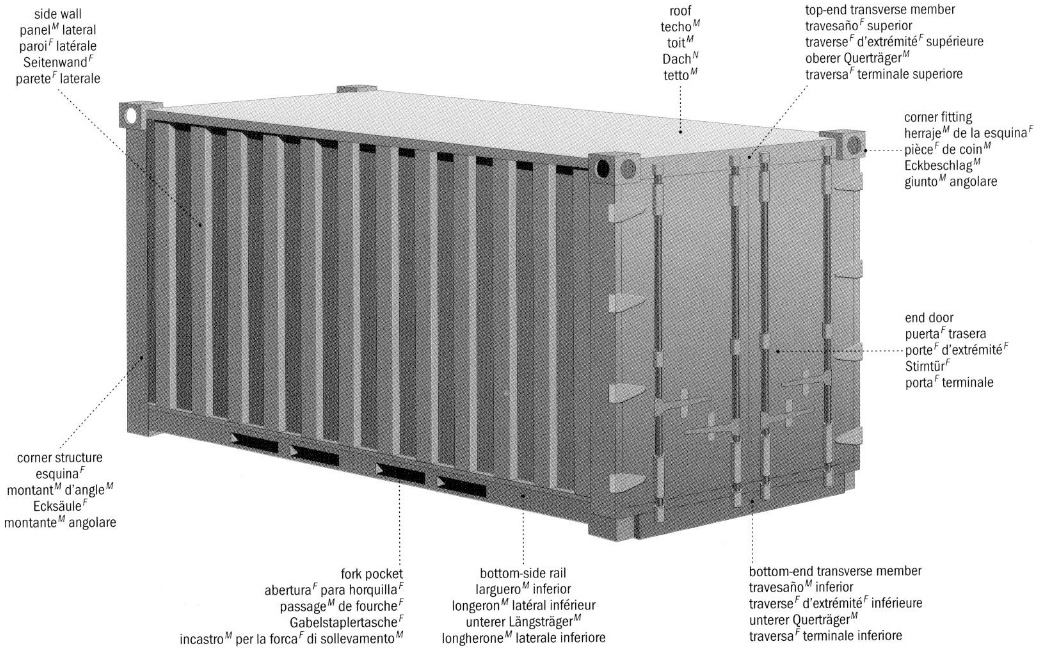

side wall
panel^M lateral
paroi^F latérale
Seitenwand^F
parete^F laterale

roof
techo^M
toit^M
Dach^N
tetto^M

top-end transverse member
travesaño^F superior
traverse^F d'extrémité^F supérieure
oberer Querträger^M
traversa^F terminale superiore

corner fitting
herraje^M de la esquina^F
pièce^F de coin^M
Eckbeschlag^M
giunto^M angolare

end door
puerta^F trasera
porte^F d'extrémité^F
Stirntür^F
porta^F terminale

corner structure
esquina^F
montant^M d'angle^M
Ecksäule^F
montante^M angolare

fork pocket
abertura^F para horquilla^F
passage^M de fourche^F
Gabelstaplertasche^F
incastro^M per la forca^F di sollevamento^M

bottom-side rail
larguero^M inferior
longeron^M latéral inférieur
unterer Längsträger^M
longherone^M laterale inferiore

bottom-end transverse member
travesaño^M inferior
traverse^F d'extrémité^F inférieure
unterer Querträger^M
traversa^F terminale inferiore

bulldozer

bulldozer[M] | bouteur[M] | Planierraupe[F] | bulldozer[M]

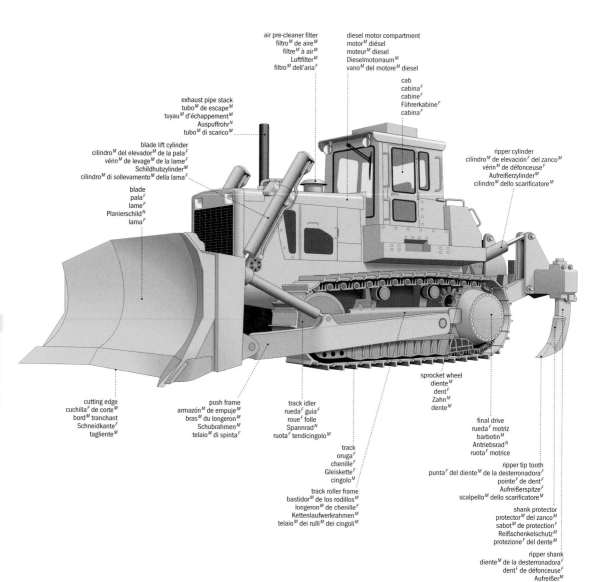

air pre-cleaner filter
filtro[M] de aire[M]
filtre[M] à air[M]
Luftfilter[M]
filtro[M] dell'aria[F]

diesel motor compartment
motor[M] diésel
moteur[M] diesel
Dieselmotorraum[M]
vano[M] del motore[M] diesel

cab
cabina[F]
cabine[F]
Führerkabine[F]
cabina[F]

exhaust pipe stack
tubo[M] de escape[M]
tuyau[M] d'échappement[M]
Auspuffrohr[N]
tubo[M] di scarico[M]

ripper cylinder
cilindro[M] de elevación[F] del zanco[M]
vérin[M] de défonceuse[F]
Aufreißerzylinder[M]
cilindro[M] dello scarificatore[M]

blade lift cylinder
cilindro[M] del elevador[M] de la pala[F]
vérin[M] de levage[M] de la lame[F]
Schildhubzylinder[M]
cilindro[M] di sollevamento[M] della lama[F]

blade
pala[F]
lame[F]
Planierschild[N]
lama[F]

cutting edge
cuchilla[F] de corte[M]
bord[M] tranchant
Schneidkante[F]
tagliente[M]

push frame
armazón[M] de empuje[M]
bras[M] du longeron[M]
Schubrahmen[M]
telaio[M] di spinta[F]

track idler
rueda[F] guía[F]
roue[F] folle
Spannrad[N]
ruota[F] tendicingolo[M]

sprocket wheel
diente[M]
dent[F]
Zahn[M]
dente[M]

final drive
rueda[F] motriz
barbotin[M]
Antriebsrad[N]
ruota[F] motrice

track
oruga[F]
chenille[F]
Gleiskette[F]
cingolo[M]

ripper tip tooth
punta[F] del diente[M] de la desterronadora[F]
pointe[F] de dent[F]
Aufreißerspitze[F]
scalpello[M] dello scarificatore[M]

track roller frame
bastidor[M] de los rodillos[M]
longeron[M] de chenille[F]
Kettenlaufwerkrahmen[M]
telaio[M] dei rulli[M] dei cingoli[M]

shank protector
protector[M] del zanco[M]
sabot[M] de protection[F]
Reißschenkelschutz[M]
protezione[F] del dente[M]

ripper shank
diente[M] de la desterronadora[F]
dent[F] de défonceuse[F]
Aufreißer[M]
dente[M] dello scarificatore[M]

crawler tractor
tractor[M] de orugas[F]
tracteur[M] à chenilles[F]
Gleiskettenschlepper[M]
trattore[M] cingolato

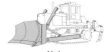

blade
pala[F]
lame[F]
Planierschaufel[F]
lama[F]

ripper
zanco[M]
défonceuse[F]
Aufreißer[M]
scarificatore[M]

wheel loader

cargadora^F-retroexcavadora^F | chargeuse^F-pelleteuse^F | Radlader^M | terna^F

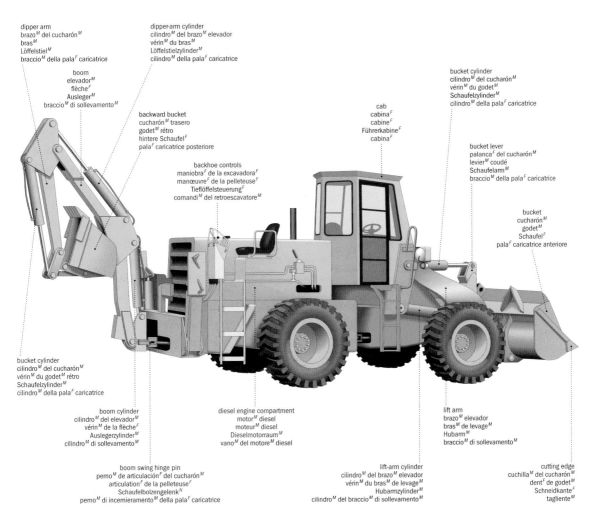

dipper arm
brazo^M del cucharón^M
bras^M
Löffelstiel^M
braccio^M della pala^F caricatrice

dipper-arm cylinder
cilindro^M del brazo^M elevador
vérin^M du bras^M
Löffelstielzylinder^M
cilindro^M della pala^F caricatrice

boom
elevador^M
flèche^F
Ausleger^M
braccio^M di sollevamento^M

backward bucket
cucharón^M trasero
godet^M rétro
hintere Schaufel^F
pala^F caricatrice posteriore

backhoe controls
maniobra^F de la excavadora^F
manœuvre^F de la pelleteuse^F
Tieflöffelsteuerung^F
comandi^M del retroescavatore^M

bucket cylinder
cilindro^M del cucharón^M
vérin^M du godet^M
Schaufelzylinder^M
cilindro^M della pala^F caricatrice

cab
cabina^F
cabine^F
Führerkabine^F
cabina^F

bucket lever
palanca^F del cucharón^M
levier^M coudé
Schaufelarm^M
braccio^M della pala^F caricatrice

bucket
cucharón^M
godet^M
Schaufel^F
pala^F caricatrice anteriore

bucket cylinder
cilindro^M del cucharón^M
vérin^M du godet^M rétro
Schaufelzylinder^M
cilindro^M della pala^F caricatrice

boom cylinder
cilindro^M del elevador^M
vérin^M de la flèche^F
Auslegerzylinder^M
cilindro^M di sollevamento^M

diesel engine compartment
motor^M diesel
moteur^M diesel
Dieselmotorraum^M
vano^M del motore^M diesel

lift arm
brazo^M elevador
bras^M de levage^M
Hubarm^M
braccio^M di sollevamento^M

boom swing hinge pin
perno^M de articulación^F del cucharón^M
articulation^F de la pelleteuse^F
Schaufelbolzengelenk^N
perno^M di incernieramento^M della pala^F caricatrice

lift-arm cylinder
cilindro^M del brazo^M elevador
vérin^M du bras^M de levage^M
Hubarmzylinder^M
cilindro^M del braccio^M di sollevamento^M

cutting edge
cuchilla^M del cucharón^M
dent^F de godet^M
Schneidkante^F
tagliente^M

front-end loader
cargador^M delantero
chargeuse^F frontale
Schaufellader^M
pala^F caricatrice anteriore

wheel tractor
tractor^M de ruedas^F
tracteur^M
Radtraktor^M
trattore^M gommato

backhoe
excavadora^F
pelleteuse^F
Tieflöffel^M
retroescavatore^M

scraper

raspador^M | décapeuse^F | Schrapper^M | ruspa^F

gooseneck
cuello^M de ganso^M
col^M-de-cygne^M
Schwanenhals^M
collo^M d'oca^F

steering cylinder
cilindro^M de dirección^F
vérin^M de direction^F
Lenkzylinder^M
cilindro^M direzionale

tractor engine compartment
motor^M del tractor^M
tracteur^M-remorqueur^M
Motorraum^M
vano^M del motore^M di traino^M

elevator
eyector^M
éjecteur^M
Auswerfer^M
eiettore^M

draft tube
barra^F de arrastre^M
palonnier^M
Saugrohr^N
tubo^M di posizionamento^M

bowl
contenedor^M
benne^F
Schürfkübel^M
cassone^M

cutting edge
cuchilla^F de corte^M
lame^F racleuse
Schneidkante^F
tagliente^M

draft arm
brazo^M de arrastre^M
brancard^M
Saugarm^M
braccio^M di posizionamento^M

hydraulic shovel

pala^F hidráulica | pelle^F hydraulique | Hydraulik-Hochlöffelbagger^M | escavatore^M idraulico

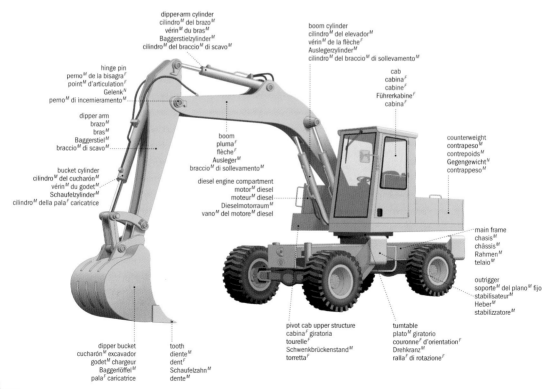

dipper-arm cylinder
cilindro^M del brazo^M
vérin^M du bras^M
Baggerstielzylinder^M
cilindro^M del braccio^M di scavo^M

boom cylinder
cilindro^M del elevador^M
vérin^M de la flèche^F
Auslegerzylinder^M
cilindro^M del braccio^M di sollevamento^M

hinge pin
perno^M de la bisagra^F
point^M d'articulation^F
Gelenk^N
perno^M di incernieramento^M

cab
cabina^F
cabine^F
Führerkabine^F
cabina^F

dipper arm
brazo^M
bras^M
Baggerstiel^M
braccio^M di scavo^M

counterweight
contrapeso^M
contrepoids^M
Gegengewicht^N
contrappeso^M

boom
pluma^F
flèche^F
Ausleger^M
braccio^M di sollevamento^M

bucket cylinder
cilindro^M del cucharón^M
vérin^M du godet^M
Schaufelzylinder^M
cilindro^M della pala^F caricatrice

diesel engine compartment
motor^M diesel
moteur^M diesel
Dieselmotorraum^M
vano^M del motore^M diesel

main frame
chasis^M
châssis^M
Rahmen^M
telaio^M

outrigger
soporte^M del plano^M fijo
stabilisateur^M
Heber^M
stabilizzatore^M

dipper bucket
cucharón^M excavador
godet^M chargeur
Baggerlöffel^M
pala^F caricatrice

tooth
diente^M
dent^F
Schaufelzahn^M
dente^M

pivot cab upper structure
cabina^F giratoria
tourelle^F
Schwenkbrückenstand^M
torretta^F

turntable
plato^M giratorio
couronne^F d'orientation^F
Drehkranz^M
ralla^F di rotazione^F

TRANSPORT AND MACHINERY

grader

niveladora^F | niveleuse^F | Straßenhobel^M | livellatrice^F

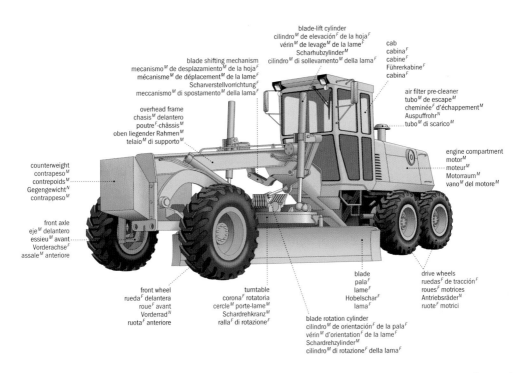

blade-lift cylinder
cilindro^M de elevación^F de la hoja^F
vérin^M de levage^M de la lame^F
Scharhubzylinder^M
cilindro^M di sollevamento^M della lama^F

cab
cabina^F
cabine^F
Führerkabine^F
cabina^F

blade shifting mechanism
mecanismo^M de desplazamiento^M de la hoja^F
mécanisme^M de déplacement^M de la lame^F
Scharverstellvorrichtung^F
meccanismo^M di spostamento^M della lama^F

air filter pre-cleaner
tubo^M de escape^M
cheminée^F d'échappement^M
Auspuffrohr^N
tubo^M di scarico^M

overhead frame
chasis^M delantero
poutre^F-châssis^M
oben liegender Rahmen^M
telaio^M di supporto^M

engine compartment
motor^M
moteur^M
Motorraum^M
vano^M del motore^M

counterweight
contrapeso^M
contrepoids^M
Gegengewicht^N
contrappeso^M

front axle
eje^M delantero
essieu^M avant
Vorderachse^F
assale^M anteriore

blade
pala^F
lame^F
Hobelschar^F
lama^F

drive wheels
ruedas^F de tracción^F
roues^F motrices
Antriebsräder^N
ruote^F motrici

front wheel
rueda^F delantera
roue^F avant
Vorderrad^N
ruota^F anteriore

turntable
corona^F rotatoria
cercle^M porte-lame^M
Schardrehkranz^M
ralla^F di rotazione^F

blade rotation cylinder
cilindro^M de orientación^F de la pala^F
vérin^M d'orientation^F de la lame^F
Schardrehzylinder^M
cilindro^M di rotazione^F della lama^F

dump truck

volcadora^F | camion^M-benne^F | Muldenkipper^M | autocarro^M a cassone^M ribaltabile

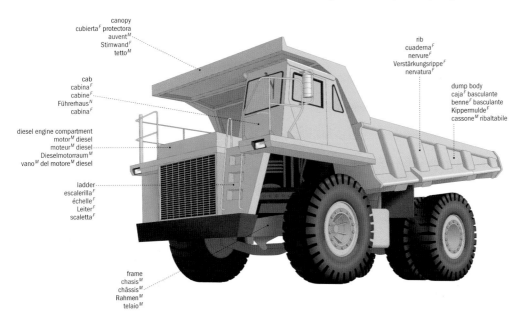

canopy
cubierta^F protectora
auvent^M
Stirnwand^F
tetto^M

rib
cuaderna^F
nervure^F
Verstärkungsrippe^F
nervatura^F

cab
cabina^F
cabine^F
Führerhaus^N
cabina^F

dump body
caja^F basculante
benne^F basculante
Kippermulde^F
cassone^M ribaltabile

diesel engine compartment
motor^M diesel
moteur^M diesel
Dieselmotorraum^M
vano^M del motore^M diesel

ladder
escalerilla^F
échelle^F
Leiter^F
scaletta^F

frame
chasis^M
châssis^M
Rahmen^M
telaio^M

tractor

tractor^M | tracteur^M agricole | Traktor^M | trattore^M

tractor: rear view
tractor^M : vista^F trasera
tracteur^M agricole : vue^F arrière
Traktor^M: Hinteransicht^F
trattore^M: vista^F posteriore

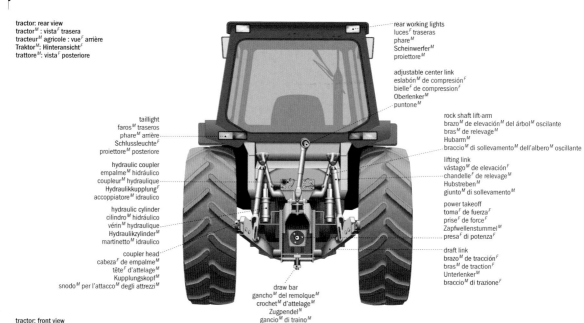

rear working lights
luces^F traseras
phare^M
Scheinwerfer^M
proiettore^M

adjustable center link
eslabón^M de compresión^F
bielle^F de compression^F
Oberlenker^M
puntone^M

taillight
faros^M traseros
phare^M arrière
Schlussleuchte^F
proiettore^M posteriore

rock shaft lift-arm
brazo^M de elevación^M del árbol^M oscilante
bras^M de relevage^M
Hubarm^M
braccio^M di sollevamento^M dell'albero^M oscillante

hydraulic coupler
empalme^M hidráulico
coupleur^M hydraulique
Hydraulikkupplung^F
accoppiatore^M idraulico

lifting link
vástago^M de elevación^F
chandelle^F de relevage^M
Hubstreben^M
giunto^M di sollevamento^M

hydraulic cylinder
cilindro^M hidráulico
vérin^M hydraulique
Hydraulikzylinder^M
martinetto^M idraulico

power takeoff
toma^F de fuerza^F
prise^F de force^F
Zapfwellenstummel^M
presa^F di potenza^F

coupler head
cabeza^F de empalme^M
tête^F d'attelage^M
Kupplungskopf^M
snodo^M per l'attacco^M degli attrezzi^M

draft link
brazo^M de tracción^F
bras^M de traction^F
Unterlenker^M
braccio^M di trazione^F

draw bar
gancho^M del remolque^M
crochet^M d'attelage^M
Zugpendel^N
gancio^M di traino^M

tractor: front view
tractor^M : vista^F frontal
tracteur^M agricole : vue^F avant
Traktor^M: Vorderansicht^F
trattore^M: vista^F anteriore

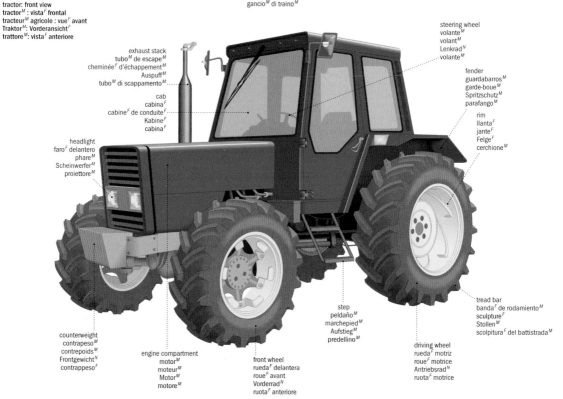

steering wheel
volante^M
volant^M
Lenkrad^N
volante^M

exhaust stack
tubo^M de escape^M
cheminée^F d'échappement^M
Auspuff^M
tubo^M di scappamento^M

fender
guardabarros^M
garde-boue^M
Spritzschutz^M
parafango^M

cab
cabina^F
cabine^F de conduite^F
Kabine^F
cabina^F

rim
llanta^F
jante^F
Felge^F
cerchione^M

headlight
faro^F delantero
phare^M
Scheinwerfer^M
proiettore^M

tread bar
banda^F de rodamiento^M
sculpture^F
Stollen^M
scolpitura^F del battistrada^M

counterweight
contrapeso^M
contrepoids^M
Frontgewicht^N
contrappeso^F

engine compartment
motor^M
moteur^M
Motor^M
motore^M

front wheel
rueda^F delantera
roue^F avant
Vorderrad^N
ruota^F anteriore

step
peldaño^M
marchepied^M
Aufstieg^M
predellino^M

driving wheel
rueda^F motriz
roue^F motrice
Antriebsrad^N
ruota^F motrice

agricultural machinery

maquinaria^F agrícola | machinerie^F agricole | landwirtschaftliche Maschinen^F | macchine^F agricole

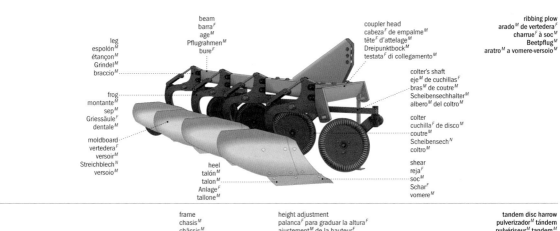

beam
barra^F
age^M
Pflugrahmen^M
bure^F

leg
espolón^M
étançon^M
Grindel^M
braccio^M

frog
montante^M
sep^M
Griessäule^F
dentale^M

moldboard
vertedera^F
versoir^M
Streichblech^N
versoio^M

heel
talón^M
talon^M
Anlage^F
tallone^M

coupler head
cabeza^F de empalme^M
tête^F d'attelage^M
Dreipunktbock^M
testata^F di collegamento^M

colter's shaft
eje^M de cuchillas^F
bras^M de coutre^M
Scheibensechhalter^M
albero^M del coltro^M

colter
cuchilla^F de disco^M
coutre^M
Scheibensech^N
coltro^M

shear
reja^F
soc^M
Schar^F
vomere^M

ribbing plow
arado^M de vertedera^F
charrue^F à soc^M
Beetpflug^M
aratro^M a vomere-versoio^M

frame
chasis^M
châssis^M
Rahmen^M
telaio^M

disc arm
brazo^M de disco^M
bras^M
Scheibenarm^M
braccio^M del disco^M

disc
disco^M
disque^M
Scheibe^F
disco^M

height adjustment
palanca^F para graduar la altura^F
ajustement^M de la hauteur^F
Hubwerk^N
regolazione^F dell'altezza^F

hydraulic hose
manguera^F hidráulica
conduit^M hydraulique
Hydraulikschlauch^M
tubo^M idraulico flessibile

draw bar hitch
cabeza^F de enganche^M
tête^F d'attelage^M
Anhängemaul^N
attacco^M della barra^F di traino^M

tandem disc harrow
pulverizador^M tándem
pulvériseur^M tandem^M
Tandemscheibenegge^F
erpice^M doppio a dischi^M

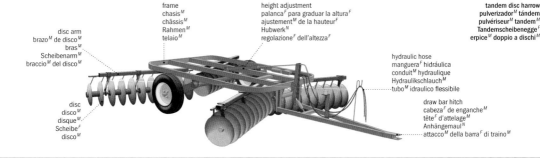

frame
bastidor^M
châssis^M
Rahmen^M
telaio^M

rotary hoe
azadón^M rotatorio
houe^F rotative
Sternscheibe^F
zappa^F rotante

tine
púa^F de muelle^M
dent^F
Zinke^F
rebbio^M

cultivator
cultivador^M
cultivateur^M
Grubber^M
coltivatore^M

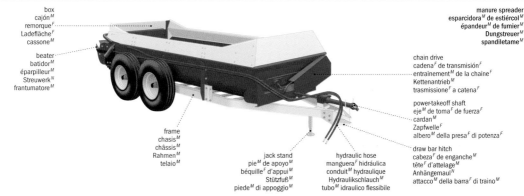

box
cajón^M
remorque^F
Ladefläche^F
cassone^M

beater
batidor^M
éparpilleur^M
Streuwerk^N
frantumatore^M

frame
chasis^M
châssis^M
Rahmen^M
telaio^M

jack stand
pie^M de apoyo^M
béquille^F d'appui^M
Stützfuß^M
piede^M di appoggio^M

hydraulic hose
manguera^F hidráulica
conduit^M hydraulique
Hydraulikschlauch^M
tubo^M idraulico flessibile

manure spreader
esparcidora^M de estiércol^M
épandeur^M de fumier^M
Dungstreuer^M
spandiletame^M

chain drive
cadena^F de transmisión^F
entraînement^M de la chaine^F
Kettenantrieb^M
trasmissione^F a catena^F

power-takeoff shaft
eje^M de toma^F de fuerza^F
cardan^M
Zapfwelle^F
albero^M della presa^F di potenza^F

draw bar hitch
cabeza^F de enganche^M
tête^F d'attelage^M
Anhängemaul^N
attacco^M della barra^F di traino^M

rake
rastrillo^M
râteau^M
Schubrechwender^M
rastrello^M meccanico

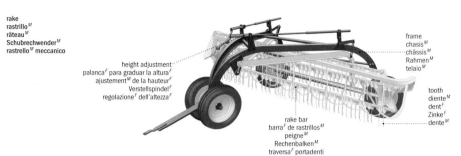

height adjustment
palanca^F para graduar la altura^F
ajustement^M de la hauteur^F
Verstellspindel^F
regolazione^F dell'altezza^F

frame
chasis^M
châssis^M
Rahmen^M
telaio^M

tooth
diente^M
dent^F
Zinke^F
dente^M

rake bar
barra^F de rastrillos^M
peigne^M
Rechenbalken^M
traversa^F portadenti

flail mower
segadora^F
faucheuse^F-conditionneuse^F
Anhängemähwerk^N
falciacondizionatrice^F

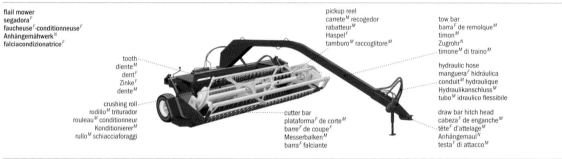

pickup reel
carrete^M recogedor
rabatteur^M
Haspel^F
tamburo^M raccoglitore^M

tow bar
barra^F de remolque^M
timon^M
Zugrohr^N
timone^M di traino^M

tooth
diente^M
dent^F
Zinke^F
dente^M

hydraulic hose
manguera^F hidráulica
conduit^M hydraulique
Hydraulikanschluss^M
tubo^M idraulico flessibile

crushing roll
rodillo^M triturador
rouleau^M conditionneur
Konditionierer^M
rullo^M schiacciaforaggi

cutter bar
plataforma^F de corte^M
barre^F de coupe^F
Messerbalken^M
barra^F falciante

draw bar hitch head
cabeza^F de enganche^M
tête^F d'attelage^M
Anhängemaul^N
testa^F di attacco^M

hay baler
empacadora^F de heno^M
ramasseuse^F-presse^F
Hochdruckpresse^F
imballatrice^F

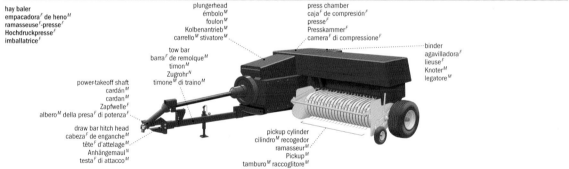

plungerhead
émbolo^M
foulon^M
Kolbenantrieb^M
carrello^M stivatore^M

press chamber
caja^F de compresión^F
presse^F
Presskammer^F
camera di compressione^F

binder
agavilladora^F
lieuse^F
Knoter^M
legatore^M

tow bar
barra^F de remolque^M
timon^M
Zugrohr^N
timone^M di traino^M

power-takeoff shaft
cardán^M
cardan^M
Zapfwelle^F
albero^M della presa^F di potenza^F

draw bar hitch head
cabeza^F de enganche^M
tête^F d'attelage^M
Anhängemaul^N
testa^F di attacco^M

pickup cylinder
cilindro^M recogedor
ramasseur^M
Pickup^M
tamburo^M raccoglitore^M

forage harvester
cosechera^F de forraje^M
fourragère^F
Feldhäcksler^M
raccoglitrice^F di foraggio^M

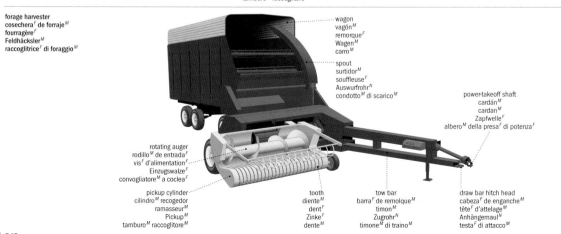

wagon
vagón^M
remorque^F
Wagen^M
carro^M

spout
surtidor^M
souffleuse^F
Auswurfrohr^N
condotto^M di scarico^M

power-takeoff shaft
cardán^M
cardan^M
Zapfwelle^F
albero^M della presa^F di potenza^F

rotating auger
rodillo^M de entrada^F
vis^F d'alimentation^F
Einzugswalze^F
convogliatore^M a coclea^F

pickup cylinder
cilindro^M recogedor
ramasseur^M
Pickup^M
tamburo^M raccoglitore^M

tooth
diente^M
dent^F
Zinke^F
dente^M

tow bar
barra^F de remolque^M
timon^M
Zugrohr^N
timone^M di traino^M

draw bar hitch head
cabeza^F de enganche^M
tête^F d'attelage^M
Anhängemaul^N
testa^F di attacco^M

seed drill
sembradora^F a chorrillo^M
semoir^M en lignes^F
Drillmaschine^F
seminatrice^F

grain tube
tubo^M para el grano^M
tube^M d'ensemencement^M
Fallrohr^N
tubo^M di caduta^F del seme^M

ensiling tube
tubo^M de ensilaje^M
tuyau^M d'ensilage^M
Sammelrohr^N
condotto^M di insilamento^M

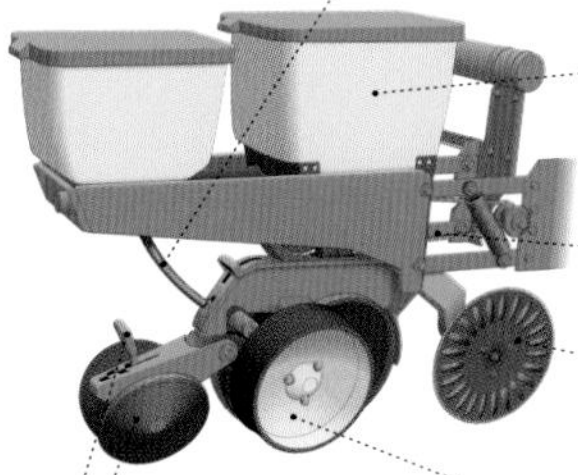

forage blower
aventador^M de forraje^M
souffleuse^F de fourrage^M
Abladegebläse^N
insilatrice^F

hopper
tolva^F
trémie^F
Saatgutbehälter^M
tramoggia^F

maneuvering bar
barra^F de maniobra^F
barre^F de manœuvre^F
Bedienungshebel^M
barra^F di manovra^F

chain drive
cadena^F de transmisión^F
chaîne^F d'entraînement^M
Antrieb^M
trasmissione^F a catena^F

fan's tube
tubo^M de ventilación^F
tuyau^M du ventilateur^M
Gebläserohr^N
condotto^M del ventilatore^M

colter
cuchilla^F
coutre^M
Sech^N
coltro^M

fan
ventilador^M
ventilateur^M
Gebläse^N
ventilatore^M

covering disk
disco^M tapador
disque^M d'enterrage^M
Zustreicher^M
disco^M di copertura^F

press wheel
rueda^F compresora
roue^F de pression^F
Druckrolle^F
rullo^M di compressione^F

feed table
mesa^F alimentadora
table^F d'alimentation^F
Dosierteller^M
alimentatore^M

hopper
tolva^F
trémie^F
Behälter^M
tramoggia^F

disk spacing lever
palanca^F de espaciamiento^M de los discos^M
levier^M d'écartement^M
Einstellhebel^M
leva^F spaziatrice dei dischi^M

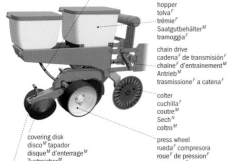

rotating auger
rodillo^M de entrada^F
vis^F d'alimentation^F
Einzugsschnecke^F
convogliatore^M a coclea^F

cab
cabina^F
cabine^F de conduite^F
Kabine^F
cabina^F

grain elevator
elevador^M
élévateur^M à grain^M
Kornelevator^M
elevatore^M della granella^F

grain tank
depósito^M del grano^M
réservoir^M à grain^M
Korntank^M
serbatoio^M della granella^F

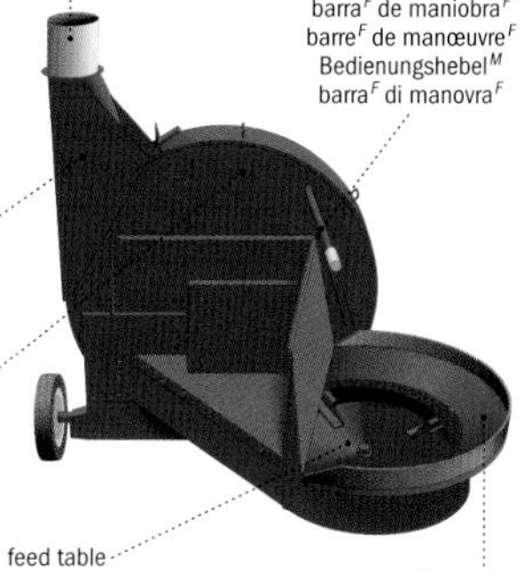

combine harvester
cosechadora^F trilladora^F
moissonneuse^F-batteuse^F
Mähdrescher^M
mietitrebbiatrice^F

divider
separador^M
diviseur^M
Halmteiler^M
separatore^M

unloading tube
tubo^M de descarga^F
tube^M de déchargement^M
Auslaufrohr^N
tubo^M di scarico^M

straw spreader
esparcidor^M de paja^F
éparpilleur^M de paille^F
Strohverteiler^M
spargitore^M di paglia^F

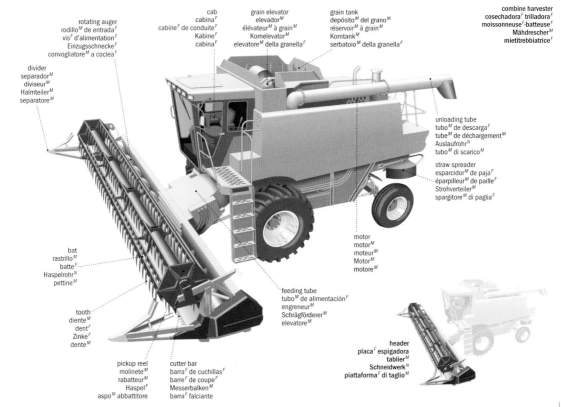

bat
rastrillo^M
batte^F
Haspelrohr^N
pettine^M

motor
motor^M
moteur^M
Motor^M
motore^M

tooth
diente^M
dent^F
Zinke^F
dente^M

feeding tube
tubo^M de alimentación^F
engreneur^M
Schrägförderer^M
elevatore^M

pickup reel
molinete^M
rabatteur^M
Haspel^F
aspo^M abbattitore

cutter bar
barra^F de cuchillas^F
barre^F de coupe^F
Messerbalken^M
barra^F falciante

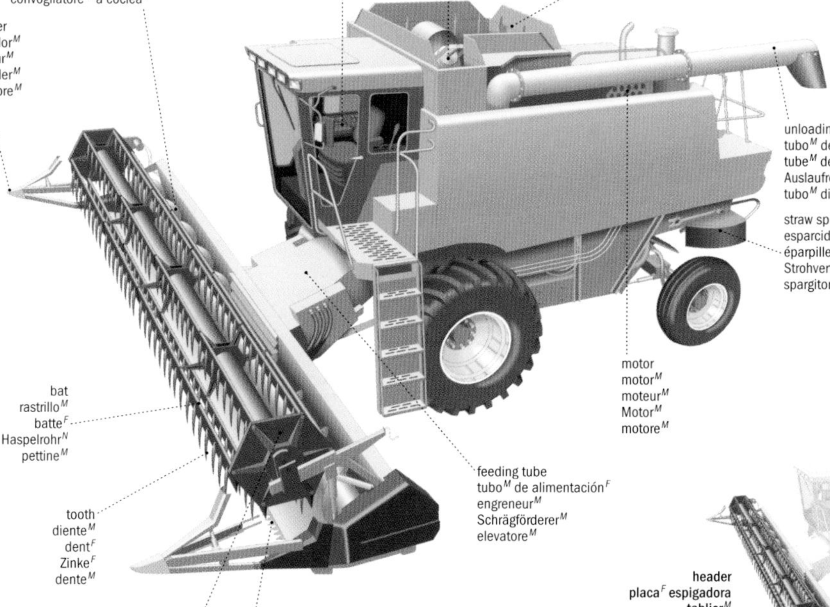

header
placa^F espigadora
tablier^M
Schneidwerk^N
piattaforma^F di taglio^M

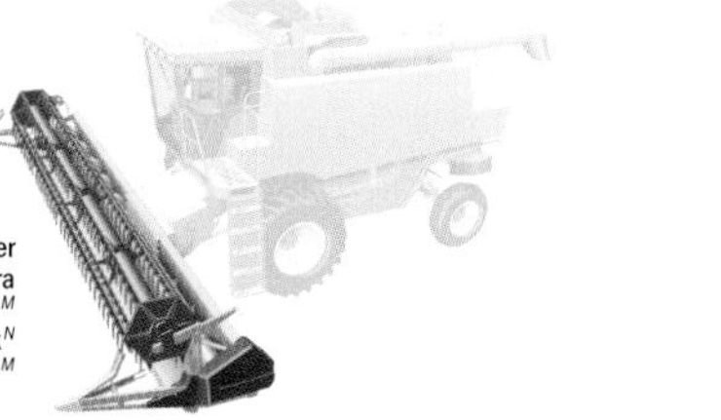

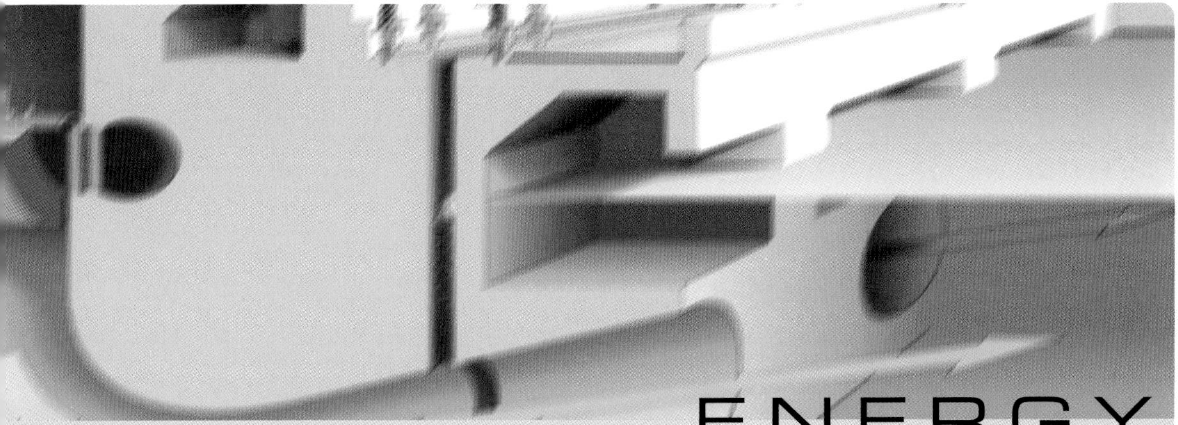

ENERGY

ENERGÍA | ÉNERGIES | ENERGIE | ENERGIA

production of electricity from geothermal energy

producción^F de electricidad^F por energía^F geotérmica | production^F d'électricité^F par énergie^F géothermique | geothermischer Energie^F | energia^F geotermica

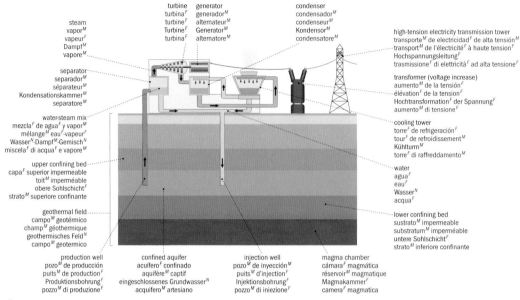

turbine
turbina^F
turbine^F
Turbine^F
turbina^F

generator
generador^M
alternateur^M
Generator^M
alternatore^M

condenser
condensador^M
condenseur^M
Kondensor^M
condensatore^M

steam
vapor^M
vapeur^F
Dampf^M
vapore^F

high-tension electricity transmission tower
transporte^M de electricidad^F de alta tensión^M
transport^M de l'électricité^F à haute tension^F
Hochspannungsleitung^F
trasmissione^F di elettricità^F ad alta tensione^F

separator
separador^M
séparateur^M
Kondensationskammer^M
separatore^M

transformer (voltage increase)
aumento^M de la tensión^F
élévation^F de la tension^F
Hochtransformation^F der Spannung^F
aumento^M di tensione^F

water-steam mix
mezcla^F de agua^F y vapor^M
mélange^M eau^F-vapeur^F
Wasser^N-Dampf^M-Gemisch^N
miscela^F di acqua^F e vapore^M

cooling tower
torre^F de refrigeración^F
tour^F de refroidissement^M
Kühlturm^M
torre^F di raffreddamento^M

upper confining bed
capa^F superior impermeable
toit^M imperméable
obere Sohlschicht^F
strato^M superiore confinante

water
agua^F
eau^F
Wasser^N
acqua^F

geothermal field
campo^M geotérmico
champ^M géothermique
geothermisches Feld^N
campo^M geotermico

lower confining bed
sustrato^M impermeable
substratum^M imperméable
untere Sohlschicht^F
strato^M inferiore confinante

production well
pozo^M de producción
puits^M de production^F
Produktionsbohrung^F
pozzo^M di produzione^F

confined aquifer
acuífero^F confinado
aquifère^M captif
eingeschlossenes Grundwasser^N
acquifero^M artesiano

injection well
pozo^M de inyección^M
puits^M d'injection^F
Injektionsbohrung^F
pozzo^M di iniezione^F

magma chamber
cámara^F magmática
réservoir^M magmatique
Magmakammer^F
camera^F magmatica

thermal energy

energía^F térmica | énergie^F thermique | Wärmeenergie^F | energia^F termica

geothermal energy
energía^F geotérmica
énergie^F géothermique
Elektrizitätserzeugung^F aus Wärmeenergie^F
geotermica

crusher
trituradora^F
broyeur^M
Zerkleinerungswerk^N
frantumatore^M

stack
chimenea^F
cheminée^F
Schornstein^M
ciminiera^F

cooling tower
torre^F de refrigeración^F
tour^F de refroidissement^M
Kühlturm^M
torre^F di raffreddamento^M

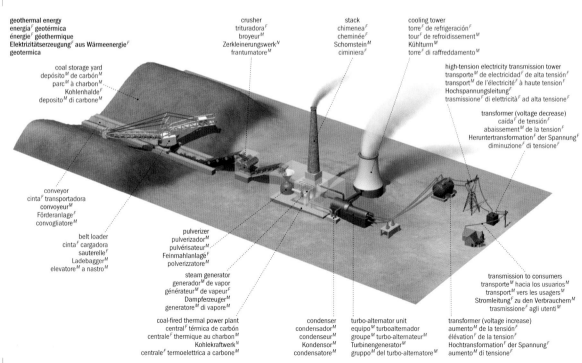

coal storage yard
depósito^M de carbón^M
parc^M à charbon^M
Kohlenhalde^F
deposito^M di carbone^M

high-tension electricity transmission tower
transporte^M de electricidad^F de alta tensión^M
transport^M de l'électricité^F à haute tension^F
Hochspannungsleitung^F
trasmissione^F di elettricità^F ad alta tensione^F

transformer (voltage decrease)
caída^F de tensión^F
abaissement^M de la tension^F
Heruntertransformation^F der Spannung^F
diminuzione^F di tensione^F

conveyor
cinta^F transportadora
convoyeur^F
Förderanlage^F
convogliatore^M

belt loader
cinta^F cargadora
sauterelle^F
Ladebagger^M
elevatore^M a nastro^M

pulverizer
pulverizador^M
pulvérisateur^M
Feinmahlanlage^F
polverizzatore^M

transmission to consumers
transporte^M hacia los usuarios^M
transport^M vers les usagers^M
Stromleitung^F zu den Verbrauchern^M
trasmissione^F agli utenti^M

steam generator
generador^M de vapor
générateur^M de vapeur^F
Dampferzeuger^M
generatore^M di vapore^M

coal-fired thermal power plant
central^F térmica de carbón
centrale^F thermique au charbon^M
Kohlekraftwerk^N
centrale^F termoelettrica a carbone^M

condenser
condensador^M
condenseur^M
Kondensor^M
condensatore^M

turbo-alternator unit
equipo^M turboalternador
groupe^M turbo-alternateur^M
Turbinengenerator^M
gruppo^M del turbo-alternatore^M

transformer (voltage increase)
aumento^M de la tensión^F
élévation^F de la tension^F
Hochtransformation^F der Spannung^F
aumento^M di tensione^F

coal mine

minas^F de carbón^M | mine^F de charbon^M | Kohlebergwerk^N | miniera^F di carbone^M

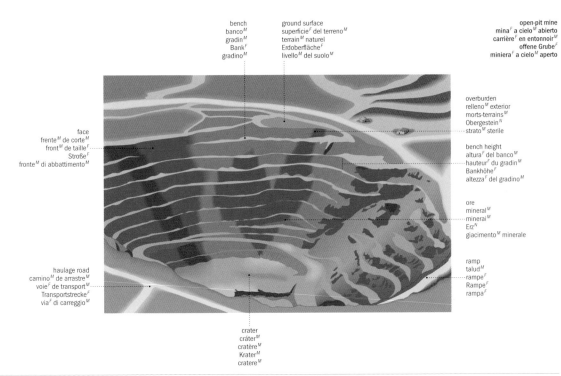

bench
banco^M
gradin^M
Bank^F
gradino^M

ground surface
superficie^F del terreno^M
terrain^M naturel
Erdoberfläche^F
livello^M del suolo^M

open-pit mine
mina^F a cielo^M abierto
carrière^F en entonnoir^M
offene Grube^F
miniera^F a cielo^M aperto

overburden
relleno^M exterior
morts-terrains^M
Obergestein^N
strato^M sterile

face
frente^M de corte^M
front^M de taille^F
Stroße^F
fronte^M di abbattimento^M

bench height
altura^F del banco^M
hauteur^F du gradin^M
Bankhöhe^F
altezza^F del gradino^M

ore
mineral^M
minerai^M
Erz^N
giacimento^M minerale

ramp
talud^M
rampe^F
Rampe^F
rampa^F

haulage road
camino^M de arrastre^M
voie^F de transport^M
Transportstrecke^F
via^F di carreggio^M

crater
cráter^M
cratère^M
Krater^M
cratere^M

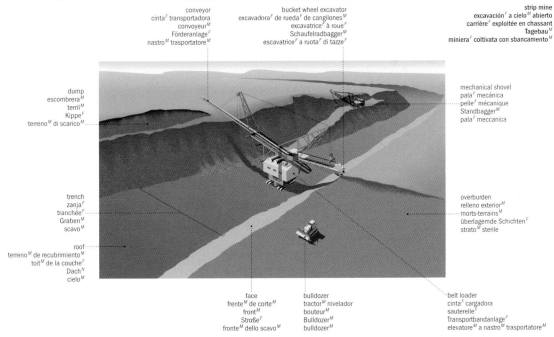

conveyor
cinta^F transportadora
convoyeur^M
Förderanlage^F
nastro^M trasportatore^M

bucket wheel excavator
excavadora^F de rueda^F de cangilones^M
excavatrice^F à roue^F
Schaufelradbagger^M
escavatrice^F a ruota^F di tazze^F

strip mine
excavación^F a cielo^M abierto
carrière^F exploitée en chassant
Tagebau^M
miniera^F coltivata con sbancamento^M

dump
escombrera^M
terril^M
Kippe^F
terreno^M di scarico^M

mechanical shovel
pala^F mecánica
pelle^F mécanique
Standbagger^M
pala^F meccanica

trench
zanja^F
tranchée^F
Graben^M
scavo^M

overburden
relleno exterior^M
morts-terrains^M
überlagemde Schichten^F
strato^M sterile

roof
terreno^M de recubrimiento^M
toit^M de la couche^F
Dach^N
cielo^M

face
frente^M de corte^M
front^M
Stroße^F
fronte^M dello scavo^M

bulldozer
tractor^M nivelador
bouteur^M
Bulldozer^M
bulldozer^M

belt loader
cinta^F cargadora
sauterelle^F
Transportbandanlage^F
elevatore^M a nastro^M trasportatore^M

ENERGY

coal mine

jackleg drill
perforadora^F con empujador^M neumático
marteau^M perforateur à poussoir^M pneumatique
Bohrhammer^M
martello^M perforatore con servosostegno^M

hammer drill
taladro^M percutor
marteau^M perforateur
Schlagbohrer^M
martello^M perforatore^M

water hose
manguera^F de agua^F
flexible^M d'eau^F
Wasserschlauch^M
tubo^M flessibile per l'acqua^F

bit
broca^F
taillant^M
Bohrkopf^M
tagliente^M

drill rod
barrena^F
fleuret^M
Bohrstange^F
fioretto^M

air leg
cilindro^M neumático
poussoir^M pneumatique
Druckluft-Bohrknecht^M
servosostegno^M

air hose
manguera^F de aire^M
flexible^M d'air^M
Luftschlauch^M
tubo^M flessibile per l'aria^F compressa

water separator
separador^M de agua^F
séparateur^M d'eau^F
Wasserabscheider^M
separatore^M dell'acqua^F

oiler
aceitera^F
graisseur^M
Öler^M
oliatore^M

maintenance shop
taller^M de mantenimiento^M
atelier^M d'entretien^M
Maschinenhaus^N
officina^F riparazioni^F

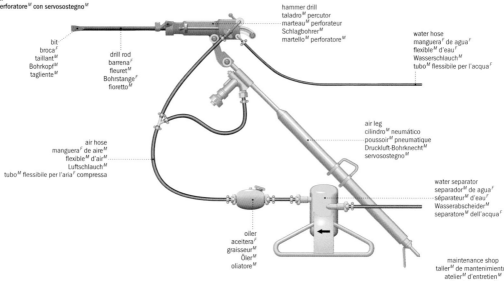

pithead
planta^F exterior de una mina^F
carreau^M de mine^F
Übertageanlage^F
esterno^M della miniera^F

dump
escombrera^M
terril^M
Schlackenhalde^F
terreno^M di scarico^M

main fan
ventilador^M principal
ventilateur^M principal
Hauptlüfter^M
ventilatore^M principale

loading bunker
silo^M de carga^F
silo^M de chargement^M
Verladebunker^M
silo^M del minerale^M

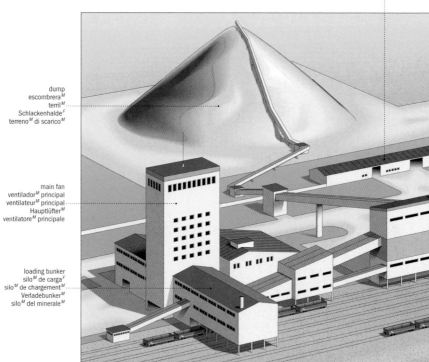

GEOTHERMAL AND FOSSIL ENERGY | ENERGÍA GEOTÉRMICA Y FÓSIL
GÉOTHERMIE ET ÉNERGIE FOSSILE | GEOTHERMISCHE UND FOSSILE ENERGIE | ENERGIA GEOTERMICA E FOSSILE

coal mine

pneumatic jackhammer
martillo^M neumático
marteau^M pneumatique
Pressluftbohrer^M
piccone^M pneumatico

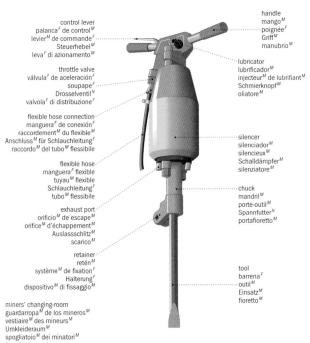

control lever
palanca^F de control^M
levier^M de commande^F
Steuerhebel^M
leva^F di azionamento^M

handle
mango^M
poignée^F
Griff^M
manubrio^M

lubricator
lubrificador^M
injecteur^M de lubrifiant^M
Schmierknopf^M
oliatore^M

throttle valve
válvula^F de aceleración^F
soupape^F
Drosselventil^N
valvola^F di distribuzione^F

flexible hose connection
manguera^F de conexión^F
raccordement du flexible^M
Anschluss^M für Schlauchleitung^F
raccordo^M del tubo^M flessibile

silencer
silenciador^M
silencieux^M
Schalldämpfer^M
silenziatore^M

flexible hose
manguera^F flexible
tuyau^M flexible
Schlauchleitung^F
tubo^M flessibile

chuck
mandril^M
porte-outil^M
Spannfutter^N
portafioretto^M

exhaust port
orificio^M de escape^M
orifice^M d'échappement^M
Auslassschlitz^M
scarico^M

retainer
retén^M
système^M de fixation^F
Halterung^F
dispositivo^M di fissaggio^M

tool
barrena^F
outil^M
Einsatz^M
fioretto^M

shaft head
pozo^M principal
tête^F de puits^M
Schachtgerüsteingang^M
entrata^F del pozzo^M

miners' changing-room
guardarropa^M de los mineros^M
vestiaire^M des mineurs^M
Umkleideraum^M
spogliatoio^M dei minatori^M

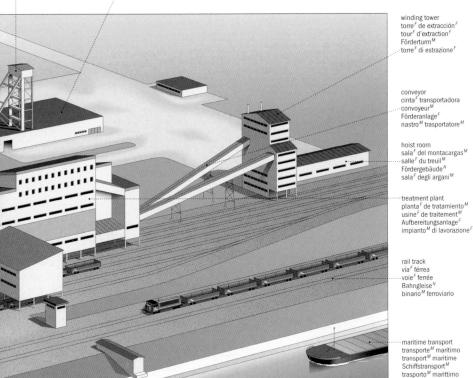

winding tower
torre^F de extracción^F
tour^F d'extraction^F
Förderturm^M
torre^F di estrazione^F

conveyor
cinta^F transportadora
convoyeur^M
Förderanlage^F
nastro^M trasportatore^M

hoist room
sala^F del montacargas^M
salle^F du treuil^M
Fördergebäude^N
sala^F degli argani^M

treatment plant
planta^F de tratamiento^M
usine^F de traitement^M
Aufbereitungsanlage^F
impianto^M di lavorazione^F

rail track
vía^F férrea
voie^F ferrée
Bahngleise^N
binario^M ferroviario

maritime transport
transporte^M marítimo
transport^M maritime
Schiffstransport^M
trasporto^M marittimo

ENERGY

GEOTHERMAL AND FOSSIL ENERGY | ENERGÍA GEOTÉRMICA Y FÓSIL
GÉOTHERMIE ET ÉNERGIE FOSSILE | GEOTHERMISCHE UND FOSSILE ENERGIE | ENERGIA GEOTERMICA E FOSSILE

coal mine

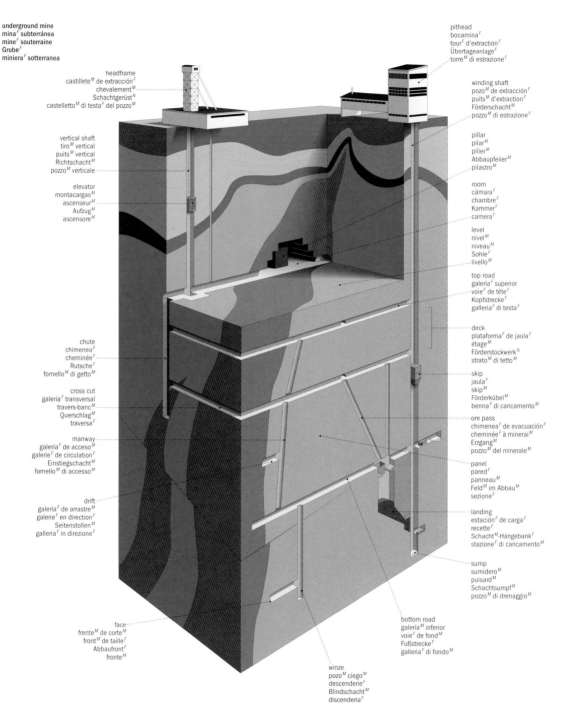

underground mine
mina^F subterránea
mine^F souterraine
Grube^F
miniera^F sotterranea

headframe
castillete^M de extracción^F
chevalement^M
Schachtgerüst^N
castelletto^M di testa^F del pozzo^M

vertical shaft
tiro^M vertical
puits^M vertical
Richtschacht^M
pozzo^M verticale

elevator
montacargas^M
ascenseur^M
Aufzug^M
ascensore^M

chute
chimenea^F
cheminée^F
Rutsche^F
fornello^M di getto^M

cross cut
galería^F transversal
travers-banc^M
Querschlag^M
traversa^F

manway
galería^F de acceso^M
galerie^F de circulation^F
Einstiegschacht^M
fornello^M di accesso^M

drift
galería^F de arrastre^M
galerie^F en direction^F
Seitenstollen^M
galleria^F in direzione^F

face
frente^M de corte^M
front^M de taille^F
Abbaufront^F
fronte^M

pithead
bocamina^F
tour^F d'extraction^F
Übertageanlage^F
torre^F di estrazione^F

winding shaft
pozo^M de extracción^F
puits^M d'extraction^F
Förderschacht^M
pozzo^M di estrazione^F

pillar
pilar^M
pilier^M
Abbaupfeiler^M
pilastro^M

room
cámara^F
chambre^F
Kammer^F
camera^F

level
nivel^M
niveau^M
Sohle^F
livello^M

top road
galería^F superior
voie^F de tête^F
Kopfstrecke^F
galleria^F di testa^F

deck
plataforma^F de jaula^F
étage^M
Förderstockwerk^N
strato^M di tetto^M

skip
jaula^F
skip^M
Förderkübel^M
benna^F di caricamento^M

ore pass
chimenea^F de evacuación^F
cheminée^F à minerai^M
Erzgang^M
pozzo^M del minerale^M

panel
pared^F
panneau^M
Feld^M im Abbau^M
sezione^F

landing
estación^F de carga^F
recette^F
Schacht^M-Hängebank^F
stazione^F di caricamento^M

sump
sumidero^M
puisard^M
Schachtsumpf^M
pozzo^M di drenaggio^M

bottom road
galería^M inferior
voie^F de fond^M
Fußstrecke^F
galleria^F di fondo^M

winze
pozo^M ciego^M
descenderie^F
Blindschacht^M
discenderia^F

oil

petróleo^M | pétrole^M | Erdöl^N | petrolio^M

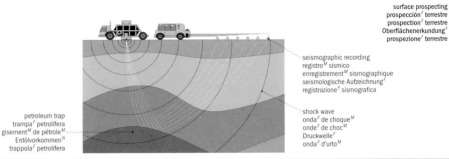

surface prospecting
prospección^F terrestre
prospection^F terrestre
Oberflächenerkundung^F
prospezione^F terrestre

seismographic recording
registro^M sísmico
enregistrement^M sismographique
seismologische Aufzeichnung^F
registrazione^F sismografica

petroleum trap
trampa^F petrolífera
gisement^M de pétrole^M
Erdölvorkommen^N
trappola^F petrolifera

shock wave
onda^F de choque^M
onde^F de choc^M
Druckwelle^F
onda^F d'urto^M

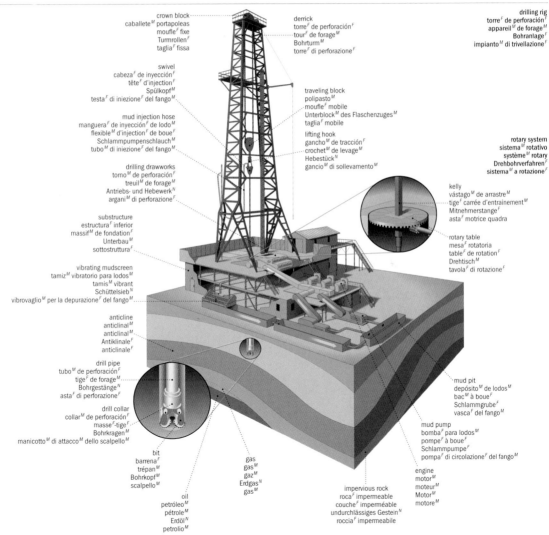

crown block
caballete^M portapoleas
moufle^F fixe
Turmrollen^F
taglia^F fissa

derrick
torre^F de perforación^F
tour^F de forage^M
Bohrturm^M
torre^F di perforazione^F

drilling rig
torre^F de perforación^F
appareil^M de forage^M
Bohranlage^F
impianto^M di trivellazione^F

swivel
cabeza^F de inyección^F
tête^F d'injection^F
Spülkopf^M
testa^F di iniezione^F del fango^M

traveling block
polipasto^M
moufle^F mobile
Unterblock^M des Flaschenzuges^M
taglia^F mobile

mud injection hose
manguera^F de inyección^F de lodo^M
flexible^M d'injection^F de boue^F
Schlammpumpenschlauch^M
tubo^M di iniezione^F del fango^M

lifting hook
gancho^M de tracción^F
crochet^F de levage^M
Hebestück^N
gancio^M di sollevamento^M

rotary system
sistema^M rotativo
système^M rotary
Drehbohrverfahren^F
sistema^M a rotazione^F

drilling drawworks
torno^M de perforación^F
treuil^M de forage^M
Antriebs- und Hebewerk^N
argani^M di perforazione^F

kelly
vástago^M de arrastre^M
tige^F carrée d'entrainement^M
Mitnehmerstange^F
asta^F motrice quadra

substructure
estructura^F inferior
massif^M de fondation^F
Unterbau^M
sottostruttura^F

rotary table
mesa^F rotatoria
table^F de rotation^F
Drehtisch^M
tavola^F di rotazione^F

vibrating mudscreen
tamiz^M vibratorio para lodos^M
tamis^M vibrant
Schüttelsieb^N
vibrovaglio^M per la depurazione^F del fango^M

anticline
anticlinal^M
anticlinal^M
Antiklinale^F
anticlinale^F

drill pipe
tubo^M de perforación^F
tige^F de forage^M
Bohrgestänge^N
asta^F di perforazione^F

mud pit
depósito^M de lodos^M
bac^M à boue^F
Schlammgrube^F
vasca^F del fango^M

drill collar
collar^M de perforación^F
masse^F-tige^F
Bohrkragen^M
manicotto^M di attacco^M dello scalpello^M

mud pump
bomba^F para lodos^M
pompe^F à boue^F
Schlammpumpe^F
pompa^F di circolazione^F del fango^M

bit
barrena^F
trépan^M
Bohrkopf^M
scalpello^M

gas
gas^M
gaz^M
Erdgas^N
gas^M

engine
motor^M
moteur^M
Motor^M
motore^M

oil
petróleo^M
pétrole^M
Erdöl^N
petrolio^M

impervious rock
roca^F impermeable
couche^F imperméable
undurchlässiges Gestein^N
roccia^F impermeabile

ENERGY

oil

ENERGY

production platform
plataforma^F de producción^F
plate-forme^F de production^F
Förderplattform^F
piattaforma^F di produzione^F

crane
grúa^F
grue^F
Kran^M
gru^F

oil/gas separator
separador^M de petróleo^M y gas^M
séparateur^M de gaz^M
Öl-/Gasabscheider^M
separatore^M gas^M / petrolio^M

derrick
torre^F de perforación^F
tour^F de forage^M
Bohrturm^M
torre^F di perforazione^F

gas lift module
módulo^M de inyección^F de gas^M
module^M d'injection^F de gaz^M
Druckgasförderanlage^F
modulo^M di sollevamento^M a mezzo gas^M

oil-processing area
área^F de procesamiento^M del petróleo^M
section^F raffinerie^F
Ölverarbeitungsbereich^M
area^F di lavorazione^F del greggio^M

flare
quemador^M
torche^F
Abfackelung^F
torcia^F

helipad
helipuerto^M
hélisurface^F
Hubschrauberlandeplatz^M
eliporto^M

radio mast
antena^F de radio^M
antenne^F radio^F
Funkmast^M
antenna^F radio^F

lifeboat
bote^M salvavidas
canot^M de sauvetage^M
Rettungsboot^N
lancia^F di salvataggio^M

hull column
columna^F de estabilización^F
colonne^F de stabilisation^F
Tragsäule^F
colonna^F di stabilizzazione^F

anchor wires
cables^M de anclaje^M
chaînes^F d'ancrage^M
Ankerketten^F
cavi^M di ancoraggio^M

pontoon
pontón^M
ponton^M
Ponton^M, Schwimmkörper^M
galleggiante^M

production/export riser system
sistema^M de tuberia de producción^F/expedición^F
tubage^M de production^F/expédition^F
Förder-/Exportsteigsystem^N
tubazione^F di produzione^F e di spedizione^F

tubular member
estructura^F tubular
section^F tubulaire
Rohrquerstrebe^F
elemento^M tubolare

export pipeline
oleoducto^M de exportación^M
oléoduc^M d'évacuation^F
Exportpipeline^F
oleodotto^M di spedizione^F

manifold
colector^M
manifold^M
Rohrverteilerstück^N
collettore^M

surface pipe
tubería^F del caudal^M del pozo^M
tube^M conducteur
Leitrohr^N
tubazione^F di superficie^F

Christmas tree
árbol^M de Navidad^F
arbre^M de Noël^M
Erdöleruptionskreuz^N
albero^M di Natale^M

well flow line
línea^F de flujo^M del pozo^M
tubage^M de production^F
Produktionsbohrung^F
condotta^F di raccolta^F

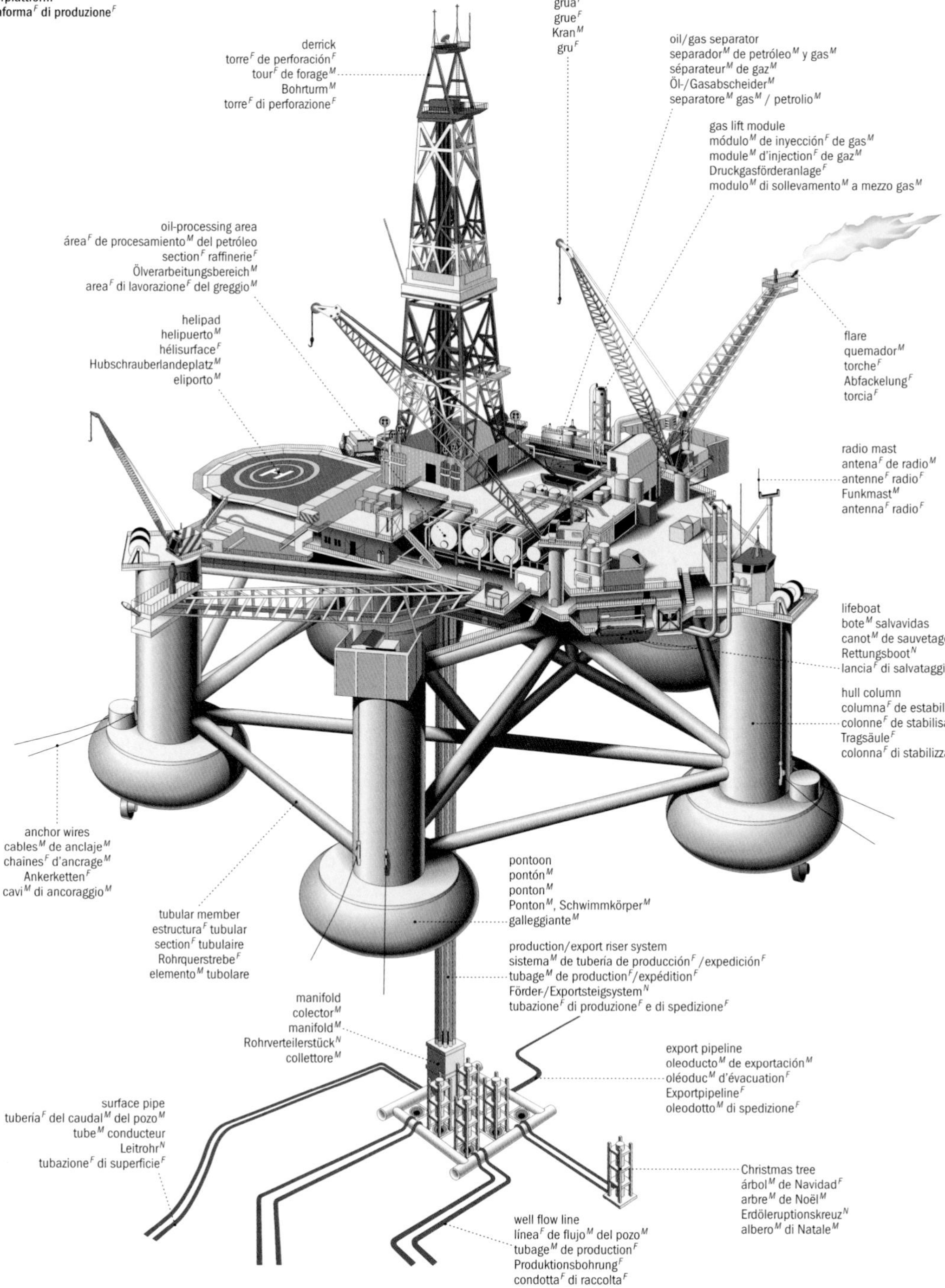

GEOTHERMAL AND FOSSIL ENERGY | ENERGÍA GEOTÉRMICA Y FÓSIL
GÉOTHERMIE ET ÉNERGIE FOSSILE | GEOTHERMISCHE UND FOSSILE ENERGIE | ENERGIA GEOTERMICA E FOSSILE

oil

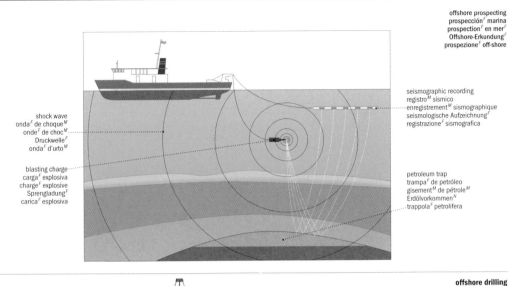

offshore prospecting
prospección^F marina
prospection^F en mer^F
Offshore-Erkundung^F
prospezione^F off-shore

seismographic recording
registro^M sísmico
enregistrement^M sismographique
seismologische Aufzeichnung^F
registrazione^F sismografica

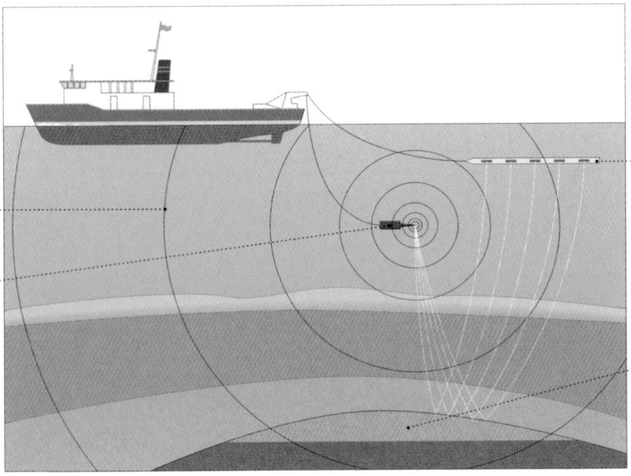

shock wave
onda^F de choque^M
onde^F de choc^M
Druckwelle^F
onda^F d'urto^M

blasting charge
carga^F explosiva
charge^F explosive
Sprengladung^F
carica^F esplosiva

petroleum trap
trampa^F de petróleo
gisement^M de pétrole^M
Erdölvorkommen^N
trappola^F petrolifera

offshore drilling
perforación^F marina
forage^M en mer^F
Offshore-Bohrung^F
perforazione^F off-shore

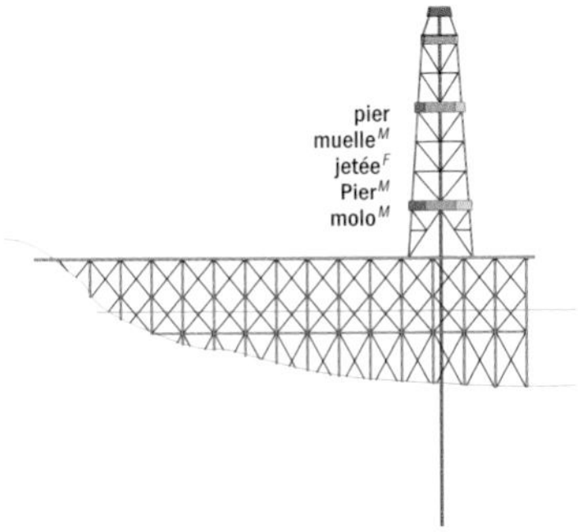

pier
muelle^M
jetée^F
Pier^M
molo^M

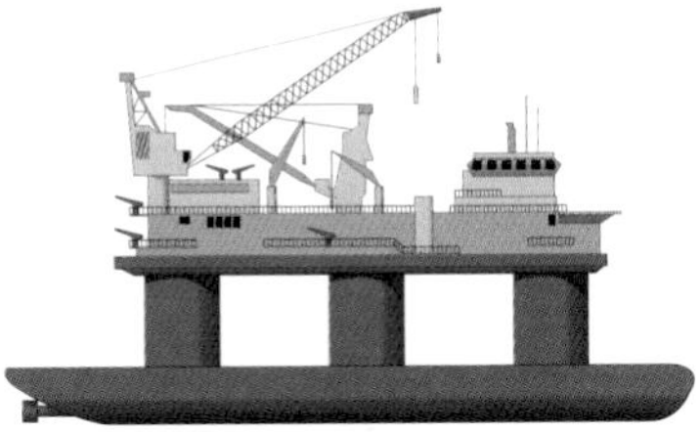

emergency support vessel
embarcación^F de emergencia^F
barge^F de service^M d'urgence^F
Hilfs- und Rettungsschiff^N
nave^F appoggio^M

ENERGY

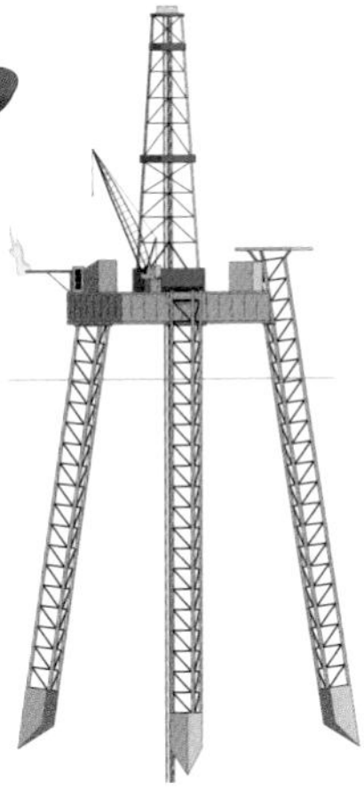

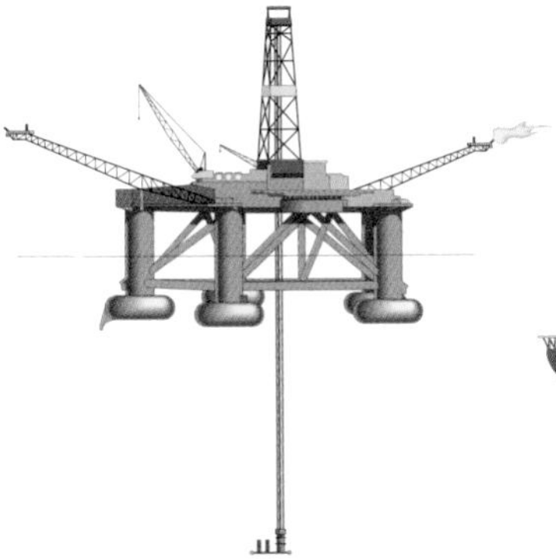

semisubmersible platform
plataforma^F petrolera semisumergida
plate-forme^F semi-submersible
Halbtaucher^M
piattaforma^F semisommergibile

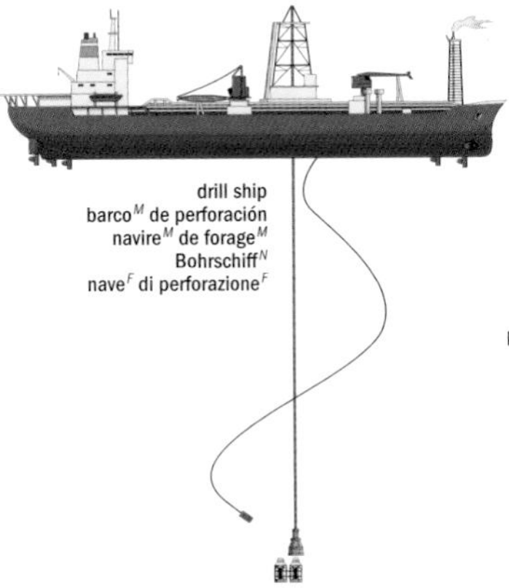

drill ship
barco^M de perforación
navire^M de forage^M
Bohrschiff^N
nave^F di perforazione^F

jack-up platform
plataforma^F montada en gatos^M mecánicos
plate-forme^F auto-élévatrice
Hubplattform^F
piattaforma^F autoelevatrice

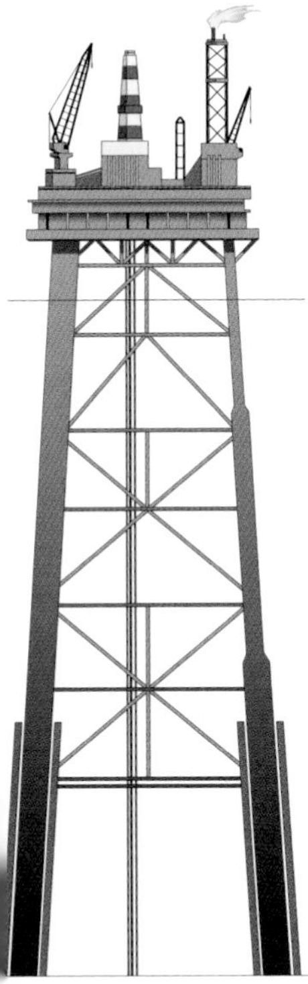

fixed platform
plataforma^F fija
plate-forme^F fixe
Festplattform^F
piattaforma^F fissa

oil

ENERGY

Christmas tree
árbol^M de Navidad^F
arbre^M de Noël^M
Erdöleruptionskreuz^N
albero^M di Natale^M

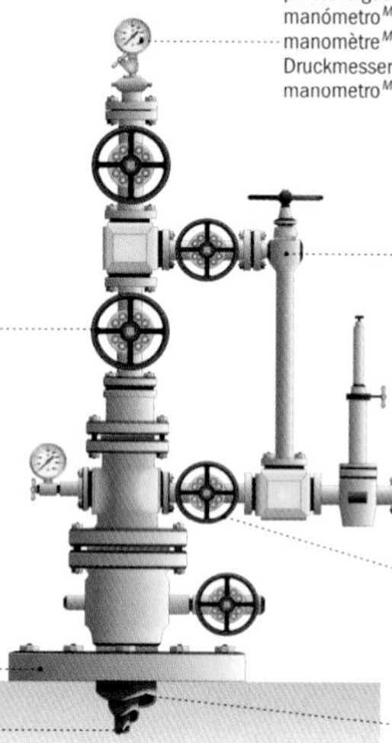

pressure gauge
manómetro^M
manomètre^M
Druckmesser^M
manometro^M

flow bean
reductor^M de flujo^M
duse^F
Eruptionsdüse^F
valvola^F di regolazione^F

master gate valve
válvula^F maestra
vanne^F maîtresse
Hauptschieberventil^N
valvola^F a saracinesca^F principale

pipeline
oleoducto^M
oléoduc^M
Pipeline^F
oleodotto^M

tubing head
cabeza^F de la tubería^F
tête^F de puits^M
Steigrohrkopf^M
testa^F della condotta^F di produzione^F

tubing valve
válvula^F de la tubería^F
vanne^F de production^F
Steigrohrventil^N
valvola^F di produzione^F

tubing
tubería^F
colonne^F de production^F
Steigrohr^N
condotta^F di produzione^F

casing first string
recubrimiento^M de la primera tubería^F
tubage^M de surface^F
Rohrfahrteingang^M
colonna^F di superficie^F

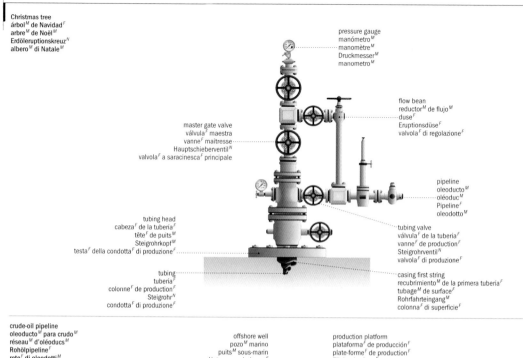

crude-oil pipeline
oleoducto^M para crudo^M
réseau^M d'oléoducs^M
Rohölpipeline^F
rete^F di oleodotti^M

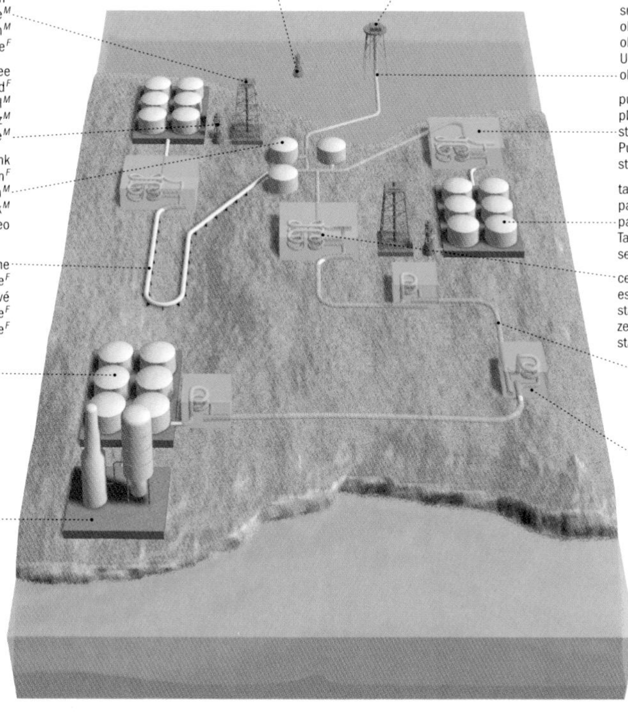

offshore well
pozo^M marino
puits^M sous-marin
Unterwasserbohrung^F
pozzo^M off-shore

production platform
plataforma^F de producción^F
plate-forme^F de production^F
Förderplattform^F
piattaforma^F di produzione^F

derrick
torre^F de perforación^F
tour^F de forage^M
Bohrturm^M
torre^F di perforazione^F

submarine pipeline
oleoducto^M submarino
oléoduc^M sous-marin
Unterwasserpipeline^F
oleodotto^M sottomarino

Christmas tree
árbol^M de Navidad^F
arbre^M de Noël^M
Erdöleruptionskreuz^M
albero^M di Natale^M

pumping station
planta^F de bombeo^M
station^F de pompage^M
Pumpstation^F
stazione^F di pompaggio^M

buffer tank
tanque^M de regulación^F de presión^F
réservoir^M tampon^M
Puffertank^M
serbatoio^M di stoccaggio^M temporaneo

tank farm
patio^M de tanques^M
parc^M de stockage^M
Tankanlage^F
serbatoi^M di stoccaggio^M

aboveground pipeline
oleoducto^M de superficie^F
oléoduc^M surélevé
überirdische Pipeline^F
oleodotto^M di superficie^F

central pumping station
estación^F central de bombeo^M
station^F de pompage^M principale
zentrale Pumpstation^F
stazione^F di pompaggio^M principale

terminal
terminal^M
parc^M de stockage^M terminal
Erdölterminal^N
stazione^F terminale

pipeline
oleoducto^M
oléoduc^M
Pipeline^F
oleodotto^M

refinery
refinería^F
raffinerie^F
Raffinerie^F
raffineria^F

intermediate booster station
planta^F intermedia de refuerzo^M
station^F de pompage^M intermédiaire
Druckverstärkerpumpanlage^F
stazione^F di pompaggio^M intermedia

GEOTHERMAL AND FOSSIL ENERGY | ENERGÍA GEOTÉRMICA Y FÓSIL
GÉOTHERMIE ET ÉNERGIE FOSSILE | GEOTHERMISCHE UND FOSSILE ENERGIE | ENERGIA GEOTERMICA E FOSSILE

oil

tanks^M
tanques^M
réservoirs^M
Tanks^M
serbatoi^M

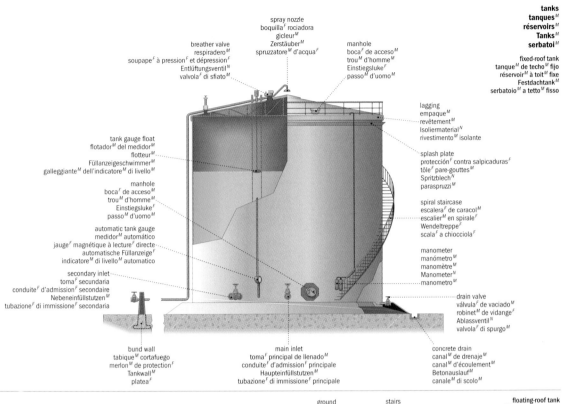

spray nozzle
boquilla^F rociadora
gicleur^M
Zerstäuber^M
spruzzatore^M d'acqua^F

breather valve
respiradero^M
soupape^F à pression^F et dépression^F
Entlüftungsventil^N
valvola^F di sfiato^M

manhole
boca^F de acceso^M
trou^M d'homme^M
Einstiegsluke^F
passo^M d'uomo^M

fixed-roof tank
tanque^M de techo^M fijo
réservoir^M à toit^M fixe
Festdachtank^M
serbatoio^M a tetto^M fisso

lagging
empaque^M
revêtement^M
Isoliermaterial^N
rivestimento^M isolante

tank gauge float
flotador^M del medidor^M
flotteur^M
Füllanzeigeschwimmer^M
galleggiante^M dell'indicatore^M di livello^M

splash plate
protección^F contra salpicaduras^F
tôle^F pare-gouttes^M
Spritzblech^N
paraspruzzi^M

manhole
boca^F de acceso^M
trou^M d'homme^M
Einstiegsluke^F
passo^M d'uomo^M

spiral staircase
escalera^F de caracol^M
escalier^F en spirale^F
Wendeltreppe^F
scala^F a chiocciola^F

automatic tank gauge
medidor^M automático
jauge^F magnétique à lecture^F directe
automatische Füllanzeige^F
indicatore^M di livello^M automatico

manometer
manómetro^M
manomètre^M
Manometer^N
manometro^M

secondary inlet
toma^F secundaria
conduite^F d'admission^F secondaire
Nebeneinfüllstutzen^M
tubazione^F di immissione^F secondaria

drain valve
válvula^F de vaciado^M
robinet^M de vidange^F
Ablassventil^N
valvola^F di spurgo^M

bund wall
tabique^M cortafuego
merlon^M de protection^F
Tankwall^M
platea^F

main inlet
toma^F principal de llenado^M
conduite^F d'admission^F principale
Haupteinfüllstutzen^M
tubazione^F di immissione^F principale

concrete drain
canal^M de drenaje^M
canal^M d'écoulement^M
Betonauslauf^M
canale^M di scolo^M

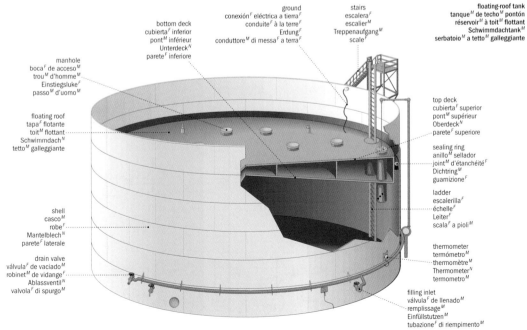

floating-roof tank
tanque^M de techo^M pontón
réservoir^M à toit^M flottant
Schwimmdachtank^M
serbatoio^M a tetto^M galleggiante

bottom deck
cubierta^F inferior
pont^M inférieur
Unterdeck^N
parete^F inferiore

ground
conexión^F eléctrica a tierra^F
conduite^F à la terre^F
Erdung^F
conduttore^M di messa^F a terra^F

stairs
escalera^F
escalier^M
Treppenaufgang^M
scale^F

manhole
boca^F de acceso^M
trou^M d'homme^M
Einstiegsluke^F
passo^M d'uomo^M

top deck
cubierta^F superior
pont^M supérieur
Oberdeck^N
parete^F superiore

floating roof
tapa^F flotante
toit^M flottant
Schwimmdach^N
tetto^M galleggiante

sealing ring
anillo^M sellador
joint^M d'étanchéité^F
Dichtring^M
guarnizione^F

ladder
escalerilla^F
échelle^F
Leiter^F
scala^F a pioli^M

shell
casco^M
robe^F
Mantelblech^N
parete^F laterale

thermometer
termómetro^M
thermomètre^M
Thermometer^N
termometro^M

drain valve
válvula^F de vaciado^M
robinet^M de vidange^F
Ablassventil^N
valvola^F di spurgo^M

filling inlet
válvula^F de llenado^M
remplissage^M
Einfüllstutzen^M
tubazione^F di riempimento^M

ENERGY

oil

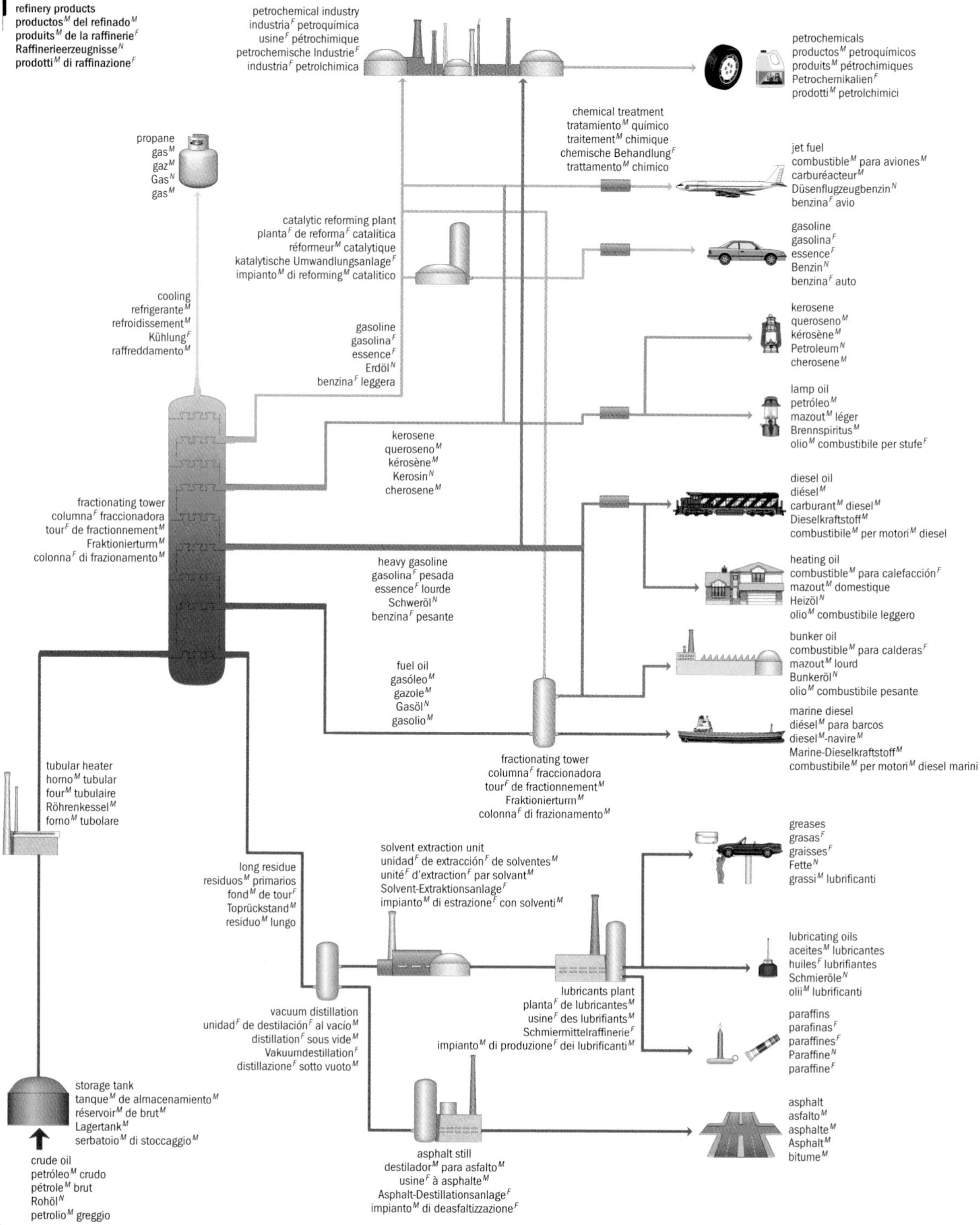

refinery products
productos^M del refinado^M
produits^M de la raffinerie^F
Raffinerieerzeugnisse^N
prodotti^M di raffinazione^F

petrochemical industry
industria^F petroquímica
usine^F pétrochimique
petrochemische Industrie^F
industria^F petrolchimica

petrochemicals
productos^M petroquímicos
produits^M pétrochimiques
Petrochemikalien^F
prodotti^M petrolchimici

propane
gas^M
gaz^M
Gas^N
gas^M

chemical treatment
tratamiento^M químico
traitement^M chimique
chemische Behandlung^F
trattamento^M chimico

jet fuel
combustible^M para aviones^M
carburéacteur^M
Düsenflugzeugbenzin^N
benzina^F avio

catalytic reforming plant
planta^F de reforma^F catalítica
réformeur^M catalytique
katalytische Umwandlungsanlage^F
impianto^M di reforming^M catalitico

gasoline
gasolina^F
essence^F
Benzin^N
benzina^F auto

cooling
refrigerante^M
refroidissement^M
Kühlung^F
raffreddamento^M

gasoline
gasolina^F
essence^F
Erdöl^N
benzina^F leggera

kerosene
queroseno^M
kérosène^M
Petroleum^N
cherosene^M

lamp oil
petróleo^M
mazout^M léger
Brennspiritus^M
olio^M combustibile per stufe^F

kerosene
queroseno^M
kérosène^M
Kerosin^N
cherosene^M

fractionating tower
columna^F fraccionadora
tour^F de fractionnement^M
Fraktionierturm^M
colonna^F di frazionamento^M

diesel oil
diésel^M
carburant diesel^M
Dieselkraftstoff^M
combustibile^M per motori^M diesel

heavy gasoline
gasolina^F pesada
essence^F lourde
Schweröl^N
benzina^F pesante

heating oil
combustible^M para calefacción^F
mazout^M domestique
Heizöl^N
olio^M combustibile leggero

fuel oil
gasóleo^M
gazole^M
Gasöl^N
gasolio^M

bunker oil
combustible^M para calderas^F
mazout^M lourd
Bunkeröl^N
olio^M combustibile pesante

marine diesel
diésel^M para barcos^M
diesel^M-navire^M
Marine-Dieselkraftstoff^M
combustibile^M per motori^M diesel marini

fractionating tower
columna^F fraccionadora
tour^F de fractionnement^M
Fraktionierturm^M
colonna^F di frazionamento^M

tubular heater
horno^M tubular
four^M tubulaire
Röhrenkessel^M
forno^M tubolare

long residue
residuos^M primarios
fond^M de tour^F
Toprückstand^M
residuo^M lungo

solvent extraction unit
unidad^F de extracción^F de solventes^M
unité^F d'extraction^F par solvant^M
Solvent-Extraktionsanlage^F
impianto^M di estrazione^F con solventi^M

greases
grasas^F
graisses^F
Fette^N
grassi^M lubrificanti

lubricating oils
aceites^M lubricantes
huiles^F lubrifiantes
Schmieröle^N
olii^M lubrificanti

vacuum distillation
unidad^F de destilación^F al vacío^M
distillation^F sous vide^M
Vakuumdestillation^F
distillazione^F sotto vuoto^M

lubricants plant
planta^F de lubricantes^M
usine^F des lubrifiants^M
Schmiermittelraffinerie^F
impianto^M di produzione^F dei lubrificanti^M

paraffins
parafinas^F
paraffines^F
Paraffine^N
paraffine^F

storage tank
tanque^M de almacenamiento^M
réservoir^M de brut^M
Lagertank^M
serbatoio^M di stoccaggio^M

asphalt still
destilador^M para asfalto^M
usine^F à asphalte^M
Asphalt-Destillationsanlage^F
impianto^M di deasfaltizzazione^F

asphalt
asfalto^M
asphalte^M
Asphalt^M
bitume^M

crude oil
petróleo^M crudo
pétrole^M brut
Rohöl^N
petrolio^M greggio

ENERGY

hydroelectric complex

complejo^M hidroeléctrico | complexe^M hydroélectrique | Wasserkraftwerk^N | impianto^M idroelettrico

crest of spillway
cresta^F del aliviadero^M
seuil^M de déversoir^M
Überlaufkrone^F
soglia^F dello sfioratore^M

spillway gate
compuerta^F del aliviadero
vanne^F
Verschluss^F des Hochwasserentlastungswehrs^N
paratoia^F dello sfioratore^M

top of dam
cresta^F de la presa^F
crête^F
Dammkrone^F
coronamento^M

reservoir
embalse^M
réservoir^M
Stausee^M
bacino^M

headbay
embalse^M a monte^M
bief^M d'amont^M
Oberwasser^N
bacino^M a monte

spillway
aliviadero^M
déversoir^M
Hochwasserentlastungswehr^N
sfioratore^M

penstock
tubería^F de carga^F
conduite^F forcée
Fallleitung^F
condotta^F forzata

gantry crane
grúa^F de caballete^M
portique^M
Bockkran^M
gru^F a portale^M

ENERGY

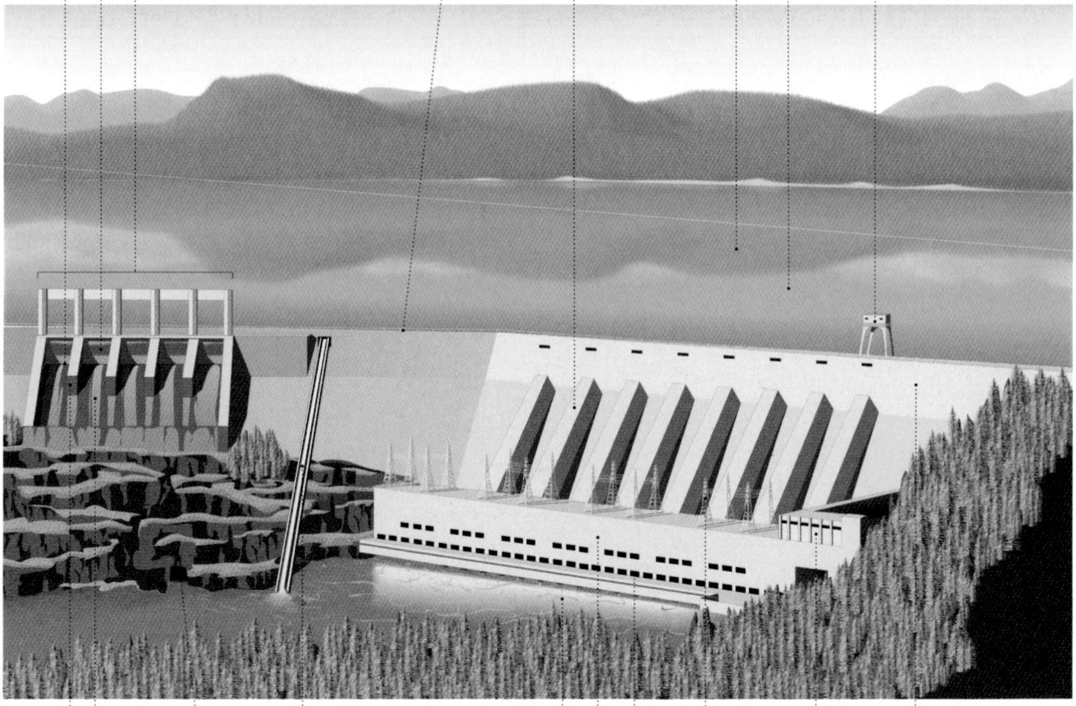

diversion canal
canal^M de derivación^F
canal^M de dérivation^F
Ablenkkanal^M
canale^M di derivazione^F

afterbay
embalse^M de compensación^F
bief^M d'aval^M
Ausgleichsbecken^N
bacino^M a valle

control room
sala^F de control^M
salle^F de commande^F
Steuerzentrale^F
sala^F di controllo^M

spillway chute
canal^M del aliviadero^M
coursier^M d'évacuateur^M
Überfallrinne^F
scivolo^M dello sfioratore^M

power plant
central^F eléctrica
centrale^F
Speicherkraftwerk^N
centrale^F elettrica

bushing
boquilla^F
traversée^F de transformateur^M
Durchführung^F
stazione^F di trasformazione^F

training wall
muro^M de encauzamiento^M
mur^M bajoyer^M
Leitwerk^N
muro^M di sponda^F

log chute
rebosadero^M
passe^F à billes^F
Trift^F
scivolo^M per tronchi^M d'albero^M

machine hall
sala^F de máquinas^F
salle^F des machines^F
Maschinenhalle^F
sala^F macchine^F

dam
presa^F
barrage^M
Damm^M
diga^F

hydroelectric complex

cross section of a hydroelectric power plant
sección^F transversal de una central^F hidroeléctrica
coupe^F d'une centrale^F hydroélectrique
Wasserkraftwerk^N im Querschnitt^M
sezione^F trasversale di una centrale^F idroelettrica

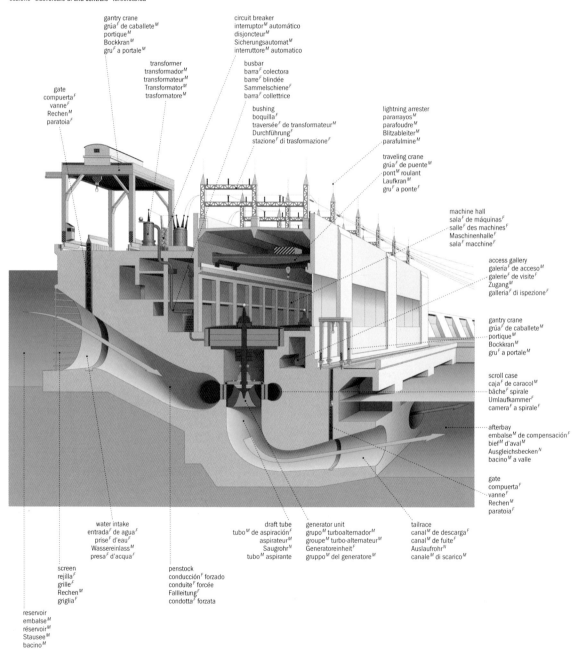

gantry crane
grúa^F de caballete^M
portique^M
Bockkran^M
gru^F a portale^M

circuit breaker
interruptor^M automático
disjoncteur^M
Sicherungsautomat^M
interruttore^M automatico

transformer
transformador^M
transformateur^M
Transformator^M
trasformatore^M

busbar
barra^F colectora
barre^F blindée
Sammelschiene^F
barra^F collettrice

gate
compuerta^F
vanne^F
Rechen^M
paratoia^F

bushing
boquilla^F
traversée^F de transformateur^M
Durchführung^F
stazione^F di trasformazione^F

lightning arrester
pararrayos^M
parafoudre^M
Blitzableiter^M
parafulmine^M

traveling crane
grúa^F de puente^M
pont^M roulant
Laufkran^M
gru^F a ponte^F

machine hall
sala^F de máquinas^F
salle^F des machines^F
Maschinenhalle^F
sala^F macchine^F

access gallery
galería^F de acceso^M
galerie^F de visite^F
Zugang^M
galleria^F di ispezione^F

gantry crane
grúa^F de caballete^M
portique^M
Bockkran^M
gru^F a portale^M

scroll case
caja^F de caracol^M
bâche^F spirale
Umlaufkammer^F
camera^F a spirale^F

afterbay
embalse^M de compensación^F
bief^M d'aval^M
Ausgleichsbecken^N
bacino^M a valle

gate
compuerta^F
vanne^F
Rechen^M
paratoia^F

water intake
entrada^F de agua^F
prise^F d'eau^F
Wassereinlass^M
presa^F d'acqua^F

draft tube
tubo^M de aspiración^F
aspirateur^M
Saugrohr^N
tubo^M aspirante

generator unit
grupo^M turboalternador^M
groupe^M turbo-alternateur^M
Generatoreinheit^F
gruppo^M del generatore^M

tailrace
canal^M de descarga^F
canal^M de fuite^F
Auslaufrohr^N
canale^M di scarico^M

screen
rejilla^F
grille^F
Rechen^M
griglia^F

penstock
conducción^F forzado
conduite^F forcée
Fallleitung^F
condotta^F forzata

reservoir
embalse^M
réservoir^M
Stausee^M
bacino^M

generator unit

grupo^M turboalternador^M | groupe^M turbo-alternateur^M | Stromgenerator^M | gruppo^M generatore^M

thrust bearing
cojinete^M de empuje^M
palier^M de butée^F
Drucklager^N
cuscinetto^M assiale

gate operating ring
anillo^M regulador
cercle^M de vannage^M
Ringschütz^M
cuscinetto^M reggispinta

runner blade
paleta^F de la turbina^F
aube^F de roue^F
Läuferblatt^N
pala^F della girante^F

turbine headcover
cubierta^F superior de la turbina^F
couvercle^M de la turbine^F
Turbinenummantelung^F
coperchio^M della turbina^F

rotor
rotor^M
rotor^M
Rotor^M
rotore^M

collector
colector^M
collecteur^M
Kollektor^M
collettore^M

stator
estator^M
stator^M
Stator^M
statore^M

generator
generador^M
alternateur^M
Generator^M
generatore^M

shaft
árbol^M
arbre^M
Welle^F
albero^M

spiral case
caja^F espiral
bâche^F spirale
Spiralgehäuse^N
camera^F a spirale

stay vane blade
paletas^F de la turbina^F
aube^F avant-directrice
Schaufelblatt^N
pala^F direttrice

wicket gate
álabe^M
aube^F directrice
Leitschaufel^F
distributore^M

runner
rodete^M
roue^F
Laufrad^N
girante^F

stay ring
anillo^M distribuidor
avant-distributeur^M
Stützring^M
anello^M di ancoraggio^M

bottom ring
anillo^M inferior
flasque^M inférieur
Grundring^M
anello^M di fondo^M

draft tube
tubo^M de aspiración^F
aspirateur^M
Saugrohr^N
tubo^M aspirante

draft tube liner
calza^F de descarga^F
blindage^M d'aspirateur^M
Ausströmmantel^M
camicia^F di scarico^M

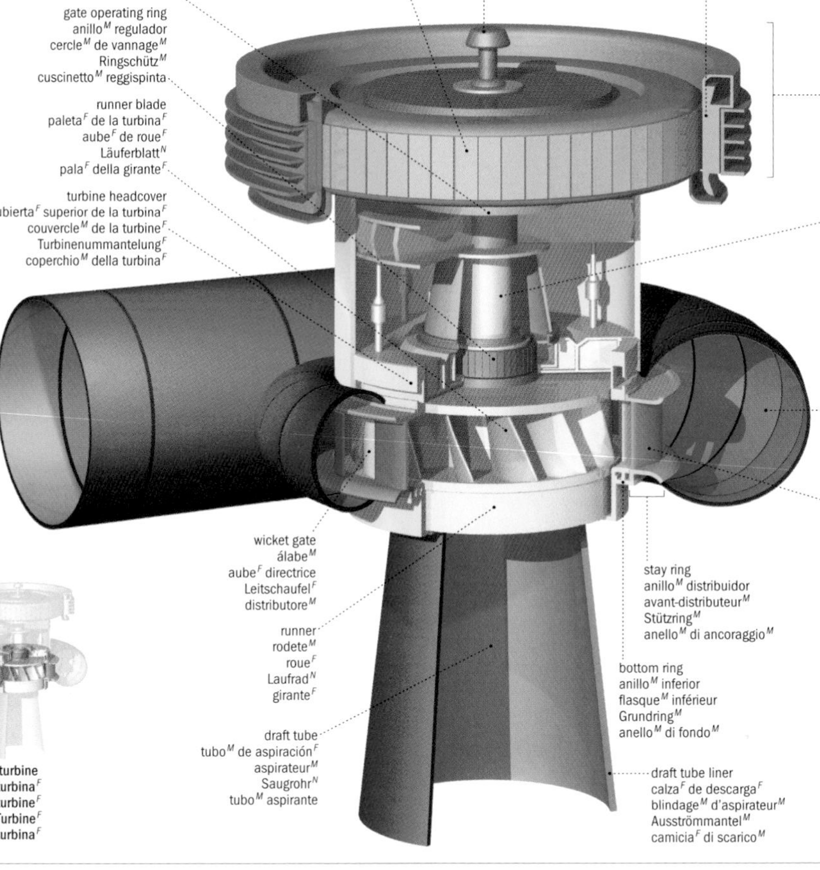

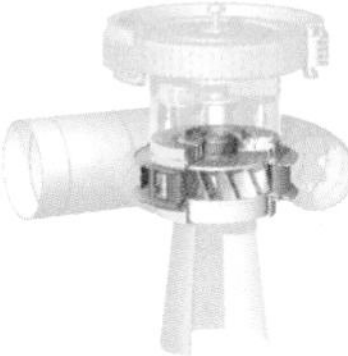

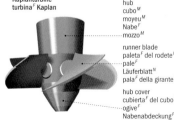

turbine
turbina^F
turbine^F
Turbine^F
turbina^F

ENERGY

Kaplan runner
turbina^F Kaplan
roue^F Kaplan
Kaplanturbine^F
turbina^F Kaplan

hub
cubo^M
moyeu^M
Nabe^F
mozzo^M

runner blade
paleta^F del rodete^M
pale^F
Läuferblatt^N
pala^F della girante^F

hub cover
cubierta^F del cubo^M
ogive^M
Nabenabdeckung^F
ogiva^F

bucket
álabe^M
auget^M
Zelle^F
cucchiaio^M

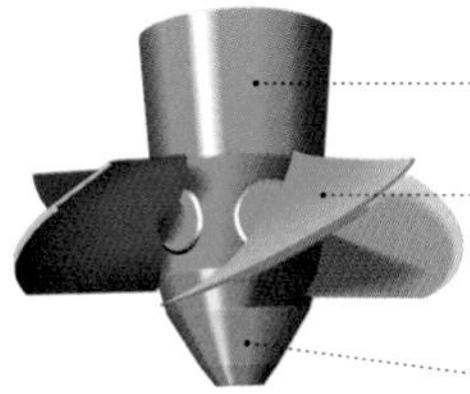

Pelton runner
turbina^F Pelton
roue^F Pelton
Peltonturbine^F
turbina^F Pelton

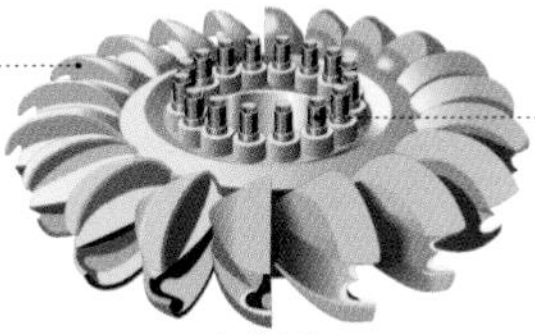

bucket ring
rueda^F de alabes^M
couronne^F d'aubage^M
Zellenring^M
ruota^F dei cucchiai^M

coupling bolt
perno^M de acoplamiento^M
boulon^M d'accouplement^M
Kupplungsbolzen^M
bullone^M di accoppiamento^M

runners
rodetes^M
roues^F
Turbinen^F
giranti^F

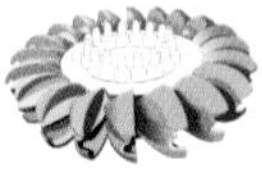

Francis runner
turbina^F Francis
roue^F Francis
Francisturbine^F
turbina^F Francis

blade
paleta^F
aube^F
Blatt^N
pala^F

ring
anillo^M
flasque^M
Ring^M
anello^M

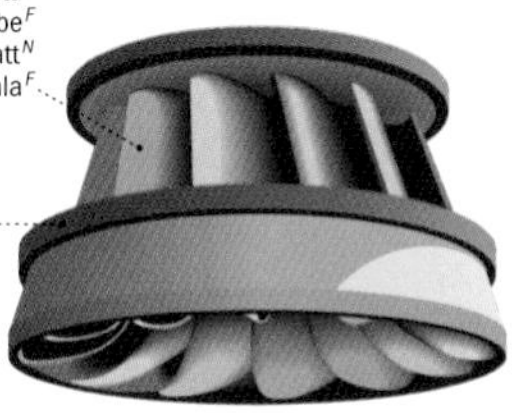

examples of dams

ejemplos^M de presas^F | exemples^M de barrages^M | Beispiele^N für Staudämme^M | esempi^M di dighe^F

buttress dam
presa^F de contrafuertes^M
barrage^M à contreforts^M
Stützpfeilerstaudamm^M
diga^F a contrafforti^M

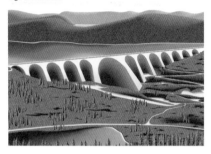

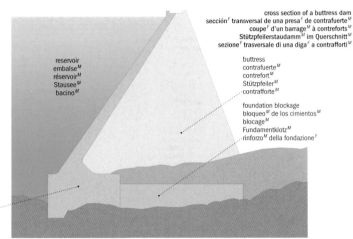

cross section of a buttress dam
sección^F transversal de una presa^F de contrafuerte^M
coupe^F d'un barrage^M à contreforts^M
Stützpfeilerstaudamm^M im Querschnitt^M
sezione^F trasversale di una diga^F a contrafforti^M

reservoir
embalse^M
réservoir^M
Stausee^M
bacino^M

buttress
contrafuerte^M
contrefort^M
Stützpfeiler^M
contrafforte^M

foundation blockage
bloqueo^M de los cimientos^M
blocage^M
Fundamentklotz^M
rinforzo^M della fondazione^F

foundation
cimientos^M
fondation^F
Fundament^N
fondazione^F

embankment dam
presa^F de tierra^F
barrage^M en remblai^M
Uferdamm^M
diga^F in terra^F

ENERGY

cross section of an embankment dam
sección^F transversal de una presa^F de tierra^F
coupe^F d'un barrage^M en remblai^M
Uferdamm^M im Querschnitt^M
sezione^F trasversale di una diga^F in terra^F

top of dam
coronación^F
crête^F
Dammkrone^F
coronamento^M

berm
berma^F
risberme^F
Berme^F
berma^F

downstream shoulder
talud^M de aguas^F abajo
recharge^F aval
Unterstützmauer^F
spalla^F a valle

wave wall
parapeto^M contra olas^F
mur^M de batillage^M
Wellenmauer^F
frangiflutti^M

clay core
núcleo^M de arcilla^F
noyau^M d'argile^F
Lehmkern^M
nucleo^M centrale di argilla^F

drainage layer
capa^F drenante
couche^F drainante
Drainage-Schicht^F
strato^M drenante

drainage blanket
plantilla^F de desagüe^M
tapis^M drainant
Drainage-Decke^F
strato^M di sabbia^F drenante

reservoir
embalse^M
réservoir^M
Stausee^M
bacino^M

downstream toe
pie^M del talud^M
pied^M aval
Trockenseite^F
piede^M a valle

pitching
revestimiento^M
perré^M
Neigung^F
rivestimento^M

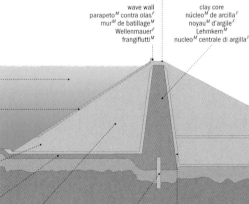

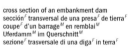

upstream toe
pie^M del talud^M
pied^M amont
Dammbrust^F
piede^M a monte

upstream blanket
capa^F de arcilla^F
tapis^M amont
Oberwasserdecke^F
strato^M di sabbia^F a monte

upstream shoulder
talud^M de aguas^F contenidas
recharge^F amont
Oberstützmauer^F
spalla^F a monte

cut-off trench
cortina^F de inyecciones^F
parafouille^M
Abdichtungsgraben^M
taglione^M

sand
arena^F
sable^M
Sand^M
sabbia^F

foundation of dam
cimientos^M de una presa^F
terrain^M de fondation^F
Dammsockel^M
platea^F di fondazione^F

cross section of an arch dam
sección^F transversal de una presa^F de bóveda
coupe^F d'un barrage^M-voûte^F
Bogenstaudamm^M im Querschnitt^M
sezione^F trasversale di una diga^F a volta^F

arch dam
presa^F de bóveda^F
barrage^M-voûte^F
Bogenstaudamm^M
diga^F a volta^F

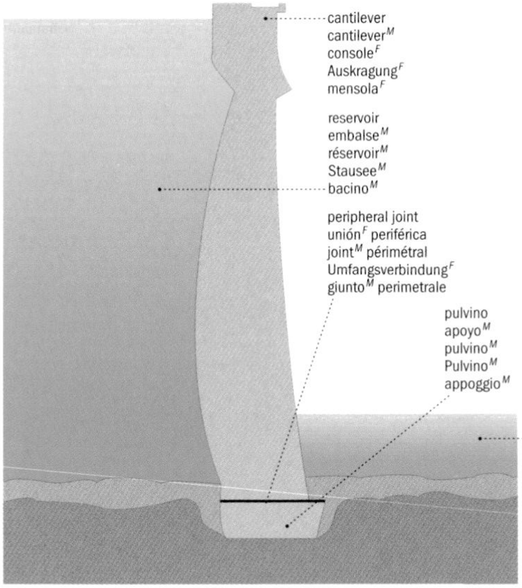

cantilever
cantilever^M
console^F
Auskragung^F
mensola^F

reservoir
embalse^M
réservoir^M
Stausee^M
bacino^M

peripheral joint
unión^F periférica
joint^M périmétral
Umfangsverbindung^F
giunto^M perimetrale

pulvino
apoyo^M
pulvino^M
Pulvino^M
appoggio^M

afterbay
embalse^M de compensación^F
bief^M aval
Ausgleichsbecken^N
bacino^M a valle

soil
suelo^M
sol^M
Erdreich^N
suolo^M

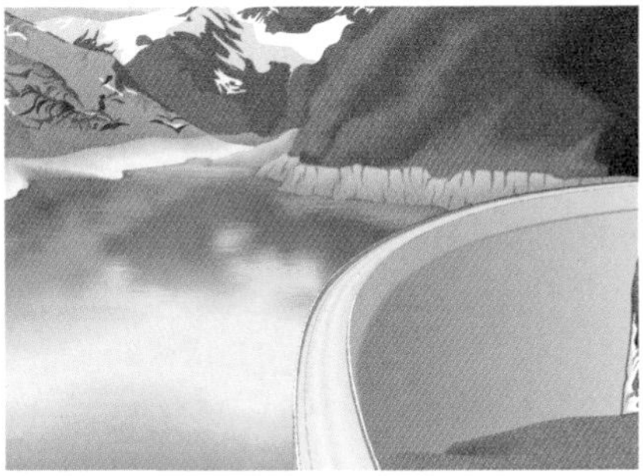

cross section of a gravity dam
sección^M transversal de una presa^F de gravedad^F
coupe^F d'un barrage^M-poids^M
Schwergewichtsstaudamm^M im Querschnitt^M
sezione^F trasversale di una diga^F a gravità^F

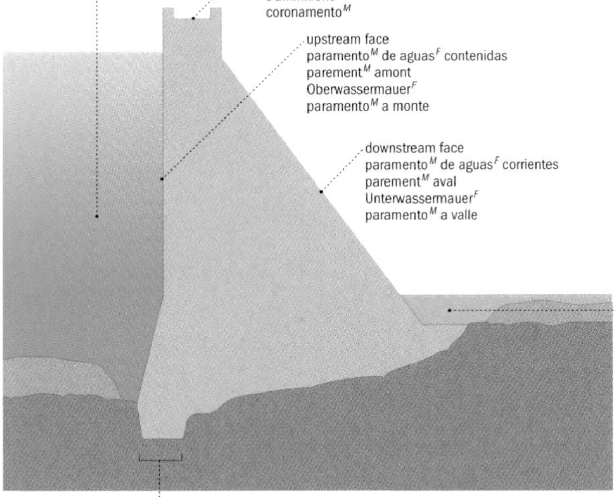

gravity dam
presa^F
barrage^M-poids^M
Gewichtsstaudamm^M
diga^F a gravità^F

reservoir
embalse^M
réservoir^M
Stausee^M
bacino^M

top of dam
coronamiento^M
couronnement^M
Dammkrone^F
coronamento^M

upstream face
paramento^M de aguas^F contenidas
parement^M amont
Oberwassermauer^F
paramento^M a monte

downstream face
paramento^M de aguas^F corrientes
parement^M aval
Unterwassermauer^F
paramento^M a valle

afterbay
embalse^M de compensación^F
bief^M aval
Ausgleichsbecken^N
bacino^M a valle

cut-off trench
cortina^F de inyecciones^F
parafouille^M
Dichtungsschleier^M
taglione^M

ENERGY

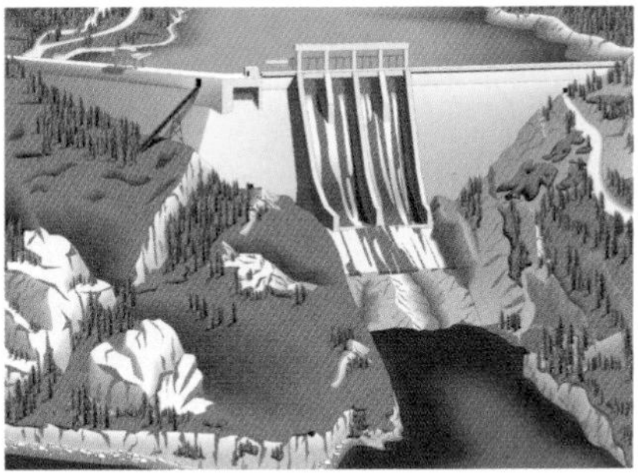

steps in production of electricity

etapas^F de la producción^F de electricidad^F | étapes^F de production^F de l'électricité^F | Einzelschritte^M bei der Elektrizitätserzeugung^F | fasi^F della produzione^F di elettricità^F

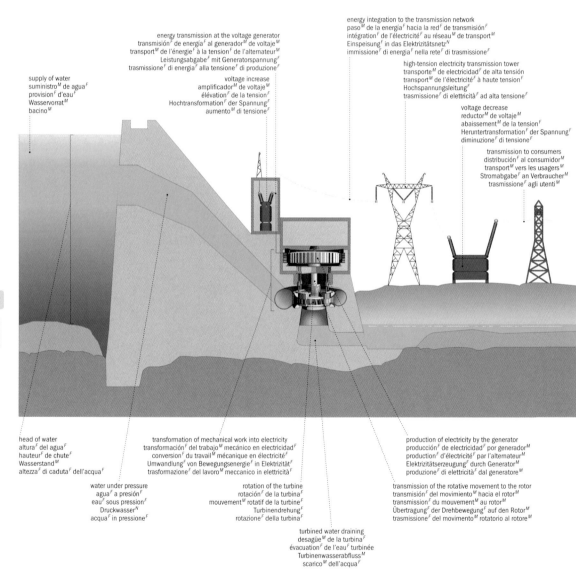

energy transmission at the voltage generator
transmisión^F de energía^F al generador^M de voltaje^M
transport^M de l'énergie^F à la tension^F de l'alternateur^M
Leistungsabgabe^F mit Generatorspannung^F
trasmissione^F di energia^F alla tensione^F di produzione^F

energy integration to the transmission network
paso^M de la energía^F hacia la red^F de transmisión^F
intégration^F de l'électricité^F au réseau^M de transport^M
Einspeisung^F in das Elektrizitätsnetz^N
immissione^F di energia^F nella rete^F di trasmissione^F

high-tension electricity transmission tower
transporte^M de electricidad^F de alta tensión
transport^M de l'électricité^F à haute tension^F
Hochspannungsleitung^F
trasmissione^F di elettricità^F ad alta tensione^F

supply of water
suministro^M de agua^F
provisión^F d'eau^F
Wasservorrat^M
bacino^M

voltage increase
amplificador^M de voltaje^M
élévation^F de la tension^F
Hochtransformation^F der Spannung^F
aumento^M di tensione^F

voltage decrease
reductor^M de voltaje^M
abaissement^M de la tension^F
Heruntertransformation^F der Spannung^F
diminuzione^F di tensione^F

transmission to consumers
distribución^F al consumidor^M
transport^M vers les usagers^M
Stromabgabe^F an Verbraucher^M
trasmissione^F agli utenti^M

head of water
altura^F del agua^F
hauteur^F de chute^F
Wasserstand^M
altezza^F di caduta^F dell'acqua^F

transformation of mechanical work into electricity
transformación^F del trabajo^M mecánico en electricidad^F
conversion^F du travail^M mécanique en électricité^F
Umwandlung^F von Bewegungsenergie^F in Elektrizität^F
trasformazione^F del lavoro^M meccanico in elettricità^F

production of electricity by the generator
producción^F de electricidad^F por generador^M
production^F d'électricité^F par l'alternateur^M
Elektrizitätserzeugung^F durch Generator^M
produzione^F di elettricità^F dal generatore^M

water under pressure
agua^F a presión^F
eau^F sous pression^F
Druckwasser^N
acqua^F in pressione^F

rotation of the turbine
rotación^F de la turbina^F
mouvement^M rotatif de la turbine^F
Turbinendrehung^F
rotazione^F della turbina^F

transmission of the rotative movement to the rotor
transmisión^F del movimiento^M hacia el rotor^M
transmission^F du mouvement^M au rotor^M
Übertragung^F der Drehbewegung^F auf den Rotor^M
trasmissione^F del movimiento^M rotatorio al rotore^M

turbined water draining
desagüe^M de la turbina^F
évacuation^F de l'eau^F turbinée
Turbinenwasserabfluss^M
scarico^M dell'acqua^F

ENERGY

electricity transmission

transporte^M de electricidad^F | transport^M de l'électricité^F | Elektrizitätsverteilung^F | trasmissione^F di elettricità^F

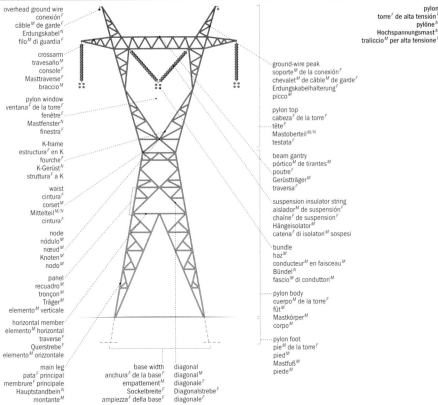

medium-tension distribution line
línea^F de distribución^F de media tensión^F
ligne^F de distribution^F à moyenne tension^F
Mittelspannungsleitung^F
linea^F di distribuzione^F a media tensione^F

hot line connector
conector^M de línea^F cargada
connecteur^M à serrage^M mécanique
Anschluss^M für Hochspannungsleitung^F
connettore^M della linea^F attiva

insulator
aislador^M
isolateur^M
Isolator^M
isolatore^M

overhead connection
acometida^F aérea
branchement^M aérien
Freileitung^F
connessione^F aerea

crossarm
travesaño^M
traverse^F
Traverse^F
braccio^M

brace
puntal^M
contrefiche^F
Stütze^F
controvento^M

lightning arrester
pararrayos^M
parafoudre^M
Blitzableiter^M
parafulmine^M

fuse
fusible^M
fusible^M
Sicherung^F
fusibile^M

fuse cutout
placa^F para fusibles^M
coupe-circuit^M
Sicherungsabschnitt^M
interruttore^M automatico

bushing
boquilla^F
traversée^F
Durchführung^F
guaina^F isolante

fuse holder
portafusible^M
porte-fusible^M
Sicherungsträger^M
portafusibili^M

transformer
transformador^M
transformateur^M
Transformator^M
trasformatore^M

terminal
terminal^M
borne^F
Endableitung^F
terminale^M

low-tension distribution line
cables^M de baja tensión^F
ligne^F de distribution^F à basse tension^F
Niedrigspannungsleitung^F
linea^F di distribuzione^F a bassa tensione^F

supply point
cables^M de suministro^M
point^M d'alimentation^F
Stromanschlusspunkt^M
punto^M di alimentazione^F

insulator
aislador^M
isolateur^M
Isolator^M
isolatore^M

overhead ground wire
conexión^F
câble^M de garde^F
Erdungskabel^N
filo^M di guardia^F

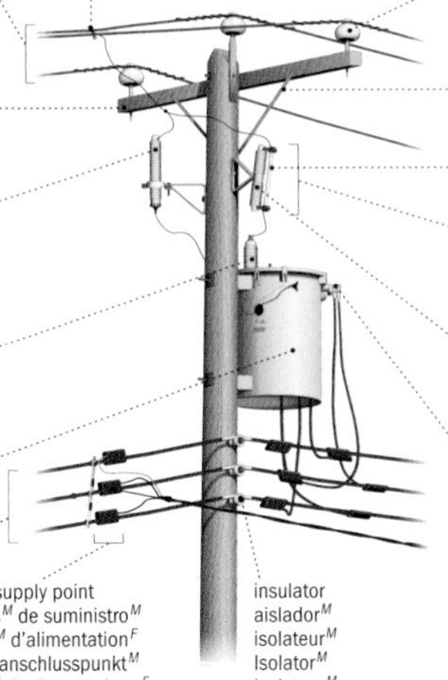

pylon
torre^F de alta tensión^F
pylône^M
Hochspannungsmast^M
traliccio^M per alta tensione^F

crossarm
travesaño^M
console^F
Masttraverse^F
braccio^M

ground-wire peak
soporte^M de la conexión^F
chevalet^M de câble^M de garde^F
Erdungskabelhalterung^F
picco^M

pylon window
ventana^F de la torre^F
fenêtre^F
Mastfenster^N
finestra^F

pylon top
cabeza^F de la torre^F
tête^F
Mastoberteil^{M/N}
testata^F

K-frame
estructura^F en K
fourche^F
K-Gerüst^N
struttura^F a K

beam gantry
pórtico^M de tirantes^M
poutre^F
Gerüstträger^M
traversa^F

waist
cintura^F
corset^M
Mittelteil^{M/N}
cintura^F

suspension insulator string
aislador^M de suspensión^F
chaîne^F de suspension^F
Hängeisolator^M
catena^F di isolatori^M sospesi

node
nódulo^M
nœud^M
Knoten^M
nodo^M

bundle
haz^M
conducteur^M en faisceau^M
Bündel^N
fascio^M di conduttori^M

panel
recuadro^M
tronçon^M
Träger^M
elemento^M verticale

pylon body
cuerpo^M de la torre^F
fût^M
Mastkörper^M
corpo^M

horizontal member
elemento^M horizontal
traverse^F
Querstrebe^F
elemento^M orizzontale

pylon foot
pie^M de la torre^F
pied^M
Mastfuß^M
piede^M

main leg
pata^F principal
membrure^F principale
Hauptstandbein^N
montante^M

base width
anchura^F de la base^F
empattement^M
Sockelbreite^F
ampiezza^F della base^F

diagonal
diagonal^M
diagonale^F
Diagonalstrebe^F
diagonale^F

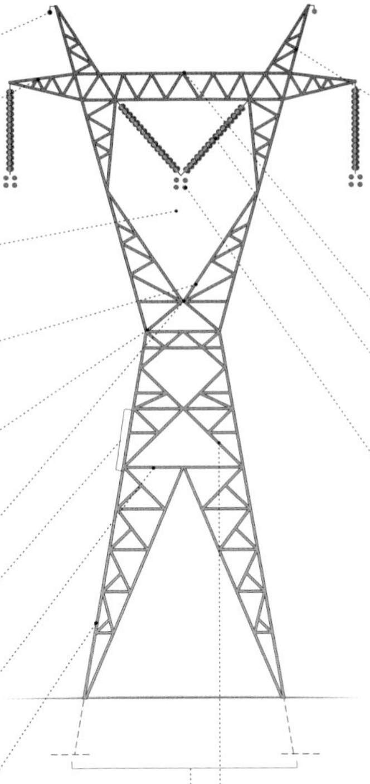

tidal power plant

planta^F de energía^F maremotriz | usine^F marémotrice | Gezeitenkraftwerk^N | centrale^F elettrica mareomotrice

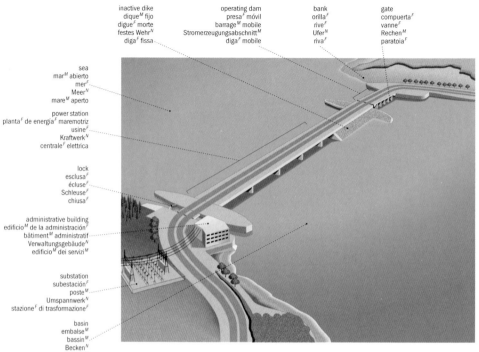

inactive dike
dique^M fijo
digue^F morte
festes Wehr^N
diga^F fissa

operating dam
presa^F móvil
barrage^M mobile
Stromerzeugungsabschnitt^M
diga^F mobile

bank
orilla^F
rive^F
Ufer^N
riva^F

gate
compuerta^F
vanne^F
Rechen^M
paratoia^F

sea
mar^M abierto
mer^F
Meer^N
mare^M aperto

power station
planta^F de energía^F maremotriz
usine^F
Kraftwerk^N
centrale^F elettrica

lock
esclusa^F
écluse^F
Schleuse^F
chiusa^F

administrative building
edificio^M de la administración^F
bâtiment^M administratif
Verwaltungsgebäude^N
edificio^M dei servizi^M

substation
subestación^F
poste^M
Umspannwerk^N
stazione^F di trasformazione^F

basin
embalse^M
bassin^M
Becken^N
bacino^M

cross section of a power plant
sección^F transversal de una central^F eléctrica
coupe^F de l'usine^F
Kraftwerk^N im Querschnitt^M
sezione^F trasversale di una centrale^F elettrica

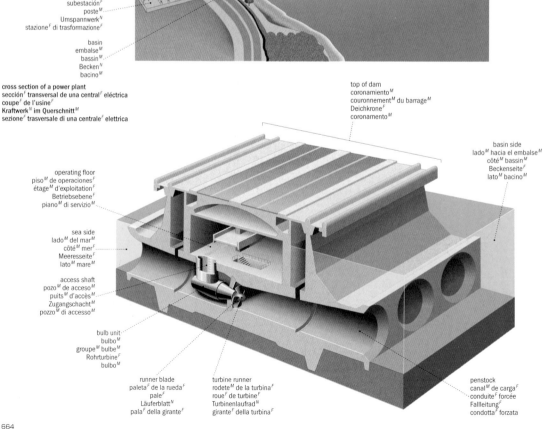

top of dam
coronamiento^M
couronnement^M du barrage^M
Deichkrone^F
coronamento^M

basin side
lado^M hacia el embalse^M
côté^M bassin^M
Beckenseite^F
lato^M bacino^M

operating floor
piso^M de operaciones^F
étage^M d'exploitation^F
Betriebsebene^F
piano^M di servizio^M

sea side
lado^M del mar^M
côté^M mer^F
Meeresseite^F
lato^M mare^M

access shaft
pozo^M de acceso^M
puits^M d'accès^M
Zugangschacht^M
pozzo^M di accesso^M

bulb unit
bulbo^M
groupe^M bulbe^M
Rohrturbine^F
bulbo^M

runner blade
paleta^F de la rueda^F
pale^F
Läuferblatt^N
pala^F della girante^F

turbine runner
rodete^M de la turbina^F
roue^F de turbine^F
Turbinenlaufrad^N
girante^F della turbina^F

penstock
canal^M de carga^F
conduite^F forcée
Fallleitung^F
condotta^F forzata

production of electricity from nuclear energy

producción[F] de electricidad[F] por energía[F] nuclear | production[F] d'électricité[F] par énergie[F] nucléaire | Elektrizitätserzeugung[F] aus Kernenergie[F] | produzione[F] di elettricità[F] da energia[F] nucleare

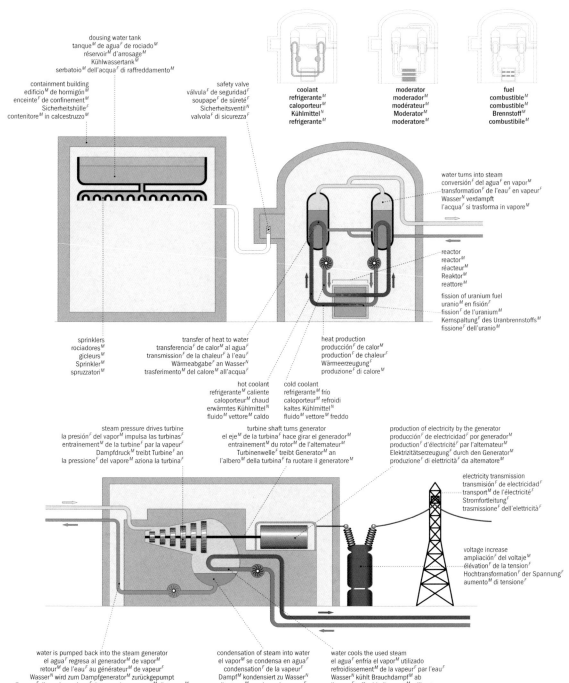

dousing water tank
tanque[M] de agua[F] de rociado[M]
réservoir[M] d'arrosage[M]
Kühlwassertank[M]
serbatoio[M] dell'acqua[F] di raffreddamento[M]

containment building
edificio[M] de hormigón[M]
enceinte[F] de confinement[M]
Sicherheitshülle[F]
contenitore[M] in calcestruzzo[M]

safety valve
válvula[F] de seguridad[F]
soupape[F] de sûreté[F]
Sicherheitsventil[N]
valvola[F] di sicurezza[F]

coolant
refrigerante[M]
caloporteur[M]
Kühlmittel[N]
refrigerante[M]

moderator
moderador[M]
modérateur[M]
Moderator[M]
moderatore[M]

fuel
combustible[M]
combustible[M]
Brennstoff[M]
combustibile[M]

water turns into steam
conversión[F] del agua[F] en vapor[M]
transformation[F] de l'eau[F] en vapeur[F]
Wasser[N] verdampft
l'acqua[F] si trasforma in vapore[M]

reactor
reactor[M]
réacteur[M]
Reaktor[M]
reattore[M]

fission of uranium fuel
uranio[M] en fisión[F]
fission[F] de l'uranium[M]
Kernspaltung[F] des Uranbrennstoffs[M]
fissione[F] dell'uranio[M]

sprinklers
rociadores[M]
gicleurs[M]
Sprinkler[M]
spruzzatori[M]

transfer of heat to water
transferencia[F] de calor[M] al agua[F]
transmission[F] de la chaleur[F] à l'eau[F]
Wärmeabgabe[F] an Wasser[N]
trasferimento[M] del calore[M] all'acqua[F]

heat production
producción[F] de calor[M]
production[F] de chaleur[F]
Wärmeerzeugung[F]
produzione[F] di calore[M]

hot coolant
refrigerante[M] caliente
caloporteur[M] chaud
erwärmtes Kühlmittel[N]
fluido[M] vettore[M] caldo

cold coolant
refrigerante[M] frío
caloporteur[M] refroidi
kaltes Kühlmittel[N]
fluido[M] vettore[M] freddo

steam pressure drives turbine
la presión[F] del vapor[M] impulsa las turbinas[F]
entraînement[M] de la turbine[F] par la vapeur[F]
Dampfdruck[M] treibt Turbine[F] an
la pressione[F] del vapore[M] aziona la turbina[F]

turbine shaft turns generator
el eje[M] de la turbina[F] hace girar el generador[M]
entraînement[M] du rotor[M] de l'alternateur[M]
Turbinenwelle[F] treibt Generator[M] an
l'albero[M] della turbina[F] fa ruotare il generatore[M]

production of electricity by the generator
producción[F] de electricidad[F] por generador[M]
production[F] d'électricité[F] par l'alternateur[M]
Elektrizitätserzeugung[F] durch den Generator[M]
produzione[F] di elettricità[F] da alternatore[M]

electricity transmission
transmisión[F] de electricidad[F]
transport[M] de l'électricité[F]
Stromfortleitung[F]
trasmissione[F] dell'elettricità[F]

voltage increase
ampliación[F] del voltaje[M]
élévation[F] de la tension[F]
Hochtransformation[F] der Spannung[F]
aumento[M] di tensione[F]

water is pumped back into the steam generator
el agua[F] regresa al generador[M] de vapor[M]
retour[M] de l'eau[F] au générateur[M] de vapeur[F]
Wasser[N] wird zum Dampfgenerator[M] zurückgepumpt
l'acqua[F] di condensazione[F] ritorna nel generatore[M] di vapore[M]

condensation of steam into water
el vapor[M] se condensa en agua[F]
condensation[F] de la vapeur[F]
Dampf[M] kondensiert zu Wasser[N]
il vapore[M] condensa in acqua[F]

water cools the used steam
el agua[F] enfría el vapor[M] utilizado
refroidissement[M] de la vapeur[F] par l'eau[F]
Wasser[N] kühlt Brauchdampf[M] ab
l'acqua[F] raffredda il vapore[M] utilizzato

ENERGY

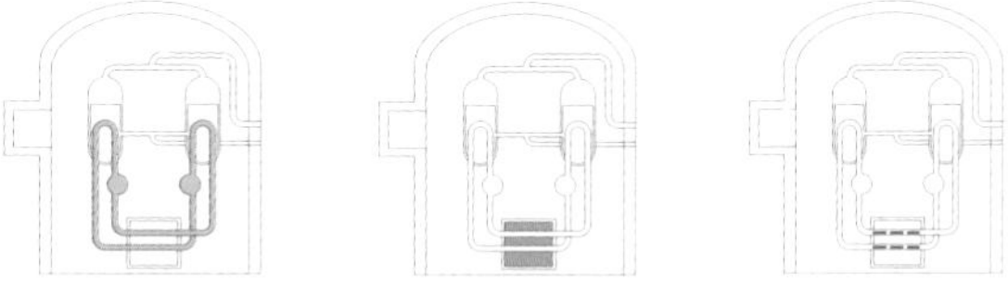

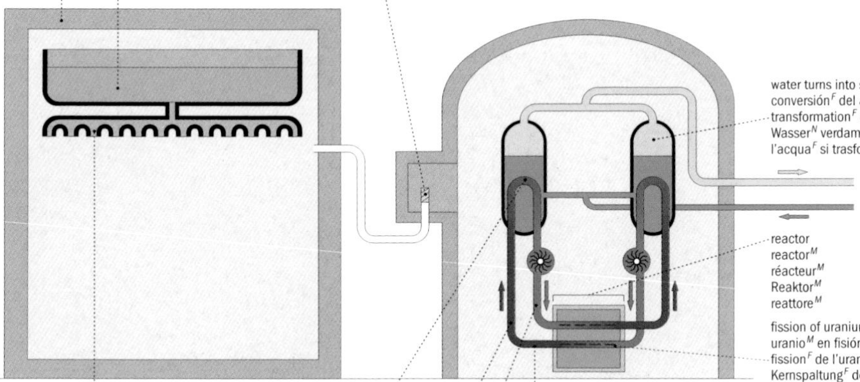

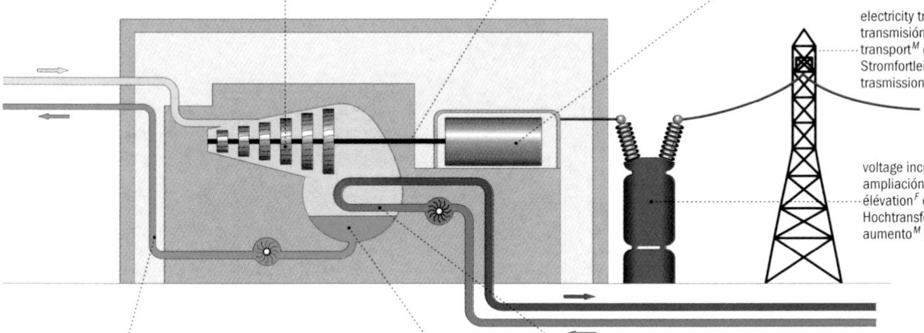

fuel handling sequence

secuencia^F en el manejo^M de combustible^M | séquence^F de manipulation^F du combustible^M | Brennstabbeschickung^F | manipolazione^F del combustibile^M

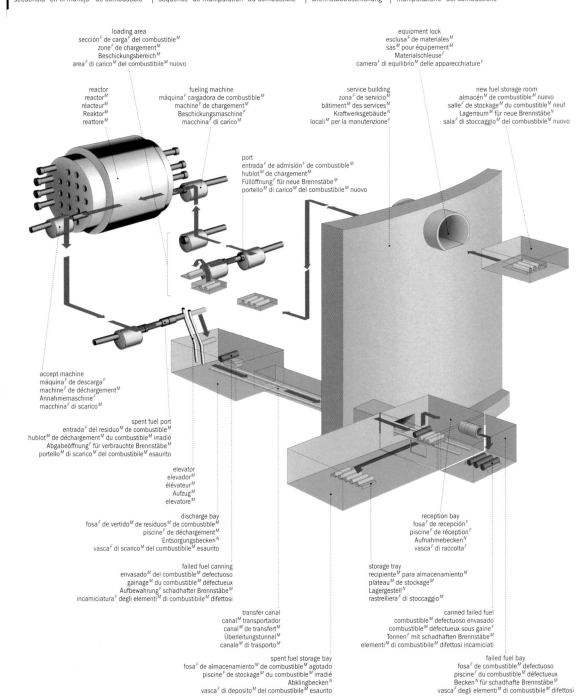

loading area
sección^F de carga^F del combustible^M
zone^F de chargement^M
Beschickungsbereich^M
area^F di carico^M del combustibile^M nuovo

equipment lock
esclusa^F de materiales^M
sas^M pour équipement^M
Materialschleuse^F
camera^F di equilibrio^M delle apparecchiature^F

reactor
reactor^M
réacteur^M
Reaktor^M
reattore^M

fueling machine
máquina^F cargadora de combustible^M
machine^F de chargement^M
Beschickungsmaschine^F
macchina^F di carico^M

service building
zona^F de servicio^M
bâtiment^M des services^M
Kraftwerksgebäude^N
locali^M per la manutenzione^F

new fuel storage room
almacén^M de combustible^M nuevo
salle^F de stockage^F du combustible^M neuf
Lagerraum^M für neue Brennstäbe^N
sala^F di stoccaggio^M del combustibile^M nuovo

port
entrada^F de admisión^F de combustible^M
hublot^M de chargement^M
Füllöffnung^F für neue Brennstäbe^M
portello^M di carico^M del combustibile^M nuovo

accept machine
máquina^F de descarga^F
machine^F de déchargement^M
Annahmemaschine^F
macchina^F di scarico^M

spent fuel port
entrada^F del residuo^M de combustible^M
hublot^M de déchargement^M du combustible^M irradié
Abgabeöffnung^F für verbrauchte Brennstäbe^M
portello^M di scarico^M del combustibile^M esaurito

elevator
elevador^M
élévateur^M
Aufzug^M
elevatore^M

discharge bay
fosa^F de vertido^M de residuos^M de combustible^M
piscine^F de déchargement^M
Entsorgungsbecken^N
vasca^F di scarico^M del combustibile^M esaurito

reception bay
fosa^F de recepción^F
piscine^F de réception^F
Aufnahmebecken^N
vasca^F di raccolta^F

failed fuel canning
envasado^M del combustible^M defectuoso
gainage^M du combustible^M défectueux
Aufbewahrung^F schadhafter Brennstäbe^M
incamiciatura^F degli elementi^M di combustibile^M difettosi

storage tray
recipiente^M para almacenamiento^M
plateau^M de stockage^M
Lagergestell^N
rastrelliera^F di stoccaggio^M

transfer canal
canal^M transportador
canal^M de transfert^M
Überleitungstunnel^M
canale^M di trasporto^M

canned failed fuel
combustible^M defectuoso envasado
combustible^M défectueux sous gaine^F
Tonnen^F mit schadhaften Brennstäbe^M
elementi^M di combustibile^M difettosi incamiciati

spent fuel storage bay
fosa^F de almacenamiento^M de combustible^M agotado
piscine^F de stockage^M du combustible^M irradié
Abklingbecken^N
vasca^F di deposito^M del combustibile^M esaurito

failed fuel bay
fosa^F de combustible^M defectuoso
piscine^F du combustible^M défectueux
Becken^N für schadhafte Brennstäbe^M
vasca^F degli elementi^M di combustibile^M difettosi

ENERGY

fuel bundle

elemento^M de combustible^M | grappe^F de combustible^M | Brennstabbündel^N | elemento^M di combustibile^M

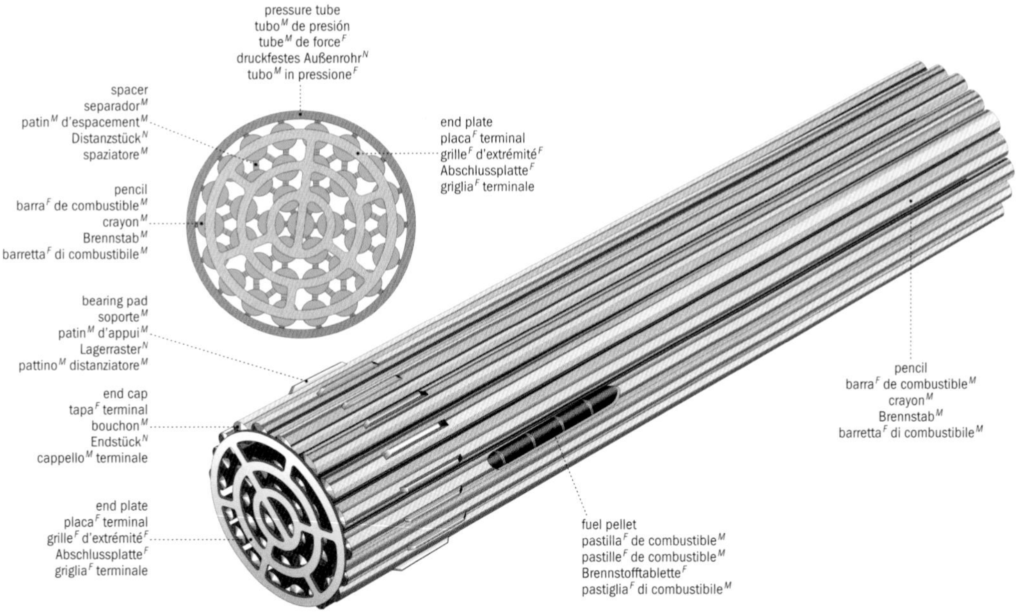

spacer
separador^M
patin^M d'espacement^M
Distanzstück^N
spaziatore^M

pressure tube
tubo^M de presión
tube^M de force^F
druckfestes Außenrohr^N
tubo^M in pressione^F

end plate
placa^F terminal
grille^F d'extrémité^F
Abschlussplatte^F
griglia^F terminale

pencil
barra^F de combustible^M
crayon^M
Brennstab^M
barretta^F di combustibile^M

bearing pad
soporte^M
patin^M d'appui^M
Lagerraster^N
pattino^M distanziatore^M

pencil
barra^F de combustible^M
crayon^M
Brennstab^M
barretta^F di combustibile^M

end cap
tapa^F terminal
bouchon^M
Endstück^N
cappello^M terminale

end plate
placa^F terminal
grille^F d'extrémité^F
Abschlussplatte^F
griglia^F terminale

fuel pellet
pastilla^F de combustible^M
pastille^F de combustible^M
Brennstofftablette^F
pastiglia^F di combustibile^M

nuclear reactor

carga^F del reactor^M nuclear | réacteur^M nucléaire | Kernreaktor^M | reattore^M nucleare

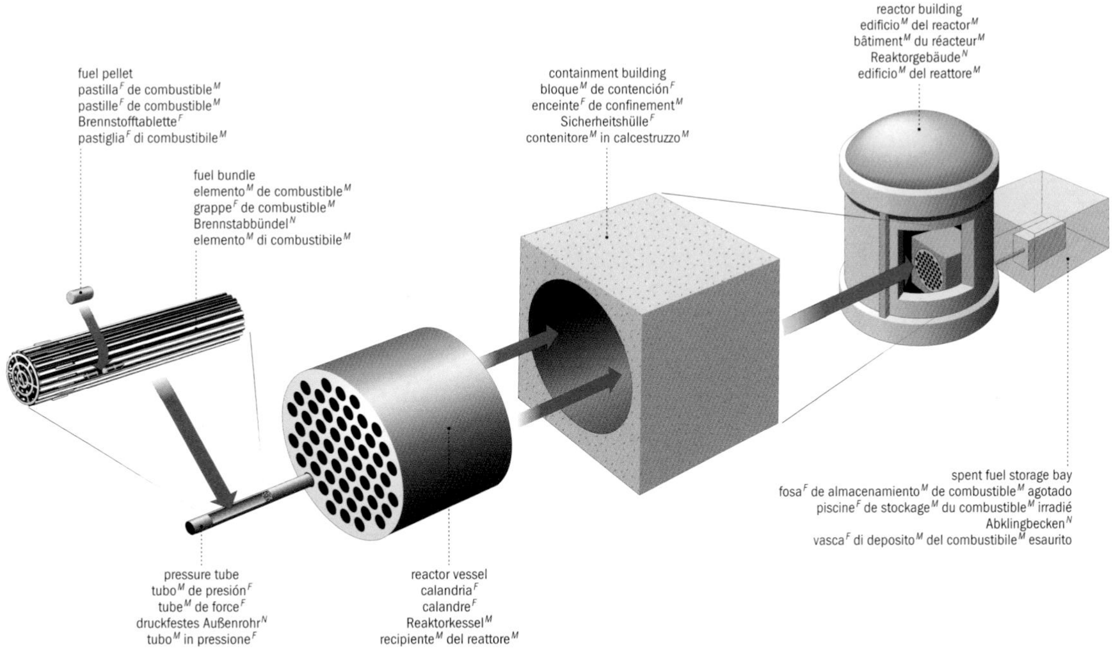

fuel pellet
pastilla^F de combustible^M
pastille^F de combustible^M
Brennstofftablette^F
pastiglia^F di combustibile^M

fuel bundle
elemento^M de combustible^M
grappe^F de combustible^M
Brennstabbündel^N
elemento^M di combustibile^M

containment building
bloque^M de contención^F
enceinte^F de confinement^M
Sicherheitshülle^F
contenitore^M in calcestruzzo^M

reactor building
edificio^M del reactor^M
bâtiment^M du réacteur^M
Reaktorgebäude^N
edificio^M del reattore^M

pressure tube
tubo^M de presión^F
tube^M de force^F
druckfestes Außenrohr^N
tubo^M in pressione^F

reactor vessel
calandria^F
calandre^F
Reaktorkessel^M
recipiente^M del reattore^M

spent fuel storage bay
fosa^F de almacenamiento^M de combustible^M agotado
piscine^F de stockage^M du combustible^M irradié
Abklingbecken^N
vasca^F di deposito^M del combustibile^M esaurito

nuclear power plant

central^F nuclear | centrale^F nucléaire | Kernkraftwerk^N | centrale^F elettronucleare

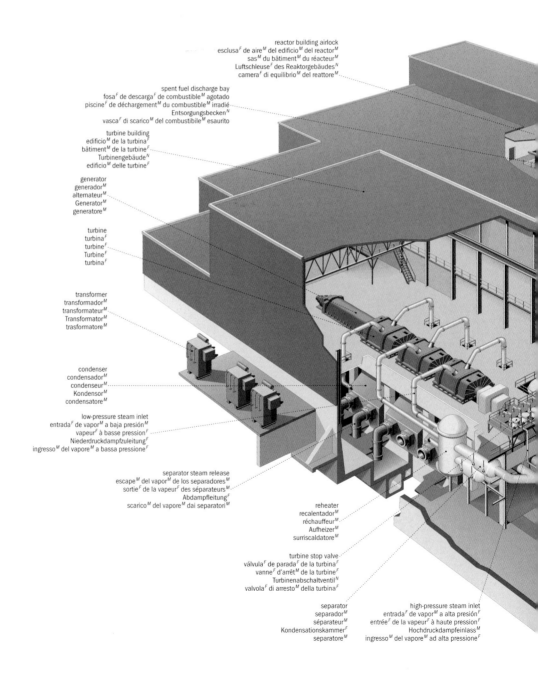

reactor building airlock
esclusa^F de aire^M del edificio^M del reactor^M
sas^M du bâtiment^M du réacteur^M
Luftschleuse^F des Reaktorgebäudes^N
camera^F di equilibrio^M del reattore^M

spent fuel discharge bay
fosa^F de descarga^F de combustible^M agotado
piscine^F de déchargement^M du combustible^M irradié
Entsorgungsbecken^N
vasca^F di scarico^M del combustibile^M esaurito

turbine building
edificio^M de la turbina^F
bâtiment^M de la turbine^F
Turbinengebäude^N
edificio^M delle turbine^F

generator
generador^M
alternateur^M
Generator^M
generatore^M

turbine
turbina^F
turbine^F
Turbine^F
turbina^F

transformer
transformador^M
transformateur^M
Transformator^M
trasformatore^M

condenser
condensador^M
condenseur^M
Kondensor^M
condensatore^M

low-pressure steam inlet
entrada^F de vapor^M a baja presión^M
vapeur^F à basse pression^F
Niederdruckdampfzuleitung^F
ingresso^M del vapore^M a bassa pressione^F

separator steam release
escape^M del vapor^M de los separadores^M
sortie^F de la vapeur^F des séparateurs^M
Abdampfleitung^F
scarico^M del vapore^M dai separatori^M

reheater
recalentador^M
réchauffeur^M
Aufheizer^M
surriscaldatore^M

turbine stop valve
válvula^F de parada^F de la turbina^F
vanne^F d'arrêt^M de la turbine^F
Turbinenabschaltventil^N
valvola^F di arresto^M della turbina^F

separator
separador^M
séparateur^M
Kondensationskammer^F
separatore^M

high-pressure steam inlet
entrada^F de vapor^M a alta presión^F
entrée^F de la vapeur^F à haute pression^F
Hochdruckdampfeinlass^M
ingresso^M del vapore^M ad alta pressione^F

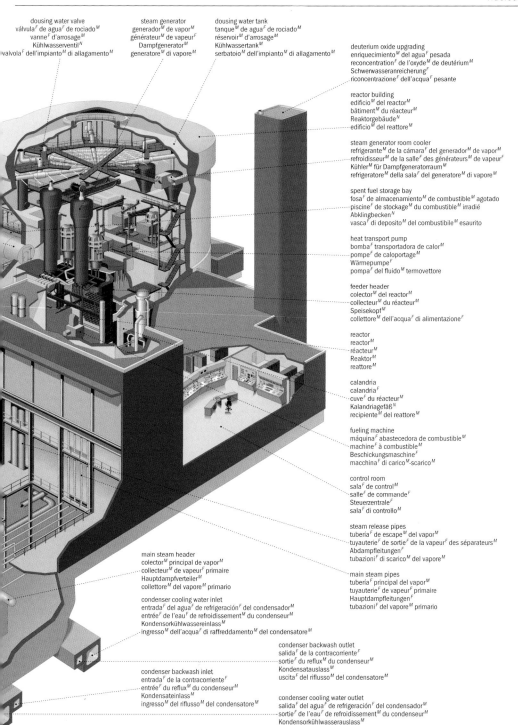

dousing water valve
válvula^F de agua^F de rociado^M
vanne^F d'arrosage^M
Kühlwasserventil^N
valvola^F dell'impianto^M di allagamento^M

steam generator
generador^M de vapor^M
générateur^M de vapeur^F
Dampfgenerator^M
generatore^F di vapore^M

dousing water tank
tanque^M de agua^F de rociado^M
réservoir^M d'arrosage^M
Kühlwassertank^M
serbatoio^M dell'impianto^M di allagamento^M

deuterium oxide upgrading
enriquecimiento^M del agua^F pesada
reconcentration^F de l'oxyde^M de deutérium^M
Schwerwasseranreicherung^F
riconcentrazione^F dell'acqua^F pesante

reactor building
edificio^M del reactor^M
bâtiment^M du réacteur^M
Reaktorgebäude^N
edificio^M del reattore^M

steam generator room cooler
refrigerante^M de la cámara^F del generador^M de vapor^M
refroidisseur^M de la salle^F des générateurs^M de vapeur^F
Kühler^M für Dampfgeneratorraum^M
refrigeratore^M della sala^F del generatore^M di vapore^M

spent fuel storage bay
fosa^F de almacenamiento^M de combustible^M agotado
piscine^F de stockage^M du combustible^M irradié
Abklingbecken^N
vasca^F di deposito^M del combustibile^M esaurito

heat transport pump
bomba^F transportadora de calor^M
pompe^F de caloportage^M
Wärmepumpe^F
pompa^F del fluido^M termovettore

feeder header
colector^M del reactor^M
collecteur^M du réacteur^M
Speisekopf^M
collettore^M dell'acqua^F di alimentazione^F

reactor
reactor^M
réacteur^M
Reaktor^M
reattore^M

calandria
calandria^F
cuve^F du réacteur^M
Kalandriagefäß^N
recipiente^M del reattore^M

fueling machine
máquina^F abastecedora de combustible^M
machine^F à combustible^M
Beschickungsmaschine^F
macchina^F di carico^M-scarico^M

control room
sala^F de control^M
salle^F de commande^F
Steuerzentrale^F
sala^F di controllo^M

steam release pipes
tubería^F de escape^M del vapor^M
tuyauterie^F de sortie^F de la vapeur^F des séparateurs^M
Abdampfleitungen^F
tubazioni^F di scarico^M del vapore^M

main steam header
colector^M principal de vapor^M
collecteur^M de vapeur^F primaire
Hauptdampfverteiler^M
collettore^M del vapore^M primario

main steam pipes
tubería^F principal del vapor^M
tuyauterie^F de vapeur^F primaire
Hauptdampfleitungen^F
tubazioni^F del vapore^M primario

condenser cooling water inlet
entrada^F del agua^F de refrigeración^F del condensador^M
entrée^F de l'eau^F de refroidissement^M du condenseur^M
Kondensorkühlwassereinlass^M
ingresso^M dell'acqua^F di raffreddamento^M del condensatore^M

condenser backwash inlet
entrada^F de la contracorriente^F
entrée^F du reflux^M du condenseur^M
Kondensateinlass^M
ingresso^M del riflusso^M del condensatore^M

condenser backwash outlet
salida^F de la contracorriente^F
sortie^F du reflux^M du condenseur^M
Kondensatauslass^M
uscita^F del riflusso^M del condensatore^M

condenser cooling water outlet
salida^F del agua^F de refrigeración^F del condensador^M
sortie^F de l'eau^F de refroidissement^M du condenseur^M
Kondensorkühlwasserauslass^M
uscita^F dell'acqua^F di raffreddamento^M del condensatore^M

carbon dioxide reactor

reactor^M de bióxido^M de carbono^M | réacteur^M au gaz^M carbonique | Kohlendioxidreaktor^M | reattore^M ad anidride^F carbonica

fuel: natural uranium
combustible^M : uranio^M natural
combustible^M : uranium^M naturel
Brennstoff^M: Natururan^N
combustibile^M: uranio^M naturale

moderator: graphite
moderador^M : grafito^M
modérateur^M : graphite^M
Moderator^M: Graphit^M
moderatore^M: grafite^F

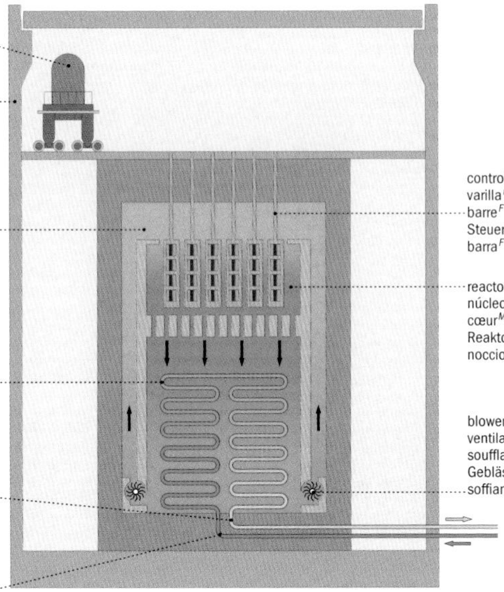

coolant: carbon dioxide
refrigerante^M : dióxido^M de carbono^M
caloporteur^M : gaz^M carbonique
Kühlmittel^N: Kohlendioxid^N
fluido^M refrigerante: anidride^F carbonica

fueling machine
máquina^F cargadora del combustible^M
machine^F de chargement^M
Beschickungsmaschine^F
macchina^F di carico^M-scarico^M

concrete shielding
blindaje^M de hormigón^M
enceinte^F en béton^M
Betonmantel^M
schermatura^F in calcestruzzo^M

carbon dioxide gas coolant
gas^M refrigerante de dióxido^M de carbono^M
gaz^M carbonique de refroidissement^M
Kohlendioxidkühlgas^N
anidride^F carbonica di raffreddamento^M

heat exchanger
intercambiador^M de calor^M
échangeur^M de chaleur^F
Wärmetauscher^M
scambiatore^M di calore^M

steam outlet
salida^F de vapor^M
sortie^F de la vapeur^F
Dampfauslass^M
uscita^F del vapore^M

feedwater
alimentación^F de agua^M
alimentation^F en eau^F
Speisewasser^N
acqua^F di alimentazione^F

control rod
varilla^F de control^M
barre^F de contrôle^M
Steuerstab^M
barra^F di controllo^M

reactor core
núcleo^M del reactor^M
cœur^M du réacteur^M
Reaktorkern^M
nocciolo^M del reattore^M

blower
ventilador^M del evaporador^M
soufflante^F
Gebläse^N
soffiante^M

heavy-water reactor

reactor^M de agua^F pesada | réacteur^M à eau^F lourde | Schwerwasserreaktor^M | reattore^M ad acqua^F pesante

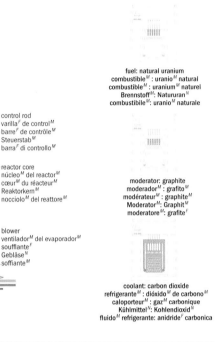

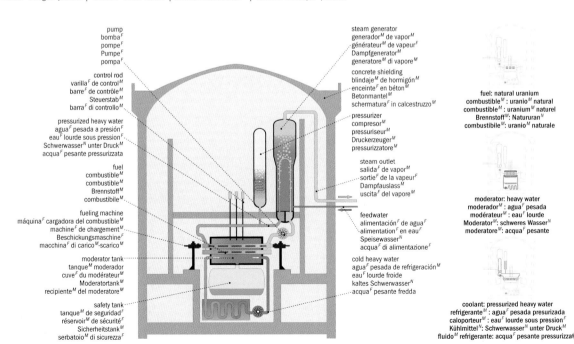

pump
bomba^F
pompe^F
Pumpe^F
pompa^F

control rod
varilla^F de control^M
barre^F de contrôle^M
Steuerstab^M
barra^F di controllo^M

pressurized heavy water
agua^F pesada a presión^F
eau^F lourde sous pression^F
Schwerwasser^N unter Druck^M
acqua^F pesante pressurizzata

fuel
combustible^M
combustible^M
Brennstoff^M
combustibile^M

fueling machine
máquina^F cargadora del combustible^M
machine^F de chargement^M
Beschickungsmaschine^F
macchina^F di carico^M-scarico^M

moderator tank
tanque^M moderador
cuve^F du modérateur^M
Moderatortank^M
recipiente^M del moderatore^M

safety tank
tanque^M de seguridad^F
réservoir^M de sécurité^F
Sicherheitstank^M
serbatoio^M di sicurezza^F

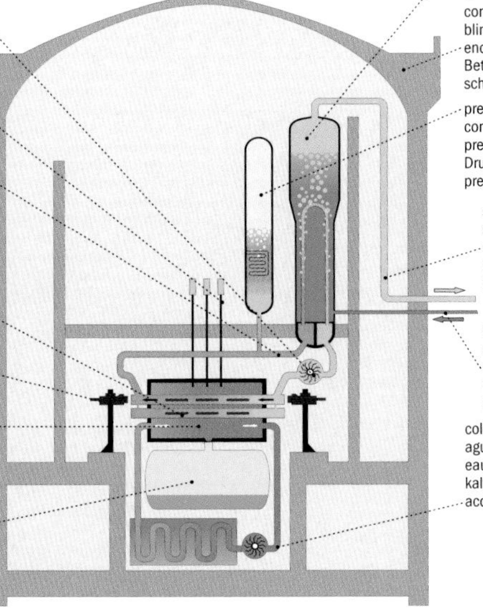

steam generator
generador^M de vapor^M
générateur^M de vapeur^F
Dampfgenerator^M
generatore^M di vapore^M

concrete shielding
blindaje^M de hormigón^M
enceinte^F en béton^M
Betonmantel^M
schermatura^F in calcestruzzo^M

pressurizer
compresor^M
pressuriseur^M
Druckerzeuger^M
pressurizzatore^M

steam outlet
salida^F de vapor^M
sortie^F de la vapeur^F
Dampfauslass^M
uscita^F del vapore^M

feedwater
alimentación^F de agua^F
alimentation^F en eau^F
Speisewasser^N
acqua^F di alimentazione^F

cold heavy water
agua^F pesada de refrigeración^M
eau^F lourde froide
kaltes Schwerwasser^N
acqua^F pesante fredda

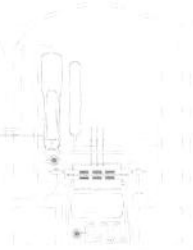

fuel: natural uranium
combustible^M : uranio^M natural
combustible^M : uranium^M naturel
Brennstoff^M: Natururan^N
combustibile^M: uranio^M naturale

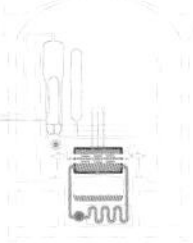

moderator: heavy water
moderador^M : agua^F pesada
modérateur^M : eau^F lourde
Moderator^M: schweres Wasser^N
moderatore^M: acqua^F pesante

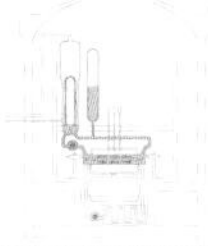

coolant: pressurized heavy water
refrigerante^M : agua^F pesada presurizada
caloporteur^M : eau^F lourde sous pression^F
Kühlmittel^N: Schwerwasser^N unter Druck^M
fluido^M refrigerante: acqua^F pesante pressurizzata

ENERGY

pressurized-water reactor

reactor^M de agua^F a presión^F | réacteur^M à eau^F sous pression^F | Druckwasserreaktor^M | reattore^M ad acqua^F pressurizzata

fuel: enriched uranium
combustible^M : uranio^M enriquecido
combustible^M : uranium^M enrichi
Brennstoff^M: angereichertes Uran^N
combustibile^M: uranio^M arricchito

moderator: natural water
moderador^M : agua^F natural
modérateur^M : eau^F naturelle
Moderator^M: leichtes Wasser^N
moderatore^M: acqua^F naturale

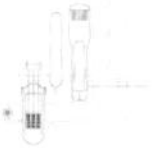

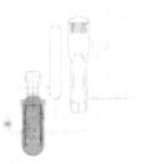

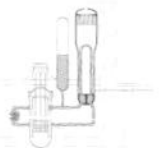

coolant: pressurized water
refrigerante^M : agua^F presurizada
caloporteur^M : eau^F sous pression^F
Kühlmittel^N: Druckwasser^N
fluido^M refrigerante: acqua^F pressurizzata

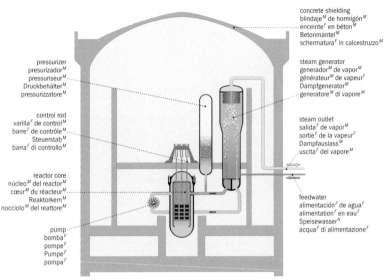

pressurizer
presurizador^M
pressuriseur^M
Druckbehälter^M
pressurizzatore^M

control rod
varilla^F de control^M
barre^F de contrôle^F
Steuerstab^M
barra^F di controllo^M

reactor core
núcleo^M del reactor^M
cœur^M du réacteur^M
Reaktorkern^M
nocciolo^M del reattore^M

pump
bomba^F
pompe^F
Pumpe^F
pompa^F

concrete shielding
blindaje^M de hormigón^M
enceinte^F en béton^M
Betonmantel^M
schermatura^F in calcestruzzo^M

steam generator
generador^M de vapor^M
générateur^F de vapeur^F
Dampfgenerator^M
generatore^M di vapore^M

steam outlet
salida^F de vapor^M
sortie^F de la vapeur^F
Dampfauslass^M
uscita^F del vapore^M

feedwater
alimentación^F de agua^F
alimentation^F en eau^F
Speisewasser^N
acqua^F di alimentazione^F

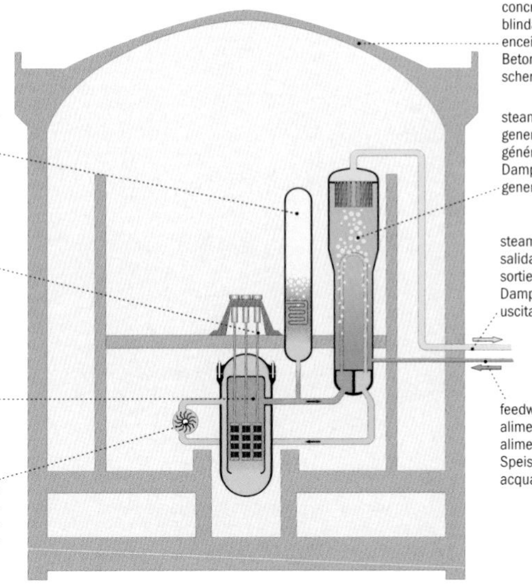

boiling-water reactor

reactor^M de agua^F hirviente | réacteur^M à eau^F bouillante | Siedewasserreaktor^M | reattore^M ad acqua^F bollente

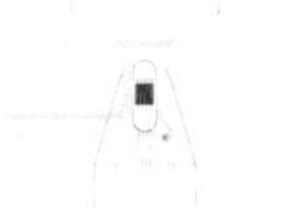

fuel: enriched uranium
combustible^M : uranio^M enriquecido
combustible^M : uranium^M enrichi
Brennstoff^M: angereichertes Uran^N
combustibile^M: uranio^M arricchito

moderator: natural water
moderador^M : agua^F natural
modérateur^M : eau^F naturelle
Moderator^M: leichtes Wasser^N
moderatore^M: acqua^F naturale

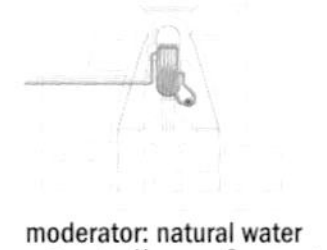

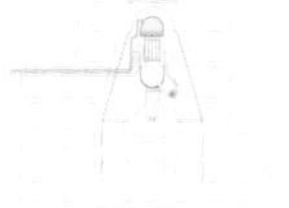

coolant: boiling water
refrigerante^M : agua^F hirviente
caloporteur^M : eau^F bouillante
Kühlmittel^N: Siedewasser^N
fluido^M refrigerante: acqua^F bollente

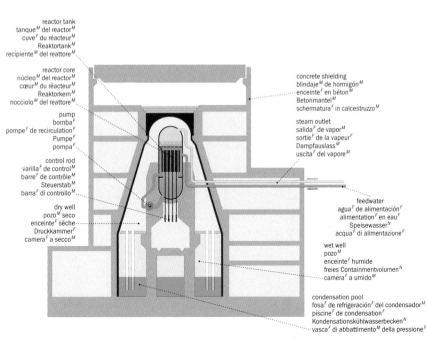

reactor tank
tanque^M del reactor^M
cuve^F du réacteur^M
Reaktortank^M
recipiente^M del reattore^M

reactor core
núcleo^M del reactor^M
cœur^M du réacteur^M
Reaktorkern^M
nocciolo^M del reattore^M

pump
bomba^F
pompe^F de recirculation^F
Pumpe^F
pompa^F

control rod
varilla^F de control^M
barre^F de contrôle^M
Steuerstab^M
barra^F di controllo^M

dry well
pozo^M seco
enceinte^F sèche
Druckkammer^F
camera^F a secco^M

concrete shielding
blindaje^M de hormigón^M
enceinte^F en béton^M
Betonmantel^M
schermatura^F in calcestruzzo^M

steam outlet
salida^F de vapor^M
sortie^F de la vapeur^F
Dampfauslass^M
uscita^F del vapore^M

feedwater
agua^F de alimentación^F
alimentation^F en eau^F
Speisewasser^N
acqua^F di alimentazione^F

wet well
pozo^M
enceinte^F humide
freies Containmentvolumen^N
camera^F a umido^M

condensation pool
fosa^F de refrigeración^F del condensador^M
piscine^F de condensation^F
Kondensationskühlwasserbecken^N
vasca^F di abbattimento^M della pressione^F

ENERGY

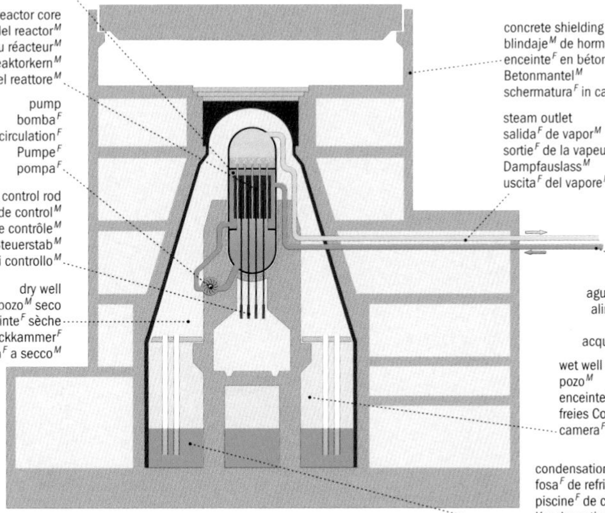

solar cell

célula^F solar | photopile^F | Solarzelle^F | cella^F solare

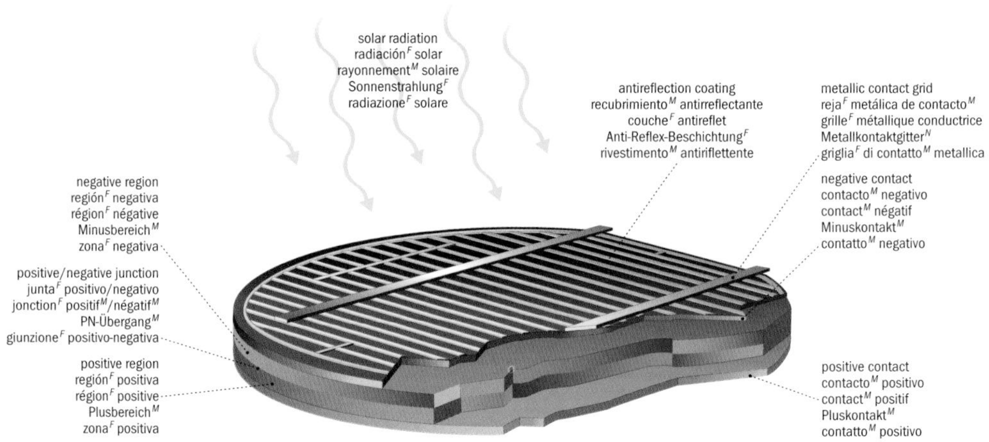

solar radiation
radiación^F solar
rayonnement^M solaire
Sonnenstrahlung^F
radiazione^F solare

antireflection coating
recubrimiento^M antirreflectante
couche^F antireflet
Anti-Reflex-Beschichtung^F
rivestimento^M antiriflettente

metallic contact grid
reja^F metálica de contacto^M
grille^F métallique conductrice
Metallkontaktgitter^N
griglia^F di contatto^M metallica

negative region
región^F negativa
région^F négative
Minusbereich^M
zona^F negativa

negative contact
contacto^M negativo
contact^M négatif
Minuskontakt^M
contatto^M negativo

positive/negative junction
junta^F positivo/negativo
jonction^F positif^M/négatif^M
PN-Übergang^M
giunzione^F positivo-negativa

positive region
región^F positiva
région^F positive
Plusbereich^M
zona^F positiva

positive contact
contacto^M positivo
contact^M positif
Pluskontakt^M
contatto^M positivo

flat-plate solar collector

colector^M solar plano | capteur^M solaire plan | Flachkollektor^M | collettore^M solare piatto

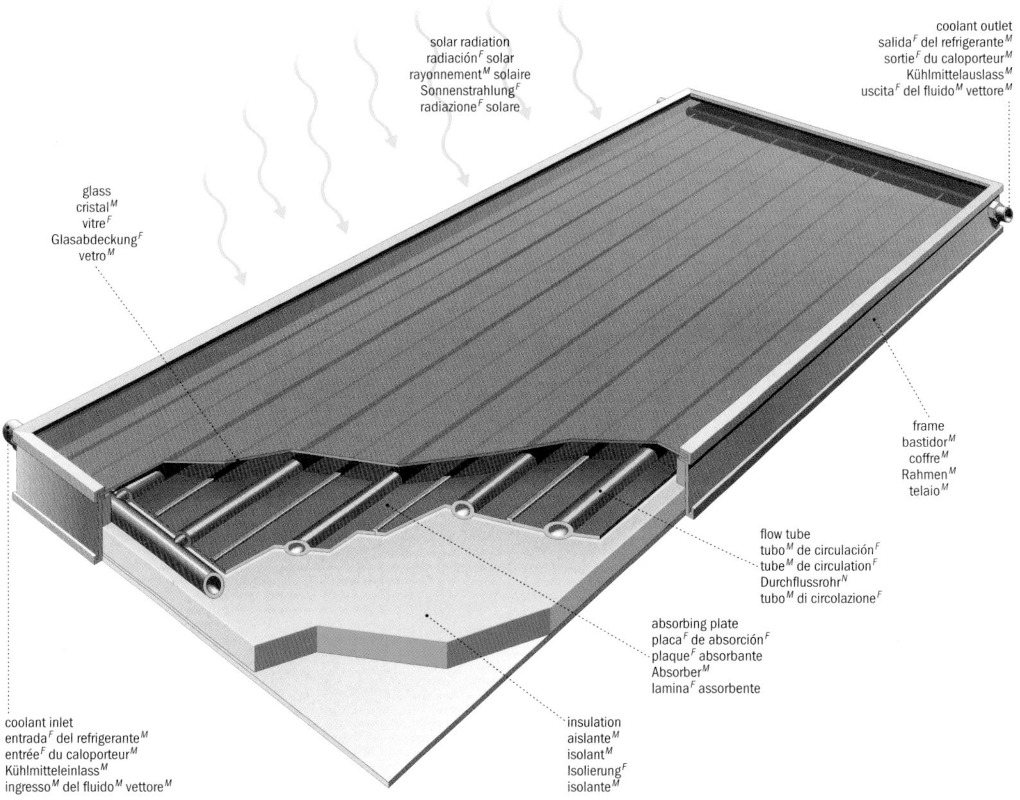

solar radiation
radiación^F solar
rayonnement^M solaire
Sonnenstrahlung^F
radiazione^F solare

coolant outlet
salida^F del refrigerante^M
sortie^F du caloporteur^M
Kühlmittelauslass^M
uscita^F del fluido^M vettore^M

glass
cristal^M
vitre^F
Glasabdeckung^F
vetro^M

frame
bastidor^M
coffre^M
Rahmen^M
telaio^M

flow tube
tubo^M de circulación^F
tube^M de circulation^F
Durchflussrohr^N
tubo^M di circolazione^F

absorbing plate
placa^F de absorción^F
plaque^F absorbante
Absorber^M
lamina^F assorbente

coolant inlet
entrada^F del refrigerante^M
entrée^F du caloporteur^M
Kühlmitteleinlass^M
ingresso^M del fluido^M vettore^M

insulation
aislante^M
isolant^M
Isolierung^F
isolante^M

solar-cell system

sistema^M de células^F solares | circuit^M de photopiles^F | Solarzellensystem^N | sistema^M a celle^F solari

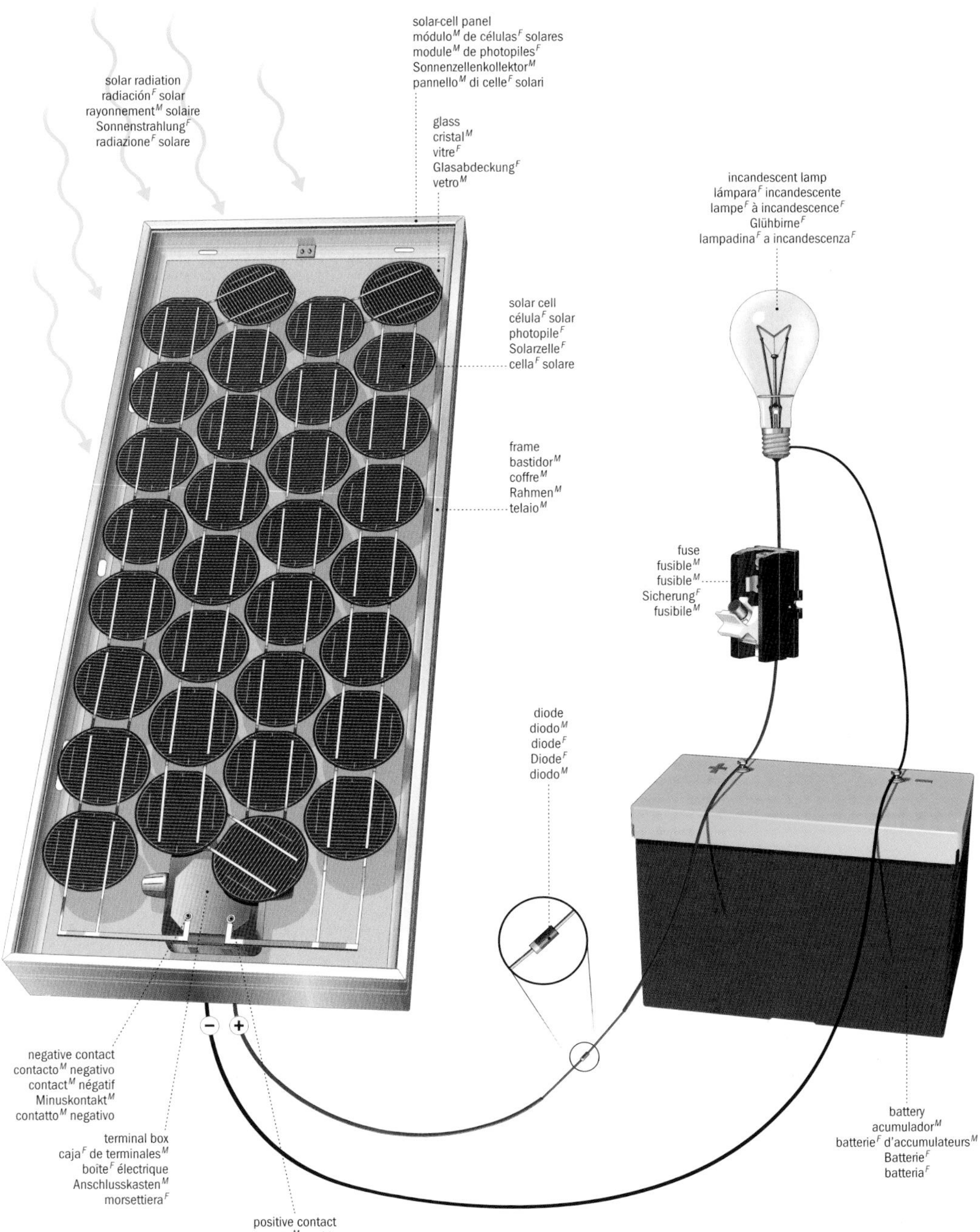

solar-cell panel
módulo^M de células^F solares
module^M de photopiles^F
Sonnenzellenkollektor^M
pannello^M di celle^F solari

solar radiation
radiación^F solar
rayonnement^M solaire
Sonnenstrahlung^F
radiazione^F solare

glass
cristal^M
vitre^F
Glasabdeckung^F
vetro^M

incandescent lamp
lámpara^F incandescente
lampe^F à incandescence^F
Glühbirne^F
lampadina^F a incandescenza^F

solar cell
célula^F solar
photopile^F
Solarzelle^F
cella^F solare

frame
bastidor^M
coffre^M
Rahmen^M
telaio^M

fuse
fusible^M
fusible^M
Sicherung^F
fusibile^M

diode
diodo^M
diode^F
Diode^F
diodo^M

negative contact
contacto^M negativo
contact^M négatif
Minuskontakt^M
contatto^M negativo

battery
acumulador^M
batterie^F d'accumulateurs^M
Batterie^F
batteria^F

terminal box
caja^F de terminales^M
boîte^F électrique
Anschlusskasten^M
morsettiera^F

positive contact
contacto^M positivo
contact^M positif
Pluskontakt^M
contatto^M positivo

ENERGY

673

solar furnace

horno^M solar | four^M solaire | Sonnenofen^M | forno^M solare

solar radiation
radiación^F solar
rayonnement^M solaire
Sonnenstrahlung^F
radiazione^F solare

solar ray reflected
rayo^M solar reflejado
rayon^M solaire réfléchi
reflektierte Sonnenstrahlen^M
raggio^M solare riflesso

target area
punto^M de concentración^F
foyer^M
Zielgebiet^N
zona^F focale

furnace
horno^M
four^M
Ofen^M
forno^M

parabolic mirror
espejo^M parabólico
miroir^M parabolique
Parabolspiegel^M
specchio^M parabolico

tower
torre^F
tour^F
Turm^M
torre^F

hill
colina^F
pente^F
Anhöhe^F
collina^F

reflecting surface
superficie^F reflectante
surface^F réfléchissante
Sonnenspiegel^M
superficie^F riflettente

bank of heliostats
terraplén^M de los helióstatos^M
champ^M d'héliostats^M
Anordnung^F von Sonnenspiegeln^M
batteria^F di eliostati^M

production of electricity from solar energy

producción^F de electricidad^F por energía^F solar | production^F d'électricité^F par énergie^F solaire | Elektrizitätserzeugung^F aus Sonnenenergie^F | produzione^F di elettricità^F da energia^F solare

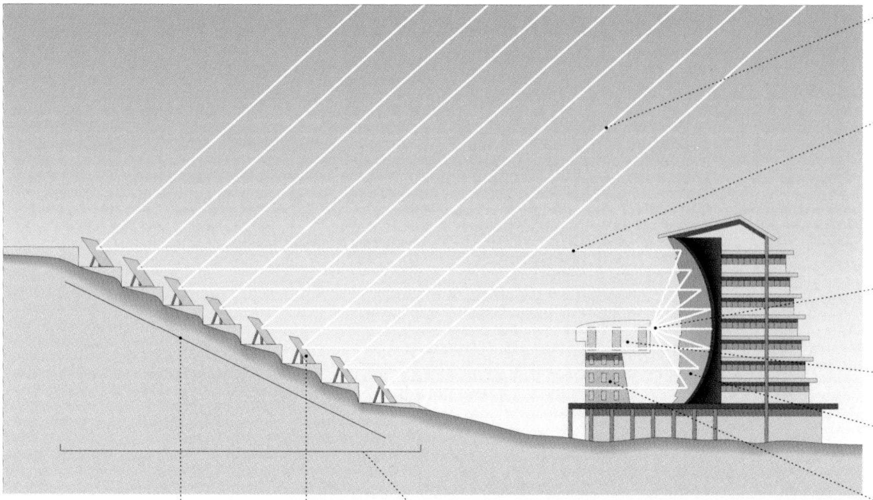

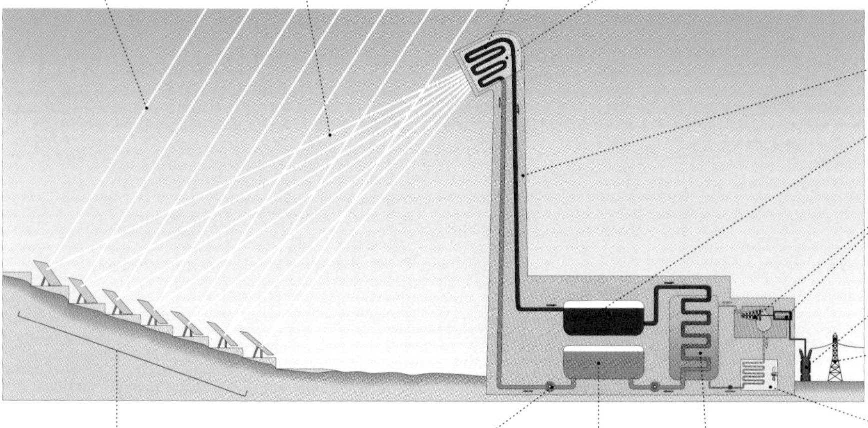

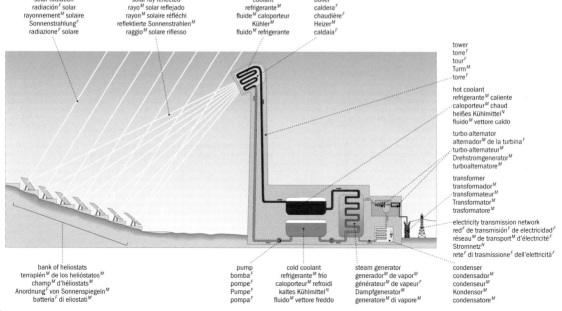

solar radiation
radiación^F solar
rayonnement^M solaire
Sonnenstrahlung^F
radiazione^F solare

solar ray reflected
rayo^M solar reflejado
rayon^M solaire réfléchi
reflektierte Sonnenstrahlen^M
raggio^M solare riflesso

coolant
refrigerante^M
fluide^M caloporteur
Kühler^M
fluido^M refrigerante

boiler
caldera^F
chaudière^F
Heizer^M
caldaia^F

tower
torre^F
tour^F
Turm^M
torre^F

hot coolant
refrigerante^M caliente
caloporteur^M chaud
heißes Kühlmittel^N
fluido^M vettore caldo

turbo-alternator
alternador^M de la turbina^F
turbo-alternateur^M
Drehstromgenerator^M
turboalternatore^M

transformer
transformador^M
transformateur^M
Transformator^M
trasformatore^M

electricity transmission network
red^F de transmisión^F de electricidad^F
réseau^M de transport^M d'électricité^F
Stromnetz^N
rete^F di trasmissione^F dell'elettricità^F

bank of heliostats
terraplén^M de los helióstatos^M
champ^M d'héliostats^M
Anordnung^F von Sonnenspiegeln^M
batteria^F di eliostati^M

pump
bomba^F
pompe^F
Pumpe^F
pompa^F

cold coolant
refrigerante^M frío
caloporteur^M refroidi
kaltes Kühlmittel^N
fluido^M vettore freddo

steam generator
generador^M de vapor^M
générateur^M de vapeur^F
Dampfgenerator^M
generatore^M di vapore^M

condenser
condensador^M
condenseur^M
Kondensor^M
condensatore^M

solar powered house

casa^F solar | maison^F solaire | Solarhaus^N | casa^F solare

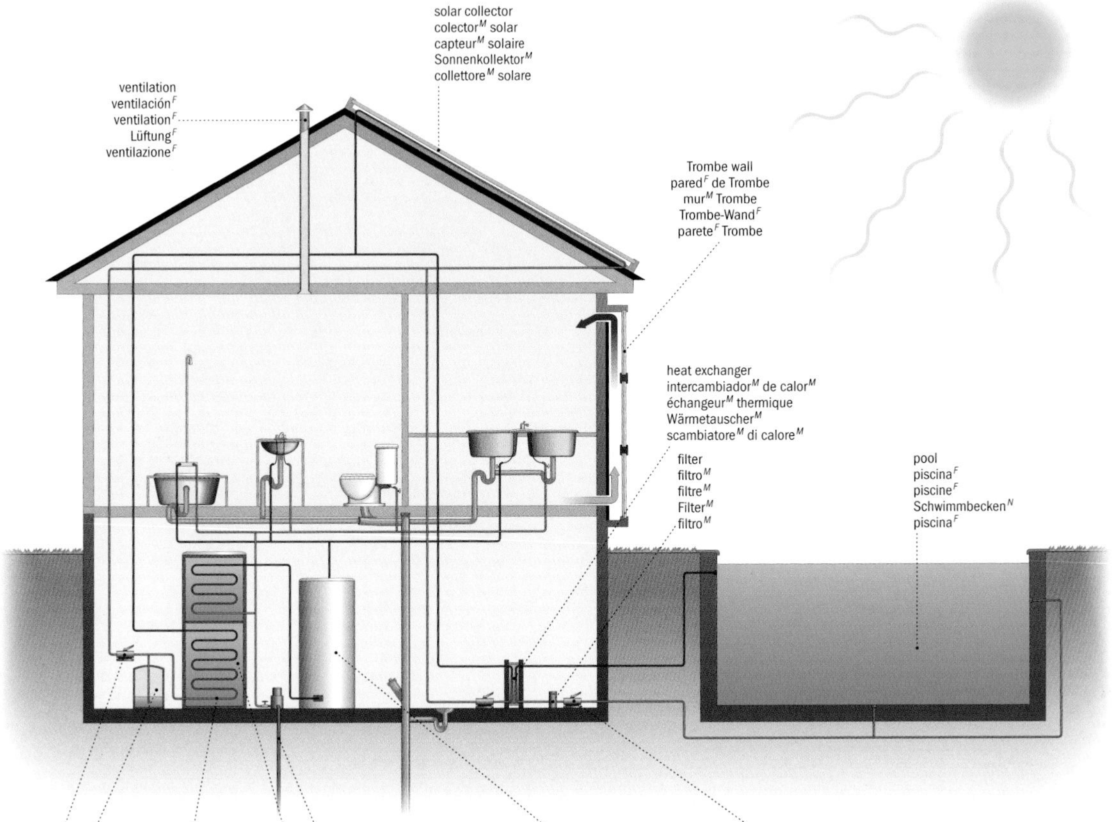

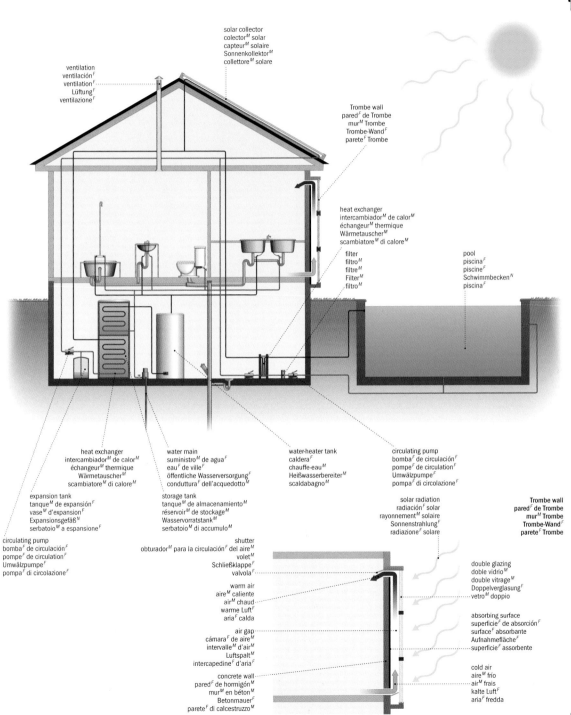

solar collector
colector^M solar
capteur^M solaire
Sonnenkollektor^M
collettore^M solare

ventilation
ventilación^F
ventilation^F
Lüftung^F
ventilazione^F

Trombe wall
pared^F de Trombe
mur^M Trombe
Trombe-Wand^F
parete^F Trombe

heat exchanger
intercambiador^M de calor^M
échangeur^M thermique
Wärmetauscher^M
scambiatore^M di calore^M

filter
filtro^M
filtre^M
Filter^M
filtro^M

pool
piscina^F
piscine^F
Schwimmbecken^N
piscina^F

heat exchanger
intercambiador^M de calor^M
échangeur^M thermique
Wärmetauscher^M
scambiatore^M di calore^M

water main
suministro^M de agua^F
eau^F de ville^F
öffentliche Wasserversorgung^F
conduttura^F dell'acquedotto^M

water-heater tank
caldera^F
chauffe-eau^M
Heißwasserbereiter^M
scaldabagno^M

circulating pump
bomba^F de circulación^F
pompe^F de circulation^F
Umwälzpumpe^F
pompa^F di circolazione^F

expansion tank
tanque^M de expansión^F
vase^M d'expansion^F
Expansionsgefäß^N
serbatoio^M a espansione^F

storage tank
tanque^M de almacenamiento^M
réservoir^M de stockage^M
Wasservorratstank^M
serbatoio^M di accumulo^M

solar radiation
radiación^F solar
rayonnement^M solaire
Sonnenstrahlung^F
radiazione^F solare

Trombe wall
pared^F de Trombe
mur^M Trombe
Trombe-Wand^F
parete^F Trombe

circulating pump
bomba^F de circulación^F
pompe^F de circulation^F
Umwälzpumpe^F
pompa^F di circolazione^F

shutter
obturador^M para la circulación^F del aire^M
volet^M
Schließklappe^F
valvola^F

warm air
aire^M caliente
air^M chaud
warme Luft^F
aria^F calda

air gap
cámara^F de aire^M
intervalle^M d'air^M
Luftspalt^M
intercapedine^F d'aria^F

concrete wall
pared^F de hormigón^M
mur^M en béton^M
Betonmauer^F
parete^F di calcestruzzo^M

double glazing
doble vidrio^M
double vitrage^M
Doppelverglasung^F
vetro^M doppio

absorbing surface
superficie^F de absorción^F
surface^F absorbante
Aufnahmefläche^F
superficie^F assorbente

cold air
aire^M frío
air^M frais
kalte Luft^F
aria^F fredda

ENERGY

675

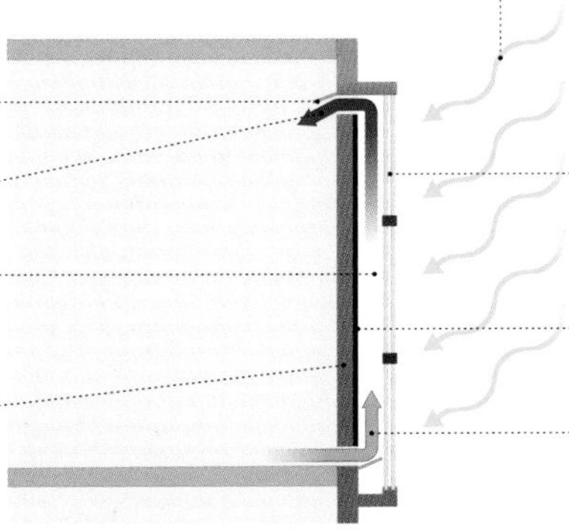

windmill

molino^M de viento^M | moulin^M à vent^M | Windmühle^F | mulino^M a vento^M

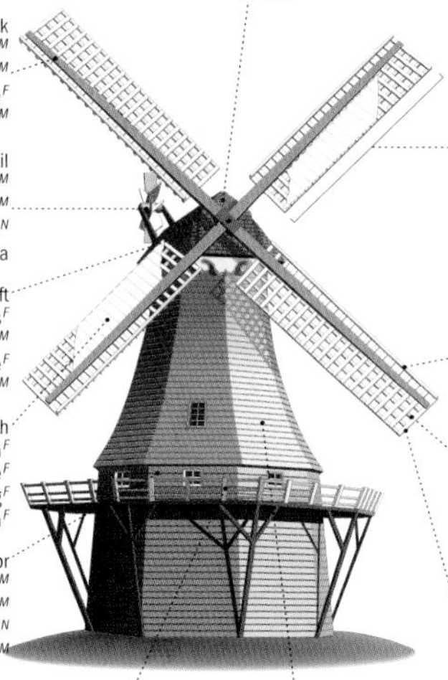

tower mill
molino^M de torre^F
moulin^M tour^F
Turmwindmühle^F
mulino^M a torre^F

cap
casquete^M
calotte^F
Windmühlenhaube^F
calotta^F

rotor
rotor^M
rotor^M
Rotor^M
rotore^M

post mill
molino^M de plataforma^F giratoria
moulin^M pivot^M
Bockmühle^F
mulino^M a pilastro^M

stock
larguero^M
bras^M
Windrute^F
braccio^M

sail
aspa^F
aile^F
Flügel^M
pala^F

tail pole
puntal^M trasero
queue^F
Stert^M
timone^M

fantail
molinete^M
gouvernail^M
Seitenrad^N
pala^F ausiliaria

hemlath
lama^F
cotret^M
Saumlatte^F
barra^F

windshaft
eje^M de las aspas^F
arbre^M
Welle^F
albero^M

sail cloth
lona^F
voile^F
Segeltuchbespannung^F
tela^F

sailbar
travesaño^M
latte^F
Segelstange^F
listello^M

floor
piso^M
étage^M
Sockelgeschoß^N
piano^M

gallery
corredor^M
galerie^F
Galerie^F
balcone^M

tower
torre^F
tour^F
Turm^M
torre^F

frame
armazón^M
cadre^M
Rahmen^M
telaio^M

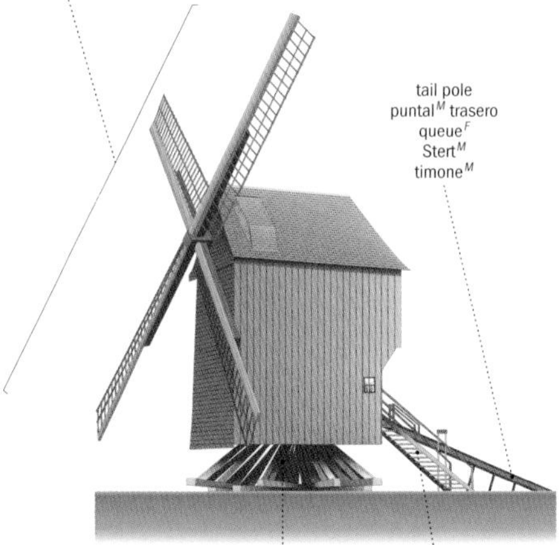

post
soporte^M de la plataforma^F
pivot^M
Königsbaum^M
pilastro^M

steps
escalera^F
escalier^M
Treppe^F
scala^F

wind turbines and electricity production

turbinas^F de viento^M y producción^F eléctrica | éoliennes^F et production^F d'électricité^F | Windkraftwerke^N und Elektrizitätserzeugung^F | turbine^F eoliche e produzione^F di elettricità^F

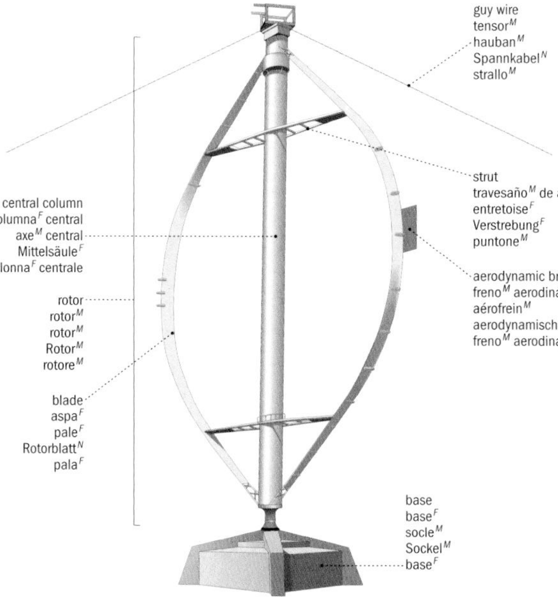

vertical-axis wind turbine
turbina^F de viento^M de eje^M vertical
éolienne^F à axe^M vertical
Windkraftwerk mit vertikaler Achse^F
turbina^F ad asse^M verticale

guy wire
tensor^M
hauban^M
Spannkabel^N
strallo^M

central column
columna^F central
axe^M central
Mittelsäule^F
colonna^F centrale

strut
travesaño^M de apoyo^M
entretoise^F
Verstrebung^F
puntone^M

aerodynamic brake
freno^M aerodinámico
aérofrein^M
aerodynamische Bremse^F
freno^M aerodinamico

rotor
rotor^M
rotor^M
Rotor^M
rotore^M

blade
aspa^F
pale^F
Rotorblatt^N
pala^F

base
base^F
socle^M
Sockel^M
base^F

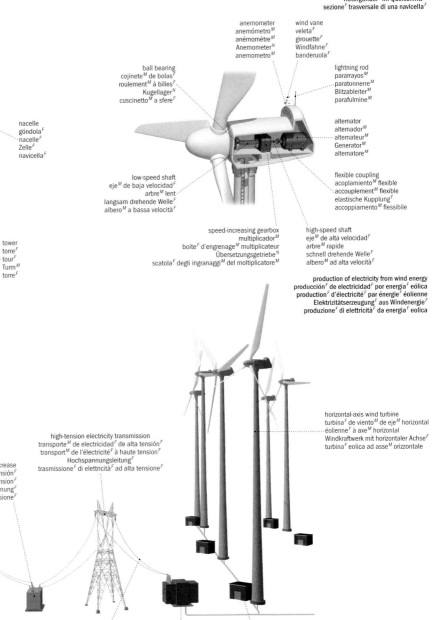

horizontal-axis wind turbine
turbina^F de viento^M de eje^M horizontal
éolienne^F à axe^M horizontal
Windkraftwerk mit horizontaler Achse^F
turbina^F eolica ad asse^M orizzontale

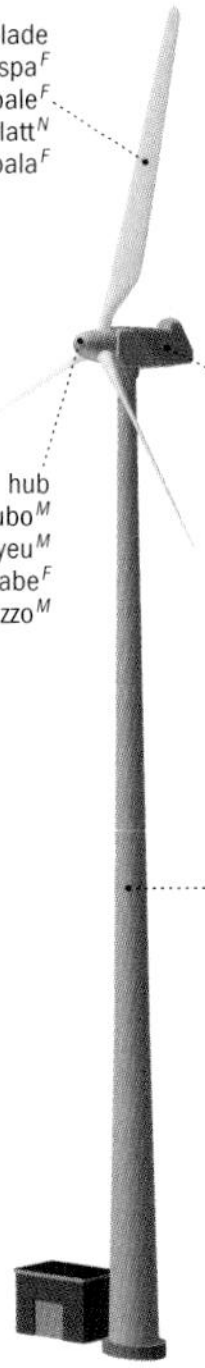

nacelle cross-section
sección^F transversal de la góndola^F
coupe^F de la nacelle^F
Rotorgondel^F im Querschnitt^M
sezione^F trasversale di una navicella^F

blade
aspa^F
pale^F
Rotorblatt^N
pala^F

anemometer
anemómetro^M
anémomètre^M
Anemometer^N
anemometro^M

wind vane
veleta^F
girouette^F
Windfahne^F
banderuola^F

ball bearing
cojinete^M de bolas^F
roulement^M à billes^F
Kugellager^N
cuscinetto^M a sfere^F

lightning rod
pararrayos^M
paratonnerre^M
Blitzableiter^M
parafulmine^M

nacelle
góndola^F
nacelle^F
Zelle^F
navicella^F

alternator
alternador^M
alternateur^M
Generator^M
alternatore^M

hub
cubo^M
moyeu^M
Nabe^F
mozzo^M

low-speed shaft
eje^M de baja velocidad^F
arbre^M lent
langsam drehende Welle^F
albero^M a bassa velocità^F

flexible coupling
acoplamiento^M flexible
accouplement^M flexible
elastische Kupplung^F
accoppiamento^M flessibile

tower
torre^F
tour^F
Turm^M
torre^F

speed-increasing gearbox
multiplicador^M
boite^F d'engrenage^M multiplicateur
Übersetzungsgetriebe^N
scatola^F degli ingranaggi^M del moltiplicatore^M

high-speed shaft
eje^M de alta velocidad^F
arbre^M rapide
schnell drehende Welle^F
albero^M ad alta velocità^F

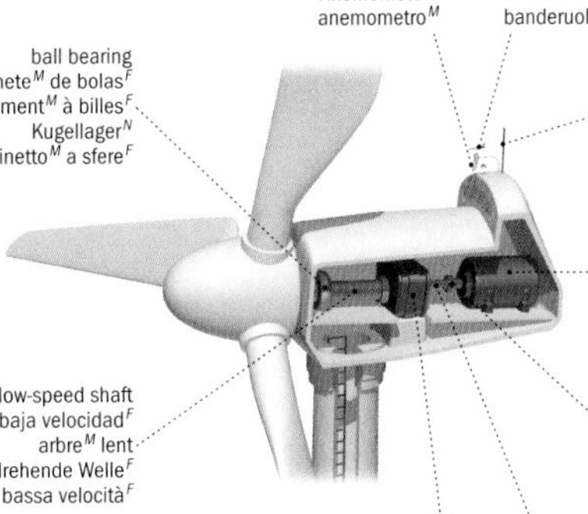

production of electricity from wind energy
producción^F de electricidad^F por energía^F eólica
production^F d'électricité^F par énergie^F éolienne
Elektrizitätserzeugung^F aus Windenergie^F
produzione^F di elettricità^F da energia^F eolica

high-tension electricity transmission
transporte^M de electricidad^F de alta tensión^F
transport^M de l'électricité^F à haute tension^F
Hochspannungsleitung^F
trasmissione^F di elettricità^F ad alta tensione^F

horizontal-axis wind turbine
turbina^F de viento^M de eje^M horizontal
éolienne^F à axe^M horizontal
Windkraftwerk mit horizontaler Achse^F
turbina^F eolica ad asse^M orizzontale

voltage decrease
disminución^F de la tensión^F
abaissement^M de la tension^F
Heruntertransformation^F der Spannung^F
diminuzione^F di tensione^F

transmission to consumers
transporte^M hacia los usuarios^M
transport^M vers les usagers^M
Stromleitung^F an die Verbraucher^M
trasmissione^F agli utenti^M

energy integration to the transmission network
integración^F de energía^F a la red^F de transporte^M
intégration^F de l'électricité^F au réseau^M de transport^M
Einspeisung^F in das Leitungsnetz^N
integrazione^F di energia^F alla rete^F di trasmissione^F

second voltage increase
segundo aumento^M de tensión^F
seconde élévation^F de la tension^F
zweite Spannungserhöhung^F
secondo aumento^M di tensione^F

first voltage increase
primer aumento^M de la tensión^F
première élévation^F de la tension^F
erste Spannungserhöhung^F
primo aumento^M di tensione^F

ENERGY

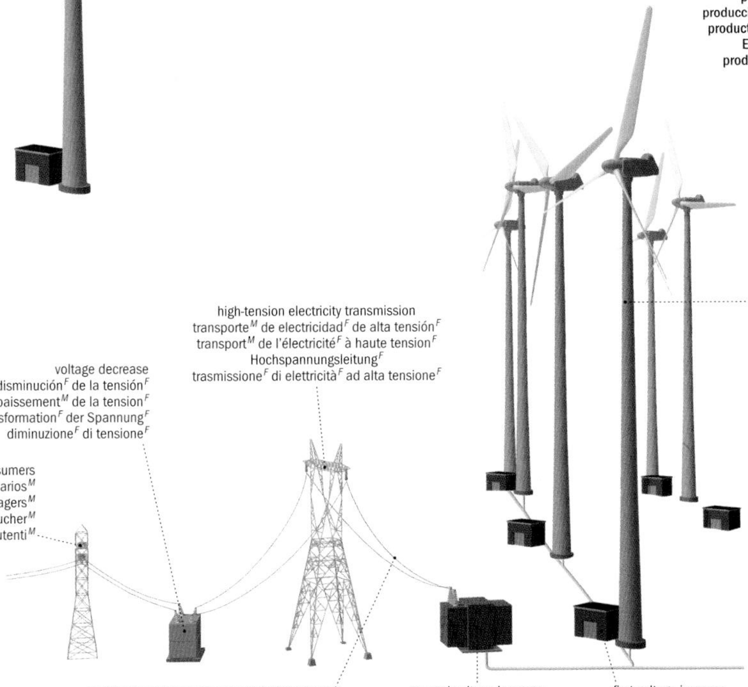

Sc Ti V Cr Mn Fe Co
Y Zr Nb Mo Tc Ru Rh
W Re Os Ir

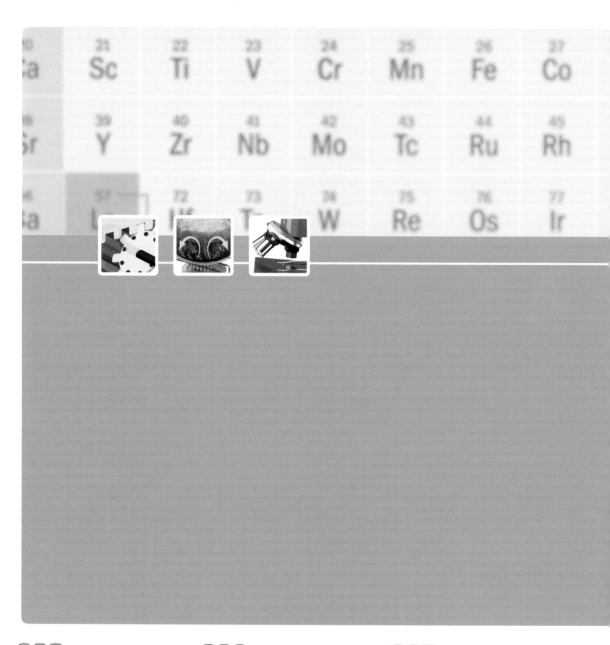

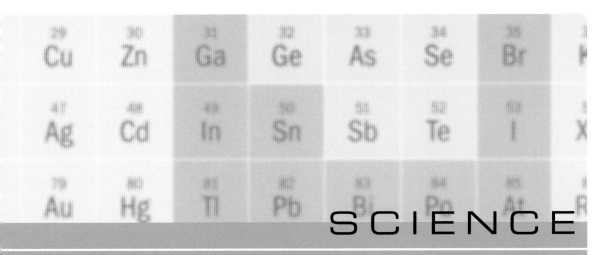

SCIENCE

CIENCIA | SCIENCE | WISSENSCHAFT | SCIENZA

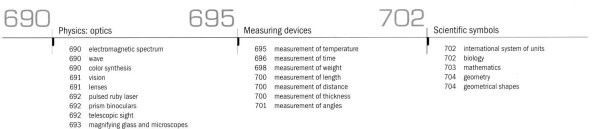

matter

materia[F] | matière[F] | Materie[F] | materia[F]

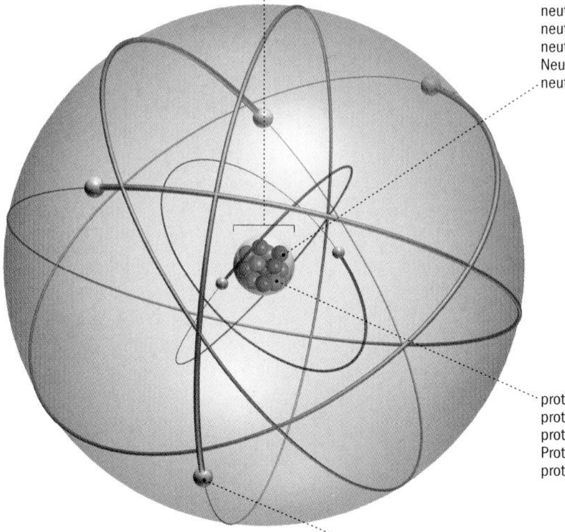

atom
átomo[M]
atome[M]
Atom[N]
atomo[M]

nucleus
núcleo[M]
noyau[M]
Atomkern[M]
nucleo[M]

neutron
neutrón[M]
neutron[M]
Neutron[N]
neutrone[M]

proton
protón[M]
proton[M]
Proton[N]
protone[M]

electron
electrón[M]
électron[M]
Elektron[N]
elettrone[M]

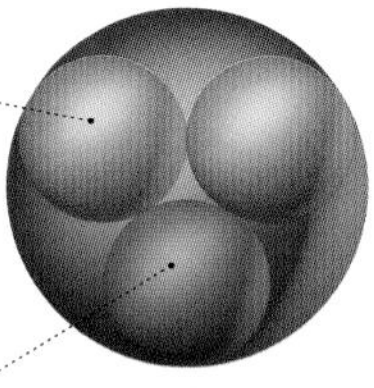

d quark
quark[M] d
quark[M] d
Down-Quark[N]
quark[M] d

u quark
quark[M] u
quark[M] u
Up-Quark[N]
quark[M] u

neutron
neutrón[M]
neutron[M]
Neutron[N]
neutrone[M]

proton
protón[M]
proton[M]
Proton[N]
protone[M]

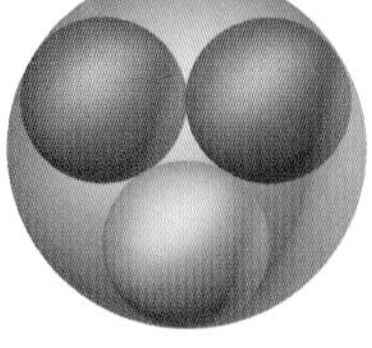

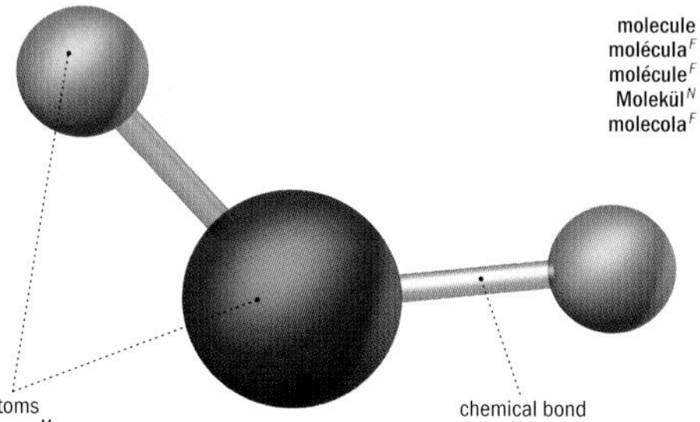

molecule
molécula[F]
molécule[F]
Molekül[N]
molecola[F]

atoms
átomos[M]
atomes[M]
Atome[N]
atomi[M]

chemical bond
enlace[M] químico
liaison[F] chimique
chemische Bindung[F]
legame[M] chimico

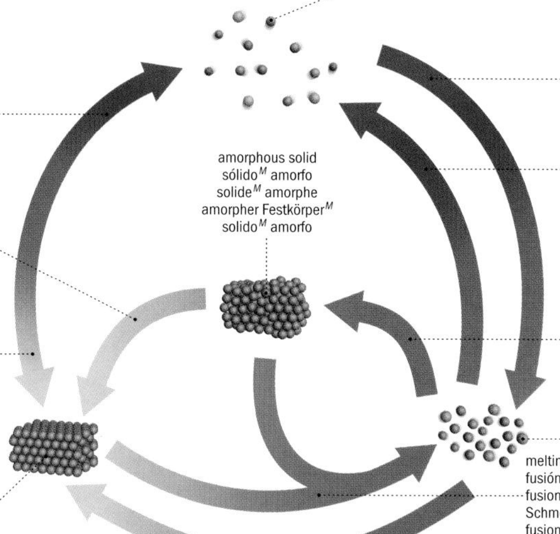

states of matter
estados[M] de la materia[F]
états[M] de la matière[F]
Aggregatzustände[M]
stati[M] della materia[F]

gas
gas[M]
gaz[M]
Gas[N]
gas[M]

sublimation
sublimación[F]
sublimation[F]
Sublimation[F]
sublimazione[F]

condensation
condensación[F]
condensation[F]
Kondensieren[N]
condensazione[F]

amorphous solid
sólido[M] amorfo
solide[M] amorphe
amorpher Festkörper[M]
solido[M] amorfo

evaporation
evaporación[F]
vaporisation[F]
Verdampfen[N]
evaporazione[F]

crystallization
cristalización[F]
cristallisation[F]
Kristallisation[F]
cristallizzazione[F]

supercooling
sobrefusión[F]
surfusion[F]
Unterkühlen[N]
soprafusione[F]

condensation
condensación[F]
condensation[F]
Kondensieren[N]
condensazione[F]

liquid
líquido[M]
liquide[M]
Flüssigkeit[F]
liquido[M]

melting
fusión[F]
fusion[F]
Schmelzen[N]
fusione[F]

solid
sólido[M]
solide[M]
Festkörper[M]
solido[M]

freezing
solidificación[F]
solidification[F]
Erstarren[N]
solidificazione[F]

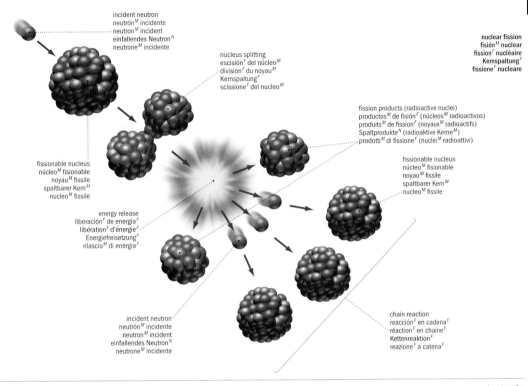

incident neutron
neutrón^M incidente
neutron^M incident
einfallendes Neutron^N
neutrone^M incidente

nucleus splitting
escisión^F del núcleo^M
division^F du noyau^M
Kernspaltung^F
scissione^F del nucleo^M

nuclear fission
fisión^M nuclear
fission^F nucléaire
Kernspaltung^F
fissione^F nucleare

fission products (radioactive nuclei)
productos^M de fisión^F (núcleos^M radioactivos)
produits^M de fission^F (noyaux^M radioactifs)
Spaltprodukte^N (radioaktive Kerne^M)
prodotti^M di fissione^F (nuclei^M radioattivi)

fissionable nucleus
núcleo^M fisionable
noyau^M fissile
spaltbarer Kern^M
nucleo^M fissile

fissionable nucleus
núcleo^M fisionable
noyau^M fissile
spaltbarer Kern^M
nucleo^M fissile

energy release
liberación^F de energía^F
libération^F d'énergie^F
Energiefreisetzung^F
rilascio^M di energia^F

chain reaction
reacción^F en cadena^F
réaction^F en chaine^F
Kettenreaktion^F
reazione^F a catena^F

incident neutron
neutrón^M incidente
neutron^M incident
einfallendes Neutron^N
neutrone^M incidente

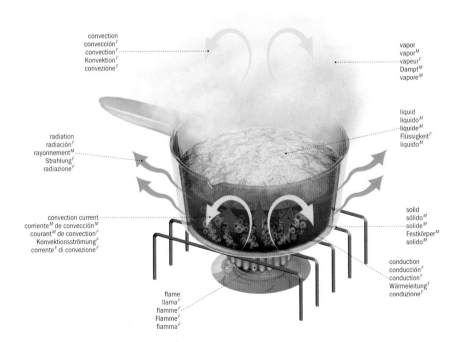

heat transfer
transmisión^F de calor^M
transfert^M de la chaleur^F
Wärmeübertragung^F
trasferimento^M di calore^M

convection
convección^F
convection^F
Konvektion^F
convezione^F

vapor
vapor^M
vapeur^F
Dampf^M
vapore^M

liquid
líquido^M
liquide^M
Flüssigkeit^F
liquido^M

radiation
radiación^F
rayonnement^M
Strahlung^F
radiazione^F

convection current
corriente^M de convección^M
courant^M de convection^F
Konvektionsströmung^F
corrente^F di convezione^F

solid
sólido^M
solide^M
Festkörper^M
solido^M

conduction
conducción^F
conduction^F
Wärmeleitung^F
conduzione^F

flame
llama^F
flamme^F
Flamme^F
fiamma^F

SCIENCE

chemical elements

elementos^M químicos | éléments^M chimiques | chemische Elemente^N | elementi^M chimici

table of elements
tabla^F periódica de los elementos^M
tableau^M périodique des éléments^M
Periodensystem^N
tavola^F periodica degli elementi^M

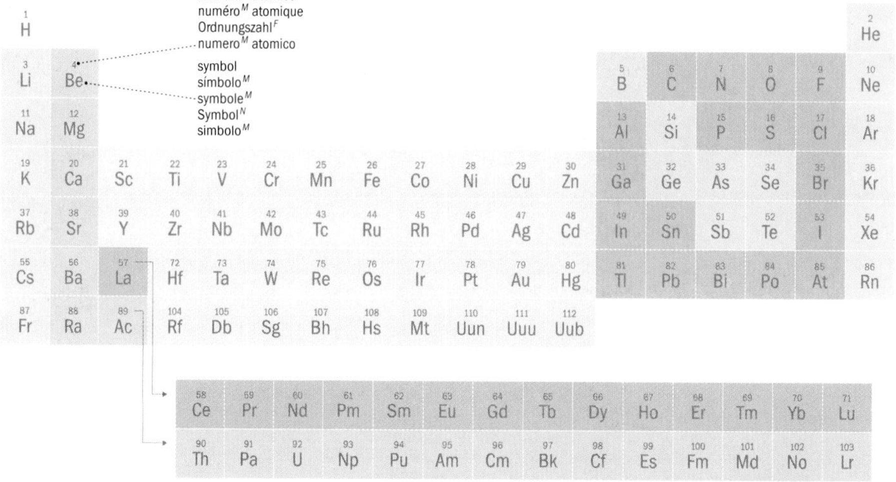

atomic number
número^M atómico
numéro^M atomique
Ordnungszahl^F
numero^M atomico

symbol
símbolo^M
symbole^M
Symbol^N
simbolo^M

hydrogen
hidrógeno^M
hydrogène^M
Wasserstoff^M
idrogeno^M

$_1$ H

alkali metals
metales^M alcalinos
métaux^M alcalins
Alkalimetalle^N
metalli^M alcalini

$_3$ Li
lithium
litio^M
lithium^M
Lithium^N
litio^M

$_{11}$ Na
sodium
sodio^M
sodium^M
Natrium^N
sodio^M

$_{19}$ K
potassium
potasio^M
potassium^M
Kalium^N
potassio^M

$_{37}$ Rb
rubidium
rubidio^M
rubidium^M
Rubidium^N
rubidio^M

$_{55}$ Cs
cesium
cesio^M
césium^M
Cäsium^N
cesio^M

$_{87}$ Fr
francium
francio^M
francium^M
Franzium^N
francio^M

alkaline earth metals
metales^M alcalinotérreos
métaux^M alcalino-terreux
Erdalkalimetalle^N
metalli^M alcalino-terrosi

$_4$ Be
beryllium
berilio^M
béryllium^M
Beryllium^N
berillio^M

$_{12}$ Mg
magnesium
magnesio^M
magnésium^M
Magnesium^N
magnesio^M

$_{20}$ Ca
calcium
calcio^M
calcium^M
Kalzium^N
calcio^M

$_{38}$ Sr
strontium
estroncio^M
strontium^M
Strontium^N
stronzio^M

$_{56}$ Ba
barium
bario^M
baryum^M
Barium^N
bario^M

$_{88}$ Ra
radium
radio^M
radium^M
Radium^N
radio^M

semi-metals (metalloids)
semimetales^M (metaloides^M)
semi-métaux^M (métalloïdes^M)
Halbmetalle^N (Metalloide^N)
semimetalli^M (metalloidi^M)

$_5$ B
boron
boro^M
bore^M
Bor^N
boro^M

$_{14}$ Si
silicon
silicio^M
silicium^M
Silizium^N
silicio^M

$_{32}$ Ge
germanium
germanio^M
germanium^M
Germanium^N
germanio^M

$_{33}$ As
arsenic
arsénico^M
arsenic^M
Arsen^N
arsenico^M

$_{34}$ Se
selenium
selenio^M
sélénium^M
Selen^N
selenio^M

$_{51}$ Sb
antimony
antimonio^M
antimoine^M
Antimon^N
antimonio^M

$_{52}$ Te
tellurium
telurio^M
tellure^M
Tellur^N
tellurio^M

other metals
otros metales^M
autres métaux^M
andere Metalle^N
altri metalli^M

$_{13}$ Al
aluminum
aluminio^M
aluminium^M
Aluminium^N
alluminio^M

$_{31}$ Ga
gallium
galio^M
gallium^M
Gallium^N
gallio^M

$_{49}$ In
indium
indio^M
indium^M
Indium^N
indio^M

$_{50}$ Sn
tin
estaño^M
étain^M
Zinn^N
stagno^M

$_{81}$ Tl
thallium
talio^M
thallium^M
Thallium^N
tallio^M

$_{82}$ Pb
lead
plomo^M
plomb^M
Blei^N
piombo^M

$_{83}$ Bi
bismuth
bismuto^M
bismuth^M
Wismut^N
bismuto^M

$_{84}$ Po
polonium
polonio^M
polonium^M
Polonium^N
polonio^M

transition metals
metales^M de transición
métaux^M de transition^F
Übergangsmetalle^N
metalli^M di transizione^F

21 Sc
scandium
escandio^M
scandium^M
Scandium^N
scandio^M

22 Ti
titanium
titanio^M
titane^M
Titan^N
titanio^M

23 V
vanadium
vanadio^M
vanadium^M
Vanadium^N
vanadio^M

24 Cr
chromium
cromo^M
chrome^M
Chrom^N
cromo^M

25 Mn
manganese
manganeso^M
manganèse^M
Mangan^N
manganese^M

26 Fe
iron
hierro^M
fer^M
Eisen^N
ferro^M

27 Co
cobalt
cobalto^M
cobalt^M
Kobalt^N
cobalto^M

28 Ni
nickel
níquel^M
nickel^M
Nickel^N
nichel^M

29 Cu
copper
cobre^M
cuivre^M
Kupfer^N
rame^M

30 Zn
zinc
cinc^M
zinc^M
Zink^N
zinco^M

39 Y
yttrium
itrio^M
yttrium^M
Yttrium^N
ittrio^M

40 Zr
zirconium
zirconio^M
zirconium^M
Zirkonium^N
zirconio^M

41 Nb
niobium
niobio^M
niobium^M
Niob^N
niobio^M

42 Mo
molybdenum
molibdeno^M
molybdène^M
Molybdän^N
molibdeno^M

43 Tc
technetium
tecnecio^M
technétium^M
Technetium^N
tecnezio^M

44 Ru
ruthenium
rutenio^M
ruthénium^M
Ruthenium^N
rutenio^M

45 Rh
rhodium
rodio^M
rhodium^M
Rhodium^N
rodio^M

46 Pd
palladium
paladio^M
palladium^M
Palladium^N
palladio^M

47 Ag
silver
plata^F
argent^M
Silber^N
argento^M

48 Cd
cadmium
cadmio^M
cadmium^M
Cadmium^N
cadmio^M

72 Hf
hafnium
hafnio^M
hafnium^M
Hafnium^N
afnio^M

73 Ta
tantalum
tántalo^M
tantale^M
Tantal^N
tantalio^M

74 W
tungsten
tungsteno^M
tungstène^M
Wolfram^N
tungsteno^M

75 Re
rhenium
renio^M
rhénium^M
Rhenium^N
renio^M

76 Os
osmium
osmio^M
osmium^M
Osmium^N
osmio^M

77 Ir
iridium
iridio^M
iridium^M
Iridium^N
iridio^M

78 Pt
platinum
platino^M
platine^M
Platin^N
platino^M

79 Au
gold
oro^M
or^M
Gold^N
oro^M

80 Hg
mercury
mercurio^M
mercure^M
Quecksilber^N
mercurio^M

104 Rf
rutherfordium
rutherfodio^M
rutherfordium^M
Rutherfordium^N
rutherfordio^M

105 Db
dubnium
dubnio^M
dubnium^M
Dubnium^N
dubnio^M

106 Sg
seaborgium
seaborgio^M
seaborgium^M
Seaborgium^N
seaborgio^M

107 Bh
bohrium
bohrio^M
bohrium^M
Bohrium^N
bohrio^M

108 Hs
hassium
hassio^M
hassium^M
Hassium^N
hassio^M

109 Mt
meitnerium
meitnerio^M
meitnerium^M
Meitnerium^N
meitnerio^M

110 Uun
ununnilium
ununnilio^M
ununnilium^M
Ununnilium^N
ununnilio^M

111 Uuu
ununnunium
ununnunio^M
or^M
Ununnunium^N
ununnunio^M

112 Uub
ununbium
ununbio^M
ununbium^M
Ununbium^N
ununbio^M

non-metals
no metales^M
non-métaux^M
Nichtmetalle^N
non metalli^M

6 C
carbon
carbón^M
carbone^M
Kohlenstoff^M
carbonio

7 N
nitrogen
nitrógeno^M
azote^M
Stickstoff^M
azoto^M

8 O
oxygen
oxígeno^M
oxygène^M
Sauerstoff^M
ossigeno^M

9 F
fluorine
flúor^M
fluor^M
Fluor^N
fluoro^M

15 P
phosphorus
fósforo^M
phosphore^M
Phosphor^M
fosforo^M

16 S
sulfur
azufre^M
soufre^M
Schwefel^M
zolfo^M

17 Cl
chlorine
cloro^M
chlore^M
Chlor^N
cloro^M

35 Br
bromine
bromo^M
brome^M
Brom^N
bromo^M

53 I
iodine
yodo^M
iode^M
Jod^N
iodio^M

85 At
astatine
ástato^M
astate^M
Astat^N
astato^M

SCIENCE

chemical elements

noble gases
gases[M] **nobles**
gaz[M] **rares**
Edelgase[N]
gas[M] **nobili**

2 **He**	helium helio[M] hélium[M] Helium[N] elio[M]	10 **Ne**	neon neón[M] néon[M] Neon[N] neo[M]	18 **Ar**	argon argón[M] argon[N] Argon[N] argo[M]	36 **Kr**	krypton criptón[M] krypton[M] Krypton[N] cripto[M]

| 54 **Xe** | xenon
xenón[M]
xénon[M]
Xenon[N]
xeno[M] | 86 **Rn** | radon
radón[M]
radon[M]
Radon[N]
radon[M] |

lanthanides (rare earth)
lantánidos[M] **(tierras**[F] **raras)**
lanthanides[M] **(terres**[F] **rares)**
Lanthanoide[N] **(Seltenerdmetalle**[N]**)**
lantanidi[M] **(terre**[F] **rare)**

57 **La**	lanthanum lantano[M] lanthane[M] Lanthan[N] lantanio[M]	61 **Pm**	promethium promecio[M] prométhium[M] Promethium[N] promezio[M]	65 **Tb**	terbium terbio[M] terbium[M] Terbium[N] terbio[M]	69 **Tm**	thulium tulio[M] thulium[M] Thulium[N] tulio[M]
58 **Ce**	cerium cerio[M] cérium[M] Cer[N] cerio[M]	62 **Sm**	samarium samario[M] samarium[M] Samarium[N] samario[M]	66 **Dy**	dysprosium disprosio[M] dysprosium[M] Dysprosium[N] disprosio[M]	70 **Yb**	ytterbium iterbio[M] ytterbium[M] Ytterbium[N] itterbio[M]
59 **Pr**	praseodymium praseodimio[M] praséodyme[M] Praseodym[N] praseodimio[M]	63 **Eu**	europium europio[M] europium[M] Europium[N] europio[M]	67 **Ho**	holmium holmio[M] holmium[M] Holmium[N] olmio[M]	71 **Lu**	lutetium lutecio[M] lutécium[M] Lutetium[N] lutezio[M]
60 **Nd**	neodymium neodimio[M] néodyme[M] Neodym[N] neodimio[M]	64 **Gd**	gadolinium gadolinio[M] gadolinium[M] Gadolinium[N] gadolinio[M]	68 **Er**	erbium erbio[M] erbium[M] Erbium[N] erbio[M]		

actinides
actínidos[M] **(tierras**[F] **raras)**
actinides[M]
Actinoide[N] **(Seltenerdmetalle**[N]**)**
attinidi[M]

89 **Ac**	actinium actino[M] actinium[M] Actinium[N] attinio[M]	93 **Np**	neptunium neptunio[M] neptunium[M] Neptunium[N] nettunio[M]	97 **Bk**	berkelium berquelio[M] berkélium[M] Berkelium[N] berchelio[M]	101 **Md**	mendelevium mendelevio[M] mendélévium[M] Mendelevium[N] mendelevio[M]
90 **Th**	thorium torio[M] thorium[M] Thorium[N] torio[M]	94 **Pu**	plutonium plutonio[M] plutonium[M] Plutonium[N] plutonio[M]	98 **Cf**	californium californio[M] californium[M] Californium[N] californio[M]	102 **No**	nobelium nobelio[M] nobélium[M] Nobelium[N] nobelio[M]
91 **Pa**	protactinium protactinio[M] protactinium[M] Protactinium[N] protoattinio[M]	95 **Am**	americium americio[M] américium[M] Americium[N] americio[M]	99 **Es**	einsteinium einstenio[M] einsteinium[M] Einsteinium[N] einsteinio[M]	103 **Lr**	lawrencium laurencio[M] lawrencium[M] Lawrencium[N] laurenzio[M]
92 **U**	uranium uranio[M] uranium[M] Uran[N] uranio[M]	96 **Cm**	curium curio[M] curium[M] Curium[N] curio[M]	100 **Fm**	fermium fermio[M] fermium[M] Fermium[N] fermio[M]		

chemistry symbols

símbolos[M] químicos | symboles[M] de chimie[F] | chemische Symbole[N] | simboli[M] chimici

negative charge
elemento[M] negativo
négatif[M]
negativ geladen
carica[F] negativa

positive charge
elemento[M] positivo
positif[M]
positiv geladen
carica[F] positiva

reversible reaction
reacción[F]
réaction[F] réversible
reversible Reaktion[F]
reazione[F] reversibile

reaction direction
dirección[F]
direction[F] d'une réaction[F]
Reaktionsrichtung[F]
direzione[F] della reazione[F]

SCIENCE

laboratory equipment

material^M de laboratorio^M | matériel^M de laboratoire^M | Laborgeräte^N | strumenti^M di laboratorio^M

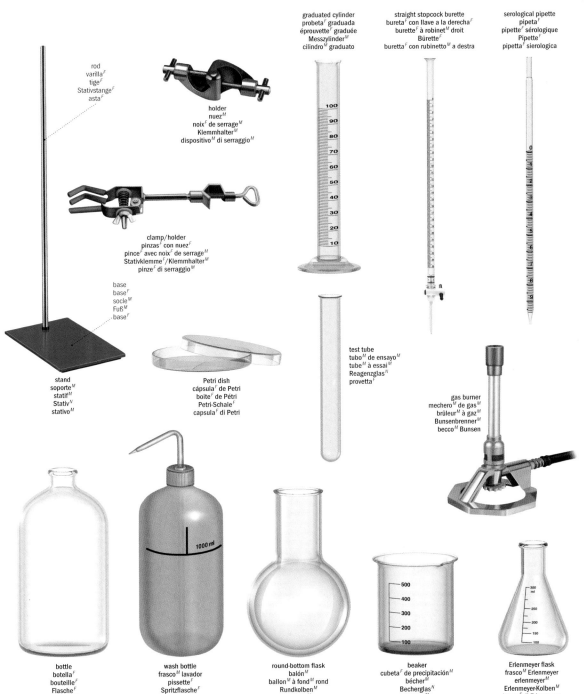

rod
varilla^F
tige^F
Stativstange^F
asta^F

holder
nuez^M
noix^F de serrage^M
Klemmhalter^M
dispositivo^M di serraggio^M

graduated cylinder
probeta^F graduada
éprouvette^F graduée
Messzylinder^M
cilindro^M graduato

straight stopcock burette
bureta^F con llave a la derecha^F
burette^F à robinet^M droit
Bürette^F
buretta^F con rubinetto^M a destra

serological pipette
pipeta^F
pipette^F sérologique
Pipette^F
pipetta^F sierologica

clamp/holder
pinzas^F con nuez^F
pince^F avec noix^F de serrage^M
Stativklemme^F/Klemmhalter^M
pinze^F di serraggio^M

base
base^F
socle^M
Fuß^M
base^F

stand
soporte^M
statif^M
Stativ^N
stativo^M

Petri dish
cápsula^F de Petri
boite^F de Pétri
Petri-Schale^F
capsula^F di Petri

test tube
tubo^M de ensayo^M
tube^M à essai^M
Reagenzglas^N
provetta^F

gas burner
mechero^M de gas^M
brûleur^M à gaz^M
Bunsenbrenner^M
becco^M Bunsen

bottle
botella^F
bouteille^F
Flasche^F
bottiglia^F

wash bottle
frasco^M lavador
pissette^F
Spritzflasche^F
spruzzetta^F

round-bottom flask
balón^M
ballon^M à fond^M rond
Rundkolben^M
pallone^M

beaker
cubeta^F de precipitación^M
bécher^M
Becherglas^N
becher^M

Erlenmeyer flask
frasco^M Erlenmeyer
erlenmeyer^M
Erlenmeyer-Kolben^M
beuta^F di Erlenmeyer

gearing systems

sistemas^M de engranajes^F | engrenages^M | Zahnradgetriebe^N | sistemi^M di ingranaggio^M

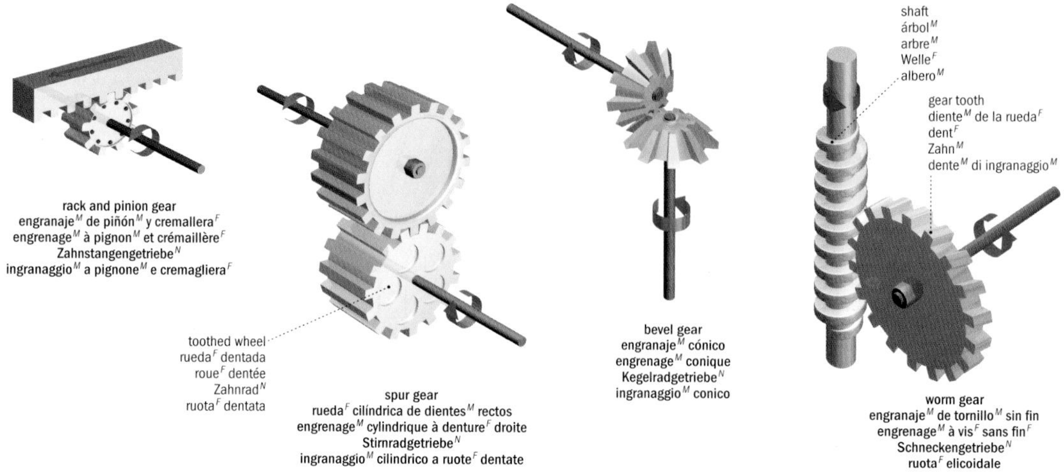

shaft
árbol^M
arbre^M
Welle^F
albero^M

gear tooth
diente^M de la rueda^F
dent^F
Zahn^M
dente^M di ingranaggio^M

rack and pinion gear
engranaje^M de piñón^M y cremallera^F
engrenage^M à pignon^M et crémaillère^F
Zahnstangengetriebe^N
ingranaggio^M a pignone^M e cremagliera^F

toothed wheel
rueda^F dentada
roue^F dentée
Zahnrad^N
ruota^F dentata

spur gear
rueda^F cilíndrica de dientes^M rectos
engrenage^M cylindrique à denture^F droite
Stirnradgetriebe^N
ingranaggio^M cilindrico a ruote^F dentate

bevel gear
engranaje^M cónico
engrenage^M conique
Kegelradgetriebe^N
ingranaggio^M conico

worm gear
engranaje^M de tornillo^M sin fin
engrenage^M à vis^F sans fin^F
Schneckengetriebe^N
ruota^F elicoidale

double pulley system

sistema^F de doble polea^F | système^M à deux poulies^F | einfacher Flaschenzug^M | sistema^M a doppia puleggia^F

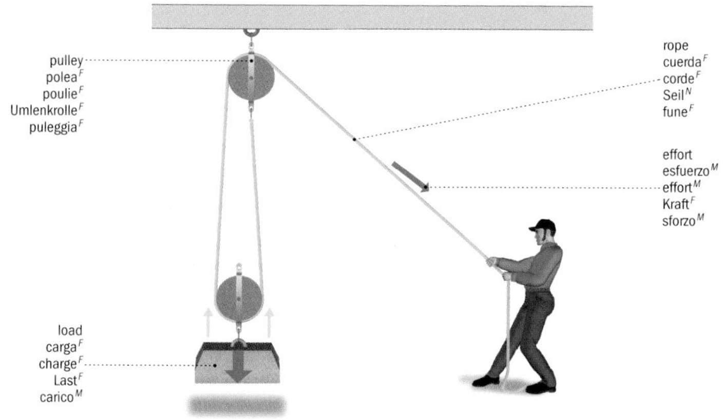

pulley
polea^F
poulie^F
Umlenkrolle^F
puleggia^F

rope
cuerda^F
corde^F
Seil^N
fune^F

effort
esfuerzo^M
effort^M
Kraft^F
sforzo^M

load
carga^F
charge^F
Last^F
carico^M

lever

palanca^F | levier^M | Hebel^M | leva^F

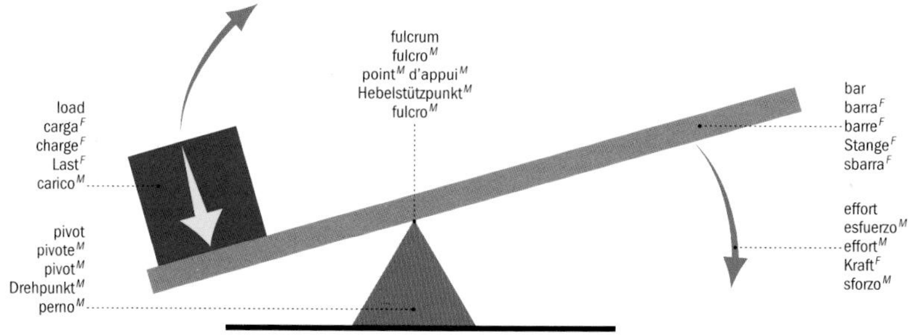

load
carga^F
charge^F
Last^F
carico^M

fulcrum
fulcro^M
point^M d'appui^M
Hebelstützpunkt^M
fulcro^M

bar
barra^F
barre^F
Stange^F
sbarra^F

pivot
pivote^M
pivot^M
Drehpunkt^M
perno^M

effort
esfuerzo^M
effort^M
Kraft^F
sforzo^M

magnetism

magnetismo ^{M} | magnétisme ^{M} | Magnetismus ^{M} | magnetismo ^{M}

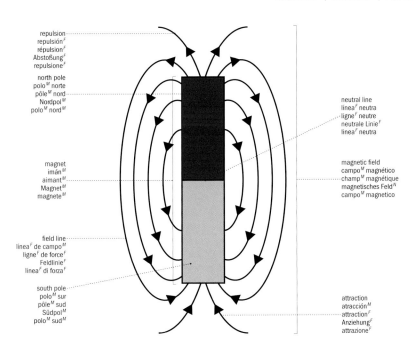

repulsion
repulsión ^{F}
répulsion ^{F}
Abstoßung ^{F}
repulsione ^{F}

north pole
polo ^{M} norte
pôle ^{M} nord
Nordpol ^{M}
polo ^{M} nord ^{M}

magnet
imán ^{M}
aimant ^{M}
Magnet ^{M}
magnete ^{M}

field line
línea ^{F} de campo ^{M}
ligne ^{F} de force ^{F}
Feldlinie ^{F}
linea ^{F} di forza ^{F}

south pole
polo ^{M} sur
pôle ^{M} sud
Südpol ^{M}
polo ^{M} sud ^{M}

neutral line
línea ^{F} neutra
ligne ^{F} neutre
neutrale Linie ^{F}
linea ^{F} neutra

magnetic field
campo ^{M} magnético
champ ^{M} magnétique
magnetisches Feld ^{N}
campo ^{M} magnetico

attraction
atracción ^{M}
attraction ^{F}
Anziehung ^{F}
attrazione ^{F}

parallel electrical circuit

circuito ^{M} eléctrico en paralelo ^{M} | circuit ^{M} électrique en parallèle ^{F} | Parallelschaltung ^{F} | circuito ^{M} elettrico parallelo

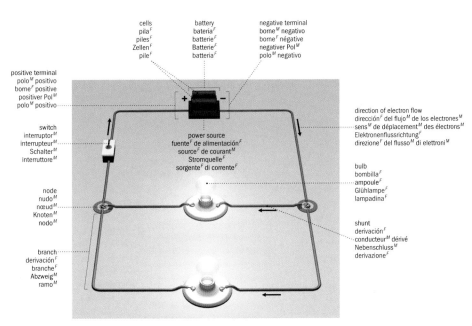

cells
pila ^{F}
piles ^{F}
Zellen ^{F}
pile ^{F}

battery
batería ^{F}
batterie ^{F}
Batterie ^{F}
batteria ^{F}

negative terminal
borne ^{M} negativo
borne ^{F} négative
negativer Pol ^{M}
polo ^{M} negativo

positive terminal
polo ^{M} positivo
borne ^{F} positive
positiver Pol ^{M}
polo ^{M} positivo

switch
interruptor ^{M}
interrupteur ^{M}
Schalter ^{M}
interruttore ^{M}

node
nudo ^{M}
nœud ^{M}
Knoten ^{M}
nodo ^{M}

branch
derivación ^{F}
branche ^{F}
Abzweig ^{M}
ramo ^{M}

power source
fuente ^{F} de alimentación ^{F}
source ^{F} de courant ^{M}
Stromquelle ^{F}
sorgente ^{F} di corrente ^{F}

direction of electron flow
dirección ^{F} del flujo ^{M} de los electrones ^{M}
sens ^{M} de déplacement ^{M} des électrons ^{M}
Elektronenflussrichtung ^{F}
direzione ^{F} del flusso ^{M} di elettroni ^{M}

bulb
bombilla ^{F}
ampoule ^{F}
Glühlampe ^{F}
lampadina ^{F}

shunt
derivación ^{F}
conducteur ^{M} dérivé
Nebenschluss ^{M}
derivazione ^{F}

SCIENCE

generators

generadores^M | générateurs^M | Generatoren^M | generatori^M

dynamo
dinamo^M
dynamo^F
Dynamo^M
dinamo^F

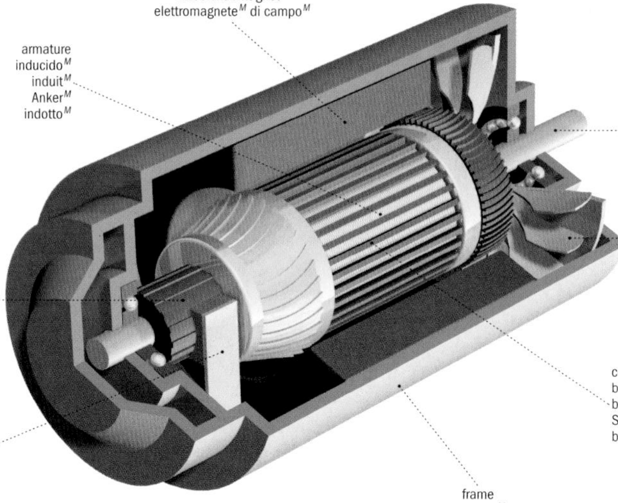

field electromagnet
electroimán^M
inducteur^M à électroaimant^M
Feldelektromagnet^M
elettromagnete^M di campo^M

armature
inducido^M
induit^M
Anker^M
indotto^M

shaft
árbol^M
arbre^M
Welle^F
albero^M

fan wheel
hélice^F de ventilación^F
hélice^F de ventilation^F
Ventilator^M
elica^F di ventilazione^F

commutator
conmutador^M
collecteur^M
Kommutator^M
collettore^M

coil
bobinado^M
bobinage^M
Spule^F
bobina^F

brush
escobilla^F
balai^M
Bürste^F
spazzola^F

frame
bastidor^M
carcasse^F
Gehäuse^N
telaio^M

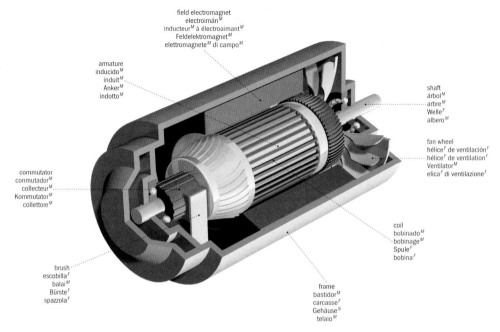

alternator
alternador^M
alternateur^M
Wechselstromgenerator^M
alternatore^M

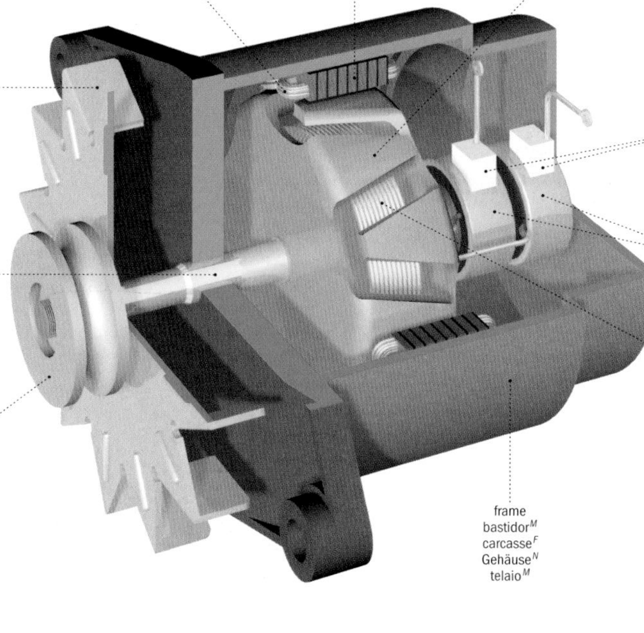

armature winding
devanado^F de inducido^M
enroulement^M d'induit^M
Ankerwicklung^F
avvolgimento^M dell'indotto^M

armature core
núcleo^M del inducido^M
noyau^M d'induit^M
Ankerkern^M
nucleo^M dell'indotto^M

claw-pole rotor
rotor^M de dientes^M
rotor^M à griffes^F
Klauenpolrad^N
rotore^M a griffa^F

fan wheel
hélice^F de ventilación^F
hélice^F de ventilation^F
Ventilator^M
elica^F di ventilazione^F

brushes
escobillas^F
balais^M
Bürsten^F
spazzole^F

collector rings
anillos^M colectores
bagues^F collectrices
Schleifringe^M
anelli^M collettori

shaft
árbol^M
arbre^M
Welle^F
albero^M

field winding
devanado^M inductor
enroulement^M inducteur
Feldwicklung^F
avvolgimento^M induttore^M

drive pulley
polea^F de tracción^M
poulie^F d'entraînement^M
Antriebslagerschild^N
puleggia^F conduttrice

frame
bastidor^M
carcasse^F
Gehäuse^N
telaio^M

dry cells

pilas^F secas | piles^F sèches | Trockenelemente^N | pile^F a secco^M

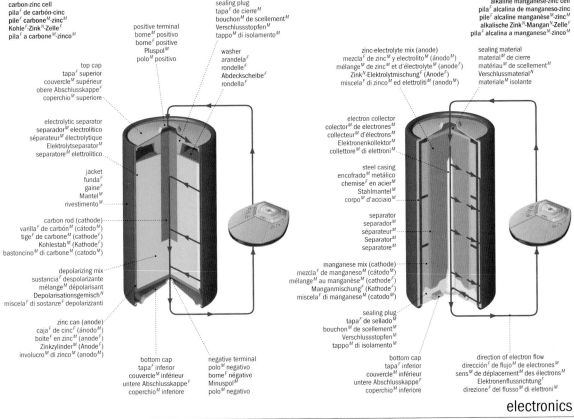

carbon-zinc cell
pila^F de carbón-cinc
pile^F carbone^M-zinc^M
Kohle^F-Zink^N-Zelle^F
pila^F a carbone^M-zinco^M

top cap
tapa^F superior
couvercle^M supérieur
obere Abschlusskappe^F
coperchio^M superiore

electrolytic separator
separador^M electrolítico
séparateur^M électrolytique
Elektrolytseparator^M
separatore^M elettrolitico

jacket
funda^F
gaine^F
Mantel^M
rivestimento^M

carbon rod (cathode)
varilla^F de carbón^M (cátodo^M)
tige^F de carbone^M (cathode^F)
Kohlestab^M (Kathode^F)
bastoncino^M di carbone^M (catodo^M)

depolarizing mix
sustancia^F despolarizante
mélange^M dépolarisant
Depolarisationsgemisch^N
miscela^F di sostanze^F depolarizzanti

zinc can (anode)
caja^F de cinc^F (ánodo^M)
boite^F en zinc^M (anode^F)
Zinkzylinder^M (Anode^F)
involucro^M di zinco^M (anodo^M)

sealing plug
tapa^F de cierre^M
bouchon^M de scellement^M
Verschlussstopfen^M
tappo^M di isolamento^M

positive terminal
borne^M positivo
borne^F positive
Pluspol^M
polo^M positivo

washer
arandela^F
rondelle^F
Abdeckscheibe^F
rondella^F

bottom cap
tapa^F inferior
couvercle^M inférieur
untere Abschlusskappe^F
coperchio^M inferiore

negative terminal
polo^M negativo
borne^F négative
Minuspol^M
polo^M negativo

alkaline manganese-zinc cell
pila^F alcalina de manganeso-zinc
pile^F alcaline manganèse^M-zinc^M
alkalische Zink^N-Mangan^N-Zelle^F
pila^F alcalina a manganese^M-zinco^M

zinc-electrolyte mix (anode)
mezcla^F de zinc^M y electrolito^M (ánodo^M)
mélange^M de zinc^M et d'électrolyte (anode^F)
Zink^N-Elektrolytmischung^F (Anode^F)
miscela^F di zinco^M ed elettroliti^M (anodo^M)

sealing material
material^M de cierre
matériau^M de scellement^M
Verschlussmaterial^N
materiale^M isolante

electron collector
colector^M de electrones^M
collecteur^M d'électrons^M
Elektronenkollektor^M
collettore^M di elettroni^M

steel casing
encofrado^M metálico
chemise^F en acier^M
Stahlmantel^M
corpo^M d'acciaio^M

separator
separador^M
séparateur^M
Separator^M
separatore^M

manganese mix (cathode)
mezcla^F de manganeso^M (cátodo^M)
mélange^M au manganèse^M (cathode^F)
Manganmischung^F (Kathode^F)
miscela^F di manganese^M (catodo^M)

sealing plug
tapa^F de sellado^M
bouchon^M de scellement^M
Verschlussstopfen^M
tappo^M di isolamento^M

bottom cap
tapa^F inferior
couvercle^M inférieur
untere Abschlusskappe^F
coperchio^M inferiore

direction of electron flow
dirección^F de flujo^M de electrones^M
sens^M de déplacement^M des électrons^M
Elektronenflussrichtung^F
direzione^F del flusso^M di elettroni^M

electronics

electrónica^F | électronique^F | Elektronik^F | elettronica^F

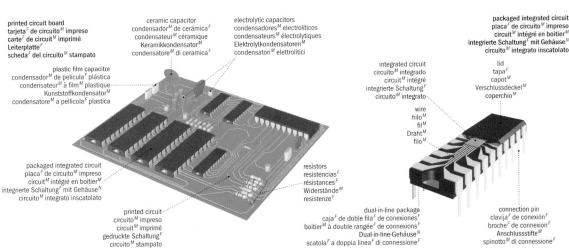

printed circuit board
tarjeta^F de circuito^M impreso
carte^F de circuit^M imprimé
Leiterplatte^F
scheda^F del circuito^M stampato

plastic film capacitor
condensador^M de película^F plástica
condensateur^M à film^M plastique
Kunststoffkondensator^M
condensatore^M a pellicola^F plastica

packaged integrated circuit
placa^F de circuito^M impreso
circuit^M intégré en boitier^M
integrierte Schaltung^F mit Gehäuse^N
circuito^M integrato inscatolato

printed circuit
circuito^M impreso
circuit^M imprimé
gedruckte Schaltung^F
circuito^M stampato

ceramic capacitor
condensador^M de cerámica^F
condensateur^M céramique
Keramikkondensator^M
condensatore^M di ceramica^F

electrolytic capacitors
condensadores^M electrolíticos
condensateurs^M électrolytiques
Elektrolytkondensatoren^M
condensatori^M elettrolitici

integrated circuit
circuito^M integrado
circuit^M intégré
integrierte Schaltung^F
circuito^M integrato

wire
hilo^M
fil^M
Draht^M
filo^M

resistors
resistencias^F
résistances^F
Widerstände^M
resistenze^F

dual-in-line package
caja^F de doble fila^F de conexiones^F
boitier^M à double rangée^F de connexions^F
Dual-in-line-Gehäuse^N
scatola^F a doppia linea^F di connessione^F

packaged integrated circuit
placa^F de circuito^M impreso
circuit^M intégré en boitier^M
integrierte Schaltung^F mit Gehäuse^N
circuito^M integrato inscatolato

lid
tapa^F
capot^M
Verschlussdeckel^M
coperchio^M

connection pin
clavija^F de conexión^F
broche^F de connexion^F
Anschlussstifte^M
spinotto^M di connessione^F

SCIENCE

electromagnetic spectrum

espectro^M electromagnético | spectre^M électromagnétique | elektromagnetisches Spektrum^N | spettro^M elettromagnetico

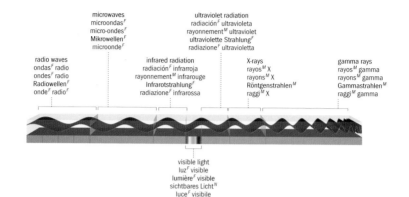

microwaves
microondas^F
micro-ondes^F
Mikrowellen^F
microonde^F

ultraviolet radiation
radiación^F ultravioleta
rayonnement^M ultraviolet
ultraviolette Strahlung^F
radiazione^F ultravioletta

radio waves
ondas^F radio
ondes^F radio
Radiowellen^F
onde^F radio^F

infrared radiation
radiación^F infrarroja
rayonnement^M infrarouge
Infrarotstrahlung^F
radiazione^F infrarossa

X-rays
rayos^M X
rayons^M X
Röntgenstrahlen^M
raggi^M X

gamma rays
rayos^M gamma
rayons^M gamma
Gammastrahlen^M
raggi^M gamma

visible light
luz^F visible
lumière^F visible
sichtbares Licht^N
luce^F visibile

wave

onda^F | onde^F | Welle^F | onda^F

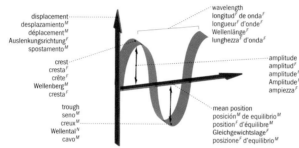

displacement
desplazamiento^M
déplacement^M
Auslenkungsrichtung^F
spostamento^M

wavelength
longitud^F de onda^F
longueur^F d'onde^F
Wellenlänge^F
lunghezza^F d'onda^F

crest
cresta^F
crête^F
Wellenberg^M
cresta^F

amplitude
amplitud^F
amplitude^F
Amplitude^F
ampiezza^F

trough
seno^M
creux^M
Wellental^N
cavo^M

mean position
posición^M de equilibrio^M
position^F d'équilibre^M
Gleichgewichtslage^F
posizione^F d'equilibrio^M

color synthesis

síntesis^F de los colores^M | synthèse^F des couleurs^F | Farbmischung^F | sintesi^F dei colori^M

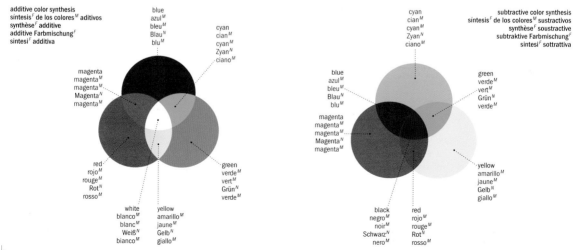

additive color synthesis
síntesis^F de los colores^M aditivos
synthèse^F additive
additive Farbmischung^F
sintesi^F additiva

blue
azul^M
bleu^M
Blau^N
blu^M

cyan
cian^M
cyan^M
Zyan^N
ciano^M

magenta
magenta^M
magenta^M
Magenta^N
magenta^M

red
rojo^M
rouge^M
Rot^N
rosso^M

green
verde^M
vert^M
Grün^N
verde^M

white
blanco^M
blanc^M
Weiß^N
bianco^M

yellow
amarillo^M
jaune^M
Gelb^N
giallo^M

cyan
cian^M
cyan^M
Zyan^N
ciano^M

subtractive color synthesis
síntesis^F de los colores^M sustractivos
synthèse^F soustractive
subtraktive Farbmischung^F
sintesi^F sottrattiva

blue
azul^M
bleu^M
Blau^N
blu^M

green
verde^M
vert^M
Grün^N
verde^M

magenta
magenta^M
magenta^M
Magenta^N
magenta^M

yellow
amarillo^M
jaune^M
Gelb^N
giallo^M

black
negro^M
noir^M
Schwarz^N
nero^M

red
rojo^M
rouge^M
Rot^N
rosso^M

vision

visión^F | vision^F | Sehen^N | vista^F

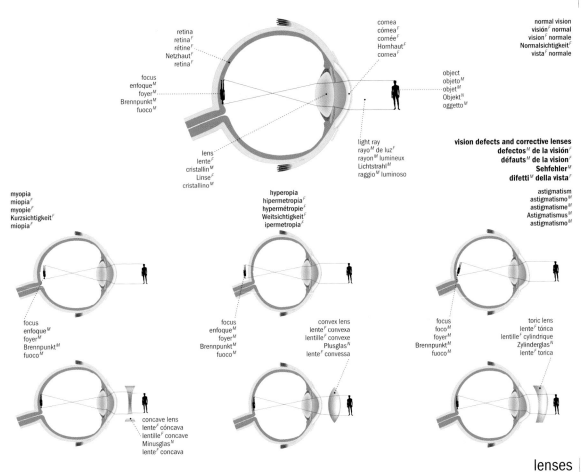

retina
retina^F
rétine^F
Netzhaut^F
retina^F

cornea
córnea^F
cornée^F
Hornhaut^F
cornea^F

focus
enfoque^M
foyer^M
Brennpunkt^M
fuoco^M

object
objeto^M
objet^M
Objekt^N
oggetto^M

lens
lente^F
cristallin^M
Linse^F
cristallino^M

light ray
rayo^M de luz^F
rayon^M lumineux
Lichtstrahl^M
raggio^M luminoso

normal vision
visión^F normal
vision^F normale
Normalsichtigkeit^F
vista^F normale

vision defects and corrective lenses
defectos^M de la visión^F
défauts^M de la vision^F
Sehfehler^M
difetti^M della vista^F

myopia
miopía^F
myopie^F
Kurzsichtigkeit^F
miopia^F

hyperopia
hipermetropía^F
hypermétropie^F
Weitsichtigkeit^F
ipermetropia^F

astigmatism
astigmatismo^M
astigmatisme^M
Astigmatismus^M
astigmatismo^M

focus
enfoque^M
foyer^M
Brennpunkt^M
fuoco^M

focus
enfoque^M
foyer^M
Brennpunkt^M
fuoco^M

convex lens
lente^F convexa
lentille^F convexe
Plusglas^N
lente^F convessa

focus
foco^M
foyer^M
Brennpunkt^M
fuoco^M

toric lens
lente^F tórica
lentille^F cylindrique
Zylinderglas^N
lente^F torica

concave lens
lente^F cóncava
lentille^F concave
Minusglas^N
lente^F concava

lenses

lentes^F | lentilles^F | Linsen^F | lenti^F

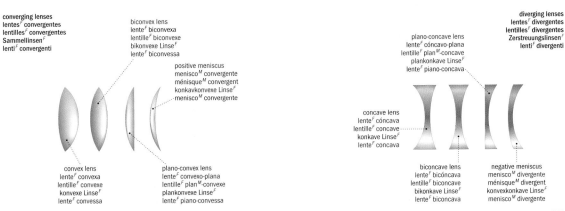

converging lenses
lentes^F convergentes
lentilles^F convergentes
Sammellinsen^F
lenti^F convergenti

biconvex lens
lente^F biconvexa
lentille^F biconvexe
bikonvexe Linse^F
lente^F biconvessa

positive meniscus
menisco^M convergente
ménisque^M convergent
konkavkonvexe Linse^F
menisco^M convergente

diverging lenses
lentes^F divergentes
lentilles^F divergentes
Zerstreuungslinsen^F
lenti^F divergenti

plano-concave lens
lente^F cóncavo-plana
lentille^F plan^M-concave
plankonkave Linse^F
lente^F piano-concava

concave lens
lente^F cóncava
lentille^F concave
konkave Linse^F
lente^F concava

convex lens
lente^F convexa
lentille^F convexe
konvexe Linse^F
lente^F convessa

plano-convex lens
lente^F convexo-plana
lentille^F plan^M-convexe
plankonvexe Linse^F
lente^F piano-convessa

biconcave lens
lente^F bicóncava
lentille^F biconcave
bikonkave Linse^F
lente^F biconcava

negative meniscus
menisco^M divergente
ménisque^M divergent
konvexkonkave Linse^F
menisco^M divergente

SCIENCE

pulsed ruby laser

láser^M de rubí^M pulsado | laser^M à rubis^M pulsé | Rubin^M-Impulslaser^M | laser^M a rubino^M pulsato

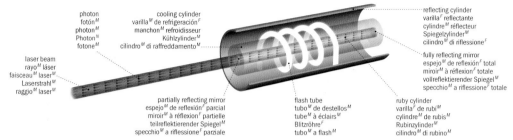

photon
fotón^M
photon^M
Photon^N
fotone^M

cooling cylinder
varilla^M de refrigeración^F
manchon^M refroidisseur
Kühlzylinder^M
cilindro^M di raffreddamento

reflecting cylinder
varilla^F reflectante
cylindre^M réflecteur
Spiegelzylinder^M
cilindro^M di riflessione^F

laser beam
rayo^M láser
faisceau^M laser^M
Laserstrahl^M
raggio^M laser^M

fully reflecting mirror
espejo^M de reflexión^F total
miroir^F à réflexion^F totale
vollreflektierender Spiegel^M
specchio^M a riflessione^F totale

partially reflecting mirror
espejo^M de reflexión^F parcial
miroir^F à réflexion^F partielle
teilreflektierender Spiegel^M
specchio^M a riflessione^F parziale

flash tube
tubo^M de destellos^M
tube^M à éclairs^M
Blitzröhre^F
tubo^M a flash^M

ruby cylinder
varilla^F de rubí^M
cylindre^M de rubis^M
Rubinzylinder^M
cilindro^M di rubino^M

prism binoculars

prismáticos^M binoculares | jumelles^F à prismes^M | Prismenfernglas^N | binocolo^M prismatico

eyepiece
ocular^M
oculaire^M
Okular^N
oculare^M

lens system
sistema^M de lentes^F
système^M de lentilles^F
Linsensystem^N
sistema^M di lenti^F

Porro prism
prisma^M de Porro
prisme^M de Porro
Porro-Prisma^N
prisma^M di Porro

hinge
bisagra^F
charnière^F
Scharnier^N
cerniera^F

objective lens
objetivo^M
lentille^F objectif^M
Objektiv^N
lente^F obiettivo^M

focusing ring
anillo^M de enfoque^M
bague^F de correction^F dioptrique
Scharfstellring^M
anello^M di regolazione^F diottrica

central focusing wheel
rueda^F central de enfoque^M
molette^F de mise^F au point^M
zentrales Scharfstellrad^N
rotella^F centrale di messa^F a fuoco^M

bridge
puente^M
pont^M
Brücke^F
ponte^M

body
tubo^M
tube^M
Tubus^M
corpo^M

telescopic sight

visor^M telescópico | lunette^F de visée^F | Zielfernrohr^N | cannocchiale^M di mira^F

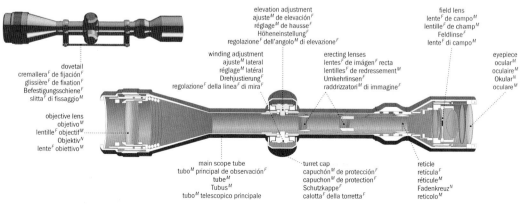

elevation adjustment
ajuste^M de elevación^F
réglage^M de hausse^F
Höheneinstellung^F
regolazione^F dell'angolo^M di elevazione^F

field lens
lente^F de campo^M
lentille^F de champ^M
Feldlinse^F
lente^F di campo^M

winding adjustment
ajuste^M lateral
réglage^M latéral
Drehjustierung^F
regolazione^F della linea^F di mira^F

erecting lenses
lentes^F de imágen^F recta
lentilles^F de redressement^M
Umkehrlinsen^F
raddrizzatori^M di immagine^F

eyepiece
ocular^M
oculaire^M
Okular^N
oculare^M

dovetail
cremallera^F de fijación^F
glissière^F de fixation^F
Befestigungsschiene^F
slitta^F di fissaggio^M

objective lens
objetivo^M
lentille^F objectif^M
Objektiv^N
lente^F obiettivo^M

main scope tube
tubo^M principal de observación^F
tube^M
Tubus^M
tubo^M telescopico principale

turret cap
capuchón^M de protección^F
capuchon^M de protection^F
Schutzkappe^F
calotta^F della torretta^F

reticle
reticula^F
réticule^M
Fadenkreuz^N
reticolo^M

SCIENCE

magnifying glass and microscopes

lupa^F y microscopios^M | loupe^F et microscopes^M | Lupe^F und Mikroskope^N | lente^F di ingrandimento^M e microscopi^M

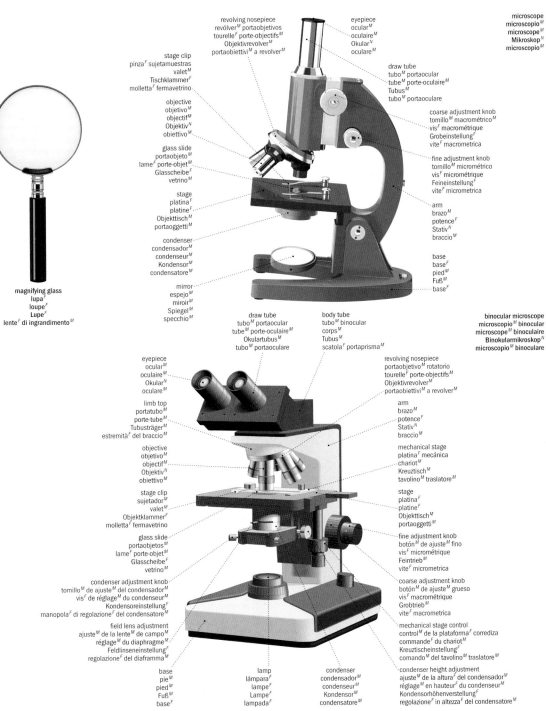

microscope
microscopio^M
microscope^M
Mikroskop^N
microscopio^M

revolving nosepiece
revólver^M portaobjetivos
tourelle^F porte-objectifs^M
Objektivrevolver^M
portaobiettivi^M a revolver^M

eyepiece
ocular^M
oculaire^M
Okular^N
oculare^M

stage clip
pinza^F sujetamuestras
valet^M
Tischklammer^F
molletta^F fermavetrino

draw tube
tubo^M portaocular
tube^M porte-oculaire^M
Tubus^M
tubo^M portaoculare

objective
objetivo^M
objectif^M
Objektiv^N
obiettivo^M

coarse adjustment knob
tornillo^M macrométrico^M
vis^F macrométrique
Grobeinstellung^F
vite^F macrometrica

glass slide
portaobjeto^M
lame^F porte-objet^M
Glasscheibe^F
vetrino^M

fine adjustment knob
tornillo^M micrométrico
vis^F micrométrique
Feineinstellung^F
vite^F micrometrica

stage
platina^F
platine^F
Objekttisch^M
portaoggetti^M

arm
brazo^M
potence^F
Stativ^N
braccio^M

condenser
condensador^M
condenseur^M
Kondensor^M
condensatore^M

base
base^F
pied^M
Fuß^M
base^F

mirror
espejo^M
miroir^M
Spiegel^M
specchio^M

magnifying glass
lupa^F
loupe^F
Lupe^F
lente^F di ingrandimento^M

draw tube
tubo^M portaocular
tube^M porte-oculaire^M
Okulartubus^M
tubo^M portaoculare

body tube
tubo^M binocular
corps^M
Tubus^M
scatola^F portaprisma^M

binocular microscope
microscopio^M binocular
microscope^M binoculaire
Binokularmikroskop^N
microscopio^M binoculare

eyepiece
ocular^M
oculaire^M
Okular^N
oculare^M

revolving nosepiece
portaobjetivo^M rotatorio
tourelle^F porte-objectifs^M
Objektivrevolver^M
portaobiettivi^M a revolver^M

limb top
portatubo^M
porte-tube^M
Tubusträger^M
estremità^F del braccio^M

arm
brazo^M
potence^F
Stativ^N
braccio^M

objective
objetivo^M
objectif^M
Objektiv^N
obiettivo^M

mechanical stage
platina^F mecánica
chariot^M
Kreuztisch^M
tavolino^M traslatore^M

stage clip
sujetador^M
valet^M
Objektklammer^F
molletta^F fermavetrino

stage
platina^F
platine^F
Objekttisch^M
portaoggetti^M

glass slide
portaobjetos^M
lame^F porte-objet^M
Glasscheibe^F
vetrino^M

fine adjustment knob
botón^M de ajuste^M fino
vis^F micrométrique
Feintrieb^M
vite^F micrometrica

condenser adjustment knob
tornillo^M de ajuste^M del condensador^M
vis^F de réglage^M du condensateur^M
Kondensoreinstellung^F
manopola^F di regolazione^F del condensatore^M

coarse adjustment knob
botón^M de ajuste^M grueso
vis^F macrométrique
Grobtrieb^M
vite^F macrometrica

field lens adjustment
ajuste^M de la lente^M de campo^M
réglage^M du diaphragme^M
Feldlinseneinstellung^F
regolazione^F del diaframma^M

mechanical stage control
control^M de la plataforma^F corrediza
commande^F du chariot^M
Kreuztischeinstellung^F
comando^M del tavolino^M traslatore^M

base
pie^M
pied^M
Fuß^M
base^F

lamp
lámpara^F
lampe^F
Lampe^F
lampada^F

condenser
condensador^M
condenseur^M
Kondensor^M
condensatore^M

condenser height adjustment
ajuste^M de la altura^F del condensador^M
réglage^M en hauteur^F du condenseur^M
Kondensorhöhenverstellung^F
regolazione^F in altezza^F del condensatore^M

SCIENCE

magnifying glass and microscopes

cross section of an electron microscope
corte^M transversal de un microscopio^M de electrones^M
coupe^F d'un microscope^M électronique
Elektronenmikroskop^N im Querschnitt^M
sezione^F di un microscopio^M elettronico

electron gun
cañón^M de electrones^M
canon^M à électrons^M
Elektronenkanone^F
cannone^M elettronico

vacuum manifold
canalización^F de vacío^M
canalisation^F de pompage^M
Vakuumrohr^N
collettore^M a vuoto^M

condenser
condensador^M
condenseur^M
Kondensor^M
condensatore^M

aperture changer
abertura^F para el cambio^M de gases^M
commande^F de sélection^F de l'ouverture^F
Blendeneinstellung^F
cambiaaperture^M

aperture diaphragm
abertura^F del diafragma^M
diaphragme^M d'ouverture^F
Aperturblende^F
diaframma^M di apertura^F

stage
platina^F
porte-spécimen^M
Objekttisch^M
portaoggetti^M

electron beam
haz^M de electrones^M
faisceau^M d'électrons^M
Elektronenstrahl^M
fascio^M elettronico

electron beam positioning
posición^F del haz^M de electrones^M
alignement^M du faisceau^M dans l'axe^M
Elektronenstrahljustierung^F
posizionamento^M del fascio^M rispetto all'asse^F

beam diameter reduction
reducción^F del diámetro^M del haz^M
concentration^F du faisceau^M
Verminderung^F des Strahldurchmessers^M
riduzione^F del diametro^M del fascio^M

focusing lenses
lentes^F de enfoque^M
lentilles^F de mise^F au point^M
elektronenoptische Linsen^F
lenti^F di focalizzazione^F

visual transmission
transmisión^F visual
transmission^F de l'image^F
Einblicklupe^F
trasmissione^F dell'immagine^F

vacuum chamber
cámara^F de vacío^M
chambre^F à vide^M
Vakuumkammer^F
camera^F a vuoto^M

electron microscope elements
elementos^M del microscopio^M de electrones^M
composantes^F d'un microscope^M électronique
Teile^N des Elektronenmikroskops^M
elementi^M del microscopio^M elettronico

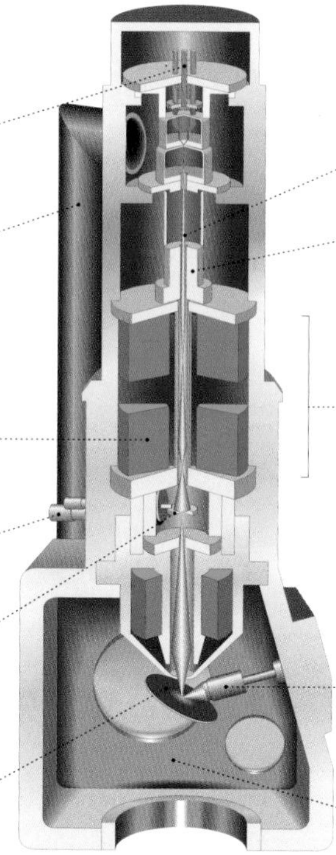

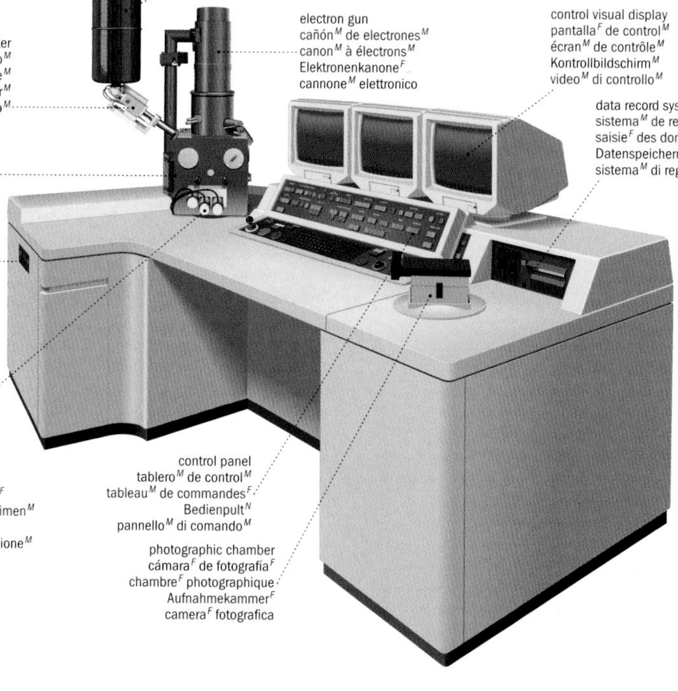

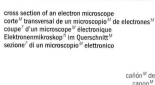

liquid nitrogen tank
tanque^M del nitrógeno^M
réservoir^M d'azote^M liquide
Behälter^M mit flüssigem Stickstoff^M
serbatoio^M di azoto^M liquido

spectrometer
espectrómetro^M
spectromètre^M
Spektrometer^M
spettrometro^M

specimen chamber
cámara^F para la muestra^F
chambre^F d'observation^F
Probenkammer^F
camera^F portacampioni

vacuum system console
consola^F para el sistema^M de vacío^M
bâti^M de la pompe^F à vide^M
Vakuumpumpe^F
console^F per il vuoto^M

electron gun
cañón^M de electrones^M
canon^M à électrons^M
Elektronenkanone^F
cannone^M elettronico

control visual display
pantalla^F de control^M
écran^M de contrôle^M
Kontrollbildschirm^M
video^M di controllo^M

data record system
sistema^M de registro^M de la información^F
saisie^F des données^F
Datenspeicherung^F
sistema^M di registrazione^F dei dati^M

specimen positioning control
control^M de posición^F de la muestra^F
commande^F de positionnement^M du spécimen^M
Positionskontrolle^F der Probe^F
manopola^F di posizionamento^M del campione^M

control panel
tablero^M de control^M
tableau^M de commandes^F
Bedienpult^N
pannello^M di comando^M

photographic chamber
cámara^F de fotografía^F
chambre^F photographique
Aufnahmekammer^F
camera^F fotografica

SCIENCE

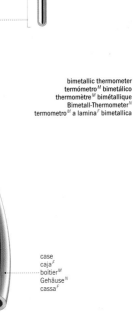

thermometer
termómetro^M
thermomètre^M
Thermometer^N
termometro^M

Fahrenheit scale
escala^F Fahrenheit
échelle^F Fahrenheit
Fahrenheitskala^F
scala^F Fahrenheit

Celsius scale
escala^F Celsius
échelle^F Celsius
Celsiusskala^F
scala^F Celsius

temperature measured in Fahrenheit
grados^M F
°F
Grad^M Fahrenheit
gradi^M Fahrenheit

temperature measured in Celsius
grados^M C
°C
Grad^M Celsius
gradi^M Celsius

alcohol column
columna^F de alcohol^M
colonne^F d'alcool^M
Alkoholsäule^F
colonna^F d'alcool^M

alcohol bulb
cubeta^F de alcohol^M
réservoir^M d'alcool^M
Alkoholkolben^M
bulbo^M d'alcool^M

expansion chamber
cámara^F de expansión^F
chambre^F d'expansion^F
Ausdehnungskammer^F
camera^F di espansione^F

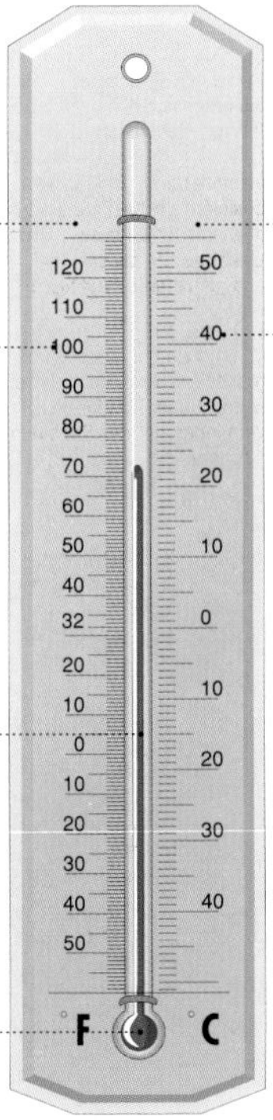

clinical thermometer
termómetro^M clínico
thermomètre^M médical
Fieberthermometer^N
termometro^M clínico

capillary bore
tubo^M capilar
tube^M capillaire
Kapillarröhrchen^N
tubo^M capillare

scale
escala^F de temperaturas^F
graduation^F
Skala^F
scala^F graduata

column of mercury
columna^F de mercurio^M
colonne^F de mercure^M
Quecksilbersäule^F
colonna^F di mercurio^M

stem
tubo^M de cristal^M
tige^F
Röhre^F
asta^F

constriction
estrechamiento^M
étranglement^M
Verengung^F
strozzatura^F

mercury bulb
cubeta^F de mercurio^M
réservoir^M de mercure^M
Quecksilberkolben^M
bulbo^M di mercurio^M

SCIENCE

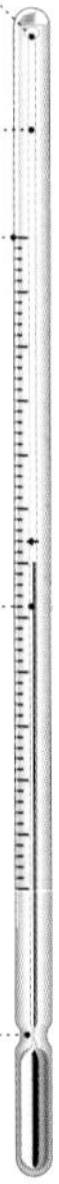

bimetallic thermometer
termómetro^M bimetálico
thermomètre^M bimétallique
Bimetall-Thermometer^N
termometro^M a lamina^F bimetallica

pointer
aguja^F
aiguille^F
Zeiger^M
indice^M

dial
cuadrante^M
cadran^M
Anzeigeskala^F
quadrante^M

case
caja^F
boitier^M
Gehäuse^N
cassa^F

shaft
barra^F
arbre^M
Welle^F
albero^M

bimetallic helix
hélice^F bimetálica
élément^M bimétallique hélicoïdal
Bimetallspirale^F
spirale^F bimetallica

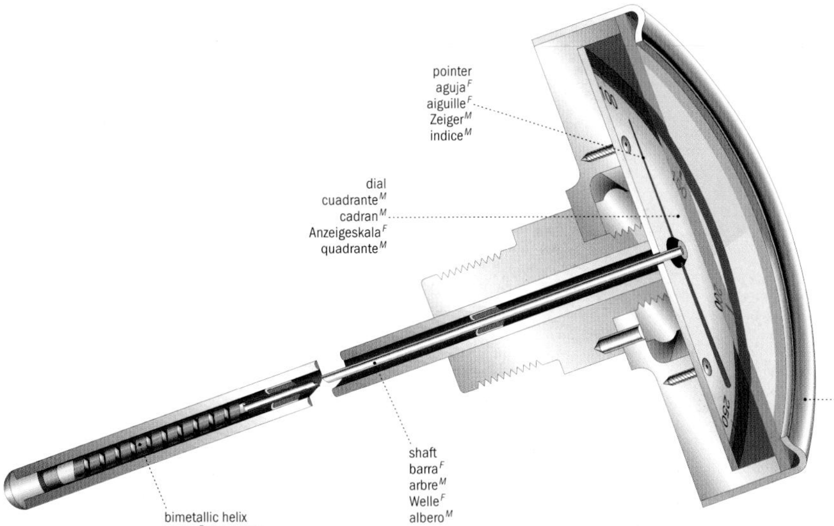

measurement of time

medición^F del tiempo^M | mesure^F du temps^M | Zeitmessung^F | misura^F del tempo^M

stopwatch
cronómetro^M
chronomètre^M
Stoppuhr^F
cronometro^M

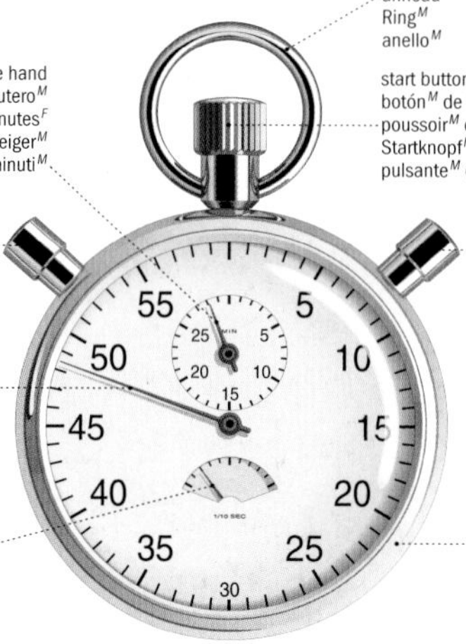

ring
anilla^F
anneau^M
Ring^M
anello^M

minute hand
minutero^M
aiguille^F des minutes^F
Minutenzeiger^M
lancetta^F dei minuti^M

start button
botón^M de inicio^M de marcha^F
poussoir^M de mise^F en marche^F
Startknopf^M
pulsante^M di partenza^F

reset button
botón^M de inicio^M del contador^M
poussoir^M de remise^F à zéro^M
Rückstellknopf^M
pulsante^M di azzeramento^M

stop button
botón^M de parada^F
poussoir^M d'arrêt^M
Stoppknopf^M
pulsante^M di arresto^M

second hand
segundero^M
trotteuse^F
Sekundenzeiger^M
lancetta^F dei secondi^M

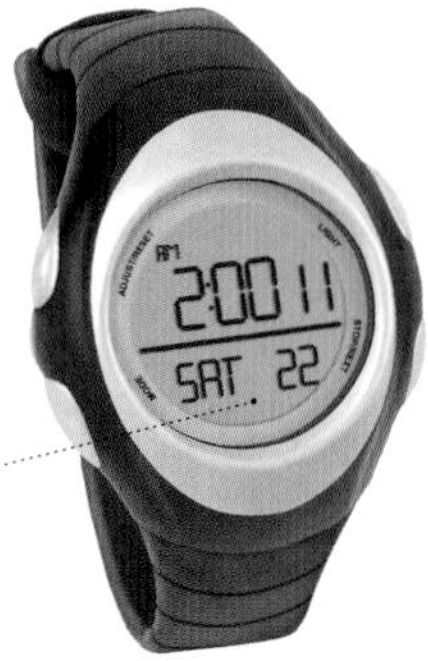

liquid-crystal display
registro^M de cristal^M líquido
cristaux^M liquides
LCD-Anzeige^F
quadrante^M a cristalli^M liquidi

1/10 second hand
aguja^F de décimas^F de segundo^M
aiguille^F des dixièmes^M de seconde^F
Zehntelsekundenzeiger^M
lancetta^F dei decimi^M di secondo^M

case
estuche^M
boîtier^M
Gehäuse^N
cassa^F

digital watch
reloj^M digital
montre^F à affichage^M numérique
Digitaluhr^F
orologio^M digitale

analog watch
reloj^M de pulsera^F
montre^F à affichage^M analogique
Analoguhr^F
orologio^M analogico

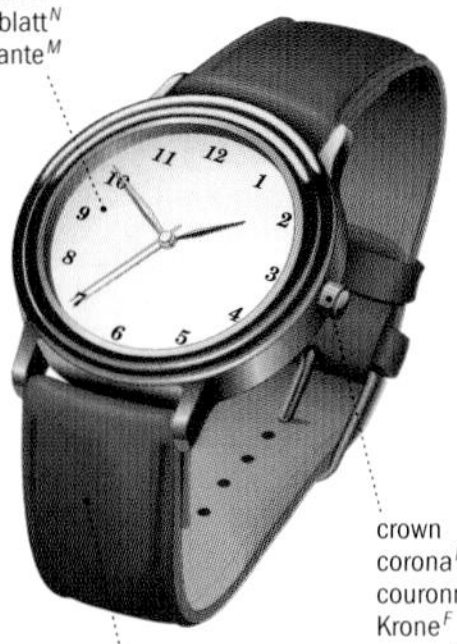

dial
cuadrante^M
cadran^M
Zifferblatt^N
quadrante^M

mechanical watch
reloj^M mecánico
montre^F mécanique
mechanische Uhr^F
orologio^M meccanico

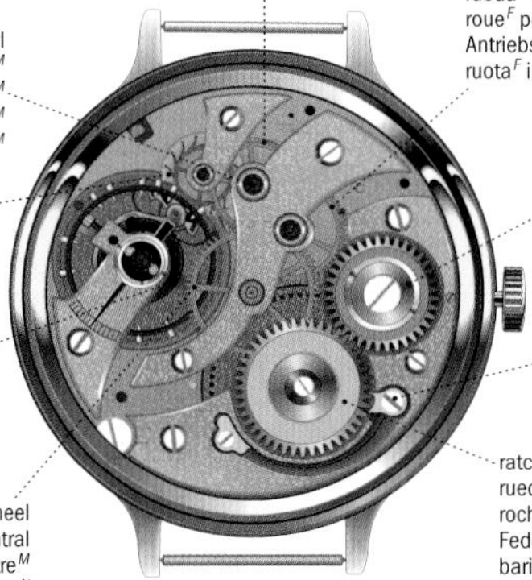

fourth wheel
rueda^F de los segundos^M
roue^F de champ^M
Ankerrad^N
ruota^F dei secondi^M

third wheel
rueda^F media
roue^F petite moyenne
Antriebswerk^N
ruota^F intermedia

jewel
rubí^M
rubis^M
Stein^M
rubino^M

winder
cuerda^F
remontoir^M
Aufzugsrad^N
ruota^F di carica^F

escape wheel
rueda^F de escape^M
roue^F d'échappement^M
Hemmungsrad^N
ruota^F di scappamento^M

click
trinquete^M
cliquet^M
Sperrstift^M
cricchetto^M

hairspring
espiral^M
spiral^M
Spiralfeder^F
molla^F a spirale^M

crown
corona^F
couronne^F
Krone^F
corona^F

ratchet wheel
rueda^F de trinquete^M
rochet^M
Federhaus^N
bariletto^M

center wheel
rueda^F central
roue^F de centre^M
Spannrad^N
ruota^F di centro^M

strap
correa^F
bracelet^M
Uhrband^N
cinturino^M

sundial
reloj^M de sol^M
cadran^M solaire
Sonnenuhr^F
meridiana^F

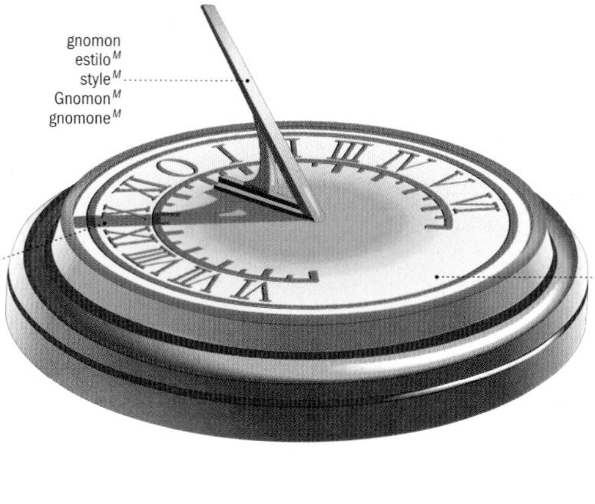

gnomon
estilo^M
style^M
Gnomon^M
gnomone^M

shadow
sombra^F
ombre^F
Schatten^M
ombra^F

dial
cuadrante^M
cadran^M
Zifferblatt^N
quadrante^M

SCIENCE

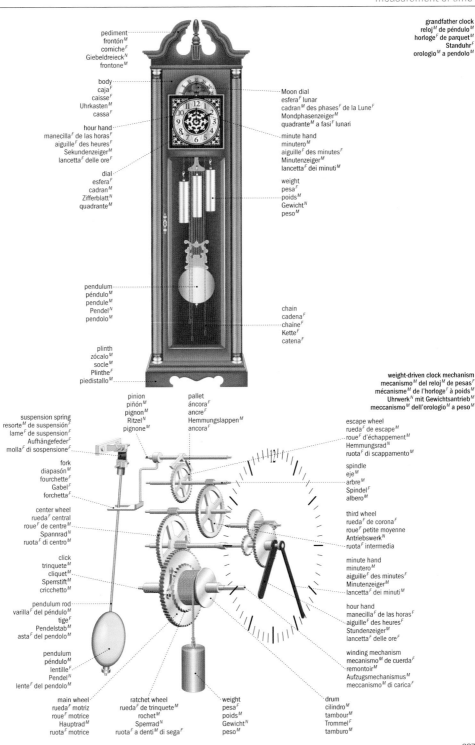

grandfather clock
reloj^M de péndulo^M
horloge^F de parquet^M
Standuhr^F
orologio^M a pendolo^M

pediment
frontón^M
corniche^F
Giebeldreieck^N
frontone^M

body
caja^F
caisse^F
Uhrkasten^M
cassa^F

Moon dial
esfera^F lunar
cadran^M des phases^F de la Lune^F
Mondphasenzeiger^M
quadrante^M a fasi^F lunari

hour hand
manecilla^F de las horas^F
aiguille^F des heures^F
Sekundenzeiger^M
lancetta^F delle ore^F

minute hand
minutero^M
aiguille^F des minutes^F
Minutenzeiger^M
lancetta^F dei minuti^M

dial
esfera^F
cadran^M
Zifferblatt^N
quadrante^M

weight
pesa^F
poids^M
Gewicht^N
peso^M

pendulum
péndulo^M
pendule^M
Pendel^N
pendolo^M

chain
cadena^F
chaîne^F
Kette^F
catena^F

plinth
zócalo^M
socle^M
Plinthe^F
piedistallo^M

weight-driven clock mechanism
mecanismo^M del reloj^M de pesas^F
mécanisme^M de l'horloge^F à poids^M
Uhrwerk^N mit Gewichtsantrieb^M
meccanismo^M dell'orologio^M a peso^M

pinion
piñón^M
pignon^M
Ritzel^N
pignone^M

pallet
áncora^F
ancre^F
Hemmungslappen^M
ancora^F

suspension spring
resorte^M de suspensión^F
lame^F de suspension^F
Aufhängefeder^F
molla^F di sospensione^F

escape wheel
rueda^F de escape^M
roue^F d'échappement^M
Hemmungsrad^N
ruota^F di scappamento^M

fork
diapasón^M
fourchette^F
Gabel^F
forchetta^F

spindle
eje^M
arbre^M
Spindel^F
albero^M

center wheel
rueda^F central
roue^F de centre^M
Spannrad^N
ruota^F di centro^M

third wheel
rueda^F de corona^F
roue^F petite moyenne
Antriebswerk^N
ruota^F intermedia

click
trinquete^M
cliquet^M
Sperrstift^M
cricchetto^M

minute hand
minutero^M
aiguille^F des minutes^F
Minutenzeiger^M
lancetta^F dei minuti^M

hour hand
manecilla^F de las horas^F
aiguille^F des heures^F
Stundenzeiger^M
lancetta^F delle ore^F

pendulum rod
varilla^F del péndulo^M
tige^F
Pendelstab^M
asta^F del pendolo^M

winding mechanism
mecanismo^M de cuerda^F
remontoir^M
Aufzugsmechanismus^M
meccanismo^M di carica^F

pendulum
péndulo^M
lentille^F
Pendel^N
lente^F del pendolo^M

main wheel
rueda^F motriz
roue^F motrice
Hauptrad^M
ruota^F motrice

ratchet wheel
rueda^F de trinquete^M
rochet^M
Sperrrad^N
ruota^F a denti^M di sega^F

weight
pesa^F
poids^M
Gewicht^N
peso^M

drum
cilindro^M
tambour^M
Trommel^F
tamburo^M

measurement of weight

medición[F] del peso[M] | mesure[F] de la masse[F] | Wiegen[N] | misura[F] del peso[M]

beam balance
balanza[F] de astil[M]
balance[F] à fléau[M]
Balkenwaage[F]
bilancia[F] di precisione[F]

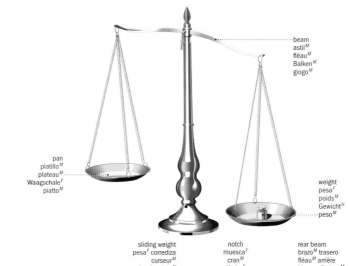

beam
astil[M]
fléau[M]
Balken[M]
giogo[M]

pan
platillo[M]
plateau[M]
Waagschale[F]
piatto[M]

weight
pesa[F]
poids[M]
Gewicht[N]
peso[M]

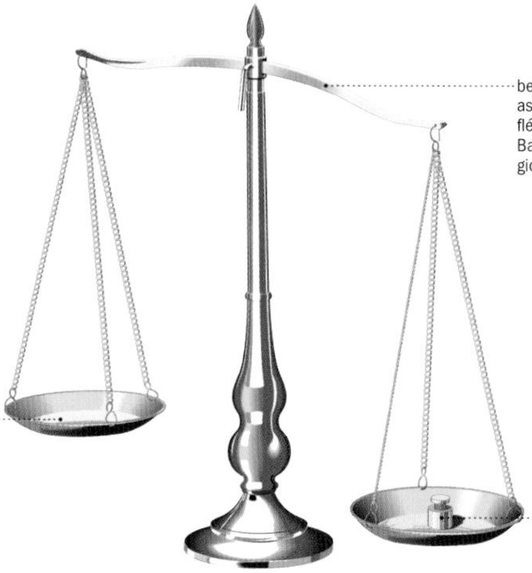

steelyard
báscula[F] romana
balance[F] romaine
Handwaage[F]
stadera[F]

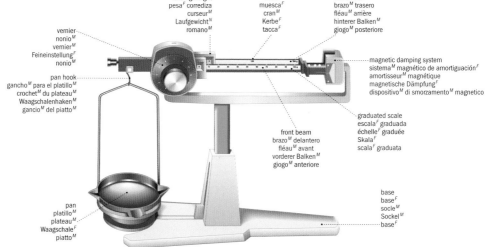

sliding weight
pesa[F] corrediza
curseur[M]
Laufgewicht[N]
romano[M]

notch
muesca[F]
cran[M]
Kerbe[F]
tacca[F]

rear beam
brazo[M] trasero
fléau[M] arrière
hinterer Balken[M]
giogo[M] posteriore

vernier
nonio[M]
vernier[M]
Feineinstellung[F]
nonio[M]

magnetic damping system
sistema[M] magnético de amortiguación[F]
amortisseur[M] magnétique
magnetische Dämpfung[F]
dispositivo[M] di smorzamento[M] magnetico

pan hook
gancho[M] para el platillo[M]
crochet[M] du plateau[M]
Waagschalenhaken[M]
gancio[M] del piatto[M]

graduated scale
escala[F] graduada
échelle[F] graduée
Skala[F]
scala[F] graduata

front beam
brazo[M] delantero
fléau[M] avant
vorderer Balken[M]
giogo[M] anteriore

pan
platillo[M]
plateau[M]
Waagschale[F]
piatto[M]

base
base[F]
socle[M]
Sockel[M]
base[F]

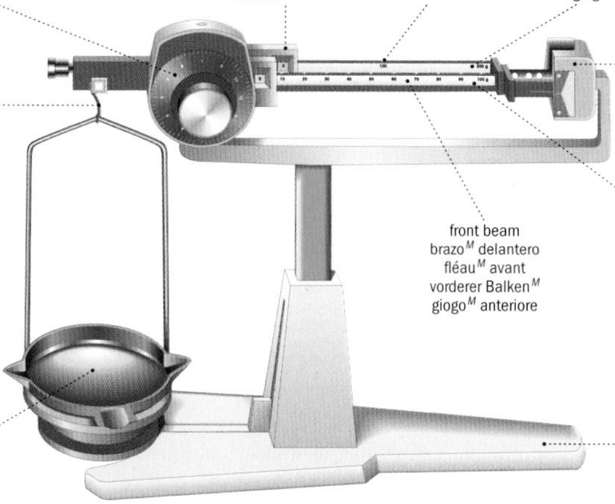

Roberval's balance
balanza[F] de Roberval
balance[F] de Roberval
Roberval-Waage[F]
bilancia[F] a sospensione[F] inferiore

pointer
fiel[M]
aiguille[F]
Zeiger[M]
indice[M]

dial
esfera[F]
cadran[M]
Anzeige[F]
quadrante[M]

weight
pesa[F]
poids[M]
Gewicht[N]
peso[M]

pan
platillo[M]
plateau[M]
Waagschale[F]
piatto[M]

beam
astil[M]
fléau[M]
Balken[M]
giogo[M]

base
base[F]
socle[M]
Sockel[M]
base[F]

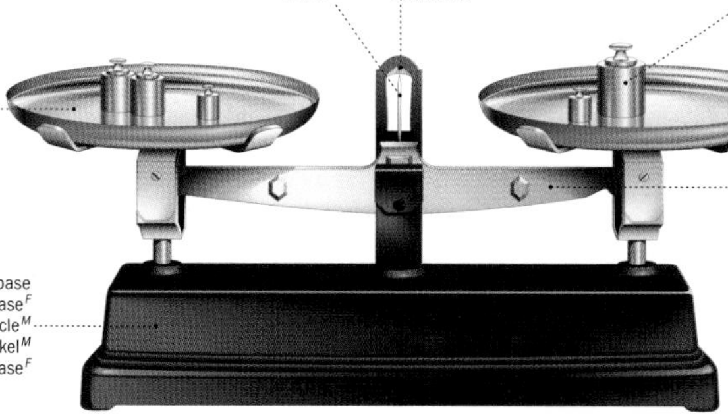

SCIENCE

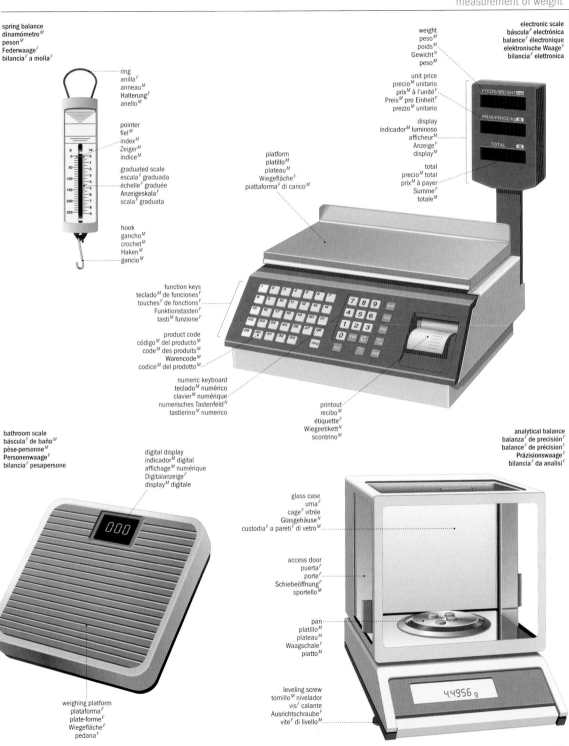

spring balance
dinamómetro[M]
peson[M]
Federwaage[F]
bilancia[F] a molla[F]

ring
anilla[F]
anneau[M]
Halterung[F]
anello[M]

pointer
fiel[M]
index[M]
Zeiger[M]
indice[M]

graduated scale
escala[F] graduada
échelle[F] graduée
Anzeigeskala[F]
scala[F] graduata

hook
gancho[M]
crochet[M]
Haken[M]
gancio[M]

weight
peso[M]
poids[M]
Gewicht[N]
peso[M]

unit price
precio[M] unitario
prix[M] à l'unité[F]
Preis[M] pro Einheit[F]
prezzo[M] unitario

display
indicador[M] luminoso
afficheur[M]
Anzeige[F]
display[M]

total
precio[M] total
prix[M] à payer
Summe[F]
totale[M]

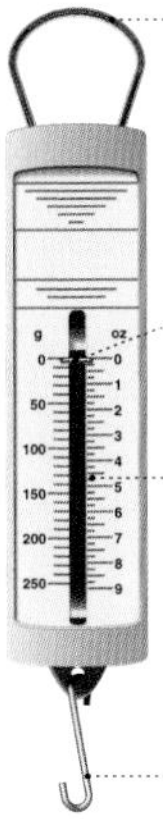

electronic scale
báscula[F] electrónica
balance[F] électronique
elektronische Waage[F]
bilancia[F] elettronica

FOIDS/WEIGHT kg

PRIX/PRICE/kg $

TOTAL $

platform
platillo[M]
plateau[M]
Wiegefläche[F]
piattaforma[F] di carico[M]

function keys
teclado[M] de funciones[F]
touches[F] de fonctions[F]
Funktionstasten[F]
tasti[M] funzione[F]

product code
código[M] del producto[M]
code[M] des produits[M]
Warencode[M]
codice[M] del prodotto[M]

numeric keyboard
teclado[M] numérico
clavier[M] numérique
numerisches Tastenfeld[N]
tastierino[M] numerico

printout
recibo[M]
étiquette[F]
Wiegeetikett[N]
scontrino[M]

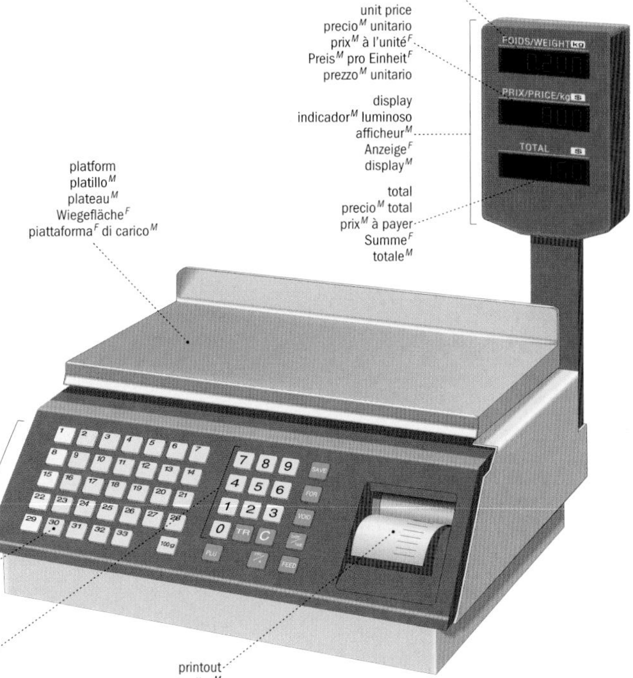

bathroom scale
báscula[F] de baño[M]
pèse-personne[M]
Personenwaage[F]
bilancia[F] pesapersone

digital display
indicador[M] digital
affichage[M] numérique
Digitalanzeige[F]
display[M] digitale

analytical balance
balanza[F] de precisión[F]
balance[F] de précision[F]
Präzisionswaage[F]
bilancia[F] da analisi[F]

SCIENCE

glass case
urna[F]
cage[F] vitrée
Glasgehäuse[N]
custodia[F] a pareti[F] di vetro[M]

access door
puerta[F]
porte[F]
Schiebeöffnung[F]
sportello[M]

pan
platillo[M]
plateau[M]
Waagschale[F]
piatto[M]

4.4956 g

leveling screw
tornillo[M] nivelador
vis[F] calante
Ausrichtschraube[F]
vite[F] di livello[M]

weighing platform
plataforma[F]
plate-forme[F]
Wiegefläche[F]
pedana[F]

measurement of length

medición^F de la longitud^F | mesure^F de la longueur^F | Längenmessung^F | misura^F della lunghezza^F

ruler
regla^F graduada
règle^F graduée
Lineal^N
righello^M

scales
escala^F graduada
graduation^F
Skala^F
scala^F graduata

measurement of distance

medición^F de la distancia^F | mesure^F de la distance^F | Entfernungsmessung^F | misura^F della distanza^F

pedometer
odómetro^M
podomètre^M
Schrittzähler^M/Pedometer^N
pedometro^M

reset button
botón^M de inicio^M del contador^M
bouton^M de remise^F à zéro^M
Rückstellknopf^M
pulsante^M di azzeramento^M

distance traveled
distancia^F recorrida
distance^F parcourue
zurückgelegte Strecke^F
distanza^F percorsa

clip
pinza^F
agrafe^F
Klemme^F
clip^F

step setting
contador^M
réglage^M du pas^M
Schrittlängeneinstellung^F
regolazione^F del passo^M

case
caja^F
boîtier^M
Gehäuse^N
involucro^M

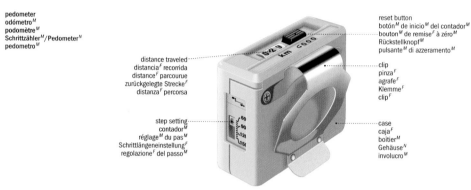

measurement of thickness

medición^F del espesor^M | mesure^F de l'épaisseur^F | Dickemessung^F | misura^F dello spessore^M

vernier caliper
escala^F graduada de vernier^M, pico^M de rey^M
pied^M à coulisse^F à vernier^M
Schieblehre^F/Meßschieber^M
calibro^M a corsoio^M con nonio^M

clamping screws
tornillos^M de bloqueo^M
vis^F de blocage^M
Feststellschrauben^F
viti^F di bloccaggio^M

clamping block
bloqueo^M
bloc^M de pression^F
Klemmvorrichtung^F
blocco^M di chiusura^F

main scale
escala^F de la regla^F
graduation^F de la règle^F
Hauptmaßstab^M
scala^F graduata del righello^M

vernier
vernier^M
vernier^M
Nonius^M
nonio^M

fixed jaw
mandíbula^F fija
bec^M fixe
feststehender Meßschnabel^M
espansione^F fissa

vernier scale
escala^F graduada de vernier^M/pico^M de rey^M
graduation^F du vernier^M
Schieber^M
scala^F graduata del nonio^M

fine adjustment wheel
tornillo^M micrométrico
molette^F d'ajustage^M
Feineinstellung^F
rotella^F di regolazione^F

ruler
escala^F graduada
règle^F
Lineal^N
righello^M

sliding jaw
mandíbula^F deslizante
bec^M mobile
verschiebbarer Meßschnabel^M
espansione^F mobile

anvil
tope^M fijo
touche^F fixe
Anschlag^M
contropunta^F

spindle
tope^M móvil
touche^F mobile
Meßspindel^F
asta^F mobile

finely threaded screw
rosca^F
vis^F micrométrique
Filigrangewinde^N
vite^F micrometrica

micrometer caliper
micrómetro^M
micromètre^M palmer^M
Mikrometerschraube^F
micrometro^M a vite^F

ratchet knob
husillo^M
bouton^M à friction^F
Sperrdrehknopf^M
nottolino^M a scatto^M

frame
cuerpo^M
corps^M
Meßbügel^M
archetto^M

lock nut
tuerca^F de bloqueo^M
bague^F de blocage^M
Feststellschraube^F
ghiera^F di bloccaggio^M

thimble
tambor^M
tambour^M
Meßtrommel^F
tamburo^M

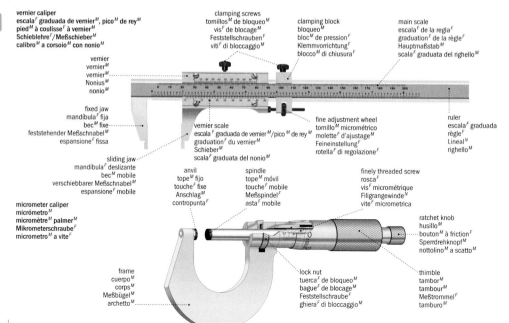

measurement of angles

medición^F de ángulos^M | mesure^F des angles^M | Winkelmessung^F | misura^F degli angoli^M

theodolite
teodolito^M
théodolite^M
Theodolit^M
teodolite^M

optical sight
visor^M
viseur^M
Mikroskopokular^N
collimatore^M ottico

alidade
alidada^F móvil
alidade^F
Alhidade^F
alidada^F

telescope
telescopio^M
lunette^F
Fernrohr^N
cannocchiale^M

adjustment for vertical-circle image
botón^M para ajustar la imágen^F verticalmente
ajustement^M de l'image^F du cercle^M vertical
Höhenfeintrieb^M
regolazione^F dell'immagine^F del cerchio^M zenitale

illumination mirror
espejo^M iluminador
miroir^M d'éclairage^M
Beleuchtungsspiegel^M
lente^F di illuminazione^F

micrometer screw
tornillo^M micrométrico
bouton^M de réglage^F du micromètre^M optique
Mikrometerknopf^M
manopola^F di regolazione^F del micrometro^M

alidade level
nivelador^M de la alidada^F
nivelle^F d'alidade^F
Alhidadenebene^F
livella^F fissata all'alidada^F

adjustment for horizontal-circle image
botón^M para ajustar la imágen^F horizontalmente
ajustement^M de l'image^F du cercle^M horizontal
Seitenfeintrieb^M
regolazione^F dell'immagine^F del cerchio^M azimutale

leveling head locking knob
botón^M de fijación^F del nivel^M principal
bouton^M de verrouillage^M de l'embase^F
Ausrichtkopfblockierung^F
manopola^F di bloccaggio^M del basamento^M

horizontal clamp
tornillo^M de fijación^F horizontal
blocage^M du pivotement^M
Seitenklemme^F
morsetto^M dei movimenti^M azimutali

leveling screw
tornillo^M nivelador
vis^F calante
Ausrichtschraube^F
vite^F di livello^M

leveling head level
nivelador^M principal
nivelle^F d'embase^F
Ausrichtkopfebene^F
livella^F del basamento^M

leveling head
nivelación^F principal
embase^F
Ausrichtkopf^M
basamento^M

base plate
placa^F de fijación^F
plaque^F de fixation^F
Sockelplatte^F
piastra^F di base^F

bevel square
falsa escuadra^F
fausse-équerre^F
Schmiege^F
squadra^F falsa

protractor
transportador^M
rapporteur^M d'angle^M
Winkelmesser^M
goniometro^M

international system of units

sistema[M] internacional de unidades[F] de medida[F] | système[M] international d'unités[F] | internationales Einheitensystem[N] | sistema[M] internazionale di unità[F] di misura[F]

unit of frequency	unit of electric potential difference	unit of electric charge	unit of energy
unidad[F] de medida[F] de frecuencia[F]	unidad[F] de medida[F] de la diferencia[F] de potencial[M] eléctrico	unidad[F] de medida[F] de carga[F] eléctrica	unidad[F] de medida[F] de energía[F]
mesure[F] de la fréquence[F]	mesure[F] de la différence[F] de potentiel[M] électrique	mesure[F] de la charge[F] électrique	mesure[F] de l'énergie[F]
Maßeinheit[F] der Frequenz[F]	Maßeinheit[F] der elektrischen Spannung[F]	Maßeinheit[F] der elektrischen Ladung[F]	Maßeinheit[F] der Energie[F]
unità[F] di misura[F] della frequenza[F]	unità[F] di misura[F] della differenza[F] di potenziale[M] elettrico	unità[F] di misura[F] della carica[F] elettrica	unità[F] di misura[F] dell'energia[F]

Hz	V	C	J
hertz	volt	coulomb	joule
hercio[M]	voltio[M] , volt[M]	culombio[M]	julio[M]
hertz[M]	volt[M]	coulomb[M]	joule[M]
Hertz[N]	Volt[N]	Coulomb[N]	Joule[N]
hertz[M]	volt[M]	coulomb[M]	joule[M]

unit of power	unit of force	unit of electric resistance	unit of electric current
unidad[F] de medida[F] de potencia[F] eléctrica	unidad[F] de medida[F] de fuerza[F]	unidad[F] de medida[F] de resistencia[F] eléctrica	unidad[F] de medida[F] de corriente[F] eléctrica
mesure[F] de la puissance[F]	mesure[F] de la force[F]	mesure[F] de la résistance[F] électrique	mesure[F] du courant[M] électrique
Maßeinheit[F] der Leistung[F]	Maßeinheit[F] der Kraft[F]	Maßeinheit[F] des elektrischen Widerstands[M]	Maßeinheit[F] der elektrischen Stromstärke[F]
unità[F] di misura[F] della potenza[F] elettrica	unità[F] di misura[F] della forza[F]	unità[F] di misura[F] della resistenza[F] elettrica	unità[F] di misura[F] della corrente[F] elettrica

W	N	Ω	A
watt	newton	ohm	ampere
vatio[M]	newton[M]	ohmnio[M]/ohm[M]	amperio[M]
watt[M]	newton[M]	ohm[M]	ampère[M]
Watt[N]	Newton[N]	Ohm[N]	Ampere[N]
watt[M]	newton[M]	ohm[M]	ampere[M]

unit of length	unit of mass	unit of temperature	unit of thermodynamic temperature
unidad[F] de medida[F] de longitud[F]	unidad[F] de medida[F] de masa[F]	unidad[F] de medida[F] de la temperatura[F]	unidad[F] de medida[F] de temperatura[F] termodinámica
mesure[F] de la longueur[F]	mesure[F] de la masse[F]	mesure[F] de la température[F]	mesure[F] de la température[F] thermodynamique
Maßeinheit[F] der Länge[F]	Maßeinheit[F] der Masse[F]	Maßeinheit[F] Temperatur[F]	Maßeinheit[F] der thermodynamischen Temperatur[F]
unità[F] di misura[F] della lunghezza[F]	unità[F] di misura[F] della massa[F]	unità[F] di misura[F] della temperatura[F]	unità[F] di misura[F] della temperatura[F] termodinamica

m	kg	°C	K
meter	kilogram	degree Celsius	kelvin
metro[M]	kilogramo[M]	grado[M] Celsius	kelvin[M]
mètre[M]	kilogramme[M]	degré[M] Celsius	kelvin[M]
Meter[M]	Kilogramm[N]	Grad[M] Celsius	Kelvin[N]
metro[M]	kilogrammo[M]	grado[M] Celsius	kelvin[M]

unit of amount of substance	unit of radioactivity	unit of pressure	unit of luminous intensity
unidad[F] de medida[F] de cantidad[F] de materia[F]	unidad[F] de medida[F] de radioactividad[F]	unidad[F] de medida[F] de presión[F]	unidad[F] de medida[F] de intensidad[F] luminosa
mesure[F] de la quantité[F] de matière[F]	mesure[F] de la radioactivité[F]	mesure[F] de la pression[F]	mesure[F] de l'intensité[F] lumineuse
Maßeinheit[F] der Stoffmenge[F]	Maßeinheit[F] der Radioaktivität[F]	Maßeinheit[F] des Drucks[M]	Maßeinheit[F] der Lichtstärke[F]
unità[F] di misura[F] della quantità[F] di sostanza[F]	unità[F] di misura[F] della radioattività[F]	unità[F] di misura[F] della pressione[F]	unità[F] di misura[F] dell'intensità[F] luminosa

mol	Bq	Pa	cd
mole	becquerel	pascal	candela
mole[M]	becquerel[M]	pascal[M]	candela[M]
mole[F]	becquerel[M]	pascal[M]	candela[M]
Mol[N]	Becquerel[N]	Pascal[N]	Candela[F]
mole[F]	becquerel[M]	pascal[M]	candela[F]

biology

biología[F] | biologie[F] | Biologie[F] | biologia[F]

female
femenino[M]
femelle[F]
weiblich
femminile

male
masculino[M]
mâle[M]
männlich
maschile

Rh+

blood factor RH positive
factor[M] RH positivo
facteur[M] Rhésus positif
Rhesusfaktor[M] positiv
fattore[M] Rh positivo

Rh-

blood factor RH negative
factor[M] RH negativo
facteur[M] Rhésus négatif
Rhesusfaktor[M] negativ
fattore[M] Rh negativo

†

death
muerte[F]
mort[F]
gestorben
morte[F]

birth
nacimiento[M]
naissance[F]
geboren
nascita[F]

mathematics

matemáticas[F] | mathématiques[F] | Mathematik[F] | matematica[F]

minus/negative
resta[F]
soustraction[F]
Subtraktion[F]
sottrazione[F]

plus/positive
suma[F]
addition[F]
Addition[F]
addizione[F]

multiplied by
multiplicación[F]
multiplication[F]
Multiplikation[F]
moltiplicazione[F]

divided by
división[F]
division[F]
Division[F]
divisione[F]

equals
igual a
égale
ist gleich
uguale a

is not equal to
no es igual a
n'égale pas
ist ungleich
diverso da

is approximately equal to
casi igual a
égale à peu près
ist annähernd gleich
approssimativamente uguale a

is equivalent to
equivalente a
équivaut à
ist äquivalent mit
equivalente a

is identical to
idéntico a
est identique à
ist identisch mit
coincide con

is not identical to
no es idéntico a
n'est pas identique à
ist nicht identisch mit
non coincide con

plus or minus
más[M] o menos[M]
plus ou moins
plus oder minus
più o meno

is less than or equal to
igual o menor que
égal ou plus petit que
ist gleich oder kleiner als
minore o uguale a

is greater than
mayor que
plus grand que
ist größer als
maggiore di

is greater than or equal to
igual o mayor que
égal ou plus grand que
ist gleich oder größer als
maggiore o uguale a

is less than
menor que
plus petit que
ist kleiner als
minore di

empty set
conjunto[M] vacío
ensemble[M] vide
leere Menge[F]
insieme[M] vuoto

union of two sets
unión[F]
réunion[F]
Mengenvereinigung[F]
unione[F]

intersection of two sets
intersección[F]
intersection[F]
Mengenschnitt[M]
intersezione[F]

is included in/is a subset of
inclusión[F]
inclusion[F]
echte Teilmenge[F] von
contenuto in

percent
porcentaje[M]
pourcentage[M]
Prozent[N]
percento[M]

is an element of
pertenece a
appartenance[F]
Element[N] von
appartiene a

is not an element of
no pertenece a
non-appartenance[F]
nicht Element[N] von
non appartiene a

sum
suma[F]
sommation[F]
Summe[F]
sommatoria[F]

square root of
raíz[F] cuadrada de
racine[F] carrée de
Quadratwurzel[F] aus
radice[F] quadrata di

fraction
fracción[M]
fraction[F]
Bruch[M]
frazione[F]

infinity
infinito[M]
infini[M]
unendlich
infinito[M]

integral
integral
intégrale[F]
Integral[N]
integrale[M]

factorial
factorial
factorielle[F]
Fakultät[F]
fattoriale[M]

Roman numerals
números[M] romanos
chiffres[M] romains
römische Ziffern[F]
numeri[M] romani

I

one
uno
un[M]
Eins[F]
uno

V

five
cinco
cinq[M]
Fünf[F]
cinque

X

ten
diez
dix[M]
Zehn[F]
dieci

L

fifty
cincuenta
cinquante[M]
Fünfzig[F]
cinquanta

C

one hundred
mil
cent[M]
Hundert[F]
cento

D

five hundred
quinientos
cinq cents[M]
Fünfhundert[F]
cinquecento

M

one thousand
cien
mille[M]
Tausend[F]
mille

geometry

geometría[F] | géométrie[F] | Geometrie[F] | geometria[F]

○
degree
grado[M]
degré[M]
Grad[M]
grado[M]

ˈ
minute
minuto[M]
minute[F]
Bogenminute[F]
primo[M]

ˈˈ
second
segundo[M]
seconde[F]
Bogensekunde[F]
secondo[M]

π
pi
pi[M]
pi[M]
Pi[N]
pi[M] greco

⊥
perpendicular
perpendicular[F]
perpendiculaire[F]
ist senkrecht zu
perpendicolare

‖
is parallel to
es paralelo a
parallèle
ist parallel zu
parallelo a

⫮
is not parallel to
no es paralelo a
non-parallèle
ist nicht parallel zu
non parallelo a

∟
right angle
ángulo[M] recto
angle[M] droit
rechter Winkel[M]
angolo[M] retto

⦦
obtuse angle
ángulo[M] obtuso
angle[M] obtus
stumpfer Winkel[M]
angolo[M] ottuso

∠
acute angle
ángulo[M] agudo
angle[M] aigu
spitzer Winkel[M]
angolo[M] acuto

geometrical shapes

formas[F] geométricas | formes[F] géométriques | geometrische Formen[F] | forme[F] geometriche

examples of angles
ejemplos[M] de ángulos[M]
exemples[M] d'angles[M]
Beispiele[N] für Winkel[M]
esempi[M] di angoli[M]

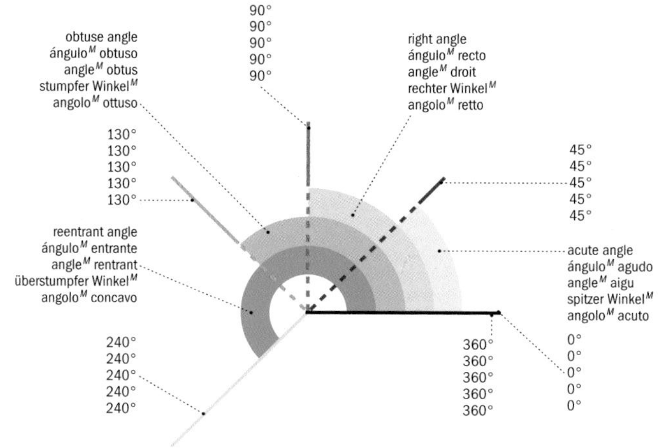

obtuse angle
ángulo[M] obtuso
angle[M] obtus
stumpfer Winkel[M]
angolo[M] ottuso

90°
90°
90°
90°
90°

right angle
ángulo[M] recto
angle[M] droit
rechter Winkel[M]
angolo[M] retto

130°
130°
130°
130°
130°

45°
45°
45°
45°
45°

reentrant angle
ángulo[M] entrante
angle[M] rentrant
überstumpfer Winkel[M]
angolo[M] concavo

acute angle
ángulo[M] agudo
angle[M] aigu
spitzer Winkel[M]
angolo[M] acuto

240°
240°
240°
240°
240°

360°
360°
360°
360°
360°

0°
0°
0°
0°
0°

plane surfaces
superficies[F]
surfaces[F]
ebene Flächen[F]
superfici[F]

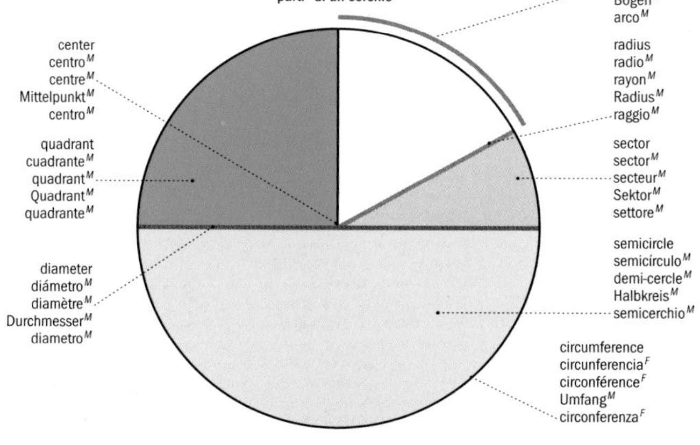

parts of a circle
partes[M] de un círculo[M]
parties[F] d'un cercle[M]
Teile[M] eines Kreises[M]
parti[F] di un cerchio[M]

center
centro[M]
centre[M]
Mittelpunkt[M]
centro[M]

arc
arco[M]
arc[M]
Bogen[M]
arco[M]

radius
radio[M]
rayon[M]
Radius[M]
raggio[M]

quadrant
cuadrante[M]
quadrant[M]
Quadrant[M]
quadrante[M]

sector
sector[M]
secteur[M]
Sektor[M]
settore[M]

diameter
diámetro[M]
diamètre[M]
Durchmesser[M]
diametro[M]

semicircle
semicírculo[M]
demi-cercle[M]
Halbkreis[M]
semicerchio[M]

circumference
circunferencia[F]
circonférence[F]
Umfang[M]
circonferenza[F]

geometrical shapes

polygons
polígonos[M]
polygones[M]
Vielecke[N]
poligoni[M]

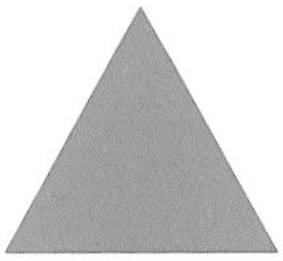

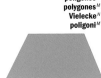

triangle
triángulo[M]
triangle[M]
Dreieck[N]
triangolo[M]

square
cuadrado[M]
carré[M]
Quadrat[N]
quadrato[M]

rectangle
rectángulo[M]
rectangle[M]
Rechteck[N]
rettangolo[M]

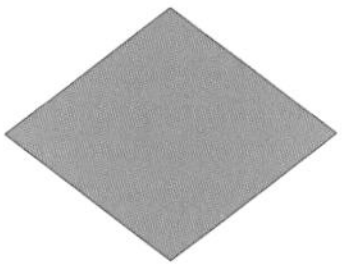

rhombus
rombo[M]
losange[M]
Rhombus[M]
rombo[M]

trapezoid
trapecio[M]
trapèze[M]
unregelmäßiges Trapez[N]
trapezio[M]

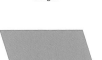

parallelogram
paralelogramo[M]
parallélogramme[M]
Parallelogramm[N]
parallelogramma[M]

quadrilateral
cuadrilátero[M]
quadrilatère[M]
Viereck[N]
quadrilatero[M]

regular pentagon
pentágono[M] regular
pentagone[M] régulier
regelmäßiges Fünfeck[N]
pentagono[M] regolare

regular hexagon
hexágono[M] regular
hexagone[M] régulier
regelmäßiges Sechseck[N]
esagono[M] regolare

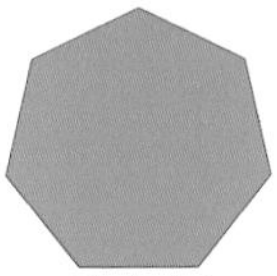

regular heptagon
heptágono[M] regular
heptagone[M] régulier
regelmäßiges Siebeneck[N]
ettagono[M] regolare

regular octagon
octágono[M] regular
octogone[M] régulier
regelmäßiges Achteck[N]
ottagono[M] regolare

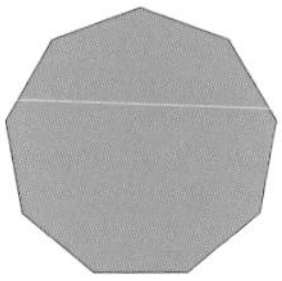

regular nonagon
nonágono[M] regular
ennéagone[M] régulier
regelmäßiges Neuneck[N]
enneagono[M] regolare

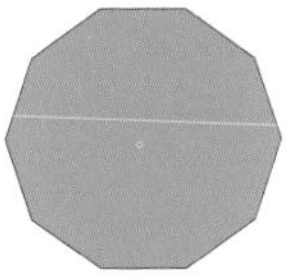

regular decagon
decágono[M] regular
décagone[M] régulier
regelmäßiges Zehneck[N]
decagono[M] regolare

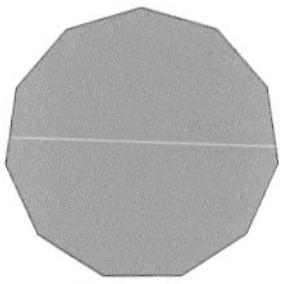

regular hendecagon
endecágono[M] regular
hendécagone[M] régulier
regelmäßiges Elfeck[N]
endecagono[M] regolare

regular dodecagon
dodecágono[M] regular
dodécagone[M] régulier
regelmäßiges Zwölfeck[N]
dodecagono[M] regolare

solids
cuerpos[M] **sólidos**[M]
volumes[M]
Körper[M]
solidi[M]

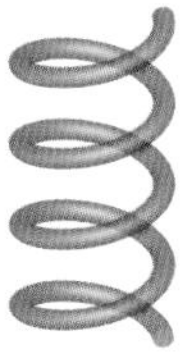

helix
hélice[F]
hélice[F]
Helix[F]
elica[F]

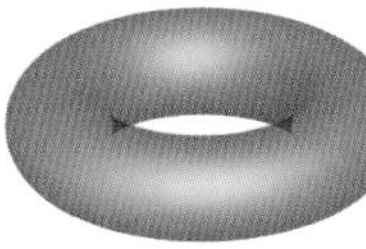

torus
toro[M]
tore[M]
Torus[M]
toro[M]

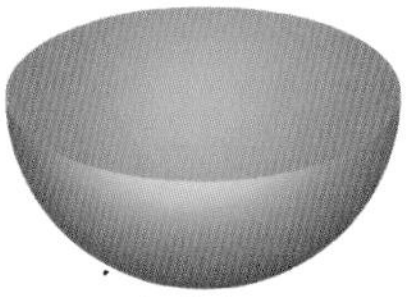

hemisphere
hemisferio[M]
hémisphère[M]
Halbkugel[F]
semisfera[F]

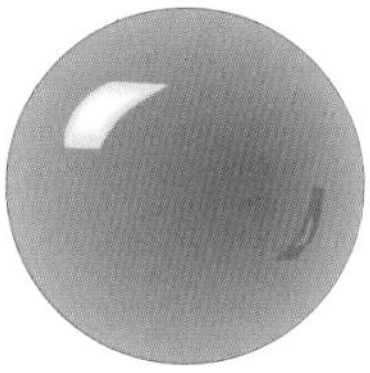

sphere
esfera[F]
sphère[F]
Kugel[F]
sfera[F]

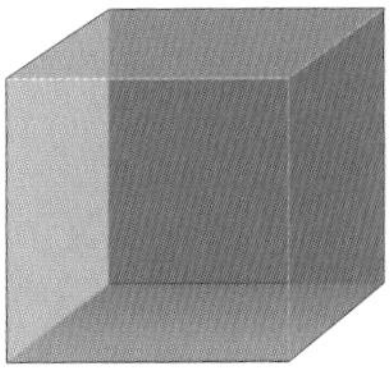

cube
cubo[M]
cube[M]
Würfel[M]
cubo[M]

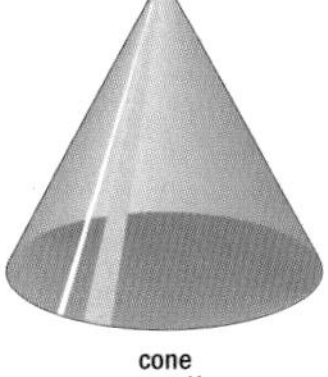

cone
cono[M]
cône[M]
Kegel[M]
cono[M]

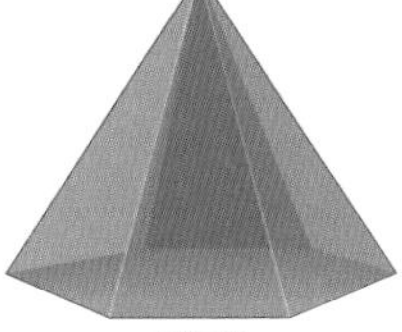

pyramid
pirámide[F]
pyramide[F]
Pyramide[F]
piramide[F]

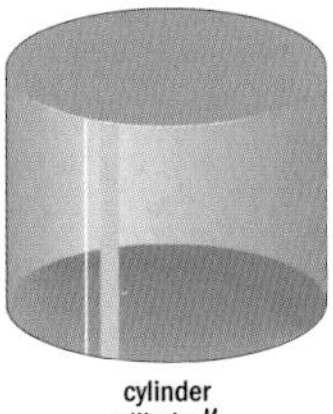

cylinder
cilindro[M]
cylindre[M]
Zylinder[M]
cilindro[M]

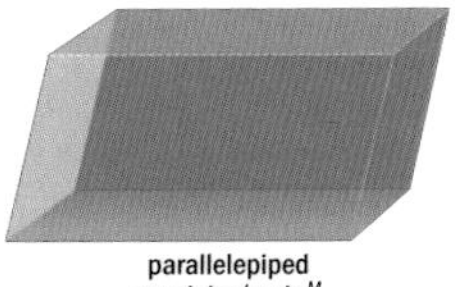

parallelepiped
paralelepipedo[M]
parallélépipède[M]
Parallelepiped[N]
parallelepipedo[M]

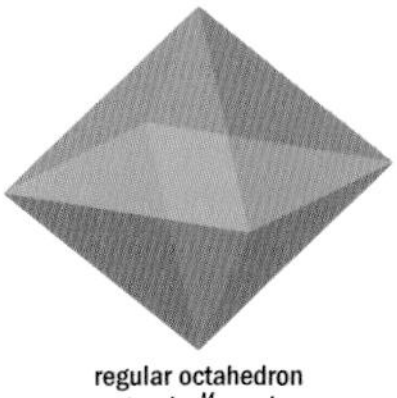

regular octahedron
octaedro[M] regular
octaèdre[M] régulier
regelmäßiges Oktaeder[N]
ottaedro[M] regolare

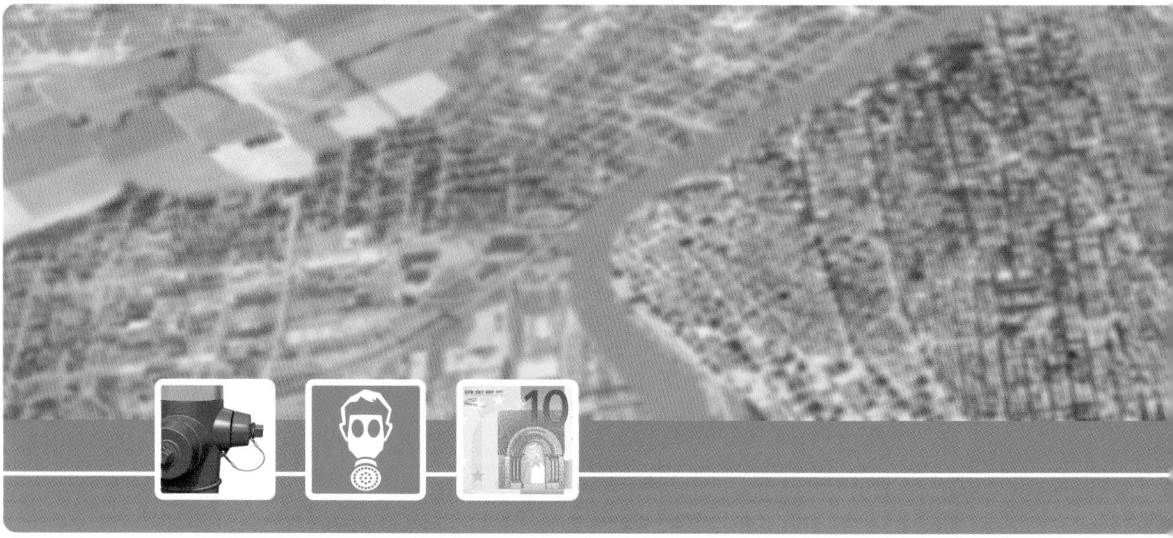

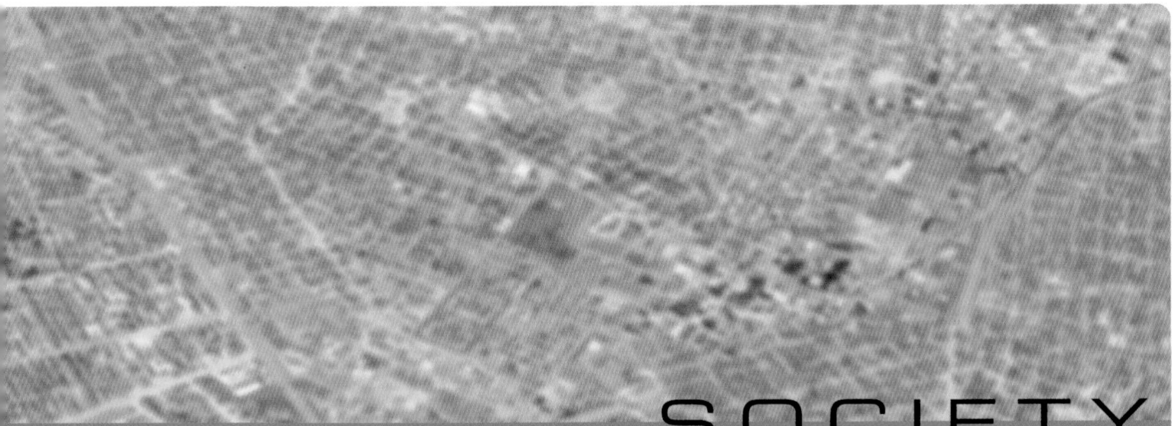

SOCIETY

SOCIEDAD | SOCIÉTÉ | GESELLSCHAFT | SOCIETÀ

agglomeration

conurbación^F | agglomération^F | Ballungsgebiet^N | conurbazione^F

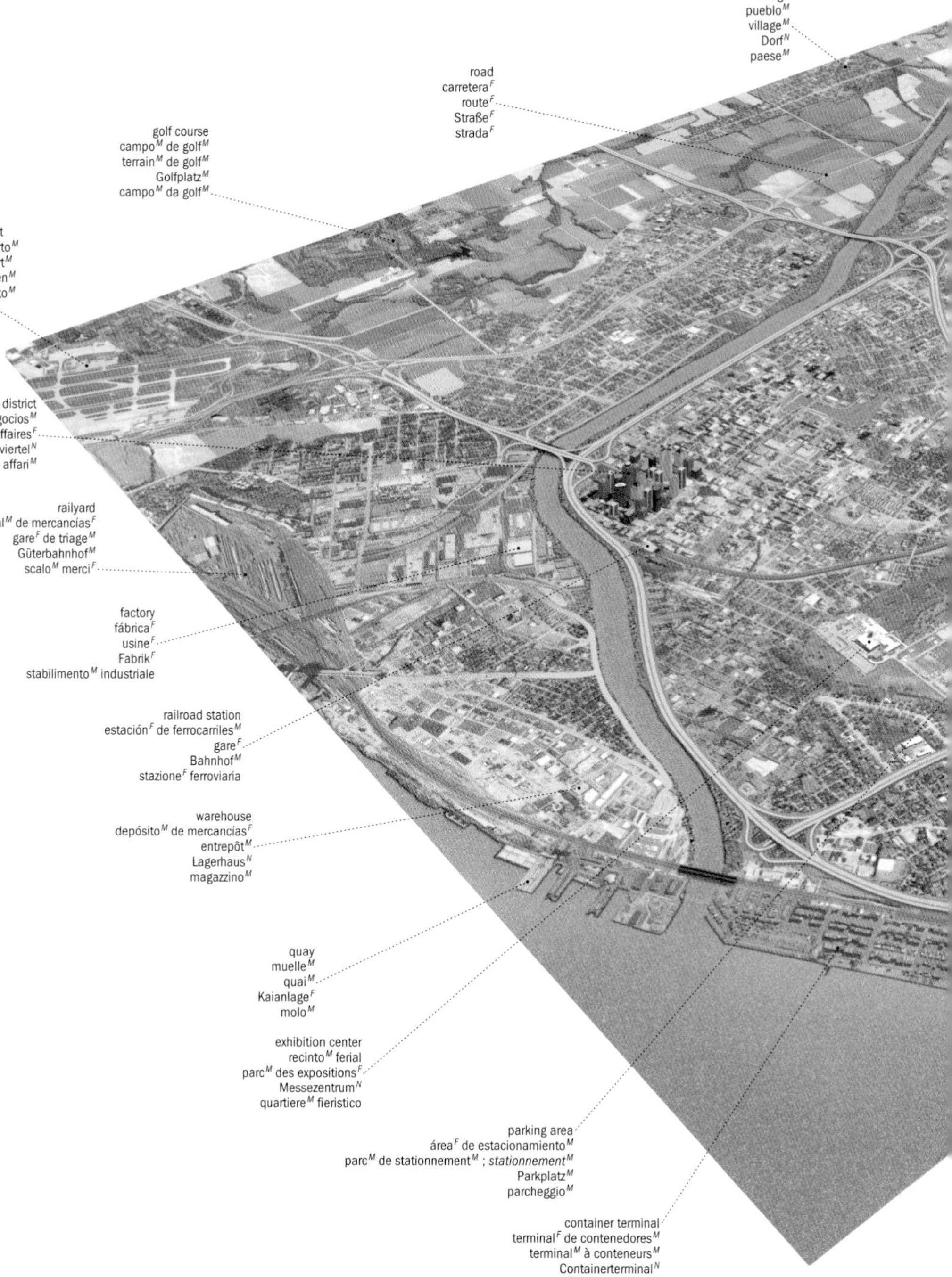

village
pueblo^M
village^M
Dorf^N
paese^M

road
carretera^F
route^F
Straße^F
strada^F

golf course
campo^M de golf^M
terrain^M de golf^M
Golfplatz^M
campo^M da golf^M

airport
aeropuerto^M
aéroport^M
Flughafen^M
aeroporto^M

business district
centro^M de negocios^M
quartier des affaires^F
Geschäftsviertel^N
quartiere^M degli affari^M

railyard
terminal^M de mercancías^F
gare^F de triage^M
Güterbahnhof^M
scalo^M merci^F

factory
fábrica^F
usine^F
Fabrik^F
stabilimento^M industriale

railroad station
estación^F de ferrocarriles^M
gare^F
Bahnhof^M
stazione^F ferroviaria

warehouse
depósito^M de mercancías^F
entrepôt^M
Lagerhaus^N
magazzino^M

quay
muelle^M
quai^M
Kaianlage^F
molo^M

exhibition center
recinto^M ferial
parc^M des expositions^F
Messezentrum^N
quartiere^M fieristico

parking area
área^F de estacionamiento^M
parc^M de stationnement^M ; *stationnement*^M
Parkplatz^M
parcheggio^M

container terminal
terminal^F de contenedores^M
terminal^M à conteneurs^M
Containerterminal^N
deposito^M per containers^M

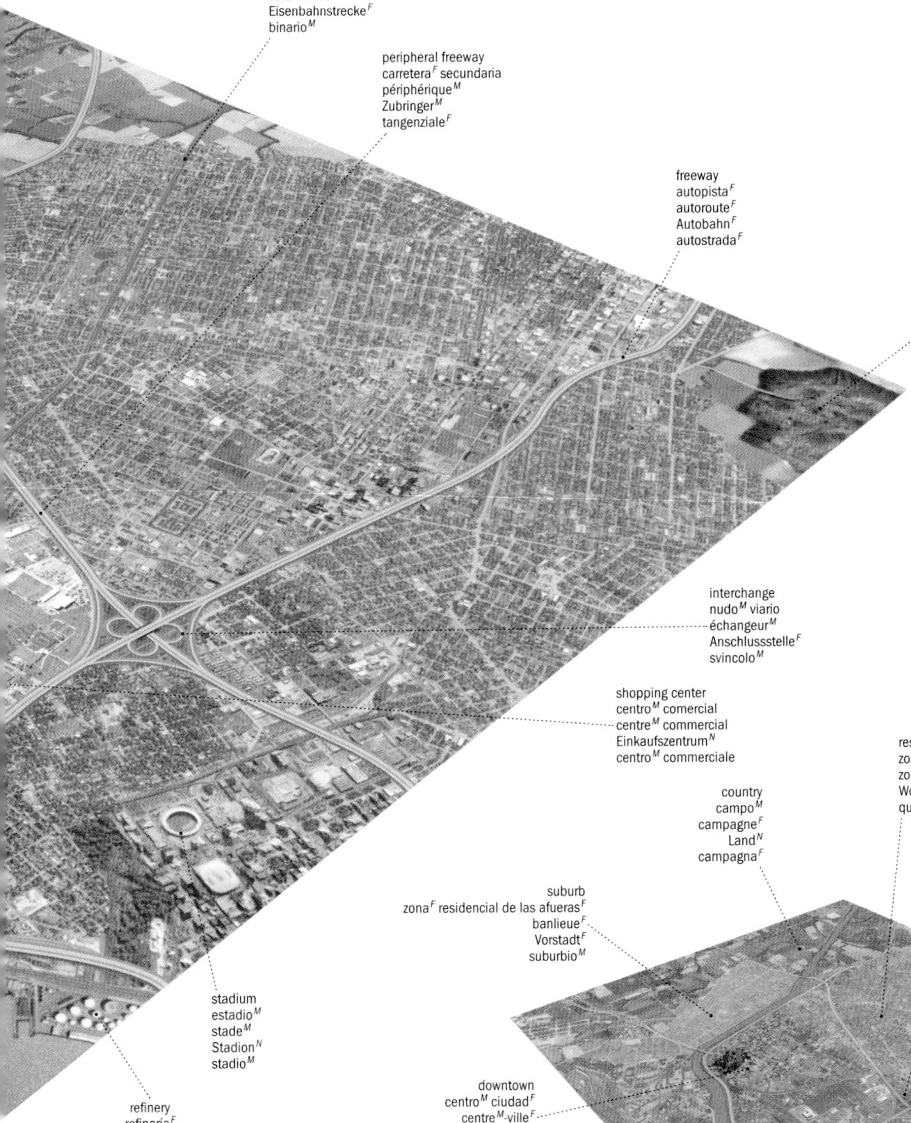

track
vía^F ferroviaria
voie^F ferrée
Eisenbahnstrecke^F
binario^M

peripheral freeway
carretera^F secundaria
périphérique^M
Zubringer^M
tangenziale^F

freeway
autopista^F
autoroute^F
Autobahn^F
autostrada^F

landfill
vertedero^M
décharge^F
Mülldeponie^F
discarica^F

interchange
nudo^M viario
échangeur^M
Anschlussstelle^F
svincolo^M

shopping center
centro^M comercial
centre^M commercial
Einkaufszentrum^N
centro^M commerciale

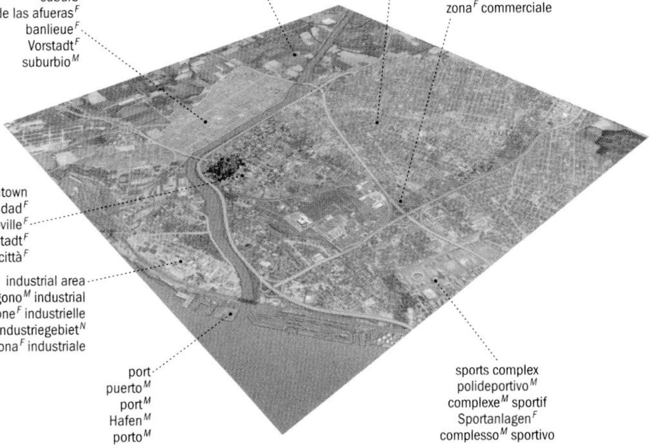

residential district
zona^F residencial
zone^F résidentielle
Wohngebiet^N
quartiere^M residenziale

country
campo^M
campagne^F
Land^N
campagna^F

commercial zone
zona^F comercial
zone^F commerciale
Gewerbegebiet^N
zona^F commerciale

suburb
zona^F residencial de las afueras^F
banlieue^F
Vorstadt^F
suburbio^M

stadium
estadio^M
stade^M
Stadion^N
stadio^M

downtown
centro^M ciudad^F
centre^M-ville^F
Innenstadt^F
centro^M della città^F

refinery
refinería^F
raffinerie^F
Raffinerie^F
raffineria^F

industrial area
polígono^M industrial
zone^F industrielle
Industriegebiet^N
zona^F industriale

port
puerto^M
port^M
Hafen^M
porto^M

sports complex
polideportivo^M
complexe^M sportif
Sportanlagen^F
complesso^M sportivo

SOCIETY

709

downtown

centro^M ciudad^F | centre^M-ville^F | Innenstadt^F | centro^M della città^F

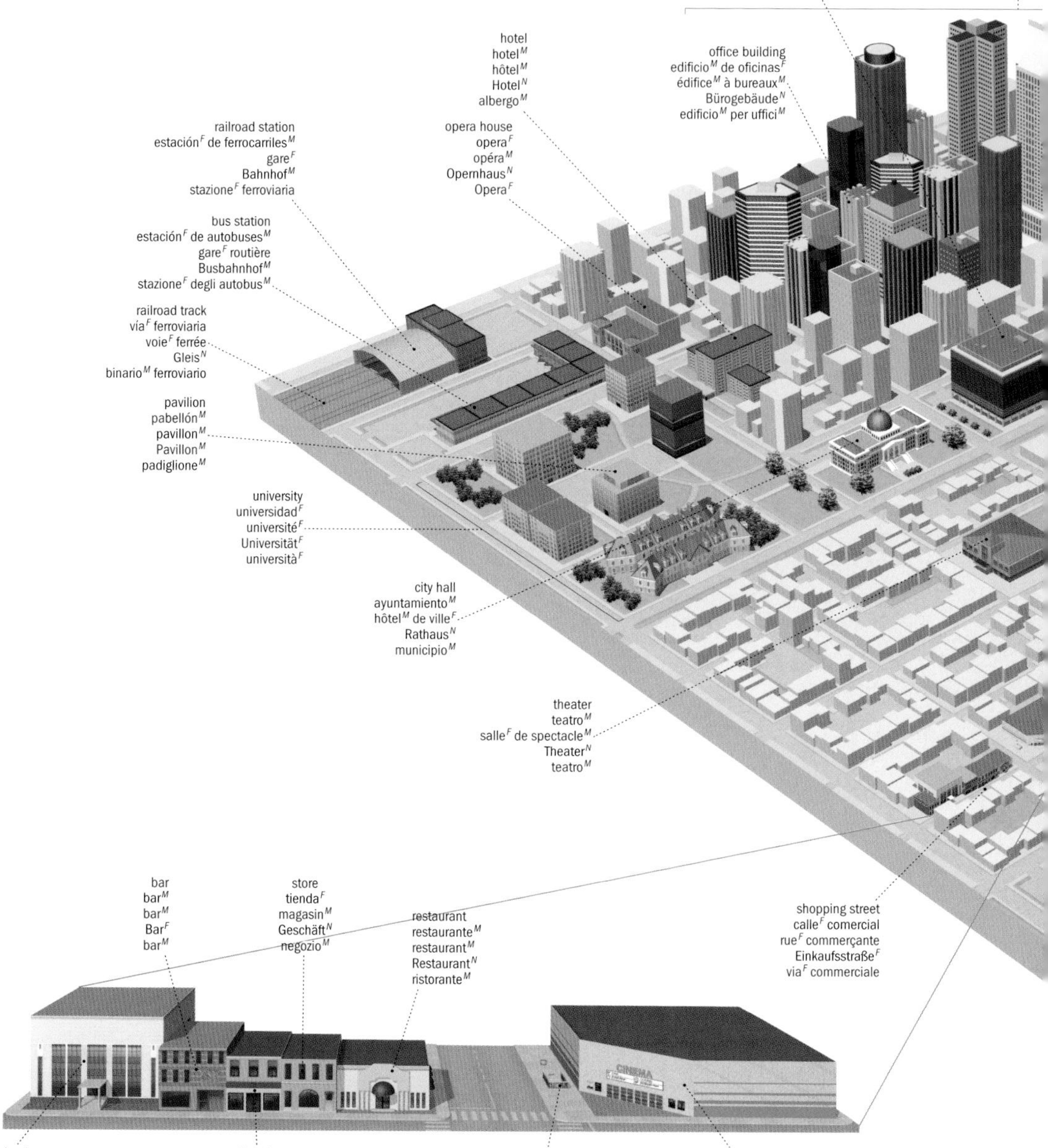

courthouse
Palacio^M de Justicia^F
palais^M de justice^F
Gerichtsgebäude^N
palazzo^M di giustizia^F

business district
centro^M de negocios^M
quartier^M des affaires^F
Geschäftsviertel^N
quartiere^M degli affari^M

hotel
hotel^M
hôtel^M
Hotel^N
albergo^M

office building
edificio^M de oficinas^F
édifice^M à bureaux^M
Bürogebäude^N
edificio^M per uffici^M

railroad station
estación^F de ferrocarriles^M
gare^F
Bahnhof^M
stazione^F ferroviaria

opera house
opera^F
opéra^M
Opernhaus^N
Opera^F

bus station
estación^F de autobuses^M
gare^F routière
Busbahnhof^M
stazione^F degli autobus^M

railroad track
vía^F ferroviaria
voie^F ferrée
Gleis^N
binario^M ferroviario

pavilion
pabellón^M
pavillon^M
Pavillon^M
padiglione^M

university
universidad^F
université^F
Universität^F
università^F

city hall
ayuntamiento^M
hôtel^M de ville^F
Rathaus^N
municipio^M

theater
teatro^M
salle^F de spectacle^M
Theater^N
teatro^M

shopping street
calle^F comercial
rue^F commerçante
Einkaufsstraße^F
via^F commerciale

bar
bar^M
bar^M
Bar^F
bar^M

store
tienda^F
magasin^M
Geschäft^N
negozio^M

restaurant
restaurante^M
restaurant^M
Restaurant^N
ristorante^M

bank
banco^M
banque^F
Bank^F
banca^F

coffee shop
cafetería^F
café^M
Café^N
caffè^M

subway station
estación^F de metro^M
station^F de métro^M
U-Bahn^F-Station^F
stazione^F della metropolitana^F

movie theater
cine^M
cinéma^M
Kino^N
cinema^M

SOCIETY

convention center
palacio^M de congresos^M
palais^M des congrès^M
Kongresszentrum^N
palazzo^M dei congressi^M

educational institution
centro^M educativo
établissement^M scolaire
Bildungseinrichtung^F
complesso^M scolastico

boulevard
bulevar^M
boulevard^M
Boulevard^M
boulevard

street
calle^F
rue^F
Straße^F
via^F

avenue
avenida^F
avenue^F
Querstraße^F/Allee^F
avenue

fire station
parque^M de bomberos^M
caserne^F de pompiers^M
Feuerwache^F
caserma^F dei vigili^M del fuoco^M

cemetery
cementerio^M
cimetière^M
Friedhof^M
cimitero^M

church
iglesia^F
église^F
Kirche^F
chiesa^F

lane
callejón^M
ruelle^F
Gasse^F
vicolo^M

apartment building
bloque^M de apartamentos^M
immeuble^M résidentiel
Wohnblock^M
condominio^M

police station
comisaria^F de policia^F
poste^M de police^F
Polizeirevier^N
stazione^F di polizia^F

park
parque^M
parc^M
Park^M
parco^M

library
biblioteca^F
bibliothèque^F
Bibliothek^F
biblioteca^F

post office
oficina^F de correos^M
bureau^M de poste^F
Postamt^N
ufficio^M postale

service station
estación^F de servicio^M
station^F-service^M
Tankstelle^F
stazione^F di servizio^M

supermarket
supermercado^M
supermarché^M
Supermarkt^M
supermercato^M

museum
museo^M
musée^M
Museum^N
museo^M

car dealer
concesionario^M de automóviles
concessionnaire^M d'automobiles^F
Autohaus^N
concessionaria^F di automobili^M

theater
teatro^M
théâtre^M
Theater^N
teatro^M

hospital
hospital^M
hôpital^M
Krankenhaus^N
ospedale^M

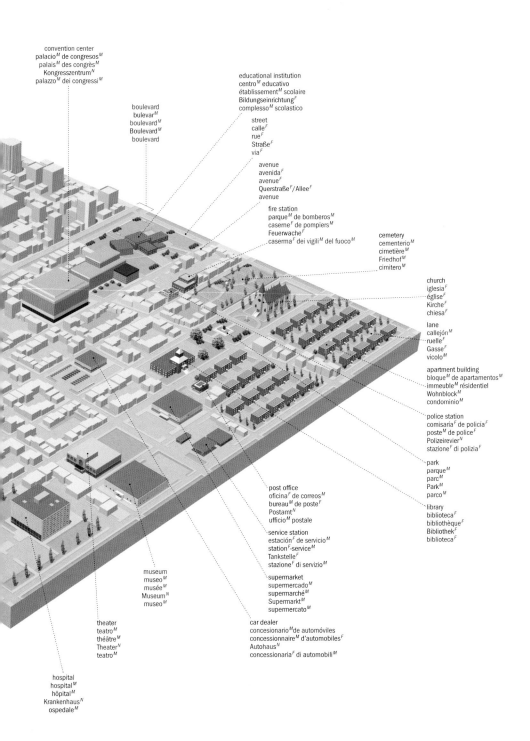

cross section of a street

vista^F transversal de una calle^F | coupe^F d'une rue^F | Straße^F im Querschnitt^M | sezione^F trasversale di una strada^F

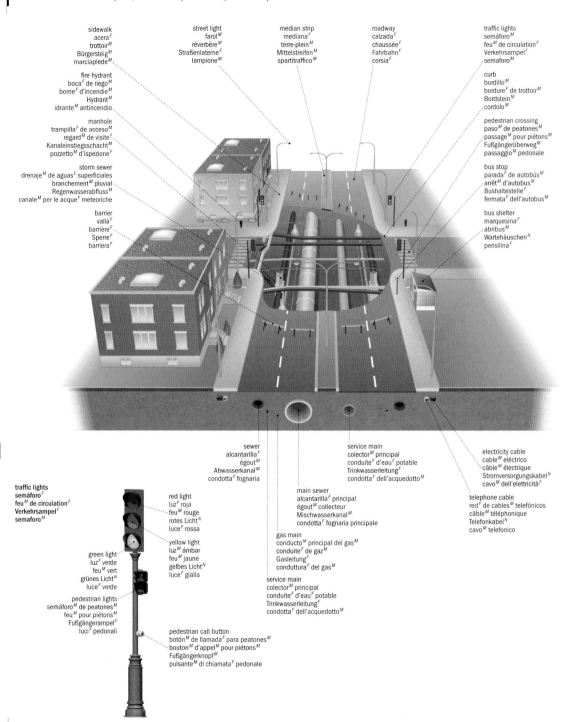

sidewalk
acera^F
trottoir^M
Bürgersteig^M
marciapiede^M

fire hydrant
boca^F de riego^M
borne^F d'incendie^M
Hydrant^M
idrante^M antincendio

manhole
trampilla^F de acceso^M
regard^M de visite^F
Kanaleinstiegsschacht^M
pozzetto^M d'ispezione^F

storm sewer
drenaje^M de aguas^F superficiales
branchement^M pluvial
Regenwasserabfluss^M
canale^M per le acque^F meteoriche

barrier
valla^F
barrière^F
Sperre^F
barriera^F

street light
farol^M
réverbère^M
Straßenlaterne^F
lampione^M

median strip
mediana^F
terre-plein^M
Mittelstreifen^M
spartitraffico^M

roadway
calzada^F
chaussée^F
Fahrbahn^F
corsia^F

traffic lights
semáforo^M
feu^F de circulation^F
Verkehrsampel^F
semaforo^M

curb
bordillo^M
bordure^F de trottoir^M
Bordstein^M
cordolo^M

pedestrian crossing
paso^M de peatones^M
passage^M pour piétons^M
Fußgängerüberweg^M
passaggio^M pedonale

bus stop
parada^F de autobús^M
arrêt^M d'autobus^M
Bushaltestelle^F
fermata^F dell'autobus^M

bus shelter
marquesina^F
abribus^M
Wartehäuschen^N
pensilina^F

sewer
alcantarilla^F
égout^M
Abwasserkanal^M
condotta^F fognaria

service main
colector^M principal
conduite^F d'eau^F potable
Trinkwasserleitung^F
condotta^F dell'acquedotto^M

electricity cable
cable^M eléctrico
câble^M électrique
Stromversorgungskabel^N
cavo^M dell'elettricità^F

traffic lights
semáforo^F
feu^M de circulation^F
Verkehrsampel^F
semaforo^M

main sewer
alcantarilla^F principal
égout^M collecteur
Mischwasserkanal^M
condotta^F fognaria principale

red light
luz^F roja
feu^M rouge
rotes Licht^N
luce^F rossa

telephone cable
red^F de cables^M telefónicos
câble^M téléphonique
Telefonkabel^N
cavo^M telefonico

yellow light
luz^M ámbar
feu^M jaune
gelbes Licht^N
luce^F gialla

gas main
conducto^M principal del gas^M
conduite^F de gaz^M
Gasleitung^F
conduttura^F del gas^M

green light
luz^F verde
feu^M vert
grünes Licht^N
luce^F verde

service main
colector^M principal
conduite^F d'eau^F potable
Trinkwasserleitung^F
condotta^F dell'acquedotto^M

pedestrian lights
semáforo^M de peatones^M
feu^M pour piétons^M
Fußgängerampel^F
luci^F pedonali

pedestrian call button
botón^M de llamada^F para peatones^M
bouton^M d'appel^M pour piétons^M
Fußgängerknopf^M
pulsante^M di chiamata^F pedonale

office building

edificio^M de oficinas^F | édifice^M à bureaux^M | Bürogebäude^N | edificio^M per uffici^M

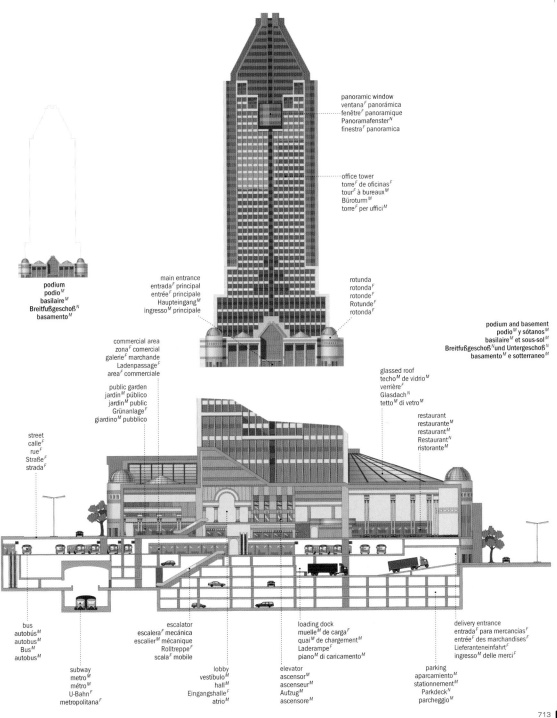

panoramic window
ventana^F panorámica
fenêtre^F panoramique
Panoramafenster^N
finestra^F panoramica

office tower
torre^F de oficinas^F
tour^F à bureaux^M
Büroturm^M
torre^F per uffici^M

rotunda
rotonda^F
rotonde^F
Rotunde^F
rotonda^F

main entrance
entrada^F principal
entrée^F principale
Haupteingang^M
ingresso^M principale

podium
podio^M
basilaire^M
Breitfußgeschoß^N
basamento^M

podium and basement
podio^M y sótanos^M
basilaire^M et sous-sol^M
Breitfußgeschoß^N und Untergeschoß^N
basamento^M e sotterraneo^M

commercial area
zona^F comercial
galerie^F marchande
Ladenpassage^F
area^F commerciale

glassed roof
techo^M de vidrio^M
verrière^F
Glasdach^N
tetto^M di vetro^M

public garden
jardín^M público
jardin^M public
Grünanlage^F
giardino^M pubblico

restaurant
restaurante^M
restaurant^M
Restaurant^N
ristorante^M

street
calle^F
rue^F
Straße^F
strada^F

bus
autobús^M
autobus^M
Bus^M
autobus^M

escalator
escalera^F mecánica
escalier^M mécanique
Rolltreppe^F
scala^F mobile

loading dock
muelle^M de carga^F
quai^M de chargement^M
Laderampe^F
piano^M di caricamento^M

delivery entrance
entrada^F para mercancías^F
entrée^F des marchandises^F
Lieferanteneinfahrt^F
ingresso^M delle merci^F

subway
metro^M
métro^M
U-Bahn^F
metropolitana^F

lobby
vestíbulo^M
hall^M
Eingangshalle^F
atrio^M

elevator
ascensor^M
ascenseur^M
Aufzug^M
ascensore^M

parking
aparcamiento^M
stationnement^M
Parkdeck^N
parcheggio^M

SOCIETY

shopping center

centro^M comercial | centre^M commercial | Einkaufszentrum^N | centro^M commerciale

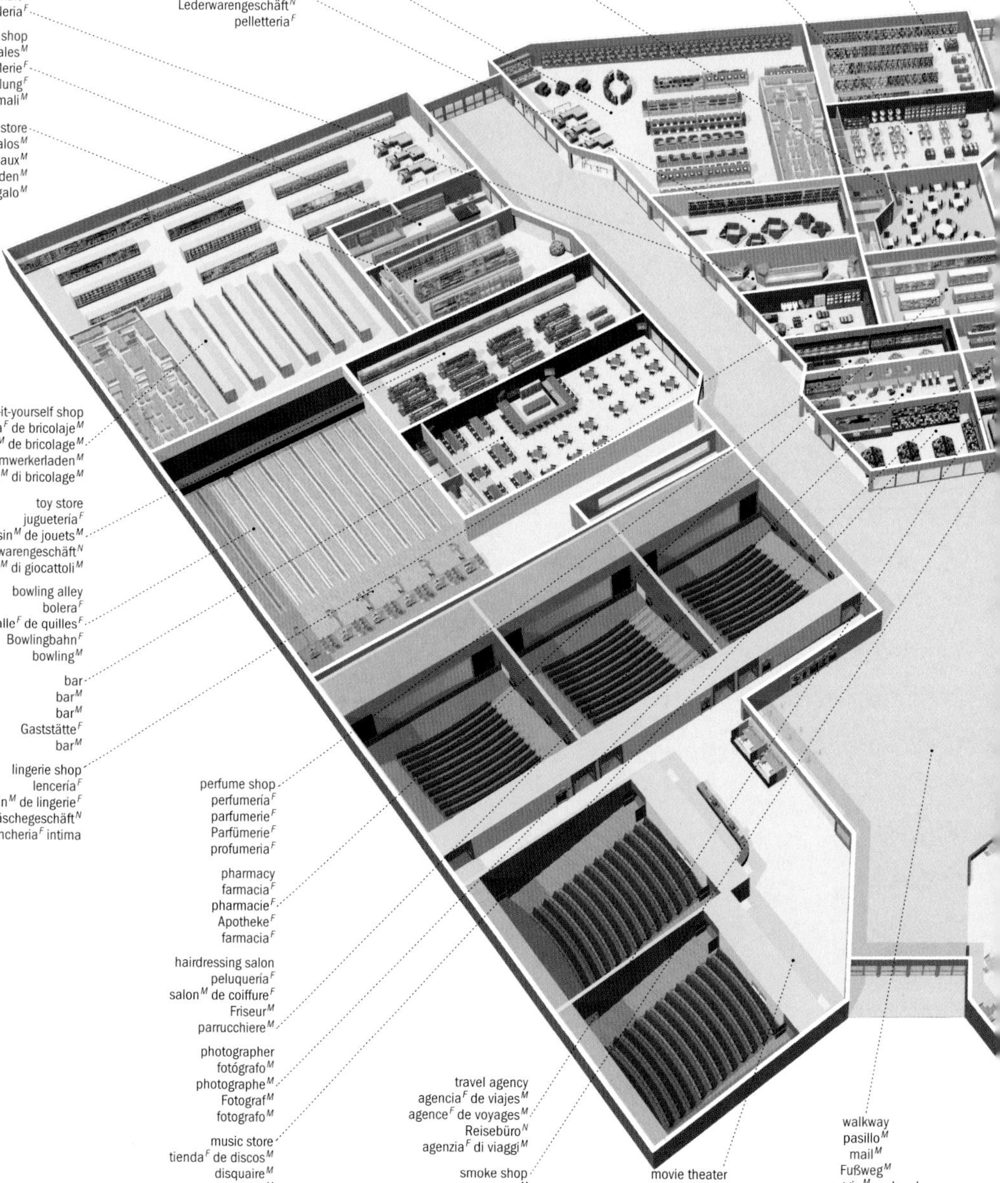

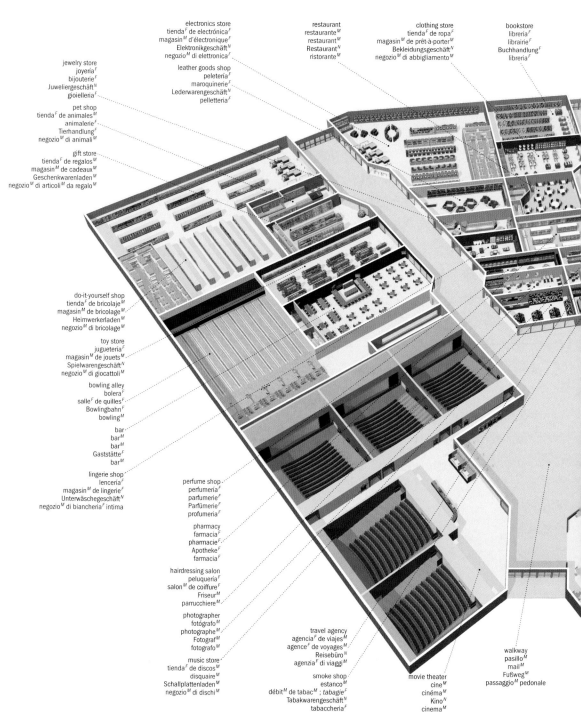

electronics store
tienda^F de electrónica^F
magasin^M d'électronique^F
Elektronikgeschäft^N
negozio^M di elettronica^F

restaurant
restaurante^M
restaurant^M
Restaurant^N
ristorante^M

clothing store
tienda^F de ropa^F
magasin^M de prêt-à-porter^M
Bekleidungsgeschäft^N
negozio^M di abbigliamento^M

bookstore
libreria^F
librairie^F
Buchhandlung^F
libreria^F

jewelry store
joyería^F
bijouterie^F
Juweliergeschäft^N
gioielleria^F

leather goods shop
peletería^F
maroquinerie^F
Lederwarengeschäft^N
pelletteria^F

pet shop
tienda^F de animales^M
animalerie^F
Tierhandlung^F
negozio^M di animali^M

gift store
tienda^F de regalos^M
magasin^M de cadeaux^M
Geschenkwarenladen^M
negozio^M di articoli^M da regalo^M

do-it-yourself shop
tienda^F de bricolaje^M
magasin^M de bricolage^M
Heimwerkerladen^M
negozio^M di bricolage^M

toy store
juguetería^F
magasin^M de jouets^M
Spielwarengeschäft^N
negozio^M di giocattoli^M

bowling alley
bolera^F
salle^F de quilles^F
Bowlingbahn^F
bowling^M

bar
bar^M
bar^M
Gaststätte^F
bar^M

lingerie shop
lencería^F
magasin^M de lingerie^F
Unterwäschegeschäft^N
negozio^M di biancheria^F intima

perfume shop
perfumería^F
parfumerie^F
Parfümerie^F
profumeria^F

pharmacy
farmacia^F
pharmacie^F
Apotheke^F
farmacia^F

hairdressing salon
peluquería^F
salon^M de coiffure^F
Friseur^M
parrucchiere^M

photographer
fotógrafo^M
photographe^M
Fotograf^M
fotografo^M

travel agency
agencia^F de viajes^M
agence^F de voyages^M
Reisebüro^N
agenzia^F di viaggi^M

music store
tienda^F de discos^M
disquaire^M
Schallplattenladen^M
negozio^M di dischi^M

smoke shop
estanco^M
débit^M de tabac^M ; tabagie^F
Tabakwarengeschäft^N
tabaccheria^F

movie theater
cine^M
cinéma^M
Kino^N
cinema^M

walkway
pasillo^M
mail^M
Fußweg^M
passaggio^M pedonale

SOCIETY

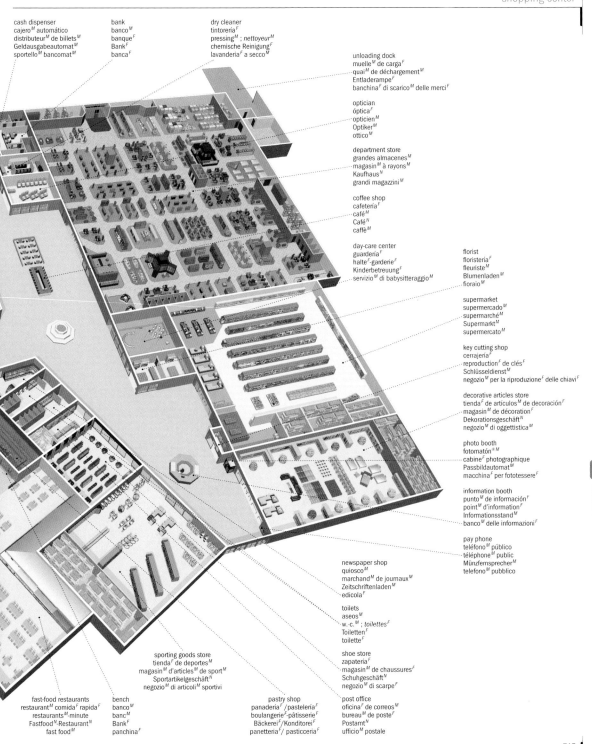

cash dispenser
cajero^M automático
distribuidor^M de billets^M
Geldausgabeautomat^M
sportello^M bancomat^M

bank
banco^M
banque^F
Bank^F
banca^F

dry cleaner
tintorería^F
pressing^M ; nettoyeur^M
chemische Reinigung^F
lavanderia^F a secco^M

unloading dock
muelle^M de carga^F
quai^M de déchargement^M
Entladerampe^F
banchina^F di scarico^M delle merci^F

optician
óptica^F
opticien^M
Optiker^M
ottico^M

department store
grandes almacenes^M
magasin^M à rayons^M
Kaufhaus^N
grandi magazzini^M

coffee shop
cafetería^F
café^M
Café^N
caffè^M

day-care center
guardería^F
halte^F-garderie^F
Kinderbetreuung^F
servizio^M di babysitteraggio^M

florist
floristería^F
fleuriste^M
Blumenladen^M
fioraio^M

supermarket
supermercado^M
supermarché^M
Supermarkt^M
supermercato^M

key cutting shop
cerrajería^F
reproduction^F de clés^F
Schlüsseldienst^M
negozio^M per la riproduzione^F delle chiavi^F

decorative articles store
tienda^F de artículos^M de decoración^F
magasin^M de décoration^F
Dekorationsgeschäft^N
negozio^M di oggettistica^M

photo booth
fotomatón*^M
cabine^F photographique
Passbildautomat^M
macchina^F per fototessere^F

information booth
punto^M de información^F
point^M d'information^F
Informationsstand^M
banco^M delle informazioni^F

pay phone
teléfono^M público
téléphone^M public
Münzfernsprecher^M
telefono^M pubblico

newspaper shop
quiosco^M
marchand^M de journaux^M
Zeitschriftenladen^M
edicola^F

toilets
aseos^M
w.-c.^M ; toilettes^F
Toiletten^F
toilette^F

shoe store
zapatería^F
magasin^M de chaussures^F
Schuhgeschäft^N
negozio^M di scarpe^F

sporting goods store
tienda^F de deportes^M
magasin^M d'articles^M de sport^M
Sportartikelgeschäft^N
negozio^M di articoli^M sportivi

fast-food restaurants
restaurant^M comida^F rapida^F
restaurants^M-minute
Fastfood^N-Restaurant^N
fast food^M

bench
banco^M
banc^M
Bank^F
panchina^F

pastry shop
panadería^F /pastelería^F
boulangerie^F-pâtisserie^F
Bäckerei^F/Konditorei^F
panetteria^F/ pasticceria^F

post office
oficina^F de correos^M
bureau^M de poste^F
Postamt^N
ufficio^M postale

SOCIETY

715

department store

grandes almacenes^M | magasin^M à rayons^M | Kaufhaus^N | grandi magazzini^M

men's underwear
ropa^F interior de hombre^M
sous-vêtements^M d'hommes^M
Herrenunterwäsche^F
biancheria^F intima per uomo^M

swimsuits
trajes^M de baño^M
vêtements^M de bain^M
Bademoden^F
costumi^M da bagno^M

lingerie
lencería^F
lingerie^F
Unterwäsche^F
biancheria^F intima per donna^F

women's suits
trajes^M sastre de señora^F
tailleurs^M
Damenkostüme^N
abiti^M da donna^F

women's nightwear
ropa^F de noche de mujer^F
vêtements^M de nuit^M de femmes^F
Damen^F-Nachtwäsche^F
biancheria^F da notte^F per donna^F

women's shoes
zapatos^M de mujer^F
chaussures^F de femmes^F
Damenschuhe^M
scarpe^F da donna^F

men's suits
trajes^M de hombre^M
costumes^M
Herrenanzüge^M
abiti^M da uomo^M

men's accessories
accesorios^M de hombre^M
accessoires^M d'hommes^M
Herren^M-Accessoires^N
accessori^M da uomo^M

men's shoes
zapatos^M de hombre^M
chaussures^F d'hommes^M
Herrenschuhe^M
scarpe^F da uomo^M

men's pants
pantalones^M
pantalons^M d'hommes^M
Hosen^F
pantaloni^M

men's shirts
camisas^F
chemises^F d'hommes^M
Hemden^N
camicie^F

neckties
corbatas^F
cravates^F
Krawatten^F
cravatte^F

women's casual wear
ropa^F informal de mujer^F
vêtements^M décontractés de femmes^F
Damen^F-Freizeitbekleidung^F
abbigliamento^M casual femminile

stockroom
almacén^M
magasin^M
Lager^N
magazzino^M

running shoes
zapatillas^M de deporte^M
chaussures^F de sport^M
Sportschuhe^M
scarpe^F da ginnastica^F

mattresses and box springs
colchones^M y somieres^M
matelas^M et sommiers^M
Matratzen^F und Matratzenrahmen^M
materassi^M e reti^F

household linen
ropa^F para el hogar^M
linge^M de maison^F
Haushaltswäsche^F
biancheria^F per la casa^F

audiovisual equipment
material^M audiovisual
matériel^M audiovisuel
Audio- und Videobedarf^M
materiale^M audiovisivo

kitchen articles
artículos^M de cocina^F
articles^M de cuisine^F
Haushaltswaren^F
articoli^M da cucina^F

receiving area
área^F de recepción^F
aire^F de réception^F
Warenannahmebereich^M
area^F di ricevimento^M delle merci^F

women's coats
abrigos^M de mujer^F
manteaux^M de femmes^F
Damenjacken^F und -mäntel^M
soprabiti^M da donna^F

women's sweaters
jerséis^M de mujer^F
tricots^M de femmes^F
Damenpullover^M
maglie^F da donna^F

checkouts
cajas^F
caisses^F
Kassen^F
casse^F

unloading docks
muelle^M de carga^F
quais^M de déchargement^M
Entladerampen^F
banchine^F di scarico^M delle merci^F

fitting room
probador^M
cabine^F d'essayage^M
Ankleidekabine^F
camerino^M

women's sportswear
ropa^F de deporte^M de mujer^F
vêtements^M de sport^M de femmes^F
Damen^F-Sportbekleidung^F
abbigliamento^M sportivo femminile

decorative accessories
accesorios^M de decoración^F
accessoires^M de décoration^F
Dekorationsartikel^M
oggettistica^F

major domestic appliances
grandes electrodomésticos^M
gros appareils^M électroménagers
große Elektrohaushaltsgeräte^N
grandi elettrodomestici^M

luggage
maletas^F
bagages^M
Koffer^M und Reisetaschen^F
valigie^F

watches and jewelry
relojes^M y joyería^F
montres^F et bijoux^M
Uhren^F und Schmuck^M
orologi^M e gioielli^M

women's accessories
accesorios^M femeninos
accessoires^M de femmes^F
Damen^F-Accessoires^N
accessori da donna^F

cosmetics
cosméticos^M
cosmétiques^M
Kosmetikartikel^M
prodotti^M di bellezza^F

perfume
perfumes^M
parfum^M
Parfümerie^F
profumeria^F

men's coats
abrigos^M de hombre^M
manteaux^M d'hommes^M
Herrenjacken^F und -mäntel^M
soprabiti^M da uomo^M

men's nightwear
pijamas^M de hombre^M
vêtements^M de nuit^F d'hommes^M
Herren^M-Nachtwäsche^F
biancheria^F da notte^F per uomo^M

men's sportswear
ropa^F de deportes^M de hombre^M
vêtements^M de sport^M d'hommes^M
Herren^M-Sportbekleidung^F
abbigliamento^M sportivo da uomo^M

men's sweaters
jerséis^M de hombre^M
tricots^M d'hommes^M
Herrenpullover^M
maglioni^M da uomo^M

men's casual wear
ropa^F informal de hombre^M
vêtements^M décontractés d'hommes^M
Herren^M-Freizeitbekleidung^F
abbigliamento^M casual maschile

children's shoes
zapatos^M de niños^M
chaussures^F d'enfants^M
Kinderschuhe^M
scarpe^F per bambini^M

girls' wear size 7 to 17
ropa^F para niñas^F de 7 a 17 años^M
vêtements^M de filles^F de 7 à 17 ans^M
Mädchenbekleidung^F 7 bis 17 Jahre^N
abbigliamento^M per ragazze^F dai 7 ai 17 anni^M

boys' wear size 7 to 17
ropa^F para niños^M de 7 a 17 años^M
vêtements^M de garçons^M de 7 à 17 ans^M
Knabenbekleidung^F 7 bis 17 Jahre^N
abbigliamento^M per ragazzi^M dai 7 ai 17 anni^M

boys' wear size 2 to 6
ropa^F para niños^M de 2 a 6 años^M
vêtements^M de garçons^M de 2 à 6 ans^M
Knabenbekleidung^F 2 bis 6 Jahre^N
abbigliamento^M per bambini^M dai 2 ai 6 anni^M

girls' wear size 2 to 6
ropa^F para niñas^F de 2 a 6 años^M
vêtements^M de filles^F de 2 à 6 ans^M
Mädchenbekleidung^F 2 bis 6 Jahre^N
abbigliamento^M per bambine^F dai 2 ai 6 anni^M

children's sportswear
ropa^F de deportes^M para niños^M
vêtements^M de sport^M d'enfants^M
Kinder^N-Sportbekleidung^F
abbigliamento^M sportivo per bambini^M

baby wear
ropa^F de bebé^M
vêtements^M de bébés^M
Babybekleidung^F
abbigliamento^M per bebè^M

candies
confitería^F
confiserie^F
Süßwaren^F
dolciumi^M

checkouts
cajas^F
caisses^F
Kassen^F
casse^F

lobby
vestíbulo^M
vestibule^M
Eingangsbereich^M
atrio^M

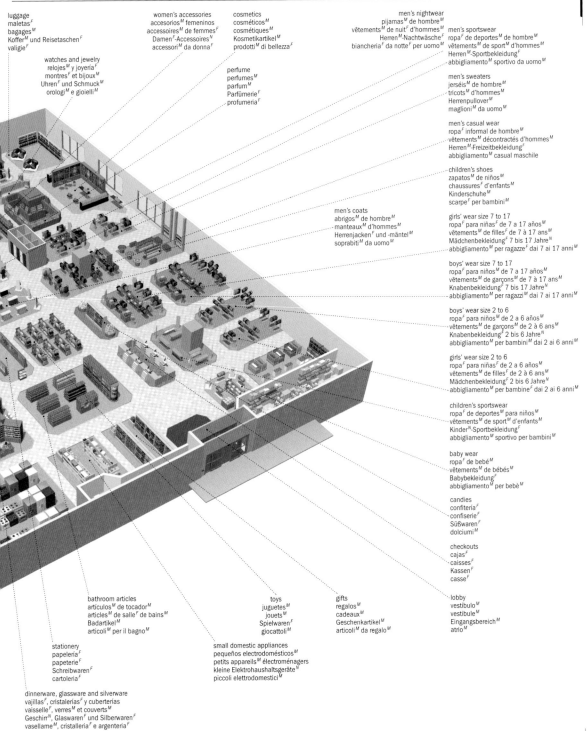

bathroom articles
artículos^M de tocador^M
articles^M de salle^F de bains^M
Badartikel^M
articoli^M per il bagno^M

stationery
papelería^F
papeterie^F
Schreibwaren^F
cartoleria^F

dinnerware, glassware and silverware
vajillas^F, cristalerías^F y cuberterías^F
vaisselle^F, verres^M et couverts^M
Geschirr^N, Glaswaren^F und Silberwaren^F
vasellame^M, cristalleria^F e argenteria^F

toys
juguetes^M
jouets^M
Spielwaren^F
giocattoli^M

small domestic appliances
pequeños electrodomésticos^M
petits appareils^M électroménagers
kleine Elektrohaushaltsgeräte^N
piccoli elettrodomestici^M

gifts
regalos^M
cadeaux^M
Geschenkartikel^M
articoli^M da regalo^M

convention center

palacio^M de congresos^M | palais^M des congrès^M | Kongresszentrum^N | palazzo^M dei congressi^M

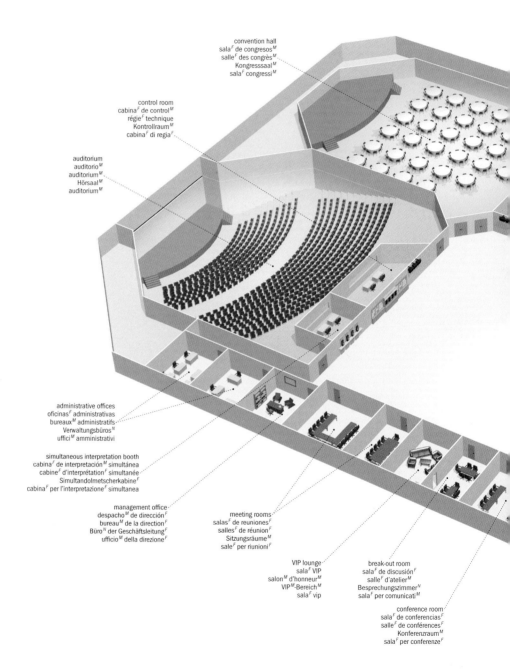

convention hall
sala^F de congresos^M
salle^F des congrès^M
Kongresssaal^M
sala^F congressi^M

control room
cabina^F de control^M
régie^F technique
Kontrollraum^M
cabina^F di regia^F

auditorium
auditorio^M
auditorium^M
Hörsaal^M
auditorium^M

administrative offices
oficinas^F administrativas
bureaux^M administratifs
Verwaltungsbüros^N
uffici^M amministrativi

simultaneous interpretation booth
cabina^F de interpretación^M simultánea
cabine^F d'interprétation^F simultanée
Simultandolmetscherkabine^F
cabina^F per l'interpretazione^F simultanea

management office
despacho^M de dirección^F
bureau^M de la direction^F
Büro^N der Geschäftsleitung^F
ufficio^M della direzione^F

meeting rooms
salas^F de reuniones^F
salles^F de réunion^F
Sitzungsräume^M
sale^F per riunioni^F

VIP lounge
sala^F VIP
salon^M d'honneur^M
VIP^M-Bereich^M
sala^F vip

break-out room
sala^F de discusión^F
salle^F d'atelier^M
Besprechungszimmer^N
sala^F per comunicati^M

conference room
sala^F de conferencias^F
salle^F de conférences^F
Konferenzraum^M
sala^F per conferenze^F

organizers' offices
oficinas^F de los organizadores^M
bureaux^M des organisateurs^M
Veranstalterbüros^N
uffici^M degli organizzatori^M

exhibition stand
stand^M de exposición^F
stand^M d'exposition^F
Ausstellungsstand^M
stand^M espositivo

movable panel
tabique^M móvil
cloison^F mobile
versetzbare Trennwand^F
pannello^M mobile

exhibit hall
sala^F de exposición^F
salle^F d'exposition^F
Ausstellungsraum^M
sala^F delle esposizioni^F

unloading dock
muelle^M de carga^F
quai^M de déchargement^M
Entladerampe^F
banchina^F di scarico^M

kitchen
cocina^F
cuisine^F
Küche^F
cucina^F

bar
bar^M
bar^M
Bar^F
bar^M

restaurant
restaurante^M
restaurant^M
Restaurant^N
ristorante^M

hall
vestíbulo^M
hall^M
Halle^F
hall^F

toilets
aseo^M
w.-c.^M ; *toilettes*^F
Toilette^F
toilette^F

cloakroom
guardarropa^M
vestiaire^M
Garderobe^F
guardaroba^M

information desk
punto^M de información^F
comptoir^M de renseignements^M
Informationsschalter^M
banco^M delle informazioni^F

ticket office
taquilla^F
billetterie^F
Kasse^F
biglietteria^F

security service
servicio^M de seguridad^F
service^M de sécurité^F
Sicherheitsdienst^M
servizio^M di sicurezza^F

manual revolving doors
puertas^F giratorias manuales
portes^F à tambour^M manuelles
Drehtüren^F
porte^F girevoli manuali

entrance
entrada^F
entrée^F
Eingang^M
entrata^F

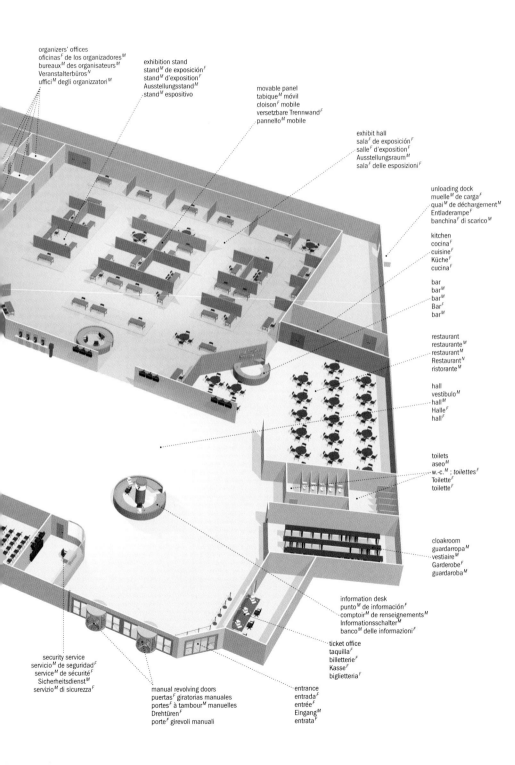

restaurant

restaurante ^{M} | restaurant ^{M} | Restaurant ^{M} | ristorante ^{M}

store room
despensa ^{F}
salle ^{F} d'entreposage ^{M}
Lagerraum ^{M}
magazzino ^{M}

office
oficina ^{F}
bureau ^{M}
Büro ^{N}
ufficio ^{M}

refrigerated display case
mostrador ^{M} frigorífico
présentoir ^{M} réfrigéré
Kühlvitrine ^{F}
armadio ^{M} frigorifero ^{M}

customer's restrooms
aseos ^{M} para los clientes ^{M}
w.-c. ^{M} ; toilettes ^{F}
Gästetoiletten ^{F}
toilette ^{F} per i clienti ^{M}

wine steward
sumiller ^{M}
sommelier ^{M}
Weinkellner ^{M}, Sommelier ^{M}
sommelier ^{M}

refrigerator
frigorífico ^{M}
réfrigérateur ^{M}
Kühlschrank ^{M}
frigorifero ^{M}

wine cellar
bodega ^{F}
cave ^{F} à vins ^{M}
Weinkeller ^{M}
cantina ^{F} dei vini ^{M}

service table
mesa ^{F} de servicio ^{M}
table ^{F} de service ^{M}
Serviertisch ^{M}
tavolo ^{M} di servizio ^{M}

customers' cloakroom
guardarropa ^{M} de los clientes ^{M}
vestiaire ^{M} des clients ^{M}
Gästegarderobe ^{F}
guardaroba ^{M} dei clienti ^{M}

freezer
congelador ^{M}
congélateur ^{M}
Gefrierschrank ^{M}
congelatore ^{M}

buffet
buffet ^{M}
buffet ^{M}
Buffet ^{N}
buffet ^{M}

staff entrance
entrada ^{F} del personal ^{M}
entrée ^{F} du personnel ^{M}
Personaleingang ^{M}
ingresso ^{M} del personale ^{M}

maître d'hôtel
maître ^{M}
maître ^{M} d'hôtel ^{M}
Oberkellner ^{M}
maître ^{M}

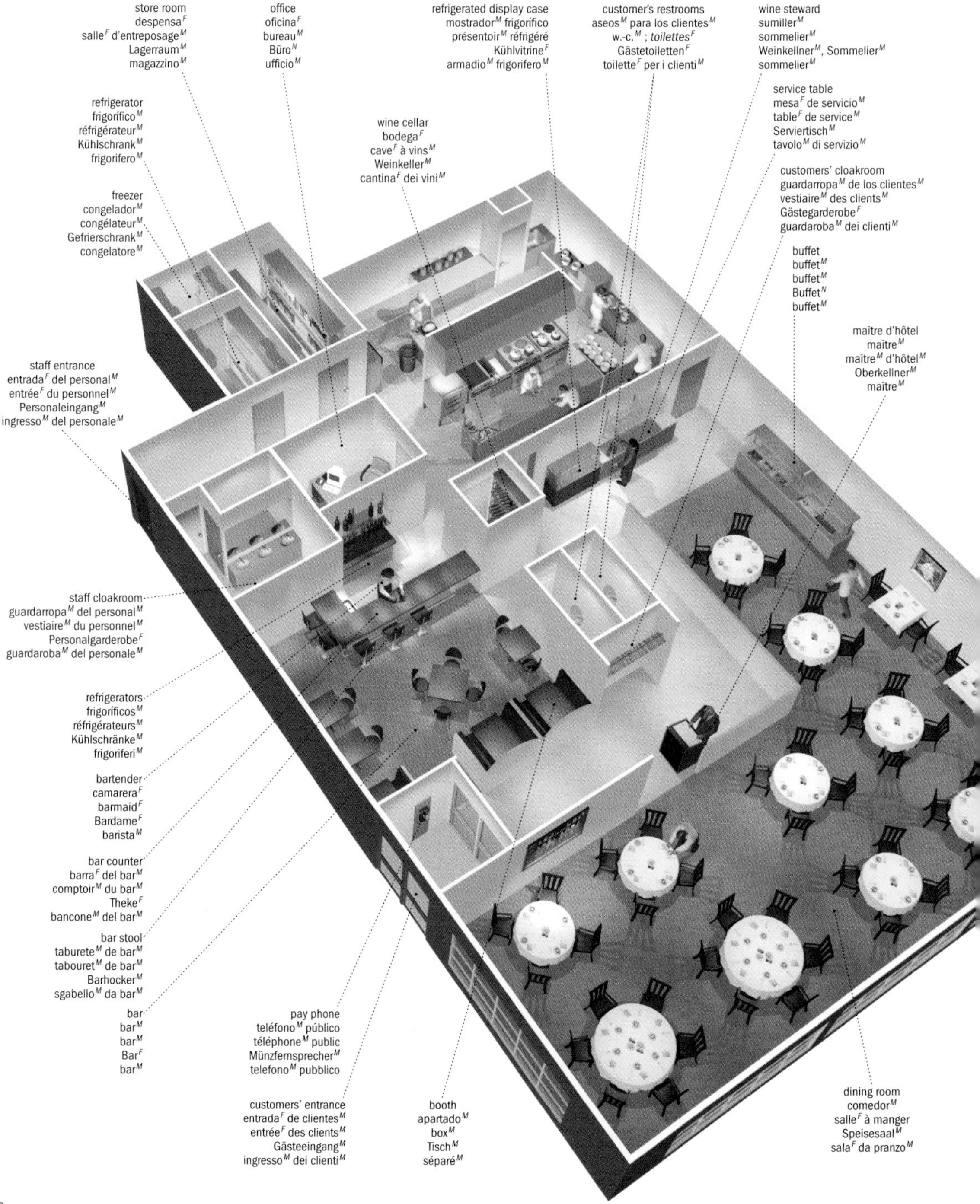

staff cloakroom
guardarropa ^{M} del personal ^{M}
vestiaire ^{M} du personnel ^{M}
Personalgarderobe ^{F}
guardaroba ^{M} del personale ^{M}

refrigerators
frigoríficos ^{M}
réfrigérateurs ^{M}
Kühlschränke ^{M}
frigoriferi ^{M}

bartender
camarera ^{F}
barmaid ^{F}
Bardame ^{F}
barista ^{M}

bar counter
barra ^{F} del bar ^{M}
comptoir ^{M} du bar ^{M}
Theke ^{F}
bancone ^{M} del bar ^{M}

bar stool
taburete ^{M} de bar ^{M}
tabouret ^{M} de bar ^{M}
Barhocker ^{M}
sgabello ^{M} da bar ^{M}

bar
bar ^{M}
bar ^{M}
Bar ^{M}
bar ^{M}

pay phone
teléfono ^{M} público
téléphone ^{M} public
Münzfernsprecher ^{M}
telefono ^{M} pubblico

customers' entrance
entrada ^{F} de clientes ^{M}
entrée ^{F} des clients ^{M}
Gästeeingang ^{M}
ingresso ^{M} dei clienti ^{M}

booth
apartado ^{M}
box ^{M}
Tisch ^{M}
séparé ^{M}

dining room
comedor ^{M}
salle ^{F} à manger
Speisesaal ^{M}
sala ^{F} da pranzo ^{M}

kitchen
cocina^F
cuisine^F
Küche^F
cucina^F

hood
campana^F
hotte^F
Dunstabzugshaube^F
cappa^F

pot-and-pan sink
fregadero^M para las cazuelas^F
évier^M à batterie^F de cuisine^F
Spülbecken^N für Töpfe^M und Pfannen^F
lavandino^M per le pentole^F

dishwasher
lavavajillas^M
lave-vaisselle^F
Geschirrspüler^M
lavastoviglie^F

station chef
chef^M
chef^M de partie^F
Koch^M
aiuto^M cuoco^M

cleaning supplies
productos^M de limpieza^F
produits^M de nettoyage^M
Putzmittel^N
prodotti^M per la pulizia^F

dishwasher
lavavajillas^M
plongeur^M
Spüler^M
lavapiatti^M

work top
encimera^F
plan^M de travail^M
Arbeitsplatte^F
piano^M di lavoro^M

prerinse sink
fregadero^M de prelavado^M
évier^M de prérinçage^M
Vorspülbecken^N
lavandino^M per il prelavaggio^M

ice machine
máquina^F de hielo
machine^F à glaçons^M
Eismaschine^F
macchina^F del ghiaccio^M

dirty dish table
mesa^F para la vajilla^F sucia
table^F pour la vaisselle^F sale
Ablage^F für schmutziges Geschirr^N
tavolo^M per i piatti^M sporchi

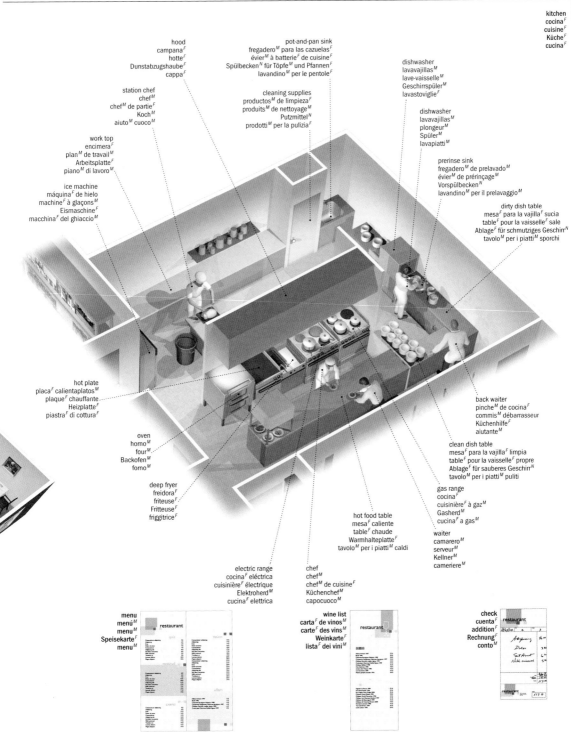

hot plate
placa^F calientaplatos^M
plaque^F chauffante
Heizplatte^F
piastra^F di cottura^F

back waiter
pinche^F de cocina^F
commis^M débarrasseur
Küchenhilfe^F
aiutante^F

oven
horno^M
four^M
Backofen^M
forno^M

clean dish table
mesa^F para la vajilla^F limpia
table^F pour la vaisselle^F propre
Ablage^F für sauberes Geschirr^N
tavolo^M per i piatti^M puliti

deep fryer
freidora^F
friteuse^F
Fritteuse^F
friggitrice^F

gas range
cocina^F
cuisinière^F à gaz^M
Gasherd^M
cucina^F a gas^M

hot food table
mesa^F caliente
table^F chaude
Warmhalteplatte^F
tavolo^M per i piatti^M caldi

waiter
camarero^M
serveur^M
Kellner^M
cameriere^M

electric range
cocina^F eléctrica
cuisinière^F électrique
Elektroherd^M
cucina^F elettrica

chef
chef^M
chef^M de cuisine^F
Küchenchef^M
capocuoco^M

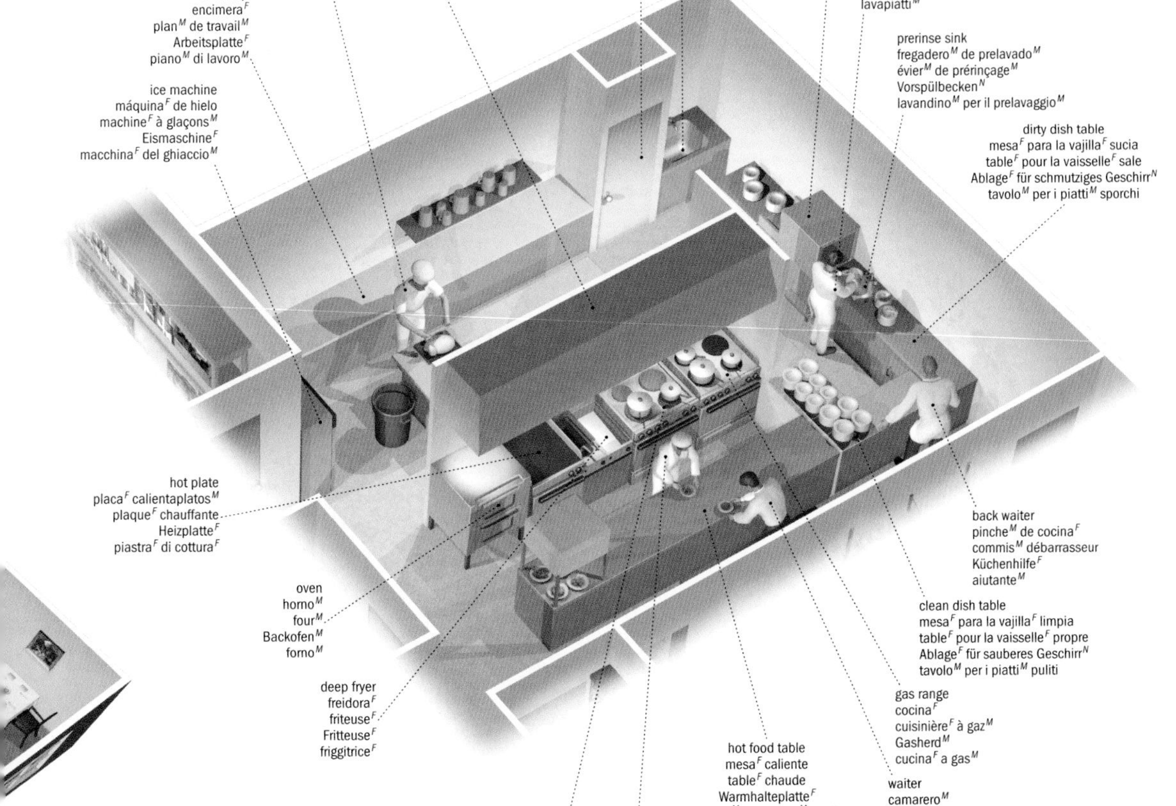

menu
menú^M
menu^M
Speisekarte^F
menu^M

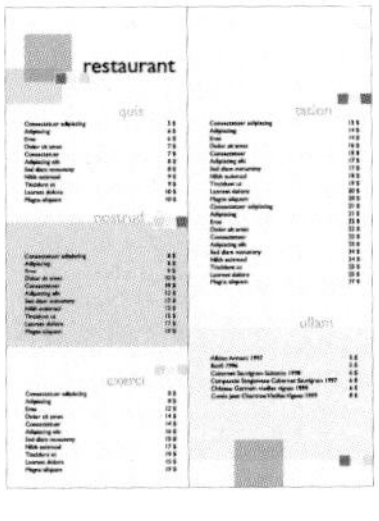

wine list
carta^F de vinos^M
carte^F des vins^M
Weinkarte^F
lista^F dei vini^M

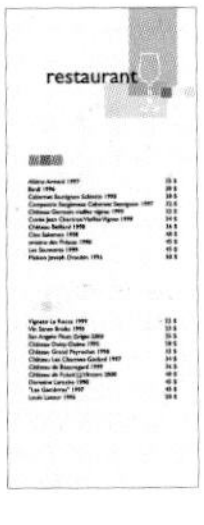

check
cuenta^F
addition^F
Rechnung^F
conto^M

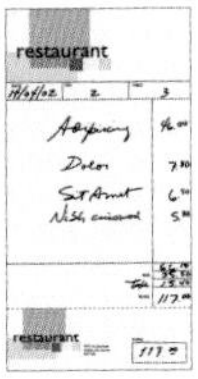

self-service restaurant/cafeteria

restaurante^M de autoservicio^M | restaurant^M libre-service | Selbstbedienungsrestaurant^N | self-service^M

work top
encimera^F
plan^M de travail^M
Arbeitsplatte^F
piano^M di lavoro^M

sink
fregadero^M
évier^M
Spülbecken^N
lavandino^M

bread and cheese
pan^M y queso^M
pain^M et fromage^M
Brot^N und Käse^M
pane^M e formaggio^M

hot food
platos^M calientes
mets^M chauds
warme Speisen^F
piatti^M caldi

cooking utensils
batería^F de cocina^F
batterie^F de cuisine^F
Kochgeschirr^N
batteria^F da cucina^F

soup
sopa^F
soupe^F
Suppe^F
minestra^F

cold room
cámara^F fría
chambre^F froide
Kühlraum^M
cella^F frigorifera

store room
despensa^F
salle^F d'entreposage^M
Lagerraum^M
magazzino^M

hors d'oeuvres and cold food
entremeses^M y platos^M fríos
hors-d'œuvre^M et mets^M froids
Vorspeisen^F und kalte Gerichte^N
antipasti^M e piatti^M freddi

salads
ensaladas^F
salades^F
Salate^M
insalate^F

self-service display case
mostrador^M de autoservicio^M
comptoir^M libre-service
Selbstbedienungstheke^F
banco^M del self-service^M

trays
bandejas^M
plateaux^M
Tabletts^N
vassoi^M

refrigerator
frigorífico^M
réfrigérateur^M
Kühlschrank^M
frigorifero^M

range hood
campana^F
hotte^F
Dunstabzugshaube^F
cappa^F

silverware and napkins
cubiertos^M y servilletas^F
couverts^M et serviettes^F
Besteck^N und Servietten^F
posate^F e tovaglioli^M

steamer
vaporera^F
cuiseur^M-vapeur^F
Dampfkocher^M
cucina^F a vapore^M

counter
barra^F
comptoir^M
Theke^F
bancone^M

oven
horno^M
four^M
Backofen^M
forno^M

stool
taburete^M
tabouret^M
Hocker^M
sgabello^M

range
cocina^F
cuisinière^F
Herd^M
cucina^F

cooking area
área^F de cocina^F
centre^M de cuisson^F
Kochbereich^M
zona^F cottura

cooking plate
placa^F de cocina^F
plaque^F de cuisson^F
Kochplatte^F
piastra^F di cottura^F

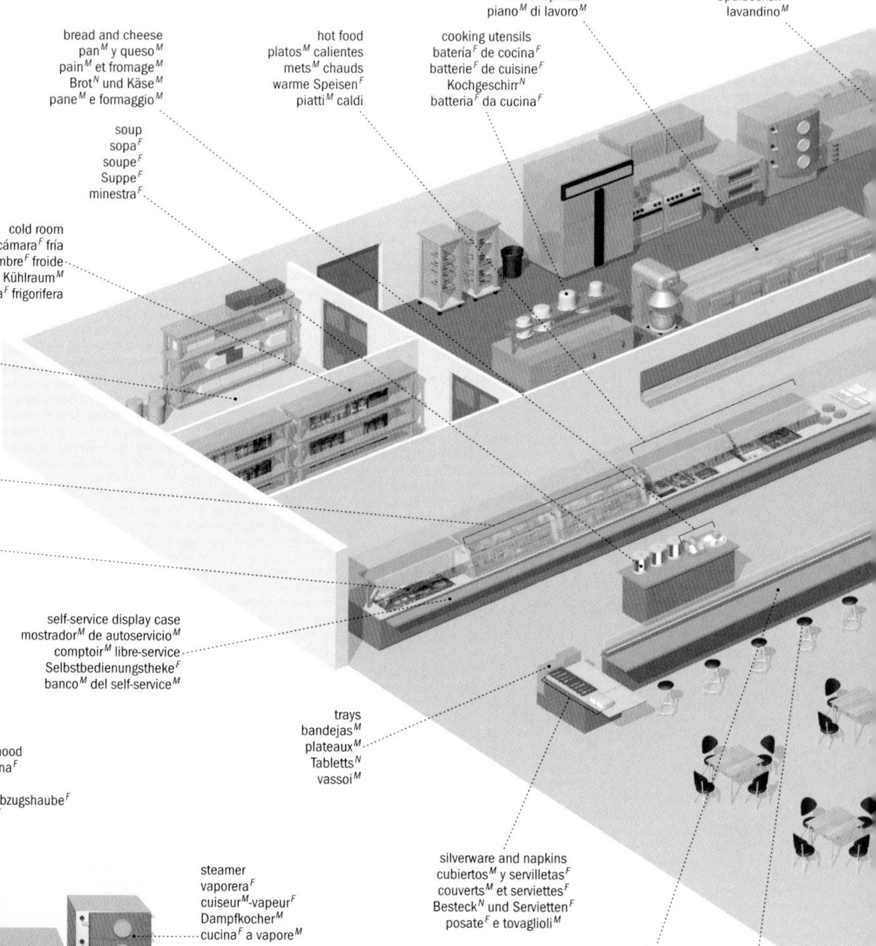

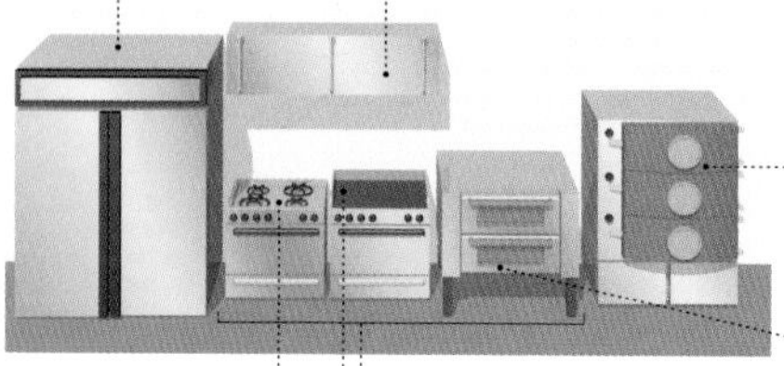

SOCIETY

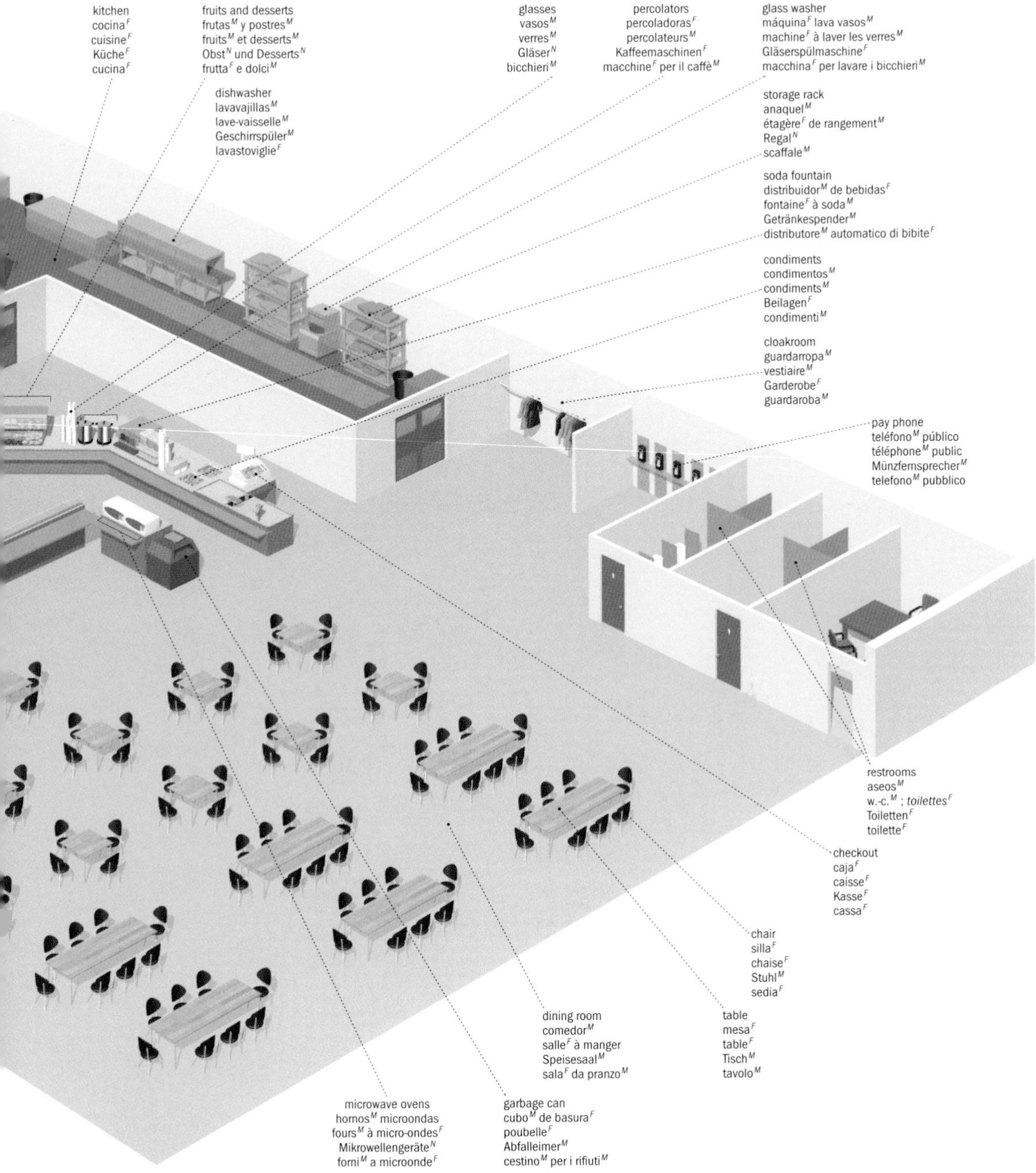

kitchen
cocina^F
cuisine^F
Küche^F
cucina^F

fruits and desserts
frutas^M y postres^M
fruits^M et desserts^M
Obst^N und Desserts^N
frutta^F e dolci^M

dishwasher
lavavajillas^M
lave-vaisselle^F
Geschirrspüler^M
lavastoviglie^F

glasses
vasos^M
verres^M
Gläser^N
bicchieri^M

percolators
percoladoras^F
percolateurs^M
Kaffeemaschinen^F
macchine^F per il caffè^M

glass washer
máquina^F lava vasos^M
machine^F à laver les verres^M
Gläserspülmaschine^F
macchina^F per lavare i bicchieri^M

storage rack
anaquel^M
étagère^F de rangement^M
Regal^N
scaffale^M

soda fountain
distribuidor^M de bebidas^F
fontaine^F à soda^M
Getränkespender^M
distributore^M automatico di bibite^F

condiments
condimentos^M
condiments^M
Beilagen^F
condimenti^M

cloakroom
guardarropa^M
vestiaire^M
Garderobe^F
guardaroba^M

pay phone
teléfono^M público
téléphone^M public
Münzfernsprecher^M
telefono^M pubblico

restrooms
aseos^M
w.-c.^M ; *toilettes^F*
Toiletten^F
toilette^F

checkout
caja^F
caisse^F
Kasse^F
cassa^F

chair
silla^F
chaise^F
Stuhl^M
sedia^F

table
mesa^F
table^F
Tisch^M
tavolo^M

dining room
comedor^M
salle^F à manger
Speisesaal^M
sala^F da pranzo^M

microwave ovens
hornos^M microondas
fours^M à micro-ondes^F
Mikrowellengeräte^N
forni^M a microonde^F

garbage can
cubo^M de basura^F
poubelle^F
Abfalleimer^M
cestino^M per i rifiuti^M

SOCIETY

723

hotel

hotel^M | hôtel^M | Hotel^N | albergo^M

reception level
nivel^M de la recepción^F
niveau^M de la réception^F
Empfangsebene^F
piano^M della reception^F

kitchen
cocina^F
cuisine^F
Küche^F
cucina^F

food reserves
despensa^F
réserves^F alimentaires
Vorratsschrank^M
dispensa^F

janitor's closet
portería^F
local^M d'entretien^M
Portierszimmer^N
stanzino^M del portiere^M

unloading dock
carga^F y descarga^F
quai^M de déchargement^M
Entladerampe^F
banchina^F di scarico^M delle merci^F

laundry
lavandería^F
buanderie^F
Wäscherei^F
lavanderia^F

linen room
lencería^F
lingerie^F
Wäschekammer^F
locale^M per la biancheria^F

gentlemen's restroom
aseo^M de caballeros^M
w.-c.^M hommes^M ; toilettes^F hommes^M
Herrentoilette^F
toilette^F degli uomini^M

dining room
comedor^M
salle^F à manger
Speisesaal^M
sala^F da pranzo^M

screen
pantalla^F
écran^M
Leinwand^F
schermo^M

meeting room
sala^F de reuniones^F
salle^F de réunion^F
Sitzungssaal^M
sala^F per riunioni^F

ladies' restroom
aseo^M de señoras^F
w.-c.^M femmes^F ; toilettes^F femmes^F
Damentoilette^F
toilette^F delle donne^F

cocktail lounge
salón^M bar
bar^M-salon^M
Cocktailbar^F
sala^F per i cocktail^M

office
despacho^M
bureau^M
Büro^N
ufficio^M

stairs
escaleras^F
escalier^M
Treppe^F
scale^F

elevator
ascensor^M
ascenseur^M
Aufzug^M
ascensore^M

front desk
recepción^F
réception^F
Empfang^M
reception^F

lounge
salón^M
salon^M d'attente^F
Aufenthaltsraum^M
salotto^M

hall
vestíbulo^M
hall^M
Empfangshalle^F
hall^F

lobby
entrada^F
vestibule^M
Vorhalle^F
atrio^M

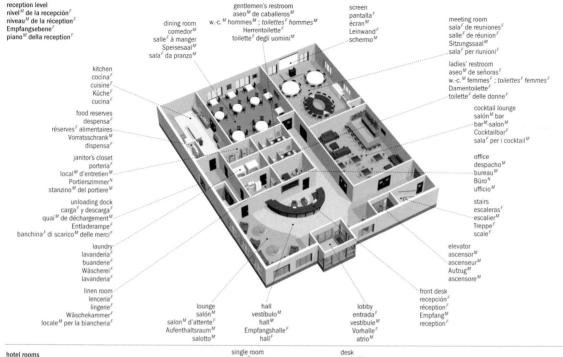

hotel rooms
habitación^F de hotel^M
chambres^F d'hôtel^M
Hotelzimmer^N
camera^F d'albergo^M

television set
televisión^F
téléviseur^M
Fernsehgerät^N
televisione^F

mirror
espejo^M
miroir^M
Spiegel^M
specchio^M

bathroom
baño^M
salle^F de bains^M
Bad^N
stanza^F da bagno^M

sink
lavabo^M
lavabo^M
Waschtisch^M
lavandino^M

toilet
inodoro^M
w.-c.^M ; toilette^F
WC^N
water^M

bath and shower
bañera^F y ducha^F
baignoire^F et douche^F
Badewanne^F und Dusche^F
vasca^F da bagno^M e doccia^F

single room
habitación^F individual
chambre^F simple
Einzelzimmer^N
camera^F matrimoniale

double bed
cama^F doble
lit^M à deux places^F
Doppelbett^N
letto^M matrimoniale

desk
escritorio^M
bureau^M
Schreibtisch^M
scrivania^F

bedside lamp
lámpara^F de cabecera^F
lampe^F de chevet^M
Nachttischlampe^F
lampada^F da comodino^M

telephone
teléfono^M
téléphone^M
Telefon^N
telefono^M

bedside table
mesilla^F de noche^F
table^F de chevet^M
Nachttisch^M
comodino^M

single bed
cama^F individual
lit^M à une place^F
Einzelbett^N
letto^M singolo

love seat
sofá^M de dos plazas^F
causeuse^F
zweisitziges Sofa^N
divano^M a due posti^M

double room
habitación^M doble
chambre^F double
Doppelzimmer^N
camera^F doppia

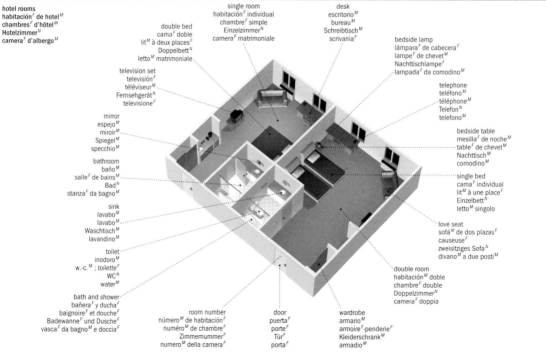

room number
número^M de habitación^F
numéro^M de chambre^F
Zimmernummer^F
numero^M della camera^F

door
puerta^F
porte^F
Tür^F
porta^F

wardrobe
armario^M
armoire^F-penderie^F
Kleiderschrank^M
armadio^M

common symbols

simbolos[M] de uso[M] común | symboles[M] d'usage[M] courant | allgemeine Zeichen[N] | simboli[M] comuni

men's restroom
aseoss[M] de caballeros[M]
toilettes[F] pour hommes[M]
Toiletten[F] (Herren[M])
toilette[F] (uomini[M])

women's restroom
aseos[M] de señoras[F]
toilettes[F] pour dames[F]
Toiletten[F] (Damen[F])
toilette[F] (donne[F])

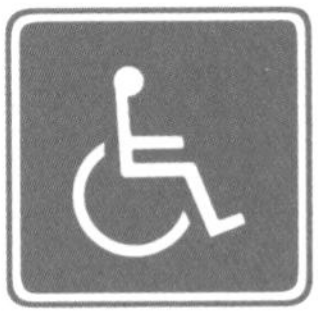

wheelchair access
acceso[M] para minusválidos[M]
accès[M] pour handicapés[M] physiques
Zugang[M] für Behinderte[M]
accesso[M] per i portatori[M] di handicap[M]

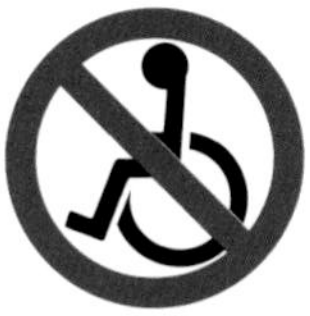

no wheelchair access
prohibido usar silla[F] de ruedas[F]
ne pas utiliser avec un fauteuil[M] roulant
Verbot für Rollstuhlfahrer[M]
accesso[M] non consentito alle sedie[F] a rotelle[M]

camping (trailer and tent)
zona[F] para acampar y para caravanas[F]
camping[M] et caravaning[M]
Camping[N] für Zelte[N] und Wohnwagen[M]
area[F] per campeggio[M] e caravan[M]

picnic area
zona[F] de comidas[F] campestres
pique-nique[M]
Rastplatz[M]
area[F] per pic-nic[M]

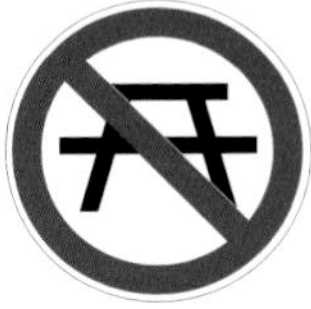

picnics prohibited
prohibido hacer comidas[F] campestres
pique-nique[M] interdit
Picknick[N] verboten
vietato fare pic-nic[M]

camping (tent)
zona[F] para acampar
camping[M]
Zeltplatz[M]
campeggio[M]

camping prohibited
prohibido acampar
camping[M] interdit
Zelten[N] verboten
vietato fare campeggio[M]

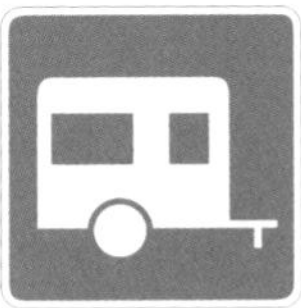

camping (trailer)
zona[F] para caravanas[F]
caravaning[M]
Camping[N] für Wohnwagen[M]
area[F] per caravan[M]

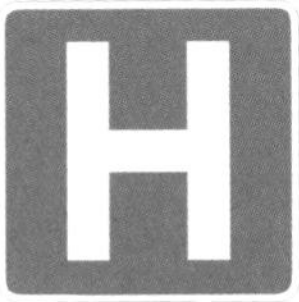

hospital
hospital[M]
hôpital[M]
Krankenhaus[N]
ospedale[M]

coffee shop
cafeteria[F]
casse-croûte[M]
Cafeteria[F]
punto[M] di ristoro[M]

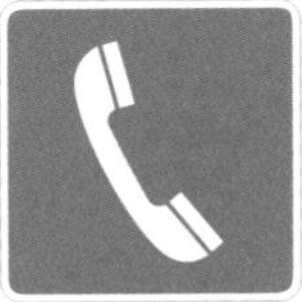

telephone
teléfono[M]
téléphone[M]
Telefon[N]
telefono[M]

restaurant
restaurante[M]
restaurant[M]
Restaurant[N]
ristorante[M]

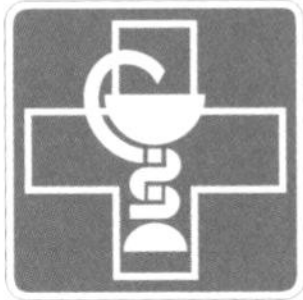

pharmacy
farmacia[F]
pharmacie[F]
Apotheke[F]
farmacia[F]

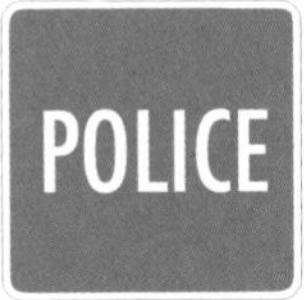

police
policia[F]
police[F]
Polizei[F]
polizia[F]

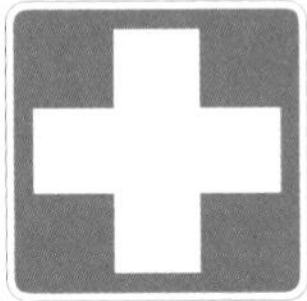

first aid
puesto[M] de socorro[M]
premiers soins[M]
Erste Hilfe[F]
pronto soccorso[M]

service station
gasolinera[F]
poste[M] de carburant[M]
Tankstelle[F]
stazione[F] di rifornimento[M]

fire extinguisher
extintor[M] de incendios[M]
extincteur[M] d'incendie[M]
Feuerlöscher[M]
estintore[M]

information
información[F]
renseignements[M]
Information[F]
informazioni[F]

information
información[F]
renseignements[M]
Information[F]
informazioni[F]

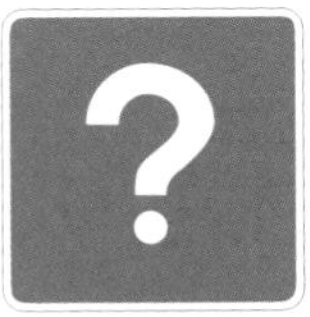

lost and found articles
oficina[F] de objetos[M] perdidos
articles[M] perdus et retrouvés
Fundbüro[N]
oggetti[M] smarriti

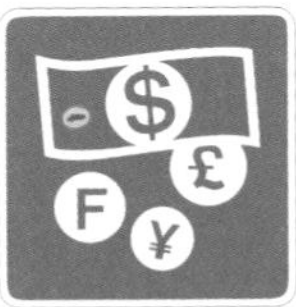

currency exchange
cambio[M]
change[M]
Geldwechsel[M]
cambio[M]

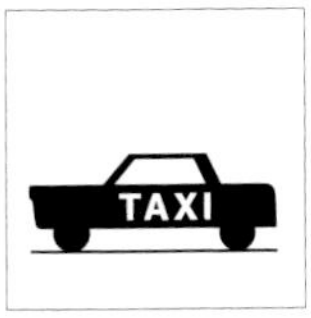

taxi transportation
servicio[M] de taxis[M]
transport[M] par taxi[M]
Taxi[N]
taxi[M]

SOCIETY

725

prison

cárcel^F | prison^F | Justizvollzugsanstalt^F | carcere^M

control of staff entries and exits
control^M de entrada^F y salida^F del personal^F
contrôle^M des entrées^F et sorties^F du personnel^M
Personalein- und -ausgangskontrolle^F
controllo^M dell'entrata^F e dell'uscita^F del personale^M

staff entrance
entrada^F del personal^M
entrée^F du personnel^M
Personaleingang^M
ingresso^M del personale^M

library
biblioteca^F
bibliothèque^F
Bibliothek^F
biblioteca^F

governor's office
despacho^F del director^M
bureau^M du directeur^M
Büro^N des Direktors^M
ufficio^M del direttore^M

assistant governor's office
despacho^F del subdirector^M
bureau^M du directeur^M adjoint
Büro^N des stellvertretenden Direktors^M
ufficio^M del vicedirettore^M

office
oficina^F
bureau^M
Büro^N
ufficio^M

visitors' front office
oficina^F de recepción^F de visitantes^M
bureau^M d'accueil^M des visiteurs^M
Empfangsraum^M für Besucher^M
ufficio^M di accettazione^F dei visitatori^M

visitors' entrance
entrada^M de los visitantes^M
entrée^F des visiteurs^M
Besuchereingang^M
ingresso^M dei visitatori^M

walk-through metal detector
pórtico^M detector^M de metales^M
portique^M détecteur de métal^M
Durchgangsmetalldetektor^M
metal detector^M a porta^F

visitors' waiting room
sala^F de espera^F de visitantes^M
salle^F d'attente^F des visiteurs^M
Warteraum^M für Besucher^M
sala^F d'attesa^F dei visitatori^M

coatroom
guardarropa^M
vestiaire^M
Garderobe^F
guardaroba^M

patrol wagon
coche^M celular
voiture^F cellulaire
Gefangenentransporter^M
cellulare^M

garage
garaje^M
garage^M
Garage^F
garage^M

inmates' entrance
entrada^M de detenidos^M
entrée^F des détenus^M
Insasseneingang^M
ingresso^M dei detenuti^M

inmates' admission office
oficina^F de admisión^F de los detenidos^M
bureau^M d'admission^F des détenus^M
Insassenaufnahme^F
ufficio^M d'ammissione^F dei detenuti^M

laundry
lavandería^F
buanderie^F
Wäscherei^F
lavanderia^F

workshop
taller^M
atelier^M
Werkstatt^F
laboratorio^M

chapel
capilla^M
chapelle^F
Kapelle^F
cappella^F

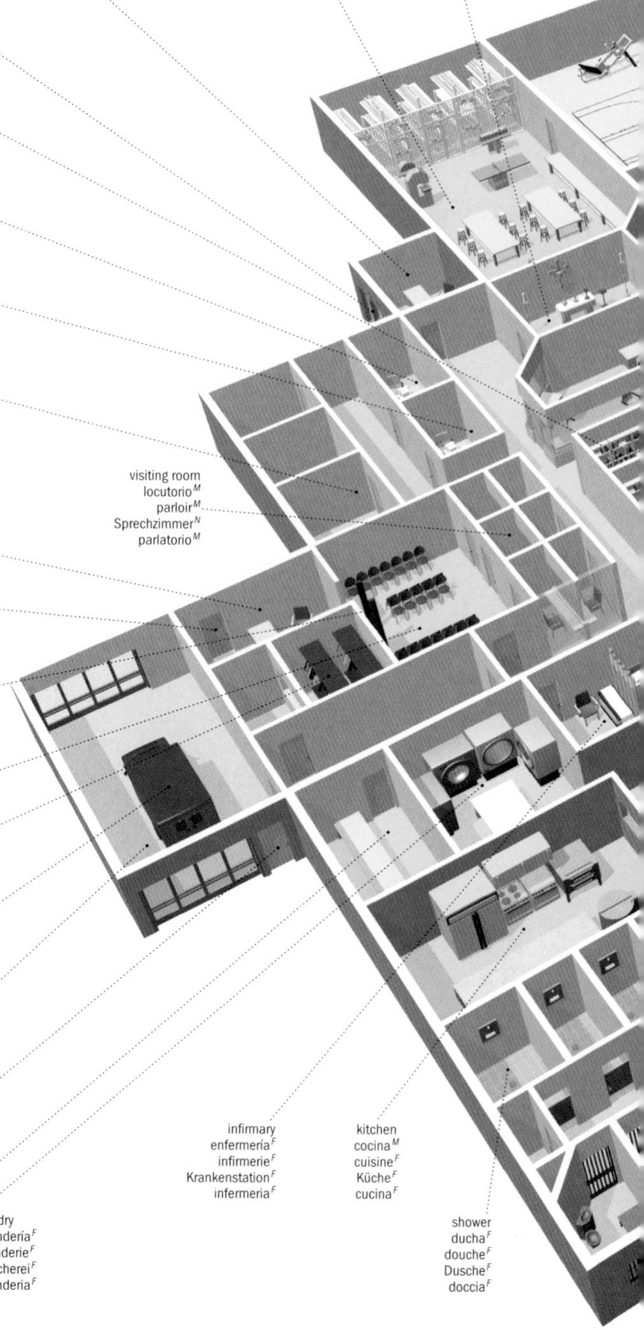

visiting room
locutorio^M
parloir^M
Sprechzimmer^N
parlatorio^M

infirmary
enfermería^F
infirmerie^F
Krankenstation^F
infermeria^F

kitchen
cocina^M
cuisine^F
Küche^F
cucina^F

shower
ducha^F
douche^F
Dusche^F
doccia^F

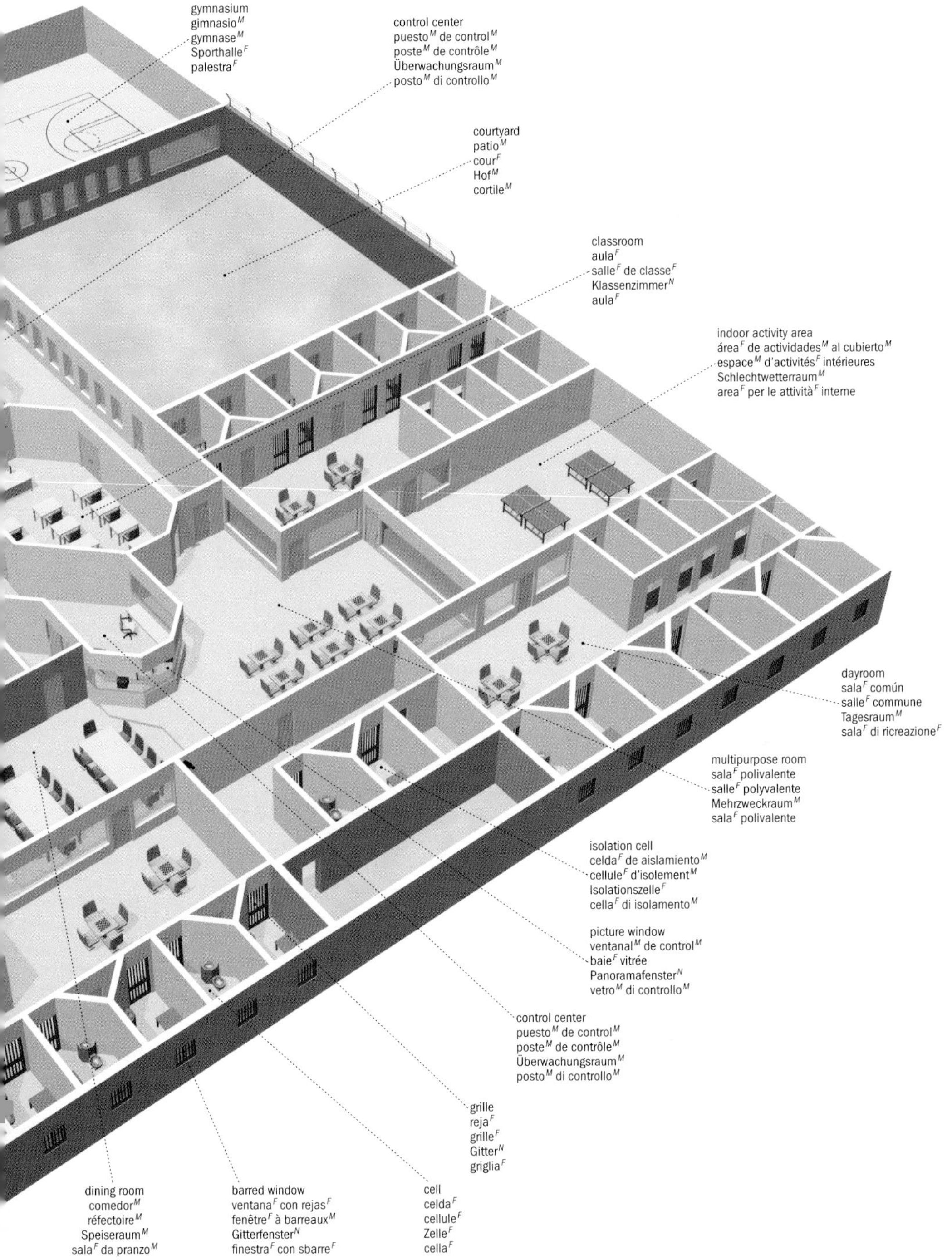

gymnasium
gimnasio^M
gymnase^M
Sporthalle^F
palestra^F

control center
puesto^M de control^M
poste^M de contrôle^M
Überwachungsraum^M
posto^M di controllo^M

courtyard
patio^M
cour^F
Hof^M
cortile^M

classroom
aula^F
salle^F de classe^F
Klassenzimmer^N
aula^F

indoor activity area
área^F de actividades^M al cubierto^M
espace^M d'activités^F intérieures
Schlechtwetterraum^M
area^F per le attività^F interne

dayroom
sala^F común
salle^F commune
Tagesraum^M
sala^F di ricreazione^F

multipurpose room
sala^F polivalente
salle^F polyvalente
Mehrzweckraum^M
sala^F polivalente

isolation cell
celda^F de aislamiento^M
cellule^F d'isolement^M
Isolationszelle^F
cella^F di isolamento^M

picture window
ventanal^M de control^M
baie^F vitrée
Panoramafenster^N
vetro^M di controllo^M

control center
puesto^M de control^M
poste^M de contrôle^M
Überwachungsraum^M
posto^M di controllo^M

grille
reja^F
grille^F
Gitter^N
griglia^F

dining room
comedor^M
réfectoire^M
Speiseraum^M
sala^F da pranzo^M

barred window
ventana^F con rejas^F
fenêtre^F à barreaux^M
Gitterfenster^N
finestra^F con sbarre^F

cell
celda^F
cellule^F
Zelle^F
cella^F

SOCIETY

727

court

tribunal^M | tribunal^M | Gericht^N | tribunale^M

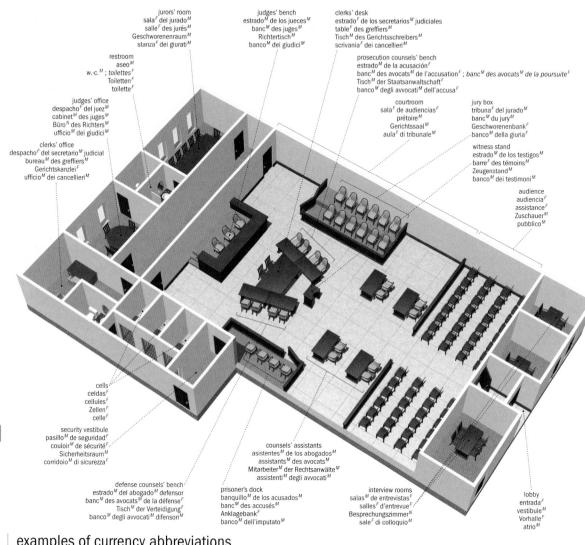

jurors' room
sala^F del jurado^M
salle^F des jurés^M
Geschworenenraum^M
stanza^F dei giurati^M

judges' bench
estrado^M de los jueces^M
banc^M des juges^M
Richtertisch^M
banco^M dei giudici^M

clerks' desk
estrado^F de los secretarios^M judiciales
table^F des greffiers^M
Tisch^M des Gerichtsschreibers^M
scrivania^F dei cancellieri^M

restroom
aseo^M
w.-c.^M ; toilettes^F
Toiletten^F
toilette^F

prosecution counsels' bench
estrado^M de la acusación^F
banc^M des avocats^M de l'accusation^F ; banc^M des avocats^M de la poursuite^F
Tisch^M der Staatsanwaltschaft^F
banco^M degli avvocati^M dell'accusa^F

judges' office
despacho^F del juez^M
cabinet^M des juges^M
Büro^N des Richters^M
ufficio^M dei giudici^M

courtroom
sala^F de audiencias^F
prétoire^M
Gerichtssaal^M
aula^F di tribunale^M

jury box
tribuna^F del jurado^M
banc^M du jury^M
Geschworenenbank^F
banco^M della giuria^F

clerks' office
despacho^F del secretario^M judicial
bureau^M des greffiers^M
Gerichtskanzlei^F
ufficio^M dei cancellieri^M

witness stand
estrado^M de los testigos^M
barre^F des témoins^M
Zeugenstand^M
banco^M dei testimoni^M

audience
audiencia^F
assistance^F
Zuschauer^M
pubblico^M

cells
celdas^F
cellules^F
Zellen^F
celle^F

security vestibule
pasillo^M de seguridad^F
couloir^M de sécurité^F
Sicherheitsraum^M
corridoio^M di sicurezza^F

counsels' assistants
asistentes^M de los abogados^M
assistants^M des avocats^M
Mitarbeiter^M der Rechtsanwälte^M
assistenti^M degli avvocati^M

defense counsels' bench
estrado^M del abogado^M defensor
banc^M des avocats^M de la défense^F
Tisch^M der Verteidigung^F
banco^M degli avvocati^M difensori^M

prisoner's dock
banquillo^M de los acusados^M
banc^M des accusés^M
Anklagebank^F
banco^M dell'imputato^M

interview rooms
salas^M de entrevistas^F
salles^F d'entrevue^F
Besprechungszimmer^N
sale^F di colloquio^M

lobby
entrada^F
vestibule^M
Vorhalle^F
atrio^M

examples of currency abbreviations

ejemplos^M de abreviaciones^F de monedas^F | exemples^M d'unités^F monétaires | Beispiele^N für Währungsabkürzungen^F | esempi^M di simboli^M di valute^F

cent
centavo^M
cent^M
Cent^M
cent^M

euro
euro^M
euro^M
Euro^M
euro^M

peso
peso^M
peso^M
Peso^M
peso^M

pound
libra^F
livre^F
Pfund^N
sterlina^F

dollar
dólar^M
dollar^M
Dollar^M
dollaro^M

rupee
rupia^F
roupie^F
Rupie^F
rupia^F

new shekel
nuevo shekel^M
nouveau shekel^M
neuer Schekel^M
nuovo shekel^M

yen
yen^M
yen^M
Yen^M
yen^M

money and modes of payment

dinero^M y modos^M de pago^M | monnaie^F et modes^M de paiement^M | Geld^N und Zahlungsmodalitäten^F | denaro^M e metodi^M di pagamento^M

coin: obverse
moneda^F: anverso^M
pièce^F : avers^M
Münze^F: Vorderseite^F
moneta^F: diritto^M

date
fecha^F
millésime^M
Jahreszahl^F
anno^M

edge
canto^M
tranche^F
Rand^M
contorno^M

coin: reverse
moneda^F: reverso^M
pièce^F : revers^M
Münze^F: Rückseite^F
moneta^F: rovescio^M

outer ring
cordoncillo^M
couronne^F
Außenring^M
corona^F

denomination
valor^M
valeur^F
Wertangabe^F
indicación^F del valore^M

initials of the issuing bank
iniciales^F del banco^M emisor
initiales^F de la banque^F émettrice
Kürzel^N der Ausgabebank^F
iniziali^F della banca^F di emissione^F

security thread
hilo^M de seguridad^F
fil^M de sécurité^F
Sicherheitsfaden^M
filo^M di sicurezza^F

official signature
firma^F oficial
signature^F officielle
amtliche Unterschrift^F
firma^F ufficiale

portrait
retrato^M
effigie^F
Porträt^N
effigie^F

serial number
número^M de serie^F
numéro^M de série^F
Seriennummer^F
numero^M di serie^F

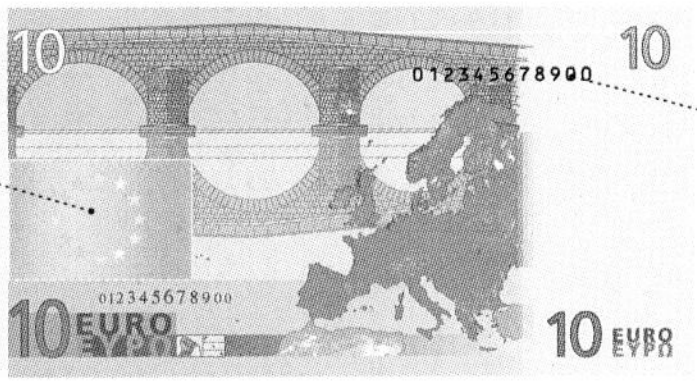

flag of the European Union
bandera^F de la Unión^F Europea
drapeau^M de l'Union^F Européenne
Flagge^F der Europäischen Union^F
bandiera^F dell'Unione^F Europea

banknote: front
billete^M: recto^M
billet^M de banque^F : recto^M
Banknote^F: Vorderseite^F
banconota^F: dritto^M

hologram foil strip
banda^F holográfica metalizada
bande^F métallisée holographique
metallisiertes Hologramm^N
banda^F olografica

watermark
filigrana^F
filigrane^M
Wasserzeichen^N
filigrana^F

color shifting ink
tinta^F de color^M cambiante
encre^F à couleur^F changeante
metallische Tinte^F
inchiostro^M a colori^M cangianti

banknote: back
billete^M : verso^M
billet^M de banque^F : verso^M
Banknote^F: Rückseite^F
banconota^F: rovescio^M

serial number
número^M de serie^F
numéro^M de série^F
Seriennummer^F
numero^M di serie^F

motto
lema^M
devise^F
Leitspruch^M
motto^M

denomination
valor^M
valeur^F
Wertangabe^F
indicación^F del valore^M

name of the currency
nombre^M de la moneda^F
nom^M de la monnaie^F
Währungsangabe^F
nome^M della valuta^F

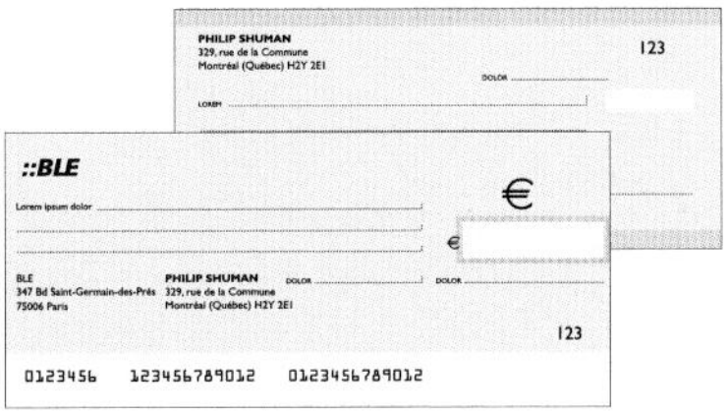

magnetic stripe
banda^F magnética
bande^F magnétique
Magnetstreifen^M
banda^F magnetica

cardholder's signature
firma^M del titular^M
signature^F du titulaire^M
Unterschrift^F des Inhabers^M
firma^F del titolare^M

checks
cheques^M
chèques^M
Schecks^M
assegni^M

traveler's check
cheque^M de viaje^M
chèque^M de voyage^M
Travellerscheck^M
traveller's cheque^M

credit card
tarjeta^F de crédito^M
carte^F de crédit^M
Kreditkarte^F
carta^F di credito^M

card number
número^M de la tarjeta^F
numéro^M de carte^F
Kartennummer^F
numero^M della carta^F

cardholder's name
nombre^M del titular^M
nom^M du titulaire^M
Name^M des Inhabers^M
nome^M del titolare^M

expiration date
fecha^F de vencimiento^M
date^F d'expiration^F
Verfallsdatum^N
data^F di scadenza^F

SOCIETY

bank

banco^M | banque^F | Bank^F | banca^F

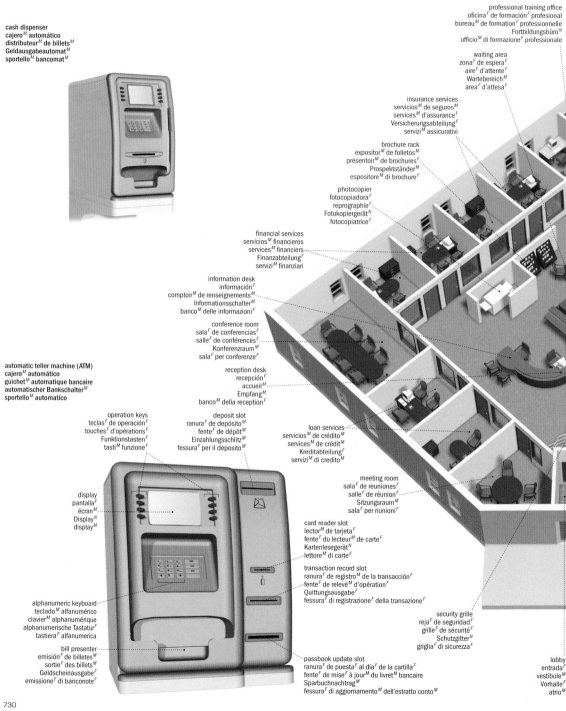

cash dispenser
cajero^M automático
distribuidor^M de billets^M
Geldausgabeautomat^M
sportello^M bancomat^M

professional training office
oficina^F de formación^F profesional
bureau^M de formation^F professionnelle
Fortbildungsbüro^N
ufficio^M di formazione^F professionale

waiting area
zona^F de espera^F
aire^F d'attente^F
Wartebereich^M
area^F d'attesa^F

insurance services
servicios^M de seguros^M
services^M d'assurance^F
Versicherungsabteilung^F
servizi^M assicurativi

brochure rack
expositor^M de folletos^M
présentoir^M de brochures^F
Prospektständer^M
espositore^M di brochure^F

photocopier
fotocopiadora^F
reprographie^F
Fotokopiergerät^N
fotocopiatrice^F

financial services
servicios^M financieros
services^M financiers
Finanzabteilung^F
servizi^M finanziari

information desk
información^F
comptoir^M de renseignements^M
Informationsschalter^M
banco^M delle informazioni^F

conference room
sala^F de conferencias^F
salle^F de conférences^F
Konferenzraum^M
sala^F per conferenze^F

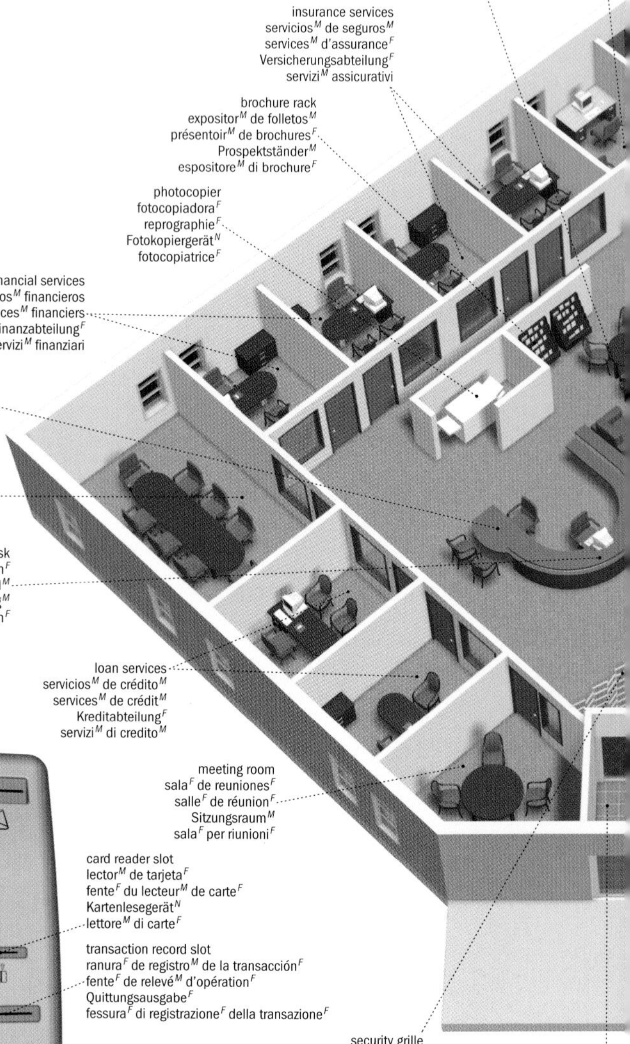

automatic teller machine (ATM)
cajero^M automático
guichet^M automatique bancaire
automatischer Bankschalter^M
sportello^M automatico

reception desk
recepción^F
accueil^M
Empfang^M
banco^M della reception^F

operation keys
teclas^F de operación^F
touches^F d'opérations^F
Funktionstasten^F
tasti^M funzione^F

deposit slot
ranura^F de depósito^M
fente^F de dépôt^M
Einzahlungsschlitz^M
fessura^F per il deposito^M

loan services
servicios^M de crédito^M
services^M de crédit^M
Kreditabteilung^F
servizi^M di credito^M

meeting room
sala^F de reuniones^F
salle^F de réunion^F
Sitzungsraum^M
sala^F per riunioni^F

display
pantalla^F
écran^M
Display^N
display^M

card reader slot
lector^M de tarjeta^F
fente^F du lecteur^M de carte^F
Kartenlesegerät^N
lettore^M di carte^F

transaction record slot
ranura^F de registro^M de la transacción^F
fente^F de relevé^M d'opération^F
Quittungsausgabe^F
fessura^F di registrazione^F della transazione^F

alphanumeric keyboard
teclado^M alfanumérico
clavier^M alphanumérique
alphanumerische Tastatur^F
tastiera^F alfanumerica

bill presenter
emisión^F de billetes^M
sortie^F des billets^M
Geldscheinausgabe^F
emissione^F di banconote^F

security grille
reja^F de seguridad^F
grille^F de sécurité^F
Schutzgitter^N
griglia^F di sicurezza^F

passbook update slot
ranura^F de puesta^F al día^F de la cartilla^F
fente^F de mise^F à jour^M du livret^M bancaire
Sparbuchnachtrag^M
fessura^F di aggiornamento^M dell'estratto conto^M

lobby
entrada^F
vestibule^M
Vorhalle^F
atrio^M

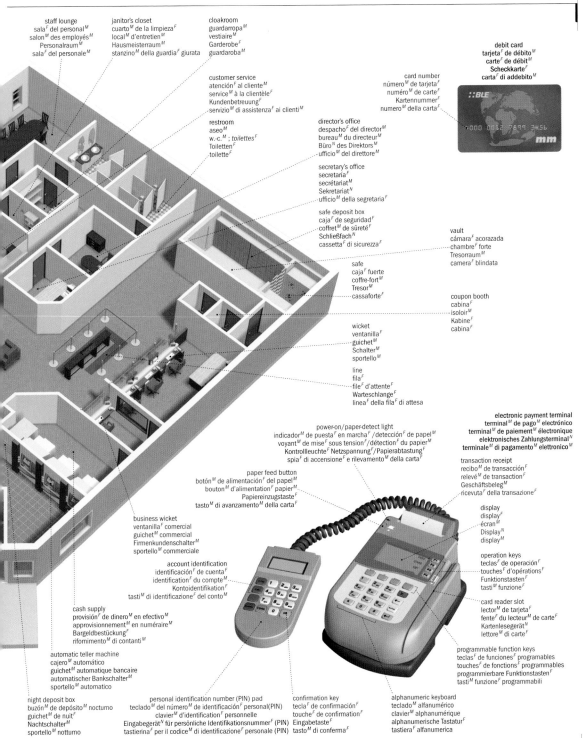

staff lounge
sala^F del personal^M
salon^M des employés^M
Personalraum^M
sala^F del personale^M

janitor's closet
cuarto^M de la limpieza^F
local^M d'entretien^M
Hausmeisterraum^M
stanzino^M della guardia^F giurata

cloakroom
guardarropa^M
vestiaire^M
Garderobe^F
guardaroba^M

debit card
tarjeta^F de débito^M
carte^F de débit^M
Scheckkarte^F
carta^F di addebito^M

customer service
atención^F al cliente^M
service^M à la clientèle^F
Kundenbetreuung^F
servizio^M di assistenza^F ai clienti^M

card number
número^M de tarjeta^F
numéro^M de carte^F
Kartennummer^F
numero^M della carta^F

restroom
aseo^M
w.-c.^{M} ; toilettes^F
Toiletten^F
toilette^F

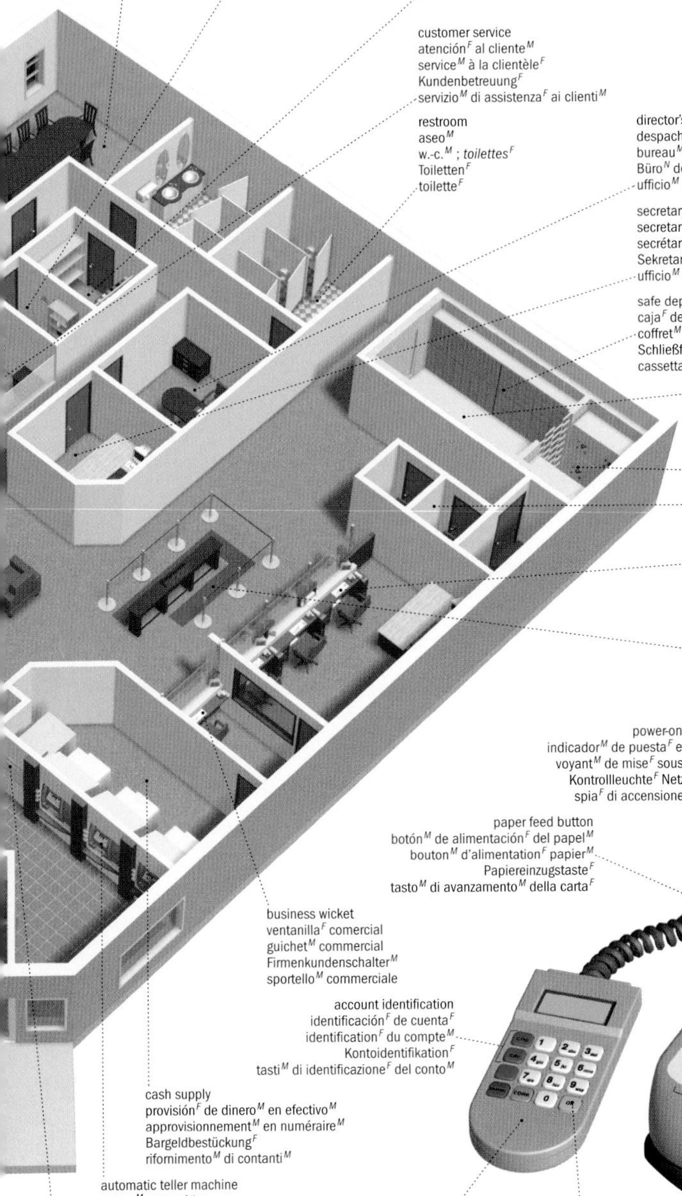

director's office
despacho^F del director^M
bureau^M du directeur^M
Büro^N des Direktors^M
ufficio^M del direttore^M

secretary's office
secretaría^F
secrétariat^M
Sekretariat^N
ufficio^M della segretaria^F

safe deposit box
caja^F de seguridad^F
coffret^M de sûreté^F
Schließfach^N
cassetta^F di sicurezza^F

vault
cámara^F acorazada
chambre^F forte
Tresorraum^M
camera^F blindata

safe
caja^F fuerte
coffre-fort^M
Tresor^M
cassaforte^F

coupon booth
cabina^F
isoloir^M
Kabine^F
cabina^F

wicket
ventanilla^F
guichet^M
Schalter^M
sportello^M

line
fila^F
file^F d'attente^F
Warteschlange^F
linea^F della fila^F di attesa

electronic payment terminal
terminal^M de pago^M electrónico
terminal^M de paiement^M électronique
elektronisches Zahlungsterminal^N
terminale^M di pagamento^M elettronico^M

power-on/paper-detect light
indicador^M de puesta^F en marcha^F /detección^F de papel^M
voyant^M de mise^F sous tension^F/détection^F du papier^M
Kontrollleuchte^F Netzspannung^F/Papierabtastung^F
spia^F di accensione^F e rilevamento^M della carta^F

transaction receipt
recibo^M de transacción^F
relevé^M de transaction^F
Geschäftsbeleg^M
ricevuta^F della transazione^F

paper feed button
botón^M de alimentación^F del papel^M
bouton^M d'alimentation^F papier^M
Papiereinzugstaste^F
tasto^M di avanzamento^M della carta^F

display
display^F
écran^M
Display^N
display^M

business wicket
ventanilla^F comercial
guichet^M commercial
Firmenkundenschalter^M
sportello^M commerciale

operation keys
teclas^F de operación^F
touches^F d'opérations^F
Funktionstasten^F
tasti^M funzione^F

account identification
identificación^F de cuenta^F
identification^F du compte^M
Kontoidentifikation^F
tasti^M di identificazione^F del conto^M

card reader slot
lector^M de tarjeta^F
fente^F du lecteur^M de carte^F
Kartenlesegerät^N
lettore^M di carte^F

cash supply
provisión^F de dinero^M en efectivo^M
approvisionnement^M en numéraire^M
Bargeldbestückung^F
rifornimento^M di contanti^M

programmable function keys
teclas^F de funciones^F programables
touches^F de fonctions^F programmables
programmierbare Funktionstasten^F
tasti^M funzione^F programmabili

automatic teller machine
cajero^M automático
guichet^M automatique bancaire
automatischer Bankschalter^M
sportello^M automatico

night deposit box
buzón^M de depósito^M nocturno
guichet^M de nuit^F
Nachtschalter^M
sportello^M notturno

personal identification number (PIN) pad
teclado^M del número^M de identificación^F personal(PIN)
clavier^M d'identification^F personnelle
Eingabegerät^N für persönliche Identifikationsnummer^F (PIN)
tastierina^F per il codice^M di identificazione^F personale (PIN)

confirmation key
tecla^F de confirmación^F
touche^F de confirmation^F
Eingabetaste^F
tasto^M di conferma^F

alphanumeric keyboard
teclado^M alfanumérico
clavier^M alphanumérique
alphanumerische Tastatur^F
tastiera^F alfanumerica

::BLE
1000 0012 7899 3456
mm

library

biblioteca^F | bibliothèque^F | Bibliothek^F | biblioteca^F

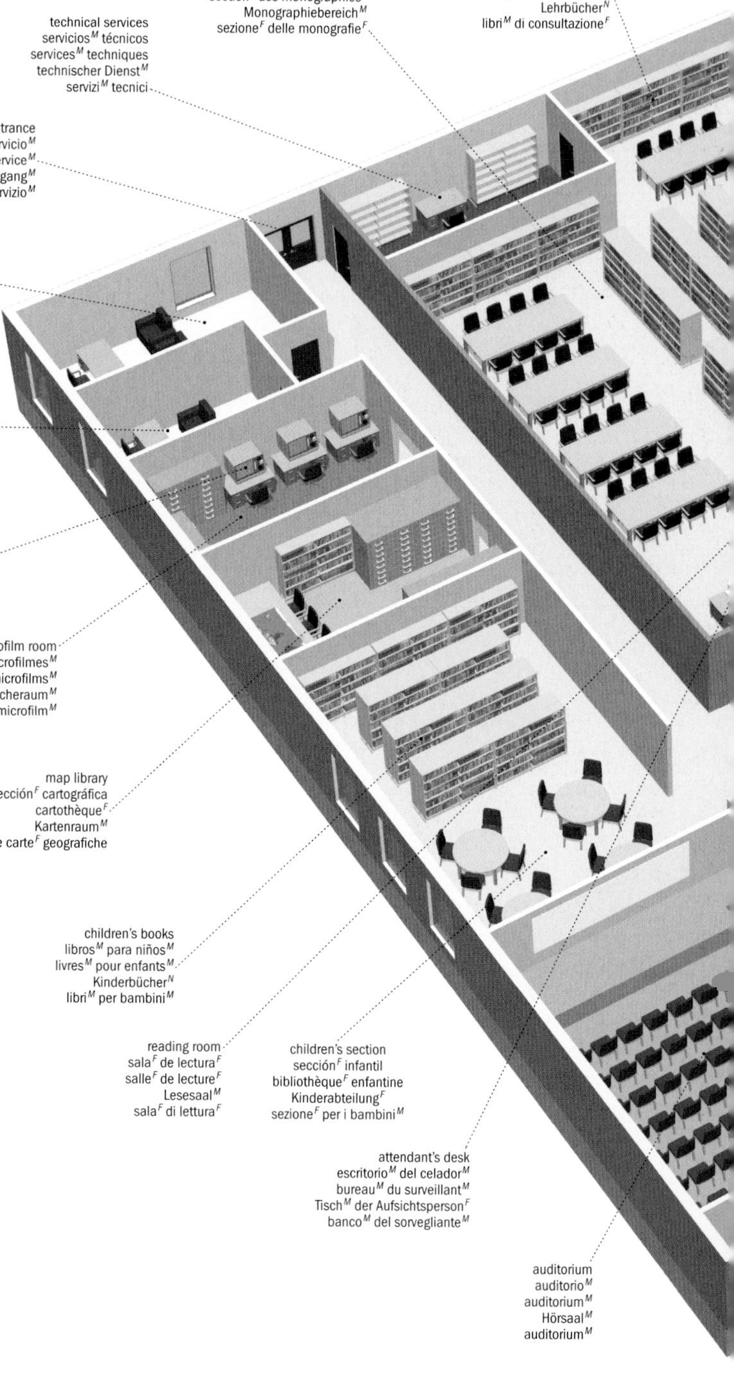

monograph section
sección^M de monografías^F
section^F des monographies^F
Monographiebereich^M
sezione^F delle monografie^F

reference books
libros^M de consulta^F
ouvrages^M de référence^F
Lehrbücher^N
libri^M di consultazione^F

technical services
servicios^M técnicos
services^M techniques
technischer Dienst^M
servizi^M tecnici

service entrance
entrada^F de servicio^M
entrée^F de service^M
Diensteingang^M
entrata^F di servizio^M

director's office
despacho^M del director^M
bureau^M du directeur^M
Büro^N des Direktors^M
ufficio^M del direttore^M

librarian's office
despacho^M del bibliotecario^M
bureau^M du bibliothécaire^M
Büro^N des Bibliothekars^M
ufficio^M del bibliotecario^M

microfilm reader
lector^M de microfilmes^M
lecteur^M de microfilm^M
Mikrofichelesegerät^N
lettore^M di microfilm^M

microfilm room
sala^F de microfilmes^M
salle^F des microfilms^M
Mikroficheraum^M
stanza^F dei microfilm^M

map library
sección^F cartográfica
cartothèque^F
Kartenraum^M
sezione^F delle carte^F geografiche

children's books
libros^M para niños^M
livres^M pour enfants^M
Kinderbücher^N
libri^M per bambini^M

reading room
sala^F de lectura^F
salle^F de lecture^F
Lesesaal^M
sala^F di lettura^F

children's section
sección^F infantil
bibliothèque^F enfantine
Kinderabteilung^F
sezione^F per i bambini^M

attendant's desk
escritorio^M del celador^M
bureau^M du surveillant^M
Tisch^M der Aufsichtsperson^F
banco^M del sorvegliante^M

auditorium
auditorio^M
auditorium^M
Hörsaal^M
auditorium^M

SOCIETY

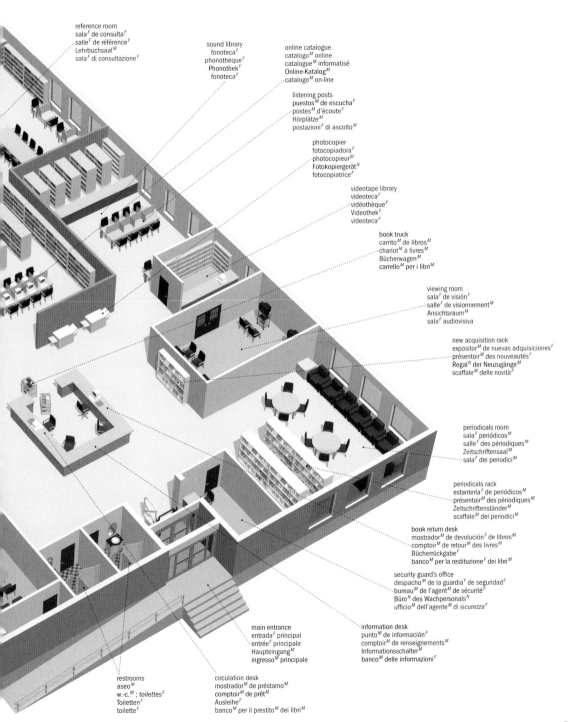

reference room
sala^F de consulta^F
salle^F de référence^F
Lehrbuchsaal^M
sala^F di consultazione^F

sound library
fonoteca^F
phonothèque^F
Phonothek^F
fonoteca^F

online catalogue
catalogo^M online
catalogue^M informatisé
Online-Katalog^M
catalogo^M on-line

listening posts
puestos^M de escucha^F
postes^M d'écoute^F
Hörplätze^F
postazioni^F di ascolto^M

photocopier
fotocopiadora^F
photocopieur^M
Fotokopiergerät^N
fotocopiatrice^F

videotape library
videoteca^F
vidéothèque^F
Videothek^F
videoteca^F

book truck
carrito^M de libros^M
chariot^M à livres^M
Bücherwagen^M
carrello^M per i libri^M

viewing room
sala^F de visión^F
salle^F de visionnement^M
Ansichtsraum^M
sala^F audiovisiva

new acquisition rack
expositor^M de nuevas adquisiciones^F
présentoir^M des nouveautés^F
Regal^N der Neuzugänge^M
scaffale^M delle novità^F

periodicals room
sala^F periódicos^M
salle^F des périodiques^M
Zeitschriftensaal^M
sala^F dei periodici^M

periodicals rack
estantería^F de periódicos^M
présentoir^M des périodiques^M
Zeitschriftenständer^M
scaffale^M dei periodici^M

book return desk
mostrador^M de devolución^F de libros^M
comptoir^M de retour^M des livres^M
Bücherrückgabe^F
banco^M per la restituzione^F dei libri^M

security guard's office
despacho^M de la guardia^F de seguridad^F
bureau^M de l'agent^M de sécurité^F
Büro^N des Wachpersonals^N
ufficio^M dell'agente^M di sicurezza^F

information desk
punto^M de información^F
comptoir^M de renseignements^M
Informationsschalter^M
banco^M delle informazioni^F

main entrance
entrada^F principal
entrée^F principale
Haupteingang^M
ingresso^M principale

circulation desk
mostrador^M de préstamo^M
comptoir^M de prêt^M
Ausleihe^F
banco^M per il prestito^M dei libri^M

restrooms
aseo^M
w.-c.^{M} ; toilettes^F
Toiletten^F
toilette^F

school

colegio^M | école^F | Schule^F | scuola^F

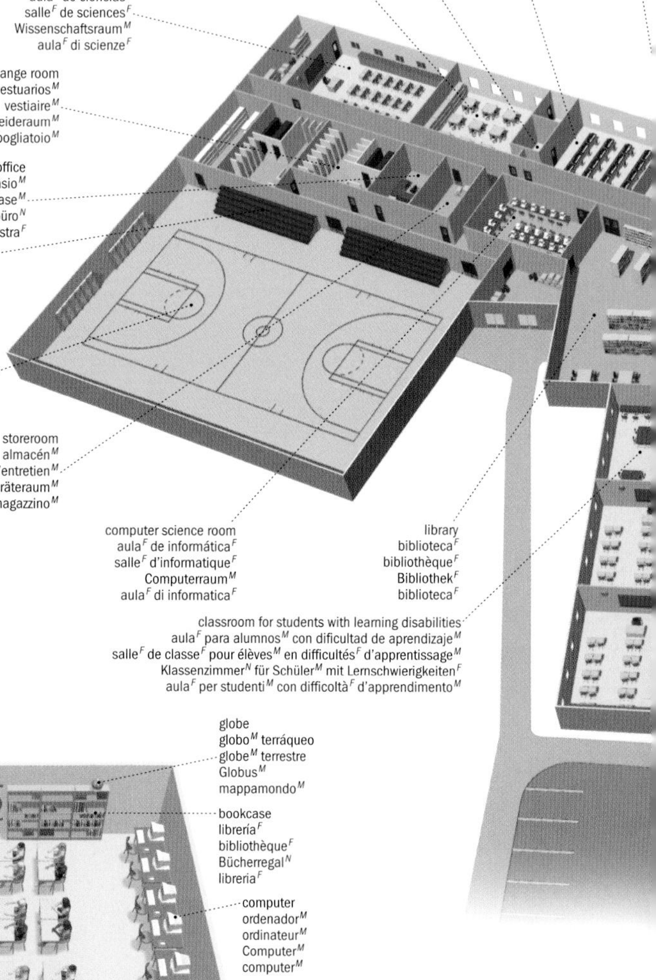

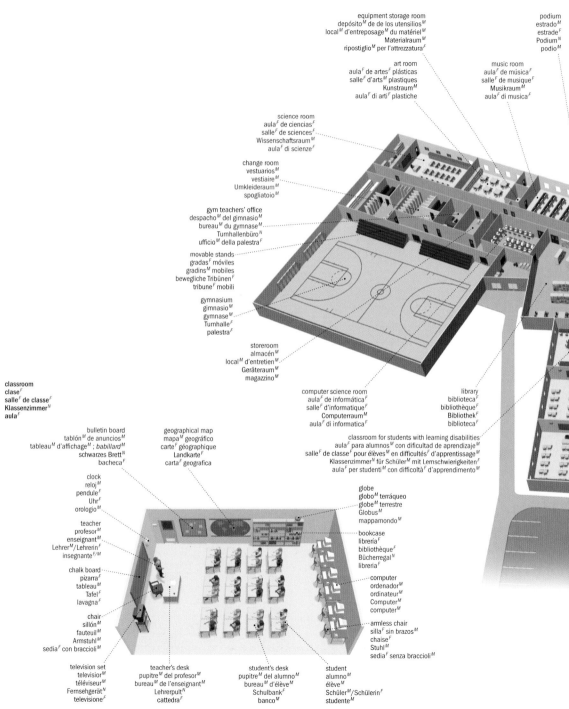

equipment storage room
depósito^M de de los utensilios^M
local^M d'entreposage^M du matériel^M
Materialraum^M
ripostiglio^M per l'attrezzatura^F

podium
estrado^M
estrade^F
Podium^N
podio^M

art room
aula^F de artes^F plásticas
salle^F d'arts^M plastiques
Kunstraum^M
aula^F di arti^F plastiche

music room
aula^F de música^F
salle^F de musique^F
Musikraum^M
aula^F di musica^F

science room
aula^F de ciencias^F
salle^F de sciences^F
Wissenschaftsraum^M
aula^F di scienze^F

change room
vestuarios^M
vestiaire^M
Umkleideraum^M
spogliatoio^M

gym teachers' office
despacho^M del gimnasio^M
bureau^M du gymnase^M
Turnhallenbüro^N
ufficio^M della palestra^F

movable stands
gradas^F móviles
gradins^M mobiles
bewegliche Tribünen^F
tribune^F mobili

gymnasium
gimnasio^M
gymnase^M
Turnhalle^F
palestra^F

storeroom
almacén^M
local^M d'entretien^M
Geräteraum^M
magazzino^M

computer science room
aula^F de informática^F
salle^F d'informatique^F
Computerraum^M
aula^F di informatica^F

library
biblioteca^F
bibliothèque^F
Bibliothek^F
biblioteca^F

classroom
clase^F
salle^F de classe^F
Klassenzimmer^N
aula^F

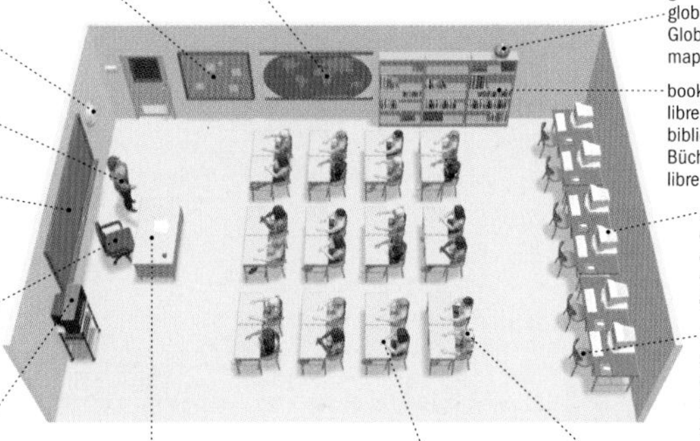

bulletin board
tablón^M de anuncios^M
tableau^M d'affichage^M ; babillard^M
schwarzes Brett^N
bacheca^F

geographical map
mapa^M geográfico
carte^F géographique
Landkarte^F
carta^F geografica

classroom for students with learning disabilities
aula^F para alumnos^M con dificultad de aprendizaje^M
salle^F de classe^F pour élèves^M en difficultés^F d'apprentissage^M
Klassenzimmer^N für Schüler^M mit Lernschwierigkeiten^F
aula^F per studenti^M con difficoltà^F d'apprendimento^M

clock
reloj^M
pendule^F
Uhr^F
orologio^M

globe
globo^M terráqueo
globe^M terrestre
Globus^M
mappamondo^M

teacher
profesor^M
enseignant^M
Lehrer^M/Lehrerin^F
insegnante^F/M

bookcase
librería^F
bibliothèque^F
Bücherregal^N
libreria^F

chalk board
pizarra^F
tableau^M
Tafel^F
lavagna^F

computer
ordenador^M
ordinateur^M
Computer^M
computer^M

chair
sillón^M
fauteuil^M
Armstuhl^M
sedia^F con braccioli^M

armless chair
silla^F sin brazos^M
chaise^F
Stuhl^M
sedia^F senza braccioli^M

television set
televisor^M
téléviseur^M
Fernsehgerät^N
televisione^F

teacher's desk
pupitre^M del profesor^M
bureau^M de l'enseignant^M
Lehrerpult^N
cattedra^F

student's desk
pupitre^M del alumno^M
bureau^M d'élève^F
Schulbank^F
banco^M

student
alumno^M
élève^F
Schüler^M/Schülerin^F
studente^M

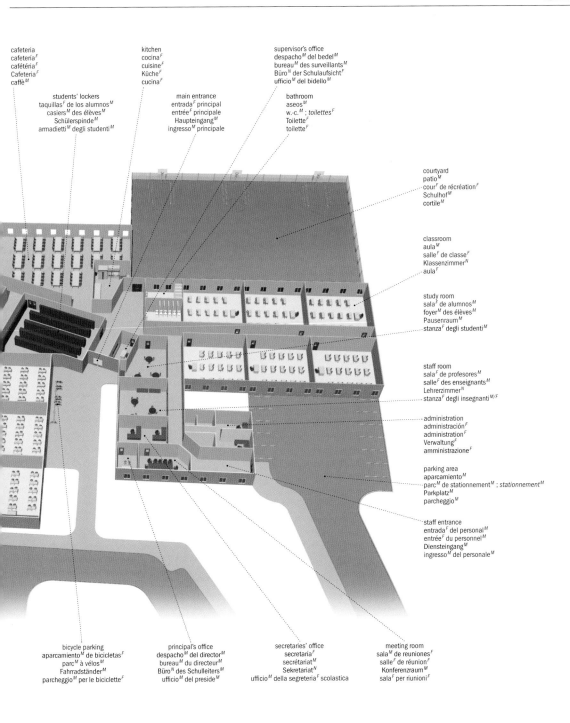

cafeteria
cafetería^F
cafétéria^F
Cafeteria^F
caffè^M

kitchen
cocina^F
cuisine^F
Küche^F
cucina^F

supervisor's office
despacho^M del bedel^M
bureau^M des surveillants^M
Büro^N der Schulaufsicht^F
ufficio^M del bidello^F

students' lockers
taquillas^F de los alumnos^M
casiers^M des élèves^M
Schülerspinde^M
armadietti^M degli studenti^M

main entrance
entrada^F principal
entrée^F principale
Haupteingang^M
ingresso^M principale

bathroom
aseos^M
w.-c.^M ; *toilettes*^F
Toilette^F
toilette^F

courtyard
patio^M
cour^F de récréation^F
Schulhof^M
cortile^M

classroom
aula^M
salle^F de classe^F
Klassenzimmer^N
aula^F

study room
sala^F de alumnos^M
foyer^M des élèves^M
Pausenraum^M
stanza^F degli studenti^M

staff room
sala^F de profesores^M
salle^F des enseignants^M
Lehrerzimmer^N
stanza^F degli insegnanti^{M/F}

administration
administración^F
administration^F
Verwaltung^F
amministrazione^F

parking area
aparcamiento^M
parc^M de stationnement^M ; *stationnement*^M
Parkplatz^M
parcheggio^M

staff entrance
entrada^F del personal^M
entrée^F du personnel^M
Diensteingang^M
ingresso^M del personale^M

bicycle parking
aparcamiento^M de bicicletas^F
parc^M à vélos^M
Fahrradständer^M
parcheggio^M per le biciclette^F

principal's office
despacho^M del director^M
bureau^M du directeur^M
Büro^N des Schulleiters^M
ufficio^M del preside^M

secretaries' office
secretaría^F
secrétariat^M
Sekretariat^N
ufficio^M della segreteria^F scolastica

meeting room
sala^F de reuniones^F
salle^F de réunion^F
Konferenzraum^M
sala^F per riunioni^F

chronology of religions

Cronología^F de algunas Religiones^F del mundo^M | chronologie^F des religions^F | Chronologie^F eineger Weltreligionen^F | cronologia^F de certi religioni^F

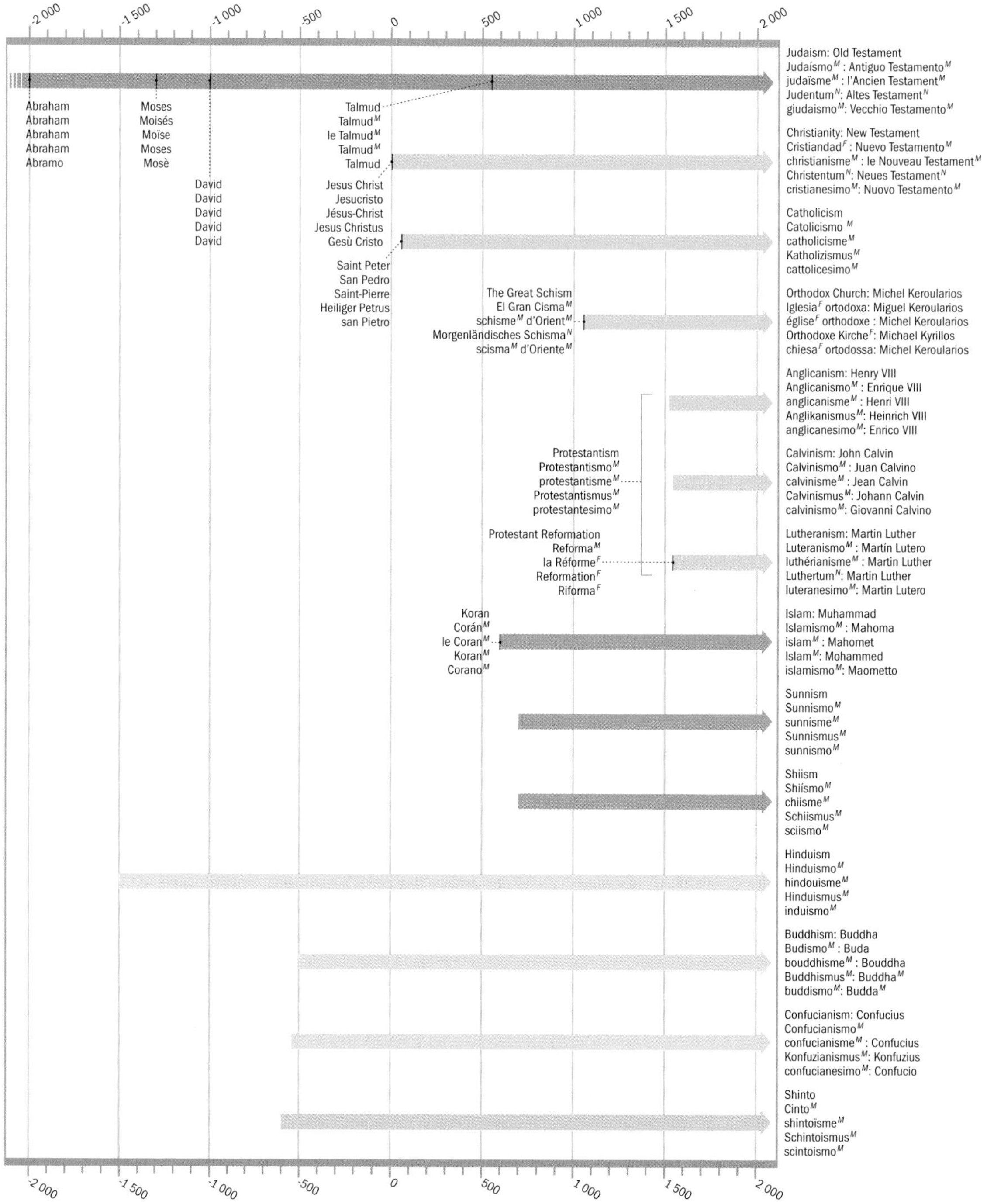

Judaism: Old Testament
Judaísmo^M : Antiguo Testamento^M
judaisme^M : l'Ancien Testament^M
Judentum^N: Altes Testament^N
giudaismo^M: Vecchio Testamento^M

Abraham — Moses — Talmud
Abraham — Moisés — Talmud^M
Abraham — Moïse — le Talmud^M
Abraham — Moses — Talmud^M
Abramo — Mosè — Talmud

Christianity: New Testament
Cristiandad^F : Nuevo Testamento^M
christianisme^M : le Nouveau Testament^M
Christentum^N: Neues Testament^N
cristianesimo^M: Nuovo Testamento^M

David — Jesus Christ
David — Jesucristo
David — Jésus-Christ
David — Jesus Christus
David — Gesù Cristo

Catholicism
Catolicismo^M
catholicisme^M
Katholizismus^M
cattolicesimo^M

Saint Peter
San Pedro
Saint-Pierre
Heiliger Petrus
san Pietro

Orthodox Church: Michel Keroularios
Iglesia^F ortodoxa: Miguel Keroularios
église^F orthodoxe : Michel Keroularios
Orthodoxe Kirche^F: Michael Kyrillos
chiesa^F ortodossa: Michel Keroularios

The Great Schism
El Gran Cisma^M
schisme^M d'Orient^M
Morgenländisches Schisma^N
scisma^M d'Oriente^M

Anglicanism: Henry VIII
Anglicanismo^M : Enrique VIII
anglicanisme^M : Henri VIII
Anglikanismus^M: Heinrich VIII
anglicanesimo^M: Enrico VIII

Protestantism
Protestantismo^M
protestantisme^M
Protestantismus^M
protestantesimo^M

Calvinism: John Calvin
Calvinismo^M : Juan Calvino
calvinisme^M : Jean Calvin
Calvinismus^M: Johann Calvin
calvinismo^M: Giovanni Calvino

Protestant Reformation
Reforma^M
la Réforme^F
Reformation^F
Riforma^F

Lutheranism: Martin Luther
Luteranismo^M : Martín Lutero
luthérianisme^M : Martin Luther
Luthertum^N: Martin Luther
luteranesimo^M: Martin Lutero

Koran
Corán^M
le Coran^M
Koran^M
Corano^M

Islam: Muhammad
Islamismo^M : Mahoma
islam^M : Mahomet
Islam^M: Mohammed
islamismo^M: Maometto

Sunnism
Sunnismo^M
sunnisme^M
Sunnismus^M
sunnismo^M

Shiism
Shiísmo^M
chiisme^M
Schiismus^M
sciismo^M

Hinduism
Hinduismo^M
hindouisme^M
Hinduismus^M
induismo^M

Buddhism: Buddha
Budismo^M : Buda
bouddhisme^M : Bouddha
Buddhismus^M: Buddha^M
buddismo^M: Budda^M

Confucianism: Confucius
Confucianismo^M
confucianisme^M : Confucius
Konfuzianismus^M: Konfuzius
confucianesimo^M: Confucio

Shinto
Cinto^M
shintoïsme^M
Schintoismus^M
scintoismo^M

SOCIETY

Catholic church

iglesia^F | église^F | Kirche^F | chiesa^F

secondary altar
altar^M lateral
autel^M secondaire
Nebenaltar^M
altare^M secondario

communion rail
comulgatorio^M
table^F de communion^F
Kommunionbank^F
balaustra^F della comunione^F

baptismal font
pila^F bautismal
fonts^M baptismaux
Taufbecken^N
fonte^F battesimale

bell tower
campanario^M
clocher^M
Glockenturm^M
campanile^M

lectern
atril^M
lutrin^M
Pult^N
leggio^M

ex-voto
exvoto^M
ex-voto^M
Weihgabe^F
ex voto^M

stained glass window
vidriera^F
vitrail^M
Kirchenfenster^N
vetrata^F

confessionals
confesionarios^M
confessionnal^M
Beichtstuhl^M
confessionale^M

sanctuary lamp
lámpara^F del santuario^M
lampe^F de sanctuaire^M
Chorlampe^F
lampada^F del presbiterio^M

crucifix
crucifijo^M
crucifix^M
Kruzifix^N
crocifisso^M

altarpiece
retablo^M
retable^M
Altarbild^N
pala^F dell'altare^M

tabernacle
tabernáculo^M
tabernacle^M
Tabernakel^{M/N}
tabernacolo^M

statue
estatua^F
statue^F
Statue^F
statua^F

frontal
frontal^M
devant^M d'autel^M
Antependium^N
paliotto^M

altar cross
cruz^F del altar^M
croix^F d'autel^M
Altarkreuz^N
croce^F dell'altare^M

censer
incensario^M
encensoir^M
Weihrauchkessel^M
turibolo^M

sacristy
sacristía^F
sacristie^F
Sakristei^F
sacrestia^F

pulpit
púlpito^M
chaire^F
Kanzel^F
pulpito^M

holy water font
pila^F de agua^M bendita
bénitier^M
Weihwasserbecken^N
acquasantiera^F

pew
banco^M
banc^M
Kirchenbank^F
panca^F

high altar
altar^M mayor
maître-autel^M
Hochaltar^M
altare^M maggiore

candle
vela^F
cierge^M
Kerze^F
candela^F

chalice
cáliz^M
calice^M
Kelch^M
calice^M

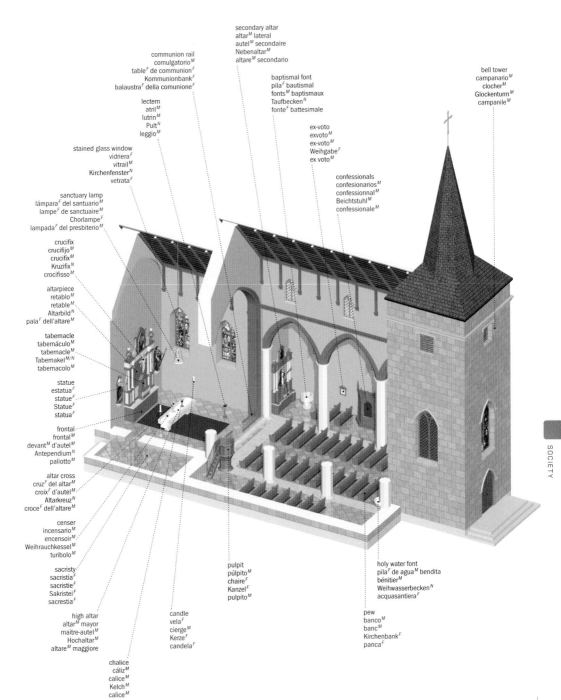

SOCIETY

synagogue

sinagoga[F] | synagogue[F] | Synagoge[F] | sinagoga[F]

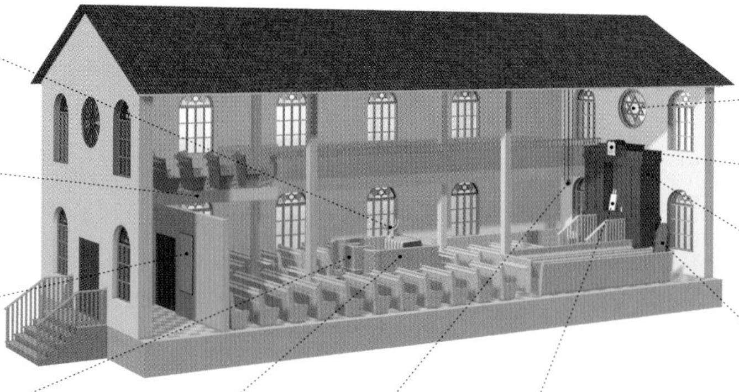

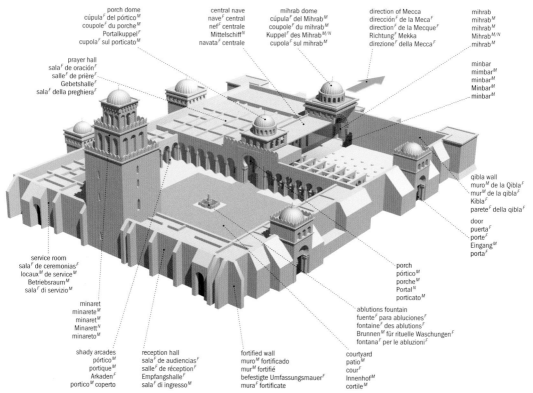

menorah
menorah[F]
menora[F]
Menora[F]
menorah[F]

balcony
balcón[M]
balcon[M]
Galerie[F]
balconata[F]

memorial board
lápida[F] conmemorativa
tableau[M] du souvenir[M]
Gedenktafel[F]
lapide[F] commemorativa

pulpit
púlpito[M]
table[F] de lecture[F]
Kanzel[F]
pulpito[M]

bimah
bimah[F]
bimah[F]
Bimah[F]
bimah[F]

eternal light
llama[F] perpetua
lumière[F] perpétuelle
Ewiges Licht[N]
luce[F] perpetua

Torah scrolls
rollos[M] de la Torá[F]
rouleaux[M] de la Torah[F]
Thorarollen[F]
rotoli[M] della Torah[F]

Star of David
estrella[F] de David
étoile[F] de David
Davidstern[M]
stella[F] di David

Ten Commandments
diez mandamientos[M]
les dix commandements[M]
Zehn Gebote[N]
dieci comandamenti[M]

ark
arca[M]
arche[F]
Thoraschrein[M]
arca[F]

rabbi's seat
asiento[M] del rabino[M]
siège[M] du rabbin[M]
steinerner Ehrensessel[M]
seggio[M] del rabbino[M]

mosque

mezquita[F] | mosquée[F] | Moschee[F] | moschea[F]

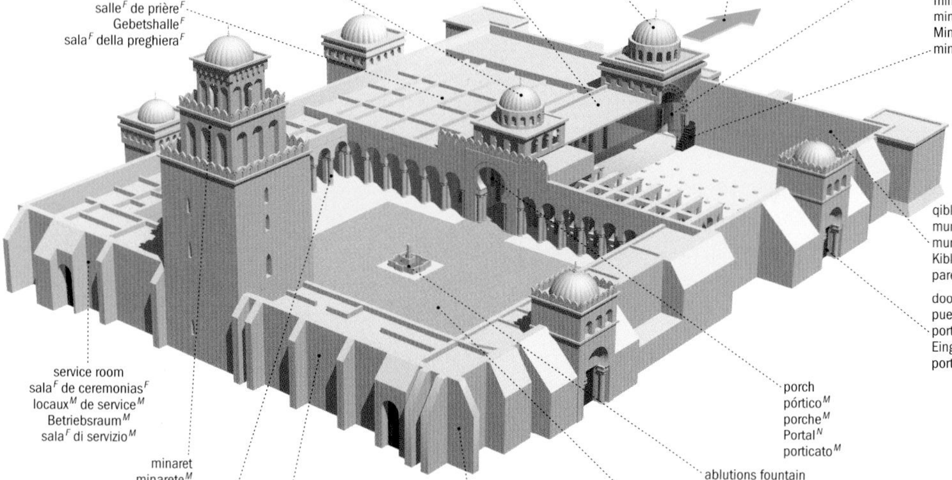

porch dome
cúpula[F] del pórtico[M]
coupole[F] du porche[M]
Portalkuppel[F]
cupola[F] sul porticato[M]

prayer hall
sala[F] de oración[F]
salle[F] de prière[F]
Gebetshalle[F]
sala[F] della preghiera[F]

central nave
nave[F] central
nef[F] centrale
Mittelschiff[N]
navata[F] centrale

mihrab dome
cúpula[F] del Mihrab[M]
coupole[F] du mihrab[M]
Kuppel[F] des Mihrab[M/N]
cupola[F] sul mihrab[M]

direction of Mecca
dirección[F] de la Meca[F]
direction[F] de la Mecque[F]
Richtung[F] Mekka
direzione[F] della Mecca[F]

mihrab
mihrab[M]
mihrab[M]
Mihrab[M/N]
mihrab[M]

minbar
mimbar[M]
minbar[M]
Minbar[M]
minbar[M]

qibla wall
muro[M] de la Qibla[F]
mur[M] de la qibla[F]
Kibla[F]
parete[F] della qibla[F]

door
puerta[F]
porte[F]
Eingang[M]
porta[F]

service room
sala[F] de ceremonias[F]
locaux[M] de service[M]
Betriebsraum[M]
sala[F] di servizio[M]

minaret
minarete[M]
minaret[M]
Minarett[N]
minareto[M]

shady arcades
pórtico[M]
portique[M]
Arkaden[F]
portico[M] coperto

reception hall
sala[F] de audiencias[F]
salle[F] de réception[F]
Empfangshalle[F]
sala[F] di ingresso[M]

fortified wall
muro[M] fortificado
mur[M] fortifié
befestigte Umfassungsmauer[F]
mura[F] fortificate

courtyard
patio[M]
cour[F]
Innenhof[M]
cortile[M]

porch
pórtico[M]
porche[M]
Portal[N]
porticato[M]

ablutions fountain
fuente[F] para abluciones[F]
fontaine[F] des ablutions[F]
Brunnen[M] für rituelle Waschungen[F]
fontana[F] per le abluzioni[F]

SOCIETY

heraldry

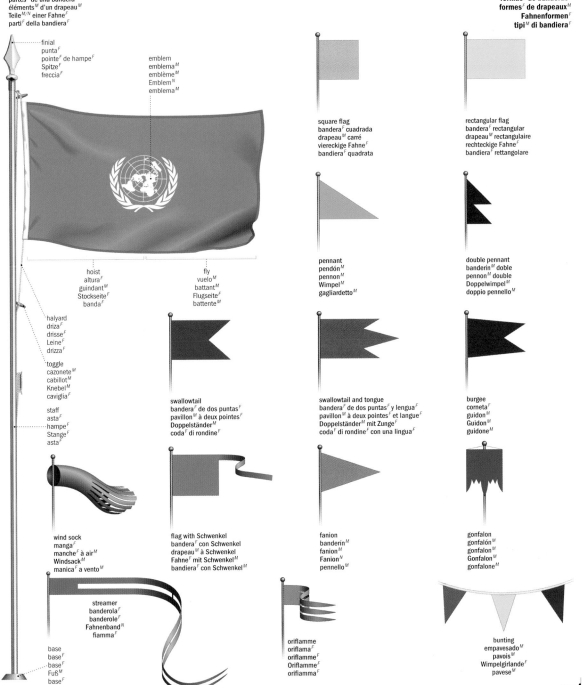

parts of a flag
partes^F de una bandera^F
éléments^M d'un drapeau^M
Teile^{M/N} einer Fahne^F
parti^F della bandiera^F

finial
punta^F
pointe^F de hampe^F
Spitze^F
freccia^F

emblem
emblema^M
emblème^M
Emblem^N
emblema^M

hoist
altura^F
guindant^M
Stockseite^F
banda^F

fly
vuelo^M
battant^M
Flugseite^F
battente^F

halyard
driza^F
drisse^F
Leine^F
drizza^F

toggle
cazonete^M
cabillot^M
Knebel^M
caviglia^F

staff
asta^F
hampe^F
Stange^F
asta^F

wind sock
manga^F
manche^F à air^M
Windsack^M
manica^F a vento^M

flag with Schwenkel
bandera^F con Schwenkel
drapeau^M à Schwenkel
Fahne^F mit Schwenkel^M
bandiera^F con Schwenkel^M

streamer
banderola^F
banderole^F
Fahnenband^N
fiamma^F

base
base^F
base^F
Fuß^M
base^F

square flag
bandera^F cuadrada
drapeau^M carré
viereckige Fahne^F
bandiera^F quadrata

pennant
pendón^M
pennon^M
Wimpel^M
gagliardetto^M

swallowtail
bandera^F de dos puntas^F
pavillon^M à deux pointes^F
Doppelständer^M
coda^F di rondine^F

swallowtail and tongue
bandera^F de dos puntas^F y lengua^F
pavillon^M à deux pointes^F et langue^F
Doppelständer^M mit Zunge^F
coda^F di rondine^F con una lingua^F

fanion
banderín^M
fanion^M
Fanion^N
pennello^M

oriflamme
oriflama^F
oriflamme^F
Oriflamme^F
orifiamma^F

flag shapes
formas^F de banderas^F
formes^F de drapeaux^M
Fahnenformen^F
tipi^M di bandiera^F

rectangular flag
bandera^F rectangular
drapeau^M rectangulaire
rechteckige Fahne^F
bandiera^F rettangolare

double pennant
banderín^M doble
pennon^M double
Doppelwimpel^M
doppio pennello^M

burgee
corneta^F
guidon^M
Guidon^M
guidone^M

gonfalon
gonfalón^M
gonfalon^M
Gonfalon^M
gonfalone^M

bunting
empavesado^M
pavois^M
Wimpelgirlande^F
pavese^M

SOCIETY

heraldry

shield divisions
divisiones^F de los escudos^M
divisions^F de l'écu^M
Schildplätze^M
divisioni^M dello scudo^M

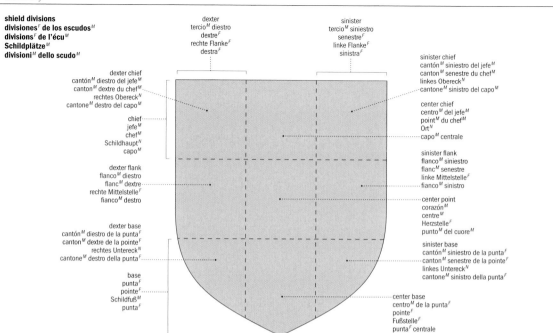

dexter
tercio^M diestro
dextre^F
rechte Flanke^F
destra^F

sinister
tercio^M siniestro
senestre^F
linke Flanke^F
sinistra^F

sinister chief
cantón^M siniestro del jefe^M
canton^M senestre du chef^M
linkes Obereck^N
cantone^M sinistro del capo^M

dexter chief
cantón^M diestro del jefe^M
canton^M dextre du chef^M
rechtes Obereck^N
cantone^M destro del capo^M

center chief
centro^M del jefe^M
point^M du chef^M
Ort^N
capo^M centrale

chief
jefe^M
chef^M
Schildhaupt^N
capo^M

sinister flank
flanco^M siniestro
flanc^M senestre
linke Mittelstelle^F
fianco^M sinistro

dexter flank
flanco^M diestro
flanc^M dextre
rechte Mittelstelle^F
fianco^M destro

center point
corazón^M
centre^M
Herzstelle^F
punto^M del cuore^M

dexter base
cantón^M diestro de la punta^F
canton^M dextre de la pointe^F
rechtes Untereck^N
cantone^M destro della punta^F

sinister base
cantón^M siniestro de la punta^F
canton^M senestre de la pointe^F
linkes Untereck^N
cantone^M sinistro della punta^F

base
punta^F
pointe^F
Schildfuß^M
punta^F

center base
centro^M de la punta^F
pointe^F
Fußstelle^F
punta^F centrale

examples of partitions
ejemplos^M de particiones^F
exemples^M de partitions^F
Teilungsbeispiele^N
esempi^M di partizioni^F

per fess
escudo^M cortado
coupé
blaues Schildhaupt^N in Silber
troncato

party
escudo^M partido
parti
gespalten
partito

per bend
escudo^M tronchado
tranché
schräg geteilt
trinciato

quarterly
escudo^M acuartelado
écartelé
geviert
inquartato

examples of ordinaries
ejemplos^M de piezas^F honorables
exemples^M de pièces^F honorables
Beispiele^N für Heroldsbilder^N
esempi^M di pezze^F onorevoli^M

chief
jefe^M
chef^M
Hauptrand^M
capo^M

chevron
cheurón^M
chevron^M
Sparren^M
scaglione^M

pale
palo^M
pal^M
Pfahl^M
palo^M

cross
cruz^F
croix^F
Kreuz^N
croce^F

SOCIETY

examples of metals
ejemplos^M de metales^M
exemples^M de métaux^M
Beispiele^N für Metall^N
esempi^M di metalli^M

examples of furs
ejemplos^M de forros^M
exemples^M de fourrures^F
Beispiele^N für Pelzwerk^N
esempi^M di pellicce^F

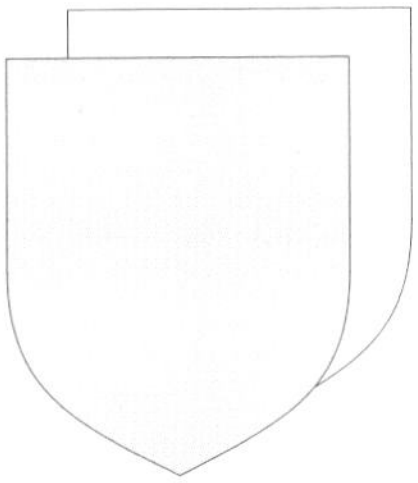

argent
plata^F
argent^M
Silber^N
argento^M

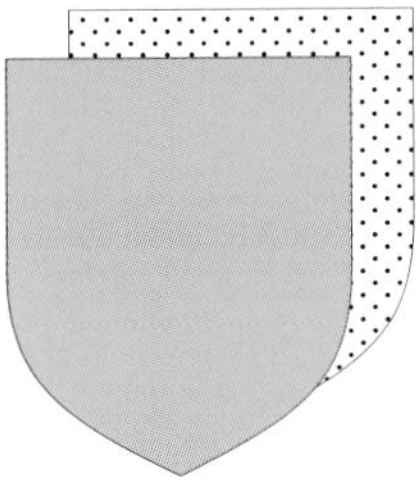

or
oro^M
or^M
Gold^N
oro^M

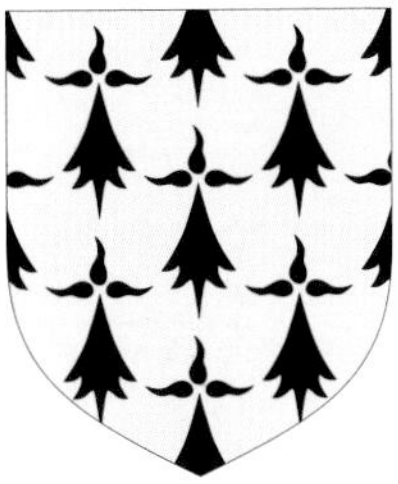

ermine
armiño^M
hermine^F
Hermelin^M
ermellino^M

vair
cerros^M
vair^N
Eishutfeh^N
vaio^M

examples of charges
ejemplos^M de muebles^M
exemples^M de meubles^M
Beispiele^N für Wappenzeichen^N
esempi^M di figure^F

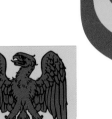

fleur-de-lis
flor^F de lis^F
fleur^F de lis^M
Lilie^F
giglio^M

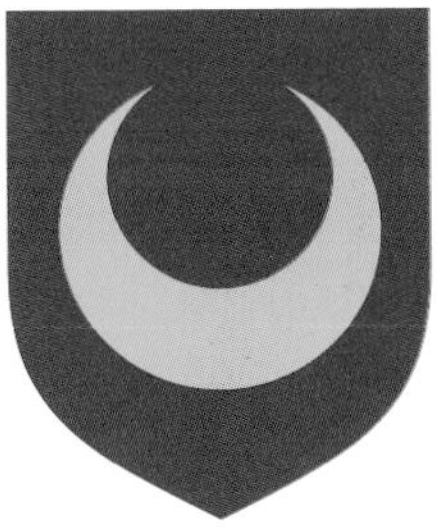

crescent
creciente^M
croissant^M
Mondsichel^F
crescente^M

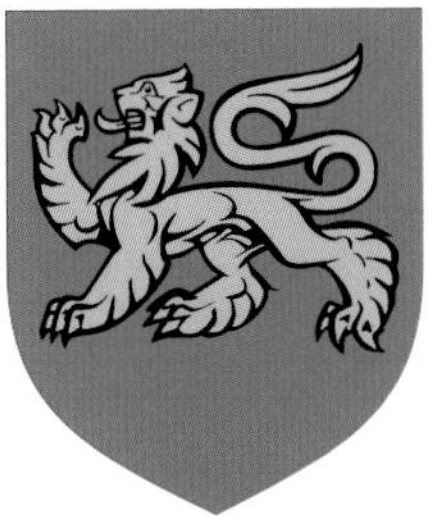

lion passant
león^M pasante
lion^M passant
schreitender Löwe^M
leone^M passante

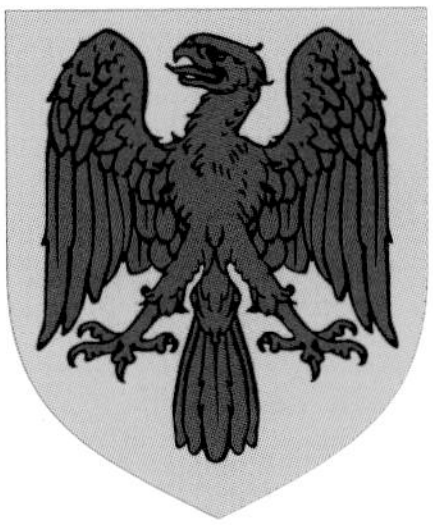

eagle
águila^F
aigle^F
Adler^M
aquila^F

mullet
estrella^F
étoile^F
Stern^M
stella^F

examples of colors
ejemplos^M de colores^M
exemples^M de couleurs^F
Farbbeispiele^N
esempi^M di colori^M

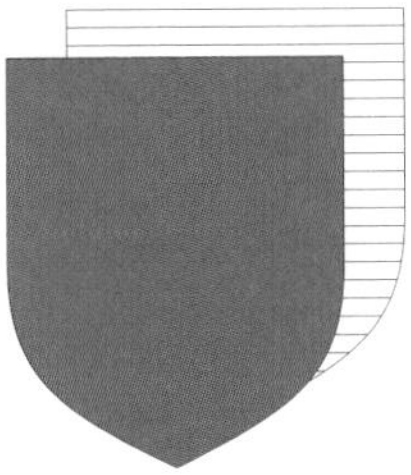

azure
azur^M
azur^M
blau
azzurro^M

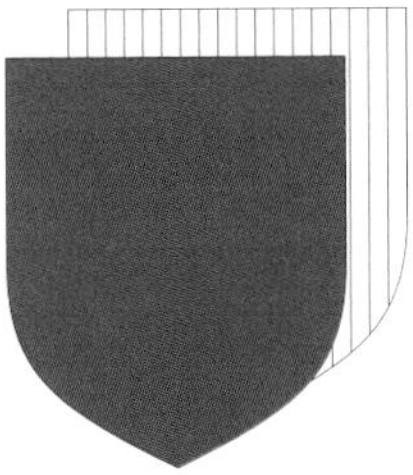

gules
gules^M
gueules^M
rot
rosso^M

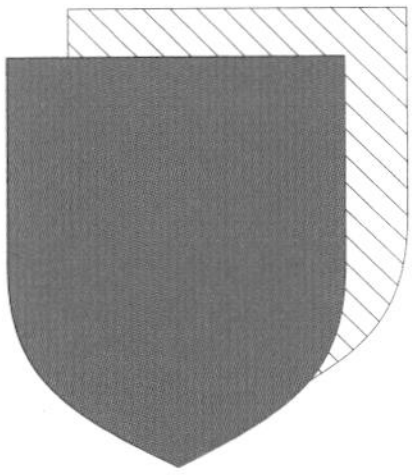

vert
sinople^M
sinople^M
grün
verde^M

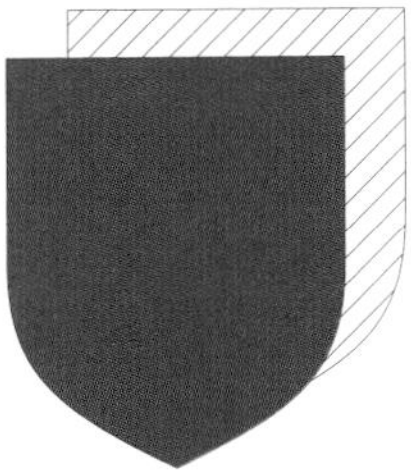

purpure
púrpura^M
pourpre^M
purpurn
porpora^M

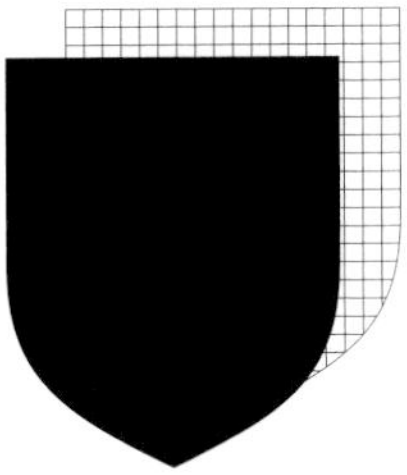

sable
sable^M
sable^M
schwarz
nero^M

flags

banderas[F] | drapeaux[M] | Flaggen[F] | bandiere[F]

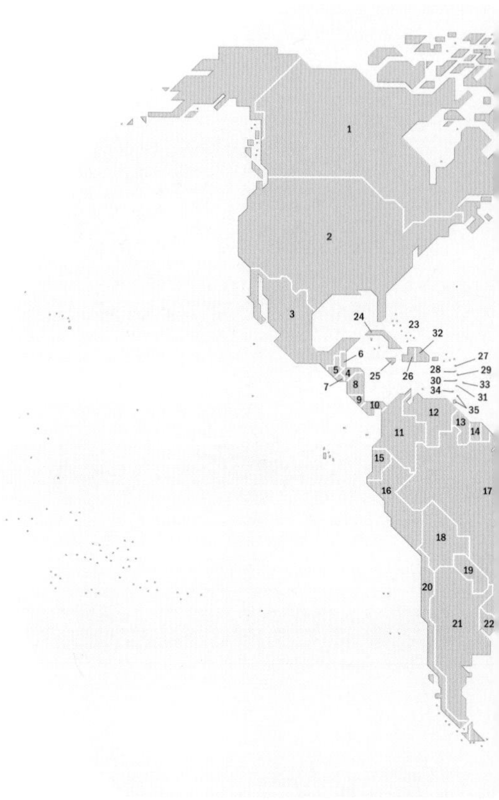

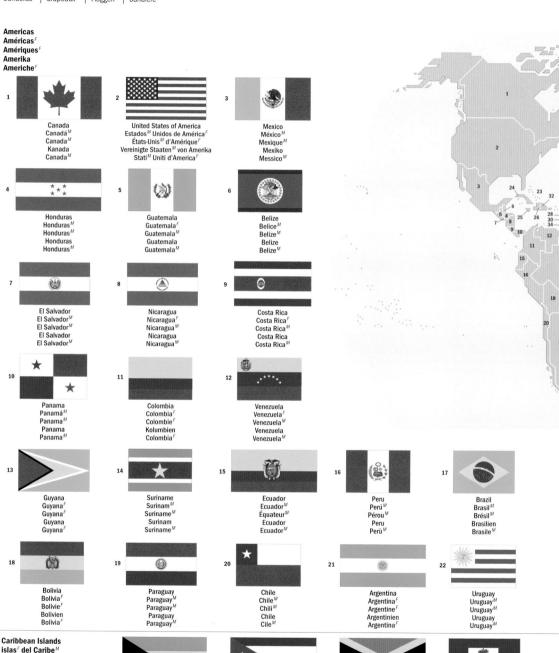

Americas
Américas[F]
Amériques[F]
Amerika
Americhe[F]

1 Canada
Canadá[M]
Canada[M]
Kanada
Canada[M]

2 United States of America
Estados[M] Unidos de América[F]
États-Unis[M] d'Amérique[F]
Vereinigte Staaten[M] von Amerika
Stati[M] Uniti d'America[F]

3 Mexico
México[M]
Mexique[M]
Mexiko
Messico[M]

4 Honduras
Honduras[M]
Honduras[M]
Honduras
Honduras[M]

5 Guatemala
Guatemala[F]
Guatemala[M]
Guatemala
Guatemala[M]

6 Belize
Belice[M]
Belize[M]
Belize
Belize[M]

7 El Salvador
El Salvador[M]
El Salvador[M]
El Salvador
El Salvador[M]

8 Nicaragua
Nicaragua[F]
Nicaragua[M]
Nicaragua
Nicaragua[M]

9 Costa Rica
Costa Rica[F]
Costa Rica[M]
Costa Rica
Costa Rica[M]

10 Panama
Panamá[M]
Panama[M]
Panama
Panama[M]

11 Colombia
Colombia[F]
Colombie[F]
Kolumbien
Colombia[F]

12 Venezuela
Venezuela[F]
Venezuela[M]
Venezuela
Venezuela[M]

13 Guyana
Guyana[F]
Guyana[F]
Guyana
Guyana[F]

14 Suriname
Surinam[M]
Suriname[M]
Surinam
Suriname[M]

15 Ecuador
Ecuador[M]
Équateur[M]
Ecuador
Ecuador[M]

16 Peru
Perú[M]
Pérou[M]
Peru
Perù[M]

17 Brazil
Brasil[M]
Brésil[M]
Brasilien
Brasile[M]

18 Bolivia
Bolivia[F]
Bolivie[F]
Bolivien
Bolivia[F]

19 Paraguay
Paraguay[M]
Paraguay[M]
Paraguay
Paraguay[M]

20 Chile
Chile[M]
Chili[M]
Chile
Cile[M]

21 Argentina
Argentina[F]
Argentine[F]
Argentinien
Argentina[F]

22 Uruguay
Uruguay[M]
Uruguay[M]
Uruguay
Uruguay[M]

Caribbean Islands
islas[F] **del Caribe**[M]
Antilles[F]
Karibische Inseln[F]
Isole[F] **delle Antille**[F]

23 The Bahamas
Bahamas[F]
Bahamas[F]
Bahamas[F]
Bahama[F]

24 Cuba
Cuba[F]
Cuba[F]
Kuba
Cuba[F]

25 Jamaica
Jamaica[F]
Jamaique[F]
Jamaika
Giamaica[F]

26 Haiti
Haiti[M]
Haiti[M]
Haiti
Haiti[F]

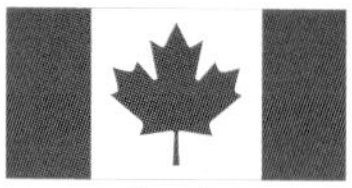

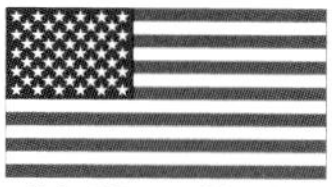

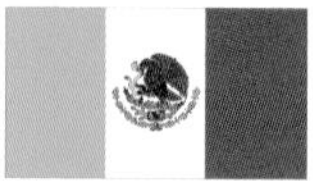

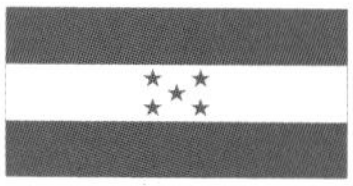

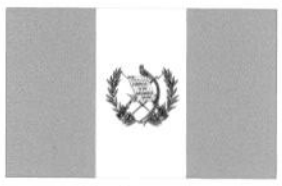

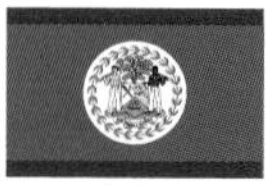

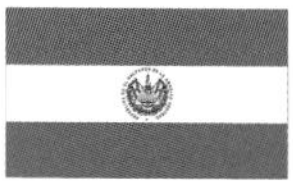

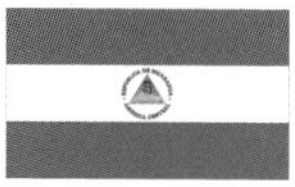

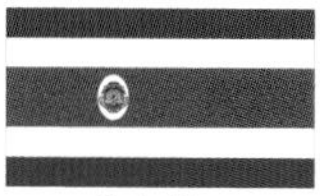

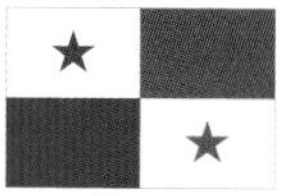

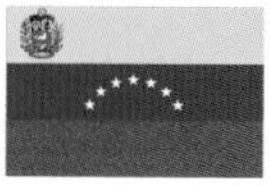

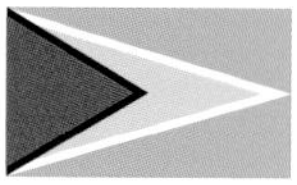

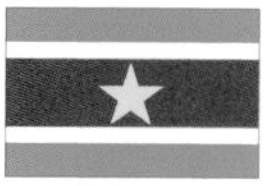

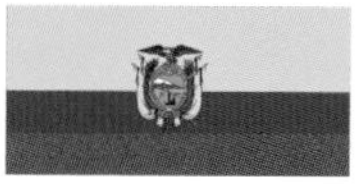

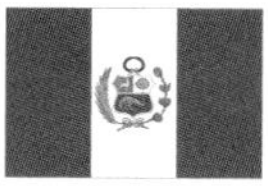

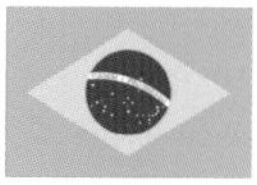

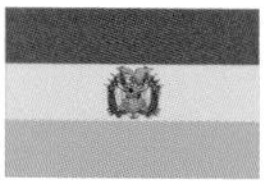

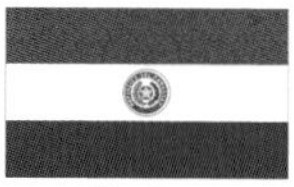

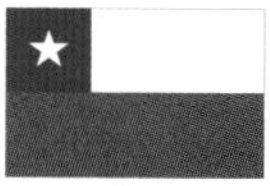

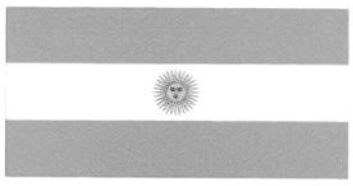

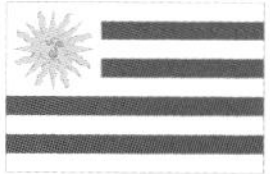

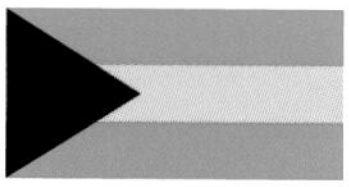

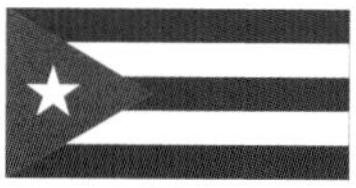

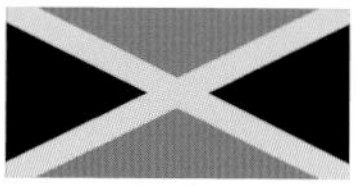

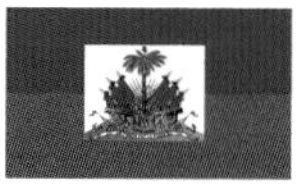

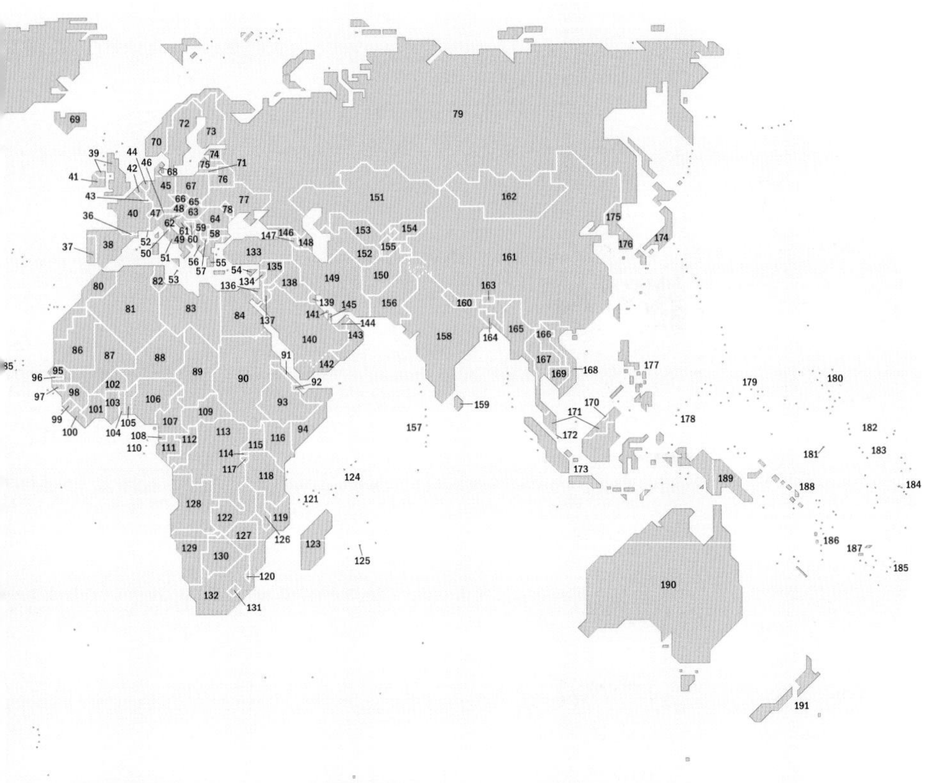

27

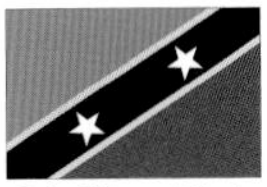

Saint Kitts and Nevis
Saint Kitts and Nevis[M]
Saint-Kitts-et-Nevis[M]
Saint Kitts und Nevis
Saint Kitts e Nevis[F]

28

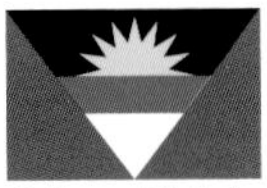

Antigua and Barbuda
Antigua[F] y Barbuda[F]
Antigua-et-Barbuda[F]
Antigua und Barbuda
Antigua e Barbuda[F]

29

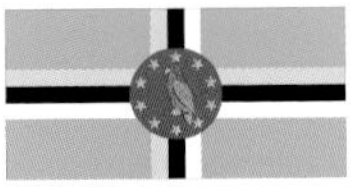

Dominica
Dominica[F]
Dominique[F]
Dominica
Dominica[F]

30

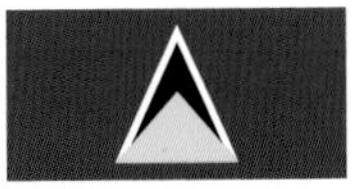

Saint Lucia
Santa Lucía[F]
Sainte-Lucie[F]
St. Lucia
Saint Lucia[F]

31

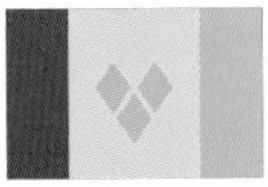

Saint Vincent and the Grenadines
San Vicente y las Granadinas[F]
Saint-Vincent[M]-et-les Grenadines[F]
Saint Vincent und die Grenadinen
Saint Vincent e Grenadine[F]

32

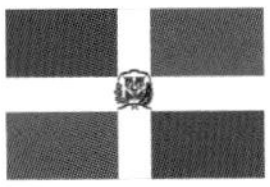

Dominican Republic
República[F] Dominicana
République[F] dominicaine
Dominikanische Republik[F]
Repubblica[F] Dominicana

33

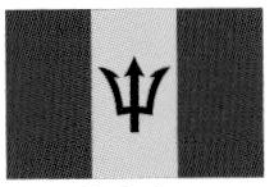

Barbados
Barbados[F]
Barbade[F]
Barbados
Barbados[F]

34

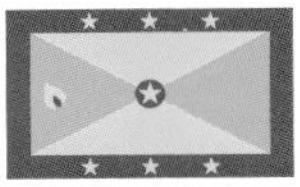

Grenada
Granada[F]
Grenade[F]
Grenada
Grenada[F]

35

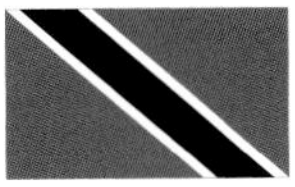

Trinidad and Tobago
Trinidad[F] y Tobago[M]
Trinité-et-Tobago[F]
Trinidad und Tobago
Trinidad[F] e Tobago[F]

Europe
Europa[F]
Europe[F]
Europa
Europa[F]

36

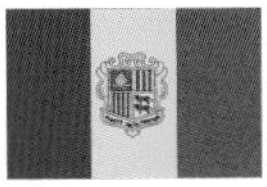

Andorra
Principado[M] de Andorra[F]
Andorre[F]
Andorra
Andorra[F]

37

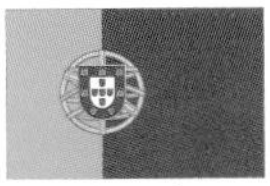

Portugal
Portugal[M]
Portugal[M]
Portugal
Portogallo[M]

38

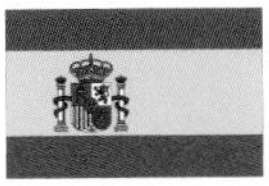

Spain
España[F]
Espagne[F]
Spanien
Spagna[F]

39

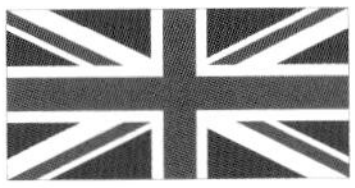

United Kingdom
Reino[M] Unido de Gran Bretaña[F] e Irlanda[F] del Norte[M]
Royaume-Uni[M] de Grande-Bretagne[F] et d'Irlande[F] du Nord[M]
Vereinigtes Königreich[N] von Großbritannien und Nordirland
Regno[M] Unito di Gran Bretagna[F] e Irlanda[F] del Nord[M]

40

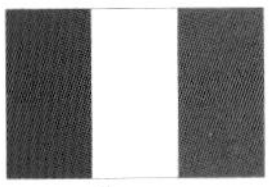

France
Francia[F]
France[F]
Frankreich
Francia[F]

41

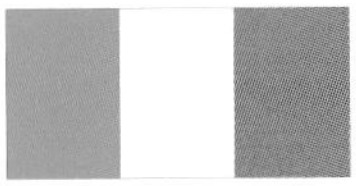

Ireland
Irlanda[F]
Irlande[F]
Irland
Irlanda[F]

42

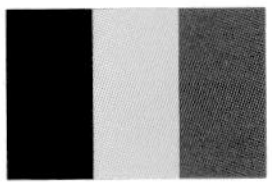

Belgium
Bélgica[F]
Belgique[F]
Belgien
Belgio[M]

43

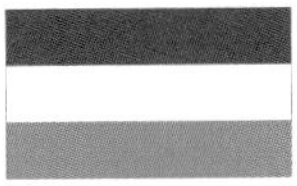

Luxembourg
Luxemburgo[M]
Luxembourg[M]
Luxemburg
Lussemburgo[M]

44

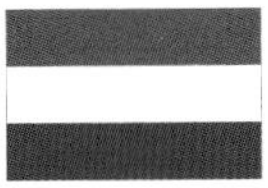

Netherlands
Países[M] Bajos
Pays-Bas[M]
Niederlande[F]
Paesi[F] Bassi

SOCIETY

743

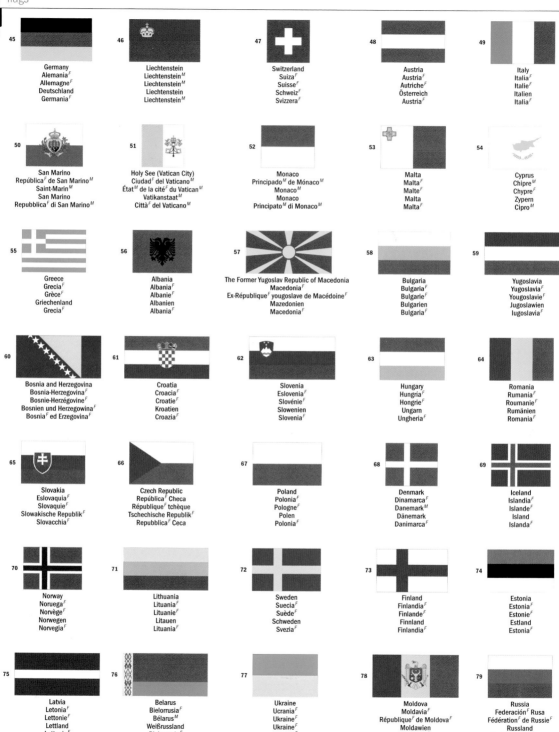

45 Germany
Alemania[F]
Allemagne[F]
Deutschland
Germania[F]

46 Liechtenstein
Liechtenstein[M]
Liechtenstein[M]
Liechtenstein
Liechtenstein[M]

47 Switzerland
Suiza[F]
Suisse[F]
Schweiz[F]
Svizzera[F]

48 Austria
Austria[F]
Autriche[F]
Österreich
Austria[F]

49 Italy
Italia[F]
Italie[F]
Italien
Italia[F]

50 San Marino
República[F] de San Marino[M]
Saint-Marin[M]
San Marino
Repubblica[F] di San Marino[M]

51 Holy See (Vatican City)
Ciudad[F] del Vaticano[M]
État[M] de la cité[F] du Vatican[M]
Vatikanstaat[M]
Città[F] del Vaticano[M]

52 Monaco
Principado[M] de Mónaco[M]
Monaco[M]
Monaco
Principato[M] di Monaco[M]

53 Malta
Malta[F]
Malte[F]
Malta
Malta[F]

54 Cyprus
Chipre[M]
Chypre[F]
Zypern
Cipro[M]

55 Greece
Grecia[F]
Grèce[F]
Griechenland
Grecia[F]

56 Albania
Albania[F]
Albanie[F]
Albanien
Albania[F]

57 The Former Yugoslav Republic of Macedonia
Macedonia[F]
Ex-République[F] yougoslave de Macédoine[F]
Mazedonien
Macedonia[F]

58 Bulgaria
Bulgaria[F]
Bulgarie[F]
Bulgarien
Bulgaria[F]

59 Yugoslavia
Yugoslavia[F]
Yougoslavie[F]
Jugoslawien
Iugoslavia[F]

60 Bosnia and Herzegovina
Bosnia-Herzegovina[F]
Bosnie-Herzégovine[F]
Bosnien und Herzegowina[F]
Bosnia[F] ed Erzegovina[F]

61 Croatia
Croacia[F]
Croatie[F]
Kroatien
Croazia[F]

62 Slovenia
Eslovenia[F]
Slovénie[F]
Slowenien
Slovenia[F]

63 Hungary
Hungría[F]
Hongrie[F]
Ungarn
Ungheria[F]

64 Romania
Rumania[F]
Roumanie[F]
Rumänien
Romania[F]

65 Slovakia
Eslovaquia[F]
Slovaquie[F]
Slowakische Republik[F]
Slovacchia[F]

66 Czech Republic
República[F] Checa
République[F] tchèque
Tschechische Republik[F]
Repubblica[F] Ceca

67 Poland
Polonia[F]
Pologne[F]
Polen
Polonia[F]

68 Denmark
Dinamarca[F]
Danemark[M]
Dänemark
Danimarca[F]

69 Iceland
Islandia[F]
Islande[F]
Island
Islanda[F]

70 Norway
Noruega[F]
Norvège[F]
Norwegen
Norvegia[F]

71 Lithuania
Lituania[F]
Lituanie[F]
Litauen
Lituania[F]

72 Sweden
Suecia[F]
Suède[F]
Schweden
Svezia[F]

73 Finland
Finlandia[F]
Finlande[F]
Finnland
Finlandia[F]

74 Estonia
Estonia[F]
Estonie[F]
Estland
Estonia[F]

75 Latvia
Letonia[F]
Lettonie[F]
Lettland
Lettonia[F]

76 Belarus
Bielorrusia[F]
Bélarus[M]
Weißrussland
Bielorussia[F]

77 Ukraine
Ucrania[F]
Ukraine[F]
Ukraine[F]
Ucraina[F]

78 Moldova
Moldavia[F]
République[F] de Moldova[F]
Moldawien
Moldavia[F]

79 Russia
Federación[F] Rusa
Fédération[F] de Russie[F]
Russland
Federazione[F] Russa

POLITICS | POLÍTICA
POLITIQUE | POLITIK | POLÍTICA

flags

Africa
África^F
Afrique^F
Afrika
Africa^F

80 Morocco
Marruecos^M
Maroc^M
Marokko
Marocco^M

81 Algeria
Argelia^F
Algérie^F
Algerien
Algeria^F

82 Tunisia
Túnez^M
Tunisie^F
Tunesien
Tunisia^F

83 Lybia
Libia^F
Jamahiriya^F arabe libyenne
Libyen
Libia^F

84 Egypt
Egipto^M
Égypte^F
Ägypten
Egitto^M

85 Cape Verde
islas^F de Cabo^M Verde
Cap-Vert^M
Kap Verde
Capo Verde^M

86 Mauritania
Mauritania^F
Mauritanie^F
Mauretanien
Mauritania^F

87 Mali
República^F de Malí
Malí^M
Mali
Repubblica^F del Mali^M

88 Niger
Níger^M
Niger^M
Niger^M
Niger^M

89 Chad
Chad^M
Tchad^M
Tschad^M
Ciad^M

90 Sudan
Sudán^M
Soudan^M
Sudan^M
Sudan^M

91 Eritrea
Eritrea^F
Érythrée^F
Eritrea
Eritrea^F

92 Djibouti
Yibouti^M
Djibouti^M
Dschibuti
Gibuti^M

93 Ethiopia
Etiopía^F
Éthiopie^F
Äthiopien
Etiopia^F

94 Somalia
Somalia^F
Somalie^F
Somalia
Somalia^F

95 Senegal
Senegal^M
Sénégal^M
Senegal^N
Senegal^M

96 The Gambia
Gambia^M
Gambie^F
Gambia
Gambia^M

97 Guinea-Bissau
Guinea-Bissau^F
Guinée-Bissau^F
Guinea-Bissau
Guinea Bissau^F

98 Guinea
Guinea^F
Guinée^F
Guinea
Guinea^F

99 Sierra Leone
Sierra^F Leona
Sierra Leone^F
Sierra Leone
Sierra Leone^F

100 Liberia
Liberia^F
Libéria^M
Liberia
Liberia^F

101 Côte d'Ivoire
Costa de Marfil^F
Côte d'Ivoire^F
Elfenbeinküste
Costa d'Avorio^F

102 Burkina Faso
Burkina Faso^M
Burkina Faso^M
Burkina Faso
Burkina Faso^M

103 Ghana
Ghana^F
Ghana^M
Ghana
Ghana^M

104 Togo
Togo^M
Togo^M
Togo
Togo^M

105 Benin
Benín^M
Bénin^M
Benin
Benin^M

106 Nigeria
Nigeria^F
Nigeria^M
Nigeria
Nigeria^F

107 Cameroon
Camerún^M
Cameroun^M
Kamerun
Camerun^M

108 Equatorial Guinea
Guinea^F Ecuatorial
Guinée^F équatoriale
Äquatorialguinea
Guinea^F Equatoriale

109 Central African Republic
República^F Centroafricana
République^F centrafricaine
Zentralafrikanische Republik^F
Repubblica^F Centrafricana

110 Sao Tome and Principe
Santo Tomé y Príncipe^M
São Tomé-et-Príncipe^M
São Tomé und Principe
São Tomé e Principe^M

111 Gabon
Gabón^M
Gabon^M
Gabun
Gabon^M

112 Republic of the Congo
Congo^M
Congo^M
Kongo^M
Congo^M

113 Democratic Republic of the Congo
República^F Democrática del Congo^M
République^F démocratique du Congo^M
Republik^F Kongo^M
Repubblica^F Democratica del Congo^M

114 Rwanda
Ruanda^M
Rwanda^M
Ruanda
Ruanda^M

115 Uganda
Uganda^F
Ouganda^M
Uganda
Uganda^F

116 Kenya
Kenia^F
Kenya^M
Kenia
Kenya^M

117 Burundi
Burundi^M
Burundi^M
Burundi
Burundi^M

118 Tanzania
Tanzanía^F
République^F-Unie de Tanzanie^F
Tansania
Tanzania^F

SOCIETY

745

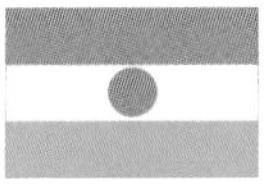

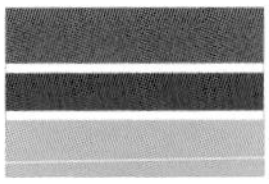

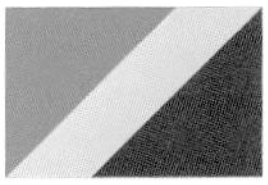

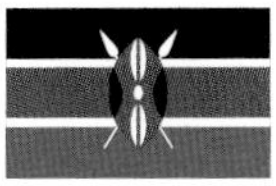

flags

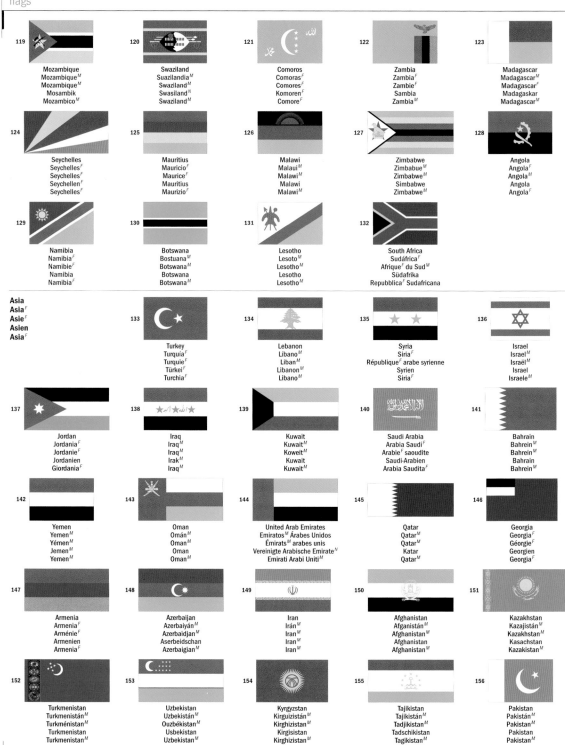

119
Mozambique
Mozambique[M]
Mozambique[M]
Mosambik
Mozambico[M]

120
Swaziland
Suazilandia[M]
Swaziland[M]
Swasiland[N]
Swaziland[M]

121
Comoros
Comoras[F]
Comores[F]
Komoren[F]
Comore[F]

122
Zambia
Zambia[F]
Zambie[F]
Sambia
Zambia[F]

123
Madagascar
Madagascar[M]
Madagascar[F]
Madagaskar
Madagascar[M]

124
Seychelles
Seychelles[F]
Seychelles[F]
Seychellen[F]
Seychelles[F]

125
Mauritius
Mauricio[F]
Maurice[F]
Mauritius
Maurizio[F]

126
Malawi
Malaui[M]
Malawi[F]
Malawi
Malawi[M]

127
Zimbabwe
Zimbabue[M]
Zimbabwe[M]
Simbabwe
Zimbabwe[M]

128
Angola
Angola[F]
Angola[M]
Angola
Angola[F]

129
Namibia
Namibia[F]
Namibie[F]
Namibia
Namibia[F]

130
Botswana
Bostuana[M]
Botswana[M]
Botswana
Botswana[M]

131
Lesotho
Lesoto[M]
Lesotho[M]
Lesotho
Lesotho[M]

132
South Africa
Sudáfrica[F]
Afrique[F] du Sud[M]
Südafrika
Repubblica[F] Sudafricana

Asia
Asia[F]
Asie[F]
Asien
Asia[F]

133
Turkey
Turquía[F]
Turquie[F]
Türkei[F]
Turchia[F]

134
Lebanon
Líbano[M]
Liban[M]
Libanon[M]
Libano[M]

135
Syria
Siria[F]
République[F] arabe syrienne
Syrien
Siria[F]

136
Israel
Israel[M]
Israël[M]
Israel
Israele[M]

137
Jordan
Jordania[F]
Jordanie[F]
Jordanien
Giordania[F]

138
Iraq
Iraq[M]
Iraq[M]
Irak[M]
Iraq[M]

139
Kuwait
Kuwait[M]
Koweit[M]
Kuwait
Kuwait[M]

140
Saudi Arabia
Arabia Saudí[F]
Arabie[F] saoudite
Saudi-Arabien
Arabia Saudita[F]

141
Bahrain
Bahrein[M]
Bahrein[M]
Bahrain
Bahrein[M]

142
Yemen
Yemen[M]
Yémen[M]
Jemen
Yemen[M]

143
Oman
Omán[M]
Oman[M]
Oman
Oman[M]

144
United Arab Emirates
Emiratos[M] Árabes Unidos
Émirats[M] arabes unis
Vereinigte Arabische Emirate[N]
Emirati Arabi Uniti[M]

145
Qatar
Qatar[M]
Qatar[M]
Katar
Qatar[M]

146
Georgia
Georgia[F]
Géorgie[F]
Georgien
Georgia[F]

147
Armenia
Armenia[F]
Arménie[F]
Armenien
Armenia[F]

148
Azerbaijan
Azerbaiyán[M]
Azerbaidjan[M]
Aserbeidschan
Azerbaigian[M]

149
Iran
Irán[M]
Iran[M]
Iran[M]
Iran[M]

150
Afghanistan
Afganistán[M]
Afghanistan[M]
Afghanistan
Afghanistan[M]

151
Kazakhstan
Kazajistán[M]
Kazakhstan[M]
Kasachstan
Kazakistan[M]

152
Turkmenistan
Turkmenistán[M]
Turkménistan[M]
Turkmenistan
Turkmenistan[M]

153
Uzbekistan
Uzbekistán[M]
Ouzbékistan[M]
Usbekistan
Uzbekistan[M]

154
Kyrgyzstan
Kirguizistán[M]
Kirghizistan[M]
Kirgisistan
Kirghizistan[M]

155
Tajikistan
Tajikistán[M]
Tadjikistan[M]
Tadschikistan
Tagikistan[M]

156
Pakistan
Pakistán[M]
Pakistan[M]
Pakistan
Pakistan[M]

157

Maldives
Maldivas[F]
Maldives[F]
Malediven[F]
Maldive[F]

158

India
India[F]
Inde[F]
Indien
India[F]

159

Sri Lanka
Sri Lanka[M]
Sri Lanka[M]
Sri Lanka
Sri Lanka[M]

160

Nepal
Nepal[M]
Népal[M]
Nepal
Nepal[M]

161

China
China[F]
Chine[F]
China
Cina[F]

162

Mongolia
Mongolia[F]
Mongolie[F]
Mongolei[F]
Mongolia[F]

163

Bhutan
Bután[M]
Bhoutan[M]
Bhutan
Bhutan[M]

164

Bangladesh
Bangladesh[M]
Bangladesh[M]
Bangladesch
Bangladesh[M]

165

Burma
Myanmar[M]
Myanmar[M]
Myanmar
Myanmar[M]

166

Laos
Laos[M]
République[F] démocratique populaire lao
Laos
Laos[M]

167

Thailand
Tailandia[F]
Thailande[F]
Thailand
Tailandia[F]

168

Vietnam
Vietnam[M]
Viet Nam[M]
Vietnam
Vietnam[M]

169

Cambodia
Camboya[F]
Cambodge[M]
Kambodscha
Cambogia[F]

170

Brunei
Brunei[F]
Brunéi Darussalam[M]
Brunei
Brunei[M]

171

Malaysia
Malasia[F]
Malaisie[F]
Malaysia
Malaysia[F]

172

Singapore
Singapur[M]
Singapour[F]
Singapur
Singapore[F]

173

Indonesia
Indonesia[F]
Indonésie[F]
Indonesien
Indonesia[F]

174

Japan
Japón[M]
Japon[M]
Japan
Giappone[M]

175

North Korea
Republica[F] Democrática Popular de Corea[F]
République[F] populaire démocratique de Corée[F]
Nord-Korea
Repubblica[F] Democratica Popolare di Corea[F]

176

South Korea
República[F] de Corea[F]
République[F] de Corée[F]
Süd-Korea
Repubblica[F] di Corea[F]

177

Philippines
Filipinas[F]
Philippines[F]
Philippinen[F]
Filippine[F]

178

Palau
Palau[M]
Palaos[M]
Palau
Palau[M]

179

Federated States of Micronesia
Micronesia[F]
Micronésie[F]
Mikronesien
Micronesia[F]

Oceania and Polynesia
Oceanía[F] y Polinesia[F]
Océanie[F] et Polynésie[F]
Ozeanien und Polynesien
Oceania[F] e Polinesia[F]

180

Marshall Islands
Islas[F] Marshall
Îles[F] Marshall
Marshallinseln[F]
Isole Marshall[F]

181

Nauru
Nauru[M]
Nauru[F]
Nauru
Nauru[M]

182

Kiribati
Kiribati[M]
Kiribati[F]
Kiribati
Kiribati[M]

183

Tuvalu
Tuvalu[M]
Tuvalu[M]
Tuvalu
Tuvalu[M]

184

Samoa
Samoa[F]
Samoa[F]
Samoa
Samoa[F]

185

Tonga
Tonga[M]
Tonga[F]
Tonga
Tonga[M]

186

Vanuatu
Vanuatu[M]
Vanuatu[M]
Vanuatu
Vanuatu[M]

187

Fiji
Fiji[F]
Fidji[F]
Fidschi
Figi[F]

188

Solomon Islands
Islas Salomón[F]
Îles[F] Salomon
Salomoninseln[F]
Isole[F] Salomone

189

Papua New Guinea
Papua Nueva Guinea[F]
Papouasie-Nouvelle-Guinée[F]
Papua-Neuguinea
Papua Nuova Guinea[F]

190

Australia
Australia[F]
Australie[F]
Australien
Australia[F]

191

New Zealand
Nueva Zelanda[F]
Nouvelle-Zélande[F]
Neuseeland
Nuova Zelanda[F]

weapons in the Stone Age

armas^F de la Edad^F de Piedra^F | armes^F de l'âge^M de pierre^F | Steinzeitwaffen^F | armi^F dell'età^F della pietra^F

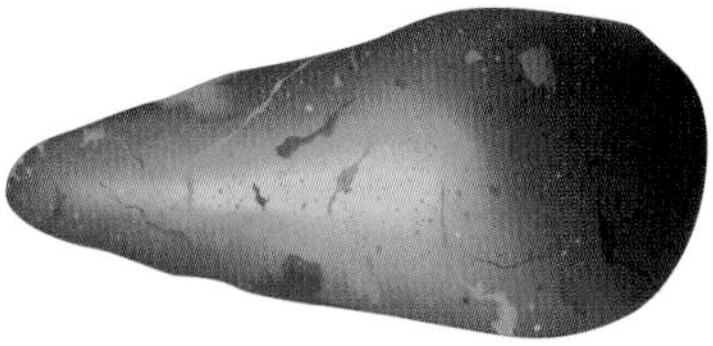

polished stone hand axe
hacha^F de piedra^F pulida
hache^F en pierre^F polie
polierter Steinfaustkeil^M
ascia^F levigata

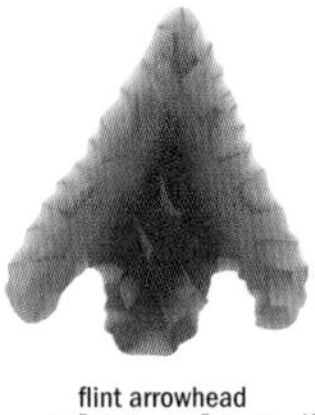

flint arrowhead
punta^F de flecha^F de sílex^M
pointe^F de flèche^F en silex^M
Pfeilspitze^F aus Feuerstein^M
punta^F di freccia^F in selce^F

flint knife
cuchillo^M de sílex^M
couteau^M en silex^M
Messer^N aus Feuerstein^M
coltello^M di selce^F

weapons in the age of the Romans

armas^F del imperio^M romano | armes^F de l'époque^F romaine | Waffen^F in der Römerzeit^F | armi^F al tempo^M dei Romani^M

Roman legionary
legionario^M romano
légionnaire^M romain
römischer Legionär^M
legionario^M romano

Gallic warrior
guerrero^M galo
guerrier^M gaulois
gallischer Krieger^M
guerriero^M gallico

crest
penacho^M
cimier^M
Helmbusch^M
cimiero^M

cuirass
loriga^F
cuirasse^F
Kürass^M
lorica^F

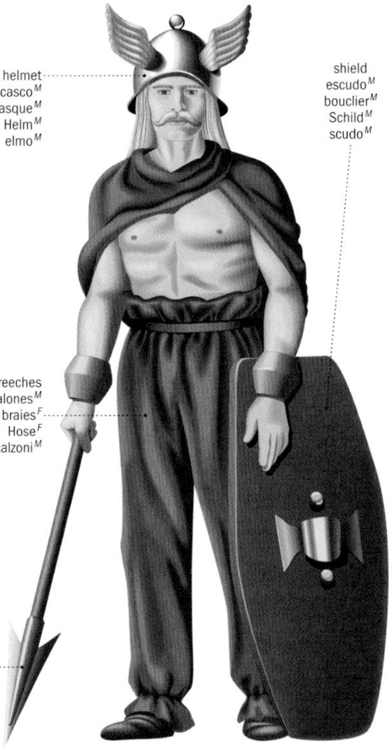

helmet
casco^M
casque^M
Helm^M
elmo^M

shield
escudo^M
bouclier^M
Schild^M
scudo^M

shield
escudo^M
bouclier^M
Schild^M
scudo^M

gladius
espada^F
glaive^M
Kurzschwert^N
gladio^M

javelin
jabalina^F
javelot^M
Lanze^F
giavellotto^M

breeches
pantalones^M
braies^F
Hose^F
calzoni^M

tunic
túnica^F
tunique^F
Tunika^F
tunica^F

sandal
sandalia^F
sandale^F
Sandale^F
sandalo^M

spear
lanza^F
lance^F
Speer^M
lancia^F

SOCIETY

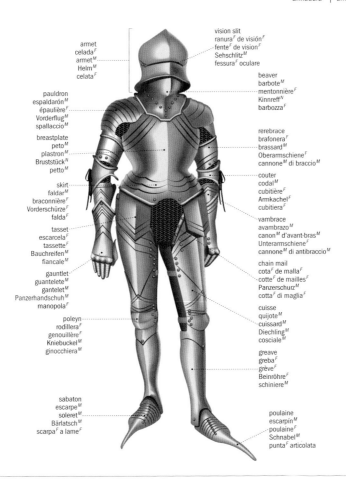

armet
celada^F
armet^M
Helm^M
celata^F

vision slit
ranura^F de visión^F
fente^F de vision^F
Sehschlitz^M
fessura^F oculare

beaver
barbote^M
mentonnière^F
Kinnreff^N
barbozza^F

pauldron
espaldarón^M
épaulière^F
Vorderflug^M
spallaccio^M

rerebrace
brafonera^F
brassard^M
Oberarmschiene^F
cannone di braccio^M

breastplate
peto^M
plastron^M
Bruststück^N
petto^M

couter
codal^M
cubitière^F
Armkachel^F
cubitiera^F

skirt
faldar^M
braconnière^F
Vorderschürze^F
falda^F

vambrace
avambrazo^M
canon^M d'avant-bras^M
Unterarmschiene^F
cannone^M di antibraccio^M

tasset
escarcela^F
tassette^F
Bauchreifen^M
fiancale^M

chain mail
cota^F de malla^F
cotte^F de mailles^F
Panzerschurz^M
cotta^F di maglia^F

gauntlet
guantelete^M
gantelet^M
Panzerhandschuh^M
manopola^F

cuisse
quijote^M
cuissard^M
Diechling^M
cosciale^M

poleyn
rodillera^F
genouillère^F
Kniebuckel^M
ginocchiera^M

greave
greba^F
grève^F
Beinröhre^F
schiniere^M

sabaton
escarpe^M
soleret^M
Bärlatsch^M
scarpa^F a lame^F

poulaine
escarpín^M
poulaine^F
Schnabel^M
punta^F articolata

armet
yelmo^M
armet^M
Helm^M
elmo^M

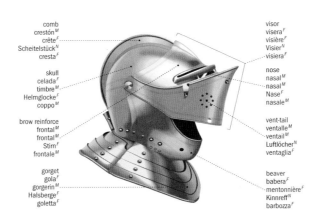

comb
crestón^M
crête^F
Scheitelstück^N
cresta^F

visor
visera^F
visière^F
Visier^N
visiera^F

skull
celada^F
timbre^M
Helmglocke^F
coppo^M

nose
nasal^M
nasal^M
Nase^F
nasale^M

brow reinforce
frontal^M
frontal^M
Stirn^F
frontale^M

vent-tail
ventalle^M
ventail^M
Luftlöcher^N
ventaglia^F

gorget
gola^F
gorgerin^M
Halsberge^F
goletta^F

beaver
babera^F
mentonnière^F
Kinnreff^N
barbozza^F

SOCIETY

bows and crossbow

arcos^M y ballesta^F | arcs^M et arbalète^F | Bogen^M und Armbrust^F | archi^M e balestra^F

crossbow
ballesta^F
arbalète^F
Armbrust^F
balestra^F

bow
arco^M
arc^M
Bügel^M
arco^M

stirrup
estribera^F
étrier^M
Steigbügel^M
staffa^F

tiller
cureña^F
arbrier^M
Abzugstange^F
teniere^M

nut
nuez^F
noix^F
Nuss^F
noce^F

pulley block
cierre^M de polea^F
moufle^F
Rollkloben^M
ponte^M

trigger
gatillo^M
détente^F
Abzug^M
manetta^F

bolt
flecha^F
carreau^M d'arbalète^F
Bolzen^M
dardo^M

groove
canal^M
rainure^F
Rinne^F
scanalatura^F

crank
manivela^F
manivelle^F
Drehschwengel^M
manovella^F

pulley
polea^F
poulie^F
Winde^F
carrucola^F

bowstring
cuerda^F
corde^F
Bogensehne^F
corda^F

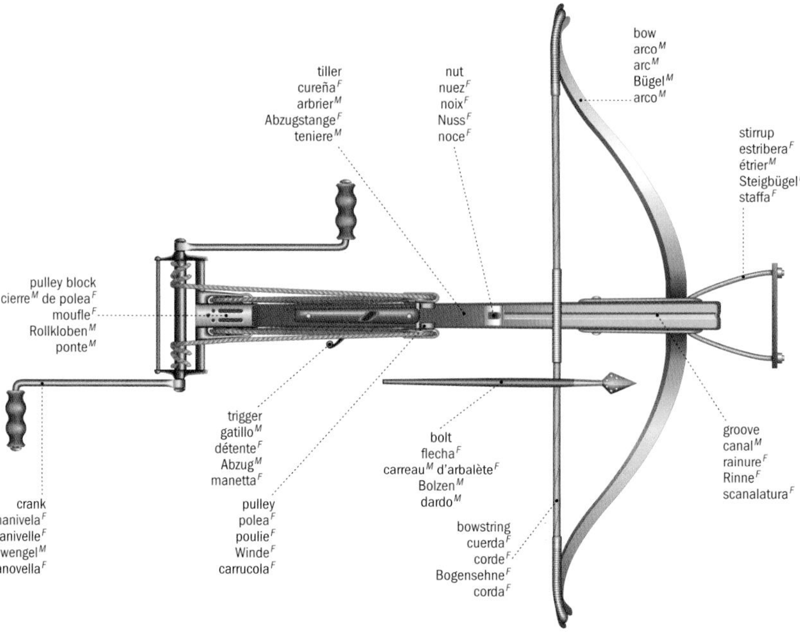

bow
arco^M
arc^M
Bogen^M
arco^M

nock
muesca^F
encoche^F
Nocke^F
cocca^F

upper limb
rama^F superior
branche^F supérieure
oberer Wurfarm^M
braccio^M superiore

handle
empuñadura^F
poignée^F
Handgriff^M
impugnatura^F

back
dorso^M
dos^M
Bogen^M
dorso^M

lower limb
rama^F inferior
branche^F inférieure
unterer Wurfarm^M
braccio^M inferiore

bowstring
cuerda^F
corde^F
Bogensehne^F
corda^F

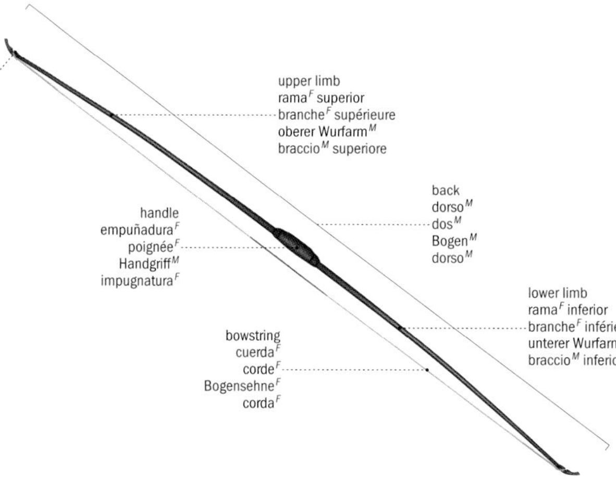

modern bow
arco^M moderno
arc^M moderne
moderner Bogen^M
arco^M moderno

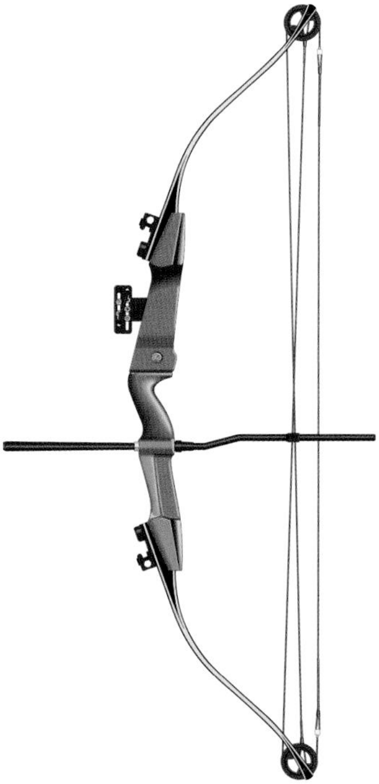

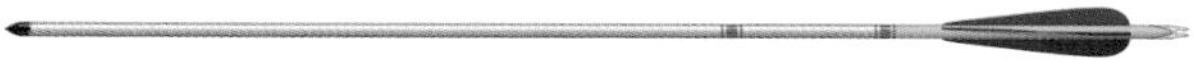

arrow
flecha^F
flèche^F
Pfeil^M
freccia^F

thrusting and cutting weapons

armas^F blancas | armes^F blanches | Hieb- und Stichwaffen^F | armi^F da lancio^M e da taglio^M

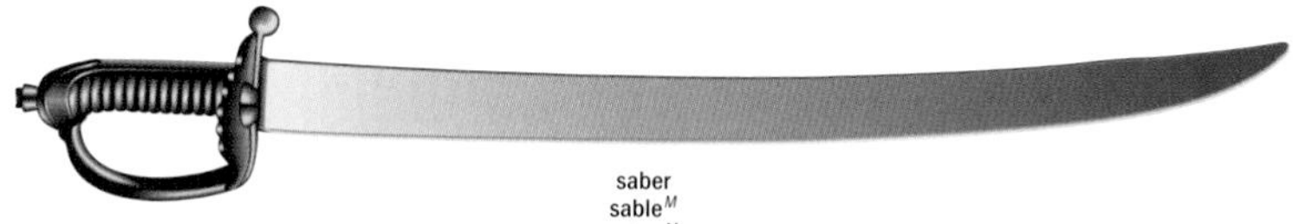

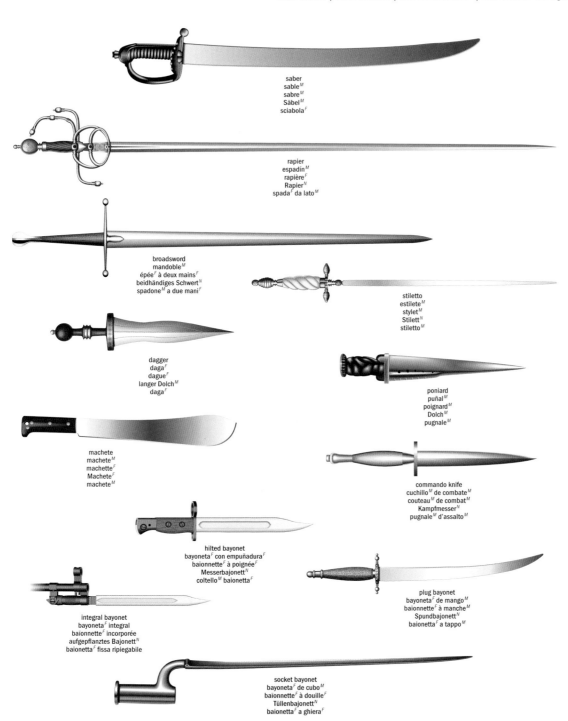

saber
sable^M
sabre^M
Säbel^M
sciabola^F

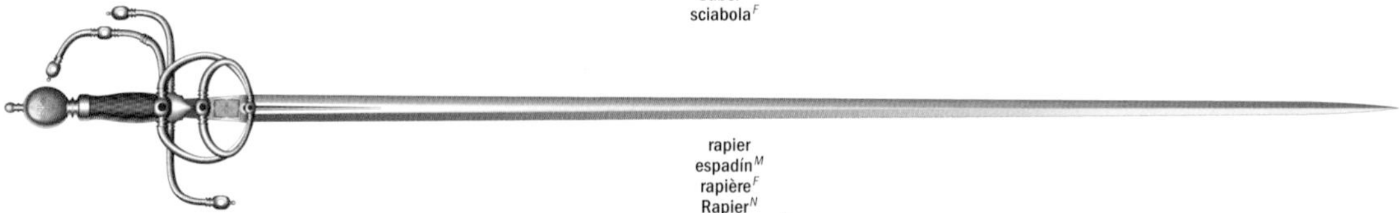

rapier
espadín^M
rapière^F
Rapier^N
spada^F da lato^M

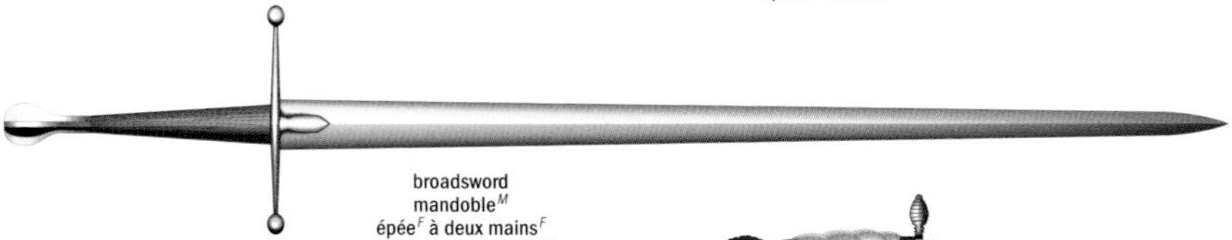

broadsword
mandoble^M
épée^F à deux mains^F
beidhändiges Schwert^N
spadone^M a due mani^F

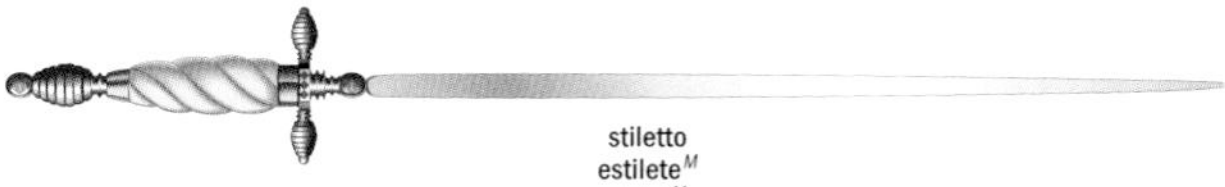

stiletto
estilete^M
stylet^M
Stilett^N
stiletto^M

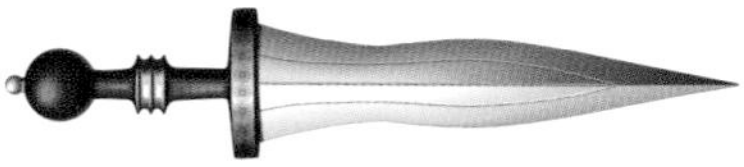

dagger
daga^F
dague^F
langer Dolch^M
daga^F

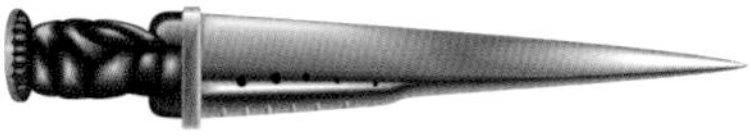

poniard
puñal^M
poignard^M
Dolch^M
pugnale^M

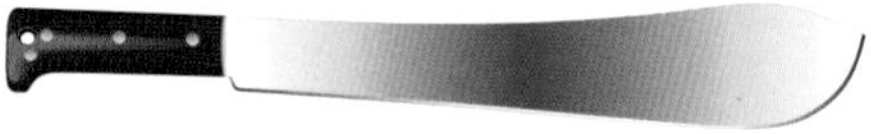

machete
machete^M
machette^F
Machete^F
machete^M

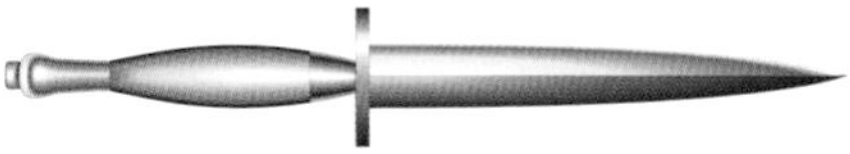

commando knife
cuchillo^M de combate^M
couteau^M de combat^M
Kampfmesser^N
pugnale^M d'assalto^M

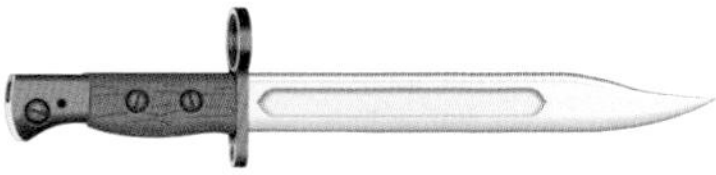

hilted bayonet
bayoneta^F con empuñadura^F
baionnette^F à poignée^F
Messerbajonett^N
coltello^M baionetta^F

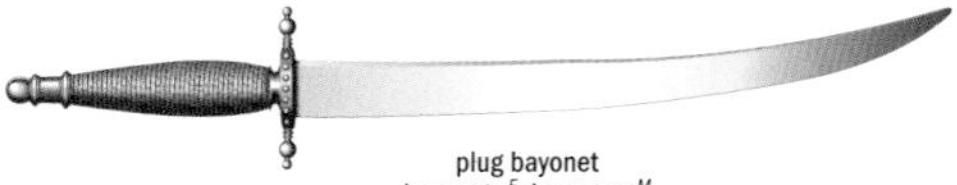

plug bayonet
bayoneta^F de mango^M
baionnette^F à manche^M
Spundbajonett^N
baionetta^F a tappo^M

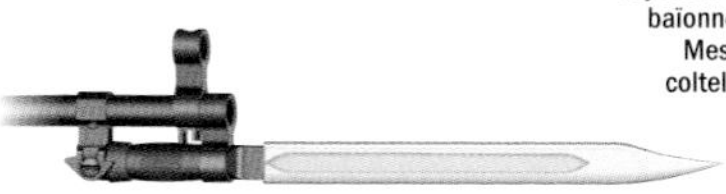

integral bayonet
bayoneta^F integral
baionnette^F incorporée
aufgepflanztes Bajonett^N
baionetta^F fissa ripiegabile

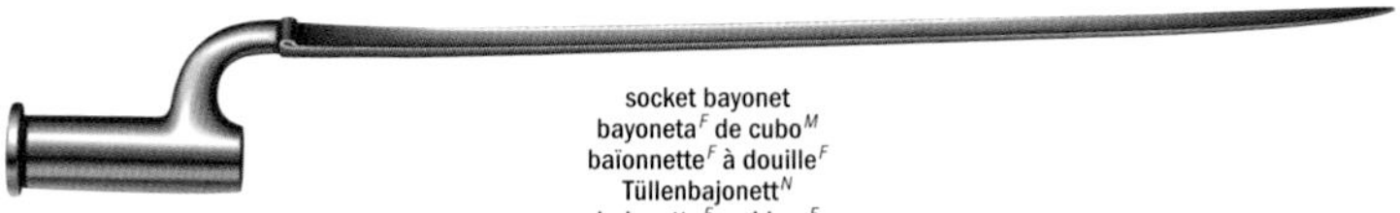

socket bayonet
bayoneta^F de cubo^M
baionnette^F à douille^F
Tüllenbajonett^N
baionetta^F a ghiera^F

SOCIETY

harquebus

arcabuz[M] | arquebuse[F] | Arkebuse[F] | archibugio[M]

steel
eslabón[M]
batterie[F]
Stahl[M]
acciarino[M]

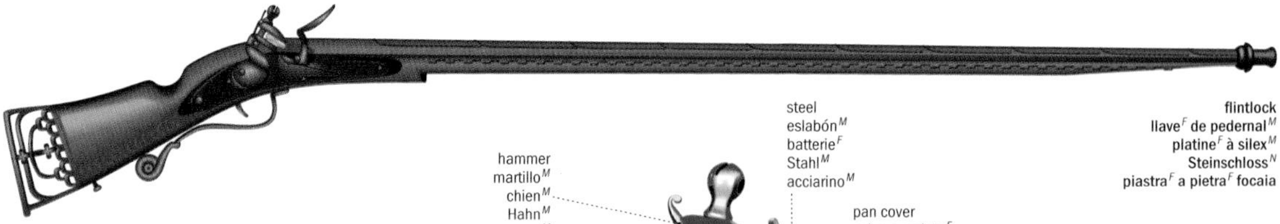

flintlock
llave[F] de pedernal[M]
platine[F] à silex[M]
Steinschloss[N]
piastra[F] a pietra[F] focaia

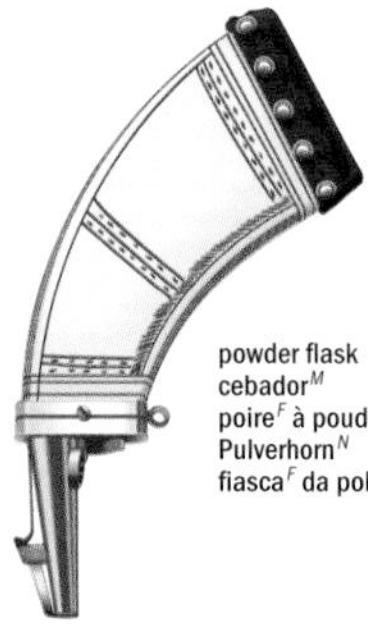

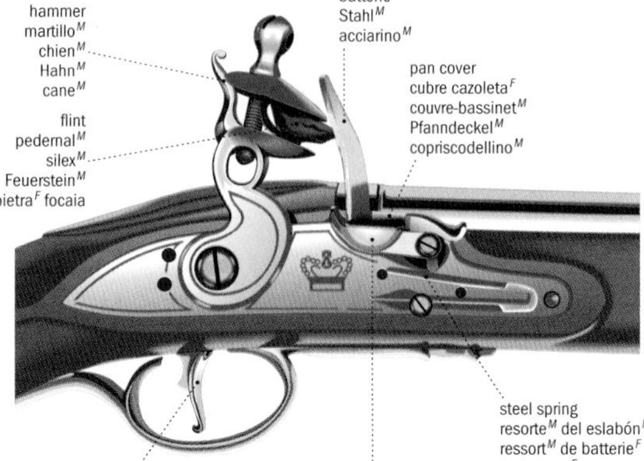

hammer
martillo[M]
chien[M]
Hahn[M]
cane[M]

pan cover
cubre cazoleta[F]
couvre-bassinet[M]
Pfanndeckel[M]
copriscodellino[M]

flint
pedernal[M]
silex[M]
Feuerstein[M]
pietra[F] focaia

powder flask
cebador[M]
poire[F] à poudre[F]
Pulverhorn[N]
fiasca[F] da polvere[F]

steel spring
resorte[M] del eslabón[M]
ressort[M] de batterie[F]
Stahlfeder[F]
molla[F] dell'acciarino[M]

ball
bala[F]
balle[F]
Kugel[F]
pallottola[F]

trigger
gatillo[M]
détente[F]
Abzug[M]
grilletto[M]

pan
cazoleta[F]
bassinet[M]
Pfanne[F]
scodellino[M]

seventeenth century cannon and mortar

cañón[M] y mortero[M] del siglo[M] XVII | canon[M] et mortier[M] du XVIIe siècle[M] | Kanone[F] und Mörser[M] aus dem 17. Jahrhundert[N] | cannone[M] e mortaio[M] del XVII° secolo[M]

firing accessories
accesorios[M] de disparo[M]
accessoires[F] de mise[F] à feu[M]
Geschosszubehör[N]
accessori[M] per il tiro[M]

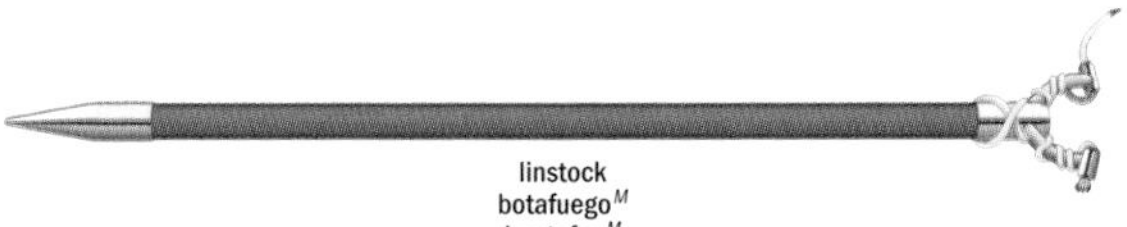

linstock
botafuego[M]
boutefeu[M]
Luntenstock[M]
buttafuoco[M]

sponge
escobillón[M]
écouvillon[M]
Schwamm[M]
scovolo[M]

ladle
cucharón[M]
lanterne[F]
Ladeschaufel[F]
cucchiaia[F]

worm
sacatrapos[M]
tire-bourre[M]
Spirale[F]
cavastracci[M]

rammer
atacador[M]
refouloir[M]
Ladestock[M]
calcatoio[M]

projectiles
proyectiles[M]
projectiles[M]
Projektile[N]
proietti[M]

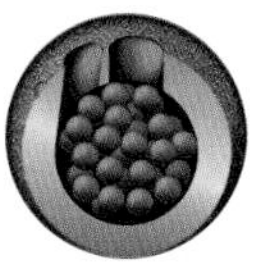

hollow shot
bala[F] con perdigones[M]
boulet[M] creux
Hohlladungsgeschoss[N]
palla[F] cava

solid shot
bala[F] sólida
boulet[M]
Vollgeschoss[N]
palla[F]

bar shot
bala[F] de barra[F]
boulet[M] ramé
Stangenkugel[F]
palla[F] ramata

grapeshot
metralla[F]
grappe[F] de raisin[M]
Kartätsche[F]
mitraglia[F]

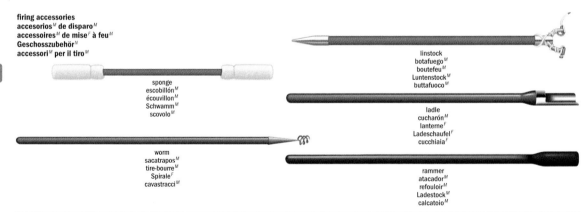

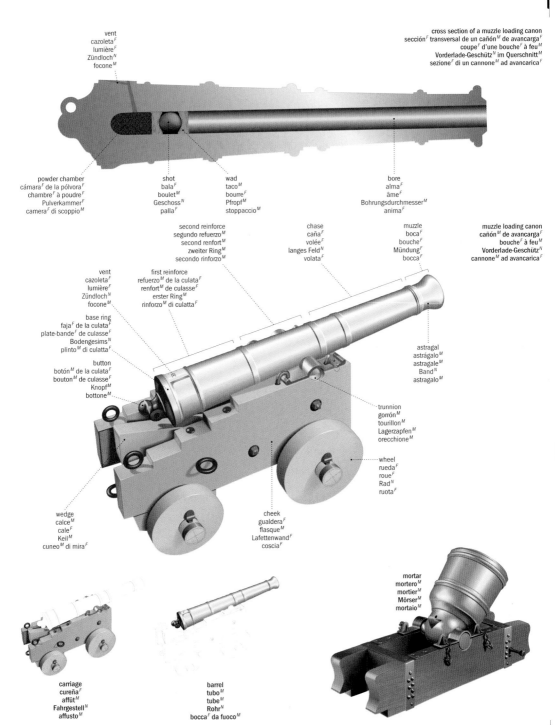

cross section of a muzzle loading canon
sección^F transversal de un cañón^M de avancarga^F
coupe^F d'une bouche^F à feu^M
Vorderlade-Geschütz^M im Querschnitt^M
sezione^F di un cannone^M ad avancarica^F

vent
cazoleta^F
lumière^F
Zündloch^N
focone^M

powder chamber
cámara^F de la pólvora^F
chambre^F à poudre^F
Pulverkammer^F
camera^F di scoppio^M

shot
bala^F
boulet^M
Geschoss^N
palla^F

wad
taco^M
bourre^F
Pfropf^M
stoppaccio^M

bore
alma^F
âme^F
Bohrungsdurchmesser^M
anima^F

second reinforce
segundo refuerzo^M
second renfort^M
zweiter Ring^M
secondo rinforzo^M

chase
caña^F
volée^F
langes Feld^N
volata^F

muzzle
boca^F
bouche^F
Mündung^F
bocca^F

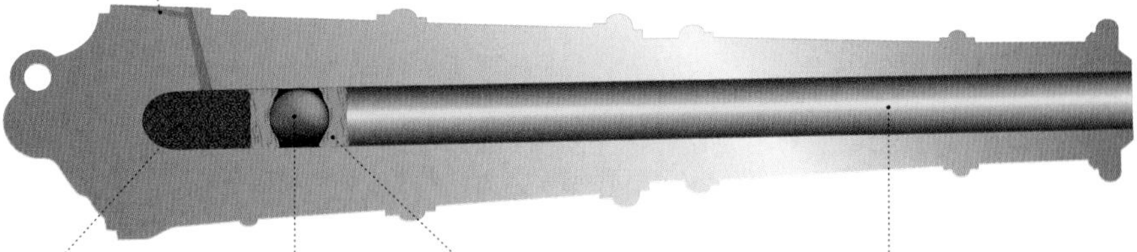

muzzle loading canon
cañón^M de avancarga^F
bouche^F à feu^M
Vorderlade-Geschütz^N
cannone^M ad avancarica^F

vent
cazoleta^F
lumière^F
Zündloch^N
focone^M

first reinforce
refuerzo^M de la culata^F
renfort^M de culasse^F
erster Ring^M
rinforzo^M di culatta^F

base ring
faja^F de la culata^F
plate-bande^F de culasse^F
Bodengesims^N
plinto^M di culatta^F

button
botón^M de la culata^F
bouton^M de culasse^F
Knopf^M
bottone^M

astragal
astrágalo^M
astragale^M
Band^N
astragalo^M

trunnion
gorrón^M
tourillon^M
Lagerzapfen^M
orecchione^M

wheel
rueda^F
roue^F
Rad^N
ruota^F

wedge
calce^F
cale^F
Keil^M
cuneo^M di mira^F

cheek
gualdera^F
flasque^M
Lafettenwand^F
coscia^F

mortar
mortero^M
mortier^M
Mörser^M
mortaio^M

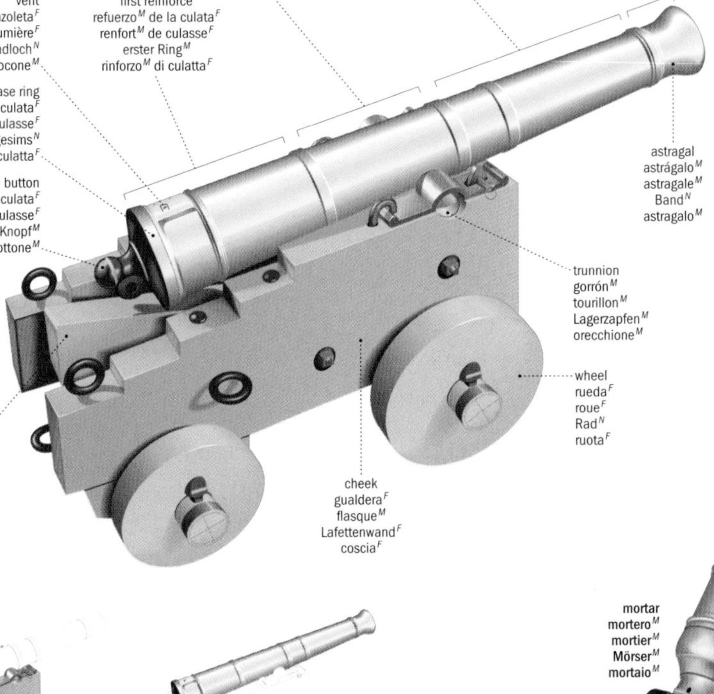

carriage
cureña^F
affût^M
Fahrgestell^N
affusto^M

barrel
tubo^M
tube^M
Rohr^N
bocca^F da fuoco^M

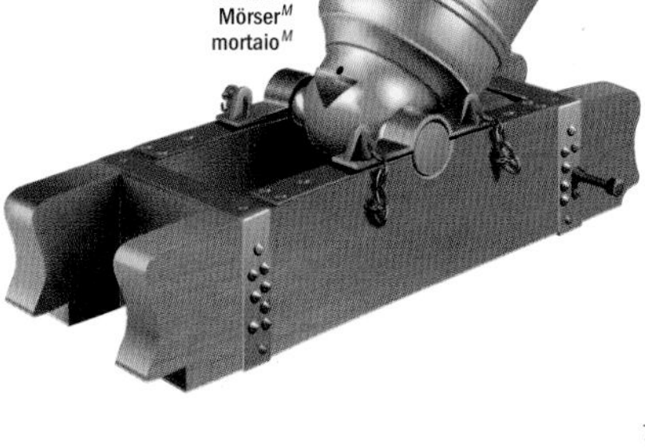

SOCIETY

submachine gun

metralleta^F | pistolet^M mitrailleur^M | Maschinenpistole^F | pistola^F mitragliatrice^F

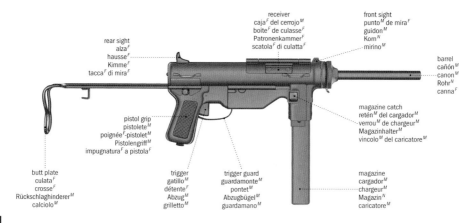

receiver
caja^F del cerrojo^M
boite^F de culasse^F
Patronenkammer^F
scatola^F di culatta^F

front sight
punto^M de mira^F
guidon^M
Korn^N
mirino^M

rear sight
alza^F
hausse^F
Kimme^F
tacca^F di mira^F

barrel
cañón^M
canon^M
Rohr^N
canna^F

pistol grip
pistolete^M
poignée^F-pistolet^M
Pistolengriff^M
impugnatura^F a pistola^F

magazine catch
retén^M del cargador^M
verrou^M de chargeur^M
Magazinhalter^M
vincolo^M del caricatore^M

butt plate
culata^F
crosse^F
Rückschlaghinderer^M
calciolo^M

trigger
gatillo^M
détente^F
Abzug^M
grilletto^M

trigger guard
guardamonte^M
pontet^M
Abzugbügel^M
guardamano^M

magazine
cargador^M
chargeur^M
Magazin^N
caricatore^M

pistol

pistola^F | pistolet^M | Pistole^F | pistola^F semiautomatica

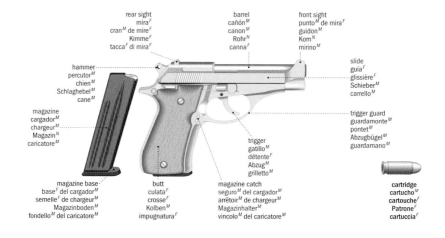

rear sight
mira^F
cran^M de mire^F
Kimme^F
tacca^F di mira^F

barrel
cañón^M
canon^M
Rohr^N
canna^F

front sight
punto^M de mira^F
guidon^M
Korn^N
mirino^M

hammer
percutor^M
chien^M
Schlaghebel^M
cane^M

slide
guía^F
glissière^F
Schieber^M
carrello^M

magazine
cargador^M
chargeur^M
Magazin^N
caricatore^M

trigger guard
guardamonte^M
pontet^M
Abzugbügel^M
guardamano^M

trigger
gatillo^M
détente^F
Abzug^M
grilletto^M

magazine base
base^F del cargador^M
semelle^F de chargeur^M
Magazinboden^M
fondello^M del caricatore^M

butt
culata^F
crosse^F
Kolben^M
impugnatura^F

magazine catch
seguro^M del cargador^M
arrêtoir^M de chargeur^M
Magazinhalter^M
vincolo^M del caricatore^M

cartridge
cartucho^M
cartouche^F
Patrone^F
cartuccia^F

revolver

revólver^M | revolver^M | Revolver^M | pistola^F a tamburo^M

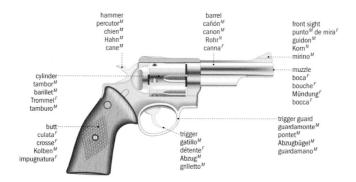

hammer
percutor^M
chien^M
Hahn^M
cane^M

barrel
cañón^M
canon^M
Rohr^N
canna^F

front sight
punto^M de mira^F
guidon^M
Korn^N
mirino^M

cylinder
tambor^M
barillet^M
Trommel^F
tamburo^M

muzzle
boca^F
bouche^F
Mündung^F
bocca^F

butt
culata^F
crosse^F
Kolben^M
impugnatura^F

trigger
gatillo^M
détente^F
Abzug^M
grilletto^M

trigger guard
guardamonte^M
pontet^M
Abzugbügel^M
guardamano^M

SOCIETY

automatic rifle

fusil^M automático | fusil^M automatique | automatisches Gewehr^N | fucile^M automatico

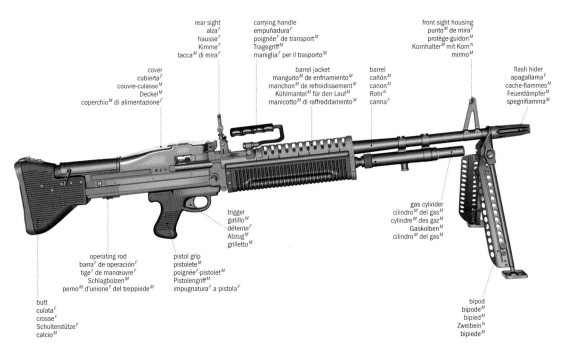

receiver
caja^F del cerrojo^M
boîte^F de culasse^F
Patronenkammer^F
scatola^F di culatta^F

rear sight
alza^F
hausse^F
Kimme^F
tacca^M di mira^F

barrel
cañón^M
canon^M
Rohr^N
canna^F

bolt assist mechanism
mecanismo^M asistido de descarga^F
mécanisme^M d'assistance^F de la culasse^F
Schlagbolzenmechanismus^M
meccanismo^M di chiusura^F, caricamento^M e sparo^M

ejection port
ventana^F de eyección^F
fenêtre^F d'éjection^F
Hülsenauswurf^M
feritoia^F di espulsione^F

barrel jacket
manguito^M de enfriamiento^M
manchon^M de refroidissement^M
Kühlmantel^M für den Lauf^M
manicotto^M di raffreddamento^M

front sight housing
punto^M de mira^F
protège-guidon^M
Kornhalter^M mit Korn^N
mirino^M

charging handle
palanca^F del cerrojo^M
levier^M d'armement^M
Durchladegriff^M
manetta^F di caricamento^M

handguard
guardamano^M
garde-main^M
Handschutz^M
copricanna^M

flash hider
apagallama^F
cache-flammes^M
Feuerdämpfer^M
spegnifiamma^M

pistol grip
pistolete^M
poignée^F-pistolet^M
Pistolengriff^M
impugnatura^F a pistola^F

magazine
cargador^M
chargeur^M
Magazin^N
caricatore^M

butt
culata^F
crosse^F
Schulterstütze^F
calciolo^M

trigger
gatillo^M
détente^F
Abzug^M
grilletto^M

safety
seguro^M
verrou^M de sûreté^F
Sicherung^F
sicura^F

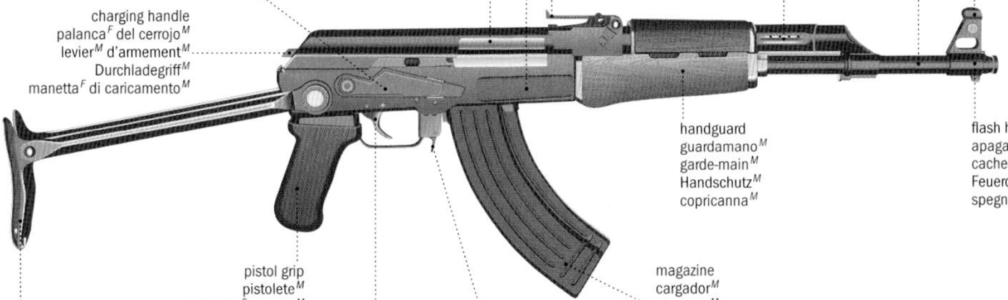

light machine gun

fusil^M ametrallador | fusil^M mitrailleur^M | leichtes Maschinengewehr^N | mitragliatrice^F leggera

rear sight
alza^F
hausse^F
Kimme^F
tacca^M di mira^F

carrying handle
empuñadura^F
poignée^F de transport^M
Tragegriff^M
maniglia^F per il trasporto^M

front sight housing
punto^M de mira^F
protège-guidon^M
Kornhalter^M mit Korn^N
mirino^M

cover
cubierta^F
couvre-culasse^F
Deckel^M
coperchio^M di alimentazione^F

barrel jacket
manguito^M de enfriamiento^M
manchon^M de refroidissement^M
Kühlmantel^M für den Lauf^M
manicotto^M di raffreddamento^M

barrel
cañón^M
canon^M
Rohr^N
canna^F

flash hider
apagallama^F
cache-flammes^M
Feuerdämpfer^M
spegnifiamma^M

trigger
gatillo^M
détente^F
Abzug^M
grilletto^M

gas cylinder
cilindro^M del gas^M
cylindre^M des gaz^M
Gaskolben^M
cilindro^M del gas^M

operating rod
barra^F de operación^F
tige^F de manœuvre^F
Schlagbolzen^M
perno^M d'unione^F del treppiede^M

pistol grip
pistolete^M
poignée^F-pistolet^M
Pistolengriff^M
impugnatura^F a pistola^F

butt
culata^F
crosse^F
Schulterstütze^F
calcio^M

bipod
bipode^M
bipied^M
Zweibein^N
bipiede^M

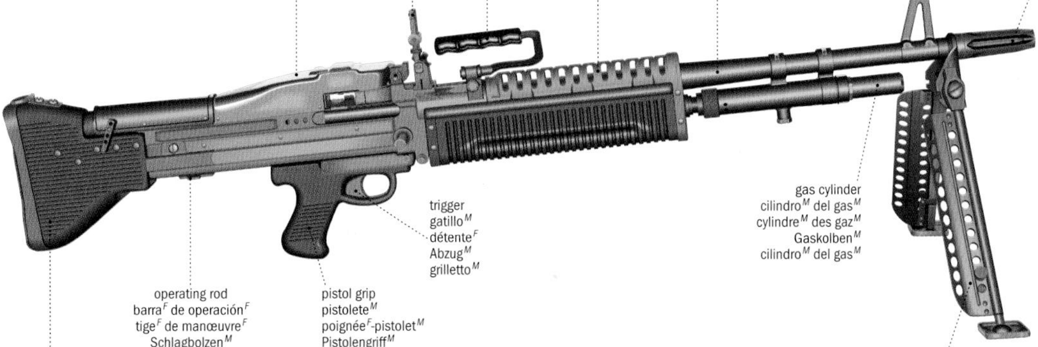

modern howitzer

obús^M moderno | obusier^M moderne | moderne Haubitze^F | obice^M moderno

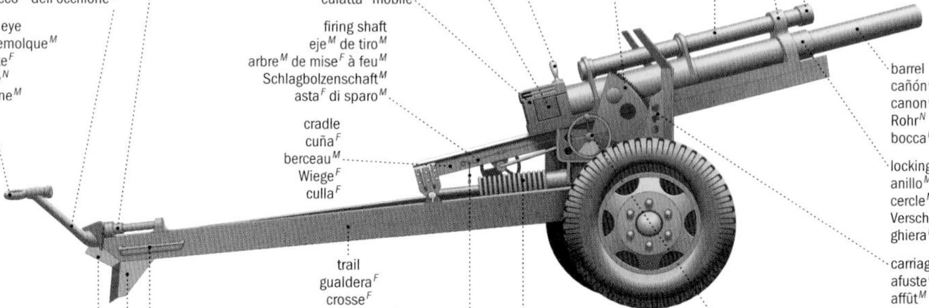

breechblock operating lever assembly
palanca^F de accionamiento^M de la recámara^F
levier^M de manœuvre^F de la culasse^F
Bedienungshebel^M für Verschlussblock^M
leva^F di manovra^F dell'otturatore^M

recuperator cylinder
cilindro^M de recuperación^F
cylindre^M récupérateur
Vorholer^M
cilindro^M ricuperatore

recoil sleigh
patín^M de retroceso^M
glissoire^F de recul^M
Rohrrücklauf^M
slitta^F di rinculo^M

drawbar lock
seguro^M de la barra^F de tracción^F
verrou^M de barre^F d'attelage^M
Zugstangenverschluss^M
fermo^M del braccio^M d'attacco^M dell'occhione^M

breechblock
bloque^M de cierre^M de la recámara^F
culasse^F
Verschlussblock^M
prisma^M otturatore^M

elevating arc
arco^M de elevación^F
crémaillère^F de pointage^M
Zahnbogen^M
arco^M dentato di elevazione^F

recuperator cylinder front head
cabeza^F delantera del cilindro^M de recuperación^F
tête^F avant du cylindre^M récupérateur
Vorholervorderteil^N
testa^F del cilindro^M ricuperatore

drawbar
barra^F de tracción^F
barre^F d'attelage^M
Zugstange^F
braccio^M d'attacco^M dell'occhione^M

sliding breech
placa^F de la culata^F
manchon^M de culasse^F
Schubkurbelverschluss^M
culatta^F mobile

towing eye
argolla^F de remolque^M
lunette^F
Auge^N
occhione^M

firing shaft
eje^M de tiro^M
arbre^M de mise^F à feu^M
Schlagbolzenschaft^M
asta^F di sparo^M

barrel
cañón^M
canon^M
Rohr^N
bocca^F da fuoco^M

cradle
cuña^F
berceau^M
Wiege^F
culla^F

locking ring
anillo^M de bloqueo^M
cercle^M de verrouillage^M
Verschlussring^M
ghiera^F di bloccaggio^M

carriage
afuste^M
affût^M
Fahrgestell^N
affusto^M

trail
gualdera^F
crosse^F
Schleppstange^F
coda^F

float
flotador^M
flotteur^M
Schwimmer^M
dente^M di roccia^F

lifting handle
asa^F de levantamiento^M
poignée^F de soulèvement^M
Hebegriff^M
maniglia^F di sollevamento^M

equilibrator
estabilizador^M
équilibreur^M
Gewichtsausgleicher^M
equilibratore^M

elevating hand-wheel
rueda^F de elevación^F
manivelle^F de pointage^M en hauteur^F
Höhenrichtwerk^N
volantino^M di puntamento^M in elevazione^F

spade
pala^F
bêche^F
Spaten^M
vomere^M

firing lanyard
cuerda^F de disparo^M
cordon^M tire-feu^M
Abzugsleine^F
funicella^F di sparo^M

modern mortar

mortero^M moderno | mortier^M moderne | Granatwerfer^M | mortaio^M moderno

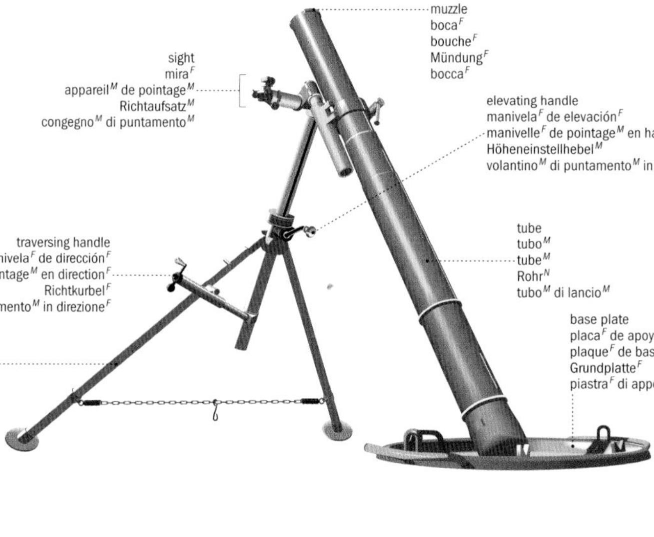

muzzle
boca^F
bouche^F
Mündung^F
bocca^F

sight
mira^F
appareil^M de pointage^M
Richtaufsatz^M
congegno^M di puntamento^M

elevating handle
manivela^F de elevación^F
manivelle^F de pointage^M en hauteur^F
Höheneinstellhebel^M
volantino^M di puntamento^M in elevazione^F

traversing handle
manivela^F de dirección^F
manivelle^F de pointage^M en direction^F
Richtkurbel^F
volantino^M di puntamento^M in direzione^F

tube
tubo^M
tube^M
Rohr^N
tubo^M di lancio^M

bipod
bípode^M
bipied^M
Zweibein^N
bipiede^M

base plate
placa^F de apoyo^M
plaque^F de base^F
Grundplatte^F
piastra^F di appoggio^M

hand grenade

granada^F de mano^F | grenade^F à main^F | Handgranate^F | bomba^F a mano^F

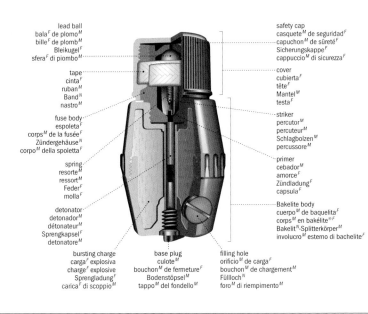

lead ball
bala^F de plomo^M
bille^F de plomb^M
Bleikugel^F
sfera^F di piombo^M

tape
cinta^F
ruban^M
Band^N
nastro^M

fuse body
espoleta^F
corps^M de la fusée^F
Zündergehäuse^N
corpo^M della spoletta^F

spring
resorte^M
ressort^M
Feder^F
molla^F

detonator
detonador^M
détonateur^M
Sprengkapsel^F
detonatore^M

safety cap
casquete^M de seguridad^F
capuchon^M de sûreté^F
Sicherungskappe^F
cappuccio^M di sicurezza^F

cover
cubierta^F
tête^F
Mantel^M
testa^F

striker
percutor^M
percuteur^M
Schlagbolzen^M
percussore^M

primer
cebador^M
amorce^F
Zündladung^F
capsula^F

Bakelite body
cuerpo^M de baquelita^F
corps^M en bakélite^{®F}
Bakelit^N-Splitterkörper^M
involucro^M esterno di bachelite^F

bursting charge
carga^F explosiva
charge^F explosive
Sprengladung^F
carica^F di scoppio^M

base plug
culote^M
bouchon^M de fermeture^F
Bodenstöpsel^M
tappo^M del fondello^M

filling hole
orificio^M de carga^F
bouchon^M de chargement^M
Füllloch^N
foro^M di riempimento^M

bazooka

bazuca^F | bazooka^M | Panzerfaust^F | bazooka^M

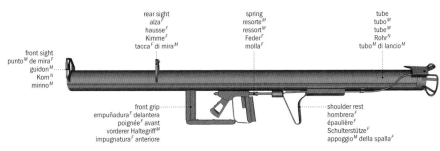

rear sight
alza^F
hausse^F
Kimme^F
tacca^F di mira^M

spring
resorte^M
ressort^M
Feder^F
molla^F

tube
tubo^M
tube^M
Rohr^N
tubo^M di lancio^M

front sight
punto^M de mira^F
guidon^M
Korn^N
mirino^M

front grip
empuñadura^F delantera
poignée^F avant
vorderer Haltegriff^M
impugnatura^F anteriore

shoulder rest
hombrera^F
épaulière^F
Schulterstütze^F
appoggio^M della spalla^F

recoilless rifle

cañón^M sin retroceso^M | canon^M sans recul^M | rückstoßfreies Geschütz^N | cannone^M senza rinculo^M

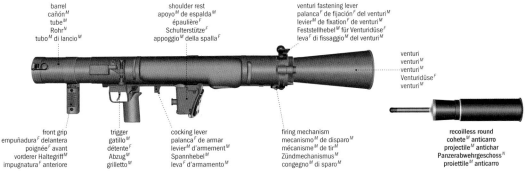

barrel
cañón^M
tube^M
Rohr^N
tubo^M di lancio^M

shoulder rest
apoyo^M de espalda^F
épaulière^F
Schulterstütze^F
appoggio^M della spalla^F

venturi fastening lever
palanca^F de fijación^F del venturi^M
levier^M de fixation^F de venturi^M
Feststellhebel^M für Venturidüse^F
leva^F di fissaggio^M del venturi^M

venturi
venturi^M
venturi^M
Venturidüse^F
venturi^M

front grip
empuñadura^F delantera
poignée^F avant
vorderer Haltegriff^M
impugnatura^F anteriore

trigger
gatillo^M
détente^F
Abzug^M
grilletto^M

cocking lever
palanca^F de armar
levier^M d'armement^M
Spannhebel^M
leva^F d'armamento^M

firing mechanism
mecanismo^M de disparo^M
mécanisme^M de tir^M
Zündmechanismus^M
congegno^M di sparo^M

recoilless round
cohete^M anticarro
projectile^M antichar
Panzerabwehrgeschoss^N
proiettile^M anticarro

antipersonnel mine

mina^M antipersona | mine^F antipersonnel | Antipersonenmine^F | mina^F antiuomo

pressure plate
platillo^M de presión^F
plateau^M de pression^F
Druckzünder^M
piastra^F di pressione^F

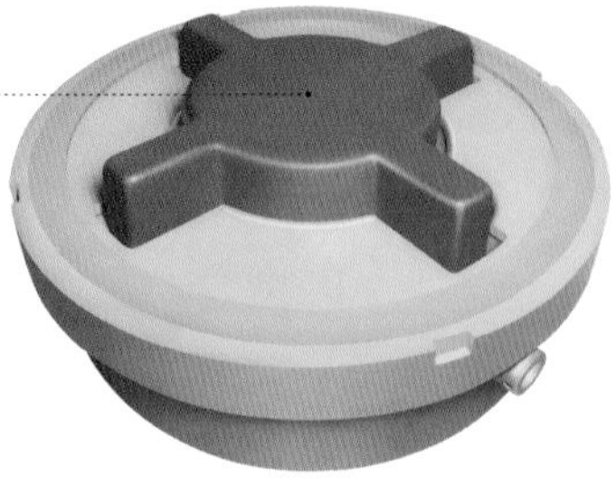

tank

carro^M de combate^M | char^M d'assaut^M | Panzer^M | carro^M armato

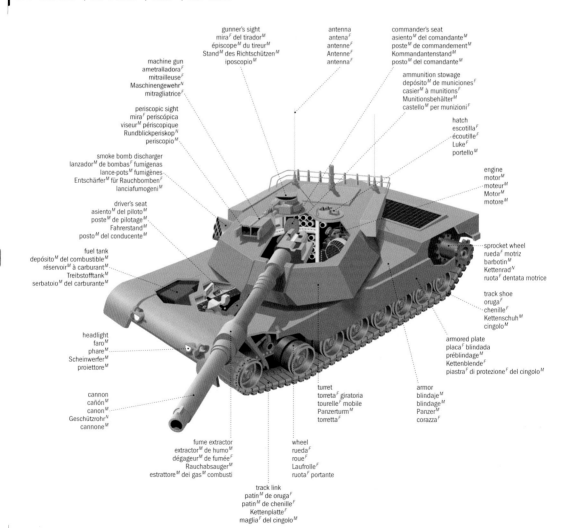

gunner's sight
mira^F del tirador^M
épiscope^M du tireur^M
Stand^M des Richtschützen^M
iposcopio^M

antenna
antena^F
antenne^F
Antenne^F
antenna^F

commander's seat
asiento^M del comandante^M
poste^M de commandement^M
Kommandantenstand^M
posto^M del comandante^M

machine gun
ametralladora^F
mitrailleuse^F
Maschinengewehr^N
mitragliatrice^F

ammunition stowage
depósito^M de municiones^F
casier^M à munitions^F
Munitionsbehälter^M
castello^M per munizioni^F

periscopic sight
mira^F periscópica
viseur^M périscopique
Rundblickperiskop^N
periscopio^M

hatch
escotilla^F
écoutille^F
Luke^F
portello^M

smoke bomb discharger
lanzador^M de bombas^F fumígenas
lance-pots^M fumigènes
Entschärfer^M für Rauchbomben^F
lanciafumogeni^M

engine
motor^M
moteur^M
Motor^M
motore^M

driver's seat
asiento^M del piloto^M
poste^M de pilotage^M
Fahrerstand^M
posto^M del conducente^M

fuel tank
depósito^M del combustible^M
réservoir^M à carburant^M
Treibstofftank^M
serbatoio^M del carburante^M

sprocket wheel
rueda^F motriz
barbotin^M
Kettenrad^N
ruota^F dentata motrice

track shoe
oruga^F
chenille^F
Kettenschuh^M
cingolo^M

headlight
faro^M
phare^M
Scheinwerfer^M
proiettore^M

armored plate
placa^F blindada
préblindage^M
Kettenblende^F
piastra^F di protezione^F del cingolo^M

cannon
cañón^M
canon^M
Geschützrohr^N
cannone^M

turret
torreta^F giratoria
tourelle^F mobile
Panzerturm^M
torretta^F

armor
blindaje^M
blindage^M
Panzer^M
corazza^F

fume extractor
extractor^M de humo^M
dégageur^M de fumée^F
Rauchabsauger^M
estrattore^M dei gas^M combusti

wheel
rueda^F
roue^F
Laufrolle^F
ruota^F portante

track link
patín^M de oruga^F
patin^M de chenille^F
Kettenplatte^F
maglia^F del cingolo^M

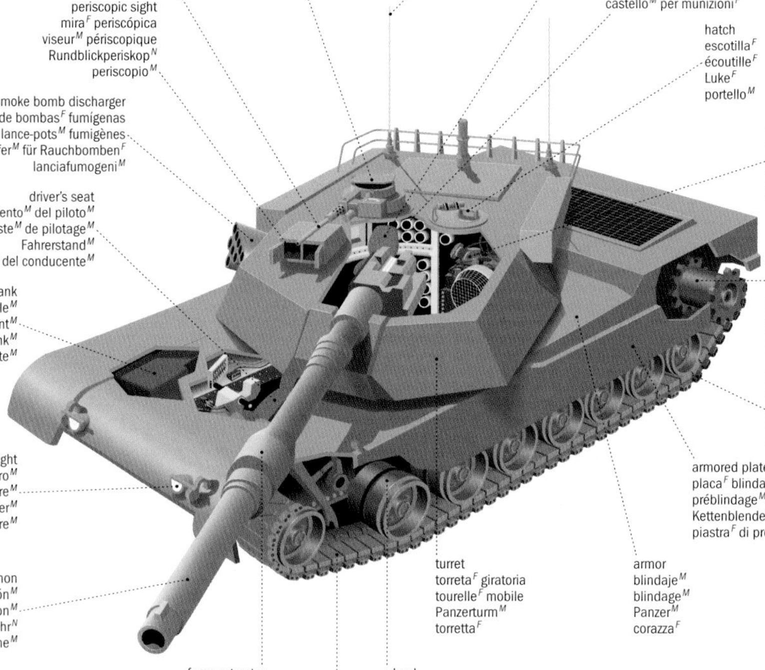

SOCIETY

missiles

proyectiles[M] | missiles[M] | Flugkörper[M] | missili[M]

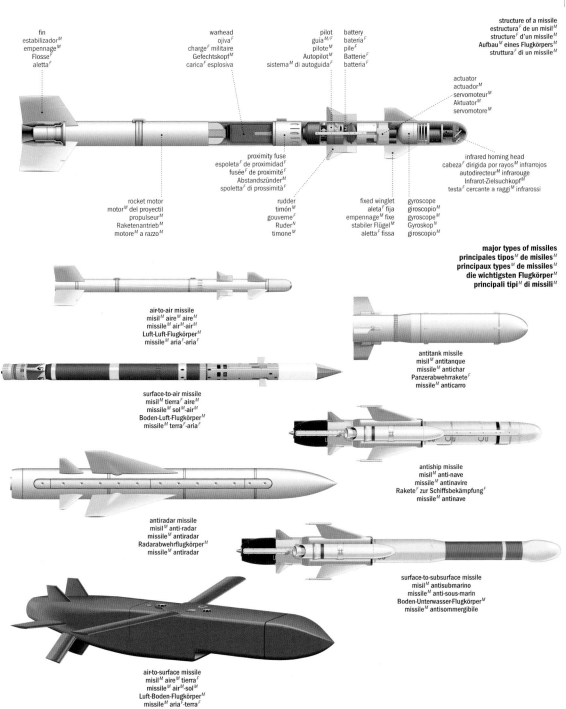

structure of a missile
estructura[F] de un misil[M]
structure[F] d'un missile[M]
Aufbau[M] eines Flugkörpers[M]
struttura[F] di un missile[M]

fin
estabilizador[M]
empennage[M]
Flosse[F]
aletta[F]

warhead
ojiva[F]
charge[F] militaire
Gefechtskopf[M]
carica[F] esplosiva

pilot
guía[M/F]
pilote[M]
Autopilot[M]
sistema[M] di autoguida[F]

battery
batería[F]
pile[F]
Batterie[F]
batteria[F]

actuator
actuador[M]
servomoteur[M]
Aktuator[M]
servomotore[M]

proximity fuse
espoleta[F] de proximidad[F]
fusée[F] de proximité[F]
Abstandszünder[M]
spoletta[F] di prossimità[F]

infrared homing head
cabeza[F] dirigida por rayos[M] infrarrojos
autodirecteur[M] infrarouge
Infrarot-Zielsuchkopf[M]
testa[F] cercante a raggi[M] infrarossi

rocket motor
motor[M] del proyectil
propulseur[M]
Raketenantrieb[M]
motore[M] a razzo[M]

rudder
timón[M]
gouverne[F]
Ruder[N]
timone[M]

fixed winglet
aleta[F] fija
empennage[M] fixe
stabiler Flügel[M]
aletta[F] fissa

gyroscope
giroscopio[M]
gyroscope[M]
Gyroskop[N]
giroscopio[M]

major types of missiles
principales tipos[M] de misiles[M]
principaux types[M] de missiles[M]
die wichtigsten Flugkörper[M]
principali tipi[M] di missili[M]

air-to-air missile
misil[M] aire[M] aire[M]
missile[M] air[M]-air[M]
Luft-Luft-Flugkörper[M]
missile[M] aria[F]-aria[F]

surface-to-air missile
misil[M] tierra[M] aire[M]
missile[M] sol[M]-air[M]
Boden-Luft-Flugkörper[M]
missile[M] terra[F]-aria[F]

antiradar missile
misil[M] anti-radar
missile[M] antiradar
Radarabwehrflugkörper[M]
missile[M] antiradar

antitank missile
misil[M] antitanque
missile[M] antichar
Panzerabwehrrakete[F]
missile[M] anticarro

antiship missile
misil[M] anti-nave
missile[M] antinavire
Rakete[F] zur Schiffsbekämpfung[F]
missile[M] antinave

surface-to-subsurface missile
misil[M] antisubmarino
missile[M] anti-sous-marin
Boden-Unterwasser-Flugkörper[M]
missile[M] antisommergibile

air-to-surface missile
misil[M] aire[M] tierra[F]
missile[M] air[M]-sol[M]
Luft-Boden-Flugkörper[M]
missile[M] aria[F]-terra[F]

SOCIETY

759

combat aircraft

avión^M de combate^M | avion^M de combat^M | Kampfflugzeug^N | aeroplano^M da combattimento^M

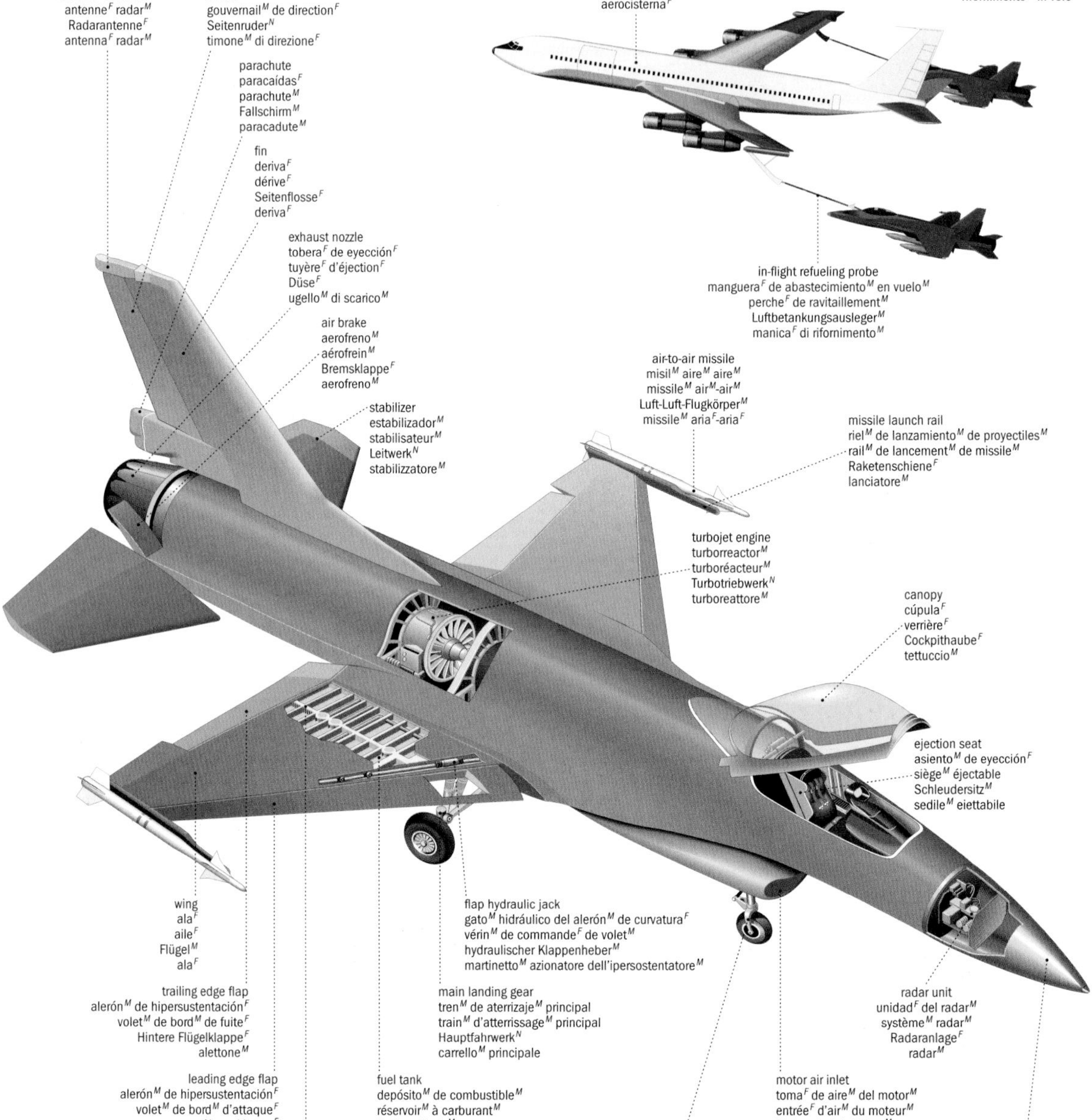

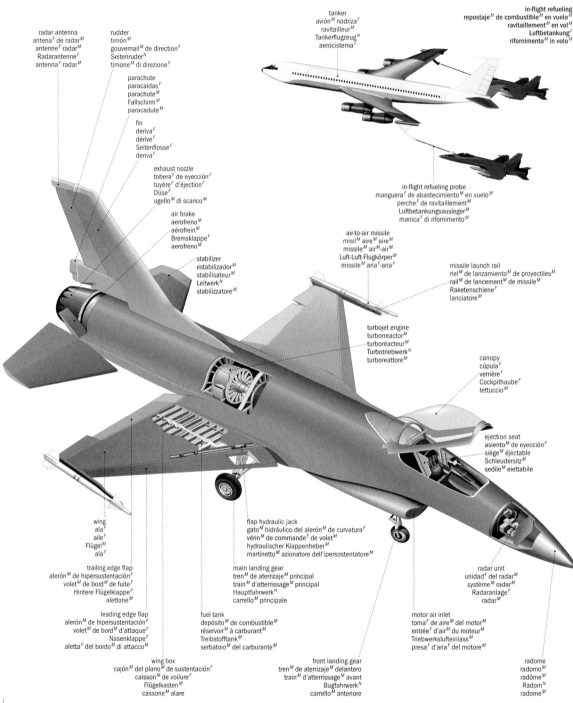

tanker
avión^M nodriza^F
ravitailleur^M
Tankerflugzeug^N
aerocisterna^F

in-flight refueling
repostaje^M de combustible^M en vuelo^M
ravitaillement^M en vol^M
Luftbetankung^F
rifornimento^M in volo^M

radar antenna
antena^F de radar^M
antenne^F radar^M
Radarantenne^F
antenna^F radar^M

rudder
timón^M
gouvernail^M de direction^F
Seitenruder^N
timone^M di direzione^F

parachute
paracaídas^F
parachute^M
Fallschirm^M
paracadute^M

fin
deriva^F
dérive^F
Seitenflosse^F
deriva^F

exhaust nozzle
tobera^F de eyección^F
tuyère^F d'éjection^F
Düse^F
ugello^M di scarico^M

in-flight refueling probe
manguera^F de abastecimiento^M en vuelo^M
perche^F de ravitaillement^M
Luftbetankungsausleger^M
manica^F di rifornimento^M

air brake
aerofreno^M
aérofrein^M
Bremsklappe^F
aerofreno^M

air-to-air missile
misil^M aire^F aire^M
missile^M air^M-air^M
Luft-Luft-Flugkörper^M
missile^M aria^F-aria^F

stabilizer
estabilizador^M
stabilisateur^M
Leitwerk^N
stabilizzatore^M

missile launch rail
riel^M de lanzamiento^M de proyectiles^M
rail^M de lancement^M de missile^M
Raketenschiene^F
lanciatore^M

turbojet engine
turborreactor^M
turboréacteur^M
Turbotriebwerk^N
turboreattore^M

canopy
cúpula^F
verrière^F
Cockpithaube^F
tettuccio^M

ejection seat
asiento^M de eyección^F
siège^M éjectable
Schleudersitz^M
sedile^M eiettabile

wing
ala^F
aile^F
Flügel^M
ala^F

flap hydraulic jack
gato^M hidráulico del alerón^M de curvatura^F
vérin^M de commande^F de volet^M
hydraulischer Klappenheber^M
martinetto^M azionatore dell'ipersostentatore^M

trailing edge flap
alerón^M de hipersustentación^F
volet^M de bord^M de fuite^F
Hintere Flügelklappe^F
alettone^M

main landing gear
tren^M de aterrizaje^M principal
train^M d'atterrissage^M principal
Hauptfahrwerk^N
carrello^M principale

radar unit
unidad^F del radar^M
système^M radar^M
Radaranlage^F
radar^M

leading edge flap
alerón^M de hipersustentación^F
volet^M de bord^M d'attaque^F
Nasenklappe^F
aletta^F del bordo^M di attacco^M

fuel tank
depósito^M de combustible^M
réservoir^M à carburant^M
Treibstofftank^M
serbatoio^M del carburante^M

motor air inlet
toma^F de aire^M del motor^M
entrée^F d'air^M du moteur^M
Triebwerkslufteinlass^M
presa^F d'aria^F del motore^M

wing box
cajón^M del plano^M de sustentación^F
caisson^M de voilure^F
Flügelkasten^M
cassone^M alare

front landing gear
tren^M de aterrizaje^M delantero
train^M d'atterrissage^M avant
Bugfahrwerk^N
carrello^M anteriore

radome
radomo^M
radôme^M
Radom^N
radome^M

aircraft carrier

portaaviones[M] | porte-avions[M] | Flugzeugträger[M] | portaerei[F]

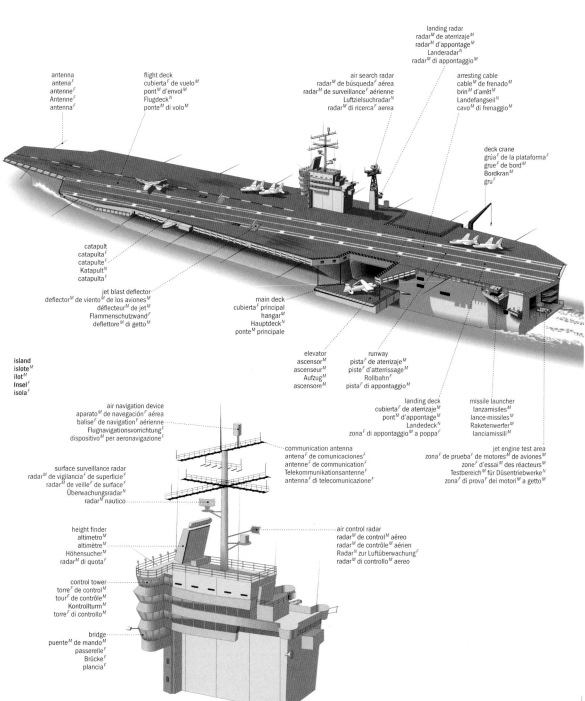

landing radar
radar[M] de aterrizaje[M]
radar[M] d'appontage[M]
Landeradar[N]
radar[M] di appontaggio[M]

antenna
antena[F]
antenne[F]
Antenne[F]
antenna[F]

flight deck
cubierta[F] de vuelo[M]
pont[M] d'envol[M]
Flugdeck[N]
ponte[M] di volo[M]

air search radar
radar[M] de búsqueda[F] aérea
radar[M] de surveillance[F] aérienne
Luftzielsuchradar[N]
radar[M] di ricerca[F] aerea

arresting cable
cable[M] de frenado[M]
brin[M] d'arrêt[M]
Landefangseil[N]
cavo[M] di frenaggio[M]

deck crane
grúa[F] de la plataforma[F]
grue[F] de bord[M]
Bordkran[M]
gru[F]

catapult
catapulta[F]
catapulte[F]
Katapult[N]
catapulta[F]

jet blast deflector
deflector[M] de viento[M] de los aviones[M]
déflecteur[M] de jet[M]
Flammenschutzwand[F]
deflettore[M] di getto[M]

main deck
cubierta[F] principal
hangar[M]
Hauptdeck[N]
ponte[M] principale

island
islote[M]
ilot[M]
Insel[F]
isola[F]

elevator
ascensor[M]
ascenseur[M]
Aufzug[M]
ascensore[M]

runway
pista[F] de aterrizaje[M]
piste[F] d'atterrissage[M]
Rollbahn[F]
pista[F] di appontaggio[M]

landing deck
cubierta[F] de aterrizaje[M]
pont[M] d'appontage[M]
Landedeck[N]
zona[F] di appontaggio[M] a poppa[F]

missile launcher
lanzamisiles[M]
lance-missiles[M]
Raketenwerfer[M]
lanciamissili[M]

air navigation device
aparato[M] de navegación[F] aérea
balise[F] de navigation[F] aérienne
Flugnavigationsvorrichtung[F]
dispositivo[M] per aeronavigazione[F]

jet engine test area
zona[F] de prueba[F] de motores[M] de aviones[M]
zone[F] d'essai[M] des réacteurs[M]
Testbereich[M] für Düsentriebwerke[N]
zona[F] di prova[F] dei motori[M] a getto[M]

communication antenna
antena[F] de comunicaciones[F]
antenne[F] de communication[F]
Telekommunikationsantenne[F]
antenna[F] di telecomunicazione[F]

surface surveillance radar
radar[M] de vigilancia[F] de superficie[F]
radar[M] de veille[F] de surface[F]
Überwachungsradar[N]
radar[M] nautico

air control radar
radar[M] de control[M] aéreo
radar[M] de contrôle[M] aérien
Radar[N] zur Luftüberwachung[F]
radar[M] di controllo[M] aereo

height finder
altímetro[M]
altimètre[M]
Höhensucher[M]
radar[M] di quota[F]

control tower
torre[F] de control[M]
tour[F] de contrôle[M]
Kontrollturm[M]
torre[F] di controllo[M]

bridge
puente[M] de mando[M]
passerelle[F]
Brücke[F]
plancia[F]

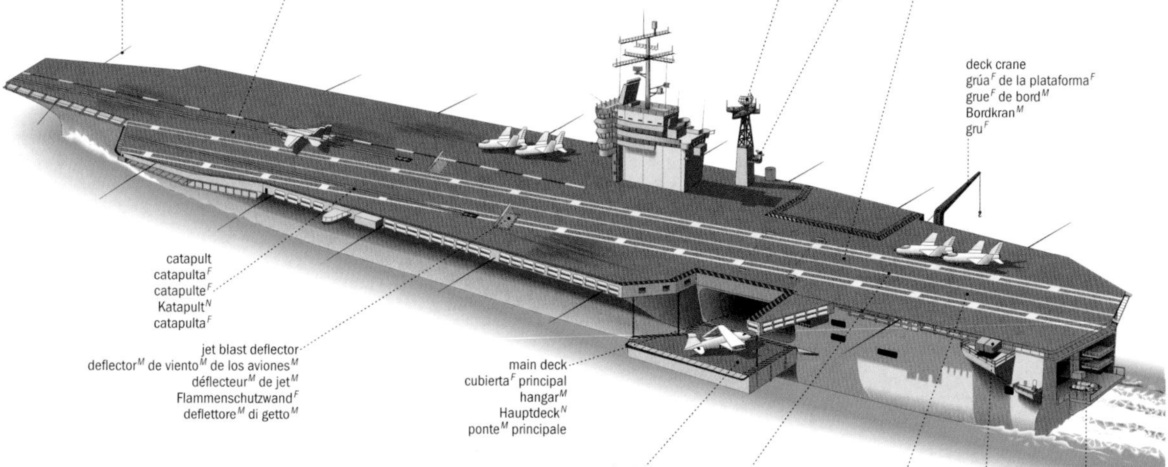

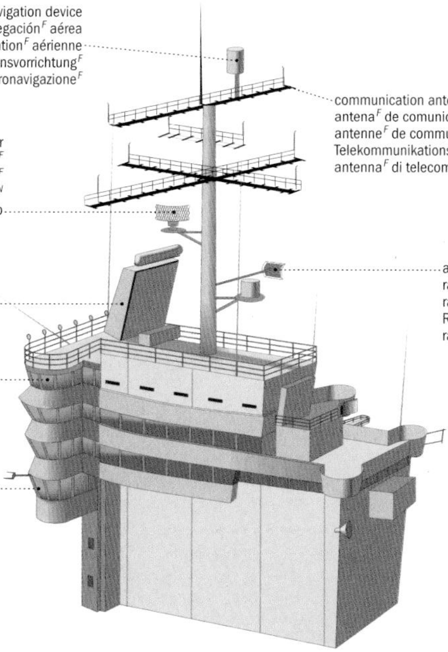

frigate

fragata^F | frégate^F | Fregatte^F | fregata^F

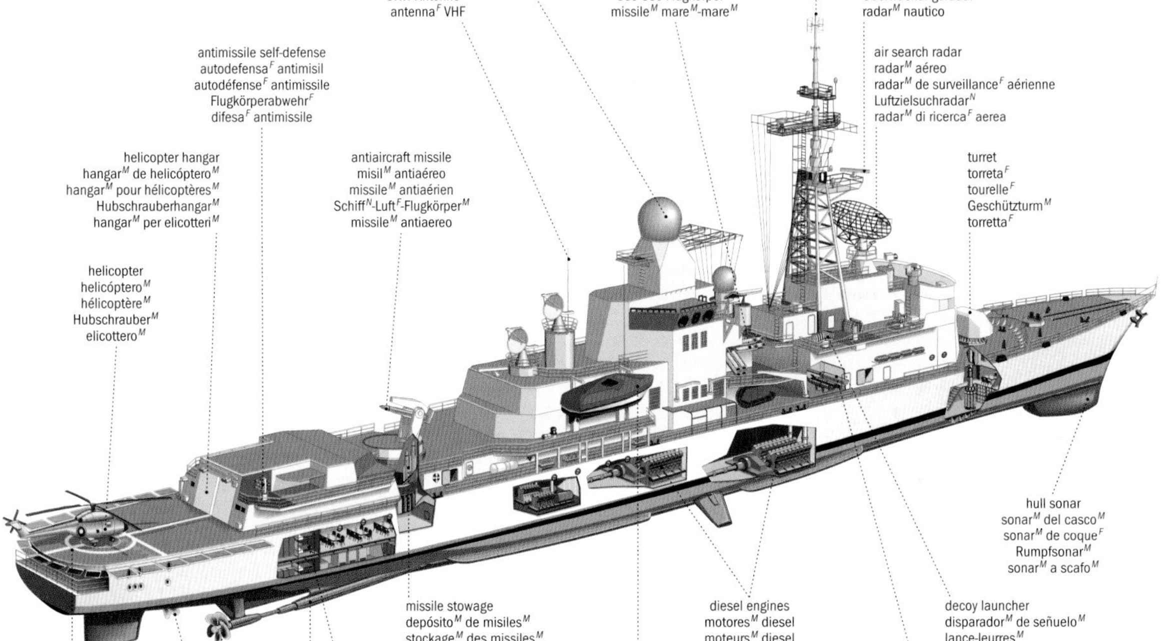

telecommunication antenna
antena^F de telecomunicaciones^F
antenne^F de télécommunication^F
Telekommunikationsantenne^F
antenna^F di telecomunicazione^F

target detection radar
radar^M de detección de blancos^M
radar^M de détection^F
Radar^N zur Zielverfolgung^F
radar^M di acquisizione^F del bersaglio^M

VHF antenna
antena^F VHF
antenne^F VHF
UKW-Antenne^F
antenna^F VHF

sea-to-sea missile
misil^M mar^M a mar^M
missile^M mer^F-mer^F
See-See-Flugkörper^M
missile^M mare^M-mare^M

surface surveillance radar
radar^M de vigilancia^F de superficie^F
radar^M de veille^F de surface^F
Überwachungsradar^N
radar^M nautico

antimissile self-defense
autodefensa^F antimisil
autodéfense^F antimissile
Flugkörperabwehr^F
difesa^F antimissile

antiaircraft missile
misil^M antiaéreo
missile^M antiaérien
Schiff^N-Luft^F-Flugkörper^M
missile^M antiaereo

air search radar
radar^M aéreo
radar^M de surveillance^F aérienne
Luftzielsuchradar^N
radar^M di ricerca^F aerea

turret
torreta^F
tourelle^F
Geschützturm^M
torretta^F

helicopter hangar
hangar^M de helicóptero^M
hangar^M pour hélicoptères^M
Hubschrauberhangar^M
hangar^M per elicotteri^M

helicopter
helicóptero^M
hélicoptère^M
Hubschrauber^M
elicottero^M

hull sonar
sonar^M del casco^M
sonar^M de coque^F
Rumpfsonar^N
sonar^M a scafo^M

missile stowage
depósito^M de misiles^M
stockage^M des missiles^M
Raketendepot^N
deposito^M dei missili^M

diesel engines
motores^M diesel
moteurs^M diesel
Dieselmotoren^M
motori^M diesel

decoy launcher
disparador^M de señuelo^M
lance-leurres^F
Köderlauncher^M
lanciarazzi^M civetta^F

propellers
hélices^F
hélices^F
Schrauben^F
eliche^F

officers' quarters
camarotes^M de los oficiales^M
logement^M des officiers^M
Offiziersquartiere^N
alloggio^M degli ufficiali^M

ship's motor boat
lancha^F de motor^M
vedette^F
Motorbeiboot^N
scialuppa^M

surface-to-subsurface missile
misil^M antisubmarino
missile^M anti-sous-marin
Boden-Unterwasser-Flugkörper^M
missile^M antisommergibile

shaft
eje^M
arbre^M
Welle^F
asse^M portaelica

helicopter flight deck
plataforma^F de vuelo^M del helicóptero^M
hélisurface^F
Hubschrauberlandeplatz^M
piattaforma^F di appontaggio^M per elicotteri^M

nuclear submarine

submarino^M nuclear | sous-marin^M nucléaire | Atom^N-Unterseeboot^N | sottomarino^M nucleare

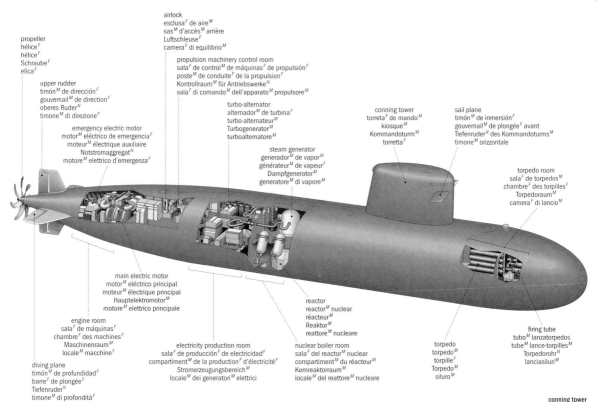

propeller
hélice^F
hélice^F
Schraube^F
elica^F

upper rudder
timón^M de dirección^F
gouvernail^M de direction^F
oberes Ruder^N
timone^M di direzione^F

emergency electric motor
motor^M eléctrico de emergencia^F
moteur^M électrique auxiliaire
Notstromaggregat^N
motore^M elettrico d'emergenza^F

airlock
esclusa^F de aire^M
sas^M d'accès^M arrière
Luftschleuse^F
camera^F di equilibrio^M

propulsion machinery control room
sala^F de control^M de máquinas^F de propulsión^F
poste^M de conduite^F de la propulsion^F
Kontrollraum^M für Antriebswerke^N
sala^F di comando^M dell'apparato^M propulsore^M

turbo-alternator
alternador^M de turbina^F
turbo-alternateur^M
Turbogenerator^M
turboalternatore^M

steam generator
generador^M de vapor^M
générateur^M de vapeur^F
Dampfgenerator^M
generatore^M di vapore^M

conning tower
torreta^F de mando^M
kiosque^M
Kommandoturm^M
torretta^F

sail plane
timón^M de inmersión^F
gouvernail^M de plongée^F avant
Tiefenruder^N des Kommandoturms^M
timone^M orizzontale

torpedo room
sala^F de torpedos^M
chambre^F des torpilles^F
Torpedoraum^M
camera^F di lancio^M

main electric motor
motor^M eléctrico principal
moteur^M électrique principal
Hauptelektromotor^M
motore^M elettrico principale

engine room
sala^F de máquinas^F
chambre^F des machines^F
Maschinenraum^M
locale^M macchine^F

diving plane
timón^M de profundidad^F
barre^F de plongée^F
Tiefenruder^N
timone^M di profondità^F

electricity production room
sala^F de producción^F de electricidad^F
compartiment^M de la production^F d'électricité^F
Stromerzeugungsbereich^M
locale^M dei generatori^M elettrici

reactor
reactor^M nuclear
réacteur^M
Reaktor^M
reattore^M nucleare

nuclear boiler room
sala^F del reactor^M nuclear
compartiment^M du réacteur^M
Kernreaktorraum^M
locale^M del reattore^M nucleare

torpedo
torpedo^M
torpille^F
Torpedo^M
siluro^M

firing tube
tubo^M lanzatorpedos
tube^M lance-torpilles^F
Torpedorohr^N
lanciasiluri^M

conning tower
torreta^F
kiosque^M
Kommandoturm^M
torretta^F

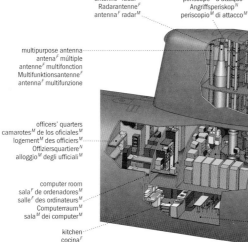

radar antenna
antena^F de radar^M
antenne^F radar^M
Radarantenne^F
antenna^F radar^M

attack periscope
periscopio^M de ataque^M
périscope^M d'attaque^F
Angriffsperiskop^N
periscopio^M di attacco^M

radio antenna
antena^F de radio^F
antenne^F radio^F
Funkantenne^F
antenna^F radio^F

navigation periscope
periscopio^M de navegación^F
périscope^M de veille^F
Navigationsperiskop^N
periscopio^M di esplorazione^F

multipurpose antenna
antena^F múltiple
antenne^F multifonction
Multifunktionsantenne^F
antenna^F multifunzione

officers' quarters
camarotes^M de los oficiales^M
logement^M des officiers^M
Offiziersquartiere^N
alloggio^M degli ufficiali^M

operation control room
sala^F de control^M de operaciones^F
poste^M de commandement^M
Operationszentrale^F
camera^F di manovra^F

computer room
sala^F de ordenadores^M
salle^F des ordinateurs^M
Computerraum^M
sala^M dei computer^M

kitchen
cocina^F
cuisine^F
Kombüse^F
cambusa^F

dining room
comedor^M
salle^F à manger
Messe^F, Speiseraum^M
mensa^F

fire prevention

prevención^F de incendios^M | prévention^F des incendies^M | Brandbekämpfung^F | prevenzione^F degli incendi^M

fire station
parque^M de bomberos^M
caserne^F de pompiers^M
Feuerwehrzentrale^F
caserma^F dei vigili^M del fuoco^M

officers' dormitory
dormitorio^M de los oficiales^M
chambre^F des officiers^M
Offiziersraum^M
camera^F degli ufficiali^M

documentation center
centro^M de documentación^F
centre^M de documentation^F
Dokumentationszentrum^N
centro^M di documentazione^F

chief's office
despacho^M del jefe^M de bomberos^M
bureau^M du chef^M
Büro^N des Kommandanten^M
ufficio^M del comandante^M

firefighters' dormitory
dormitorio^M de los bomberos^M
dortoir^M des pompiers^M
Mannschaftsschlafsaal^M
dormitorio^M dei vigili^M del fuoco^M

administrative office
oficina^F administrativa
bureau^M administratif
Verwaltungsbüro^N
ufficio^M amministrativo

fire prevention education officer's office
despacho^M del inspector^F de prevención^F de incendios^M
bureau^M de l'inspecteur^M en prévention^F-incendie^M
Büro^N des Brandschutzbeauftragten^M
ufficio^M dell'ufficiale^M addetto alla formazione^F dei vigili^M del fuoco^M

officers' washrooms and showers
aseos^M y duchas^F de los oficiales^M
toilettes^F et douches^F des officiers^M
Duschen^F und Toiletten^F der Offiziere^M
bagno^M e doccia^F degli ufficiali^M

meeting room
sala^F de reuniones^F
salle^F de réunion^F
Sitzungsraum^M
sala^F riunioni^F

firefighters' washrooms and showers
aseos^M y duchas^F de los bomberos^M
toilettes^F et douches^F des pompiers^M
Mannschaftsduschen^F und
bagno^M e doccia^F dei vigili^M del fuoco^M

turnouts
trajes^M de intervención^F
tenue^F d'intervention^F
Dienstkleidung^F
divise^F di servizio^M

locker room
vestuario^M
vestiaire^M
Umkleideraum^M
spogliatoio^M

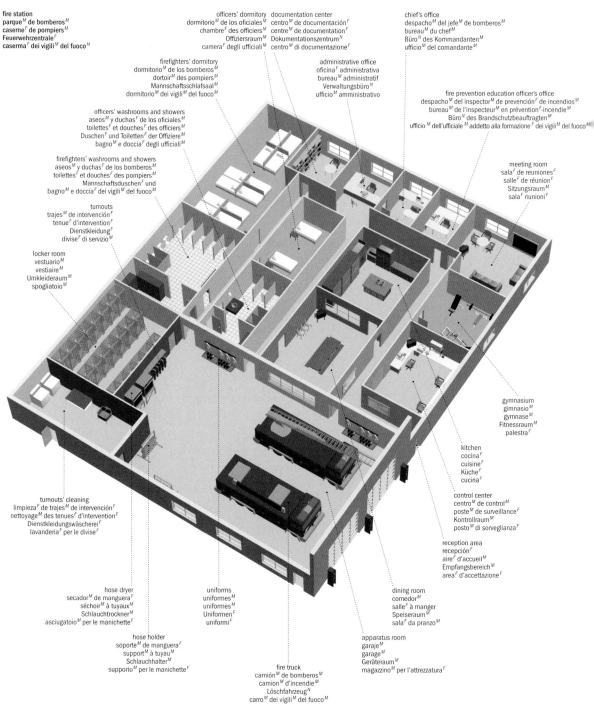

gymnasium
gimnasio^M
gymnase^M
Fitnessraum^M
palestra^F

kitchen
cocina^F
cuisine^F
Küche^F
cucina^F

control center
centro^M de control^M
poste^M de surveillance^F
Kontrollraum^M
posto^M di sorveglianza^F

reception area
recepción^F
aire^F d'accueil^M
Empfangsbereich^M
area^F d'accettazione^F

turnouts' cleaning
limpieza^F de trajes^M de intervención^F
nettoyage^M des tenues^F d'intervention^F
Dienstkleidungswäscherei^F
lavanderia^F per le divise^F

hose dryer
secador^M de manguera^F
séchoir^M à tuyaux^M
Schlauchtrockner^M
asciugatoio^M per le manichette^F

uniforms
uniformes^M
uniformes^M
Uniformen^F
uniformi^F

dining room
comedor^M
salle^F à manger
Speiseraum^M
sala^F da pranzo^M

hose holder
soporte^M de manguera^F
support^M à tuyau^M
Schlauchhalter^M
supporto^M per le manichette^F

fire truck
camión^M de bomberos^M
camion^M d'incendie^M
Löschfahrzeug^N
carro^M dei vigili^M del fuoco^M

apparatus room
garaje^M
garage^M
Geräteraum^M
magazzino^M per l'attrezzatura^F

SOCIETY

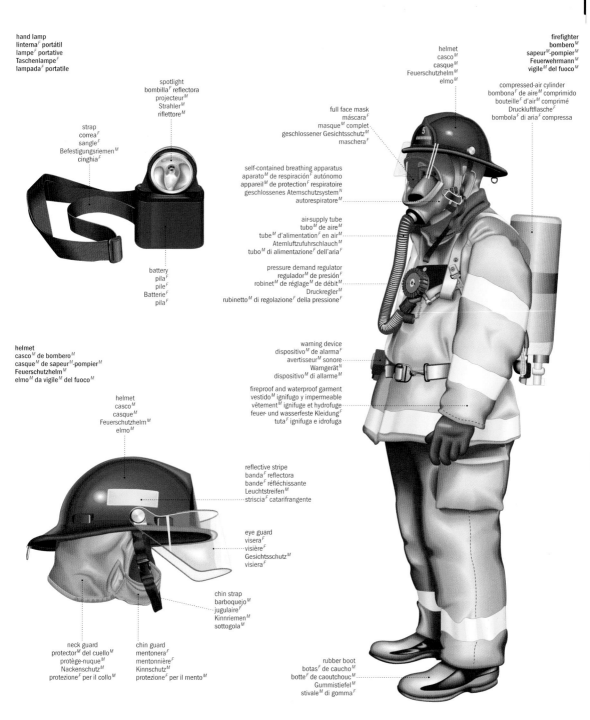

hand lamp
linterna^F portátil
lampe^F portative
Taschenlampe^F
lampada^F portatile

spotlight
bombilla^F reflectora
projecteur^M
Strahler^M
riflettore^M

strap
correa^F
sangle^F
Befestigungsriemen^M
cinghia^F

battery
pila^F
pile^F
Batterie^F
pila^F

helmet
casco^M de bombero^M
casque^M de sapeur^M-pompier^M
Feuerschutzhelm^M
elmo^M da vigile^M del fuoco^M

helmet
casco^M
casque^M
Feuerschutzhelm^M
elmo^M

reflective stripe
banda^F reflectora
bande^F réfléchissante
Leuchtstreifen^M
striscia^F catarifrangente

eye guard
visera^F
visière^F
Gesichtsschutz^M
visiera^F

chin strap
barboquejo^M
jugulaire^F
Kinnriemen^M
sottogola^M

neck guard
protector^M del cuello^M
protège-nuque^M
Nackenschutz^M
protezione^F per il collo^M

chin guard
mentonera^F
mentonnière^F
Kinnschutz^M
protezione^F per il mento^M

helmet
casco^M
casque^M
Feuerschutzhelm^M
elmo^M

full face mask
máscara^F
masque^M complet
geschlossener Gesichtsschutz^M
maschera^F

self-contained breathing apparatus
aparato^M de respiración^F autónomo
appareil^M de protection^F respiratoire
geschlossenes Atemschutzsystem^N
autorespiratore^M

air-supply tube
tubo^M de aire^M
tube^M d'alimentation^F en air^M
Atemluftzufuhrschlauch^M
tubo^M di alimentazione^F dell'aria^F

pressure demand regulator
regulador^M de presión^F
robinet^M de réglage^M de débit^M
Druckregler^M
rubinetto^M di regolazione^F della pressione^F

warning device
dispositivo^M de alarma^F
avertisseur^M sonore
Warngerät^N
dispositivo^M di allarme^M

fireproof and waterproof garment
vestido^M ignifugo y impermeable
vêtement^M ignifuge et hydrofuge
feuer- und wasserfeste Kleidung^F
tuta^F ignifuga e idrofuga

firefighter
bombero^M
sapeur^M-pompier^M
Feuerwehrmann^M
vigile^M del fuoco^M

helmet
casco^M
casque^M
Feuerschutzhelm^M
elmo^M

compressed-air cylinder
bombona^F de aire^M comprimido
bouteille^F d'air^M comprimé
Druckluftflasche^F
bombola^F di aria^F compressa

rubber boot
botas^F de caucho^M
botte^F de caoutchouc^M
Gummistiefel^M
stivale^M di gomma^F

SOCIETY

fire engines
camiones^M **de bomberos**^M
véhicules^M **d'incendie**^M
Löschfahrzeuge^N
carri^M **dei pompieri**^M

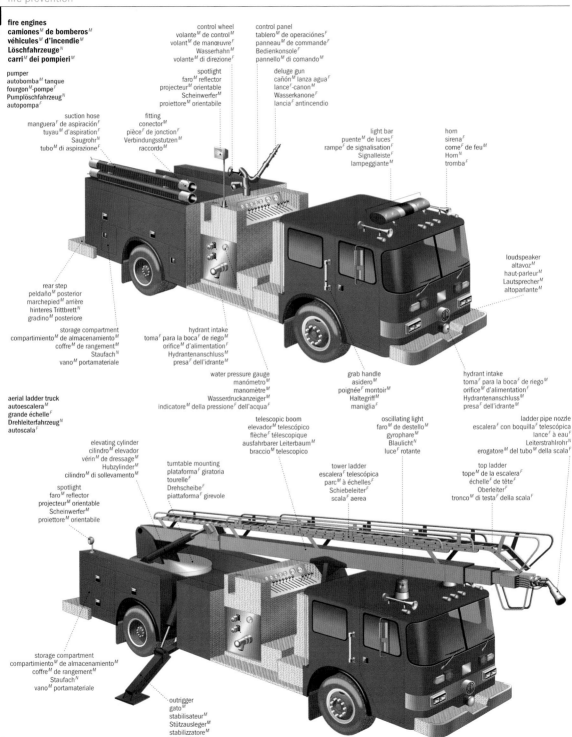

pumper
autobomba^M tanque
fourgon^M-pompe^F
Pumplöschfahrzeug^N
autopompa^F

control wheel
volante^M de control
volant^M de manœuvre^F
Wasserhahn^M
volante^M di direzione

control panel
tablero^M de operaciónes^F
panneau^M de commande^F
Bedienkonsole^F
pannello^M di comando^M

spotlight
faro^M reflector
projecteur^M orientable
Scheinwerfer^M
proiettore^M orientabile

deluge gun
cañón^M lanza agua^F
lance^F-canon^M
Wasserkanone^F
lancia^F antincendio

suction hose
manguera^F de aspiración^F
tuyau^M d'aspiration^F
Saugrohr^N
tubo^M di aspirazione^F

fitting
conector^M
pièce^F de jonction^F
Verbindungsstutzen^M
raccordo^M

light bar
puente^M de luces^F
rampe^F de signalisation^F
Signalleiste^F
lampeggiante^M

horn
sirena^F
corne^F de feu^M
Horn^N
tromba^F

loudspeaker
altavoz^M
haut-parleur^M
Lautsprecher^M
altoparlante^M

rear step
peldaño^M posterior
marchepied^M arrière
hinteres Trittbrett^N
gradino^M posteriore

storage compartment
compartimiento^M de almacenamiento^M
coffre^M de rangement^M
Staufach^N
vano^M portamateriale

hydrant intake
toma^F para la boca^F de riego^M
orifice^F d'alimentation^F
Hydrantenanschluss^M
presa^F dell'idrante^M

water pressure gauge
manómetro^M
manomètre^M
Wasserdruckanzeiger^M
indicatore^M della pressione^F dell'acqua^F

grab handle
asidero^M
poignée^F montoir^M
Haltegriff^M
maniglia^F

hydrant intake
toma^F para la boca^F de riego^M
orifice^M d'alimentation^F
Hydrantenanschluss^M
presa^F dell'idrante^M

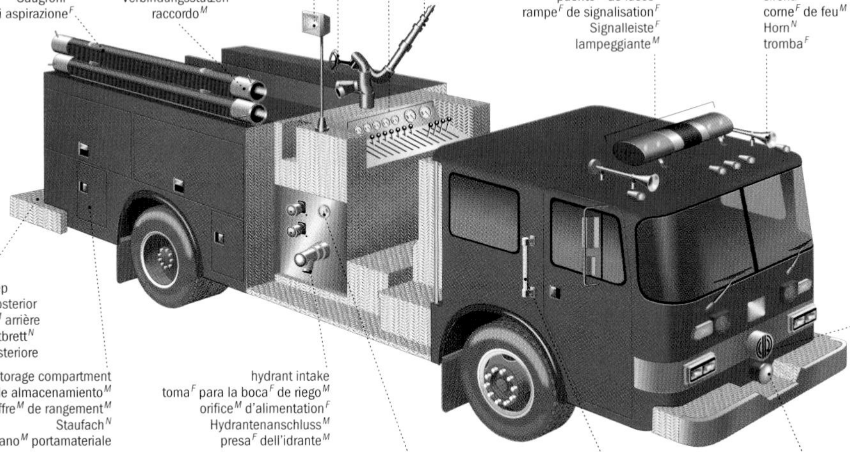

aerial ladder truck
autoescalera^F
grande échelle^F
Drehleiterfahrzeug^N
autoscala^F

elevating cylinder
cilindro^M elevador
vérin^M de dressage^M
Hubzylinder^M
cilindro^M di sollevamento^M

telescopic boom
elevador^M telescópico
flèche^F télescopique
ausfahrbarer Leiterbaum^M
braccio^M telescopico

oscillating light
faro^M de destello^M
gyrophare^F
Blaulicht^N
luce^F rotante

ladder pipe nozzle
escalera^F con boquilla^F telescópica
lance^F à eau^F
Leiterstrahlrohr^N
erogatore^M del tubo^M della scala^F

turntable mounting
plataforma^F giratoria
tourelle^F
Drehscheibe^F
piattaforma^F girevole

tower ladder
escalera^F telescópica
parc^M à échelles^F
Schiebeleiter^F
scala^F aerea

top ladder
tope^M de la escalera^F
échelle^F de tête^F
Oberleiter^F
tronco^M di testa^F della scala^F

spotlight
faro^M reflector
projecteur^M orientable
Scheinwerfer^M
proiettore^M orientabile

storage compartment
compartimiento^M de almacenamiento^M
coffre^M de rangement^M
Staufach^N
vano^M portamateriale

outrigger
gato^M
stabilisateur^M
Stützausleger^M
stabilizzatore^M

SOCIETY

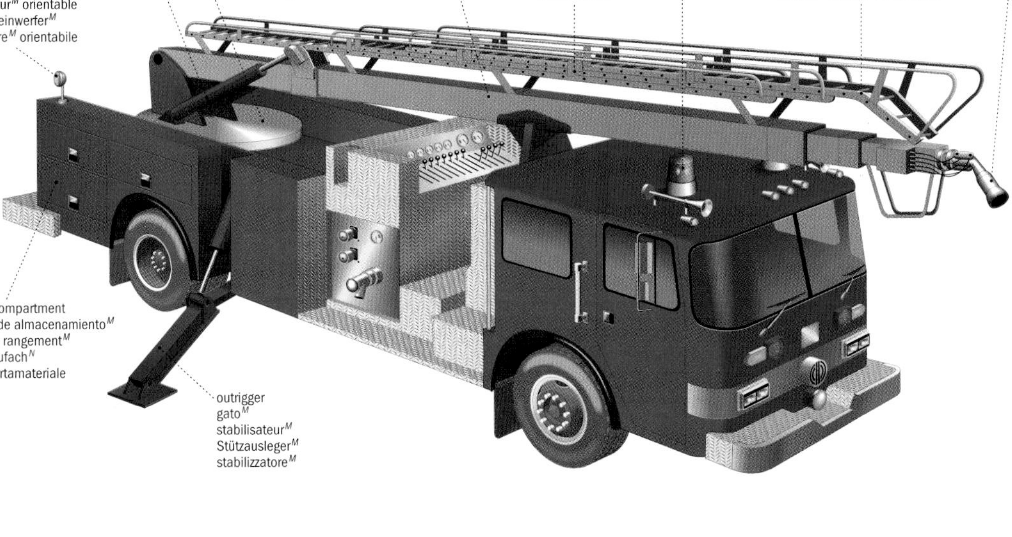

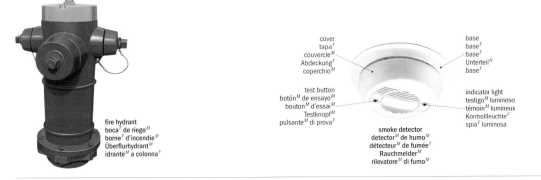

fire hydrant
boca^F de riego^M
borne^F d'incendie^M
Überflurhydrant^M
idrante^M a colonna^F

cover
tapa^F
couvercle^M
Abdeckung^F
coperchio^M

base
base^F
base^F
Unterteil^N
base^F

test button
botón^M de ensayo^M
bouton^M d'essai^M
Testknopf^M
pulsante^M di prova^F

indicator light
testigo^M luminoso
témoin^M lumineux
Kontrollleuchte^F
spia^F luminosa

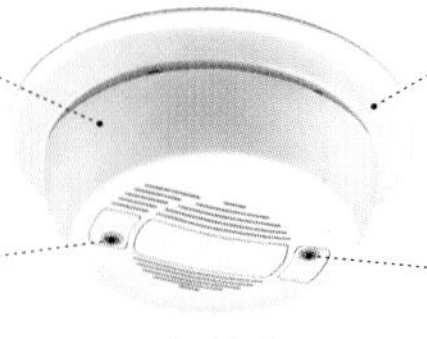

smoke detector
detector^M de humo^M
détecteur^M de fumée^F
Rauchmelder^M
rilevatore^M di fumo^M

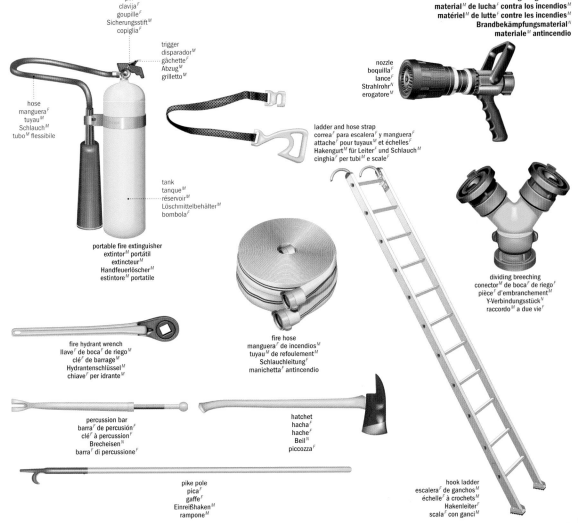

pin
clavija^F
goupille^F
Sicherungsstift^M
copiglia^F

trigger
disparador^M
gâchette^F
Abzug^M
grilletto^M

hose
manguera^F
tuyau^M
Schlauch^M
tubo^M flessibile

tank
tanque^M
réservoir^M
Löschmittelbehälter^M
bombola^F

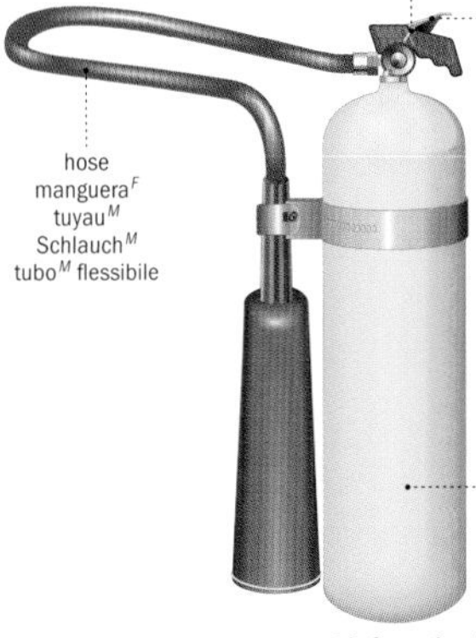

portable fire extinguisher
extintor^M portátil
extincteur^M
Handfeuerlöscher^M
estintore^M portatile

fire-fighting materials
material^M de lucha^F contra los incendios^M
matériel^M de lutte^F contre les incendies^M
Brandbekämpfungsmaterial^N
materiale^M antincendio

nozzle
boquilla^F
lance^F
Strahlrohr^M
erogatore^M

ladder and hose strap
correa^F para escalera^F y manguera^F
attache^F pour tuyaux^M et échelles^F
Hakengurt^M für Leiter^F und Schlauch^M
cinghia^F per tubi^M e scale^F

dividing breeching
conector^M de boca^F de riego^F
pièce^F d'embranchement^M
Y-Verbindungsstück^N
raccordo^M a due vie^F

fire hydrant wrench
llave^F de boca^F de riego^M
clé^F de barrage^M
Hydrantenschlüssel^M
chiave^F per idrante^M

fire hose
manguera^F de incendios^M
tuyau^M de refoulement^M
Schlauchleitung^F
manichetta^F antincendio

percussion bar
barra^F de percusión^F
clé^F à percussion^F
Brecheisen^N
barra^F di percussione^F

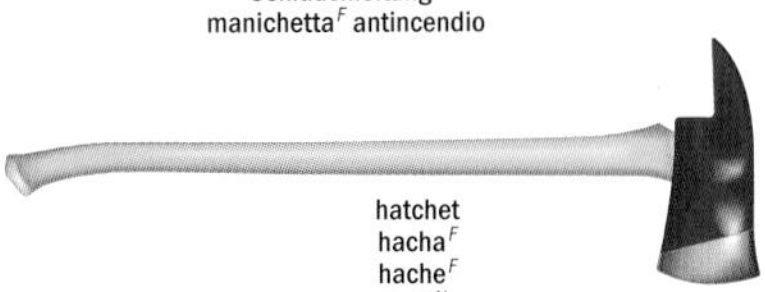

hatchet
hacha^F
hache^F
Beil^N
piccozza^F

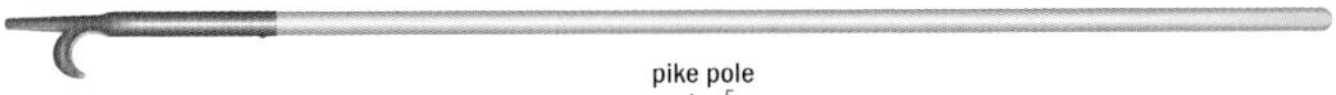

pike pole
pica^F
gaffe^F
Einreißhaken^M
rampone^M

hook ladder
escalera^F de ganchos^M
échelle^F à crochets^M
Hakenleiter^F
scala^F con ganci^M

SOCIETY

crime prevention

prevención^F de la criminalidad^F | prévention^F de la criminalité^F | vorbeugende Verbrechensbekämpfung^F | prevenzione^F del crimine^M

police station
estación^F de policía^F
poste^M de police^F
Polizeirevier^M
stazione^F di polizia^F

men's cell
celda^F de hombres^M
cellule^F pour hommes^M
Männerzelle^F
cella^F per gli uomini^M

women's cell
celda^F de mujeres^M
cellule^F pour femmes^F
Frauenzelle^F
cella^F per le donne^F

prisoners' shower
duchas^M de los presos^M
douche^F des détenus^M
Häftlingsdusche^F
doccia^F dei detenuti^M

identification section
sección^M de identificación^F
section^F de l'identité^F
Erkennungsdienstbereich^M
sezione^F di riconoscimento^M

control room
sala^F de control^M
poste^M de contrôle^M
Kontrollraum^M
posto^M di controllo^M

staff restroom
aseo^M del personal^M
w.-c.^M du personnel^M ; toilettes^F du personnel^M
Personaltoiletten^F
bagno^M del personale^M

staff lounge
sala^F del personal^M
salon^M du personnel^M
Personalraum^M
sala^F del personale^M

staff locker room
guardarropa^M del personal^M
vestiaire^M du personnel^M
Personalumkleideraum^M
spogliatoio^M del personale^M

chief officer's office
despacho^M del oficial^M superior
bureau^M de l'officier^M supérieur
Büro^N des Dienststellenleiters^M
ufficio^M del comandante^M

staff entrance
entrada^F del personal^M
entrée^F du personnel^M
Personaleingang^M
ingresso^M del personale^M

report writing room
sala^F de redacción^F de informes^M
salle^F de rédaction^F des rapports^M
Protokollraum^M
stanza^F per stilare i rapporti^M

junior officer's office
despacho^F del oficial^M subalterno
bureau^M de l'officier^M subalterne
Büro^N des stellvertretenden Dienststellenleiters^M
ufficio^M del vicecomandante^M

cell for minors
celda^F de menores^M
cellule^F pour mineurs^M
Minderjährigenzelle^F
cella^F per i minori^M

interrogation room
sala^F de interrogatorios^M
salle^F d'interrogatoire^M
Verhörraum^M
stanza^F per gli interrogatori^M

complaints office
oficina^F de quejas^F
bureau^M des plaintes^F
Anzeigenaufnahme^F
ufficio^M per le denunce^F

waiting room
sala^F de espera^F
salle^F d'attente^F
Warteraum^M
sala^F d'attesa^F

main entrance
entrada^F principal
entrée^F principale
Haupteingang^M
ingresso^M principale

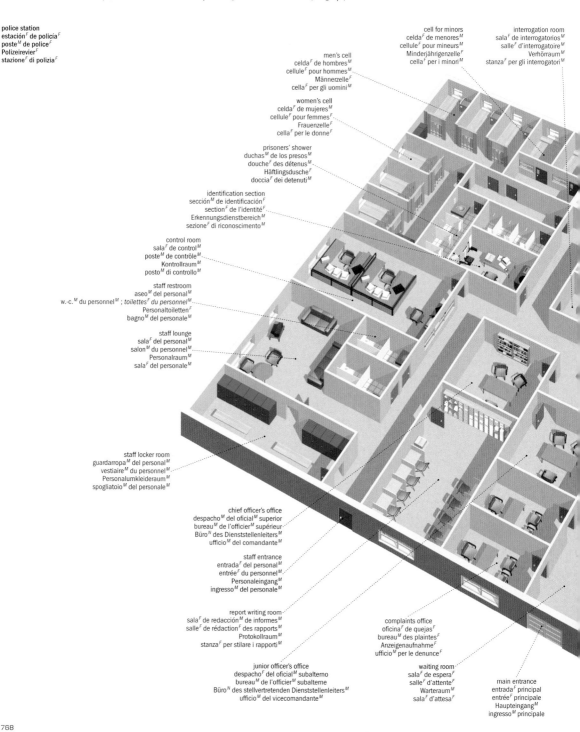

SOCIETY

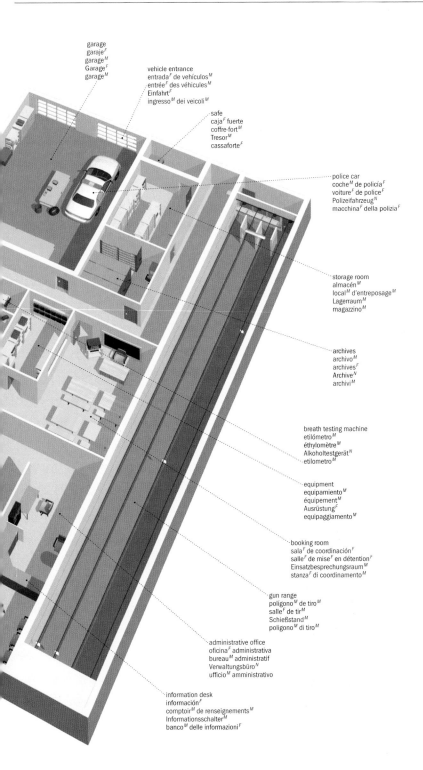

garage
garaje^F
garage^M
Garage^F
garage^M

vehicle entrance
entrada^F de vehículos^M
entrée^F des véhicules^M
Einfahrt^F
ingresso^M dei veicoli^M

safe
caja^F fuerte
coffre-fort^M
Tresor^M
cassaforte^F

police car
coche^M de policía^F
voiture^F de police^F
Polizeifahrzeug^N
macchina^F della polizia^F

storage room
almacén^M
local^M d'entreposage^M
Lagerraum^M
magazzino^M

archives
archivo^M
archives^F
Archive^N
archivi^M

breath testing machine
etilómetro^M
éthylomètre^M
Alkoholtestgerät^N
etilometro^M

equipment
equipamiento^M
équipement^M
Ausrüstung^F
equipaggiamento^M

booking room
sala^F de coordinación^F
salle^F de mise^F en détention^F
Einsatzbesprechungsraum^M
stanza^F di coordinamento^M

gun range
polígono^M de tiro^M
salle^F de tir^M
Schießstand^M
poligono^M di tiro^M

administrative office
oficina^F administrativa
bureau^M administratif
Verwaltungsbüro^N
ufficio^M amministrativo

information desk
información^F
comptoir^M de renseignements^M
Informationsschalter^M
banco^M delle informazioni^F

SOCIETY

crime prevention

police officer
agente^M de policía^F
agent^M de police^F
Polizeibeamter^M
agente^M di polizia^F

cap
gorra^F
casquette^F
Mütze^F
berretto^M

badge
insignia^F
insigne^M
Abzeichen^N
distintivo^M

shoulder strap
hombrera^F
patte^F d'épaule^F
Schulterklappe^F
spallina^F

rank insignia
insignia^F de grado^M
insigne^M de grade^M
Dienstgradabzeichen^N
gradi^M

identification badge
placa^F de identificación^F
insigne^M d'identité^F
Namensschild^N
cartellino^M di identificazione^F

uniform
uniforme^M
uniforme^M
Uniform^F
uniforme^F

duty belt
cinturón^M de servicio^M
ceinturon^M de service^M
Dienstgürtel^M
cintura^F di servizio^M

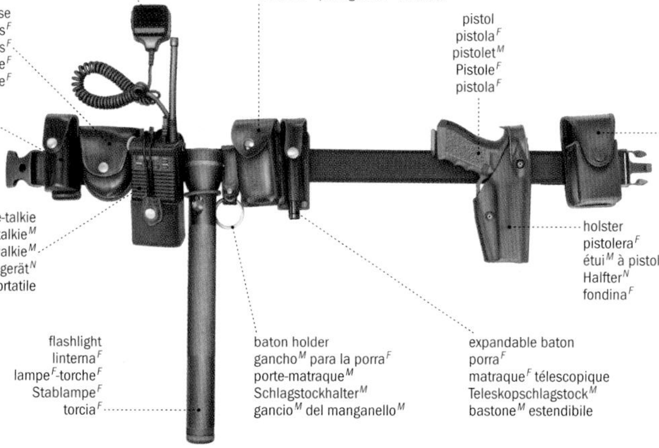

microphone
micrófono^M
microphone^M
Mikrofon^N
microfono^M

latex glove case
funda^F de guantes^M de látex^M
étui^M pour gants^M de latex^M
Tasche^F für Latexhandschuhe^M
astuccio^M per i guanti^M di lattice^M

handcuff case
estuche^M de las esposas^F
étui^M à menottes^F
Handschellentasche^F
astuccio^M delle manette^F

pistol
pistola^F
pistolet^M
Pistole^F
pistola^F

ammunition pouch
cartuchera^F
cartouchière^F
Patronentasche^F
cartucciera^F

pepper spray
aerosol^M de pimienta^F
vaporisateur^M de poivre^M
Pfefferspray^N
spray^M al peperoncino^M

walkie-talkie
walkie-talkie^M
talkie-walkie^M
Hand^F-Funksprechgerät^N
radiotelefono^M portatile

holster
pistolera^F
étui^M à pistolet^M
Halfter^N
fondina^F

flashlight
linterna^F
lampe^F-torche^F
Stablampe^F
torcia^F

baton holder
gancho^M para la porra^F
porte-matraque^F
Schlagstockhalter^M
gancio^M del manganello^M

expandable baton
porra^F
matraque^F télescopique
Teleskopschlagstock^M
bastone^M estendibile

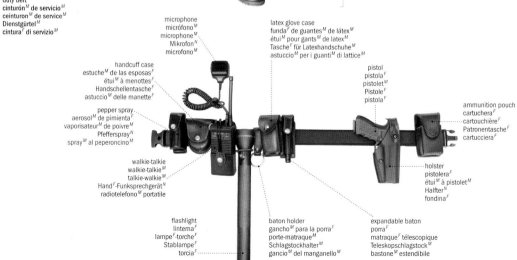

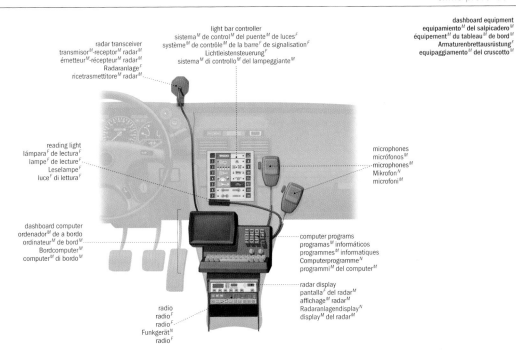

dashboard equipment
equipamiento^M del salpicadero^M
équipement^M du tableau^M de bord^M
Armaturenbrettausrüstung^F
equipaggiamento^M del cruscotto^M

light bar controller
sistema^M de control^M del puente^M de luces^F
système^M de contrôle^M de la barre^F de signalisation^F
Lichtleistensteuerung^F
sistema^M di controllo^M del lampeggiante^M

radar transceiver
transmisor^M-receptor^M radar^M
émetteur^M-récepteur^M radar^M
Radaranlage^F
ricetrasmettitore^M radar^M

microphones
micrófonos^M
microphones^M
Mikrofon^N
microfoni^M

reading light
lámpara^F de lectura^F
lampe^F de lecture^F
Leselampe^F
luce^F di lettura^F

dashboard computer
ordenador^M de a bordo
ordinateur^M de bord^M
Bordcomputer^M
computer^M di bordo^M

computer programs
programas^M informáticos
programmes^M informatiques
Computerprogramme^N
programmi^M del computer^M

radar display
pantalla^F del radar^M
affichage^M radar^M
Radaranlagendisplay^N
display^M del radar^M

radio
radio^F
radio^F
Funkgerät^N
radio^F

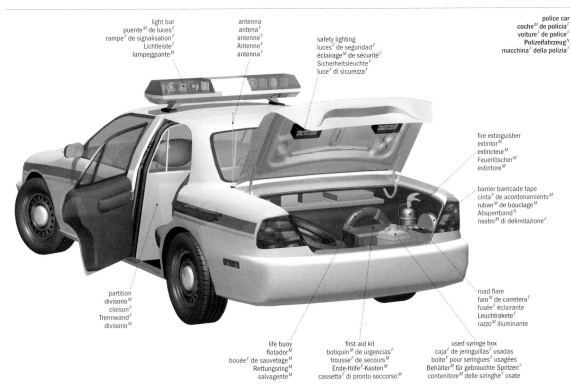

police car
coche^M de policía^F
voiture^F de police^F
Polizeifahrzeug^N
macchina^F della polizia^F

light bar
puente^M de luces^F
rampe^F de signalisation^F
Lichtleiste^F
lampeggiante^M

antenna
antena^F
antenne^F
Antenne^F
antenna^F

safety lighting
luces^F de seguridad^F
éclairage^M de sécurité^F
Sicherheitsleuchte^F
luce^F di sicurezza^F

fire extinguisher
extintor^M
extincteur^M
Feuerlöscher^M
estintore^M

barrier barricade tape
cinta^F de acordonamiento^M
ruban^M de bouclage^M
Absperrband^N
nastro^M di delimitazione^F

road flare
faro^M de carretera^F
fusée^F éclairante
Leuchtrakete^F
razzo^M illuminante

partition
divisorio^M
cloison^F
Trennwand^F
divisorio^M

life buoy
flotador^M
bouée^F de sauvetage^M
Rettungsring^M
salvagente^M

first aid kit
botiquín^M de urgencias^F
trousse^F de secours^M
Erste-Hilfe^F-Kasten^M
cassetta^F di pronto soccorso^M

used syringe box
caja^F de jeringuillas^F usadas
boîte^F pour seringues^F usagées
Behälter^M für gebrauchte Spritzen^F
contenitore^M delle siringhe^F usate

SOCIETY

ear protection

protección^F para los oídos^M | protection^F de l'ouïe^F | Gehörschutz^M | protezione^F per le orecchie^F

safety earmuffs
cascos^M de seguridad^F
serre-tête^M antibruit
Ohrenschützer^M
cuffie^F di sicurezza^F

headband
diadema^F
serre-tête^M
Kopfband^N
supporto^M elastico

earplugs
tapones^M para los oídos^M
protège-tympan^M
Ohrstöpsel^M
tappi^M per le orecchie^F

foam cushion
protector^M de espuma^F
coussinet^M en mousse^F
Schaumgummipolsterung^F
cuscinetti^M antirumore

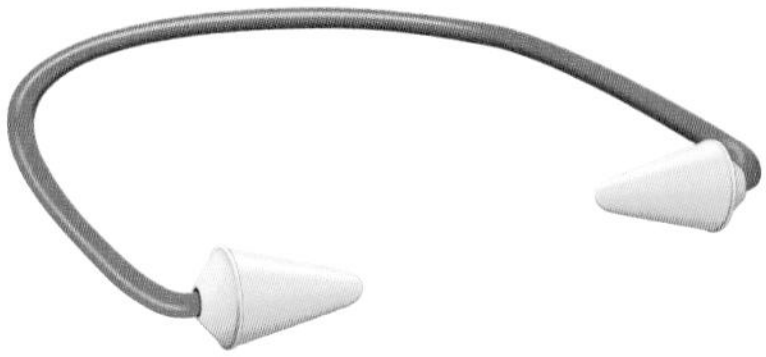

eye protection

protección^F para los ojos^M | protection^F des yeux^M | Augenschutz^M | protezione^F per gli occhi^M

safety glasses
gafas^F de seguridad^F
lunettes^F de sécurité^F
Schutzbrille^F
occhiali^M di protezione^F con ripari^M laterali

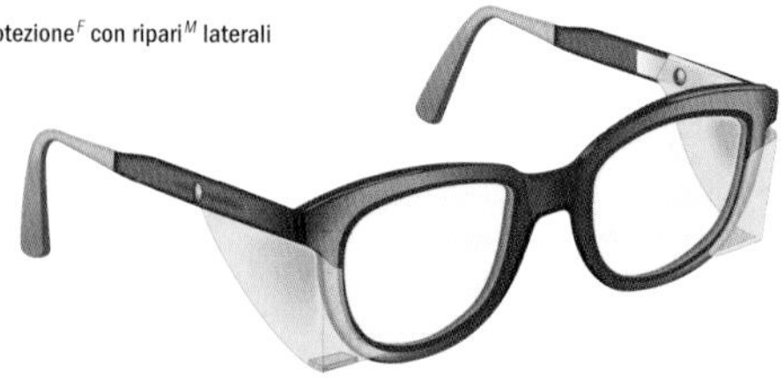

safety goggles
gafas^F protectoras
lunettes^F de protection^F
Schutzmaske^F
occhiali^M di protezione^F panoramici

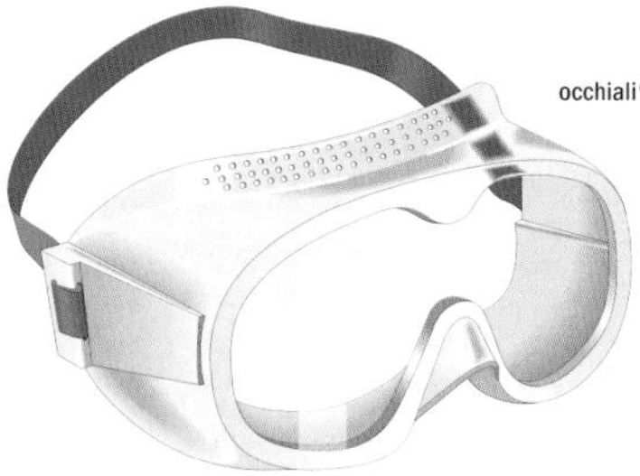

head protection

protección^F para la cabeza^F | protection^F de la tête^F | Kopfschutz^M | protezione^F per la testa^F

SOCIETY

hard hat
casco^M de seguridad^F
casque^M de sécurité^F
Schutzhelm^M
elmetto^M

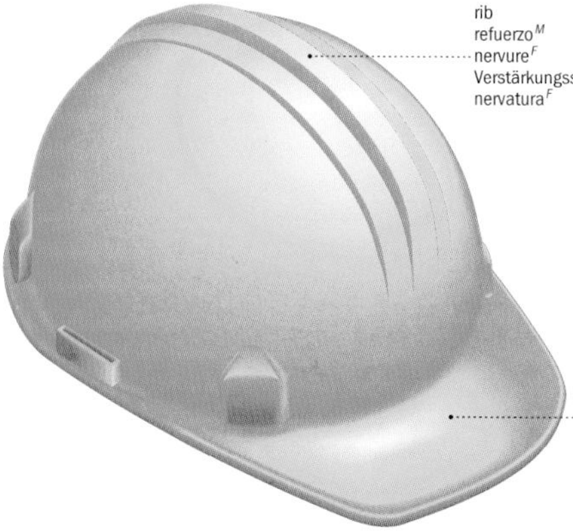

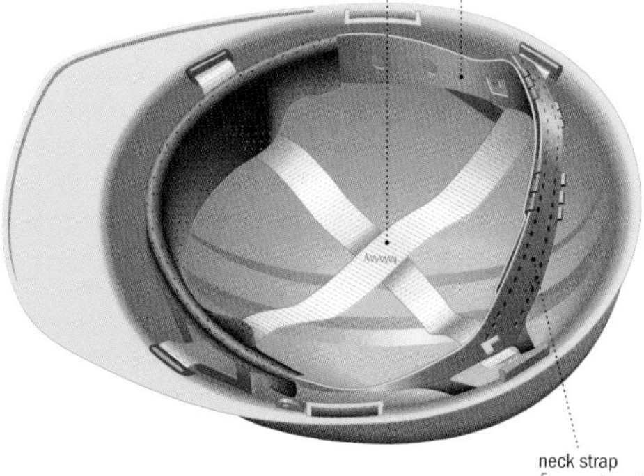

suspension band
banda^F de suspensión^F
sangle^F d'amortissement^M
Trageband^N
fascia^F di sospensione^F

headband
cinta^F
tour^M de tête^F
Kopfband^N
fascia^F stringitesta

rib
refuerzo^M
nervure^F
Verstärkungsschwelle^F
nervatura^F

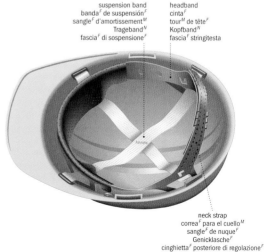

peak
visera^F
visière^F
Schild^N
visiera^F

neck strap
correa^F para el cuello^M
sangle^F de nuque^F
Genicklasche^F
cinghietta^F posteriore di regolazione^F

respiratory system protection

protección^F para el sistema^M respiratorio^M | protection^F des voies^F respiratoires | Atemschutz^M | protezione^F per le vie^F respiratorie

respirator
máscara^F antigás^M
masque^M respiratoire
Gasmaske^F
maschera^F a pieno facciale^M bifiltro

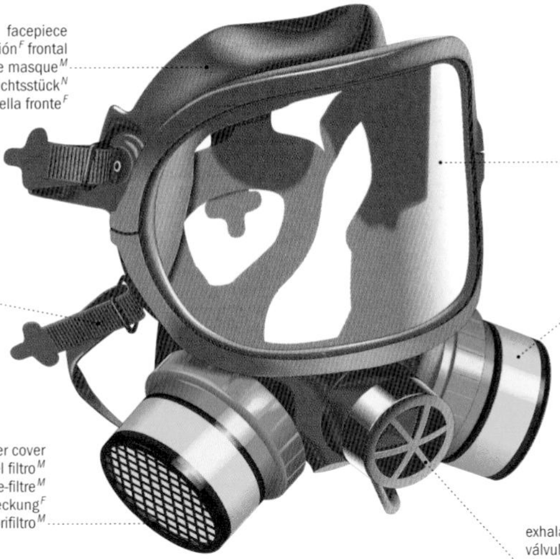

facepiece
sección^F frontal
jupe^F de masque^M
Gesichtsstück^N
fascia^F protettiva della fronte^F

visor
careta^F
oculaire^M
Visier^N
visore^M

head harness
correas^F
jeu^M de brides^F
Kopfriemen^M
elastico^M regolabile per il capo^M

cartridge
cartucho^M
cartouche^F
Kartusche^F
filtro^M

inhalation valve
válvula^F de inhalación^F
soupape^F inspiratoire
Einatmungsventil^N
valvola^F di inspirazione^F

filter cover
tapa^F del filtro^M
couvre-filtre^M
Filterabdeckung^F
coprifiltro^M

exhalation valve
válvula^F de exhalación^F
soupape^F expiratoire
Ausatmungsventil^N
valvola^F di espirazione^F

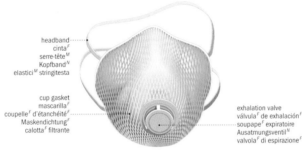

half-mask respirator
máscara^F para el polvo^M
masque^M bucco-nasal
leichte Atemschutzmaske^F
mascherina^F

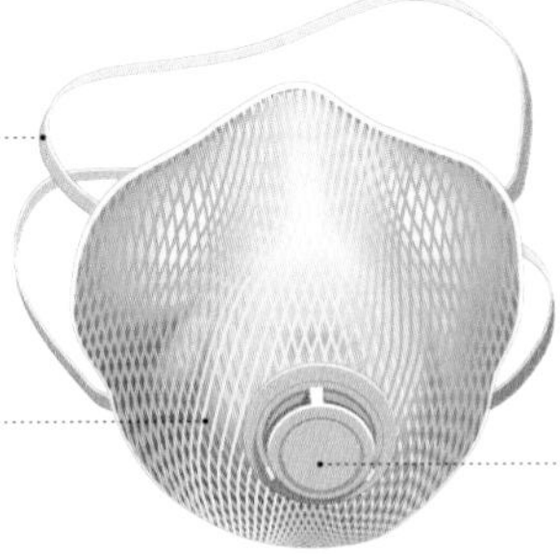

headband
cinta^F
serre-tête^M
Kopfband^N
elastici^M stringitesta

cup gasket
mascarilla^F
coupelle^F d'étanchéité^F
Maskendichtung^F
calotta^F filtrante

exhalation valve
válvula^F de exhalación^F
soupape^F expiratoire
Ausatmungsventil^N
valvola^F di espirazione^F

foot protection

protección^F para los pies^M | protection^F des pieds^M | Fußschutz^M | protezione^F per i piedi^M

safety boot
bota^F de seguridad^F
brodequin^M de sécurité^F
Sicherheitsschuh^M
scarponcino^M di sicurezza^F

toe guard
puntera^F protectora
protège-orteils^M
Zehenschützer^M
puntale^M di protezione^F

reinforced toe
tope^M
embout^M de protection^F
Stahlkappe^F
puntale^M rinforzato

safety symbols

símbolos^M de seguridad^F | symboles^M de sécurité^F | Warn- und Gebotszeichen^N | simboli^M di sicurezza^F

hazardous materials
materiales^M peligrosos
matières^F dangereuses
gefährliche Substanzen^F
materiali^M pericolosi

corrosive
corrosivo
matières^F corrosives
ätzend
materiale^M corrosivo

electrical hazard
alto voltaje^M
danger^M électrique
elektrische Spannung^F
alta tensione^F

explosive
explosivo
matières^F explosives
explosionsgefährlich
materiale^M esplosivo

flammable
inflamable
matières^F inflammables
leicht entzündlich
materiale^M infiammabile

radioactive
radioactivo
matières^F radioactives
radioaktiv
materiale^M radioattivo

poison
veneno^M
matières^F toxiques
Gift^N
materiale^M tossico

protection
protección^F
protection^F
Schutzmaßnahmen^F
misure^F di protezione^F obbligatorie

eye protection
protección^F de los ojos^M
protection^F obligatoire de la vue^F
Augenschutz^M tragen
protezione^F per gli occhi^M

ear protection
protección^F de los oídos^M
protection^F obligatoire de l'ouïe^F
Gehörschutz^M tragen
protezione^F per le orecchie^F

head protection
protección^F de la cabeza^F
protection^F obligatoire de la tête^F
Schutzhelm^M tragen
protezione^F per la testa^F

hand protection
protección^F de las manos^F
protection^F obligatoire des mains^F
Schutzhandschuhe^M tragen
protezione^F per le mani^F

foot protection
protección^F de los pies^M
protection^F obligatoire des pieds^M
Schutzschuhe^M tragen
protezione^F per i piedi^M

respiratory system protection
protección del sistema^M respiratorio
protection^F obligatoire des voies^F respiratoires
Atemschutz^M tragen
protezione^F per le vie^F respiratorie

SOCIETY

ambulance

ambulancia^F | ambulance^F | Rettungswagen^M | ambulanza^F

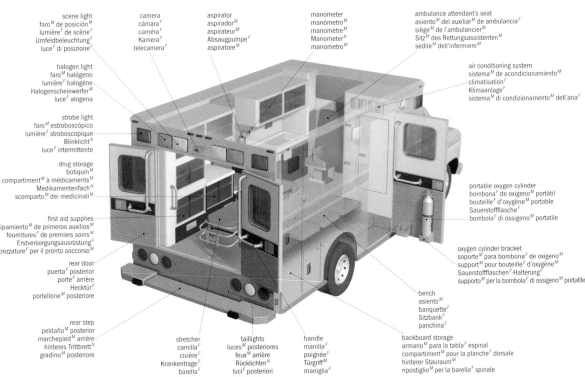

scene light
faro^M de posición^M
lumière^F de scène^F
Umfeldbeleuchtung^F
luce^F di posizione^F

camera
cámara^F
caméra^F
Kamera^F
telecamera^F

aspirator
aspirador^M
aspirateur^M
Absaugpumpe^F
aspiratore^M

manometer
manómetro^M
manomètre^M
Manometer^N
manometro^M

ambulance attendant's seat
asiento^M del auxiliar^M de ambulancia^F
siège^M de l'ambulancier^M
Sitz^M des Rettungsassistenten^M
sedile^M dell'infermiere^M

halogen light
faro^M halógeno
lumière^F halogène
Halogenscheinwerfer^M
luce^F alogena

air conditioning system
sistema^M de acondicionamiento^M
climatisation^F
Klimaanlage^F
sistema^M di condizionamento^M dell'aria^F

strobe light
faro^M estroboscópico
lumière^F stroboscopique
Blinklicht^N
luce^F intermittente

portable oxygen cylinder
bombona^F de oxigeno^M portátil
bouteille^F d'oxygène^M portable
Sauerstoffflasche^F
bombola^F di ossigeno^M portatile

drug storage
botiquín^M
compartiment^M à médicaments^M
Medikamentenfach^N
scomparto^M dei medicinali^M

first aid supplies
equipamiento^M de primeros auxilios^M
fournitures^F de premiers soins^M
Erstversorgungsausrüstung^F
attrezzature^F per il pronto soccorso^M

oxygen cylinder bracket
soporte^M para bombona^F de oxigeno^M
support^M pour bouteille^F d'oxygène^M
Sauerstoffflaschen^F-Halterung^F
supporto^M per la bombola^F di ossigeno^M portatile

rear door
puerta^F posterior
porte^F arrière
Hecktür^F
portellone^M posteriore

bench
asiento^M
banquette^F
Sitzbank^F
panchina^F

rear step
peldaño^M posterior
marchepied^M arrière
hinteres Trittbrett^N
gradino^M posteriore

stretcher
camilla^F
civière^F
Krankentrage^F
barella^F

taillights
luces^M posteriores
feux^M arrière
Rücklichter^N
luci^F posteriori

handle
manilla^F
poignée^F
Türgriff^M
maniglia^F

backboard storage
armario^M para la tabla^F espinal
compartiment^M pour la planche^F dorsale
hinterer Stauraum^M
ripostiglio^M per la barella^F spinale

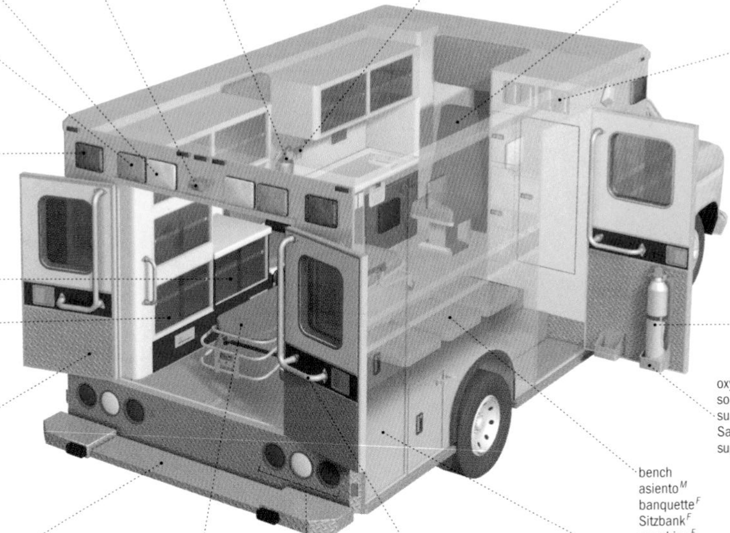

first aid equipment

equipo^M de primeros auxilios^M | matériel^M de secours^M | Notfallausrüstung^F | strumenti^M per il pronto soccorso^M

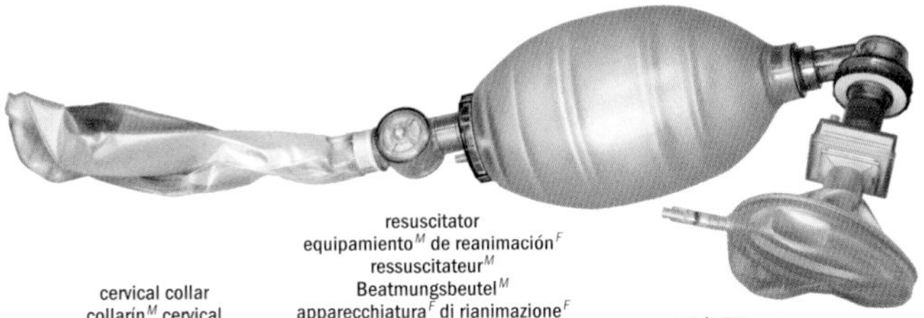

resuscitator
equipamiento^M de reanimación^F
ressuscitateur^M
Beatmungsbeutel^M
apparecchiatura^F di rianimazione^F

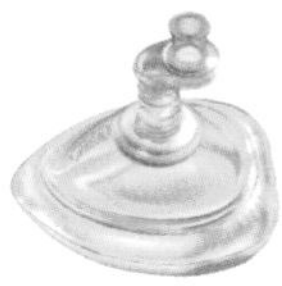

oxygen mask
máscara^F de oxigeno^M
masque^M à oxygène^M
Sauerstoff^M-Atemmaske^F
maschera^F per l'ossigeno^M

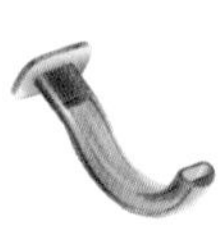

oropharyngeal airway
cánula^F orofaringea
canule^F oropharyngée
Oropharyngealtubus^M
cannula^F orofaringea

cervical collar
collarín^M cervical
collier^M cervical
Nackenstütze^F
collarino^M

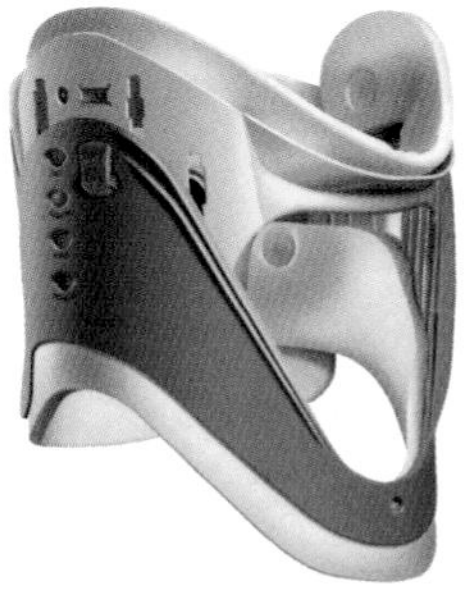

aspirator
aspirador^M
aspirateur^M
Absauger^M
aspiratore^M

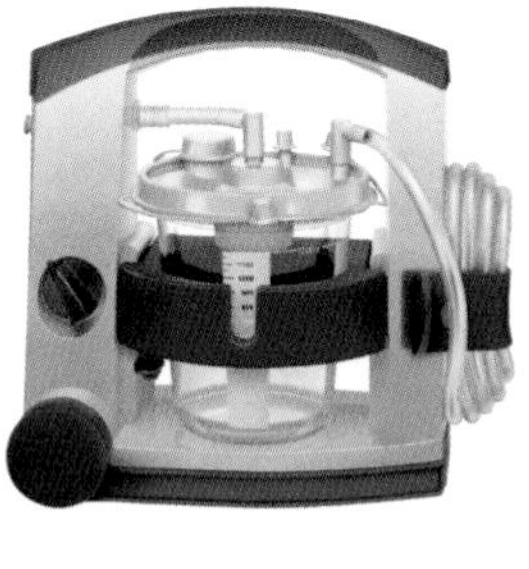

defibrillator
desfibrilador^M
défibrillateur^M
Defibrillator^M
defibrillatore^M

SOCIETY

775

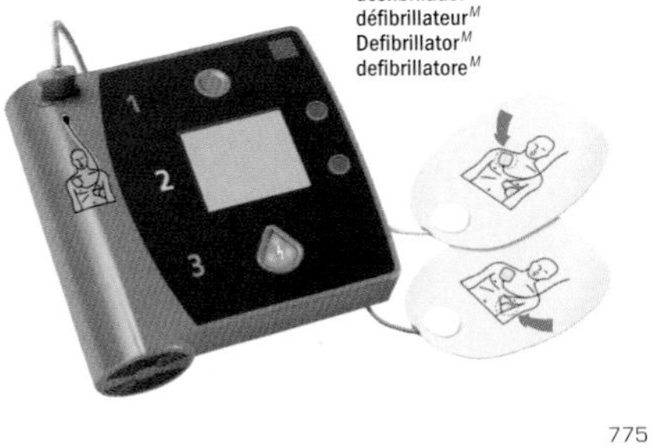

first aid equipment

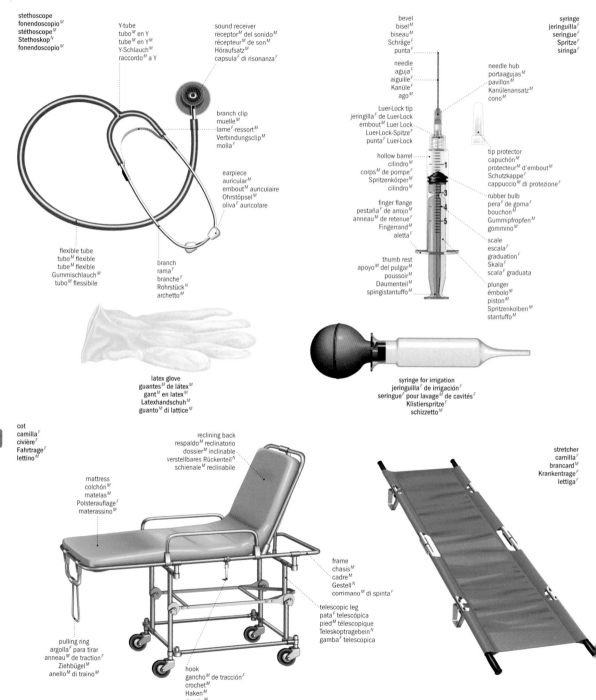

stethoscope
fonendoscopio^M
stéthoscope^M
Stethoskop^N
fonendoscopio^M

Y-tube
tubo^M en Y
tube^M en Y^M
Y-Schlauch^M
raccordo^M a Y

sound receiver
receptor^M del sonido^M
récepteur^M de son^M
Höraufsatz^M
capsula^F di risonanza^F

bevel
bisel^M
biseau^M
Schräge^F
punta^F

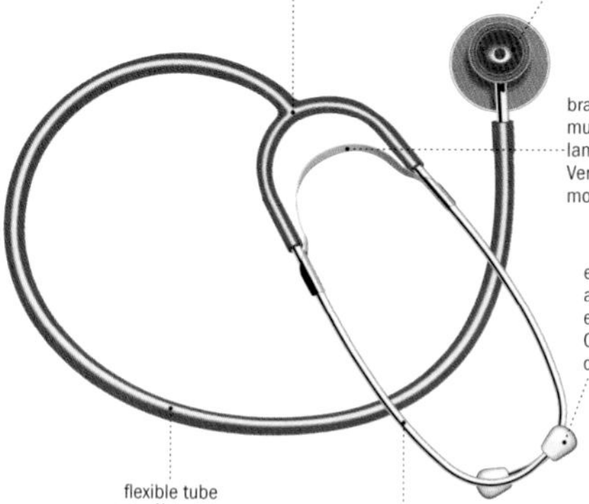

syringe
jeringuilla^F
seringue^F
Spritze^F
siringa^F

needle
aguja^F
aiguille^F
Kanüle^F
ago^M

needle hub
portaagujas^M
pavillon^M
Kanülenansatz^M
cono^M

branch clip
muelle^M
lame^F-ressort^M
Verbindungsclip^M
molla^F

Luer-Lock tip
jeringilla^F de Luer-Lock
embout^M Luer Lock
Luer-Lock-Spitze^F
punta^F Luer-Lock

earpiece
auricular^M
embout^M auriculaire
Ohrstöpsel^M
oliva^F auricolare

tip protector
capuchón^M
protecteur^M d'embout^M
Schutzkappe^F
cappuccio^M di protezione^F

hollow barrel
cilindro^M
corps^M de pompe^F
Spritzenkörper^M
cilindro^M

rubber bulb
pera^F de goma^F
bouchon^M
Gummipfropfen^M
gommino^M

finger flange
pestaña^F de arrojo^M
anneau^M de retenue^F
Fingerrand^M
aletta^F

scale
escala^F
graduation^F
Skala^F
scala^F graduata

flexible tube
tubo^M flexible
tube^M flexible
Gummischlauch^M
tubo^M flessibile

branch
rama^F
branche^F
Rohrstück^N
archetto^M

thumb rest
apoyo^M del pulgar^M
poussoir^M
Daumenteil^M
spingistantuffo^M

plunger
émbolo^M
piston^M
Spritzenkolben^M
stantuffo^M

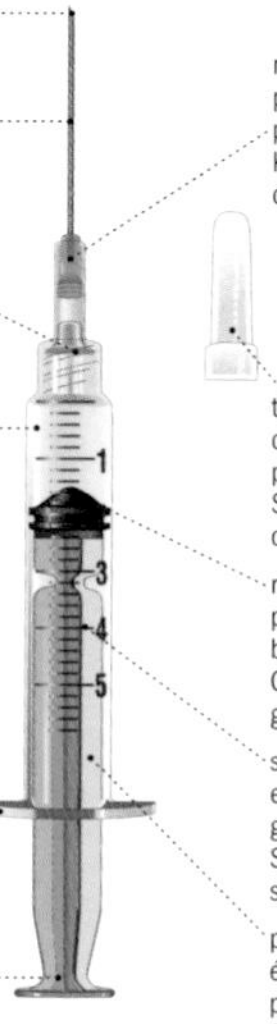

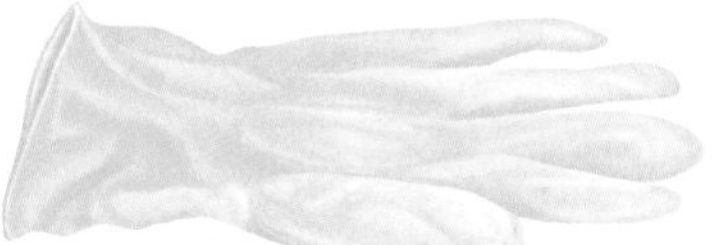

latex glove
guantes^M de látex^M
gant^M en latex^M
Latexhandschuh^M
guanto^M di lattice^M

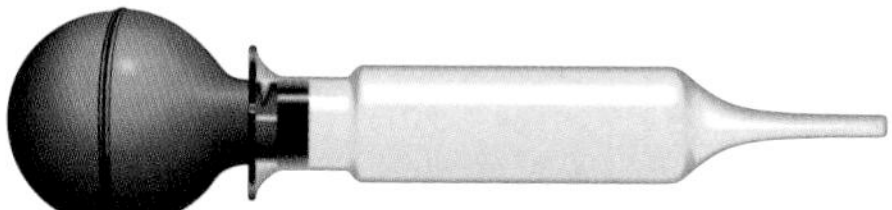

syringe for irrigation
jeringuilla^F de irrigación^F
seringue^F pour lavage^M de cavités^F
Klistierspritze^F
schizzetto^M

cot
camilla^F
civière^F
Fahrtrage^F
lettino^M

reclining back
respaldo^M reclinatorio
dossier^M inclinable
verstellbares Rückenteil^N
schienale^M reclinabile

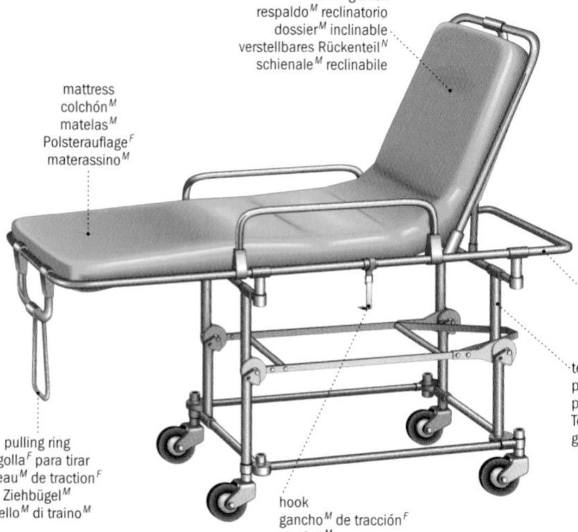

stretcher
camilla^F
brancard^M
Krankentrage^F
lettiga^F

mattress
colchón^M
matelas^M
Polsterauflage^F
materassino^M

frame
chasis^M
cadre^M
Gestell^N
corrimano^M di spinta^F

telescopic leg
pata^F telescópica
pied^M télescopique
Teleskoptragebein^N
gamba^F telescopica

pulling ring
argolla^F para tirar
anneau^M de traction^F
Ziehbügel^M
anello^M di traino^M

hook
gancho^M de tracción^F
crochet^M
Haken^M
gancio^M

SOCIETY

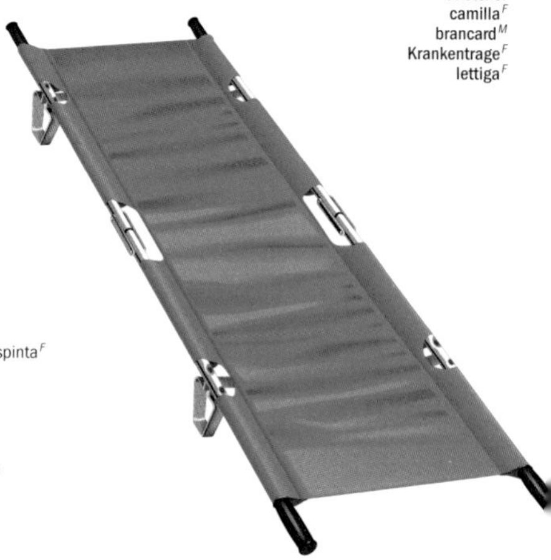

first aid kit

botiquín^M de primeros auxilios^M | trousse^F de secours^M | Erste-Hilfe-Kasten^M | cassetta^F di pronto soccorso^M

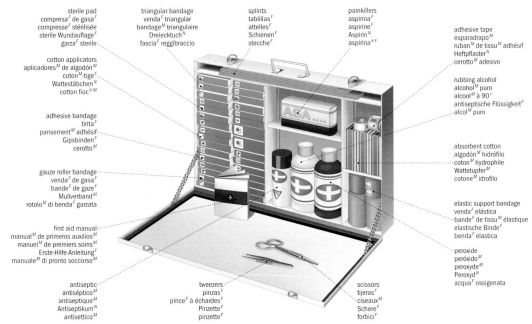

sterile pad
compresa^F de gasa^F
compresse^F stérilisée
sterile Wundauflage^F
garza^F sterile

cotton applicators
aplicadores^M de algodón^M
coton^M-tige^F
Wattestäbchen^N
cotton fioc$^{®M}$

adhesive bandage
tirita^F
pansement^M adhésif
Gipsbinden^F
cerotto^M

gauze roller bandage
venda^F de gasa^F
bande^F de gaze^F
Mullverband^M
rotolo^M di benda^F garzata

first aid manual
manual^M de primeros auxilios^M
manuel^M de premiers soins^M
Erste-Hilfe-Anleitung^F
manuale^M di pronto soccorso^M

antiseptic
antiséptico^M
antiseptique^M
Antiseptikum^N
antisettico^M

triangular bandage
venda^F triangular
bandage^M triangulaire
Dreiecktuch^N
fascia^F reggibraccio

tweezers
pinzas^F
pince^F à échardes^F
Pinzette^F
pinzette^F

splints
tablillas^F
attelles^F
Schienen^F
stecche^F

painkillers
aspirina^F
aspirine^F
Aspirin^N
aspirina$^{®F}$

adhesive tape
esparadrapo^M
ruban^M de tissu^M adhésif
Heftpflaster^N
cerotto^M adesivo

rubbing alcohol
alcohol^M puro
alcool^M à 90°
antiseptische Flüssigkeit^F
alcol^M puro

absorbent cotton
algodón^M hidrófilo
coton^M hydrophile
Wattetupfer^M
cotone^M idrofilo

elastic support bandage
venda^F elástica
bande^F de tissu^M élastique
elastische Binde^F
benda^F elastica

peroxide
peróxido^M
peroxyde^M
Peroxyd^N
acqua^F ossigenata

scissors
tijeras^F
ciseaux^M
Schere^F
forbici^F

clinical thermometers

termómetros^M clínicos | thermomètres^M médicaux | Fieberthermometer^N | termometri^M clinici

digital thermometer
termómetro^M digital
thermomètre^M numérique
Digitalthermometer^N
termometro^M digitale

mercury thermometer
termómetro^M de mercurio^M
thermomètre^M à mercure^M
Quecksilberthermometer^N
termometro^M a mercurio^M

SOCIETY

blood pressure monitor

tensiómetro^M | tensiomètre^M | Blutdruckmessgerät^N | monitor^M della pressione^F sanguigna

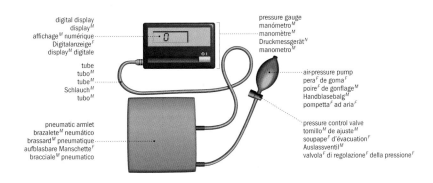

digital display
display^M
affichage^M numérique
Digitalanzeige^F
display^M digitale

tube
tubo^M
tube^M
Schlauch^M
tubo^M

pneumatic armlet
brazalete^M neumático
brassard^M pneumatique
aufblasbare Manschette^F
bracciale^M pneumatico

pressure gauge
manómetro^M
manomètre^M
Druckmessgerät^N
manometro^M

air-pressure pump
pera^F de goma^F
poire^F de gonflage^M
Handblasebalg^M
pompetta^F ad aria^F

pressure control valve
tornillo^M de ajuste^M
soupape^F d'évacuation^F
Auslassventil^M
valvola^F di regolazione^F della pressione^F

hospital

hospital^M | hôpital^M | Krankenhaus^N | ospedale^M

emergency
urgencias^F
urgences^F ; *urgence^F*
Unfallstation^F
pronto soccorso^M

family waiting room
sala^F de espera^F para la familia^F
salle^F d'attente^F des familles^F
Warteraum^M für Angehörige^M
sala^F d'attesa^F dei familiari^M

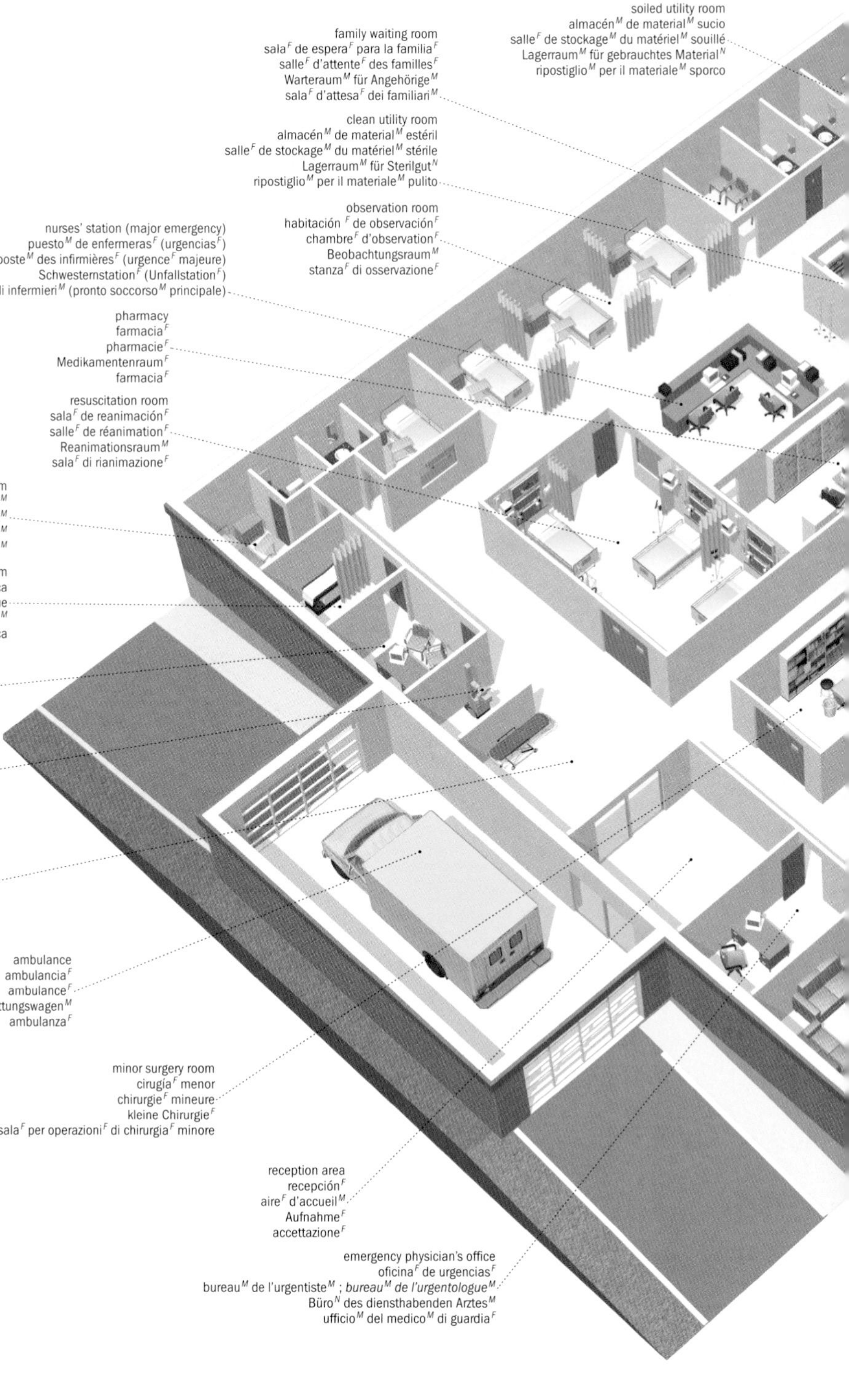

soiled utility room
almacén^M de material^M sucio
salle^F de stockage^M du matériel^M souillé
Lagerraum^M für gebrauchtes Material^N
ripostiglio^M per il materiale^M sporco

clean utility room
almacén^M de material^M estéril
salle^F de stockage^M du matériel^M stérile
Lagerraum^M für Sterilgut^N
ripostiglio^M per il materiale^M pulito

observation room
habitación^F de observación^F
chambre^F d'observation^F
Beobachtungsraum^M
stanza^F di osservazione^F

nurses' station (major emergency)
puesto^M de enfermeras^F (urgencias^F)
poste^M des infirmières^F (urgence^F majeure)
Schwesternstation^F (Unfallstation^F)
postazione^F degli infermieri^M (pronto soccorso^M principale)

pharmacy
farmacia^F
pharmacie^F
Medikamentenraum^F
farmacia^F

resuscitation room
sala^F de reanimación^F
salle^F de réanimation^F
Reanimationsraum^M
sala^F di rianimazione^F

isolation room
habitación^F de aislamiento^M
chambre^F d'isolement^M
Isolierraum^M
stanza^F di isolamento^M

psychiatric observation room
sala^F de observación^F psiquiátrica
chambre^F d'observation^F psychiatrique
psychiatrischer Beobachtungsraum^M
stanza^F per osservazione^F psichiatrica

psychiatric examination room
examen^M psiquiátrico
examen^M psychiatrique
psychiatrischer Untersuchungsraum^M
stanza^F per esame^M psichiatrico

mobile X-ray unit
unidad^F móvil de rayos^M X
appareil^M de radiographie^F mobile
fahrbares Röntgengerät^N
unità^F radiologica mobile

stretcher area
zona^F de camillas^F
secteur^M des civières^F
Tragen^F-Abstellraum^M
deposito^M delle barelle^F

ambulance
ambulancia^F
ambulance^F
Rettungswagen^M
ambulanza^F

minor surgery room
cirugía^F menor
chirurgie^F mineure
kleine Chirurgie^F
sala^F per operazioni^F di chirurgia^F minore

reception area
recepción^F
aire^F d'accueil^M
Aufnahme^F
accettazione^F

emergency physician's office
oficina^F de urgencias^F
bureau^M de l'urgentiste^M ; *bureau^M de l'urgentologue^M*
Büro^N des diensthabenden Arztes^M
ufficio^M del medico^M di guardia^F

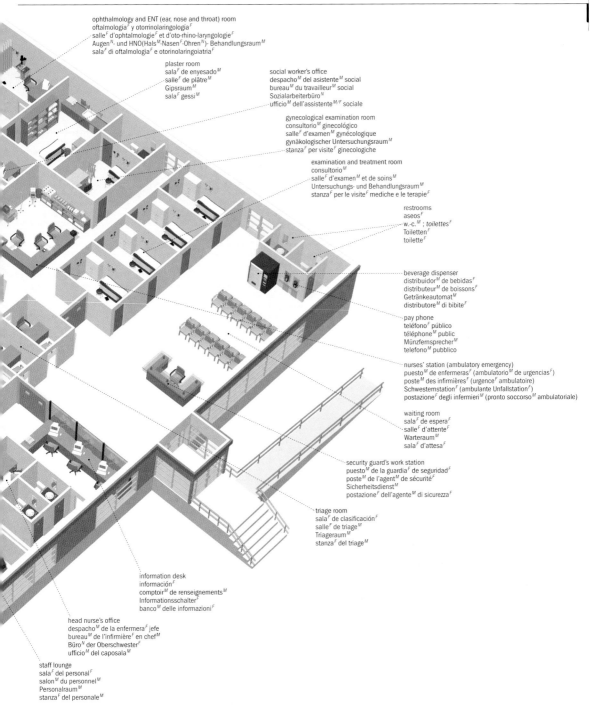

ophthalmology and ENT (ear, nose and throat) room
oftalmología^F y otorrinolaringología^F
salle^F d'ophtalmologie^F et d'oto-rhino-laryngologie^F
Augen^N- und HNO(Hals^M-Nasen^F-Ohren^N)- Behandlungsraum^M
sala^F di oftalmologia^F e otorinolaringoiatria^F

plaster room
sala^F de enyesado^M
salle^F de plâtre^M
Gipsraum^M
sala^F gessi^M

social worker's office
despacho^M del asistente^M social
bureau^M du travailleur^M social
Sozialarbeiterbüro^N
ufficio^M dell'assistente$^{M/F}$ sociale

gynecological examination room
consultorio^M ginecológico
salle^F d'examen^M gynécologique
gynäkologischer Untersuchungsraum^M
stanza^F per visite^F ginecologiche

examination and treatment room
consultorio^M
salle^F d'examen^M et de soins^M
Untersuchungs- und Behandlungsraum^M
stanza^F per le visite^F mediche e le terapie^F

restrooms
aseos^F
w.-c.^{M} ; toilettes^F
Toiletten^F
toilette^F

beverage dispenser
distribuidor^M de bebidas^F
distributeur^M de boissons^F
Getränkeautomat^M
distributore^M di bibite^F

pay phone
teléfono^F público
téléphone^M public
Münzfernsprecher^M
telefono^M pubblico

nurses' station (ambulatory emergency)
puesto^M de enfermeras^F (ambulatorio^M de urgencias^F)
poste^M des infirmières^F (urgence^F ambulatoire)
Schwesternstation^F (ambulante Unfallstation^F)
postazione^F degli infermieri^M (pronto soccorso^M ambulatoriale)

waiting room
sala^F de espera^F
salle^F d'attente^F
Warteraum^M
sala^F d'attesa^F

security guard's work station
puesto^M de la guardia^F de seguridad^F
poste^M de l'agent^M de sécurité^F
Sicherheitsdienst^M
postazione^F dell'agente^M di sicurezza^F

triage room
sala^F de clasificación^F
salle^F de triage^M
Triageraum^M
stanza^F del triage^M

information desk
información^F
comptoir^M de renseignements^M
Informationsschalter^F
banco^M delle informazioni^F

head nurse's office
despacho^M de la enfermera^F jefe
bureau^M de l'infirmière^F en chef^M
Büro^N der Oberschwester^F
ufficio^M del caposala^M

staff lounge
sala^F del personal^M
salon^M du personnel^M
Personalraum^M
stanza^F del personale^M

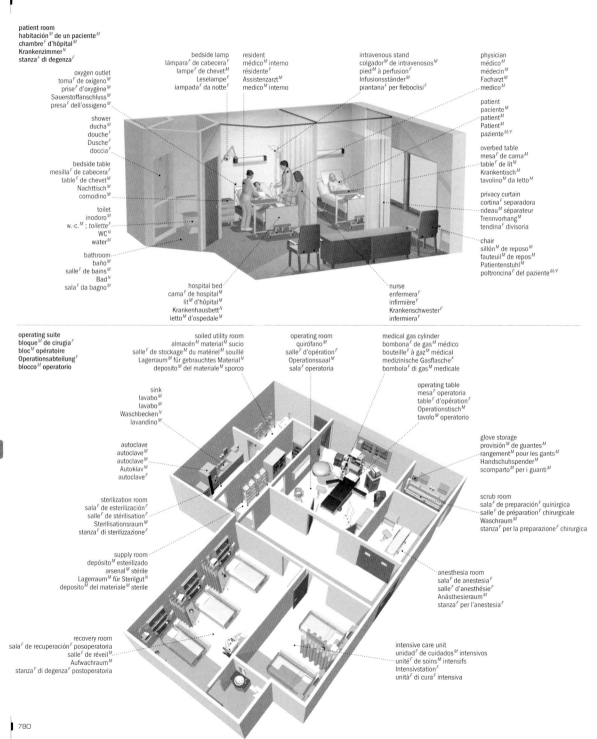

patient room
habitación^M de un paciente^M
chambre^F d'hôpital^M
Krankenzimmer^N
stanza^F di degenza^F

bedside lamp
lámpara^F de cabecera^F
lampe^F de chevet^M
Leselampe^F
lampada^F da notte^F

resident
médico^M interno
résidente^F
Assistenzarzt^M
medico^M interno

intravenous stand
colgador^M de intravenosos^M
pied^M à perfusion^F
Infusionsständer^M
piantana^F per flebolcisi^F

physician
médico^M
médecin^M
Facharzt^M
medico^M

oxygen outlet
toma^F de oxígeno^M
prise^F d'oxygène^M
Sauerstoffanschluss^M
presa^F dell'ossigeno^M

patient
paciente^M
patient^M
Patient^M
paziente$^{M/F}$

shower
ducha^F
douche^F
Dusche^F
doccia^F

overbed table
mesa^F de cama^M
table^F de lit^M
Krankentisch^M
tavolino^M da letto^M

bedside table
mesilla^F de cabecera^F
table^F de chevet^M
Nachttisch^M
comodino^M

privacy curtain
cortina^F separadora
rideau^M séparateur
Trennvorhang^M
tendina^F divisoria

toilet
inodoro^M
w.-c.^{M} ; toilette^F
WC^N
water^M

chair
sillón^M de reposo^M
fauteuil^M de repos^M
Patientenstuhl^M
poltroncina^F del paziente$^{M/F}$

bathroom
baño^M
salle^F de bains^M
Bad^N
sala^F da bagno^M

hospital bed
cama^F de hospital^M
lit^M d'hôpital^M
Krankenhausbett^N
letto^M d'ospedale^M

nurse
enfermera^F
infirmière^F
Krankenschwester^F
infermiera^F

operating suite
bloque^M de cirugía^F
bloc^M opératoire
Operationsabteilung^F
blocco^M operatorio

soiled utility room
almacén^M material^M sucio
salle^F de stockage^M du matériel^M souillé
Lagerraum^M für gebrauchtes Material^N
deposito^M del materiale^M sporco

operating room
quirófano^M
salle^F d'opération^F
Operationssaal^M
sala^F operatoria

medical gas cylinder
bombona^F de gas^M médico
bouteille^F à gaz^M médical
medizinische Gasflasche^F
bombola^F di gas^M medicale

sink
lavabo^M
lavabo^M
Waschbecken^N
lavandino^M

operating table
mesa^F operatoria
table^F d'opération^F
Operationstisch^M
tavolo^M operatorio

autoclave
autoclave^M
autoclave^M
Autoklav^M
autoclave^F

glove storage
provisión^M de guantes^M
rangement^M pour les gants^M
Handschuhspender^M
scomparto^M per i guanti^M

sterilization room
sala^F de esterilización^F
salle^F de stérilisation^F
Sterilisationsraum^M
stanza^F di sterilizzazione^F

scrub room
sala^F de preparación^F quirúrgica
salle^F de préparation^F chirurgicale
Waschraum^M
stanza^F per la preparazione^F chirurgica

supply room
depósito^M esterilizado
arsenal^M stérile
Lagerraum^M für Sterilgut^N
deposito^M del materiale^M sterile

anesthesia room
sala^F de anestesia^F
salle^F d'anesthésie^F
Anästhesieraum^M
stanza^F per l'anestesia^F

recovery room
sala^F de recuperación^F posoperatoria
salle^F de réveil^M
Aufwachraum^M
stanza^F di degenza^F postoperatoria

intensive care unit
unidad^F de cuidados^M intensivos
unité^F de soins^M intensifs
Intensivstation^F
unità^F di cura^F intensiva

specimen collection center waiting room
sala^F de espera^F del centro^M de extracción^F de sangre^M
salle^F d'attente^F du centre^M de prélèvements^M
Wartebereich^M für den Entnahmeraum^M
sala^F d'attesa^F del centro^M prelievi^M

pathology laboratory
laboratorio^M patológico
laboratoire^F de pathologie^F
pathologisches Labor^N
laboratorio^M di anatomia^F patologica

sterilization room
sala^F de esterilización^F
salle^F de stérilisation^F
Sterilisationsraum^M
sala^F di sterilizzazione^F

surgeon's sink
lavabo^M de cirujano^M
lavabo^M du chirurgien^M
Chirurgen^M-Waschraum^M
lavandino^M del chirurgo^M

ambulatory care unit
ambulatorio^M
unité^F de soins^M ambulatoires
Poliklinik^F
poliambulatorio^M

operating room
quirófano^M
salle^F d'opération^F
Operationssaal^M
sala^F operatoria

undressing booth
cabina^F para desvestirse
cabine^F de déshabillage^M
Entkleidungsraum^M
spogliatoio^M

observation room
consultorio^M
chambre^F d'observation^F
Beobachtungsraum^M
stanza^F di osservazione^F

secondary waiting room
sala^F de espera^F
salle^F d'attente^F secondaire
zweiter Warteraum^M
sala^F d'attesa^F secondaria

restrooms
aseos^M
w.-c.^M ; toilettes^F
Toiletten^F
toilette^F

social services
servicios^M sociales
services^M sociaux
Sozialdiensträume^M
servizi^M sociali

staff change room
guardarropa^M del personal^M
vestiaire^M du personnel^M
Personalumkleideraum^M
spogliatoio^M del personale^M

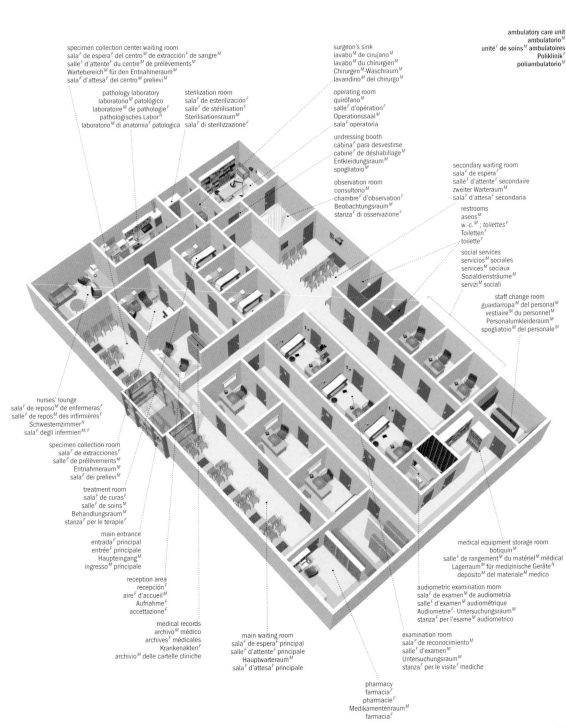

nurses' lounge
sala^F de reposo^M de enfermeras^F
salle^F de repos^M des infirmières^F
Schwesternzimmer^N
sala^F degli infermieri^{M/F}

specimen collection room
sala^F de extracciones^F
salle^F de prélèvements^M
Entnahmeraum^M
sala^F dei prelievi^M

treatment room
sala^F de curas^F
salle^F de soins^M
Behandlungsraum^M
stanza^F per le terapie^F

main entrance
entrada^F principal
entrée^F principale
Haupteingang^M
ingresso^M principale

reception area
recepción^F
aire^F d'accueil^M
Aufnahme^F
accettazione^F

medical records
archivo^M médico
archives^F médicales
Krankenakten^F
archivio^M delle cartelle cliniche

main waiting room
sala^F de espera^F principal
salle^F d'attente^F principale
Hauptwarteraum^M
sala^F d'attesa^F principale

pharmacy
farmacia^F
pharmacie^F
Medikamentenraum^M
farmacia^F

examination room
sala^F de reconocimiento^M
salle^F d'examen^M
Untersuchungsraum^M
stanza^F per le visite^F mediche

audiometric examination room
sala^F de examen^M de audiometria
salle^F d'examen^M audiométrique
Audiometrie^F- Untersuchungsraum^M
stanza^F per l'esame^M audiometrico

medical equipment storage room
botiquín^M
salle^F de rangement^M du matériel^M médical
Lagerraum^M für medizinische Geräte^N
deposito^M del materiale^M medico

SOCIETY

walking aids

auxiliares^M ortopédicos para caminar | aides^F à la marche^F | Gehhilfen^F | supporti^M per camminare

forearm crutch
muleta^F de antebrazo^M
béquille^F d'avant-bras^M
Gehkrücke^F
stampella^F canadese

underarm crutch
muleta^F de sobaco^M
béquille^F commune
Achselkrücke^F
gruccia^F

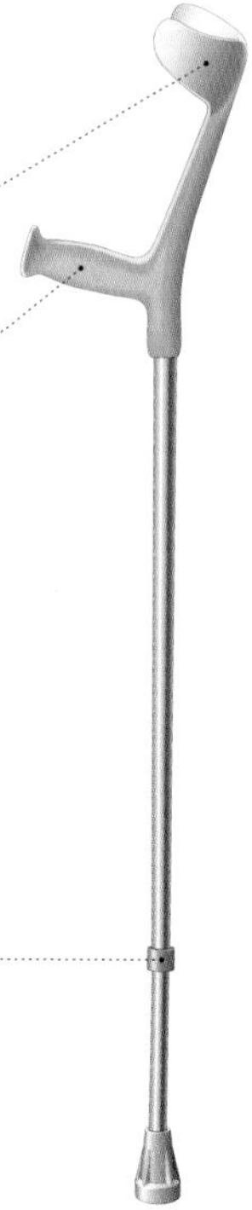

forearm support
soporte^M para el antebrazo^M
embrasse^F
Unterarmstütze^F
supporto^M per il braccio^M

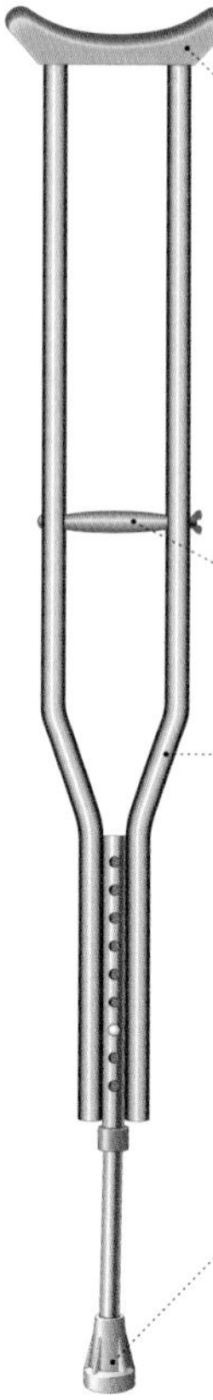

underarm rest
soporte^M para el sobaco^M
crosse^F
Achselstütze^F
supporto^M sottoascellare

handgrip
empuñadura^F
poignée^F
Griff^M
impugnatura^F

crosspiece
travesaño^M
traverse^F
Querstück^N
appoggiamano^M

upright
montante^M
montant^M
Holm^M
telaio^M

adjuster
tubo^M ajustable
réglage^M
Längenverstellung^F
regolatore^M

rubber tip
contera^F de caucho^M
embout^M de caoutchouc^M
Gummikappe^F
puntale^M

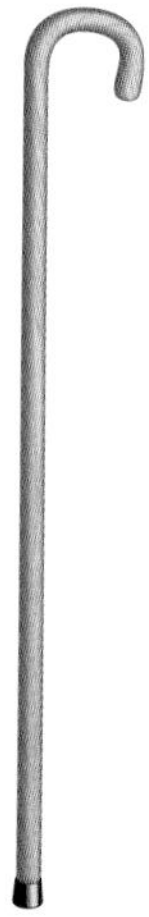

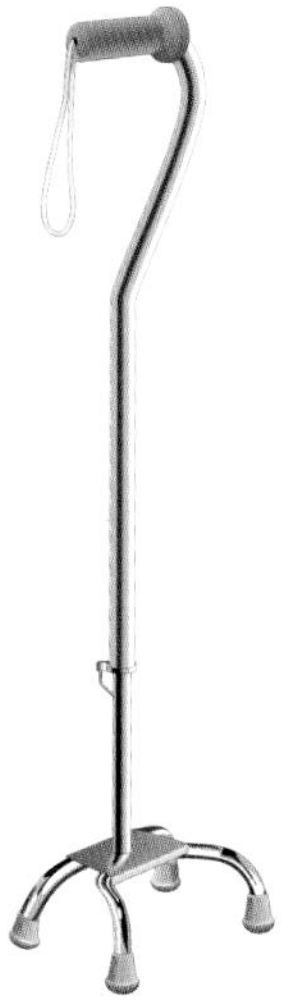

English cane
bastón^M inglés
canne^F en T^M
englischer Stock^M
bastone^M inglese

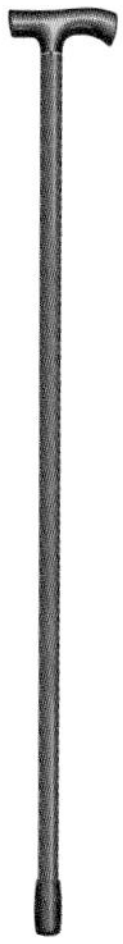

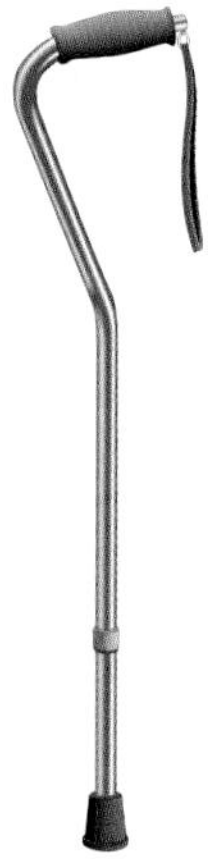

walker
andador^M
cadre^M de marche^F
Gehgestell^N
deambulatore^M

quad cane
bastón^M cuadrangular
canne^F avec quadripode^M
vierfüßiger Stock^M
quadripode^M

ortho-cane
bastón^M ortopédico
canne^F avec poignée^F orthopédique
orthopädischer Stock^M
bastone^M con manico^M anatomico

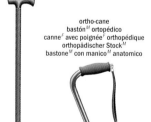

walking stick
bastón^M para caminar
canne^F en C^M
Spazierstock^M
bastone^M da passeggio^M

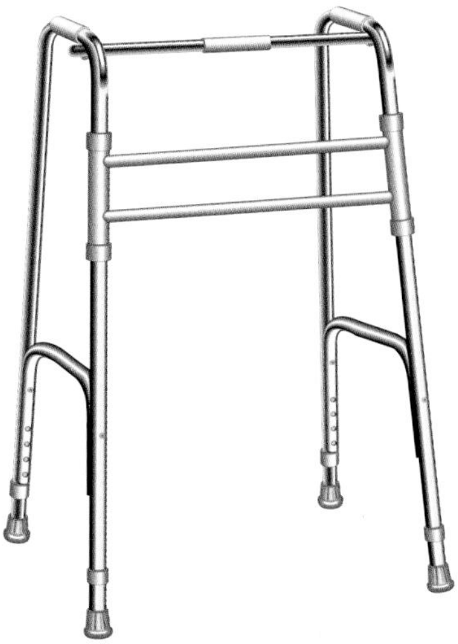

wheelchair

silla^F de ruedas^F | fauteuil^M roulant | Rollstuhl^M | sedia^F a rotelle^F

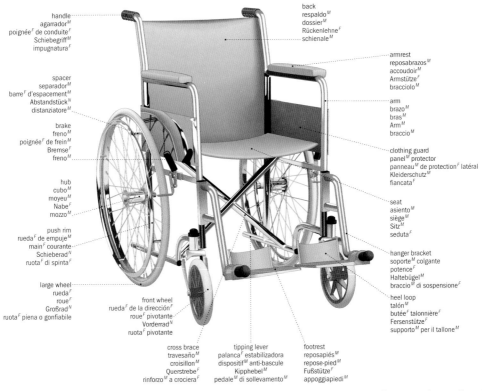

handle
agarrador^M
poignée^F de conduite^F
Schiebegriff^M
impugnatura^F

spacer
separador^M
barre^F d'espacement^M
Abstandstück^N
distanziatore^M

brake
freno^M
poignée^F de frein^M
Bremse^F
freno^M

hub
cubo^M
moyeu^M
Nabe^F
mozzo^M

push rim
rueda^F de empuje^M
main^F courante^F
Schieberad^N
ruota^F di spinta^F

large wheel
rueda^F
roue^F
Großrad^N
ruota^F piena o gonfiabile

back
respaldo^M
dossier^M
Rückenlehne^F
schienale^M

armrest
reposabrazos^M
accoudoir^M
Armstütze^F
bracciolo^M

arm
brazo^M
bras^M
Arm^M
braccio^M

clothing guard
panel^M protector
panneau^M de protection^F latéral
Kleiderschutz^M
fiancata^F

seat
asiento^M
siège^M
Sitz^M
seduta^F

hanger bracket
soporte^M colgante
potence^F
Haltebügel^M
braccio^M di sospensione^F

heel loop
talón^M
butée^F talonnière^F
Fersenstütze^F
supporto^M per il tallone^M

front wheel
rueda^F de la dirección^F
roue^F pivotante
Vorderrad^N
ruota^F pivotante

cross brace
travesaño^M
croisillon^M
Querstrebe^F
rinforzo^M a crociera^F

tipping lever
palanca^F estabilizadora
dispositif^M anti-bascule
Kipphebel^M
pedale^M di sollevamento^M

footrest
reposapiés^M
repose-pied^M
Fußstütze^F
appoggiapiedi^M

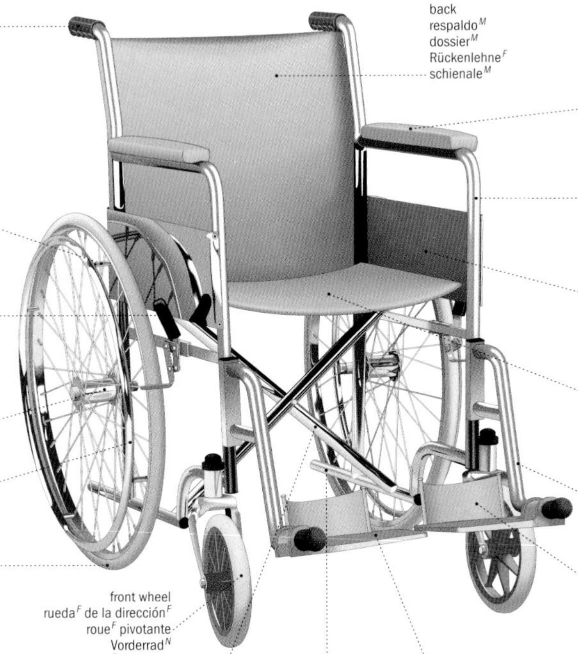

forms of medications

formas^F farmacéuticas de medicamentos^M | formes^F pharmaceutiques des médicaments^M | Arzneimittel^N-Darreichungsformen^F | confezioni^F farmaceutiche di medicinali^M

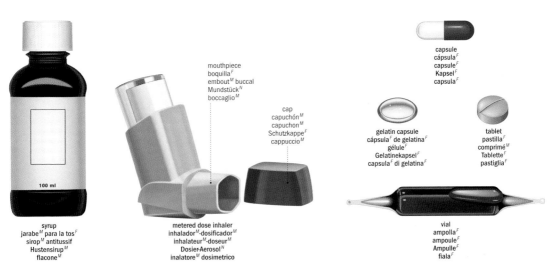

mouthpiece
boquilla^F
embout^M buccal
Mundstück^N
boccaglio^M

cap
capuchón^M
capuchon^M
Schutzkappe^F
cappuccio^M

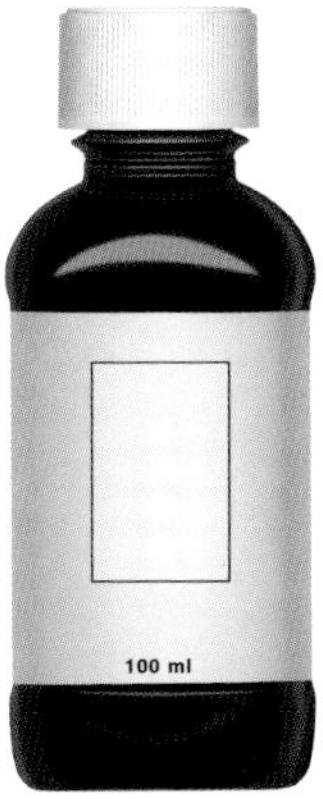

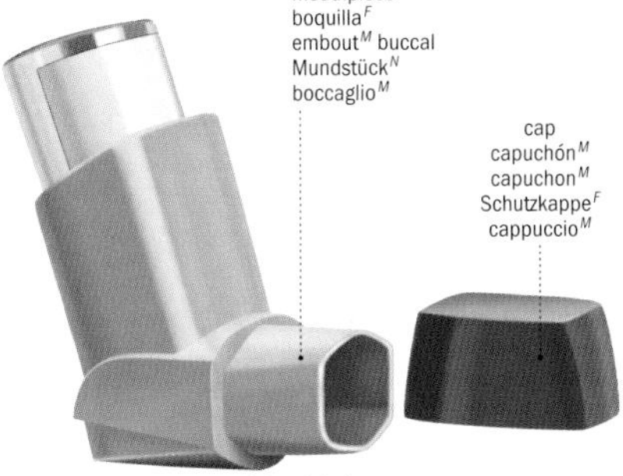

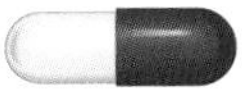

capsule
cápsula^F
capsule^F
Kapsel^F
capsula^F

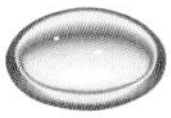

gelatin capsule
cápsula^F de gelatina^F
gélule^F
Gelatinekapsel^F
capsula^F di gelatina^F

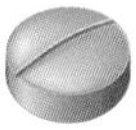

tablet
pastilla^F
comprimé^M
Tablette^F
pastiglia^F

100 ml

syrup
jarabe^M para la tos^F
sirop^M antitussif
Hustensirup^M
flacone^M

metered dose inhaler
inhalador^M-dosificador^M
inhalateur^M-doseur^M
Dosier-Aerosol^N
inalatore^M dosimetrico

vial
ampolla^F
ampoule^F
Ampulle^F
fiala^F

SOCIETY

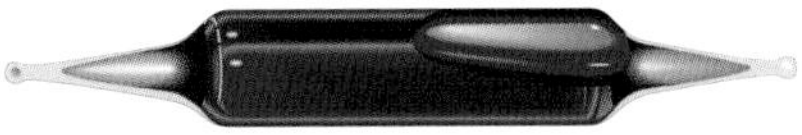

family relationships

vínculos^M familiares | liens^M de parenté^F | Verwandtschaftsbeziehungen^F | vincoli^M di parentela^F

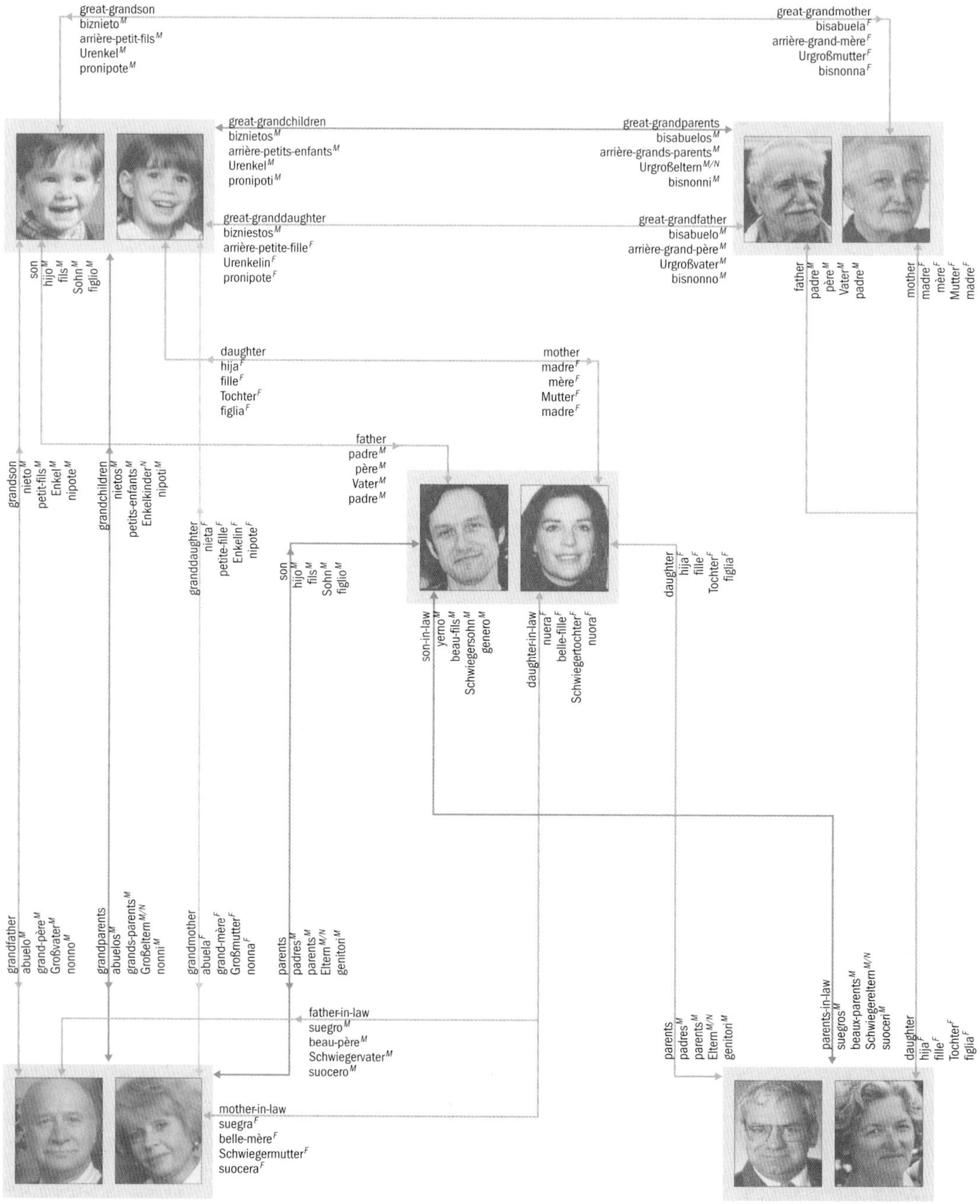

great-grandson
biznieto^M
arrière-petit-fils^M
Urenkel^M
pronipote^M

great-grandmother
bisabuela^F
arrière-grand-mère^F
Urgroßmutter^F
bisnonna^F

great-grandchildren
biznietos^M
arrière-petits-enfants^M
Urenkel^M
pronipoti^M

great-grandparents
bisabuelos^M
arrière-grands-parents^M
UrgroßelternM/N
bisnonni^M

great-granddaughter
bizniestos^M
arrière-petite-fille^F
Urenkelin^F
pronipote^F

great-grandfather
bisabuelo^M
arrière-grand-père^M
Urgroßvater^M
bisnonno^M

son
hijo^M
fils^M
Sohn^M
figlio^M

father
padre^M
père^M
Vater^M
padre^M

mother
madre^F
mère^F
Mutter^F
madre^F

daughter
hija^F
fille^F
Tochter^F
figlia^F

mother
madre^F
mère^F
Mutter^F
madre^F

father
padre^M
père^M
Vater^M
padre^M

grandson
nieto^M
petit-fils^M
Enkel^M
nipote^M

grandchildren
nietos^M
petits-enfants^M
EnkelkinderM/N
nipoti^M

granddaughter
nieta^F
petite-fille^F
Enkelin^F
nipote^F

son
hijo^M
fils^M
Sohn^M
figlio^M

daughter
hija^F
fille^F
Tochter^F
figlia^F

son-in-law
yerno^M
beau-fils^M
Schwiegersohn^M
genero^M

daughter-in-law
nuera^F
belle-fille^F
Schwiegertochter^F
nuora^F

grandfather
abuelo^M
grand-père^M
Großvater^M
nonno^M

grandparents
abuelos^M
grands-parents^M
GroßelternM/N
nonni^M

grandmother
abuela^F
grand-mère^F
Großmutter^F
nonna^F

parents
padres^M
parents^M
ElternM/N
genitori^M

father-in-law
suegro^M
beau-père^M
Schwiegervater^M
suocero^M

mother-in-law
suegra^F
belle-mère^F
Schwiegermutter^F
suocera^F

parents
padres^M
parents^M
ElternM/N
genitori^M

parents-in-law
suegros^M
beaux-parents^M
SchwiegerelternM/N
suoceri^M

daughter
hija^F
fille^F
Tochter^F
figlia^F

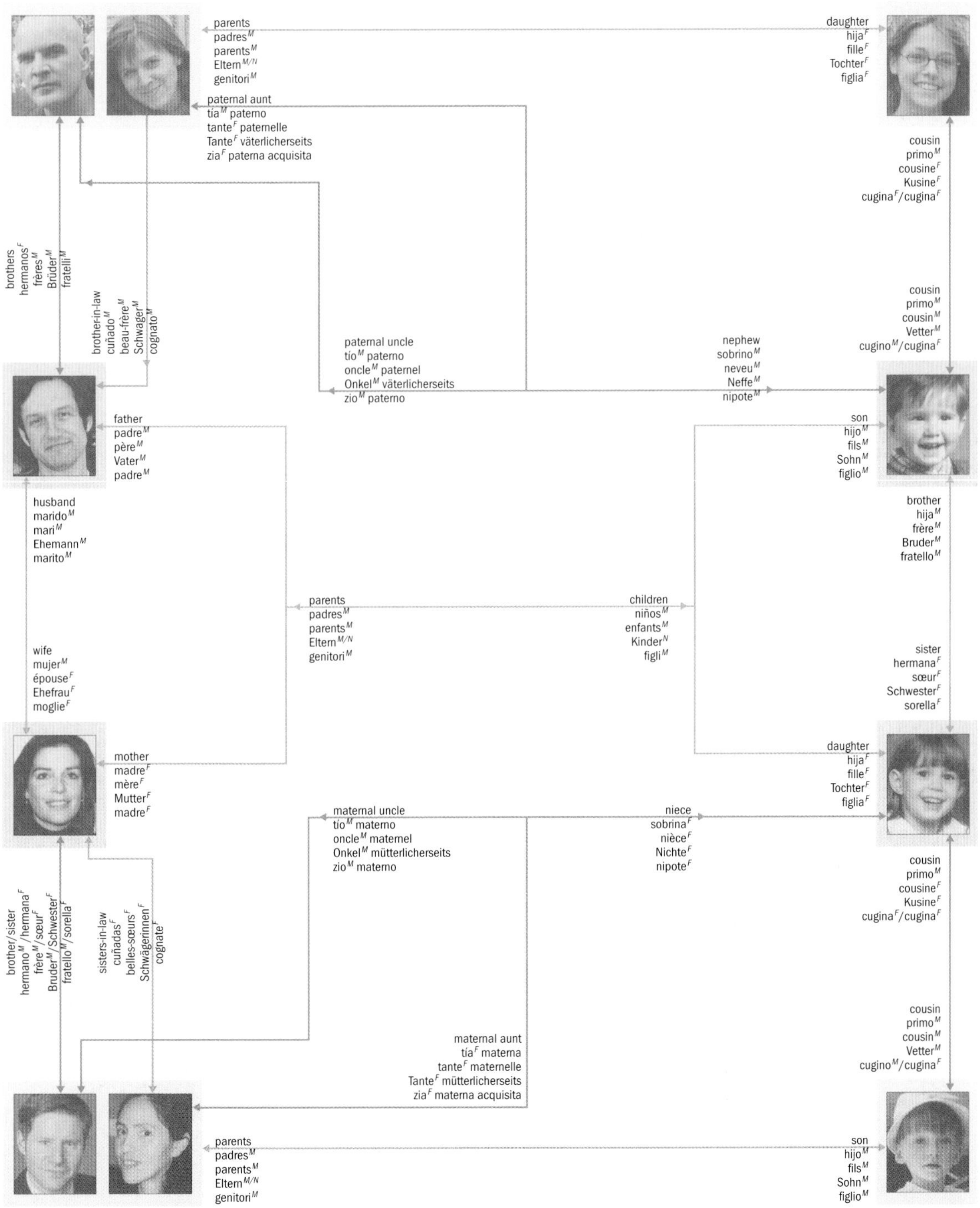

parents
padres ^{M}
parents ^{M}
Eltern $^{M/li}$
genitori ^{M}

daughter
hija ^{F}
fille ^{F}
Tochter ^{F}
figlia ^{F}

paternal aunt
tía ^{M} paterno
tante ^{F} paternelle
Tante ^{F} väterlicherseits
zia ^{F} paterna acquisita

cousin
primo ^{M}
cousine ^{F}
Kusine ^{F}
cugina ^{F}/cugina ^{F}

brothers
hermanos ^{F}
frères ^{M}
Brüder ^{M}
fratelli ^{M}

brother-in-law
cuñado ^{M}
beau-frère ^{M}
Schwager ^{M}
cognato ^{M}

cousin
primo ^{M}
cousin ^{M}
Vetter ^{M}
cugino ^{M}/cugina ^{F}

paternal uncle
tío ^{M} paterno
oncle ^{M} paternel
Onkel ^{M} väterlicherseits
zio ^{M} paterno

nephew
sobrino ^{M}
neveu ^{M}
Neffe ^{M}
nipote ^{M}

father
padre ^{M}
père ^{M}
Vater ^{M}
padre ^{M}

son
hijo ^{M}
fils ^{M}
Sohn ^{M}
figlio ^{M}

husband
marido ^{M}
mari ^{M}
Ehemann ^{M}
marito ^{M}

brother
hija ^{M}
frère ^{M}
Bruder ^{M}
fratello ^{M}

parents
padres ^{M}
parents ^{M}
Eltern $^{M/N}$
genitori ^{M}

children
niños ^{M}
enfants ^{M}
Kinder ^{N}
figli ^{M}

wife
mujer ^{M}
épouse ^{F}
Ehefrau ^{F}
moglie ^{F}

sister
hermana ^{F}
sœur ^{F}
Schwester ^{F}
sorella ^{F}

mother
madre ^{F}
mère ^{F}
Mutter ^{F}
madre ^{F}

daughter
hija ^{F}
fille ^{F}
Tochter ^{F}
figlia ^{F}

maternal uncle
tío ^{M} materno
oncle ^{M} maternel
Onkel ^{M} mütterlicherseits
zio ^{M} materno

niece
sobrina ^{F}
nièce ^{F}
Nichte ^{F}
nipote ^{F}

cousin
primo ^{M}
cousine ^{F}
Kusine ^{F}
cugina ^{F}/cugina ^{F}

brother/sister
hermano ^{M}/hermana ^{F}
frère ^{M}/sœur ^{F}
Bruder ^{M}/Schwester ^{F}
fratello ^{M}/sorella ^{F}

sisters-in-law
cuñadas ^{F}
belles-sœurs ^{F}
Schwägerinnen ^{F}
cognate ^{F}

maternal aunt
tía ^{F} materna
tante ^{F} maternelle
Tante ^{F} mütterlicherseits
zia ^{F} materna acquisita

cousin
primo ^{M}
cousin ^{M}
Vetter ^{M}
cugino ^{M}/cugina ^{F}

parents
padres ^{M}
parents ^{M}
Eltern $^{M/N}$
genitori ^{M}

son
hijo ^{M}
fils ^{M}
Sohn ^{M}
figlio ^{M}

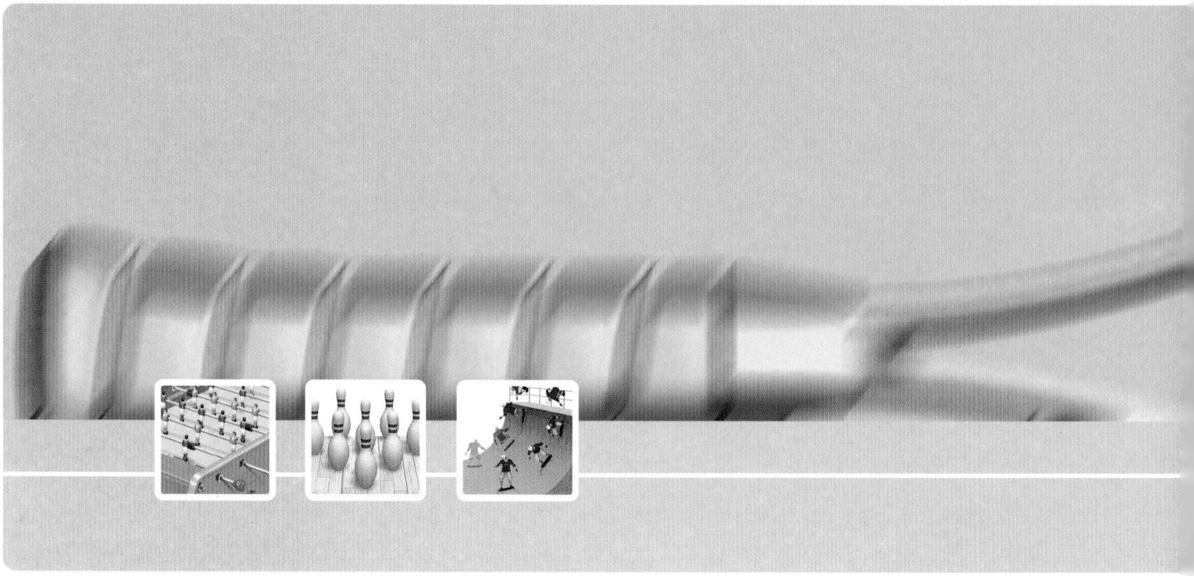

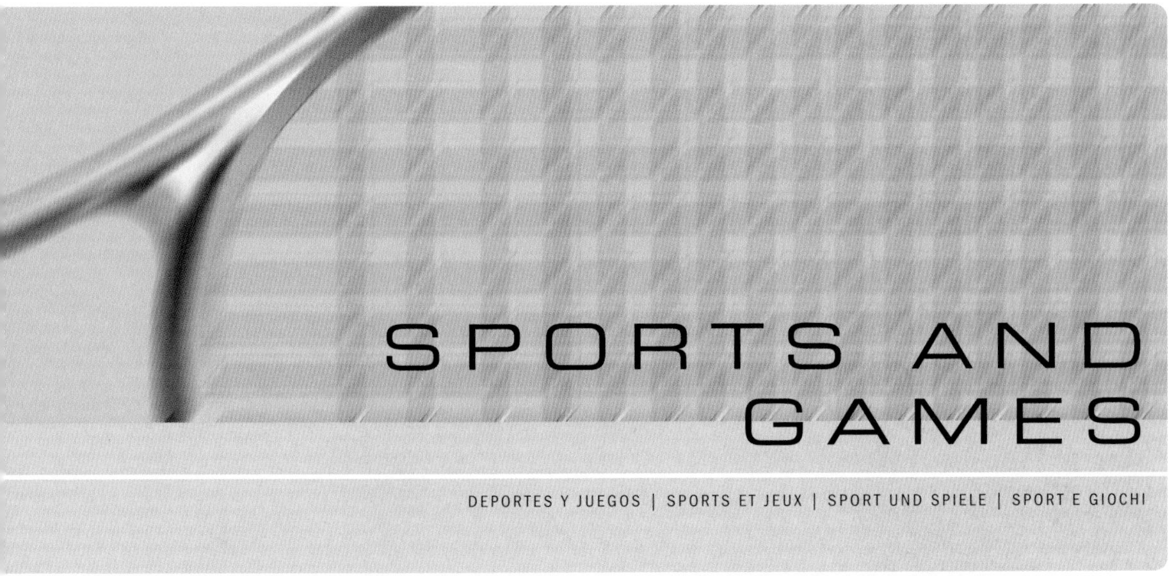

SPORTS AND GAMES

DEPORTES Y JUEGOS | SPORTS ET JEUX | SPORT UND SPIELE | SPORT E GIOCHI

sports complex

polideportivo^M | complexe^M sportif | Sportanlagen^F | complesso^M sportivo

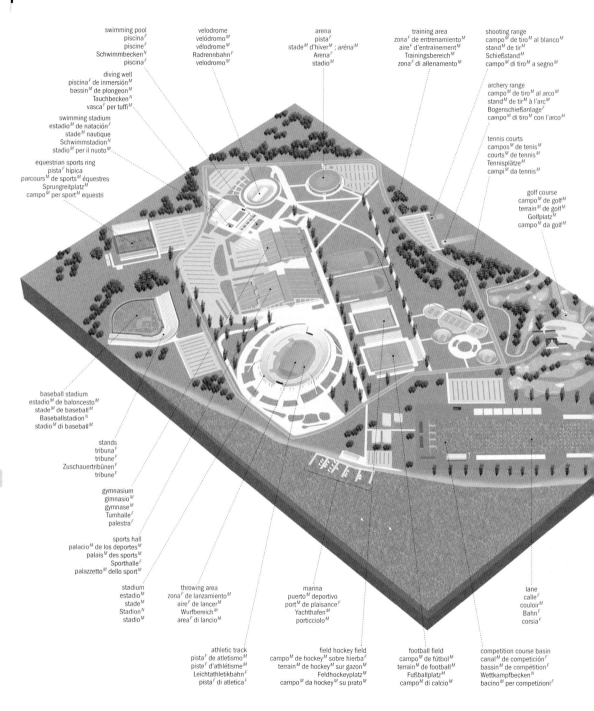

swimming pool
piscina^F
piscine^F
Schwimmbecken^N
piscina^F

diving well
piscina^F de inmersión^M
bassin^M de plongeon^M
Tauchbecken^N
vasca^F per tuffi^M

swimming stadium
estadio^M de natación^F
stade^M nautique
Schwimmstadion^N
stadio^M per il nuoto^M

equestrian sports ring
pista^F hípica
parcours^M de sports^M équestres
Sprungreitplatz^M
campo^M per sport^M equestri

velodrome
velódromo^M
vélodrome^M
Radrennbahn^F
velodromo^M

arena
pista^F
stade^M d'hiver^M ; aréna^M
Arena^F
stadio^M

training area
zona^F de entrenamiento^M
aire^F d'entraînement^M
Trainingsbereich^M
zona^F di allenamento^M

shooting range
campo^M de tiro^M al blanco^M
stand^M de tir^M
Schießstand^M
campo^M di tiro^M a segno^M

archery range
campo^M de tiro^M al arco^M
stand^M de tir^M à l'arc^M
Bogenschießanlage^F
campo^M di tiro^M con l'arco^M

tennis courts
campos^M de tenis^M
courts^M de tennis^M
Tennisplätze^M
campi^M da tennis^M

golf course
campo^M de golf^M
terrain^M de golf^M
Golfplatz^M
campo^M da golf^M

baseball stadium
estadio^M de baloncesto^M
stade^M de baseball^M
Baseballstadion^N
stadio^M di baseball^M

stands
tribuna^F
tribune^F
Zuschauertribünen^F
tribune^F

gymnasium
gimnasio^M
gymnase^M
Turnhalle^F
palestra^F

sports hall
palacio^M de los deportes^M
palais^M des sports^M
Sporthalle^F
palazzetto^M dello sport^M

stadium
estadio^M
stade^M
Stadion^N
stadio^M

throwing area
zona^F de lanzamiento^M
aire^F de lancer^M
Wurfbereich^M
area^F di lancio^M

marina
puerto^M deportivo
port^M de plaisance^F
Yachthafen^M
porticciolo^M

lane
calle^F
couloir^M
Bahn^F
corsia^F

athletic track
pista^F de atletismo^M
piste^F d'athlétisme^M
Leichtathletikbahn^F
pista^F di atletica^F

field hockey field
campo^M de hockey^M sobre hierba^F
terrain^M de hockey^M sur gazon^M
Feldhockeyplatz^M
campo^M da hockey^M su prato^M

football field
campo^M de fútbol^M
terrain^M de football^M
Fußballplatz^M
campo^M di calcio^M

competition course basin
canal^M de competición^F
bassin^M de compétition^F
Wettkampfbecken^N
bacino^M per competizioni^F

scoreboard

marcador^M | tableau^M indicateur | Anzeigetafel^F | tabellone^M segnapunti

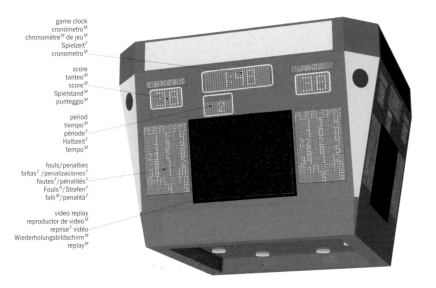

game clock
cronómetro^M
chronomètre^M de jeu^M
Spielzeit^F
cronometro^M

score
tanteo^M
score^M
Spielstand^M
punteggio^M

period
tiempo^M
période^F
Halbzeit^F
tempo^M

fouls/penalties
faltas^F/penalizaciones^F
fautes^F/pénalités^F
Fouls^N/Strafen^F
falli^M/penalità^F

video replay
reproductor de video^M
reprise^F vidéo
Wiederholungsbildschirm^M
replay^M

competition

competición^F | compétition^F | Wettkampf^M | competizione^F

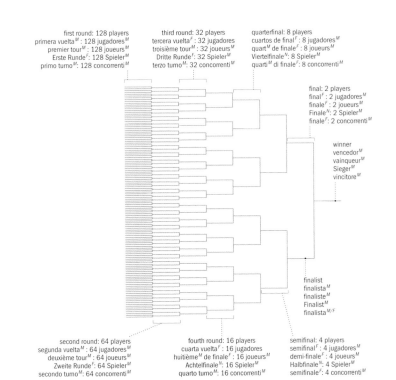

draw
empate^M
tableau^M de tournoi^M
K.O.-System^N
elenco^M dei concorrenti^M

first round: 128 players
primera vuelta^M: 128 jugadores^M
premier tour^M: 128 joueurs^M
Erste Runde^F: 128 Spieler^M
primo turno^M: 128 concorrenti^M

third round: 32 players
tercera vuelta^F: 32 jugadores^M
troisième tour^M: 32 joueurs^M
Dritte Runde^F: 32 Spieler^M
terzo turno^M: 32 concorrenti^M

quarterfinal: 8 players
cuartos de final^F: 8 jugadores^M
quart^M de finale^F: 8 joueurs^M
Viertelfinale^N: 8 Spieler^M
quarti di finale^F: 8 concorrenti^M

final: 2 players
final^F: 2 jugadores^M
finale^F: 2 joueurs^M
Finale^N: 2 Spieler^M
finale^F: 2 concorrenti^M

winner
vencedor^M
vainqueur^M
Sieger^M
vincitore^M

finalist
finalista^M
finaliste^M
Finalist^M
finalista^{M/F}

second round: 64 players
segunda vuelta^M: 64 jugadores^M
deuxième tour^M: 64 joueurs^M
Zweite Runde^F: 64 Spieler^M
secondo turno^M: 64 concorrenti^M

fourth round: 16 players
cuarta vuelta^F: 16 jugadores^M
huitième^M de finale^F: 16 joueurs^M
Achtelfinale^N: 16 Spieler^M
quarto turno^M: 16 concorrenti^M

semifinal: 4 players
semifinal^F: 4 jugadores^M
demi-finale^F: 4 joueurs^M
Halbfinale^N: 4 Spieler^M
semifinale^F: 4 concorrenti^M

arena

estadio^M | stade^M | Stadion^N | stadio^M

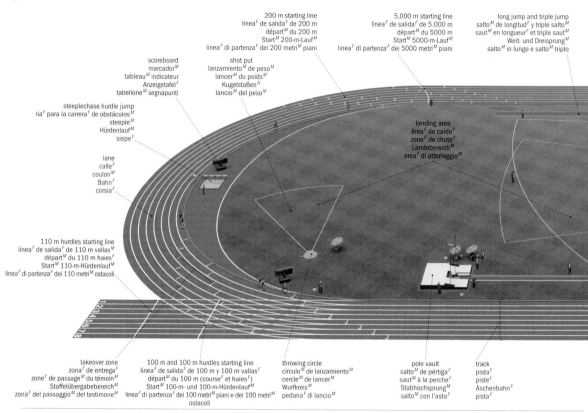

200 m starting line
línea^F de salida^F de 200 m
départ^M du 200 m
Start^M 200-m-Lauf^M
línea^F di partenza^F dei 200 metri^M piani

5,000 m starting line
línea^F de salida^F de 5.000 m
départ^M du 5000 m
Start^M 5000-m-Lauf^M
línea^F di partenza^F dei 5000 metri^M piani

long jump and triple jump
salto^M de longitud^F y triple salto^M
saut^M en longueur^F et triple saut^M
Weit- und Dreisprung^M
salto^M in lungo e salto^M triplo

scoreboard
marcador^M
tableau^M indicateur
Anzeigetafel^F
tabellone^M segnapunti

shot put
lanzamiento^M de peso^M
lancer^M du poids^M
Kugelstoßen^N
lancio^M del peso^M

landing area
área^F de caída^F
zone^F de chute^F
Landebereich^N
area^F di atterraggio^M

steeplechase hurdle jump
ria^F para la carrera^F de obstáculos^M
steeple^M
Hürdenlauf^M
siepe^F

lane
calle^F
couloir^M
Bahn^F
corsia^F

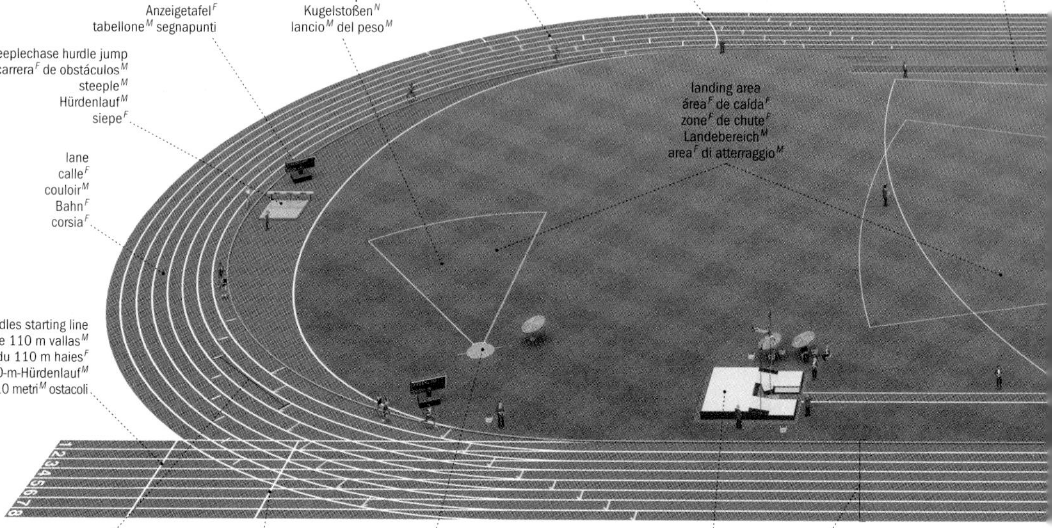

110 m hurdles starting line
línea^F de salida^F de 110 m vallas^M
départ^M du 110 m haies^F
Start^M 110-m-Hürdenlauf^M
línea^F di partenza^F dei 110 metri^M ostacoli

takeover zone
zona^F de entrega^F
zone^F de passage^M du témoin^M
Staffelübergabebereich^M
zona^F del passaggio^M del testimone^M

100 m and 100 m hurdles starting line
línea^F de salida^F de 100 m y 100 m vallas^F
départ^M du 100 m (course^F et haies^F)
Start^M 100-m- und 100-m-Hürdenlauf^M
línea^F di partenza^F dei 100 metri^M piani e dei 100 metri^M
ostacoli

throwing circle
círculo^M de lanzamiento^M
cercle^M de lancer^M
Wurfkreis^M
pedana^F di lancio^M

pole vault
salto^M de pértiga^F
saut^M à la perche^F
Stabhochsprung^M
salto^M con l'asta^F

track
pista^F
piste^F
Aschenbahn^F
pista^F

equipment
equipamiento^M
équipement^M
Geräte^N
attrezzatura^F

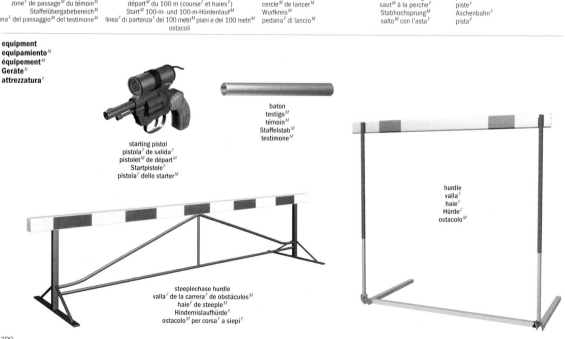

baton
testigo^M
témoin^M
Staffelstab^M
testimone^M

starting pistol
pistola^F de salida^F
pistolet^M de départ^M
Startpistole^F
pistola^F dello starter^M

hurdle
valla^F
haie^F
Hürde^F
ostacolo^M

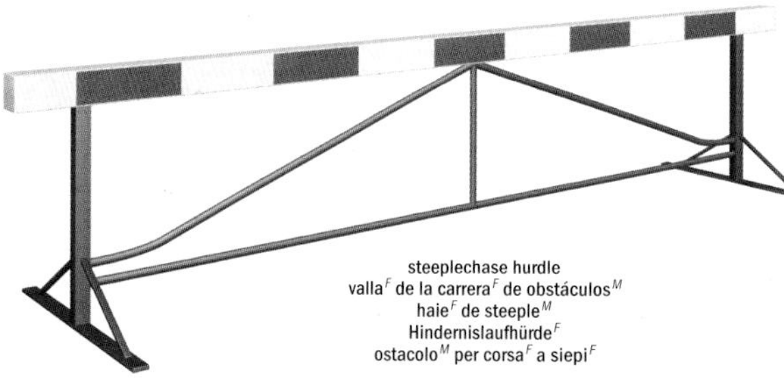

steeplechase hurdle
valla^F de la carrera^F de obstáculos^M
haie^F de steeple^M
Hindernislaufhürde^F
ostacolo^M per corsa^F a siepi^F

SPORTS AND GAMES

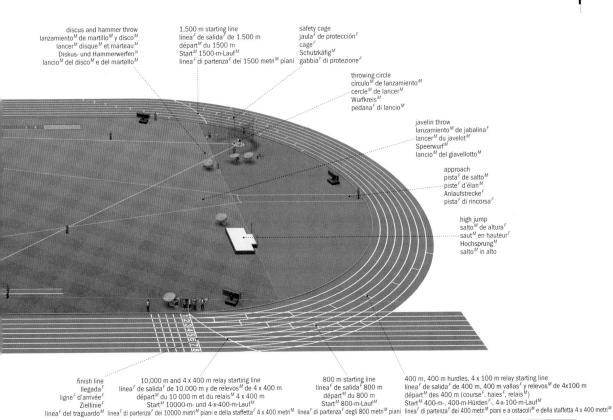

discus and hammer throw
lanzamiento^M de martillo^M y disco^M
lancer^M disque^M et marteau^M
Diskus- und Hammerwerfen^N
lancio^M del disco^M e del martello^M

1,500 m starting line
línea^F de salida^F de 1.500 m
départ^M du 1500 m
Start^M 1500-m-Lauf
línea^F di partenza^F dei 1500 metri^M piani

safety cage
jaula^F de protección^F
cage^F
Schutzkäfig^M
gabbia^F di protezione^F

throwing circle
círculo^M de lanzamiento^M
cercle^M de lancer^M
Wurfkreis^M
pedana^F di lancio^M

javelin throw
lanzamiento^M de jabalina^F
lancer^M du javelot^M
Speerwurf^M
lancio^M del giavellotto^M

approach
pista^F de salto^M
piste^F d'élan^F
Anlaufstrecke^F
pista^F di rincorsa^F

high jump
salto^M de altura^F
saut^M en hauteur^F
Hochsprung^M
salto^M in alto

finish line
llegada^F
ligne^F d'arrivée^F
Ziellinie^F
línea^F del traguardo^M

10,000 m and 4 x 400 m relay starting line
línea^F de salida^F de 10.000 m y de relevos^M de 4 x 400 m
départ^M du 10 000 m et du relais^M 4 x 400 m
Start^M 10000-m- und 4-x-400-m-Lauf^M
línea^F di partenza^F dei 10000 metri^M piani e della staffetta^F 4 x 400 metri^M

800 m starting line
línea^F de salida^F 800 m
départ^M du 800 m
Start^M 800-m-Lauf^M
línea^F di partenza^F degli 800 metri^M piani

400 m, 400 m hurdles, 4 x 100 m relay starting line
línea^F de salida^F de 400 m, 400 m vallas^F y relevos^M de 4x100 m
départ^M des 400 m (course^F, haies^F, relais^M)
Start^M 400-m-, 400-m-Hürden^F-, 4-x-100-m-Lauf^M
línea^F di partenza^F dei 400 metri^M piani e a ostacoli^M e della staffetta 4 x 400 metri^M

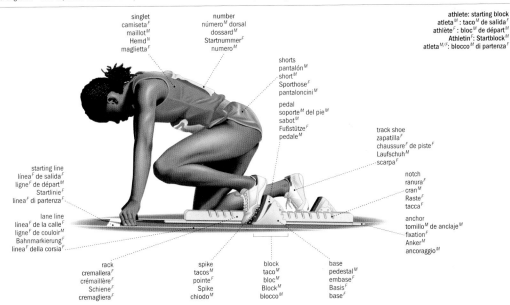

singlet
camiseta^F
maillot^M
Hemd^N
maglietta^F

number
número^M dorsal
dossard^M
Startnummer^F
numero^M

athlete: starting block
atleta^M : taco^M de salida^F
athlète^F : bloc^M de départ^M
Athletin^F: Startblock^M
atleta$^{M/F}$: blocco^M di partenza^F

shorts
pantalón^M
short^M
Sporthose^F
pantaloncini^M

pedal
soporte^M del pie^M
sabot^M
Fußstütze^F
pedale^M

track shoe
zapatilla^F
chaussure^F de piste^F
Laufschuh^M
scarpa^F

notch
ranura^F
cran^M
Raste^F
tacca^F

starting line
línea^F de salida^F
ligne^F de départ^M
Startlinie^F
línea^F di partenza^F

anchor
tornillo^M de anclaje^M
fixation^F
Anker^M
ancoraggio^M

lane line
línea^F de la calle^F
ligne^F de couloir^M
Bahnmarkierung^F
línea^F della corsia^F

rack
cremallera^F
crémaillère^F
Schiene^F
cremagliera^F

spike
tacos^M
pointe^F
Spike
chiodo^M

block
taco^M
bloc^M
Block^M
blocco^M

base
pedestal^M
embase^F
Basis^F
base^F

jumping

saltos^M | sauts^M | Sprungwettbewerbe^M | salti^M

high jump
salto^M de altura^F
saut^M en hauteur^F
Hochsprung^M
salto^M in alto

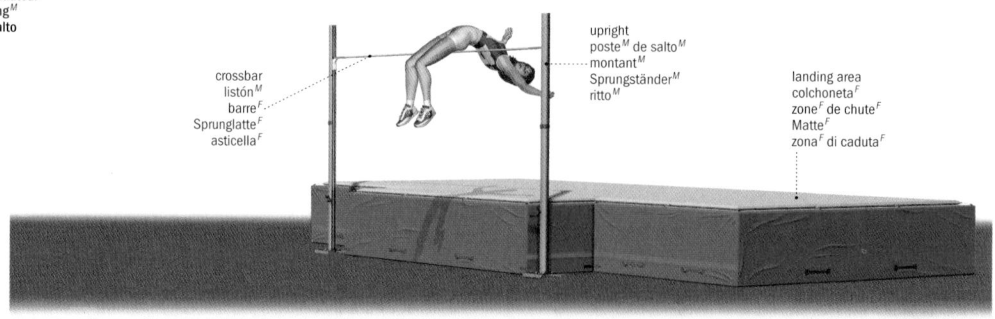

upright
poste^M de salto^M
montant^M
Sprungständer^M
ritto^M

crossbar
listón^M
barre^F
Sprunglatte^F
asticella^F

landing area
colchoneta^F
zone^F de chute^F
Matte^F
zona^F di caduta^F

pole vault
salto^M de pértiga^F
saut^M à la perche^F
Stabhochsprung^M
salto^M con l'asta^F

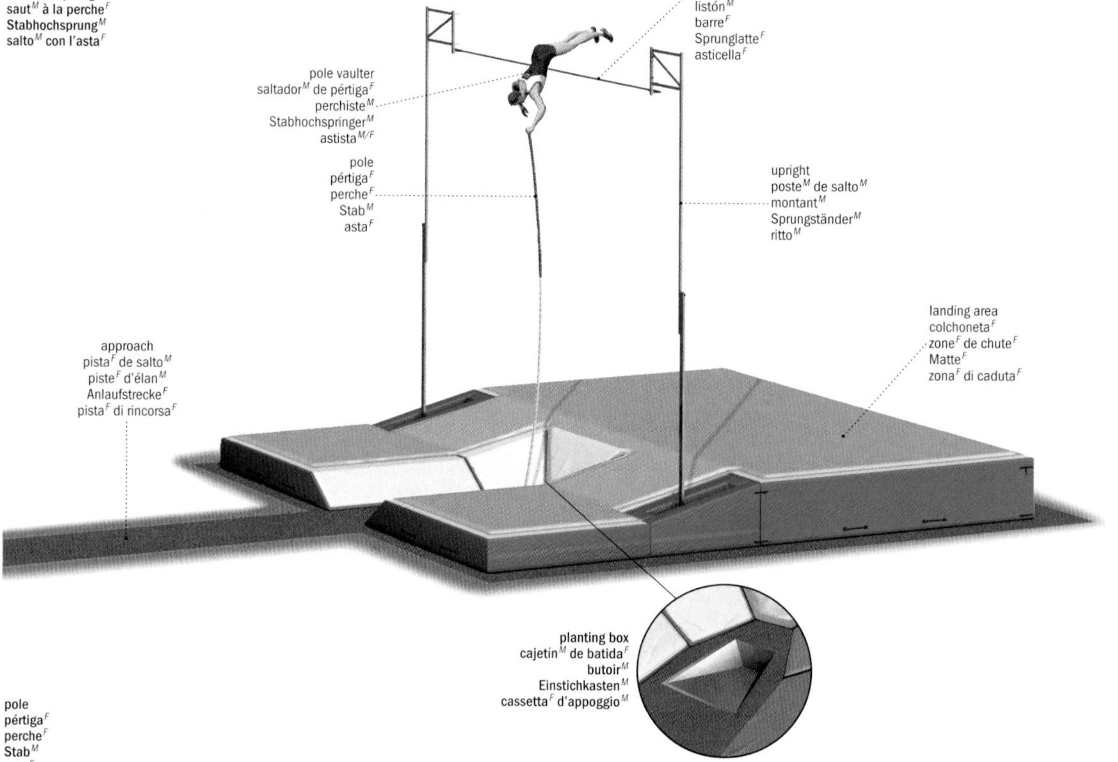

crossbar
listón^M
barre^F
Sprunglatte^F
asticella^F

pole vaulter
saltador^M de pértiga^F
perchiste^M
Stabhochspringer^M
astista^{M/F}

pole
pértiga^F
perche^F
Stab^M
asta^F

upright
poste^M de salto^M
montant^M
Sprungständer^M
ritto^M

landing area
colchoneta^F
zone^F de chute^F
Matte^F
zona^F di caduta^F

approach
pista^F de salto^M
piste^F d'élan^M
Anlaufstrecke^F
pista^F di rincorsa^F

planting box
cajetin^M de batida^F
butoir^M
Einstichkasten^M
cassetta^F d'appoggio^M

pole
pértiga^F
perche^F
Stab^M
asta^F

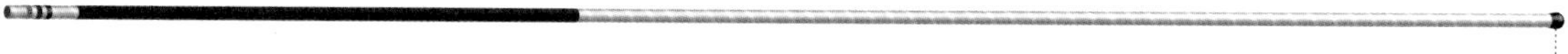

tip
punta^F
embout^M
Spitze^F
punta^F

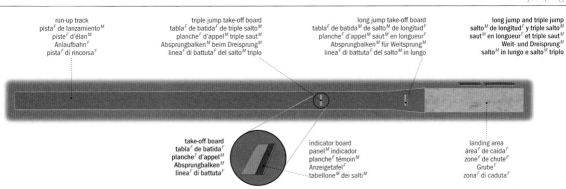

run-up track
pista^F de lanzamiento^M
piste^F d'élan^M
Anlaufbahn^F
pista^F di rincorsa^F

triple jump take-off board
tabla^F de batida^F de triple salto^M
planche^F d'appel^M triple saut^M
Absprungbalken^M beim Dreisprung^M
linea^F di battuta^F del salto^M triplo

long jump take-off board
tabla^F de batida^M de salto^M de longitud^F
planche^F d'appel^M saut en longueur^F
Absprungbalken^M für Weitsprung^M
linea^F di battuta^F del salto^M in lungo

long jump and triple jump
salto^M de longitud^F y triple salto^M
saut^M en longueur^F et triple saut^M
Weit- und Dreisprung^M
salto^M in lungo e salto^M triplo

take-off board
tabla^F de batida^F
planche^F d'appel^M
Absprungbalken^M
linea^F di battuta^F

indicator board
panel^M indicador
planche^F témoin^F
Anzeigetafel^F
tabellone^M dei salti^M

landing area
área^F de caida^F
zone^F de chute^F
Grube^F
zona^F di caduta^F

throwing

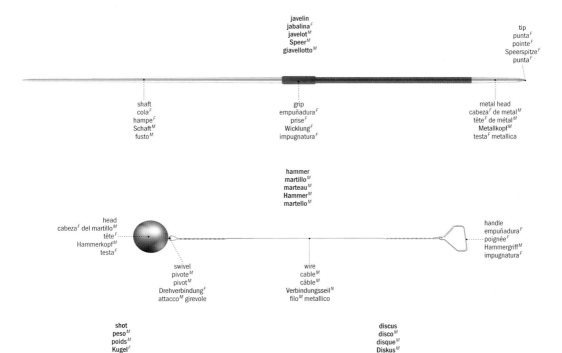

javelin
jabalina^F
javelot^M
Speer^M
giavellotto^M

tip
punta^F
pointe^F
Speerspitze^F
punta^F

shaft
cola^F
hampe^F
Schaft^M
fusto^M

grip
empuñadura^F
prise^F
Wicklung^F
impugnatura^F

metal head
cabeza^F de metal^M
tête^F de métal^M
Metallkopf^M
testa^F metallica

hammer
martillo^M
marteau^M
Hammer^M
martello^M

head
cabeza^F del martillo^M
tête^F
Hammerkopf^M
testa^F

handle
empuñadura^F
poignée^F
Hammergriff^M
impugnatura^F

swivel
pivote^M
pivot^M
Drehverbindung^F
attacco^M girevole

wire
cable^M
câble^M
Verbindungsseil^N
filo^M metallico

shot
peso^M
poids^M
Kugel^F
peso^M

discus
disco^M
disque^M
Diskus^M
disco^M

rim
canto^M
jante^F
Rand^M
bordo^M

weight
peso^M
poids^M
Gewicht^N
peso^M

body
cuerpo^M
corps^M
Korpus^M
corpo^M

baseball

béisbol^M | baseball^M | Baseball^M | baseball^M

player positions
posición^F de los jugadores^M
position^F des joueurs^M
Spielerpositionen^F
posizioni^F dei giocatori^M

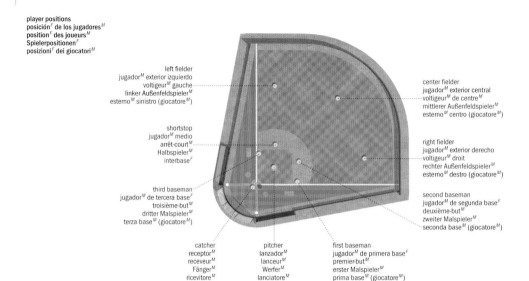

left fielder
jugador^M exterior izquierdo
voltigeur^M gauche
linker Außenfeldspieler^M
esterno^M sinistro (giocatore^M)

center fielder
jugador^M exterior central
voltigeur^M de centre^M
mittlerer Außenfeldspieler^M
esterno^M centro (giocatore^M)

shortstop
jugador^M medio
arrêt-court^M
Halbspieler^M
interbase^F

right fielder
jugador^M exterior derecho
voltigeur^M droit
rechter Außenfeldspieler^M
esterno^M destro (giocatore^M)

third baseman
jugador^M de tercera base^F
troisième-but^M
dritter Malspieler^M
terza base^F (giocatore^M)

second baseman
jugador^M de segunda base^F
deuxième-but^M
zweiter Malspieler^M
seconda base^M (giocatore^M)

catcher
receptor^M
receveur^M
Fänger^M
ricevitore^M

pitcher
lanzador^M
lanceur^M
Werfer^M
lanciatore^M

first baseman
jugador^M de primera base^F
premier-but^M
erster Malspieler^M
prima base^M (giocatore^M)

field
campo^M
terrain^M
Spielfeld^N
campo^M

third base
tercera base^F
troisième but^M
drittes Mal^N
terza base^F (posizione^F)

foul line
línea^F de foul^M
ligne^F de jeu^M
Foullinie^F
linea^F di fuoricampo^M

backstop
pantalla^F de protección^F
écran^M de protection^F
Ballfangzaun^M
schermo^M di protezione^F

dugout
banquillo^M de jugadores^M
abri^M des joueurs^M
Spielerbank^F
panchina^F dei giocatori^M

coach's box
banquillo^M del entrenador^M
rectangle^M des instructeurs^M
Coach-Box^F
zona^F dell'allenatore^M

on-deck circle
círculo^M de espera^F
cercle^M d'attente^F
On-Deck-Circle^M
cerchio^M del battitore^M successivo

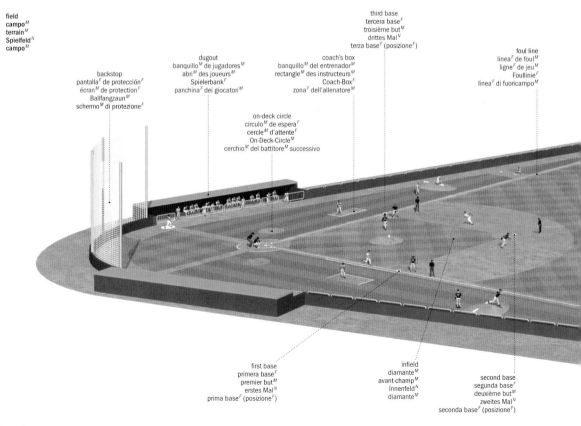

first base
primera base^F
premier but^M
erstes Mal^N
prima base^F (posizione^F)

infield
diamante^M
avant-champ^M
Innenfeld^N
diamante^M

second base
segunda base^F
deuxième but^M
zweites Mal^N
seconda base^F (posizione^F)

pitch
lanzamiento[M]
lancer[M]
Wurf[M]
lancio[M]

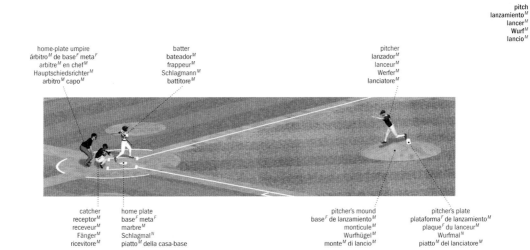

home-plate umpire
árbitro[M] de base[F] meta[F]
arbitre en chef[M]
Hauptschiedsrichter[M]
arbitro[M] capo[M]

batter
bateador[M]
frappeur[M]
Schlagmann[M]
battitore[M]

pitcher
lanzador[M]
lanceur[M]
Werfer[M]
lanciatore[M]

catcher
receptor[M]
receveur[M]
Fänger[M]
ricevitore[M]

home plate
base[F] meta[F]
marbre[M]
Schlagmal[N]
piatto[M] della casa-base

pitcher's mound
base[F] de lanzamiento[M]
monticule[M]
Wurfhügel[M]
monte[M] di lancio[M]

pitcher's plate
plataforma[F] de lanzamiento[M]
plaque[F] du lanceur[M]
Wurfmal[N]
piatto[M] del lanciatore[M]

outfield fence
vallado[M] del campo[M]
clôture[F] du champ[M] extérieur
Outfieldzaun[M]
recinzione[F]

left field
exterior[M] izquierdo
champ[M] gauche
linkes Feld[N]
esterno[M] sinistro (posizione[F])

center field
exterior[M]
champ[M] centre[M]
Mittelfeld[N]
esterno[M] centro (posizione[F])

right field
exterior[M] derecho
champ[M] droit
rechtes Feld[N]
esterno[M] destro (posizione[F])

foul post
poste[M] de foul[M]
poteau[M] de ligne[F] de jeu[M]
Foullinienpfosten[M]
palo[M] della linea[F] di fuoricampo[M]

warning track
zona[F] de atención[F]
piste[F] d'avertissement[M]
Zuschauergrenze[F]
limite[M] del campo[M]

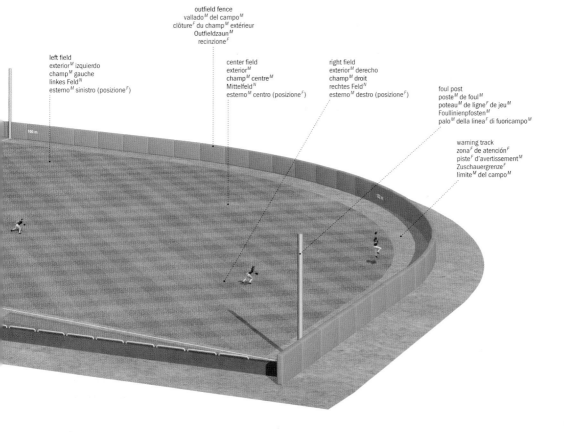

bat
bate[M]
bâton[M]
Schläger[M]
mazza[F]

batter's helmet
casco[M] del bateador[M]
casque[M] de frappeur[M]
Helm[M]
casco[M]

batter
bateador[M]
frappeur[M]
Schlagmann[M]
battitore[M]

baseball
béisbol[M]
balle[F] de baseball[M]
Baseball[M]
palla[F]

catcher
receptor[M]
receveur[M]
Fänger[M]
ricevitore[M]

throat protector
protector[M] de la garganta[F]
protège-gorge[M]
Halsschutz[M]
paragola[M]

mask
máscara[F]
masque[M]
Maske[F]
maschera[F]

frame
armazón[M] de la máscara[F]
grille[F]
Visiergestell[N]
griglia[F] per casco[M]

chest protector
peto[M]
plastron[M]
Brustschutz[M]
pettorina[F] di protezione[F]

catcher's glove
guante[M] del receptor[M]
gant[M] de receveur[M]
Fanghandschuh[M]
guanto[M]

team shirt
camiseta[F]
maillot[M] d'équipe[F]
Mannschaftstrikot[N]
maglia[F] della squadra[F]

undershirt
camiseta[F] interior
maillot[M] de corps[M]
Unterhemd[N]
prima maglia[F]

batting glove
guante[M] de bateo[M]
gant[M] de frappeur[M]
Schlaghandschuh[M]
guanto[M]

pants
pantalón[M]
pantalon[M]
Hose[F]
pantaloni[M]

stirrup sock
calcetín[M] con tirante[M]
chaussette[F]-étrier[M]
Stutzen[M]
calza[F] con reggicalze[M]

spiked shoe
zapatilla[F] con tacos[M]
chaussure[F] à crampons[M]
Stollenschuh[M]
scarpa[F] con tacchetti[M]

toe guard
protector[M] del pie[M]
protège-orteils[M]
Zehenschützer[M]
parapunta[M]

leg guard
espinillera[F]
jambière[F]
Beinschutz[M]
schiniere[M]

knee pad
rodillera[F]
genouillère[F]
Knieschützer[M]
ginocchiera[F]

ankle guard
tobillera[F]
protège-cheville[M]
Knöchelschutz[M]
parastinchi[M]

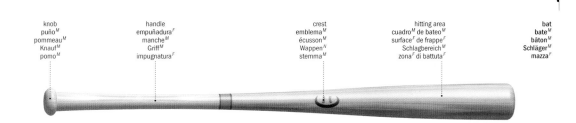

knob
puño^M
pommeau^M
Knauf^M
pomo^M

handle
empuñadura^F
manche^M
Griff^M
impugnatura^F

crest
emblema^M
écusson^M
Wappen^N
stemma^M

hitting area
cuadro^M de bateo^M
surface^F de frappe^F
Schlagbereich^M
zona^F di battuta^F

bat
bate^M
bâton^M
Schläger^M
mazza^F

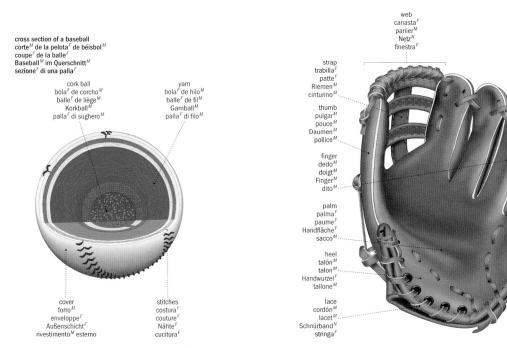

cross section of a baseball
corte^M de la pelota^F de béisbol^M
coupe^F de la balle^F
Baseball^M im Querschnitt^M
sezione^F di una palla^F

cork ball
bola^F de corcho^M
balle^F de liège^M
Korkball^M
palla^F di sughero^M

yarn
bola^F de hilo^M
balle^F de fil^M
Garnball^M
palla^F di filo^M

web
canasta^F
panier^M
Netz^N
finestra^F

fielder's glove
guante^M de recogida^F
gant^M
Handschuh^M
guanto^M del difensore^M

strap
trabilla^F
patte^F
Riemen^M
cinturino^M

thumb
pulgar^M
pouce^M
Daumen^M
pollice^M

finger
dedo^M
doigt^M
Finger^M
dito^M

palm
palma^F
paume^F
Handfläche^F
sacco^M

heel
talón^M
talon^M
Handwurzel^F
tallone^M

lace
cordón^M
lacet^M
Schnürband^N
stringa^F

cover
forro^M
enveloppe^F
Außenschicht^F
rivestimento^M esterno

stitches
costura^F
couture^F
Nähte^F
cucitura^F

softball
softball^M | softball^M | Softball^M | softball^M

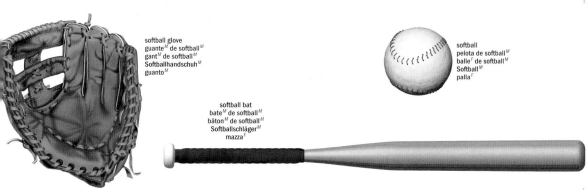

softball glove
guante^M de softball^M
gant^M de softball^M
Softballhandschuh^M
guanto^M

softball
pelota de softball^M
balle^F de softball^M
Softball^M
palla^F

softball bat
bate^M de softball^M
bâton^M de softball^M
Softballschläger^M
mazza^F

SPORTS AND GAMES

cricket

cricket[M] | cricket[M] | Cricket[N] | cricket[M]

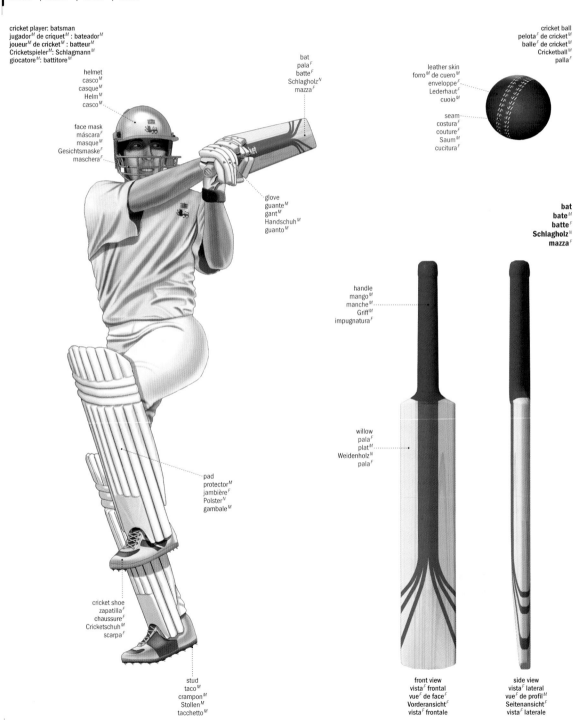

cricket player: batsman
jugador[M] de criquet[M] : bateador[M]
joueur[M] de cricket[M] : batteur[M]
Cricketspieler[M]: Schlagmann[M]
giocatore[M]: battitore[M]

cricket ball
pelota[F] de cricket[M]
balle[F] de cricket[M]
Cricketball[M]
palla[F]

bat
pala[F]
batte[F]
Schlagholz[N]
mazza[F]

leather skin
forro[M] de cuero[M]
enveloppe[F]
Lederhaut[F]
cuoio[M]

seam
costura[F]
couture[F]
Saum[M]
cucitura[F]

helmet
casco[M]
casque[M]
Helm[M]
casco[M]

face mask
máscara[F]
masque[M]
Gesichtsmaske[F]
maschera[F]

glove
guante[M]
gant[M]
Handschuh[M]
guanto[M]

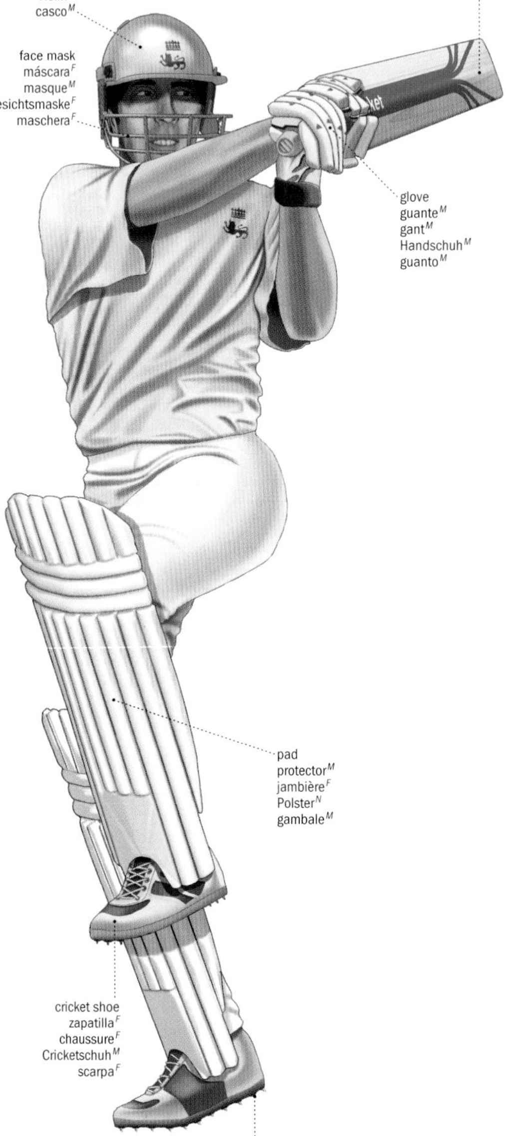

bat
bate[M]
batte[F]
Schlagholz[N]
mazza[F]

handle
mango[M]
manche[M]
Griff[M]
impugnatura[F]

willow
pala[F]
plat[M]
Weidenholz[N]
pala[F]

pad
protector[M]
jambière[F]
Polster[N]
gambale[M]

cricket shoe
zapatilla[F]
chaussure[F]
Cricketschuh[M]
scarpa[F]

stud
taco[M]
crampon[M]
Stollen[M]
tacchetto[M]

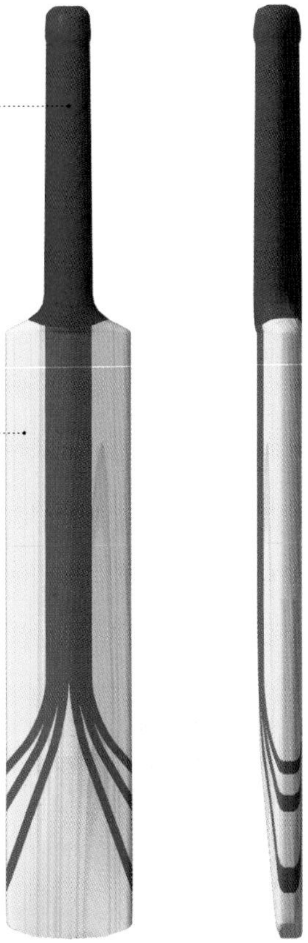

front view
vista[F] frontal
vue[F] de face[F]
Vorderansicht[F]
vista[F] frontale

side view
vista[F] lateral
vue[F] de profil[M]
Seitenansicht[F]
vista[F] laterale

**field
campo**[M]
terrain[M]
Feld[N]
campo[M]

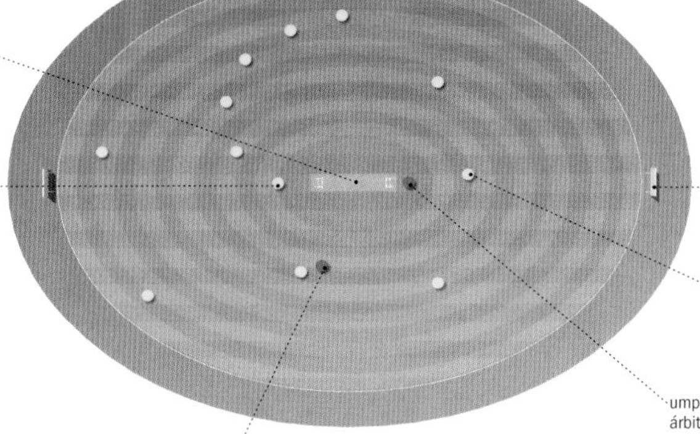

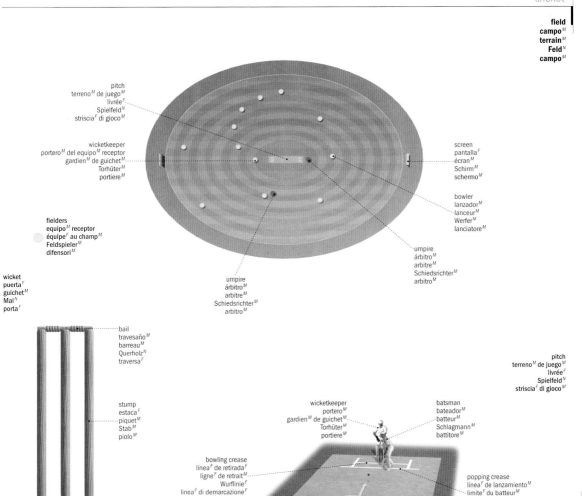

pitch
terreno[M] de juego[M]
livrée[F]
Spielfeld[N]
striscia[F] di gioco[M]

wicketkeeper
portero[M] del equipo[M] receptor
gardien[M] de guichet[M]
Torhüter[M]
portiere[M]

screen
pantalla[F]
écran[M]
Schirm[M]
schermo[M]

bowler
lanzador[M]
lanceur[M]
Werfer[M]
lanciatore[M]

fielders
equipo[M] receptor
équipe[F] au champ[M]
Feldspieler[M]
difensori[M]

umpire
árbitro[M]
arbitre[M]
Schiedsrichter[M]
arbitro[M]

umpire
árbitro[M]
arbitre[M]
Schiedsrichter[M]
arbitro[M]

wicket
puerta[F]
guichet[M]
Mal[N]
porta[F]

bail
travesaño[M]
barreau[M]
Querholz[N]
traversa[F]

stump
estaca[F]
piquet[M]
Stab[M]
piolo[M]

pitch
terreno[M] de juego[M]
livrée[F]
Spielfeld[N]
striscia[F] di gioco[M]

wicketkeeper
portero[M]
gardien[M] de guichet[M]
Torhüter[M]
portiere[M]

batsman
bateador[M]
batteur[M]
Schlagmann[M]
battitore[M]

bowling crease
línea[F] de retirada[F]
ligne[F] de retrait[M]
Wurflinie[F]
linea[F] di demarcazione[F]

popping crease
línea[F] de lanzamiento[M]
limite[F] du batteur[M]
Schlagmallinie[F]
linea[F] del battitore[M]

bowler
lanzador[M]
lanceur[M]
Werfer[M]
lanciatore[M]

delivery
lanzamiento[M]
lancer[M]
Wurf[M]
lancio[M]

return crease
línea[F] de devolución[F]
limite[F] de retour[M]
Rückwurflinie[F]
linea[F] di rimando[M]

umpire
árbitro[M]
arbitre[M]
Schiedsrichter[M]
arbitro[M]

wicket
puerta[F]
guichet[M]
Mal[N]
porta[F]

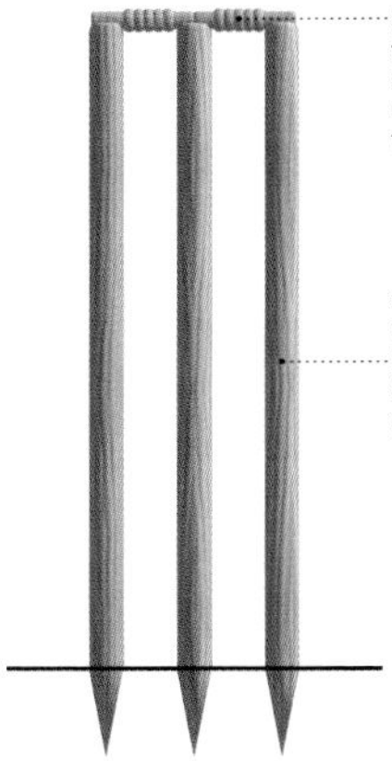

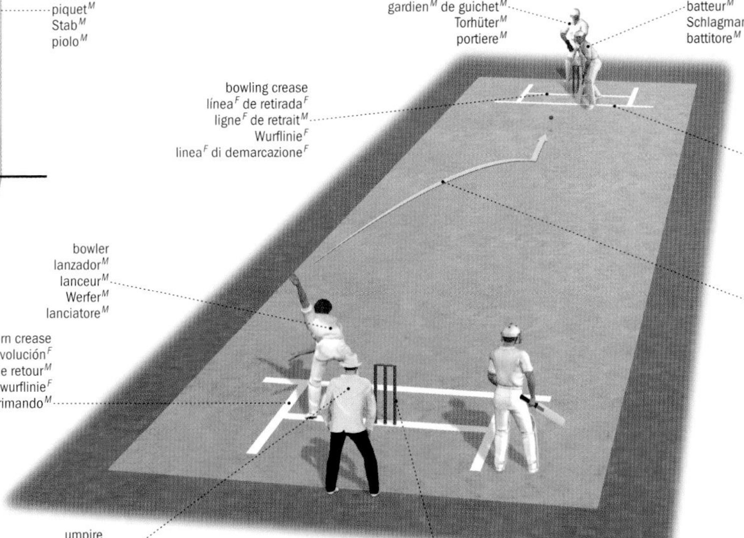

field hockey

hockey^M sobre hierba^F | hockey^M sur gazon^M | Hockey^N | hockey^M su prato^M

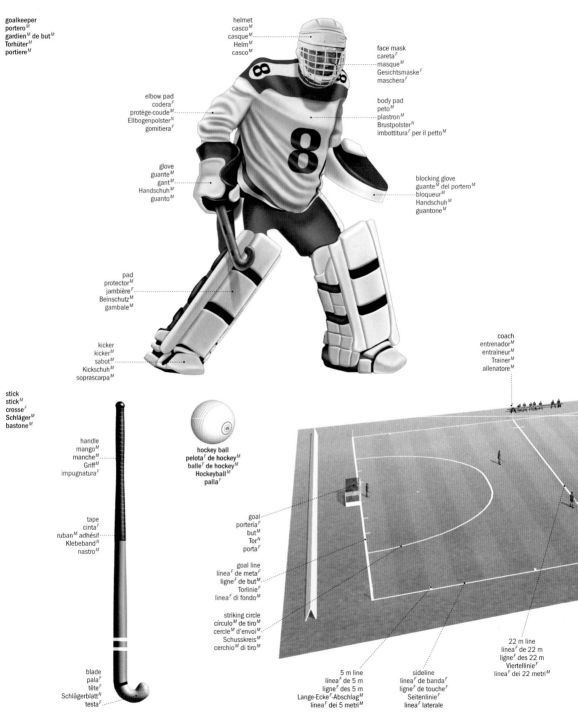

goalkeeper
portero^M
gardien^M de but^M
Torhüter^M
portiere^M

helmet
casco^M
casque^M
Helm^M
casco^M

face mask
careta^F
masque^M
Gesichtsmaske^F
maschera^F

elbow pad
codera^F
protège-coude^M
Ellbogenpolster^N
gomitiera^F

body pad
peto^M
plastron^M
Brustpolster^N
imbottitura^F per il petto^M

glove
guante^M
gant^M
Handschuh^M
guanto^M

blocking glove
guante^M del portero^M
bloqueur^M
Handschuh^M
guantone^M

pad
protector^M
jambière^F
Beinschutz^M
gambale^M

kicker
kicker^M
sabot^M
Kickschuh^M
soprascarpa^F

coach
entrenador^M
entraineur^M
Trainer^M
allenatore^M

stick
stick^M
crosse^F
Schläger^M
bastone^M

handle
mango^M
manche^M
Griff^M
impugnatura^F

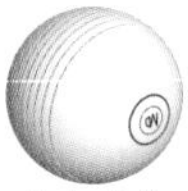

hockey ball
pelota^F de hockey^M
balle^F de hockey^M
Hockeyball^M
palla^F

tape
cinta^F
ruban^M adhésif
Klebeband^N
nastro^M

goal
portería^F
but^M
Tor^N
porta^F

goal line
línea^F de meta^F
ligne^F de but^M
Torlinie^F
linea^F di fondo^M

striking circle
círculo^M de tiro^M
cercle^M d'envoi^M
Schusskreis^M
cerchio^M di tiro^M

blade
pala^F
tête^F
Schlägerblatt^N
testa^F

5 m line
línea^F de 5 m
ligne^F des 5 m
Lange-Ecke^F-Abschlag^M
linea^F dei 5 metri^M

sideline
línea^F de banda^F
ligne^F de touche^F
Seitenlinie^F
linea^F laterale

22 m line
línea^F de 22 m
ligne^F des 22 m
Viertellinie^F
linea^F dei 22 metri^M

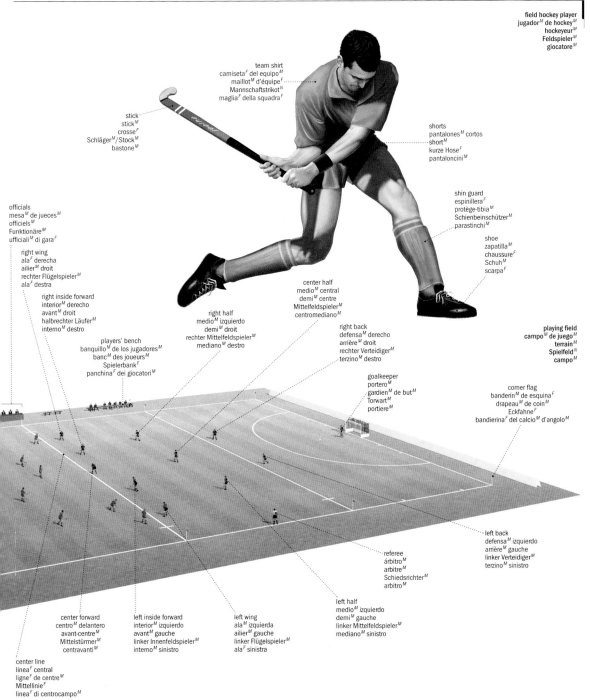

field hockey player
jugador^M de hockey^M
hockeyeur^M
Feldspieler^M
giocatore^M

team shirt
camiseta^F del equipo^M
maillot^M d'équipe^F
Mannschaftstrikot^N
maglia^F della squadra^F

stick
stick^M
crosse^F
Schläger^M/Stock^M
bastone^M

shorts
pantalones^M cortos
short^M
kurze Hose^F
pantaloncini^M

shin guard
espinillera^F
protège-tibia^M
Schienbeinschützer^M
parastinchi^M

shoe
zapatilla^M
chaussure^F
Schuh^M
scarpa^F

officials
mesa^M de jueces^M
officiels^M
Funktionäre^M
ufficiali^M di gara^F

right wing
ala^F derecha
ailier^M droit
rechter Flügelspieler^M
ala^F destra

right inside forward
interior^M derecho
avant^M droit
halbrechter Läufer^M
interno^M destro

center half
medio^M central
demi^M centre
Mittelfeldspieler^M
centromediano^M

players' bench
banquillo^M de los jugadores^M
banc^M des joueurs^M
Spielerbank^F
panchina^F dei giocatori^M

right half
medio^M izquierdo
demi^M droit
rechter Mittelfeldspieler^M
mediano^M destro

right back
defensa^M derecho
arrière^M droit
rechter Verteidiger^M
terzino^M destro

playing field
campo^M de juego^M
terrain^M
Spielfeld^N
campo^M

goalkeeper
portero^M
gardien^M de but^M
Torwart^M
portiere^M

corner flag
banderín^M de esquina^F
drapeau^M de coin^M
Eckfahne^F
bandierina^F del calcio^M d'angolo^M

left back
defensa^M izquierdo
arrière^M gauche
linker Verteidiger^M
terzino^M sinistro

referee
árbitro^M
arbitre^M
Schiedsrichter^M
arbitro^M

center forward
centro^M delantero
avant-centre^M
Mittelstürmer^M
centravanti^M

left inside forward
interior^M izquierdo
avant^M gauche
linker Innenfeldspieler^M
interno^M sinistro

left wing
ala^M izquierda
ailier^M gauche
linker Flügelspieler^M
ala^F sinistra

left half
medio^M izquierdo
demi^M gauche
linker Mittelfeldspieler^M
mediano^M sinistro

center line
línea^F central
ligne^F de centre^M
Mittellinie^F
linea^F di centrocampo^M

SPORTS AND GAMES

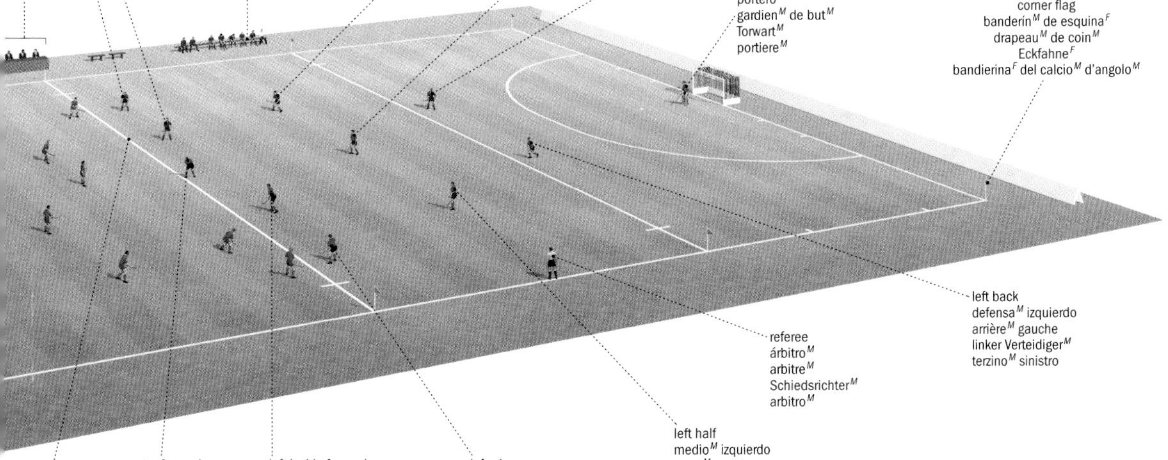

soccer

fútbol^M | football^M | Fußball^M | calcio^M

soccer player
futbolista^{M/F}
footballeur^M
Fußballspieler^M
calciatore^M

team shirt
camiseta^F del equipo^M
maillot^M d'équipe^F
Mannschaftstrikot^N
maglia^F della squadra^F

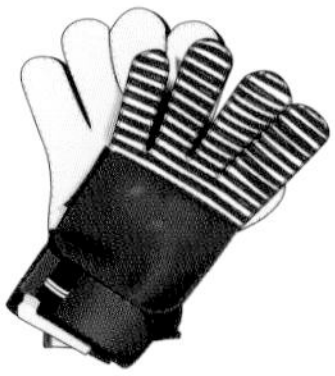

goalkeeper's gloves
guantes^M del portero^M
gants^M de gardien^M de but^M
Torwarthandschuhe^M
guanti^M del portiere^M

shorts
pantalones^M
short^M
Hose^F
pantaloncini^M

interchangeable studs
tacos^F de rosca^F
crampons^M interchangeables
Schraubstollen^M
tacchetti^M intercambiabili

soccer shoe
bota^F de fútbol^M
chaussure^F de football^M
Fußballschuh^M
scarpa^F

shin guard
espinillera^F
protège-tibia^M
Schienbeinschützer^M
parastinchi^M

sock
calcetín^M
chaussette^F
Stulpen^F
calzettone^M

soccer ball
balón^M de fútbol^M
ballon^M de football^M
Fußball^M
pallone^M

playing field
campo^M
terrain^M
Spielfeld^N
campo^M di gioco^M

goal area
área^F pequeña
surface^F de but^M
Torraum^M
area^F di porta^F

penalty spot
punto^M de penalti^M
point^M de réparation^F
Elfmeterpunkt^M
dischetto^M del rigore^M

center flag
banderín^M de línea^M de centro^M
drapeau^M de centre^M
Mittelfahne^F
bandierina^F centrale

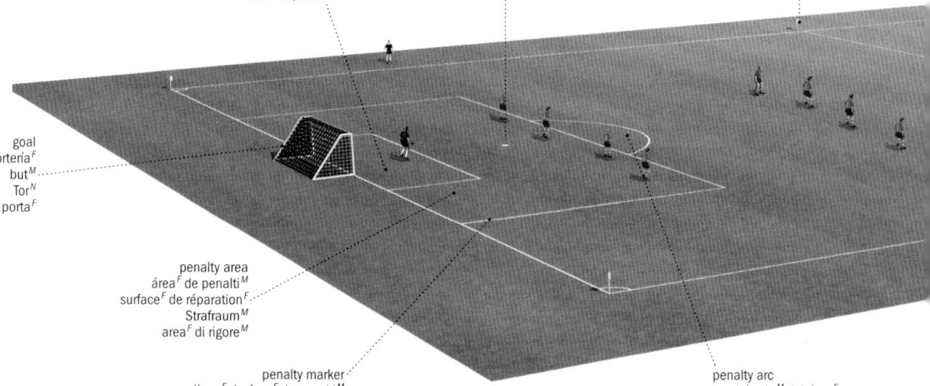

goal
portería^F
but^M
Tor^N
porta^F

penalty area
área^F de penalti^M
surface^F de réparation^F
Strafraum^M
area^F di rigore^M

penalty marker
línea^F de área^F de penalti^M
ligne^F de surface^F de réparation^F
Strafraumlinie^F
linea^F dell'area^F di rigore^M

penalty arc
semicírculo^M del área^F
arc^M de cercle^M
Strafraumbogen^M
lunetta^F

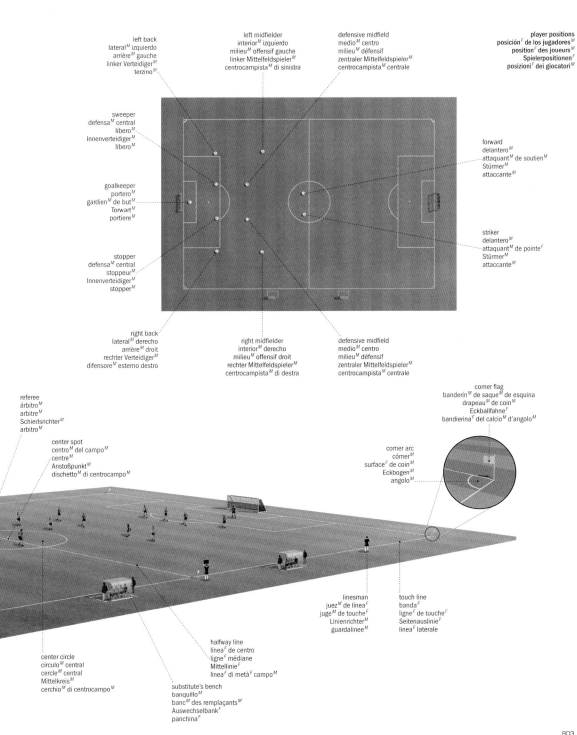

left back
lateral^M izquierdo
arrière^M gauche
linker Verteidiger^M
terzino^M

left midfielder
interior^M izquierdo
milieu^M offensif gauche
linker Mittelfeldspieler^M
centrocampista^M di sinistra

defensive midfield
medio^M centro
milieu^M défensif
zentraler Mittelfeldspieler^M
centrocampista^M centrale

player positions
posición^F de los jugadores^M
position^F des joueurs^M
Spielerpositionen^F
posizioni^F dei giocatori^M

sweeper
defensa^M central
líbero^M
Innenverteidiger^M
líbero^M

forward
delantero^M
attaquant^M de soutien^M
Stürmer^M
attaccante^M

goalkeeper
portero^M
gardien^M de but^M
Torwart^M
portiere^M

striker
delantero^M
attaquant^M de pointe^F
Stürmer^M
attaccante^M

stopper
defensa^M central
stoppeur^M
Innenverteidiger^M
stopper^M

right back
lateral^M derecho
arrière^M droit
rechter Verteidiger^M
difensore^M esterno destro

right midfielder
interior^M derecho
milieu^M offensif droit
rechter Mittelfeldspieler^M
centrocampista^M di destra

defensive midfield
medio^M centro
milieu^M défensif
zentraler Mittelfeldspieler^M
centrocampista^M centrale

referee
árbitro^M
arbitre^M
Schiedsrichter^M
arbitro^M

center spot
centro^M del campo^M
centre^M
Anstoßpunkt^M
dischetto^M di centrocampo^M

corner flag
banderín^M de saque^M de esquina
drapeau^M de coin^M
Eckballfahne^F
bandierina^F del calcio^M d'angolo^M

corner arc
córner^M
surface^F de coin^M
Eckbogen^M
angolo^M

linesman
juez^M de línea^F
juge^M de touche^F
Linienrichter^M
guardalinee^M

touch line
banda^F
ligne^F de touche^F
Seitenauslinie^F
linea^F laterale

center circle
círculo^M central
cercle^M central
Mittelkreis^M
cerchio^M di centrocampo^M

halfway line
línea^F de centro
ligne^F médiane
Mittellinie^F
linea^F di metà^F campo^M

substitute's bench
banquillo^M
banc^M des remplaçants^M
Auswechselbank^F
panchina^F

SPORTS AND GAMES

803

rugby

rugby[M] | rugby[M] | Rugby[N] | rugby[M]

players' positions
posición[F] de los jugadores[M]
position[F] des joueurs[M]
Spielerpositionen[F]
posizioni[F] dei giocatori[M]

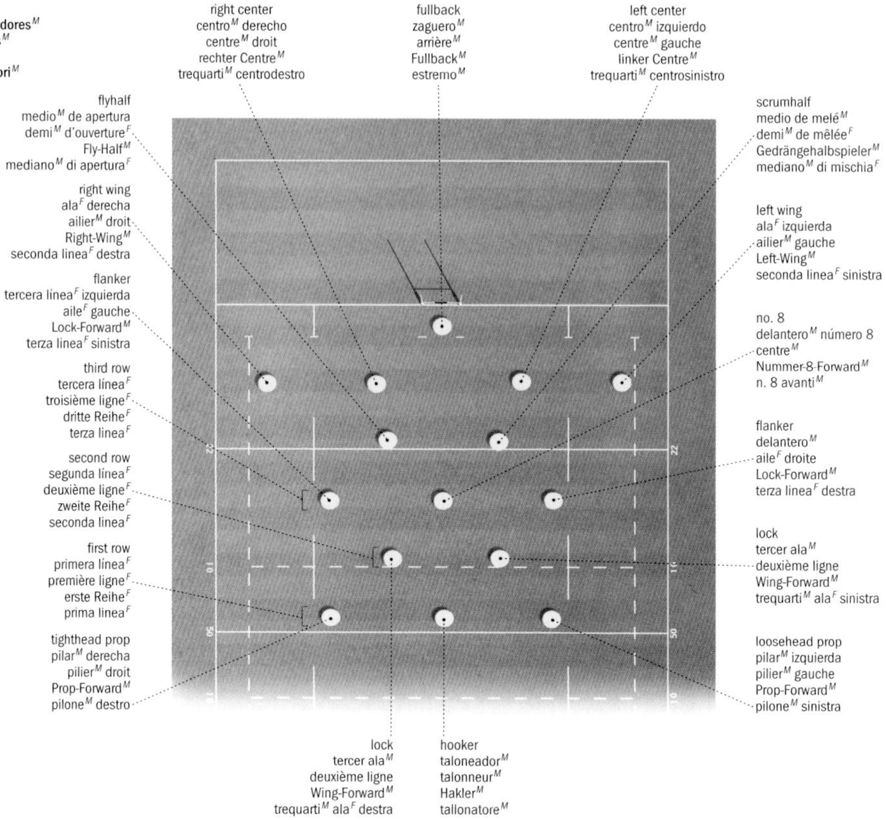

right center
centro[M] derecho
centre[M] droit
rechter Centre[M]
trequarti[M] centrodestro

fullback
zaguero[M]
arrière[M]
Fullback[M]
estremo[M]

left center
centro[M] izquierdo
centre[M] gauche
linker Centre[M]
trequarti[M] centrosinistro

flyhalf
medio[M] de apertura
demi[F] d'ouverture[F]
Fly-Half[M]
mediano[M] di apertura[F]

scrumhalf
medio de melé[M]
demi[F] de mêlée[F]
Gedrängehalbspieler[M]
mediano[M] di mischia[F]

right wing
ala[F] derecha
ailier[M] droit
Right-Wing[M]
seconda linea[F] destra

left wing
ala[F] izquierda
ailier[M] gauche
Left-Wing[M]
seconda linea[F] sinistra

flanker
tercera línea[F] izquierda
aile[F] gauche
Lock-Forward[M]
terza linea[F] sinistra

no. 8
delantero[M] número 8
centre[M]
Nummer-8-Forward[M]
n. 8 avanti[M]

third row
tercera línea[F]
troisième ligne[F]
dritte Reihe[F]
terza linea[F]

flanker
delantero[M]
aile[F] droite
Lock-Forward[M]
terza linea[F] destra

second row
segunda línea[F]
deuxième ligne[F]
zweite Reihe[F]
seconda linea[F]

first row
primera línea[F]
première ligne[F]
erste Reihe[F]
prima linea[F]

lock
tercer ala[M]
deuxième ligne
Wing-Forward[M]
trequarti[M] ala[F] sinistra

tighthead prop
pilar[M] derecha
pilier[M] droit
Prop-Forward[M]
pilone[M] destro

loosehead prop
pilar[M] izquierda
pilier[M] gauche
Prop-Forward[M]
pilone[M] sinistra

field
campo[M] de juego[M]
terrain[M]
Spielfeld[N]
campo[M]

lock
tercer ala[M]
deuxième ligne
Wing-Forward[M]
trequarti[M] ala[F] destra

hooker
taloneador[M]
talonneur[M]
Hakler[M]
tallonatore[M]

10 m line
línea[F] de 10 m
ligne[F] des 10 m
10-m-Linie[F]
linea[F] dei 10 metri[M]

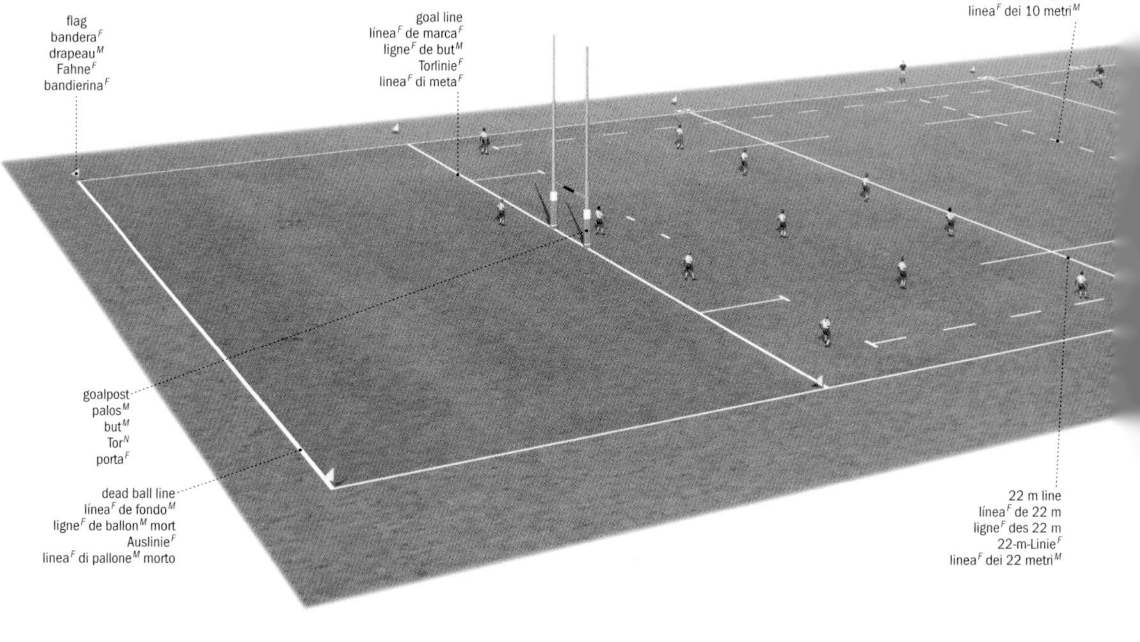

flag
bandera[F]
drapeau[M]
Fahne[F]
bandierina[F]

goal line
línea[F] de marca[F]
ligne[F] de but[M]
Torlinie[F]
linea[F] di meta[F]

goalpost
palos[M]
but[M]
Tor[N]
porta[F]

dead ball line
línea[F] de fondo[M]
ligne[F] de ballon[M] mort
Auslinie[F]
linea[F] di pallone[M] morto

22 m line
línea[F] de 22 m
ligne[F] des 22 m
22-m-Linie[F]
linea[F] dei 22 metri[M]

rugby player
jugador^M de rugby^M
rugbyman^M
Rugbyspieler^M
giocatore^M

rugby shirt
camiseta^F
maillot^M
Trikot^N
maglia^F

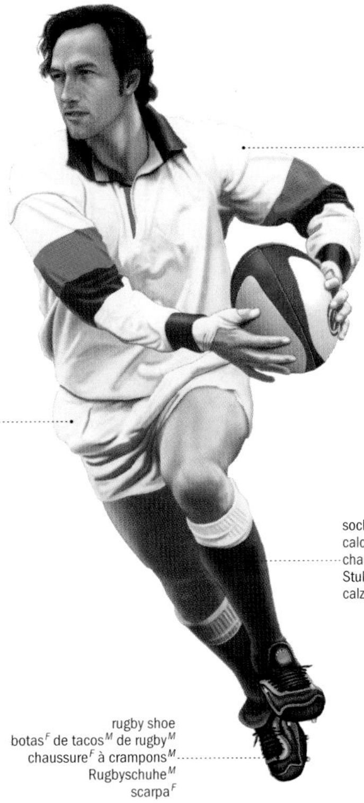

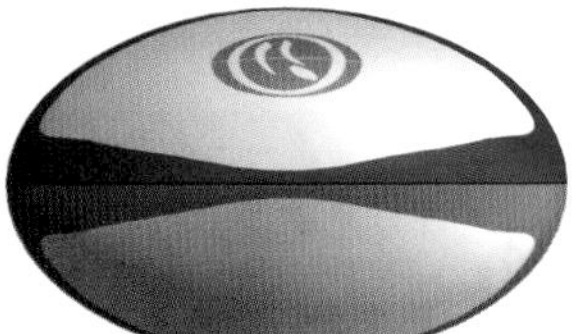

rugby ball
balón^M de rugby^M
ballon^M de rugby^M
Rugbyball^M
palla^F ovale

shorts
pantalones^M cortos
short^M
kurze Hose^F
pantaloncini^M

sock
calcetine^M alto
chaussette^F haute
Stulpen^F
calzettono^M

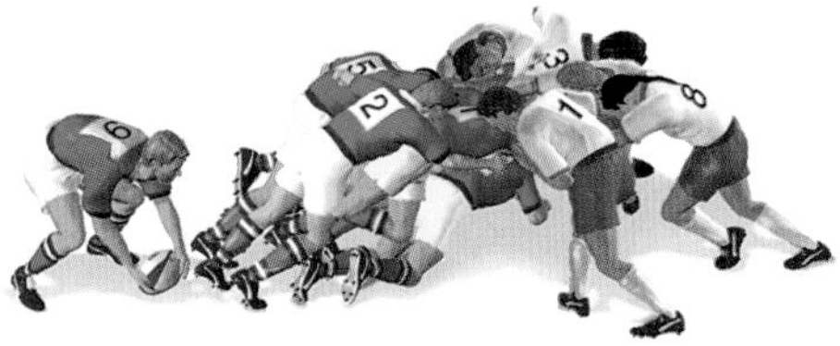

ruck
melé^F espontánea
mêlée^F spontanée
Gedränge^N
mischia^F spontanea

rugby shoe
botas^F de tacos^M de rugby^M
chaussure^F à crampons^M
Rugbyschuhe^M
scarpa^F

referee
árbitro^M
arbitre^M
Schiedsrichter^M
arbitro^M

15 m line
linea^F de 15 m
ligne^F des 15 m
15-m-Linie^F
linea^F dei 15 metri^M

in goal area
zona^F de marca^F
en-but^M
Torbereich^M
area^F di meta^F

5 m line
linea^F de 5 m
ligne^F des 5 m
5-Meter-Linie^F
linea^F dei 5 metri^M

touch judge
juez^M de línea^F
juge^M de touche^F
Seitenrichter^M
giudice^M di línea^F

touchline
línea^F de «touche»^{F}
ligne^F de touche^F
Seitenlinie^F
linea^F di uscita^F laterale

halfway dash line
línea^F de medio campo^M
ligne^F médiane
Mittellinie^F
linea^F di metà^F campo^M

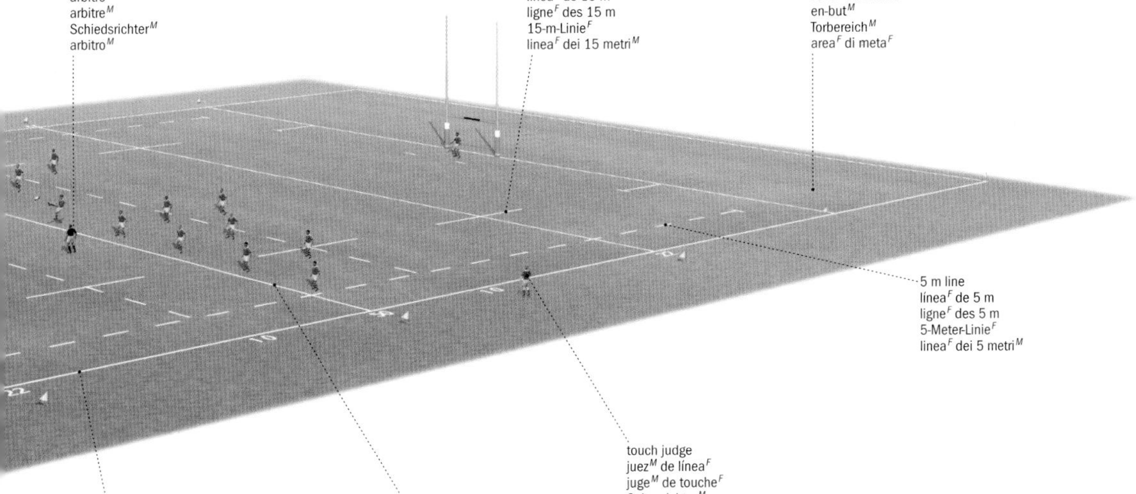

American football

fútbol^M americano | football^M américain | American Football^M | football^M americano

scrimmage: defense
melé^F: defensa^F
mêlée^F : défense^F
Gedränge^N: Verteidigung^F
mischia^F: difesa^F

right defensive end
ala^M defensivo derecho
ailier^M défensif droit
rechter Defensive End^M
difensore^M ala^F destra

right cornerback
esquinero^M derecho
demi^M de coin^M droit
rechter Corner Back^M
terzino^M di destra

right defensive tackle
tackle^M defensivo derecho
plaqueur^M droit
rechter Defensive Tackle^M
placcatore^M destro

outside linebacker
apoyador^M exterior
secondeur^M extérieur droit
äußerer Linebacker^M
linebacker^M esterno

left defensive tackle
tackle^M defensivo izquierdo
plaqueur^M gauche
linker Defensive Tackle^M
placcatore^M sinistro

right safety
safety^M débil
demi^M de sûreté^F droit
rechter Safety^M
estremo^M di destra

right (strong) safety
apoyador^M
secondeur^M intérieur
mittlerer Linebacker^M
linebacker^M centrale

inside linebacker
apoyador^M interior
secondeur^M extérieur gauche
Middle Linebacker^M
linebacker^M interno

left defensive end
ala^M defensivo izquierdo
ailier^M défensif gauche
linker Defensive End^M
difensore^M ala^F sinistra

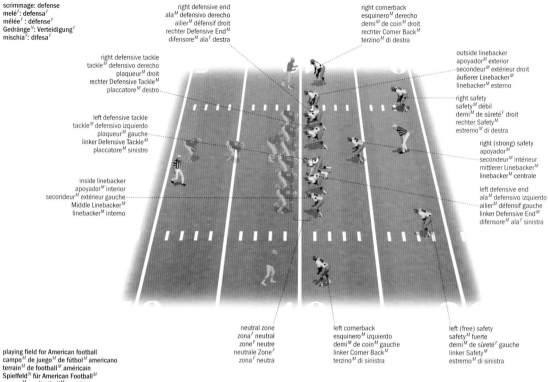

playing field for American football
campo^M de juego^M de fútbol^M americano
terrain^M de football^M américain
Spielfeld^N für American Football^M
campo^M per football^M americano

neutral zone
zona^F neutral
zone^F neutre
neutrale Zone^F
zona^F neutra

left cornerback
esquinero^M izquierdo
demi^M de coin^M gauche
linker Corner Back^M
terzino^M di sinistra

left (free) safety
safety^M fuerte
demi^M de sûreté^F gauche
linker Safety^M
estremo^M di sinistra

inbounds line
linea^F límite^M de inicio^M de jugada^F
trait^M de mise^F au jeu^M
Inbound-Linie^F
linea^F di messa^F in gioco^M

goal line
linea^F de gol^M
ligne^F de but^M
Torlinie^F
linea^F di meta^F

fifty-yard line
linea^F media
ligne^F de centre^M
Mittellinie^F
linea^F di centrocampo^M

end zone
zona^F de anotación^F
zone^F de but^M
Endzone^F
area^F di meta^F

end line
linea^F de fondo^M
ligne^F de fond^M
Endlinie^F
linea^F di fondo^M

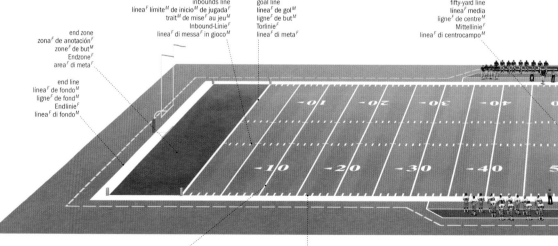

yard line
linea^F yardas^F
ligne^F des verges^F
Yardlinie^F
linea^F delle yards^F

sideline
banda^F
ligne^F de touche^F
Seitenlinie^F
linea^F laterale

SPORTS AND GAMES

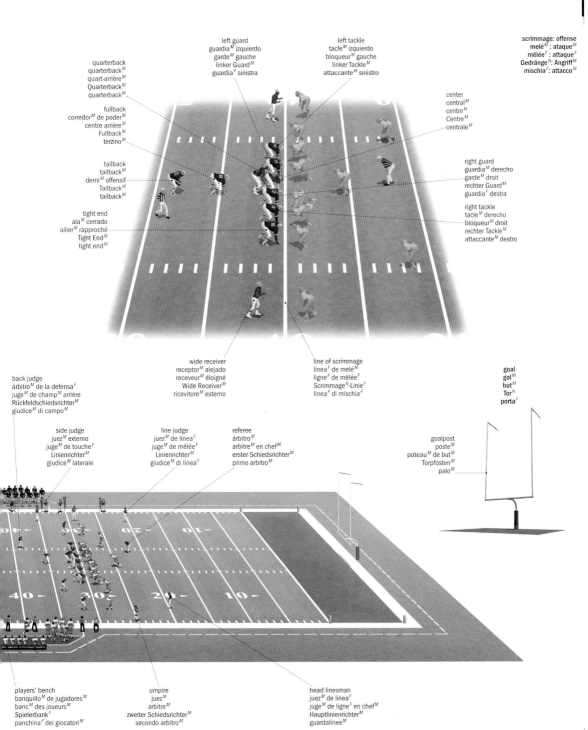

scrimmage: offense
melé ^{M} : ataque ^{M}
mêlée ^{F} : attaque ^{F}
Gedränge ^{N} : Angriff ^{M}
mischia ^{F} : attacco ^{M}

left guard
guardia ^{M} izquierdo
garde ^{M} gauche
linker Guard ^{M}
guardia ^{F} sinistra

left tackle
tacle ^{M} izquierdo
bloqueur ^{M} gauche
linker Tackle ^{M}
attaccante ^{M} sinistro

center
central ^{M}
centre ^{M}
Centre ^{M}
centrale ^{M}

quarterback
quarterback ^{M}
quart-arrière ^{M}
Quarterback ^{M}
quarterback ^{M}

fullback
corredor ^{M} de poder ^{M}
centre arrière ^{M}
Fullback ^{M}
terzino ^{M}

right guard
guardia ^{M} derecho
garde ^{M} droit
rechter Guard ^{M}
guardia ^{F} destra

tailback
tailback ^{M}
demi ^{M} offensif
Tailback ^{M}
tailback ^{M}

right tackle
tacle ^{M} derecho
bloqueur ^{M} droit
rechter Tackle ^{M}
attaccante ^{M} destro

tight end
ala ^{M} cerrado
ailier ^{M} rapproché
Tight End ^{M}
tight end ^{M}

wide receiver
receptor ^{M} alejado
receveur ^{M} éloigné
Wide Receiver ^{M}
ricevitore ^{M} esterno

line of scrimmage
línea ^{F} de melé ^{M}
ligne ^{F} de mêlée ^{F}
Scrimmage ^{N}-Linie ^{F}
linea ^{F} di mischia ^{F}

goal
gol ^{M}
but ^{M}
Tor ^{N}
porta ^{F}

back judge
árbitro ^{M} de la defensa ^{F}
juge ^{M} de champ ^{M} arrière
Rückfeldschiedsrichter ^{M}
giudice ^{M} di campo ^{M}

goalpost
poste ^{M}
poteau ^{M} de but ^{M}
Torpfosten ^{M}
palo ^{M}

side judge
juez ^{M} externo
juge ^{M} de touche ^{F}
Linienrichter ^{M}
giudice ^{M} laterale

line judge
juez ^{M} de línea ^{F}
juge ^{M} de mêlée ^{F}
Linienrichter ^{M}
giudice ^{M} di linea ^{F}

referee
árbitro ^{M}
arbitre ^{M} en chef ^{M}
erster Schiedsrichter ^{M}
primo arbitro ^{M}

players' bench
banquillo ^{M} de jugadores ^{M}
banc ^{M} des joueurs ^{M}
Spielerbank ^{F}
panchina ^{F} dei giocatori ^{M}

umpire
juez ^{M}
arbitre ^{M}
zweiter Schiedsrichter ^{M}
secondo arbitro ^{M}

head linesman
juez ^{M} de línea ^{F}
juge ^{M} de ligne ^{F} en chef ^{M}
Hauptlinienrichter ^{M}
guardalinee ^{M}

SPORTS AND GAMES

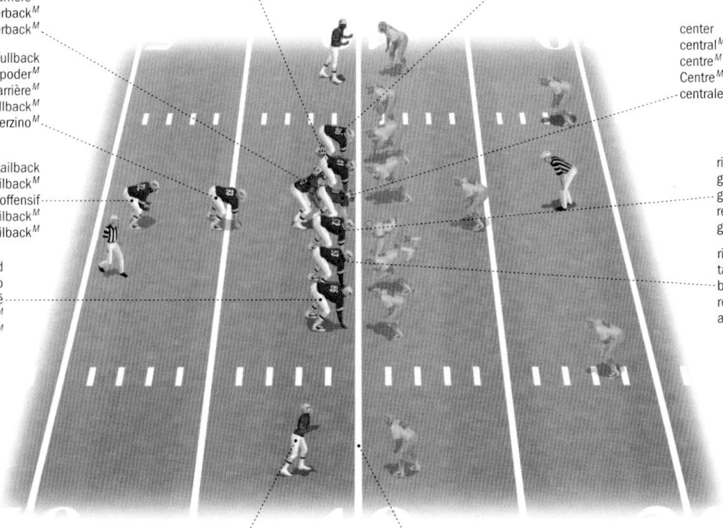

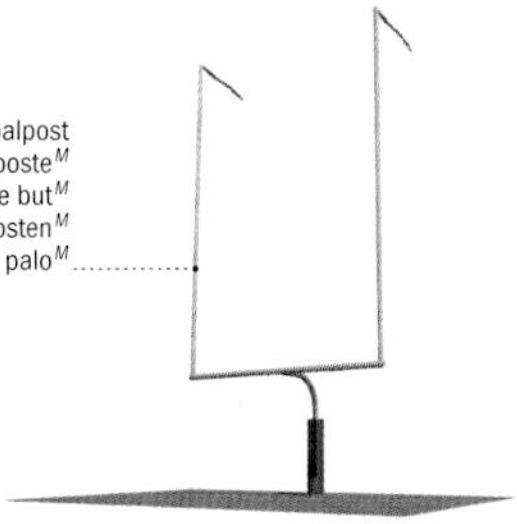

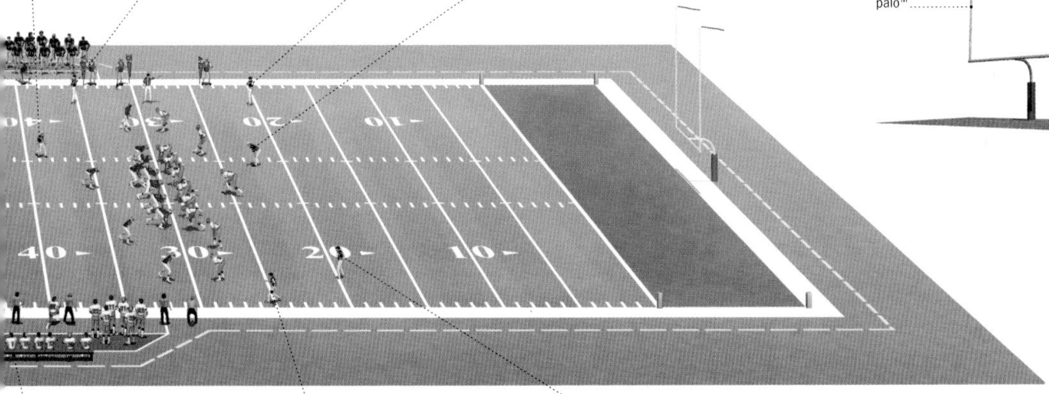

American football

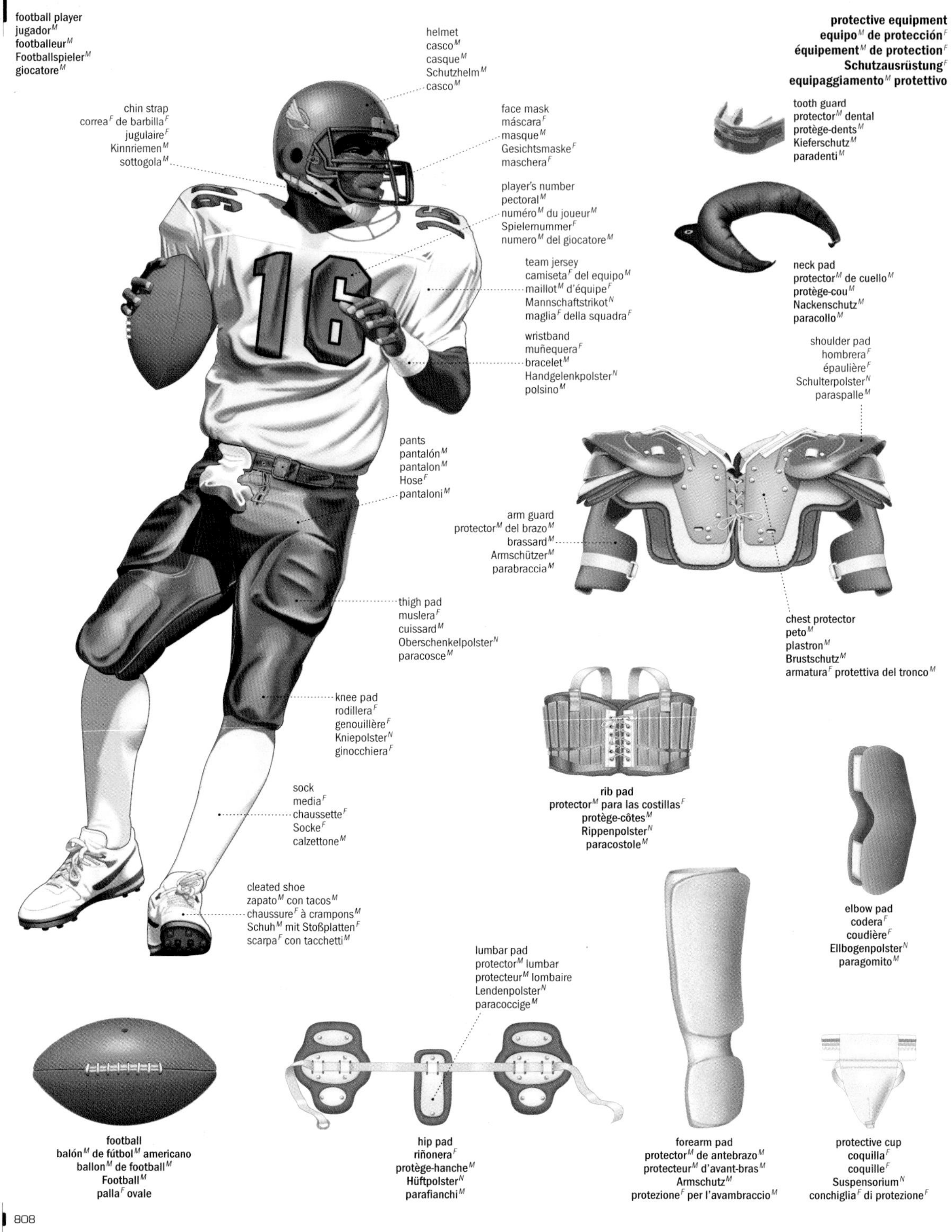

football player
jugador[M]
footballeur[M]
Footballspieler[M]
giocatore[M]

helmet
casco[M]
casque[M]
Schutzhelm[M]
casco[M]

chin strap
correa[F] de barbilla[F]
jugulaire[F]
Kinnriemen[M]
sottogola[M]

face mask
máscara[F]
masque[M]
Gesichtsmaske[F]
maschera[F]

player's number
pectoral[M]
numéro[M] du joueur[M]
Spielernummer[F]
numero[M] del giocatore[M]

team jersey
camiseta[F] del equipo[M]
maillot[M] d'équipe[F]
Mannschaftstrikot[N]
maglia[F] della squadra[F]

wristband
muñequera[F]
bracelet[M]
Handgelenkpolster[N]
polsino[M]

pants
pantalón[M]
pantalon[M]
Hose[F]
pantaloni[M]

arm guard
protector[M] del brazo[M]
brassard[M]
Armschützer[M]
parabraccia[M]

thigh pad
muslera[F]
cuissard[M]
Oberschenkelpolster[N]
paracosce[M]

knee pad
rodillera[F]
genouillère[F]
Kniepolster[N]
ginocchiera[F]

sock
media[F]
chaussette[F]
Socke[F]
calzettone[M]

cleated shoe
zapato[M] con tacos[M]
chaussure[F] à crampons[M]
Schuh[M] mit Stoßplatten[F]
scarpa[F] con tacchetti[M]

protective equipment
equipo[M] de protección[F]
équipement[M] de protection[F]
Schutzausrüstung[F]
equipaggiamento[M] protettivo

tooth guard
protector[M] dental
protège-dents[M]
Kieferschutz[M]
paradenti[M]

neck pad
protector[M] de cuello[M]
protège-cou[M]
Nackenschutz[M]
paracollo[M]

shoulder pad
hombrera[F]
épaulière[F]
Schulterpolster[N]
paraspalle[M]

chest protector
peto[M]
plastron[M]
Brustschutz[M]
armatura[F] protettiva del tronco[M]

rib pad
protector[M] para las costillas[F]
protège-côtes[M]
Rippenpolster[N]
paracostole[M]

elbow pad
codera[F]
coudière[F]
Ellbogenpolster[N]
paragomito[M]

lumbar pad
protector[M] lumbar
protecteur[M] lombaire
Lendenpolster[N]
paracoccige[M]

football
balón[M] de fútbol[M] americano
ballon[M] de football[M]
Football[M]
palla[F] ovale

hip pad
riñonera[F]
protège-hanche[M]
Hüftpolster[N]
parafianchi[M]

forearm pad
protector[M] de antebrazo[M]
protecteur[M] d'avant-bras[M]
Armschutz[M]
protezione[F] per l'avambraccio[M]

protective cup
coquilla[F]
coquille[F]
Suspensorium[N]
conchiglia[F] di protezione[F]

Canadian football

fútbol^M canadiense | football^M canadien | kanadischer Football^M | football^M canadese

playing field for Canadian football
campo^M de juego^M de fútbol^M canadiense
terrain^M de football^M canadien
Spielfeld^N für kanadischen Football^M
campo^M per football^M canadese

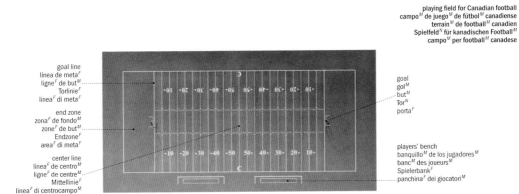

goal line
línea de meta^F
ligne^F de but^M
Torlinie^F
linea^F di meta^F

end zone
zona^F de fondo^M
zone^F de but^M
Endzone^F
area^F di meta^F

center line
línea^F de centro^M
ligne^F de centre^M
Mittellinie^F
linea^F di centrocampo^M

goal
gol^M
but^M
Tor^N
porta^F

players' bench
banquillo^M de los jugadores^M
banc^M des joueurs^M
Spielerbank^F
panchina^F dei giocatori^M

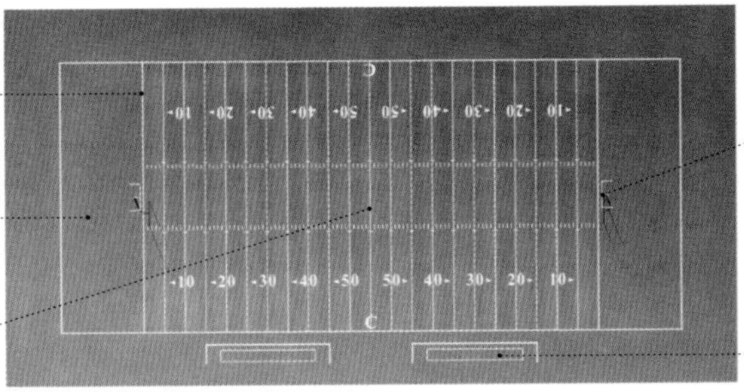

netball

netball^M | netball^M | Korbball^M | netball^M

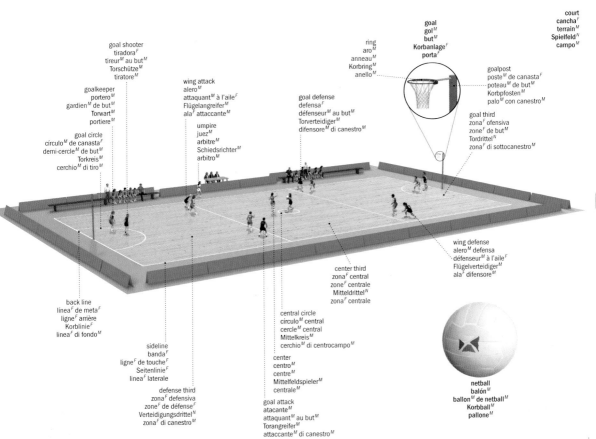

court
cancha^F
terrain^M
Spielfeld^N
campo^M

goal shooter
tiradora^F
tireur^M au but^M
Torschütze^M
tiratore^M

wing attack
alero^M
attaquant^M à l'aile^F
Flügelangreifer^M
ala^F attaccante^M

goal defense
defensa^F
défenseur^M au but^M
Torverteidiger^M
difensore^M di canestro^M

goalkeeper
portero^M
gardien^M de but^M
Torwart^M
portiere^M

umpire
juez^M
arbitre^M
Schiedsrichter^M
arbitro^M

goal circle
círculo^M de canasta^F
demi-cercle^M de but^M
Torkreis^M
cerchio^M di tiro^M

ring
aro^M
anneau^M
Korbring^M
anello^M

goal
gol^M
but^M
Korbanlage^F
porta^F

goalpost
poste^M de canasta^F
poteau^M de but^M
Korbpfosten^M
palo^M con canestro^M

goal third
zona^F ofensiva
zone^F de but^M
Tordrittel^N
zona^F di sottocanestro^M

wing defense
alero^M defensa
défenseur^M à l'aile^F
Flügelverteidiger^M
ala^F difensore^M

back line
línea^F de meta^F
ligne^F arrière
Korblinie^F
linea^F di fondo^M

center third
zona^F central
zone^F centrale
Mitteldrittel^N
zona^F centrale

central circle
círculo^M central
cercle^M central
Mittelkreis^M
cerchio^M di centrocampo^M

sideline
banda^F
ligne^F de touche^F
Seitenlinie^F
linea^F laterale

center
centro^M
centre^M
Mittelfeldspieler^M
centrale^M

defense third
zona^F defensiva
zone^F de défense^F
Verteidigungsdrittel^N
zona^F di canestro^M

goal attack
atacante^M
attaquant^M au but^M
Torangreifer^M
attaccante^M di canestro^M

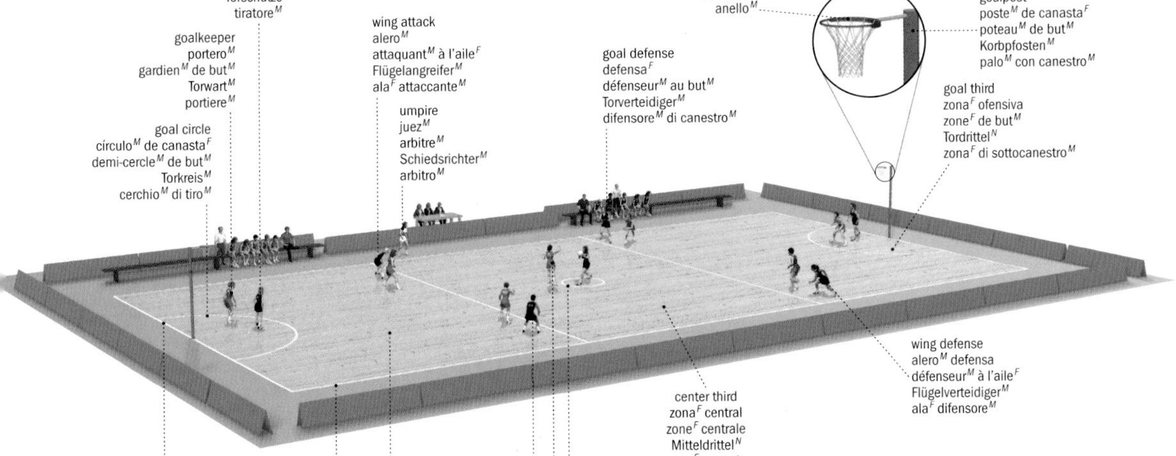

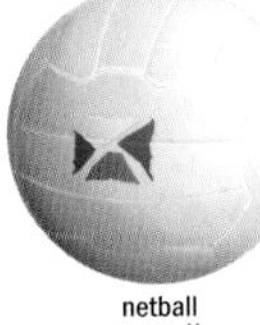

netball
balón^M
ballon^M de netball^M
Korbball^M
pallone^M

SPORTS AND GAMES

basketball

baloncesto[M] | basketball[M] | Basketballspiel[N] | pallacanestro[F]

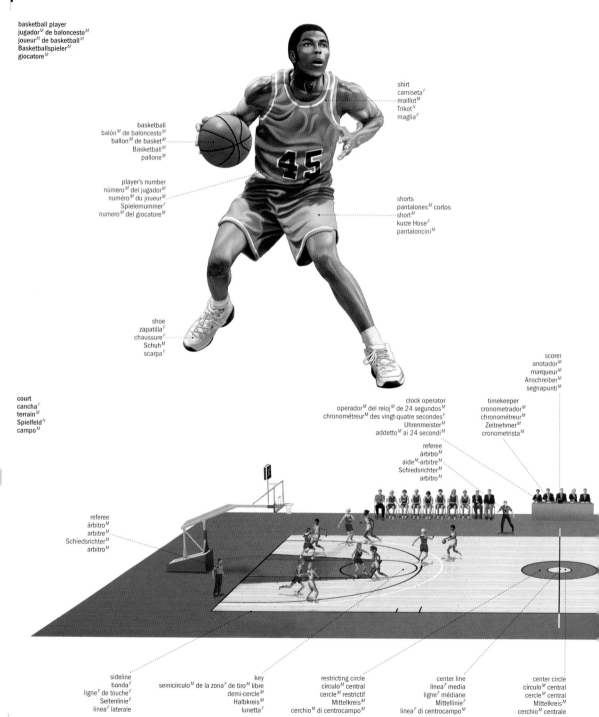

basketball player
jugador[M] de baloncesto[M]
joueur[M] de basketball[M]
Basketballspieler[M]
giocatore[M]

shirt
camiseta[F]
maillot[M]
Trikot[N]
maglia[F]

basketball
balón[M] de baloncesto[M]
ballon[M] de basket[M]
Basketball[M]
pallone[M]

player's number
número[M] del jugador[M]
numéro[M] du joueur[M]
Spielernummer[F]
numero[M] del giocatore[M]

shorts
pantalones[M] cortos
short[M]
kurze Hose[F]
pantaloncini[M]

shoe
zapatilla[F]
chaussure[F]
Schuh[M]
scarpa[F]

scorer
anotador[M]
marqueur[M]
Anschreiber[M]
segnapunti[M]

court
cancha[F]
terrain[M]
Spielfeld[N]
campo[M]

clock operator
operador[M] del reloj[M] de 24 segundos[M]
chronométreur[M] des vingt-quatre secondes[F]
Uhrenmeister[M]
addetto[M] ai 24 secondi[M]

timekeeper
cronometrador[M]
chronométreur[M]
Zeitnehmer[M]
cronometrista[M]

referee
árbitro[M]
aide[M]-arbitre[M]
Schiedsrichter[M]
arbitro[M]

referee
árbitro[M]
arbitre[M]
Schiedsrichter[M]
arbitro[M]

sideline
banda[F]
ligne[F] de touche[F]
Seitenlinie[F]
linea[F] laterale

key
semicírculo[M] de la zona[F] de tiro[M] libre
demi-cercle[M]
Halbkreis[M]
lunetta[F]

restricting circle
círculo[M] central
cercle[M] restrictif
Mittelkreis[M]
cerchio[M] di centrocampo[M]

center line
línea[F] media
ligne[F] médiane
Mittellinie[F]
linea[F] di centrocampo[M]

center circle
círculo[M] central
cercle[M] central
Mittelkreis[M]
cerchio[M] centrale

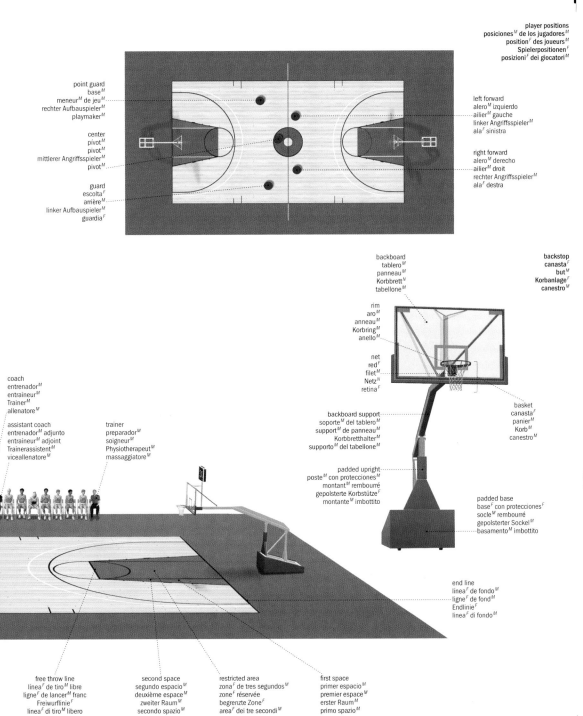

player positions
posiciones^M de los jugadores^M
position^F des joueurs^M
Spielerpositionen^F
posizioni^F dei giocatori^M

point guard
base^M
meneur^M de jeu^M
rechter Aufbauspieler^M
playmaker^M

center
pívot^M
pivot^M
mittlerer Angriffsspieler^M
pivot^M

guard
escolta^F
arrière^M
linker Aufbauspieler^M
guardia^F

left forward
alero^M izquierdo
ailier^M gauche
linker Angriffsspieler^M
ala^F sinistra

right forward
alero^M derecho
ailier^M droit
rechter Angriffsspieler^M
ala^F destra

backboard
tablero^M
panneau^M
Korbbrett^N
tabellone^M

backstop
canasta^F
but^M
Korbanlage^F
canestro^M

rim
aro^M
anneau^M
Korbring^M
anello^M

net
red^F
filet^M
Netz^N
retina^F

coach
entrenador^M
entraineur^M
Trainer^M
allenatore^M

assistant coach
entrenador^M adjunto
entraineur^M adjoint
Trainerassistent^M
viceallenatore^M

trainer
preparador^M
soigneur^M
Physiotherapeut^M
massaggiatore^M

basket
canasta^F
panier^M
Korb^M
canestro^M

backboard support
soporte^M del tablero^M
support^M de panneau^M
Korbbretthalter^M
supporto^M del tabellone^M

padded upright
poste^M con protecciones^M
montant^M rembourré
gepolsterte Korbstütze^F
montante^M imbottito

padded base
base^F con protecciones^F
socle^M rembourré
gepolsterter Sockel^M
basamento^M imbottito

end line
línea^F de fondo^M
ligne^F de fond^M
Endlinie^F
linea^F di fondo^M

free throw line
línea^F de tiro^M libre
ligne^F de lancer^M franc
Freiwurflinie^F
linea^F di tiro^M libero

second space
segundo espacio^M
deuxième espace^M
zweiter Raum^M
secondo spazio^M

restricted area
zona^F de tres segundos^M
zone^F réservée
begrenzte Zone^F
area^F dei tre secondi^M

first space
primer espacio^M
premier espace^M
erster Raum^M
primo spazio^M

SPORTS AND GAMES

volleyball

voleibol^M | volleyball^M | Volleyballspiel^N | pallavolo^F

court
cancha^F
terrain^M
Spielfeld^N
campo^M

left attacker
delantero^M izquierdo
attaquant^M gauche
linker Außenangreifer^M
attaccante^M sinistro

end line
línea^F de fondo^M
ligne^F de fond^M
Endlinie^F
linea^F di fondo^M

libero
libero^M
libero^M
Libero^M
libero^M

umpire
segundo árbitro^M
second arbitre^M
zweiter Schiedsrichter^M
secondo arbitro^M

white tape
banda^F blanca
bande^F blanche
Netzkante^F
nastro^M bianco

clear space
zona^F libre
zone^F libre
Freiraum^M
zona^F libera

scorer
anotador^M
marqueur^M
Anschreiber^M
segnapunti^M

left back
zaguero^M izquierdo
arrière^F gauche
linker Abwehrspieler^M
difensore^M sinistro

antenna
antena^F
antenne^F
Antenne^F
antenna^F

linesman
juez^M de línea^F
juge^M de ligne^F
Linienrichter^M
giudice^M di línea^F

players' bench
banquillo^M de jugadores^M
banc^M des joueurs^M
Spielerbank^F
panchina^F dei giocatori^M

sideline
banda^F
ligne^F de côté^M
Seitenlinie^F
línea^F laterale

back zone
zona^F de defensa^F
zone^F de défense^F
Verteidigungszone^F
zona^F di difesa^F

post
poste^M
poteau^M
Pfosten^M
palo^M

referee
primer árbitro^M
premier arbitre^M
erster Schiedsrichter^M
primo arbitro^M

center back
zaguero^M medio
arrière^M centre
mittlerer Abwehrspieler^M
difensore^M centrale^M

vertical side band
banda^F lateral de la red^F
bande^F verticale de côté^M
vertikales Seitenband^N
nastro^M verticale laterale

attack line
línea^F de ataque^M
ligne^F d'attaque^F
Angriffslinie^F
línea^F di attacco^M

net
red^F
filet^M
Netz^N
rete^F

right back
zaguero^M derecho
arrière^M droit
rechter Abwehrspieler^M
difensore^M destro

right attacker
delantero^M derecho
attaquant^M droit
rechter Außenangreifer^M
alzatore^M destro

center attacker
delantero^M medio
attaquant^M central
Mittelangreifer^M
attaccante^M centrale^M

attack zone
zona^F de ataque^M
zone^F d'attaque^F
Angriffszone^F
zona^F di attacco^M

volleyball
voleibol^M
ballon^M de volleyball^M
Volleyball^M
pallone^M

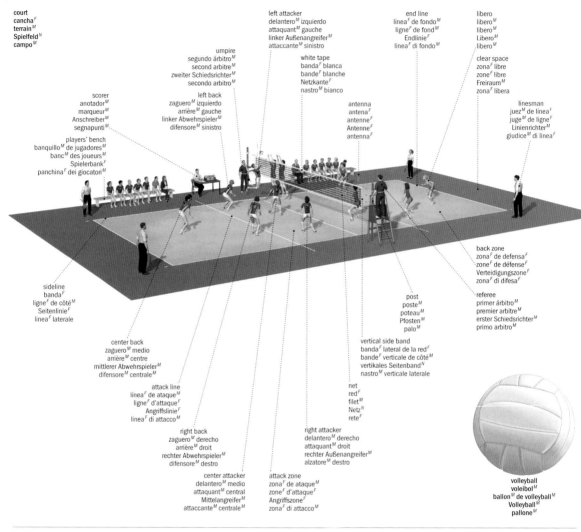

techniques
técnicas^F
techniques^F
Techniken^F
tecniche^F

dig
plancha^F
récupération^F
Hechtabwehr^F
tuffo^M

bump
rebote^M
manchette^F
baggern
bagher^M

serve
saque^M
service^M
Aufschlag^M
servizio^M

beach volleyball
voley^M playa^M
volleyball^M de plage^F
Beachvolleyball^M
beach volley^M

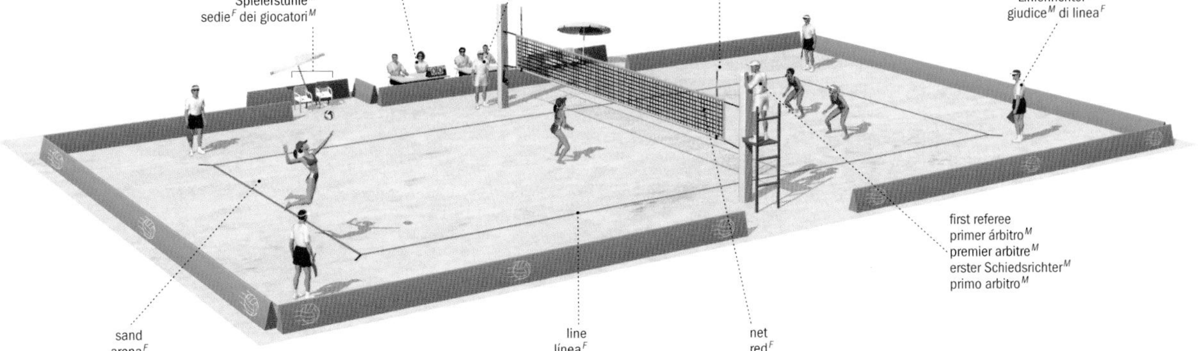

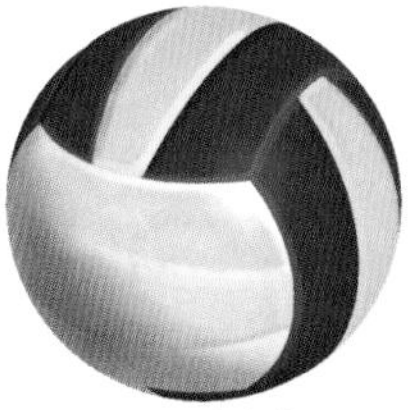

scorer
anotador^M
marqueur^M
Anschreiber^M
segnapunti^M

second referee
segundo árbitro^M
second arbitre^M
zweiter Schiedsrichter^M
secondo arbitro^M

free zone
zona^F libre
zone^F libre
Freiraum^M
zona^F libera

court
cancha^F
terrain^M
Spielfeld^N
campo^M

players' chairs
sillas^F de los jugadores^M
chaises^F des joueurs^M
Spielerstühle^M
sedie^F dei giocatori^M

line judge
juez^M de linea^F
juge^M de ligne^F
Linienrichter^M
giudice^M di linea^F

first referee
primer árbitro^M
premier arbitre^M
erster Schiedsrichter^M
primo arbitro^M

sand
arena^F
sable^M
Sand^M
sabbia^F

line
linea^F
ligne^F
Linie^F
linea^F

net
red^F
filet^M
Netz^N
rete^F

beach volleyball
voley^M playa^M
ballon^M de volleyball^M de plage^F
Beachvolleyball^M
pallone^M

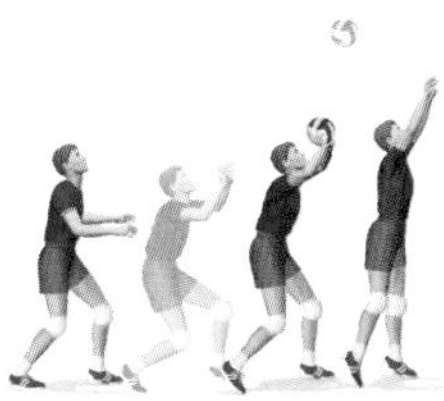

tip
toque^M
touche^F
pritschen
palleggio^M

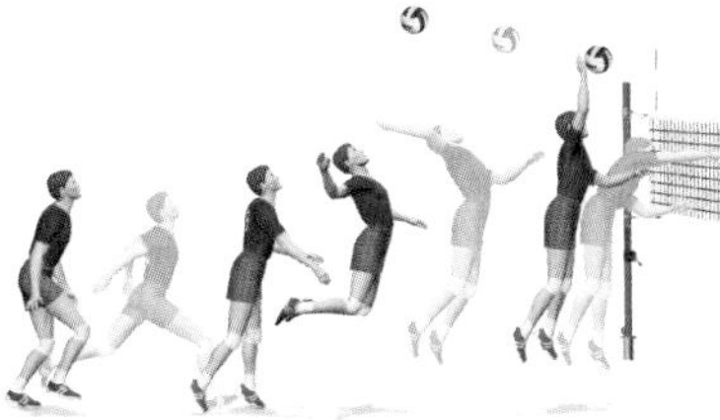

spike
remate^M
smash^M
Schmetterball^M
schiacciata^F

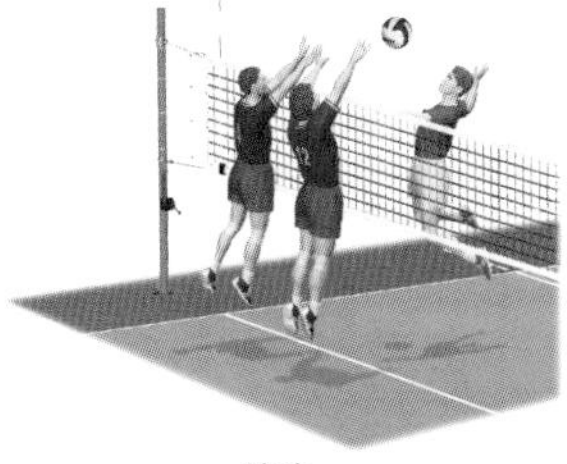

block
tapón^M
contre^M
blocken
muro^M

handball

balonmano[M] | handball[M] | Handball[M] | pallamano[F]

player positions
posición[F] de los jugadores[F]
position[F] des joueurs[M]
Spielerpositionen[F]
posizioni[F] dei giocatori[M]

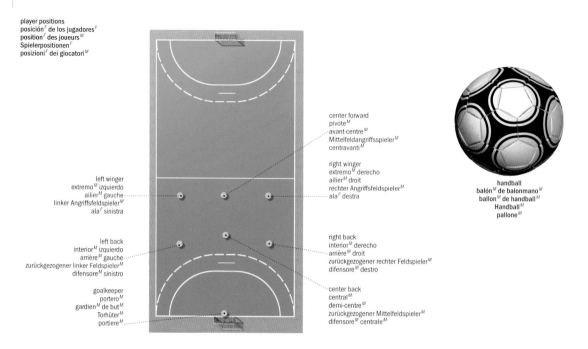

center forward
pivote[M]
avant-centre[M]
Mittelfeldangriffsspieler[M]
centravanti[M]

right winger
extremo[M] derecho
ailier[M] droit
rechter Angriffsfeldspieler[M]
ala[F] destra

left winger
extremo[M] izquierdo
ailier[M] gauche
linker Angriffsfeldspieler[M]
ala[F] sinistra

left back
interior[M] izquierdo
arrière[M] gauche
zurückgezogener linker Feldspieler[M]
defensore[M] sinistro

right back
interior[M] derecho
arrière[M] droit
zurückgezogener rechter Feldspieler[M]
defensore[M] destro

goalkeeper
portero[M]
gardien[M] de but[M]
Torhüter[M]
portiere[M]

center back
central[M]
demi-centre[M]
zurückgezogener Mittelfeldspieler[M]
difensore[M] centrale[M]

handball
balón[M] de balonmano[M]
ballon[M] de handball[M]
Handball[M]
pallone[M]

court
cancha[F]
terrain[M]
Spielfeld[N]
campo[M]

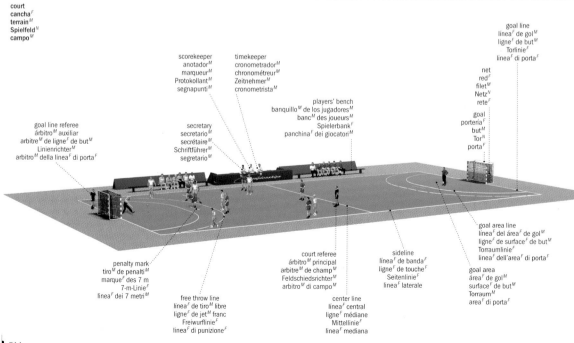

scorekeeper
anotador[M]
marqueur[M]
Protokollant[M]
segnapunti[M]

timekeeper
cronometrador[M]
chronométreur[M]
Zeitnehmer[M]
cronometrista[M]

goal line
línea[F] de gol[M]
ligne[F] de but[M]
Torlinie[F]
linea[F] di porta[F]

net
red[F]
filet[M]
Netz[N]
rete[F]

players' bench
banquillo[M] de los jugadores[M]
banc[M] des joueurs[M]
Spielerbank[F]
panchina[F] dei giocatori[M]

goal
portería[F]
but[M]
Tor[N]
porta[F]

goal line referee
árbitro[M] auxiliar
arbitre[M] de ligne[F] de but[M]
Linienrichter[M]
arbitro[M] della linea[F] di porta[F]

secretary
secretario[M]
secrétaire[M]
Schriftführer[M]
segretario[M]

goal area line
línea[F] del área[F] de gol[M]
ligne[F] de surface[F] de but[M]
Torraumlinie[F]
linea[F] dell'area[F] di porta[F]

goal area
área[F] de gol[M]
surface[F] de but[M]
Torraum[M]
area[F] di porta[F]

penalty mark
tiro[M] de penalti[M]
marque[F] des 7 m
7-m-Linie[F]
linea[F] dei 7 metri[M]

free throw line
línea[F] de tiro[M] libre
ligne[F] de jet[M] franc
Freiwurflinie[F]
linea[F] di punizione[F]

court referee
árbitro[M] principal
arbitre[M] de champ[M]
Feldschiedsrichter[M]
arbitro[M] di campo[M]

center line
línea[F] central
ligne[F] médiane
Mittellinie[F]
linea[F] mediana

sideline
línea[F] de banda[F]
ligne[F] de touche[F]
Seitenlinie[F]
linea[F] laterale

table tennis

tenis^M de mesa^F | tennis^M de table^F | Tischtennis^N | tennis^M da tavolo^M

white tape
cinta^F blanca
ruban^M blanc
weißes Band^N
nastro^M bianco

mesh
malla^F
maille^F
Maschen^F
maglia^F

table
mesa^F
table^F
Tischtennisplatte^F
tavolo^M

sideline
línea^F de banda^F
ligne^F latérale
Seitenlinie^F
línea^F laterale

net
red^F
filet^M
Netz^N
rete^F

upper edge
moldura^F superior
arête^F supérieure
Oberkante^F
bordo^M superiore

center line
línea^F divisoria central
ligne^F centrale
Mittellinie^F
línea^F centrale

leg
pata^F de la mesa^F
pied^M
Bein^N
gamba^F

end line
línea^F de fondo
ligne^F de fond^M
Endlinie^F
línea^F di fondo^M

playing surface
superficie^F de juego^M
surface^F de jeu^M
Spielfläche^F
superficie^F di gioco^M

net support
soporte^M de la red^F
support^M
Netzhalter^M
supporto^M della rete^F

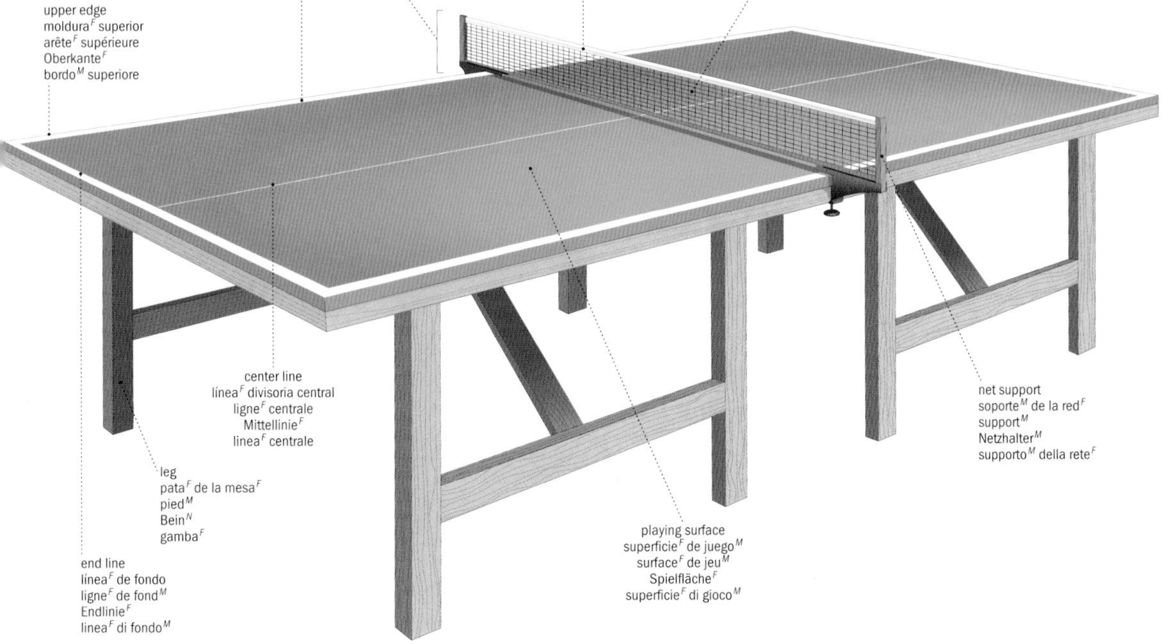

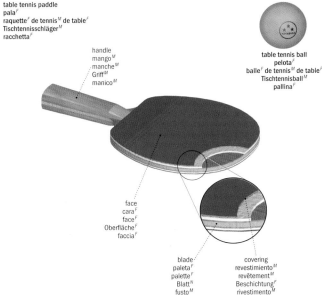

table tennis paddle
pala^F
raquette^F de tennis^M de table^F
Tischtennisschläger^M
racchetta^F

handle
mango^M
manche^M
Griff^M
manico^M

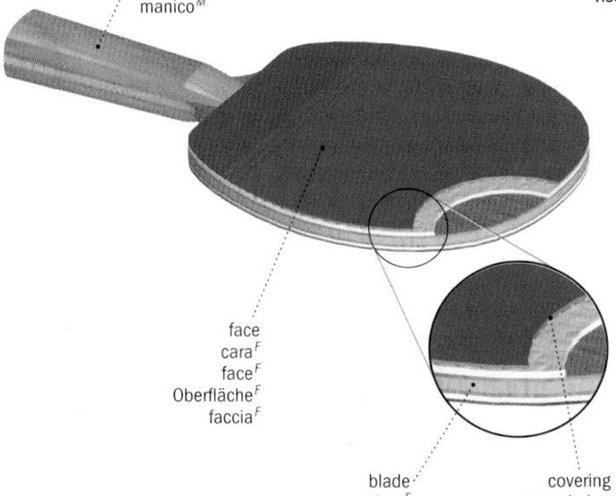

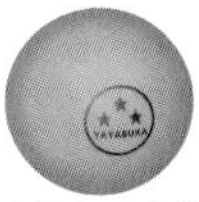

table tennis ball
pelota^F
balle^F de tennis^M de table^F
Tischtennisball^M
pallina^F

face
cara^F
face^F
Oberfläche^F
faccia^F

blade
paleta^F
palette^F
Blatt^N
fusto^M

covering
revestimiento^M
revêtement^M
Beschichtung^F
rivestimento^M

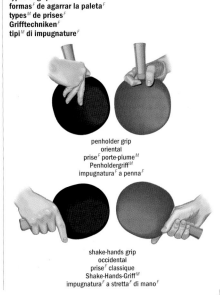

types of grips
formas^F de agarrar la paleta^F
types^M de prises^F
Grifftechniken^F
tipi^M di impugnature^F

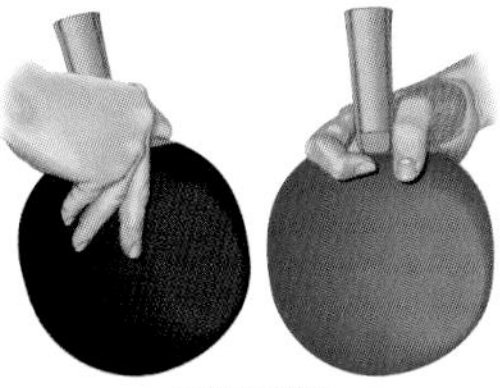

penholder grip
oriental
prise^F porte-plume^M
Penholdergriff^M
impugnatura^F a penna^F

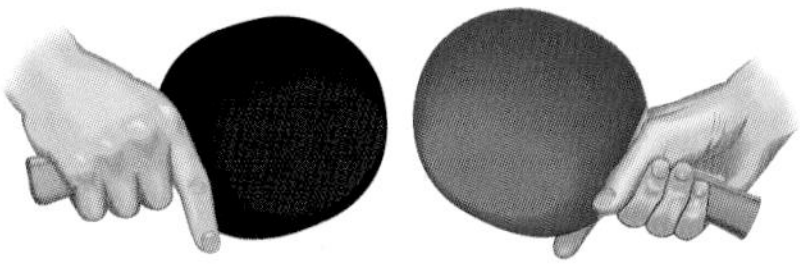

shake-hands grip
occidental
prise^F classique
Shake-Hands-Griff^M
impugnatura^F a stretta^F di mano^F

SPORTS AND GAMES

badminton

bádminton^M | badminton^M | Badminton^N | gioco^M del volano^M

court
cancha^F
terrain^M
Badmintonplatz^M
campo^M

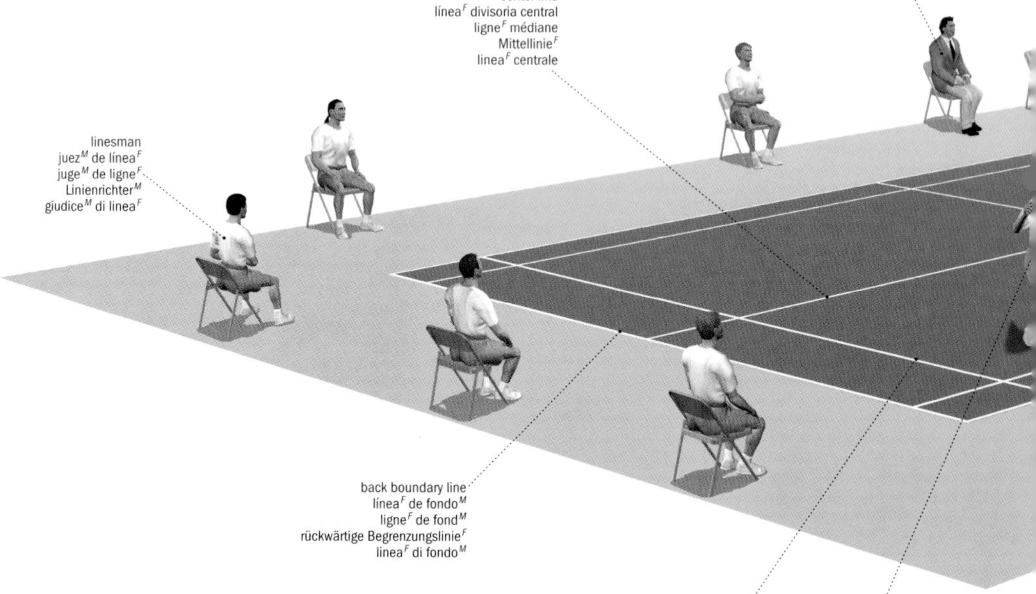

service judge
juez^M de servicio^M
juge^M de service^M
Aufschlagrichter^M
giudice^M di servizio^M

center line
línea^F divisoria central
ligne^F médiane
Mittellinie^F
linea^F centrale

linesman
juez^M de linea^F
juge^M de ligne^F
Linienrichter^M
giudice^M di linea^F

back boundary line
línea^F de fondo^M
ligne^F de fond^M
rückwärtige Begrenzungslinie^F
linea^F di fondo^M

long service line
línea^F de servicio^M largo
ligne^F de service^M long
hintere Aufschlaglinie^F für das Doppelspiel^N
linea^F di servizio^M lungo

server
jugador^M de saque^M
serveur^M
Aufgeber^M
battitore^M

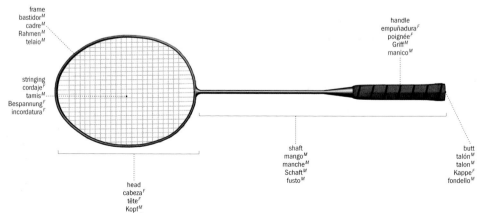

badminton racket
raqueta^F de bádminton^M
raquette^F de badminton^M
Badmintonschläger^M
racchetta^F

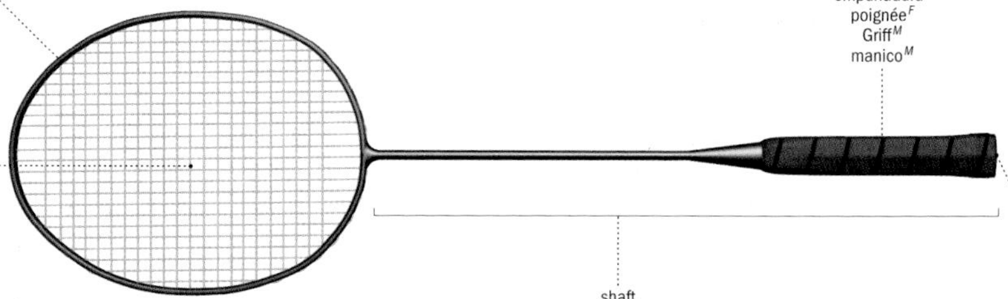

frame
bastidor^M
cadre^M
Rahmen^M
telaio^M

handle
empuñadura^F
poignée^F
Griff^M
manico^M

stringing
cordaje^M
tamis^M
Bespannung^F
incordatura^F

shaft
mango^M
manche^M
Schaft^M
fusto^M

butt
talón^M
talon^M
Kappe^F
fondello^M

head
cabeza^F
tête^F
Kopf^M
testa^F

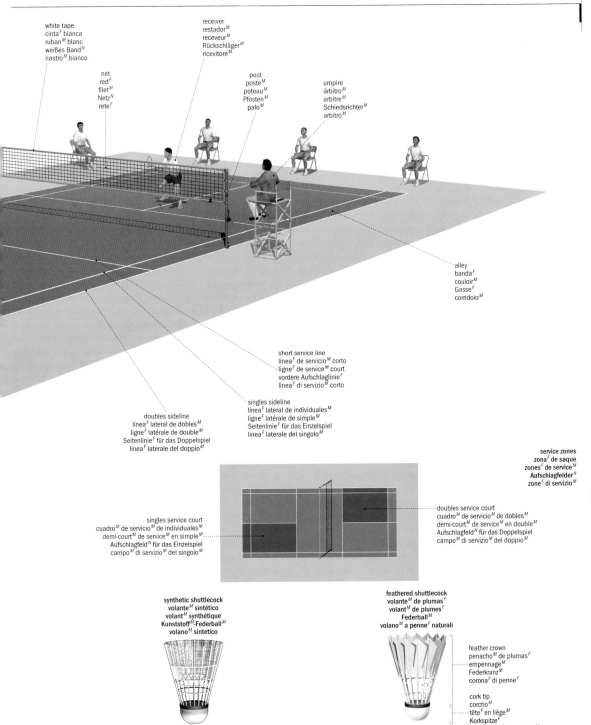

white tape
cinta^F blanca
ruban^M blanc
weißes Band^N
nastro^M bianco

receiver
restador^M
receveur^M
Rückschläger^M
ricevitore^M

net
red^F
filet^M
Netz^N
rete^F

post
poste^M
poteau^M
Pfosten^M
palo^M

umpire
árbitro^M
arbitre^M
Schiedsrichter^M
arbitro^M

alley
banda^F
couloir^M
Gasse^F
corridoio^M

short service line
línea^F de servicio^M corto
ligne^F de service^M court
vordere Aufschlaglinie^F
linea^F di servizio^M corto

singles sideline
línea^F lateral de individuales^M
ligne^F latérale de simple^M
Seitenlinie^F für das Einzelspiel
linea^F laterale del singolo^M

doubles sideline
línea^F lateral de dobles^M
ligne^F latérale de double^M
Seitenlinie^F für das Doppelspiel
linea^F laterale del doppio^M

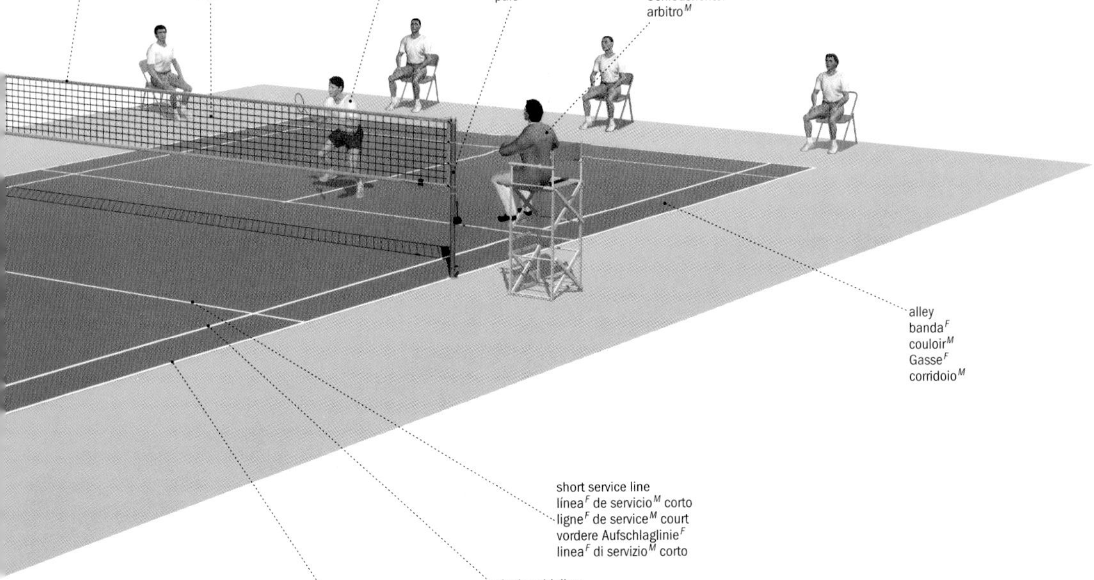

service zones
zona^F de saque
zones^F de service^M
Aufschlagfelder^N
zone^F di servizio^M

singles service court
cuadro^M de servicio^M de individuales^M
demi-court^M de service^M en simple^M
Aufschlagfeld^N für das Einzelspiel
campo^M di servizio^M del singolo^M

doubles service court
cuadro^M de servicio^M de dobles^M
demi-court^M de service^M en double^M
Aufschlagfeld^N für das Doppelspiel
campo^M di servizio^M del doppio^M

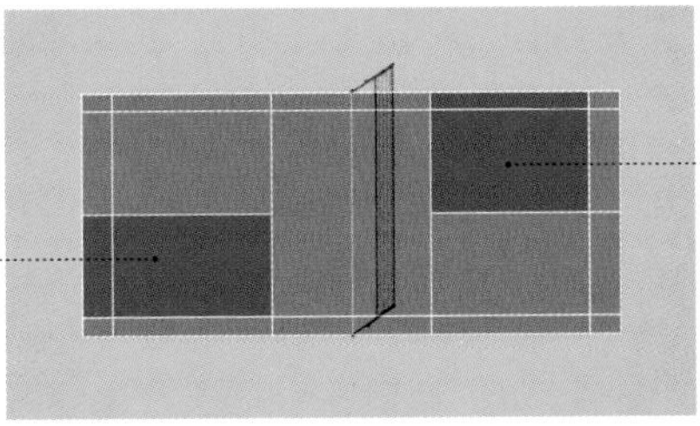

synthetic shuttlecock
volante^M sintético
volant^M synthétique
Kunststoff^M-Federball^M
volano^M sintetico

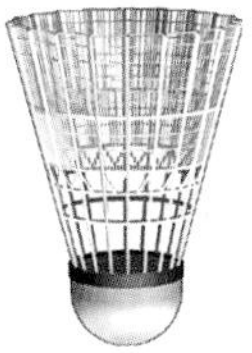

feathered shuttlecock
volante^M de plumas^F
volant^M de plumes^F
Federball^M
volano^M a penne^F naturali

feather crown
penacho^M de plumas^F
empennage^M
Federkranz^M
corona^F di penne^F

cork tip
corcho^M
tête^F en liège^M
Korkspitze^F
mezza sfera^F di sughero^M

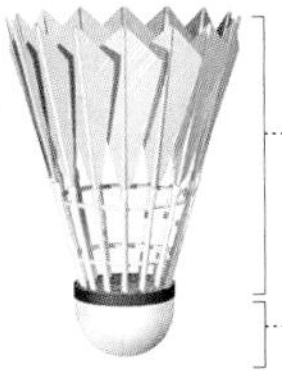

racquetball

raquetball^M | racquetball^M | Racquetballspiel^N | racquetball^M

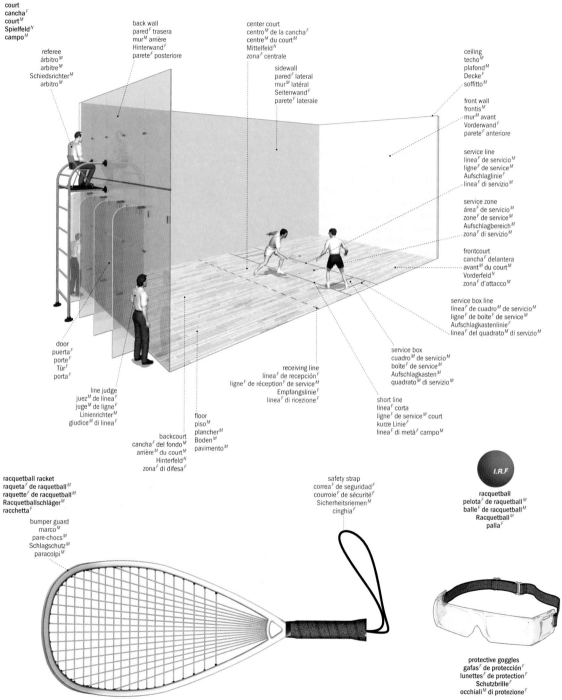

court
cancha^F
court^M
Spielfeld^N
campo^M

back wall
pared^F trasera
mur^M arrière
Hinterwand^F
parete^F posteriore

center court
centro^M de la cancha^F
centre^M du court^M
Mittelfeld^N
zona^F centrale

referee
árbitro^M
arbitre^M
Schiedsrichter^M
arbitro^M

sidewall
pared^F lateral
mur^M latéral
Seitenwand^F
parete^F laterale

ceiling
techo^M
plafond^M
Decke^F
soffitto^M

front wall
frontis^M
mur^M avant
Vorderwand^F
parete^F anteriore

service line
línea^F de servicio^M
ligne^F de service^M
Aufschlaglinie^F
linea^F di servizio^M

service zone
área^F de servicio^M
zone^F de service^M
Aufschlagbereich^M
zona^F di servizio^M

frontcourt
cancha^F delantera
avant^M du court^M
Vorderfeld^N
zona^F d'attacco^M

service box line
línea^F de cuadro^F de servicio^M
ligne^F de boîte^F de service^M
Aufschlagkastenlinie^F
linea^F del quadrato^M di servizio^M

door
puerta^F
porte^F
Tür^F
porta^F

service box
cuadro^M de servicio^M
boîte^F de service^M
Aufschlagkasten^M
quadrato^M di servizio^M

line judge
juez^M de línea^F
juge^M de ligne^F
Linienrichter^M
giudice^M di linea^F

receiving line
línea^F de recepción^F
ligne^F de réception^F de service^M
Empfangslinie^F
linea^F di ricezione^F

short line
línea^F corta
ligne^F de service^M court
kurze Linie^F
linea^F di metà^F campo^M

floor
piso^M
plancher^M
Boden^M
pavimento^M

backcourt
cancha^F del fondo^M
arrière^M du court^M
Hinterfeld^N
zona^F di difesa^F

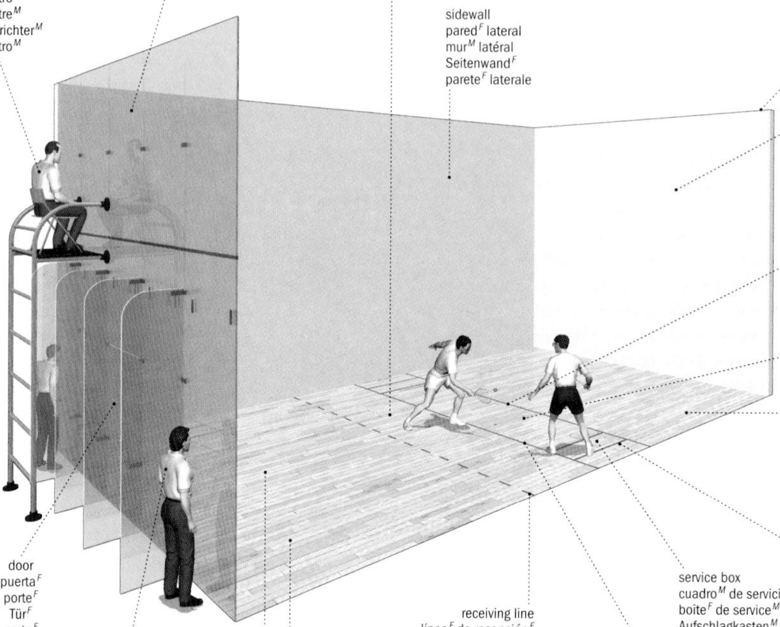

racquetball racket
raqueta^F de raquetball^M
raquette^F de racquetball^M
Racquetballschläger^M
racchetta^F

bumper guard
marco^M
pare-chocs^M
Schlagschutz^M
paracolpi^M

safety strap
correa^F de seguridad^F
courroie^F de sécurité^F
Sicherheitsriemen^M
cinghia^F

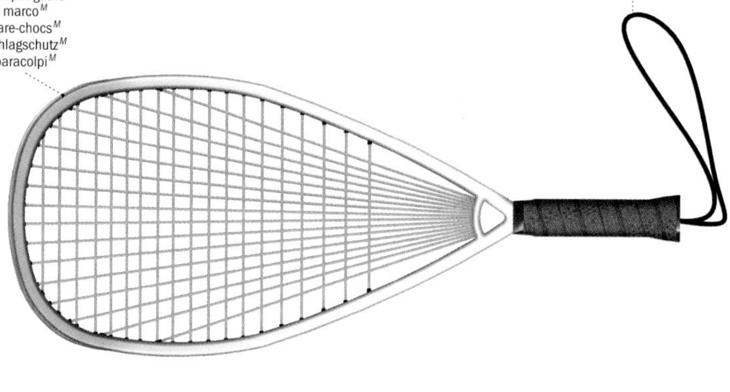

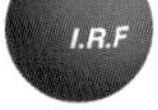

racquetball
pelota^F de raquetball^M
balle^F de racquetball^M
Racquetball^M
palla^F

I.R.F

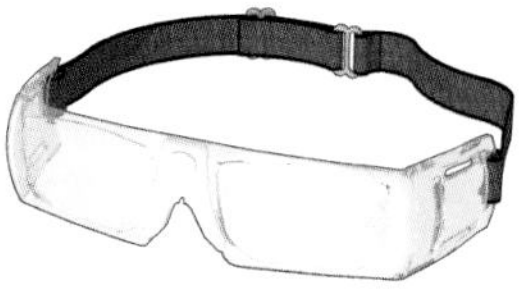

protective goggles
gafas^F de protección^F
lunettes^F de protection^F
Schutzbrille^F
occhiali^M di protezione^F

squash

squash^M | squash^M | Squash^N | squash^M

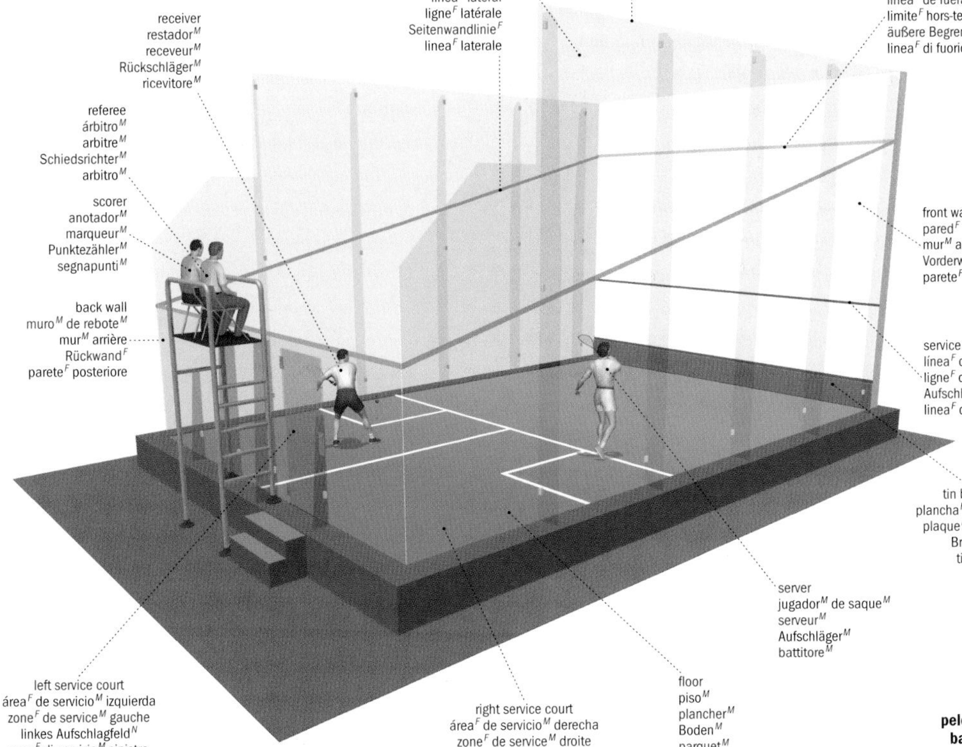

sidewall
pared^F lateral
mur^M latéral
Seitenwand^F
parete^F laterale

ceiling
techo^M
plafond^M
Decke^F
soffitto^M

court
cancha^F
court^M
Spielfeld^N
campo^M

sidewall line
línea^F lateral
ligne^F latérale
Seitenwandlinie^F
linea^F laterale

outer boundary line
línea^F de fuera^F
limite^F hors-terrain
äußere Begrenzungslinie^F
linea^F di fuoricampo^M

receiver
restador^M
receveur^M
Rückschläger^M
ricevitore^M

referee
árbitro^M
arbitre^M
Schiedsrichter^M
arbitro^M

scorer
anotador^M
marqueur^M
Punktezähler^M
segnapunti^M

front wall
pared^F frontal
mur^M avant
Vorderwand^F
parete^F frontale

back wall
muro^M de rebote^M
mur^M arrière
Rückwand^F
parete^F posteriore

service line
línea^F de servicio^M
ligne^F de service^M
Aufschlaglinie^F
linea^F di servizio^M

tin board
plancha^F de chapa
plaque^F de tôle^F
Brett^N
tin^M

server
jugador^M de saque^M
serveur^M
Aufschläger^M
battitore^M

floor
piso^M
plancher^M
Boden^M
parquet^M

left service court
área^F de servicio^M izquierda
zone^F de service^M gauche
linkes Aufschlagfeld^N
area^F di servizio^M sinistro

right service court
área^F de servicio^M derecha
zone^F de service^M droite
rechtes Aufschlagfeld^N
area^F di servizio^M destro

squash balls
pelotas^F de squash^M
balles^F de squash^M
Squashbälle^M
palle^F

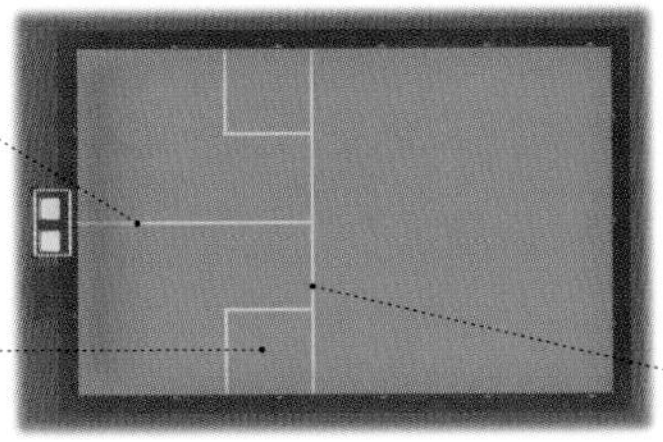

half court line
línea^F divisoria central
ligne^F de demi-court^F
Mittellinie^F
linea^F di metà^F campo^M

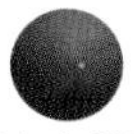

training (soft) ball
pelota^F de entrenamiento^M
balle^F d'entraînement^M
Trainingsball^M
palla^F da allenamento^M

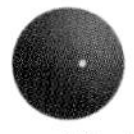

tournament (hard) ball
pelota^F de torneo^M
balle^F de tournoi^M
Turnierball^M
palla^F da gara^F

service box
cuadro^M de servicio^M
carré^M de service^M
Angaberaum^M
quadrato^M di servizio^M

short line
línea^F de servicio^M
ligne^F de service^M court
Shortline^F
linea^F corta

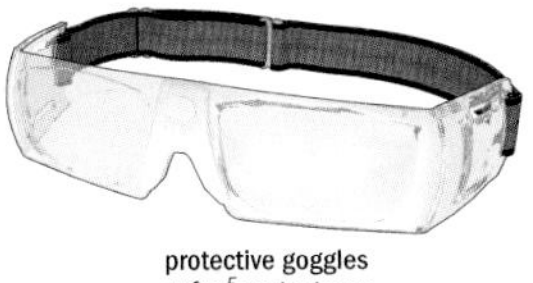

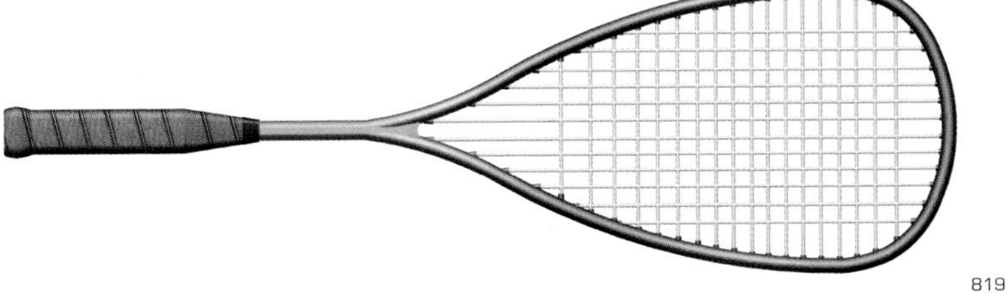

squash racket
raqueta^F de squash^M
raquette^F de squash^M
Squashschläger^M
racchetta^F

protective goggles
gafas^F protectoras
lunettes^F de protection^F
Schutzbrille^F
occhiali^M di protezione^F

tennis

tenis^M | tennis^M | Tennis^N | tennis^M

court
cancha^F
court^M
Tennisplatz^M
campo^M

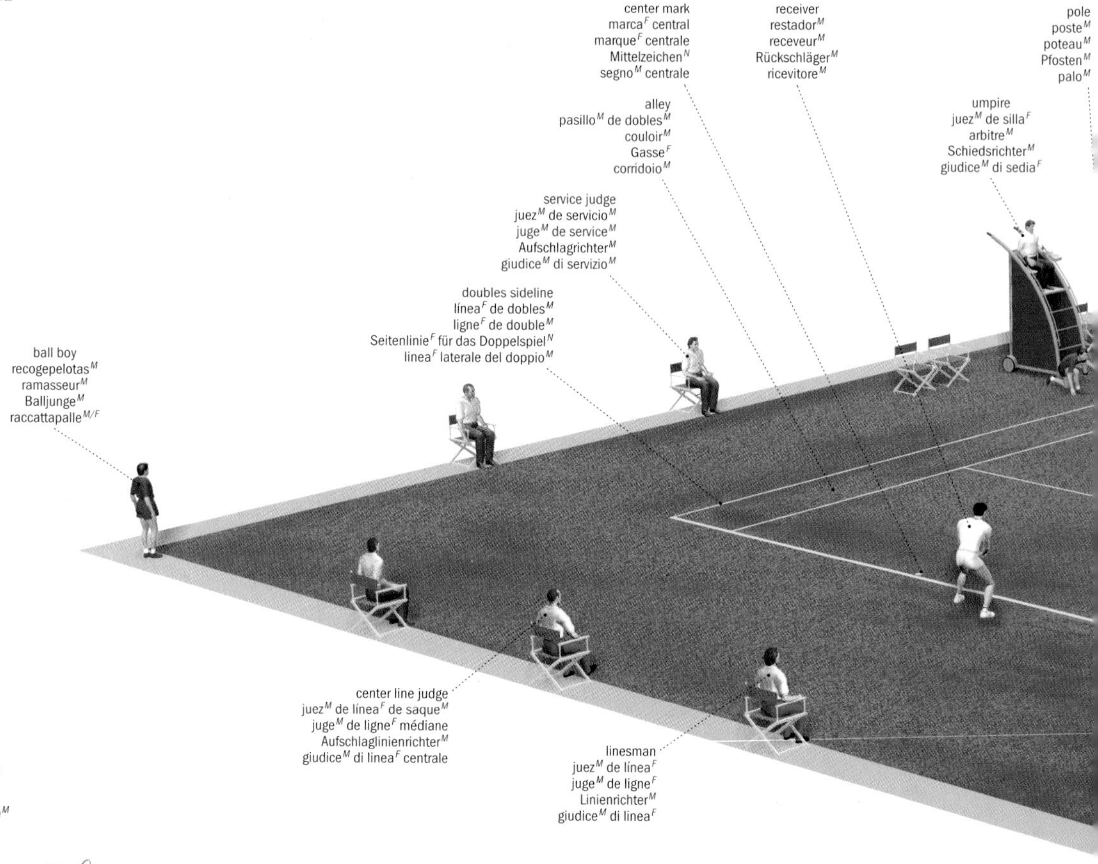

center mark
marca^F central
marque^F centrale
Mittelzeichen^N
segno^M centrale

receiver
restador^M
receveur^M
Rückschläger^M
ricevitore^M

pole
poste^M
poteau^M
Pfosten^M
palo^M

alley
pasillo^M de dobles^M
couloir^M
Gasse^F
corridoio^M

umpire
juez^M de silla^F
arbitre^M
Schiedsrichter^M
giudice^M di sedia^F

service judge
juez^M de servicio^M
juge^M de service^M
Aufschlagrichter^M
giudice^M di servizio^M

doubles sideline
linea^F de dobles^M
ligne^F de double^M
Seitenlinie^F für das Doppelspiel^N
linea^F laterale del doppio^M

ball boy
recogepelotas^M
ramasseur^M
Balljunge^M
raccattapalle^{M/F}

center line judge
juez^M de línea^F de saque^M
juge^M de ligne^F médiane
Aufschlaglinienrichter^M
giudice^M di linea^F centrale

linesman
juez^M de línea^F
juge^M de ligne^F
Linienrichter^M
giudice^M di linea^F

strokes
golpes^M
coups^M
Schläge^M
colpi^M

SPORTS AND GAMES

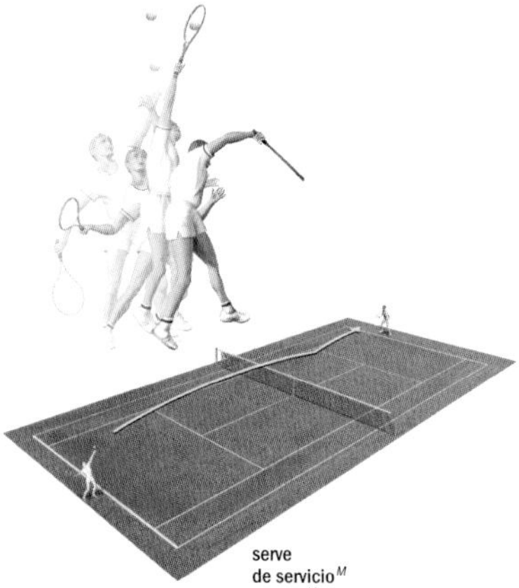

serve
de servicio^M
service^M
Aufschlag^M
servizio^M

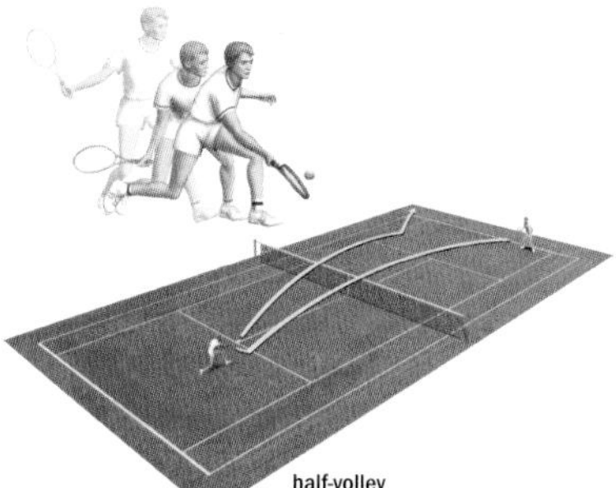

half-volley
media volea^F
demi-volée^F
Halbvolleyball^M
demi-volée^F

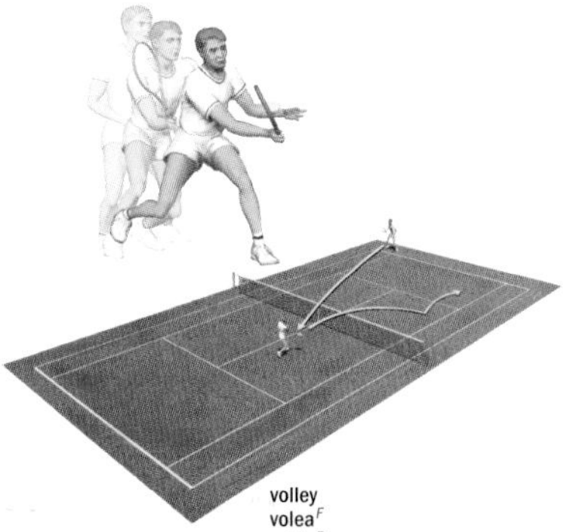

volley
volea^F
volée^F
Flugball^M
volée^F

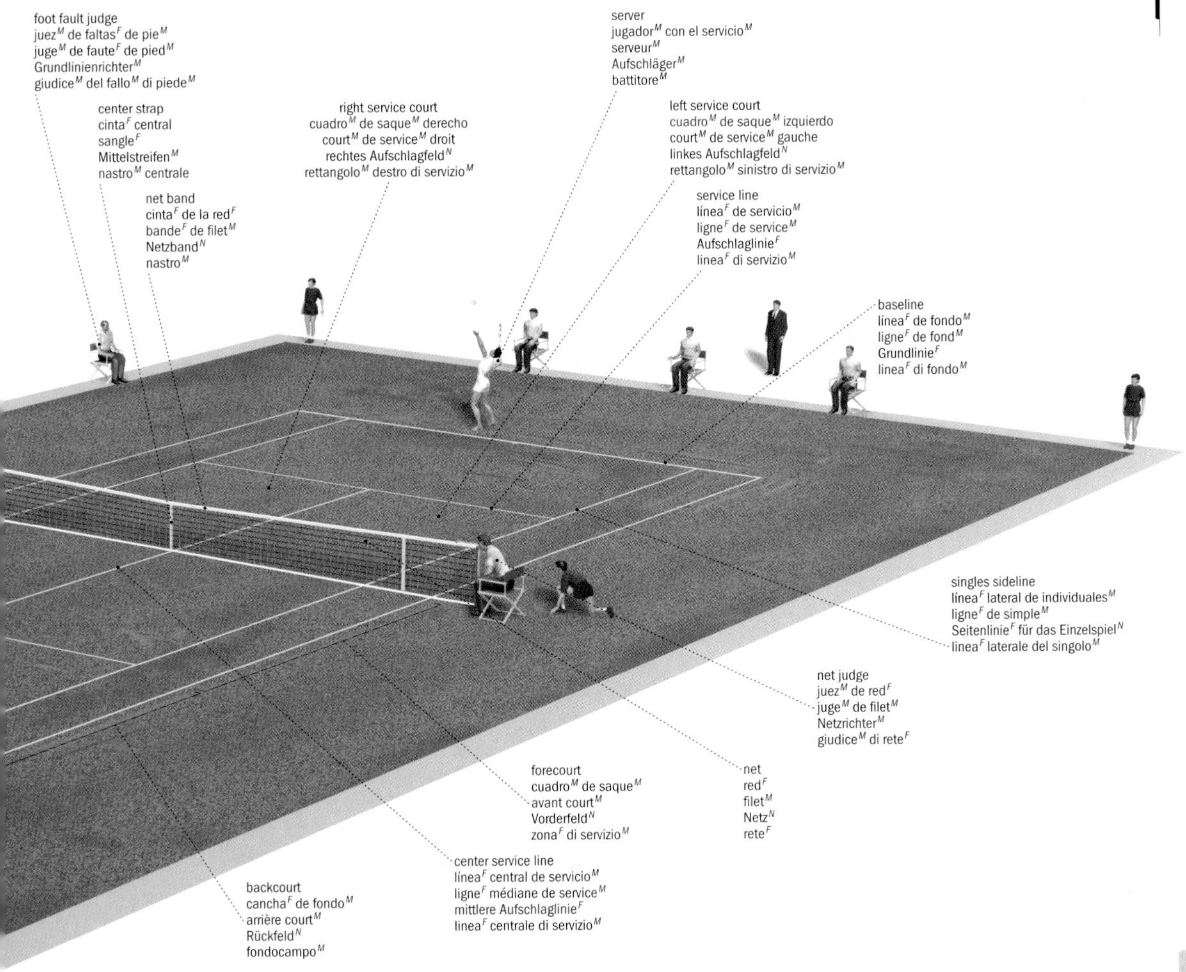

foot fault judge
juez^M de faltas^F de pie^M
juge^M de faute^F de pied^M
Grundlinienrichter^M
giudice^M del fallo^M di piede^M

center strap
cinta^F central
sangle^F
Mittelstreifen^M
nastro^M centrale

net band
cinta^F de la red^F
bande^F de filet^M
Netzband^N
nastro^M

right service court
cuadro^M de saque^M derecho
court^M de service^M droit
rechtes Aufschlagfeld^N
rettangolo^M destro di servizio^M

server
jugador^M con el servicio^M
serveur^M
Aufschläger^M
battitore^M

left service court
cuadro^M de saque^M izquierdo
court^M de service^M gauche
linkes Aufschlagfeld^N
rettangolo^M sinistro di servizio^M

service line
línea^F de servicio^M
ligne^F de service^M
Aufschlaglinie^F
linea^F di servizio^M

baseline
línea^F de fondo^M
ligne^F de fond^M
Grundlinie^F
linea^F di fondo^M

singles sideline
línea^F lateral de individuales^M
ligne^F de simple^M
Seitenlinie^F für das Einzelspiel^N
linea^F laterale del singolo^M

net judge
juez^M de red^F
juge^M de filet^M
Netzrichter^M
giudice^M di rete^F

forecourt
cuadro^M de saque^M
avant court^M
Vorderfeld^N
zona^F di servizio^M

net
red^F
filet^M
Netz^N
rete^F

center service line
línea^F central de servicio^M
ligne^F médiane de service^M
mittlere Aufschlaglinie^F
linea^F centrale di servizio^M

backcourt
cancha^F de fondo^M
arrière court^M
Rückfeld^N
fondocampo^M

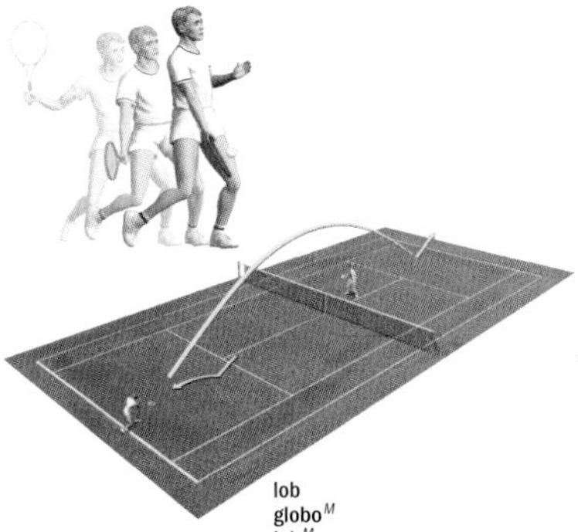

lob
globo^M
lob^M
Lob^M
pallonetto^M

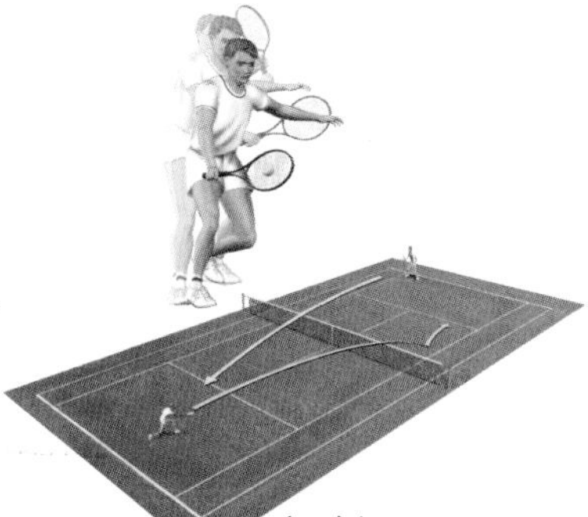

drop shot
dejada^F
amorti^M
Stoppball^M
smorzata^F

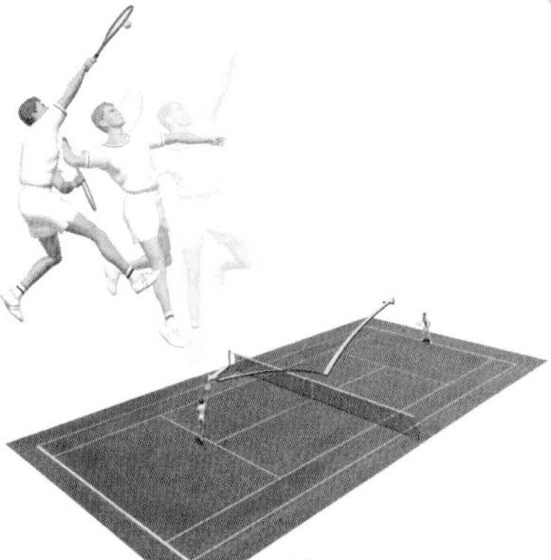

smash
smash^M
smash^M
Schmetterball^M
schiacciata

tennis

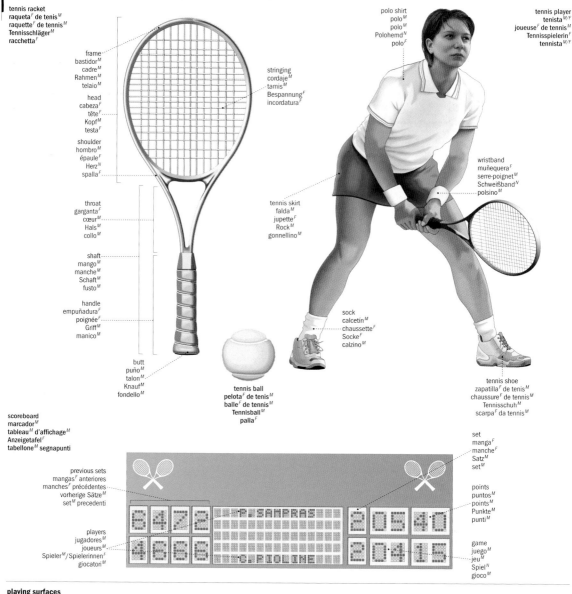

tennis racket
raqueta^F de tenis^M
raquette^F de tennis^M
Tennisschläger^M
racchetta^F

frame
bastidor^M
cadre^M
Rahmen^M
telaio^M

head
cabeza^F
tête^F
Kopf^M
testa^F

shoulder
hombro^M
épaule^F
Herz^N
spalla^F

throat
garganta^F
cœur^M
Hals^M
collo^M

shaft
mango^M
manche^M
Schaft^M
fusto^M

handle
empuñadura^F
poignée^F
Griff^M
manico^M

butt
puño^M
talon^M
Knauf^M
fondello^M

stringing
cordaje^M
tamis^M
Bespannung^F
incordatura^F

polo shirt
polo^M
polo^M
Polohemd^N
polo^F

tennis player
tenista^{M/F}
joueuse^F de tennis^M
Tennisspielerin^F
tennista^{M/F}

wristband
muñequera^F
serre-poignet^M
Schweißband^N
polsino^M

tennis skirt
falda^F
jupette^F
Rock^M
gonnellino^M

sock
calcetín^M
chaussette^F
Socke^F
calzino^M

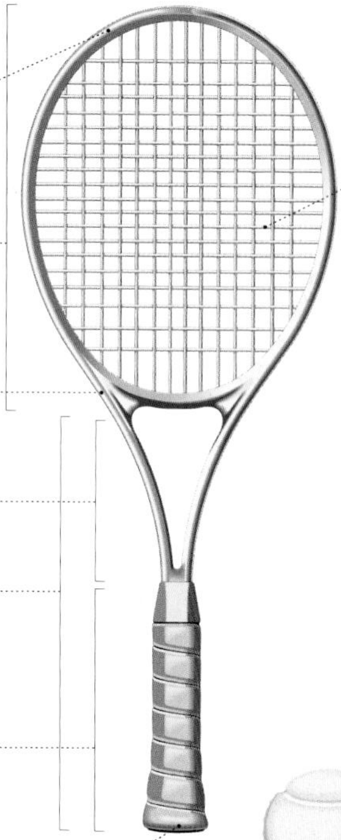

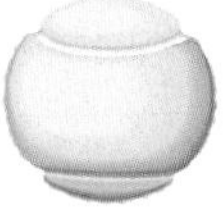

tennis ball
pelota^F de tenis^M
balle^F de tennis^M
Tennisball^M
palla^F

tennis shoe
zapatilla^F de tenis^M
chaussure^F de tennis^M
Tennisschuh^M
scarpa^F da tennis^M

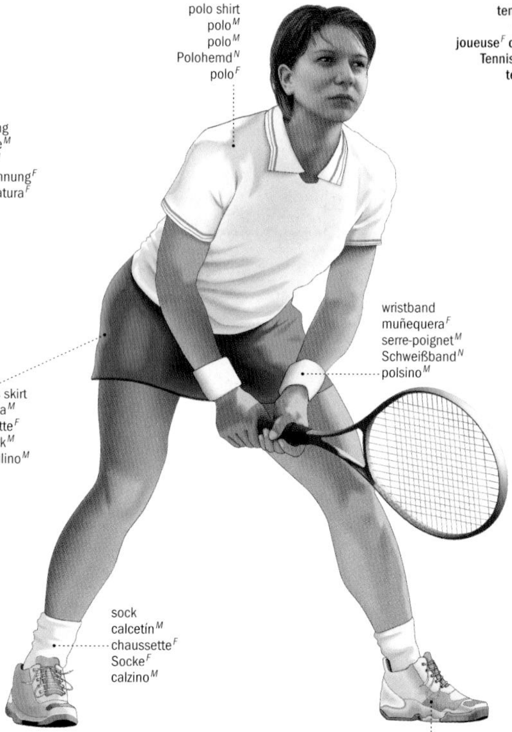

scoreboard
marcador^M
tableau^M d'affichage^M
Anzeigetafel^F
tabellone^M segnapunti

previous sets
mangas^F anteriores
manches^F précédentes
vorherige Sätze^M
set^M precedenti

players
jugadores^M
joueurs^M
Spieler^M/Spielerinnen^F
giocatori^M

set
manga^F
manche^F
Satz^M
set^M

points
puntos^M
points^M
Punkte^M
punti^M

game
juego^M
jeu^M
Spiel^N
gioco^M

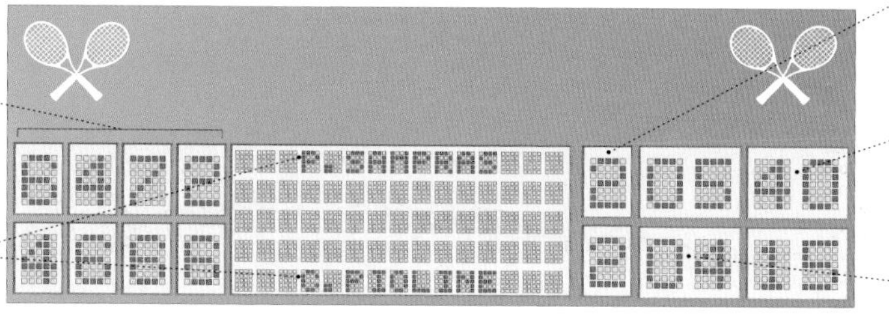

playing surfaces
superficies^F de juego^M
surfaces^F de jeu^M
Spielfeldbeläge^M
superfici^F di gioco^M

grass
hierba^F
gazon^M
Rasen^M
erba^F

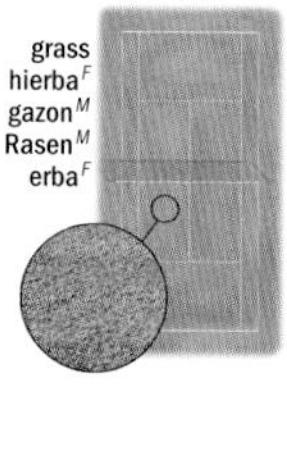

clay
tierra^F batida
terre^F battue
Sand^M
terra^F battuta

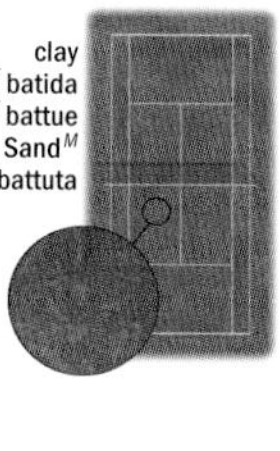

hard surface (cement)
superficie^F dura (cemento^M)
surface^F dure (ciment^M)
Hartplatz^M (Zement^M)
superficie^F dura (cemento^M)

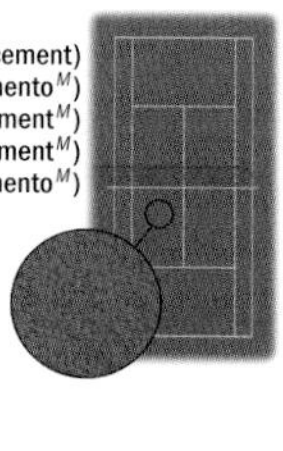

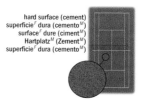

synthetic surface
superficie^F sintética
revêtement^M synthétique
Kunststoffboden^M
superficie^F sintetica

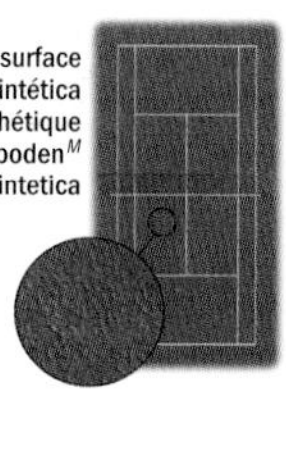

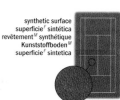

rhythmic gymnastics

gimnasia^F rítmica | gymnastique^F rythmique | rhythmische Sportgymnastik^F | ginnastica^F ritmica

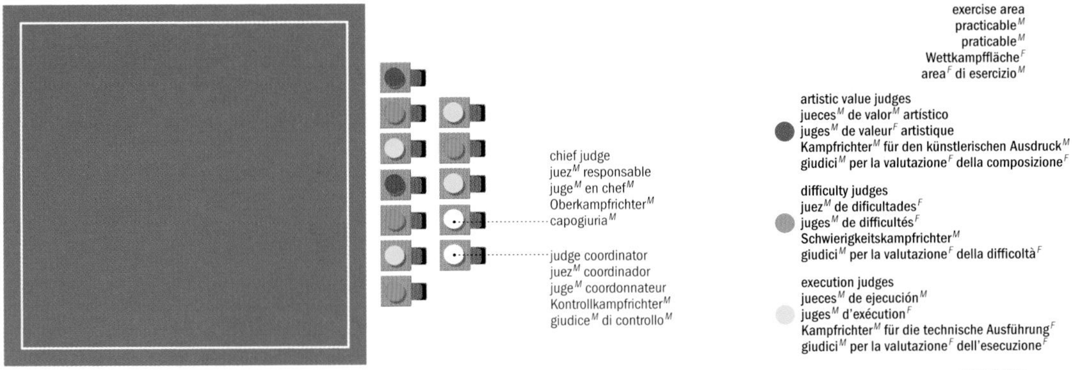

exercise area
practicable^M
praticable^M
Wettkampffläche^F
area^F di esercizio^M

artistic value judges
jueces^M de valor^M artistico
juges^M de valeur^F artistique
Kampfrichter^M für den künstlerischen Ausdruck^M
giudici^M per la valutazione^F della composizione^F

difficulty judges
juez^M de dificultades^F
juges^M de difficultés^F
Schwierigkeitskampfrichter^M
giudici^M per la valutazione^F della difficoltà^F

execution judges
jueces^M de ejecución^M
juges^M d'exécution^F
Kampfrichter^M für die technische Ausführung^F
giudici^M per la valutazione^F dell'esecuzione^F

chief judge
juez^M responsable
juge^M en chef^M
Oberkampfrichter^M
capogiuria^M

judge coordinator
juez^M coordinador
juge^M coordonnateur
Kontrollkampfrichter^M
giudice^M di controllo^M

apparatus
aparatos^M
engins^M
Handgeräte^N
attrezzi^M

clubs
mazas^F
massues^F
Keulen^F
clavette^F

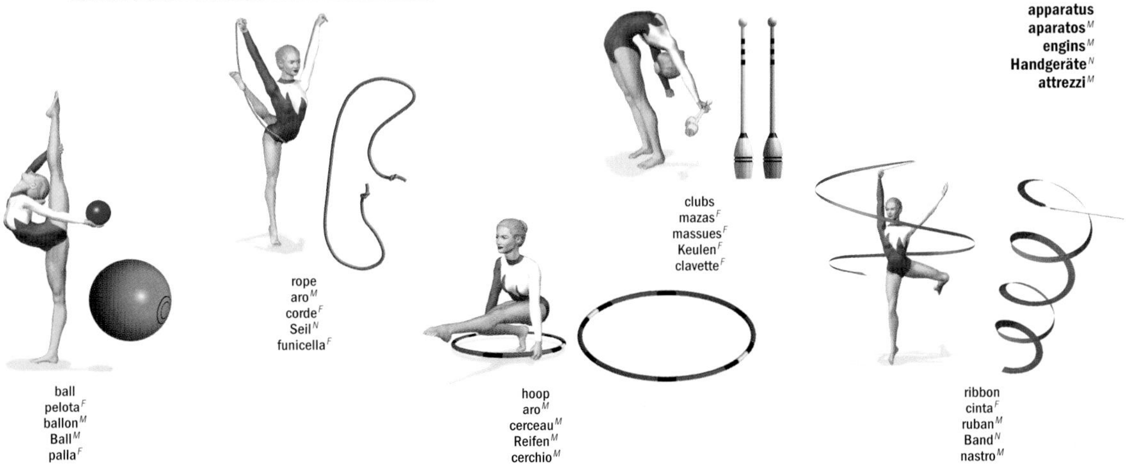

rope
aro^M
corde^F
Seil^N
funicella^F

ball
pelota^F
ballon^M
Ball^M
palla^F

hoop
aro^M
cerceau^M
Reifen^M
cerchio^M

ribbon
cinta^F
ruban^M
Band^N
nastro^M

trampoline

trampolín^M | trampoline^M | Trampolin^N | trampolino^M

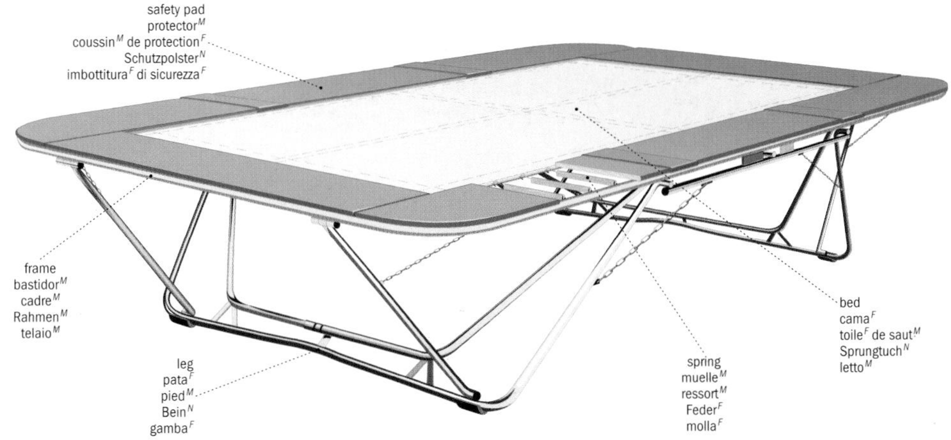

safety pad
protector^M
coussin^M de protection^F
Schutzpolster^N
imbottitura^F di sicurezza^F

frame
bastidor^M
cadre^M
Rahmen^M
telaio^M

leg
pata^F
pied^M
Bein^N
gamba^F

spring
muelle^M
ressort^M
Feder^F
molla^F

bed
cama^F
toile^F de saut^M
Sprungtuch^N
letto^M

gymnastics

gimnasia^F | gymnastique^F | Geräteturnen^N | ginnastica^F

event platform
área^F de competición^F
podium^M des épreuves^F
Geräteturnanlage^F
pedana^F

balance beam
barra^F de equilibrio^M
poutre^F
Schwebebalken^M
trave^F di equilibrio^M

floor exercise area
practicable^M para ejercicios^M de suelo^M
praticable^M pour exercices^M au sol^M
Bodenturnfläche^F
pedana^F per il corpo^M libero

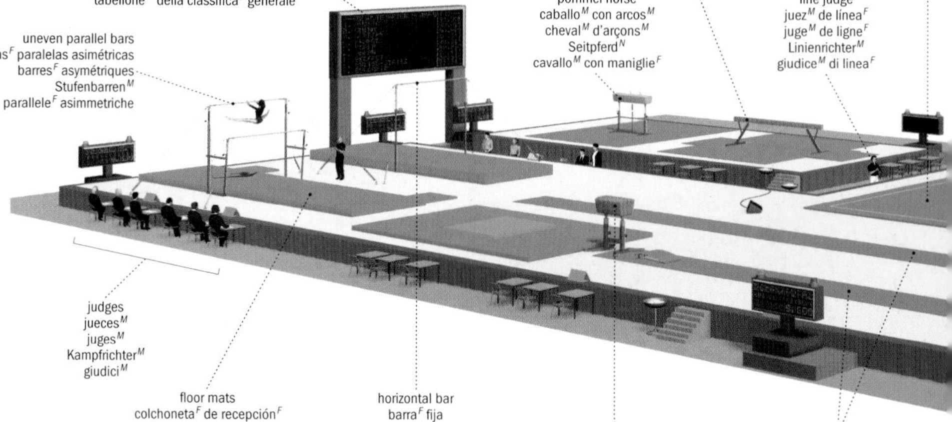

overall standings scoreboard
marcador^M de clasificación^F general
tableau^M de classement^M général
Anzeigetafel^F für das Gesamtergebnis^N
tabellone^M della classifica^F generale

pommel horse
caballo^M con arcos^M
cheval^M d'arçons^M
Seitpferd^N
cavallo^M con maniglie^F

line judge
juez^M de línea^F
juge^M de ligne^F
Linienrichter^M
giudice^M di linea^F

uneven parallel bars
barras^F paralelas asimétricas
barres^F asymétriques
Stufenbarren^M
parallele^F asimmetriche

judges
jueces^M
juges^M
Kampfrichter^M
giudici^M

floor mats
colchoneta^F de recepción^F
tapis^M de réception^F
Matten^F
materassi^M

horizontal bar
barra^F fija
barre^F fixe
Reck^N
sbarra^F orizzontale

vaulting horse
potro^M
cheval^M sautoir
Sprungpferd^N
cavallo^M per volteggi^M

approach runs
pistas^F de carreras^F
pistes^F d'élan^M
Anlaufbahn^F
pedane^F di rincorsa^F

uneven parallel bars
barras^F paralelas asimétricas
barres^F asymétriques
Stufenbarren^M
parallele^F asimmetriche

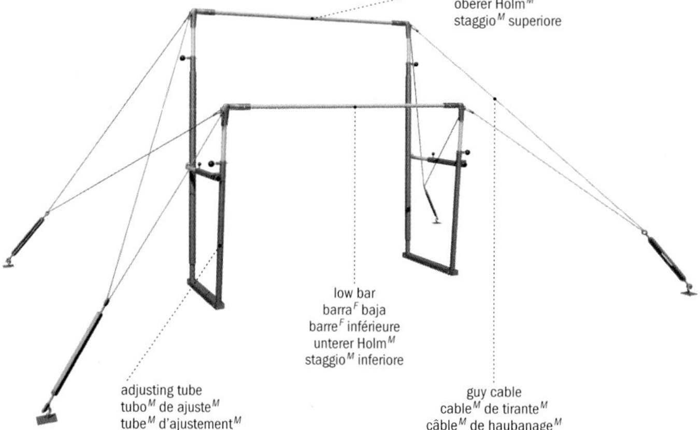

top bar
barra^F alta
barre^F supérieure
oberer Holm^M
staggio^M superiore

low bar
barra^F baja
barre^F inférieure
unterer Holm^M
staggio^M inferiore

adjusting tube
tubo^M de ajuste^M
tube^M d'ajustement^M
Rohrführung^F mit Verstellmöglichkeit^F
montante^M scorrevole

guy cable
cable^M de tirante^M
câble^M de haubanage^M
Spannseil^N
tirante^M

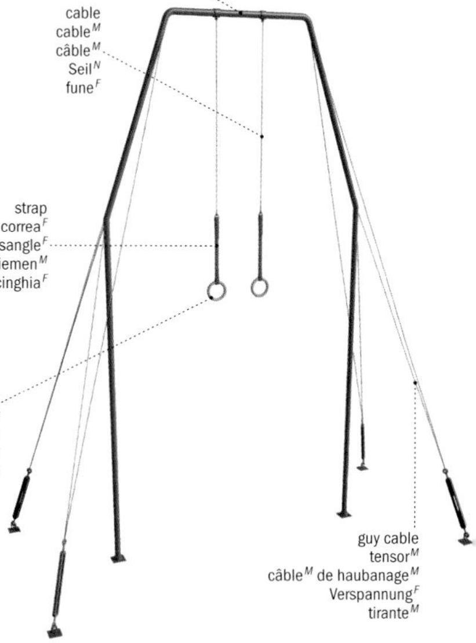

frame
bastidor^M
portique^M
Rahmen^M
telaio^M

rings
anillas^M
anneaux^M
Ringe^M
anelli^M

cable
cable^M
câble^M
Seil^N
fune^F

strap
correa^F
sangle^F
Riemen^M
cinghia^F

ring
anilla^F
anneau^M
Ring^M
anello^M

guy cable
tensor^M
câble^M de haubanage^M
Verspannung^F
tirante^M

SPORTS AND GAMES

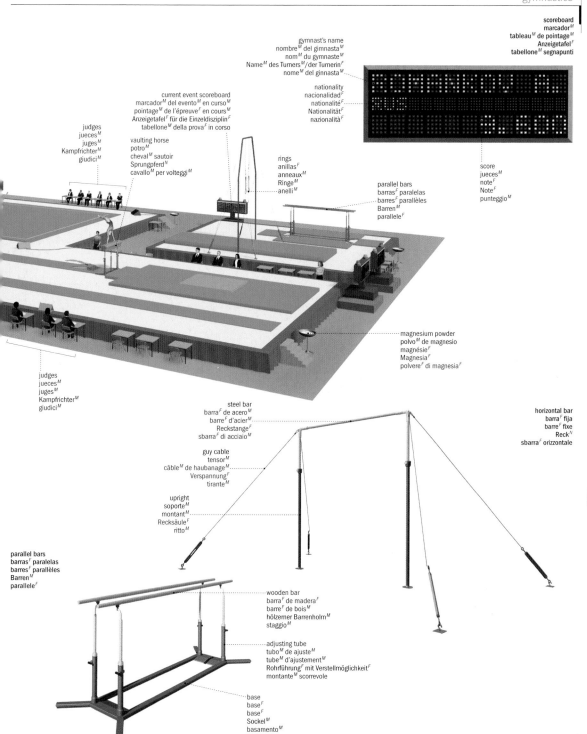

scoreboard
marcador[M]
tableau[M] de pointage[M]
Anzeigetafel[F]
tabellone[M] segnapunti

gymnast's name
nombre[M] del gimnasta[M]
nom[M] du gymnaste[F]
Name[M] des Turners[M]/der Turnerin[F]
nome[M] del ginnasta[M]

nationality
nacionalidad[F]
nationalité[F]
Nationalität[F]
nazionalità[F]

current event scoreboard
marcador[M] del evento[M] en curso[M]
pointage[M] de l'épreuve[F] en cours[M]
Anzeigetafel[F] für die Einzeldisziplin[F]
tabellone[M] della prova[F] in corso

judges
jueces[M]
juges[M]
Kampfrichter[M]
giudici[M]

vaulting horse
potro[M]
cheval[M] sautoir
Sprungpferd[N]
cavallo[M] per volteggi[M]

rings
anillas[F]
anneaux[M]
Ringe[M]
anelli[M]

score
jueces[M]
note[F]
Note[F]
punteggio[M]

parallel bars
barras[F] paralelas
barres[F] parallèles
Barren[M]
parallele[F]

magnesium powder
polvo[M] de magnesio
magnésie[F]
Magnesia[F]
polvere[F] di magnesia[F]

judges
jueces[M]
juges[M]
Kampfrichter[M]
giudici[M]

steel bar
barra[F] de acero[M]
barre[F] d'acier[M]
Reckstange[F]
sbarra[F] di acciaio[M]

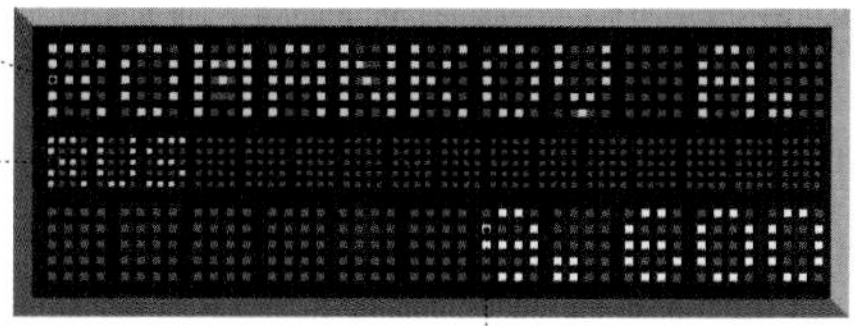

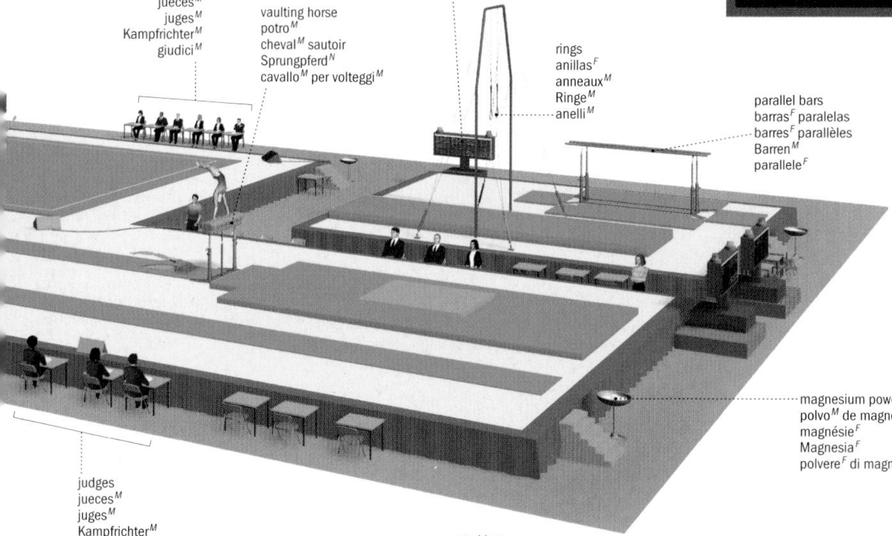

horizontal bar
barra[F] fija
barre[F] fixe
Reck[N]
sbarra[F] orizzontale

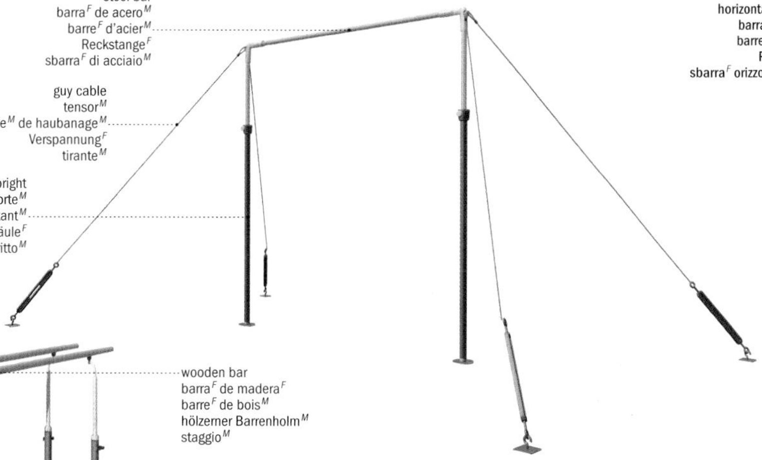

guy cable
tensor[M]
câble[M] de haubanage[M]
Verspannung[F]
tirante[M]

upright
soporte[M]
montant[M]
Recksäule[F]
ritto[M]

parallel bars
barras[F] paralelas
barres[F] parallèles
Barren[M]
parallele[F]

wooden bar
barra[F] de madera[F]
barre[F] de bois[M]
hölzerner Barrenholm[M]
staggio[M]

adjusting tube
tubo[M] de ajuste[M]
tube[M] d'ajustement[M]
Rohrführung[F] mit Verstellmöglichkeit[F]
montante[M] scorrevole

base
base[F]
base[F]
Sockel[M]
basamento[M]

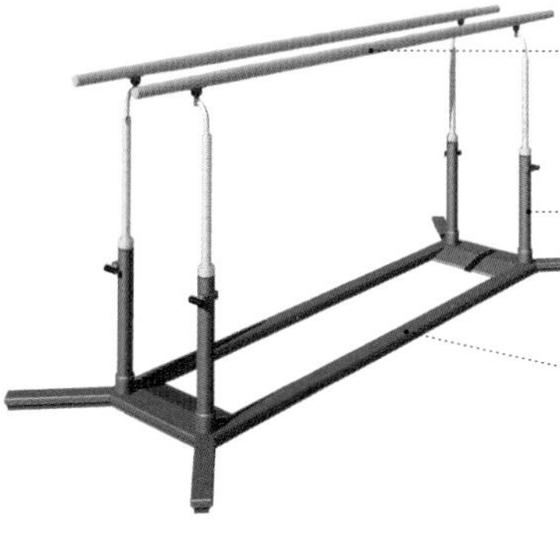

gymnastics

pommel horse
caballo^M con aros^M
cheval^M d'arçons^M
Seitpferd^N
cavallo^M con maniglie^F

saddle
silla^F
selle^F
Sattel^M
sella^F

pommel
arzón^M
arçon^M
Pausche^F
maniglia^F

neck
cabeza^F
cou^M
Hals^M
testa^F

croup
grupa^F
croupe^F
Kruppe^F
groppa^F

horse
caballo^M
cheval^M
Pferd^N
cavallo^M

tightener
tensor^M
tendeur^M
Spanner^M
tenditore^M rapido

height adjustment
regulador^M de altura^F
réglage^M de la hauteur^F
Höhenverstellung^F
sistema^M di regolazione^F dell'altezza^F

base
base^F
piètement^M
Sockel^M
base^F

upright
soporte^M
montant^M
Stütze^F
montante^M

chain
cadena^F
chaine^F
Kette^F
catena^F

antislip shoe
zapata^F antideslizante
patin^M antidérapant
rutschfester Sockel^M
piede^M antisdrucciolo

balance beam
barra^F de equilibrio^M
poutre^F d'équilibre^M
Schwebebalken^M
trave^F di equilibrio^M

height adjustment
regulador^M de altura^F
réglage^M de la hauteur^F
Höhenverstellung^F
sistema^M di regolazione^F dell'altezza^F

beam
barra^F
poutre^F
Balken^M
trave^F

upright
montante^M
montant^M
Ständer^M
montante^M

vaulting horse
potro^M
cheval^M sautoir^M
Sprungpferd^N
cavallo^M per volteggi

springboard
plancha^F de muelles^M
tremplin^M
Sprungbrett^N
pedana^F elastica

water polo

waterpolo^M | water-polo^M | Wasserballspiel^N | pallanuoto^F

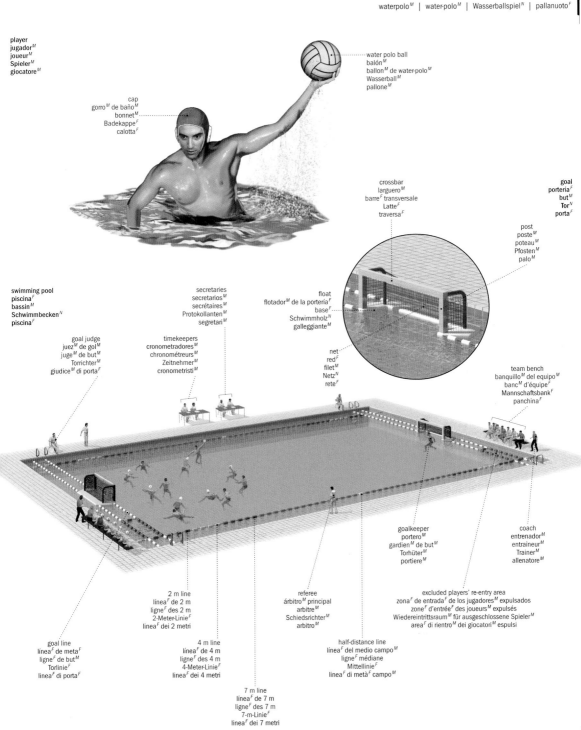

player
jugador^M
joueur^M
Spieler^M
giocatore^M

water polo ball
balón^M
ballon^M de water-polo^M
Wasserball^M
pallone^M

cap
gorro^M de baño^M
bonnet^M
Badekappe^F
calotta^F

crossbar
larguero^M
barre^F transversale
Latte^F
traversa^F

goal
portería^F
but^M
Tor^N
porta^F

post
poste^M
poteau^M
Pfosten^M
palo^M

swimming pool
piscina^F
bassin^M
Schwimmbecken^N
piscina^F

secretaries
secretarios^M
secrétaires^M
Protokollanten^M
segretari^M

float
flotador^M de la portería^F
base^F
Schwimmholz^N
galleggiante^M

goal judge
juez^M de gol^M
juge^M de but^M
Torrichter^M
giudice^M di porta^F

timekeepers
cronometradores^M
chronométreurs^M
Zeitnehmer^M
cronometristi^M

net
red^F
filet^M
Netz^N
rete^F

team bench
banquillo^M del equipo^M
banc^M d'équipe^F
Mannschaftsbank^F
panchina^F

goalkeeper
portero^M
gardien^M de but^M
Torhüter^M
portiere^M

coach
entrenador^M
entraineur^M
Trainer^M
allenatore^M

goal line
línea^F de meta^F
ligne^F de but^M
Torlinie^F
linea^F di porta^F

2 m line
línea^F de 2 m
ligne^F des 2 m
2-Meter-Linie^F
linea^F dei 2 metri

4 m line
línea^F de 4 m
ligne^F des 4 m
4-Meter-Linie^F
linea^F dei 4 metri

referee
árbitro^M principal
arbitre^M
Schiedsrichter^M
arbitro^M

excluded players' re-entry area
zona^F de entrada^F de los jugadores^M expulsados
zone^F d'entrée^F des joueurs^M expulsés
Wiedereintrittsraum^M für ausgeschlossene Spieler^M
area^F di rientro^M dei giocatori^M espulsi

half-distance line
línea^F del medio campo^M
ligne^F médiane
Mittellinie^F
linea^F di metà^F campo^M

7 m line
línea^F de 7 m
ligne^F des 7 m
7-m-Linie^F
linea^F dei 7 metri

SPORTS AND GAMES

diving

saltos^M | plongeon^M | Kunstspringen^N | tuffi^M

starting positions
posiciones^F de salto^M
positions^F de départ^M
Startpositionen^F
posizioni^F di partenza^F

flights
saltos^M
vols^M
Sprungfiguren^F
voli^M

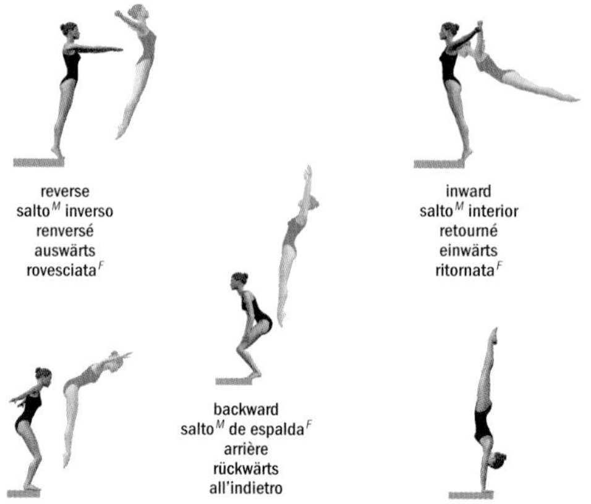

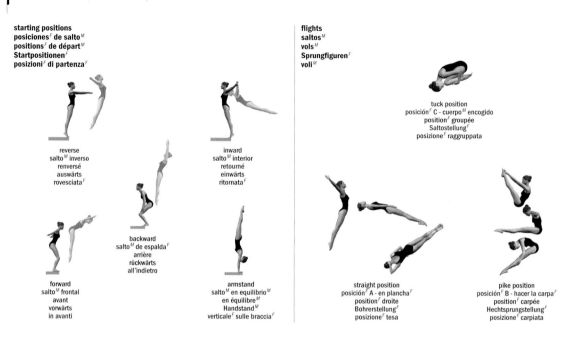

reverse
salto^M inverso
renversé
auswärts
rovesciata^F

inward
salto^M interior
retourné
einwärts
ritornata^F

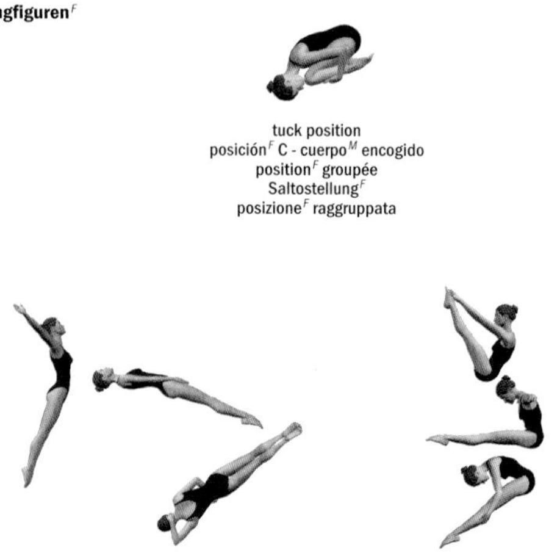

tuck position
posición^F C - cuerpo^M encogido
position^F groupée
Saltostellung^F
posizione^F raggruppata

backward
salto^M de espalda^F
arrière
rückwärts
all'indietro

forward
salto^M frontal
avant
vorwärts
in avanti

armstand
salto^M en equilibrio^M
en équilibre^M
Handstand^M
verticale^F sulle braccia^F

straight position
posición^F A - en plancha^F
position^F droite
Bohrerstellung^F
posizione^F tesa

pike position
posición^F B - hacer la carpa^F
position^F carpée
Hechtsprungstellung^F
posizione^F carpiata

diving installations
torre^F de saltos^M
plongeoir^M
Springeinrichtungen^F
strutture^F per i tuffi^M

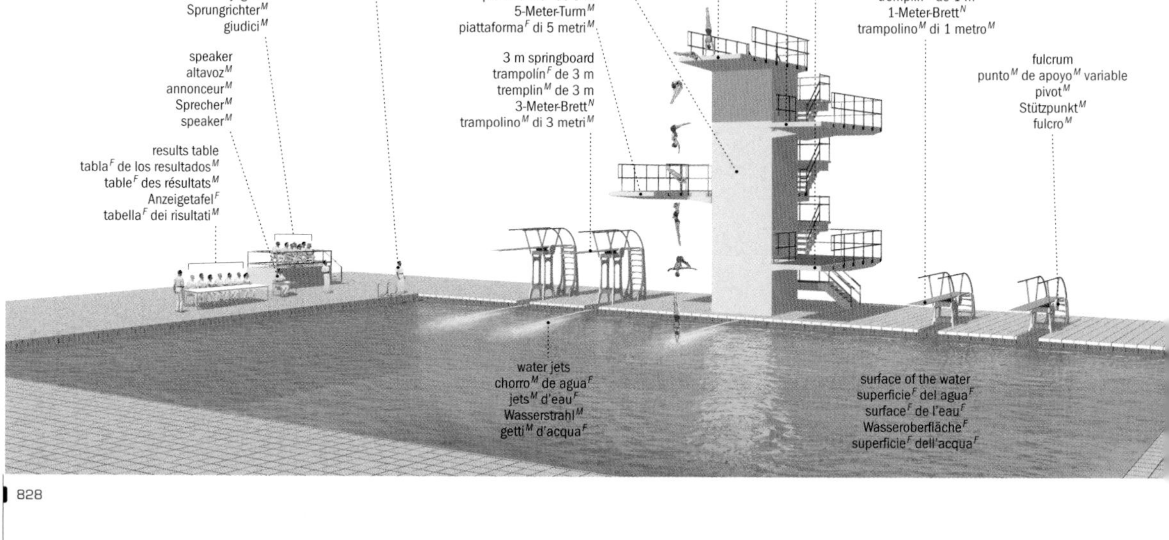

10 m platform
plataforma^F de 10 m
plate-forme^F de 10 m
10-Meter-Turm^M
piattaforma^F di 10 metri^M

7.5 m platform
plataforma^F de 7,5 m
plate-forme^F de 7,5 m
7,5-Meter-Turm^M
piattaforma^F di 7,5 metri^M

referee
juez-árbitro^M
juge^M-arbitre^M
Schiedsrichter^M
arbitro^M

diving tower
torre^F de saltos^M
tour^F du plongeoir^M
Sprungturm^M
torre^F per i tuffi^M

3 m platform
plataforma^F de 3 m
plate-forme^F de 3 m
3-Meter-Turm^M
piattaforma^F di 3 metri^M

judges
jueces^M
juges^M
Sprungrichter^M
giudici^M

5 m platform
plataforma^F de 5 m
plate-forme^F de 5 m
5-Meter-Turm^M
piattaforma^F di 5 metri^M

1 m springboard
trampolín^F de 1 m
tremplin^M de 1 m
1-Meter-Brett^N
trampolino^M di 1 metro^M

speaker
altavoz^M
annonceur^M
Sprecher^M
speaker^M

3 m springboard
trampolín^F de 3 m
tremplin^M de 3 m
3-Meter-Brett^N
trampolino^M di 3 metri^M

fulcrum
punto^M de apoyo^M variable
pivot^M
Stützpunkt^M
fulcro^M

results table
tabla^F de los resultados^M
table^F des résultats^M
Anzeigetafel^F
tabella^F dei risultati^M

water jets
chorro^M de agua^F
jets^M d'eau^F
Wasserstrahl^M
getti^M d'acqua^F

surface of the water
superficie^F del agua^F
surface^F de l'eau^F
Wasseroberfläche^F
superficie^F dell'acqua^F

AQUATIC AND NAUTICAL SPORTS | DEPORTES ACUÁTICOS Y NÁUTICOS
SPORTS AQUATIQUES ET NAUTIQUES | WASSERSPORT | SPORT ACQUATICI E NAUTICI

diving

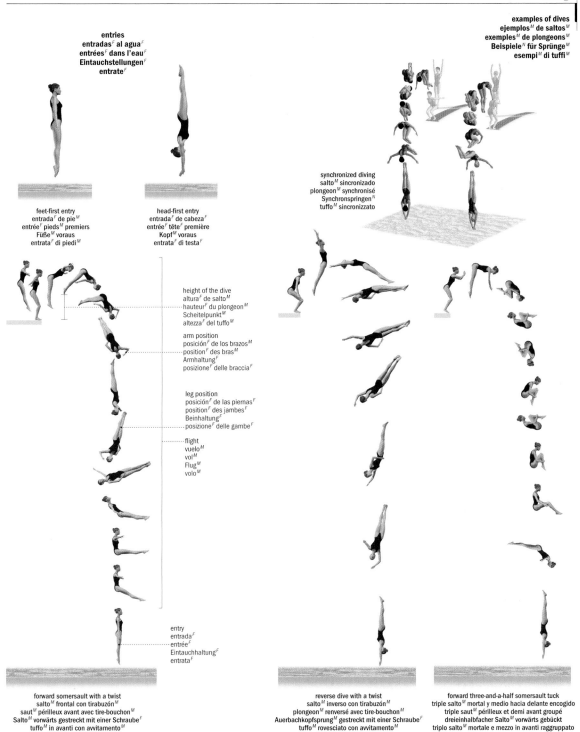

examples of dives
ejemplos^M de saltos^M
exemples^M de plongeons^M
Beispiele^N für Sprünge^M
esempi^M di tuffi^M

entries
entradas^F al agua^F
entrées^F dans l'eau^F
Eintauchstellungen^F
entrate^F

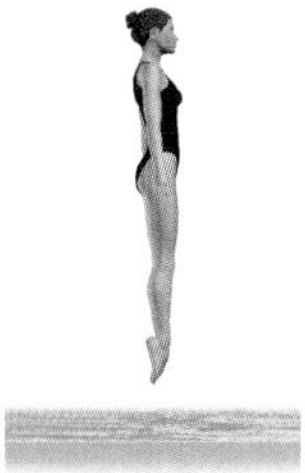

feet-first entry
entrada^F de pie^M
entrée^F pieds^M premiers
Füße^M voraus
entrata^F di piedi^M

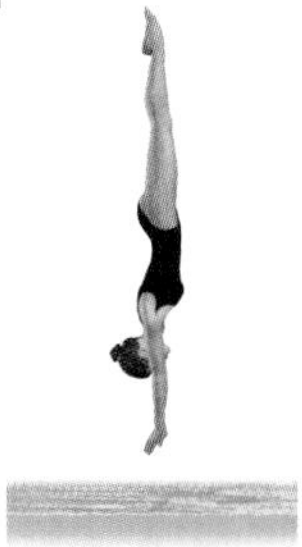

head-first entry
entrada^F de cabeza^F
entrée^F tête^F première
Kopf^M voraus
entrata^F di testa^F

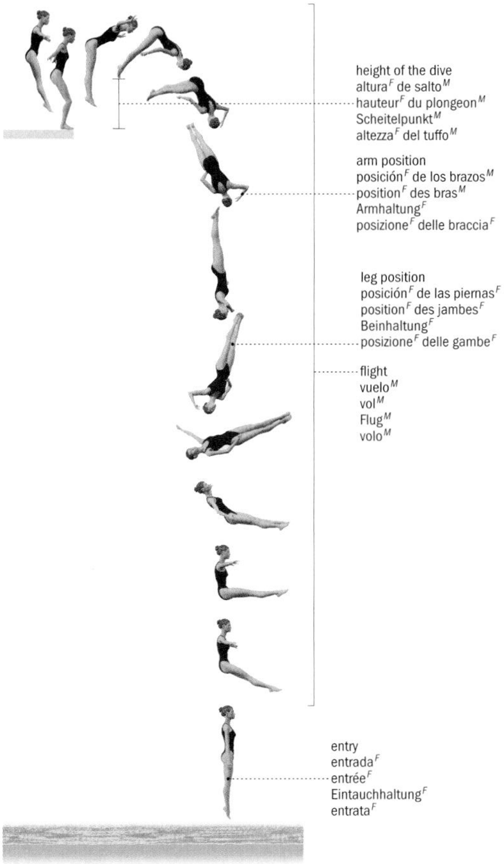

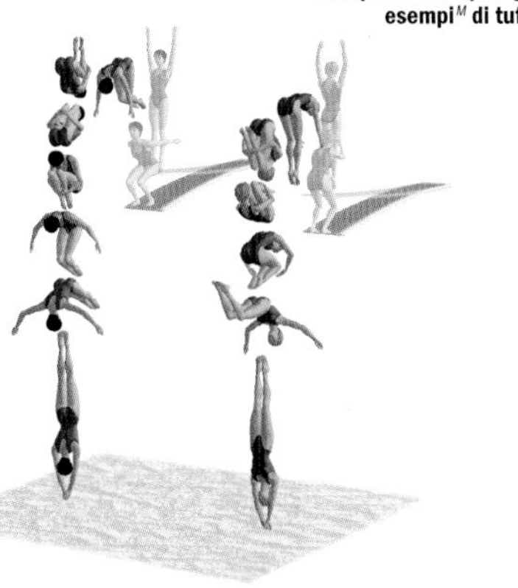

synchronized diving
salto^M sincronizado
plongeon^M synchronisé
Synchronspringen^N
tuffo^M sincronizzato

height of the dive
altura^F de salto^M
hauteur^F du plongeon^M
Scheitelpunkt^M
altezza^F del tuffo^M

arm position
posición^F de los brazos^M
position^F des bras^M
Armhaltung^F
posizione^F delle braccia^F

leg position
posición^F de las piernas^F
position^F des jambes^F
Beinhaltung^F
posizione^F delle gambe^F

flight
vuelo^M
vol^M
Flug^M
volo^M

entry
entrada^F
entrée^F
Eintauchhaltung^F
entrata^F

forward somersault with a twist
salto^M frontal con tirabuzón^M
saut^M périlleux avant avec tire-bouchon^M
Salto^M vorwärts gestreckt mit einer Schraube^F
tuffo^M in avanti con avvitamento^M

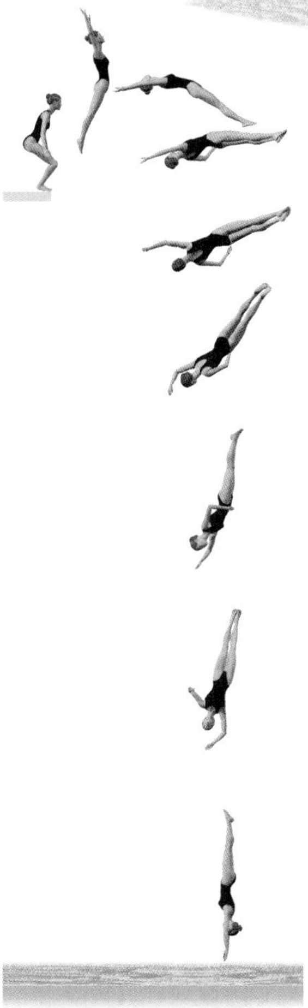

reverse dive with a twist
salto^M inverso con tirabuzón^M
plongeon^M renversé avec tire-bouchon^M
Auerbachkopfsprung^M gestreckt mit einer Schraube^F
tuffo^M rovesciato con avvitamento^M

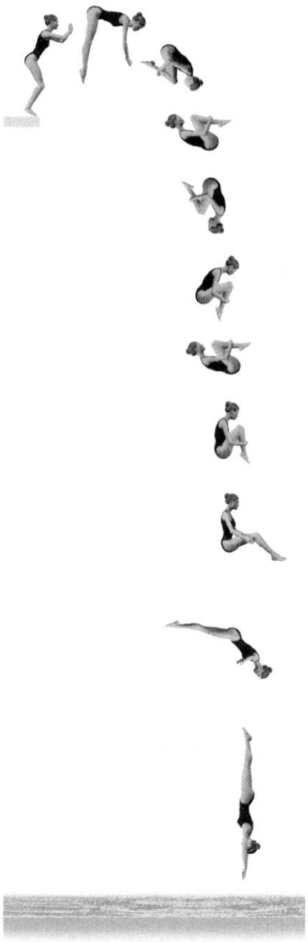

forward three-and-a-half somersault tuck
triple salto^M mortal y medio hacia delante encogido
triple saut^M périlleux et demi avant groupé
dreieinhalbfacher Salto^M vorwärts gebückt
triplo salto^M mortale e mezzo in avanti raggruppato

swimming

natación^F | natation^F | Schwimmen^N | nuoto^M

starting block
plataforma^F de salida^F
plot^M de départ^M
Startblock^M
blocco^M di partenza^F

swimsuit
traje^M de baño^M
maillot^M de bain^M
Badehose^F
costume^M da bagno^M

cap
gorro^M de baño^M
bonnet^M
Badekappe^F
cuffia^F

platform
plataforma^F de salida^F
plate-forme^F
Plattform^F
piattaforma^F

swimming goggles
gafas^F de baño^M
lunettes^F de nage^F
Schwimmbrille^F
occhialini^M da nuoto^M

starting grip (backstroke)
asidero^M : (espalda^F)
poignée^F de départ^M (dos^M)
Startgriffe^M (Rückenschwimmen^N)
barra^F di partenza^F (dorso^M)

referee
árbitro^M
juge^M arbitre^M
Schiedsrichter^M
arbitro^M

starter
juez^M de salida^F
juge^M de départ^M
Starter^M
starter^M

stroke judge
juez^M de brazado^M
juge^M de nage^F
Zugrichter^M
giudice^M di stile^M

false start rope
cuerda^F de salida^F falsa
corde^F de faux départ^M
Fehlstartleine^F
fune^F di falsa partenza^F

finish wall
muro^M de llegada^F
mur^M d'arrivée^F
Ziel^N
parete^F di arrivo^M

lane timekeeper
cronometrador^M de calle^F
chronométreur^M de couloir^M
Bahnzeitnehmer^M
cronometrista^{M/F} di corsia^F

lane
calle^F
couloir^M
Bahn^F
corsia^F

starting block
podio^M de salida^F
plot^M de départ^M
Startblock^M
blocco^M di partenza^F

chief timekeeper
jefe^M de cronometradores^M
chronométreur^M en chef^M
Hauptzeitnehmer^M
cronometrista^M capo^M

placing judge
juez^M de llegada^F
juge^M de classement^M
Platzierungsrichter^M
giudice^M di arrivo^M

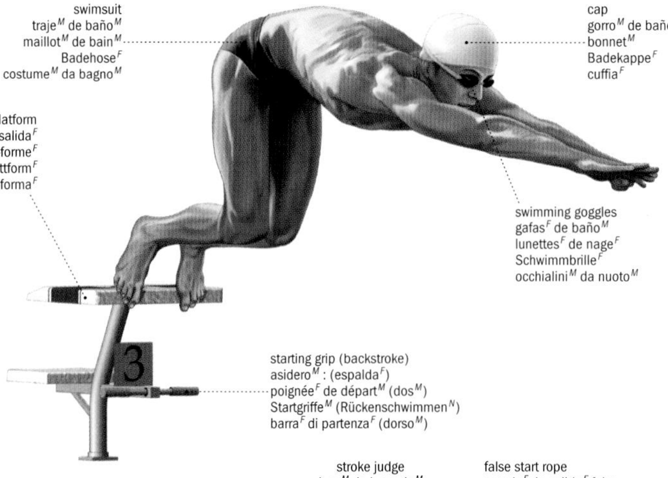

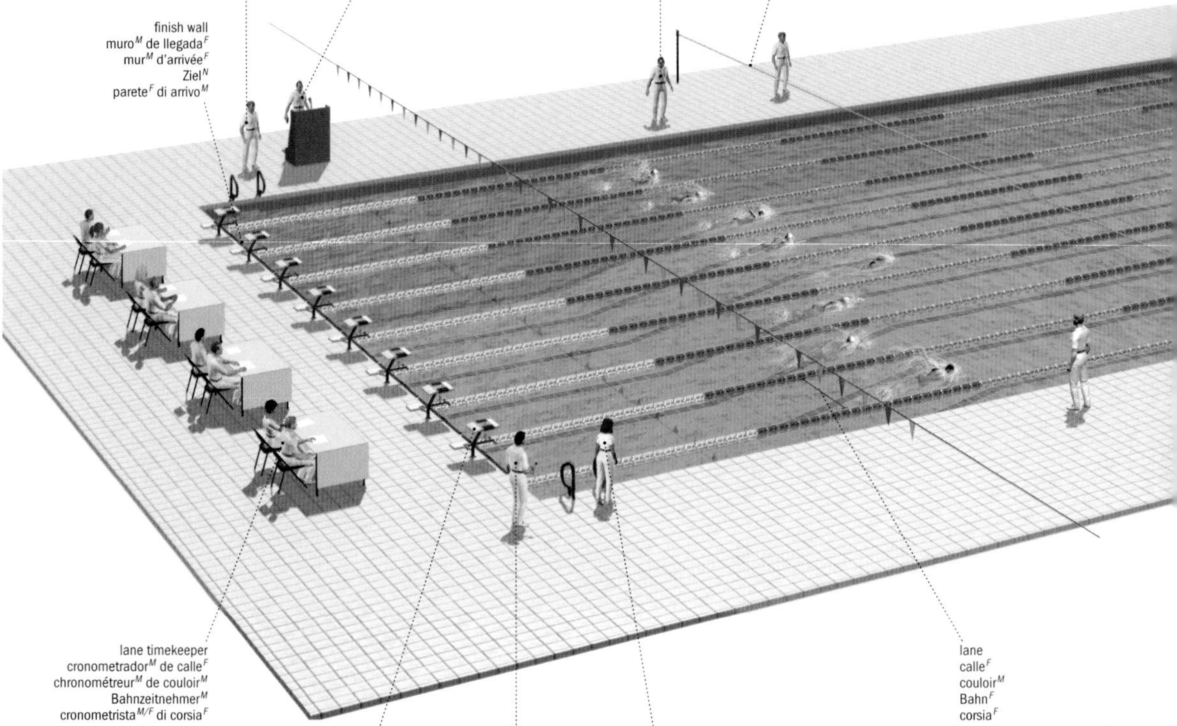

AQUATIC AND NAUTICAL SPORTS | DEPORTES ACUÁTICOS Y NÁUTICOS
SPORTS AQUATIQUES ET NAUTIQUES | WASSERSPORT | SPORT ACQUATICI E NAUTICI

swimming

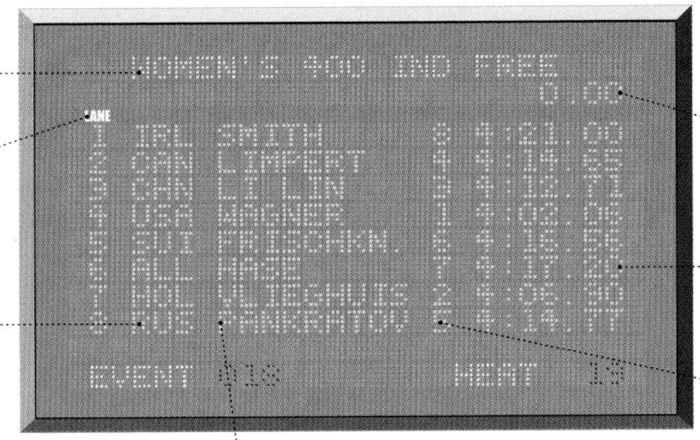

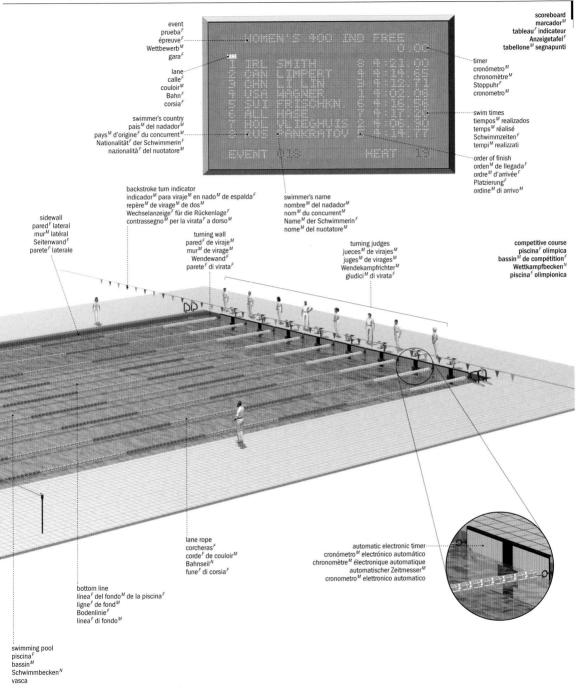

event
prueba^F
épreuve^F
Wettbewerb^M
gara^F

lane
calle^F
couloir^M
Bahn^F
corsia^F

swimmer's country
país^M del nadador^M
pays^M d'origine^F du concurrent^M
Nationalität^F der Schwimmerin^F
nazionalità^F del nuotatore^M

scoreboard
marcador^M
tableau^F indicateur
Anzeigetafel^F
tabellone^M segnapunti

timer
cronómetro^M
chronomètre^M
Stoppuhr^F
cronometro^M

swim times
tiempos^M realizados
temps^M réalisé
Schwimmzeiten^F
tempi^M realizzati

order of finish
orden^M de llegada^F
ordre^M d'arrivée^F
Platzierung^F
ordine^M di arrivo^M

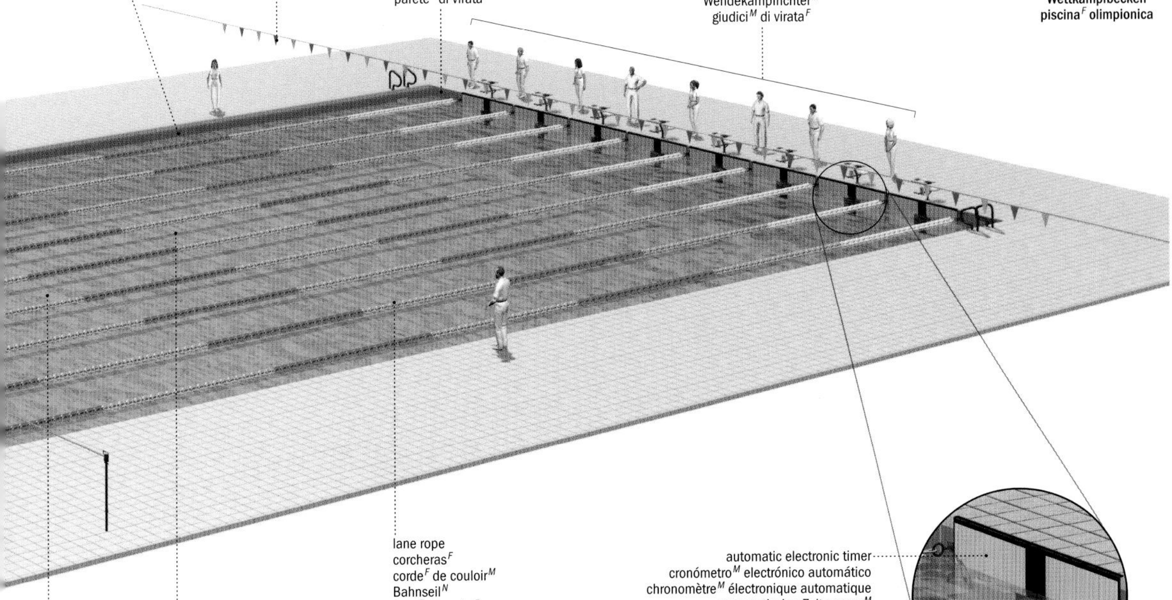

backstroke turn indicator
indicador^M para viraje^M en nado^M de espalda^F
repère^M de virage^M de dos^M
Wechselanzeige^F für die Rückenlage^F
contrassegno^M per la virata^F a dorso^M

sidewall
pared^F lateral
mur^M latéral
Seitenwand^F
parete^F laterale

turning wall
pared^F de viraje^M
mur^M de virage^M
Wendewand^F
parete^F di virata^F

swimmer's name
nombre^M del nadador^M
nom^M du concurrent^M
Name^M der Schwimmerin^F
nome^M del nuotatore^M

turning judges
jueces^M de virajes^M
juges^M de virages^M
Wendekampfrichter^M
giudici^M di virata^F

competitive course
piscina^F olímpica
bassin^M de compétition^F
Wettkampfbecken^N
piscina^F olimpionica

lane rope
corcheras^F
corde^F de couloir^M
Bahnseil^N
fune^F di corsia^F

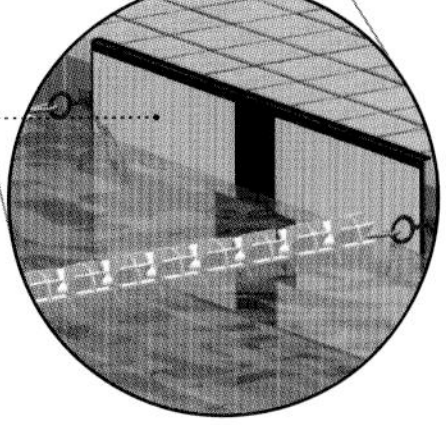

automatic electronic timer
cronómetro^M electrónico automático
chronomètre^M électronique automatique
automatischer Zeitmesser^M
cronometro^M elettronico automatico

bottom line
línea^F del fondo^M de la piscina^F
ligne^F de fond^M
Bodenlinie^F
linea^F di fondo^M

swimming pool
piscina^F
bassin^M
Schwimmbecken^N
vasca

swimming

types of strokes
estilos^M de natación^F
types^M de nages^F
verschiedene Schwimmstile^M
stili^M di nuoto^M

front crawl
crol^M
crawl^M
Kraulen^N
stile^M libero o crawl^M

breathing in
inhalación^F
inspiration^F
Einatmen^N
inspirazione^F

starting dive
salto^M de salida^F
plongeon^M de départ^M
Startsprung^M
tuffo^M di partenza^F

breathing out
exhalación^F
expiration^F
Ausatmen^N
espirazione^F

turning wall
pared^F de viraje^M
mur^M de virage^M
Wendewand^F
parete^F di virata^F

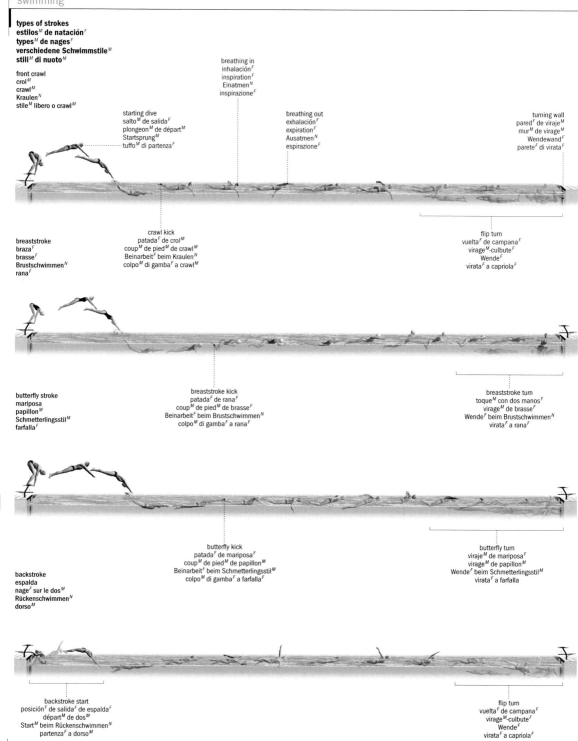

breaststroke
braza^F
brasse^F
Brustschwimmen^N
rana^F

crawl kick
patada^F de crol^M
coup^M de pied^M de crawl^M
Beinarbeit^F beim Kraulen^N
colpo^M di gamba^F a crawl^M

flip turn
vuelta^F de campana^F
virage^M-culbute^F
Wende^F
virata^F a capriola^F

butterfly stroke
mariposa
papillon^M
Schmetterlingsstil^M
farfalla^F

breaststroke kick
patada^F de rana^F
coup^M de pied^M de brasse^F
Beinarbeit^F beim Brustschwimmen^N
colpo^M di gamba^F a rana^F

breaststroke turn
toque^M con dos manos^F
virage^M de brasse^F
Wende^F beim Brustschwimmen^N
virata^F a rana^F

backstroke
espalda
nage^F sur le dos^M
Rückenschwimmen^N
dorso^M

butterfly kick
patada^F de mariposa^F
coup^M de pied^M de papillon^M
Beinarbeit^F beim Schmetterlingsstil^M
colpo^M di gamba^F a farfalla^F

butterfly turn
viraje^M de mariposa^F
virage^M de papillon^M
Wende^F beim Schmetterlingsstil^M
virata^F a farfalla

backstroke start
posición^F de salida^F de espalda^F
départ^M de dos^M
Start^M beim Rückenschwimmen^N
partenza^F a dorso^M

flip turn
vuelta^F de campana^F
virage^M-culbute^F
Wende^F
virata^F a capriola^F

sailing

vela^F | voile^F | Segelsport^M | vela^F

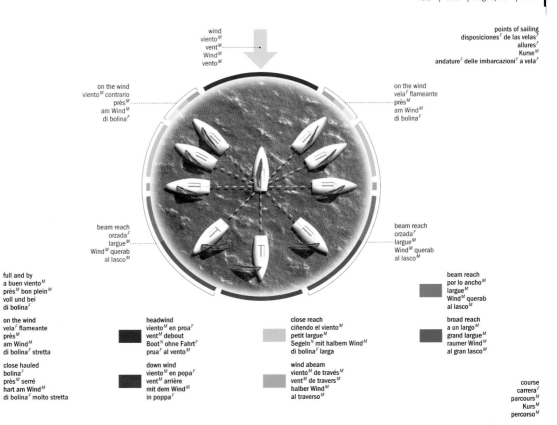

points of sailing
disposiciones^F de las velas^F
allures^F
Kurse^M
andature^F delle imbarcazioni^F a vela^F

wind
viento^M
vent^M
Wind^M
vento^M

on the wind
viento^M contrario
près^M
am Wind^M
di bolina^F

on the wind
vela^F flameante
près^M
am Wind^M
di bolina^F

beam reach
orzada^F
largue^M
Wind^M querab
al lasco^M

beam reach
orzada^F
largue^M
Wind^M querab
al lasco^M

full and by
a buen viento^M
près^M bon plein^M
voll und bei
di bolina^F

on the wind
vela^F flameante
près^M
am Wind^M
di bolina^F stretta

close hauled
bolina^F
près^M serré
hart am Wind^M
di bolina^F molto stretta

headwind
viento^M en proa^F
vent^M debout
Boot^N ohne Fahrt^F
prua^F al vento^M

down wind
viento^M en popa^F
vent^M arrière
mit dem Wind^M
in poppa^F

close reach
ciñendo el viento^M
petit largue^M
Segeln^N mit halbem Wind^M
di bolina^F larga

wind abeam
viento^M de través^M
vent^M de travers^M
halber Wind^M
al traverso^M

beam reach
por lo ancho^M
largue^M
Wind^M querab
al lasco^M

broad reach
a un largo^M
grand largue^M
raumer Wind^M
al gran lasco^M

course
carrera^F
parcours^M
Kurs^M
percorso^M

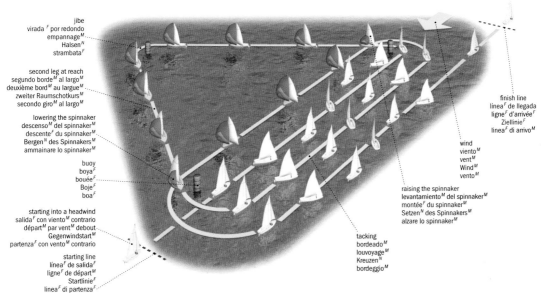

jibe
virada^F por redondo
empannage^M
Halsen^N
strambata^F

second leg at reach
segundo borde^M al largo^M
deuxième bord^M au largue^M
zweiter Raumschotkurs^M
secondo giro^M al largo^M

lowering the spinnaker
descenso^M del spinnaker^M
descente^F du spinnaker^M
Bergen^N des Spinnakers^M
ammainare lo spinnaker^M

buoy
boya^F
bouée^F
Boje^F
boa^F

starting into a headwind
salida^F con viento^M contrario
départ^M par vent^M debout
Gegenwindstart^M
partenza^F con vento^M contrario

starting line
línea^F de salida^F
ligne^F de départ^M
Startlinie^F
linea^F di partenza^F

finish line
línea^F de llegada
ligne^F d'arrivée^F
Ziellinie^F
linea^F di arrivo^M

wind
viento^M
vent^M
Wind^M
vento^M

raising the spinnaker
levantamiento^M del spinnaker^M
montée^F du spinnaker^M
Setzen^N des Spinnakers^M
alzare lo spinnaker^M

tacking
bordeado^M
louvoyage^M
Kreuzen^N
bordeggio^M

sailing

sailboat
velero[M]
dériveur[M]
Segelboot[N]
barca[F] a vela[F]

wind indicator
veleta[F] (grímpola)
girouette[F]
Verklicker[M]
segnavento[M]

mast
mástil[M]
mât[M]
Mast[M]
albero[M]

batten pocket
funda[F] del sable[M]
gousset[M] de latte[F]
Lattentasche[F]
tasca[F] per la stecca[F]

forestay
estay[M] de proa[F]
étai[M] avant
Vorstag[M]
strallo[M] di prua[F]

batten
sable[M]
latte[F]
Segellatte[F]
stecca[F]

jib
foque[M]
foc[M]
Fock[F]
fiocco[M]

mainsail
vela[F] mayor
grand-voile[F]
Großsegel[N]
randa[F]

shroud
obenque[M]
hauban[M]
Want[F]
sartia[F]

sail panel
panel[M] de la vela[F]
laize[F]
Segelkleid[N]
ferzo[M]

crosstree
cruceta[F]
barre[F] de flèche[F]
Saling[F]
crocetta[F]

telltale
axiómetro[M]
pennon[M]
Wantenverklicker[M]
segnavento[M]

boom vang
botavara[F]
halebas[M]
Halstalje[F]
caricabbasso[M]

boom
botalón[M]
bôme[F]
Baum[M]
boma[M/F]

jibsheet
escota[F] foque[M]
écoute[F] de foc[M]
Vorschot[F]
scotta[F] del fiocco[M]

mainsheet
escota[F] mayor
écoute[F] de grand-voile[F]
Großschot[N]
scotta[F] della randa[F]

cleat
escota[F]
taquet[M]
Klampe[F]
galloccia[F]

traveler
escotero[M]
barre[F] d'écoute[F]
Traveller[M]
rotaia[F] del carrello[M] di scotta[F]

tiller
caña[F] del timón[M]
barre[F]
Pinne[F]
barra[F] del timone[M]

rudder
pala[F] del timón[M]
gouvernail[M]
Ruder[N]
timone[M]

bow
proa[F]
étrave[F]
Bug[M]
prua[F]

hull
casco[M]
coque[F]
Rumpf[M]
scafo[M]

cockpit
bañera[F]
cockpit[M]
Cockpit[N]
pozzetto[M]

centerboard
orza[F] de quilla[F]
dérive[F]
Schwert[N]
deriva[F]

SPORTS AND GAMES

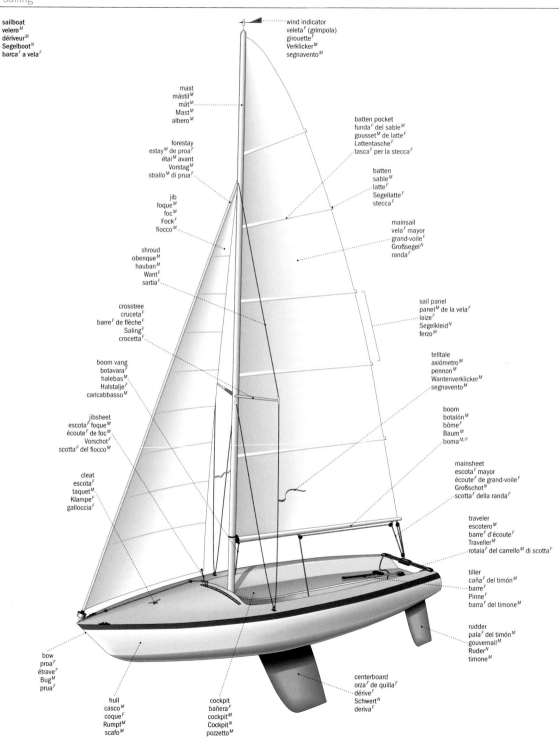

AQUATIC AND NAUTICAL SPORTS | DEPORTES ACUÁTICOS Y NÁUTICOS
SPORTS AQUATIQUES ET NAUTIQUES | WASSERSPORT | SPORT ACQUATICI E NAUTICI

sailing

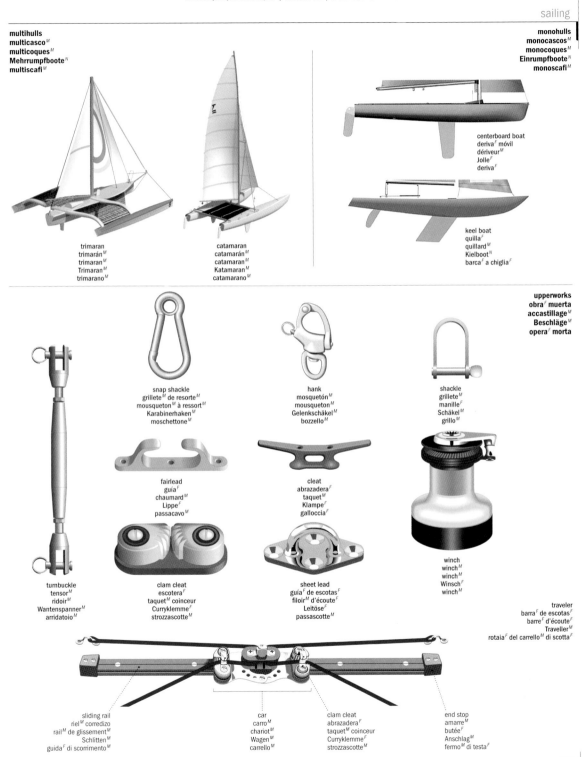

multihulls
multicasco^M
multicoques^M
Mehrrumpfboote^N
multiscafi^M

monohulls
monocascos^M
monocoques^M
Einrumpfboote^N
monoscafi^M

centerboard boat
deriva^F móvil
dériveur^M
Jolle^F
deriva^F

keel boat
quilla^F
quillard^M
Kielboot^N
barca^F a chiglia^F

trimaran
trimarán^M
trimaran^M
Trimaran^M
trimarano^M

catamaran
catamarán^M
catamaran^M
Katamaran^M
catamarano^M

upperworks
obra^F **muerta**
accastillage^M
Beschläge^M
opera^F **morta**

snap shackle
grillete^M de resorte^M
mousqueton^M à ressort^M
Karabinerhaken^M
moschettone^M

hank
mosquetón^M
mousqueton^M
Gelenkschäkel^M
bozzello^M

shackle
grillete^M
manille^F
Schäkel^M
grillo^M

fairlead
guía^F
chaumard^M
Lippe^F
passacavo^M

cleat
abrazadera^F
taquet^M
Klampe^F
galloccia^F

winch
winch^M
winch^M
Winsch^F
winch^M

turnbuckle
tensor^M
ridoir^M
Wantenspanner^M
arridatoio^M

clam cleat
escotera^F
taquet^M coinceur
Curryklemme^F
strozzascotte^M

sheet lead
guía^F de escotas^F
filoir^M d'écoute^F
Leitöse^F
passascotte^M

traveler
barra^F de escotas^F
barre^F d'écoute^F
Traveller^M
rotaia^F del carrello^M di scotta^F

sliding rail
riel^M corredizo
rail^M de glissement^M
Schlitten^M
guida^F di scorrimento^M

car
carro^M
chariot^M
Wagen^M
carrello^M

clam cleat
abrazadera^F
taquet^M coinceur
Curryklemme^F
strozzascotte^M

end stop
amarre^M
butée^F
Anschlag^M
fermo^M di testa^F

sailboard

windsurf^M | planche^F à voile^F | Surfbrett^N | windsurf^M

sail
vela^F
voile^F
Segel^N
vela^F

masthead
cabeza^F de mástil^M
tête^F de mât^M
Mastspitze^F
testa^F d'albero^M

mast sleeve
funda^F de mástil^M
fourreau^M
Masttasche^F
calza^F dell'albero^M

batten
sable^M
latte^F
Segellatte^F
stecca^F

batten pocket
funda^F del sable^M
gousset^M de latte^F
Segeltasche^F
tasca^F della stecca^F

luff
caída^F de proa^F
guindant^M
Vorliek^N
caduta^F di prua^F

leech
caída^F de popa^F
chute^F
Latte^F
caduta^F di poppa^F

window
ventana^F
fenêtre^F
Fenster^N
finestra^F

wishbone boom
botavara^F
wishbone^M
Gabelbaum^M
boma^{M/F}

clew
puño^M de escota^F
point^M d'écoute^F
Horn^N
bugna^F

mast
mástil^M
mât^M
Mast^M
albero^M

foot
pujamen^M
bordure^F
Fuß^M
bordame^M

uphaul
tirante^M de la botavara^F
tire-veille^M
Strang^M
cima^F di recupero^M

tack
puño^M de amura^F
point^M d'amure^F
Hals^M
punto^M di mura^F

mast foot
cojinete^M móvil
pied^M de mât^M
Mastlager^N
piede^M d'albero^M

daggerboard well
caja^F orza^F de quilla^F
puits^M de dérive^F
Hauptschwerteinzug^M
scassa^F di deriva^F

foot strap
correa^F
arceau^M
Fußschlaufe^F
cinghia^F per i piedi^M

stern
popa^F
poupe^F
Heck^N
poppa^F

bow
proa^F
proue^F
Bug^M
prua^F

board
tabla^F de surf^M
flotteur^M
Brett^N
tavola^F

daggerboard
orza^F de quilla^F
dérive^F
Hauptschwert^N
deriva^F a scomparsa^F

skeg
orza^F de popa^F
aileron^M
Hilfsschwert^N
pinna^F

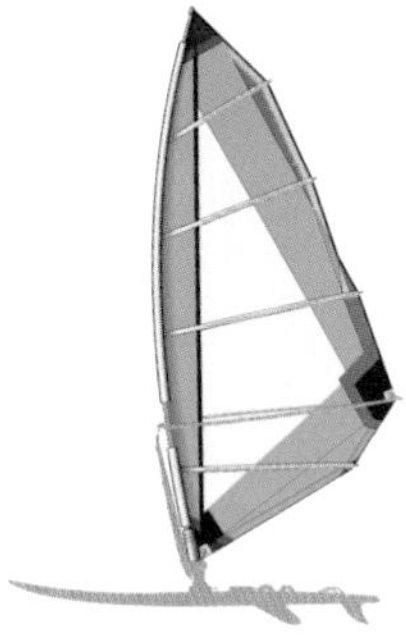

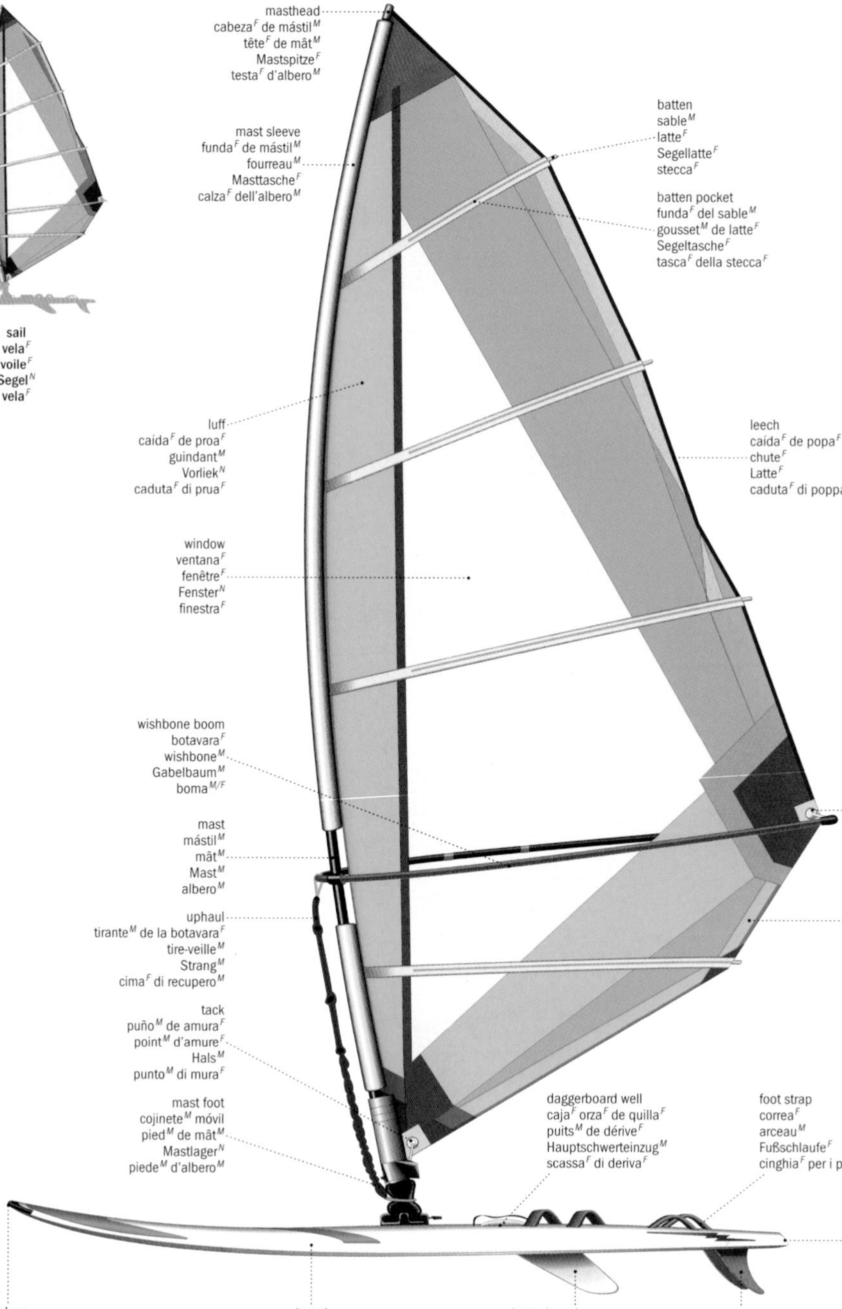

canoe-kayak: whitewater

canoa^F-kayak^M : aguas^F bravas | canoë^M-kayak^M : eaux^F vives | Kanu^N-Kajak$^{M/N}$: Wildwasser^N | canoa^F e kayak^M: rapide^F

canoe
canoa^F
canoë^M
Kanu^N
canoa^F

single-bladed paddle
remo^M de una sola pala^F
pagaie^F simple
Stechpaddel^N
pagaia^F a pala^F singola

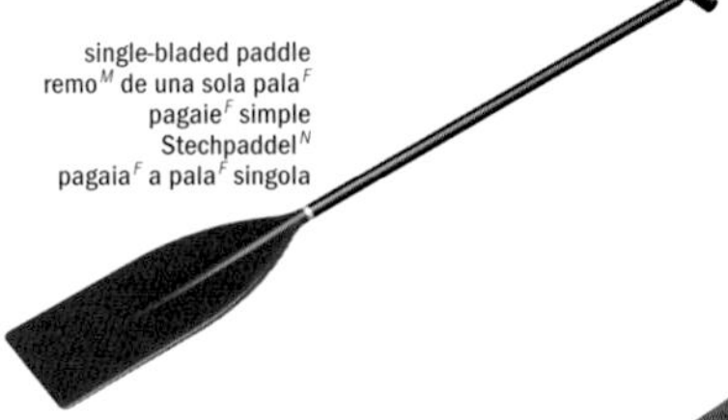

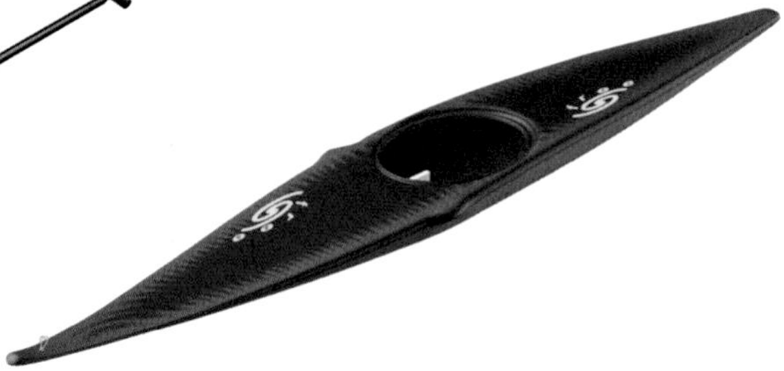

kayak
kayak^M
kayak^M
Kajak$^{M/N}$
kayak^M

double-bladed paddle
remo^M de dos palas^F
pagaie^F double
Doppelpaddel^N
pagaia^F a doppia pala^F

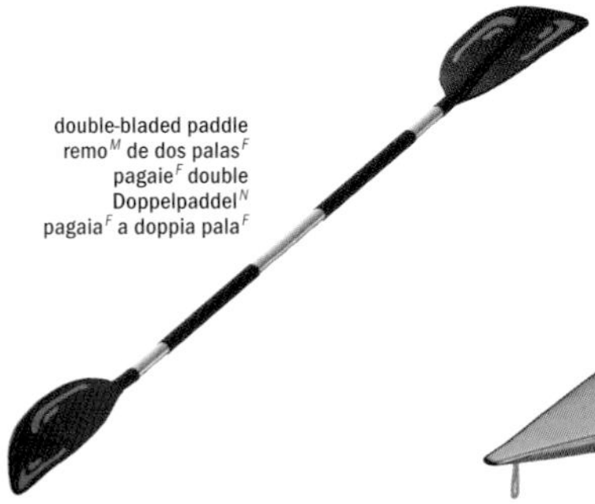

spray skirt
cubrebañeras^M
jupe^F ; jupette^F
Spritzschutz^M
paraspruzzi^M

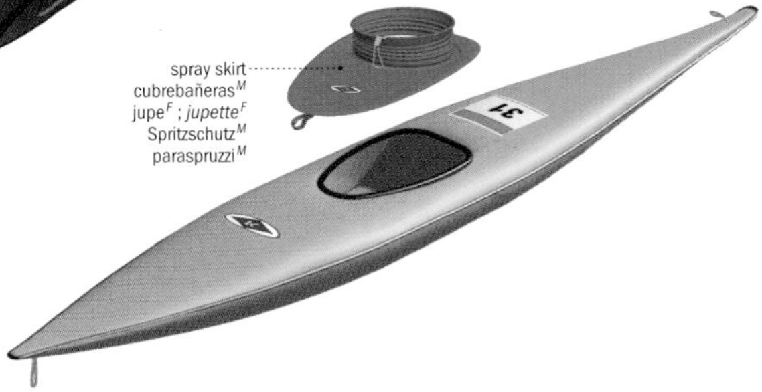

whitewater
aguas^F bravas
eaux^F vives
Wildwasser^N
rapide^F

upstream gate
puerta^F de ascenso^M
porte^F en remontée^F
Aufwärtstor^N
porta^F in risalita^F

gate judge
juez^M de puerta^M
juge^M de porte^F
Streckenschiedsrichter^M
giudice^M di partenza^F

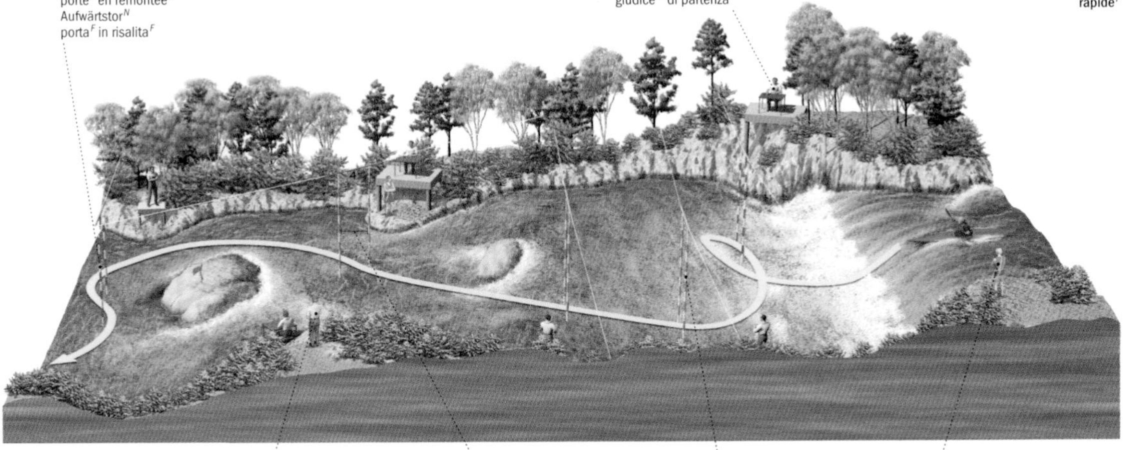

chief judge
árbitro^M principal
juge^M en chef^M
Hauptschiedsrichter^M
giudice^M principale

course gate
puerta^F de recorrido^M
porte^F du parcours^M
Richtungstor^N
porta^F

downstream gate
puerta^F de descenso^M
porte^F en descente^F
Abwärtstor^N
porta^F in discesa^F

safety officer
personal^M de la seguridad^F
responsable^M de la sécurité^F
Rettungswart^M
responsabile^M della sicurezza^F

SPORTS AND GAMES

rowing and sculling

remo^M | aviron^M | Rudern^N und Skullen^N | canottaggio^M con uno e due remi^M

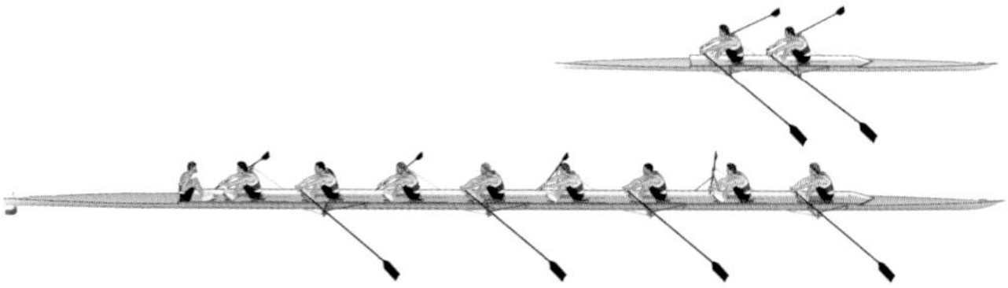

sculling (two oars)
scull^M
aviron^M à couple^M
Skullen^N (zwei Skulls^N)
canottaggio^M di coppia^F (due remi^M)

rowing (one oar)
remo^M en punta^F
aviron^M en pointe^F
Rudern^N (ein Riemen^M)
canottaggio^M di punta^F (un remo^M)

types of oars
tipos de remos^M
types^M d'avirons^M
Riemenarten^F
tipi^M di remi^M

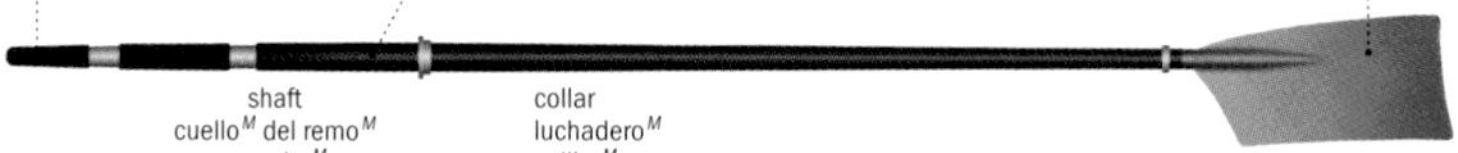

grip
guión^M
poignée^F
Griff^M
impugnatura^F

rubber sheath
funda^F de goma
manchon^M
Innenhebel^M
fasciatura^F in gomma^F

blade
pala^F
pelle^F
Blatt^N
pala^F

sculling oar
scull^M
aviron^M de couple^M
Skull^N
remo^M di coppia^F

shaft
cuello^M del remo^M
manche^M
Schaft^M
asta^F

collar
luchadero^M
collier^M
Klemmring^M
collare^M

blade
pala^F
pelle^F
Blatt^N
pala^F

sweep oar
remo^M en punta^F
aviron^M de pointe^F
Riemen^M
remo^M di punta^F

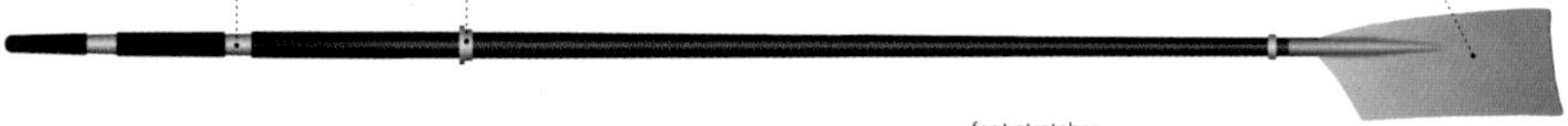

parts of a boat
partes^F de una embarcación^F
parties^F d'un bateau^M
Teile^M eines Boots^N
parti^F di una imbarcazione^F

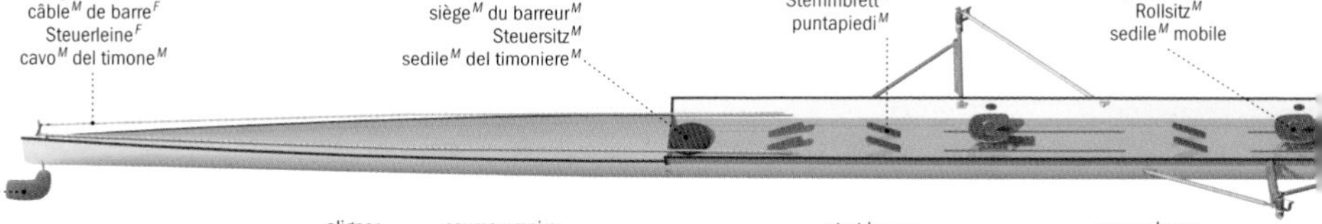

rudder cable
guardín^M
câble^M de barre^F
Steuerleine^F
cavo^M del timone^M

coxswain's seat
asiento^M del timonel^M
siège^M du barreur^M
Steuersitz^M
sedile^M del timoniere^M

foot stretcher
soportes^M para los pies^M
planche^F de pied^M
Stemmbrett^N
puntapiedi^M

sliding seat
carro^M deslizante
siège^M coulissant
Rollsitz^M
sedile^M mobile

rudder
timón^M
gouvernail^M
Steuer^N
timone^M

basin
canal^F
bassin^M
Becken^N
bacino^M

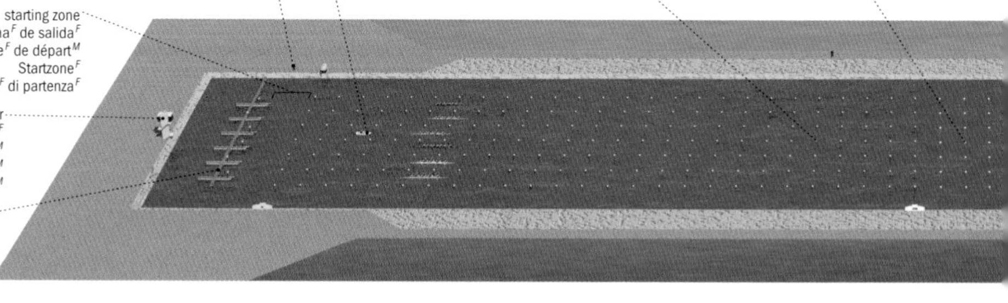

aligner
alineador^M
aligneur^M
Seitenrichter^M
allineatore^M

course umpire
árbitro^M de recorrido^M
arbitre^M de parcours^M
Streckenschiedsrichter^M
arbitro^M di percorso^M

start buoys
boyas^F de salida^F
bouées^F de départ^M
Startbojen^N
boe^F di partenza^F

course buoys
boyas^F de recorrido^M
bouées^F de parcours^M
Bahnbojen^N
boe^F di percorso^M

starting zone
zona^F de salida^F
zone^F de départ^M
Startzone^F
zona^F di partenza^F

starter
juez^M de salida^F
juge^M au départ^M
Starter^M
starter^M

starting jetty
pontón^M de salida^F
ponton^M de départ^M
Ablegepritsche^F
pontile^M di partenza^F

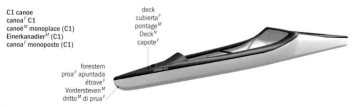

canoe-kayak: flatwater racing

canoa^F-kayak^M : regata^F | canoë^M-kayak^M : course^F en ligne^F | Kanu^N-Kajak^M/N: Flachwasserrennen^N | canoa^F e kayak^M: regate^F fluviali

C1 canoe
canoa^F C1
canoë^M monoplace (C1)
Einerkanadier^M (C1)
canoa^F monoposto (C1)

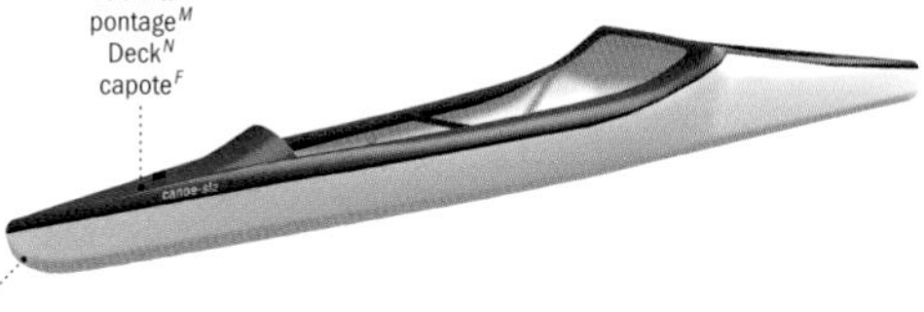

deck
cubierta^F
pontage^M
Deck^N
capote^F

forestem
proa^F apuntada
étrave^F
Vordersteven^M
dritto^M di prua^F

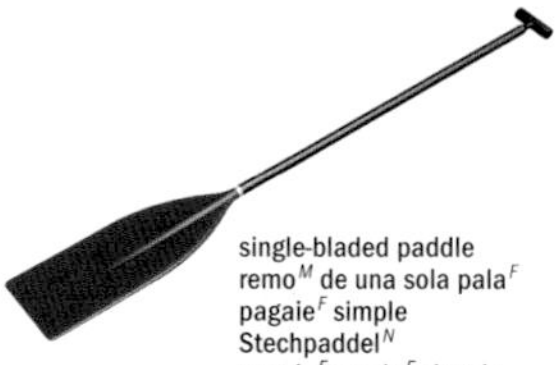

single-bladed paddle
remo^M de una sola pala^F
pagaie^F simple
Stechpaddel^N
pagaia^F a pala^F singola

rowing and sculling

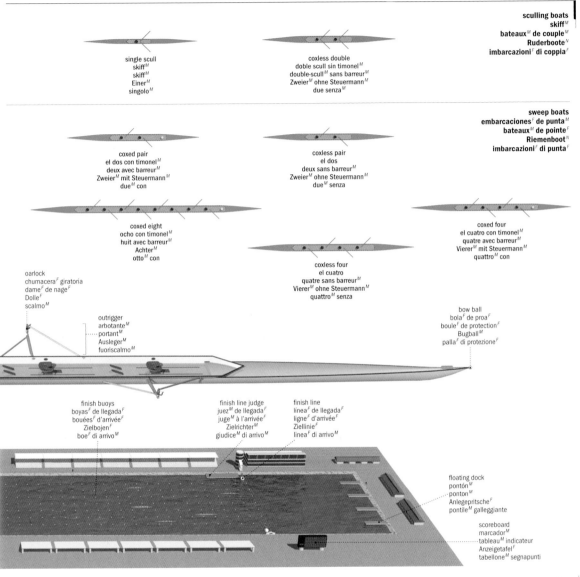

sculling boats
skiff^M
bateaux^M **de couple**^{M}
Ruderboote^N
imbarcazioni^F **di coppia**^{F}

single scull
skiff^M
skiff^M
Einer^M
singolo^M

coxless double
doble scull sin timonel^M
double-scull^M sans barreur^M
Zweier^M ohne Steuermann^M
due senza^M

sweep boats
embarcaciones^F **de punta**^{M}
bateaux^M **de pointe**^{F}
Riemenboot^N
imbarcazioni^F **di punta**^{F}

coxed pair
el dos con timonel^M
deux avec barreur^M
Zweier^M mit Steuermann^M
due^M con

coxless pair
el dos
deux sans barreur^M
Zweier^M ohne Steuermann^M
due^M senza

coxed eight
ocho con timonel^M
huit avec barreur^M
Achter^M
otto^M con

coxed four
el cuatro con timonel^M
quatre avec barreur^M
Vierer^M mit Steuermann^M
quattro^M con

coxless four
el cuatro
quatre sans barreur^M
Vierer^M ohne Steuermann^M
quattro^M senza

oarlock
chumacera^F giratoria
dame^F de nage^F
Dolle^F
scalmo^M

outrigger
arbotante^M
portant^M
Ausleger^M
fuoriscalmo^M

bow ball
bola^F de proa^F
boule^F de protection^F
Bugball^M
palla^F di protezione^F

finish buoys
boyas^F de llegada^F
bouées^F d'arrivée^F
Zielbojen^F
boe^F di arrivo^M

finish line judge
juez^M de llegada^F
juge^M à l'arrivée^F
Zielrichter^M
giudice^M di arrivo^M

finish line
linea^F de llegada^F
ligne^F d'arrivée^F
Ziellinie^F
linea^F di arrivo^M

floating dock
pontón^M
ponton^M
Anlegepritsche^F
pontile^M galleggiante

scoreboard
marcador^M
tableau^M indicateur
Anzeigetafel^F
tabellone^M segnapunti

canoe-kayak: flatwater racing

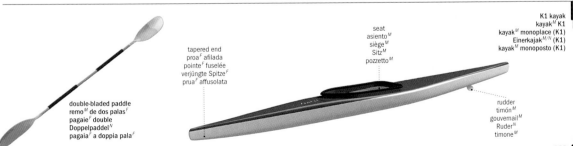

K1 kayak
kayak^M K1
kayak^M monoplace (K1)
Einerkajak$^{M/N}$ (K1)
kayak^M monoposto (K1)

seat
asiento^M
siège^M
Sitz^M
pozzetto^M

tapered end
proa^F afilada
pointe^F fuselée
verjüngte Spitze^F
prua^F affusolata

double-bladed paddle
remo^M de dos palas^F
pagaie^F double
Doppelpaddel^N
pagaia^F a doppia pala^F

rudder
timón^M
gouvernail^M
Ruder^N
timone^M

water skiing

esquí^M acuático | ski^M nautique | Wasserski^N | sci^M nautico

examples of skis
ejemplos^M de esquís^M
exemples^M de skis^M
Beispiele^N für Skier^M
esempi^M di sci^M nautici

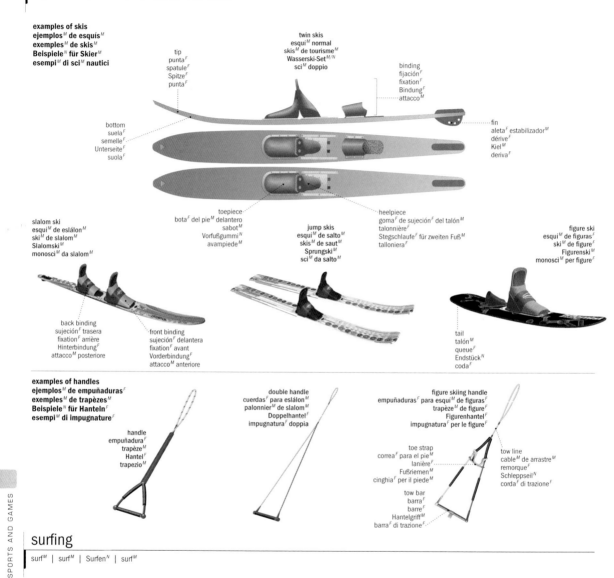

twin skis
esqui^M normal
skis^M de tourisme^M
Wasserski-Set^{M/N}
sci^M doppio

tip
punta^F
spatule^F
Spitze^F
punta^F

binding
fijación^F
fixation^F
Bindung^F
attacco^M

bottom
suela^F
semelle^F
Unterseite^F
suola^F

fin
aleta^F estabilizador^M
dérive^F
Kiel^M
deriva^F

toepiece
bota^F del pie^M delantero
sabot^M
Vorfußgummi^N
avampiede^M

heelpiece
goma^F de sujeción^F del talón^M
talonnière^F
Stegschlaufe^F für zweiten Fuß^M
talloniera^F

slalom ski
esquí^M de eslálon^M
ski^M de slalom^M
Slalomski^M
monosci^M da slalom^M

jump skis
esqui^M de salto^M
skis^M de saut^M
Sprungski^M
sci^M da salto^M

figure ski
esquí^M de figuras^F
ski^M de figure^F
Figurenski^M
monosci^M per figure^F

back binding
sujeción^F trasera
fixation^F arrière
Hinterbindung^F
attacco^M posteriore

front binding
sujeción^F delantera
fixation^F avant
Vorderbindung^F
attacco^M anteriore

tail
talón^M
queue^F
Endstück^N
coda^F

examples of handles
ejemplos^M de empuñaduras^F
exemples^M de trapèzes^M
Beispiele^N für Hanteln^F
esempi^M di impugnature^F

handle
empuñadura^F
trapèze^M
Hantel^F
trapezio^M

double handle
cuerdas^F para eslálon^M
palonnier^M de slalom^M
Doppelhantel^F
impugnatura^F doppia

figure skiing handle
empuñaduras^F para esquí^M de figuras^F
trapèze^M de figure^F
Figurenhantel^F
impugnatura^F per le figure^F

toe strap
correa^F para el pie^M
lanière^F
Fußriemen^M
cinghia^F per il piede^M

tow line
cable^M de arrastre^M
remorque^F
Schleppseil^N
corda^F di trazione^F

tow bar
barra^F
barre^F
Hantelgriff^M
barra^F di trazione^F

surfing

surf^M | surf^M | Surfen^N | surf^M

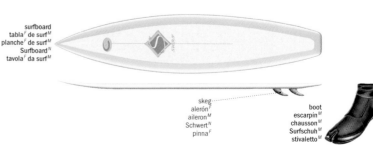

surfboard
tabla^F de surf^M
planche^F de surf^M
Surfboard^N
tavola^F da surf^M

surfer
surfista^M
surfeur^M
Surfer^M
surfista^{M/F}

skeg
alerón^F
aileron^M
Schwert^N
pinna^F

boot
escarpín^M
chausson^M
Surfschuh^M
stivaletto^M

AQUATIC AND NAUTICAL SPORTS | DEPORTES ACUÁTICOS Y NÁUTICOS
SPORTS AQUATIQUES ET NAUTIQUES | WASSERSPORT | SPORT ACQUATICI E NAUTICI

scuba diving

buceo^M | plongée^F sous-marine | Tauchen^N | pesca^F subacquea

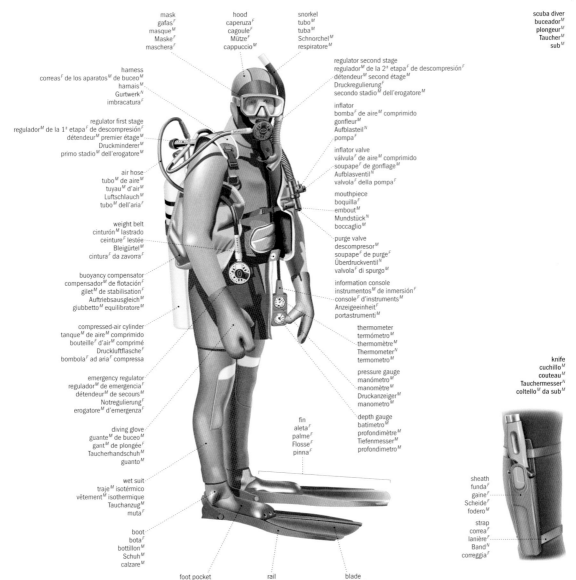

mask
gafas^F
masque^M
Maske^F
maschera^F

hood
caperuza^F
cagoule^F
Mütze^F
cappuccio^M

snorkel
tubo^M
tuba^F
Schnorchel^M
respiratore^M

scuba diver
buceador^M
plongeur^M
Taucher^M
sub^M

regulator second stage
regulador^M de la 2ª etapa^F de descompresión^F
détendeur^M second étage^M
Druckregulierung^F
secondo stadio^M dell'erogatore^M

harness
correas^F de los aparatos^M de buceo^M
harnais^M
Gurtwerk^N
imbracatura^F

inflator
bomba^F de aire^M comprimido
gonfleur^M
Aufblasteil^N
pompa^F

regulator first stage
regulador^M de la 1ª etapa^F de descompresión^F
détendeur^M premier étage^M
Druckminderer^M
primo stadio^M dell'erogatore^M

inflator valve
válvula^F de aire^M comprimido
soupape^F de gonflage^M
Aufblasventil^N
valvola^F della pompa^F

air hose
tubo^M de aire^M
tuyau^M d'air^M
Luftschlauch^M
tubo^M dell'aria^F

mouthpiece
boquilla^F
embout^M
Mundstück^N
boccaglio^M

weight belt
cinturón^M lastrado
ceinture^F lestée
Bleigürtel^M
cintura^F da zavorra^F

purge valve
descompresor^M
soupape^F de purge^F
Überdruckventil^N
valvola^F di spurgo^M

buoyancy compensator
compensador^M de flotación^F
gilet^M de stabilisation^F
Auftriebsausgleich^M
giubbetto^M equilibratore^M

information console
instrumentos^M de inmersión^F
console^F d'instruments^M
Anzeigeeinheit^F
portastrumenti^M

compressed-air cylinder
tanque^M de aire^M comprimido
bouteille^F d'air^M comprimé
Druckluftflasche^F
bombola^F ad aria^F compressa

thermometer
termómetro^M
thermomètre^M
Thermometer^M
termometro^M

knife
cuchillo^M
couteau^M
Tauchermesser^N
coltello^M da sub^M

pressure gauge
manómetro^M
manomètre^M
Druckanzeiger^M
manometro^M

emergency regulator
regulador^M de emergencia^F
détendeur^M de secours^M
Notregulierung^F
erogatore^M d'emergenza^F

depth gauge
batímetro^M
profondimètre^M
Tiefenmesser^M
profondimetro^M

fin
aleta^F
palme^F
Flosse^F
pinna^F

diving glove
guante^M de buceo^M
gant^M de plongée^F
Taucherhandschuh^M
guanto^M

sheath
funda^F
gaine^F
Scheide^F
fodero^M

wet suit
traje^M isotérmico
vêtement^M isothermique
Tauchanzug^M
muta^F

strap
correa^F
lanière^F
Band^N
correggia^F

boot
bota^F
bottillon^M
Schuh^M
calzare^M

foot pocket
bota^F de la aleta^F
chausson^M
Fußteil^N
scarpetta^F

rail
borde^M
nervure^F
Rand^M
costolatura^F

blade
palma^F
voilure^F
Blatt^N
pala^F

speargun
arpón^M submarino
fusil^M à air^M comprimé
Harpune^F
fucile^M subacqueo

boxing

boxeo^M | boxe^F | Boxen^N | pugilato^M

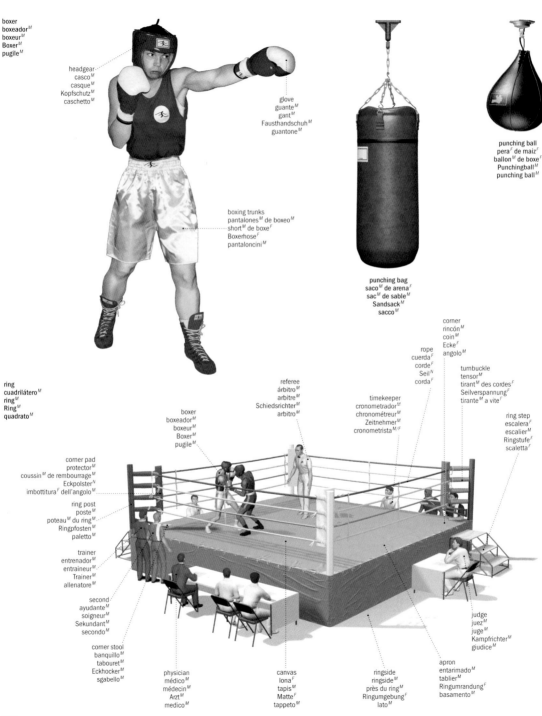

boxer
boxeador^M
boxeur^M
Boxer^M
pugile^M

headgear
casco^M
casque^M
Kopfschutz^M
caschetto^M

glove
guante^M
gant^M
Fausthandschuh^M
guantone^M

punching ball
pera^F de maíz^F
ballon^M de boxe^F
Punchingball^M
punching ball^M

boxing trunks
pantalones^M de boxeo^M
short^M de boxe^F
Boxerhose^F
pantaloncini^M

punching bag
saco^M de arena^F
sac^M de sable^M
Sandsack^M
sacco^M

corner
rincón^M
coin^M
Ecke^F
angolo^M

rope
cuerda^F
corde^N
Seil^N
corda^F

turnbuckle
tensor^M
tirant^M des cordes^F
Seilverspannung^F
tirante^M a vite^F

ring
cuadrilátero^M
ring^M
Ring^M
quadrato^M

referee
árbitro^M
arbitre^M
Schiedsrichter^M
arbitro^M

boxer
boxeador^M
boxeur^M
Boxer^M
pugile^M

timekeeper
cronometrador^M
chronométreur^M
Zeitnehmer^M
cronometrista^M/F

ring step
escalera^F
escalier^M
Ringstufe^F
scaletta^F

corner pad
protector^M
coussin^M de rembourrage^M
Eckpolster^N
imbottitura^F dell'angolo^M

ring post
poste^M
poteau^M du ring^M
Ringpfosten^M
paletto^M

trainer
entrenador^M
entraineur^M
Trainer^M
allenatore^M

second
ayudante^M
soigneur^M
Sekundant^M
secondo^M

judge
juez^M
juge^M
Kampfrichter^M
giudice^M

corner stool
banquillo^M
tabouret^M
Eckhocker^M
sgabello^M

physician
médico^M
médecin^M
Arzt^M
medico^M

canvas
lona^F
tapis^M
Matte^F
tappeto^M

ringside
ringside^M
près du ring^M
Ringumgebung^F
lato^M

apron
entarimado^M
tablier^M
Ringumrandung^F
basamento^M

lace
cordones[M]
lacet[M]
Schnürsenkel[M]
stringa[F]

boxing gloves
guantes[M] de boxeo[M]
gants[M] de boxe[F]
Boxhandschuhe[M]
guantoni[M]

bandage
vendaje[M]
bandage[M]
Bandage[F]
bendaggio[M]

protective cup
coquilla[F]
coquille[F] de protection[F]
Suspensorium[N]
conchiglia[F] di protezione[F]

mouthpiece
protector[M] bucal
protège-dents[M]
Mundschutz[M]
paradenti[M]

wrestling

lucha[F] | lutte[F] | Ringen[N] | lotta[F]

starting positions
posiciones[M] iniciales
positions[F] de départ[M]
Startpositionen[F]
posizioni[F] di partenza[F]

wrestler
luchador[M]
lutteur[M]
Ringer[M]
lottatore[M]

singlet
camiseta[F]
maillot[M]
Trikot[N]
costume[M]

crouching position (freestyle wrestling)
posición[F] en guardia[F] : (lucha[F] libre)
garde[F] basse (lutte[F] libre)
gebückter Stand[M] (Freistil[M])
guardia[F] bassa (lotta[F] libera)

standing position (Greco-Roman wrestling)
posición[F] vertical: (lucha[F] greco-romana)
garde[F] haute (lutte[F] gréco-romaine)
aufrechter Stand[M] (griechisch-römischer Stil[M])
guardia[F] in piedi[M] (lotta[F] greco-romana)

wrestling shoe
botas[F] de lucha[F]
chaussure[F] de lutte[F]
Ringerschuh[M]
scarpa[F]

wrestling area
área[F] de lucha[F] libre
aire[F] de combat[M]
Wettkampffläche[F]
area[F] di combattimento[M]

passivity zone
zona[F] de pasividad[F]
zone[F] de passivité[F]
Passivitätszone[F]
zona[F] di passività[F]

wrestler
luchador[M]
lutteur[M]
Ringer[M]
lottatore[M]

protection area
superficie[F] de protección[F]
surface[F] de protection[F]
Schutzfläche[F]
area[F] di sicurezza[F]

judge
juez[M]
juge[M]
Punktrichter[M]
giudice[M]

referee
árbitro[M]
arbitre[M]
Kampfrichter[M]
arbitro[M]

central wrestling area
zona[F] de lucha[F]
surface[F] centrale de lutte[F]
zentrale Kampffläche[F]
superficie[F] centrale di lotta[F]

mat chairperson
jefe[M] de tapiz[M]
chef[M] de tapis[M]
Hauptkampfrichter[M]
presidente[M] di tappeto[M]

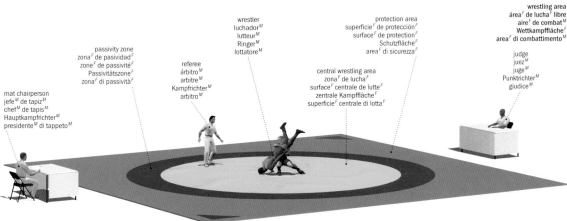

judo

judo^M | judo^M | Judo^N | judo^M

mat
tatami^M
tapis^M
Matte^F
tappeto^M

scorers and timekeepers
anotadores^M y cronometradores^M
marqueurs^M et chronométreurs^M
Registratoren^M und Zeitnehmer^M
segnapunti^M e cronometristi^M

scoreboard
marcador^M
tableau^M d'affichage^M
Anzeigetafel^F
tabellone^M segnapunti

medical team
equipo^M médico
équipe^F médicale
Ärzteteam^N
staff^M medico

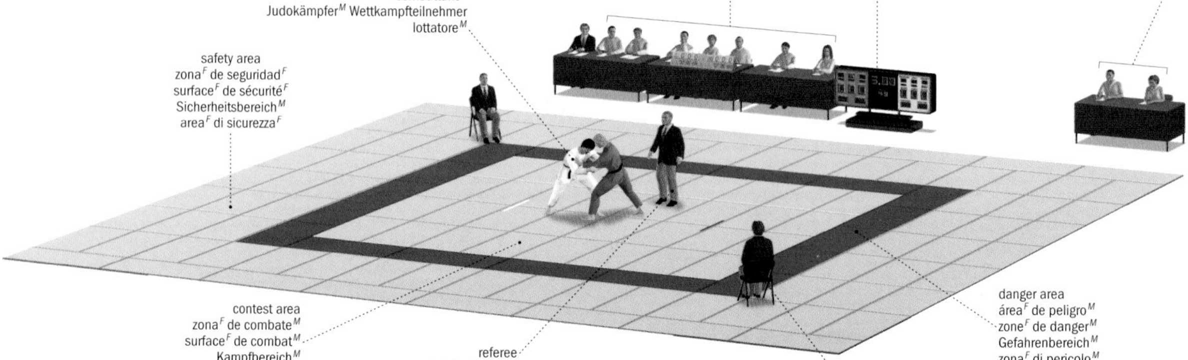

contestant
uke (defensor^M)
combattant^M
Judokämpfer^M Wettkampfteilnehmer
lottatore^M

safety area
zona^F de seguridad^F
surface^F de sécurité^F
Sicherheitsbereich^M
area^F di sicurezza^F

contest area
zona^F de combate^M
surface^F de combat^M
Kampfbereich^M
area^F di combattimento^M

referee
judoka^M neutral
arbitre^M
Schiedsrichter^M
arbitro^M

danger area
área^F de peligro^M
zone^F de danger^M
Gefahrenbereich^M
zona^F di pericolo^M

judge
juez^M
juge^M
Kampfrichter^M
giudice^M

judogi
traje^M de judo (judoji^M)
judogi^M
Judogi^M
judogi^M

jacket
kimono^M
veste^F
Jacke^F
giacca^F

examples of holds and throws
ejemplos^M de llaves^F
exemples^M de prises^F
Griff- und Wurfbeispiele^N
esempi^M di prese^F

trousers
pantalón^M
pantalon^M
Hose^F
pantaloni^M

belt
cinturón^M
ceinture^F
Gürtel^M
cintura^F

holding
inmovilización^F
immobilisation^F
Haltegriffe^M
presa^F a terra^F

sweeping hip throw
proyección^F primera de cadera^F
hanche^F ailée
Hüftwurf^M
spazzata^F d'anca^F

major outer reaping throw
osoto-gari (gran siega^F) exterior
grand fauchage^M extérieur
Große Außensichel^F
grande falciata^F esterna

stomach throw
proyección^F en círculo^M
projection^F en cercle^M
Kopfwurf^M
rovesciata^F all'indietro

major inner reaping throw
gran siega^F interior
grand fauchage^M intérieur
Große Innensichel^F
grande falciata^F interna

naked strangle
estrangulación^F
étranglement^M
Halsumklammerung^F
presa^F di strangolamento^M

arm lock
inmovilización^F de brazo^M
clé^F de bras^M
Armhebel^M
presa^F a croce^F

one-arm shoulder throw
proyección^F por encima del hombro^M con una mano^F
projection^F d'épaule^F par un côté^M
einarmiger Schulterwurf^M
proiezione^F di spalla^F e braccio^M

SPORTS AND GAMES

karate

karate^M | karaté^M | Karate^N | karatè^M

karateka
karateka^M
karatéka^F
Karateka^M
karateka^{M/F}

karate-gi
karategi^M
karatégi^M
Karategi^M
karategi^M

contest area
zona^F de combate^M
surface^F de combat^M
Wettkampfbereich^M
area^F di combattimento^M

obi
obi^M
obi^F
Obi^M
obi^M

referee's line
línea^F de árbitro^M
ligne^F de l'arbitre^M
Hauptkampfrichterlinie^F
linea^F dell'arbitro^M

competitors' line
linea de los competidores^M
ligne^F des compétiteurs^M
Kämpferlinie^F
linea^F dei karateka^M

competition area
zona^F de competición^F
aire^F de compétition^F
Wettkampffläche^F
area^F di gara^F

arbitration committee
comité^M de arbitraje^M
comité^M d'arbitrage^M
Kampfgericht^N
collegio^M arbitrale

corner judge
juez^M de ángulo^M
juge^M de coin^M
Seitenkampfrichter^M
giudice^M d'angolo^M

scorekeeper
anotador^M
marqueur^M
Listenführer^M
segnapunti^M

timekeeper
cronometrador^M
chronométreur^M
Zeitnehmer^M
cronometrista^{M/F}

referee
árbitro^M
arbitre^M
Hauptkampfrichter^M
arbitro^M

karateka
karateka^M
karatéka^M
Karateka^M
karateka^M

SPORTS AND GAMES

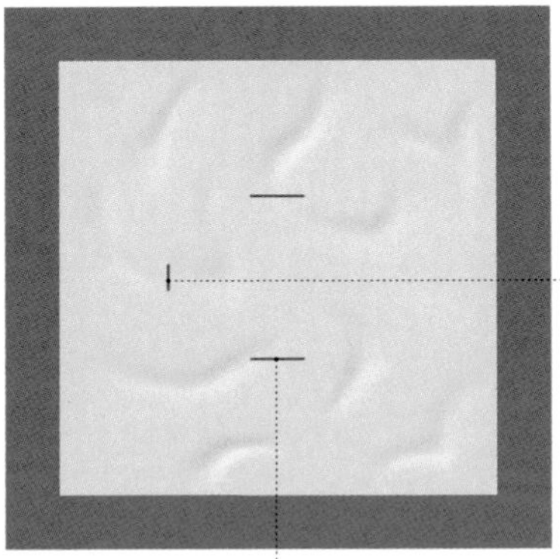

kung fu

kung fu^M | kung-fu^M | Kung-Fu^N | kung fu^M

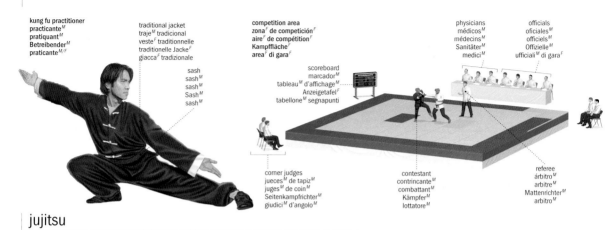

kung fu practitioner
practicante
pratiquant^M
Betreibender^M
praticante$^{M/F}$

traditional jacket
traje^M tradicional
veste^F traditionnelle
traditionelle Jacke^F
giacca^F tradizionale

sash
sash^M
sash^M
Sash^M
sash^M

competition area
zona^F **de competición**^{F}
aire^F **de compétition**^{F}
Kampffläche^F
area^F **di gara**^{F}

scoreboard
marcador^M
tableau^M d'affichage^M
Anzeigetafel^F
tabellone^M segnapunti

physicians
médicos^M
médecins^M
Sanitäter^M
medici^M

officials
oficiales^M
officiels^M
Offizielle^M
ufficiali^M di gara^F

corner judges
jueces^M de tapiz^M
juges^M de coin^M
Seitenkampfrichter^M
giudici^M d'angolo^M

contestant
contrincante^M
combattant^M
Kämpfer^M
lottatore^M

referee
árbitro^M
arbitre^M
Mattenrichter^M
arbitro^M

jujitsu

ju-jitsu^M | ju-jitsu^M | Jujutsu^N | jujutsu^M

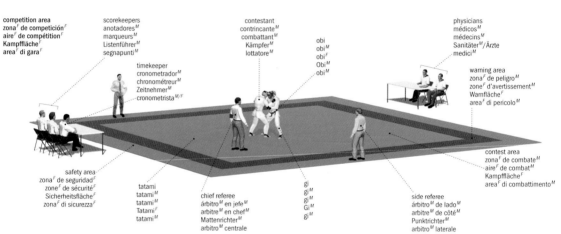

competition area
zona^F **de competición**^{F}
aire^F **de compétition**^{F}
Kampffläche^F
area^F **di gara**^{F}

scorekeepers
anotadores^M
marqueurs^M
Listenführer^M
segnapunti^M

timekeeper
cronometrador^M
chronométreur^M
Zeitnehmer^M
cronometrista$^{M/F}$

contestant
contrincante^M
combattant^M
Kämpfer^M
lottatore^M

obi
obi^M
obi^M
Obi^M
obi^M

physicians
médicos^M
médecins^M
Sanitäter^M/Ärzte
medici^M

warning area
zona^F de peligro^M
zone^F d'avertissement^M
Warnfläche^F
area^F di pericolo^M

safety area
zona^F de seguridad^F
zone^F de sécurité^F
Sicherheitsfläche^F
zona^F di sicurezza^F

tatami
tatami^M
tatami^M
Tatami^F
tatami^M

chief referee
árbitro^M en jefe^M
arbitre^M en chef^M
Mattenrichter^M
arbitro^M centrale

gi
gi^M
gi^M
Gi^M
gi^M

side referee
árbitro^M de lado^M
arbitre^M de côté^M
Punktrichter^M
arbitro^M laterale

contest area
zona^F de combate^M
aire^F de combat^M
Kampffläche^F
area^F di combattimento^M

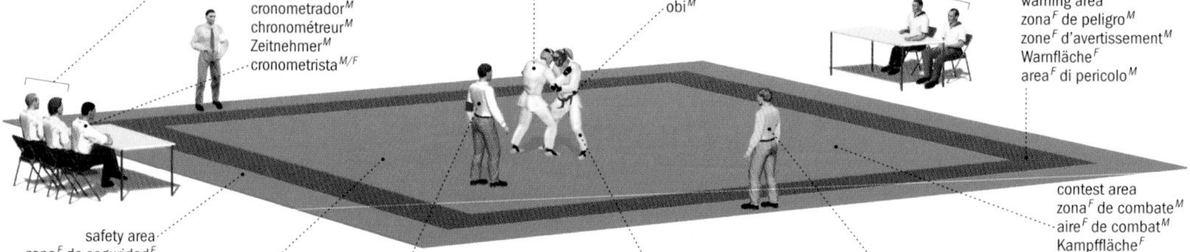

aikido

aikido^M | aïkido^M | Aikido^N | aikido^M

aikidoka
aikidoka^M
aikidoka^M
Aikidoka^M
aikidoka$^{M/F}$

obi
obi^M
obi^F
Obi^M
obi^M

aikidogi
aikidogi^M
aïkidogi^M
Aikidogi^M
aikidogi^M

hakama
hakama^M
hakama^M
Hakama^M
hakama^M

jo
bastón^M
bâton^M
Jo^M
bastone^M

bokken
bokken^M
bokken^M
Bokken^M
bokken^M

kendo

kendo^M | kendo^M | Kendo^N | kendo^M

kendoka
kendoka^M
kendoka^M
Kendoka^M
kendoka^{M/F}

men
men^M
men^M
Men^M
men^M

shinai
shinai^M
shinai^M
Shinai^M
shinai^M

do
do^M
do^M
Do^M
do^M

kote
kote^M
kote^M
Kote
kote^M

tare
tare^M
tare^M
Tare^M
tare^M

hakama
hakama^M
hakama^M
Hakama^M
hakama^M

competition area
área^F de competición^F
aire^F de compétition^F
Kampffläche^F
area^F di gara^F

center
centro^M
centre^M
Mitte^F
centro^M

danger zone
zona^F de peligro
zone^F de danger^M
Gefahrenzone^F
zona^F di pericolo^M

competitors' line
línea^F de competición
ligne^F des compétiteurs^M
Kämpferlinie^F
linea^F dei kendoka^M

assistant referee
árbitro^M auxiliar
arbitre^M auxiliaire
Schiedsrichter^M
arbitro^M ausiliario

scorekeepers
marcadores^M
marqueurs^M
Listenführer^M
segnapunti^M

timekeeper
cronometrador^M
chronométreur^M
Zeitnehmer^M
cronometrista^{M/F}

chief referee
árbitro^M en jefe^M
arbitre^M en chef^M
Hauptschiedsrichter^M
arbitro^M

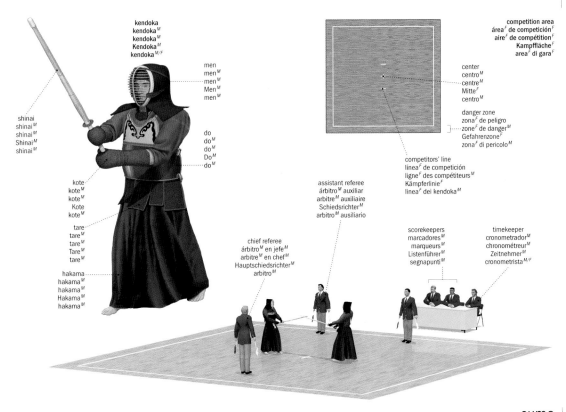

sumo

sumo^M | sumo^M | Sumo^N | sumo^M

dohyo
dohyo^M
dohyo^M
Dohyo^M
dohyo^M

mawashi
mawashi^M
mawashi^M
Mawashi^M
mawashi^M

gyoji
gyogi^M
gyoji^M
Gyoji^M
gyoji^M

mage
mage^M
mage^M
Mage^M
mage^M

sumotori
sumotori^M
sumotori^M
Sumoringer^M
sumotori^M

sagari
sagari^M
sagari^M
Sagari
sagari^M

salt
sal^M
sel^M
Salzkorb^M
sale^M

step
peldaño^M
marche^F
Stufe^F
gradino^M

water
agua^M
eau^F
Wassertrog^M
acqua^F

SPORTS AND GAMES

847

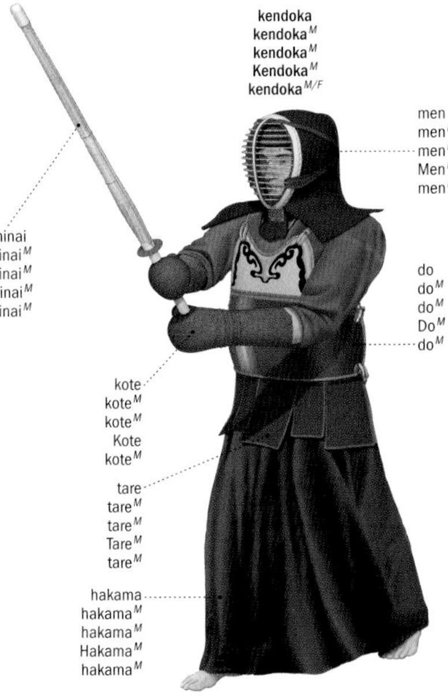

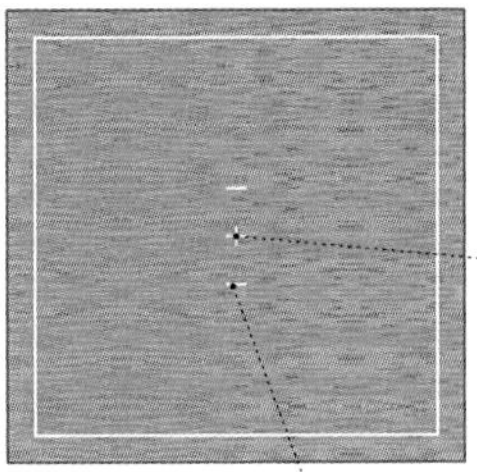

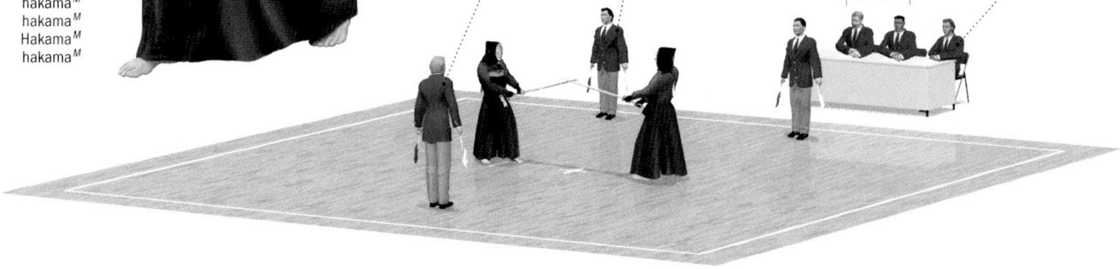

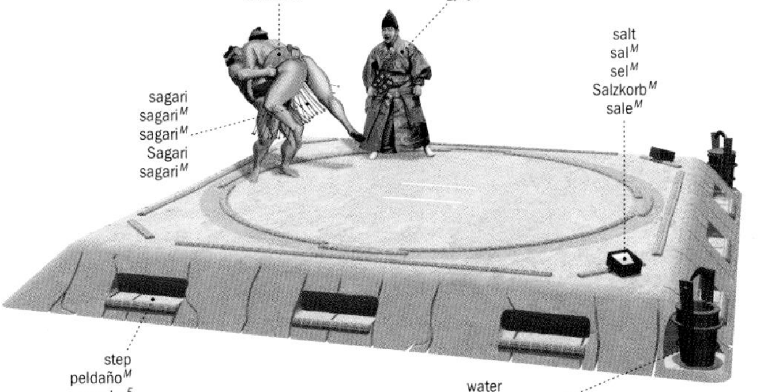

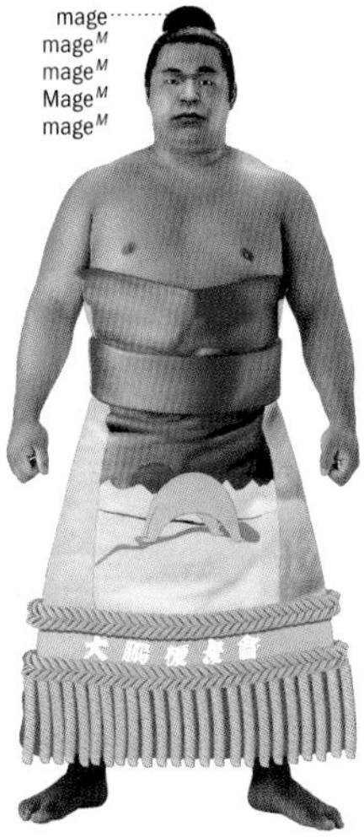

fencing

esgrima^F | escrime^F | Fechtsport^M | scherma^F

fencer
esgrimista^M
escrimeur^M
Fechter^M
schermidore^M

mask
careta^F de esgrima^F
masque^M
Fechtmaske^F
maschera^F

bib
gola^F
bavette^F
Latz^M
gorgiera^F

jacket
chaqueta^F blanca de esgrima^F
veste^F
Fechtjacke^F
giubbotto^M

glove
guante^M de esgrima^F
gant^M
Fechthandschuh^M
guanto^M

metallic plastron
peto^M metálico
plastron^M métallique
Elektroweste^F
coprigiubbotto^M metallico

cuff
manga^F
crispin^M
Ärmelaufschlag^M
manica^F

stocking
media^F
chaussette^F
Kniestrumpf^M
calzettone^M

breeches
calzón^M
culotte^F
Fechthose^F
calzoni^M

fencing shoe
zapatillas^F de esgrima^F
chaussure^F d'escrime^F
Fechtschuh^M
scarpetta^F

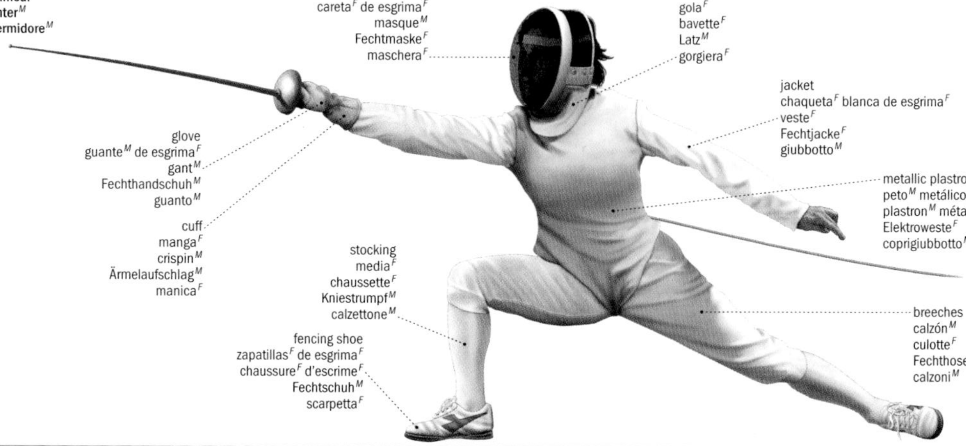

target areas
áreas^F válidas de tocado^M
cibles^F
Treffflächen^F
aree^F di bersaglio^M

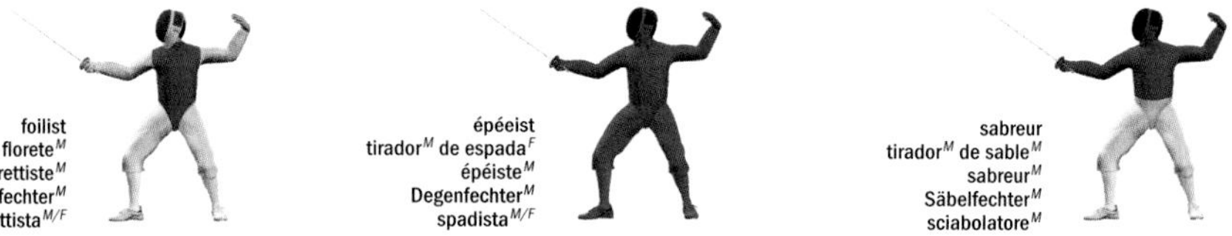

foilist
tirador^M de florete^M
fleurettiste^M
Florettfechter^M
fiorettista^{M/F}

épéeist
tirador^M de espada^F
épéiste^M
Degenfechter^M
spadista^{M/F}

sabreur
tirador^M de sable^M
sabreur^M
Säbelfechter^M
sciabolatore^M

piste
pista^F de esgrima^F
piste^F
Fechtbahn^F
pedana^F

timekeeper
cronometrador^M
chronométreur^M
Zeitnehmer^M
cronometrista^{M/F}

electric foil
florete^M eléctrico
fleuret^M électrique
Elektroflorett^N
fioretto^M elettrico

foil warning line
línea^F de puesta^F en guardia^F de florete^M
ligne^F d'avertissement^M- fleuret^M
Warnlinie^F beim Florettfechten^N
linea^F di avvertimento^M per il fioretto^M

scoring light
lámpara indicadora de tocado^M
lampe^F-témoin^M
Trefferanzeige^F
luce^F segnapunti

electrical scoring apparatus
equipo^M marcador electrónico
compte-touches^M électrique
Elektrometer^M
dispositivo^M segnapunti elettrico

reel
carrete^M del cable^M
enrouleur^M
Kabelrolle^F
bobina^F

judge
juez^M
juge^M
Kampfrichter^M
giudice^M

on guard line
línea^F de puesta^F en guardia^F
ligne^F de mise^F en garde^F
Startlinie^F
linea^F di messa in guardia^F

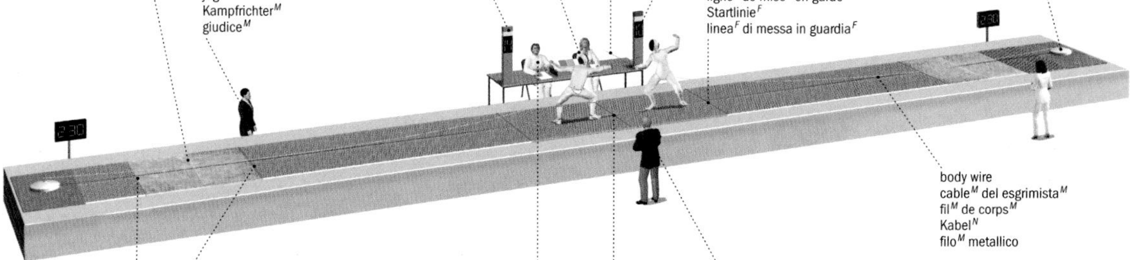

body wire
cable^M del esgrimista^M
fil^M de corps^M
Kabel^N
filo^M metallico

saber and épée warning line
línea^F de puesta^F en guardia^F de sable^M y espada^F
ligne^F d'avertissement^M- épée^F et sabre^M
Warnlinie^F beim Säbel- und Degenfechten^N
linea^F di avvertimento^M per la sciabola^F e la spada^F

president
presidente^M
président^M
Obmann^M
presidente^M

rear limit line
línea^F límite^M de salida^F
ligne^F de limite^F arrière
hintere Begrenzungslinie^F
linea^F di limite^M posteriore

scorer
marcador^M
marqueur^M
Anschreiber^M
segnapunti^M

center line
línea^F del centro^M
ligne^F médiane
Mittellinie^F
linea^F centrale

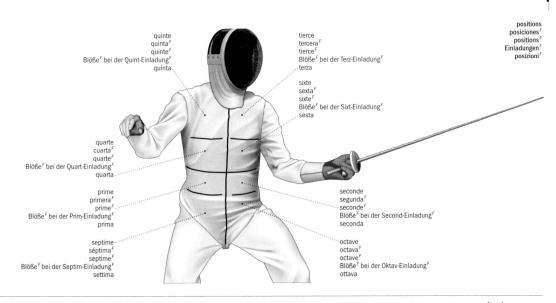

positions
posiciones^F
positions^F
Einladungen^F
posizioni^F

quinte
quinta^F
quinte^F
Blöße^F bei der Quint-Einladung^F
quinta

tierce
tercera^F
tierce^F
Blöße^F bei der Terz-Einladung^F
terza

sixte
sexta^F
sixte^F
Blöße^F bei der Sixt-Einladung^F
sesta

quarte
cuarta^F
quarte^F
Blöße^F bei der Quart-Einladung^F
quarta

prime
primera^F
prime^F
Blöße^F bei der Prim-Einladung^F
prima

seconde
segunda^F
seconde^F
Blöße^F bei der Second-Einladung^F
seconda

septime
séptima^F
septime^F
Blöße^F bei der Septim-Einladung^F
settima

octave
octava^F
octave^F
Blöße^F bei der Oktav-Einladung^F
ottava

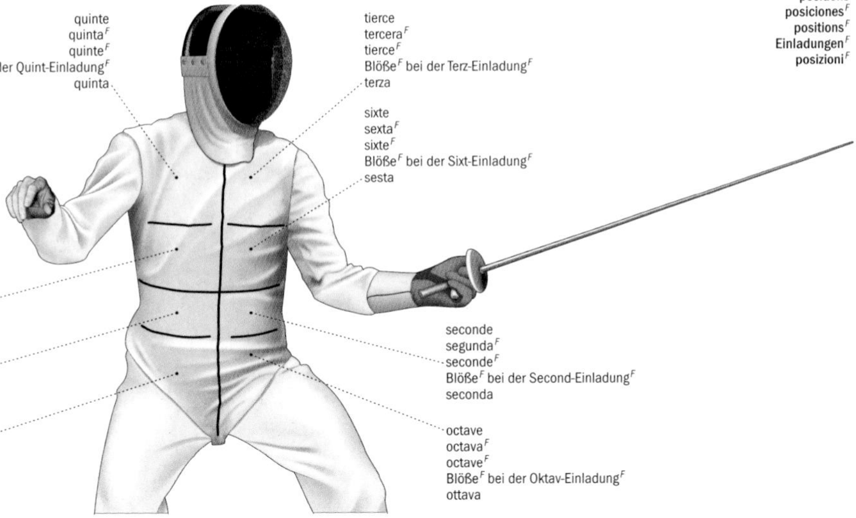

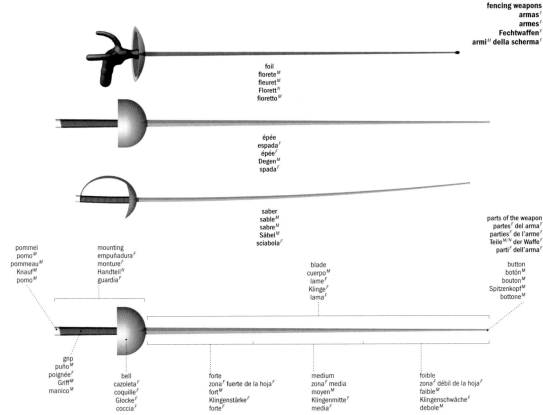

fencing weapons
armas^F
armes^F
Fechtwaffen^F
armi^M della scherma^F

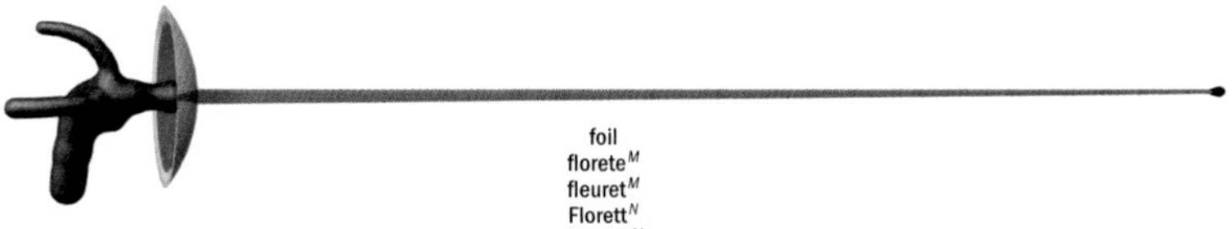

foil
florete^M
fleuret^M
Florett^N
fioretto^M

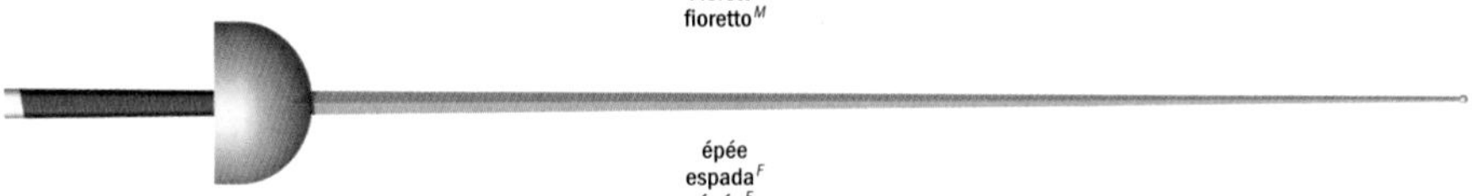

épée
espada^F
épée^F
Degen^M
spada^F

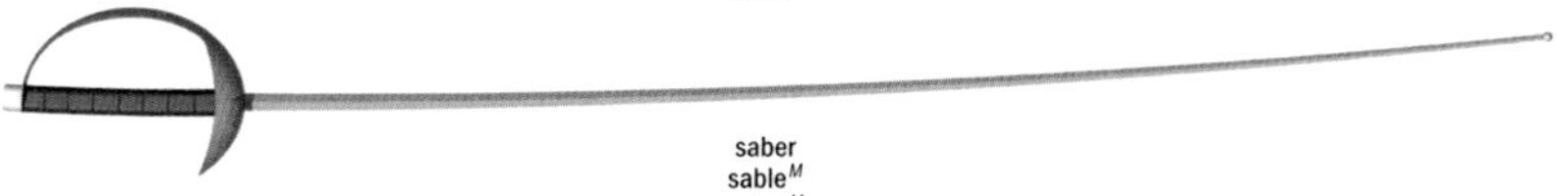

saber
sable^M
sabre^M
Säbel^M
sciabola^F

parts of the weapon
partes^F del arma^F
parties^F de l'arme^F
Teile^{M/N} der Waffe^F
parti^F dell'arma^F

pommel
pomo^M
pommeau^M
Knauf^M
pomo^M

mounting
empuñadura^F
monture^F
Handteil^N
guardia^F

blade
cuerpo^M
lame^F
Klinge^F
lama^F

button
botón^M
bouton^M
Spitzenkopf^M
bottone^M

grip
puño^M
poignée^F
Griff^M
manico^M

bell
cazoleta^F
coquille^F
Glocke^F
coccia^F

forte
zona^F fuerte de la hoja^F
fort^M
Klingenstärke^F
forte^F

medium
zona^F media
moyen^M
Klingenmitte^F
media^F

foible
zona^F débil de la hoja^F
faible^M
Klingenschwäche^F
debole^M

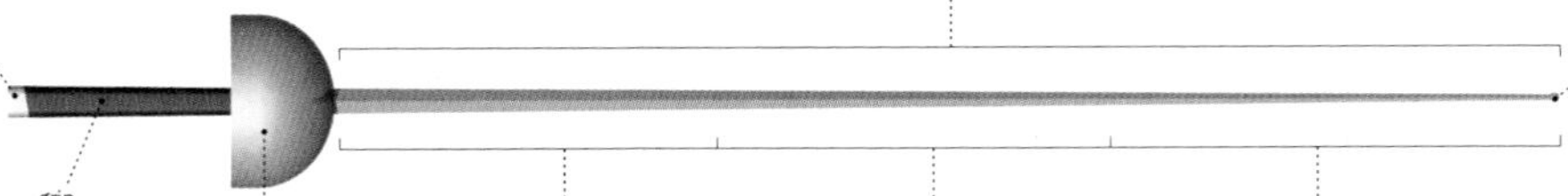

weightlifting

halterofilia^F | haltérophilie^F | Gewichtheben^N | sollevamento^M pesi^M

barbell
barra^F con pesas^F
haltère^M long
Scheibenhantel^F
bilanciere^M

wristband
muñequera^F
poignet^M de force^F
Handgelenksbandage^F
polsino^M

weightlifting belt
cinturón^M
ceinture^F d'haltérophilie^F
Gewichthebergürtel^M
cintura^F da sollevamento^M pesi^M

sleeveless jersey
camiseta^F sin mangas^F
maillot^M de corps^M
ärmelloses Sporthemd^N
canottiera^F

trunks
pantalón^M
culotte^F
Hose^F
pantaloncini^M

knee wrap
rodillera^F
genouillère^F
Kniebandage^F
ginocchiera^F

strap
correa^F
lanière^F
Riemen^M
cinturino^M

weightlifting shoe
zapatilla^F
chaussure^F d'haltérophilie^F
Gewichtheberschuh^M
scarpa^F

clean and jerk
envión^M
épaulé^M-jeté^M
Stoßen^N
slancio^M

snatch
arranque^M
arraché^M
Reißen^N
strappo^M

fitness equipment

aparatos^M de ejercicios^M | appareils^M de conditionnement^M physique | Fitnessgeräte^N | attrezzi^M ginnici

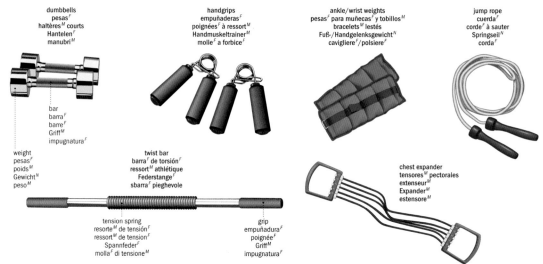

dumbbells
pesas^F
haltères^M courts
Hanteln^F
manubri^M

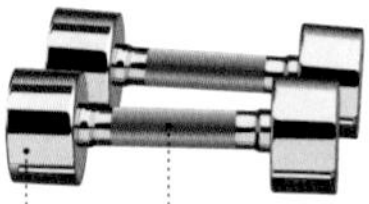

handgrips
empuñaderas^F
poignées^F à ressort^M
Handmuskeltrainer^M
molle^F a forbice^F

ankle/wrist weights
pesas^F para muñecas^F y tobillos^M
bracelets^M lestés
Fuß-/Handgelenksgewicht^N
cavigliere^F/polsiere^F

jump rope
cuerda^F
corde^F à sauter
Springseil^N
corda^F

bar
barra^F
barre^F
Griff^M
impugnatura^F

weight
pesas^F
poids^M
Gewicht^N
peso^M

twist bar
barra^F de torsión^F
ressort^M athlétique
Federstange^F
sbarra^F pieghevole

chest expander
tensores^M pectorales
extenseur^F
Expander^M
estensore^M

tension spring
resorte^M de tensión^F
ressort^M de tension^F
Spannfeder^F
molla^F di tensione^M

grip
empuñadura^F
poignée^F
Griff^M
impugnatura^F

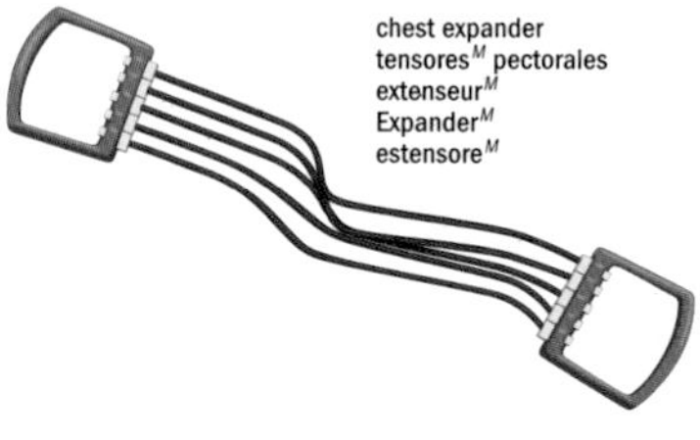

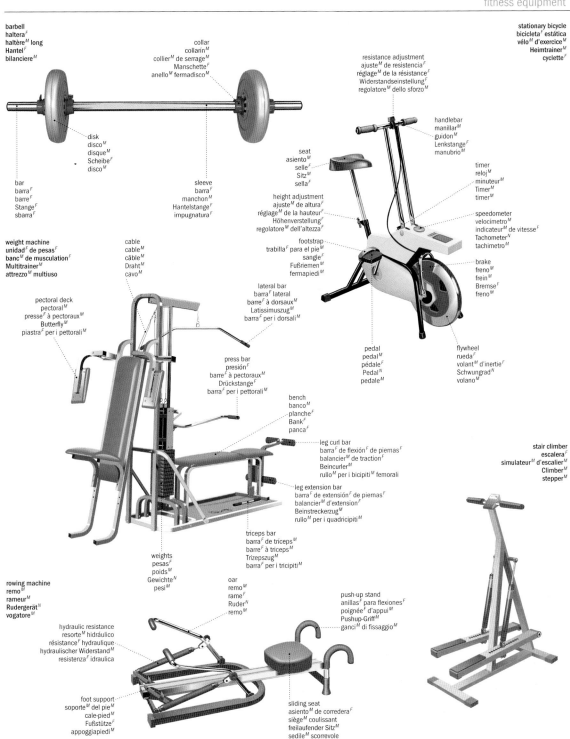

barbell
haltera^F
haltère^M long
Hantel^F
bilanciere^M

collar
collarín^M
collier^M de serrage^M
Manschette^F
anello^M fermadisco^M

stationary bicycle
bicicleta^F estática
vélo^M d'exercice^M
Heimtrainer^M
cyclette^F

resistance adjustment
ajuste^M de resistencia^F
réglage^M de la résistance^F
Widerstandseinstellung^F
regolatore^M dello sforzo^M

handlebar
manillar^M
guidon^M
Lenkstange^F
manubrio^M

disk
disco^M
disque^M
Scheibe^F
disco^M

seat
asiento^M
selle^F
Sitz^M
sella^F

timer
reloj^M
minuteur^M
Timer^M
timer^M

bar
barra^F
barre^F
Stange^F
sbarra^F

sleeve
barra^F
manchon^M
Hantelstange^F
impugnatura^F

height adjustment
ajuste^M de altura^F
réglage^M de la hauteur^F
Höhenverstellung^F
regolatore^M dell'altezza^F

speedometer
velocímetro^M
indicateur^M de vitesse^F
Tachometer^N
tachimetro^M

weight machine
unidad^F de pesas^F
banc^M de musculation^F
Multitrainer^M
attrezzo^M multiuso

cable
cable^M
câble^M
Draht^M
cavo^M

footstrap
trabilla^F para el pie^M
sangle^F
Fußriemen^M
fermapiedi^M

brake
freno^M
frein^M
Bremse^F
freno^M

pectoral deck
pectoral^M
presse^F à pectoraux^M
Butterfly^M
piastra^F per i pettorali^M

lateral bar
barra^F lateral
barre^F à dorsaux^M
Latissimuszug^M
barra^F per i dorsali^M

press bar
presión^F
barre^F à pectoraux^M
Drückstange^F
barra^F per i pettorali^M

pedal
pedal^M
pédale^F
Pedal^N
pedale^M

flywheel
rueda^F
volant^M d'inertie^F
Schwungrad^N
volano^M

bench
banco^M
planche^F
Bank^F
panca^F

stair climber
escalera^F
simulateur^M d'escalier^M
Climber^M
stepper^M

leg curl bar
barra^F de flexión^F de piernas^F
balancier^M de traction^F
Beincurler^M
rullo^M per i bicipiti^M femorali

leg extension bar
barra^F de extensión^F de piernas^F
balancier^M d'extension^F
Beinstreckerzug^M
rullo^M per i quadricipiti^M

triceps bar
barra^F de triceps^M
barre^F à triceps^M
Trizepszug^M
barra^F per i tricipiti^M

weights
pesas^F
poids^M
Gewichte^N
pesi^M

rowing machine
remo^M
rameur^M
Rudergerät^N
vogatore^M

oar
remo^M
rame^F
Ruder^N
remo^M

push-up stand
anillas^F para flexiones^F
poignée^F d'appui^M
Pushup-Griff^M
ganci^M di fissaggio^M

hydraulic resistance
resorte^M hidráulico
résistance^F hydraulique
hydraulischer Widerstand^M
resistenza^F idraulica

foot support
soporte^M del pie^M
cale-pied^M
Fußstütze^F
appoggiapiedi^M

sliding seat
asiento^M de corredera^F
siège^M coulissant
freilaufender Sitz^M
sedile^M scorrevole

show-jumping

salto^M de obstáculos^M | saut^M d'obstacle^M | Springreiten^N | salto^M ostacoli^M

obstacles
obstáculos^M
obstacles^M
Hürden^F
ostacoli^M

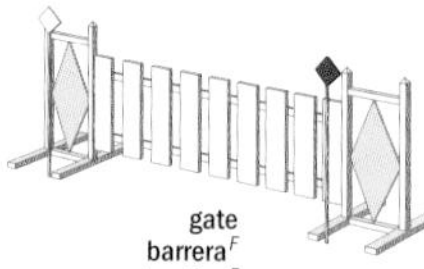

gate
barrera^F
barrière^F
Gatter^N
cancello^M

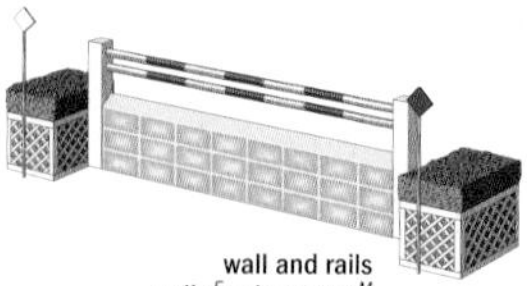

wall and rails
valla^F sobre muro^M
mur^M barré
Mauer^F mit Stangen^F
muro^M con barriere^F

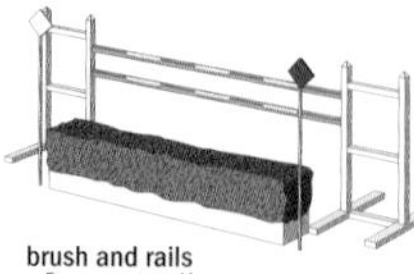

brush and rails
valla^F sobre seto^M
haie^F barrée
Bürste^F mit Stangen^F
siepe^F con barriere^F

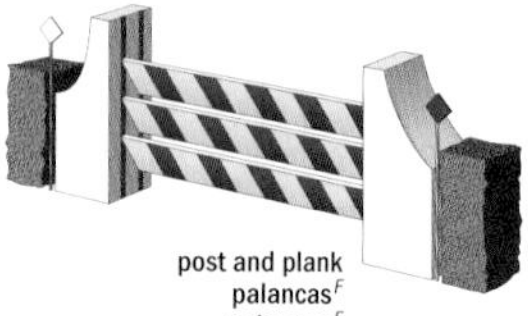

post and plank
palancas^F
palanque^F
Pfosten^M mit Latte^F
tavole^F

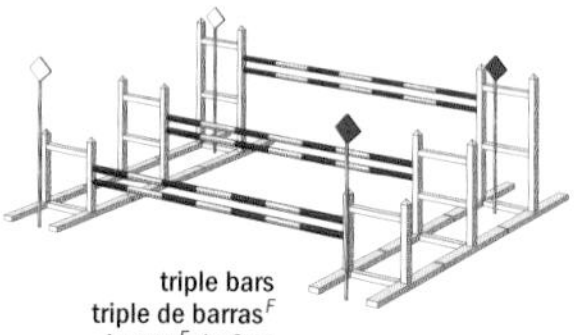

triple bars
triple de barras^F
barres^F de Spa
Dreifachbalken^M
triplice^M

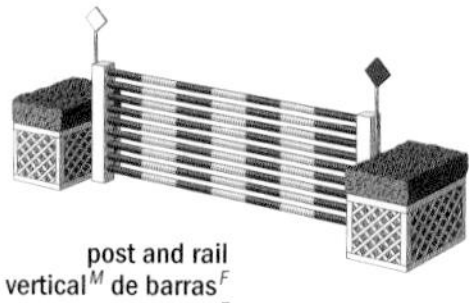

post and rail
vertical^M de barras^F
stationata^F
Pfosten^M mit Stange^F
barriere^F

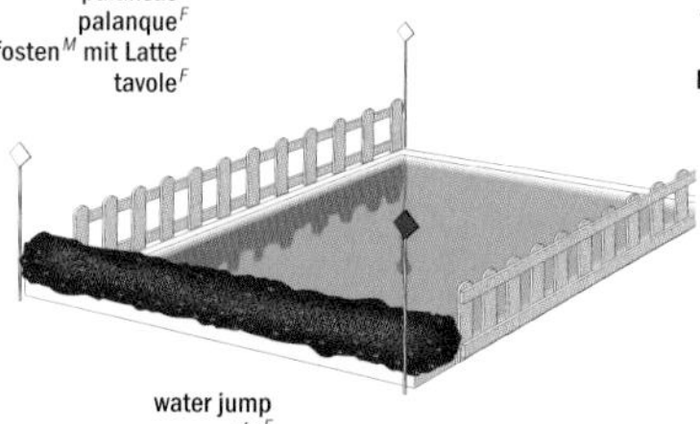

water jump
ría^F
haie^F rivière^F
Wassergraben^M
riviera^F

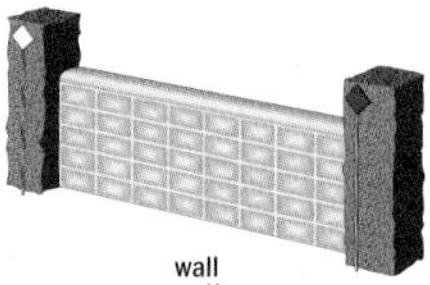

wall
muro^M
mur^M
Mauer^F
muro^M

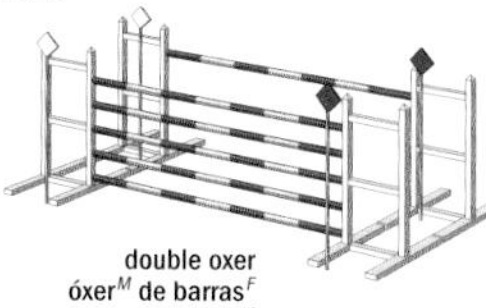

double oxer
óxer^M de barras^F
oxer^M
Doppeloxer^M
oxer^M

competition ring
pista^F para salto^M de obstáculos^M
parcours^M d'obstacles^M
Sprungreitparcours^M
campo^M di gara^F

wall
muro^M
mur^M
Mauer^F
muro^M

post and plank
palancas^F
palanque^F
Pfosten^M mit Latte^F
tavole^F

combination
combinación^F
combinaison^F
Kombination^F
combinazione^F

jump judge
juez^M de obstáculos^M
juge^M aux obstacles^M
Hindernisrichter^M
commissario^M agli ostacoli^M

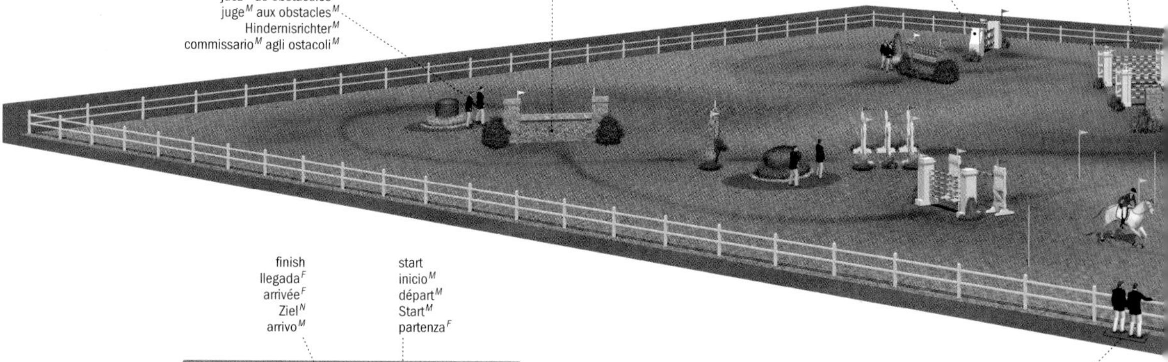

finish
llegada^F
arrivée^F
Ziel^N
arrivo^M

start
inicio^M
départ^M
Start^M
partenza^F

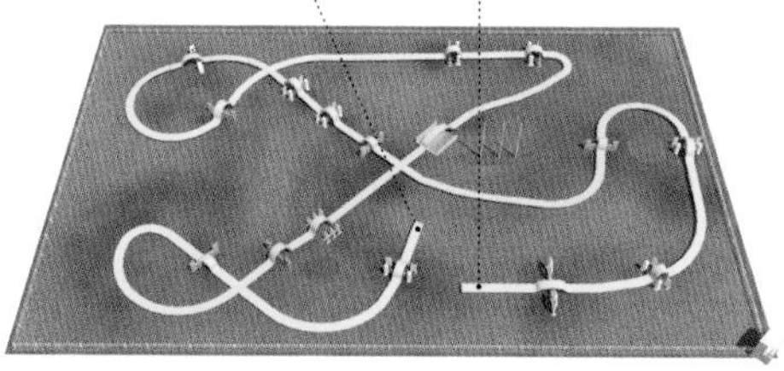

veterinarians
veterinarios^M
vétérinaires^M
Veterinäre^M
veterinari^M

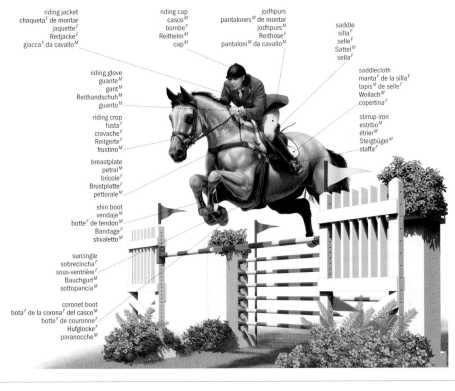

riding jacket
chaqueta^F de montar
jaquette^F
Reitjacke^F
giacca^F da cavallo^M

riding cap
casco^M
bombe^F
Reithelm^M
cap^M

jodhpurs
pantalones^M de montar
jodhpurs^M
Reithose^F
pantaloni^M da cavallo^M

saddle
silla^F
selle^F
Sattel^M
sella^F

rider
jinete^M
cavalier^M
Reiter^M
cavaliere^M

riding glove
guante^M
gant^M
Reithandschuh^M
guanto^M

saddlecloth
manta^F de la silla^F
tapis^M de selle^F
Woilach^M
copertina^F

riding crop
fusta^F
cravache^F
Reitgerte^F
frustino^M

stirrup iron
estribo^M
étrier^M
Steigbügel^M
staffa^F

breastplate
petral^M
bricole^F
Brustplatte^F
pettorale^M

shin boot
vendaje^M
botte^F de tendon^M
Bandage^F
stivaletto^M

surcingle
sobrecincha^F
sous-ventrière^F
Bauchgurt^M
sottopancia^F

coronet boot
bota^F de la corona^F del casco^M
botte^F de couronne^F
Hufglocke^F
paranocche^M

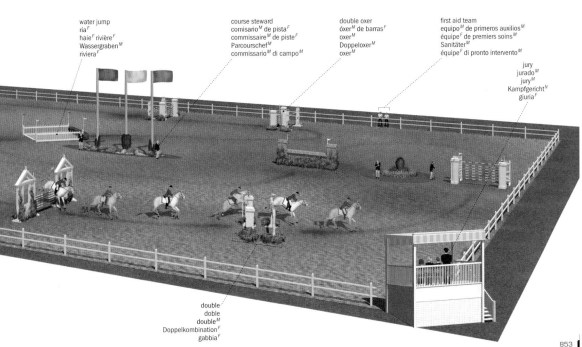

water jump
ria^F
haie^F rivière^F
Wassergraben^M
riviera^F

course steward
comisario^M de pista^F
commissaire^M de piste^F
Parcourschef^M
commissario^M di campo^M

double oxer
óxer^M de barras^F
oxer^M
Doppeloxer^M
oxer^M

first aid team
equipo^M de primeros auxilios^M
équipe^F de premiers soins^M
Sanitäter^M
équipe^F di pronto intervento^M

jury
jurado^M
jury^M
Kampfgericht^N
giuria^F

double
doble
double^M
Doppelkombination^F
gabbia^F

SPORTS AND GAMES

853

riding

equitación^F | équitation^F | Reiten^N | equitazione^F

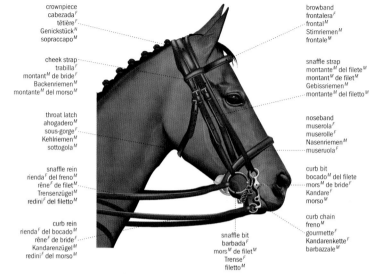

bridle
brida^F
bride^F
Zaumzeug^N
briglia^F

crownpiece
cabezada^F
tétière^F
Genickstück^N
sopraccapo^M

browband
frontalera^F
frontal^M
Stirnriemen^M
frontale^M

cheek strap
trabilla^F
montant^M de bride^F
Backenriemen^M
montante^M del morso^M

snaffle strap
montante^M del filete^M
montant^M de filet^M
Gebissriemen^M
montante^M del filetto^M

throat latch
ahogadero^M
sous-gorge^F
Kehlriemen^M
sottogola^M

noseband
muserola^F
muserolle^F
Nasenriemen^M
museruola^F

snaffle rein
rienda^F del freno^M
rêne^F de filet^M
Trensenzügel^M
redini^F del filetto^M

curb bit
bocado^M del filete
mors^M de bride^F
Kandare^F
morso^M

curb rein
rienda^F del bocado^M
rêne^F de bride^F
Kandarenzügel^M
redini^F del morso^M

curb chain
freno^M
gourmette^F
Kandarenkette^F
barbazzale^M

snaffle bit
barbada^F
mors^M de filet^M
Trense^F
filetto^M

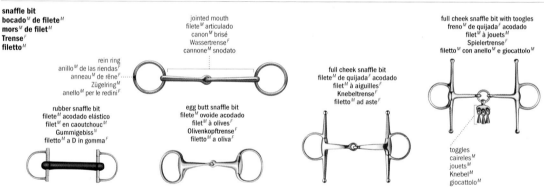

snaffle bit
bocado^M de filete^M
mors^M de filet^M
Trense^F
filetto^M

jointed mouth
filete^M articulado
canon^M brisé
Wassertrense^F
cannone^M snodato

full cheek snaffle bit with toogles
freno^M de quijada^F acodado
filet^M à jouets^M
Spielertrense^F
filetto^M con anello^M e giocattolo^M

rein ring
anillo^M de las riendas^F
anneau^M de rêne^F
Zügelring^M
anello^M per le redini^F

full cheek snaffle bit
filete^M de quijada^F acodado
filet^M à aiguilles^F
Knebeltrense^F
filetto^M ad aste^F

rubber snaffle bit
filete^M acodado elástico
filet^M en caoutchouc^M
Gummigebiss^N
filetto^M a D in gomma^F

egg butt snaffle bit
filete^M ovoide acodado
filet^M à olives^F
Olivenkopftrense^F
filetto^M a oliva^F

toggles
caireles^M
jouets^M
Knebel^M
giocattolo^M

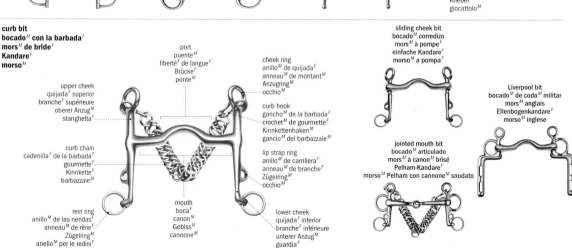

curb bit
bocado^M con la barbada^F
mors^M de bride^F
Kandare^F
morso^M

port
puente^M
liberté^F de langue^F
Brücke^F
ponte^M

cheek ring
anillo^M de quijada^F
anneau^M de montant^M
Anzugring^M
occhio^M

sliding cheek bit
bocado^M corredizo
mors^M à pompe^F
einfache Kandare^F
morso^M a pompa^M

upper cheek
quijada^F superior
branche^F supérieure
oberer Anzug^M
stanghetta^F

curb hook
gancho^M de la barbada^F
crochet^M de gourmette^F
Kinnkettenhaken^M
gancio^M del barbazzale^M

Liverpool bit
bocado^M de codo^M militar
mors^M anglais
Ellenbogenkandare^F
morso^M inglese

curb chain
cadenilla^F de la barbada^F
gourmette^F
Kinnkette^F
barbazzale^M

lip strap ring
anillo^M de carrillera^F
anneau^M de branche^F
Zügelring^M
occhio^M

jointed mouth bit
bocado^M articulado
mors^M à canon^M brisé
Pelham-Kandare^F
morso^M Pelham con cannone^M snodato

rein ring
anillo^M de las riendas^F
anneau^M de rêne^F
Zügelring^M
anello^M per le redini^F

mouth
boca^F
canon^M
Gebiss^N
cannone^M

lower cheek
quijada^F inferior
branche^F inférieure
unterer Anzug^M
guardia^F

saddle
silla^F de montar
selle^F
Sattel^M
sella^F

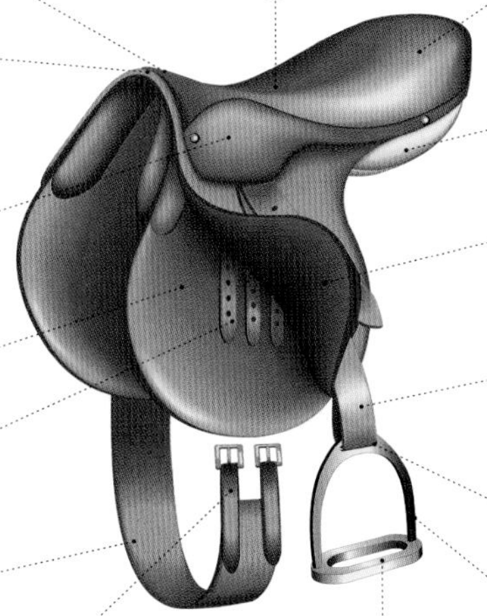

pommel
borrén^M
pommeau^M
Vorderzwiesel^M
pomo^M

seat
sillín^M
siège^M
Sitz^M
seggio^M

cantle
borrén^M trasero
troussequin^M
Hinterzwiesel^F
paletta^F

tree
arzón^M
arcade^F
Baum^M
archetto^M d'arcione^M

panel
forro^M
matelassure^F
Sattelpolster^N
cuscino^M

skirt
faldoncillo^M
petit quartier^M
Schnallenabdeckung^F
piccolo quartiere^M

flap
hoja^F del faldón^M lateral
quartier^M
Pausche^F
quartiere^M

knee roll
rodillera^F
faux quartier^M
Schweißblatt^N
falso quartiere^M

stirrup leather
correa^F
étrivière^F
Bügelriemen^M
staffile^M

tab
latiguillo^M
contre-sanglon^M
Gurtstrippe^F
riscontro^M

eye
ojo^M
œil^M
Auge^N
occhio^M

girth
cincha^F
sangle^F
Sattelgurt^M
sottopancia^M

girth strap
correa^F de la cincha^F
sanglon^M
Gurtschnalle^F
fibbia^F del sottopancia^M

tread
hondón^M
plancher^M
Trittfläche^F
panca^F

branch
aro^M
branche^F
Bügel^M
arco^M

dressage
doma^F | dressage^M | Dressurreiten^N | dressage^M

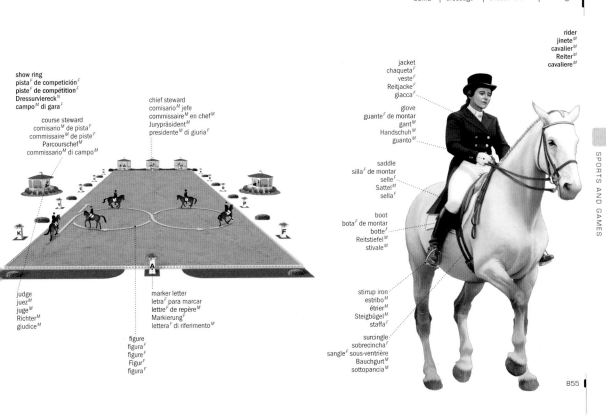

show ring
pista^F de competición^F
piste^F de compétition^F
Dressurviereck^N
campo^M di gara^M

chief steward
comisario^M jefe
commissaire^M en chef^M
Jurypräsident^M
presidente^M di giuria^F

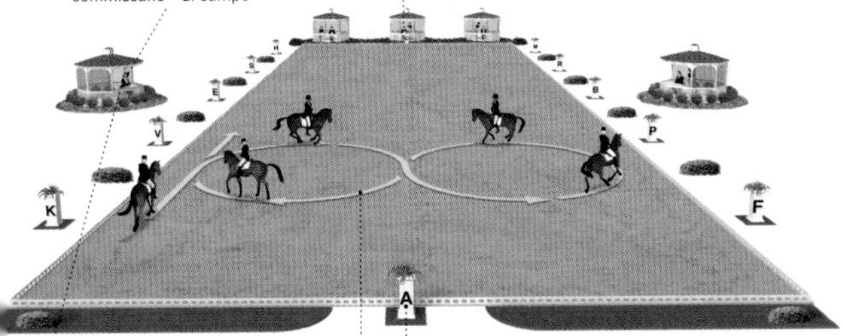

course steward
comisario^M de pista^F
commissaire^M de piste^F
Parcourschef^M
commissario^M di campo^M

rider
jinete^M
cavalier^M
Reiter^M
cavaliere^M

jacket
chaqueta^F
veste^F
Reitjacke^F
giacca^F

glove
guante^F de montar
gant^M
Handschuh^M
guanto^M

saddle
silla^F de montar
selle^F
Sattel^M
sella^F

boot
bota^F de montar
botte^F
Reitstiefel^M
stivale^M

judge
juez^M
juge^M
Richter^M
giudice^M

marker letter
letra^F para marcar
lettre^F de repère^M
Markierung^F
lettera^F di riferimento^M

figure
figura^F
figure^F
Figur^F
figura^F

stirrup iron
estribo^M
étrier^M
Steigbügel^M
staffa^F

surcingle
sobrecincha^F
sangle^F sous-ventrière
Bauchgurt^M
sottopancia^M

SPORTS AND GAMES

855

horse racing: turf

carrera^F de caballos^M : turf^M | course^F de chevaux^M : turf^M | Pferderennen^N: Galopprennen^N | corse^F dei cavalli^M: galoppo^M

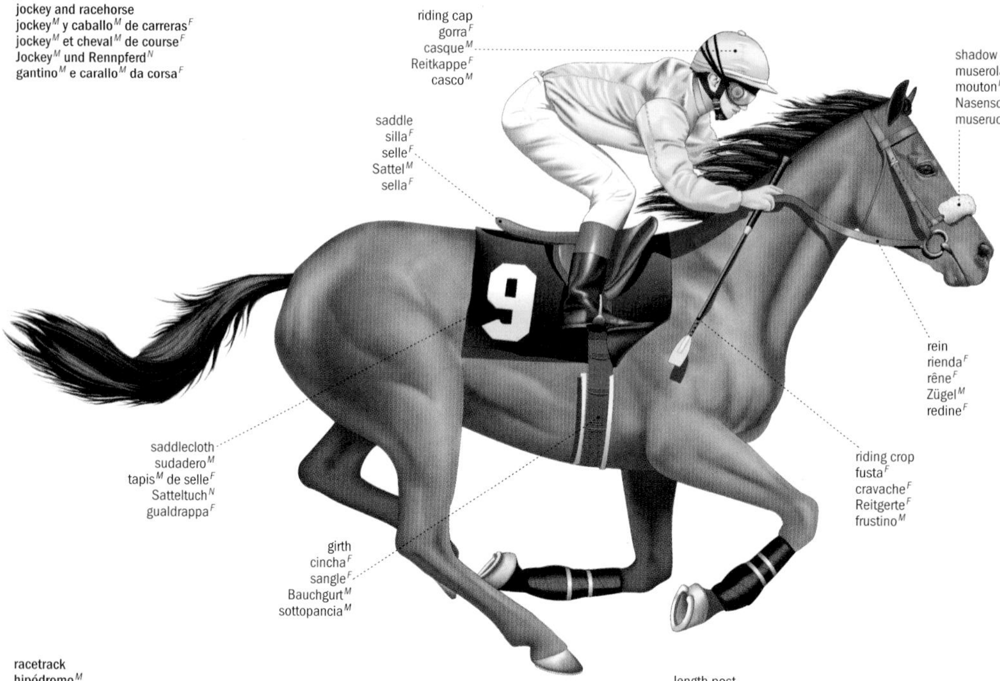

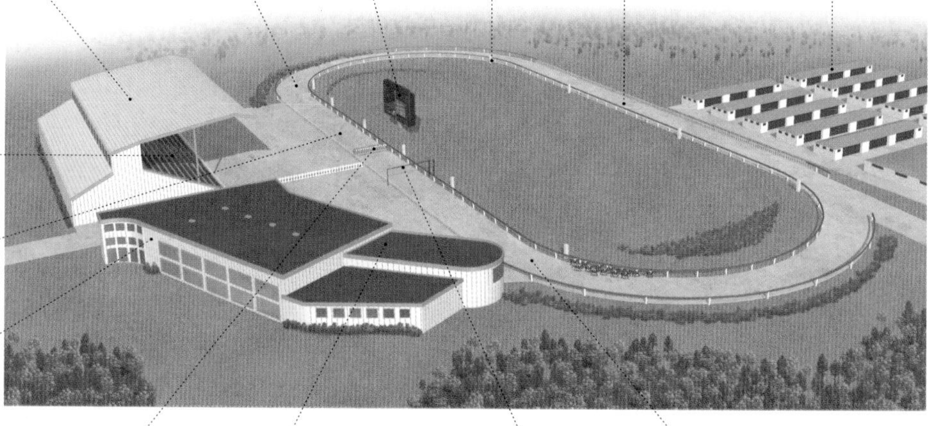

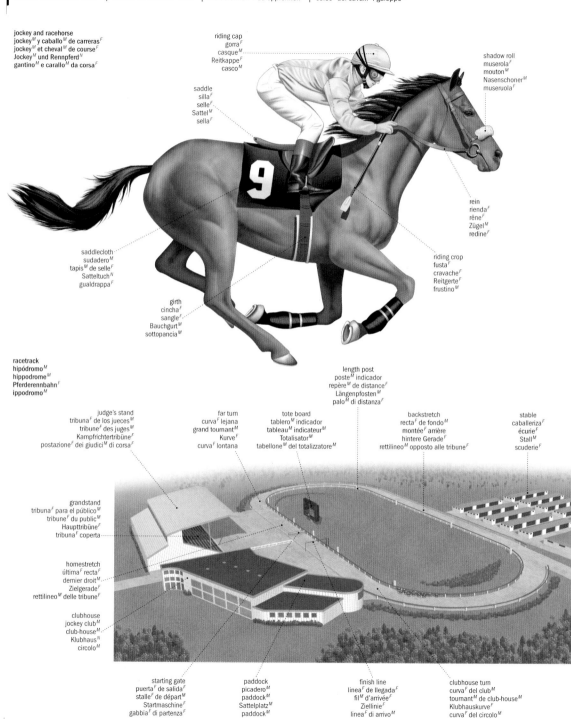

horse racing: harness racing

carrera^F de caballos^M : carreras^F con arneses^M | course^F de chevaux^M : course^F attelée | Pferderennen^N: Trabrennen^N | corse^F dei cavalli: trotto^M e ambio^M

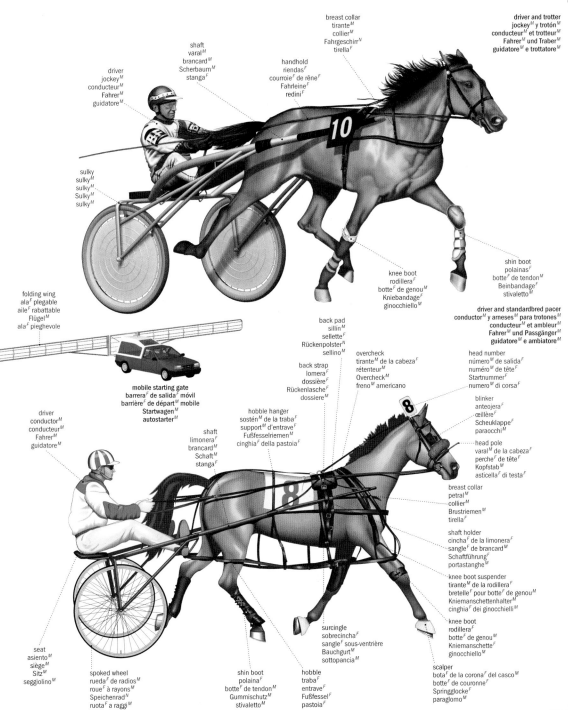

breast collar
tirante^M
collier^M
Fahrgeschirr^N
tirella^F

driver and trotter
jockey^M y trotón^M
conducteur^M et trotteur^M
Fahrer^M und Traber^M
guidatore^M e trottatore^M

shaft
varal^M
brancard^M
Scherbaum^M
stanga^F

handhold
riendas^F
courroie^F de rêne^F
Fahrleine^F
redini^F

driver
jockey^M
conducteur^M
Fahrer^M
guidatore^M

sulky
sulky^M
sulky^M
Sulky^M
sulky^M

folding wing
ala^F plegable
aile^F rabattable
Flügel^M
ala^F pieghevole

knee boot
rodillera^F
botte^F de genou^M
Kniebandage^F
ginocchiello^M

shin boot
polainas^F
botte^F de tendon^M
Beinbandage^F
stivaletto^M

driver and standardbred pacer
conductor^M y arneses^M para trotones^M
conducteur^M et ambleur^M
Fahrer^M und Passgänger^M
guidatore^M e ambiatore^M

back pad
sillín^M
sellette^F
Rückenpolster^M
sellino^M

overcheck
tirante^M de la cabeza^F
rétenteur^M
Overcheck^M
freno^M americano

head number
número^M de salida^F
numéro^M de tête^F
Startnummer^F
numero^M di corsa^F

back strap
lomera^F
dossière^F
Rückenlasche^F
dossiere^M

mobile starting gate
barrera^F de salida^F móvil
barrière^F de départ^M mobile
Startwagen^M
autostarter^M

blinker
anteojera^F
œillère^F
Scheuklappe^F
paraocchi^M

hobble hanger
sostén^M de la traba^F
support^M d'entrave^F
Fußfesselriemen^M
cinghia^F della pastoia^F

head pole
varal^M de la cabeza^F
perche^F de tête^F
Kopfstab^M
asticella^F di testa^F

driver
conductor^M
conducteur^M
Fahrer^M
guidatore^M

shaft
limonera^F
brancard^M
Schaft^M
stanga^F

breast collar
petral^M
collier^M
Brustriemen^M
tirella^F

shaft holder
cincha^F de la limonera^F
sangle^F de brancard^M
Schaftführung^F
portastanghe^M

knee boot suspender
tirante^M de la rodillera^F
bretelle^F pour botte^F de genou^M
Kniemanschettenhalter^M
cinghia^F dei ginocchielli^M

knee boot
rodillera^F
botte^F de genou^M
Kniemanschette^F
ginocchiello^M

surcingle
sobrecincha^F
sangle^F sous-ventrière^F
Bauchgurt^M
sottopancia^M

hobble
traba^F
entrave^F
Fußfessel^F
pastoia^F

scalper
bota^F de la corona^F del casco^M
botte^F de couronne^F
Springglocke^F
paraglomo^M

seat
asiento^M
siège^M
Sitz^M
seggiolino^M

spoked wheel
rueda^F de radios^M
roue^F à rayons^M
Speichenrad^N
ruota^F a raggi^M

shin boot
polaina^F
botte^F de tendon^M
Gummischutz^M
stivaletto^M

857

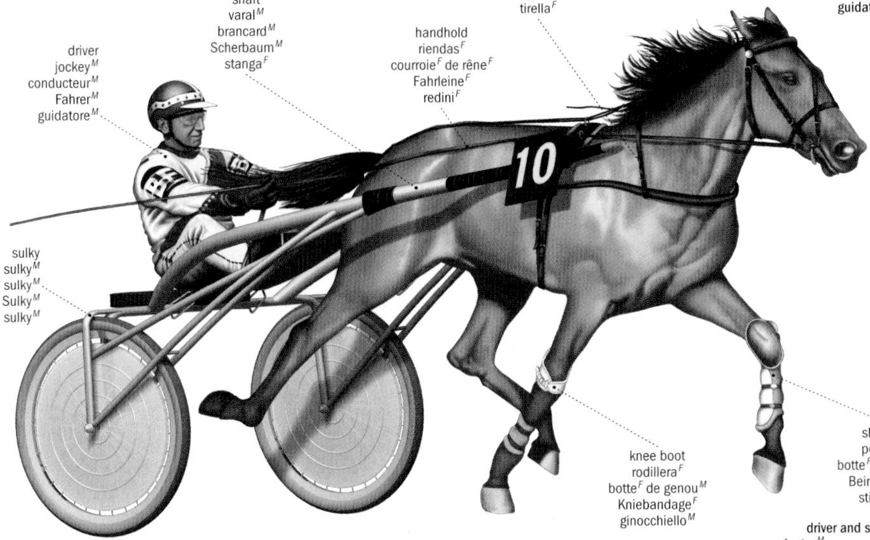

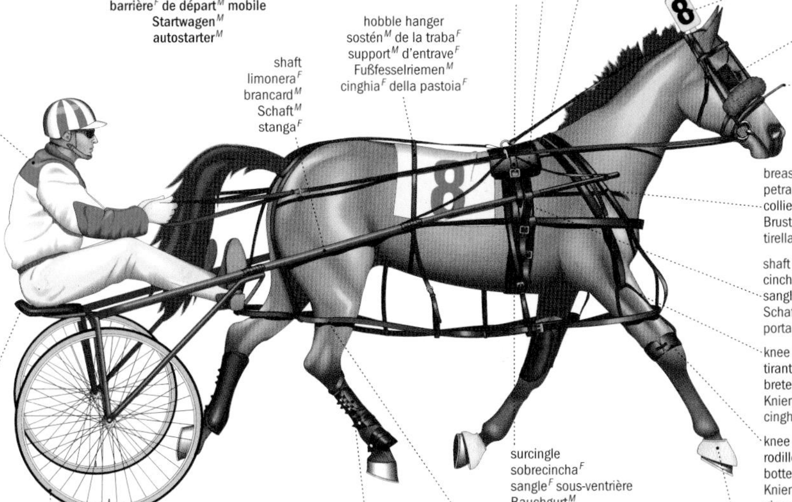

polo

polo^M | polo^M | Polo^N | polo^M

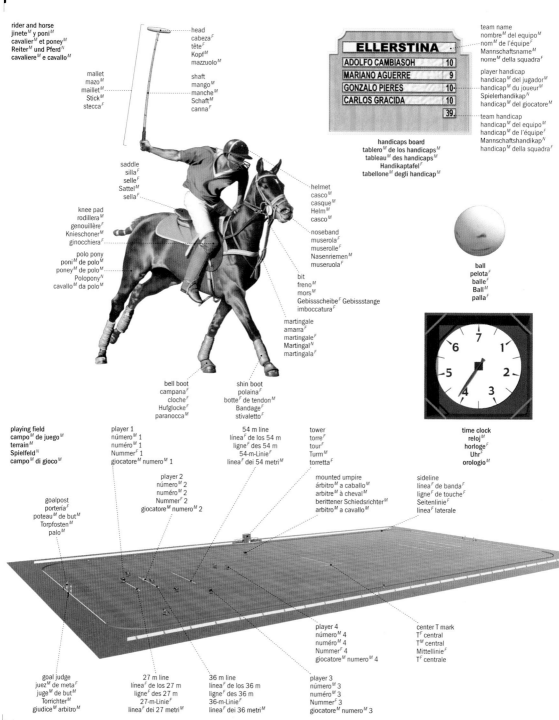

rider and horse
jinete^M y poni^M
cavalier^M et poney^M
Reiter^M und Pferd^N
cavaliere^M e cavallo^M

head
cabeza^F
tête^F
Kopf^M
mazzuolo^M

mallet
mazo^M
maillet^M
Stick^M
stecca^F

shaft
mango^M
manche^M
Schaft^M
canna^F

saddle
silla^F
selle^F
Sattel^M
sella^F

helmet
casco^M
casque^M
Helm^M
casco^M

knee pad
rodillera^M
genouillère^F
Knieschoner^M
ginocchiera^F

noseband
muserola^F
muserolle^F
Nasenriemen^M
museruola^F

polo pony
poni^M de polo^M
poney^M de polo^M
Polopony^N
cavallo^M da polo^M

bit
freno^M
mors^M
Gebissscheibe^F Gebissstange
imboccatura^F

martingale
amarra^F
martingale^F
Martingal^N
martingala^F

bell boot
campana^F
cloche^F
Hufglocke^F
paranocca^M

shin boot
polaina^F
botte^F de tendon^M
Bandage^F
stivaletto^F

team name
nombre^M del equipo^M
nom^M de l'équipe^F
Mannschaftsname^M
nome^M della squadra^F

ELLERSTINA
ADOLFO CAMBIASOH	10
MARIANO AGUERRE	9
GONZALO PIERES	10
CARLOS GRACIDA	10
	39

player handicap
handicap^M del jugador^M
handicap^M du joueur^M
Spielerhandikap^N
handicap^M del giocatore^M

team handicap
handicap^M del equipo^M
handicap^M de l'équipe^F
Mannschaftshandikap^N
handicap^M della squadra^F

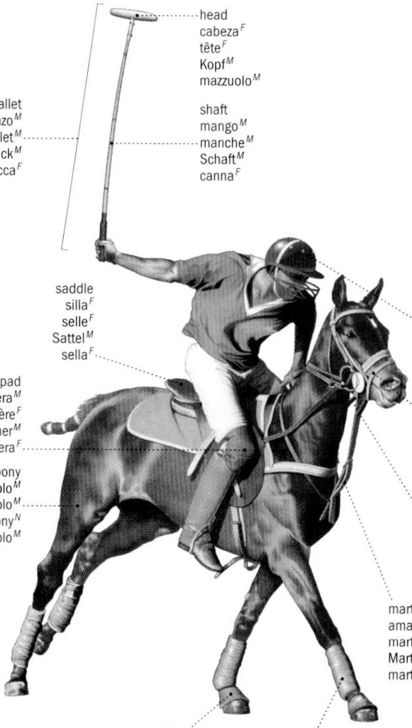

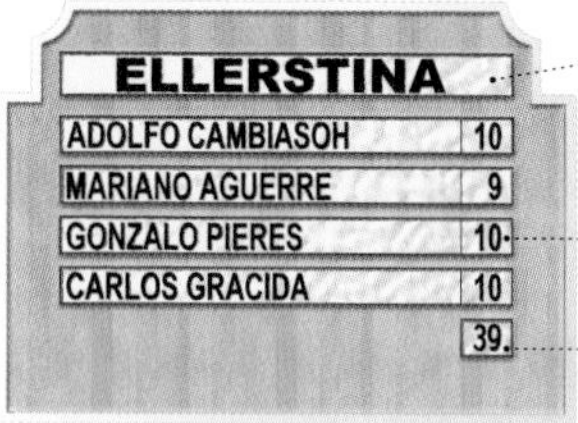

handicaps board
tablero^M de los handicaps^M
tableau^M des handicaps^M
Handikaptafel^F
tabellone^M degli handicap^M

ball
pelota^F
balle^F
Ball^M
palla^F

time clock
reloj^M
horloge^F
Uhr^F
orologio^M

playing field
campo^M de juego^M
terrain^M
Spielfeld^N
campo^M di gioco^M

player 1
número^M 1
numéro^M 1
Nummer^F 1
giocatore^M numero^M 1

54 m line
línea^F de los 54 m
ligne^F des 54 m
54-m-Linie^F
linea^F dei 54 metri^M

tower
torre^F
tour^F
Turm^M
torretta^F

player 2
número^M 2
numéro^M 2
Nummer^F 2
giocatore^M numero^M 2

mounted umpire
árbitro^M a caballo^M
arbitre^M à cheval^M
berittener Schiedsrichter^M
arbitro^M a cavallo^M

sideline
línea^F de banda^F
ligne^F de touche^F
Seitenlinie^F
linea^F laterale

goalpost
portería^F
poteau^M de but^M
Torpfosten^M
palo^M

player 4
número^M 4
numéro^M 4
Nummer^F 4
giocatore^M numero^M 4

center T mark
T^F central
T^M central
Mittellinie^F
T^F centrale

goal judge
juez^M de meta^F
juge^M de but^M
Torrichter^M
giudice^M arbitro^M

27 m line
línea^F de los 27 m
ligne^F des 27 m
27-m-Linie^F
linea^F dei 27 metri^M

36 m line
línea^F de los 36 m
ligne^F des 36 m
36-m-Linie^F
linea^F dei 36 metri^M

player 3
número^M 3
numéro^M 3
Nummer^F 3
giocatore^M numero^M 3

SPORTS AND GAMES

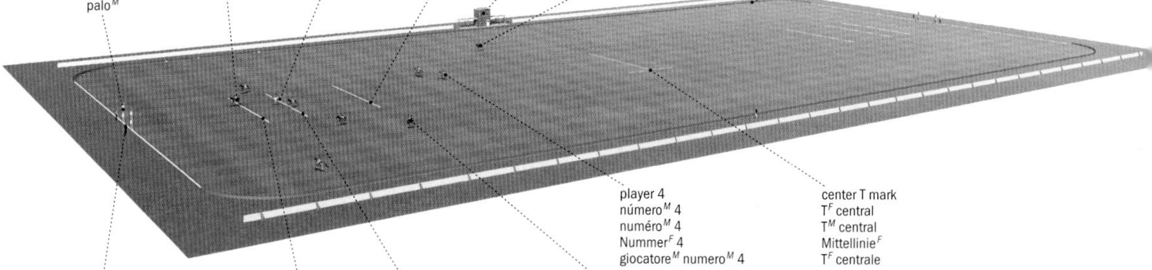

PRECISION AND ACCURACY SPORTS | DEPORTES DE PRECISIÓN Y PUNTERÍA
SPORTS DE PRÉCISION | PRÄZISIONSSPORT | SPORT DI PRECISIONE

archery

tiro^M con arco^M | tir^M à l'arc^M | Bogenschießen^N | tiro^M con l'arco^M

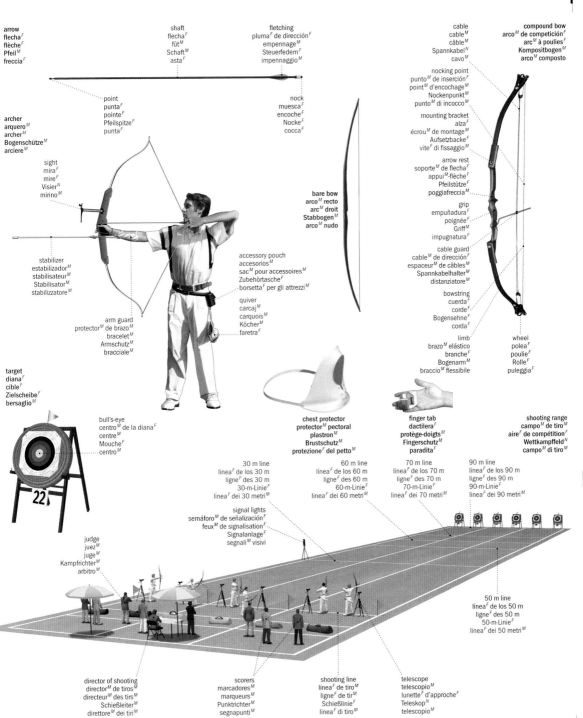

arrow
flecha^F
flèche^F
Pfeil^M
freccia^F

shaft
flecha^F
fût^M
Schaft^M
asta^F

fletching
pluma^F de dirección^F
empennage^M
Steuerfedern^F
impennaggio^M

cable
cable^M
câble^M
Spannkabel^N
cavo^M

compound bow
arco^M de competición^F
arc^M à poulies^F
Kompositbogen^M
arco^M composto

point
punta^F
pointe^F
Pfeilspitze^F
punta^F

nock
muesca^F
encoche^F
Nocke^F
cocca^F

nocking point
punto^M de inserción^F
point^M d'encochage^M
Nockenpunkt^M
punto^M di incocco^M

archer
arquero^M
archer^M
Bogenschütze^M
arciere^M

mounting bracket
alza^F
écrou^M de montage^M
Aufsetzbacke^F
vite^F di fissaggio^M

sight
mira^F
mire^F
Visier^N
mirino^M

arrow rest
soporte^M de flecha^F
appui^M-flèche^F
Pfeilstütze^F
poggiafreccia^M

bare bow
arco^M recto
arc^M droit
Stabbogen^M
arco^M nudo

grip
empuñadura^F
poignée^F
Griff^M
impugnatura^F

stabilizer
estabilizador^M
stabilisateur^M
Stabilisator^M
stabilizzatore^M

accessory pouch
accesorios^M
sac^M pour accessoires^M
Zubehörtasche^F
borsetta^F per gli attrezzi^M

cable guard
cable^M de dirección^F
espaceur^M de câbles^M
Spannkabelhalter^M
distanziatore^M

quiver
carcaj^M
carquois^M
Köcher^M
faretra^F

bowstring
cuerda^F
corde^F
Bogensehne^F
corda^F

arm guard
protector^M de brazo^M
bracelet^M
Armschutz^M
bracciale^M

limb
brazo^M elástico
branche^F
Bogenarm^M
braccio^M flessibile

wheel
polea^F
poulie^F
Rolle^F
puleggia^F

target
diana^F
cible^F
Zielscheibe^F
bersaglio^M

bull's-eye
centro^M de la diana^F
centre^M
Mouche^F
centro^M

chest protector
protector^M pectoral
plastron^M
Brustschutz^M
protezione^F del petto^M

finger tab
dactilera^F
protège-doigts^M
Fingerschutz^M
paradita^F

shooting range
campo^M de tiro^M
aire^F de compétition^F
Wettkampffeld^N
campo^M di tiro^M

30 m line
linea^F de los 30 m
ligne^F des 30 m
30-m-Linie^F
linea^F dei 30 metri^M

60 m line
linea^F de los 60 m
ligne^F des 60 m
60-m-Linie^F
linea^F dei 60 metri^M

70 m line
linea^F de los 70 m
ligne^F des 70 m
70-m-Linie^F
linea^F dei 70 metri^M

90 m line
linea^F de los 90 m
ligne^F des 90 m
90-m-Linie^F
linea^F dei 90 metri^M

signal lights
semáforo^M de señalización^F
feux^M de signalisation^F
Signalanlage^F
segnali^M visivi

judge
juez^M
juge^M
Kampfrichter^M
arbitro^M

50 m line
linea^F de los 50 m
ligne^F des 50 m
50-m-Linie^F
linea^F dei 50 metri^M

director of shooting
director^M de tiros^M
directeur^M des tirs^M
Schießleiter^M
direttore^M dei tiri^M

scorers
marcadores^M
marqueurs^M
Punktrichter^M
segnapunti^M

shooting line
linea^F de tiro^M
ligne^F de tir^M
Schießlinie^F
linea^F di tiro^M

telescope
telescopio^M
lunette^F d'approche^F
Teleskop^N
telescopio^M

22

shotgun shooting

tiro^M al plato^M | tir^M au fusil^M | Wurftaubenschießen^N | tiro^M con fucile^M

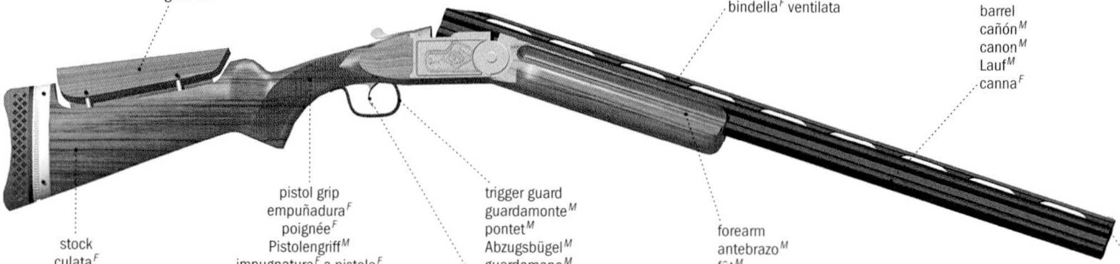

shotgun
escopeta^F calibre^M 12
fusil^M calibre^M 12
Schrotflinte^F
fucile^M

cheek piece
apoyo mejilla^F
appui^M-joue^F
Backe^F
guancia^F

ventilated rib
banda^F de ventilación^F
bande^F ventilée
ventilierte Laufschiene^F
bindella^F ventilata

barrel
cañón^M
canon^M
Lauf^M
canna^F

pistol grip
empuñadura^F
poignée^F
Pistolengriff^M
impugnatura^F a pistola^F

trigger guard
guardamonte^M
pontet^M
Abzugsbügel^M
guardamano^M

forearm
antebrazo^M
fût^M
Schaft^M
asta^F

stock
culata^F
crosse^F
Kolben^M
calcio^M

trigger
gatillo^M
détente^F
Abzug^M
grilletto^M

muzzle
boca^F
bouche^F
Mündung^F
bocca^F

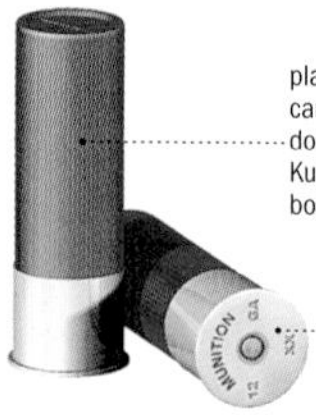

plastic case
cartucho^M de plástico^M
douille^F de plastique^M
Kunststoffhülse^F
bossolo^M

clay target
plato^M
plateau^M
Wurfscheibe^F
piattello^M

base
casquillo^M
culot^M
Hülsenboden^M
fondello^M

cartridges
cartuchos^M
cartouches^F
Patronen^F
cartucce^F

clay target
plato^M
plateau^M
Wurfscheibe^F
piattello^M

trap machine
lanzaplatos^M
appareil^M de lancement^M
Wurfmaschine^F
macchina^F di lancio^M dei piattelli^M

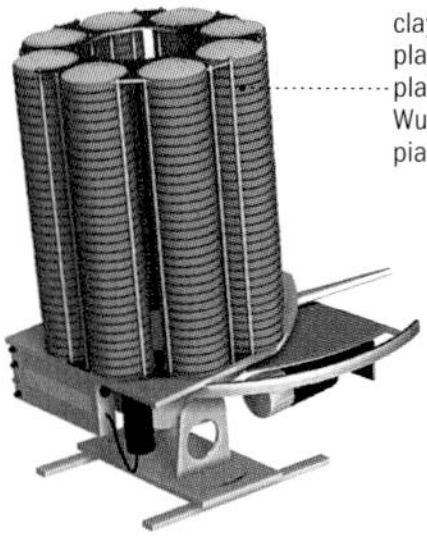

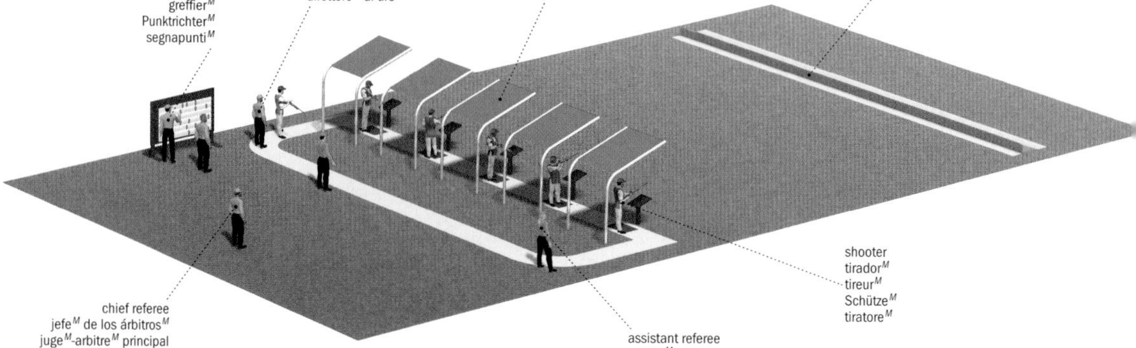

shooting range
campo^M de tiro^M
pas^M de tir^M
Schießanlage^F
campo^M di tiro^M

chief range officer
juez-árbitro de tiro^M
juge^M-arbitre^M de pas^M de tir^M
Schießleiter^M
direttore^M di tiro^M

shooting station
campo^M de tiro^M
poste^M de tir^M
Schießstand^M
pedana^F di tiro^M

trench
foso^M de tiro^M
fosse^F de tir^M
Schießgraben^M
fossa^F di tiro^M

scorer
anotador^M
greffier^M
Punktrichter^M
segnapunti^M

chief referee
jefe^M de los árbitros^M
juge^M-arbitre^M principal
leitender Kampfrichter^M
arbitro^M

assistant referee
árbitro^M auxiliar
arbitre^M auxiliaire
Kampfrichter^M
arbitro^M ausiliario

shooter
tirador^M
tireur^M
Schütze^F
tiratore^M

rifle shooting

tiro^M al blanco^M | tir^M à la carabine^F | Gewehrschießen^N | tiro^M con carabina^F

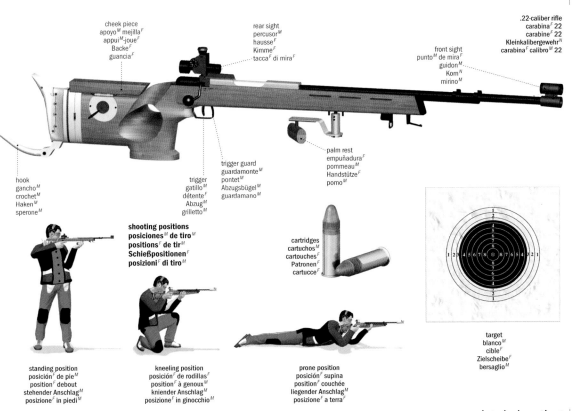

cheek piece
apoyo^M mejilla^F
appui^M-joue^F
Backe^F
guancia^F

rear sight
percusor^M
hausse^F
Kimme^F
tacca^F di mira^F

.22-caliber rifle
carabina^F 22
carabine^F 22
Kleinkalibergewehr^N
carabina^F calibro^M 22

front sight
punto^M de mira^F
guidon^M
Korn^N
mirino^M

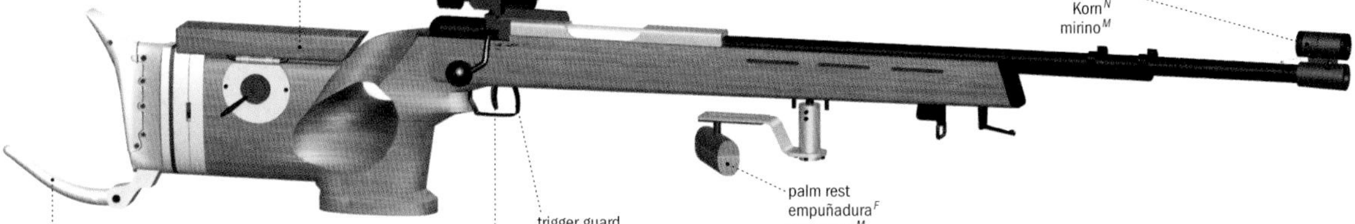

palm rest
empuñadura^F
pommeau^M
Handstütze^F
pomo^M

hook
gancho^M
crochet^M
Haken^M
sperone^M

trigger
gatillo^M
détente^F
Abzug^M
grilletto^M

trigger guard
guardamonte^M
pontet^M
Abzugsbügel^M
guardamano^M

**shooting positions
posiciones^M de tiro^M
positions^F de tir^M
Schießpositionen^F
posizioni^F di tiro^M**

cartridges
cartuchos^M
cartouches^F
Patronen^F
cartucce^F

standing position
posición^F de pie^M
position^F debout
stehender Anschlag^M
posizione^F in piedi^M

kneeling position
posición^F de rodillas^F
position^F à genoux^M
kniender Anschlag^M
posizione^F in ginocchio^M

prone position
posición^F supina
position^F couchée
liegender Anschlag^M
posizione^F a terra^F

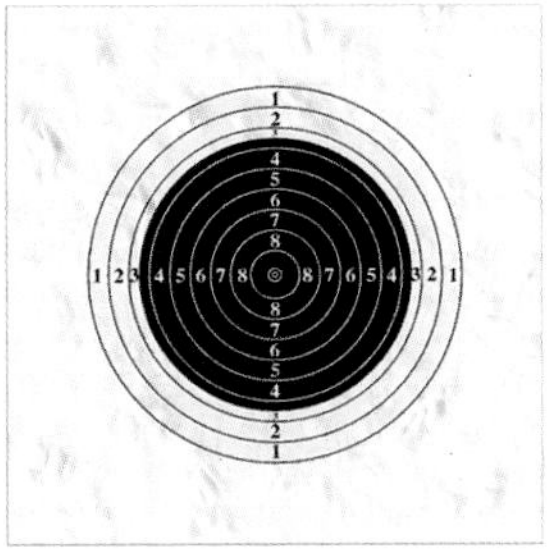

target
blanco^M
cible^F
Zielscheibe^F
bersaglio^M

pistol shooting

tiro^M de pistola^F | tir^M au pistolet^M | Pistolenschießen^N | tiro^M con pistola^F

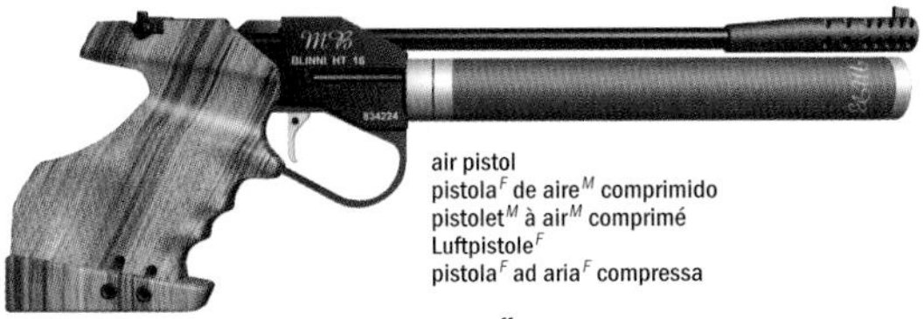

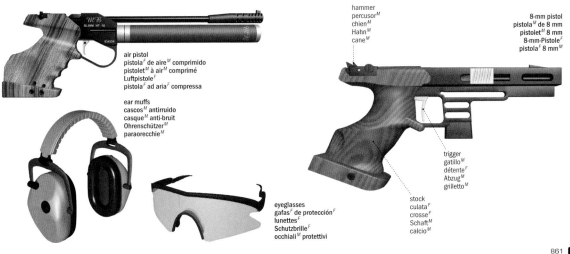

air pistol
pistola^F de aire^M comprimido
pistolet^M à air^M comprimé
Luftpistole^F
pistola^F ad aria^F compressa

hammer
percusor^M
chien^M
Hahn^M
cane^M

8-mm pistol
pistola^F de 8 mm
pistolet^M 8 mm
8-mm-Pistole^F
pistola^F 8 mm^M

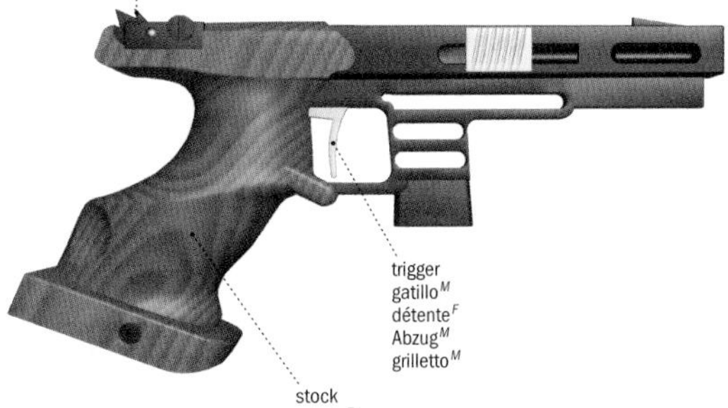

ear muffs
cascos^M antirruido
casque^M anti-bruit
Ohrenschützer^M
paraorecchie^M

trigger
gatillo^M
détente^F
Abzug^M
grilletto^M

eyeglasses
gafas^F de protección^F
lunettes^F
Schutzbrille^F
occhiali^M protettivi

stock
culata^F
crosse^F
Schaft^M
calcio^M

SPORTS AND GAMES

billiards

billar^M | billard^M | Billard^N | biliardo^M

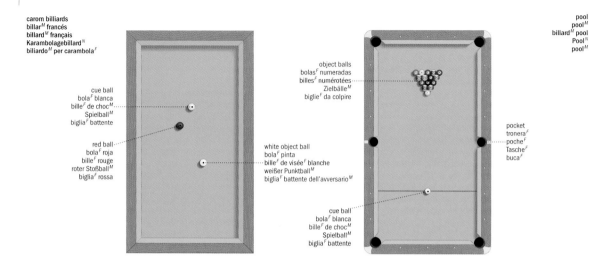

carom billiards
billar^M francés
billard^M français
Karambolagebillard^N
biliardo^M per carambola^F

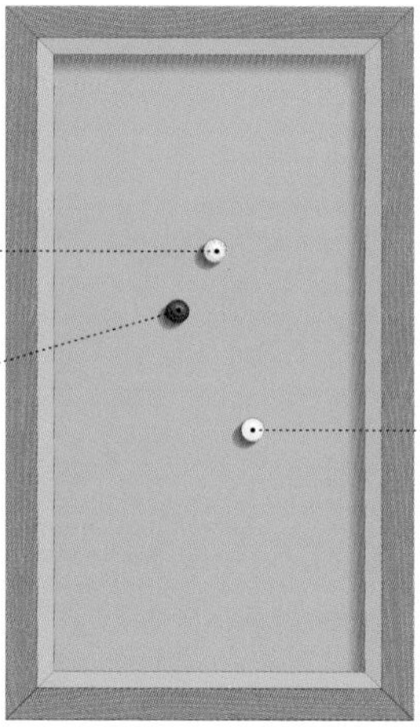

pool
pool^M
billard^M pool
Pool^N
pool^M

object balls
bolas^F numeradas
billes^F numérotées
Zielbälle^M
biglie^F da colpire

cue ball
bola^F blanca
bille^F de choc^M
Spielball^M
biglia^F battente

pocket
tronera^F
poche^F
Tasche^F
buca^F

red ball
bola^F roja
bille^F rouge
roter Stoßball^M
biglia^F rossa

white object ball
bola^F pinta
bille^F de visée^F blanche
weißer Punktball^M
biglia^F battente dell'avversario^M

cue ball
bola^F blanca
bille^F de choc^M
Spielball^M
biglia^F battente

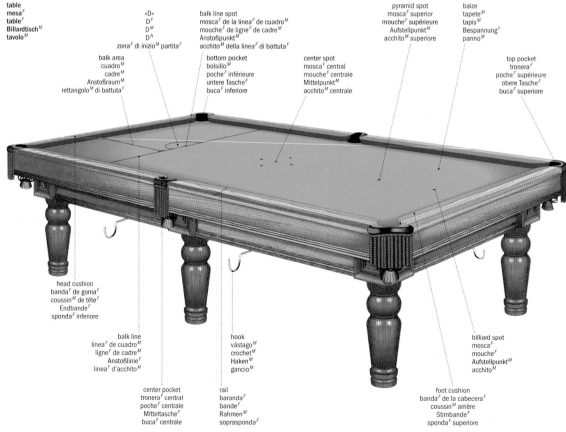

table
mesa^F
table^F
Billardtisch^M
tavolo^M

«D»
D^F
D^M
D^N
zona^F di inizio^M partita^F

balk line spot
mosca^F de la línea^F de cuadro^M
mouche^F de ligne^F de cadre^M
Anstoßpunkt^M
acchito^M della línea^F di battuta^F

pyramid spot
mosca^F superior
mouche^F supérieure
Aufstellpunkt^M
acchito^M superiore

baize
tapete^M
tapis^M
Bespannung^F
panno^M

balk area
cuadro^M
cadre^M
Anstoßraum^M
rettangolo^M di battuta^F

bottom pocket
bolsillo^M
poche^F inférieure
untere Tasche^F
buca^F inferiore

center spot
mosca^F central
mouche^F centrale
Mittelpunkt^M
acchito^M centrale

top pocket
tronera^F
poche^F supérieure
obere Tasche^F
buca^F superiore

head cushion
banda^F de goma^F
coussin^M de tête^F
Endbande^F
sponda^F inferiore

balk line
línea^F de cuadro^M
ligne^F de cadre^M
Anstoßlinie^F
linea^F d'acchito^M

hook
vástago^M
crochet^M
Haken^M
gancio^M

billiard spot
mosca^F
mouche^F
Aufstellpunkt^M
acchito^M

center pocket
tronera^F central
poche^F centrale
Mittelstasche^F
buca^F centrale

rail
baranda^F
bande^F
Rahmen^M
soprasponda^F

foot cushion
banda^F de la cabecera^F
coussin^M arrière
Stirnbande^F
sponda^F superiore

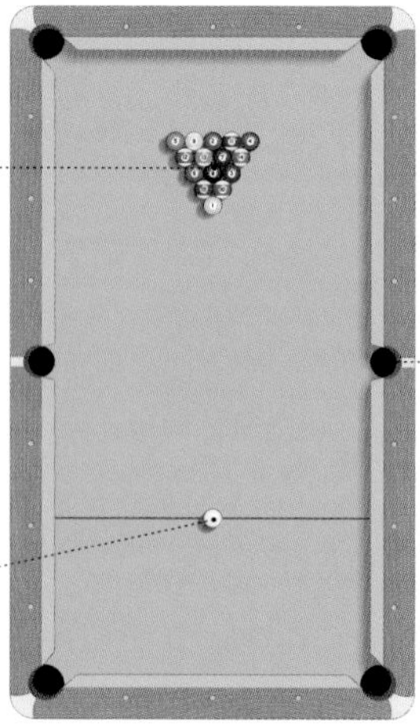

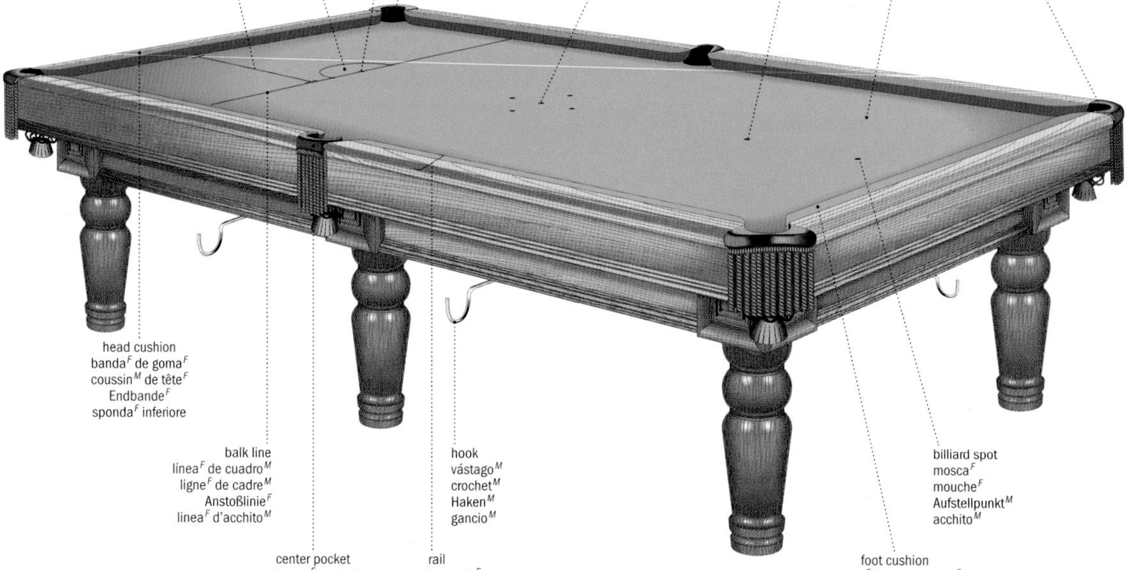

PRECISION AND ACCURACY SPORTS | DEPORTES DE PRECISIÓN Y PUNTERÍA
SPORTS DE PRÉCISION | PRÄZISIONSSPORT | SPORT DI PRECISIONE

billiards

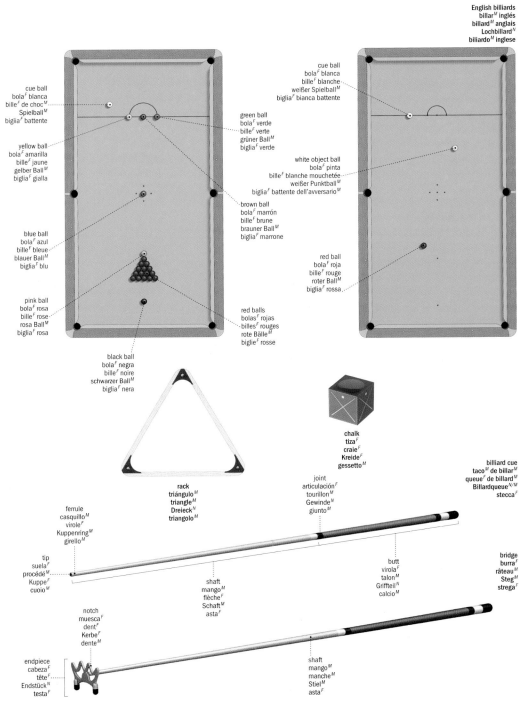

snooker
snooker^M
snooker^M
Snooker^N
snooker^M

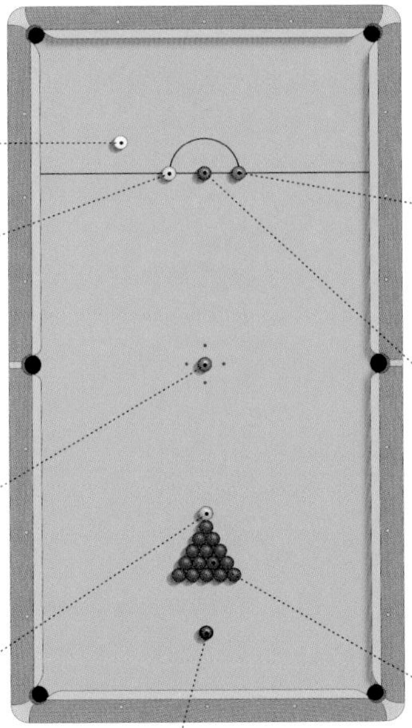

English billiards
billar^M inglés
billard^M anglais
Lochbillard^N
biliardo^M inglese

cue ball
bola^F blanca
bille^F de choc^M
Spielball^M
biglia^F battente

cue ball
bola^F blanca
bille^F blanche
weißer Spielball^M
biglia^F bianca battente

green ball
bola^F verde
bille^F verte
grüner Ball^M
biglia^F verde

yellow ball
bola^F amarilla
bille^F jaune
gelber Ball^M
biglia^F gialla

white object ball
bola^F pinta
bille^F blanche mouchetée
weißer Punktball^M
biglia^F battente dell'avversario^M

brown ball
bola^F marrón
bille^F brune
brauner Ball^M
biglia^F marrone

blue ball
bola^F azul
bille^F bleue
blauer Ball^M
biglia^F blu

red ball
bola^F roja
bille^F rouge
roter Ball^M
biglia^F rossa

pink ball
bola^F rosa
bille^F rose
rosa Ball^M
biglia^F rosa

red balls
bolas^F rojas
billes^F rouges
rote Bälle^M
biglie^F rosse

black ball
bola^F negra
bille^F noire
schwarzer Ball^M
biglia^F nera

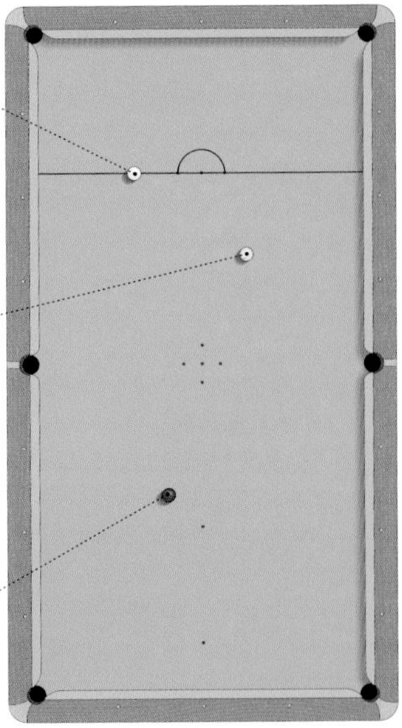

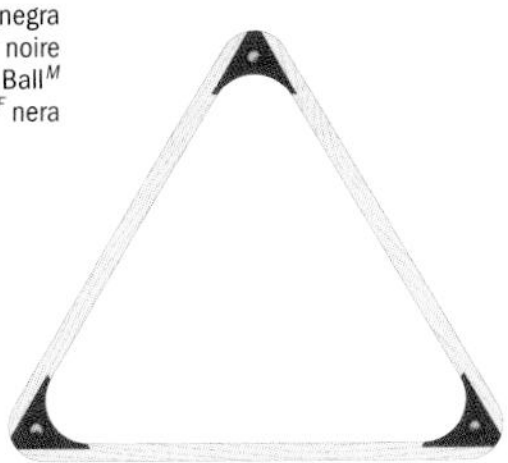

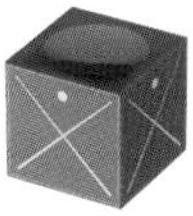

chalk
tiza^F
craie^F
Kreide^F
gessetto^M

rack
triángulo^M
triangle^M
Dreieck^N
triangolo^M

joint
articulación^F
tourillon^M
Gewinde^N
giunto^M

billiard cue
taco^M de billar^M
queue^F de billard^M
Billardqueue^{N/M}
stecca^F

ferrule
casquillo^M
virole^F
Kuppenring^M
girello^M

tip
suela^F
procédé^M
Kuppe^F
cuoio^M

shaft
mango^M
flèche^F
Schaft^M
asta^F

butt
virola^F
talon^M
Griffteil^N
calcio^M

bridge
burra^F
râteau^M
Steg^M
strega^F

notch
muesca^F
dent^F
Kerbe^F
dente^M

endpiece
cabeza^F
tête^F
Endstück^N
testa^F

shaft
mango^M
manche^M
Stiel^M
asta^F

SPORTS AND GAMES

863

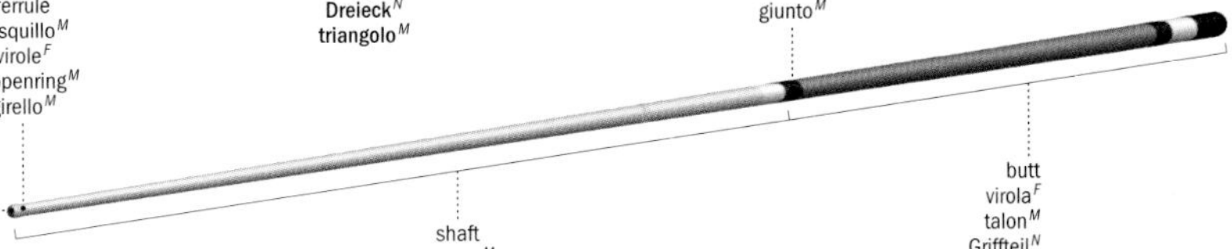

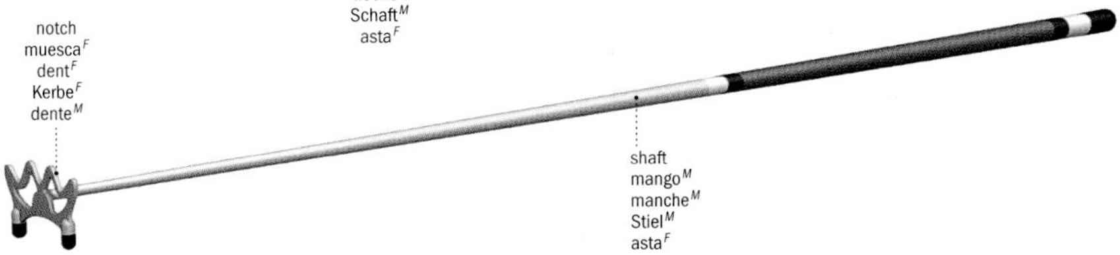

lawn bowling

bolos^M sobre hierba^F | boulingrin^M | Boule^N | bowling^M su prato^M

bowling technique
lanzamiento^M
technique^F du lancer^M
Schießen^N
lancio^M

bowls
bolos^M
boules^F
Kugeln^F
bocce^F

jack
boliche^M
cochonnet^M
Zielkugel^F
pallino^M

forward swing
impulso^M de lanzamiento^M
élan^M
Schwungholen^N
slancio^M in avanti

delivery
lanzamiento^M
lancer^M
Aufsetzen^N
lancio^M

follow-through
seguimiento^M de la bola^F
accompagnement^M
Abwurf^M
accompagnamento^M

green
bolera^F
pelouse^F
Grün^N
campo^M

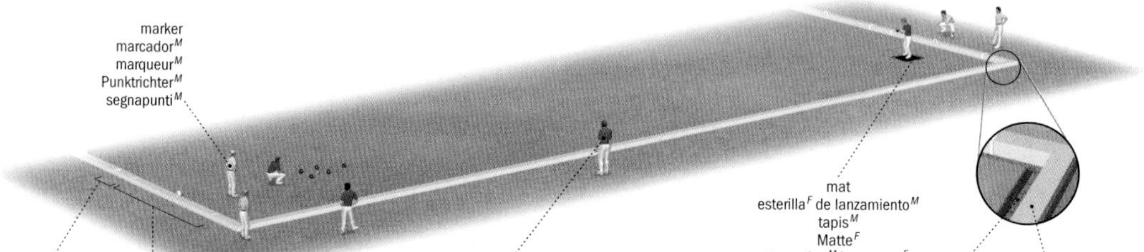

marker
marcador^M
marqueur^M
Punktrichter^M
segnapunti^M

mat
esterilla^F de lanzamiento^M
tapis^M
Matte^F
tappetino^M in gomma^F

dead bowl area
calle^F
zone^F de boule^F morte
Ausbereich^M
area^F di fuorigioco^M

rink
pista^F
surface^F de jeu^M
Abwurfstelle^F
corsia^F di gioco^M

umpire
árbitro^M
arbitre^M
Schiedsrichter^M
arbitro^M

ditch
cuneta^F
rigole^F
Graben^M
fossato^M

bank
bordillo^M
muret^M
Bande^F
sponda^F

petanque

petanca^F | pétanque^F | Petanque^N | petanque^M

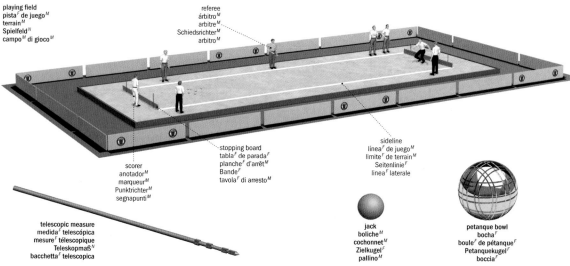

playing field
pista^F de juego^M
terrain^M
Spielfeld^N
campo^M di gioco^M

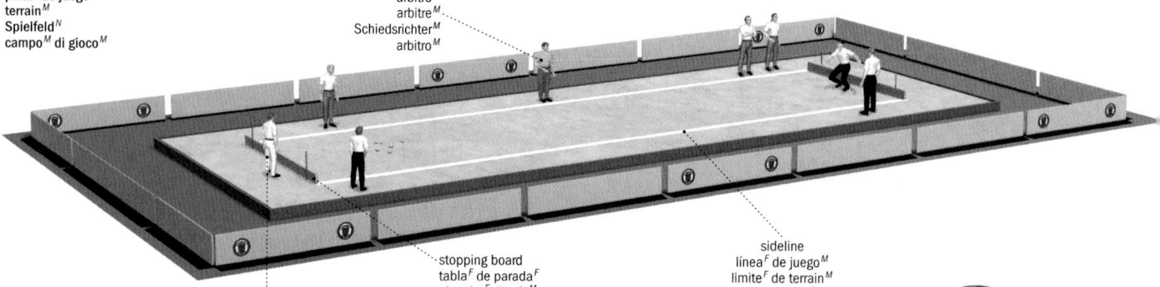

referee
árbitro^M
arbitre^M
Schiedsrichter^M
arbitro^M

stopping board
tabla^F de parada^F
planche^F d'arrêt^M
Bande^F
tavola^F di arresto^M

sideline
línea^F de juego^M
limite^F de terrain^M
Seitenlinie^F
linea^F laterale

scorer
anotador^M
marqueur^M
Punktrichter^M
segnapunti^M

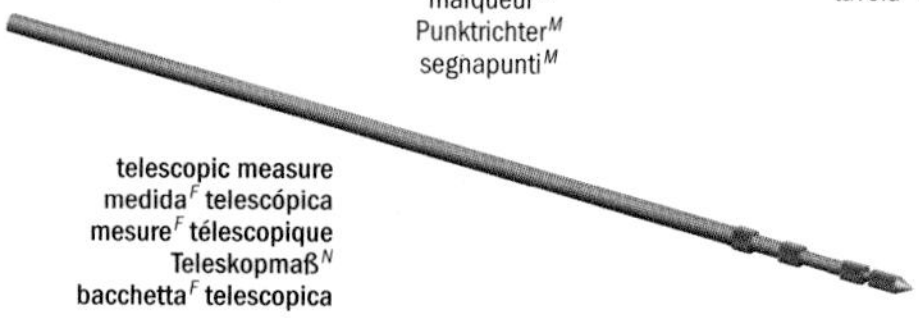

telescopic measure
medida^F telescópica
mesure^F télescopique
Teleskopmaß^N
bacchetta^F telescopica

jack
boliche^M
cochonnet^M
Zielkugel^F
pallino^M

petanque bowl
bocha^F
boule^F de pétanque^F
Petanquekugel^F
boccia^F

bowling

juego^M de bolos^M | jeu^M de quilles^F | Bowling^N | bowling^M

examples of pins
ejemplos^M de bolos^M
exemples^M de quilles^F
Beispiele^N für Kegel^M
esempi^M di birilli^M

American duckpin
bolo^M chico
Dauphine^F américaine
Duckpin^M
birillo^M americano

tenpin
bolo^M
grosse quille^F
Zehnerpin^M
birillo^M grosso

candlepin
bolo^M cilíndrico
quille^F chandelle^F
Candlepin^M
birillo^M a candela^F

fivepin
bolo^M pequeño
petite quille^F
Fünferpin^M
birillo^M piccolo

Canadian duckpin
bolo^M chico
Dauphine^F canadienne
Duckpin^M
birillo^M canadese

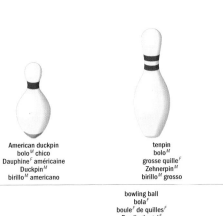

bowling ball
bola^F
boule^F de quilles^F
Bowlingkugel^F
boccia^F

headpin
bolo^M delantero
quille^F-reine^F
Vordereckpin^M
birillo^M centrale

setup
disposición^F de los bolos^M
quillier^M
Aufstellung^F
disposizione^F dei birilli^M

shoe
zapato^M
chaussure^F
Bowlingschuh^M
scarpa^F

pin
bolo^M
quille^F
Pin^M
birillo^M

pocket
separación^F entre bolos^M
poche^F
Gasse^F
spazio^M

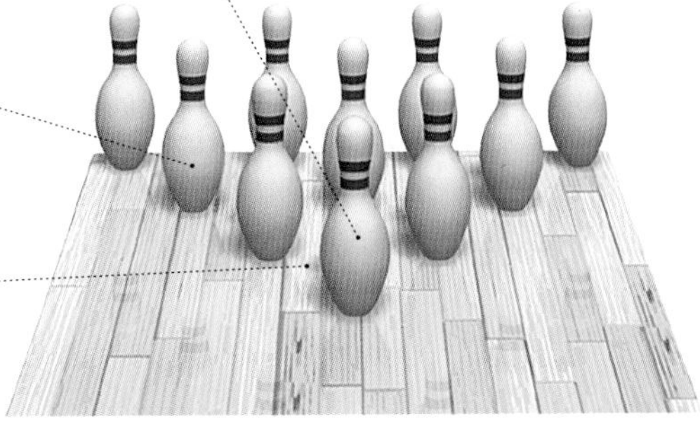

ball return
devolvedor^M
monte-boules^M
Kugelrücklaufkasten^M
ritomabocce^M

score console
marcador^M
tableau^M marqueur^M
Punktekonsole^F
console^F del punteggio^M

ball
bola^F
boule^F
Kugel^M
boccia^F

bowler
jugadora^F de bolos^M
quilleuse^F
Bowlerin^F
lanciatrice^F

keyboard
teclado^M
clavier^M
Kontrollkonsole^F
tastiera^F

ball stand
stand^M de bolos^M
boulier^M
Kugelträger^M
corsia^F d'appoggio^M

setup
disposición^F de los bolos^M
quillier^M
Aufstellmaschine^F
riposizionatore^M automatico

bowling alley
pista^F de bolos^M
allée^F de quilles^F
Bowlingbahn^F
pista^F da bowling

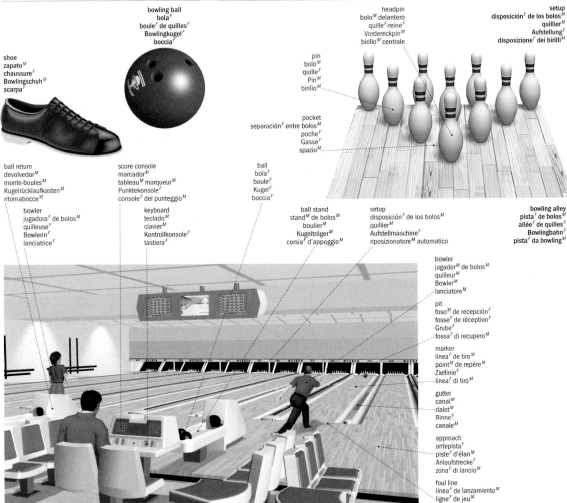

bowler
jugador^M de bolos^M
quilleur^M
Bowler^M
lanciatore^M

pit
foso^M de recepción^F
fosse^F de réception^F
Grube^F
fossa^F di recupero^M

marker
linea^F de tiro^M
point^M de repère^F
Ziellinie^F
linea^F di tiro^M

gutter
canal^M
dalot^M
Rinne^F
canale^M

approach
antepista^F
piste^F d'élan^M
Anlaufstrecke^F
zona^F di lancio^M

foul line
linea^F de lanzamiento^M
ligne^F de jeu^M
Foullinie^F
linea^F di fallo^M

golf

accesorios^M de golf^M | golf^M | Golfspiel^N | golf^M

course
campo^M de golf^M
parcours^M
Golfplatz^M
percorso^M

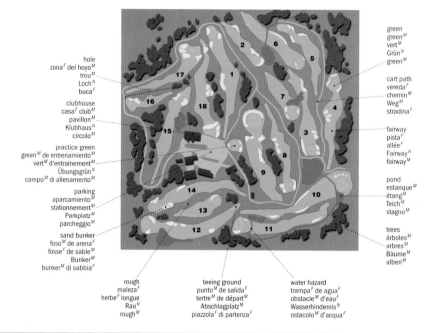

green
green^M
vert^M
Grün^N
green^M

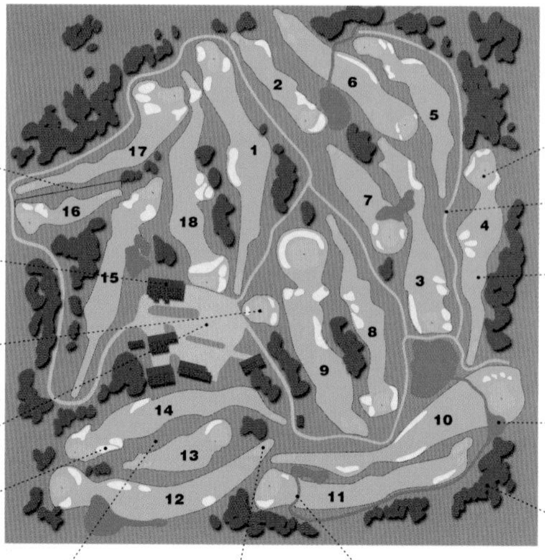

hole
zona^F del hoyo^M
trou^M
Loch^N
buca^F

cart path
vereda^F
chemin^M
Weg^M
stradina^F

clubhouse
casa^F club^M
pavillon^M
Klubhaus^N
circolo^M

fairway
pista^F
allée^F
Fairway^N
fairway^M

practice green
green^M de entrenamiento^M
vert^M d'entraînement^M
Übungsgrün^N
campo^M di allenamento^M

parking
aparcamiento^M
stationnement^M
Parkplatz^M
parcheggio^M

pond
estanque^M
étang^M
Teich^M
stagno^M

sand bunker
foso^M de arena^F
fosse^F de sable^M
Bunker^M
bunker^M di sabbia^F

trees
árboles^M
arbres^M
Bäume^M
alberi^M

rough
maleza^F
herbe^F longue
Rau^N
rough^M

teeing ground
punto^M de salida^F
tertre^M de départ^M
Abschlagplatz^M
piazzola^F di partenza^F

water hazard
trampa^F de agua^F
obstacle^M d'eau^F
Wasserhindernis^N
ostacolo^M d'acqua^F

holes
hoyos^M
trous^M
Löcher^N
buche^F

par 3 hole
hoyo^M de par 3
trou^M de normale^F 3
Par^N-3-Loch^N
buca^F par 3

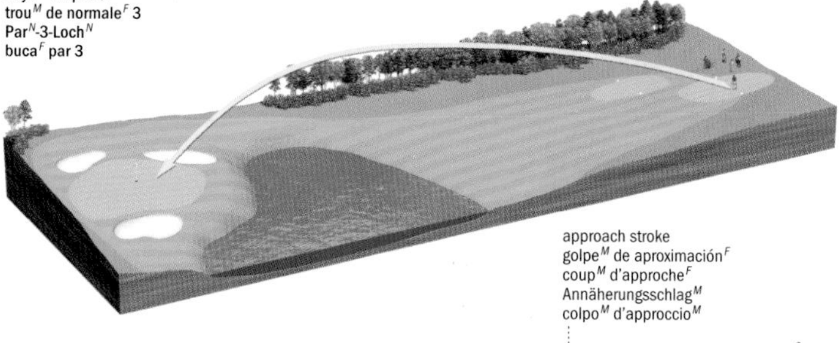

approach stroke
golpe^M de aproximación^F
coup^M d'approche^F
Annäherungsschlag^M
colpo^M d'approccio^M

tee-off stroke
tee^M de salida^F
coup^M de départ^M
Abschlag^M
colpo^M d'inizio^M

par 4 hole
hoyo^M de par 4
trou^M de normale^F 4
Par^N-4-Loch^N
buca^F par 4

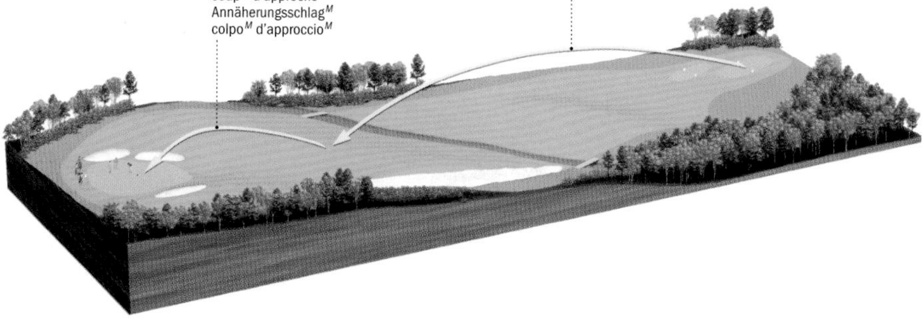

PRECISION AND ACCURACY SPORTS | DEPORTES DE PRECISIÓN Y PUNTERÍA
SPORTS DE PRÉCISION | PRÄZISIONSSPORT | SPORT DI PRECISIONE

golf

types of golf clubs
bastones[M]
types[M] de bâtons[M] de golf[M]
Arten[F] von Golfschläger[M]
tipi[M] di mazze[F]

golf ball
pelota[F] de golf[M]
balle[F] de golf[M]
Golfball[M]
palla[F]

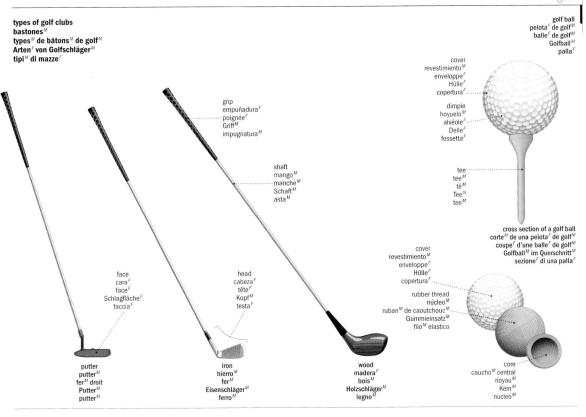

grip
empuñadura[F]
poignée[F]
Griff[M]
impugnatura[M]

shaft
mango[M]
manche[M]
Schaft[M]
asta[M]

cover
revestimiento[M]
enveloppe[F]
Hülle[F]
copertura[F]

dimple
hoyuelo[M]
alvéole[F]
Delle[F]
fossetta[F]

tee
tee[M]
té[M]
Tee[N]
tee[M]

face
cara[F]
face[F]
Schlagfläche[F]
faccia[F]

head
cabeza[F]
tête[F]
Kopf[M]
testa[F]

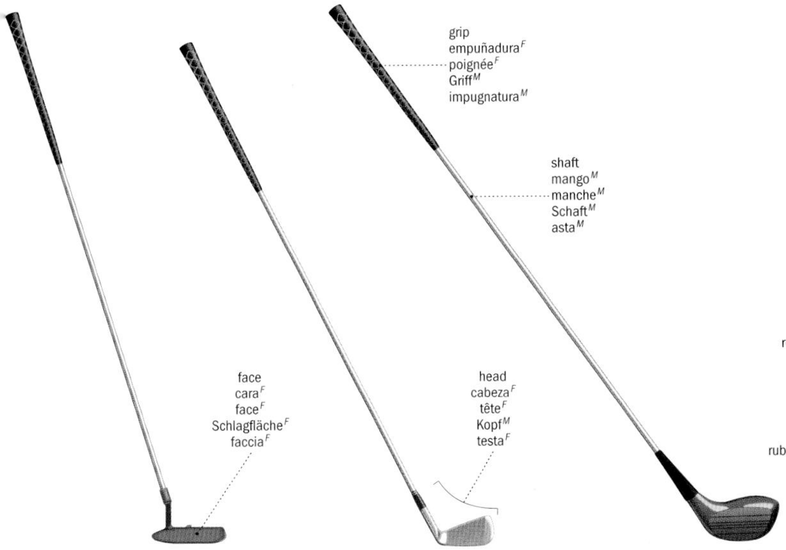

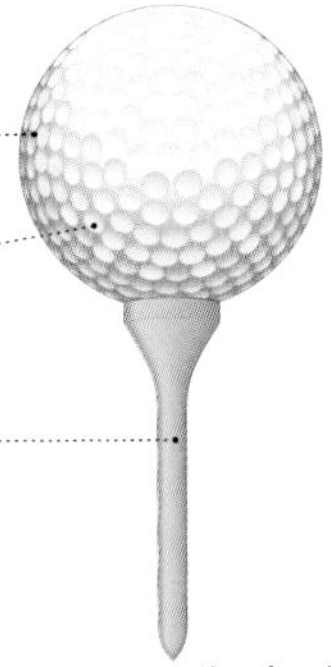

cross section of a golf ball
corte[M] de una pelota[F] de golf[M]
coupe[F] d'une balle[F] de golf[M]
Golfball[M] im Querschnitt[M]
sezione[F] di una palla[F]

cover
revestimiento[M]
enveloppe[F]
Hülle[F]
copertura[F]

rubber thread
núcleo[M]
ruban[M] de caoutchouc[M]
Gummieinsatz[M]
filo[M] elastico

putter
putter[M]
fer[M] droit
Putter[M]
putter[M]

iron
hierro[M]
fer[M]
Eisenschläger[M]
ferro[M]

wood
madera[F]
bois[M]
Holzschläger[M]
legno[M]

core
caucho[M] central
noyau[M]
Kern[M]
nucleo[M]

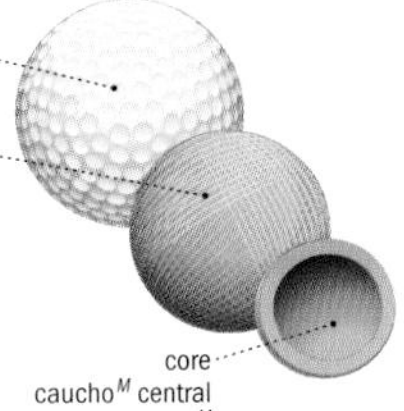

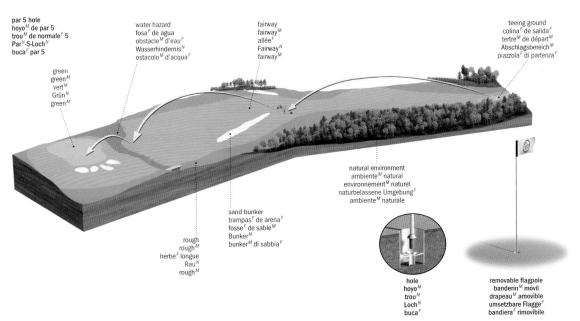

par 5 hole
hoyo[M] de par 5
trou[M] de normale[F] 5
Par[N]-5-Loch[N]
buca[F] par 5

water hazard
fosa[F] de agua
obstacle[M] d'eau[F]
Wasserhindernis[N]
ostacolo[M] d'acqua[F]

fairway
fairway[M]
allée[F]
Fairway[N]
fairway[M]

teeing ground
colina[F] de salida[F]
tertre[M] de départ[M]
Abschlagsbereich[M]
piazzola[F] di partenza[F]

green
green[M]
vert[M]
Grün[N]
green[M]

natural environment
ambiente[M] natural
environnement[M] naturel
naturbelassene Umgebung[F]
ambiente[M] naturale

rough
rough[M]
herbe[F] longue
Rau[N]
rough[M]

sand bunker
trampas[F] de arena[F]
fosse[F] de sable[M]
Bunker[M]
bunker[M] di sabbia[F]

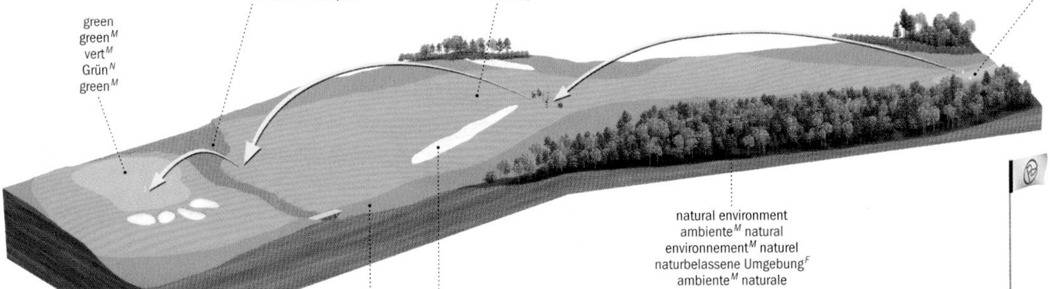

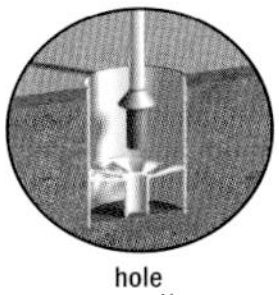

hole
hoyo[M]
trou[M]
Loch[N]
buca[F]

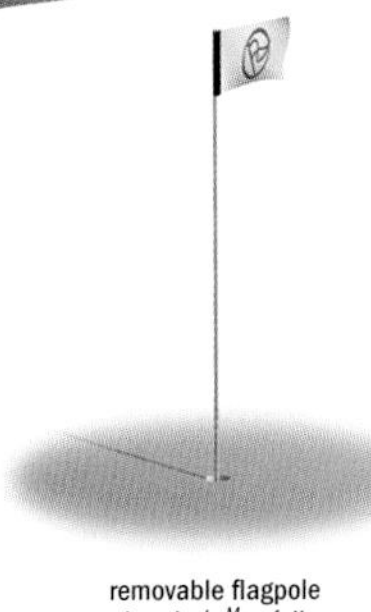

removable flagpole
banderín[M] móvil
drapeau[M] amovible
umsetzbare Flagge[F]
bandiera[F] rimovibile

SPORTS AND GAMES

golf

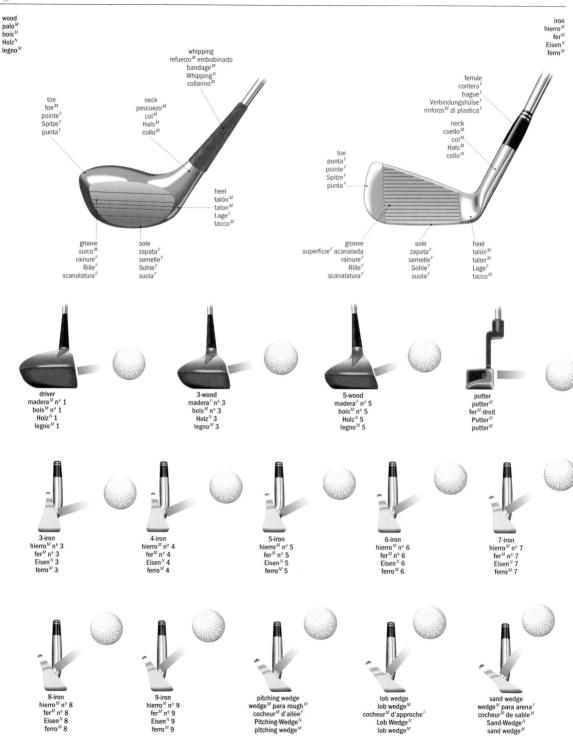

wood
palo^M
bois^M
Holz^N
legno^M

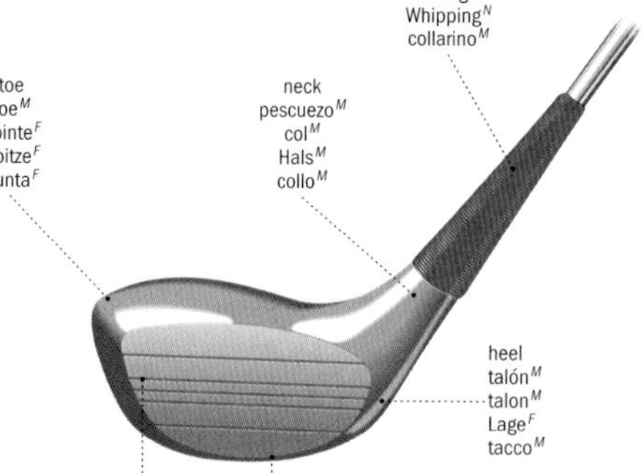

iron
hierro^M
fer^M
Eisen^N
ferro^M

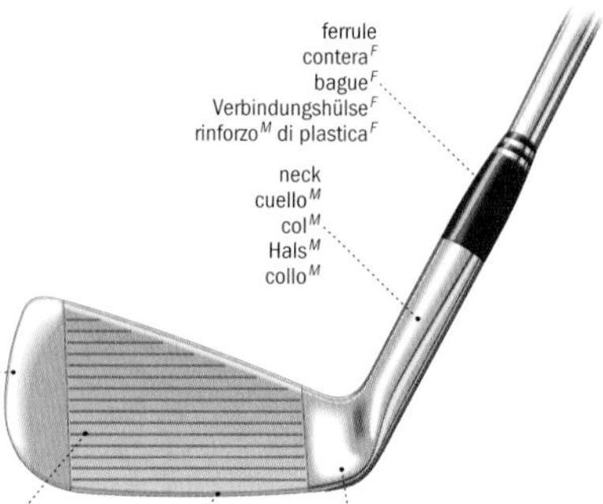

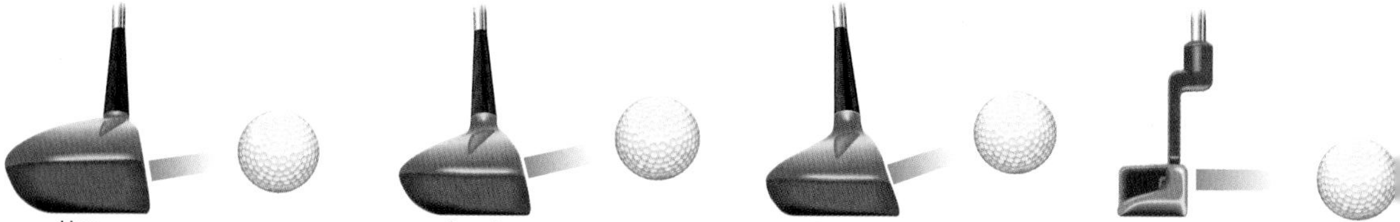

whipping
refuerzo^M embobinado
bandage^M
Whipping^N
collarino^M

ferrule
contera^F
bague^F
Verbindungshülse^F
rinforzo^M di plastica^F

toe
toe^M
pointe^F
Spitze^F
punta^F

neck
pescuezo^M
col^M
Hals^M
collo^M

neck
cuello^M
col^M
Hals^M
collo^M

toe
punta^F
pointe^F
Spitze^F
punta^F

heel
talón^M
talon^M
Lage^F
tacco^M

groove
surco^M
rainure^F
Rille^F
scanalatura^F

sole
zapata^F
semelle^F
Sohle^F
suola^F

groove
superficie^F acanalada
rainure^F
Rille^F
scanalatura^F

sole
zapata^F
semelle^F
Sohle^F
suola^F

heel
talón^M
talon^M
Lage^F
tacco^M

driver
madera^M n° 1
bois^M n° 1
Holz^N 1
legno^M 1

3-wood
madera^F n° 3
bois^M n° 3
Holz^N 3
legno^M 3

5-wood
madera^F n° 5
bois^M n° 5
Holz^N 5
legno^M 5

putter
putter^M
fer^M droit
Putter^M
putter^M

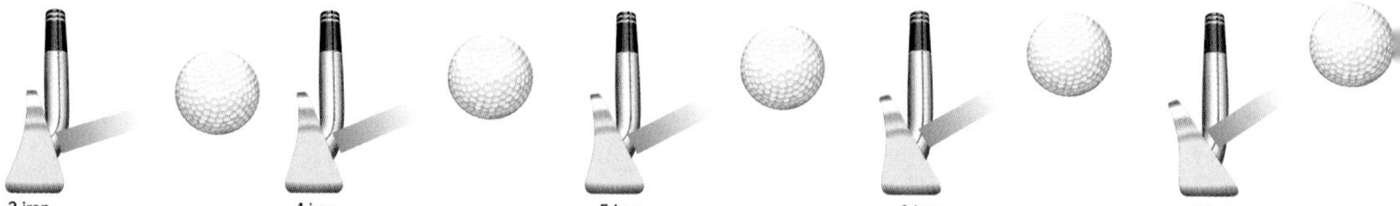

3-iron
hierro^M n° 3
fer^M n° 3
Eisen^N 3
ferro^M 3

4-iron
hierro^M n° 4
fer^M n° 4
Eisen^N 4
ferro^M 4

5-iron
hierro^M n° 5
fer^M n° 5
Eisen^N 5
ferro^M 5

6-iron
hierro^M n° 6
fer^M n° 6
Eisen^N 6
ferro^M 6

7-iron
hierro^M n° 7
fer^M n° 7
Eisen^N 7
ferro^M 7

8-iron
hierro^M n° 8
fer^M n° 8
Eisen^N 8
ferro^M 8

9-iron
hierro^M n° 9
fer^M n° 9
Eisen^N 9
ferro^M 9

pitching wedge
wedge^M para rough^M
cocheur^M d'allée^F
Pitching-Wedge^N
pitching wedge^M

lob wedge
lob wedge^M
cocheur^M d'approche^F
Lob Wedge^N
lob wedge^M

sand wedge
wedge^M para arena^F
cocheur^M de sable^M
Sand-Wedge^N
sand wedge^M

SPORTS AND GAMES

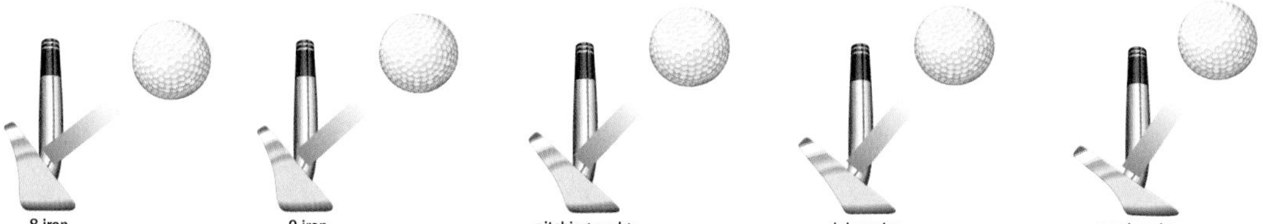

PRECISION AND ACCURACY SPORTS | DEPORTES DE PRECISIÓN Y PUNTERÍA
SPORTS DE PRÉCISION | PRÄZISIONSSPORT | SPORT DI PRECISIONE

golf

shoulder strap
correa^F
sangle^F
Schultergurt^M
tracolla^F

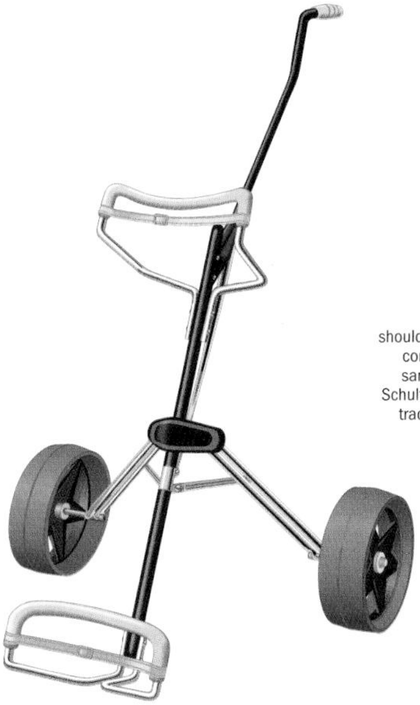

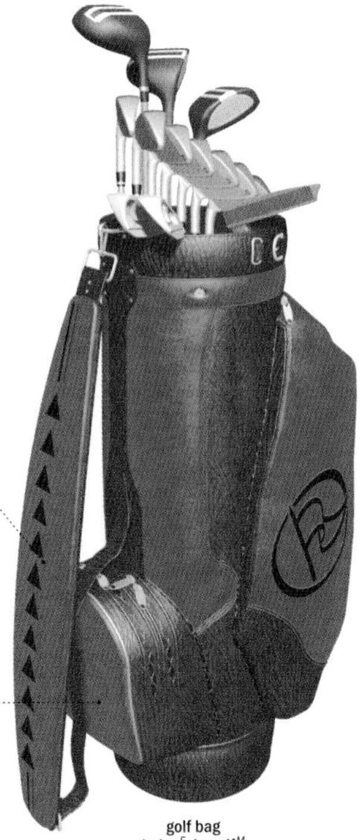

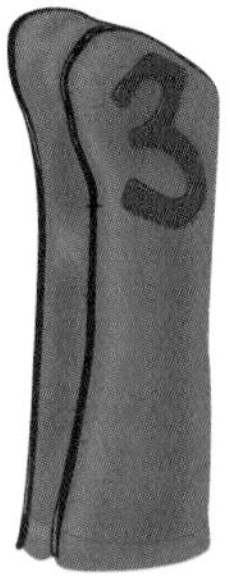

head cover
capuchón^M de bastones^M
capuchon^F
Schlägerabdeckung^F
coprilegno^M

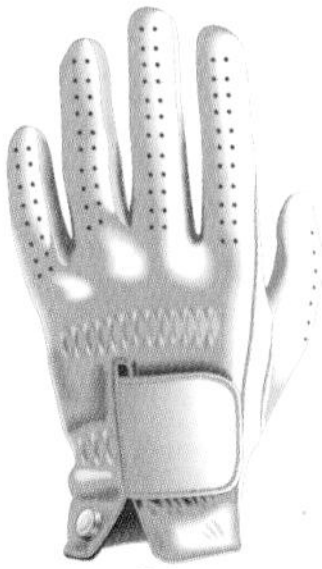

golf glove
guante^M de golf^M
gant^M de golf^M
Golfhandschuh^M
guanto^M

golf cart
carrito^M de golf^M
chariot^M
Golfwagen^M
carrello^M

pocket
bolsillo^M
poche^F
Seitentasche^F
tasca^F

golf bag
bolsa^F de golf^M
sac^M de golf^M
Golftasche^F
sacca^F

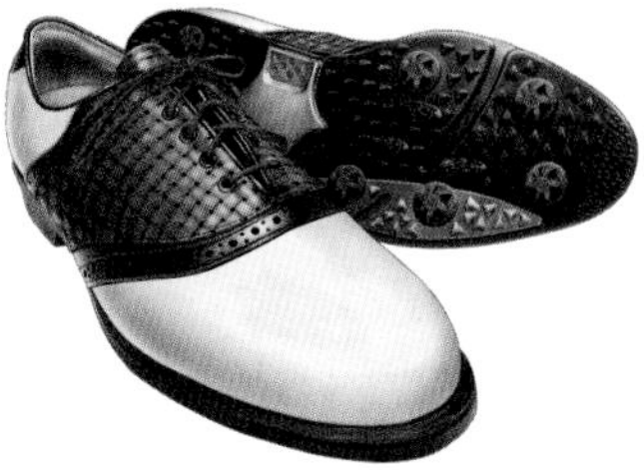

golf shoes
zapatos^M de golf^M
chaussures^F de golf^M
Golfschuhe^M
scarpe^F

bag well
portabolsa^F
porte-sac^M
Taschenträger^M
portasacca^M

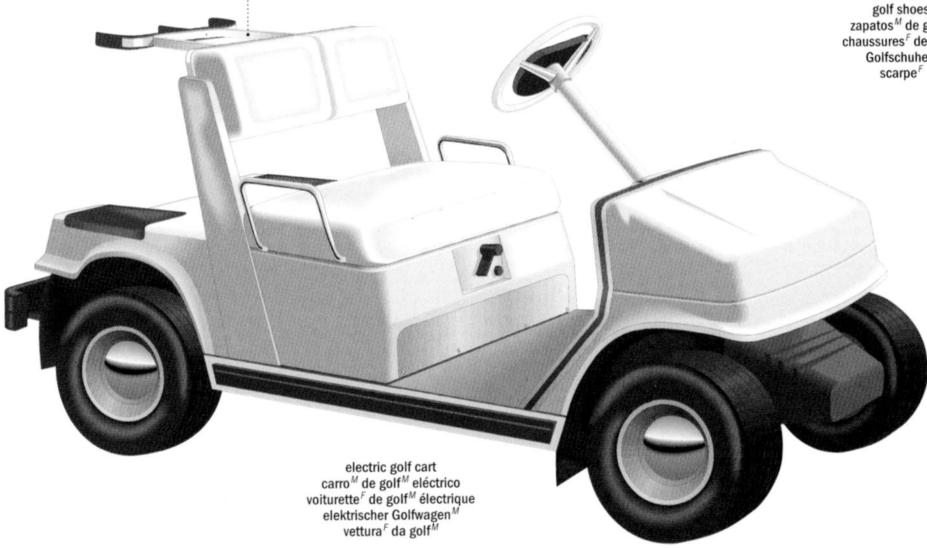

electric golf cart
carro^M de golf^M eléctrico
voiturette^F de golf^M électrique
elektrischer Golfwagen^M
vettura^F da golf^M

SPORTS AND GAMES

road racing

ciclismo^M por carretera^F | cyclisme^M sur route^F | Straßenradsport^M | ciclismo^M su strada^F

road-racing bicycle and cyclist
bicicleta^F de carreras^F y ciclista^M
vélo^M de course^F et cycliste^M
Straßenrennrad^N und Fahrer^M
bicicletta^F da corsa^F e ciclista$^{M/F}$

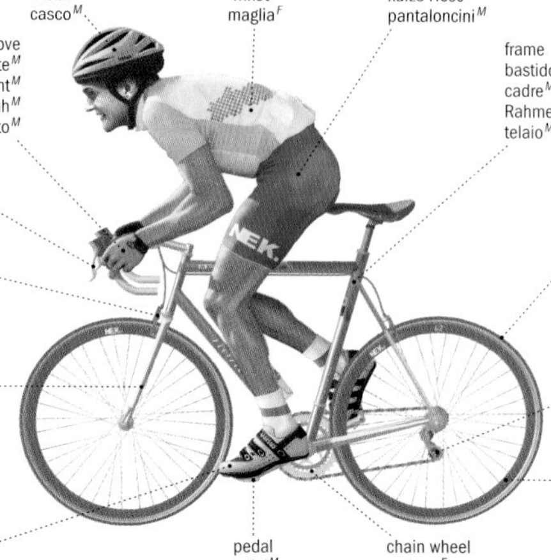

helmet
casco^M
casque^M
Helm^M
casco^M

jersey
malla^F
maillot^M
Trikot^N
maglia^F

shorts
pantalones^M elásticos
cuissard^M
kurze Hose^F
pantaloncini^M

glove
guante^M
gant^M
Handschuh^M
guanto^M

frame
bastidor^M
cadre^M
Rahmen^M
telaio^M

brake lever and shifter
palanca^F del freno^M y cambio^M de velocidades^F
poignée^F de frein^M et manette^F de dérailleur^M
Bremsgriff^M und Schalthebel^M
leva^F del freno^M e del cambio^M

tire
neumático^M
pneu^M
Reifen^M
pneumatico^M

brake
freno^M
frein^M
Bremse^F
freno^M

derailleur
cambio^M de velocidades^F
dérailleur^M
Umwerfer^M
deragliatore^M

fork
horquilla^F
fourche^F
Radgabel^F
forcella^F

wheel
rueda^F
roue^F
Rad^N
ruota^F

shoe
zapato^M
chaussure^F
Schuh^M
scarpa^F

pedal
pedal^M
pédale^F
Pedal^N
pedale^M

chain wheel
cadena^F
plateau^M
Kettenrad^M
ruota^F della moltiplica^F

road cycling competition
competición^M de ciclismo^M por carretera^F
compétition^F de cyclisme^M sur route^F
Straßenradrennen^N
gara^F di ciclismo^M su strada^F

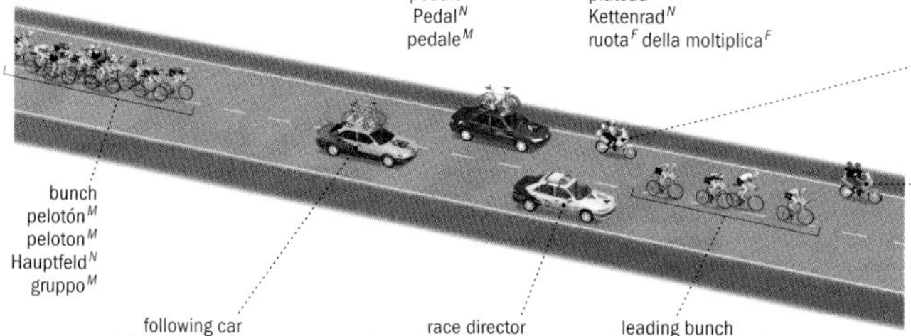

motorcycle-mounted camera
moto cámara^F
moto^F-caméra^F
Motorradkamera^F
motocicletta con telecamera^F

leading motorcycle
moto^M de cabeza^F
moto^F de tête^F
Führungsmotorrad^N
motocicletta^F di testa^F

bunch
pelotón^M
peloton^M
Hauptfeld^N
gruppo^M

following car
coche^M del equipo^M
voiture^F suiveuse
Verfolgerauto^N
ammiraglia^F

race director
director^M de carrera^F
directeur^M de course^F
Rennleiter^M
direttore^M della corsa^F

leading bunch
pelotón^M de cabeza^F
peloton^M de tête^F
Führungsgruppe^F
gruppo^M di testa^F

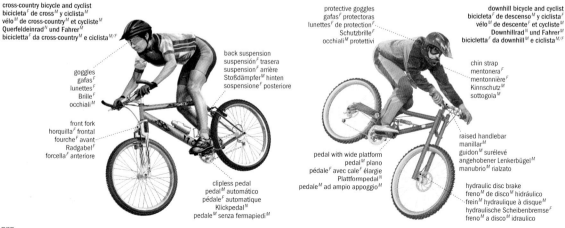

mountain biking

ciclismo^M de montaña^F | vélo^M de montagne^F | Mountainbike^N | mountain bike^F

cross-country bicycle and cyclist
bicicleta^F de cross^M y ciclista^M
vélo^M de cross-country^M et cycliste^M
Querfeldeinrad^N und Fahrer^M
bicicletta^F da cross-country^M e ciclista$^{M/F}$

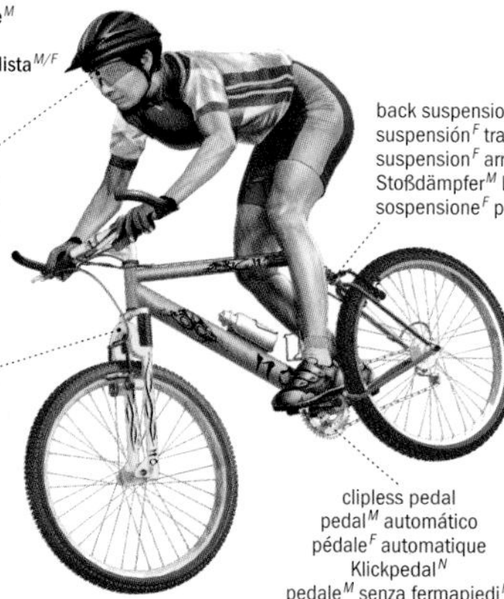

goggles
gafas^F
lunettes^F
Brille^F
occhiali^M

front fork
horquilla^F frontal
fourche^F avant
Radgabel^F
forcella^F anteriore

back suspension
suspensión^F trasera
suspension^F arrière
Stoßdämpfer^M hinten
sospensione^F posteriore

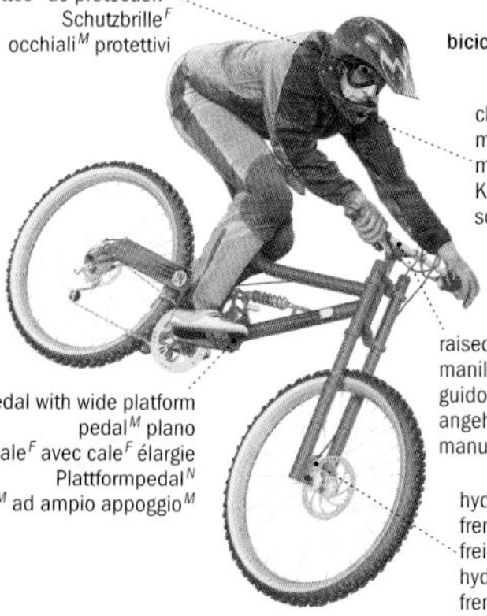

protective goggles
gafas^F protectoras
lunettes^F de protection^F
Schutzbrille^F
occhiali^M protettivi

downhill bicycle and cyclist
bicicleta^F de descenso^M y ciclista^F
vélo^M de descente^F et cycliste^F
Downhillrad^N und Fahrer^M
bicicletta^F da downhill^M e ciclista$^{M/F}$

chin strap
mentonera^F
mentonnière^F
Kinnschutz^M
sottogola^M

raised handlebar
manillar^M
guidon^M surélevé
angehobener Lenkerbügel^M
manubrio^M rialzato

clipless pedal
pedal^M automático
pédale^F automatique
Klickpedal^N
pedale^M senza fermapiedi^M

pedal with wide platform
pedal^M plano
pédale^F avec cale^F élargie
Plattformpedal^N
pedale^M ad ampio appoggio^M

hydraulic disc brake
freno^M de disco^M hidráulico
frein^M hydraulique à disque^M
hydraulische Scheibenbremse^F
freno^M a disco^M idraulico

track cycling

ciclismo^M en pista^F | cyclisme^M sur piste^F | Bahnradsport^M | ciclismo^M su pista^F

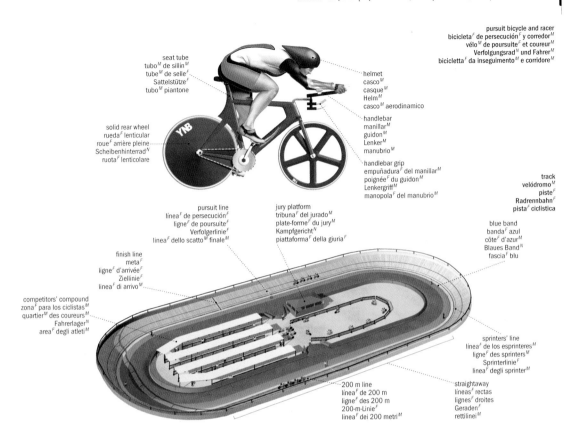

pursuit bicycle and racer
bicicleta^F de persecución^F y corredor^M
vélo^M de poursuite^F et coureur^M
Verfolgungsrad^M und Fahrer^M
bicicletta^F da inseguimento^M e corridore^M

seat tube
tubo^M de sillín^M
tube^M de selle^F
Sattelstütze^F
tubo^M piantone

helmet
casco^M
casque^M
Helm^M
casco^M aerodinamico

solid rear wheel
rueda^F lenticular
roue^F arrière pleine
Scheibenhinterrad^N
ruota^F lenticolare

handlebar
manillar^M
guidon^M
Lenker^M
manubrio^M

handlebar grip
empuñadura^F del manillar^M
poignée^F du guidon^M
Lenkergriff^M
manopola^F del manubrio^M

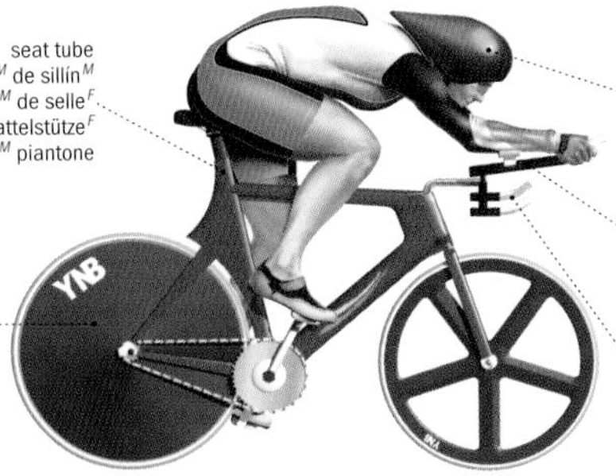

track
velódromo^M
piste^F
Radrennbahn^F
pista^F ciclistica

pursuit line
linea^F de persecución^F
ligne^F de poursuite^F
Verfolgerlinie^F
linea^F dello scatto^M finale

jury platform
tribuna^F del jurado^M
plate-forme^F du jury^M
Kampfgericht^N
piattaforma^F della giuria^F

blue band
banda^F azul
côte^F d'azur^F
Blaues Band^N
fascia^F blu

finish line
meta^F
ligne^F d'arrivée^F
Ziellinie^F
linea^F di arrivo^M

competitors' compound
zona^F para los ciclistas^M
quartier^M des coureurs^M
Fahrerlager^N
area^M degli atleti^M

sprinters' line
linea^F de los esprinteres^M
ligne^F des sprinters^M
Sprinterlinie^F
linea^F degli sprinter^M

200 m line
línea^F de 200 m
ligne^F des 200 m
200-m-Linie^F
linea^F dei 200 metri^M

straightaway
líneas^F rectas
lignes^F droites
Geraden^F
rettilinei^M

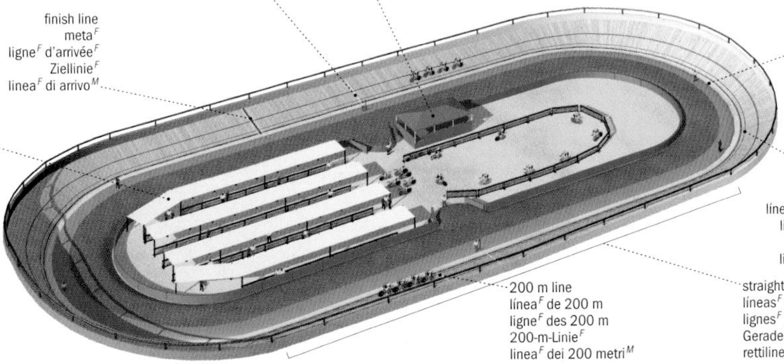

BMX

ciclocross^M | bicross^M | BMX^N | mountain bike^F da cross

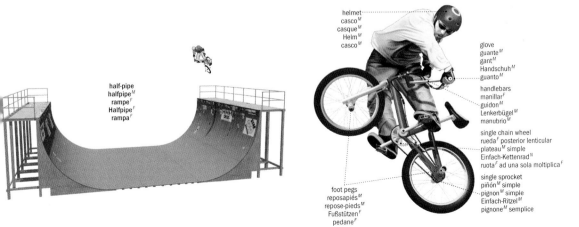

helmet
casco^M
casque^M
Helm^M
casco^M

half-pipe
halfpipe^M
rampe^F
Halfpipe^F
rampa^F

glove
guante^M
gant^M
Handschuh^M
guanto^M

handlebars
manillar^M
guidon^M
Lenkerbügel^M
manubrio^M

single chain wheel
rueda^F posterior lenticular
plateau^M simple
Einfach-Kettenrad^N
ruota^F ad una sola moltiplica^F

single sprocket
piñón^M simple
pignon^M simple
Einfach-Ritzel^M
pignone^M semplice

foot pegs
reposapiés^M
repose-pieds^M
Fußstützen^F
pedane^F

SPORTS AND GAMES

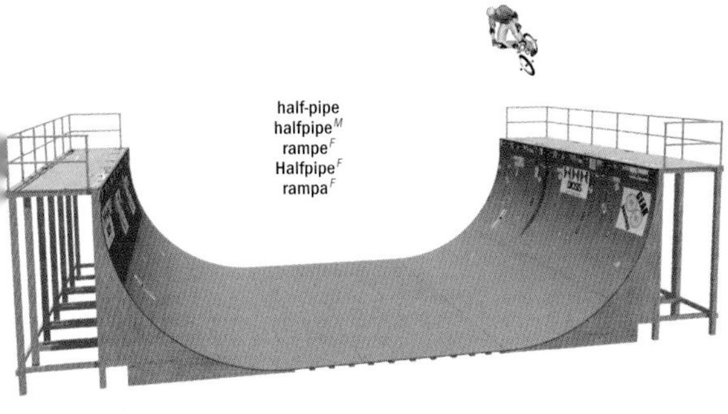

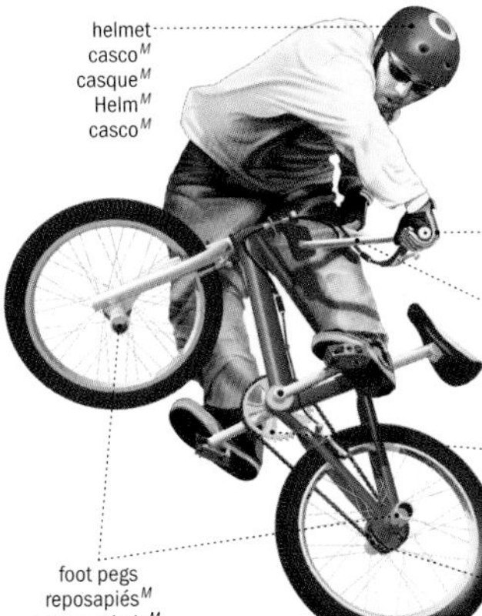

car racing

carreras^F de coches^M | course^F automobile | Autorennen^N | automobilismo^M

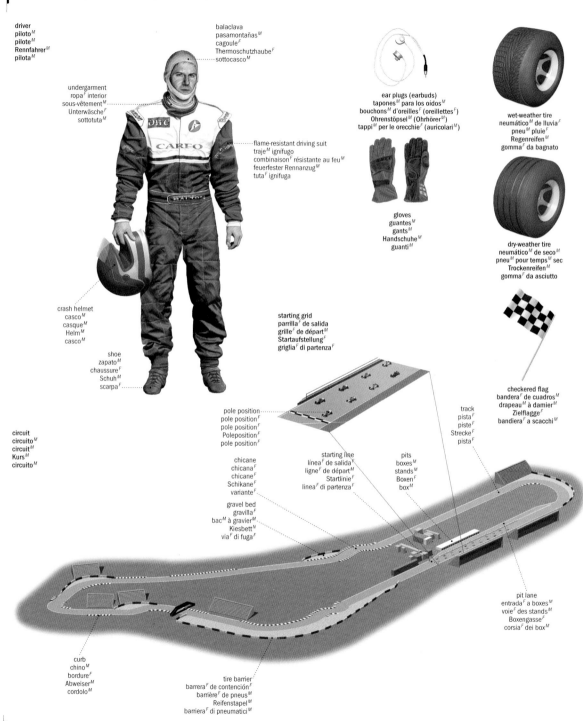

driver
piloto^M
pilote^M
Rennfahrer^M
pilota^M

balaclava
pasamontañas^M
cagoule^F
Thermoschutzhaube^F
sottocasco^M

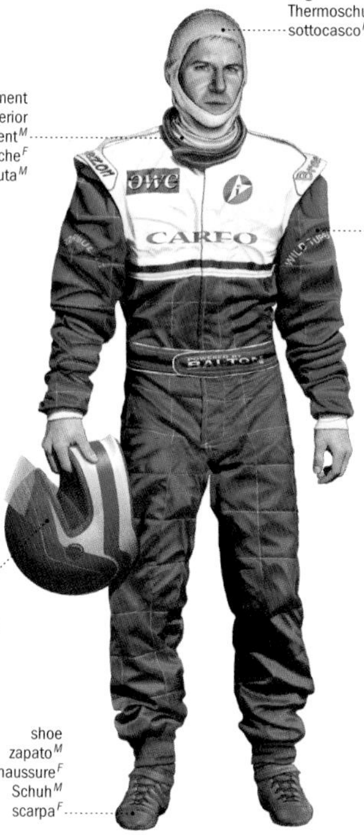

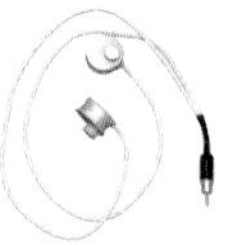

ear plugs (earbuds)
tapones^M para los oídos^M
bouchons^M d'oreilles^F (oreillettes^F)
Ohrenstöpsel^M (Ohrhörer^M)
tappi^M per le orecchie^F (auricolari^M)

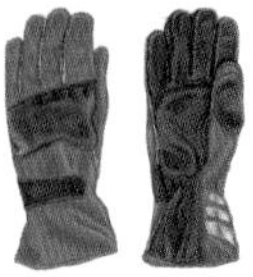

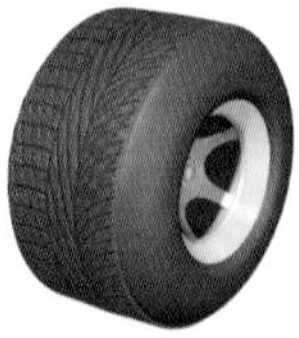

wet-weather tire
neumático^M de lluvia^F
pneu^M pluie^F
Regenreifen^M
gomma^F da bagnato

undergarment
ropa^F interior
sous-vêtement^M
Unterwäsche^F
sottotuta^M

flame-resistant driving suit
traje^M ignífugo
combinaison^F résistante au feu^M
feuerfester Rennanzug^M
tuta^F ignifuga

gloves
guantes^M
gants^M
Handschuhe^M
guanti^M

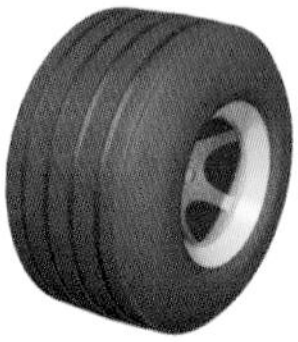

dry-weather tire
neumático^M de seco^M
pneu^M pour temps^M sec
Trockenreifen^M
gomma^F da asciutto

crash helmet
casco^M
casque^M
Helm^M
casco^M

starting grid
parrilla^F de salida
grille^F de départ^M
Startaufstellung^F
griglia^F di partenza^F

shoe
zapato^M
chaussure^F
Schuh^M
scarpa^F

checkered flag
bandera^F de cuadros^M
drapeau^M à damier^M
Zielflagge^F
bandiera^F a scacchi^M

pole position
pole position^F
pole position^F
Poleposition^F
pole position^F

track
pista^F
piste^F
Strecke^F
pista^F

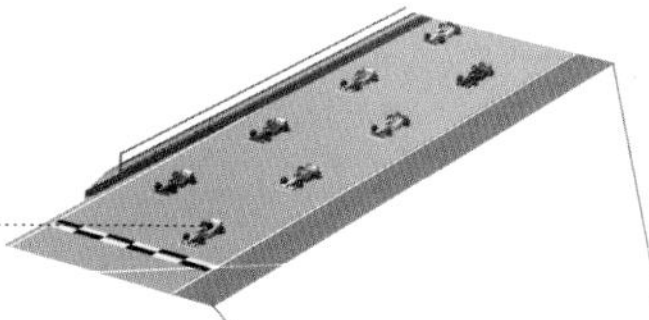

circuit
circuito^M
circuit^M
Kurs^M
circuito^M

chicane
chicana^F
chicane^F
Schikane^F
variante^F

starting line
línea^F de salida
ligne^F de départ^M
Startlinie^F
línea^F di partenza^F

pits
boxes^M
stands^M
Boxen^F
box^M

gravel bed
gravilla^F
bac^M à gravier^M
Kiesbett^N
via^F di fuga^F

pit lane
entrada^F a boxes^M
voie^F des stands^M
Boxengasse^F
corsia^F dei box^M

curb
chino^M
bordure^F
Abweiser^M
cordolo^M

tire barrier
barrera^F de contención^F
barrière^F de pneus^M
Reifenstapel^M
barriera^F di pneumatici^M

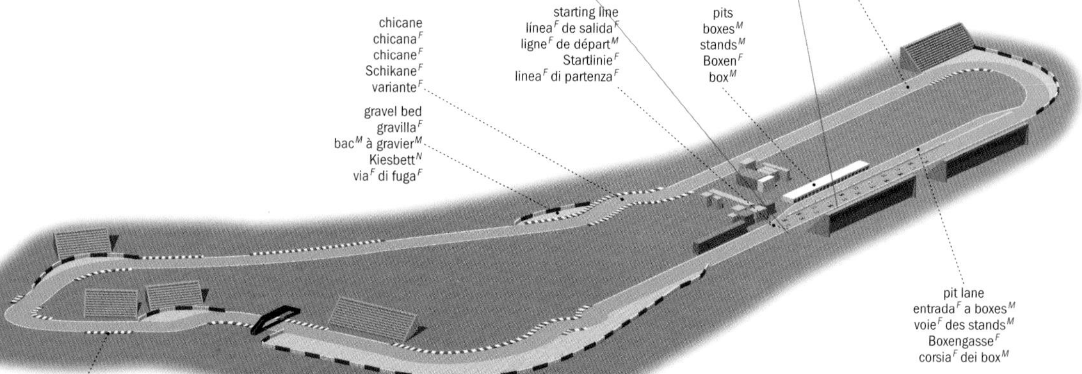

SPORTS AND GAMES

Formula 1® car
coche^M de Fórmula 1
voiture^F de Formule^F 1
Formel-1-Auto^N
auto^F da formula^F 1

wing
alerón^M
aileron^M
Flügel^M
alettone^M

camera
cámara^F
caméra^F
Kamera^F
telecamera^F

cockpit
habitáculo^M
habitacle^M
Cockpit^N
abitacolo^M

radio antenna
antena^F de radio^F
antenne^F radio^F
Funkantenne^F
antenna^F radio^F

Pitot tube
tubo^M de Pitot
tube^M de Pitot
Pitot-Rohr^N
tubo^M di Pitot

side fairings
alerón^M
ponton^M
Seitenkästen^M
carenatura^F laterale

roll structure
estructura^F protectora
structure^F anti-tonneau
Überrollschutz^M
struttura^F protettiva

safety belt
cinturón^M de seguridad^F
ceinture^F de sécurité^F
Sicherheitsgurt^M
cintura^F di sicurezza^F

steering wheel
volante^M
volant^M
Lenkrad^N
volante^M

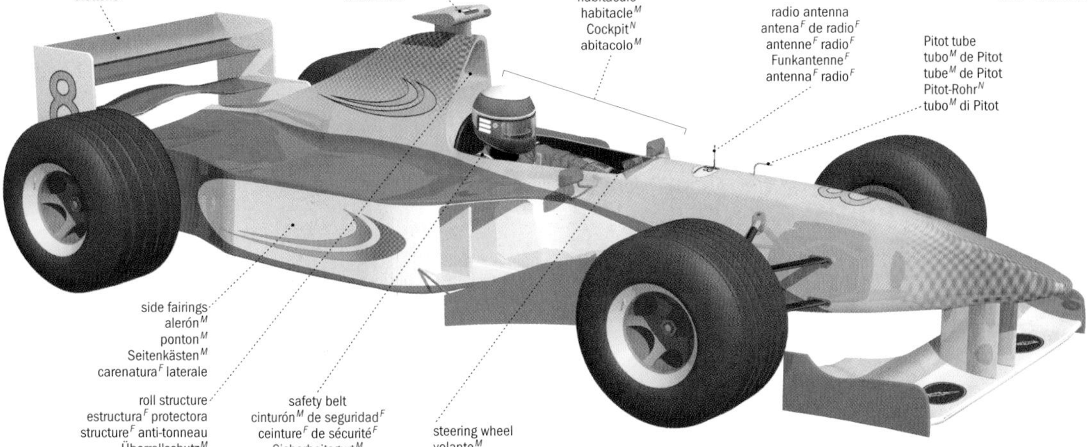

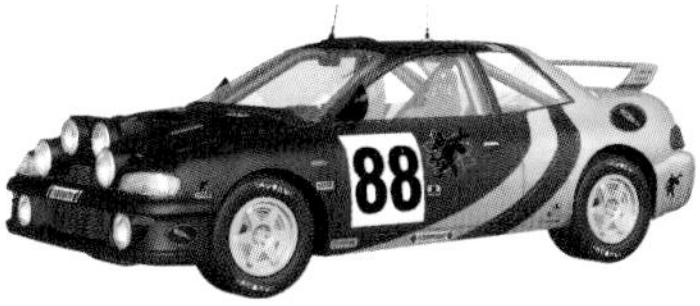

rally car
coche^M de rally
voiture^F de rallye^M
Geländefahrzeug^N
auto^F da rally^M

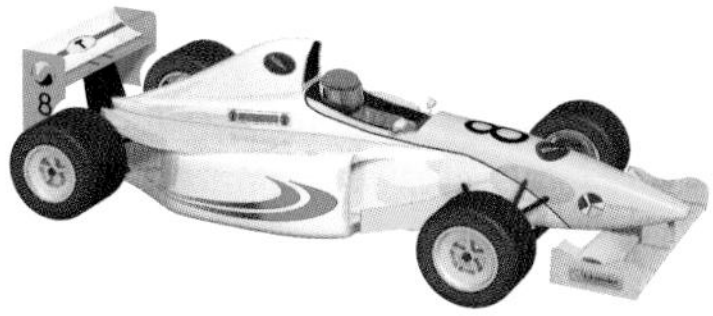

Formula 3000 car
coche^M de fórmula 3000
voiture^F de formule^F 3000
Formel-3000-Auto^N
auto^F da formula^F 3000

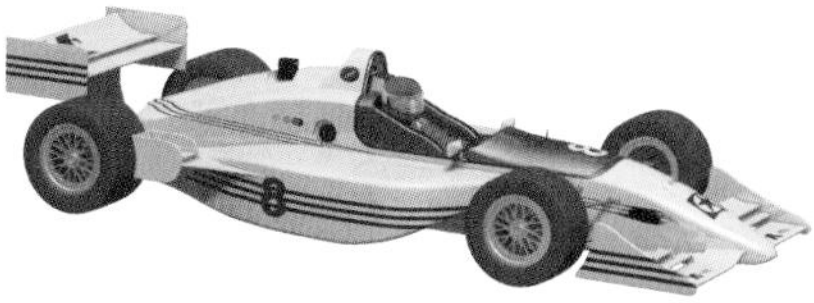

Indycar®
coche^M de Indy
voiture^F de formule^F Indy
Formel-Indy-Auto^N
auto^F da formula^F Indy

pit stop
pit stop^M
arrêt^M au stand^M
Boxenstopp^M
sosta^F ai box^M

refueler
repostador^M
ravitailleur^M
Betanker^M
addetto^M al rifornimento^M

starter mechanic
mecánico^M de arranque^M
responsable^M du démarreur^M
Start-Mechaniker^M
meccanico^M dello start^M

refueling device
tanque^M para repostar
dispositif^M de ravitaillement^M
Tankanlage^F
serbatoio^M per il rifornimento^M

compressed-air tank
bombona^F de aire^M comprimido
réservoir^M d'air^M comprimé
Drucklufttank^M
bombola^F ad aria^F compressa

jack
gato^M
cric^M
Wagenheber^M
martinetto^M

mechanic
mecánico^M
mécanicien^M
Mechaniker^M
meccanico^M

pneumatic drill
taladro^M neumático
pistolet^M pneumatique
Schlagschrauber^M
avvitatore^M pneumatico

chief mechanic
jefe^M de mecánicos^M
chef^M mécanicien^M
Chef-Mechaniker^M
capo^M meccanico^M

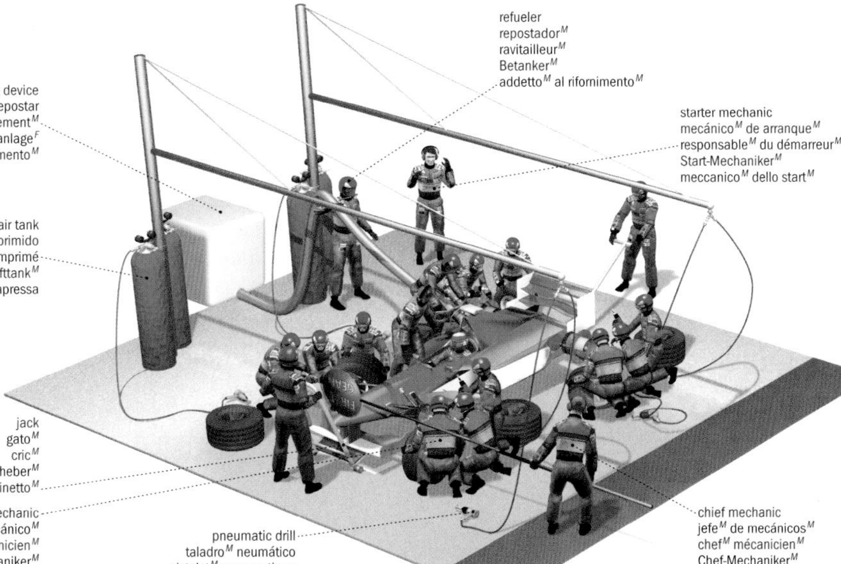

motorcycling

motocicleta[F] | motocyclisme[M] | Motorradsport[M] | motociclismo[M]

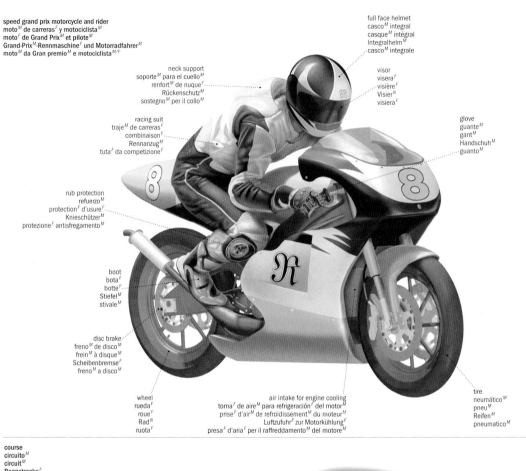

speed grand prix motorcycle and rider
moto[M] de carreras[F] y motociclista[M]
moto[F] de Grand Prix[M] et pilote[M]
Grand-Prix[M]-Rennmaschine[F] und Motorradfahrer[M]
moto[M] da Gran premio[M] e motociclista[M/F]

full face helmet
casco[M] integral
casque[M] intégral
Integralhelm[M]
casco[M] integrale

neck support
soporte[M] para el cuello[M]
renfort[M] de nuque[F]
Rückenschutz[M]
sostegno[M] per il collo[M]

visor
visera[F]
visière[F]
Visier[N]
visiera[F]

racing suit
traje[M] de carreras[F]
combinaison[F]
Rennanzug[M]
tuta[F] da competizione[F]

glove
guante[M]
gant[M]
Handschuh[M]
guanto[M]

rub protection
refuerzo[M]
protection[F] d'usure[F]
Knieschützer[M]
protezione[F] antisfregamento[M]

boot
bota[F]
botte[F]
Stiefel[M]
stivale[M]

disc brake
freno[M] de disco[M]
frein[M] à disque[M]
Scheibenbremse[F]
freno[M] a disco[M]

wheel
rueda[F]
roue[F]
Rad[N]
ruota[F]

air intake for engine cooling
toma[F] de aire[M] para refrigeración[F] del motor[M]
prise[F] d'air[M] de refroidissement[M] du moteur[M]
Luftzufuhr[F] zur Motorkühlung[F]
presa[F] d'aria[F] per il raffreddamento[M] del motore[M]

tire
neumático[M]
pneu[M]
Reifen[M]
pneumatico[M]

course
circuito[M]
circuit[M]
Rennstrecke[F]
circuito[M]

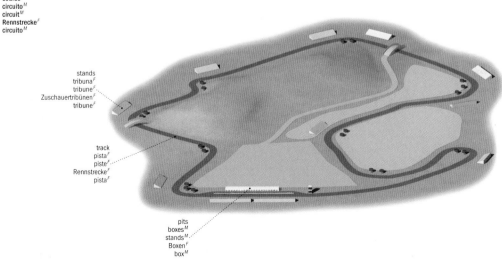

stands
tribuna[F]
tribune[F]
Zuschauertribünen[F]
tribune[F]

track
pista[F]
piste[F]
Rennstrecke[F]
pista[F]

pits
boxes[M]
stands[M]
Boxen[F]
box[M]

motocross and supercross motorcycle
moto^M de motocross^M y supercross^M
moto^F de motocross^M et supercross^M
Motocross^N- und Supercross^N-Motorrad^N
motocicletta^F da motocross^M e supercross^M

trial motorcycle
moto^F de trial^M
moto^F de trial^M
Trial^N-Motorrad^N
motocicletta^F da trial^M

protective suit
traje^M de protección^F
combinaison^F de protection^F
Schutzanzug^M
tuta^F protettiva

glove
guante^M
gant^M
Handschuh^M
guanto^M

pants
pantalones^M
pantalon^M
Hose^F
pantaloni^M

helmet
casco^M
casque^M
Helm^M
casco^M per cross

protective goggles
guantes^M protectores
lunettes^F de protection^F
Schutzbrille^F
occhiali^M protettivi

hand protector
protector^M de mano^F
protège-main^M
Handschutz^M
paramano^M

number plate
placa^F de número^M
plaque^F-numéro^M
Startnummer^F
numero^M di gara^F

fork
horquilla^F
fourche^F
Gabel^F
forcella^F

rally motorcycle
moto^M de rally^M
moto^F de rallye^M
Rallye^F-Motorrad^N
motocicletta^F da rally^M

nubby tire
neumático^M de tacos^M
pneu^M à crampons^M
Stollenreifen^M
pneumatico^M scolpito

boot
bota^F
botte^F
Stiefel^M
stivale^M

protective plate
placa^F protectora
plaque^F de protection^F
Schutzplatte^F
piastra^F di protezione^F

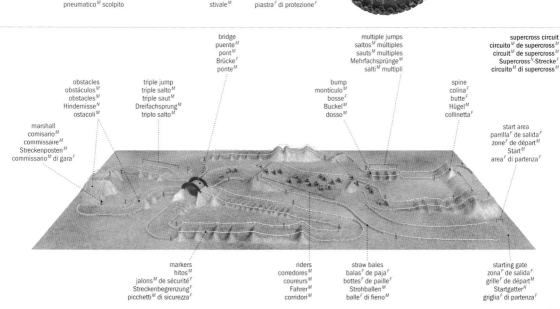

bridge
puente^M
pont^M
Brücke^F
ponte^M

multiple jumps
saltos^M múltiples
sauts^M multiples
Mehrfachsprünge^M
salti^M multipli

supercross circuit
circuito^M de supercross^M
circuit^F de supercross^M
Supercross^N-Strecke^F
circuito^M di supercross^M

obstacles
obstáculos^M
obstacles^M
Hindernisse^N
ostacoli^M

triple jump
triple salto^M
triple saut^M
Dreifachsprung^M
triplo salto^M

bump
monticulo^M
bosse^F
Buckel^M
dosso^M

spine
colina^F
butte^F
Hügel^M
collinetta^F

marshall
comisario^M
commissaire^M
Streckenposten^M
commissario^M di gara^F

start area
parrilla^F de salida^F
zone^F de départ^M
Start^M
area^F di partenza^F

markers
hitos^M
jalons^M de sécurité^F
Streckenbegrenzung^F
picchetti^M di sicurezza^F

riders
corredores^M
coureurs^M
Fahrer^M
corridori^M

straw bales
balas^F de paja^F
bottes^F de paille^F
Strohballen^M
balle^F di fieno^M

starting gate
zona^F de salida^F
grille^F de départ^M
Startgatter^N
griglia^F di partenza^F

personal watercraft

moto^F acuática | scooter^M de mer^F ; *motomarine^F* | Jetski^M | acquascooter^M

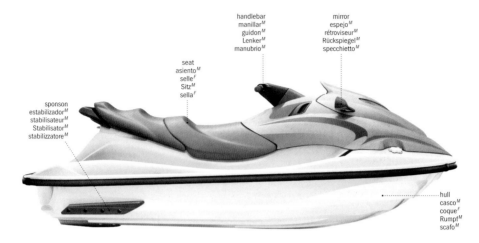

handlebar
manillar^M
guidon^M
Lenker^M
manubrio^M

mirror
espejo^M
rétroviseur^M
Rückspiegel^M
specchietto^M

seat
asiento^M
selle^F
Sitz^M
sella^F

sponson
estabilizador^M
stabilisateur^M
Stabilisator^M
stabilizzatore^M

hull
casco^M
coque^F
Rumpf^M
scafo^M

snowmobile

moto^M nieve | motoneige^F | Schneemobil^N | gatto^M delle nevi^F

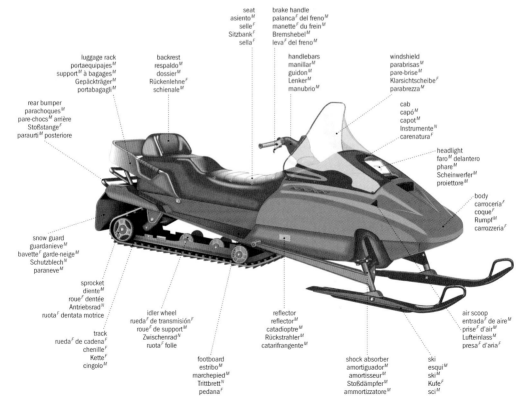

seat
asiento^M
selle^F
Sitzbank^F
sella^F

brake handle
palanca^F del freno^M
manette^F du frein^M
Bremshebel^M
leva^F del freno^M

luggage rack
portaequipajes^M
support^M à bagages^M
Gepäckträger^M
portabagagli^M

backrest
respaldo^M
dossier^M
Rückenlehne^F
schienale^M

handlebars
manillar^M
guidon^M
Lenker^M
manubrio^M

windshield
parabrisas^M
pare-brise^M
Klarsichtscheibe^F
parabrezza^M

rear bumper
parachoques^M
pare-chocs^M arrière
Stoßstange^F
paraurti^M posteriore

cab
capó^M
capot^M
Instrumente^N
carenatura^F

headlight
faro^M delantero
phare^M
Scheinwerfer^M
proiettore^M

body
carrocería^F
coque^F
Rumpf^M
carrozzeria^F

snow guard
guardanieve^M
bavette^F garde-neige^M
Schutzblech^N
paraneve^M

sprocket
diente^M
roue^F dentée
Antriebsrad^N
ruota^F dentata motrice

idler wheel
rueda^F de transmisión^F
roue^F de support^M
Zwischenrad^N
ruota^F folle

reflector
reflector^M
catadioptre^M
Rückstrahler^M
catarifrangente^M

air scoop
entrada^F de aire^M
prise^F d'air^M
Lufteinlass^M
presa^F d'aria^F

track
rueda^F de cadena^F
chenille^F
Kette^F
cingolo^M

footboard
estribo^M
marchepied^M
Trittbrett^N
pedana^F

shock absorber
amortiguador^M
amortisseur^M
Stoßdämpfer^M
ammortizzatore^M

ski
esquí^M
ski^M
Kufe^F
sci^M

curling

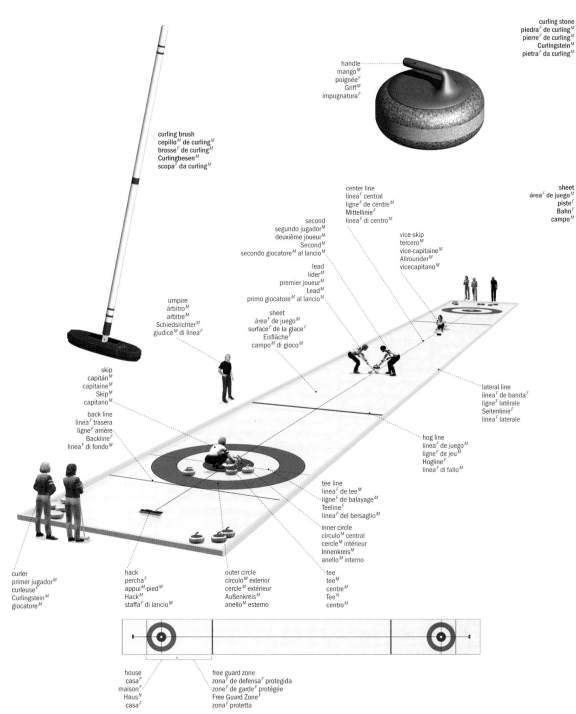

curling stone
piedra^F de curling^M
pierre^F de curling^M
Curlingstein^M
pietra^F da curling^M

handle
mango^M
poignée^F
Griff^M
impugnatura^F

curling brush
cepillo^M de curling^M
brosse^F de curling^M
Curlingbesen^M
scopa^F da curling^M

center line
línea^F central
ligne^F de centre^M
Mittellinie^F
linea^F di centro^M

sheet
área^F de juego^M
piste^F
Bahn^F
campo^M

second
segundo jugador^M
deuxième joueur^M
Second^M
secondo giocatore^M al lancio^M

vice-skip
tercero^M
vice-capitaine^M
Allrounder^M
vicecapitano^M

lead
líder^M
premier joueur^M
Lead^M
primo giocatore^M al lancio^M

umpire
árbitro^M
arbitre^M
Schiedsrichter^M
giudice^M di linea^F

sheet
área^F de juego^M
surface^F de la glace^F
Eisfläche^F
campo^M di gioco^M

lateral line
línea^F de banda^F
ligne^F latérale
Seitenlinie^F
linea^F laterale

skip
capitán^M
capitaine^M
Skip^M
capitano^M

back line
línea^F trasera
ligne^F arrière
Backline^F
linea^F di fondo^M

hog line
línea^F de juego^M
ligne^F de jeu^M
Hogline^F
linea^F di fallo^M

tee line
línea^F de tee^M
ligne^F de balayage^M
Teeline^F
linea^F del bersaglio^M

inner circle
círculo^M central
cercle^M intérieur
Innenkreis^M
anello^M interno

curler
primer jugador^M
curleuse^F
Curlingstein^M
giocatore^M

hack
percha^F
appui^M-pied^M
Hack^M
staffa^F di lancio^M

outer circle
círculo^M exterior
cercle^M extérieur
Außenkreis^M
anello^M esterno

tee
tee^M
centre^M
Tee^N
centro^M

house
casa^F
maison^F
Haus^N
casa^F

free guard zone
zona^F de defensa^F protegida
zone^F de garde^F protégée
Free Guard Zone^F
zona^F protetta

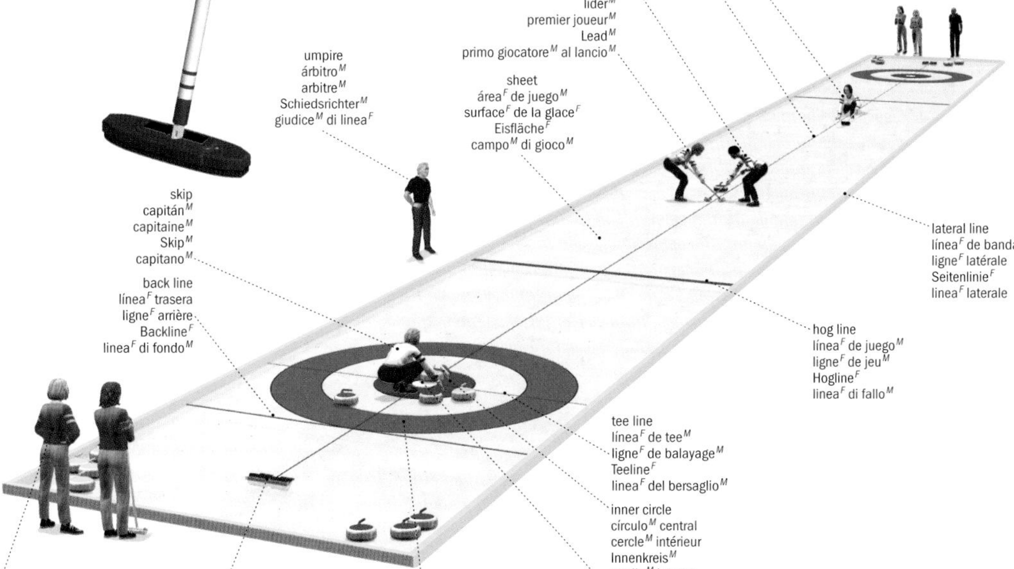

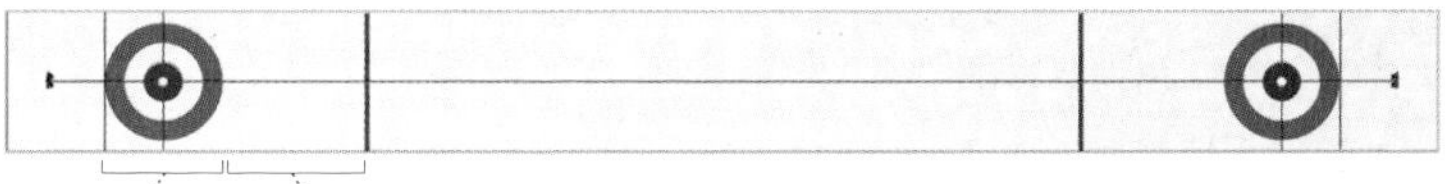

ice hockey

hockey^M sobre hielo^M | hockey^M sur glace^F | Eishockey^N | hockey^M su ghiaccio^M

ice hockey player
jugador^M
hockeyeur^M
Eishockeyspieler^M
giocatore^M

visor
visera^F
visière^F
Gesichtsschutz^M
visiera^F

helmet
casco^M
casque^M
Schutzhelm^M
casco^M

team's emblem
emblema^M del equipo^M
emblème^M d'équipe^F
Mannschaftsabzeichen^N
simbolo^M della squadra^F

player's number
número^M del jugador^M
numéro^M du joueur^M
Spielemummer^F
numero^M del giocatore^M

glove
guante^M
gant^M
Handschuh^M
guanto^M

pants
pantalónes^M
culotte^F
Hose^F
pantaloni^M

stocking
calcetines^M
bas^M
Stutzen^M
calzettone^M

skate
bota^F
patin^M
Schlittschuh^M
pattino^M

blade
cuchilla^F
lame^F
Kufe^F
lama^F

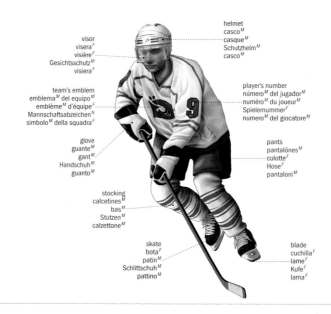

rink
pista^F
patinoire^F
Eisfläche^F
campo^M

face-off spot
punto^M de saque^M
point^M de mise^F au jeu^M
Anspielpunkt^M
punto^M di ingaggio^M

right defense
defensa^M derecho
défenseur^M droit
rechter Verteidiger^M
difensore^M destro

left defense
defensa^M izquierdo
défenseur^M gauche
linker Verteidiger^M
difensore^M sinistro

goal line
línea^F de gol^M
ligne^F de but^M
Torlinie^F
linea^F di porta^F

glass protector
cristal^M de protección^M
vitre^F de protection^F
Schutzwand^F
vetro^M di protezione^F

players' bench
banquillo^M de los jugadores^M
banc^M des joueurs^M
Spielerbank^F
panchina^F dei giocatori^M

rink corner
esquina^F
coin^M de patinoire^F
Ecke^F
angolo^M della pista^F

goal judge
juez^M de gol^M
juge^M de but^M
Torrichter^M
giudice^M di porta^F

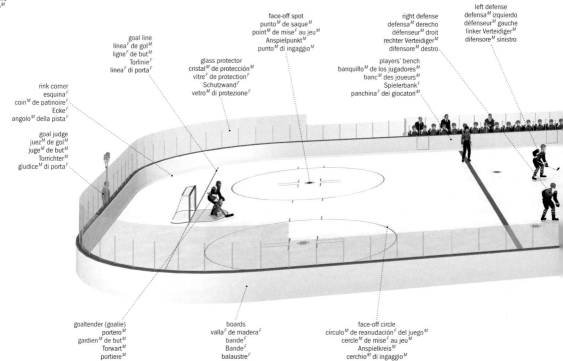

goaltender (goalie)
portero^M
gardien^M de but^M
Torwart^M
portiere^M

boards
valla^F de madera^F
bande^F
Bande^F
balaustre^F

face-off circle
círculo^M de reanudación^M del juego^M
cercle^M de mise^F au jeu^M
Anspielkreis^M
cerchio^M di ingaggio^M

goaltender (goalie)
portero^M
gardien^M de but^M
Torwart^M
portiere^M

face mask
protector^M facial
masque^M
Gesichtsschutzmaske^F
maschera^F

blocking glove
escudo^M
bouclier^M
Abwehrhandschuh^M
guanto^M da respinta^F

catching glove
guante^M rígido
mitaine^F
Fanghandschuh^M
guanto^M da presa^F

goaltender's pad
protector^M de piernas^F
jambière^F de gardien^M de but^M
Beinpolster^N
paragambe^M

goaltender's stick
bastón^M del portero^M
crosse^F de gardien^M de but^M ; bâton^M de gardien^M de but^M
Torwartschläger^M
bastone^M

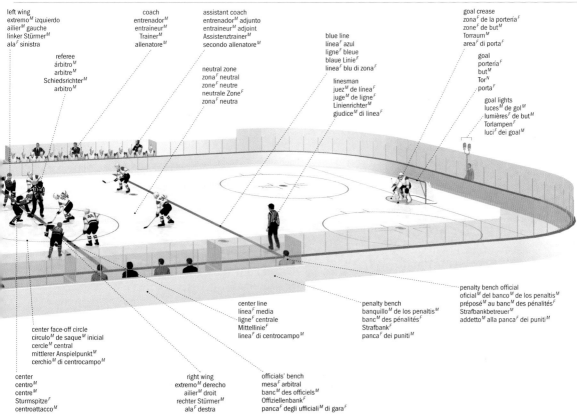

left wing
extremo^M izquierdo
ailier^M gauche
linker Stürmer^M
ala^F sinistra

coach
entrenador^M
entraîneur^M
Trainer^M
allenatore^M

assistant coach
entrenador^M adjunto
entraîneur^M adjoint
Assistenztrainer^M
secondo allenatore^M

referee
árbitro^M
arbitre^M
Schiedsrichter^M
arbitro^M

neutral zone
zona^F neutral
zone^F neutre
neutrale Zone^F
zona^F neutra

blue line
línea^F azul
ligne^F bleue
blaue Linie^F
linea^F blu di zona^F

linesman
juez^F de línea^F
juge^M de ligne^F
Linienrichter^M
giudice^M di linea^F

goal crease
zona^F de la portería^F
zone^F de but^M
Torraum^M
area^F di porta^F

goal
portería^F
but^M
Tor^N
porta^F

goal lights
luces^F de gol^M
lumières^F de but^M
Torlampen^F
luci^F dei goal^M

penalty bench official
oficial^M del banco^M de los penaltis^M
préposé^M au banc^M des pénalités^F
Strafbankbetreuer^M
addetto^M alla panca^F dei puniti^M

penalty bench
banquillo^M de los penaltis^M
banc^M des pénalités^F
Strafbank^F
panca^F dei puniti^M

center face-off circle
círculo^M de saque^M inicial
cercle^M central
mittlerer Anspielpunkt^M
cerchio^M di centrocampo^M

center line
línea^F media
ligne^F centrale
Mittellinie^F
linea^F di centrocampo^M

center
centro^M
centre^F
Sturmspitze^F
centroattacco^M

right wing
extremo^M derecho
ailier^M droit
rechter Stürmer^M
ala^F destra

officials' bench
mesa^F arbitral
banc^M des officiels^M
Offiziellenbank^F
panca^F degli ufficiali^M di gara^F

SPORTS AND GAMES

ice hockey

player's stick
palo^M del jugador^M
crosse^F de joueur^M ; bâton^M de joueur^M
Eishockeyschläger^M
bastone^M del giocatore^M

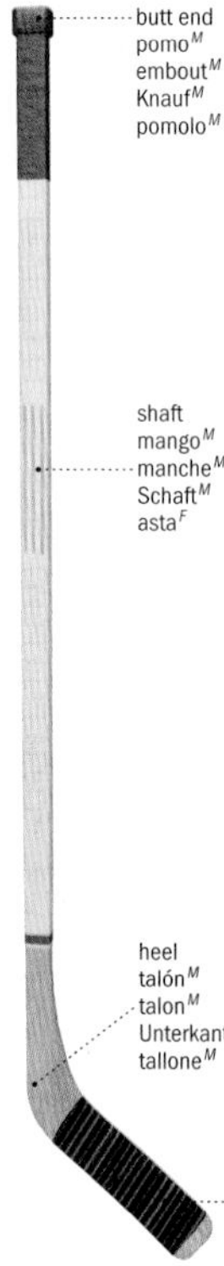

goaltender's stick
palo^M del portero^M
crosse^F de gardien^M de but^M ; bâton^M de gardien^M de but^M
Torwartschläger^M
bastone^M del portiere^M

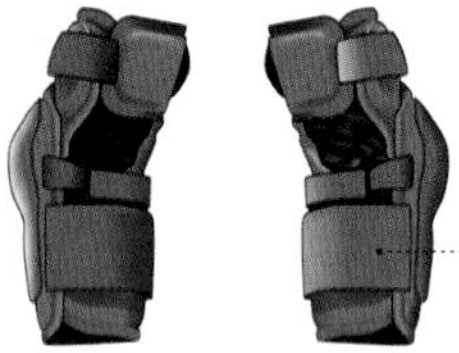

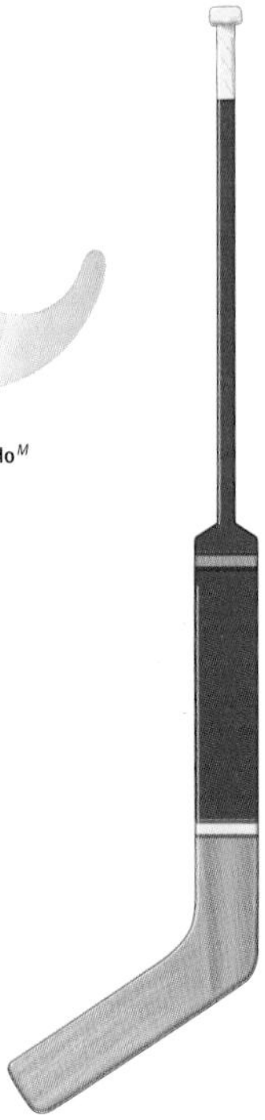

butt end
pomo^M
embout^M
Knauf^M
pomolo^M del bastone^M

cuff
muñequera^F
manchette^F
Manschette^F
copripolso^M

throat protector
protector^M de cuello^M
protège-gorge^F
Halsschutz^M
paracollo^M

elbow pads
codera^F
protège-coude^M
Ellbogenpolster^N
paragomiti^M

shaft
mango^M
manche^M
Schaft^M
asta^F

throat protector
protector^M del cuello^M
protège-gorge^F
Halsschutz^M
paragola^M

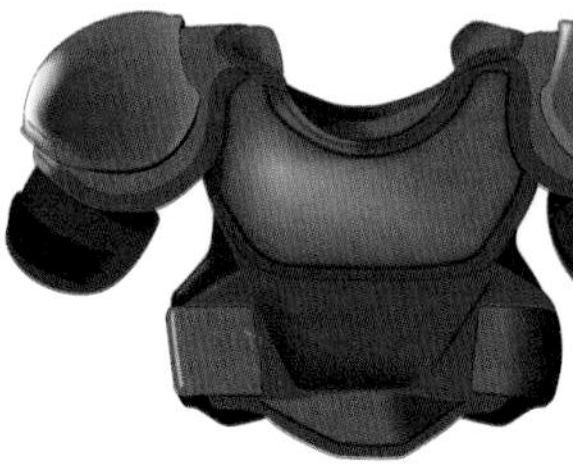

shoulder pads
hombrera^F
épaulière^F
Schulterpolster^N
paraspalle^M

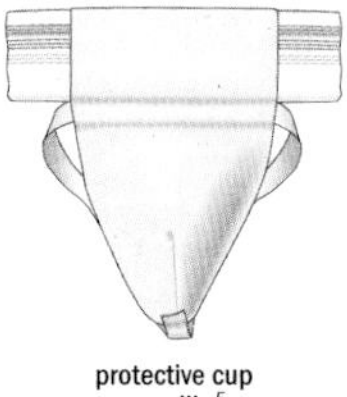

protective cup
coquilla^F
coquille^F
Suspensorium^N
conchiglia^F di protezione^F

heel
talón^M
talon^M
Unterkante^F
tallone^M

blade
pala^F del stick^M
lame^F
Blatt^N
pala^F

puck
disco^M
palet^M ; rondelle^F
Puck^M
dischetto^M

arm pad
protector^M del brazo^M
brassard^M
Ampolster^N
parabraccia^M

knee pad
rodillera^F
genouillère^F
Kniepolster^N
ginocchiera^F

player's skate
patín^M
patin^M
Schlittschuh^M
pattino^M

goaltender's chest pad
peto^M del portero^M
plastron^M de gardien^M de but^M
Torwartbrustschutz^M
pettorina^F del portiere^M

tendon guard
protector^M del tendón^M
protège-tendon^M
Sehnenschützer^M
proteggitendine^M

toe box
puntera^F reforzada
renfort^M de pointe^F
Kappe^F
rinforzo^M di cuoio^M

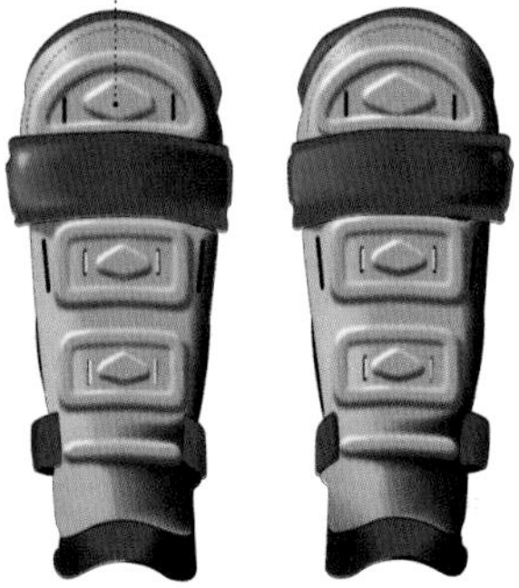

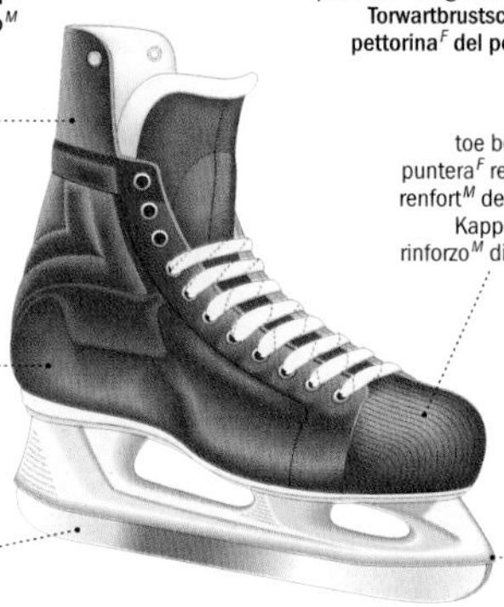

goaltender's skate
patín^M del portero^M
patin^M de gardien^M de but^M
Torwartschlittschuh^M
pattino^M del portiere^M

boot
bota^F
chaussure^F
Stiefel^M
scarpa^F

point
puntera^F
pointe^F
Spitze^F
punta^F

blade
hoja^F de cuchilla^F
lame^F
Kufe^F
lama^F

pads
tobillera^F
jambières^F
Schienbeinschützer^M
paragambe^M

figure skating

patinaje^M artistico | patinage^M artistique | Eiskunstlauf^M | pattinaggio^M artistico

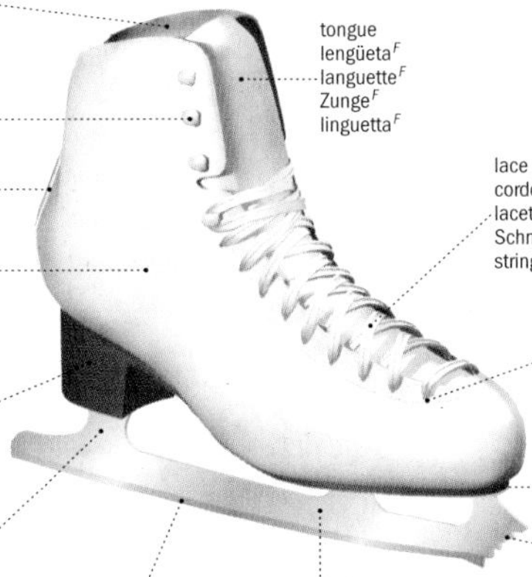

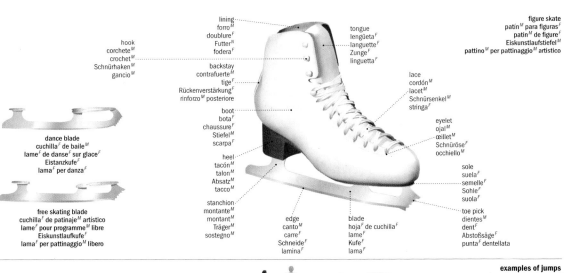

lining
forro^M
doublure^F
Futter^N
fodera^F

hook
corchete^M
crochet^M
Schnürhaken^M
gancio^M

backstay
contrafuerte^M
tige^F
Rückenverstärkung^F
rinforzo^M posteriore

tongue
lengüeta^F
languette^F
Zunge^F
linguetta^F

figure skate
patín^M para figuras^F
patín^M de figure^F
Eiskunstlaufstiefel^M
pattino^M per pattinaggio^M artistico

lace
cordón^M
lacet^M
Schnürsenkel^M
stringa^F

boot
bota^F
chaussure^F
Stiefel^M
scarpa^F

eyelet
ojal^M
œillet^M
Schnüröse^F
occhiello^M

dance blade
cuchilla^F de baile^M
lame^F de danse^F sur glace^F
Eistanzkufe^F
lama^F per danza^F

heel
tacón^M
talon^M
Absatz^M
tacco^M

sole
suela^F
semelle^F
Sohle^F
suola^F

stanchion
montante^M
montant^M
Träger^M
sostegno^M

edge
canto^M
carre^F
Schneide^F
lamina^F

blade
hoja^F de cuchilla^F
lame^F
Kufe^F
lama^F

toe pick
dientes^M
dent^F
Abstoßsäge^F
punta^F dentellata

free skating blade
cuchilla^F de patinaje^M artistico
lame^F pour programme^M libre
Eiskunstlaufkufe^F
lama^F per pattinaggio^M libero

examples of jumps
ejemplos^M de piruetas^F
exemples^M de sauts^M
Beispiele^N für Sprünge^M
esempi^M di salti^M

axel
axel^M
axel^M
Axel^M
axel^M

salchow
salchow^M
salchow^M
Salchow^M
salchow^M

toe loop
loop^M de puntera^F
boucle^F piquée
Toeloop^M
loop^M di punta^F

flip
flip^M
flip^M
Flip^M
flip^M

lutz
lutz^M
lutz^M
Lutz^M
lutz^M

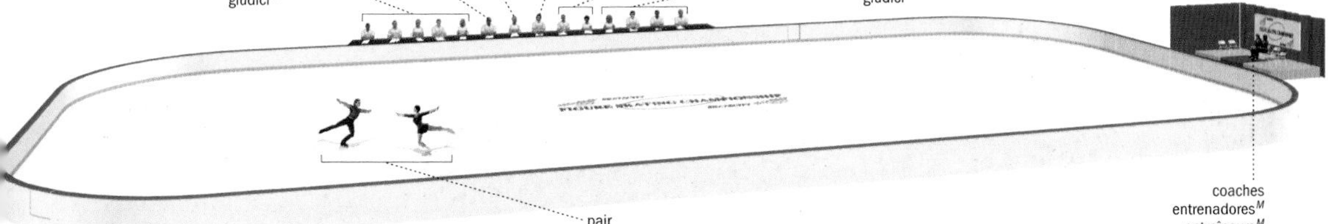

timekeeper
cronometrador^M
chronométreur^M
Zeitnehmer^M
cronometrista$^{M/F}$

referee
presidente^M de jurado^M
arbitre^M
Oberschiedsrichter^M
presidente^M di giuria^F

assistant referee
asistente^M de presidente^M del jurado^M
arbitre^M adjoint
Assistenzschiedsrichter^M
assistente^M del presidente^M di giuria^F

technical delegates
delegados^M técnicos
délégués^M techniques
technische Delegierte^M
referenti^M tecnici

rink
pista^F de patinaje^M sobre hielo^M
patinoire^F
Eisfläche^F
pista^F di pattinaggio^M

judges
jueces^M
juges^M
Kampfrichter^M
giudici^M

judges
jueces^M
juges^M
Kampfrichter^M
giudici^M

coaches
entrenadores^M
entraineurs^M
Trainer^M
allenatori^M

pair
pareja^F
couple^M
Paar^N
coppia^F

SPORTS AND GAMES

881

speed skating

patinaje^M de velocidad^F | patinage^M de vitesse^F | Eisschnelllauf^M | pattinaggio^M di velocità^F

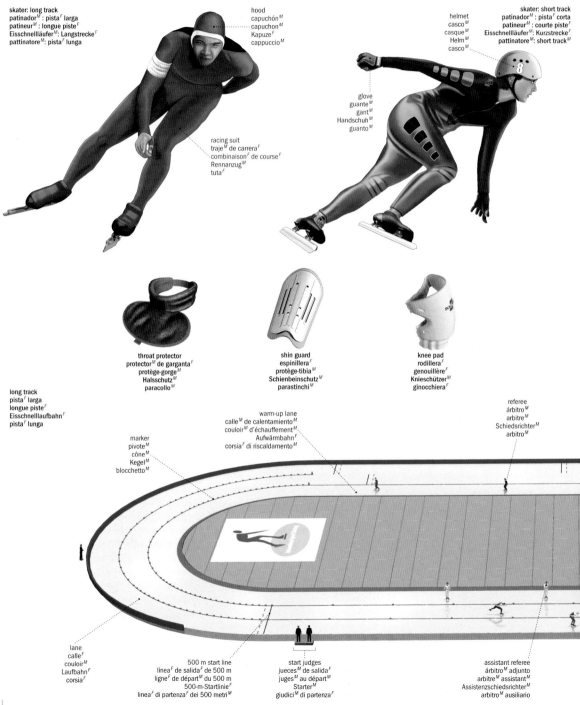

skater: long track
patinador^M : pista^F larga
patineur^M : longue piste^F
Eisschnellläufer^M: Langstrecke^F
pattinatore^M: pista^F lunga

hood
capuchón^M
capuchon^M
Kapuze^F
cappuccio^M

helmet
casco^M
casque^M
Helm^M
casco^M

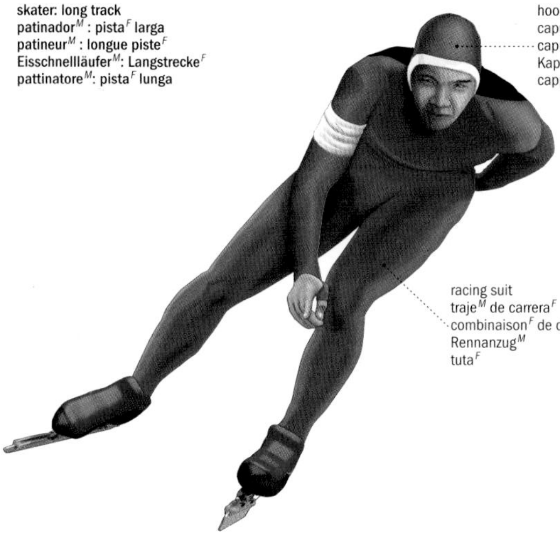

skater: short track
patinador^M : pista^F corta
patineur^M : courte piste^F
Eisschnellläufer^M: Kurzstrecke^F
pattinatore^M: short track^M

glove
guante^M
gant^M
Handschuh^M
guanto^M

racing suit
traje^M de carrera^F
combinaison^F de course^F
Rennanzug^M
tuta^F

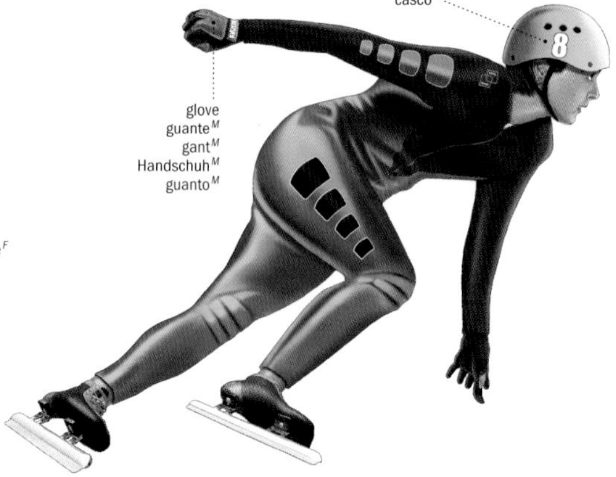

throat protector
protector^M de garganta^F
protège-gorge^M
Halsschutz^M
paracollo^M

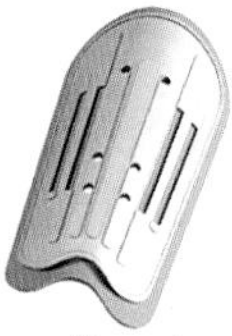

shin guard
espinillera^F
protège-tibia^M
Schienbeinschutz^M
parastinchi^M

knee pad
rodillera^F
genouillère^F
Knieschützer^M
ginocchiera^F

long track
pista^F larga
longue piste^F
Eisschnelllaufbahn^F
pista^F lunga

referee
árbitro^M
arbitre^M
Schiedsrichter^M
arbitro^M

warm-up lane
calle^M de calentamiento^M
couloir^M d'échauffement^M
Aufwärmbahn^F
corsia^F di riscaldamento^M

marker
pivote^M
cône^M
Kegel^M
blocchetto^M

lane
calle^F
couloir^M
Laufbahn^F
corsia^F

500 m start line
línea^F de salida^F de 500 m
ligne^F de départ^M du 500 m
500-m-Startlinie^F
linea^F di partenza^F dei 500 metri^M

start judges
jueces^M de salida^F
juges^M au départ^M
Starter^M
giudici^M di partenza^F

assistant referee
árbitro^M adjunto
arbitre^M assistant^M
Assistenzschiedsrichter^M
arbitro^M ausiliario

SPORTS AND GAMES

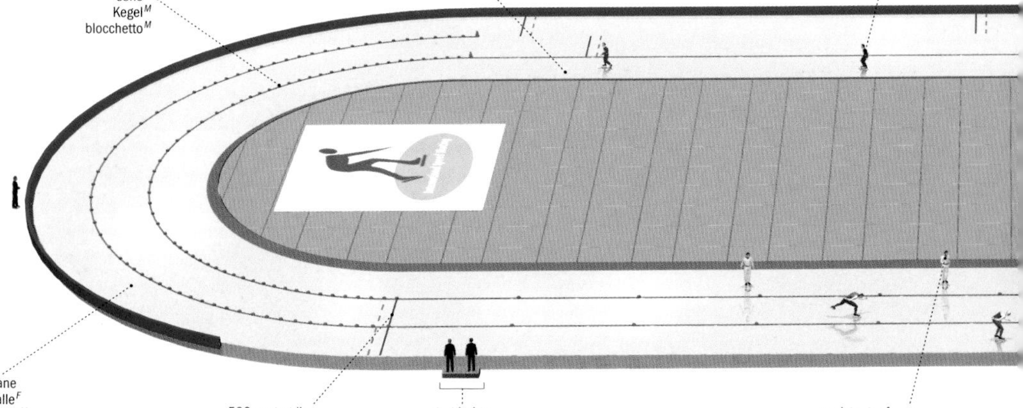

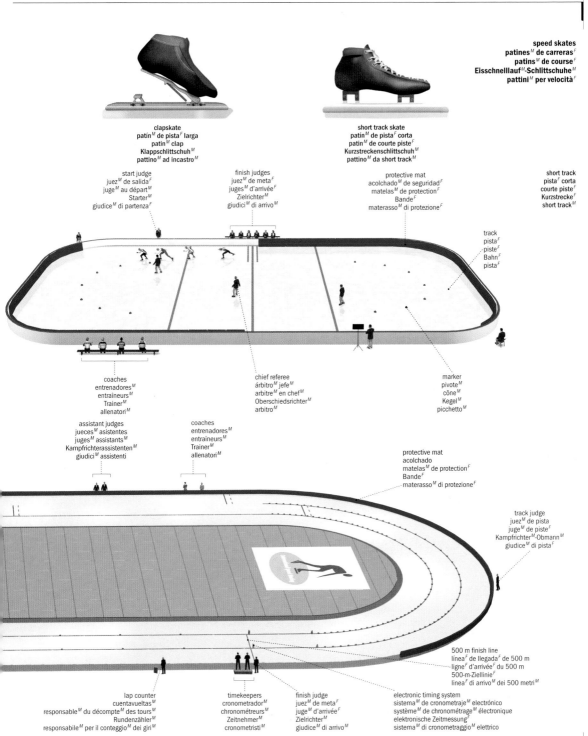

speed skates
patines^M de carreras^F
patins^M de course^F
Eisschnelllauf^M-Schlittschuhe^M
pattini^M per velocità^F

clapskate
patín^M de pista^F larga
patín^M clap
Klappschlittschuh^M
pattino^M ad incastro^M

short track skate
patín^M de pista^F corta
patín^M de courte piste^F
Kurzstreckenschlittschuh^M
pattino^M da short track^M

short track
pista^F corta
courte piste^F
Kurzstrecke^F
short track^M

start judge
juez^M de salida^F
juge^M au départ^M
Starter^M
giudice^M di partenza^F

finish judges
juez^M de meta^F
juges^M d'arrivée^F
Zielrichter^M
giudici^M di arrivo^M

protective mat
acolchado^M de seguridad^F
matelas^M de protection^F
Bande^F
materasso^M di protezione^F

track
pista^F
piste^F
Bahn^F
pista^F

coaches
entrenadores^M
entraineurs^M
Trainer^M
allenatori^M

chief referee
árbitro^M jefe^M
arbitre^M en chef^M
Oberschiedsrichter^M
arbitro^M

marker
pivote^M
cône^M
Kegel^M
picchetto^M

assistant judges
jueces^M asistentes
juges^M assistants^M
Kampfrichterassistenten^M
giudici^M assistenti

coaches
entrenadores^M
entraineurs^M
Trainer^M
allenatori^M

protective mat
acolchado^M
matelas^M de protection^F
Bande^F
materasso^M di protezione^F

track judge
juez^M de pista^F
juge^M de piste^F
Kampfrichter^M-Obmann^M
giudice^M di pista^F

500 m finish line
línea^F de llegada^F de 500 m
ligne^F d'arrivée^F du 500 m
500-m-Ziellinie^F
linea^F di arrivo^M dei 500 metri^M

lap counter
cuentavueltas^M
responsable^M du décompte^M des tours^M
Rundenzähler^M
responsabile^M per il conteggio^M dei giri^M

timekeepers
cronometrador^M
chronométreurs^M
Zeitnehmer^M
cronometristi^M

finish judge
juez^M de meta^F
juge^M d'arrivée^F
Zielrichter^M
giudice^M di arrivo^M

electronic timing system
sistema^M de cronometraje^M electrónico
système^M de chronométrage^M électronique
elektronische Zeitmessung^F
sistema^M di cronometraggio^M elettrico

bobsled

bobsleigh ^{M} | bobsleigh ^{M} | Bobschlitten ^{M} | bob ^{M}

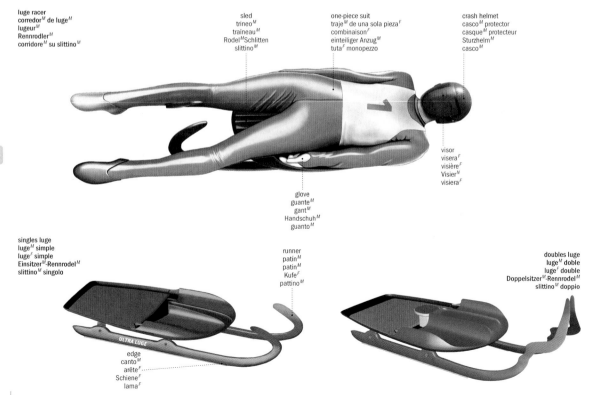

four-person bobsled
bobsleigh ^{M} a cuatro
bobsleigh ^{M} à quatre
Viererbob ^{M}
bob ^{M} a quattro

brakeman
guardafrenos ^{M}
freineur ^{M}
Bremser ^{M}
frenatore ^{M}

captain
capitán ^{M}
capitaine ^{M}
Steuermann ^{M}
capitano ^{M}

handle
asa ^{F}
poignée ^{F}
Griff ^{M}
maniglia ^{F}

shell
bob ^{M}
coque ^{F}
Gehäuse ^{N}
carena ^{F}

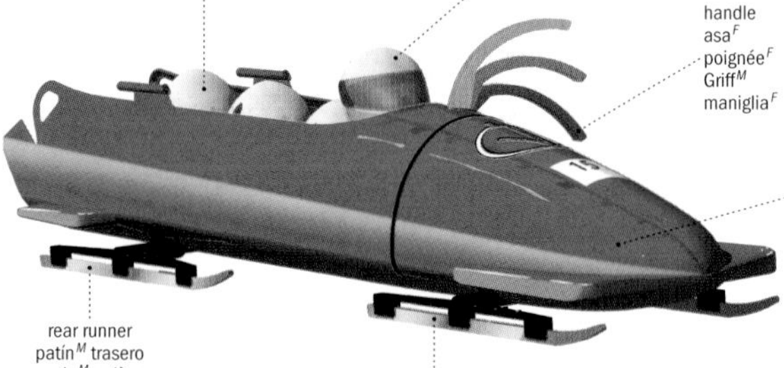

two-person bobsled
bobsleigh ^{M} de dos
bobsleigh ^{M} à deux
Zweierbob ^{M}
bob ^{M} a due

rear runner
patín ^{M} trasero
patín ^{M} arrière
hintere Kufe ^{F}
pattino ^{M} posteriore

front runner
patín ^{M} delantero
patín ^{M} avant
vordere Kufe ^{F}
pattino ^{M} anteriore

luge

luge ^{M} | luge ^{F} | Rennrodel ^{M} | slittino ^{M}

luge racer
corredor ^{M} de luge ^{M}
lugeur ^{M}
Rennrodler ^{M}
corridore ^{M} su slittino ^{M}

sled
trineo ^{M}
traîneau ^{M}
Rodel ^{M}Schlitten ^{M}
slittino ^{M}

one-piece suit
traje ^{M} de una sola pieza ^{F}
combinaison ^{F}
einteiliger Anzug ^{M}
tuta ^{F} monopezzo

crash helmet
casco ^{M} protector
casque ^{M} protecteur
Sturzhelm ^{M}
casco ^{M}

visor
visera ^{F}
visière ^{F}
Visier ^{N}
visiera ^{F}

glove
guante ^{M}
gant ^{M}
Handschuh ^{M}
guanto ^{M}

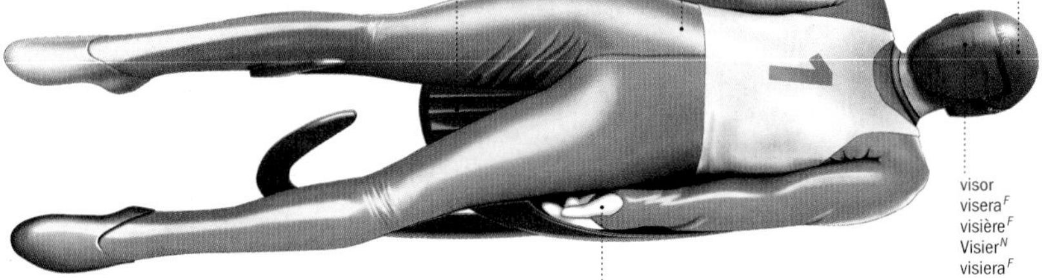

singles luge
luge ^{M} simple
luge ^{F} simple
Einsitzer ^{M}-Rennrodel ^{M}
slittino ^{M} singolo

runner
patín ^{M}
patín ^{M}
Kufe ^{F}
pattino ^{M}

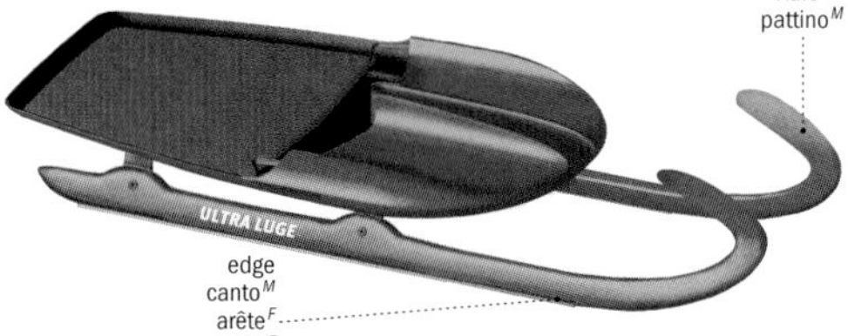

doubles luge
luge ^{M} doble
luge ^{F} double
Doppelsitzer ^{M}-Rennrodel ^{M}
slittino ^{M} doppio

ULTRA LUGE

edge
canto ^{M}
arête ^{F}
Schiene ^{F}
lama ^{F}

skeleton

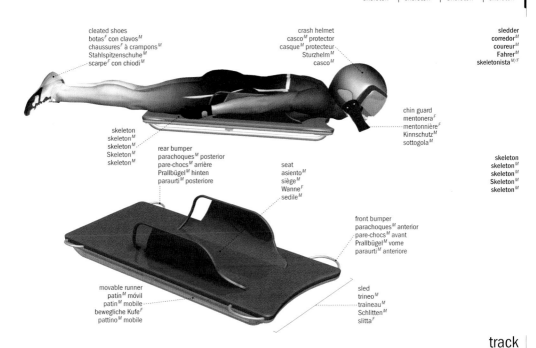

cleated shoes
botas[F] con clavos[M]
chaussures[F] à crampons[M]
Stahlspitzenschuhe[M]
scarpe[F] con chiodi[M]

crash helmet
casco[M] protector
casque[M] protecteur
Sturzhelm[M]
casco[M]

sledder
corredor[M]
coureur[M]
Fahrer[M]
skeletonista[M/F]

chin guard
mentonera[F]
mentonnière[F]
Kinnschutz[M]
sottogola[M]

skeleton
skeleton[M]
skeleton[M]
Skeleton[M]
skeleton[M]

rear bumper
parachoques[M] posterior
pare-chocs[M] arrière
Prallbügel[M] hinten
paraurti[M] posteriore

seat
asiento[M]
siège[M]
Wanne[F]
sedile[M]

skeleton
skeleton[M]
skeleton[M]
Skeleton[M]
skeleton[M]

front bumper
parachoques[M] anterior
pare-chocs[M] avant
Prallbügel[M] vorne
paraurti[M] anteriore

movable runner
patín[M] móvil
patin[M] mobile
bewegliche Kufe[F]
pattino[M] mobile

sled
trineo[M]
traîneau[M]
Schlitten[M]
slitta[F]

track

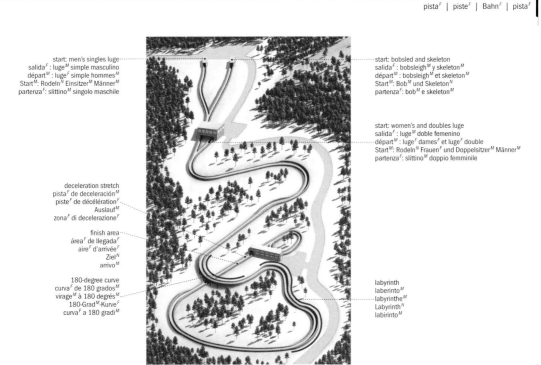

start: men's singles luge
salida[F] : luge[M] simple masculino
départ[M] : luge[F] simple hommes[M]
Start[M]: Rodeln[N] Einsitzer[M] Männer[M]
partenza[F]: slittino[M] singolo maschile

start: bobsled and skeleton
salida[F] : bobsleigh[M] y skeleton[M]
départ[M] : bobsleigh[M] et skeleton[M]
Start[M]: Bob[M] und Skeleton[N]
partenza[F]: bob[M] e skeleton[M]

start: women's and doubles luge
salida[F] : luge[M] doble femenino
départ[M] : luge[F] dames[F] et luge[F] double
Start[M]: Rodeln[N] Frauen[F] und Doppelsitzer[M] Männer[M]
partenza[F]: slittino[M] doppio femminile

deceleration stretch
pista[F] de deceleración[M]
piste[F] de décélération[F]
Auslauf[M]
zona[F] di decelerazione[F]

finish area
área[F] de llegada[F]
aire[F] d'arrivée[F]
Ziel[N]
arrivo[M]

180-degree curve
curva[F] de 180 grados[M]
virage[F] à 180 degrés[M]
180-Grad[M]-Kurve[F]
curva[F] a 180 gradi[M]

labyrinth
laberinto[M]
labyrinthe[M]
Labyrinth[N]
labirinto[M]

SPORTS AND GAMES

ski resort

estación^F de esquí | station^F de ski^M | Skigebiet^N | stazione^F sciistica

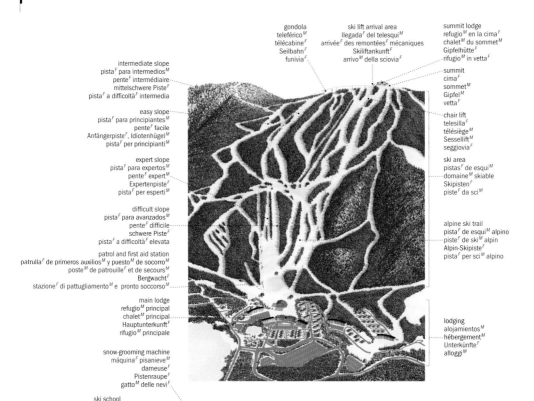

gondola
teleférico^M
télécabine^F
Seilbahn^F
funivia^F

ski lift arrival area
llegada^F del telesquí^M
arrivée^F des remontées^F mécaniques
Skiliftankunft^F
arrivo^M della sciovia^F

summit lodge
refugio^M en la cima^F
chalet^M du sommet^M
Gipfelhütte^F
rifugio^M in vetta^F

intermediate slope
pista^F para intermedios^M
pente^F intermédiaire
mittelschwere Piste^F
pista^F a difficoltà^F intermedia

summit
cima^F
sommet^M
Gipfel^M
vetta^F

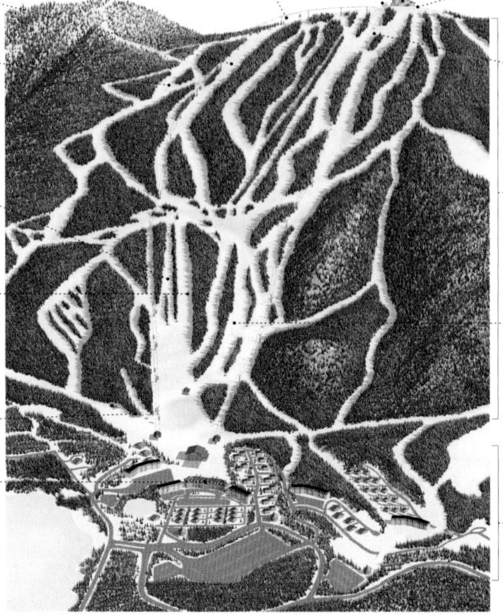

easy slope
pista^F para principiantes^M
pente^F facile
Anfängerpiste^F, Idiotenhügel^M
pista^F per principianti^M

chair lift
telesilla^F
télésiège^M
Sessellift^M
seggiovia^F

expert slope
pista^F para expertos^M
pente^F expert^M
Expertenpiste^F
pista^F per esperti^M

ski area
pistas^F de esquí^M
domaine^M skiable
Skipisten^F
piste^F da sci^M

difficult slope
pista^F para avanzados^M
pente^F difficile
schwere Piste^F
pista^F a difficoltà^F elevata

alpine ski trail
pista^F de esquí^M alpino
piste^F de ski^M alpin
Alpin-Skipiste^F
pista^F per sci^M alpino

patrol and first aid station
patrulla^F de primeros auxilios^M y puesto^M de socorro^M
poste^M de patrouille^F et de secours^M
Bergwacht^F
stazione^F di pattugliamento^M e pronto soccorso^M

main lodge
refugio^M principal
chalet^M principal
Hauptunterkunft^F
rifugio^M principale

lodging
alojamientos^M
hébergement^M
Unterkünfte^F
alloggi^M

snow-grooming machine
máquina^F pisanieve^M
dameuse^F
Pistenraupe^F
gatto^M delle nevi^F

ski school
escuela^F de esquí^M
école^F de ski^M
Skischule^F
scuola^F di sci^M

chair lift departure area
embarque^M del telesilla^M
départ^M des télésièges^M
Sesselliftabfahrt^F
partenza^F della seggiovia^F

T-bar
telesquí^M
téléski^M biplace
Schlepplift^M
sciovia^F

cross-country ski trail
pista^F de fondo^M
piste^F de ski^M de fond^M
Langlaufloipe^F
pista^F da fondo^M

skiers' lodge
hospedería^F para esquiadores^M
pavillon^M des skieurs^M
Skihütte^F
ristoro^M per sciatori^M

gondola departure area
embarque^M teleférico^M
départ^M des télécabines^F
Seilbahnabfahrt^F
partenza^F della funivia^F

condominiums
bloque^M de apartamentos^M
copropriété^F
Appartements^N
appartamenti^M

ice rink
pista^F de patinaje^M
patinoire^F
Eislaufplatz^M
pista^F di pattinaggio^M

mountain lodge
refugio^M de montaña^F
chalet^M de montagne^F
Berghütte^F
baita^F di montagna^F

hotel
hotel^M
hôtel^M
Hotel^N
albergo^M

information desk
punto^M de información^F
renseignements^M
Informationsschalter^M
ufficio^M delle informazioni^F

village
pueblo^M
village^M
Dorf^N
villaggio^M

parking
aparcamiento^M
parc^M de stationnement^M ; stationnement^M
Parkplatz^M
parcheggio^M

snowboarding

snowboard^M | surf^M des neiges^F | Snowboarden^N | snowboard^M

helmet
casco^M
casque^M
Helm^M
casco^M

coveralls
traje^M de esquí^M
combinaison^F
Skianzug^M
tuta^F

goggles
gafas^F de esquí^M
lunettes^F
Skibrille^F
occhiali^M

snowboarder
snowboarder^M
surfeur^M
Snowboarder^M
snowboardista^{M/F}

shin guard
tobillera^F
protège-tibia^M
Schienbeinschützer^M
parastinchi^M

snowboard
snowboard^M
surf^M des neiges^F
Snowboard^N
snowboard^M

glove
guante^M
gant^M
Handschuh^M
guanto^M

hard boot
bota^F rigida
botte^F rigide
Hardboots^M
scarpone^M rigido

flexible boot
bota^F blanda
botte^F souple
Softboots^M
scarpone^M morbido

freestyle snowboard
tabla^F de freestyle^M
surf^M acrobatique
Freestyleboard^N
snowboard^M per freestyle^M

plate binding
fijaciones^F
fixation^F à plaque^F
Plattenbindung^F
attacco^M

alpine snowboard
tabla^F alpina
surf^M alpin
Alpinboard^N
snowboard^M per sci^M alpino

soft binding
fijaciones^M blandas
fixation^F à coque^F
Softbindung^F
attacco^M morbido

tail
cola^F
talon^M
Brettende^N
coda^F

nose
cabeza^F
spatule^F
Brettspitze^F
punta^F

edge
borde^M
carre^F
Kante^F
bordo^M

competition site: half-pipe
pista^F de competición^F : half-pipe^M
aire^F de compétition^F : demi-lune^F
Wettkampfplatz^M: Halfpipe^F
pista^F di gara^F: half-pipe^M

judges' stand
posición^F del jurado^M
cabine^F des juges^M
Wettkampfgericht^N
postazione^F dei giudici^M di gara^F

start
salida^F
départ^M
Start^M
partenza^F

half-pipe
half-pipe^M
demi-lune^F
Halfpipe^F
half-pipe^M

finish area
meta^F
aire^F d'arrivée^F
Zielbereich^M
arrivo^M

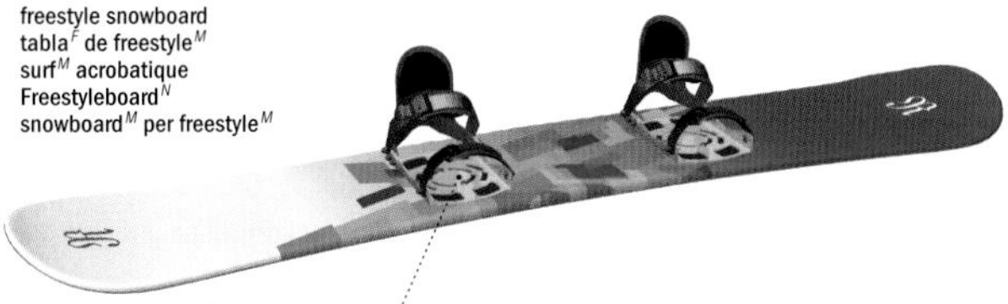

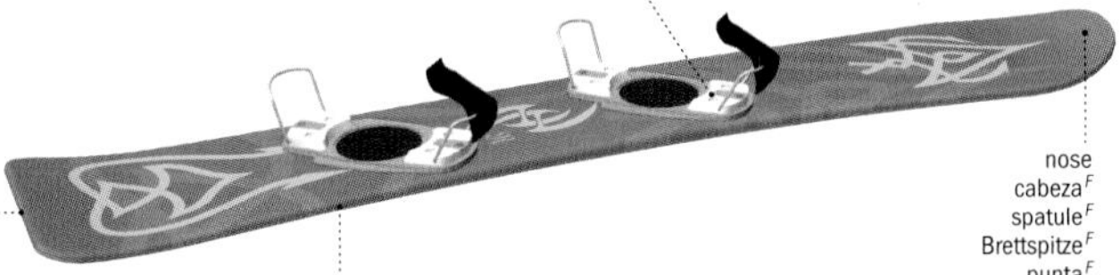

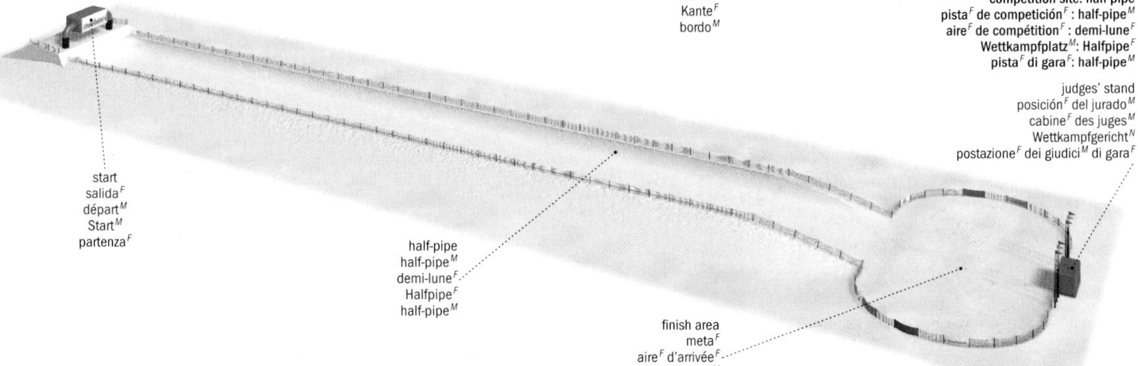

alpine skiing

esquí[M] alpino | ski[M] alpin | alpines Skilaufen[N] | sci[M] alpino

alpine skier
esquiador[M] alpino
skieur[M] alpin
alpiner Skiläufer[M]
sciatore[M]

ski goggles
gafas[F] de esquí[M]
lunettes[F] de ski[M]
Skibrille[F]
occhiali[M]

ski suit
traje[M] de esquí[M]
combinaison[F] de ski[M]
Skianzug[M]
tuta[F]

ski glove
guante[M] de esquí[M]
gant[M] de ski[M]
Skihandschuhe[M]
guanto[M]

basket
arandela[F]
rondelle[F]
Stockteller[M]
rotella[F]

helmet
casco[M]
casque[M]
Sturzhelm[M]
casco[M]

ski pole
bastón[M] de esquí[M]
bâton[M] de ski[M]
Skistock[M]
racchetta[F]

ski boot
bota[F]
chaussure[F] de ski[M]
Skistiefel[M]
scarpone[M]

wrist strap
correa[F] para la mano[F]
dragonne[F]
Handschlaufe[F]
cappio[M]

handle
empuñadura[F]
poignée[F]
Griff[M]
impugnatura[F]

groove
ranura[F] guía[F]
rainure[F]
Führungsrille[F]
scanalatura[F]

ski
esquí[M]
ski[M]
Ski[M]
sci[M]

bottom
superficie[F] de deslizamiento[M]
semelle[F]
Laufsohle[F]
suola[F]

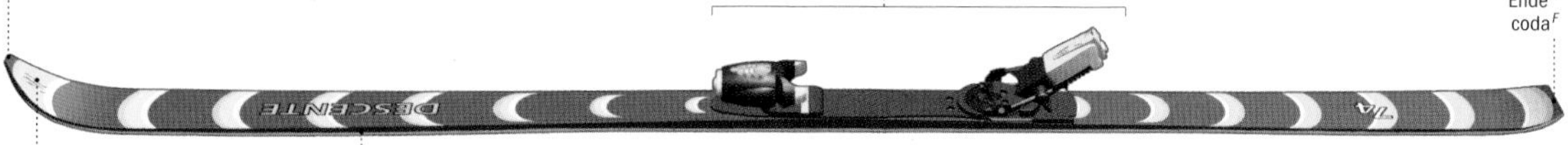

safety binding
fijaciones[F]
fixation[F] de sécurité[F]
Sicherheitsbindung[F]
attacco[M] di sicurezza[F]

tip
punta[F]
pointe[F]
Spitze[F]
punta[F]

tail
cola[F]
talon[M]
Ende[N]
coda[F]

shovel
pala[F]
spatule[F]
Schaufel[F]
spatola[F]

edge
canto[M]
carre[F]
Stahlkante[F]
lamina[F]

ski
esquí[M]
ski[M]
Ski[M]
sci[M]

examples of skis
ejemplos[M] de esquís[M]
exemples[M] de skis[M]
Beispiele[N] für Skier[M]
esempi[M] di sci[M]

slalom ski
esquí[M] de eslalon[M]
ski[M] de slalom[M]
Slalomski[M]
sci[M] da slalom[M]

giant slalom ski
esquí[M] de eslalon[M] gigante
ski[M] de grand slalom[M]
Riesenslalomski[M]
sci[M] da slalom[M] gigante

downhill and Super-G ski
esquí[M] de descenso[M] /eslalon[M]
ski[M] de descente[F]/super-G[M]
Abfahrts- und Superriesenslalom[M]-Ski[M]
sci[M] da discesa[F] libera e supergigante[M]

technical events
pruebas^F
épreuves^F
Disziplinen^F
specialità^F

ski boot
botas^F para esquiar
chaussure^F de ski^M
Skistiefel^M
scarpone^M

inner boot
botín^M interior
chausson^M intérieur
Innenstiefel^M
scarpetta^F interna

upper cuff
guarnición^F
collier^M
obere Manschette^F
bordo^M della scarpetta^F

tongue
lengüeta^F
languette^F
Zunge^F
linguettone^M

upper
alto^M de caña^F
tige^F
Rücklagenstütze^F
appoggio^M del polpaccio^M

upper strap
correa^F de ajuste^M
courroie^F de tige^F
oberes Verschlussband^N
fascia^F di chiusura^F

upper shell
bota^F externa
coque^F supérieure
obere Schale^F
gambale^M

adjusting catch
ajustador^M de la bota^F
cran^M de réglage^M
Einstellkerbe^F
dispositivo^M di regolazione^F

buckle
hebilla^F
boucle^F
Verschluss^M
gancio^M

sole
suela^F rígida
semelle^F
Sohle^F
suola^F

hinge
pivote^M
charnière^F
Gelenk^N
snodo^M

lower shell
contrafuerte^M
coque^F inférieure
untere Schale^F
scafo^M

downhill
descenso^M
descente^F
Abfahrtslauf^M
discesa^M libera

super giant (super-G) slalom
eslalon^M supergigante
super-géant^M
Superriesenslalom^M
slalom^M supergigante

giant slalom
eslalon^M gigante
slalom^M géant
Riesenslalom^M
slalom^M gigante

special slalom
eslalon^M especial
slalom^M spécial
Spezialslalom^M
slalom^M speciale

safety binding
fijación^F de seguridad^F del esquí^M
fixation^F de sécurité^F
Sicherheitsbindung^F
attacco^M di sicurezza^F

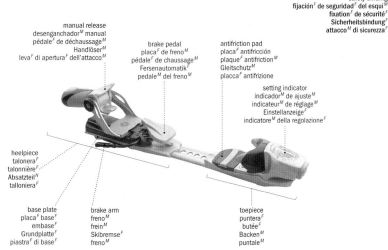

manual release
desenganchador^M manual
pédale^F de déchaussage^F
Handlöser^M
leva^F di apertura^F dell'attacco^M

brake pedal
placa^F de freno^M
pédale^F de chaussage^M
Fersenautomatik^F
pedale^M del freno^M

antifriction pad
placa^F antifricción
plaque^F antifriction^M
Gleitschutz^M
placca^F antifrizione

setting indicator
indicador^M de ajuste^M
indicateur^M de réglage^M
Einstellanzeige^F
indicatore^M della regolazione^F

heelpiece
talonera^F
talonnière^F
Absatzteil^N
talloniera^F

base plate
placa^F base^F
embase^F
Grundplatte^F
piastra^F di base^F

brake arm
freno^M
frein^M
Skibremse^F
freno^M

toepiece
puntera^F
butée^F
Backen^M
puntale^M

SPORTS AND GAMES

freestyle skiing

esquí^M artístico | ski^M acrobatique | Freestyle^N | freestyle^M

course: moguls competition
pista^F : saltos^M
piste^F : descente^F de bosses^F
Buckelpiste^F
pista^F: specialità^F moguls

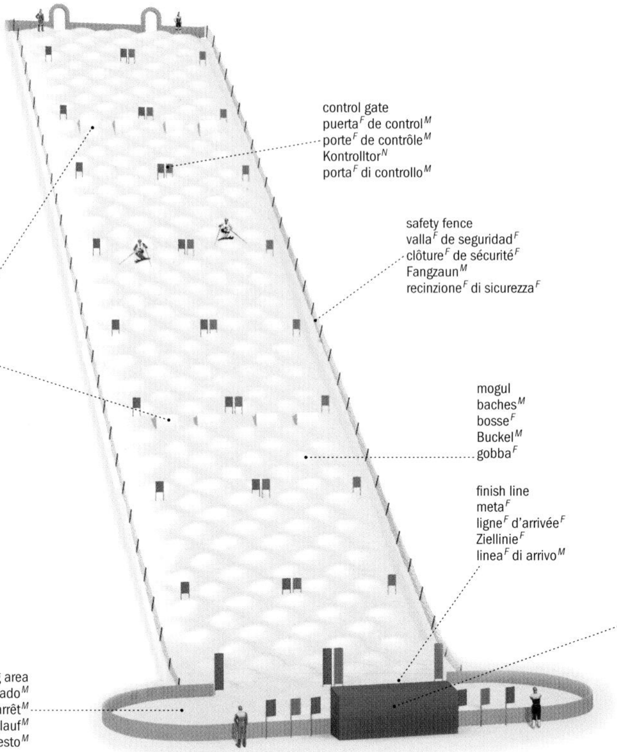

control gate
puerta^F de control^M
porte^F de contrôle^M
Kontrolltor^N
porta^F di controllo^M

safety fence
valla^F de seguridad^F
clôture^F de sécurité^F
Fangzaun^M
recinzione^F di sicurezza^F

kickers
kickers^M
tremplins^M
Sprungschanzen^F
trampolini^M

mogul
baches^M
bosse^F
Buckel^M
gobba^F

finish line
meta^F
ligne^F d'arrivée^F
Ziellinie^F
linea^F di arrivo^M

judges' stand
tribuna^F del jurado^M
tribune^F des juges^M
Kampfrichterstand^M
tribuna^F dei giudici^M

stopping area
zona^F de frenado^M
aire^F d'arrêt^M
Auslauf^M
area^F di arresto^M

aerial site
zona^F de salto^M
site^M de saut^M
Sprunganlage^F
area^F del salto^M

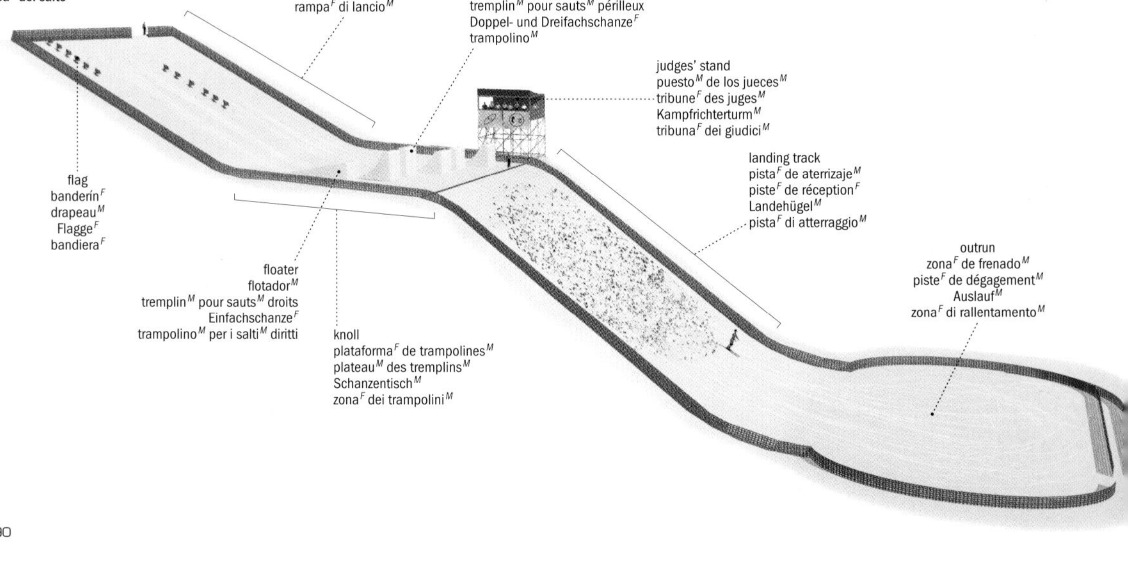

inrun
pista^F de despegue^M
piste^F d'élan^M
Anlauf^M
rampa^F di lancio^M

kicker
kicher^M
tremplin^M pour sauts^M périlleux
Doppel- und Dreifachschanze^F
trampolino^M

judges' stand
puesto^M de los jueces^M
tribune^F des juges^M
Kampfrichterturm^M
tribuna^F dei giudici^M

landing track
pista^F de aterrizaje^M
piste^F de réception^F
Landehügel^M
pista^F di atterraggio^M

flag
banderín^F
drapeau^M
Flagge^F
bandiera^F

floater
flotador^M
tremplin^M pour sauts^M droits
Einfachschanze^F
trampolino^M per i salti^M diritti

knoll
plataforma^F de trampolines^M
plateau^M des tremplins^M
Schanzentisch^M
zona^F dei trampolini^M

outrun
zona^F de frenado^M
piste^F de dégagement^M
Auslauf^M
zona^F di rallentamento^M

ski jumping

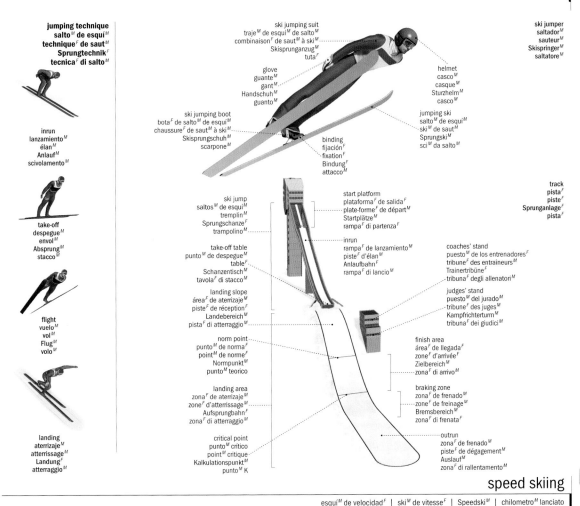

jumping technique
salto^M de esquí^M
technique^F de saut^M
Sprungtechnik^F
tecnica^F di salto^M

inrun
lanzamiento^M
élan^M
Anlauf^M
scivolamento^M

take-off
despegue^M
envol^M
Absprung^M
stacco^M

flight
vuelo^M
vol^M
Flug^M
volo^M

landing
aterrizaje^M
atterrissage^M
Landung^F
atterraggio^M

ski jumping suit
traje^M de esquí^M de salto^M
combinaison^F de saut^M à ski^M
Skisprunganzug^M
tuta^F

glove
guante^M
gant^M
Handschuh^M
guanto^M

ski jumping boot
bota^F de salto^M de esquí^M
chaussure^F de saut^M à ski^M
Skisprungschuh^M
scarpone^M

ski jumper
saltador^M
sauteur^M
Skispringer^M
saltatore^M

helmet
casco^M
casque^M
Sturzhelm^M
casco^M

jumping ski
salto^M de esquí^M
ski^M de saut^M
Sprungski^M
sci^M da salto^M

binding
fijación^F
fixation^F
Bindung^F
attacco^M

ski jump
saltos^M de esquí^M
tremplin^M
Sprungschanze^F
trampolino^M

take-off table
punto^M de despegue^M
table^F
Schanzentisch^M
tavola^F di stacco^M

landing slope
área^F de aterrizaje^M
piste^F de réception^F
Landebereich^M
pista^F di atterraggio^M

norm point
punto^M de norma^F
point^M de norme^F
Normpunkt^M
punto^M teorico

landing area
zona^F de aterrizaje^M
zone^F d'atterrissage^M
Aufsprungbahn^F
zona^F di atterraggio^M

critical point
punto^M crítico
point^M critique
Kalkulationspunkt^M
punto^M K

start platform
plataforma^F de salida^F
plate-forme^F de départ^M
Startplätze^M
rampa^F di partenza^F

inrun
rampa^F de lanzamiento^M
piste^F d'élan^M
Anlaufbahn^F
rampa^F di lancio^M

track
pista^F
piste^F
Sprunganlage^F
pista^F

coaches' stand
puesto^M de los entrenadores^F
tribune^F des entraineurs^M
Trainertribüne^F
tribuna^F degli allenatori^M

judges' stand
puesto^M del jurado^M
tribune^F des juges^M
Kampfrichterturm^M
tribuna^F dei giudici^M

finish area
área^F de llegada^F
zone^F d'arrivée^F
Zielbereich^M
zona^F di arrivo^M

braking zone
zona^F de frenado^M
zone^F de freinage^M
Bremsbereich^M
zona^F di frenata^F

outrun
zona^F de frenado^M
piste^F de dégagement^M
Auslauf^M
zona^F di rallentamento^M

speed skiing

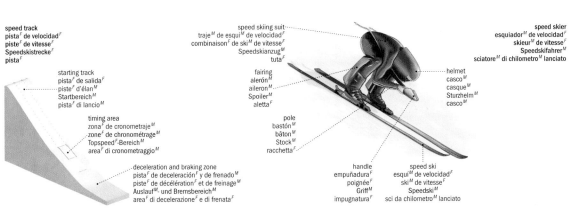

speed track
pista^F de velocidad^F
piste^F de vitesse^F
Speedskistrecke^F
pista^F

starting track
pista^F de salida^F
piste^F d'élan^M
Startbereich^M
pista^F di lancio^M

timing area
zona^F de cronometraje^M
zone^F de chronométrage^M
Topspeed^F-Bereich^M
area^F di cronometraggio^M

deceleration and braking zone
pista^F de deceleración^F y de frenado^M
piste^F de décélération^F et de freinage^M
Auslauf^M- und Bremsbereich^M
area^F di decelerazione^F e di frenata^F

speed skiing suit
traje^M de esquí^M de velocidad^F
combinaison^F de ski^M de vitesse^F
Speedskianzug^M
tuta^F

fairing
alerón^M
aileron^M
Spoiler^M
aletta^F

pole
bastón^M
bâton^M
Stock^M
racchetta^F

handle
empuñadura^F
poignée^F
Griff^M
impugnatura^F

speed skier
esquiador^M de velocidad^F
skieur^M de vitesse^F
Speedskifahrer^M
sciatore^M di chilometro^M lanciato

helmet
casco^M
casque^M
Sturzhelm^M
casco^M

speed ski
esquí^M de velocidad^F
ski^M de vitesse^F
Speedski^M
sci^M da chilometro^M lanciato

cross-country skiing

esquí de fondo^M | ski^M de fond^M | Skilanglauf^M | sci^M da fondo^M

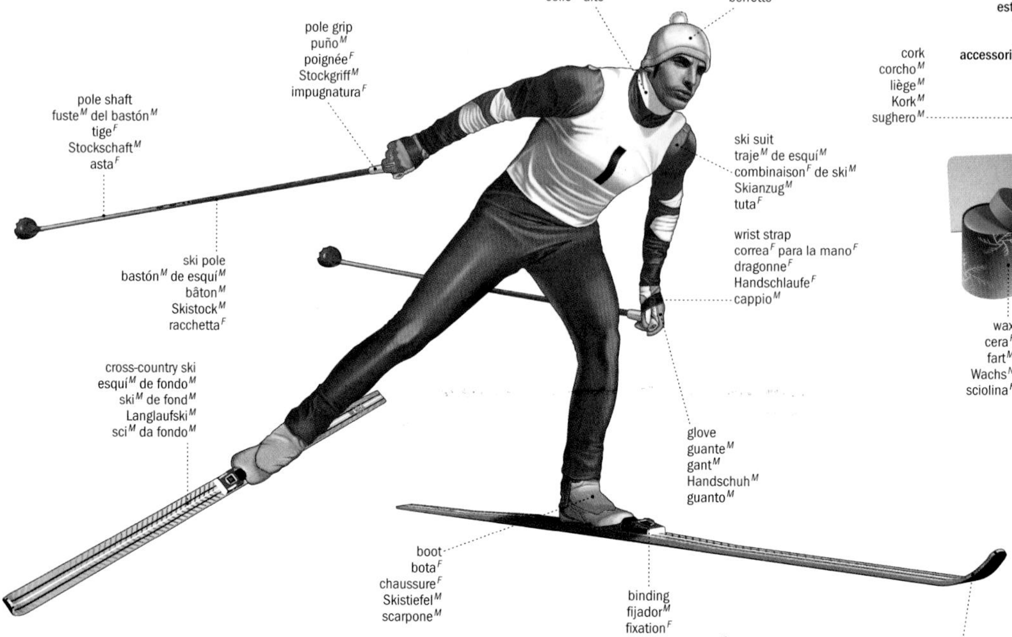

cross-country skier
fondista^M
skieur^M de fond^M
Langläufer^M
fondista^M/F

turtleneck
jersey^M de cuello^M de cisne^M
col^M roulé
Rollkragen^M
collo^M alto

ski hat
gorro^M
bonnet^M ; tuque^F
Skimütze^F
berretto^M

waxing kit
estuche^M de encerado^M
trousse^F de fartage^M
Wachsausrüstung^F
accessori^M per la sciolinatura^F

pole grip
puño^M
poignée^F
Stockgriff^M
impugnatura^F

cork
corcho^M
liège^M
Kork^M
sughero^M

pole shaft
fuste^M del bastón^M
tige^F
Stockschaft^M
asta^F

ski suit
traje^M de esquí^M
combinaison^F de ski^M
Skianzug^M
tuta^F

ski pole
bastón^M de esquí^M
bâton^M
Skistock^M
racchetta^F

wrist strap
correa^F para la mano^F
dragonne^F
Handschlaufe^F
cappio^M

wax
cera^F
fart^M
Wachs^N
sciolina^F

cross-country ski
esquí^M de fondo^M
ski^M de fond^M
Langlaufski^M
sci^M da fondo^M

glove
guante^M
gant^M
Handschuh^M
guanto^M

scraper
rasqueta^F
racloir^M
Abziehklinge^F
raschietto^M metallico

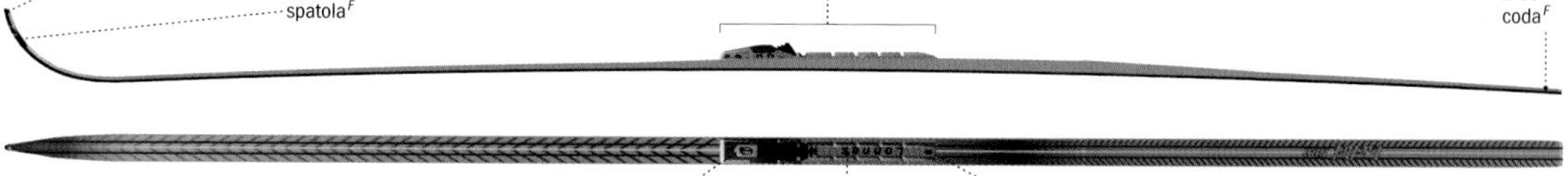

boot
bota^F
chaussure^F
Skistiefel^M
scarpone^M

binding
fijador^M
fixation^F
Langlauf-Rattenfallbindung^F
attacco^M

shovel
punta^F
spatule^F
Schaufel^F
spatola^F

cross-country ski
esquí^M de fondo^M
ski^M de fond^M
Langlaufski^M
sci^M da fondo^M

ski tip
punta^F del esquí^M
pointe^F de ski^M
Skispitze^F
punta^F dello sci^M

toe binding
fijación^F para el pie^M
fixation^F à butée^F avant
Vorfußbindung^F
attacco^M

tail
cola^F
talon^M
Ende^N
coda^F

shovel
punta^F
spatule^F
Schaufel^F
spatola^F

skating step
paso^M de patinador^M
pas^M de patineur^M
Schlittschuhschritt^M
passo^M pattinato

clamp
ratonera^F
fourchette^F
Backen^M
morsetto^M anteriore

toeplate
apoyo^M para el pie^M
étrier^F
Vorfußplatte^F
staffa^F

heelplate
pieza^F de talón^M
talonnière^F
Absatzplatte^F
talloniera^F

diagonal step
paso^M alternativo
pas^M alternatif
diagonaler Schlittschuhschritt^M
passo^M alternato

skating kick
golpe^M de patín^M
coup^M de patin^M
Doppelstockschub^M
colpo^M di pattino^M

gliding phase
fase^F de impulsión^F
phase^F de glisse^F
Gleitphase^F
fase^F di scivolamento^M

pushing phase
fase^F de impulsión^F
phase^F de poussée^F
Schubphase^F
fase^F di spinta^F

gliding phase
fase^F de deslizamiento^M
phase^F de glisse^F
Schubphase^F
fase^F di scivolamento^M

pushing phase
fase^F de impulso^F
phase^F de poussée^F
Schubphase^F
fase^F di spinta^F

biathlon

biathlon[M] | biathlon[M] | Biathlon[N] | biathlon[M]

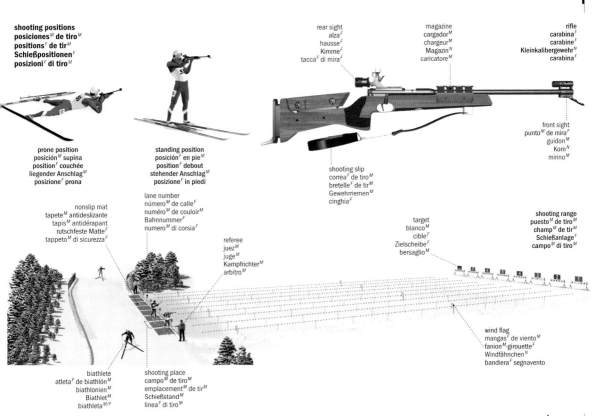

shooting positions
posiciones[M] de tiro[M]
positions[F] de tir[M]
Schießpositionen[F]
posizioni[F] di tiro[M]

rear sight
alza[F]
hausse[F]
Kimme[F]
tacca[F] di mira[F]

magazine
cargador[M]
chargeur[M]
Magazin[N]
caricatore[M]

rifle
carabina[F]
carabine[F]
Kleinkalibergewehr[N]
carabina[F]

prone position
posición[M] supina
position[F] couchée
liegender Anschlag[M]
posizione[F] prona

standing position
posición[F] en pie[M]
position[F] debout
stehender Anschlag[M]
posizione[F] in piedi

front sight
punto[M] de mira[F]
guidon[M]
Korn[N]
mirino[M]

shooting slip
correa[F] de tiro[M]
bretelle[F] de tir[M]
Gewehrriemen[M]
cinghia[F]

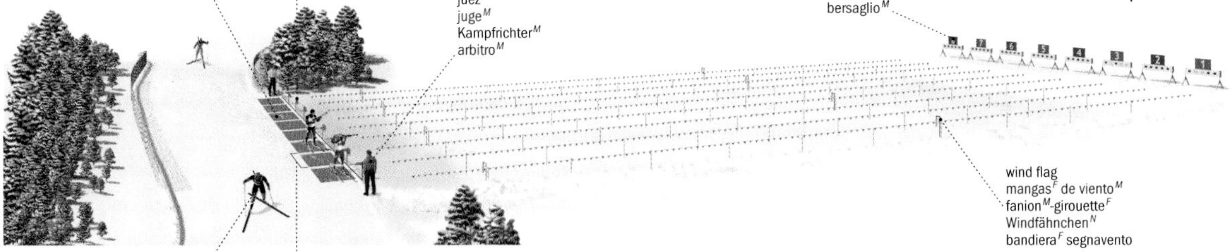

nonslip mat
tapete[M] antideslizante
tapis[M] antidérapant
rutschfeste Matte[F]
tappeto[M] di sicurezza[F]

lane number
número[M] de calle[F]
numéro[M] de couloir[M]
Bahnnummer[F]
numero[M] di corsia[F]

referee
juez[M]
juge[M]
Kampfrichter[M]
arbitro[M]

target
blanco[M]
cible[F]
Zielscheibe[F]
bersaglio[M]

shooting range
puesto[M] de tiro[M]
champ[M] de tir[M]
Schießanlage[F]
campo[M] di tiro[M]

wind flag
mangas[F] de viento[M]
fanion[M]-girouette[F]
Windfähnchen[N]
bandiera[F] segnavento

biathlete
atleta[F] de biathlón[M]
biathlonien[M]
Biathlet[M]
biathleta[M/F]

shooting place
campo[M] de tiro[M]
emplacement[M] de tir[M]
Schießstand[M]
linea[F] di tiro[M]

snowshoes

raqueta[F] | raquettes[F] | Schneeschuh[M] | racchetta[F] da neve[F]

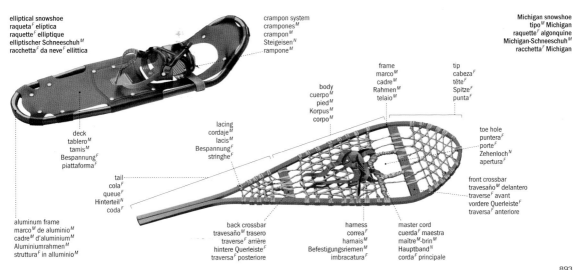

elliptical snowshoe
raqueta[F] elíptica
raquette[F] elliptique
elliptischer Schneeschuh[M]
racchetta[F] da neve[F] ellittica

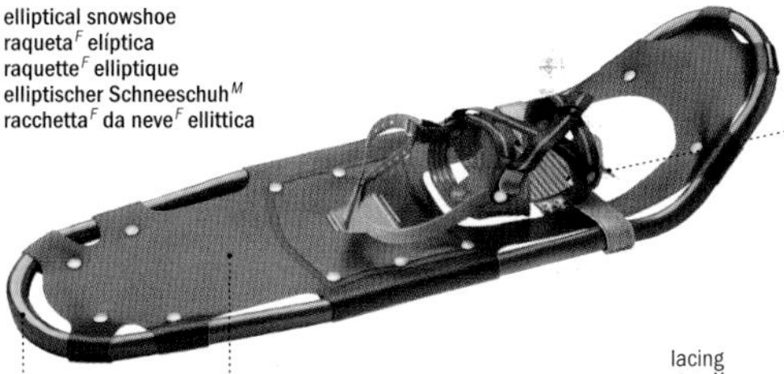

crampon system
crampones[M]
crampon[M]
Steigeisen[N]
rampone[M]

Michigan snowshoe
tipo[M] Michigan
raquette[F] algonquine
Michigan-Schneeschuh[M]
racchetta[F] Michigan

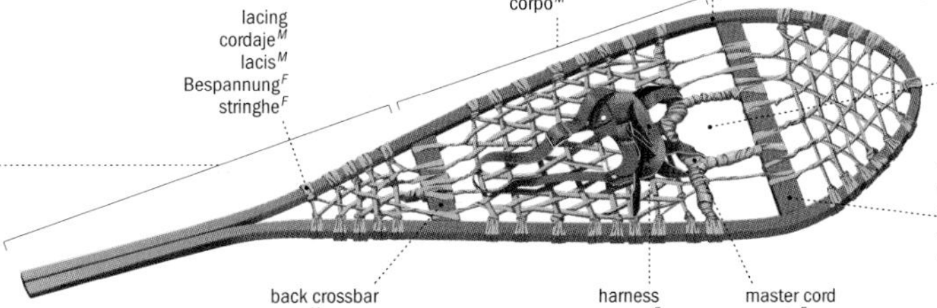

frame
marco[M]
cadre[M]
Rahmen[M]
telaio[M]

tip
cabeza[F]
tête[F]
Spitze[F]
punta[F]

body
cuerpo[M]
pied[M]
Korpus[M]
corpo[M]

lacing
cordaje[M]
lacis[M]
Bespannung[F]
stringhe[F]

deck
tablero[M]
tamis[M]
Bespannung[F]
piattaforma[F]

toe hole
puntera[F]
porte[F]
Zehenloch[N]
apertura[F]

tail
cola[F]
queue[F]
Hinterteil[N]
coda[F]

front crossbar
travesaño[M] delantero
traverse[F] avant
vordere Querleiste[F]
traversa[F] anteriore

aluminum frame
marco[M] de aluminio[M]
cadre[M] d'aluminium[M]
Aluminiumrahmen[M]
struttura[F] in alluminio[M]

back crossbar
travesaño[M] trasero
traverse[F] arrière
hintere Querleiste[F]
traversa[F] posteriore

harness
correa[F]
harnais[M]
Befestigungsriemen[M]
imbracatura[F]

master cord
cuerda[F] maestra
maître[M]-brin[M]
Hauptband[N]
corda[F] principale

skateboarding

skateboard ^{M} | planche ^{F} à roulettes ^{F} | Skateboarding ^{N} | skateboard ^{M}

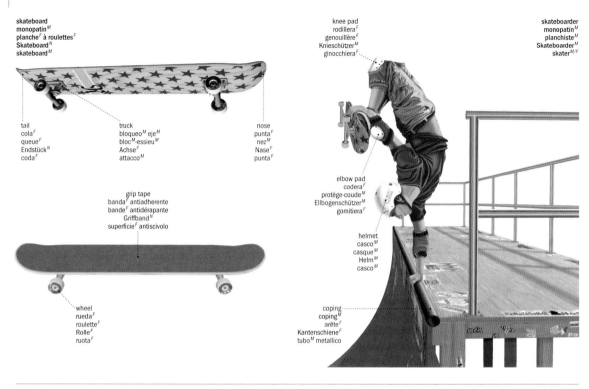

skateboard
monopatín ^{M}
planche ^{F} à roulettes ^{F}
Skateboard ^{N}
skateboard ^{M}

knee pad
rodillera ^{F}
genouillère ^{F}
Knieschützer ^{M}
ginocchiera ^{F}

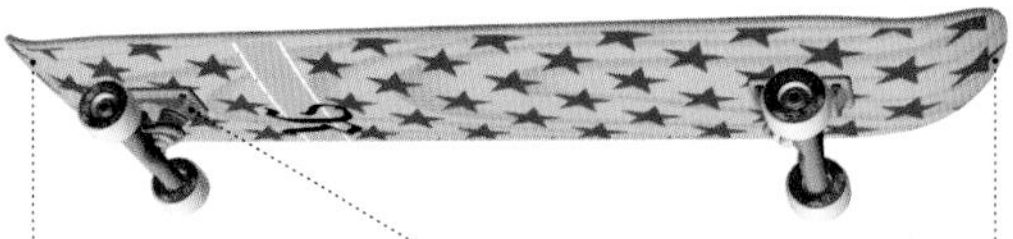

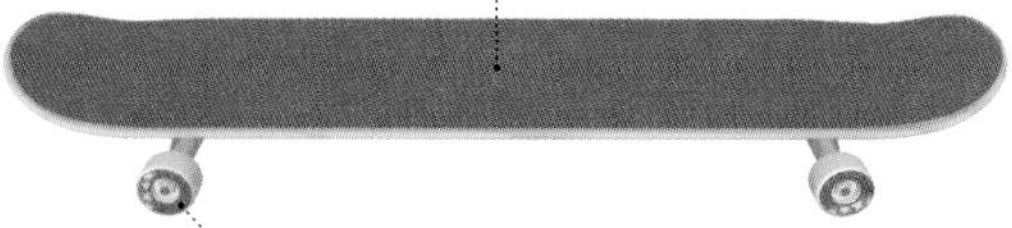

skateboarder
monopatín ^{M}
planchiste ^{M}
Skateboarder ^{M}
skater $^{M/F}$

tail
cola ^{F}
queue ^{F}
Endstück ^{N}
coda ^{F}

truck
bloqueo ^{M} eje ^{M}
bloc ^{M}-essieu ^{M}
Achse ^{F}
attacco ^{M}

nose
punta ^{F}
nez ^{M}
Nase ^{F}
punta ^{F}

grip tape
banda ^{F} antiadherente
bande ^{F} antidérapante
Griffband ^{N}
superficie ^{F} antiscivolo

elbow pad
codera ^{F}
protège-coude ^{M}
Ellbogenschützer ^{M}
gomitiera ^{F}

helmet
casco ^{M}
casque ^{M}
Helm ^{M}
casco ^{M}

wheel
rueda ^{F}
roulette ^{F}
Rolle ^{F}
ruota ^{F}

coping
coping ^{M}
arête ^{F}
Kantenschiene ^{F}
tubo ^{M} metallico

ramp
medio tubo ^{M}
rampe ^{F}
Rampe ^{F}
rampa ^{F}

guard rail
barandilla ^{F}
rambarde ^{F}
Geländer ^{N}
guardrail ^{M}

platform
plataforma ^{F}
plate-forme ^{F}
Plattform ^{F}
piattaforma ^{F}

coping
coping ^{M}
arête ^{F}
Kantenschiene ^{F}
tubo ^{M} metallico

flat
piso ^{M}
fond ^{M}
Flachstück ^{N}
piano ^{M}

vertical section
sección ^{F} vertical
surface ^{F} verticale
Vertikale ^{F}
superficie ^{F} verticale

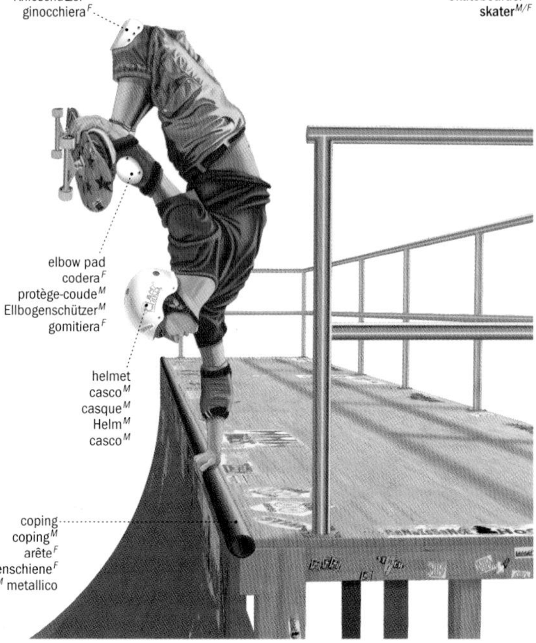

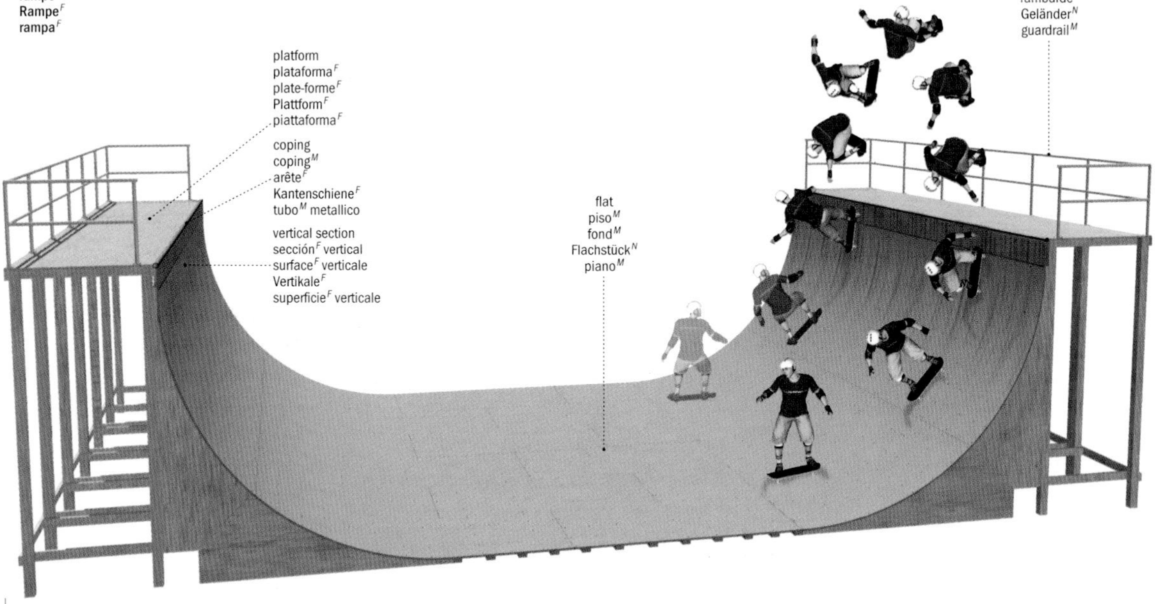

in-line skating

patinaje^M en línea^F | patin^M à roues^F alignées | Inlineskating^N | pattinaggio^M in linea^F

acrobatic skate
patinaje^M acrobático
patin^M acrobatique
Stuntskate^M
pattino^M acrobatico

inner boot
botín^M interior
chausson^M intérieur
Innenstiefel^M
scarpetta^F interna

upper shell
bota^F externa
coque^F supérieure
Schalenschuh^M
gambale^M

frame
bastidor^M
platine^F
Schiene^F
telaio^M

wheel
rueda^F
roue^F
Rolle^F
rotella^F

skater
patinador^M
patineuse^F
Skaterin^F
pattinatore^M

helmet
casco^M
casque^M
Helm^M
casco^M

elbow pad
codera^F
coudière^F
Ellbogenschützer^M
gomitiera^F

knee pad
rodillera^F
genouillère^F
Knieschützer^M
ginocchiera^F

in-line speed skate
patín^M en línea^F
patin^M de vitesse^F
Speedskate^M
pattino^M da velocità^F

wrist guard
muñequera^F
protège-poignet^M
Handgelenkschützer^M
polsiera^F

in-line skate
patín^M en línea^F
patin^M à roues^F alignées
Rollschuh^M
pattino^M a rotelle^F

upper shell
bota^F externa
coque^F supérieure
Oberschale^F
gambale^M

inner boot
botín^F interior
chausson^M intérieur
Innenstiefel^M
scarpetta^F interna

adjusting buckle
hebilla^F de ajuste^M
boucle^F de réglage^M
Einstellspanner^M
dispositivo^M di regolazione^F

in-line hockey skate
patín en línea^F de hockey^M
patin^M de hockey^M
Hockeyskate^M
pattino^M da hockey^M

axle
eje^M
essieu^M
Achse^F
assale^M

boot
bota^F
chaussure^F
Stiefel^M
scarpa^F

heel stop
freno^M trasero
frein^M de talon^M
Absatzstopper^M
freno^M a tampone^M

wheel
rueda^F
roue^F
Rolle^F
ruota^F

truck
bogie^M
bloc^M-essieu^M
Wagen^M
carrello^M

SPORTS AND GAMES

895

skydiving

paracaidismo^M en caída^F libre | chute^F libre | Fallschirmspringen^N | paracadutismo^M in caduta^F libera

skydiver
paracaidista^{M/F}
sauteur^M
Fallschirmspringer^M
paracadutista^{M/F}

reserve parachute
paracaídas^M de reserva^F
parachute^M de secours^M
Reservefallschirm^M
paracadute^M di riserva^F

main parachute
paracaídas^M principal
parachute^M principal
Hauptfallschirm^M
paracadute^M principale

helmet
casco^M
casque^M de saut^M
Schutzhelm^M
casco^M

boot
bota^F
botte^F de saut^M
Springerstiefel^M
scarpone^M

goggles
gafas^F
lunettes^F de vol^M
Schutzbrille^F
occhiali^M

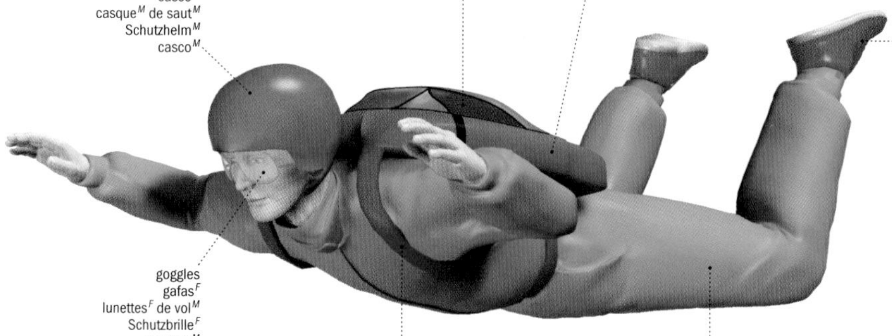

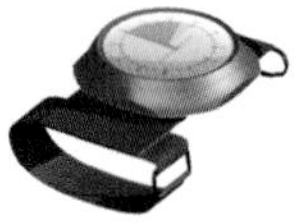

altimeter
altímetro^M
altimètre^M
Höhenmesser^M
altimetro^M

harness
arnés^M
harnais^M
Gurtwerk^N
imbracatura^F

one-piece coverall
traje^M de vuelo^M
combinaison^F de vol^M
einteiliger Overall^M
combinazione^F di volo^M

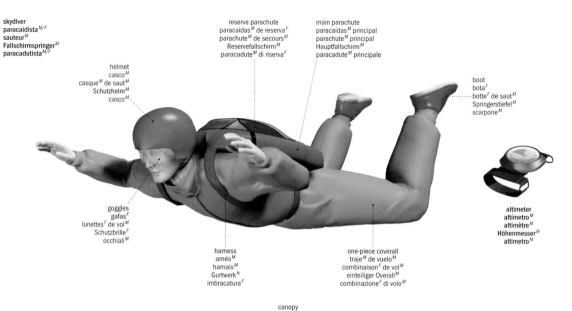

canopy
vela^F
voile^F
Fallschirmkappe^F
vela^F

parachute
paracaídas^M
parachute^M
Fallschirmspringen^N
paracadute^M

stabilizer
estabilizador^M
stabilo^M
Stabilisierungsfläche^F
stabilizzatore^M

pilot chute
paracaídas^M piloto
extracteur^M
Ausziehschirm^M
calottino^M estrattore

suspension line
cuerdas^F de suspensión^F
suspentes^F
Fangleinen^F
cordini^M di sospensione^F

slider
deslizador^M
glisseur^M
Slider^M
slider^M

brake loop
mando^M de los frenos^M
commande^F des freins^M
Bremsleine^F
comando^M del freno^M

harness
arnés^M
harnais^M
Gurtzeug^N
imbracatura^F

skydiver
paracaidista^{M/F}
parachutiste^M
Fallschirmspringer^M
paracadutista^{M/F}

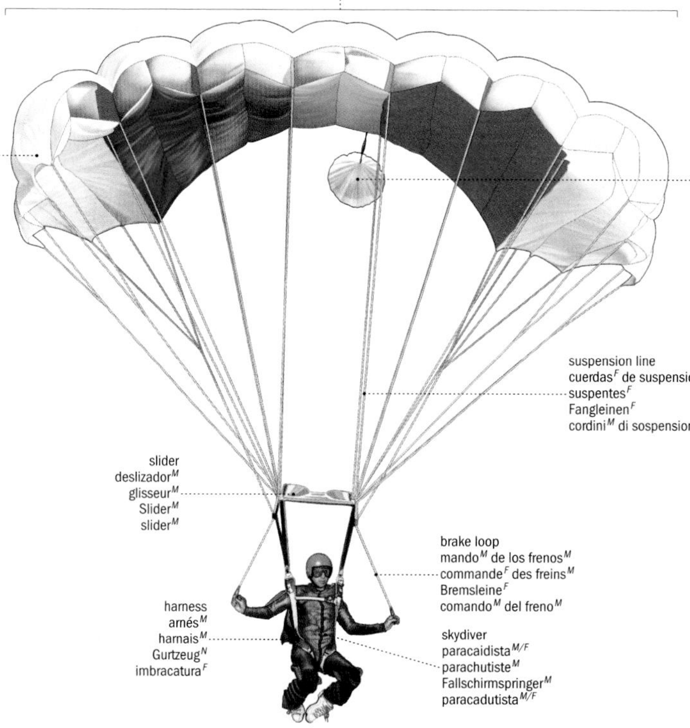

paragliding

parapente^M | parapente^M | Gleitschirmfliegen^N | parapendio^M

canopy
velamen^M
aile^F
Gleitschirm^M
velatura^F

canopy
velamen^M
voile^F
Schirm^M
vela^F

half cell
célula^F
demi-caisson^M
Schirmsegment^N
cella^F

trailing edge
borde^M de salida^F
bord^M de fuite^F
Endkante^F
bordo^M di fuga^F

paragliding pilot
parapentista^{M/F}
parapentiste^M
Gleitflieger^M
pilota^M

leading edge
borde^M de ataque^M
bord^M d'attaque^F
Vorderkante^F
bordo^M di attacco^M

helmet
casco^M de salto^M
casque^M
Schutzhelm^M
casco^M

riser
correa^F principal de sustentación^F
élévateur^M
Haupttragegurt^M
bretella^F

brake loop
correa^F de amortiguación^F
commande^F des freins^M
Bremsleine^F
comando^M del freno^M

harness
arnés^M
harnais^M
Gurtwerk^N
imbracatura^F

stabilizer
estabilizador^M
stabilo^M
Stabilisator^M
stabilizzatore^M

saddle
silla^F
sellette^F
Sitz^M
selletta^F

suspension line
cuerdas^F de suspensión^F
suspentes^F
Hängeleinen^F
cordini^M di sospensione^F

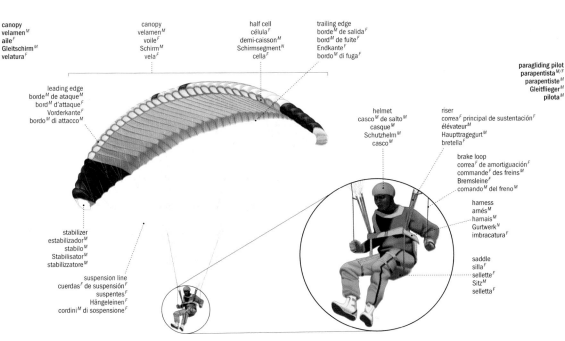

hang gliding

vuelo^M libre | vol^M libre | Drachenfliegen^N | deltaplano^M

crossbar
barra^F transversal
tube^M transversal
Querstange^F
tubo^M trasversale

sail
ala^F delta
voilure^F
Tragsegel^N
vela^F

leading edge tube
tubo^M del borde^M de ataque^M
tube^M de bord^M d'attaque^F
Vorderstangentasche^F
tubo^M del bordo^M di attacco^M

hang glider
ala^F delta
aile^F libre
Flugdrachen^M
deltaplano^M

hang gliding pilot
piloto^M
pilote^M
Pilot^M
pilota^M

batten
sable^M
latte^F
Längslatte^F
stecca^F

king post
mástil^M
mât^M
Spannmast^M
puntale^M

airframe
trapecio^M
trapèze^M
Steuerbügel^M
trapezio^M

keel
quilla^F
quille^F
Kielstange^F
chiglia^F

nose
proa^F
nez^M
Nase^F
muso^M

hang point
arzón^M de amarre^M
point^M d'ancrage^M
Aufhängepunkt^M
punto^M di sospensione^F

flight bag
saco^M de pilotaje^M
fourreau^M
Sack^M mit Rettungssystem^N
sacco^M imbottito

rigging wire
tirante^M de fijación^F
hauban^M
Rigg-Stahlseil^N
cavo^M del sartiame^M

wing
ala^F
aile^F
Flügel^M
ala^F

harness
arnés^M
harnais^M
Gurtwerk^N
imbracatura^F

trailing edge
caída^F de popa^F
bord^M de fuite^F
Endkante^F
bordo^M di fuga^F

tip
punta^F del ala^F
bout^M d'aile^F
Flügelspitze^F
punta^F dell'ala^F

control bar
barra^F de dirección^F
barre^F de commande^F
Lenkstange^F
barra^F di controllo^M

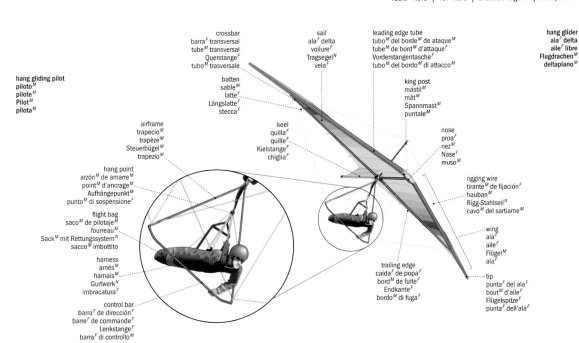

SPORTS AND GAMES

glider

planeador^M | planeur^M | Segelflugzeug^N | aliante^M

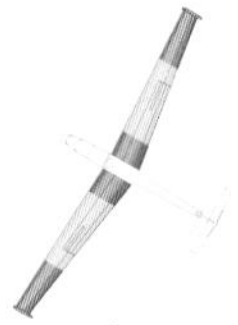

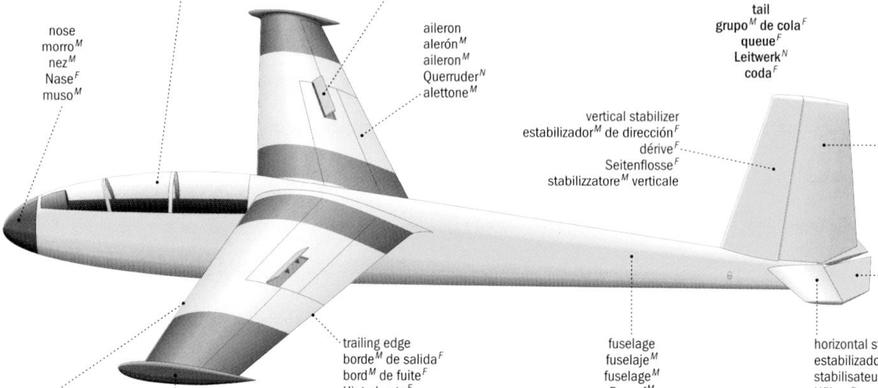

cockpit canopy
cubierta^F de la cabina^F
verrière^F
Kanzel^F
calotta^F della cabina^F di pilotaggio^M

air brake
freno^M aerodinámico
aérofrein^M
Bremsklappe^F
freno^M aerodinamico

tail
grupo^M de cola^F
queue^F
Leitwerk^N
coda^F

wings
ala^F
ailes^F
Flügel^M
ala^F

nose
morro^M
nez^M
Nase^F
muso^M

aileron
alerón^M
aileron^M
Querruder^N
alettone^M

vertical stabilizer
estabilizador^M de dirección^F
dérive^F
Seitenflosse^F
stabilizzatore^M verticale

rudder
timón^M de dirección^F
gouvernail^M de direction^F
Seitenruder^N
timone^M di direzione^F

elevator
timón^M de profundidad^F
gouvernail^M de profondeur^F
Höhenruder^N
timone^M di profondità^F

trailing edge
borde^M de salida^F
bord^M de fuite^F
Hinterkante^F
bordo^M di fuga^F

fuselage
fuselaje^M
fuselage^M
Rumpf^M
fusoliera^F

horizontal stabilizer
estabilizador^M horizontal
stabilisateur^F
Höhenflosse^F
stabilizzatore^M orizzontale

leading edge
borde^M de ataque^M
bord^M d'attaque^F
Vorderkante^F
bordo^M di attacco^M

wing tip
borde^M marginal
saumon^M d'aile^F
Flügelspitze^F
punta^F dell'ala^F

cockpit
cabina^F del piloto^M
cabine^F de pilotage^M
Cockpit^N
cabina^F di pilotaggio^M

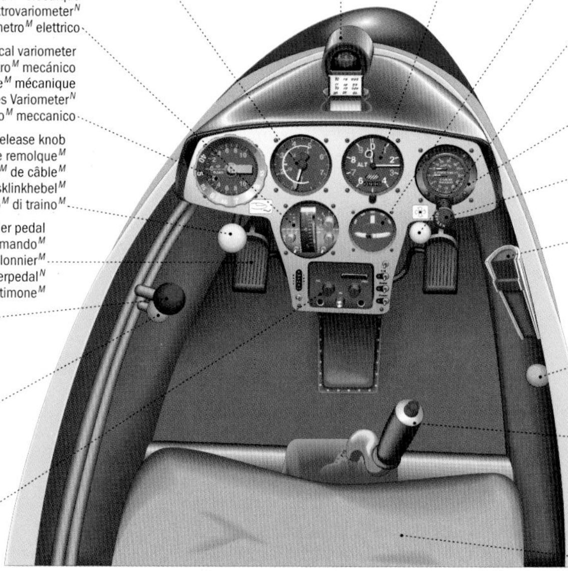

airspeed indicator
anemómetro^M
anémomètre^M
Geschwindigkeitsanzeige^F
anemometro^M

compass
brújula^F
compas^M
Kompass^M
bussola^F

altimeter
altímetro^M
altimètre^M
Höhenmesser^M
altimetro^M

turn and slip indicator
indicador^M de viraje^M y de inclinación^F
indicateur^M de virage^M et d'inclinaison^F latérale
Wendezeiger^M
indicatore^M di virata^F e di inclinazione^F

electric variometer
variómetro^M eléctrico
variomètre^M électrique
Elektrovariometer^N
variometro^M elettrico

cockpit ventilation
ventilador^M de cabina^F
ventilation^F de la cabine^F
Frischluftzufuhr^F
manopola^F per l'aerazione^F della cabina^F

mechanical variometer
variómetro^M mecánico
variomètre^M mécanique
mechanisches Variometer^N
variometro^M meccanico

oxygen feeding control
control^M de alimentador^M de oxígeno^M
contrôle^M d'alimentation^F en oxygène^M
Sauerstoffzufuhranzeige^F
indicatore^M dell'alimentazione^F di ossigeno^M

tow release knob
liberador^M del cable^M de remolque^M
commande^F de largage^M de câble^M
Ausklinkhebel^M
manopola^F di sgancio^M del cavo^M di traino^M

oxygen feeding knob
palanca^F de alimentador^M de oxígeno^M
commande^F d'alimentation^F en oxygène^M
Sauerstoffzufuhrregler^M
regolatore^M dell'alimentazione^F di ossigeno^M

rudder pedal
pedal^M del timón^M de mando^M
pédale^F de palonnier^M
Seitenruderpedal^N
pedale^M del timone^M

microphone
micrófono^M
microphone^M
Mikrofon^N
microfono^M

air brake handle
mando^M del freno^M aerodinámico
commande^F d'aérofrein^M
Bremsklappenhebel^M
comando^M del freno^M aerodinamico

canopy release knob
eyector^M de la cubierta^F de cabina^F
commande^F de largage^M de la verrière^F
Kanzellösehebel^M
manopola^F per l'apertura^F della calotta^F

turn and slip knob
mando^M de viraje^M y de inclinación^F
commande^F de virage^M et d'inclinaison^F latérale
Wendehebel^M
comando^M di virata^F e di inclinazione^F

control stick
palanca^F de mando^M
manche^M à balai^M
Steuerknüppel^M
cloche^F

radio
radio^M
radio^F
Funkgerät^N
radio^F

seat
asiento^M
siège^M
Sitz^M
sedile^M

ballooning

vuelo[M] en globo[M] | montgolfière[F] | Freiballonsport[M] | mongolfiera[F]

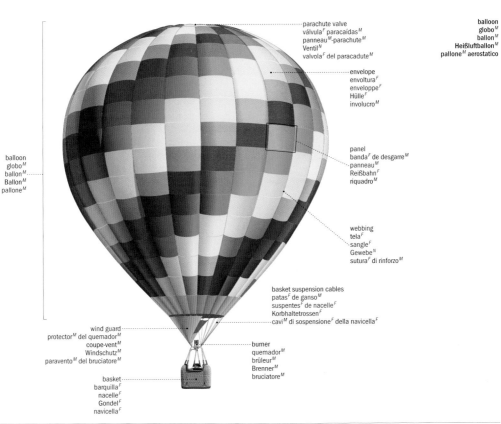

parachute valve
válvula[F] paracaídas[M]
panneau[M]-parachute[M]
Ventil[N]
valvola[F] del paracadute[M]

balloon
globo[M]
ballon[M]
Heißluftballon[M]
pallone[M] aerostatico

envelope
envoltura[F]
enveloppe[F]
Hülle[F]
involucro[M]

panel
banda[F] de desgarre[M]
panneau[M]
Reißbahn[F]
riquadro[M]

balloon
globo[M]
ballon[M]
Ballon[M]
pallone[M]

webbing
tela[F]
sangle[F]
Gewebe[N]
sutura[F] di rinforzo[M]

basket suspension cables
patas[F] de ganso[M]
suspentes[F] de nacelle[F]
Korbhaltetrossen[F]
cavi[M] di sospensione[F] della navicella[F]

wind guard
protector[M] del quemador[M]
coupe-vent[M]
Windschutz[M]
paravento[M] del bruciatore[M]

burner
quemador[M]
brûleur[M]
Brenner[M]
bruciatore[M]

basket
barquilla[F]
nacelle[F]
Gondel[F]
navicella[F]

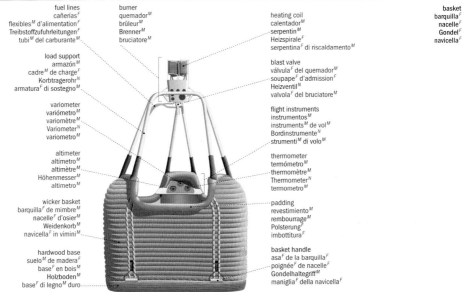

fuel lines
cañerías[F]
flexibles[M] d'alimentation[F]
Treibstoffzufuhrleitungen[F]
tubi[M] del carburante[M]

burner
quemador[M]
brûleur[M]
Brenner[M]
bruciatore[M]

heating coil
calentador[M]
serpentin[M]
Heizspirale[F]
serpentina[F] di riscaldamento[M]

basket
barquilla[F]
nacelle[F]
Gondel[F]
navicella[F]

load support
armazón[M]
cadre[M] de charge[F]
Korbtragerohr[N]
armatura[F] di sostegno[M]

blast valve
válvula[F] del quemador[M]
soupape[F] d'admission[F]
Heizventil[N]
valvola[F] del bruciatore[M]

variometer
variómetro[M]
variomètre[M]
Variometer[N]
variometro[M]

flight instruments
instrumentos[M]
instruments[M] de vol[M]
Bordinstrumente[N]
strumenti[M] di volo[M]

altimeter
altímetro[M]
altimètre[M]
Höhenmesser[M]
altimetro[M]

thermometer
termómetro[M]
thermomètre[M]
Thermometer[N]
termometro[M]

wicker basket
barquilla[F] de mimbre[M]
nacelle[F] d'osier[M]
Weidenkorb[M]
navicella[F] in vimini[M]

padding
revestimiento[M]
rembourrage[M]
Polsterung[F]
imbottitura[F]

hardwood base
suelo[M] de madera[F]
base[F] en bois[M]
Holzboden[M]
base[F] di legno[M] duro

basket handle
asa[F] de la barquilla[F]
poignée[F] de nacelle[F]
Gondelhaltegriff[M]
maniglia[F] della navicella[F]

rock climbing

escalada^F | escalade^F | Sportklettern^N | arrampicata^F

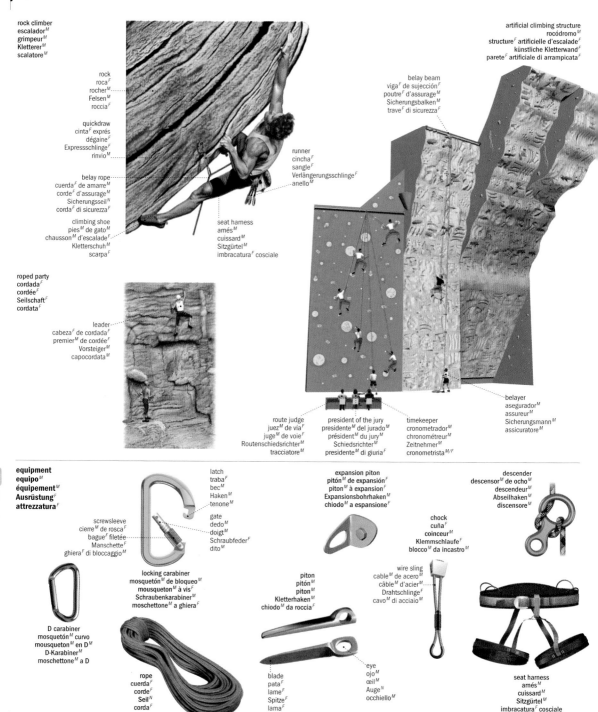

rock climber
escalador^M
grimpeur^M
Kletterer^M
scalatore^M

rock
roca^F
rocher^M
Felsen^M
roccia^F

quickdraw
cinta^F exprés
dégaine^F
Expressschlinge^F
rinvio^M

belay rope
cuerda^F de amarre^M
corde^F d'assurage^M
Sicherungsseil^N
corda^F di sicurezza^F

climbing shoe
pies^M de gato^M
chausson^M d'escalade^F
Kletterschuh^M
scarpa^F

roped party
cordada^F
cordée^F
Seilschaft^F
cordata^F

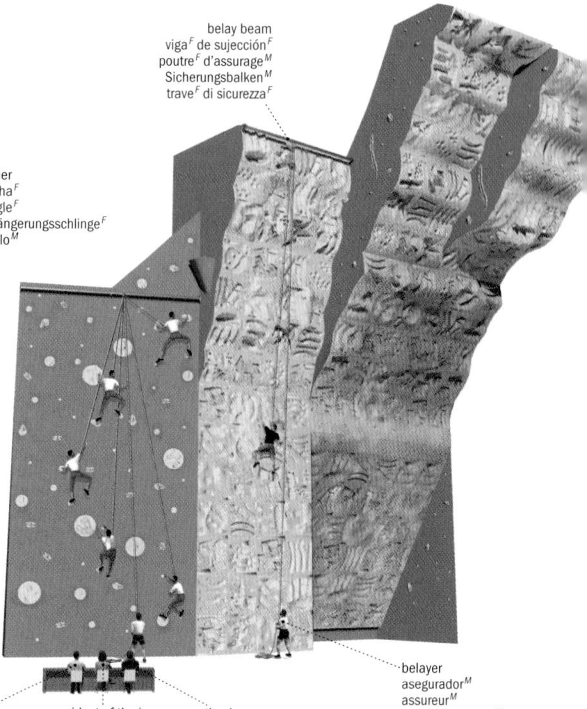

leader
cabeza^F de cordada^F
premier^M de cordée^F
Vorsteiger^M
capocordata^M

runner
cincha^F
sangle^F
Verlängerungsschlinge^F
anello^M

seat harness
arnés^M
cuissard^M
Sitzgürtel^M
imbracatura^F cosciale

artificial climbing structure
rocódromo^M
structure^F artificielle d'escalade^F
künstliche Kletterwand^F
parete^F artificiale di arrampicata^F

belay beam
viga^F de sujección^F
poutre^F d'assurage^M
Sicherungsbalken^M
trave^F di sicurezza^F

belayer
asegurador^M
assureur^M
Sicherungsmann^M
assicuratore^M

route judge
juez^M de vía^F
juge^M de voie^F
Routenschiedsrichter^M
tracciatore^M

president of the jury
presidente^M del jurado^M
président^M du jury^M
Schiedsrichter^M
presidente^M di giuria^F

timekeeper
cronometrador^M
chronométreur^M
Zeitnehmer^M
cronometrista$^{M/F}$

equipment
equipo^M
équipement^M
Ausrüstung^F
attrezzatura^F

screwsleeve
cierre^M de rosca^F
bague^F filetée
Manschette^F
ghiera^F di bloccaggio^M

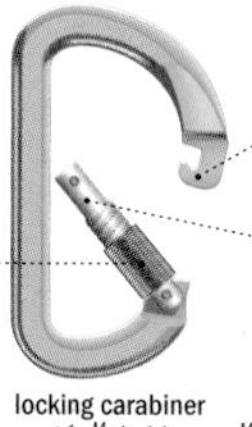

latch
traba^F
bec^M
Haken^M
tenone^M

gate
dedo^M
doigt^M
Schraubfeder^F
dito^M

locking carabiner
mosquetón^M de bloqueo^M
mousqueton^M à vis^F
Schraubenkarabiner^M
moschettone^M a ghiera^F

D carabiner
mosquetón^M curvo
mousqueton^M en D^M
D-Karabiner^M
moschettone^M a D

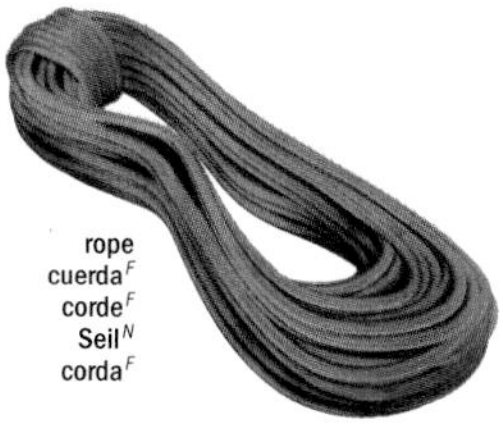

rope
cuerda^F
corde^F
Seil^N
corda^F

expansion piton
pitón^M de expansión^F
piton^M à expansion^F
Expansionsbohrhaken^M
chiodo^M a espansione^F

piton
pitón^F
piton^M
Kletterhaken^M
chiodo^M da roccia^F

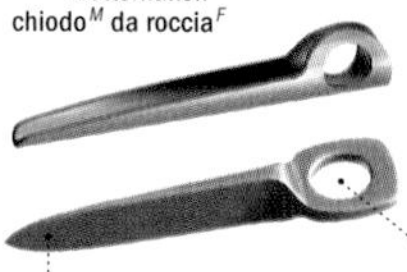

blade
pata^F
lame^F
Spitze^F
lama^F

eye
ojo^M
œil^M
Auge^N
occhiello^M

chock
cuña^F
coinceur^M
Klemmschlaufe^F
blocco^M da incastro^M

wire sling
cable^M de acero^M
câble^M d'acier^M
Drahtschlinge^F
cavo^M di acciaio^M

descender
descensor^M de ocho^M
descendeur^M
Abseilhaken^M
discensore^M

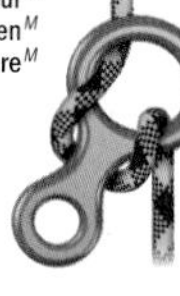

seat harness
arnés^M
cuissard^M
Sitzgürtel^M
imbracatura^F cosciale

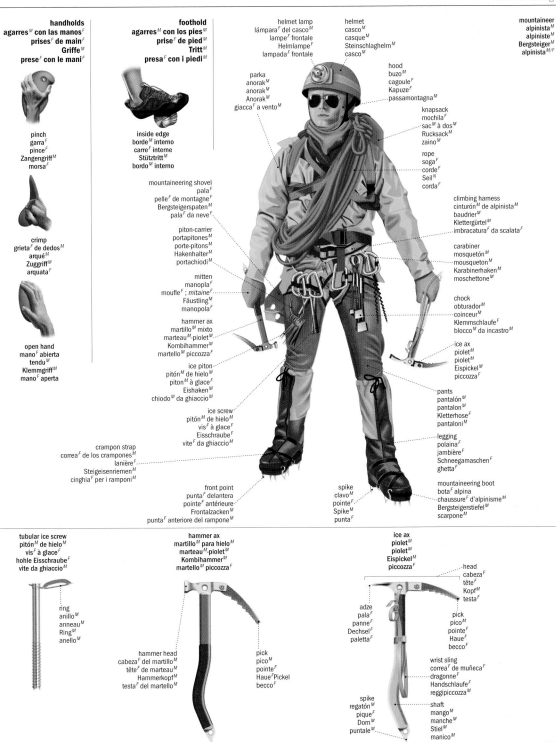

handholds
agarres^M con las manos^F
prises^F de main^F
Griffe^M
prese^F con le mani^F

pinch
garra^F
pince^F
Zangengriff^M
morsa^F

crimp
grieta^F de dedos^M
arqué^F
Zuggriff^M
arquata^F

open hand
mano^F abierta
tendu^M
Klemmgriff^M
mano^F aperta

foothold
agarres^M con los pies^M
prise^F de pied^M
Tritt^M
presa^F con i piedi^M

inside edge
borde^M interno
carre^F interne
Stütztritt^M
bordo^M interno

mountaineering shovel
pala^F
pelle^F de montagne^F
Bergsteigerspaten^M
pala^F da neve^F

piton-carrier
portapitones^M
porte-pitons^M
Hakenhalter^M
portachiodi^M

mitten
manopla^F
moufle^F ; mitaine^F
Fäustling^M
manopola^F

hammer ax
martillo^M mixto
marteau^M-piolet^M
Kombihammer^M
martello^M piccozza^F

ice piton
pitón^M de hielo^M
piton^M à glace^F
Eishaken^M
chiodo^M da ghiaccio^M

ice screw
pitón^M de hielo^M
vis^F à glace^F
Eisschraube^F
vite^F da ghiaccio^M

crampon strap
correa^F de los crampones^M
lanière^F
Steigeisenriemen^M
cinghia^F per i ramponi^M

front point
punta^F delantera
pointe^F antérieure
Frontalzacken^M
punta^F anteriore del rampone^M

helmet lamp
lámpara^F del casco^M
lampe^F frontale
Helmlampe^F
lampada^F frontale

parka
anorak^M
anorak^M
Anorak^M
giacca^F a vento^M

helmet
casco^M
casque^M
Steinschlaghelm^M
casco^M

hood
buzo^M
cagoule^F
Kapuze^F
passamontagna^M

knapsack
mochila^F
sac^M à dos^M
Rucksack^M
zaino^M

rope
soga^F
corde^F
Seil^N
corda^F

climbing harness
cinturón^M de alpinista^M
baudrier^M
Klettergürtel^M
imbracatura^F da scalata^F

carabiner
mosquetón^M
mousqueton^M
Karabinerhaken^M
moschettone^M

chock
obturador^M
coinceur^M
Klemmschlaufe^F
blocco^M da incastro^M

ice ax
piolet^M
piolet^M
Eispickel^M
piccozza^F

pants
pantalón^M
pantalon^M
Kletterhose^F
pantaloni^M

legging
polaina^F
jambière^F
Schneegamaschen^F
ghetta^F

mountaineering boot
bota^F alpina
chaussure^F d'alpinisme^M
Bergsteigerstiefel^M
scarpone^M

spike
clavo^M
pointe^F
Spike^M
punta^F

mountaineer
alpinista^M
alpiniste^M
Bergsteiger^M
alpinista$^{M/F}$

---

tubular ice screw
pitón^M de hielo^M
vis^F à glace^F
hohle Eisschraube^F
vite da ghiaccio^M

ring
anillo^M
anneau^M
Ring^M
anello^M

hammer ax
martillo^M para hielo^M
marteau^M-piolet^M
Kombihammer^M
martello^M piccozza^F

hammer head
cabeza^F del martillo^M
tête^F de marteau^M
Hammerkopf^M
testa^F del martello^M

pick
pico^M
pointe^F
Haue^F Pickel
becco^F

ice ax
piolet^M
piolet^M
Eispickel^M
piccozza^F

head
cabeza^F
tête^F
Kopf^M
testa^F

adze
pala^F
panne^F
Dechsel^F
paletta^F

pick
pico^M
pointe^F
Haue^F
becco^F

wrist sling
correa^F de muñeca^F
dragonne^F
Handschlaufe^F
reggipiccozza^M

spike
regatón^M
pique^F
Dorn^M
puntale^M

shaft
mango^M
manche^M
Stiel^M
manico^M

camping

acampada^F | camping^M | Camping^N | campeggio^M

examples of tents
ejemplos^M de tiendas^F de campaña^F
exemples^M de tentes^F
Beispiele^N für Zelte^N
esempi^M di tende^F

rainfly
doble techo^M
double toit^M
Überdach^N
telo^M esterno

two-person tent
tienda^F para dos
tente^F deux places^F
Zweipersonenzelt^N
tenda^F a due posti^M

door
puerta^F
porte^F
Eingang^M
porta^F

canopy
toldo^M delantero
auvent^M
Vordach^N
tettoia^F

guy line
viento^M
hauban^M
Zeltspannleine^F
tirante^M

stake
estaquilla^F
piquet^M
Hering^M
picchetto^M

strainer
fiador^M
tendeur^M
Spanner^M
regolatore^M del tirante^M

zipper
cierre^M
fermeture^F à glissière^F
Reißverschluss^M
cerniera^F lampo

inner tent
tienda^F interior
tente^F intérieure
Innenzelt^N
tenda^F interna

elastic strainer
fiador^M elástico
Sandow$^{®\,M}$
Gummispannring^M
elastico^M

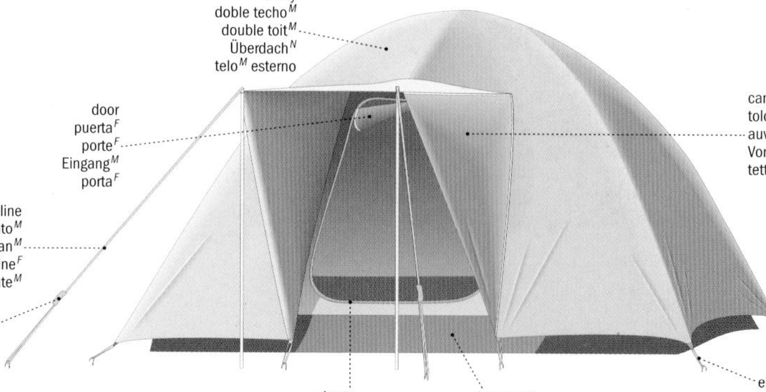

family tent
tienda^F de campaña^F tamaño^M familiar
tente^F familiale
Familienzelt^N
tenda^F di tipo^M familiare

window canopy
toldo^M de ventana^F
auvent^M de fenêtre^F
Fensterüberdachung^F
tenda^F coprifinestra

living room
cuarto^M de estar
séjour^M
Wohnraum^M
zona^F abitabile

guy line
viento^M
hauban^M
Zeltspannleine^F
tirante^M

elastic strainer
fiador^M elástico
Sandow$^{®\,M}$
Gummispannring^M
elastico^M

bedroom
dormitorio^M
chambre^F
Schlafraum^M
camera^F da letto^M

sewn-in floor
piso^M cosido
tapis^M de sol^M cousu
eingenähter Boden^M
fondo^M

wall
muro^M
mur^M
Zeltwand^F
parete^F

stake loop
presilla^F de estaquilla^F
boucle^F de piquet^M
Heringsschlaufe^F
asola^F per il picchetto^M

canvas divider
lona^F de separación^F
cloison^F
Raumteiler^M
divisorio^M di tela^F

frame
armadura^F
armature^F
Gestänge^N
intelaiatura^F

screen window
ventana^F-mosquitero^M
fenêtre^F moustiquaire^F
Fliegenfenster^N
finestra^F zanzariera

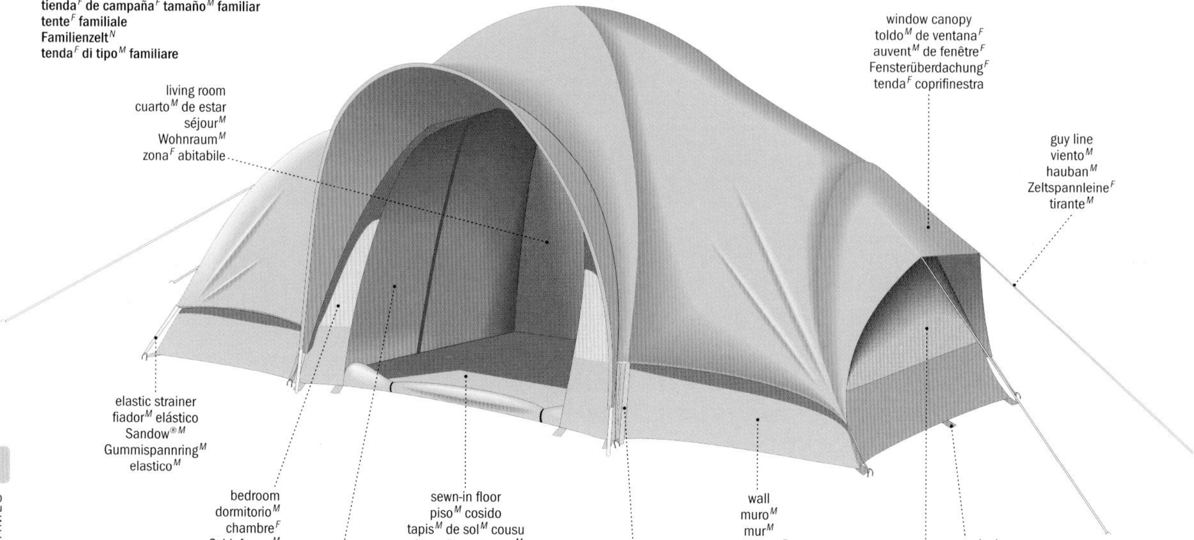

wagon tent
tienda^F tipo^M vagón^M
tente^F grange^F
Mannschaftszelt^N
tenda^F da cucina^F

wall tent
tienda^F rectangular
tente^F rectangulaire
Steilwandzelt^N
tenda^F da campo^M

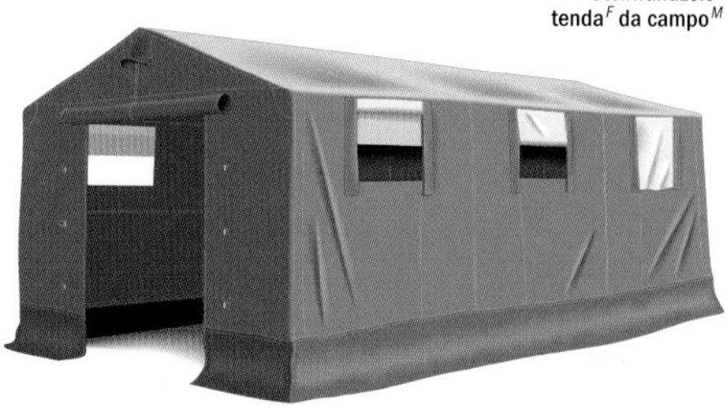

pup tent
tienda^F de campaña^F clásica
tente^F canadienne
Hauszelt^N
tenda^F canadese

rainfly
doble toldo^M
double toit^M
Überdach^N
telo^M esterno

roof pole
palo^M de la tienda^F
mât^M de toit^M
Zeltstange^F
palo^M frontale

inner tent
tienda^F interior
tente^F intérieure
Innenzelt^N
tenda^F interna

elastic strainer
fiador^M elástico
Sandow®^{M}
Gummispannring^M
elastico^M

door
puerta^F
porte^F
Eingang^M
porta^F

stake loop
presilla^F de estaquilla^F
boucle^F de piquet^M
Heringsschlaufe^F
asola^F per il picchetto^M

sewn-in floor
piso^M cosido
tapis^M de sol^M cousu
eingenähter Boden^M
fondo^M

stake
estaquilla^F
piquet^M
Hering^M
picchetto^M

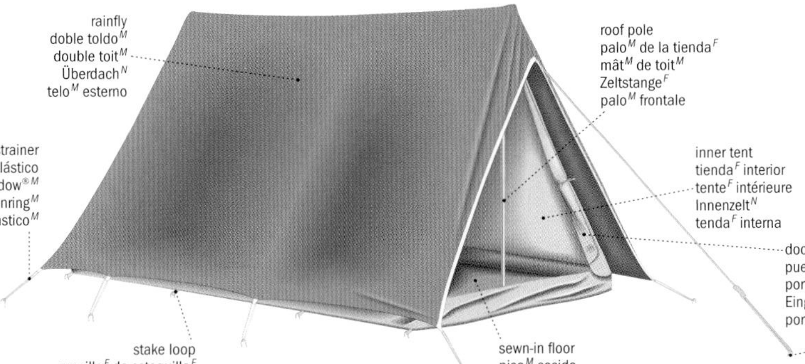

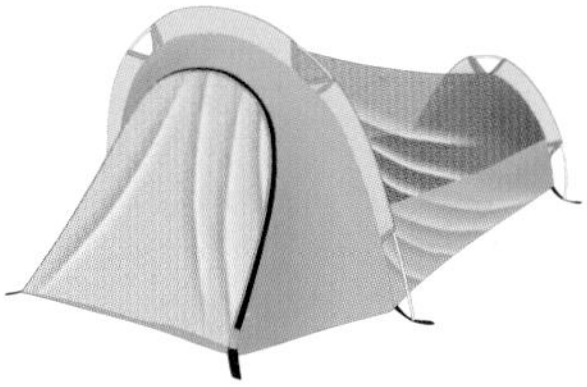

one-person tent
tienda^F unipersonal
tente^F individuelle
Einpersonenzelt^N
tenda^F a un posto^M

dome tent
tienda^F tipo^M domo^M
tente^F dôme^M
Kuppelzelt^N
tenda^F a cupola^F

pop-up tent
tienda^F tipo^M iglú^M
tente^F igloo^M
Igluzelt^N
tenda^F a igloo^M

lantern
linterna^F
lanterne^F
Lampe^F
lanterna^F

globe
globo^M
globe^M
Glas^N
globo^M di vetro^M

pump
bomba^F
pompe^F
Pumpe^F
pompa^F

burner frame
armazón^M del quemador^M
bâti^M du brûleur^M
Brennsockel^M
telaio^M del bruciatore^M

pressure regulator
regulador^M de presión^F
régulateur^M de pression^F
Gasstromregulierung^F
regolatore^M di luminosità^F

leakproof cap
tapón^M hermético
bouchon^F antifuite
Dichtverschluss^M
capsula^F ermetica

tank
tanque^M
réservoir^M
Gasbehälter^M
bombola^F

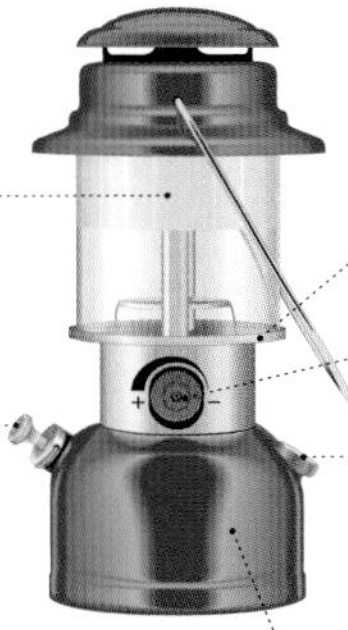

propane or butane accessories
equipos^M de gas^M
accessoires^M au propane^M ou au butane^M
Propan- oder Butangas-Geräte^N
accessori^M a propano^M o butano^M

heater
calentador^M
chaufferette^F
Heizstrahler^M
stufa^F a gas^M

double-burner camp stove
cocina^F de campo^M
réchaud^M à deux feux^M
zweiflammiger Gasbrenner^M
fornello^M da campo^M a due fuochi^M

tank
bombona^F de gas^M
réservoir^M
Gasbehälter^M
bombola^F

burner
quemador^M
brûleur^M
Brenner^M
bruciatore^M

wire support
parrilla^F estabilizadora
grille^F stabilisatrice
Metallaufsatz^M
griglia^F

single-burner camp stove
hornillo^M
réchaud^M à un feu^M
einflammiger Gasbrenner^M
fornello^M da campo^M con un bruciatore^M

control valve
válvula^F de control^M
robinet^M relais^M
Reglerventil^N
manopola^F di regolazione^F del gas^M

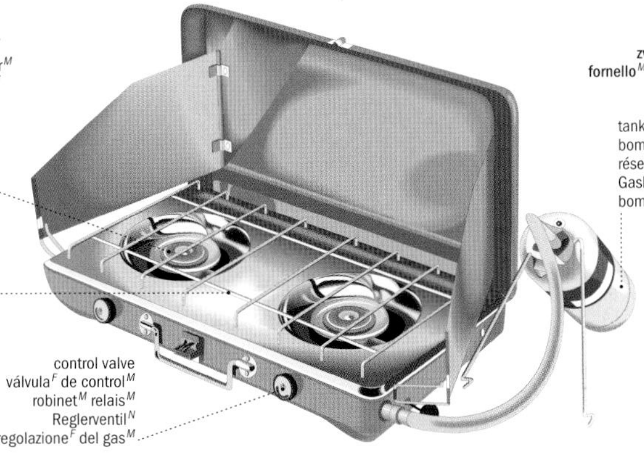

camping

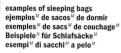

examples of sleeping bags
ejemplos^M de sacos^M de dormir
exemples^M de sacs^M de couchage^M
Beispiele^N für Schlafsäcke^M
esempi^M di sacchi^M a pelo^M

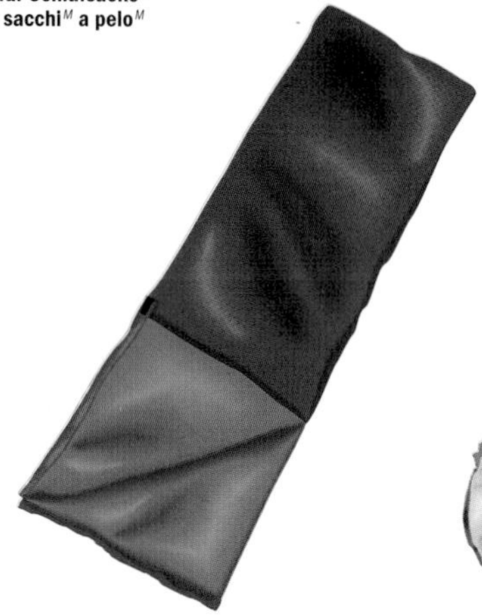

rectangular
saco^M rectangular
rectangulaire
Rechteckschlafsack^M
rettangolare

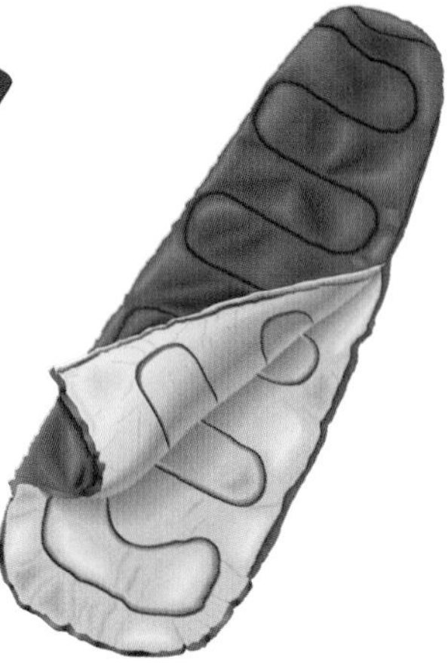

semi-mummy
saco^M semirrectangular
semi-rectangulaire
Halbmumienschlafsack^M
semi-mummia^F

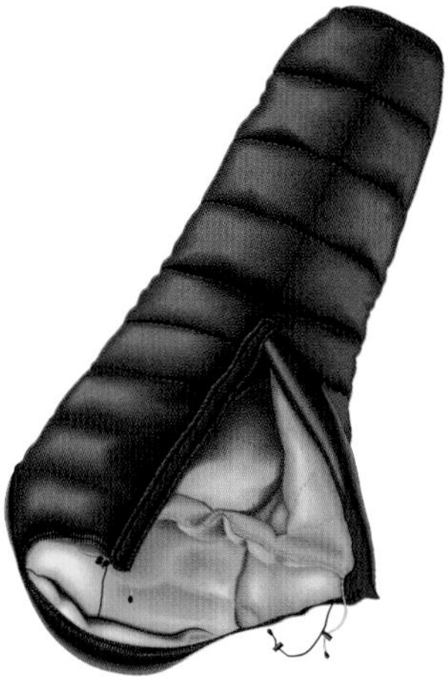

mummy
de momia^F
à cagoule^F
Mumienschlafsack^M
mummia^F

bed and mattress
camas^F y colchonetas^F
lit^M et matelas^M
Bett^N mit Matratze^F
branda^F e materassino^M

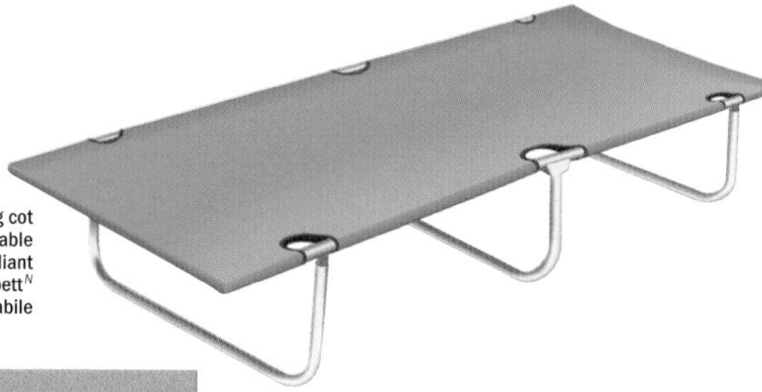

folding cot
catre^M desmontable
lit^M de camp^M pliant
Feldbett^N
brandina^F smontabile

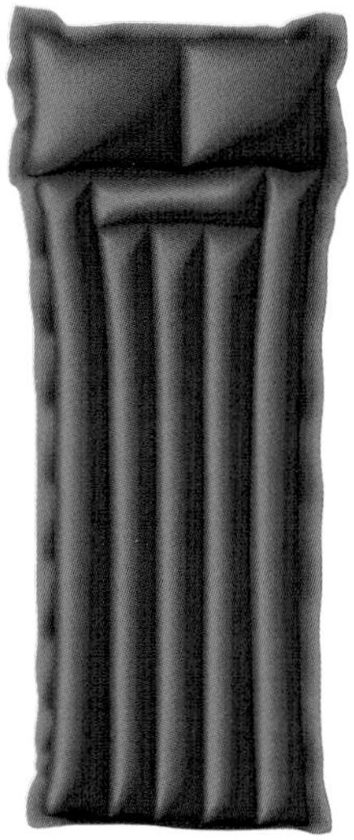

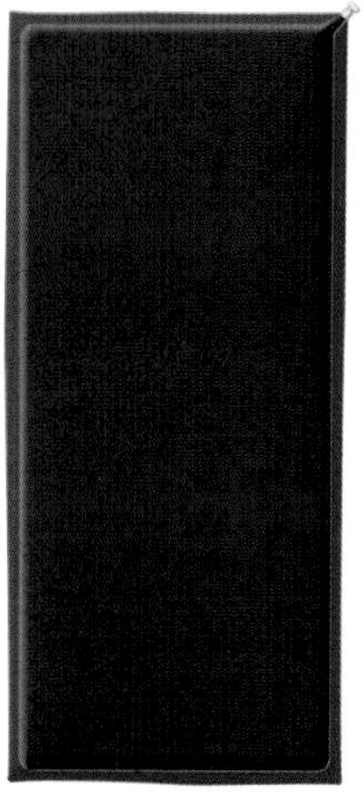

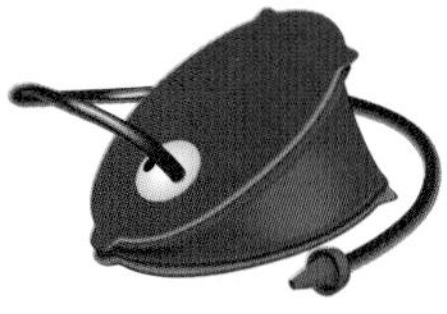

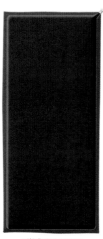

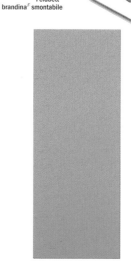

inflator-deflator
muelle^M para inflar y desinflar
gonfleur^M-dégonfleur^M
Kombipumpe^F
gonfiatore^M a soffietto^M

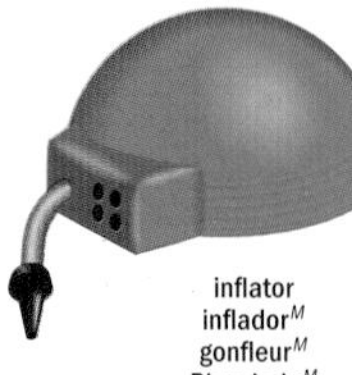

inflator
inflador^M
gonfleur^M
Blasebalg^M
gonfiatore^M

air mattress
colchoneta^F de aire^M
matelas^M pneumatique
Luftmatratze^F
materassino^M pneumatico

self-inflating mattress
colchoneta^F aislante
matelas^M autogonflant
selbstaufblasbare Luftmatratze^F
materassino^M autogonfiante

foam pad
colchoneta^F de espuma^F
matelas^M mousse^F
Schaumgummimatratze^F
materassino^M isolante

SPORTS AND GAMES

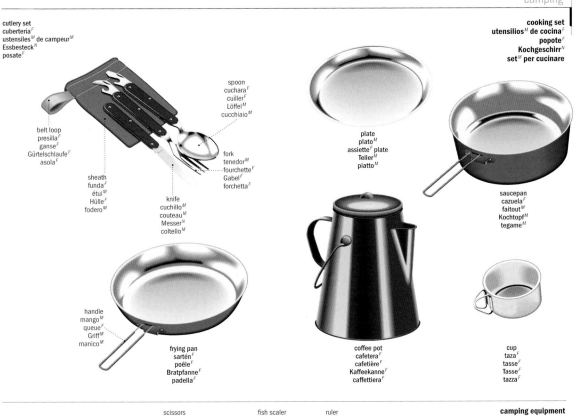

cutlery set
cubertería^F
ustensiles^M de campeur^M
Essbesteck^N
posate^F

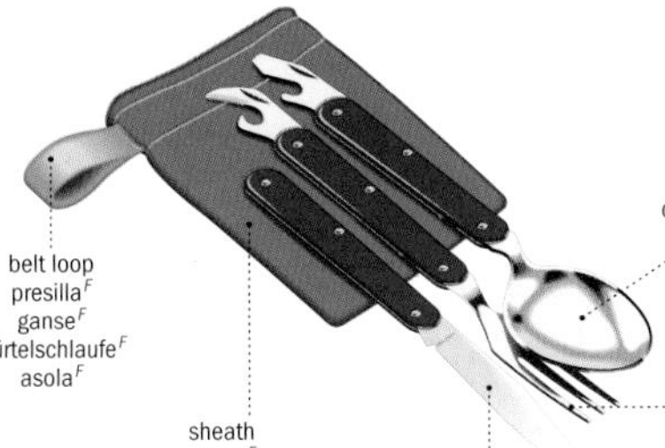

cooking set
utensilios^M de cocina^F
popote^F
Kochgeschirr^N
set^M per cucinare

spoon
cuchara^F
cuiller^F
Löffel^M
cucchiaio^M

belt loop
presilla^F
ganse^F
Gürtelschlaufe^F
asola^F

fork
tenedor^M
fourchette^F
Gabel^F
forchetta^F

sheath
funda^F
étui^M
Hülle^F
fodero^M

knife
cuchillo^M
couteau^M
Messer^N
coltello^M

plate
plato^M
assiette^F plate
Teller^M
piatto^M

saucepan
cazuela^F
faitout^M
Kochtopf^M
tegame^M

handle
mango^M
queue^F
Griff^M
manico^M

frying pan
sartén^F
poêle^F
Bratpfanne^F
padella^F

coffee pot
cafetera^F
cafetière^F
Kaffeekanne^F
caffettiera^F

cup
taza^F
tasse^F
Tasse^F
tazza^F

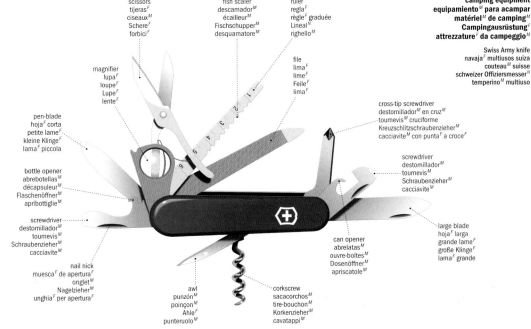

scissors
tijeras^F
ciseaux^M
Schere^F
forbici^F

fish scaler
descamador^M
écailleur^M
Fischschupper^M
desquamatore^M

ruler
regla^F
règle^F graduée
Lineal^N
righello^M

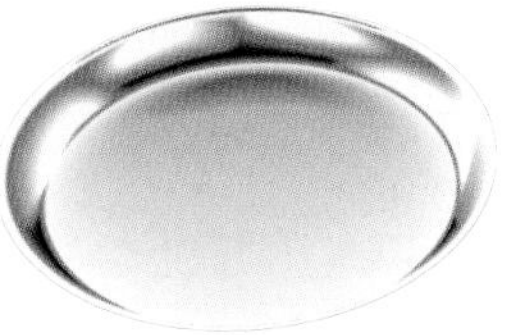

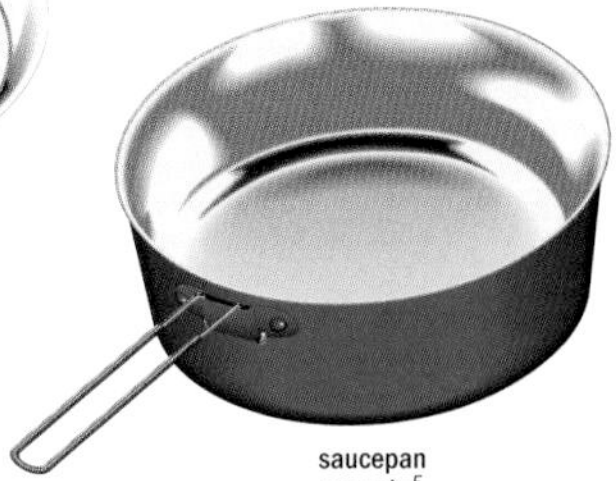

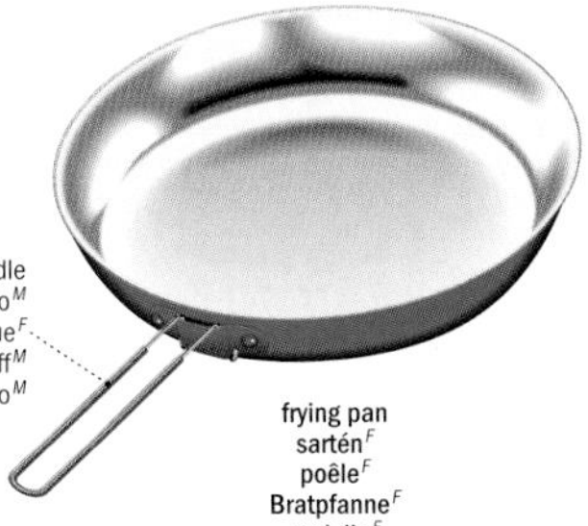

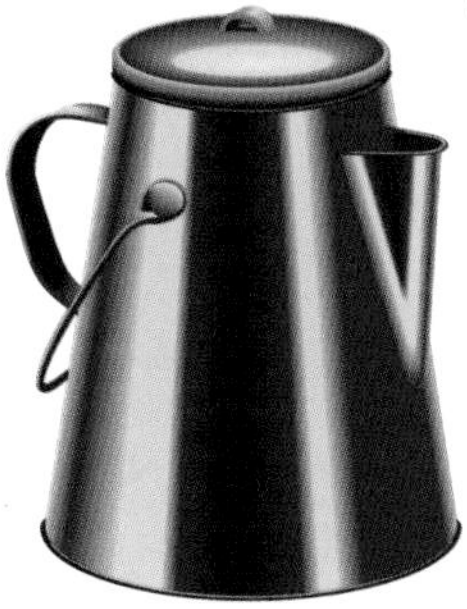

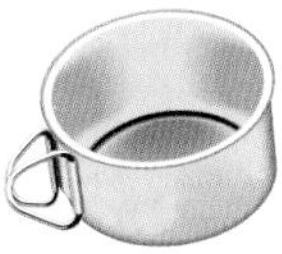

camping equipment
equipamiento^M para acampar
matériel^M de camping^M
Campingausrüstung^F
attrezzature^F da campeggio^M

magnifier
lupa^F
loupe^F
Lupe^F
lente^F

file
lima^F
lime^F
Feile^F
lima^F

Swiss Army knife
navaja^F multiusos suiza
couteau^M suisse
schweizer Offiziersmesser^N
temperino^M multiuso

pen-blade
hoja^F corta
petite lame^F
kleine Klinge^F
lama^F piccola

cross-tip screwdriver
destornillador^M en cruz^M
tournevis^M cruciforme
Kreuzschlitzschraubenzieher^M
cacciavite^M con punta^F a croce^F

bottle opener
abrebotellas^M
décapsuleur^M
Flaschenöffner^M
apribottiglie^M

screwdriver
destornillador^M
tournevis^M
Schraubenzieher^M
cacciavite^M

screwdriver
destornillador^M
tournevis^M
Schraubenzieher^M
cacciavite^M

large blade
hoja^F larga
grande lame^F
große Klinge^F
lama^F grande

nail nick
muesca^F de apertura^F
onglet^M
Nagelzieher^M
unghia^F per apertura^F

can opener
abrelatas^M
ouvre-boîtes^M
Dosenöffner^M
apriscatole^M

awl
punzón^M
poinçon^M
Ahle^F
punteruolo^M

corkscrew
sacacorchos^M
tire-bouchon^M
Korkenzieher^M
cavatappi^M

SPORTS AND GAMES

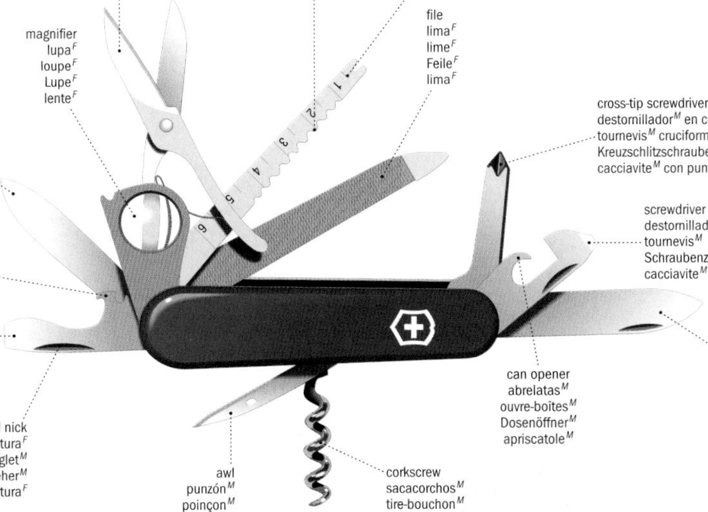

camping

backpack
mochila^F
sac^M à dos^M
Rucksack^M
zaino^M

top flap
solapa^F
rabat^M
Deckeltasche^F
patta^F di chiusura^F

shoulder strap
espaldera^F
bretelle^F
Schultergurt^M
spallaccio^M

tightening buckle
hebilla^F de regulación^F
boucle^F de réglage^M
Schließe^F
fibbia^F di regolazione^F

side compression strap
correa^F de compresión^F
sangle^F de compression^F
seitlicher Kompressionsgurt^M
cinghia^F di compressione^F laterale

front compression strap
correa^F de cierre^M
sangle^F de fermeture^F
vorderer Straffergurt^M
cinghia^F di compressione^F frontale

strap loop
pasador^M
passe-sangle^M
Riemenschlaufe^F
passacinghia^M

hip belt
cinturón^M
ceinture^F
Hüftgurt^M
cintura^F a vita^F

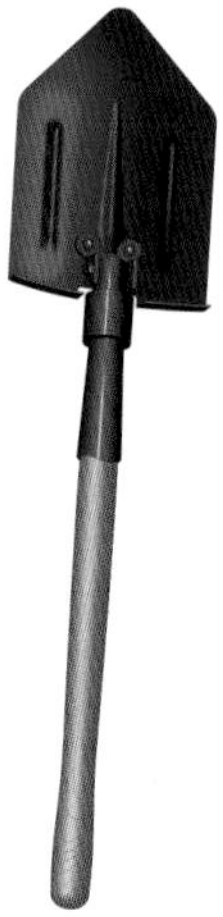

folding shovel
pala^F plegable
pelle^F-pioche^F pliante
Klappspaten^M
badile^M pieghevole

hurricane lamp
lámpara^F de petróleo^M
lampe^F-tempête^F
Sturmlampe^F
lampada^F a petrolio^M

vacuum bottle
termo^M
bouteille^F isolante
Thermosflasche^F
thermos^M

bottle
botella^F del termo^M
bouteille^F
Flasche^F
bottiglia^F

stopper
tapón^M
bouchon^M
Verschluss^M
tappo^M

cup
taza^F
tasse^F
Becher^M
bicchiere^M

canteen
cantimplora^F
gourde^F
Feldflasche^F
borraccia^F

cooler
nevera^F
glacière^F
Kühlbox^F
frigo^M portatile

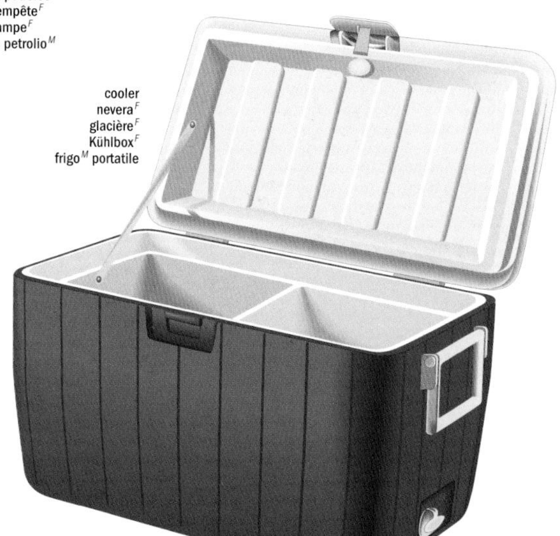

water carrier
termo^M con llave^F de servicio^M
cruche^F
Wasserkanister^M
contenitore^M termico

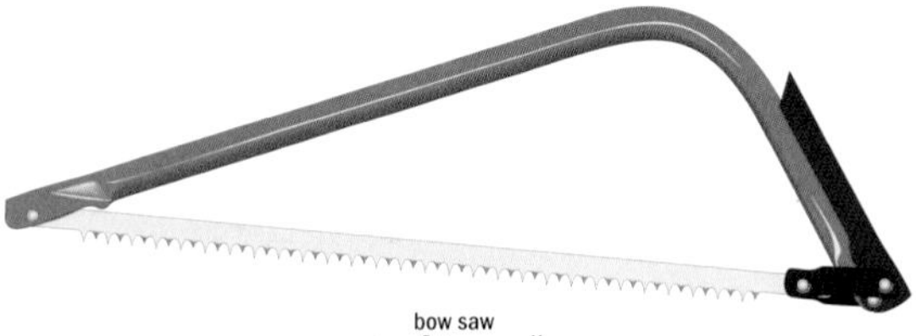

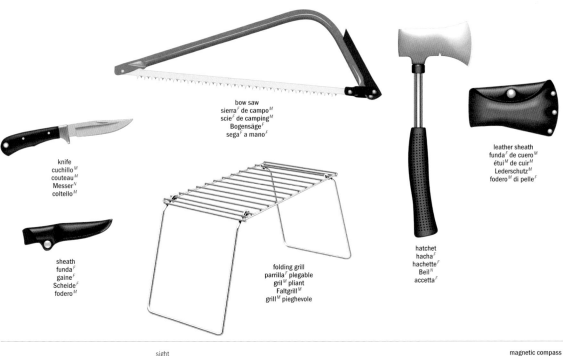

bow saw
sierra^F de campo^M
scie^F de camping^M
Bogensäge^F
sega^F a mano^F

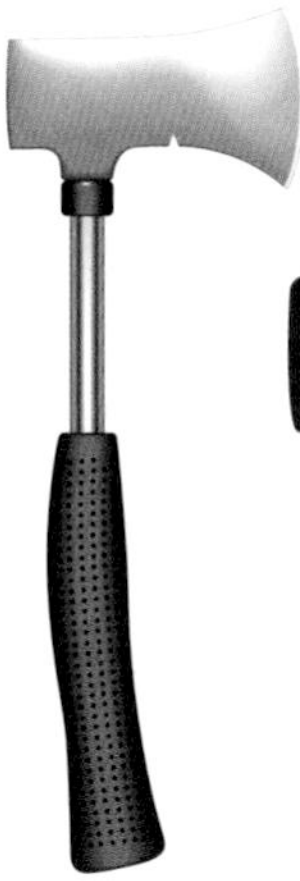

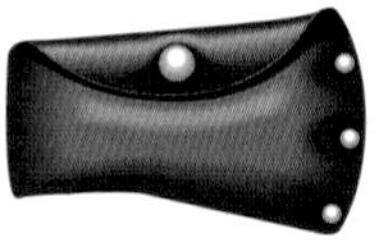

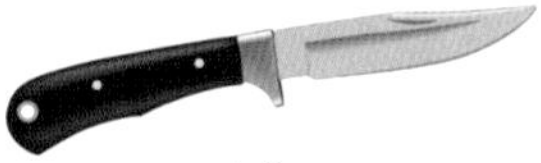

knife
cuchillo^M
couteau^M
Messer^N
coltello^M

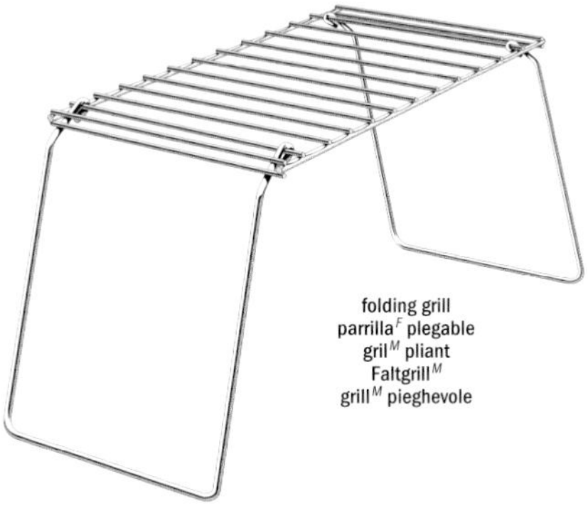

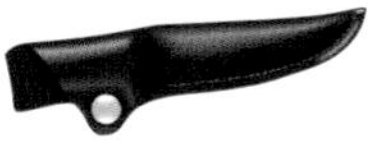

sheath
funda^F
gaine^F
Scheide^F
fodero^M

folding grill
parrilla^F plegable
gril^M pliant
Faltgrill^M
grill^M pieghevole

leather sheath
funda^F de cuero^M
étui^M de cuir^M
Lederschutz^M
fodero^M di pelle^F

hatchet
hacha^F
hachette^F
Beil^N
accetta^F

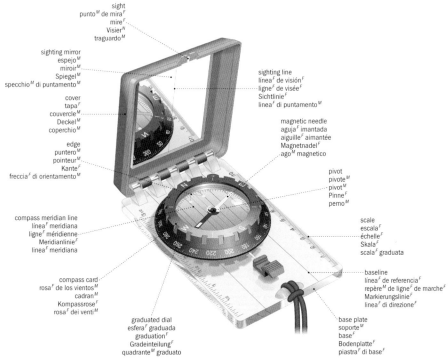

sight
punto^M de mira^F
mire^F
Visier^N
traguardo^M

sighting mirror
espejo^M
miroir^M
Spiegel^M
specchio^M di puntamento^M

cover
tapa^F
couvercle^M
Deckel^M
coperchio^M

edge
puntero^M
pointeur^M
Kante^F
freccia^F di orientamento^M

compass meridian line
línea^F meridiana
ligne^F méridienne
Meridianlinie^F
linea^F meridiana

compass card
rosa^F de los vientos^M
cadran^M
Kompassrose^F
rosa^F dei venti^M

graduated dial
esfera^F graduada
graduation^F
Gradeinteilung^F
quadrante^M graduato

sighting line
línea^F de visión^F
ligne^F de visée^F
Sichtlinie^F
linea^F di puntamento^M

magnetic needle
aguja^F imantada
aiguille^F aimantée
Magnetnadel^F
ago^M magnetico

pivot
pivote^M
pivot^M
Pinne^F
perno^M

scale
escala^F
échelle^F
Skala^F
scala^F graduata

baseline
línea^F de referencia^F
repère^M de ligne^F de marche^F
Markierungslinie^F
linea^F di direzione^F

base plate
soporte^M
base^F
Bodenplatte^F
piastra^F di base^F

magnetic compass
brújula^F magnética
boussole^F magnétique
Magnetkompass^M
bussola^F magnetica

SPORTS AND GAMES

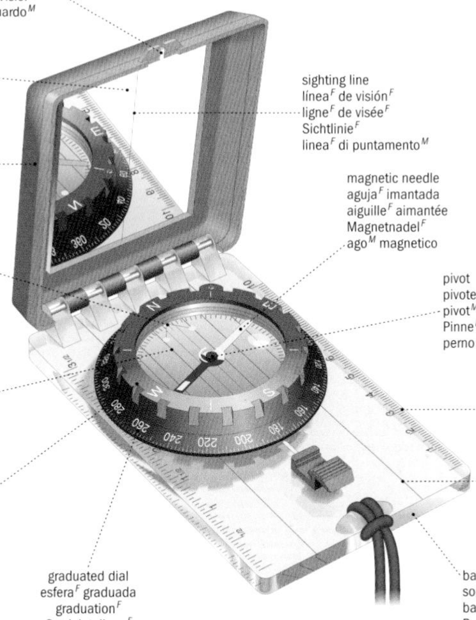

knots

nudos^M | nœuds^M | Knoten^M | nodi^M

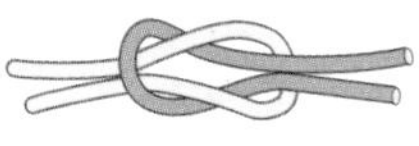

square knot
nudo^M de rizo^M
nœud^M plat
Kreuzknoten^M
nodo^M piano

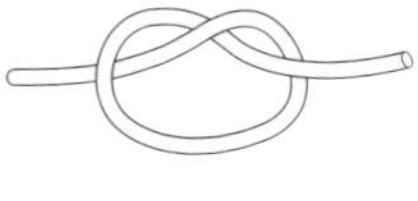

overhand knot
nudo^M llano
nœud^M simple
Hausfrauenknoten^M
nodo^M semplice

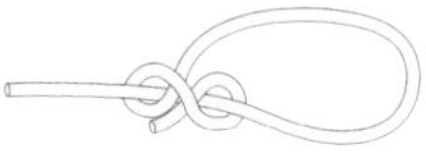

running bowline
balso^M
nœud^M coulant
laufender Pahlstek^M
nodo^M scorsoio

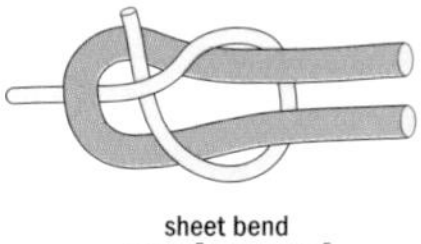

sheet bend
vuelta^F de escota^F
nœud^M d'écoute^F simple
einfacher Schotstek^M
nodo^M di scotta^F semplice

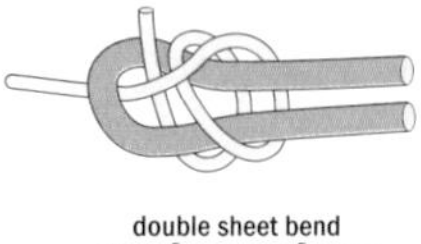

double sheet bend
vuelta^F de escota^F doble
nœud^M d'écoute^F double
doppelter Schotstek^M
nodo^M di scotta^F doppio

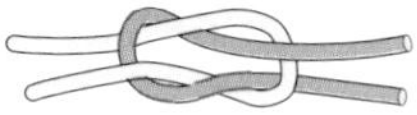

granny knot
nudo^M de tejedor^M
nœud^M de vache^F
Altweiberknoten^M
nodo^M vaccaio

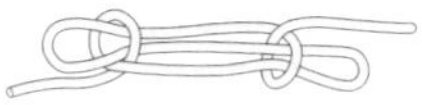

sheepshank
margarita^F
nœud^M de jambe^F de chien^M
Verkürzungsstek^M
nodo^M a margherita^F

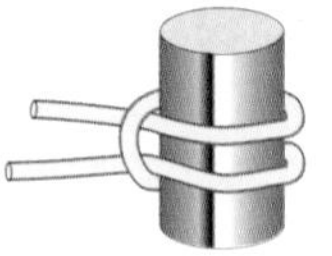

cow hitch
vuelta^F de cabo^M
demi-clé^F renversée
Kuhstek^M
nodo^M bocca^F di lupo^M

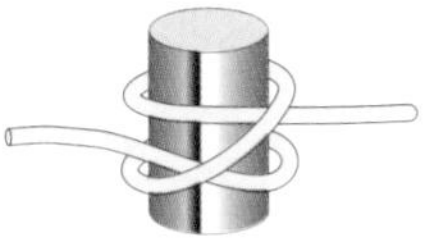

clove hitch
nudo^M de dos cotes^M
nœud^M de cabestan^M
Slipstek^M
nodo^M parlato semplice

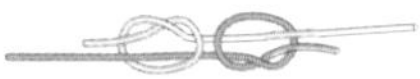

fisherman's knot
nudo^M de pescador^M
nœud^M de pêcheur^M
Fischerknoten^M
nodo^M del pescatore^M

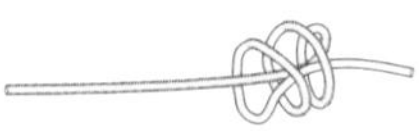

heaving line knot
nudo^M de guía^F
nœud^M de Franciscain^M
Wurflinienknoten^M
nodo^M parlato doppio

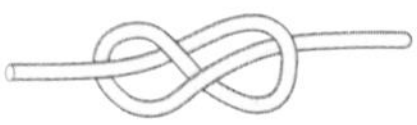

figure-eight knot
lasca^F doble
nœud^M d'arrêt^M
Achtknoten^M
nodo^M Savoia

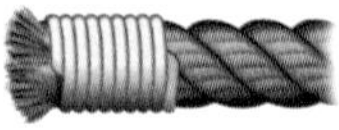

common whipping
sobrenudo^M
surliure^F
einfacher Takling^M
impalmatura^F normale

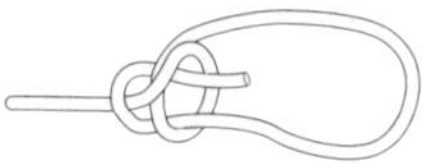

bowline
as^M de guía^F
nœud^M de chaise^F simple
Pahlstek^M
gassa^F d'amante^M

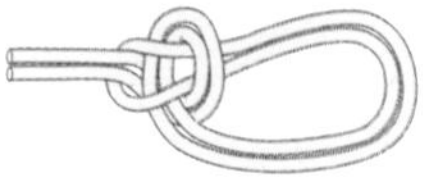

bowline on a bight
as^M de guía^F de eslinga^F doble
nœud^M de chaise^F double
doppelter Pahlstek^M
gassa^F d'amante^M doppia

---

short splice
empalmadura^F
épissure^F courte
Spleiß^M
impiombatura^F corta

forming
conformación^F
début^M
Flechten^N
avvio^M

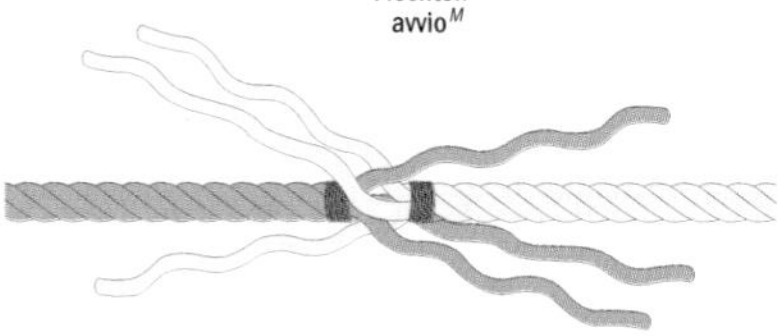

completion
acabado^M
fin^F
fertige Verbindung^F
completamento^M

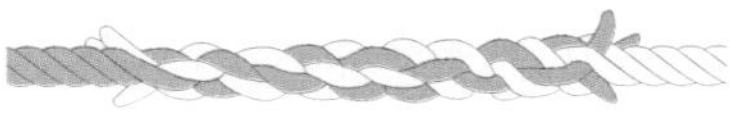

cable
cable^M
câble^M
Tauwerk^N
cavo^M

twisted rope
cable^M torcido
cordage^M commis
gedrehtes Seil^N
corda^F attorcigliata

braided rope
cable^M trenzado
cordage^M tressé
geflochtenes Seil^N
corda^F intrecciata

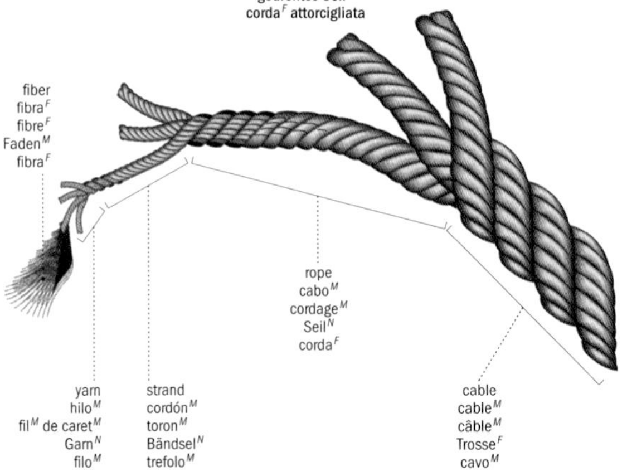

fiber
fibra^F
fibre^F
Faden^M
fibra^F

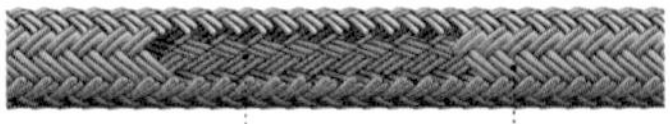

core
núcleo^M
âme^F
Kern^M
anima^F

sheath
forro^M
gaine^F
Mantel^M
guaina^F di protezione^F

rope
cabo^M
cordage^M
Seil^N
corda^F

yarn
hilo^M
fil^M de caret^M
Garn^N
filo^M

strand
cordón^M
toron^M
Bändsel^N
trefolo^M

cable
cable^M
câble^M
Trosse^F
cavo^M

fishing

pesca^F | pêche^F | Sportfischerei^F | pesca^F

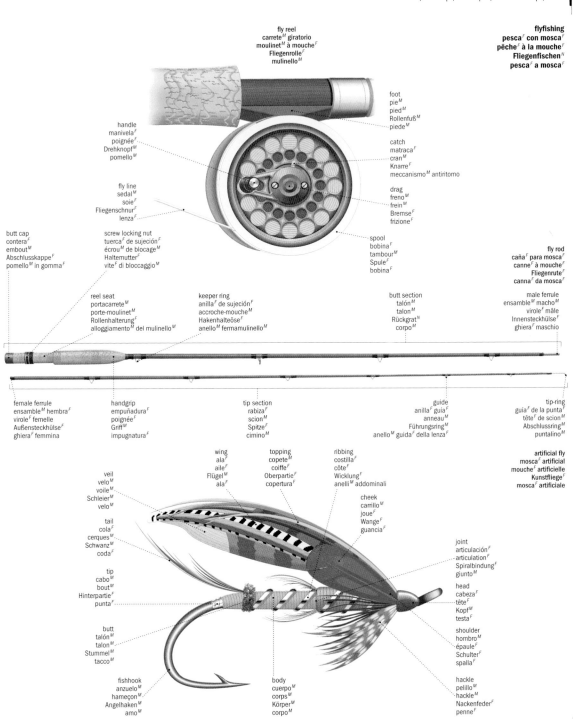

fly reel
carrete^M giratorio
moulinet^M à mouche^F
Fliegenrolle^F
mulinello^M

flyfishing
pesca^F con mosca^F
pêche^F à la mouche^F
Fliegenfischen^N
pesca^F a mosca^F

foot
pie^M
pied^M
Rollenfuß^M
piede^M

handle
manivela^F
poignée^F
Drehknopf^M
pomello^M

catch
matraca^F
cran^M
Knarre^F
meccanismo^M antiritorno

fly line
sedal^M
soie^F
Fliegenschnur^F
lenza^F

drag
freno^M
frein^M
Bremse^F
frizione^F

butt cap
contera^F
embout^M
Abschlusskappe^F
pomello^M in gomma^F

screw locking nut
tuerca^F de sujeción^F
écrou^M de blocage^M
Haltemutter^F
vite^F di bloccaggio^M

spool
bobina^F
tambour^M
Spule^F
bobina^F

fly rod
caña^F para mosca^F
canne^F à mouche^F
Fliegenrute^F
canna^F da mosca^F

reel seat
portacarrete^M
porte-moulinet^M
Rollenhalterung^F
alloggiamento^M del mulinello^M

keeper ring
anilla^F de sujeción^F
accroche-mouche^F
Hakenhalteöse^F
anello^M fermamulinello^M

butt section
talón^M
talon^M
Rückgrat^N
corpo^M

male ferrule
ensamble^M macho^M
virole^F mâle
Innensteckhülse^F
ghiera^F maschio

female ferrule
ensamble^M hembra^F
virole^F femelle
Außensteckhülse^F
ghiera^F femmina

handgrip
empuñadura^F
poignée^F
Griff^M
impugnatura^F

tip section
rabiza^F
scion^M
Spitze^F
cimino^M

guide
anilla^F guía^F
anneau^M
Führungsring^M
anello^M guida^F della lenza^F

tip-ring
guía^F de la punta^F
tête^F de scion^M
Abschlussring^M
puntalino^M

wing
ala^F
aile^F
Flügel^M
ala^F

topping
copete^M
coiffe^F
Oberpartie^F
copertura^F

ribbing
costilla^F
côte^F
Wicklung^F
anelli^M addominali

artificial fly
mosca^F artificial
mouche^F artificielle
Kunstfliege^F
mosca^F artificiale

veil
velo^M
voile^F
Schleier^M
velo^M

cheek
carrillo^M
joue^F
Wange^F
guancia^F

tail
cola^F
cerques^M
Schwanz^M
coda^F

joint
articulación^F
articulation^F
Spiralbindung^F
giunto^M

tip
cabo^M
bout^M
Hinterpartie^F
punta^F

head
cabeza^F
tête^F
Kopf^M
testa^F

butt
talón^M
talon^M
Stummel^M
tacco^M

shoulder
hombro^M
épaule^F
Schulter^F
spalla^F

fishhook
anzuelo^M
hameçon^M
Angelhaken^M
amo^M

body
cuerpo^M
corps^M
Körper^M
corpo^M

hackle
pelillo^M
hackle^M
Nackenfeder^F
penne^F

SPORTS AND GAMES

909

fishing

casting
pesca^F de lanzado^M
pêche^F au lancer^M
Casting^N
pesca^F al lancio^M

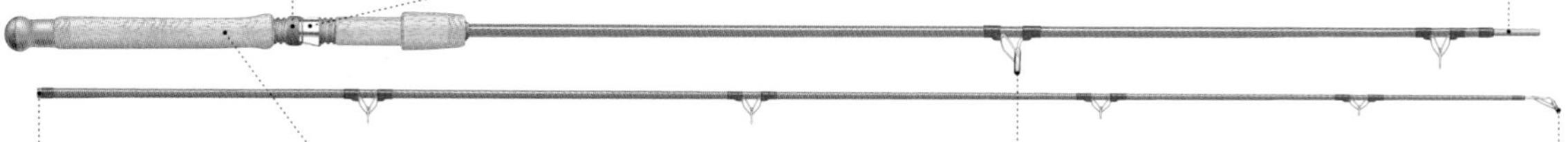

spinning rod
caña^F para lanzado^M
canne^F à lancer^M
Spinnrute^F
canna^F da lancio^M

screw locking nut
fijador^M de carrete^M
écrou^M de blocage^M
Haltemutter^F
vite^F di bloccaggio^M

reel seat
portacarrete^M
porte-moulinet^M
Rollenhalterung^F
alloggiamento^M del mulinello^M

male ferrule
virola^F macho
virole^F mâle
Außengewinde^N
ghiera^F maschio

female ferrule
virola^F hembra
virole^F femelle
Innengewinde^N
ghiera^F femmina

butt grip
mango^M posterior
poignée^F arrière
Rutengriff^M
impugnatura^F

butt guide
anilla^F para lanzado^M largo
anneau^M de départ^M
erster Führungsring^M
anello^M guida^F della lenza^F

tip-ring
guía^F de la punta^F
anneau^M de tête^F
Abschlussring^M
puntalino^M

open-face spinning reel
carrete^M de bobina^F fija
moulinet^M à tambour^M fixe
offene Spinnrolle^F
mulinello^M a bobina^F fissa

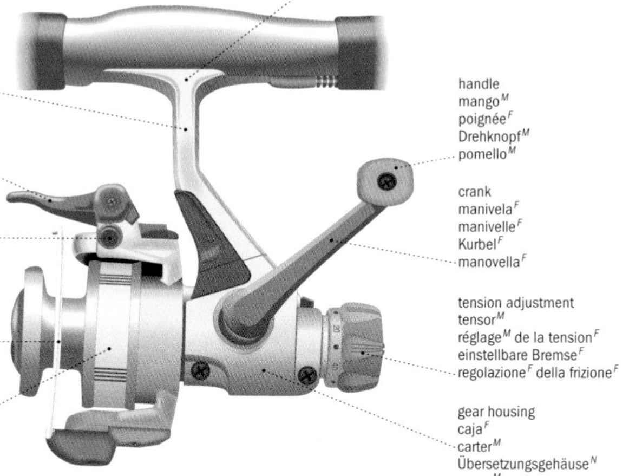

foot
talón^M
talon^M
Rollenhaltepartie^F
piede^M

leg
pata^F
pied^M
Rollenfuß^M
gambo^M

bail arm opening mechanism
freno^M
mécanisme^M d'ouverture^F de l'anse^F
Bügelspannmechanismus^M
meccanismo^M di apertura^F dell'archetto^M

line guide
asa^F
guide-ligne^M
Schnurlauffröllchen^N
guida^F del filo^M

bail arm
devanador^M
anse^F
Schnurfangbügel^M
archetto^M

spool
bobina^F
tambour^M
Spule^F
bobina^F

handle
mango^M
poignée^F
Drehknopf^M
pomello^M

crank
manivela^F
manivelle^F
Kurbel^F
manovella^F

tension adjustment
tensor^M
réglage^M de la tension^F
einstellbare Bremse^F
regolazione^F della frizione^F

gear housing
caja^F
carter^M
Übersetzungsgehäuse^N
carter^M

baitcasting reel
carrete^M de tambor^M
moulinet^M à tambour^M tournant
Multirolle^F
mulinello^M a bobina^F rotante

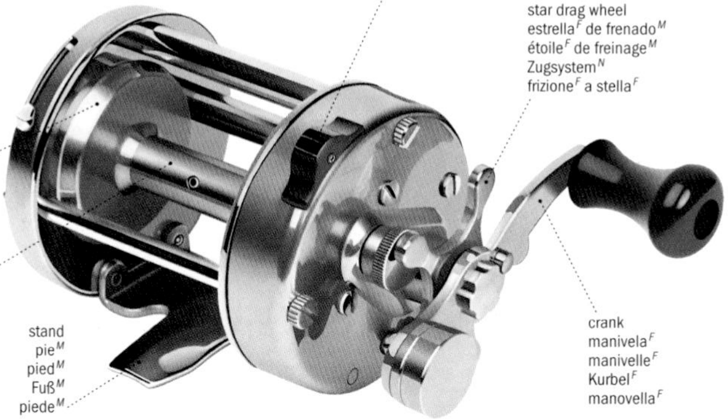

spool-release mechanism
disparador^M del tambor^M
mécanisme^M de débrayage^M du tambour^M
Schnappmechanismus^M
meccanismo^M di rilascio^M della bobina^F

star drag wheel
estrella^F de frenado^M
étoile^F de freinage^M
Zugsystem^N
frizione^F a stella^F

spool
tambor^M
tambour^M
Spule^F
bobina^F

spool axle
eje^M del tambor^M
axe^M de tambour^M
Spulenachse^F
asse^M della bobina^F

stand
pie^M
pied^M
Fuß^M
piede^M

crank
manivela^F
manivelle^F
Kurbel^F
manovella^F

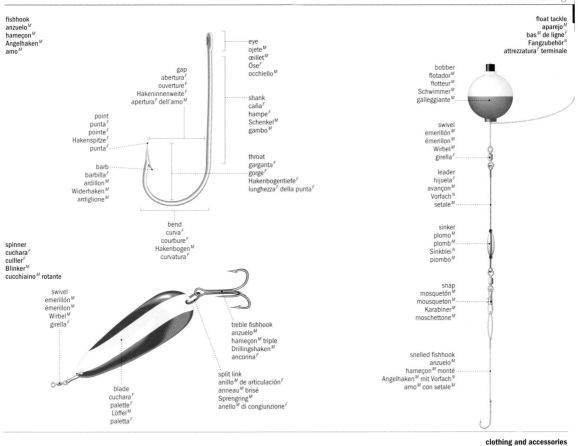

fishhook
anzuelo^M
hameçon^M
Angelhaken^M
amo^M

eye
ojete^M
œillet^M
Öse^F
occhiello^M

gap
abertura^F
ouverture^F
Hakeninnenweite^F
apertura^F dell'amo^M

shank
caña^F
hampe^F
Schenkel^M
gambo^M

point
punta^F
pointe^F
Hakenspitze^F
punta^F

throat
garganta^F
gorge^F
Hakenbogentiefe^F
lunghezza^F della punta^F

barb
barbilla^F
ardillon^M
Widerhaken^M
ardiglione^M

bend
curva^F
courbure^F
Hakenbogen^M
curvatura^F

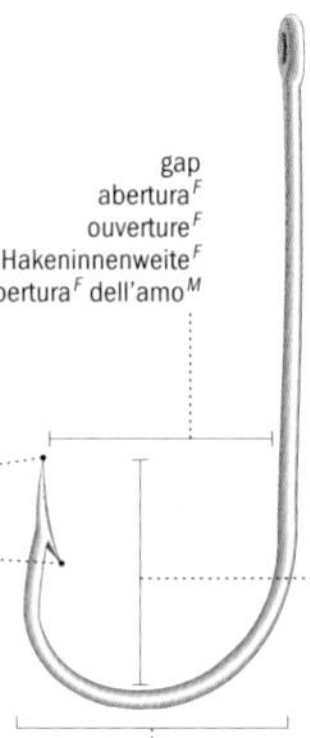

spinner
cuchara^F
cuiller^F
Blinker^M
cucchiaino^M rotante

swivel
emerillón^M
émerillon^M
Wirbel^M
girella^F

treble fishhook
anzuelo^M
hameçon^M triple
Drillingshaken^M
ancorina^F

split link
anillo^M de articulación^F
anneau^M brisé
Sprengring^M
anello^M di congiunzione^F

blade
cuchara^F
palette^F
Löffel^M
paletta^F

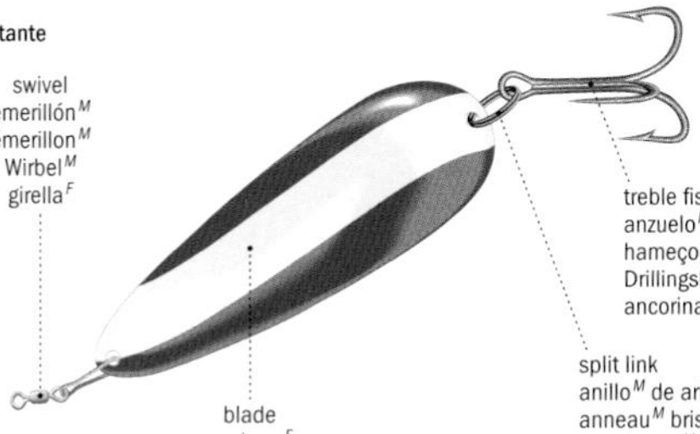

float tackle
aparejo^M
bas^M de ligne^F
Fangzubehör^N
attrezzatura^F terminale

bobber
flotador^M
flotteur^M
Schwimmer^M
galleggiante^M

swivel
emerillón^M
émerillon^M
Wirbel^M
girella^F

leader
hijuela^F
avançon^M
Vorfach^N
setale^M

sinker
plomo^M
plomb^M
Sinkblei^N
piombo^M

snap
mosquetón^M
mousqueton^M
Karabiner^M
moschettone^M

snelled fishhook
anzuelo^M
hameçon^M monté
Angelhaken^M mit Vorfach^N
amo^M con setale^M

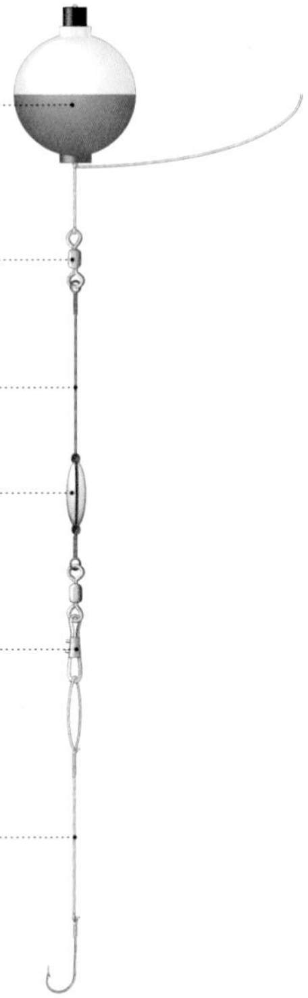

clothing and accessories
ropa^F y accesorios^M
vêtements^M et accessoires^M
Kleidung^F und Zubehör^N
abbigliamento^M e accessori^M

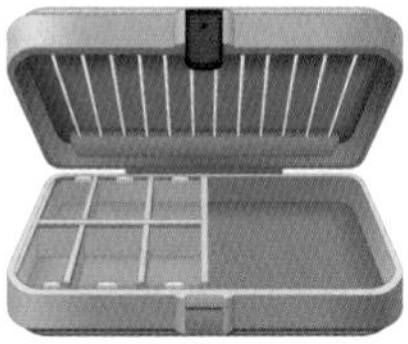

tackle box
caja^F de pesca^F
boîte^F à leurres^M
Spinnerschachtel^F
scatola^F portaesche^F

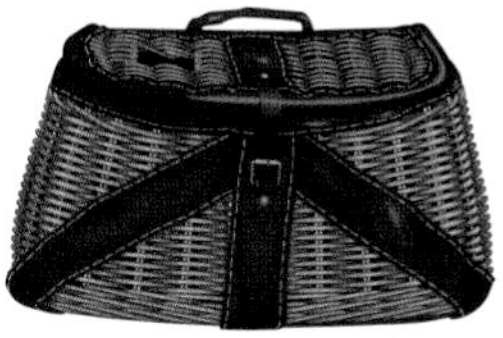

creel
cesta^F de pescador^M
panier^M
Fischkorb^M
cestino^M

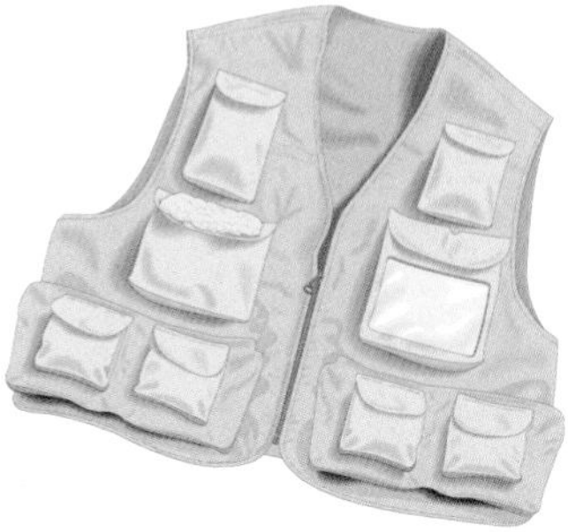

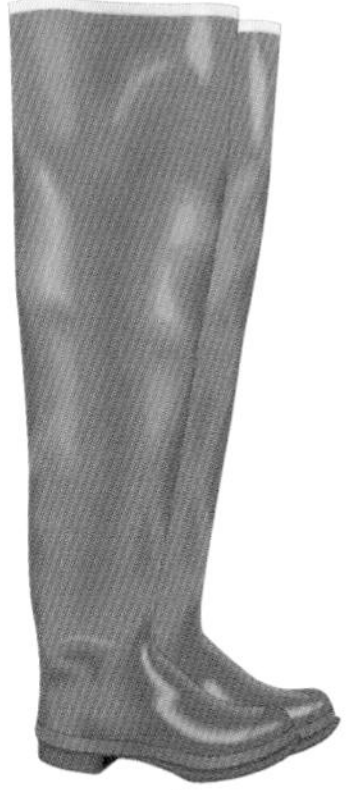

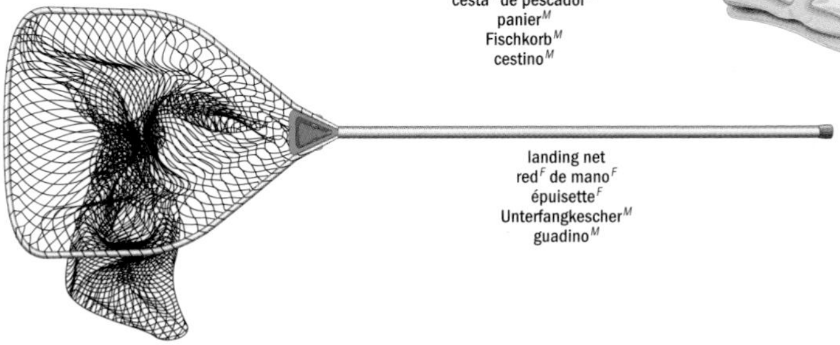

landing net
red^F de mano^F
épuisette^F
Unterfangkescher^M
guadino^M

fishing vest
chaleco^M de pescador^M
veste^F de pêche^F
Anglerweste^F
giubbotto^M da pescatore^M

waders
botas^F altas
cuissardes^F
Watstiefel^M
stivaloni^M impermeabili

hunting

caza[F] | chasse[F] | Jagen[N] | caccia[F]

rifle (rifled bore)
rifle[M]
carabine[F] (canon[M] rayé)
Gewehr[N] (gezogener Lauf[M])
fucile[M] a canna[F] rigata

pistol grip
empuñadura[F]
poignée[F]
Kolbenhals[M]
impugnatura[F] a pistola[F]

butt plate
cantonera[F]
plaque[F] de couche[F]
Rückschlaghinderer[M]
calciolo[M]

breechblock
bloque[M] de cierre[M] de la recámara[F]
bloc[M] de culasse[F]
Verschlussstück[N]
blocco[M] della culatta[F]

hammer
percutor[M]
chien[M]
Hahn[M]
cane[M]

telescopic sight
mira[F] telescópica
lunette[F] de visée[F]
Zielfernrohr[N]
mirino[M] a cannocchiale[M]

rear sight
alza[F]
hausse[F]
Kimme[F]
tacca[F] di mira[F]

muzzle
boca[F]
bouche[F]
Mündung[F]
bocca[F]

front sight
punto[M] de mira[F]
guidon[M]
Korn[N]
mirino[M]

trigger guard
guardamonte[M]
pontet[M]
Abzugbügel[M]
paragrilletto[M]

barrel
cañón[M]
canon[M]
Rohr[N]
canna[F]

stock
culata[F]
crosse[F]
Schäftung[F]
calcio[M]

lever
palanca[F]
levier[M]
Bügelhebel[M]
leva[F]

trigger
gatillo[M]
détente[F]
Abzug[M]
grilletto[M]

muzzle
boca[F]
bouche[F]
Mündung[F]
bocca[F]

shotgun (smooth-bore)
escopeta[F]
fusil[M] (canon[M] lisse)
Schrotflinte[F] (glatter Lauf[M])
fucile[M] a canna[F] liscia

pistol grip
empuñadura[F]
poignée[F]
Pistolengriff[M]
impugnatura[F] a pistola[F]

hammer
percutor[M]
chien[M]
Hahn[M]
cane[M]

ventilated rib
banda[F] de ventilación[F]
bande[F] ventilée
Laufschiene[F]
bindella[F] ventilata

front sight
punto[M] de mira[F]
guidon[M]
Korn[N]
mirino[M]

butt plate
cantonera[F]
plaque[F] de couche[F]
Rückschlaghinderer[M]
calciolo[M]

breechblock
bloque[M] de cierre[M] de recámara[F]
bloc[M] de culasse[F]
Verschlussstück[N]
blocco[M] della culatta[F]

forearm
caña[F]
fût[M]
Vorderschaft[M]
asta[F]

barrel
cañón[M]
canon[M]
Rohr[N]
canna[F]

stock
culata[F]
crosse[F]
Schäftung[F]
calcio[M]

trigger guard
guardamonte[M]
pontet[M]
Abzugbügel[M]
paragrilletto[M]

trigger
gatillo[M]
détente[F]
Abzug[M]
grilletto[M]

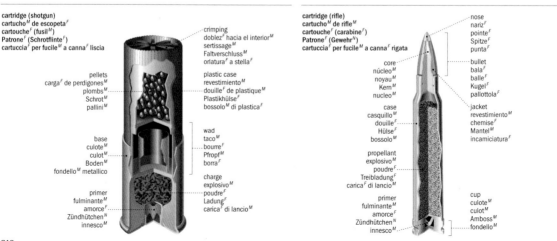

cartridge (shotgun)
cartucho[M] de escopeta[F]
cartouche[F] (fusil[M])
Patrone[F] (Schrotflinte[F])
cartuccia[F] per fucile[M] a canna[F] liscia

crimping
doblez[M] hacia el interior[M]
sertissage[M]
Faltverschluss[M]
orlatura[F] a stella[F]

pellets
carga[F] de perdigones[M]
plombs[M]
Schrot[M]
pallini[M]

plastic case
revestimiento[M]
douille[F] de plastique[M]
Plastikhülse[F]
bossolo[M] di plastica[F]

base
culote[M]
culot[M]
Boden[M]
fondello[M] metallico

wad
taco[M]
bourre[F]
Pfropf[M]
borra[F]

charge
explosivo[M]
poudre[F]
Ladung[F]
carica[F] di lancio[M]

primer
fulminante[M]
amorce[F]
Zündhütchen[N]
innesco[M]

cartridge (rifle)
cartucho[M] de rifle[M]
cartouche[F] (carabine[F])
Patrone[F] (Gewehr[N])
cartuccia[F] per fucile[M] a canna[F] rigata

nose
nariz[F]
pointe[F]
Spitze[F]
punta[F]

core
núcleo[M]
noyau[M]
Kern[M]
nucleo[M]

bullet
bala[F]
balle[F]
Kugel[F]
pallottola[F]

case
casquillo[M]
douille[F]
Hülse[F]
bossolo[M]

jacket
revestimiento[M]
chemise[F]
Mantel[M]
incamiciatura[F]

propellant
explosivo[M]
poudre[F]
Treibladung[F]
carica[F] di lancio[M]

primer
fulminante[M]
amorce[F]
Zündhütchen[N]
innesco[M]

cup
culote[M]
culot[M]
Amboss[M]
fondello[M]

jaws
mordazas ^{F}
mâchoires ^{F}
Bügel ^{M}
ganasce ^{F}

pan
paleta ^{F}
palette ^{F}
Teller ^{M}
perno ^{M}

spring
muelle ^{M}
ressort ^{M}
Feder ^{F}
molla ^{F}

spring
resorte ^{M}
ressort ^{M}
Feder ^{F}
molla ^{F}

dog
perro ^{M}
chien ^{M}
Trittplatte ^{F}
cane ^{M}

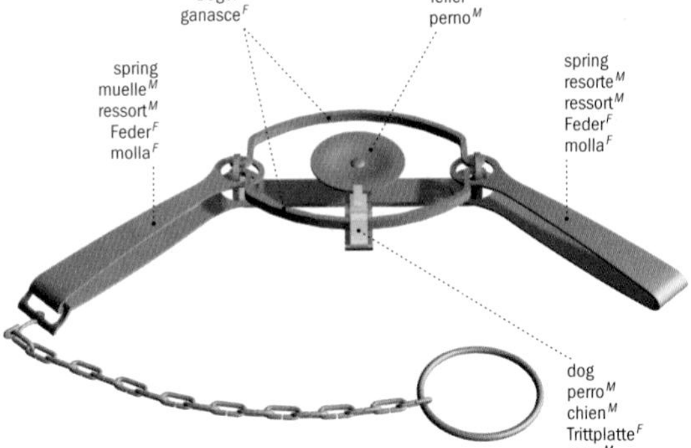

leghold trap
cepo ^{M}
piège ^{M} à patte ^{F} à mâchoires ^{F}
Tellereisen ^{N}
tagliola ^{F}

steel cable
cable ^{M} de acero ^{M}
câble ^{M} d'acier ^{M}
Stahldraht ^{M}
cavetto ^{M} di acciaio ^{M}

locking device
dispositivo ^{M} de cierre ^{M}
dispositif ^{M} de fermeture ^{F}
Verschluss ^{M}
dispositivo ^{M} di chiusura ^{F}

swivel
eslabón ^{M} giratorio
émerillon ^{M}
Wirbelschäkel ^{M}
girella ^{F}

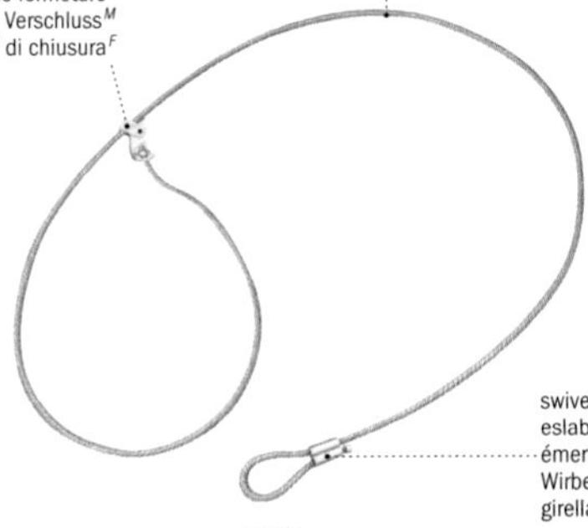

snare
lazo ^{M}
collet ^{M}
Schlinge ^{F}
laccio ^{M}

clip
enganche ^{M}
attache ^{F}
Öse ^{F}
anello ^{M} di attacco ^{M}

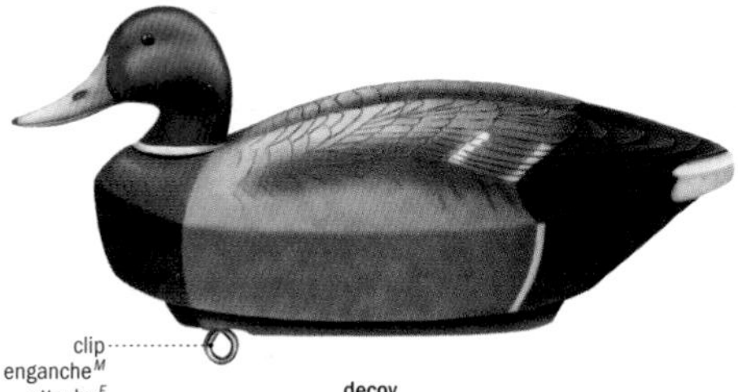

decoy
señuelo ^{M}
appeau ^{M}
Lockente ^{F}
richiamo ^{M}

compound bow
arco ^{M} de poleas ^{F}
arc ^{M} à poulies ^{F}
Kompositbogen ^{M}
arco ^{M} composto

wheel
polea ^{F}
poulie ^{F}
Rolle ^{F}
puleggia ^{F}

nocking point
punto de empulgada ^{F}
point ^{M} d'encochage ^{M}
Nockpunkt ^{M}
punto ^{M} di incocco ^{M}

mounting bracket
tornillo ^{M} de montaje ^{M}
écrou ^{M} de montage ^{M}
Stellmutter ^{F}
vite ^{F} di fissaggio ^{M}

sight
mira ^{F}
mire ^{F}
Visier ^{N}
mirino ^{M}

arrow rest
apoya-flecha ^{M}
appui ^{M}-flèche ^{F}
Pfeilanlagepunkt ^{M}
poggiafreccia ^{M}

grip
empuñadura ^{F}
poignée ^{F}
Griff ^{M}
impugnatura ^{F}

cable guard
separacables ^{M}
espaceur ^{M} de câbles ^{M}
Kabelschutz ^{M}
distanziatore ^{M}

bowstring
cuerda ^{F}
corde ^{F}
Sehne ^{F}
corda ^{F}

cable
cable ^{M}
câble ^{M}
Kabel ^{N}
cavo ^{M}

limb
pala ^{F}
branche ^{F}
Bogenarm ^{M}
flettente ^{M}

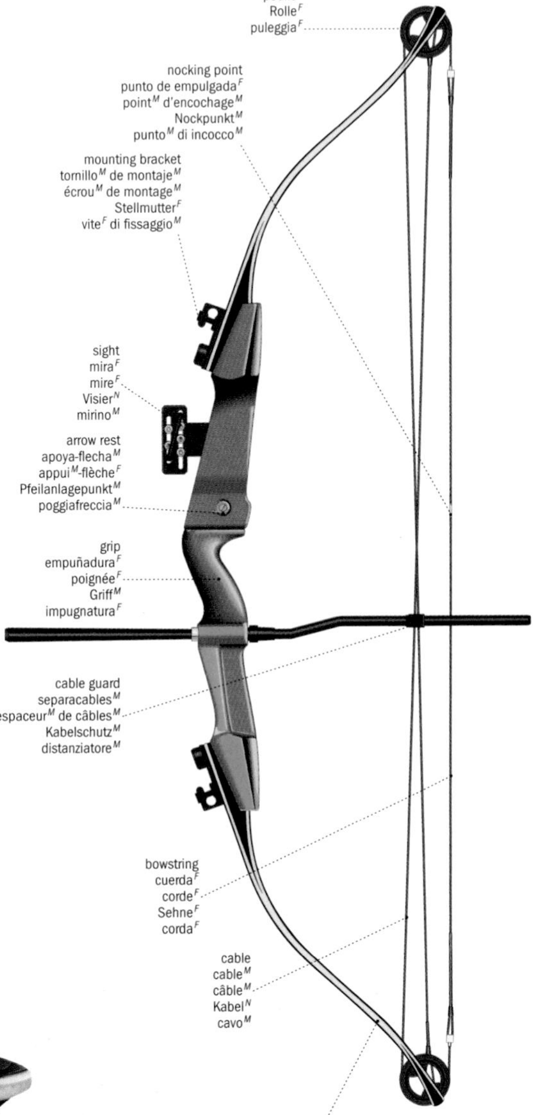

dice and dominoes

dados^M y dominós^M | dés^M et dominos^M | Würfel^M und Dominosteine^M | dadi^M e domino^M

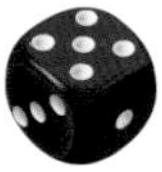

ordinary die
dado^M común
dé^M régulier
gewöhnlicher Würfel^M
dado^M comune

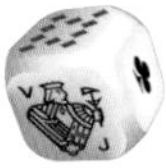

poker die
dado^M de póquer^M
dé^M à poker^M
Pokerwürfel^M
dado^M da poker^M

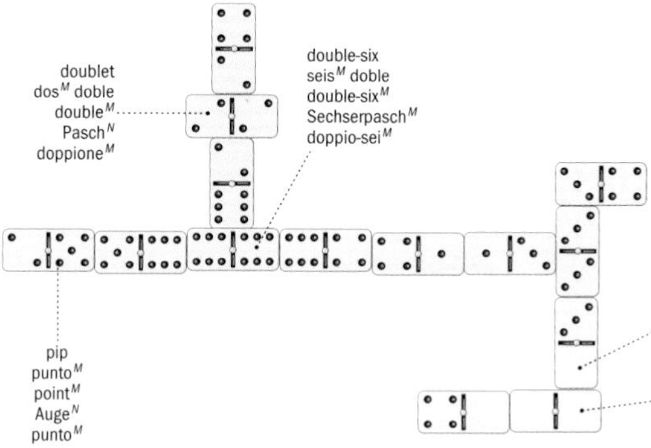

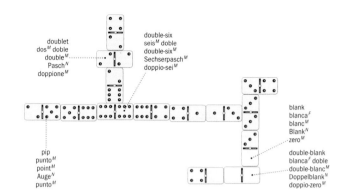

doublet
dos^M doble
double^M
Pasch^N
doppione^M

double-six
seis^M doble
double-six^M
Sechserpasch^M
doppio-sei^M

blank
blanca^F
blanc^M
Blank^N
zero^M

double-blank
blanca^F doble
double-blanc^M
Doppelblank^N
doppio-zero^M

pip
punto^M
point^M
Auge^N
punto^M

cards

baraja^F | cartes^F | Kartenspiele^N | giochi^M di carte^F

symbols
simbolos^M
symboles^M
Farben^F
simboli^M

heart
corazón^M
cœur^M
Herz^N
cuori^M

diamond
diamante^M
carreau^M
Karo^N
quadri^M

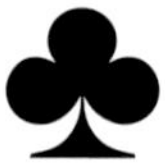

club
trébol^M
trèfle^M
Kreuz^N
fiori^M

spade
espada^F
pique^M
Pik^N
picche^M

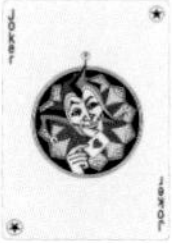

joker
comodín^M
Joker^M
Joker^M
jolly^M

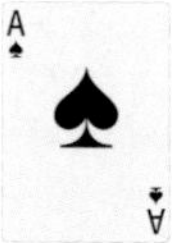

ace
as^M
As^M
Ass^N
asso^M

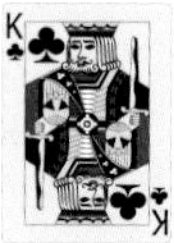

king
rey^M
Roi^M
König^M
re^M

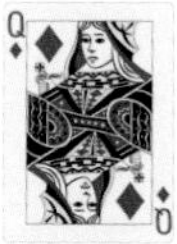

queen
reina^F
Dame^F
Dame^F
donna^F

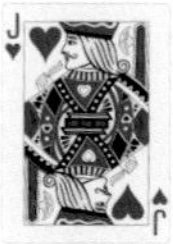

jack
jota^F
Valet^M
Bube^M
fante^M

standard poker hands
manos^F de póquer^M
combinaisons^F au poker^M
normale Pokerblätter^N
combinazioni^F del poker^M

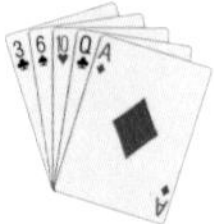

high card
cartas^F altas
carte^F isolée
höchste Karte^F
carta^F più alta

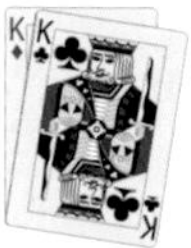

one pair
un par^M
paire^F
ein Pärchen^F
coppia^F

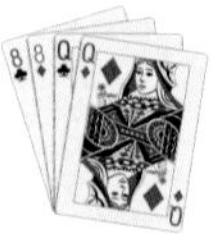

two pairs
dos pares^M
double paire^F
zwei Pärchen^N
doppia coppia^F

three-of-a-kind
trío^M
brelan^M
Drilling^M
tris^M

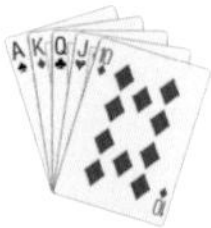

straight
escalera^F
séquence^F
Straße^F
scala^F

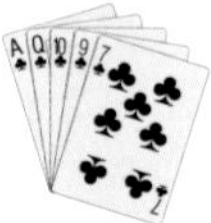

flush
color^M
couleur^F
Flush^M
colore^M

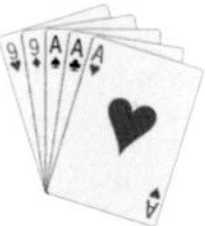

full house
full^M
main^F pleine
Full House^N
full^M

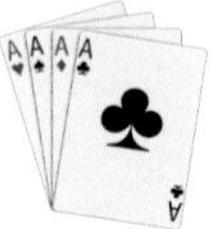

four-of-a-kind
póquer^M
carré^F
Vierling^M
poker^M

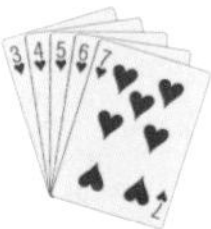

straight flush
escalera^F de color^M
quinte^F
Straight Flush^M
scala^F reale

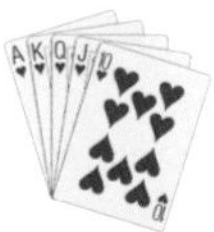

royal flush
escalera^F real
quinte^F royale
Royal Flush^M
scala^F reale massima

board games

juegos^M de mesa^F | jeux^M de plateau^M | Brettspiel^N | giochi^M da tavola^F

backgammon
backgammon^M
jacquet^M
Backgammon^N
backgammon^M

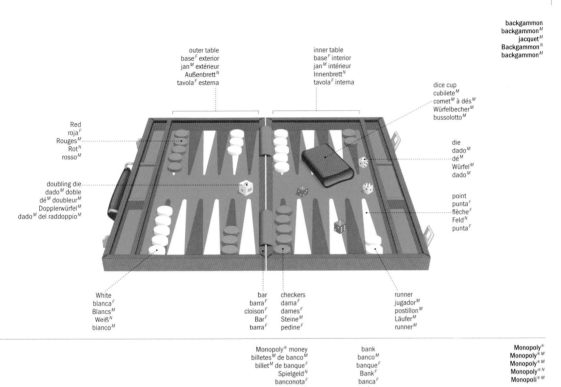

outer table
base^F exterior
jan^M extérieur
Außenbrett^N
tavola^F esterna

inner table
base^F interior
jan^M intérieur
Innenbrett^N
tavola^F interna

dice cup
cubilete^M
cornet^M à dés^M
Würfelbecher^M
bussolotto^M

Red
roja^F
Rouges^M
Rot^N
rosso^M

die
dado^M
dé^M
Würfel^M
dado^M

doubling die
dado^M doble
dé^M doubleur
Dopplerwürfel^M
dado^M del raddoppio^M

point
punta^F
flèche^F
Feld^N
punta^F

White
blanca^F
Blancs^M
Weiß^N
bianco^M

bar
barra^F
cloison^F
Bar^F
barra^F

checkers
dama^F
dames^F
Steine^M
pedine^F

runner
jugador^M
postillon^M
Läufer^M
runner^M

Monopoly®
Monopoly^{® M}
Monopoly^{® M}
Monopoly^{® N}
Monopoli^{® M}

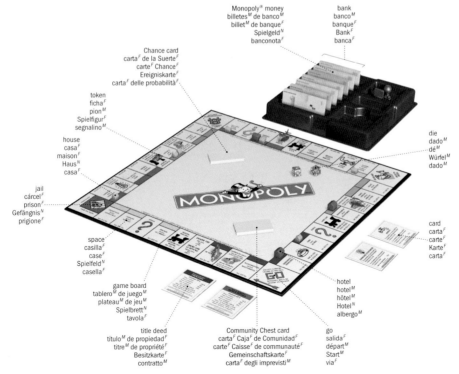

Monopoly® money
billetes^M de banco^M
billet^M de banque^F
Spielgeld^N
banconota^F

bank
banco^M
banque^F
Bank^F
banca^F

Chance card
carta^F de la Suerte^F
carte^F Chance^F
Ereigniskarte^F
carta^F delle probabilità^F

token
ficha^F
pion^M
Spielfigur^F
segnalino^M

die
dado^M
dé^M
Würfel^M
dado^M

house
casa^F
maison^F
Haus^N
casa^F

jail
cárcel^F
prison^F
Gefängnis^N
prigione^F

card
carta^F
carte^F
Karte^F
carta^F

space
casilla^F
case^F
Spielfeld^N
casella^F

hotel
hotel^M
hôtel^M
Hotel^N
albergo^M

game board
tablero^M de juego^M
plateau^M de jeu^M
Spielbrett^N
tavola^F

title deed
título^M de propiedad^F
titre^M de propriété^F
Besitzkarte^F
contratto^M

Community Chest card
carta^F Caja^F de Comunidad^F
carte^F Caisse^F de communauté^F
Gemeinschaftskarte^F
carta^F degli imprevisti^M

go
salida^F
départ^M
Start^M
via^F

SPORTS AND GAMES

915

board games

chess
ajedrez^M
échecs^M
Schach^N
scacchi^M

chessboard
tablero^M de ajedrez^M
échiquier^M
Schachbrett^N
scacchiera^F

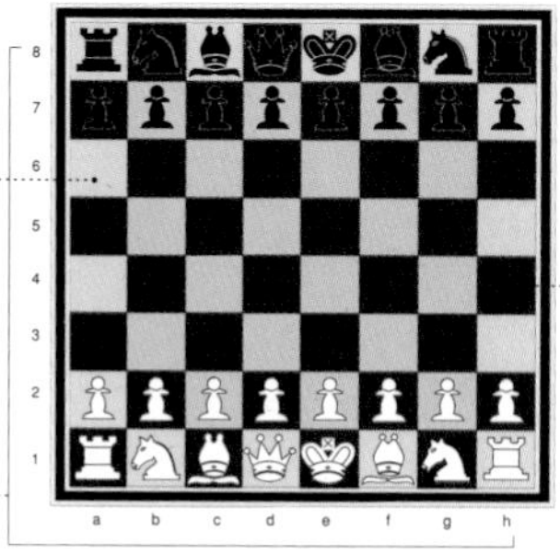

queen's side
lado^M de la reina^F
aile^F Dame^F
Damenflanke^F
lato^M della regina^F

king's side
lado^M del rey^M
aile^F Roi^M
Königsflanke^F
lato^M del re^M

chess pieces
piezas^F
pièces^F
Schachfiguren^F
pezzi^M

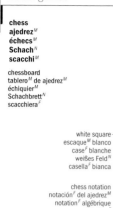

Black
negras^F
Noirs^M
Schwarz^N
neri^M

white square
escaque^M blanco
case^F blanche
weißes Feld^N
casella^F bianca

black square
escaque^M negro
case^F noire
schwarzes Feld^N
casella^F nera

chess notation
notación^F del ajedrez^M
notation^F algébrique
Notation^F
notazione^F degli scacchi^M

White
blancas^F
Blancs^M
Weiß^N
bianchi^M

types of movements
tipos^M de movimientos^M
types^M de déplacements^M
Zugarten^F
tipi^M di movimenti^M

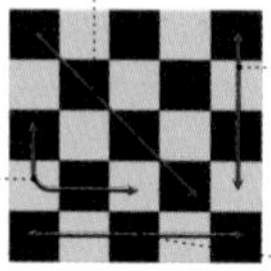

diagonal movement
movimiento^M diagonal
déplacement^M diagonal
diagonaler Zug^M
movimento^M diagonale

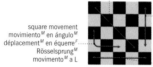

vertical movement
movimiento^M vertical
déplacement^M vertical
vertikaler Zug^M
movimento^M verticale

square movement
movimiento^M en ángulo^M
déplacement^M en équerre^F
Rösselsprung^M
movimento^M a L

horizontal movement
movimiento^M horizontal
déplacement^M horizontal
horizontaler Zug^M
movimento^M orizzontale

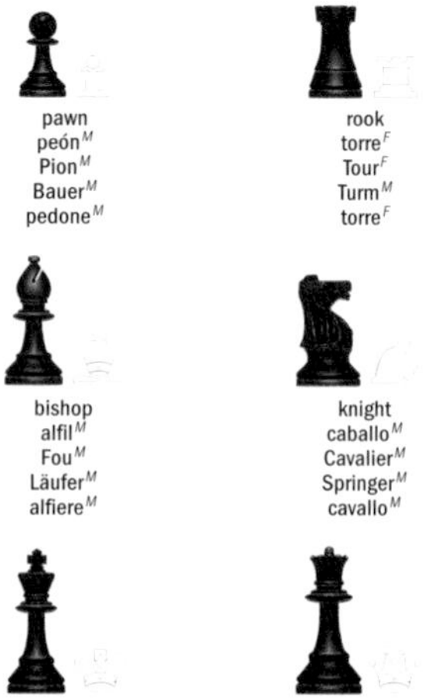

pawn
peón^M
Pion^M
Bauer^M
pedone^M

rook
torre^F
Tour^F
Turm^M
torre^F

bishop
alfil^M
Fou^M
Läufer^M
alfiere^M

knight
caballo^M
Cavalier^M
Springer^M
cavallo^M

king
rey^M
Roi^M
König^M
re^M

queen
reina^F
Dame^F
Dame^F
regina^F

go
go (sun-tse)^M
go^M
Go^N
go^M

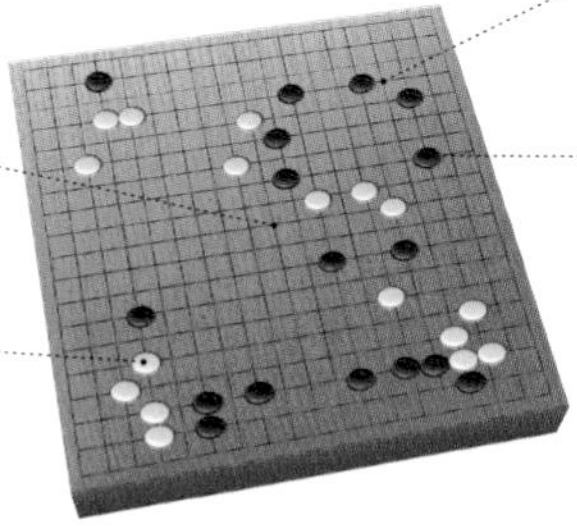

board
tablero^M
terrain^M
Spielbrett^N
scacchiera^F

major motions
principales movimientos^M
principaux mouvements^M
Hauptspielzüge^M
mosse^F principali

handicap spot
obstáculo^M
point^M de handicap^M
schwacher Punkt^M
punto^M di handicap^M

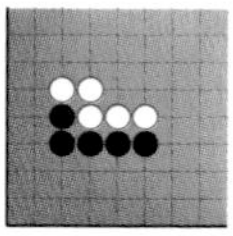

connection
conexión^F
connexion^F
Verbindung^F
gruppo^M

center
centro^M
centre^M
Mittelpunkt^M
centro^M

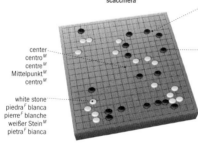

black stone
piedra^F negra
pierre^F noire
schwarzer Stein^M
pietra^F nera

white stone
piedra^F blanca
pierre^F blanche
weißer Stein^M
pietra^F bianca

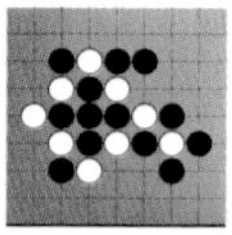

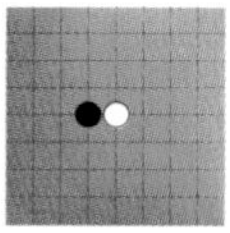

contact
contacto^M
contact^M
Berührung^F
contatto^M

capture
captura^F
capture^F
Fangen^N
cattura^F

checkers
damas^F
jeu^M de dames^F
Dame^F
dama^F

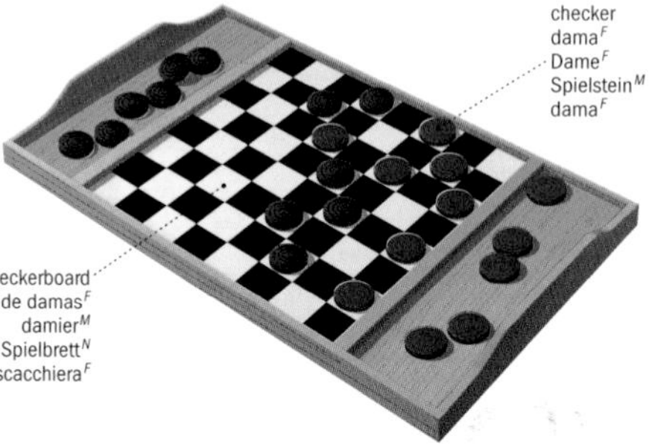

checker
dama^F
Dame^F
Spielstein^M
dama^F

checkerboard
tablero^M de damas^F
damier^M
Spielbrett^N
scacchiera^F

jigsaw puzzle

puzle^M | puzzle^M ; *casse-tête^M* | Puzzle^N | puzzle^M

piece
pieza^F
pièce^F
Puzzleteil^N
tessera^F

picture
imagen^F
image^F
Bild^N
immagine^F

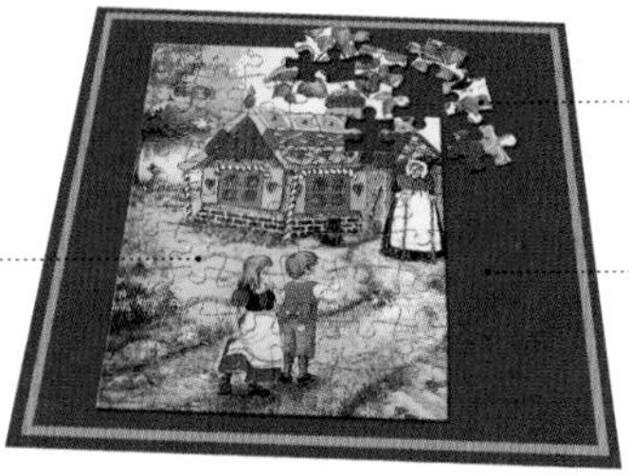

board
tablero^M
plateau^M
Unterlage^F
tavola^F

mah-jongg

mah-jongg^M | mah-jong^M | Mah-Jongg^N | mah-jongg^M

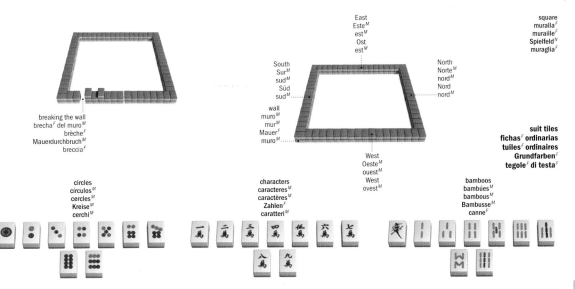

East
Este^M
est^M
Ost
est^M

square
muralla^F
muraille^F
Spielfeld^N
muraglia^F

South
Sur^M
sud^M
Süd
sud^M

North
Norte^M
nord^M
Nord
nord^M

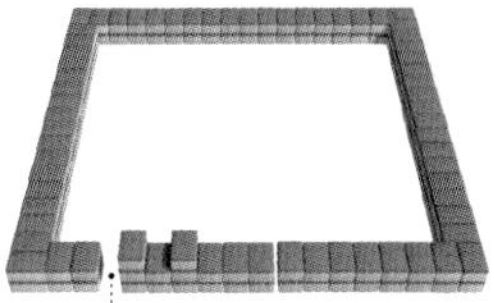

breaking the wall
brecha^F del muro^M
brèche^F
Mauerdurchbruch^M
breccia^F

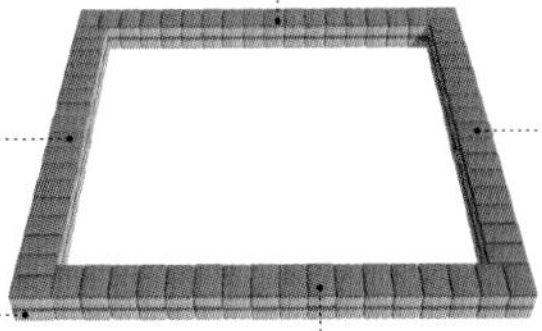

wall
muro^M
mur^M
Mauer^F
muro^M

West
Oeste^M
ouest^M
West
ovest^M

suit tiles
fichas^F ordinarias
tuiles^F ordinaires
Grundfarben^F
tegole^F di testa^F

circles
círculos^M
cercles^M
Kreise^M
cerchi^M

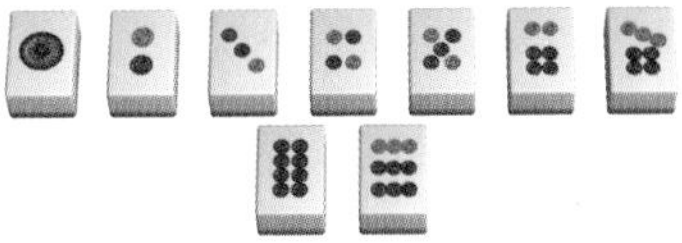

characters
caracteres^M
caractères^M
Zahlen^F
caratteri^M

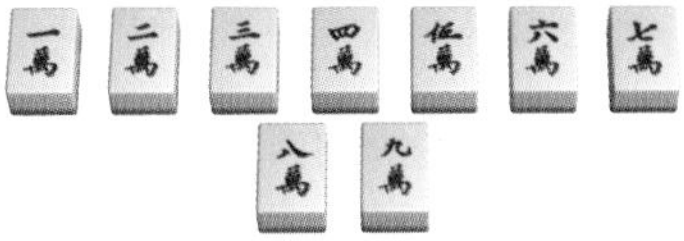

bamboos
bambúes^M
bambous^M
Bambusse^M
canne^F

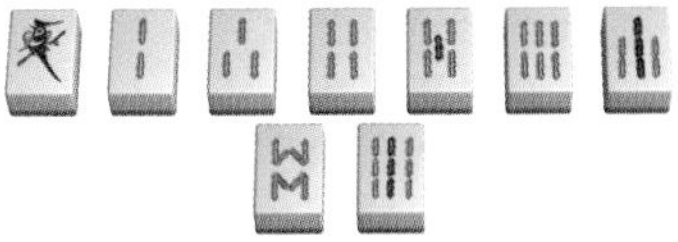

honor tiles
fichas^F de honor^M
honneurs^M
Trumpffarben^F
onori^M supremi

winds
vientos^M
vents^M
Winde^M
venti^M

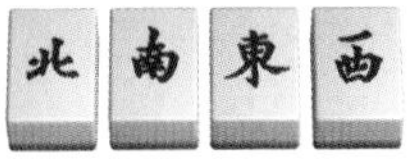

dragons
dragones^M
dragons^M
Drachen^M
dragoni^M

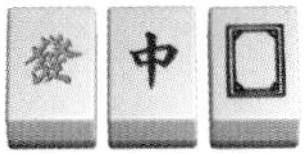

flowers
fichas^F de beneficio^M
tuiles^F de bonification^F
Hasardsteine^M
tegole^F bonus

flower tiles
fichas^F de flores^F
fleurs^F
Blumenziegel^M
fiori^M

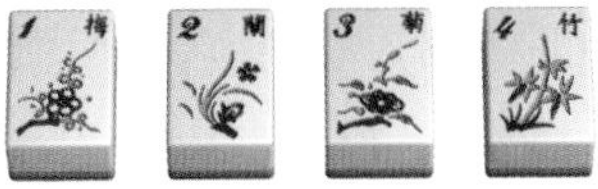

season tiles
fichas^F de estaciones^F
saisons^F
Jahreszeitenziegel^M
stagioni^F

SPORTS AND GAMES

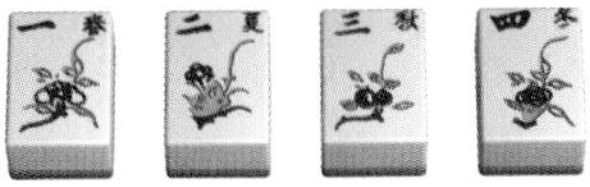

video entertainment system

videojuego^M | système^M de jeux^M vidéo | Videospielsystem^N | videogioco^M

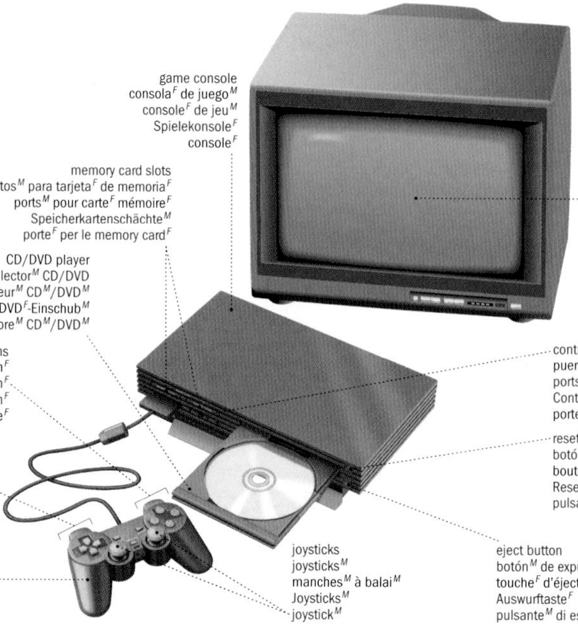

game console
consola^F de juego^M
console^F de jeu^M
Spielekonsole^F
console^F

memory card slots
puertos^M para tarjeta^F de memoria^F
ports^M pour carte^F mémoire^F
Speicherkartenschächte^M
porte^F per i memory card^F

CD/DVD player
lector^M CD/DVD
lecteur^M CD^M/DVD^M
CD^F-/DVD^F-Einschub^M
lettore^M CD^M/DVD^M

action buttons
botones^M de acción^F
touches^F d'action^F
Aktionstasten^F
pulsanti^M di azione^F

directional buttons
botones^M de dirección^F
touches^F directionnelles
Richtungstasten^F
pulsanti^M direzionali

controller
mando^M
manette^F de jeu^M
Controller^M
manopola^F di controllo^M

visual display
pantalla^F
écran^M
Monitor^M
video^M

controller ports
puertos^M para el mando^M
ports^M pour manette^F
Controller^M-Schnittstellen^F
porte^F di controllo^M

reset button
botón^M de reset^M
bouton^M de réinitialisation^F
Resettaste^F
pulsante^M di reset^M

eject button
botón^M de expulsión^F
touche^F d'éjection^F
Auswurftaste^F
pulsante^M di espulsione^F

joysticks
joysticks^M
manches^M à balai^M
Joysticks^M
joystick^M

darts

juego^M de dardos^M | jeu^M de fléchettes^F | Dartspiel^N | freccette^F

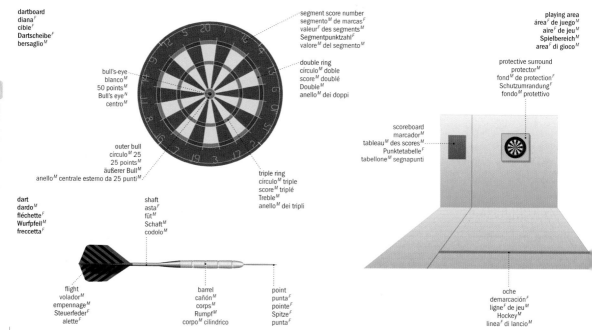

dartboard
diana^F
cible^F
Dartscheibe^F
bersaglio^M

bull's-eye
blanco^M
50 points^M
Bull's eye^N
centro^M

outer bull
círculo^M 25
25 points^M
äußerer Bull^M
anello^M centrale esterno da 25 punti^M

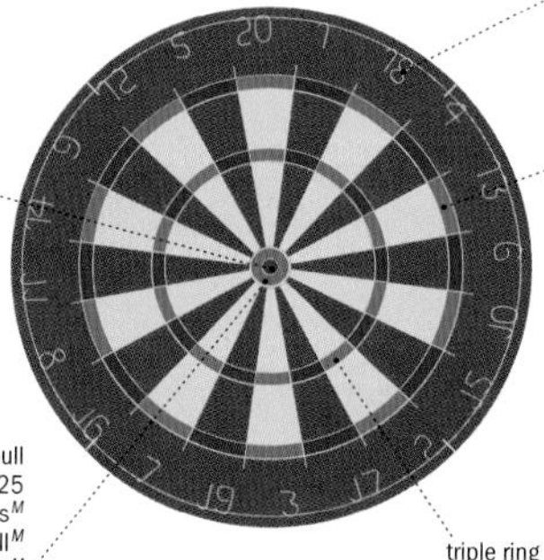

segment score number
segmento^M de marcas^F
valeur^F des segments^M
Segmentpunktzahl^F
valore^M del segmento^M

double ring
círculo^M doble
score^F doublé
Double^F
anello^M dei doppi

triple ring
círculo^M triple
score^M triplé
Treble^M
anello^M dei tripli

playing area
área^F de juego^M
aire^F de jeu^M
Spielbereich^M
area^F di gioco^M

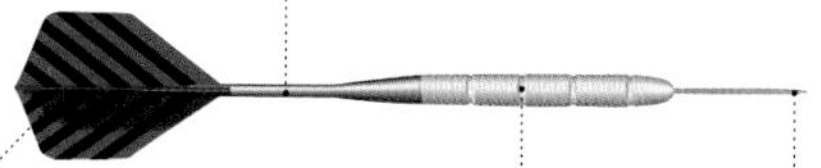

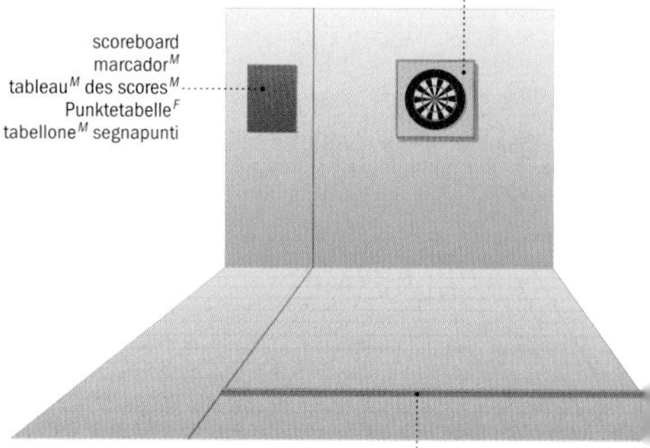

protective surround
protector^M
fond^M de protection^F
Schutzumrandung^F
fondo^M protettivo

scoreboard
marcador^M
tableau^M des scores^M
Punktetabelle^F
tabellone^M segnapunti

dart
dardo^M
fléchette^F
Wurfpfeil^M
freccetta^F

shaft
asta^F
fût^M
Schaft^M
codolo^M

flight
volador^M
empennage^M
Steuerfeder^F
alette^F

barrel
cañón^M
corps^M
Rumpf^M
corpo^M cilindrico

point
punta^F
pointe^F
Spitze^F
punta^F

oche
demarcación^F
ligne^F de jeu^M
Hockey^M
linea^F di lancio^M

SPORTS AND GAMES

roulette table

mesa^F de la ruleta^F | table^F de roulette^F | Roulettespieltisch^M | tavolo^M da roulette^F

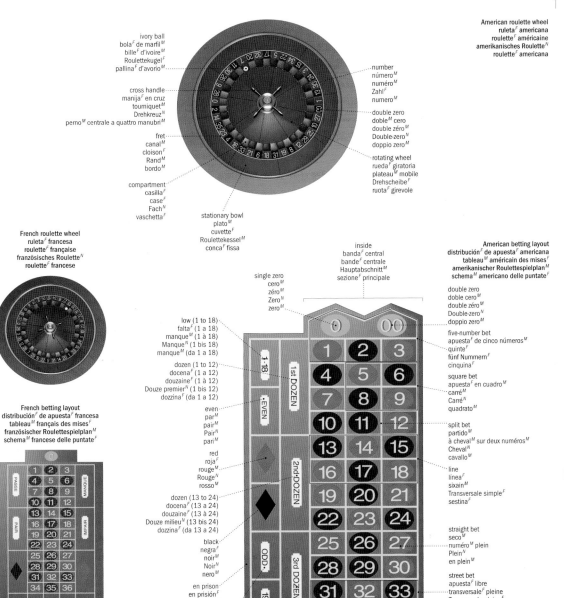

American roulette wheel
ruleta^F americana
roulette^F américaine
amerikanisches Roulette^N
roulette^F americana

ivory ball
bola^F de marfil^M
bille^F d'ivoire^M
Roulettekugel^F
pallina^F d'avorio

number
número^M
numéro^M
Zahl^F
numero^M

cross handle
manija^F en cruz
tourniquet^M
Drehkreuz^N
perno^M centrale a quattro manubri^M

double zero
doble^M cero
double zéro^M
Double-zero^N
doppio zero^M

fret
canal^M
cloison^F
Rand^M
bordo^M

rotating wheel
rueda^F giratoria
plateau^M mobile
Drehscheibe^F
ruota^F girevole

compartment
casilla^F
case^F
Fach^N
vaschetta^F

stationary bowl
plato^M
cuvette^F
Roulettekessel^M
conca^F fissa

French roulette wheel
ruleta^F francesa
roulette^F française
französisches Roulette^N
roulette^F francese

inside
banda^F central
bande^F centrale
Hauptabschnitt^M
sezione^F principale

American betting layout
distribución^F de apuesta^F americana
tableau^M américain des mises^F
amerikanischer Roulettespielplan^M
schema^M americano delle puntate^F

single zero
cero^M
zéro^M
Zero^N
zero^M

double zero
doble cero^M
double zéro^M
Double-zero^N
doppio zero^M

low (1 to 18)
falta^F (1 a 18)
manque^M (1 à 18)
Manque^N (1 bis 18)
manque^M (da 1 a 18)

five-number bet
apuesta^F de cinco números^M
quinte^F
fünf Nummern^F
cinquina^F

French betting layout
distribución^F de apuesta^F francesa
tableau^M français des mises^F
französischer Roulettespielplan^M
schema^M francese delle puntate^F

dozen (1 to 12)
docena^F (1 a 12)
douzaine^F (1 à 12)
Douze premier^N (1 bis 12)
dozzina^F (da 1 a 12)

square bet
apuesta^F en cuadro^M
carré^M
Carré^N
quadrato^M

even
par^M
pair^M
Pair^N
pari^M

split bet
partido^M
à cheval^F sur deux numéros^M
Cheval^N
cavallo^M

red
roja^F
rouge^M
Rouge^N
rosso^M

line
linea^F
sixain^M
Transversale simple^F
sestina^F

dozen (13 to 24)
docena^F (13 a 24)
douzaine^F (13 à 24)
Douze milieu^N (13 bis 24)
dozzina^F (da 13 a 24)

black
negra^F
noir^M
Noir^N
nero^M

straight bet
seco^M
numéro^M plein
Plein^N
en plein^M

en prison
en prisión^F
en prison^F
en prison
in prigione^F

street bet
apuesta^F libre
transversale^F pleine
Transversale pleine^F
terzina^F

odd
impar^M
impair^M
Impair^N
dispari^M

two columns split bet
apuesta^F sobre dos columnas^F
à cheval^M sur deux colonnes^F
zwei Kolonnen Cheval^N
cavallo^M su due colonne^F

high (19 to 36)
pasa^F (19 a 36)
passe^F (19 à 36)
Passe^N (19 bis 36)
passe^M (da 19 a 36)

dozen (25 to 36)
docena^F (25 a 36)
douzaine^F (25 à 36)
Douze dernier^N (25 bis 36)
dozzina^F (da 25 a 36)

column
columna^F
colonne^F
Kolonne^F
colonna^F

dozen (13 to 24)

slot machine

máquina^F tragaperras | machine^F à sous^M | einarmiger Bandit^M | slot-machine^F

cross section
corte^M transversal
coupe^F
Querschnitt
sezione^F trasversale

casing
caja^F
boitier^M
Gehäuse^N
cassa^F

coin slot
ranura^F para monedas^F
fente^F à monnaie^F
Münzeinwurf^M
fessura^F per l'introduzione^F delle monete^F

reel
tambor^M
rouleau^M
Glücksrad^N
rullo^M

reel plate
engranaje^M
plaque^F de rouleau^M
Drehkranz^M
piastra^F del rullo^M

coin reject slot
devolución^F de monedas^F rechazadas
réceptacle^M pour les pièces^F refusées
Münzrückgabe^F
fessura^F per la restituzione^F delle monete^F

payout trigger
disparador^M de pago^M
déclencheur^M de paiement^M
Auszahlungshebel^M
levetta^F di erogazione^F della vincita^F

symbol
símbolo^M
symbole^M
Symbol^N
simbolo^M

lever
palanca^F
bras^M
Hebel^M
leva^F

jackpot feed
selector^M del premio^M
alimentation^F jackpot^M
Jackpot-Leitung^F
alimentazione^F del premio^M

spring linkage
resorte^M del sistema^M articulado
levier^M à ressort^M
Federverbindung^F
collegamento^M a molla^F

winning line
combinación^F ganadora
combinaison^F gagnante
Gewinnkombination^F
combinazione^F vincente

coin chute
conducto^M de monedas^F
conduite^F des pièces^F
Münzleitung^F
slitta^F delle monete^F

strongbox
caja^F fuerte
caisse^F blindée
Gehäuseverstärkung^F
cassa^F

payout tray
bandeja^F de pago^M
plateau^M réceptacle^M de paiement^M
Auszahlungsschale^F
vassoio^M delle vincite^F

jackpot box
casilla^F del dinero^M
boite^F jackpot^M
Jackpot-Kasten^M
scatola^F del premio^M

electrical payout linkage
control^M eléctrico de pago^M
commande^F électrique de paiement^M
elektrisches Auszahlungselement^N
comando^M elettrico di erogazione^F della vincita^F

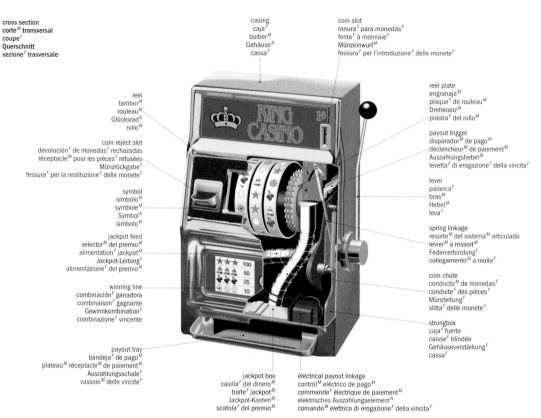

soccer table

futbolín^M | baby-foot^M | Tischfußball^M | calcio^M balilla

score counter
anotador^M
boulier^M-compteur^M
Toranzeige^F
segnapunti^M

rubber bumper
amortiguador^M de caucho^M
amortisseur^M en caoutchouc^M
Stoßfänger^M
paracolpi^M di gomma^F

player
jugador^M
joueur^M
Spieler^M
giocatore^M

goal
gol^M
but^M
Tor^N
porta^F

telescopic rod
barra^F telescópica
barre^F télescopique
Teleskopstangen^F
asta^F telescopica

playing field
campo^M de juego^M
terrain^M de jeu^M
Spielfeld^N
campo^M di gioco^M

ball
bola^F
balle^F
Ball^M
pallina^F

handle
empuñadura^F
poignée^F
Griff^M
manopola^F

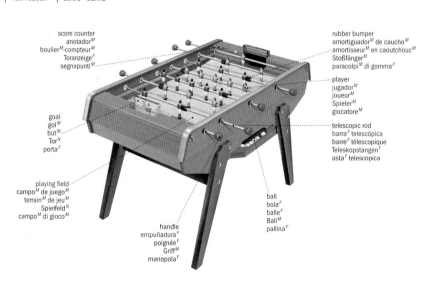

English Index

ENGLISH INDEX

ASTRONOMY > 2-25;   EARTH > 26-71;   VEGETABLE KINGDOM > 72-89;   ANIMAL KINGDOM > 90-143;   HUMAN BEING > 144-177;   FOOD AND KITCHEN > 178-241;   HOUSE > 242-295;
DO-IT-YOURSELF AND GARDENING > 296-333;   CLOTHING > 334-371;   PERSONAL ADORNMENT AND ARTICLES > 372-391;   ARTS AND ARCHITECTURE > 392-465;   COMMUNICATIONS AND
OFFICE AUTOMATION > 466-535;   TRANSPORT AND MACHINERY > 536-643;   ENERGY > 644-677;   SCIENCE > 678-705;   SOCIETY > 706-785;   SPORTS AND GAMES > 786-920

923

ASTRONOMY > 2–25; EARTH > 26–71; VEGETABLE KINGDOM >72-89; ANIMAL KINGDOM > 90-143; HUMAN BEING > 144-177; FOOD AND KITCHEN > 178-241; HOUSE > 242-295; DO-IT-YOURSELF AND GARDENING > 296-333; CLOTHING > 334-371; PERSONAL ADORNMENT AND ARTICLES > 372-391; ARTS AND ARCHITECTURE > 392-465; COMMUNICATIONS AND OFFICE AUTOMATION > 466-535; TRANSPORT AND MACHINERY > 536-643; ENERGY > 644-677; SCIENCE > 678-705; SOCIETY > 706-785; SPORTS AND GAMES > 786-920

ASTRONOMY > 2-25;   EARTH > 26-71;   VEGETABLE KINGDOM >72-89;   ANIMAL KINGDOM > 90-143;   HUMAN BEING > 144-177;   FOOD AND KITCHEN > 178-241;   HOUSE > 242-295;
DO-IT-YOURSELF AND GARDENING > 296-333;   CLOTHING > 334-371;   PERSONAL ADORNMENT AND ARTICLES > 372-391;   ARTS AND ARCHITECTURE > 392-465;   COMMUNICATIONS AND
OFFICE AUTOMATION > 466-535;   TRANSPORT AND MACHINERY > 536-643;   ENERGY > 644-677;   SCIENCE > 678-705;   SOCIETY > 706-785;   SPORTS AND GAMES > 786-920

927

ASTRONOMY > 2-25; EARTH > 26-71; VEGETABLE KINGDOM > 72-89; ANIMAL KINGDOM > 90-143; HUMAN BEING > 144-177; FOOD AND KITCHEN > 178-241; HOUSE > 242-295;
DO-IT-YOURSELF AND GARDENING > 296-333; CLOTHING > 334-371; PERSONAL ADORNMENT AND ARTICLES > 372-391; ARTS AND ARCHITECTURE > 392-465; COMMUNICATIONS AND
OFFICE AUTOMATION > 466-535; TRANSPORT AND MACHINERY > 536-643; ENERGY > 644-677; SCIENCE > 678-705; SOCIETY > 706-785; SPORTS AND GAMES > 786-920;

931

ENGLISH INDEX

ENGLISH INDEX

ASTRONOMY > 2-25; EARTH > 26-71; VEGETABLE KINGDOM > 72-89; ANIMAL KINGDOM > 90-143; HUMAN BEING > 144-177; FOOD AND KITCHEN > 178-241; HOUSE > 242-295; DO-IT-YOURSELF AND GARDENING > 296-333; CLOTHING > 334-371; PERSONAL ADORNMENT AND ARTICLES > 372-391; ARTS AND ARCHITECTURE > 392-465; COMMUNICATIONS AND OFFICE AUTOMATION > 466-535; TRANSPORT AND MACHINERY > 536-643; ENERGY > 644-677; SCIENCE > 678-705; SOCIETY > 706-785; SPORTS AND GAMES > 786-920

ASTRONOMY > 2-25; EARTH > 26-71; VEGETABLE KINGDOM >72-89; ANIMAL KINGDOM > 90-143; HUMAN BEING > 144-177; FOOD AND KITCHEN > 178-241; HOUSE > 242-295;
DO-IT-YOURSELF AND GARDENING > 296-333; CLOTHING > 334-371; PERSONAL ADORNMENT AND ARTICLES > 372-391; ARTS AND ARCHITECTURE > 392-465; COMMUNICATIONS AND
OFFICE AUTOMATION > 466-535; TRANSPORT AND MACHINERY > 536-643; ENERGY > 644-677; SCIENCE > 678-705; SOCIETY > 706-785; SPORTS AND GAMES > 786-920

933

ENGLISH INDEX

ENGLISH INDEX

ASTRONOMY > 2-25;   EARTH > 26-71;   VEGETABLE KINGDOM >72-89;   ANIMAL KINGDOM > 90-143;   HUMAN BEING > 144-177;   FOOD AND KITCHEN > 178-241;   HOUSE > 242-295;
DO-IT-YOURSELF AND GARDENING > 296-333;   CLOTHING > 334-371;   PERSONAL ADORNMENT AND ARTICLES > 372-391;   ARTS AND ARCHITECTURE > 392-465;   COMMUNICATIONS AND
OFFICE AUTOMATION > 466-535;   TRANSPORT AND MACHINERY > 536-643;   ENERGY > 644-677;   SCIENCE > 678-705;   SOCIETY > 706-785;   SPORTS AND GAMES > 786-920

935

ASTRONOMY > 2-25;   EARTH > 26-71;   VEGETABLE KINGDOM >72-89;   ANIMAL KINGDOM > 90-143;   HUMAN BEING > 144-177;   FOOD AND KITCHEN > 178-241;   HOUSE > 242-295;
DO-IT-YOURSELF AND GARDENING > 296-333;   CLOTHING > 334-371;   PERSONAL ADORNMENT AND ARTICLES > 372-391;   ARTS AND ARCHITECTURE > 392-465;   COMMUNICATIONS AND
OFFICE AUTOMATION > 466-535;   TRANSPORT AND MACHINERY > 536-643;   ENERGY > 644-677;   SCIENCE > 678-705;   SOCIETY > 706-785;   SPORTS AND GAMES > 786-920

937

ENGLISH INDEX

ENGLISH INDEX

ASTRONOMY > 2-25;   EARTH > 26-71;   VEGETABLE KINGDOM >72-89;   ANIMAL KINGDOM > 90-143;   HUMAN BEING > 144-177;   FOOD AND KITCHEN > 178-241;   HOUSE > 242-295;
DO-IT-YOURSELF AND GARDENING > 296-333;   CLOTHING > 334-371;   PERSONAL ADORNMENT AND ARTICLES > 372-391;   ARTS AND ARCHITECTURE > 392-465;   COMMUNICATIONS AND
OFFICE AUTOMATION > 466-535;   TRANSPORT AND MACHINERY > 536-643;   ENERGY > 644-677;   SCIENCE > 678-705;   SOCIETY > 706-785;   SPORTS AND GAMES > 786-920

939

ENGLISH INDEX

ASTRONOMY > 2-25;   EARTH > 26-71;   VEGETABLE KINGDOM >72-89;   ANIMAL KINGDOM > 90-143;   HUMAN BEING > 144-177;   FOOD AND KITCHEN > 178-241;   HOUSE > 242-295;
DO-IT-YOURSELF AND GARDENING > 296-333;   CLOTHING > 334-371;   PERSONAL ADORNMENT AND ARTICLES > 372-391;   ARTS AND ARCHITECTURE > 392-465;   COMMUNICATIONS AND
OFFICE AUTOMATION > 466-535;   TRANSPORT AND MACHINERY > 536-643;   ENERGY > 644-677;   SCIENCE > 678-705;   SOCIETY > 706-785;   SPORTS AND GAMES > 786-920

ENGLISH INDEX

941

ASTRONOMY > 2-25;   EARTH > 26-71;   VEGETABLE KINGDOM >72-89;   ANIMAL KINGDOM > 90-143;   HUMAN BEING > 144-177;   FOOD AND KITCHEN > 178-241;   HOUSE > 242-295;
DO-IT-YOURSELF AND GARDENING > 296-333;   CLOTHING > 334-371;   PERSONAL ADORNMENT AND ARTICLES > 372-391;   ARTS AND ARCHITECTURE > 392-465;   COMMUNICATIONS AND
OFFICE AUTOMATION > 466-535;   TRANSPORT AND MACHINERY > 536-643;   ENERGY > 644-677;   SCIENCE > 678-705;   SOCIETY > 706-785;   SPORTS AND GAMES > 786-920;

ENGLISH INDEX

943

ENGLISH INDEX

ASTRONOMY > 2-25;   EARTH > 26-71;   VEGETABLE KINGDOM > 72-89;   ANIMAL KINGDOM > 90-143;   HUMAN BEING > 144-177;   FOOD AND KITCHEN > 178-241;   HOUSE > 242-295;
DO-IT-YOURSELF AND GARDENING > 296-333;   CLOTHING > 334-371;   PERSONAL ADORNMENT AND ARTICLES > 372-391;   ARTS AND ARCHITECTURE > 392-465;   COMMUNICATIONS AND
OFFICE AUTOMATION > 466-535;   TRANSPORT AND MACHINERY > 536-643;   ENERGY > 644-677;   SCIENCE > 678-705;   SOCIETY > 706-785;   SPORTS AND GAMES > 786-920

949

ENGLISH INDEX

ENGLISH INDEX

ASTRONOMY > 2-25;   EARTH > 26-71;   VEGETABLE KINGDOM >72-89;   ANIMAL KINGDOM > 90-143;   HUMAN BEING > 144-177;   FOOD AND KITCHEN > 178-241;   HOUSE > 242-295;
DO-IT-YOURSELF AND GARDENING > 296-333;   CLOTHING > 334-371;   PERSONAL ADORNMENT AND ARTICLES > 372-391;   ARTS AND ARCHITECTURE > 392-465;   COMMUNICATIONS AND
OFFICE AUTOMATION > 466-535;   TRANSPORT AND MACHINERY > 536-643;   ENERGY > 644-677;   SCIENCE > 678-705;   SOCIETY > 706-785;   SPORTS AND GAMES > 786-920

951

ENGLISH INDEX

Indice español

ASTRONOMÍA > 2-25; TIERRA > 26-71; REINO VEGETAL >72-89; REINO ANIMAL > 90-143; SER HUMANO > 144-177; PRODUCTOS ALIMENTARIOS Y DE COCINA > 178-241; CASA > 242-295; BRICOLAJE Y JARDINERÍA > 296-333; VESTIDO > 334-371; ACCESORIOS Y ARTÍCULOS PERSONALES > 372-391; ARTE Y ARQUITECTURA > 392-465; COMUNICACIONES Y AUTOMATIZACIÓN DE OFICINA > 466-535; TRANSPORTE Y VEHÍCULOS > 536-643; ENERGÍA > 644-677; CIENCIA > 678-705; SOCIEDAD > 706-785; DEPORTES Y JUEGOS > 786-920

953

INDICE ESPAÑOL

954

ASTRONOMÍA > 2-25;   TIERRA > 26-71;   REINO VEGETAL >72-89;   REINO ANIMAL > 90-143;   SER HUMANO > 144-177;   PRODUCTOS ALIMENTARIOS Y DE COCINA > 178-241;   CASA > 242-295;
BRICOLAJE Y JARDINERÍA > 296-333;   VESTIDO > 334-371;   ACCESORIOS Y ARTÍCULOS PERSONALES > 372-391;   ARTE Y ARQUITECTURA > 392-465;   COMUNICACIONES Y AUTOMATIZACIÓN DE
OFICINA > 466-535;   TRANSPORTE Y VEHÍCULOS > 536-643;   ENERGÍA > 644-677;   CIENCIA > 678-705;   SOCIEDAD > 706-785;   DEPORTES Y JUEGOS > 786-920

955

ÍNDICE ESPAÑOL

ASTRONOMÍA > 2-25;   TIERRA > 26-71;   REINO VEGETAL >72-89;   REINO ANIMAL > 90-143;   SER HUMANO > 144-177;   PRODUCTOS ALIMENTARIOS Y DE COCINA > 178-241;   CASA > 242-295; BRICOLAJE Y JARDINERÍA > 296-333;   VESTIDO > 334-371;   ACCESORIOS Y ARTÍCULOS PERSONALES > 372-391;   ARTE Y ARQUITECTURA > 392-465;   COMUNICACIONES Y AUTOMATIZACIÓN DE OFICINA > 466-535;   TRANSPORTE Y VEHÍCULOS > 536-643;   ENERGÍA > 644-677;   CIENCIA > 678-705;   SOCIEDAD > 706-785;   DEPORTES Y JUEGOS > 786-920

ASTRONOMÍA > 2-25; TIERRA > 26-71; REINO VEGETAL > 72-89; REINO ANIMAL > 90-143; SER HUMANO > 144-177; PRODUCTOS ALIMENTARIOS Y DE COCINA > 178-241; CASA > 242-295;
BRICOLAJE Y JARDINERÍA > 296-333; VESTIDO > 334-371; ACCESORIOS Y ARTÍCULOS PERSONALES > 372-391; ARTE Y ARQUITECTURA > 392-465; COMUNICACIONES Y AUTOMATIZACIÓN DE
OFICINA > 466-535; TRANSPORTE Y VEHÍCULOS > 536-643; ENERGÍA > 644-677; CIENCIA > 678-705; SOCIEDAD > 706-785; DEPORTES Y JUEGOS > 786-920

959

ÍNDICE ESPAÑOL

INDICE ESPAÑOL

ASTRONOMÍA > 2-25;   TIERRA > 26-71;   REINO VEGETAL >72-89;   REINO ANIMAL > 90-143;   SER HUMANO > 144-177;   PRODUCTOS ALIMENTARIOS Y DE COCINA > 178-241;   CASA > 242-295;
BRICOLAJE Y JARDINERÍA > 296-333;   VESTIDO > 334-371;   ACCESORIOS Y ARTÍCULOS PERSONALES > 372-391;   ARTE Y ARQUITECTURA > 392-465;   COMUNICACIONES Y AUTOMATIZACIÓN DE
OFICINA > 466-535;   TRANSPORTE Y VEHÍCULOS > 536-643;   ENERGÍA > 644-677;   CIENCIA > 678-705;   SOCIEDAD > 706-785;   DEPORTES Y JUEGOS > 786-920

965

INDICE ESPAÑOL

ASTRONOMÍA > 2-25; TIERRA > 26-71; REINO VEGETAL >72-89; REINO ANIMAL > 90-143; SER HUMANO > 144-177; PRODUCTOS ALIMENTARIOS Y DE COCINA > 178-241; CASA > 242-295;
BRICOLAJE Y JARDINERÍA > 296-333; VESTIDO > 334-371; ACCESORIOS Y ARTÍCULOS PERSONALES > 372-391; ARTE Y ARQUITECTURA > 392-465; COMUNICACIONES Y AUTOMATIZACIÓN DE
OFICINA > 466-535; TRANSPORTE Y VEHÍCULOS > 536-643; ENERGÍA > 644-677; CIENCIA > 678-705; SOCIEDAD > 706-785; DEPORTES Y JUEGOS > 786-920

969

molde redondo con muelles 232
moldeador de cutículas 377
moldes de pastas 232
moldura 253, 560
moldura lateral 551
moldura superior 815
mole 702
molécula 680
molibdeno 683
molinete 643, 676
molinillo de café 240
molino de plataforma giratoria 676
molino de torre 676
molino de viento 676
molleja 116
mollejas 212
moluscos 104, 217
moneda : anverso 729
moneda, anverso 729
moneda, reverso 729
moneda: reverso 729
monedero 387
Mongolia 747
monitor 507
monitor de efectos video/digitales 491
monitor de la producción técnica 491
monitor de producción 489
monitor de salida 491
monitor de sonido 489, 491
monitor de vídeo 518
monitor de visualización previa 489
monitor del sonido 490
monitor principal de visualización previa
   491
monitores de entrada 491
monitores de visualización previa 491
monitors de control del director 428
mono 369
mono de esquí con capucha 369
monocascos 835
monóculo 385
monopatín 894
monopatín 894
Monopoly® 915
monovolumen 549
montacargas 634, 650
montagnais 469
montaña 45, 886
montaña alta, climas 61
Montañas Rocosas 30
montante 246, 252, 371, 424, 425,
   460, 461, 628, 629, 641, 782, 826,
   881
montante central 247, 249, 278, 551
montante de la bisagra 247
montante de la cerradura 247
montante del filete 854
montante del muro 253
montante embarillado 249
montante esquinero 252
montante quicial 249
monte de Venus 170
Monte Everest 53
monte marino 49
Montes Apalaches 30
Montes Cárpatos 32
Montes transantárticos 29
Montes Urales 32
montículo 875
montura 385
montura de bayoneta 478
montura de cartón 483
montura de la hebilla 350
montura del objetivo 477
montura en herradura 17
monumento 39
moqueta 254
moras 192
morcilla 216
morcillo 214
mordaza 302, 303, 306, 307, 308,
   310, 312, 317, 377
mordaza curva 310
mordaza fija 311, 312
mordaza móvil 311, 312
mordaza recta 310
mordazas 312, 913
mordente 435
morfología de un bogavante 107
morfología de un caballo 124
morfología de un canguro hembra 143
morfología de un caracol 104
morfología de un delfín 136
morfología de un gato 133
morfología de un gorila 139
morfología de un murciélago 140
morfología de un pájaro 115

morfología de un perro 130
morfología de un pulpo 106
morfología de un tiburón hembra 108
morfología de un topo 121
morfología de una abeja trabajadora 98
morfología de una araña 103
morfología de una concha bivalva 105
morfología de una concha univalva 105
morfología de una estrella de mar 95
morfología de una mariposa 96
morfología de una perca 108
morfología de una rana 110
morfología de una rata 122
morfología de una serpiente venenosa:
   cabeza 112
morfología de una tortuga 113
morilla 183
morillos 257
morral 388
morrena central 46
morrena de fondo 46
morrena frontal 46
morrena lateral 46
morrena terminal 46
morrillo 298
morro 624, 898
morro abatible 629
morsa 137
mortadela 216
mortero 298, 612, 753
mortero del siglo XVII 752
mortero moderno 756
mosaico 406
Mosca 11
mosca 101, 862
mosca artificial 909
mosca central 862
mosca de la línea de cuadro 862
mosca superior 862
mosca tsetsé 101
mosquetón 835, 901, 911
mosquetón curvo 900
mosquetón de bloqueo 900
mosquito 101
mostaza 84
mostaza alemana 200
mostaza americana 200
mostaza blanca 198
mostaza de Dijon 200
mostaza en grano 200
mostaza en polvo 200
mostaza inglesa 200
mostaza negra 198
mostrador 620
mostrador de autoservicio 722
mostrador de carne de autoservicio 180
mostrador de carne fresca 180
mostrador de devolución de libros 733
mostrador de préstamo 733
mostrador de quesos 181
mostrador frigorífico 720
mostrador, carne 180
mostrador, quesos 181
mostrador 327
moto acuática 876
moto cámara 870
moto de cabeza 870
moto de carreras y motociclista 874
moto de motocross 875
moto de rally 875
moto de trial 875
moto nieve 876
moto, motociclista 874
motocicleta 574, 874
motocicleta : vista desde lo alto 576
motocicleta de turismo 577
motocicleta todo terreno 577
motocicletas, ejemplos 577
motocultor 327
motor 236, 237, 240, 261, 288, 292,
   293, 294, 304, 307, 308, 320, 323,
   327, 332, 384, 574, 639, 640, 643,
   651, 758
motor a reacción 60
motor de arranque 332
motor de aterrizaje 18
motor de cuatro tiempos 564
motor de elevación diésel 605
motor de gasolina 553, 563, 566
motor de la bomba 263
motor de propulsión diésel 605
motor del brazo actuador 521
motor del cohete 24
motor del disco 521
motor del proyectil 759
motor del tractor 638
motor del ventilador 258, 261
motor diesel 586, 637, 638, 639

motor diésel 636
motor eléctrico 259, 331, 332, 561,
   563
motor eléctrico de emergencia 763
motor eléctrico principal 763
motor fueraborda 607
motor principal 23
motor turbocompresor 564
motor, bogie 585
motores diesel 762
motores, tipos 564
movimiento diagonal 916
movimiento en ángulo 916
movimiento horizontal 916
movimiento horizontal del suelo 43
movimiento vertical 916
movimiento vertical del suelo 43
movimientos de un avión 630
Mozambique 746
mozzarella 210
mucosa olfatoria 175
mueble bar 279
muebles contenedores 278, 510
muebles de oficina 510
muebles de trabajo 511
muebles infantiles 281
muebles, ejemplos 741
muela 308
muela del juicio 159
muelle 249, 596, 653, 708, 776, 823,
   913
muelle de carga 395, 713, 715, 716,
   719
muelle helicoidal 553
muelle para inflar y desinflar 904
muerte 702
muesca 348, 362, 698, 750, 859, 863
muesca de apertura 905
muescas 424
muestra 458
muestreador 450
muflón 128
muguete 80
mujer 148
mujer, guantes 346
mujer, ropa 355
mujer, sombreros 341
mujer, zapatos 343
mújol 220
mula 128
muleta de antebrazo 782
muleta de sobaco 782
multicasco 835
multiplicación 703
multipack 223
multiplicador 677
mundo, climas 61
mundo, lenguas 468
muñeca 140, 147, 149, 156, 173
muñequera 808, 822, 850, 880, 895
munster 211
muralla 408, 409, 917
murciélago 140
murciélago hoja de lanza 141
murciélago vampiro 141
murciélago, morfología 140
muro 7, 246, 852, 902, 917
muro de abordaje 597
muro de cimentación 252
muro de encauzamiento 657
muro de la Qibla 738
muro de ladrillos 253, 298
muro de llegada 830
muro de nubes 63
muro de piedras 298
muro de rebote 819
muro del ojo 63
muro fortificado 738
muro lateral 597
musaraña 121
músculo aductor anterior 105
músculo aductor posterior 105
músculo bulbocavernoso 169
músculo erector del pelo 172
músculo papilar 162
músculo recto inferior 177
músculo recto superior 177
músculos 150
músculos del manto 106
muselina 231
museo 394, 711
museo, tienda 394
muserola 854, 856, 858
musgo 75
musgo, estructura 75
musgos, ejemplos 75
música 432

muslera 808
muslo 115, 124, 130, 147, 149, 169,
   170
muslo, aductor 150
muslo, recto interno 151
musola 218
mútulo 404
Myanmar 747

N

nabiza 187
nabo 189
nabo sueco 189
nacimiento 702
nacionalidad 825
nadador, país 831
nahualt 469
nalga 147, 149, 169, 170
Namibia 746
naos 403
naranja 194, 400
naranja amarillento 400
naranja china 194
naranja rojizo 400
naranja, corte 82
narciso 80
narina 108, 110, 112, 115
nariz 122, 148, 175, 912
nariz, aleta 175
nariz, dorso 175
nariz, ventana 175
narval 137
nasal 749
nasofaringe 175
nata 210
nata agria 210
nata de montar 210
natación 788, 830
Nauru 747
navaja 217
navaja de barbero 383
navaja de injertar 330
navaja jardinera 330
navaja multiusos suiza 905
navaja para entresacar 381
navajo 469
nave 41, 411
nave central 738
nave espacial 53
nave lateral 411
navegación, instrumentos 612
navegador 524
navicular 155, 156
Nazca, Placa 43
NEAR 19
neblina 57, 65
nebulosa planetaria 8
neceser 388, 389
necrológico 471
nectarina 192
nefridio 107
negativo 485
negativos, armario de secado 484
negra 435, 919
negras 916
negrita 472
negro 472, 690
neodimio 684
neón 684
Nepal 747
neptunio 684
Neptuno 4, 5
nervadura central 84
nervadura principal 79
nervadura secundaria 79
nervio 172, 426
nervio abdominogenital mayor 166
nervio abdominogenital menor 166
nervio auditivo 174
nervio central 75
nervio ciático mayor 166
nervio ciático menor del muslo 166
nervio ciático poplíteo externo 166
nervio ciático poplíteo interno 166
nervio circunflejo 166
nervio crural 166
nervio cubital 166
nervio de vela estay 602
nervio diagonal 410
nervio digital 166
nervio espinal 167
nervio femorocutáneo 166
nervio glúteo 166
nervio intercostal 166
nervio mediano 166
nervio musculocutáneo de la pierna 166

nervio obturador 166
nervio olfativo 109
nervio olfatorio 175
nervio óptico 177
nervio radial 166
nervio raquídeo 168
nervio safeno externo 166
nervio safeno interno 166
nervio secundario 410
nervio tibial anterior 166
nervio transversal 410
nervio vestibular 174
nervios craneales 166
nervioso, sistema 166
netball 809
neumático 551, 560, 570, 579, 870,
   874
neumático de capas al sesgo 561
neumático de invierno 560
neumático de lluvia 872
neumático de rendimiento 560
neumático de seco 872
neumático de tacos 560, 577, 875
neumático de todas las estaciones 560
neumático de turismo 560
neumático radial 561
neumático radial con cinturones 561
neumáticos, ejemplos 560
neurona motora 168
neurona sensorial 168
neuronas, cadena 168
neutrón 680
neutrón incidente 681
neuzes del Brasil 193
nevera 548, 906
neviza 46
newton 702
Nicaragua 742
nicho de seguridad 543
niebla 57, 65
nieta 784
nieto 784
nietos 784
nieve 64
nieve ácida 70
nieve fuerte continua 57
nieve fuerte intermitente 57
nieve ligera continua 57
nieve ligera intermitente 57
nieve moderada continua 57
nieve moderada intermitente 57
nieves perpetuas 45
Níger 745
Nigeria 745
Nilo 34
nimbostrato 56
nimbostratos 62
niños 785
niños, ropa 369
niobio 683
níquel 683
nísperos 193
Nissl, cuerpos 168
nitrógeno 683
nivel 650
nivel de agua 241, 261
nivel de aire 313
nivel de equilibrio del agua 49
nivel de la recepción 724
nivel del agua 261, 288
nivel del mar 42, 49, 53
nivel del mar, presión barométrica 55
nivel el agua, indicador 239
nivel freático 47
nivel inferior 597
nivel superior 597
nivelación principal 701
nivelador 309
nivelador de la alidada 701
nivelador principal 701
niveladora 639
nivómetro 58, 59
no blanquear con cloro 347
no es idéntico a 703
no es igual a 703
no es paralelo a 704
no lavar 347
no metales 683
no pertenece a 703
no planchar 347
no secar en secadora mecánica 347
nobelio 684
nódulo 663
nódulo de Ranvier 168
nogal 88
nombre de la estación 592
nombre de la moneda 729

ASTRONOMÍA > 2-25;   TIERRA > 26-71;   REINO VEGETAL > 72-89;   REINO ANIMAL > 90-143;   SER HUMANO > 144-177;   PRODUCTOS ALIMENTARIOS Y DE COCINA > 178-241;   CASA > 242-295;
BRICOLAJE Y JARDINERÍA > 296-333;   VESTIDO > 334-371;   ACCESORIOS Y ARTÍCULOS PERSONALES > 372-391;   ARTE Y ARQUITECTURA > 392-465;   COMUNICACIONES Y AUTOMATIZACIÓN DE
OFICINA > 466-535;   TRANSPORTE Y VEHÍCULOS > 536-643;   ENERGÍA > 644-677;   CIENCIA > 678-705;   SOCIEDAD > 706-785;   DEPORTES Y JUEGOS > 786-920

981

ÍNDICE ESPAÑOL

ASTRONOMÍA > 2-25; TIERRA > 26-71; REINO VEGETAL > 72-89; REINO ANIMAL > 90-143; SER HUMANO > 144-177; PRODUCTOS ALIMENTARIOS Y DE COCINA > 178-241; CASA > 242-295; BRICOLAJE Y JARDINERÍA > 296-333; VESTIDO > 334-371; ACCESORIOS Y ARTÍCULOS PERSONALES > 372-391; ARTE Y ARQUITECTURA > 392-465; COMUNICACIONES Y AUTOMATIZACIÓN DE OFICINA > 466-535; TRANSPORTE Y VEHÍCULOS > 536-643; ENERGÍA > 644-677; CIENCIA > 678-705; SOCIEDAD > 706-785; DEPORTES Y JUEGOS > 786-920

INDICE ESPAÑOL

985

Index français

ASTRONOMIE > 2-25; TERRE > 26-71; RÈGNE VÉGÉTAL >72-89; RÈGNE ANIMAL > 90-143; ÊTRE HUMAIN > 144-177; ALIMENTATION ET CUISINE > 178-241; MAISON > 242-295;
BRICOLAGE ET JARDINAGE > 296-333; VÊTEMENTS > 334-371; PARURE ET OBJETS PERSONNELS > 372-391; ARTS ET ARCHITECTURE > 392-465; COMMUNICATIONS ET BUREAUTIQUE > 466-535;
TRANSPORT ET MACHINERIE > 536-643; ÉNERGIES > 644-677; SCIENCE > 678-705; SOCIÉTÉ > 706-785; SPORTS ET JEUX > 786-920;

987

ASTRONOMIE > 2-25;   TERRE > 26-71;   RÈGNE VÉGÉTAL > 72-89;   RÈGNE ANIMAL > 90-143;   ÊTRE HUMAIN > 144-177;   ALIMENTATION ET CUISINE > 178-241;   MAISON > 242-295;
BRICOLAGE ET JARDINAGE > 296-333;   VÊTEMENTS > 334-371;   PARURE ET OBJETS PERSONNELS > 372-391;   ARTS ET ARCHITECTURE > 392-465;   COMMUNICATIONS ET BUREAUTIQUE > 466-535;
TRANSPORT ET MACHINERIE > 536-643;   ÉNERGIES > 644-677;   SCIENCE > 678-705;   SOCIÉTÉ > 706-785;   SPORTS ET JEUX > 786-920;

989

ASTRONOMIE > 2-25;   TERRE > 26-71;   RÈGNE VÉGÉTAL >72-89;   RÈGNE ANIMAL > 90-143;   ÊTRE HUMAIN > 144-177;   ALIMENTATION ET CUISINE > 178-241;   MAISON > 242-295;
BRICOLAGE ET JARDINAGE > 296-333;   VÊTEMENTS > 334-371;   PARURE ET OBJETS PERSONNELS > 372-391;   ARTS ET ARCHITECTURE > 392-465;   COMMUNICATIONS ET BUREAUTIQUE > 466-535;
TRANSPORT ET MACHINERIE > 536-643;   ÉNERGIES > 644-677;   SCIENCE > 678-705;   SOCIÉTÉ > 706-785;   SPORTS ET JEUX > 786-920

991

ASTRONOMIE > 2-25;   TERRE > 26-71;   RÈGNE VÉGÉTAL >72-89;   RÈGNE ANIMAL > 90-143;   ÊTRE HUMAIN > 144-177;   ALIMENTATION ET CUISINE > 178-241;   MAISON > 242-295;
BRICOLAGE ET JARDINAGE > 296-333;   VÊTEMENTS > 334-371;   PARURE ET OBJETS PERSONNELS > 372-391;   ARTS ET ARCHITECTURE > 392-465;   COMMUNICATIONS ET BUREAUTIQUE > 466-535;
TRANSPORT ET MACHINERIE > 536-643;   ÉNERGIES > 644-677;   SCIENCE > 678-705;   SOCIÉTÉ > 706-785;   SPORTS ET JEUX > 786-920

993

ASTRONOMIE > 2-25; TERRE > 26-71; RÈGNE VÉGÉTAL >72-89; RÈGNE ANIMAL > 90-143; ÊTRE HUMAIN > 144-177; ALIMENTATION ET CUISINE > 178-241; MAISON > 242-295;
BRICOLAGE ET JARDINAGE > 296-333; VÊTEMENTS > 334-371; PARURE ET OBJETS PERSONNELS > 372-391; ARTS ET ARCHITECTURE > 392-465; COMMUNICATIONS ET BUREAUTIQUE > 466-535;
TRANSPORT ET MACHINERIE > 536-643; ÉNERGIES > 644-677; SCIENCE > 678-705; SOCIÉTÉ > 706-785; SPORTS ET JEUX > 786-920

995

INDEX FRANÇAIS

ASTRONOMIE > 2-25; TERRE > 26-71; RÈGNE VÉGÉTAL >72-89; RÈGNE ANIMAL > 90-143; ÊTRE HUMAIN > 144-177; ALIMENTATION ET CUISINE > 178-241; MAISON > 242-295;
BRICOLAGE ET JARDINAGE > 296-333; VÊTEMENTS > 334-371; PARURE ET OBJETS PERSONNELS > 372-391; ARTS ET ARCHITECTURE > 392-465; COMMUNICATIONS ET BUREAUTIQUE > 466-535;
TRANSPORT ET MACHINERIE > 536-643; ÉNERGIES > 644-677; SCIENCE > 678-705; SOCIÉTÉ > 706-785; SPORTS ET JEUX > 786-920

INDEX FRANÇAIS

997

INDEX FRANÇAIS

ASTRONOMIE > 2-25;   TERRE > 26-71;   RÈGNE VÉGÉTAL > 72-89;   RÈGNE ANIMAL > 90-143;   ÊTRE HUMAIN > 144-177;   ALIMENTATION ET CUISINE > 178-241;   MAISON > 242-295;
BRICOLAGE ET JARDINAGE > 296-333;   VÊTEMENTS > 334-371;   PARURE ET OBJETS PERSONNELS > 372-391;   ARTS ET ARCHITECTURE > 392-465;   COMMUNICATIONS ET BUREAUTIQUE > 466-535;
TRANSPORT ET MACHINERIE > 536-643;   ÉNERGIES > 644-677;   SCIENCE > 678-705;   SOCIÉTÉ > 706-785;   SPORTS ET JEUX > 786-920

999

INDEX FRANÇAIS

ASTRONOMIE > 2-25;   TERRE > 26-71;   RÈGNE VÉGÉTAL >72-89;   RÈGNE ANIMAL > 90-143;   ÊTRE HUMAIN > 144-177;   ALIMENTATION ET CUISINE > 178-241;   MAISON > 242-295;
BRICOLAGE ET JARDINAGE > 296-333;   VÊTEMENTS > 334-371;   PARURE ET OBJETS PERSONNELS > 372-391;   ARTS ET ARCHITECTURE > 392-465;   COMMUNICATIONS ET BUREAUTIQUE > 466-535;
TRANSPORT ET MACHINERIE > 536-643;   ÉNERGIES > 644-677;   SCIENCE > 678-705;   SOCIÉTÉ > 706-785;   SPORTS ET JEUX > 786-920

INDEX FRANÇAIS

1003

INDEX FRANÇAIS

ASTRONOMIE > 2-25; TERRE > 26-71; RÈGNE VÉGÉTAL > 72-89; RÈGNE ANIMAL > 90-143; ÊTRE HUMAIN > 144-177; ALIMENTATION ET CUISINE > 178-241; MAISON > 242-295;
BRICOLAGE ET JARDINAGE > 296-333; VÊTEMENTS > 334-371; PARURE ET OBJETS PERSONNELS > 372-391; ARTS ET ARCHITECTURE > 392-465; COMMUNICATIONS ET BUREAUTIQUE > 466-535;
TRANSPORT ET MACHINERIE > 536-643; ÉNERGIES > 644-677; SCIENCE > 678-705; SOCIÉTÉ > 706-785; SPORTS ET JEUX > 786-920

1007

INDEX FRANÇAIS

INDEX FRANÇAIS

ASTRONOMIE > 2-25; TERRE > 26-71; RÈGNE VÉGÉTAL > 72-89; RÈGNE ANIMAL > 90-143; ÊTRE HUMAIN > 144-177; ALIMENTATION ET CUISINE > 178-241; MAISON > 242-295;
BRICOLAGE ET JARDINAGE > 296-333; VÊTEMENTS > 334-371; PARURE ET OBJETS PERSONNELS > 372-391; ARTS ET ARCHITECTURE > 392-465; COMMUNICATIONS ET BUREAUTIQUE > 466-535;
TRANSPORT ET MACHINERIE > 536-643; ÉNERGIES > 644-677; SCIENCE > 678-705; SOCIÉTÉ > 706-785; SPORTS ET JEUX > 786-920

INDEX FRANÇAIS

1009

ASTRONOMIE > 2-25; TERRE > 26-71; RÈGNE VÉGÉTAL >72-89; RÈGNE ANIMAL > 90-143; ÊTRE HUMAIN > 144-177; ALIMENTATION ET CUISINE > 178-241; MAISON > 242-295;
BRICOLAGE ET JARDINAGE > 296-333; VÊTEMENTS > 334-371; PARURE ET OBJETS PERSONNELS > 372-391; ARTS ET ARCHITECTURE > 392-465; COMMUNICATIONS ET BUREAUTIQUE > 466-535;
TRANSPORT ET MACHINERIE > 536-643; ÉNERGIES > 644-677; SCIENCE > 678-705; SOCIÉTÉ > 706-785; SPORTS ET JEUX > 786-920

1011

INDEX FRANÇAIS

INDEX FRANÇAIS

ASTRONOMIE > 2-25; TERRE > 26-71; RÈGNE VÉGÉTAL > 72-89; RÈGNE ANIMAL > 90-143; ÊTRE HUMAIN > 144-177; ALIMENTATION ET CUISINE > 178-241; MAISON > 242-295;
BRICOLAGE ET JARDINAGE > 296-333; VÊTEMENTS > 334-371; PARURE ET OBJETS PERSONNELS > 372-391; ARTS ET ARCHITECTURE > 392-465; COMMUNICATIONS ET BUREAUTIQUE > 466-535;
TRANSPORT ET MACHINERIE > 536-643; ÉNERGIES > 644-677; SCIENCE > 678-705; SOCIÉTÉ > 706-785; SPORTS ET JEUX > 786-920

1013

INDEX FRANÇAIS

INDEX FRANÇAIS

ASTRONOMIE > 2-25;   TERRE > 26-71;   RÈGNE VÉGÉTAL > 72-89;   RÈGNE ANIMAL > 90-143;   ÊTRE HUMAIN > 144-177;   ALIMENTATION ET CUISINE > 178-241;   MAISON > 242-295;
BRICOLAGE ET JARDINAGE > 296-333;   VÊTEMENTS > 334-371;   PARURE ET OBJETS PERSONNELS > 372-391;   ARTS ET ARCHITECTURE > 392-465;   COMMUNICATIONS ET BUREAUTIQUE > 466-535;
TRANSPORT ET MACHINERIE > 536-643;   ÉNERGIES > 644-677;   SCIENCE > 678-705;   SOCIÉTÉ > 706-785;   SPORTS ET JEUX > 786-920   1015

INDEX FRANÇAIS

INDEX FRANÇAIS

ASTRONOMIE > 2-25;   TERRE > 26-71;   RÈGNE VÉGÉTAL >72-89;   RÈGNE ANIMAL > 90-143;   ÊTRE HUMAIN > 144-177;   ALIMENTATION ET CUISINE > 178-241;   MAISON > 242-295;
BRICOLAGE ET JARDINAGE > 296-333;   VÊTEMENTS > 334-371;   PARURE ET OBJETS PERSONNELS > 372-391;   ARTS ET ARCHITECTURE > 392-465;   COMMUNICATIONS ET BUREAUTIQUE > 466-535;
TRANSPORT ET MACHINERIE > 536-643;   ÉNERGIES > 644-677;   SCIENCE > 678-705;   SOCIÉTÉ > 706-785;   SPORTS ET JEUX > 786-920;

1017

INDEX FRANCAIS

INDEX FRANÇAIS

Deutsches Register

ASTRONOMIE > 2-25;   ERDE > 26-71;   PFLANZENREICH >72-89;   TIERREICH > 90-143;   MENSCH > 144-177;   NAHRUNGSMITTEL UND KÜCHE > 178-241;   HAUS > 242-295;
HEIMWERKEN UND GARTENARBEIT > 296-333;   KLEIDUNG > 334-371;   PERSÖNLICHE AUSSTATTUNG > 372-391;   KUNST UND ARCHITEKTUR > 392-465;   KOMMUNIKATION UND BÜROTECHNIK > 466-535;
TRANSPORT UND FAHRZEUGE > 536-643;   ENERGIE > 644-677;   WISSENSCHAFT > 678-705;   GESELLSCHAFT > 706-785;   SPORT UND SPIELE > 786-920

1019

ASTRONOMIE > 2-25; ERDE > 26-71; PFLANZENREICH >72-89; TIERREICH > 90-143; MENSCH > 144-177; NAHRUNGSMITTEL UND KÜCHE > 178-241; HAUS > 242-295;
HEIMWERKEN UND GARTENARBEIT > 296-333; KLEIDUNG > 334-371; PERSÖNLICHE AUSSTATTUNG > 372-391; KUNST UND ARCHITEKTUR > 392-465; KOMMUNIKATION UND BÜROTECHNIK > 466-535;
TRANSPORT UND FAHRZEUGE > 536-643; ENERGIE > 644-677; WISSENSCHAFT > 678-705; GESELLSCHAFT > 706-785; SPORT UND SPIELE > 786-920

1021

DEUTSCHES REGISTER

ASTRONOMIE > 2-25; ERDE > 26-71; PFLANZENREICH >72-89; TIERREICH > 90-143; MENSCH > 144-177; NAHRUNGSMITTEL UND KÜCHE > 178-241; HAUS > 242-295;
HEIMWERKEN UND GARTENARBEIT > 296-333; KLEIDUNG > 334-371; PERSÖNLICHE AUSSTATTUNG > 372-391; KUNST UND ARCHITEKTUR > 392-465; KOMMUNIKATION UND BÜROTECHNIK > 466-535;
TRANSPORT UND FAHRZEUGE > 536-643; ENERGIE > 644-677; WISSENSCHAFT > 678-705; GESELLSCHAFT > 706-785; SPORT UND SPIELE > 786-920

DEUTSCHES REGISTER

1025

1030

ASTRONOMIE > 2-25;   ERDE > 26-71;   PFLANZENREICH >72-89;   TIERREICH > 90-143;   MENSCH > 144-177;   NAHRUNGSMITTEL UND KÜCHE > 178-241;   HAUS > 242-295; HEIMWERKEN UND GARTENARBEIT > 296-333;   KLEIDUNG > 334-371;   PERSÖNLICHE AUSSTATTUNG > 372-391;   KUNST UND ARCHITEKTUR > 392-465;   KOMMUNIKATION UND BÜROTECHNIK > 466-535; TRANSPORT UND FAHRZEUGE > 536-643;   ENERGIE > 644-677;   WISSENSCHAFT > 678-705;   GESELLSCHAFT > 706-785;   SPORT UND SPIELE > 786-920

ASTRONOMIE > 2-25;   ERDE > 26-71;   PFLANZENREICH >72-89;   TIERREICH > 90-143;   MENSCH > 144-177;   NAHRUNGSMITTEL UND KÜCHE > 178-241;   HAUS > 242-295;
HEIMWERKEN UND GARTENARBEIT > 296-333;   KLEIDUNG > 334-371;   PERSÖNLICHE AUSSTATTUNG > 372-391;   KUNST UND ARCHITEKTUR > 392-465;   KOMMUNIKATION UND BÜROTECHNIK > 466-535;
TRANSPORT UND FAHRZEUGE > 536-643;   ENERGIE > 644-677;   WISSENSCHAFT > 678-705;   GESELLSCHAFT > 706-785;   SPORT UND SPIELE > 786-920

DEUTSCHES REGISTER

1031

DEUTSCHES REGISTER

DEUTSCHES REGISTER

ASTRONOMIE > 2-25;   ERDE > 26-71;   PFLANZENREICH >72-89;   TIERREICH > 90-143;   MENSCH > 144-177;   NAHRUNGSMITTEL UND KÜCHE > 178-241;   HAUS > 242-295;
HEIMWERKEN UND GARTENARBEIT > 296-333;   KLEIDUNG > 334-371;   PERSÖNLICHE AUSSTATTUNG > 372-391;   KUNST UND ARCHITEKTUR > 392-465;   KOMMUNIKATION UND BÜROTECHNIK > 466-535;
TRANSPORT UND FAHRZEUGE > 536-643;   ENERGIE > 644-677;   WISSENSCHAFT > 678-705;   GESELLSCHAFT > 706-785;   SPORT UND SPIELE > 786-920

DEUTSCHES REGISTER

1035

Litze 391
Litzen 460, 461
Litzenstab 461
Lob 821
Lob Wedge 868
Loch 423, 866, 867
Loch, gestanztes 342, 350
Loch, Par-3 866
Loch, Par-4 866
Loch, Par-5 867
Lochbillard 863
Locher 533
Löcher 866
Lochrohr 263
Lochschlitten 456
Lochziegel 298
Lock-Forward 804
Lockennadel 380
Lockenstab 381
Lockente 913
Lockenwickler 380
Löffel 227, 905, 911
Löffel, Beispiele 228
Löffeleisen 401
Löffelstiel 637
Löffelstielzylinder 637
Loge 431
Lokale Station 486
Lokomotive 585
Lokomotive, dieselelektrische 586
Lokschuppen 583
Lokverkehrsgleis 589
Longanfrucht 196
Longdrinkglas 225
Lorbeer 202
Lorgnette 385
Löschen 515
löschender Rückschritt 515
Löschfahrzeug 764
Löschfahrzeuge 766
Löschflugzeug 628
Löschhubschrauber 631
Löschmittelbehälter 767
Löschpapier 531
Löschtaste 477, 501, 508, 515, 529
loser Puder 378
loser Vorhang 283
Löshebel 310
Lötkolben 318
Lötlampe 314, 319
Lötpistole 318
Lötspitze 318
Lötwerkzeuge 318
Lötzinn 318
Lounge 608
Löwe 13, 135
Löwe, schreitender 741
Löwenzahn 187
Luchs 12, 134
Luer-Lock-Spitze 776
Luffaschwamm 379
Luft 565
Luft, absinkende kalte 63
Luft, aufsteigende warme 63
Luft, kalte 64, 675
Luft, warme 64, 675
Luft-Boden-Flugkörper 759
Luft-Luft-Flugkörper 759, 760
Luftansaugrohr 605
Luftaufbereitung 261
Luftaustrittsöffnung 260, 382
Luftaustrittsschlitz 289
Luftbefeuchter 261
Luftbetankung 760
Luftbetankungsausleger 760
Luftdatenrechner 626
Luftdruck 55
Luftdruck in Meereshöhe 55
Luftdruck, Messung 59
Luftdruckänderung 55
Luftdüse 556
Lufteinlass 320, 567, 568, 575, 605, 876
Lufteinlauf 631
Luftentfeuchter 261
Lüfter 497, 526, 552, 561, 563, 566
Lüfterkopf 614
Luftfahrt 487
Luftfeuchtigkeit 261
Luftfeuchtigkeit, Messung 59
Luftfilter 261, 331, 552, 586, 636
Luftkammer 117
Luftkissenfahrzeug 605
Luftklappe 571
Luftkompressor 585, 586
Luftkühler 564
Luftloch 390, 470

Luftlöcher 749
Luftmasse 55
Luftmatratze 904
Luftmatratze, selbstaufblasbare 904
Luftpistole 861
Luftpolster 370, 531
Luftpolsterumschlag 531
Luftpost 475
Luftpropeller 605
Luftpumpe 11, 578
Luftreiniger 261
Luftröhre 116, 125, 163
Luftschacht 402
Luftschadstoffe 69
Luftschlauch 398, 648, 841
Luftschleuse 23, 763
Luftschleuse des Reaktorgebäudes 668
Luftspalt 675
Luftsport 896
Luftsprudler 268
Luftstrom 398
Luftstromrichtdüse 382
Luftstromschalter 382
Lufttemperatur 55
Lüftung 594, 675
Lüftungsgitter 258
Lüftungsschlitz 261
Luftventil 320, 398
Luftverkehr 618
Luftverschmutzung 69
Luftwege 163
Luftwiderstand 504
Luftzielsuchradar 761, 762
Luftzufuhr 874
Luftzufuhrregler 256
Luggersegel 601
Luke 758
Lunge 104, 110, 112, 116, 125
Lunge, linke 161, 163
Lunge, rechte 161, 163
Lungen 163
Lungenarterie 160, 163
Lungenarterienstamm 162
Lungenfell 163
Lungenmittellappen 163
Lungenoberlappen 163
Lungenunterlappen 163
Lungenvene 160
Lungenvene, linke 162
Lungenvene, rechte 162
Luntenstock 752
Lunula 105
Lupe 693, 905
Lupine 190
Lutetium 684
Luthertum 736
Lutz 881
Luxemburg 743
Luzerne, blaue 190
Lyra 433
Lysosom 94

Mäander 48
Macadamianussen 193
Macchie 66
Machete 751
Mackenzie 30
Madagaskar 34, 746
Mädchenbekleidung 2 bis 6 Jahre 717
Mädchenbekleidung 7 bis 17 Jahre 717
Madreporenplatte 95
Magazin 754, 755, 893
Magazinbalg 445
Magazinboden 754
Magazinhalter 754
Mage 847
Magellan 19
Magen 95, 104, 105, 106, 109, 110, 112, 113, 125, 161, 164
Magenmund 107
Magenpförtner 107
Magenstütze 367
Magenta 690
mager 472
Magma 44, 49
Magmakammer 44, 646
Magnesia 825
Magnesium 682
Magnet 45, 488, 534, 687
Magnetband 495
Magnetbaumaschine 488
magnetische Dämpfung 698
magnetische Dichtung 291
magnetische Trennung 71
magnetischer Deckelhalter 240

magnetisches Feld 494, 687
Magnetismus 687
Magnetkompass 907
Magnetnadel 907
Magnetometer 60
Magnetstreifen 729
Mah-Jongg 917
Mähdrescher 643
Mähne 124
Mähwerk 333
Mähwerkaushebung 333
Maiglöckchen 80
Maikäfer 101
Maine Coon 132
Mais 85, 203
Maismehl 204
Maisöl 209
Maissirup 209
Majuskel 472
Makak 139
Make-up 378
Makrele 219
Makronukleus 94
Makroobjektiv 478
Mal 799
Mal, drittes 794
Mal, zweites 794
Malagasy 469
malaiopolynesische Sprachen 469
Malawi 746
Malawisee 34
Malaysia 747
Malediven 747
Malen 396
Malerpinsel 320
Malerstaffelei 11
Mali 745
Malpappe 400
Malpighi-Gefäß 99
Malpighi-Gefäße 97
Malspachtel 397
Malspieler, dritter 794
Malspieler, erster 794
Malspieler, zweiter 794
Malstock 399
Malta 744
Malzessig 201
Mammut 93
Mandarine 194
Mandel 174
Mandeln 193
Mandoline 433
Mangan 683
Manganmischung (Kathode) 689
Mango 197
Mangochutney 201
Mangold 185
Mangostane 196
Maniküre 377
Maniok 184
Mann 146
Männerzelle 768
männlich 702
männliche Blütenstände 89
männliche Geschlechtsorgane 169
Mannschaftsabzeichen 878
Mannschaftsbank 827
Mannschaftsduschen 764
Mannschaftshandikap 858
Mannschaftsname 858
Mannschaftsschlafsaal 764
Mannschaftstrikot 796, 801, 802, 808
Mannschaftszelt 902
Manometer 655, 775
Manövriereinheit, bemannte 20
Manque (1 bis 18) 919
Mansardendach 414
Mansardenfenster 244
Manschette 349, 851, 880, 900
Manschette, aufblasbare 777
Manschettenknopf 361
Mantel 105, 106, 352, 355, 689, 757, 908, 912
Mäntel 352, 355
Mantel, oberer 42
Mantel, unterer 42
Mantelblech 655
Mantelhöhle 106
Mantelkleid 356
Mantelmauer 408
Mantelmuskeln 106
Mantelstromführung 627
Manual 445
Manual für das Hauptwerk 444
Manual für das Oberwerk 444
Manual für das Rückpositiv 444
Manuale 444

Manuell-/Automatikeinstellung 465
manuelle Aussteuerung 499
manuelle Diawahl 483
manuelle Scharfeinstellung 483
Manxkatze 133
Maori 469
Marcato-Zeichen 435
Marconikutter 601
Marder 134
Margarine 209
Marginalschild 113
Marianengraben 50
Marie-Byrd-Land 29
Marienkäfer 101
Marine-Dieselkraftstoff 656
Mariner 19
Mariniergewürze 199
maritim 61
Mark 87, 165, 200, 212
Mark, verlängertes 167
Markenadel 390
Marker 397, 470
Markhöhle 154
Markierschnur 313
Markierung 855
Markierung für Filmanfang 476
Markierungslinie 907
Markierungspunkt 455
Markscheide 154
Markstrahlen 87
Marokko 745
Mars 4, 5
Mars Odyssey 19
Marshallinseln 747
Marsstenge 602
Martin Luther 736
Martingal 858
Mascara, flüssiges 378
Mascarabürstchen 378
Mascarastein 378
Maschen 815
Maschenanschlag 457
Maschenprobe 458
Maschinen, landwirtschaftliche 641
Maschinengewehr 758
Maschinengewehr, leichtes 755
Maschinenhalle 657, 658
Maschinenhaus 648
Maschinenpistole 754
Maschinenraum 606, 608, 763
Maschinenwäsche 347
Maschinist 428
Maserung 300
Maske 796, 841
Maskenbildner 428
Maskendichtung 773
Massagebürste 379
Massagehandschuh 379
Massagespitze 384
Masse 43, 272
Masse, Maßeinheit 702
Masseelektrode 562
Massekabel 318
Massekontakt 497
Massengut-Terminal 596
Massenversand 475
massereiche Sterne 8
Massezange 318
massiver Korpus 441
Mast 792, 842, 844, 864
Mastdarm 164, 169, 170
Mastfenster 663
Mastfuß 663
Masthalterung 493
Mastkörper 663
Mastlager 836
Mastoberteil 663
Mastspitze 836
Maststeuerhebel 632, 633
Maststasche 836
Masttraverse 663
Maß 231
Maßband 313, 454
Maßeinheit der elektrischen Ladung 702
Maßeinheit der elektrischen Spannung 702
Maßeinheit der elektrischen Stromstärke 702
Maßeinheit der Energie 702
Maßeinheit der Frequenz 702
Maßeinheit der Kraft 702
Maßeinheit der Länge 702
Maßeinheit der Leistung 702
Maßeinheit der Lichtstärke 702
Maßeinheit der Masse 702
Maßeinheit der Radioaktivität 702
Maßeinheit der Stoffmenge 702

Maßeinheit der thermodynamischen Temperatur 702
Maßeinheit der Zeit 702
Maßeinheit des Drucks 702
Maßeinheit des elektrischen Widerstands 702
Maßeinheit Temperatur 702
mäßiger Regen 64
Maßwerk 411
Matchbeutel 388
Material, radarabsorbierendes 629
Materialraum 734
Materialschleuse 666
Materie 680
Mathematik 703
Matratze 280, 281
Matratzen 716
Matratzenauflage 280
Matratzenrahmen 716
Matrosenbluse 359
Matrosenkragen 362
Matte 792, 842, 844, 864
Matte, rutschfeste 893
Matten 824
Mattenisolierung 299
Mattenrichter 846
Mattscheibe 477
Mauer 852, 917
Mauer mit Stangen 852
Mauerdurchbruch 917
Mauernagel 301
Mauersegler 118
Mauerturm 408
Mauertürmchen 408
Mauerwerk 253
Maul 108, 124, 136
Maul-Ringschlüssel 311
Maultier 128
Maultrommel 433
Maulwurf 121
Maulwurf, äußere Merkmale 121
Maulwurf, Skelett 121
Maurerhammer 315
Maurerkelle 315
Maurerwerkzeuge 315
Mauretanien 745
Mauritius 746
Maus, mechanische 516
Maus, optische 516
Mauspad 516
Mausschnittstelle 513, 518
Mawashi 847
Maximumthermometer 59
Maya 469
Mazedonien 744
Mechanik 686
Mechaniker 873
mechanische Maus 516
mechanische Uhr 696
mechanische Verbindungen 269
mechanisches Variometer 898
Medaillon 374
mediane Zungenfurche 176
Medikamentenfach 775
Medikamentenraum 778, 781
mediterrane Subtropen 61
medizinische Gasflasche 780
medizinische Geräte, Lagerraum 781
Meer 38, 664
Meer, Arabisches 33
Meer, Japanisches 33
Meer, Kaspisches 33
Meer, Mare 7
Meer, Ostchinesisches 33
Meer, Rotes 33, 34
Meer, Schwarzes 33
Meer, Südchinesisches 33
Meeräsche 220
Meerbarbe, rote 219
Meerbusen, Bottnischer 32
Meerenge 38
Meeresalgen 183
Meeresboden 49
Meeressäugetiere 136
Meeressäugetiere, Beispiele 137
Meeresseite 664
Meeresspiegel 42, 49, 53
Meerkohl 186
Meerneunauge 219
Meerohr 217
Meerrettich 189
Meersalat 183
Meersalz 201
Meerschweinchen 123
Meganeura 92
Megazostrodon 93
Mehl 204

ASTRONOMIE > 2-25;   ERDE > 26-71;   PFLANZENREICH >72-89;   TIERREICH > 90-143;   MENSCH > 144-177;   NAHRUNGSMITTEL UND KÜCHE > 178-241;   HAUS > 242-295;
HEIMWERKEN UND GARTENARBEIT > 296-333;   KLEIDUNG > 334-371;   PERSÖNLICHE AUSSTATTUNG > 372-391;   KUNST UND ARCHITEKTUR > 392-465;   KOMMUNIKATION UND BÜROTECHNIK > 466-535;
TRANSPORT UND FAHRZEUGE > 536-643;   ENERGIE > 644-677;   WISSENSCHAFT > 678-705;   GESELLSCHAFT > 706-785;   SPORT UND SPIELE > 786-920

1037

ASTRONOMIE > 2-25; ERDE > 26-71; PFLANZENREICH >72-89; TIERREICH > 90-143; MENSCH > 144-177; NAHRUNGSMITTEL UND KÜCHE > 178-241; HAUS > 242-295;
HEIMWERKEN UND GARTENARBEIT > 296-333; KLEIDUNG > 334-371; PERSÖNLICHE AUSSTATTUNG > 372-391; KUNST UND ARCHITEKTUR > 392-465; KOMMUNIKATION UND BÜROTECHNIK > 466-535;
TRANSPORT UND FAHRZEUGE > 536-643; ENERGIE > 644-677; WISSENSCHAFT > 678-705; GESELLSCHAFT > 706-785; SPORT UND SPIELE > 786-920

1039

DEUTSCHES REGISTER

ASTRONOMIE > 2-25; ERDE > 26-71; PFLANZENREICH >72-89; TIERREICH > 90-143; MENSCH > 144-177; NAHRUNGSMITTEL UND KÜCHE > 178-241; HAUS > 242-295;
HEIMWERKEN UND GARTENARBEIT > 296-333; KLEIDUNG > 334-371; PERSÖNLICHE AUSSTATTUNG > 372-391; KUNST UND ARCHITEKTUR > 392-465; KOMMUNIKATION UND BÜROTECHNIK > 466-535;
TRANSPORT UND FAHRZEUGE > 536-643; ENERGIE > 644-677; WISSENSCHAFT > 678-705; GESELLSCHAFT > 706-785; SPORT UND SPIELE > 786-920

1045

DEUTSCHES REGISTER

ASTRONOMIE > 2-25;   ERDE > 26-71;   PFLANZENREICH >72-89;   TIERREICH > 90-143;   MENSCH > 144-177;   NAHRUNGSMITTEL UND KÜCHE > 178-241;   HAUS > 242-295;
HEIMWERKEN UND GARTENARBEIT > 296-333;   KLEIDUNG > 334-371;   PERSÖNLICHE AUSSTATTUNG > 372-391;   KUNST UND ARCHITEKTUR > 392-465;   KOMMUNIKATION UND BÜROTECHNIK > 466-535;
TRANSPORT UND FAHRZEUGE > 536-643;   ENERGIE > 644-677;   WISSENSCHAFT > 678-705;   GESELLSCHAFT > 706-785;   SPORT UND SPIELE > 786-920

1047

DEUTSCHES REGISTER

DEUTSCHES REGISTER

ASTRONOMIE > 2-25; ERDE > 26-71; PFLANZENREICH >72-89; TIERREICH > 90-143; MENSCH > 144-177; NAHRUNGSMITTEL UND KÜCHE > 178-241; HAUS > 242-295;
HEIMWERKEN UND GARTENARBEIT > 296-333; KLEIDUNG > 334-371; PERSÖNLICHE AUSSTATTUNG > 372-391; KUNST UND ARCHITEKTUR > 392-465; KOMMUNIKATION UND BÜROTECHNIK > 466-535;
TRANSPORT UND FAHRZEUGE > 536-643; ENERGIE > 644-677; WISSENSCHAFT > 678-705; GESELLSCHAFT > 706-785; SPORT UND SPIELE > 786-920

1051

DEUTSCHES REGISTER

ASTRONOMIE > 2-25;   ERDE > 26-71;   PFLANZENREICH >72-89;   TIERREICH > 90-143;   MENSCH > 144-177;   NAHRUNGSMITTEL UND KÜCHE > 178-241;   HAUS > 242-295;
HEIMWERKEN UND GARTENARBEIT > 296-333;   KLEIDUNG > 334-371;   PERSÖNLICHE AUSSTATTUNG > 372-391;   KUNST UND ARCHITEKTUR > 392-465;   KOMMUNIKATION UND BÜROTECHNIK > 466-535;
TRANSPORT UND FAHRZEUGE > 536-643;   ENERGIE > 644-677;   WISSENSCHAFT > 678-705;   GESELLSCHAFT > 706-785;   SPORT UND SPIELE > 786-920

Indice delle voci italiane

ASTRONOMIA > 2-25; TERRA > 26-71; REGNO VEGETALE > 72-89; REGNO ANIMALE > 90-143; ESSERE UMANO > 144-177; GENERI ALIMENTARI E CUCINA > 178-241; CASA > 242-295;
FAI DA TE E GIARDINAGGIO > 296-333; ABBIGLIAMENTO > 334-371; ACCESSORI E ARTICOLI PERSONALI > 372-391; ARTE E ARCHITETTURA > 392-465; COMUNICAZIONI E BUROTICA > 466-535;
TRASPORTI E VEICOLI > 536-643; ENERGIA > 644-677; SCIENZA > 678-705; SOCIETÀ > 706-785; SPORT E GIOCHI > 786-920

1057

INDICE DELLE VOCI ITALIANE

INDICE DELLE VOCI ITALIANE

ASTRONOMIA > 2-25;   TERRA > 26-71;   REGNO VEGETALE >72-89;   REGNO ANIMALE > 90-143;   ESSERE UMANO > 144-177;   GENERI ALIMENTARI E CUCINA > 178-241;   CASA > 242-295;
FAI DA TE E GIARDINAGGIO > 296-333;   ABBIGLIAMENTO > 334-371;   ACCESSORI E ARTICOLI PERSONALI > 372-391;   ARTE E ARCHITETTURA > 392-465;   COMUNICAZIONI E BUROTICA > 466-535;
TRASPORTI E VEICOLI > 536-643;   ENERGIA > 644-677;   SCIENZA > 678-705;   SOCIETÀ > 706-785;   SPORT E GIOCHI > 786-920

1059

INDICE DELLE VOCI ITALIANE

INDICE DELLE VOCI ITALIANE

ASTRONOMIA > 2-25; TERRA > 26-71; REGNO VEGETALE >72-89; REGNO ANIMALE > 90-143; ESSERE UMANO > 144-177; GENERI ALIMENTARI E CUCINA > 178-241; CASA > 242-295;
FAI DA TE E GIARDINAGGIO > 296-333; ABBIGLIAMENTO > 334-371; ACCESSORI E ARTICOLI PERSONALI > 372-391; ARTE E ARCHITETTURA > 392-465; COMUNICAZIONI E BUROTICA > 466-535;
TRASPORTI E VEICOLI > 536-643; ENERGIA > 644-677; SCIENZA > 678-705; SOCIETÀ > 706-785; SPORT E GIOCHI > 786-920

1065

INDICE DELLE VOCI ITALIANE

ASTRONOMIA > 2-25; TERRA > 26-71; REGNO VEGETALE >72-89; REGNO ANIMALE > 90-143; ESSERE UMANO > 144-177; GENERI ALIMENTARI E CUCINA > 178-241; CASA > 242-295; FAI DA TE E GIARDINAGGIO > 296-333; ABBIGLIAMENTO > 334-371; ACCESSORI E ARTICOLI PERSONALI > 372-391; ARTE E ARCHITETTURA > 392-465; COMUNICAZIONI E BUROTICA > 466-535; TRASPORTI E VEICOLI > 536-643; ENERGIA > 644-677; SCIENZA > 678-705; SOCIETÀ > 706-785; SPORT E GIOCHI > 786-920

1067

INDICE DELLE VOCI ITALIANE

ASTRONOMIA > 2-25;   TERRA > 26-71;   REGNO VEGETALE >72-89;   REGNO ANIMALE > 90-143;   ESSERE UMANO > 144-177;   GENERI ALIMENTARI E CUCINA > 178-241;   CASA > 242-295;
FAI DA TE E GIARDINAGGIO > 296-333;   ABBIGLIAMENTO > 334-371;   ACCESSORI E ARTICOLI PERSONALI > 372-391;   ARTE E ARCHITETTURA > 392-465;   COMUNICAZIONI E BUROTICA > 466-535;
TRASPORTI E VEICOLI > 536-643;   ENERGIA > 644-677;   SCIENZA > 678-705;   SOCIETÀ > 706-785;   SPORT E GIOCHI > 786-920

ASTRONOMIA > 2-25;   TERRA > 26-71;   REGNO VEGETALE >72-89;   REGNO ANIMALE > 90-143;   ESSERE UMANO > 144-177;   GENERI ALIMENTARI E CUCINA > 178-241;   CASA > 242-295;
FAI DA TE E GIARDINAGGIO > 296-333;   ABBIGLIAMENTO > 334-371;   ACCESSORI E ARTICOLI PERSONALI > 372-391;   ARTE E ARCHITETTURA > 392-465;   COMUNICAZIONI E BUROTICA > 466-535;
TRASPORTI E VEICOLI > 536-643;   ENERGIA > 644-677;   SCIENZA > 678-705;   SOCIETÀ > 706-785;   SPORT E GIOCHI > 786-920;

1069

INDICE DELLE VOCI ITALIANE

ASTRONOMIA > 2-25;　TERRA > 26-71;　REGNO VEGETALE >72-89;　REGNO ANIMALE > 90-143;　ESSERE UMANO > 144-177;　GENERI ALIMENTARI E CUCINA > 178-241;　CASA > 242-295;
FAI DA TE E GIARDINAGGIO > 296-333;　ABBIGLIAMENTO > 334-371;　ACCESSORI E ARTICOLI PERSONALI > 372-391;　ARTE E ARCHITETTURA > 392-465;　COMUNICAZIONI E BUROTICA > 466-535;
TRASPORTI E VEICOLI > 536-643;　ENERGIA > 644-677;　SCIENZA > 678-705;　SOCIETÀ > 706-785;　SPORT E GIOCHI > 786-920

1071

INDICE DELLE VOCI ITALIANE

ASTRONOMIA > 2-25; TERRA > 26-71; REGNO VEGETALE >72-89; REGNO ANIMALE > 90-143; ESSERE UMANO > 144-177; GENERI ALIMENTARI E CUCINA > 178-241; CASA > 242-295;
FAI DA TE E GIARDINAGGIO > 296-333; ABBIGLIAMENTO > 334-371; ACCESSORI E ARTICOLI PERSONALI > 372-391; ARTE E ARCHITETTURA > 392-465; COMUNICAZIONE E BUROTICA > 466-535;
TRASPORTI E VEICOLI > 536-643; ENERGIA > 644-677; SCIENZA > 678-705; SOCIETÀ > 706-785; SPORT E GIOCHI > 786-920

ASTRONOMIA > 2-25;   TERRA > 26-71;   REGNO VEGETALE >72-89;   REGNO ANIMALE > 90-143;   ESSERE UMANO > 144-177;   GENERI ALIMENTARI E CUCINA > 178-241;   CASA > 242-295;
FAI DA TE E GIARDINAGGIO > 296-333;   ABBIGLIAMENTO > 334-371;   ACCESSORI E ARTICOLI PERSONALI > 372-391;   ARTE E ARCHITETTURA > 392-465;   COMUNICAZIONI E BUROTICA > 466-535;
TRASPORTI E VEICOLI > 536-643;   ENERGIA > 644-677;   SCIENZA > 678-705;   SOCIETÀ > 706-785;   SPORT E GIOCHI > 786-920

1073

ASTRONOMIA > 2-25;   TERRA > 26-71;   REGNO VEGETALE >72-89;   REGNO ANIMALE > 90-143;   ESSERE UMANO > 144-177;   GENERI ALIMENTARI E CUCINA > 178-241;   CASA > 242-295;
FAI DA TE E GIARDINAGGIO > 296-333;   ABBIGLIAMENTO > 334-371;   ACCESSORI E ARTICOLI PERSONALI > 372-391;   ARTE E ARCHITETTURA > 392-465;   COMUNICAZIONI E BUROTICA > 466-535;
TRASPORTI E VEICOLI > 536-643;   ENERGIA > 644-677;   SCIENZA > 678-705;   SOCIETÀ > 706-785;   SPORT E GIOCHI > 786-920

1077

INDICE DELLE VOCI ITALIANE

ASTRONOMIA > 2-25; TERRA > 26-71; REGNO VEGETALE > 72-89; REGNO ANIMALE > 90-143; ESSERE UMANO > 144-177; GENERI ALIMENTARI E CUCINA > 178-241; CASA > 242-295;
FAI DA TE E GIARDINAGGIO > 296-333; ABBIGLIAMENTO > 334-371; ACCESSORI E ARTICOLI PERSONALI > 372-391; ARTE E ARCHITETTURA > 392-465; COMUNICAZIONI E BUROTICA > 466-535;
TRASPORTI E VEICOLI > 536-643; ENERGIA > 644-677; SCIENZA > 678-705; SOCIETÀ > 706-785; SPORT E GIOCHI > 786-920

1079

INDICE DELLE VOCI ITALIANE

ASTRONOMIA > 2-25; TERRA > 26-71; REGNO VEGETALE >72-89; REGNO ANIMALE > 90-143; ESSERE UMANO > 144-177; GENERI ALIMENTARI E CUCINA > 178-241; CASA > 242-295;
FAI DA TE E GIARDINAGGIO > 296-333; ABBIGLIAMENTO > 334-371; ACCESSORI E ARTICOLI PERSONALI > 372-391; ARTE E ARCHITETTURA > 392-465; COMUNICAZIONI E BUROTICA > 466-535;
TRASPORTI E VEICOLI > 536-643; ENERGIA > 644-677; SCIENZA > 678-705; SOCIETÀ > 706-785; SPORT E GIOCHI > 786-920

1081

INDICE DELLE VOCI ITALIANE

ASTRONOMIA > 2-25; TERRA > 26-71; REGNO VEGETALE >72-89; REGNO ANIMALE > 90-143; ESSERE UMANO > 144-177; GENERI ALIMENTARI E CUCINA > 178-241; CASA > 242-295;
FAI DA TE E GIARDINAGGIO > 296-333; ABBIGLIAMENTO > 334-371; ACCESSORI E ARTICOLI PERSONALI > 372-391; ARTE E ARCHITETTURA > 392-465; COMUNICAZIONI E BUROTICA > 466-535;
TRASPORTI E VEICOLI >536-643; ENERGIA > 644-677; SCIENZA > 678-705; SOCIETÀ > 706-785; SPORT E GIOCHI > 786-920

1083

INDICE DELLE VOCI ITALIANE

INDICE DELLE VOCI ITALIANE

ASTRONOMIA > 2-25; TERRA > 26-71; REGNO VEGETALE >72-89; REGNO ANIMALE > 90-143; ESSERE UMANO > 144-177; GENERI ALIMENTARI E CUCINA > 178-241; CASA > 242-295;
FAI DA TE E GIARDINAGGIO > 296-371; ABBIGLIAMENTO > 334-371; ACCESSORI E ARTICOLI PERSONALI > 372-391; ARTE E ARCHITETTURA > 392-465; COMUNICAZIONI E BUROTICA > 466-535;
TRASPORTI E VEICOLI > 536-643; ENERGIA > 644-677; SCIENZA > 678-705; SOCIETÀ > 706-785; SPORT E GIOCHI > 786-920;

INDICE DELLE VOCI ITALIANE

ASTRONOMIA > 2-25; TERRA > 26-71; REGNO VEGETALE >72-89; REGNO ANIMALE > 90-143; ESSERE UMANO > 144-177; GENERI ALIMENTARI E CUCINA > 178-241; CASA > 242-295; FAI DA TE E GIARDINAGGIO > 296-333; ABBIGLIAMENTO > 334-371; ACCESSORI E ARTICOLI PERSONALI > 372-391; ARTE E ARCHITETTURA > 392-465; COMUNICAZIONI E BUROTICA > 466-535; TRASPORTI E VEICOLI > 536-643; ENERGIA > 644-677; SCIENZA > 678-705; SOCIETÀ > 706-785; SPORT E GIOCHI > 786-920

1089

U

V

ASTRONOMIA > 2-25; TERRA > 26-71; REGNO VEGETALE >72-89; REGNO ANIMALE > 90-143; ESSERE UMANO > 144-177; GENERI ALIMENTARI E CUCINA > 178-241; CASA > 242-295;
FAI DA TE E GIARDINAGGIO > 296-333; ABBIGLIAMENTO > 334-371; ACCESSORI E ARTICOLI PERSONALI > 372-391; ARTE E ARCHITETTURA > 392-465; COMUNICAZIONI E BUROTICA > 466-535;
TRASPORTI E VEICOLI > 536-643; ENERGIA > 644-677; SCIENZA > 678-705; SOCIETÀ > 706-785; SPORT E GIOCHI > 786-920;

1091

INDICE DELLE VOCI ITALIANE